online resource centre
www.oxfordtextbooks.co.uk/orc/jones_sufrin5e/

This book is accompanied by an **Online Resource Centre** offering additional resources and materials to support learning and to ensure that the book meets its many readers' needs.

- A full chapter on **State Aid** is available online

- An **interactive map** of the European Union provides useful factual information on each country's involvement in the EU

- A timeline tracing the evolution of EU legal history

- **Regular updates** are an indispensable resource providing easy access to the latest changes and developments in the law

- **Annotated web links** are also offered to facilitate further study into different jurisdictions and areas of research

Please visit **www.oxfordtextbooks.co.uk/orc/jones_sufrin5e/** to find the resources. To access the additional chapter on State Aid, please enter

Username: jones_sufrin5e

Password: JS_state

EU COMPETITION LAW

TEXT, CASES, AND MATERIALS

Fifth Edition

ALISON JONES

Solicitor, Professor of Law, King's College London

AND

BRENDA SUFRIN

Solicitor, Emeritus Professor of Law, University of Bristol

OXFORD
UNIVERSITY PRESS

OXFORD

UNIVERSITY PRESS

Great Clarendon Street, Oxford, OX2 6DP,
United Kingdom

Oxford University Press is a department of the University of Oxford.
It furthers the University's objective of excellence in research, scholarship,
and education by publishing worldwide. Oxford is a registered trade mark of
Oxford University Press in the UK and in certain other countries

Published in the United States of America by Oxford University Press
198 Madison Avenue, New York, NY 10016, United States of America

British Library Cataloguing in Publication Data

Data available

Library of Congress Control Number: 2013946494

ISBN 978–0–19–966032–2

Printed and bound by CPI Group (UK) Ltd, Croydon, CR0 4YY

PREFACE

The last edition of this book was being written as the Treaty of Lisbon came into force. It has now become apparent that the decision to omit from the body of the amended EC Treaty (the TFEU) a reference to a 'system ensuring that competition is not distorted', and to place it instead in a Protocol, has not had the calamitous effect feared by some. Rather, the Court of Justice has confirmed that it is 'business as usual'; there has been no diminution in the enforcement of the competition rules or slowing down of developments in the law which, on the contrary, have proceeded again at breath-taking pace.

Since the publication of the last edition the Court of Justice, the European Court of Human Rights, the Commission, and the national courts and national competition authorities of the Member States have all been extremely active publishing judgments, decisions, regulations, and other measures (draft or final) which have had, or will have, significant impact on virtually every aspect of EU competition law discussed in this book. For example, the Commission has: adopted new block exemption Regulations on R&D and specialisation and published new Guidelines on horizontal cooperation agreements; is consulting on changes to the technology transfer regime which need to be put in place before May 2014; published a new draft de minimis Notice for consultation; published a draft Directive (and other measures) designed to facilitate damages actions before national courts; and, within the field of mergers, commenced a review of the working and operation of the simplified procedure and a broader review of the system of merger regulation focusing, in particular, on the question of whether to apply merger control rules to deal with the anti-competitive effects stemming from acquisitions of, non-controlling minority interests, and the effectiveness and smoothness of the case referral system.

The Commission's proposal to amend the de minimis Notice was stated to be to take account of the Court of Justice's 2012 *Expedia* judgment. *Expedia*, like *T-Mobile, Pierre Fabre, Allianz Hungária Biztosító Zrt, and Generali-Providencia Biztosító Zrt v. Gazdasági Versenyhivatal*, is yet another case in which the Court has had to deal with the vitally important question of when an agreement infringes Article 101(1) because it is restrictive of competition by object. The last three years have also been a rich period for Article 102 judgments. In *TeliaSonera, Deutsche Telekom, Telefónica, Tomra, Post Danmark*, and *AstraZeneca* the EU Courts have variously dealt, inter alia, with margin squeeze, predatory and selective pricing, abuses in respect of the patent system and other regulatory procedures, the relationship between the application of the competition rules and national sector regulation, the concept of super-dominance, justification on grounds of efficiencies, and the 'as efficient competitor standard'. The judgments raise interesting questions about the influence of the Commission's Guidance Paper on Enforcement Priorities in Applying Article 102 to Exclusionary Conduct. At the time of writing the General Court judgment in *Intel*, which we had hoped to include in this edition, is still pending. The EU Courts have also heard numerous cartel appeal cases.

It is nearly 10 years since the 'modernisation' of the enforcement of Articles 101 and 102, the effects of which are now becoming clearer. The Commission has not yet made use of its powers to make findings of inapplicability pursuant to Article 10 of Regulation 1/2003 and has never issued informal guidance on a novel question. The EU Courts no longer hear appeals from refusals or granting of exemptions, or against conditions on exemptions, so those types of case have disappeared. As the Commission continues to pursue an aggressive enforcement policy against cartels, however, the EU Courts hear an enormous number of appeals from infringement decisions, mainly concerned with procedural matters, fines, and leniency but also with issues which span the procedural/substantive divide such as the liability of parents for the conduct of their subsidiaries. The most striking feature of the Commission's anti-cartel activity is the importance of the leniency regime and that, together with the settlement procedure which was introduced in 2008, allows significant scope for negotiation during cartel proceedings. The question of whether EU competition procedures, and the judicial review exercised by the General Court, are compatible and sufficient to satisfy human rights provisions, remains a live issue despite the European Court of Human Rights ruling in *Menarini* and the Court of Justice's *KME* and *Chalkor* judgments. In an attempt to meet some of the criticism levied at its procedures, the Commission has sought to make them more transparent, both with the publication of its 'Best Practices' documents and its internal Manual of Procedure.

A significant proportion of the cases arising, post-modernisation, before the Court of Justice which do not involve cartels or mergers are now Article 267 references from national courts. These references arise not only from private litigation in national courts involving competition law issues but also from cases in which national courts are hearing appeals from the decisions of national competition authorities. Although national competition authorities are playing an increasingly important role in the enforcement of the EU competition law provisions, the limitations on their powers in the decentralised system were made clear in *Tele2Polska*. Private litigation in the national courts is also increasing and the Commission's policy of encouraging it has received a further boost with the publication, in June 2013, of its proposal for a Directive designed to remove a number of practical difficulties confronted by claimants when instigating damages claims, a practical guide on the quantification of harm for damages to assist national courts and a recommendation of non-binding principles for collective redress mechanisms for Member States. These proposals also seek to optimise the delicate interaction between public and private enforcement. The problems of reconciling the facilitation of private actions without compromising public enforcement systems were vividly demonstrated in *Pfleiderer* in respect of access to leniency statements.

An extremely significant development since 2004 in the application of the competition rules in antitrust (non-merger) cases has also been the increasing use of the commitments decision procedure provided for in Article 9 of Regulation 1/2003. The wide discretion of the Commission in taking commitments was confirmed by the Court of Justice in *Alrosa* in 2010 and the Commission has taken full advantage of this. It is seen throughout this edition that, outside the cartel area, Commission infringement decisions under Article 7 of Regulation 1/2003 are now a rarity. In particular, the Commission regularly uses commitments decisions in Article 102 cases, where they have been notably employed in respect of the energy sector, and in cases in the IT sector arising from complaints about each other from the global giants of the digital economy. This evolution of the non-cartel parts of public enforcement into a system of negotiated outcomes deprives the EU Courts of any opportunity to consider what are often highly contentious and/or novel issues and means that there is not even a Commission decision definitively finding the relevant conduct or agreement to be a breach of the competition rules.

The developments outlined have, along with others, demanded once again much rewriting, rethinking, and restructuring of the chapters in this edition. We have attempted to process all of the changes and to consider their wider implications for the development of EU competition law and policy fully, whilst at the same time keeping the book manageable. We have also changed the chapter order to render it more logical. Our aim with this edition, as ever, is to provide students, and others interested in competition law, with as comprehensive as possible a package of text, commentary, and materials given the confines of space. That task becomes more difficult with each edition, given not only the ever-expanding body of the law but also the ever-increasing body of literature and commentary on it. The last three years has seen a wealth of new literature, including the publication of a number of scholarly monographs, practitioner volumes, books combining law and economics, and the launch of new specialist competition law journals. This is evidence of the continuing dynamism, excitement and commercial importance of this area of law, and its inter-disciplinary nature which sits at the interface of law and economics. As always some things we would have liked to have included have been left on the cutting-room floor but we have attempted to give readers at least a flavour of the main debates and ideas, and to provide references and further reading indicating where these may be pursued.

We would like to extend our thanks to everyone who has assisted us in the preparation of this edition. In particular, we wish to thank Baskaran Balasingham, Natalie St Cyr Clarke, and Lisa Daniel who have helped us with research and the Centre of European Law at King's College London for its generous research funding. We also owe an enormous debt of gratitude to Abbey Nelms, Sarah Stephenson, Emily Uecker and their colleagues at OUP, our copy-editor Susan Faircloth, and our proofreader, Fiona Tatham, for their helpfulness and efficiency.

Our intention is to state the law as at 31 May 2013. With the cooperation and forbearance of OUP, however, we have been able to include a note at least of some later developments up until the beginning of July 2013. Further developments which occurred too late may be found on a companion website that accompanies this book. The main objective of this website is to set out a list of recent developments in the law, to publish the online State Aid chapter and to provide links to helpful websites where further information can be obtained. The website can be accessed at www.oxfordtextbooks.co.uk/orc/jones_sufrin5e/.

The authors would like to dedicate this edition to Jack, Matilda, and Holly Keen, and to Madoc Vaughan Lowe John, born 28 July 2013.

Alison Jones
Brenda Sufrin
31 July 2013

CITATION AND TERMINOLOGY FOLLOWING THE TREATY OF LISBON

When the Treaty of Lisbon came into force on 1 December 2009, the European Community ceased to exist and was replaced and succeeded by the European Union. Further, the EC Treaty (the Treaty of Rome as amended) was renamed the Treaty on the Functioning of the European Union (TFEU) and both the Treaty on European Union (TEU) and the TFEU were amended and renumbered. These amendments made a substantial number of changes of substance to the Treaties, although not to the main competition articles, which are now contained in the TFEU. The modifications have led to important changes of terminology, including the change in the title of the Court of First Instance (CFI) to the 'General Court'. In this edition we deal with these changes by broadly continuing the practices we adopted in the fourth edition.

- In the text the competition articles are referred to by the new numbers (Articles 101–109 TFEU) even when speaking historically, i.e., discussing cases or events occurring before 1 December 2009.

- Other articles of the Treaties are referred to in the text by their new numbers where the wording is unchanged or the change is cosmetic or insignificant in substance (e.g., the article providing for the preliminary reference procedure, Article 234 EC, is referred to as Article 267 TFEU). Where there are more significant changes this is explained in the text and the old and new numbering used appropriately.

- In quotations and extracts, unless otherwise indicated, we replace the old number with the new number placed in square brackets, i.e., 'Article [101 TFEU]' or '[Article 101] replaces 'Article 81 EC', 'Article 85 EC' and 'Article 85 EEC'.

- References to Article 3(1)(g) EC (and Articles 3(g) and 3(f) as it formerly was) are left unaltered.

- The titles of Union legislation and other documents have been left unaltered, as have the titles of books, articles and other publications.

- The abbreviation of the Merger Regulation, Regulation 139/2004, is changed to EUMR.

- The Community Courts previously comprised the Court of Justice (usually abbreviated in English as 'ECJ') and the Court of First Instance (CFI). The Courts are now together called the Court of Justice of the European Union (CJEU). The CFI is now the 'General Court'. We have changed the name of the CFI historically and refer to it as the General Court from its inception. In quotations and extracts this is denoted by the use of square brackets, i.e., '[General Court]'. In this edition we have adopted the abbreviation 'CJ' for the Court of Justice.

Visit the main OUP Law website for access to full tables of equivalence showing the numbering changes made to the EU's governing treaties: www.oxfordtextbooks.co.uk/orc/eulaw/.

ACKNOWLEDGEMENTS

Grateful acknowledgement is made to all the authors and publishers of copyright material that appear in this book, and in particular to the following for permission to reprint material from the sources indicated:

Extracts from UK Competition Law Reports (UKCLR) and Office of Fair Trading Research Paper 2: Barriers to Entry and Exit in Competition Policy are Crown copyright material and are reproduced under Class Licence Number C01P0000148 with the permission of the Controller of HMSO and the Queen's Printer for Scotland.

Extracts from the reports of the European Court of Justice and Court of First Instance (ECR) are taken from www.curia.europa.eu. These are unauthenticated reports and are reproduced free of charge. The definitive versions are published in Reports of Cases before the Court of Justice or the Official Journal of the European Union.

American Bar Association: extracts from P. Areeda: 'Essential Facilities: An Epithet in Need of Limiting Principles', 58 Antitrust Law Journal 841 (1990).

Basic Books, a member of Perseus Books Group: extracts from Robert H. Bork: The Antitrust Paradox: A Policy at War with Itself (Basic Books, 1993), copyright © 1978 by Basic Books, LLC.

The Competition Law Review and the author: extracts from A. P. Komninos: 'Public and Private Antitrust Enforcement in Europe: Complement? Overlap?' 3 The Competition Law Review 3 (2006).

The Court of Justice of the European Free Trade Association States: extracts from the judgment in Case E-15/10 Posten Norge AS v. EFTA Surveillance Authority, 18 April 2012.

European Commission: extracts from 'Fighting Cartels Why and How? Why Should we be Concerned with Cartels and Collusive Behaviour?', a speech given by Commissioner Mario Monti at the 3rd Nordic Competition Policy Conference, Stockholm, 11–12 September 2000, as published on the Commission's website http://europa.eu/rapid/press-release_SPEECH-00-295_en.htm.

Hart Publishing: extracts from G. Amato: Antitrust and the Bounds of Power (Hart, 1997); and R. O'Donoghue and A. J. Padilla: The Law and Economics of Article 82 EC (Hart, 2006).

Harvard Law Review Association: extracts from W. S. Comanor: 'Vertical price-fixing, vertical market restrictions, and the new antitrust policy', 98 Harvard LR 983 (1985), copyright © 1985 The Harvard Law Review Association.

Wolters Kluwer Law & Business: extracts from Common Market Law Review: Giorgio Monti: 'Article 81 EC and Public Policy', CMLRev (2002) 1057, 'The Scope of Collective Dominance under Article 82C', 38 CMLRev (2001) 131; and extracts from World Competition: D. Hildebrand: 'The European School in EC Competition Law', 25 World Competition 3 (2002); L. Peeperkorn: 'IP Licences and Competition Rules: Striking the Right Balance', 26 World Competition (2003) . . . 527.

The Michigan Law Review Association and the author: extracts from H. Hovenkamp: 'Antitrust Policy After Chicago', 84 Mich LR 213 (1985), copyright © 1985 by Michigan Law Review Association.

New York University Law School: extract from Eleanor M. Fox and Lawrence A. Sullivan: 'Antitrust—Retrospective and Prospective: Where Are We Coming From? Where Are We Going?', 62 New York University Law Review 936 (1987).

Oxford University Press: extracts from S. D. Anderman and J. Kallauagher: Technology. Transfer and the New EU Competition Rules: Intellectual Property Licensing after Modernization (OUP, 2006); J. Faull and A. Nikpay (eds): The EC Law of Competition (2nd edn, OUP, 2007); C. Harding and J. Joshua: Regulating

Cartels in Europe (2nd edn, OUP, 2010); and from the Journal of European Competition Law and Practice: B. Meyring: 'T-Mobile: Further confusion on information exchanges between competitors: Case C-8/08 *T-Mobile Netherlands and others* [2009] ECR I-4529, *JECLAP* 30 (2010).

Sweet & Maxwell Ltd: extracts from S. Bishop and M. Walker: *The Economics of EC Competition Law: Concepts, Application and Measurement* (3rd edn, Sweet & Maxwell, 2010); extracts from European Competition Law Review: J. P. Azevedo and M. Walker: 'Dominance: Meaning and Measurement', *ECLR* 363 (2002); C. Gauer and M. Jaspers, 'Designing a European Solution for a "One Stop Leniency Shop"' *ECLR* 685 (2006); and A. Jones and D. Beard: 'Co-contractors, Damages and Article 81: The ECJ Finally Speaks' *ECLR* 246 (2002); extracts from European Law Review: P. Nebbia: 'Damages Actions for the Infringement of EC Competition Law: Compensation or Deterrence?', *ELRev* (2008); J Temple Lang: 'How Can the Problems of Exclusionary Abuses under Article 102 TFEU be resolved?', *ELRev* (2012); extracts from Global Competition Litigation Review: R. Nazzini: 'The Objective of Private Remedies in EU Competition Law' *Global Competition Litigation Review* (2011); and extracts from Common Market Law Reports (CMLR).

Thomson West: extracts from H. Hovenkamp: *Federal Antitrust Policy: The Law of Competition and its Practice* (4th edn, West, 2011).

Every effort has been made to trace and contact copyright holders prior to publication but this has not been possible in every case. If notified, the publisher will undertake to rectify any errors or omissions at the earliest opportunity.

OUTLINE CONTENTS

Table of European Cases   xxvii

Table of International Cases   lxx

Table of Legislation   lxxii

Table of European and International Treaties, Conventions, and Charters   xcii

Bibliography   xcvii

List of Abbreviations   xcviii

1. INTRODUCTION TO COMPETITION LAW   1

2. THE EUROPEAN UNION AND ITS COMPETITION LAW AND INSTITUTIONS   98

3. ARTICLE 101 TFEU: THE ELEMENTS   122

4. THE RELATIONSHIP BETWEEN ARTICLE 101(1) AND ARTICLE 101(3) TFEU   192

5. INTRODUCTION TO ARTICLE 102 TFEU   269

6. ARTICLE 102 TFEU: DOMINANT POSITION   297

7. ARTICLE 102 TFEU: CONDUCT WHICH CAN BE AN ABUSE   365

8. COMPETITION, THE STATE, AND PUBLIC UNDERTAKINGS: ARTICLE 106 TFEU   597

9. CARTELS AND OLIGOPOLY   659

10. HORIZONTAL COOPERATION AGREEMENTS   731

11. VERTICAL AGREEMENTS   768

12. LICENSING AGREEMENTS AND OTHER AGREEMENTS INVOLVING INTELLECTUAL PROPERTY RIGHTS   846

13. PUBLIC ENFORCEMENT BY THE COMMISSION AND THE NATIONAL COMPETITION AUTHORITIES OF THE ANTITRUST PROVISIONS   922

14. PRIVATE ENFORCEMENT   1082

15. MERGERS   1128

16. INTERNATIONAL ASPECTS   1258

Index   1299

OUTLINE CONTENTS

CONTENTS

Table of European Cases   xxvii
Table of International Cases   lxx
Table of Legislation   lxxii
Table of European and International Treaties, Conventions, and Charters   xcii
Bibliography   xcvii
List of Abbreviations   xcviii

1. INTRODUCTION TO COMPETITION LAW   1

    1. Central Issues   1
    2. Introduction   1
    3. The Objectives of Competition Law   4
        A. Economic Efficiency and Welfare   4
        B. Other Objectives of Competition Law   15
        C. Conclusions   18
    4. US Law   19
    5. Schools of Competition Analysis and Theories and Concepts Relevant to
        Competition Law   21
        A. The Structure → Conduct → Performance Paradigm and the Harvard School   21
        B. The Chicago School, Post-Chicago, and Neo-Chicago   22
        C. Game Theory   30
        D. Contestable Markets Theory   31
        E. Raising Rivals' Costs   31
        F. Transaction Cost Economics   31
        G. Workable Competition   32
        H. The Austrian School   32
        I. Effective Competition   33
    6. Ordoliberalism   33
    7. EU Competition Law   34
        A. General   34
        B. The Objectives of the EU and the Role of the Competition Rules   35
        C. The Objectives of EU Competition Law   38
        D. EU Competition Law and Regulation   52
        E. The New Economy   54
    8. Competition Law and the International Context   56

9. The Techniques and Tools of Competition Law 56
   A. General 56
   B. Form or Effects and Theories of Harm 56
   C. Over- and Under-Enforcement: Type 1 and Type 2 Errors 57
   D. The Use of Economic Analysis 58
10. Market Power, Market Definition, and Barriers to Entry 59
   A. Market Power 59
   B. Market Definition and EU Competition Law 61
   C. Barriers to Entry and Expansion 85
11. Conclusions 93
12. Further Reading 94

2. THE EUROPEAN UNION AND ITS COMPETITION LAW AND INSTITUTIONS 98
1. Central Issues 98
2. Introduction 99
3. Introduction to the European Union 99
   A. The European Union and the European Community 99
   B. The EU Treaties 100
   C. The Non-Judicial EU Institutions 101
   D. EU Acts 104
   E. The EU Courts 105
   F. General Principles of Union Law and Human Rights 107
   G. The EU Legal Order 108
4. The Competition Provisions 109
   A. General 109
   B. The Substantive Competition Provisions of the TFEU 114
   C. The Procedural Provisions 115
   D. The Merger Regulation 117
   E. Other Relevant Treaty Provisions 117
5. Notices and Guidelines 118
6. The Competition Rules and the European Economic Area 119
7. Modernisation 119
8. Conclusions 120
9. Further Reading 121

3. ARTICLE 101 TFEU: THE ELEMENTS 122
1. Central Issues 122
2. Introduction 122
3. The Text of Article 101 123
4. The Scheme of Article 101 124
   A. The Three Paragraphs 124

	B.	The Consequences of Infringement	125
	C.	Burden and Standard of Proof	126
5.		The Interpretation and Application of Article 101(1)	127
	A.	'Undertaking' and 'Associations of Undertakings'	127
	B.	The Meaning of 'Agreement', 'Decision', and 'Concerted Practice'	149
	C.	Object or Effect of the Prevention, Restriction, or Distortion of Competition	179
	D.	An Appreciable Effect on Competition and Trade	180
	E.	An Appreciable Effect on Trade Between Member States	181
	F.	Agreements Required by National Legislation or Encouraged by National Governments	186
	G.	Commission Notices	188
	H.	Extraterritoriality	188
6.		Article 101(2)	189
7.		Exclusions	189
8.		Conclusions	190
9.		Further Reading	191

4. THE RELATIONSHIP BETWEEN ARTICLE 101(1) AND ARTICLE 101(3) TFEU — 192

1.		Central Issues	192
2.		Introduction and Background	192
	A.	Article 101(1) and Article 101(3)	192
	B.	Possible Ways of Reconciling Article 101(1) and Article 101(3)	193
	C.	The Interpretation of 'Object or Effect is the Prevention, Restriction, or Distortion of Competition'—The Broad Approach	194
	D.	The Drawbacks of a Broad Interpretation of Article 101(1): The Need for a More Economic Approach?	195
	E.	Section 1 of the Sherman Act	197
	F.	Modernisation	198
3.		Article 101(1), Agreements Which Have as their Object or Effect the Prevention, Restriction, or Distortion of Competition	203
	A.	General	203
	B.	Object or Effect	204
	C.	Agreements that Restrict Competition by Object: Restraints Which, 'By their Very Nature', Restrict Competition	205
	D.	Identifying the Category of Object Restraints	205
	E.	Agreements that Restrict Competition by Effect	232
	F.	Ancillary Restraints	242
	G.	Conclusions on the Approach Required under Article 101(1): Is Any Weighing or Balancing Required?	246

4. Article 101(3)   249
   A. Application of Article 101(3)   249
   B. Burden and Standard of Proof   250
   C. Any Agreement May in Principle Benefit from Article 101(3)   251
   D. The Article 101(3) Criteria   252
   E. Block Exemptions   263
   F. Unilateral Action and Article 101(3)   266
5. Conclusions   267
6. Further Reading   267

5. INTRODUCTION TO ARTICLE 102 TFEU   269
1. Central Issues   269
2. Introduction   269
3. The Text of Article 102   270
4. The Scheme of Article 102   271
   A. The Prohibition   271
   B. The Enforcement of Article 102   272
5. The Interpretation and Application of Article 102   276
   A. The Meaning of One or More Undertakings   276
   B. A Dominant Position   281
   C. A Dominant Position Within a Substantial Part of the Internal Market   281
   D. Abuse   283
   E. An Effect on Trade Between Member States   283
6. The Review of Article 102   287
   A. The Inauguration of the Review   287
   B. The Staff Discussion Paper   288
   C. The Guidance Paper   289
7. The Relationship Between Article 102 and Article 101   293
8. Conclusions   295
9. Further Reading   295

6. ARTICLE 102 TFEU: DOMINANT POSITION   297
1. Central Issues   297
2. Introduction   297
3. The Definition of a Dominant Position   298
   A. The Definition of a Dominant Position in the Case Law   298
   B. Dominant Position in the Guidance Paper   302
   C. Effects-Based Analysis and the Concept of Dominance   303
4. Establishing Dominance   304
5. Market Definition in Article 102 Cases   305
   A. General   305

	B.	The Product Market	306
	C.	The Geographic Market	326
	D.	The Temporal Market	330
	E.	The *Tetra Pak II* Case	331
6.		Assessing Market Power	335
	A.	General	335
	B.	Market Shares	336
	C.	Other Factors Indicating Dominance and Barriers to Entry	344
	D.	Countervailing Buyer Power	359
	E.	Dominant Positions in the New Economy	361
7.		Conclusions	363
8.		Further Reading	363

7. ARTICLE 102 TFEU: CONDUCT WHICH CAN BE AN ABUSE — 365

1.		Central Issues	365
2.		Introduction	366
3.		The Meaning of Abuse	366
	A.	General	366
	B.	Types of Abuse	367
	C.	The Broad Nature of the Concept of Abuse	372
	D.	Exclusionary Abuses: Distinguishing Illegitimate from Legitimate Conduct	378
	E.	Form- and Effects-Based Analysis	382
4.		The Commission's Approach to Exclusionary Abuses in the Guidance Paper: The Adoption of the 'Anti-Competitive Foreclosure' Concept	382
5.		Objective Justification, Efficiency, and Other Defences	385
	A.	General	385
	B.	Objective Justification in the Case Law	386
	C.	The Burden of Proof	388
	D.	Justification in the Guidance Paper	389
	E.	Comments	390
	F.	Protecting the Undertaking's Own Commercial Interests	391
	G.	The 'Meeting Competition' Defence	392
6.		Dominance and Abuse on Different Markets	393
7.		General Issues in Respect of Abuses Concerning Prices	396
	A.	Exploitative and Exclusionary Pricing Policies	396
	B.	Price Discrimination	396
	C.	Costs Levels	398
	D.	The General Approach in the Guidance Paper to Price-Based Exclusionary Conduct: the 'As Efficient Competitor' Standard	399
	E.	The General Approach of the EU Courts to Pricing Abuses	401

8. Predatory Pricing   401
   - A. General   401
   - B. The Areeda–Turner Test   403
   - C. The Test Laid Down in *AKZO*   404
   - D. The *Post Danmark* Case   408
   - E. The 'Meeting Competition' Defence and Predatory Pricing   411
   - F. Recoupment   412
   - G. Predatory Pricing in the Guidance Paper and the Sacrifice Principle   417
   - H. Predatory Pricing and New Economy Markets   419
   - I. Selective Above-Cost Pricing   420

9. Margin Squeeze   426
   - A. General   426
   - B. The Case Law   427
   - C. Cases and Decisions Outside the Telecommunications Sector   444
   - D. Margin Squeeze in the Guidance Paper   445
   - E. US Law on Margin Squeeze   445
   - F. Comment   446
   - G. Summary   449

10. Exclusive Purchasing (Single Branding) Contracts and Discount and Rebate Schemes   450
   - A. General   450
   - B. The Case Law on Exclusive Purchasing   450
   - C. Exclusive Purchasing in the Guidance Paper   453
   - D. Discount and Rebate Schemes   454

11. Tying and Bundling   485
   - A. General   485
   - B. The Commercial Rationale for Tying and Bundling   487
   - C. The Economic Arguments over Tying and Bundling   487
   - D. Tying and Bundling and Article 102   489
   - E. The Case Law   489

12. Refusal to Supply   510
   - A. General   510
   - B. The *Commercial Solvents* Case: Refusal to Supply Existing Customers in Order to Exclude Competitors from Downstream Markets   511
   - C. Refusal to Supply on a Downstream Market and the 'Essential Facilities' Concept   513
   - D. Refusal to Supply and Intellectual Property Rights   526
   - E. Refusal to Supply in Response to an Attack on the Dominant Undertaking's Commercial Interests   548
   - F. Refusal to Supply and Parallel Trade   550
   - G. Refusal to Supply in the Guidance Paper   550
   - H. Refusal to Supply and the 'Essential Facilities' Doctrine in US Law   553

13. Other Exclusionary Practices 556

    A. General 556

    B. The Acquisition of Intellectual Property Rights 557

    C. The Misuse of Intellectual Property Rights or Other Regulatory Procedures 558

    D. Pursuit of Legal Proceedings, Vexatious Litigation, and Enforcing Legal Rights 564

    E. Search Engine Practices 565

    F. Vertical and Horizontal Integration 567

14. Discrimination Contrary to Article 102(c) 567

    A. General 567

    B. The Application of Article 102(c) to Primary Line Injury and Exclusionary Conduct 568

    C. Article 102(c) and Non-vertically Integrated Undertakings 568

    D. Vertically Integrated Undertakings 569

    E. Geographical Price Discrimination 570

    F. Competitive Disadvantage and Article 102(c) 572

15. Exploitative Abuses 575

    A. Unfairly High or Low Pricing 575

    B. Imposing Unfair Trading Conditions and Entering into Restrictive Agreements 582

    C. Inefficiency and Limiting Production 583

16. Refusal to Supply, Export Bans, and Other Conduct Hindering Inter-Member State Trade 584

17. Abuse and Collective Dominance 590

18. Conclusions 591

19. Further Reading 591

8. COMPETITION, THE STATE, AND PUBLIC UNDERTAKINGS: ARTICLE 106 TFEU 597

    1. Central Issues 597

    2. Introduction 598

        A. General 598

        B. The Limits of Competition Law 600

    3. Article 4 TEU 601

    4. Article 106 602

        A. The Objectives of Article 106 603

        B. The Format of Article 106 603

    5. Article 106(1) 604

        A. Definitions 604

        B. Measures Which Are Forbidden by Article 106(1) 607

        C. Summary of the Measures Which Make Abuse Unavoidable or Create a Situation in Which the Undertaking is Led to Abuse its Dominant Position 628

    6. Article 106(2) 630

        A. The Institutional Setting of Services of General Economic Interest 630

B. The Concepts and Terminology of 'Services of General Economic Interest' and 'Services of General Interest'   632

C. The Purpose of Article 106(2)   634

D. Undertakings Having the Character of a Revenue-producing Monopoly   634

E. Undertakings Entrusted with the Operation of Services of General Economic Interest   634

F. No Effect on Trade Contrary to the Interests of the Union   652

7. The Direct Effect of Article 106(1) and (2)   652

     A. Article 106(1)   652

     B. Article 106(2)   652

8. Article 106(3)   653

     A. The Ambit of the Provision   653

     B. Decisions   653

     C. Directives   654

9. Services of General Economic Interest and State Aid   656

10. Conclusion on Services of General Economic Interest   656

11. Conclusions   657

12. Further Reading   657

9. CARTELS AND OLIGOPOLY   659

1. Central Issues   659

2. Introduction   659

     A. Cartels and Oligopoly   659

     B. Explicit and Tacit Collusion   660

     C. Competition Law and Collusion (Explicit and Tacit)   673

3. Cartels   675

     A. Introduction   675

     B. Scope of Article 101   675

     C. Price-Fixing, Restrictions on Output, Market-Sharing, and Collusive Tendering   678

     D. Restrictions on Non-Price Trading Conditions, Advertising, and Promotion and Information-Sharing Agreements   696

4. Oligopoly   709

     A. Oligopoly and Article 101   709

     B. Oligopoly and Article 102   716

     C. Alternative Methods for Dealing with Oligopolistic Markets Under EU Law   727

5. Conclusions   729

6. Further Reading   730

10. HORIZONTAL COOPERATION AGREEMENTS   731

1. Central Issues   731

2. Introduction   731

3. Joint Ventures 733
   A. What is a Joint Venture? 733
   B. Competition Concerns in Respect of Joint Ventures 733
   C. Joint Ventures and the Merger Regulation 734
   D. The Development of the Commission's Approach to the Assessment of Joint Ventures Under Article 101 734
4. The Contents of the Guidelines 739
5. The General Approach to Horizontal Cooperation Agreements in the Guidelines 739
6. Information Agreements 741
7. Research and Development Agreements 741
   A. The Application of Article 101(1) 741
   B. The Application of Article 101(3) 742
8. Production Agreements 746
   A. General 746
   B. The Application of Article 101(1) 746
   C. The Application of Article 101(3) 747
9. Purchasing Agreements 749
   A. The Nature of Joint Purchasing and its Treatment in the Guidelines 749
   B. Cases on Joint Purchasing 752
10. Commercialisation Agreements 754
   A. General 754
   B. The Application of Article 101(1) 754
   C. The Application of Article 101(3) 756
11. Standardisation Agreements 757
   A. Standardisation and Standard-Setting 757
   B. Standard Terms 762
12. Agreements in Particular Sectors 763
   A. General 763
   B. Insurance 763
   C. Payment Services 764
   D. Sport 764
13. Conclusions 767
14. Further Reading 767

11. VERTICAL AGREEMENTS 768
1. Central Issues 768
2. Introduction 768
   A. General 768
   B. Methods of Distribution 769
   C. Competition Rules and Distribution 773
3. The EU Approach—An Overview 784
   A. The Background: The Single Market Project and Restrictions on Economic Freedom 784

		B.	Criticisms of this Approach	784
		C.	The More Economic Approach: the Block Exemption and Reform	785
		D.	Methodology	786
	4.	Distribution Agreements and Article 101(1) of the Treaty		788
		A.	Vertical Agreements which Restrict Competition by Object	788
		B.	Analysing the Restrictive 'Effect' of Vertical Restraints	801
	5.	Article 101(3)		817
		A.	General	817
		B.	The Old Block Exemptions	817
		C.	The Verticals Regulation—Regulation 330/2010	818
		D.	The Motor Vehicle Distribution Block Exemption	834
		E.	Article 101(3)—Individual Assessment	834
	6.	Sub-contracting Agreements		841
	7.	Article 102 and Distribution		842
	8.	Conclusions		842
	9.	Further Reading		845

12. LICENSING AGREEMENTS AND OTHER AGREEMENTS INVOLVING INTELLECTUAL PROPERTY RIGHTS — 846

	1.	Central Issues		846
	2.	Introduction		847
		A.	General	847
		B.	Types of Intellectual Property Rights	848
		C.	The Relationship between Intellectual Property Rights and Competition Law	851
		D.	The Relationship between Intellectual Property Rights and the Free Movement Rules	853
	3.	Exploiting Intellectual Property Rights by Licensing		854
		A.	General	854
		B.	Commercial Considerations in Licences	855
		C.	Development of Competition Policy Towards Licensing of Intellectual Property Rights	858
		D.	The Adoption of the 2004 TTBER and the Technology Transfer Guidelines	867
	4.	Regulation 772/2004, the Technology Transfer Block Exemption		874
		A.	General	874
		B.	The Scheme of the TTBER	875
		C.	Principal Features of the TTBER	875
		D.	Scope of the TTBER	876
		E.	Safe Harbour: the Market Share Thresholds	880
		F.	Hardcore Restrictions	884
		G.	Excluded Restrictions	891
		H.	Withdrawal and Disapplication of the Block Exemption	893
		I.	Duration of the Exemption	894

5. The Application of Article 101 to Licensing Agreements Falling Outside
the TTBER 894
   A. General Principles 894
   B. The Application of the TTBER and the Guidelines to Specific Provisions ... 898
   C. Technology Pools 906
6. Trade Mark Licences 908
   A. General 908
   B. The *Campari* Decision 909
   C. The *Moosehead/Whitbread* Decision 912
   D. The Current Position 913
7. Trade Mark Delimitation Agreements 913
8. Copyright (Other Than Software) Licences 914
   A. General 914
   B. Performance Copyright 914
   C. Collective Licensing of Copyright 919
9. The Application of Article 102 to Intellectual Property Rights 920
10. Conclusions 920
11. Further Reading 921

13. PUBLIC ENFORCEMENT BY THE COMMISSION AND THE NATIONAL
COMPETITION AUTHORITIES OF THE ANTITRUST PROVISIONS 922

1. Central Issues 922
2. Introduction 923
3. The Change to the Enforcement Regime in May 2004 923
4. The Old Enforcement Regime Set Up by Regulation 17 924
5. Modernisation 925
   A. The Modernisation White Paper 925
   B. The Modernisation 'Package' 927
6. The European Competition Network 932
7. The Best Practices Notice and the Manual of Procedures 932
8. Enforcement by the Commission 933
   A. General 933
   B. The Investigation Stage of the Administrative Procedure: Fact-Finding by the
Commission 939
   C. The Second, 'Inter Partes', Stage of the Procedure 966
   D. Commission Decisions 979
   E. The Settlement Procedure in Cartel Cases 992
   F. Informal Settlements 993
   G. Fines and Periodic Penalty Payments 994
   H. Sector Inquiries 1028
   I. The Powers of the Commission and Due Process 1028
9. Proceedings Before the Court of Justice of the European Union 1029
   A. Judicial Review 1029
   B. Actions for Damages Under Article 340 TFEU 1050

10. Enforcement by the National Competition Authorities Within
    the European Competition Network   1051
    A. General   1051
    B. Division of Work   1052
    C. Consistent Application of Articles 101 and 102   1060
    D. EU and National Competition Law   1061
11. The Relationship Between EU and National Competition Law   1061
12. Criminalisation and Sanctions Against Individuals   1064
13. Complaints   1066
    A. General   1066
    B. Where to Complain   1067
    C. Standing   1068
    D. The Procedure   1071
    E. The Three-Stage Procedure   1071
    F. Rejection of the Complaint   1071
    G. Acting on a Complaint   1076
    H. Judicial Review Proceedings   1077
    I. Complaints and the Merger Regulation   1078
14. Conclusions   1078
15. Further Reading   1078

14. PRIVATE ENFORCEMENT   1082
    1. Central Issues   1082
    2. Introduction   1083
        A. General   1083
        B. Direct Effect, the Principle of National Procedural Autonomy,
            and 'EU' Remedies   1083
        C. A Paucity of Antitrust Litigation in Europe?   1085
        D. The relationships between Private and Public Enforcement: Should
            Private Actions Be Encouraged?   1087
        E. Uniform and Concurrent Application of Articles 101 and 102 1094
    3. The Enforceability of Agreements Infringing Articles 101 or 102 1097
        A. Article 101   1097
        B. Article 102   1099
    4. Remedies: Damages Actions and Injunctions   1100
        A. Damages   1100
        B. Injunctions   1125
    5. Conclusions   1126
    6. Further Reading   1127

15. MERGERS   1128
    1. Central Issues   1128
    2. Introduction   1129
        A. What is a Merger?   1129

	B.	The Purposes of Merger Control	1129
	C.	The History of the European Merger Control Regulation	1134
	D.	Scheme of the European Union Merger Regulation	1139
3.		Jurisdiction	1140
	A.	Concentrations	1140
	B.	EU Dimension	1149
	C.	Concentrations with an EU Dimension: a One-Stop Shop?	1157
	D.	Concentrations without a Community—an EU—Dimension	1168
	E.	A Residual Role for Articles 101 and 102 of the Treaty	1171
4.		Procedure	1172
	A.	Notification	1172
	B.	Pre-Notification Reasoned Submissions	1174
	C.	Suspension	1176
	D.	Phase I Investigation	1177
	E.	Phase II	1178
	F.	Conduct of Merger Investigations	1179
5.		Substantive Appraisal of Concentrations Under the EU Merger Regulation	1180
	A.	Background	1180
	B.	Reform and the New Substantive Test	1182
	C.	Burden and Standard of Proof and Counterfactual	1184
	D.	A Significant Impediment to Effective Competition, in Particular by the Creation or Strengthening of a Dominant Position	1187
	E.	Article 2(4), (5), Joint Ventures	1241
	F.	Restrictions Directly Related and Necessary to the Concentration	1244
	G.	Commitments or Remedies	1245
6.		EUMR Statistics	1252
7.		Appeals	1253
8.		International Issues	1254
	A.	The Long Arm of the EUMR	1254
	B.	Reciprocity	1256
9.		Conclusions	1256
10.		Further Reading	1257
16.		**INTERNATIONAL ASPECTS**	**1258**
1.		Central Issues	1258
2.		Introduction	1258
3.		The Position in US Law	1259
	A.	General	1259
	B.	The Effects Doctrine	1260
	C.	Enforcement and the Reactions of Other States	1263
	D.	Foreign Plaintiffs in US Courts	1265
	E.	Discovery in US Courts	1269
	F.	The Effects Doctrine and Foreign Conduct Affecting Exports	1269

4. International Law 1270
5. The Position in EU Law 1271
    A. General 1271
    B. The *Dyestuffs* Case 1272
    C. The *Wood Pulp* Case 1274
    D. The Merger Regulation 1278
    E. Enforcement Jurisdiction 1286
6. International Cooperation 1286
    A. General 1286
    B. EU Bilateral Agreements 1287
    C. Multilateral Cooperation 1292
7. Conclusions 1296
8. Further Reading 1296

Index 1299

TABLE OF EUROPEAN CASES

[Page references in **bold** indicate that the item is given particular prominence in the text.]

COMMISSION DECISIONS

1998 World Cup Finals [2000] OJ L5/55, [2000] 4 CMLR 963 ... 111, 128, 371, 376, 378, 583

Accor/Barrière/Colony (Case M.3373), [2004] OJ C196/8 ... 1162

Acrylic Glass (methacrylates) IP/06/698, 31 May 2006 ... 1028

AEI/Reyrolle Parsons re Vacuum Interrupters [1977] OJ L48/32, [1977] 1 CMLR D 67 ... 182, **735–736**

Aérospatiale-Alenia/de Havilland (Case IV/M.53) [1991] OJ L334/42, [1992] 4 CMLR M2 ... 1189, **1210**, 1217, **1240**

Aggregate Industries/Foster Yeoman (Case M.4298) ... 1162–1163

Agreement of Davide Campari-Milano SpA, Re the *see* Campari

Agreements of Davidson Rubber Co, Re [1972] OJ L143/31 ... 860

AICIA v. CNSD [1993] OJ L203/27 ... 128, 174, 217

Air France/KLM (Case M.3280) ... 1197

Air Liquide/BOC (Case M. 1630), [2004] OJ L92/1 ... 1209

Airtours/First Choice (Case IV/M.1524) [2000] OJ L93/1, [2000] 5 CMLR 494 ... 723, 1036, 1182, 1203

Albertis/Autostrada (Case COMP/M.4249) IP/06/1244 ... 1028, 1167

Alcatel/AEG Kabel (Case IV/M.165) [1992] OJ C6/23 ... 1162, 1200

Alcatel/Telettra (Case IV/M.42) [1991] OJ L122/48, [1991] 4 CMLR 778 ... 1191, 1209, 1251

Alpha Flight Services/Aéroports de Paris [1998] OJ L230/10, [1998] 5 CMLR 611 ... 283

Aluminium Imports from Eastern Europe [1985] OJ L92/1, [1987] 3 CMLR 813 ... 129, 150

Amer/Salomon (Case M.3765) ... 1195

American Cyanamid/Shell (Case IV/M.354) [1993] OJ C273/6 ... 1191

Amino Acid (Lysine) Cartel [2001] OJ L152/24, [2001] 5 CMLR 322 ... 685, 942, 1008

Anglo American/Tarmac (Case M.1779) ... 1162

Animal Feed Phosphates Producers (Case COMP/38.866), 20 July 2010, IP/10/985, OJ C111/19 ... 993, 1017

Anseau [1982] OJ L167/39, [1982] 2 CMLR 193 ... 173–174, 697

Antalis/MAP (Case M.4753) ... 1206

AOIP v. Beyrard [1976] OJ L6/8, [1976] 1 CMLR D14 ... 860

AP Moller (Case M.969), [1999] OJ L183/29 ... 1177

Arjomari/Wiggins Teape (Case IV/M.25) [1990] OJ C321/16 ... 1142

AROW/BNIC [1982] OJ L379/1, [1983] 2 CMLR 240 ... 150

Aster 2/Flint Ink (Case M.3886) ... 1216

Astra/Zeneca, IP/05/737 ... 380

Athens International Airport (Case COMP/38.469) ... 1075

Austrian Banks (Lombard Club) [2004] OJ L56/1 ... 62–63, 682

B&W Loudspeakers IP/00/1418 (opening of proceedings) and IP/02/916 (comfort letter) ... 830, 834

Bananas (Case COMP/39188) ... 169, 700–701

Bandengroothandel Frieschebebrug BV/Nederlandsche Banden-Michelin NV [1981] OJ L353/33, [1982] 1 CMLR 643 ... 311, 326

Barretts & Baird (Wholesale) v IPCS [1987] IRLR 3 ... 1119

BASF/Pantochim/Eurodial (Case IV/M.2314) IP/01/984 ... **1220**

Bass [1999] OJ L186/1, [1999] 5 CMLR 782 ... 786, 804, 1096

Bayer Dental [1990] OJ L351/46, [1992] 4 CMLR 61 ... 999

BBI/Boosey & Hawkes [1987] OJ L286/36, [1988] 4 CMLR 67 ... 345–346, 358, 392, 550, 556, 564, 992

Beecham/Parke, Davis, [1979] OJ L70/11 ... 195, 253

Behringwerke/Armour Pharmaceutical, (Case IV/M.495) ... 359

BELASCO [1986] OJ L232/15, [1991] 4 CMLR 130 ... 174, 664, 675–676, 684, 698

Belgian Brewers [2003] OJ L 200/1 ... 168, 675, 688

Bleaching Chemicals (hydrogen peroxide and perborate), IP/06/560, 3 May 2006 ... 681, 1028

Blokker/Toys'R'Us (Case IV/M.890) ... 1169

BMG/Sony [2005] OJ L65/30 ... 70, 1207

BMW [1975] OJ L29/1 ... 810

BMW Belgium NV and Belgian BMW Dealers [1978] OJ L46/33 ... 258

Boeing/McDonnell Douglas (Case M.877), [1997] OJ L336/16 ... 1189, **1199**, 1250, 1255, **1284–1285**, 1290

Bosch/Rexroth (Case M.2060) ... 1248

Boussois/Interpane [1987] OJ L50/30 ... 863

BP/E.ON (Case COMP/M.2533) ... 1158, 1162, 1184

BP/Erdölchemie (Case M.2624), [2004] OJ L91/40 ... 1179

BPB Industries [1989] OJ L10/50, [1990] 4 CMLR 464 ... 328, 355, 451, 464

BPCL [1984] OJ L212/1 ... 749

British Aerospace/GEC Marconi (Case IV/M.1438) OJ [1999] C241/8 ... **1166–1167**

British Aerospace/Lagardère SCA (Case M.820), [1997] OJ C22/6 ... 1166

British Aerospace/VSEL (Case M.528) ... 1166

British Airways/Dan Air merger (Case IV/M.278) [1993] 5 CMLR M61 ... 1169

British Midland/Aer Lingus [1992] OJ L96/34, [1993] 4 CMLR 596 ... 283, 327, 355, 358, 514–515, 531

British Telecom-MCI [1994] OJ L52/51, [1995] 5 CMLR 301 ... 1136

Bronbemaling v. Heidemaatschappij [1975] OJ L249/27, [1975] 2 CMLR D67 ... 860

Brussels National Airport (Zaventem) [1995] OJ L216/8, [1996] 4 CMLR 232 ... 569

BSCH/A.Champaliaud (Case M.1616), [1999] OJ C306/37 ... 1165

BSG/Universe (Case M.4662) ... 1206

BSkyB/Kirsch (Case IV/Jv. 37) ... 1250

BT/AT&T (Case IV/Jv. 15) ... 1243–1244

Building and Construction Industry in the Netherlands [1992] OJ L92/1, [1993] 5 CMLR 135 ... 690, 699, 1068

Burroughs/Deplanque [1972] OJ L13/50 [1972] CMLR D67 ... 860

Butadiene Rubber and Emulsion Styrene Butadiene Rubber Cartel (Case COMP/F/38.638) ... 966, 1013

Calcium Carbide cartel (Case COMP/39.396), [2009] OJ C301/18, IP/09/1169 ... 1013, 1016

Campari [1978] OJ L70/69, [1978] 2 CMLR 397 ... 195, 254, **909–911**, 913

Candle Waxes Cartel (Case COMP/C.39181) [2009] OJ C 295/17 ... 63, 1277

Cannes Extension Agreement IP/06/1311 ... 983

Carlsberg/Interbrew, XXIVth Report on Competition Policy ... 557

Cartel in Aniline Dyes, Re [1969] OJ L195/11, [1969] CMLR D23 ... 710, 1272

Cartonboard [1994] OJ L243/1, [1995] 5 CMLR 547 ... 681, 685, 714, 716, 1019, 1050, 1216

Cast Iron and Steel Rolls [1983] OJ L317/1, [1984] 1 CMLR 694 ... 679, 695

Caterpillar/MWM (Case M.6106) ... 1169

CCIE/GTE (Case M.258) ... 1142

Cement cartel [1994] OJ L343/1, [1995] 4 CMLR 327 ... 1030, 1037, 1047, 1050

Centradia IP 02/943 ... 709

CEPI/Cartonboard [1996] OJ C310/3 ... 705

CEWAL [1993] OJ L34/2, [1995] 5 CMLR 198 ... 287, 421, 423, 718, 720–724

Charles Jourdan [1989] OJ L35/31 ... 816

Chiquita/Fyffes IP(92)461 ... 913

Cimbell, Re [1972] OJ L303/24 ... 703

CISAC Agreement, 16 July 2008 ... 147

CISC Agreement (Case COMP/38.698) [2009] 4 CMLR 577 ... 635, 757, 920

Clearstream Banking AG and Clearstream International SA, COMP/38.096. IP/04/705, 2 June 2004 ... 74, 523, 999

CNSD [1993] OJ L203/27 ... 138

Cobelpa/VNP [1977] OJ L242/10 ... 703

Coca-Cola [2005] OJ L253/21 ... 492

Coca-Cola Company/Carlsberg A/S (Case M.833), [1998] OJ L145/41 ... 1188, 1209–1210, 1230

Coca-Cola Enterprises/Amalgamated Beverages (Case IV/M.794) [1997] OJ L218/15 ... 462, 1230

Coca-Cola, XIXth Report on Competition Policy ... 462

Compagnie Maritime Belge [2005] OJ L171/28 ... 422, 724, 1045

Concordato Incendio [1990] OJ L15/25, [1991] 4 CMLR 199 ... 696, 763

Concrete Reinforcing Bars *see* Italian Concrete Reinforcing Bars

Connex/DNVBVG (Case COMP/M.2370) ... 1161–1162

Consumer Detergents, 13 April 2011 ... **175**, 232, 257, 695, 697

Continental Can Co Inc., Re [1972] OJ L7/25, [1972] CMLR D11 ... 277, 299, 355, 367

Covisint IP/01/1155 ... 709

Danone/Numico (Case COMP/M.4842) ... **1199**

Danone/Numico (Case M.4842) ... 1197

Davidson Rubber Co, Re Agreements of [1972] OJ L143/31 [1972] CMLR D52 ... 860

De Beers/ALROSA (Case COMP/B-2/38.381) [2006] OJ L205/24 ... 273, **983–984**

De Laval-Stork, [1977] OJ L215/11 ... 195, 253

De Poste-La Poste [2002] OJ L61/32, [2002] 4 CMLR 1426 … 393–394, 652

Decca Navigator [1989] OJ L43/7, [1990] 4 CMLR 627 … 355

Deloitte & Touche/Andersen (UK (Case IV/M.2810) … 1220

Deutsche Bahn/EWS (Case M.4746) … 1199

Deutsche Börse/NYSE Euronext (Case M.6166) … 51, 1198, 1255

Deutsche Bundesligia [2005] OJ L134/46, [2005] 5 CMLR 1715 … 113

Deutsche Post AG [2001] OJ L125/27, [2001] 5 CMLR 99 … 407, 417, 419, 458

Deutsche Post AG [2001] OJ L331/40, [2002] 4 CMLR 598 Interception of cross-border mail … 375, 510, 569, 578

DFB [2005] OJ L134/46 … 766

Digital Undertaking, Commission Press Release IP/97/868 … 273, 492, 567, 993

Distillers Company Ltd [1978] OJ L50/16 … 792

Distillers Company plc (Red Label) [1983] OJ C245/3, [1983] 3 CMLR 173 … 792

Distribution of Package Tours During the 1990 World Cup [1992] OJ L326/31 … 127–128, 138

Distrigaz (Case COMP/B-1/337.96)6 [2008] OJ C9/8 … 273, 983

DONG/Elsam/Energie E2 (Case COMP/M.3868) … 1240

Dow Chemical Company (Case IV/M.663) … 144

DRAMS (Case COMP/38.511), IP/10/586 … 993

DSD [2001] OJ L166/1 … 580, 582

DSD (exemption) [2001] OJ L319/1, [2002] 4 CMLR 405 … 257–258, 762

Duales System Deutschland AG (DSD) [2001] OJ L166/1, [2001] 5 CMLR 609 … 579, 582–583, 999

Dutch Courier Services [1990] OJ L10/47, [1990] 4 CMLR 947 … 637, 641

Dutch Cranes [1995] OJ L 312/79 … 760

Dutch Express Delivery Services [1994] OJ L10/47 … 584, 628

Dutch Industrial and Medical Gases [2003] OJ L84/1 … 151

Ebooks (Case 39.847), IP/12/1367 … 982

Eco-Emballages [2001] OJ L233/37 … 257, 762

ECS/AKZO: interim measures [1985] OJ L374/1, [1986] 3 CMLR 273 … 358, 404, 406

EDF/London Electricity (Case M.1346) … 1165

EDF - Long Term Electricity Contracts in France Commitments Decision 17 March 2010, IP/10/290 … 273, 983

EDP/ENI/GDP (Case COMP/M.3440) … 1225

EFIM (Case COMP/C-3/39.391), 20 May 2009 … 321

Electrabel/CNR (Case M.4994) … 1142

Electrolux/AEG (Case IV/M.458) … 75

Elopak Italia/Tetra Pak [1991] OJ L72/1, [1992] 4 CMLR 551 … 319, 330–331, 347, 491, 556

ENEL/DT/FT (Case IV/Jv. 2) … 1242

ENI (Case COMP/39.315), 29 September 2010 … 273, 386, 521–522

Enso/Stora (Case M.1225), [1999] OJ L254/9 … 359, 1191, 1209, 1216

E.ON (Case COMP/B-1/39.326) Press Release IP/08/2008 … 948

E.On/Endesa (Case COMP/M.4110) … 1151, 1167

E.ON/MOL (Case COMP/M.3696) … 1225

EPH (Case COMP/39.793), IP/12/319 … 943, 947

Ernst & Young/Andersen Germany (Case IV/M.2824) … 1220

Ernst & Young France/Andersen France and (Case IV/M.2816) … 1220

Eurex IP/02/4 … 709

Eurocheque: Helsinki Agreement [1992] OJ L95/50, [1993] 5 CMLR 323 … 682, 691

Eurofirma, Re [1973] CMLR D217 … 300

Eurofix-Bauco/Hilti [1988] OJ L65/19, [1989] 4 CMLR 677 … 319, **353–354**, 356–358, 421, 486–487, **490–491**, 584

Europay (Eurocard-MasterCard), 19 December 2007 … 147, 221

European Champions League case *see* Joint Selling of commercial rights to the UEFA Champions League

European Council of Manufacturers of Domestic Appliances [2000] OJ L187/47 … 257, 695, 697, 761

European Night Services [1994] OJ L259/20, [1995] 5 CMLR 76 … 517, 675, 734

European Sugar Cartel, Re [1973] OJ L140/17, [1973] CMLR D65 … 689

Eutilia/Endorsia IP/01/1775 … 709

Express Dairies/Arla Foods (Case COMP/M.3130) … 1163

Exxon/Shell [1994] OJ L144/20 … 257

Fabricants de Papiers Peints de Belgique [1974] OJ L237/3, [1974] 2 CMLR D102 … 696

FAG-Flughafen Frankfurt/Main AG [1998] OJ L72/30, [1998] 4 CMLR 779 … 283

Film Purchases by German Television Stations [1989] OJ L284/96, [1990] 4 CMLR 841 … 916

Fine Art Auction Houses IP/02/1585, COMP/E-2/37.784, [2006] 4 CMLR 90 … 682, 695

Fire Insurance [1985] OJ L35/20 … 763

Flat Glass [1989] OJ L33/44 … 278

Flat Glass IP/07/1781 … 280, **717–718**, **723**, 1202

Football World Cup 1998 *see* 1998 World Cup Finals

Ford/Volkswagen [1993] OJ L20/14 ... 253, 256

French Beef [2003] OJ L209/12, [2005] 5 CMLR 891 ... 128, 187, 681

French State/Suralmo, IXth Report on Competition Policy (Commission, 1979), part 114 ... 857

French-West African Shipowners' Committees [1992] OJ L134/1, [1993] 5 CMLR 446 ... 279, 718, 723

Fujitsu/Siemens (Case IV/Jv. 22), [1999] OJ C318/15 ... **1242–1244**

Gas [2009] OJ C248/5 ... 688

Gas Insulated Switchgear cartel COMP/38.899, IP/07/80, 24 January 2007 ... 672, 682, 690

Gas Natural/Endesa (Case COMP/M.3986) ... 1167

Gaz de France/Suez (Case M.4180) ... 1240

GDF commitments decision, gas markets in France (Case COMP/39.316) [2009] C57/13, IP/09/1872 ... 273, 522, 983

GE/AGFA NDT (Case M.3136), IP/03/1666 ... 1169

GE/Honeywell (Case COMP/M.2220) ... 1214, 1223–1224, 1226, **1230–1232**, 1234, **1250**, 1255, **1285–1286**, 1290

GE/Instrumentarium Case (Case COMP/M.3083), IP/03/1193 ... 1195, 1199, **1250**

GE/Smiths Group (Case COMP/M.4561) ... 1165

GEAE/P&W [2000] OJ L58/16 ... 749

GEES/Unison (Case M.2738) ... 1169

GEMA [1971] OJ L134/15, [1971] CMLR D35 ... 583, 635

Gencor/Lonrho (Case IV/M.619) [1997] OJ L11/30, [1999] 4 CMLR 107 ... 70, 1174, 1189, 1206, 1255, **1279**

Generics/AstraZeneca (Case COMP/A.37.507.F3), IP/05/737 ... 82, 322, 360, 374, 558, 565

German Banks [2003] OJ L15/1, [2003] 4 CMLR 842 ... 682

German Electricity Balancing Markets (E.ON) (Case COMP/39.389) [2009] OJ C 36/8 ... 273, 522, 584, 983

German Electricity Wholesale Markets (Case COMP/39.388) ... 584, 983

Goodyear Italiana-Euram, [1975] OJ L38/10 ... 195, 254

Google (Case COMP/39.740), IP/13/371, MEMO/13/383, 25 April 2013 ... 81, 91, 273–274, 357, 565–566, 569, 983, 1226, 1237

Google/DoubleClick (Case M.4371) ... 1237

Google/Motorola (Case M.6381) ... 1226, 1247

Gosmé/Martell-DMP [1991] OJ L185/21 ... 146

Govia/Connex South Central (Case COMP/M.2446) ... 1161

Graphite Electrodes [2002] OJ L100/1, [2002] 5 CMLR 829 ... 177, 681, 956, 1004

Greek Lignite and Electricity Markets (Case COMP/38.700), [2009] 4 CMLR 495 ... 285, 447, 605, 618–620, 630

Grohe [1985] OJ L19/17, [1988] 4 CMLR 612 ... 809–810

Groupement des Cartes Bancaires (Case COMP/38.606) ... 764

Grundig [1985] OJ L233/1, renewed [1994] OJ L20/15, [1995] 4 CMLR 658 ... 809–811

Grundig [1994] OJ L20/15 ... 811

Guinness/Grand Metropolitan (Case IV/M.938) [1998] OJ L288/24 ... 70, 1230, **1237–1238**

GVG\fS [2004] OJ L11/17, [2004] CMLR 1446 ... 522

GVL [1981] OJ L370/49 ... 335

Haniel/Fels (Case M.2495) ... 1162

Haniel/Ytong (Case M.2568) ... 1162

Hasselblad AG [1982] OJ L161/18, [1982] 2 CMLR 233 ... 792, 810–812

Hershey/Schiffers, Commission Press Release IP/90/87 ... 913

Hoffmann-La Roche/Boehringer Mannheim (Case M.950) ... 1251

Holdercim/Cedest (Case M.460) ... 1163

HP/Compaq (Case M.2609) ... 1209

Hutchinson 3G Austria/Orange Austria (Case M.6497) ... 1192, 1195–1196

IAG/bmi (Case M.6447) ... 1196

Iberia/British Airways (Case M.5747) ... 1196

IBM [1984] OJ L118/24, [1984] 2 CMLR 342 ... 493, 810, 1031

IBM Maintenance Services (Case COMP/39.692), 13 December 2011 ... 273, 510, 521, 525, 582, 982–983

IFTRA Aluminium OJ 1975 L228/3 ... 703

IFTRA Rules on Glass Containers [1974] OJ L160/1, [1974] 2 CMLR D50 ... 679, 691, 703

IJsselcentrale [1991] OJ L28/3 ... 146

Ilmailulaitos/Luftsfartverket (Finnish Airports) [1999] OJ L69/24, [1999] 5 CMLR 90 ... 283

Inco/Falconbridge (Case COMP/M.4000) ... 1216

Independent Watches Repairers, (COMP/39.097), IP/11/952 ... 80

Industrial Gases Cartel decision [2003] OJ L84/1 ... 1017

Ineos/Kerling (Case M.4734) ... 1176, 1179, 1193

Info-LabCase IV/36431 ... 320–321, 521

Inreon IP/02/761 ... 709

Intel (Case COMP/C-3/37.990), [2010] OJ C227/13, [2010] 4 CMLR 314 ... 273, 293, 304, 340, 354, 356, 358–359, 385, 456, **482–483**, **557**, 975, 999, 1012

Intel/McAfee (Case M.5984)...1238, 1250, 1255

Interbrew/Bass (Case IV/M.2044) [2000] OJ C293/11, IP/00/940...1163

International Energy Program [1983] OJ L376/30...708

IRI/Nielsen, XXXVIth Report on Competition Policy (1996) part 64...451

Irish Continental Group v. CCI Morlaix (Port of Roscoff) [1995] 5 CMLR 177...**282–283**, 515–516

Irish Sugar [1997] OJ L258/1, [1997] 5 CMLR 666...187, 327, 423, 443, 462, 464, 557, 571, 718, 720, 724–725, 1202

Italian Concrete Reinforcing Bars (Case COMP/37.956), 30 September 2009...110, 1033

Italian GSM [1995] OJ L280/49...628

Italian Raw Tobacco, Comp/38.2101, [2006] 4 CMLR 1766...1020

J&J/Pfizer (Case M.4314)...**1230**

Jaz/Peter [1969] OJ L195/5, [1970] CMLR 129...746

JCB [2002] OJ L69/1, [2002] 4 CMLR 1458...792

JCI/FIAMM (Case COMP/M.4381)...1198

Johnson & Johnson/Guidant (Case COMP/M.3687)...1209

Joint selling of commercial rights to the UEFA Champions League [2003] OJ L291/25, [2004] 4 CMLR 9...693, 919

Joint selling of the media rights to the FA Premier League, 22 March 2006, [2006] 5 CMLR 1430...113

Junghans [1977] OJ L30/10...810

Kabel und Metallwerke Neumeyer AG and Etablissements Luchaire SA Agreement [1975] OJ L222/34...259

Kali und Salz/MdK/Treuhand (Case IV/M.308) [1994] OJ L186/30, [1994] 4 CMLR 526...1201, **1217–1218**, 1250

KarstadtQuelle/MyTravel (Case M.4601)...1184, 1206

Kesko/Tuko (Case M.784), [1997] OJ L174/47...1169, 1179

KLM/Martinair (Case M.1328)...1196

Kodak [1970] OJ L142/24, [1970] CMLR D19...812, 1269

Konica [1988] OJ L78/34...792

Konsortium ECR 900 [1990] OJ L228/31, [1992] 4 CMLR 54...738

Körsnäs/AssiDomän Cartonboard (Case COMP/M.4057), IP/06/610...1209, **1216**

Kronospan/Constantia (Case M.4525)...1198

Kyowa/Saitama Banks [1992] 4 CMLR 1186...1278

La Banque Postale, les Caisses d'Épargne et de Prévoyance and the Crédit Mutuel, for the distribution of the Livret A and Livret Bleu Commission Decision C (2007) 2110 Final of 10 May 2007...637

La Poste/Swiss Post/JV (Case M.6503)...1248

Lagardère/Natexis/VUP (Case M.2978), 7 January 2004...1148, 1163

Langnese-Iglo [1993] OJ L183/19, [1994] 4 CMLR 51...265, 803–804

Langnese-Iglo GmbH [1993] OJ L183/19...803–804

LdPE cartel (low-density polyethylene [1989] OJ L74/21, [1990] 4 CMLR 382...1035

Liberty Global/Kabel Baden-Württemberg (Case M.5900)...1162

Liptons Cash Registers/Hugin [1978] OJ L22/23, [1978] CMLR D19...318

London European-Sabena [1988] OJ L317/47, [1989] 4 CMLR 662...327, 514–515

London Stock Exchange/LCH Clearnet Group (Case M.6502)...1175

Lufthansa/Eurowings (Case M.3940)...1197

Lufthansa/SN Airholding (Brussels Airline) (Case M.5335)...1196

Lufthansa/Swiss (Case M.3280)...1197

Lundbeck (Case COMP/39226) 19 June 2013...906

Luxembourg Brewers [2002] OJ L253/21...184, 688, 690, 1004

Lyonnaise des Eaux SA/Northumbrian Water Group (Case IV/M.567)...1165

McCormick/CPC/Ostmann (Case M.330)...1161

MCI WorldCom/Sprint (Case COMP/M.1741)...1148, **1198–1199**, 1222

Magill TV Guide [1989] OJ L78/43, [1989] 4 CMLR 757...**528**

Maize Seeds [1978] OJ L286/23, [1978] 3 CMLR 434...**859–860**

Mannesmann/Hoesch (Case IV/M.222) [1993] OJ L114/34...1162

Mannesmann/Vallourec/Ilva (Case IV/M.315) [1994] OJ L102/15, [1994] 4 CMLR 529...1210, 1240

Marine Hoses Cartel (Case COMP/39.406) [2010] 4 CMLR 148...952, 1009

MasterCard, 19 December 2007, COMP/34.579 [2009] OJ C264/8...72, 81, 764, 1269

Matsushita/MCA [1992] 4 CMLR M36...1278

MBB/Aerospatiale (Case M.17) [1991] OJ C59/13...1142

Meldoc [1986] OJ L348/50...690

Mercedes-Benz [2002] OJ L257/1...792–793

Mercedes-Benz/Kässbohrer (Case IV/M.477) [1995] OJ L211/1, [1995] 4 CMLR 600...1209

Metal Box/Elopak (ODIN) [1990] OJ L209/15, [1991] 4 CMLR 832...738

Methionine Cartel [2003] OJ L255/1...1028

Methylglucamine [2004] OJ L38/18, [2004] 4 CMLR 1591...688, 699, 1014

Metso/Aker Kvoerner (Case COMP/M.4187)...1216

Michelin [1981] OJ L353/33, [1982] 1 CMLR 643...311, 326

Michelin [2001] OJ L143/1, [2002] 5 CMLR 388 (Michelin II)...73, 288, 311–312, 328–329, 339, 454, **463–464**, 468–470, 483

Microsoft, Commission Decision of 12 July 2006, C(2006)4420, IP/06/076...996

Microsoft, COMP/C-3/37.792...45, 67, 74, 78, 289, 317, 340, 345, 358, 362, 396, **493–494**, 516, 537, 580, 981, 996

Microsoft IP(94)653 17 July 1994, [1994] 5 CMLR 143...582

Microsoft/Skype (Case M.6281)...1238, 1253

Microsoft (Tying) (Case COMP/39.530), IP/13/2013...273, 982–983, 989, 996

Moosehead/Whitbread [1990] OJ L100/32, [1991] 4 CMLR 391...877, **912–913**

Morgan Stanley/Visa (Case COMP/37.860)...81, 764, 980, 1076

Morgan Stanley/Visa International and Visa Europe (Case COMP/C), 3 October 2007...980, 1076

Motorola (Case COMP/39.986), IP/12/345...273, 565, 908

Motorola Mobility, IP/13/406, 6 May 2013...564, 732, 758

MSG Media Service GmbH (Case M.469), [1994] OJ L364/1...1240, 1248

Murat [1983] OJ L348/20...810

Napier Brown/British Sugar [1988] OJ L284/41, [1990] 4 CMLR 196...327, 408, 426, 489, 507, 510, 513

National Carbonising [1976] OJ L35/6, [1976] 1 CMLR D82...426, 444, 515

National Sulphuric Acid [1980] OJ L260/24...174, 754

NDC Health/IMS Health: Interim Measures [2002] OJ L59/18, [2002] 4 CMLR 111...358, **531–532**, 535, 991–992

Nestlé/Gerber Case (Case COMP/M.4688)...1191, **1238**

Nestlé/Perrier (Case IV/M.190) [1992] OJ L356/1, [1993] 4 CMLR M17...64, 70, 91, 327, 358, 719, 1191, 1200

Nestlé/Ralston Purina (Case IV/M.2337), IP/01/1136...**1251**

Newitt/Dunlop Slazenger International [1992] OJ L131/32, [1993] 5 CMLR 352...792

Newscorp/Telepiù (Case IV/M.2876) IP/03/478...82, 1220–1221, 1251

Newspaper Publishing (Case IV/M.423)...1165

Nintendo [2003] OJ L255/33, [2004] 4 CMLR 421...793, 835, 1015–1016

Nokia/Navteq (Case COMP/M.4942)...1226

Nordic Satellite Distribution (Case IV/M.490) [1990] OJ L53/21, [1995] CMLR 258...1248

Northrop Grumman/Litton Industries (Case COMP/M.2308), IP/01/438...1167

Novalliance/Systemform [1997] OJ L47/11, [1997] 4 CMLR 876...792

Novartis/Hexal (Case M.3658)...1195

Nuovo CEGAM [1984] OJ L99/29, [1984] 2 CMLR 484...150, 763

Nutreco/BASF (Case M.4617)...1191

Olympic Air/Aegean Airlines (Case M.5830)...1196, 1211

Omya/ Huber (Case M.3796), IP/06/1017...1169

ONP (Case COMP/39.510)...997

Opel Nederland [2001] OJ L59/1...1040

Optical Fibres [1986] OJ L236/30...**736–737**

Oracle/Sun Microsystems (Case M.5529)...1231, 1247

Organic Peroxides [2005] OJ L110/44...666, 675, 973, 999

Outokumpu/Inoxum (Case M.6471)...1248

Oxford University Press, Burlington Books, and Pearson PLC (Case COMP/39771) 10 October 2012...844

P & I Clubs [1985] OJ L376/2, [1989] 4 CMLR 178...128, 252

P and I Clubs [1999] OJ L125/12...584

P&O Princess/Carnival (Case M.2706)...1158

Parfums Givenchy [1992] OJ L236/11, [1993] 5 CMLR 579...809–812, 832

Pelikan/Kyocera (1995) XXVth Competition Report part 87, [1997] OJ C372/5...320–321, 493

PepsiCo/General Mills (Case M.232)...1188

Peroxygen Products [1985] OJ L35/1, [1985] 1 CMLR 481...666, 687

Peugeot IP/05/1227...792, 844

Philips/Osram [1994] OJ l378/37...749

Philips VCR (Case IV/29/151)...760

Pioneer [1980] OJ L60/1, [1980] 1 CMLR 457...172, 933, 968, 998, 1000–1002, 1005, 1014, 1017, 1040

Plasterboard [2005] OJ L166/8...679

PO Video Games (Case COMP./35.38)7, [2003] OJ L255/33, [2004] 4 CMLR 421...793, 835, 1015–1016

Polaroid/SSI XIIIth Report on Competition Policy (Commission, 1983)...584

Polypropylene Cartel [1986] OJ L230/1, [1988] 4 CMLR 347...165, 167, 170, 177, 679, 942, 1002, 1035

Port of Rødby [1994] OJ L55/52, [1994] 5 CMLR 457...283, 515–516, 629–630, 654

Port of Roscoff see Irish Continental Group v. CCI Morlaix

Pre-Insulated Pipe Cartel [1999] OJ L24/1, [1998] 4 CMLR 402 ... 137, 690, 757, 1005

Procter & Gamble/Gillette (Case COMP/M.3732) ... 1209, 1216

Professional Videotape (Case COMP/38.432) ... 1015–1016

Prokent/Tomra, COMP/38.113, IP/06/398, 29 March 2006 ... 337, 339, 345, **360**, 478, 483

Pronuptia [1987] OJ L13/39, [1989] 4 CMLR 355 ... 816

ProSiebenSat.1/RTL/JV (Case M.5881) ... 1162

Publishers' Association-Net Book Agreement [1989] OJ L22/12, [1989] 4 CMLR 825 ... 680

PVC Cartel II [1994] OJ L239/14 ... 168, 950, 955, 968, 970–971, 994, 997, 1003, 1035, 1047

Quinine Cartel [1969] OJ L192/5, [1969] CMLR D41 ... 684, 1000

RAI/UNITEL [1978] OJ L157/39 ... 128

Rambus, commitments decision COMP/38.636, 9 September 2009, [2010] OJ C30/17 ... 273, 563, 581, 732, 758, 908, 982, 989

Raymond/Nagoya [1972] OJ L143/39, [1972] CMLR D45 ... 860

Redland/Lefarge (Case M.1030) ... 1162

Renault/Volvo (Case IV/M.4) [1990] OJ C281/2 ... 1191, 1209

Repsol Butano/Shell Gas (Case M.3664) ... 1216

Reuter/BASF [1976] OJ L254/40 ... 128

Reuters/Telerate (Case M.3692) ... 1207

Rewe/Meinl (Case M.1221), [1999] OJ L274/1 ... 1221

Roberts/Greene King IP/98/967 ... 805

Rockwood/Süd-Chemie (Case COMP/M.3910) ... 1220

RTL/Veronica/Endemol (Case M.553), [1996] OJ L294/14 ... 1169

RWE - Gas Foreclosure (Case COMP/39.402), 18 March 2009 ... 273, 445, 511, 522, 983

Ryanair/Aer Lingus [2008] 4 CMLR 667 ... 70

Ryanair/Aer Lingus (Case COMP/M.4439) ... 1143, 1193, **1196–1198, 1210–1211, 1216**

Ryanair/Aer Lingus (Case M.6663) ... 1193, **1196**

Saab/Celsius (Case COMP/M.1797) IP/00/118 ... 1167

Saint Gobain/Wacker-Chemie/NOM (Case IV/M.774) [1997] OJ L247/1, [1997] 4 CMLR 25 ... 1220

Saint Gobain/Wacker-Chemie/NOM (Case M.774), [1997] OJ L247/1 ... 1209

Samsung [1999] OJ L225/12, [1998] 4 CMLR 494 ... 1284

Samsung (Case IV/M. 920) ... 1176

Samsung, IP/12/1448, 21 December 2012 ... 564, 732, 758

Sandoz [1987] OJ L222/28 ... 159, **999**

Sanitec/Sphinx (Case M.1578), [2000] OJ L294/1 ... 1189, 1217

Santander/Bradford & Bingley (Case M.5363) ... 1176

SAS/Maersk [2001] OJ L265/15, [2001] 5 CMLR 1119 ... 687, 952

Scandlines Sverige v. Port of Helsingborg (Case COMP/36.568) [2006] 4 CMLR 1298 ... 579–580

Schneider/Legrand (Case COMP/M.2282), IP/01/1393 ... 1050, 1176, 1178–1179, 1234, **1248**

Schneider /Legrand II (Case COMP/M.2283) ... 1234

Schöller Lebensmittel GmbH & Co KG [1993] OJ L183/1, [1994] 4 CMLR 51 ... 803–804

SCJ/Sara Lee (Insecticides and Airfresheners) (Cases M.5969 and M.5895) ... 1169

Scottish and Newcastle [1999] OJ L186/28 ... 1096

Sea Containers Ltd v. Stena Sealink Ports [1994] OJ L15/8, [1995] 4 CMLR 84 ... 282, 515, 992

Scalink/B&I Holyhead: Interim Measures [1992] 5 CMLR 255 ... 282, 327, 355, 510, **514–515**, 992

Seamless Steel Tubes [2003] OJ L140/1 ... 687, 955

SEB/Moulinex (Case COMP/M.2621), IP/02/22 ... 1163, 1220

Secit/Holderbank/Cimpor (Case COMP/M.2054) ... 1165

ServiceMaster [1988] OJ L332/38 ... 816

SFR/Télé 2 France (Case COMP/M.4504) ... 1225

Shell/DEA (Case COMP/M.2398) ... 1158, 1184

Shell/Montecatani (Case M.269), [1994] OJ L332/48 ... 1189, 1210

Ship Classification (Case COMP/39.416), COMP/39.416 Commitments decision, 14 October 2009 ... 760

Sicasov [1999] OJ L4/27, [1999] 4 CMLR 192 ... 864

Siemens/Philips (Case M.238), [1993] OJ C11/5 ... 1162

Siemens/VA Tech (Case M.3653) ... 1249

Sirdar/Phildar [1975] OJ L125/27 ... 913

Skanska/Scancem (Case IV/M.1157) [1999] OJ L183/1 ... 1210

Slovakian Hybrid Mail Services decision (Case COMP/39.562), [2009] 4 CMLR 663 ... 584, 610, 616, 629, 651

Société Générale de Belgique/Générale de Banque (Case IV/M.343) ... 1142

Soda Ash [1991] OJ L152/1, [1994] 4 CMLR 454, readopted [2003] OJ L10/1 ... 150–151, 347, 357, 459, 666, 687, 1035

Soda-Ash-ICI [2003] OJ L10/33 ... 450, 459

Soda Ash-Solvay [2003] OJ L10/10 ... 150–151, 347, 357, 459, 666, 687, 1035

Sogecable/Canalsatelite Digital/Via Digital (Case COMP/M.2845) ... 1220

Solvay/LaPorte (Case M.197), [1992] OJ C165/26 ... 1153

Sony/Mubsadala/EMI Music (Case M.6459)...1208

Sony/SonyBMG (Case COMP.M/5272)...1207

Sovion/HMG (Case M.3605)...82

Spanish Airports [2000] OJ L208/36, [2000] 5 CMLR 967...283, 569

Spanish Courier Services [1990] OJ L233/19, [1991] 4 CMLR 560...129, 610, 637, 654

Spanish GSM [1997] OJ L79/19...628

Spring [2000] OJ L195/49, [2000] 5 CMLR 948...786

Standard & Poor's (US International Securities Identification Numbering) (Case COMP/39.592), 15 December 2011...273, 581

Steel Beams COMP.38/907, 8 November 2006...1035

Steetley plc/Tarmac (Case IV/M.180) [1992] 4 CMLR 337...1161–1162

Stichting Baksteen [1994] OJ L131/15...257

Stichting Certificatie Kraanverhuurbedrijf and Federatie van Nederlandse Kraanbedrijven [1995] OJ L312/79...174, 184

STX/Aker Yards (Case COMP/M.4956)...1176

Südzucker/ED&F MAN (Case M.6286)...1249

Sun Alliance/Royal Insurance (Case COMP/M.759)...1165

Supporters Juventus Turin-FIGC-CONI-UEFA-FIFA (Case COMP/39.464)...113

Svenska Tobaks, XXVIIth Report on Competition Policy...557

SWIFT, XXVIIth Report on Competition Policy...523

Synthetic Fibres [1984] OJ L207/17, [1985] 1 CMLR 787...257, 260

Synthetic Rubber IP/06/1851...680, 688

T-Mobile/tele.ring (Case COMP/M.3916)...**1195–1196**

Telekomunikacja Polska (Case COMP/39.525, 22 June 2011...337, 357, 385, 387, 510, 521

Telenor/Canal+/Canal Digital 29 December 2003...840

Telia/Telenor/Schibsted (Case IV/Jv. 2), [1999] OJ C178/15...**1242**

Telos (Case IV/29.895), [1982] OJ L58/19...1179

Tesco/Carrefour (Case M.3905)...1162

Tetra Laval/Sidel (Case COMP/M.2416), IP/01/1516...1179, 1188, 1223, **1230**, **1234–1235**, 1250, 1253

Tetra Laval/SIG Simonazzi (Case M.3746)...1195

Tetra Pak/Alfa Laval (Case IV/M.68) [1991] OJ L290/35, [1992] 4 CMLR M81...1191, 1210

Tetra Pak/BTG [1988] OJ L272/27...265, 294, 326, 332

Tetra Pak I [1988] OJ L272/37, [1990] 4 CMLR 97...358

Tetra Pak II [1992] OJ L72/1, [1992] 4 CMLR 551...486–487, 490–492, 1002, 1188

Thales/DCN (Case M.4191)...1167

Thomas Cook/CGL and Midland (Case M.5996)...1162

Thomson CSF/Racal (Case M.1858), IP/00/628...1165, 1167

Thyssen/Krupp (Case M.1080)...1167

Time-Warner/AOL (Case COMP/M.1845), IP/00/1145...**1225**, 1249

Toltecs/Dorcet [1982] OJ L379/19, [1983] 1 CMLR 412...913

TomTom/Tele Atlas (Case COMP/M.4854)...1226

Torras/Sarrio, Case IV/M.166 (1992)...75

Total/PetroFina (Case M.1388)...1162

Total/Sasol/JV (Case M.3637)...1198

Transatlantic Conference Agreement (TACA) [1999] OJ L95/1, [1999] 4 CMLR 1415...279–280, 557, 718, 722–725, 1019, 1034–1035

Transocean Marine Paint Associations [1967] OJ L/10...835

Travelport/Worldspan Case (Case COMP/M4523)...1193

Tretorn [1994] OJ L378/45...792

TUI/First Choice (Case COMP/M.4600)...1184, 1191, 1206

UEFA [1999] OJ C363/2...113

UEFA Champions League [2003] OJ L291/25, [2004] 4 CMLR 549...693, 766

UIP [1989] OJ L226/25...757

UK Agricultural Tractor Exchange [1992] OJ L68/19, [1994] 3 CMLR 358...174, 703–704

Ukwal [1992] OJ L121/45, [1993] 5 CMLR 632...1286

Uniform Eurocheques [1985] OJ L35/43, [1985] 3 CMLR 434...635, 682

Universal/BMG (Case M.4404)...1193

Universal/EMI Music (Case M.6458)...1208

Universal Music Group/EMI (Case M.6458)...1207–1208

UPM.Myllykoski/ Rhein Papier (Case M.6101)...1198

UPS/TNT Express (Case M.6570)...1248, 1255

UTC/Goodrich (Case M.6410)...1248

Vaassen BV/Moris [1979] OJ L19/32, [1979] 1 CMLR 511...128, 486–487

Vacuum Interrupters, [1977] OJ L48/32...195, 735

Van den Bergh (Irish Ice Cream) [1998] OJ L246/1, [1998] 5 CMLR 539...73, 263, 294, 317, 451, 999

Varta/Bosch (Case IV/M.12) [1991] OJ L320/26, [1992] 5 CMLR M1...1162, 1191

VBBB and VBVB [1982] OJ L54/36...260

VEBA/Degusa (Case M.492), [1994] OJ C303/5...1249

Vegetable Parchment [1978] OJ L70/54...999

Villeroy & Bosch [1985] OJ L 376/15, [1998] 4 CMLR 461...810–811

Virgin/BA [2000] OJ L30/1, [2000] 4 CMLR 999 ... 323, 359, 394, 398, 454, 463, **469–470**, 505, 572, 1033

Visa (Case COMP/39.398) ... 764, 1269

Visa International-Multilateral Interchange Fee [2002] OJ L318/17, [2003] 4 CMLR 283 ... 147, 221, 691, 764

Vitamins [2003 OJ L6/1, [2003] 4 CMLR 1030 ... 682, 1015, 1265

Vodafone/Airtouch (Case M.1430) ... 1210

Volkswagen [1998] OJ L124/60, [1998] 5 CMLR 33 ... 155, 162, 792–793, 834, 1004

Volvo/Scania (Case IV/M.1672) [2001] OJ L143/74 ... 70, 1195, 1240

Votorantim/ Fischer (Case M.5907) ... 1198

VW-Passat [2001] OJ L262/14, [2001] 5 CMLR 1309 ... 162

Wanadoo COMP/38.233, [2005] 5 CMLR 120 ... 74, 78, 312, 337, 406, 420

Wanadoo España/Telefónica COMP/38.784 ... 45, 354, 357, 392, 427, 441, 522

Water Portal IP/02/956 ... 709

Welded Steel Mesh cartel [1989] OJ L260/1, [1991] 4 CMLR 13 ... 994, 1003

Whitbread [1999] OJ L88/26, [1999] 5 CMLR 118 ... 786, 804, 877, 912, 1096

Windsurfing International [1982] OJ L229/1, [1984] 1 CMLR 1 ... 865

Wirtschaftsvereinigung Stahl [1998] OJ L1/10, [1998] 4 CMLR 450 ... 706

Wood Pulp [1985] OJ L85/1, [1985] 3 CMLR 474 ... 1275, 1286

Wood Pulp Cartel, Re see Ahlström Oy

Wood Pulp Producers [1985] OJ L85/1, [1985] 3 CMLR 474 ... 712, 1046, 1275

WorldCom/MCI (Case IV/M.1069) [1999] OJ L116/1, [1999] 5 CMLR 876 ... 82

Worldspan/Travelport (Case M.4523) ... 1206

X/Open Group (Case IV/31.458) ... 760

Yamaha IP/03/1028 ... 789, 792

Yara/Kemira GrowHow (Case COMP/M.4730) ... 1142–1143, 1176

Yves Rocher [1987] OJ L8/49 ... 816

Yves Saint Laurent [1992] OJ L12/24 ... 810–812

Zanussi [1978] OJ L322/26 ... 792

Zinc Phosphate [2003] OJ L153/1 ... 685

Zinc Producer Group [1984] OJ L220/7, [1985] 2 CMLR 108 ... 680, 703, 711

GENERAL COURT (ALPHABETICAL TABLE)

AC-Treuhand AG v. Commission (Case T-99/04) [2008] ECR II-1501 ... 102, 150, 153–155, 171, 176, 199, 292, 675, 933, 938, 999

Adriatica di Navigazione v. Commission (Case T-61/99) [2003] ECR II-5349 ... 63

Aer Lingus v. Commission (Case T-411/07) [2010] ECR II-3457 ... 1143, 1196

Aeroporia Aigaiou Aeroporiki v. Commission (Case T-202/11) (pending) ... 1196, 1211

Aeroports de Paris v. Commission (Case T-128/98) [2000] ECR II-3929, [2001] 4 CMLR 611 ... 569

Air France v. Commission (Case T-2/93) [1994] ECR II-323 ... 1142, 1253

Air Inter v. Commission (Case T-260/94) [1997] ECR II-997, [1997] 5 CMLR 851 ... **648–649**

Airtours plc v. Commission (Case T-342/99) [2002] ECR II-2585, [2002] 5 CMLR 317 ... 57, 102–103, 106, 278, 280, 719, 722–724, 1036, 1182, 1185, **1186-1187**, **1200–1204**, 1205–1208

Akzo Nobel Chemicals Ltd v. Commission (Cases T-125/03 R and T-253/03 R) [2004] 4 CMLR 744 ... 961, 963, 965–966

Akzo Nobel v. Commission (Case T-112/05) [2007] ECR II-5049 ... 146

Akzo Nobel v. Commission (Case T-345/12 R) [2012] ECR II-00, 16 November 2012 ... 975, 1049

ALROSA v. Commission (Case T-170/06) [2007] ECR II-2601 ... 273, 453, 979, **984**, 1031

Amann & Söhne GmbH & Co KG v. Commission (Case T-446/05 P) [2010] ECR II-1255 ... 63–65, 76, 85, 118, 1015

Amministrazione Autonoma dei Monopoli di Stato (AAMS) v. Commission (Case T-139/98) [2001] ECR II-3413, [2002] 4 CMLR 302 ... 583–584

Aragonesas Industrias y Energía, SAU v. Commission, (Case T-348/08) 25 October 2011 ... 126

Arcelor Mittal v. Commission (Case T-405/06) 31 March 2009 ... 110, 1033

Archer Daniels Midlands Company and Archer Daniels Ingredients Ltd v. Commission (Case T-224/00) [2003] ECR II-2597 ... 685, 942, 1008

Areva and Alstom v. Commission (Cases T-117/07 and 121/07) [2011] ECR II-633 ... 938

Arkema France v. Commission (Case T-343/08) [2011] ECR II-2287 ... 938

Asia Motor France v. Commission (Case T-154/98) [2000] ECR II-3453 ... 187

Associazione 'Giùlemanidallajuve' v. Commission (Case T-273/09) [2011] ECR II-000, 19 March 2012 ... 113

AstraZeneca v. Commission (Case T-321/05) [2010] ECR II-2805 ... 67, 69, 82, 302, 322–323, 339, 346–347, 356, 360, 374, 377, 380, 560–561

Atlantic Container Line v. Commission (Case T-395/94) [2002] ECR II-875, [2002] 4 CMLR 1232 ... 294, 338, 980–981

Atlantic Container Line AB v. Commission (Cases T-191 and T-214/98) [2003] II-3275, [2005] 5 CMLR 1283 ... **187**, 277, 279–280, 326, 344, 392, 557, 718, 722, 724, 975, 1035, 1049–1050

Atochem v. Commission (Case T-3/89) [1991] ECR II-867 ... 154, 177

Automec Srl v. Commission (Automec I) (Case T-64/89) [1990] ECR II-367, [1991] 4 CMLR 177 ... 1075

Automec Srl v. Commission (Automec II) (Case T-24/90) [1992] ECR II-2223, [1992] 5 CMLR 431 ... 292–293, 812, 933, **1072–1074**, 1075

Avebe v. Commission (Case T-314/01) [2006] ECR II-3085 ... 144–145

Balloré v. Commission (Cases T-109/02 etc.) 27 April 2007 ... 669, 671, 968

BASF v. Commission (Cases T-79/89 etc.) [1992] ECR II-315, [1992] 4 CMLR 357 ... 1032–1033, 1035

BASF v. Commission (Cases T-15 and 26/02) [2006] ECR II-497 ... 669, 672, 682, 1015, 1026

BASF v. Commission (Cases T-101/05 and 111/05) [2007] ECR II-4949 ... 177, 671, 1041

Bayer AG v. Commission (Case T-41/96) [2000] ECR II-3383, [2001] 4 CMLR 126 ... 150, **156–160**, 510, 792–793, 1049

BEMIM v. Commission (Case T-114/92) [1995] ECR II-147, [1996] 4 CMLR 305 ... 1068

BEUC v. Commission (Case T-37/92) [1994] ECR II-285 ... 1069, 1077

Böel v. Commission (Case T-142/89) [1995] ECR II-867 ... 163

BPB Industries and British Gypsum v. Commission (Case T-65/89) [1993] ECR II-389, [1993] 5 CMLR 32 ... 285, 328, 356, 376, 392–393, 424, 451, 459, 464, 486, 523, 568, 582, 998

Brasserie Nationale NA v. Commission (Cases T-49/02 and T-51/02) [2005] ECR II-3033, [2006] 4 CMLR 8 ... 216, 688, 690, 1004

Britannia Alloys v. Commission (Case T-33/02) [2005] ECR II-4973 ... 997, 1017

British Airways v. Commission (Case T-219/99) [2003] ECR II-5917, [2004] 4 CMLR 1008 ... 64, 287–288, 305–306, 312, **323–325**, 326, **328–330**, 339, **341–343**, 359, 398, 454, 456, 469–470, 483, 572, 933, 1033–1034

British Plasterboard v. Commission (Case T-53/03) [2008] ECR II-1333 ... 126, 154, 177, 584, 973, 1002–1004, 1012, 1015, 1039, 1046

Buchmann v. Commission (Case T-295/94) [1994] ECR II-1265 ... 1050

BUPA v. Commission (Case T-289/03) [2008] ECR II-18 ... **634–640**

BVBA Kruidvat v. Commission (Case T-87/92) [1996] ECR II-1851, [1997] 4 CMLR 1046 ... 1031

Cableuropa v. Commission (Cases T-346 and 347/02) 30 September 2003 ... 1164

Cañas v. Commission (Case T-508/09) [2012] ECR II-000, 26 March 2012 ... 113

CB v. Commission (Case T-491/07) [2102] ECR II-000, 24 November 2012 ... 764

CCE de la Société générale des grandes sources and others v. Commission (Case T-96/92 R) [1995] ECR II-1213 ... 1253

CDC Hydrogen Peroxide v. Commission (Case T-437/08) [2011] ECR II-000, 15 December 2011 ... 978, 1086

Cementbouw Handel & Industrie BV v. Commission (Case T-282/02) [2006] ECR II-319 ... 1141, 1143

Chalkor v. Commission (Case T-21/05) [2010] ECR II-1895 ... 1041

Cimenteries CBR SA v. Commission (Cases T-10-12, 14-15/92) [1992] ECR II-2667 ... 149, 970

Cimenteries CBR SA v. Commission (Cases T-25, 26, 30–2, 34–9, 42–6, 48, 50–71, 87, 88, 103, and 104/95) ... 148–149

Cisco Systems and Management v. Commission (Case T-79/12) (judgment pending) ... 1238, 1253

Clearstream Banking AG v. Commission (Case T-301/04) 9 September 2009 ... 64, 74, 81, 311, 317, 326, 376–377, 388, 392, 510, 521, **523–525**, 568–569, 999

Coating AG v. Commission (Case T-175/95 BASF) [1999] ECR II-1581, [2000] 4 CMLR 33 ... 792

Coca-Cola v. Commission (Cases T-125 and 127/97) [2000] ECR II-1733, [2000] 5 CMLR 467 ... 271, 305, 1188

Comité Central d'Enterprise de la Société Anonyme Vittel v. Commission (Case T-12/93) [1995] ECR II-1247 ... 1239

Commission v. Tetra Laval (Case T-5/02) [2002] ECR II-4381 ... 1223

Compagnie Générale Maritime v. Commission (Case T-86/95) [2002] ECR. II-1011 ... 259

Compagnie Maritime Belge (Case T-276/04) [2008] ECR II-1277 ... 422, 1045

Compagnie Maritime Belge Transports SA v. Commission (Cases T-24/93 etc.) [1996] ECR II-1201 ... 279, 421, 423, 470

Confédération européenne des associations d'horlogers-réparateurs (CEAHR) v. Commission (Case T-427/08) [2010] ECR II-5865 ... 63–64, 66, 74, 80, 293, 321, 507, 525, 1075

Consiglio Nazionale degli Spedizionieri Doganali v. Commission (Case T-513/93) [2000] ECR II-1807 ... 187

Daimler Chrysler AG v. Commission (Case T-325/01) [2005] ECR II-3319 ... 139, 774–776, 792–793

Dansk Rørindustri (Case T-21/99) ... 179

Degussa (Case T-279/02) [2006] ECR II-897 ... 1017, 1028

Deltafina v. Commission [2011] ECR II-000, (Case T-12/06 P) 9 September 2011 ... 1020

Der Grüne Punkt-Duales System Deutschland judgment (Case T-151/01) [2007] ECR II-1607 ... 583, 999

Der Grüne Punkt-Duales System Deutschland v. Commission (Case T-289/01) 24 May 2007 ... 580, 762

Deutsche Bahn AG v. Commission (Case T-229/94) [1997] ECR II-1689, [1998] 4 CMLR 220 ... 83, 359, 567–569

Deutsche Telekom v. Commission (Case T-271/03) [2008] ECR II-477 ... 54, 289, 291, 427–428, 447–448, 522

Dimosia Epicheirisi Ilektrismou AE (DEI) v. Commission (Case T-169/08) [2012] ECR I-000, 12 September 2012 ... 285, 447, 605, **618–619**, 630

Dole Food and Dole Germany v. Commission (Case T-588/08 P) (judgment pending) ... 169, 700–701

Dow Chemical Company v. Commission, (Case T-77/08) 2 February 2012 ... 144, 146

Dunlop Slazenger v. Commission (Cases T-38 and 43/92) [1994] ECR II-441, [1993] 5 CMLR 352 ... 158, 172, 791–792

EasyJet Airline Co. Ltd v. Commission (Case T-177/04) [2006] ECR II-1913 ... 66, 1197, 1253

EDP v. Commission (Case T-87/05) [2005] ECR II-3745 ... 1184, 1225, 1246, 1254

Electrabel v. Commission (Case T-332/09) 12 December 2012 ... 1142, 1177

Elf Aquitaine v. Commission, (Case T-299/08) 17 May 2011 ... 143, 932

EMC v. Commission (Case T-432/05) [2010] ECR II-1629 ... 758, 1075

EnBW Energie Baden-Württemberg v. Commission (Case T-344/08) [2012] ECR I-000, 22 May 2012 ... 978, **1026–1027**

Endemol Entertainment Holding BV v. Commission (Case T-221/95) [1999] ECR II-1299 ... 974, 1169–1170, 1253

Endesa SA v. Commission (Case T-41/07) [2006] ECR II-2533 ... 49, 1167

Endesa v. Commission (Case T-417/05) [2006] ECR II-2533 ... 1151

Energetický a průmyslový holding v. Commission, (Case T-272/12) judgment pending ... 947

ENI v. Commission, (Case T-39/07) 13 July 2011 ... 966

Enichem Anic SpA v. Commission (Case T-6/89) [1991] ECR II-1623 ... 177

Enso Española v. Commission (Case T-348/94) [1998] ECR II-1875 ... 1039

E.ON Energie AG v. Commission (Case T-141/08) [2010] ECR II-5761 ... 948

E.ON Ruhrgas AG v. Commission, (Case T-360/09) 29 June 2012 ... 206, 210, 245, 688, 790

Esso and ors v. Commission (Case T-540/08), judgment pending ... 63, 1277

European Federation of Ink and Ink Cartridge Manufacturers (EFIM) v. Commission (Case T-296/09) [2011] ECR II-000 ... 321

European Night Services v. Commission (Cases T-374, 375, 384 and 388/94) [1998] ECR II-3141, [1998] 5 CMLR 718 ... 62, 85, 180, 199, 204, 206, 237–238, 242, 246, 331, **517–518**, 524, 675, 732, 734, 738, 895, 1037, 1045

F91 Diddeleng (Case T-341/10) [2012] ECR II-000, 16 April 2012 ... 113

Fédération Française des Sociétés d'assurances (FFSA) (Case T-106/95) [1997] ECR II-0229 ... 656

Fédération nationale de l'industrie et des commerces en gros des viandes (FNICGV) v. Commission (Case T-252/03) [2004] ECR II-3795 ... 1039

FENIN v. Commission [2003] (Case T-319/99) ECR II-357 ... 51, **134**, 583

FENIN v. Commission (Case T-319/99) [2003] ECR II-357, [2003] 5 CMLR 34 ... 582

Ferriere Nord SpA v. Commission (Case T-153/04) 27 September 2006 ... 994

Ferriere Nord v. Commission (Case T-143/89) [1995] ECR II-917 ... 998, 1004

Fiatagri and Ford New Holland v. Commission (Case T-34/92) [1994] ECR II-905 ... 174, 704

Fiskeby Board AB v. Commission (Case T-319/94) [1998] ECR II-1331 ... 1019

FNSEA v. Commission (Cases T-217/03 and T-245/03) [2008] ECR I-10193 ... 128, 681

France Télécom SA v. Commission (Case T-340/03) [2007] ECR II-107 ... 289, **312–314**, 315, 337, 357, 362, 376, 392, 406, 408, 411–412, 415, 420, 947

Fred Olsen v Commission (Case T-17/02) ... 638

Fresh Del Monte Produce v. Commission, (Case T-587/08) 14 March 2013 ... 141, 143, 145–146, 165, 169, 178, 212, 700–702, 1015

Fuji Electric System Co. Ltd v. Commission, (Case T-132/07) 12 July 2011 ... 144, 146, 938

Gencor Ltd v. Commission (Case T-102/96) [1999] ECR II-753 … 370, 719–720, 1135–1136, **1200–1202**, 1206–1207, 1248, **1255–1256**, 1256, 1262, **1278–1283**

General Electric Company v. Commission (Case T-210/01) [2005] ECR II-5575 … 299–300, 339, 486, 489, **1229**, **1232–1234**, 1285

General Motors Nederland BV and Opel Nederland BV v. Commission, (Case T-368/00) [2003] ECR II-4491 … 157–158, 162, 215, 1040

General Technic-Otis Sàrl v. Commission (Cases T-141/07, etc.) [2011] ECR II-000, 13 July 2011 … 938

GlaxoSmithKline Services Unlimited v. Commission (Case T-168/01) [2006] ECR II-2969 … 33, 39, 46–47, 108, 223, **252**, 254, 571, 585, 835, 1037, 1045

Groupe Danone v. Commission (Case T-38/02) [2005] ECR II-4407 … 675, 688

Groupement d'Achat Edouard Leclerc v. Commission (Case T-19/92) [1996] ECR II-1851, [1997] 4 CMLR 968 … 807–808, 810–812

Groupement d'Achat Édouard Leclerc v. Commission (Case T-88/92) [1996] ECR II-1961 … 810–812, 815

Groupement des Cartes Bancaires and Europay v. Commission (Cases T-39/92 and T-40/92) [1994] ECR II-49 … 682, 691, 838

Groupement des Cartes Bancaires CB v. Commission (Case T-275/94) [1995] ECR II-216 … 1019

Guérin Automobiles v. Commission (Case T-186/94) [1995] ECR II-1753 … **1076**

Gyproc Benelux v. Commission (Case T-50/03) [2008] ECR II-114 … 679

Herlitz AG v. Commission (Case T-66/92) [1994] ECR II-531, [1995] 5 CMLR 458 … 140

HFB Holdings v. Commission (Case T-102/92) [2002] ECR II-1487 … 141, 690

Hilti v. Commission (Case T-30/89) [1991] ECR II-1439, [1992] 4 CMLR 16 … 317, **319–320**, 338, 353, 386, 490–492, 496–497, 500, 965

Hoechst GmbH v. Commission (Case T-410/03) [2008] ECR II-881 … 980, 1017–1018

Hoek Loos NV v. Commission (Cases T-303 and 304/02) [2006] ECR II-1887, [2006] 5 CMLR 8 … 151, 681, 1017

Holcim v. Commission (Case T-28/03) [2005] ECR II-1357 … 1050

Honeywell v. Commission and General Electric Company v. Commission (Cases T-209 and 210/01) [2005] ECR II-5527 and 5575 … 1214, 1223, 1226, 1229–1232, 1250, 1255

Hynix v. Commission (Case T-149/10) (judgment pending) … 908

ICF v. Commission, (Case T-406/08) judgment pending … 1012

ICI v. Commission (Case T-36/91) [1995] ECR II-1847 … 970

IECC v. Commission (Cases T-133 and 204/95) [1998] ECR II-3645 … 1068

Imperial Chemical Industries plc v. Commission (Case T-13/89) [1992] ECR II-757 … 222, 680

IMS Health v. Commission (Case T-184/01) [2001] ECR II-3193, [2002] 4 CMLR 58 … 532, 991–992, 1032, 1048–1049

Independent Music Publishers and Labels Association (Impala) v. Commission (Case T-464/04) [2006] ECR II-2289, [2006] 5 CMLR 19 … 719, 969, 1200, 1204, **1207–1208**, 1253–1254

Industrie des poudres sphériques SA v. Commission of the European Communities (Case T-5/97) [2000] ECR II-3755 … 426

Intel v. Commission (Case T-286/09) judgment pending … 273, 304, 340, 354, 356, 358, 475, 482, 484, 999, 1012

International Confederation of Societies of Authors and Composers (CISAC) v. Commission (Case T-442/08) 12 April 2013 … 126, 147, 635, 757, 920

Irish Sugar plc v. Commission (Case T-228/97) [1999] ECR II-2969, [1999] 5 CMLR 1300 … 280, 344, 359–360, 373–374, 376, 384–385, 392, 397, **421–424**, 456, 458, 462, 556, 568, 572, 584, 720, 724–725, 1202–1203

Itochu v. Commission (Case T-12/03) [2009] ECR II-883 … 793, 835

ITT Promedia NV v. Commission (Case T-111/96) [1998] ECR II-2937, [1998] 5 CMLR 491 … 187, 374, 376–377, 559, **564–565**

JCB Service v. Commission (Case T-67/01) [2004] ECR II-49, [2004] 4 CMLR 1346 … 157, 162, 195, 789, 792, 827

Jégo-Quéré v. Commission (Case T-177/01) [2002] ECR II-665 … 106

John Deere Ltd v. Commission (Case T-35/92) [1994] ECR II-957 … 174, 229, **704–707**

Joynson v. Commission (Case T-231/99) [2002] ECR II-2085, [2002] 5 CMLR 123 … 786

Jungbunzlauer v Commission (Case T-43/02) … 179

Kaučuk v. Commission (Cases T-44 and 45/07) 13 July 2011 … 672, 681, 688

Kesko Oy v. Commission (Case T-22/97) [1999] ECR II-3755 … 1168–1169

Kish Glass and Co Ltd v. Commission (Case T-65/96) [2000] ECR II-1885 … 64, 75, 274, 312, 323, 1038–1039

KME v. Commission (Case T-127/04) [2009] ECR II-1167 … 1041

Koelman v. Commission (Case T-575/93) [1996] ECR II-1, [1996] 4 CMLR … 1071

La Cinq SA v. Commission (Case T-44/90) [1992] ECR II-1 ... 991

Lagardère SCA and Canal+ SA v. Commission (Case T-251/00) [2002] ECR II-4825, [2003] 4 CMLR 965 ... 1244

L'Air liquide SA v. Commission, (Case T-185/06) 6 June 2011 ... 143

Langnese-Iglo & Schöller Lebensmittel v. Commission (Cases T-7 and 9/93) [1995] ECR II-1533 ... 803–804, 980

Laurent Piau v. Commission (Case T-193/02) [2005] ECR II-209 ... 112, 148, 219, 256, 278, 281, 344, 722

Limburgse Vinyl Maatschappij NV v. Commission (PVC Cartel II) (Cases T-305-7, 313-16, 318, 325, 328-9, 335/94) [1999] ECR I-931 ... 968, 970–972, 994, **997–998**, 1003, 1035

LR AF 1998 A/S v. Commission (Case T-23/99) [2002] ECR II-1705, [2002] 5 CMLR 571 ... 1001

MCI v. Commission (Case T-310/00) [2004] ECR II-3253 ... 1148, 1198

Mannesmannröhren-Werke AG v. Commission (Case T-112/98) [2001] ECR II-729 ... 955–956, 1056

Mannesmannröhren-Werke AG v. Commission (Case T-44/00) [2004] ECR II-2223 ... 687

Manufacture Française des Pneumatiques Michelin v. Commission (Case T-203/01) [2004] 4 CMLR 923 ... 73, 288, 312, 376, 392, 401, 423, 452, 454, 456, **464–468**, 500–501, 523–524, 974, 1013

Martinelli v. Commission (Case T-150/89) [1995] ECR II-1165 ... 1002

MasterCard Inc, MasterCard International Inc, and MasterCard Europe SPRL v. Commission (Case T-111/08) [2012] ECR II-000, 24 May 2012 ... 63, 72, 81, 147, 199, 215, **221–222**, **245–246**, 250–251, 253, 692, 764

Matra Hachette v. Commission (Case T-17/93) [1994] ECR II-595 ... 200, 205, 251–252, **254–256**, 690–691, 834, 838, 976

max.mobil v. Commission (Case T-54/99) [2002] ECR II-313 ... 653, 1075

Meca-Medina v. Commission (Case T-313/02) [2004] ECR II-3291 ... 220

Menarini v Commission (Case T-179/00) ... 1039

Métropole Télévision SA v. Commission (Cases T-528, 542, 543 and 546/93) [1996] ECR II-649, [1996] 5 CMLR 386 ... 113, 250, 256, 732, **752–754**, 834, 1031, 1037

Métropole Télévision SA v. Commission (Case T-206/99) [2001] 4 CMLR 1423 ... 113

Métropole Télévision SA v. Commission (Case T-206/99) [2001] ECR II-1057 ... 113

Métropole Télévision SA (M6) v. Commission (Case T-112/99) [2001] ECR II-2459, [2001] 5 CMLR 1236 ... **199–200**, 232, 245–246, 248, 732

Métropole Télévision SA (M6) and others v. Commission (Cases T-185, 216, 299 and 300/00) [2002] ECR II-3805 ... 113, 732, 752–753

Microsoft v. Commission (Case T-167/08) [2012] ECR II-000, 27 June 2012 ... 516, 537, 580, 996

Microsoft v. EC Commission (Case T-201/04) [2007] ECR II-3601 ... 15, 41, 55, 67, 73–74, 77, 79, 81, 271, **273–275**, 289, 317, 322, 337, 362, 366, 370–371, **373–376**, 380, 386, **388**, 391, 395–396, 400, 483, 486, 489, **495–504**, 506–508, 516, 523, 525, **538–546**, 551, 553, 580, 979, 981, 996, 1033, 1036–1039, 1048–1049

Monty Program AB (Case T-292/10) (judgment pending) ... 1247

MyTravel v. Commission (Case T-212/03) [2008] ECR II-1967 ... 1050, **1254**

MyTravel v. Commission (Case T-403/05) [2008] ECR II-2027 ... 977, 1253

Nederlandse Valbond Varkenshouders v. Commission (Case T-151/05) [2009] ECR II-1219 ... 67, 69, 82, 1185

Nexans France SAS v. Commission (Case T-135/09) [2012] ECR I-000, 14 November 2012 ... 935, 940, 942–**945**, **945–949**

Nintendo and Nintendo of Europe v. Commission (Case T-13/03) [2009] ECR II-975 ... 793, 835, 1015, 1020

Nintendo v. Commission (Case T-1/03), 30 April 2009 ... 1015

Novácke Chemické Závody v. Commission (Case T-352/09) [2012] ECR I-000, 12 December 2012 ... 1016

O2 (Germany) GmbH & Co. OHG v. Commission (Case T-328/03) [2006] ECR II-1231, [2006] 5 CMLR 5 ... 199, 237–238

Omnis v. Commission (Case T-74/11) [2013] ECR II-000, 30 May 2013 ... 1075

Omya v. Commission (Case T-145/06) [2009] ECR II-145 ... 1178

Ordre National des Pharmaciens en France (ONP) v. Commission, (Case T-90/11) judgment pending ... 997

Österreichische Postsparkasse AG v. Commission (Cases T-213/01 and 214/01) [2006] ECR II-1601 ... 46, **1069–1070**

Parker ITR and Parker-Hannifin v. Commission (Cases T-146/09 etc.) [2013] ECR I-000, 17 May 2013 ... 952, 1009

Parker Pen Ltd v. Commission (Case T-77/92) [1994] ECR II-549, [1995] 5 CMLR 435 ... 139–140, 146, 790, 792

Pergan Hilfsstoffe für Industrielle Prozesse GmbH v. Commission (Case T-474/04) [2007] ECR II-4225 ... 973

Peróxiidos Orgánicos SA v. Commission 16 Nov 2006, (Case T-120/04 etc) [2007] 4 CMLR 4...666, 675

Petrofina SA v. Commission (Case T-2/89) [1991] ECR II-1087...177, 679

Peugeot v. Commission (Case T-450/05) [2009] ECR II-2533...792

Pfizer Animal Health v Council (Case T-13/99)...275, 1038

Postbank NV v. Commission, (Case T-353/94) [1996] ECR II-921...973, 1120

Prysmian SpA v. Commission (Case T-140/09) [2012] ECR I-000, 14 November 2012...944

Publishers' Association v. Commission (Case T-66/89) [1992] ECR II-1995, [1992] 5 CMLR 120...680, 1034

Raiffeisen Zentralbank Österreich v. Commission (Cases T-259-264 and 271/02) [2006] ECR II-5169...63, 682

Rhône-Poulenc and ors v Commission (Cases T-1-4/89 and 6-15/89) [1991] ECR II-869...170, 177, 937

Romana Tabacchi v. Commission (Cases T-11-12/06) 5 October 2011...680

Royal Philips Electronics v. Commission (Case T-119/02) [2003] ECR II-1433, [2003] 5 CMLR 53...1163, 1253–1254

RTE, ITP, BBC v. EC Commission (Cases T-69-70/89, 76/89) [1991] ECR II-485, [1991] 4 CMLR 586...356, 514–515, 524, 526–528, 920, 1047

Ryanair v. Commission (Case T-342/07) [2010] ECR II-3457...1196–1197, 1210, 1216

SA Hercules NV v. Commission (Case T-7/89) [1991] ECR II-1711, [1992] 4 CMLR 84...150, 158, 166, 170, 177, 675, 679–680, 970

Sarrio SA v. Commission (Case T-334/94) [1998] ECR II-1439, [1998] 5 CMLR 195...681, 703

SCA Holding v. Commission (Case T-327/94) [1998] ECR II-549, [1998] 5 CMLR 435...1001

Scandinavian Airlines System AB v. Commission (Case T-241/01) [2005] ECR II-2917, [2005] 5 CMLR 18...687, 1040

Schindler Holding v. Commission (Cases T-138/07, etc.,) 13 July 2011...690

Schneider Electric SA v. Commission (Case T-310/01) [2002] ECR II-4071, [2003] 4 CMLR 768...57, 103, 106, 1176, 1178–1180, 1185, 1234, 1248, **1254**

Schneider v. Commission (Case T-351/03) [2007] ECR II-2237...1050, 1254

Schunk and Schunk Kohlenstoff-Technik v. Commission (Case T-69/04) [2008] ECR II-2567...1014

Scippacercola and Terezakis v. Commission (Case T-306/05) [2008] ECR II-4...1075

Scottish Football Association v. Commission (Case T-46/92) [1994] ECR II-1039...941

SELEX Sistemi Integrati SpA v. Commission (Case T-155/04) 12 December 2006, [2007] 4 CMLR 372...**136**, 378

SEP v. Commission (Case T-39/90) [1991] ECR II-1497, [1992] 5 CMLR 33...940

SGL Carbon v. Commission (Case T-68/04) [2008] ECR II-2511...1013, 1017

Shaw v. Commission (Case T-131/99) [2002] ECR II-2023, [2002] 5 CMLR 81...786, 1096

Shell International Chemical Co Ltd v. Commission (Case T-11/89) [1992] ECR II-884...137–138, 680, 968, 1039

Shell Petroleum v. Commission, (Case T-343/06) 27 September 2012...142, 145

Slovenská Pošta v. Commission, (Case T-556/08) judgment pending...610, 629, 651

Società Italiana Vetro, Fabbrica Pisana and PPG Vernante Pennitalia v. Commission ('Flat Glass') (Cases T-68, 77 and 78/89) [1992] ECR II-1403, [1992] 5 CMLR 302...127, 145, 277, 421, **717**, 723, 1036–1037, **1200–1203**

Société d'Hygiène Dermatologique de Vichy v. Commission (Case T-19/91) [1992] ECR II-415...809, 811–812

Sodima v. Commission (Cases T-190/95 and T-45/96) [1999] ECR II-3617...1077

Solvay v. Commission (Cases T-30/91, etc.) [1995] ECR II-1775, [1996] 5 CMLR 57...459, 666, 686–687, 970–971, 1034–1035

Solvay v. Commission (Case T-57/01) [2009] ECR II-4621...452, 459, 568–569, 666, 687, 972–973

SP v. Commission, (Cases T-472/09, etc.) judgment pending...110

Spain v. Commission (Case T-65/08) (judgment pending)...1167

Spain v. European Commission (Case T-398/07) [2012] ECR I-000, 29 March 2012...54, 442

SPO v. Commission (Case T-29/92) [1996] ECR II-289...260, 690, 699, 838

SP SpA v. Commission (Cases T-27/03 etc.) [2007] ECR II-4331...110, 1033

Stichting Certificatie Kraanverhuurbedrijf (SCK) and Federatie van Nederlandse Kraanverhuurbedrijven (FNK) v. Commission (Cases T-213/95 and T-18/96) [1997] ECR II-1739, [1998] 4 CMLR 259...174, 997

Sun Chemical Group v. Commission (Case T-282/06) [2007] ECR II-2149...1187, **1192–1193**

Tate & Lyle, Napier Brown and British Sugar (Cases T-202/98, etc.) [2001] ECR II-2035...169, 679, 700

Telefónica and Telefónica de España v. European Commission (Case T-336/07) [2012] ECR I-000, 29 March 2012...54, 354, 392, 401, 427, **441–449**, 522, 553

Telekomunikacja Polska, (Case T-486/11) judgment pending...337, 357, 385, 387, 510, 521

Tetra Laval BV v. Commission (Case T-5/02) [2002] ECR II-4381, [2002] 5 CMLR 1182...57, 103, 448, 974, 1180, 1185, 1223, **1226–1227**, 1230, **1235–1236**, 1250, 1254

Tetra Pak International SA v. Commission (Case T-83/91) [1994] ECR II-755, [1997] 4 CMLR 726...**319–320**, **329–334**, 338, 355–356, 375, 394, 408, 414, 423, 491, 496–498, 571, 1003

Tetra Pak Rausing SA (Tetra Pak I) v. Commission (Case T-51/89) [1990] ECR II-309, [1991] 4 CMLR 334...83, 326, 358, 376, 392, 557

Thyssen Stahl AG v. Commission (Case T-141/94) [1999] ECR II-347...154, 700, 704

ThyssenKrupp Stainless AG v. Commission (Case T-24/07) [2009] ECR II-2309...1033

Tierce Ladbroke SA v. Commission (Case T-504/93) [1997] ECR II-923, [1975] 5 CMLR 309...**531–532**

Tokai Carbon v. Commission (Cases T-236, 239, 244-246, 251-252/01) [2004] ECR II-1181, [2004] 5 CMLR 28...682, 956, 1012, 1025, 1041

Tokai Carbon Co Ltd v. Commission (Cases T-71, 74, 87 and 91/03) [2005] ECR II-10...63, 179, 1012

Tomra Systems v. Commission (Case T-155/06) [2010] ECR II-4361...337–339, 344–345, 360, 452, 454, 475, **478–482**

Tréfileurope Sales SARL v. Commission (Case T-141/89) [1995] ECR II-791...144

Tréfilunion v. Commission (Case T-148/89) [1995] ECR II-1063...200, 246, 1003

Trelleborg Industrie v. Commission (Case T-147 and 148/09) 17 May 2013...**178–179**

Tremblay v. Commission (Case T-5/93) [1995] ECR II-185...1032, 1086

Tremblay v. Commission (Case T-224/95) [1997] ECR II-2215...919

Union Française de l'Express v. Commission (Case T-60/05) [2007] ECR II-3397...1075

UPM-Kymmene v. Commission (Case T-53/06) [2012] ECR I-000, 6 March 2012...1016

Van den Bergh Foods Ltd v. Commission (Case T-65/98) [2004] 4 CMLR 1...73, 199, 232, 249–250, 263, 316–317, 451–452, 803–804, **837–840**, 1037, 1048–1049

Verein für Konsumenteninformation (Case T-2/03) [2005] ECR II-1121...978, 1086

Viho Europe BV v. Commission (Case T-102/92) [1995] ECR II-117...139, 141, 146

Visa Europe v. Commission (Case T-461/07) [2011] ECR II-000, 14 April 2011...81, 764, 938, 980, 1076

Volkswagen AG v. Commission (Case T-62/98) [2000] ECR II-2707, [2000] 5 CMLR 853...62, 150, 155, 162, 792–793, 834

Volkswagen v. Commission (Case T-208/01) [2003] ECR II-5141, [2004] 4 CMLR 72...157, 162, 789–790, 792

Weichert (Case T-2/09)...169, 700

Wieland-Werke AG v. Commission (Case T-116/04) [2009] ECR II-1087...**1040**

Wirtschaftskammer Kärnten and best connect Ampere Strompool v. Commission (Case T-350/03) [2006] ECR II-68...1253

Wirtschaftsvereinigung Stahl (Case T-16/98) [2000] ECR II-1217, [2001] 5 CMLR 3...706

World Wide Tobacco España v. Commission (Cases T-37/05 etc.) (judgment pending)...680

WWF UK v. Commission (Case T-105/95)...**564–565**

Zunis Holding v. Commission (Case T-83/92) [1993] ECR II-1169...1253

GENERAL COURT (NUMERICAL TABLE)

T-1-4/89 and 6-15/89 Rhône-Poulenc and ors v Commission [1991] ECR II-869...170, 177, 937

T-2/89 Petrofina SA v. Commission [1991] ECR II-1087...177, 679

T-3/89 Atochem v. Commission [1991] ECR II-867...154, 177

T-6/89 Enichem Anic SpA v. Commission [1991] ECR II-1623...177

T-7/89 SA Hercules NV v. Commission [1991] ECR II-1711, [1992] 4 CMLR 84...150, 158, 166, 170, 177, 675, 679–680, 970

T-11/89 Shell International Chemical Co Ltd v. Commission [1992] ECR II-884...137–138, 680, 968, 1039

T-13/89 Imperial Chemical Industries plc v. Commission [1992] ECR II-757...222, 680

T-14/89 Montedipe v. Commission [1992] ECR II-1155...200

T-30/89 Hilti v. Commission [1991] ECR II-1439, [1992] 4 CMLR 16...317, **319–320**, 338, 353, 386, 491–492, 496–497, 500, 965

T-51/89 Tetra Pak Rausing SA (Tetra Pak I) v. Commission [1990] ECR II-309, [1991] 4 CMLR 334...83, 326, 358, 376, 392, 557

T-64/89 Automec Srl v. Commission (Automec I) [1990] ECR II-367, [1991] 4 CMLR 177...1074–1075

T-65/89 BPB Industries and British Gypsum v. Commission [1993] ECR II-389, [1993] 5 CMLR 32...285, 328, 356, 376, 392–393, 424, 451, 459, 464, 486, 523, 568, 582, 998

T-66/89 Publishers' Association v. Commission [1992] ECR II-1995, [1992] 5 CMLR 120...680, 1034

T-68, 77 and 78/89, Società Italiana Vetro, Fabbrica Pisana and PPG Vernante Pennitalia v. Commission ('Flat Glass') [1992] ECR II-1403 ... 127, 145, 277, 421, **717**, 723, 1036–1037, **1200–1203**

T-69-70/89, 76/89 RTE, ITP, BBC v. EC Commission [1991] ECR II-485, [1991] 4 CMLR 586 ... 356, 514–515, 524, 526–528, 920, 1047

T-79/89 etc BASF v. Commission [1992] ECR II-315, [1992] 4 CMLR 357 ... 1032–1033, 1035

T-141/89 Tréfileurope Sales SARL v. Commission [1995] ECR II-791 ... 144

T-143/89 Ferriere Nord v. Commission [1995] ECR II-917 ... 998, 1004

T-148/89 Tréfilunion v. Commission [1995] ECR II-1063 ... 200, 246, 1003

T-150/89 Martinelli v. Commission [1995] ECR II-1165 ... 1002

T-24/90 Automec Srl v. Commission (Automec II) [1992] ECR II-2223, [1992] 5 CMLR 431 ... 292–293, 812, 933, **1072–1074**, 1075

T-39/90 SEP v. Commission [1991] ECR II-1497, [1992] 5 CMLR 33 ... 940

T-44/90 La Cinq SA v. Commission [1992] ECR II-1 ... 991

T-19/91 Société d'Hygiène Dermatologique de Vichy v. Commission [1992] ECR II-415 ... 809, 811–812

T-30/91, etc. Solvay v. Commission [1995] ECR II-1775, [1996] 5 CMLR 57 ... 459, 665–666, 686–687, 970–971, 1034–1035

T-36/91 ICI v. Commission [1995] ECR II-1847 ... 970

T-83/91 Tetra Pak International SA v. Commission [1994] ECR II-755, [1997] 4 CMLR 726 ... **319–320**, **329–334**, 338, 355–356, 375, 394, 408, 414, 423, 491, 496–498, 571, 1003

T-10-12, 14-15/92 Cimenteries CBR SA v. Commission [1992] ECR II-2667 ... 970

T-19/92 Groupement d'Achat Edouard Leclerc v. Commission [1996] ECR II-1851, [1997] 4 CMLR 968 ... 807–808, 810–812

T-29/92 SPO v. Commission [1996] ECR II-289 ... 260, 690, 699, 838

T-34/92, Fiatagri and Ford New Holland v. Commission [1994] ECR II-905 ... 174, 704

T-35/92 John Deere Ltd v. Commission [1994] ECR II-957 ... 174, **704–707**

T-37/92 BEUC v. Commission [1994] ECR II-285 ... 1069, 1077

T-38 and 43/92 Dunlop Slazenger v. Commission [1994] ECR II-441, [1993] 5 CMLR 352 ... 158, 172, 791–792

T-39/92 and T-40/92 Groupement des Cartes Bancaires and Europay v. Commission [1994] ECR II-49 ... 682, 691, 838

T-46/92 Scottish Football Association v. Commission [1994] ECR II-1039 ... 940

T-66/92 Herlitz AG v. Commission [1994] ECR II-531, [1995] 5 CMLR 458 ... 140

T-77/92 Parker Pen Ltd v. Commission [1994] ECR II-549, [1995] 5 CMLR 435 ... 139–140, 146, 790, 792

T-83/92 Zunis Holding v. Commission [1993] ECR II-1169 ... 1253

T-87/92 BVBA Kruidvat v. Commission [1996] ECR II-1851, [1997] 4 CMLR 1046 ... 1031

T-88/92 Groupement d'Achat Édouard Leclerc v. Commission [1996] ECR II-1961 ... 810–812, 815

T-96/92 R, CCE de la Société générale des grandes sources and others v. Commission [1995] ECR II-1213 ... 1253

T-102/92, Viho Europe BV v. Commission [1995] ECR II-117 ... 139, 141, 146

T-114/92 BEMIM v. Commission [1995] ECR II-1427 ... 1068

T-144/92 BEMIM v. Commission [1995] ECR II-147, [1996] 4 CMLR 305 ... 1068

T-2/93 Air France v. Commission [1994] ECR II-323 ... 1142, 1253

T-5/93 Roger Tremblay v. Commission [1995] ECR II-185 ... 1032, 1086

T-7 and 9/93 Langnese-Iglo & Schöller Lebensmittel v. Commission [1995] ECR II-1533 ... 803–804, 980

T-12/93 Comité Central d'Enterprise de la Société Anonyme Vittel v. Commission [1995] ECR II-1247 ... 1239

T-17/93 Matra Hachette v. Commission [1994] ECR II-595 ... 200, 205, 251–252, **254–256**, 691, 834, 838, 976

T-24/93 etc., Compagnie Maritime Belge Transports SA v. Commission [1996] ECR II-1201 ... 392, 421, 423, 470, 718

T-450/93 Listeral [1994] ECR II-1177 ... 991

T-504/93 Tierce Ladbroke SA v. Commission [1997] ECR II-923, [1975] 5 CMLR 309 ... **531–532**

T-513/93 Consiglio Nazionale degli Spedizionieri Doganali v. Commission [2000] ECR II-1807 ... 187

T-528, 542, 543 and 546/93 Métropole Télévision SA v. Commission [1996] ECR II-649, [1996] 5 CMLR 386 ... 113, 250, 256, 732, **752–754**, 834, 1031, 1037

T-575/93 Koelman v. Commission [1996] ECR II-1, [1996] 4 CMLR ... 1071

T-141/94 Thyssen Stahl AG v. Commission [1999] ECR II-347 ... 154, 700, 704

T-186/94 Guérin Automobiles v. Commission [1995] ECR II-1753 ... **1076**

T-229/94 Deutsche Bahn AG v. Commission [1997] ECR II-1689, [1998] 4 CMLR 220 ... 83, 359, 567–569

T-260/94 Air Inter v. Commission [1997] ECR II-997, [1997] 5 CMLR 851 ... **648-649**

T-275/94 Groupement des Cartes Bancaires CB v. Commission [1995] ECR II-216 ...1019

T-295/94 R Buchmann v. Commission [1994] ECR II-1265 ...1050

T-305-7, 313-16, 318, 325, 328-9, 335/94 Limburgse Vinyl Maatschappij NV v. Commission (PVC Cartel II) [1999] ECR I-931 ...950, 968, 970–972, 994, **997–998**, 1003, 1035

T-319/94 Fiskeby Board AB v. Commission [1998] ECR II-1331 ...1019

T-327/94 SCA Holding v. Commission [1998] ECR II-549, [1998] 5 CMLR 435 ...1001

T-334/94 Sarrio SA v. Commission [1998] ECR II-1439, [1998] 5 CMLR 195 ...681, 703

T-348/94 Enso Española v. Commission [1998] ECR II-1875 ...1039

T-353/94 Postbank NV v. Commission, [1996] ECR II-921 ...973, 1120

T-374, 375, 384 and 388/94 European Night Services v. Commission [1998] ECR II-3141, [1998] 5 CMLR 718 ...62, 85, 180, 199, 204, 206, 237, 242, 246, 331, **517–518**, 524, 675, 732, 734, 738, 895, 1037, 1045

T-395/94 Atlantic Container Line v. Commission [2002] ECR II-875, [2002] 4 CMLR 1232 ...294, 338, 980–981

T-86/95 Compagnie Générale Maritime v. Commission [2002] ECR. II-1011 ...259

T-105/95 WWF UK v. Commission ...564

T-106/95 Fédération Française des Sociétés d'assurances (FFSA) [1997] ECR II-0229 ...655

T-133 and 204/95 IECC v. Commission [1998] ECR II-3645 ...1068

T-175/95 BASF Coating AG v. Commission [1999] ECR II-1581, [2000] 4 CMLR 33 ...792

T-190/95 and T-45/96 Sodima v. Commission [1999] ECR II-3617 ...1077

T-213/95 and T-18/96 Stichting Certificatie Kraanverhuurbedrijf (SCK) and Federatie van Nederlandse Krannverhuurbedrijven (FNK) v. Commission [1997] ECR II-1739, [1998] 4 CMLR 259 ...174, 997

T-221/95 Endemol Entertainment Holding BV v. Commission [1999] ECR II-1299 ...974, 1169–1170, 1253

T-224/95 Tremblay v. Commission [1997] ECR II-2215 ...919

T-41/96 Bayer AG v. Commission [2000] ECR II-3383, [2001] 4 CMLR 126 ...150, **156–160**, 510, 792–793, 1049

T-65/96 Kish Glass and Co Ltd v. Commission [2000] ECR II-1885 ...64, 75, 274, 312, 323, 1038–1039

T-102/96 Gencor Ltd v. Commission [1999] ECR II-753 ...370, 719–720, 1135–1136, **1200–1202**, 1206–1207, 1248, **1255–1256**, 1256, 1262, **1278–1283**

T-111/96 ITT Promedia NV v. Commission [1998] ECR II-2937, [1998] 5 CMLR 491 ...187, 374, 376–377, 559, 564

T-5/97 Industrie des poudres sphériques SA v. Commission of the European Communities [2000] ECR II-3755 ...426

T-22/97 Kesko Oy v. Commission [1999] ECR II-3755 ...1168–1169

T-125 and 127/97 Coca-Cola v. Commission [2000] ECR II-1733, [2000] 5 CMLR 467 ...271, 305, 1188

T-228/97 Irish Sugar plc v. Commission [1999] ECR II-2969, [1999] 5 CMLR 1300 ...280, 344, 359–360, 373–374, 376, 384–385, 392, 397, **421–424**, 456, 458, 462, 556, 568, 572, 584, 720, 724–725, 1202–1203

T-16/98 Wirtschaftsvereinigung Stahl [2000] ECR II-1217, [2001] 5 CMLR 3 ...706

T-62/98 Volkswagen AG v. Commission [2000] ECR II-2707, [2000] 5 CMLR 853 ...62, 150, 155, 162, 792–793, 834

T-65/98 Van den Bergh Foods Ltd v. Commission [2004] 4 CMLR 1 ...73, 199, 232, 249–250, 263, 316–317, 451–452, 803–804, **837–840**, 1037, 1048–1049

T-112/98 Mannesmannröhren-Werke AG v. Commission [2001] ECR II-729 ...955, 1056

T-128/98 Aeroports de Paris v. Commission [2000] ECR II-3929, [2001] 4 CMLR 611 ...569

T-139/98 Amministrazione Autonoma dei Monopoli di Stato (AAMS) v. Commission [2001] ECR II-3413, [2002] 4 CMLR 302 ...583–584

T-154/98 Asia Motor France v. Commission [2000] ECR II-3453 ...187

T-191/98 and T-214/98 Atlantic Container Line AB v. Commission [2003] II-3275, [2005] 5 CMLR 1283 ...**187**, 277, 279–280, 326, 344, 392, 557, 718, 722, 724, 975, 1035, 1049–1050

T-202/98, etc., Tate & Lyle, Napier Brown and British Sugar [2001] ECR II-2035 ...169, 679, 700

T-9/99 HFB Holdings v. Commission [2002] ECR II-1487 ...141, 690

T-13/99 Pfizer Animal Health v Council ...275, 1038

T-21/99 Dansk Rørindustri ...179

T-23/99 LR AF 1998 A/S v. Commission [2002] ECR II-1705, [2002] 5 CMLR 571 ...1001

T-25/99 Roberts v. Commission [2001] ECR, II-1881, [2001] 5 CMLR 828 ...804

T-54/99 max.mobil v. Commission [2002] ECR II-313 ...653, 1075

T-61/99 Adriatica di Navigazione v. Commission [2003] ECR II-5349 ...63

T-112/99 Métropole Télévision SA (M6) v. Commission [2001] ECR II-2459, [2001] 5 CMLR 1236 ... **199–200**, 232, 245–246, 248, 732

T-131/99 Shaw v. Commission [2002] ECR II-2023, [2002] 5 CMLR 81 ... 786, 1096

T-206/99 Métropole Télévision SA v. Commission [2001] ECR II-1057 ... 113

T-219/99 British Airways v. Commission [2003] ECR II-5917, [2004] 4 CMLR 1008 ... 64, 287–288, 305–306, 312, **323–325**, 326, **328–330**, 339, **341–343**, 359, 398, 454, 456, 469–470, 483, 572, 933, 1033–1034

T-231/99 Joynson v. Commission [2002] ECR II-2085, [2002] 5 CMLR 123 ... 786

T-319/99 FENIN v. Commission [2003] ECR II-357 ... 51, **134**, 583

T-342/99 Airtours plc v. Commission [2002] ECR II-2585, [2002] 5 CMLR 317 ... 106, 719, 1182, **1200–1204**, 1202

T-44/00 Mannesmannröhren-Werke AG v. Commission [2004] ECR II-2223 ... 687

T-179/00 A. Menarini v Commission ... 275, 1039

T-185/00, T-216/00, T-299/00 and T-300/00 Métropole Télévision SA (M6) and others v. Commission [2002] ECR II-3805 ... 113, 732, 752–753

T-224/00 Archer Daniels Midlands Company and Archer Daniels Ingredients Ltd v. Commission [2003] ECR II-2597 ... 685, 942, 1008

T-251/00 Lagardère SCA and Canal+ SA v. Commission [2002] ECR II-4825, [2003] 4 CMLR 965 ... 1244

T-310/00 MCI v. Commission [2004] ECR II-3253 ... 1148, 1198

T-342/00 Airtours v. Commission [2002] ECR II-2585, [2002] 5 CMLR 317 ... 1182

T-368/00 General Motors Nederland BV and Opel Nederland BV v. Commission, [2003] ECR II-4491 ... 157–158, 162, 215, 1040

T-57/01 Solvay v. Commission [2009] ECR II-4621 ... 452, 459, 568–569, 666, 687, 972–973

T-67/01 JCB Service v. Commission [2004] ECR II-49, [2004] 4 CMLR 1346 ... 157, 162, 195, 789, 792, 827

T-151/01 Der Grüne Punkt-Duales System Deutschland judgment [2007] ECR II-1607 ... 583, 999

T-168/01, GlaxoSmithKline Services Unlimited v. Commission [2006] ECR II-2969 ... 33, 39, 46–47, 108, 223, **252**, 254, 571, 585, 835, 1037, 1045

T-177/01 Jégo-Quéré v. Commission [2002] ECR II-665 ... 106

T-184/01 R IMS Health v. Commission [2001] ECR II-3193, [2002] 4 CMLR 58 ... 532, 991–992, 1032, 1048–1049

T-203/01 Manufacture Française des Pneumatiques Michelin v. Commission [2004] 4 CMLR 923 ... 73, 288, 312, 376, 392, 401, 423, 452, 454, 456, **464–468**, 500–501, 523–524, 974, 1013

T-208/01 Volkswagen v. Commission [2003] ECR II-5141, [2004] 4 CMLR 72 ... 157, 162, 789–790, 792

T-209 and 210/01 Honeywell v. Commission and General Electric Company v. Commission [2005] ECR II-5527 and 5575 ... 1214, 1223, 1226, 1229–1232, 1250, 1255

T-210/01 General Electric Company v. Commission [2005] ECR II-5575 ... 299–300, 339, 486, 489, **1229, 1232–1234**, 1285

T-213/01 and 214/01 Österreichische Postsparkasse AG v. Commission [2006] ECR II-1601 ... 46, **1069–1070**

T-236, 239, 244-246, 251-252/01 Tokai Carbon v. Commission [2004] ECR II-1181, [2004] 5 CMLR 28 ... 682, 956, 1012, 1025, 1041

T-241/01 Scandinavian Airlines System AB v. Commission [2005] ECR II-2917, [2005] 5 CMLR 18 ... 687, 1040

T-289/01 Der Grüne Punkt-Duales System Deutschland v. Commission, 24 May 2007 ... 580, 762

T-310/01 Schneider Electric SA v. Commission [2002] ECR II-4071, [2003] 4 CMLR 768 ... 57, 103, 106, 1176, 1178–1180, 1185, 1234, 1248, 1254

T-314/01, Avebe v. Commission [2006] ECR II-3085 ... 144–145

T-325/01 Daimler Chrysler AG v. Commission [2005] ECR II-3319 ... 139, 774–776, 792–793

T-5/02 Tetra Laval BV v. Commission [2002] ECR II-4381, [2002] 5 CMLR 1182 ... 57, 103, 448, 974, 1180, 1185, 1223, **1226–1227**, 1230, **1235–1236**, 1250, 1254

T-15 and 26/02, BASF v. Commission [2006] ECR II-497 ... 672, 682, 1015, 1026

T-17/02 Fred Olsen v Commission ... 638

T-33/02 Britannia Alloys v. Commission [2005] ECR II-4973 ... 997–998, 1004, 1017

T-38/02 Groupe Danone v. Commission [2005] ECR II-4407 ... 675, 688

T-43/02 Jungbunzlauer v Commission ... 179

T-49/02 and T-51/02 Brasserie Nationale NA v. Commission [2005] ECR II-3033, [2006] 4 CMLR 8 ... 216, 688, 690, 1004

T-109/02 etc. Balloré v. Commission, 27 April 2007 ... 669, 671, 968

T-119/02 Royal Philips Electronics v. Commission [2003] ECR II-1433, [2003] 5 CMLR 53 ... 1163–1164, 1253–1254

T-193/02 Laurent Piau v. Commission [2005] ECR II-209 ... 112, 148, 219, 256, 278, 281, 344, 722

T-259-264 and 271/02 Raiffeisen Zentralbank Österreich v. Commission [2006] ECR II-5169 ... 63, 682, 1069

T-279/02 Degussa [2006] ECR II-897 ... 1017, 1028

T-282/02 Cementbouw Handel & Industrie BV v. Commission [2006] ECR II-319 ... 1141, 1143

T-303 and 304/02 Hoek Loos NV v. Commission [2006] ECR II-1887, [2006] 5 CMLR 8 ... 151, 681, 1017

T-313/02 Meca-Medina v. Commission [2004] ECR II-3291 ... 220

T-346 and 347/02 Cableuropa v. Commission, 30 September 2003 ... 1164

T-1/03 Nintendo v. Commission, 30 April 2009 ... 1015

T-2/03 Verein für Konsumenteninformation [2005] ECR II-1121 ... 978, 1086

T-12/03 Itochu v. Commission [2009] ECR II-909 ... 793, 835

T-13/03 Nintendo and Nintendo of Europe v. Commission [2009] ECR II-975 ... 793, 835, 1015, 1020

T-27/03 etc. SP SpA v. Commission [2007] ECR II-4331 ... 110, 1033

T-28/03 Holcim v. Commission [2005] ECR II-1357 ... 1050

T-50/03 Gyproc Benelux v. Commission [2008] ECR II-114 ... 679

T-53/03 British Plasterboard v. Commission [2008] ECR II-1333 ... 126, 154, 177, 584, 973, 1002–1004, 1012, 1015, 1039, 1046

T-71/03, T-74/03, T-87/03 and T-91/03 Tokai Carbon Co Ltd v. Commission [2005] ECR II-10 ... 63, 179, 1012

T-125/03 R and T-253/03 R Akzo Nobel Chemicals Ltd v. Commission [2004] 4 CMLR 744 ... 961, 963, 965–966

T-212/03 My Travel v. Commission [2008] ECR II-1967 ... 1050, 1254

T-217/03 and T-245/03 FNSEA v. Commission [2008] ECR I-10193 ... 128, 681

T-252/03 Fédération nationale de l'industrie et des commerces en gros des viandes (FNICGV) v. Commission [2004] ECR II-3795 ... 1039

T-271/03 Deutsche Telekom v. Commission [2008] ECR II-477 ... 54, 289, 291, 427–428, 448, 522

T-289/03 BUPA v. Commission [2008] ECR II-18 ... **634–640**

T-328/03 O2 (Germany) GmbH & Co. OHG v. Commission [2006] ECR II-1231, [2006] 5 CMLR 5 ... 199, 237–238

T-340/03 France Télécom SA v. Commission [2007] ECR II-107 ... 289, **312–314**, 315, 337, 357, 362, 376, 392, 406, 408, 411–412, 415, 420, 947

T-350/03 Wirtschaftskammer Kärnten and best connect Ampere Strompool v. Commission [2006] ECR II-68 ... 1253

T-351/03 Schneider v. Commission [2007] ECR II-2237 ... 1050, 1254

T-410/03 Hoechst GmbH v. Commission [2008] ECR II-881 ... 980, 1017–1018

T-68/04 SGL Carbon v. Commission [2008] ECR II-2511 ... 1013, 1017

T-69/04 Schunk and Schunk Kohlenstoff-Technik v. Commission [2008] ECR II-2567 ... 1014

T-99/04 AC-Treuhand AG v. Commission [2008] ECR II-1501 ... 102, 150, 153–155, 171, 176, 199, 292, 675, 933, 938, 999

T-116/04 Wieland-Werke AG v. Commission [2009] ECR II-1087 ... **1040**

T-120/04 etc Peróxidos Orgánicos SA v. Commission 16 Nov 2006, [2007] 4 CMLR 4 ... 666, 675

T-127/04 KME v. Commission [2009] ECR II-1167 ... 1041

T-155/04 SELEX Sistemi Integrati SpA v. Commission 12 December 2006, [2007] 4 CMLR 372 ... **136**, 378

T-177/04 EasyJet Airline Co. Ltd v. Commission [2006] ECR II-1913 ... 66, 1197, 1253

T-201/04 Microsoft v. EC Commission [2007] ECR II-3601 ... 15, 41, 55, 67, 74, 77, 79, 81, 271, **273–275**, 289, 317, 322, 337, 362, 366, 370–371, 373–375, 380, 386, **388**, 391, 395–396, 400, 483, 486, 489, **495–504**, 506–508, 516, 523, 525, **538–546**, 548, 551, 553, 580, 979, 981, 996, 1033, 1036–1039, 1048–1049

T-276/04 Compagnie Maritime Belge [2008] ECR II-1277 ... 422, 1045

T-301/04 Clearstream Banking AG v. Commission, 9 September 2009 ... 64, 74, 81, 311, 317, 326, 376–377, 388, 392, 510, 521, **523–525**, 568–569, 999

T-464/04 Independent Music Publishers and Labels Association (Impala) v. Commission [2006] ECR II-2289, [2006] 5 CMLR 19 ... 719, 969, 1200, 1204, **1207–1208**, 1253–1254

T-474/04 Pergan Hilfsstolle für Industrielle Prozesse GmbH v. Commission [2007] ECR II-4225 ... 973

T-21/05 Chalkor v. Commission [2010] ECR II-1895 ... 1041

T-37/05 etc World Wide Tobacco España v. Commission (judgment pending) ... 680

T-60/05 Union Française de l'Express v. Commission [2007] ECR II-3397 ... 1075

T-87/05 EDP v. Commission [2005] ECR II-3745 ... 1184, 1225, 1246, 1254

T-101/05 and 111/05, BASF v. Commission [2007] ECR II-4949 ... 177, 671, 1041

T-112/05, Akzo Nobel v. Commission [2007] ECR II-5049 ... 146

T-151/05 Nederlandse Valbond Varkenshouders v. Commission [2009] ECR II-1219 ... 67, 69, 82, 1185

T-306/05 Scippacercola and Terezakis v. Commission [2008] ECR II-4 ... 1075

T-321/05, AstraZeneca v. Commission [2010] ECR II-2805 ... 67, 69, 82, 302, 322–323, 339, 346–347, 356, 360, 374, 377, 380, 560–561

T-403/05 MyTravel v. Commission [2008] ECR II-2027 ... 977, 1253

T-417/05 Endesa v. Commission [2006] ECR II-2533 ... 1151

T-432/05 EMC v. Commission [2010] ECR II-1629 ... 758, 1075

T-446/05 P, Amann & Söhne GmbH & Co KG v. Commission [2010] ECR II-1255 ... 63–65, 76, 85, 118, 1015

T-450/05 Peugeot v. Commission [2009] ECR II-2533 ... 792

T-11-12/06 Romana Tabacchi v. Commission, 5 October 2011 ... 680

T-12/06 P Deltafina v. Commission [2011] ECR II-000, 9 September 2011 ... 1020

T-53/06 UPM-Kymmene v. Commission [2012] ECR I-000, 6 March 2012 ... 1016

T-145/06 Omya v. Commission [2009] ECR II-145 ... 1032, 1178

T-155/06 Tomra Systems v. Commission [2010] ECR II-4361 ... 337–339, 344–345, 360, 452, 454, 475, **478–482**

T-170/06 ALROSA v. Commission [2007] ECR II-2601 ... 273, 453, 979, **984**, 1031

T-185/06 L'Air liquide SA v. Commission, 6 June 2011 ... 143

T-282/06 Sun Chemical Group v. Commission [2007] ECR II-2149 ... 1187, **1192–1193**

T-343/06, Shell Petroleum v. Commission, 27 September 2012 ... 142, 145

T-405/06 Arcelor Mittal v. Commission, 31 March 2009 ... 110, 1033

T-24/07 ThyssenKrupp Stainless AG v. Commission [2009] ECR II-2309 ... 1033

T-39/07 ENI v. Commission, 13 July 2011 ... 966

T-41/07 Endesa SA v. Commission [2006] ECR II-2533 ... 1167

T-44 and 45/07 Kaučuk v. Commission, 13 July 2011 ... 672, 681, 688

T-117/07 and 121/07 Areva and Alstom v. Commission [2011] ECR II-633 ... 938

T-132/07, Fuji Electric System Co. Ltd v. Commission, 12 July 2011 ... 144, 146, 938

T-138/07, etc., Schindler Holding v. Commission, 13 July 2011 ... 690

T-141/07, etc., General Technic-Otis Sàrl v. Commission [2011] ECR II-000, 13 July 2011 ... 938

T-336/07, Telefónica and Telefónica de España v. European Commission [2012] ECR I-000, 29 March 2012 ... 54, 354, 392, 401, 427, **441–449**, 522, 553

T-342/07 Ryanair v. Commission [2010] ECR II-3457 ... 1196–1197, 1210, 1216

T-398/07, Spain v. European Commission [2012] ECR I-000, 29 March 2012 ... 54, 442

T-411/07 Aer Lingus v. Commission [2010] ECR II-3457 ... 1143, 1196

T-461/07 Visa Europe v. Commission [2011] ECR II-000, 14 April 2011 ... 81, 764, 938, 980, 1076

T-491/07 CB v. Commission [2102] ECR II-000, 24 November 2012 ... 764

T-65/08 Spain v. Commission (judgment pending) ... 1167

T-77/08 The Dow Chemical Company v. Commission, 2 February 2012 ... 144, 146

T-111/08, MasterCard Inc, MasterCard International Inc, and MasterCard Europe SPRL v. Commission [2012] ECR II-000, 24 May 2012 ... 63, 72, 81, 147, 199, 215, **221–222**, **245–246**, 250–251, 253, 692, 764

T-141/08 E.ON Energie AG v. Commission [2010] ECR II-5761 ... 948

T-167/08 Microsoft v. Commission [2012] ECR I-000, 27 June 2012 ... 516, 537, 580, 996

T-169/08, Dimosia Epicheirisi Ilektrismou AE (DEI) v. Commission [2012] ECR I-000, 12 September 2012 ... 285, 447, 605, **618–619**, 630

T-299/08, Elf Aquitaine v. Commission, 17 May 2011 ... 143, 932

T-343/08 Arkema France v. Commission [2011] ECR II-2287 ... 938

T-344/08 EnBW Energie Baden-Württemberg v. Commission [2012] ECR I-000, 22 May 2012 ... 978, **1026–1027**

T-348/08, Aragonesas Industrias y Energía, SAU v. Commission, 25 October 2011 ... 126

T-406/08 ICF v. Commission, judgment pending ... 1012

T-427/08, Confédération européenne des associations d'horlogers-réparateurs (CEAHR) v. Commission [2010] ECR II-5865 ... 63–64, 66, 74, 80, 293, 321, 507, 525, 1075

T-437/08 CDC Hydrogen Peroxide v. Commission [2011] ECR II-000, 15 December 2011 ... 978, 1086

T-442/08, International Confederation of Societies of Authors and Composers (CISAC) v. Commission, 12 April 2013 ... 126, 147, 635, 757, 920

T-540/08, Esso and ors v. Commission, judgment pending ... 63, 1277

T-556/08 Slovenská Postă v. Commission, judgment pending...610, 629, 651

T-587/08, Fresh Del Monte Produce v. Commission, 14 March 2013...141, 143, 145–146, 165, 169, 178, 212, 700–702, 1015

T-588/08 P Dole Food and Dole Germany v. Commission (judgment pending)...169, 700–701

T-2/09 Weichert...169, 700

T-135/09 Nexans France SAS v. Commission [2012] ECR I-000, 14 November 2012...935, 940, 942–**945**, **945–949**

T-140/09 Prysmian SpA v. Commission [2012] ECR I-000, 14 November 2012...944

T-146/09 etc. Parker ITR and Parker-Hannifin v. Commission [2013] ECR I-000, 17 May 2013...952, 1009

T-147 and 148/09 Trelleborg Industriev. Commission 17 May 2013...**178–179**

T-273/09, Associazione 'Giùlemanidallajuve' v. Commission, 19 March 2012...113

T-286/09 Intel v. Commission (judgment pending)...273, 304, 340, 354, 356, 358, 475, 482, 484, 999, 1012

T-296/09, European Federation of Ink and Ink Cartridge Manufacturers (EFIM) v. Commission [2011] ECR II-000...321

T-332/09 Electrabel v. Commission, 12 December 2012...1142, 1177

T-352/09 Nováck Chemické Závody v. Commission [2012] ECR I-000, 12 December 2012...1016

T-360/09 E.ON Ruhrgas AG v. Commission, 29 June 2012...206, 210, 245, 688, 790

T-472/09, etc., SP v. Commission, judgment pending...110

T-508/09, Cañas v. Commission [2012] ECR II-000, 26 March 2012...113

T-149/10 Hynix v. Commission (judgment pending)...908

T-292/10 Monty Program AB (judgment pending)...1247

T-341/10, F91 Diddeleng [2012] ECR II-000, 16 April 2012...113

T-74/11 Omnis v. Commission [2013] ECR II-000, 30 May 2013...1075

T-90/11 Ordre National des Pharmaciens en France (ONP) v. Commission, judgment pending...997

T-202/11 Aeroporia Aigaiou Aeroporiki v. Commission (pending)...1196, 1211

T-486/11 Telekomunikacja Polska, judgment pending...337, 357, 385, 387, 510, 521

T-79/12 Cisco Systems and Management v. Commission (judgment pending)...1238, 1253

T-272/12 Energetický a průmyslový holding v. Commission, judgment pending...947

T-345/12 R, Akzo Nobel v. Commission [2012] ECR II-00, 16 November 2012...975, 1049

COURT OF JUSTICE (ALPHABETICAL TABLE)

Aalborg Portland A/S v. Commission (Cement) (Cases C-204, 205, 211, 213, 217 and 219/00 P) [2004] I-123, [2005] 4 CMLR 251...126, **154–155**, 163, 178–179, 252, 679, 686–687, 690–691, **971–973**, 1018, 1029–1030, 1037, 1042, **1046–1047**

AB Volvo v. Erik Veng (Case 238/87) [1988] ECR 6211, [1989] 4 CMLR 122...318, 515, **525–527**, 533

ACF Chemiefarma NV v. Commission (Quinine Cartel) (Case 41/69) [1970] ECR 661...150, 158, 177, 684

Adams v. Commission (Case 53/84) [1985] ECR 3595...1050

Adams v. Commission (Case 145/83) [1985] ECR 3539, [1986] 1 CMLR 506...973

ADBHU (Case 240/83) [1985] ECR 531...656

AEG-Telefunken AG v. Commission (Case 107/82) [1983] ECR 3151, [1984] 3 CMLR 325...144, 156–159, 162, 182, 789, 812–813, 968, 972, 1019

Aeroports de Paris v. Commission (Case C-82/01) [2002] ECR I-9297, [2003] 4 CMLR 609...569

AG2R Prévoyance v. Beaudout Père et Fils SARL, (Case C-437/09) 31 March 2011...133, 153, 601, 605, 611, 628, 648

Ahlström Osakeyhtiö and Others v. Commission (Cases C-89, 104, 114, 116–117/85 and 125 to 129/85) [1988] ECR 5193, [1993] ECR I-1307...126, 165, 170, 172, 187, 701, 710–**712**, **712–715**, 1036–1037, 1046, 1272, **1274–1276**

Ahmed Saeed Flugreisen and Silver Line Reisebüro GmbH v. Zentrale zur Bekämpfung unlauteren Wettbewerbs eV (Case 66/86) [1989] ECR 803, [1990] 4 CMLR 102...140, 283, 583, 605, 636–637, 641, 653

AKZO v. Commission (Case 5/85) [1986] ECR 2585, [1987] 3 CMLR 716...942, 1032–1033

AKZO v. Commission (Case 53/85) [1986] ECR 1965, [1987] 1 CMLR 231...942, 976, 990–991

AKZO v. Commission (Case C-62/86) [1991] ECR I-3359...305, 315–316, 326–327, 338, 344–345, 358, 371–372, 377, 380, 395, 401, **403–407**, 408, 416, 419–420, 422–423, 430, 436, 565, 1068, 1189–1190

Akzo Nobel Chemicals Ltd v. Commission (Case
C-550/07 P) [2010] ECR I-8301 ... 938, **961–965**

AKZO Nobel NV v. Commission, 10 September
2009, (Case C-97/08 P) [2009] ECR 000 ... 137, 141,
143–144, 146

Albany International BV v. Stichting
Bedrijfspensioenfonds Textielindustrie (Case
C-67/96) [1999] ECR I-5751, [2000] 4 CMLR
446 ... 51, 127, 129, 133, 137–138, 153, 219, 601,
614, **621–624**, 629–630, 636–637, 644–645,
647–648

Allianz Hungária Biztosító Zrt, Generali-Providencia
Biztosító Zrt v. Gazdasági Versenyhivatal,
(Case C-32/11) 14 March 2013 ... 212,
794–796, 1099

Alsatel v. Novasam (Case 247/86) [1988] ECR 5987,
[1990] 4 CMLR 434 ... 328, 579

Altair Chimica (Case C-207/01) ... 187

Altmark Trans GmbH, Regierungspräsidium
Magdeburg v. Nahverkehrsgesellschaft Altmark
GmbH (Case C-280/00) [2003] ECR I-7747 ... 599,
632, 635, 656

AM&S Ltd v. Commission (Case 155/79) [1982] ECR
1575, [1982] 2 CMLR 264 ... 940, **958–960**

Ambulanz Glöckner v. Landkreis Südwestpflaz (Case
C-475/99) [2001] ECR I-8089, [2002] 4 CMLR
726 ... 127, 136, 584, 606, **627–629**, 637, **650–651**

Amministrazione delle Finanze dello Stato v. San
Giorgio SpA (Case 199/82) [1983] ECR 3595, [1985]
2 CMLR 658 ... 1084

Amministrazione delle Finanze dello Stato
v. Simmenthal SpA (Case 106/77) [1978] ECR 629,
[1978] 3 CMLR 263 ... 108, 1102

AOK Bundesverband v. Ichthyol-Gesellschaft Cordes,
Hermani & Co (Cases C-264, 306, 354 & 355/01)
[2004] ECR I-2493, [2004] 4 CMLR 126 ... 51, 129,
132–135, 601

Arbed SA v. Commission (Case C-176/99 P) [2003] ECR
I-10687 ... 1035

Arcaro (Case C-168/95) [1996] ECR I-4705 ... 1007

Arcelor Mittal v. Commission (Cases C-201/09
and C-216/09 P) [2011] ECR I-2239 ... 110, 143,
146, 1033

Archer Daniels Midland Co (Case C-511/06 P), 9 July
2009 ... 934, 968, 1012

Archer Daniels Midland Co v. Commission (Case
C-397/03 P) [2006] ECR I-4429, [2006] 5 CMLR
230 ... 118, 242, 685, 942, 1008, 1018, 1040, 1043

Archer Daniels Midland Co v. Commission (Case
C-510/06 P) [2009] ECR I-1843 ... 154, 1003,
1008, 1012

Aristrain v. Commission (Case C-196/99 P) [2003] ECR
I-11005 ... 1005

ASBL Vereniging van Vlaamse Reisbureaus v. ASBL
Sociale Dienst van de Plaatselijke en Gewestelijke
Overheidsdiensten (Case 311/85) [1987] ECR 3801,
[1989] 4 CMLR 213 ... 679, 773–774

Asnef-Equifax, Servicios de Información sobre
Solvencia y Crédito, SL v. Asociación de Usuarios
de Servicios Bancarios (Ausbanc) (Case C-238/05)
[2006] ECR I-11125 ... 149, 229, 259, 702, 704,
707–708

AstraZeneca v. Commission (Case C-457/10 P) [2012]
ECR I-000, 6 December 2012 ... 69, 82, 90, 299, 302,
322, 338–339, 346–347, 355–356, 360, 373–374,
378, 380, 382, 388, **558–562**, 729

Auto24 SARL v. Jaguar Land Rover France SAS, (Case
C-158/11) 14 June 2012 ... 809, 834

Autotrasporti Librandi v. Cuttica Spedizioni (Case
C-38/97) [1998] ECR I-5955, [1998] 5 CMLR
966 ... 164

Bagnasco v. Banca Popolare di Novarra (NPN) and
Cassa di Risparmio di Genova e Imperia (Carige)
(Case C-215/96) [1999] ECR I-135 [1999] 4 CMLR
624 ... 184, 229–230

Banchero (Case C-387/93) [1995] ECR
I-4663 ... 607, 621

BASF v. Commission (Dyestuffs) (Case 49/69) [1972]
ECR 619 ... 976, 978

BAT and Reynolds v. Commission (Cases 142 and
156/84) [1987] ECR 4487, [1988] 4 CMLR 24 ... 969,
1039, 1073, 1136

BAT v. Commission (Case 35/83) [1985] ECR 363,
[1985] 2 CMLR 470 ... 913

Baustahlgewebe v. Commission (Case C-185/95 P)
[1998] ECR I-8422 ... 937, 970, 1046, 1048

Bayer AG and Maschinenfabrik Hennecke v. Heinz
Süllhöfer (Case 65/86) [1988] ECR 5249, [1990] 4
CMLR 182 ... 527, 913

Béguelin Import v. GL Import-Export (Case 22/71)
[1971] ECR 949, [1972] CMLR 81 ... 138, 180, 226,
720, 1102, **1272**

Belgische Radio en Televisie v. SV SABAM (Case
127/73) [1974] ECR 51, [1974] 2 CMLR 23 ... 116,
128, 275, 282, 634, 652, 1102

Benedetti v. Munari (Case 52/76) [1977] ECR 163 ... 604

Benzine en Petroleum Handelsmaatschappij BV
v. Commission (Case 77/77) (ABG Oil) [1978] ECR
1513, [1978] 3 CMLR 174 ... 281–282, 331, 510, 589

Bergaderm and Goupil v. Commission (Case C-352/98 P)
[2000] ECR I-5291 ... 1047, 1050

Bertelsmann AG, Sony Corporation of America (Case
C-413/06 P) [2008] ECR I-4951 ... 719, 969, 1184–
1185, 1201, **1204–1205**, 1207–1208, 1253–1254

Bilger v. Jehle (Case 43/69) [1970] ECR 127 ... 235

BMV v. ALD (Case C-70/93) [1995] ECR I-3429 ... 159

BMW Belgium v. Commission (Cases 32/78, 36/78 to 82/78) [1979] ECR 2435, [1980] 1 CMLR 370 ... 155, 159, 224, 812

BNIC v. Clair (Case 123/83) [1985] ECR 391, [1985] 2 CMLR 430 ... 147, 182, 429, 604

BPB Industries plc and British Gypsum Ltd v. Commission (Case C-310/93 P) [1995] ECR I-865, [1997] 4 CMLR 238 ... 328, 394, 459, 464, 568, 582, 584, 974, 1048

Brasserie de Haecht SA v. Wilkin (No. 1) (Case 23/67) [1967] ECR 407, [1968] CMLR 26 ... 197, 233–235, 1108

Brentjens' Handelsonderneming BV v. Stichting Bedrijfspensioenfonds voor de Handel in Bouwmaterialen (Cases C-115-17/97) [1999] ECR I-6025, [2000] 4 CMLR 566 ... 153, 623

British Airways plc v. Commission (Case C-95/04 P) [2006] ECR I-2331 ... 42, 47, 81–82, 271, 289, 292, 300, 305–306, 323, 370, 372, 377, 382, 386–387, 394, 398, 401, 416, 439, 454, 456, 459, **470–475**, 483, 568, **573–575**, 586–587

British Leyland plc v. Commission (Case 226/84) [1986] ECR 3263, [1987] 1 CMLR 185 ... 81, 282, 327, 355, 372, 577–578, 584, 586–587

British Sugar plc v. Commission (Case C-359/01 P) [2004] ECR I-4933, [2004] 5 CMLR 329 ... 169, 679, 700, 1047–1048

Bundeskartellamt v. Volkswagen AG and VAG Leasing GmbH (Case C-266/93) [1995] ECR I-3477 ... 138, 773–775

Bundesverband der Arzneimittel- Importeure EV and Commission v. Bayer AG (Cases C-2 & 3/01 P) [2004] ECR I-23, [2004] 4 CMLR 653 ... 149–150, 156–158, **160–162**, 272, 510, 585, 791–793, 1036, 1049

Bundeswettbewerbsbehörde and Bundeskartellanwalt v. Schenker (Case C-681/11) [2013] ECR I-000, 18 June 2013 ... 998

Bundeswettbewerbsbehörde v. Donau Chemie AG (Case C-536/11) [2013] ECR I-000, 6 June 2013 ... 1027, 1060, 1092

Cadillon (Case 1/71) ... 229–230

Cañas v. Commission, (Case C-269/12 P), judgment pending ... 113

Centrafarm BV and Adnaan De Peijper v. Sterling Drug Inc (Case 15/74) [1974] ECR 1183, [1974] 2 CMLR 480 ... 138–141, 277

Centre Belge d'Etudes du Marché-Télémarketing (CBEM) v. Compagnie Luxembourgeoise de Télédiffusion SA and Information Publicité Benelux SA (Case 311/84) [1985] ECR 3261, [1986] 2 CMLR 558 ... 275, 355, 386–387, 393–394, 489, 506, 510, 515, 519, 525, 537, 609, 611–612, 614, 616

Centro Servizi Spediporto v. Spedizioni Maritima del Golfo srl (Case C-96/94) [1995] ECR I-2883, [1996] 4 CMLR 613 ... 164, 281, 718

CEPSA Estaciones de Servicio SA v. LV Tobar e Hojos Sl ('CEPSA') (Case C-279/06) [2008] ECR I-6681 ... 138, 774–776

Chemische Afvalstoffen Dusseldorp BV v. Minister van Volkshuisvesting, Ruimtelijke Ordening en Milieubeheer (Case C-203/96) [1998] ECR I-4075, [1998] 3 CMLR 873 ... 619, 627, 634–638, 644–645

CICCE v. Commission (Case 298/83) [1985] ECR 1105, [1986] 1 CMLR 486 ... 300, 581, 1073

CICCRA v. Renault (Case 53/87) [1988] ECR 6039, [1990] 4 CMLR 265 ... 318, 515, 525–526, 579

CILFIT Srl and Lanificio de Gavardo SpA v. Ministry of Health (Case 283/81) [1982] ECR 3415, [1983] CMLR 472 ... 105

Cipolla v. Fazari (Cases C-94/04 and C-202/04) ECR I-1142 ... 187

Cisal di Battistello Venanzio & Co v. Istituto Nazionale per L'Assicurazione Contro Glifortuni Sul Lavoro (INAIL) (Case C-218/00) [2002] ECR I-691, [2002] 4 CMLR 24 ... **132–134**, 601

CNL-Sucal v. HAG GF AG ('Hag II') (Case C-10/89) [1990] ECR I-3711, [1990] 3 CMLR 571 ... 105, 231

Coditel v. Ciné Vog Films (Case 62/79) [1980] ECR 881, [1981] 2 CMLR 362 (Coditel I) ... 211, 854, 914

Coditel v. Ciné Vog Films (Case 262/81) [1982] ECR 3381, [1983] 1 CMLR 49 (Coditel II) [1982] ECR 3382, [1983] 1 CMLR 49 ... 215, 753, 854, 864–865, 914, **914–916**, 918

Commission and France v. Ladbroke Racing (Cases C-359/95 P and C-379/95 P) [1997] ECR I-6265 ... 187, 428

Commission v. Agrofert Holding a.s. (Case C-477/10 P) [2012] ECR I-000, 28 June 2012 ... 977, 1180, 1253

Commission v. Anic (Case C-49/92 P) [1999] ECR I-4125, [2001] 4 CMLR 17 ... 149–150, 154, 169–170, 177

Commission v. Assidomän Kraft Products AB (Case C-310/97 P) [1999] ECR I-5363, [1999] 5 CMLR 1253 ... 1030, 1046, 1048

Commission v. Atlantic Container Line and others (Case C-149/95 P(R)) [1995] ECR I-2165 ... 1048

Commission v. BASF (Case C-137/92 P) [1994] ECR I-2555 ... 979, **1033–1035**, 1048

Commission v. Council (ERTA) (Case 22/70) [1971] ECR 263 ... 104, 1032

Commission v. DEI, (Case C-553/12 P) judgment pending ... 630

Commission v. DEI, (Case C-554/12 P) judgment pending ... 285, 605, 619

Commission v. Éditions Odile Jacob (Case C-404/10 P) [2012] ECR I-000, 28 June 2012 ... 977–978, 1148, 1180, 1253

Commission v. EnBW Energie Baden-Württemberg, (Case C-365/12 P) judgment pending ... 978, 1026

Commission v. Finland (Case C-284/05) [2009] ECR
I-11705...113

Commission v. France (Re Electricity and Gas Imports)
(Case C-159/94) [1997] ECR I-5815...652

Commission v. Germany (Case C-280/93 R) [1993] ECR
I-3667...1048

Commission v. GlaxoSmithKline Services Unlimited
(Cases C-501, 513, 515 and 519/06 P) [2009] ECR
000, para. 61...40, 158, 223, 254, 289, 585

Commission v. ICI (Cases C-286-288/95)P [2000] ECR
I-2341...1035

Commission v. Ireland (Case 249/81) [1982] ECR
4005...607

Commission v. Ireland (Case C-221/08) [2010] ECR
I-1669...49

Commission v. Italy (Case 39/72) [1973] ECR
101...1103–1104

Commission v. Italy (Case 42/83) [1985] ECR
873...129

Commission v. Italy (Case C-138/11) [1998] ECR
I-3851, [1998] 5 CMLR 889...127, 135, 147

Commission v. Jégo-Quéré (Case C-263/02 P) [2004]
ECR I-3425...106

Commission v. Lisrestal (Case C-32/95 P) [1996] ECR
I-5373...966

Commission v. Netherlands (Re Electricity Imports)
(Case C-157/94) [1997] ECR I-5699...637, **643**,
646–647, 652

Commission v. Scheider Electric, (Case C-440/07 P) 16
July 2009...1050, 1254

Commission v. Solvay (Cases C-286-8/96 P) [2000] ECR
I-2391, [2000] 5 CMLR 454...459

Commission v. Stichting Administratiekantoor
Portielje and Gosselin Group NV (Case C-440/11
P)...146

Commission v. Technische Glaswerke Ilmenau (Case
C-139/07 P) [2010] ECR I-5885...977

Commission v. Tetra Laval (Case C-12/03 P) [2005]
ECR I-987...57, 102–103, 448, 538, 1038, 1042,
1184–1187, 1223, **1226–1228**, 1230, 1235–1236,
1248, 1250

Commission v Trenker (Case C-459/00 P(R))...1039

Commission v. Volkswagen AG (Case C-74/04 P)
[2006] ECR I-6585...157, 162–164, 272, 789–790,
792, 1036

Compagnie Commerciale de l'Ouest (Cases C-78-83/90)
[1992] ECR I-1847...622

Compagnie Maritime Belge Transports SA
v. Commission (Cases C-395 and 396/96 P) [2000]
ECR I-1365, [2000] 4 CMLR 1076...277–280, 293,
344, 370, 375, 377, 380, 392, 397, 406, 413–415,
421–423, 425, 464, 471, 557, 565, 590, **720–722**,
724, 968, 1039, 1045

Compagnie Royale Asturienne des Mines SA and
Rheinzink GmbH v. Commission (Cases 29
and 30/83) [1984] ECR 1679, [1985] 1 CMLR
688...126, 1036

Compañía española para la fabricación de aceros
inoxidables SA (Acerinox) v. Commission (Case
C-57/02 P) [2005] ECR I-6689...1046, 1048

Compass-Datenbank GmbH v. Republik Österreich,
(Case C-138/11) 12 July 2012...127, 129, 131

Competition Authority v. Beef Industry
Development Society Ltd (BIDS) and Barry Brothers
(Carrigmore) Meals Ltd (Case C-209/07) [2008] ECR
I-8637...187, 204–206, 211–212, 215–216, 224, 231,
675, 694

Confederación Española de Empresarios de Estaciones
de Servicio v. Compañia Española de Petróleos SA
(Case C-217/05) [2006] ECR I-11987...137–138,
774–776

Connect Austria Gesellschaft für Telekommunikation
GmbH v. Telekom-Control-Kommission (Case
C-462/99) [2003] ECR I-5147...618–619

Consorzio Industrie Fiammiferi (CIF) v. Autorità
Garante della Concorrenza e del Mercato (Case
C-198/01) [2003] ECR I-8055; [2003] 5 CMLR
829...187, 428, 1063–1064

Coop de France Bétail and Viande v. Commission,
FNSEA v. Commission (Cases C-101 and 110/07)
[2008] ECR I-10193...128, 187, **225–226**, 675,
680–682, 1018

Corbeau (Case C-320/91) [1993] ECR I-2533, [1995]
4 CMLR 621...**620–621**, 625–626, 630, 634, 637,
641–647, 649–650, 652–653

Corinne Bodson v. Pompes Funèbres des Régions
Libérées SA (Case 30/87) [1988] ECR 2479, [1989]
4 CMLR 984...130, 139–140, 277, 282, 355, 578,
603, 605

Corsica Ferries France SA v. Gruppo Antichi
Ormeggiatori del Porto di Genova Coop arl [1998]
ECR I-3949, (Case C-266/96) [1998] 5 CMLR
402...283, 601, 622, 629, 637, **645–646**

Corsica Ferries Italia Srl v. Corpo dei Piloti del Porto di
Genovo (Case C-18/93) [1994] ECR I-1783...568,
572, 581, 614, 622

Corus UK v. Commission (Case C-199/99) [2003] ECR
I-000 [RB1]0...972

Courage Ltd v. Crehan (Case C-453/99) [2001] ECR
I-6297, [2001] 5 CMLR 28...39, 125, 1027, 1092,
1098, **1102–1104**, **1108**, 1119, 1122

Criminal Proceedings against Becu (Case C-22/98)
[1999] ECR I-5665, [2001] 4 CMLR 968...137–138

Dansk Rørindustri A/S v. Commission (Cases C-189,
202, 208 and 213/02 P) [2005] ECR I-5425, [2005] 5
CMLR 796...65, 102, 118, 143, 230, 291, 690, **933**,
1000, **1005–1008**, 1013–1014, 1016–1017, 1040,
1042, 1048

Delimitis v. Henninger Bräu (Case C-234/89) [1991] ECR I-935, [1992] 5 CMLR 210…184, 197, 200, 204, **234–238**, 242, 452, 772, **802–805**, 875, 1072, 1094–1097, 1108

Deltafina v. Commission, (Case C-578/11) judgment pending…1020

Demo-Studio Schmidt v. Commission (Case 210/81) [1983] ECR 3045, [1984] 1 CMLR 63…1068, 1073

Der Grüne Punkt-Duales System Deutschland GmbH v. Commission (Case C-385/07) 16 July 2009…327, 580, 582, 999

Deutsche Bahn AG v. Commission (Case C-436/97) [1999] ECR I-2387…569

Deutsche Grammophon v. Metro (Case 78/70) [1971] ECR 487, [1971] CMLR 631…579, 853

Deutsche Post AG v. Gesellschaft für Zahlungssysteme mbH (GZS) and Citicorp Kartenservice GmbH (Cases C-147-8/97) [2000] ECR I-825…578, 624, **624–626**, 630, 637, 649

Deutsche Telekom v. Commission (Case C-280/08 P) [2010] ECR I-9555…48, 53–54, 91, 271, 289, 291, 370–373, 380, 382, 401, **427–434**, 434–437, 439–441, 444–449, 556

Diego Cali e Figli SrL v. SEPG (Case C-343/95) [1997] ECR I-1547, [1997] 5 CMLR 484…130–131, 601, 604

DIP v. Commune di Bassano del Grappa and Commune di Chioggia (Cases C-140-142/94) [1995] ECR I-3257, [1996] 4 CMLR 157…280–281, 601

Distillers Company v. Commission (Case 30/78) [1980] ECR 2229, [1980] 3 CMLR 121…792, 835

Dorsch Consult (Case C-54/96) [1997] ECR I-4961…106

Doulamis (Case C-466/05) [1998] ECR I-1377…187

Dow Chemical Company v. Commission, (Case C-179/12) judgment pending…144

DSR-Senator Lines v. Commission (Case C-364/99 P(R)) [1999] ECR I-8733…1050

Eco Swiss China Time Ltd v. Benetton International NV (Case C-126/97) [1999] ECR I-3055, [2000] 5 CMLR 816…39, 1102

Electrabel v. Commission (Case C-84/13 P) (judgment pending)…1142, 1177

Ellinki Radiophonia Tileorassi-Anonimi Etairia (ERT-AE) v. Dimotiki Etairia Pliroforissis (DEP) (Case C-260/89) [1991] ECR I-2925, [1994] 4 CMLR 540…107, 393, 515, 599–600, 605, **611–617**, 620, 623–625, 629, 645, 653

EMC Development AB v. Commission (Case C-367/10 P) [2011] ECR I-000, 31 March 2011…1075

Eni SpA v. Commission, (Case C-508/11) 8 May 2013…143

Entreprenørforeningens Affalds (FFAD) v. Københavns Kommune (Case C-209/98) [2000] ECR-3743, [2001] 2 CMLR 936…605, 637, 624

E.ON Energie AG v. Commission, (Case C-89/11 P) 22 November 2012…948

Erauw-Jacquéry Sprl v. La Hesbignonne Société Coopérative (Case 27/87) [1988] ECR 1999, [1988] 4 CMLR 576…196, 211, 215, **863–864**, 896

Erste Group Bank AG v. Commission (Cases C-125, 113, 135 and 137/07 P) [2009] ECR I-8681…63, 682, 1069

ETA Fabriques d'Ebauches v. DK Investments SA (Case 31/85) [1985] ECR 3933, [1986] 2 CMLR 674…792, 810, 812

Etablissements Consten SA & Grundig-Verkaufs-GmbH v. Commission (Cases 56 and 58/64) [1966] ECR 299, [1966] CMLR 418…39, 123, 138, **151–153**, 183, 196, **205–211**, 223, 230–231, 239, 252–253, 790–791, 805, 822, 835, 838–839, 854, 860, 871, 909, 970, 1036, 1108

ETI and others (Case C-280/06) [2007] ECR I-10893…141

European Commission v. Alrosa (Case C-441/07 P) [2010] ECR I-5949…273, 453, 966, **985–989**, 1031, 1048

European Federation of Ink and Ink Cartridge Manufacturers (EFIM) v. Commission, (Case C-59/12 P) judgment pending…321

European Parliament v. Council ('Chernobyl') (Case C-70/88) [1990] ECR I-2041, [1992] 1 CMLR 91…105, 231

European Sugar Cartel, Re the; Cooperatiëve Vereniging Suiker Unie v. EC Commission (Cases 40-8, 50, 54-6, 111, 113, and 114/73) [1975] ECR 1663…110, 165, 168, 174, 281, 423, 428, **456–457**, 461, 464, 471, 574, 583–584, 700, **710–712**, 774

Europemballage & Continental Can v. Commission (Cases 6/72 and 7/72) [1973] ECR 215 [1973] CMLR 199…37, 46, 61–63, 66, 74, 109, 141, 143, 255, 270–272, 277, 288, 299, 304, **325**, 326, 332, **367–370**, 373, 416, 422, 471, 500, 567, 981, 1036–1037, 1135–1136, 1286

Evonik Degussa GmbH v. Commission (Case C-266/06 P) [2008] ECR I-81…1017

Expedia Inc. v. Autorité de la Concurrence (Case C-226/11) [2012] ECR I-000, 13 December 2012…118, 226, **228–231**, 242, 795

Factortame (Case C-213/89) [1990] ECR I-2433…1102, **1125–1126**

Federación Nacional de Empresas de Instrumentación Científica, Médica, Técnica y Dental (FENIN) v. Commission, 11 July 2006, (Case C-205/03 P) [2006] ECR I-6295, [2006] 5 CMLR 7…51, 127, **133–135**, 583

Fédération Française des Sociétés d'Assurance v. Ministère de l'Agriculture et de la Pêche (Case C-244/94) [1995] ECR I-4013, [1996] 4 CMLR 536…133, 601

Ferriere Nord v. Commission (Case C-219/95 P) [1997] ECR I-4411 ... 994, 1048

Ferring (Case C-53/00) [2001] ECR I-9067 ... 656

Flaminio Costa v. ENEL (Case 6/64) [1964] ECR 585, 593-4, [1964] CMLR 425 ... 108, 598, 1102

Football Association Premier League v. QC Leisure and Karen Murphy v. Media Protection Services Ltd (Cases C-403/08 and 429/08) [2011] ECR I-000 ... 39–40, 112, 206, 211, 215, 224, 256, 791, 854, 864, 917

Ford and Ford Europe v. Commission (Cases 25 and 26/84) [1985] ECR 2725 ... 158, 161

Ford Werke AG and Ford of Europe Inc v. Commission (Cases 228 and 229/82) [1984] ECR 1129, [1984] 1 CMLR 649 ... 157, 162, 266–267, 812, 991

Foto-Frost v. Hauptzollamt Lübeck-Ost (Case 314/85) [1987] ECR 4199 ... 1095, 1120

France v. Commission (Case C-202/88) [1991] ECR I-1223 (the Telecommunications Equipment case) ... 600, 604–605, **607–608**, 614–617, 629, 637, 647, **654–655**, 1033

France v. Commission (Case C-327/91) [1994] ECR I-3641, [1994] 5 CMLR 517 ... 1287

France and others v. Commission (Kali und Salz) (Case C-30/95) [1998] ECR I-1375 ... 719–722, 1179, 1187, 1200, 1205–1206, 1217, 1246, 1250, 1253

France, Italy and the UK v. Commission (Cases 188-90/80) [1982] ECR 2545, [1982] 3 CMLR 144 ... 604, 653–654

France Télécom v. Commission (Case C-202/07 P) [2009] 4 CMLR 1149 ... 73–74, 289, 312, 362, 372, 374, 378, 392, 406, 408, **411–412, 415–417**, 419–420, 430, 562, 1041, 1047

Francovich v. Italy (Cases C-6 and 9/90) [1991] ECR I-5357, [1993] 2 CMLR 66 ... 1084, 1102

French Republic and Société commerciale des potasses et de l'azote (SCPA) and Entreprise minière et chimique (EMC) v. Commission (Cases C-68/94 and 30/95) [1998] ECR I-1375 ... 37, 106, 109, 255, 280, 370, 719–722, 966, 1036–1037, 1180, 1188, **1200–1201**, 1206, **1217–1219**, 1247, 1250, 1253

Fresh Del Monte Produce v. Commission (Cases C-293 and 294/13 P) (judgments pending) ... 178, 700

FRUBO v. Commission (Case 71/74) [1975] ECR 563, [1975] 2 CMLR 123 ... 110

Gabalfrisa and Others [2000] (Cases C-110/98 to C-147/98) ECR I-1577 ... 106

Geigy v. Commission (Case 52/69) [1972] ECR 787 ... 143, 1286

GEMA v. Commission (Case 125/78) [1979] ECR 3173 ... 300, 581, 1072–1073

Gemeente Almelo v. NV Energiebedrijf Ijsselmij (Case C-393/92) [1994] ECR I-1477 ... 280, 635–637, **643–644**, 652, 718, 721

General Motors BV v. Commission (Case C-551/03 P) [2006] ECR I-3173 ... 157–158, 162, 216, 588

General Motors Continental NV v. Commission (Case 26/75) [1975] ECR 1367, [1976] 1 CMLR 95 ... 81, 282, 327, 577, 587

General Química SA v. Commission, (Case C-90/09 P) 20 January 2011 ... 142

Germany v. Commission (Case 24/62) [1963] ECR 63, [1963] CMLR 347 ... 1034

GlaxoSmithKline Services Unlimited v. Commission (Case C-501/06 P) [2009] ECR I-9291 ... 14, 40, 47, 54, 123, 158, 206, **222–225**, 250–251, 254, 289, 579, 585, 788, 790, 792, 798, 813, 835, 895–896, 918, 1038, 1048

Gøttrup-Klim Grovvareforening v. Dansk Landbrugs Grovvareselskab AmbA (DLG) (Case C-250/92) [1994] ECR I-5641, [1996] 4 CMLR 191 ... 128, 138, 147, 197, 199–200, 215, 218, **244**, 248, 343, 750, 752

Groupe Danone v. Commission (Case C-3/06 P) 8 February 2007 ... 675, 687–688, 964, 1004–1005, 1040

GT-Link A/S v. De Danske Statsbaner (DSB) (Case C-242/95) [1997] ECR I-4449, [1997] 5 CMLR 601 ... 516, 630, 638, 1084

Guérin Automobiles v. Commission (Case C-282/95 P) [1997] ECR I-1503 ... 1102

Gutmann v. Commission of the EAEC (Cases 18 and 35/65) [1966] ECR 149 ... 1018

GVL v. Commission (Case 7/82) [1983] ECR 483, [1983] 3 CMLR 645 ... 510, 583

Hasselblad (GB) Ltd v. Commission (Case 86/82) [1984] ECR 883, [1984] 1 CMLR 559 ... 172, 206, 702, 793, 810–812

Hilti AG v. EC Commission (Case C-53/92 P) [1994] ECR I-667, [1994] 4 CMLR 614 ... **319–320**, 338, 353, 389, 487, 489–492, 494–495, 500–501, 507, 1041, 1046

H. J. Banks v. British Coal Corporation (Case C-128/92) [1994] ECR I-1209, [1994] 5 CMLR à ... 275

Hoechst AG v. Commission (Cases 46/87 and 227/88) [1989] ECR 2859, [1991] 4 CMLR 410 ... 46, 942, 944, 947, 949–950, 954

Hoffmann-La Roche & Co AG v. Commission (Case 85/76) [1979] ECR 461, [1979] 3 CMLR 211 ... 33, 63, 277, 288, 293, **299**, 302, **313–314**, 315, 332, **336–339**, 341, 344–347, **351**, 355, 359, **372–373**, 376, 378, 405, 415, 423, 430, 433, 450–451, **455–458**, 460–461, 464, 467, 469, 471–473, 475, 480, 483, 523, 543, 568, 717, 725, 972, **974**, 999

Hoffmann-La Roche (Case 102/77) ... 717

Höfner and Elser v. Macroton GmbH (Case C-41/90) [1991] ECR I-1979, [1993] 4 CMLR 306 ... 127, **129–130**, 135, 181, 584, 599–600, 605, **609–610**, 611–614, 622, 641, 645, 650–652

Holcim (Deutschland) AG v. Commission (Case C-282/05 P) [2007] ECR I-2941 ... 1050

Hugin Kassaregister AB and Hugin Cash Registers Ltd v. Commission (Case 22/78) [1979] ECR 1869, [1979] 3 CMLR 345 ... 181, 282, 284, 318, 356, 371, 525, 527, 567

Hüls AG v. Commission (Case C-199/92 P) [1999] ECR I-4287, [1999] 5 CMLR 1016 ... 126, 154, **165–167**, 169–170, 177, 675, 679–680, 685, 937, 1041, 1046

Hydrotherm Gerätebau GmbH v. Compact de Dott Ing Mario Adredi & CSAS (Case 170/83) [1984] ECR 2999, [1985] 3 CMLR 224 ... 137–141, 146

IAZ International Belgium SA v. Commission (Cases 96 to 102, 104, 105, 108 and 110/82) [1983] ECR 3369, [1984] 3 CMLR 276 ... 128, 138, 148, 173–174, 224, 429, 588, 675, 697, 757, 1016

IBM v. Commission (Case 60/81) [1981] ECR 2639, [1981] 3 CMLR 635 ... 106, 968–969, 1031–1032

ICI v. Commission (Dyestuffs) (Cases 48, 49, and 51-7/69) [1972] ECR 619, [1972] CMLR 557 ... 140–143, 146, 165, 170, 173, 678–679, **710–711**, 715, 1033, **1272–1274**, 1286

ICI plc v. Commission (Case C-200/92 P) [1999] ECR I-4399, [1999] 5 CMLR 1110 ... 177, 680

IMS Health GmbH & Co. OHG v. NDC Health GmbH & Co. KG (Case C-418/01) [2004] ECR I-5039, [2004] 4 CMLR 1543 ... 41, 81, 275, 322, 356, 391, 526, **531–535**, 537, 539–540, 543, 545, 991–992, 1032, 1048–1049

Inspecteur van de Belastingdienst v. Commission (Case C-429/07), 11 June 2009 ... 1019

Ireks-Arkady v. Council and Commission (Case 238/78) [1979] ECR 2955 ... 1103

Irish Sugar plc v. Commission (Case C-497/99 P) [2001] ECR I-5333, [2001] 5 CMLR 1082 ... 344, 421, 423, 456, 465–466, 542

Istituto Chemioterapico Italiano Spa and Commercial Solvents Corp v. EC Commission (Cases 6 and 7/73) [1974] ECR 223, [1974] 1 CMLR 309 ... 80, 144, 182, 277, 284, 317, 321–322, 332–333, 355, 370–371, 393–394, **510–515**, 519–520, 525, 529–531, 537, 567, 586, 980–981, 1068

Italy v. Commission (Case 41/83) [1985] ECR 873, [1985] 2 CMLR 368 ... 428, 639, 641

Italy v. Sacchi (Case 155/73) [1974] ECR 409, [1974] 2 CMLR 177 ... 127, 130, 604–605, 609, 611–612, 648, 653

Javico International and Javico AF v. Yves Saint Laurent Parfums SA (Case C-306/96) [1998] ECR I-1983, [1998] 5 CMLR 172 ... 180, 183, 229, 588

JCB Service v. Commission (Case C-167/04) [2006] ECR I-8935, [2006] 5 CMLR 23 ... 157, 162, 195, 789, 792

Job Centre (Case C-55/96) [1997] ECR I-7119, [1998] 4 CMLR 708 ... 584, 610, 617, 628, 651

John Deere Ltd v. Commission (Case C-7/95 P) [1998] ECR I-3111, [1998] 5 CMLR 311 ... 174, 229, 704–706, 1041, 1046

Johnston v. Chief Constable of the Royal Ulster Constabulary (Case 222/84) [1986] ECR 1651 ... 564

Just I/S v. Danish Ministry for Fiscal Affairs (Case 68/79) [1980] ECR 501 ... 1103

Kanal 5 Ltd v. Föreningen Svenska Tonsättares Internationella Musikbyrå (STIM) upa (Case C-52/07) [2008] ECR I-9275 ... 304, 386, 574, 581, 919

Kattner Stahlbau GmbH v. Maschinenbau -und Metall-Berufsgenossenschaft (Case C-350/07) [2009] ECR I-1513 ... 132–133, 601

Keck and Mithouard, Criminal Proceedings against (Cases C-267 and 268/91) [1993] ECR I-6097, [1995] 1 CMLR 101 ... 105, 231

Ker-Optika (Case C-108/09) [2010] ECR I-0000 ... 814–815

Keurkoop v. Nancy Kean Gifts (Case 144/81) [1982] ECR 2853, [1983] 2 CMLR 47 ... 848

Kingdom of Sweden v. Commission (Case C-506/08P) [2011] ECR I-75, 21 July 2011 ... 977

Kish Glass and Co Ltd v. Commission (Case C-241/00) [2001] ECR I-7159 ... 75, 274, 323, 1038–1039

Klopp (Case 107/83) [1984] ECR 2971 ... 217

KME Germany AG v. Commission (Case C-272/09 P) [2011] ECR I-000, 8 December 2011 ... 100, 231, 934, 937, 1029, 1032, 1037, 1039, **1041–1043**, 1044

Knauf Gips v. Commission (Case C-407/08P) [2010] ECR I-6375 ... 100, 938, 968

Kohl (Case C-158/96) [1998] ECR I-1931 ... 133

Köllensperger and Atzwanger (Case C-103/97) [1999] ECR I-551 ... 106

Kolpinghuis Nijmegen (Case 80/86) [1987] ECR 3969 ... 1007

Konkurrensverket v. TeliaSonera Sverige AB (Case C-52/09) [2011] ECR I-527 ... 38, 43, 46, 48, 109, 292, 299, 366, **373–376**, 377, 380, 382, 386–387, 395, 396, 401, 424, 427, **434–441**, 443–449, 521–522, 551, 553, 580

Langnese-Iglo v. Commission (Case C-279/95 P) [1998] ECR I-5609, [1998] 5 CMLR 933 ... 266, 980–981

Laurent Piau v. Commission (Case C-171/05 P) [2006] ECR I-37 ... 219, 256

Lestelle v. Commission (Case C-30/91 P) [1992] ECR I-3755 ... 225

Limburgse Vinyl Maatschappij NV v. Commission (Cases C-238, 244-5, 247, 250, 251-2 and 254/99) [2002] ECR I-8375 ... 938, 950, 956, 966, 971–972, 1018, 1035, 1043, 1047

L'Oréal NV and L'Oréal SA v. De Nieuwe AMCK Puba (Case 31/80) [1980] ECR 3775, [1981] 2 CMLR 235 ... 309, 808–809, 814

Lück v. Hauptzollamt Köln (Case 34/67) [1968] ECR 245 ... 1084

Maatschappij Drijvende Bokken BV v. Stichting Pensioenfonds voor de Vervoer-en Havenbedrijven (Case C-219/97) [1999] ECR I-6121, [2000] 4 CMLR 599...623

Mac Quen (Case C-108/96) [2001] ECR I-837...218

Magill *see* RTE & ITP v. Commission (Magill) (Cases C-241-242/91 P) [1995] ECR I-743

Manfredi v. Lloyd Adriatico Assicurazioni SpA (Cases C-295-98/04) [2006] ECR I-6619, [2006] 5 CMLR 17...125, 1092, 1097, **1104**, 1106–1107, 1109

Marshall v. Southampton and South-West Hampshire Area Health Authority (Teaching) (No. 2) (Case C-271/91) [1993] ECR I-4367, [1993] 3 CMLR 293...1084

MasterCard Inc, MasterCard International Inc, and MasterCard Europe SPRL v. Commission (Case C-382/12 P), (pending)...63, 81, 147, 199, 221, 245, 764

Masterfoods v. HB Ice Cream Ltd (Case C-344/98) [2000] ECR I-11369...429, 1095

max.mobil (Case C-141/02 P) [2005] ECR I-1283...653

Meca-Medina and Majcen v. Commission, (Case C-519/04 P) [2006] ECR I-6991 [2006] 5 CMLR 1023 1023...51, 112, 128, 220, 247, 249, 764, 1047–1048

Merci Convenzionali Porto di Genova SpA v. Siderurgica Gabrielli SpA (Case C-179/90) [1991] ECR I-5889, [1994] 4 CMLR 422...283, 584, 599, 605, 607, **613**, 617, 620, 622–623, 625, 638, 641, 645

Merck and Co Inc v. Primecrown Ltd (Merck II) (Cases C-267 and 268/95) [1996] ECR I-6285, [1997] 1 CMLR 83...854

Metro v. Cartier (Case C-372/02) [1994] ECR I-15, [1994] 5 CMLR 331...792

Metro-SB-Grossmärkte GmbH v. Commission (No. 1) (Case 26/76) [1977] ECR 1875, [1978] 2 CMLR 1...32, 246, 255–256, 789, **807–812**, 814, 1031, 1077

Metro-SB-Grossmärkte GmbH v. Commission (No. 2) (Case 75/84) [1986] ECR 3021, [1987] 1 CMLR 118...**807–810**, 1031

Miller International Schallplaten v. Commission (Case 19/77) [1978] ECR 131, [1978] 2 CMLR 334...224, 792, 795, **998**

Ministère Public v. Lucas Asjes (Nouvelles Frontières) (Cases 209-213/84) [1986] ECR 1425, [1986] 3 CMLR 173...116

Ministère Public v. Tournier (Case 395/87) [1989] ECR 2521, [1991] 4 CMLR 248...579, 919

Ministère Public of Luxembourg v. Muller (Case 10/71) [1971] ECR 723...637, 653

Moccia Irme and Others v. Commission (Cases C-280/99 P to C-2102/99 P)...1047

Montecatini v. Commission (Case C-235/92 P) [1999] ECR I-4539...200

Motosykletistiki Omospondia Ellados NPID (MOTOE) (Greek Motorcycling Federation) v. Elliniko Dimosio (Case C-49/07) [2008] ECR I-4863...112, 128, 136, 276, **616–617**, 629, 764

Musik-Vertrieb Membran v. GEMA (Cases 55 and 57/80) [1981] ECR 147, [1981] 2 CMLR 44...853

Musique Diffusion Française SA v. Commission (Pioneer) (Cases 100-103/80) [1983] ECR 1825, [1983] 3 CMLR 221...102, 172, 933, 968, 972, 998, **1000–1001**, 1014, 1017, 1039–1040

National Panasonic v. Commission (Case 136/79) [1980] ECR 2033, [1980] CMLR 169...**942–944**

Nederlandsche Banden-Industrie Michelin v. Commission (Michelin I) (Case 322/81) [1983] ECR 3461, [1985] I CMLR 282...64, 73, 79, 285, 300, 306, **309**–311, 311–312, 323, **326–328**, 330–331, 339, 345, 347, **352–353**, 373–374, 379, 394, 416, 423, 428, **460–462**, 465–466, 471–473, 480, 483, 528, 568, 609–610, 612, 954, 972, 1002

Nederlandse Federatieve Vereniging voor de Groothandel op Elektrotechnisch Gebied v. Commission (Case C-105/04 P) [2006] ECR I-8725...178–179, 206, 938

Neste Markkinointi Oy v. Yötuuli (Case C-214/99) [2000] ECR I-1121, [2000] 4 CMLR 993...804

Netherlands and Koninklijke PTT Netherland v. Commission (Cases C-48 and 66/90) [1992] ECR I-565, [1993] 5 CMLR 316...653

Nexans France SAS v. Commission, (Case C-37/13) judgment pending...944, 947

Nintendo Co and Nintendo of Europe GmbH v. Commission (Case C-260/09 P) [2011] ECR I-419...156, 793

Nold v. Commission (Case 4/73) [1974] ECR 491, [1974] CMLR 338...105, 231, 943

Nungesser v. Commission (Case 258/78) [1982] ECR 2015, [1983] 1 CMLR 27...138, 196, 199–200, 211, **859**–863, 863–864, 872–873, 896, 899

NV GB-INNO-BM v. ATAB (Case 13/77) [1977] ECR 2115...**601–602**, 606, 609, 612

NV L'Oreal and SA L'Oreal v. PVBA De Nieuwe AMCK (Case 31/90) [1980] ECR 3775...309

Ojha v. Commission (Case C-294/95 P) [1996] ECR I-5863...225

Ordem dos Técnicos Oficiais de Contas (OTOC) v. Autoridade da Concorrência, (Case C-1/12) 28 February 2013...128, 148–149, 219, 260–261, 619, 651

Orkem SA v. Commission (Case 374/87) [1989] ECR 3283, [1991] 4 CMLR 502...940–941, **954**, 957, 1056

Oscar Bronner GmbH & Co KG v. Mediaprint (Case C-7/97) [1998] ECR I-7791, [1999] 4 CMLR 112...42, 106, 275, 304, 322, 391, 437–438, 441–444, 446, **518**–520, 520–522, 524–526, 533–535, 537–538, 554, 556

Österreichischer Gewerkschaftsbund (Case C-195/98) [2000] ECR I-10497 ... 106

Oude Luttikhuis v. Verenigde Cooperatieve Melkindustrie (Case C-399/93) [1995] ECR I-1415 ... 200

Papierfabrik August Koehler AG v. Commission (Cases C-322, C-327 and C-338/07 P), 3 September 2009 ... 968

Parke Davis v. Probel (Case 24/67) [1968] ECR 55 ... 355, 579

Parliament v. Bieber (Case C-284/98 P) [2000] ECR I-1527 ... 1047

Pavlov v. Stichting Pensioenfonds Medische Specialisten (Cases C-180-184/98) [2000] ECR I-6451, [2001] 4 CMLR 30 ... 127, 133, 136–138, 147, 153, 601, 627

Pedro IV Servicios (Case C-260/07) [2009] ECR I-2437 ... 229, 796

Pfleiderer AG v. Bundeskartellamt (Case C-360/09) [2011] ECR I-5161 ... 118, 230, 1027, 1060, 1084, **1090–1092**, 1120

Pierre Fabre Dermo-Cosmétique SAS v. Président de l'Autorité de la concurrence (Case C-439/09) [2011] ECR I-000, 13 October 2011 ... 40, 213, 220, 232, 263, 789, **793–795**, **812–814**, 818, 829

Plaumann & Co v. Commission (Case 25/62) [1963] ECR 95, [1964] CMLR 29 ... 1031

Portelange (Case 10/69) [1969] ECR 309 ... 1102

Portugal v. Commission (Case C-163/99) [2001] ECR I-2613, [2002] 2 CMLR 1319 ... 283, 456, 464–466, 568–569, 573, 629, 653–654

Post Danmark A/S v. Konkurrencerådet (C-209/10) [2012] ECR I-000, 27 March 2012 ... 46, 48, 272–273, 292, 366–367, **373**, 374, 376, **378–380**, 382, 385, **387**, 389–391, 398–399, 401, 406, **408–411**, 421, 425, 447, 725

Poucet and Pistre v. Assurances Générales de France (Cases C-159-160/91) [1993] ECR I-637 ... 127, 132, 601, 604

Premier League Ltd v. QC Leisure and Murphy v. Media Protection Services Ltd, (Cases C-403 and 429/08) 4 October 2011 ... 39–40, 112, 206, 211, 215, 224, 256, 791, 854, 864, **917–919**

Prezes Urzędu Ochrony Konkurencji i Konsumentów v. Tele 2 Polska sp. z o.o., now Netia SA (Case C-375/09) [2011] ECR I-3055 ... 274, 1051

Pronuptia de Paris GmbH v. Pronuptia de Paris Irmgard Schillgallis (Case 161/84) [1986] ECR 353, [1986] 1 CMLR 414 ... 183, 197, 199–200, **243**, 789, **815–816**, 879

Protimonopolný úrad Slovenskej republiky v. Slovenská sporiteľňa a.s. (Case C-68/12) [2013] ECR I-000, 7 February 2013 ... 47, 123, 164, 206, 250, 261

Prym and Prym Consumer v Commission (Case C-534/07 P) ... 1042–1043

Pubblico Ministero della Repubblica Italiana v. Società Agricola Industria Latte (SAIL) (Case 82/71) [1972] ECR 119 ... 604

Publishers' Association v. Commission (Case 56/89 R) [1989] ECR 1693 ... 1049

Publishers' Association v. Commission (Case C-360/92 P) [1995] ECR I-23; [1995] 5 CMLR 33 ... 680, 1034, 1048, 1062

Quin Barlo Ltd v. Commission (Case C-70/12 P) [2013] ECR I-00, 30 May 2013 ... 1039, 1047

Reisebüro Broede (Case C-3/95) [1996] ECR I-6511 ... 217–218, 248

Remia BV and Verenigde Bedrijven Nutricia v. Commission (Case 42/84) [1985] ECR 2545, [1987] 1 CMLR 1 ... 128, 196, **243**, 252, 274, 1036–1038

Rewe-Handelsgesellschaft Nord mbH v. Hauptzollamt Kiel (Case 158/80) [1981] ECR 1805, [1981] 1 CMLR 449 ... 1084

Rewe-Zentralfinanz eG and Rewe-Zentral AG v. Landwirtschaftskammer für das Saarland (Case 33/76) [1976] ECR 1989 ... 1083–1084

Rheinmühlen-Düsseldorf (Case 166/73) v. Einfuhr und Vorratsstelle für Getreide und Futtermittel [1974] ECR 33 ... 109

Roofing Felt Cartel, Re: BELASCO v. Commission (Case 246/86) [1989] ECR 2117, [1991] 4 CMLR 96 ... 173–174, 184, 664, 675–676, 684–685, 698

Roquette Frères SA v. Directeur Général de la Concurrence, de la Consommation et de la Répression des Fraudes (Case C-94/00) [2002] ECR I-9011, [2003] 4 CMLR 46 ... 38, 46, 48, 945, 949–950

Roquette Frères v. Council (Case 138/79) [1980] ECR 3333 ... 1034

RTE v. Commission (Cases 76-7 and 91/89 R) [1989] ECR 1141, [1989] 4 CMLR 749 ... 169, 679, 700, 994, 1047–1049

RTE & ITP v. Commission (Magill) (Cases C-241-242/91 P) [1995] ECR I-743 ... 41, 322, 355–356, 387, 410, 515, 518–521, 526, **528–533**, 536–541, 543, 545–546, 548, 848–849, 981

RTT v. GB-INNO-BM SA (Case C-18/88) [1991] ECR I-5973 ... 515, 600, **614–615**, 616–617, 620, 623, 625, 627, 629, 641

SA Binon & Cie v. SA Agence et Messageries de la Presse (Case 243/83) [1985] ECR 2015, [1985] 3 CMLR 800 ... 211, 232, 789, 795, 810, 812, **835**, 895

SA Brasserie de Haecht II v. Wilkin Janssen (Case 48/72) [1973] ECR 77 ... 938, 1102

SA Hercules NV v. Commission (Case C-51/92 P) [1999] ECR I-4235, [1999] 5 CMLR 976 ... 165, 177, 675, 679–680, 685, 969–972, 1043

San Marco v. Commission (Case C-19/95 P) [1996] ECR I-4435 ... 973, 1046

Sandoz Prodotti Farmaceutici SpA v. Commission (Case C-277/87) [1990] ECR I-45 ... 150, 157–158, 161, 792, 999

Sarrió v. Commission (Case C-291/98 P) [2000] ECR I-9991 ... 155, 170

SAT Fluggesellschaft v. Eurocontrol (Case C-364/92) [1994] ECR I-43, [1994] 5 CMLR 208 ... 127, 130–131, 136, 601, 604

Schmid (Case C-516/99) [2002] ECR I-4573 ... 106

Schneider Electric SA v. Commission (Case C-188/06 P) [2007] ECR I-35 ... 1178, 1253

SELEX Sistemi Integrati SpA v. Commission (Case C-113/07) [2009] ECR I-2207 ... 130, **136**, 276, 601, 1048

SEP v. Commission (Case C-36/92 P) [1994] ECR I-1911 ... 940

SFEI v. Commission (Case C-39/93 P) [1994] ECR I-2681 ... 1077

SGL Carbon AG v. Commission (Case C-328/05 P) [2007] ECR I-3921 ... 968

SGL Carbon AG v. Commission (Case C-564/08 P), 12 November 2009 ... 1013, 1017, 1019

SGL v. Commission (Cases C-301/04 and 308/04) [2006] ECR I-5915, [2006] 5 CMLR 15 ... 681–682, **956–957**, 1016

Shell International Chemical Co Ltd v. Commission (Case C-234/92 P) [1999] ECR I-4501, [1999] 5 CMLR 1142 ... 680, 1035

Showa Denko v. Commission (Case C-289/04 P) [2006] 5 CMLR 840 ... 964, 1002, 1004, 1012, 1014, 1018

Silvano Raso (Case C-163/96) [1998] ECR I-533, [1998] 4 CMLR 73 ... 613, 616, 623, 629, 645

Smanor and Others v. Commission (Case C-317/97 P) ... 1047

Société Civile Agricole du Centre d'Insémination de la Crespelle v. Coopérative d'Elevage et d'Insemination Artificielle du Département de la Mayenne (Case C-323/93) [1994] ECR I-5077 ... 282, 604–605, 617, **621–623**, 645

Société de Vente de Ciments et Bétons de l'Est SA v. Kerpen & Kerpen GmbH & Co KG (Case 319/82) [1983] ECR 4173, [1985] 1 CMLR 511 ... 189, 242, 1097, 1099

Société La Technique Minière (STM) v. Maschinebau Ulm GmbH (Case 56/65) [1966] ECR 234, [1966] CMLR 357 ... 124, 181–182, 189, 196, 199–200, 204, 208, 224, 232–233, **238–240**, 248, **805–806**, 813, 1097

Sodemare v. Regione Lombardia (Case C-70/95) [1997] ECR I-3395, [1998] 4 CMLR 667 ... 132, 281, 601, 718

Solvay SA v. European Commission (Case C-109/10 P) [2011] ECR I-000, 25 October 2011 ... 292, 452, 459, 568, 938, 966, 973, 1034

Sot. Lelos kai Sia EE and others v. GlaxoSmithKline AEVE Farmakeftikon Proionton (Glaxo Greece) (Cases C-468 to 478/06) [2008] ECR I-7139 ... 40, 54, 106, 158, 225, 275, 289, 291, 372, 392, 431, 550, 575, 579, **585–590**, 918

Spain, Belgium & Italy v. Commission (Cases C-271, 281, and 289/90) [1992] ECR I-5833 ... 600, 603–606, 654–655, 1033

Spain v. Commission (Case C-196/07) [2008] ECR I-41 ... 49, 1167

SSI v. Commission (Cases 240-2, 261and 262/82) [1985] ECR 3831, [1987] 3 CMLR 661 ... 150–151, 681, 1017

Star Fruit v. Commission (Case 247/87) [1989] ECR 291 ... 1072

Stora Kopparbergs Berlgslags AB v. Commission (Case C-286/98 P) [2000] ECR I-9925 ... 143, 681, 716

Sumitomo Metal Industries Ltd v. Commission (Cases C-403 and 405/04 P) [2007] ECR I-729 ... 687, 1048

Syndicat National des Fabricants Raffineurs d'Huile de Graissage v. Inter Huiles (Case 172/82) [1983] ECR 555 ... 653

Synetairismos Farmakopoion Aitolias & Akarnanias (Syfait) v. Glaxosmithkline AEVE (Case C-53/03) [2005] ECR I-4609, [2005] 5 CMLR 1 ... 106, 389, 585

T-5/02 Commission v. Tetra Laval [2002] ECR II-4381 ... 1223

T-Mobile Netherlands BV v. Raad van bestuur van de Nederlandse Mededingingsautoriteit (Case C-8/08) [2009] ECR 000 ... 47, **167–169**, 170, 204–206, **211–212**, 214–215, 222–225, 231, 700, 702, 794–795, 917–918

Technische Unie v Commission (Case C-113/04 P) ... 179

Telefónica and Telefónica de España v. European Commission (Case C-295/12), (pending) ... 54, 354, 427, 442, 444, 522

Tepea BV v. Commission (Case 28/77) [1978] ECR 1391, [1978] 3 CMLR 392 ... 150

Tetra Pak International SA v. Commission (Tetra Pak II) (Case C-333/94 P) [1996] ECR I-5951, [1997] 4 CMLR 662 ... 271, 316–317, 319, 330–331, 338, 347, 356, 370, 375–376, 386, **394–396**, 406, **414–415**, 419, 422–423, 471, 486–487, **491–492**, 493–494, 496–500, 507, 570, 582, 584, 980, 999, 1003, 1188

Thyssen Stahl AG v. Commission (Case C-194/99 P) [2003] ECR I-10821 ... 154, 1043

ThyssenKrupp Nirosta v. Commission (Case C-352/09 P) [2011] ECR I-2359 ... 938, 1033

ThyssenKrupp Stainless AG v. Commission (Cases C-65/02 P and C-73/02 P) [2005] ECR I-6773 ... 1035

Tipp-Ex GmbH v. Commission (Case C-279/87) [1990] ECR I-261 ... 157

Tomra Systems v. Commission (Case C-549/10 P) [2012] ECR I-000, 19 April 2012 ... 291, 339, 345, 373, **376–378**, 382, 401, 447, 452, 454, 456, **460**, **478–482**

Toshiba v. Úřad pro ochranu hospodářské soutěže, (Case C-17/10) [2012] ECR I-000, 14 February 2012 ... 100, 1018

Transocean Marine Paint Association v. Commission (No. 2) (Case 17/74) [1974] ECR 1063, [1974] 2 CMLR 459 ... 966, 1033

Unilever Bestfoods (Ireland) Ltd v. EC Commission (Case C-552/03 P) [2006] 5 CMLR 1494 ... 73, 199, 232, 249–250, 263, 316–317, 437, 452, 803–804, 837–838, 1037–1038, 1049

Union Royale Belge des Sociétés de Football Association v. Bosman (Case C-415/93) [1995] ECR I-4921, [1996] 1 CMLR 645 ... 39, 112

United Brands and United Brands Continentaal v. Commission (Case 27/76) [1978] ECR 207, [1978] 1 CMLR 429 ... 32–33, 64–65, 73, 76–77, 82, 92, 270, 297, **299–300**, 302, **306–308**, 327, 331, 338–339, 341, 344–346, **348–351**, 354–355, 357–359, 372, 387, 391–392, 397, 410, 423, 464, 510, **549, 570–571**, 572, **575–577**, 579, 584, 586–587, 589, 626, **998**, 1048–1049

United Kingdom v. Council (Case 68/86) [1988] ECR 855, [1988] 2 CMLR 543 ... 1034

Upjohn Ltd v. The Licensing Authority established by the Medicines Act 1968 (Case C-120/97) [1999] ECR I-223 ... 275, 1038

Van Eycke v. ASPA NV (Case 267/86) [1988] ECR 4769, [1990] 4 CMLR 330 ... 601

Van Gend en Loos v. Nederlandse Administratie der Belastingen (Case 26/62) [1963] ECR 1, 12, [1963] CMLR 105 ... 108, 1102

Van Landewyck v. Commission (Cases 209-215 and 218/78) [1980] ECR 3125 ... 147–148, 150, 158–159, 1039

VBVB and VBBB v. Commission (Cases 43 & 63/82) [1984] ECR 19, [1985] 1 CMLR 27 ... 150–151, 252, 260, 680, 970

VdS v. Commission (Case 45/85) [1987] ECR 405,

[1988] 4 CMLR 264 ... 763

Vereeniging van Cementhandelaren v. Commission (Case 8/72) [1972] ECR 977, [1973] CMLR 7 ... 174, 184, 679, 980

Versalis SpA v. Commission, (Case C-511/11) [2013] ECR I-000, 13 June 2013 ... 1015

Viho Europe BV v. Commission (Case C-73/95 P) [1996] ECR I-5457, [1997] 4 CMLR 419 ... **139–141**, 145–146, 151, 155–156, 277

Völk v. Vervaecke (Case 5/69) [1969] ECR 295, 302, [1969] CMLR 273, 282 ... **180**, 182, **226–230**

Volkswagen AG v. Commission (Case C-338/00 P) [2003] ECR I-9189, [2004] 4 CMLR 351 ... 150, 155, 162, 792–793, 834, 997

Von Colson and Kamann v. Land Nordrhein-Westfalen (Case 14/83) [1984] ECR 1891, [1986] 2 CMLR 430 ... 1084

VZW Vereniging van Vlaamse Reisbureaus v. VZW Sociale Dienst van de Plaatselijke en Gewestelijke Overheidsdiensten (Case 311/87) [1987] ECR 3801, [1989] 4 CMLR 213 ... 324

Wachauf v. Federal Republic of Germany (Case 5/88) [1989] ECR 2609, [1990] 1 CMLR 328 ... 107

Walrave & Koch v. Association Union Cycliste Internationale (Case 36/74) [1974] ECR 1405 ... 39, 112

Walt Wilhelm v. Bundeskartellamt (Case 14/68) [1969] ECR 1 ... 109, 1061–1062

Weichert (Case C-73/10 P) ... 169, 700

Windsurfing International v. EC Commission (Case 193/83) [1986] ECR 611, [1986] 3 CMLR 489 ... 185, 865, 898

Wouters v. Algemene Raad van de Nederlandse Order van Advocaten (Case C-309/99) [2002] ECR I-1577, [2002] 4 CMLR 913 ... 39–40, 51, 111, 128–129, 147–148, 181, **216–221**, 247–249, 276, 280, 685, 697, 722, 815

X (criminal proceedings) (Case C-373/90) [1992] ECR I-131 ... 587

Züchner v. Bayerische Vereinsbank (Case 172/80) [1981] ECR 2021, [1982] 1 CMLR 313 ... 181, **710–712**

COURT OF JUSTICE (NUMERICAL TABLE)

24/62 Germany v. Commission [1963] ECR 63, [1963] CMLR 347 ... 1034

25/62 Plaumann & Co v. Commission [1963] ECR 95, [1964] CMLR 29 ... 1031

26/62 Van Gend en Loos v. Nederlandse Administratie der Belastingen [1963] ECR 1, 12, [1963] CMLR 105 ... 108, 1102

6/64 Flaminio Costa v. ENEL [1964] ECR 585, 593-4, [1964] CMLR 425 ... 108, 598, 1102

56 and 58/64 Etablissements Consten SA & Grundig-Verkaufs-GmbH v. Commission [1966] ECR 299, [1966] CMLR 418 ... 39, 123, 138, **151–153**, 183, 196, **205–211**, 223, 230–231, 239, 252–253, 790–791, 805, 822, 835, 838–839, 854, 860, 871, 909, 970, 1036, 1108

18 and 35/65 Gutmann v. Commission of the EAEC [1966] ECR 149 … 1018

56/65 Société La Technique Minière (STM) v. Maschinebau Ulm GmbH [1966] ECR 234, [1966] CMLR 357 … 124, 181–182, 189, 196, 199–200, 204, 208, 224, 232–233, **238–240**, 248, **805–806**, 813, 1097

23/67 Brasserie de Haecht SA v. Wilkin (No. 1) [1967] ECR 407, [1968] CMLR 26 … 197, 233–235, 1108

24/67 Parke Davis v. Probel [1968] ECR 55 … 355, 579

34/67 Lück v. Hauptzollamt Köln [1968] ECR 245 … 1084

14/68 Walt Wilhelm v. Bundeskartellamt [1969] ECR 1 … 109, 1061–1062

5/69 Völk v. Vervaecke [1969] ECR 295 … **180**, 182, **226–230**

10/69 Portelange [1969] ECR 309 … 1102

41/69 ACF Chemiefarma NV v. Commission (Quinine Cartel) [1970] ECR 661 … 150, 158, 177, 684

43/69 Bilger v. Jehle [1970] ECR 127 … 235

48, 49, and 51-7/69 ICI v. Commission (Dyestuffs) [1972] ECR 619, [1972] CMLR 557 … 140–143, 146, 165, 170, 173, 678–679, **710–711**, 715, 1033, **1272–1274**, 1286

49/69 BASF v. Commission (Dyestuffs) [1972] ECR 619 … 976, 978

52/69 Geigy v. Commission [1972] ECR 787 … 143, 1286

22/70 Commission v. Council (ERTA) [1971] ECR 263 … 104, 1032

78/70 Deutsche Grammophon v. Metro [1971] ECR 487, [1971] CMLR 631 … 579, 853

1/71 Cadillon … 229–230

10/71 Ministère Public of Luxembourg v. Muller [1971] ECR 723 … 637, 653

22/71 Béguelin Import v. GL Import-Export [1971] ECR 949, [1972] CMLR 81 … 138, 180, 226, 720, 1102, **1272**

82/71 Pubblico Ministero della Repubblica Italiana v. Società Agricola Industria Latte (SAIL) [1972] ECR 119 … 604

6/72 and 7/72 Europemballage & Continental Can v. Commission [1973] ECR 215 [1973] CMLR 199 … 37, 46, 61–63, 66, 74, 109, 141, 143, 255, 270–272, 277, 288, 299, 303–304, **325**, 326, 332, **367–370**, 373, 416, 422, 471, 500, 567, 981, 1036–1037, 1135–1136, 1286

8/72 Vereeniging van Cementhandelaren v. Commission [1972] ECR 977, [1973] CMLR 7 … 174, 184, 679, 980

39/72 Commission v. Italy [1973] ECR 101 … 1103–1104

48/72 SA Brasserie de Haecht II v. Wilkin Janssen [1973] ECR 77 … 938, 1102

4/73 Nold v. Commission [1974] ECR 491, [1974] CMLR 338 … 105, 231, 943

6 and 7/73 Istituto Chemioterapico Italiano Spa and Commercial Solvents Corp v. EC Commission [1974] ECR 223, [1974] 1 CMLR 309 … 80, 144, 182, 277, 284, 317, 321–322, 332–333, 355, 370–371, 393–394, **510–515**, 519–520, 525, 529–531, 537, 567, 586, 980–981, 1068

40-8, 50, 54-6, 111, 113, and 114/73 European Sugar Cartel, Re the; Cooperatiëve Vereniging Suiker Unie v. EC Commission [1975] ECR 1663 … 110, 165, 168, 174, 281, 423, 428, 456–457, 461, 464, 471, 574, 583–584, 700, **710–712**, 774

127/73 Belgische Radio en Televisie v. SV SABAM [1974] ECR 51, [1974] 2 CMLR 23 … 116, 128, 275, 282, 634, 652, 1102

155/73 Italy v. Sacchi [1974] ECR 409, [1974] 2 CMLR 177 … 127, 130, 604–605, 609, 611–612, 648, 653

166/73 Rheinmühlen-Düsseldorf v. Einfuhr und Vorratsstelle für Getreide und Futtermittel [1974] ECR 33 … 109

15/74 Centrafarm BV and Adnaan De Peijper v. Sterling Drug Inc [1974] ECR 1183, [1974] 2 CMLR 480 … 138–141, 277

17/74 Transocean Marine Paint Association v. Commission (No. 2) [1974] ECR 1063, [1974] 2 CMLR 459 … 966, 1033

36/74 Walrave & Koch v. Association Union Cycliste Internationale [1974] ECR 1405 … 39, 112

71/74 FRUBO v. Commission [1975] ECR 563, [1975] 2 CMLR 123 … 110

26/75 General Motors Continental NV v. Commission [1975] ECR 1367, [1976] 1 CMLR 95 … 81, 282, 327, 577–578, 587

26/76 Metro-SB-Grossmärkte GmbH v. Commission (No. 1) [1977] ECR 1875, [1978] 2 CMLR 1 … 32, 246, 255–256, 789, **807–812**, 814, 1031, 1077

27/76 United Brands v. Commission [1978] ECR 207 … 32–33, 64–65, 73, 76–77, 82, 92, 270, 297, **299–300**, 302, **306–308**, 327, 331, 338–339, 341, 344–346, **348–351**, 354–355, 357–359, 372, 387, 391–392, 397, 410, 423, 464, 510, **549, 570–571**, 572, **575–577**, 579, 584, 586–587, 589, 626, **998**, 1048–1049

33/76 Rewe-Zentralfinanz eG and Rewe-Zentral AG v. Landwirtschaftskammer für das Saarland [1976] ECR 1989 … 1083–1084

52/76 Benedetti v. Munari [1977] ECR 163 … 604

85/76 Hoffmann-La Roche & Co AG v. Commission [1979] ECR 461, [1979] 3 CMLR 21115, 526 … 33, 63, 277, 288, 293, **299**, 302, **313–314**, 315, 332, **336–339**, 341, 344–347, **351**, 355, 359, **372–373**, 376, 378, 405, 415, 423, 430, 433, 450–451, **455–458**, 460–461, 464, 467, 469, 471–473, 475, 480, 483, 523, 543, 568, 717, 725, 972, **974**, 999

13/77 NV GB-INNO-BM v. ATAB [1977] ECR 2115 ... **601–602**, 606, 609, 612

19/77 Miller International Schallplaten v. Commission [1978] ECR 131, [1978] 2 CMLR 334 ... 224, 792, 795, **998**

28/77, Tepea BV v. Commission [1978] ECR 1391 ... 150

77/77 Benzine en Petroleum Handelsmaatschappij BV (ABG Oil) v. Commission [1978] ECR 1513, [1978] 3 CMLR 174 ... 281–282, 331, 510, 589

102/77 Hoffmann-La Roche ... 717

106/77 Amministrazione delle Finanze dello Stato v. Simmenthal SpA [1978] ECR 629, [1978] 3 CMLR 263 ... 108, 1102

22/78 Hugin Kassaregister AB and Hugin Cash Registers Ltd v. Commission [1979] ECR 1869, [1979] 3 CMLR 345 ... 181, 282, 284, 318, 356, 371, 525, 527, 567

32/78, 36/78 to 82/78 BMW Belgium v. Commission [1979] ECR 2435, [1980] 1 CMLR 370 ... 155, 159, 224, 812

125/78 GEMA v. Commission [1979] ECR 3173 ... 1072

209-215 and 218/78 Van Landewyck v. Commission [1980] ECR 3125 ... 148, 150, 158–159, 1039

238/78 Ireks-Arkady v. Council and Commission [1979] ECR 2955 ... 1103

258/78 Nungesser v. Commission [1982] ECR 2015, [1983] 1 CMLR 27 ... 138, 196, 199–200, 211, **859–**863, 863–864, 872–873, 896, 899

62/79 Coditel v. Ciné Vog Films [1980] ECR 881, [1981] 2 CMLR 362 (Coditel I) ... 211, 854, 914

68/79 Just I/S v. Danish Ministry for Fiscal Affairs [1980] ECR 501 ... 1103

136/79 National Panasonic v. Commission [1980] ECR 2033, [1980] CMLR 169 ... **942–944**

138/79 Roquette Frères v. Council [1980] ECR 3333 ... 1034

155/79 AM&S Ltd v. Commission [1982] ECR 1575, [1982] 2 CMLR 264 ... 940, **958–960**

31/80 L'Oréal NV and L'Oréal SA v. De Nieuwe AMCK Puba [1980] ECR 3775, [1981] 2 CMLR 235 ... 309, 808–809, 814

55 and 57/80 Musik-Vertrieb Membran v. GEMA [1981] ECR 147, [1981] 2 CMLR 44 ... 853

100-103/80 Musique Diffusion Française SA v. Commission (Pioneer) [1983] ECR 1825, [1983] 3 CMLR 221 ... 102, 172, 933, 968, 972, 998, **1000–1001**, 1014, 1017, 1039–1040

158/80 Rewe-Handelsgesellschaft Nord mbH v. Hauptzollamt Kiel [1981] ECR 1805, [1981] 1 CMLR 449 ... 1084

172/80 Züchner v. Bayerische Vereinsbank [1981] ECR 2021, [1982] 1 CMLR 313 ... 181, **710–712**

188-90/80 France, Italy and the UK v. Commission [1982] ECR 2545, [1982] 3 CMLR 144 ... 604, 653–654

60/81 IBM v. Commission [1981] ECR 2639, [1981] 3 CMLR 635 ... 106, 968–969, 1031–1032

144/81 Keurkoop v. Nancy Kean Gifts [1982] ECR 2853, [1983] 2 CMLR 47 ... 848

210/81 Demo-Studio Schmidt v. Commission [1983] ECR 3045, [1984] 1 CMLR 63 ... 1068, 1073

249/81 Commission v. Ireland [1982] ECR 4005 ... 607

262/81 Coditel v. Ciné Vog Films [1982] ECR 3381, [1983] 1 CMLR 49 (Coditel II) [1982] ECR 3382, [1983] 1 CMLR 49 ... 215, 753, 854, 864–865, 914, **914–916**, 918

283/81 CILFIT Srl and Lanificio de Gavardo SpA v. Ministry of Health [1982] ECR 3415, [1983] CMLR 472 ... 105

322/81 Nederlandsche Banden-Industrie Michelin v. Commission (Michelin I) [1983] ECR 3461, [1985] I CMLR 282 ... 64, 73, 79, 285, 300, 306, **309**–311, 311–312, 323, **326–328**, 330–331, 339, 345, 347, **352–353**, 373–374, 379, 394, 416, 423, 428, **460–462**, 465–466, 471–473, 480, 483, 528, 568, 609–610, 612, 954, 972, 1002

7/82 GVL v. Commission [1983] ECR 483, [1983] 3 CMLR 645 ... 510, 583

43 and 63/82, VBVB and VBBB v. Commission [1984] ECR 19 ... 150–151, 252, 260, 680, 970

86/82 Hasselblad (GB) Ltd v. Commission [1984] ECR 883, [1984] 1 CMLR 559 ... 172, 206, 702, 793, 810–812

96 to 102, 104, 105, 108 and 110/82 IAZ International Belgium SA v. Commission [1983] ECR 3369, [1984] 3 CMLR 276 ... 128, 138, 148, 173–174, 224, 429, 588, 675, 697, 757, 1016

107/82 AEG-Telefunken AG v. Commission [1983] ECR 3151, [1984] 3 CMLR 325 ... 144, 156–159, 162, 182, 789, 812–813, 968, 972, 1019

172/82 Syndicat National des Fabricants Raffineurs d'Huile de Graissage v. Inter Huiles [1983] ECR 555 ... 653

199/82 Amministrazione delle Finanze dello Stato v. San Giorgio SpA [1983] ECR 3595, [1985] 2 CMLR 658 ... 1084

228 and 229/82 Ford Werke AG and Ford of Europe Inc v. Commission [1984] ECR 1129, [1984] 1 CMLR 649 ... 157, 162, 266–267, 812, 991

240-2, 261and 262/82 SSI v. Commission [1985] ECR 3831, [1987] 3 CMLR 661 ... 150

319/82 Société de Vente de Ciments et Bétons de l'Est SA v. Kerpen & Kerpen GmbH & Co KG [1983] ECR 4173, [1985] 1 CMLR 511 ... 189, 242, 1097, 1099

14/83 Von Colson and Kamann v. Land Nordrhein-Westfalen [1984] ECR 1891, [1986] 2 CMLR 430 ... 1084

29 and 30/83 Compagnie Royale Asturienne des Mines SA and Rheinzink GmbH v. Commission [1984] ECR 1679, [1985] 1 CMLR 688 ... 126, 1036

35/83 BAT v. Commission [1985] ECR 363, [1985] 2 CMLR 470 ... 913

41/83 Italy v. Commission [1985] ECR 873, [1985] 2 CMLR 368 ... 428, 639, 641

42/83 Commission v. Italy [1985] ECR 873 ... 129

123/83 BNIC v. Clair [1985] ECR 391, [1985] 2 CMLR 430 ... 147, 182, 429, 604

145/83 Adams v. Commission [1985] ECR 3539, [1986] 1 CMLR 506 ... 973

170/83 Hydrotherm Gerätebau GmbH v. Compact de Dott Ing Mario Adredi & CSAS [1984] ECR 2999, [1985] 3 CMLR 224 ... 137–141, 146

193/83 Windsurfing International v. EC Commission [1986] ECR 611, [1986] 3 CMLR 489 ... 185, 865, 898

240/83 ADBHU [1985] ECR 531 ... 656

243/83 SA Binon & Cie v. SA Agence et Messageries de la Presse [1985] ECR 2015 ... 211, 232, 789, 795, 810, 812, **835**, 895

298/83 CICCE v. Commission [1985] ECR 1105, [1986] 1 CMLR 486 ... 300, 581, 1073

25 and 26/84 Ford and Ford Europe v. Commission [1985] ECR 2725 ... 158, 161

42/84 Remia BV and Verenigde Bedrijven Nutricia v. Commission [1985] ECR 2545, [1987] 1 CMLR 1 ... 128, 196, **243**, 252, 274, 1036–1038

53/84 Stanley Adams v. Commission [1985] ECR 3595 ... 1050

75/84 Metro-SB-Grossmärkte GmbH v. Commission (No. 2) [1986] ECR 3021, [1987] 1 CMLR 118 ... **807–810**, 1031

142 and 156/84 BAT and Reynolds v. Commission [1987] ECR 4487, [1988] 4 CMLR 24 ... 969, 1039, 1073, 1136

161/84 Pronuptia de Paris GmbH v. Pronuptia de Paris Irmgard Schillgallis [1986] ECR 353, [1986] 1 CMLR 414 ... 183, 197, 199–200, **243**, 789, **815–816**, 879

209-213/84 Ministère Public v. Lucas Asjes (Nouvelles Frontières) [1986] ECR 1425, [1986] 3 CMLR 173 ... 116

222/84 Johnston v. Chief Constable of the Royal Ulster Constabulary [1986] ECR 1651 ... 564

226/84 British Leyland plc v. Commission [1986] ECR 3263, [1987] 1 CMLR 185 ... 81, 282, 327, 355, 372, 577–578, 584, 586–587

311/84 Centre Belge d'Etudes du Marché-Télémarketing (CBEM) v. Compagnie Luxembourgeoise de Télédiffusion SA and Information Publicité Benelux SA [1985] ECR 3261, [1986] 2 CMLR 558 ... 275, 355, 386–387, 393–394, 489, 506, 510, 515, 519, 525, 537, 609, 611–612, 614, 616

5/85 AKZO v. Commission [1986] ECR 2585, [1987] 3 CMLR 716 ... 942, 1032–1033

31/85 ETA Fabriques d'Ebauches v. DK Investments SA [1985] ECR 3933, [1986] 2 CMLR 674 ... 792, 810, 812

45/85 VdS v. Commission [1987] ECR 405, [1988] 4 CMLR 264 ... 763

53/85 AKZO v. Commission [1986] ECR 1965, [1987] 1 CMLR 231 ... 942, 976, 990–991

311/85 ASBL Vereniging van Vlaamse Reisbureaus v. ASBL Sociale Dienst van de Plaatselijke en Gewestelijke Overheidsdiensten [1987] ECR 3801, [1989] 4 CMLR 213 ... 679, 773–774

314/85 Foto-Frost v. Hauptzollamt Lübeck-Ost [1987] ECR 4199 ... 1095, 1120

C-89, 104, 114, 116-117/85 and 125 to 129/85, Ahlström Osakeyhtiö and Others v. Commission [1988] ECR 5193, [1993] ECR I-1307 ... 126, 165, 170, 172, 187, 701, 710–**712**, **712**, **715**, 1036–1037, 1046, 1272, **1274–1276**

65/86 Bayer AG and Maschinenfabrik Hennecke v. Heinz Süllhöfer [1988] ECR 5249, [1990] 4 CMLR 182 ... 527, 913

66/86 Ahmed Saeed Flugreisen and Silver Line Reisebüro GmbH v. Zentrale zur Bekämpfung unlauteren Wettbewerbs eV [1989] ECR 803, [1990] 4 CMLR 102 ... 140, 283, 583, 605, 636–637, 641, 653

68/86 United Kingdom v. Council [1988] ECR 855, [1988] 2 CMLR 543 ... 1034

80/86 Kolpinghuis Nijmegen [1987] ECR 3969 ... 1007

246/86 Roofing Felt Cartel, Re: BELASCO v. Commission [1989] ECR 2117, [1991] 4 CMLR 96 ... 173–174, 184, 664, 675–676, 684–685, 698

247/86 Alsatel v. Novasam [1988] ECR 5987, [1990] 4 CMLR 434 ... 328, 579

267/86 Van Eycke v. ASPA NV [1988] ECR 4769, [1990] 4 CMLR 330 ... 601

C-62/86 AKZO v. Commission [1991] ECR I-3359 ... 305, 315–316, 326–327, 338, 344–345, 358, 371–372, 377, 380, 395, 401, **403–407**, 408, 416, 419–420, 422–423, 430, 436, 565, 1068, 1189–1190

27/87 Erauw-Jacquéry Sprl v. La Hesbignonne Société Coopérative [1988] ECR 1999, [1988] 4 CMLR 576 ... 196, 211, 215, **863–864**, 896

30/87 Corinne Bodson v. Pompes Funèbres des Régions Libérées SA [1988] ECR 2479, [1989] 4 CMLR 984 ... 130, 139–140, 277, 282, 355, 578, 603, 605

46/87 and 227/88 Hoechst AG v. Commission [1989] ECR 2859, [1991] 4 CMLR 410 ... 46, 942, 944, 947, 949–950, 954

53/87 CICCRA v. Renault [1988] ECR 6039, [1990] 4 CMLR 265 ... 318, 515, 525–526, 579

238/87 AB Volvo v. Erik Veng [1988] ECR 6211, [1989] 4 CMLR 122 ... 318, 515, **525–527**, 533

247/87 Star Fruit v. Commission [1989] ECR
291 ... 1073

311/87 VZW Vereniging van Vlaamse Reisbureaus
v. VZW Sociale Dienst van de Plaatselijke en
Gewestelijke Overheidsdiensten [1987] ECR 3801,
[1989] 4 CMLR 213 ... 324

374/87 Orkem SA v. Commission [1989] ECR 3283,
[1991] 4 CMLR 502 ... 940–941, **954**, 957, 1056

395/87 Ministère Public v. Tournier [1989] ECR 2521,
[1991] 4 CMLR 248 ... 579, 919

C-277/87 Sandoz Prodotti Farmaceutici SpA
v. Commission [1990] ECR I-45 ... 150, 157–158,
161, 792, 999

C-279/87, Tipp-Ex GmbH v. Commission [1990] ECR
I-261 ... 157

5/88 Wachauf v. Federal Republic of Germany [1989]
ECR 2609, [1990] 1 CMLR 328 ... 107

C-18/88 RTT v. GB-INNO-BM SA [1991] ECR
I-5973 ... 515, 600, **614–615**, 616–617, 620, 623,
625, 627, 629, 641

C-70/88 European Parliament v. Council ('Chernobyl')
[1990] ECR I-2041, [1992] 1 CMLR 91 ... 105, 231

C-202/88 France v. Commission [1991] ECR I-1223
(the Telecommunications Equipment case) ... 600,
604–605, **607–608**, 614–617, 629, 637, 647,
654–655, 1033

56/89 R Publishers' Association v. Commission [1989]
ECR 1693 ... 1049

76-7 and 91/89 R RTE v. Commission [1989] ECR 1141,
[1989] 4 CMLR 749 ... 169, 679, 700, 994, 1047–1049

C-10/89 CNL-Sucal v. HAG GF AG ('Hag II') [1990] ECR
I-3711, [1990] 3 CMLR 571 ... 105, 231

C-213/89 Factortame [1990] ECR I-2433 ... 1102,
1125–1126

C-234/89 Delimitis v. Henninger Bräu [1991] ECR
I-935, [1992] 5 CMLR 210 ... 184, 197, 200, 204,
234–238, 242, 452, 772, **802–805**, 875, 1072,
1094–1097, 1108

C-260/89 Ellinki Radiophonia Tileorassi-Anonimi
Etairia (ERT-AE) v. Dimotiki Etairia Pliroforissis
(DEP) [1991] ECR I-2925, [1994] 4 CMLR 540 ... 107,
393, 515, 599–600, 605, **611–617**, 620, 623–625,
629, 645, 653

C-6 and 9/90 Francovich v. Italy [1991] ECR I-5357,
[1993] 2 CMLR 66 ... 1084, 1102

C-41/90 Höfner and Elser v. Macroton GmbH [1991]
ECR I-1979, [1993] 4 CMLR 306 ... 127, **129–130**,
135, 181, 584, 599–600, 605, **609–610**, 611–614,
622, 641, 645, 650–652

C-48 and 66/90 Netherlands and Koninklijke PTT
Netherland v. Commission [1992] ECR I-565, [1993]
5 CMLR 316 ... 653

C-78-83/90 Compagnie Commerciale de l'Ouest [1992]
ECR I-1847 ... 622

C-179/90 Merci Convenzionali Porto di Genova SpA
v. Siderurgica Gabrielli SpA [1991] ECR I-5889,
[1994] 4 CMLR 422 ... 283, 584, 599, 605, 607, **613**,
617, 620, 622–623, 625, 638, 641, 645

C-271, 281, and 289/90 Spain, Belgium & Italy
v. Commission [1992] ECR I-5833 ... 600, 603–606,
654–655, 1033

C-373/90 X (criminal proceedings) [1992] ECR
I-131 ... 587

C-30/91 P Lestelle v. Commission [1992] ECR
I-3755 ... 225

C-159-160/91 Poucet and Pistre v. Assurances
Générales de France [1993] ECR I-637 ... 127, 132,
601, 604

C-241-242/91 P RTE & ITP v. Commission [1995] ECR
I-743 ... 41, 322, 355–356, 387, 410, 515, 518–521,
526, **528–533**, 536–541, 543, 545–546, 548,
848–849, 981

C-267 and 268/91 Keck and Mithouard, Criminal
Proceedings against [1993] ECR I-6097, [1995] 1
CMLR 101 ... 105, 231

C-271/91 Marshall v. Southampton and South-West
Hampshire Area Health Authority (Teaching) (No.
2) [1993] ECR I-4367 ... 1084

C-320/91 Corbeau [1993] ECR I-2533, [1995] 4 CMLR
621 ... **620–621**, 625–626, 630, 634, 637, **641–647**,
649–650, 652–653

C-327/91 France v. Commission [1994] ECR I-3641,
[1994] 5 CMLR 517 ... 1287

C-36/92 P SEP v. Commission [1994]
ECR I-1911 ... 940

C-49/92 P Commission v. Anic [1999] ECR I-4125,
[2001] 4 CMLR 17 ... 149–150, 154, 169–170, 177

C-51/92 P SA Hercules NV v. Commission [1999]
ECR I-4235, [1999] 5 CMLR 976 ... 165, 177, 675,
679–680, 685, 969–972, 1043

C-53/92 P Hilti AG v. EC Commission [1994] ECR I-667,
[1994] 4 CMLR 614 ... **319–320**, 338, 353, 389, 487,
489–492, 494–495, 500–501, 507, 1041, 1046

C-128/92 H. J. Banks v. British Coal Corporation [1994]
ECR I-1209, [1994] 5 CMLR à ... 275

C-137/92 P Commission v. BASF [1994] ECR
I-2555 ... 979, **1033–1035**, 1048

C-199/92 P Hüls AG v. Commission [1999] ECR I-4287,
[1999] 5 CMLR 1016 ... 126, 154, **165–167**,
169–170, 177, 675, 679–680, 685, 937, 1041, 1046

C-200/92 P ICI plc v. Commission [1999] ECR I-4399,
[1999] 5 CMLR 1110 ... 177, 680

C-234/92 P Shell International Chemical Co Ltd
v. Commission [1999] ECR I-4501, [1999] 5 CMLR
1142 ... 680, 1036

C-235/92 P Montecatini v. Commission [1999] ECR
I-4539 ... 200

C-250/92 Gøttrup-Klim Grovvareforening v. Dansk Landbrugs Grovvareselskab AmbA (DLG) [1994] ECR I-5641, [1996] 4 CMLR 191 ... 128, 138, 147, 197, 199–200, 215, 218, **244**, 343, 750, 752

C-360/92 P Publishers' Association v. Commission [1995] ECR I-23; [1995] 5 CMLR 33 ... 680, 1034, 1048, 1062

C-364/92 SAT Fluggesellschaft v. Eurocontrol [1994] ECR I-43, [1994] 5 CMLR 208 ... 127, 130–131, 136, 601, 604

C-393/92 Gemeente Almelo v. NV Energiebedrijf Ijsselmij [1994] ECR I-1477 ... 280, 635–637, **643–644**, 652, 718, 721

C-18/93 Corsica Ferries Italia Srl v. Corpo dei Piloti del Porto di Genovo [1994] ECR I-1783 ... 568, 572, 581, 614, 622

C-39/93 P SFEI v. Commission [1994] ECR I-2681 ... 1077

C-70/93 BMV v. ALD [1995] ECR I-3429 ... 159

C-266/93 Bundeskartellamt v. Volkswagen AG and VAG Leasing GmbH [1995] ECR I-3477 ... 138, 773–775

C-280/93 R Commission v. Germany [1993] ECR I-3667 ... 1048

C-310/93 P BPB Industries plc and British Gypsum Ltd v. Commission [1995] ECR I-865, [1997] 4 CMLR 238 ... 328, 394, 459, 464, 568, 582, 584, 974, 1048

C-323/93 Société Civile Agricole du Centre d'Insémination de la Crespelle v. Coopérative d'Elevage et d'Insemination Artificielle du Département de la Mayenne [1994] ECR I-5077 ... 282, 604–605, 617, **621–623**, 645

C-387/93 Banchero [1995] ECR I-4663 ... 607, 621

C-399/93 Oude Luttikhuis v. Verenigde Cooperatieve Melkindustrie [1995] ECR-I 1415 ... 200

C-415/93 Union Royale Belge des Sociétés de Football Association v. Bosman [1995] ECR I-4921, [1996] 1 CMLR 645 ... 39, 112

C-68/94 and 30/95 French Republic and Société commerciale des potasses et de l'azote (SCPA) and Entreprise minière et chimique (EMC) v. Commission [1998] ECR I-1375 ... 37, 106, 109, 255, 280, 370, 719–722, 966, 1036–1037, 1180, 1188, **1200–1201**, 1206, **1217–1219**, 1247, 1250, 1253

C-96/94 Centro Servizi Spediporto v. Spedizioni Maritima del Golfo srl [1995] ECR I-2883, [1996] 4 CMLR 613 ... 164, 281, 718

C-140-142/94 DIP v. Commune di Bassano del Grappa and Commune di Chioggia [1995] ECR I-3257, [1996] 4 CMLR 157 ... 280–281, 601

C-157/94 Commission v. Netherlands (Re Electricity Imports) [1997] ECR I-5699 ... 637, **643**, 646–647, 652

C-159/94 Commission v. France (Re Electricity and Gas Imports) [1997] ECR I-5815 ... 652

C-244/94 Fédération Française des Sociétés d'Assurance v. Ministère de l'Agriculture et de la Pêche [1995] ECR I-4013, [1996] 4 CMLR 536 ... 133, 601

C-333/94 P Tetra Pak International SA v. Commission (Tetra Pak II) [1996] ECR I-5951, [1997] 4 CMLR 662 ... 271, 316–317, 319, 330–331, 338, 347, 356, 370, 375–376, 386, **394–396**, 406, **414–415**, 419, 422–423, 471, 486–487, **491–492**, 493–494, 496–500, 507, 570, 582, 584, 980, 999, 1003, 1188

C-3/95 Reisebüro Broede [1996] ECR I-6511 ... 217–218, 248

C-7/95 P John Deere Ltd v. Commission [1998] ECR I-3111, [1998] 5 CMLR 311 ... 174, 229, 704–706, 1041, 1046

C-19/95 P San Marco v. Commission [1996] ECR I-4435 ... 973, 1046

C-30/95, France and others v. Commission (Kali und Salz) [1998] ECR I-1375 ... 719–722, 1179, 1187, 1200, 1205–1206, 1217, 1246, 1250, 1253

C-32/95 P, Commission v. Lisrestal [1996] ECR I-5373 ... 966

C-70/95 Sodemare v. Regione Lombardia [1997] ECR I-3395, [1998] 4 CMLR 667 ... 132, 281, 601, 718

C-73/95 P Viho Europe BV v. Commission [1996] ECR I-5457, [1997] 4 CMLR 419 ... **139–141**, 145–146, 151, 155–156, 277

C-149/95 P(R) Commission v. Atlantic Container Line and others [1995] ECR I-2165 ... 994, 1048

C-168/95 Arcaro [1996] ECR I-4705 ... 1007

C-185/95 P Baustahlgewebe v. Commission [1998] ECR I-8422 ... 937, 970, 1046, 1048

C-219/95 P Ferriere Nord v. Commission [1997] ECR I-4411 ... 994, 1048

C-242/95 GT-Link A/S v. De Danske Statsbaner (DSB) [1997] ECR I-4449, [1997] 5 CMLR 601 ... 516, 630, 638, 1084

C-261/95 Palmisani [1997] ECR I-4025 ... 1103

C-267 and 268/95 Merck and Co Inc v. Primecrown Ltd (Merck II) [1996] ECR I-6285, [1997] 1 CMLR 83 ... 854

C-279/95 P Langnese-Iglo v. Commission [1998] ECR I-5609, [1998] 5 CMLR 933 ... 266, 980–981

C-282/95 P Guérin Automobiles v. Commission [1997] ECR I-1503 ... 1102

C-286-288/95 P Commission v. ICI [2000] ECR I-2341 ... 1035

C-294/95 P Ojha v. Commission [1996] ECR I-5863 ... 225

C-343/95 Diego Cali e Figli SrL v. SEPG [1997] ECR I-1547, [1997] 5 CMLR 484 ... 130–131, 601, 604

C-359/95 P and C-379/95 P Commission and France v. Ladbroke Racing [1997] ECR I-6265 ... 187, 428

C-35/96 Commission v. Italy [1998] ECR I-3851, [1998] 5 CMLR 889 ... 127, 135, 147

C-54/96 Dorsch Consult [1997] ECR I-4961 ... 106

C-55/96 Job Centre [1997] ECR I-7119, [1998] 4 CMLR 708 ... 584, 610, 617, 628, 651

C-67/96 Albany International BV v. Stichting Bedrijfspensioenfonds Textielindustrie [1999] ECR I-5751, [2000] 4 CMLR 446 ... 51, 127, 129, 133, 137–138, 153, 219, 601, 614, **621–624**, 629–630, 636–637, 644–645, **647–648**

C-108/96 Mac Quen [2001] ECR I-837 ... 218

C-158/96 Kohl [1998] ECR I-1931 ... 133

C-163/96 Silvano Raso [1998] ECR I-533, [1998] 4 CMLR 73 ... 613, 616, 623, 629, 645

C-203/96 Chemische Afvalstoffen Dusseldorp BV v. Minister van Volkshuisvesting, Ruimtelijke Ordening en Milieubeheer [1998] ECR I-4075, [1998] 3 CMLR 873 ... 619, 627, 634–638, 644–645

C-215/96 Bagnasco v. Banca Popolare di Novarra (NPN) and Cassa di Risparmio di Genova e Imperia (Carige) [1999] ECR I-135 [1999] 4 CMLR 624 ... 184, 229–230

C-266/96 Corsica Ferries France SA v. Gruppo Antichi Ormeggiatori del Porto di Genova Coop arl [1998] ECR I-3949, [1998] 5 CMLR 402 ... 283, 601, 622, 629, 637, **645–646**

C-306/96 Javico International and Javico AF v. Yves Saint Laurent Parfums SA [1998] ECR I-1983, [1998] 5 CMLR 172 ... 180, 183, 229, 588

C-395 and 396/96 P Compagnie Maritime Belge Transports SA v. Commission [2000] ECR I-1365, [2000] 4 CMLR 1076 ... 277–280, 293, 344, 370, 375, 377, 380, 392, 397, 406, 413–415, **421–423**, 425, 464, 471, 557, 565, 590, **720–722**, 724, 968, 1039, 1045

C-7/97 Oscar Bronner GmbH & Co KG v. Mediaprint [1998] ECR I-7791, [1999] 4 CMLR 112 ... 42, 106, 275, 304, 322, 391, 437–438, 441–444, 446, **518**–520, 520–522, 524–526, 533–535, 537–538, 554, 556

C-38/97 Autotrasporti Librandi v. Cuttica Spedizion [1998] ECR I-5955, [1998] 5 CMLR 966 ... 164

C-103/97 Köllensperger and Atzwanger [1999] ECR I-551 ... 106

C-115-17/97 Brentjens' Handelsonderneming BV v. Stichting Bedrijfspensioenfonds voor de Handel in Bouwmaterialen [1999] ECR I-6025, [2000] 4 CMLR 566 ... 153, 623

C-120/97 Upjohn Ltd v. The Licensing Authority established by the Medicines Act 1968 [1999] ECR I-223 ... 275, 1038

C-126/97 Eco Swiss China Time Ltd v. Benetton International NV [1999] ECR I-3055, [2000] 5 CMLR 816 ... 39, 1098, 1102

C-147-8/97 Deutsche Post AG v. Gesellschaft für Zahlungssysteme mbH (GZS) and Citicorp Kartenservice GmbH [2000] ECR I-825 ... 578, 624, **624–626**, 630, 637, 649

C-219/97 Maatschappij Drijvende Bokken BV v. Stichting Pensioenfonds voor de Vervoer-en Havenbedrijven [1999] ECR I-6121, [2000] 4 CMLR 599 ... 623

C-310/97 P Commission v. Assidomän Kraft Products AB [1999] ECR I-5363, [1999] 5 CMLR 1253 ... 1030, 1046, 1048

C-317/97 P Smanor and Others v. Commission ... 1047

C-436/97 Deutsche Bahn AG v. Commission [1999] ECR I-2387 ... 569

C-22/98 Criminal Proceedings against Becu [1999] ECR I-5665, [2001] 4 CMLR 968 ... 137–138

C-110/98 to C-147/98 Gabalfrisa and Others [2000] ECR I-1577 ... 106

C-180-184/98 Pavlov v. Stichting Pensioenfonds Medische Specialisten [2000] ECR I-6451, [2001] 4 CMLR 30 ... 127, 133, 136–138, 147, 153, 601, 627

C-195/98 Österreichischer Gewerkschaftsbund [2000] ECR I-10497 ... 106

C-209/98 Entreprenørforeningens Affalds (FFAD) v. Københavns Kommune [2000] ECR-3743, [2001] 2 CMLR 936 ... 605, 637, 624

C-284/98 P Parliament v. Bieber [2000] ECR I-1527 ... 1047

C-286/98 P Stora Kopparbergs Berlgslags AB v. Commission [2000] ECR I-9925 ... 143, 681, 716

C-291/98 P Sarrió v. Commission [2000] ECR I-9991 ... 155, 170

C-344/98 Masterfoods v. HB Ice Cream Ltd [2000] ECR I-11369 ... 429, 1095

C-352/98 P Bergaderm and Goupil v. Commission [2000] ECR I-5291 ... 1047, 1050

C-441/98 and C-442/98 Michaïlidis [2000] ECR I-7145 ... 1103

C-163/99 Portugal v. Commission [2001] ECR I-2613, [2002] 2 CMLR 1319 ... 283, 456, 464–466, 568–569, 573, 629, 653–654

C-176/99 P Arbed SA v. Commission [2003] ECR I-10687 ... 1035

C-194/99 P Thyssen Stahl AG v. Commission [2003] ECR I-10821 ... 163, 1043

C-196/99 P Aristrain v. Commission [2003] ECR I-11005 ... 1005

C-199/99 Corus UK v. Commission [2003] ECR I-000 [RB1]0 ... 971

C-214/99 Neste Markkinointi Oy v. Yötuuli [2000] ECR I-1121, [2000] 4 CMLR 993 ... 804

C-238, 244-5, 247, 250, 251-2 and 254/99, Limburgse Vinyl Maatschappij NV v. Commission [2002] ECR I-8375 ... 938, 950, 956, 966, 971–972, 1018, 1035, 1043, 1047

C-280/99 P to C-2102/99 P Moccia Irme and Others v. Commission ... 1047

C-309/99 Wouters v. Algemene Raad van de Nederlandse Order van Advocaten [2002] ECR I-1577, [2002] 4 CMLR 913 ... 39–40, 51, 111, 128–129, 147–148, 181, **216–221**, 247–249, 276, 280, 685, 697, 722, 815

C-453/99 Courage Ltd v. Crehan [2001] ECR I-6297, [2001] 5 CMLR 28 ... 39, 125, 1027, 1092, 1098, **1102–1104**, **1108**, 1119, 1122

C-462/99 Connect Austria Gesellschaft für Telekommunikation GmbH v. Telekom-Control-Kommission [2003] ECR I-5147 ... 618

C-475/99 Ambulanz Glöckner v. Landkreis Südwestpflaz [2001] ECR I-8089, [2002] 4 CMLR 726 ... 127, 136, 584, 606, **627–629**, 637, **650–651**

C-497/99 P Irish Sugar plc v. Commission [2001] ECR I-5333, [2001] 5 CMLR 1082 ... 344, 421, 423, 456, 465–466, 542

C-516/99 Schmid [2002] ECR I-4573 ... 106

C-53/00 Ferring [2001] ECR I-9067 ... 656

C-94/00 Roquette Frères SA v. Directeur Général de la Concurrence, de la Consommation et de la Répression des Fraudes [2002] ECR I-9011, [2003] 4 CMLR 46 ... 38, 46, 48, 945, 949–950

C-204, 205, 211, 213, 217 and 219/00 P Aalborg Portland A/S v. Commission (Cement) [2004] I-123, [2005] 4 CMLR 251 ... 126, **154–155**, 163, 178–179, 252, 679, 686–687, 690–691, **971–973**, 1018, 1029–1030, 1037, 1042, **1046–1047**

C-218/00 Cisal di Battistello Venanzio & Co v. Istituto Nazionale per L'Assicurazione Contro Glifortuni Sul Lavoro (INAIL) [2002] ECR I-691, [2002] 4 CMLR 24 ... **132–134**, 601

C-241/00 Kish Glass and Co Ltd v. Commission [2001] ECR I-7159 ... 75, 274, 323, 1038–1039

C-280/00 Altmark Trans GmbH, Regierungspräsidium Magdeburg v. Nahverkehrsgesellschaft Altmark GmbH [2003] ECR I-7747 ... 599, 632, 635, 656

C-338/00 P Volkswagen AG v. Commission [2003] ECR I-9189, [2004] 4 CMLR 351 ... 150, 155, 162, 792–793, 834, 997

C-459/00 P(R) Commission v Trenker ... 275, 1038

C-2 & 3/01 P Bundesverband der Arzneimitte-Importeure EV and Commission v. Bayer AG [2004] ECR I-23, [2004] 4 CMLR 653 ... 149–150, 156–158, **160–162**, 272, 510, 585, 791–793, 1036, 1049

C-198/01 Consorzio Industrie Fiammiferi (CIF) v. Autorità Garante della Concorrenza e del Mercato [2003] ECR I-8055; [2003] 5 CMLR 829 ... 187, 428, 1063–1064

C-207/01 Altair Chimica ... 187

C-264, 306, 354 & 355/01 AOK Bundesverband v. Ichthyol-Gesellschaft Cordes, Hermani & Co [2004] ECR I-2493, [2004] 4 CMLR 126 ... 51, 129, **132–135**, 601

C-359/01 P British Sugar plc v. Commission [2004] ECR I-4933, [2004] 5 CMLR 329 ... 169, 679, 700, 1047–1048

C-418/01 IMS Health GmbH & Co. OHG v. NDC Health GmbH & Co. KG [2004] ECR I-5039, [2004] 4 CMLR 1543 ... 41, 81, 275, 322, 356, 391, 526, **531–535**, 537, 539–540, 543, 545, 991–992, 1032, 1048–1049

C-57/02 P Compañía española para la fabricación de aceros inoxidables SA (Acerinox) v. Commission [2005] ECR I-6689 ... 1046, 1048

C-65/02 P and C-73/02 P ThyssenKrupp Stainless AG v. Commission [2005] ECR I-6773 ... 1035

C-141/02 P, max.mobil [2005] ECR I-1283 ... 653

C-189/02P, 202/02 P, 208/02 P and 213/02 P Dansk Rørindustri A/S v. Commission [2005] ECR I-5425, [2005] 5 CMLR 796 ... 65, 102, 118, 143, 230, 291, 690, **933**, 937, 1000, **1005–1008**, 1013–1014, 1016–1017, 1040, 1042, 1048

C-263/02 P Commission v. Jégo-Quéré [2004] ECR I-3425 ... 106

C-372/02 Metro v. Cartier [1994] ECR I-15, [1994] 5 CMLR 331 ... 792

C-12/03 P Commission v. Tetra Laval [2005] ECR I-987 ... 57, 102–103, 448, 538, 1038, 1042, **1184–1187**, 1223, **1226–1228**, 1230, 1235–1236, 1248, 1250

C-53/03 Synetairismos Farmakopoion Aitolias & Akarnanias (Syfait) v. GlaxoSmithKline AEVE [2005] ECR. I-4609, [2005] 5 CMLR 1 ... 106, 389, 585

C-205/03 P Federación Nacional de Empresas de Instrumentación Científica, Médica, Técnica y Dental (FENIN) v. Commission, 11 July 2006, [2006] ECR I-6295, [2006] 5 CMLR 7 ... 51, 127, **133–135**, 583

C-397/03 P Archer Daniels Midland Company v. Commission [2006] ECR I-4429, [2006] 5 CMLR 230 ... 118, 242, 685, 942, 1008, 1018, 1040, 1043

C-551/03 P General Motors BV v. Commission [2006] ECR I-3173 ... 157–158, 162, 216, 588

C-552/03 P Unilever Bestfoods (Ireland) Ltd v. EC Commission [2006] 5 CMLR 1494 ... 73, 199, 232, 249–250, 263, 316–317, 437, 452, 803–804, 837–838, 1037–1038, 1049

C-74/04 P Commission v. Volkswagen AG [2006] ECR I-6585 ... 157, 162–164, 272, 789–790, 792, 1036

C-94/04 and C-202/04 Cipolla v. Fazari ECR I-1142 ... 187

C-95/04 P, British Airways v. Commission [2007] ECR I-2331 ... 42, 47, 81–82, 271, 289, 292, 300, 305–306, 323, 370, 372, 377, 382, 386–387, 394, 398, 401, 416, 439, 454, 456, 459, **470–475**, 483, 568, **573–575**, 586–587

C-105/04 P Nederlandse Federatieve Vereniging voor de Groothandel op Elektrotechnisch Gebied v. Commission [2006] ECR I-8725 ... 178–179, 206, 938

C-113/04 P Technische Unie v Commission ... 179

C-167/04 JCB Service v. Commission [2006] ECR I-8935, [2006] 5 CMLR 23 ... 157, 162, 195, 789, 792

C-289/04 P Showa Denko v. Commission [2006] 5 CMLR 840 ... 964, 1002, 1004, 1012, 1014, 1018

C-295-98/04 Manfredi v. Lloyd Adriatico Assicurazioni SpA [2006] ECR I-6619, [2006] 5 CMLR 17 ... 125, 1092, 1097, **1104**, 1106–1107, 1109

C-301/04 and 308/04 SGL v. Commission [2006] ECR I-5915, [2006] 5 CMLR 15 ... 681–682, **956–957**, 1016

C-403 and 405/04 P, Sumitomo Metal Industries Ltd v. Commission [2007] ECR I-729 ... 687, 1048

C-519/04 P Meca-Medina and Majcen v. Commission, [2006] ECR I-6991 [2006] 5 CMLR 1023 ... 51, 112, 128, 220, 247, 249, 764, 1047–1048

C-171/05 P Laurent Piau v. Commission [2006] ECR I-37 ... 219, 256

C-217/05 Confederación Española de Empresarios de Estaciones de Servicio v. Compañia Española de Petróleos SA [2006] ECR I-11987 ... 137–138, 774–776

C-238/05 Asnef-Equifax, Servicios de Información sobre Solvencia y Crédito, SL v. Asociación de Usuarios de Servicios Bancarios (Ausbanc) (2006) ECR I-11125 ... 149, 229, 259, 702, 704, **707 708**

C-282/05 P, Holcim (Deutschland) AG v. Commission [2007] ECR I-2941 ... 1050

C-284/05, Commission v. Finland [2009] ECR I-11705 ... 113

C-328/05 P, SGL Carbon AG v. Commission [2007] ECR I-3921 ... 969

C-466/05 Criminal Proceedings against Doulamis [1998] ECR I-1377 ... 187

C-3/06 P Groupe Danone v. Commission, 8 February 2007 ... 675, 687–688, 964, 1004–1005, 1040

C-188/06 P Schneider Electric SA v. Commission [2007] ECR I-35 ... 1178, 1253

C-266/06 P Evonik Degussa GmbH v. Commission [2008] ECR I-81 ... 1017

C-279/06 CEPSA Estaciones de Servicio SA v. LV Tobar e Hojos Sl ('CEPSA') [2008] ECR I-6681 ... 138, 774–776

C-413/06 P Bertelsmann AG, Sony Corporation of America [2008] ECR I-4951 ... 719, 969, 1184–1185, 1201, **1204–1205**, 1207–1208, 1253–1254

C-468 to 478/06 Sot. Lelos kai Sia EE and others v. GlaxoSmithKline AEVE Farmakeftikon Proionton (Glaxo Greece) [2008] ECR I-7139 ... 40, 54, 106, 158, 225, 275, 289, 291, 372, 392, 431, 550, 575, 579, **585–590**, 918

C-501/06 P GlaxoSmithKline Services Unlimited v. Commission [2009] ECR I-9291 ... 14, 40, 47, 54, 123, 158, 206, **222–225**, 250–251, 254, 289, 579, 585, 788, 790, 792, 798, 813, 835, 895–896, 918, 1038, 1048

C-510/06 P Archer Daniels Midland Co v. Commission [2009] ECR I-1843 ... 154, 1003, 1008, 1012

C-511/06 P Archer Daniels Midland [2009] ECR I-5843, 9 July 2009 ... 934, 968, 1012

C-49/07 Motosykletistiki Omospondia Ellados NPID (MOTOE) (Greek Motorcycling Federation) v. Elliniko Dimosio [2008] ECR I-4863 ... 112, 128, 136, 276, **616–617**, 629, 764

C-52/07, Kanal 5 Ltd v. Föreningen Svenska Tonsättares Internationella Musikbyrå (STIM) upa [2008] ECR I-9275 ... 304, 386, 574, 581, 919

C-101 and 110/07 Coop de France Bétail and Viande v. Commission, FNSEA v. Commission [2008] ECR I-10193 ... 128, 187, **225–226**, 675, 681, 1018

C-113/07 SELEX Sistemi Integrati SpA v. Commission [2009] ECR I-2207 ... 130, **136**, 276, 601, 1048

C-125, 113, 135 and 137/07 P, Erste Group Bank AG v. Commission [2009] ECR I-8681 ... 63, 682, 1069

C-139/07 P Commission v. Technische Glaswerke Ilmenau [2010] ECR I-5885 ... 977

C-196/07 Spain v. Commission [2008] ECR I-41 ... 49, 1167

C-202/07 P France Télécom v. Commission [2009] 4 CMLR 1149 ... 73–74, 289, 312, 362, 372, 374, 378, 392, 406, 408, **411–412**, **415–417**, 419–420, 430, 562, 1047

C-209/07 Competition Authority v. Beef Industry Development Society Ltd (BIDS) and Barry Brothers (Carrigmore) Meals Ltd [2008] ECR I-8637 ... 187, 204–206, 211–212, 215–216, 224, 231, 675, 694

C-260/07 Pedro IV Servicios [2009] ECR I-2437 ... 229, 796

C-322/07 P, C-327/07 P and C-338/07 P, Papierfabrik August Koehler AG v. Commission, 3 September 2009 ... 968

C-350/07, Kattner Stahlbau GmbH v. Maschinenbau -und Metall- Berufsgenossenschaft [2009] ECR I-1513 ... 132–133, 601

C-385/07 Der Grüne Punkt-Duales System Deutschland GmbH v. Commission 16 July 2009 ... 327, 580, 582, 999

C-429/07 Inspecteur van de Belastingdienst v. Commission, 11 June 2009 ... 1019

C-440/07 P Commission v. Scheider Electric, 16 July 2009 ... 1050, 1254

C-441/07 P, European Commission v. Alrosa [2010] ECR I-5949 ... 273, 453, 966, **985–989**, 1031, 1048

C-534/07 P Prym and Prym Consumer v Commission ... 1042–1043

C-550/07 P Akzo Nobel Chemicals Ltd v. Commission [2010] ECR I-8301 ... 938, **961–965**

C-8/08 T-Mobile Netherlands BV v. Raad van bestuur van de Nederlandse Mededingingsautoriteit [2009] ECR 000 ... 47, **167–169**, 170, 204–206, **211–212**, 215, 222–224, 700, 702, 794, 917

C-97/08 P AKZO Nobel NV v. Commission, 10 September 2009, [2009] ECR 000 ... 137, 141, **143–144**, 146

C-221/08, Commission v. Ireland [2010] ECR I-1669 ... 49

C-280/08 P, Deutsche Telekom v. Commission [2010] ECR I-9555 ... 48, 53–54, 91, 271, 289, 291, 370–373, 380, 382, 401, **427**–434, 434–437, 439–441, 444–449, 556

C-403 and 429/08, Premier League Ltd v. QC Leisure and Murphy v. Media Protection Services Ltd, 4 October 2011 ... 39–40, 112, 206, 211, 215, 224, 256, 791, 854, 864, **917–919**

C-407/08 P, Knauf Gips v. Commission [2010] ECR I-6375 ... 100, 938, 968

C-506/08 P Kingdom of Sweden v. Commission [2011] ECR I-75, 21 July 2011 ... 977

C-564/08 P SGL Carbon AG v. Commission, 12 November 2009 ... 1013, 1017, 1019

C-52/09, Konkurrensverket v. TeliaSonera Sverige AB [2011] ECR I-527 ... **38**, 43, 46, 48, 109, 292, 299, 366, 373–375, 377, 380, 382, 386–387, 395, 396, 401, 424, 427, **434–441**, 443–449, 521–522, 551, 553, 580

C-90/09 P, General Química SA v. Commission, 20 January 2011 ... 142

C-108/09 Ker-Optika [2010] ECR I-0000 ... 814–815

C-201/09 and C-216/09 P Arcelor Mittal v. Commission [2011] ECR I-2239 ... 110, 143, 146, 1033

C-260/09 P Nintendo Co and Nintendo of Europe GmbH v. Commission [2011] ECR I-419 ... 156, 793

C-272/09 P, KME Germany AG v. Commission [2011] ECR I-000, 8 December 2011 ... 100, 231, 934, 937, 1029, 1032, 1037, 1039, **1041–1043**, 1044

C-352/09 P ThyssenKrup Nirosta v. Commision [2011] ECR I-2359 ... 938, 1033

C-360/09, Pfleiderer AG v. Bundeskartellamt [2011] ECR I-5161 ... 118, 230, 1027, 1060, 1084, **1090–1092**, 1120

C-375/09 Prezes Urzędu Ochrony Konkurencji i Konsumentów v. Tele 2 Polska sp. z o.o., now Netia SA [2011] ECR I-3055 ... 274, 1051

C-437/09, AG2R Prévoyance v. Beaudout Père et Fils SARL, 31 March 2011 ... 133, 153, 601, 605, 611, 628, 648

C-439/09, Pierre Fabre Dermo-Cosmétique SAS v. Président de l'Autorité de la concurrence [2011] ECR I-000, 13 October 2011 ... 40, 213, 220, 232, 263, 789, **793–795**, **812–814**, 818, 829

C-17/10, Toshiba v. Úřad pro ochranu hospodá?ské soutěže, [2012] ECR I-000, 14 February 2012 ... 100, 1018

C-73/10 P Weichert ... 169, 700

C-109/10 P, Solvay SA v. European Commission [2011] ECR I-000, 25 October 2011 ... 292, 452, 459, 568, 938, 966, 973, 1034

C-209/10, Post Danmark A/S v. Konkurrencerådet [2012] ECR I-000, 27 March 2012 ... 46, 48, 272–273, 292, 366–367, **373**, 374, 376, **378–380**, 382, 385, **387**, 389–391, 398–399, 401, 406, **408–411**, 421, 425, 447, 725

C-367/10 P EMC Development AB v. Commission [2011] ECR I-000, 31 March 2011 ... 1075

C-404/10 P Commission v. Éditions Odile Jacob [2012] ECR I-000, 28 June 2012 ... 977–978, 1148, 1180, 1253

C-457/10 P, AstraZeneca v. Commission, [2012] ECR I-000, 6 December 2012 ... 69, 82, 90, 299, 302, 322, 338–339, 346–347, 355–356, 360, 373–374, 378, 380, 382, 388, **558–562**, 729

C-477/10 P Commission v. Agrofert Holding a.s. [2012] ECR I-000, 28 June 2012 ... 977, 1180, 1253

C-549/10 P, Tomra Systems v. Commission [2012] ECR I-000, 19 April 2012 ... 291, 339, 345, 373, **376–378**, 382, 401, 447, 452, 454, 456, **460**, **478–482**

C-32/11 Allianz Hungária Biztosító Zrt, Generali-Providencia Biztosító Zrt v. Gazdasági Versenyhivatal, 14 March 2013 ... 212, **794–796**, 1099

C-89/11 P E.ON Energie AG v. Commission, 22 November 2012 ... 948

C-138/11 Compass-Datenbank GmbH v. Republik Österreich, 12 July 2012 ... 127, 129, 131

C-158/11 Auto24 SARL v. Jaguar Land Rover France SAS, 14 June 2012 ... 809, 834

C-226/11, Expedia Inc. v. Autorité de la Concurrence [2012] ECR I-000 ... 118, 226, **228–231**, 242, 795

C-440/11 P, Commission v. Stichting Administratiekantoor Portielje and Gosselin Group NV ... 146

C-508/11 Eni SpA v. Commission, 8 May 2013 ... 143

C-511/11 Versalis SpA v. Commission, [2013] ECR I-000, 13 June 2013 ... 1015

C-536/11 Bundeswettbewerbsbehörde v. Donau Chemie AG [2013] ECR I-000, 6 June 2013 ... 1027, 1060, 1092

C-578/11 Deltafina v. Commission, judgment pending ... 1020

C-681/11 Bundeswettbewerbsbehörde and Bundeskartellanwalt v. Schenker [2013] ECR I-000, 18 June 2013 ... 998

C-1/12, Ordem dos Técnicos Oficiais de Contas (OTOC) v. Autoridade da Concorrência, 28 February 2013 ... 128, 148–149, 219, 260–261, 619, 651

C-59/12 P, European Federation of Ink and Ink Cartridge Manufacturers (EFIM) v. Commission, judgment pending ... 321

C-68/12, Protimonopolný úrad Slovenskej republiky v. Slovenská sporiteľňa a.s. [2013] ECR I-000, 7 February 2013 ... 47, 123, 164, 206, 250, 261

C-70/12 P Quin Barlo Ltd v. Commission [2013] ECR I-00, 30 May 2013 ... 1039, 1047

C-179/12 The Dow Chemical Company v. Commission, judgment pending ... 144

C-269/12 P, Cañas v. Commission, judgment pending ... 113

C-295/12 Telefónica and Telefónica de España v. European Commission (pending) ... 54, 354, 427, 442, 444, 522

C-365/12 P Commission v. EnBW Energie Baden-Württemberg, judgment pending ... 978, 1026

C-382/12 P MasterCard Inc, MasterCard International Inc, and MasterCard Europe SPRL v. Commission (pending) ... 63, 81, 147, 199, 221, 245, 764

C-553/12 P, Commission v. DEI, judgment pending ... 630

C-554/12 P, Commission v. DEI, judgment pending ... 285, 605, 619

C-37/13 Nexans France SAS v. Commission, judgment pending ... 944, 947

C-84/13 P Electrabel v. Commission (judgment pending) ... 1142, 1177

C-293 and 294/13 P Fresh Del Monte Produce v. Commission (judgments pending) ... 178, 700

EFTA COURT

Posten Norge v. EFTA Surveillance Authority, (Case E-15/10) 18 April 2012 ... **1044–1045**

EUROPEAN COURT OF HUMAN RIGHTS

Bendenoun v. France Series A, No. 284, (1994) 18 EHRR 54 ... 936

Benham v. UK 1996-III No. 10, (1996) 22 EHRR 293 ... 936

Cantoni v France, 15 November 1996, Reports of Judgments and Decisions, 1996-V, °° 29 to 32 ... 1006–1007

Coëme and Others v Belgium, 22 June 2000, Reports, 2000-VII, ° 145 ... 1006

Colas Est and Others v. France, 16 April, 2002, not yet published in the Reports of Judgments and Decisions ... 950

Colas Est Case No. 37971/97, Reports of Judgments and Decisions 2002-II ... 950–951

Engel v. Netherlands Series A, No. 22, (1976) 1 EHRR 647 ... 936–937

Funke v. France, Series A, No. 256-A, (1993) 16 EHRR 297 ... 955

Heaney and McGuinness v. Ireland (2001) 33 EHRR 12 ... 955

Jussila v. Finland 2006-XIV, (2007) 45 EHRR 39 ... 935–937, 1044

Kerojärvi v. Finland, 19 July 1995, Series A, No. 322, ° 42 ... 972

Le Compte, Van Leuven, and De Meyere v. Belgium Series A, No. 54, (1983) 5 EHRR 183 ... 936

Mantovanelli v. France, 18 March 1997, Reports of Judgments and Decisions 1997-II, § 33 ... 972

Menarini Diagnostics S.R.L. v. Italy, App 43509/08, judgment 27 September 2011 ... 670, 937

Niemitz v. Germany, Series A, No. 251-B, (1992) 16 EHRR 97 ... 934, 950

Özturk v. Germany Series A, No 73, (1984) 6 EHRR 409 ... 936

Saunders v. UK [1997] 23 EHRR 313 ... 935, 955

Société Bouygues Telecom v. France, Applicant 2324/08 ... 937

Société Stenuit v. France (1992) 14 EHRR 509 ... 937

S.W. v. United Kingdom and C.R. v. United Kingdom, judgments of 22 November 1995, Series A, Nos 335-B and 335-C ... 1006

NATIONAL COURTS OF THE MEMBER STATES

IRELAND

Masterfoods v. HB Ice Cream [1992] 3 CMLR 830 ... 1120

SWEDEN

Boliden Mineral AB v. Birka, 23 December 2004 ... 1099

Scandinavian Airlines System (SAS) v. Swedish Board of Aviation (unreported), Swedish Court of Appeal ... 1100

UNITED KINGDOM

AAH Pharmaceuticals Ltd and Others v. Pfizer Ltd and UniChem Ltd [2007] EWHC 565 ... 1095

Adidas-Salomon v. Lawn Tennis Association and Others [2006] EWHC 1318 (Ch) ... 1126

Albion Water Ltd v. Dwr Cymru Cyfyngedig, [2010] CAT 30, [2013] CAT 6 ... 1121, 1123

American Cyanamid Co v Ethicon [1975] AC 396 ... 1126

Application des Gaz SA v Falks Veritas Ltd [1974] Chap 381 ... 1119

Argos Limited and Littlewoods Limited v. OFT, JJB Sports plc v. OFT [2006] EWCA 1318 ... 125

Arkin v. Borchard Lines Ltd [2000] EuLR 232 (preliminary issues), [2003] EWHC 687 (Comm Ct) (final judgment) ... 1120, 1122

Attheraces Ltd v. British Horseracing Board [2007] EWCA Civ 38 ... 724, 1087, 1122

BCL Old Co Ltd v. BASF AG [2008] CAT 24, [2009] EWCA 434, [2009] CAT 29, [2010] CAT 5, [2010] EWCA Civ 1258, [2012] UKSC 45 ... 1121

Bettercare Group Limited v. DGFT [2002] CAT 7, [2002] CompAR 299 ... 135

Bookmakers Afternoon Greyhound Services Ltd v. Amalgamated Racing Ltd [2008] EWHC 2688 (Ch), [2009] EWCA Civ 750 ... 1122

British Leyland Motor Corp Ltd v TI Silencers Ltd [1981] FSR 213 (CA) ... 1098

British Nylon Spinners Ltd v ICI Ltd [1955] Ch 37 ... 1264

Calor Gas Ltd v. Express Fuels (Scotland) Ltd [2008] ScotCS CSOH 13, 25 Jan 2008 ... 1098

Capital Meters Ltd v. National Grid plc (Case 1199/5/7/12) ... 1121

Chemidus Wavin Ltd v. TERI [1978] 3 CMLR 514 ... 1098

Chester City Council v. Arriva plc [2007] EWHC 1373 ... 1120, 1122

Cooper Tire & Rubber v. Shell Chemicals [2009] EWHC 2609, [2010] EWCA Civ 864 ... 142, 1120–1121

Courage v. Crehan [2004] EWCA Civ 637 ... 1099

Courage Ltd v. Crehan [1999] EuLR 834 ... 1101

Crehan v. Inntrepreneur Pub Company [2003] EWHC 1510 (Ch), [2004] EWCA Civ 637 (CA) ... 1096, 1119–1120, 1122

Crehan v. Inntrepreneur Pub Company [2004] EWCA Civ 1318 ... 1122

Cutsforth v. Mansfield Inns [1986] I CMLR 1 ... 1126

Devenish Nutrition Ltd v. Sanofi Aventis SA [2007] EWHC 2394, [2008] EWCA Civ 10 ... 1000, 1123

Emerald Supplies Ltd v. British Airways plc [2009] EWHC 741 (Ch) ... 1121

Emerson Electric Co v. Morgan Crucible Company plc Case 1077/5/7/07 ... 1121

English Welsh & Scottish Railway Limited v E.ON UK plc [2007] EWHC 599 ... 275, 1100

Enron Coal Services Ltd (in liquidation) v. English Welsh & Scottish Railway [2009] CAT 18, [2011] EWCA Civ 2 ... 1122

Enron Coal Services Ltd (in liquidation) v. English Welsh & Scottish Railway Ltd [2009] CAT 7, [2009] EWCA Civ 647, [2009] CAT 36, [2011] EWCA Civ 2 ... 1121

FA Premier League [2006] 5 CMLR 1430 ... 113, 302, 766, 983

Football Association Premier League Ltd v. QC Leisure [2008] EWHC 44 (Ch), [2008] EWHC 1411 ... 916, 1098

Freightliner Ltd and Freightliner Heavy Haul Ltd v. English Welsh and Scottish Railways Ltd (Case 1105/5/7/08) ... 1124

Garden Cottage Foods Ltd v. Milk Marketing Board [1984] AC 130 ... 1119, 1126

Genzyme CA 98/03/03, [2003] UKCLR 950 ... 360

Genzyme Ltd v. OFT [2004] CAT 4, [2004] CompAR 358 ... 360

Getmapping plc v. Ordnance Survey [2002] UKCLR 410 ... 1126

Gibbs Mew plc v Gemmell [1999] 1 EGLR 43, [1998] EuLR 588 ... 1098, 1100–1101

Goldsoll v Goldman [1914] 2 Chap. 603 ... 1098

Grampian County Food Group v. Sanofi-Aventis SA and Devenish Nutrition Ltd v. Sanofi Aventis SA [2008] EWCA Civ 10 ... 1121

Healthcare at Home Ltd v. Genzyme [2006] CAT 29 ... 1121

Holman v. Johnson (1775) 1 Cowp. 341 ... 1099

Independent Television Publications v. Time Out [1984] FSR 64 ... 528

Inewos Vinyls Ltd v. Huntsman Petrochemicals (UK) Ltd [2006] EWHC 1241 (Ch) ... 1122

Inntrepreneur Estates (CPC) plc v. Milne, unreported, 30 July 1993 ... 1101

Inntrepreneur Estates (GL) Ltd v. Boyes [1993] 2 EGLR 112 ... 1098

Inntrepreneur Estates Ltd v. Mason [1993] 2 CMLR 293 ... 1098

Inntrepreneur Pub Company v. Crehan [2006] UKHL 38 ... 804, 1096

Integraph Corporation v. Solid Systems CAD Services Ltd [1995] ECC 53 (ChD) ... 1098

Intel Corporation v. VIA Technologies [2002] EWCA Civ 1905, [2002] All ER (D) 346 ... 1098, 1126

JB v. Switzerland [2001] Crim. L.R. 748 ... 955

JJ Burgess & Sons v. OFT [2005] CAT 25 ... 1121

JJB Sports plc v. Office of Fair Trading (Case 1022/1/1/03) [2004] CAT 17, [2006] EWCA Civ 1318 ... 126, 163, 171–172, 680

Matthew Brown plc v. Campbell [1998] EuLR 530 ... 1101

Moy Park Ltd v. Degussa (Case No 1147/5/7/09) ... 1121, 1123

Moy Park Ltd v. Tessenderlo Chemie NV (Case 1202/5/7/12) ... 1121

Murphy v. Media Protection Services Ltd [2008] EWHC 1666 (Admin) ... 916

Murray v. Schooner Charming Betsy, 2 Cranch 64, 118 (1804) ... 1266

Napp v. DGFT Case 1001/1/1/01 [2002] CAT 1 ... 1120

National Grid [2011] EWHC 1717 (Ch), [2012] EWHC 869 (Ch) v. ABB ... 1120

National Grid Electricity Transmission Plc v. ABB Ltd [2009] EWHC 1326 (Ch) ... 1121, 1124

Network Multimedia Television Ltd v. Jobserve Ltd Ch D, judgment of 5 April 2001, CA (Civ Div) 21 December 2001 ... 1126

Norris v. Government of the United States of America [2010] UKSC 9 ... 1265

Oakdale (Richmond) Ltd v. National Westminster Bank plc [1997] EuLR 7, [1997] 3 CMLR 815 ... 1098

Panayiotou v. Sony Music Entertainment (UK) Ltd [1994] ECC 395 ... 1098

Passmore v. Morland plc [1993] 3 All ER 1005 ... 189, 1099

Philips Electronics NV v. Ingman Ltd [1999] FSR 112 (ChD) ... 1098

Pitney Bowes Inc. v. Francotyp-Postalia GmbH [1991] FSR 72 (ChD) ... 1098

Plessey Co plc v. General Electric Co plc [1988] ECC 384 ... 1126

Provimi v. Aventis [2003] EWHC 961 ... 142, 1123

R v. Ghosh [1982] 2 All ER 689 ... 1065

R v. Whittle and ors [2008] EWCA Crim 2560 ... 668, 952

Racecourse Association, The v. OFT (Case 1035/1/04) [2005] CAT 29 ... 216, 247

Rio Tinto Zinc Corp v. Westinghouse Electric Corp [1978] AC 547 ... 1264

SanDisk Corporation v. Koninklijki Philips Electronics N.v. [2007] EWHC 332 (Ch) ... 1123

Scottish Courage Ltd v. McCabe [2007] EWHC 538 ... 1098

Shearson Lehmann v. McLaine Watson [1989] 2 Lloyd's Rep 570 ... 1120

Siemens plc v. National Grid plc (Case 1198/5/7/12) ... 1121

Sirdar Ltd v. Les Fils de Louis Mulliez and Orsay Knitting Wools Ltd [1975] FSR 309 (ChD) ... 1098

Society of Lloyd's v. Clementson [1995] 1 CMLR 693 ... 1098

Software Cellular Network Limited v. T-Mobile (UK) Ltd [2007] EWHC 1790 (Ch) ... 1126

Tobacco, Case CE/2596-03, 15 April 2010 ... 797

Toshiba Carrier UK Ltd v. KME Yorkshire Ltd [2012] EWCA Civ 1190 ... 142, 1120, 1123

Travel Group plc (in liquidation) v. Cardiff City Transport Services Ltd [2012] CAT 19 ... 1123

Trent Taverns Ltd v. Sykes [1998] EuLR 571, [1999] EuLR 492 ... 1098, 1101

W.H. Newson Holding Ltd and others v. IMI plc (Case 1194/5/7/12) ... 1121

Wilson v. Lancing College Ltd (Case 1008/5/7/08) ... 1121, 1124

TABLE OF INTERNATIONAL CASES

[Page references in **bold** indicate that the item is given particular prominence in the text]

INTERNATIONAL COURTS

Lotus case (1927), PCIJ, Ser.A, No. 10 … **1270**

Japan-Measures Affecting Consumer Photographic Film and Paper (WTO Panel) WT/DS44/R, 31 March 1998 … 1270

UNITED STATES

AT & T Corp v. Iowa Utilities Bd., 525 US 428, 119 S.Ct. 721 … 555

Albrecht v. Herald Co 390 US 145 (1968) … 797

Alcoa, 274 US 268, 47 S. Ct 592 (1927) … 1262, 1270

American Banana Co v. United Fruit Co, 213 US 347, 356, 29 S.Ct 511, 512 (1909) … 1260

Arizona v. Maricopa County Medical Society, 457 US 332, 344 (1982) … 197

Aspen Skiing Co v. Aspen Highlands Skiing Corp., 472 US 585, 105 S.Ct. 2847, 86 L.Ed.2d 467 … 555

Atlantic Richfield Co v. USA Petroleum Co. 495 US 329 (1990) … 1122

Broadcast Music, Inc. v. Columbia Broadcasting Sys., Inc., 441 US 1 (1979) … 221

Brooke Group Ltd v. Brown & Williamson Tobacco Corp 509 US 209, 113 S.Ct. 2578, 125 L.Ed.2d 168 (1993) … 412–413, 445, 556, 725

Brown Shoe Co v. United States, 370 US 294, 82 S.Ct 1502 (1962) … 22, 1211

Brunswick Corp v. Pueblo Bowl-O-Mat Inc 429 US 477 (1977) … 1122

Chicago Board of Trade v. US, 246 US 231, 238 (1918) … 197–198

Citizen Publishing Co. v. United States, 394 US 131, 138, 89 S.Ct 927, 931 (1969) … 1217

Continental TV, Inc. v. GTE Slyvania Inc., 433 US 36 (1977) … 198, 797

Continental TV Inc v. GTE Sylvania Inc., 694 F.2d 1132 (9th Cir. 1982) … 798

Copperweld Corp v. Independence Tube Corp. 467 US 36 … 139

Dr Miles Medical Co v. John D Park & Sons Co 220 US 373 (1911) … 797

Eastman Kodak Co v. Image Technical Services Inc 504 US 451, 112 S.Ct 2072 (1992) … 303, 492

EEOC v. Arabian Amercian Oil Co., 499 US 244 … 1260

F.Hoffmann-La Roche Ltd v. Empagran SA 315 F.3d 338 (DC Cir. 2003), 542 US 155(2004) … 1125, 1259, **1265–1268**

Federal Trade Commission v. Actavis, Inc, 17 June 2013 … 906

FTC v. Consolidated Foods Corp 380 US 592, 85 S.Ct 1221965 … 22

FTC v. Indiana Federation of Dentists, 476 US 447 (1986) … 206

FTC v. Procter & Gamble Co, 386 US 568, 87 S.Ct 1221967 … 22

Hanover Shoe v. United Shoe Machinery Corp 392 US 481 (1968) … 1110

Hartford Fire Insurance Co v. California, 509 US 764, 113 S.Ct 2891 (1993) … **1262–1263**, 1266–1268, 1276, 1283–1284, 1287

Illinois Brick Co v. Illinois 431 US 720 (1997) … 1111

Intel Corp. v. Advanced Micro Device Inc 542 US, S.Ct. 2466 (2004) … 1025, **1269**

Jefferson Parish Hospital District No. 2 v. Hyde 466 US 2 (1984) … 487

Keifer-Stewart Co v. Joseph E Seagram & Sons Inc 340 US 211 (1951) … 797

Lauritzen v. Larsen 345 U.S. 571 (1953) … 1266

Leegin Creative Leather Products Inc. v. PSKS, Inc., DBA Kay's Kloset…Kay's Shoes, 551 US 887 (2007) … 798–799

McCulloch v. Sociedad Nacional de Marineros de Honduras, 372 U.S. 10 (1963) … 1266

Mannington Mills Inc v. Congoleum Corp, 595 F.2D 1287 (3rd Cir. 1979) … 1261, 1268

Matsushita Elec. Indust. Co Ltd v. Zenith Radio Corp, 475 US 574, 106 S.Ct. 1348, 89 L.Ed.2d 538 (1986) … 402, 413, 555

Merritt v. Faulkner, 697 F. 2d 767th Cir … 28

Methionine Antitrust Litigation, In re 221 F.R.D. 1 (N.D.Cal.2002) … 1025

Monosodium Glutamate Antitrust Litigation, In re 477 F.3d 535 (8th Cir, 2007) ... 1125, 1268

Morrison v. National Australia Bank Ltd, 130 S.Ct 2869 (2010) ... 1260

National Society of Professional Engineers v. United States, 435 US 679 (1978) ... 197

NCAA v. Board of Regents of Univ. of Okla., 468 US 85, 104 (1984) ... 197, 221

Norris v. Government of the US [2008] UKHL 16, [2008] 1 AC 920 ... 1065, 1265

Northern Pac R Co v. United States, 356 US 1, 5 (1958) ... 197

Pacific Bell Telephone Company v. linkLine Communications Inc. 129 S.Ct. 1109 ... 445

Payment Card Interchange Fee and Merchant Discount Antitrust Litigation, Re MDL Docket No. 1720, Master File No. 1:05 md-1720-JG-JO, District Court of the Eastern District of New York ... **1269**

Perma Life Mufflers Inc v. International Parts Corporation, 392 US 134 (1968) ... 1101

Polygram Holding, Inc v. Federal Trade Commission, 416 F.3d 29, 35 (D.C. Cir. 2005) ... 197–198

Romero v. International Terminal Operating Co., 358 U.S. 354 (1959) ... 1266

Schor v. Abbott Laboratoires No. 05-3344 (US Court of Appeals, 7th Circuit, 2006) ... **487–488**

Société Nationale Industrielle Aérospatiale v. United States District Court for the Southern District of Iowa 482 US 522 ... 1263, 1269

Sosa v. Alvarez-Machain, 542 US 2004 ... 1260

Standard Oil Co of New Jersey v. United States, 221 US 1 (1911) ... 197, 298

State Oil v. Khan, 522 US 3, 20 (1997) ... 231, 798

Theatre Enterprises v. Paramount Film Distributing Corporation, 346 US 537 (1954) ... 674

Timberlane Lumber Co. v. Bank of America, 549 F.2d 597 at 613 (9th Cir. 1976) ... **1260–1261**, 1263

United States v. Aluminum Co of America, 148 F.2d 416 (2d Cir. 1945) ... 1260, 1267

United States v. American Tobacco Co, 221 US 106 (1911) ... 197

United States v. AMR Corporation and American Airlines, 335 F.3d 1109 (2003) ... 380–381

United States v. Arnold, Schwinn & Co, 388 US 365, 87 S.Ct 1851967 ... 22, 797

United States v. Colgate & Co, 250 US 300, 307, 39 S.Ct 465 (1919) ... 555

United States v. Dentsply International Inc 399 F. 3d 181 ... 381

United States v. EI du Pont de Nemours & Co 351 US 377 (1956) ... 71, 298

United States v. Grinnell Corp, 384 US 563 (1966) ... 298

United States v. ICI Ltd 105 F.Supp 215 (1952) ... **1263–1264**

United States v. Microsoft Corp 87 F.Supp.2d 30, (D.D.C.2000), 253 F.3d 34 (D.C.Cir.) ... 495, 555

United States v. Nippon Paper Industries Co., 109 F.3d (1st Cir. 1997) ... **1263**, 1268

United States v. Pilkington (1994-2) Trade Cases ... 1269

United States v. Sisal Sales Corporation, 274 US 268, 47 S.Ct 592 (1927) ... 1260

United States v. Socony-Vaccuum Oil Co, 310 US 150 (1940) ... 197

United States v. Trans-Missouri Freight Association., 166 US 290 (1897) ... 197

United States v. Trenton Potteries Co, 273 US 392 (1927) ... 197

Verizon Communications Inc v. Trinko LLP, 540 US 398, 124 S.Ct 872 (2004) ... 54, 445, 517, 536, **554–556**, 575, 667

Virgin Atl. Airways Ltd v. British Airways plc, 257 F.3d 256 (2d Cir. 2001) ... 484

Vitamins Antitrust Litigation, In re 217 F.R.D 229 (DDC 2002) ... 1025

TABLE OF LEGISLATION

[Page references in **bold** indicate that the item is reproduced or otherwise given particular prominence]

EUROPEAN SECONDARY LEGISLATION

REGULATIONS

17/62 Regulation implementing Articles 85 and 86 of the Treaty [1956–60] OJ Spec. Ed. 87 . . . 34, 98, 99, 101, 113, 115, 125, 251, 273, 294, 671, 769, 922, 923, 924, 925, 926, 927, 931, 947, 949, 954, 956, 957, **958, 959, 960,** 961, 971, **974,** 981, 991, 993, 994, 1001, 1002, 1004, 1005, 1008, 1033, 1040, 1061, 1067, 1072, **1073,** 1097

Art. 2 . . . 271, 924

Art. 3 . . . 511, 980, 981, 991, 1068, **1070, 1072, 1073**

Art. 3(1) . . . 981

Art. 3(2) . . . 1069, **1070**

Art. 3(2)(b) . . . 1031

Art. 4 . . . 195, 220, 247

Art. 4(1) . . . 924

Art. 4(2) . . . 924, 925

Art. 4(2)(b) . . . 859

Art. 6(1) . . . 925

Art. 8(1) . . . 924

Art. 8(2) . . . 924

Art. 8(3) . . . 294, 924, 931

Art. 9 . . . 114, 219

Art. 9(1) . . . 125, 195, 924

Art. 11 . . . 939, 940, **957, 958**

Art. 11(1) . . . **956**

Art. 11(2) . . . **954, 957**

Art. 11(4) . . . 955, **956**

Art. 11(5) . . . **954,** 956, **957**

Art. 12 . . . 727, 728

Art. 12(1) . . . 727

Art. 14 . . . 939, **943, 944,** 951, **958, 960**

Art. 14(1) . . . 947, **958**

Art. 14(1)(a) . . . **964**

Art. 14(1)(b) . . . **964**

Art. 14(1)(c) . . . 948

Art. 14(2) . . . **958**

Art. 14(3) . . . 404, 943, **944,** 949, 952, **958, 960,** 991, 1020, 1022, 1033

Art. 14(6) . . . 949

Art. 15 . . . 997, 1001

Art. 15(1) . . . 995

Art. 15(1)(b) . . . 940

Art. 15(2) . . . **429,** 996, 1000, 1001, 1002, 1005, 1013, 1040, 1042

Art. 15(4) . . . 937

Art. 15(5) . . . 924

Art. 15(6) . . . 174, 924

Art. 16(1) . . . 996

Art. 17 . . . **1043**

Art. 19(1) . . . **944,** 966, 970

Art. 19(2) . . . 970

Art. 19(3) . . . 113, 1031

Art. 20 . . . **974**

26/62 Council Reg. applying competition rules to production of trade and agricultural products [1959–62] OJ Spec. Ed. 129 . . . 110

27/62 Reg. implementing Reg. 17 [1959–1962] OJ Spec. Ed. 132 . . . 924

141/62 Council Regulation exempting transport from the application of Regulation 17 [1962] OJ L124/2751 . . . 931

99/63/EEC Regulation on the hearings provided for in Art. 19(1) and (2) of Regulation 17 [1962–64] OJ Spec. Ed. 47 . . . 944, 967, 970, 1072, **1073**

Art. 3 . . . 970

Art. 6 . . . **1073**

Arts 7–9 . . . 970

19/65 Council Reg. applying Art. 85(3) to agreements and concerted practices [1965–1966] OJ Spec. Ed. Series 1, p. 35 . . . 264, 876

67/67/EEC Reg. applying Art. 85(3) to exclusive dealing agreements [1967] OJ Spec. Ed. 10 . . . 817, 909, 911

1017/68/EEC Council Reg. applying competition rules to transport [1968] OJ L241/10 . . . 1157

2821/71 Reg. applying Art. 85(3) to agreements and concerted practices [1971] OJ Spec. Ed., 1032 . . . 264

2988/74 Reg. on limitation periods in proceedings relating to competition and transport

[1974] OJ L319/1 . . . 994

1983/83 Reg. applying Art. 85(3) to exclusive distribution agreements [1983] OJ L173/1 . . . 817, 820

1984/83 Regulation applying Art. 85(3) to exclusive purchasing agreements [1983]

OJ L173/7 . . . 265, 817, 980

Recital 5 . . . **839**

2349/84 Regulation on patent licensing agreements [1984] OJ L219/15 . . . 557, 860, 866

417/85 Regulation on specialisation agreements [1985] OJ L53/1 . . . 735

418/85 Regulation on research and development agreements [1985] OJ L53/5 ... 735

4056/86 Council Regulation applying Arts 85 and 86 to maritime transport [1986] OJ L378/1 ... 279, 421, **422**, 423, 718, 1157
Art. 1(3)(b) ... **422**
Art. 3 ... 279
Art. 8 ... 421, **717**
Art. 8(2) ... **717**, 718

3597/87/EEC Reg ... 157

3975/87 Reg. on the air transport sector [1987] OJ L374/1 ... 1033

4087/88 Reg. applying Art. 85(3) to franchise agreements [1988] OJ L359/46 ... 817, 909

556/89 Regulation on know-how agreements [1989] OJ L61/1 ... 866, 877

4064/89/EEC Merger Reg. [1989] OJ L395/1 ... 33, 42, 45, 65, 101, 102, 110, 117, 189, 237, 278, 719, 723, 732, 969, 1137, 1138, 1147, 1151, 1152, 1154, 1172, 1181, 1182, 1183, 1200, 1232, 1239, 1278, **1280**, **1281**, **1283**
Recitals 1–5 ... **1280**
Recital 9 ... **1280**
Recital 11 ... 1278, **1280**
Recital 13 ... 1239
Recital 30 ... **1280**
Art. 1 ... **1280**, 1283, 1284
Art. 1(2) ... **1280**
Art. 1(4) ... 1137, 1152
Art. 2 ... 370
Art. 2(2) ... **1181**
Art. 2(3) ... **1181**, **1281**
Art. 3 ... 1168
Art. 3(2) ... 1145
Art. 6 ... 1252
Art. 6(1)(c) ... 1284
Art. 7(4) ... 1252
Art. 8 ... 1252
Art. 8(2) ... 1252
Art. 22(3)–(5) ... 1168
Art. 22(4) ... 1252
Art. 24 ... **1280**

2367/90 Reg. on the control of concentrations between undertakings [1990] OJ L219/5 ... 1137

1534/91 Council Reg. empowering the Commission to adopt block exemptions for certain types of agreements in the insurance sector [1991] OJ L143/1 ... 116, 264

1768/92 Council Reg. on protection certificates for medicinal products [1992] OJ L182/1 ... 848

2408/92 Reg. on access for air carriers to intra-Community air routes [1992] OJ L240/8 ... **649**

3932/92 Reg. on the insurance sector [1992] OJ L398/7 ... 763

151/93 Commission Reg. [1993] OJ L21/8 ... 735

3666/93 Reg. on categories of specialization agreements, R&D agreements, patent licensing agreements and know-how licensing agreements [1993] OJ L21/8 ... 1137

40/94/EEC Council Reg. on Community Trade Mark Regulation [1994] OJ L11/1 ... 847, 849

2100/94 Council Regulation on plant variety rights [1994] OJ L227/1 ... 850
Art. 8 ... 863
Art. 9 ... 863
Art. 21 ... 863

3385/94 Reg. [1994] OJ L377/28 ... 924

240/96 Commission Reg. on technology transfer agreements [1996] OJ L31/2 ... 141, 557, 860, 866, 867, 868, 874, 875, 890, 894, 924
Art. 12 ... 867

1103/97 Council Reg. [1997] OJ L162/1 ... 1151
Art. 2(1) ... 994

1310/97 Council Reg. [1997] OJ L180/1 ... 110, 117, 189, 237, 370, 719, 723, 1137, 1151, 1168, 1181
Art. 1(1)(a) ... 1151
Art. 1(1)(b) ... 1151

2236/97 Commission Reg. [1997] OJ L306/12 ... 735

447/98 Commission Reg. on the notifications, time limits, and hearings provided for in Council Reg. 4064/89 on the control of concentrations between undertakings [1998] OJ L61/1 ... 1137

2842/98 Hearing Reg. [1998] OJ L354/18 ... 932, 967, 932, 967

2843/98 Commission Reg. on the transport sector [1998] OJ L354/22 ... 924

1215/1999 Council Regulation applying Art. 81(3) to agreement and concerted practices [1999] OJ L148/1 ... 264

1216/1999 Council Reg. implementing Arts 81 and 82 [1999] OJ L148/5 ... 859, 924

2790/99 First Verticals Commission Reg. [1999] OJ L336/21 ... 42, 265 768, 769, 785, 817, 818, 823, 833, 867, 879, 891
Art. 1(b) ... 451
Art. 2(3) ... 879
Art. 2(5) ... 879
Art. 4(b) ... 890, 891

1216/2000 Council Reg. [1999] OJ L 148/5264

2658/2000 Commission Reg. on specialisation agreements [2001] OJ L304/3 ... 42, 732, 735, 867, 879

2659/2000 Commission Reg. on categories of research and development agreements [2001] OJ L304/7 ... 42, 732, 735, 746, 867, 879

2887/2000 Reg. on unbundled access to the local loop [2000] OJ L336/4 ... 435

44/2001 Council Reg. on jurisdiction and the recognition and enforcement of judgments in civil and commercial matters (Brussels Regulation) [2001] OJ L12/1 ... 1123

Art. 2 . . . 1123
Art. 6(1) . . . 1123

1049/2001 Transparency Reg. [2001] OJ
L145/43 . . . 932, 976, 977, 978, 1026, **1027**, 1253
Recital 4 . . . **1027**
Art. 2 . . . 976
Art. 2(1) . . . 976
Art. 2(3) . . . 976
Art. 4 . . . 976, **977**, **1027**
Art. 4(1) . . . 976, **977**
Art. 4(2) . . . 976, **977**, **1026**, **1027**
Art. 4(3) . . . 976, **977**, 978, 1026
Art. 4(4) . . . **977**

6/2002 Council Reg. on Community designs [2002] OJ
L3/1 . . . 850

1400/2002 Commission Reg. on Motor Vehicle
Distribution [2002] OJ L203/30 . . . 787, 823, 834

1/2003/EC Council Reg. implementing Arts 81 and
82 [2003] OJ L1/1 . . . 39, 41, 48, 53, 98, 99, 100, 101,
104, 109, 110, 114, 115, 116, 118, 119, 120, 125, 174,
195, 198, 249, 265, 266, 273, 274, 287, 294, 653, 668,
671, 676, 727, 767, 922, 923, 924, 927, 929, 931, 932,
933, 938, 948, 952, 953, 957, 961, **964**, 966, 967, 976,
978, 979, 983, **985**, **986**, **987**, **988**, 991, 994, 995,
1000, 1027, 1028, 1031, 1033, 1045, 1051, 1052,
1053, **1056**, 1067, 1068, 1075, 1078, **1091**, **1092**,
1093, 1094, 1095, 1157, 1168, 1172, 1179
Recital 8 . . . **1062**
Recital 9 . . . 1063
Recital 12 . . . 726, 981
Recital 13 . . . 982, **985**
Recital 14 . . . 933, 990
Recital 25 . . . 948, **964**
Recital 26 . . . 952, **964**
Recital 34 . . . 108
Recital 37 . . . **934**, 984
Recital 38 . . . **927**, 933
Ch I . . . 929
Ch II . . . 930
Ch III . . . 930, 939
Ch IV . . . 930, 1052
Ch V . . . 930
Ch VI . . . 930
Ch VII . . . 930
Ch VIII . . . 930
Ch IX . . . 930
Ch X . . . 931
Ch XI . . . 931
Art. 1 . . . 124, 198, 929, 1093, 1120
Art. 2 . . . 126, 249, 250, 388, 893, 929
Art. 2(1) . . . 939
Art. 3 . . . 109, 185, 186, 198, 287, 929, **1062**,
1093, 1145
Art. 3(1) . . . **229**, **1062**, 1063
Art. 3(2) . . . **229**, **231**, 287, **1062**, 1063, 1068, **1070**
Art. 3(3) . . . **1062**, 1063
Art. 4 . . . 930
Art. 5 . . . 198, 273, 930, **1051**, 1067, 1172
Art. 6 . . . 930, 1093

Art. 7 . . . vi, 273, 511, 674, 726, 930, 933, 967, **979**,
980, 982, 983, 984, **985**, **986**, **988**, 989, 995,
1066, 1067
Art. 7(1) . . . 980, 981, 984, **985**, **986**, 989, 993
Art. 7(2) . . . 930, 1031, 1068, 1069, 1070
Arts 7–10 . . . 198
Art. 8 . . . 930, 967, **991**, 992, 995, 996, 1076
Art. 9 . . . vi, 250, 273, 445, 565, 692, 732, 764, 766,
923, 930, 939, 966, **982**, 983, 984, **985**, **986**, **988**,
989, 990, 993, 994, 995, 996, 1031
Art. 9(1) . . . 939, **982**, 984, **986**, **988**, 989
Art. 9(2) . . . **982**, 983
Art. 10 . . . v, 250, 271, 733, 930, 933, 939, **990**,
1145, 1031
Art. 11 . . . 930, 1057, 1060, **1092**
Art. 11(1) . . . 1060
Art. 11(3) . . . 1054
Art. 11(4) . . . 1060, 1061
Art. 11(5) . . . 1060
Art. 11(6) . . . 938, 990, 1055, 1059, 1061
Arts 11–16 . . . 1052
Art. 12 . . . 930, 1023, **1056**, 1057, 1060, **1092**
Art. 12(1) . . . 1055, **1056**
Art. 12(2) . . . 1055, **1056**
Art. 12(3) . . . 1055, **1056**
Art. 13 . . . 930, 1055, 1067, **1068**, 1075, 1093
Art. 14 . . . 104, 930
Art. 15 . . . 726, 930, 1093, 1094
Art. 15(1) . . . 1086
Art. 15(2) . . . 1095
Art. 15(3) . . . 257, 1094
Art. 16 . . . 930, 1089, 1093, 1095, 1120
Art. 16(1) . . . 939, **1116**
Art. 17 . . . 111, 727, 729, 905, 930, 982, 995, 1028
Art. 17(1) . . . **728**
Art. 17(2) . . . 728
Arts 17–22 . . . 973
Art. 18 . . . 930, 939, 940, 941, 953, 995, 1028, 1286
Art. 18(1) . . . 940
Art. 18(2) . . . **940**, 941, 942, 995, 1286
Art. 18(3) . . . 941, 942, 990, 995, 1286
Art. 18(5) . . . 941, 1286
Art. 18(6) . . . 940
Arts 18–21 . . . 1055
Art. 19 . . . 930, 940, 949, **953**, 1023, 1028
Art. 19(1) . . . **953**
Art. 19(2) . . . **953**
Art. 20 . . . 934, 939, 940, 941, 949, 951, 952, 953,
964, 995, 1022, 1028, 1064, 1265, 1283
Art. 20(1) . . . 941
Art. 20(2) . . . **941**, 947, 949
Art. 20(2)(a) . . . 947
Art. 20(2)(b) . . . 947
Art. 20(2)(c) . . . 947, 948
Art. 20(2)(d) . . . 948, 951, 995
Art. 20(2)(e) . . . 948, 953, 995
Art. 20(3) . . . 941, 942
Art. 20(4) . . . 940, 942, 943, 944, 945, **946**, 948, 965,
990, 991, 995, 1020
Art. 20(5) . . . 941, 949

Art. 20(6) . . . 941, 947, **949**
Art. 20(7) . . . 949
Art. 20(8) . . . **949**, 952
Art. 21 . . . 930, 934, 940, 945, 951, 952, 953, 1023, 1028, 1064, 1286
Art. 21(1) . . . **952**
Art. 21(3) . . . 952
Art. 22 . . . 930, 1028
Art. 23 . . . 125, 930, 941, 952, 967, 997, 1028, 1039, 1066
Art. 23(1) . . . 937, 940, 947, 994, **995**
Art. 23(1)(a) . . . 940
Art. 23(1)(c) . . . 996
Art. 23(1)(d) . . . 948
Art. 23(1)(e) . . . 948
Art. 23(2) . . . 142, 937, 994, **996**, 997, 1000, 1002, 1005, 1011, 1013
Art. 23(2)(c) . . . 983
Art. 23(3) . . . **996**, 1041
Art. 23(4) . . . 995, **996**, 997
Art. 23(5) . . . 668, 937, **997**
Art. 24 . . . 930, 937, 941, 994, **995**, 1028
Art. 24(1)(d) . . . 941
Art. 25 . . . 930, 994, 1030
Art. 26 . . . 930, 994
Art. 27 . . . 930, 976, 992
Art. 27(1) . . . 966
Art. 27(2) . . . 930, 966, 970, 973, 975, 984, **988**
Art. 27(4) . . . 939, 966, 983, 984
Art. 28 . . . 930, 973, **1055**, **1056**
Art. 28(2) . . . 973
Art. 29 . . . 294, 930, 1072
Art. 29(1) . . . 265, 832, 893
Art. 29(2) . . . 266, 832, 893
Art. 30 . . . 931, 973
Art. 31 . . . 931, **994**, 1039, 1041, **1043**
Art. 32 . . . 115
Art. 33 . . . 931, 1067
Art. 34 . . . 931
Art. 35 . . . 273, 931, 1051, 1052
Art. 36–42 . . . 931
Art. 43 . . . 931
Art. 44 . . . 931
Art. 45 . . . 931

358/2003 Commission Reg. on the insurance sector [2003] OJ L53/8 . . . 763

139/2004 Council Reg. on European Mergers (EUMR — European Merger Regulation) [2004] OJ L124/1 . . . viii, 33, 42, 45, 46, 49, 51, 56, 62, 70, 101, 104, 108, 109, 110, 117, 119, 120, 144, 189, 237, 243, 277, 278, 287, 297, 448, 567, 659, 674, 718, 719, 720, 721, 722, 723, 727, 728, 729, 731, 732, 733, 734, 923, 969, 977, 995, 1059, 1078, 1129, 1132, 1133, 1134, 1135, 1136, 1138, 1139, 1140, 1143, 1144, 1145, 1148, 1149, 1150, 1151, 1152, 1153, 1154, 1157, 1158, 1161, 1163, 1166, 1167, 1168, 1171, 1172, 1173, 1174, 1176, 1177, 1178, 1180, 1182, 1183, 1187, 1189, 1203, 1211, 1214, 1235, 1239, 1241, 1242, 1244, 1247, 1252, 1253, 1254, 1255, 1256, 1258, 1271, 1278, 1279, 1284, 1285

Recital 8 . . . 1149
Recital 10 . . . 1278
Recital 11 . . . **1160**
Recital 14 . . . 1161, 1173
Recital 17 . . . 1172
Recital 19 . . . 1166
Recital 20 . . . 1140
Recital 21 . . . 1244
Recital 23 . . . 1239
Recital 25 . . . **1183**
Recital 26 . . . **1183**
Recital 28 . . . 1187
Recital 29 . . . 45, 1215
Recital 30 . . . **1246**, 1247
Recital 32 . . . 343
Recital 34 . . . 1173
Art. 1 . . . 1150, 1154, 1168, 1278
Art. 1(1) . . . **1150**, 1168
Art. 1(2) . . . **1150**, 1151, 1152, 1154, 1156, 1174, 1278
Art. 1(3) . . . 1150, 1151, **1152**, 1154, 1156, 1159, 1174, 1278
Art. 1(4) . . . 1139
Art. 2 . . . 1159, 1214, 1239, 1240, 1278
Art. 2(1) . . . 1183, 1215, 1239
Art. 2(1)(b) . . . 45, 1214
Art. 2(2) . . . 278, 723, 1183, 1187, **1219**, **1235**, 1241
Art. 2(3) . . . 33, 278, 723, 733, **1182**, 1183, 1186, 1187, **1235**, 1241
Art. 2(4) . . . 733, 734, 1147, 1184, **1241**, 1242
Art. 2(5) . . . 1147, 1184, **1241**, 1245
Art. 3 . . . 1129, 1140, 1157, 1168, 1241
Art. 3(1) . . . **1140**
Art. 3(1)(a) . . . 1141
Art. 3(1)(b) . . . 1140, 1141, **1142**, 1144
Art. 3(2) . . . **1141**, 1154
Art. 3(4) . . . 734, **1140**, 1144, 1145
Art. 3(5) . . . 1147, 1148
Art. 3(5)(a) . . . 1148
Art. 4 . . . **1172**, 1176, 1284
Art. 4(1) . . . **1172**
Art. 4(2) . . . 1172, 1173
Art. 4(3) . . . 1177
Art. 4(4) . . . 1157, 1159, 1160, 1164, 1174, 1175, 1252
Art. 4(5) . . . 1150, 1157, 1170, 1171, 1174, 1175, 1176, 1252
Art. 5 . . . 1154, 1155, 1278
Art. 5(1) . . . 1153, 1278
Art. 5(2) . . . 1153, 1156
Art. 5(3) . . . 1153
Art. 5(4) . . . 1153, **1154**
Art. 5(4)(b) . . . **1154**
Art. 5(5)(b) . . . 1154
Art. 6 . . . 1177, 1252
Art. 6(1) . . . 1177, 1244, 1278
Art. 6(1)(a) . . . 1177, 1252
Art. 6(1)(b) . . . 1176, 1177, 1244, 1252
Art. 6(1)(c) . . . 1148, **1149**, 1177, 1178, 1246, 1252
Art. 6(2) . . . 1177, 1246, 1252
Art. 6(3) . . . 1179, 1251, 1252

Art. 7 . . . 1170
Art. 7(1) . . . 1176
Art. 7(2) . . . 1176
Art. 7(3) . . . 1176, 1252
Art. 7(4) . . . 1176
Art. 8 . . . 1148, 1178
Art. 8(1) . . . 1176, 1178, 1244, 1252
Art. 8(2) . . . 1176, 1178, 1244, 1246, 1252
Art. 8(3) . . . 1252
Art. 8(4) . . . 1143, 1176, 1179, 1252
Art. 8(5) . . . 1176, 1179
Art. 8(6) . . . 1178, 1179, 1251, 1252
Art. 8(7) . . . 1251
Art. 9 . . . 1157, 1159, **1160**, 1161, 1162, 1163, 1164,
    1174, 1175, 1177, 1252, 1278
Art. 9(1) . . . **1160**
Art. 9(2) . . . 1159, **1160**
Art. 9(2)(a) . . . 1161, 1163
Art. 9(2)(b) . . . 1161
Art. 9(3) . . . 1159, **1160**, 1161, 1252
Art. 9(4) . . . 1161
Art. 9(5) . . . 1159
Art. 9(6) . . . 1161
Art. 9(6)–(9) . . . 1174
Art. 9(7) . . . 1162
Art. 9(8) . . . 1159, 1162
Art. 10 . . . 1177
Art. 10(1) . . . 1161, 1177
Art. 10(3) . . . 1178
Art. 10(5) . . . 1253
Art. 10(6) . . . 1176, 1178
Art. 11 . . . 1179
Art. 12 . . . 1179
Art. 13 . . . 1179
Art. 14 . . . 995, 1179, 1252
Art. 14(1) . . . 1179
Art. 14(2)(a) . . . 1176
Art. 14(2)(b) . . . 1176
Art. 14(2)(d) . . . 1251
Art. 15 . . . 1179
Art. 15(1)(c) . . . 1251
Art. 16 . . . 1253
Art. 17(2) . . . 1172
Art. 18(1) . . . 1179
Art. 18(2) . . . 1179
Art. 18(3) . . . 1179
Art. 19 . . . 104
Art. 21 . . . 1134, 1157, 1165, 1167, 1252
Art. 21(1) . . . 1147, **1157**, 1168, 1171, 1244
Art. 21(1)–(3) . . . **1157**
Art. 21(2) . . . **1157**
Art. 21(3) . . . **1157**, 1159, 1168
Art. 21(4) . . . 51, 1157, 1159, **1164**, 1165, 1166, 1167
Art. 22 . . . 1150, 1157, 1159, 1160, 1168, 1169, 1170,
    1171, 1175, 1252
Art. 22(1) . . . **1168**
Art. 22(3) . . . 1176, 1252
Art. 22(4) . . . 1165
Art. 22(5) . . . 1170
Art. 24 . . . 1256
Art. 24(3) . . . 1256

411/2004 Council Reg. on air transport [2004] OJ
L68/1 . . . 115, 116, 1157

772/2004 Commission Reg. on Technology Transfer
(TTBER) [2004] OJ L123/11 . . . 76, 264, 265, 557,
748, 822, 823, 846, 847, 848, 850, 851, **852**, 855, 859,
860, 866, 867, 868, 869, 870, 872, 874, 875, 876, 877,
878, 879, 880, 881, 882, 883, 884, 891, 892, 893, 894,
895, 898, 899, 900, 901, 902, 903, 904, 905, 906, 907,
908, 909, 913, 914, 916, 920, 921
Recital 4 . . . **874**
Art. 1 . . . 875
Art. 1(1)(b) . . . 855, 875, 876, 877, 894, 908, 914
Art. 1(1)(c) . . . 885
Art. 1(1)(d) . . . 885
Art. 1(1)(h) . . . 875, 877
Art. 1(1)(i) . . . 850, 877
Art. 1(1)(j) . . . 883
Art. 1(1)(j)(i) . . . **883**
Art. 1(1)(j)(ii) . . . 881, **883**
Art. 1(2) . . . 876
Art. 2 . . . 141, 875, 876, 878, 880, 885, 888, 891, 892
Art. 2(1) . . . **894**
Art. 3 . . . 875, 880
Art. 3(1) . . . **880**
Art. 3(2) . . . **880**
Art. 3(3) . . . 881, 882
Art. 4 . . . 875, 876, 884, 895
Art. 4(1) . . . 884, **885**
Art. 4(1)(a) . . . 865, **885**, 886, 898
Art. 4(1)(b) . . . **885**, 886, 901
Art. 4(1)(c) . . . **885**, 886, 899, 900, 901
Art. 4(1)(c)(i) . . . **885**, 886, 902
Art. 4(1)(c)(ii) . . . **885**, 886
Art. 4(1)(c)(iii) . . . **885**, 886
Art. 4(1)(c)(iv) . . . **885**, 887, 900
Art. 4(1)(c)(v) . . . **885**, 887, 900
Art. 4(1)(c)(vi) . . . **885**, 887
Art. 4(1)(c)(vii) . . . **885**, 887
Art. 4(1)(d) . . . **885**, 888, 898
Art. 4(2) . . . 884, **888–889**
Art. 4(2)(a) . . . **888–889**
Art. 4(2)(b) . . . **889**, 901
Art. 4(2)(b)(i) . . . **889**, 900
Art. 4(2)(b)(ii) . . . **889**, 890, 900
Art. 4(2)(b)(iii) . . . **889**, 890
Art. 4(2)(b)(iv) . . . **889**, 890
Art. 4(2)(b)(v) . . . **889**, 890
Art. 4(2)(b)(vi) . . . **889**, 890
Art. 4(2)(c) . . . **889**, 891
Art. 4(3) . . . 884
Art. 5 . . . 875, **891–892**, 894, 904
Art. 5(1)(a) . . . **891**, 892
Art. 5(1)(b) . . . **892**
Art. 5(1)(c) . . . **892**
Art. 5(2) . . . **892**, 893, 904
Art. 6 . . . 875, 893
Art. 6(1) . . . 893
Art. 6(2) . . . 893
Art. 7 . . . 875, 893
Art. 8 . . . 875, 881

Art. 8(1) ... 882
Art. 8(2) ... 884
Art. 9 ... 875
Art. 10 ... 875
Art. 11 ... 875

773/2004 Commission on the conduct of proceedings by the Commission pursuant to Articles 101 and 102 (the Implementing Regulation) [2004] OJ L123/18 ... 116, 927, 931, 932, 967, 968, 970, 1115
Ch IV ... 1067
Art. 2 ... 939
Art. 2(1) ... **939**
Art. 2(3) ... 939
Art. 2(4) ... 939
Art. 3 ... **953**
Art. 4(2) ... 948
Art. 4(3) ... **948**
Art. 5 ... 1071
Art. 5(1) ... 1071
Art. 6 ... 1076
Art. 6(1) ... **974**
Art. 7 ... 1032
Art. 7(1) ... **974**, 1071, 1075
Art. 7(2) ... 1075
Art. 9 ... **1068**
Art. 10(1) ... 968
Art. 10(2) ... 968, **974**
Arts 10–14 ... 970
Art. 11(2) ... 968
Art. 12 ... 978
Art. 13 ... 978
Art. 13(1) ... **974**
Art. 13(3) ... **974**
Art. 14(4) ... 978
Art. 14(5) ... 978
Art. 14(6) ... 978
Art. 14(8) ... 978
Art. 15 ... 970
Art. 15(2) ... 973, 975
Art. 16 ... 970, 974
Art. 16(1) ... **973**
Art. 16(2) ... **974**, 975
Art. 16(3) ... 975
Art. 17(3) ... 948, 953
Annex ... 939

802/2004 Commission Implementing Reg. [2004] OJ L133/1 ... 1138, 1150, 1173
Art. 3(2) ... 1173
Arts 7–10 ... 1177
Art. 11(1)(b) ... 1180
Art. 11(1)(c) ... 1180
Art. 13(2) ... 1179
Art. 13(3) ... 1179
Art. 14 ... 1179
Art. 15 ... 1179
Art. 17(1) ... 1179
Art. 19(1) ... 1177, 1246
Art. 19(2) ... 1178, 1246

1184/2006 Council Reg. applying competition rules to agricultural products [2006] OJ L 214/7 ... 51, 110, 189

Art. 2(1) ... 110

1419/2006 Council Reg. on maritime transport [2006] OJ L269/1 ... 115, 421

1234/2007 Single CMO Reg. [2007] OJ L299/1110

622/2008 Commission Reg. on the conduct of settlement procedures in cartel cases [2008] OJ L171/3 ... 931, 992, 1076

169/2009 Council Reg. [2009] OJ L61/1 ... 264

207/2009/EC Reg. OJ [2009] L78/1 ... 847, 849

246/2009 Council Reg. on liner shipping companies (consortia) [2009] OJ L79/1 ... 111, 116, 264

487/2009 Council Reg. on the air transport sector [2009] OJ L148/1 ... 111, 264

906/2009 Commission Reg. on liner shipping companies (consortia) [2009] OJ L256/31 ... 111, 116, 264

1211/2009 Reg. establishing the BEREC [2009] OJ L337/1 ... 52

267/2010 Commission Reg. on the insurance sector [2010] OJ L83/1 ... 116, 264, 763
Art. 2 ... 763
Art. 3 ... 763
Art. 5 ... 763
Art. 6 ... 763

330/2010 Commission Reg. on the application of Article 101(3) to categories of vertical agreements and concerted practices (Verticals Regulation) [2010] OJ L102/1 ... 61, 76, 115, 264, 265, 294, 455, 745, 746, 750, 754, 769, 776, 786, 787, 789, 801, 807, 809, 818, 819, 820, 821, 822, 823, 824, 825, 826, 828, 829, 830, 831, 832, 833, 834, 841, 842, 844, 867, 875, 879, 889, 891, 893, 909, 914, 921, 1224
Recital 6 ... 818
Recital 7 ... 818
Recital 8 ... 818
Recitals ... 818
Art. 1 ... 818, 821
Art. 1(1)(a)–(i) ... **820**
Art. 1(b) ... 451,
Art. 1(1)(d) ... 455
Art. 1(1)(g) ... 832
Art. 1(2) ... 820
Art. 2 ... 820, 824, 825, 831
Art. 2(1) ... 819
Art. 2(2) ... 822
Art. 2(3) ... 819, 822, 909
Art. 2(4) ... 754, 819, 821
Art. 2(5) ... 819, 823
Art. 3 ... 823, **824**
Art. 3(1) ... 819
Art. 4 ... 793, 819, 825, 827, 830, 843, 888
Art. 4(a) ... 826
Art. 4(a)–(e) ... **825–826**
Art. 4(b) ... 827, 829, 830, 843
Art. 4(c) ... 828, 829, 830
Art. 4(d) ... 829
Art. 4(e) ... 827, 830
Art. 5 ... 825, 830, **831**, 838, 843
Art. 5(1) ... 831
Art. 5(1)(c) ... 832

Art. 5(3) ... 832
Art. 6 ... 833
Art. 6(2) ... 833
Art. 7 ... 824, 833
Art. 7(d) ... 833
Art. 8 ... 833
Art. 9 ... 833
Art. 10 ... 834

461/2010 Commission Reg. [2010] OJ L129/52 ... 116, 264, 834

1217/2010 Commission Reg. on research and development agreements [2010] OJ L335/36 ... v, 61, 76, 116, 264, 294, 731, 732, 735, 741, 742, 747, 867
Art. 1 ... 742
Art. 1(1)(a) ... **742–743**
Art. 1(1)(b) ... 743

Art. 1(1)(b)(g) ... 743
Art. 1(1)(m)(i) ... **743, 744, 745**
Art. 1(1)(m)(ii) ... **743, 744, 745**
Art. 2 ... 742, 743, 744, 745, 747
Art. 3 ... 742, **743**, 746, 747
Art. 4 ... 742, **744**, 747
Art. 4(1) ... **744**
Art. 4(2) ... **744**
Art. 5 ... 742, **744–745**, 746, 747
Art. 5(a) ... **744**, 745
Art. 5(b) ... **744**, 745

DIRECTIVES

65/65 Directive [1965–1966 OJ Spec. Ed. 24 ... 560, 561, 562
Art. 4 ... **562**

70/50 Directive on quantitative restrictions on imports [1970] OJ Spec. Ed. 17 ... 607

77/249/EEC Council Directive on lawyers' freedom to provide services [1977] OJ L78/17 ... 960

80/723/EEC Commission Directive Transparency Directive [1980] OJ L195/35 ... 604, 654, 655

85/413 Commission Directive on transparency of financial relations between Member States and public undertakings [1985] OJ L229/20 ... 604, 654

86/653 Council Directive on the coordination of the laws of the Member States relating to self-employed commercial agents [1986] OJ L382/17 ... 770
Art. 1(2) ... 770
Art. 19 ... 770

87/54 Council Directive on legal protection of topographies and semiconductor products [1987] OJ L24/36 ... 850

88/301 Directive on telecommunications terminal equipment [1988] OJ L131/73 ... 605, 606, 608, 654, 655
Art. 2 ... 605, 606

Art. 5(c) ... **745**
Art. 5(d)–(g) ... **745**
Art. 6 ... 742, **745**
Art. 7 ... 655, 744
Art. 8 ... 655
Recital 2 ... 741

1218/2010 Commission Reg. on specialisation agreements [2010] OJ L335/43 ... 61, 76, 116, 264, 294, 731, 732, 735, 747, 748, 867
Art. 1 ... **747, 748**
Art. 2 ... **748**
Art. 2(2) ... **748**
Art. 2(3)(a) ... **748**
Art. 2(3)(b) ... **748**
Art. 3 ... **748**
Art. 4 ... **748–749**

360/2012 De minimis Reg. [2012] OJ L114/8 ... 632

Commission Proposal for a Regulation of the Council on the control of concentrations between undertakings, [1973] OJ C92/1
Art. 1(1) ... 1255

Commission Proposal for a Council Regulation on the control of concentrations between undertakings [2003] OJ C20/4 ... 297, 1138
Recitals 55–57 ... 297
Art. 2(2) ... 297

89/104/EEC Council Directive to approximate the laws of the Member States relating to Trade Marks (First Trade Mark Directive) [1989] OJ L40/1 ... 847, 849

89/105 Council Directive on transparency of measures regulating the prices of medicinal products for human use and their inclusion in the scope of national health insurance systems [1989] OJ L40/8 ... 54

90/387 Council Directive on Open Network Provision [1990] OJ L192/1 ... 655

90/388/EEC Directive on competition in the markets for telecommunications services [1990] OJ L192/10 ... 427, 606, 654

91/250 Directive on the legal protection of computer programs [1991] OJ L122/42 ... **546**, 850

91/440 Council Directive on railways [1991] OJ L237/25 ... 518

93/13/EEC Council Directive on unfair terms in consumer contracts [1993] OJ L95/29 ... 583

94/46 Directive on satellite communications [1994] OJ L268/15 ... 606
Preamble ... 606
Art. 1(2)(b) ... **918**

96/9 Directive on legal protection of databases [1996] OJ L77/20 ... 849, 850

97/67 Postal Directive [1998] OJ L15/14 . . . 651

98/49/EC Council Directive on pension rights of employed and self-employed persons [1998] OJ L209/46 . . . 647

98/71 Directive on the legal protection of designs [1998] OJ L289/28 . . . 850

2001/29/EC Directive on Copyright and Related Rights in the Information Society [2001] OJ L167/10 . . . 849

2001/83/EC Directive on the Community code relating to medicinal products for human use [2001] OJ L211/67 . . . 54
Art. 81 . . . **589**

2002/21/EC Directive on a common regulatory framework for electronic communications networks and services (Electronic Communications Directive) [2002] OJ L108/33 . . . 52, 53

2002/22 Directive on electronic communications (Universal Service Directive) [2002] OJ L108/51 . . . 52

2002/58 Directive on privacy and electronic communications [2002] OJ L201/37 . . . 52

2006/111 Commission Directive on the transparency of financial relations between Member States and public undertakings as well as on financial transparency within certain undertakings (Transparency Directive) [2006] OJ L318/17 . . . 604
Art. 2(b) . . . **604**

2006/116/EC Directive on the term of protection of copyright and certain related rights [2006] OJ L372/12 . . . 849

2007/58 Directive on railways [2007] OJ L315/44 . . . 111

2008/95/EC Directive to approximate the laws of the Member States relating to Trade Marks [2008] OJ L299/25 . . . 847, 848
Art. 4(1)(b) . . . 848

2009/24/EC Directive [2009] OJ L111/16 . . . 850

2009/136 Directive on electronic communications networks and data [2009] OJ L337/11 . . . 52

2009/140/EC Directive on a common regulatory framework for electronic communications (Electronic Communications Directive) [2009] OJ L337/3 . . . 52, 53
Recital 5 . . . 53

Proposal for a Directive amending Directive 98/71 on the legal protection of designs (COM/2004/582) . . . 850

Proposal for a Directive of the European Parliament and of the Council on certain rules governing actions for damages under national law for infringements of the competition law provision of the Member States and the European Union COM(2013) 404 final . . . 1082, 1087, 1094, 1108, 1113, 1114
Chap I . . . **1114**
Chap II . . . **1114**
Chap III . . . **1116**
Chap IV . . . **1117**
Chap V . . . **1117–1118**
Chap VI . . . **1118**
Arts. 1–4 . . . **1114**
Art. 2 . . . **1114**
Art. 3 . . . **1114**
Arts. 5–8 . . . **1114**
Arts. 9–11 . . . **1116**
Arts. 12–15 . . . **1117**
Art. 16 . . . **1117–1118**
Arts. 17–18 . . . **1118**

Proposal by the Commission for a Directive on damages actions, 11 June 2013, IP/13/525 . . . 1025, 1027

Proposal for a Directive amending Directive 98/71 on the legal protection of designs (COM/2004/582) . . . 850

Proposal for a Directive designed to remove a number of practical difficulties confronted by victims of infringements of the EU antitrust rules when instigating damages claims . . . vi, 1082, 1087, 1113

DECISIONS

58/255 Council Decision . . . 113

72/403 Commission Decision relating to a proceeding under Article 85 of the EEC Treaty [1972] OJ L272/35 . . . 774

81/969/EEC Commission Decision relating to a proceeding under Article 86 of the EEC Treaty [1981] OJ L353/33 . . . 465

83/462/EEC Commission Decision relating to a proceeding under Article 86 of the EEC Treaty [1983] OJ L252/13 . . . 411

89/205/EEC Commission Decision relating to a proceeding under Article 86 of the EEC Treaty [1989] OJ L78/43
Recital 23 . . . 541

94/601/EC Commission Decision . . . **1006**

94/810 Commission Decision on terms of reference of hearing officers [1994] OJ L330/67 . . . 969

97/624 Commission Decision relating to a proceeding under Article 86 of the EEC Treaty [1997] OJ L258/1 paras. 120–122 . . . 557

2001/462 Commission Decision on the terms of reference of hearing officers (Hearing Officer Mandate) [2001] OJ L162/21 . . . 969
Recital 6 . . . 969
Art. 2(2) . . . 969

2002/165 Commission Decision relating to a proceeding under Article 82 of the EC Treaty [2002] OJ L59/18
para. 15 . . . 535

2003/741 Commission Decision relating to a proceeding under Article 82 of the EC Treaty [2003] OJ L268/69 . . . 532

2004/407 Council Decision amending the Protocol on the Statute of the ECJ [2004] OJ L132/5 . . . 1037

2005/842 Commission Decision on the application of Art. 86(2) to State aid [2005] OJ L312/67 . . . 656

2011/695 Commission Decision of the President of the European Commission of 13 October 2011 on the function and terms of reference of the hearing officer in certain competition proceedings [2011] OJ L275/29 (the 'HO Terms of Reference') . . . 969
    Recital 3–8 . . . 969

Art. 1(2) . . . 969
Art. 2(2) . . . 969
Art. 7 . . . 975
Art. 8 . . . 975, 991
Art. 10 . . . 978
Art. 13(1) . . . 978
Art. 14(1) . . . 978
Art. 16 . . . 979

2012/21 Commission Decision specifying that certain types of compensation paid by Member States to undertakings dealing with services of general economic interest are compatible with Article 106(2) and exempt from the State aid notification obligation under Article 108 [2012] OJ L7/3 . . . 632, 656

NOTICES ETC.

Draft Guidelines on the application of Article 101 TFEU to technology transfer agreements, 20 February 2013 . . . 43
    para. 5 . . . 43
    para. 22 . . . 79
    para. 26 . . . 78

Guidance on the Commission's Enforcement Priorities in Applying Article 82 [now Article 102 TFEU] of the EC Treaty to Abusive Exclusionary Conduct by Dominant Undertakings [2009] OJ C45/2 (Guidance Paper) . . . v, 43, 118, 269, 289, 290, 291, 292, 293, 302, 335, 336, 339, **340**, **343**, 344, **348**, 359, 360, 363, 365, 366, 372, 380, 381, 382, 383, 384, 385, 386, 387, 388, **389**, **390**, 391, 396, 399, **400**, 402, **417**, **418**, 421, 425, 445, 446, 450, 453, 454, 457, 476, 477, 478, 479, 480, 482, 483, 484, 485, 487, 489, 506, 507, 508, 509, 522, 550, 551, 552, 553, 586, 591, 740, 1008
    para. 1 . . . 378
    paras. 1–8 . . . 290
    para. 2 . . . 290, 291
    para. 3 . . . 290
    para. 5 . . . 43, **290**
    para. 6 . . . **290**, 378
    para. 7 . . . 40, 290
    para. 9 . . . **302**
    paras. 9–18 . . . 336
    paras. 9–31 . . . 291
    para. 10 . . . 60, **303**
    para. 11 . . . 59, 60, 302, **303**, 383
    para. 12 . . . 336, 347, 359
    para. 13 . . . 61, 339, **340**
    para. 14 . . . **343–344**
    para. 15 . . . **340**
    para. 16 . . . 347, **348**
    para. 17 . . . 347, **348**, 354, 359
    para. 18 . . . **360**
    para. 19 . . . 46, **383**, 384, 385
    para. 20 . . . **383**, 384, 508
    para. 21 . . . 384
    para. 22 . . . 380, 381, **385**
    para. 23 . . . 381, **400**
    paras. 23–27 . . . 399

    para. 24 . . . 381, 399, **400**, 425
    para. 25 . . . **400**
    para. 26 . . . **400**
    para. 26, n.2 . . . 398, 399, 418
    para. 26, n.3 . . . 407
    para. 27 . . . **400**
    para. 28 . . . 389
    paras. 28–31 . . . 477
    para. 29 . . . **389**
    para. 30 . . . **390**, 391, 418, 509
    para. 31 . . . **390**
    para. 32 . . . 450
    paras. 32–46 . . . 450
    paras. 32–90 . . . 291
    para. 33 . . . 451
    paras. 33–36 . . . 452
    para. 34 . . . 453
    para. 36 . . . 453
    para. 37 . . . 476
    para. 37, n. 3 . . . 476
    paras. 37–45 . . . 476
    paras. 37–46 . . . 456
    para. 39 . . . 477
    para. 40 . . . 456
    paras. 41–42 . . . 477
    para. 43 . . . 477
    para. 44 . . . 477
    para. 45 . . . 477
    para. 46 . . . 454, 477
    paras. 47–74 . . . 506
    para. 48 . . . 486
    para. 48, n. 2 . . . 486
    para. 49 . . . 489
    para. 50 . . . 506
    para. 50, n. 3 . . . 487
    para. 51 . . . **507**
    para. 52 . . . 509
    para. 53 . . . 508
    paras. 53–58 . . . 508
    para. 54 . . . 509
    para. 55 . . . 509
    para. 56 . . . **509**

para. 57 . . . 509
para. 58 . . . 509
paras. 59–61 . . . 455, 509
para. 61 . . . 509
para. 62 . . . 509
para. 63 . . . **418**, 419, 425
para. 64 . . . **418**
paras. 64–65 . . . 381
para. 65 . . . **418**
para. 66 . . . **418**
para. 67 . . . **418**
para. 68 . . . **418**
para. 69 . . . **419**
para. 70 . . . **417**
para. 71 . . . **417**
para. 72 . . . **419**, 421, 425
para. 73 . . . **419**
para. 74 . . . 418, **419**
para. 75 . . . 586
paras. 75–90 . . . 445, 550
para. 77 . . . 291, 511, 550
para. 78 . . . 551
para. 79 . . . 551
para. 80 . . . 442, **445**, 551
para. 80, fn 8 . . . 445
para. 80, fn 9 . . . 445
para. 81 . . . 551, 552
para. 82 . . . 442, 445, **552**
para. 83 . . . 551
para. 84 . . . 552
para. 85 . . . 551
para. 87 . . . 552
para. 89 . . . 553
para. 90 . . . 553

Guidelines on the applicability of Article 101 of the
  Treaty on the Functioning of the European Union
  to horizontal co-operation agreements (Horizontal
  Cooperation Guidelines) [2011] OJ C11/01 . . . 111,
  118, 188, 250, 699, 700, 701, 731, 732, 734, 735, 739,
  740, 741, 742, 746, 747, 749, 750, 754, 757, 758, 761,
  762, 767, 908
para. 1 . . . 739
para. 10 . . . **739**
para. 11 . . . 145, 146
paras. 13–14 . . . 739
paras. 20–53 . . . 740
para. 21 . . . **734**
paras. 23–31 . . . 740
para. 28 . . . **740**
para. 28–29 . . . 740
para. 29 . . . **740**
para. 30 . . . **740**
paras. 32–38 . . . 740
para. 34 . . . 740
paras. 35–37 . . . 740
para. 38 . . . 740
paras. 39–47 . . . 741
para. 46 . . . 738
para. 47 . . . 738
para. 48 . . . 741

para. 55 . . . 171, 700
paras. 55–110 . . . 741
paras. 57–58 . . . 699
para. 58 . . . 741
para. 59 . . . **741**
para. 60 . . . 700
para. 62 . . . 169
paras. 64–71 . . . 699
para. 65 . . . 699
paras. 69–71 . . . 700
paras. 72–74 . . . 701
para. 73 . . . 701
para. 75 . . . 702
para. 77 . . . 704
paras. 86–94 . . . 703
para. 89 . . . 703
para. 94 . . . 704
para. 111 . . . **741**
para. 112 . . . 741
paras. 114–126 . . . 742
paras. 116–117 . . . 79
paras. 116–118 . . . 742
para. 119 . . . 78
paras. 119–122 . . . 742
para. 129 . . . 742
para. 130 . . . 742
paras. 132–133 . . . 742
para. 134 . . . 740
paras. 141–149 . . . 746
para. 142 . . . 746
para. 143 . . . 746, 754
para. 145 . . . 746
para. 146 . . . 746
paras. 147–149 . . . 746
paras. 157–159 . . . 746
paras. 162–182 . . . 747
para. 163 . . . 747
para. 167 . . . 747
paras. 168–169 . . . 747
para. 169 . . . 740
para. 170 . . . 740
paras. 175–176 . . . 747
para. 183 . . . 749
para. 184 . . . 749
para. 185 . . . 749
para. 186 . . . 749
paras. 187–193 . . . 749
para. 194 . . . 749, 750
para. 196 . . . 750
paras. 197–199 . . . 750
para. 204 . . . 750
para. 206 . . . **750**
para. 207 . . . **750**
para. 208 . . . 740
paras. 208–209 . . . 750
para. 210 . . . 750
para. 212 . . . **751**
para. 213 . . . 751
para. 216 . . . **751**
para. 217 . . . **751**
para. 218 . . . **751**

para. 219 . . . **751**
para. 220 . . . **752**
para. 225 . . . **754**
paras. 225–256 . . . 754
para. 227 . . . 754
para. 228 . . . 754
para. 230 . . . **755**
para. 231 . . . **755**
para. 232 . . . **755**
para. 233 . . . **755**
para. 234–235 . . . 755
para. 237 . . . **755**
para. 238 . . . **755**
para. 239 . . . **755**
para. 240 . . . 740, 756
paras. 240–241 . . . 756
paras. 242–243 . . . 756
paras. 244–245 . . . 756
para. 246 . . . **756**
para. 247 . . . **756**
para. 248 . . . **756**
para. 249 . . . **756**
para. 250 . . . **756**
para. 257 . . . 757, 908
para. 257, n.1 . . . 757
para. 258 . . . 757
para. 259 . . . 762
para. 261 . . . 757
para. 262 . . . 762
paras. 264–268 . . . 757
para. 269 . . . **758**
paras. 270–271 . . . 762
para. 272 . . . 762
paras. 273–276 . . . 757
para. 276 . . . 762
para. 279 . . . 758
para. 280 . . . **759**
paras. 280–291 . . . 758
para. 281 . . . **759**
para. 282 . . . **759**
para. 283 . . . **759**
paras. 283–287 . . . 563
para. 284 . . . **759**
para. 285 . . . **759**
para. 286 . . . **759**
para. 287 . . . **759**
paras. 292–299 . . . 759
paras. 300–307 . . . 762
para. 308 . . . **760**
para. 309 . . . **760**
para. 310 . . . **760**
para. 311 . . . **760**
para. 312 . . . **762**
para. 313 . . . **762**
para. 314 . . . **760**
para. 315 . . . **760**
para. 316 . . . **760**
para. 317 . . . **760**
para. 318 . . . 760, **761**
para. 319 . . . **761**
para. 320 . . . **762**

para. 321 . . . **761**
para. 322 . . . **762**
para. 323 . . . **763**
para. 324 . . . **761**, 763

Guidelines on the applicability of Article 101 to
horizontal cooperation agreements [2001] OJ
C3/2 . . . 42, 731, 732, 735, 739, 758, 1242

Guidelines on the application of Article 101 to maritime transport [2008] OJ C245/2 . . . 111, 700

Guidelines on the application of Article 101 to technology transfer agreements (Technology Transfer
Guidelines) [2004] OJ C101/2 . . . 188, 250, 847, 848,
852, 853, 856, 857, 859, 867, 868, **869**, 870, 872, 879,
881, 884, 894, 895, 896, 897, 898, 901, 902, 903, 904,
906, 909, 914, 916, 920, 921
para. 4 . . . 870
para. 5 . . . **870–871**
para. 6 . . . **871**
para. 7 . . . **871**
para. 8 . . . **871**
para. 9 . . . **871**
paras. 10–18 . . . 872, 895
para. 12(a) . . . **872**
para. 12(b) . . . **872**, 873, 900
para. 17 . . . 896
para. 18 . . . 896
para. 19 . . . 881, 893
paras. 19–22 . . . 876
para. 21 . . . 881
para. 22 . . . 79, 881
para. 23 . . . 881
para. 25 . . . 78, 881
para. 26 . . . 883
para. 27 . . . **883**
para. 28 . . . 883
para. 30 . . . 884
para. 31 . . . 878, 884
para. 32 . . . 883
para. 33 . . . 884
para. 36 . . . 870
para. 39 . . . 876
para. 40 . . . 894
para. 42 . . . 878, 894
para. 43 . . . 878
para. 44 . . . 878
para. 45 . . . 878, 894
para. 47 . . . 850, 877
para. 48 . . . 877
para. 49 . . . 878
paras. 49–50 . . . 877
para. 50 . . . 908
paras. 50–52 . . . 877
para. 51 . . . 894, 914
para. 52 . . . 894, 914, 916
para. 53 . . . 894, 909
paras. 56–64 . . . 879
paras. 59–60 . . . 879
paras. 62–63 . . . 879
para. 64 . . . 879
para. 66 . . . 883

para. 68...884
para. 69...880
para. 70...882
para. 71...882, 910
paras. 74–76...884
para. 77...900, 902
para. 79...886
paras. 79–81...886
para. 81...865, 898
para. 84...886
para. 86...886
para. 88...886
para. 89...887
para. 90...902
para. 92...887
para. 93...887
para. 94...888
para. 97...889
para. 98...889
para. 99...889
para. 100...889
para. 101...890
para. 102...886
para. 104...890
para. 108...892
para. 109...892, 904, 905
para. 110...905
paras. 110–111...892
para. 112...904
para. 113...904
para. 121...893
para. 122...893
paras. 123–129...893
paras. 130–132...895
para. 131... 879, 880, **895**
para. 132...897
para. 133...897
para. 134...897
para. 135...897
para. 136...897
para. 137...897
para. 138...897
para. 139...897
para. 140...898
para. 141...895
para. 146...896
para. 147...897
para. 148...896
para. 149...896
para. 150...896
para. 151...897
para. 155...898
para. 156...898
para. 157...898
para. 158...899
para. 159...898
para. 160...899
para. 162...856
para. 163...899
para. 164...899
para. 165...899

para. 166...899
para. 167...900
para. 169...900
paras. 170–171...900
para. 172...900
para. 173...900
para. 174...900
para. 175...901
para. 176...901
para. 177...901
para. 178...901
para. 179...857
para. 180...857
para. 183...902
para. 184...902
para. 185...902
para. 187...902
para. 188...902
para. 189...902
para. 190...903
para. 191...857
para. 193...903
para. 194...903
para. 199...904
para. 200...904
paras. 201–203...904
para. 204...905
para. 207...905
para. 208...905
para. 209...904, 906
para. 210...906
paras. 210–235...878, 906
paras. 215–216...907
paras. 217–222...907
paras. 219–222...907
para. 224...**907**
paras. 225–229...907
paras. 230–235...907

Guidelines on the application of Article 81(3) [now
    Article 101(3)] [2004] OJ C101/97 (Article 101(3)
    Guidelines)...39, 40, 43, 52, 93, 118, 123, 188, 193,
    204, 223, 238, 242, 244, 247, 250, 254, 258, 259, 260,
    261, 262, 266, 288, 390, 735, 786, 801, 806, 837, 869,
    872, 873, 894, 909, 921, 927, 1242
para. 2.2.3...244
para. 13...40, 123
para. 16...43
para. 17...204, 239
paras. 17–24...238
para. 18...204, 238, 239, 261, 740
para. 18(2)...240, 806
para. 21...43
para. 22...207, 223
para. 23...232
para. 24...233, 238, 801
paras. 24–27...238
para. 25...43
paras. 25–26...233, 801
para. 26...238
paras. 28–29...243

paras. 28–31 . . . 233, 801
para. 30 . . . 246
para. 33 . . . 251
para. 42 . . . 254
para. 43 . . . 259
para. 44 . . . 250
para. 45 . . . 253
para. 46 . . . 252
para. 48 . . . 252
para. 51 . . . 253
paras. 52–59 . . . 253
paras. 59–72 . . . 253
paras. 64–68 . . . 253
paras. 69–72 . . . 253
para. 73 . . . **261**
para. 74 . . . **261**
para. 79 . . . 260
para. 80 . . . 260
paras. 83–104 . . . 258
para. 84 . . . 46
para. 85 . . . 259
paras. 86–89 . . . 260
paras. 90–91 . . . 260
para. 105 . . . 262
para. 106 . . . 262, 263, 294
paras. 114–115 . . . 93
para. 115 . . . 263
para. 116 . . . 263

Guidelines on the assessment of horizontal mergers
  under the Council Regulation on the control of
  concentrations between undertakings (Horizontal
  Merger Guidelines) [2004] OJ C31/03 . . . 43, 93, 118,
  335, 389, 1133, 1138, 1183, 1189, 1190, 1191, 1193,
  1199, 1200, 1205, 1207, 1209, 1215, 1221
Pt III . . . 1190
Pt IV . . . 1190
Pts V–VII . . . 1190
Pt VIII . . . 1190
para. 1 . . . 1187
para. 4 . . . 1187
para. 5 . . . 1133, 1183, 1189, 1215
para. 8 . . . 43, 1189
para. 9 . . . 1184
para. 10 . . . 1188
para. 14 . . . 340, 1190
paras. 14–21 . . . 1191
para. 16 . . . 1190
para. 17 . . . **1190–1191**
paras. 17–18 . . . 1190
para. 18 . . . **1191**
paras. 19–21 . . . 1191
para. 21 . . . 1191
para. 25 . . . 1193
para. 27 . . . 1193
paras. 27–30 . . . 1193
para. 31 . . . 1198
paras. 32–35 . . . 1198
para. 35 . . . 1198
para. 36 . . . 1198
paras. 37–38 . . . 1199

para. 39. **1199**
para. 40 . . . **1200**
para. 41 . . . 1200
para. 42 . . . 1196
paras. 45–57 . . . 1207
para. 68 . . . 1209
para. 73 . . . 1210
para. 74 . . . 1210
para. 75 . . . 1210
para. 76 . . . 1215
para. 77 . . . 1215
para. 78 . . . 1215
paras. 79–84 . . . 1215
paras. 80–81 . . . 43
para. 84 . . . 1215, 1216
para. 85 . . . 389, 1215, **1216**
paras. 86–88 . . . 1215
para. 87 . . . 1215
para. 89 . . . 1217, **1221**
para. 90 . . . **1221**
para. 91 . . . **1221**

Guidelines on the assessment of non-horizontal
  mergers under the Council Regulation on the
  control of concentrations between undertakings
  (Non-Horizontal Merger Guidelines) [2008] OJ
  C265/6 . . . 43, 1132, 1138, 1187, 1223, 1224, 1225,
  1229, 1230, 1236, 1237, 1238
para. 10 . . . 43
paras. 11–13 . . . 1223
para. 12 . . . **1223**
para. 13 . . . **1223–1224**
para. 14 . . . **1224**
para. 16 . . . 1224
paras. 25–26 . . . 1224
para. 27 . . . 1224
para. 46 . . . **1229**
paras. 55–57 . . . 1225
para. 78 . . . 1225
paras. 90–91 . . . 1230
para. 92 . . . 1236
paras. 93–118 . . . 1236
para. 118 . . . 1237
para. 119 . . . **1239**
para. 120 . . . **1239**
para. 121 . . . **1239**

Guidelines on the assessment of significant market
  power under the Community regulatory framework
  for electronic communications, networks and services [2002] OJ C165/6 . . . 336, 344

Guidelines on the effect on trade concept contained in
  Articles 81 and 82 of the Treaty (Guidelines on the
  effect on trade concept) [2004] OJ C101/81 . . . 181,
  188, 226, 269, 271, **285**, 286, 927
para. 3 . . . 181
para. 5 . . . 181
para. 13 . . . 181
para. 17 . . . **285**
para. 19 . . . 181
paras. 25–32 . . . 182
para. 26 . . . 182

paras. 33–35 . . . 182
paras. 36–43 . . . 182
para. 43 . . . 182
paras. 44–57 . . . 185
para. 46 . . . 185
para. 50 . . . 185, 186
paras. 50–57 . . . 185
para. 52 . . . 185, 186
para. 53 . . . 186
para. 54 . . . 186
paras. 58–109 . . . 181
para. 60 . . . 184
paras. 61–72 . . . 184
paras. 73–76 . . . 285
para. 90 . . . 286
para. 91 . . . 286
para. 93 . . . 285
para. 94 . . . **285–286**
para. 95 . . . **286**
para. 96 . . . **286**
para. 101 . . . 287
para. 103 . . . 287
paras. 106–109 . . . 287

Guidelines on the method of setting fines imposed pursuant to Article 23(2)(a) of Regulation 1/2003 [2006] OJ C210/2 (Fining Guidelines) . . . 118, 1000, 1005, **1006**, **1007**, **1008**, 1009, 1012, 1013, 1014, 1015, 1028, 1036, 1039, 1040, 1041, **1042**, **1043**
para. 4 . . . 1015
para. 6 . . . 1012
para. 13 . . . **1009**, 1012
para. 14 . . . **1009**
para. 15 . . . **1009**
para. 16 . . . **1009**
para. 17 . . . **1009**
para. 18 . . . **1009**
para. 19 . . . **1009**
para. 20 . . . **1010**
para. 21 . . . **1010**, 1012
para. 22 . . . **1010**
para. 23 . . . **1010**
para. 24 . . . **1010**, 1013
para. 25 . . . **1010**, 1013
para. 26 . . . **1010**
para. 27 . . . **1010**
para. 28 . . . **1010**, 1015, 1028
para. 29 . . . **1011**, 1012, 1015
para. 30 . . . **1011**, 1013
para. 31 . . . **1011**, 1014
para. 32 . . . **1011**
para. 33 . . . **1011**
para. 34 . . . **1011**
para. 35 . . . **1011**, 1016, 1017
para. 37 . . . 1012
para. 38 . . . 1005

Guidelines on the method of setting fines pursuant to Regulation 17, Art. 15(2) and Art. 65(5) of the ECSC Treaty [1998] OJ C9/3 . . . 1000, 1004, 1005, 1008, 1012, 1013, 1014, 1016
Section 2 . . . 1004

Section 3 . . . 1004
para. 1 . . . 1004
para. 2 . . . 1014

Guidelines on vertical restraints [2000] OJ C291/1 (Verticals Guidelines) . . . 42, 450, 451, 456, 768, 769
para. 7 . . . 42
para. 152 . . . 456

Guidelines on vertical restraints [2010] OJ C130/10 (Verticals Guidelines) . . . 40, 43, 118, 188, 250, 450, 451, 746, 750, 754, 769, 770, 772, 775, 776, 779, 780, 783, 786, 789, 800, 801, 804, 806, 815, 816, 818, 822, 824, 825, 827, 828, 834, 836, 837, 838, 842, 844, 879, 909, 919
para. 6 . . . 779
para. 7 . . . 40, 43, 782
para. 12 . . . 770
paras. 12–21 . . . 774
para. 13 . . . 774
para. 14 . . . 775
para. 15 . . . 775
paras. 18–19 . . . 776
paras. 18–21 . . . 776
para. 20 . . . 776
para. 21 . . . 773
paras. 23–73 . . . 818
para. 25 . . . 821
para. 26 . . . 821
para. 27 . . . 822
para. 28 . . . 821
para. 29 . . . 822
para. 31 . . . 822
para. 33 . . . 822
paras. 43–45 . . . 822
para. 44 . . . 822
para. 45 . . . **823**
para. 47 . . . 836
paras. 47–59 . . . 825
para. 48 . . . **826**
para. 49 . . . 826
para. 50 . . . 827
para. 51 . . . 828
para. 52 . . . 828, 829
para. 53 . . . 829, 830
para. 54 . . . 830
para. 56 . . . 830
para. 57 . . . 830
para. 58 . . . 830
para. 60 . . . 836
paras. 60–64 . . . 836
para. 61 . . . 220, **836**
para. 62 . . . **836**
paras. 63–64 . . . 836
para. 67 . . . 832
para. 69 . . . 832
para. 72 . . . 825
paras. 75–76 . . . 832
para. 77 . . . 832
para. 78 . . . 832
para. 80 . . . 833
para. 81 . . . 833

para. 82 ... 833
para. 83 ... 833
paras. 84–85 ... 833
paras. 96–230 ... 801
para. 98 ... 786
para. 100 ... **783**, 802
para. 101 ... **783**, 833
para. 102 ... **783**
para. 103 ... **783**
para. 104 ... 780, **783**
para. 105 ... 780, **784**
para. 106 ... 779
paras. 106–109 ... 779
para. 107 ... 780
para. 109 ... **837**
para. 110 ... 787
para. 111 ... **802**
paras. 111–121 ... 802
para. 112 ... **802**
paras. 113–121 ... 802
para. 120 ... 266
para. 129 ... 772
para. 130 ... 803
paras. 131–136 ... 837
paras. 132–133 ... 804
para. 133 ... 450, 804
paras. 139–226 ... 837
para. 141 ... 804
para. 143 ... 804
para. 151 ... 805
paras. 151–167 ... 805
para. 153 ... 806
para. 154 ... 806
para. 155 ... 838
para. 158 ... 838
para. 161 ... **806**
para. 162 ... 772
paras. 168–173 ... 817
para. 171 ... 838
para.174 ... 771
paras. 174–188 ... 809
para. 175 ... 807, 808, 811
para. 187 ... 811
para. 189 ... **815**
paras. 189–191 ... 816
paras. 192–202 ... 817
paras. 203–208 ... 817
para. 205 ... 772
paras. 209–210 ... 772
paras. 209–213 ... 817
para. 211 ... 171
paras. 214–222 ... 816
para. 223 ... 836
paras. 223–229 ... 836
para. 224 ... 799, **800**
para. 225 ... 836
para. 226 ... 826
para. 227 ... 789
paras. 227–229 ... 828

Consolidated Jurisdictional Notice under Council Regulation 139/2004/EC on the control of concentrations between undertakings (Jurisdictional Notice) [2008] OJ C95/1 ... 733, 734, 1138, 1140, 1143, **1145**, **1146**, 1148, 1149, 1153, 1154
para. 9 ... 1141
para. 10 ... 1141
para. 16 ... **1141–1142**
para. 20 ... 145
para. 35 ... 1148
para. 54 ... 1142, 1143
para. 56 ... 1142
para. 57 ... 1142
paras. 59–60 ... 1142
para. 62 ... **1143–1144**
para. 63 ... **1144**
paras. 64–82 ... 1144
paras. 83–90 ... 1144
para. 84 ... 1144
paras. 91–109 ... 734, 1145
para. 94 ... 1145
para. 95 ... **1145**
para. 96 ... **1146**
para. 97 ... **1146**
paras. 98–100 ... 1146
para. 103 ... **1146–1147**
para. 104 ... **1147**
para. 105 ... **1147**
paras. 106–109 ... 1147
paras. 110–118 ... 1147
para. 114 ... 1148
para. 119 ... **1149**
paras. 119–120 ... 1149
para. 120 ... **1149**
para. 124 ... 1149
para. 132 ... **1153**
para. 133 ... **1153**
paras. 134–153 ... 1153
paras. 154–156 ... 1173
paras. 157–174 ... 1153
para. 175 ... **1154**
para. 176 ... **1154**
para. 177 ... **1154**
para. 187 ... 1155

Notice concerning agreements, decisions and concerted practices in the field of cooperation between enterprises [1968] JO C75/3 ... 734
para. II(8) ... 697

Notice concerning agreements, decisions and concerted practices of minor importance which do not fall under Art. 85(1) [1970] OJ C64/1 ... 226, 676

Notice concerning the Alliance Agreement between British Airways and American Airlines [1996] OJ C288/4 ... 117

Notice concerning the assessment of certain subcontracting agreements in relation to Article 85(1) (Subcontracting Notice) [1979] OJ C1/20032 ... 188, 746, 841, 878

para. 1 ... 841
para. 2 ... 841

Notice concerning the assessment of the cooperative
joint ventures pursuant to Art. 85 [1993] OJ C43/2
733, 734, 738
para. 1 ... 733
para. 7 ... 735

Notice on a simplified procedure for the treatment of
certain concentrations under Council Regulation
139/2004 [2005] OJ C56/32 ... 1138, 1150
para. 17 ... 1150

Notice on access agreements in the telecommunications sector [1998] OJ C265/2 ... 522

Notice on agreements of minor importance which do
not appreciably restrict competition under Article
81(1) [Article 101(1)] (De minimis Notice) [2001]
OJ C368/13 ... 76, 118, 142, 226, 227, 228, **241**, 242,
740, 786, 1242
para. 2 ... **241**, 242
para. 4 ... **241**, 242
para. 5 ... **241**
para. 6 ... **241**
para. 7 ... **241**
para. 8 ... 241
para. 9 ... 242
para. 12 ... 142, 240

Notice on agreements of minor importance which do
not fall within the meaning of Art. 85(1) [1997] OJ
C372/13 ... 242

Notice on Agreements to Reduce Capacity, 16 June
2011 ... 695

Notice on Best Practices for the Conduct of Proceedings
(Best Practices) [2011] OJ C308/6 ... 932, 967, 975,
982, 983, 1017, 1248, 1289, 1290
para. 2 ... 1290
para. 6 ... 932
paras. 9–11 ... 933
paras. 47–52 ... 965
paras. 51–68 ... 965
paras. 60–61 ... 967
paras. 60–66 ... 967
para. 61 ... 967
para. 65 ... 967
para. 66 ... 967
paras. 67–69 ... 967
para. 70 ... 967
paras. 81–91 ... 968
para. 83 ... 968
para. 84 ... 968
para. 88 ... 1017
para. 96 ... 975
paras. 97–98 ... 976
para. 100 ... 968
paras. 106–108 ... 978
paras. 109–111 ... 968
paras. 115–133 ... 983
para. 116 ... 982
paras. 129–133 ... 983

Notice on calculation of turnover under Council
Regulation 4064/89 on the control of concentrations
between undertakings [1998] OJ C66/25 ... 1138

Notice on case allocation under the referral rules of the
Merger Regulation [2005] OJ C56/2 ... 1138, 1157,
1158, 1164, 1170, 1174, 1175
Pt III ... 1159
para. 3 ... 1157
para. 5 ... 1157
para. 8 ... **1158**
paras. 8–14 ... 1174
para. 9 ... **1158**
paras. 9–13 ... 1160
para. 10 ... **1158**
para. 11 ... **1158**
para. 12 ... **1158**
para. 13 ... **1159**
para. 14 ... **1159**
paras. 19–23 ... 1174
paras. 25–32 ... 1175
para. 37 ... 1161
paras. 38–41 ... 1161
paras. 42–45 ... 1168
para. 45 ... 1170

Notice on cooperation between national courts and the
Commission in applying Articles 85 and 86 Treaty
[1993] OJ C39/6 ... 1074
paras. 13–15 ... 1074
para. 14 ... 1074

Notice on cooperation between the Commission and
the courts of the EU Member States in the application of Articles 81 and 82 (Cooperation Notice)
[2004] OJ C101/54 ... 118, 927, 932, 950, 1067,
1074, 1105
paras. 9–10 ... 1105
paras. 11–13 ... 1095
para. 29 ... 1094
para. 40 ... 952

Notice on cooperation within the Network of
Competition Authorities (Cooperation Notice)
[2004] OJ C101/43 ... 48, 118, 927, 932, 938, 990,
1052, **1053**, 1057, 1060, 1061
para. 5 ... 1052
para. 8 ... **1053**
para. 9 ... **1053**
para. 10 ... **1054**
para. 11 ... **1054**
para. 12 ... **1054**
para. 13 ... **1054**
para. 14 ... **1054**
para. 15 ... **1054**
para. 18 ... 1054
para. 19 ... 1055
para. 28(a) ... 973, **1055–1056**
para. 28(b) ... **1056**
para. 28(c) ... **1056**
para. 37 ... 1057
paras. 39–42 ... 1057
para. 41 ... **1057**

para. 43 . . . 1060
para. 51 . . . 990, 1061
para. 52 . . . 938
para. 54(d) . . . 990
para. 58 . . . 104

Notice on immunity from fines and reduction of
fines in cartel cases (Leniency Notice) [2002] OJ
C45/3 . . . 677, 1020, 1022

Notice on Immunity from Fines and Reduction of
Fines in Cartel Cases (Leniency Notice) [2006] OJ
C298/17 . . . 45, 118, 677, 976, 982, 1009, 1020,
1021, 1022, **1023**, **1024**, 1025, 1026, 1027, 1042,
1059, 1060
para. 3 . . . 45
para. 8 . . . **1021**
para. 8(a) . . . **1021**, 1022, 1059
para. 8(b) . . . **1021**, 1022, 1059
para. 9 . . . **1021**
para. 9(a) . . . **1021**
para. 9(b) . . . **1021**
para. 10 . . . **1021**
para. 11 . . . **1021**
para. 12 . . . 1020, **1022**
para. 13 . . . **1022**, 1028
para. 15 . . . **1023**
para. 16 . . . **1023**
para. 23 . . . **1024**
para. 24 . . . **1024**
para. 25 . . . **1025**
para. 26 . . . **1025**
para. 31 . . . 1025
paras. 31–35 . . . 1020
para. 32 . . . 1026
paras. 33–34. 976
para. 34 . . . 1026

Notice on informal guidance relating to novel questions concerning Articles 81 [101] and 82 [102] of
the EC Treaty that arise in individual cases (informal
guidance letters) [2004] OJ C101/78 . . . 118, 733,
926, 926, 928, 929, 933
para. 1 . . . 928
para. 2 . . . 933
para. 3 . . . 926, 928
para. 4 . . . 928
para. 5 . . . **928**
para. 7 . . . 928
para. 8 . . . **928**
para. 8(a) . . . **928**, 929
para. 8(b) . . . 733, **928**, 929
para. 8(c) . . . **928**, 929
para. 9 . . . 929
para. 10 . . . 929
para. 11 . . . 929
para. 14 . . . 929
para. 21 . . . 929
para. 23 . . . 929
para. 24 . . . 929
para. 45 . . . 929

para. 48 . . . 929

Notice on patent licensing agreements (Christmas message) [1962–1963] JO 2922/62 . . . 859

Notice on remedies acceptable under Council
Regulation 4064/89 and under Regulation 447/98
(Remedies Notice) [2001] OJ C68/3 . . . 118,
1247, 1248
Pt IV . . . 1248
paras. 31–32 . . . 1248

Notice on remedies acceptable under Council
Regulation 139/2004 and under Commission
Regulation 802/2004 (Remedies Notice) [2008] OJ
C267/1 . . . 1138, 1247, 1249, 1250
para. 1.4 . . . 1249
para. 3 . . . 1247
paras. 13–14 . . . 1250
para. 22 . . . 1248
paras. 53–57 . . . 1248
para. 66 . . . 1250
para. 69 . . . 1250, 1251

Notice on restrictions directly related and necessary to
concentrations [2001] OJ C188/5 . . . 245, 1244

Notice on restrictions directly related and necessary to
concentrations [2005] OJ C56/24 . . . 188, 244, 245,
1138, 1244, 1245
Pt II . . . 1245
Pt III . . . 1245
Pt IV . . . 1245
paras. 3–6 . . . 1245
para. 20 . . . 1245
para. 21 . . . 1245
paras. 22–23 . . . 1245
para. 26 . . . 1245
paras. 27–35 . . . 1245
para. 36 . . . 1245
paras. 42–43 . . . 1245

Notice on the application of the competition rules to
access agreements in the telecommunications sector
framework, relevant markets and principles [1998]
OJ C265/12 417
para. 114 . . . 417
para. 115 . . . 417
paras. 117–119 . . . 426

Notice on the application of the competition rules to
the postal sector [1998] OJ C39/2 . . . 188

Notice on the application of the competition
rules to cross-border credit transfers [1995] OJ
C251/3 . . . 523

Notice on the concept of concentration under Council
Regulation 4064/89 on the control of concentrations
between undertakings [1998] OJ C66/5 . . . 1138

Notice on the concept of full-function ventures under
Council Regulation 4064/89 on the control of
concentrations between undertakings [1998] OJ
C66/1 . . . 733, 1138
para. 3 . . . 733

Notice on the concept of undertakings concerned under Council Regulation 4064/89 on the control of concentrations between undertakings [1998] OJ C66/14...1138

Notice on the conduct of settlement procedures in view of the adoption of Decisions pursuant to Art. 7 and Art. 23 of Council Regulation 1/2003 in cartel cases [2008] OJ C167/1...923, 992
para. 20...992

Notice on the Definition of the Relevant Market for the Purposes of Community Competition Law [1997] OJ C372/5...42, **65**, **66**, 67, **68**, 69, 72, 73, 74, 75, 76, 77, 79, **83**, 85, 118, 313, 314, 326, 330, **337**, 824, 881, 1188
para. 1...65
para. 2...65
para. 4...65
para. 5...65
para. 7...**65**, 66
para. 8...**65**
para. 12...**85**
para. 13...66, 306
para. 14...**66**
paras. 13–14...66
para. 15...**68**
paras. 15–19...69
para. 16...**68**
para. 17...**68**
para. 18...**68**
para. 19...**68**, 71
para. 20...75
paras. 20–23...**66**, 76, 326
para. 21...75
para. 22...75
para. 23...**75**, 76
paras. 25–52...69
para. 28...**83**
para. 29...**83**
para. 30...**83**
para. 36...**73**, 74
para. 38...70
para. 39...69
para. 42...**71**
para. 43...65, **78**, 309, 360
para. 44...**83**
para. 45...**84**
para. 46...**84**
para. 47...**84**
para. 48...**84**
para. 49...**84**
para. 50...**84**
para. 51...**84**
para. 52...**84**
para. 53...**337**
para. 54...**337**
para. 55...**337**

para. 56...**68**, 79, 80
para. 57...76, **77**, 316
para. 58...**68**, 76, **77**

Notice on the Handling of Complaints by the Commission under Articles 81 and 82 of the EC Treaty [2004] OJ C101/65 (Complaints Notice)...118, 927, 932, **1067**, **1068**, 1093
para. 17...1093
para. 18...1093
paras. 19–25...1067
para. 21...1067
para. 23...**1067–1068**
para. 24...**1068**
para. 25...**1068**
para. 35...**1068–1069**
para. 36...**1069**
para. 37...**1069**
para. 38...1068, **1069**
para. 39...**1069**
para. 40...**1069**
para. 42...1072
para. 44...**1074**, 1093
para. 54...1071
para. 55...1071
para. 56...1071
para. 57...1071
paras. 64–67...1076
para. 80...1076
Annex...1071

Notice on the non-imposition or reduction of fines in cartel cases (Leniency Notice or Whistleblower's Notice) [1996] OJ C204/14...677, 1015, 1019, 1020

Notice on the rules for access to the Commission file in cases pursuant to Arts 81 and 82 of the EC Treaty, Arts 53, 54 and 57 of the EEA Agreement and Council Regulation 139/2004 (Notice on access to the file) [2005] OJ C325/07...969, 970, 974, 975, 1026, 1138
para. 12...975
para. 13...975
para. 15...975
para. 16...975
para. 18...974
para. 19...974
paras. 30–31...976
paras. 35–38...975
para. 42...975
para. 44...970
para. 47...975

Notice published pursuant to Art. 27(4) of Council Regulation 1/2003 (Market Test Notice) [2005] OJ C136/32...984

Notice regarding restrictions ancillary to concentrations [1990] OJ C203/5...245

RECOMMENDATIONS

96/280/EC Commission Recommendation on the definition of SMEs [1996] OJ L107/4 . . . 241
  Annex . . . **241**

Commission Recommendation on common principles for injunctive and compensatory collective redress mechanisms in the Member States concerning violations of rights granted under Union law C(2013) 3539/3 . . . 1087

Commission Recommendation on relevant product and service markets within the electronic communications sector susceptible to ex ante regulation in accordance with Directive 2002/21/EC on a common regulatory framework for electronic communications networks and services [2007] OJ L344/65 . . . 53

UNITED KINGDOM LEGISLATION

STATUTES

Broadcasting Act 1990
  s. 176 . . . 528

Communications Act 2003 . . . 52

Company Directors Disqualification Act 1986 . . . 1066

Competition Act 1998 . . . 53, 56, 67, 189, 797, 949, 1120
  Chapter I . . . 189, 247, 1066, 1120
  Chapter II . . . 1066, 1100, 1120
  ss. 26–28 . . . 1054
  ss. 42–44 . . . 1065
  s. 47A . . . 1119, 1120, 1121
  s. 47B . . . 1119, 1121
  s. 50 . . . 189
  s. 60 . . . 247, 1274
  Schs 1–4 . . . 189
  Sch 2 . . . 189
  Sch 3 . . . 189

Copyright Act 1956 . . . 528

Copyright, Designs and Patents Act . . . 1988
  s. 3(1) . . . 528
  ss. 77–85 . . . 849
  s. 213 . . . 850
  s. 265 . . . 849
  s. 297(1) . . . 916

Enterprise Act 2002 . . . 53, 189, 581, 730, 952, 1063, 1065, 1165, 1264
  Pt 3 . . . 1162
  Pt 6 . . . 125, 668
  s. 131 . . . 18

s. 188 . . . 1065, 1264
s. 190(4) . . . 1065
s. 191 . . . 668, 1264
s. 204 . . . 125, 668, 1066
s. 243 . . . 1264

Enterprise and Regulatory Reform Act 2013 . . . 668

European Communities Act . . . 1972
  s. 2 . . . 1119

Evidence (Proceedings in Other Jurisdictions) Act 1975 . . . 1264

Fair Trading Act 1973 . . . 451, 1162
  ss. 57–62 . . . 1165

Plant Varieties and Seeds Act . . . 1997
  s. 4(2) . . . 863
  s. 22 . . . 863

Prevention of Fraud (Investments) Act . . . 1958
  s. 13(1)(a)(i) . . . 955

Protection of Trading Interest Act 1980 . . . 1264
  s. 1 . . . 1264
  s. 2 . . . 1264
  s. 5 . . . 1264
  s. 6 . . . 1264

Registered Designs Act . . . 1949
  s. 1B(1) . . . 849

Restrictive Trade Practices Act 1976 . . . 56

Trade Marks Act 1994 . . . 847, 849

STATUTORY INSTRUMENTS

Civil Procedure Rules 1998 (SI 1998/3132)
  r. 19.6 . . . 1121

Competition Act 1998 (Land Agreements Exclusion and Revocation) Order 2004 (SI 2004/1260) . . . 189

Competition Act 1998 (Land and Vertical Agreements Exclusion) Order 2000 (SI 2000/310) . . . 189

Copyright and Related Rights Regulations 2003 (SI 2003/2498) . . . 849

Design Right (Semi-conductor Topographies) Regulations 1989 (SI 1989/1100) . . . 850

EC Competition Law (Arts 88 and 89) Enforcement Regulations 1996 (SI 1996/ 2199) . . . 116

European Communities (Enforcement of Community Judgments) Order 1972 (SI 1972/1590) . . . 1019

Registered Designs Regulations 2001 (SI 2001/3949) . . . 849

Registered Designs Regulations 2003 (SI 2003/550) . . . 849

FOREIGN LEGISLATION

CANADA

Act for the Prevention and Suppression of
  Combinations Formed in Restraint of Trade
  1889 . . . 19

CHINA

Anti-Monopoly Law 2008 . . . 1291
  Art. 1 . . . 17

GERMANY

Civil Code . . . 130

Criminal Code
  s. 298 . . . 689

Law on the Promotion of Employment (AFG) . . . **129**,
  130, **609**
  Art. 3 . . . **130**

RettDG 1991 . . . **627**, **650**
  para. 18(3) . . . **627**, **628**, **651**

GREECE

Road Traffic Code . . . **616**

Art. 49 . . . 616, 617

KOREA

Monopoly Regulation and Fair Trade Act . . . 1980
  Art. 1 . . . 17

SOUTH AFRICA

Competition Act no. 89 of . . . 1998
  s. 2(f) . . . 17

UNITED STATES

Antitrust Enforcement Guidelines for International
  Operations (Antitrust and Trade Reg. Rep. (BNA),
  Special Supplement (6 Apr. 1995) . . . 1263
  para. 3.1222 . . . 1269

Alien Tort Statute 1789 . . . 1260

Antitrust Criminal Penalty Enhancement and Reform
  Act 2004 . . . 678, 1259, 1265

Celler-Kefauver Act 1950 . . . 19

Clayton Act 1914 . . . 19
  s. 4 . . . 669, 1083, 1085
  s. 5(a) . . . 1085
  s. 15 . . . 1259
  s. 16 . . . 1083, 1085

Fair Trade Acts . . . 800

Federal Trade Commission Act 1914 . . . 19

Foreign Sovereign Immunities Act 1976 . . . 1262

Foreign Trade Antitrust Improvements
  Act 1982 . . . 1261, 1262, 1265, **1266**, **1267**,
  1268, 1269

Hart-Scott-Rodino Antitrust Improvements Act
  1976 . . . 19

Iran Freedom and Counter-Proliferation Act
  2012 . . . 1260

Iran–Libya Sanctions Act 1996 . . . 1260

Iran Sanctions At 2006 . . . 1260

National Labour Relations Act 1935 . . . **1266**

Restatement (Third) of Foreign Relations Law
  1986 . . . 1266
  § 402 . . . **1267**
  § 403(1) . . . **1266**
  § 403(2) . . . **1266**, **1267**

Robinson-Patman Act 1936 . . . 19, 413
  § 13(a) . . . 413

Securities and Exchange Act 1934 . . . 1260

Sherman Act 1890 . . . 2, 19, 20, 26, 197, 554, **555**, 678,
  1064, 1259, 1260, **1261**, 1262, 1263, 1265, 1266,
  1267, 1268, 1269, 1276
  s. 1 . . . **19**, 20, 197, 231, 674, 797, 1264
  s. 2 . . . **19**, 20, 21, 54, 339, 371, 381, 403, 413, 445,
  483, 553, **554**, **555**, 591

Telecommunications Act 1996 . . . **554**, **555**

Trade Act . . . 1974
  s. 301 . . . 1270

US Horizontal Merger Guidelines 2010 . . . 61, 1132,
  1211, 1213, 1217
  § 10 . . . 1211, 1213
  § 11 . . . 1217
  § 12.9, 545 . . . 1217

Webb-Pomerone Act 1918 . . . **1276**

TABLE OF EUROPEAN AND INTERNATIONAL TREATIES, CONVENTIONS, AND CHARTERS

[Page references in **bold** indicate that the item is given particular prominence in the text]

African Caribbean and Pacific Agreement (ACP), Cotonou Agreement 2003 ... 1292
Art. 45 ... 1292

Agreement between the Government of the US and the Commission of the European Communities regarding the application of their Competition Laws 1991 [1991] 4 CMLR 823, 30 ILM 1487 ... 1284, 1287, 1289, 1293
Art. II ... 1287
Art. III ... 1287
Art. IV ... 1287
Art. V ... **1287–1288**, 1290
Art. VI ... 1284, 1287, **1288**, 1290
Art. VII ... 1290
Art. IX ... 1290

Berne Convention for the Protection of Literary and Artistic Works 1886 ... 849, 850

Charter of Fundamental Rights of the European Union 2000 ... 98, 100, 101, 107, 597, 600, 632, 922, 934, 937, 1035, 1036, 1044, 1075, 1078
Ch. IV ... 632
Art. 7 ... **934**, 935, 950
Art. 20 ... 938, **962**
Art. 21 ... 938, **962**
Art. 36 ... 600, **632**
Art. 41 ... 973
Art. 41(1) ... 938
Art. 41(2) ... 938, 984
Art. 41(2)(a) ... 973
Art. 41(2)(b) ... 973
Art. 47 ... 934, **935**, 937, 938, 968, 1029, 1039, **1042**, **1043**, 1044
Art. 48(1) ... 935, 938
Art. 48(2) ... 935, **964**, **1116**
Art. 49(1) ... 938
Art. 50 ... 938, 1018
Art. 52 ... 934
Art. 52(3) ... **100**

Constitutional Treaty 2004 ... 655

Copyright Treaty 1996 (WIPO) ... 849

Declaration 1 to the Treaties ... 100

EC/US Cooperation Agreement 1991, *see* Agreement between the Government of the US and the Commission of the European Communities regarding the application of their Competition Laws ... 1991

EU/Brazil Memorandum of Understanding on Cooperation 2009 ... 1291

EU/Canada Bilateral Agreement 1999 ... 1290
Art. V ... 1290
Art. VI ... 1290

EU/Japan Bilateral Agreement 2003 ... 1291

EU/Korea Bilateral Agreement 2009 ... 1291

EU/Russian Federation Memorandum of Understanding on Cooperation 2011 ... 1291

EU/Switzerland Cooperation Agreement 2013 ... 1291

EU/US Positive Comity Agreement 1998 [1998] OJ L173/28, [1999] 4 CMLR 502 ... 1289
Art. II(4)(a) ... 1289
Art. III ... 1289
Art. IV ... 1289
Art. V ... 1290
Art. VI ... 1290
Art. VII ... 1290
Art. IX ... 1290

Euro-Mediterranean Agreements ... 1291

European Convention for the Protection of Human Rights and Fundamental Freedoms (ECHR) 1950 ... 100, 101, 107, 670, 922, 934, 950, 952, 997, **1007**, 1078
Art. 6 ... 126, **564**, 934, **935**, 936, 937, 938, **954**, 955, 1039, **1044**, 1120
Art. 6(1) ... 126, **935**, 936, 937, 938, **954**, 955, **972**, 979, 1029, 1039, 1042, 1044, **1045**, 1048
Art. 6(2) ... 126, **935**, 937
Art. 6(3) ... **935**
Art. 7(1) ... **1006**, **1007**, 1014
Art. 8 ... **934**, 943, 950, 951, 952
Art. 8(1) ... **934**, **943**, 950
Art. 8(2) ... **934**, **943**, 950
Art. 13 ... **564**
Protocol 7, Art. 4 ... 1018

European Economic Area (EEA) Agreement 1992 ... 119
Art. 53 ... 119
Art. 54 ... 119
Art. 56(1)(a) ... 119
Art. 56(1)(b) ... 119
Art. 56 (1)(c) ... 119
Art. 56(3) ... 119
Art. 57 ... 119
Art. 59 ... 119
Art. 108(2) ... 119
Protocol 28 ... 854

European Patent Convention (EPC) 1973 ... 847, 848

International Covenant on Civil and Political
Rights ... 1966
Art. 14 ... **954**
Art. 14(3)(g) ... **954**

Lomé Agreement ... 1292

Lugano Convention ... 1123

Partnership and Cooperation Agreements ... 1291

Performances and Phonograms Treaty 1996
(WIPO) ... 849

Protocols attached to the TEU and TFEU Treaties by the
Treaty of Lisbon
Protocol ... 597
Protocol 3 ... 105, 106
Protocol 26 on Services of General Interest ... 600,
630, 631, 632
Protocol 26, Art. 1 ... **631**
Protocol 26, Art. 2 ... **631**
Protocol 27 on Internal Market and
Competition ... 37, **38**, 109, 120, 370
Protocol 30 ... 100

Single European Act 1986 ... 36

Stabilization and Association Agreements ... 1291

Statute of the Court of Justice of the EAEC
Protocol, Art. 17 ... **959**

Statute of the Court of Justice of the ECSC
Protocol, Art. 20 ... **959**

Statute of the Court of Justice of the EEC
Protocol, Art. 17 ... **959**

Statute of the Court of Justice of the European Union
(CJEU), *see also* Protocol 3 of the TEU and TFEU
Treaties
Art. 19 ... **962**
Art. 49 ... 105
Art. 51 ... 106, 1037, **1046**, **1047**
Art. 58 ... 1046
Art. 61 ... 105, 1047

Treaty Establishing the European Atomic Energy
Community 1957 (Euratom Treaty) ... 51, 99, 110

Treaty Establishing the European Coal and Steel
Community 1951 (Treaty of Paris) ... 99, 110, 368,
426, 1033, 1134
Art. 65 ... 34, 154, 706
Art. 65(1) ... 110, 1033
Art. 66 ... 34
Art. 66(7) ... 275, 1134

Treaty Establishing the European Community
(pre-Amsterdam) (EEC) 1957 (Treaty of Rome) ... 1,
32, 34, 46, 368, 599, 600, 782, **943**, 1134
Preamble ... 36
Art. 2 ... **36**, 37, **140**, 368, **369**, 1134
Art. 3 ... 36, 37, 38, 369

Treaty Establishing the European Community
(post-Amsterdam) (EC) 1999 ... 33, 36, 49, 99, 100,
110, 114, 119, 630, **985**, 1050, **1091**, **1158**
Art. 2 ... 1239
Art. 3 ... 630

Art. 3(1)(g) ... viii, 1, 33, 37, 39, 46, 109, 120, **140**,
368, 379, **415**, **475**, 512, **549**, **574**, **587**, **602**,
611, **615**, **626**, **943**, **958**, 1063, **1102**, **1280**
Art. 16 ... 630, 631

Treaty of Amsterdam 1999 ... 18, 36, 37, 99, 117, 600,
630, 631

Treaty of Lisbon 2007 ... v, viii, 1, 18, 33, 36, 37, **38**, 49,
98, 100, 105, 110, 114, 117, 600, 630, 631, 655, 1078
Protocols, *see* Protocols attached to the TEU and
TFEU Treaties

Treaty of Nice 2001 ... 107, 1034
Art. 7 ... 1070

Treaty of Paris, *see* Treaty Establishing the European
Coal and Steel Community

Treaty on European Union (TEU) 1993 (Maastricht
Treaty) ... viii, 36, 37, 49, 98, 99, 100, 107, 109,
110, 1035
Art. 1 ... 100
Art. 2 ... **36**, 37, 631
Art. 3 ... 37
Art. 3(1) ... 18, **36**, 48
Art. 3(1)(b) ... 107
Art. 3(3) ... **36**, 37, **38**
Art. 4 ... 601, 603, 607, **622**, 631, 1061
Art. 4(3) ... 276, 597, 601, **602**, 1084
Art. 5 ... 107, **638**
Art. 5(1) ... 107
Art. 5(4) ... 107
Art. 6 ... 100, 1036
Art. 6(2) ... 101
Art. 6(3) ... **107**
Art. 17 ... 102, 105, 653
Art. 17(1) ... **1073**
Art. 45 ... 1047
Art. 51 ... 37
Art. 56 ... 1048
Protocols, *see* Protocols attached to the TEU and
TFEU Treaties by the Treaty of Lisbon

Treaty on the Functioning of the European Union
(TFEU) ... v, viii, 1, 18, 36, 37, 49, 98, 100, 104, 107,
108, 109, 110, 114, 115, 117, 119, 183, 216, 255, 603,
631, 853, 854, 1035, 1187, 1253
Preamble ... 36
Title VII, Ch 1 ... 109, 120
Title XII on Education, vocational, training, youth
and sport ... 111–112
Section 1 ... 109
Section 2 ... 109
Art. 1 ... 124
Art. 2 ... 119
Art. 3 ... 631
Art. 3(1)(b) ... **38**, 107, 109
Art. 7 ... 49
Art. 8 ... 49
Arts 8–13 ... 49, 255
Art. 9 ... 49
Art. 10 ... 49
Art. 11 ... 49
Art. 12 ... 49

Art. 13 . . . 49
Art. 14 . . . 597, 600, 630, 631, 632, **638**
Art. 15(1) . . . 976
Art. 15(2) . . . 976
Art. 16 . . . 632
Art. 18 . . . 583, 602, 603, 607, **622**
Art. 26 . . . 36
Art. 34 . . . **248**, **602**, 607, 853
Arts 34–36 . . . 117
Art. 35 . . . **602**, 853
Art. 36 . . . 530, 652, **853**, 854, **914**, **915**
Art. 37 . . . 114, 115, 634
Art. 39 . . . 110, 190
Art. 45 . . . 607
Art. 56 . . . **248**, **854**, **915**
Arts 56–62 . . . 117
Art. 57 . . . **915**
Art. 90–100 . . . 111
Art. 93 . . . 631, 633
Art. 101 . . . v, viii, 20, 33, 38, 39, 40, 42, 43, 46, 47,
    51, 56, 57, 62, 63, 65, 72, 85, 98, 99, 114, 115, 116,
    117, 119, 120, 122, **123–124**, 125, 127, 128, 130,
    132, 138, 139, 141, 143, 145, 146, 148, 149, 151,
    152, **153**, 155, 156, 160, 161, 164, 165, 168, 169,
    172, 175, 177, **180**, 181, 182, 183, 185, 186, **187**,
    188, 189, 190, 192, 193, 195, 196, 197, 198, 199,
    200, 201, 203, 211, 213, 215, 216, 221, 223, **225**,
    228, **229**, **230**, 232, 233, **234**, 241, 243, 244, **248**,
    249, 250, 254, 255, 259, 263, 265, 266, 267, 269,
    270, **274**, 275, 276, 277, 278, 279, 283, 284, 287,
    289, 293, 294, 295, 343, 367, **428**, 451, 452, **458**,
    468, **512**, 583,, 517, 526, 557, 585, **588**, 597, 600,
    601, 604, 607, **611**, **612**, 619, **620**, 652, 655, 659,
    660, 673, 674, 675, 676, 679, 680, 683, 684, 700,
    702, 709, **713**, 715, 716, **717**, 718, 719, 721, 723,
    724, **726**, 727, **728**, 729, 731, 732, 733, 734, 735,
    740, 741, 742, 764, 768, 769, 774, 785, 786, 787,
    790, 796, 797, 802, 808, 810, 812, 814, 815, 816,
    819, 822, 829, 831, 837, 842, 843, 844, 846, 847,
    850, 852, 853, 859, 868, **869**, **870**, 871, 872, 873,
    874, 879, 880, 887, 890, 891, 894, 895, 897, 898,
    902, 903, 904, 906, 907, 908, 909, **915**, 916, **917**,
    919, 920, 921, 922, 923, 925, **928**, 929, 930, 931,
    932, 933, 939, 942, **943**, **944**, **949**, 952, **958**, **959**,
    960, 966, 968, **974**, **979**, 980, 984, **987**, **988**,
    990, 991, 995, 996, 998, 999, **1005**, **1006**, **1010**,
    1022, 1038, 1048, 1049, **1051**, 1055, 1057, 1060,
    1061, **1062**, 1063, 1064, 1066, 1067, **1070**, **1073**,
    1074, 1076, 1077, 1082, 1083, 1084, 1085, 1086,
    1088, **1089**, **1091**, 1092, 1093, 1094, 1095, 1096,
    1097, 1098, 1099, 1100, 1101, **1102**, **1103**, 1104,
    1106, **1107**, **1108**, **1109**, **1111**, 1112, 1113,
    1116, **1118**, 1119, 1120, 1121, 1122, 1135, 1136,
    1144, 1145, 1147, 1157, 1168, 1171, 1172, 1176,
    1191, **1199**, 1200, 1205, 1239, 1241, 1242, 1244,
    1271, 1272, **1275**, **1276**, 1277, **1280**, 1286
Art. 101(1) . . . v, 40, 47, 61, 63, 108, 110, 114, 115,
    122, **123**, 124, 125, 126, 127, 128, 137, **139**, **140**,
    145, 146, 147, 148, 149, 150, 151, **152**, **153**, 154,
    155, 156, 157, **158**, **159**, 161, **162**, 164, 165, **166**,
    167, 173, 174, 177, 179, **180**, 182, 183, 184, 186,

188, 189, 190, 192, 193, 194, 195, 196, 197, 198,
    199, 200, 201, 203, 204, 205, 206, 207, 208, **209**,
    210, 211, 212, 213, 215, 216, 217, **218**, 219, 220,
    221, **222**, 223, 224, **225**, 226, 227, 228, **229**, **230**,
    231, 232, 233, **234**, **236**, **237**, 238, 239, 240, **241**,
    242, 243, 244, 245, 246, 247, **248**, 249, 250, 251,
    255, 258, 259, 260, 264, 265, 266, 267, 271, 272,
    278, 279, 294, 389, **468**, 487, 673, 675, 676, 678,
    679, 680, 682, 683, 685, 687, 689, 691, 692, 694,
    695, 696, 697, 698, 700, 702, 703, 704, 706, **707**,
    708, 709, 710, 711, 712, 715, **717**, 718, **721**, 724,
    729, 731, 734, 735, 736, 738, 740, 741, 742, **748**,
    750, 751, 752, **753**, 754, **755**, 758, 759 760, 761,
    762, 764, **765**, 768, 769, 773, 774, 775, 776, 777,
    784, 785, 786, 787, 788, 789, 790, 794, **796**, 797,
    800, 801, 802, 803, 804, 805, 806, **807**, **808**, 809,
    810, 811, 812, **813**, **814**, 815, 816, 817, 818, 819,
    820, 823, 824, 825, 826, 829, 830, 832, 834, **835**,
    836, **839**, 840, 841, 843, 844, 846, 847, 859, 860,
    861, **862**, 863, **864**, 865, 866, 868, 869, 870, 871,
    872, 875, 876, 878, 890, 893, 894, 895, 896, 898,
    899, 900, 902, 904, 905, 906, 907, 909, 910, **911**,
    912, 913, 914, 916, **917**, **918**, **919**, 920, 924, 925,
    926, 958, 970, 980, 990, 998, 1036, 1037, 1038,
    1041, 1061, **1062**, 1063, 1064, 1070, **1073**, 1086,
    1096, 1097, 1098, 1099, 1100, **1102**, 1103, 1104,
    1106, **1108**, 1120, 1121, 1122, 1136, 1184, 1241,
    1244, 1272, **1273**, 1275
Art. 101(1)(a) . . . **222**, 696
Art. 101(1)(b) . . . 217, 218, 279, 684, 685, 686
Art. 101(1)(c) . . . 279, 686
Art. 101(2) . . . 114, **123**, 124, 125, 189, 239, 925,
    1097, 1098, **1102**, 1103, 1136
Art. 101(3) . . . 14, 39, 43, 45, 47, 48, 49, 51, 52, 62,
    108, 114, 115, 116, 120, 122, **123–124**, 125, 126,
    149, **152**, 157, 179, 186, 188, 190, 192, 193, 194,
    195, 196, 198, 199, 200, 201, 203, 204, 205, 206,
    212, 213, **214**, 216, 219, 221, 223, 232, 233, **245**,
    246, 247, 248, 249, 250, 251, **252**, 253, 254, **255**,
    256, 257, 258, 259, 260, 261, **262**, 263, 265, 266,
    267, 271, 279, 288, 293, 294, 385, 388, 389, 391,
    448, 451, 458, 676, 678, 680, 691, 692, 693, 694,
    695, 696, 704, 708, 718, 721, 731, 734, 735, **736**,
    738, 740, 741, 742, 746, **748**, 749, 750, **751**, **752**,
    753, 754, **756**, **757**, 758, **760**, 761, 762, 763, 764,
    766, 768, 769, 777, 780, 784, 785, 786, 787, 800,
    801, 803, 804, 806, **807**, **808**, 809, 811, 812, 816,
    817, 818, 819, 824, 825, 832, 834, **835**, 836, 837,
    838, 839, 840, 842, 843, 844, 846, 859, 860, **862**,
    863, 864, 866, 868, 869, 870, 871, 873, 876, 884,
    893, 895, 896, 897, 898, 899, 900, 901, 902, 905,
    907, **910**, 913, 916, 917, **919**, 920, 922, 924, 925,
    926, 927, 928, 929, 958, 966, 980, 990, 1031, 1037,
    1038, 1045, 1061, **1062**, 1063, 1070, **1073**, 1086,
    1097, 1099, **1102**, 1120, 1127, 1184, 1241, 1244
Arts 101–106 . . . 36, 109
Arts 101–109 . . . viii, 100, **602**, 603, **609**, **622**
Art. 102 . . . v, vi, 21, 33, 35, **38**, 40, 41, 42, 43, **44**, 45,
    46, 47, 48, 54, 56, 61, 62, 63, 64, 65, 72, 74, 76, 78,
    79, 80, 81, 90, 91, 93, 98, 99, 105, 106, 109, 110,
    111, 114, 115, 116, 117, 118, 120, 119, 120, 125,

127, 128, 131, 132, 140, 142, 145, 151, **152**, **153**, 155, 160, 161, 181, 182, 186, **187**, 238, 259, 263, 269, **270–271**, 272, 273, 274, 275, 276, 277, 278, 279, 280, 281, 282, 283, 284, **285**, 286, 287, 288, 289, 290, 291, 292, 293, 294, 295, 297, 298, 300, **302**, **303**, 304, 305, 306, **307**, 317, 318, 319, **324**, 335, 336, 339, **340**, 341, 343, 344, 348, 355, 363, 365, 366, 367, **368**, 370, 371, 372, **373**, 374, **375**, **376**, **377**, 378, **379**, **380**, 382, **383**, 385, **387**, **388**, 389, 390, 391, 393, **394**, **395**, 396, 403, 404, **405**, **410**, **411**, **412**, 415, 416, 419, 421, **422**, **423**, 425, 426, **428**, **429**, **430**, **431**, 432, 433, 434, **435**, **436**, **437**, **438**, 442, **443**, **444**, 445, **446**, 448, 449, 450, 451, 452, 453, 454, 456, **457**, **460**, **461**, **462**, 463, **464**, **465**, **466**, **467**, **468**, 469, **470**, **471**, **473**, **474**, **475**, 478, **479**, **480**, **481**, 484, **485**, 486, 487, 489, 491, 492, 493, **494**, 495, **496**, **497**, **498**, **499**, **500**, **501**, **505**, 506, 510, 511, **512**, 513, **515**, 516, 517, 518, **519**, **520**, 522, **523**, **524**, 525, 526, **527**, 528, **529**, **530**, 532, **535**, **539**, **540**, **543**, **544**, 546, 547, 548, **549**, 551, 554, 557, **559**, 560, 561, **562**, 563, **564**, **565**, 567, 568, 570, 572, **573**, **574**, 575, 576, **577**, 578, 579, 580, 582, 583, 584, 585, **586**, 587, **588**, **590**, 591, 597, 600, **602**, 603, 604, 607, **609**, **610**, **611**, **612**, **613**, **614**, 615, 616, **617**, 618, 619, **620**, 621, **622**, **623**, **624**, **625**, **626**, **627**, **628**, 630, 634, **645**, **646**, 648, 652, **655**, 659, 660, 674, 709, 716, 717, 718, **720**, 721, 722, 723, 724, **726**, **728**, 729, 758, 764, **765**, 769, 785, 815, 842, 843, 847, 848, 849, 852, 871, 906, 908, 919, 920, 922, 923, 925, **928**, 929, 930, 931, 932, 933, 939, 942, **943**, **949**, 952, **958**, **959**, **960**, 968, **974**, **979**, 980, 982, 983, 984, 985, **987**, **988**, 989, **990**, 991, 992, 995, 996, 998, 999, **1005**, **1010**, 1036, 1037, 1038, 1044, 1048, **1051**, 1055, 1060, 1061, **1062**, 1063, 1064, 1066, 1067, **1070**, **1073**, **1074**, 1076, 1077, 1082, 1083, 1084, 1085, 1086, 1088, **1089**, **1091**, 1093, 1094, 1095, 1098, 1099, 1100, **1102**, 1104, **1106**, **1107**, **1109**, **1111**, 1112, 1113, **1116**, **1118**, 1119, 1120, 1122, 1125, 1135, 1136, 1157, 1168, 1171, 1172, 1182, 1188, 1190, 1191, 1200, 1203, 1226, **1227**, **1228**, **1229**, 1244, 1258, 1271, 1277, **1280**, 1286

Art. 102(a) ... **366**, 367, **430**, **435**, **443**, 575, 576, 580, 582, **613**, 614

Art. 102(a)–(d) ... 271

Art. 102(b) ... 45, 47, 279, **366**, 370, 454, **470**, **471**, 474, **475**, **530**, 535, 538, **541**, **543**, **545**, 547, 568, 583, **586**, **587**, **587**, **610**, **613**, 614, **626**, **628**, 629

Art. 102(c) ... **366**, 372, 398, 454, 457, 459, **471**, 531, **567**, 568, 569, 570, 572, **573**, **574**, 582, 583, **587**, **613**, 614, 622, **626**

Art. 102(d) ... **366**, **489**, 491, 492, 499, **500**, **501**, 507

Art. 103 ... 102, 115, 116, 117, 120, **654**, **655**, **1073**, 1135, 1137, **1280**

Art. 103(1) ... **115**, **958**

Art. 103(2) ... **115**

Art. 103(2)(b) ... 117

Art. 104 ... **116**, 117, 120, 1171, 1172

Art. 105 ... **117**, 120, 1171, 1172

Art. 105(1) ... **117**, **1073**

Art. 105(2) ... **117**

Art. 105(3) ... **117**

Art. 106 ... 114, 116, 119, 120, 219, 393, 447, 516, 584, 597, 598, **602**, 603, **608**, **609**, **611**, **615**, 616, **617**, 619, **620**, **623**, **625**, **627**, **628**, 631, **642**, 648, 653, **654**, **655**, 729

Art. 106(1) ... 276, 516, 597, **602**, 603, 604, 605, 607, **608**, **609**, **610**, **611**, **612**, **613**, 614, **615**, **617**, 618, 619, **620**, 621, **622**, **623**, 624, **625**, 627, 628, 629, 630, 634, **635**, 641, 643, **645**, **646**, 647, 652, **656**

Art. 106(2) ... 51, 114, 129, **130**, 132, 190, 219, 276, 386, 569, 578, 597, 599, 600, **602**, 603, **609**, **611**, **612**, **614**, **615**, **617**, 618, **620**, **621**, **624**, **625**, **626**, 627, 628, 629, 630, 632, 634, **635**, **636**, 637, 638, 639, 641, 643, 644, 645, 646, **647**, 648, **649**, **650**, **651**, 652, 653, **656**, 1037

Art. 106(3) ... 52, 105, 116, 597, **603**, 604, 605, **608**, 628, 653, 654, **655**, 656, 1033

Art. 107 ... 631, 656

Art. 107(3) ... 46

Arts 107–109 ... 109

Art. 108 ... 656

Art. 114 ... 52, 117, **654**, **655**

Art. 115 ... 117, 654

Art. 119 ... 599

Art. 165(1) ... 111

Art. 168 ... 638

Art. 168(1) ... 49

Art. 173 ... 50, 599

Art. 173(1) ... 50

Art. 173(3) ... 50

Art. 179(2) ... 741

Art. 219 ... 102

Art. 228 ... 104

Art. 234. 1034

Art. 246 ... 1034

Art. 256 ... 106

Art. 256(1) ... 106

Art. 257 ... 107

Art. 258 ... 49, 449, 603, 653, **1073**

Art. 261 ... 994, 1029, 1039, 1041, 1044

Art. 263 ... 106, **807**, **958**, 965, 969, 987, 1029, **1030**, 1032, 1036, 1039, 1041, **1042**, **1043**, 1044, 1048, 1055, 1187, 1201, 1253

Art. 263(2) ... 1030

Art. 263(4) ... 1030, 1031

Art. 264 ... 1045

Art. 265 ... 1077

Art. 266 ... **1045**

Art. 267 ... vi, viii, 106, 109, **130**, 216, **230**, 244, 273, 275, 292, 386, 387, 434, 518, 525, 526, 576, 585, 599, **611**, **613**, **616**, 707, 718, 917, 1019, 1049, 1090, 1094, 1100, 1116

Art. 278 ... **943**, **944**, **960**, 965, **1048**

Art. 279 ... **960**, 965, 1048

Art. 288 ... 104, 264, **1073**

Arts. 289–290 ... 104

Arts 289–296 ... 115

Arts 289–297 ... 604, 654

Art. 295 . . . 101
Art. 296 . . . 101, 1034, **1074**
Art. 299 . . . 1019
Art. 300 . . . 101
Art. 308 . . . 1137
Art. 326 . . . 113
Art. 339 . . . **973**
Art. 340 . . . 974, **1050**, 1254
Art. 340(2) . . . 1254
Art. 345 . . . 452, 599, 853
Art. 346 . . . 51, 1159, 1166, 1167
Art. 346(1)(b) . . . 113, 190, **1166**, **1167**
Art. 346(2) . . . **1166**
Art. 352 . . . 37, 102, 117, 120, 1135, **1280**
Annex 1 . . . 110

Protocols, *see* Protocols attached to the TEU and
TFEU Treaties by the Treaty of Lisbon

UK/US Mutual Legal Assistance Treaty
2001 . . . 1264

Universal Postal Convention (UPC) 1989 . . . 624, 625,
626, 627, 637
Art. 1 . . . **625**
Art. 25 . . . **624, 625**
Art. 25(1) . . . **626**
Art. 25(2) . . . **626**
Art. 25(3) . . . **626**

World Trade Organization (WTO) Charter
1995 . . . 1293

BIBLIOGRAPHY

The following are general works on EU competition law which cover the material dealt with in this book. Specialised reading is listed at the end of each chapter in the 'Further Reading' section.

ALLAN, W., FURSE, M., and SUFRIN, B. (eds.), *Butterworths Competition Law* (Butterworths, looseleaf)

AMATO, G., and EHLERMANN, C.-D., *EC Competition Law, A Critical Assessment* (Hart Publishing, 2007)

BAEL, I. van, and BELLIS, J.-F., *Competition Law of the European Community* (5th edn, Kluwer, 2009)

BELLAMY, G., and CHILD, G. (V. Rose and D. Bailey, eds.), *European Community Law of Competition* (7th edn, Oxford University Press, 2013)

BISHOP, S., and WALKER, M., *The Economics of EC Competition Law* (3rd edn, Sweet & Maxwell, 2010)

EZRACHI, A., *EU Competition Law, An Analytical Guide to the Leading Cases* (3rd edn, Hart Publishing, 2012)

FAULL, J., and NIKPAY, A. (eds.), *The EC Law of Competition* (2nd edn, Oxford University Press, 2007, 3rd edn forthcoming, 2014)

GOYDER, J., and ALBORS-LLORENS, A., *Goyder's EC Competition Law* (5th edn, Oxford University Press, 2009)

KOKKORIS, I., *Competition Cases from the European Union* (2nd edn, Sweet & Maxwell, 2010

KORAH, V., and LIANOS, I., *Competition Law, Text Cases and Materials* (Hart Publishing, 4th edn, 2014)

MARCO COLINO, S., *Competition Law of the EU and UK* (7th edn, Oxford University Press, 2011)

MONTI, G., *EC Competition Law* (Cambridge University Press, 2007)

MOTTA, M., *Competition Policy: Theory and Practice* (Cambridge University Press, 2004)

RODGER, B., and MACCULLOCH, A., *Competition Law and Policy in the EU and UK* (4th edn, Cavendish Publishing, 2013)

SLOT, P. J., and JOHNSTON, A., *An Introduction to Competition Law* (2nd edn, Hart Publishing, 2013)

WHISH, R., and BAILEY, D., *Competition Law* (7th edn, OUP, 2012)

BLOGS

http://chillingcompetition.com (Nicolas Petit and Alfonso Lamadrid de Pablo)
http://professorgeradin.blogs.com/professor_geradins_weblog/

LIST OF ABBREVIATIONS

AAC	average avoidable cost
AC	Appeal Cases
AIC	average incremental cost
AJIL	*American Journal of International Law*
All ER	All England Law Reports
Ant Bull	*Antitrust Bulletin*
Antitrust LJ	*Antitrust Law Journal*
ATC	average total cost
ATP	absolute territorial protection
AVC	average variable cost
Bell J Econ	*Bell Journal of Economics*
BER	Block Exemption Regulation
BEREC	Body of European Regulators for Electronic Communications
BYIL	*British Yearbook of International Law*
CAP	Common Agricultural Policy
CAT	Competition Appeal Tribunal
CBI	Confederation of British Industry
CDE	*Cahiers de Droit Europeén*
CFI	Court of First Instance (renamed as General Court (GC) by the Treaty of Lisbon)
Charter	Charter of Fundamental Rights of the European Union
CISAC	International Confederation of Societies of Authors and Composers
CJ	Court of Justice
CJEU	Court of Justice of the European Union
CLP	*Current Legal Problems*
CMLR	Common Market Law Reports
CMLRev	*Common Market Law Review*
CMO	Common Organisation of Agricultural Markets
Colum LR	*Columbia Law Review*
CompAR	Competition Appeal Reports
Comp Law	*Competition Law Journal*
Cornell LR	*Cornell Law Review*
Cowp	Cowper's King's Bench Report
DG Comp	EC Commission Competition Directorate-General
DGFT	Director General for Fair Trading
DOJ	Department of Justice (US)
EAGCP	European Advisory Group on Competition Policy
EBU	European Broadcasting Union
EC	European Community
ECC	European Commercial Cases
ECHR	European Convention for the Protection of Human Rights
ECJ	European Court of Justice
ECLR	*European Competition Law Review*
ECN	European Competition Network
ECR	European Court Reports
ECSC	European Coal and Steel Community

ECtHR	European Court of Human Rights
Edinburgh LR	*Edinburgh Law Review*
EEA	European Economic Area
EEC	European Economic Community
EFTA	European Free Trade Area
EG	*Estates Gazette*
EGLR	Estates Gazette Law Reports
EHRR	European Human Rights Reports
EIPR	*European Intellectual Property Review*
ELRev	*European Law Review*
EMU	Economic and Monetary Union
EPC	European Patent Convention (1973)
ESA	EFTA Surveillance Authority
ETSI	European Telecommunications Standards Institute
EU	European Union
EuLR	European Law Reports
EUMR	European Union Merger Regulation
Euratom	European Atomic Energy Community
EWCA Civ	England and Wales Court of Appeal (Civil)
EWHC	England and Wales High Court
FIFA	International Federation of Association Football
Fordham Corp L Inst	Fordham Corporate Law Institute
Fordham Int'l LJ	*Fordham International Law Journal*
FRAND	fair, reasonable, and non-discriminatory
FTAIA	Foreign Trade Antitrust Improvements Act
FTC	Federal Trade Commission (US)
GC	General Court (formerly the Court of First Instance)
GWB	Gesetz gegen Wettbewerbsbeschrankungen (German competition law system)
Harvard LR	*Harvard Law Review*
HHI	Herfindahl-Hirschman index
HMG	Horizontal Merger Guidelines
HMT	Hypothetical Monopolist Test
ICLQ	*International and Comparative Law Quarterly*
ICN	International Competition Network
ICT	Information and Communications Technology
ILM	*International Legal Materials*
Indus & Corp Change	*Industrial and Corporate Change*
IO	industrial organisation
IOC	International Olympic Committee
IP	intellectual property
IPAC	International Competition Advisory Committee
IPRs	intellectual property rights
IRLR	*Industrial Relations Law Reports*
JBL	Journal of Business Law
JECLAP	*Journal of Competition Law and Practice*
JIEL	*Journal of International Economic Law*
JO	Journal Officiel
LIEI	*Legal Issues in European Integration/Legal Issues in Economic Integration*
LME	London Metals Exchange
LRAIC	long run average incremental cost
MES	minimum efficient scale

MFN	Most Favoured Nation
Mich LR	Michigan Law Review
MIF	Multilateral Interchange Fee
MLE	Model Leniency Programme
MLR	*Modern Law Review*
MPV	multipurpose vehicle
NAAT	not appreciably affect trade
NCAs	national competition authorities
New York Univ LR	*New York University Law Review*
NHMG	Non-horizontal Merger Guidelines
OECD	Organization for Economic Co-operation and Development
OFCOM	Communications Regulator (UK)
OFGEM	Office of Gas and Electricity Markets (UK)
OFT	Office of Fair Trading (UK)
OFWAT	Office of Water Services (UK)
OJ	Official Journal
OPEC	Organisation of Petroleum Exporting Countries
P&I	Protection and Indemnity Clubs
PEC	promotion equalization charge
PPI	pricing pressure indices
PPO	Public Postal Operators
QB	Queen's Bench
Quart J of Econ	*Quarterly Journal of Economics*
R&D	research and development
RdC	Receuil des Cours de l'Academie de drior international de la Haye
RPM	resale price maintenance
RTPA	Restrictive Trade Practices Act 1976
SEA	Single European Act 1986
SEP	standard-essential patent
SIEC	significant impediment to effective competition
SLC	substantial lessening of competition
SME	small and medium-sized enterprises
SO	Statement of Objections
SRMC	short run marginal cost
SSNIP	Small but Significant Non-transitory Increase in Price
Stan LR	*Stanford Law Review*
TEU	Treaty on European Union ('Maastricht')
TFEU	Treaty on the Functioning of the European Union
TTBER	Technology Transfer Block Exemption Regulation (Reg. 772/2004) (or BER)
UCLA LR	*University of California Los Angeles Law Review*
UKCLR	United Kingdom Competition Law Reports
UNCTAD	United Nations Conference on Trade and Development
Univ Chic LR	University of Chicago Law Review
Univ Mich LR	*University of Michigan Law Review*
U Pa LR	*University of Pennsylvania Law Review*
UPP	upward pricing pressure
USO	Universal Service Obligation
WIPO	World Intellectual Property Organisation
WTO	World Trade Organisation
Yale LJ	*Yale Law Journal*
YEL	*Yearbook of European Law*

1
INTRODUCTION TO COMPETITION LAW

1. CENTRAL ISSUES

1. Competition law is concerned with ensuring that firms (undertakings) operating in the free market economy do not restrict or distort competition in a way that prevents the market from functioning optimally.

2. The belief that competition amongst undertakings produces the best outcomes for society is based on economic theory that employs models of perfect competition and monopoly, and concepts of welfare and efficiency.

3. It is possible for systems of competition law to pursue objectives other than the economic ones of welfare and efficiency. Whether they should and, if so, what other objectives are or should be pursued, is extremely controversial.

4. Even if it is accepted that welfare and efficiency should be the sole or main goal of competition law, there is much debate as to what the welfare standard should be (social welfare or consumer welfare), how markets work and when, and on what basis, competition authorities should intervene. Three main 'schools' of competition analysis are known as Harvard, Chicago, and Post-Chicago.

5. A system of competition law was provided for in the EC Treaty (the Treaty of Rome). Article 3(1)(g) EC provided that the activities of the EC included 'a system ensuring that competition in the internal market is not distorted'. The provision is now in a Protocol to the Treaty on European Union (TEU) and the Treaty on the Functioning of the European Union (TFEU) which have governed the European Union since the coming into force of the Treaty of Lisbon, and the Court of Justice (CJ) has recognised that this has the same effect as Article 3(1)(g) EC.

6. A school of political theory in Europe (and more particularly, Germany) called ordoliberalism contained ideas about competition law which have been influential in EU competition law.

7. EU competition law has been undergoing a process of modernisation. This has led to the competition rules being applied in a more economically rigorous way, based on welfare and efficiency standards.

8. Three central concepts used in competition law are market power, market definition, and barriers to entry.

2. INTRODUCTION

'What *is* competition law?' is the first question any book on competition law must address.

The starting point is that competition law exists to protect competition in a free market economy. The terms competition *policy* and competition *law* are often used synonymously but competition law can be described as the means by which competition policy is implemented in respect of firms operating in the marketplace. Adherence to a belief in the free market economy leads to great importance being attached to competition policy and competition laws. The former senior official of the

European Commission's Competition Directorate-General has described the role of EU competition policy as follows:[1]

Competition policy must therefore act on a number of fronts at the same time. First, it must enforce competition law whenever there are harmful effects on Europe's citizens or businesses. But second, it must also ensure that the regulatory environment fosters competitive markets. It needs to screen proposed and existing legislation. Thirdly, it must help shape global economic governance through promoting the convergence of substantive competition rules, strengthening cooperation with other jurisdictions and promoting a shift of emphasis from trade regulation to competition regulation in the WTO. Finally, it must develop a competition culture in the society in which it operates. This is in itself one of the principal elements which can guarantee the competitiveness of an economy in the longer term.

A free market economy is an economic system in which the allocation of resources is determined by supply and demand in free markets and is not directed by government regulation. States which adopt a market economy do so because they consider it to be the form of economic organisation which brings the greatest benefits to society. The basis of a free market is competition between firms, and competition is considered—for the reasons explored later—to deliver efficiency and welfare. At the other end of the spectrum is an economy which is run by central government planning, such as that which existed in Soviet Russia.

The foundation of free market theory is usually located in the work of Adam Smith in the eighteenth century.[2] He thought that governments should remove artificial obstacles to the operation of free markets, such as price controls, and allow competition to flourish. Individuals pursuing their own self-interest competing in the marketplace would be led by the 'invisible hand' to achieve the general good:

Every individual necessarily labours to render the annual revenue of the society as great as he can. He generally neither intends to promote the public interest, nor knows how much he is promoting it…He intends only his own gain, and he is in this, as in many other cases, led by an invisible hand to promote an end which was no part of his intention. Nor is it always the worse for society that it was no part of his intention. By pursuing his own interest he frequently promotes that of the society more effectually than when he really intends to promote it. I have never known much good done by those who affected to trade for the public good.[3]

From this developed the concept of the market as an efficient and self-regulating mechanism with which governments should not interfere. Faith in the market was shaken to its core by the Great Depression of the 1930s,[4] but it recovered to become in the latter part of the twentieth century the great organising principle of western economies, exported around the world, particularly after the fall of the Communist regimes of the Soviet Union and eastern Europe which was celebrated as the triumph of free market capitalism over central planning. The high priests of the free market were those belonging to the 'Chicago School' of economics, which also had a profound influence on the development of competition law and is discussed later.[5]

The financial crisis which began in 2007 shattered any belief that markets are omniscient. The financial crisis was a failure of financial markets, but its effects have been felt throughout the 'real', i.e. non-financial, economy.[6] It has been shown that enlightened self-interest in the banking sector

---

[1] P. Lowe, 'The Design of Competition Policy Institutions for the 21st Century—the Experience of the European Commission and DG Competition' (2008) 3 *Competition Policy Newsletter* 1, 6.

[2] See Adam Smith, *The Wealth of Nations* (1776, reprinted Penguin, 1999).

[3] *The Wealth of Nations* (cited in n. 2), Book IV.

[4] It is taken to have started with the US stock market crash on 29 October 1929.

[5] See Section 5.B, p. 22 ff.

[6] At least in the West, including the EU and the US. Some of the world's burgeoning economies did not experience the financial crisis in the same way.

does not lead to the general good. However, Adam Smith never thought it would. He did not apply the 'invisible hand' concept to banks. Rather, he set out the 'real-bills' doctrine which would lead to prudent lending policies.[7] In contrast to this caution, from the 1960s onwards, financial economists developed theories such as the efficient-market hypothesis[8] and rational expectations theory[9] which posited financial markets as rational, self-correcting organisms. These ideas have been largely discredited.[10] It is now recognised that financial markets are different in that they cannot be allowed to fail and need a special type and degree of regulation.[11] As Adam Smith prophetically put it, justifying his suggested restrictions on banks:

> Such regulations may, no doubt, be considered as in some respects a violation of natural liberty. But these exertions of the natural liberty of a few individuals, which might endanger the security of the whole society, are, and ought to be, restrained by the laws of all governments, of the most free, as well as the most despotical.[12]

The crisis has led to a widespread loss of faith in the robustness of the market and a rejection of some of the wilder excesses of free market capitalism.

The adoption of a free market economy does not mean leaving every sector to unbridled competition. Even Adam Smith believed that governments should provide for certain public institutions which individuals would have no interest in undertaking as they would not yield profit. Furthermore, sectors such as health services or the provision of basic utilities may be subject to governmental intervention or government controls for reasons of public policy even though they can be operated for profit. Different States may have different views about how far the free market should be tempered or supplemented by a social component. The situation on this in the EU is discussed later in this book.[13]

It may seem ironic that competition laws seek to control and interfere with the freedom of conduct of firms in order to promote free competition. However, similar paradoxes face democratic governments in other spheres, such as the perennial question of how far the liberties of individuals should be constrained in order to uphold liberty itself.

In the competition context regulatory rules are necessary to deal with market imperfections and failures. In particular, left alone to determine their own conduct, firms are likely to combine or collude in a way which is profitable to them but which works to the detriment of society as a whole. Adam Smith himself described the tendency of those operating within the same trade to conspire to fix prices.[14] Cartels are an age-old phenomenon. Further, competition between firms may produce a 'winner' which dominates the market, or 'natural' monopolies may exist on a market. In these situations it may be thought necessary for competition law to restrain the dominant firm's behaviour. Monopolies may also be created if competitors are allowed to merge freely with one another. Competition law may thus aim to preclude mergers where necessary to preserve the competitive process on the market.

---

[7] *The Wealth of Nations* (cited in n. 2), 402.

[8] Efficient-market hypothesis is particularly associated with Professor Eugene Fama, see e.g. E. Fama, 'Efficient Capital Markets: A Review of Theory and Empirical Work' (1970) 25 *Journal of Finance* 383–41.

[9] See J. Muth, 'Rational Expectations and the Theory of Price Movements' (1961) 29 *Econometrica* 315–33; R. Lucas, 'Expectations and the Neutrality of Money' (1972) 4 *Journal of Economic Theory* 103–12. His work on rational expectation theory won Robert Lucas the Nobel Prize in 1995.

[10] Only largely discredited, since they are still defended in the arguments raging amongst economists in the wake of the financial crisis. For a general overview of the financial crisis and the relevant theories of the economics of financial markets see J. Cassidy, *How Markets Fail: The Logic of Economic Calamities* (Allen Lane, 2009).

[11] See e.g. R. A. Posner, *A Failure of Capitalism* (Harvard University Press, 2009). Judge Posner is a leading American antitrust scholar of the Chicago School.

[12] *The Wealth of Nations* (cited in n. 2), 402.

[13] See Section 7 and Chap. 8.

[14] *The Wealth of Nations* (cited in n. 4).

The previous discussion assumes that the objective of competition law is to achieve economic goals. However, there is much disagreement about what goals should be pursued through the application of the competition rules. Some argue that competition law should pursue solely economic goals, others that there should be a wider range of objectives. Section 3 discusses the possible objectives of competition law.

In respect of terminology it should be noted that in general parlance competition law is often called by its American name, 'antitrust law'. However, the European Commission (the EU competition authority) now uses the term 'antitrust' to denote the areas of competition law other than merger control and State aid.[15] The reader will find, nevertheless, that many of the sources quoted in this book use 'antitrust' in its more general meaning.

3. THE OBJECTIVES OF COMPETITION LAW

There are a number of possible objectives which competition law may pursue.[16]

A. ECONOMIC EFFICIENCY AND WELFARE

(i) Efficiency

One possible objective of competition law is economic efficiency. Efficiency is not an end in itself but it can lead to the maximisation of 'welfare'—a concept which is discussed later[17] and, in the EU context, it can be a means of promoting the objectives of the Union. This section seeks to show why competition is thought to achieve efficiency and produce the greatest benefits to society in the form of welfare.[18] To facilitate the understanding of these issues it is necessary to understand some basic concepts of microeconomics and welfare economics.[19]

(ii) Basic Economic Concepts

a. Demand Curves and Consumer and Producer Surplus

Consumers are all different. They place different values on things, have different preferences and different incomes, and will consequently be willing to pay different prices for a particular product. The maximum amount a consumer is willing to pay for a product is his reservation price.

Although suppliers might like to charge each consumer his individual reservation price, in practice this is not normally feasible. The supplier must therefore consider the relationship between the consumer's willingness to pay and the quantity which will be bought on the market as a whole. If only buyers with very high reservation prices are supplied, the quantity produced will be smaller than if buyers with lower reservation prices are supplied. Conversely, if greater quantities are produced the price will have to fall to incorporate buyers with lower reservation prices. The relationship between price and supply is represented by the market demand curve. The demand curve normally slopes downwards from left to right.

[15] See, e.g., the website of the Directorate-General responsible for competition policy, <http://www.ec.europa.eu/competition/index_en.html>.

[16] See e.g. G. Monti, *EC Competition Law* (Cambridge University Press, 2007), Ch 2; K. Coates, *Competition Law and Regulation of Technology Markets* (Oxford University Press, 2011), Ch 2.

[17] See Section 3.A.vii, p. 12.

[18] See D. Geradin, A. Layne-Farrar and N. Petit, *EU Competition Law and Economics* (Oxford University Press, 2012), 2.10–2.34.

[19] Welfare economics is the branch of economics which deals with the desirability of the social consequences of the arrangement of economic activities. Welfare economics is described as 'normative' as it depends on value judgements about how well the economy works.

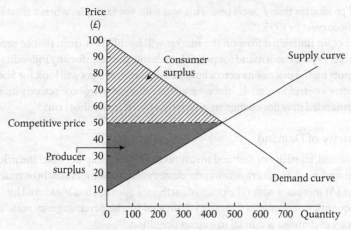

Figure 1.1 Demand curve and consumer and producer surplus

If we assume that the market price is £50 we can see that some consumers will be paying £50 for a product for which they would have paid more. This results in what is known as *consumer surplus* and is shown by the hatched area in Fig. 1.1. It is the difference between the buyers' reservation price and the market price.[20]

The supply curve shows the marginal cost[21] of production. In Fig. 1.1 we see that the producer is selling the output for more than it costs to produce. This results in what is known as *producer surplus* and is shown by the shaded area in Fig. 1.1.

b. Elasticity of Demand (Own Price Elasticity)

The amount by which the quantity demanded increases as price reduces (and vice versa) will depend on the market in question and the elasticity of demand for the product.

Price elasticity of demand measures the sensitivity of the quantity demanded to the price. Demand is said to be *inelastic* if an increase in price leads to an insignificant fall in demand. Conversely, demand is *elastic* if an increase in price leads to a significant fall in demand.

Technically, price elasticity of demand is the percentage change in the quantity of a product demanded divided by the corresponding percentage change in its price. The result will be a negative figure as the fall in demand will be expressed as a negative figure from the starting point. If demand for widgets[22] falls by 2 per cent as a result of a 1 per cent price increase the change in demand will be expressed as −2 per cent. The demand elasticity is then −2 divided by 1 (the price increase), which is −2.[23] Typically, elasticity falls as one moves down the demand curve, so that at higher prices demand is more elastic. Economic theory puts the dividing line between elastic and inelastic demand at −1. Demand is elastic at a figure below, or more negative, than −1. It is inelastic between −1 and 0. In markets where demand is inelastic shortages will lead to higher prices. So a bad harvest may be

---

[20] The concept of consumer surplus was first described by Alfred Marshall, *Principles of Economics* (8th edn, Macmillan, 1920).

[21] See Section 3.A.iii.a, p. 7 for an explanation of marginal cost.

[22] A widget is traditionally a mythical product with no specific characteristics used in competition law examples. Despite the recent use of 'widget' to describe (i) a device in the bottom of cans which introduces nitrogen into the liquid and therefore puts a head on canned beer (it won the Queen's Award for Industry in 1991) and (ii) a stand-alone application that can be embedded into third-party web-pages (such as Facebook) it still retains its characterless role as the Everyman of competition law discourse.

[23] Economists often express this figure without using the minus (as it is always negative). The bigger the negative number the 'higher' the elasticity, e.g., elasticity of −5 is higher than elasticity of −1.

better for food producers than a good one. This was true, for example, when a frost disaster struck the Brazil coffee harvest in 1995.[24]

The position of an individual firm on the market will be different from that of producers on the market as a whole. Even if the demand for petrol is inelastic, the price for any individual brand will be elastic. If Esso puts up the price of its petrol but Shell does not, drivers will look for Shell garages and purchase the latter's petrol instead. If, however, all the sellers of petrol collectively increase the price the quantity demanded may not change significantly, at least in the short run.[25]

c. Cross-elasticity of Demand

As already explained, elasticity of demand measures the relationship between the price of the product and the demand for it. In contrast, *cross price elasticity of demand* measures how much the demand for one product (A) increases when the price of *another* (B) goes up. It is measured by the percentage change in the quantity demanded of product A divided by the percentage increase in the price of B. Cross-elasticity of demand is crucial to market definition.[26]

Cross price elasticity is positive if the price increase in B leads to an increase in demand for A, and this suggests that A and B are substitute products. The Brazil coffee shortage, although leading to an increase in the price of coffee, did not cause consumers to stop purchasing coffee and to purchase tea instead. This indicated that consumers did not consider tea was a substitute for coffee. An important point to note when considering two products is that there may be cross price elasticity in one direction and not in the other. Although coffee drinkers may not purchase tea when the price of coffee increases, this does not mean that tea drinkers would not purchase coffee if there was a similar price rise in tea. If products are complements of each other, rather than substitutes, the cross price elasticity figure will be negative rather than positive. If the price of petrol goes up the demand for big-engine gas-guzzling cars may go down.

d. Profit Maximisation

An assumption is made for the purposes of welfare economics that firms act rationally and in a way which maximises profits.[27] Whether firms do always behave in this way is doubtful.[28] It will be seen later that, in particular where a firm has a monopoly, the managers may prefer a 'quiet life' to profit maximisation. Nevertheless, welfare economics is predicated on this basis. It is certainly a safe assumption that a firm will be concerned not to make long-term losses, otherwise it will ultimately

---

[24] D. Begg, G. Vernasca, S. Fischer, and R. Dornbusch, *Economics* (10th edn, McGraw-Hill, 2011), 76–77.

[25] The demand for petrol is not totally inelastic, although elasticity is low. Arguments about whether governments should take action on the environment by discouraging driving through higher petrol taxes are predicated on the assumption of some elasticity in the demand for petrol. In the long run consumers may change their travelling habits, lifestyle, and/or buy more fuel-efficient or electric cars.

[26] See Section 10.B, pp. 61 ff.

[27] Profits represent the difference between the total cost of producing goods or providing a service and the revenue earned by selling them.

[28] There is an enormous literature on this subject. The seminal work was A. A. Berle and G. C. Means, *The Modern Corporation and Private Property* (revised edn 1968, Harcourt Brace and World, 1932). For an extensive discussion see J. E. Parkinson, *Corporate Power and Responsibility* (Oxford University Press, 1993), particularly chs 2–4. This doubt arises partly because of the separation of ownership from control in all but the smallest companies. In the layers of complex organisation which make up modern businesses, decisions may be made by managers and executives facing uncertain future events and a large number of variables. Their expectations may be misplaced, they may be averse to risk-taking, and they may be most concerned with corporate or individual survival or the growth of the company rather than its profitability. Management may pursue a policy of 'satisficing'. This is a theory of firm behaviour that is contrary to that of profit maximisation. 'Satisficing' is when management adopts certain goals for profits, sales, etc. and tries to meet, but not necessarily exceed, them. The goals may not be set high in the first place, so that management will not seem a failure if it does not achieve them, and it is unwilling to be in a position where the shareholders demand ever higher goals in the future. See H. A. Simon, 'Theories of Decision-making in Economic and Behavioral Sciences' (1959) 49 *American Economic Review* 253 and Parkinson, *Corporate Power and Responsibility*, 66–67.

have to leave the market. Also, a firm which does not deliver profits to its shareholders will be attractive to a predator and so vulnerable to a take-over bid.[29]

e. Economies of Scale and Scope

Economies of scale occur when the average cost of producing a commodity falls as more is produced. If a widget factory produces only one widget that one widget must bear the whole cost of establishing and running the factory. If it produces 100,000 widgets, however, the costs are spread over 100,000 widgets instead of one. Some costs (variable costs) may increase with production (energy and labour for example, although they may not increase proportionately to the number of extra units). However, some costs may not increase at all: for example, the driver of a lorry delivering widgets will be paid the same whether the lorry is full or half empty.

Economies of scale result where efficiency in production is achieved as output is increased. There inevitably comes a point, however, when the average cost ceases to fall and economies of scale can no longer be reaped. That point is called the minimum efficient scale (MES). The MES is of great significance in competition law since it has important repercussions for market structure. Where the MES is very large in relation to the market, i.e. a producer has to supply a large quantity of products on the market before the MES is reached, only a few firms, possibly only one, will be able to operate efficiently on the market. A 'natural monopoly' is where it is less costly for just one firm to serve the market than for the market to be divided between more players. On a competitive market, however, the MES is low in comparison to overall demand so that numerous firms can operate efficiently on the market.

Economies of scope occur where it is cheaper to produce two different products jointly than each separately. This may result from factors such as shared assembly lines or shared personnel which enable the firm to make costs savings by producing a range of goods rather than the individual products on their own. Economies of scope may mean that a multi-product firm has lower unit costs than a single-product firm.

(iii) Perfect Competition and Efficiency

a. Perfect Competition

The theory of perfect competition presents a model of a market in which efficiency is maximised and cannot, therefore, be improved by the application of competition rules.

A perfectly competitive market is one in which there is a large number of buyers and sellers (firms with very small market shares can operate at minimal costs since the MES is small in comparison to the size of the market); the product is homogeneous; all the buyers and sellers have perfect information;[30] there are no barriers to entry or exit so that sellers can come on to, and leave, the market freely;[31] there are no transaction costs (buyers and sellers do not incur costs or fees to participate in the market); and there are no externalities (firms do not impose uncompensated costs on others but rather, each bears the full cost of its production process). The result is that each seller is insignificant in relation to the market as a whole and has no influence on the product's price. Consequently, sellers are described as price-takers, not price-makers.

In a perfectly competitive market the price does not exceed marginal cost. The marginal cost to a firm is the cost of producing one extra unit of the product. So if it costs £100 to produce ten widgets but £105 to produce 11, the marginal cost is £5. On such a market the firm will always be able to add to profit where the marginal cost of producing a unit is less than the price. The producer will therefore increase production until the price obtained per unit equals marginal cost. If the price is

---

[29] See Parkinson (cited in n. 28), 113–132.

[30] Buyers and sellers know of every change in price or demand and so respond immediately to such changes.

[31] For a discussion of barriers to entry, see Section 10.C, pp. 85 ff.

below marginal cost the firm will have to respond by reducing output. In other words, in a perfectly competitive market a firm's marginal revenue (the rise in what the firm earns by one extra unit of output) equals marginal cost.[32]

Where the price charged for a product is at marginal cost this does not mean that the firm makes no profit. It does, but only a 'normal' one, that is, a rate of profit that is just sufficient to keep the firm in the industry. All the factors of production used to make the product must be taken into account when computing the cost, including the capital. The firm has to make enough of a return on the capital employed in the business to make it worthwhile staying on the market. When economists talk of zero profits they mean that there is no profit above the 'normal' level, which is assessed in relation to the 'opportunity cost'. Opportunity costs are the value of what has to be given up to do something else. The capital employed in the business must therefore reap a profit to compensate the business for the profit which would come from a different outlay. If the firm does not do this it will leave the market.

The relationship between marginal and average cost is also an important one. The average cost is the costs of the firm evened out over all the units produced.[33] When the marginal cost of the next unit exceeds the average cost of the existing units, producing the next unit raises average costs. In that case the firm can decrease costs by reducing supply. If, on the other hand, the marginal cost of the next unit is less than the average cost of the existing units, an extra unit reduces average costs. In that case the firm can decrease costs by increasing supply. So the producer will produce at the point at which the average cost curve and the marginal cost curve intersect.

b. Allocative Efficiency

The fact that on a perfectly competitive market the market price equals the marginal cost is said to lead to *allocative efficiency*.

Allocative efficiency results from the fact that goods are produced in the quantities valued by society. The supplier will expand production to the point where market price and marginal cost coincide. The supplier will not make more but neither, if it is acting rationally to maximise profits, will it make less. Everyone who is willing and able to purchase the product at its cost of production will therefore be able to do so. The result is a market which is in equilibrium. Allocative efficiency is a state in which none of the players, sellers or buyers, could be made better off without someone being made worse off. It is sometimes known as Pareto optimal after the Italian economist, Vilfredo Pareto (1848–1923), who first developed the theory.

c. Productive Efficiency

Similarly, *productive* (or technical) efficiency results from perfectly competitive markets. Goods are produced at the lowest possible cost. Every firm has to produce at minimum cost or it will lose its custom to others, make losses, and eventually be obliged to leave the market. Given the perfect information in the market any cost-cutting techniques will be copied by the other firms and the market price will be lowered generally. There is therefore downward pressure on costs and cost reductions are passed on to customers because of the competitive pressure from other suppliers.

d. Dynamic Efficiency

Dynamic efficiency is a third type of efficiency. Allocative and productive efficiency describe static situations, but dynamic efficiency is concerned with how well a market delivers innovation and technological progress. The relation of dynamic efficiency to the concept of perfectly competitive

---

[32] The reason for this is that although the *industry's* demand curve is downward sloping, the demand curve for *each individual firm* is horizontal, which means that however much it sells it will get the market price. For further explanation of this, see Begg et al. *Economics* (cited in n. 24), Chap. 8; D. W. Carlton and J. M. Perloff, *Modern Industrial Organization* (4th edn, Pearson Addison Wesley, 2005), Chap. 3.

[33] See further, Chap. 7 for a discussion of costs in relation to pricing abuses.

markets is complex for, as we see later,[34] it can be argued that innovation may be better delivered by monopolistic rather than competitive markets and that the ability to achieve market power is an important spur to innovation. Many economists argue that dynamic efficiency is the most important kind of efficiency for increasing the 'welfare' which is discussed later.

(iv) Monopoly

At the opposite end of the spectrum to perfect competition lies monopoly. A monopoly is a market where there is only one seller. This may be because there are barriers which prevent other firms from entering the market or because there is a natural monopoly as the MES of production means that only one undertaking can operate profitably on the market.

Theory predicts that as the firm is not constrained by any competitors it will price as high as possible. The monopoly price will be above the competitive market price. However, the price that the monopolist charges is still affected by demand and is constrained to some extent by products from outside the market. As the price rises some customers will not purchase the product but will use their resources to purchase something else instead. The firm usually faces a downward-sloping demand curve, so the higher the price it charges the lower the demand for its product.

If a monopolist sells just one unit it may receive a very high price for that unit but that price is unlikely to cover its costs. The monopolist will therefore wish to sell more units but in order to do so it must lower the price in order to attract customers with lower reservation prices. Unless the monopolist can *price discriminate* between customers, the monopolist must lower the price on all units, not just the extra ones. The producer's marginal revenue is the extra amount the monopolist obtains from selling the extra unit, but because it involves lowering the price across the board the marginal revenue is less than the selling price. This means that the monopolist will sell units only up to the point at which the marginal revenue equals the marginal cost. A monopolist's marginal revenue is below the market price. This in turn means that the quantity supplied of the product will be less than that which would be supplied on a competitive market. Thus prices are higher than those resulting on a competitive market and output is restricted. This is illustrated in Fig. 1.2.

Figure 1.2 shows that, in the absence of price discrimination, the marginal revenue curve is always under the demand curve.[35] Because price is above the competitive price the monopolist makes abnormal profits but some consumers who would have paid the competitive (marginal cost) price are deprived of the product. Some of the consumer surplus identified in Fig. 1.1 is therefore transferred to the producer as monopoly profit but some is lost altogether. The horizontally hatched triangle in Fig. 1.2 shows this *deadweight loss of monopoly*, the loss of consumer surplus which is not turned into profit for the producer.

According to this theory, therefore, the main distinction between perfect competition and pure monopoly is that the monopolist's price exceeds marginal cost, while the competitor's price equals marginal cost. This monopoly pricing leads to a transfer of wealth from consumer to producer (the vertically hatched area in Fig. 1.2). It is for this reason that firms operating on a competitive market may wish to emulate the effect of monopoly by colluding, for example, to set their prices at above the competitive level and by reducing output.

From an efficiency point of view the transfer of wealth to the monopolist may be immaterial. The behaviour does not, however, simply lead to a redistribution of income but also results in the misallocation in resources and a deadweight loss. It is this loss to efficiency as a whole that is of greatest concern.

---

[34] See Section 3.A.viii, p. 14.

[35] If the monopolist is able to practise perfect price discrimination, i.e. charge each customer his reservation price, the marginal revenue curve and the demand curve are the same.

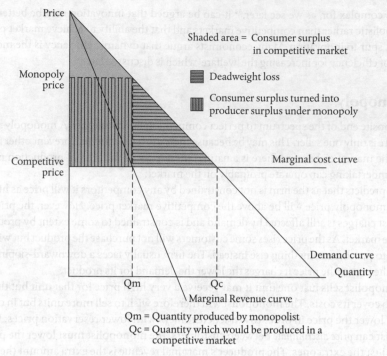

Price

Shaded area = Consumer surplus
in competitive market

▭ Deadweight loss

▤ Consumer surplus turned into
producer surplus under monopoly

Monopoly
price

Competitive
price

Marginal cost curve

Demand curve

Quantity

Qm   Qc

Marginal Revenue curve

Qm = Quantity produced by monopolist
Qc = Quantity which would be produced in a
competitive market

Figure 1.2 The deadweight loss due to monopoly

This seeming technicality, so trivial at first glance, is the basis of the economist's most general condemnation of monopoly: it leads to an allocation of resources that is inefficient in the sense of failing to satisfy consumer wants as completely as possible.[36]

In this respect, therefore, the objection to monopoly is not the popular concern—that the monopolist is able to charge excessively for its product—but that monopoly is inefficient.[37] Consumers who would have bought the product at the competitive price will spend their money on other things and welfare is not maximised as allocative inefficiency occurs. However, it is also possible to consider that the redistribution of benefits to producers from consumers who buy at above the competitive price is itself a form of inefficiency—distributive inefficiency[38].

Another important objection to monopoly is that a monopolist will not have the same pressure as firms operating on a competitive market to reduce its costs. This was identified by Leibenstein as, and has become known as, 'X-inefficiency'. It describes internal inefficiencies and rising costs due, for example, to high salaries, excessive perks, over-manning, and the lack of need to minimise the cost of production.[39] A monopolist may also waste resources, for example, defending its monopoly

---

[36] F. M. Scherer and D. Ross, *Industrial Market Structure and Economic Performance* (3rd edn, Houghton Mifflin, 1990), 23.

[37] Economists have often sought to quantify the deadweight loss. The starting point was Harberger's article in 1954 in which he calculated the loss in the US as less than 0.1% of national income: see A. C. Harberger, 'Monopoly and Resource Allocation' (1954) 44 *American Economic Review* 77–87. In a mass of further studies this has been found to be a great under-estimate (for the literature on this, see Scherer and Ross, *Industrial Market Structure and Economic Performance* (cited in n. 36), 661–667). Cowling and Mueller calculated it as 7%: see K. Cowling and D. C. Mueller, 'The Social Costs of Monopoly Power' (1978) 88 *Economic Journal* 724–748, although Scherer and Ross, *Industrial Market Structure and Economic Performance* (cited in n. 36), describe these results as 'exaggerated'. In this, as in much else in economics, there are wide differences in views.

[38] Geradin et al., *EU Competition Law and Economics* (cited in n. 18), 2.29.

[39] H. Leibenstein, 'Allocative efficiency vs. "X-efficiency"' (1966) 56 *American Economic Review* 392–415.

position, maintaining excess capacity, and indulging in excessive product differentiation.[40] These inefficiencies will be reflected in higher prices. Another possible inefficiency is that a monopolist not subject to competitive pressures will have little incentive to innovate and to improve its production methods. However, as we have already said, it can be argued that the opposite will be true on some markets.[41]

(v) Oligopoly

Oligopoly is a market structure lying between perfect competition and monopoly on the spectrum. On an oligopolistic market there are only a few leading firms, so the market is 'concentrated'. Given their small number they know each other's identity and recognise that they are affected by the output and pricing decisions of the others. They are not only competitors but rivals too. This mutual awareness may lead on some markets to tacit (that is, understood or implied without being stated) collusion between them. It may also lead them to collude expressly. However, other oligopolistic markets are characterised by fierce competition. Thus in some markets the price appears to be set above the competitive level and to approximate monopoly pricing, but in others it is not. A wealth of economic literature has been produced setting out economic models of oligopoly to explain why this occurs. The differences in behaviour on these markets also cause problems for those responsible for drafting and applying the competition rules. The mainstream explanations of oligopolistic behaviour and the way in which EU competition law attempts to deal with oligopolistic markets are described in Chapter 9. It is important to note, however, that many markets are oligopolistic and present a major problem for competition authorities.

(vi) Perfect Competition, Monopoly, and Competition in the Real World

Monopolies and oligopolies do exist. Monopolies may be created and maintained by state regulation (utilities and transport markets, for example) and/or may be natural. Pure monopoly is relatively rare outside these circumstances but some markets, although not a hundred per cent monopolised, may be dominated by one firm which holds a very large share of the market. Other markets may be oligopolistic, dominated by two, three, or four sellers. Even though there may be a fringe of smaller sellers on this type of market, they may present the same concerns for competition law as those arising on a monopolistic market, as explained in Section 3.A.v.[42]

This analysis of perfectly competitive markets presents a number of problems. The main problem is that in the real world perfectly competitive markets hardly ever exist.[43] Rather, the model of perfect competition is just that—a model. It is a useful starting point because it demonstrates the concepts of productive and allocative efficiency. In reality, however, markets do not possess all the characteristics of perfect competition. It is very unlikely that an infinite number of firms will be operating at identical costs levels, that producers will not benefit from economies of scale, and that sellers and buyers have perfect information across an atomistic market. Important caveats must thus be attached to the theory that the perfectly competitive market is superior. In particular, in most markets economies of scale make the attainment of perfect competition impossible and in some

---

[40]   See, e.g., R. Posner, 'The Social Costs of Monopoly and Regulation' (1975) *Journal of Political Economy* 83.

[41]   And see Section 3.A.viii, pp. 14.

[42]   For a more detailed discussion see, Chs. 5–7 and 9.

[43]   D. W. Carlton and J. M. Perloff, *Modern Industrial Organization* (4th edn, Pearson Addison Wesley, 2005), 84, suggest that the buying and selling of shares on the New York Stock Exchange comes close to satisfying the assumptions for perfect competition.

monopolies are 'natural' because of the MES. Further, it is not actually clear[44] that profit maximisation is the policy which firms always pursue.

The reality is that most markets lie somewhere between perfect competition and monopoly, in a state of 'imperfect' or 'monopolistic' competition where firms make differentiated or heterogeneous products[45] which consumers regard as imperfect substitutes, so that each firm has some degree of market power in that if it raises its prices it will not lose all its customers. The model of perfect competition is nonetheless still useful as a benchmark against which to measure the competitiveness of real markets. The difference between the perfectly competitive and monopolistic (or oligopolistic) market focuses attention on the crucial question: whether the firm or firms have sufficient market power to raise prices above the competitive level and keep them there. As Hovenkamp says:

The value of any model lies not in the absolute fidelity of each element to real world phenomena, but in the model's ability to make useful predictions and, more importantly, its ability to give us meaningful verbal accounts of our observations.[46]

(vii) The Concept of Welfare: Social (Total) Welfare, Consumer Welfare, and Efficiency Trade-offs

Welfare is the measure of how well a market is performing. A perfectly competitive market maximises welfare because it leads to efficiency. However, there are different concepts of welfare: social (otherwise called *total*) welfare and consumer welfare.

We have already seen that producer surplus is the profit a producer makes by selling goods above the cost of production. Consumer surplus is the difference between what consumers would be prepared to pay for goods and what they do pay. *Social (total) welfare* is the sum of these two surpluses. The objection to monopoly, it will be recalled, is that it does not just transfer some consumer surplus to producers but that some surplus (the deadweight) is totally lost to the market. That is a loss to social welfare.

Consumer welfare can for present purposes be equated with consumer surplus (the aggregate measure of the surplus of all consumers).[47] If competition policy is concerned with consumer welfare rather than social welfare it will be concerned with the transfer of surplus from producers to consumers.[48] However, *social* welfare may be maximised by such a transfer. In other words, prohibiting conduct and transactions which reduce consumer welfare may not allow efficiency gains which maximise social welfare.[49] Efficiency and consumer welfare may pull in different directions. In contrast, a competition policy which chooses to pursue social welfare as an objective is concerned only with the loss of efficiency represented by the deadweight 'triangle' and is not concerned about the redistributive effects of efficiency gains.[50] This is sometimes called 'the constant dollar' (or constant euro) philosophy, as no value judgement is made as to who, producer or consumer, has the dollar. In this respect it should be noted that producing undertakings may have shareholders who include institutions such as pension funds and life assurance firms whose members and policyholders benefit from the company profits. Employees too may benefit from increased profits. It is not necessarily

---

[44] See n. 28.

[45] Or products which consumers think of as differentiated. The differentiation and heterogeneity may mainly be in their minds, perhaps as the result of clever branding or advertising.

[46] H. Hovenkamp, *Federal Antitrust Policy: The Law of Competition and its Practice* (4th edn, West, 2011), 39.

[47] See M. Motta, *Competition Policy* (Cambridge University Press, 2004), 18.

[48] See R. J. Van den Bergh and P. D. Camesasca, *European Competition Law and Economics: A Comparative Perspective* (2nd edn, Sweet & Maxwell, 2006), 37. As noted in Section 5.B.i, p. 25 the influential American commentator Robert Bork used the terminology 'consumer welfare' differently.

[49] See P. Akman, *The Concept of Abuse in EU Competition Law* (Hart Publishing, 2012), 37–44.

[50] Compensating redistribution can be achieved by other policies, such as taxation, if thought desirable.

justifiable to privilege the buyer (the consumer) above the seller (the producer) as if the welfare of one is inherently more precious than that of the other.[51] Furthermore, as we shall see, the term 'consumers' in EU competition law includes customers on intermediate markets,[52] so where the customers are not final consumers but intermediate buyers a consumer welfare standard favours the buying *firm* over the selling one.

Moreover, although theory accords prime position to allocative efficiency, improving overall efficiency may require a trade-off between different types of efficiencies, which may have an effect on the relationship between producer and consumer surplus. This is discussed in the following extract, which explains what is meant by a *potential Pareto* (or *Kaldor Hicks*) *improvement*. Whereas a *Pareto improvement* is an action by which nobody loses and at least one person benefits, *a potential Pareto improvement* is a concept which deals with a situation where different efficiency goals are not consistent with each other, by providing that where there are both winners and losers the winners must win more than the losers lose.

R. J. Van den Bergh and P. D. Camesasca, *European Competition Law and Economics: A Comparative Perspective* (2nd edn, Sweet & Maxwell, 2006), 29–30

In some cases, allocative efficiency may conflict with other efficiency goals: productive efficiency and dynamic efficiency . . . Productive or technical efficiency implies that output is maximised by using the most effective combination of inputs; hence internal slack (also called X-inefficiency) is absent. The goal of productive efficiency implies that more efficient firms, which produce at lower costs, should not be prevented from taking business away from less efficient ones. Obviously, the achievement of productive efficiency is not a Pareto improvement since the less efficient firms are made worse off. Dynamic efficiency is achieved through the invention, development and diffusion of new products and production processes that increase social welfare. Whereas productive efficiency and allocative efficiency are static notions, progressiveness or dynamic efficiency refers to the rate of technological progress. Again, there will be losers in the dynamic competitive struggle, so that Pareto improvements cannot be reached. To enable policy decisions when the different efficiency goals are not consistent with each other, welfare economics offers the alternative criterion of Kaldor-Hicks efficiency.

A Kaldor-Hicks improvement allows changes in which there are both winners and losers, but requires that the gainers gain more than the losers lose. This condition being satisfied, the winners could compensate the losers . . . and still have a surplus left for themselves . . . A Kaldor-Hicks improvement is also referred to as a potential Pareto improvement, since actual compensation would again satisfy the Pareto criterion. The central value judgment underlying Kaldor-Hicks efficiency is that an exchange of money has a neutral impact on aggregate well-being, which may not be the case when the incomes of gainers and losers differ. By using the Kaldor-Hicks criterion total welfare is maximised. This welfare notion may allow clearing mergers that enable the merging firms to achieve important scale economies and thus improve productive efficiency, but at the same time enable previously independent firms to collude and raise prices above competitive levels. In terms of total welfare, it is irrelevant that producers rather than consumers capture the surplus produced by achieving efficiencies, as the monopoly overcharge paid by purchasers to stockholders is treated as a transfer from one member of a society to another and so is ignored in the balance.

[51] Akman, *The Concept of Abuse in EU Competition Law* (cited in n. 49), 39; J. Farrell and M. L. Katz, 'The Economics of Welfare Standards in Antitrust' (2006) 2(2) *Competition Policy International* 3.

[52] See Section 7.C.ii.b, p. 45.

The question of trade-off between efficiencies and the relationship between efficiency and consumer welfare poses difficult problems for EU competition law. These issues are discussed further in the following chapters of this book.[53]

(viii) Dynamic Competition

The trade-off between different types of efficiencies already mentioned is particularly acute when dynamic efficiencies are concerned:

… an improvement in terms of dynamic efficiency does not satisfy the Pareto criterion, since this will harm less innovative firms which will lose customers to their technically superior competitors. However, such improvements may satisfy the Kaldor-Hicks criterion since benefits both to pioneering firms and consumers may outweigh losses to non-innovative firms.[54]

It is often said that monopolies have fewer incentives to innovate than firms in competitive markets but it is also argued that substantial market power is an incentive to innovate. The Austrian economist Joseph Schumpeter took issue with the idea that competition is a better spur to innovation than monopoly. He considered that a monopolist may be more willing to bear the risks and costs of invention and technical development.[55] Schumpeter's argument is that competition in innovation is more important than price competition because it is a more effective means of obtaining an advantage over one's competitors. This is known as 'Schumpterian rivalry', where firms compete in a constant race to bring new products on to the market in 'gales of creative destruction', competition is dynamic, and positions of market power are short term as further innovation hands the advantage to another player. This involves accepting that short-term positions of substantial market power may arise but that this is not necessarily inimical to consumer welfare. The following extract from an article by an economist explains why this is so.

D. Hildebrand, 'The European School in EC Competition Law' (2002) 25 *World Competition* 3, 8–9

In the static welfare analysis of market power, it is evidenced that a consumer surplus loss will occur where the consumer willing to pay the marginal cost is not supplied. Indeed this normally occurs when there is an unregulated monopoly that raises price above marginal cost of supply. A measure of the static inefficiency that results is analysed in terms of the actual cost of production in comparison with the minimum production cost (productive inefficiency), and in terms of price set above marginal cost of supply (allocative inefficiency)…In this static analysis there is a clear total welfare loss associated with the exercise of market power. The static analysis, however, has no time dimension because it is looking at an equilibrium situation. Such an analysis is unable to explain or incorporate technological development or product and process innovation: it is concerned solely with the allocation of resources in the context of fixed technology and a given cost situation. In the real world, product markets evolve over time because of new technological discoveries and the introduction of new and improved products. Such innovation generates welfare gains due to dynamic efficiencies. This means that a proper welfare analysis

---

[53] See in particular Chap. 4 (Art. 101(3)), Chap. 7 in relation to abuses of a dominant position), and Chap. 15 (mergers).

[54] Van den Bergh and Camesasca, *European Competition Law and Economics: A Comparative Perspective* (cited in n. 48), 31. And see the litigation culminating in Case C-501/06 P, *GlaxoSmithKline Services Unlimited* v. *Commission* [2009] ECR I-9291, discussed in Chap. 4, where it was argued that increased prices to consumers were outweighed by dynamic efficiencies resulting from the undertaking concerned having more profit to plough back into the research and development of pharmaceuticals.

[55] J. A. Schumpeter, *Capitalism, Socialism and Democracy* (Harper, 1942).

of market power needs to take into account both the static and dynamic efficiencies—and any trade-off between them.

Where dynamic efficiency aspects are introduced into the competition analysis, it is evident that the presumption that market power leads to a loss of allocative efficiency and to a loss in consumer welfare is crucially predicated on the assumptions that the costs of the firm concerned do not fall due to production rationalization or that product innovation does not occur. According to the European School, the following conclusion can be drawn: market power may speed productivity and growth and reduce the costs of the growth process despite a tendency to a less than optimal allocation of resources in static equilibrium.

Dynamic efficiency is analysed in terms of how total surplus, consumer plus producer surplus, evolves over time with the introduction of a product of process innovation. A new product satisfied a demand that was not catered for before. If the product was supplied at its short run marginal production cost then none of the suppliers would recover their original research and development (R & D) investment. The anticipation of this by suppliers would mean that there would be no incentive to make the investment and develop a new product. Even in a competitive market situation, a firm invests in a project if the net present value of future returns matches the investment outlay and initial losses. The competitive firm's assessment will include the need for at least a normal rate of profit as an equilibrium condition. Suppliers are indifferent between investing and not, if they subsequently earn profits that exactly recover their outlay as well as the normal return on the investment. Product innovation only occurs if firms earn more than just enough to offset their investment. They will only actually invest if they anticipate making profits in excess. Such profits, however, mean pricing above short run minimal average total costs either because there are barriers to entry or because the innovating firm has market power. The market, when it is functioning well, solves this difficult balance by accommodating the creation of temporary positions of market dominance, the resulting super profits attracting all manner and types of entrepreneurial factor which bids away the excessive profit such that in equilibrium the marginal investment will be just offset by the present value of future normal profit.

Nevertheless, recent research has shown that monopolies and tight oligopolies are less conducive to innovation than less concentrated markets.[56] Concepts of dynamic efficiency and dynamic competition are particularly important in respect of the 'new economy' of high technology markets.[57]

B. OTHER OBJECTIVES OF COMPETITION LAW

(i) Introduction

Competition laws may pursue a variety of goals. Different jurisdictions may have different goals, and may change their goals over time. Even if one accepts that the goal of competition law is efficiency and welfare there is the question whether this should be the *only* objective.

Once this has been resolved it has to be decided exactly what competition law should be adopted and *how* it should be applied in pursuit of these goals. We look first at what other goals competition law might pursue.

[56] P. Aghion, N. Bloom, R. Blundell, R. Griffith, and P. Howitt, 'Competition and Innovation: An Inverted-U Relationship', (2005) 120 *Quart J of Economics* 701, cited by the DG Comp, Alexander Italianer, 'Level Playing-field and Innovation in Technology Markets', Conference on Antitrust in Technology, Palo Alto, 28 January 2013, <http://www.ec.europa.eu/competition/speeches/text/sp2013_01_en.pdf>.

[57] See Section 7.E, pp. 54 ff. and e.g. the *Microsoft* case, Case T-201/04, *Microsoft v. Commission* [2007] ECR II-3601, discussed in Chap. 7.

(ii) Preservation of Liberty and Dispersal of Economic Power

The use of the competition rules to preserve competitive markets may also uphold the foundations of liberal democracy. Competitive markets will generally preclude the creation of excessive private power.

G. Amato, *Antitrust and the Bounds of Power* (Hart Publishing, 1997), 2–3

Antitrust law was, as we know, invented neither by the technicians of commercial law (though they became its first specialists) nor by economists themselves (though they supplied its most solid cultural background). It was instead desired by politicians and (in Europe) by scholars attentive to the pillars of the democratic systems, who saw it as an answer (if not indeed 'the' answer) to a crucial problem for democracy: the emergence from the company or firm, as an expression of the fundamental freedom of individuals, of the opposite phenomenon of private power; a power devoid of legitimation and dangerously capable of infringing not just the economic freedom of other private individuals, but also the balance of public decisions exposed to its domineering strength. On the basis of the principles of liberal democracy, the problem was twofold and constituted a real dilemma. Citizens have the right to have their freedoms acknowledged and to exercise them; but just because they are freedoms they must never become coercion, an imposition on others. Power in liberal democratic societies is, in the public sphere, recognized only in those who hold it legitimately on the basis of law, while, in the private sphere, it does not go beyond the limited prerogatives allotted within the firm to its owner. Beyond these limits, private power in a liberal democracy (by contrast with what had occurred, and continues to occur, in societies of other inspirations) is in principle seen to be abusive, and must be limited so that no-one can take decisions that produce effects on others without their assent being given.

The question whether government regulation or the private power of the firm is more to be feared is an ideological one which pervades many arguments in competition law. However, one of the most important arguments in favour of a competitive market structure, where the individual sellers and buyers are insignificant in relation to the size of the market, is that it decentralises and disperses private power and protects individual freedom.[58] This conception of the value of competition is central to the ideas of ordoliberalism, as described later.[59] The preservation of liberty may in some markets result in economic efficiency. In other cases the goals may be inimical.

(iii) Economic Freedom and Protecting Competitors and Fair Competition

Competition laws which aim at the dispersal of power as a matter of ideology may favour small businesses and seek to protect them from big business. Instead of protecting the process of competition the law may protect *competitors* and the structure of the market. For example, competition law can be used to protect small firms from the dominant firm's (efficient) low pricing, or to force a dominant firm to give access to resources it controls to a smaller firm in order to allow the latter to compete with it. In some situations it may be necessary to protect competitors in order to protect competition as a way of preventing a loss to consumer welfare. However, there is a crucial distinction between on the one hand protecting competitors and the competitive process as a means of achieving economic

---

[58] See Scherer and Ross, *Industrial Market Structure and Economic Performance* (cited in n. 36), 18.
[59] See Section 6, p. 33.

welfare and, on the other hand, protecting competitors for their own sake or maintaining a particular market structure as a matter of principle.

A policy which seeks to protect competitors and market structure is often called a policy of 'economic freedom' or labelled as 'ordoliberal' after the school of thought described below which prizes economic freedom as a value in itself.[60] Economic freedom means that individuals should be free to participate in the market as competitors or consumers, unhindered by the economic power of other market participants.[61] Such a policy may accord with popular sentiment which is distrustful of 'large' firms.[62] It can be described as 'populist', as we shall see,[63] and may protect 'fair' rather than 'free' competition. 'Fairness' in this sense includes the idea that small firms should have equal opportunities to compete and that they should be protected from discriminatory practices. A competition policy based on economic freedom enables a government to nurture small businesses, and to promote a society in which citizens are encouraged to be their own boss, run their own business, and behave in an entrepreneurial manner. The dispersal of market power may prevent the redistribution of wealth from consumers to firms with market power but the protection of small and inefficient businesses may also take wealth from consumers and lead to a loss in economic welfare.

(iv) Public Policy and Socio-Political Factors

Competition law may also be used to service other policies, such as social, employment, industrial, environmental, and/or regional policy (for example, by prohibiting mergers which will cause job losses, or allowing restrictive agreements which will preserve declining industries for a little longer or produce environmental benefits). The pursuit of such policies may be inconsistent with the pursuit of efficiency. In some countries socio-political objectives are set out in the competition legislation. For example, South Africa's competition law has six purposes, one of which is 'to promote the greater spread of ownership, in particular to increase the ownership stakes of historically disadvantaged persons';[64] China's competition law is stated to be enacted for the purpose, inter alia, of 'promoting the healthy development of the socialist market economy';[65] and the purpose of Korea's competition law is, inter alia, 'to strive for the balanced development of the national economy'.[66]

(v) Productivity Growth

A leading American economist has argued that the primary goal of competition law should be the growth of the economy. He therefore considers that competition law should first and foremost pursue dynamic efficiency because it is innovation that drives economic growth.[67]

(vi) Happiness

It is being seriously suggested, in the wake of the economic crisis, that competition law should promote 'happiness' in the sense of citizens' opportunities to increase well-being, and that in

---

[60] See Section 6, p. 33.

[61] See the discussion on economic freedom in Monti, *EC Competition Law* (cited in n. 16), 22–25.

[62] See Section 5.B.i.

[63] See n. 82.

[64] Competition Act no. 89 of 1998, s. 2(f).

[65] Anti-Monopoly Law, Art. 1; see M. Furse, *Antitrust Law in China, Korea, and Vietnam* (Oxford University Press, 2009), ch 2-1.

[66] Monopoly Regulation and Fair Trade Act 1980, Article 1; see Furse, *Antitrust Law in China, Korea, and Vietnam* (cited in n. 65), Chap. 1-1.

[67] Michael Porter, 'Competition and Antitrust: A Productivity-Based Approach' in C. Weller (ed.), *Unique Value: Competition Based on Innovation Creating Unique Value for Antitrust, the Economy, Education and Beyond* (Innovation Press, LLC, 2005).

post-industrial, wealthy countries competition policy should advance economic, social, and democratic values rather than mere economic welfare objectives.[68] This idea has something in common with the ordoliberal concept of economic freedom and the EU's aim of 'well-being'.[69]

(vii) The EU Dimension of the Single Market

In the EU there is a special dimension. The competition rules are set out in the TFEU which is the former EC Treaty as amended by the Treaty of Lisbon. The competition rules must therefore be viewed in the context of the aims and objectives of the EU, in particular the integration of the single market. The history of the EC Treaty, the EC, and the EU is explained in Chapter 2. The aims of the EU and the EU competition rules are, however, introduced in Section 5.

C. CONCLUSIONS

There seems to be a general consensus at present amongst economists, competition lawyers, and policy-makers, at least in Europe, North America, and Australasia, that competition law should be adopted and applied in pursuance of economic efficiency and welfare. There are differences of opinion, however, as to whether the appropriate welfare standard is social welfare or consumer welfare and it will be seen throughout this book that there are different views as to how competition law rules can best achieve welfare objectives.

Nevertheless, the extent to which competition laws should rather or also be used to pursue other goals such as economic freedom, or should take account of public policy considerations, remains a live issue. The argument has intensified in the maelstrom of the economic crisis which has affected the economies of many countries (including those of the EU). Of greatest importance in the EU context is the stance of the EU Courts, which have not embraced a consumer welfare standard as the sole objective. In some countries public policy objectives are written into the legislation. The pursuit of these other goals may favour small firms, individuals, or environmental concerns at the expense of consumer welfare.[70] Supporting small businesses for their own sake at the expense of more efficient competitors will be a drag on the economy. Similarly, the prevention of a merger which would result in efficiencies because it may save jobs in the short term may mean that the individual companies are unable to compete effectively on the market in the long run, and allowing an anti-competitive agreement between firms in an industry in historic decline may ensure the firms' survival for a time but cause inefficiency. It may be better for nature to take its course. The most efficient will survive and the remaining resources can be used in new industries which will create future prosperity.

This is not to say that there should not be social, regional, employment, environmental, or other policies. It is a matter of whether, and to what extent, these may be or should be pursued as part of a *competition* policy and how far competition can be isolated from other policies. The question of what concerns competition law should encompass, and whether it should serve narrow economic ends and be devoid of other values, is ultimately a matter of political choice, and we return to

---

[68] See M. E. Stucke, 'Should Competition Policy Promote Happiness', SSRN: <http://papers.ssrn.com/sol3/papers.cfm?abstract_id=2203533>.

[69] See Section 7.B, p. 36. One of the aims of the EU is to promote the 'well-being of its peoples', TEU, Art. 3(1).

[70] A good example of the tension between a popular distrust of large and powerful firms coupled with sentimentality towards small businesses on the one hand, and a popular liking for low prices and plenty of choice on the other, can be seen in the debate in the UK over supermarkets which culminated in the market investigation reference of the grocery sector by the Office of Fair Trading (OFT) to the Competition Commission under s. 131 of the Enterprise Act 2002 in May 2006; see *The Grocery Market, the OFT's reasons for making a reference to the Competition Commission*, OFT 845 and the Competition Commission Final Report, *Groceries Market Investigation*, 30 April 2008. Similarly, although a society may object to the ability of a large company with market power to make excessive profits at the expense of consumers, the shareholders in the monopolist may be institutions such as pension funds and assurance companies which are investing on behalf of the consumers in their role as workers or policyholders, as already noted.

the matter when looking at the 'Chicago School' in Section 5.B and at the current objectives of EU competition law.

4. US LAW

It is impossible to discuss EU competition law without some reference to US law because of the influence which American legal scholars, lawyers, and economists, working with reference to the American system, have had on competition law thinking.

The US was one of the first jurisdictions to adopt a proper 'modern' system of competition law.[71] The US Congress passed the Sherman Act in 1890.[72] It is still in force. Section 1[73] states:

Every contract, combination in the form of trust or otherwise, or conspiracy, in restraint of trade or commerce among the several States, or with foreign nations, is hereby declared to be illegal. Every person who shall make any contract or engage in any combination or conspiracy hereby declared to be illegal shall be deemed guilty of a felony...

Section 2 states:

Every person who shall monopolize, or attempt to monopolize, or combine or conspire with any other person or persons, to monopolize any part of the trade or commerce among several States, or with foreign nations, shall be deemed guilty of a felony...

None of the expressions used in the Sherman Act, such as 'in restraint of trade' or 'monopolize' were defined.

The most popular explanation for the passing of the Sherman Act is that it was to combat the power of the 'trusts'. It had become common for the owners of stocks held in competing companies to transfer the stocks to trustees who then controlled the activities of those competitors and consequently lessened competition between them (this is why it has become known as 'antitrust' law). The activities of the railroad companies gave rise to particular concern. It is also claimed, however, that the Sherman Act was more of a protectionist measure passed in response to pressure by farmers, small businesses, or those desiring to stop the transfer of wealth from consumers to big business.[74] The Chicago School[75] view is that it was passed to preserve economic efficiency, but since the theories of allocative efficiency, dead-weight loss, and Pareto-efficiency had not then been invented it cannot have been articulated in exactly this way.[76] The argument about the conception of US antitrust is not merely about history, but is important when considering what the objective of that law is

---

[71] Canada was the first (Act for the Prevention and Suppression of Combinations Formed in Restraint of Trade, 1889). For a historical survey of rules in respect of monopolies and cartels, see N. Green, 'From Rome to Rome: The Evolution of Competition Law into a Twenty-First Century Religion' [2010] *Comp Law* 7; the UK courts developed a doctrine of restraint of trade at common law, but this never developed into a system of competition law: see *Chitty On Contracts* (29th edn, Sweet & Maxwell, 2006), ch 16.

[72] 'An Act to protect trade and commerce against unlawful restraints and monopolies', 15 USC, 2 July 1890. It was supplemented by later statutes, the Clayton Act (1914), the Federal Trade Commission Act (1914), the Robinson-Patman Act (1936), the Celler-Kefauver Act (1950) and the Hart-Scott-Rodino Antitrust Improvements Act 1976.

[73] See also Chap. 4.

[74] See E. T. Sullivan (ed.), *The Political Economy of the Sherman Act* (Oxford University Press, 1991) for a collection of essays written between 1959 and 1989 on the Sherman Act, published to mark the centenary of the Act. The articles display the wide divergence of views between some of the most eminent names in antitrust thinking, as well as historians and Department of Justice officials.

[75] For the Chicago School, see 5.B. For Robert Bork's Chicago view of the intention of Congress see R. H. Bork, *The Antitrust Paradox* (Basic Books, 1978, reprinted with a new Introduction and Epilogue, 1993), Chap. 2.

[76] Alfred Marshall's *Principles of Economics* (Macmillan, 1890) was first published in 1890 and Pareto published his theory in 1909. For a good account of the history of the US legislation, see E. Gellhorn, W. E. Kovacic, and S. Calkins, *Antitrust Law and Economics* (5th edn, West, 2004), 22–36.

now and in the 'struggle for the soul of antitrust'. It may seem to the neutral observer that in passing the Sherman Act Congress made a law without a discernible policy behind it and that the policy only emerged later. However, according to Richard Posner, a leading exponent of the Chicago School, the motives of the legislators of 1890 are irrelevant.[77]

US law developed in a series of judicial decisions in the half-century following the Sherman Act in a rather ad hoc manner and reflected the experiences of the American economy as it went through an industrial revolution, the Depression (when antitrust enforcement was relaxed),[78] and the New Deal.[79] In the 1940s and 1950s the 'workable competition' hypothesis[80] was influential.[81] In the 1950s the Structure → Conduct → Performance (S→C→P) paradigm was developed by what is called the Harvard School. This led to a belief that markets were fragile and to an antitrust policy which intervened to protect small businesses against large firms.[82] Chicago School thinking[83] had a profound impact on the development of antitrust enforcement in the US from the 1970s onwards and has influenced the thinking about competition law in Europe and around the world. The Bush administrations (2000–2008) took a non-interventionist stance towards the conduct of big business, particularly in respect of merger control and the application of s. 2 of the Sherman Act. This culminated in the 2008 report of the Department of Justice (DOJ) setting out a policy of restrained enforcement of s. 2.[84] In 2009 the Obama administration repudiated this policy and withdrew the report, and the newly appointed Assistant Attorney General of the Antitrust Division of the DOJ (the top US antitrust official) announced that the Obama administration would be pursuing vigorous antitrust enforcement.[85]

There are three particular features of US antitrust law which should be noted as differing from EU law.[86] These need to be borne in mind when looking at US cases or reading American commentators. First, the US competition authorities, the DOJ Antitrust Division and the FTC, enforce the antitrust laws by bringing actions before the ordinary federal courts: they are primarily prosecutors rather than decision-makers (although the FTC does have administrative adjudication powers and both agencies shape the application of the law by the issuing of guidelines, making speeches, negotiating settlements, and so on). The DOJ may bring criminal as well as civil proceedings for violations of the Sherman Act. The state governments (through their attorneys general) may also prosecute federal antitrust infringements and the states have their own state antitrust laws. This is in contrast to the EU competition authority, the Commission, which enforces the rules by taking decisions binding

---

[77] R. A. Posner, *Antitrust Law* (2nd edn, University of Chicago Press, 2001), 24–26.

[78] It has been claimed that this prolonged the Depression, see J. D. Harkrider, 'Lessons from the Great Depression' (2009) 23(2) *Antitrust* 6.

[79] The New Deal was a federal policy begun under President Roosevelt in 1933 to aid those thrown out of employment in the Depression. Collusion between competitors was first encouraged and then prosecuted; see P. Freeman, 'We Are Here In A Very Melancholy State: Financial Crisis And Competition', speech 3 November 2009, <http://www.competition-commission.org.uk/our_role/speeches/pdf/freeman_031009.pdf>.

[80] See Section 5.G, pp. 32.

[81] See the Report of the Attorney General's National Committee to Study the Antitrust Laws (1955).

[82] A policy which Posner describes as 'populist' because he sees it as based on 'a hostility towards wealth and power and a suspicion of capitalism but a suspicion that falls short of an endorsement of socialism': Posner, *Antitrust Law* (cited in n. 77), 24. 'Populism' is a term that has been attached to various political movements in different countries (e.g., late nineteenth-century Russia) but in general means the preferences of 'ordinary people'. It is characterised by the defence of the little man against powerful organisations, such as governments, large firms, and trade unions.

[83] See Section 5.B.

[84] *Competition and Monopoly: Single-Firm Conduct Under Section 2 of the Sherman Act*, United States Department of Justice (2008). The Federal Trade Commission (FTC) did not endorse the report and three of the four Commissioners disassociated themselves from its conclusions, see FTC Press Release, 8 September 2008.

[85] Christine A. Varney, 'Vigorous Antitrust Enforcement In This Challenging Era', 11 May 2009, speech available on the DOJ website, <http://www.justice.gov/atr/public/speeches/245711.htm>.

[86] There are more than three differences of course (e.g., s. 1 of the Sherman Act is structured differently from the EU counterpart, Art. 101) but the three mentioned here are particularly crucial.

on the firms concerned, acting as both prosecutor and judge.[87] Secondly, in the US the antitrust laws are the subject of a very significant amount of private litigation, again before the ordinary federal courts. This contrasts with the position in Europe where private litigation has hitherto been relatively rare.[88] The result of these two factors is that US law has been developed on a case by case basis by the courts, while in the EU it has been primarily developed by an administrative authority with the EU Courts acting only to review the legality of the authority's actions or to interpret the law on references from national courts. The third matter to note at the outset is that s. 2 of the Sherman Act forbids 'monopolization' and attempts to 'monopolize'. It is thus crucially different from the corresponding provision in EU law, Article 102, which forbids the 'abuse of a dominant position'. So in the US anti-competitive conduct by which market power is *acquired* is an offence, whereas Article 102 can be applied only against the conduct of firms which are already in a dominant position. In Chapter 7 we see that at present the law on matters such as refusal to supply, predatory pricing, margin squeeze, rebates, and tying is not the same in the EU as in the US.

5. SCHOOLS OF COMPETITION ANALYSIS AND THEORIES AND CONCEPTS RELEVANT TO COMPETITION LAW

A. THE STRUCTURE → CONDUCT → PERFORMANCE PARADIGM AND THE HARVARD SCHOOL

The S→C→P paradigm holds that the structure of the market determines the firm's conduct and that conduct determines market performance, for example, profitability, efficiency, technical progress, and growth. The model thus sought to establish that certain industry structures lead to certain types of conduct which then lead to certain kinds of economic performance. In particular, highly concentrated industries cause conduct which leads to poor economic performance, especially reduced output and monopoly prices.

These views stemmed mainly from work done at Harvard University. The initial work was done in the 1930s, particularly by E. S. Mason,[89] and was developed by his pupil J. S. Bain in the 1950s.[90] The theory was developed through empirical studies of American industries (20 manufacturing industries were studied in the early 1950s) rather than from theoretical models. The conclusion that market structure dictated performance caused a belief that competition law should be concerned with *structural* remedies rather than *behavioural* remedies. The focus of attention was, therefore, on concentrated industries. Bain considered that most industries were more concentrated than was necessary (economies of scale were not substantial in most industries); that barriers to entry were widespread and very high and so new firms were prevented from entering markets; and that the monopoly pricing associated with oligopolies began to occur at relatively low levels of concentration. These influential conclusions coincided with a general trend of US Congressional policies which sought to protect small businesses and which were suspicious of business expansion. This led in the 1960s to

---

[87] See Chs 2 and 13.

[88] The 'modernisation' of EU law, which came into effect on 1 May 2004, aims, inter alia, to encourage greater private enforcement, and the European Commission has reviewed how private actions may be facilitated: see further Chs 2 and 14.

[89] See E. S. Mason, *Economic Concentration and the Monopoly Problem* (Harvard University Press, 1957).

[90] See J. S. Bain, *Barriers to New Competition* (Harvard University Press, 1956) and *Industrial Organization* (2nd edn, Wiley, 1968).

an interventionist antitrust enforcement policy in the US.[91] Criticism of the Bainian analysis, led by the Chicago School (discussed in Section 5.B), centred particularly on the fact that the conclusions drawn from the empirical studies were flawed;[92] that they wrongly found barriers to entry to be pervasive and wrongly found economies of scale to be rare. Consequently, the policy of condemning so many business practices as anti-competitive was misconceived. Despite the rise of the Chicago School, the S→C→P paradigm remains a basic tool of competition analysis. Although mainstream economists no longer believe that structure *dictates* performance, it accepts that structure is important to the ability of firms to behave anti-competitively. As Hovenkamp says:

The S-C-P paradigm left certain marks that seem all but indelible—for example, the greatly increased attention to market definition, barriers to entry, and proof of market power that even the most convinced members of the Chicago School acknowledge to be important. Antitrust without structural analysis has become impossible, thanks largely to the S-C-P writers. To be sure, they may have gone too far in emphasizing structure over conduct, but that is a question of balance, not of basic legitimacy. Not even S-C-P's most vehement critics would roll the clock back completely.[93]

B. THE CHICAGO SCHOOL, POST-CHICAGO, AND NEO-CHICAGO

(i) The Chicago School

It is important to recognise that 'Chicago' antitrust theory does not exist in a vacuum. Rather, it is part of what is known as Chicago economics, a school of neo-classical, libertarian, free-market economics, called after the university where many of its originators and adherents did (and still do) their work.[94] Put very simply, Chicago economics holds that people are rational and that markets work and are self-correcting. Chicago thinking has had a lasting influence on the economic policies of governments throughout the world. In particular it inspired the economic policies of the Reagan and Bush administrations in the US and of the Conservative government of Margaret Thatcher in the UK. However, the financial crisis has caused many to believe that the theoretical, mathematical models of perfect markets in which so many institutions and governments put their faith have proved deficient and the painful realities of the financial crisis have led to a reconsideration of their foundations.

The foundations of Chicago competition analysis are rigorously theoretical. Even while the S→C→P paradigm was becoming established as the dominant ideology of the day Chicago scholars were decrying it and developing an alternative model based on neoclassical price theory. Although the S→C→P model has never been entirely eclipsed, Chicago School economics produced a 'revolution' in competition thinking in the US and then around the world.[95] Although, in its turn, it has

---

[91] e.g., *Brown Shoe Co* v. *United States*, 370 US 294, 82 S.Ct 1502 (1962); *FTC* v. *Consolidated Foods Corp* 380 US 592, 85 S.Ct 1220 (1965); *FTC* v. *Procter & Gamble Co*, 386 US 568, 87 S.Ct 1224 (1967); *United States* v. *Arnold, Schwinn & Co*, 388 US 365, 87 S.Ct 1856 (1967).

[92] Inter alia, in that they used accounting rates of return to calculate profits although they are unreliable indicators of monopoly profits; that they used cross-sectional data rather than data on a particular industry; that they were not a proper test unless based on long-run rather than short-run performance; and that the researchers did not always consider that the structural variables were not exogenous i.e. that the concentration was itself determined by the economic conditions of the industry. There is modern work with the S→C→P model (notably by John Sutton) which takes account in particular of this last, very serious concern: see further Carlton and Perloff, *Modern Industrial Organization* (cited in n. 43), 246–274.

[93] Hovenkamp, *Federal Antitrust Policy: The Law of Competition and its Practice* (cited in n. 46), 45.

[94] The description here relates to the Chicago School from the 1960s. The macroeconomist Milton Friedman, who opposed Keynesianism and developed monetarism during the 1960s worked at Chicago from 1944 to 1977. Other eminent Chicagoans include George Stigler, Robert Lucas, and Eugene Fama.

[95] See generally R. Posner, 'The Chicago School of Antitrust Analysis' (1979) 127 *Univ. Pa. LR* 92. The main proponents of its antitrust ideas, besides Posner, include George Stigler, Harold Demsetz (although he worked after 1971 at the University of California), Yale Brozen, and Robert Bork.

been strongly criticised, its influence on competition law is profound. In the US the ascendancy of Chicago during the 1970s and 1980s led to a change of direction in the application of antitrust law.[96]

The fundamental Chicago view[97] is that the pursuit of efficiency, by which is meant allocative efficiency[98] as defined by the market, should be the sole goal of competition law. Chicago does not espouse sentimentality for small businesses or the corner store but places trust in the market, which it holds to be robust when it comes to competition. The identity of the winners or losers is irrelevant so long as efficiency is achieved. Indeed, since the writers consider that few barriers to entry exist, that industries frequently benefit from economies of scale, and that businesses are profit-maximisers, the Chicago School places much belief in the ability of the market to correct and achieve efficiency itself without interference from governments or competition laws.

Hovenkamp sets out the basic tenets of the Chicago School in the following extract from an article written in 1985. Although critical of some of the views, Hovenkamp nonetheless describes himself as a 'fellow traveler'.

H. Hovenkamp, 'Antitrust Policy After Chicago' [1985] *Univ. Mich. LR* 213, 226–229

…the following discussion summarizes a few of the model's basic assumptions and principles that have been particularly important in Chicago School antitrust scholarship.

(1) Economic efficiency, the pursuit of which should be the exclusive goal of the antitrust laws, consists of two relevant parts: allocative efficiency and productive efficiency … Occasionally practices that increase a firm's productive efficiency reduce the market's allocative efficiency. For example, construction of a large plant and acquisition of large market share may increase a firm's productive efficiency by enabling it to achieve economies of scale; however, these actions may simultaneously reduce allocative efficiency by facilitating monopoly pricing. A properly defined antitrust policy will attempt to maximize net efficiency gains…

(2) Most markets are competitive, even if they contain a relatively small number of sellers. Furthermore, product differentiation tends to undermine competition far less than was formerly presumed. As a result, neither high market concentration nor product differentiation are the anti-competitive problems earlier oligopoly theorists believed them to be…

(3) Monopoly, when it exists, tends to be self-correcting; that is, the monopolist's higher profits generally attract new entry into the monopolist's market, with the result that the monopolist's position is quickly eroded. About the best that the judicial process can do is hasten the correction process…

(4) 'Natural' barriers to entry are more imagined than real. As a general rule investment will flow into any market where the rate of return is high. The one significant exception consists of barriers to entry that are not natural—that is, barriers that are created by government itself. In most markets the government would be best off if it left entry and exit unregulated…

(5) Economies of scale are far more pervasive than economists once believed, largely because earlier economists looked only at intra-plant or production economics, and neglected economies of distribution.

---

[96] See generally R. Pitofsky (ed.), *How Chicago Overshot the Mark: The Effect of Conservative Economic Analysis on US Antitrust* (Oxford University Press, 2008); D. Crane, 'Chicago, Post-Chicago and Neo-Chicago' (2009) 76 *Univ. Chicago LR* 191 (a review of the Pitofsky book). For a highly critical view of the influence of Chicago on US antitrust policy, see C. E. Mueller, 'Antitrust Economics and the "The Flying Dutchman": How Economists Ruined Antitrust in Reagan's 1980s' (2008) 32 *Antitrust Law and Economics Review* 1.

[97] We can only describe here the views of Chicago School scholars generally. There are considerable divergences of view among them, see further e.g. D. Crane, 'Chicago, Post-Chicago and Neo-Chicago' (cited in n. 96).

[98] Chicago theory holds that the market itself punishes those who are productively inefficient. As the conditions for Pareto-efficiency can rarely be fulfilled, Chicago usually uses 'potential' Pareto-efficiency as the guide, which means a policy whereby the total gains of all those who gain should be greater than the total losses of all those who lose, see Section 3.A.vii, p. 12 ff.

As a result, many more industries than were formerly thought may operate most economically only at fairly high concentration levels...

(6) Business firms are profit-maximizers. That is, their managers generally make decisions that they anticipate will make the firm more profitable than any alternative decision would. The model would not be undermined, however, if it should turn out that many firms are not profit maximizers, but are motivated by some alternative goal, such as revenue maximization, sales maximization, or 'satisficing.'...[99] The integrity of the market efficiency model requires only that a few firms be profit-maximizers. In that case, the profits and market shares of these firms will grow at the expense of other firms in the market...

(7) Antitrust enforcement should be designed in such a way as to penalize conduct precisely to the point that it is inefficient, but to tolerate or encourage it when it is efficient...During the Warren Court era,[100] antitrust enforcement was excessive, and often penalized efficient conduct...

(8) The decision to make the neoclassical market efficiency model the exclusive guide for antitrust policy is nonpolitical.

A clear statement of the view that 'efficiency is all' is set out in Robert Bork's celebrated polemic, *The Antitrust Paradox*.[101]

R. H. Bork, *The Antitrust Paradox: A Policy at War with Itself* (Basic Books, 1978, reprinted with a new Introduction and Epilogue, 1993), 90–91

Antitrust is about the effects of business behavior on consumers. An understanding of the relationship of that behavior to consumer well-being can be gained only through basic economic theory. The economic models involved are essential to all antitrust analysis, but they are simple and require no previous acquaintance with economics to be comprehended. Indeed, since we can hardly expect legislators, judges, and lawyers to be sophisticated economists as well, it is only the fact that the simple ideas of economics are powerful and entirely adequate to this field that makes it conceivable for the law to frame and implement useful policy.

Consumer welfare is greatest when society's economic resources are allocated so that consumers are able to satisfy their wants as fully as technological constraints permit. Consumer welfare, in this sense, is merely another term for the wealth of the nation. Antitrust thus has a built-in preference for material prosperity, but it has nothing to say about the ways prosperity is distributed or used. Those are matters for other laws. Consumer welfare, as the term is used in antitrust, has no sumptuary or ethical component, but permits consumers to define by their expression of wants in the marketplace what things they regard as wealth. Antitrust litigation is not a process for deciding who should be rich or poor, nor can it decide how much wealth should be expended to reduce pollution or undertake to mitigate the anguish of the cross-country skier at the desecration wrought by snowmobiles. It can only increase collective wealth by requiring that many lawful products, whether skis or snowmobiles, be produced and sold under conditions most favorable to consumers.

The role of the antitrust laws, then, lies at that stage of the economic process in which production and distribution of goods and services are organized in accordance with the scale of values that consumers

---

[99] For 'satisficing' see n. 28.

[100] Earl Warren was Chief Justice of the Supreme Court from 1953 until 1968.

[101] Robert Bork (1927–2012) was President Reagan's nominee for the Supreme Court in 1987 but he was rejected by the Senate.

choose by their relative willingness to purchase. The law's mission is to preserve, improve, and reinforce the powerful economic mechanisms that compel businesses to respond to consumers. 'From a social point of view,' as Frank H. Knight puts it, 'this process may be viewed under two aspects, (a) the assignment or allocation of the available productive forces and materials among the various lines of industry, and (b) the effective *co-ordination* of the various means of production in each industry into such groupings as will produce the greatest result.' ...

These two factors may conveniently be called *allocative efficiency* and *productive efficiency* ... These two types of efficiency make up the overall efficiency that determines the level of our society's wealth, or consumer welfare. The whole task of antitrust can be summed up as the effort to improve allocative efficiency without impairing productive efficiency so greatly as to produce either no gain or a net loss in consumer welfare. That task must be guided by basic economic analysis, otherwise the law acts blindly upon forces it does not understand and produces results it does not intend.

It should be noted from the second paragraph of this extract that Bork equates 'consumer welfare' with the 'wealth of the nation'. Thus his conception of 'consumer welfare' is what is usually called 'social' or 'total' welfare.[102] The confusion arising from this use of the term 'consumer welfare' has been called the 'Chicago trap' and should be borne in mind when reading Chicago School sources.[103] Bork pursued his conception of consumer welfare in the extract from the Epilogue to his book when it was reprinted in 1993. Critics had argued that efficiency could not be the sole pursuit of competition law without becoming inconsistent with other government policies, such as those pursuing distributive goals. Bork made a riposte to this.

R. H. Bork, *The Antitrust Paradox: A Policy at War with Itself* (Basic Books, 1978, reprinted with a new Introduction and Epilogue, 1993), 426–429

Of the two, the issue of the goals of antitrust seems to have fared somewhat better than the law's capacity to deal with economics. Fifteen years ago, the question of what goals antitrust serves, and hence what factors a judge may properly consider in deciding an antitrust case, had not been addressed in any systemic fashion. The answers given by courts and commentators were hardly more than slogans of a more or less appealing variety, depending on your taste for populist rhetoric. Though the preservation of competition was often cited as the aim of the law, there seemed no agreed definition of what, for the purposes of antitrust, competition is.

'Competition,' the courts assured us, meant the preservation or comfort of small businesses, the advancement of first amendment values, the preservation of political democracy, the preservation of local ownership, and so on ad infinitum. Judges could and did choose among the items they had invented and placed in this grab bag in order to legislate freely. Cornucopias have their attractions but, when it comes to finding and applying a policy to guide adjudication, horns of plenty make anything resembling a rule of law impossible.

The argument of this book, of course, is that competition must be understood as the maximization of consumer welfare or, if you prefer, economic efficiency. That requires economic reasoning because courts must balance, when they conflict, possible losses of efficiency in the allocation of resources with possible gains in the productive use of those resources. In a word, the goal is maximum economic efficiency

---

[102] See Section 3.A.vii, p. 12.

[103] See K. Cseres, *Competition Law and Consumer Protection* (Kluwer Law International, 2005) 331–332; P. Akman, 'Consumer versus "Customer": the Devil in the Detail' (2010) 37 *Journal of Law and Society* 315.

to make us as wealthy as possible. The distribution of that wealth or the accomplishment of noneconomic goals are the proper subjects of other laws and not within the competence of judges deciding antitrust cases.

By and large, with some ambiguity at times, the more recent cases have adopted a consumer welfare model. Aside from some explicit statements to that effect, the best evidence for the proposition is that courts now customarily speak the language of economics rather than pop sociology and political philosophy. If the conversion from a multi-goal jurisprudence is not complete, it is nevertheless very substantial. Explicit opposition to the consumer welfare thesis comes less from judges than from the academics. The objections are generally of two kinds: denial that an exclusive consumer welfare focus is to be found in the various antitrust statutes; and insistence that such a policy is not desirable.

…A different line of attack comes from those who observe, quite correctly, that people value things other than consumer welfare, and, therefore, quite incorrectly, that antitrust ought not be confined to advancing that goal. As non sequiturs go, that one is world class. There may be someone identified with the Chicago School who thinks all human activity can be analyzed in terms of economics and efficiency, but that is not true of most Chicagoans and certainly constitutes no part of my argument. No one body of law can protect everything that people value. If antitrust could, we would need no other statutes. If we trace the implications of the proposition, it results in judges deciding cases as if the Sherman Act said: 'A restraint of trade shall consist of any contract, combination, or conspiracy that fails to produce, in the eyes of the court, the optimum mix of consumer welfare and other good things that Americans want.' That is inevitably the result of bringing into judicial consideration an open-ended list of attractive-sounding goals to be weighed against consumer welfare.

Nor is there any force to the argument that the consumer welfare cannot be the exclusive mission of antitrust since that mission will be rendered less effective unless all other government policies pursue the same goal. Of course, antitrust will be less effective in promoting consumer welfare if government simultaneously subsidizes small business. A tariff policy designed to keep American companies viable will be less effective if government allows foreign competitors to set up manufacturing operations in the United States. That fact does not state a reason for a judge to alter the way he construes the tariff laws or other laws that apply to foreign companies' operations here. Many statutory policies conflict to some degree with other statutory policies. Whether or not they should do so, and to what degree, is a subject for legislation rather than adjudication.

In any event, no matter what policy goals or combination of goals one attributes to antitrust, the effectiveness of the law in forwarding those policies will be diminished by other public policies. That fact tells us nothing about how judges should go about deciding cases under the antitrust statutes.

The following extract is from the 2001 second edition of Posner's seminal book first published in 1976. The author is taking issue with the 'populist' view that would seek to use competition laws to promote goals other than efficiency and addresses the issue of using competition law to promote the interests of small business.

R. A. Posner, *Antitrust Law* (2nd edn, University of Chicago Press, 2001), 25

Antitrust enforcement is not only an ineffectual, but a perverse, instrument for trying to promote the interests of small business as a whole. Antitrust objectives and the objectives of small business people are incompatible at a very fundamental level. The best overall antitrust policy from a small-business standpoint is no antitrust policy. By driving a wedge between the prices and the costs of the larger firms in the market (a market cannot be effectively cartelized unless the large firms in it participate in the cartel), monopoly enables the smaller firms to survive even if their costs are higher than those of the large firms. The only kind of antitrust policy that would benefit small business would be one that sought to prevent large firms from underpricing less efficient small firms by sharing their lower costs with consumers in the form of lower prices. Apart from raising in acute form the question whether society should promote small business at the expense of the consumer, such a policy would be unworkable because it would require comprehensive and continuing supervision of the prices of large firms. There are no effective shortcuts. For example, if mergers between large firms are forbidden because of concern that they will enable the firms resulting from such mergers to take advantage of economies of scale and thereby underprice smaller firms operating at a less efficient scale, one or more of the larger firms will simply expand until the efficient scale of operation is reached.

Perhaps the most contentious of all Chicago School claims is that the pursuit of efficiency as the sole goal of competition law is non-political. The essential argument is that since competition policy is dictated only by microeconomics it is ideology-free. The adoption of such a policy is, however, in itself ideological. Chicago proclaims itself as neutral because it believes only in market forces. The idea that this is an apolitical stance is challenged by Fox and Sullivan in an article published in 1987. In particular, the authors stress that the law should not only be about economics. Rather, economics should be used as a tool to support the system which is aimed at supporting consumers and a dynamic system of competition law. The Chicagoans' view of economics itself reflects a vision of what society we should live in.

E. M. Fox and L. A. Sullivan, 'Antitrust—Retrospective and Prospective: Where Are We Coming From? Where Are we Going?' (1987) 62 *New York Univ LR* 936, 956–959

Economists have both praised and criticized mainstream antitrust law. Many economists, especially those with Chicago leanings, think that because antitrust is about markets, as is microeconomics, antitrust law should be economics. They react as though the law is out of kilter whenever it diverges from their particular economic insight; and they so react regardless of whether the law diverges because empirical processes have not validated factual assumptions, or because the law has identified social goals other than or in addition to allocative efficiency. Law is not economics. Nor were the antitrust laws adopted to squeeze the greatest possible efficiency out of business. Nonetheless, we would not want an antitrust system that hurts consumers rather than helps them. Most people agree that economics is a tool that can help keep the system on course to help consumers and to facilitate dynamic competition. Economic analysts have provided important insights into why business acts the way it does, and what the probable effect of a practice will be on the marketplace. Despite the consensus that economics can play a supporting role, the Chicago School, in the name of law and economics, has waged ideological warfare, assaulting antitrust itself. Commitment and belief fuel the debate on both sides. While others seem aware that the debate is about values, Chicagoans seem not to be. They often claim the imperative of science for their policy prescriptions. But on points of basic difference between Chicagoans on the one hand and realists or traditionalists on the other, the Chicago assertions are not provable. They are not matters of fact. They cannot be derived from economics. The basic difference between Chicagoans and traditionalists is a difference of vision about what kind of society we are and should strive to be . . .

. . . The Chicago beliefs are compatible with only the most minimal law. In antitrust, the most minimal law, given the existence of the statutes, is law that proscribes only clear cartel agreements and mergers that would create a monopoly in a market that included all perceptible potential competition. Let us review the characteristics that underlie this minimalist approach to antitrust.

First, the Chicago School claims that it has the right prescription for efficiency. This is unprovable; some would say highly suspect, and others would say wrong. Economic experts have intense debates as to what scheme is likely to produce a more efficient or a more dynamic, inventive economy. Economics does not provide a conclusive answer. Within a wide range, the answer is indeterminate…

Second, the Chicago School always opts for norms that presuppose that markets are robust and that firms, imbued with perfect knowledge and risk neutrality, move their resources quickly and easily to the most profitable opportunity. Data about how people actually behave belie these assumptions…Yet Chicagoans continue to press for legal rules that accept these assumptions as true…It is this mind-set that led Judge Posner to dissent in a recent case in which a prisoner was blinded in jail and sued prison authorities for neglect…A majority of the appellate court thought that appointment of counsel was improperly denied to the prisoner, but Judge Posner disagreed…Assuming the existence of a market for lawyers that would function like a Chicago model market, Judge Posner argued that if the prisoner's case was any good, a lawyer would have taken it on contingency. The fact that no lawyer did 'proved' that the prisoner's case lacked merit…[104]

Third, the Chicago School defines competition in terms of efficiency; defines efficiency as the absence of inefficiency; defines inefficiency in terms of artificial output restraint;…and thus concludes that any activity that does not demonstrably limit output is efficient and therefore pro-competitive. Thus, it 'proves' that almost all business activity is efficient—a neat trick.

Fox and Sullivan thus question (long before the financial crisis) the bases of many of the views on which the Chicago concept of efficiency is hung and hence challenge its faith in the ability of the market to correct itself. Criticisms have also been made of the Chicagoans' belief that barriers to entry are rare outside government regulation,[105] that potential competition polices the market as well as existing competitors because, in the absence of barriers to entry, monopolists will be challenged by new entrants if they reap monopoly profits, and that most markets are competitive. The Chicago model is criticised for being 'static' and concentrating too much on long-term effects rather than on short-term effects and of competition as a process. Above all, it is argued that the neoclassical market efficiency model of Chicago is too simple to account for or predict business behaviour in the real world. However, note should be taken of the views of the American scholar in the extract[106] that one should be wary of over-simplistic depictions of the Chicago School as some kind of extremist ideology. Whatever criticisms can be and have been made of the Chicago School, it undeniably changed competition law thinking profoundly. It placed rigorous economic analysis at the centre of competition law. After Chicago it is impossible to accept the S→C→P paradigm without qualification, or not to think of efficiency as a central concern. It shed new light on many matters.

(ii) Post-Chicago

'Post-Chicago School' scholars recognise that economics may give indications of what questions to ask, but does not always yield definitive answers, and certainly not answers which are necessarily value-free. Post-Chicago (or 'new industrial economics') stresses the effect that the strategic conduct of firms can have in different market situations. Post-Chicago makes heavy use of game theory (see Section 5.C) to examine how firms may indulge in strategic entry deterrence. So, for example, the Chicago belief that predatory pricing is rarely rational conduct[107] is replaced in Post-Chicago analysis by considering that in some circumstances it can be adopted as a rational strategy to prevent

---

[104] The case concerned was *Merritt v. Faulkner*, 697 F. 2d 761 (7th Cir.).

[105] See the discussion of barriers to entry in Section 10.C, p. 85 ff.

[106] Kovacic in Section 5.B.iv.

[107] Chicago scholars differ about this: Bork said 'never' rational, but others are less absolutist.

new competitors entering the market,[108] and the Chicago 'single monopoly profit theorem' has been countered with new thinking about leverage.[109] In short, Post-Chicago competition scholarship admits of more complexities than either the Harvard or Chicago approaches and 'helps observers understand why conduct thought benign in light of Chicago School teaching might in fact lessen competition'.[110] It also attempts to deal with the importance of dynamic competition.[111] However, Post-Chicago analysis is heavily theoretical and makes greater demands on competition authorities and decision-makers because of the very wealth of models and theories that may fall to be considered, and it is has been criticised for offering little by way of empirical verification and therefore of being of limited practical utility.[112]

(iii) Neo-Chicago

'Neo-Chicago' is a recently coined term to describe those who are faithful to the core tenets of the Chicago School but take on board the criticisms made of it and present an intellectually reinvigorated Chicago.[113]

(iv) Conclusion

The debate about the ideas of Chicago wages as passionately as ever. The recent book edited by Pitofsky[114] elicited a fierce defence from those who consider that Pitofsky (as distinct from some of the contributors to that volume) perpetuated the misrepresentation of Chicago as an extremist conservative ideology. Many scholars take the view that labels of 'Chicago', 'Post-Chicago', and so on are no longer helpful and should be abandoned other than in a historical context. There is much to be said for this. The distinction between Harvard, Chicago, and Post-Chicago could always be drawn too starkly. A leading American scholar and member (and former Chairman) of the FTC has counselled caution against seeing the history of US antitrust in rigid Harvard/Chicago/Post-Chicago terms and considers that doing so distorts the understanding not only of the evolution of US antitrust but also of its relationship with EU antitrust policy. Rather, many scholars and judges have held more nuanced views and cannot be as neatly pigeon-holed as some descriptions of their work have suggested.

William E. Kovacic, 'The Intellectual DNA of Modern U.S. Competition Law For Dominant Firm Conduct: The Chicago/ Harvard Double Helix' [2007] 1(1) *Columbia Business Law Review* 8–10

More recent developments in trans-Atlantic competition policy have accentuated my doubts about the conventional Chicago/Post-Chicago framework. In reading the work of foreign scholars … and participating

---

[108] See Chap. 7.

[109] Important in the debate about practices such as 'tying' by dominant undertakings, see Chap. 7.

[110] E. Gellhorn, W. Kovacic, S. Calkins, *Antitrust Law and Economics* (5th edn, West, 2004), 97; see further A. Cucinotta, R. Pardolesi, and R. van Denley Bergh, *Post-Chicago Developments in Antitrust Law* (Edward Elgar, 2002).

[111] See Section 3.A.viii, p. 14.

[112] See Crane, 'Chicago, Post-Chicago and Neo-Chicago' (cited in n. 96); B. H. Kobayashi and T. J. Muris, 'Chicago, Post-Chicago, and Beyond: Time to Let Go of the 20th Century' (2012) 78 *Antitrust LJ* 147; cf. D. Rubenfield, 'On the Foundations of Antitrust Law and Economics' in Pitofsky, (ed.), *How Chicago Overshot the Mark* (cited in n. 96), 51, 55, who considers that 'This new post-Chicago School perspective should be given substantial credit for its influence on courts and the competition authorities' (i.e. the courts and authorities of the US).

[113] D. S. Evans and A. Jorge Padilla, 'Designing Antitrust Rules for Assessing Unilateral Practices: A Neo-Chicago Approach' (2005) 72 *U. Chi. LR* 7; Crane, 'Chicago, Post-Chicago and Neo-Chicago' (cited in n. 96).

[114] Pitofsky, (ed.), *How Chicago Overshot the Mark* (cited in n. 96).

in international conferences I have become convinced that the Chicago/Post-Chicago School framework seriously distorts discussions about U.S. abuse of dominance policy and its relationship to EU competition policy. The tendency is to explain U.S. experience in terms of a Chicago/Post-Chicago dialectic and the subsequent preoccupation with branding ideas with Chicago or Post-Chicago labels prevents Americans and Europeans from understanding why the U.S. system developed as it did and from seeing more accurately why their systems differ...

...The first problem is the implication that Chicago and Post-Chicago perspectives have little in common. The frequently-voiced suggestion that the Chicago School and the Post-Chicago School are antonyms overlooks important connections between the two bodies of thought. Many Post-Chicago School scholars build upon theoretical or empirical propositions advanced by Chicago School exponents...Some Chicago scholars appear to acknowledge the value of Post-Chicago ideas, at least so far as finding similarities between the modern Post-Chicago scholarship and early Chicago School views on antitrust policy...The tendency to focus on differences between these schools obscures how developments in competition policy, both in theory and practice, often are incremental and cumulative, with significant borrowings across bodies of thought that sometimes, or often, are depicted as being distinct and self-contained...

...A second problem with explaining modern U.S. antitrust experience as a Chicago School/Post-Chicago School contest is the suggestion that each school is monolithic and single-minded. Neither body of literature features such a uniformity of preferences...

...A third problem with framing the modern policy debate in terms of a Chicago School/Post-Chicago School dialectic is that it incorrectly attributes antitrust perspectives to a single source when they instead stemmed from more diverse intellectual influences. The perceived origins of ideas can affect views about whether the ideas are legitimate. One way to discredit an idea is to depict its brand and the originators of the brand as violating norms of reasonable thought. In modern discourse about competition policy, commentators sometimes depict Chicago School advocates as extremists, close-minded fanatics, or mere "ideologues"...If one agrees that Chicago School views are unduly extreme, it is a short step to conclude that a competition policy system assumed to be guided chiefly by Chicago School views is itself extremist, unsoundly ideological, and unworthy of emulation.

From the point of view of EU competition law what is important is not the labels and the politics, but the ideas, theories, and insights which this rich period of (mainly) American discourse has yielded and which inform so many of the debates which rage over the application of the EU rules, as discussed in the subsequent chapters of this book.

C. GAME THEORY

Game theory is central to much modern industrial organisation theory and stems from work done in the 1940s by von Neumann and Morgenstern.[115] It models the strategic interactions between firms—their conflict and cooperation—as 'games' in which each firm plans its own strategy, for example with regard to pricing or output, in the light of assumptions about the strategy which will be adopted by its competitors. Game theory is in particular an important tool in analysing the conduct of oligopolies and is dealt with further in that context in Chapter 9. It is important in Post-Chicago analysis, as already explained.[116]

---

[115] J. von Neumann and O. Morgenstern, *The Theory of Games and Economic Behaviour* (Princeton University Press, 1944).

[116] In Section 5.B.ii.

D. CONTESTABLE MARKETS THEORY

The theory of contestable markets[117] places the main emphasis on freedom of entry to, and exit from, a market. It attaches importance not to the structure of the market but to its contestability. So long as 'hit-and-run' entry by competitors is possible the behaviour of firms operating on the market will be constrained and they will perform efficiently and price competitively. The minimum conditions for a contestable market are instantaneous entry and costless exit and, crucially, the inability of the incumbent to respond to entry by another competitor by lowering its prices. This last point is vital because otherwise the incumbent firm can keep its prices at monopoly level and only lower them when it needs to respond to competition. In reality, again, the conditions for perfect contestability are not often found.[118] However, the term 'contestable market', meaning one with low barriers to entry and exit where the threat of entry does significantly constrain the incumbent, is used more loosely and is now often found in competition law discussion.[119]

E. RAISING RIVALS' COSTS

Raising rivals' costs describes strategic behaviour of a firm which is designed to raise the costs of its rivals relative to its own.[120] It normally requires some degree of market power (or, for some strategies, political power or influence). It includes interfering with the production or selling methods of rivals, lobbying for or supporting government regulation which has a differential impact on the rivals' costs, raising the price of inputs, tying, raising switching costs (so that customers find it difficult or expensive to change to the rival's goods or services), and indulging in rapid product innovation in primary markets.[121] Some behaviour which raises rivals' costs may also increase welfare and whether competition law should sanction or allow it often depends on the particular circumstance of the case. In the following chapters of this book we will come across many examples of behaviour which can raise rivals' costs.

F. TRANSACTION COST ECONOMICS

Transaction cost economics is based on the theory first developed by Ronald Coase in *The Nature of the Firm*.[122] Transaction costs are the costs a firm incurs by trading with other parties. Coase's argument was that a firm can choose to organise its activities by doing things itself (so internalising the costs) or by using other parties to do them (i.e. using the market). A firm producing widgets may therefore have a choice between producing the inputs necessary for widget production itself or obtaining them from other parties. Similarly it may have a choice between doing its own distribution or using independent distributors. The first of these options in each case involves vertical integration while the second involves agreements with others. Which is chosen will depend on its comparative efficiency. The insight from transaction cost economics for competition law is that competition law should not be designed so as to force firms to take less efficient options for doctrinaire reasons of promoting more competitive markets.

---

[117] W. J. Baumol, J. Panzar, and R. Willig, *Contestable Markets and the Theory of Industry Structure* (Harcourt Brace Jovanovich, 1982); W. J. Baumol, 'Contestable Markets: An Uprising in the Theory of Industry Structure' (1982) 72 *Amer. Economic Rev.* 1.

[118] Sunk costs, for example, will be a hindering factor, see Section 10.C.iii.a, p. 89.

[119] S. Bishop and M. Walker, *The Economics of EC Competition Law* (3rd edn, Sweet & Maxwell, 2010), 3.35.

[120] T. G. Krattenmaker and S. C. Salop, 'Anti-competitive Exclusion; Raising Rivals' Costs to Achieve Power Over Price' (1986) 96 *Yale LJ* 209.

[121] See D. W. Carlton and J. M. Perloff, *Modern Industrial Organization* (4th edn, Pearson Addison Wesley, 2005), 371–379.

[122] (1937) 4 *Economica* 38. See also the work of Oliver Williamson, particularly 'Transaction Cost Economics' in R. Schmalensee and R. D. Willig (eds.), *1 Handbook of Industrial Organization* (1989) 135.

Transaction cost research has identified efficiency reasons for which firms use various forms of internal organization and has underscored the importance of contractual techniques in curbing opportunistic behavior that, if left unchecked, undermines business arrangements that increase efficiency. By showing that the main purpose of many forms of economic organization—for example, joint ventures, vertical integration, and restrictive distribution contracts—often is to reduce costs, transaction costs scholars have spurred a reevaluation of antitrust doctrines that have treated such arrangements with hostility.[123]

Transaction cost economics was taken on board by the Post-Chicago School, but in contrast to other ideas which Post-Chicago adopts, such as the anti-competitive effects of strategic behaviour, transaction cost economics points to a *less* expansive application of competition rules.

G. WORKABLE COMPETITION

The theory of 'workable competition' was developed in the 1940s.[124] It was associated with the Harvard School and held that as perfect competition was usually impossible to attain competition policy should aim to produce the best competitive arrangement practically attainable. This too presented difficulties. The criteria by which workability can be assessed may be divided into structure, conduct, and performance criteria but it may be hard to assess whether or not they have been satisfied in any particular industry; and if some are satisfied and some not, it may be hard to decide whether workability has been attained without making subjective value judgements.[125] Workable competition, in short, does not provide a very workable basis for developing a sound competition policy. The Court of Justice (CJ) referred to workable competition in 1976 in *Metro I*, equating it with 'the degree of competition necessary to ensure the observance of the basic requirements and the attainment of the objectives of the EEC Treaty'.[126]

H. THE AUSTRIAN SCHOOL

The Austrian School embraces a theory of dynamic competition which goes beyond that advanced by Schumpeter.[127] As with Chicago, the Austrian School's conception of competition policy is just one facet of a wider school of economic theory,[128] one of whose most influential voices in the twentieth century was von Hayek.[129] von Hayek believed in untrammelled free markets and the ability of potential competition to prevent the long-run exploitation of monopoly power. The implications of this were that competition laws should not interfere with the competitive process, not even by prohibiting cartels.[130]

---

[123] E. Gellhorn, W. Kovacic, S. Calkins, *Antitrust Law and Economics* (5th edn, West, 2004), 101. See also Van den Bergh and Camesasca, *European Competition Law and Economics: A Comparative Perspective* (cited in n. 48), 94–98; P. L. Joskow, 'The Role of Transaction Cost Economics in Antitrust and Public Utility Regulatory Policies' (1991) 7 *JL Economic & Org* 53.

[124] J. M. Clark, 'Towards a Concept of Workable Competition' (1940) 30 *American Economic Review* 241–256; see also S. Sosnick, 'A Critique of Concepts of Workable Competition' (1958) 72 *Quarterly Journal of Economics* 380–423.

[125] See further F. M. Scherer and D. Ross, *Industrial Market Structure and Economic Performance* (3rd edn, Houghton Mifflin, 1990), 52–55; Van den Bergh and Camesasca, *European Competition Law and Economics: A Comparative Perspective* (cited in n. 48), 70–73.

[126] Case 26/76, *Metro v. Commission (No. 1)* [1977] ECR 1875, para. 20.

[127] See Section 3.A.viii, p. 14.

[128] Originating with Carl Menger, Professor of Economics at the University of Vienna, 1873–1903.

[129] Friedrich von Hayek held chairs from 1931 at various universities: in London (the London School of Economics), Germany, and Austria and, from 1950 to 1962, at the University of Chicago.

[130] See further Van den Bergh and Camesasca, *European Competition Law and Economics: A Comparative Perspective* (cited in n. 48), 88.

I. EFFECTIVE COMPETITION

The concept of *effective competition* is important in EU competition law. A dominant position is defined for the purposes of Article 102[131] as involving an undertaking's power to 'prevent effective competition being maintained on the relevant market'[132] and under the EU Merger Regulation the grounds for the prohibition of a merger are that it would 'significantly impede effective competition'.[133] The General Court (GC) said in *GlaxoSmithKline* that 'the competition referred to in Article 3(1)(g) EC[134] and Article 81 EC [now Article 101 TFEU] is taken to mean effective competition, that is to say, the degree of competition necessary to ensure the attainment of the objectives of the Treaty'.[135] Bishop and Walker explain that 'effective competition' should be outcome-based.

> ### S. Bishop and M. Walker, *The Economics of EC Competition Law* (3rd edn, Sweet & Maxwell, 2010), 20–21
>
> 2-008 ... The economic goal of EC competition law is the protection and promotion of effective competition. But this is a goal only because of the benefits that it delivers to European consumers. What matters therefore are the outcomes for consumers that competition in a particular market delivers—not the particular form that the competition process takes. Whether a market is characterized by effective competition or not therefore depends on the outcomes it produces.
>
> This raises the question of what outcomes are produced by effective competition and how can they be distinguished from those produced by less than effective competition. The practical application of competition law ought to be interested less in outcomes that are desirable in some theoretical, abstract sense and more in outcomes that are feasible for regulatory intervention to achieve... To draw this distinction requires consideration of the various economic models of competition and the implications each type of model has for consumer welfare.

Effective competition is therefore the means to an end, not the end itself.

6. ORDOLIBERALISM

Ordoliberalism is not a just school of competition or economic theory but an entire political and economic philosophy. However, it has important implications for competition policy and it is therefore convenient to mention it here before looking in Section 7, and in later chapters, at its influence on EU competition law.

Ordoliberalism was conceived in Germany in the 1930s and nurtured at the University of Freiburg during the Nazi era.[136] It became a key element of post-war thinking in Germany, envisaging a new

---

[131] One of the two main EU competition law articles, previously Art. 82 (and before 1999, Art. 86). See Chaps. 5–7.

[132] Case 2/76, *United Brands* v. *Commission* [1978] ECR 207, para. 65; Case 85/76, *Hoffmann-La Roche & Co AG* v. *Commission* [1979] ECR 461, para. 38.

[133] Council Reg. 139/2004 [2004] OJ L124/1, Art. 2(3). The previous Merger Regulation, Council Reg. 4064/89 [1990] OJ L257/13, also employed the concept of 'effective competition', see Chap. 15.

[134] For the fate of Art. 3(1)(g) under the Treaty of Lisbon see Section 7.B, p. 37–38 ff.

[135] Case T-168/01, *GlaxoSmithKline Services Unlimited* v. *Commission* [2006] ECR II-2969, para. 109. The Treaty referred to here was the EC Treaty. For the objectives of the EC Treaty, see Section 7.B, p. 36 ff.

[136] Hence its alternative name of the 'Freiburg School'. The leading ordoliberal theorists were the economist Walter Eucken and the lawyers Franz Böhm and Hanns Grossmann-Doerth. See further D. Gerber, 'Constitutionalizing the Economy: German Neo-liberalism, Competition Law and the 'New Europe' (1994) 42 *American Journal of Comparative Law* 25.

relationship between law and the economic system and holding that competition is necessary for economic well-being and that economic freedom is necessary for political freedom.[137] It advocates an 'economic constitution' whereby competition and economic freedom are embedded into the law so that there is neither unconstrained private power nor discretionary governmental intervention in the economy. Competition law, it holds, should create and protect the conditions of competition. It follows from this that competition is a value in itself and not just a means by which purely economic objectives—such as efficiency—are to be achieved. An ordoliberal approach leads to the kind of competition policy already described where competitors and small and medium-sized enterprises are protected for their own sake regardless of the effects on efficiency and firms with market power have to behave 'as if' the market was competitive. Ordoliberalism prizes the freedom of all citizens to be able to enter and compete on markets. This is often called the principle of 'economic freedom', as already explained.

7. EU COMPETITION LAW

A. GENERAL

The first European competition rules were Articles 65 and 66 of the Treaty of Paris of 1951, which created the European Coal and Steel Community (ECSC).[138] The Treaty of Rome, which established the European Economic Community (EEC), and the competition rules set within it came into force in 1958. However, the EEC competition rules were not enforced by the Community institutions until after Regulation 17 was passed four years later.[139]

We have already seen that there are many different objectives which competition laws can pursue. One of the most extraordinary things about EU competition law is that 50 years after Regulation 17 came into force there is still no consensus about which of these it is trying to achieve (apart from the single market dimension, a concern unique to EU law).[140] The search for the objectives of EU competition law is not a theoretical pursuit of merely academic interest but a matter of crucial practical importance as it affects how the competition rules are interpreted and how they are applied and enforced in individual cases. As Bork wrote in relation to US law: 'Antitrust policy cannot be made rational until we are able to give a firm answer to one question: What is the point of the law—what are its goals?'[141] The overall purpose of EU competition law is to contribute to achieving the aims of the Union; the issue, therefore, is what objectives competition law pursues in order to do this. It

---

[137] W. Möschel, 'Competition Policy from an Ordo Point of View' in A. Peacock and H. Willgerodt (eds.), *German Neo-Liberals and the Social Market Economics* (MacMillan, 1989), 142.

[138] They were based on a draft prepared, at the behest of Jean Monnet, by the Harvard antitrust lawyer Robert Bowie, who was an adviser to John McCloy, the US High Commissioner for Germany and a close ally of Monnet. Monnet, a French economist and public official (Deputy Secretary-General of the League of Nations 1919–1923) is considered to be, with Robert Schuman, one of the founding fathers of the EU. For an account of the history of the ECSC see D. Spiernburg and R. Poidevin, *The History of the High Authority of the European Coal and Steel Community: Supranationality in Operation* (Weidenfeld & Nicolson, 1994). The ECSC competition provisions were the pattern for the later EEC ones.

[139] [1959–62] OJ Spec. Ed. 87. See Chap. 2. The EU competition rules also apply to the EEA, see Chap. 2.

[140] P. Akman, 'The Role of "Freedom" in EU Competition Law' (2013) 33 *Legal Studies* (December). See generally e.g. C.-D. Ehlermann and L. Laudati (eds.), *European Competition Law Annual 1997: Objectives of Competition Policy* (Hart Publishing, 1998); and more recently L. Parret, 'The Objectives of EU Competition Law and Policy' (2010) 6 *European Competition Journal* 339; R. Nazzini, *The Foundations of European Union Competition Law, The Objectives and Principles of Article 10* (Oxford University Press, 2011); P. Akman, *The Concept of Abuse in EU Competition Law* (Hart Publishing, 2012). For the history of the EU competition rules see D. Gerber, 'Constitutionalizing the Economy: German Neo-liberalism, Competition Law and the New Europe' (1994) 42 *American Journal of Comparative Law* 25; D. Gerber, *Law and Competition in Twentieth Century Europe: Protecting Prometheus* (Clarendon Press, 1998); A. Weitbrecht, 'From Freiburg to Chicago and beyond—the first 50 years of European competition law' (2008) *ECLR* 81.

[141] R. Bork, *The Antitrust Paradox: A Policy at War With Itself* (Basic Books, 1978, reprinted with a new Introduction and Epilogue, 1993), 50.

has been pointed out that it is useful to distinguish between ultimate and intermediate goals.[142] The ultimate objective might be social welfare, consumer welfare, or economic freedom, for example, whereas intermediate goals might be to maintain an effective competitive structure, or protect the process of competition, in order to achieve that ultimate objective.

In the last 50 years the economic and political environment has dramatically changed, as the Commission said in its 2010 Report on Competition Policy. That means that competition policy rules and procedures have undergone a constant process of adaptation in order to contribute to the major objectives of the EU (there described by the Commission as 'building the single market, making it deliver for consumers and achieving a competitive social market').[143] Whether that means that the *objectives* of competition law have changed is another matter. It has been persuasively argued that '[i]f the Member States have assigned certain objectives and a given content to the EU competition rules, it is for the Member States alone to change those objectives and that content, and not for bureaucrats or judges backed up by the vocal support of certain quarters of private practice, business, and academia'.[144] The difficulty, however, is ascertaining what objective(s) the Member States *did* assign to the competition rules in the Treaties.

For a long time it was thought that there was a strong ordoliberal influence from the German delegation on the drafting of the EEC competition provisions (particularly what is now Article 102)[145] but recent meticulous research on the *travaux préparatoires* has shown that this has been overstated.[146] The *travaux préparatoires* suggest that ordoliberal goals are not embedded in the rules. The arguments still rage on, however. A division between those who consider that the objectives are (or should be) confined to efficiency and welfare and those who believe that the rules should espouse other goals is over-simplistic. One commentator, for example, argues that the ultimate objective is long-tern social welfare, but incorporates economic freedom and fairness within that concept of welfare.[147] It is submitted that there is much to be said for the conclusion that:

The EC Treaty was indeed a collective work, moulded by various influences, all of which are reflected in the various provisions referring to competition policy. In other words, the Treaty's commitment to 'undistorted competition' enshrines a multi-faceted concept.[148]

The European Commission comes down on one side of the argument. Since the mid-2000s it has adopted the consumer welfare standard in respect of its enforcement of the competition rules. The EU Courts, however, continue to take a broader view of the objectives. In the remainder of this section we examine the objectives of EU competition law in the context of the EU Treaties, the current approach of the Commission, and the case law of the EU Courts. Throughout the remaining chapters of this book we see the arguments about objectives played out in the application of the competition rules in individual cases and in Union instruments.

B. THE OBJECTIVES OF THE EU AND THE ROLE OF THE COMPETITION RULES

An examination of the *raison d'être* of the EU is beyond the scope of a book on competition law. However, it is necessary to look briefly at the aims and objectives of the EU in order to understand the context within which the competition rules are set.

---

[142] L. Parret, 'The Objectives of EU Competition Law and Policy' (cited in n. 140), 340.

[143] Commission Report on Competition Policy 2010, COM(2011) 328 final, 10.6.2011, para. 1.

[144] Nazzini, *The Foundations of European Union Competition Law* (cited in n. 140), 12. This is a comment on the adoption of the consumer welfare standard.

[145] See e.g. Gerber, *Law and Competition in Twentieth Century Europe* (cited in n. 140), 7–8.

[146] P. Akman, 'Searching for the Long-Lost Soul of Article 82' (2009) 29 *OJLS* 267.

[147] Nazzini, *The Foundations of European Union Competition Law* (cited in n. 140).

[148] Geradin et al., *EU Competition Law and Economics* (cited in n. 18), 1.70.

The Preamble to the Treaty of Rome, which established the original entity, the EEC (later the EC),[149] included the recognition that 'the removal of existing obstacles calls for concerted action in order to guarantee steady expansion, balanced trade and fair competition' (this now appears in the Preamble to the TFEU). The objectives of the (E)EC were set out in Article 2 of the Treaty of Rome, which in its final form stated:[150]

The Community shall have as its task, by establishing a common market and an economic and monetary union and by implementing the common policies or activities referred to in Articles 3 and 4, to promote throughout the Community a harmonious, balanced and sustained development of economic activities, a high level of employment and of social protection, equality between men and women, sustainable and non-inflationary growth, a high degree of competitiveness and convergence of economic performance, a high level of protection and improvement of the quality of the environment, the raising of the standard of living and quality of life, and economic and social cohesion and solidarity among Member States.

The Community therefore had a number of wide-ranging and aspirational goals which it sought to achieve through economic integration. The creation of the common market was not an end in itself, but one of the means of achieving the promotion of the matters listed in Article 2. The 'common market', often used colloquially as a synonym for the Community (and now for the EU), means an area where direct and indirect barriers to trade between Member States are removed and a common import and export policy adopted toward the outside world as far as commercial transactions are concerned. The single market is the 'internal' aspect of the common market, and is now defined in Article 26 of the Treaty on the Functioning of the European Union (TFEU):[151]

The internal market shall comprise an area without internal frontiers in which the free movement of goods, persons, services and capital is ensured in accordance with the provisions of these Treaties.[152]

The economic integration of the Member States was taken further by progress towards Economic and Monetary Union (EMU).[153] The single internal market, however, remains the core concept on which economic integration is founded.

The Treaty of Lisbon subsumed the EC into the EU and amended both the TEU and the EC Treaty, now renamed the Treaty on the Functioning of the European Union (TFEU), as from 1 December 2009.[154] The objectives of the EU are now set out in Article 3(1) TEU:

The Union's aim is to promote peace, its values and the well-being of its peoples.

The reference to 'values' relates to Article 2 TEU which states:

The Union is founded on the values of respect for human dignity, freedom, democracy, equality, the rule of law and respect for human rights, including the rights of persons belonging to minorities. These values are common to the Member States in a society in which pluralism, non-discrimination, tolerance, justice, solidarity and equality between women and men prevail.

Article 3(3) states:

The Union shall establish an internal market. It shall work for the sustainable development of Europe based on balanced economic growth and price stability, a highly competitive social market economy, aiming at full

---

[149] See Chap. 2.

[150] Following the coming into force of the Treaty of Amsterdam on 1 May 1999.

[151] Previously Art. 14(2) of the Treaty of Rome (ex Art. 7a). The concept of the 'internal market' was first formally enshrined in the Treaty by the Single European Act 1986 (SEA), which provided for its completion by the end of 1992.

[152] 'These Treaties' refers to the TFEU and the Treaty on European Union (TEU).

[153] The third and final stage of EMU entailed the adoption of a single currency, the Euro.

[154] The specific competition provisions (Articles 101–106) remain substantively unchanged by Lisbon, other than minor amendments such as replacing 'common market' with 'internal market' and an addition to one of the procedural articles, Art. 105 (ex Art. 85 EC), see Chap. 2.

employment and social progress, and a high level of protection and improvement of the quality of the environment. It shall promote scientific and technological advance.

It shall combat social exclusion and discrimination, and shall promote social justice and protection, equality between women and men, solidarity between generations and protection of the rights of the child.

It shall promote economic, social and territorial cohesion, and solidarity among Member States.

It shall respect its rich cultural and linguistic diversity, and shall ensure that Europe's cultural heritage is safeguarded and enhanced.

The new Articles 2 and 3 in the TEU have more to do with social values and aims than purely economic objectives.[155] The words 'highly competitive social market economy' should be noted in particular. It is possible to interpret this as a shift away from 'neo-American' or 'Anglo-Saxon' capitalism towards a more 'Rhine model' capitalism.[156] On taking up office as the new Competition Commissioner in February 2010, Joaquín Almunia said in his Mandate statement:[157]

My vision for competition policy in Europe is linked to my political vision of Europe as an area of peace and stability, freedom and democracy. I see competition policy as a means of strengthening our social market economy, and enhancing its efficiency and fairness.

Article 3 of the Treaty of Rome set out a broad range of the 'activities' of the Community necessary for the purposes set out in Article 2. This included a highly significant provision, Article 3(1)(g), (originally Article 3(f))[158] which stated that the activities should include:

a system ensuring that competition in the internal market is not distorted.

Article 3(1)(g) was of great importance because it embedded the principle of undistorted competition in the fundamental provisions of the Treaty. The Court saw it as the foundation for the specific competition rules and has consistently referred to it in interpreting those rules, most famously in *Continental Can*.[159]

Neither the TEU nor the TFEU replicates Article 3(1)(g). As can be seen from Article 3(3), the provision in the TEU on the establishment of the internal market contains nothing about competition. There is therefore no Treaty provision proclaiming adherence to the principle of undistorted competition.[160] However, the principle *does* appear in one of the Protocols annexed to and forming 'an integral part'[161] of the Treaties. Protocol No. 27 on the Internal Market And Competition states that the High Contracting Parties,

Considering that the internal market as set out in Article 3 of the Treaty on European Union includes a system ensuring that competition is not distorted, Have agreed that: To this end, the Union shall, if necessary, take action under the provisions of the Treaties, including under Article 352 of the Treaty on the Functioning of the European Union.

---

[155] See P. Syrpis, 'The Treaty of Lisbon: Much Ado...But About What?' (2008) 37 *Industrial Law Journal* 219.

[156] Broadly 'Rhine model' capitalism can be characterised by collective achievement, public consensus, and social welfare while 'neo-American' or 'Anglo-Saxon' capitalism is individualistic, unregulated, based on short-term profits, and with a minimal social component: see M. Albert, *Capitalism Against Capitalism* (Whurr Publishers Ltd, 1993).

[157] <http://ec.europa.eu/commission_2010-2014/almunia/about/mandate/index_en.htm>.

[158] And then Art. 3(g). The renumbering was brought about by the Treaties of Maastricht (the TEU) and Amsterdam in 1993 and 1999 respectively. In this book the provision is referred to as 'Art. 3(1)(g)' throughout, unless otherwise indicated. Until the 1993 amendments it read: '*the institution of* a system ensuring that competition in the common market is not distorted' (emphasis added).

[159] Case 6/72, *Europemballage & Continental Can* v. *Commission* [1973] ECR 215, discussed further in Chaps. 5 and 7. See also C-68/94, *French Republic* v. *Commission* [1998] ECR I-1375.

[160] The removal of the reference to free and undistorted competition from the body of the Treaties is attributed to the insistence of President Sarkozy of France. The provision disappeared on the night of 21 June 2007 during the final last-minute negotiations on the Treaty of Lisbon. President Sarkozy was reported as saying at the time, 'Competition as an ideology, as a dogma: what has it done for Europe?', *Financial Times*, 26 June 2007, p. 12.

[161] Article 51 TEU.

Moreover, Article 3(1)(b) TFEU states that one of the areas in which the Union has exclusive competence is:

The establishing of the competition rules necessary for the functioning of the internal market.

It was generally thought by competition lawyers that the cumulative effect of these provisions was to leave the position in respect of 'undistorted competition' unchanged. When the Lisbon Treaty was agreed the Commission immediately issued a Press Release declaring that it would carry on enforcing competition policy as before.[162] That the position is indeed unchanged was confirmed by the CJ in *TeliaSonera*, in giving judgment in a preliminary reference concerning the interpretation of one of the competition articles, Article 102.[163]

Case C-52/09, *Konkurrensverket* v. *TeliaSonera Sverige AB* [2011] ECR I-527

Court of Justice

20 In order to answer those questions, it must be observed at the outset that Article 3(3) TEU states that the European Union is to establish an internal market, which, in accordance with Protocol No 27 on the internal market and competition, annexed to the Treaty of Lisbon (OJ 2010 C 83, p. 309), is to include a system ensuring that competition is not distorted.

21 Article 102 TFEU is one of the competition rules referred to in Article 3(1)(b) TFEU which are necessary for the functioning of that internal market.

22 The function of those rules is precisely to prevent competition from being distorted to the detriment of the public interest, individual undertakings and consumers, thereby ensuring the well-being of the European Union (see, to that effect, Case C-94/00 *Roquette Frères*...paragraph 42).

In describing the major developments in competition policy and enforcement over the last 40 years the Commission said in its 2010 report that there had been a constant process of adaptation in order to contribute to the major objectives of the EU:

Building the Single Market, making it deliver for consumers and achieving a competitive social market economy.[164]

C. THE OBJECTIVES OF EU COMPETITION LAW

The ultimate objective of the competition articles, Articles 101 and 102, must be the same, although the intermediate goals and the way in which they go about achieving them may vary.

(i) The Single Market

As we have seen, competition policy was included in the list of Community activities set out in Article 3 of the Treaty of Rome from the inception of the Community in 1958. It was embedded

---

[162] Memo 07/250, 23 June 2007. For the Commission, the competition community, and some Member States, the inclusion of free and undistorted competition among the Union's fundamental provisions was taken for granted. It was not foreseen that it would be a sticking point in the Treaty negotiations. The episode was a salutary reminder that for some Member States the concept of competition as a central organising principle of European integration was still open to question.

[163] For the substantive issues in this case, see Chap. 7.

[164] Commission Report on Competition Policy 2010, COM(2011)328 final, 10.6.2011, para. 1.

in the Treaty right from the start as part of a set of wide policy instruments oriented towards the objective of European economic integration.[165] Competition policy was thought necessary to underpin the internal market aspect of the common market because there was no point in dismantling, by means of the free movement provisions, State measures which divided the Community territorially and compartmentalised the market if private undertakings could erect and maintain barriers to trade between Member States by carving up markets between them and indulging in anti-competitive practices. Economic integration was therefore promoted both by free movement and by competition.[166]

The EU Courts have repeatedly stressed the fundamental nature of the competition rules in the light of Article 3(1)(g) in achieving the single market. The CJ said in *Eco Suisse*:

However, according to Article [3(1)(g)] EC... Article [101] constitutes a fundamental provision which is essential for the accomplishment of the tasks entrusted to the Community and, in particular, for the functioning of the internal market.[167]

The role of competition policy as an instrument of single market integration is absolutely crucial to an understanding of EU competition law. It differentiates EU law from any other system of competition law, whether in the Member States, the US, or elsewhere. This is seen very clearly, for example, in respect of the law on vertical restraints.[168]

The Commission's Annual Report on Competition Policy for 2000 talked of two objectives of competition policy:

The first objective of competition policy is the maintenance of competitive markets...

The second is the single market objective.... Moreover, the objectives of competition policy have been integrated into the Commission's new strategy for the European single market adopted on 24 November.[169] The aim is to prevent anti-competitive practices from undermining the single market's achievements.

In the 2004 Guidelines on the application of what is now Article 101(3)[170] the Commission formulated the objectives of competition law in a way which conceptualises competition and market

---

[165] See Gerber, *Law and Competition in Twentieth Century Europe* (cited in n. 140), 347–348.

[166] See J. Baquero Cruz, *Between Competition and Free Movement: The Economic Constitutional Law of the European Community* (Hart Publishing, 2002). In general it is true to say that the free movement provisions apply to State measures and the competition provisions to those of private actors. However, this statement masks a number of complexities. First, in some cases the free movement provisions can bind private parties, in particular where 'collective' private action is concerned in the area of free movement of persons and services, such as Case 36/74, *Walrave & Koch v. Association Union Cycliste Internationale* [1974] ECR 1405 and Case 415/93, *Union Royal Belge des Sociétés de Football Association ASBL & others v. Jean-Marc Bosman* [1995] ECR I-4921, (both cases concerned the rules of sporting organisations). Secondly, some situations raise both free movement and competition issues e.g. *Bosman* (on the right of professional football players to move between clubs when out of contract) and *FAPL*, Cases 403/08 and 429/08, *Football Association Premier League v. QC Leisure* and *Karen Murphy v. Media Protection Services Ltd* [2011] ECR I-9083 on the selling of TV rights to the Premier League); see also Case C-303/99, *Wouters v. Algemene Raad van de Nederlandse Order van Advocaten* [2002] ECR I-1577, on the rules of the Dutch Bar, discussed in Chap. 3. Thirdly, it is possible to impugn some State measures on competition grounds and the application of the competition rules to State action has become a significant aspect of competition law in the EU, as discussed in Chap. 8.

[167] Case C-126/97, *Eco Swiss China Time Ltd v. Benetton International NV* [1999] ECR I-3055, [2000] 5 CMLR 816, para. 36. Art. 101 is one of the two main substantive competition articles. See also Case C-453/99, *Courage Ltd v. Crehan* [2001] ECR I-6297, para. 20; Case T-168/01, *GlaxoSmithKline Services Unlimited v. Commission* [2006] ECR II-2969, para. 11 'indispensable for the achievement of the missions entrusted to the Community'.

[168] From Cases 56 & 58/64, *Etablissements Consten SA & Grundig-Verkaufs-GmbH v. Commission* [1966] ECR 299 onwards; see Chap. 11.

[169] This is a reference to the Commission's communication of 24 November 199COM(1999) 642, endorsed by the Helsinki Council, Bull. 12-1999), setting out the strategic objectives of the internal market for the next five years (2000–2004), which were to improve the citizens' quality of life, enhance the efficiency of the EU's product and capital markets, improve the business environment, and exploit the achievements of the internal market in a changing world.

[170] [2004] OJ C101/97, published as part of the package of Notices accompanying Regulation 1/2003.

integration as serving a common end, rather than seeing competition as a means of advancing the single market.[171] They contain an important statement of the objectives of Article 101:[172]

The objective of Article [101] is to protect competition on the market as a means of enhancing consumer welfare and of ensuring an efficient allocation of resources. Competition and market integration serve these ends since the creation and preservation of an open single market promotes an efficient allocation of resources throughout the Community for the benefit of consumers.

This sees both competition and the creation and preservation of the single market as promoting consumer welfare and an efficient allocation of resources[173] (although there are cases where the goals of market integration and consumer welfare have been in conflict). In the Verticals Guidelines (2010) the Commission says:

The objective of Article 101 is to ensure that undertakings do not use agreements—in this context vertical agreements—to restrict competition on the market to the detriment of consumers. Assessing vertical restraints is also important in the context of the wider objective of achieving an integrated internal market. Market integration enhances competition in the European Union. Companies should not be allowed to re-establish private barriers between Member States where State barriers have been successfully abolished.[174]

The continuing importance of the single market goal to competition law is a striking feature of recent case law. In *GlaxoSmithKline* the CJ confirmed that agreements limiting parallel imports have the object of restricting competition contrary to Article 101(1),[175] referring to 'the Treaty's objective of achieving the integration of national markets through the establishment of a single market'.[176] In *Sot. Lélos* the CJ held a dominant undertaking's refusal to supply in order to prevent parallel trade between Member States is *prima facie* an abuse under Article 102 although capable of objective justification;[177] *Pierre Fabre* was driven by the wish to stop contractual provisions (*in casu* selling over the internet) from preventing inter-Member State trade;[178] and the finding in *Football Association Premier League* that the arrangements for selling Premier League TV rights contravened Article 101 as well as the free movement of services provisions was because they resulted in the artificial partitioning of the single market.[179] Further, in the Guidance on Article 102[180] the Commission says that in addition to exclusionary abuses (the subject of the Guidance) it may intervene in relation to 'certain behaviour that undermines the efforts to achieve an integrated internal market'.

---

[171] See n. 173.

[172] 2004 Guidelines [2004] OJ C101/97, para. 13.

[173] As said, e.g., in the quotation from the Commission's 2000 Report on Competition Policy already quoted. For the development of the convergence of competition and market integration see C. D. Ehlermann, 'The Contribution of EC competition policy to the Single Market' (1992) 29 *CMLRev* 257; K. Mortelmans, 'Towards Convergence of the Rules on Free Movement and Competition' (2001) 38 *CMLRev* 613; R. O'Loughlin, 'EC Competition Rules and Free Movement Rules: An Examination of the Parallels and their furtherance by the ECJ *Wouters* Decision' [2003] *ECLR* 62; J. Baquero Cruz, *Between Competition and Free Movement* (cited in n. 166). This does not mean, however, that the single market does not have a *political* function as well.

[174] Guidelines on vertical restraints [2010] OJ C130/1, para. 7.

[175] Case C-501/06 P, *GlaxoSmithKline Services Unlimited* v. *Commission* [2009] ECR I-9291, paras. 59–62, disapproving on this point the judgment of the GC, see Chap. 4.

[176] Case C-501/06 P, *GlaxoSmithKline Services Unlimited* v. *Commission* [2009] ECR I-9291, para. 61.

[177] Case C-468-478/06, *Sot. Lélos kai Sia EE and others* v. *GlaxoSmithKline AEVE Farmakeftikon Proionton* [2008] ECR I-7139, see Chap. 7.

[178] Case C-439/09, *Pierre Fabre Dermo-Cosmétique SAS* v. *Président de l'Autorité de la concurrence* [2011] ECR I-9419, 13 October 2011.

[179] Cases 403/08 and 429/08, *Football Association Premier League* v. *QC Leisure* and *Karen Murphy* v. *Media Protection Services Ltd* [2011] ECR I-9083, 4 October 2011; see the comments of the Commissioner on this in the speech 'Competition—What's in it for Consumers?', European Competition and Consumer Day, Poznan, 24 November 2011, SPEECH/11/803.

[180] Guidance on the Commission's Enforcement Priorities in Applying Article 82 of the EC Treaty to Abusive Exclusionary Conduct by Dominant Undertakings [2009] OJ C45/2, para. 7 (discussed in Chaps. 5–7).

(ii) The Development of the Law

a. Ordoliberalism and other Non-Welfare Issues

We have noted that it has been argued that the drafting of the competition rules was less the product of ordoliberalism than previously thought.[181] As far as the *development* of EU competition law is concerned the established view is that it has been greatly influenced by ordoliberal ideas.[182] Ordoliberalism, it will be recalled, prizes individual economic freedom and is hostile to monopoly not because of its effects on efficiency but because it embodies private economic power. The ordoliberal influence on both the EU Courts and the Commission has been acknowledged by a previous Director General of Competition:

> The case-law of the European courts and also the decisional practice of the Commission were initially influenced by ordoliberal thought which has its origin in the so-called Freiburg School... The protection of individual economic freedom—as a value in itself—was regarded as the primary objective of competition policy.[183]

The conventional view has been challenged by a commentator who found, on a quantitative analysis, relatively few references in the case law to 'economic freedom', 'freedom to compete', or analogous terms.[184] The references increased, rather than diminished, over time, a trend which runs counter to the view that the ordoliberal influence was stronger in the early days of competition law. Three of such references were in major Article 102 cases on refusal to supply.[185] However, although not couched in expressly in 'freedom' terms many judgments, in particular on Article 102, have reflected ordoliberal principles in interpreting and applying Article 102 to protect competitors themselves rather than competition, to favour small or medium-sized enterprises, to keep markets open and to achieve 'fairness'.[186]

This raises the issue of how far, if at all, EU competition law can accommodate considerations such as the environment or employment. The matter is considered later.[187] We see that the Commission, in adopting the consumer welfare standard, has eschewed the use of the competition rules to protect or advance other interests, but the case law of the EU Courts, and the decisional practice of the Commission (at least in the past), is not so clear.

b. The 'Modernisation' of EU Competition Law and the Consumer Welfare Standard

'Modernisation' is often used to describe the major reform in the enforcement of EU competition law which took place in 2004 when Regulation 1/2003 came into force.[188] However, it should be understood as a wider and deeper phenomenon. During the 1990s the Commission began a move towards a realignment of competition law in line with the modern economic thinking on efficiency and welfare previously discussed.[189] 'Modernisation' therefore encompasses the gradual revolution in

---

[181] See Section 7.A, p. 35.

[182] Due in part to the powerful presence of German officials in the Competition Directorate-General and the influence of German domestic competition law, see D. Gerber, *Law and Competition in Twentieth Century Europe: Protecting Prometheus* (Clarendon Press, 1998), 331–333.

[183] P. Lowe, 'Consumer Welfare and Efficiency—New Guiding Principles of Competition Policy?', 13th International Competition and 14th European Competition Day, Munich, 27 March 2007, <http://ec.europa.eu/competition/speeches/index_2007.html>.

[184] P. Akman, 'The Role of "Freedom" in EU Competition Law' (2013) 33 *Legal Studies* (cited in n. 140).

[185] Cases C-241-241/91 P, *RTE & ITP v. Commission (Television Listings/Magill)* [1995] ECR I-743; Case C-418/01 *IMS Health GmbH & Co. OHG v. NDC Health GmbH & Co.KG* [2004] ECR I-5039; Case T-201/04, *Microsoft v. EC Commission* [2007] ECR II-3601.

[186] See Chap. 7, and Geradin et al., *EU Competition Law and Economics* (cited in n. 18), 1.63–1.64.

[187] See Section 7.C.ii.d, p. 48 ff.

[188] Council Reg. 1/2003 [2003] OJ L1/1 and the accompanying secondary legislation and Notices.

[189] See Section 3.A.iii, p. 7 ff.

the interpretation and application of the substantive law which has taken place both before 2004[190] and afterwards. This is often called the 'more economic' approach. The effect of modernisation in this sense on the application of the competition provisions, Articles 101 and 102, and the Merger Regulation[191] is seen throughout this book.

As modernisation progressed the speeches, publications, and 'soft law' documents emanating from the Commission proclaimed the belief that the competition rules should promote efficiency and consumer welfare.[192] An early manifestation was the statement in the Commission Guidelines on vertical restraints in 2000 that '[t]he protection of competition is the primary objective of EC competition policy, as this enhances consumer welfare and creates an efficient allocation of resources'.[193] In a speech in July 2001 Commissioner Monti said:[194]

...the goal of competition policy, in all its aspects, is to protect consumer welfare by maintaining a high degree of competition in the common market. Competition should lead to lower prices, a wider choice of goods, and technological innovation, all in the interest of the consumer.

The fact that he said that the protection of consumer welfare was *the* goal rather than *a* goal was acclaimed by the then Deputy Assistant Attorney General of the US DOJ Antitrust Division who said that '[w]e in the United States applaud Commissioner Monti's bold leadership in embracing the consumer welfare model of competition policy'.[195] Adherence to the consumer welfare standard continued under the next Commissioner, Neelie Kroes, who said, for example:[196]

Consumer welfare is now well established as the standard the Commission applies when assessing mergers and infringements of the Treaty rules on cartels and monopolies. Our aim is simple: to protect competition in the market as a means of enhancing consumer welfare and ensuring an efficient allocation of resources. An effects-based approach, grounded in solid economics, ensures that citizens enjoy the benefits of a competitive, dynamic market economy.

The policy is maintained under Commissioner Joaquín Almunia:

[190] This could be discerned first of all in the approach to the assessment of mergers under the regime which came into operation in 1990 (pursuant to the original European Merger Regulation, Council Reg. 4064/89 [1990] OJ L257/13, now Reg. 139/2004 [2004] OJ L24/1, see Chap. 15). See also the adoption by the Commission of a Notice on the definition of the relevant market in 1997 (Commission Notice on the definition of the relevant market for the purposes of Community competition law [1997] OJ C372/51); the Green Paper on vertical restraints (COM (96) 721 final) paving the way for the reform of the Commission's much-criticised policy towards vertical restraints in 1999 (Commission Regulation 2790/99 [1999] OJ L336/21 and the Commission Notice, Guidelines on vertical restraints [2000] OJ C291/1 (since amended), see Chap. 11); the 1999 White Paper on the modernisation of enforcement and procedure (Commission White Paper on modernisation of the rules implementing Articles 81 and 82 of the EC Treaty [1999] OJ C132/1); Guidelines and block exemptions on horizontal cooperation agreements in 2000 (Guidelines on the applicability of Article 81 of the EC Treaty to horizontal cooperation agreements [2001] OJ C3/2; Commission Reg. 2658/2000 on specialisation agreements [2000] OJ L304/3; Commission Reg. 2659/2000 on categories of research and development agreements [2000] OJ L304/7), since amended).

[191] Reg. 4064/89 [1990] OJ L257/13.

[192] Particularly after the appointment of an economist, Mario Monti, as Commissioner responsible for competition in 1999, see e.g M. Monti, 'European Competition Policy for the 21st Century' SPEECH/00/389, 20 October 2000, <http://www.ec.europa.eu./competition/speeches/> and in B. Hawk (ed.) [2000] *Fordham Corp L Inst*, Chap. 15. In 1998 Advocate-General Jacobs reminded the CJ that 'the primary purpose of Art. [102] is to prevent distortion of competition—and in particular to safeguard the interests of consumers—rather than to protect the position of particular competitors', Case C-7/97, *Oscar Bronner GmbH & Co KG v. Mediaprint* [1998] ECR I-7791, para. 58 of his Opinion, see Chap. 7.

[193] [2000] OJ C291/1 (the 'Verticals Guidelines'), para. 7.

[194] M. Monti, 'The Future for Competition Policy in the European Union', Merchant Taylor's Hall, London, 9 July 2001, SPEECH/01/340, <http://www.ec.europa.eu/competition/speeches/>.

[195] William J. Kolasky, 'North Atlantic Competition Policy: Converging Towards What?', Address given at the BIICL 2nd Annual International and Comparative Law Conference, London, 17 May 2002, available on the DOJ website, <http://www.usdoj.gov/atr/public/speeches/speech_kolasky.htm>.

[196] 'Delivering Better Markets and Better Choices', European Consumer and Competition Day, London, 15 September 2005, SPEECH/05/512, <http://ec.europa.eu/competition/speeches/>.

Consumer welfare is not just a catchy phrase. It is the cornerstone, the guiding principle of EU competition policy.[197]

We saw[198] that in the Guidelines on Article 101(3) the Commission states that '[t]he objective of Article [101] is to protect competition on the market as a means of enhancing consumer welfare and of ensuring an efficient allocation of resources'. Documents such as the Horizontal Merger Guidelines (2004),[199] the Non-horizontal Merger Guidelines (2008),[200] and the Verticals Guidelines (2010)[201] all proclaim the role of competition law in preventing detriment to consumers. The Guidance Paper on the Commission's enforcement priorities in applying Article 102 (2009) states that the Commission will focus on those types of conduct that are most harmful to consumers.[202] The Article 101(3) Guidelines passage was repeated in the draft Guidelines on technology transfer in February 2013 with only minor textual amendments ('The aim of Article 101 as a whole is to protect competition on the market with a view to promoting consumer welfare and an efficient allocation of resources')[203] which is notable as the draft post-dates the judgment of the CJ in *TeliaSonera*, discussed in Section 7.C.(ii)c. Furthermore, the whole rhetoric of the Commission in its press releases, speeches by officials, policy documents, reports, and all other publications is to stress that its activities are for the benefit of European *consumers*.

The consumer welfare standard means that competition law is applied to prevent *detriment* to consumer welfare, as competition law normally acts to prevent restrictive agreements and anti-competitive conduct and mergers rather than to force undertakings to take action to increase welfare. The modernised 'more economics' approach taken by the Commission entails not just the adoption of a consumer welfare standard but also an 'effects' approach to applying that standard.[204] However, when the Commission actually comes down to translating the consumer welfare standard into actual tests with which to analyse individual cases it can be criticised for continued over-reliance on effects on competitors rather than concentrating solely on harm to consumers.[205]

'Consumer detriment' appears to consist of higher prices, reduced output, less choice or lower quality of goods or services, or diminished innovation, while consumer *benefit* consists of the reverse (lower prices, greater output, greater choice, higher quality, more innovation).[206] Adopting the consumer welfare standard means that the Commission has formally rejected not only broader objectives such as economic freedom[207] and the protection of competitors, as already discussed, but also the social welfare standard. The Commission is concerned with distributive effects. There is support for this in the wording of Article 101(3) which demands that a 'fair share' of the efficiency gains

---

[197] 'Competition—what's in it for consumers?', Poznan, 24 November 2011, SPEECH/1/2003803, <http://ec.europa.eu/competition/speeches/>.

[198] See Section 7.C.i, p. 40.

[199] Guidelines on the assessment of horizontal mergers [2004] OJ C31/03, para. 8.

[200] Guidelines on the assessment of non-horizontal mergers [2008] OJ C265/7, para. 10.

[201] Guidelines on vertical restraints [2010] OJ C130/1, para. 7, discussed in text at n. 174.

[202] Guidance on the Commission's Enforcement Priorities in Applying Article 82 of the EC Treaty to Abusive Exclusionary Conduct by Dominant Undertakings [2009] OJ C 45/2, para. 5.

[203] Draft Guidelines on the application of Article 101 TFEU to technology transfer agreements, 20 February 2013, para. 5.

[204] See Section 9.B, p. 56.

[205] See P. Marsden, 'Some Outstanding Issues from the European Commission's Guidance on Article 102 TFEU: Not-So-Faint Echoes of Ordoliberalism' in F. Etro and I. Kokkoris (eds.), *Competition Law and the Enforcement of Article 102* (Oxford University Press, 2010), Chap. 3.

[206] See P. Marsden and P. Whelan, 'Consumer Detriment and its Application in EC and UK Competition Law' [2006] ECLR 569, and e.g. Guidelines on the application of Article 81(3) [now Article 101(3)] [2004] OJ C101/97, particularly paras. 16, 21, 25; Guidelines on the assessment of horizontal mergers [2004] OJ C31/3, paras. 8, 80–81; Guidance Paper on Commission's Enforcement Priorities in Applying Article 82, para. 5; Guidelines on the assessment of non-horizontal mergers [2008] OJ C265/7, para. 10.

[207] See generally L. Lovdahl Gormesen, 'The Conflict between Economic Freedom and Consumer Welfare in the Modernisation of Article 82' (2007) 3 *European Competition Journal* 329.

resulting from anti-competitive agreements must be passed on to consumers.[208] A commentator gives three reasons for the Commission choosing consumer welfare rather than social welfare.

R. Nazzini, *The Foundations of European Union Competition Law, The Objectives and Principles of Article 102* (Oxford University Press, 2011), 44–45

First, consumer welfare, as a test, is easier to apply than social welfare. It is more straightforward to argue—although not necessarily to prove—that as a result of the exclusion of a competitor or of an agreement between firms prices will be higher, than to explain why the aggregate producer and consumer surplus will be lower. ...

Secondly, consumer welfare is a politically acceptable way of arguing for an economic approach to competition law. The very mention of the word 'consumer' evokes ideas of fairness, redistribution, and protection of the many and vulnerable, making this rhetoric attractive to politicians, policy-makers, and competition officials. On the other hand, the consumer welfare objective may be applied so that, in many circumstances, it leads to precisely the same consequences as a social welfare objective ... Consumer welfare can be used as a populist slogan to sell, to the public, an economic approach to competition law.

Thirdly, consumer welfare is a politically acceptable way to disguise a non-interventionist agenda. It would be more difficult politically to argue that a tying practice by a dominant undertaking should be allowed because it does not make any difference to the sum of industry profits and consumer surplus than to argue that it should be allowed because an integrated product is good for consumers.

Bishop and Walker state that the economic goal of EU competition law is concerned with improving allocative efficiency in ways that do not impair productive efficiency to the prejudice of consumer welfare. They explain that regulators (i.e. competition authorities) must be careful to see consumer welfare in a dynamic rather than static context. They also explain that productive efficiency is important but that competition law is mainly concerned with allocative efficiency. Further, they make the important point that in most cases the distinction between consumer welfare and social (total) welfare is not significant.

S. Bishop and M. Walker, *The Economics of EC Competition Law* (3rd edn, Sweet & Maxwell, 2010), 31–32

2-019

There is a potential danger with the consumer welfare standard if it is not understood properly. If regulators treat the pursuit of consumer welfare in an entirely static framework, then this can lead to significantly sub-optimal outcomes. In particular, problems can arise when the pursuit of consumer welfare leads to an attitude or belief that any profits earned by firms must be at the cost of consumer welfare. Such an attitude might be reasonable in a static framework ... but is not reasonable in a dynamic framework in which firms invest and innovate to the ultimate benefit of consumers. A regulatory focus on short-run consumer welfare can be damaging to the incentives that firms face to invest. Firms invest and innovate because they expect to be able to earn profits from doing so. When investments are risky, the return to successful investments must compensate firms for the risk taken. If regulators treat the profitability of firms with

---

[208] See Chap. 4.

too much suspicion, they may be tempted to remove the rewards to risky investment by forcing firms that have successfully taken risks to lower prices. If regulators do this consistently, firms will be deterred from investing or innovating. In short, consumer welfare needs to be maximised within a dynamic, not static, framework.

A different issue to the relative importance of consumer and producer welfare is the relative importance of allocative efficiency and productive efficiency. Allocative efficiency more directly benefits consumers (since it implies that prices are at marginal costs, not higher), but we would expect productive efficiency to also benefit consumers. Reductions in marginal cost feed through into reductions in price even under monopoly.... However, despite the fact that the welfare losses arising from productive inefficiency are potentially of equal magnitude to those resulting from allocative inefficiency, most competition inquiries are more concerned with allocative efficiency.... The economic goal of EC competition law appears to be concerned with improving allocative efficiency in ways that do not impair productive efficiency so greatly as to produce no increase (or even net reduction) in total consumer welfare. Given that competition law enforcement should not, in general, be concerned with detailed micro-regulation of industries, this is a reasonable policy objective. Direct regulation of a firm's efficiency is likely to be fraught with difficulty and, given the informational constraints under which regulators usually work, is likely to be prone to substantial errors.

So the conclusion...is that the welfare standard for EC competition law is consumer welfare, not social welfare, but that in most cases the distinction is not important because maximising consumer welfare and maximising social welfare require the same outcomes. However, there are times when it does matter (for instance, in some mergers), and on these occasions the focus is on consumer welfare.

The decisions that the Commission has taken since modernisation, however, can often be criticised from a consumer welfare perspective. This is particularly true of Article 102 decisions, such as *Microsoft*,[209] and *Télefonica*[210] as seen in Chapter 7. Furthermore, the application of the consumer welfare standard in EU law is confused by the meaning given to the word 'consumers'. The word appears twice in the competition provisions, in Article 101(3) and in Article 102(b) where one example of an abuse of a dominant position is 'limiting production, markets or technical development to the prejudice of consumers'. Consumers also feature in the Merger Regulation (EUMR), Article 2(1)(b) of which says that in appraising a merger the Commission shall take into account, inter alia, 'the interests of the intermediate and ultimate consumers, and the development of technical and economic progress provided that it is to consumers' advantage and does not form an obstacle to competition'.[211] The normal (and popular) conception of a 'consumer' is a private (natural person) end-user and the current Commission rhetoric emphasises the benefits that the enforcement of the competition rules has for individual citizens. Moreover, the 2006 Leniency Notice (setting out the rewards for whistle-blowing cartel members) justifies the leniency policy on the grounds that '[t]he interests of consumers *and citizens* in ensuring that secret cartels are detected and punished outweigh the interest in fining those undertakings that enable the Commission to detect and prohibit such practices'[212] (emphasis added). This suggests that European citizens have an interest in the enforcement of the competition rules that goes beyond their role as consumers. However, 'consumers' has long been interpreted in EU competition law as encompassing all indirect and direct users and not just private end-users, i.e. it includes intermediate customers as well, as can be seen from the passage

---

[209] COMP/C-3/37.792, [2005] 4 CMLR 965.

[210] COMP/38.784.

[211] Council Reg. 139/2004 [2004] OJ L24/1 (the EUMR). Exactly the same provision appeared in the original Merger Regulation, 4064/89 [1990] OJ L257/13. Note also that Recital 29 of Reg. 139/2004 refers to a merger's potential efficiencies counteracting the effects on competition and 'in particular the potential harm to consumers' (there was no similar recital in 4064/89).

[212] Commission Notice on immunity from fines and reduction of fines in cartel cases [2006] OJ C298/17, para. 3, see Chap. 13.

from the Merger Regulation quoted earlier in this paragraph.[213] The problems with this are that the interests of intermediate customers and end-users may well not coincide, and intermediate customers may be competitors of the supplier in downstream markets. This can cause complications,[214] particularly in Article 102 cases.

What has already been said in respect of the consumer welfare standard applies to the antitrust and merger control aspects of EU competition policy. It does not apply to State aid policy. This was explained by the then Director General of Competition who said that in respect of State aid it was *social* welfare and equated this to the notion of 'common interest' found in the State aid provisions:[215]

However, a consumer welfare standard cannot be transposed directly to the world of State aid. In fact, beyond any justification it may have in terms of allocative efficiency, State aid can be justified on the basis of non-economic grounds such as reducing social disparities which consumer welfare does not measure. Whether the rationale for State aid is efficiency or equity, the correct welfare standard for State aid policy— expressed in economic terms—would seem to be the social welfare of the European Union, which is equivalent to the notion of common interest found in Article [107(3) TFEU].

c. The Objectives of Competition Law and the Case Law of the Court

The adoption by the Commission of the consumer welfare standard has not been unambiguously followed by the EU Courts.[216] Given that, it cannot properly be said that the objective of EU competition law is consumer welfare.

In *Continental Can* in 1974 the CJ said:

Article [102] is not only aimed at practices which may cause damage to consumers directly, but also at those which are detrimental to them through their impact on an effective competition structure such as is mentioned in Article [3(1)(g)] of the [EC] Treaty.[217]

This principle looks to the protection of the market structure because of indirect possible long-term effects on consumers, and not just at immediate direct effects on them. The EU Courts have repeated the 'indirect as well as direct' principle on subsequent occasions but in many cases looked to the protection of the market structure without making clear the relationship of that to the welfare of consumers, as discussed in Chapter 7. The impact on consumers, however, has recently been given more emphasis in *TeliaSonera*[218] and *Post Danmark*.[219]

In 2000 the CJ said in *Hoechst* that the function of the competition rules 'is, as follows from the fourth preamble to the Treaty, Article 3[(1)(g)] and Articles [101] and [102], to prevent competition being distorted to the detriment of the public interest, individual undertakings and consumers'.[220] It repeated this in *Roquette Frères* in 2002.[221] In 2006, however, the GC gave two judgments in which it identified the 'well-being' or 'welfare' of the final consumer as the objective. The first was *Österreichische Postsparkasse*:[222]

---

[213]   See as well as the EUMR, Guidelines on the application of Article 81(3) [now Article 101(3)] [2004] OJ C101/97, para. 84 (direct or indirect users…including producers that use the products as an input…In other words…customers of the parties to the agreement and subsequent purchasers); Guidance Paper on Article 102, para. 19, n. 2.

[214]   See P. Akman, '"Consumer" versus "Customer": the Devil in the Detail' (2010) 37 *Journal of Law and Society* 315.

[215]   P. Lowe, 'The Design of Competition Policy Institutions for the 21st Century—the Experience of the European Commission and DG Competition' (2008) 3 *Competition Policy Newsletter* 1, 6.

[216]   With the exception of the GC in Case T-168/01, *GlaxoSmithKline Services Unlimited* [2006] ECR II-2969.

[217]   Case 6/72, *Europemballage & Continental Can v. EV Commission* [1973] ECR 215, para. 12.

[218]   Case C-52/09, *Konkurrensverket v. TeliaSonera Sverige AB* [2011] ECR I-527.

[219]   Case C-209/10, *Post Danmark A/S v. Konkurrencerådet*, 27 March 2012; see Chap. 7.

[220]   Cases 46/87 and 227/88, *Hoechst v. EC Commission* [1989] ECR 2859, para. 25. The Treaty referred to is the Treaty of Rome. For the fourth preamble see Section 7.B, p. 36.

[221]   Case C-94/00 *Roquette Frères* [2002] ECR I-9011, para. 42.

[222]   Cases T-213/01 and T-214/01, *Österreichische Postsparkasse AG v. Commission* and *Bank für Arbeit und Wirtschaft AG v. Commission* [2006] ECR II-1601, para. 115.

It should be pointed out in this respect that the ultimate purpose of the rules that seek to ensure that competition is not distorted in the internal market is to increase the well-being of consumers. That purpose can be seen in particular from the wording of Article [101]. Whilst the prohibition laid down in Article [101] may be declared inapplicable in the case of cartels which contribute to improving the production or distribution of the goods in question or to promoting technical or economic progress, that possibility, for which provision is made in Article [101(3)] is inter alia subject to the condition that a fair share of the resulting benefit is allowed for users of those products. Competition law and competition policy therefore have an undeniable impact on the specific economic interests of final customers who purchase goods or services.

This was followed by the judgment in *GlaxoSmithKline* where the GC said:[223]

However, as the objective of the Community competition rules is to prevent undertakings, by restricting competition between themselves or with third parties, from reducing the welfare of the final consumer of the products in question…

In *GlaxoSmithKline* this formulation of the objective of the rules was crucial to one of the findings in the case, as it prevented an agreement from falling within the prohibition of anti-competitive agreements in Article 101(1) by reason of its object alone. Although the object of the agreement was to restrict parallel trade the GC held that could not, on the facts of the case, be equated with the object of reducing the welfare of the final consumer.[224]

Advocate-General Kokott's Opinion in *British Airways*, delivered in February 2006, described Article 102 as not being 'only or primarily designed to protect the immediate interests of individual competitors or consumers but to protect the structure of the market and thus competition as such (as an institution)…'.[225] The CJ's judgment in that case, which took a very 'conservative' line towards the application of Article 102, did not gainsay that statement.[226] Rather, the CJ said that the GC had been entitled to find an infringement of Article 102(b) in respect of one alleged abuse without examining whether consumers had been prejudiced.[227] In a preliminary reference ruling in 2009, *T-Mobile Netherlands*, the CJ said, agreeing with its Advocate-General (Kokott AG again):

In any event, as the Advocate General pointed out at point 58 of her Opinion, Article [101], like the other competition rules of the Treaty, is designed to protect not only the immediate interests of individual competitors or consumers but also to protect the structure of the market and thus competition as such.[228]

The CJ reprised this in the judgment on the appeal from the GC in *GlaxoSmithKline* when it firmly disapproved of the GC views on the object of agreements and parallel trade:

…it must be borne in mind that the Court has held that, like other competition rules laid down in the Treaty, Article 81 EC aims to protect not only the interests of competitors or of consumers, but also the structure of the market and, in so doing, competition as such. Consequently, for a finding that an agreement has an anti-competitive object, it is not necessary that final consumers be deprived of the advantages of effective competition in terms of supply or price (see, by analogy, *T-Mobile Netherlands and Others*, cited above, paragraphs 38 and 39).[229]

The CJ repeated this in 2013 in *Protimonopolný úrad Slovenskej republiky* v. *Slovenská sporiteľňa a.s.*[230]

---

[223] Case T-168/01, *GlaxoSmithKline Services Unlimited* v. *Commission* [2006] ECR II-2969, para. 118.

[224] See further Chap. 4.

[225] Opinion of Kokott A-G in Case C-95/04 P, *British Airways* v. *Commission* [2007] ECR I-2331, para. 86.

[226] See further Chap. 7.

[227] *British Airways*, para. 107.

[228] Case C-8/08, *T-Mobile Netherlands BV* v. *Raad van bestuur van de Nederlandse Mededingingsautoriteit* [2009] ECR I-4529, para. 38.

[229] Case C-501/06 P, *GlaxoSmithKline Services Unlimited* v. *Commission* [2009] ECR I-9291, para. 63.

[230] Case C-68/12, *Protimonopolný úrad Slovenskej republiky* v. *Slovenská sporiteľňa a.s.*, 7 February 2013, para. 18.

A striking thing about these statements of the CJ is that they appear to assume that the aim is the protection of competitors as well as consumers (without any indication that the interests of the two groups might conflict) and stress that they also protect the market structure and 'competition as such'. The latter phrase refers to the ordoliberal belief in the competition as a value in itself. AG Kokott herself interpreted this in *British Airways* as meaning competition as 'an institution'.

In *Deutsche Telekom* in 2010 the CJ held that an undertaking was committing an abuse of its dominant position contrary to Article 102 even though avoiding the abuse would entail *increasing* its prices to consumers.[231] In *TeliaSonera* in 2011, as has been seen in the extract quoted,[232] the CJ stated that the function of the competition rules is:

precisely to prevent competition from being distorted to the detriment of the public interest, individual undertakings and consumers, thereby ensuring the well-being of the European Union (see, to that effect, Case C-94/00 *Roquette Frères*...paragraph 42).[233]

The phrase 'well-being of the Union' is a clear reference to the aims of the EU set out in Article 3(1) TEU ('well-being of its peoples').[234] It is not just detriment to consumers from distortions of competition which must be prevented to achieve this, but detriment to the public interest and individual undertakings also. Some commentators have interpreted this as long-term social welfare.[235] In the subsequent case of *Post Danmark*[236] the Grand Chamber of the CJ gave a judgment which although containing no express statement about the objectives of the law, did focus heavily on effects on consumers.

Although the EU Courts are concerned with the welfare of consumers, therefore, it is but one concern amongst others. The EU Courts and the Commission have not always been singing from the same hymn sheet as the saying goes. *Post Danmark* may, however, signal a clearer focus in which the Courts' thinking will be more aligned with that of the Commission's declared policy. Time will tell.

d. Public Policy Considerations and the EU's Industrial Policy

The question of the objectives of EU competition law inevitably raises the issue of how far, if at all, factors other than those relating to welfare and efficiency should be taken into account in the application of the law to individual cases.[237] It will be seen in the subsequent chapters of this book that on numerous occasions in the past, cases and decisions have taken account of public policy considerations,[238] particularly those embodied in other Union policies, but that contradictory messages on this have been sent out by the EU Courts and the Commission.

The adoption by the Commission of the consumer welfare standard makes it difficult to simultaneously take other considerations into account, unless a conception of consumer welfare is adopted which includes some general notion of the 'well-being' of citizens. As we have seen, the whole philosophy of the modern 'economic' approach to competition policy is that it should be concerned only with welfare and efficiency. Moreover, the 2004 reforms, which decentralised the enforcement of EU competition law to the national competition authorities of the Member States[239]

---

[231] Case C-280/08 P, *Deutsche Telekom* v. *Commission* [2010] ECR I-9555, para. 181. The abuse concerned was a margin squeeze. The CJ considered that in the longer term competitive pressure would lead to a reduction in prices (para. 182). See further Chap. 7.

[232] In Section 7.B.

[233] Case C-52/09, *Konkurrensverket* v. *TeliaSonera Sverige AB* [2011] ECR I-527, para. 22.

[234] As set out in Section 7.B.

[235] Nazzini, *The Foundations of European Union Competition Law* (cited in n. 140), 5.

[236] Case C-209/10, *Post Danmark A/S* v. *Konkurrencerådet*, 27 March 2012.

[237] See G. Monti, 'Article 81 EC and Public Policy' (2002) 30 *CMLRev* 1057; A. C. Witt, 'Public Policy Goals under EU Competition Law' (2012) 8 *European Competition Journal* 443.

[238] See in particular the application of Art. 101(3), discussed in Chap. 4.

[239] Council Reg. 1/2003 [2003] OJ L1/1; Commission Notice on cooperation within the network of competition authorities [2004] OJ C101/43.

and gave encouragement to the private enforcement of the competition rules in the national courts, made the exclusion of other considerations attractive on expediency grounds. It is one thing for the Commission to balance competition against other Union policies, but quite another for national courts and authorities to do so.[240]

EU competition policy does not stand alone in splendid isolation. It was stated in the EC Treaty to be one of a number of activities undertaken to achieve the objectives of the Treaty, and its role has not changed under the Treaty of Lisbon. The EC Treaty in its final form contained a number of horizontal 'policy-linking' ('flanking') provisions, and this is an even more prominent feature post-Lisbon in the TEU and TFEU. Article 7 TFEU provides generally for consistency between all EU policies and activities:

The Union shall ensure consistency between its policies and activities, taking all of its objectives into account and in accordance with the principle of conferral of powers.

Articles 8–13 TFEU set out specific matters that must be taken into account. Article 8 provides that 'in all its activities, the Union shall aim to eliminate inequalities and to promote equality, between men and women'.[241] The promotion of a high level of employment, the guarantee of social protection, the fight against social exclusion, and a high level of education, training, and protection of human health has to be taken into account by the Union in 'defining and implementing its policies and activities';[242] as does consumer protection,[243] combating discrimination based on gender, racial or ethnic origin, religion or belief, disability, age, or sexual orientation,[244] and ensuring a high level of human health protection.[245] Environmental protection, in particular promoting sustainable development, must be 'integrated into the definition and implementation of Union policies and activities'.[246] As far as, inter alia, the internal market is concerned animal welfare has to be regarded.[247]

The effect of these provisions on competition law is a matter of debate. For example, Odudu argues that 'definition and implementation' does not include enforcement in a particular case[248] whereas Townley argues that they can provide a legal base for non-efficiency considerations in competition cases.[249] Hitherto the EU Courts have not addressed the legal effect of the policy-linking clauses.

There is a particular question of the relationship of competition law to the EU's industrial policy.[250] 'Industrial policy' can be defined in many ways, but at its widest it includes all State acts and

---

[240] In the Commission White Paper on modernisation of the rules implementing Articles 81 and 82 of the EC Treaty [1999] OJ C132/1, the Commission first proposed decentralisation and turned its face against using Art. 101(3) to take into account public policy: see Chap. 4. Member States do pursue objectives which do not fit with the efficiency approach. In 2006 Member State governments interfered with merger transactions in the energy sector in order to protect national companies from 'foreign' take-overs, thus incurring the wrath of the Commission which considered the actions contrary to the EUMR, Reg. 139/2004 [2004] OJ L24/22. The Commission took infringement proceedings under Art. 258 TFEU against Spain in respect of the conditions the Spanish energy regulator had imposed on the take-over of the Spanish energy company Endesa by the German company E.ON, Case C-196/07, *Spain v. Commission* [2008] ECR I-41 (summary, the full judgment is available only in Spanish and French): see Press Release IP/06/1426.

[241] Known as 'gender mainstreaming'.

[242] Art. 9 TFEU.

[243] Art.12 TFEU.

[244] Art. 10 TFEU.

[245] Art. 168(1).

[246] Art. 11 TFEU.

[247] Art. 13 TFEU. The internal market includes competition policy. The other policies listed are agriculture, fisheries, transport, research and technological development, and space.

[248] Relying on the minimum price for tobacco products case, Case C-221/08, *Commission v. Ireland* [2010] ECR I-1669, in which what is now Art. 168(1) TFEU was argued, and on the apparent lack of direct effect: O. Odudu, 'The Wider Concerns of Competition Law' (2010) 30 *OJLS* 599, 606–607.

[249] C. Townley, *Article 81 EC and Public Policy* (Hart Publishing, 2009), 50–54. See also G. Monti, *EC Competiton Law* (Cambridge University Press, 2007), 90–91.

[250] See W. Sauter, *Competition Law and Industrial Policy in the EU* (Oxford University Press, 1997); N. Petit and N. Neyrinck, 'Industrial Policy and Competition Enforcement: Is there, Could There and Should There Be a Nexus?', Global Competition Law Centre Conference 2012, <http://papers.ssrn.com/sol3/papers.cfm?abstract_id=2225903>.

policies which relate to industry. It can encompass such policies as employment, protecting domestic industry from foreign competition, regional development, encouraging 'national champions', and fostering particular sectors. Industrial policy may also be 'horizontal' and aimed at 'competitiveness' across the whole economy.[251] The EU's industrial policy provision is now Article 173 TFEU.[252] It adopts a competitiveness strategy:

The Union and the Member States shall ensure that the conditions necessary for the competitiveness of the Union's industry exist.[253]

This entails speeding up the adjustment of industry to structural changes; encouraging an environment favourable to initiative and to the development of small and medium-sized undertakings (SMEs); encouraging an environment favourable to cooperation between undertakings; and fostering better exploitation of the industrial potential of policies of innovation, research, and technological development.[254] However, nothing in Article 173 can provide a basis for Union measures which, inter alia, 'could lead to a distortion of the competition'.[255]

In 2004 the Commission issued a Communication, *A pro-active competition policy for a competitive Europe*,[256] which set competition at the heart of industrial policy rather than in opposition to it. The Commission said that '[T]he goal of a pro-active competition policy is to support the competitive process in the internal market and to induce firms to engage in competitive and dynamically efficiency-enhancing behaviour'. The Commissioner elaborated on this in a speech in September 2006, in which she gave her own definition of 'industrial policy':

This afternoon I would like us to try to rethink industrial policy! I think it makes no sense to speak of industrial policy and competition policy as distinct one from the other, let alone as antagonistic policies. I would rather define industrial policy as one which frames the structural conditions necessary to ensure economic success in a globalising economy. And I therefore have no qualms in saying that competition policy forms—or should form—a central plank in any industrial policy.[257]

This statement must be seen in the context of the Lisbon Strategy[258] whereby the EU set itself the strategic goal of becoming the most competitive and dynamic knowledge-based economy in the world by 2010, capable of sustainable economic growth and more and better jobs and greater social cohesion. The 2004 Communication said of competition and the Lisbon Strategy:

Competition policy is one of a number of Community policies impacting upon the economic performance of Europe. It is a key element of a coherent and integrated policy to foster the competitiveness of Europe's industries and to attain the goals of the Lisbon strategy.

The Lisbon Agenda has been replaced for the current decade with the 'EU 2020' strategy. The Consultation Paper launching the strategy referred to the EU needing 'well functioning markets where competition and consumer access stimulate growth and innovation' in order to gear the single market to serve the goals of EU 2020;[259] and in the 2011 Competition Report the Commission said:

[251] See N. Petit and N. Neyrinck, 'Industrial Policy and Competition Enforcement' (cited in n. 250), for an account of the different forms of industrial policies.

[252] Previously Art. 157 EC.

[253] Art. 173(1).

[254] Art. 173(1).

[255] Art. 173(3).

[256] COM(2004)293 final.

[257] Neelie Kroes, 'Industrial Policy and Competition Law & Policy', speech at Fordham University School of Law, 14 September 2006, <http://ec.europa.eu/competition/speeches/index_speeches_by_the_commissioner.html>.

[258] Originally declared at the Lisbon European Council in March 2000 and relaunched in February 2005 in the Communication of the Commission to the Spring European Council, *Working together for growth and jobs: A new start for the Lisbon Strategy* COM(2005)24, 2 February 2005.

[259] Commission Working Document 'Consultation on the Future "EU 2020" Strategy' COM(2009)647 final, 9–10.

Competition enforcement and advocacy also serve other wider longer-term objectives such as enhancing consumer welfare, supporting the EU's growth, jobs and competitiveness in line with the Europe 2020 Strategy for smart, sustainable and inclusive growth.[260]

EU competition law does not provide mechanisms by which undertakings can be forced to take positive action to promote competitiveness or other socio-political goals. Rather, competition law *prohibits* anti-competitive agreements, conduct (on the part of dominant firms), and mergers. It therefore comes down to the question of whether such agreements, conduct, or mergers can nevertheless be permitted because they deliver socio-political benefits.

There are in practice two ways in which non-welfare or efficiency issues and other Union policies can be taken into account.[261] A matter may be excluded from the scope of competition law altogether,[262] or the matter may be covered by the competition rules but other considerations may be taken into account in their application in what has been described as a compromise or 'balancing' exercise.[263] Examples of the former are the CJ's exclusion of collective bargaining agreements between employer and employees on the ground that such arrangements fall within the ambit of social policy,[264] and cases finding that an entity is not an 'undertaking' and its agreements or conduct therefore not subject to the competition rules.[265]

The EU Merger Regulation contains specific provisions on the ability of Member States to take account of certain public policy considerations in respect of mergers to which the Regulation applies.[266] An analysis of possible industrial policy influence on Commission merger decisions has not shown industrial policy considerations to systematically override competition-related ones.[267]

The main context in which the 'compromise' or 'balancing' route arises is in respect of Article 101 (which prohibits anti-competitive agreements) which is examined in Chapter 4, where we see that the EU Courts have sometimes taken account of wider considerations, as has the Commission itself. Public policy considerations may result in a finding that the agreement does not infringe the prohibition in the first place, such as in *Wouters* where the CJ held that the rules of the Dutch Bar pursued public interest objectives,[268] but public policy considerations are usually raised in the context of Article 101(3), which provides an exemption from the prohibition for restrictive agreements which satisfy four conditions. As part of the 'modernisation' and the adoption of the consumer welfare standard

---

[260] Commission Report on Competition Policy for 2011, 9. See also Commissioner Almunia, 'Industrial policy and Competition policy: Quo vadis Europa?', 10 February 2012, SPEECH/12/83, <europa.eu/rapid/press-release_SPEECH-12-83_en.pdf>.

[261] See generally O. Odudu, *The Boundaries of EC Competition Law* (Oxford University Press, 2006), Chap. 7; C. Townley, *Article 81 EC and Public Policy* (Hart Publishing, 2009).

[262] Some matters are excluded from the competition rules by the Treaties themselves: national security connected with the production or trade in arms (Art. 346 TFEU; for the application of this in the context of mergers, see Chap. 15) and nuclear energy (inasmuch as it is covered by the Euratom Treaty). The competition provisions now apply to agriculture subject to the three exceptions set out in Council Reg. 1184/2006 [2006] OJ L214/7. For the position of undertakings entrusted with services of general economic interest see Art. 106(2) TFEU, discussed in Chap. 8.

[263] See Townley, *Article 81 EC and Public Policy* (cited in n. 261), Chap. 2.

[264] Case C-67/96, *Albany International BV v. Stichting Bedrijfspensioenfonds Textielindustrie* [1999] ECR I-6025: see Chap. 3.

[265] e.g., Case C-205/03 P, *Federación Nacional de Empresas de Instrumentación Científica, Médica, Técnica y Dental (FENIN) v. Commission*, [2006] ECR I-6295 (ECJ), aff'g Case T-319/99 *FENIN v. Commission* [2003] ECR II-357; Cases C-264, 306, 354, & 355/01, *AOK Bundesverband and others v. Ichtyol-Gesellschaft Cordes and others* [2004] ECR I-2493: see further Chaps. 3 and 8.

[266] Council Regulation 139/2004 [2004] OJ L124/1, Art. 21(4); see Chap. 15.

[267] Petit and Neyrinck, 'Industrial Policy and Competition Enforcement' (cited in n. 250), 25–29. The Commissioner commented on the prohibited merger between Deutsche Börse and NYSE Euronext (M.6166, IP/12/94, 1 February 2012) that the price of creating a European champion would have been harm to customers (SPEECH/12/131, 28 February 2012). There is evidence, however, that the Commission has used its merger regulation powers to open up the market in network industries, see Petit and Neyrinck, at 28.

[268] Case C-309/99, *Wouters v. Algemene Raad van der Nederlandse Orde van Advocaten* [2002] ECR I-1577; see also Case C-519/04 P, *Meca-Medina and Majcen v. Commission* [2006] ECR I-6991.

the Commission construes Article 101(3) as a pure 'efficiency defence' and considers that factors other than efficiencies cannot normally be taken into account in deciding whether the conditions are satisfied. This approach is set out in the Guidelines on Article 101(3) published by the Commission in 2004.[269] There is considerable debate about whether the Commission can or should adopt this approach given the case law.[270]

D. EU COMPETITION LAW AND REGULATION

In the last 30 years there has been a revolution in the way in which public services are owned and run. Throughout Europe many State-owned, and often vertically integrated, monopolies have been wholly or partly privatised.[271] The opening up of sectors previously monopolised by State enterprises legally protected from competition is known as liberalisation. The EU has pursued a far-reaching programme of liberalisation and harmonisation in respect of the transport, postal services, energy, and telecommunications (electronic communications) markets.[272] However liberalisation can lead, at least in the short term, to private monopolies replacing public ones. This does not necessarily benefit consumers. There are particular problems in sectors where the provision of services depends on the use of a network (such as railway lines or telephone lines) which cannot feasibly be duplicated and where control of the network may create a 'bottleneck' monopoly which hinders downstream competitors. Moreover, some services—such as the supply of water, sewage, and basic postal services—may need to be the subject of a public service obligation such as 'universal service' (USO). As the market does not provide satisfactory outcomes to these problems the liberalised sectors are often subject to 'regulation'. Regulation 'consists of public interventions which affect the operation of markets through command and control'.[273] This typically involves setting up a regulatory body which implements controls on prices and quality, fixes terms of contracts, mandates and polices access by downstream competitors, and oversees the obligations of the undertaking such as the USO.[274] There are at present no EU-wide regulators[275] but EU law imposes duties on national sector regulators in the Member States. The relevant EU sector legislation may require the establishment of an independent national regulatory authority (NRA) and specify in detail the powers and duties it must possess. Under the 2009 electronic telecommunications reform package[276] the Commission may become closely involved in regulatory remedies chosen by the NRAs.

---

[269] Guidelines on the application of Article 81(3) [now Article 101(3)] of the Treaty [2004] C 101/97 ('the Article 101(3) Guidelines'), see further Chap. 4.

[270] See e.g. Witt, 'Public Policy Goals under EU Competition Law' (cited in n. 237), 469–471, Petit and Neyrinck, 'Industrial Policy and Competition Enforcement' (cited in n. 250), 13.

[271] Private rather than public ownership is a major plank of the 'neoliberal' ideology which drives globalised capitalism.

[272] It has been pursued through directives adopted under the special procedure laid down in Art. 106(3) TFEU (ex Art. 86(3) EC) and through Council harmonisation directives under Art. 114 TFEU (ex Art. 95 EC).

[273] T. Prosser, *Law and the Regulators* (Oxford University Press, 1997), 4.

[274] Prosser, *Law and the Regulators* (cited in n. 273), 5–6. Obviously this is a generality. The functions of the regulators differ between sectors and different States organise regulation differently. The regulators in the UK include OFWAT (water), OFGEM (energy), the Rail Regulator, and, pursuant to the Communications Act 2003, OFCOM.

[275] Though note that the expression 'regulator' is often used loosely to mean 'competition authority'. As far as EU-wide sector regulators are concerned, the Commission proposed an EU-wide authority for electronic communications during negotiations on the reform of the electronic communications legislation. The Member States did not accept this. Instead a new body, the Body of European Regulators for Electronic Communications (BEREC) consisting of the heads of the 27 Member States' NCAs, has been created, Reg. 1211/2009 [2009] OJ L239/1.

[276] See Directive 2009/140/EC [2009] OJ L337/3 on a common regulatory framework for electronic communications, and Directive 2009/136 [2009] OJ L137/11, which amend the electronics communications directives of 2002 (21/2002, 22/2002, 58/2002).

There are some major differences between regulation and competition law,[277] although it has been persuasively argued that competition law is 'conceptually very similar' to some types of regulation, namely the type of regulation that encourages or promotes competitive markets, rather than that which pursues public policy objectives (some regulation pursues both).[278] First, there is the oft-cited difference that regulation acts *ex ante* (in advance) whereas competition law (other than merger control) normally acts *ex post* (reacting to conduct which is taking place or has taken place).[279] Where prices are concerned, for example, a regulator sets out in advance what the undertaking may charge while a competition authority will step in only if and when it appears that an undertaking's pricing infringes the competition rules. On the other hand, the desire of undertakings to comply with competition laws means that in practice competition law does have considerable *ex ante* effect.[280] Secondly, regulatory agencies often possess more extensive and detailed information about the whole industry and the wider issues affecting the market than do competition authorities. The latter concentrate on the specific conduct in issue. Thirdly, competition authorities generally try to avoid behavioural remedies whereas sector regulators provide detailed rules on matters such as prices and conditions which require close monitoring. Regulation is more *dirigiste* than competition law. Fourthly, the position of a regulator may be affected by its closeness to the market players and to the government (despite liberalisation many States retain a financial stake in former state-owned monopolies). Fifthly, regulation may be a transitory phase which is replaced by competition law in the long term.

The last point is important. Sector regulation should be put in place only where competition law is unable to deal with market failures. The European Commission may ultimately veto the decision of a national regulatory authority to subject a particular market to *ex ante* regulation if it thinks it unnecessary. The Commission favours the replacement of regulation with competition law whenever possible.[281] In the 2009 electronic communications directive[282] the Commission looked forward to a time when the sector is no longer subject to *ex ante* regulation:

The aim is progressively to reduce *ex-ante* sector specific rules as competition in the markets develops and, ultimately, for electronic communications to be governed by competition law only. Considering that the markets for electronic communications have shown strong competitive dynamics in recent years, it is essential that *ex-ante* regulatory obligations only be imposed where there is no effective and sustainable competition.

Competition laws can apply to regulated sectors alongside regulatory regimes. Member States vary as to whether NRAs may apply competition rules as well as regulatory rules.[283] The relationship

---

[277] P.-A. Buigues and R. Klotz, 'Margin Squeeze in Regulated Industries: The CFI Judgment in the *Deutsche Telekom* Case' (2008) *GCP* (July (1)) 1, 17; J. C. Laguna de Paz, 'Regulation and Competition Law' [2012] *ECLR* 77.

[278] K. Coates, *Competition Law and Regulation of Technology Markets* (Oxford University Press, 2011), 2.03–2.04.

[279] Monopoly control is generally *ex post*, and so, in the current regime under Reg. 1/2003, is the control of anti-competitive agreements (although there is the possibility of interim measures or injunctions). Merger control is *ex ante* (the EU merger regime requires prior notification of mergers with a 'Community dimension', see Chap. 15). For the differences between competition and regulation, see further R. O'Donoghue and A. J. Padilla, *The Law and Economics of Article 102* (2nd edn, Hart Publishing, 2013), pp. 44–47.

[280] Coates, *Competition Law and Regulation of Technology Markets* (cited in n. 278), 2.2.17–2.19.

[281] For example, see Commission Recommendation on relevant product and service markets within the electronic communications sector susceptible to *ex ante* regulation in accordance with Directive 2002/21/EC on a common regulatory framework for electronic communications networks and services [2007] OJ L344/65, which sets out three cumulative criteria to be applied in determining whether a market is one in which *ex ante* regulation may be warranted.

[282] Directive 2009/140/EC (cited in n. 276), recital 5.

[283] In the UK the sector regulators have concurrent powers to apply the Competition Act 1998 and the Enterprise Act 2002 in their sectors. See generally *Butterworths Competition Law* (Butterworths, looseleaf), Div. IX.

between sector-specific regulation and EU competition law was clarified in *Deutsche Telekom*[284] and *Telefónica*[285] in which the EU Courts held that an undertaking could infringe Article 102 by applying a pricing policy which constituted an abusive 'margin squeeze' even though the prices had been approved by the national telecommunications regulator, as the competition rules supplemented by *ex post* review the legislative framework adopted by the Union legislator for *ex ante* regulation of the telecommunications market.[286] The CJ and GC held that regulatory approval does not remove an undertaking's liability for infringing the competition rules unless the restrictive effects of its conduct are caused wholly by the national law and the undertaking has no room for manoeuvre.[287] The Commission cannot be bound by a decision taken by a national body[288] which, although bound to respect the Treaty provisions, operates under national law which might have different sectoral objectives to Union law.[289] The position is different in the US where the Supreme Court has declined to apply ordinary competition law (s. 2 of the Sherman Act) to conduct in the regulated telecommunications sector on the grounds that it is the regulatory regime which is designed to deter and remedy anti-competitive harm.[290] The Supreme Court does not want to impose upon undertakings intervention from two different sources. However, the US has a federal sector regulation regime[291] so the dynamics of the relationship with federal antitrust law are different from those of the relationship between EU competition law and national regulation in the Member States.

In the EU the pharmaceutical sector is also subject to regulation but not in the way, and for the reasons, previously discussed. Regulation of the pharmaceutical sector arises from the operation of the national healthcare systems in the Member States and the resulting interest of the Member States in controlling, directly or indirectly, the price of pharmaceuticals. The differing national regimes of price controls lead to wide variations in prices between Member States.[292] The degree of price regulation in this sector is a major factor in competition cases concerning parallel trade in pharmaceuticals.[293]

E. THE NEW ECONOMY

The 'new economy' is a term which includes the telecommunications (electronic communications), media, and information technology sectors[294] and high technology industries such as internet-based

---

[284] Case C-280/08 P, *Deutsche Telekom v. Commission* [2010] ECR I-9555. See D. Geradin and R. O'Donoghue, 'The Concurrent Application of Competition Law and Regulation: The Case of Margin Squeeze Abuses in the Telecommunications Sector' (2005) 1 *Journal of Competition Law and Economics* 355, GCLC Working Paper 04/05, pp. 51–65.

[285] Case T-336/07, *Telefónica and Telefónica de España v. European Commission*, 29 March 2012, on appeal Case C-295/12 P, judgment pending; Case T-398/07, *Spain v. European Commission*, 29 March 2012.

[286] Case C-280/08 P, *Deutsche Telekom v. Commission* [2010] ECR I-9555, para. 92. See further Chap. 7.

[287] Case C-280/08 P, *Deutsche Telekom v. Commission* [2010] ECR I-9555, paras. 80–89.

[288] Case C-280/08 P, *Deutsche Telekom v. Commission* [2010] ECR I-9555, para. 90.

[289] Case T-271/03, *Deutsche Telekom v. Commission* [2008] ECR II-477, para. 113 (GC).

[290] *Verizon Communications Inc v. Trinko LLP* 540 US 398, 124 S Ct 872 (2004), see Chap. 7,

[291] See Hovenkamp, *Federal Antitrust Policy: The Law of Competition and its Practice* (cited in n. 46), and Chap. 19.

[292] There are also EU harmonisation measures in the pharmaceutical sector, see particularly Directive 2001/83/EC on the Community code relating to medicinal products for human use [2001] OJ L211/67 and Council Directive 89/105 on transparency of measures regulating the prices of medicinal products for human use and their inclusion in the scope of national health insurance systems [1989] OJ L40/8.

[293] Case C-468–478/06, *Sot. Lélos kai Sia EE and others v. GlaxoSmithKline AEVE Farmakeftikon Proionton* [2008] ECR I-7139; Case C-501/06 P, *GlaxoSmithKline Services Unlimited v. Commission* [2009] ECR I-9291.

[294] Which have converged to such an extent that they have to be regulated as a whole, see European Commission, 'Towards an Information Society Approach', Green Paper on the convergence of the telecommunications, media and information technology sectors, and the implication for regulation, COM (97)623 final (Brussels, 1997).

businesses (e.g. B2B marketplaces),[295] computer software and hardware, biotechnology, and aero-space. The characteristics of these markets include very rapid innovation and technological change; the creation, exploitation of, and reliance on intellectual property rights; the need for complemen-tary products, services, or platforms to work together; and a high degree of technical complexity. In some markets such as electronic communications 'network effects' (the platform or network becomes more valuable the more users it has) are an important feature.[296] new economy industries pose particular problems for competition laws. For example, competition between undertakings is not so much on price as on innovation; the usual ways of defining markets may not work well;[297] and competition may not be in markets but *for* markets (markets may 'tip' towards one firm whose prod-ucts become the standard, rendering the firm dominant—Microsoft is the obvious instance[298]—and competition will be aimed at replacing the dominant firm). Regulation can be applied to some mar-kets, as in the case of electronic communications, to deal with some of the issues but there is much debate about the extent to which 'ordinary' competition law can be satisfactorily applied to the new economy.[299] It is crucially important that competition law is applied in new economy markets to promote dynamic efficiency and that competition law does not reduce the incentives for firms to innovate. It is often argued that the application of competition rules should be revised to fully allow for the dynamic competition in these markets. EU competition law does not apply the rules differ-ently, however. The European Commission does not refrain from enforcing competition law in the new economy. The Director General for Competition has said:[300]

we sometimes hear that there is no need for antitrust intervention in high-tech markets. Allegedly, the constant and rapid pace of technological innovation would make entrenched positions of market power impossible to maintain.

Well, if there are such characteristics present in a market, we will fully acknowledge them in our cases... But we do not think that 'high-tech' markets—however their boundaries may be defined—should be generally immune from antitrust intervention.

In reality, these markets may often have characteristics which actually increase the likelihood of entrenched market power over time. These could for instance be network effects, sunk costs, tipping, lock-in and so on. Entrenched market positions can thus be used anti-competitively, to exclude existing competitors or to pre-vent other potential ones from entering the market.

In the later chapters of this book we see many examples of cases and merger decisions involving new economy markets.

---

[295] Software systems whereby parties transact business online through a central node.

[296] For a case where network effects were an important issue, see Case T-201/04, *Microsoft v. Commission* [2007] ECR II-3601, discussed in Chap.7.

[297] For market definition tests, see Section 10.B

[298] Note also the battle in the early 1980s between the Betamax and VHS video formats, which was won by VHS to the total extinction of Betamax.

[299] See, e.g., J. Temple Lang, 'European Community Antitrust Law—Innovation Markets and High Technology Industries' [1996] *Fordham Corp L Inst*, 519; C. Veljanovski, 'EC Antitrust in the New Economy: Is the European Commission's View of the Network Economy Right?' [2001] *ECLR* 115; C. Ahlborn, D. S. Evans, and A. J. Padilla, 'Competition Policy in the New Economy: Is European Competition Law up to the Challenge?' [2001] *ECLR* 156; M. Monti, 'Defining the Boundaries, Competition Policy in High Tech Sectors', speech at UBS Warburg Conference, Barcelona, 11 September 2001; D. S. Evans and R. Schmalensee, 'Some Economic Aspects of Antitrust Analysis in Dynamically Competitive Industries', NBER Working Paper 8268, May 2001; R. Lind and P. Muysert, 'Innovation and Competition Policy: Challenges for the New Millennium', [2003] *ECLR* 87.

[300] Alexander Italianer, 'Level Playing-field and Innovation in Technology Markets', Conference on Antitrust in Technology, Palo Alto, 28 January 2013, <http://www.ec.europa.eu/competition/speeches/text/sp2013_01_en.pdf>.

8. COMPETITION LAW AND THE INTERNATIONAL CONTEXT

The effects of anti-competitive practices and the exercise of monopoly power can be felt in States far away from that in which the undertaking concerned is located. Many undertakings in today's globalised economy are truly 'multinational' in the sense that they have a presence throughout the world. One of the most important issues in competition law is the international application and enforcement of competition laws and there are increasing developments in international cooperation in competition matters. States throughout the world, including many developing countries, have put in place systems of competition law. The international aspects of competition law arise throughout this book, but are discussed as a whole in Chapter 16.

9. THE TECHNIQUES AND TOOLS OF COMPETITION LAW

A. GENERAL

The discussion in Section 3 suggests that appropriate competition rules should be framed:

(i) to deal with the prejudicial consequences of market power;

(ii) to deal with oligopolistic markets;

(iii) to prevent mergers which lead to a concentration in market power;

(iv) to prevent restrictive agreements between competitors (horizontal agreements); and

(v) to prevent restrictive vertical agreements which have anti-competitive consequences.

How such rules are interpreted and applied will be crucial to the pursuit of those goals.

B. FORM OR EFFECTS AND THEORIES OF HARM

It is possible for a system of competition law to be 'form' based. This entails a prohibitory approach based on the form that agreement or conduct takes, or the size or similar characteristic of parties to a merger.[301]

EU competition law is not form based. It is essentially an 'effects-based' law. The provisions are drafted in broad terms. Thus Article 101 TFEU broadly aims to prevent 'restrictive' agreements ((iv) and (v) in the list in Section 9.A); Article 102 broadly aims to prevent abuses of market power, in the terms of Article 102 'abuses of a dominant position' ((i) in the list in Section 9.A); and the Merger Regulation is intended to preclude mergers which would significantly impede effective competition, in particular by the creation or strengthening of a dominant position ((ii) and (iii) in the list in Section 9.A).[302] Ironically, despite the form of the provisions, the EU competition authorities have often been

---

[301] A clear example of such a system was that which existed in the UK under what, in its final form, was the Restrictive Trade Practices Act (RTPA) 1976. The legislation proscribed certain types of agreements between certain types of party concerning the matters listed in the Act. There was no possibility of examining the effects of agreements to see if they did in fact restrict competition. The matter was deliberately denuded of economic content and the law reduced to a number of formal propositions. The perverse result was that many harmless and even pro-competitive agreements were caught and some which were seriously anti-competitive allowed. See R. Whish, *Competition Law* (3rd edn, Butterworths, 1993), Chap. 5. The RTPA was repealed and replaced by the Competition Act 1998.

[302] These Articles are described in greater detail in Chap. 2 and are discussed fully in subsequent chapters. The control of oligopolistic markets, outside the merger context, is problematic: see Chap. 9.

criticised for failing to take a sufficiently economically rigorous approach to the application of competition law and for having instead adopted a formalistic one. They have sometimes operated on the assumption that certain things should be prohibited as a matter of course because they are bound to have an anti-competitive effect. The process of 'modernisation' has included a move towards the application of a proper 'effects-based' approach and the European Commission, which enforces the EU competition rules,[303] has displayed a greater determination to use rigorous economic analysis in its decision-making. Indeed, it will be seen in Chapter 4 that in respect of Article 101 it was the EU Courts which took the lead in moving away from a form-based approach to a more effects-based analysis. The Commission's commitment to a 'more economics' approach was epitomised by the creation of the new post of Chief Competition Economist in 2003,[304] in the wake of a number of merger cases in which the GC annulled prohibition decisions of the Commission for inadequate reasoning. An effects-based approach means that in considering a particular agreement, merger, or practice the Commission should examine the actual or likely anti-competitive effects on the basis of the actual facts before it. In other words, it is incumbent on the party alleging that the competition rules have been infringed to spell out a convincing *theory of harm*. In the following extract two economists set out the characteristics of a well-developed theory of harm.

H. Zenger and M. Walker, 'Theories of Harm in European Competition Law: A Progress Report' in J. Bourgeois and D. Waelbrock (eds.), *Ten Years of Effects-based Approach in EU Competition Law* **(Bruylant, 2012), 185 and available at SSRN: <http://ssrn.com/abstract=2009296>**

The requirement to present a theory of harm imposes a logically consistent approach to the assessment of anti-competitive behaviour. If the theory of harm is made explicit by competition authorities, then this makes it much harder for internally inconsistent or speculative competition concerns to survive the process of assessment.

A well-developed theory of harm has the following characteristics:

- it should articulate how competition, and, ultimately, consumers will be harmed relative to an appropriately defined counter-factual;
- it should be internally logically consistent;
- it should be consistent with the incentives that the various parties face; and
- it should be consistent with (or at least not inconsistent with) the available empirical evidence.

C. OVER- AND UNDER-ENFORCEMENT: TYPE 1 AND TYPE 2 ERRORS

One reason for using effects-based analysis is to achieve an optimal level of enforcement of the competition rules. Ideally EU law should avoid both over- and under-enforcement. Over-enforcement means prohibiting agreements, conduct, or mergers where there is no actual or likely anti-competitive harm. These are called Type 1 errors, or 'false positives'.[305] Under-enforcement means failing to

---

[303] See Chap. 2.

[304] Case T-342/99 *Airtours plc* v. *Commission* [2002] ECR II-2585; Case T-310/01 *Schneider Electric SA* v. *Commission* [2002] ECR II-4071; Case T-5/02 *Tetra Laval BV* v. *Commission* [2002] ECR II-4381, *aff'd* Case C-12/03P *Commission* v. *Tetra Laval* [2005] ECR I-987.

[305] The way the terminology 'Type 1' and 'Type 2' errors is used is not standardised. Some commentators use the labels the other way round. However, this book uses Type 1 errors to describe false positives and Type 2 to describe under-enforcement.

prohibit such things where there is anti-competitive harm. These are called Type 2 errors, or 'false negatives'. It is important to realise that over-enforcement of competition rules may be as harmful as under-enforcement. Indeed, the prevailing view is that it is *more* harmful because preventing things which are in reality not anti-competitive chills pro-competitive activity and stunts innovation. Whether a competition law system is equally, or more, worried about Type 1 or Type 2 errors will affect the entire way in which the law is applied.

D. THE USE OF ECONOMIC ANALYSIS

Economic analysis is not, however, a panacea. It does not necessarily tell the competition authority what the outcome of any given agreement or conduct will be. Economics itself employs assumptions, economists may come to different conclusions on any given matter, and economics does not provide the answer to every question. The applicability of the law may turn, for example, on the question whether or not a particular firm has market power. There may, however, be disagreement about what market the firm operates on (are pink widgets really substitutes for yellow widgets?) and about whether barriers to entry exist[306] to prevent other undertakings entering that market and challenging that firm's strong position. The economic view that monopoly is inefficient presents, therefore, only a starting point to the application of the law in any particular case. Furthermore, even if there is agreement that competition law should achieve consumer welfare, there can be disagreement about how allocative, productive, and dynamic efficiencies should be weighed against one another, what are the welfare implications of certain practices, or whether the protection of competitors in the short term is necessary to protect competition, and thus consumer welfare, in the longer term. We see these debates played out in the cases discussed throughout this book. Merger control, for example, discussed in Chapter 15, involves predicting the future effects of transactions that have not yet taken place.

It was seen in Section 5 that there are fashions in economic theory and schools of antitrust analysis, and that today's orthodoxy may be overtaken by new ideas. Nevertheless, given that competition policy is concerned with economic structures, conduct, and effects, it must be correct that its application should be as economically literate as possible. Faull and Nikpay explains the advantages and limitations of economic analysis in competition cases.[307]

J. Faull and A. Nikpay (eds.), *The EC Law of Competition* (2nd edn, Oxford University Press, 2007), 4

1.02 The growing acceptance and importance of economics in competition policy raises questions regarding the usefulness of economics, both for devising competition rules and for deciding on competition cases. A word of caution is appropriate in this respect. Economic thinking and economic models have proved not to be perfect guides....

1.03 Economic theories and models are built on and around assumptions. This approach has the benefit of making explicit the various elements relied upon in arriving at a particular conclusion or insight. At the same time, these assumptions by definition do not cover (all) real world situations. In addition, when the assumptions are changed the outcomes of the models may look very different. It is for these reasons that the application of economic theories may not always be able to give a clear and definitive answer, for

---

[306] See Section 10.C, p. 85 ff.

[307] See also J. Briones, 'A Balance of the Impact of Economic Analysis on the EU Competition Policy' (2009) 32 *World Competition* 27; S. Bishop, 'Snake-Oil with Mathematics is Still Snake-Oil: Why Recent Trends in the Application of So-Called "Sophisticated" Economics is Hindering Good Competition Enforcement' (2013) 9 *European Competition Journal* 67.

example as to what will happen in a market when companies merge, or when companies try to collude or engage in specific types of conduct.

1.04 The best that the application of economic principles can do in general is to provide a coherent framework of analysis, to provide relevant lines of reasoning, to identify the main issues to be checked in the context of certain theories of competitive harm, and possibly to exclude certain outcomes. In other words, it helps to tell the most plausible story. In individual cases it will be necessary first to find the concepts and the model that best fit the actual market conditions of the case and then to proceed with the analysis of the actual or possible competition consequences. Economic insights can also be useful in the formulation of policy rules, indicating under what conditions anti-competitive outcomes are very unlikely, very likely, or rather likely, and helping to devise safe harbours.

In Section 10 we introduce some of the basic economic concepts used in antitrust analysis.

10. MARKET POWER, MARKET DEFINITION, AND BARRIERS TO ENTRY

A. MARKET POWER

Economists usually define market power as the ability to price above short-run marginal cost.[308] So firms that, individually or collectively, are able to restrict output, increase prices above the competitive level, and earn monopoly profits are said to have market power. Concomitantly, they can influence the variety or quality of goods or services, innovation, and the other parameters of competition.[309] Most firms have some market power in the short term,[310] but it is 'substantial' market power which endures for a significant period of time that matters.

There are other concepts of market power, such as the power to exclude competitors, which are also relevant to competition law.[311] This is explained in the following extract.

S. Bishop and M. Walker, *The Economics of EC Competition Law* (3rd edn, Sweet & Maxwell, 2010), 3-041

The question arises as to whether there is a genuine distinction between pricing power and exclusionary power. It might be argued that exercising exclusionary power is a way of reducing the degree of competition and thereby allowing firms to raise prices. In general this is true. However, it has been argued that there are occasions where there are genuine differences between the two types of market power and that there are (more) occasions when the analysis is simplified by thinking primarily in terms of exclusionary power. This argument holds that consumers can be harmed in more ways than just by being required to pay higher prices than they would under conditions of effective competition. For instance, they might be harmed by behaviour that limits the ability of competitors to introduce new, innovative products that, as a

---

[308] See D. W. Carlton and J. M. Perloff, *Modern Industrial Organization* (4th edn, Pearson Addison Wesley, 2005), 642; Bishop and Walker, *The Economics of EC Competition Law* (cited in n. 119), 3-002; J. Faull and A. Nikpay, *The EC Law of Competition* (2nd edn, Oxford University Press, 2007), 1.19. For market power in EU competition law generally, see L. Ortiz Blanco, *Market Power in EU Antitrust Law* (Hart Publishing, 2012).

[309] Guidance Paper, see n. 202, at para. 11.

[310] For instance, customers and competitors will need time to react to the price increase.

[311] See Chap. 6; Monti, *EC Competition Law* (cited in n. 16), 124–127.

result of anti-competitive behaviour by an incumbent, never make it to the market. Behaviour of this type by an incumbent can harm consumers and increase the incumbent's profits relative to what they would be absent the anti-competitive behaviour, without necessarily raising the prices of any products in the market....

Certainly, it is noteworthy that most allegations of an abuse of a dominant position under EU law focus on what are referred to as exclusionary abuses rather than directly on what are referred to as exploitative abuses. The former include abuses such as refusing to supply, some vertical restraints and predation, whilst the latter refer to abuses such as excessive pricing and price discrimination. Further, the concept of exclusionary power is also consistent with the legal definition of 'dominance' which holds that dominance involves, inter alia, the power to act independently of competitors. This is consistent with the notion of being able to exclude competitors.

It is, however, power over price which is now the usual starting point for competition authorities.[312] In this section we introduce the concepts of market definition and barriers to entry which are central to the assessment of market power in EU competition law and to the discussion throughout this book.

In 1981 a seminal paper by William Landes and Richard Posner triggered a continuing debate about the assessment of market power, and the point at which the degree of market power warrants antitrust proceedings.[313] Landes and Posner advocated the use of the Lerner index to assess market power.[314] This expresses the concept of market power 'as the setting of price in excess of marginal cost by measuring the proportional deviation of price at the firm's profit-maximizing output from the firm's marginal costs at that output'.[315]

There are two ways of measuring a firm's market power, 'direct' and 'indirect'. The 'direct' method involves estimating the market power by using econometric methods, particularly the residual demand curve (the demand curve facing a single firm).[316] However, this requires data which is often not available and even if it is the estimation of market power in this way may prove problematic.[317]

The 'indirect' method involves a structural approach. First the 'relevant market' is defined and secondly the power on that market of the undertaking under review is assessed using market share and 'barriers to entry' analysis. Barriers to entry are vital to the determination of market power by this method since it is these which enable a firm already in the market to earn monopoly profits without attracting other firms to enter that market. The definition, identification, and significance of barriers to entry is discussed later.[318] The 'indirect' method is the one most commonly used by competition

---

[312] See Article 102 Guidance Paper, paras. 10 and 11; The OFT in its Guideline *Assessment of Market Power*, para. 1.4, expressly takes power over price as a convenient description of market power while recognising that it may consist in the ability and incentive to harm competition in other ways.

[313] W. M. Landes and R. A. Posner, 'Market Power in Antitrust Cases' (1981) 94 *Harvard L Rev* 937. See the discussion in J. Vickers, 'Market Power in Competition Cases' (2006) 2 *European Competition Journal* 3.

[314] A. P. Lerner, 'The Concept of Monopoly and the Measurement of Monopoly Power' (1934) *Rev. Economic Studies*, 157.

[315] Van den Bergh and Camesasca, *European Competition Law and Economics: A Comparative Perspective* (cited in n. 48), 110, give the simplest formulation as $L = (P − MC)/P$. See also J. Vickers, 'Market Power in Competition Cases' (2006) 2 *European Competition Journal* 3, 4–6.

[316] Called 'residual' as it is demand not met by other firms in the market: see Carlton and Perloff, *Modern Industrial Organization* (cited in n. 308), 66–69.

[317] Motta, *Competition Policy* (cited in n. 47), 116–117; Vickers, 'Market Power in Competition Cases' (cited in n.316), 7. See also J. B. Baker and T. F. Bresnahan, 'Estimating the Residual Demand Curve Facing a Single Firm' (1988) 6 *International Journal of Industrial Organization*, 283; G. Monti, *EC Competition Law* (cited in n. 16), 290, 150–153; J. A. Keyte and N. R. Stoll, 'Markets? We Don't Need No Stinking Markets! The FTC and Market Definition' (2004) 49 *Antitrust Bulletin* 593.

[318] See Section 10.C and Chap. 6.

authorities throughout the world.[319] It is used by the European Commission.[320] Moreover, it has the imprimatur of the CJ.[321]

Under the 'indirect' method, therefore, the determination of the relevant market (or 'antitrust market'[322]) is of crucial importance. This raises the important question of how a market is identified and defined.[323]

The size of a firm's market share both in absolute terms and relative to those of its competitors is the usual starting point for assessing market power.[324] It is not normally sufficient on its own for, as already noted, a more detailed analysis of the economic features of the market, such as barriers to entry, will also be required in order to determine the competitive constraints to which the firm is subject. However, in some areas of EU competition law market share stands proxy for market power. The current thinking of the Commission, in line with economic theory, is that many agreements between undertakings are not anti-competitive unless a degree of market power is present, although that degree may be less than that required to put an undertaking into a 'dominant position' for the purpose of the competition rules.[325] Block exemption regulations, which exempt categories of agreements from the prohibition in Article 101(1) TFEU, are therefore drafted to apply only to situations in which the undertakings' market shares are below certain thresholds.[326] This approximation of market share with market power is simplistic but considered the most practicable way of enabling the block exemptions to be applied. The use of market share as the sole determinant is likely to over-estimate rather than under-estimate the market power of the undertakings concerned.[327]

B. MARKET DEFINITION AND EU COMPETITION LAW

(i) The Importance of Market Definition

It is only by defining the relevant market that a firm's market power can be assessed by the 'indirect' method. The purpose of defining the relevant market is to identify which products and services are

---

[319] However, the revised US Horizontal Merger Guidelines published by the DOJ in 2010 introduced Upward Pricing Pressure as an alternative to market definition in the assessment of mergers of firms producing differentiated products (Section 6.1). The Upward Pricing Pressure concept was developed in the work of Farrell and Shapiro (see the updated version, J. Farrell and C. Shapiro, 'Antitrust Evaluation of Horizontal Mergers: An Economic Alternative to Market Definition' Working Paper, February 5 2010, <http://faculty.haas.berkeley.edu/shapiro/alternative.pdf>). It uses the value of diverted sales to measure the extent of the competitive constraint on a merging firm's product that is eliminated by the merger; see e.g. OECD Policy Roundtable on market definition DAF/COMP(2012)19, <http://www.oecd.org/daf/competition/Marketdefinition2012.pdf>, 5.1; G. das Varma, 'Will Use of the Upward Pressure Test Lead to an Increase in the Level of Merger Enforcement?' (2009) 24 (1) *Antitrust* 27; J. J. Simons and M. B. Coate, 'Upward Pressure on Price Analysis: Issues and Implications for Merger Policy' (2010) *European Competition Journal* 377.

[320] Commissioner Almunia has said that 'snazzier analytical tools' do not make the intermediate step of market definitions unnecessary, but that these tools are complementary. He gave the example of the *Unilever/Sara Lee* merger as a case in which market definition and various economic methods were all used. SPEECH 11/561, 8 September 2011.

[321] Case 6/72, *Europemballage Corp and Continental Can Co Inc v. Commission* [1973] ECR 215, para. 32 and subsequent case law: see Section 10.B.ii, p. 62, and Chap. 6.

[322] Including markets in merger cases, although, the Commission now uses 'antitrust' to denote areas of competition law other than mergers.

[323] On market definition generally, see the OECD Roundtable document, DAF/COMP(2012) 19 (cited in n. 319). See also, in respect of Article 102 TFEU, the discussion in Chap. 6.

[324] See the Guidance Paper [2009] OJ C45/2, para. 13 and Chap. 6. Market share measures 'the relative size of a firm in an industry or market, in terms of the proportion of total output, sales or capacity it accounts for': Commission Glossary of terms used in EU competition policy (Brussels, July 2002).

[325] Under Art. 102 TFEU undertakings in a 'dominant position' can infringe the rules by 'abusing' that position. See Chaps. 5–7.

[326] So below the threshold there is a 'safe harbour'. See e.g. Commission Reg. 330/2010 [2010] OJ L102/1 on vertical restraints, Chap. 11; Commission Reg. 1217/2010 [2010] OJ L335/36 on research and development agreements, and Commission Reg. 1218/2010 [2010] OJ L335/43 on specialisation agreements, Chap. 10.

[327] For the reasons why this is so see Section 10.C.i, p. 85.

such close substitutes for one another that they operate as a competitive constraint on the behaviour of the suppliers of those respective products and services. Suppose, for example, you are suspicious that Y, the only producer of yellow widgets, is exercising market power and engaging in monopoly pricing. A preliminary question which must be asked is whether or not the product has substitutes to which customers could easily turn. If it does, then if Y raises prices it will lose customers. If customers can buy blue widgets, which are perfect substitutes, from other firms a rise in the price of yellow widgets will lead customers to buy (cheaper) blue ones instead. Saying that Y has a 'monopoly' over the sale of yellow widgets is meaningless in economic terms. Similarly, suppose Y is the sole manufacturer of all colours of widgets. Y will still not be able to raise prices without losing customers if blodgets, which are made by other firms, are perfect substitutes for widgets. The problem of market definition is that it is often difficult to decide which products or services are in the same market. It is obvious, for example, that steel beams and chewing-gum are not in the same market, but what about coffee and tea, vodka and whisky, bananas and apples, Eurostar and cross-Channel ferries?

It is important to remember that market definition is not an end in itself. Rather, it is 'a tool for aiding the competitive assessment by identifying those substitute products or services which provide an effective constraint on the competitive behaviour of the products or services being offered in the market by the parties under investigation'.[328] So the guiding principle is that a relevant market is 'something worth monopolising'.[329]

We now consider how the relevant market has been defined for the purposes of EU competition law. We also outline the way in which the EU institutions go about, or should go about, actually determining what the relevant market is in any given case. Greater detail of the way in which the market has actually been determined by the EU authorities in specific contexts is set out in the relevant chapters later in this book.

(ii) The Definition of the Relevant Market

The importance of market definition has been recognised by the EU Courts. They have stressed that it is necessary to define the relevant market before a breach of Article 102 TFEU can be established[330] as the application of the Article requires the existence of a dominant position in a given market 'which presupposes that such a market has already been defined'.[331] It is also essential to the application of the Merger Regulation.[332] In respect of Article 101 TFEU the determination of the market is ordinarily necessary before it can be determined whether or not an agreement has as its effect the prevention, restriction, or distortion of competition;[333] to the determination of whether or not an agreement *appreciably* restricts competition or trade, to the determination of whether or not an agreement substantially eliminates competition in the internal market for the purposes of Article 101(3), and, in most cases, whether a block exemption is applicable or not. However, the GC noted in the *Lombard Club* judgment that market definition plays a different role in Article 101 cases

---

[328] Bishop and Walker, *The Economics of EC Competition Law* (cited in n. 119) 4-002.

[329] Bishop and Walker, *The Economics of EC Competition Law* (cited in n. 119), 4-005.

[330] Case 6/72, *Europemballage Corp and Continental Can Co Inc* v. *Commission* [1973] ECR 215, para. 32. On the other hand, if the conduct complained of would not amount to an abuse even if the undertaking concerned *was* in a dominant position it may not be necessary to define the market.

[331] Case T-62/98, *Volkswagen AG* v. *Commission* [2002] ECR II-2707, para. 231.

[332] Council Reg. 139/2004 [2004] OJ L24/1. See further Chap. 15.

[333] Cases T-374, 375, 384 and 388/94, *European Night Services* v. *Commission* [1998] ECR II-3141, paras. 93–95 and 105. In L. Kaplow, 'Why (Ever) Define Markets?' (2010) 124 *Harv. L. Review* 437 the author argues that 'the market definition process is incoherent as a matter of basic economic principle and hence should be abandoned entirely'. See the discussion of this article in *Antitrust Bulletin* Special Issue: Louis Kaplow, 'Why (Ever) Define Markets?' [2012] 57(4) *Antitrust Bulletin*.

from that in Article 102 cases.[334] In Article 101 cases concerning horizontal price-fixing, for example, it may be unnecessary for the Commission to define the market precisely. In the *Lombard Club* case, which concerned a horizontal cartel, it was justified for the Commission to use a broad market definition including many banking products that might in other contexts have belonged to separate markets, provided that an effect on competition in that market could be shown. In cartel cases the Commission is entitled to use as the relevant market the group of products over which the undertakings have colluded.[335] In *Mastercard* the GC said:[336]

171 It must also be noted that the definition of the relevant market differs according to whether Article [101] or Article [102] is to be applied. For the purposes of Article [102], the proper definition of the relevant market is a necessary precondition for any judgment as to allegedly anti-competitive behaviour, since, before an abuse of a dominant position is ascertained, it is necessary to establish the existence of a dominant position on a given market, which presupposes that such a market has already been defined. For the purposes of applying Article [101], the reason for defining the relevant market is to determine whether the agreement, the decision by an association of undertakings or the concerted practice at issue is liable to affect trade between Member States and has as its object or effect the prevention, restriction or distortion of competition within the common market. That is why, for the purposes of Article [101(1)], the objections to the definition of the market adopted by the Commission cannot be seen in isolation from those concerning the impact on trade between Member States and the impairing of competition. It has also been held that the objection to the definition of the relevant market is of no consequence provided that the Commission has rightly concluded, on the basis of the documents referred to in the contested decision, that the agreement in question distorted competition and was liable to have an appreciable effect on trade between Member States (see Case T-61/99 *Adriatica di Navigazione* v. *Commission* ... paragraph 27 ...).

The EU Courts define the relevant market in terms of substitutability ('interchangeability'). The CJ has thus adopted a definition of a relevant market which describes the market as consisting of products[337] which are interchangeable with each other but not (or only to a limited extent) interchangeable with those outside it. This interchangeability may be with other products (widgets as substitutes for blodgets) or with the same products from elsewhere (widgets from France as substitutes for widgets from the UK). The relevant market therefore has both a product aspect (the product market) and a geographical aspect (the geographic market).

The CJ has given the following definitions of the *relevant product market*:

the definition of the relevant market is of essential significance, for the possibilities of competition can only be judged in relation to those characteristics of the products in question by virtue of which those products are particularly apt to satisfy an inelastic need and are only to a limited extent interchangeable with other products.[338]

The concept of the relevant market in fact implies that there can be effective competition between the products which form part of it and this presupposes that there is a sufficient degree of interchangeability between all the products forming part of the same market insofar as a specific use of such products is concerned.[339]

---

[334] Cases T-259/02 to 264/02 and T-271/02, *Raiffeisen Zentralbank Österreich and Others* v. *Commission* [2006] ECR II-5169 (aff'd on appeal, Cases C-125, 113, 135 and 137/07 P, *Erste Group Bank AG* v. *Commission* [2009] ECR I-8681, paras. 62–63); see also Case T-61/99 *Adriatica di Navigazione* v. *Commission* [2003] ECR II-5349.

[335] See e.g. Cases T-71/03, 74/03, 87/03, and 93/03, *Tokai Carbon Co Ltd* v. *Commission* [2005] ECR II-10, para. 90; COMP/C.39181 *Candle Waxes Cartel* [2009] OJ C295/17, para. 263, on appeal Case T-540/08, *Esso and ors* v. *Commission*, judgment pending.

[336] Case T-111/08, *MasterCard Inc, MasterCard International Inc, and MasterCard Europe SPRL* v. *Commission*, 24 May 2012, on appeal Case C-382/12 P, judgment pending.

[337] Or services. The words 'products' and 'product market' encompass both products and services, as appropriate.

[338] Case 6/72, *Europemballage Corp and Continental Can Co Inc* v. *Commission* [1973] ECR 215, para. 32.

[339] Case 85/76, *Hoffmann-La Roche & Co AG* v. *EC Commission* [1979] ECR 461, para. 28; Case T-446/05 P, *Amann & Söhne GmbH & Co KG* v. *Commission* [2010] ECR II-1255, para. 55; Case T-427/08, *Confédération européenne des associations d'horlogers-réparateurs (CEAHR)* v. *Commission* [2010] ECR II-5865, para. 67.

for the purposes of investigating the possibly dominant position of an undertaking on a given market, the possibilities of competition must be judged in the context of the market comprising the totality of the products which, with respect to their characteristics, are particularly suitable for satisfying constant needs and are only to a limited extent interchangeable with other products.[340]

This approach to product market definition uses a 'functional interchangeability' yardstick based on the 'qualitative' criteria of characteristics, price, and intended use. In some cases this approach has led to controversial decisions delineating very narrow markets. In *United Brands*, for example, the CJ upheld the finding that the market for bananas was separate from the market for other fruit.[341] The Commission and the EU Courts have (at least in the past) been criticised for focusing too much attention on characteristics, price, and use. If too much attention is placed on factors which in reality tell us little about a relevant market then decisions are of course likely to be arbitrary. In particular, if the market is not determined scientifically, reference to factors such as product characteristics, intended use, and consumer preference may mean that too much subjectivity is introduced into the determination. In many circumstances this may result in the adoption of too narrow a market definition. In some cases, moreover, characteristics and intended use are not particularly useful to the determination of the relevant market. They will not shed light when trying to determine, for example, whether or not sparkling mineral water is in the same market as still mineral water, tap water, orange juice, or tonic water. All of these products have similar characteristics and uses.[342] Likewise, the fact that two products serving the same function have significantly different prices (as is the case, for example, with many consumer products such as watches, pens, perfumes, handbags) does not necessarily put them into different markets. Consumers commonly make a trade-off between price and (actual or perceived) quality and the existence of different versions may constrain the pricing decisions of the producers.

In *United Brands* the CJ set out the following definition of the *relevant geographic market*:[343]

The opportunities for competition under Article [102 TFEU] must be considered having regard to the particular features of the product in question and with reference to a clearly defined geographic area in which it is marketed and where the conditions of competition are sufficiently homogeneous for the effect of the economic power of the undertaking concerned to be able to be evaluated.... The conditions for the application of Article [102] to an undertaking in a dominant position presuppose the clear delimitation of the substantial part of the Common Market in which it may be able to engage in abuses which hinder effective competition and this is an area where the objective conditions of competition applying to the product in question must be the same for all traders.

In some cases there may also be a temporal aspect, although this is usually considered as a feature of the product and therefore part of the delineation of the product market.

The European Commission plays the key role in the enforcement of the EU competition rules and insofar as the definition of the relevant market involves complex economic assessments by the Commission it is subject to only limited review by the EU Courts.[344]

---

[340] Case 322/81, *Nederlandsche Banden-Industrie Michelin v. Commission* [1983] ECR 3461, para. 37; Case T-219/99, *British Airways v. Commission* [2003] ECR II-5917, para. 91; Case T-301/04, *Clearstream Banking AG v. Commission* [2009] ECR II-5917, para. 49; Case T-446/05 P, *Amann & Söhne GmbH & Co KG v. Commission* [2010] ECR II-1255, para. 55.

[341] See Chap. 6.

[342] See the *Nestlé/Perrier* merger case [1993] 4 CMLR M17, discussed in Chap. 15.

[343] Case 27/76, *United Brands v. Commission* [1978] ECR 207, paras. 11 and 44.

[344] Case T-65/96, *Kish Glass v. Commission* [2000] ECR II-1885, para. 64; Case T-446/05 P, *Amann & Söhne GmbH & Co KG v. Commission* [2010] ECR II-1255, para. 54; Case T-427/08, *Confédération européenne des associations d'horlogers-réparateurs (CEAHR) v. Commission* [2010] ECR II-586, para. 66.

(iii) The Commission Notice on the Definition of the Relevant Market for the Purposes of EU Competition Law

a. The Publication of the Notice

In 1997 the Commission published a Notice on the definition of the relevant market for the purposes of Community competition law.[345] The Commission had previously been criticised for taking an approach to market definition in Article 101 and Article 102 cases which was insufficiently economically rigorous and the Notice provides a 'modernised' framework for determining the relevant market on economic principles. It reflected the new practice the Commission had developed in the area of merger control after the Merger Regulation came into force in 1990.[346] The Notice is still current.

The Notice states that its purpose is to 'provide guidance as to how the Commission applies the concept of relevant product and geographic market in its ongoing enforcement of [Union] competition law' (para. 1). The Commission states that market definition is a tool to identify and define the boundaries of competition between firms and that it serves to establish the framework within which the Commission applies competition policy (para. 2).

The Notice indicates that it seeks to render public the procedures the Commission follows and the evidence which it relies upon in reaching decisions on market definition. By doing this the Commission hoped to increase transparency and assist undertakings (paras. 4 and 5), rendering more transparent the Commission's practices and leading to greater consistency in its decisions. The GC confirmed this role of the Notice in *Amann & Söhne*.[347] As in respect of other Notices, by adopting and publishing its rules of conduct the Commission has imposed a limit on the exercise of its discretion and must not depart from them on pain of being penalised for breach of fundamental principles of law such as equal treatment or protection of legitimate expectations.[348]

The Commission's approach set out in the Notice is outlined in this chapter since it describes the economic analysis which should be used to define the relevant market in all competition cases. The case law and the relevant Commission decisions in specific contexts are described in context in subsequent chapters.[349]

b. The Definition of the Relevant Market in the Notice

The definition of the relevant market adopted by the Commission in the Notice on market definition is based on that of the CJ, as already set out.

> ## Commission Notice on the Definition of the Relevant Market for the Purposes of Community Competition Law [1997] OJ C372/5
>
> 7.... A relevant product market comprises all those products and/or services which are regarded as interchangeable or substitutable by the consumer, by reason of the products' characteristics, their prices and their intended use.
>
> 8.... The relevant geographic market comprises the area in which the undertakings concerned are involved in the supply and demand of products or services, in which the conditions of competition are

---

[345] [1997] OJ C372/5.

[346] See Chaps. 6 and 15.

[347] Case T-446/05 P, *Amann & Söhne GmbH & Co KG* v. *Commission* [2010] ECR II-1255, paras. 137–139.

[348] *Amann & Söhne*, para. 137, following Cases C-189/02P, 202/02 P, 208/02 P, and 213/02 P, *Dansk Rørindustri A/S and Others* v. *Commission* [2005] ECR I-5425, paras. 209–211, see Chap. 2, Section 5, p. 118.

[349] It should be noted here, however, that the process described in the Notice is at odds with previous Commission decisions and some of the case law of the EU Courts, e.g., the treatment of 'unique suitability' in para. 43 of the Notice differs from that of the CJ in Case 27/76, *United Brands* v. *Commission* [1978] ECR 207, discussed in Section 10.B.vii.b, p. 77 and Chap. 6.

sufficiently homogeneous and which can be distinguished from neighbouring areas because the conditions of competition are appreciably different in those areas.

Paragraph 7 was cited by the GC in *CEAHR*.[350] The problem, of course, is to identify what products are considered substitutes by consumers.

(iv) Demand and Supply Substitution

We have seen that the relevant market depends on the determination of which products in which areas are substitutes for one another. If a product has perfect substitutes the sole producer of such a product has no market power, because if that supplier tries to exploit his monopoly by raising the price his customers will turn to the substitutes. There are two aspects to substitutability. *Demand substitution* is concerned with the ability of users of the product to switch to substitute products. *Supply substitution* is concerned with the ability of producers of similar products to switch to producing the relevant product. *Potential competition* is also important. The behaviour of an undertaking on a market will be constrained if potential competitors are easily able to enter the market. Potential competition is, however, ordinarily taken into account not at the stage of market definition but later on in the competitive assessment when considering an undertaking's position on the already defined market.[351]

When defining the relevant market both demand and supply substitutability have to be considered.[352] The Commission's Notice indicates however that the Commission mainly focuses on demand-side substitution.

Commission Notice on the Definition of the Relevant Market for the Purposes of Community Competition Law [1997] OJ C372/5

13.... From an economic point of view, for the definition of the relevant market, demand substitution constitutes the most immediate and effective disciplinary force on the suppliers of a given product, in particular in relation to their pricing decisions. A firm or a group of firms cannot have a significant impact on the prevailing conditions of sale, such as prices, if its customers are in a position to switch easily to available substitute products or to suppliers located elsewhere. Basically, the exercise of market definition consists in identifying the effective alternative sources of supply for the customers of the undertakings involved, in terms both of products/services and of geographic location of suppliers.

14. The competitive constraints arising from supply side substitutability other than those described in paragraphs 20 to 23 and from potential competition are in general less immediate and in any case require an analysis of additional factors. As a result such constraints are taken into account at the assessment stage of competition analysis.

Paragraph 13 was approved by the GC in *easyjet*.[353]

---

[350] *CEAHR*, para. 68,

[351] See Chap. 6.

[352] The Commission lost Case 6/72, *Europemballage Corp & Continental Can Co Inc v. Commission* [1973] ECR 215 on the issue of demand substitution, see Chap. 6.

[353] Case T-177/04, *easyjet v. Commission* [2006] ECR II- 1931, para. 99.

(v) Demand Substitution

a. Ways of Measuring Demand Substitution

Demand substitution identifies which products a consumer considers to be substitutes for another. Unless products are totally homogeneous there will be no perfect substitutes. On the other hand, most products do have substitutes of some kind. Whether or not products are substitutes for one another is dependent on a number of factors, particularly customer preference, whether customers can switch immediately or need time to adapt, whether there is similarity in quality or price, and whether the substitutes are available. The matter may be complicated if some customers can switch to substitutes but others cannot or if a product has several uses and there are substitutes for some of those uses but not for others. As already explained, products may be substitutes in one direction and not in the other (asymmetrical substitution). For example, in *Microsoft*[354] the Commission found that while a streaming media player was a substitute for a media player which delivered less functionality, substitution the other way round was not readily available as less powerful media players did not satisfy consumer demand for features such as streaming or video playback. In *AstraZeneca* purchasers had only gradually switched from one product to another but it could not be concluded from this that the first product exercised a significant competitive constraint over the other.[355]

b. The SSNIP Test

Interchangeability is gauged by measuring 'cross-elasticity of demand', as described earlier.[356] The primary method now favoured by the Commission for measuring the cross-elasticity of demand, set out in its Notice on market definition, is the hypothetical monopolist test (HMT), put into effect by using the SSNIP test. This is a 'quantitative' test that reflects the more economically rigorous approach adopted by the Commission to market definition.

SSNIP stands for a Small but Significant Non-transitory Increase in Price.[357] The test[358] has been adopted by competition authorities around the world, including the US (where it was pioneered by the DOJ in 1982), Canada, New Zealand, Australia, and the UK.[359] It is an approach which reflects contemporary economic analysis. The test is as follows: a small (5–10 per cent) rise in the price of widgets is assumed. It is then asked whether this price increase would cause widget customers to purchase blodgets, or to purchase widgets from another area, to such an extent that the price rise is unprofitable. If the answer is yes, then blodgets and/or widgets from the other area form part of the same market. The test is then repeated for that bigger bundle of products until the point is reached when the price rise would be profitable. Customers who are able and willing to switch are called 'marginal' customers.

---

[354] COMP/C-3/37.792, [2005] 4 CMLR 965, para. 415, on appeal Case T-201/04, *Microsoft* v. *Commission* [2007] ECR II-3601.

[355] Case T-321/05, *AstraZeneca* v. *Commission* [2010] ECR II-2805, paras. 89–107. The products were respectively H2 blockers and proton pump inhibitors (PPIs) for gastro-intestinal conditions. The latter gradually became the preferred treatment of choice for the more severe conditions. See Chap. 6, p. 322.

[356] See Section 3.A.ii, p. 6.

[357] Note that where buying (procurement) markets are concerned, the test may involve a postulated *reduction* in price, as in the merger case, Case T- 151/05, *Nederlandse Vakbond Varkenshouders (NVV)* v. *Commission* [2009] ECR II-1219 where in defining the geographic market the question arose as to whether a reduction in the prices paid for pigs by slaughterhouses in some areas would lead to pig farmers exporting their pigs to slaughterhouses in other areas.

[358] Van den Bergh and Camesasca, *European Competition Law and Economics: A Comparative Perspective* (cited in n. 48), 131, say that, 'The so-called SSNIP test is not a test in itself but a conceptual framework, within which several quantitative tests can be employed to address the market delineation question'.

[359] See the OFT Guideline 403, *Market Definition*, setting out the principles of market definition for the purposes of the Competition Act 1998 and, further, the report prepared for the OFT by National Economic Research Associates (S. Bishop and S. Baker), *The role of market definition in monopoly and dominance inquiries* (Economic Discussion Paper 2, July 2001, OFT 342).

Commission Notice on the Definition of the Relevant Market for the Purposes of Community Competition Law [1997] OJ C372/5

15. The assessment of demand substitution entails a determination of the range of products which are viewed as substitutes by the consumer. One way of making this determination can be viewed as a speculative experiment, postulating a hypothetical small, lasting change in relative prices and evaluating the likely reactions of customers to that increase. The exercise of market definition focuses on prices for operational and practical purposes, and more precisely on demand substitution arising from small, permanent changes in relative prices. This concept can provide clear indications as to the evidence that is relevant in defining markets.

16. Conceptually, this approach means that, starting from the type of products that the undertakings involved sell and the area in which they sell them, additional products and areas will be included in, or excluded from, the market definition depending on whether competition from these other products and areas affect or restrain sufficiently the pricing of the parties' products in the short term.

17. The question to be answered is whether the parties' customers would switch to readily available substitutes or to suppliers located elsewhere in response to a hypothetical small (in the range 5 to 10 per cent) but permanent relative price increase in the products and areas being considered. If substitution were enough to make the price increase unprofitable because of the resulting loss of sales, additional substitutes and areas are included in the relevant market. This would be done until the set of products and geographical areas is such that small, permanent increases in relative prices would be profitable. The equivalent analysis is applicable in cases concerning the concentration of buying power, where the starting point would then be the supplier and the price test serves to identify the alternative distribution channels or outlets for the supplier's products. In the application of these principles, careful account should be taken of certain particular situations as described within paragraphs 56 and 58.

18. A practical example of this test can be provided by its application to a merger of, for instance, soft-drink bottlers. An issue to examine in such a case would be to decide whether different flavours of soft drinks belong to the same market. In practice, the question to address would be whether consumers of flavour A would switch to other flavours when confronted with a permanent price increase of 5 to 10 per cent for flavour A. If a sufficient number of consumers would switch to, say, flavour B, to such an extent that the price increase for flavour A would not be profitable owing to the resulting loss of sales, then the market would compromise at least flavours A and B. The process would have to be extended in addition to other available flavours until a set of products is identified for which a price rise would not induce a sufficient substitution in demand.

19. Generally, and in particular for the analysis of merger cases, the price to take into account will be the prevailing market price. This may not be the case where the prevailing price has been determined in the absence of sufficient competition. In particular for the investigation of abuses of dominant positions, the fact that the prevailing price might already have been substantially increased will be taken into account.[360]

An economist explains the significance and advantages of the Commission's use of the SSNIP test when defining markets as follows:[361]

The success of the SSNIP is no accident. The question that it asks goes to the core of why we care about market definition in the first place. We can only answer the question of whether, for instance, a 70 per cent share of a 'market' is likely to give a company market power if that 'market' is an economically meaningful market. The key question is whether substitution to other products or other geographic regions is a substantial, or

---

[360] This is a recognition of the so-called 'cellophane fallacy'. See the discussion in Section 10.B.v.d, p. 71 ff.

[361] W. Bishop, 'Editorial: The Modernisation of DGIV' [1997] ECLR 481. This was written when the Notice was in draft form. The final version, however, did not differ in any material respect relevant here.

only a trivial, limitation on the conduct of the parties offering those products. We want to include within the market everything that offers substitution to the products at issue for significant numbers of consumers and to exclude from the market all those things that are not realistic substitutes. The SSNIP test is a convenient way of doing this.

The EU Courts have approved the use of the SSNIP test, for example in *AstraZeneca*.[362]

The practical problem, however, is actually applying the SSNIP test. How are customers' reactions to the hypothetical price rise to be gauged? The Commission attempts to answer this question in paragraphs 25–52 of the Notice. It stresses that it has an open approach to empirical evidence and recognises that the types of evidence which will be relevant and influential will depend on the industry, product, or services in question. The Commission states that it can ordinarily establish the potential market from preliminary information available or submitted by firms involved. Frequently, the matter may boil down to a question as simple as 'Is product A in the same market as product B?' Where this is so, the case may be determined without a precise definition of the market being necessary. Where greater precision in market definition is necessary, the Commission may contact the main customers and companies in the industry, professional associations, and companies in upstream markets to ascertain their views. It may address written requests for information to the market players (including asking their views on reactions to hypothetical price increases and on market boundaries), enter into discussions with them, and even carry out visits to or inspections of the premises of the parties and/or their customers and competitors. Where consumers are concerned it is recognised that asking hypothetical questions may lead to biased results and that interviewees may behave in practice differently from how they answer survey questions.[363] Research on consumer behaviour has led economists to favour 'conjoint analysis' whereby the 'trade-offs' which consumers make when confronted with different products (between, e.g., price and quality, reliability and trendiness) can be built into the analysis.[364]

The Commission states in the Notice[365] that it will consider quantitative tests devised by economists for the purpose of delineating markets. These include elasticity estimates, tests based on similarity of price movements over time (price correlation analysis),[366] causality calculations,[367] and price convergence analysis. In particular, it will consider evidence of recent substitution in the past available as a result of actual events or shocks in the market ('shock analysis'), including the entry of other competitors into the market or the introduction of new products.[368] Indeed, the Commission indicates that

---

[362] Case T-321/05, *AstraZeneca v. Commission* [2010] ECR II-2805, paras. 86–7 where the GC said, '[i]n order to evaluate the merits of the applicants' arguments, both in principle and in the specific circumstances of this case, it is necessary to place them in the theoretical framework adopted by the Commission in the Notice on market definition for the purposes of determining competitive constraints' and went on to refer to paras. 15–19 of the Notice. On appeal, Case C-457/10 P, *AstraZeneca v. Commission*, 6 December 2012, the market definition point was not taken. See also Case T-151/05, *NVV v. Commission* [2009] ECR II-1219.

[363] As anyone who has ever been asked to take part in a market research exercise will know. And see M. Hughes and N. Beale, 'Customer Surveys in UK Merger Cases—the Art and Science of Asking the Right People the Right Questions' [2005] *ECLR* 297.

[364] See B. Dunbow, 'Understanding Consumers: The Value of Stated Preferences in Antitrust Proceedings' [2003] 24 *ECLR* 141; D. Hildebrand, *The Role of Economic Analysis in the EC Competition Rules* (Kluwer Law International, 2002), 329–331; D. Hildebrand, 'The European School in EC Competition Law' (2002) 25 *World Competition* 3; D. Hildebrand, 'Using Conjoint Analysis for Market Definition: Application of Modern Market Research Tools to Implement the Hypothetical Monopolist Test' (2006) 29(2) *World Competition* 315.

[365] Para. 39.

[366] See G. J. Stigler and R. A. Sherwin, 'The Extent of the Market' (1985) 28 *Journal of Law and Economics* 555.

[367] Causality tests try to determine if there is causation from one series of prices to another, or if they mutually determine each other. The most widely accepted testing procedure recently has been 'Granger causality', a method set out in C. Granger, 'Investigating Causal Relations by Econometric Models and Cross-Spectral Methods' (1969) 37 *Econometrica* 424, see Van den Bergh and Camesasca, *European Competition Law and Economics: A Comparative Perspective* (cited in n. 48), 137.

[368] As well as things like natural disasters, strikes, sudden exchange rate changes, regulatory intervention, and the introduction of new technology.

'this sort of information will normally be fundamental for market definition'.[369] Evidence of the consequences of past launches of new products on the sales of existing products is also described as useful.

The wide range of tests that can be employed in the attempt to define markets were discussed in a 1999 report prepared by an economics consultancy for the UK competition authority, the OFT.[370] The report demonstrated that there are problems of some kind with all the tests (although these are being continually refined and improved). For example:

> Generally, tests based on price trends alone should be treated with caution, as they do not allow an assessment of whether prices could be profitably raised by market participants. However, the paucity of the data available often prevents the analyst from estimating more appropriate demand models, so that antitrust markets are defined on the basis of price tests alone.[371]

Bishop and Walker accept that price correlation analysis has several weaknesses[372] but consider that nevertheless it can provide useful information to aid market definition. One of its attractions is that it has 'relatively low information requirements and ease of use'[373] which is particularly important when, as in merger investigations, competition authorities are working to very tight deadlines.[374] There is general agreement that price correlation, Granger causality, and cointegration[375] tests may identify economic markets but do not necessarily establish antitrust markets, i.e. do not answer the question 'Is this market worth monopolising?'[376] The HMT can also be implemented through critical loss analysis.[377] This seeks to identify the smallest percentage of sales which, if lost, would make a SSNIP unprofitable[378] i.e. 'the critical loss is the point where the two opposing effects of a price increase offset each other so that the net effect in profits is nil'.[379] Critical loss analysis has drawbacks and in particular is unsuitable in two-sided markets.[380]

---

[369] Para. 38. Economics is not an experimental science. The consequences of something happening which really affects the products available on the market (e.g., a shortage arising from a natural disaster) are therefore particularly significant.

[370] OFT 266, *Quantitative techniques in competition analysis*, Research Paper 17, prepared by LECG Ltd.

[371] OFT 266, para. 2.25.

[372] Price correlation analysis is based on the idea that if two products are in the same market their prices will move in the same way over time. Similarity, however, may result from products in different markets being subject to the same changes in external forces (common shocks), such as the increase in the price of a raw material needed for both. This could result in a spurious correlation: see Motta, *Competition Policy* (cited in n. 47), 108.

[373] Bishop and Walker, *The Economics of EC Competition Law* (cited in n. 119), para. 10.02.

[374] See Chap. 15 for the time periods applicable under the EC Merger Regulation. Price correlation analysis was used, inter alia, in the leading merger cases of *Nestlé/Perrier* [1992] OJ L356/1, *Guinness/Grand Metropolitan* [1998] OJ L288/24, *Lonrho/Gencor* [1997] OJ L11/30, *Ryanair/Aer Lingus* [2008] 4 CMLR 667, *BMG/Sony* [2005] OJ L65/30. Merger simulation, which attempts to directly calculate how much prices are likely to rise post-merger may also be used in merger cases, as it was in *Volvo/Scania* [2001] OJ L143/74.

[375] Cointegration analysis looks at the relationship between economic data series, such as price series, and examines whether it is stable over the long term.

[376] OFT 266, para. 8.7; Bishop and Walker, *The Economics of EC Competition Law* (cited in n. 119), para. 10-73; H. Wills, 'Market Definition: How Stationarity Tests Can Improve Accuracy' [2002] *ECLR* 4.

[377] See Van den Bergh and Camesasca, *European Competition Law and Economics: A Comparative Perspective* (cited in n. 48), 137–140; Faull and Nikpay, *The EC Law of Competition* (cited in n. 308), 1.277–1.282; Geradin et al., *EU Competition Law and Economics* (cited in n. 18), 4.35-4.36; OECD Roundtable on market definition (cited in n.319), 3.2.3; D. P. O'Brien and A. L. Wickelgreen, 'A Critical Analysis of Critical Loss Analysis' (2003) 70 *Antitrust Law Journal* 161; B. Harris and C. Veljanovski, 'Critical Loss Analysis: Its Growing Use in Competition Law' [2003] *ECLR* 213; I. Kokkoris, 'Critical Loss Analysis: Critically Ill?' [2005] *ECLR* 518; Ø. Daljord, 'An Exact Arithmetic SSNIP Test for Asymmetric Products' (2009) 5(3) *JCL & E* 563; K. Hüschelrath, 'Critical Loss Analysis in Market Definition and Merger Control (2009) 3 *European Competition Journal* 757; A. Ten Kate and G. Niels, 'The Concept of Critical Loss for a Group of Differentiated Products' (2010) 6(2) *JCL & E* 321.

[378] G. Bellamy and G. Child (V. Rose and D. Bailey, eds.), *European Law of Competition* (7th edn, Oxford University Press, 2013), 4.039.

[379] O'Donoghue and Padilla, *The Law and Economics of Article 102* (cited in n. 279), 110.

[380] Geradin et al., *EU Competition Law and Economics* (cited in n. 18), 4.36. For two-sided markets, see Section 10.B.vii.j, p. 81

However, as the OFT report concluded, although quantitative techniques are not 'magic bullets' they can, when used correctly and rigorously, be helpful tools.[381] Faull and Nikpay conclude that the value of the SSNIP test is in directing the attention to asking the right questions:

In our view, the complexity of the SSNIP test should, however, not be overemphasised. The most important aspect of the SSNIP is its conceptual side, not its quantitative side...Even when no detailed data are available, it is useful to think of the market definition question in terms of SSNIP. By asking a question which is directly linked to the purpose of antitrust analysis (is the exercise of market power an issue for this collection of products or not?), it brings a certain structure and consistency to the market definition exercise. The SSNIP concept provides for a framework within which to consider the question of economic substitution.[382]

c. Switching Costs

The Commission will not consider two *prima facie* demand substitutes as belonging to one market if it sees that there are obstacles which will prevent or hinder customers from changing. Paragraph 42 of the Notice discusses 'switching costs':

42. *Barriers and costs associated with switching demand to potential substitutes.*

There are a number of barriers and costs that might prevent the Commission from considering two prima facie demand substitutes as belonging to one single product market. It is not possible to provide an exhaustive list of all the possible barriers to substitution and of switching costs. These barriers or obstacles might have a wide range of origins, and in its decisions, the Commission has been confronted with regulatory barriers or other forms of State intervention, constraints arising in downstream markets, need to incur specific capital investment or loss in current output in order to switch to alternative inputs, the location of customers, specific investment in production process, learning and human capital investment, retooling costs of other investments, uncertainty about quality and reputation of unknown suppliers, and others.

Switching costs are therefore the price which consumers pay for changing to another product. They are not necessarily financial but cover inconvenience and hassle as well. Switching costs may also act as barriers to entry[383] and may be created or increased by incumbent firms as an exclusionary tactic.

d. The Cellophane Fallacy

A major problem with the SSNIP test is known as the 'cellophane fallacy'. Paragraph 19 of the Notice recognises the difficulties presented by the cellophane fallacy (although it does not refer to it as such). The fallacy arises from the fact that the SSNIP test cannot identify whether the current price is already a monopoly price resulting from the exercise of market power. It is named after the subject matter of a US case in which the Supreme Court is said to have failed to recognise it, in that it erroneously accepted Du Pont's argument that cellophane was not a separate relevant market but competed directly and closely with other flexible packaging materials such as aluminium foil, polythene, and wax paper.[384]

The difficulty is that a profit-maximising firm will price as high as it can. If X is the sole supplier of widgets it will normally set the price of widgets at a level where other products constrain it. If the marginal cost of a widget is £5 but blodgets, which perform the same function as widgets, are sold at their marginal cost of £10, X will sell widgets at just under £10. That way X still makes a supra-normal profit and does not lose out to the blodget manufacturers. At the price of £10 blodgets and widgets are substitutes, and X can argue, as Du Pont did in *Cellophane*, that since it cannot raise

---

[381] OFT 266, para. 18.12.

[382] Faull and Nikpay, *The EC Law of Competition* (cited in n. 308), 1.14L. Peeperkorn and V. Verouden).

[383] See Section 10.C.iii, p. 88 ff.

[384] *United States v. EI du Pont de Nemours & Co* 351 US 377 (1956).

the price without losing sales it must be operating on a competitive market. Yet X is already making a monopoly profit. It may have no substitutes at its competitive price of £5 but will at £10. In the *Cellophane* case the Supreme Court found that the market was that for all flexible wrapping materials as other materials competed with cellophane at its current price. It did not ask, however, whether or not cross-elasticity between cellophane and other materials was only high *because Du Pont was already exercising market power*. The Notice recognises this difficulty. The Commission states that using the prevailing market price as the base figure from which to hypothesise the 5–10 per cent price rise of the SSNIP test may be inappropriate where that price has been determined in the absence of competition. This means that great care will have to be exercised if using the SSNIP test to determine whether or not an incumbent on a market has a 'dominant position' (or market power) for the purposes of Article 102. Recognition of the cellophane fallacy prevented the Commission using the SSNIP test in the Article 101 case *MasterCard*.[385]

In contrast, in merger cases it has only to be decided whether or not the merger will create or increase market power. The SSNIP test is thus much more reliable since the prevailing market price is the appropriate starting point from which to assess the effects of the merger.

The cellophane fallacy is a great problem because in very many markets prices do reflect some degree of market power and the failings of the SSNIP test in dealing with these is a serious limitation on its utility in non-merger cases. Furthermore, it is not just an issue where prices are already set above the competitive level, but also where the prevailing price is too low.[386] However, although the Notice recognises the problem it makes no suggestions for dealing with it. Geradin, Layne-Farrar, and Petit suggest how the problem should be approached.

D. Geradin, A. Layne-Farrar, and N. Petit, *EU Competition Law and Economics* (Oxford University Press, 2012), 185–186

4.46 To guard against the cellophane fallacy, one could estimate the competitive price before conducting a hypothetical monopolist test with a SSNIP or a critical loss test. In practice, however, if determining the competitive price were easy, we would not need to conduct any other tests. We could simply compare the actual price the undertaking was charging in the marketplace with the competitive one to assess that undertaking's market power—we would not need any HMT or critical loss estimation. Alternatively, one could ignore the HMT test and instead rely on qualitative evidence to determine the relevant market. The point of the HMT and critical loss tests, however, is to provide meaningful structure to the assessment of markets, to ensure that physically similar products are included in the same market only when consumers view them as substitutes, and to identify those seemingly dissimilar products that should be included in a market because consumers substitute among them. It is difficult to impossible to achieve those goals through qualitative analysis alone. As a result, the Commission's Discussion Paper observes that '[t]he SSNIP test at prevailing prices remains useful in the sense that it is indicative of substitution patterns at those prices'.[387]

The best approach, then, is to conduct a SSNIP or critical loss test, but compare the results against other measures to ensure that the market has not been defined too broadly and thus falsely indicated a lack of market power. One way to do [that] is to consider multiple tests with qualitative checks, where consistent results among all of the evidence would offer the most reliable market definition.

---

[385] COMP/C.34.579, *MasterCard*, 19 December 2007, on appeal Case T-111/08, *MasterCard Inc, MasterCard International Inc, and MasterCard Europe SPRL v. Commission*, 24 May 2012.

[386] See P. Crocioni, 'The Hypothetical Monopolist Test: What it can and cannot tell you' [2002] *ECLR* 355.

[387] This is a reference to the Commission Staff Discussion Paper on the application of Article 82 to exclusionary abuses, Brussels, 9 December 2005, para. 15. For the Discussion Paper, see Chap. 5.

e. Characteristics and Intended Use

In paragraph 36 of the Notice the Commission recognises the limited usefulness of analysing the characteristics and intended use of a product when defining the market. The Notice indicates, however, that such an analysis may be useful as a preliminary step when considering the possible substitutes for a product.

Commission Notice on the Definition of the Relevant Market for the Purposes of Community Competition Law [1997] OJ C372/5

36. An analysis of the product characteristics and its intended use allows the Commission, as a first step, to limit the field of investigation of possible substitutes. However, product characteristics and intended use are insufficient to show whether two products are demand substitutes. Functional interchangeability or similarity in characteristics may not, in themselves, provide sufficient criteria, because the responsiveness of customers to relative price changes may be determined by other considerations as well. For example, there may be different competitive constraints in the original equipment market for car components and in spare parts, thereby leading to a separate delineation of two relevant markets. Conversely, differences in product characteristics are not in themselves sufficient to exclude demand substitutability, since this will depend to a large extent on how customers value different characteristics.

However, as has already been noted, in the past an analysis of the characteristics and use of the product were the usual criteria for identifying substitutability and it was above all the experience of the Commission in defining markets for the purpose of merger control which led it to favour the more economic SSNIP test. The case law of the EU Courts and the decisions of the Commission discussed in this book are replete with considerations of characteristics and use in market definition.[388] It is the examination of the characteristics of the product which have given rise to the greatest criticisms, as in the *United Brands* case, where the CJ famously had to decide whether bananas were in a separate market from fruit.[389] In some cases, however, a consideration of the use of the product can be crucial because it can then be determined that it has no substitutes. Since the publication of the Notice the Commission itself has continued to use characteristics and use where appropriate, in particular where there is insufficient data to apply the SSNIP test, as is often the case.[390] In its *Michelin* decision of 2001 (*Michelin II*),[391] the Commission held, without mentioning the SSNIP test, that the market for new replacement tyres for lorries and buses was separate to that for retreads. It took into account the 'analysis of their specific characteristics and their uses by final consumers'[392] based on surveys

---

[388]   See particularly Chap. 6.

[389]   Case 2/76, *United Brands v. Commission* [1978] ECR 207.

[390]   See, for example, *Van den Bergh Foods Ltd* [1998] OJ L246/1, particularly paras. 130–138, where the Commission held that impulse ice cream (bought as individual portions in shops for immediate consumption) and take-home ice cream (multi-packs of single items designed for storage and consumption at home) were in different markets (it also distinguished catering ice cream, sold in bulk to catering establishments, from impulse and take-home ice cream, and it distinguished between the markets for industrial (produced for wide-scale distribution) and 'artisan' (produced, distributed, and consumed locally on a small scale) ice cream. The decision was upheld in Case T-65/98, *Van den Bergh Foods Ltd v. Commission* [2003] ECR II-4653, where the GC said that the 'distinction on the basis of the consumer's intended purpose in purchasing the ice cream in turn determines the differences in characteristics and price between impulse and take-home products' (para. 132).

[391]   [2002] OJ L58/25, [2002] 5 CMLR 388, upheld by the GC on appeal, Case T-203/01, *Michelin v. Commission* [2003] ECR II-4071. The case was, in effect, a sequel to the 1981 case, Case 322/81, *Nederlandsche Banden-Industrie Michelin v. Commission* [1983] ECR 3461: see further Chap. 6.

[392]   *Michelin II*, para. 116.

of those consumers (the haulier firms). In three more recent Article 102 decisions, *Microsoft*,[393] *Wanadoo*,[394] and *Clearstream*,[395] the Commission relied heavily on qualitative analysis, although in *Wanadoo* it also referred to the SSNIP test.[396] In short, the examination of characteristics and use is often not in practice confined to the 'first step' as suggested in paragraph 36 of the Notice, particularly in view of the very real difficulties caused by the cellophane fallacy in so many non-merger cases.

f. Price

The price of products may affect whether or not they are in the same market. Price may be a reflection of a product's characteristics. This is so with products which are available in cheap utility and in luxury versions, such as pens, watches, cosmetics, and perfume, where the price difference relates to characteristics which do not necessarily affect use and function. In such cases the utility and luxury versions may be in separate product markets. For example, in *CEAHR* the GC accepted the Commission's distinction between cheap watches and luxury/prestige watches costing 60 to 160 times as much.[397] However, cheap and luxury products may also be part of a continuous chain of substitution in which a rise in the price of the cheapest model may lead consumers to switch to the next cheapest, and so on.[398] An example of a case where price put products into different markets is *Microsoft* where the Commission held that higher-level operating systems and basic workgroup server systems were in different markets because it would be 'extremely cost inefficient' for a customer to buy a (more expensive) higher-level system just to fulfil basic workgroup functions.[399]

(vi) Supply Substitution

In *Continental Can*[400] the CJ stated that the market must be defined by reference both to supply-side and demand-side substitutability. If a manufacturer of one product can readily switch production to another product then both products may be in the same market.[401] The difficulty is to distinguish supply-side substitutability from potential competition. The Commission considers this dilemma in the Notice and concludes that it is a question of time scale. If a producer of one product can switch production to another in the short term, without significant cost or risk, then those two products will be found to be in the same market. If a producer can enter the market but only in the longer term and after incurring some cost, then that producer is not relevant at the stage of market definition. It will be important, however, when assessing market power: if the producer can enter the market then it is a potential competitor and its existence will have a constraining effect on those operating on the market. Supply substitution is likely to be possible only where producers make products which,

---

[393] COMP/C-3/37.792, *Microsoft* [2005] 4 CMLR 965, *aff'd* Case T-201/04, *Microsoft* v. *Commission* [2007] ECR II-3601.

[394] COMP/38.233, [2005] 5 CMLR 120, *aff'd* Case C-202/07 P, *France Télécom* v. *Commission* [2009] ECR I-2369.

[395] COMP/38/096, [2005] 5 CMLR 1302, *aff'd* Case T-301/04, *Clearstream Banking* v. *Commission* [2009] ECR II-3155.

[396] See further Chap. 6.

[397] Case T-427/08, *Confédération européenne des associations d'horlogers-réparateurs (CEAHR)* v. *Commission* [2010] ECR II-5865, paras. 73–74. The phrase 'luxury/prestige' was the Commission's interpretation of the description 'watches worth repairing' contained in the complaint whose rejection was the subject of the case.

[398] For chains of substitution, see Section 10.B.vii.a, p. 76.

[399] COMP/C-3/37.792, *Microsoft* [2005] 4 CMLR 965, para. 376.

[400] Case 6/72, *Europemballage Corp & Continental Can Co Inc* v. *Commission* [1973] ECR 215.

[401] The SSNIP test can be applied to supply-side substitution by postulating whether the price increase would be rendered unprofitable by other suppliers moving to produce the product; see G. Niels, 'The SSNIP Test: Some Common Misconceptions' (2004) *Competition Law Journal* 267; Bellamy and Child, *European Law of Competition* (cited in n. 378), 4.053.

while not substitutes for one another from the consumer's perspective are, nonetheless, similar. An example, given by the Commission in its Notice, is markets for paper.[402]

Commission Notice on the Definition of the Relevant Market for the Purposes of Community Competition Law [1997] OJ C372/5

20. Supply-side substitutability may also be taken into account when defining markets in those situations in which its effects are equivalent to those of demand substitution in terms of effectiveness and immediacy. This means that suppliers are able to switch production to the relevant products and market them in the short term.... without incurring significant additional costs or risks in response to small and permanent changes in relative prices. When these conditions are met, the additional production that is put on the market will have a disciplinary effect on the competitive behaviour of the companies involved. Such an impact in terms of effectiveness and immediacy is equivalent to the demand substitution effect.

21. These situations typically arise when companies market a wide range of qualities or grades of one product; even if, for a given final customer or group of consumers, the different qualities are not substitutable, the different qualities will be grouped into one product market, provided that most of the suppliers are able to offer and sell the various qualities immediately and without the significant increases in costs described above. In such cases, the relevant product market will encompass all products that are substitutable in demand and supply, and the current sales of those products will be aggregated so as to give the total value or volume of the market. The same reasoning may lead to group different geographic areas.

22. A practical example of the approach to supply-side substitutability when defining product markets is to be found in the case of paper. Paper is usually supplied in a range of different qualities, from standard writing paper to high quality papers to be used, for instance, to publish art books. From a demand point of view, different qualities of paper cannot be used for any given use, i.e., an art book or a high quality publication cannot be based on lower quality papers. However, paper plants are prepared to manufacture the different qualities, and production can be adjusted with negligible costs and in a short time-frame. In the absence of particular difficulties in distribution, paper manufacturers are able therefore, to compete for orders of the various qualities, in particular if orders are placed with sufficient lead time to allow for modification of production plans. Under such circumstances, the Commission would not define a separate market for each quality of paper and its respective use. The various qualities of paper are included in the relevant market, and their sales added up to estimate total market value and volume.

23. When supply-side substitutability would entail the need to adjust significantly existing tangible and intangible assets, additional investments, strategic decisions or time delays, it will not be considered at the stage of market definition. Examples where supply-side substitution did not induce the Commission to enlarge the market are offered in the area of consumer products, in particular for branded beverages. Although bottling plants may in principle bottle different beverages, there are costs and lead times involved (in terms of advertising, product testing and distribution) before the products can actually be sold. In these cases, the effects of supply-side substitutability and other forms of potential competition would then be examined at a later stage.

---

[402] In Case IV/M.166, *Torras/Sarrio* (1992) the Commission relied upon supply-side substitution in considering a merger in the paper sector, see M. Furse, *The Law of Merger Control in the EC and the UK* (Hart Publishing, 2007), 33. See also Case IV/M.458, *Electrolux/AEG* (all models and sizes of washing machines found to be in the same market, ditto for dishwashers, fridges, microwaves, and so on); Case T-65/96, *Kish Glass and Co Ltd v. Commission* [2000] ECR II-1885, *aff'd* Case C-241/00 P, *Kish Glass and Co Ltd v. Commission* [2001] ECR I-7159 where the market definition point was not pleaded (different thicknesses of glass in the same market).

The GC referred to paragraphs 20–23 in *Amann & Söhne*, to determine 'in the light of those considerations, whether the Commission correctly applied the criterion of supply-side substitutability'.[403] That case concerned industrial thread. The Commission concluded that there were two markets from the point of view of the supply side, automotive (for use in the motor industry) and non-automotive (for use in clothing, embroidery, footwear, etc). Automotive thread is manufactured to higher specifications, to comply with ISO standards, although it can be used in the non-automotive sector also. The Commission found that non-automotive thread producers would have no interest in incurring the higher costs associated with automotive thread production solely on the ground that it might sell that thread to motor industry customers. The GC confirmed that the Commission had committed no manifest error in finding that there was no supply substitution here and that the automotive and non-automotive markets were distinct.[404]

Whether supply-side issues are taken into account at the market definition stage can be of utmost importance in cases where the only issue is market share and there is no 'later stage' as referred to at the end of paragraph 23 of the Notice. As already explained, a feature of recent block exemption regulations is that they apply only to agreements where the parties have market shares below a particular threshold.[405] Supply-side substitution taken into account at the market definition stage may widen the market and enable the parties concerned to take advantage of the block exemption, while they may have too large a share of a narrower market. Furthermore, in cases where the question is whether an undertaking is in a dominant position, too little emphasis on supply-side substitutability may lead to over-narrow definitions of the market, a matter which is not necessarily remedied by taking into account potential competition at the next stage of the assessment of market power. In particular, a presumption of dominance for the purposes of Article 102 is triggered at a market share of 50 per cent so the dynamics of the assessment may be skewed by omitting supply-side substitutability.[406]

(vii) Particular Issues in Market Definition

a. Chains of Substitution

Demand-side substitutability can be complicated by the existence of a 'chain of substitution', where B is a substitute for A and C is a substitute for B, etc. This can occur in geographic as well as product markets.[407] For example, two shops may compete for the customers who live between them, but for customers who live the far side of either of them the substitute may be different:

Shop A ← customer 1 → **Shop B** ← customer 2 → **Shop C** ← customer 3 → **Shop D**

In this example, shops A and B are substitutes for customer 1, shops B and C are substitutes for customer 2, and shops C and D are substitutes for customer 3. Shops A and D, A and C, B and D are not direct substitutes for any customer. How then are the boundaries of the geographic market to be drawn? In product markets chains of substitution can arise from products with multiple uses or from versions of products sold at different prices as noted earlier. The Commission's Notice discusses the chain of substitution problem in paragraphs 57 and 58, and at the end of 57 concludes that the real question is how far the existence of substitutes has a constraining influence on an undertaking's pricing policy. So a chain of substitution can place a series of products into a single market if

---

[403] Case T-446/05 P, *Amann & Söhne GmbH & Co KG v. Commission* [2010] ECR II-1255, para. 73.

[404] Case T-446/05 P, *Amann & Söhne GmbH & Co KG v. Commission* [2010] ECR II-1255, paras 74–88.

[405] See p. 61 and e.g. Commission Reg. 330/2010 [2010] OJ L102/1 on vertical restraints, Chap. 11; Commission Reg. 1218/2010 [2010] OJ L335/43 on specialisation agreements, Commission Reg. 1217/2010 [2010] OJ L335/36 on research and development agreements, Chap. 10; Commission Reg. 772/2004 [2004] OJ L123/11 on technology transfer agreements, Chap. 12. The Notice on agreements of minor importance [2001] OJ C368/13, Chap. 3, also uses market share thresholds.

[406] For a more detailed discussion of this see Chap. 6.

[407] For geographic market definition, see further Section 10.B.viii, p. 82.

a SSNIP in respect of products in one part of the chain would be unprofitable because customers would switch to products elsewhere in the chain.

57. In certain cases, the existence of chains of substitution might lead to the definition of a relevant market where products or areas at the extreme of the market are not directly substitutable. An example might be provided by the geographic dimension of a product with significant transport costs. In such cases, deliveries from a given plant are limited to a certain area around each plant by the impact of transport costs. In principle, such an area could constitute the relevant geographic market. However, if the distribution of plants is such that there are considerable overlaps between the areas around different plants, it is possible that the pricing of those products will be constrained by a chain substitution effect, and lead to the definition of a broader geographic market. The same reasoning may apply if product B is a demand substitute for products A and C. Even if products A and C are not direct demand substitutes, they might be found to be in the same relevant product market since their respective pricing might be constrained by substitution to B.

58. From a practical perspective, the concept of chains of substitution has to be corroborated by actual evidence, for instance related to price inter-dependence at the extremes of the chains of substitution, in order to lead to an extension of the relevant market in an individual case. Price levels at the extremes of the chains would have to be of the same magnitude as well.[408]

Chains of substitution are discussed further in Chapter 6.

b. Distinct Groups of Customers

Customers as a whole have different preferences and priorities but exercises in market definition have to recognise that some customers may be able to turn to a substitute in response to a price rise while for others it is impossible. A person who cannot drive, for example, cannot respond to an increase in rail fares by driving him- or herself in a car, and customers may be 'locked in' because of previous choices they have made. The most (in)famous case of this problem in EU law is *United Brands*[409] in which the CJ confirmed the Commission's finding that there was a market for bananas separate from that for other fruit partly on the grounds that for some consumers (the very young, the old, and the sick) bananas were a uniquely suitable fruit (they can be mashed up for babies, are easily digestible, are easy to handle, and can be eaten by people with no teeth). This reasoning, however, is incorrect. The fact that bananas satisfy a unique need of a particular class of customers does not mean that bananas constitute a separate market if the average customer is not so limited in their choice of fruit and can respond to a price rise in bananas by buying other fruit. Although it may be possible at point of sale to discriminate *in favour* of certain customers (such as students or old age pensioners) on production of identification, it is generally not possible to discriminate in the same way *against* individuals, for example pensioners, and to charge them a higher price. If it is impossible to discriminate against the 'infra-marginal' customers who cannot switch—the young, old, and sick—by charging them a higher price, then the behaviour of marginal customers (who are able to switch) must be taken into account. It is the marginal customers who affect a supplier's pricing decisions and whose behaviour is, consequently, crucial in the determination of the market. One group of customers which has a particular need for the product is difficult to exploit unless it can somehow be kept separate from other customers and the other customers can be prevented from making sales on to the special class or the profits from the special class outweigh the loss of the marginal customers.

In its Notice on market definition the Commission recognises (despite the *United Brands* judgment) that a distinct group of customers will be relevant to market definition only where they constitute a separate market and price discrimination between the different groups of customers is possible:

---

[408] Bellamy and Child, *European Law of Competition* (cited in n. 378), 4.063, n. 246 point out that the last sentence of para. 58 only applies to chains in geographic markets.

[409] Case 2/76, *United Brands v. Commission* [1978] ECR 207.

43. The extent of the product market might be narrowed in the presence of distinct groups of customers. A distinct group of customers for the relevant product may constitute a narrower, distinct market when such a group could be subject to price discrimination. This will usually be the case when two conditions are met: (a) it is possible to identify clearly which group an individual customer belongs to at the moment of selling the relevant products to him, and (b) trade among customers or arbitrage by third parties should not be feasible.

United Brands is examined in Chapter 6.

c. Markets in the New Economy

One of the problems in applying competition law to the 'new economy' is the application of the usual principles of market definition. The SSNIP test tries to identify short-term demand substitutability by positing a small but significant price rise. However, as we have seen,[410] the high technology markets of the new economy are characterised by dynamic competition, where the threat to existing products comes from new products. The implicit assumption underlying the SSNIP test, however, is that the products are homogeneous and competitors compete on price. Concentrating on hypothetical price rises instead of the competitive constraints stemming from product innovation may lead in dynamically competitive industries to the identification of over-narrow markets.

Application of the SSNIP test in an industry where competition is performance-based (almost always true when product innovation is present) rather than purely price-related is likely to create a downward bias in the definition of the size of the relevant product market, and a corresponding upward bias in the assessment of market power.[411]

It has therefore been argued that the importance of market definition should be down-played where new economy markets are concerned and that over-reliance on market shares should be avoided.[412] Market definition in the new economy is a particular problem in merger cases, where the merging parties may be hoping to produce innovative products which do not yet exist.[413] The concept of an 'innovation market' may be useful here. An innovation market consists of the research and development (R & D) directed to a particular new or improved product or process and its close substitutes. Bishop and Walker consider that (i) where possible it is probably better to define standard product markets than more speculative innovation markets, (ii) there are competition issues that are best analysed using the innovation market concept but (iii) where the issue *is* best analysed using innovation markets, market shares should be interpreted with great care.[414]

d. Technology Markets

There can be a market in the technology used in the production of a product which is distinct from the market for the product itself. Technology markets are relevant in respect of technology licensing agreements[415] and R & D horizontal cooperation agreements.[416] They consist of the

---

[410] See Section 7.D.

[411] D. Teece and M. Coleman, 'The Meaning of Monopoly: Antitrust Analysis in High-technology Industries' [1998] *Antitrust Bulletin* 801, 827–828.

[412] Over-reliance on market shares is criticised in relation to all markets, as discussed in Chap. 6, but in the new economy context it is considered particularly damaging.

[413] See Chap. 15. For further discussion of the issue in respect of Art. 102 cases such as *Microsoft* (cited in n. 393) and *Wanadoo* (cited in n. 394), see Chap. 6.

[414] Bishop and Walker, *The Economics of EC Competition Law* (cited in n. 119), 4-44. The Commission uses the concept 'innovation and new products markets' in the Horizontal Cooperation Guidelines [2010] OJ C11/1, para. 119, and 'innovation markets' in the 2004 Technology Transfer Guidelines [2004] OJ C101/2, para. 25. However, the wording in the corresponding paragraph to the 2004 Guidelines in the Draft Technology Transfer Guidelines of 20 February 2013 (para. 26) has been changed to 'competition in innovation' rather than 'innovation markets'.

[415] Chap. 12.

[416] Chap. 10.

technology which is licensed or marketed by the parties and the substitutes to which licensees or customers could switch in response to a SSNIP.[417]

e. The Structure of Supply and Demand

The structure of supply and demand may be important in determining the relevant market and may cause identical products to fall into different markets because the dynamics of the transactions concerning them differ. The structure of supply and demand may also create 'sub-markets'. This is seen further in Chapter 6.

f. One Market or Two?

Special problems of market definition arise where products are connected with one another but are not substitutes. Demand substitutability does not help with the issue of determining whether certain products are one whole product (or 'system') or whether they are separate. One aspect of this is the matter of 'aftermarkets'. In other situations the products may be supplied at the same time, or may be part of a range sold together. What, for instance, about size 38 and size 42 shoes (they are not substitutes for one another, so does that mean there are separate product markets for each size of shoe?).[418] Is a pair of shoes one product or two (a right and left shoe are not substitutes for one another)? What about the shoes and the laces (again, they are not substitutes for one another)? The division of products into separate markets can be crucial in cases concerning allegations of 'tying' or 'bundling' which may constitute an abuse of a dominant position contrary to Article 102.[419] In *Microsoft* the GC held that the criterion for assessing the distinctiveness of products in Article 102 cases is consumer demand.[420]

g. Aftermarkets

An 'aftermarket' is a market comprising complementary ('secondary') products or services that are purchased after another ('primary') product to which they relate. Many durable goods, such as cars, need compatible spare parts and some, such as vacuum cleaners or photocopiers, need a constant supply of 'consumables': some cleaners need bags or filters, photocopiers need toner cartridges and paper, and so on. Furthermore, durables may need to be serviced and repaired. The customer may be 'locked in'—the owner of a Ford Focus needs spare parts which fit a Ford Focus, not those which fit a Honda Civic. The Commission Notice, paragraph 56 says that this is an area 'where the application of the principles above has to be undertaken with care'. It recognises that 'constraints on substitution imposed by conditions in the connected markets' must be taken into account. Although the normal approach to market definition may result in an aftermarket consisting of one brand of spare parts where compatibility with a primary product is important, that may not be, in certain situations, a 'relevant product market' for the purpose of the competition rules. The Notice says that:[421]

a different market definition may result if significant substitution between secondary products is possible or if the characteristics of the primary products make quick and direct consumer responses to relative price increases of the secondary products feasible.

This recognises that if customers can see the costs they will incur in the aftermarket when buying the primary product (i.e. they can estimate the 'whole-life' cost of the primary and secondary

---

[417] See the Horizontal Cooperation Guidelines, n. 414, paras. 116–117; Draft Technology Transfer Guidelines, para. 22, repeating para. 22 of the Technology Transfer Guidelines 2004, n. 414; and further Chaps. 10 and 12.

[418] See the definition of the tyre market in Case 322/81, *NV Nederlandsche Banden-Industrie Michelin* v. *Commission* [1983] ECR 3461, discussed in Chap. 6.

[419] See further Chap. 7.

[420] Case T-201/04, *Microsoft* v. *Commission* [2007] ECR II-3601, para. 917.

[421] OJ [1997] C 372/5, para. 56.

products together) the decision as to which brand of primary product to purchase may be influenced by those costs. In such a case the primary and secondary products will comprise one single unified ('system') market and the competition is between the 'systems'. Paragraph 56 was cited by the GC in CEAHR.[422] In the Discussion Paper on Article 102[423] the Commission said that one brand of secondary products will not be a relevant product market first, where customers can switch to the secondary products of other producers and secondly, where it is possible to switch to another primary product and thus avoid the higher prices in the aftermarket. The Commission repeated this in its CEAHR decision.[424]

In CEAHR the GC confirmed this approach to market definition in respect of aftermarkets[425] although it annulled the Commission decision, inter alia for failing to apply it correctly.[426] The Commission had rejected a complaint from a confederation of national associations of independent watch repairers about the alleged collusive behaviour of luxury/prestige watch manufacturers in refusing to supply them with spare parts. The Commission took the view that there were no separate markets in spare parts for, and the repair and maintenance of, luxury/prestige watches (those costing between €1500 and €4000 when bought new). Rather, they were part of the highly competitive primary product market. The GC found that the Commission had not satisfactorily established whether the different brands of spare parts were substitutes for one another or that consumers could or would reasonably switch to another primary product in order to avoid a price increase for spare parts. In respect of the latter:

The factors raised by the Commission merely indicate a purely theoretical possibility of switching to another primary product, which is not a sufficient demonstration for the purposes of the definition of the relevant market. That definition is based on the concept that effective competition exists, which presupposes that a sufficient number of consumers would actually switch to another primary product in the event of a moderate price increase for spare parts in order to make such an increase unprofitable.[427]

Further, the Commission argued that purchasers of the primary product (the watch) were influenced by price increases in the repair and maintenance market when making their original choice between the luxury brands, thus making this a 'systems' market. The GC held that the Commission had not shown this to be so, and indeed had said itself that the cost of repairs was minor and insignificant compared to the price of the watch.[428]

h. Markets for Raw Materials and 'Inputs'

A raw material may constitute a separate product market even though the derivative product made from it forms part of a wide product market which has a number of substitutes. This was established in Commercial Solvents.[429] There may also be a market consisting of a resource or facility which an undertaking does not market to third parties but uses solely for its own production purposes. The EU Courts have held that this 'input' may constitute a potential or hypothetical market separate from

---

[422] Case T-427/08, CEAHR v. Commission [2010] ECR II-5865, para. 70.

[423] Commission Staff Discussion Paper on the application of Article 82 to exclusionary abuses, Brussels, 9 December 2005, paras. 247–249.

[424] C (2008) 3600, 10 July 2008.

[425] CEAHR, n. 422.

[426] The decision was also annulled because the Commission had not sufficiently explained why it had concluded that there was not enough Community interest to pursue the investigation: see further Chap. 13.

[427] Case T-427/08, CEAHR v. Commission [2010] ECR II-5865, at para. 102.

[428] Para. 22 of the Commission decision. One instinctively feels that this was not a systems market. Neither a person buying a €4000 watch as a gift nor one buying it for themselves is likely to worry about the minor cost of repairs. Nevertheless, it is possible that one might be rich enough to discard a watch and buy another rather than bother to have the first one repaired. This would not, however, be because of an increase in price. On the annulment of the decision rejecting the complaint the Commission opened proceedings against the watch manufacturers, COMP/39.097, Independent Watches Repairers, IP/11/952.

[429] Cases 6 & 7/73, Istituto Chemioterapico Italiano Spa & Commercial Solvents v. EC Commission [1974] ECR 223.

that for the product or service in which it is used.[430] The point is important in cases of refusal to supply under Article 102 where the existence of two markets, rather than one, is crucial.[431]

i. Markets Created by State Regulation

A relevant market may be affected by State regulation. Legislation may, for example, define a statutory market. Such regulation may mean that no substitutes are permitted for a particular product or service. In *General Motors*[432] and *British Leyland*[433] national regulations required conformity or type-approval certificates from importers of motor vehicles and provided that they could only be issued by the vehicle manufacturer. In both cases the CJ held that the provision of the certificates was a separate market and not part of the motor car market.

j. Two-Sided Markets (Platforms)

A two-sided market (or platform) is one where the firms have to compete simultaneously for two groups of customers.[434] Examples include game machine manufacturers who need customers to buy the consoles and game developers to write games for them, newspapers and other media which need to attract both advertisers and readers/viewers, and estate agents who need both buyers and sellers. For a two-sided market to work there must be customers on both sides. A price rise to one side may lose sales to both groups and, indeed, it may be necessary to subsidise one side in order to keep attracting the other. One side may even use the platform for free (estate agents may levy fees only on the successful seller for example). This is true of search engines, where the searches are free to Internet users. Search engines are not just two-sided, but *multi-sided*, as they involve Internet users, advertisers, and content providers.[435] The conclusion is that the usual market definition tests are of little use in two (or multi)-sided markets: if the SSNIP test or critical loss analysis is applied in the usual way it leads to incorrect definitions. In *MasterCard MIF*, which concerned MasterCard's multilateral interchange fees for cross-border payment card transactions, the two sides were an upstream market where the different card schemes competed in persuading financial institutions to join their schemes and where they provided services to those institutions,[436] and a downstream market where the financial institutions competed for acquiring services, i.e. contracting with merchants (such as retailers) so that they would accept payments by card. The Commission held that the relevant market was the downstream one for acquiring payment cards.[437]

k. Markets in the Pharmaceutical Sector

The Commission defines markets in the pharmaceutical sector by reference to the third level of the WHO/EphMRA Anatomical Therapeutical Chemical (ATC) classification which groups medicines

---

[430] Case C-418/01, *IMS Health GmbH & Co. OHG v. NDC Health GmbH & Co. KG* [2004] ECR I-5039, paras. 43–45; Case T-201/04, *Microsoft v. Commission* [2007] ECR II-3601, para. 335; Case T-301/04, *Clearstream Banking v. Commission* [2009] ECR II-3155, paras. 65–66.

[431] See Chap. 7

[432] Case 26/75, *General Motors v. Commission* [1975] ECR 1367.

[433] Case 226/84, *British Leyland v. Commission* [1986] ECR 3263.

[434] There is a large literature on two-sided markets. See e.g. B. Caillaud and B. Julien, 'Chicken and Egg: Competition Among Intermediation Service Providers' (2003) 34(2) *RAND Journal of Economics* 309; J -C. Rochet and J. Tirole, 'Two-Sided Markets: A Progress Report (2006) 35(3) *RAND Journal of Economics* 645.

[435] See the *Google* case, in which the Commission took a Commitments Decision so the market definition issue was not tested, Chap.7.

[436] COMP/34.579, *MasterCard*, 19 December 2007, Summary [2009] OJ C264/8, para. 281, appeal dismissed; Case T-111/08, *MasterCard Inc, MasterCard International Inc, and MasterCard Europe SPRL v. Commission*, 24 May 2012, on appeal Case C-382/12 P, judgment pending.

[437] COMP/34.579, *MasterCard*, 19 December 2007, Summary [2009] OJ C264/8, para. 316. These markets were national in scope (para. 329), see Section 10.B.viii for geographic markets. See also COMP/37.860, *Morgan Stanley/Visa International and Visa Europe* 3 October 2007, appeal dismissed Case T-461/07, *Visa Europe v. Commission* [2011] ECR II-1729, 14 April 2011. In the *Google* case, the Commission took the Commitments Decision route, so the market definition issue was not tested, Chap. 7, p. 566.

in terms of therapeutic indications, i.e. intended use. Where appropriate in the circumstances of the case, however, an analysis may be carried out at another level, such as four (mode of action) or five (individual active substances).[438] The GC in *AstraZeneca* approved the Commission's approach.[439] *AstraZeneca* also established that pharmaceutical markets can be narrowly delineated by reference to the *means* by which the treatment is effected, rather than to the condition being treated.[440] Furthermore *AstraZeneca* shows that the general principles of market definition apply in the pharmaceutical sector and that they are not excluded by regulation in the sector or by reimbursement of the cost of medicine by national health systems.

l. Markets on the Buying Side (Procurement Markets)

The previous discussion is predicated on markets defined on the supply side. However, it is also possible to define markets on the demand side, that is, in terms of what is being bought. This is illustrated in the *British Airways* case, discussed in Chapters 6 and 7.[441] A number of merger cases have involved procurement markets, for example *NewsCorp/Telepiù*,[442] and *NVV v. Commission*.[443] The SSNIP test is applied by postulating a 5–10 per cent *reduction* in price in buying markets.

(viii) The Geographic Market

It is normally essential that the geographic market is defined. The CJ in *United Brands* stressed the importance of defining the market from a geographic perspective.[444] Because market definition is determined by reference to substitutability it is possible that even firms producing identical products will not operate in the same market if they operate within mutually exclusive geographic areas. However where, for example, a customer in England may be able to substitute French widgets for English ones the English producer will not have market power if the small but significant price rise causes his customers to purchase French widgets instead. Whether or not geographic areas are mutually exclusive—whether the geographic market in a particular product is global,[445] local, or something in between—will depend on a number of factors, most notably the cost of transport, the nature of the product, and legal regulation (including intellectual property rights). If transport costs are high relative to the value of the product, as in the case of paving slabs or concrete tiles, a geographic market may be small, perhaps even local. There may be chains of substitution in geographic markets, as explained earlier.[446]

The Commission sets out its approach to geographical market definition in the Notice. In paragraph 8[447] it describes the geographic market as comprising an area 'in which the conditions of competition are sufficiently homogeneous', faithfully following the CJ's definition in *United Brands*,[448] although the rest of the Notice does not stress this aspect. Rather the Commission appears to

---

[438] COMP/A.37.507/F3, *AstraZeneca* [2006] 5 CMLR 287, 15 June 2005, para. 3.

[439] Case T-321/05, *AstraZeneca v. Commission* [2010] ECR II-2805; *aff'd* Case C-457/10 P, *AstraZeneca v. Commission*, 6 December 2012. See J. Westin, 'Defining Relevant Market in the Pharmaceutical Sector in the Light of the Losec Case—Just How Different is the Pharmaceutical Market?' [2011] *ECLR* 57.

[440] See further Chap. 6.

[441] Case C-95/04 P, *British Airways v. Commission* [2007] ECR I-2331.

[442] M.2876, [2004] OJ L110/73 (broadcasting rights).

[443] Case T-151/05, *Nederlandse Vakbond Varkenshoudes (NVV) v. Commission* [2009] ECR II-1219, the appeal from M.3605, *Sovion/HMG* (purchase of pigs by slaughterhouses, see n. 357).

[444] Case 27/76, *United Brands v. Commission* [1978] ECR 207.

[445] As it was, e.g., in the merger case, Case IV/M.1069, *WorldCom/MCI* [1999] OJ L116/1.

[446] See Section 10.B.vii.a, p. 76.

[447] See Section 10.B.iii.b, p. 65.

[448] Case 2/76, *United Brands v. Commission* [1978] ECR 207, at para. 11.

recognise that the behaviour of undertakings may be constrained by imports from areas where the conditions of competition are not the same.[449] In *Deutsche Bahn*[450] the GC held that 'the definition of the geographical market does not require the objective conditions of competition between traders to be perfectly homogenous. It is sufficient if they are "similar" or "sufficiently homogeneous" and accordingly, only areas in which the objective conditions of competition are "heterogeneous" may not be considered to constitute a uniform market.'

In the Notice the Commission adopts the SSNIP test for determining the geographic as well as the product market. The Notice indicates the type of evidence that it considers to be relevant to the determination of the geographic market. Note that techniques such as critical loss analysis may be used here as well.

Commission Notice on the Definition of the Relevant Market for the Purposes of Community Competition Law [1997] OJ C372/5

28. The Commission's approach to geographic market definition might be summarized as follows: it will take a preliminary view of the scope of the geographic market on the basis of broad indications as to the distribution of market shares between the parties and their competitors, as well as a preliminary analysis of pricing and price differences at national and Community or EEA level. This initial view is used basically as a working hypothesis to focus the Commission's enquiries for the purposes of arriving at a precise geographic market definition.

29. The reasons behind any particular configuration of prices and market shares need to be explored. Companies might enjoy high market shares in their domestic markets just because of the weight of the past, and conversely, a homogeneous presence of companies throughout the EEA might be consistent with national or regional geographic markets. The initial working hypothesis will therefore be checked against an analysis of demand characteristics (importance of national or local preferences, current patterns of purchases of customers, product differentiation/brands, other) in order to establish whether companies in different areas do indeed constitute a real alternative source of supply for consumers. The theoretical experiment is again based on substitution arising from changes in relative prices, and the question to answer is again whether the customers of the parties would switch their orders to companies located elsewhere in the short term and at a negligible cost.

30. If necessary, a further check on supply factors will be carried out to ensure that those companies located in differing areas do not face impediments in developing their sales on competitive terms throughout the whole geographic market. This analysis will include an examination of requirements for a local presence in order to sell in that area the conditions of access to distribution channels, costs associated with setting up a distribution network, and the presence or absence of regulatory barriers arising from public procurement, price regulations, quotas and tariffs limiting trade or production, technical standards, monopolies, freedom of establishment, requirements for administrative authorizations, packaging regulations, etc. In short, the Commission will identify possible obstacles and barriers isolating companies located in a given area from the competitive pressure of companies located outside that area, so as to determine the precise degree of market interpenetration at national, European or global level.

...

44. The type of evidence the Commission considers relevant to reach a conclusion as to the geographic market can be categorized as follows:

---

[449] And see V. Korah, *An Introductory Guide to EC Competition Law and Practice* (9th edn, Hart Publishing, 2007), para. 4.3.1.2.

[450] Case T-229/94, *Deutsche Bahn AG v. Commission* [1997] ECR II-1689, para. 92; see also Case T-51/89, *Tetra Pak Rausing SA v. Commission* [1990] ECR II-309, paras. 91 and 92.

45. *Past evidence of diversion of orders to other areas.* In certain cases, evidence on changes in prices between different areas and consequent reactions by customers might be available. Generally, the same quantitative tests used for product market definition might as well be used in geographic market definition, bearing in mind that international comparisons of prices might be more complex due to a number of factors such as exchange rate movements, taxation and product differentiation.

46. *Basic demand characteristics.* The nature of demand for the relevant product may in itself determine the scope of the geographical market. Factors such as national preferences or preferences for national brands, language, culture and life style, and the need for a local presence have a strong potential to limit the geographic scope of competition.

47. *Views of customers and competitors.* Where appropriate, the Commission will contact the main customers and competitors of the parties in its enquiries, to gather their views on the boundaries of the geographic market as well as most of the factual information it requires to reach a conclusion on the scope of the market when they are sufficiently backed by factual evidence.

48. *Current geographic pattern of purchases.* An examination of the customers' current geographic pattern of purchases provides useful evidence as to the possible scope of the geographic market. When customers purchase from companies located anywhere in the Community or the EEA on similar terms, or they procure their supplies through effective tendering procedures in which companies from anywhere in the Community or the EEA submit bids, usually the geographic market will be considered to be Community-wide.

49. *Trade flows/pattern of shipments.* When the number of customers is so large that it is not possible to obtain through them a clear picture of geographic purchasing patterns, information on trade flows might be used alternatively, provided that the trade statistics are available with a sufficient degree of detail for the relevant products. Trade flows, and above all, the rationale behind trade flows provide useful insights and information for the purpose of establishing the scope of the geographic market but are not in themselves conclusive.

50. *Barriers and switching costs associated to divert orders to companies located in other areas.* The absence of trans-border purchases or trade flows, for instance, does not necessarily mean that the market is at most national in scope. Still, barriers isolating the national market have to be identified before it is concluded that the relevant geographic market in such a case is national. Perhaps the clearest obstacle for a customer to divert its orders to other areas is the impact of transport costs and transport restrictions arising from legislation or from the nature of the relevant products. The impact of transport costs will usually limit the scope of the geographic market for bulky, low-value products, bearing in mind that a transport disadvantage might also be compensated by a comparative advantage in other costs (labour costs or raw materials). Access to distribution in a given area, regulatory barriers still existing in certain sectors, quotas and custom tariffs might also constitute barriers isolating a geographic area from the competitive pressure of companies located outside that area. Significant switching costs in procuring supplies from companies located in other countries constitute additional sources of such barriers.

51. On the basis of the evidence gathered, the Commission will then define a geographic market that could range from a local dimension to a global one, and there are examples of both local and global markets in past decisions of the Commission.

52. The paragraphs above describe the different factors which might be relevant to define markets. This does not imply that in each individual case it will be necessary to obtain evidence and assess each of these factors. Often in practice the evidence provided by a subset of these factors will be sufficient to reach a conclusion, as shown in the past decisional practice of the Commission.

In *Amman & Söhne* the Commission defined a supply-side EEA-wide geographic market for automotive thread as motor manufacturers commonly have factories located in several different countries and in order to reduce costs need a uniform thread which can be used in all of them. The relevant market in industrial thread for other sectors, where these features were not present, was regional only (Benelux and the Nordic countries).[451]

The Commission says in the Notice that the methodology it sets out there 'might lead to different results depending on the nature of the competition issue being examined'. In particular:[452]

the scope of the geographic market might be different when analysing a concentration, where the analysis is essentially prospective, from an analysis of past behaviour. The different time horizon considered in each case might lead to the result that different geographic markets are defined for the same products depending on whether the Commission is examining a change in the structure of supply, such as a concentration or a cooperative joint venture, or examining issues relating to certain past behaviour.

It will be seen in later chapters that the EU's approach to the geographic market has been criticised in the past for failing to give sufficient attention to substitutability between different geographic areas. As in the case of the product market the geographic market has often been drawn narrowly. Commissioner Almunia addressed some of these criticisms in a speech in 2011 when he said:[453]

The debate in Europe, instead, is not about the demise of market definition at the hand of snazzier analytical tools,[454] but about the geographic scope of markets. Often companies tell us that our market definitions are too narrow and that we should broaden them because of globalisation and of new competition from emerging markets. This is a fair point, because defining the markets affected by a merger which involves companies and competitors with operations in several regions of the world can be a very complex exercise. However, we try to respond to the challenge by constantly adjusting our market definitions to changing market realities. In telecommunication equipment and enterprise software applications, for instance, our definitions have become EU-wide if not worldwide. Also, in the pharmaceutical sector, some ingredients are now usually considered to be sold on a worldwide basis.

And then, there is another point to make. I do not believe that globalisation makes all markets automatically worldwide—that depends on the prevailing competitive conditions. For example, the scope of the markets for electricity distribution or for consumer goods does not change simply because some suppliers—utilities and retailers—extend their operations into more countries. Customers in these countries may still be faced with very different prices and choices. In sum, when it comes to the geographic scope of markets, we apply a simple maxim: we take the markets as we find them.

(ix) The Temporal Market

The Commission Notice does not refer to a separate temporal dimension of the market, i.e. the time over which the market operates.[455] Many markets do not have a temporal aspect and where they do it may be an inherent part of the definition of the product market and analysed as such. The temporal dimension may be particularly relevant when considering transport markets.[456]

C. BARRIERS TO ENTRY AND EXPANSION

(i) The Role of Barriers to Entry

Barriers to entry or expansion are crucial when determining whether or not a firm is a monopolist or has significant market power on a market. Even a firm with a 100 per cent share of a market may

---

[451] Case T-446/05 P, *Amann & Söhne GmbH & Co KG v. Commission* [2010] ECR II-1255, paras 78–80.

[452] Market Definition Notice, para. 12.

[453] Joaquín Almunia, 'Policy Objectives in Merger Control' SPEECH/11/561, Fordham, New York, 8 September 2011.

[454] The Commissioner was referring to economic tests such as upward pressure pricing, see n. 319.

[455] See Bellamy and Child, *European Law of Competition* (cited in n. 378), 4.087–4.088.

[456] In Cases T-374–375, 384, and 388/94, *European Night Services v. Commission* [1998] ECR II-3141, where the GC annulled an Art. 101 Commission decision on a joint venture, the Commission raised during the appeal the matter of confining the business transport market to early morning and late evening rather than all round the clock.

not, in economic terms, have a monopoly. Market shares tell us nothing about why the firm has such a high market share or about potential competition. It tells us only about the current state of competition. A firm will not be able to charge monopoly prices if other firms can freely enter the market and compete with it. Excessive prices indicate to others that entry to the market is profitable. Whether or not a firm really does have a monopolist's power over price is, therefore, dependent on how vulnerable it is to new entrants. Such vulnerability to new entrants is dependent upon 'barriers to entry'. A firm can exercise market power for a significant time only if barriers to entry exist. As Bork states:[457] '[t]he concept of barriers to entry is crucial to antitrust debate... The ubiquity and potency of the concept are undeniable.'

It is difficult to give even the loosest definition of what 'barriers to entry' means without taking sides in the debate which has been ongoing for many years between different schools of economic thought.[458] To put it as neutrally as possible, however, a barrier to entry may be described as something which prevents or hinders the emergence of potential competition which would otherwise constrain the incumbent undertaking. A barrier to expansion is something which prevents or hinders an existing competitor from expanding output. The term 'barriers to entry' is used in the present discussion to include barriers to entry *and* barriers to expansion, unless the context otherwise requires. However, it should be noted that barriers to entry may be high although barriers to expansion are low.[459] The height of barriers to entry, as well as their existence, must always be taken into account.

(ii) The Definition of a Barrier to Entry

The seminal work on barriers to entry was that of J. S. Bain[460] who belonged to the Harvard School.[461] Bain described barriers to entry as:

the extent to which, in the long run, established firms can elevate their selling prices above the minimal average costs of production and distribution... without inducing potential entrants to enter the industry.

This defines barriers to entry in an effects-based way. In contrast, Stigler, a leading exponent of the Chicago School,[462] adopted a narrower definition, focusing on the differences in demand and cost conditions suffered by incumbent firms and potential entrants respectively. He defined a barrier to entry as:

a cost of producing (at some or every rate of output) which must be borne by a firm which seeks to enter the industry but is not borne by firms already in the industry.[463]

---

[457] R. Bork, *The Antitrust Paradox: A Policy at War With Itself* (Basic Books, 1978, reprinted with a new Introduction and Epilogue, 1993), 310–311.

[458] See Section 5.

[459] See Geradin et al., *EU Competition Law and Economics* (cited in n. 18), 4.69; entry may require large capital investment while expansion of existing plant does not.

[460] J. S. Bain, 'Economies of Scale, Concentration, and the Condition of Entry in Twenty Manufacturing Industries' (1954) 44 *American Economic Review* 15, *Barriers to New Competition* (Harvard University Press, 1956), and *Industrial Organization* (2nd edn, John Wiley, 1968).

[461] See Section 5.A.

[462] See Section 5.B, p. 22.

[463] G. J. Stigler, *The Organization of Industry* (Irwin, 1968), 67; see also W. Baumol and R. Willig, 'Fixed Costs, Sunk Costs, Entry Barriers and Sustainability of Monopoly' (1981) 95 *Quarterly Journal of Economics* 405, 408, and C. von Weizsäcker, 'A Welfare Analysis of Barriers to Entry' (1980) 11 *Bell J Econ* 399, 400. D. Carlton, 'Why Barriers to Entry are Barriers to Understanding', (2004) 94(2) *American Economic Review*, May, 466, 468, says that 'Although Stigler's definition of "barrier" as a differential cost is concise and unambiguous, it does raise the question of why it should be called a "barrier". Why not call it "differential cost advantage?" This may seem overly pedantic, but introduction of unnatural use of language can lead to confusion. Consider, for example, an industry where the government restricts the numbers of firms to 100. It issues 100 licences to operate that are then sold in an open market. The entry restriction is likely to be inefficient, but as long as all firms have access to the (artificially) scarce license at

Gilbert's definition follows Bain but emphasises 'first-mover advantages'(the advantages the firm derives simply from being on the market before its potential competitors) rather than absolute costs advantages:[464]

a barrier to entry is a rent that is derived from incumbency. It is the additional profit that a firm can earn as a sole consequence of being established in an industry.

The essential debate remains whether the definition of Bain or of Stigler and the Chicago School is the more appropriate or accurate. The Bain approach results in many things being identified as barriers. Conversely, the definition adopted by Stigler means that very few things constitute barriers to entry.[465] For example, Bain's approach, unlike Stigler's, accepts that market conduct may operate as a barrier to entry because the definition is effects-based.[466] Further, Bain's definition admits that economies of scale may operate as a barrier to entry, since they deter new entrants and so allow prices to remain above minimum unit cost. Stigler's definition does not, however, accept that economies of scale operate as a barrier since both incumbents and new competitors have to face them at the time they enter the market.[467] There is therefore a lack of the asymmetry which the Stigler definition demands.

It is the Bain approach which today has the greatest influence in industrial economics and which is ordinarily used in competition law decisions in both the EU and the US.[468] Herbert Hovenkamp explains why this is so.

H. Hovenkamp, *Federal Antitrust Policy: The Law of Competition and its Practice* (4th edn, West, 2011), 39–40

The difference between the two definitions of entry barriers can be quite substantial. For example, under the Bainian definition economies of scale is a qualifying barrier to entry. If scale economies are significant, then incumbent firms with established markets may have a large advantage over any new entrant, who will enter the market at a low rate of output. As a result, scale economies can permit incumbent firms to earn monopoly returns up to a certain point without encouraging new entry.

By contrast, scale economies are not a qualifying entry barrier under the Stiglerian definition. Both incumbent firms and new entrants had to deal with them at the time of entry; so scale economies are not a cost that applies only to new entrants.

The Stiglerian conception of entry barriers is based on a powerful analytic point: entry barrier analysis should distinguish desirable from undesirable entry. If prospective entrants face precisely the same costs that incumbents faced but still find entry unprofitable, then this market has probably already attained the appropriate number of players, even though monopoly profits are being earned. For example, suppose that minimum efficient scale (MES) in a market requires a 30% market share. Such a market has room for only

the market-clearing price, there is no entry barrier according to Stigler's definition. All firms earn a normal rate of return. Yet there is a restriction to entry. It seems to mangle the English language to refuse to call this entry restriction a "barrier to entry".'

[464] R. Gilbert, 'Mobility Barriers and the Value of Incumbency' in R. Schmalensee and R. Willig (eds.), *Handbook of Industrial Organization* (North Holland, 1989), 478. For absolute costs advantages, see Section 10.C.iii, p. 89.

[465] All Stiglerian entry barriers are Bainian entry barriers as well, but not vice versa.

[466] R. P. McAfee, H. M. Mialon, and M. A. Williams, 'What is a Barrier to Entry?' (2004) 94(2) *American Economic Review*, May, 461, 462 comment that 'Bain's definition is flawed in that it builds the consequences of the definition into the definition itself'.

[467] McAfee et al., 'What is a Barrier to Entry?' (cited in n. 466), say that the present tense 'is' in Stigler's definition is confusing as '[l]iterally, the definition implies that a cost that only entrants (not incumbents) have to bear today is an entry barrier, even if incumbents had to bear it in the past (when they entered the market)'.

[468] See the US *Horizontal Merger Guidelines* (2010, replacing the 1992 Guidelines revised 1997, <http://justice.gov/atr/public/guidelines/hmg-2010.pdf>) issued by the DOJ and the FTC.

three MES firms—and a three-firm market is quite likely to perform oligopolistically or else be conducive to collusion. The Stiglerian approach to entry barriers would say that, although monopoly profits are being earned in the industry, entry barriers should not be counted as high because entry by a fourth firm is not socially desirable. Additional entry would force at least one firm to be of suboptimal size, and eventually one of the four would probably exit the market.... The socially desirable solution to the problem of oligopoly performance in this market is not to force entry of a fourth, inefficiently small firm; but rather to look for alternative measures that make collusion more difficult.

Nevertheless, antitrust analysis has mainly used the Bainian rather than the Stiglerian definition of entry barriers. The Bainian definition is written into the 2010 Horizontal Merger Guidelines promulgated by the Justice Department's Antitrust Division and the Federal Trade Commission (FTC)...In all antitrust decisions except for a few in the FTC, tribunals have relied on the Bainian definition...

Although the Stiglerian approach to entry barriers offers a useful insight into the relationship between market structure and socially desirable entry, there are nevertheless good reasons for antitrust policy to prefer the Bainian approach. In particular, the Bainian definition is free of the value judgment of what constitutes socially desirable entry. This is important because the existence of entry barriers is not itself an antitrust violation. The antitrust policy maker does not use entry barrier analysis in order to consider whether further entry into a market is socially desirable; the market itself will take care of that question. Rather, the question is whether a particular practice is plausibly anti-competitive. This distinction is critically important because we know so little about the minimum efficient scale of operation in any given market.

The various definitions of barriers to entry are summed up in the OECD's Roundtable report of 2005.[469] The debate about barriers to entry is not some theoretical discussion akin to mediaeval theologians debating the number of angels on the head of a pin. It is absolutely vital to the determination of market power. If factors are too readily identified as entry barriers a firm may be wrongly found to have market power and its conduct may then be constrained by competition laws. Similarly a merger between two firms may be prohibited even though it does not lead to the firms acquiring market power. This may mean that the competitive process is actually harmed by competition law since it interferes with and impedes the behaviour of firms operating on a competitive market. On the other hand, if the possibility of entry barriers is too easily dismissed, undertakings which do have market power might escape the prohibitions of competition law and mergers which create or strengthen market power might be allowed.

(iii) Types of Barrier to Entry

We have seen[470] that Post-Chicago and modern industrial organisation (IO) theory stresses the strategic conduct of undertakings. It looks to the effect which conduct has on structure, rather than vice versa, and considers that whether a new entrant will enter a market will depend, at least in part, on the conditions of competition it will face post-entry. Thus predatory behaviour by the incumbent firm may constitute a barrier to entry. The theory also emphasises the importance that 'sunk costs' may have on a firm's decision to enter a market. Sunk costs are costs which cannot be recovered on exiting a market.[471]

The list of barriers to entry considered in sections a. to c. follows that in the OECD report.[472] The OECD divides barriers to entry into two types, but notes that '[s]ome arguably spill over from one

---

[469] OECD Policy Roundtable on barriers to entry DAF/COMP(2005)42, available at <http://www.oecd.org/regreform/sectors/36344429.pdf>, 2.2.

[470] At Section 5.B.ii, p. 28.

[471] See R. Schmalensee, 'Sunk Costs and Antitrust Barriers to Entry' (2004) 94(2) *American Economic Review*, May.

[472] See also the 'slightly adapted version' of the list in Geradin et al., *EU Competition Law and Economics* (cited in n. 18), 2.104–2.124. See also OFT Research Paper 2, 'Barriers to Entry and Exit in Competition Policy'; OFT 1282, 'Barriers to Entry, Expansion and Exit in Retail Banking' (2010).

category to the other, and none of them should be viewed in isolation because they can interact with and magnify each other'.[473] The two types it identifies are structural and strategic. Sunk costs are considered separately because they 'permeate the whole discussion'. The report describes sunk costs, and structural and strategic barriers to entry.

a. Sunk Costs[474]

Sunk costs can generally affect entry in two ways. First, because the money has already gone an incumbent undertaking can rationally ignore sunk costs when making pricing decisions so it may deter some entrants that are equally, and maybe even more, efficient. Secondly, sunk costs make entry more risky as if entry turns out to be a failure the sunk costs will be irrecoverable. Examples of sunk costs are:[475]

- Start-up phase losses;
- Investments in human capital such as recruiting and training costs;
- Investments in highly specialised equipment or buildings with limited resale value;
- Advertising and promotion costs;
- R & D that does not yield results with alternative uses;
- Expenses of complying with government regulations.

b. Structural Barriers[476]

Structural barriers arise from the basic conditions in the industry and are normally factors out of the incumbents' direct control or originate from their general efforts to compete and not from specific entry-deterring strategies. They include:

- *Absolute costs advantages*,[477] which are advantages which the incumbent enjoys but which are not available to entrants, such as exclusive access to necessary resources or technology.[478]
- *Economies of scale and scope*.[479] In the absence of a requirement for sunk costs economies of scale and scope do not deter or prevent entry.
- *High capital costs*. The OECD says that 'high' has two meanings: absolute and relative.[480] Whether high capital costs constitute a barrier to entry is a matter of debate. Bain considered that capital requirements could give rise to barriers to entry because of the amount a new entrant would need to enter the market at an efficient scale.[481] However, in Bork's view:[482]

---

[473]   OECD Policy Roundtable on barriers to entry DAF/COMP(2005)42 (cited in n. 471), section 3.

[474]   OECD Policy Roundtable on barriers to entry DAF/COMP(2005)4 (cited in n. 469), section 3.1.

[475]   OECD Policy Roundtable on barriers to entry DAF/COMP(2005)4 (cited in n. 469), section 3.1.

[476]   OECD Policy Roundtable on barriers to entry DAF/COMP(2005)4 (cited in n. 469), section 3.2.

[477]   OECD Policy Roundtable on barriers to entry DAF/COMP(2005)4 (cited in n. 469), section 3.2.1.

[478]   They have been described as arising 'if some factor of production is denied to the potential entrant and, but for this omitted factor, the latter firm would be as efficient as the incumbent firm', Van den Bergh and Camesasca, *European Competition Law and Economics: A Comparative Perspective* (cited in n. 48), 142, referring to R. J. Gilbert, 'Mobility Barriers and the Value of Incumbency', in R. Schmalensee and R. D. Willig (eds.), *The Handbook of Industrial Organization I* (North Holland, 1989). Cost advantages may not endure in high technology markets with a rapid rate of innovation, and in those markets the timescale of change will be important.

[479]   OECD Roundtable on barriers to entry DAF/COMP(2005)4 (cited in n. 469), sections 3.2.2 and 3.2.3. For economies of scale and scope see Section 3.A.ii, p. 7.

[480]   OECD Policy Roundtable on barriers to entry DAF/COMP(2005)4 (cited in n. 469), section 3.2.4.

[481]   J. S. Bain, *Barriers to New Competition* (Harvard University Press, 1956) where he reported on a survey of 20 US industries. Capital requirements are therefore linked to economies of scale.

[482]   R. H. Bork, *The Antitrust Paradox* (Basic Books, 1978), 320.

Capital requirements exist and certainly inhibit entry—just as talent requirements for playing professional football exist and inhibit entry. Neither barrier is in any sense artificial or the proper subject of special concern for antitrust policy.

The Commission explained in the Discussion Paper on Article 102 that:48[3]

in some cases [financial strength] may be one of the factors that contribute to a finding of a dominant position, in particular in those cases where (i) finance is relevant to the competitive process in the industry under review; (ii) there are significant asymmetries between competitors in terms of their internal financing capabilities; and (iii) particular features of the industry make it difficult for firms to attract external funds.

The OECD says that it is probably most useful to think about how capital costs affect a potential entrant's decision.484

- *Reputational effects* whereby the incumbent has a strong reputation for reliability or quality. The effects will be greater where customers will incur significant risk, inconvenience, or expense in trying new products.[485]

- *Network effects.*[486] Network effects are discussed earlier.[487] They have been described as 'among the determinants of the conditions of entry in many industries, and they can create a truly formidable entry obstacle, sufficient to permit prices to persist above competitive level[s] for a substantial period of time without attracting entry'.[488]

- *Legal and regulatory barriers*[489] include all kinds of rules, restrictions, and conditions imposed by governments on entry on to or operation within, a market. They include intellectual property rights (IPRs). The Chicago School views them as the most substantial barriers to entry. If legal and regulatory barriers are manipulated by incumbents they can be seen as strategic barriers too.[490]

- *Barriers to exit.*[491] The costs of exiting a market may deter undertakings from entering it in the first place. High costs of exit (including sunk costs) make entry riskier. The OECD report points out that high barriers to exit may make incumbents respond more aggressively to entrants, thus creating more barriers to entry.

- *First mover advantages*[492] are the advantages that the incumbent derives from being the first in the market and which mean that subsequent entrants cannot compete on equal terms. First mover advantages include some of the barriers to entry already mentioned, such as network effects, reputation, and IPRs.

- *Vertical integration* means that an undertaking operates at more than one stage of the production and distribution chain.[493] It may be difficult for an entrant to enter at only one stage and the

---

[483] Commission Staff Discussion Paper on the application of Article 82 to exclusionary abuses, Brussels, 9 December 2005, para. 40.

[484] OECD Roundtable on barriers to entry DAF/COMP(2005)4 (cited in n. 469), section 3.2.4., citing Schmalensee's 'pragmatic approach' in R. Schmalensee, 'Horizontal Merger Policy: Problems and Changes' (1987) 1 *Economic Perspectives* 4, that if business people think the cost of capital is a barrier to entry, then that will affect their decisions about entry and become a *de facto* barrier.

[485] OECD Roundtable on barriers to entry DAF/COMP(2005)4 (cited in n. 469), section 3.2.5.

[486] OECD Roundtable on barriers to entry DAF/COMP(2005)4 (cited in n. 469), section 3.2.6.

[487] See Section 7.E, p. 54.

[488] G. J. Werden, 'Network Effects and Conditions of Entry: Lessons from the Microsoft Case' (2001) 69 *ALJ* 8 (Werden is discussing the action against Microsoft in the US, not the EU case).

[489] OECD Roundtable on barriers to entry DAF/COMP(2005)4 (cited in n. 469), section 3.2.7.

[490] See e.g. Case C-457/10 P, *AstraZeneca* v. *Commission*, 6 December 2012, discussed in Chap. 7.

[491] OECD Roundtable on barriers to entry DAF/COMP(2005)4 (cited in n. 469), section 3.2.8.

[492] OECD Roundtable on barriers to entry DAF/COMP(2005)4 (cited in n. 469), section 3.2.9.

[493] OECD Roundtable on barriers to entry DAF/COMP(2005)4 (cited in n. 469), section 3.2.10.

vertical integration may endow the incumbent with advantages that can be replicated only by a similarly integrated entrant. It can be argued, however, that when vertical integration takes place barriers to entry are only added up and are not multiplied. Vertical integration may therefore accompany monopoly but is not an indicator of it.[494] Vertically integrated firms may discriminate in favour of their own downstream operations, which becomes a strategic barrier, as in the cases on margin squeeze discussed in Chapter 7.[495]

c. Strategic Behaviour by Incumbents

The OECD says[496] that strategies which deter entry may be intentionally created or enhanced for that purpose. Sometimes the strategies are used to pre-empt entry and sometimes they are used in retaliation against entry that has already occurred. Threats are an effective deterrent if (and only if) they are credible. Many of the practices listed are discussed in Chapter 7 as they constitute conduct which can amount to an abuse of a dominant position for the purposes of Article 102 insofar as they 'foreclose' the market, i.e. have exclusionary effects.

- *Predatory pricing*[497] is where an incumbent prices below cost to deter entrants or drive out competitors. See further Chapter 7.

- *Limit pricing* is where the incumbent does not price below cost but deliberately fails to maximise short-term profit, so that it leaves too little residual demand for entry to be profitable. It normally works only if there are economies of scale or scope, because it depends on the entrant being unable to operate efficiently at the available level of demand.[498] The potential entrants also need to believe that the incumbent will maintain that level of output whether or not the new entry occurs.

- *Intentional over-investment in capacity and sunk costs*.[499] An incumbent undertaking may over-invest in sunk assets so that it operates with significant spare capacity. The threat of this spare capacity being used may deter a potential entrant, as the incumbent may be able to manufacture large quantities of the product using that spare capacity at a very low unit cost.

- *Fidelity (loyalty) and bundled rebates*[500] comprise pricing practices whereby undertakings give discounts and rebates to customers in exchange for the customers' loyalty in not buying elsewhere or for buying certain amounts. See further Chapter 7.

- *Product differentiation and advertising*.[501] There is an extensive economics literature about the extent to which advertising, reputation, and goodwill may operate as barriers to entry. There can be economies of scale in advertising and advertising expenditures will usually be sunk costs.[502]

---

[494] See C. Baden Fuller, 'Art. 86 EEC: Economic Analysis of the Existence of a Dominant Position' (1979) 4 *ELRev* 423, 440 and the economic literature cited there; D. Harbord and T. Hoehn, 'Barriers to Entry and Exit in European Competition Policy' (1994) 14 *International Review of Law and Economics* 411, 419; V. Korah, 'Concept of a Dominant Position Within The Meaning of Art. 86' (1980) 17 *CMLRev* 395, 408.

[495] For example, Case C-280/08 P, *Deutsche Telekom* v. *Commission* [2010] ECR I-9555. See also the *Google* case, COMP/39.*Google*, IP/13/371, MEMO/13/383, 25 April 2013.

[496] OECD Roundtable on barriers to entry DAF/COMP(2005)4 (cited in n. 469), section 3.3.

[497] OECD Roundtable on barriers to entry DAF/COMP(2005)4 (cited in n. 471), section 3.3.1.

[498] OECD Roundtable on barriers to entry DAF/COMP(2005)4 (cited in n. 469), section 3.3.2.

[499] OECD Roundtable on barriers to entry DAF/COMP(2005)4 (cited in n. 469), section 3.3.3, which cites A. M. Spence, 'Entry, Capacity, Investment and Oligopolistic Pricing', (1977) 8 *Bell Journal of Economics* 53 and A. Dixit, 'The Role of Investment in Entry Deterrence' (1980) 90 *Economic Journal* 9 on the theory of this strategy.

[500] OECD Roundtable on barriers to entry DAF/COMP(2005)4 (cited in n. 469), section 3.3.4.

[501] OECD Roundtable on barriers to entry DAF/COMP(2005)4 (cited in n. 469), section 3.3.5.

[502] Although a brand image built up by advertising might be deployable in a separate market, e.g., the name Virgin is applied to many different products and services. The Commission described advertising and promotion as sunk costs in the merger decision *Nestlé/Perrier* [1992] OJ L356/1, [1993] 4 CMLR M17, para. 97.

Bain considered advertising a barrier to entry.[503] Advertising builds up goodwill and reputation, and the first brand in the market may enjoy a classic first-mover advantage which will operate as a barrier to entry to later entrants.[504] Stigler's view, however, was that advertising is not a barrier to entry: it reduces consumer search costs and is pro-competitive.[505] Advertising and brand reputation may contribute to rendering the undertaking's product a 'must-stock' item, which can in turn make the undertaking an 'unavoidable trading partner' There is also a significant literature on brand proliferation and product differentiation as barriers to entry.[506] Van den Bergh and Camesasca explain that the insights of modern IO theory show that advertising and product differentiation can reduce consumer welfare in some circumstances.

R. J. Van den Bergh and P. D. Camesasca, *European Competition Law and Economics: A Comparative Perspective* (2nd edn, Sweet & Maxwell, 2006), 145–146

Recent work in modern industrial organisation has further contributed to our understanding of product differentiation and advertising as entry barriers. It now appears that a cautious approach is warranted. Product differentiation and advertising can, under certain conditions, reduce consumer welfare. Advertising may be used either to increase the objective knowledge of products or to create consumers' preferences for a particular brand, thereby making the demand for those products less elastic and market entry by newcomers more difficult. However, to qualify as an entry barrier and not just as an entry impediment, the effects of advertising must last sufficiently long to enable incumbent firms to earn super-normal profits persistently. On the latter point the relevant empirical evidence is mixed: some researchers found that the effects of advertising lasted for several years, whereas others found that advertising effects are gone within a year…. Modern industrial organisation stresses the importance of sunk costs in assessing whether advertising may function as a barrier to entry. Sunk costs are central to the calculations of potential entrants: advertising costs to build consumer loyalty are normally sunk costs unless an exiting firm could either sell its brand name or use it somewhere else without a loss. The higher advertising and promotion expenditures that cannot be recovered on exiting a particular market, the more entry will be deterred…. Recent literature in industrial organisation on product differentiation also includes the view that it may be used as an instrument to obstruct market entry. To deter entrants looking for unfulfilled product design or brand image niches, established sellers might seek to crowd product space with enough brands (brand proliferation) so that no room for profitable new entry remains….

The Commission Staff Discussion Paper said:[507]

it may be difficult to enter an industry where experience or reputation is necessary to compete effectively, both of which may be difficult to obtain as an entrant. Factors such as consumer loyalty to a particular

---

[503] J. S. Bain, *Barriers to New Competition* (Harvard University Press, 1956). See also M. Spence, 'Notes on Advertising, Economies of Scale and Entry Barriers' (1980) 95 *Quarterly Journal of Economics* 493; J. Sutton, *Sunk Costs and Market Structure: Price Competition, Advertising, and the Evolution of Concentration* (MIT Press, 1991).

[504] See R. Schmalensee, 'Entry Deterrence in the Ready-to-eat Breakfast Cereal Industry' (1978) 9 *Bell Journal of Economics* 305.

[505] G. Stigler, 'The Economics of Information' (1961) 69 *J. Polit. Economy* 213; see Van den Bergh and Camesasca, *European Competition Law and Economics: A Comparative Perspective* (cited in n. 48), 144–145.

[506] See Bain (cited in n. 219); R. Schmalensee, 'Product Differentiation Advantages of Pioneering Brands' (1981) 72 *American Economic Review* 349. Bain considered product differentiation a barrier to entry but the Chicago School does not.

[507] Commission Staff Discussion Paper on the application of Article 82 to exclusionary abuses, Brussels, 9 December 2005, para. 40.

brand, the closeness of relationships between suppliers and customers, the importance of promotion or advertising, or other reputation advantages will be taken into account. Advertising and other investments in reputation are often sunk costs which cannot be recovered in the case of exit and which therefore make entry more risky.

- *Tying.*[508] Tying and bundling, whereby a dominant undertaking makes the purchase of one product conditional on the purchase of another, or 'bundles' them together, are discussed in Chapter 7.

- *Exclusive dealing arrangements*[509] are vertical arrangements whereby customers contract with an incumbent undertaking to purchase all their requirements of the relevant product from that undertaking. They raise similar issues to fidelity rebates, which may have the same effect. They are discussed in Chapter 7. The OECD report notes that an incumbent undertaking operating on a market where it is necessary to use distributors may sign exclusive contracts with enough of the available distributors (rather than directly with the customers) to mean that new entrants would need in effect to vertically integrate, a requirement that would render entry riskier and therefore less likely.

- *Patent hoarding.*[510] Although IPRs can be structural barriers (both as legal and regulatory barriers and as first mover advantages) the way in which they are used by their holders can also be strategic barriers. The OECD mentions the practice of 'patent hoarding' whereby an undertaking acquires numerous patents that block the feasible methods of competing and thereby builds a 'fortress' around its market position. These may be patents that the undertaking has no intention of exploiting commercially, but are simply deterrents to entry.[511]

Although not specifically listed in the OECD Roundtable document, switching costs, discussed earlier in respect of their possible effect on market definition, can also constitute barriers to entry. Switching costs are structural barriers but can also be exploited by undertakings and so form strategic barriers. Furthermore, opportunity costs can act as barriers. Opportunity costs, the value of what has to be given up to do something else,[512] can be classed as an absolute cost advantage for the incumbent.

The European Commission sets out the forms that barriers to entry can take in the 2004 Horizontal Merger Guidelines, which are discussed in Chapter 12.[513] In the Notice the Commission takes a broad view of barriers to entry, considering that they can comprise legal or technical advantages or may exist because of the established position of the incumbent firms on the market. The Commission also deals with barriers to entry in the Guidance Paper, discussed in Chapter 6—where the decisional practice of the Commission and the case law in respect of Article 102 are discussed.

11. CONCLUSIONS

1. Competition law upholds the workings of the free market economy by policing the conduct of firms as they compete in the market. Whether anti-competitive harm should be judged by the effects

---

[508] OECD Roundtable on barriers to entry DAF/COMP(2005)4 (cited in n. 469), section 3.3.6.

[509] OECD Roundtable on barriers to entry DAF/COMP(2005)4 (cited in n. 469), section 3.3.7.

[510] OECD Roundtable on barriers to entry DAF/COMP(2005)4 (cited in n. 469), section 3.3.8. The practice is also addressed in in the OECD Roundtable report *Intellectual Property Rights*, DAF(2004)24, <http://www.oecd.org/daf/competition/abuse/34306055.pdf>.

[511] The abuse of IPRs is discussed in Chap. 7.

[512] See Section 3.A.iii.

[513] [2004] OJ C31/5. See also the Commission Guidelines on the application of Article 81(3) [now Article 101(3)] of the Treaty [2004] OJ C101/97, paras. 114–115.

on competitors, on the structure of competition, on consumers, on society in some broader sense, or by some combination of these, is a matter of long-standing debate and controversy.

2. There is currently a consensus in mainstream economics that competition law systems should be designed to maximise 'welfare' although there are differences of opinion as to whether this should be 'total welfare' or 'consumer welfare'. In the past (at least) EU competition law has sought to achieve a more diffuse range of objectives. The debate about the aims of EU competition law is affected by the fact that competition is but one of a range of policies pursued by the EU and that EU competition policy serves as a tool of the single market. At present the view of the European Commission, the EU competition authority, is that competition law should be directed at consumer welfare. The EU Courts currently tend to express the objectives of EU competition law in rather wider terms.

3. The belief that competition produces the best outcomes for society is based on neoclassical economic theory. This teaches that in competitive markets prices are kept down, and other benefits, such as quality, choice, and innovation, flow to consumers, whereas in markets which are monopolised output is reduced, prices rise, and consumers are deprived of choice, quality, and innovation. Competition is said to produce 'efficiency'. The matter is complicated by the fact that there are different aspects to efficiency and, in particular, the need to take account of dynamic efficiencies may make the application of competition law in any specific situation a complex exercise. Even where there is agreement about the ultimate objectives of competition law there is much debate about how to achieve efficiency and maximise consumer welfare and in any particular case there may be room for argument about the analysis of the market, the effects of the transaction or conduct under review, and the desirability of intervention.

4. A central concept of competition law is 'market power'. Market power is usually defined as the ability to profitably raise prices above the competitive level for a significant period of time but may also be described in terms of the power to exclude.

5. Market definition and barriers to entry are both employed in assessing market power. There are difficulties involved in defining markets and identifying (and even defining) a barrier to entry. The imprecise nature of these concepts should be borne in mind in all cases where the application of competition rules is being considered. If markets are wrongly defined and barriers to entry imagined the application of the competition rules can take a wrong turn and prohibit conduct which might otherwise achieve economic efficiency.

12. FURTHER READING

A. BOOKS

AKMAN, P., *The Concept of Abuse in EU Competition Law* (Hart Publishing, 2012), Chap. 1

AMATO, G., *Antitrust and the Bounds of Power* (Hart Publishing, 1997)

BAIN, J. S., *Barriers to New Competition* (Harvard University Press, 1956)

—— *Industrial Organization* (2nd edn, John Wiley, 1968)

BAQUERO CRUZ, J., *Between Competition and Free Movement* (Hart Publishing, 2002)

BEGG, D., VERNASCA, G., FISCHER, S., and DORNBUSCH, R., *Economics* (10th edn, McGraw-Hill, 2011)

BISHOP, S., and WALKER, M., *The Economics of EC Competition Law: Concepts, Application and Measurement* (3rd edn, Sweet & Maxwell, 2010)

BORK, R. H., *The Antitrust Paradox: A Policy at War with Itself* (Basic Books, 1978, reprinted with a new Introduction and Epilogue, 1993)

CARLTON, D. W., and PERLOFF, J. M., *Modern Industrial Organization* (4th edn, Pearson Addison Wesley, 2005)

CASSIDY, J., *How Markets Fail: The Logic of Economic Calamities* (Allen Lane, 2009)

CINI, M., and MCGOWAN, L., *Competition Policy in the European Union* (Macmillan, 1998)

COATES, K., *EC Competition Law in Technology Markets* (Oxford University Press, 2010), Chap. 2

CSERES, K., *Competition Law and Consumer Protection* (Kluwer Law International, 2005) 331–332

CUCINOTTA, A., PARDOLESI R., and VAN DENLEY BERGH, R., *Post-Chicago Developments in Antitrust Law* (Edward Elgar, 2002)

ELHAUGE, F., and GERADIN, D., *Global Competition Law and Economics* (2nd edn, Hart Publishing, 2011), Chap. 1

FATUR, A. *EU Competition Law and the Information and Communication Technology Network Industries* (Hart Publishing, 2012)

FAULL, J., and NIKPAY, A. (eds.), *The EC Law of Competition* (2nd edn, Oxford University Press, 2007), Chap. 1

GAL, M. S., *Competition Policy for Small Market Economies* (Harvard University Press, 2003)

GELLHORN, E., KOVACIC, W. E., and CALKINS, S., *Antitrust Law and Economics* (5th edn, West, 2004)

GERADIN, D., LAYNE-FARRAR, A., and PETIT, N., *EU Competition Law and Economics* (Oxford University Press, 2012)

GERBER, D., *Law and Competition in Twentieth Century Europe: Protecting Prometheus* (Oxford University Press, 1998)

HILDEBRAND, D., *The Role of Economics Analysis in the EC Competition Rules* (Kluwer Law International, 2002)

HOVENKAMP, H., *The Antitrust Enterprise, Principle and Execution* (Harvard University Press, 2005)

—— *Federal Antitrust Policy: The Law of Competition and its Practice* (4th edn, West, 2011)

JACQUEMIN, A. P., and DE JONG, H. W., *European Industrial Organisation* (Macmillan, 1997)

LIANOS, I., and SOKOL, D., *The Global Limits of Competition Law* (Stanford University Press, 2012)

MERCURO, N., and MEDEMA, S. G., *Economics and the Law: From Posner to Post-Modernism* (Princeton University Press, 1999)

MOTTA, M., *Competition Policy* (Cambridge University Press, 2004)

NAZZINI, R., *The Foundations of European Union Competition Law, The Objectives and Principles of Article 102* (Oxford University Press, 2011), Chap. 2

NIELS, G., and JENKINS, H., *Economics for Competition Lawyers* (Oxford University Press, 2011)

ODUDU, O., *The Boundaries of EC Competition Law* (Oxford University Press, 2006), Chap. 2

ORTIZ BLANCO, L., *Market Power in EU Antitrust Law* (Hart Publishing, 2012)

PATEL, K. K., and SCHWEITZER, H., *The Historical Foundations of EU Competition Law* (Oxford University Press, 2013)

PITOFSKY, R., (ed.), *How Chicago Overshot the Mark: The Effect of Conservative Economic Analysis on US Antitrust* (Oxford University Press, 2008)

POSNER, R. A., *Antitrust Law* (2nd edn, University of Chicago Press, 2001)

—— *A Failure of Capitalism* (Harvard University Press, 2009)

—— *The Crisis of Capitalist Democracy* (Harvard University Press, 2010)

SAUTER, W., *Competition Law and Industrial Policy in the EU* (Oxford University Press, 1997)

SCHERER, F. M., and ROSS, D., *Industrial Market Structure and Economic Performance* (3rd edn, Houghton Mifflin, 1990), Chaps. 1, 2, and 4

STIGLER, G. J., *The Organization of Industry* (Irwin, 1968)

STIGLITZ, J., *Freefall: Free Markets and the Sinking of the Global Economy* (Penguin, 2010)

TOWNLEY, C., *Article 81 EC and Public Policy* (Hart Publishing, 2009)

VAN DEN BERGH, R. J., and CAMESASCA, P. D., *European Competition Law and Economics: A Comparative Perspective* (2nd edn, Sweet & Maxwell, 2006)

VIVES, X. (ed.), *Competition Policy in the EU: Fifty Years on from the Treaty of Rome* (Oxford University Press, 2009)

WILLIAMSON, O. E., *Anti-Trust Economics* (Basil Blackwell, 1987)

ZIMMER, D. (ed.), *The Goals of Competition Law* (Edward Elgar, 2012)

B. CHAPTERS IN BOOKS

MÖSCHEL, W., 'Competition Policy from an Ordo Point of View', in A. Peacock and H. Willgerodt (eds.), *German Neo-Liberals and the Social Market Economics* (Macmillan, 1989), 142

ZENGER, H., and WALKER, M., 'Theories of Harm in European Competition Law: A Progress Report', available at http://ssrn.com/abstract=2009296 and in J. Bourgeois and D. Waelbrock (eds.), *Ten Years of Effects-based Approach in EU Competition Law* (Bruylant, 2012) 185

C. ARTICLES

AKMAN, P., 'Searching for the Long-Lost Soul of Article 82' (2009) 29 *OJLS* 267

—— '"Consumer" versus "Customer": the Devil in the Detail' (2010) 37 *Journal of Law and Society* 315

—— 'The Role of Freedom in EU Competition Law' (2013) *Legal Studies* (December)

—— 'The Role of "Freedom" in EU Competition Law' (2013) 33 *Legal Studies* forthcoming

ANDRIYCHUK, O. 'The Dialectics of Competition Law: Sketching the Ordo-Austrian Approach to Antitrust' (2012) 35(2) *World Competition* 355

ANTITRUST BULLETIN SPECIAL ISSUE: Louis Kaplow, 'Why (Ever) Define Markets?' [2012] 57(4) *Antitrust Bulletin*

BAIN, J. S., 'Economies of Scale, Concentration, and the Condition of Entry in Twenty Manufacturing Industries' (1954) 44 *American Economic Review* 15

BISHOP, S., 'Snake-Oil with Mathematics is Still Snake-Oil: Why Recent Trends in the Application of So-Called "Sophisticated" Economics is Hindering Good Competition Enforcement' (2013) 9 *European Competition Journal* 67

BRIONES, J., 'A Balance of the Impact of Economic Analysis on the EU Competition Policy' (2009) 32 *World Competition* 27

CAILLAUD, B., and JULIEN, B., 'Chicken and Egg: Competition Among Intermediation Service Providers' (2003) 34(2) *RAND Journal of Economics* 309

CRANE, D., 'Chicago, Post-Chicago and Neo-Chicago' (2009) 76 *U. Chi. L. Rev.* 1911

CROCIONI, P., 'The Hypothetical Monopolist Test: What it can and cannot tell you' [2002] *ECLR* 355

DUNBOW, B., 'Understanding Consumers: The Value of Stated Preferences in Antitrust Proceedings' [2003] *ECLR* 141

EASTERBROOK, F.H., 'The Limits of Antitrust' (1984) 63(6) *Texas Law Review*

FARRELL, J., and KATZ, M. L., 'The Economics of Welfare Standards in Antitrust' (2006) 2(2) *Competition Policy International* 3

FOX, E. M., 'The New American Competition Policy: From Antitrust to Pro-efficiency?' [1981] *ECLR* 439

—— 'The Modernisation of Antitrust: A New Equilibrium' (1981) 66 *Cornell LR*

—— 'Consumer Beware Chicago' (1984–1985) 84 *Mich LR* 1714

—— 'What is Harm to Competition? Exclusionary Practices and Anti-competitive Effect' (2002) 70 *ALJ* 371

—— and SULLIVAN, L. A., 'Antitrust—Retrospective and Prospective: Where Are We Coming From? Where Are we Going?' (1987) 62 *New York Univ LR* 936

FRAZER, T., 'Competition Policy after 1992: The Next Step' (1990) 53 *MLR* 609

GERBER, D., 'Constitutionalizing the Economy: German Neo-liberalism, Competition Law and the "New Europe"' (1994) 42 *American Journal of Comparative Law* 25

GREEN, N., 'From Rome to Rome: The Evolution of Competition Law into a Twenty-first Century Religion' [2010] *Comp Law* 25

HARBORD, D., and HOEHN, T., 'Barriers to Entry and Exit in European Competition Policy' (1994) 14 *International Review of Law and Economics* 41

HILDEBRAND, D., 'The European School in EC Competition Law' (2002) 25 *World Competition* 3

HOVENKAMP, H., 'Antitrust after Chicago' (1984–1985) 84 *Mich LR* 213

HÜSCHELRATH, K., 'Critical Loss Analysis in Market Definition and Merger Control (2009) 3 *European Competition Journal* 757

—— 'The Costs and Benefits of Antitrust Enforcement: Identification and Measurement' (2012) 35(1) *World Competition* 121

KAPLOW, L., 'Why (Ever) Define Markets?' (2010) 124 *Harv. L. Review* 437

KOVACIC, W., 'The Intellectual DNA of Modern U.S. Competition Law For Dominant Firm Conduct: The Chicago/Harvard Double Helix' (2007) 1 *Columbia Business Law Review* 1

LANDES, W. M., and POSNER, R. A., 'Market Power in Antitrust Cases' (1981) 94 *Harvard LR* 937

LEIBENSTEIN, H., 'Allocative Efficiency vs. "X-efficiency"' (1966) 56 *American Economic Review* 392

LOWE, P., 'The Design of Competition Policy Institutions for the 21st Century—the Experience of the European Commission and DG Competition' (2008) 3 *Competition Policy Newsletter* 1

MANNE, G. A., and WRIGHT, J. D., 'Innovation and the Limits of Antitrust' (2010) 1 *Journal of Competition Law and Economics*, Special Issue, 'The Limits of Antitrust Revisited'

MARSDEN, P., and WHELAN, P, 'Consumer Detriment and its Application in EC and UK Competition Law' [2006] *ECLR* 569

MUELLER, C.E., 'Antitrust Economics and the "The Flying Dutchman": How Economists Ruined Antitrust in Reagan's 1980s' (2008) 34 (2) *Antitrust Law and Economics Review* 1

PARRET, L., 'The Objectives of EU Competition Law and Policy' (2010) 6 *European Competition Journal* 339

PETIT, N., and NEYRINCK, N., 'Industrial Policy and Competition Enforcement: Is there, Could There and Should There Be a Nexus?', available at http://ssrn.com/abstract=2225903

POSNER, R. A., 'The Social Costs of Monopoly and Regulation' [1975] *Journal of Political Economy* 83

—— 'The Chicago School of Antitrust Analysis' (1979) 127 *Univ Pa LR* 925

ROCHET, J.-C., and TIROLE, J., 'Two-Sided
Markets: A Progress Report (2006) 35(3) *RAND Journal of Economics* 645

THÉPOT, F., 'Market Power in Online Search and Social
Networking: A Matter of Two-Sided Markets' (2013)
World Comp (2) 33

TOWNLEY, C., 'Which Goals Count in Article 101
TFEU?: Public Policy and its Discontents' [2011]
ECLR 441

VELJANOVSKI, C., 'Markets without
Substitutes: Substitution versus Constraints as the
Key to Market Definition' [2010] *ECLR* 122

WEITBRECHT, A., 'From Freiburg to Chicago and
beyond—the first 50 years of European competition
law' [2008] *ECLR* 81

WITT, A. C., 'Public Policy Goals under EU Competition
Law' (2012) 8 *European Competition Journal* 443

2

THE EUROPEAN UNION AND ITS COMPETITION LAW AND INSTITUTIONS

1. CENTRAL ISSUES

1. The entity now called the European Union (EU) was originally called the European Economic Community (EEC), which was created by the Treaty of Rome in 1957. The EEC later became the EC, the major 'pillar' of the European Union. On 1 December 2009 the Treaty of Lisbon came into force and the EU replaced and succeeded the EC. The EC has ceased to exist.

2. The Treaties governing the EU are the Treaty on European Union (TEU), the Treaty on the Functioning of the European Union (TFEU) and the Charter of Fundamental Rights of the European Union (the Charter). The competition rules were previously contained in the Treaty of Rome, and so before 1 December 2009 competition law was 'EC' rather than 'EU' law. It is now 'EU' law. The competition rules are contained in the TFEU.

3. The Council has played a relatively minor role in the development of competition law. In 1962 Council Regulation 17 gave wide powers to enforce and apply the competition rules to the Commission. Regulation 17 was replaced by Regulation 1/2003, which took effect on 1 May 2004.

4. The Commission is divided into Directorates-General. One of these, the Directorate-General for Competition (DG Comp) is responsible for competition policy. One Commissioner has responsibility for the competition portfolio.

5. The national competition authorities (NCAs) of the Member States and the national courts share the responsibility for the application and enforcement of the EU competition rules with the Commission.

6. The Court of Justice of the European Union (CJEU) comprises the Court of Justice (CJ) and the General Court (GC), previously the Court of First Instance (CFI)). These are together referred to in this book as the 'EU Courts'. They play an important part in developing the competition rules, through hearing appeals from Commission decisions and (at present only as regards the CJ) by hearing preliminary references from the national courts of the Member States. The CJEU is responsible for the interpretation of EU law.

7. The doctrines of the EU legal order such as direct applicability and supremacy apply in the field of competition law as to all other areas of EU law. The general principles of EU law and fundamental human rights (now largely embodied in the Charter) apply, and are particularly important in competition law, which entails the imposition of penalties and sanctions upon legal persons.

8. Two main provisions, Articles 101 and 102 TFEU, set out the competition rules. These are amplified by rafts of delegated legislation, notices, and other instruments, by Commission decisions in individual cases, and by the case law of the EU Courts.

9. The EU and three other states form the European Economic Area (EEA) and in effect the EU competition rules apply throughout the EEA, and not just to the EU.

10. The 'modernisation' of EU competition law, of which the linchpin is Regulation 1/2003, took EU competition law into a new era.

2. INTRODUCTION

In this chapter we give a brief outline of the history of the EU and its institutions in order to set the competition rules in context. We then set out the competition provisions themselves and briefly explain the way in which those rules are applied and enforced. Public and private enforcement of the competition rules are discussed more fully in Chapter 13 and Chapter 14. As the printed edition of this book does not deal with the State aid rules this chapter discusses the legal provisions and the powers of the institutions in respect only to antitrust and mergers, and the word 'competition' should be understood in this sense unless the context otherwise requires.[1]

It is important to note that on 1 May 2004 a fundamental change took place in the way that EU competition law is applied and enforced. Council Regulation 17,[2] the first regulation implementing what are now Articles 101 and 102, which had governed enforcement since 1962, was replaced by Council Regulation 1/2003.[3] Regulation 1/2003 is the main legislative plank in the process of the 'modernisation' of EU competition law enforcement.[4] Other reforms and developments both before and after 1 May 2004 are also part of the modernisation programme.[5]

3. INTRODUCTION TO THE EUROPEAN UNION

A. THE EUROPEAN UNION AND THE EUROPEAN COMMUNITY

The EU has its foundation in the EEC. After the Second World War, three European Communities were created: the European Coal and Steel Community (ECSC), 1951, created by the Treaty of Paris; the European Atomic Energy Community (Euratom), 1957; and the EEC, created by the Treaty of Rome, 1957. The ECSC Treaty was concluded for only 25 years and expired on 23 July 2002.[6] Euratom is under the control of the EU but is a legally distinct entity.[7]

The Treaty of Rome governing the EEC was amended several times, including by the Treaty of Amsterdam in 1999 which effected a renumbering of the articles of the Treaty. The most significant amendments were made by the Treaty on European Union (TEU)[8] which entered into force on 1 November 1993. The TEU created a new entity, the European Union (EU), which marked a new stage in the process of European integration. The EU comprised three 'pillars': (i) the existing three Communities, (ii) cooperation in the Common Foreign and Security Policy, and (iii) cooperation in Justice and Home Affairs. The TEU expanded the ambit of the EEC to include more powers, particularly in the fields of economic and monetary union and citizenship, and renamed it the European Community (EC).[9]

---

[1] See the separate Online Resource Centre for a chapter on State aid. The powers of the institutions in respect of State aid are dealt with fully there.

[2] [1959–62] OJ Spec. Ed. 87.

[3] [2003] OJ L1/1.

[4] A new regulation to replace Reg.17 was first proposed by the Commission in the 1999 Commission White Paper on modernisation of the rules implementing Arts 81 and 82 of the EC Treaty [1999] OJ C132/1, [1999] 5 CMLR 208.

[5] See Chap. 1, Section 7.C.ii.b, p. 41.

[6] For the effect of this on the competition rules applicable to the coal and steel sectors see Section 4.A.iii, p. 110.

[7] See further <http://ec.europa.eu//euratom/index.html>.

[8] Known as 'Maastricht' after the Dutch town where it was signed. At the time the number of Member States had risen, through successive waves of accessions, to 12.

[9] The Treaty of Amsterdam, which came into force on 1 May 1999, moved some matters from the third pillar to the first.

The Treaty of Lisbon came into force on 1 December 2009. Lisbon amended both the TEU and the EC Treaty. The EC was subsumed into the EU which replaced and succeeded it[10] so that the 'European Community' ceased to exist. After 1 December 2009, therefore, we speak of EU competition law rather than EC competition law. The amended EC Treaty was renamed the Treaty on the Functioning of the Union (TFEU).[11] The TEU and the TFEU, which have the 'same legal value',[12] are together referred to in this book as 'the Treaties'.

As of 1 July 2013, with the accession of Croatia, the EU comprises 28 Member States, ten of which entered in 2004.[13] The implication of the 2004 enlargement for the enforcement of competition law was one of the reasons for the 'decentralisation' in the modernisation Regulation, Regulation 1/2003.

B. THE EU TREATIES

The TEU establishes the EU, states its values and objectives, sets out the respective competences of the EU and the Member States, and provides for the EU institutions and for the Common Defence and Security policy. The TFEU, as its name implies, contains more detailed provisions and also the rules of substantive law. The competition rules, including the State aid rules, are set out in Articles 101–109 TFEU. The aims and objectives of the EC Treaty, and now the TEU and the TFEU, have provided the context for the application of the competition rules. In particular, the single market objective influences the way in which the competition rules are interpreted and applied.

The Charter of Fundamental Rights was 'solemnly proclaimed' in 2000[14] but was not expressed to be legally binding. However, under the Treaty of Lisbon the Charter has been made legally binding by the amended Article 6 TEU which states that it has the same legal value as the TEU and TFEU.[15] The Charter can 'perhaps best be described as a creative distillation of the rights contained in the various European and international agreements and national constitutions on which the ECJ had for some years already drawn'.[16] Chief amongst those European and international agreements is the European Convention for the Protection of Human Rights and Fundamental Freedoms (European Convention on Human Rights, ECHR) and many of the Charter's provisions directly correspond to those in the ECHR. Article 52 (3) of the Charter says:

In so far as this Charter contains rights which correspond to rights guaranteed by the Convention for the Protection of Human Rights and Fundamental Freedoms, the meaning and scope of those rights shall be the same as those laid down by the said Convention. This provision shall not prevent Union law providing more extensive protection.

---

[10] Art. 1 TEU, as amended by the Treaty of Lisbon.

[11] For the full consolidated texts of the TEU, as amended, and the TFEU, see [2008] OJ C115/1.

[12] Art. 1 TEU.

[13] The original Member States were Belgium, France, Germany, Italy, Luxembourg, and the Netherlands; Denmark, Ireland, and the UK acceded in 1973; Greece in 1981; Spain and Portugal in 1986; Austria, Finland, and Sweden in 1995; Cyprus, the Czech Republic, Estonia, Hungary, Latvia, Lithuania, Malta, Poland, Slovakia, and Slovenia in 2004; Bulgaria and Romania in 2007; and Croatia in 2013. As at 1 July 2013 five countries have been granted 'official candidate' status: the Former Yugoslav Republic of Macedonia, Iceland, Montenegro, Serbia, and Turkey. See <http://ec.europa.eu/enlargement/index_en.htm>.

[14] By the Council, Parliament, and Commission. It was politically approved by the Member States at the Nice European Council summit in December 2000: [2000] OJ C364/1.

[15] See also Declaration 1 to the Treaties. The UK and Poland have an opt-out from the Charter, Protocol 30 to the Treaties.

[16] P. Craig and G. de Búrca, *EU Law: Text, Cases and Materials* (5th edn, Oxford University Press, 2011), 395. The CJ cited the Charter for the first time in Case C-540/03, *European Parliament* v. *Council* [2006] ECR I-5769, para. 38. It has been applied in a number of competition cases, such as Case C-407/08P, *Knauf Gips* v. *Commission* [2010] ECR I-6375, Case C-272/09 P, *KME Germany AG* v. *Commission*, 8 December 2011 and Case C-17/10, *Toshiba* v. *Úřad pro ochranu hospodářské soutěže*, 14 February 2012.

The Charter (and the ECHR) contain several provisions relating to effective judicial protection which are of importance in EU competition procedure, such as the right to a fair trial and the rights of defence.[17] Article 6(2) TEU provides that the EU will accede to the ECHR.[18]

C. THE NON-JUDICIAL EU INSTITUTIONS

(i) Introduction

The Treaties establish the EU's autonomous institutions and the rules governing them. They confer legislative, executive, and judicial powers upon the institutions in order that the EU's tasks can be achieved. The main institutions of the EU are the European Parliament, the Council, the Commission, the Court of Justice of the European Union, the European Central Bank, and the Court of Auditors.[19] In this section we consider the roles of the Council and the Commission, focusing particularly on the responsibilities of those institutions within the sphere of EU competition policy, and noting also the Advisory Committees provided for by Regulation 1/2003 and Regulation 139/2004, and the Ombudsman.[20] The EU Courts are considered in Section 3.E.[21]

(ii) The Council

The Council, which is comprised of representatives of the individual Member States, is the most powerful of the EU's political institutions. For example, it takes the final step in the passing of primary EU legislation,[22] concludes agreements with foreign countries, and plays a key role in the EU budget. In the sphere of EU competition law it does not, however, play a role on a day-to-day basis. Nonetheless, it has been responsible for the adoption of a number of important legislative acts within the competition sphere. In particular, through Regulation 17 and Regulation 1/2003, the Council conferred power on the Commission to enforce the competition rules.[23] Further, it has given the Commission power to adopt regulations exempting groups of agreements from the application of the competition rules (block exemptions),[24] and it adopted the Merger Regulation, conferring power on the Commission to rule on the compatibility with the internal market of mergers above certain turnover thresholds.[25]

The delegation to the Commission of the routine enforcement of the rules has had the advantage that the development of competition policy and the enforcement of the competition rules has not generally been subject to the delays and compromises that have been encountered in other areas of activity. Where the Council plays a significant role progress is dependent on the political will of the individual Member States, reflecting their differing views and interests. The Commission

---

[17] These were already protected by the general principles of law and fundamental rights developed by the EU Courts, which reflected the provisions of the ECHR. See further Chap. 13.

[18] A draft accession agreement between the EU and the Council of Europe was agreed at the beginning of April 2013.

[19] Note also the advisory bodies, the Economic and Social Committee and the Committee of the Regions: Art. 300 TFEU; see Craig and de Búrca, EU Law: Text, Cases and Materials (cited in n. 16), 68–69.

[20] The role of the European Parliament in the legislative process in the sphere of competition policy is generally limited to a consultative role. Nonetheless, it can be influential.

[21] Section 3.E, p. 105 ff.

[22] In many matters it does this in concert with the European Parliament: see the legislative procedures now set out in Arts 295 and 296 TFEU.

[23] And, in Council Reg. 1/2003, on the NCAs of the Member States.

[24] See Chap. 4.

[25] Reg. 139/2004 [2004] OJ L24/1, replacing Reg. 4064/89 [1989] OJ L395/1.

has been vigorous in its enforcement of the competition rules since the early days of the EEC. In contrast, the introduction of the original Merger Regulation[26] took 16 years to reach the statute book. Even then the Regulation represented a political compromise and has required significant amendment.[27]

(iii) The Commission and DG Comp

The Commission is headed by the Commissioners, unelected individuals who represent the interests of the EU.[28] The Commission has a number of different functions. It formulates most proposals for legislation, mediates between the individual Member States, and as the 'guardian of the Treaties' is responsible for the enforcement of EU rules.[29] It is the key enforcer of the competition rules.[30] It has power, for example, to take decisions finding an infringement of the EU competition rules and fining those responsible. EU law is primarily applied through a 'public' enforcement system rather than through private litigation[31] and for over 50 years the Commission has both enforced the competition rules and played the central role in formulating and developing the law.

One of the Commissioners has responsibility for competition. Since 10 February 2010 it has been Joaquín Almunia. The three previous Competition Commissioners were Neelie Kroes, 2004–2010, Mario Monti, 1999–2004, and Karel Van Miert, 1993–1999. Administratively the European Commission is divided into separate Directorates-General. Before 1999 the Directorate-General dealing with competition was known as DG IV. It is now called the Competition Directorate-General, known as DG Comp. It is headed by a Director-General,[32] has three Deputy Directors-General[33] and a Chief Economist, and is divided into Directorates. One of the Directorates is dedicated to the investigation and prosecution of cartels.

Although one Commissioner is responsible for the competition portfolio, formal decisions taken by the Commission must be adopted by the College of Commissioners as a whole,[34] subject to some limited possibilities for delegation.[35] The significance of DG Comp being part of the Commission as a whole and not just a stand-alone body was explained by the then Director-General in the following passage.[36]

---

[26] The legal basis for the merger regulation is Art. 103 TFEU (ex Art. 83 EC), which requires a qualified majority, and Art. 352 TFEU (ex Art. 308 EC), which requires unanimous approval in the Council and the consent of Parliament.

[27] See Chap. 15.

[28] Art. 17 TEU.

[29] Art. 17 TEU.

[30] The Commission is 'required to ensure the application of the principles' laid down in the competition Articles, Case T-99/04, *AC-Treuhand AG* v. *Commission* [2008] ECR II-1501, para. 163; Cases C-189/02 P, 202/02 P, 208/02 P and 213/02 P, *Dansk Rørindustri A/S and others* v. *Commission* [2005] ECR I-5425, para. 170; Cases 100–103/80, *Musique Diffusion Française SA* v. *Commission (Pioneer)* [1983] ECR 11025, para. 105.

[31] Although the latter is now actively encouraged; see Chap. 14.

[32] As at 1 July 2013, Alexander Italianer.

[33] One responsible for each of Antitrust and Mergers, Operations, and State Aid.

[34] Decisions may be passed by a simple majority: Art. 219 TFEU. The Legal Service of the Commission also plays an important role in competition matters.

[35] See Chap. 13.

[36] But see Chap. 13 for criticism of the fact that Commission decisions are taken by a (political) body (the College of Commissioners) which has had no part in the proceedings.

P. Lowe, 'The Design of Competition Policy Institutions for the 21st Century—the Experience of the European Commission and DG Competition' (2008) 3 *Competition Policy Newsletter* 1, 6

The European Commission finds itself in a substantially different position to a national authority. In the first place, its institutional independence should not be in question. As reflected in the EU treaties, its independence from national and political interests is fundamental to its mission of promoting the 'common interest' of the European Union as a whole.

Secondly, the Commission has delegated fully its powers to investigate a case, and manage the due process, to DG Competition. The Commissioner for Competition is in addition empowered to take decisions on cases and problems which raise no significant policy issue. These arrangements offer a solid guarantee of the integrity and impartiality of investigations and their conclusions, while reserving all key decisions on cases and policy for the college of Commissioners as a whole.

Thirdly, a competition authority certainly needs to be independent and impartial. But it should not be isolated or uninformed. It needs to be fully aware of the market and the regulatory environment around competition law enforcement. And it needs to be in a position to influence legislators and regulators, particularly when competition problems can be better addressed by new or amended regulation. This only underlines the advantage of EU competition policy of having the work of the Competition Commissioner and DG Competition fully embedded within the Commission. Finally, it is worth underlining again that the Commission as an institution, and not just DG Competition, retains the role of Europe's competition authority.

Since 2008, when DG Comp has been particularly concerned with the application of the State aid rules during the financial crisis, it has worked in close cooperation with the Directorates-General for Financial Markets and for Economic and Monetary Affairs.

The office of Chief Economist was created in 2003, mainly in response to a series of judgments annulling Commission merger decisions[37] which convinced the Commission that their decisions should be subjected to a more rigorous internal regime of economic oversight. The role of the Chief Economist and his team is to give guidance on methodological issues of economics and econometrics in the application of the competition rules; to give general guidance in individual competition cases from their early stages; to give detailed guidance in the most important competition cases involving complex economic issues, in particular those requiring sophisticated quantitative analysis; and to contribute to the development of general policy instruments with an economic content.[38] He is also responsible for coordinating the activities of the Economic Advisory Group on Competition Policy (EAGCP).[39]

Details of DG Comp, its Directorates, and staff can be found on its website.[40] DG Comp's website is the source of other information critical to those studying or practising EU competition law. For example, relevant legislation, Commission decisions, daily news, press releases, speeches, articles,

[37] Case T-342/99, *Airtours plc* v. *Commission* [2002] ECR II-2585; Case T-310/01, *Schneider Electric SA* v. *Commission* [2002] ECR II-4071; Case T-5/02, *Tetra Laval BV* v. *Commission* [2002] ECR II-4381, *aff'd* by the CJ, Case C-12/03 P, *Commission* v. *Tetra Laval* [2005] ECR I-987. See further Chap. 15.

[38] The Chief Economist heads a team of economists. The first Chief Economist was Professor Lars-Hendrik Röller; the second was Professor Damian Neven. As at 1 July 2013 it is Professor Kai-Uwe Kühn.

[39] EAGCP is a group of academic industrial organisation economists whose members represent different fields of research and academic research centres in Europe. They are nominated to the group by the Commissioner on the proposal of the Chief Economist. EAGCP's role is to support DG Comp's economic reasoning in competition policy analysis. The Commissioner or the Director-General may also ask EAGCP members on an ad hoc basis to provide economic advice on particular issues (see, e.g., EAGCP's July 2005 opinion on the reform of Art. 82, discussed in Chaps. 5 and 6).

[40] <http://ec.europa.eu/competition/index_en.html>.

proposals, the Commission's newsletter,[41] and annual reports can be found on the website. The site also provides links to competition judgments handed down by the EU Courts and to the sites of the Member States' NCAs, the European Competition Network (ECN), the competition authorities of third countries, the International Competition Network (ICN), and other international organisations concerned with competition policy, such as the Organization for Economic Cooperation and Development (OECD), the World Trade Organization (WTO), and the United Nations Conference on Trade and Development (UNCTAD).

Under the regime brought into effect on 1 May 2004 by Council Regulation 1/2003[42] to modernise the enforcement of the EC competition rules, the NCAs and national courts of the Member States share the enforcement of the competition rules with the Commission. The ECN was created by the Commission and NCAs to achieve, amongst other things, a harmonious and consistent application of the competition rules.

(iv) The Advisory Committee on Restrictive Practices and Dominant Positions and the Advisory Committee on Concentrations

Regulation 1/2003 provides for an Advisory Committee on Restrictive Practices and Dominant Positions.[43] It is 'the forum where experts from the various [national] competition authorities[44] discuss individual cases and general issues of Community competition law'.[45] A similar Advisory Committee on Concentrations has functions under the EU Merger Regulation.[46]

The role and powers of the Advisory Committee were strengthened by Regulation 1/2003.[47]

(v) The European Ombudsman

Article 228 TFEU provides for a European Ombudsman, elected by the European Parliament, empowered to deal with complaints in respect of maladministration by EU institutions (other than the CJEU acting in a judicial capacity). This includes complaints against the Commission in its enforcement of the competition rules.[48]

D. EU ACTS

EU acts adopted by the autonomous EU institutions (the Council, the Commission, and the European Parliament), such as regulations, directives, decisions, recommendations, and opinions, flesh out the basic principles set out in the Treaties.[49] Most general legislative acts, intended to apply in all of the Member States, are adopted by regulation or directive.

It has already been seen that a number of regulations have been adopted by the Council to ensure that the objectives of the European competition rules are carried out. In the field of competition the

---

[41] *Competition Policy Newsletter.*

[42] [2003] OJ L1/1: see Chap. 13.

[43] Art. 14.

[44] Those of the Member States.

[45] Commission Notice on cooperation within the Network of Competition Authorities [2004] OJ L123/18, para. 58.

[46] Reg. 139/2004, Art. 19.

[47] See further Chap. 13.

[48] The first decision on such a complaint was issued on 30 September 2008, case 1881/2006/JF; see Chap. 13.

[49] Art. 288 TFEU (ex Art. 249 EC) defines the main characteristics of each of these measures. The CJ has, however, recognised that other *sui generis* acts adopted by one of the Community (now Union) institutions may be capable of producing legal effects: Case 22/70, *Commission v. Council (ERTA)* [1971] ECR 263. Under the TFEU there is a distinction between 'legislative' and 'non-legislative' acts: see Arts 289–290.

Commission has adopted a number of regulations under powers delegated to it by the Council and applies the competition rules to undertakings by means of decisions.[50]

E. THE EU COURTS

The EU's judicial system comprises the CJEU which includes the CJ and the GC.[51] They are together referred to in this book as 'the EU Courts'. Provision is also made for specialist courts. The GC was called the Court of First Instance (CFI) until the Treaty of Lisbon came into force. The CFI was originally set up in 1989. The CJ is assisted by Advocates-General. An Advocate General delivers an Opinion on a case before the CJ gives judgment.[52] The EU Courts have the task of interpreting the law set out in the Treaties and secondary legislation[53] and ensuring that the law is observed. The difficulties of interpretation are compounded by the fact that each language text of an EU provision is relevant to the determination (all provisions are translated into each of the 24 EU languages).[54] Each text has equal status and is equally authentic.[55] The approach of the EU Courts is to adopt a 'teleological' interpretation of Treaty provisions or EU acts, which are construed in the context of the EU's objectives and activities.[56] On occasion the CJ has gone so far as to ignore clear words of the Treaty or act if that construction will ensure an interpretation which best accords with the broad objectives of the Treaty.[57] A number of instances in which the CJ has adopted an extremely broad interpretation of the competition rules or one which does not accord with the clear wording of the text will be seen in this book.

The EU Courts have no system of precedent as understood in common law systems. In practice, however, they strive for consistency.[58] It is only on rare occasions that previous rulings of the CJ have been expressly reversed.[59] The GC does not consider itself bound by its own previous decisions and neither generally does it consider itself bound by the CJ.[60] As there is, however, an appeal from the

---

[50] The Commission also has powers under Art. 106(3) TFEU (ex Art. 86(3), which deals with public undertakings and those to whom Member States grant special or exclusive rights, to adopt directives (addressed to Member States) without the participation of the Council: see Chap. 8.

[51] The CJEU 'shall ensure that in the interpretation and application of the Treaties the law is observed': Art. 17 TEU. For the EU Courts generally, see A. Arnull, *The European Union and its Court of Justice* (2nd edn, Oxford University Press, 2006).

[52] The Opinion is not binding but can be very valuable in illuminating the case and the issues it raises. The GC can appoint an Advocate General on an ad hoc basis from among its members: Statute of the CJEU Art. 49, attached as Protocol 3 to the TEU and TFEU.

[53] And Notices, insofar as these have some binding effect. See Section 5.

[54] These were, as at 1 July 2013, Bulgarian, Czech, Croatian, Danish, Dutch, English, Estonian, Finnish, French, German, Greek, Hungarian, Irish, Italian, Latvian, Lithuanian, Maltese, Polish, Portuguese, Romanian, Spanish, Slovakian, Slovenian, and Swedish. Irish became a full official and working language on 1 January 2007 but not all EU documents are translated into Irish.

[55] Case 283/81, *CILFIT Srl and Lanificio de Gavardo SpA* v. *Ministry of Health* [1982] ECR 3415, para. 18.

[56] See Chap. 1.

[57] See, e.g., Case C-70/88, *European Parliament* v. *Council* ('Chernobyl') [1990] ECR I-2041.

[58] Case 4/73, *Nold* v. *Commission* [1974] ECR 491. See also A. Arnull, 'Owning up to Fallibility: Precedent and the Court of Justice' (1993) 30 *CML Rev.* 247.

[59] See, e.g., Case C-70/88, *European Parliament* v. *Council* ('Chernobyl') [1990] ECR I-2041; Case C-10/89, *CNL-Sucal* v. *HAG GF AG* ('Hag II') [1990] ECR I-3711; and Cases C-267 and 268/91, *Keck and Mithouard, Criminal Proceedings Against* [1993] ECR I-6097, paras. 15–16. On some (unsatisfactory) occasions the CJ has departed from its previous case law without explaining what it was doing but in others it has distinguished the case before it from the precedents in a way more familiar to common lawyers: see further Arnull, *The European Union and its Court of Justice* (cited in n. 51), 625–633. The (un)willingness of the CJ to depart from its previous decisions is an issue in respect of a modernised approach to Art. 102, see Chaps. 5 and 7.

[60] Unless there are exceptional circumstances, such as the previous judgment having the status of res judicata, or where the Statute of the Court decrees it, e.g. where the CJ overturns a judgment of the GC on a point of law and refers the case back to the GC for judgment, Art. 61 decrees that the GC is bound by the CJ on points of law. See Arnull, *The European Union and its Court of Justice* (cited in n. 51), 633–637.

GC to the CJ on a point of law, it is open to the CJ to reverse the GC if it does not agree with the lower court's departure from precedent. In a famous example of the GC striking out on its own, *Jégo-Quéré*, the CJ overturned the GC on appeal and restored the status quo, but did not gainsay the GC's right not to follow the CJ's previous decisions.[61]

In the context of EU competition law the EU Courts hear two main types of action. First, Article 263 TFEU (ex Article 230 EC) specifically provides for the review of the legality of acts adopted by the EU institutions. This includes challenging the legality of the Commission's competition decisions. Further, it allows for challenges to a number of other administrative acts of the Commission which are capable of affecting the interests of individuals. Challenges are normally made in the first instance to the GC.[62] A fast-track procedure is available in certain cases.[63] Competition cases form a significant part of the GC's work and the GC has developed considerable competition law expertise. Nevertheless, the intensity (or lack of it) with which the GC reviews Commission competition decisions is a major issue in the enforcement of EU competition law which has human rights implications.[64] Appeals on points of law can be made from the GC to the CJ.[65] The CJ takes a limited view of its role in such appeals[66] and it is often necessary to look at the GC judgment rather than that of the CJ to find a fuller analysis of the issues.

Secondly, the national courts apply the EU competition rules, which are directly applicable. Article 267 TFEU (ex Article 234 EC) provides a procedure whereby a national court or tribunal may (and in some circumstances must) request the CJ to give a preliminary ruling on a question on the interpretation or validity of EU law where a decision on the question is necessary to enable that court or tribunal to give judgment.[67] At present these references are still made directly to the CJ and are not dealt with by the GC.[68] The CJ refuses to give a ruling on a reference from a body that does not constitute a 'court or tribunal' within the criteria laid down in the case law.[69] On these grounds it refused to rule on a reference from the Greek competition authority on an important point concerning the application of Article 102 but accepted a reference on the same issue from a Greek court.[70] The CJ does give rulings on points of EU law which are crucial to the interpretation of domestic law in the case before the referring court. This is important in competition law where most Member States have domestic laws which deliberately mirror the EU rules and are interpreted in line with them. Leading rulings in EU competition law have been given in such cases.[71]

---

[61] Case T-177/01, *Jégo-Quéré v. Commission* [2002] ECR II-665, *rev'd* by the CJ, Case C-263/02 P, *Commission v. Jégo-Quéré* [2004] ECR I-3425. The case concerned the matter of when an individual had standing under Art. 230(4) EC to challenge an act of general application (the standing rule has been amended in the equivalent TFEU provision, Art. 263 TFEU).

[62] See Art. 256(1) TFEU and the Protocol on the Statute of the CJEU, Art. 51, see further Chap. 13 and Cases C-68/95 and C-30/95, *France v. Commission* [1998] ECR I-1375.

[63] Codified rules of the GC as amended, Art. 76a.

[64] See Chap. 13.

[65] Protocol on the Statute of the Court of Justice, Art. 51.

[66] See Chap. 13.

[67] Final courts must refer. For a full discussion, see Craig and de Búrca, *EU Law: Text, Cases and Materials* (cited in n. 16) and Chap. 13.

[68] Art. 256 TFEU provides that the GC shall have jurisdiction to give preliminary rulings 'in specific areas laid down by the Statute'. The Statute of the Court does not yet lay down any such areas and all preliminary rulings therefore continue to go to the CJ.

[69] See in particular Case C-54/96, *Dorsch Consult* [1997] ECR I-4961; Cases C-110/98 to C-147/98, *Gabalfrisa and Others* [2000] ECR I-1577; Case C-195/98, *Österreichischer Gewerkschaftsbund* [2000] ECR I-10497; Case C-516/99, *Schmid* [2002] ECR I-4573; Case C-103/97, *Köllensperger and Atzwanger* [1999] ECR I-551.

[70] Case C-53/03, *Synetairismos Farmakopoion Aitolias & Akarnanias (Syfait) v. GlaxoSmithKline* [2005] ECR I-4609 (reference refused); Case C-468-478/06, *Sot. Lélos kai Sia and others EE v. GlaxoSmithKline AEVE Farmakeftikon Proionton* [2008] ECR I-7139.

[71] E.g. the refusal to supply case, Case C-7/97, *Oscar Bronner GmbH & Co KG v. Mediaprint* [1998] ECR I-7791.

The EU Courts' volume of work can cause severe delays for litigants. This problem is particularly acute in the sphere of mergers where timing will be of the essence to the parties. The introduction of the expedited procedure before the GC ameliorates these difficulties to some extent but there is still criticism of the delays and calls for the creation of a specialist competition court to remedy the problem.[72] In 2003 provision was made for specialist courts to be attached to the GC[73] and this is now contained Article 257 TFEU.[74] However, the Civil Service Tribunal (2005), which deals with staff cases, is so far the only one to have been established. The issue of whether the judicial architecture should be reformed to encompass a specialist competition court has also arisen in the context of the debate about whether the current arrangements for judicial review of Commission proceedings is adequate and in particular whether it satisfies the requirements of the ECHR.[75]

F. GENERAL PRINCIPLES OF UNION LAW AND HUMAN RIGHTS

We have seen in Section 3 that the EU has its own Charter of Fundamental Rights which is of 'equal value' to the TEU and TFEU. Prior to that the EU Courts had already developed a body of law known as the general principles of law and human rights, now given expression by the Charter, which are principles, based on national laws of Member States and international treaties to which the Member States are signatories, especially the ECHR, in accordance with which EU law is interpreted. The principles are important when determining the boundaries of proper and lawful action of EU and national institutions (when the latter are acting within the sphere of EU law).[76]

Article 6(3) TEU states:

Fundamental rights, as guaranteed by the European Convention for the Protection of Human Rights and Fundamental Freedoms and as they result from the constitutional traditions common to the Member States, shall constitute general principles of the Union's law.

The general principles include legitimate expectation, legal certainty, proportionality,[77] effective judicial protection, good administration, equality, and non-discrimination. All are important in competition law where the actions of institutions applying and enforcing the EU competition rules (both the Commission and the NCAs) must respect the general principles of law and ensure that their administrative procedures comply with them. As we see in Chapter 13 in many appeals from competition decisions the parties have alleged that the Commission has failed to observe these principles.

Subsidiarity, the principle whereby the Union does not take action unless it is more effective than action taken at national, regional, or local level is also a general principle of EU law and is now enshrined in Article 5 TEU. It applies only to areas not within the exclusive competence of the Union, and by Article 3(1)(b) TFEU, 'the establishing of the competition rules necessary for the

---

[72] The UK's Confederation of British Industry (CBI) called for the creation of specialist competition panels in the GC, see CBI Report, 15 June 2006. The question of whether there is a need for the creation of a distinct European competition court as a panel of the GC was examined by the House of Lords European Union Select Committee. The Select Committee concluded that there was no such need at that time (Select Committee on the European Union, 15th Report, 27 March 2007).

[73] Art. 225a EC, inserted by the Treaty of Nice. The term used there was 'judicial panels'.

[74] Which actually refers to 'specialist courts' rather than 'judicial panels'.

[75] See Chap. 13.

[76] See, e.g., Case 5/88, *Wachauf v. Federal Republic of Germany* [1989] ECR 2609, [1990] 1 CMLR 328; Case C-260/89, *Ellinki Radiophonia Tileorassi—Anonimi Etairia (ERT-AE) v. Dimotiki Etairia Pliroforissis (DEP)* [1991] ECR I-2925.

[77] Proportionality is described in Art. 5(4) TEU as requiring that 'the content and form of Union action shall not exceed what is necessary to achieve the objectives of the Treaties'. Article 5(1) states that 'the use of Union competences is governed by the principles of subsidiarity and proportionality'.

functioning of the internal market' is an area of exclusive Union competence. However, the institutional arrangements in Regulation 1/2003 set up to effect the modernisation of competition law inter alia by decentralising enforcement to Member States were specifically expressed to be in accordance with the principle of subsidiarity.[78] It should be noted that the EU competition rules apply only to agreements and practices when they *affect trade between Member States* or to mergers that have an *EU [previously Community] dimension*[79] (matters that do not have such effect or dimension are of national concern only as they do not concern the functioning of the internal market) and the GC said in *GlaxoSmithKline* that the limitation of Article 101(1) to agreements which may affect inter-Member State trade gives 'concrete form' to the principle of subsidiarity.[80]

G. THE EU LEGAL ORDER

(i) Direct Applicability

Although founded on treaties which are international agreements, the EU has developed its own unique legal system, with its own institutions and enforcement mechanisms.

International law and international treaties traditionally impose obligations only on States and do not impose obligations or confer rights on private individuals. However, very early in the Community's development the CJ ruled that rights and obligations created by Community (now EU) law were capable of enforcement by and against private individuals and not just the Member States. This applies both to Treaty provisions[81] and Regulations, provided that they meet certain conditions.[82] Individuals are therefore entitled to rely on rights that they derive from these measures before national courts even if they have not been implemented by national legislation. The only requirement is that the EU measure is *capable of direct effect*. The main competition provisions set out in the TFEU are directly applicable and can be relied upon by or against private individuals in actions in national courts. One of these provisions, Article 101(3) of the Treaty, has only been directly applicable since 1 May 2004. The implications of the previous lack of direct applicability and the significance of the change made by Regulation 1/2003 are seen in other parts of this book. The provisions of regulations are likewise directly applicable. Regulations both of the Council and of the Commission are important in EU competition law.

(ii) Supremacy

Where there is a conflict between a directly effective EU provision and national law, the former must prevail.[83] The principle of supremacy ensures the full effectiveness and uniform application of directly effective EU law.[84]

Before 1 May 2004 the position was that the doctrine of supremacy did not ordinarily mean that national competition legislation could not be applied where Community competition rules

---

[78] Council Reg. 1/2003 [2003] OJ L1/1, recital 34.

[79] As at 1 July 2013 the relevant wording of the Merger Regulation had not been changed to reflect the demise of the EC. However, in this book the terminology 'EU dimension' or 'Union dimension' is used.

[80] Case T-168/01, *GlaxoSmithKline Services Unlimited* [2006] ECR II-2969, para. 201.

[81] Case 26/62, *Van Gend en Loos v. Nederlandse Administratie der Belastingen* [1963] ECR 1, 1229.

[82] The provision relied upon must be sufficiently precise and unconditional.

[83] Case 6/64, *Costa v. ENEL* [1964] ECR 585, 593–594, 456.

[84] A national court faced with national rules or legislation that conflict with EU law has an obligation to give immediate precedence to the EU provisions. If necessary it must refuse to apply the provisions of national legislation even if subsequently adopted: see Case 106/77, *Amministrazione delle Finanze dello Stato v. Simmenthal SpA* [1978] ECR 6293, para. 24.

applied,[85] but where there was a *conflict* between national and Community law, the latter had to prevail.[86] Regulation 1/2003, Article 3,[87] however, makes specific provision for the relationship between EU and national competition law in the sphere of anti-competitive agreements and conduct. The position under Regulation 1/2003 is discussed in Chapter 13. The EU Merger Regulation also specifically deals with the relationship between EU and national merger regimes.[88]

(iii) Article 267 TFEU

It is Article 267 TFEU (ex Article 234 EC) which enables the enforcement of the EU rules at the national level through the principles of direct effect and supremacy without compromising the uniformity of EU law. As seen in Section 3.E, it provides for the CJ to give rulings on questions of EU law referred to it by national courts of the Member States. The procedure was said by the CJ in 1974 to be 'essential for the preservation of the Community character of the law established by the Treaty and has the object of ensuring that in all circumstances the law is the same in all states of the Community'.[89] It has been critical in the sphere of competition law.

4. THE COMPETITION PROVISIONS

A. GENERAL

(i) Article 3(1)(g) of the EC Treaty

The omission of an equivalent provision in the body of the TEU or TFEU to Article 3(1)(g) of the EC Treaty is discussed in Chapter 1.[90] It was explained there that the relegation of the words 'a system ensuring that competition is not distorted' to a Protocol is of no significance.[91] When looking at the way in which the EU Courts have hitherto interpreted the competition provisions it is impossible to ignore Article 3(1)(g). Article 3(1)(g) was crucial to the judgment in *Continental Can*, the seminal competition case in 1973 on what is now Article 102 TFEU.[92] The words of Article 3(1)(g), now in Protocol 27, must therefore always be borne in mind when looking at the provisions which set out the competition rules in greater detail.

(ii) The Main Treaty Provisions and the Merger Regulation

According to Article 3(1)(b) TFEU the establishment of competition rules necessary for the functioning of the internal market is an area of exclusive Union competence. The main competition rules are contained in Chapter 1 of Title VII of the TFEU. Section 1 (Articles 101–106, ex Articles 81–86 EC) deals with rules applying to undertakings.[93] Section 2 (Articles 107–109, ex Articles 87–89) deals

---

[85] But see the provisions dealing with mergers, Chap. 15.

[86] Case 14/68, *Walt Wilhelm v. Bundeskartellamt* [1969] ECR 1. There were, however, potential complications where national law applied more strictly to agreements authorised by EC law, see the discussion in the 1st edn of this book, pp. 1008–1015.

[87] [2003] OJ L1/1.

[88] See Chap. 15.

[89] Case 166/73, *Rheinmühlen-Düsseldorf v. Einfuhr und Vorratsstelle für Getreide und Futtermittel* [1974] ECR 33.

[90] See Chap. 1, Section 7.B.

[91] Case C-52/09, *Konkurrensverket v. TeliaSonera Sverige AB* [2011] ECR I-527, paras. 20–22.

[92] Case 6/72, *Europemballage Corporation and Continental Can Co Inc v. Commission* [1973] ECR 215, para. 23. See Chaps. 5 and 7. See also Case C-68/94, *French Republic v. Commission* [1998] ECR I-1375.

[93] Broadly, any entity engaged in commercial activities: see Chap. 3.

with State aid. Merger control has never been expressly contained in any Treaty provision. It is provided for in Council Regulation 139/2004.[94]

(iii) Special Sectors

The basic position is that the competition rules cover all areas of the economy. However, the following should be noted about the special position of certain sectors.

a. Coal and Steel

Until 23 July 2002 the coal and steel industries were governed by the European Coal and Steel Community Treaty. Upon the expiry of that Treaty coal and steel passed into the scope of the EC Treaty and thence into that of the TEU and TFEU.[95] In the appeal from the *Reinforcing Bars Cartel* decision[96] the GC annulled a decision in respect of a breach of Article 65(1) ECSC which the Commission had purported to adopt after the expiry of the Treaty. The GC confirmed that upon the expiry of the Treaty the coal and steel sectors had passed within the *lex generalis* of the EC Treaty but held that this did not give the Commission competence to take a decision under provisions that had expired.[97]

b. Atomic Energy

The Euratom Treaty of 1957 established the European Atomic Energy Community in respect of the non-military use of nuclear energy. Article 305(2) EC provided that the EC competition provisions applied to nuclear energy insofar as they did not derogate from the Euratom Treaty. That article was repealed by the Treaty of Lisbon. The sector is therefore subject to no special provisions. The Commission took a number of decisions on horizontal cooperation agreements in the industry despite Article 305(2).

c. Agriculture

In 1962 Regulation 26[98] modified the competition rules in respect of agriculture, and there is some tension between the objectives of the common agricultural policy (CAP)[99] and competition policy. Currently the agriculture sector is governed by two Regulations, Regulation 1184/2006[100] and Regulation 1234/2007 (the Single CMO Regulation).[101] The effect of these Regulations is that Article 102 applies to the production and trade of agricultural products and Article 101(1) applies as well, but with three exceptions in the case of the latter.[102] These are: (i) agreements, decisions, and practices which form an integral part of national market organisations, (ii) agreements, decisions, and practices which are necessary for the attainment of the objectives of the CAP, and (iii) agreements

---

[94] [2004] OJ L24/1, replacing Council Reg. 4064/89[1989] OJ L395/1, as amended by Council Reg. 1310/97 [1997] OJ L180/1.

[95] The Commission issued a Communication in June 2002 explaining how the EC rules would in future apply to coal and steel: [2002] OJ C152/5. It stated that it did not intend to initiate proceedings under the EC rules in respect of agreements it had previously authorised under the ECSC regime unless 'owing to substantial factual or legal developments' they were clearly not eligible for exemption under the EC Treaty:[2002] OJ C152/5, paras. 28–29. For the differences between the ECSC and EC regimes, see the 3rd edn of this book, p. 109, n. 3 and G. Bellamy and G. Child, *European Law of Competition* (5th edn, Sweet & Maxwell, 2001).

[96] COMP/37.956 on appeal Cases T-27/03 etc., *SP SpA* v. *Commission* [2007] ECR II-4331. The Commission readopted the *Concrete Reinforcing Bars* decision under Reg.1/2003, COMP/37.956 [2009], 30 September 2009 (on appeal Cases T-472/09 etc., *SP* v. *Commission*, judgment pending).

[97] See also Case C-201/09 P, *Arcelor Mittal* v. *Commission* [2011] ECR I-2239; see further Chap. 13.

[98] [1959–62] OJ Spec. Ed. 129.

[99] Art. 39 TFEU (ex Art. 33 EC).

[100] [2006] OJ L214/7.

[101] [2007] OJ L 299/1. CMO stands for common organisation of agricultural markets.

[102] The agricultural products to which the regulations apply are set out in TFEU Annex I. The exceptions are contained in Art. 2 (1) of Reg. 1184/2006.

between farmers or associations of farmers belonging to a single Member State not involving an obligation to charge identical prices.[103]

d. Transport

The transport sector, once characterised by national legal monopolies in respect of rail and air transport, has gradually been liberalised and brought within the general competition regime.[104] In the rail sector, freight was fully liberalised from 1 January 2007 and international passenger services as from 1 January 2010.[105] Council Regulation 487/2009[106] provides for block exemptions in the air transport sector but currently there are no such exemptions. The maritime transport sector was previously subject to a specially generous regime but this has been significantly amended and curtailed.[107]

e. Other Sectors Subject to Liberalisation

The EU embarked on programmes of liberalisation and/or harmonisation of the energy, telecommunications, broadcasting, and financial services sectors with the aim of opening them up to greater competition. The issue of the relationship between competition law and the specific regulatory regimes which apply to these sectors was discussed in Chapter 1.[108] There has been little sympathy for the claims that these sectors should receive favourable treatment and should be protected from the competitive process and there has been a plethora of recent competition decisions concerning them.[109] The Commission is also much concerned with the application of the competition rules to professional services.[110]

f. Sport

Next, there is the question of sport.[111] Article 165(1) TFEU (in Title XII on 'Education, vocational, training, youth and sport') says:

---

[103] R. Whish and D. Bailey, *Competition Law* (7th edn, Oxford University Press, 2012), 964 consider the provision on farmers' associations not to be a further exception but an embellishment of the rest of the provision, cf. Bellamy and Child, *European Law of Competition* (7th edn, Oxford University Press, 2013), 12.157.

[104] The EU provisions on transport generally are set out in Arts 90–100 TFEU. Council Reg. 487/2009 now gives the Commission power to issue block exemptions in the air transport sector.

[105] Directive 2007/58/EC [2007] OJ L315/44. See Commission Press Release IP/09/2001 (30 December 2009).

[106] [2009] OJ L148/1.

[107] Council Reg. 246/2009 [2009] OJ L79/1 gives the Commission power to adopt block exemptions in respect of international liner consortia. The Commission adopted Reg. 906/2009 [2009] OJ L256/31 pursuant to this. The Commission issued Guidelines on the application of Art. 101 to maritime transport services in 2008, [2008] OJ C245/2. These expired on 26 September 2013 and, following a public consultation in 2012, the Commission decided not to renew them, but rather to rely on the general law, including the Horizontal Cooperation Guidelines [2011] OJ C11/1.

[108] See Chap. 1, Section 7.D, p. 52.

[109] See Chap. 7. The Commission has undertaken sector enquiries under Reg. 1/2003, Art. 17 in respect of the energy sector and the financial services sector (payment cards, retail banking, and business insurance). Article 102 is being rigorously applied to the energy sector in order to make liberalisation effective. See P. Cameron, *Competition in Energy Markets* (2nd edn, Oxford University Press, 2007) on energy markets. For 'universal service' obligations, see further Chap. 8.

[110] The Commission has produced two reports: *Report on Competition in Professional Services* COM/2004/0083 final, February 2004; and *Professional Services—Scope for More Reform* COM/2005/0405 final, in September 2005. As a follow-up to these reports the European Parliament passed a resolution in December 2006 supporting the Commission's moves to rid the professional services sector of overly restrictive regulation (which is often put in place, or maintained, by the actions of Member States). For a discussion of the regulation of the legal profession in the Netherlands, see the discussion of Case C-303/99, *Wouters v. Algemene Raad van de Nederlandse Orde van Advocaten* [2002] ECR I-1577 in Chap. 4.

[111] See Annex 1 to the Staff Working Document accompanying the Commission White Paper on Sport of July 2007, 'The EU and Sport: Background and Context' (SEC(2007)935), accompanying the White Paper, COM(2007) 391 final; P. Kienapfel and A. Stein, 'The Application of Articles 81 and 82 EC in the Sports Sector (2007) *Competition*

…The Union shall contribute to the promotion of European sporting issues, while taking account of the specific nature of sport, its structures based on voluntary activity and its social and educational function.

Early case law on EU law and sport concerned the application of the free movement provisions to sporting rules. The CJ established that the practice of sport was subject to Community law only insofar as it constituted an economic activity.[112] In the watershed case of *Bosman* the CJ applied the free movement provisions to the football transfer system.[113] More recently the free movement of services provisions, as well as the competition rules, have been applied to the licensing of television rights to football.[114] Bodies regulating sports may be in a dominant[115] or collectively dominant[116] position. In *Meca-Medina*[117] the CJ recognised that sporting regulatory bodies may have rules which are necessary for regulating sporting activity even if they limit competition because such a limitation is 'inherent in the organisation and proper conduct of competitive sport and its very purpose is to ensure healthy rivalry between athletes'.[118] It nevertheless held that EU law must be the judge of whether the rules are compatible with the competition rules, in that they must comply with the principle of proportionality and not apply excessive penalties, for instance. The CJ said:[119]

…it is apparent that the mere fact that a rule is purely sporting in nature does not have the effect of removing from the scope of the Treaty the person engaging in the activity governed by that rule or the body which has laid it down.

If the sporting activity in question falls within the scope of the Treaty, the conditions for engaging in it are subject to all the obligations which result from the various provisions of the Treaty….

Competition law is applied to the undoubtedly commercial aspects of sport[120] which have huge economic impact in the EU, as the Commission says on its website, and the Commission has been

Policy Newsletter (3)6; E. Szyszcak, 'Competition and Sport' (2007) 32 *ELRev* 95; S. Van den Bogaert and A. Vermeersch, 'Sport and the EC Treaty: a tale of uneasy bedfellows?' (2006) 31 *ELRev* 821; S. Weatherill, '"Fair Play Please": Recent Developments in the Application of EC Law to Sport' (2003) 40 *CMLRev* 51.

[112] Case 36/74, *Walrave and Koch v. Association Union Cycliste Internationale* [1974] ECR 1405; see also Case 13/76, *Donà v. Mantero* [1976] ECR 1333.

[113] Case C-415/93, *Union Royale Belge des Sociétés de Football Association v. Bosman* [1995] ECR I-4921, which altered fundamentally the professional game in Europe.

[114] Cases 403/08 and 429/08, *Football Association Premier League v. QC Leisure* and *Karen Murphy v. Media Protection Services Ltd*, [2011] ECR I-9083, 4 October 2011, see further, text at n. 121.

[115] See e.g. Case C-49/07, *Motosykletistiki Omospondia Ellados NPID (MOTOE) v. Elliniko Dimosio* [2008] ECR I-4863 (Greek Motorcycling Federation), discussed in Chap. 8.

[116] See Case T-193/02, *Laurent Piau v. Commission* [2005] ECR II-209 (FIFA).

[117] Case C-519/04, *Meca-Medina and Majcen v. Commission* [2006] ECR I-6991. The case concerned the Olympic swimming doping rules of the International Olympic Committee (IOC) and is discussed further in Chap. 3. For the Commission's policy on the application of competition law to sporting rules generally, see Annex 1 to the Commission Staff Working Document, section 2 (cited in n. 111); Mario Monti, 'Sport and Competition', speech given at a Commission-organised conference on sports, Brussels, 17 April 2000; Mario Monti, 'Competition and Sport the Rules of the Game', speech given at European Olympic Committee Conference on 'Governance in Sport', Féderation Internationale de l'Automobile, Brussels, 26 February 2001; Alexander Schaub, 'Sports and Competition: Broadcasting Rights for Sports Events', European Competition Day, Madrid, 26 February 2002: all available on DG Comp's website, <http://ec.europa.eu/competition/index_en.html>.

[118] Case C-519/04, *Meca-Medina and Majcen v. Commission* [2006] ECR I-6991, para. 45.

[119] *Meca Medina*, paras. 27–28; see Annex 1 to the Commission Staff Working Document, section 2.1.5 (cited in n. 111). See further Case T-193/02, *Laurent Piau v. Commission* [2005] ECR II-209; E. Szyszcak, 'Competition and Sport' (cited in n. 111).

[120] See section 3 of Annex 1 to the Commission Staff Working Document (cited in n. 111) and, e.g., the application of Art. 102 to the ticketing arrangements for the 1998 World Cup in 1998 *Football World Cup* [2000] OJ L5/55, [2000] 4 CMLR 963; the Commission dealt with Formula One racing in a lengthy investigation which culminated in a separation of the functions of the FIA and the FAO, IP/01/120.

particularly concerned with the sale of media rights to sporting events.[121] However, it does not interfere with what it considers to be pure sporting issues[122] and cooperates with sporting bodies in trying to reach a consensus on issues which straddle the commercial/purely sporting divide. For example, in 2012 Commissioner Almunia and the President of UEFA, Michel Platini, issued a joint statement on UEFA's Financial Fair Play policy (clubs' football-related income should at least match football-related expenditure).[123] The Commission is disinclined to become involved in policing sports disputes and the GC has backed it up on this. In 2012 the GC dismissed three appeals against Commission rejections of complaints, one of which concerned the sanctions imposed on Juventus in the Italian match-rigging scandal.[124] The Commission has a section of its website devoted to competition law and sport, which also covers the application of the State Aid rules, which are relevant, for example, where public authorities give support to sports infrastructure and/or financial benefits to undertakings concerned with sport.[125]

g. Security Connected with Military Equipment

Article 346(1)(b)[126] provides that the Treaty provisions shall not preclude any Member State from taking 'such measures as it considers necessary for the protection of the essential interests of its security which are connected with the production of or trade in arms, munitions and war material; such measures shall not adversely affect the conditions of competition in the internal market regarding products which are not intended for specifically military purposes'. This provision has, for example, been used by Member States to retain jurisdiction over mergers with a military significance.[127] A list of the products covered by Article 346(1)(b) is contained in a Council decision of 1958.[128] The provision has to be interpreted strictly[129] and it is for the Member State seeking to rely on it to prove that it is necessary to have recourse to it in order to protect its essential security interests.[130]

---

[121] As well as the *FAPL* and *Murphy* case (cited in n. 114), see *Joint selling of the commercial rights of the UEFA Champions League* [2003] OJ L291/25, [2004] 4 CMLR 9; *Deutsche Bundesliga* [2005] OJ L134/46, [2005] 5 CMLR 1715; *FA Premier League* [2006] 5 CMLR 1430; and Annex 1 to the Commission Staff Working Document, section 3 (cited in n. 111). The saga of litigation over the rules of the European Broadcasting Union (EBU) was largely to do with the television rights to sporting events: Cases T-528, 542, 543, and 546/93, *Métropole Télévision SA v. Commission* [1996] ECR II-649; Case T-206/99, *Métropole Télévision SA v. Commission* [2001] ECR II-1057; Cases T-185, 216, 299 & 300/00, *Métropole Télévision SA (M6) v. Commission* [2002] ECR II-3805. For the sale of media rights, see also T. Toft, 'Developments in European Law', Speech to the Sports and Law Congress, Berlin, 28 April 2006, <http://ec.europa.eu/competition/speeches/text/sp2006_003_en.pdf>.

[122] See *UEFA* [1999] OJ C363/2 where the Commission published an Art. 19(3) Notice under Reg. 17 setting out its initial view that a UEFA rule precluding more than one club belonging to the same owner from taking part in the same competition did not fall within the competition rules and the Commission's rejection of a complaint against UEFA's 'at home and away from home' rule (each club must play its home matches at its own ground) on the grounds that it was a purely sporting rule and as such outside the competition rules, IP/99/965.

[123] 21 March 2012.

[124] Case T-273/09, *Associazione 'Giùlemanidallajuve' v. Commission*, 19 March 2012; the decision was in the case COMP/39.464, *Supporters Juventus Turin—FIGC-CONI-UEFA-FIFA*; the scandal involved certain Italian teams influencing referee appointments. Juventus were, inter alia, relegated to Serie B (along with Lazio and Fiorentina), forfeited two Serie A titles, and were excluded from the 2006–2007 Champions League (they immediately gained promotion back to Serie A the next season). The other two cases were Case T-508/09, *Cañas v. Commission*, 26 March 2012, on appeal Case C-269/12 P, judgment pending (anti-doping sanctions in tennis) and Case T-341/10, *F91 Diddeleng*, 16 April 2012 (rules of the Luxembourg FA).

[125] The Commission is reported to be investigating State aid allegedly given to Real Madrid in connection with property transactions. It is investigating the public funding of five dutch clubs, including PSV Eindhoven, IP/13/192.

[126] Ex Art. 296(1)(b)EC.

[127] See Chap. 15. For Art. 326 generally, see P. Koutrakos, *Trade, Foreign Policy and Defence in EU Constitutional Law* (Hart Publishing, 2001).

[128] Council decision 255/58. It has never been officially published in the OJ but the list is reproduced in the materials volume (Vol. II) of Bellamy and Child, *European Law of Competition*, (cited in n. 103), Appendix A7, para. 43.

[129] Case C-284/05, *Commission v. Finland* [2009] ECR I-11705, para. 46.

[130] Case C-284/05, *Commission v. Finland* [2009] ECR I-11705, para. 49.

B. THE SUBSTANTIVE COMPETITION PROVISIONS OF THE TFEU

The substantive competition provisions of the TFEU are summarised here.[131] The provisions are dealt with more fully in later chapters.

(i) Article 101 TFEU (ex Article 81 EC, ex Article 85 EC)

Article 101 is set out in three parts: Article 101(1) prohibits agreements, decisions of associations of undertakings and concerted practices which have as their object or effect the prevention, restriction, or distortion of competition and which may affect trade between Member States. Article 101(2) states that such agreements are void. Article 101(3) provides, however, that Article 101(1) may be 'declared inapplicable' in respect of agreements, decisions, or concerted practices or of categories of such agreements which are on balance beneficial since they satisfy the criteria set out in that provision. The provisions governing the analysis of an agreement are split, therefore, between Article 101(1) and Article 101(3). This 'bifurcation' of Article 101 has caused great difficulties.[132]

The wording in Article 101(3) that Article 101(1) 'may...be declared inapplicable' to certain agreements left open, deliberately perhaps, the question of how and by whom this declaration was to be made. The Council in 1962 conferred exclusive power on the Commission to exempt agreements from the prohibition of Article 101(1),[133] and later enabled it to adopt 'block exemption' regulations exempting categories of agreements from the prohibition.[134] In 1999, however, the Commission proposed in its White Paper on modernisation[135] that the system of individual exemption should be abandoned. This proposal was adopted by the Council in Regulation 1/2003[136] and from 1 May 2004 Article 101(3) has had direct effect and is applied directly by the Commission, national courts, and NCAs as an exception to the Article 101(1) prohibition.

(ii) Article 102 TFEU (ex Article 82 EC, ex Article 86 EC)

Article 102 prohibits an undertaking which holds a dominant position in the internal market, or a substantial part of it, from abusing that position insofar as it may affect inter-Member State trade. It contains no express provision for exception or exemption.

(iii) Articles 106 and 37 TFEU (ex Articles 86 and 31 EC, ex Articles 90 and 31 EC)

Article 106 deals with the application of the competition rules (and other rules of the Treaties) to public undertakings and those given special or exclusive rights by Member States. It contains a limited exemption (Article 106(2)) from the Treaty rules for such undertakings. That limitation has, however, been construed narrowly.

---

[131] Note that in these Articles the Treaty of Lisbon has replaced the words 'common market' in the EC Treaty with 'internal market'. This makes no substantive difference.

[132] See Chap. 4.

[133] Reg. 17 [1959–62] OJ Spec. Ed. 87, Art. 9.

[134] See Chap. 13.

[135] Commission White Paper on modernisation of the rules implementing Arts 81 and 82 of the EC Treaty [1999] OJ C132/1, [1999] 5 CMLR 208, paras. 11–13.

[136] [2003] OJ L1/1.

Article 37 is situated in the part of the TFEU concerned with the free movement of goods. It requires Member States which have State monopolies of a commercial character to eliminate discrimination between nationals of Member States regarding the conditions under which goods are procured and marketed.

C. THE PROCEDURAL PROVISIONS

(i) Article 103 TFEU (ex Article 87 EC)

Article 103 confers a general power on the Council to adopt secondary legislation to give effect to the principles laid down in Articles 101 and 102. It provides:[137]

1. The appropriate regulations or directives to give effect to the principles set out in Articles 101 and 102 shall be laid down by the Council on a proposal from the Commission and after consulting the European Parliament.

2. The regulations or directives referred to in paragraph 1 shall be designed, in particular:

   (a) to ensure compliance with the prohibitions laid down in Article 101(1) and in Article 102 by making provision for fines and periodic penalty payments;

   (b) to lay down detailed rules for the application of Article 101(3), taking into account the need to ensure effective supervision on the one hand, and to simplify administration to the greatest possible extent on the other;

   (c) to define, if need be, in the various branches of the economy, the scope of the provisions of Articles 101 and 102;

   (d) to define the respective functions of the Commission and of the Court of Justice of the European Union in applying the provisions laid down in this paragraph;

   (e) to determine the relationship between national laws and the provisions contained in this Section or adopted pursuant to this Article.

a. Implementing Legislation

The Council has adopted regulations pursuant to Article 103 implementing Articles 101 and 102. The most important of these regulations is Regulation 1/2003, which replaced Regulation 17 of 1962 on 1 May 2004. Regulation 1/2003 confers power to enforce the competition rules on the Commission and on the NCAs of the Member States.[138]

b. Block Exemptions

The Council has adopted regulations delegating power to the Commission to adopt regulations granting block exemptions, by which Article 101(1) is declared to be inapplicable to specified types of agreements.[139] The Commission has issued a number of block exemptions under these delegated powers. Some of these are general (such as those on vertical restraints[140] and horizontal cooperation

---

[137] The wording is slightly altered from Art. 83 EC by the removal of the reference to qualified majority voting in the Council and should now be read in the light of the provisions of the TFEU pertaining to legislative procedures, Arts 289–296.

[138] The exclusion of certain maritime transport services from Reg. 1/2003 by Art. 32 was removed by Council Reg. 1419/2006 [2006] OJ L269/1. Until Reg. 411/2004 [2004] OJ L68/1 the competition rules did not apply to aviation between the EU and third countries. Reg. 1/2003 now applies to the enforcement of the competition rules in the transport sector.

[139] See Chap. 4.

[140] Commission Reg. 330/2010 [2010] OJ L1021.

agreements[141]) and some relate only to special sectors (for example, motor vehicle distribution,[142] insurance,[143] and maritime transport[144]).

c. Other Regulations and Measures Adopted by the Commission

The Commission has also adopted secondary legislation which implements Council Regulation 1/2003. For example, Regulation 773/2004[145] governs proceedings by the Commission, covering matters such as the Commission's powers while carrying out investigations under Regulation 1/2003, the handling of complaints[146] by the Commission, and the hearings that Regulation 1/2003 requires the Commission to carry out. Directives are rarely used in the area of competition policy. However, very unusually, the Commission has power under Article 106 to issue directives in order to ensure the application of that Article (directives are normally primary legislation issued by the Council).[147]

(ii) Article 104 TFEU (ex Article 84 EC, ex Article 88 EC)

Article 104 enables Member States to apply Articles 101 and 102 in certain circumstances:

Until the entry into force of the provisions adopted in pursuance of Article 103, the authorities in Member States shall rule on the admissibility of agreements, decisions and concerted practices and on abuse of a dominant position in the internal market in accordance with the law of their country and with the provisions of Article 101, in particular paragraph 3, and of Article 102.

This article confers power on 'authorities in Member States' to apply the competition rules prior to the Council's adoption of implementing rules. In *Nouvelles Frontières*[148] the CJ held that the term authorities 'refers to either the administrative authorities entrusted, in most Member States, with the task of applying domestic legislation on competition subject to the review of legality carried out by competent courts, or else the courts to which, in other Member States, the task has been especially entrusted'. This provision does not, however, apply to an ordinary national court before which the direct effect of an EU competition provision is pleaded.[149]

Article 104 appears to have been designed as a transitional provision. It remained significant in conferring power on the NCAs to act whenever EU implementing legislation does not apply. An example of this prior to 1 May 2004 was international flights between Community and non-Community airports.[150] All sectors of the economy are now subject to Regulation 1/2003.

---

[141] Commission Reg. 1217/2010 on research and development agreements [2010] OJ L 335/36; Commission Reg. 1218/2010 on specialisation agreements [2010] OJ L335/43.

[142] Commission Reg. 461/2010 [2010] OJ L129/52.

[143] See Commission Reg. 267/2010 [2010] OJ L83/1, made pursuant to Council Reg. 1534/91 [1991] OJ L143/1 empowering the Commission to adopt block exemptions for certain types of agreements in the insurance sector.

[144] Commission Reg. 906/2009 [2009] OJ L256/31, adopted pursuant to Council Reg. 246/2009.

[145] [2004] OJ L123/18.

[146] This means complaints to the Commission that undertakings have infringed the competition rules. Complaints play an important role in the enforcement of competition law. See Chap. 13.

[147] Or by the Council and Parliament. For Art. 106(3), see Chap. 8.

[148] Cases 209–213/84, *Ministère Public v. Lucas Asjes (Nouvelles Frontières)* [1986] ECR 1425, para. 55.

[149] Case 127/73, *BRT v. SABAM* [1974] ECR 51.

[150] The UK adopted regulations, the EC Competition Law (Arts 88 and 89) Enforcement Regulations 1996 (SI 1996/2199), to enable the competition authorities to act in such cases and asserted jurisdiction over the proposed alliance between British Airways and American Airlines on this basis. The Commission now enjoys powers of investigation and enforcement with respect to the applications of Arts 101 and 102 to air transport between the Community and third countries, under Reg. 411/2004, [2004] OJ L68/1.

(iii) Article 105 TFEU (ex Article 89 EC)

Article 105 imposes a general duty on the Commission to ensure compliance with the competition rules:

1. Without prejudice to Article 104, the Commission shall ensure the application of the principles laid down in Articles 101 and 102. On application by a Member State or on its own initiative, and in co-operation with the competent authorities in the Member States, who shall give it their assistance, the Commission shall investigate cases of suspected infringement of these principles. If it finds that there has been an infringement, it shall propose appropriate measures to bring it to an end.

    2. If the infringement is not brought to an end, the Commission shall record such infringement of the principles in a reasoned decision. The Commission may publish its decision and authorise Member States to take the measures, the conditions and details of which it shall determine, needed to remedy the situation.

    3. The Commission may adopt regulations relating to the categories of agreement in respect of which the Council has adopted a regulation or a directive pursuant to Article 103(2)(b).

Article 105 originally included the words 'as soon as it takes up its duties' between the words 'shall' and 'ensure' in the first line. This suggested that it was merely a transitional provision enabling the Commission to enforce Articles 101 and 102 prior to the adoption of implementing legislation. The change of wording (effected by the Treaty of Amsterdam) recognises that it is not a temporary measure, but confers on the Commission a permanent residual power to intervene. The Commission was forced to assert jurisdiction under Article 105 when concerned about a proposed alliance between British Airways and American Airlines at the time when air transport between a Community airport and a non-Member State was not covered by the relevant legislation[151]

Article 105(3) was added by the Treaty of Lisbon. It gives the Commission a general power to adopt regulations governing categories of agreements, i.e. block exemptions,[152] although it is dependent on a prior Council regulation. Previously the Commission could only do this following specific ad hoc Council regulations.

D. THE MERGER REGULATION

The present Merger Regulation, 139/2004, was adopted by the Council pursuant to Article 103 and Article 352 TFEU (ex Article 308 EC). It replaced, with effect from 1 May 2004, the original Merger Regulation, Regulation 4064/89.[153] The Merger Regulation applies to concentrations with a 'Community [now EU] dimension'.[154]

E. OTHER RELEVANT TREATY PROVISIONS

Other provisions of the TFEU may interact with the competition provisions. For example, the provisions relating to the free movement of goods, Articles 34–36, and relating to the free movement of services, Articles 56–62. There is a significant interface between the free movement rules and the competition provisions. The free movement rules are also of particular importance when dealing with intellectual property rights. Articles 114 and 115 permit the Union institutions to adopt measures to achieve the approximation of national rules which affect the establishment and functioning of an internal market.

---

[151] Commission Notice concerning the Alliance Agreement between British Airways and American Airlines [1996] OJ C288/4.

[152] For block exemptions generally, see Chap. 4.

[153] [1989] OJ L395/1, as amended by Council Reg. 1310/97 [1997] OJ L180/1. Article 352, the residual legislative power, was used as one of the bases for both Reg. 4064/89 and Reg. 139/2004 as it was thought that, on its own, Art. 103 was an inadequate basis for legislation to control mergers: see Chap. 15.

[154] For the terminology see n. 79.

5. NOTICES AND GUIDELINES

The Commission issues Communications and Notices (some of which are called 'Guidelines')[155] which play a significant role in EU competition law. They are important statements of how the Commission deals with certain matters and help undertakings build an understanding of how the competition rules will be applied in practice. The Notices may constitute a clarification of the substantive law and explain the approach the Commission takes to particular kinds of agreements, practices, or mergers[156] or set out the principles by which the Commission exercises its administrative discretion.[157] A number of Notices were issued to accompany Regulation 1/2003 and its flanking legislation in order to flesh out the details of the new enforcement system.[158] Most of the Notices are crucial to complete an overall picture of a particular competition rule and in practice they influence the way in which firms conduct business. The Notices do not have legislative force and are sometimes referred to as 'soft law'.[159] However, that underplays their real effects as the CJ has held that they may form rules of practice from which the Commission cannot depart in an individual case without breaching general principles of law such as equal treatment and legitimate expectation.[160] We see throughout this book instances in which cases before the EU Courts are fought on the issue of whether the Commission did or did not properly follow or apply one of more of its Notices.[161] Particular issues arise in respect of the Notice which the Commission issued in December 2009 on its enforcement priorities in the application of Article 102 to exclusionary abuses.[162] This is dealt with in Chapters 5 to 7. The Notices are not binding on the courts or NCAs of the Member States.[163]

---

[155] e.g., the Notice on the definition of the relevant market [1997] OJ C372/5; Notice on agreements of minor importance [2001] OJ C368/13; Notice on remedies acceptable under the Merger Regulation [2001] OJ C168/3.

[156] Such as the Guidelines on vertical restraints [2010] OJ C130/1; Guidelines on horizontal cooperation agreements [2011] OJ C11/1; Guidelines on the assessment of horizontal mergers [2004] C 31/5.

[157] Such as the Guidelines on the method of setting fines imposed pursuant to Article 23(2)(a) of Regulation No. 1/2003 [2006] OJ C210/5 and Commission Notice on Immunity from Fines and Reduction of Fines in Cartel Cases [2006] OJ C298/17 (the Leniency Notice).

[158] Notice on cooperation within the network of competition authorities [2004] OJ C101/43; Notice on cooperation between the Commission and the courts of the EU Member States [2004] OJ C101/54; Notice on the handling of complaints by the Commission [2004] OJ C101/65; Notice on informal guidance relating to novel questions [2004] OJ C101/78; Notice on the effect on trade concept in Article 81 and Article 82 [2004] OJ C101/81; Guidelines on the application of Article 81(3) [2004] OJ C101/97.

[159] L. Senden, *Soft Law in European Community Law* (Hart Publishing, 2004); S. Lefevre, 'Interpretative Communications and the Implementation of Community Law at National Level' (2004) 29 *ELRev* 808; H. A. Cosma and R. Whish, 'Soft Law in the Field of EU Competition Policy' (2003) *European Business Law Review*, 25; N. Petit and M. Rato, 'From Hard to Soft Enforcement of EC Competition Law—A Bestiary of "Sunshine" Enforcement Instruments', <http://ssrn.com/abstract=1270109>. The European Parliament was extremely critical in 2007 of the widespread use of 'soft law', see European Parliament Resolution of 4 September 2007 on institutional and legal implications of the use of 'soft law' instruments (2007/2028(INI)).

[160] Cases C-189/02P, 202/02 P, 208/02 P and 213/02 P, *Dansk Rørindustri A/S and Others* v. *Commission* [2005] ECR I-5425, paras. 209–213; Case C-397/03 P, *Archer Daniels Midland Company* v. *Commission* [2006] ECR I-4429; Case C-226/11, *Expedia Inc.* v. *Autorité de la Concurrence*, 13 December 2012, para. 28; Case T-446/05 P, *Amann & Söhne GmbH & Co KG* v. *Commission* [2010] ECR II-1255, paras. 137–139; H. C. H. Hofman, 'Negotiated and Non-Negotiated Administrative Rule-making: The Example of EC Competition Policy', (2006) 43 *CMLRev* 153; Senden, *Soft Law in European Community Law* (cited in n. 159).

[161] Particularly in respect of the Fining Guidelines (currently [2006] OJ C210/2) and the Leniency Notice (currently [2006] OJ C298/17) (cited in n. 157), and see Chap. 13.

[162] Guidance on Commission's Enforcement Priorities in Applying Article 82 of the EC Treaty to Abusive Exclusionary Conduct by Dominant Undertakings [2009] OJ C45/2.

[163] Case C-360/09, *Pfleiderer AG* v. *Bundeskartellamt* [2011] ECR I-5161; Case C-226/11, *Expedia Inc.* v. *Autorité de la Concurrence*, 13 December 2012.

The Commission also issues a plethora of other material, such as press releases, memos, 'frequently asked questions', speeches by the Commissioner and Commission officials, the Annual Report on Competition Policy, and the *Competition Policy Newsletter* which contains articles by officials on recent decisions and other developments.[164]

6. THE COMPETITION RULES AND THE EUROPEAN ECONOMIC AREA

The agreement establishing the EEA came into force on 1 January 1994. The EEA creates a free trade area between the EU and the European Free Trade Area (EFTA) countries with the exception of Switzerland.[165] The competition rules in the EEA are modelled on those in the EC Treaty (now the TFEU). References to trade between the contracting parties, however, replace references to trade between Member States. The agreement effectively extends to the territory of the relevant EFTA States the EU competition rules and all the rules governing the internal market, including intellectual property.

Article 53 EEA is modelled on Article 101 TFEU, Article 54 EEA is modelled on Article 2, Article 59 EEA is modelled on Article 106, and Article 57 EEA effectively applies the rules set out in the EU Merger Regulation to the EEA.

The EFTA Surveillance Authority (ESA) is entrusted, together with the Commission, with the enforcement of the EEA competition rules. The EEA Agreement sets out when the ESA or the Commission has jurisdiction over a particular case. Essentially the ESA has jurisdiction where:

(i) only trade between the EFTA States is affected; or

(ii) trade between one or more EFTA States and the EU is affected and the turnover of the undertakings concerned in the EFTA States is one-third or more of the total turnover of those undertakings in the EEA as a whole.[166] Where, however, trade in the EU is affected to an appreciable extent the Commission and not the ESA has jurisdiction.[167] The Commission has jurisdiction in all other cases.

The EEA Agreement also established an EFTA Court. This court has jurisdiction in competition matters to deal with appeals from the ESA, infringement actions brought by the ESA against EFTA States, and the settlement of disputes between two or more EFTA States.[168]

7. MODERNISATION

As already explained, on 1 May 2004 Council Regulation 1/2003[169] brought in a new era in EU competition law. Regulation 1/2003 is a decentralising measure whereby a greater role than previously is given to the NCAs and national courts of the Member States to share with the Commission the enforcement and application of the competition rules.

---

[164] See Petit and Rato, 'From Hard to Soft Enforcement of EC Competition Law' (cited in n. 159).

[165] Switzerland did not join the EEA after membership was rejected in a referendum. As Austria, Finland, and Sweden joined the EU on 1 January 1995, the only States which are in the EEA and not also in the EU are Liechtenstein, Iceland, and Norway. Switzerland has special arrangements with the EU.

[166] EEA Agreement, Art. 56(1)(a) and (b).

[167] EEA Agreement, Art. 56(1)(c) and (3).

[168] EEA Agreement, Art. 108(2).

[169] [2003] OJ L1/1.

Regulation 1/2003 did not, in itself, change the substantive law but, as will be seen throughout this book, the mechanisms for enforcement and application have impacted on the development of the substantive law and an appreciation of how the law is, and has been, enforced is necessary to a proper understanding of it. Many of the cases discussed in this book were decided under the previous enforcement system. The previous enforcement system, along with the reasons for its reform, is described, where the context requires, when the present system is examined. In Chapter 4 we look at the linchpin of the reforms, the rendering of Article 101(3) directly applicable.

The 'modernisation' contained in Regulation 1/2003 was a matter of great controversy. One striking feature, however, should be noted initially: Regulation 1/2003 contains the voluntary surrender by the European Commission of some of its monopoly powers. It is rare for a body to initiate and orchestrate the divestment of its own monopoly. One has to admire the boldness of the Commission in conceiving the reforms and carrying them through. Nevertheless, it must be stressed that despite the changes brought into effect by Regulation 1/2003 the Commission remains at the heart of the system, at the centre of the development and application of EU competition law and policy, as it has been since 1962.[170]

8. CONCLUSIONS

1. The EU competition rules are primarily contained in Title VII, Chapter 1 of the TFEU.

2. The two main competition articles are Article 101 TFEU which applies to agreements between undertakings and Article 102 which applies to the conduct of undertakings in a 'dominant position'.

3. Articles 101 and 102 are supplemented by Article 106 (public undertakings and undertakings with special or exclusive rights) and by articles concerned with powers and procedures (Articles 103, 104 and 105).

4. The competition articles were held by the CJ to be a specific working out of Article 3(1)(g) EC which in effect now appears in Protocol 27 to the TEU and TFEU.

5. The control of mergers is governed by Council Regulation 139/2004 (the EUMR) made under what are now Articles 103 and 352 TFEU.

6. The EU competition rules are primarily enforced by administrative bodies by way of 'public' enforcement.

7. The European Commission enforces the EU competition rules through DG Comp, the Competition Directorate-General. However, the modernisation embodied in Regulation 1/2003 decentralised enforcement to the NCAs of the Member States which form, together with the Commission, the European Competition Network (ECN).

8. The competition rules are directly applicable and can be enforced in national courts.

9. The enforcement and application of the competition rules must be seen in the context of the EU legal order as whole.

---

[170] Indeed, it has been argued that the Commission in fact executed a 'strategic coup', by marginalising national laws and in effect centralising rather than decentralising control of the application of the competition rules: see S. Wilkes, 'Agency Escape: Decentralization or Dominance of the European Commission in the Modernisation of Competition Policy' (2005) 18(3) *Governance* 431.

9. FURTHER READING

A. BOOKS

ARNULL, A., *The European Union and its Court of Justice* (2nd edn, Oxford University Press, 2006)

BELLAMY and CHILD (V. Rose and D. Bailey, eds.), *European Law of Competition* (7th edn, Oxford University Press, 2013), 1.001–1.081

CHALMERS, D., DAVIES, G., and MONTI, G., *European Union Law* (2nd edn, Cambridge University Press, 2010)

CRAIG, P., and DE BÚRCA, G., *EU Law: Text, Cases and Materials* (5th edn, Oxford University Press, 2011)

DASHWOOD, A., DOUGAN, M., RODGER, B., SPAVENTA, E., and WYATT, D., *Wyatt and Dashwood's European Union Law* (6th edn, Sweet & Maxwell, 2011)

GOYDER, J., and ALBORS-LLORENS, A., *Goyder's EC Competition Law* (5th edn, Oxford University Press, 2009), Chaps. 2–5.

HARTLEY, T. C., *The Foundations of European Community Law* (7th edn, Oxford University Press, 2010)

SENDEN, L., *Soft Law in European Community Law* (Hart Publishing, 2004)

WARD, I., *A Critical Introduction to European Law* (3rd edn, Cambridge University Press, 2009)

B. ARTICLES

COSMA, H. A., and WHISH, R., 'Soft Law in the Field of EU Competition Policy' (2003) *European Business Law Review*, 25

LEFEVRE, S., 'Interpretative Communications and the Implementation of Community Law at National Level' (2004) 29 *ELRev* 808

SYRPIS, P., 'The Treaty of Lisbon: Much Ado…But About What?' (2008) 37 *Industrial Law Journal* 219

3

ARTICLE 101 TFEU: THE ELEMENTS

1. CENTRAL ISSUES

1. Chapters 3 and 4 set out and introduce the core elements of Article 101. The way in which this provision applies to specific types of business agreements (e.g. cartels, horizontal cooperation agreements, distribution agreements, and intellectual property licensing agreements) is discussed in greater detail in later chapters.

2. Article 101(1) prohibits agreements or other collusion between two or more independent undertakings which has as its object or effect the prevention, restriction, or distortion of competition and which affects trade between Member States.

3. Article 101(1) applies only to agreements which appreciably affect competition and trade.

4. Article 101(3) provides that the Article 101(1) prohibition may be declared inapplicable to agreements which fulfil its four criteria (two positive and two negative), broadly where beneficial aspects of the agreement outweigh its restrictive effect.

5. Chapter 3 focuses on the following issues:

(a) *Who* Article 101 applies to, i.e. which entities constitute an 'undertaking' and are consequently bound to comply with the competition rules;

(b) What constitutes *joint* conduct caught by Article 101(1) and how this is distinguished from unilateral conduct falling outside of its scope; and

(c) When an agreement appreciably *affects trade* between Member States and so falls within the jurisdictional scope of Article 101(1).

6. Chapter 4 focuses on the question of *which* agreements are prohibited by Article 101. In particular:

(a) When an agreement appreciably 'restricts' competition for the purposes of Article 101(1); and

(b) When the beneficial aspects of the agreement enable it to satisfy the conditions of Article 101(3) and 'trump' the restrictive effects identified under Article 101(1).

2. INTRODUCTION

Article 101 precludes certain restrictive agreements between independent market operators, whether 'horizontal' (between parties operating at the same level of the economy, often actual or potential competitors) or 'vertical' (between parties operating at different levels, for example, an agreement between a manufacturer and its distributor). In this chapter the scheme of Article 101, the consequences of infringing it, and some of the key elements of Article 101(1) are considered. Chapter 4 focuses on the relationship between Article 101(1) and Article 101(3) and the substantive question of which agreements restrict competition and/or meet the Article 101(3) criteria.

How the provisions of Article 101 are interpreted depends, of course, upon the policy objectives being pursued in its enforcement. It has been seen in Chapter 1 that the answer to the question of 'what are the goals of Article 101?' is not entirely straightforward. The view reiterated by the Commission in recent years, and set out in its guidelines on the application of Article 101(3) (the 'Article 101(3) Guidelines'), is that the goal of Article 101 should be consumer welfare:[1]

> The objective of Article [101] is to protect competition on the market as a means of enhancing consumer welfare and of ensuring an efficient allocation of resources. Competition and market integration serve these ends since the creation and preservation of an open single market promotes an efficient allocation of resources throughout the Community for the benefit of consumers.[2]

It is not clear, however, whether it is possible to isolate EU competition law and policy in this way from other EU goals and objectives. Indeed, in *GlaxoSmithKline*, an important case dealing with the application of Article 101 to distribution arrangements, the CJ held that not only are the competition rules designed to achieve 'the Treaty's objective of achieving the integration of national markets through the establishment of a single market'[3] but that:

> like other competition rules laid down in the Treaty, Article [101] aims to protect not only the interests of competitors or of consumers, but also the structure of the market and, in so doing, competition as such. Consequently, for a finding that an agreement has an anti-competitive object, it is not necessary that final consumers be deprived of the advantages of effective competition in terms of supply or price.[4]

Further, it will be seen that some judgments of the EU Courts support the view that, in certain circumstances, public policy considerations should form part of the substantive appraisal under Article 101.

3. THE TEXT OF ARTICLE 101

Article 101 provides:

(1) The following shall be prohibited as incompatible with the common market: all agreements between undertakings, decisions by associations of undertakings and concerted practices which may affect trade between Member States and which have as their object or effect the prevention, restriction or distortion of competition within the common market, and in particular those which:

    (a) directly or indirectly fix purchase or selling prices or any other trading conditions;

    (b) limit or control production, markets, technical development, or investment;

    (c) share markets or sources of supply;

    (d) apply dissimilar conditions to equivalent transactions with other trading parties, thereby placing them at a competitive disadvantage;

    (e) make the conclusion of contracts subject to acceptance by the other parties of supplementary obligations which, by their nature or according to commercial usage, have no connection with the subject of such contracts.

(2) Any agreements or decisions prohibited pursuant to this Article shall be automatically void.

(3) The provisions of paragraph 1 may, however, be declared inapplicable in the cases of:

    — any agreement or category of agreements between undertakings;

    — any decision or category of decisions by associations of undertakings;

---

[1] [2004] OJ C101/97, para. 13.

[2] See Guidelines on the application of Article 81(3) [now Article 101(3)] of the Treaty (the Article 101(3) Guidelines) [2004] OJ C101/97, para. 13.

[3] Cases C-501, 513, 515, and 519/06 P, [2009] ECR I-9291, para. 61. See also, e.g., Cases 56 and 58/64, *Établissements Consten SA & Grundig-Verkaufs-GmbH* v. *Commission (Consten and Grundig)* [1966] ECR 299.

[4] Cases C-501, 513, 515, and 519/06 P, [2009] ECR I-9291, para. 63. See also e.g., Case C-68/12, *Protimonopolný úrad Slovenskej republiky* v. *Slovenská sporiteľňa as*, 7 February 2013, para. 18.

— any concerted practice or category of concerted practices,

which contributes to improving the production or distribution of goods or to promoting technical or economic progress, while allowing consumers a fair share of the resulting benefit, and which does not:

(a) impose on the undertakings concerned restrictions which are not indispensable to the attainment of these objectives;

(b) afford such undertakings the possibility of eliminating competition in respect of a substantial part of the products in question.

4. THE SCHEME OF ARTICLE 101

A. THE THREE PARAGRAPHS

It can be seen from the text that Article 101 is in three parts.

(i) The Prohibition

For the prohibition in Article 101(1) to apply the following must be established:

(a) collusion or joint conduct—an agreement or concerted practice between two or more under-takings or a decision by an association of undertakings;

(b) collusion which appreciably[5] restricts competition—that is which has as its object or effect the prevention, restriction, or distortion of competition. An illustrative, but not exhaustive list of examples of such preventions, restrictions, or distortions is set out; and

(c) an appreciable effect on trade between Member States.[6]

(ii) Nullity

Although Article 101(2) specifically states that an agreement, decision, or concerted practice prohibited by Article 101(1) is automatically void, the CJ has held that the nullity affects *only* the clauses in the agreement prohibited by the provision.[7] The agreement as a whole is void only if the prohibited clauses cannot be severed from the remaining terms of the agreement. The nullity is automatic and is not dependent upon any prior decision to that effect.[8]

(iii) Legal Exception—Declaration of Inapplicability

The Article 101(1) prohibition may be declared inapplicable to an agreement, etc.,[9] which fulfils the four criteria (two positive and two negative) set out in Article 101(3). Between 1962 and 2004, agreements could benefit from Article 101(3) only if they were specifically 'exempted' from the Article 101(1) prohibition by virtue of either an *individual exemption*, granted by the Commission following notification of the agreement to it, or a *block exemption*, granted by EU regulation to certain categories

---

[5] Art. 101 itself does not provide that the effect on competition and trade must be an appreciable one. The CJ has, however, held that an agreement falls outside the prohibition if its effect on competition and trade is insignificant, see Section 5.D and E., pp. 180–186.

[6] See Section 5.E.

[7] Case 56/65, *Société Technique Minière* v. *Maschinenbau Ulm GmbH* [1966] ECR 235. See Section 6 and Chap. 14.

[8] See Reg. 1/2003, Art. 1.

[9] In this chapter unless the context otherwise requires or the discussion is specifically about one or other category of collusion the word 'agreement' is used as shorthand to cover agreements, decisions, and concerted practices.

of agreement. The Commission had *sole* power to declare Article 101(1) inapplicable to individual agreements pursuant to Article 101(3).[10] From 1 May 2004, however, it has not been possible to gain an individual exemption for an agreement from the Commission (although block exemptions remain) and the Commission's exclusive competence to apply Article 101(3) has been removed.[11] The Commission, the national competition authorities (NCAs), or national courts may now apply Article 101(3) individually to agreements whenever an agreement's compatibility with the provision is questioned.

B. THE CONSEQUENCES OF INFRINGEMENT

Severe consequences may result for parties to an agreement which contravenes Article 101(1) but which does not meet the four criteria set out in Article 101(3).

It has already been seen that provisions in an agreement that violate Article 101(1) are automatically void where the agreement does not meet the conditions of Article 101(3). Article 101(2) may, therefore, render carefully negotiated clauses in an agreement void and unenforceable. The sanction of nullity will not be much of a threat to some parties to a prohibited agreement, however. Members of a cartel, for example, are unlikely to be concerned about their inability to enforce the agreement in court.[12] Cartels and other serious infringements are, in contrast, more likely to be deterred by the risk of a fine being imposed following an investigation by a public authority or by an order to pay damages following private litigation.

The Commission takes the central role in enforcing the EU competition law rules. It has broad powers to investigate suspected infringements of Article 101, to order those found to have violated the provision to put an end to the breach, and to impose fines (often huge fines) on undertakings that have committed a breach of the rules.[13] Until 2004, the NCAs and national courts played a relatively minor role in the enforcement process, partly at least, in consequence of their inability to apply Article 101(3).[14] Since 2004, however, Regulation 1/2003 has enabled, and in some circumstances required, the NCAs, and the national courts, to share in the enforcement of Article 101 and to apply it in its entirety.[15] Compliance with Article 101 is thus policed not only by the Commission, but by NCAs[16] and private litigants bringing tortious or other proceedings before a national court. NCAs may be able to impose fines, and/or other more severe sanctions, on undertakings or individuals found to have been involved in a breach of the rules.[17] In addition, although there has, until recently, been relatively little antitrust litigation in Europe, in *Courage Ltd v. Crehan*[18] the CJ made it clear that an

[10] This monopoly was conferred on the Commission by the Council in Reg. 17 [1959–62] OJ Spec. Ed. 87, Art. 9(1), see Chaps. 2, 4, and 13.

[11] See Reg. 1/2003 and Chap. 13.

[12] They are likely to have their own mechanisms in place for the enforcement of the cartel, see Chap. 9.

[13] Fines may be imposed of up to 10% of an undertaking's turnover in the preceding year of business, and in cases of serious violations of the rules have tended to be large, Reg. 1/2003, Art. 23, see Chaps. 9 and 13.

[14] The exclusive right to apply Art. 101(3) was reserved to the Commission, see Reg. 17, cited in n. 10.

[15] Reg. 1/2003 provides that NCAs applying Arts 101 and 102 may adopt decisions ordering an infringement to be brought to an end, ordering interim measures, accepting commitments and imposing fines, periodic penalty payments, or imposing any other penalty provided for in their national law.

[16] In some Member States national regulatory authorities may also be able to enforce the competition rules in the sectors for which they are responsible.

[17] In the UK, for example, in addition to corporate fines, sanctions against *individuals* are available (imprisonment, fines, and/or disqualification from acting as a director) in certain circumstances, see Enterprise Act 2002, Part 6, s. 204 and Chap. 9.

[18] Case C-453/99, *Courage Ltd v. Crehan* [2001] ECR I-6297. See also Cases 295–298/04, *Manfredi v. Lloyd Adriatico Assicurazioni SpA* [2006] ECR I-6619 and Chap. 14.

individual who has suffered loss due to another's breach of the competition rules must, in principle, be able to recover damages. A number of steps are being taken to encourage 'private' enforcement of the competition rules and such claims are increasingly becoming a reality. Public and private enforcement are considered in detail in Chapters 13 and 14 respectively.

C. BURDEN AND STANDARD OF PROOF

Although the Commission's antitrust proceedings are administrative, it is clear that, because they may culminate in the imposition of punitive fines, those fines are treated as *de facto* criminal charges for the purposes of Article 6(1) of the ECHR. It is seen in Chapter 13 that this has important consequences for the procedures carried out by the Commission and the standard of review of its decisions that must be conducted by the EU Courts. In addition, the CJ has confirmed that 'the presumption of innocence resulting in particular from Article 6(2) of the ECHR ... applies to the procedures relating to infringements of the competition rules applicable to undertakings that may result in the imposition of fines or periodic penalties payments'.[19] The burden is therefore clearly on the Commission, or other person, alleging an infringement of Article 101(1) to prove the same. Once this is established, the burden shifts on to the undertakings claiming the benefit of Article 101(3) to establish that the agreement meets its criteria.[20]

The CJ has held that, given the significant fines which may accompany an infringement decision and the non-negligible stigma attached to a finding of infringement for the legal or natural person involved, the Commission must establish 'sufficiently precise and coherent proof'[21] of an infringement—the Commission must provide 'a firm, precise and consistent body of evidence' to justify its view.[22] A breach of the competition rules appears, therefore, to have to be established only on the balance of probabilities and the Commission does not have 'to adduce proof beyond reasonable doubt of the existence of the infringement'.[23] However, 'any doubt of the Court must benefit the undertaking' to which an infringement decision is addressed.[24] 'The Court cannot therefore conclude that the Commission has established the existence of the infringement at issue to the requisite legal standard if it still entertains doubts on that point, in particular in proceedings for the annulment of a decision imposing a fine'.[25]

---

[19]   Case C-199/92 P, *Hüls AG* v. *Commission* [1999] ECR I-4287, paras. 149–150.

[20]   See Reg. 1/2003, Art. 2. In Cases C-204, 205, 211, 213, 217, and 219/00 P, *Aalborg Portland A/S* v. *Commission (Cement)* [2004] ECR I-123, para. 78 and Chap. 13.

[21]   Cases 29 and 30/83, *Compagnie Royale Asturienne des Mines SA and Rheinzink GmbH* v. *Commission* [1984] ECR 1679. The standard of proof in civil litigation will be a matter for the national courts of the relevant Member State, see Chap. 14.

[22]   Cases C-89/85, C-104/85, C-114/85, C-116/85, C-117/85, and C-125/85 to C-129/85, *Ahlström Osakeyhtiö and Others* v. *Commission* [1993] ECR I-1307, para. 127.

[23]   Case T-53/03, *British Plasterboard* v. *Commission* [2008] ECR II-1333. In the UK, the Competition Appeal Tribunal (CAT) has held that although Office of Fair Trading (OFT) proceedings (under EU antitrust law or its UK equivalent) may lead to the imposition of a penalty (involving a 'criminal charge' for the purposes of Article 6 of the ECHR) this does not mean that the standard of proof is proof beyond reasonable doubt (the criminal standard established in domestic cases). Rather, it has held that the standard of proof to be applied is the civil standard—the preponderance or balance of probabilities applied taking account of the gravity of the offence, see, e.g. Case 1022/1/1/03, *JJB Sports plc* v. *Office of Fair Trading* [2004] CAT 17, aff'd [2006] EWCA Civ 1318 and further Chap. 13.

[24]   Case T-442/08, *International Confederation of Societies of Authors and Composers (CISAC)* v. *Commission*, 12 April 2013, para. 91.

[25]   Case T-348/08, *Aragonesas Industrias y Energía, SAU* v. *Commission*, 25 October 2011, paras. 92–93.

5. THE INTERPRETATION AND APPLICATION OF ARTICLE 101(1)

A. 'UNDERTAKING' AND 'ASSOCIATIONS OF UNDERTAKINGS'

(i) Every Entity Engaged in an Economic Activity: the Constituent Elements of an Undertaking

Article 101 applies to agreements and concerted practices between *undertakings* and decisions by *associations of undertakings*. Undertaking has the same meaning for the purposes of both Article 101 and Article 102[26] so the concept determines 'the categories of actors to which the competition rules apply'.[27] The term 'undertaking' is not defined in the Treaty but it is settled in the case law that it 'encompasses every entity engaged in an economic activity, regardless of the legal status of the entity and the way in which it is financed'.[28] Entities engaged in economic activity must respect the principles of competition, whilst entities performing tasks in the public interest fall outside the scope of the rules.[29] The critical question, therefore, which is explored in the series of cases in this section, is what constitutes 'economic activity'. The fine distinctions that have been drawn in the cases have turned on the *functions* performed by the particular bodies involved in the case. The cases seem to establish, however, that the characteristic features of an 'economic activity' is (1) the offering of goods or services on the market,[30] (2) where that activity 'could, at least in principle, be carried on by a private undertaking in order to make profits'.[31] If these requirements are satisfied it is irrelevant that the body is not in fact profit making[32] or that it is not set up for an economic purpose.[33]

---

[26] See Cases T-68, 77 and 78/89, *Società Italiana Vetro SpA v. Commission* [1992] ECR II-1403, para. 358. Many of the cases discussed in this chapter concerned Art. 102, not Art. 101.

[27] Case C-67/96, *Albany International BV v. Stichting Bedrijfspensioenfonds Textielindustrie* [1999] ECR I-5751, Jacobs AG, para. 206.

[28] Case C-41/90, *Höfner and Elser v. Macrotron GmbH* [1991] ECR I-1979, para. 21. This definition has been consistently repeated by the Court, see, e.g., Cases C-159 and 160/91, *Poucet and Pistre v. Assurances Générales de France* [1993] ECR I-637, para. 17; Case 364/92, *SAT Fluggesellschaft mbH v. Eurocontrol* [1994] ECR I-43, para. 18, Cases C-180–184/98, *Pavlov v. Stichting Pensioenfonds Medische Specialisten* [2000] ECR I-6451, para. 74, and Case C-138/11, *Compass-Datenbank GmbH v. Republik Österreich*, 12 July 2012, para. 35.

[29] For the view that the Treaty contains a public/ private divide and that the different treatment of these entities is 'justified by a presumption underlying the rules of the private sphere that its occupants are self-interested and the presumption underlying rules of the public sphere that its occupants operate in pursuit of the public interest', see O. Odudu, *The Boundaries of EC Competition Law: The Scope of Article 81* (Oxford University Press, 2006), 45–56.

[30] See, e.g., Case C-475/99, *Firma Ambulanz Glöckner v. Landkreis Südwestpfalz* [2001] ECR I-8089, para. 19, Case C-35/96 *Commission v. Italy* [1998] ECR I-3851, para. 36 and Case C-205/03 P, *FENIN v. Commission*, [2006] ECR I-6295, para. 25.

[31] Case C-67/96, *Albany International BV v. Stichting Bedrijfspensioenfonds Textielindustrie* [1999] ECR I-5751, Jacobs AG, para. 311. Cases C-180–184/98, *Pavlov v. Stichting Pensioenfonds Medische Specialisten* [2000] ECR I-6451, para. 201. See Odudu, *The Boundaries of EC Competition Law: The Scope of Article 81* (cited in n. 29), 26–45 (the three positive requirements of economic activity are that the entity must: 'offer goods or services to the market; bear the economic or financial risk of the enterprise; and have the potential to make profit from the activity').

[32] Cases 96-102, 104, 105, 108, and 110/82, *NV IAZ International Belgium SA v. Commission* [1983] ECR 3369; Case C-67/96, *Albany International BV v. Stichting Bedrijfspensioenfonds Textielindustrie* [1999] ECR I-5751. In the UK the OFT investigated price fixing by private schools, many of which are non-profit-making charitable organisations, see *Independent Schools*, 20 November 2006.

[33] Case 155/73, *Italy v. Sacchi* [1974] ECR 409. See also *The Distribution of Package Tours During the 1990 World Cup* [1992] OJ L326/31 discussed in n. 36 and accompanying text.

(ii) The Legal Status or Form or the Entity is Immaterial

Because the notion of an undertaking focuses on the nature of the activity carried out by the entity concerned (a functional approach is adopted),[34] the legal personality of the entity is not decisive. The notion may encompass natural persons, legal persons, and/or State and public bodies (even if they supply public services or if the entity is subject to a public service obligation). As well as companies and partnerships, therefore, individuals,[35] sporting bodies or bodies carrying out activities having a connection with sport,[36] trade associations,[37] agricultural cooperatives,[38] P & I clubs,[39] collecting societies,[40] and professional bodies[41] have been held to be undertakings for the purposes of the rules. The fact that the business occupation of a body is viewed as a liberal profession is not inconsistent with the fact that it may be an undertaking or an association of undertakings engaged in an economic activity.[42] In *Wouters v. Algemene Raad van de Nederlandse Orde van Advocaten*,[43] for example, the CJ made it clear that members of the Bar which offered, for a fee, services in the form of legal assistance carried out an economic activity and so were undertakings for the purposes of the rules. Neither the complex and technical nature of the services provided nor the fact that the profession was regulated altered this conclusion.[44] Similarly, in *Ordem dos Técnicos Oficiais de Contas v. Autoridade da Concorrência*,[45] the CJ confirmed that chartered accountants, who offer accounting services for remuneration and assume the financial risks related to the exercise of those activities, carry on economic activity and are therefore undertakings.

The importance of the function, and not the nature, of the entity is illustrated by a case concerning the 1990 World Cup. In this case the Commission held that sporting and other associations, the international football federation (FIFA), the Italian FA (FIGC), and the local organising committee, which carried out economic activities, were all undertakings within the meaning of Article 101(1).[46] Although in some circumstances it may be inappropriate to apply the competition rules to functions carried out by sporting bodies,[47] they may apply where the body is carrying out economic activities.[48]

[34] Focusing on the activity carried out rather than the nature of the actor that performed it, see O. Odudu, 'The Meaning of Undertaking within Article 101' (2005) 7 *Cambridge Yearbook of European Legal Studies* 209 citing A. Deringer, *The Competition Law of the European Economic Community: A Commentary on the EEC Rules of Competition (Articles 85 to 90) Including the Implementing Regulations and Directives* (New York: Commerce Clearing House, 1968), 5.

[35] E.g., *RAI/UNITEL* [1978] OJ L157/39, *Reuter/BASF* [1976] OJ L254/40, *French Beef* [2003] OJ L209/12, *aff'd* (but fines reduced) in Cases T-217 and 245/03, *FNSEA v. Commission* [2004] ECR II-271, Cases C-101 and 110/07, *Coop de France bétail et viande v. Commission*, *FNSEA v. Commission* [2008] ECR I-10193, but not, it seems, employees, see Section 5.A.v. See also Case 42/84, *Remia BV and others v. Commission* [1985] ECR 2545; *Vaessen BV/Moris* [1979] OJ L19/32.

[36] *Distribution of Package Tours During the 1990 World Cup* [1992] OJ L326/31, paras. 43–58.

[37] Case 96/82, *NV IAZ International Belgium v. Commission* [1983] ECR 3369.

[38] See Case C-250/92, *Gøttrup-Klim e.a. Grovvareforeninger and Others v. Dansk Landbrugs Grovvareselskab AmbA* [1994] ECR I-5641.

[39] Protection and Indemnity clubs, *P & I Clubs* [1985] OJ L376/2.

[40] Which engage in the commercial provision of services, see e.g. Case 127/73, *Belgische Radio en Televisie v. SV SABAM* [1974] ECR 313.

[41] See generally M. Monti, 'Competition in Professional Services: New Light and New Challenges', 21 March 2003, available at <http://ec.europa.eu/competition/speeches/text/sp2003_070_en.pdf>.

[42] *AICIA v. CNSD* [1993] OJ L203/27, para. 40.

[43] Case C-309/99, [2002] ECR I-1577.

[44] Case C-309/99, [2002] ECR I-1577, paras. 46–49, 64.

[45] Case C-1/12, 28 February 2013.

[46] *The Distribution of Package Tours During the 1990 World Cup* [1992] OJ L326/31. French organisers of the 1998 World Cup were also found to have infringed Art. 102 by discriminating on grounds of nationality: *1998 World Cup Finals* [2000] OJ L5/55.

[47] For the discussion of when rules inherent in sport are subject to Art. 101, see Chap. 2.

[48] *The Distribution of Package Tours During the 1990 World Cup* [1992] OJ L326/31, especially paras. 44–60. See also Case C-519/04 P, *Meca-Medina v. Commission* [2006] ECR I-6991, and Case C-49/07, *Motosykletistiki Omospondia Ellados NPID (MOTOE) v. Elliniko Dimosio* [2008] ECR I-4863.

(iii) Public Bodies and Bodies Performing Public Functions which are not Economic

a. Distinction between Economic Activities and Activities which must Necessarily be Carried out by the State or which fulfil a Social Function[49]

It is seen in Section 5.A.ii that the conclusion that any entity engaged in economic activity constitutes an undertaking raises the possibility that the agreements and conduct of public bodies or corporations can be scrutinised for compatibility with the rules. Indeed, an entity may be an undertaking even where it does not have an independent legal personality but forms part of a State's general administration.[50] In determining which entities constitute 'undertakings', the case law draws a distinction between activities classified as 'economic' in character, and those which are not economic—where the entity 'acts in the exercise of official authority'—or those connected with the exercise of 'public powers'. An entity, public or private, which performs non-economic tasks will not be an undertaking and will be immune from the application of the rules. Entities, public or private, engaged in economic activity, which can be separated from the exercise of public powers,[51] will act as an undertaking and will need to consider the application of the competition rules.[52]

It has been seen that the core issue in determining of whether an entity is engaged in economic activities or tasks of a public nature appears to depend upon whether the offering of goods or services on the market could be carried out by a private firm to make a profit. 'If there were no possibility of a private undertaking carrying on a given activity, there would be no purpose in applying the competition rules to it.'[53] The tendency of States to contract out what were considered to be public tasks to private entities has made this distinction a difficult one to draw in practice. In determining what constitutes an undertaking the CJ in *Höfner and Elser* v. *Macrotron*, focused on the responsibilities of the relevant entity, holding that employment procurement activities were economic in nature since they had not always been, and are not necessarily, carried out by public entities.

Case C-41/90, *Höfner and Elser* v. *Macrotron* [1991] ECR I-1979

Under German law on the promotion of employment (the AFG) the Bundesanstalt für Arbeit (Federal Office for Employment, the Bundesanstalt), a public agency, had a monopoly in employment recruitment. Nevertheless the Bundesanstalt tolerated private agencies dealing with the recruitment of business executives. This case concerned a dispute which arose in the German courts between a private recruitment agency and a company for which it had provided recruitment services in breach of the Bundesanstalt's exclusive right. The private agency sought to recover fees payable under the terms of the recruitment contract. The German courts took the view that the claim should fail on the grounds that the contract had

---

[49] See also Chap. 8.

[50] *Spanish Courier Services* [1990] OJ L233/19; *Aluminium Products* [1985] OJ L92/1. See also Case 42/83, *Commission v. Italy* [1985] ECR 873, paras. 16–20 and Case C-138/11, *Compass-Datenbank GmbH v. Republik Österreich*, 12 July 2012, para. 35.

[51] See Section 5.A.iv, pp. 136–137.

[52] But see e.g. Case C-67/96, *Albany International BV* v. *Stichting Bedrijfspensioenfonds Textielindustrie* [1999] ECR I-5751, Case C-309/99, *Wouters v. Algemene Raad van de Nederlandse Orde van Advocaten* [2002] ECR I-577, and Art. 106(2) (which provides that undertakings entrusted with the operation of services of general economic interest or having the character of a revenue-producing monopoly are subject to the competition rules only insofar as the application of the rules does not obstruct the performance of the tasks assigned to them). Article 106(2), like all derogations from the main Treaty objectives, is construed narrowly, see Chap. 8. A finding that an entity is not an undertaking obviates the need for reliance on Art. 106(2).

[53] Cases C-264, 306, 354, and 355/01, *AOK Bundesverband v. Ichthyol-Gesellschaft Cordes, Hermani & Co* [2004] ECR I-2493, Jacobs AG, para. 27.

been concluded in breach of German law and was void. The German Civil Code provides that any legal act which infringes a statutory prohibition is void (the prohibition applies to employment procurement activities carried out in breach of the AFG). The Oberlandesgericht München nevertheless considered that the outcome of the dispute might be dependent on EU law and referred a number of questions to the CJ under Article 267 TFEU. In particular, it asked whether the Bundesanstalt had committed an abuse of a dominant position.[54] This necessitated consideration of whether the Bundesanstalt was an undertaking for the purposes of the competition rules.

Court of Justice

21. It must be observed, in the context of competition law, first that the concept of an undertaking encompasses every entity engaged in an economic activity, regardless of the legal status of the entity and the way in which it is financed and, secondly, that employment procurement is an economic activity.

22. The fact that employment procurement activities are normally entrusted to public agencies cannot affect the economic nature of such activities. Employment procurement has not always been, and is not necessarily, carried out by public entities. That finding applies in particular to executive recruitment.

23. It follows that an entity such as a public employment agency engaged in the business of employment procurement may be classified as an undertaking for the purpose of applying the Community competition rules.

24. It must be pointed out that a public employment agency which is entrusted, under the legislation of a Member State, with the operation of services of general economic interest, such as those envisaged in Article 3 of the AFG, remains subject to the competition rules pursuant to Article [106(2)] unless and to the extent to which it is shown that their application is incompatible with the discharge of its duties: see Case 155/73, *Sacchi*…

The EU Courts have, however, sought to balance the need to protect competition against the need to respect the powers of the individual Member States. The rules do not apply, therefore, to the exercise of sovereign powers of the state, tasks performed in the public interest or administrative functions. In *Bodson*,[55] the competition rules were not applicable because the local authority was carrying out an administrative duty, granting concessions for funeral services. The CJ stressed that Article 101 would not apply to communes acting in their capacity as public authorities and entrusted with the 'operation of a public service'.[56] Similarly, in *SAT Fluggesellschaft mbH* v. *Eurocontrol*,[57] the CJ indicated that Eurocontrol (European Organisation for the Safety of Air Navigation), which performed tasks which were in the public interest (maintaining and improving air navigation safety), was not an undertaking even though it collected route charges (which were set not by it but by the Contracting States). The supervision of airspace was a duty typically reserved to public authorities. In the later case of *SELEX Sistemi Integrati SpA* v. *Commission*,[58] the CJ confirmed that Eurocontrol would not act as an undertaking even when conducting economic activities if those activities were connected with, and inseparable from, the exercise of its public powers.[59]

In *Diego Calì*,[60] the CJ referred to *Eurocontrol* when dealing with a case concerning anti-pollution surveillance and intervention entrusted by the national port authority at Genoa to a *private* limited

---

[54] This aspect of the case is discussed in Chaps. 7 and 8.

[55] Case 30/87, *Corinne Bodson* v. *SA Pompes funèbres des régions libérées* [1988] ECR 2479.

[56] Case 30/87, *Corinne Bodson* v. *SA Pompes funèbres des régions libérées* [1988] ECR 2479, para. 18.

[57] Case C-364/92, [1994] ECR I-43.

[58] Case C-113/07, *SELEX Sistemi Integrati SpA* v. *Commission* [2009] ECR I-2207.

[59] See also discussion of Case C-113/07, *SELEX Sistemi Integrati SpA* v. *Commission* [2009] ECR I-2207 in Section 5.A.iv, pp. 136–137.

[60] Case C-343/95, *Diego Calì e Figli Srl* v. *SEPG* [1997] ECR I-1547.

company, SEPG. A port user, Diego Calì, challenged charges levied on it by SEPG in respect of services provided, on the grounds that SEPG had abused its dominant position contrary to Article 102. The CJ found that SEPG was not an undertaking since it carried out services relating to the protection of the environment which were not of an economic nature but which were essential functions of the State. The purpose of the activity was to guarantee safety and to protect the port environment and to ensure public assets were properly protected in the interest of the State and citizens.[61]

22. The anti-pollution surveillance for which SEPG was responsible in the oil port of Genoa is a task in the public interest which forms part of the essential functions of the State as regards protection of the environment in maritime areas.

23. Such surveillance is connected by its nature, its aim and the rules to which it is subject with the exercise of powers relating to the protection of the environment which are typically those of a public authority. It is not of an economic nature justifying the application of the Treaty rules on competition…

24. The levying of a charge by SEPG for preventive anti-pollution surveillance is an integral part of its surveillance activity in the maritime area of the port and cannot affect the legal status of that activity (Case C-364/92 *SAT Fluggesellschaft* v. *Eurocontrol*…paragraph 28). Moreover, as stated in paragraph 8 of this judgment, the tariffs applied by SEPG have been approved by the public authorities.

The outcome of *Eurocontrol*, and *Diego Calì* thus turned upon the CJ's assessment that these tasks, in contrast to those carried out in *Höfner and Elser*, could only be performed by or on behalf of a public body.[62] The cases clarify that the fact that a product or a service supplied by a public entity is provided in return for remuneration is not sufficient for the activity to be classified as an economic one, especially if it is not independently set by the entity. Similarly, in *Compass-Datenbank GmbH* v. *Republik Österreich*,[63] the CJ held that a 'data collection activity in relation to undertakings, on the basis of a statutory obligation on those undertakings to disclose the data and power of enforcement related thereto, falls within the exercise of public powers'.[64] Consequently, a public authority which stored such data did not constitute an undertaking even though it allowed persons to search for that data and/or provided print-outs for it and charged for the service:[65]

42. With regard to the fact that the making available to interested persons of the data in such a database is remunerated, it should be noted that…to the extent that the fees or payments due for the making available to the public of such information are not laid down directly or indirectly by the entity concerned but are provided for by law, the charging of such remuneration can be regarded as inseparable from that making available of data. Thus, the charging by the Republik Österreich of fees or payments due for the making available to the public of that information cannot change the legal classification of that activity, meaning that it does not constitute an economic activity.

In a line of cases concerning pension funds and social security schemes (for example, relating to healthcare or accident insurance), the CJ has drawn a distinction between entities which operate in the same way as, or in competition with, ordinary commercial enterprises in the same sector (which are undertakings even if the scheme has a social objective) and entities which, fulfilling an exclusively social function, carry out an activity which is based on the principle of solidarity and is subject to

---

[61] Case C-343/95, *Diego Calì e Figli Srl* v. *SEPG* [1997] ECR I-1547, Cosmas AG, paras. 44–46.

[62] Odudu states that it is not feasible to profit from the provision of public goods and services and that '[b]oth *Eurocontrol* and *Diego Calì* show recognition that effective provision of a public good is impossible absent the coercive power of the state'. He identifies the two characteristics of public goods that make profit impossible: such goods are non-rivalrous in consumption (once produced, an infinite number of consumers can enjoy them without increased production cost or diminished enjoyment by others); and the benefits are non-excludable (it is not possible to prevent people from enjoying the benefits once the good is produced)', Odudu, *The Boundaries of EC Competition Law: The Scope of Article 81* (cited in n. 29), 42–45.

[63] Case C-138/11, 12 July 2012.

[64] Case C-138/11, 12 July 2012, para. 40.

[65] The fact that the public entity relied on intellectual property rights to protect the data also did not mean that it necessarily acted as an undertaking, Case C-138/11, 12 July 2012, paras. 47–50.

State supervision.[66] The principle of solidarity has been described as: 'the redistribution of income between those who are better off and those who, in view of their resources...would be deprived'[67] or 'the inherently uncommercial act of involuntary subsidization of one social group by another'.[68]

In a number of cases, it has been found that an entity is not an undertaking because: (i) the scheme it operates applies the principle of solidarity or involves an element of cross-subsidy, for example, because benefits paid or the scope of coverage are not proportionate to contributions, contributions are not proportionate to risk, benefits may be payable even though contributions due have not been paid; and (ii) the scheme is subject to State supervision and the State exercises control over how the scheme functions. Thus in *Poucet et Pistre*,[69] it was held that a French body running a compulsory social security scheme was not an undertaking. In this case, benefits received under the scheme administered were not proportionate to contributions and contributions made were proportionate to income (there was an element of cross-subsidy).

18. Sickness funds, and the organizations involved in the management of the public social security system, fulfil an exclusively social function. That activity is based on the principle of national solidarity and is entirely non-profit-making. The benefits paid are statutory benefits bearing no relation to the amount of contributions.

19. Accordingly, that activity is not an economic activity and, therefore, the organizations to which it is entrusted are not undertakings within the meaning of Articles [101] and [102].

Similarly, in:

- *Cisal v. INAIL*,[70] the CJ found that an institution providing compulsory insurance against accidents at work and occupational diseases applied the principle of solidarity and did not carry out an economic activity for the purposes of competition law. (It was financed by contributions which were not systematically set at a rate proportionate to the risk of insurance, the amount of benefits paid were not necessarily proportionate to earnings, there was no direct link between the contributions paid and the benefits granted, and the amount of benefits and contributions were, in the last resort, fixed by the State. The compulsory affiliation of the scheme was essential to its financial balance and for the application of the principle of solidarity[71]);

- In *AOK Bundesverband*,[72] the CJ held that sickness funds fulfilled 'an exclusively social function, which is founded on the principle of national solidarity and is entirely non-profit making'.[73] In particular, the funds were obliged to offer benefits to members which were not dependent upon the amount of contributions, and an equalisation of costs and risks was operated between the funds. This conclusion was not affected by the fact that latitude was available to the funds when

---

[66] See Case C-350/07, *Kattner Stahlbau GmbH v. Maschinenbau -und Metall- Berufsgenossenschaft* [2009] ECR I-1513 (a body to which firms in an industry must be affiliated in respect of insurance against accidents at work and occupational diseases is not an undertaking, but fulfils a social function, where such a body operates within the framework of a scheme which applies the principle of solidarity and is subject to State supervision).

[67] Cases C-159–160/91, *Poucet et Pistre v. Assurances Générales de France* [1993] ECR I-637, para. 10.

[68] Case C-70/95, *Sodemare SA v. Regione Lombardia* [1997] ECR I-3395, Fennelly AG, para. 29. In his book, Odudu considers that a number of elements possessed by redistributive activity can be identified: (a) compulsion; (b) control over cost; (c) control over price; and (d) absence of link between cost and price, see Odudu, *The Boundaries of EC Competition Law: The Scope of Article* 81 (cited in n. 29), 39–42.

[69] Cases C-159–160/91, *Poucet et Pistre v. Assurances Générales de France* [1993] ECR I-637.

[70] C-218/00, *Cisal di Battistello Venanzio & Co v. Istituto nazionale per l'assicurazione contro gli infortuni sul lavoro (INAIL)* [2002] ECR I-691.

[71] C-218/00, *Cisal di Battistello Venanzio & Co v. Istituto nazionale per l'assicurazione contro gli infortuni sul lavoro (INAIL)* [2002] ECR I-691, paras. 31–46, Jacobs AG, paras. 71–82. See also Case C-350/07, *Kattner Stahlbau GmbH v. Maschinenbau- und Metall-Berufsgenossenschaft* [2009] ECR I-1513.

[72] Cases C-264, 306, 354, and 355/01, *AOK Bundesverband v. Ichthyol-Gesellschaft Cordes, Hermani & Co* [2004] ECR I-2493. The CJ rejected the view of its Advocate-General that the funds were undertakings and that their 'purchasing cartel' was subject to the competition rules unless exempt by virtue of Art. 106(2), see Chap. 8.

[73] Cases C-264, 306, 354, and 355/01, *AOK Bundesverband v. Ichthyol-Gesellschaft Cordes, Hermani & Co* [2004] ECR I-2493, para. 51.

setting their contribution rate and that some competition with one another did exist.[74] Further, the Court held that the fund associations' practice of fixing maximum purchasing amounts was linked to their social functions and did not, therefore, constitute an activity of an economic nature.[75]

Although EU law does not detract from the powers of the Member States to organise their social security systems,[76] the fact that such a system has a social aim is not in itself sufficient to preclude the activity in question from being classified as economic activity. It must therefore be examined whether the scheme can be 'regarded as applying the principle of solidarity and to what extent it is subject to supervision by the State' before it can be determined whether the given activity is economic.[77] In *Fédération Française des Sociétés d'Assurance*,[78] a non-profit-making body operating a pension scheme was found to be an undertaking. The entity operated in the same way as other insurance companies, the rules were like those of private schemes, and there was no mutuality or cross-subsidy between the beneficiaries. The CJ further considered these cases in *Albany*.[79] This case concerned a supplementary pension fund. Essentially, affiliation to the fund was compulsory in the textile industry. A dispute broke out between the fund and Albany, a textile business, which wished to be exempted from the affiliation. On a reference to it the CJ stressed the economic functions carried out by the pension fund. It found the fund to be an undertaking even though: affiliation to the scheme was compulsory; the supplementary pension scheme was designed to top up an extremely limited statutory pension; the sectoral pension fund was non-profit-making; and the pension fund was obliged to accept all workers without a medical examination.[80] The CJ accepted that the social objectives which the pension fund was required to pursue might make the service it provided less competitive than those offered by other insurance companies. These factors did not, however, detract from the fact that the activities it engaged in were economic ones. The pension fund determined the amount of contributions made and benefits received (the latter were dependent upon the results of the investments made by it) and it could, in certain circumstances, grant exemption from affiliation to the fund. The social objectives were relevant, however, to the CJ's finding that the public authority could nonetheless confer on a pension fund the exclusive right to manage a supplementary pension scheme in a given sector.[81]

In *AG2R Prévoyance v. Beaudout Père et Fils SARL*,[82] the CJ held that an undertaking operating a scheme based on the principle of solidarity might be an undertaking if it enjoyed a degree of autonomy and was free from State control. It was for the national court, however, to determine whether the entity at issue, although non-profit-making and acting on the basis of the principle of solidarity, was in fact an undertaking chosen on the basis of financial and economic considerations from other undertakings with which it competed on the provident services market.

[74] Contrast the Opinion of Jacobs AG in Cases C-264, 306, 354, and 355/01, *AOK Bundesverband v. Ichthyol-Gesellschaft Cordes, Hermani & Co* [2004] ECR I-2493, para. 42.

[75] See also the discussion of Case C-205/03 P, *FENIN v. Commission* [2006] ECR I-6295 in Section 5.A.iii.b.

[76] C-218/00, *Cisal di Battistello Venanzio & Co v. Istituto nazionale per l'assicurazione contro gli infortuni sul lavoro (INAIL)* [2002] ECR I-691, para. 31 (relying in particular on Case C-158/96, *Kohl* [1998] ECR I-1931, para. 17). See also Case C-350/07, *Kattner Stahlbau GmbH v. Maschinenbau- und Metall-Berufsgenossenschaft* [2009] ECR I-1513, para. 37.

[77] Case C-350/07, *Kattner Stahlbau GmbH v. Maschinenbau- und Metall-Berufsgenossenschaft* [2009] ECR I-1513, paras. 42–43.

[78] Case C-244/94, *Fédération Française des Sociétés d'Assurance and Others v. Ministère de l'Agriculture et de la Pêche* [1995] ECR I-4013.

[79] Case C-67/96, *Albany International BV v. Stichting Bedrijfspensioenfonds Textielindustrie* [1999] ECR I-5751.

[80] Case C-67/96, *Albany International BV v. Stichting Bedrijfspensioenfonds Textielindustrie* [1999] ECR I-5751, paras. 77–87. In Cases C-180–184, *Pavlov v. Stichting Pensioenfonds Medische Specialisten* [2000] ECR I-6451, the CJ also concluded that a pension fund which was compulsory for members of the Dutch medical profession was an undertaking. It was carrying out an economic activity and the facts that the Fund was non-profit-making and that it had solidarity aspects were not sufficient to relieve the Fund of its status as an undertaking.

[81] See discussion of the case in Chap. 8.

[82] Case C-437/09, 31 March 2011, paras. 53–65.

b. Purchasing of Goods and Services by an Entity not Engaged in Economic Activity

In *Federación Nacional de Empresas de Instrumentación Científica, Médica, Técnica y Dental (FENIN)* v. *Commission*,[83] it had to be considered when 'purchasing' of goods and services by a public entity that discharges social functions might constitute economic activity. In this case, an association of the undertakings which marketed medical goods and equipment to bodies forming part of the Spanish Health Service (SNS), complained to the Commission that SNS organisations were guilty of an abuse of a dominant position, in particular because they systematically took an average of 300 days to pay their debts. The Commission rejected the complaint on the ground that the organisations in question were not undertakings when they participated in the management of the national health service. Consequently, they were not acting as undertakings when they purchased medical goods and supplies. On appeal, the GC affirmed that bodies forming part of the SNS did not act as an undertaking when *purchasing* medical goods and equipment for the purpose either of using them for activities of a purely social nature (to provide free health services to SNS members) or of offering goods and services as part of an economic activity.[84] The Court stressed that it was the *supply* function (the offering of goods and services on a market) of the entity that was important when determining whether economic activity was carried out and not the purchasing function.[85] In the context of the former, SNS operated according to the principle of solidarity. It was funded from social security contributions and other State funding and it provided services free of charge to its members on the basis of universal cover. If the activity for which the entity purchased goods was not an economic one, it made no difference that the entity might wield very considerable economic power, even giving rise to a monopsony.[86] The GC did not consider whether the fact that SNS did charge some patients (not covered by SNS) for care would alter the conclusion on the undertaking question. Although this point was raised on appeal it had not been put to the Commission and so was held not to be relevant for the purposes of reviewing the legality of the Commission's decision.[87]

On appeal, the CJ,[88] in a very short judgment, upheld the decision of the GC and rejected FENIN's argument that the GC had adopted too narrow a definition of economic activity since it had failed to consider whether purchasing activity is in itself an economic activity which may be dissociated from the service subsequently provided or because the subsequent activity, the provision of medical treatment, was itself an economic activity. Again, the CJ stressed that the characteristic feature of an economic activity consists in offering of goods and services on a given market.

Case C-205/03, *Federación Nacional de Empresas de Instrumentación Científica, Médica, Técnica y Dental (FENIN)* v. *Commission* [2006] ECR I-6295

Court of Justice

23 In support of the first part of its plea, FENIN argues that the [GC] adopted a definition of economic activity which is too narrow, holding that that activity necessarily consists of the offer of goods or services

---

[83] Case C-205/03 P, *FENIN* v. *Commission* [2006] ECR I-6295, Case T-319/99, [2003] ECR II-351.

[84] See also Cases C-264, 306, 354, and 355/01, *AOK Bundesverband* v. *Ichthyol-Gesellschaft Cordes, Hermani & Co* [2004] ECR I-2493.

[85] Case T-319/99, [2003] ECR II-351, para. 36.

[86] Case T-319/99, *FENIN* v. *Commission* [2003] ECR II-351, para. 37. Contrast the view of Jacobs AG in Case C-218/00, *Cisal di Battistello Venanzio & Co* v. *Istituto nazionale per l'assicurazione contro gli infortuni sul lavoro (INAIL)* [2002] ECR I-691, para. 71.

[87] Case T-319/99, *FENIN* v. *Commission* [2003] ECR II-351, paras. 40–43.

[88] Case C-205/03 P, *FENIN* v. *Commission* [2006] ECR I-6295.

on a given market and excluding all purchasing activity from that definition. FENIN submits that the approach of the [GC] would enable many bodies to avoid the competition rules of the Treaty, even though competition is affected by the conduct of such bodies.

24 The Commission submits that it is precisely the act of placing goods or services on a given market which characterises the concept of economic activity and not purchasing activity as such. Accordingly, there is no need to dissociate the purchase from the use to which the purchased goods are put.

Findings of the Court

25 The [GC] rightly held, in paragraph 35 of the judgment under appeal, that in Community competition law the definition of an 'undertaking' covers any entity engaged in an economic activity, regardless of the legal status of that entity and the way in which it is financed (Case C-41/90 *Höfner and Elser*..., paragraph 21, and Joined Cases C-264/01, C-306/01, C-354/01, and C-355/01 *AOK-Bundesverband*..., paragraph 46). In accordance with the case-law of the Court of Justice, the [GC] also stated, in paragraph 36 of the judgment under appeal, that it is the activity consisting in offering goods and services on a given market that is the characteristic feature of an economic activity (Case C-35/96 *Commission v. Italy*..., paragraph 36).

26 The [GC] rightly deduced, in paragraph 36 of the judgment under appeal, that there is no need to dissociate the activity of purchasing goods from the subsequent use to which they are put in order to determine the nature of that purchasing activity, and that the nature of the purchasing activity must be determined according to whether or not the subsequent use of the purchased goods amounts to an economic activity.

27 It follows that the first part of the single plea raised by FENIN in support of its appeal, that the purchasing activity of the SNS management bodies constitutes an economic activity in itself, dissociable from the service subsequently provided and which, as such, should have been examined separately by the [GC], must be dismissed as unfounded.

The judgment in *FENIN* thus makes it clear that *purchasing* for consumption is not economic activity and that purchasing will only constitute an economic activity if the goods and services acquired are subsequently used as an input for an economic activity, the offering of goods and services on a market.[89] This means that public bodies (even if wielding substantial purchasing power) will escape the reach of competition law unless the goods or services are bought for an economic activity. In so concluding, the Court was perhaps mindful of the 'dangerous territory' it enters when seeking to determine whether an activity carried on by the State or a State entity is of an economic nature 'since it must find a balance between the need to protect undistorted competition on the common market and respect for the power of the Member States'.[90] The decision reached in this case will inevitably

---

[89] Contrast the view of the UK's Competition Appeal Tribunal, in *Bettercare Group Ltd v. DGFT* [2002] CAT 7 (the conclusion of commercial contracts with private sector bodies was an economic activity and that it made no difference whether the entity acted as purchaser, rather than the supplier, of the services in question (especially where the purchaser was in a position to generate the effects which the competition rules seek to prevent)).

[90] Case C-205/03 P, *FENIN v. Commission* [2006] ECR I-6295, Maduro AG, para. 26. For the view that economic activity depends equally on buyers and sellers so that there is no reason why the concept of an undertaking should apply only to one side of the equation, and that although this approach to public procurement might bring short-term savings (adopting unfair and anti-competitive practices to increase efficiency of its purchasing) it may ultimately cause the disappearance of innovative and competitive suppliers in a number of areas of importance to public welfare, see J. Skilbeck, 'The EC Judgment in AOK: Can a major public sector purchaser control the prices it pays or is it subject to competition law?' (2004) 44 *PPLR* NA95–97 and J. Skilbeck, 'Just when is a public body an "Undertaking": FENIN and Bettercare compared' (2003) 4 *PPLR* NA75–77. This conclusion is hard on suppliers, particularly in markets where there are few other customers, as arguably this means that they will be made to make sacrifices in the name of the principle of solidarity, see, e.g. L. Montana and J. Jellis, 'The Concept of Undertakings in EC Competition Law and its Application to Public Bodies: Can you Buy your way into Article 82?' [2003] *Comp Law* 110 and Chap. 8.

lead to difficult questions of when purchasing in a particular case is sufficiently closely linked to the provision[91] of goods or services by the purchaser to constitute economic activity[91] and how purchasing should be treated when only some or a small proportion of the goods acquired are used in connection with an economic activity.

(iv) The Notion of an Undertaking is a Relative Concept

As the notion of undertaking focuses on the nature of the activity carried out by the entity concerned, it is clear that it is 'a relative concept in the sense that a given entity might be regarded as an undertaking for one part of its activities while the rest fall outside the competition rules'.[92] Thus 'the fact that, for the exercise of part of its activities, an entity is vested with public powers does not, in itself, prevent it from being classified as an undertaking ... in respect of the remainder of its economic activities'.[93] In each case therefore it is necessary to identify the particular 'activity' carried out by the entity in question, as insofar as it engages in economic activities which are not connected with the exercise of public powers it will be subject to the competition law rules.[94]

In *SELEX Sistemi Integrati SpA v. Commission*,[95] for example, the Commission argued that Eurocontrol was not an undertaking, relying on a previous finding of the CJ that:

'[t]aken as a whole, Eurocontrol's activities, by their nature, their aim and the rules to which they are subject, are connected with the exercise of powers relating to the control and supervision of air space which are typically those of a public authority (air space management and development of air safety)'.[96]

On appeal, the GC stressed that the Court's previous ruling had been based exclusively on a review of Eurocontrol's activities at issue in the previous case, namely the creation and collection of route charges on behalf of the Contracting States from users of air navigation services. Since the competition provisions applied to activities of an entity which could be severed from those in which it engages as a public authority, the various activities of Eurocontrol relevant in that case had to be considered individually to determine whether they were economic in nature. On the facts, the GC considered that in exercising some of the relevant activities, such as assisting the national administrations, Eurocontrol was acting as an undertaking.[97] The CJ, however, held that the GC had made an assessment that was erroneous in law, that Eurocontrol's activity of assisting the national administrations was connected with the exercise of public powers so that, in carrying out that activity, the organisation was not acting as an undertaking.[98] In contrast, in *Motosykletistiki Omospondia Ellados NPID (MOTOE) v. Elliniko Dimosio*,[99] the CJ held that a legal (non-profit-making) person which organised motorcycling events and entered into sponsorship, advertising, and insurance contracts designed to exploit those events commercially *was* an undertaking even though it was also vested

---

[91] See, e.g. Cases C-180–4/98, *Pavlov v. Stichting Pensioenfonds Medische Specialisten* [2000] ECR I-6451.

[92] Case C-475/99, *Firma Ambulanz Glöckner v. Landkreis Südwestpfalz* [2001] ECR I-8089, Jacobs AG, para. 72. Some of the activities carried out by medical aid organisations in this case were economic in character and others were not (e.g., the power to grant or refuse authority for the provision of independent ambulance services).

[93] Case C-49/07 *Motosykletistiki Omospondia Ellados NPID (MOTOE) v. Elliniko Dimosio* [2008] ECR I-4863, para. 25.

[94] Where an economic activity is connected with (and inseparable from) the exercise of public powers, however, the entity will not be treated as an undertaking, see Case C-113/07 P, *SELEX Sistemi Integrati SpA v. Commission* [2009] ECR I-2207.

[95] Case T-155/04, [2006] ECR II-4797, Case C-113/07 P, [2009] ECR I-2207.

[96] Case C-364/92, *SAT Fluggesellschaft mbH v. Eurocontrol* [1994] ECR I-43, para. 30.

[97] Case T-155/04, *SELEX Sistemi Integrati SpA v. Commission* [2006] ECR II-4797, paras. 50–94.

[98] Case C-113/07 P, *SELEX Sistemi Integrati SpA v. Commission* [2009] ECR I-2207.

[99] Case C-49/07, *Motosykletistiki Omospondia Ellados NPID (MOTOE) v. Elliniko Dimosio* [2008] ECR I-4863.

with public powers (authorising the organisation of motorcycling events) and carried out activities which were not of an economic nature.

(v) Employees and Trade Unions

Although individuals may act as independent economic actors and constitute an undertaking, it seems that employees are not undertakings for the purposes of the competition rules (although the actions of the employee may be attributable to the employer). Rather, employees in an employment relationship and which do not bear the financial risks of the business, but perform work for and under the direction of their employers do not 'in themselves constitute "undertakings" within the meaning of Community competition law'.[100] In *Albany*, Advocate-General Jacobs clearly set out his view that the competition rules were not designed to cover the activities of employees.[101] They were not structured to be applicable to employees and employees did not perform the 'functions' of undertakings. Rather, he considered work and labour to be distinct from the provision of goods or services. Consequently, trade unions would not be characterised as undertakings (or associations of undertakings) insofar as they acted as agents for their members (employees).[102]

(vi) Single Economic Units[103]

a. What is a Single Economic Unit? Natural Persons, Legal Persons, and Principal-Agent and Parent-Subsidiary Relationships

It has been seen that a functional approach is taken to the concept of an undertaking and that it encompasses any entity engaged in economic activity, regardless of its legal personality or status or the way in which it is financed. It has also been long accepted, however, that the term undertaking is not necessarily synonymous with natural or legal personality[104] but denotes 'an economic unit for the purpose of the subject-matter of the agreement in question even if in law that economic unit consists of several persons, natural or legal'.[105] The concept of an undertaking is aimed at economic units 'which consist of a unitary organization of personal, tangible and intangible elements which pursues a specific economic aim on a long-term basis and can contribute to the commission of an infringement'.[106]

---

[100] Case C-22/98, *Criminal Proceedings Against Becu* [1999] ECR I-5665, para. 26. See further discussion of economic units in Section 5.A.vi.

[101] See also his opinion in Cases C-180–184/98, *Pavlov v. Stichting Pensioenfonds Medische Specialisten* [2000] ECR I-6451. The CJ in Case C-67/96, *Albany International BV v. Stichting Bedrijfspensioenfonds Textielindustrie* [1999] ECR I-5751 did not rule specifically on whether or not, or when, employees or trade unions qualify as undertakings for the purposes of the competition rules, ruling that collective agreements concluded between trade unions and employers relating to conditions of employment and working conditions fell outside Art. 101(1) altogether, see Section 5.B.ii.c, pp. 153–154.

[102] If the employee does not constitute an undertaking, the trade union could not constitute an association of undertakings.

[103] See further, W. P. J. Wils, 'The Undertaking as Subject of E.C. Competition Law and the Imputation of Infringements to Natural or Legal Persons' (2000) 25 *ELRev* 99 and A. Jones, 'The Boundaries of an Undertaking in EU Competition Law' (2012) 8(2) *European Competition Journal* 301.

[104] *Pre-insulated Pipe Cartel* [1999] OJ L24/1, para. 154 ('The subject of the competition rules in the Treaty is the "undertaking", a concept not necessarily identical with the notion of corporate legal personality in national commercial company or fiscal law').

[105] Case 170/83, *Hydrotherm Gerätebau GmbH v. Compact de Dott Ing Mario Adredi & CSAS* [1984] ECR 2999, para. 11; Case C-97/08 P, *Akzo Nobel v. Commission* [2009] ECR I-8237, para. 55. This suggests that the assessment must be made in the context of the specific agreement concluded so that the same entity might be considered to be acting unilaterally or jointly depending on the nature of the agreement. See also Case C-217/05, *Confederación Española de Empresarios de Estaciones de Servicio v. Compañia Española de Petróleos SA* [2006] ECR I-11987.

[106] Case T-11/89, *Shell International Chemical Company v. Commission* [1992] ECR II-757, para. 311.

An undertaking may thus be comprised simply of a natural person (a single individual), a legal person, or groups of persons (made up of natural or legal persons such as two or more companies within a corporate group).

- individual sole traders (natural persons) may constitute an undertaking;[107]

- legal persons, such as companies and partnerships,[108] made up of a collection of individual persons, may also be undertakings. In this context, the cases do not seem to look behind the legal personality but individuals working within the legal person, and not accepting individual risk, are treated as constituent elements of it.[109] Thus in *Becu*, for example, the CJ held that dock workers, performing work for and under the direction of their employers, were to be viewed as being incorporated into the undertaking concerned and forming part of the 'economic unit';[110]

- the close economic links which exist in many relationships between principal and agent have led the CJ to recognise that an independently owned agent may lose its character as an independent trader and operate as an auxiliary organ 'forming an integral part of the principal's undertaking'[111] where the agent does not take on any (or only a negligible portion of) financial and commercial risk linked to sales of goods to third parties on behalf of the principal (even it seems if the agent acts for more than one principal);[112]

- in the context of parent-subsidiary relationships, the entities will constitute an economic unit if the subsidiary 'enjoys no economic independence'[113] or if the entities 'form an economic unit within which the subsidiary has no real freedom to determine its course of action on the market'[114] but carries out the instructions issued by the parent company controlling it. The formal separation of those entities resulting from distinct legal identity is not therefore decisive. The

---

[107] See n. 35.

[108] See e.g., Case 258/78, *Nungesser v. Commission* [1982] ECR 2015 and *Breeders' rights: roses* [1985] OJ L369/9. See also sporting bodies (*Distribution of Package Tours During the 1990 World Cup* [1992] OJ L326/31, paras. 43–58), trade associations (Case 96/82, NV IAZ *International Belgium v. Commission* [1983] ECR 3369), and agricultural cooperatives (Case C-250/92, *Gøttrup-Klim e.a. Grovvareforeninger and Others v. Dansk Landbrugs Grovvareselskab AmbA* [1994] ECR I-5641). See also n. 109.

[109] There is thus a difficult line to be drawn between legal entities, economic units, and cartels. Firms such as companies and partnerships inevitably eliminate competition, and result in price fixing and market-sharing competition, between individuals within them. Characterisation of a partnership as an undertaking renders such arrangements per se legal under Article 101. In contrast an agreement between independent competing undertakings to fix prices and share markets is almost invariably illegal under Article 101, see e.g., R. H. Bork, *The Antitrust Paradox: A Policy at War with Itself* (Basic Books, 1978, reprinted with a new Introduction and Epilogue, 1993), 264–265 and H. Hovenkamp and C. R. Leslie, 'The Firm as Cartel Manager' (2011) 64(3) *Vanderbilt Law Review* 813, 818 ('[t]he lines between firms, cartels and joint ventures are notoriously indistinct').

[110] Case C-22/98, *Criminal Proceedings Against Becu* [1999] ECR I-5665, para. 26. See also the view of Jacobs AG in Case 67/96, *Albany International BV v. Stichting Bedrijfspensioenfonds Textielindustrie* [1996] ECR I-05457 (cited in nn. 100–102 and accompanying text and, e.g., *CNSD* [1993] OJ L203/27, Cases C-180–184/98, *Pavlov v. Stichting Pensioenfonds Medische Specialisten* [2000] ECR I-6451).

[111] Case C-266/93, *Bundeskartellamt v. Volkswagen and VAG Leasing GmbH* [1995] ECR I-3477, paras. 18–19. See also Case C-279/06, *CEPSA* [2008] ECR I-6681, para. 35 relying on Case C-217/05, *CEES* [2006] ECR I-11987, para. 38. Contrast Cases 46 and 58/64, *Consten and Grundig* [1966] ECR 299, 340 where the CJ rejected the argument that vertical agreements did not constitute agreements between undertakings as the supplier and distributor were not on an equal footing and were not competitors, and distinguished this situation from that in which a producer includes within his undertaking the distribution of his own products by some means, e.g., through a commercial representative.

[112] Case C-279/06, *CEPSA* [2008] ECR I-6681, para. 36. Agency relationships are discussed in Chap 11.

[113] Case 22/71, *Béguelin Import Co. v. S.A.G.L. Import Export* [1971] ECR 949, para. 8.

[114] Case 15/74, *Centrafarm BV and Adriaan De Peijper v. Sterling Drug Inc* [1974] ECR 1183, para. 41. See also Case 170/83, *Hydrotherm Gerätebau GmbH v. Compact de Dott. Ing. Mario Adreoli & C. Sas* [1984] ECR 2999, para. 11, Case T-11/89, *Shell v. Commission* [1992] ECR II-757, para. 311 and generally Wils, 'The Undertaking as Subject of E.C. Competition Law and the Imputation of Infringements to Natural or Legal Persons' (cited in n. 103), 99.

relevant question is not whether two given companies are separate legal persons but, rather, whether they behave together as a single unit on the market.[115]

b. Consequences of the Single Economic Unit Doctrine

The economic unit doctrine has a number of important consequences. First, it affects the substantive reach of Article 101: agreements and concerted practices between the parent and subsidiary (or other entities) forming part of the same economic unit, and concerned merely with the internal allocation of tasks between them,[116] fall outside of Article 101 (as they are part of the same undertaking, such arrangements are intra-undertaking rather than arrangements between independent undertakings). In *Viho*,[117] for example, the CJ confirmed that the Commission had been correct to reject a complaint that Parker's distribution agreements concluded with its 100 per cent owned subsidiaries infringed Article 101. Parker controlled the sales, advertising, and marketing policy of its subsidiaries which had no real autonomy to determine their course of action. Consequently, agreements and arrangements between these companies were not caught by Article 101(1): the activity constituted internal allocation of functions of a single enterprise and not the collusive action required to trigger Article 101.[118]

Case C-73/95 P, *Viho Europe BV* v. *Commission* [1996] ECR I-5457

Parker Pen Ltd is a company incorporated under English law which produces writing utensils. This case concerned a complaint made by a Dutch company, Viho, which marketed office equipment on a wholesale basis. Viho had been unable to obtain Parker products on conditions equivalent to those granted to Parker's subsidiaries and independent distributors. It complained to the Commission that Parker's distribution system (which prohibited exports between Member States, divided the common market into national markets, and maintained artificially high prices on those national markets) was in breach of Article 101(1). Parker sold its products through subsidiary companies in Germany, Belgium, France, Spain, and the Netherlands of which it owned 100 per cent of the shares. Sales and marketing of the products through the subsidiaries were controlled by an area team of three directors.

After an investigation the Commission informed Viho that it was rejecting the complaint. Parker's subsidiary companies were wholly dependent on it, enjoyed no real autonomy, and the distribution system did not go beyond the normal allocation of tasks within a group of undertakings. Viho appealed against the Commission's rejection of the complaint to the GC which upheld the decision.[119] Viho appealed to the CJ which confirmed that the Commission and the GC had correctly classified the Parker Group as one economic unit within which the subsidiaries did not enjoy real autonomy in determining their course of action in the market.

---

[115] Case T-325/01, *DaimlerChrysler AG* v. *Commission* [2005] ECR II-3319, para. 85.

[116] Case 15/74, *Centrafarm BV and Adriaan De Peijper* v. *Sterling Drug Inc* [1974] ECR 1183, para. 41. See also Case 170/83, *Hydrotherm Gerätebau GmbH* v. *Compact de Dott. Ing. Mario Adreoli*, para. 41 (the Commission had submitted that Art. 101 was not applicable to agreements where their sole object was the allocation of tasks within the same economic unit but that it would apply to agreements having a wider scope, see also Trabucchi AG) and Case 30/87 *Bodson* v. *Pompes Funèbres* [1988] ECR 2479, para. 19.

[117] Case C-73/95 P, *Viho Europe BV* v. *Commission* [1996] ECR I-5457.

[118] The US Supreme Court in *Copperweld Corp* v. *Independence Tube Corp.* 467 US 36 (1984) has held that since a parent and a wholly owned subsidiary have a complete unity of interest and because a parent can assert full control at any moment if a subsidiary fails to act in a parent's interest, the parent and subsidiary have a unity of purpose or common design that belies the existence of an agreement for antitrust purposes.

[119] Case T-102/92, [1995] ECR II-17 (holding that Art. 101(1) referred only to relations between economic entities which were capable of competing with one another. It did not cover agreements or concerted practices between entities belonging to the same group if they formed an economic unit).

Court of Justice

13. The appellant claims that the fact that the conduct in question occurs within a group of companies does not preclude the application of Article [101(1)], since the division of responsibilities between the companies in the Parker group aims to maintain and partition national markets by means of absolute territorial protection. The evaluation of such conduct, which has harmful effects on competition, should not therefore depend on whether it takes place within a group or between Parker and its independent distributors. The appellant points out that such territorial protection prevents third parties such as itself from obtaining supplies freely within the Community from the subsidiary which offers the best commercial terms, so as to be able to pass such benefits on to the customer.

14. Consequently, the appellant considers that Article [101(1)], interpreted in the light of Articles 2 and [3(1)(c) and (g)][120]...must apply, since the referral policy in question goes far beyond a mere internal allocation of tasks within the Parker group.

15. It should be noted, first of all, that it is established that Parker holds 100 per cent of the shares of its subsidiaries in Germany, Belgium, Spain, France and the Netherlands and that the sales and marketing activities of its subsidiaries are directed by an area team appointed by the parent company and which controls, in particular, sales targets, gross margins, sales costs, cash flow and stocks. The area team also lays down the range of products to be sold, monitors advertising and issues directives concerning prices and discounts.

16. Parker and its subsidiaries thus form a single economic unit within which the subsidiaries do not enjoy real autonomy in determining their course of action in the market, but carry out the instructions issued to them by the parent company controlling them (Case 48/69, *ICI* v. *E.C. Commission*...; Case 15/74, *Centrafarm* v. *Sterling Drug*...; Case 16/74, *Centrafarm* v. *Winthrop*...; Case 30/87, *Bodson* v. *Pompes Funèbres*...; and Case 66/86, *Ahmed Saeed Flugreisen and Others* v. *Zentrale zur Bekämpfung unlauteren Wettbewerbs*...).

17. In those circumstances, the fact that Parker's policy of referral, which consists essentially in dividing various national markets between its subsidiaries, might produce effects outside the ambit of the Parker group which are capable of affecting the competitive position of third parties cannot make Article [101(1)] applicable....On the other hand, such unilateral conduct could fall under Article [102] if the conditions for its application, as laid down in that article[,] were fulfilled.

18. The [GC] was therefore fully entitled to base its decision solely on the existence of a single economic unit in order to rule out the application of Article [101(1)] to the Parker group.

This case establishes that truly unilateral behaviour of an undertaking, even if within a group of connected companies, will escape the ambit of the competition rules unless that undertaking holds a dominant position and commits an infringement of Article 102. In contrast, arrangements which go beyond internal allocation of duties and distribution arrangements concluded between independent undertakings will be caught by Article 101(1) if they restrict or distort competition. For example, the complaints lodged by Viho about the arrangements between Parker and its *independent distributors*, i.e. firms which were not connected to Parker by any type of ownership or control,culminated with a Commission decision finding that the distribution arrangements were in breach of Article 101(1) and with the parties being fined.[121]

In *Hydrotherm Gerätebau GmbH* v. *Compact del Dott Ing Mario Andreoli & C Sas*,[122] the CJ also confirmed that a natural person, a limited partnership, and another firm constituted (and so counted as) a single economic unit when they were all controlled by the same natural person.[123] This could be

---

[120] See Chaps. 1 and 2.

[121] See the appeals to the GC in Case T-66/92, *Herlitz AG* v. *Commission* [1994] ECR II-531, and Case T-77/92, *Parker Pen Ltd* v. *Commission* [1994] ECR II-549.

[122] Case 170/83, *Hydrotherm Gerätebau GmbH* v. *Compact de Dott Ing Mario Adredi & CSAS* [1984] ECR 2999.

[123] See also n. 105 and accompanying text. The terminology used in this case is rather confusing however as the judgment also refers to the partnership and the firm as undertakings and so concludes that the block exemption

relevant, for example, to the application of the technology transfer block exemption which permits only 'bilateral' agreements.[124]

Although the rationale underpinning this line of judgments has not been made explicit, in *Hydrotherm* the CJ stated that where entities form part of the same economic unit, competition between the parties is impossible.[125] The Court thus seems to consider that the arrangements between such entities resemble the internal workings of the firm and that the unity of purpose that they pursue renders meaningless the application of Article 101 to agreements between them (there is no competition to be protected[126]). If the subsidiary's strategy is determined by the parent, the parent and subsidiary will pursue a common course irrespective of the existence of any agreement between them: 'the unified conduct on the market of the parent company and its subsidiaries takes precedence over the formal separation between those companies as a result of their separate legal personalities'.[127]

The doctrine has, however, more controversially, been relied on as a mechanism for attributing liability and responsibility for an infringement of the competition law rules committed by a subsidiary to its parent company ('attribution of liability' cases).[128] Although the Article 101 (and 102) prohibition is directed at 'undertakings', decisions penalising breaches of competition rules must be addressed to, and fines imposed on, persons, natural or legal.[129] The economic unit doctrine allows[130] the conduct of a subsidiary which has infringed the competition rules to be imputed to the parent which forms part of the same undertaking. As the 'parent company and its subsidiary form a single economic unit and therefore a single undertaking' a decision imposing fines can be addressed 'to the parent company, without having to establish the personal involvement of the latter in the infringement'.[131] Responsibility for the competition law infringement falls to the undertaking/economic unit as a whole.[132]

regulation can be applied 'even if several legally independent undertakings participate in the agreement as one contracting party provided that those undertakings constitute an economic unit for the purposes of the agreement', para. 12. This seems to suggest that the undertaking as an economic unit can be comprised of a number of undertakings, which are natural or legal persons, see also Case 15/74, *Centrafarm BV and Adriaan De Peijper v. Sterling Drug Inc* [1974] ECR 1183, para. 32 and Case T-102/92, *Viho Europe BV v. Commission* [1995] ECR II-117, paras. 47–53.

[124] See Reg. 772/2004 [2004] OJ L123/11, Art. 2 (replacing Reg. 240/96 [1996] OJ L31/2) and Case 170/83, *Hydrotherm Gerätebau GmbH v. Compact del Dott. Ing. Mario Adreoli & C. Sas* [1984] ECR 2999. The 2004 technology transfer block exemption specifically provides that the term undertaking includes 'connected undertakings' as defined therein, see Chap. 12.

[125] Case 170/83, *Hydrotherm Gerätebau GmbH v. Compact de Dott Ing Mario Adredi & CSAS* [1984] ECR 2999, para. 11, but see also n. 111.

[126] For an interesting account of the cases dealing with this issue and the principles underpinning them see Lenz AG in Case C-73/95 P, *Viho Europe BV v. Commission* [1996] ECR I-5457, paras. 31–73, especially para. 67.

[127] Case T-102/92, *Viho Europe BV v. Commission* [1995] ECR II-117, para. 50. See also Case T-9/99, *HFB Holdings v. Commission* [2002] ECR II-1487, paras. 54–68 and Case C-97/08 P, *Akzo Nobel v. Commission* [2009] ECR I-8237, para. 55.

[128] Some have complained that such a use of the concept of an undertaking is unconvincing, illogical, and breaches fundamental principles, in particular the principle of personal responsibility, the presumption of innocence, and of limited liability, see, e.g., J. Joshua, Y. Botteman, and L. Atlee, '"You Can't Beat the Percentage"—The Parental Liability Presumption in EU Cartel Enforcement' in *Global Competition Review—The European Antitrust Review 2012*, 3, S. Thomas, 'Guilty of a Fault that One has not Committed. The Limits of the Group-Based Sanction Policy Carried out by the Commission and the European Courts in EU-Antitrust Law' [2012] *JECLAP* 11, K. Hofstetter and M. Ludescher, 'Fines against Parent Companies in EU Antitrust Law: Setting Incentives for "Best Practice Compliance"' (2010) 33 *World Competition* 55, and M. Bronckers and A. Vallery, 'No Longer Presumed Guilty? The Impact of Fundamental Rights on Certain Dogmas of EU Competition Law' (2011) 34 *World Competition* 535.

[129] E.g., natural persons, corporations, partnerships, or charities, etc.

[130] See Case 48/69, *Imperial Chemical Industries v. Commission (Dyestuffs)* [1972] ECR 619, paras. 11 and 131–140 and Case 6/72, *Europemballage and Continental Can v. Commission* [1973] ECR 215.

[131] Case C-97/08 P, *Akzo Nobel v. Commission* [2009] ECR I-8237, paras. 58–59.

[132] Case T-587/08, *Fresh Del Monte Produce v. Commission*, 14 March 2013, para. 53. 'The parent's awareness of, still less its participation in, the subsidiaries' wrongdoing has nothing to do with it. The acid test is whether together they compose one and the same undertaking', Joshua et al., '"You Can't Beat the Percentage"' (cited in n. 128), 3.

It is clear that the Commission's policy in many cartel infringement cases is now, wherever possible, to hold parent companies (and indeed top group holding companies) jointly and severally liable with their subsidiaries (Chapter 13 discusses fining policy more fully).[133] This policy maximises the total level of fines both by augmenting the maximum cap on the level of fines which can be imposed (which is 10 per cent of the turnover of the undertaking as a whole[134]) and by enhancing the risk of an uplift in the fine for recidivism or deterrence.[135] A competition authority may also be particularly keen to attribute responsibility to a parent company where, for example, the subsidiary may be unable to pay any fine imposed or where it wishes to impose liability on a parent company which operated the agreement, and concocted the breach, outside the EU. In *ICI v. Commission (Dyestuffs)*,[136] for example, the CJ rejected the applicant's argument that the Commission was not empowered to impose fines on it in respect of actions taken outside the EU. By the use of its power to control its subsidiaries established in the EU, the applicant had been able to ensure that its decisions were implemented on that market. The subsidiary did not enjoy autonomy and its actions could be attributed to the parent. In this way the single economic entity doctrine avoids the need for the extraterritorial application of EU competition law. The doctrine enables the competition rules to be applied to companies outside the jurisdiction without recourse to the more controversial 'implementation' or 'effects' doctrines.[137]

The single economic unit doctrine has also been relied upon by claimants in private litigation before the English courts, to anchor an action for damages in the UK by bringing it against a member of the economic unit domiciled in the UK (a UK subsidiary) where another member of that unit (for example, a non-UK parent) has committed the violation of the competition law rules.[138]

Some EU secondary legislation and Commission Notices also utilise a similar idea. For example, most of the block exemptions[139] and the Commission's Notice on agreements of minor importance[140] apply only to firms which do not exceed specified market shares. These provisions require that, when calculating market shares, the shares of all entities closely 'connected' (as defined therein) to the entity that actually entered into the agreement must be taken into account.[141] Similarly, the activities of the whole group must be considered when determining whether or not the parties to the agreement are competing undertakings.[142] Although the definition of connected entities in these provisions is designed to provide legal certainty, some of the language used within them is confusing, as it suggests an approach to the concept of undertaking which is not evidently consistent with the notion of an undertaking as defined by the EU Courts.[143]

---

[133] '[T]he existence of intermediary companies between the subsidiary and the parent company does not affect the possibility of applying the presumption that the parent company in fact exercises decisive influence over the subsidiary', Case T-343/06, *Shell Petroleum v. Commission*, 27 September 2012, para. 52. See also Case C-90/09 P, *General Química SA v. Commission*, 20 January 2011, paras. 88–89.

[134] See Reg 1/2003 [2003] OJ L1/1, art 23(2) and Chap. 14.

[135] The Commission has a discretion as to whether to hold the parent jointly and severally liable with the corporate entity directly involved in the infringement. To maximise the deterrent effect of fines, the Commission's 'invariable policy today is to hold a group parent automatically responsible for cartel infringements committed down the line by its wholly owned subsidiaries', Joshua et al., '"You Can't Beat the Percentage"' (cited in n. 128), 3–4.

[136] Cases 48, 49, and 51–7/69, [1972] ECR 619, paras. 125–146.

[137] The extraterritorial application of the competition rules is discussed in Chap. 16.

[138] See, in particular, *Provimi v. Aventis* [2003] EWHC 961, *Cooper Tire & Rubber v. Shell Chemicals* [2009] EWHC 2609 (Comm), [2010] EWCA Civ 864 (appeal dismissed), and *Toshiba Carrier UK Ltd v. KME Yorkshire Ltd* [2012] EWCA Civ 1190.

[139] See Chap. 4.

[140] Commission Notice on agreements of minor importance which do not appreciably restrict competition under Article [101(1)] [2001] OJ C368/13.

[141] See e.g. Commission Notice on agreements of minor importance which do not appreciably restrict competition under Article [101(1)] [2001] OJ C368/13, para. 12.

[142] See e.g. Chap. 10.

[143] See A. Jones, 'The Boundaries of an Undertaking' [2012] *European Competition Journal* 301.

c. The Boundaries of the Economic Unit

Given the significant consequences that flow from the acceptance of the single economic unit doctrine, a critical issue is exactly how broadly the concept of an economic unit extends and, in particular, exactly when a subsidiary has sufficient independence to prevent the doctrine from applying. Although there is relatively little case law which deals with the question of when an agreement falls outside the ambit of Article 101 on this basis (and so when the concept of an undertaking affects the substantive reach of Article 101), there are a greater number of 'attribution of liability' cases which shed light on the question of how, in this context at least, it is determined whether or not the subsidiary and parent constitute part of the same economic unit. The key issue identified in these latter cases is whether the parent is able to, *and does actually*, exercise decisive influence over the policy and direct the conduct of its subsidiary, so that the subsidiary does not enjoy real autonomy or independence in determining its course of action in the market.[144] Critically, the cases establish:

(i) that where a parent holds a 100 per cent shareholding in a subsidiary, or a de minimis amount less than 100 per cent,[145] a rebuttable presumption that the parent does in fact exercise decisive influence over the commercial policy and conduct of its subsidiary applies.[146] In such cases joint and several liability for the parent firm follows unless it adduces sufficient evidence to show that the subsidiary acted independently.[147] This point was clearly established in *Akzo Nobel*.

Case C-97/08P, *Akzo Nobel NV and Others* v. *Commission*, 10 September 2009

Court of Justice

58. It is clear from settled case-law that the conduct of a subsidiary may be imputed to the parent company in particular where, although having a separate legal personality, that subsidiary does not decide independently upon its own conduct on the market, but carries out, in all material respects, the instructions given to it by the parent company (see, to that effect, *Imperial Chemical Industries* v. *Commission*, paragraphs 132 and 133; *Geigy* v. *Commission*, paragraph 44; Case 6/72 *Europemballage and Continental Can* v. *Commission...*, paragraph 15; and *Stora*, paragraph 26), having regard in particular to the economic, organisational and legal links between those two legal entities (see, by analogy, *Dansk Rørindustri and Others* v. *Commission*, paragraph 117, and *ETI and Others*, paragraph 49).

59. That is the case because, in such a situation, the parent company and its subsidiary form a single economic unit and therefore form a single undertaking...Thus, the fact that a parent company and its subsidiary constitute a single undertaking within the meaning of Article [101] enables the Commission to address a decision imposing fines to the parent company, without having to establish the personal involvement of the latter in the infringement.

---

[144] Case 48/69, *Imperial Chemical Industries* v. *Commission (Dyestuffs)* [1972] ECR 619, paras. 125–146.

[145] See e.g., Case T-299/08, *Elf Aquitaine* v. *Commission*, 17 May 2011 and Case C-508/11 *Eni SpA* v. *Commission*, 8 May 2013.

[146] Case C-286/98 P, *Stora Kopparbergs Bergslags AB* v. *Commission* [2000] ECR I-9925, para. 29 and Case C-97/08 P, *Akzo Nobel NV* v. *Commission* [2009] ECR I-8237, para. 60, Cases C-201 and 216/09 P, *ArcelorMittal Luxembourg SA* v. *Commission*, 29 March 2011, and *AEG* v. *Commission* [1983] ECR 3151, para. 50. It is for the parent to rebut the presumption by submitting evidence relating to the organisational, economic, and legal links between its subsidiary and itself which are apt to demonstrate that they do not constitute a single economic entity: Case C-97/08P, *Akzo Nobel NV and Others* v. *Commission*, 10 September 2009, para. 65. The Commission is obliged to consider the rebuttal evidence and if it fails to do so its decision will be overturned, see e.g. Case T-185/06, *L'Air liquide SA* v. *Commission*, 6 June 2011.

[147] Case T-587/08, *Fresh Del Monte Produce* v. *Commission*, 14 March 2013, para. 58. It has been questioned whether this presumption is in fact rebuttable in practice, see Joshua et al., '"You Can't Beat the Percentage"' (cited in n. 128), 3 and R. Burnley, 'Group Liability for Antitrust Infringements: Responsibility and Accountability' (2010) 33 *World Competition* 595, but see, e.g., Case C-508/11 *Eni SpA* v. *Commission*, 8 May, 2013.

60. In the specific case where a parent company has a 100% shareholding in a subsidiary which has infringed the Community competition rules, first, the parent company can exercise a decisive influence over the conduct of the subsidiary (see, to that effect, *Imperial Chemical Industries* v. *Commission*, paragraphs 136 and 137) and, second, there is a rebuttable presumption that the parent company does in fact exercise a decisive influence over the conduct of its subsidiary (see, to that effect, *AEG-Telefunken* v. *Commission*, paragraph 50, and *Stora*, paragraph 29).

61. In those circumstances, it is sufficient for the Commission to prove that the subsidiary is wholly owned by the parent company in order to presume that the parent exercises a decisive influence over the commercial policy of the subsidiary. The Commission will be able to regard the parent company as jointly and severally liable for the payment of the fine imposed on its subsidiary, unless the parent company, which has the burden of rebutting that presumption, adduces sufficient evidence to show that its subsidiary acts independently on the market (see, to that effect, *Stora*, paragraph 29).

(ii) the ability to and actual exercise of decisive influence can be ascertained in other situations 'on the basis of a body of factual evidence, including, in particular, any management power exercised by the parent company or companies over their subsidiary',[148] for example where: the parent holds a majority interest in a subsidiary[149] or a minority interest which is allied to rights greater than those normally granted to minority shareholders;[150] or a parent has negative control[151] over its subsidiary, at least where two or more parents have negative control over a joint venture ('JV')[152] and so cooperate to determine the JV's commercial policy—that is, in situations where the parents have the power to exercise, and have actually exercised, *joint control* over a JV.[153] In *Dow*,[154] for example, the GC upheld the Commission's finding that Dow (and the other parent EI Du Pont) was jointly and severally liable for the infringement of its JV and formed part of the same economic unit with it.[155] The Court relied amongst other things[156] on the fact that the Commission had found that they had acquired joint control of the JV when appraising it on its creation under the EUMR.[157] It thus accepted that the parents had been found to have the power to jointly control their JV and further that, in the light of all the economic, legal, and organisational links, control had actually been exercised.

In some cases the GC has even gone so far as to hold that where two companies are placed in a position analogous to that in which a single company owns the entire share capital of its subsidiary,

---

[148] Case T-132/07, *Fuji Electric System Co. Ltd* v. *Commission*, 12 July 2011, para. 181, relying on Case T-314/01, *Avebe* v. *Commission* [2006] ECR II-3085, para. 136.

[149] Case T-141/89 *Tréfileurope Sales SARL* v. *Commission* [1995] ECR II-791. See also Cases 6,7/73, *Istituto Chemioterapico Italiano S.p.A. and Commercial Solvents Corporation* v. *Commission* [1974] ECR 223 (parent and subsidiary in which the parent held a 51 per cent shareholding were to be treated as an economic unit).

[150] Case T-132/07, *Fuji Electric System Co Ltd* v. *Commission*, 12 July 2011, para. 183.

[151] The EUMR also applies to changes in the quality of control.

[152] The term JV can be used to describe a wide spectrum of commercial arrangements between firms. In competition law, it is frequently used to describe an entity which (i) constitutes a separate business entity, and (ii) is jointly controlled by at least two parents.

[153] See, especially, Case T-314/01, *Avebe* v. *Commission* [2006] ECR II-3085, Case T-132/07, *Fuji Electric System Co. Ltd* v. *Commission*, 12 July 2011, Case T-77/08, *The Dow Chemical Company* v. *Commission*, 2 February 2012, Case C-179/12 P, judgment pending and Case T-76/08, *EI du Pont de Nemours* v. *Commission*, 2 February 2012, Case C-172/12 P, judgment pending.

[154] Case T-77/08, *The Dow Chemical Company* v. *Commission*, 2 February 2012, Case C-179/12 P, judgment pending.

[155] Case IV/M.663.

[156] E.g., the facts that each had the right to participate on a Members' Committee which approved certain matters pertaining to the strategic direction of the JV, that they had both withdrawn from the chloroprene rubber market and participated on it only through their JV. Net profits or losses of the JV were allocated in equal proportions to the two parents.

[157] Case IV/M.663.

it is possible to apply the *presumption* that a parent company in fact exercises decisive influence over its subsidiary. In *Avebe*, for example, it held that a JV, on the one hand, and its parents, on the other 'do form an economic unit...in the context of which the unlawful conduct of the subsidiary may be imputed to the parent companies, who become liable by virtue of the fact that they in reality control its marketing policy'[158] and in *Shell Petroleum NV v. Commission*[159] the Court endorsed the Commission's view that the situation (notwithstanding the coexistence of two legal parent entities) was analogous to that in which a single parent company controls fully its subsidiary, so entitling the Commission to rely on the *Akzo* presumption.

What is not entirely clear, however, is whether the concept of an undertaking developed in the attribution of liability lines of cases is identical to that developed in the substantive reach cases. If the notions are the same, the consequences are far-reaching and the doctrine potentially excludes a relatively wide spectrum of behaviour from Article 101(1) altogether, in particular, agreements between:

- persons bound together by a contractual relationship which results in one person working for and under the direction of another and so being integrated within that other (for example, an employment or agency contract) or one person controlling the behaviour of another;[160]
- a parent and a subsidiary, where the latter has no freedom to determine its course of action or economic independence as the parent has sufficient rights to exercise, and does actually exercise, positive control over its behaviour;
- (possibly) a parent and a subsidiary, where the latter has sufficient rights to veto strategic decisions of the latter, and actually exercises such negative control over its behaviour;
- subsidiaries/sister companies[161] which are controlled (within the meaning set out earlier) by the same parent; and
- a JV and its parent(s) or between parents which have the power to, and do actually, exercise jointly control and decisive influence over the JV's behaviour.

Because of the functional approach taken to the concept of an undertaking, however, it would seem that even if such a broad exclusion from Article 101 potentially applies, it would relate only to conduct which relates to the internal working of, or the internal allocation of responsibilities within, the economic unit.[162]

Support certainly can be found for the view that the concept of an undertaking is the same in the two lines of cases. Not only do the cases all hinge on the interpretation of the term 'undertaking', without any suggestion that the concept should be considered differently in differing scenarios but in *Flat Glass*[163] the GC clarified that the term 'undertaking' has the same meaning in Article 102 as the

---

[158] Case T-314/01, *Avebe v. Commission* [2006] ECR II-3085, para. 141.

[159] Case T-343/06, 27 September 2012

[160] See also, e.g., Commission Consolidated Jurisdictional Notice under Council Regulation (EC) No. 139/2004 on the control of concentrations between undertakings [2008] C95/1, para. 20, the Commission's decision in *Bananas* (12 October 2008) where the Commission found that the combination of a partnership, capital links, and a distribution agreement was sufficient to give Del Monte the possibility to exercise decisive influence on the way Weichert ran its business and that Del Monte did exercise such influence, paras. 383–385, *aff'd* Case T-587/08 *Fresh Del Monte Produce v. Commission*, 14 March 2013.

[161] Commission Guidelines on the applicability of Article 101 of the Treaty on the Functioning of the European Union to horizontal co-operation agreements [2011] OJ C11/1, para. 11 ('Horizontal Cooperation Guidelines') ('the same is true for sister companies, that is to say companies over which decisive influence is exercised by the same parent company. They are consequently not considered to be competitors even if they are both active on the same relevant product and geographic markets.').

[162] But see Case C-73/95 P, *Viho Europe BV v. Commission* [1996] ECR I-5457, paras. 14–18 and Wils, 'The Undertaking as Subject of E.C. Competition Law and the Imputation of Infringements to Natural or Legal Persons' (cited in n. 103), 107.

[163] Joined Cases T-68, 77-78/89, *Società Italiano Vetro SpA v. Commission* [1992] ECR II-1403, at paras. 357–8. See also

one given to it in the context of Article 101; and in *Hydrotherm*[164] the CJ held that 'in competition law, the term "undertaking" must be understood as designating an economic unit...'. Further, in both *Dyestuffs*[165] and *Viho*,[166] the CJ held that the consequence of the economic doctrine was both that Article 101(1) was inapplicable to arrangements between entities within the economic unit (intra-undertaking agreements) and that the actions of the subsidiary could be attributed to the parent company[167] and in some cases there has been cross-referral between the lines of cases.[168] It could also be argued that a single concept would provide the greatest coherence to the system.

A case could, however, also be constructed that there should be a context-specific approach to the concept of an undertaking.[169] Not only have the attribution of liability cases considerably expanded the concept of an undertaking without specific reference to the underlying objectives of the doctrine or to its consequences for the reach and scope of Article 101, but the objectives underpinning the doctrine in the two lines of cases are, arguably, quite different. This might suggest different interpretations of the concept in the different contexts (in attribution of liability cases the issue is when it is appropriate to ignore the legal personality of the entity that committed the infringement and to impose liability on a parent for an infringement it did not itself commit—when can the parent be said to have 'personal responsibility' for the violation?—but in substantive reach cases the policy is to take outside the scope of Article 101 only arrangements which resemble the internal workings of a firm and/or arrangements between entities which are in any event bound to pursue a common policy on a market). Indeed, in *Del Monte* the GC held that when determining whether the conduct of one firm (Weichert) could be imputed to another (Del Monte), the applicant's reference to *Suiker Unie* and *BMW* were irrelevant

since those judgments concern legal issues and have factual backgrounds that differ from those of the present case. *Suiker Unie and Others v. Commission* concerns the applicability of Article [101] to agreements concluded between trade representatives and principals. *BMW Belgium and Others v. Commission* concerns direct responsibility in the light of a fine which the Commission imposed on car dealers for having agreed on an export prohibition. In neither of those decisions was the Court required to examine and determine the question whether the conditions for the imputation to one undertaking of an infringement committed by another were satisfied.[170]

In addition, the broad interpretation of the concept in attribution of liability cases seems to conflict with decisions adopted by the Commission in cases which specifically dealt with the substantive reach of Article 101, see for example, *IJsselcentrale*,[171] *Gosmé/Martell-DMP*,[172] and with jurisprudence

---

[164] Case 170/83, *Hydrotherm Gerätebau GmbH v. Compact de Dott Ing Mario Adredi & CSAS* [1984] ECR 2999, para. 11. See also Horizontal Co-operation Guidelines, para. 11, n. 8.

[165] Case 48/69, *Imperial Chemical Industries v. Commission (Dyestuffs)* [1972] ECR 619, paras. 132–136.

[166] Case C-73/95 P, *Viho Europe BV v. Commission* [1996] ECR I-5457, para. 16. In Case T-102/92, *Viho Europe BV v. Commission* [1995] ECR II-117 the GC also relied on cases concerning parental liability in its judgment upholding the Commission's conclusion that agreements between Parker Pen and its subsidiaries fell outside of Art. 101(1). Indeed it concluded that the Commission had been correct in finding that because the subsidiaries' conduct could be *imputed* to the parent the integrated distribution system fell outside of Art. 101.

[167] See also Kokott AG in Case C-440/11 P, *Commission v. Stichting Administratiekantoor Portielje and Gosselin Group NV*, para. 31 and Bot AG in Cases C-201&216/09 P, *ArcelorMittal Luxembourg SA v. Commission*, para. 178.

[168] See e.g. Case T-112/05, *Akzo Nobel v. Commission* [2007] ECR II-5049, paras. 63–64, aff'd Case C-97/08 P, *Akzo Nobel v. Commission* [2009] ECR I-8237, paras. 72–78, Case T-132/07, *Fuji Electric System Co Ltd v. Commission*, 12 July 2011, para. 180 and Case T-77/08, *The Dow Chemical Company v. Commission*, 2 February 2012, para. 73.

[169] In e.g. Singapore, the Competition Commission has held that two entities may not form a single economic entity in one context (e.g. where the issue is whether agreements between the entities should be excluded from its prohibition of anti-competitive agreements) even though they may do so in another context (e.g. where the issue is whether to hold one of the companies liable for the other's competition infringement or whether to treat them as a single economic entity for the purposes of analysing the competitive effects of a merger), see CCS 400/003/06, *Qantas-Orangestar Cooperation Agreement*, 5 March 2007.

[170] Case T-587/08, *Fresh Del Monte Produce v. Commission*, 14 March 2013, para. 151.

[171] [1991] OJ L28/3.

[172] [1991] OJ L185/21. Each parent held 50% of the capital and half the supervisory board had to be drawn from each parent's shareholders.

dealing with 'associations of undertakings' which have generally interpreted this concept broadly to encompass entities used as an institutionalised mechanism for coordinating the members/shareholders' conduct (see Section 5.A.vii.a).

(vii) Associations of Undertakings

a. Institutionalised Forms of Cooperation

It has been seen that Article 101(1) applies not only to agreements and concerted practices between undertakings, but to decisions by associations of undertakings. It seems that the principal reason for such a reference is to enable 'those applying Article [101(1)] to hold associations liable for the anti-competitive behaviour of their members'.[173] In *Wouters v. Algemene Raad van de Nederlandse Orde van Advocaten*,[174] Advocate General Léger stated that the concept

seeks to prevent undertakings from being able to evade the rules on competition on account simply of the form in which they coordinate their conduct on the market. To ensure that this principle is effective, Article [101(1)] covers not only direct methods of coordinating conduct between undertakings (agreements and concerted practices) but also institutionalised forms of cooperation, that is to say, situations in which economic operators act through a collective structure or a common body.[175]

An association of undertakings 'consists of undertakings of the same general type and makes itself responsible for representing and defending their common interests *vis-à-vis* other economic operators, government bodies and the public in general'.[176] Thus it has been found to apply to: trade associations (which may provide a forum for competitors in a particular industry to get together and to discuss matters which may be to their mutual interest and a perfect vehicle through which undertakings in a specific industry coordinate action), agricultural cooperatives,[177] an association of collecting societies,[178] a body set up by statute and with public functions if they represent the trading interests of the members (even if there are some members appointed by the government or another public authority),[179] and professional associations (even if governed by a public law statute).[180] It has also been found that *Visa*[181] and *MasterCard*[182] are associations of undertakings. Such a categorisation means that their recommendations, rules, and other unilateral acts designed to coordinate the

---

[173] J. Faull and A. Nikpay (eds.), *The EC Law of Competition* (2nd edn, Oxford University Press, 2007), para. 3.102.

[174] Case C-309/99, [2002] ECR I-1577.

[175] Case C-309/99, *Wouters v. Algemene Raad van de Nederlandse Orde van Advocaten* [2002] ECR I-577, Léger AG, para. 62. Relying on M. Waelbroek and A. Frignani, *Commentaire J. Megret, Le Droit de la CE*, Vol. 4, *Concurrence* (Éditions de l'Université de Bruxelles, 2nd edn, 1997), para. 128.

[176] Case C-309/99, *Wouters v. Algemene Raad van de Nederlandse Orde van Advocaten* [2002] ECR I-577, Léger AG, para. 61.

[177] Case C-250/92, *Gøttrup-Klim e.a. Grovvareforeninger and Others v. Dansk Landbrugs Grovvareselskab AmbA* [1994] ECR I-5641.

[178] See *CISAC Agreement*, 16 July 2008, partially annulled on appeal, Case T-442/08, *International Confederation of Societies of Authors and Composers (CISAC) v. Commission*, 12 April 2013, see Chap. 9.

[179] Case 123/83, *BNIC v. Clair* [1985] ECR 391.

[180] See Case C-35/96, *Commission v. Italy* [1998] ECR I-3851, paras. 36–38 (*CNSD*) (dealing with a professional association of custom agents); Cases C-180–184/98, *Pavlov v. Stichting Pensioenfonds Medische Specialisten* [2000] ECR I-6451, paras. 73–77, and Case C-309/99, *Wouters v. Algemene Raad van de Nederlandse Orde van Advocaten* [2002] ECR I-577, para. 65.

[181] E.g. *Visa International* [2002] OJ L318/17.

[182] See *Europay (Eurocard-MasterCard)*, 19 December 2007. In this case the Commission rejected MasterCard's argument that its public listing on the New York Stock Exchange had changed the organisation's governance so fundamentally that any decision of its board no longer qualified as a decision of an association (an institutionalised form of coordination of the banks' conduct) but rather constituted a 'unilateral' act which each member bank bilaterally agrees to abide by, *aff'd* Case T-111/08, *MasterCard Inc v. Commission*, 24 May 2012, paras. 241–260, on appeal Case C-382/12 P (judgment pending).

behaviour of members constitute decisions which are brought within Article 101 without separate proof of a concerted practice or agreement between the individual members of the association.

b. The Relationship between Associations of Undertakings and Undertakings

A particular feature of Article 101, which applies to agreements between undertakings and the decisions of associations of undertakings, is that an entity has sometimes been found to be acting both jointly with its parents/members (as an association of undertakings) and unilaterally as a single undertaking at the same time. In *Laurent Piau*,[183] for example, the GC held that although a sporting association constituted an association of undertakings it also constituted an undertaking insofar as it engaged in economic activity in a market itself. This reasoning is not entirely easy, however. If the association is viewed as an undertaking and a single economic actor, the parents/members are viewed as part of that economic unit and not as separate undertakings. But if the parents are not undertakings, the sporting association cannot be an association of undertakings.

A further question arising is whether an association of undertakings which carries out non-economic activity should be subject to the competition rules. It would seem that such non-economic activity should not be caught as, in essence, the conduct of the association is treated as the joint conduct of its members/shareholders (whose actions are not caught unless they are economic in nature).[184] Indeed, in *Wouters v. Algemene Raad van de Nederlandse Orde van Advocaten*,[185] the CJ suggests that a functional approach should be adopted to the concept of an association of undertakings in the same way as it applies to the concept of an undertaking. In that case it was argued that the Bar of the Netherlands, a body governed by public law, should not constitute an association of undertakings when exercising regulatory powers in order to perform a task of public interest. The CJ held that the 'rules of competition do not apply to activity which, by its nature, its aim and the rules to which it is subject does not belong to the sphere of economic activity . . . or which is connected with the exercise of the powers of a public authority . . .'.[186] It held, however, that in adopting the regulatory rules the association was neither fulfilling a social function based on the principle of solidarity nor exercising powers which are typically those of a public authority. Rather, it was acting as the regulatory body of a profession, the practice of which constitutes an economic activity. It thus concluded that the Bar of the Netherlands must be regarded as an association of undertakings within the meaning of Article 101(1) when adopting a regulation such as one which prohibited certain multidisciplinary partnerships. 'Such a regulation constitutes the expression of the intention of the delegates of the members of a profession that they should act in a particular manner in carrying on their economic activity'.[187] Similarly, in *Ordem dos Técnicos Oficiais de Contas (OTOC) v. Autoridade da Concorrência*,[188] the CJ held that a professional association of chartered accountants was to be regarded as an association of undertakings when it adopted a regulation providing that

---

[183] Case T-193/02, *Piau v. Commission* [2005] ECR II-209, para. 69.

[184] But for the view that '[i]f the functional definition of undertaking given in *Höfner* captures all economic activity then associations of undertakings must be addressed when engaged in non-economic activity, otherwise the association would be an undertaking in its own right and "associations of undertakings" otiose', see Odudu, *The Boundaries of EC Competition Law: The Scope of Article 81* (cited in n. 29), 52–53. See also Cases 209–215 nd 218/78, *Van Landewyck and Others v. Commission* [1980] ECR 3125, paras. 87–88; Cases 96–102, 104, 105, 108, and 110/82, *NV IAZ International Belgium SA v. Commission* [1983] ECR 3369, paras. 19–20 and Cases T-25, 26, 30–32, 34–39, 42–46, 48, 50–71, 87, 88, 103, and 104/95, *Cimenteries CBR v. Commission* [2000] ECR II-491, para. 1320.

[185] Case C-309/99, [2002] ECR I-1577.

[186] Case C-309/99, [2002] ECR I-1577, para. 57.

[187] Case C-309/99, [2002] ECR I-1577, para. 64. The Court found this view to be supported by the facts: that the governing body of the Bar was composed exclusively of members of the Bar elected solely by members of the profession and that when adopting regulatory measures it was not required to do so by reference to specified public-interest criteria (it was authorised to act where to do so would be in the interest of the proper practice of the profession); and given the influence the regulation had on the conduct of the members of the Bar of the Netherlands on the market in legal services (which indicated it did not fall outside the sphere of economic activity).

[188] Case C-1/12, 28 February 2013.

certain compulsory training to be undertaken by chartered accountants could be provided only by OTOC. Even though OTOC was regulated by public law and required to adopt binding rules putting in place a system of compulsory training for its members and to ensure a quality service, it could not be regarded when adopting the rules as exercising powers which are typically those of a public authority and the rules at issue could not be regarded as not belonging to the sphere of economic activity (they had a direct impact on the market for compulsory training for chartered account-ants[189]). The CJ also held that it was immaterial that OTOC did not seek to make a profit: 'that does not prevent an entity which carries out operations on the market from being considered an under-taking, where the corresponding offer of services exists in competition with that of other operators which do seek to make a profit'.[190]

B. THE MEANING OF 'AGREEMENT', 'DECISION', AND 'CONCERTED PRACTICE'

(i) Introduction

Article 101(1) prohibits joint not individual conduct. The reference to 'agreements between under-takings, decisions by associations of undertakings and concerted practices' thus requires some element of 'collusion' between independent undertakings. The different types of collusion are distin-guishable from each other only by their intensity and the forms in which they manifest themselves and must be understood in the light of the concept inherent in the Treaty competition rules that each economic operator must determine independently the policy which it intends to adopt.

In effect, while that provision distinguishes between 'concerted practices', 'agreements between undertak-ings' and 'decisions by associations of undertakings', the aim is to have the prohibitions of that article catch different forms of coordination and collusion between undertakings (see Case C-49/92 P, *Commission* v. *Anic Partecipazioni*..., paragraph 112). Accordingly...a precise characterisation of the nature of the cooperation at issue in the main proceedings is not liable to alter the legal analysis to be carried out under Article [101].[191]

In many Article 101 cases the existence of an agreement is not in doubt. There may be doubt, how-ever, as to the precise terms of the agreement or as to whether the terms can be said to restrict compe-tition. In other cases, frequently where it is suspected that a serious violation of the competition rules has been committed (for example, horizontal or vertical price fixing), evidence that independent undertakings agreed or concerted to fix prices will, effectively, prove a violation of Article 101(1).[192] If detected, a large fine may be imposed on the undertakings proved to have been party to the infringement. In such cases, the parties who have been 'colluding' are likely to do so in an amor-phous way and to try and conceal the existence of the practices rather than attempt to try to defend their legitimacy under Article 101(3). The challenge for the competition authorities in such cases therefore is to uncover such covert operations and, where evidence is skimpy, to determine whether or not the behaviour on the market results from collusion, which is prohibited under Article 101, or independent behaviour, which is not.

Although the terms agreement, decision, and concerted practice may overlap and nothing turns legally on whether the conduct results from one or the other, collectively they draw a critical dividing

---

[189] It did not matter therefore that the rules would not affect competition on the market on which the members of the professional association practise their profession as it could do so on the market on which the professional association itself has an economic activity, Case C-1/12, 28 February 2013, para. 45.

[190] Case C-1/12, 28 February 2013, para. 57

[191] Case C-238/05, *Asnef-Equifax, Servicios de Información sobre Solvencia y Crédito, SL* v. *Asociación de Usuarios de Servicios Bancarios (Ausbanc)* [2006] ECR I-11125.

[192] As the agreement has as its 'object' the restriction of competition, its anti-competitive 'effect' does not need to be demonstrated, see Chap. 4.

line between lawful independent behaviour and illegitimate collusive practices. The terms are interpreted broadly but not so broadly that policy or behaviour that is determined *independently* on the market is incorporated within them.

(ii) Agreement

a. A Concurrence of Wills

The term 'agreement' has been given a liberal construction. In *Bayer AG* v. *Commission*,[193] the GC set out what has now become the classic definition of the concept, holding that proof of an agreement must be founded upon 'the existence of the subjective element that characterizes the very concept of the agreement, that is to say a concurrence of wills between economic operators on the implementation of a policy, the pursuit of an objective, or the adoption of a given line of conduct on the market'.[194] It is 'clear from the case-law that in order for there to be an agreement…it is sufficient that the undertakings in question should have expressed their joint intention to conduct themselves on the market in a specific way'.[195]

Proof of an agreement must, therefore, be founded upon the direct or indirect finding of a concurrence of wills between economic operators. So long as there is a concurrence of wills, constituting the faithful expression of the parties' intention,[196] its form is unimportant. The concept catches agreements whether or not they amount to a contract under national rules, whether or not they are intended to be legally binding, whether or not sanctions are provided for a breach, and whether they are in writing or oral.[197] It covers 'gentlemen's agreements',[198] standard conditions of sale,[199] trade association rules (which are treated as an agreement between the members to abide by the rules),[200] and agreements entered into to settle disputes, such as trade mark delimitation agreements.[201] An agreement exists once the parties agree on 'good neighbour rules' or 'establish practice and ethics' or 'certain rules of the game which it is in the interests of all of us to follow'.[202] Further, an agreement which has been terminated may be caught by Article 101(1) in respect of the period after termination if the effects of the agreement continue to be felt.[203] Agreements may be caught even if they are encouraged or approved by national law[204] or entered into after consultation with the national authorities.[205]

---

[193] Case T-41/96, [2000] ECR II-3383, *aff'd* on appeal Cases C-2 and 3/01 P, [2004] ECR I-23.

[194] Case T-41/96, [2000] ECR II-3383, *aff'd* on appeal Cases C-2 and 3/01 P, [2004] ECR I-23.

[195] Case T-41/96, *Bayer AG* v. *Commission* [2000] ECR II-3383, para. 67, *aff'd* on appeal Cases C-2 and 3/01 P, [2004] ECR I-23, relying on, e.g., Case 41/69, *ACF Chemiefarma NV* v. *Commission (the Quinine Cartel)* [1970] ECR 661, para. 112. See also Case C-49/92, *Commission* v. *Anic Partecipazioni* [1999] ECR I-4125, paras. 79 and 122 and Case T-99/04, *AC-Treuhand AG* v. *Commission* [2008] ECR II-1501, para. 118.

[196] Case T-41/96, *Bayer AG* v. *Commission* [2000] ECR II-3383, para. 69, *aff'd* on appeal Cases C-2 and 3/01 P, [2004] ECR I-23. See also Case T-62/98, *Volkswagen AG* v. *Commission* [2000] ECR II-2707, *aff'd* Case C-338/00 P, *Volkswagen AG* v. *Commission* [2003] ECR I-9189.

[197] See e.g. Case 28/77, *Tepea BV* v. *Commission* [1978] ECR 1391.

[198] Case 41/69, *ACF Chemiefarma NV* v. *Commission (the Quinine Cartel)* [1970] ECR 661. In this case undertakings operated an export cartel but extended its terms within the EU through a gentlemen's agreement. The CJ held that so long as the parties had declared themselves willing to abide by the gentleman's agreement that was sufficient.

[199] Case C-277/87, *Sandoz prodotti farmaceutici SpA* v. *Commission* [1990] ECR I-45.

[200] *Nuovo Cegam* [1984] OJ L99/29.

[201] See Chap. 12.

[202] Cases 209–15 and 218/78, *Van Landewyck* v. *Commission* [1980] ECR 3125, paras. 85 and 86 and *Cement* [1994] OJ L343/1, para. 45(6).

[203] Case T-7/89, *SA Hercules Chemicals NV* v. *Commission* [1991] ECR II-1711. Whether or not an agreement has been terminated may be difficult to determine, see *Soda-ash—Solvay* [1991] OJ L152/1.

[204] See Cases 43 and 63/88, *VBVB & VBBB* v. *Commission* [1984] ECR 19; *Aluminium Imports from Eastern Europe* [1985] OJ L92/1; *AROW/BNIC* [1982] OJ L379/1.

[205] Cases 240–242, 261, and 262/82, *SSI* v. *Commission* [1985] ECR 3831. For the position where the State *requires* or encourages undertakings to enter into anti-competitive agreements, see Section 5.F and Chap. 8.

It is no defence that an undertaking was bullied into concluding the agreement,[206] or that an undertaking had cheated or never intended to implement or to adhere to the terms of the agreement. This point was made forcefully by the Commission in *Industrial and Medical Gases*.[207] In this case, two of the undertakings alleged to be members of a cartel, Air Liquide and Westfalen, argued that they had not taken part in the agreements or implemented them. Rather, they had acted as a 'tough competitor' on the market or had pursued an 'aggressive commercial policy' towards competitors. The Commission rejected these arguments:

351. The Commission notes that the fact that Air Liquide and Westfalen participated in several meetings, and that the object of these meetings was to restrict competition, is confirmed by the documentary evidence in the Commission's file. The finding that the behaviour described constitutes agreements within the meaning of Article [101(1)] is not altered even if it is established that one or more participants had no intention to implement the joint intentions expressed by them. Having regard to the manifestly anti-competitive nature of the meetings at which intentions were expressed, the undertakings concerned, by taking part without publicly distancing themselves, gave the other participants the impression that they subscribed to what was discussed and would act in conformity with it. The notion of 'agreement' is objective in nature. The actual motives (and hidden intentions) which underlay the behaviour adopted are irrelevant.

b. Agreements between Undertakings Operating at Different Levels of the Economy or in Separate Markets

Article 101(1) applies to agreements concluded between two or more undertakings (bilateral or multilateral agreements). It has been seen that it is not applicable, however, where agreements are concluded between companies forming part of a single economic entity and that it is not generally applicable to agency agreements.[208] In the course of argument in *Consten and Grundig* v. *Commission*[209] it was suggested that, in a similar way, Article 101(1) should not be applied to agreements concluded between undertakings operating at different levels of the economy. If a producer could restrict the actions of its commercial representative[210] without triggering the operation of Article 101(1) it should also be able to restrict the action of independent distributors. Article 101 should not be concerned with agreements concluded between entities which were not competitors and which were not on an equal footing. Rather, any such conduct considered to be restrictive of competition should be dealt with under Article 102. The CJ rejected these arguments, holding that Article 101(1) could apply to vertical arrangements.[211] The wording of the provision did not suggest that a distinction between horizontal and vertical agreements should be drawn. The agreement had not been concluded between a manufacturer and an entity integrated within it but had been concluded between independent undertakings. Further, the fact that the agreement was not concluded between competitors was immaterial. Article 101 applied to all agreements between undertakings which had the potential to distort competition within the common market.

Cases 56 and 58/64, *Etablissements Consten SA & Grundig-Verkaufs-GmbH* v. *Commission...*, 339–40

In 1957 Grundig, a German manufacturer of radios, tape recorders, dictaphones, and televisions, appointed Consten as its exclusive agent for France. Consten agreed, amongst other things, not to

---

[206] Case T-25/95, *Cimenteries CBR SA* v. *Commission* [2000] ECR II-491, para. 2557.
[207] [2003] OJ L84/1, *aff'd* on appeal Case T-304/02, *Hoek Loos NV* v. *Commission* [2006] ECR II-1887.
[208] Case C-73/95 P, *Viho Europe BV* v. *Commission* [1996] ECR I-5457, and Chap. 11.
[209] Cases 56 and 58/64, *Consten and Grundig* [1966] ECR 299.
[210] See the discussion of agency in Chap. 11.
[211] Distribution agreements are discussed further in Chap. 11.

handle any competing products, to order a minimum quantity of Grundig products, to stock accessories and spare parts and to provide after-sales services. In return, Grundig agreed not to deliver the product for sale in France and imposed export and re-export restrictions on all distributors in other Member States. The Grundig trade mark, Gint, was registered in France in Consten's name. Under the agreements Consten, therefore, had absolute territorial protection. No one else was entitled to sell Grundig products in France either actively or passively. In fact, UNEF, a Parisian company, started importing and selling Grundig products at more favourable prices in France. Consten commenced proceedings in the French courts contending that UNEF had failed to respect its contract with Grundig, that it was indulging in unfair competition, and that it was infringing Consten's trade mark rights. It also brought proceedings against Leissner in Strasbourg which had obtained Grundig products for resale in France. UNEF complained to the Commission and, in 1963, the agreement was notified to the Commission for examination. The French court adjourned its proceedings to await the Commission's decision.

The Commission concluded that the agreements did infringe Article 101(1) and could not be individually exempted under Article 101(3). Consten and Grundig appealed to the Court of Justice. One of their pleas was that Article 101(1) applied only to 'horizontal' and not 'vertical' agreements. This argument was supported by the Italian Government.

Court of Justice

The complaints concerning the applicability of Article [101(1)] to sole distributorship contracts

The applicants submit that the prohibition in Article [101(1)] applies only to so-called horizontal agreements. The Italian Government submits furthermore that sole distributorship contracts do not constitute 'agreements between undertakings' within the meaning of that provision, since the parties are not on a footing of equality. With regard to these contracts, freedom of competition may only be protected by virtue of Article [102].

Neither the wording of Article [101] nor that of Article [102] gives any ground for holding that distinct areas of application are to be assigned to each of the two Articles according to the level in the economy at which the contracting parties operate. Article [101] refers in a general way to all agreements which distort competition within the Common Market and does not lay down any distinction between those agreements based on whether they are made between competitors operating at the same level in the economic process or between non-competing persons operating at different levels. In principle, no distinction can be made where the Treaty does not make any distinction.

Furthermore, the possible application of Article [101] to a sole distributorship contract cannot be excluded merely because the grantor and the concessionnaire are not competitors inter se and not on a footing of equality. Competition may be distorted within the meaning of Article [101(1)] not only by agreements which limit it as between the parties, but also by agreements which prevent or restrict the competition which might take place between one of them and third parties. For this purpose, it is irrelevant whether the parties to the agreement are or are not on a footing of equality as regards their position and function in the economy. This applies all the more, since, by such an agreement, the parties might seek, by preventing or limiting the competition of third parties in respect of the products, to create or guarantee for their benefit an unjustified advantage at the expense of the consumer or user, contrary to the general aims of Article [101].

It is thus possible that, without involving an abuse of a dominant position, an agreement between economic operators at different levels may affect trade between Member States and at the same time have as its object or effect the prevention, restriction or distortion of competition, thus falling under the prohibition of Article [101(1)].

In addition, it is pointless to compare on the one hand the situation, to which Article [101] applies, of a producer bound by a sole distributorship agreement to the distributor of his products with on the other hand that of a producer who includes within his undertaking the distribution of his own products by some means, for example, by commercial representatives, to which Article [101] does not apply. These situations are distinct in law and, moreover, need to be assessed differently, since two marketing organizations, one of which is [i]ntegrated into the manufacturer's undertaking whilst the other is not, may not necessarily have the same efficiency. The wording of Article [101] causes the prohibition to apply, provided that the other conditions are met, to an agreement between several undertakings. Thus it does not apply where a sole undertaking integrates its own distribution network into its business organization. It does not thereby follow, however, that the contractual situation based on an agreement between a manufacturing and a distributing undertaking is rendered legally acceptable by a simple process of economic analogy—which is in any case incomplete and in contradiction with the said Article. Furthermore, although in the first case the Treaty intended in Article [101] to leave untouched the internal organization of an undertaking and to render it liable to be called in question, by means of Article [102], only in cases where it reaches such a degree of seriousness as to amount to an abuse of a dominant position, the same reservation could not apply when the impediments to competition result from agreement between two different undertakings which then as a general rule simply require to be prohibited.

Finally, an agreement between producer and distributor which might tend to restore the national divisions in trade between Member States might be such as to frustrate the most fundamental objectives of the Community. The Treaty, whose preamble and content aim at abolishing the barriers between States, and which in several provisions gives evidence of a stern attitude with regard to their reappearance, could not allow undertakings to reconstruct such barriers. Article [101(1)] is designed to pursue this aim, even in the case of agreements between undertakings placed at different levels in the economic process.

The submissions set out above are consequently unfounded.

In *AC-Treuhand AG v. Commission*[212] the GC also made it clear that Article 101(1) catches agreements between undertakings, even where the purpose of the agreement is to restrict competition on a market on which one of the undertakings is not active. In this case, the GC upheld a fine imposed on AC-Treuhand which assisted in the implementation of a cartel by, for example, storing secret documents relating to the cartel and organising meetings. In so doing, it rejected the applicant's argument that 'a consultancy firm cannot be regarded as a co-perpetrator of an infringement—because it does not carry out an economic activity on the relevant market affected by the restriction of competition and because its contribution to the cartel is merely subordinate...'.[213]

c. Collective Bargaining Agreements

Article 101(1) *does not* apply to collective agreements between workers and employers intended to improve working conditions which belong to the realm of social policy. In *Albany International BV v. Stichting Bedrijfspensioenfonds Textielindustrie*[214] the CJ held that agreements concluded by representatives of employers and workers in a sector would not be caught by Article 101(1) insofar as those agreements related to the improvement of conditions of work and employment. Not only was it an objective of the Treaty to ensure that competition in the common market was not distorted, but one of the Treaty's objectives was to achieve a high level of employment and social protection. The latter objective would be thwarted if Article 101(1) applied to agreements adopted by management and

[212] Case T-99/04, *AC-Treuhand AG v. Commission* [2008] ECR II-1501.

[213] Case T-99/04, *AC-Treuhand AG v. Commission* [2008] ECR II-1501, para. 136.

[214] Case C-67/96, *Albany International BV v. Stichting Bedrijfspensioenfonds Textielindustrie* [1999] ECR I-5751, see especially paras. 46–64. See also Cases C-115–117/97, *Brentjens' Handelsonderneming BV v. Stichting Bedrijfspensioenfonds voor de Handel in Bouwmaterialen* [1999] ECR I-6025, para. 57, Cases C-180–184/98, *Pavlov v. Stichting Pensioenfonds Medische Specialisten* [2000] ECR I-6451, para. 67 and Case C-437/09, *AG2R Prévoyance v. Beaudout Père et Fils SARL*, 31 March 2011, paras. 28–36.

labour to improve conditions of work and employment. Consequently, such agreements fell outside the scope of Article 101(1) of the Treaty altogether.

d. Participation in Meetings—Acceptance of an Offer to Collude

Any regular participant in a meeting at which an anti-competitive agreement is concluded will be taken to have participated in that agreement, unless it can establish that it did not have any anti-competitive intention when it attended the meeting, and that the other participants were aware of this.[215] It appears, therefore, that the participant tacitly accepts an offer to collude by not publicly distancing itself further from the agreement. It is no defence that the participant did not put the initiatives into effect. Evidence of prices or other behaviour not reflecting those discussed at the meeting are not, therefore, sufficient to prove that it had not participated in the scheme.[216] The CJ set this position out clearly in *Cement*.[217]

Cases C-204, 205, 211, 213, 217, and 219/00 P, *Aalborg Portland AS* v. *Commission* [2004] ECR I-123

Court of Justice

81. According to settled case-law, it is sufficient for the Commission to show that the undertaking concerned participated in meetings at which anti-competitive agreements were concluded, without manifestly opposing them, to prove to the requisite standard that the undertaking participated in the cartel. Where participation in such meetings has been established, it is for that undertaking to put forward evidence to establish that its participation in those meetings was without any anti-competitive intention by demonstrating that it had indicated to its competitors that it was participating in those meetings in a spirit that was different from theirs (see Case C-199/92 P, *Hüls* v. *Commission*..., paragraph 155, and Case C-49/92 P, *Commission* v. *Anic*..., paragraph 96).

82. The reason underlying that principle of law is that, having participated in the meeting without publicly distancing itself from what was discussed, the undertaking has given the other participants to believe that it subscribed to what was decided there and would comply with it.

83. The principles established in the case-law cited at paragraph 81 of this judgment also apply to participation in the implementation of a single agreement. In order to establish that an undertaking has participated in such an agreement, the Commission must show that the undertaking intended to contribute by its own conduct to the common objectives pursued by all the participants and that it was aware of the actual conduct planned or put into effect by other undertakings in pursuit of the same objectives or that it could reasonably have foreseen it and that it was prepared to take the risk (*Commission* v. *Anic*, paragraph 87).

---

[215] See e.g., Case C-510/06 P, *Archer Daniels Midland Co* v. *Commission* [2009] ECR I-1843, paras. 119–120 and Case T-3/89, *Atochem* v. *Commission* [1991] ECR II-867, paras. 53–54, *Steel Beams* (proceedings under Art. 65 of the ECSC Treaty), Case T-141/94, *Thyssen Stahl AG* v. *Commission* [1999] ECR II-347, para. 177 *aff'd* Case C-194/99 P, [2003] ECR I-10821.

[216] Case T-3/89, *Atochem* v. *Commission* [1991] ECR II-867, para. 100 and Case T-53/03, *British Plasterboard* v. *Commission* [2008] ECR II-1333, para. 85 ('[W]here an undertaking participates, even without taking an active part, in meetings between undertakings with an anti-competitive object and does not publicly distance itself from what occurred at those meetings, thus giving the impression to the other participants that it subscribes to the results of the meetings and will act in conformity with them, it may be considered as established that it participates in the cartel resulting from those meetings').

[217] Cases C-204, 205, 211, 213, 217, and 219/00 P, *Aalborg Portland AS* v. *Commission* [2004] I-123. See also Case T-99/04, *AC-Treuhand AG* v. *Commission* [2008] ECR II-1501 (an undertaking which assisted in the implementation of a cartel agreement violated Art. 101(1). The fact that it attended cartel meetings without manifesting an opposition to them was sufficient to prove that it had participated in the cartel. The fact that it did not take part in all aspects of the cartel scheme or played only a minor in the aspects in which it did participate was not material to the establishment of an infringement but would have an influence on the assessment of the extent of the liability and the severity of the penalty, see paras. 129–132).

84. In that regard, a party which tacitly approves of an unlawful initiative, without publicly distancing itself from its content or reporting it to the administrative authorities, effectively encourages the continuation of the infringement and compromises its discovery. That complicity constitutes a passive mode of participation in the infringement which is therefore capable of rendering the undertaking liable in the context of a single agreement.

85. Nor is the fact that an undertaking does not act on the outcome of a meeting having an anti-competitive purpose such as to relieve it of responsibility for the fact of its participation in a cartel, unless it has publicly distanced itself from what was agreed in the meeting (see Case C-291/98 P, *Sarrió v. Commission...*, paragraph 50).

86. Neither is the fact that an undertaking has not taken part in all aspects of an anti-competitive scheme or that it played only a minor role in the aspects in which it did participate material to the establishment of the existence of an infringement on its part. Those factors must be taken into consideration only when the gravity of the infringement is assessed and if and when it comes to determining the fine (see, to that effect, *Commission v. Anic*, paragraph 90).

e. Vertical Agreements and Unilateral Conduct

It is clear that the word 'agreement' catches terms and conditions even if imposed by one party on another. If the terms are accepted the fact that one of the parties was unwilling to accept them does not prevent the agreement from being formed (although fines may be reserved for the principal beneficiaries of the activity involved).[218] In *BMW*,[219] an agreement was found to have been concluded which incorporated export bans imposed on reluctant BMW dealers. A further related question is the extent to which the term agreement can encompass what, at first sight at least, appears to be a purely unilateral policy or unilateral conduct pursued by one of the parties to an agreement. The question of when behaviour is truly unilateral (where the aims can be achieved without participation of another) and when unilateral behaviour is merely *apparent* (receiving explicit or tacit acquiescence by another) is an important and difficult one which has provoked considerable litigation. The former, even if restrictive of competition or hindering parallel imports, falls outside of Article 101 and the scope of the competition rules unless conducted by a dominant firm.[220] Where, however, the act or conduct, albeit apparently unilateral, is the expression of the concurrence of wills of at least two parties an agreement will be established.[221]

Take, for example, a vertical agreement between a supplier and a dealer. Such agreements are unlikely to incorporate provisions imposing resale price maintenance or incorporating an export ban as these generally constitute clear violations of Article 101(1).[222] What would be the position, therefore, if on its face an agreement appears to comply with Article 101 but the supplier subsequently unilaterally announces that it will not deal with dealers that do not adhere to minimum recommended prices or who sell outside their allotted territory *or* it is understood that if dealers do not

---

[218] The Commission may, therefore, decline to impose a fine on a party that has acted unwillingly, against its own economic interest, or under duress, see, e.g., *Volkswagen* [1998] OJ L124/60, on appeal Case T-62/98, *Volkswagen AG v. Commission* [2000] ECR II-2707, the appeal to the CJ was dismissed, Case C-338/00 P, *Volkswagen AG v. Commission* [2003] ECR I-9189. See Chap. 13 for a discussion of the Commission's fining policy.

[219] Case 32/78, *BMW v. Commission* [1979] ECR 2435.

[220] Art. 101 applies only to cases where there is an agreement or other concertation between two or more undertakings. Although Art. 102 may apply to unilateral anti-competitive acts of an undertaking it does so *only* where the undertaking is dominant. The Treaty thus envisages that a non-dominant firm may act unilaterally, even if it thereby restricts competition or hinders parallel imports, without infringing either Art. 101 or Art. 102. See also the discussion, in Section 5.A.vi.b, of Case C-73/95 P, *Viho Europe BV v. Commission* [1996] ECR I-5457.

[221] Case T-99/04, *AC-Treuhand AG v. Commission* [2008] ECR II-1501, para. 118.

[222] Such agreements are generally presumed to infringe Article 101(1) and not to meet the conditions of Article 101(3), see Chaps. 4 and 11.

adhere to minimum recommended prices and/or if they sell outside their allotted territory, they will not be supplied? Can an agreement to adhere to minimum resale prices or an export ban between the supplier and dealers be established and/or can a dealer that continues to accept supply be said to have 'tacitly' acquiesced in the supplier's policy and to have agreed to adhere to the anti-competitive terms? Does it make any difference whether or not the dealers do in fact adhere to the terms or whether they price cut or make sales outside of their territory and/or whether the policy manifests itself before or after the agreement was concluded?

The Commission has been prepared in a number of cases to infer the existence of an agreement, whether or not the provisions found to be an integral part of the agreement operate to the advantage of the other party to the contract. In *Bayer AG v. Commission*,[223] however, the CJ made it clear that such a finding will not be upheld in the absence of evidence of a concurrence of wills between the undertakings. Thus in the absence of any direct documentary evidence of a written agreement incorporating the policy, the Commission (or other person trying to prove a violation) will have to establish to the requisite legal standard that there was a concurrence of wills sufficient to trigger Article 101(1). A unilateral announcement of policy by one party to the contract combined with continued participation in the business arrangement by the other, may not therefore on its own be sufficient to establish the existence of an agreement or concurrence of wills. The cases demonstrate, however, that great care will need to be exercised by firms in this area and that this requirement does not provide a mechanism for parties to avoid the application of Article 101 by operating an agreement informally—if it can be established that an invitation to pursue the policy has been accepted, at least tacitly, or acquiesced in by the other party to the contract, the actions may be found to have spilled over into an agreement. In *Activision Blizzard Germany GmbH v. Commission*,[224] the CJ expressly clarified that the standard of proof required for the purposes of establishing an anti-competitive agreement is the same whether in the framework of a vertical or a horizontal relationship.[225] Although an important difference is that in the framework of a vertical relationship between a manufacturer and a distribution a certain measure of contact between the parties is lawful, in each case it is still necessary to ask whether an agreement can be inferred from all the evidence having regard to all the relevant factors, and the economic and legal context specific to the case.[226]

An early case is *AEG*.[227] In this case, AEG-Telefunken (a developer and manufacturer of consumer electronic products) notified its selective distribution system to the Commission[228] which indicated to AEG that the system did not infringe Article 101(1). Subsequently, however, the Commission received numerous complaints alleging that AEG was not operating the scheme in the manner notified. AEG had refused to supply certain resellers which satisfied the stipulated objective criteria, but which would not adhere to a policy of charging minimum prices (and so in effect the agreement incorporated a resale price maintenance provision).[229] AEG argued that the acts complained of were not part of its agreement with resellers, but were decisions that it had taken unilaterally. Both the Commission and the Court rejected this argument. The CJ held that a refusal to approve distributors who satisfied the qualitative criteria necessary to become a member of the selective distribution system would be unlawful. This behaviour

on the part of the manufacturer does not constitute, on the part of the undertaking, unilateral conduct which, as AEG claims, would be exempt from the prohibition contained in Article [101(1)]. On the contrary, it forms part of the contractual relations between the undertaking and resellers. Indeed, in the case of the admission

---

[223] Case T-41/96, [2000] ECR II-3383, and Cases C-2 and 3/01 P, [2004] ECR I-23.

[224] Case C-260/09 P, [2011] ECR I-419.

[225] Case C-260/09 P, [2011] ECR I-419, para. 71.

[226] Case C-260/09 P, [2011] ECR I-419, para. 72.

[227] Case 107/82, *AEG-Telefunken v. Commission* [1983] ECR 3151.

[228] A selective distribution system is one where the supplier limits the number or, more usually, the type of outlets that sell its products. They are discussed in greater detail in Chap. 11.

[229] See Chaps. 4 and 11.

of a distributor, approval is based on the acceptance, tacit or express, by the contracting parties of the policy pursued by AEG which requires *inter alia* the exclusion from the network of all distributors who are qualified for admission but are not prepared to adhere to that policy.[230]

The Court thus found that the resellers' admission to the network was dependent upon their acceptance, express or tacit, of AEG's policy.

A similar approach has been adopted in other cases, many involving export bans imposed on distributors. In *Ford*,[231] the Commission refused an individual exemption to a selective distribution system for the distribution and sale of Ford products in Germany. Ford had stopped supplying right-hand-drive cars to its German dealers in order to prevent those distributors from exporting the cars into the UK (where its car prices were higher). The Commission considered that Ford's decision to cease supply of right-hand-drive cars was an integral part of the agreements with its German dealers. This act was taken into account when determining whether or not Article 101(1) was infringed and whether the agreement should benefit from Article 101(3). The CJ upheld the finding that the decision on the part of Ford formed part of the contractual relations between the undertakings and its dealers. Admission to the Ford AG dealer network implied acceptance by the contracting parties of the policy pursued by Ford with regard to the models delivered to the German market.

In *Sandoz*,[232] the CJ affirmed the Commission's view that Sandoz's policy of sending invoices to customers with the words 'export prohibited' upon them did not constitute unilateral conduct, but, on the contrary, formed part of the general framework of commercial relations which the undertaking maintained with its customers. The Court stressed the uniform and systematic repetition of this practice noting that customers

were sent the same standard invoice after each individual order... The repeated orders of the products and the successive payments without protest by the customer of the prices indicated on the invoice bearing the words "export prohibited", constituted a tacit acquiescence on the part of the latter in the clauses stipulated in the invoice.[233]

In each of these cases the CJ accepted that apparently unilateral conduct could be read into an agreement even though, in the export ban cases at least, it did not operate to the dealer's advantage. Although the Commission may look favourably on the dealer, when deciding whether to impose fines on a party to a contract, that party could become liable for damages to anyone who can prove loss suffered in consequence of the infringement.[234] Caution needs to be exercised therefore to ensure that an agreement is not found where none really exists.[235]

In both *Bayer AG v. Commission*[236] and *Volkswagen v. Commission*,[237] however, the GC annulled the Commission's decisions, finding that unilateral conduct formed part of an agreement.[238]

---

[230] Case 107/82, *AEG-Telefunken v. Commission* [1983] ECR 3151, para. 38.

[231] Cases 228 and 229/82, *Ford Werke AG and Ford of Europe Inc v. Commission* [1984] ECR 1129. See also Case C-279/87, *Tipp-Ex GmbH v. Commission* [1990] ECR I-261.

[232] Case C-277/87, *Sandoz prodotti farmaceutici SpA v. Commission* [1990] ECR I-45.

[233] Case C-277/87, *Sandoz prodotti farmaceutici SpA v. Commission* [1990] ECR I-45, paras. 7–12.

[234] See Chap. 14.

[235] See, e.g., H. H. Lidgard, 'Unilateral Refusal to Supply: An Agreement in Disguise?' [1997] *ECLR* 354.

[236] Case T-41/96, *Bayer AG v. Commission* [2000] ECR II-3383, *aff'd* Cases C-2 and 3/01 P, [2004] ECR I-23.

[237] Case T-208/01, [2003] ECR II-5141, *aff'd* Case C-74/04P, [2006] ECR I-6585.

[238] See also Case T-368/00, *General Motors Nederland BV and Opel Nederland BV v. Commission* [2003] ECR II-4491 (annulling a finding of the Commission that Opel and dealers in the Netherlands had agreed to a policy of preventing exports), *aff'd* Case C-551/03 P, *General Motors BV v. Commission* [2006] ECR I-3173 and T-67/01, *JCB Service v. Commission* [2004] ECR II-49, *aff'd*, Case C-167/04, *JCB Service v. Commission* [2006] ECR I-8935 (annulling a finding of an agreement to fix retail prices and discounts) discussed further in Chap. 11.

In *Bayer/Adalat*[239] the Commission had imposed a fine of three million Euro on Bayer AG for taking action to prevent parallel imports in the pharmaceutical market. In this case, parallel imports into the UK had apparently led to the sale of Adalat by Bayer's UK subsidiary falling by almost a half. Bayer responded by reducing the volumes of the drug supplied to its French and Spanish distributors. As the dealers had obligations to supply their home markets' requirements, this had the effect of curbing their ability to engage in parallel trade and sales of the drug Adalat into the UK. The Commission found that the export ban was an integral element in the continuous commercial relations between Bayer and its wholesalers (which were aware of Bayer's policy and continued to place and renew orders for the product).

On appeal the GC[240] considered that the Commission had pushed the concept of an agreement too far when deciding that the wholesalers' continuation of commercial relations with Bayer amounted to their acquiescence in its restrictive supply policy. In fact, their actual conduct was contrary to that policy—a concurrence of wills between Bayer and the wholesalers, designed to prevent or limit exports of Adalat, had not been established. The GC drew a distinction between cases in which a genuinely unilateral measure had been adopted (without express or implied participation of another) and those in which the unilateral character of the measure was merely apparent, receiving at least the tacit acquiescence of the dealers.[241] It also held that the Commission could not rely on case law precedents, in which a concurrence of wills had been found, to call into question the Court's conclusion that neither agreement nor acquiescence in Bayer's policy had been established. In distinguishing *AEG* and *Ford* the GC stressed that the practices of the manufacturers in those cases, refusing to approve distributors who satisfied the qualitative criteria, were not unilateral but part of the contractual relations between the manufacturers and resellers since *admission* to the selective distribution networks[242] in those cases was based on the acceptance, tacit or express, by the contracting parties, of the policy pursued by the supplier.[243]

Case T-41/96, *Bayer AG* v. *Commission* [2000] ECR II-3383

General Court

B. The concept of an agreement within the meaning of Article [101(1)]

66. The case-law shows that, where a decision on the part of a manufacturer constitutes unilateral conduct of the undertaking, that decision escapes the prohibition in Article [101(1)] (Case 107/82 *AEG* v. *Commission*..., paragraph 38; Joined Cases 25/84 and 26/84 *Ford and Ford Europe* v. *Commission*..., paragraph 21; Case T-43/92 *Dunlop Slazenger* v. *Commission*..., paragraph 56).

67. It is also clear from the case-law that in order for there to be an agreement within the meaning of Article [101(1)] it is sufficient that the undertakings in question should have expressed their joint intention to conduct themselves on the market in a specific way (Case 41/69 *ACF Chemiefarma* v. *Commission*..., paragraph 112; Joined Cases 209/78 to 215/78 and 218/78 *Van Landewyck and Others* v. *Commission*..., paragraph 86; Case T-7/89 *Hercules Chemicals* v. *Commission*..., paragraph 256).

---

[239] [1996] OJ L201/1. See also discussion of Cases C-501, 513, 515, and 519/06 P, *GlaxoSmithKline Services* v. *Commission*, 6 October 2009, Chap. 4, and Case C-468–478/06, *Sot. Lélos kai Sia EE* v. *GlaxoSmithKline AEVE* [2008] ECR I-7139, Chap. 7.

[240] Case T-41/96, [2000] ECR II-3383, *aff'd* Cases C-2 and 3/01 P, 6 [2004] ECR I-23. See also Case T-368/00, *General Motors Nederland BV and Opel Nederland BV* v. *Commission* [2003] ECR II-4491, *aff'd* Case C-551/03 P, *General Motors BV* v. *Commission* [2006] ECR I-3173, para. 58.

[241] Case T-41/96, [2000] ECR II-3383, paras. 66–71, *aff'd* Cases C-2 and 3/01 P, [2004] ECR I-23.

[242] See n. 228.

[243] Case 107/82, *AEG-Telefunken AG* v. *Commission* [1983] ECR 3151, para. 38.

68. As regards the form in which that common intention is expressed, it is sufficient for a stipulation to be the expression of the parties' intention to behave on the market in accordance with its terms (see, in particular, *ACF Chemiefarma*, paragraph 112, and *Van Landewyck*, paragraph 86), without its having to constitute a valid and binding contract under national law (*Sandoz*, paragraph 13).

69. It follows that the concept of an agreement within the meaning of Article [101(1)], as interpreted by the case-law, centres around the existence of a concurrence of wills between at least two parties, the form in which it is manifested being unimportant so long as it constitutes the faithful expression of the parties' intention.

70. In certain circumstances, measures adopted or imposed in an apparently unilateral manner by a manufacturer in the context of his continuing relations with his distributors have been regarded as constituting an agreement within the meaning of Article [101(1)] (Joined Cases 32/78, 36/78 to 82/78 *BMW Belgium and Others* v. *Commission*..., paragraphs 28 to 30; *AEG*, paragraph 38; *Ford and Ford Europe*, paragraph 21;...*Metro II*..., paragraphs 72 and 73; *Sandoz*, paragraphs 7 to 12; Case C-70/93 *BMW* v. *ALD*..., paragraphs 16 and 17).

71. That case-law shows that a distinction should be drawn between cases in which an undertaking has adopted a genuinely unilateral measure, and thus without the express or implied participation of another undertaking, and those in which the unilateral character of the measure is merely apparent. Whilst the former do not fall within Article [101(1)], the latter must be regarded as revealing an agreement between undertakings and may therefore fall within the scope of that article. That is the case, in particular, with practices and measures in restraint of competition which, though apparently adopted unilaterally by the manufacturer in the context of its contractual relations with its dealers, nevertheless receive at least the tacit acquiescence of those dealers.

72. It is also clear from that case-law that the Commission cannot hold that apparently unilateral conduct on the part of a manufacturer, adopted in the context of the contractual relations which he maintains with his dealers, in reality forms the basis of an agreement between undertakings within the meaning of Article [101(1)] if it does not establish the existence of an acquiescence by the other partners, express or implied, in the attitude adopted by the manufacturer (*BMW Belgium*, paragraphs 28 to 30; *AEG*, paragraph 38; *Ford and Ford Europe*, paragraph 21; *Metro II*, paragraphs 72 and 73; *Sandoz*, paragraphs 7 to 12; *BMW* v. *ALD*, paragraphs 16 and 17).

In addition, the GC held that the Commission had *not* shown that Bayer had sought to obtain agreement or acquiescence from its wholesalers to adhere to its policy or that the wholesalers had acquiesced explicitly or implicitly, in the policy.[244] Further, the case-law precedents cited did not support its decision.[245]

Case T-41/96, *Bayer AG* v. *Commission* [2000] ECR II-3383

General Court

151. Examination of the attitude and actual conduct of the wholesalers shows that the Commission has no foundation for claiming that they aligned themselves on the applicant's policy designed to reduce parallel imports.

152. The argument based on the fact that the wholesalers concerned had reduced their orders to a given level in order to give Bayer the impression that they were complying with its declared intention

[244] Case 107/82, *AEG-Telefunken AG* v. *Commission* [1983] ECR 3151, paras. 66–185. In the context of a selective distribution system admission to the network may be based on acceptance by the distributors of the policy pursued by the producers, para. 170.

[245] Case 107/82, *AEG-Telefunken AG* v. *Commission* [1983] ECR 3151, paras. 158–171.

thereby to cover only the needs of their traditional market, and that they acted in that way in order to avoid penalties, must be rejected, because the Commission has failed to prove that the applicant demanded or negotiated the adoption of any particular line of conduct on the part of the wholesalers concerning the destination for export of the packets of Adalat which it had supplied, and that it penalised the exporting wholesalers or threatened to do so.

153. For the same reasons, the Commission cannot claim that the reduction in orders could be understood by Bayer only as a sign that the wholesalers had accepted its requirements, or maintain that it is because they satisfied Bayer's requirements that they had to procure extra quantities destined for export from wholesalers who were not suspect in Bayer's eyes and whose higher orders were therefore fulfilled without difficulty.

154. Moreover, it is obvious from the recitals of the Decision examined above that the wholesalers continued to try to obtain packets of Adalat for export and persisted in that line of activity, even if, for that purpose, they considered it more productive to use different systems to obtain supplies, namely the system of distributing orders intended for export among the various agencies on the one hand, and that of placing orders indirectly through small wholesalers on the other. In those circumstances, the fact that the wholesalers changed their policy on orders and established various systems for breaking them down or diversifying them, by placing them through indirect means, cannot be construed as evidence of their intention to satisfy Bayer or as a response to any request from Bayer. On the contrary, that fact could be regarded as demonstrating the firm intention on the part of the wholesalers to continue carrying on parallel exports of Adalat.

155. In the absence of evidence of any requirement on the part of the applicant as to the conduct of the wholesalers concerning exports of the packets of Adalat supplied, the fact that they adopted measures to obtain extra quantities can be construed only as a negation of their alleged acquiescence. For the same reasons, the Court must also reject the Commission's argument that, in the circumstances of the case, it is normal that certain wholesalers should have tried to obtain extra supplies by circuitous means since they had to undertake to Bayer not to export and thus to order reduced quantities, not capable of being exported.

156. Nor, finally, has the Commission proved that the wholesalers wished to pursue Bayer's objectives or wished to make Bayer believe that they did. On the contrary, the documents examined above demonstrate that the wholesalers adopted a line of conduct designed to circumvent Bayer's new policy of restricting supplies to the level of traditional orders.

157. The Commission was therefore wrong in holding that the actual conduct of the wholesalers constitutes sufficient proof in law of their acquiescence in the applicant's policy designed to prevent parallel imports.

The GC thus stressed that the Commission was not at liberty to widen the scope of the rules in the way it had done. It was not entitled to prohibit truly unilateral behaviour which did not abuse a dominant position, even if the aim of this conduct was to hinder parallel imports, to restrict competition, and affect trade between Member States. It was not 'open to the Commission to achieve a result, such as the harmonization of prices in the medicinal products markets, by enlarging or straining the scope' of the Treaty rules.[246]

The GC's judgment was upheld by the CJ. The CJ started by stating that its judgment was confined to the question of whether there was an agreement within the meaning of Article 101. 'It should be made clear, therefore, that neither the possible application of other aspects of Article [101], nor Article [102]…, nor any other possible definitions of the relevant market are at issue in these proceedings.'[247] The CJ did not therefore deny that Article 102 proceedings might have been possible, if a position of dominance had been established.[248] Like the GC, the CJ stressed that it was not open for

---

[246] Case T-41/96, [2000] ECR II-3383, para. 179.

[247] Cases C-2 and 3/01 P, [2004] ECR I-23, para. 42.

[248] See discussion of refusal to deal in Chap. 7.

the Commission automatically to assume that the expression of a unilateral policy by one of the parties established an agreement. Such a broad approach would confuse Article 101 with Article 102. It also considered that the GC had been correct to find that the Commission could not rely on the case-law precedents to call into question the analysis leading the GC to conclude that, in this case, acquiescence by the wholesalers in Bayer's policy was not established. It thus distinguished cases such as *AEG* and *Ford* on the basis that admission to the network in those cases was based on adherence to the manufacturer's policy.

Cases C-2 and 3/01 P, *Bundesverband der Arzneimittel-Importeure EV and Commission* v. *Bayer AG* [2004] ECR I-23

Court of Justice

102. For an agreement within the meaning of Article [101(1)] to be capable of being regarded as having been concluded by tacit acceptance, it is necessary that the manifestation of the wish of one of the contracting parties to achieve an anti-competitive goal constitute an invitation to the other party, whether express or implied, to fulfil that goal jointly, and that applies all the more where, as in this case, such an agreement is not at first sight in the interests of the other party, namely the wholesalers.

103. Therefore, the [GC] was right to examine whether Bayer's conduct supported the conclusion that the latter had required of the wholesalers, as a condition of their future contractual relations, that they should comply with its new commercial policy.

...

141....[I]t is important to note that this case raises the question of the existence of an agreement prohibited by Article [101(1)]. The mere concomitant existence of an agreement which is in itself neutral and a measure restricting competition that has been imposed unilaterally does not amount to an agreement prohibited by that provision. Thus, the mere fact that a measure adopted by a manufacturer, which has the object or effect of restricting competition, falls within the context of continuous business relations between the manufacturer and its wholesalers is not sufficient for a finding that such an agreement exists.

142. The case of *Sandoz* concerned an export ban imposed by a manufacturer in the context of continuous business relations with wholesalers. The Court of Justice held that there was an agreement prohibited by Article [101(1)]. However, as the [GC] points out in paragraphs 161 and 162 of the judgment under appeal, that conclusion was based upon the existence of an export ban imposed by the manufacturer which had been tacitly accepted by the wholesalers. In that regard, at paragraph 11 of the *Sandoz* judgment, the Court of Justice held that [t]he repeated orders of the products and the successive payments without protest by the customer of the prices indicated on the invoices, bearing the words export prohibited, constituted a tacit acquiescence on the part of the latter in the clauses stipulated in the invoice and the type of commercial relations underlying the business relations between Sandoz PF and its clientele. The existence of a prohibited agreement in that case therefore rested not on the simple fact that the wholesalers continued to obtain supplies from a manufacturer which had shown its intention to prevent exports, but on the fact that an export ban had been imposed by the manufacturer and tacitly accepted by the wholesalers. Therefore, the appellants cannot usefully rely on the *Sandoz* judgment in support of their plea that the [GC] erred in law by requiring acquiescence of the wholesalers in the measures imposed by the manufacturer.

143. Nor can the appellants rely on *AEG*, *Ford* and *BMW Belgium*, arguing that business relations in the wholesale trade in pharmaceutical products are comparable to a selective distribution system such as that which was at issue in those cases. As has been stated in paragraph 141 of this judgment, the relevant question is that of the existence of an agreement within the meaning of Article [101(1)].

144. As has been stated in paragraph 106 of this judgment, in the *AEG* and *Ford* judgments the need to demonstrate the existence of an agreement within the meaning of Article [101(1)] was not at issue. The

existence of an agreement capable of infringing that provision having already been established, the question raised was whether the measures adopted by the manufacturer formed part of that agreement and therefore had to be taken into account when examining the compatibility of that agreement with Article [101(1)]. In that regard, the [GC] rightly pointed out that, in those judgments, the Court of Justice had held that, at the time of a distributor's admission, its authorisation was based on its adherence to the policy pursued by the manufacturer…

145. A similar analysis must be drawn from the judgment in *BMW Belgium*, in which the question was whether Article [101(1)] of the [EC] Treaty must be interpreted as [prohibiting] a motor vehicle manufacturer which sells its vehicles through a selective distribution system from agreeing with its authorised dealers that they are not to supply vehicles to independent leasing companies where, without granting an option to purchase, those companies make them available to lessees residing or having their seat outside the contract territory of the authorised dealer in question, or from calling on such dealers to act in such a way (paragraph 14).

In *Volkswagen v. Commission*,[249] the GC also annulled a Commission decision in which the Commission had found that VW had set the selling price of the VW Passat in Germany in an agreement with its dealers.[250] The GC reiterated the critical distinction between agreements (based on the concurrence of wills) and unilateral measures taken without the participation (explicit, tacit, or implied) of the undertakings to which they were addressed.[251] It was not sufficient for the Commission to conclude that unilateral calls by the manufacturer, intended to influence the dealer,[252] provided sufficient evidence of an agreement between them. 'In doing so, the Commission is seeking to impose a new legal approach which not only enlarges the meaning of agreement, but also changes the rules on the burden of proof in its favour.'[253] Further, the GC held that the Commission was wrong to conclude that acquiescence in the supplier's policy could be inferred simply from the dealer being part of a selective distribution network and that signature of an agreement which complies with competition law implied tacit acceptance of *future* unlawful variations of the agreement.[254] Rather, acquiescence and the existence of an agreement had to be established and the Commission had not done so in this case. In contrast: in *AEG*,[255] such acquiescence had been established since admission to the network was on the basis of acceptance of AEG's policy; in *Ford*,[256] the dealers had clearly implemented the terms of the circular sent by Ford and which was linked to the dealership agreement; and in *Volkswagen*,[257] the Italian dealers had

---

[249] Case T-208/01, [2003] ECR II-5141, *aff'd* Case C-74/04 P, [2006] ECR I-6585.

[250] [2001] OJ L262/14. It imposed a fine of €30.96 million on Volkswagen in respect of the infringement.

[251] Case T-208/01, [2003] ECR II-5141, paras. 30–35, *aff'd* Case C-74/04 P, [2006] ECR I-6585.

[252] By definition the calls were intended to influence the dealer in the performance of the contract, Case T-208/01, [2003] ECR II-5141, para. 57.

[253] Case T-208/01, [2003] ECR II-5141, para. 19, *aff'd* on appeal Case C-74/04, [2006] ECR I-6585, para. 38. In Case T-67/01, *JCB Service v. Commission* [2004] ECR II-49, the GC also annulled a Commission finding that a supplier's policy of drawing up lists of recommended retail prices amounted to resale price maintenance. The GC considered that these price scales were not binding and that there was nothing to indicate that JCB's efforts to influence dealers and discourage them from agreeing on lower sales prices involved coercion, see especially paras. 121–133. This finding of the GC was not challenged before the CJ which broadly upheld the judgment of the GC, Case C-167/04, *JCB Service v. Commission* [2006] ECR I-8935. See also, e.g., Case T-368/00, *General Motors Nederland BV and Opel Nederland BV v. Commission* [2003] ECR II-4491, *aff'd* Case C-551/03 P, *General Motors BV v. Commission* [2006] ECR I-3173.

[254] The Commission's case amounted to a claim that a dealer who signed a dealership which complies with competition law is deemed to have accepted in advance a later unlawful variation of the contract.

[255] Case 107/82, *AEG-Telefunken AG v. Commission* [1983] ECR 3151.

[256] Cases 228–229/82, *Ford Werke AG and Ford of Europe Inc v. Commission* [1984] ECR 1129.

[257] This was a different Volkswagen case involving export bans, *Volkswagen* [1998] OJ L124/60, on appeal Case T-62/98, *Volkswagen AG v. Commission* [2000] ECR II-2707, the appeal to the CJ was dismissed, Case C-338/00 P, *Volkswagen AG v. Commission* [2003] ECR I-9189, see further Chap. 11.

accepted the anti-competitive initiative and refused to sell to foreign customers and the dealership agreement provided for the possibility of limiting deliveries.

On appeal, the Commission argued that it was 'settled' law that a request by a manufacturer to authorised dealers did not constitute a unilateral act but an agreement if it formed part of a set of continuous business relations governed by a general agreement drawn up in advance.[258] However, the CJ[259] upheld the conclusion of the GC (and the annulment of the Commission's decision), ruling that a request by a manufacturer did not relieve the Commission of its obligation to prove that there was a concurrence of wills on the part of the parties to the dealership agreement (established either from the clauses of the dealership agreement or from the conduct of the parties, in particular from tacit acquiescence by the dealers in the manufacturer's request).[260] Although the CJ held that the GC had erred in law in making an assumption that contractual clauses complying with the competition rules could not be regarded as authorising requests which are contrary to those rules,[261] it concluded that this error had not affected the soundness of the conclusion reached.

Both the *Bayer* and *Volkswagen* judgments thus admonish the Commission for too easily finding an agreement where none existed. It is now apparent that simply continuing to participate in a selective distribution system or accepting supplies under the terms of a distribution agreement will not be sufficient to establish liability. A dealer that signs up to a distribution agreement or selective distribution network in no way binds itself to accept future variations in the way the agreement is operated. Where, however, the dealer knows of the supplier's policy at the time it enters contractual relations, it may then be concluded that the contract was dependent upon the dealer accepting that policy.

f. Hub and Spoke Arrangements

Anti-competitive agreements (or concerted practices) may have both horizontal and vertical elements. For example, collusion between retailers as to the price at which they will sell a particular product could be achieved, directly or indirectly, through the intermediary of a supplier. In such a case it could be critical to determine both whether a vertical price fixing agreement exists (between the supplier and the relevant retailers) and/or whether there is in fact an agreement or a concerted practice between the supplier and retailers to fix the retail prices of the product (see Section 5.B.viii.d). In the latter scenario, the violation has a horizontal element and so may become an even more serious infringement of the competition rules.[262]

g. Agreements Concluded by Employees

An agreement (or concerted practice) can arise from the actions of employees acting within the scope of their employment. EU law holds that the undertaking will be liable even if the employees were not authorised or instructed to act in that way by senior management—personal conduct on the part of, or the assent of, a representative authorised under the undertaking's constitution

---

[258] It had been thought by many commentators that, at least as far as selective distribution systems were concerned, dealers involved in ongoing business relationships would be found to have agreed to whatever sale policies the manufacturer had chosen to adopt by the very fact of agreeing to become part of a network, see Faull and Nikpay, *The EC Law of Competition*) (cited in n. 173), para. 3.68.

[259] Case C-74/04 P, [2006] ECR I-6585.

[260] Case C-74/04 P, [2006] ECR I-6585, paras. 39–56. In this case the Commission had not attempted to show that the dealers had tacitly acquiesced in the manufacturer's request but had argued that the concurrence was part of the dealership agreement.

[261] Rather, clauses had to be examined individually to determine whether the requests at issue were part of the overall commercial relationship between VW and its dealers.

[262] See, e.g., discussion of Case 1022/1/1/03, *JJB Sports plc v. Office of Fair Trading* [2004] CAT 17, *aff'd* [2006] EWCA Civ 1318 at n. 303 and accompanying text.

is not required. In *Protimonopolný úrad Slovenskej republiky* v. *Slovenská sporiteľňa as*, the CJ thus clarified that:

it is not necessary for there to have been action by, or even knowledge on the part of, the partners or principal managers of the undertaking concerned; action by a person who is authorised to act on behalf of the undertaking suffices.[263]

This is particularly relevant in situations where employees have entered into secret collusive conspiracies to rig markets. Undertakings should have in place, and should enforce, a compliance programme to prevent breaches of the competition rules.[264] Although EU law does not provide sanctions (disqualification, fines, and/or imprisonment) for the individual employees, such sanctions are available in some EU Member States.

h. Recommendations by Bodies Constituted under Statutory Powers

Several cases have raised the question of whether there is an 'agreement' where undertakings are represented on a body constituted under statutory powers to make recommendations in respect of a certain industry, etc. The CJ has held that there is not an agreement even when the trade representatives are in the majority on the committee, provided that the public authorities have not delegated their power of decision and that the matters to be fixed (e.g., tariffs) are fixed with due regard for public-interest criteria.[265]

i. Proving an Agreement

In addition to knowing how the concept of an agreement is defined it is essential to know how it is proved. The previous discussion establishes that an agreement may be founded on a 'direct or indirect finding' of the existence of a concurrence of wills. Thus, both direct evidence,[266] which will frequently be lacking in cases involving serious violations of the rules, and indirect or circumstantial evidence from which the agreement may be inferred may be relied upon to establish the concurrence of wills. The line of cases dealing with vertical agreements establishes that care must be taken when determining whether the requisite will can be found either from the clauses of the agreement in question and/or from the conduct of the parties in question.[267]

(iii) Concerted Practices

a. Description of a Concerted Practice

Article 101(1) is aimed at explicit collusion whatever form it takes, whether a formal agreement between undertakings to coordinate their behaviour and reduce effective competition between them or through more informal arrangements. The term concerted practice[268] is thus designed to provide a safety net, catching looser forms of collusion. It aims to forestall the possibility of undertakings evading the application of Article 101 by colluding in a manner falling short of an agreement.

---

[263] Case C-68/12, 7 February 2013, para. 25.

[264] See further Chap. 13.

[265] See, e.g., Case C-96/94, *Centro Servizi Spediporto Srl* v. *Spedizioni Marittima del Golfo Srl* [1995] ECR I-2883; Case C-38/97, *Autotrasporti Librandi Snc di Librandi F. & C.* v. *Cuttica spedizioni servizi internationali Srl* [1998] ECR I-5955, see Chap. 8. See also the discussion of decisions by association of undertakings in Section 5.B.iv.

[266] i.e. smoking gun evidence which does not require inferences to establish the agreement alleged. Written or parol evidence may be used. The Commission has broad investigative powers which may help it uncover direct evidence of an agreement and the Commission's leniency programme is designed to encourage participants to come forward with direct evidence necessary to prove the existence of an agreement, see Chaps. 9 and 13.

[267] The CJ stated in Case C-74/04, *Commission* v. *Volkswagen AG* [2006] ECR I-6585, para. 39 that the will of the parties might result both from the clauses of the agreement in question and from the conduct of the parties. See n. 228 and accompanying text.

[268] The definition of concerted practice is explored further in Chap. 9.

Classic descriptions of a concerted practice were set out by the CJ in *ICI v. Commission (Dyestuffs)*[269] and *Suiker Unie*.[270] In *Dyestuffs*, it held that the purpose of the term was to preclude:

co-ordination between undertakings which, without having reached the stage where an agreement, properly so called, has been concluded, knowingly substitutes practical co-operation between them for the risks of competition.[271]

In *Suiker Unie*, it confirmed that the concept in no way required 'the working out of an actual plan'.[272] Further, it is clear that although the concept 'does not deprive economic operators of a right to adapt intelligently to the existing and anticipated conduct of their competitors',[273] it does:

preclude any direct or indirect contact between such operators, the object or effect whereof is either to influence the conduct on the market of an actual or potential competitor or to disclose to such a competitor the course of conduct which they themselves have decided to adopt or contemplate adopting on the market.[274]

Although, therefore, the concept does not require an actual plan or a 'meeting of the minds'[275] it does seem to require *reciprocal* cooperation or a joint intention to conduct themselves in a specific way, disclosed through direct or indirect contact, designed to influence the conduct of an actual or potential competitor or to reveal to them the course of conduct that will or may be adopted on the market. Where therefore firms engage in conduct designed to remove strategic uncertainty about each other's future conduct on the market, they are not acting independently or unilaterally and so their conduct is subject to Article 101:

[T]he criteria of coordination and cooperation necessary for determining the existence of concerted practice are understood in the light of the notion inherent in the Treaty provisions on competition, according to which an economic operator must determine independently the policy which he intends to adopt on the common market.[276]

b. The Need for the Concertation to be Implemented on the Market

One important difference between the concept of an agreement and the concept of a concerted practice is that the latter term implies a requirement that the concertation should be practised or implemented on the market. This matter arose in the appeals from the Commission's decision in *Polypropylene*[277] where one of the issues to be decided was if it mattered whether the parties' conduct was characterised as an agreement or a concerted practice. One of the arguments raised by some of the parties was that although an agreement would be caught by Article 101(1) even if it was not implemented, as intended, on the market, direct or indirect conduct which has not been

---

[269] Cases 48, 49, and 51–57/69, *ICI v. Commission* [1972] ECR 619.

[270] Cases 40–48, 50, 54–56, 111, and 113–114/73, *Re the European Sugar Cartel; Coöperatieve Vereniging 'Suiker Unie' UA v. Commission* [1975] ECR 1663.

[271] Cases 48, 49, 51–57/69, *ICI v. Commission* [1972] ECR 619, paras. 64 and 65.

[272] Cases 40–48, 50, 54–56, 111, and 113–114/73, *Re the European Sugar Cartel; Coöperatieve Vereniging 'Suiker Unie' UA v. Commission* [1975] ECR 1663, para. 173.

[273] Case C-89/85, *Ahlström Osakeyhtiö v. Commission* [1993] ECR I-1307, para. 71.

[274] Cases 40–48, 50, 54–56, 111, and 113–114/73, *Re the European Sugar Cartel; Coöperatieve Vereniging 'Suiker Unie' UA v. Commission* [1975] ECR 1663, para. 174.

[275] Case T-587/08, *Fresh Del Monte Produce v. Commission*, 14 March 2013, para. 300 ('the intervener's complaint that the contested decision does not mention a meeting of minds between it and Dole or the existence of a common course of conduct is irrelevant, since the conduct in question falls within the specific legal classification of a concerted practice and not of an anti-competitive agreement').

[276] Case T-587/08, *Fresh Del Monte Produce v. Commission*, 14 March 2013, para. 301.

[277] *Polypropylene* [1986] OJ L230/1, appeals substantially dismissed by both the GC and the CJ: see, e.g., Case C-51/92 P, *SA Hercules Chemicals NV v. Commission* [1999] ECR I-4235, and Case C-199/92 P, *Hüls AG v. Commission* [1999] ECR I-4287.

implemented on a market did not amount to a concerted practice. An agreement, however informal and whether or not successful or acted upon, is a consensual act. In contrast, the word 'practice', in the concept of concerted practice, implied proof not only of concertation but *also* of the fact that steps have been taken to give effect to the concertation. There would, therefore, be no actual concerted *practice* if the parties only *plotted* to coordinate their behaviour but did not carry out that plot by conduct on the market. The arguments supporting this view and academic writings on this issue are fully reviewed in the Opinion of Advocate-General Vesterdorf designated by the President of the GC.[278] The CJ accepted that the concept of a concerted practice does require both concertation between the undertakings *and* 'subsequent conduct on the market, and a relationship of cause and effect between the two'.[279] However, it held that once evidence had been adduced of concertation it is presumed that undertakings taking part in the concerted action and remaining active on the market—especially where the concertation takes place on a regular basis—take account of the information exchanged with competitors in determining their conduct on the market. It is therefore for the undertaking to establish that concertation had not been followed by conduct on the market.

Case C-199/92 P, *Hüls AG* v. *Commission (Polypropylene)* [1999] ECR I-4287

Court of Justice

158. The Court of Justice has consistently held that a concerted practice refers to a form of co-ordination between undertakings which, without having been taken to a stage where an agreement properly so-called has been concluded, knowingly substitutes for the risks of competition practical co-operation between…

159. The criteria of co-ordination and co-operation must be understood in the light of the concept inherent in the provisions of the Treaty relating to competition, according to which each economic operator must determine independently the policy which he intends to adopt on the market…

160. According to that case law, although that requirement of independence does not deprive economic operators of the right to adapt themselves intelligently to the existing and anticipated conduct of their competitors, it does however strictly preclude any direct or indirect contact between such operators, the object or effect whereof is either to influence the conduct on the market of an actual or potential competitor or to disclose to such a competitor the course of conduct which they themselves have decided to adopt or contemplate adopting on the market, where the object or effect of such contact is to create conditions of competition which do not correspond to the normal conditions of the market in question, regard being had to the nature of the products or services offered, the size and number of the undertakings and the volume of the said market…

161. It follows, first, that the concept of a concerted practice, as it results from the actual terms of Article [101(1)], implies, besides undertakings' concerting with each other, subsequent conduct on the market, and a relationship of cause and effect between the two.

162. However, subject to proof to the contrary, which the economic operators concerned must adduce, the presumption must be that the undertakings taking part in the concerted action and remaining active on the market take account of the information exchanged with their competitors for the purposes of determining

---

[278] See [1991] ECR I-1711, 1923–1946. The AG was appointed following the order of the CJ referring this and other cases to the GC soon after its establishment. It was the view of the AG that failed attempts to concert would not be caught by Art. 101(1). The GC did not specifically address this point, since it took the view that having participated in and having obtained information from meetings with competitors an undertaking would be bound to take it into account, directly or indirectly, when determining its conduct on the market. The Court assumed that information acquired as a result of a concerted practice always influences the market conduct of the participants: see, e.g., Case T-7/89, *SA Hercules Chemicals NV* v. *Commission* [1991] ECR II-1711, para. 260.

[279] Case C-199/92 P, *Hüls AG* v. *Commission* [1999] ECR I-4287, para. 161.

their conduct on that market. That is all the more true where the undertakings concert together on a regular basis over a long period, as was the case here, according to the findings of the [GC].

163. Secondly, contrary to Hüls's argument, a concerted practice as defined above is caught by Article [101(1)], even in the absence of anti-competitive effects on the market.

164. First, it follows from the actual text of that provision that, as in the case of agreements between undertakings and decisions by associations of undertakings, concerted practices are prohibited, regardless of their effect, when they have an anti-competitive object.

165. Next, although the very concept of a concerted practice presupposes conduct by the participating undertakings on the market, it does not necessarily mean that that conduct should produce the specific effect of restricting, preventing or distorting competition.

166. Lastly, that interpretation is not incompatible with the restrictive nature of the prohibition laid down in Article [101(1)]...since, far from extending its scope, it corresponds to the literal meaning of the terms used in that provision.

167. Consequently, contrary to Hüls's argument, the [GC] was not in breach of the rules applying to the burden of proof when it considered that, since the Commission had established to the requisite legal standard that Hüls had taken part in polypropylene producers' concerting together for the purpose of restricting competition, it did not have to adduce evidence that their concerting together had manifested itself in conduct on the market or that it had had effects restrictive of competition; on the contrary, it was for Hüls to prove that that did not have any influence whatsoever on its own conduct on the market.

It can be seen from this extract that the Court emphasised that the question whether or not the parties had engaged in a concerted practice was distinct from the question whether or not that concertation had restricted competition[280] and clarifies that although a concerted practice requires concertation *and also* subsequent conduct, there is a presumption that concertation has been followed by conduct and has been taken into account where the undertakings concerned remained active on the market. This is true whether the undertakings concert together on a regular basis over a long period or whether the concerted practice stems from a single meeting.[281] This presumption of a causal connection stems from Article 101 and so forms an integral part of EU law.[282] As it is very hard to envisage circumstances in which an undertaking can establish that its conduct was *not* influenced by information acquired through concerting with others, the most important question appears to be whether or not there was collusion.

The importance of the concept of a concerted practice does not thus result so much from the distinction between it and an agreement as from the distinction between forms of collusion falling under Article [101(1)] and mere parallel behaviour with no element of concertation.[283]

The following are examples of the type of conduct which might be used to establish that the parties involved have engaged in a 'concerted practice'.

c. Direct Contact—Frequent or Isolated Exchanges, or Disclosure, of Information

Even if undertakings do not agree to fix prices or share markets, etc., the sharing or exchange of sensitive information may constitute a mechanism for substituting practical cooperation between them for the risks of competition, for example, reciprocal exchanges of strategic information (even if only

---

[280] Where the object of the concerted practice is to restrict competition it is not necessary to show that the conduct has the *effect* of restricting, preventing, or distorting competition, see Chap. 4.

[281] Case C-8/08, *T-Mobile Netherlands BV v. Raad van bestuur van de Nederlandse Mededingingsautoriteit* [2009] ECR I-4529.

[282] Case C-8/08, *T-Mobile Netherlands BV v. Raad van bestuur van de Nederlandse Mededingingsautoriteit* [2009] ECR I-4529, para. 52. See also A. Gerbandy, Case Comment [2010] 47 *CMLRev* 1199.

[283] *Polypropylene* [1986] OJ L230/1, para. 87.

on a single occasion).[284] In *Suiker Unie*,[285] for example, documents established that the parties had contacted each other and that they pursued the aim of removing in advance any uncertainty about the future conduct of their competitors. This conduct facilitated the coordination of their commercial behaviour.

In *PVC*,[286] the Commission considered that the term concerted practice was particularly apt to cover the involvement of some undertakings, for example, Shell. Shell, whilst not a full member of the cartel, had cooperated with it. It was thus able to adapt its own market behaviour in the light of this contact. Similarly, in *Belgian Brewers*[287] the Commission took the view that, in respect of one of the cartels it found to be operating on the Belgian market, the private label cartel, it could not establish an agreement from available evidence, but that a concerted practice was proven. Meetings between the brewers had clearly served to influence the market behaviour of the competitors and to report on market behaviour to competitors.

At the meetings not only was information exchanged but prices and customers were discussed. From statements…it is clear that the aim of the meetings was, firstly, to prevent a price war and adopt a position on prices and, secondly, to share out customers by not making (real) offers to the customers of other brewers.[288]

Further, in *T-Mobile Netherlands BV v. Raad van bestuur van de Nederlandse Mededingingsautoriteit*,[289] the CJ confirmed that a concerted practice could result not only from meetings which occurred on a regular basis over a long period but from an isolated exchange of information. In this case competing mobile telephone network operators had met only on a single occasion and discussed the reduction of certain standard dealer remunerations for postpaid subscriptions (packages whereby customers pay a fixed subscription charge and are invoiced subsequently for the number of minutes called). The CJ stressed that Article 101 precluded contact between firms which might influence the conduct on the market of competitors or disclose to them its decisions or intentions concerning its own conduct on the market.[290] The number, frequency, and form of meetings between competitors required to concert, however, depended on both the subject matter of the concerted action and the particular market conditions. The CJ also confirmed that the presumption that a concerted practice would influence the conduct of the undertakings participating in the practice where they remain active on that market was an integral part of EU law which had to be applied by a national court.

Case C-8/08, *T-Mobile Netherlands BV v. Raad van bestuur van de Nederlandse Mededingingsautoriteit*, 4 June 2009

Court of Justice

59. Depending on the structure of the market, the possibility cannot be ruled out that a meeting on a single occasion between competitors…may, in principle, constitute a sufficient basis for the participating

---

[284] Case C-8/08, *T-Mobile Netherlands BV v. Raad van bestuur van de Nederlandse Mededingingsautoriteit* [2009] ECR I-4529, paras. 54–62.

[285] Cases 40–48, 50, 54–56, 111, and 113–114/73, *Re the European Sugar Cartel; Coöperatieve Vereniging 'Suiker Unie' UA v. Commission* [1975] ECR 1663.

[286] [1994] OJ L239/14.

[287] [2003] OJ L200/1.

[288] [2003] OJ L200/1, para. 254.

[289] Case C-8/08, *T-Mobile Netherlands BV v. Raad van bestuur van de Nederlandse Mededingingsautoriteit* [2009] ECR I-4529.

[290] Case C-8/08, *T-Mobile Netherlands BV v. Raad van bestuur van de Nederlandse Mededingingsautoriteit* [2009] ECR I-4529, paras. 32–35.

undertakings to concert their market conduct and thus successfully substitute practical cooperation between them for competition and the risks that that entails...

60.... [T]he number, frequency, and form of meetings between competitors needed to concert their market conduct depend on both the subject-matter of that concerted action and the particular market conditions. If the undertakings concerned establish a cartel with a complex system of concerted actions in relation to a multiplicity of aspects of their market conduct, regular meetings over a long period may be necessary. If, on the other hand... the objective of the exercise is only to concert action on a selective basis in relation to a one-off alteration in market conduct with reference simply to one parameter of competition, a single meeting between competitors may constitute a sufficient basis on which to implement the anti-competitive object which the participating undertakings aim to achieve.

61. In those circumstances, what matters is not so much the number of meetings held between the participating undertakings as whether the meeting or meetings which took place afforded them the opportunity to take account of the information exchanged with their competitors in order to determine their conduct on the market in question and knowingly substitute practical cooperation between them for the risks of competition. Where it can be established that such undertakings successfully concerted with one another and remained active on the market, they may justifiably be called upon to adduce evidence that that concerted action did not have any effect on their conduct on the market in question.

In *Bananas*,[291] the Commission also found that three banana importers, Chiquita, Dole, and Weichert, which had engaged in direct bilateral pre-pricing communications (prior to setting their weekly quotation prices), had taken part in a concerted practice to coordinate quotation prices for bananas. They repeatedly communicated over a two-year period in relation to price-setting factors (factors relevant for setting of quotation prices) before quotation prices were set. As the communications were about future pricing policies the participants could not fail to take the information into account when determining the policy which they intended to pursue on the market. Further, the Commission held that the bilateral exchange of quotation prices after they had been set provided a monitoring mechanism for the pre-pricing communications. It thus considered that it had demonstrated cooperation (that the parties had knowingly adopted or adhered to collusive devices which facilitated the coordination of their commercial behaviour) and subsequent conduct on the market sufficient to establish the existence of a concerted practice.

The concept of a concerted practice may also encompass a disclosure of strategic information by one undertaking to a competitor (whether by, for example, mail, email, phone call, or orally at a meeting) where the recipient requests the information or accepts it.[292] A recipient of such strategic information will be presumed to have accepted the information tendered to it in this way, and to have altered its conduct accordingly, unless it publicly distances itself from, and clearly states that it does not wish to receive, it:

mere attendance at a meeting where a company discloses its pricing plans to competitors is likely to be caught by Article 101, even in the absence of an explicit agreement to raise prices. When a company receives strategic information from a competitor (be it in a meeting, by mail or electronically), it will be presumed to have accepted the information and adapted its market conduct accordingly unless it responds with a clear statement that it does not wish to receive such data.[293]

---

[291] Case COMP/39188 *Bananas*, 15 October 2008, *aff'd* Cases T-587/08, *Fresh Del Monte Produce v. Commission*, 14 March 2013 and T-588/08 P *Dole Food and Dole Germany v. Commission* (judgment pending). The appeal by Weichert, Case T-2/09, was dismissed as manifestly inadmissible as it was lodged out of time, *aff'd* Case C-73/10 P.

[292] See, e.g., Cases T-25/95, etc., *Cimenteries CBR SA v. Commission* [2000] ECR II-491, Cases T-202/98, etc., *Tate & Lyle, Napier Brown and British Sugar* [2001] ECR II-2035 *aff'd*, Case C-359/01P, *British Sugar* [2004] ECR I-4933.

[293] Horizontal Cooperation Guidelines, para. 62, relying on *Tate & Lyle* (cited in n. 292), para. 54, Case C-199/92, *Hüls v. Commission* [1999] ECR I-4287, para. 162 and Case C-49/92 P, *Anic v. Commission* [1999] ECR I-4125, para. 121.

In *Polypropylene*,[294] for example, although the Commission had concluded that an agreement existed between the undertakings, the GC[295] confirmed that the Commission had been correct to classify the meetings in the alternative as a concerted practice. The clear purpose of the competing undertakings participating in meetings, during which information was exchanged about, for example, prices and sales volumes, was to disclose to each other the course of conduct which each of the producers itself contemplated adopting on the market.[296] Participants clearly had the aim of eliminating any uncertainty about the future conduct of their competitors. They were bound to take into account the course of conduct upon which other participants had decided.

Even if, therefore, parties have not actually agreed to exchange price information its simple exchange may be prohibited where the behaviour of the undertakings eliminates 'the risks of competition and the hazards of competitors' spontaneous reactions ...'.[297] The exchange of sensitive information exacerbates the problems of, and increases transparency on, oligopolistic markets where there is already limited opportunity for competition.[298]

d. Indirect Contact/Sharing of Information and Hub and Spoke Arrangements

More difficult to categorise are situations where undertakings do not directly pass information to each other but disclose information which is nonetheless received by competitors, for example because the information was published publicly by an undertaking (perhaps on a website or to investors[299]) or because the information was received and published or transferred by an intermediary (such as a newspaper or trade journal, an independent consultant, a trade association, or a mutual customer or supplier). In such situations it is necessary to assess carefully on the facts whether or not the undertakings have acted independently, adapting their conduct to that of their competitors, or whether they have engaged in indirect contact designed to influence the conduct of their competitors.

While it is correct to say that this requirement of independence does not deprive economic operators of the right to adapt themselves intelligently to the existing or anticipated conduct of their competitors, it does, none the less, strictly preclude any direct or indirect contact between such operators by which an undertaking may influence the conduct on the market of its actual or potential competitors or disclose to them its decisions or intentions concerning its own conduct on the market where the object or effect of such contact is to create conditions of competition which do not correspond to the normal conditions of the market in question, regard being had to the nature of the products or services offered, the size and number of the undertakings involved and the volume of that market...[300]

In *Wood Pulp*,[301] for example, the CJ found that no collusion had been established where undertakings had announced their price increases in advance and the information had been rapidly transferred between both buyers and sellers by means of publication in the trade press.

---

[294] *Polypropylene* [1986] OJ L230/1.

[295] The judgments of the CJ focused mainly on procedural arguments, but see, e.g., Case C-199/92 P, *Hüls AG v. Commission* [1999] ECR I-4287, discussed in Section 5.B.iii.b, 165–167.

[296] e.g., Case T-7/89, *SA Hercules Chemicals NV v. Commission* [1992] ECR II-1711, para. 259, see Case C-199/92 P, *Hüls v. Commission* [1999] ECR I-4287, para. 155; Case C-49/92 P, *Commission v. Anic* [1999] ECR I-4125, para. 96; Case C-291/98 P, *Sarrió SA v. Commission* [2000] ECR I-9991, para. 50.

[297] Cases 48, 49, and 51–57/69, *ICI v. Commission (Dyestuffs)* [1972] ECR 619, para. 119. But such conduct may be hard to distinguish from a unilateral decision, e.g. to send a price list to the press for publication or to make a price announcements in advance, see discussion in Chap. 9 and especially the discussion of Cases C-89, 104, 114, 116–117, and 125–129/85, *Wood Pulp* [1993] ECR I-1307.

[298] See Chap. 9.

[299] E.g., earnings calls with industry analysts are often monitored by competitors.

[300] Case C-8/08, *T-Mobile Netherlands BV v. Raad van bestuur van de Nederlandse Mededingingsautoriteit* [2009] ECR I-4529, para. 33.

[301] Cases C-89, 104, 114, 116–117, and 125–129/85, *Re Wood Pulp Cartel: Ahlström Osakeyhtiö v. Commission (Wood Pulp II)* [1993] ECR I-1307, see further Chap. 11.

Exchanges of information between competitors (A and C) may also take place through the intermediary of a common customer or supplier (B). For example B might act as a 'hub' collating and distributing competitively sensitive information relating to its retailers (A and C, the 'spokes'). Information exchanged in this way may be of a type which reduces the uncertainty over the pricing intentions or output of rival retailers; for example, it may reveal future pricing intentions. The question of exactly when a vertical information exchange (a frequent and often necessary practice in many supplier/customer relationships) may also support the existence of a concerted practice involving competitors at the upstream or downstream level is controversial.[302] Although an agreement or concerted practice can be presumed where a competitor discloses strategic information directly to another competitor and the latter accepts it (and does not publicly distance itself from it), such a presumption should, arguably, not be made simply because A passed strategic information (for example about its intended retail pricing) to B, who then passed the information to C, as there may have been valid business justification for A sharing this information with B. Although there is no EU case law which deals with this issue the matter has been considered by the UK courts. In *JJB Sports plc v. Office of Fair Trading*,[303] for example, the appellant sought to challenge the OFT's finding that it unlawfully participated in various price-fixing arrangements. In relation to an allegation that it had participated in indirect exchanges of price information with competing retailers through the intermediary of Umbro, the CAT held that:

642. The fact that only one participant reveals his future intentions or other competitive information does not exclude the possibility of a concerted practice, since the recipient of the information in question cannot morally fail to take that information into account when formulating its policy on the market.

Building on this, the CAT later indicated that a concerted practice might be found where a retailer disclosed its pricing intentions to a supplier in circumstances where it was reasonably foreseeable that that information might be used to influence market conditions:

659. If one retailer A privately discloses to a supplier B its future pricing intentions in circumstances where it is reasonably foreseeable that B might make use of that information to influence market conditions, and B then passes that pricing information on to a competing retailer C, then in our view A, B and C are all to be regarded on those facts as parties to a concerted practice having as its object or effect the prevention, restriction or distortion of competition. The prohibition on direct *or indirect* contact between competitors on prices has been infringed.

660. As regards A, the position might in our view be different only if it could be shown that retailer A revealed its future pricing intentions to its supplier B for some legitimate purpose not related in any way to competition, and could not reasonably have foreseen that such information would be used by B in a way capable of affecting market conditions. It seems to us that such disclosure by a retailer to a supplier will rarely be legitimate, otherwise resale price maintenance could be reintroduced by the back door.

It is doubtful whether this broad interpretation of a concerted practice is consistent with the requirement set out in *Dyestuffs* that the parties to the concerted practice should *knowingly* substitute practical cooperation for the risks of competition and the requirement of reciprocal contact in concerted practices.[304] Indeed, on appeal, the Court of Appeal, although upholding the finding of liability, did indicate that this broad statement of the CAT, if taken out of context, went too far. The Court of Appeal considered that reasonable foresight was not enough to find a concerted practice. Rather, it favoured a more subjective test for the imposition of liability in which retailer A intended that the

[302] See also, e.g., Commission's Guidelines on Vertical Restraints [2010] OJ C130/01, para. 211; Horizontal Cooperation Guidelines, para. 55.

[303] Case 1022/1/1/03, [2004] CAT 17 (Judgment on Liability).

[304] See generally A. Albors-Lorens, 'Horizontal Agreements and Concerted Practices in EC Competition Law: Unlawful and Legitimate Contacts between Competitors' [2006] 51 *Ant Bull* 837.

information be passed on by B and that retailer C knew that the information had been provided by A to B and used that information in setting its prices.

The Tribunal may have gone too far if it intended that suggestion to extend to cases in which A did not, in fact, foresee that B would make use of the pricing information to influence market conditions or in which C did not, in fact, appreciate that the information was being passed to him with A's concurrence.[305]

e. Parallel Behaviour

Market data may show that undertakings have acted in parallel (for example, that competing undertakings increased prices at the same moment, offered the same discounts and/or terms and conditions to customers, etc.)

For the purposes of Article 101, a crucial question is whether such parallel behaviour results from independent or concerted action. Undertakings that operate on an oligopolistic market with only a few players and transparent conditions will know how their competitors are likely to behave and react to their actions. On such markets the operators may have no need to agree to disclose information giving away their contemplated course of conduct, since their actions are mutually interdependent. Alignment of conduct and parallel behaviour (tacit collusion) may be a rational response to characteristics of the relevant market even if the parties do not explicitly collude. The question of whether parallel behaviour, such as identical simultaneous price rises, constitutes a concerted practice or will furnish proof of a concerted practice. The CJ's important judgment in *Wood Pulp*[306] is examined in Chapter 9. Chapter 9 also explores further the circumstances in which exchanges of information (direct or indirect) between undertakings may constitute an infringement of the rules.

f. Concerted Practice and Vertical Arrangements

A concerted practice may be operated horizontally between colluding competitors but also vertically between a manufacturer and its distributors. In *Pioneer*,[307] for example, the Commission found that Pioneer and its European exclusive distributors had engaged in concerted practices to prevent the parallel import of Pioneer products from the UK and Germany into France.

(iv) Decisions by Associations of Undertakings

a. Medium for a Cartel

Of course, trade and other associations perform a plethora of legitimate functions which promote the competitiveness of the industry as a whole. However, membership of an association, particularly a trade association, may also tempt the undertakings meeting within its auspices to collude together and to coordinate their action. Indeed, studies have shown that where players wish to coordinate their action on a market, coordination through a trade association or some other vehicle may be critical when there are a relatively large number of players on the market.

Trade associations can play a particularly important role when [a] cartel involves a large number of firms. Hay and Delley (1974) found that trade associations were involved in more than 80 per cent of the cartels they studied that had more than 15 members, and in 100 per cent of cartels with more than 25 members. Levenstein and Suslow (2006) found that 29 per cent of the cartels in their sample involved trade associations.

---

[305] *Argos Ltd and Littlewoods Ltd* v. *OFT, JJB Sports plc* v. *OFT* [2006] EWCA Civ 1318, para. 91. The Court of Appeal held, however, that the higher substantive test was satisfied on the facts.

[306] Case C-89/85, *Ahlström Osakeyhtiö* v. *Commission* [1993] ECR I-1307.

[307] [1980] OJ L60/1. The finding that Pioneer had participated in the concerted practices was upheld on appeal: see Cases 100–103/80, *SA Musique Diffusion française SA* v. *Commission* [1983] ECR 1825, see especially paras. 75–76. See also Case 86/82, *Hasselblad (GB) Ltd* v. *Commission* [1984] ECR 883, paras. 24–29 and Case T-43/92, *Dunlop Slazenger International Ltd* v. *Commission* [1994] ECR-II 441 and, in the UK, Case 1022/1/1/03, *JJB Sports plc* v. *Office of Fair Trading* [2004] CAT 17, paras. 150–163, 637–670 aff'd [2006] EWCA Civ 1318.

In 2003 the Commission found Treuhand AG, a Swiss consultancy, guilty of cartel behaviour because it facilitated a cartel even though it did not itself produce or sell the relevant product. The actual cartel was for organic peroxides and included Akzo Group, Atofina SA and Peroxid Chemic GmbH. The Commission found that AC-Treuhand had actively organised the cartel and provided support to it, such as organising meetings, providing and sharing information and storing contracts.[308]

In *Re Belgian Roofing Felt Cartel*,[309] for example, an agreement was discovered between members of Belasco (Société Coopérative des Asphalteurs Belges) which was intended to ensure control of the Belgian roofing market. The parties had agreed, amongst other things, to adopt a common price list and minimum selling prices for roofing felt, to set quotas for sales on the Belgian market, and to advertise jointly their 'Belasco' products. The agreement was implemented by resolutions passed at the general meeting of Belasco. Belasco actively participated in the operations in a number of ways: in particular, it employed an accountant who monitored compliance with quotas at the end of each year so that penalties could be levied on members which had exceeded their quotas. Further, Belasco financed the joint advertising of the 'Belasco' trade mark which fostered users' impression of a homogeneous product. Members were not, therefore, able to compete by differentiating their products.

It may be that the conduct adopted by the members may be characterised as a decision or an agreement or a concerted practice. However, conduct may be prohibited even if technically speaking no agreement or concerted practice has been concluded. The prohibition of decisions as well as agreements and concerted practices may therefore facilitate the proof and prohibition of collusive devices operated through associations. The concept has been interpreted broadly to catch conduct designed to coordinate the conduct of the members contrary to Article 101(1),[310] whether engaged in through resolutions of the association, recommendations, the operation of certification schemes, or through the association's constitution itself.

b. Trade Association Recommendations

A recommendation by an association to its members, which has no binding effect, will constitute a decision, if in reality it is intended to determine, or is likely to have the effect of determining, the members' conduct. In *IAZ*,[311] a recommendation made by an association of water-supply undertakings that its members should not connect 'unauthorised' appliances (without a conformity label supplied by another Belgian trade association) to the mains systems was held to be a binding decision capable of restricting competition within the meaning of Article 101(1). The practice discriminated against non-Belgian producers of the appliances. Similarly, in *FENEX*,[312] the Commission held that the recommendation of tariffs by a Dutch association to its member forwarding companies constituted a decision by an association of undertakings within the meaning of Article 101(1). Although the tariffs merely took the form of recommendations, the procedure for drawing up and circulating the tariffs was a habitual activity of the association and was accompanied by circulars drafted in more mandatory terms. The Commission concluded that the circulation of the tariffs had to be interpreted as a faithful reflection of the association's resolve to coordinate the conduct of its members on the relevant market.

c. Medium for Exchange of Information

More subtly, the association may simply collect and disseminate sensitive information and facilitate its exchange between competitors. Were the association to be used, for example, as a vehicle for

---

[308] S. Bishop and M. Walker, *The Economics of EC Competition Law: Concepts, Application and Measurement* (3rd edn, Sweet & Maxwell, 2010), para. 5.016, see also Chap. 9.

[309] Case 246/86, *Re Roofing Felt Cartel: S.C. Belasco v. Commission* [1989] ECR 2117.

[310] Case 96/82, *NV IAZ International Belgium v. Commission* [1983] ECR 3369.

[311] *Anseau* [1982] OJ L167/39, on appeal Case 96/82, *NV IAZ International Belgium v. Commission* [1983] ECR 3369.

[312] [1996] OJ L181/28.

exchanging information on the prices that the members intended to charge for their products, etc., the parties would inevitably be found to be operating a concerted practice.[313]

d. Certification Schemes

Certification schemes operated by members of an association may, in reality, be designed to exclude non-members from business opportunities or to preclude foreign undertakings from penetrating the domestic market of the association's members.[314] The word 'decision', in addition to catching acts of the association which are binding on its members, may also catch these types of more informal methods of coordinating members' actions. In *Stichting Certificatie Kraanverhuurbedrijf and the Federatie van Nederlandse Kraanbedrijven v. Commission*,[315] the Commission fined both FNK and SCK after an examination of agreements that they had notified.[316] Not only did the rules of FNK (the rules constituted a decision by an association of undertakings) providing for the charging of 'reasonable' rates by its members infringe Article 101(1), but SCK's rules on the certification of the crane-hire trade were also caught. The prohibition on the certificate holders from hiring cranes from non-affiliated firms without valid certification plates (and not affiliated to SCK) restricted competition between affiliated firms and substantially restricted access to the market by other firms.

The individual members themselves may be fined where membership coincides with participation in the agreement. Further, where the Commission finds that there has been a 'decision' by an association of undertakings, the association may be fined independently. In *Re Belgian Roofing Felt Cartel*,[317] for example, fines were imposed on both Belasco itself and the individual members of the cartel.[318]

e. The Trade Association's Constitution

The constitution and rules of a trade association may themselves qualify as a decision (and an agreement) within Article 101(1).[319]

f. Governmental Intervention

The fact that a governmental body has either approved of or even imposed an obligation on an association to adopt a scale of compulsory tariffs for the association's members does not alter any resolution's (or other decision's) status as a decision of an association of undertakings.[320]

(v) Complex Arrangements and Single Continuous Infringements

A cartel operated through an agreement or concerted practice can consist of a whole complex set of arrangements spread out over a number of different countries and over a lengthy period

---

[313] See Cases 40–48, 50, 54–56, 111, and 113–114/73, *Re the European Sugar Cartel; Coöperatieve Vereniging 'Suiker Unie' UA v. Commission* [1975] ECR 1663. See also *UK Agricultural Tractor Exchange* [1992] OJ L68/19, upheld on appeal, Case T-34/92, *Fiatagri and Ford New Holland v. Commission* [1994] ECR II-905, and Case T-35/92, *John Deere Ltd v. Commission* [1994] ECR II-957, on appeal to the CJ Case C-7/95 P, *John Deere Ltd v. Commission* [1998] ECR I-3111, see Chap 9.

[314] As in *Anseau* [1982] OJ L167/39, on appeal Case 96/82, *IAZ International Belgium NV v. Commission* [1983] ECR 3369. See also Case 8/72, *Vereeniging van Cementhandelaren v. Commission* [1972] ECR 977.

[315] *Stichting Certificatie Kraanverhuurbedrijf and Federatie van Nederlandse Kraanbedrijven* [1995] OJ L312/79; on appeal Cases T-213/95 and T-18/96, *Stichting Certificatie Kraanverhuurbedrijf and Federatie van Nederlandse Kraanbedrijven v. Commission* [1997] ECR II-1739.

[316] After a preliminary examination of the agreements ([1994] OJ L117/30), the Commission had suspended the parties' immunity from fines that arose on the notification of an agreement to the Commission (Reg. 17 [1959–62] OJ Spec. Ed. 87, Art. 15(6)).

[317] [1986] OJ L232/15; on appeal Case 246/86, *Re Roofing Felt Cartel: S.C. Belasco v. Commission* [1989] ECR 2117.

[318] Reg. 1/2003 altered the fining system to make it more effective against trade associations, see Chap. 13.

[319] *National Sulphuric Acid* [1980] OJ L260/24.

[320] *AICIA v. CNSD* [1993] OJ L203/27, paras. 42–44.

of time. Where a cartel operates, for example, on a global basis it may also involve a number of sub-agreements operated in different countries and some firms may leave and others may join during its tenure. In such cases it may be necessary to determine the scope of the cartel (in terms of product and geographical reach) as well as the time period over which it operated and its members—for example, whether the arrangements are sufficiently linked that it can be said that there is one global cartel or whether there are a number of smaller national cartels. The concept of a single continuing infringement is '[d]esigned to capture the dynamic of one and the same cartel under Article [101] '[321] operated over a period of time (as opposed to multiple separate cartel agreements). The Commission summarised the nature of the concept in the *Consumer Detergents* case:[322]

36. A complex cartel may properly be viewed as a single and continuous infringement for the time frame in which it existed. The General Court has pointed out that the concept of 'single agreement' or 'single infringement' presupposes a complex of practices adopted by various parties in pursuit of a single anti-competitive economic aim. The cartel may well be varied from time to time, or its mechanisms adapted or strengthened to take account of new developments. It would be artificial to split up such continuous conduct, characterised by a single purpose, by treating it as consisting of several separate infringements, when what was involved was a single infringement which progressively would manifest itself in both agreements and concerted practices.

37. The mere fact that each participant in a cartel may play the role which is appropriate to its own specific circumstances does not exclude its responsibility for the infringement as a whole, including acts committed by other participants but which share the same anticompetitive object or effect. An undertaking which takes part in the common unlawful enterprise by actions which contribute to the realisation of the shared objective is equally responsible, for the whole period of its adherence to the common scheme, for the acts of the other participants pursuant to the same infringement. This is certainly the case where it is established that the undertaking in question was aware of the unlawful behaviour of the other participants or could have reasonably foreseen it and was prepared to take the risk.

Harding and Joshua note the huge significance of the concept, some of its salient features, the difficulties in definition, and that, because of the consequences that follow, the finding of a wider single continuous cartel is usually in the interest of the Commission.

C. Harding and J. Joshua, *Regulating Cartels in Europe* (Oxford University Press, 2nd edn, 2010), 175–177

Aggregation into a single infringement may well increase the size of the market and extent of trade affected, increase the number of participants, and perhaps extend the duration, all of which would add to the gravity of the infringement and justify higher fines. For the participants, there may be exposure to additional legal risks, notably prosecution in other jurisdictions, the transfer of the liability of core players to minor actors, and increased exposure to consequent civil liability claims. Time bars may be removed in relation to earlier activities, now joined to more recent cartel operations. The only possible consolation for cartel participants would be the capping of penalties in terms of the maximum which might be imposed for a single infringement...

---

[321] J. Joshua, 'Single Continuous Infringement of Article 81 EC: Has the Commission Stretched the Concept Beyond the Limit of its Logic?' (2009) 5 *European Competition Journal* 451, 451. The author states at 452: '[d]eriving its rationale from the temporal dimension of the common law conspiracy as "an agreement with a continuance in time", the continuing infringement concept was also intended, by focusing on bad conduct as much as on the element of consensus, to capture and translate to an EC context the "offensiveness" implicit in criminal conspiracy'. See also D. Bailey, 'Single, Overall Agreement in EU Competition Law' [2010] 47 *CMLRev* 473

[322] IP/11/473, 13 April 2011, paras. 36–37.

On the other hand, the consequences of disaggregation or decortications into multiple separate cartels are various. On the whole it is likely to increase prosecution effort and costs, it may multiply the involvement of different enforcement agencies, and complicate the legal process, especially the management of leniency applications... There is likely to be a larger number of smaller fines, which may or may not in aggregate match the larger single fine resulting from the single infringement. On the other hand, there may be a prosecutorial advantage in disaggregation, if this allows large corporate structures to be broken down, so that different companies within the same group may be dealt with in relation to separate cartels according to their different involvement in the same market.

Such considerations confirm the significance of the criteria for cartel definition and deciding whether there may be a single or multiple cartels. In... reviewing the activities of alleged cartel participants, the [GC] has used a vocabulary of 'complementary' action as descriptive of single infringement and cartel: the acts must be 'closely linked', an 'integrated set of arrangements', 'interwoven and uninterrupted', or be bound together by a 'sufficient definite and decisive causal link'. Evidence of such complementarity would include, in the Court's view, the period of application, the objective, and the content, including the methods used. More specifically, the Commission in its decisions on cartels has identified a number of 'objective elements' as indicia of a single infringement: common objective; similarity of products or services; similarity of behaviour in different geographical areas, commonality of membership, modus operandi, personnel, and the nature of meetings. But the factual complexities of and variations as between actual cases may render the organization of such criteria for purposes of overall assessment a difficult matter. As Joshua has commented:

...rarely does the Commission explain how the components are interlinked or what degree of knowledge is required. No doubt the Commission often reaches the 'right' solution intuitively. The danger is that if the exercise becomes a mere recitation, it fuels accusation that the result is 'political'. It also does not help that, to the extent the Commission has developed and articulated any principled test, its application on the ground is not entirely consistent... if the distinction between a single and many conspiracies is clear enough conceptually, its empirical application is beset with difficulty.

Part of the problem is the organizational complexity of some cartels, which may have core and minor memberships, national or regional subsets, and an overarching or 'global' coordination, all of which may be matters of evidential difficulty. Some cartels may resemble 'hub and spoke' conspiracies, with which there may be little awareness on the spoke of the main or core conspiracy at the hub. It may be necessary for regulators and courts to master a complex factual scenario in order to define the limits of a cartel and thus the extent of liability.

It may be argued that a convincing and reliable test may be based on elements of interdependence and knowledge. 'Interdependence' describes well the idea of a chain of activities which all contribute in a necessary and decisive way to the goals of the cartel organization—the resulting network of activity of linked but crucial actions defines the infrastructure and scope of the cartel. But it is also necessary for this interdependent activity to be performed with knowledge of its purpose and significance, an awareness which characterizes the action and also supplies a justifiable mental element as a basis for liability. Thus in the *Treuhand* case, the consultancy firm was aware that its servicing of the cartel's activities was a necessary part of the success of those activities. On the other hand, in the *Choline Chloride Cartel*...[t]he earlier involvement of the American and Canadian companies was not necessary or decisive for the later operation of the cartel in Europe. A *knowing interdependence* may therefore be put forward as a test of cartel scope and perpetrator liability, separating 'core' involvement from acts of ancillary, unknowing, and uninformed support for minor actors who are thus outside the cartel and not liable in a significant way for the cartel's activity.

Cartel identification and definition is thus an issue of some complexity, but one that must be mastered, since the existence and identify of the cartel must first be proven for the offence or infringement to be properly prosecuted. A crucial problem would seem to be that of sorting the peripheral accessory players and their activities from the essential participation.

The concept of a single continuous infringement was first used in *Polypropylene*,[323] a case concerning a long-lasting cartel in the petrochemical industry. Fifteen firms were held by the Commission to have infringed the competition rules by participating in a framework agreement to fix prices and sales volumes. The Commission considered that the cartel, which was based on an overall framework agreement or a common and detailed plan manifested in a series of more detailed sub-agreements worked out from time to time, constituted a single continuing agreement for the purpose of Article 101(1). Some firms claimed they were not liable as they had not participated in all aspects of the arrangements. The GC held that the Commission was justified in treating the entire course of the collusion as one single agreement. For there to be an 'agreement' for the purposes of Article 101(1) it was sufficient for the undertakings to have 'expressed their joint intention to conduct themselves on the market in a specific way'.[324] In this case the undertakings had, throughout the whole course of the arrangements, pursued the single economic aim of distorting the polypropylene market.

Since then the Commission has frequently relied on the concept which has facilitated the application of Article 101 to cartels 'which are "not born fully grown" but develop organically as the members conceive ever more sophisticated ways to achieve their objectives while reducing the risk of detection'.[325] It may also avoid the application of the five-year limitation period by finding that old conduct forms part of an agreement which has endured over a long period.[326] In the *Graphite Electrodes*[327] cartel, the Commission explained that:

A complex cartel may thus properly be viewed [as] a single continuing infringement for the time frame in which it existed. The agreement may well be varied from time to time, or its mechanisms adapted or strengthened to take account of new developments. The validity of this assessment is not affected by the possibility that one or more elements of a series of actions or of a continuous course of conduct could individually and in themselves constitute a violation of Article 101(1) of the Treaty.[328]

In *Bananas*, the GC also confirmed that three competitors which had engaged in bilateral price communications with each other (between A and B, A and C, and B and C) were party to a single anti-competitive arrangement even if individually they had not been aware of communications exchanged between the others (for example A was not aware of exchanges between B and C):

an undertaking which has participated in a single and complex infringement by its own conduct, which [met] the definition of an agreement or concerted practice having an anti-competitive object within the meaning of Article [101(1)] and was intended to help bring about the infringement as a whole, may also be responsible for the conduct of other undertakings followed in the context of the same infringement throughout the period of its participation in the infringement ....

Further, it held that it is 'clear that the concept of single infringement can be applied to the legal characterisation of anti-competitive conduct consisting of agreements, of concerted practices and of decisions of associations of undertakings, but also to the personal nature of liability for the

---

[323] *Polypropylene* [1986] OJ L230/1; on appeal Cases T-1/89, *Rhône-Poulenc v. Commission* [1991] ECR II-867; T-2/89, *Petrofina SA v. Commission* [1991] ECR II-1087; T-3/89 *Atochem v. Commission* [1991] ECR II-1177; T-6/89, *Enichem Anic SpA v. Commission* [1991] ECR II-1623; T-7/89, *SA Hercules Chemicals NV v. Commission* [1991] ECR II-1711, etc. The appeals by the companies to the CJ were broadly dismissed: see Case C-51/92 P, *Hercules Chemicals NC v. Commission* [1999] ECR I-4235; Case C-199/92 P, *Hüls AG v. Commission* [1999] ECR I-4287; *ICI v. Commission* [1999] ECR I-4399, etc., although the appeal by the Commission against the partial annulment of its decision against Enichem was mainly successful, Case C-49/92 P, *Commission v. Anic Partecipazioni* [1999] ECR I-4125.

[324] See especially Case T-1/89, *Rhône-Poulenc v. Commission* [1991] ECR II-867, para. 120, relying on Case 41/69, *ACF Chemiefarma NV v. Commission* [1970] ECR 661, para. 112.

[325] Joshua, 'Single Continuous Infringement of Article 81 EC', cited in n. 321, at 459.

[326] But see Cases T-101/05, etc., *BASF v. Commission* [2007] ECR II-4949 where the Commission's finding of a single continuous agreement was not upheld and the decision found to be time-barred. Occasionally, fines may be maximised by finding not a single cartel but a series of cartels over a number of different markets, see Chap. 13.

[327] *Graphite Electrodes* [2002] OJ L100/1. See also, e.g., T-53/03, *British Plasterboard v. Commission* [2008] ECR II-1333.

[328] [2002] OJ L100/1, para. 103.

infringement of the competition law rules'.[329] Where therefore the infringement results from a series of acts or from continuous conduct forming part of an overall plan, with the same object of distorting competition, the Commission may be entitled to attribute liability on the basis of participation in the infringement as a whole, even if it is established that the undertaking concerned directly participated in only one of some of the constituent elements of the infringement. This will be the case, for example, where the undertaking concerned intended to contribute by its own conduct to the common objectives pursued by all the participants and was aware of the actual conduct planned or put into effect by the other undertakings in pursuit of the same objectives or that it could reasonably have foreseen it and that it was prepared to take the risk.

In *Trelleborg Industrie v. Commission*,[330] an appeal from the Commission's *Marine Hoses* decision, the GC set out the salient features of a single and continuous infringement and distinguished these from single, repeated infringements. The GC explained that as in cartel cases the existence of an infringement frequently had to be pieced together from fragmentary evidence (see further Chapter 9), coincidences and indicia might be relied on to provide information not only about the mere existence of anti-competitive practices or agreements, but also about their duration or the period of application. Thus the Commission might be entitled to support a finding of continuous infringement by relying on evidence that actions formed part of an overall plan—for example, establishing the identical nature of the objectives of the practices at issue, the identical nature of the undertakings which participated in the infringement, the identical nature of the detailed rules for its implementation, the fact that the natural persons involved on behalf of the undertakings and/or the geographical scope of the practices are identical—even if evidence of the infringement has not been produced in relation to all specific periods.[331]

Cases T-147 and 148/09 *Trelleborg Industrie* v. *Commission* 17 May 2013

General Court

– The existence of a continuous infringement

57 It should be borne in mind that, in most cases, the existence of an anti-competitive practice or agreement must be inferred from a number of coincidences and indicia which, taken together, may, in the absence of another plausible explanation, constitute evidence of an infringement of the competition rules. Such coincidences and indicia, when evaluated overall, may provide information not just about the mere existence of anti-competitive practices or agreements, but also about the duration of continuous anti-competitive practices or the period of application of anti-competitive agreements (see, to that effect, *Aalborg Portland and Others* v *Commission*, paragraph 52 above, paragraph 57, and Case C-105/04 P *Nederlandse Federatieve Vereniging voor de Groothandel op Elektrotechnisch Gebied* v *Commission* . . ., paragraphs 94 to 96 . . .).

58 Furthermore, such an infringement may be the consequence not only of an isolated act but also of a series of acts or indeed of continuous conduct. That interpretation cannot be challenged on the ground that one or more elements of that series of acts or of that continuous conduct might also constitute in themselves, and taken in isolation, an infringement of the competition rules. Where the various actions form part of an 'overall plan', owing to their identical object, which distorts competition within the common market, the Commission is entitled to impute liability for those actions

---

[329] Cases T-587/08 *Fresh Del Monte Produce v. Commission*, 14 March 2013, paras. 587–588, on appeal Cases C-293 and 294/13 P (judgments pending).

[330] Cases T-147 and 148/09, 17 May 2013.

[331] Cases T-147 and 148/09, 17 May 2013, paras. 50–71.

according to participation in the infringement considered as a whole (see *Aalborg Portland and Others* v *Commission*, ... paragraph 258 and *Nederlandse Federatieve Vereniging voor de Groothandel op Elektrotechnisch Gebied* v *Commission*, ... paragraph 110).

59 As regards the lack of evidence that there was an agreement during certain specific periods or, at least, the lack of evidence of its implementation by an undertaking during a given period, it should be recalled that the fact that evidence of the infringement has not been produced in relation to certain specific periods does not preclude the infringement from being regarded as established during a longer overall period than those periods, provided that such a finding is supported by objective and consistent indicia. In the context of an infringement extending over a number of years, the fact that a cartel is shown to have applied during different periods, which may be separated by longer or shorter periods, has no effect on the existence of the cartel, provided that the various actions which form part of the infringement pursue a single purpose and fall within the framework of a single and continuous infringement (*Nederlandse Federatieve Vereniging voor de Groothandel op Elektrotechnisch Gebied* v *Commission*, ... paragraphs 97 and 98; see also, to that effect, *Aalborg Portland and Others* v *Commission*, ... paragraph 260).

60 In that regard, several criteria have been identified by the case-law as relevant for assessing whether there is a single infringement, namely the identical nature of the objectives of the practices at issue (Case T-21/99 *Dansk Rørindustri* v *Commission* ... paragraph 67; see also, to that effect, Case C-113/04 P *Technische Unie* v *Commission* ... paragraphs 170 and 171; and Case T-43/02 *Jungbunzlauer* v *Commission* ... paragraph 312), the identical nature of the goods or services concerned (see, to that effect, judgment of 15 June 2005 in Joined Cases T-71/03, T-74/03, T-87/03 and T-91/03 *Tokai Carbon and Others* v *Commission*, ... paragraphs 118, 119 and 124, and *Jungbunzlauer* v *Commission*, paragraph 312), the identical nature of the undertakings which participated in the infringement (*Jungbunzlauer* v *Commission*, paragraph 312), and the identical nature of the detailed rules for its implementation (*Dansk Rørindustri* v *Commission*, paragraph 68). Furthermore, whether the natural persons involved on behalf of the undertakings are identical and whether the geographical scope of the practices at issue is identical are also factors which may be taken into consideration for the purposes of that examination.

61 The case-law therefore permits the Commission to assume that the infringement—or the participation of an undertaking in the infringement—has not been interrupted, even if it has no evidence of the infringement in relation to certain specific periods, provided that the various actions which form part of the infringement pursue a single purpose and are capable of falling within the framework of a single and continuous infringement; such a finding must be supported by objective and consistent indicia showing that an overall plan exists.

62 If those conditions are satisfied, the concept of continuous infringement ... allows the Commission to impose a fine in respect of the whole of the period of infringement taken into consideration and establishes the date on which the limitation period begins to run, namely the date on which the continuous infringement ceased.

63 However, the undertakings accused of collusion may attempt to rebut that presumption by submitting indicia and evidence proving that, on the contrary, the infringement—or their participation in it—did not continue during those same periods.

C. OBJECT OR EFFECT OF THE PREVENTION, RESTRICTION, OR DISTORTION OF COMPETITION

Agreements and other collusive practices are not prohibited unless they have as their object or the effect the prevention, restriction, or distortion of competition. The way in which this phrase is interpreted determines the types of agreements which are prohibited and the scope of application of Article 101(1). Further, the way in which Article 101(1) is interpreted has a crucial impact on the role played by and the interpretation of Article 101(3)—as the latter excepts from the Article 101(1) prohibition agreements which satisfy its conditions. The relationship and interaction of these two paragraphs and the question of what issues should be considered under each Article has caused enormous controversy and is fully explored in Chapter 4.

D. AN APPRECIABLE EFFECT ON COMPETITION AND TRADE

The CJ has held that 'in order to come within the prohibition imposed by Article [101], the agreement must affect trade between Member States and the free play of competition to an appreciable extent'.[332] The concept of appreciability was accepted by the CJ in *Völk v. Vervaecke*.

Case 5/69, *Völk* v. *Vervaecke* [1969] ECR 295, 302

The case concerned an exclusive distribution agreement concluded between Mr Völk, the owner of a company, Erd & Co, which manufactured washing machines, and Vervaecke, a Belgian company which distributed household electrical appliances. Under the agreement, Vervaecke had the exclusive right to sell Völk's products in Belgium and Luxembourg. According to the Commission, Erd & Co had only 0.08 per cent of the market for the production of washing machines EU wide, 0.2 per cent of the market in Germany and 0.6 per cent of the market in Belgium and Luxembourg. Following a dispute which raised the validity of the agreement before the German courts, the Oberlandesgericht in Munich made an Article 234 reference to the EU Courts. In particular, it asked the CJ whether, in considering if an agreement fell within Article 101(1), regard had to be had to the proportion of the market that the grantor had.

Court of Justice

If an agreement is to be capable of affecting trade between Member States it must be possible to foresee with a sufficient degree of probability on the basis of a set of objective factors of law or of fact that the agreement in question may have an influence, direct or indirect, actual or potential, on the pattern of trade between Member States in such a way that it might hinder the attainment of the objectives of a single market between States. Moreover the prohibition in Article [101(1)] is applicable only if the agreement in question also has as its object or effect the prevention, restriction or distortion of competition within the common market. Those conditions must be understood by reference to the actual circumstances of the agreement. Consequently an agreement falls outside the prohibition in Article [101] when it has only an insignificant effect on the markets, taking into account the weak position which the persons concerned have on the market of the product in question. Thus an exclusive dealing agreement, even with absolute territorial protection, may, having regard to the weak position of the persons concerned on the market in the products in question in the area covered by the absolute protection, escape the prohibition laid down in Article [101(1)].

This case clarifies that EU law is not concerned with agreements, even those containing severe restraints,[333] concluded between parties that hold a weak position on the market and which have an insignificant effect on intra-community trade and/or on competition. The insignificant position held by the undertakings causes the EU institutions to take the view that the agreement cannot possibly

---

[332] Case 22/71, *Béguelin Import Co.* v. *S.A.G.L. Import Export* [1971] ECR 949, para. 16. The text of Art. 101(1) does not require that the effect on competition or trade should be appreciable.

[333] In *Völk*, the distributor had been granted absolute territorial protection, which has as its object the restriction of competition, Case 5/69, *Völk* v. *Vervaecke* [1969] ECR 295, 302. See also Case C-306/96, *Javico International and Javico AG* v. *Yves Saint Laurent Parfums SA* [1998] ECR I-1983, para. 17. Object restraints and appreciability are discussed more fully in Chap. 4.

threaten the EU objectives.[334] The Commission's interpretation of appreciability is now fleshed out in two separate notices—one dealing with the effect on trade concept (see further Section 5.E.viii) and one dealing with agreements of minor importance which do not appreciably restrict competition (see Chapter 4).

E. AN APPRECIABLE EFFECT ON TRADE BETWEEN MEMBER STATES

(i) Jurisdictional Limit

The concept of an effect on trade between Member States sets out a jurisdictional limit to the prohibition laid down in Article 101 (it is also a requirement that any abuse of a dominant position should affect trade for the purposes of Article 102). The criterion confines the scope of the application of Articles 101 and 102 to agreements having a minimum level of cross-border effects within the EU, hence the practices must *appreciably* affect trade between Member States.[335] Since the requirement is merely viewed as a jurisdictional matter, it has been interpreted broadly, although it is accepted that the EU has no jurisdiction over cases in which the effects of an agreement, or conduct, are confined to one Member State.[336] The meaning of an effect on trade has been clarified in the case law. The Commission has also prepared a notice on the concept of effect on trade between Member States[337] which seeks to set out the principles developed by the Court and to spell out when agreements and conduct may 'appreciably' affect trade between Member States. It aims 'to set out the methodology for the application of the effect on trade concept and to provide guidance on its application in frequently occurring situations'.[338] In paragraphs 58–109 of the guidelines it applies the general principles set out in the cases to common types of agreements and abuses, for example: different types of agreements and abuse covering or implemented in several Member States; agreements and abuses covering a single or only part of a Member State; agreements and abuses involving imports and exports with undertakings located in third countries; and agreements and practices involving undertakings located in third countries. The guidelines are, of course, without prejudice to the interpretation given to the concept by the EU Courts.[339]

(ii) The Tests

The Commission's notice stresses, relying on case law of the Court,[340] that '[t]he concept of "trade" is not limited to traditional exchanges of goods and services across borders. It is a wider concept, covering all cross-border economic activity, including establishment. This interpretation is consistent with the fundamental objective of the Treaty to promote free movement of goods, services, persons and capital'.[341] An agreement will be found to 'affect trade' if it interferes with the pattern of trade between Member States.[342] There must be an impact on the flow of goods and services or

---

[334] Rather, it is more appropriate that they should be examined, if at all, within the framework of national competition legislation.

[335] Guidelines on the effect on trade concept contained in Arts 81 and 82 of the Treaty (Guidelines on the effect on trade concept) [2004] OJ C101/81, para. 13.

[336] Case 22/78, *Hugin v. Commission* [1979] ECR 1869.

[337] [2004] OJ C101/81.

[338] Guidelines on the effect on trade concept, para. 3.

[339] Guidelines on the effect on trade concept, para. 5.

[340] See, e.g., Case 172/80, *Zürchner v. Bayerische Vereinsbank AG* [1981] ECR 2021, para. 18, and Case C-309/99, *Wouters v. Algemene Raad van de Nederlandse Orde van Advocaten* [2002] ECR I-1577, Case C-41/90, *Höfner and Elser v. Macrotron* [1991] ECR I-1979.

[341] Guidelines on the effect on trade concept, para. 19.

[342] Case 56/65, *Société Technique Minière v. Maschinenbau Ulm GmbH* [1966] ECR 235.

other relevant economic activities involving at least two Member States. An agreement or practice may also be found to affect trade if it is liable to interfere with the structure of competition in the common market, for example where it eliminates or threatens to eliminate competitors operating within the Union. This latter structural test is more commonly used in the context of Article 102 than Article 101.[343]

(iii) Pattern of Trade Test

In *Société Technique Minière* v. *Maschinenbau Ulm*,[344] the CJ set out a broad interpretation of the requirement that an agreement should affect trade so that it is easily satisfied. All that is necessary is that 'it must be possible to foresee with a sufficient degree of probability on the basis of a set of objective factors of law or of fact that the agreement in question may have an influence, direct or indirect, actual or potential, on the pattern of trade between Member States …'.[345]

The test requires the following to be shown:

(a) a sufficient degree of probability on the basis of a set of objective factors of law of fact;[346]

(b) an influence on the pattern of trade between Member States;[347]

(c) a direct or indirect, actual or potential influence on the pattern of trade.[348]

An agreement will, therefore, be caught even if it is not established that the agreement will affect the pattern of trade if it can be shown that it is *capable* of having such an effect,[349] for example, if it is anticipated that it will affect the pattern of trade in the future. As it is only a jurisdictional criterion it is not necessary to establish that it actually has cross-border effects. Relevant factors to the determination will be: the nature of the agreement and practice; the nature of the products; and the position and importance of the undertakings involved.

The fact that the influence on trade need only be direct, indirect, actual, or potential means that a broad range of agreements will be caught including, for example: agreements affecting goods or services that are not traded, but which are used in the supply of a final product, which is traded;[350] agreements which do not actually affect trade but which, taking account of foreseeable market developments, may affect trade in the future. In *AEG* v. *Commission*,[351] the CJ held that the fact that there was little inter-State trade did not mean that Article 101(1) was inapplicable if it could reasonably be expected that the patterns of trade in the future might change. The Commission states, however, that the inclusion of indirect and potential effects in the analysis of effects on trade between Member States does not mean that the analysis can be based on remote, hypothetical, or speculative effects.

For instance, an agreement that raises the prices of a product which is not tradable reduces the disposable income of consumers. As consumers have less money to spend they may purchase fewer products imported from other Member States. However, the link between such income effects and trade between Member States is generally in itself too remote to establish [EU] law jurisdiction.[352]

---

[343] See Case 6–7/73, *Istituto Chemioterapico Italiano SpA and Commercial Solvents Corp* v. *Commission* [1974] ECR 223, especially para. 5, and Chap. 5.

[344] Case 56/65, [1966] ECR 235.

[345] Case 56/65, *Société Technique Minière* v. *Maschinenbau Ulm GmbH* [1966] ECR 235, 249, and Case 5/69, *Völk* v. *Vervaecke* [1969] ECR 295, 302.

[346] Guidelines on the effect on trade concept, paras. 25–32.

[347] Guidelines on the effect on trade concept, paras. 33–35.

[348] Guidelines on the effect on trade concept, paras. 36–43.

[349] Guidelines on the effect on trade concept, para. 26.

[350] Case 123/83, *BNIC* v. *Clair* [1985] ECR 391, para. 29.

[351] Case 107/82, [1983] ECR 3151, para. 60; see also *AEI/Reyrolle Parsons re Vacuum Interrupters* [1977] OJ L48/32.

[352] Guidelines on the effect on trade concept, para. 43.

(iv) An Increase in Trade

In *Consten and Grundig*,[353] the parties argued before the CJ that their distribution agreement did not produce an effect on trade within the meaning of Article 101(1) since it increased trade between Member States (in the absence of the agreement, Grundig products might not have been sold in France at all). This argument was partially supported by a textual analysis of the Treaty since, in at least one language (Italian), the text suggested that the effect on trade should be a harmful or prejudicial one. The CJ[354] rejected this argument, ruling that 'the fact that an agreement encourages an increase, even a large one, in the volume of trade between states is not sufficient to exclude the possibility that the agreement may "affect" such trade…'.[355] Rather, it examined the contract, which precluded anyone other than Consten from importing Grundig products into France, and prohibited Consten from re-exporting the products into other Member States, concluding that it 'indisputably affects trade between Member States'. Instead of attempting to adopt a literal interpretation of the provision the CJ adopted an interpretation which respected the aims and spirit of the Treaty. It was important that agreements such as the exclusive distribution agreement at issue in that case should be capable of being scrutinised under the provisions. The aim of the Treaty was not to increase trade as an end in itself, but to create a system of undistorted competition. The CJ concluded that Article 101 applied to any agreement which might threaten the freedom of trade between Member States in a manner which might harm the attainment of the single market. The term pattern of trade is neutral, it is not a condition that trade is restricted or reduced.

(v) Partitioning of the Common Market

Many vertical agreements are capable of an effect on trade between Member States because of their tendency to incorporate territorial restrictions and their ability to partition the common market. It was seen in the extract in Section 5.B.ii.b that the CJ in *Consten and Grundig* found that the nature of the territorial restrictions was to affect trade. Similarly, other agreements concerning imports or exports, containing provisions sharing markets between a manufacturer and its distributor or between distributors *inter se* are capable of affecting trade between Member States.[356]

Even an agreement covering third countries and undertakings located in third countries may appreciably affect trade between Member States where it is capable of affecting cross-border economic activity inside the Union, for example an agreement preventing a distributor appointed for a territory outside the EU from making sales outside its contractual territory (and, consequently, into the EU). If, in the absence of the agreement, resale to the EU would be both possible and likely, it may be capable of affecting patterns of trade inside the EU.[357] Whether or not an agreement with an undertaking outside the EU will affect trade will depend on factors such as the object of the agreement (whether the object of the agreement is to restrict competition within the EU), the prices for the contractual products charged in the EU and those charged outside the EU, the level of customs duties, and transport costs.[358] Further, the product volumes exported compared to the total market for those products in the territory of the common market must not be insignificant.[359]

It is also possible that an agreement may have an effect on trade even if it does not appear to do so at first sight. The impact on inter-State trade may be revealed on a closer examination of the agreement.

[353] Cases 56 and 58/64, *Consten and Grundig* [1966] ECR 299.

[354] The argument was, however, supported by Roemer AG. He took the view that the effect on trade would have to be an unfavourable one before the prohibition applied.

[355] Cases 56 and 58/64, *Consten and Grundig* [1966] ECR 299, 341.

[356] Case 161/84, *Pronuptia de Paris GmbH v. Pronuptia de Paris Irmgard Schillgallis* [1986] ECR 353, para. 27.

[357] Case C-306/96, *Javico International and Javico AF v. Yves Saint Laurent Parfums SA* [1998] ECR I-1983, paras. 15–29.

[358] Case C-306/96, *Javico International and Javico AF v. Yves Saint Laurent Parfums SA* [1998] ECR I-1983, paras. 15–29.

[359] Case C-306/96, *Javico International and Javico AF v. Yves Saint Laurent Parfums SA* [1998] ECR I-1983, paras. 15–29.

In *Delimitis v. Henninger Bräu*,[360] for example, a beer-supply agreement between a German brewer and a German café proprietor imposed an obligation on the latter to purchase beer only from the brewer. In derogation from this obligation, however, it included an access clause permitting the café proprietor to purchase competing beer from suppliers in other Member States. The CJ ruled that the national court would have to examine the agreement in greater detail. It was critical to determine whether or not this 'access' clause was hypothetical or real. The contract obliged the café proprietor to purchase a specific quantity of the brewer's beer each year. It had to be determined, therefore, whether or not this clause stipulating the minimum quantity of the brewer's beer to be purchased in reality left the café proprietor with a real opportunity to purchase beer from brewers in other Member States. If it did not, the agreement would produce an effect on inter-State trade, despite the access clause. On the other hand, if the agreement left a real possibility for foreign brewers to supply the outlet, the agreement was not in principle capable of affecting trade between Member States.

(vi) Agreements Operating in One Member State

It tends to be assumed that an agreement between parties situated in different Member States affects trade between Member States.[361] It can be seen from *Delimitis* that an agreement which operates in only one Member State is also quite capable of affecting trade between Member States.

Similarly, national cartels, especially those dominating the whole or a large part of a market, tend to reinforce compartmentalisation and make it more difficult for undertakings from other Member States to penetrate the market.[362] The CJ has consistently held that the fact that a cartel relates only to the marketing of products in a single Member State is not sufficient to exclude the possibility that trade between Member States might be affected.[363] Indeed, the cartel is likely to be successful only if the members can defend themselves against foreign competition. If they do not, and the product covered by the agreement is tradable, the cartel is likely to be undermined by competition from undertakings in other Member States. The agreement in *Belasco*,[364] for example, specifically provided for protective and defensive measures to be taken against foreign undertakings. Where the relevant product or service affected by the cartel is easily transmissible across borders it is likely that an effect on trade will be found. A Dutch cartel agreement which operated in order to restrict competition in the market for mobile cranes was held to have an effect on intra-Union trade. Since the cranes could travel at speeds of between 63 and 78 k.p.h., the agreement was likely to affect German and Belgian firms operating near the Dutch border.[365] The Commission reached a similar conclusion in *Luxembourg Brewers*[366] in respect of a cartel designed to insulate the Luxembourg market against imports of beer from other Member States.

In *Carlo Bagnasco v. BPN*[367] and *Dutch Banks*,[368] the CJ and Commission respectively concluded that purely national banking agreements were not capable of affecting trade between Member States. *Bagnasco*, for example, concerned retail banking services (guarantees for current account credit

---

[360] Case C-234/89, [1991] ECR I-935.

[361] See, e.g., Guidelines on the effect on trade concept, paras. 61–72.

[362] Case 8/72, *Vereeniging van Cementhandelaren v. Commission* [1972] ECR 997. In Cases C-215 and 216/96, *Bagnasco v. Banca Popolare di Novara (BPN) and Cassa di Risparmio di Genova e Imperia SpA (Carige)* [1999] ECR I-135, paras. 38–53, however, the CJ held that standard bank conditions relating to the provision of general guarantees required to secure the opening of current account credit facilities in Italy did not have an appreciable effect on intra-Community trade within the meaning of Article 101(1).

[363] Case C-246/86, *S.C. Belasco v. Commission* [1989] ECR 2117, para. 33.

[364] Case C-246/86, *S.C. Belasco v. Commission* [1989] ECR 2117, paras. 35–38.

[365] *Stichting Certificatie Kraanverhuurbedrijf and Federatie van Nederlandse Kraanbedrijven* [1995] OJ L312/79.

[366] [2002] OJ L253/21, paras. 77–81.

[367] Case C-215/96, [1999] ECR I-135. See also Guidelines on the effect on trade concept, para. 60.

[368] [1991] OJ L271/28.

facilities) and the CJ considered that trade was not capable of being appreciably affected because the potential for trade in the products was very limited. The market was not particularly susceptible to imports and retail banking services were not an important factor affecting the choice made by undertakings from other Member States when determining whether or not to establish themselves in another Member State. Although somewhat out of line with other case law and decisions setting out extensive EU jurisdiction, the cases may be explicable by virtue of a reluctance to apply EU law to cases which essentially have a national impact and so can be dealt with at a national level. Post-modernisation, of course, such cases may be appraised by the appropriate NCA under Article 101 (if an effect on trade is found) as well as domestic law.[369]

(vii) Restrictions on Competition and Restrictions on Trade

It is clear that so long as the agreement as a whole affects trade between Member States it is immaterial that the clause (or clauses) which restricts competition does not itself affect trade.[370]

(viii) Agreements which Appreciably Affect Trade between Member States

The Commission's notice dealing with the effect on trade concept also deals with the quantitative element of the criterion, the question of when an agreement will *appreciably* affect trade between Member States.[371] It states that EU law limits jurisdiction to agreements and practices capable of having effects on trade of a certain magnitude. In particular, appreciability can be appraised by reference to the position and importance of the undertakings on the relevant market. The Commission considers that appreciability can be measured both in absolute terms (turnover) and in relative terms, comparing the position of the relevant undertakings with others on the market (market share).[372] In paragraphs 50–57, the Commission seeks to quantify appreciability, stressing however that the assessment depends on the circumstances of each individual case. It does, however, indicate when trade is normally not capable of being appreciably affected. It sets out a negative rebuttable presumption, defining the absence of an appreciable effect on trade between Member States (the NAAT-rule). In contrast to its notice on agreements of minor importance, the Commission states that the rule applies to *all* agreements irrespective of the restrictions contained within them (i.e. it applies even to agreements containing hardcore restraints).[373] Agreements which do not fall within its negative definition of appreciability do not, however, necessarily appreciably affect trade.

At paragraph 52 the Commission states its view that 'in principle agreements are not capable of appreciably affecting trade between Member States when the following *cumulative* conditions are met' (emphasis added):[374]

(a) The aggregate market share of the parties on any relevant market within the Community affected by the agreement does not exceed 5 per cent, and

---

[369] But see discussion of Reg. 1/2003, Art. 3 in Chap. 13.

[370] See Case 193/83, *Windsurfing International Inc v. Commission* [1986] ECR 611. This case is discussed in Chap. 12.

[371] Commission Guidelines on the effect on trade concept, paras. 44–57.

[372] Commission Guidelines on the effect on trade concept, para. 46.

[373] Commission Guidelines on the effect on trade concept, para. 50.

[374] The NAAT-rule does not apply in emerging markets. In such cases appreciability may have to be assessed on the basis of the position of the parties on related product markets or their strength in technologies relating to the agreement.

(b) In the case of horizontal agreements, the aggregate annual Community turnover of the undertakings concerned in the products covered by the agreement does not exceed 40 million Euro.[375] In case of agreements concerning joint buying of products the relevant turnover shall be the parties' combined purchases of the products covered by the agreement.

In the case of vertical agreements, the aggregate annual Community turnover of the supplier in the products covered by the agreement does not exceed 40 million Euro. In the case of licence agreements the relevant turnover shall be the aggregate turnover of the licensees in the products incorporating the licensed technology and the licensor's own turnover in such products. In cases involving agreements concluded between a buyer and several suppliers the relevant turnover shall be the buyer's combined purchase of the products covered by the agreement.

Paragraph 52 also provides marginal relief for those that outgrow the notice in two successive calendar years. In cases where the presumption applies the Commission will not normally institute proceedings. Further, where undertakings assumed in good faith that an agreement is covered by the negative presumption, the Commission will not impose fines.[376]

In contrast, paragraph 53 states that for agreements that, by their very nature, are capable of affecting trade between Member States, such as agreements concerning imports and exports or covering several Member States, there is a *rebuttable positive presumption* that the effects on trade are appreciable when the turnover of the parties exceeds 40 million Euro. It may also often be presumed that effects are appreciable where the 5 per cent threshold is exceeded. These rebuttable presumptions will obviously be of central importance when these issues are litigated before national courts.

(ix) The Relationship between EU and National Law

The breadth of the effect on trade criterion determines the scope of Regulation 1/2003, Article 3, which determines the relationship between Articles 101 and 102 and national law. The effect on trade criterion can therefore have a substantive outcome. Essentially, Article 3 provides that whenever an NCA or national court applies national competition laws to an agreement or practice that affects trade between Member States, it must also apply Articles 101 and 102. The application of national competition law may not, however, lead to the prohibition of agreements which affect trade between Member States but which do not restrict competition within the meaning of Article 101(1), or which fulfil the conditions of Article 101(3) or which are covered by an EU block exemption. Further, a national authority cannot authorise an agreement prohibited by EU law. The relationship between EU and national law is dealt with more fully in Chapter 13.

F. AGREEMENTS REQUIRED BY NATIONAL LEGISLATION OR ENCOURAGED BY NATIONAL GOVERNMENTS

National law or national regulatory regimes may affect competition in a market. Case law makes it clear that Article 101 is not applicable to anti-competitive activities of a firm if the restrictive effects on competition originate solely from the implementation of national law, for example, where national law requires an agreement or creates a framework eliminating any possible competitive conduct.[377] In such a case the anti-competitive effect results not from the autonomous conduct of

---

[375] The turnover threshold is calculated on the basis of total EU sales excluding tax during the last financial year by the undertakings concerned. Sales between entities that form part of the same undertaking are excluded, Commission Guidelines on the effect on trade concept, para. 54.

[376] Commission Guidelines on the effect on trade concept, para. 50.

[377] Where a Member State takes measures which lead to an infringement of the antitrust rules by a firm, the Commission may be able to issue an infringement decision against that State, see Chap. 8.

the firms but from the national law and not the agreement.[378] Article 101 is concerned with the conduct of undertakings and not with laws or regulations of Member States.[379]

Where, however, national law leaves room for competition, firms must comply with the competition rules. This position is clearly spelt out by the GC in its judgment in *Atlantic Container Line*.

Cases T-191 and 212–214/98, *Atlantic Container Line* v. *Commission* [2003] ECR II-3275, para. 1130

General Court

1130. According to the case-law, Articles [101] and [102] apply only to anti-competitive conduct in which undertakings engage on their own initiative. If anti-competitive conduct is required of undertakings by national law or if the latter creates a legal framework eliminating any possibility of competitive conduct on their part, Articles [101] and [102] do not apply. In such a situation, the restriction of competition is not attributable, as is implied by those provisions, to the autonomous conduct of the undertakings. Articles [101] and [102] may apply, by contrast, if it is found that the national legislation does not preclude undertakings from engaging in autonomous conduct which prevents, restricts or distorts competition (Joined Cases C-359/95 P and C-379/95 P *Commission and France* v. *Ladbroke Racing* . . ., paragraph 33; . . . in Case C-198/01 *Consorzia Industrie Fiammiferi*, paragraphs 52 to 55, and Case C-207/01 *Altair Chimica*, paragraphs 30, 35 and 36; Case T-111/96 *ITT Promédia* v. *Commission* . . ., paragraph 96; *Irish Sugar* . . ., paragraph 130; Case T-513/93 *Consiglio Nazionale degli Spedizionieri Doganali* v. *Commission* . . ., paragraphs 58 and 59; and Case T-154/98 *Asia Motor France and Others* v. *Commission* . . ., paragraphs 78 to 91). Consequently, if a national law merely allows, encourages or makes it easier for undertakings to engage in autonomous anti-competitive conduct, those undertakings remain subject to the Treaty competition rules (see *inter alia* Joined Cases 89/85, 104/85, 114/85, 116/85, 117/85 and 125/85 to 129/85 *Ahlström* v. *Commission* . . ., paragraph 20, and *Consorzia Industrie Fiammiferi*, cited above, paragraph 56).

Agreements between undertakings may therefore be caught even if they are encouraged or approved by national law or entered into after consultation with the national authorities.[380] Indeed, in both *Competition Authority* v. *Beef Industry Development Society Ltd (BIDS)*[381] and *Coop de France bétail et viande* v. *Commission*[382] undertakings were found to have violated Article 101 even though national governments had some knowledge of, or involvement with, the relevant agreements concluded.[383]

---

[378] See, e.g., Cases C-94/04 and 202/04, *Cipolla* v. *Fazari* [2006] ECR I-11421. A Member State may violate its EU obligations, however, 'where a Member State requires or encourages the adoption of agreements; contrary to Article [101] or reinforces their effects, or where it divests its own rules of the character of legislation by delegating to private economic operators responsibility for taking decisions affecting the economic sphere', para. 47. But contrast Case C-466/05, *Criminal Proceedings against Doulamis* [1998] ECR I-1377, paras. 19–22 (legislation prohibiting dental care providers from advertising does not infringe EU law where there is no evidence that it encourages, reinforces, or codifies concerted practices or decisions by undertakings or delegates responsibility to private operators). A national authority is duty bound to disapply national legislation which violates EU law, see Case C-198/01, *Consorzio Industrie Fiammiferi (CIF)* v. *Autorità Garante della Concorrenza e del Mercato* [2003] ECR I-8055 discussed in Chap. 13.

[379] See Cases C-94 and 202/04 *Cipolla* v. *Fazari* [2006] ECR I-11421.

[380] See further Chap. 1.

[381] Case C-209/07, *Competition Authority* v. *Beef Industry Development Society Ltd and Barry Brothers (Carrigmore) Meals Ltd* [2008] ECR I-8637.

[382] Cases C-101 and 110/07 P, *Coop de France bétail et viande* v. *Commission* [2008] ECR I-10193.

[383] The type of intervention that occurred in these cases is perhaps reflective of a general problem faced by some competition agencies that the government or its agencies may put forward or encourage firms to conclude voluntary agreements to achieve 'laudable and important health, environmental or other policy objectives'. A government might, therefore, be sympathetic to, and encourage, arrangements put together by entities operating in an industry

G. COMMISSION NOTICES

In addition to the Notice on agreements of minor importance and the Guidelines on the effect of trade concept, the Commission has issued other notices/guidelines which indicate that certain agreements may not infringe Article 101(1), in particular because they do not restrict competition. The Commission started issuing notices in 1962 in order to clarify specific matters arising under Article 101, including circumstances in which certain restrictive practices would fall outside Article 101(1). As in the case of the notices already discussed, these notices provide useful guidance for parties. Although they are not rules of law which the Commission (or a court) is always bound to observe, they nevertheless form rules of practice from which the Commission itself may not depart without giving reasons that are compatible with the principle of equal treatment.[384] The following notices are of particular significance in determining the application of Article 101(1) to agreements:[385]

- Commission Notice concerning its assessment of certain subcontracting agreements;[386]
- Guidelines on Vertical Restraints;[387]
- Guidelines on the application of Article 81 [now Article 101] to horizontal cooperation agreements;[388]
- Guidelines on the application of Article 81 of the EC Treaty [now Article 101] to technology transfer agreements;[389]
- Commission Notice on restrictions directly related and necessary to the concentration;[390]
- Guidelines on the application of Article 81(3) of the Treaty [now Article 101(3)].[391]

H. EXTRATERRITORIALITY

The question of when and in what circumstances the competition rules may be applied to the acts of overseas undertakings (which are not established in the EU) is controversial and politically sensitive. The answer to this question does, of course, have an impact on the scope of Article 101(1). The extraterritorial reach of Article 101(1) and the other EU competition rules is explored in Chapter 16.

in crisis. Some competition agencies are concerned that governmental encouragement of voluntary agreements undermines compliance with competition law by sending mixed signals to businesses as to what is permitted and what is prohibited. Competition agencies thus increasingly engage in advocacy with government departments providing advice on the effects of, and alternatives to, restrictions of competition in any aspect of the law or a proposed change in the law and play a role in ensuring that government agencies do not send out these confusing messages and/or adopt legislation which will result in a restriction of competition, without consciously weighing the resulting harm against another conflicting policy objective. Indeed, John Fingleton, then Chief Executive of the UK's OFT, stated that it is critical for competition agencies during a financial and economic crisis to protect government from populist measures and has stated that, 'It is our role, and duty, to repeatedly emphasize the importance for long-term business investment and decision-making of a consistent and clear framework of competition and consumer enforcement. See J. Fingleton, 'Competition Policy in Troubled Times', 20 January 2009.

[384] See Chap. 2, Section 5, pp. 118–119.

[385] See also, e.g., Notice on the application of the competition rules to the postal sector [1998] OJ C39/2.

[386] [1979] OJ C1/2, see Chap. 11.

[387] The Guidelines on Vertical Restraints [2010] OJ C130/10.

[388] [2011] OJ C11/01.

[389] [2004] OJ C101/2, see Chap. 12.

[390] [2005] OJ C56/24. Although this notice applies to merger cases, it provides guidance on the question of when contractual restraints fall outside Art. 101(1) on the grounds that they are 'ancillary' to a pro-competitive merger or agreement, see Chaps. 4 and 15.

[391] [2004] OJ C101/97, discussed in Chap. 4.

6. ARTICLE 101(2)

It has already been seen that despite the clear wording of Article 101(2), the nullity provided for in that provision applies only to individual *clauses* in the agreement affected by the Article 101(1) prohibition. In *Société Technique Minière v. Maschinenbau Ulm GmbH*,[392] the CJ held that the agreement as a whole is void only where those clauses are not severable from the remaining terms of the agreement. It thus interpreted Article 101(2) with reference only to its purpose in EU law and to ensure compliance with the Treaty. The English Court of Appeal has taken the view that the nullity imposed by Article 101(2) is not absolute. Rather, it has only the same temporaneous or transient effect as the prohibition in Article 101(1) (an agreement will cease to be void if the agreement itself ceases to restrict competition or to affect trade within the meaning of Article 101(1)).[393]

The CJ has held that the question whether any null clause or clauses in an agreement can be severed from the rest of the agreement must be determined by national, not EU, law.[394] Each national court will, therefore, have to apply its own national rules on severance to determine the impact of Article 101(2) on the arrangements before it.[395]

7. EXCLUSIONS

In the UK, the Competition Act 1998 (CA 1998) provides that the Chapter I prohibition (modelled on Article 101(1)) does not apply to agreements 'excluded' by, or as a result of, other provisions of the Act.[396] For example, transactions that constitute mergers under the Enterprise Act 2002 merger regime or concentrations with an EU dimension under the EU Merger Regulation are excluded as are: agreements subject to competition scrutiny under special enactments;[397] land agreements;[398] agreements required to comply with planning obligations or a legal requirement; certain agreements made by an undertaking entrusted with the operation of services of general economic interest or of a revenue-producing monopoly;[399] and certain agreements relating to agricultural products.[400]

Although Article 101 does not itself refer to any express exclusions, in practice a number of agreements are excluded from its scope in a similar way. For example, the scheme of the EU Merger Regulation is such that, with certain limited exceptions, merger transactions that constitute a 'concentration' are assessed either under any applicable national competition legislation, or, where the transaction has an EU dimension, under the provisions of the Merger Regulation itself. The idea is that concentrations, which include certain joint venture agreements, should not generally be appraised under Article 101.[401] In addition, Regulation 1184/2006[402] provides that the competition

---

[392] Case 56/65, [1966] ECR 234, 250.

[393] *Passmore v. Morland plc* [1999] 3 All ER 1005.

[394] See also Case 319/82, *Société de Vente de Ciments et Bétons de l'Est v. Kerpen & Kerpen GmbH & Co KG* [1983] ECR 4173, para. 11. See Chap. 14.

[395] See further, Chap. 14 and, e.g., C. Cauffman, 'The Impact of Voidness for Infringements of Article 101TFEU on Related Contracts' [2012] *European Competition Journal* 95.

[396] See especially s. 50 of and Schs 1–4 to the Act.

[397] See CA 1998, Sch. 2.

[398] See the Competition Act 1998 (Land and Vertical Agreements Exclusion) Order 2000 (SI 2000/310) and the Competition Act 1998 (Land Agreements Exclusion and Revocation) Order 2004 (SI 2004/1260).

[399] CA 1998, Sch. 3.

[400] CA 1998, Sch. 3.

[401] For discussion of the complicated question of which transactions fall to be assessed within the procedure of the Merger Reg., Council Reg. 139/2004 [2004] OJ L24/1 (replacing Council Reg. 4064/89 [1989] OJ L395/1, as amended by Council Reg. 1310/97 [1997] OJ L180/1)) and not under Art. 101 see Chaps. 10 and 15.

[402] [2006] OJ L214/7.

rules shall not apply to certain agricultural agreements, for example, those of farmers, farmers' associations, or associations of such associations belonging to a single Member State which concern the production or sale of agricultural products or the use of joint facilities for the storage, treatment, or processing of agricultural products, and under which there is no obligation to charge identical prices (unless the Commission finds that competition is thereby excluded or that the objectives of Article 39 TFEU are jeopardised). Article 346(1)(b) TFEU provides that nothing in the Treaty shall preclude the application by Member States of measures 'it considers necessary for the protection of the essential interests of its security which are connected with the production of or trade in arms, munitions, and war material'. Further, it has been mentioned that Article 106(2) TFEU provides that the competition rules do not apply to some activities of public bodies or bodies entrusted with public services. It has also been seen that in interpreting the elements of Article 101(1), the CJ has excluded from its ambit agreements belonging to the realm of social policy, agreements concluded by firms when carrying out tasks of a public or social nature, agreements between entities which form part of the same undertaking or economic unit, agreements required by national legislation and matters which are of a purely sporting interest and, as such, have nothing to do with economic activity.

8. CONCLUSIONS

Agreements that infringe Article 101(1) and which do not meet the conditions of Article 101(3) are prohibited. Severe consequences potentially flow for those that violate Article 101. It is therefore of utmost importance for a firm to know whether any agreement it concludes may violate Article 101(1).

The following provides a checklist of agreements (or conduct) which may fall outside Article 101(1) and escape the prohibition altogether:

1. Agreements which are not concluded by two or more entities engaged in economic activity;
2. Agreements between entities which are part of the same economic unit, for example, certain parent and subsidiary or principal and agent relationships;
3. Collective agreements between employers and workers;
4. Unilateral conduct not explicitly or tacitly accepted by another or by another party to a contract;
5. Agreements which constitute a 'concentration' within the meaning of the Merger Regulation;
6. Agreements which relate to the production of or trade in certain agricultural products;
7. Agreements which do not have as their object or effect the prevention, restriction, or distortion of competition;[403]
9. Agreements which do not appreciably or significantly restrict competition;
10. Agreements which do not appreciably affect trade between Member States (although such agreements may be subject to national competition law);
11. Agreements which are necessary for the performance of a task of general economic interest entrusted to them by a Member State (see Article 106(2));
12. Agreements required by national law; and
13. Agreements which are truly extraterritorial.

---

[403] See Chap. 4. In addition to case law, various Commission notices and guidelines provide both general and specific guidance on this issue.

9. FURTHER READING

A. BOOKS

HARDING, C., and JOSHUA, J., *Regulating Cartels in Europe* (2nd edn, Oxford University Press, 2010)

ODUDU, O., *The Boundaries of EC Competition Law: The Scope of Article 81* (Oxford University Press, 2006)

TOWNLEY, C., *Article 81 EC and Public Policy* (Hart Publishing, 2009)

B. ARTICLES

ALBORS-LLORENS, A., 'Horizontal Agreements and Concerted Practices in EC Competition Law: Unlawful and Legitimate Contacts between Competitors' (2006) 51 *Ant Bull* 837

BAILEY, D., 'Single, Overall Agreement in EU Competition Law' [2010] *CMLRev* 473

CAUFFMAN, C., 'The Impact of Voidness for Infringements of Article 101TFEU on Related Contracts' [2012] *European Competition Journal* 95

JONES, A., 'The boundaries of an undertaking in EU Competition Law' (2012) 8 *European Competition Journal* 301

JOSHUA, J., 'Single Continuous Infringement of Article 81 EC: Has the Commission Stretched the Concept Beyond the Limit of its Logic?' (2009) 5 *European Competition Journal* 451

JOSHUA, J., BOTTEMAN, Y., AND ATLEE, L., '"You Can't Beat the Percentage"—The Parental Liability

Presumption in EU Cartel Enforcement' in *Global Competition Review The European Antitrust Review 2012*, 3

THOMAS, S., 'Guilty of a Fault that One has not Committed. The Limits of the Group-Based Sanction Policy Carried out by the Commission and the European Courts in EU-Antitrust Law' [2012] *JECLAP* 11

WESSELY, T., 'Polyproplyene appeal cases' (2001) 38 *CMLRev* 739

WICKIHALDER, U., 'The distinction between an "agreement" within the meaning of Article 81(1) of the EC Treaty and unilateral conduct' [2006] *European Competition Journal* 87

WILS, W. P. J., 'The Undertaking as Subject of EC Competition Law and the Imputation of Infringements to Natural or Legal Persons' (2000) 25 *ELRev* 99

4

THE RELATIONSHIP BETWEEN ARTICLE 101(1) AND ARTICLE 101(3) TFEU

1. CENTRAL ISSUES

1. It is seen in Chapter 3 that, essentially, the scheme of Article 101 is that Article 101(1) prohibits agreements between undertakings which appreciably affect trade between Member States and which have as their object or effect the restriction of competition whilst Article 101(3) provides that the prohibition may be declared inapplicable to any agreement which satisfies its four conditions.

2. In this chapter the relationship between Article 101(1) and Article 101(3) is explored. Essentially, it focuses on the substantive question of *which* agreements contravene the objectives of Article 101 and so should be prohibited.

3. In conducting substantive assessment it is necessary to consider how the analysis should be divided between Article 101(1) and Article 101(3). This issue is of enormous importance, since the burden of proving a breach of Article 101(1) rests on the person alleging the same, whilst the burden of establishing that the Article 101(3) criteria are established rests on those undertakings claiming its benefit.

4. The Commission now takes an economic approach to Article 101 based on a consumer

welfare objective. It states that Article 101(1) is about identifying the anti-competitive effects of an agreement (agreements which adversely affect competition by restricting inter-brand or intra-brand competition) whilst Article 101(3) allows the balancing of offsetting efficiencies against these restrictive effects. The case law of the EU Courts suggests, however, that broader objectives may be relevant under both Article 101(1) and Article 101(3).

5. Acute difficulties in this area are that:

- the procedural framework between 1962 and 2004, conferring exclusive competence on the Commission to rule on the compatibility of Article 101(3), led to distortions in interpretation of both Article 101(1) and Article 101(3); and

- different cases suggest different approaches to the analysis required under Article 101(1) and Article 101(3) respectively.

6. This means that there is no crystal-clear answer to the question of which agreements are prohibited by Article 101 and, correspondingly, what analysis is required under Article 101(1) and Article 101(3) respectively.

2. INTRODUCTION AND BACKGROUND

A. ARTICLE 101(1) AND ARTICLE 101(3)

This chapter examines the question of which agreements contravene the objectives of Article 101 and so should be prohibited. It has been seen that substantive analysis under Article 101 is conducted in two parts. First, an agreement has to be scrutinised to determine whether it infringes Article

101(1), i.e. whether it has as its object or effect the restriction[1] of competition. If it does not, that is the end of the story. If it does, it must, secondly, be determined whether or not the agreement meets the criteria set out in Article 101(3). Article 101(1) may be declared inapplicable to any agreement which provides specified benefits (broadly, it improves the production or distribution of goods or services or promotes technical or economic progress), allows consumers a fair share of the benefit, does not contain any indispensable restrictions, and does not eliminate competition in a substantial part of the products in question.

The discussion in this chapter establishes that the Commission's interpretation of Article 101 and view of how Article 101(1) and Article 101(3) interact has evolved considerably over time. Indeed, in its early application of Article 101 the Commission adopted a formalistic approach to Article 101, taking the view that many agreements violated Article 101(1) and so were prohibited unless 'exempted' under Article 101(3). This method led to uncertainty for business, treatment of agreement by form rather than effect and meant that pro-competitive business practices may have been deterred (and that Type I errors occurred). At the end of the 1990s, however, the Commission recognised the problems that this approach created for businesses and over a number of years reviewed and rethought its analysis under both Article 101(1) and Article 101(3). In particular, it has become willing to accept that more complex analysis should be conducted before an agreement is found to infringe Article 101—there should be a shift from rules based on the form of the agreement to ones which focus on its effects. In 2004 the Commission set out a new, more coherent framework of analysis in its Guidelines on the application of Article 81(3) [now Article 101(3)] of the Treaty (the Article 101(3) Guidelines)[2] (which is elucidated further in specific Guidelines dealing with horizontal cooperation, vertical agreements, and technology transfer agreements) respectively.[3] Although this framework represents an enormous advancement on the earlier position, it will be seen that it is not entirely possible to reconcile it with all of the case law and decisional practice under Article 101. In particular, the Commission's view that the objective of Article 101 is consumer welfare and efficiency, as well as the creation and preservation of an open single market, does not appear to be fully supported by the Court.

This section starts by examining possible ways of reconciling the two parts of Article 101 and how the Commission's methodology has evolved over time. It outlines the Commission's initial approach, the problems this created and how, and why, modernisation occurred. Section 3 then examines more closely the analysis of agreements under Article 101(1) and when they may be found to be restrictive of competition by object or effect, whilst Section 4 considers the analysis required under Article 101(3).

B. POSSIBLE WAYS OF RECONCILING ARTICLE 101(1) AND ARTICLE 101(3)

The bifurcated structure of Article 101 has, to some extent, complicated its interpretation and led to uncertainty as to the correct role for, and analysis required by, each part. Key questions arising are what objectives influence the interpretation of Article 101 and what factors are taken into account at each stage, i.e.: (i) what constitutes a restriction of competition for the purposes of Article 101(1); and (ii), in what circumstances should such restrictions be 'trumped' by Article 101(3) benefits? If many agreements are found to restrict competition within the meaning of Article 101(1), numerous agreements will be prohibited *unless* saved by Article 101(3) (which becomes the main vehicle

---

[1] The words 'prevention, restriction, or distortion' are intended to cover any interference with competition, and are synonymous, so the term 'restriction' will be used as shorthand in this text to cover all three.

[2] See Guidelines on the application of Article 81(3) [now Article 101(3)] of the Treaty (the Article 101(3) Guidelines) [2004] OJ C101/97.

[3] See Chaps. 10–12.

for authorising agreements). If, however, a narrower interpretation is adopted when determining whether or not a contractual provision restricts competition and infringes Article 101(1), the role played by Article 101(3) is more limited. Finding the right balance between the application of Article 101(1) and Article 101(3) has proved to be extremely difficult.

The wording of Article 101(1) and Article 101(3) itself does not define their relationship. A number of different approaches may be adopted, or advocated, as to how they should be reconciled. For example:

(1) One way of reconciling the two parts is to adopt a literal or broad interpretation of Article 101(1), bringing many agreements within its net, and conducting a more detailed analysis of the anti-competitive, pro-competitive, and other aspects of the agreement within the more structured framework of Article 101(3). In this scenario the requirement that the agreement restricts competition serves a jurisdictional function (bringing within its ambit all potentially problematic agreements). The rigorous substantive assessment is then completed under Article 101(3).

(2) A second approach is to conduct a more detailed analysis when determining whether an agreement has as its object or effect the 'restriction' of competition (Article 101(1)) and to thereby confine the role of Article 101(3). An assessment of a presumed (in object cases), actual, or likely (in effect cases) adverse impact on consumer welfare is made when determining whether it restricts competition. Article 101(3) then plays a more limited role, excepting agreements presumed to restrict competition[4] *and*, perhaps, allowing other demonstrable public policy benefits (such as benefits to environment, health, industry, culture, or employment) to be balanced against identified anti-competitive effects.

(3) A third approach is to divide the substantive appraisal more evenly between the two parts. There are a number of ways in which this division could be effected, but one method could be to use Article 101(1) to identify presumed, actual, or likely anti-competitive effects and Article 101(3) to enable the parties to establish that the agreement achieves offsetting efficiencies or pro-competitive effects. For example, Article 101(1) could become concerned with allocative efficiency (and, essentially, deadweight loss resulting from contrived restrictions of output) whilst Article 101(3) could become a productive and dynamic efficiency inquiry, available to allow the parties to demonstrate that the restraints in the agreement are necessary to achieve efficiencies which will be passed on to consumers and compensate them for the resulting allocative inefficiencies.[5]

The discussion in Sections C–F establishes that the Commission initially adopted an approach close to (1) but that many commentators urged it to take an approach closer to (2). Further, that although neither the Commission nor the EU Courts' current approach equates *exactly* to any of those outlined the Commission's modern approach most closely resembles (3).

C. THE INTERPRETATION OF 'OBJECT OR EFFECT IS THE PREVENTION, RESTRICTION, OR DISTORTION OF COMPETITION'—THE BROAD APPROACH

One of the most strident criticisms made of the Commission's application of the competition rules in the past was its failure to adopt a sufficiently realistic economic interpretation of Article 101(1), in particular, when determining whether or not an agreement restricts competition. The broad criticism was that, in accordance with the ordoliberal philosophy, it tended to take the view that certain restrictions on a party's conduct (restraints on economic freedom) were tantamount to restrictions on competition. Further, that any restriction which might interfere with the single market

---

[4] Where there is a presumption of anti-competitive effects (see discussion of object restraints in Section 3, especially pp. 203–232, Art. 101(3) could be relied upon to demonstrate that the agreement in fact produces pro-competitive effects.

[5] See, e.g., O. Odudu, *The Boundaries of EC Competition Law: The Scope of Article 81* (Oxford University Press, 2006), Chaps. 5–7.

objective amounted to a restriction of competition.[6] In short, the Commission found, after a formalistic assessment, that many agreements, whether distribution, intellectual property licensing, or joint venture or other horizontal collaboration agreements, were caught within the widely cast net of Article 101(1) but subsequently completed its analysis, by authorising (or exempting) many agreements, using Article 101(3)[7] (the analysis thus resembled approach 1 set out in Section 2.B). Arguably, the Commission conducted much of the analysis when scrutinising an agreement for its compliance with the requirements set out in Article 101(3) which it could in fact have conducted earlier when determining whether or not the agreement restricted competition under Article 101(1).

This approach seems to have been motivated both by ideology and practicalities. The Commission utilised Article 101 to limit restrictions on conduct, to promote rivalry between undertakings operating on a market, and to prevent interferences with the single market project.[8] It considered that rivalry between firms produced the best results, and was the best stimulant of economic activity.[9] Further, a broad jurisdictional interpretation of Article 101(1) cemented the Commission's central role in the development of EU competition policy since it had the exclusive right to apply Article 101(3) through the system of 'notification and exemption'.[10] The impact of this arrangement has been enduring, both on the interpretation of Article 101 and on the Commission's special and influential role in the moulding and shaping of competition policy.

D. THE DRAWBACKS OF A BROAD INTERPRETATION OF ARTICLE 101(1): THE NEED FOR A MORE ECONOMIC APPROACH?

At first sight, it may appear immaterial whether or not the more rigorous scrutiny of the agreement is conducted under Article 101(1) or Article 101(3) if the outcome is the same. This is not just an academic point, however.

First, the broad approach raised conceptual difficulties: businesses found it hard to understand why their agreement was characterised as restrictive of competition, simply because it imposed restrictions on the conduct of one of the parties.[11] Indeed, commentators complained that the method failed to provide transparent, predictable, and operable criteria for businesses to apply.[12] Secondly, until 1 May 2004 when Regulation 1/2003 came into force, negative procedural consequences resulted from this approach. Parties fearful that their agreement might infringe Article 101(1) had either to notify their agreement to the Commission (which had the exclusive right to grant individual exemptions)[13] or draft it to fall within one of the block exemptions.[14] The Commission's

---

[6] See Chap. 1 and e.g., J. Faull and A. Nikpay (eds.), *The EC Law of Competition* (2nd edn, Oxford University Press, 2007), paras. 3.132–3.144.

[7] See, e.g., *Goodyear Italiana-Euram*, [1975] OJ L38/10, *Campari*, [1978] OJ L70/69 para. 7, part IIA, *Vacuum Interrupters*, [1977] OJ L48/32, *De Laval-Stork*, [1977] OJ L215/11 para. 6, and *Beecham/Parke, Davis*, [1979] OJ L70/11.

[8] See Chap. 1.

[9] See Faull and Nikpay (eds.), *The EC Law of Competition* (cited in n. 6), paras. 3.132–3.134.

[10] See Reg. 17, [1959–1962] OJ Spec. Ed. 87, Arts 9(1) and 4. This enabled it to influence the form and way in which agreements were operated through its application of Article 101(3). In contrast, had it adopted a narrower, more economic approach to Article 101(1), greater enforcement of agreements would have been delegated to the national level and the uniform interpretation of the competition rules might have been compromised.

[11] Especially if, in subsequently exempting the agreement, the Commission essentially accepted that the agreement was a pro-competitive one.

[12] See, e.g., B. E. Hawk, 'System Failure: Vertical Restraints and EC Competition Law' (1995) 32 *CMLRev* 973.

[13] Reg. 17 [1959–1962] OJ Spec. Ed. 87, Art. 9(1). Notification was a time- and cost-consuming exercise and the Commission could not grant more than a few individual exemptions each year (see e.g., Case T-67/01, *JCB Service v. Commission* [2004] ECR II-49 (*aff'd* Case C-167/04, [2006] ECR I-8935) concerning an agreement notified to the Commission in 1973 but not dealt with until 2000.

[14] See Section 4.E, pp. 263–266.

monopoly over Art. 101(3) effectively also excluded national courts and National Competition Authorities (NCAs) from the enforcement process.

Because of these difficulties, the Commission was urged to take a more economically sophisticated approach in assessing in the first place whether or not an agreement restricted competition within the meaning of Article 101(1).[15] It was argued that Article 101(1) should not generally be applied formalistically to an agreement (or provisions within it) which did not have an appreciable adverse effect on competition. A number of arguments were thus presented in support of the need for a more sophisticated economic approach to be taken to Article 101(1). In particular it was contended that:

- the legal rules followed by the Commission under Article 101(1) were overbroad (wrongly favouring the freedom of individual traders over consumer welfare) and did not provide sufficiently precise and operable criteria to determine which agreements restricted competition;

- the approach led to the condemnation under Article 101(1) of innocuous agreements which did not in fact restrict competition through anti-competitive effects.[16] The analysis conducted by the Commission when scrutinising an agreement for its compliance with the requirements set out in Article 101(3) was more appropriate to the determination of whether or not the agreement restricted competition under Article 101(1). Because of the unlikelihood of gaining an exemption, pro-competitive agreements may have been deterred and Type I errors may have occurred;

- if a consideration of anti- and pro-competitive effects was conducted under Article 101(1), many of the procedural problems experienced in the application of Article 101 would fall away. Fewer agreements would need *either* to be notified and subjected to the interminable delay involved in gaining Commission authorisation *or* drafted to comply with rigid block exemptions which encouraged formalism and treatment of agreement by category rather than effect. In addition, the Commission's resources would be freed to deal with the more serious violations of the competition rules and the rarer cases which would demand scrutiny under Article 101(3); and critically

- the advocated approach was necessitated by the case law of the EU Courts which had not interpreted the concept of a restriction of competition under Article 101(1) so broadly as the Commission. Although it has been clear since the CJ's judgment in *Établissements Consten S.à.R.L and Grundig-Verkaufs-GmbH* v. *Commission*[17] that there is no need to take account of the effects of an agreement if its *object* is to restrict competition, it was maintained that in 'effect' cases, a series of judgments commencing with *Société Technique Minière* v. *Maschinenbau Ulm GmbH* (*STM*)[18] (and including cases such as *Nungesser* v. *Commission*,[19] *Erauw-Jacquéry Sprl* v. *La Hesbignonne Société Coopérative*,[20] *Remia BV and NV Verenigde Bedrijven Nutricia* v. *Commission*,[21] *Pronuptia de Paris GmbH*

---

[15] See, e.g., R. Joliet, *The Rule of Reason in Antitrust Law* (Nijhof, 1967); I. Forrester and C. Norall, 'The Laïcization of Community Law: Self-help and the Rule of Reason: How Competition is and could be Applied' (1984) 21 *CMLRev* 11; V. Korah, 'EEC Competition Policy—Legal Form or Economic Efficiency?' [1986] 39 *CLP* 85; B.E. Hawk, 'System Failure: Vertical Restraints and EC Competition Law' (1995) 32 *CMLRev* 973; James S. Venit, 'Pronuptia: Ancillary Restraints or Unholy Alliances' 11 *ELRev* 213 (1986); R. Whish and B. Sufrin, 'Article 85 and the Rule of Reason' (1987) 7 *YEL* 1. See also, more recently, A. Jones, 'Analysis of Agreements under US and EC Antitrust Law—Convergence or Divergence?' (2006) 51 *Ant Bull* 691.

[16] Since many of the agreements prohibited created or increased competition they should not have required authorisation under Art. 101(3), see, e.g., the Opinion of AG Roemer in Cases 56 and 58/64, *Consten and Grundig* [1966] ECR 299.

[17] Cases 56 and 58/64, [1966] ECR 299.

[18] Case 56/65, [1966] ECR 235.

[19] Case 258/78, [1982] ECR 2015.

[20] Case 27/87, [1988] ECR 1919.

[21] Case 42/84, [1985] ECR 2545.

v. *Pronuptia de Paris Irmgard Schillgallis*,[22] *Brasserie de Haecht (No. 1)*,[23] *Gøttrup-Klim Grovvareforeninger and Others v. Dansk Landbrugs Grovvareselskab AmbA*,[24] and *Delimitis v. Henninger Bräu*)[25] required the drawing up of a competition balance sheet and a weighing of anti and pro-competitive effects under Article 101(1).[26]

E. SECTION 1 OF THE SHERMAN ACT

During the EU debate, reference was frequently made to the need for greater economic analysis, similar perhaps to 'rule of reason' analysis conducted in the US. Section 1 of the Sherman Act 1890 (the US equivalent of Article 101) provides that '[e]very contract, combination in the form of a trust or otherwise, or conspiracy, in restraint of trade or commerce among the several States, or with foreign nations, is declared to be illegal ...' but contains no legal exception to the prohibition.

Since the main objective of a contract is to restrain the conduct of the parties to it, the US Supreme Court soon recognised that a literal interpretation of the section might result in many (or all) agreements being held to be illegal.[27] 'Every agreement concerning trade, every regulation of trade, restrains. To bind, to restrain, is of their very essence.'[28] The US courts thus construed the section to mean that contracts must not restrain trade unreasonably.[29] Eventually, and following the emergence of a consensus that the paramount goal of the Sherman Act is consumer welfare and efficiency, this has become an enquiry into the competitive significance of the restraint.[30] In determining whether or not an agreement does restrain competition unreasonably the courts traditionally adopted two separate approaches—per se and rule of reason analysis.[31]

Some contracts are considered to be illegal per se.

There are certain agreements or practices which because of their pernicious effect on competition and lack of any redeeming virtue are conclusively presumed to be unreasonable and therefore illegal without elaborate inquiries as to the precise harm they have caused or the business excuse for their use.[32]

This bright line rule focuses *solely* on whether the conduct took place, not on its effect. Some agreements, such as naked price-fixing among competitors,[33] are automatically held to restrain competition unreasonably. They are considered to be so likely to be anti-competitive that the court will not waste time or resources requiring that anti-competitive effects must be proved and/or hearing justifications for the agreement.

By the 1960s a large number of restraints had been categorised as illegal per se. For the sake of business certainty and litigation efficiency the courts were prepared to tolerate the invalidation of some agreements that a full-blown rule of reason inquiry might have proved to be reasonable.[34] Toward

---

[22] Case 161/84, [1986] ECR 353.

[23] Case 23/67, [1967] ECR 407.

[24] Case C-250/92, [1994] ECR I-5641.

[25] Case C-234/89, [1991] ECR I-935.

[26] See Section 3.

[27] But see the approach adopted in *United States v. Trans-Missouri Freight Ass'n.*, 166 US 290 (1897).

[28] *Chicago Board of Trade v. US*, 246 US 231, 238 (1918), per Brandeis J.

[29] *Standard Oil Co of New Jersey v. US*, 221 US 1 (1911); *US v. American Tobacco Co*, 221 US 106 (1911).

[30] *National Society of Professional Engineers v. United States*, 435 US 679 (1978).

[31] As the law has developed, however, the boundary between the two categories has become increasingly blurred so that 'there is often no bright line separating per se from Rule of Reason analysis', *NCAA v. Board of Regents of Univ. of Okla.*, 468 US 85, 104 (1984). This has led some courts to conclude that there has been a move, away from fixed categories, to a continuum, *Polygram Holding, Inc., v. Federal Trade Commission*, 416 F.3d 29, 35 (D.C. Cir. 2005).

[32] *Northern Pac R Co v. United States*, 356 US 1, 5 (1958).

[33] *US v. Trenton Potteries Co*, 273 US 392 (1927); *US v. Socony-Vaccuum Oil Co*, 310 US 150 (1940).

[34] *Arizona v. Maricopa County Medical Society*, 457 US 332, 344 (1982).

the end of the 1970s, however, the Supreme Court began to retreat from this position based on form and to move to one grounded in economics, embracing rule of reason analysis. Indeed, since 1977 the presumptive and prevailing standard has been the 'rule of reason'.[35] Under this analysis, agreements are not assumed to be illegal but are assessed in their legal and economic context to determine:

> whether the restraint imposed is such as merely regulates and perhaps thereby promotes competition or whether it is such as may suppress or even destroy competition. To determine that question the court must ordinarily consider the facts peculiar to the business to which the restraint is applied; its condition before and after the restraint was imposed; the nature of the restraint and its effect, actual or probable.[36]

In short, the anti- and pro-competitive aspects of the agreement are weighed before an agreement is condemned as illegal.[37]

Not all commentators agreed that EU case law supported an approach identical or similar to the US rule of reason under Article 101(1).[38] Nonetheless, the core message was simple—a less formalistic and more economic approach was required under Article 101, especially under Article 101(1).

F. MODERNISATION

(i). Modernisation, Regulation 1/2003, and *Métropole Télévision (M6)*

Eventually, the Commission realised that the status quo was no longer tenable: the notification system was failing and some change was obligatory. It set about reformulating its approach to agreements, accepting that there should be a shift from an approach based on form to one more focused on effects.[39] Further, it sought to resolve the procedural problems arising by proposing that its monopoly over Article 101(3) should be revoked. On 1 May 2004, Regulation 1/2003 abolished the Commission's exclusive right to rule on the compatibility of an agreement with Article 101(3), rendering Article 101(3) directly applicable as a legal exception to Article 101(1).[40] It may, therefore, now be applied not only by the Commission,[41] but also by the NCAs of each of the Member States[42] and the national courts.[43]

In rethinking its stance towards agreements, the Commission has accepted that a more economic and less rigid analysis of agreements under both Article 101(1) and Article 101(3) is requisite.[44] It has therefore gradually detached itself from its earlier more interventionist policy as it has moved towards an acceptance that consumer welfare should be the benchmark against which agreements are tested. The Commission, however, has not accepted that a 'rule of reason' style analysis, balancing anti- and pro-competitive effects under Article 101(1), provides the solution. Rather, it is the Commission's view that it is Article 101(3) not Article 101(1) which provides the

---

[35] *Continental TV, Inc. v. GTE Slyvania Inc.*, 433 US 36 (1977).

[36] *Chicago Board of Trade* v. *US*, 246 US 231, 238 (1918), per Brandeis J.

[37] The rule of reason analysis has proved hard to apply in practice and there is limited guidance from the Supreme Court on this issue. The circuit courts have adopted their own methods and have developed approaches in between the per se and rule of reason approaches, tailoring the extent of the inquiry to the suspect conduct in each case, see, e.g., *Polygram Holding, Inc* v. *FTC*, 416 F.3d 29, 33–4 (DC Cir 2005).

[38] See e.g. R. Whish and B. Sufrin, 'Article 85 and the Rule of Reason', (1987) 7 YEL 1.

[39] It reviewed and overhauled the working of Article 101 between 1996 and 2004. See especially Chaps. 9–12.

[40] Reg. 1/2003, Art. 1 provides that agreements which are caught by Art. 101(1) and which do not satisfy the conditions of Art. 101(3) are prohibited, no prior decision to that effect being required. Further that agreements which are caught by Art. 101(1), but which satisfy the conditions of Art. 101(3), are not prohibited, no prior decision to that effect being required.

[41] Reg. 1/2003, Arts 7–10.

[42] Reg. 1/2003, Arts 5 and 3.

[43] The Commission is seeking to encourage greater 'private' enforcement of EU competition law, see Chap. 14.

[44] See Chaps. 9–12.

appropriate forum for weighing the restrictive effects of the agreement (identified at the Article 101(1) stage) against the economic benefits and efficiencies created by the agreement.[45] Otherwise, Article 101(3) would be rendered virtually redundant—being utilised *only* to authorise restrictive agreements found to have as their object the restriction of competition *or* to authorise agreements resulting in non-economic benefits, for example, social, industrial, environmental, employment, cultural, and/or regional benefits. Whether or not these latter socio-political factors may, or should, be taken into account when making the assessment under Article 101(3) will be discussed in Section 4.[46]

Although it will be seen that the EU cases on this issue are difficult to reconcile, a number of judgments of the GC, including *Métropole Télévision (M6) v. Commission*,[47] support the view of the Commission that Article 101(3) provides the main forum for weighing anti- and pro-competitive aspects of an agreement and, indeed, goes further.

Métropole Télévision (M6) concerned an appeal from a Commission decision holding that the creation of the joint venture, Télévision par Satellite (TPS), did not infringe Article 101(1) but that certain clauses in the notified agreements infringed Article 101(1) and could be exempted under Article 101(3) *only* for a period of three years. Amongst other things, the applicants argued that the Commission had been wrong to exempt the clauses. Rather, the reasoning adopted by the Commission indicated that these clauses *favoured* competition and did not restrict it. Had the Commission, therefore, correctly applied Article 101(1) using the rule of reason, weighing the pro- and anti-competitive effects of the agreement, the Commission should have found that the agreement did not restrict competition within the meaning of Article 101 at all.[48] The GC did not accept this argument, observing that contrary to the applicants' assertions the existence of such a rule had not been confirmed by the EU Courts. Echoing the view of the Commission, that such an interpretation would be difficult to reconcile with the rules prescribed by Article 101, it stated that Article 101(3) provided the correct forum for weighing the pro- and anti-competitive aspects of the agreement. The Court recognised that some EU cases, such as *STM*,[49] had favoured a 'more flexible' interpretation of the Article 101(1) prohibition,[50] but held that they did not establish the existence of a rule of reason. Rather, such a rule had not been confirmed by the Courts and the cases simply formed part of a broader trend in the case law according to which it is not necessary to hold, wholly abstractly, that any agreement restricting the freedom of action of one or more of the parties is necessarily caught by Article 101(1).[51]

[45] See White Paper on the Modernisation of the Rules Implementing Articles 85 and 86 of the EC Treaty [now Articles 101 and 102 TFEU] [1999] OJ C132/1, paras. 56–57. See also G. Monti, 'Article 81 EC and Public Policy' (2002) 39 *CMLRev* 1057–1099, 1061.

[46] See Section 4.D.i, pp. 252–258.

[47] Case T-112/99, *Métropole Télévision SA v. Commission* [2001] ECR II-2459. See also Case T-65/98, *Van den Bergh Foods v. Commission* [2003] ECR II-4653, aff'd Case C-552/03 P, *Unilever Bestfoods v. Commission* [2006] OJ C294/19 [ECR I-9091], Case T-328/03, *O2 (Germany) GmbH & Co. OHG v. Commission* [2006] ECR II-1231 and Case T-111/08, *MasterCard Inc v. Commission*, 24 May 2012, especially para. 80, on appeal Case C-382/12 P.

[48] Case T-112/99, *Métropole Télévision SA v. Commission* [2001] ECR II-2459, para. 69.

[49] Case 56/65, *Société Technique Minière v. Maschinenbau Ulm GmbH* [1966] ECR 235, 249. See also Case 258/78, *Nungesser and Eisele v. Commission* [1982] ECR 2015, Case 161/84, *Pronuptia de Paris GmbH v. Pronuptia de Paris Irmgard Schillgallis* [1986] ECR 353; Cases T-374, 375, 384, and 388/94, *European Night Services v. Commission* [1998] ECR II-3141; and Case C-250/92, *Gøttrup-Klim Grovvareforening and Others v. Dansk Landbrugs Grovvareselskab AmbA* [1994] ECR I-5641, paras. 31–35.

[50] Case T-112/99, *Métropole Télévision SA v. Commission* [2001] ECR II-2459, para. 75.

[51] For the argument (rejected) that Art. 101(1) could not apply as the agreement did *not* restrain the freedom of action of one of the parties to the agreement, see Case T-99/04, *AC Treuhand AG v. Commission* [2008] ECR II-1501, paras. 124–128 ('it is not therefore to be ruled out that an undertaking may participate in the implementation of such a restriction even if it does not restrict its own freedom of action on the market on which it is primarily active', para. 127).

Case T-112/99, *Métropole Télévision (M6)* v. *Commission* [2001] ECR II-2459

General Court

72. According to the applicants, as a consequence of the existence of a rule of reason in [EU] competition law, when Article [101(1)] is applied it is necessary to weigh the pro and anti-competitive effects of an agreement in order to determine whether it is caught by the prohibition laid down in that article. It should, however, be observed, first of all, that contrary to the applicants' assertions the existence of such a rule has not, as such, been confirmed by the [EU] courts. Quite to the contrary, in various judgments the Court of Justice and the [GC] have been at pains to indicate that the existence of a rule of reason in [EU] competition law is doubtful (see Case C-235/92 P *Montecatini* v. *Commission*...paragraph 133 (...even if the rule of reason did have a place in the context of Article [101(1)]of the Treaty), and Case T-14/89 *Montedipe* v. *Commission*...paragraph 265, and in Case T-148/89 *Tréfilunion* v. *Commission*...paragraph 109).

73. Next, it must be observed that an interpretation of Article [101(1)], in the form suggested by the applicants, is difficult to reconcile with the rules prescribed by that provision.

74. Article [101] expressly provides, in its third paragraph, for the possibility of exempting agreements that restrict competition where they satisfy a number of conditions, in particular where they are indispensable to the attainment of certain objectives and do not afford undertakings the possibility of eliminating competition in respect of a substantial part of the products in question. It is only in the precise framework of that provision that the pro and anti-competitive aspects of a restriction may be weighed (see, to that effect, Case 161/84 *Pronuptia*...paragraph 24, and Case T-17/93 *Matra Hachette* v. *Commission*...paragraph 48, and *European Night Services and Others* v. *Commission*...paragraph 136). Article [101(3)] would lose much of its effectiveness if such an examination had to be carried out already under Article [101(1)].

75. It is true that in a number of judgments the Court of Justice and the [GC] have favoured a more flexible interpretation of the prohibition laid down in Article [101(1)] (see, in particular, *Société technique minière* and *Oude Luttikhuis and Others*...*Nungesser and Eisele* v. *Commission* and *Coditel and Others*...*Pronuptia*...and *European Night Services and Others* v. *Commission*...as well as the judgment in Case C-250/92 *DLG*...paragraphs 31 to 35).

76. Those judgments cannot, however, be interpreted as establishing the existence of a rule of reason in [EU] competition law. They are, rather, part of a broader trend in the case-law according to which it is not necessary to hold, wholly abstractly and without drawing any distinction, that any agreement restricting the freedom of action of one or more of the parties is necessarily caught by the prohibition laid down in Article [101(1)]. In assessing the applicability of Article [101(1)] to an agreement, account should be taken of the actual conditions in which it functions, in particular the economic context in which the undertakings operate, the products or services covered by the agreement and the actual structure of the market concerned (see, in particular, *European Night Services and Others* v. *Commission*...paragraph 136, *Oude Luttikhuis*...paragraph 10, and *VGB and Others* v. *Commission*...paragraph 140, as well as the judgment in Case C-234/89 *Delimitis*...paragraph 31).

77. That interpretation, while observing the substantive scheme of Article [101] and, in particular, preserving the effectiveness of Article [101(3)], makes it possible to prevent the prohibition in Article [101(1)] from extending wholly abstractly and without distinction to all agreements whose effect is to restrict the freedom of action of one or more of the parties. It must, however, be emphasised that such an approach does not mean that it is necessary to weigh the pro and anti-competitive effects of an agreement when determining whether the prohibition laid down in Article [101(1)] applies.

In M6 the GC appears, therefore, to reject both the first two of the possible approaches set out in Section 2.B and to favour the third (one which divides the substantive appraisal between Article 101(1) and 101(3)).[52] It indicates that the Article 101 appraisal should be divided into five parts: (1) the Commission (or other person seeking to demonstrate the same) must establish that the agreement restricts competition (identify the anti-competitive aspects)—whether by object or effect;[53] when this burden is discharged the parties (or the undertakings seeking the benefit of Article 101(3)) must establish that (2) that the agreement achieves pro-competitive objectives; (3) consumers attain a fair share of those benefits; (4) the agreement is indispensable to the attainment of the benefits; and (5) there is no possibility of an elimination of competition.[54]

This supposition leads to two further questions. Was the GC correct to interpret previous case law this way? If so, exactly how is the envisaged division in analysis to be made: in particular, what constitutes a restriction of competition for the purpose of Article 101(1) and what 'pro-competitive' 'aspects of a restriction' can be weighed against them under Article 101(3)? In seeking to answer these questions the discussion in Sections 3 and 4 indicates that, unfortunately, the position is not quite as clear as the GC in M6 suggests.

(ii) The Importance of the Debate: the Relationship between Article 101(1) and Article 101(3)

The decision to render Article 101(3) directly applicable has meant that the procedural problems that followed as a result of the notification and authorisation system have fallen away. In one sense, therefore, it does not matter if a broad interpretation of Article 101(1) is adopted, since the Article 101(3) appraisal can be conducted by the Commission, an NCA, or a national court, i.e. wherever the issue arises. In substantive and practical terms, however, the debate about the role and scope of Article 101(1) still retains life. It is of paramount importance to know what appraisal should be conducted under Article 101(1) and Article 101(3) respectively. The analysis that must be conducted under Article 101(1) has a profound impact on the role and scope of Article 101(3), the burden of proof imposed on the claimant and those claiming the benefit of Article 101(3) respectively (which may be critical to the outcome of a case),[55] and the risk the parties to the agreement are perceived to take in conclusion of an agreement. The operation of an agreement that falls within Article 101(1) and requires justification under Article 101(3) is perceived, commercially, to be of greater risk than one falling outside of Article 101(1) altogether.

(iii) Categories of Analysis: Clear Rules or More Complex Standards?

Even if the Commission is correct that the goal of Article 101 is to identify agreements that harm consumer welfare and that the analysis should be divided between Article 101(1) and Article 101(3) in the way that it suggests, it still leaves the conundrum of how to achieve that objective within the Article 101 framework. How can rules or standards be constructed which will be both sufficiently:

(a) clear—so as to enable firms to comply with them and courts or other decision-makers to administer them; and

(b) accurate—identifying and prohibiting conduct which harms the objectives of Article whilst permitting those that may promote competition?

---

[52] But see, e.g., Monti, 'Article 81 EC and Public Policy' (cited in n. 45), 1057.

[53] But see also the discussion of ancillary restraints in Section 3.F, pp. 242–246.

[54] These steps have similarities to the four steps taken in US rule of reason analysis, see A. Jones, 'Analysis of Agreements under U.S. and EC Antitrust Law—Convergence or Divergence?' [2006] 51 *Ant Bull* 691.

[55] See Chap. 3, Section 4.C, p. 126.

Although at first sight it might appear necessary to ensure accuracy that any anti-competitive effects should be identified and balanced against any pro-competitive benefits in each case, such an approach is likely to impose too high a burden on firms (especially small ones), competition agencies (and other claimants) and courts, creating a risk both that pro-competitive agreements will be deterred and too little enforcement/condemnation of harmful agreements will occur. In selecting the correct approach, a trade-off may therefore need to be made between more complex standards, requiring detailed factual and economic analysis, which are more difficult and costly to apply, and simpler bright line rules, which require less sophisticated analysis and less emphasis on expert economic evidence but which may, consequently, be less accurate than one which more closely analyses the factual and economic context of the case. It may also be necessary to consider whether an approach which may sometimes condemn legitimate business practices (false positives or 'Type 1' errors) and so potentially chill pro-competitive conduct is a lesser or greater evil than one which may sometimes allow anti-competitive practices to escape antitrust prohibitions (false negatives or 'Type 2' errors).[56] The OECD has on more than one occasion stated that a desirable approach to anti-competitive practices is one which is:[57]

- accurate—based on widely accepted economic principles and yielding minimal costs from false positives and false negatives;
- administrable—it should be relatively easy to apply;
- applicable—the wider the scope of conduct the approach can cover well, the better;
- consistent—it should yield predictable results;
- objective—it should leave no room for subjective input from the decision-maker; and
- transparent—the approach and its objectives should be understandable.

In seeking to achieve these goals, most competition law systems accept that some sorting of agreements into categories is required, distinguishing between and affording different treatment to, for example:

- Agreements which are very likely to cause anti-competitive effects and unlikely to have offsetting benefits; such agreements are frequently prohibited on proof that the agreement exists (as under the per se rule in the US where a conclusive presumption of unreasonableness applies) or are *presumed* to be incompatible with the competition law rules. A per se rule or presumption of illegality against such agreements provides clarity and legal certainty and a patent deterrent to the practice at issue. It is also easier and less costly to administer and apply than a more complex standard. An inherent difficulty with any such rule is, of course, that, in spite of its benefits, its application is bound, on some occasions, to result in hard cases and/or *false positives*.[58] Best practice thus suggests that per se rules, or presumptions of illegality, should be drawn on the basis of accepted economic principles so that they yield minimal error costs (from false positives, i.e. wrongly finding that a pro-competitive agreement infringes the competition law rules);
- Agreements which are very unlikely to cause anti-competitive effects—in some systems, such agreements may benefit from a safe harbour or a presumption of compatibility with the rules; and
- Agreements whose effects are more ambiguous—which require closer individual scrutiny of anti-competitive and pro-competitive effects. Because of the complex nature of such analysis, error risks also arise.

The question of how any such categories are to be drawn, how flexibly they are applied, and which agreements fall within each category is generally controversial. It will be seen that in the EU there are four main categories of antitrust analysis (see further Figure 4.1):

---

[56] See Chap. 1, Section 9.C, p. 57.

[57] See, e.g., OECD Policy Roundtables: Resale Price Maintenance (2008), available at <http://www.oecd.org/daf/competition/43835526.pdf>.

[58] See, e.g., L. Kaplow, 'Rules Versus Standards: An Economic Analysis' (1992–1993) 42 *Duke LJ* 556.

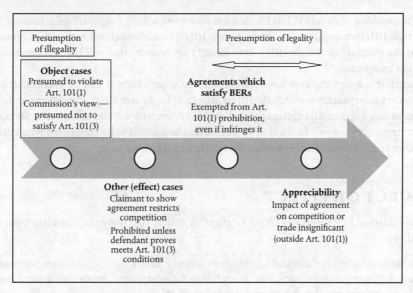

Figure 4.1 Categories of Antitrust Analysis under Article 101

(1) Agreements containing 'object' restraints—which are presumed to infringe Article 101(1) (unless their market impact is insignificant—see point (2)). The Commission's view is that they are also presumed not to satisfy the conditions of Article 101(3) (consequently, the safe harbour of a block exemption (see point (3)) will not apply). Although these presumptions are rebuttable, in practice it may be hard or impossible to do so;

(2) Agreements which do not appreciably restrict competition—EU law provides that agreements between undertaking which have a weak position on the market are unlikely to have a significant effect on competition and so fall outside of the scope of Article 101(1);

(3) Agreements benefiting from a block exemption—the block exemptions apply a presumption that agreements satisfying their conditions will produce efficiencies which offset any anticompetitive effects. Such agreements benefit from an exemption from Article 101 (a safe harbour) which can only be withdrawn prospectively;

(4) Other agreements—which have to be analysed individually to determine whether they have as their effect the restriction of competition and, if so, whether the agreement satisfies the four conditions of Article 101(3).

The question of which agreements fall within each of the categories, and so how broadly each category applies, is explored in the later sections of this chapter and later chapters of the book.

3. ARTICLE 101(1), AGREEMENTS WHICH HAVE AS THEIR OBJECT OR EFFECT THE PREVENTION, RESTRICTION, OR DISTORTION OF COMPETITION

A. GENERAL

In Section 2 it was explained that, in the past, the Commission was criticised for failing to take a sufficiently economic approach when determining whether or not an agreement restricts competition within the meaning of Article 101(1) but that it is now more willing to embark on economic analysis at the Article 101(1) stage. In particular, the Article 101(3) Guidelines clearly set out the Commission's view that the purpose of Article 101(1) is to identify agreements that will harm consumer welfare and market integration.[59]

This section surveys the case law and consider to what extent it can be reconciled with the Commission's interpretation of Article 101(1) set out in its Article 101(3) Guidelines and the GC's judgment in M6. Section 3.B explains the distinction between object and effect cases. Sections 3.C–3.E examine object cases whilst Section 3.F considers the analysis to be conducted when determining whether an agreement has as its effect the restriction of competition.

B. OBJECT OR EFFECT

The CJ has clarified that the words 'object or effect' in Article 101(1) are not cumulative but alternative conditions.

It has, since the judgment in Case 56/65 *LTM*…been settled case-law that the alternative nature of that requirement indicated by the conjunction 'or', leads, first, to the need to consider the precise purpose of the agreement, in the economic context in which it is to be applied.[60]

An agreement, decision, or concerted practice[61] is thus caught if *either* its object *or* its effect is the restriction of competition.[62]

Where…an analysis of the said clauses does not reveal the effect on competition to be sufficiently deleterious, the consequence of the agreement should then be considered and for it to be caught by the prohibition it is then necessary to find that factors are present that show that competition has in fact been prevented or restricted or distorted to an appreciable extent. The competition in question must be understood within the actual context in which it would occur in the absence of the agreement in dispute.[63]

Whether or not an agreement falls within the object or effect category has a critical impact on the likelihood of a violation being established and the burden of proof. Where it is shown that the object of an agreement is to restrict competition (and the other conditions of Article 101(1) are satisfied), a violation of Article 101 is proved unless it can be demonstrated that the agreement satisfies the Article 101(3) criteria.[64]

Where the object of the agreement is not found to restrict competition, the burden of proving that this is its *effect* is on the person alleging the breach. Only where this is established does the burden shift on to the parties to defend it under Article 101(3).

---

[59] See Art. 101(3) Guidelines, paras. 17 and 18.

[60] Case C-209/07, *Competition Authority* v. *Beef Industry Development Society Ltd and Barry Brothers (Carrigmore) Meals Ltd* (*BIDS*) [2008] ECR I-8637, para. 15.

[61] See, e.g., Case C-8/08, *T-Mobile Netherlands BV* v. *Raad van bestuur van de Nederlandse Mededingingsautoriteit* [2009] ECR I-4529.

[62] Case 56/65, *Société Technique Minière* v. *Maschinenbau Ulm GmbH* [1966] ECR 235, 249. See also Case C-234/89, *Delimitis* v. *Henninger Bräu* [1991] ECR I-935, para. 13 and Cases T-374, 375, 384, and 388/94, *European Night Services* v. *Commission* [1998] ECR II-3141, para. 136.

[63] Case 56/65, *Société Technique Minière* v. *Maschinebau Ulm GmbH* [1966] ECR 235, 249.

[64] Although it may not of course be easy to demonstrate that the agreement exists, see Chap. 3, Section 5.B.

C. AGREEMENTS[65] THAT RESTRICT COMPETITION BY OBJECT: RESTRAINTS WHICH, 'BY THEIR VERY NATURE', RESTRICT COMPETITION[66]

'The distinction between "infringements by object" and "infringements by effect" arises from the fact that certain forms of collusion between undertakings can be regarded, by their very nature, as being injurious to the proper functioning of normal competition.'[67]

Agreements containing restrictions that, in the context in which the agreement is operated,[68] are considered to be very likely to harm the objectives pursued by the competition rules are *presumed* to be injurious to competition—to be restrictive by object. This suggests that a bright line test is applied, holding that some restraints are so likely to have a 'pernicious' effect on competition and so unlikely to produce efficiencies that they are automatically assumed to restrict competition. A clear presumption against the practice is established and costs do not need to be incurred in establishing anti-competitive effects:[69] no proof or demonstration of restrictive effects is required.[70]

Only when the object of the agreement cannot be said to restrict competition is it necessary to consider whether restrictive effect can be established.

D. IDENTIFYING THE CATEGORY OF OBJECT RESTRAINTS

(i) Reference to the Content of the Agreement's Provisions, the Objectives it Seeks to Ascertain, and the Context of which it Forms Part

The case law provides that in order to determine whether conduct is 'by its very nature' injurious to competition or anti-competitive in nature, 'regard must be had inter alia to the content of its

---

[65] The criteria laid down for the purpose of determining whether conduct has as its object or effect the restriction of competition are applicable irrespective of whether the case entails an agreement, a decision, or a concerted practice, see Case C-8/08, *T-Mobile Netherlands BV v. Raad van bestuur van de Nederlandse Mededingingsautoriteit* [2009] ECR I-4529.

[66] See generally, e.g., A. Jones, 'Left Behind by Modernisation? Restrictions by Object under Article 101(1) [2010] 6(3) *European Competition Journal* 649, S. King, 'The Object Box: Law, Policy or Myth?' [2011] *European Competition Journal* 269, M. Mahtani, 'Thinking Outside the Object Box: An EU and UK Perspective' [2012] *European Competition Journal* 1, D. Bailey, 'Restrictions of Competition by Object under Article 101 TFEU' (2012) 49 *CMLRev* 559 and P Ibáñez Colomo, 'Market Failure, Transaction Costs and Articles 101(1) TFEU Case Law' [2012] *ELRev* 541.

[67] Case C-209/07, *Competition Authority v. Beef Industry Development Society Ltd and Barry Brothers (Carrigmore) Meals Ltd (BIDS)* [2008] ECR I-8637, para. 17.

[68] It is the terms of the agreement not the subjective intent of the parties that is important, see Section 3.D.iii.

[69] See Case C-8/08, *T-Mobile Netherlands BV v. Raad van bestuur van de Nederlandse Mededingingsautoriteit [2009]* ECR I-4529, AG Kokott, para. 43.

[70] '[F]or the purposes of applying Article [101(1)], there is no need to take account of the concrete effects of an agreement once it appears that it has as its object the prevention, restriction or distortion of competition', Cases 56 and 58/64, *Consten and Grundig* [1966] ECR 299, 342. It thus has similarities to the rule of per se illegality adopted in the US, see Section 1.E. Arguably, however, the parallel between the US *per se* and EU *object* cases should not be taken further than this. In contrast to the position in the US, (i) any alleged economic justifications or pro-competitive aspects of the agreement may, in the EU, be weighed against the restrictive elements at the Art. 101(3) stage (although in practice, it is rare for such agreements to meet Art. 101(3) criteria, this possibility at least remains, see Case T-17/93, *Matra Hachette* v. *Commission* [1994] ECR II-595, and Section 4.C); (ii) agreements characterised by the US courts as *per se* infringements are not identical to agreements held by the CJ to have as their object the restriction of competition; and (iii) agreements in the EU will escape prohibition in the EU if the impact of the agreement is 'insignificant' or of minor importance (see Section 3D.v and 3.E.v). These kinds of differences have led some to question whether it is useful to adopt the language of per se illegality at all under EU competition law. The differences are, however, actually more theoretical than real as agreements restricting competition by object are most unlikely to escape the Art. 101(1) prohibition on the grounds that they do not appreciably restrict competition or on the grounds that they satisfy the conditions of Art. 101(3).

provisions, the objectives it seeks to ascertain and the economic and legal context of which it forms part'.[71] Object categorisation thus appears to require an assessment of not only: (i) the content of the agreement; but also (ii) its objective; and (iii) context.[72]

(ii) Content

a. Contractual Restraints Likely to be Found to be Restrictive by Object

In this discussion, and in subsequent chapters of this book, it will be seen that jurisprudence has, over the years, established that agreements containing the following restraints[73] are highly likely to be found, in principle, to be restrictive by object:[74]

- Agreements between competitors to fix prices or to limit output or share markets (see especially *European Night Services* v. *Commission*[75]);

- Agreements between competitors to reduce capacity (see *Competition Authority* v. *Beef Industry Development Society Ltd (BIDS)*[76] where the CJ held that an agreement between beef and veal processors designed to reduce processing capacity had as its object the restriction of competition);

- Information exchanges between competitors designed, directly or indirectly, to fix purchase or selling prices (see *T-Mobile Netherlands BV* v. *Raad van bestuur van de Nederlandse Mededingingsautoriteit*);[77]

- Vertical price fixing agreements (resale price maintenance);[78]

- Vertical restraints conferring absolute territorial protection (ATP) on a distributor (see further *Consten and Grundig*) or otherwise aimed at partitioning national markets according to national borders or limiting parallel trade.[79]

---

[71] Case C-501/06 P, *GlaxoSmithKline Services Unlimited* v. *Commission*, [2009] ECR I-9291, para. 58.

[72] Object categorisation is not affected by the fact that an undertaking adversely affected and complaining about the agreement is operating illegally on the relevant market: Case C-68/12, *Protimonopolný úrad Slovenskej republiky* v. *Slovenská sporiteľňa as*, 7 February 2013, paras. 14–21.

[73] It may also be that collective exclusive dealing is restrictive by object, see *Nederlandse Federatieve Vereniging voor de Groothandel op Elektrotechnisch Gebied and Technische Unie* [2000] OJ L39/1 (collective exclusive dealing arrangements by association intended to prevent supplies to undertakings not belonging to that associations) *aff'd* Cases T5 and 6/00, *Nederlandse Federatieve Vereniging voor de Groothandel op Elektrotechnisch Gebied* v. *Commission* [2003] ECR II-5761 and Case C-105/04P, [2006] ECR I-8725. In the US, the courts distinguish between 'classic' collective boycott cases which are likely to result in predominantly anti-competitive effects, for example, where firms with market power boycott suppliers or customers in order to discourage them from doing business with competitors (illegal per se) and others which are appraised under the rule of reason, see, e.g., *FTC* v. *Indiana Federation of Dentists* 476 US 447 (1986).

[74] But see cases cited in n. 107 and discussion in Section 3.D.iii–vi, pp. 212–231.

[75] Cases T-374, 375, 384, and 388/94, [1998] ECR II-3141, para. 136 (the GC held that agreements containing obvious restrictions of competition, such as provisions in agreements between competitors fixing prices or sharing markets, will automatically be held to restrict competition within the meaning of Article 101(1)). See also Art. 101(3) Guidelines, para. 21 and Case T-360/09, *E.ON Ruhrgas AG* v. *Commission*, 29 June 2012 (agreement between actual or potential competitors not to penetrate each other's home market is restrictive by object), discussed in Chap. 9.

[76] Case C-209/07, [2008] ECR I-8637.

[77] Case C-8/08, [2009] ECR I-4529, paras. 36–43; see also the discussion of the case in Section 3.D.iii, pp. 212–214.

[78] See n. 99 and accompanying text.

[79] *Consten and Grundig* is discussed in the text accompanying n. 84. See especially Case C-501/06 P, *GlaxoSmithKline Services Unlimited* v. *Commission* [2009] ECR I-9291, para. 61, Case T-360/09, *E.ON Ruhrgas AG* v. *Commission*, 29 June 2012 and Cases C-403 and 429/08, *Premier League Ltd* v. *QC Leisure* and *Murphy* v. *Media Protection Services Ltd*, 4 October 2011. See also, e.g., Case 86/62, *Hasselblad* v. *Commission* [1984] ECR 883, para. 46 ('As the Commission rightly points out, a prohibition of sales between authorized dealers constitutes a restriction of their economic freedom and, consequently, a restriction of competition').

Further, when determining the content of the agreement it may be necessary to consider not only its express terms but the behaviour of the parties as '[t]he way in which an agreement is actually implemented may reveal a restriction of competition by object even where the formal agreement does not contain an express provision to that effect'.[80]

One of the greatest controversies about this so-called 'list' or 'box' of restraints is that it includes vertical restraints. The treatment of vertical restraints, in particular (considered further in Chapter 11) has caused considerable dispute. Since vertical agreements are not made between competitors but between providers of complementary goods and services, they are less obviously anti-competitive than horizontal agreements.[81] Some commentators have thus argued that competition law should only be concerned with vertical agreements where one of the parties to the agreement has market power and that no restraint incorporated within a vertical agreement should be treated as presumptively illegal or by its very nature injurious to competition. Indeed, some systems of competition law take a fairly relaxed or laissez-faire approach to vertical agreements.[82] In the EU, however, the cases establish that at least two categories of provision in vertical agreements, designed to eliminate competition between a supplier's distributors, will in principle be found to have as their object the restriction of competition.[83]

Since 1966 it has been established that distribution agreements which provide a distributor with an exclusive sales territory and protection from sales by others within the territory (creating ATP) have as their object the restriction of competition. This position was established by the CJ in *Consten and Grundig*[84] and has been followed in a number of cases since then. It was seen in Chapter 3 that *Consten and Grundig* concerned an agreement concluded between Grundig, a German manufacturer of radios, tape recorders, dictaphones, and televisions, and Consten. Consten was appointed exclusive distributor of Grundig's products in France. The agreement obliged Consten not to handle competing products, to order a minimum quantity of Grundig products, to stock accessories and spare parts, to provide after-sales services, and not to sell Grundig products outside France. In return, Grundig agreed not to deliver the product for sale in France itself and to prohibit all other distributors from seeking sales, actively or passively, within France. To reinforce the territorial protection Grundig assigned to Consten the rights to the Grundig trade mark GINT, in France. The provisions in the agreement were therefore intended to confer ATP upon Consten and to prevent all parallel trade in Grundig products. The parties argued that these restrictions on the conduct and/or the restriction on the sale of Grundig products by anyone else in France did not amount to restrictions of competition.

The Commission issued a decision finding that the agreement was designed to restrict and distort competition. The exclusive contract and ancillary arrangements (in particular, in relation to the trade mark) had the object of relieving Consten of the competition of other undertakings insofar as it involved the import or wholesale trade in Grundig products in France. Further, an exemption was refused. The agreement created ATP, prevented consumers obtaining a fair share of any of the benefits of the agreement, and contained restrictions which were not indispensable to the attainment of any benefit.

The parties appealed to the CJ, challenging the Commission's decision on several grounds.[85] In particular, they complained that the Commission had erred in its application of Article 101(1) since it had failed to base itself on the 'rule of reason'. It had been wrong simply to conclude that the object

---

[80] Article 101(3) Guidelines, para. 22.

[81] See Chap. 11.

[82] This was the position in the UK until 2004 (see e.g. R. Whish and D. Bailey, *Competition Law* (7th edn, Butterworths, 2012), Chap. 5) and see discussion of the position in the US in Chap. 11.

[83] But see also Chap. 11.

[84] Cases 56 and 58/64, *Consten and Grundig* [1966] ECR 299. It has been reiterated in a series of cases since then, see e.g. n. 79.

[85] One of the grounds being that Art. 101(1) did not apply to vertical agreements at all, see Chap. 3.

of its agreement was to restrict competition without considering its effect. Broadly, the parties' argument hinged on the fact that the agreement had been essential to enable Grundig to penetrate the French market and could not, therefore, be said to restrict competition.[86] The Commission had wrongly considered the transaction with hindsight, *ex post*, when matters had turned out well. If, however, it had taken account of the market at the time that the agreement was entered into, *ex ante*, when matters looked risky and uncertain, it would have been apparent that the distributor would not have proceeded without the territorial protection.[87] The exclusivity was crucial to prevent other distributors from taking a 'free ride'[88] on Consten's promotional and investment efforts. They would have been able to import the products more cheaply from Germany[89] (this was, in fact, exactly what UNEF, a Parisian company, and Leissner in Strasbourg had done).

The parties thus argued that despite the fact that the agreement resulted in the existence of only one distributor of Grundig products in France (there was a restriction on *intra-brand competition*), the agreement led to an increase in competition for electrical products in France (there was an increase in *inter-brand competition*). French consumers wishing to purchase such products now also had the option to purchase Grundig products in addition to those of the other manufacturers on the market. Consequently, the Commission had been wrong to focus solely on the restriction in intra-brand competition. It should instead have considered the effects of the disputed contract upon competition between Grundig and its competitor's products.

The notion that the Commission's decision should have been marked with greater market analysis was supported by Advocate-General Roemer,[90] who was highly critical of the Commission's approach. The Commission should have considered both whether the agreement was necessary for Grundig to penetrate the French market and whether or not there was vigorous competition between producers of competing products. Article 101(1) should not have been applied on the basis of purely theoretical considerations to a situation which might, upon closer inspection, reveal no appreciable adverse effects on competition. Article 101(1) required a consideration of the effects of the agreement on the market. This could not be established without looking at the market *in concreto* and without taking account of competition between similar products. In a case like this one, where the agreement had already been implemented, the Commission should have made a comparison between two market situations: that after making the agreement and that which would have arisen had there been no agreement.[91] If Grundig would not have found an outlet for its products in the absence of supplying a sole concessionaire, the exclusive distribution agreement clearly promoted competition. It would have been necessary for Grundig to gain access to or penetrate the new market. In the AG's view, therefore, Article 101(1) should not be applied if, in the absence of the agreement appointing a single distributor exclusively in France, Grundig would not have found an outlet for its products.

In this case the CJ did not agree with its Advocate-General but upheld the Commission's decision.[92] It held that the agreement giving Consten a monopoly over the sale of Grundig products in France (ATP) had as its *object* the restriction of competition so that an assessment of its *effect* was unnecessary. The arguments of the parties thus fell on deaf ears.

---

[86] In the absence of the promise of exclusivity, a distributor would not have been encouraged to take on the risky new venture and invest resources in promoting the new product on the French market. Such a distributor would have to persuade French consumers to purchase Grundig products instead of other competing brands of electrical products available and established on the French market.

[87] See, e.g., V. Korah, *An Introductory Guide to EC Competition Law and Practice* (9th edn, Hart Publishing, 2007), section 2.4.

[88] For a more detailed discussion of the free rider arguments, see Chap. 11.

[89] The German distributors did not, consequently, have to engage in such high levels of promotion and investment.

[90] Cases 56 and 58/64, *Consten and Grundig* [1966] ECR 299.

[91] See the CJ's judgment in Case 56/65, *Société Technique Minière v. Maschinenbau Ulm GmbH* [1966] ECR 235, discussed in Section 3.E.iv, pp. 239–240.

[92] Cases 56 and 58/64, [1966] ECR 299.

Cases 56 and 58/64, *Établissements Consten S.à.R.L. and Grundig-Verkaufs-GmbH* v. *Commission* [1966] ECR 299, 342–3

Court of Justice

The complaints concerning the criterion of restriction on competition

The applicants and the German Government maintain that since the Commission restricted its examination solely to Grundig products the decision was based upon a false concept of competition and of the rules on prohibition contained in Article [101(1)], since this concept applies particularly to competition between similar products of different makes; the Commission, before declaring Article [101(1)] to be applicable, should, by basing itself upon the 'rule of reason', have considered the economic effects of the disputed contract upon competition between the different makes. There is a presumption that vertical sole distributorship agreements are not harmful to competition and in the present case there is nothing to invalidate that presumption. On the contrary, the contract in question has increased the competition between similar products of different makes. The principle of freedom of competition concerns the various stages and manifestations of competition. Although competition between producers is generally more noticeable than that between distributors of products of the same make, it does not thereby follow that an agreement tending to restrict the latter kind of competition should escape the prohibition of Article [101(1)] merely because it might increase the former.

Besides, for the purpose of applying Article [101(1)], there is no need to take account of the concrete effects of an agreement once it appears that it has as its object the prevention, restriction or distortion of competition.

Therefore the absence in the contested decision of any analysis of the effects of the agreement on competition between similar products of different makes does not, of itself, constitute a defect in the decision.

It thus remains to consider whether the contested decision was right in founding the prohibition of the disputed agreement under Article [101(1)] on the restriction on competition created by the agreement in the sphere of the distribution of Grundig products alone. The infringement which was found to exist by the contested decision results from the absolute territorial protection created [by] the said contract in favour of Consten on the basis of French law. The applicants thus wished to eliminate any possibility of competition at the wholesale level in Grundig products in the territory specified in the contra[c]t essentially by two methods.

First, Grundig undertook not to deliver even indirectly to third parties products intended for the area covered by the contract. The restrictive nature of that undertaking is obvious if it is considered in the light of the prohibition on exporting which was imposed not only on Consten but also on all the other sole concessionnaires of Grundig, as well as the German wholesalers.

Secondly, the registration in France by Consten of the GINT trade mark, which Grundig affixes to all its products, is intended to increase the protection inherent in the disputed agreement, against the risk of parallel imports into France of Grundig products, by adding the protection deriving from the law on industrial property rights. Thus no third party could import Grundig products from other Member States of the [Union] for resale in France without running serious risks.

The defendant properly took into account the whole distribution system thus set up by Grundig. In order to arrive at a true representation of the contractual position the contract must be placed in the economic and legal context in the light of which it was concluded by the parties. Such a procedure is not to be regarded as an unwarrantable interference in legal transactions or circumstances which were not the subject of the proceedings before the Commission.

The situation as ascertained above results in the isolation of the French market and makes it possible to charge for the products in question prices which are sheltered from all effective competition. In addition, the more producers succeed in their efforts to render their own makes of product individually distinct in the eyes of the consumer, the more the effectiveness of competition between producers tend[s] to diminish. Because of the considerable impact of distribution costs on the aggregate cost price, it seems important that competition between dealers should also be stimulated. The efforts of the dealer are stimulated by competition between distributors of products of the same make. Since the agreement thus aims at isolating the French market for Grundig products and maintaining artificially, for products of a very well-known brand, separate national markets within the [EU], it is therefore such as to distort competition in the Common Market.

It was therefore proper for the contested decision to hold that the agreement constitutes an infringement of Article [101(1)]. No further considerations, whether of economic data (price differences between France and Germany, representative character of the type of appliance considered, level of overheads borne by Consten) or of the corrections of the criteria upon which the Commission relied in its comparisons between the situations of the French and German markets, and no possible favourable effects of the agreement in other respects, can in any way lead, in the face of abovementioned restrictions, to a different solution under Article [101(1)].

The judgment in *Consten and Grundig* establishes that Article 101(1) applies to horizontal and vertical agreements, to all agreements which affect trade between Member States even if the effect on trade is not a prejudicial one,[93] and, potentially, to agreements relating to the licensing of intellectual property rights,[94] and that Article 101(1) applies to an agreement which had as its object the restriction of competition irrespective of its alleged effects.[95] Although the CJ recognised the importance of competition between producers (inter-brand competition) it held that agreements which restricted competition between distributors (intra-brand competition) could also restrict competition for the purposes of Article 101(1). It was important that competition between dealers should be stimulated, and intra-brand as well as inter-brand competition maintained. In particular, restrictions on intra-brand competition might facilitate brand differentiation and diminish competition between producers. The agreement in question eliminated any possibility of competition between distributors of Grundig products and led to the isolation of the French market and so distorted competition and infringed Article 101(1). The Commission had not, therefore, erred by failing to consider the effects of the agreement for the purposes of Article 101(1).

There seems little doubt that the Court's judgment in *Consten and Grundig* was influenced not only by the pernicious effects of the agreement's provisions from a competition perspective, but also by the effects of the agreement from the single market perspective.[96] Whatever the economic justifications for the agreement the affront to the single market goal in this case was too severe.[97] Arguably, it was this factor that led to categorising the agreement as an '*object*' case. The object of the agreement was to grant *ATP* and to eliminate competition at a wholesale level in Grundig products in the territory. The French market had been isolated and the French distributor sheltered from all effective competition. The Court sent out a clear message: agreements which divide up the internal market and preclude all cross-border trade in the contract product will not be tolerated. Provisions providing for such protection in an agreement will automatically infringe Article 101(1).

---

[93] See Chap. 3.

[94] The CJ also held that the agreement relating to the GINT trade mark infringed Art. 101(1). Otherwise, Consten could have used the trade mark to achieve the objectives of the prohibited exclusive distribution agreement: see Chap. 12.

[95] The object of the agreement was to restrict competition even though the parties might have been able to show that the agreement was necessary to ensure that the supplier found an outlet for its products.

[96] See also, e.g., Case T-360/09, *E.ON Ruhrgas AG v. Commission*, 29 June 2012.

[97] See Chap. 1.

G. Amato, *Antitrust and the Bounds of Power* (Hart Publishing, 1997), 48–49

In the leading case in this area, *Consten and Grundig*, of 1966…the Commission challenged the exclusive agreement for France that Grundig had given to Consten and had strengthened by barring its wholesale distributors in Germany and other countries from selling to France, where the price of Grundig products was kept higher than elsewhere, net of French tax. The parties maintained, first before the Commission itself and then before the Court of Justice, that Article [101] referred primarily to inter-brand competition, and that as far as intra-brand restrictions went, one had to presume efficiency in promoting inter-brand competition failing proof of the contrary. This argument copied word-for-word approaches of the Chicago School, which in fact at the time the American courts themselves had rejected, in the name of protection (dropped later in the *Sylvania* case) for the right of each distributor or retailer to exercise freedom of trade without restraint. Our court did not accept the arguments either, but for very different reasons. It accepted that inter-brand competition was the most relevant for the purposes of prohibition under Article [101], but added that this did not *a priori* exempt intra-brand restrictions, with the consequence—inconceivable today (and perhaps in earlier times too) for an American court—that the fact that the Commission was not concerned to ascertain the size of inter-brand competition was irrelevant. On this basis, the absolute territorial protection by which the exclusivity for France was guaranteed was illegitimate. It is indeed true, said the Court, that imports have an effect on the supply planning that Consten may engage in and on the organization of services it may offer customers. But a margin of risk is inherent in commercial activity, and in any case 'the more manufacturers isolate themselves from each other in consumers' eyes, the more competition among them is reduced. Moreover, competition among wholesale distributors of products of one and the same brand enlivens the downstream market of sales to final consumers'.

As we can see, these are very important assertions of principle that bring the decision close to the American ones of the 1960s. But there are two important differences, one explicit and the other implicit. The explicit one is that the need for intra-brand competition is based on protection not of an individual right (freedom of trade) but of a general and objective principle (competitiveness of the market in all its segments). The implicit one is that such a pervasive and rigorous principle is asserted to the extent that it serves to protect another principle, a higher one in 1966, that of market integration. For the territory protected by Consten's rigid exclusivity coincided with that of the French State, and both the Commission and the Court saw this protection as persistence of the segmentation of economic activities along national frontiers, violating the 'Grundnorm' of the whole [EU] system.

In a series of cases the CJ has also confirmed that vertical price restraints (imposing fixed or minimum prices on a dealer so eliminating price competition between dealers) have as their object the restriction of competition.[98] In *SA Binon & Cie v. SA Agence et Messageries de la Presse*[99] the CJ stated: 'provisions which fix the prices to be observed in contracts with third parties constitute, of themselves, a restriction on competition within the meaning of Article [101(1)]'.[100]

In accordance with this approach, the CJ has also taken the view that restrictions in intellectual property licensing agreements on the determination of prices for the licensed products and providing ATP for the licensee have as their *object* the restriction of competition within the meaning of Article 101(1).[101]

---

[98] See the discussion of resale price maintenance (RPM), Chap. 11.

[99] Case 243/83, [1985] ECR 2015.

[100] Case 243/83, [1985] ECR 2015, para. 44 and Chap. 11.

[101] See Chap. 12 and, e.g., Case 258/78, *Nungesser v. Commission* [1982] ECR 2015, Case 27/87, *Erauw-Jacquéry Sprl v. La Hesbignonne Société Coopérative* [1988] ECR 1919, case 62/79, *Coditel v. Ciné Vog Films (Coditel I)* [1980] ECR 881 and Cases C-403 and 429/08, *Premier League Ltd v. QC Leisure* and *Murphy v. Media Protection Services Ltd*, 4 October 2011.

212 | EU COMPETITION LAW

b. Is there a Defined List of Object Restraints?

It is important to remember that the category of object restraints is not as simple as constituting a list.[102] The restraints set out in Section 3.D.(ii)a provide a starting point but the objectives of an agreement and the context in which it operates are also relevant to the assessment. These factors could require the category to be: expanded—to include restraints whose anti-competitive nature is apparent from the objective it pursues and/or the context in which it operates; or narrowed—to exclude agreements containing the listed restraints where it is clear from the objectives pursued and/or the context in which it operates that a presumption of anti-competitive effects is not warranted. Further, it is possible that the approach to a particular restraint could change over time to reflect, for example, changes in economic thinking (see section 3.D.vi). Although, therefore, it can be predicted that the agreements containing these restraints will ordinarily be found to have as their object the restriction of competition, it may be arguable in a given case that object categorisation is inappropriate—either generally or in relation to the specific facts/circumstances of a case.

(iii) The Objective of the Agreement and the Context in which it Operates: Expanding the List of Object Restraints

In *T-Mobile* the CJ indicated that the category of object restraints may be expanded beyond the restraints identified in Section 3.D.ii. Although the practice at issue in *T-Mobile* may have indirectly facilitated the fixing of prices, the CJ stated in very broad terms that:

in order for a concerted practice to be regarded as having an anti-competitive object, it is sufficient that it has the *potential* to have a negative impact on competition. In other words, the concerted practice must *simply be capable* in an individual case, having regard to the specific legal and economic context, of resulting in the prevention, restriction or distortion of competition … Whether and to what extent, in fact, such anti-competitive effects result can only be of relevance for determining the amount of any fine and assessing any claim for damages[103] [emphasis added].

Clearly, this type of broad statement, suggesting that any agreement with the potential to impact on competition negatively might be restrictive by object, is likely to encourage competition agencies—or others trying to establish a violation of Article 101(1)—to argue that a more expansive category of restraints is restrictive by object. In so doing, an obligation to demonstrate restrictive effects is side-stepped and the burden is shifted to the parties to defend their agreement under Article 101(3). In *Allianz Hungária Biztosító Zrt, Generali-Providencia Biztosító Zrt v. Gazdasági Versenyhivatal*,[104] for example, the Hungarian competition authority found that a number of bilateral agreements concluded between insurance companies and car repairers (or a Car Repairers' Association) might be restrictive of competition by object. Again the CJ indicated that the category of object restraints is potentially far-reaching, stating that:[105]

agreements would also amount to a restriction of competition by object in the event that the referring court found that it is likely that, having regard to the economic context, competition on that market would be eliminated or seriously weakened following the conclusion of those agreements. In order to determine the likelihood of such a result, that court should in particular take into consideration the structure of that market, the existence of alternative distribution channels and their respective importance and the market power of the companies concerned.

---

[102] See Case C-209/07, *Competition Authority v. Beef Industry Development Society Ltd and Barry Brothers (Carrigmore) Meals Ltd (BIDS)* [2008] ECR I-8637, AG Trstenjack and articles cited in n. 66.

[103] Case C-8/08, *T-Mobile Netherlands BV v. Raad van bestuur van de Nederlandse Mededingingsautoriteit [2009]* ECR I-4529, para. 31. See further Case T-587/08, *Fresh Del Monte Produce v. Commission*, 14 March 2013, para. 306 and Chap. 9.

[104] Case C-32/11, 14 March 2013.

[105] *Allianz Hungária Biztosító Zrt, Generali-Providencia Biztosító Zrt v. Gazdasági Versenyhivatal*, Case C-32/11, 14 March 2013, para. 48.

In this case the Court stressed that a restriction by object could not be ruled out simply because the agreements were vertical in nature as such agreements could have significant restrictive potential. Further, and importantly, the CJ made it clear that vertical agreements which implement or affirm a horizontal agreement which is restrictive by object will also be considered to be restrictive by object.

In *Pierre Fabre* v. *Président de l'Autorité de la concurrence*,[106] the CJ also cast doubt on the traditional view that selective distribution agreements require some form of analysis of the restrictive effects of the agreement, stating that they necessarily affect competition and 'are to be considered, in the absence of objective justification, as "restrictions by object"'.

The extent to which the object category can be stretched is thus still being tested. Arguably, however, the approach set out in *T-Mobile*, and these other cases, is overly-expansive and, indeed, rather worryingly vague and broad. In particular, the extended analysis suggested by the CJ to be necessary to determine whether the object of an agreement is to restrict competition seems to collapse or blur the distinction between object and effects cases and makes it unclear exactly how much specific market analysis is required before a conclusion that an agreement is restrictive by object can be reached (taking account of the specific legal and economic context but without having to demonstrate whether and to what extent anti-competitive effects materialise) and before full effects analysis must be conducted. Indeed, the suggestion that any agreement with the potential to have a negative impact on competition is restrictive by object could, at its broadest construction, do away with the need for effects analysis completely.

Arguably, the approach to object restrictions should be more closely in tune with the economic effects of the conduct so that only a relatively narrow category of agreements—which have been established to always or almost always be restrictive of competition—should be so defined. Such an approach would prevent technical violations of Article 101(1) from occurring which require justification under Article 101(3). Some of the difficulties with the approach of the CJ to the 'legal and economic context' of the case in *T-Mobile* are explored in the following extract from an article by Dr Meyring.

B. Meyring, 'T-Mobile: Further Confusion on Information Exchanges Between Competitors' [2010] *JECLAP* 30

Analysis

It has often been highlighted that the [*T-Mobile*] ruling makes clear that one single meeting between competitors can be enough for a serious violation of Article [101] and can trigger the presumption that participants have considered what was discussed at this meeting when they determine their market conduct. The judgment is also important in that it highlights that [Article 101] goes beyond protecting final consumers and also aims to protect competitors as well as a competitive market structure as such. Finally, the judgment contains interesting and controversial language on the assessment of information exchanges. This is the focus of this paper. At the outset, the Court summarises its approach to the distinction between violations by object and violations by effect. It points out that both concepts are alternatives and that, contrary to the national court's view, there is no need to analyse the effects of a specific practice once it is established that its object was to restrict competition.

The role of the economic context in the assessment remains, however, unclear. On the one hand, the Court holds that the conduct must be *capable* of restricting competition in its '*specific legal and economic context*', even in the framework of a restriction by object. In other words, this seems to indicate that conduct that might aim at a restriction of competition but cannot achieve this purpose because of a specific economic or regulatory context cannot be treated as a violation by object. This is in line with the statement according to which '*the intention of the parties is not an essential factor*'. On the other hand,

---

[106] Case C-439/09, 13 October 2011. See further Chap. 11

the Court reemphasises that it is irrelevant 'whether and to what extent' anti-competitive effects in fact materialise.

Even though this seems to be what point 31 says ('it is sufficient'), it would be wrong to conclude that any potential to have a negative impact is sufficient to establish that a practice is a restriction by object. First, this would do away with restrictions by effect altogether because practices that are not even capable of having anti-competitive effects will not produce such effects in any event—and all other restrictions would be restrictions by object. Second, the concept of a violation by object is a narrow one. As the Court notes in point 29, restrictions by object are only the severest forms of collusion that 'can be regarded, by their very nature, as being injurious to the proper functioning of normal competition'. These practices are hardcore cartels and it is indeed common sense that these are prohibited, whether or not they actually turn out to be effective in the individual case. In its Guidelines on the application of Article [101(3)], the Commission speaks of restrictions that 'have such a high potential of negative effects on competition that it is unnecessary . . . to demonstrate any actual effects on the market' (point 21).

Practices outside this category may or may not affect competition, depending on their economic context. They merit and require a careful analysis as to their effects on competition. It would be inappropriate to circumvent this requirement by simply classifying them as restrictions by object.

The Court argues that 'an exchange of information which is capable of removing uncertainties between participants as regards the timing, extent and details of the modifications to be adopted by the undertaking concerned must be regarded as pursuing an anticompetitive object' (point 41). This is a bold statement and it is worth recalling that, in the case at hand, the parties had discussed contemplated modifications of their standard remuneration for dealers. This discussion related to a strategic choice that would be implemented in the future. Moreover, the request for a preliminary ruling suggests that the future levels of remuneration were not unilaterally set and then exchanged but were 'discussed', which implies that the aim of the conversations was to determine the right level. Advocate General Kokott sets out in her opinion that the discussions indeed resulted in a coordination of market conduct (at point 36). It is not surprising that the Court classifies such a discussion as a restriction by object. However, it seems very odd in this context to elaborate, as the Court does, on information exchanges. Where two competitors discuss, on the basis of their market knowledge and strategic planning, how their competing products should best be priced, we would hardly speak of an information exchange but rather of a price fixing cartel. And it seems obvious to treat such a discussion as a violation by object. The legal assessment of the information exchange in this framework would be irrelevant, and would only obscure the real issue. The fact that the discussion covered other conditions should not make any difference to this part of the analysis.

The phrase 'information exchange' appears in none of the three preliminary questions, and the legal analysis of information exchanges as such seems to be irrelevant for the case that the national Court has to decide. By focusing on the exchange of confidential information, the ECJ produced statements that are confusing and far too broad. The question in this case was not when information exchanges are legal but where precisely is the line in the sand that separates violations by object from practices that turn on the analysis of their effect. The Court has missed an opportunity to provide more clarity as to the crucial question when precisely a practice is a restriction by object. It has also failed to acknowledge, like Advocate General Kokott at point 37 of her opinion, that not every exchange of information between competitors has an anticompetitive object.

E. Practical significance

The judgment leads to further confusion in the competition law analysis of information exchanges. Whereas the Court's *John Deere* judgment had used a checklist approach to analyse the effects of an information exchange between competitors, the Maritime Transport Guidelines and the cases on AC Nielsen in Finland, Norway, and Sweden have moved to a more economic approach to effects. The ECJ's judgment in *T-Mobile Netherlands* should not be misinterpreted as advocating a simplistic *per se* approach to such cases. Rather, it makes clear that an information exchange that is ancillary to a cartel must be treated together with the cartel and as a *per se* violation. The Court could have stated this more clearly.

(iv) The Objective of the Agreement and the Context in which it Operates: Narrowing the List of Object Restraints

a. General

Conversely, the CJ has occasionally accepted that an agreement containing restraints set out in the list in Section 3.D.ii.a is not restrictive by object.[107] Where a claimant alleges that an agreement is restrictive by object such an argument is, therefore, frequently countered by defendants with the argument that the objective and context in which an agreement is operated requires a *narrower* interpretation of the category of restrictions by object, for example, where (i) the parties did not intend to restrict competition; (ii) the agreement is not intended to be anti-competitive but rather is designed to achieve a pro-competitive or other legitimate objective (so that a presumption of illegality is unwarranted); and/or (iii) it is plain from the overall context in which the agreement operates that an assumption of anti-competitive effects is inappropriate (there is no credible theory of harm). These types of argument have been used to contend either simply that the restraints do not have as their object the restriction of competition (and so infringe Article 101(1) only if restrictive effects are demonstrated) or, in exceptional circumstances, that the restraints do not restrict competition at all as they are essential to the operation of a legitimate pro-competitive agreement.

b. Subjective Intention of the Parties: the Parties did not Intend to Restrict Competition

When assessing objectives, closer regard is 'paid to the wording of its provision and to the objectives which it is intended to attain'[108] than to the subjective intention of the parties.[109] It appears therefore that a subjective intent to restrict competition by object or to infringe Article 101 is not a necessary condition to a violation.[110] Conversely, the fact that the parties did not intend to restrict competition and infringe Article 101 will not necessarily deprive an agreement of an anti-competitive object. Rather, intention is determined objectively, so the parties' subjective intent cannot be relied upon to exculpate otherwise anti-competitive behaviour. In *BIDS*,[111] for example, the CJ rejected the parties' argument that by acting to reduce capacity they had not acted with an anti-competitive purpose or an intention to injure competition and the welfare of consumers, but with the intention of rationalising the beef industry and so making it more competitive by reducing, but not eliminating, production overcapacity.

c. Restrictions of Competition Essential to, or Inherent in, the Pursuit of a Legitimate (Public Policy?) Objective: the CJ's Judgment in *Wouters*

In *BIDS*,[112] the CJ also rejected the parties' justification that they had simply acted to deal with an industry crisis. Rather it held that this 'type of arrangement conflicts patently with the concept

---

[107] See, e.g., Case C-250/92, *Gøttrup-Klim Grovvareforeninger and Others v. Dansk Landbrugs Grovvareselskab AmbA* [1994] ECR I-5641 (discussed in Section 3.F.iii), Case 262/81, *Coditel v. Ciné Vog Films* [1982] ECR 3381 (*Coditel II*) and Case 27/87, *Erauw-Jacquéry v. La Hesbignonne* [1988] ECR 1919 (see Chap. 12, cf. Cases C-403 and 429/08, *Premier League Ltd v. QC Leisure* and *Murphy v. Media Protection Services Ltd*, 4 October 2011). See also discussion of Case T-111/08, *MasterCard Inc v. Commission* 24 May 2012 (in Section 3.F.iv.c).

[108] Case C-209/07, *Competition Authority v. Beef Industry Development Society Ltd and Barry Brothers (Carrigmore) Meals Ltd* [2008] ECR I-8637, para. 21

[109] Although intention can be taken into account, Case C-8/08, *T-Mobile Netherlands BV v. Raad van bestuur van de Nederlandse Mededingingsautoriteit* [2009] ECR I-4529, para. 27.

[110] Where an intent to restrict competition is found, however, this may be relevant to a determination that the agreement is restrictive by object, see e.g., Case T-368/00, *General Motors Nederland and Opel Nederland* [2003] ECR II-4491.

[111] Case C-209/07, *Competition Authority v. Beef Industry Development Society Ltd and Barry Brothers (Carrigmore) Meals Ltd* [2008] ECR I-8637.

[112] Case C-209/07, *Competition Authority v. Beef Industry Development Society Ltd and Barry Brothers (Carrigmore) Meals Ltd* [2008] ECR I-8637, para. 21, set out in text accompanying n. 114.

inherent in the [TFEU] provisions relating to competition, according to which each economic operator must determine independently the policy which it intends to adopt on the common market'.[113] Further, that an agreement could restrict competition by object even if that was not its sole aim:

In that regard, even supposing it to be established that the parties to an agreement acted without any subjective intention of restricting competition, but with the object of remedying the effects of a crisis in their sector, such considerations are irrelevant for the purposes of applying Article [101(1)]. Indeed, an agreement may be regarded as having a restrictive object even if it does not have the restriction of competition as its sole aim but also pursues other legitimate objectives (General Motors v. Commission, paragraph 64 . . .). It is only in connection with Article [101(3)] that matters such as those relied upon by BIDS may, if appropriate, be taken into consideration for the purposes of obtaining an exemption from the prohibition laid down in Article [101(1)].[114]

In some judgments, however, the CJ has held that an agreement—even one containing severe restraints which might ordinarily be considered to be restrictive by object—will not restrict competition within the meaning of Article 101(1) where those restraints do not go beyond what is necessary to achieve a legitimate objective.

In *Wouters v. Algemene Raad van de Nederlandse Orde van Advocaten*,[115] for example, the CJ had to consider the compatibility with Article 101 of rules adopted in the Netherlands which prohibited members of the Bar practising in full partnership with accountants. The question arose in national proceedings. Following a reference to it under Article 267 TFEU, the CJ found that Regulations adopted by a body such as the Bar of the Netherlands had to be regarded as a decision adopted by an association of undertakings. Further, that the regulations did not have as their object or effect the restriction of competition.

Case C-309/99, *Wouters* v. *Algemene Raad van de Nederlandse Orde van Advocaten* [2002] ECR I-1577

Court of Justice

73. By its second question the national court seeks, essentially, to ascertain whether a regulation such as the 1993 Regulation which, in order to guarantee the independence and loyalty to the client of members of the Bar who provide legal assistance in conjunction with members of other liberal professions, adopts universally binding rules governing the formation of multi-disciplinary partnerships, has the object or effect of restricting competition within the common market and is likely to affect trade between Member States.

. . .

86. It appears to the Court that the national legislation in issue in the main proceedings has an adverse effect on competition and may affect trade between Member States.

87. As regards the adverse effect on competition, the areas of expertise of members of the Bar and of accountants may be complementary. Since legal services, especially in business law, more and more frequently require recourse to an accountant, a multi-disciplinary partnership of members of the Bar and accountants would make it possible to offer a wider range of services, and indeed to propose new ones. Clients would thus be able to turn to a single structure for a large part of the services necessary for the organisation, management and operation of their business (the 'one-stop shop' advantage).

---

[113] Case C-209/07, *Competition Authority v. Beef Industry Development Society Ltd and Barry Brothers (Carrigmore) Meals Ltd* [2008] ECR I-8637, para. 34.

[114] Case C-209/07, *Competition Authority v. Beef Industry Development Society Ltd and Barry Brothers (Carrigmore) Meals Ltd* [2008] ECR I-8637, para. 21.

[115] Case C-309/99, [2002] ECR I-1577.

88. Furthermore, a multi-disciplinary partnership of members of the Bar and accountants would be capable of satisfying the needs created by the increasing interpenetration of national markets and the consequent necessity for continuous adaptation to national and international legislation.

89. Nor, finally, is it inconceivable that the economies of scale resulting from such multi-disciplinary partnerships might have positive effects on the cost of services.

90. A prohibition of multi-disciplinary partnerships of members of the Bar and accountants, such as that laid down in the 1993 Regulation, is therefore liable to limit production and technical development within the meaning of Article [101(1)(b)].

...

97. However, not every agreement between undertakings or every decision of an association of undertakings which restricts the freedom of action of the parties or of one of them necessarily falls within the prohibition laid down in Article [101(1)]. For the purposes of application of that provision to a particular case, account must first of all be taken of the overall context in which the decision of the association of undertakings was taken or produces its effects. More particularly, account must be taken of its objectives, which are here connected with the need to make rules relating to organisation, qualifications, professional ethics, supervision and liability, in order to ensure that the ultimate consumers of legal services and the sound administration of justice are provided with the necessary guarantees in relation to integrity and experience (see, to that effect, Case C-3/95 *Reisebüro Broede*...paragraph 38). It has then to be considered whether the consequential effects restrictive of competition are inherent in the pursuit of those objectives.

98. Account must be taken of the legal framework applicable in the Netherlands, on the one hand, to members of the Bar and to the Bar of the Netherlands, which comprises all the registered members of the Bar in that Member State, and on the other hand, to accountants.

99. As regards members of the Bar, it has consistently been held that, in the absence of specific Community rules in the field, each Member State is in principle free to regulate the exercise of the legal profession in its territory (Case 107/83 *Klopp*...paragraph 17, and *Reisebüro*, paragraph 37). For that reason, the rules applicable to that profession may differ greatly from one Member State to another.

100. The current approach of the Netherlands, where Article 28 of the Advocatenwet entrusts the Bar of the Netherlands with responsibility for adopting regulations designed to ensure the proper practice of the profession, is that the essential rules adopted for that purpose are, in particular, the duty to act for clients in complete independence and in their sole interest, the duty, mentioned above, to avoid all risk of conflict of interest and the duty to observe strict professional secrecy.

101. Those obligations of professional conduct have not inconsiderable implications for the structure of the market in legal services, and more particularly for the possibilities for the practice of law jointly with other liberal professions which are active on that market.

102. Thus, they require of members of the Bar that they should be in a situation of independence *vis-à-vis* the public authorities, other operators and third parties, by whom they must never be influenced. They must furnish, in that respect, guarantees that all steps taken in a case are taken in the sole interest of the client.

103. By contrast, the profession of accountant is not subject, in general, and more particularly, in the Netherlands, to comparable requirements of professional conduct.

104. As the Advocate General has rightly pointed out in paragraphs 185 and 186 of his Opinion, there may be a degree of incompatibility between the 'advisory' activities carried out by a member of the Bar and the 'supervisory' activities carried out by an accountant. The written observations submitted by the respondent in the main proceedings show that accountants in the Netherlands perform a task of certification of accounts. They undertake an objective examination and audit of their clients' accounts, so as to be able to impart to interested third parties their personal opinion concerning the reliability of those accounts. It follows that in the Member State concerned accountants are not bound by a rule of

professional secrecy comparable to that of members of the Bar, unlike the position under German law, for example.

105. The aim of the 1993 Regulation is therefore to ensure that, in the Member State concerned, the rules of professional conduct for members of the Bar are complied with, having regard to the prevailing perceptions of the profession in that State. The Bar of the Netherlands was entitled to consider that members of the Bar might no longer be in a position to advise and represent their clients independently and in the observance of strict professional secrecy if they belonged to an organisation which is also responsible for producing an account of the financial results of the transactions in respect of which their services were called upon and for certifying those accounts.

106. Moreover, the concurrent pursuit of the activities of statutory auditor and of adviser, in particular legal adviser, also raises questions within the accountancy profession itself, as may be seen from the Commission Green Paper 96/C/321/01 'The role, the position and the liability of the statutory auditor within the European Union' (OJ 1996 C 321, p. 1; see, in particular, paragraphs 4.12 to 4.14).

107. A regulation such as the 1993 Regulation could therefore reasonably be considered to be necessary in order to ensure the proper practice of the legal profession, as it is organised in the Member State concerned.

108. Furthermore, the fact that different rules may be applicable in another Member State does not mean that the rules in force in the former State are incompatible with [EU] law (see, to that effect, Case C-108/96 *Mac Quen and Others*...paragraph 33). Even if multi-disciplinary partnerships of lawyers and accountants are allowed in some Member States, the Bar of the Netherlands is entitled to consider that the objectives pursued by the 1993 Regulation cannot, having regard in particular to the legal regimes by which members of the Bar and accountants are respectively governed in the Netherlands, be attained by less restrictive means (see, to that effect, with regard to a law reserving judicial debt-recovery activity to lawyers, *Reisebüro*, paragraph 41).

109. In light of those considerations, it does not appear that the effects restrictive of competition such as those resulting for members of the Bar practising in the Netherlands from a regulation such as the 1993 Regulation go beyond what is necessary in order to ensure the proper practice of the legal profession (see, to that effect, Case C-250/92 *DLG*...paragraph 35).

110. Having regard to all the foregoing considerations, the answer to be given to the second question must be that a national regulation such as the 1993 Regulation adopted by a body such as the Bar of the Netherlands does not infringe Article [101(1)], since that body could reasonably have considered that that regulation, despite the effects restrictive of competition that are inherent in it, is necessary for the proper practice of the legal profession, as organised in the Member State concerned.

The reasoning adopted by the CJ in this case is difficult. It first stated that it appeared 'that the national legislation in issue...has an adverse effect on competition' since partnerships of lawyers and accountants would, for example, be able to offer a wider range of services, propose new ones, and result in economies of scale.[116] That being so, the prohibition of multidisciplinary partnerships was liable to limit production and technical development within the meaning of Article 101(1)(b) TFEU. Although this appears within the list of restraints typically categorised as restrictive by object, the CJ held that not every agreement between undertakings that restricted the freedom of action of the parties necessarily fell within the prohibition of Article 101(1). Rather, account had to be taken of the *objectives* of the restrictions and the overall context in which they were adopted. In this case, the objective of the rules was to ensure that the ultimate consumers of legal services and the sound administration of justice were provided with the necessary guarantees in relation to integrity and experience. For example, members of the Bar might not be in a position to advise and represent

---

[116] Case C-309/99, [2002] ECR I-1577, para. 86.

clients independently if they belonged to an organisation which was also responsible for producing an account for the financial results of the transactions in respect of which their services were called upon and for certifying those accounts. The regulation therefore did not infringe Article 101(1) 'since the association could reasonably have considered that, despite its inherent restrictive effect on competition, it was necessary for the proper practice of the legal profession as organized in the Member States concerned'.[117]

In this case, therefore, the CJ, despite appearing to find that the agreement restricted competition on account of its adverse effects on competition (in terms of the services that could be offered and economies of scope), went on to conclude that the agreement did not infringe Article 101(1) (by object or effect)[118] as the restraints were necessary for the proper practice of the legal profession.[119] As the agreement did not infringe Article 101(1), it did not have to be determined whether the rules of ethics could be excepted through the application of Article 101(3).[120] The CJ did not, as it had done with respect to collective bargaining agreements in *Albany*,[121] consider that reasonable rules relating to the regulation of the provision of professional services[122] should fall outside Article 101(1) altogether. Rather, at first sight, the Court appears to weigh the anti-competitive effects of the agreement against benefits which were *not* economic efficiency benefits.

The approach taken in *Wouters* is not easy to reconcile with all of the jurisprudence, for example, *BIDS* and the GC's judgment in *Laurent Piau*.[123] In the latter case the GC held that the actual principle of a licence, required by FIFA as a condition for carrying on the occupation of players' agent, constituted a 'barrier to access to that economic activity and therefore necessarily affects competition'. The GC consequently concluded that the conduct could be accepted 'only in so far as the conditions set out in Article [101(3)] are satisfied'.[124] Had the CJ taken this course in *Wouters*, the referring national court, which did not at this time have jurisdiction to rule on the compatibility of the agreement with Article 101(3),[125] would have been compelled to rule that the regulations, or at least the restric-

---

[117] Case C-309/99, [2002] ECR I-1577, at paras. 106–110. Contrast the Opinion of Léger AG in this case who considered, at paras. 104–105, that the rule of reason in EU competition law was strictly confined to a 'purely competitive balance-sheet of the effects of the agreement'. The reasoning of the CJ in this case, however, required the introduction into the provisions of Art. 101(1) considerations which were linked to the pursuit of a 'public-interest objective'. The AG took the view, however, that social concerns, and considerations connected with the pursuit of the public interest, were relevant only to the Art. 101(3) appraisal, see Section 4.D, pp. 252–263.

[118] The CJ had after all made it clear that the rules might have negative effects on prices, innovation, and/or the variety or quality of goods and services that could be expected.

[119] Contrast Case C-1/12, *Ordem dos Técnicos Oficiais de Contas (OTOC)* v. *Autoridade da Concorrência*, 28 February 2013, where the CJ held that rules adopted by a professional association of chartered accountants providing that certain compulsory training to be undertaken by chartered accountants could be provided only by OTOC was not necessary to achieve a legitimate objective (in that case to guarantee the quality of the services offered by chartered accountants). The rules eliminated all competition rather than putting in place criteria to ensure training bodies equal access to the market.

[120] Or, perhaps through Art. 106(2) on the grounds that the rules were necessary to the task entrusted by statute to the Dutch Bar Council. The CJ considered, however, that it was precluded from applying Art. 106(2). The Bar Council was not an entrusted undertaking or group of undertakings within the meaning of Art. 106, Case C-309/99, [2002] ECR I-1577, paras. 111–116. Contrast the Opinion of the Léger AG, see, e.g., paras. 114 and 201.

[121] Case C-67/96, *Albany International BV* v. *Stichting Bedrijfspensioenfonds Textielindustrie* [1999] ECR I-5751. See Chap. 3, Section 5.B.ii.c, pp. 153–154.

[122] The Commission is in fact concerned about the compatibility of many such regulatory rules with the EU competition provisions. In March 2003, DG Comp launched a stocktaking exercise for professional services. The purpose of the exercise is to consider the justification for and effects of restrictive rules and regulations in the professions. Details of this exercise are available on DG Comp's website, at <http://www.europa.eu.int/comm/competition/liberalization/conference/libprofconference.html>.

[123] Case T-193/02, *Laurent Piau* v. *Commission* [2005] ECR II-209 (appeal dismissed by Order of the CJ, Case C-171/05 P, [2006] ECR I-37).

[124] Case T-193/02 *Laurent Piau* v. *Commission* [2005] ECR II-209 (appeal dismissed by Order of the CJ, Case C-171/05 P, [2006] ECR I-37, para. 101).

[125] At this time only the Commission could apply Art. 101(3) in individual cases (Reg. 17, Art. 9) where notification had been made (and no notification had been made in this case), see n. 10.

tive rules within them, were void.[126] The CJ's clear view was that the Bar Association had not been unreasonable in considering that the restrictive rules were warranted by reference to the objective pursued.

One explanation for *Wouters* could be that the principle set out therein only applies to restrictions designed to achieve public policy (in that case deontological) objectives.[127] This approach could also explain the ruling in *Meca-Medina*,[128] that restraints on freedom of action resulting from anti-doping rules do not constitute a restriction of competition[129] if inherent in, and justified by, a legitimate objective: in that case the organisation and proper conduct of competitive sport. Restraints imposed by the rules had to be limited to what is necessary to ensure the proper conduct of competitive sport.[130] Further, in its Guidelines on Vertical Restraints the Commission states that severe restraints in vertical agreements 'may be objectively necessary in exceptional cases for an agreement of a particular type or nature and therefore fall outside Article 101(1). For example, a hardcore restriction may be objectively necessary to ensure that a public ban on selling dangerous substances to certain customers for reasons of safety or health is respected'.[131]

The types of arguments raised in *Wouters* have, however, sometimes been relied on by parties seeking to provide legitimate economic (as well as non-economic) explanations for provisions which appear in principle to be restrictive of competition. Indeed, in the Commission's Guidelines on Vertical Restraints the Commission also states that severe restraints (such as bans on selling outside a specified sales territory) will fall outside Article 101(1) for two years where a manufacturer needs to encourage substantial investments by a distributor in order to start developing a market—for example where the distributor needs to invest in launching and establishing a new brand on the market.[132] In *Pierre Fabre v. Président de l'Autorité de la concurrence*[133] the CJ also suggested, in rather broad terms, that *all* selective distribution agreements (not just those, like the one at issue, containing a *de facto* ban on Internet selling and selling outside a contractual area) would be considered 'in the absence of objective justification, as "restrictions by object"'.[134] On the facts, the CJ did not consider that the ban on Internet selling, which was 'liable to restrict competition',[135] constituted a proportionate measure to achieve a legitimate aim. This case and selective distribution agreements are considered further in Chapter 11.

It has also been argued that agreements incorporating severe restraints are not restrictive by object where the restraints are inherent in, or objectively necessary to, a *pro-competitive* venture, for example, where horizontal price restraints are not 'naked'[136] but are designed, and necessary, to achieve some

---

[126] Even if the parties had notified the agreement to the Commission any exemption granted would not have taken effect retrospectively, see Reg. 17, [1959–1962] OJ Spec. Ed. 87, Art. 4.

[127] See e.g., E. Rousseva and M. Marquis, 'Hell Freezes Over: A Climate change for Assessing Exclusionary Conduct under Article 102 TEFU' (2012) *JECLAP* 32, see n. 122 and accompanying text.

[128] Case C-519/04 P, *Meca-Medina v. Commission* [2006] ECR I-6991.

[129] The CJ held that 'the penal nature of the anti-doping rules...are capable of producing adverse effects on competition because they could, if penalties were ultimately to prove unjustified, result in an athlete's unwarranted exclusion from sporting events', Case C-519/04 P, *Meca-Medina v. Commission* [2006] ECR I-6991, para. 47.

[130] Case C-519/04 P, *Meca-Medina v. Commission* [2006] ECR I-6991, paras. 45–47. The CJ set aside the judgment of the GC which had held that the sporting rules had nothing to do with economic activity and so fell outside the scope of Art. 101, Case T-313/02, [2004] ECR II-3291.

[131] [2010] OJ C130/1, para. 60.

[132] Guidelines on Vertical Restraints [2010] OJ C130/1, para. 61.

[133] Case C-439/09, 13 October 2011.

[134] *Pierre Fabre v. Président de l'Autorité de la concurrence*, para. 39.

[135] *Pierre Fabre v. Président de l'Autorité de la concurrence*, para. 38.

[136] Agreements are 'naked' where 'they seek to restrict competition without producing any objective countervailing benefits', Mario Monti, 'Fighting Cartels Why and How?' 3rd Nordic Competition Policy Conference Stockholm, 11–12 September 2000, discussed in Chap. 9.

efficiency-enhancing objective.[137] Indeed, in a series of cases the question has arisen as to how the setting of multilateral interchange fees (MIFs) in payment card systems, should be analysed under Article 101 and, in particular, whether it should be treated as an integral part of the operation of the payment system which falls outside the scope of Article 101(1) altogether. In Chapter 9 it will be seen that although these arrangements involve horizontal price restraints, it has never been ruled that agreements incorporating MIFs are restrictive by object (although it has not been found either that such provisions fall outside Article 101(1) altogether).[138] Thus in *Visa International-Multilateral Interchange Fee*,[139] the Commission found that the object of the MIF was to procure efficiencies within the payment system (rather than the restriction of competition). It did, however, go on to find that it had the *effect* of restricting the freedom of banks individually to decide their own pricing policies and distorting the conditions of competition on the Visa issuing and acquiring markets).[140] Similarly, in *MasterCard*,[141] although the Commission indicated that the setting of the MIF might be restrictive of competition by object, it based its decision on a finding that the MIF provisions had restrictive effects on competition.[142] The arguments relating to the necessity of the MIF to the payment card system seemed therefore to influence the Commission to the extent that it did not find the arrangement to be restrictive by object, but were not sufficient to convince the Commission that the agreement was not restrictive of competition at all on the grounds that the restraints were ancillary—directly related, objectively necessary and proportionate—to the implementation of the main operation. The extent to which the concept of objective necessity set out in *Wouters* differs from, or overlaps with, the concept of ancillary restraints (discussed in Section 3.F) is somewhat unclear. On appeal, the GC in *MasterCard*[143] upheld the Commission's finding of restrictive effects and agreed with the Commission that the MIF provisions did not constitute ancillary restrictions which were objectively necessary for the operation of the MasterCard system[144] (it has not been demonstrated that the system was incapable of functioning without the MIF—see further the boxed extract from the judgment in Section 3.F.). It did indicate, however, that the Commission might have been able, had it chosen to do so, to base its finding of an infringement of Article 101(1) on the grounds that the agreement was restrictive by object.

Case T-111/08, *MasterCard Inc v Commission*, 24 May 2012

General Court

137 First, it must be observed that the fact—noted by the Commission in recitals 461 to 498 to the contested decision—that competition between the MasterCard system and the other bank card schemes for the banks' business resulted in upward pressure on the levels of the MIF is a relevant aspect of the

---

[137] See, e.g., the approach of the US Supreme Court (restraints escape per se categorisation and are capable of justification in the US if ancillary to an efficiency-enhancing integration, see, e.g., *Broadcast Music, Inc. v. Columbia Broadcasting Sys., Inc.*, 441 US 1 (1979) and *NCAA v. Bd. of Regents of the Univ. of Okla.*, 468 US 85 (1984)).

[138] Faull and Nikpay (eds.), *The EC Law of Competition* (cited in n. 6), para. 11.42.

[139] [2002] OJ L318/17.

[140] Nonetheless, it granted individual exemption to the MIF under Article 101(3) subject to conditions, see further Chap 11.

[141] *Europay (Eurocard-MasterCard)*, 19 December 2007.

[142] Again the Commission rejected the argument that the MIF was objectively necessary for the operation of the MasterCard system (or could operate as ancillary restrictions) taking the view that the question of whether the restrictions were desirable to the commercial success of that operation, or offered greater efficiency, could be assessed only under Article 101(3). In contrast to *Visa*, however, the Commission considered that the economic arguments put forward were inadequate to satisfy the conditions of Article 101(3).

[143] Case T-111/08, *MasterCard Inc v. Commission* 24 May 2012, on appeal Case C-382/12 P.

[144] Case T-111/08, *MasterCard Inc v. Commission* 24 May 2012, on appeal Case C-382/12 P, paras. 77–79.

economic context within the meaning of the case-law...Accordingly, the Commission was legitimately able to take it into account in its examination of the effects of the MIF on competition.

138 Secondly, it should be noted that, in recitals 401 to 407 to the contested decision, the Commission stated that the MIF 'may, by its very nature, have the potential of fixing prices' (recital 405 to the contested decision). It also, correctly, refuted the applicants' arguments based on the MIF's pursuit of legitimate objectives or on the absence of an intention to restrict competition. It nevertheless decided, in recital 407 to the contested decision, not to 'reach a definite conclusion as to whether the [MIF of the MasterCard payment organisation] is a restriction by object within the meaning of Article [101(1)]', on the ground that it was clearly established 'that the [MIF of the MasterCard payment organisation] [had] the effect of appreciably restricting and distorting competition to the detriment of merchants in the acquiring markets'.

139 The anti-competitive object and effect of a decision by an association of undertakings are not cumulative but alternative conditions for assessing whether such a decision comes within the scope of the prohibition laid down in Article [101(1)]. The alternative nature of that condition, indicated by the conjunction 'or', leads first to the need to consider the precise purpose of the decision, in the economic context in which it is to be applied. Where, however, the analysis of the content of the decision does not reveal a sufficient degree of harm to competition, the consequences of the decision should then be considered and for it to be caught by the prohibition it is necessary to find that those factors are present which show that competition has in fact been prevented, restricted or distorted to an appreciable extent. It is not necessary to examine the effects of a decision once its anti-competitive object has been established (see, to that effect, Joined Cases C-501/06 P, C-513/06 P, C-515/06 P, and C-519/06 P *GlaxoSmithKline Services and Others* v *Commission* [2009] ECR I-9291, paragraph 55).

140 In that regard, it is helpful to point out that Article [101(1)(a)] expressly provides that measures which directly or indirectly fix purchase or selling prices constitute restrictions of competition, and that, according to the case-law, the purpose of Article [101(1)(a)] is to prohibit undertakings from distorting the normal formation of prices on the markets (Case T-13/89 *ICI* v *Commission*...paragraph 311).

141 However, in so far as the Commission did not expressly rely on there being a restriction of competition by object...in order to ascertain whether the MIF constitutes a restriction of competition by effect, the competition in question should be assessed within the actual context in which it would occur in the absence of that MIF.

d. An Assumption of Anti-Competitive Effects is Inappropriate in the Context of the Case

It has been seen that the case law makes it clear that once an agreement has been characterised as restrictive by object, the actual effect of the agreement need not be considered—the agreement is simply assumed to restrict competition. It seems to follow therefore that a finding that an agreement has as its object the restriction of competition cannot be rebutted by proof that it did not have this effect.[145] It has also been seen, however, that the cases establish that in order to determine whether an agreement has an anti-competitive nature in the first place, an assessment must be made not only of the content of its provisions, but the objectives it seeks to attain and the economic and legal context of which it forms part. Further, that the objective and context of an agreement has sometimes been relied upon to expand the category of object restraints, beyond the list of those traditionally considered to fall within it. This suggests that it should also be arguable that a restraint *prima facie* appearing to have as its object the restriction of competition may escape such a characterisation

---

[145] 'Accordingly,...there is no need to consider the effects of a concerted practice where its anti-competitive object is established', Case C-8/08, *T-Mobile Netherlands BV v. Raad van bestuur van de Nederlandse Mededingingsautoriteit* [2009] ECR I-4529, para. 31.

where an examination of its context clearly indicates that an assumption of anti-competitive effects is inappropriate.[146]

This argument appears to have been accepted by the GC, but *not* the CJ, in *GlaxoSmithKline Services Unlimited* v. *Commission*[147] when the GC concluded that before an agreement could be categorised as restrictive by object, an abridged analysis of its effects had to be conducted. This case concerned the general sales conditions for the supply of certain pharmaceuticals products to Spanish wholesalers which GlaxoSmithKline Services Unlimited (GSK) had notified (under the old notification and exemption system) to the Commission, seeking confirmation that the agreement did not infringe Article 101. The arrangements incorporated (in clause 4) a dual pricing system which resulted in Spanish wholesalers being charged a higher price for drugs resold in other Member States than for those resold in Spain. GSK admitted that the purpose of this provision was to restrict parallel trade, but argued that parallel trade benefited only the intermediaries (the parallel importers and exporters). In contrast, the restriction on parallel trade benefited final consumers as it provided GSK with additional resources for investment in the research and development (R&D) of new medicines. The Commission did not accept these arguments and, in 2001, issued a decision concluding both that (1) the general sales conditions infringed Article 101(1)—they had as their object and effect the restriction of competition; and (2) they did not merit an exemption as GSK had not proved its case under Article 101(3).

The GC ruled that the Commission had been right to find that the agreement infringed Article 101(1) but annulled the decision insofar as it had rejected GSK's exemption application.[148] With regard to the violation of Article 101(1), however, the GC held that the Commission had been wrong to characterise the agreement as restrictive by object: although it held that it was true that an agreement intended to prevent parallel trade unfavourably had, in principle, to be regarded as having its object the restriction of competition, the Court stated that Article 101(1) also required an abridged analysis designed to determine whether an agreement had as its object the restriction of competition, to the detriment of the final consumers. The GC concluded that, in this case, the specific characteristics of the pharmaceutical sector, which led to prices of medicine being largely shielded from the free play of supply and demand by regulation, meant that *no* assumption could be made that parallel trade would reduce prices and increase the welfare of final consumers. It could not therefore be presumed that an agreement containing an export ban, dual pricing system, or other limitation of parallel trade, would have a negative effect on competition so that it was to be regarded as having the object of restricting competition.

Despite the special circumstances that existed in *GlaxoSmithKline*, the conclusion drawn by the GC seemed potentially to open the possibility for parties to agreements, generally considered to pursue an object restrictive of competition, to argue that they should not in fact be presumed to restrict competition because of the particular facts of the case and so to bring effects analysis into object cases.[149] In order to try and clarify exactly what analysis is required to make a finding of restriction by object, the Commission appealed this aspect of the GC's judgment. On appeal, the CJ held that the agreement was indeed restrictive by object. The Court stressed that in principle agreements aimed at prohibiting or limiting parallel trade have as their object the prevention of competition and that that principle applies in the pharmaceutical sector. Further, that an agreement tending to restore national divisions in trade between Member States might be such as to frustrate the Treaty's single

---

[146] See Article 101(3) Guidelines, para. 22.

[147] Case T-168/01, *GlaxoSmithKline Services Unlimited* v. *Commission* [2006] ECR II-2969.

[148] The GC held that the Commission had not adequately refuted GSK's evidence of efficiencies, see Section 4, pp. 249–267.

[149] Indeed, it has been seen that in *Consten and Grundig*, the parties argued passionately that their agreement conferring ATP on Consten had been essential to its operation. Advocate-General Roemer supported their view, but the CJ held that since the *object of* the agreement was to restrict competition a consideration of the effects was not necessary, Cases 56 and 58/64, *Établissements Consten S.à.R.L and Grundig-Verkaufs-GmbH* v. *Commission* [1966] ECR 299, 342–343.

market objective and that it was not necessary for an agreement to be considered to have as its object the restriction of competition, that it be presumed to deprive final consumers of the advantages of effective competition in terms of price. The CJ thus reinforced the narrow nature of the 'exceptional circumstances' in which ATP will not be found to have as its object the restriction of competition.[150]

Case C-501/06 P, *GlaxoSmithKline Services* v. *Commission*, 6 October 2009

Court of Justice

54 As the Commission, Aseprofar and EAEPC all contend that the [GC] committed an error of law in its assessment of the anti-competitive object of the agreement and ask the Court to uphold point 2 of the operative part of the judgment under appeal by effecting a replacement of grounds, it is appropriate to begin by considering their arguments before those put forward by GSK in support of its appeal.

55 First of all, it must be borne in mind that the anti-competitive object and effect of an agreement are not cumulative but alternative conditions for assessing whether such an agreement comes within the scope of the prohibition laid down in Article [101(1)]]. According to settled case-law since the judgment in Case 56/65 *LTM*…the alternative nature of that condition, indicated by the conjunction 'or', leads first to the need to consider the precise purpose of the agreement, in the economic context in which it is to be applied. Where, however, the analysis of the content of the agreement does not reveal a sufficient degree of harm to competition, the consequences of the agreement should then be considered and for it to be caught by the prohibition it is necessary to find that those factors are present which show that competition has in fact been prevented, restricted or distorted to an appreciable extent. It is also apparent from the case-law that it is not necessary to examine the effects of an agreement once its anti-competitive object has been established (see, to that effect, Case C-8/08 *T-Mobile Netherlands*…, paragraphs 28 and 30).

56 Secondly, to examine the anti-competitive object of the agreement before its anti-competitive effect is all the more justified because, if the error of law alleged by the Commission, Aseprofar and EAEPC turns out to be substantiated, GSK's appeal directed at the grounds of the judgment under appeal relating to the anti-competitive effect of the agreement will fall to be dismissed.

57 Consequently, it is appropriate to ascertain whether the [GC]'s assessment as to whether the agreement has an anti-competitive object, as referred to in paragraphs 41 to 46 of this judgment, is in accordance with the principles extracted from the relevant case-law.

58 According to settled case-law, in order to assess the anti-competitive nature of an agreement, regard must be had inter alia to the content of its provisions, the objectives it seeks to attain and the economic and legal context of which it forms a part (see, to that effect, Joined Cases 96/82 to 102/82, 104/82, 105/82, 108/82 and 110/82 *IAZ International Belgium and Others* v. *Commission*…, paragraph 25, and Case C-209/07 *Beef Industry Development Society and Barry Brothers*…, paragraphs 16 and 21). In addition, although the parties' intention is not a necessary factor in determining whether an agreement is restrictive, there is nothing prohibiting the Commission or the Community judicature from taking that aspect into account (see, to that effect, *IAZ International Belgium and Others* v. *Commission*, cited above, paragraphs 23 to 25).

59 With respect to parallel trade, the Court has already held that, in principle, agreements aimed at prohibiting or limiting parallel trade have as their object the prevention of competition (see, to that effect, Case 19/77 *Miller International Schallplaten* v. *Commission*…, paragraphs 7 and 18, and Joined Cases 32/78, 36/78 to 82/78 *BMW Belgium and Others* v. *Commission*…, paragraphs 20 to 28 and 31).

---

[150] See in particular discussion of Cases C-403 and 429/08, *Premier League Ltd* v. *QC Leisure*, 4 October 2011, in Chap. 12.

60 As observed by the Advocate General in point 155 of her Opinion, that principle, according to which an agreement aimed at limiting parallel trade is a 'restriction of competition by object', applies to the pharmaceuticals sector.

61 The Court has, moreover, held in that regard, in relation to the application of Article [101] and in a case involving the pharmaceuticals sector, that an agreement between producer and distributor which might tend to restore the national divisions in trade between Member States might be such as to frustrate the Treaty's objective of achieving the integration of national markets through the establishment of a single market. Thus on a number of occasions the Court has held agreements aimed at partitioning national markets according to national borders or making the interpenetration of national markets more difficult, in particular those aimed at preventing or restricting parallel exports, to be agreements whose object is to restrict competition within the meaning of that article of the Treaty (Joined Cases C-468/06 to C-478/06 *Sot. Lélos kai Sia and Others*..., paragraph 65 and case-law cited).

62 With respect to the [GC]'s statement that, while it is accepted that an agreement intended to limit parallel trade must in principle be considered to have as its object the restriction of competition, that applies in so far as it may be presumed to deprive final consumers of the advantages of effective competition in terms of supply or price, the Court notes that neither the wording of Article [101(1)] nor the case-law lend support to such a position.

63 First of all, there is nothing in that provision to indicate that only those agreements which deprive consumers of certain advantages may have an anti-competitive object. Secondly, it must be borne in mind that the Court has held that, like other competition rules laid down in the Treaty, Article [101] aims to protect not only the interests of competitors or of consumers, but also the structure of the market and, in so doing, competition as such. Consequently, for a finding that an agreement has an anti-competitive object, it is not necessary that final consumers be deprived of the advantages of effective competition in terms of supply or price (see, by analogy, *T-Mobile Netherlands and Others*, cited above, paragraphs 38 and 39).

64 It follows that, by requiring proof that the agreement entails disadvantages for final consumers as a prerequisite for a finding of anti-competitive object and by not finding that that agreement had such an object, the [GC] committed an error of law.

65 However, where the grounds of a judgment of the [GC] are contrary to Community law, that judgment need not be set aside if the operative part of the judgment appears to be well founded on other legal grounds (see, to that effect, Case C-30/91 P *Lestelle* v. *Commission*..., paragraph 28, and Case C-294/95 P *Ojha* v. *Commission*..., paragraph 52).

66 That is the case here. It suffices to note that in point 2 of the operative part of the judgment under appeal, the [GC] confirmed Article 1 of the contested decision, by which the Commission had found that the agreement infringed Article [101(1)]. Accordingly, it is not necessary to set aside point 2 of the operative part of the judgment under appeal.

67 In the light of all the aforegoing considerations, GSK's appeal must be dismissed as unfounded in so far as it seeks to establish that the agreement was compatible with Article [101(1)].

In *Coop de France bétail et viande* v. *Commission*[151] the CJ also clearly held that it is not necessary to analyse the effects of an agreement fixing minimum purchasing prices and suspending imports of beef into France. The parties argued that the Commission and GC should have taken account of the economic context in which it arose (in that case, that the beef industry was facing a crisis which had led the EU institutions to put an intervention system in place to help farmers subsist). The CJ ruled that the GC had taken the economic context into account when making its determination that the purpose of the agreement was to restrict competition in the single market and to distort the setting

---

[151] Cases C-101 and 110/07 P, [2008] ECR I-10193.

of prices. Furthermore, it was well established that there was no need to take account of the actual effects of an agreement once it appears that its object is to restrict competition and that 'since the [GC] concluded that it was established that the object of the Agreement... was anti-competitive, it correctly ruled... that the Commission was not bound to research the actual effects on competition of the measure'.[152]

The CJ thus seems to be more willing to allow reliance on the context of the case as a mechanism for expanding the category of object restraints than as a mechanism for narrowing it.

(v) Object Cases and Appreciability

a. Völk v. Vervaecke

In the preceding discussion it has been seen that the conclusion that an agreement has as its object the restriction of competition makes the simple assumption that, in the context in which the agreement is operated, it constitutes an obvious threat to the attainment of the Treaty's objectives, irrespective of its actual effects. The person alleging the infringement is not, therefore, generally required to demonstrate the relevant market or the existence of market power. In Chapter 3, however, it was seen that the CJ has made it clear that 'in order to come within the prohibition imposed by Article [101(1)], the agreement must affect trade between Member States and the free play of competition to an appreciable extent'.[153] in Völk the CJ clarified that EU law is not concerned with agreements, even those containing object restraints such as ATP, which have an 'insignificant effect on the market, taking into account the weak position which the persons concerned have on the market of the product in question'.[154]

b. Commission Notice on Agreements of Minor Importance which do not Appreciably Restrict Competition (De Minimis) and Expedia

The concept of appreciability is obviously of huge practical importance to undertakings, particularly small and medium-sized ones. Because of this the Commission has, over the years, issued a series of notices indicating when, in its view, an agreement is likely to be considered to be of minor importance. The current Notice (which is under review)[155] on agreements of minor importance which do not appreciably restrict competition[156] uses market share thresholds to quantify what is *not* likely to be an appreciable restriction of competition. Although the Notice provides that agreements between competitors (actual or potential) and non-competitors are likely to be of minor importance where the parties' market shares do not exceed 10 per cent and 15 per cent respectively,[157] the Notice states that it does not apply at all to agreements containing specified 'hardcore' restrictions, including:

(a) agreements between competitors which fix prices, limit output or sales, or allocate markets or customers; or

(b) agreements between non-competitors which impose fixed or minimum sale prices on buyers or restrict the territory into which, or the customers to whom, the buyer may sell.

---

[152] Cases C-101 and 110/07 P, [2008] ECR I-10193, para. 88.

[153] Case 22/71, *Béguelin Import Co. v. GL Import-Export S.A.* [1971] ECR 949. The text of Art. 101(1) does not require that the effect on competition or trade should be appreciable.

[154] 'Thus an exclusive dealing agreement, even with absolute territorial protection, may, having regard to the weak position of the persons concerned on the market in the products in question in the area covered by the absolute protection, escape the prohibition laid down in Article [101(1)]', Case 5/69, *Völk v. Vervaecke* [1969] ECR 295, 302.

[155] Commission Notice on agreements of minor importance which do not appreciably restrict competition under Article 81(1) (De minimis Notice) [2001] OJ C368/13 (replacing a notice published in 1997, -the first notice having been published in 1970, [1970] OJ C64/)1. The Commission launched a review of the notice in July 2013, see IP/13/685 and <http://ec.europa.eu/competition/consultations/2013_de_minimis_notice/index_en.html>.

[156] The question of what constitutes an appreciable effect on trade between Member States is dealt with in the separate notice on the effect on trade concept, see Chap. 3.

[157] See further Section 3.E.v, pp. 240–242.

The list of hardcore restraints in the Notice on Agreements of Minor Importance which do not Appreciably Restrict Competition mirror those set out in the horizontal and vertical block exemptions (see Chapters 10 and 11 respectively):

---

11. Points 7, 8 and 9 do not apply to agreements containing any of the following hardcore restrictions:

(1) as regards agreements between competitors as defined in point 7, restrictions which, directly or indirectly, in isolation or in combination with other factors under the control of the parties, have as their object:

    (a) the fixing of prices when selling the products to third parties;

    (b) the limitation of output or sales;

    (c) the allocation of markets or customers;

(2) as regards agreements between non-competitors as defined in point 7, restrictions which, directly or indirectly, in isolation or in combination with other factors under the control of the parties, have as their object:

    (a) the restriction of the buyer's ability to determine its sale price, without prejudice to the possibility of the supplier imposing a maximum sale price or recommending a sale price, provided that they do not amount to a fixed or minimum sale price as a result of pressure from, or incentives offered by, any of the parties;

    (b) the restriction of the territory into which, or of the customers to whom, the buyer may sell the contract goods or services, except the following restrictions which are not hardcore:

      — the restriction of active sales into the exclusive territory or to an exclusive customer group reserved to the supplier or allocated by the supplier to another buyer, where such a restriction does not limit sales by the customers of the buyer,

      — the restriction of sales to end users by a buyer operating at the wholesale level of trade,

      — the restriction of sales to unauthorised distributors by the members of a selective distribution system, and

      — the restriction of the buyer's ability to sell components, supplied for the purposes of incorporation, to customers who would use them to manufacture the same type of goods as those produced by the supplier;

    (c) the restriction of active or passive sales to end users by members of a selective distribution system operating at the retail level of trade, without prejudice to the possibility of prohibiting a member of the system from operating out of an unauthorised place of establishment;

    (d) the restriction of cross-supplies between distributors within a selective distribution system, including between distributors operating at different levels of trade;

    (e) the restriction agreed between a supplier of components and a buyer who incorporates those components, which limits the supplier's ability to sell the components as spare parts to end users or to repairers or other service providers not entrusted by the buyer with the repair or servicing of its goods;

(3) as regards agreements between competitors as defined in point 7, where the competitors operate, for the purposes of the agreement, at a different level of the production or distribution chain, any of the hardcore restrictions listed in paragraph (1) and (2) above.

An important question arising has been how this Notice relates to the CJ's judgment in *Völk* which clearly seemed to establish that even object restraints (which are generally hardcore restraints[158]) may fall outside Article 101(1) on de minimis grounds (in that case it will be remembered the parties had exceptionally small market shares of less than 1 per cent). Given (a) the non-binding nature of the

---

[158] See Section 3.E.v, pp. 240–242.

Notice,[159] (b) that the Notice does not state that agreements containing 'hardcore' restraints cannot fall outside Article 101(1) on de minimis grounds (only that they do not benefit from the limited safe harbour provided by the Notice), and (c) the clear ruling of the CJ in *Völk*, a fair assumption had been simply that the Notice provided *no* guidance on the question of when agreements containing object or hardcore restraints have an insignificant effect on competition. The Notice should not, therefore, be interpreted as meaning that they could not fall outside Article 101(1) on these grounds. Rather, it was indicative of the view that such agreements would only be considered to be of minor importance where the parties' market shares are considerably lower than those set out in the Notice (the more serious the restraint the less likely it is to be insignificant).[160]

At the end of 2012, however, the CJ handed down a judgment in *Expedia* in which it states, in paragraph 37, that an agreement which is restrictive of competition by object is so injurious to competition that it always constitutes an appreciable restriction of competition. Many now take the view that this judgment implicitly overrules the previous ruling in *Völk v. Vervaecke*. Indeed, the Commission states in a press release announcing its review of the de minimis Notice that the judgment in *Expedia* 'has established that a restriction with an anticompetitive object constitutes, by its very nature, an appreciable restriction of competition. The proposal therefore clarifies that agreements containing a restriction by object are always seen as an appreciable restriction of competition'.[161]

If the CJ did intend to overrule *Völk* in *Expedia*, however, it did not do so as clearly as it might have done.[162] In particular, prior to paragraph 37, it relies on *Völk* both as authority for the settled position that an agreement falls outside of Article 101(1) if it has only an insignificant effect on the market and also as a case in which it was found 'that an exclusive dealing agreement, even with absolute territorial protection, has only an insignificant effect on the market…taking into account the weak position which the persons concerned have in that market'.[163] Further, it concludes that an NCA can only apply Article 101(1) to an agreement, stated by the national court to be restrictive by object, 'provided that that agreement constitutes an appreciable restriction of competition'.[164]

Case C-226/11, *Expedia Inc* v. *Authorité de la Concurrence*, 13 December 2012

In this case the French competition authority had found that a joint venture created by SNCF and Expedia for the reservation and sale of train tickets over the internet infringed Article 101 and French law and

---

[159] Although it intends to make transparent the manner in which the Commission will apply Article 101 and imposes a limit on the exercise of the Commission's discretion (the Commission cannot depart from the content set out therein without being in breach of the general principles of law, for example of equal treatment and legitimate expectations), it is not a legally binding measure which is binding on the courts or NCAs. National courts and NCAs are not therefore bound to take it into account when determining whether an agreement appreciably restricts competition, Case C-226/11, *Expedia Inc* v. *Authorité de la Concurrence*, 13 December 2012, paras. 23–31. On 18 April 2013, the French Court of Appeal upheld the decision, finding an infringement of Article 101.

[160] The Commission is more willing to accept that an agreement containing hardcore restraints may escape Article 101(1) on the ground that the agreement does not appreciably affect trade (see Chap. 3). Nonetheless it seems unlikely that the Commission would allocate resources to agreements, even those containing hardcore restraints, where the parties' markets shares are very small, see Faull and Nikpay (eds.), *The EC Law of Competition* (cited in n. 6), para. 3.164.

[161] IP/13/685. The Commission does not, in its draft Notice, go as far as this statement suggests. Rather it simply provides, like the current Notice, that the market share thresholds set out in the Notice do not apply to agreements which have as their object the restriction of competition or are characterised as hardcore restrictions in any current or future block exemption (which it considers to generally constitute restrictions by object), see draft Notice, para. 12 available at <http://ec.europa.eu/competition/consultations/2013_de_minimis_notice/de_minimis_notice_en.pdf>.

[162] See n. 161.

[163] Case C-226/11, *Expedia Inc* v. *Authorité de la Concurrence*, 13 December 2012, para. 22.

[164] Case C-226/11, *Expedia Inc* v. *Authorité de la Concurrence*, 13 December 2012, para. 38.

imposed financial penalties on both SNCF and Expedia. The parties alleged on appeal that as their market shares fell below 10%, the agreement should have fallen outside of the competition rules on de minimis grounds. The Cour de Cassation concluded that the agreement at issue had an anti-competitive object but stayed proceeding to refer to the CJ the question of whether the national finding would be precluded if the parties' market shares did not reach the thresholds specified by the Commission in the de minimis notice.

Court of Justice

The question referred for a preliminary ruling

14 By its question, the referring court seeks to know, essentially, whether Article 101(1) TFEU and Article 3(2) of Regulation No 1/2003 must be interpreted as precluding a national competition authority from applying Article 101(1) TFEU to an agreement between undertakings that may affect trade between Member States, but that does not reach the thresholds specified by the Commission in its *de minimis* notice.

15 It should be noted that Article 101(1) TFEU prohibits as incompatible with the internal market all agreements between undertakings, decisions by associations of undertakings and concerted practices which may affect trade between Member States and which have as their object or effect the prevention, restriction or distortion of competition within the internal market.

16 It is settled case-law that an agreement of undertakings falls outside the prohibition in that provision, however, if it has only an insignificant effect on the market (... *Völk* v *Vervaecke* ..., paragraph 7; ... P *John Deere* v *Commission* ..., paragraph 77; ... *Bagnasco* ..., paragraph 34; and ... *Asnef-Equifax* ..., paragraph 50).

17 Accordingly, if it is to fall within the scope of the prohibition under Article 101(1) TFEU, an agreement of undertakings must have the object or effect of perceptibly restricting competition within the common market and be capable of affecting trade between Member States (... *BMW* ..., paragraph 18; ... *Javico* [1998] ..., paragraph 12; and ... *Pedro IV Servicios* ..., paragraph 68).

18 With regard to the role of Member State authorities in the enforcement of Union competition law, the first sentence of Article 3(1) of Regulation No 1/2003 establishes a close link between the prohibition of the agreements set out in Article 101 TFEU and the corresponding provisions of national competition law. Where the national competition authority applies provisions of national law prohibiting cartels to an agreement of undertakings which is capable of affecting trade between Member States within the meaning of Article 101 TFEU, the first sentence of Article 3(1) requires Article 101 TFEU also to be applied to it in parallel (... *Toshiba Corporation* ..., paragraph 77).

19 Under Article 3(2) of Regulation No 1/2003, the application of national competition law may not lead to the prohibition of such agreements if they do not restrict competition within the meaning of Article 101(1) TFEU.

20 It follows that the competition authorities of the Member States can apply the provisions of national law prohibiting cartels to an agreement of undertakings which is capable of affecting trade between Member States within the meaning of Article 101 TFEU only where that agreement perceptibly restricts competition within the common market.

21 The Court has held that the existence of such a restriction must be assessed by reference to the actual circumstances of such an agreement (Case 1/71 *Cadillon* ..., paragraph 8). Regard must be had, inter alia, to the content of its provisions, the objectives it seeks to attain and the economic and legal context of which it forms a part (... *GlaxoSmithKline Services* ..., paragraph 58). It is also appropriate to take into consideration the nature of the goods or services affected, as well as the real conditions of the functioning and the structure of the market or markets in question (see, to that effect, *Asnef-Equifax* ..., paragraph 49).

22 In its examination, the Court found, inter alia, that an exclusive dealing agreement, even with absolute territorial protection, has only an insignificant effect on the market in question, taking into account

the weak position which the persons concerned have in that market, (*Völk*, paragraph 7, and *Cadillon*, paragraph 9). In other cases, however, it did not base its decision on the position of the persons concerned in the market in question. Accordingly, in paragraph 35 of *Bagnasco and Others*, it found that an agreement between the members of a banking association which excludes the right, with regard to the opening of current-account credit facilities, to adopt a fixed interest rate cannot have an appreciable restrictive effect on competition, since any variation of the interest rate depends on objective factors, such as changes occurring in the money market.

23 It is apparent from paragraphs 1 and 2 of the *de minimis* notice that the Commission intends to quantify therein, with the help of market share thresholds, what is not an appreciable restriction of competition within the meaning of Article 101 TFEU and the case-law cited in paragraphs 16 and 17 of the present judgment.

24 With regard to the wording of the *de minimis* notice, its non-binding nature, for both the competition authorities and the courts of the Member States, is emphasised in the third sentence of paragraph 4 thereof.

...

28 It is apparent from [paragraph 4], first, that the purpose of that notice is to make transparent the manner in which the Commission, acting as the competition authority of the European Union, will itself apply Article 101 TFEU. Consequently, by the *de minimis* notice, the Commission imposes a limit on the exercise of its discretion and must not depart from the content of that notice without being in breach of the general principles of law, in particular the principles of equal treatment and the protection of legitimate expectations (see, to that effect, ... *Dansk Rørindustri and Others* v *Commission* ..., paragraph 211). Furthermore, it intends to give guidance to the courts and authorities of the Member States in their application of that article.

29 Consequently, and as the Court has already had occasion to point out, a Commission notice, such as the *de minimis* notice, is not binding in relation to the Member States (see, to that effect, ... *Pfleiderer* ..., paragraph 21).

...

31 Consequently, in order to determine whether or not a restriction of competition is appreciable, the competition authority of a Member State may take into account the thresholds established in paragraph 7 of the *de minimis* notice but is not required to do so. Such thresholds are no more than factors among others that may enable that authority to determine whether or not a restriction is appreciable by reference to the actual circumstances of the agreement.

32 Contrary to what Expedia argued during the hearing, the proceedings brought and penalties imposed by the competition authority of a Member State, on undertakings that enter into an agreement that has not reached the thresholds defined in the *de minimis* notice, cannot infringe, as such, the principles of legitimate expectations and legal certainty, having regard to the wording of paragraph 4 of that notice.

33 Furthermore, as the Advocate General pointed out in point 33 of her Opinion, the principle of the lawfulness of penalties does not require the *de minimis* notice to be regarded as a legal measure binding on the national authorities. Cartels are already prohibited by the primary law of the European Union, that is, by Article 101(1) TFEU.

34 In so far as Expedia, the French Government and the Commission have, in their written observations or during the hearing, questioned the finding made by the national court that it is not disputed that the agreement at issue in the main proceedings had an anti-competitive object, it should be remembered that, in proceedings under Article 267 TFEU, which is based on a clear separation of functions between the national courts and the Court of Justice, any assessment of the facts in the main proceedings is a matter for the national court (... *Winner Wetten* ..., paragraph 49 ...).

35 Moreover, it should be noted that, according to settled case-law, for the purpose of applying Article 101(1) TFEU, there is no need to take account of the concrete effects of an agreement once it appears that it has as its object the prevention, restriction or distortion of competition (see, to that effect, ... *Consten and*

Grundig v *Commission*...;...*KME Germany and Others* v *Commission*...paragraph 65; and...*KME Germany and Others* v *Commission*..., paragraph 75).

36 In that regard, the Court has emphasised that the distinction between 'infringements by object' and 'infringements by effect' arises from the fact that certain forms of collusion between undertakings can be regarded, by their very nature, as being injurious to the proper functioning of normal competition (...*Beef Industry Development Society and Barry Brothers ('BIDS')...,* paragraph 17, and...*T-Mobile Netherlands...,* paragraph 29).

37 It must therefore be held that an agreement that may affect trade between Member States and that has an anti-competitive object constitutes, by its nature and independently of any concrete effect that it may have, an appreciable restriction on competition.

38 In light of the above, the answer to the question referred is that Article 101(1) TFEU and Article 3(2) of Regulation No 1/2003 must be interpreted as not precluding a national competition authority from applying Article 101(1) TFEU to an agreement between undertakings that may affect trade between Member States, but that does not reach the thresholds specified by the Commission in its *de minimis* notice, provided that that agreement constitutes an appreciable restriction of competition within the meaning of that provision.

(vi) Redrawing the Boundaries of the Object Category

In the US, the Supreme Court has, despite the principle of *stare decisis*,[165] been prepared to reconsider its previous decisions to categorise certain types of agreement as illegal 'per se' under section 1 of the Sherman Act. The category of agreements considered illegal per se has, therefore, to prevent false positives and to allow antitrust scrutiny of more ambivalent agreements, changed over time (and, in fact, dramatically in the last 30 years), to reflect changes in ideology and economic thinking.[166] Similarly, it is possible that the CJ could rethink the boundaries of the 'object' category of restraints where necessary to reflect economic and other developments. The reality is, however, that EU objectives have not evolved as dramatically as they have in the US and that, despite having no formal system of precedent, the CJ strives for consistency,[167] and, consistently, reiterates and reaffirms statements set out in previous judgments. It is likely, therefore, to be only on the rarest and most exceptional of occasions that it will see fit to reverse a previous ruling and, consequently, rethink the category of restraints characterised as restraints by object.[168]

(vii) Restrictions by Object and 'Hardcore' Restraints

The previous discussion sets out the types of contractual provisions that have caused a finding that an agreement has as its object the restriction of competition. These object restraints broadly correspond with a list of 'hardcore' restraints, identified by the Commission in its Notices, Guidelines, and

[165] A system of precedent and 'a policy judgment that in most matters it is more important that the applicable rule of law be settled than that it be settled right', *State Oil* v. *Khan*, 522 US 3, 20 (1997). Although lower courts are bound to apply the law laid down by the Supreme Court, the Supreme Court does, however, have the prerogative exceptionally to overrule one of its previous judgments.

[166] See, e.g., A. Jones, 'Completion of the revolution in antitrust doctrine on restricted distribution: *Leegin* and its implications for EC competition law' [2008] 53 *Ant Bull* 903, 918–920.

[167] Case 4/73, *Nold* v. *Commission* [1974] ECR 491. See also A. Arnull, "Owning up to Fallibility: Precedent and the Court of Justice (1993) 30 *CMLRev* 247.

[168] See, e.g., Case C-70/88, *European Parliament* v. *Council ('Chernobyl')* [1990] ECR I–2041; Case C-10/89, *CNL-Sucal* v. *HAG GF AG* [1990] ECR I–3711; and Cases C-267 and 268/91, *Keck and Mithouard, Criminal Proceedings Against* [1993] ECR I–6097, paras. 15–16. See further Chap. 11.

block exemptions, as agreements presumed to infringe Article 101(1) and presumed *not* to satisfy the Article 101(3) criteria (for which reason the block exemption regulations do not apply).[169] As observed by the CJ in *Pierre Fabre* v. *Président de l'Autorité de la concurrence*,[170] however, when asked by the French Court whether the ban on Internet selling in the context of a selective distribution system constituted a 'hardcore' restriction of competition', the term 'hardcore' restriction is not used in Article 101 and was not used in the (then) block exemption applying to vertical agreements (the term is now incorporated by the Commission in the current verticals block exemption). The CJ thus reformulated the question it had been asked as a question seeking to ascertain (1) whether the contractual restraint was restrictive of competition by object (and the fact that the Commission has categorised it as a hardcore restraint does not necessarily mean that it has the object or effect of restricting competition[171]), (2) whether the contract could benefit from the block exemption and, if not, (3) whether it could nevertheless benefit from the Article 101(3) exception.

(viii) Conclusion

Object restrictions are considered so serious that, save where their impact on competition is insignificant, they are viewed as restrictions of competition. Unless the restraints are ancillary, inherent, or objectively necessary to achieve a legitimate objective, economic or other justifications may only be considered within the context of Article 101(3).[172] Although some commentators have regretted the fact that the Court has adopted this formalistic interpretation of a provision drafted in terms of economic concepts,[173] pragmatically, the finding that some contracts or contractual provisions have as their object the restriction of competition is sensible (so long as the category is realistically thought through and confined) as it eradicates the need to prove, at cost, the adverse consequences of provisions which are in practice likely to lead to inefficiency and are unlikely to have any redeeming justification. The burden is then shifted to the parties to prove its beneficial effects, relying on Article 101(3).

E. AGREEMENTS THAT RESTRICT COMPETITION BY EFFECT

(i) Rejection of the Rule of Reason

Ever since 1966, and its judgment in *Société Technique Minière* v. *Maschinenbau Ulm GmbH*,[174] the CJ has recognised that agreements which do not have as their object the restriction of competition should be assessed in their market context and an economic approach adopted when determining its effect. This position has been reiterated on many occasions. The Courts have been accepting of economic justifications and explanations for restraints contained in an agreement when determining whether they restrict competition within the meaning of Article 101(1). It has been seen, however, that the GC in *Métropole Télévision (M6)*[175] expressly rejected the argument that these judgments required a

---

[169] Article 101(3) Guidelines, para. 23. See also, e.g., *Consumer Detergents*, 13 April 2011, paras. 53–54.

[170] Case C-439/09, 13 October 2011.

[171] See Opinion of Mazák AG in Case C-439/09, *Pierre Fabre* v. *Président de l'Autorité de la concurrence*, 13 October 2011, para. 29.

[172] See Case 243/83, *SA Binon & Cie* v. *SA Agence et Messageries de la Presse* [1985] ECR 2015 (cited in n. 99), 204.

[173] V. Korah, 'EEC Competition Policy—Legal Form or Economic Efficiency?' [1986] 39 CLP 85, 92–93 ('[t]o see whether an agreement restricts competition, it is not enough to examine its provisions. One needs to know about the market and the commercial reasons for inserting restrictive provisions.').

[174] Case 56/65, [1966] ECR 235.

[175] Case T-112/99, *Métropole Télévision SA* v. *Commission* [2001] ECR II-2459, see also Case T-65/98, *Van den Bergh Foods* v. *Commission* [2003] ECR II-4653, aff'd Case C-552/03 P, *Unilever Bestfoods* v. *Commission* [2006] OJ C294/19.

US rule of reason style analysis but also held that Article 101(1) should not be applied abstractly to restrictions on freedom of action.[176] Although making these statements on how Article 101(1) is *not* to be applied, the Court did not elucidate how it is determined whether restrictions in an agreement are anti-competitive and caught by Article 101(1). What assessment then must be conducted at the Article 101(1) stage?

(ii) The Analytical Framework Set out by the Commission in the Article 101(3) Guidelines and the Importance of the Counterfactual

In its Guidelines on the application of Article 101(3), the Commission sets out its interpretation, post M6, of the relationship between Article 101(1) and Article 101(3) and in light of its statement that the objective of Article 101 is to enhance consumer welfare and to ensure an efficient allocation of resources. It commences by stressing that in Article 101(1) 'effects' cases, there is no presumption of anti-competitive effects, rather, the likely impact of the agreement on inter- or intra-brand competition must be determined. Two counterfactuals may thus need to be used:

- one to determine whether the agreement restricts inter-brand competition—whether the agreement restricts actual or potential competition that would have existed without the agreement;[177] and

- one to determine whether it restricts intra-brand competition (whether the agreement restricts actual or potential competition that would have existed in the absence of the contractual restraints).

This requires proof that the agreement either (1) affects 'actual or potential competition to such an extent that on the relevant market negative effects on prices, output, innovation or the variety or quality of goods and services can be expected with a reasonable degree of probability'[178] or (2) restricts a supplier's distributors from competing with each other, since potential competition that could have existed between the distributors absent the restraint is restricted. If, following these principles, it is concluded that the transaction is not restrictive of competition, the Commission states that restraints 'ancillary' to the main non-restrictive transaction also fall outside Article 101(1).[179]

(iii) Restraints on Inter-Brand Competition: Appraisal of an Agreement in its Legal and Economic Context

The CJ in both STM[180] and *Brasserie de Haecht (No. 1)*[181] stressed the need to examine an agreement which did not have as its object the restriction of competition in its market context to determine its effect. The latter case concerned the compatibility of a beer supply agreement, containing a beer tie, with Article 101(1). In many Member States brewers conclude agreements with outlets such as public houses, which, in return for certain benefits from the brewer, oblige the outlet to purchase beer

---

[176] Rather, account had to be taken of the impact of the agreement in the economic context in which the undertakings operated.

[177] The need to consider the impact of the agreement as against the counterfactual—the position which would have existed in the absence of the agreement—has been stressed in a number of cases, see, e.g., 56/65, *Société Technique Minière* v. *Maschinenbau Ulm GmbH* [1966] ECR 235.

[178] Article 101(3) Guidelines, para. 24. This could be because the agreement restricts actual or potential competition between the parties or between any one of the parties and third parties that could have existed absent the agreement, Article 101(3) Guidelines, paras. 25–26.

[179] Article 101(3) Guidelines, paras. 28–31.

[180] Case 56/65, *Société Technique Minière* v. *Maschinenbau Ulm GmbH* [1966] ECR 235, 249–50, set out in Section 3.E(iv).

[181] Case 23/67, *Brasserie de Haecht SA* v. *Wilkin (No. 1)* [1967] ECR 407.

(and perhaps other drinks) exclusively from the brewer (or another named supplier). The CJ held that in considering whether there was a restriction of competition, it was necessary to take account of the whole market context in which the beer supply agreement operated, including the simultaneous existence of similar contracts.

The CJ built upon the foundations set in *Brasserie de Haecht* in *Delimitis* v. *Henninger Bräu*.[182] It held that the object of a commitment to purchase beer and other drinks exclusively from named suppliers was not to restrict competition. On the contrary, the Court specifically referred to the benefits which flowed from such an agreement, for example the guarantee for a supplier of an outlet for its product; the assurance that the retailer would concentrate its sales efforts on the distribution of the contract goods; the ability of the retailer to gain access to the market on favourable terms; and the guarantee for the retailer of supply of products. Since the object of the agreement was not to restrict competition, the agreement would only be prohibited by Article 101(1) if this was its effect.

Case C-234/89, *Delimitis* v. *Henninger Bräu* [1991] ECR I-935

Delimitis and a brewer concluded an agreement in which the brewer let a public house to Delimitis. In return, Delimitis undertook to obtain beer and soft drinks from the brewer or its subsidiaries. On the termination of the agreement a dispute arose as to the agreement's compatibility with Article 101. On a preliminary reference the Court of Justice set out guidelines in order to enable the national court to assess the compatibility of the agreement with Article 101. The extract below deals with Article 101(1).

Court of Justice

The compatibility of beer supply agreements with Article [101(1)]

10. Under the terms of beer supply agreements, the supplier generally affords the reseller certain economic and financial benefits, such as the grant of loans on favourable terms, the letting of premises for the operation of a public house and the provision of technical installations, furniture and other equipment necessary for its operation. In consideration for those benefits, the reseller normally undertakes, for a predetermined period, to obtain supplies of the products covered by the contract only from the supplier. That exclusive purchasing obligation is generally backed by a prohibition on selling competing products in the public house let by the supplier.

11. Such contracts entail for the supplier the advantage of guaranteed outlets, since, as a result of his exclusive purchasing obligation and the prohibition on competition, the reseller concentrates his sales efforts on the distribution of the contract goods. The supply agreements, moreover, lead to co-operation with the reseller, allowing the supplier to plan his sales over the duration of the agreement and to organize production and distribution effectively.

12. Beer supply agreements also have advantages for the reseller, inasmuch as they enable him to gain access under favourable conditions and with the guarantee of supplies to the beer distribution market. The reseller's and supplier's shared interest in promoting sales of the contract goods likewise secures for the reseller the benefit of the supplier's assistance in guaranteeing product quality and customer service.

13. If such agreements do not have the object of restricting competition within the meaning of Article [101(1)], it is nevertheless necessary to ascertain whether they have the effect of preventing, restricting or distorting competition.

14. In its judgment in Case 23/67 *Brasserie De Haecht* v. *Wilkin*..., the Court held that the effects of such an agreement had to be assessed in the context in which they occur and where they might combine with

[182] Case C-234/89, [1991] ECR I-935. See V. Korah, 'The Judgment in Delimitis: A Milestone Towards a Realistic Assessment of the Effects of an Agreement or a Damp Squib' [1992] 14 *EIPR* 167.

others to have a cumulative effect on competition. It also follows from that judgment that the cumulative effect of several similar agreements constitutes one factor amongst others in ascertaining whether, by way of a possible alteration of competition, trade between Member States is capable of being affected.

15. Consequently, in the present case it is necessary to analyse the effects of a beer supply agreement, taken together with other contracts of the same type, on the opportunities of national competitors or those from other Member States, to gain access to the market for beer consumption or to increase their market share and, accordingly, the effects on the range of products offered to consumers.

16. In making that analysis, the relevant market must first be determined. The relevant market is primarily defined on the basis of the nature of the economic activity in question, in this case the sale of beer. Beer is sold through both retail channels and premises for the sale and consumption of drinks. From the consumer's point of view, the latter sector, comprising in particular public houses and restaurants, may be distinguished from the retail sector on the grounds that the sale of beer in public houses does not solely consist of the purchase of a product but is also linked with the provision of services, and that beer consumption in public houses is not essentially dependent on economic considerations. The specific nature of the public house trade is borne out by the fact that the breweries organize specific distribution systems for this sector which require special installations, and that the prices charged in that sector are generally higher than retail prices.

17. It follows that in the present case the reference market is that for the distribution of beer in premises for the sale and consumption of drinks. That finding is not affected by the fact that there is a certain overlap between the two distribution networks, namely inasmuch as retail sales allow new competitors to make their brands known and to use their reputation in order to gain access to the market constituted by premises for the sale and consumption of drinks.

18. Secondly, the relevant market is delimited from a geographical point of view. It should be noted that most beer supply agreements are still entered into at a national level. It follows that, in applying the [EU] competition rules, account is to be taken of the national market for beer distribution in premises for the sale and consumption of drinks.

19. In order to assess whether the existence of several beer supply agreements impedes access to the market as so defined, it is further necessary to examine the nature and extent of those agreements in their totality, comprising all similar contracts tying a large number of points of sale to several national producers (judgment in Case 43/69 *Bilger* v. *Jehle* . . .). The effect of those networks of contracts on access to the market depends specifically on the number of outlets thus tied to national producers in relation to the number of public houses which are not so tied, the duration of the commitments entered into, the quantities of beer to which those commitments relate, and on the proportion between those quantities and the quantities sold by free distributors.

20. The existence of a bundle of similar contracts, even if it has a considerable effect on the opportunities for gaining access to the market, is not, however, sufficient in itself to support a finding that the relevant market is inaccessible, inasmuch as it is only one factor, amongst others, pertaining to the economic and legal context in which an agreement must be appraised (Case 23/67 *Brasserie De Haecht*, cited above). The other factors to be taken into account are, in the first instance, those also relating to opportunities for access.

21. In that connection it is necessary to examine whether there are real concrete possibilities for a new competitor to penetrate the bundle of contracts by acquiring a brewery already established on the market together with its network of sales outlets, or to circumvent the bundle of contracts by opening new public houses. For that purpose it is necessary to have regard to the legal rules and agreements on the acquisition of companies and the establishment of outlets, and to the minimum number of outlets necessary for the economic operation of a distribution system. The presence of beer wholesalers not tied to producers who are active on the market is also a factor capable of facilitating a new producer's access to that market since he can make use of those wholesalers' sales networks to distribute his own beer.

22. Secondly, account must be taken of the conditions under which competitive forces operate on the relevant market. In that connection it is necessary to know not only the number and the size of producers present on the market, but also the degree of saturation of that market and customer fidelity to existing brands, for it is generally more difficult to penetrate a saturated market in which customers are loyal to a small number of large producers than a market in full expansion in which a large number of small producers are operating without any strong brand names. The trend in beer sales in the retail trade provides useful information on the development of demand and thus an indication of the degree of saturation of the beer market as a whole. The analysis of that trend is, moreover, of interest in evaluating brand loyalty. A steady increase in sales of beer under new brand names may confer on the owners of those brand names a reputation which they may turn to account in gaining access to the public-house market.

23. If an examination of all similar contracts entered into on the relevant market and the other factors relevant to the economic and legal context in which the contract must be examined shows that those agreements do not have the cumulative effect of denying access to that market to new national and foreign competitors, the individual agreements comprising the bundle of agreements cannot be held to restrict competition within the meaning of Article [101(1)]. They do not, therefore, fall under the prohibition laid down in that provision.

24. If, on the other hand, such examination reveals that it is difficult to gain access to the relevant market, it is necessary to assess the extent to which the agreements entered into by the brewery in question contribute to the cumulative effect produced in that respect by the totality of the similar contracts found on that market. Under the [EU] rules on competition, responsibility for such an effect of closing off the market must be attributed to the breweries which make an appreciable contribution thereto. Beer supply agreements entered into by breweries whose contribution to the cumulative effect is insignificant do not therefore fall under the prohibition under Article [101(1)].

25. In order to assess the extent of the contribution of the beer supply agreements entered into by a brewery to the cumulative sealing-off effect mentioned above, the market position of the contracting parties must be taken into consideration. That position is not determined solely by the market share held by the brewery and any group, to which it may belong, but also by the number of outlets tied to it or to its group, in relation to the total number of premises for the sale and consumption of drinks found in the relevant market.

26. The contribution of the individual contracts entered into by a brewery to the sealing-off of that market also depends on their duration. If the duration is manifestly excessive in relation to the average duration of beer supply agreements generally entered into on the relevant market, the individual contract falls under the prohibition under Article [101(1)]. A brewery with a relatively small market share which ties its sales outlets for many years may make a significant contribution to a sealing-off of the market as a brewery in a relatively strong market position which regularly releases sales outlets at shorter intervals.

27. The reply to be given to the first three questions is therefore that a beer supply agreement is prohibited by Article [101(1)], if two cumulative conditions are met. The first is that, having regard to the economic and legal context of the agreement at issue, it is difficult for competitors who could enter the market or increase their market share to gain access to the national market for the distribution of beer in premises for the sales and consumption of drinks. The fact that, in that market, the agreement in issue is one of a number of similar agreements having a cumulative effect on competition constitutes only one factor amongst others in assessing whether access to that market is indeed difficult. The second condition is that the agreement in question must make a significant contribution to the sealing-off effect brought about by the totality of those agreements in their economic and legal context. The extent of the contribution made by the individual agreement depends on the position of the contracting parties in the relevant market and on the duration of the agreement.

In determining the effect of the agreement the CJ stated that it is first necessary to define the relevant market. It must then be ascertained whether there is a concrete possibility for new competitors to penetrate the market or existing competitors to expand taking account of the number and size of producers operating on the market, the existence of networks of agreements, the saturation of the market, and brand loyalty, etc. If analysis shows that there is no denial of access to the market, an agreement cannot be found to restrict competition. Conversely, if access is inhibited it must then be assessed whether the agreement in question (which is taken to mean the agreements of that particular producer or brewer) contributes appreciably to that situation.

The analysis required by the CJ in this case highlights the importance of looking at the contractual restraint, not abstractly as a restraint, but in the context in which it operates before its effect can be determined. Irrespective of the fact that the judgment in *Delimitis* dealt only with beer supply agreements it affirmed the general need for an economic approach when determining the compatibility of an agreement with Article 101(1) and an assessment of the impact of the agreement on inter-brand competition.

In *European Night Services*[183] the GC also stressed the need for an economic approach to Article 101(1) in the context of horizontal agreements. In many cases parties operating at the same level of the economy may conclude an agreement which does not have the sole purpose of coordinating the parties' market conduct. For example, parties may create a joint venture[184] to pool their resources, perhaps to facilitate or speed up new entry into a market, to share financial risks, to achieve cost savings, or even to enable entry into a new market (each undertaking individually may not have the necessary skills or technology to make entry feasible). Obviously, such agreements may cause concern to competition authorities[185] but in *European Night Services* v. *Commission* the GC emphasised that where such an agreement does not contain obvious restrictions of competition, the actual conditions in which an agreement functions must be taken into account when considering whether or not it has the effect of restricting competition. In particular, account has to be taken of 'the economic context in which the undertakings operate, the products or services covered by the agreement and the actual structure of the market concerned'.[186] The importance of examining the conditions of competition, including existing and *potential* competition, was stressed. This was necessary:

in order to ascertain whether, in the light of the structure of the market and the economic and legal context within which it functions, there are real concrete possibilities for the undertakings concerned to compete among themselves or for a new competitor to penetrate the relevant market and compete with the undertakings already established.[187]

In *O2 (Germany) GmbH & Co OHG* v. *Commission*[188] the GC also stressed that the general method of analysis under Article 101(1) required an examination of the economic and legal context in which the agreement was concluded. In making the assessment, competition had to be understood in the context in which it would occur in the absence of the agreement in dispute.

---

[183] Cases T-374, 375, and 388/94, [1998] ECR II-3141.

[184] In some circumstances, the establishment of a joint venture amounts to a concentration for the purposes of the EU Merger Regulation, Council Reg. 139/2004 [2004] OJ L24/1, replacing Council Reg. 4064/89 [1989] OJ L395/1, as amended by Council Reg. 1310/97 [1997] OJ L180/1, discussed further in Chaps. 10 and 15.

[185] Although collaboration between such undertakings may enhance the position of the competitors on the market and lead to advantages on that market which the competitors may be unable to achieve on their own, joint venture agreements may: make it easier for the parties to collude (in particular, the collaboration may spill over outside the field of the agreement); foreclose third parties; be more restrictive than is necessary to achieve the objectives achieved; or result in a loss of actual or potential competition between the competitors, see Chap. 10.

[186] Cases T-374, 375, and 388/94, [1998] ECR II-3141, para. 136.

[187] Cases T-374, 375, and 388/94, [1998] ECR II-3141, para. 137. For joint ventures generally, see Chap. 10.

[188] Case T-328/03, [2006] ECR II-1231. See, e.g., M. Marquis, 'O2 (Germany) v. Commission and the exotic mysteries of Article 81(1) EC' [2007] 32 *ELRev* 29.

71. The examination required in the light of Article [101(1)] consists essentially in taking account of the impact of the agreement on existing and potential competition (see, to that effect, Case C-234/89, Delimitis...) and the competition situation in the absence of the agreement (Société minière et technique...), those two factors being intrinsically linked.

72. The examination of competition in the absence of an agreement appears to be particularly necessary as regards markets undergoing liberalization or emerging markets... where effective competition may be problematic owing, for example, to the presence of a dominant operator, the concentrated nature of the market structure or the existence of significant barriers to entry—factors referred to, in the present case, in the Decision.[189]

The *Delimitis, European Night Services,* and *O2* cases are reflective of an 'economic approach' which supports the Commission's view, set out in its Article 101(3) Guidelines, that a finding that actual or potential competition on the market has been restricted to an appreciable extent is facilitated by proof that the agreement has in fact led to those anti-competitive effects that are the expected consequence of a restriction of competition (i.e. a reduction in output or an increase in price).[190] However, this does not necessarily mean that 'an assessment of the positive and negative effects of the agreement from the point of view of competition must be carried out at the stage of Article [101(1)]'.[191] According to the Guidelines, potential anti-competitive effects are determined through an examination of whether the parties individually or jointly have or obtain some degree of market power and, if so, whether the agreement contributes to the creation, maintenance, or strengthening of that market power or allows the parties to exploit it.[192] Where the parties have no such market power, the agreement cannot have anti-competitive effects, and, therefore, cannot be said to restrict competition. The scarcity of the case law and economically reasoned Commission decisions in this area, however, make it difficult to draw conclusions as to the *degree* of market power required to establish anti-competitive effects.[193] The Article 101(3) Guidelines state only that the requisite degree is 'less than the degree of market power required for a finding of dominance under Article [102]'.[194] This, combined with the moderately low market share thresholds, of 20–30 per cent, that are set out in the block exemptions,[195] which *exempt* agreements from the Article 101(1) prohibition, may cause firms to be concerned that market power issues will arise under Article 101(1) where relatively low market share thresholds are exceeded (10–20 per cent for agreements between competitors and 15–30 per cent for agreements between non-competitors).

---

[189] Case T-328/03, [2006] ECR II-1231, paras. 71–72. In this case the GC found that the Commission had not carried out an economic analysis of the effect of the agreement on the competitive situation.

[190] See Article 101(3) Guidelines, paras. 18 and 24 and Case T-328/03, *O2 (Germany) GmbH & Co OHG v. Commission* [2006] ECR II-1231, para. 68.

[191] Case T-328/03, *O2 (Germany) GmbH & Co OHG v. Commission* [2006] ECR II-1231, para. 70. 'Such a method of analysis, as regards in particular the taking into account of the competition situation that would exist in the absence of the agreement, does not amount to carrying out an assessment of the pro- and anti-competitive effects of the agreement... The examination required in the light of Article [101(1) TFEU] consists essentially in taking account of the impact of the agreement on existing and potential competition... and the competition situation in the absence of the agreement' Case T-328/03, *O2 (Germany) GmbH & Co OHG v. Commission* [2006] ECR II-1231, paras. 69–71.

[192] Article 101(3) Guidelines, paras. 24–27. The Guidelines thus recognise that it is usually necessary to define the market and to examine the nature of the products, the market position of the parties, the market position of competitors and buyers, and the existence of potential competitors and barriers to entry. Such an assessment must ordinarily be made in the actual context in which competition occurs, Article 101(3) Guidelines, paras. 17–24.

[193] See the general discussion in Faull and Nikpay (eds.), *The EC Law of Competition* (cited in n. 6), paras. 3.310–3.336.

[194] Article 101(3) Guidelines, para. 26.

[195] See Section 4.E, pp. 263–266.

(iv) Restraints on Intra-brand Competition

It has already been explained that the Commission's Guidelines state that when determining what constitutes a restriction of competition within the meaning of Article 101(1), it must *also* be determined whether the agreement (or its parts) restricts *intra-brand* competition.[196]

In *Société Technique Minière* v. *Maschinenbau Ulm GmbH (STM)*,[197] for example, the CJ dealt with an exclusive distribution agreement which, in contrast to that concerned in *Consten and Grundig*, did not confer ATP (or a complete monopoly over the right to distribute in France) on the distributor. The contractual arrangements did admit the possibility of parallel imports from distributors in other Member States. In this case the CJ did not hold that the object of the agreement was to restrict competition. Rather, accepting similar arguments to those raised by the parties in *Consten and Grundig*, it indicated that an exclusive distribution agreement would not restrict competition if the appointment of an exclusive distributor was necessary in order to enable a manufacturer to penetrate a new market. Before it could be determined whether the agreement restricted competition, the agreement should be examined in the light of the competition which would occur if the agreement in question were not or had not been made. In this case it seemed that the economic justifications for the agreement might outweigh the territorial restrictions inherent in the agreement.

Case 56/65, *Société Technique Minière* v. *Maschinenbau Ulm GmbH* [1966] ECR 234, 249–50

The parties entered into an agreement by which a French company was given exclusive rights to distribute in France the equipment (levelling machines) of a German manufacturer. The French company was free to re-export the equipment outside France. The parties fell out, and in litigation in the French courts the French company claimed that the agreement was void under Article 101(2) because it infringed Article 101(1). The Cour d'Appel Paris asked the Court of Justice on a preliminary reference how it should assess the compatibility of this type of agreement with Article 101(1).

Court of Justice

The effects of the agreement on competition

…The competition in question must be understood within the actual context in which it would occur in the absence of the agreement in dispute. In particular it may be doubted whether there is an interference with competition if the said agreement seems really necessary for the penetration of a new area by an undertaking. Therefore, in order to decide whether an agreement containing a clause 'granting an exclusive right of sale' is to be considered as prohibited by reason of its object or of its effect, it is appropriate to take into account in particular the nature and quantity, limited or otherwise, of the products covered by the agreement, the position and importance of the grantor and the concessionnaire on the market for the products concerned, the isolated nature of the disputed agreement or, alternatively, its position in series of agreements, the severity of the clauses intended to protect the exclusive dealership or, alternatively, the opportunities allowed for other commercial competitors in the same products by way of parallel re-exportation and importation.

---

[196] Article 101(3) Guidelines, paras. 17 and 18. See also the discussion of Cases 56 and 58/64, *Consten and Grundig* [1966] ECR 299, 348, discussed in Section 3.D. (ii)a, pp. 206–211.

[197] Case 56/65, [1966] ECR 235.

In line with *STM* the CJ has also held that where exclusivity provisions do not give a licensee of intellectual property (IP) rights ATP, restrictions in a licensing agreement may fall outside Article 101(1) if necessary to protect the investment of the licensee.[198]

In its Guidelines the Commission relies on this line of cases as authority for the proposition that territorial or customer intra-brand restraints are caught by Article 101(1) unless 'objectively necessary' for the existence of an agreement of that type or nature.

The question is not whether the parties in their particular situation would not have accepted to conclude a less restrictive agreement, but whether given the nature of the agreement and the characteristics of the market a less restrictive agreement would not have been concluded by undertakings in a similar setting. For instance, territorial restraints in an agreement between a supplier and a distributor may for a certain period of time fall outside Article 101(1), if the restraints are objectively necessary in order for the distributor to penetrate a new market.[199]

This sweeping approach, appears to be motivated more by single market and/or economic freedom than pure competition concerns, and potentially brings many vertical and IP licensing agreements within the ambit of Article 101 whether or not the parties have market power and/or the ability to affect prices or output on the market for example, by foreclosing access to supply or distribution channels to competitors. This appears to underline the view that EU:

institutions continue to see merit in protecting, albeit to a significantly lesser degree than in the past, the process…of competition rather than focusing exclusively on the direct or probable economic effects of agreements. This means that in certain circumstances agreements which have a neutral or even *net positive* effect on consumer welfare and allocative efficiency can fall within the scope of Article [101(1)].[200]

It is not at all clear that such a sweeping approach is dictated by *STM*, which clearly seems to require an assessment of the competitive situation in the absence of the agreement in dispute *and* a determination of the strength of the parties' position on the market prior to an assessment of the compatibility of an agreement with Article 101(1).

(v) Appreciability

a. Agreements of Minor Importance: Market Share Thresholds

Where an agreement does not contain object or 'hardcore' restraints, the Commission's Notice on agreements of minor importance (currently under review) provides that the agreement is not likely to restrict competition appreciably where the aggregate market share held by the parties to the agreement does not exceed 10 per cent (for competitors) or 15 per cent (for non-competitors). Where it is difficult to classify the agreement, the 10 per cent threshold applies. For the purposes of calculating market shares, the market shares of 'connected undertakings' are included.[201]

---

[198] See Chap. 12.

[199] Article 101(3) Guidelines, para. 18(2) and Chap. 11. This statement suggests that if not objectively necessary the intra-brand restraints will have as their effect the restriction of competition, irrespective of the amount of inter-brand competition on the market (subject to the principle of appreciability).

[200] Faull and Nikpay (eds.), *The EC Law of Competition* (cited in n. 6), para. 3.142, and see Chap. 1.

[201] De minimis Notice, para. 12. The current Notice is under review, see IP/13/685 and <http://ec.europa.eu/competition/consultations/2013_de_minimis_notice/index_en.html>. The draft Notice does not propose a change to the market share thresholds.

Commission Notice on Agreements of Minor Importance which do not Appreciably Restrict Competition under Article 81(1) of the Treaty Establishing the EC [now Article 101(1)] (de minimis) [2001] OJ C368/13

1. Article [101(1)] prohibits agreements between undertakings which may affect trade between Member States and which have as their object or effect the prevention, restriction or distortion of competition within the common market. The Court of Justice…has clarified that this provision is not applicable where the impact of the agreement on intra-community trade or on competition is not appreciable.

2. In this notice the Commission quantifies, with the help of market share thresholds, what is not an appreciable restriction of competition under Article [101]. This negative definition of appreciability does not imply that agreements between undertakings which exceed the thresholds set out in this notice appreciably restrict competition. Such agreements may still have only a negligible effect on competition and may therefore not be prohibited by Article [101(1)].

3. Agreements may in addition not fall under Article [101(1)] because they are not capable of appreciably affecting trade between Member States. This notice does not deal with this issue. It does not quantify what does not constitute an appreciable effect on trade. It is however acknowledged that agreements between small and medium-sized undertakings, as defined in the Annex to Commission Recommendation 96/280/EC(3), are rarely capable of appreciably affecting trade between Member States. Small and medium-sized undertakings are currently defined in that recommendation as undertakings which have fewer than 250 employees and have either an annual turnover not exceeding EUR 40 million or an annual balance-sheet total not exceeding EUR 27 million.

4. In cases covered by this notice the Commission will not institute proceedings either upon application or on its own initiative. Where undertakings assume in good faith that an agreement is covered by this notice, the Commission will not impose fines. Although not binding on them, this notice also intends to give guidance to the courts and authorities of the Member States in their application of Article [101].

5. This notice also applies to decisions by associations of undertakings and to concerted practices.

6. This notice is without prejudice to any interpretation of Article [101] which may be given by the Court of Justice or the [GC] of the European Communities.

II

7. The Commission holds the view that agreements between undertakings which affect trade between Member States do not appreciably restrict competition within the meaning of Article [101(1)]:

(a) if the aggregate market share held by the parties to the agreement does not exceed 10 per cent on any of the relevant markets affected by the agreement, where the agreement is made between undertakings which are actual or potential competitors on any of these markets (agreements between competitors); or

(b) if the market share held by each of the parties to the agreement does not exceed 15 per cent on any of the relevant markets affected by the agreement, where the agreement is made between undertakings which are not actual or potential competitors on any of these markets (agreements between non-competitors).

Where competition in a market is restricted by the cumulative effect of agreements entered into by different suppliers and distributors, however, a reduced threshold of 5 per cent applies.[202] Access to a market is unlikely to be foreclosed by the cumulative effect of parallel networks of agreements where they cover less than 30 per cent of the market. This paragraph will be of particular importance in the context of distribution agreements for example, beer supply agreements, which operate in a

---

[202] De minimis Notice, para. 8.

similar way to other agreements on the market.[203] The Notice improves on the position set out in the previous 1997 Notice which did not apply at all where the relevant market was restricted by the cumulative effects of parallel networks of similar agreements established by several manufacturers or dealers.

b. Outgrowing the Notice

If parties outgrow the Notice by subsequently acquiring greater market shares or achieving increased turnovers, paragraph 9 of the Notice provides for some marginal relief.

9. The Commission also holds the view that agreements are not restrictive of competition if the market shares do not exceed the thresholds of respectively 10 per cent, 15 per cent and 5 per cent set out in point 7 and 8 during two successive calendar years by more than 2 percentage points.

c. Effect of the Notice

It has been seen that although the de minimis notice is not legally binding on NCAs or courts,[204] it creates legitimate expectations so that the Commission itself should not depart from them without reason without being in breach of this principle and the principle of equal treatment.[205] Indeed, the Commission states at paragraph 4 of the Notice that where an agreement falls within its ambit, it will not, generally, institute proceedings. Further, where undertakings assume in good faith that an agreement is covered by the Notice, the Commission will not impose fines. The parties cannot, however, be saved from the consequence of nullity in the event of the agreement being found to contravene Article 101(1) (although the Notice could guide the national courts in its application). Therefore, although the market shares set out in the Notice are useful in indicating the parties' position on the market, they are not conclusive. Agreements between parties with smaller market shares may produce a significant impact. Conversely, agreements between undertakings with greater shares of the market may produce insignificant results[206]—'the negative definition of the appreciability of…restriction does not imply that agreements of undertakings which exceed those thresholds appreciably restrict competition'.[207]

F. ANCILLARY RESTRAINTS

If a main transaction does not restrict inter- or intra-brand competition, the Commission states in its Article 101(3) Guidelines that individual restraints in the agreement ancillary to it (i.e. directly related and necessary to its implementation and proportionate to the main non-restrictive distribution or

---

[203] Beer supply agreements will not restrict competition at all if they do not significantly contribute to a cumulative effect caused by the network on the market, see Case 234/89, *Delimitis v. Henninger Bräu AG* [1991] ECR I-935, paras. 24–26. This aspect of the case is discussed in Section 3.E.iii.

[204] Case C-226/11, *Expedia Inc v. Autorité de la Concurrence*, 13 December 2012, paras. 23–27.

[205] The CJ has held that although guidelines are not rules of law, 'they form rules of practice from which the administration may not depart in an individual case without giving reasons that are compatible with the principle of equal treatment', Case C-397/03 P, *Archer Daniels Midland Co v. Commission* [2006] ECR I-4429, para. 91 (see Chap. 2). In practice some national courts might be willing to take the de minimis Notice into account when assessing whether or not an agreement has an appreciable effect on competition and trade within the meaning of Art. 101(1).

[206] See para. 2 of the Notice and, e.g., Case 319/82, *Société de Vente de Ciments et Bétons de l'Est SA v. Kerpen and Kerpen GmbH & Co KG* [1983] ECR 4173, para. 8. Where the parties to an agreement only slightly exceed the market shares set out in the Notice the Commission must justify a finding that the agreement nonetheless has an appreciable effect on competition and trade. Where it fails to do so the Court may quash a decision holding that an agreement falls within Art. 101(1), Cases T-374, 375, 384, and 388/94, *European Night Services v. Commission* [1998] ECR II-3141, paras 102–105.

[207] De minimis Notice, para. 2 and Case C-226/11, *Expedia Inc v. Autorité de la Concurrence*, 13 December 2012, para. 25.

joint venture agreement) will also be compatible with Article 101(1).[208] The Commission states that the following cases are examples of cases where restraints ancillary to a pro-competitive agreement have been held to be compatible with Article 101(1).

(i) *Remia and Nutricia*

In *Remia and Nutricia*[209] the CJ recognised that a non-compete clause on the sale of a business was likely to be an essential part of an agreement to sell a business. Viewed *ex post*, a non-compete clause may appear to restrict competition between the parties. However, when assessed *ex ante* it may become clear that competition is not restricted. No undertaking would be willing to purchase the business without an assurance from the vendor that it will not remain in business in such a way that it would still be able to exploit the goodwill and the customers of the business sold. Nonetheless, the Court held that the non-compete clause must be limited to what is necessary to make the transaction viable. If it is broader than required for the sale, for example, if it precludes the vendor from setting up any business within a wide geographic area for an indefinite period of time, it will restrict competition within the meaning of Article 101(1).[210]

(ii) *Pronuptia*

In *Pronuptia de Paris GmbH v. Pronuptia de Paris Irmgard Schillgallis*[211] the CJ set out Guidelines for a national court ruling on the compatibility of a distribution franchising agreement with Article 101(1). It held that restrictions essential to the successful operation of a distribution franchise agreement, which provided a means for an undertaking to derive financial benefit from its expertise without investing its own capital and a means for traders who do not have expertise to benefit from the franchisor's experience and reputation, would not restrict competition. In particular, the franchisor should be able to communicate know-how without running the risk that it would be used to benefit competitors and to take measures necessary to maintain the identity and reputation of the network.[212] The Court thus considered that restrictions within the agreement would fall outside Article 101(1) if objectively necessary to the successful operation of the franchising transaction.

The CJ did not consider, however, that all contractual restraints would be necessary to achieve these objectives. In particular, the Court held that provisions which shared markets between the franchisor and franchisees or between the franchisees or which prevented the franchisees from engaging in price competition with one another would restrict competition.[213] Clauses in the agreement which conferred territorial exclusivity upon the franchisee were not essential to the functioning of the agreement and restricted competition. The combination of an exclusivity and location clause essentially gave the franchisees ATP within their franchise area.[214]

---

[208] Article 101(3) Guidelines, paras. 28–29.

[209] Case 42/84, *Remia BV and NV Verenigde Bedrijven Nutricia v. Commission* [1985] ECR 2545. Transactions that constitute a 'concentration' (or merger) may now be dealt with under the EU Merger Regulation rather than Art. 101, see Chap. 15

[210] Case 42/84, *Remia BV and NV Verenigde Bedrijven Nutricia v. Commission* [1985] ECR 2545, paras 17–36.

[211] Case 161/84, [1986] ECR 353.

[212] Case 161/84, [1986] ECR 353, paras. 16–17, *see also* Chap. 10.

[213] Case 161/84, [1986] ECR 353, para. 23.

[214] G. Amato, *Antitrust and the Bounds of Power* (Hart Publishing, 1997), 50–51. For franchise agreements generally, see Chap. 11.

(iii) *Gøttrup-Klim*

In *Gøttrup-Klim Grovvareforening and Others v. Dansk Landbrugs Grovvareselskab AmbA*[215] the CJ was asked by a Danish court whether a clause in the statutes of Dansk Landbrugs Grovvareselskab AmbA (a Danish cooperative association distributing farm supplies, (DLG)) restricted competition within the meaning of Article 101(1). The object of DLG was to provide its members with farm supplies (such as fertiliser) at the lowest possible prices and to offer its members other services, particularly in the area of finance. In 1988 the statutes of DLG were changed because of increasing competition from the claimants in this case. Essentially, the disputed clause precluded some of DLG's members from holding membership of, or any other kind of participation in, associations, societies, or other forms of cooperative organisation in competition with DLG, with regard to the purchase and sale of fertilisers and plant protection products. The statutes provided that members which infringed this rule would be excluded from DLG (and some members were in fact excluded). DLG had notified the amendment to the Commission for negative clearance or exemption, but at the time of the proceedings before the CJ, it had still not received an answer to the letter of notification. In the proceedings before the CJ the Commission stated in reply to a question from the Court that the amendment to the statutes did not infringe the Article 101(1) prohibition.

DLG contended that the aim of the clause was not to restrict competition. On the contrary it (1) enabled the members to stand up to a few very large multinational producers of fertilisers and plant protection products in order to obtain lower purchase prices for Danish farmers, and (2) prevented competitors' representatives from taking part in the association's management bodies (shareholders' committee and board of directors) in which business secrets were discussed. The Danish authorities did not take the view that the statutes as amended infringed Danish competition law. Nonetheless, the claimants challenged the compatibility of the provision with Article 101 and sought compensation and damages in respect of the loss sustained from their exclusion from DLG. The Danish court referred the matter to the CJ using the procedure set out in Article 267 TFEU. In particular it asked whether a provision in the statutes of a commercial cooperative society excluding members that participated in a cooperative organisation which competed with it was contrary to Article 101(1). The CJ replied that it would not, so long as the provision was restricted to what was necessary to ensure that the cooperative functioned properly and maintained its contractual power in relation to producers.

The doctrine of ancillary restraints is not without difficulties, however. In particular, it appears to be limited by the Court's unwillingness to push it to its logical conclusion and to accept that any restraint—even perhaps one providing a distributor with ATP—may sometimes be ancillary to a non-restrictive agreement.[216] Further, it is by no means easy to identify whether or not a particular restraint is 'ancillary' to the operation of the particular agreement so it may be hard to apply in practice.

The Commission explains how it approaches 'ancillary restraints' in its Guidelines on the application of Article 101(3).[217] Also of relevance is a Commission Notice on restrictions directly related and necessary to concentrations,[218] which sets out guidance on how it is determined whether restrictions are ancillary to *concentrations* (merger transactions). Although specific to mergers, it appears from the GC's judgment in *M6* that this Notice will also provide guidance in pure Article 101 cases. Indeed, in *M6* the GC drew on a previous notice on restrictions directly related and necessary to

---

[215] Case C-250/92, *Gøttrup-Klim Grovvareforeninger and Others v. Dansk Landbrugs Grovvareselskab AmbA* [1994] ECR I-5641.

[216] In *Pronuptia,*for example, the Court concluded that provisions in a franchising agreement which led to the sharing of markets between the franchisor and the franchisees or between franchisees would restrict competition for the purpose of Art. 101(1).

[217] Article 101(3) Guidelines, para. 2.2.3.

[218] [2005] OJ C26/4 discussed in Chap. 15.

concentrations[219] when considering the parties' argument that two clauses should *not* have been found to infringe Article 101(1). In addition to the rule of reason argument set out earlier, the parties argued that these clauses were 'ancillary' to the operation of the non-restrictive joint venture. The two clauses were an exclusivity clause, granting TPS the exclusive right to broadcast general-interest channels and a clause, essentially, granting TPS the right of first refusal with regard to special-interest channels produced by the parties. As the Commission had found that the joint venture did *not* infringe Article 101(1), it was argued that the ancillary clauses should also have been cleared. The GC rejected this argument. It considered that the clauses were not objectively necessary for the operation of the joint venture and, even if they were, the Commission had not committed a manifest error in concluding that the restrictions were not proportionate to, or exceeded what was necessary for, the creation of the joint venture.[220]

In *MasterCard*[221] the GC also had to deal with the argument that the Commission ought to have concluded that the MIF was objectively necessary to the operation of the payment card system. The GC seems to consider the arguments of objective necessity[222] and ancillary restraints to be the same (the latter requiring restraints both to be directly related and objectively necessary to the implementation of the agreement) but rejected the argument on the facts. In so doing it explored the meaning of an ancillary restriction and how the concept relates to the rule of reason debate and the analysis required under Article 101(3).

Case T-111/08, *MasterCard, Inc* v *Commission*, 24 May 2012

General Court

a) The part of the plea in which it is alleged that the objective necessity of the MIF was incorrectly assessed

77 The concept of an ancillary restriction covers any restriction which is directly related and necessary to the implementation of a main operation (Case T-112/99 *M6*…, paragraph 104).

78 A restriction 'directly related' to implementation of a main operation must be understood to be any restriction which is subordinate to the implementation of that operation and which has an evident link with it (*M6 and Others* v *Commission*, cited in paragraph 77 above, paragraph 105).

79 The condition that a restriction be necessary implies a twofold examination. It is necessary to establish, first, whether the restriction is objectively necessary for the implementation of the main operation and, secondly, whether it is proportionate to it (*M6 and Others* v *Commission*…, paragraph 106).

80 As regards the examination of the objective necessity of a restriction, it must be observed that inasmuch as the existence of a rule of reason cannot be upheld, the requirement for objective necessity cannot be interpreted as implying a need to weigh the pro and anti-competitive effects of an agreement. Such an analysis can take place only in the specific framework of Article [101(3)]. Therefore, examination of the objective necessity of a restriction in relation to the main operation cannot but be relatively abstract. It is not a question of analysing whether, in the light of the competitive situation on the relevant market, the restriction is indispensable to the commercial success of the main operation but of determining whether, in the specific context of the main operation, the restriction is necessary to implement that operation. If,

---

[219] 1990 Notice, [1990] OJ C203/5. This notice was replaced by a 2001 Notice, [2001] OJ C188/5, and then by a Notice in 2004, [2005] OJ C56/24.

[220] Case T-112/99, *Métropole Télévision (M6)* v. *Commission* [2001] ECR II-2459, paras. 103–117.

[221] Case T-111/08, *MasterCard, Inc* v. *Commission* 24 May 2012, on appeal Case C-382/12 P. See also, e.g., Case T-360/09, *E.ON Ruhrgas AG* v. *Commission*, 29 June 2012 (finding that a side letter providing for market sharing is not ancillary to an agreement for the construction and operation of a gas pipe line), paras. 60–82.

[222] See Section 3.D.iv, pp. 215–226.

without the restriction, the main operation is difficult or even impossible to implement, the restriction may be regarded as objectively necessary for its implementation (*M6 and Others* v *Commission*..., paragraphs 107 and 109).

81 As regards the examination of the proportionate nature of the restriction in relation to implementation of the main operation, it is important to verify whether its duration and its material and geographic scope do not exceed what is necessary to implement that operation. If the duration or the scope of the restriction exceed what is necessary in order to implement the operation, it must be assessed separately under Article [101(3)] (*M6*..., paragraph 113).

82 Lastly, inasmuch as the assessment of the ancillary nature of a restriction in relation to a main operation entails complex economic assessments by the Commission, judicial review of that assessment is limited to verifying whether the relevant procedural rules have been complied with, whether the statement of the reasons for the decision is adequate, whether the facts have been accurately stated and whether there has been a manifest error of appraisal or misuse of powers (*M6*..., paragraph 114).

83 In the present case, the only point at issue is the condition relating to the objective necessity of the MIF. In essence, the applicants, supported by a number of interveners, raise two complaints. They submit that the contested decision is vitiated by an error in that the Commission applied the wrong legal criteria. They also take the view that the Commission made a manifest error of assessment in its examination of the objective necessity of that MIF.

G. CONCLUSIONS ON THE APPROACH REQUIRED UNDER ARTICLE 101(1): IS ANY WEIGHING OR BALANCING REQUIRED?

The Commission's view (supported by recent GC judgments) that no weighing of pro- and anti-competitive effects is permitted under Article 101(1) in 'effect' cases,[223] is difficult to reconcile with all of the case law, in particular that dealing with ancillary restraints doctrine and others such as STM.[224] This view requires a difficult distinction to be drawn between proportionate restraints *objectively necessary* to the implementation of a main non-restrictive operation (which would be difficult or even impossible to implement without the restriction)— which are ancillary and fall outside Article 101(1) and restraints which are indispensable to achieve efficiencies or to the commercial success of the main operation, which can only be weighed against anti-competitive effects under Article 101(3).[225]

---

[223] Case T-112/99, [2001] ECR II-2459, para. 107; Article 101(3) Guidelines, para. 30. This position arguably represents a change in direction from the position set out by the GC in Cases T-374, 375 and 388/94, *European Night Services* [1998] ECR II-3141, where the GC indicated that a balancing under Art. 101(1) might be required where restrictions by effect are involved. It stated at para. 136 that: 'in assessing an agreement under Article [101(1) TFEU], account should be taken of the actual conditions in which it functions, in particular the economic context in which the undertakings operate, the products or services covered by the agreement and the actual structure of the market concerned...unless it is an agreement containing obvious restrictions of competition such as price-fixing, market-sharing or the control of outlets (Case T-148/89, *Tréfilunion* v. *Commission* [1995] ECR II-1063, para. 109). In the latter case, such restrictions may be weighed against their claimed pro-competitive effects only in the context of Article [101(3) TFEU], with a view to granting an exemption from the prohibition in Article [101(1)].'

[224] See also, e.g., Case 26/76, *Metro-SB-Grossmärkte GmbH* v. *Commission (No. 1)* [1977] ECR 1875, especially paras. 20–22. But see e.g., J. Faull and A. Nikpay (eds.), *The EC Law of Competition* (Oxford University Press, 2nd edn, 2007), paras. 3.248–3.291. For the view that the doctrine is merely about 'administrative convenience, allowing the Commission to focus on the principal effects of an agreement, but also to control minor aspects if the ancillary restraints are excessive in duration or scope', see G. Monti, *EC Competition Law* (Cambridge University Press, 2007), 34–5.

[225] In the US, a doctrine of ancillary restraints has been used as a mechanism for distinguishing between naked restraints (demanding per se categorisation) and those related to an efficiency-enhancing integration and reasonably

If the GC and Commission are simply stating that a disputed agreement, including these restraints, does not restrict inter- or intra-brand competition and so does not infringe Article 101(1) this is not controversial.[226] However, the case law suggests that in some situations the analysis goes beyond this and that there is in fact a need to weigh pro- and anti-competitive effects of the disputed restraint: anti-competitive restraints are permitted only if ancillary to some *pro-competitive* objective. This view is supported, for example, by Advocate General Léger who, in *Wouters v. Algemene Raad van de Nederlandse Order van Advocaten*,[227] relied on these cases as evidence of a limited application of the rule of reason. 'Confronted with certain classes of agreement... [the CJ] has drawn up a competition balance-sheet and, where the balance is positive, has held that the clauses necessary to perform the agreement fell outside the prohibition laid down by Article [101(1)].'[228]

The judgments of the CJ in *Wouters v. Algemene Raad van de Nederlandse Orde van Advocaten*[229] and *Meca-Medina v. Commission*,[230] discussed in Section 3.D.iv, are also problematic to the non-weighing view. Neither of these judgments refers to the GC's judgment in *Métropole*. If the Commission's analytical framework is correct, it might have been expected that the CJ in these cases would, having stated that the agreement had clear adverse effects on competition (in terms of the services that could be offered and economies of scope), have gone on to find that the object or effect of the agreement was the restriction of competition.[231] The justifications raised by the parties could then only have been appraised when determining whether the rules of ethics could be excepted through the application of Article 101(3). The CJ did not, however, take this course. It has been seen that had it done so in *Wouters*, the referring national court, which did not at this time have jurisdiction to rule on the compatibility of the agreement with Article 101(3), would have been compelled to rule that the regulations, or at least the restrictive rules within them, were void.[232] The CJ's clear view was that the Bar Association had not been unreasonable in considering that the restrictive rules were warranted by reference to the objective pursued.

---

necessary to achieve its pro-competitive benefits (analysed under the rule of reason). Under this doctrine it must be established that the restraints (which being severe are often by their very nature considered anti-competitive) are reasonably necessary for an integration which might generate plausible cognisable efficiencies. If so, rule of reason, not per se, analysis is applied. This approach clearly requires some weighing of pro- and anti-competitive benefits both when applying the doctrine and, subsequently, when conducting rule of reason analysis, see A. Jones, 'Analysis of Agreements under U.S. and EC Antitrust Law—Convergence or Divergence?' [2006] 51 *Ant Bull* 691.

[226] Arguably in *Pronuptia*, for example, the agreement and the 'ancillary restraints' did not restrict competition at all.

[227] Case C-309/99, [2002] ECR I-1577.

[228] Case C-309/99, [2002] ECR I-1577, Léger AG, para. 103. See also Case 1035/1/1/04, *The Racecourse Association (the 'RCA') v. OFT* [2005] CAT 29, where the UK's Competition Appeal Tribunal (CAT) confessed to having 'some difficulty in reconciling' the approach in *Gøttrup-Klim* and *Wouters* with that in *Métropole*. It considered that the analysis required under Art. 101(1) by the CJ in *Gøttrup-Klim* and *Wouters* was a rather more flexible exercise than the GC had been willing to appreciate in *Métropole* (*M6*). In determining the compatibility of that agreement with Chap. I of the Competition Act 1998 (based on and generally interpreted in accordance with Art. 101(1), see s. 60 Competition Act 1998) the CAT held that it was not enough that an arrangement was apparently anti-competitive for it to have as its effect the restriction of competition. 'What those cases show is that ostensibly restrictive arrangements which are necessary to achieve a proper commercial objective will not, or may not, constitute an anti-competitive infringement at all. Whether or not they will do so requires an objective analysis of the particular arrangement entered into by the parties, assessed by reference to their subjective "wants" and against the evidence of the particular market in which they made their arrangement. The task then is to consider whether the restrictive arrangement of which complaint is made is "necessary" to achieve the objective', para. 167. A restriction could be regarded as objectively necessary for its implementation if the main operation was difficult or even impossible to implement without the restriction.

[229] Case C-309/99, [2002] ECR I-1577 (this judgment is not referred to by the Commission in its discussion of Art. 101(1) in the Article 101(3) Guidelines).

[230] Case C-519/04 P, *Meca-Medina v. Commission* [2006] ECR I-6991.

[231] The CJ had after all made it clear that the rules might have negative effects on prices, innovation, and/or the variety or quality of goods and services that could be expected.

[232] Even if the parties had notified the agreement to the Commission any exemption granted would not have taken effect retrospectively, see Reg. 17, [1959–1962] OJ Spec. Ed. 87, Art. 4.

These cases thus seem to provide support for the view that some weighing of anti-competitive and pro-competitive effects, and even *other* non-competition public interest objectives,[233] should take place under Article 101(1). Some commentators have argued that the judgment in *Wouters* did not go this far, however, and have offered other explanations for them, for example: that the CJ conflated and operated Article 101(1) and Article 101(3) as if they were a single provision;[234] that it simply applies the concept of ancillary restraints, endorsing the restraint on the grounds that it was ancillary not to some legitimate pro-competitive objective but to the regulatory aim of ensuring integrity and experience;[235] that *Wouters* is explicable by the fact that the rule was promulgated not by an undertaking but by an association of undertakings;[236] or that the CJ transposed its analysis in free movement cases to the competition sphere (or sought to align the two sets of rules), weighing non-discriminatory national rules against domestic mandatory requirements of public policy and allowing the Court to take account of non-competition factors which relate to domestic interests.[237]

G. Monti, 'Article 81 EC and Public Policy' (2002) *CMLRev* 1057, 1087–1088

This is a remarkable *ratio decidendi* for the Court intertwines principles of competition law and free movement... In simple terms, the line of reasoning followed is this: we know from *Cassis de Dijon* that an indistinctly applicable domestic rule which is an obstacle to the free movement of goods does not fall under the prohibition in Article [34] if it is necessary to satisfy a mandatory requirement relating to, for example, fairness of commercial transactions or the defence of the consumer. The same approach has been applied in relation to other freedoms. In *Wouters*, the Court relies on this line of case law, specifically referring to *Reisbüro Vroede*, a case in relation to the regulation of the legal profession in the context of Article [56] (freedom to provide services) where it held that a non-discriminatory rule of German law which infringed Article [56] might be justified in the public interest. The Court then holds that the principle created by this case law (labelled by many commentators a 'rule of reason') applies *mutatis mutandis* to Article [101]. Having transposed a rule from the free movement case law into the competition case law, the Court was free to say that the prohibition in Article [101] could not apply. This reasoning incorporates the rule of reason deployed in the free movement area as a mechanism for justifying an agreement otherwise unlawful under Article [101(1)]. It is ironic that while the Court (most explicitly in *Métropole*) has regularly refused to adopt an *American-style* rule of reason in Article [101] (whereby the legality of an agreement would depend upon whether, on balance it increased consumer welfare) it has in *Wouters* given strong indications that what I shall call the *European-style rule of reason*, developed in the free movement field, can apply to competition cases so that an anti-competitive agreement necessary to preserve a domestic mandatory requirement of public policy is allowed to escape the application of

---

[233] See n. 127.

[234] See J Goyder and A. Albors-Llorens, *Goyder's EC Competition Law* (5th edn, Oxford University Press, 2009), 115–116.

[235] Whish and Bailey, *Competition* (cited in n. 82), Chap. 3, section 4.

[236] Had the rule been adopted by an undertaking, it would have fallen outside of Art. 101 as the activity it was conducting was regulatory in nature (and regulation is not an economic activity). Once within Art. 101 the CJ had to find an appropriate standard by which to assess the non-economic regulatory activity and that the principles applied were free-movement not competition ones. See Odudu, *The Boundaries of EC Competition Law: The Scope of Article 81* (cited in n. 5), 53.

[237] Monti, 'Article 81 EC and Public Policy' (cited in n. 45), 1057, 1087–1088. See also Monti, *EC Competition Law* (cited in n. 224), 110–113. For the view that the rule in *Wouters* was to deal with market failures—information asymmetries that are typically present in professional service, see Ibáñez Colomo, 'Market Failure, Transaction Costs and Articles 101(1) TFEU Case Law' (cited in n. 66), 550.

> Article [101]. Thus *Wouters* is another in a line of cases that exemplifies what Mortelmans[238] labelled a 'convergence' in the application of the rules on free movement and competition. The purpose of convergence in this case is to allow the Court to take into account non-competition factors which relate to *domestic* interests.

There seems little doubt that the cases do not fully answer the question of exactly what analysis is required under Article 101(1) and cast doubt on the view that Article 101(1) is *not* only about identifying undue restrictions on inter- or intra-brand competition.

The difficulty with a conclusion that weighing is required under Article 101(1) is that it does not mesh well with the current Article 101 scheme. First, it has already been noted that this interpretation of Article 101(1) would confer an extremely limited role on Article 101(3). It would be relevant only in object or public policy cases.[239] Not only does this interpretation of Article 101(3) not appear to fit with its broad wording, but the question of whether other public policy objectives should be relevant to the Article 101(3) appraisal is politically charged and highly controversial (especially as it is now applied by a plethora of national courts and NCAs).[240] The Commission currently takes the view that these factors should not be taken into account in Article 101 cases. Secondly, the approach allocates similar analysis to different forums and sits awkwardly with the burden of proof allocated by Regulation 1/2003. In object cases, any justifications for the agreement could be considered only within the structured framework of Article 101(3) (where the onus lies with the parties)[241] whilst in effect cases, justifications would have to be raised and considered within the more amorphous framework of Article 101(1) (where the burden lies with the Commission or other person seeking to prove the breach). Thirdly, the conclusion does not fit well with the existence of the current overarching block exemptions. These block exemptions do *not* generally apply to agreements containing hardcore restraints (agreements which have as their object the restriction of competition) and would seem redundant, at least in their current form, in effect cases if the weighing of pro- and anti-competitive aspects of the agreement had already been concluded under Article 101(1).[242]

It is clear, therefore, why the Commission and the GC take the view that weighing of pro- and anti-competitive effects should be divided between Article 101(1) and Article 101(3). This view would seem to require, however, some clarification from the CJ, and some evolution in the case law.

4. ARTICLE 101(3)

A. APPLICATION OF ARTICLE 101(3)

Although a number of block exemptions exempt certain categories of agreement from Article 101(3) (see Section E), it has not been possible, since 2004, to notify an agreement to the Commission seeking an 'individual' exemption decision from the Commission. Article 101(3) can, however, be applied in individual cases in a variety of different ways. For example, the Commission has to consider the application of Article 101(3) in infringement proceedings where it is raised by persons seeking to rely on it. It may also have to apply Article 101(3) when adopting commitment or non-infringements

---

238 K. Mortelmans, 'Towards convergence in the application of the rules on free movement and on competition' (2001) 38 *CMLRev* 613.

239 See Section 2.B, pp. 193–194. If public policy issues may also be taken into account under Art. 101(1) (as *Wouters* and *Meca-Medina* suggest) the role of Art. 101(3) would be even more limited.

240 See Section 4.

241 Reg 1/2003, Art. 2.

242 But the block exemptions are designed to operate as safe harbours, see Section 4.E, pp. 263–266.

decisions or when providing 'informal guidance'.[243] Further, NCAs and national courts may, when considering the compatibility of an agreement with Article 101, apply that provision in its entirety. Nonetheless, since 'modernisation' there have been very few cases dealing with the application of Article 101(3) in individual cases. Consequently, there is little recent jurisprudence providing clarification of how these important criteria are interpreted. The Commission's Article 101(3) and other Guidelines provide helpful guidance to business, shedding light on how the Commission interprets the criteria.

B. BURDEN AND STANDARD OF PROOF

Agreements meeting the conditions of block exemption are presumed to meet the Article 101(3) criteria (and the benefit of a block exemption can only be withdrawn prospectively). In an individual case, however, those claiming the benefit of Article 101(3) have the burden[244] of establishing, by means of convincing argument and evidence, that *all* four[245] Article 101(3) criteria are satisfied:[246] (1) that the agreement achieves benefits; (2) that a fair share of those benefits are passed on to consumers; (3) that the agreement does not contain any indispensable restraints; and (4) that it does not eliminate competition in respect of a substantial part of the products in question. The first two criteria of Article 101(3) are positive. The second two are negative. The exception rule applies only for as long as the four conditions are met.[247]

Once undertakings have submitted evidence to support an argument that Article 101(3) is satisfied, it is for the fact finder to examine whether, on the balance of probabilities,[248] the agreement in question does meet these criteria. In its new analytical framework the Commission has narrowed the role of Article 101(1) to the identification of negative effects on competition.[249] It has also sought, correspondingly, to limit the role of Article 101(3)[250] to the determination of whether efficiencies achieved by the agreement outweigh negative effects, so that the agreement is on balance pro-competitive.

The aim of the [EU] competition rules is to protect competition on the market as a means of enhancing consumer welfare and of ensuring an efficient allocation of resources. Agreements that restrict competition may at the same time have pro-competitive effects by way of efficiency gains. Efficiencies may create additional value by lowering the cost of producing an output, improving the quality of the product or creating

---

[243] See Reg. 1/2003 [2003] OJ L1/1, Arts 9 and 10, Commission notice on informal guidance relating to novel questions concerning Articles 81 and 82 of the EC Treaty that arise in individual cases (guidance letters) [2004] OJ C101/78, and Chap. 13.

[244] Reg. 1/2003, Art 2.

[245] The requirements are cumulative, see Case T-528/93, *Métropole Télévision S.A. v. Commission* [1996] ECR II-649, para. 93 and Case T-65/98, *Van den Bergh Foods v. Commission* [2003] ECR II 4653, para. 144, *aff'd*, Case C-552/03 P, *Unilever Bestfoods v. Commission* [2006] ECR I-9091 and Case C-68/12, *Protimonopolný úrad Slovenskej republiky v. Slovenská sporiteľňa as*, 7 February 2013, paras. 31–34.

[246] Case T-168/01, *GlaxoSmithKline Services Unlimited v. Commission* [2006] ECR II-296, para. 235 and Case T-111/08, *MasterCard Inc v. Commission* 24 May 2012, para. 196.

[247] It ceases to apply when that is no longer the case, Article 101(3) Guidelines, para. 44. The parties will therefore have to continually review their agreement to ensure that is continues to satisfy the Art. 101(3) conditions. Under the old notification system an exemption would have been granted to an agreement for a specified period of time.

[248] See Case C-501/06 P, *GlaxoSmithKline Services Unlimited v. Commission* [2009] ECR I-9291, paras. 93–95 where the CJ makes it clear that parties need to demonstrate that it is more likely than not that the agreement satisfies the Art. 101(3) conditions. At the national level the standard of proof would be governed by national law.

[249] The Article 101(3) Guidelines increased the bar for those seeking to justify their agreement under Art. 101(3), in terms of the level and sophistication of evidence required. The Horizontal, Vertical and Technology Transfer Guidelines also provide more specific guidance on how the Commission considers the Art. 101(3) criteria apply to those agreements, see Chaps. 10, 11, and 12.

[250] In early cases much of the Commission's analysis was focused on Art. 101(3), on account of the broad jurisdictional interpretation of Art. 101(1). Despite this, published exemption decisions, especially the early ones, did not contain particularly lengthy or sophisticated analysis of the Art. 101(3) criteria.

a new product. When the pro-competitive effects of an agreement outweigh its anti-competitive effects the agreement is on balance pro-competitive and compatible with the objectives of the [EU] competition rules. The net effect of such agreements is to promote the very essence of the competitive process, namely to win customers by offering better products or better prices than those offered by rivals. This analytical framework is reflected in Article [101(1)] and Article [101(3)]. The latter provision expressly acknowledges that restrictive agreements may generate objective economic benefits so as to outweigh the negative effects of the restriction of competition.[251]

It is frequently argued that the Commission has, post-modernisation and in the Article 101(3) Guidelines, imposed an excessively high burden of proof on those seeking to establish that the conditions of Article 101(3) are met.[252] Challenging the Commission's approach is not easy, however, as it now rarely rules on the compatibility of an agreement with Article 101(3) and when reviewing a Commission decision, the GC will not substitute its own economic assessment for that of the Commission, but will only assess whether the evidence the Commission relies on 'is factually accurate, reliable and consistent' and also whether 'it contains all the information which must be taken into account for the purpose of assessing a complex situation and whether it is capable of substantiating the conclusions drawn from it'.[253] Deference is therefore afforded to the Commission's margin of appreciation and decisions are only overturned where, for example, the Commission has made an error of fact or the decision is inadequately reasoned (see further Chapter 13). In *MasterCard*, for example, the GC rejected the parties' arguments relating to Article 101(3), holding that the Commission had examined the arguments and evidence put forward by the parties and had properly been able to conclude that the Article 101(3) conditions were not fulfilled.[254]

C. ANY AGREEMENT MAY IN PRINCIPLE BENEFIT FROM ARTICLE 101(3)

Although the Commission considers that there is a presumption that an agreement containing hardcore, or object, restraints is unlikely to fulfil the Article 101(3) criteria, it is clear that any fact finder in a case must examine whether or not it does. Any agreement may in principle benefit from it (including agreements containing object restraints). Indeed, in *GlaxoSmithKline Services Unlimited v. Commission*,[255] the GC[256] held that the Commission (the fact finder in that case as the parties had notified the agreement to it under the old notification system set up by Regulation 17) had not adequately discharged its burden of examining the Article 101(3) arguments put forward by the parties in respect of an agreement designed to prevent parallel trade in its pharmaceutical products, and refuting them by means of substantiated evidence.[257] It has been seen that although the GC will not substitute its own economic assessment for that of the Commission, it will assess whether the evidence the Commission relies on is accurate, reliable and consistent and contains all the relevant information and is capable of substantiating the conclusions drawn.[258]

---

[251] Article 101(3) Guidelines, para. 33.

[252] See e.g. Case T-111/08, *MasterCard Inc v. Commission*, 24 May 2012, para. 194.

[253] Case T-111/08, *MasterCard Inc v. Commission* 24 May 2012, para. 202.

[254] Case T-111/08, *MasterCard Inc v. Commission* 24 May 2012, paras. 194–237.

[255] Case T-168/01 [2006] ECR II-2969, paras. 247–252, this aspect of the judgment was *aff'd* Cases C-501 and 513, 515 and 519/06 P. See also Case T-17/93 *Matra Hachette v. Commission* [1994] ECR II-595, para. 85.

[256] The CJ upheld the GC's ruling with regard to Article 101(3), Case C-501/06 P, [2009] ECR I-9291.

[257] In some respects the GC held that the Commission had sought to reject the arguments on the basis of evidence which was, to say the least, fragmentary and of limited relevance or value. These omissions were particularly severe in a market, such as pharmaceuticals, where competition was distorted by the presence of national regulation.

[258] See n. 253 and accompanying text.

> ### Case T-168/01, *GlaxoSmithKline Services Unlimited* v. *Commission* [2006] ECR II-2969
>
> #### General Court
>
> 233. Any agreement which restricts competition, whether by its effects or by its object, may in principle benefit from an exemption (*Consten and Grundig* v. *Commission*...342, 343 and 347, and Case T-17/93 *Matra Hachette* v. *Commission*...paragraph 85), as the Commission, moreover, observed at recital 153 to the Decision and at the hearing.
>
> 234. The application of that provision is subject to certain conditions, satisfaction of which is both necessary and sufficient (*Remia and Others* v. *Commission*...paragraph 38, and *Matra Hachette* v. *Commission*...paragraph 104). First, the agreement concerned must contribute to improving the production or distribution of the goods in question, or to promoting technical or economic progress; second, consumers must be allowed a fair share of the resulting benefit; third, it must not impose on the participating undertakings any restrictions which are not indispensable; and, fourth, it must not afford them the possibility of eliminating competition in respect of a substantial part of the products in question.
>
> 235. Consequently, a person who relies on Article [101(3)] must demonstrate that those conditions are satisfied, by means of convincing arguments and evidence (Joined Cases 43/82 and 63/82 *VBVB and VBBB* v. *Commission*...paragraph 52, and *Aalborg Portland and Others* v. *Commission*...paragraph 78).
>
> 236. The Commission, for its part, must adequately examine those arguments and that evidence (*Consten and Grundig* v. *Commission*...347), that is to say, it must determine whether they demonstrate that the conditions for the application of Article [101(3)] are satisfied. In certain cases, those arguments and that evidence may be of such a kind as to require the Commission to provide an explanation or justification, failing which it is permissible to conclude that the burden of proof borne by the person who relies on Article [101(3)] has been discharged (*Aalborg Portland and Others* v. *Commission*, paragraph 55 above, paragraph 79). As the Commission agrees in its written submissions, in such a case it must refute those arguments and that evidence.

It will be seen in later chapters, however, that given the Commission's presumption against hardcore restraints (and its view that the more severe the restriction the less likely it is to satisfy the Article 101(3) conditions[259]) and the dearth of guidance on when agreements containing such restraints might satisfy the Article 101(3) criteria, undertakings are reluctant in practice to incorporate such restraints within their agreements.

D. THE ARTICLE 101(3) CRITERIA

(i) Criterion 1: The Agreement Must Lead to an Improvement in the Production or Distribution of Goods or the Promotion of Technical or Economic Progress

a. Article 101(3) Benefits

Criterion 1 requires that the agreement: (1) lead to an improvement in the production of goods or services;[260] (2) lead to an improvement in the distribution of goods or services; (3) promote technical

---

[259] Article 101(3) Guidelines, para. 46. See further in particular discussion of indispensability in Section 4.D.iii.

[260] Although Art. 101(3) does not make specific reference to services, services are covered by analogy: see e.g., P & I Clubs [1985] OJ L376/2 and Article 101(3) Guidelines, para. 48.

progress; and/or (4) promote economic progress. The benefits referred to are not subjective ones that result to the parties to the agreement (for example, from the exercise of market power) and must be derived from empirical data and facts not just economic theory. The CJ has stressed that the improvement must 'show appreciable objective advantages of such a character as to compensate for the disadvantages which they cause in the field of competition'.[261] In *MasterCard*, the GC went so far as to hold that Article 101(3) would not apply since the 'primary beneficiaries' of the benefits flowing from the MasterCard system were its payment organisation and participating banks. Article 101(3) 'cannot be identified with all the advantages which the parties obtain from the agreement in their production or distribution activities'.[262]

In *MasterCard* the GC clarified that the appreciable advantages under Article 101(3) may arise 'not only for the relevant market but also for every other market on which the agreement in question might have beneficial effects'.[263]

b. Efficiency Gains

This first limb permits the parties to establish that, despite the fact that the agreement restricts competition, efficiency gains, cost efficiencies,[264] and qualitative efficiencies, creating value in the form of new or improved products (dynamic efficiencies),[265] will result from the economic activity that forms the object of the agreement (there must be a causal link between the agreement and the claimed efficiencies).[266] The Commission's Guidelines on the application of Article 101(3) state that parties must substantiate efficiency claims by showing the nature of the claimed efficiencies, the link between the agreement and the efficiencies, the likelihood and magnitude of each claimed efficiency, and how and when each claimed efficiency would be achieved.[267]

Parties may, therefore, establish that the agreement will improve production or distribution or promote technical or economic progress, for example, through cost reduction (such as those originating from: development of new production technologies and methods; synergies resulting from an integration of existing assets; economies of scale or scope; or better production planning)[268] and/or through improvement in the quality and choice of goods and services.[269] A number of joint venture agreements have, therefore, succeeded on the grounds that new or better products will be produced and that the cooperation permitted the parties to do so more quickly or cheaply and/ or through the sharing of risk or cost, through the pooling of technical expertise and/or by making the venture financially viable.[270] In *Ford/Volkswagen*,[271] for example, the Commission held that the parties' creation of a joint venture company to develop and produce a multi-purpose vehicle

---

[261] Cases 56 and 58/64, *Consten and Grundig* [1966] ECR 299, 348, *Van den Bergh Foods v. Commission*, paras. 101 and 139.

[262] Case T-111/08, *MasterCard Inc v. Commission*, 24 May 2012, para. 221.

[263] Case T-111/08, *MasterCard Inc v. Commission*, 24 May 2012, para. 228.

[264] Article 101(3) Guidelines, paras. 64–68.

[265] Article 101(3) Guidelines, paras. 69–72.

[266] Article 101(3) Guidelines, para. 45.

[267] Article 101(3) Guidelines, paras. 51 and 52–59. Examples of different types of efficiencies are given at paras. 59–72.

[268] Article 101(3) Guidelines, paras. 64–68.

[269] The enhancing potential of the agreement may not therefore be cost reduction but quality improvement resulting from technical and technological advance. Research and development, technology licensing and joint production, and distribution agreements may all be capable of realising these qualitative efficiencies, Article 101(3) Guidelines, paras. 69–72.

[270] See, e.g., *Beecham/Parke, Davis* [1979] OJ L70/11 (R&D agreement would promote 'technical progress' by creating a product for the prevention or treatment of an impairment for which there was no known marketed compound and where the pooling of research capacities was a major factor in providing a reasonable likelihood of success); *De Laval-Stork* [1977] OJ L 215/11 (R&D agreement would enable the parties to penetrate a market more easily and quickly, reach optimal size, work at greater capacity, and share the latest technical advances).

[271] [1993] OJ L20/14.

(MPV) in Portugal would improve the production of goods and promote technical development. It would rationalise product development and manufacturing and establish a new and modern manufacturing plant which would be using the latest production technology. In addition, the parties' pooling of technical knowledge would be converted into a significantly improved and innovative MPV. In the context of vertical and intellectual property licensing agreements the Commission has taken account of the fact that the agreement will improve production and distribution of products through, for example, permitting an increase in production capacity, conferring incentives to promote a product, and conferring incentives to concentrate sales efforts, and/or through reduction in transaction costs.[272] In *GlaxoSmithKline Services Unlimited v. Commission*[273] Glaxo argued that the territorial restraints in the distribution agreements were necessary to stimulate and support costly and risky global R&D in a market where inter-brand competition was driven by innovation not price and where in many Member States the prices were controlled by public authorities. The agreement would thus encourage competition upstream by encouraging innovation and on the market itself, by optimising the distribution of medicines. In particular, it was stressed that the strong competitive pressure to innovate would ensure that any additional profits made would be ploughed into investment in R&D. The GC considered that the Commission had been wrong to reject the evidence raised, which appeared 'relevant, reliable and credible' and, to some extent, to be corroborated by Commission documents.[274] On appeal, the CJ[275] ruled that the GC had not erred in law in finding that the Commission had erroneously failed to take into account certain facts highlighted by GSK in its request for exemption, including the specific structural features of the pharmaceuticals sector.

c. Non-Competition Factors

A controversial issue is whether the first head of Article 101(3) permits the parties to rely on broader public policy benefits achieved by the agreement. This question was of importance in the modernisation debate and as to the question of whether the Commission should, or could, relinquish its exclusive right to rule on the compatibility of an agreement with Article 101(3). An acceptance that Article 101(3) permitted a balancing of public and private interests and/or of conflicting EU policies might have militated against the abolition of the notification and authorisation system and defeated the modernisation proposals.[276] In its White Paper on modernisation the Commission stated that Article 101(3) is intended 'to provide a legal framework for the economic assessment of restrictive practices and not to allow the application of the competition rules to be set aside because of political considerations'.[277] In its Article 101(3) Guidelines, the discussion of the first condition of Article 101(3) is headed 'Efficiency gains' and *only* efficiency gains are discussed within it. Although it states that '[g]oals pursued by other Treaty provisions can be taken into account to the extent that they can be subsumed under the four conditions of Article [101(3)]'[278] its reliance on the ruling of the GC in *Matra Hachette* suggests that it considers that these factors may only be taken into account

---

[272] See, e.g., *Goodyear Italiana-Euram* [1975] OJ L38/10; *Campari* [1978] OJ L70/69.

[273] Case T-168/01, [2006] ECR II-2969.

[274] Case T-168/01, [2006] ECR II-2969, paras. 233–307.

[275] Cases C-501, 513, 515, 519/06 P, [2009] ECR I-9291.

[276] If the application of Art. 101(3) involves the consideration of socio-political issues, it might have been considered unwise to delegate this task to a multiplicity of bodies, including national courts.

[277] [1999] OJ C132/1, para. 56. See, e.g., C. D. Ehlermann in C. D. Ehlermann and L. Laudati (eds.), *European Competition Law Annual 1997: Objectives of Competition Policy* (Hart Publishing, 1998), 480; R. Wesseling, 'The Commission White Paper on Modernisation of EC Antitrust Law: Unspoken consequences and incomplete treatment of alternative options' [1999] *ECLR* 420; Monti, 'Article 81 EC and Public Policy' (cited in n. 45),1057.

[278] Article 101(3) Guidelines, para. 42. The following words incorporated in the draft guidelines were not repeated in the final version of the document: 'It is not, on the other hand, the role of Article [101] and the authorities enforcing this Treaty provision to allow undertakings to restrict competition in pursuit of general interest aims.'

'supererogatorily' where 'public policy considerations have been used to supplement the economic benefits which the agreement generates'.[279]

Case T-17/93, *Matra Hachette* v. *Commission* [1994] ECR II-595

General Court

139. As regards the argument based on the reference to 'exceptional circumstances', the Court observes that, although the Commission refers to them, in particular in paragraphs 23 and 28, and in paragraph 36, in which the Decision concludes its examination of the condition under review and considers the project's impact on public infrastructures and on employment, and its impact on European integration, the latter paragraph ends with the following sentence: 'This would not be enough to make an exemption possible unless the conditions of Article [101(3)] were fulfilled, but it is an element which the Commission has taken into account'. The Court considers that it is clear from the latter sentence that the 'exceptional circumstances' thus referred to in the Decision were taken into consideration by the Commission only supererogatorily. In other words, it is sufficiently established that, if those circumstances had not been referred to, the operative part of the decision adopted would have been exactly the same as that of the contested Decision. It follows that the applicant's argument that, on the contrary, the individual exemption decision granted for the project in question was adopted only on the basis of the 'exceptional circumstances' surrounding the project must be rejected.

The Commission thus seems to take the view that past practice 'has never shown that the competition rules were "set aside" for political considerations...rather public policy considerations have been used to supplement the economic benefits which the agreement generates'.[280]

A narrow view, that only improvements in economic efficiency can be taken into account under Article 101(3), is certainly the one which sits best with the Commission's view of Article 101's objectives and how Article 101(1) and (3) now interact. It is, however, arguably a somewhat disingenuous interpretation of past judgments and decisional practice. It has been seen that the CJ has, when construing the competition provisions, adopted a teleological interpretation[281] so that it is conceivable that, despite its actual wording, the criteria set out in Article 101(3) might be interpreted broadly against the backdrop of the wider EU aims and objectives.[282] Indeed, pursuit of a sole consumer welfare objective may produce results inconsistent with other EU policies and the TFEU specifically provides in some places that the formulation and implementation of *all* EU policies and actions should take account of certain 'policy-linking' clauses, such as environmental protection, employment, culture, health, consumer protection, industrial policy, and/or the elimination of regional disparities.[283] In *Metro (No 1)*,[284] the CJ took the view that the fact that an agreement might lead to stability in the labour market, was a matter which could be taken into account within the first criterion of Article 101(3). The agreement in question constituted 'a stabilizing factor with regard to the provision of employment which, since it improves the general conditions of production, especially when market

---

[279] See Faull and Nikpay (eds.), *The EC Law of Competition* (cited in n. 6), para. 3.406.

[280] Monti, 'Article 81 EC and Public Policy' (cited in n. 45),1057, 1090–1091. If the Commission is attempting to go further than this, however, and is seeking to deny even the more limited role of socio-political factors under Art. 101(3), then the view is difficult, if not impossible, to square with previous decisional practice and case law.

[281] See, e.g., Case 6/72, *Europemballage Corp. and Continental Can Co., Inc.* v. *Commission* [1973] ECR 215 (discussed in Chap. 5); Cases C-68/94 and 30/95, *France* v. *Commission* [1998] ECR I-1375 (discussed in Chaps. 9 and 15).

[282] Art. 101(3) could therefore be construed to permit authorisation of agreements which provide benefits, e.g., from a regional, social, environmental, cultural, and/or industrial perspective, see Monti, 'Article 81 EC and Public Policy' (cited in n. 45), 1057.

[283] See, Chap. 1 (and discussion of Arts 8–13 TFEU), C. Townley, *Article 101 and Public Policy* (Hart Publishing, 2009), and Odudu, *The Boundaries of EC Competition Law: The Scope of Article 81* (cited in n. 5), 161.

[284] Case 26/76, *Metro-SB-Grossmärkte GmbH* v. *Commission (No. 1)* [1977] ECR 1875.

conditions are unfavourable, comes within the framework of the objective to which reference may be had pursuant to Article [101(3)]'.[285] Further, in *Métropole Télévision S.A. v. Commission*[286] the GC stated that 'the Commission is entitled to base itself on considerations connected with the pursuit of the public interest in order to grant exemption under Article [101(3)]'.[287] Both of these judgments related, however, to the position pre-modernisation when the Commission had a monopoly over the application of Article 101(3). In addition, in *Premier League Ltd v. QC Leisure* and *Murphy v. Media Protection Services Ltd*[288] the CJ held that an exclusive broadcast licensing agreement restricted competition by object and did not meet the conditions of Article 101(3). It thus rejected the parties' argument that the agreement was justifiable under Article 101(3) (as the restraints were necessary to ensure that the intellectual property rights holder was appropriately remunerated and to encourage the public to attend football stadiums) on the facts but did not say that they were not relevant under Article 101(3).

This attitude is also reflected in a number of the Commission's older decisions (although these may not all now reflect Commission thinking). In *Ford/Volkswagen*,[289] for example, the Commission noted, in exempting the agreement, that the joint venture would lead to the creation of a number of jobs and substantial foreign investment in one of the poorest regions of the EU.[290]

36. In the assessment of this case, the Commission also takes note of the fact that the project constitutes the largest ever single foreign investment in Portugal. It is estimated to lead, *inter alia*, to the creation of about 5 000 jobs and indirectly create up to another 10 000 jobs, as well as attracting other investment in the supply industry. It therefore contributes to the promotion of the harmonious development of the [EU] and the reduction of regional disparities which is one of the basic aims of the Treaty. It also furthers European market integration by linking Portugal more closely to the [EU] through one of its important industries. This would not be enough to make an exemption possible unless the conditions of Article [101(3)] were fulfilled, but it is an element which the Commission has taken into account.

Although the Commission emphasised that these broader factors would not have caused the agreement to merit an exemption had the other conditions of Article 101(3) not been fulfilled,[291] these factors do appear to have been relevant to its final decision. Further, in an appeal from this decision the Commission argued that it was possible, when determining whether the agreement contributed to technical and economic progress, to take into account factors such as the maintenance of employment.[292] Arguably, this decision is difficult to justify on pure efficiency grounds and it symbolises the infiltrations of other policy objectives into EU competition law.[293]

In a series of decisions in the 1980s, the Commission also exempted agreements concluded between competitors designed to ensure an orderly reduction of capacity between the undertakings

---

[285] Case 26/76, *Metro-SB-Grossmärkte GmbH v. Commission (No. 1)* [1977] ECR 1875,para. 43.

[286] Cases T-528, 542, 543, and 546/93, [1996] ECR II-649. See also Case T-193/02, *Laurent Piau v. Commission* [2005] ECR II-209 (appeal dismissed by Order of the CJ, Case C-171/05 P, [2006] ECR I-37), para. 103, where the GC considered that a licence system for players' agents required by FIFA resulted in a qualitative selection, appropriate for the attainment of the objective of raising professional standards for the occupation of players' agents rather than a quantitative restriction on access to that occupation.

[287] Cases T-528, 542, 543 and 546/93, [1996] ECR II-649, para. 118.

[288] Cases C-403and429/08, 4 October 2011.

[289] [1993] OJ L20/14.

[290] The Commission found that the agreement would promote harmonious development, reduce regional disparities, and contribute to the integration of the European market [1993] OJ L20/14, paras. 23, 28, and 36; see also the Commission Press Release IP/92/1083 of 23 December 1992.

[291] [1993] OJ L20/14, para. 36.

[292] Case T-17/93, *Matra Hachette v. Commission* [1994] ECR II-595, para. 96. The GC considered that as the four criteria were fulfilled apart from the 'exceptional circumstances', there was no defect in the Decision.

[293] See Amato, *Antitrust and the Bounds of Power* (cited in n. 214), 58–63, and Chap. 10.

which were operating in an industry in crisis (crisis cartels).[294] Although it might be argued that such agreements produce demonstrable efficiencies (such as the removal of inefficient capacity from the industry and increasing capacity utilisation rate, see also Chapter 9) in some of the cases the Commission also stressed the social benefits resulting from the agreements. In *Synthetic Fibres*,[295] for example, the Commission, in authorising an agreement between competitors to reduce capacity, accepted that the decision to embark on an orderly reduction in output satisfied the first criterion of Article 101(3).[296]

In a free market economy it ought to be principally a matter for the individual undertaking to judge the point at which overcapacity becomes economically unsustainable and to take the necessary steps to reduce it ... In the present case, however, market forces by themselves had failed to achieve the capacity reductions necessary to re-establish and maintain in the longer term an effective competitive structure within the common market. The producers concerned therefore agreed to organise for a limited period and collectively, the needed structural adjustment.

The Commission thus recognised that, ordinarily, individual undertakings should make their own decision about reduction in capacity. However, in this case market forces had not achieved the reductions necessary. The agreement would enable the establishment and maintenance in the long term of effective competitive structures and would improve technical efficiency by enabling the undertakings to specialise. The eventual result would be to raise profitability and restore competitiveness.

[The] coordination of plant closures will also make it easier to cushion the social effects of the restructuring by making suitable arrangements for the retraining and redeployment of workers made redundant. It can be concluded then that the agreement contributes to improving production and promoting technical and economic progress.[297]

Similarly, in *Stichting Baksteen*[298] the Commission, when exempting an agreement for the restructuring of the Dutch brick industry, took account of the fact that the agreement allowed the restructuring to be carried out in acceptable social conditions and in a way which would lead to the redeployment of employees. The Commission held that the social advantages resulting to employees would promote economic progress for the purposes of Article 101(3).[299] In Chapter 9 it will be seen that the Commission did not take such a benevolent approach during the recent financial and economic crisis and has referred to these cases as examples of arrangements which achieved efficiency gains by removing inefficient capacity from the market.[300]

In *Exxon/Shell*[301] the Commission held that a reduction in pollution would lead to a technological improvement for the purposes of Article 101(3). Further, in *European Council of Manufacturers of Domestic Appliances (CECED)*[302] it exempted an agreement concluded between 95 per cent of the producers and importers of washing machines operating on the EU market that restricted their freedom

[294] Further, it is arguable that provisions in the Commission's specialisation block exemption, which accept that production rationalisation fulfils the Art. 101(3) criteria, reflect industrial policy rather than competition thinking: Amato, *Antitrust and the Bounds of Power* (cited in n. 214), 63–64. In the early days competition policy was influenced by industrial policy to a greater extent than it is now.

[295] [1984] OJ L207/17.

[296] [1984] OJ L207/17, paras. 30–31.

[297] [1984] OJ L207/17, paras. 37–38.

[298] [1994] OJ L131/15.

[299] [1994] OJ L131/15, paras. 27–28.

[300] See further Chap. 9 and especially e.g., the Commission's observations under Reg. 1/2003, art 15(3) in *The Competition Authority v. The Beef Industry Development Society Limited*, available at <http://ec.europa.eu/competition/court/antitrust_amicus_curiae.html>.

[301] [1994] OJ L144/20.

[302] [2000] OJ L187/47. Contrast *Consumer Detergents*, 13 April 2011, paras. 53–54. See also Faull and Nikpay (eds.), *The EC Law of Competition* (cited in n. 6), para, 3.408, *Eco-Emballages* [2001] OJ L233/37 (negative clearance), and *DSD* [2001] OJ L319/1 (exemption) and Chap. 10.

to manufacture or import the least energy-efficient washing machines. The agreement was found to restrict competition within the meaning of Article 101(1). The agreement, by restricting the parties' autonomy to produce or import less environmentally friendly machines,[303] had the object of controlling one important product characteristic on which there was competition, thereby restricting competition between the parties.[304] Nonetheless the Commission considered that the agreement met the criteria set out in Article 101(3). It would reduce the potential energy consumption of new machines and consequently lessen pollution, create more technically efficient machines, and focus future R&D on furthering energy efficiency.[305] Upon approval by the Commission, the Competition Commissioner, Mario Monti declared:

When I took office as Commissioner responsible for Competition, I stressed before the European Parliament that environmental concerns are in no way contradictory with competition policy. This decision clearly illustrates this principle, enshrined in the Treaty, provided that *restrictions of competition are proportionate and necessary to achieving the environmental objectives aimed at*, to the benefit of current and future generations [emphasis added].[306]

It also seems that the production of a product which increases safety for a consumer may constitute a technical improvement.[307]

(ii) Criterion 2: Allowing Consumers a Fair Share of the Resulting Benefit

Although the second criterion of Article 101(3) requires that it must be established that the agreement allows consumers a fair share of the benefit, the Article 101(3) Guidelines indicate that this condition should be considered only after it has been determined that the restrictions incorporated in the agreement are indispensable (see Criterion 3). This is because the requirement that consumers receive a fair share of the benefits 'implies a balancing of pro-competitive and anti-competitive effects. This balancing exercise should not include restrictions that in any event are unnecessary to achieve the efficiencies.'[308]

In early decisions (and especially where the Commission adopted a more formalistic approach under Article 101(1)), the Commission was often willing to assume that this criterion would be satisfied where the first and fourth criteria were satisfied (a benefit had been shown and where competition had not been eliminated, so that competition from competing products meant that the parties would not be interested in increasing prices or reducing output). Under the 'modernised' approach, however, many of these agreements (previously dealt with under Article 101(3)) should, in theory at least, now fall outside Article 101(1) on the grounds that the agreement does not restrict competition at all. The Article 101(3) Guidelines now make satisfaction of this requirement much more difficult, demanding that the parties establish that the agreement allows consumers a fair share of the benefit, by showing that there is a pass-on of the cost and quality efficiencies to consumers.[309]

---

[303] It did not directly restrict output as the agreement was only to cease to produce the least energy efficient machines. Limited effects on output might arise only indirectly, through reduced demand.

[304] It would result in a reduction of choice for consumers since fewer cheaper washing machines would be on the market.

[305] The Commission considered that the other elements of Art. 101(3) were also satisfied, see Chap. 9.

[306] IP/00/148. This decision thus reflects the sentiment expressed in the Commission's *XXVth Report on Competition Policy* (1995) that 'in its scrutiny of individual cases pursuant to Article [101(3)]...it weighs up the restrictions on competition that result from the agreement and the environmental objectives to be attained', SEC(1997)628. See also n. 255.

[307] *BMW Belgium NV and Belgian BMW Dealers* [1978] OJ L46/33. See also *DSD* [2001] OJ L319/1.

[308] Faull and Nikpay (eds.), *The EC Law of Competition* (cited in n. 6), para. 3.436.

[309] Article 101(3) Guidelines, paras. 83–104.

This accords with the Commission's view that the objective of Article 101 is consumer not total welfare.[310]

a. Consumer

Consumer is interpreted broadly to include not only final consumers (end-users) but also intermediate consumers, including wholesalers and retailers, that purchase products in the course of their trade or business.[311] Consumers can be undertakings or private individuals. It is clear that not all individual consumers need to derive a benefit from the agreement for Article 101(3) to apply. Rather it is the overall effect on consumers in the relevant markets that must be favourable. '[I]t is the beneficial nature of the effect on all consumers in the relevant markets that must be taken into consideration, not the effect on each member of that category of consumers.'[312]

Two further issues arising in relation to the consumer benefit requirement are (i) whether the benefits must result to the same consumers in the same market as those suffering anti-competitive effects; and (ii) whether it is possible to take account of the fact that future consumers will benefit when current consumers will be hurt by the arrangement. Although the Article 101(3) Guidelines state that the benefits must be felt by consumers in the same market as that in which the anti-competitive effects take place,[313] such a restrictive interpretation of Article 101(3) does not appear to be supported by the case law. Rather, it suggests that all pro-competitive benefits in all markets should be relevant and weighed against the agreement's anti-competitive effects.[314] A broad reading of the cases might also suggest that all consumer benefits (whether current or future) should be taken into account. Such an interpretation would also be compatible with the approach adopted under Article 102 where both the short-term and longer-term effects of a strategy may be relevant to the assessment. Clearly, however, even if future benefits to future consumers are relevant, it may be extremely difficult for the parties to provide convincing evidence that such benefits will result to consumers.[315]

b. Fair Share

The Commission describes the concept of fair share in its Article 101(3) Guidelines.

85. The concept of 'fair share' implies that the pass-on of benefits must at least compensate consumers for any actual or likely negative impact caused to them by the restriction of competition found under Article [101(1)]. In line with the overall objective of Article [101] to prevent anti-competitive agreements, the net effect of the agreement must at least be neutral from the point of view of those consumers directly or likely affected by the agreement. If such consumers are worse off following the agreement, the second condition of Article [101(3)] is not fulfilled. The positive effects of an agreement must be balanced against and compensate for its negative effects on consumers. When that is the case consumers are not harmed by the agreement. Moreover, society as a whole benefits because the efficiencies lead either to fewer resources being used to produce the output consumed or to the production of more valuable products and thus to a more efficient allocation of resources.

---

[310] See Chap. 1.

[311] *Kabel und Metallwerke Neumeyer AG and Etablissements Luchaire SA Agreement* [1975] OJ L222/34.

[312] Case C-238/05, *Asnef-Equifax v. Asociación de Usuarios de Servicios Bancarios (Ausbanc)* [2006] ECR I-11125, para. 70.

[313] Unless 'the group of consumers affected by the restriction and benefiting from the efficiency gains [on a different market] are substantially the same', Article 101(3) Guidelines, para. 43.

[314] See nn. 260 and 309 and Case T-86/95, *Compagnie Générale Maritime v. Commission* [2002] ECR. II-1011, para. 343. See also e.g., C. Townley, 'The relevant market: an acceptable limit to competition analysis?' [2011] 32(10) *ECLR* 490 (arguing that the Commission's rule against aggregating across markets runs contrary to the EU Courts' precedents, creates unacceptable uncertainty, undermines consumer welfare, and risks distorting undertakings' investment decisions).

[315] See C. Townley, 'Inter-generational impacts in competition law: remembering those not yet born' [2011] *ECLR* 580 (arguing that aggregating across generations should be allowed).

The Guidelines also explain that it is *not* necessary that consumers receive a share of each and every efficiency gain identified under the first condition, nor that the pass-on must occur immediately or within a specified period of time.[316] Further, that the pass-on will have to be greater, the greater the restriction of competition.[317]

Where consumers are forced to pay a higher price without attaining other benefits from the agreement, this criterion will not be satisfied.[318] Some agreements have been refused an exemption on the ground that consumers will not receive a fair share of the benefit. For example, in *VBBB and VBVB*[319] the Commission held that the consumers would not benefit from the parties' agreement to fix the retail prices of books. On the contrary, consumers would be forced to pay a higher price and would be deprived of the opportunity to pay lower prices. The Commission has also refused exemption to agreements that are clearly designed to restrict competition and force consumers to pay a higher price for products in the absence of other compensating benefits. In *SPO and others v. Commission*,[320] for example, the GC heard an appeal against the Commission's refusal of an exemption to a Dutch building association. The purpose of the agreement in question was to protect the members from ruinous competition. The Court upheld the Commission's decision, stating that 'by taking action to counteract what they regard as ruinous competition, the applicants necessarily restrict competition and therefore deprive consumers of its benefits'.[321] In contrast, however, to the decision it took in *SPO* the Commission in *Synthetic Fibres*[322] concluded that consumers would benefit from an agreement between competitors on a market to reduce capacity. Although prices might rise initially, there was sufficient competition on the market and considerable countervailing purchasing power to limit these increases. Further, the agreement would result in a healthier, more competitive industry in the long run.[323]

(iii) Criterion 3: Indispensable Restrictions

An agreement which satisfies the first two positive criteria set out in Article 101(3) must only contain restrictions which are indispensable to the achievement of the benefits shown to result from the agreement. It has been seen that the Commission seeks to distinguish this inquiry from that made under the doctrine of ancillary restraints by asking whether the restrictive agreement and restrictions make it possible to perform the activity in question more efficiently, i.e. 'if its absence would eliminate or significantly reduce the efficiencies that follow from the agreement or make it significantly less likely that they will materialize'.[324] The assessment of indispensability is made within the actual context in which the agreement operates.[325] Further, the Commission takes the view that restrictions may be indispensable only for a period of time. Clearly, in practice, the question of indispensability is likely to confer a considerable degree of discretion on the fact-finder.

[316] Article 101(3) Guidelines, paras. 86–89.

[317] Article 101(3) Guidelines, paras. 90–91.

[318] See, e.g., *VBBB and VBVB* [1982] OJ L54/36, *aff'd* in Cases C-43 and 63/82, *VBVB and VBBB v. Commission* [1984] ECR 19.

[319] *VBBB and VBVB* [1982] OJ L54/36, *aff'd* in Cases C-43 and 63/82, *VBVB and VBBB v. Commission* [1984] ECR 19.

[320] Case T-29/92, [1995] ECR II-289.

[321] Case T-29/92, [1995] ECR II-289, para. 294.

[322] [1984] OJ L207/17.

[323] [1984] OJ L207/17, paras. 39–41.

[324] Article 101(3) Guidelines, para. 79 (and not whether the restraint is necessary to the implementation of the agreement). But see Case C-1/12, *Ordem dos Técnicos Oficiais de Contas (OTOC) v. Autoridade da Concorrência*, 28 February 2013, where the CJ relies on the same factors to state both that the agreement went beyond what was necessary to achieve a legitimate objective (and so did not fall outside Article 101(1)) and that the restrictions could not be regarded as essential for the purposes of Article 101(3).

[325] Article 101(3) Guidelines, para. 80.

The Commission states that this condition, an application of the EU principle of proportionality,[326] implies a two-fold test.

Article 101(3) Guidelines [2004] OJ C101/97

73. According to the third condition of Article [101(3)] the restrictive agreement must not impose restrictions, which are not indispensable to the attainment of the efficiencies created by the agreement in question. This condition implies a two-fold test. First, the restrictive agreement as such must be reasonably necessary in order to achieve the efficiencies.[327] Secondly, the individual restrictions of competition that flow from the agreement must also be reasonably necessary for the attainment of the efficiencies.

74. In the context of the third condition of Article [101(3)] the decisive factor is whether or not the restrictive agreement and individual restrictions make it possible to perform the activity in question more efficiently than would have been the case in the absence of the agreement or the restriction concerned. The question is not whether in the absence of the restriction the agreement would not have been concluded, but whether more efficiencies are produced with the agreement or restriction than in the absence of the agreement.[328]

Restrictions will not therefore be indispensable if the efficiencies specific to the agreement can be achieved by other practicable and less restrictive means, or if individual restrictions are not reasonably necessary to produce the efficiencies. In *Protimonopolný úrad Slovenskej republiky v. Slovenská sporiteľňa as*,[329] for example, the CJ rejected an argument that an anti-competitive agreement was required to eliminate undertakings operating illegally on the market. The CJ stressed that even if some efficiency could be demonstrated by the parties from forcing those undertakings to comply with national law (for example, from protecting the conditions for healthy competition and so seeking to promote economic progress on the market), less restrictive measures could have been adopted. In particular, rather than taking steps to eliminate the undertaking themselves, the parties could have lodged a complaint with competent authorities.

The Commission takes the view that provisions which are 'restrictive by object' or hardcore restraints are not generally indispensable. Indeed, in its Guidelines on the application of Article 101(3) the Commission states that '[r]estrictions that are black listed in block exemption regulations or qualified as hardcore restrictions in Commission Guidelines and notices are only likely to be considered indispensable in exceptional circumstances'.[330] The black lists of the block exemptions thus provide useful guidance on the types of provisions that the Commission considers are dispensable and not essential to achieving the benefits produced by a particular type of agreement.

---

[326] The principle of proportionality essentially requires that an action (whether of the EU or of a State or, in this case, parties to an agreement) should not go beyond what is necessary to achieve the objectives of the Treaty, see discussion of principle in, e.g., P. Craig and G. De Búrca, *EU Law Text, Cases and Materials* (4th edn, Oxford University Press, 2007), Chap. 9.

[327] Or, presumably, other non-economic benefits, insofar as they are relevant, see Section 4.D.i.

[328] See Article 101(3) Guidelines, para. 18.

[329] Case C-68/12, 7 February 2013. See also Case C-1/12, *Ordem dos Técnicos Oficiais de Contas (OTOC) v. Autoridade da Concorrência*, 28 February 2013, para. 102–103.

[330] Case C-1/12, *Ordem dos Técnicos Oficiais de Contas (OTOC) v. Autoridade da Concorrência*, 28 February 2013, para. 69. See also para. 46; these types of restraints are unlikely to satisfy the first two conditions of Art. 101(3) since they neither create objective economic benefits nor benefit consumers.

> ## J. Faull and A. Nikpay (eds.), *The EC Law of Competition* (2nd edn, Oxford University Press, 2007)
>
> 3.441 Once it is found that the agreement in question is necessary in order to produce the efficiencies the indispensability of each restriction of competition flowing from the agreement must be assessed. A restriction is indispensable if its absence would eliminate or significantly reduce the efficiencies achieved by the agreement or make it significantly less likely that they will materialise. The assessment of alternative solutions must take into account the actual and potential improvement in competition by the elimination of a particular restriction or the application of a less restrictive alternative. The third condition of Article [101(3)] thus incorporates a sliding scale. The more restrictive the restraint, the stricter the test under the third condition. Restrictions that are black-listed in block exemption regulations or identified as hardcore restrictions in Commission guidelines and notices are unlikely to be considered indispensable.

It is reiterated, however, that *every* agreement is potentially capable of exemption. In later chapters of this book, it will be seen that the Commission has since the publication of these Guidelines been prepared to concede that even hardcore restraints may sometimes satisfy the Article 101(3) criteria (see especially Chapter 11) and examples will be given of some such exceptional cases.[331]

A restriction will also be indispensable 'if its absence would eliminate or significantly reduce the efficiencies that follow from the agreement or make it significantly less likely that they will materialise'.[332] In *P&O Stena Line*[333] the Commission granted an exemption to a joint venture which combined the parties' services on a particular ferry route. It accepted the argument that less restrictive alternatives, such as joint scheduling, or pooling, would not enable the parties to achieve the benefits, such as cost savings and increased frequency in service, of their joint venture. The Commission expended much effort in its exemption decisions in ensuring that agreements were not more restrictive than they needed to be to achieve their accepted benefits.

(iv) Criterion 4: The Agreement Must Not Afford the Parties the Possibility of Eliminating Competition

The last requirement is that the agreement as a whole must not lead to the elimination of competition. This criterion appears to reflect the view that short-term efficiency gains must not be outweighed by longer-term losses stemming from the elimination of competition.

The Commission states in the Article 101(3) Guidelines that '[u]ltimately the protection of rivalry and the competitive process is given priority over potentially pro-competitive efficiency gains which could result from restrictive agreements'.[334] Further, it sets out its view that rivalry between undertakings on the market should be preserved since rivalry is the essential driver of economic efficiency, including dynamic efficiency.

When competition is eliminated the competitive process is brought to an end and short-term efficiency gains are outweighed by longer-term losses stemming *inter alia* from expenditures incurred by the incumbent to maintain its position (rent seeking), misallocation of resources, reduced innovation and higher prices.[335]

---

[331] See, for example, Chaps. 9 and 11.

[332] Contrast the ancillary restraints doctrine discussed in Section 3, F., pp. 242–246.

[333] [1999] OJ L163/61.

[334] Article 101(3) Guidelines, para. 105.

[335] Article 101(3) Guidelines, para. 105.

This criterion thus requires an analysis of the competitive restraints imposed on the parties, the degree of competition existing prior to the agreement, and the impact of the agreement on competition. Sources of competition, through actual and potential competitors, must be analysed along with the impact of the agreement on these competitive constraints.

The Commission considers, in its assessment, the market shares of the parties, the incentives for actual competitors to compete, the impact of the agreement on the various parameters of competition, the actual market conduct of the parties (where the agreement has been implemented), past competitive interaction, the closeness of competition previously existing between the competitors, and the scope of potential competition.

When assessing barriers to entry the Commission stresses that it takes into account the real possibility for new entry into the market.[336] At paragraph 116 of the Guidelines the Commission sets out some hypothetical examples of how this fourth condition is applied.

The Guidelines also explore the relationship between this requirement (and Article 101(3) more generally) with Article 102.[337] The following principles are set out:

(i) The application of Article 101(3) does not prevent the application of Article 102;

(ii) Conduct which is abusive should not be permitted under Article 101(3).[338] Article 101(3) could however be used to authorise an agreement concluded by a dominant undertaking which does not constitute an abuse of a dominant position;[339]

(iii) Not all agreements infringing Article 101 constitute an abuse of a dominant position.

E. BLOCK EXEMPTIONS

(i) General

A number of EU regulations grant exemption to categories of agreements that satisfy their conditions. In *Pierre Fabre* v. *Président de l'Autorité de la concurrence*,[340] the CJ held, when interpreting the block exemption that applies to vertical agreements, that as undertakings have the option of asserting that Article 101(3) applies on an individual basis to their agreement, it is not necessary to give a broad interpretation of the block exemption provisions. The block exemptions are adopted for a specified period of time and kept under review during that period. A majority of these regulations are Commission regulations adopted following authorisation from the Council. Some have, however, been adopted directly by the Council.

(ii) Current Block Exemptions

Some block exemptions pertain to specific sectors. The Commission has, however, also adopted a number of block exemptions which apply more generally to vertical, horizontal, and technology transfer agreements respectively. These block exemptions are discussed in further detail in the later chapters. Table 4.1 sets out the block exemptions currently in force.

---

[336] Article 101(3) Guidelines, para. 115 and see Chap. 1.

[337] Article 101(3) Guidelines, para. 106.

[338] Article 101(3) Guidelines, para. 106. In *Van den Bergh Foods* [1998] OJ L264/1, upheld on appeal Case T-65/98, *Van den Bergh Foods* v. *Commission* [2003] ECR II-4653, aff'd Case C-552/03 P, *Unilever Bestfoods* v. *Commission* [2006] ECR I-9091, the Commission declined to grant an exemption to conduct found to contravene Art. 102. HB's dominant position was taken into account and influenced the Commission's decision that the agreement would substantially eliminate competition within the meaning of Art. 101(3), see paras. 242–246.

[339] Article 101(3) Guidelines, para. 106.

[340] Case C-439/09, 13 October 2011.

Table 4.1 Block Exemptions Currently in Force

Regulation	Categories of agreements covered	Enabling legislation (Council Regulation)[341] (where relevant)
Commission Regulation 772/2004[342] (under review)	Technology transfer agreements	Regulation 19/65[343] (amended by Council Regulation 1215/99 and 1216/00)[344]
Commission Regulation 330/2010[345]	Vertical agreements	
Commission Regulation 461/2010[346]	Vertical agreements and concerted practices in the motor vehicle sector	
Commission Regulation 1218/2010[347]	Specialisation agreements	Regulation 2821/71[348]
Commission Regulation 1217/2010[349]	R&D agreements	
Commission Regulation 267/2010[350]	Agreements in the insurance sector	Council Regulation 1534/91[351]
Commission Regulation 906/2009[352]	Liner shipping consortia	Council Regulation 246/2009[353]
Council Regulation 169/2009[354]	Rail, road, and inland waterway sectors	

(iii) Direct Applicability

Agreements falling within the ambit of one of the block exemptions are automatically exempt from the Article 101(1) prohibition and the national courts are, and always have been, free to apply the terms of the block exemption should the validity of the agreement be raised before such a court. Article 288 TFEU (ex Article 249 EC) specifically provides that regulations are directly applicable.

If an agreement does not fall precisely within the scope of a block exemption the national court may not extend it to cover the agreement. The general rule is that if the conditions of the block exemption are not met the regulation ceases to apply in its entirety. However, in the block exemption applying to vertical and technology transfer agreements, for example, the regulations distinguish between provisions which, if inserted, mean that the block exemption does not apply and provisions which are not covered by the block exemption but which do not prevent the remaining provisions of the agreement benefiting from the Regulation.

---

[341] Council Regulation 487/2009 [2009] OJ L148/1 authorises the granting of block exemptions in the air transport sector. There are no block exemptions currently in force in this sector, however.

[342] [2004] OJ L123/11.

[343] [1965–1966] OJ Spec. Ed., 35.

[344] [1999] OJ L148/1 and [1999] OJ L148/5.

[345] [2010] OJ L102/1.

[346] [2010] OJ L129/52.

[347] [2010] OJ L335/43.

[348] [1971] OJ Spec. Ed., 1032.

[349] [2010] OJ L335/36.

[350] [2010] OJ L83/1.

[351] [1991] OJ L143/1.

[352] [2009] OJ L256/31.

[353] [2009] OJ L79/1.

[354] [2009] OJ L61/1.

Where the conditions of a block exemption are not met, the national court will, of course, be bound to determine whether or not the agreement infringes Article 101(1) and, where it does, whether it individually meets the Article 101(3) criteria. An agreement which contains clauses specifically prohibited by a regulation is, however, unlikely to satisfy Article 101(3).

(iv) Market Share Thresholds

Until the adoption of Regulation 2790/1999[355] (the first Verticals Regulation and predecessor of Regulation 330/2010), block exemptions tended to specify a narrow category of agreements covered, a list of restrictions which it was permissible for the agreement to contain ('white list'), and a list of prohibited restrictions ('black list'). The new block exemptions, adopted since 1999, have moved away from this format, in an attempt to prevent the severe straitjacketing and limitations on the parties' autonomy which resulted from the previous formula. Reflecting the more economic approach, most now provide a rule of thumb that agreements concluded by undertakings which meet specified market share thresholds, satisfy specified conditions, and which do not contain hardcore restraints are unlikely to raise competition problems (by listing only restrictions which may *not* be included within the agreement they allow the parties the freedom to determine what other provisions the agreement should include).[356] Most block exemptions thus now contain market share thresholds. For example, Regulation 330/2010, relating to vertical agreements, applies only where the relevant undertakings' market shares are below 30 per cent, Regulation 772/2004, the technology transfer block exemption (currently under review), applies only where the parties' market shares do not exceed 20 or 30 per cent of the market (depending upon whether the parties are competitors or non-competitors), and the R&D and specialisation block exemptions apply only provided the parties do not exceed market share thresholds of 25 and 20 per cent respectively.

(v) 'Hardcore' Restraints

Most block exemptions contain a list of hardcore restraints which, if included within the agreement, preclude the application of the block exemption. This reflects the Commission's view that agreements containing hardcore restraints are presumed to violate Article 101 (it is presumed that they infringe Article 101(1) and are unlikely to satisfy the Article 101(3) conditions) and so cannot benefit from a block exemption. Rather, they must be scrutinised individually to determine their compatibility with Article 101(3).

(vi) Withdrawal of Block Exemptions

Regulation 1/2003 provides that the Commission may withdraw the benefit of any *Commission* block exemption when 'it finds that in any particular case an agreement, decision or concerted practice to which the exemption Regulation applies has certain effects which are incompatible with Article [101(3)]'.[357] Withdrawal was threatened on several occasions under some of the old regulations[358] and actually occurred in *Langnese-Iglo*.[359] The CJ made clear, however, that the benefit of the block exemption (in that case Regulation 1984/83 applying to exclusive purchasing agreements) could not

---

[355] [1999] OJ L336/21. See Chap. 11.

[356] Above those market shares, however, there is a concern that the restraints may pose competition problems on account of the market power of the undertakings involved. An individual assessment is required, see especially Chaps. 10–12.

[357] Reg. 1/2003 [2003] OJ L1/1, Art. 29(1).

[358] See, e.g., *Tetra Pak/BTG* [1988] OJ L272/27.

[359] *Langnese-Iglo* [1993] OJ L183/19.

be withheld in advance from *future* agreements.[360] The Verticals block exemption, however, now specifically provides for the Commission to withdraw the benefit of the block exemption to specified categories of agreements (rather than individual agreements) by regulation.[361]

Regulation 1/2003 also provides NCAs with power to withdraw the benefit of any Commission block exemption where the agreement, to which the regulation applies, has 'effects which are incompatible with Article [101(1)] in the territory of a Member State, or in a part thereof, which has all the characteristics of a distinct geographic market'.[362]

(vii) Safe Harbours

The block exemptions are designed to provide legal certainty for undertakings. Undertakings know that agreements satisfying their conditions are valid and compatible with Article 101. Clearly, the introduction of market share thresholds detracts somewhat from this objective,[363] although their incorporation goes hand in hand with the more economic approach adopted by the Commission to Article 101. Further, the relatively low market share thresholds set out for those wishing to benefit from the safe harbour do not fit neatly within the analytical framework constructed by the Commission in its Article 101(3) Guidelines. The block exemptions were initially adopted as an essential response to the broad interpretation given to Article 101(1). Exemption under Article 101(3) was vital to the validity of many agreements. Although it is understood that the Commission now intends the block exemptions to operate as safe harbours and considers that agreements which do not satisfy these requirements do not necessarily infringe Article 101(1),[364] it is arguable that agreements satisfying their conditions will, in most cases, be unlikely to affect actual or potential competition to such an extent that a negative effect on prices, output, innovation, or the variety or quality of goods and services can be expected on the market (and so arguably should not infringe Article 101(1)). The existence of the block exemptions, although providing welcome legal certainty, therefore concentrates attention on Article 101(3) and may confuse the question of what analysis is required under Article 101(1).

F. UNILATERAL ACTION AND ARTICLE 101(3)

It was seen in Chapter 3 that in certain circumstances seemingly unilateral conduct of one party to a contract might actually form part of the contractual arrangements between it and a co-contractor, for example where it has been explicitly or tacitly accepted by the latter.[365] In many cases the Commission has relied on such behaviour to find a breach of Article 101(1).[366] Similarly, in *Ford Werke AG* v. *Commission*[367] the Commission relied both on the terms of the agreement and on the way in which it was operated by Ford when it issued a decision refusing Ford an exemption for its selective distribution system. The CJ held that the Commission was entitled, when considering the terms of the agreement, to take account not only of the written terms of the agreement but also the way the agreement was operated. In this case Ford had essentially refused to supply right-hand drive cars to its German dealers in order to protect the higher prices which the distributors charged in the UK. That apparently unilateral decision was, in this case, found to form part of the contractual

---

[360] Case C-279/95 P, *Langnese-Iglo* v. *Commission* [1998] ECR I-5609, paras. 207–209.

[361] See Chap. 11.

[362] Reg. 1/2003 [2003] OJ L1/1, Art. 29(2). See e.g., Chap. 11.

[363] See especially Chap. 12.

[364] See the Verticals Guidelines, para. 120.

[365] See Chap. 3.

[366] See Chap. 3

[367] Cases 228, 229/82, [1984] ECR 1129.

arrangements since admission to the network involved implicit acceptance by the dealers of the terms imposed by Ford.

5. CONCLUSIONS

1. The challenge for a system of competition law is to design a set of transparent and predictable rules which can be used to determine as accurately as possible, and at a tolerable cost, which agreements are so restrictive of competition that they should be prohibited and deterred. It has been seen in this chapter that this challenge has been rendered particularly difficult in the EU both by the lack of clarity over Article 101's objectives and its bifurcated structure.

2. It is clear that the Commission has moved away from its broad, jurisdictional approach to Article 101(1) which created an expansive role for Article 101(3) and (at the time) a pressing need for block exemptions. It now adopts a more economic approach to Article 101(1) and Article 101(3) based on a consumer welfare objective.

3. In modernising its approach to Article 101, the Commission has not accepted that Article 101(1) provides the correct forum for weighing pro- and anti-competitive effects on the basis that this approach would result in Article 101(3) being 'cast aside'. Rather, the Commission considers that Article 101(1) is about identifying restrictive effects on competition (it is for the Commission, or other person trying to prove the same, to demonstrate the restriction), whilst Article 101(3) provides the forum, for the person seeking to rely on it, to prove that counteracting efficiencies resulting from the agreement outweigh the effect of those restrictions.[368]

4. The difficulty with this structure is that it requires an extremely strained view of some of the case law and past decisional practice. A number of judgments of the CJ support the view that the weighing of pro- and anti-competitive effects should be conducted within the framework of Article 101(1) (restrictions of competition necessary and proportionate to a legitimate objective fall outside Article 101(1)). Further, precedent indicates that public policy objectives may be taken into account when conducting the Article 101(3) appraisal. These cases suggest a rather different picture of the analysis to be conducted under Article 101, indicating a narrower interpretation of Article 101(1) and less emphasis on Article 101(3). Further, they suggest that both Article 101(1) and Article 101(3) may still have a role to play in the pursuit of public policy objectives.

6. FURTHER READING

A. BOOKS

AMATO, G., *Antitrust and the Bounds of Power* (Hart Publishing, 1997), Chap. 4

ODUDU, O., *The Boundaries of EC Competition Law: The Scope of Article 81* (Oxford University Press, 2006)

TOWNLEY, C., *Article 81 EC and Public Policy* (Hart Publishing, 2009)

B. ARTICLES

BAILEY, D., 'Restrictions of Competition by Object under Article 101 TFEU' (2012) 49 *CMLRev* 559

FORRESTER, I., and NORALL, C., 'The Laicization of Community Law: Self-help and the Rule of Reason: How Competition Law is and could be Applied' (1984) 21 *CMLRev* 11

HAWK, B. E., 'System Failure: Vertical Restraints and EC Competition Law' (1995) 32 *CMLRev* 973

IBÁÑEZ COLOMO, P., 'Market Failure, Transaction Costs and Articles 101(1) TFEU Case Law' [2012] *ELRev* 541

---

[368] The weighing is conducted therefore within the framework of Art. 101(3) rather than under Art. 101(1).

JONES, A., 'Analysis of Agreements under US and EC Antitrust Law—Convergence or Divergence?' (2006) 51 *Ant Bull* 691

—'Left Behind by Modernisation? Restrictions by Object under Article 101(1)' (2010) 55 *Ant Bull*

KORAH, V., 'EEC Competition Policy—Legal Form or Economic Efficiency' [1986] 39 *Current Legal Problems* 85

MONTI, G., 'Article 81 and Public Policy' (2002) 39 *CMLRev* 1057

SUFRIN, B., 'The Evolution of Article 81(3) of the EC Treaty' (2006) 51 *Ant Bull* 915

TOWNLEY, C., 'Inter-generational impacts in competition law: remembering those not yet born' [2011] *ECLR* 580

WHISH, R., and SUFRIN, B., 'Article 85 and the Rule of Reason' [1987] *YEL* 1

INTRODUCTION TO ARTICLE 102 TFEU

1. CENTRAL ISSUES

1. Article 102 TFEU (previously Article 82 EC) deals with the unilateral conduct of undertakings with substantial market power.

2. Article 102 prohibits one or more undertakings which hold a dominant position in the internal market or a substantial part of it abusing that position insofar as it may affect inter-Member State trade. For an infringement of Article 102 to be established, therefore, five cumulative elements must be established.

3. 'Undertaking' has the same meaning as it does in respect of Article 101. 'One or more undertakings' means that independent undertakings may together hold a 'collective' dominant position. The meaning of an effect on inter-Member State trade is set out in the Commission Guidelines on the effect on trade concept, which explain the case law.

4. The elements of 'dominant position' and 'abuse' are particularly difficult both to define and to establish. The holding of a 'dominant position' is not prohibited, only the 'abuse' of the dominant position. Article 102 does not apply to conduct whereby non-dominant firms achieve dominance.

5. The way in which the Commission and the EU Courts have interpreted Article 102 has been extremely controversial. Article 102 has mainly been applied to 'exclusionary abuses', i.e. to conduct which impedes effective competition by excluding (foreclosing) competitors. It has been applied in a predominantly formalistic way, focusing on the form of the conduct and drawing presumptions from that,

rather than analysing the actual effects on the market. Further, it has often been applied in order to protect competitors rather than to protect the competitive process for the benefit of consumers.

6. The Commission wishes to 'modernise' the approach to Article 102. It wishes to realign Article 102 to take an effects-based approach directed to the objective of consumer welfare. In 2003 the Commission embarked upon a review of the application of Article 102 to exclusionary abuses. The review resulted first in a DG Comp Staff Discussion Paper in 2005 and culminated in the official publication in February 2009 of Commission Guidance on its enforcement priorities in applying Article 102 to abusive exclusionary conduct (the Guidance Paper).

7. The EU Courts have been slow to depart from the established case law. Recent judgments of the Court of Justice have stated the objectives of the competition law articles to be the protection of competitors as well as consumers and the protection of competition 'as such', and to prevent competition from being distorted to the detriment of the public interest, individual undertakings and consumers.

8. The Guidance Paper states that it is not intended to constitute a statement of the law. Instead, it sets out the principles which will guide the Commission in deciding when to intervene. The Commission is concerned about conduct that has an adverse impact on consumers.

2. INTRODUCTION

Article 102 is designed to deal with monopoly and market power. It focuses not on agreements *between* undertakings (as Article 101 does) but on the unilateral behaviour of undertakings which hold a 'dominant position'.[1] It constrains the behaviour of undertakings which are not sufficiently restrained by other competitors operating on the market by prohibiting the 'abuse' of a dominant position. It is important to note that Article 102 applies only to the conduct of undertakings which are already dominant and not to any anti-competitive conduct by which an undertaking *achieves* dominance, or to any other unilateral conduct by a non-dominant firm which causes harm to consumers despite that lack of dominance.[2]

As we saw in Chapter 1, a monopolist is able to restrict output and increase prices without losing sales to competitors. It can reap monopoly profits. Article 102 prohibits an undertaking with a dominant position from exploiting that position, for example by charging unfair prices or by limiting production to the prejudice of consumers. In addition, it is clear from the case law that the provision also covers anti-competitive conduct by which a dominant undertaking excludes actual or potential competitors from the market.[3] Article 102 therefore applies to so-called 'exclusionary' conduct as well as to conduct that exploits consumers directly.

The application of Article 102 by the Commission and the EU Courts has often been highly controversial. This is principally due to the following.

- Questionable findings that an undertaking is dominant for the purposes of the Article.

- An emphasis on the *form* that the behaviour of the dominant undertaking takes, rather than on its *effects*.

- An absence of coherent and consistent principles or a clear analytical or intellectual framework of analysis in the approach to Article 102.[4] This has stemmed from a failure to identify the policy objectives being pursued in the enforcement of the prohibition. As in the case of Article 101, the objectives pursued have a huge impact on the interpretation of the provision, in particular whether or not behaviour is characterised as abusive. The application of Article 102 raises very starkly the question of whether the law should protect competitors for their own sake (in the interest of 'economic freedom' in the ordoliberal sense). In the application of Article 102 and the debate surrounding it we see played out the arguments about the purposes of competition law which we noted in Chapter 1.

- The effect that the imperative of single market integration has played.

3. THE TEXT OF ARTICLE 102

Article 102 provides:[5]

Any abuse by one or more undertakings of a dominant position within the internal market or in a substantial part of it shall be prohibited as incompatible with the internal market insofar as it may affect trade between Member States. Such abuse may, in particular, consist in:

(a) directly or indirectly imposing unfair purchase or selling prices or other unfair trading conditions;

(b) limiting production, markets or technical development to the prejudice of consumers;

---

[1] It docs, however, as explained in Section 7 and in Chap. 7, include conduct which involves entering into agreements with other parties.

[2] For comments on this 'enforcement gap' see L.-H. Roeller, 'Exploitative Abuses', in C.-D. Ehlermann and M. Marquis (eds.), *European Competition Law Annual 2007: A Reformed Approach to Article 82* (Hart Publishing, 2008); I. Kokkoris, 'Are We Underenforcing Article 102 TFEU', in F. Etro and I. Kokkoris (eds.), *Competition Law and the Enforcement of Article 102* (Oxford University Press, 2010), Chap. 9.

[3] See Case 6/72, *Europemballage Corp and Continental Can Co Inc v. Commission* [1973] ECR 215 and Chap. 7 *passim*.

[4] See e.g. J. Temple Lang and R. O'Donoghue, 'Defining Legitimate Competition: How to Clarify Pricing Abuses under Article 82EC' (2002) 26 *Fordham Int'l LJ* 83, 84.

[5] The wording of Art. 102 TFEU is unchanged from that of Art. 82 EC other than the substitution of 'internal market' for 'common market'.

(c) applying dissimilar conditions to equivalent transactions with other trading parties, thereby placing them at a competitive disadvantage;

(d) making the conclusion of contracts subject to acceptance by the other parties of supplementary obligations which, by their nature or according to commercial usage, have no connection with the subject of such contracts.

4. THE SCHEME OF ARTICLE 102

A. THE PROHIBITION

Article 102 prohibits undertakings from committing an abuse of a dominant position held within the internal market or a substantial part of it where that abuse may have an effect on trade between Member States. Although sub-paragraphs (a) to (d) set out examples of abuses, they do not provide an exhaustive list.[6]

The provision does not set out a separate procedure for declaring an undertaking to be dominant and so subject to Article 102. An undertaking is dominant simply when it satisfies the criteria for dominance and the conduct under investigation then becomes potentially subject to the prohibition. In any future proceedings the dominant position has to be established afresh as the conditions of competition may have changed.[7]

Article 102 contains no express exception provision equivalent to that in Article 101(3).[8] It is, however, open to a dominant undertaking to plead that its conduct is 'objectively justified'.[9] Further, although it must be established that the dominant position is held 'in a substantial part of the internal market' and there must be an *appreciable* effect on inter-Member State trade, there is no de minimis rule equivalent to that adopted by the ECJ in relation to Article 101(1).[10]

It can be seen from the text of Article 102 that five elements must be established before the prohibition applies. They are:

(a) one or more undertakings;

(b) a dominant position;

(c) the dominant position must be held within the internal market or a substantial part of it;

(d) an abuse; and

(e) an effect on inter-State trade.

It is often extremely difficult to determine whether or not these criteria have been satisfied, in particular whether an undertaking holds a 'dominant position' and/or whether it has committed an 'abuse' of that dominant position. The problems in the application of Article 102 have mainly concerned those two elements.

---

[6] See Case 6/72, *Europemballage Corp and Continental Can Co Inc* v. *Commission* [1973] ECR 215, [1973] CMLR 199; Case C-333/94 P, *Tetra Pak International SA* v. *Commission* [1996] ECR I-5951 (*Tetra Pak II*), para. 37; Case C-95/04 P, *British Airways* v. *Commission* [2007] ECR I-2331, para. 57; Case T-201/04, *Microsoft* v. *Commission* [2007] ECR II-3601, para. 860; Case C-280/08 P, *Deutsche Telekom* v. *Commission* [2010] ECR I-9555, para. 173.

[7] Cases T-125 and 127/97, *Coca-Cola* v. *Commission* [2000] ECR II-987, paras. 81–83.

[8] Although it was possible to apply for a negative clearance under Reg. 17, Art. 2 (JO 204/62, (1959–1962) OJ Spec. Ed. 87). It is possible under Reg. 1/2003, Art. 10 for the Commission to make a finding of inapplicability (although this has never yet been done): see Chap. 13.

[9] And/or 'objectively necessary', justified by efficiencies, or only protecting its own commercial interests, see Chap. 7, Section 5.

[10] See Chap. 3. For the appreciability of the effect on inter-Member State trade see Guidelines on the effect on trade concept contained in Articles 81 and 82 of the Treaty [2004] OJ C101/81, and Section 5.E.

The question whether an undertaking is dominant requires, according to the case law of the CJ, that the market on which the undertaking is alleged to be dominant is defined.[11] The undertaking's position on the market must then be assessed. It is crucial that these definitions and assessments are made properly. It is not an offence to hold a dominant position as Article 102 does not prohibit the holding of a dominant position per se but only an abuse of it,[12] but some behaviour which may be competitive, or at least neutral, from a competition perspective when engaged in by an undertaking on a competitive market may be prohibited when engaged in by a dominant undertaking.[13] An incorrect finding of dominance may consequently lead to a ruling that an undertaking's pro-competitive behaviour is abusive conduct prohibited by Article 102 (a Type 1 'false positive' error). Furthermore, it was seen in Chapter 3 that a firm which unilaterally acts anti-competitively by imposing export bans[14] or resale prices[15] is not prohibited from doing so by Article 101(1), which applies only to agreements. If the undertaking concerned is not dominant the conduct falls outside Article 102 as well and is therefore legal. Dominant and non-dominant firms are in crucially different positions. In addition, if the concept of an abuse is found to encompass a wide spectrum of behaviour, Article 102 may come perilously close to forbidding the dominance itself.

The question of what amounts to an 'abuse' is a vexed one. It requires a determination of what conduct can and what conduct cannot legitimately be carried out by a dominant undertaking. This, of course, depends partly upon the purposes of the whole provision. As already stated, it has not always been entirely clear what objectives have been pursued in the enforcement of Article 102.

This chapter, after setting out the consequences of infringing Article 102, considers the five elements of Article 102 in turn and deals with general issues concerning their scope, interpretation, and application. Chapters 6 and 7 respectively consider in greater detail (1) how it is ascertained whether an undertaking holds a dominant position and (2) what conduct constitutes an abuse of a dominant position. It is important to realise, however, that the different elements of Article 102 cannot always be considered separately from one another. In particular, the questions whether an undertaking is in a dominant position and whether it has committed an abuse may be interrelated and intertwined.[16] As we shall see, it has even been argued that there should be no need to establish a preliminary and separate assessment of dominance, but that the analysis of dominance and abuse should be integrated.[17]

B. THE ENFORCEMENT OF ARTICLE 102

(i) Infringement Decisions, Fines, and Other Remedies

The Commission may investigate undertakings it believes may have committed a breach of Article 102. Where the Commission finds that a violation of Article 102 has been committed, it can issue a decision ordering the undertaking to put an end to the abuse (by taking positive or negative

---

[11] Case 6/72, *Europemballage Corp and Continental Can Co Inc v. Commission* [1973] ECR 215. For the argument that market power may be able to be measured directly, rather than by going through the 'indirect method' via market definition, see Chap. 1, Section 10.A, p. 60, and Chap. 6.

[12] This point was reiterated by the CJ in Case C-209/10, *Post Danmark A/S v. Konkurrencerådet*, 27 March 2012, paras. 21–22.

[13] See Chap. 7.

[14] Cases C-2 and 3/01 P, *Bundesverband der Arzneimitte—Importeure EV and Commission v. Bayer AG* [2004] ECR I-23, 5141.

[15] Case C-74/04 P, *Commission v. Volkswagen AG* [2006] ECR I-6585.

[16] See T. Eilsmansberger, 'Dominance—The Lost Child? How the Effects-Based Rules Could and Should Change Dominance Analysis' (2006) 2 *European Law Journal* 15.

[17] Report by EAGCP, July 2005, see Chap. 6, Section 3.C, p. 303.

measures) and can, where certain conditions are met, impose structural remedies.[18] Further, it can impose fines on the undertaking of up to 10 per cent of its turnover in the preceding year of business. The Commission has imposed substantial fines on undertakings found to have committed a breach of Article 102. In *Intel*[19] the Commission imposed a fine of over €1 billion on a single undertaking.

The difficulties involved in determining whether or not an infringement of Article 102 has been committed and the controversy surrounding many of the Commission's decisions taken under Article 102 have rendered the Commission's willingness to impose heavy fines in respect of breaches of the Article extremely contentious. Moreover, as shown by *Microsoft*, behavioural remedies such as ordering an undertaking to supply may be more significant for the undertaking than even a large fine.[20]

(ii) Complaints

The great majority of Article 102 cases arise from complaints.[21] Both the Commission and National Competition Authorities (NCAs) inaugurate cases after receiving complaints, and the latter may ultimately come before the Court of Justice (CJ) in an Article 267 reference.[22] The complaints are usually made by competitors, not customers,[23] as Article 102 is increasingly deployed as a weapon in the commercial struggle between the players on the market. This has become particularly noticeable in the information and communications technologies (ICT) sector, with the Commission opening investigations, for example, after complaints from Microsoft about Google,[24] and Apple and Microsoft about Motorola.[25]

(iii) Commitments Decisions

Under Regulation 1/2003, Article 9, the Commission can take 'commitments decisions' whereby it accepts binding commitments from undertakings under investigation rather than proceeding to a final decision under Article 7.[26] Under the Regulation 17 regime the Commission brought several Article 102 proceedings to a close by accepting commitments from the parties, but it could not make these binding.[27] Since 2004 the Commission has made enthusiastic use of Article 9 commitments decisions including in energy markets where Article 102 has been applied in pursuance of liberalisation.[28] The termination of cases by commitments decisions has serious implications for the

---

[18] Reg. 1/2003, Art. 7. See Chap. 13. The power to impose remedies of a structural nature, i.e. to order divestment and break-up companies was introduced by Reg. 1/2003 and did not appear in Reg. 17.

[19] Case COMP/C-3/37.990 *Intel*, on appeal Case T-286/09, *Intel v. Commission*, judgment pending, see Chap. 7.

[20] Case T-201/04, *Microsoft v. Commission* [2007] ECR II-3601.

[21] For complaints to the Commission, see Chap. 13.

[22] As, for example, in *Post Danmark*, see n. 12.

[23] In that they relate to 'exclusionary' rather than 'exploitative' abuse, see Chap. 7.

[24] COMP/39.740, *Google*, IP/13/371, MEMO/13/383, 25 April 2013.

[25] COMP/39.986, *Motorola*, IP/12/345.

[26] See generally Chap. 13, and in particular *De Beers/ALROSA* [2006] OJ L205/24, quashed by the GC, Case T-170/06, *Alrosa v. Commission* [2007] ECR II-2601; judgment set aside Case C-441/07P, *European Commission v. Alrosa* [2010] ECR I-5949.

[27] e.g., *Digital Undertaking*, Commission Press Release IP/97/868.

[28] COMP/B-1/200337.966 *Distrigas*, 11 October 2011; COMP/39.388 *German Electricity Wholesale Markets* and *German Electricity Balancing Markets (E.ON)* Summary [2009] OJ C36/8; COMP/39.402 *RWE—Gas Foreclosure*, 18 March 2009; COMP/39.402 *RWE—Gas Foreclosure*, 18 March 2009, IP/09/410; COMP/39.316, *Gaz de France*, 3 December 2009; COMP/39.836, *Long Term Electricity Contracts in France*, 17 March 2010; COMP/39.315, *ENI*, 29 September 2010. See also COMP/38.636, *Rambus*, 9 December 2009; COMP/39.530, *Microsoft* (browser tying), 16 December 2009; COMP/39.592, *Standard & Poor's (US International Securities Identification Numbering)*, 15 December 2011; COMP/39.692, *IBM Maintenance Services*, 13 December 2011; COMP/39, *Google*, [2013] OJ C120/22, commitments market test, 25 April 2013: all discussed further in Chap. 7.

development of the law on Article 102, as the nature of the procedure means that it is never established whether according to the Commission the impugned conduct *did* amount to an infringement of Article 102 and the matter never goes before the EU Courts. This exacerbates the uncertainty surrounding the question of what conduct can constitute an abuse, particularly given the contentious nature of the subject matter of some of the cases settled in this way, and dilutes the control of the Commission by the EU Courts.[29] Nevertheless most Commission Article 102 proceedings do now terminate in commitments rather than infringement decisions, and one can appreciate the attractions to both the Commission and the parties of handling the matter in this way.[30]

(iv) Enforcement by the NCAs

Regulation 1/2003 requires Member States to empower their designated competition authorities to apply Article 102 (and Article 101).[31] Article 5 provides that the NCAs shall have powers to take infringement, commitments, and fining decisions and take interim measures. The Regulation itself does not give them the power to impose structural remedies.[32] The CJ held in *Tele2Polska* that NCAs do not have power to make a finding that there has been no infringement of Article 102. Only the Commission can do that.[33]

(v) Judicial Review in Article 102 Cases

The issue of the standard and intensity of the judicial review of the Commission's decisions in competition cases is discussed in Chapter 13.[34] However, a few preliminary points should be made here about Article 102 cases. Many of the Commission's decisions on Article 102 are extremely contentious and the extent to which they are reviewed by the General Court (GC) is therefore of great concern. The EU Courts have long allowed the Commission a 'margin of appreciation' in its assessment of complex economic matters and declined to substitute their own assessment for that of the Commission. The position was clearly restated in the *Microsoft* case.

Case T-201/04, *Microsoft* v. *EC Commission* [2007] ECR II-3601

General Court

87 The Court observes that it follows from consistent case-law that, although as a general rule the Community Courts undertake a comprehensive review of the question as to whether or not the conditions for the application of the competition rules are met, their review of complex economic appraisals made by the Commission is necessarily limited to checking whether the relevant rules on procedure and on stating reasons have been complied with, whether the facts have been accurately stated and whether there has been any manifest error of assessment or a misuse of powers (Case T-65/96 *Kish Glass v Commission*...paragraph 64, upheld on appeal by order of the Court of Justice in Case C-241/00 P *Kish Glass v Commission*....see also, to that effect, with respect to Article [101 TFEU], Case 42/84 *Remia and Others v Commission*...paragraph 34, and Joined Cases 142/84 and 156/84 *BAT and Reynolds v Commission*...paragraph 62).

---

[29] For example, the 'search neutrality' principle in *Google*.

[30] See Chap. 13, Section 8.d.(iii), p. 982 ff.

[31] Reg. 1/2003, Art. 35.

[32] See Chap. 13. National law may give the NCA such powers.

[33] Case C-375/09, *Prezes Urzędu Ochrony Konkurencji i Konsumentów v. Tele2 Polska sp. z o.o., now Netia SA* [2011] ECR I-3055.

[34] And also, in respect of merger decisions, in Chap. 15.

88 Likewise, in so far as the Commission's decision is the result of complex technical appraisals, those appraisals are in principle subject to only limited review by the Court, which means that the Community Courts cannot substitute their own assessment of matters of fact for the Commission's (see, as regards a decision adopted following complex appraisals in the medico-pharmacological sphere, order of the President of the Court of Justice in Case C-459/00 P(R) *Commission v Trenker*...paragraphs 82 and 83; see also, to that effect, Case C-120/97 Upjohn...paragraph 34 and the case-law cited; Case T-179/00 *A. Menarini v Commission*...paragraphs 44 and 45; and Case T-13/99 *Pfizer Animal Health v Council*...paragraph 323).

89 However, while the Community Courts recognise that the Commission has a margin of appreciation in economic or technical matters, that does not mean that they must decline to review the Commission's interpretation of economic or technical data. The Community Courts must not only establish whether the evidence put forward is factually accurate, reliable and consistent but must also determine whether that evidence contains all the relevant data that must be taken into consideration in appraising a complex situation and whether it is capable of substantiating the conclusions drawn from it (see, to that effect, concerning merger control, Case C-12/;03 P *Commission v Tetra Laval*...paragraph 39).

We see in Chapters 6 and 7 how this standard of review has been applied to Article 102 decisions. There is an appeal from the GC to the CJ on a point of law. It is worth noting that it is very rare for the Commission to lose Article 102 cases on the substance. As at 1 July 2013 it had not lost a single one for over 20 years.[35]

(vi) Private Actions in National Courts and Article 267 References

Article 102, like Article 101, is directly effective.[36] It is possible, therefore, that an entity injured by a breach of Article 102 may bring proceedings before a national court seeking an injunction or damages in respect of loss resulting from the breach.[37]

Further, a party to a contract concluded with a dominant undertaking may claim that clauses within it are prohibited by Article 102 and consequently void or unenforceable.[38] That party may also bring proceedings to recover benefits conferred under a prohibited provision.

National courts before which Article 102 is raised may make references to the CJ for preliminary rulings under Article 267, as explained in Chapter 2. Some leading cases on Article 102 have come before the CJ in this way.[39] The use of commitments decisions by the Commission, and the consequent paucity of appeals from Commission infringement decisions to the EU Courts, are likely to make the Article 267 route even more significant for the development of the law in future.

---

[35] C. Ahlborn and D. S. Evans, 'The *Microsoft* Judgment and its Implications for Competition Policy Towards Dominant Firms in Europe' (2008–2009) 75 *Antitrust L.J.* 887 (as at 1 July 2013 it had not lost one since that was written). Part of the *Microsoft* decision on the remedy was annulled, but not the substance, see Chap. 13, Section 9.A.v.b, p. 1033.

[36] See Case 127/73, *Belgische Radio en Télévisie and Société belge des auteurs, compositeurs et editeurs v. SV SABAM and NV Fonior* [1974] ECR 313. The equivalent Article of the ECSC Treaty, Art. 66(7), did not have direct effect because it conferred sole jurisdiction on the Commission; see Case C-128/92, *H. J. Banks & Co Ltd v. British Coal Corp* [1994] ECR I-1209, paras. 18–19.

[37] See Chap. 14.

[38] For the effect of this see e.g. *English Welsh and Scottish Railway Ltd v. E.ON UK plc* [2007] EWHC 599, 23 March 2007, in Chap. 14, Section 3.B.i, p. 1100.

[39] Such as Case 311/84, *Centre Belge d'Etudes du Marché-Télémarketing v. Compagnie Luxembourgeoise de Télédiffusion SA et Information Publicité Benelux SA* [1985] ECR 3261;Case C-7/97 *Oscar Bronner GmbH & Co KG v. Mediaprint* [1998] ECR I-7791; Case C-418/01 *IMS Health GmbH & Co. OHG v. NDC Health GmbH & Co KG* [2004] ECR I-5039; Cases C-468–478/06, *Sot. Lélos kai Sia and others EE v. GlaxoSmithKline AEVE Farmakeftikon Proionton* [2008] ECR I-7139.

5. THE INTERPRETATION AND APPLICATION OF ARTICLE 102

A. THE MEANING OF ONE OR MORE UNDERTAKINGS

(i) General

'Undertaking' is interpreted in the same way for the purpose of Article 102 as for Article 101. It has been construed broadly and 'encompasses every entity engaged in an economic activity'.[40] If an entity is not engaged in an economic activity, the fact that the members who comprise it do carry out such activity will not render the entity itself an 'undertaking' for the purposes of Article 102. In *Wouters*[41] the CJ thus held that the Dutch Bar was not itself an undertaking although the individual members of the Bar *were* undertakings for the purposes of Article 101. Two points of particular importance arise when considering the meaning of the term 'undertaking' within the context of Article 102. First, since State regulation is a frequent source of an entity's market power, it is crucial to know to what extent public bodies or bodies with a special connection with the State will be characterised as undertakings and so potentially subject to Article 102. Secondly, it must be considered what is meant by 'one or more undertakings' in Article 102. So far, in this chapter reference has been made to the problems caused by monopoly and market power held by an individual undertaking. It is clearly envisaged, however, that Article 102 should apply to the conduct of more than one undertaking. Is Article 102 confined to the conduct of undertakings which are part of the same single economic entity (in which a united policy may be pursued) or does Article 102 go further and prohibit the conduct of one or more independent undertakings?

(ii) Public Bodies and Bodies Performing Public Functions

The term 'undertaking' applies to any entity engaged in commercial activities whether or not it is a State entity, even if it has no identity separate from that of the State.[42] Further, it is clear from Article 4(3) TEU and Article 106(1) TFEU that the State itself cannot confer immunity upon undertakings from the application of those rules. The fact that an undertaking's market power has been created by State action is no defence to an action based on Article 102 unless the narrow exception set out in Article 106(2) TFEU applies. This provision states that '[u]ndertakings entrusted with the operation of services of general economic interest or having the character of a revenue-producing monopoly' are subject to the competition rules unless those rules 'obstruct the performance, in law or in fact, of the particular tasks assigned to them'. This topic is discussed in Chapter 8.

(iii) One or More Undertakings—Collective Dominance

a. The Development of the Collective Dominance Concept

Initially it was believed that the term 'one or more undertakings' referred only to bodies which were part of the same economic entity, i.e. that the purpose of the term was to ensure that the conduct of all bodies within the corporate group was taken into account when assessing whether or not a breach of Article 102 had occurred. Thus circumstances such as those which arose in *Continental*

---

[40] See Chap. 3.

[41] Case C-309/99, *Wouters v. Algemene Raad van de Nederlandse Orde van Advocaten* [2002] ECR I-1577, para. 112.

[42] See Chap. 3 and Chap. 8. For two important CJ judgments concerning the status of undertakings exercising some public powers, see Case C-113/07, *SELEX Systemi Integrati SpA v. Commission* [2009] ECR I-2207 and Case C-49/07, *Motosykletistiki Omospondia Ellados NPID (MOTOE) v. Ellinkio Dimosi* [2008] ECR I-4863.

Can and *Commercial Solvents* would be caught. In *Continental Can*[43] a US company held an 85.8 per cent share in a German company (SLW). It formed a wholly owned Belgian subsidiary through which it acquired a Dutch company which was a competitor of SLW. The Commission held that the American parent had, through SLW, a dominant position in a substantial part of the common market and that an abuse of the dominant position was committed when it used its Belgian subsidiary to take over the Dutch company.[44] Similarly, in *Commercial Solvents*[45] a US parent and its 51 per cent owned Italian subsidiary were involved in a refusal to supply a third party in Italy with a raw material produced by the parent. The subsidiary followed the policy laid down by the parent and both were held to have abused a dominant position. The view that Article 102 might be confined to situations where bodies formed part of the same economic unit or the same corporate group found support from a statement of the CJ in *Hoffmann La-Roche*.[46]

Such an interpretation would, however, have meant that the term 'undertaking' in Article 102 has a different meaning from that which it has in Article 101. In Chapter 3 it was explained that the term 'undertaking' applies to all bodies which form part of the same economic entity. Bodies within the same corporate group are treated as a single undertaking if the bodies 'form an economic unit within which the subsidiary has no real freedom to determine its course of action on the market, and if the agreements or practices are concerned merely with the internal allocation of tasks as between the undertakings'.[47] If interpreted in the same way, Article 102 would apply to the behaviour of all bodies which form an economic unit even if the Article had referred only to an abuse by *an* undertaking of a dominant position. So what interpretation should be given to the phrase 'one or more undertakings'?

It has now been established that 'one or more undertakings' can refer to legally independent undertakings which together hold a 'collective dominant position' on the market. Article 102 therefore applies both to dominant positions held by single firms and to those held collectively. However, the answer to the question of what exactly constitutes a collective (or 'joint') dominant position and how it is established has had a long and tortuous evolution, and involves not only Article 102 but also the EU Merger Regulation (EUMR).[48]

b. Situations Giving Rise to Collective Dominance

The concept of collective dominance initially arose in respect of undertakings which were linked by licences or agreements. However, in the first case in which the concept was accepted, *Flat Glass*,[49] the GC spoke of entities 'united by such economic links that ... together they hold a dominant position *vis-à-vis* the other operators on the same market'.[50] This opened the door to the possibility that a collective dominant position could be held by legally independent undertakings which operate on an oligopolistic market. Oligopolies present great problems for competition laws. We see in Chapter 3 that Article 101 applies to agreements and concerted practices between undertakings. However, as explained in Chapter 9, undertakings on oligopolistic markets may act in parallel without expressly

---

[43] Case 6/72, *Europemballage Corp and Continental Can Co Inc v. Commission* [1973] ECR 215.

[44] *Re Continental Can Co Inc* [1972] OJ L7/25, [1972] CMLR D11. The CJ annulled the Commission's decision on the ground of an erroneous definition of the market (see Chap. 6) but the point about the aggregation of the activities of the group was not doubted.

[45] Cases 6 and 7/73, *Istituto Chemioterapico Italiano SpA and Commercial Solvents Corp v. Commission* [1974] ECR 223.

[46] Case 85/76, *Hoffmann-La Roche & Co AG v. Commission* [1979] ECR 461, para. 39.

[47] Case 15/74, *Centrafarm BV and Adriaan De Peijper v. Sterling Drug Inc* [1974] ECR 1147, para. 41, repeated in Case 30/87, *Bodson v. Pompes funèbres des régions libérées SA* [1988] ECR 2479, para. 19. See Chap. 3.

[48] See Chap. 15. For collective dominance generally see G. Monti, 'The Scope of Collective Dominance Under Article 82 EC' (2001) 38 *CMLRev* 131.

[49] Cases T-68, 77, and 78/89, *Società Italiano Vetro SpA v. Commission* [1992] ECR II-1403 (the *Italian Flat Glass Cartel* appeal), paras. 357–358; Cases C-395 and 396/96P, *Compagnie Maritime Belge Transports SA v. Commission* [2000] ECR I-1365; Cases T-191/98 and 212–214/98, *Atlantic Container Line & Ors v. Commission* [2003] ECR II-3275, para. 595.

[50] Cases T-68, 77, and 78/89, *Società Italiano Vetro SpA v. Commission* [1992] ECR II-1403, para. 358.

colluding. Rather, recognising their 'interdependence' they 'tacitly' collude. Such tacit collusion (or 'tacit coordination') is not caught by Article 101. Therefore, if 'economic links' include the interdependence of undertakings on an oligopolistic market the application of Article 102 might be a way of dealing with the 'oligopoly problem'.

There is also an issue of oligopolies in respect of the regulation of mergers. The concept of a 'dominant position' appears not only in Article 102 but also in the EUMR.[51] It was important to know whether the concept in the EUMR covered collective as well as single firm dominance. If it did the EUMR could be applied to the creation and strengthening of a collective dominant position and thus could prevent anti-competitive oligopolistic market structures being created in the first place, or strengthened.[52]

Following the *Flat Glass* judgment there was a stream of cases and decisions both on Article 102 and on the EUMR. The EU Courts have cited their merger judgments in Article 102 cases and vice versa, so the development of collective dominance in the context of Article 102 cannot be separated from its development under the EUMR. The case law must be read as a whole. It establishes in effect that collective dominance is of two types:

- What has been called 'non-oligopolistic'[53] or 'expressly or pure collusive' ('traditional')[54] collective dominance where there are contractual, commercial, or structural links between the parties or direct or indirect contact. The parties may be operating on an oligopolistic market but their collusion is express rather than tacit.
- 'Oligopolistic' collective dominance which arises on tightly oligopolistic markets where the undertakings can coordinate their behaviour without express collusion and have the incentive to do so. This is the form of collective dominance that is relevant to the application of both Article 102 and the EUMR.

Interestingly, the EU Courts have sometimes made statements that have advanced the law on oligopolistic collective dominance in cases which concerned non-oligopolistic collective dominance.[55]

c. Oligopolistic Collective Dominance

Given the importance of the concept of collective dominance in respect of tacit collusion between oligopolists and of mergers, the case law is fully discussed in Chapters 9 and 15. We set out in Section 5.A.iii.d, however, some points about non-oligopolistic collective dominance.

d. Non-oligopolistic Collective Dominance

In *Flat Glass* the Commission found that three Italian flat glass producers had all infringed Article 101(1) by concluding agreements to, inter alia, fix prices and sales quotas, and had infringed Article 102 by abusing their collective dominant position (although the Commission did not adduce any evidence to establish the latter infringement apart from that relied on to establish the breach of Article 101).[56] On appeal the GC quashed the Commission's decision that there had been an infringement of Article 102 on the grounds that it was not sufficient simply to recycle the facts constituting an

---

[51] Council Regulation 139/2004 [2004] OJ L124/1, on the control of concentrations between undertakings, Art. 2(2) and (3), previously Council Regulation 4064/89 [1989] OJ L395/1.

[52] The Commission's stretching of the collective dominance concept to deal with the situation where a merger has anti-competitive effects without creating or strengthening a single dominant position was the subject of *Airtours*, Case T-342/99 *Airtours plc v. Commission* [2002] ECR II-2585. The importance of dominance in respect of the EUMR was lessened by the changes made in Article 2(2) and (3) by Reg. 139/ 2004, see further Chaps. 9 and 15.

[53] See R. Nazzini, *The Foundations of European Union Competition Law, The Objectives and Principles of Article 102* (Oxford University Press, 2011), Chap. 11.

[54] See L. Ortiz Blanco, *Market Power in EU Antitrust Law* (Hart Publishing, 2012), Chap.10.

[55] See particularly Cases C-395 and 396/96P *Compagnie Maritime Belge Transports SA v. EC Commission* [2000] ECR I-1365 and Case T-193/02, *Laurent Piau v. Commission* [2005] ECR II-209.

[56] *Flat Glass* [1989] OJ L33/44.

infringement of Article 101 in order to deduce that the behaviour constituted an abuse of a collective dominant position. Nevertheless, the GC expressed the view, as already explained, that Article 102 *could* apply to independent undertakings and that Article 102 was not confined to one or more undertakings within the same corporate group.

The Commission proceeded cautiously. In a series of decisions it applied the concept of collective dominance to undertakings bound together by contractual links. In three cases, *French-West African Shipowners' Committees*,[57] *CEWAL*,[58] and *Trans-Atlantic Conference Agreement (TACA)*,[59] the Commission used collective dominance in relation to shipowners which were members of liner conferences, and which had concluded agreements regulating the operation of trade on shipping routes. In *French-West African Shipowners' Committees* the Commission imposed fines on shipowners that had participated in cargo-sharing systems on routes between France and 11 West African States. The Committees monitored the quota systems and imposed penalties on those that exceeded the quotas without approval. The Commission found that the agreements infringed Article 101(1)[60] and could not be exempted under Article 101(3).[61] In addition, the Commission considered that the shipowners had infringed Article 102 because, as a result of the conference, they had presented themselves as a united front to shippers and, consequently, the position of the shipowners on the market for cargo between France and the African States had to be assessed collectively. Since the Committees had been set up by a group of shipowners covering virtually the entire market, the agreement resulted in the creation of a collective dominant position to their advantage. Their practices, which endeavoured to eliminate effective competition for non-Committee shipping lines, constituted an abuse of the dominant position within the meaning of Article 102(b) by limiting the supply of liner services available to shippers.[62]

Similarly, in both *CEWAL*[63] and *TACA*,[64] the Commission found that members of a liner conference were collectively dominant on certain shipping routes between ports in Northern Europe and Zaïre, and Northern Europe and the US/Canada respectively. In these cases the agreements enabled the undertakings to present a 'united front' to shippers. Although it does not seem that it was strictly necessary to use Article 102, since Article 101 was applicable (Article 102 would only have been vital had the agreement been block exempted under Article 3 of Regulation 4056/86), the cases fitted neatly within the GC's formulation in *Flat Glass*. The parties were undoubtedly united by 'economic links'. The GC in the *TACA* appeal held that these links (a tariff, enforcement provisions and penalties, a secretariat, and annual business plans of the TACA) were 'capable of justifying a collective assessment of the position on the relevant market of the members of that conference for the purposes of the application of Article [102] of the Treaty, in so far as those links are such as to allow

[57] [1992] OJ L134/1.

[58] [1993] OJ L34/20. The finding of collective dominance was upheld on appeal: Cases T-24/93 etc., *Compagnie Maritime Belge Transports SA v. Commission* [1996] ECR II-1201 and Cases C-395 and 396/96 P, *Compagnie Maritime Belge Transports SA v. Commission* [2000] ECR I-1365.

[59] *Transatlantic Conference Agreement* [1999] OJ L95/1, on appeal, Case T-191/98, *Atlantic Container Line AB v. Commission* [2003] ECR II-3275.

[60] The object and effect of the agreements was to share markets amongst the members and to limit the supply of transport services available, contrary to Art. 101(1)(c) and (b) respectively.

[61] Further, and because the objective of the agreements was not to fix common rates of the participants, it did not fall within the terms of the block exemption then in force dealing with 'liner conferences', Reg. 4056/86.

[62] Both the practice of imposing penalties on shipowners which had exceeded their quotas and the application of conditions protecting their own interests against those of newcomers wishing to serve the routes infringed Art. 102.

[63] [1993] OJ L34/20.

[64] [1999] OJ L95/1 finding that the TACA members held a collective dominant position on the relevant market and abused that collective dominant position between 1994 and 1996, first, by entering into an agreement to place restrictions on the availability and content of service contracts and secondly, by altering the competitive structure of the market so as to reinforce the TACA's dominant position. The finding of collective dominance was upheld on appeal but the finding of abuse and fines were annulled, see Cases T-191 and 214–216/98, *Atlantic Container Line AB v. Commission* [2003] ECR II-3275, but see the Commission's revised decision [2003] OJ L26/53.

them to adopt together, as a single entity which presents itself as such on the market vis-à-vis users and competitors, the same line of conduct on that market'.[65] In *Irish Sugar*[66] the Commission found Irish Sugar and one of its distributors to be collectively dominant. In this case the producer and the distributor were linked *vertically* by agreements and other factors (such as close management relationships) which created a clear parallelism of interest, such as a significant equity holding which Irish Sugar held in the distributor. The links between the companies were very strong, and only just failed to satisfy the criteria for being a single economic entity.[67]

In *Almelo* where the undertakings were all regional electricity distributors in the Netherlands the CJ said that a dominant position involved the undertakings being 'linked in such a way that they adopt the same conduct on the market'.[68] In this case the undertakings adopted uniform supply conditions drawn up by their trade association. The most significant statement of what constitutes a collective dominant position for the purposes of Article 102 was in *Compagnie Maritime Belge*,[69] the appeal from the *CEWAL* decision. There the CJ said that a collective dominant position could be held by undertakings which 'present themselves or act together on a particular market as a collective entity'.[70] That must be established by examining the economic links or factors which give rise to a connection between them.[71] It must then be decided whether that collective entity holds a dominant position.[72] As already explained, the undertakings involved in the CEWAL liner conference were linked by express agreements, but nevertheless the CJ said that the existence of an agreement or other links in law were not indispensable to a finding of collective dominance.[73] Because of the importance of this judgment in developing the application of collective dominance to the tacit collusion of oligopolists, and the fact that it drew upon the earlier CJ judgment in the merger case *France v. Commission*[74] the judgment is discussed in Chapter 9.

In the appeal from the *TACA* decision the GC stated that it was not a requirement for establishing the existence of a dominant position that the elimination of effective competition (which the GC had stipulated in the merger case *Airtours*)[75] must result in the elimination of *all* competition between the undertakings concerned.[76]

Sports organisations may hold a collective dominant position. In *Laurent Piau* the GC said that it was 'unrealistic' to claim that FIFA (the International Federation of Football Associations) could not be in a collective dominant position in respect of the market for players' agents' services. It was

---

[65] *Atlantic Container Lines AB v. Commission*, para. 602.

[66] [1997] OJ L25/1. The GC upheld the finding of collective dominance: Case T-228/97, *Irish Sugar plc v. Commission* [1999] ECR II-2969.

[67] See Chap. 3, Section 5.A.vi, p. 137 ff. 'The various terms used in the contested decision to describe the applicant's position on the market before February 1990 are the result of the special nature of its links with SDL before that date. The Commission claims to have established the existence of infringements of Article [102] of the Treaty from 1985 to February 1990 committed by the applicant alone, by SDL alone, or by both together. Having accepted the applicant's argument that it did not control the management of SDL, despite holding 51% of [SDL's] capital, the Commission decided that even if it was not possible to regard the applicant and SDL as a single economic entity, they had, together at least, held a dominant position on the market in question', Case T-228/97, *Irish Sugar plc v. Commission* [1999] ECR II-2969, para. 28.

[68] Case C-393/92, *Almelo v. NV Energiebedrijf Ijsselmij* [1994] ECR I-1477, para 42, see also Case C-140/94, *DIP v. Comune di Bassano del Grappa* [1995] ECR I-3257, para. 27.

[69] Cases C-395 and 396/96 P, *Compagnie Maritime Belge Transports SA v. Commission* [2000] ECR I-1365.

[70] Cases C-395 and 396/96 P, *Compagnie Maritime Belge Transports SA v. Commission* [2000] ECR I-1365, para. 36.

[71] Cases C-395 and 396/96 P, *Compagnie Maritime Belge Transports SA v. Commission* [2000] ECR I-1365, para. 41.

[72] Cases C-395 and 396/96 P, *Compagnie Maritime Belge Transports SA v. Commission* [2000] ECR I-1365, para. 39.

[73] Cases C-395 and 396/96 P, *Compagnie Maritime Belge Transports SA v. Commission* [2000] ECR I-1365, para. 45.

[74] Cases C-68/94 and 30/95, *France v. Commission* [1998] ECR I-1375.

[75] Case T-342/99, *Airtours plc v. Commission* [2002] ECR II-2585, para. 63.

[76] Cases T-191 and 212–214/98, *Atlantic Container Line v. EC Commission* [2003] ECR II-3275, para. 130.

irrelevant that FIFA was not itself an economic operator buying agents' services as it was the emanation of the national associations and the clubs, which did.[77]

There are also difficult cases where allegations of a collective dominant position arising from national legislation or regulation have been made. These have been rejected by the CJ, mainly on the grounds that the measures did not result in the undertakings concerned ceasing to compete with one another.[78]

B. A DOMINANT POSITION

The definition of a dominant position is set out in the case law of the CJ. Both the meaning of 'dominant position' and the way in which it is decided whether any particular undertaking holds such a position is considered in detail in Chapter 6.

C. A DOMINANT POSITION WITHIN A SUBSTANTIAL PART OF THE INTERNAL MARKET

(i) Purpose of the Requirement

The dominant position of the undertaking must be held within the internal market or within a substantial part of it. The purpose of this requirement is to exclude from the Article's scope purely localised monopoly situations in which there is no Union interest. Together with the necessity that the abuse of a dominant position has an effect on trade between Member States, the requirement determines the limit of the EU's jurisdiction.

(ii) Meaning of a Substantial Part of the Internal Market

A 'substantial part' does not simply mean substantial in geographic terms. It is not a matter of counting hectares. In *Suiker Unie* the CJ stated that:

[f]or the purpose of determining whether a specific territory is large enough to amount to a 'substantial part of the common market' within the meaning of Article [102 TFEU] the pattern and volume of the production and consumption of the said product as well as the habits and economic opportunities of vendors and purchasers must be considered.[79]

(iii) Relevance of Volume of Production

In *Suiker Unie* the CJ compared the volume of sugar production in Belgium, Luxembourg, and southern Germany to that of Community production overall. It held that each of those markets was a substantial part of the common market. The CJ has never specified whether there is a particular percentage of the EU market which could automatically be said to satisfy the 'substantial' criterion. However, Advocate-General Warner, in his Opinion in the *ABG Oil* case,[80] considered that the Dutch

---

[77] Case T-193/02, *Laurent Piau v. Commission* [2005] ECR II-209, paras. 112–116. This was a case, like *Atlantic Container Line*, discussed at n. 59 and accompanying text, where, although dealing with a situation where there were express agreements between the parties concerned, the GC made important statements which relate to tacit collusion and oligopolistic collective dominance.

[78] See Case C-96/94, *Centro Servizi Spediporto v. Spedizioni Marritima del Golfo* [1995] ECR I-2883, Case C-140/94, *DIP v. Comune di Bassano del Grappa* [1995] ECR I-3257, and Case C-70/95, *Sodemare v. Regione Lombardia* [1997] ECR I-3395.

[79] Cases 40–48, 50, 54–56, 111, 113, and 114/73, *Coöperatieve Vereniging 'Suiker Unie' UA v. Commission* [1975] ECR 1663, para. 371.

[80] Case 77/77, *Benzine en Petroleum Handelsmaatschappij BV v. Commission* [1978] ECR 1513.

petrol market, which was approximately 4.6 per cent of the overall Community (as it then was) market, was substantial. He stated that:

[t]here is...in my opinion, in this kind of field, a danger in focusing attention exclusively on percentages. The opposite of 'substantial' is 'negligible', and what may seem negligible when looked at in the terms of a percentage may seem otherwise when looked at in absolute terms. The population of Luxembourg is, I believe, about 0.23 per cent of the population of the whole Community. I would however shrink from saying that one who had a monopoly, or near monopoly, of the Luxembourg market for a particular product was exempt from the application of Article [102].[81]

(iv) A Member State is Likely to be a Substantial Part of the Internal Market

In a number of cases individual Member States have been held to be a 'substantial part'[82] of the internal market, as have parts of Member States.[83] As the EU is enlarged the concept of what is a 'substantial part' of it may alter, with previously substantial parts becoming more insignificant so that older cases on this point may no longer be a reliable guide. It is difficult to imagine, however, that a single Member State would be held not to constitute a substantial part of the internal market even in an EU of more than 28 Member States. It would be politically insensitive. This attitude is reflected in the opinion of Advocate-General Warner set out in Section 5.C.iii (although at the time there were only nine Member States). As the process of European integration proceeds, however, the delineation of geographic markets may become broader and it may become rarer for a position of dominance to be found to exist in a single Member State other than in the case of statutory monopoly.

(v) Transport Cases

What constitutes a 'substantial part' of the internal market may depend on the nature of the market in issue. For example, there have been a number of transport cases in which very small areas have been found to be substantial. In both *Sealink/B&I Holyhead: Interim Measures*[84] and *Sea Containers Ltd/Stena Sealink Ports*[85] Holyhead Harbour in Wales was held to be a substantial part of the common market. In the former case the Commission stated:

40....The port of Holyhead constitutes a substantial part of the Common Market because it is a port providing one of the main links between two member-States; more especially, it provides the direct link between Great Britain and the capital city of Ireland. It should also be noted that this is, at least for passengers and cars, the most popular ferry route between Ireland and Great Britain.

In *Port of Roscoff*[86] the Commission emphasised the importance that might be played by the catchment area served by the port.

---

[81] Case 77/77, *Benzine en Petroleum Handelsmaatschappij BV* v. *Commission* [1978] ECR 1513, 1537. The CJ held that the undertaking's conduct could not constitute an abuse and did not address the dominance issue.

[82] The UK was held to be a substantial part of the common market in Case 226/84, *British Leyland plc* v. *Commission* [1986] ECR 3263, as was Belgium in Case 127/73, *Belgische Radio en Televisie and Société belge des auteurs, compositeurs et editeurs* v. *SV SABAM and NV Fonior* [1974] ECR 313 and Case 26/75, *General Motors Continental NV* v. *Commission* [1975] ECR 1367.

[83] e.g., the south-east of England in Case 22/78, *Hugin Kassaregister AB and Hugin Cash Registers Ltd* v. *Commission* [1979] ECR 1869. A number of local markets in a Member State may be aggregated together to form a 'substantial part', as in Case C–323/93, *Société Civile Agricole du Centre d'Insémination de la Crespelle* v. *Coopérative d'Elevage et d'Insémination Artificielle du Département de la Mayenne* [1994] ECR I-5077, where there was a series of local statutory monopolies in bovine insemination services which together covered the whole of France. See also Case 30/87, *Bodson* v. *Pompes Funèbres des Régions Libérées* [1988] ECR 2479.

[84] [1992] 5 CMLR 255, Commission's *XXIInd Annual Report on Competition Policy* (Commission, 1992), point 219.

[85] [1994] OJ L15/8, [1995] 4 CMLR 84.

[86] Reported as *Irish Continental Group* v. *CCI Morlaix* [1995] 5 CMLR 177.

58. The market for the supply of port services does not exist in isolation. If there was no demand from consumers for transport services, there would be no demand for port services from ferry operators. The market for transport services between Ireland and Brittany must therefore be taken into account. The port services in Brittany are essential for the operation of ferry services between a Member State, Ireland, to which can be added part of another Member State, Northern Ireland (around five million inhabitants in total), and an important region of another Member State, Brittany (around three million inhabitants). These three regions form a substantial part of the common market. For Ireland, also, the port of Roscoff is an important entry point to the continent and the rest of the Community. It is already used by 25 per cent of ferry passengers between Ireland and France each year.

In *Merci Convenzionali* the CJ looked to the volume of traffic handled by the port of Genoa. After stressing its importance in relation to the overall volume of imports and exports by sea to and from Italy the Court held that the market 'may be regarded as constituting a substantial part of the common market'.[87] The Commission has also found the activities at the port of Rødby[88] and various airports to involve substantial parts of the internal market.[89]

The transport cases suggest, therefore, that, once it has been established that the routes or traffic concerned are significant in anything other than a purely domestic context, the 'substantial part' criterion will be satisfied.[90] Indeed, the full application of Article 102 to maritime and air transport would be impossible in the absence of such an interpretation.

D. ABUSE

As with 'dominant position' the meaning of 'abuse' is to be found in the case law of the CJ. This definition, and the issue of what conduct can amount to an abuse, is the subject of Chapter 7. However, a preliminary point to note is that a distinction is commonly made between 'exploitative' and 'exclusionary' abuses. An *exploitative* abuse is conduct whereby the dominant undertaking takes advantage of its market power to exploit its customers. An *exclusionary* abuse is conduct which impedes effective competition by excluding (foreclosing) competitors thereby indirectly prejudicing consumers.[91] The application of Article 102 has been mainly concerned with exclusionary abuses. The Commission Guidance Paper on enforcement priorities, discussed in Section 6.C, is concerned only with exclusionary abuses.

E. AN EFFECT ON TRADE BETWEEN MEMBER STATES

(i) General

Article 102 applies only if the abuse of a dominant position *appreciably* affects trade between Member States. As in the context of Article 101, this requirement marks the jurisdictional divide between EU and national law. The concept of an effect on trade is interpreted in the same way under the two Articles.[92] Thus an agreement or conduct will affect trade if it interferes with the

---

[87] Case C-179/90, *Merci Convenzionali Porto di Genova SpA v. Siderurgica Gabrielli SpA* [1991] ECR I-5889, para. 15; see also Case C-266/96, *Corsica Ferries France SA v. Gruppo Antichi Ormeggiatori del Porto di Genova Coop arl* [1998] ECR I-3949, para. 38.

[88] *Port of Rødby* [1994] OJ L55/52, [1994] 5 CMLR 457.

[89] e.g., *FAG-Flughafen Frankfurt/Main AG* [1998] OJ L72/30, [1998] 4 CMLR 779; *Alpha Flight Services/Aéroports de Paris* [1998] OJ L230/10, [1998] 5 CMLR 611; *Portuguese Airports* [1999] OJ L69/31, on appeal Case C-163/99, *Portugal v. Commission* [2001] ECR I-2613; *Ilmailulaitos/Luftfartsverket* [1999] OJ L69/24, [1999] 5 CMLR 90; *Spanish Airports* [2000] OJ L208/36, [2000] 5 CMLR 967.

[90] See Case 66/86, *Ahmed Saeed Flugreisen and Silver Line Reisebüro GmbH v. Zentrale zur Bekämpfung unlauteren Wettbewerbs eV* [1989] ECR 803; *British Midland v. Aer Lingus* [1992] OJ L96/34, [1993] 4 CMLR 596.

[91] This is a basic distinction. The complications over the categorisation of abuses are discussed in Chapter 7.

[92] See Chap. 3.

pattern of trade between Member States or if it interferes with the structure of competition on the internal market (even if there is no alteration to the flow of goods or services between Member States). The latter test is more commonly utilised in Article 102 cases and was first adopted by the Court in an Article 102 case, *Commercial Solvents*.[93] This approach is particularly germane to Article 102 cases in which abusive conduct might result in a competitor leaving the market, which was indeed the position in *Commercial Solvents*. Zoja, an Italian pharmaceutical company, claimed it was being driven out of the market for a certain type of anti-TB drug by the conduct of the dominant supplier of the necessary raw material. At the time (the early 1970s) there was an insignificant incidence of TB in the EEC and Zoja was principally manufacturing for export to the developing world.[94] The CJ said that whether or not there was trade between Member States in the drugs was immaterial:

33. The Community authorities must therefore consider all the consequences of the conduct complained of for the competitive structure in the Common Market without distinguishing between production intended for sale within the market and that intended for export. When an undertaking in a dominant position with[in] the Common Market abuses its position in such a way that a competitor in the Common Market is likely to be eliminated, it does not matter whether the conduct relates to the latter's exports or its trade within the Common Market, once it has been established that this elimination will have repercussions on the competitive structure within the Common Market.[95]

Hugin,[96] however, showed that not all abusive conduct in the internal market affects trade. This case concerned the supply of cash register spare parts by a Swedish undertaking to a servicing and repair firm in south-east England at a time prior to Sweden joining the EU. The servicing firm's activities were confined to the London area and there was no inter-State trade in the spare parts. The CJ quashed the Commission's decision on the ground that there was no effect on trade between Member States. The alteration in the competitive structure if the firm went out of business would not be felt outside one part of the UK. The CJ stated:

17.... The interpretation and application of the condition relating to effects on trade between Member States contained in Articles [101 and 102 TFEU] must be based on the purpose of that condition which is to define, in the context of the law governing competition, the boundary between the areas respectively covered by Community law and the law of the Member States. Thus Community law covers any agreement or any practice which is capable of constituting a threat to freedom of trade between Member States in a manner which might harm the attainment of the objectives of a single market between the Member States, in particular by partitioning the national markets or by affecting the structure of competition within the common market. On the other hand conduct the effects of which are confined to the territory of a single Member State is governed by the national legal order.

This case established, therefore, that before trade between Member States will be affected, the alteration in the competitive structure has to have some repercussion beyond the borders of a single Member State.

The meaning of an appreciable effect on inter-Member State trade for the purposes of Article 102 is now spelt out in the Commission Guidelines on the effect on trade concept which it adopted as part of the modernisation programme. The Guidelines explain how Article 102 applies where the dominant undertaking is pursuing several practices in an overall strategy not all of which have an effect on inter-Member State trade.

---

[93] Cases 6 and 7/73, *Istituto Chemioterapico Italiano SpA and Commercial Solvents Corp v. Commission* [1974] ECR 223.

[94] Sadly, there is now a high and increasing incidence of TB in the EU.

[95] *Commercial Solvents*, Cases 6 and 7/73, *Istituto Chemioterapico Italiano SpA and Commercial Solvents Corp v. Commission* [1974] ECR 223, para. 33.

[96] Case 22/78, *Hugin Kassaregister AB and Hugin Cash Registers Ltd v. Commission* [1979] ECR 1869.

> ## Commission Guidelines on the Effect of Trade Concept Contained in Articles 81 and 82 of the Treaty [2004] OJ C101/81
>
> 17. In the case of Article [102] it is the abuse that must affect trade between Member States. This does not imply, however, that each element of the behaviour must be assessed in isolation. Conduct that forms part of an overall strategy pursued by the dominant undertaking must be assessed in terms of its overall impact. Where a dominant undertaking adopts various practices in pursuit of the same aim, for instance practices that aim at eliminating or foreclosing competitors, in order for Article [102] to be applicable to all the practices forming part of this overall strategy, it is sufficient that at least one of these practices is capable of affecting trade between Member States.

The Guidelines then deal with four situations: abuse of a dominant position covering several Member States; abuse of a dominant position covering a single Member State; abuse of a dominant position covering only part of a Member State; and abuses involving trade with third countries or practices involving undertakings in third countries. The principles set out in the Notice are basically a summing-up of the case law.

(ii) Abuse of a Dominant Position Covering Several Member States

Not surprisingly, the Commission takes the view that both exclusionary and exploitative abuses in which a dominant undertaking engages in more than one Member State are normally by their very nature capable of affecting trade between Member States.[97]

(iii) Abuse of a Dominant Position Covering a Single Member State

Where an undertaking has a dominant position which covers the whole of a Member State the Guidelines distinguish between exclusionary and exploitative abuses. Where exclusionary abuses are concerned, trade between Member States is normally capable of being affected because the abuse will generally make it more difficult for competitors from other Member States to penetrate the market.[98] There are a number of cases that illustrate this.[99] An example is *Greek Lignite and Electricity Markets*[100] in which a State-owned electricity company in Greece had a near-monopoly of the exploitation rights of an important raw material. The Commission held that this situation discouraged potential entrants on to the market from exercising their right of establishment in Greece.[101] Also, exclusionary abuses may affect the competitive structure in a Member State in a way that affects inter-Member State trade. The Guidelines explain:

94. Exclusionary abuses that affect the competitive market structure inside a Member State, for instance by eliminating or threatening to eliminate a competitor, may also be capable of affecting trade between Member States. Where the undertaking that risks being eliminated only operates in a single Member State, the abuse will normally not affect trade between Member States. However, trade between Member States is capable of being affected where the targeted undertaking exports to or imports from other Member States... and where

---

[97] Guidelines on the effect on trade concept, paras. 73–76.

[98] Guidelines on the effect on trade concept, para. 93.

[99] e.g. Case 322/81, *NV Nederlandsche Banden-Industrie Michelin v. Commission* [1983] ECR 3461; Case T-65/89, *BPB Industries and British Gypsum* [1993] ECR II-389.

[100] COMP/38.700 *Greek Lignite and Electricity Markets* [2009] 4 CMLR 495, annulled on appeal on other grounds, Case T-169/08, *Dimosia Epicheirisi Ilektrismou AE (DEI) v. Commission*, 12 September 2012, on appeal C-554/12 P, *Commission v. DEI*, judgment pending; see further Chap. 8.

[101] COMP/38/700 *Greek Lignite and Electricity Markets* [2009] 4 CMLR 495, para. 244.

it also operates in other Member States... An effect on trade may arise from the dissuasive impact of the abuse on other competitors. If through repeated conduct the dominant undertaking has acquired a reputation for adopting exclusionary practices towards competitors that attempt to engage in direct competition, competitors from other Member States are likely to compete less aggressively, in which case trade may be affected, even if the victim in the case at hand is not from another Member State.

In the case of exploitative abuses, such as price discrimination and excessive pricing, if only domestic customers are affected there will normally be no inter-Member State trade effect. But the Guidelines explain how, nevertheless, there may be:

95. However, it may do so if the buyers are engaged in export activities and are disadvantaged by the discriminatory pricing or if this practice is used to prevent imports... Practices consisting of offering lower prices to customers that are the most likely to import products from other Member States may make it more difficult for competitors from other Member States to enter the market. In such cases trade between Member States is capable of being affected.

The Guidelines explain that once the undertaking's *dominant position* covers a whole Member State it will normally not matter whether the *abuse* affects only some of the territory or only some customers:

96. As long as an undertaking has a dominant position which covers the whole of a Member State it is normally immaterial whether the specific abuse engaged in by the dominant undertaking only covers part of its territory or affects certain buyers within the national territory. A dominant firm can significantly impede trade by engaging in abusive conduct in the areas or vis-à-vis the customers that are the most likely to be targeted by competitors from other Member States. For example, it may be the case that a particular channel of distribution constitutes a particularly important means of gaining access to broad categories of consumers. Hindering access to such channels can have a substantial impact on trade between Member States. In the assessment of appreciability it must also be taken into account that the very presence of the dominant undertaking covering the whole of a Member State is likely to make market penetration more difficult. Any abuse which makes it more difficult to enter the national market should therefore be considered to appreciably affect trade. The combination of the market position of the dominant undertaking and the anti-competitive nature of its conduct implies that such abuses have normally by their very nature an appreciable effect on trade. However, if the abuse is purely local in nature or involves only an insignificant share of the sales of the dominant undertaking within the Member State in question, trade may not be capable of being appreciably affected.

(iv) Abuse of a Dominant Position Covering only Part of a Member State

If a dominant position is held in only part of a Member State it will, of course, be a matter of whether that part is a 'substantial part of the internal market'. If so, then it is again a matter of deciding whether access by competitors from other Member States is made more difficult by the abuse. If it is, inter-Member State trade must normally be considered as being appreciably affected.[102] It should be remembered that a part of a Member State comprising only a port or airport is capable of being a substantial part of the internal market.[103]

(v) Abuses Involving Trade with Third Countries

Abuses involving trade outside the EU will be caught by Article 102 if they are implemented in the EU.[104] If the conduct relates to imports or exports to and from the EU there may be an effect on cross-border activity. Imports into one Member State may affect the conditions of competition

---

[102] Guidelines on the effect on trade concept, para. 90.

[103] Guidelines on the effect on trade concept, para. 91, and see Section 5.C.v, p. 282.

[104] See Chap. 16.

there, and this may have a knock-on effect in others.[105] Where the object is to restrict competition inside the EU the requisite effect on inter-Member State trade is more readily established than when it is predominantly to restrict competition outside it.[106] A more detailed analysis is necessary where the practice is not aimed at competition inside the EU, to identify exactly how, if at all, patterns of trade between Member States will be affected.[107] Thus, the conduct of liner conferences operating on routes between European ports and third countries was held to affect inter-Member State trade in that it obstructed the activities of competitors operating from ports in other Member States, limited the choice of services available to shippers in various Member States, and disturbed normal trade patterns in the common market.[108]

(vi) Regulation 1/2003, Article 3

The question of whether an effect on inter-Member State trade exists acquired an added significance after 1 May 2004. Regulation 1/2003, Article 3 provides that where an NCA applies national law to an abuse prohibited by Article 102 it *must* also apply Article 102. This means that if there is an effect on inter-Member State trade the NCA cannot deal with conduct which meets the other criteria of Article 102 by applying national law alone. On the other hand, it is important to note that Article 3(2) does allow stricter national laws to be applied to conduct which affects inter-Member State trade, i.e. national laws can be stricter or wider than Article 102. In the Commission's 2009 Report to the Parliament on the functioning of Regulation 1/2003, the Commission expressed reservations about Article 3(2) and a wish to re-examine it.[109] The judgment in *Tele2Polska*[110] to the effect that NCAs may not make findings that there has been no infringement of Article 102 reinforced the significance of the inter-Member State trade condition.

6. THE REVIEW OF ARTICLE 102

A. THE INAUGURATION OF THE REVIEW

In 2003 DG Comp initiated a major internal review of its policy on Article 102. The Commission had already reviewed its approach to Article 101 and mergers[111] and considered it time to look at Article 102. In particular this was thought desirable in the light of the modernisation reforms whereby under Regulation 1/2003 the NCAs have 'parallel competence' with the Commission to apply Article 102. The Commission considered that 'a policy which is clear on the substantive interpretation of the Article is essential to make the system work' and that a 'credible policy on abusive conduct must be compatible with mainstream economics'.[112] However, where the modernised, more economics-based approach to Article 101 was concerned the Court had been in the vanguard,

---

[105] Guidelines on the effect on trade concept, para. 101.

[106] Guidelines on the effect on trade concept, para. 103

[107] Guidelines on the effect on trade concept, paras. 106–109.

[108] So in *CEWAL* [1993] OJ L34/2, [1995] 5 CMLR 198, see Section 5.A.iii.d, p. 278, a liner conference operating between the North Sea ports and the coast of West Africa was held to have infringed Art. 102. The inter-Member State trade point was not appealed.

[109] Communication from the Commission to the European Parliament and the Council, Report on the Functioning of Regulation 1/2003 COM(2009) 206 final; Press Release IP/09/683, see further Chap. 13; Commission Staff Working Paper accompanying the Communication from the Commission to the European Parliament and the Council, Report on the Functioning of Regulation 1/2003 SEC(2009) 574 final, paras. 160–179.

[110] See n. 33.

[111] Culminating in the new Merger Regulation, Council Regulation 139/2004 [2004] OJ L24/1.

[112] Speech by the then Director-General of DG Comp, Philip Lowe, at Fordham Corporate Law Institute 30th Annual Conference on International Antitrust Law and Policy, 23 Oct. 2003, published by 2003 Fordham Corp L Inst (B. Hawk, ed. 2004), 163.

and the Commission was walking through an open door.[113] This was not so with regard to Article 102.[114] The fact that the Commission had been converted to a new approach to Article 102 did not mean that the EU Courts agreed.

During the review the Chief Economist of DG Comp commissioned a report from EAGCP, the Economic Advisory Group on Competition Policy, which was published in July 2005 (the 'EAGCP report').[115]

B. THE STAFF DISCUSSION PAPER

The review resulted in the publication in December 2005 of a DG Comp Staff Discussion Paper on the application of the Article to exclusionary abuses (the Discussion Paper).[116]

The Discussion Paper dealt only with the application of Article 102 to *exclusionary* abuses (defined as behaviour by a dominant undertaking which is likely to have a foreclosure effect on the market).[117] As already explained exclusionary abuses are the main focus of Article 102 enforcement.[118] The thrust of the Discussion Paper was to reorientate the application of Article 102 in exclusionary abuse cases to an 'effects-based' analysis. The Discussion Paper adopted the consumer welfare standard, stating that the objective of Article 102 with regard to exclusionary abuses was 'the protection of competition on the market as a means of enhancing consumer welfare and of ensuring an efficient allocation of resources'.[119]

The Discussion Paper worked with the definitions of dominance and abuse laid down in leading cases decades before[120] and repeated ever since, but in significant respects it took a different approach to that previously taken by the EU Courts.

The Discussion Paper was put out for public consultation and stimulated a lively, wide-ranging debate.[121] Broadly speaking the direction of the Discussion Paper was welcomed but there was much disagreement about the specific proposals and some concern as to how far undertakings would be faced with even less legal certainty about the behaviour prohibited to dominant undertakings.[122] The outcome of the consultation was widely expected to be the publication of guidelines similar to the guidelines on Article 101(3).[123] However, there was a major problem as to how any guidelines embodying a reform in the law could be reconciled with the case law unless the EU Courts themselves amended their approach.

---

[113] See Chap. 4.

[114] Exemplified by two GC judgments in 2003, Case T-203/01, *Manufacture Française des Pneumatiques Michelin v. Commission* [2003] ECR II- 4071 and Case T-219/99, *British Airways v. Commission* [2003] ECR II-5917, discussed in Chap. 7.

[115] For EAGCP, see Chap. 2. The EAGCP report is available at <http://ec.europa.eu/dgs/competition/economist/eagcp_july_21_05.pdf>.

[116] Brussels, December 2005, <http://ec.europa.eu//competition/antitrust/art82/discpaper2005.pdf>.

[117] Discussion Paper, para. 1.

[118] In Section 5.D, and see also Chap. 7. The Discussion Paper dealt specifically with only the main types of exclusionary abuses.

[119] Discussion Paper, para. 4.

[120] Case 6/72, *Europemballage Corp and Continental Can Co Inc* v. *Commission* [1973] ECR 215, and Case 85/76, *Hoffmann-La Roche & Co AG* v. *Commission* [1979] ECR 461.

[121] The Commission received more than 100 submissions in response which are available on the Commission's website, in a section dedicated to the review, <http://ec.europa.eu/competition/antitrust/art82/contributions. html>. The Commission held a public hearing on the topic in June 2006, which is also available on the website, <http://ec.europa.eu/competition/antitrust/art82/hearing.html>.

[122] '...the upswing is good but the downswing and the follow-through needs a lot of work' as the Director General said in Brussels, 14 June 2006, summing up the responses to the Discussion Paper.

[123] The Discussion Paper itself described its contents as '...possible principles for the Commission's application of Article 82...' (para. 1) and was written in a similar format to the Art. 101(3) Guidelines. The Director General said at the public hearing that the Commission was looking to take a decision about issuing draft Guidelines by the end of 2006.

C. THE GUIDANCE PAPER

(i) The Road to the Guidance Paper

Two months after the publication of the Discussion Paper, Advocate-General Kokott referred to the relationship between any new approach by the Commission to Article 102 and the case law of the Court. She said, in giving her opinion in the *British Airways* appeal:[124]

...it is immaterial how the Commission intends to define its competition policy with regard to Article [102 TFEU] *for the future*...Any reorientation in the application of Article [102] can be of relevance only for future decisions of the Commission, not for the legal assessment of a decision already taken. Moreover, even if its administrative practice were to change, the Commission would still have to act within the framework prescribed for it by Article [102] as interpreted by the Court of Justice.

The subsequent, and highly significant, judgment of the CJ in the case in March 2007 took a highly conservative approach to Article 102 including a treatment of rebates which was at odds with the effects-based analysis suggested by the Commission in the Discussion Paper.[125] The GC judgments in *Microsoft*[126] and *Deutsche Telekom*[127] were also largely formalistic.[128]

As one commentator remarked:[129]

Cynics might point out that the European courts' interpretation of Article [102] has been guided to a large extent by the Commission's historic approach, which was formalistic in nature. Subsequently, the Commission's creative leeway is restricted by its own historic analysis which was approved by the European courts. Having been embedded in the European case law, this structured analysis cannot easily be changed.

Indeed, the *British Airways* and *Deutsche Telekom* judgments were appeals from Commission decisions in 1999 and 2001 respectively in which the decisions were upheld. In *Microsoft*, however, the Commission had conducted an effects analysis and examined the consumer welfare aspects.[130]

Faced with the attitude of the EU Courts and the difficulty of drafting guidelines in an area so rife with disagreements even among those who believe in effects-based analysis and the consumer welfare objective, the Commission finally adopted in February 2009 not 'guidelines' but 'Guidance' on the Commission's *enforcement priorities* in applying Article 102 to abusive exclusionary conduct by dominant undertakings (the Guidance Paper).[131]

---

[124] Case C-95/04 P, *British Airways v. Commission* [2007] ECR I-2331 para. 28 of the Opinion of Kokott AG.

[125] Cf. Discussion Paper, paras. 134–176. The case is discussed in Chap. 7.

[126] Case T-201/04, *Microsoft v. Commission* [2007] ECR II-3601.

[127] Case T-271/03, *Deutsche Telekom v. Commission* [2008] ECR II-477, *aff'd* Case C-280/08 P, *Deutsche Telekom v. Commission* [2010] ECR I-9555.

[128] See also the CJ judgment in the *Glaxo Greece* case, Cases C-468–478/06, *Sot. Lélos kai Sia and others EE v. GlaxoSmithKline AEVE Farmakeftikon Proionton* [2008] ECR I-7139 which, although an Art. 102 case on refusal to supply, was outside the range of abusive conduct covered by the Discussion Paper. The only radical development in this period in the jurisprudence was the GC's judgment on the 'object' issue in the application of Art. 101 in *GlaxoSmithKline* against which, rather ironically in this context, the Commission appealed. The judgment was disapproved on this point by the CJ in Cases C-501, 513, 515, 519/06 P, *GlaxoSmithKline Services Unlimited v. Commission* [2009] ECR I-9291.

[129] A. Ezrachi, 'The Commission's Guidance on Article 82EC and the Effects Based Approach—Legal and Practical Challenges', in A. Ezrachi (ed.), *Article 82EC: Reflections on its Recent Evolution* (Hart Publishing, 2009), 51, 56. Or, as Hamlet put it, 'hoist with one's own petard'.

[130] COMP/C-3/37.792, *Microsoft* [2005] 4 CMLR 965, see Chap. 7.

[131] Guidance on the Commission's Enforcement Priorities in Applying Article 82 of the EC Treaty to Abusive Exclusionary Conduct by Dominant Undertakings [2009] OJ C45/2. The Guidance Paper was originally published on the Commission website in December 2008 but after minor amendments the final version appeared in the Official Journal on 9 February 2009. See generally P. Akman, 'The European Commission's Guidance on Article 102 TFEU: From *Inferno* to *Paradiso*?' (2010) 73 *MLR* 605; D. Geradin, 'Is the Guidance Paper on the Commission's Enforcement Priorities in Applying Article 102 TFEU to Abusive Exclusionary Conduct Useful?', available at <http://ssrn.com/abstract=1569502>.

(ii) The Content of the Guidance Paper

The Guidance Paper specifically states that it is not intended to be a statement of the law and that it is without prejudice to the interpretation of Article 102 by the EU Courts.[132] Rather, it sets out the *enforcement priorities* that will guide the Commission's action in applying Article 102 to exclusionary conduct by dominant undertakings.[133] So the Commission is laying out what kinds of conduct it considers egregious enough to warrant intervention. It therefore focuses on 'those types of conduct that are most harmful to consumers'.[134] It makes it clear that it is not concerned with protecting competitors but with protecting an effective competitive process because of the benefits that will deliver to consumers. In other words, the Commission is eschewing formalistic and 'ordoliberal' approaches to Article 102 and looking at effects on consumers.

Guidance on the Commission's Enforcement Priorities in Applying Article 82 of the EC Treaty to Abusive Exclusionary Conduct by Dominant Undertakings [2009] OJ C45/2

5. In applying Article [102] to exclusionary conduct by dominant undertakings, the Commission will focus on those types of conduct that are most harmful to consumers. Consumers benefit from competition through lower prices, better quality and a wider choice of new or improved goods and services. The Commission, therefore, will direct its enforcement to ensuring that markets function properly and that consumers benefit from the efficiency and productivity which result from effective competition between undertakings.

6. The emphasis of the Commission's enforcement activity in relation to exclusionary conduct is on safeguarding the competitive process in the internal market and ensuring that undertakings which hold a dominant position do not exclude their competitors by other means than competing on the merits of the products or services they provide. In doing so the Commission is mindful that what really matters is protecting an effective competitive process and not simply protecting competitors. This may well mean that competitors who deliver less to consumers in terms of price, choice, quality and innovation will leave the market.

The Commission says of the Guidance Paper on its website:

The Communication provides comprehensive guidance to stakeholders in particular the business community and competition law enforcers at national level on how the Commission uses an effects-based approach to establish its enforcement priorities under Article 102 in relation to exclusionary conduct.[135]

The Guidance Paper does not deal with exploitative abuses.[136] Nor does it deal with abuses by undertakings in a collective dominant position. It contains an introductory section setting out the purpose of the Guidance;[137] an explanation of its general approach to exclusionary conduct, including a short section on market power and dominance and a general section on price-based exclusionary

---

[132] Guidance Paper, para. 3.

[133] Guidance Paper, para. 2.

[134] Guidance Paper, para. 5.

[135] <http://ec.europa.eu/competition/antitrust/art82/index.html>. See also 'Frequently Asked Questions on Commission enforcement priorities in applying Article 82 to exclusionary conduct by dominant firms', MEMO/08/761.

[136] Guidance Paper, para. 7.

[137] Guidance Paper, paras. 1–8.

conduct;[138] and then a part applying that approach to specific forms of exclusionary conduct.[139] These are exclusive dealing, including conditional rebates; tying and bundling; predation; and some exclusionary refusals to supply, under which the Commission includes margin squeezes[140] but expressly does not cover, for example, refusals to supply to prevent parallel trade.[141]

Throughout the Guidance Paper the Commission sets out a general rule as to what will 'normally' be the situation but then leaves some 'wriggle room' by adding a proviso to cover other situations where it may wish to take enforcement action because of the particular circumstances of the case. It has thus retained a wide degree of administrative discretion. Inevitably this has been criticised as still leaving undertakings without sufficient legal certainty although the Guidance Paper says that its publication will 'help undertakings better assess whether certain behaviour is likely to result in intervention by the Commission'.[142]

The Commission's decision to issue a document on its enforcement priorities rather than fully fledged Guidelines met with a mixed response. It was said that:

In a world where the European Courts cling to old case law like castaways to a wreckage, guidelines for the Commission's enforcement priorities may be the best that can be achieved at present. The inability of the European Courts to provide intellectual leadership regarding the modernisation of these rules is all the more surprising as they have been at the forefront of modernisation in the areas of restrictive agreements and EC merger control.[143]

Needless to say the detailed provisions of the Guidance Paper have been subject to extensive analysis. The Guidance Paper is discussed further in Chapters 6 and 7.

(iii) The Effect of the Guidance Paper

As noted, the Guidance Paper cannot in any way affect the existing case law of the EU Courts.[144] Even Guidelines (if indeed there is a difference between Guidance and Guidelines) are rules of practice rather than rules of law.[145] No Guidelines or Guidance can change the law. The Guidance *could*, however, influence the way that the EU Courts approach the interpretation of Article 102.

Since the publication of the Guidance Paper the EU Courts have had to deal with appeals from Commission decisions taken before its publication. This fact has inevitably affected their approach to the arguments before them. In *Tomra*[146] the appellants argued that the Commission's treatment of rebates in the decision was not in line with the Guidance Paper.[147] The CJ said that the Guidance Paper 'has no relevance to the legal assessment of a decision, such as the contested decision, which

---

[138] Guidance Paper, paras. 9–31.

[139] Guidance Paper, paras. 32–90.

[140] But see now Case C-280/08 P, *Deutsche Telekom v.Commission* [2010] ECR I-9555.

[141] Guidance Paper, para. 77. This means that it does not deal with the situation in Cases C-468–478/06,*Sot. Lélos kai Sia and others EE* v. *GlaxoSmithKline AEVE Farmakeftikon Proionton* [2008] ECR I-7139.

[142] Guidance Paper, para. 2.

[143] Linklaters Press Release, 2 December 2008.

[144] See L. Lovdahl Gormesen, 'Why the European Commission's Enforcement Priorities on Article 82 Should Be Withdrawn' [2010]*ECLR* 45 for a trenchant argument that the Commission should not try to change the law by this means.

[145] Cases C-189/02P, 202/02P, 208/02P and 213/02P, *Dansk Rørindustri A/S and others* v. *Commission* [2005] ECR I-5425, para. 209. See Chap. 2 for the status of Notices (including Guidelines).

[146] Case C-549/10 P, *Tomra Systems* v. *Commission* [2012] ECR I-000, 19 April 2012. Case C-280/08 P, *Deutsche Telekom* v. *Commission* [2010] ECR I-9555 was another judgment where the CJ affirmed the upholding by the GC of a controversial pre-Guidance Paper decision, Case T-271/03, *Deutsche Telekom* v. *Commission* [2008] ECR II-477.

[147] In that the Commission did not determine the minimum viability threshold necessary to operate on the market and whether the part of the demand tied by Tomra's practices was large enough to have exclusionary effects on competitors, and did not examine whether Tomra's prices were below its costs, see Chap. 7, Section 10.D, p. 478 ff.

was adopted in 2006', leaving open the position of a decision published subsequently to it. In her Opinion in *Solvay* AG Kokott had made the same point about pre-Guidance decisions, but added, 'What is more, even if its administrative practice were to change, the Commission would still have to act within the framework prescribed for it by the Treaties as interpreted by the Court of Justice'.[148]

In the Article 267 reference *TeliaSonera* AG Mazák described the Guidance Paper as 'a useful point of reference'[149] and took a view on margin squeeze and refusal to supply which was in line with that of the Commission in the Guidance Paper. The CJ, however, did not take that view, and disagreed with the Advocate-General. The CJ held in effect, contrary to the Guidance Paper but without referring to it, that margin squeeze is a separate abuse from refusal to supply.[150] However, one should not conclude from this that the EU Courts are not influenced by the Guidance Paper. The judgments since its publication show a marked tendency to incorporate the principles in the Guidance Paper such as the as efficient competitor standard and more emphasis on effects. Of particular significance in this regard is the ruling in *Post Danmark*,[151] which applied the as efficient competitor standard and the use of the incremental cost standard in predatory pricing, formulated an efficiencies defence in line with that in the Guidance Paper, and generally took a robust and economically literate attitude to the application of Article 102. Although the EU Courts have not adopted the consumer welfare standard as the sole objective of Article 102 the post-Guidance Paper judgments do put the effects on consumers at the centre of the analysis, as shown in the cases discussed in Chapter 7.

Undertakings will obviously look at the Guidance Paper for enlightenment as to what conduct the Commission considers an infringement of Article 102 worth pursuing because of its impact on consumers, despite the declaration that it is not a statement of the law. However, the degree to which the Guidance Paper is riddled with caveats and exceptions will make it difficult for an undertaking to mount a challenge to action by the Commission on the ground that it has breached legitimate expectations. Moreover, *Treuhand*[152] has made it clear that legitimate expectations cannot hinder the Commission's duty to enforce the competition rules. As one commentator said:[153]

The announcement that Commission intervention against certain practices will be an enforcement priority cannot be taken as an indication of the lawfulness of other behaviour that breaches art.[102] according to settled case law. A dominant company cannot invoke a right to equal treatment to complain that the Commission did not keep its promise to focus its resources on pursuing somebody else's exclusionary abuses.

The Guidance does not assure companies that their infringing conduct will go unpunished if it does not fall under the new enforcement priorities. Therefore, it cannot give rise to legitimate expectations.

Article 102 is directly applicable and may be enforced in national courts, and the Commission is currently actively encouraging more private enforcement of the competition rules.[154] The national courts are bound by the case law and must look to that rather than to Notices from the Commission.[155]

---

[148] Case C-109/10 P, *Solvay SA* v. *European Commission* [2011] ECR I-000, 25 October 2011, para. 21 of the Opinion (the CJ set aside the GC judgment and annulled the Commission decision on procedural grounds). The AG had earlier made the same point in respect of the Commission's review of Article 102 in para. 28 of her Opinion in Case C-95/04 *British Airways* v. *EC Commission* [2007] ECR I-2331.

[149] Case C-52/09, *Konkurrensverket* v. *TeliaSonera Sverige AB* [2011] ECR I-527, fn 21 of the Opinion.

[150] See the discussion of the case in Chap. 7, Section 9, p. 426 ff.

[151] Case C-209/10, *Post Danmark A/S* v. *Konkurrencerådet*, 27 March 2012; and see E. Rousseva and M. Marquis, 'Hell Freezes Over: A Climate Change for Assessing Exclusionary Conduct under Article 102 TFEU' (2012) 4 *J'nl of European Competition Law and Practice* 32.

[152] Case T-99/04, *AC-Treuhand AG* v. *Commission* [2008] ECR II-1501, para. 163.

[153] M. Kellerbauer, 'The Commission's New Enforcement Priorities in Applying Article 82EC to Dominant Companies' Exclusionary Conduct: A Shift Towards a More Economic Approach?' [2010] *ECLR* 175, 185 (the author is a member of the Commission Legal Service but was writing in a personal capacity).

[154] See Chap. 14.

[155] In accordance with the relationship of the EU Courts with the national courts in the Member States, see, e.g., D. Chalmers, G. Davies, and G. Monti, *European Union Law* (2nd edn, Cambridge University Press, 2010), Chap. 4.

NCAs must also follow the case law and should they not do so would be liable to be overturned by their national courts applying the case law. NCAs may, however, be influenced by the Commission in the cases that they prioritise for enforcement (they may find the Guidance Paper inspiring although not binding) and some NCAs already apply an effects-based analysis to cases under both Article 102 and their domestic equivalents.[156]

As for the Commission itself, it can simply refrain from bringing cases where there is no consumer harm according to its consumer welfare/effects approach. Such inactivity could be challenged by a disgruntled complainant but the GC established in the leading *Automec* case that the Commission is entitled to set its own priorities.[157] Its approach to the enforcement of Article 102 in the light of the principles set out in the Guidance Paper is shown in the *Intel* decision discussed in Chapter 7.[158] The Commission is perfectly aware that it is bound by the case law and that if it applied some different interpretation of Article 102 in a case which it *did* bring then it would be challenged on appeal. However, it is possible that given the 'light touch' judicial review which the GC usually applies in Article 102 cases the Commission might be able to subtly move matters along because of the reluctance of the Court to interfere with its 'complex economic assessments'.[159]

In conclusion, the path to modernising what has been called 'the last of the steam-powered trains'[160] is not straightforward. Ultimately, the Commission needs the EU Courts on board if the steam-powered train is to be transformed into the TGV.

7. THE RELATIONSHIP BETWEEN ARTICLE 102 AND ARTICLE 101

Articles 101 and 102 are not mutually exclusive. In *Hoffmann-La Roche*[161] the CJ confirmed that both Articles 101 and 102 may apply to the same contractual arrangements. When dealing with an exclusive requirements contract concluded by a dominant undertaking the Commission was, therefore, at liberty to proceed under either Article 101 or Article 102. The CJ held that:

the question might be asked whether the conduct in question does not fall within Article [101] and possibly within its paragraph (3) thereof. However, the fact that agreements of this kind might fall within Article [101] and in particular within paragraph (3) thereof does not preclude the application of Article [102], since this latter article is expressly aimed in fact at situations which clearly originate in contractual relations so that in such cases the Commission is entitled, taking into account the nature of the reciprocal undertakings entered into and to the competitive position of the various contracting parties on the market or markets in which they operate to proceed on the basis of Article [101] or Article [102].[162]

---

[156] Discussion between representatives of NCAs at the GCR Conference on Dominance and Unilateral Conduct, Brussels, 9 February 2010.

[157] Case T-24/90, *Automec Srl v. Commission (Automec II)* [1992] ECR II-2223. However, the discretion of the Commission is not unlimited: see Case T-427/08, *Confédération européenne des associations d'horlogers-réparateurs (CEAHR) v. Commission* [2010] ECR II-5865, Chap. 13, Section 13.F, p. 1075, for a case in which the GC annulled the Commission's decision not to pursue a complaint because the Commission had not adequately assessed the matter. For a full discussion of this matter, see W. Wils, 'Discretion and Prioritisation in Public Antitrust Enforcement' (2011) 34(3) *World Competition* 353.

[158] Case COMP/C-3/37.990, *Intel* [2010] 4 CMLR 314, see Chap. 7.

[159] See Chap. 13, Section 9.A.vi, p. 1036 ff.

[160] B. Sher, 'The Last of the Steam-Powered Trains: Modernising Article 82' [2004] *ECLR* 243.

[161] Case 85/76, *Hoffmann-La Roche & Co AG v. Commission* [1979] ECR 461. See also Cases C-395 and 396/96 P, *Compagnie Maritime Belge Transports SA v. EC Commission* [2000] ECR I-1365, para. 33.

[162] Case 85/76, *Hoffmann-La Roche & Co AG v.Commission* [1979] ECR 461, para. 116.

The fact that Article 101 and Article 102 can be applied to the same agreements or practices is a powerful argument for aligning the approach to the two provisions.[163] One situation to be considered is that of dominant firms and block exemptions.[164] An agreement concluded by a dominant undertaking may benefit from a block exemption which does not restrict its ambit to undertakings with market shares below a specified threshold. Such block exemptions are, in fact, an increasingly rare phenomenon as the current trend is for block exemptions to contain thresholds.[165] However, where the agreement does qualify under a block exemption the Commission has power to withdraw the benefit of the exemption in particular cases.[166] It is possible, nonetheless, that even prior to the benefit of the block exemption being withdrawn a dominant undertaking may be found to have committed an abuse of a dominant position.

In *Tetra Pak I*[167] the Commission found that Tetra Pak had committed an abuse of a dominant position when it acquired an undertaking which held an exclusive patent licence. That patent licence was exempted under a block exemption. The GC confirmed that an undertaking could commit an abuse of a dominant position by operating an agreement which was exempted under a block exemption even if the benefit of the block exemption had not been withdrawn. Otherwise an exemption under Article 101(3) would also operate as an exemption from Article 102.

When Regulation 17 was in force and individual exemptions were possible the Commission was in practice unlikely to grant a dominant undertaking an individual exemption in respect of an agreement the operation of which was likely to constitute an abuse of a dominant position. It was likely to take these aspects into account before granting an exemption.[168] Under Regulation 1/2003 there are no individual exemptions. The Notice on the application of Article 101(3) states that the concept of the elimination of competition in respect of a substantial part of the products in question, which precludes the exemption of an agreement from the Article 101(1) prohibition, is an 'autonomous Community law concept specific to Article 101(3)'.[169] The Notice makes it clear that Article 101(3) cannot be applied to permit an agreement that constitutes an *abuse* of a dominant position.[170] Not all restrictive agreements entered into by dominant firms will, however, constitute an abuse. The Notice gives the example of a dominant firm's participation in a non-full-function joint venture.

It has been cogently argued that it would be preferable if only Article 101 were applied to the vertical arrangements of dominant undertakings, leaving Article 102 to deal with abusive unilateral conduct that cannot be caught by Article 101.[171] One complication which arises with the applicability of both Articles to the same conduct is the difference in the position as regards the burden of proof.[172]

---

[163] See, e.g., *Van den Bergh (Irish Ice Cream)* [1998] OJ L246/1, [1998] 5 CMLR 539, and the subsequent appeals, and exclusive dealing generally, Chap. 7, Section 10.

[164] For block exemptions generally see Chap. 4.

[165] Such as Reg. 330/2010 [2010] OJ L102/1 on vertical agreements; Reg. 1217/2010 on research and development agreements [2010] OJ L335/36; and Reg. 1218/2010 on specialisation agreements [2010] OJ L335/43.

[166] Reg. 1/2003, Art. 29, and provisions in the particular exemption regulations. In certain circumstances Member States may also withdraw the benefit of a block exemption with respect to their territory.

[167] [1988] OJ L272/27, [1990] 4 CMLR 47.

[168] Under Art. 8(3), Reg. 17 [1959–1962] OJ Spec. Ed. 87, an individual decision could be revoked, inter alia, where it was based on incorrect information or induced by deceit, or where the facts basic to the decision had changed.

[169] [2004] OJ C101/97, para. 106.

[170] Notice on the application of Article 101(3), para. 106; see Case T-395/94, *Atlantic Container Line v.Commission* [2002] ECR II-875, para. 330.

[171] See E. Rousseva, 'Modernising by Eradicating: How the Commission's New Approach to Article 81 EC Dispenses with the Need to Apply Article 82 to Vertical Restraints' (2005) 42 *CMLRev* 587; E. Rousseva, *Rethinking Exclusionary Abuses in EU Competition Law* (Hart Publishing, 2010), 460–473.

[172] See also I. Lianos, 'Categorical Thinking in Competition Law and the "Effects-based Approach" in Article 82', in A. Ezrachi (ed.), *Article 82EC: Reflections on its Recent Evolution* (Hart Publishing, 2009), 19, 26–30.

The relationship between Article 101 and Article 102 is also relevant in the context of undertakings found to be 'collectively dominant' for the purposes of Article 102.[173] Both Article 101 and Article 102 may apply to the conduct of such undertakings. It is possible that the agreement between the parties will infringe Article 101 and that the behaviour conducted in consequence of the agreement will amount to an abuse of a collective dominant position. Moreover, the collective dominant position may arise from agreements between the parties.

8. CONCLUSIONS

1. Article 102 is a powerful regulatory tool. However, its application has suffered from a lack of a proper theoretical framework and from confused policy goals. Protecting competitors for their own sake can lead to consumer detriment by penalising efficient pro-competitive conduct. Even protecting competitors in order to protect competition has often been done without sufficient analysis of the real impact on consumers. It is argued that there is a danger of too many 'false positive' errors, i.e. over-enforcement which chills competition and harms consumers.

2. The general consensus between economists and lawyers at present is that Article 102 should be applied only to enhance consumer welfare and efficiency and that this should be done by taking a rigorous 'effects-based' approach to the analysis, rather than prohibiting behaviour on the basis of the form it takes. This is the policy adopted in the Commission Guidance Paper on enforcement priorities in respect of exclusionary abuses.

3. This approach to Article 102 does not sit altogether comfortably with the case law of the EU Courts. The effect of the Guidance Paper is uncertain but it appears that the principles set out there are proving influential.

9. FURTHER READING

A. BOOKS

AKMAN, P., *The Concept of Abuse in EU Competition Law* (Hart Publishing, 2012), Chap. 2

FAULL, J., and NIKPAY, A, *The EC Law of Competition* (2nd edn, Oxford University Press, 2007), Chap. 4

JOLIET, R., *Monopolization and Abuse of Dominant Position* (Nijhoff, 1970)

NAZZINI, R., *The Foundations of European Union Competition Law, The Objectives and Principles of Article 102* (Oxford University Press, 2011), Chaps. 4 and 11

O'DONOGHUE, R., and PADILLA, A. J., *The Law and Economics of Article 102* (2nd edn, Hart Publishing, 2013), Chaps. 1 and 2

ORTIZ BLANCO, L., *Market Power in EU Antitrust Law* (Hart Publishing, 2012), Chap.10

ROUSSEVA, E., *Rethinking Exclusionary Abuses in EU Competition Law* (Hart Publishing, 2010), Chap. 1

B. CHAPTERS IN BOOKS

LIANOS, I., 'Categorical Thinking in Competition Law and the Effects-based Approach in Article 82', in

A. Ezrachi (ed.), *Article 82EC: Reflections on its Recent Evolution* (Hart Publishing, 2009), 19

C. ARTICLES

AKMAN, P., 'The European Commission's Guidance on Article 102 TFEU: From *Inferno* to *Paradiso*' (2010) 73 MLR 605

ALLAN, B., 'Article 102: A Commentary on DG Competition's Discussion Paper' [2006] *Competition Policy International* 43

---

[173] See Section 5.A.iii, p. 276.

KELLERBAUER, M., 'The Commission's New Enforcement Priorities in Applying Article 82 EC to Dominant Companies' Exclusionary Conduct: A Shift Towards a More Economic Approach?' [2010] ECLR 175

KROES, NEELIE, 'Tackling Exclusionary Practices to Avoid Exploitation of Market Power: Some Preliminary Thoughts on the Policy Review of Article 82', in B. Hawk (ed.), 2005 Fordham Corp L Inst. (2006), 381

LOVDAHL GORMESEN, L., 'Why the European Commission's Enforcement Priorities on Article 82 Should Be Withdrawn' [2010] ECLR 45

MONTI, G., 'The Scope of Collective Dominance Under Article 82 EC' (2001) 38 CMLRev 131

NAZZINI, R., 'The Wood Began to Move: An Essay on Consumer Welfare, Evidence and Burden of Proof in Article 82 EC Cases' (2006) 31 ELRev 518

SHER, B., 'The Last of the Steam-Powered Trains: Modernising Article 82' [2004] ECLR 243

6

ARTICLE 102 TFEU: DOMINANT POSITION

1. CENTRAL ISSUES

1. A 'dominant position' was defined by the CJ in *Hoffmann-La Roche* and *United Brands* in terms of an undertaking's independence and ability to prevent effective competition. Article 102 can only apply to undertakings which, singly or collectively, are in such a position.

2. Dominance can be measured 'directly' or 'indirectly'. EU law measures it 'indirectly' for the purposes of Article 102 by defining the market and then assessing the undertaking's degree of market power on that market.

3. Historically, the market has been defined in Article 102 cases by employing qualitative factors such as characteristics and intended use. The Commission now advocates the use of quantitative techniques such as the small but significant non-transitory increase in price (SSNIP) test.

4. Once the market is defined, the case law places heavy reliance on market shares in order to assess the degree of market power.

5. The case law establishes that once an undertaking has 50 per cent of the market there is a presumption that it is dominant.

6. Barriers to entry (and expansion) are also taken into account and the lower the market share, the greater the importance that is attached to them. A wide range of barriers to entry and other factors indicating dominance have been taken into account in the cases.

7. The cases do not establish a figure below which an undertaking cannot be found dominant.

8. In the Guidance Paper on the Commission's enforcement priorities in applying Article 102 to exclusionary abuses the Commission states that market shares are a 'useful first indication' of the market structure and the relative importance of the undertakings active on it. The Commission maintains the position that undertakings with market shares below 40 per cent could be considered dominant. The Guidance Paper does not establish a 'safe harbour'.

9. It is often argued that the traditional way of assessing dominance is particularly unsuitable in new economy markets.

2. INTRODUCTION

As explained in Chapter 5, Article 102 only applies to undertakings in a dominant position. Whether or not an undertaking holds a 'dominant position' is therefore of central importance to Article 102.[1] Clearly the phrase is not intended only to refer to a complete monopolist (the sole undertaking on a relevant

---

[1] The concept of a 'dominant position' is also a term employed in the EU Merger Regulation (Council Reg. 139/2004 [2004] OJ L24/1, see Chap. 15). When the Merger Regulation was being amended in the mid-2000s it was proposed to decouple the definition of dominance under the Regulation from that employed for the purposes of Art. 102 (Commission proposal for a Council Regulation on the control of concentrations between undertakings, [2003] OJ C20/4, Art. 2(2) and recitals 55–57) but ultimately that was not done. It appears, therefore, that the concept remains the same under both provisions. It is important to note, however, that the concept is 'necessarily applied from two different perspectives' (J. Faull and A. Nikpay (eds.), *The EC Law of Competition* (2nd edn, Oxford University Press, 2007), para. 4.40) because a prospective rather than retrospective a prospective analysis is usually necessary for the purposes of merger control.

market). It is intended also to encompass undertakings which have a certain degree of market power.[2] The difficulty is to determine what degree of market power is necessary before Article 102 applies.

Perfect competition is rarely encountered outside textbooks; almost all firms have some market power, though most have very little. Accordingly, the relevant question in antitrust cases is not whether market power is present, but whether it is important.[3]

An initial problem in respect of Article 102 is therefore to identify with sufficient clarity the point at which an undertaking becomes, and can know it becomes, dominant and so potentially subject to the prohibition. This will be at some point on the spectrum of market power. As we saw in Chapter 1, economists describe as substantial market power (SMP) the ability of a firm to raise prices above the competitive level without attracting new entrants and losing sales to competitors so rapidly that the price increase is unprofitable and must be rescinded.[4] The power to exclude competitors may also be significant. In US law, monopoly power for the purposes of section 2 of the Sherman Act has been defined as 'the power to control prices or to exclude competition'.[5] However, non-dominant firms can also exclude competitors from the market, by virtue of better products and lower prices, etc.[6] and so such ability does not necessarily denote dominance.[7] Nevertheless, exclusion may be a *means* by which market power is maintained and the significance of the power to exclude is discussed in the extract from Bishop and Walker reproduced in Chapter 1.[8]

The definition of the term 'dominant position' in EU law should relate to the adverse consequences which result when an undertaking has market power. The traditional objection to an undertaking with market power is its inefficiency. Allocative inefficiency results from its ability to limit output and increase price, and productive inefficiency is likely to result from the ability to lead a quiet life. These problems will not arise if consumers have an alternative choice of products/services or suppliers. The increase in price or poor quality of the product or service will prompt consumers to look elsewhere. An undertaking should be found to be dominant, therefore, only if it is in a position which enables it to harm competition.[9]

3. THE DEFINITION OF A DOMINANT POSITION

A. THE DEFINITION OF A DOMINANT POSITION IN THE CASE LAW

Rather than focusing on power over price, the Court of Justice (CJ) has defined dominance in terms of an undertaking's 'economic strength' and its ability to act independently on the market.

---

[2] Although the words 'monopoly' and 'monopolist' are sometimes used as a shorthand to cover both situations.

[3] R. Schmalensee, 'Another Look at Market Power' (1981–1982) 95 *Harvard LR* 1789, 1790.

[4] See W. Landes and R. Posner, 'Market Power in Antitrust Cases' (1980–1981) 94 *Harvard LR* 937, and Chap. 1.

[5] See *Standard Oil Co of New Jersey v. United States*, 221 US 1 (1911); *United States v. E I du Pont de Nemours & Co*, 351 US 377 (1956); *United States v. Grinnell Corp*, 384 US 563 (1966).

[6] What in the context of Art. 102 is called 'competition on the merits', see Chap. 7.

[7] D. Geradin, A. Layne-Farrar, and N. Petit, *EU Competition Law and Economics* (Oxford University Press, 2012), 4.57.

[8] S. Bishop and M. Walker, *The Economics of EC Competition Law* (3rd edn, Sweet and Maxwell, 2010), 3-041, see Chap. 1, Section 10.A, p. 59.

[9] See further the argument in R. Nazzini, *The Foundations of European Union Competition Law, The Objectives and Principles of Article 102* (Oxford University Press, 2011), 335–342.

In *United Brands* the CJ said that an undertaking would hold a dominant position where it could prevent effective competition being maintained by virtue of its ability to behave independently of the usual competitive constraints facing an entity operating on a market.[10]

Case 27/76, *United Brands* v. *Commission* [1978] ECR 207

Court of Justice

65. The dominant position referred to in this Article relates to a position of economic strength enjoyed by an undertaking which enables it to prevent effective competition being maintained on the relevant market by giving it the power to behave to an appreciable extent independently of its competitors, customers and ultimately of its consumers.

66. In general a dominant position derives from a combination of several factors which, taken separately, are not necessarily determinative.

In *Hoffmann-La Roche* in 1979 the CJ elaborated on this definition. It emphasised that a position of dominance did not preclude some competition and particularly focused on the ability of the undertaking to influence the conditions of competition occurring on the market.

Case 85/76, *Hoffmann-La Roche & Co AG* v. *Commission* [1979] ECR 461, paras. 38–39

Court of Justice

38. The dominant position thus referred to relates to a position of economic strength enjoyed by an undertaking which enables it to prevent effective competition being maintained on the relevant market by affording it the power to behave to an appreciable extent independently of its competitors, its customers and ultimately of its consumers.

39. Such a position does not preclude some competition, which it does where there is a monopoly or quasi-monopoly, but enables the undertaking which profits by it, if not to determine, at least to have an appreciable influence on the conditions under which that competition will develop, and in any case to act largely in disregard of it so long as such conduct does not operate to its detriment.

The definition of dominance in *United Brands* and *Hoffmann-La Roche* has become settled case law.[11]

---

[10] See also *Re Continental Can Co Inc* [1972] JO L7/25, [1972] CMLR D11, para. 3, where the Commission described dominance in terms of independence and power over price. On appeal, Case 6/72, *Europemballage Corp and Continental Can Co Inc* v. *Commission* [1973] ECR 215, the CJ did not expressly comment on the Commission's formulation of dominance, but it was approved by Roemer AG at [1973] ECR 215, 257 and implicitly by the Court.

[11] See recently Case C-52/09, *Konkurrensverket* v. *TeliaSonera Sverige AB* [2011] ECR I-527, para. 23, Case C-457/10 P, *AstraZeneca AB and AstraZeneca plc* v. *Commission*, 6 December 2012, para. 175. See also the merger case, Case T-210/01, *General Electric* v. *Commission* [2005] ECR II-5575, para. 117, where the GC expressed it thus: 'However, even the existence of lively competition on a particular market does not rule out the possibility that there is a dominant position on that market, since the predominant feature of such a position is the ability of the undertaking concerned to act without having to take account of this competition in its market strategy and without for that reason suffering detrimental effects from such behaviour (*Hoffmann-La Roche* v *Commission*, paragraph 70, and Case 27/76 *United Brands* v *Commission*...). Thus, the fact that there may be competition on the market is indeed among the relevant factors for the purposes of ascertaining whether a dominant position exists, but it is not in itself a decisive factor in that regard'.

The definition presupposes a dominant *supplier*. However, it is clear that the dominant position may be on the buying, rather than the selling side. In that case the issue will be one of the independence of the undertaking from its suppliers. *British Airways v. Commission*, for example, concerned the position of BA as a dominant buyer of air travel agency services.[12]

The formulation of dominance in *Hoffmann-La* Roche is problematic. The CJ test uses a concept of 'independence' which is more nebulous than power over price and, particularly as the independence has to exist only 'to an appreciable extent' and is compatible with continuing competition on the market, it brings inherent uncertainty to the operation of Article 102. Commentators have questioned whether the reference both to the ability of the undertaking to impede effective competition—which implies the power to exclude competitors—and to behave independently are two separate elements.[13] It is observed, however, that in subsequent case law the EU Courts 'have never drawn any distinction between them'.[14]

In the following passage two economists argue that the 'act independently' criterion is inherently flawed and cannot distinguish satisfactorily between dominant and non-dominant firms. Note that they refer to the 'cellophane fallacy' problem, discussed in Chapter 1, in identifying the competitive price level.[15]

J. P. Azevedo and M. Walker, 'Dominance: Meaning and Measurement' [2002] *ECLR* 363, 364

Acting independently of consumers and customers

Our first criticism of the definition is that no successful firm anywhere can act to an appreciable extent independently of its consumers. This is because of what economists refer to as the discipline of the demand curve. Firms typically face downward sloping demand curves, indicating that the lower the price of their product, the more of it they sell. Conversely, if a firm raises its price, it will sell less. It is not open to the firm to raise prices and sell the same quantity as before. The demand curve facing a firm constrains its behaviour. If a firm raises its price, it has to accept that it will sell fewer units of its product. This is true of a dominant firm just as much as it is true of a non-dominant firm. One response to this might be to say that what the ECJ really meant was that a dominant firm can profitably raise prices higher than a non-dominant firm. This may well be true (see below), but it is important to note that this possibility is not dependent so much on the behaviour of consumers as on the existence and behaviour of competitors. A firm that faces many competitors will find it harder to raise prices profitably than a firm that faces no, or only weak, competitors. An example of this situation would be a cigarette manufacturer that knows that its consumers will not readily substitute cigarettes for other goods if the price of cigarettes is increased. We can say that it faces a very *inelastic* market demand. However, because it faces strong competition from other cigarette manufacturers, this firm will not be able to significantly raise its price without losing sales to a close competitor. It is clear that what constrains the firm in this case is not consumers (the shape of the demand curve) but rather its competitors.

So it appears that trying to define dominance with respect to the ability of a firm to behave to an appreciable extent independently of its consumers will not distinguish adequately between dominant and non-dominant firms.

---

[12] Case C-95/04 P, *British Airways v. Commission* [2007] ECR I-2331. See also, e.g., *Re Eurofirma* [1973] CMLR D217; Case 298/83, *CICCE v. Commission* [1985] ECR 1105.

[13] T. Eilsmansberger, 'Dominance—The Lost Child? How the Effects-Based Rules Could and Should Change Dominance Analysis' (2006) 2 *European Law Journal* 15, 16.

[14] Geradin et al. *EU Competition Law and Economics* (cited in n. 7), 4.51.

[15] Chap. 1, Section 10.B.(v)d, p. 71.

Acting independently of competitors

We have argued above that it is not economically coherent to think of firms acting independently of consumers to an appreciable extent. The next question is whether it makes sense economically to think of firms acting independently of their competitors. There is a sense in which it does, but here we run into a measurement problem. That is, we think that it may well make sense to think of firms acting independently of their competitors, but that it will be very hard to measure whether this is happening.

Every firm that faces competitors (i.e., all firms apart from true monopolists) is constrained to some extent by those competitors. This is clearly true of firms operating in a competitive market. In these circumstances firms cannot raise their prices above the competitive price level without losing so many sales to their competitors that the price rise is not profitable. Yet this is also true for a dominant firm. This is because a dominant firm will raise prices above the competitive level to the point at which the constraints imposed on the firm by its competitors and its demand curve are binding. So the dominant firm does not act independently of its competitors. Rather, its behaviour is constrained by its competitors.

However, there is clearly an important sense in which the dominant firm has acted to an appreciable extent independently of its competitors: it has raised its price above the competitive price level. So it was not constrained from raising its prices above the competitive price level. This ability to price above the competitive price level strikes us as an important aspect of being dominant. So perhaps one test of a firm's dominance is whether the firm can profitably price above the competitive price level. However, there is a measurement problem here: how can we measure whether a firm has the ability to price above the competitive price level or to act independently of its competitors?

The competitive price level is virtually always impossible to calculate...and of course if it could be routinely calculated then we would not need to worry about whether a firm was dominant. We would instead cut straight to the heart of the matter: was the firm pricing above the competitive price level by a significant amount? Further, we cannot ask the question 'could the firm profitably raise prices above the current price level' as a proxy because the answer to this question should always be 'no', regardless of whether the firm in question is dominant or not. A dominant firm, like a non-dominant firm, will raise its prices up to the point at which the constraints imposed on it by its competitors and demand curve bite and make a further price rise unprofitable.

This measurement issue is related to the *cellophane fallacy*...It has a very important implication for the ECJ's definition of dominance: an empirical test for dominance would never find that a dominant firm was acting independently of its competitors in its pricing decisions. Since it would be pricing at the profit maximizing level given the behaviour of its competitors, if its competitors changed their prices, it would change its prices. Hence the pricing policy even of a dominant firm is dependent on the pricing of its competitors.

In many cases this problem is more fundamental than just a measurement problem. In many cases it is not clear what the competitive price level is *as a matter of economic theory*, let alone practical measurement. Economists 'know' that the competitive price level is marginal cost, but this statement begs more questions than it answers. Which marginal cost—short-run/long-run? Whose marginal cost—the most efficient firm's or the least efficient firm's? What about in the case of large fixed costs (so that marginal cost will not cover the fixed costs except in the long-run)? How should fixed costs be allocated when they are incurred jointly by two or more products?

We have concentrated so far on price as being the important dimension of competition. This is clearly not always the case: in some markets the main focus of competition is in other dimensions, such as quality, service and innovation. However, our remarks above are equally applicable to markets of this type. Firms will act in such a way that they do face constraints from competitors in each of the dimensions of competition. With price that means raising prices up to the point at which further price rises would not be profitable. With quality it might be lowering quality (and hence costs), but not price up to the point at which further reductions in quality would not be profitable. With innovation it might be slowing the pace of innovation (and hence R&D expenditures) as far as it consistent with maintaining long run profits.

Azevedo and Walker suggest that a better test would be 'the ability to restrict output substantially in the market-place'. This, they argue, would mean that the undertaking must have power over price and also that the definition would be consistent with most of the standard factors usually considered relevant in the appraisal of dominance;[16] that restricting output is the key to most anti-competitive behaviour; and that concentrating on output limitation enables cases where the observation of prices and costs cannot be achieved to be dealt with more easily.[17]

Nevertheless, it is argued that 'in effect, the traditional definition of a dominant position, based on the concept of independence, and the more modern one, which requires the capacity to maintain supra-competitive prices, basically refer to the same thing. In a market economy that focuses on profit, independence can only lead to price increases, and, at the same time, improvements in the results or the positions of the companies'.[18] The General Court (GC) equated 'independence' with the ability to maintain high prices in *AstraZeneca*:[19]

267 Next, it must in any event be pointed out that a finding of market power, that is to say the ability of an undertaking to behave to an appreciable extent independently of its competitors, its customers and, ultimately, consumers, in the sense that it is in particular able to maintain prices at a higher level while retaining a much higher market share than those of its competitors…

B. DOMINANT POSITION IN THE GUIDANCE PAPER

In the Guidance Paper the Commission has a short section on 'market power'.[20] It starts its consideration of dominance with the *United Brands/Hoffmann-La Roche* definition. It relates 'independence' to the degree of competitive constraint upon an undertaking: dominance entails insufficiently effective competitive constraints so that the undertaking has substantial market power over a period of time. An undertaking that can sustain price rises above the competitive level can generally be regarded as dominant.

It will be noted that by paragraph 11 the Commission has equated dominance with power over price.

Guidance on the Commission's Enforcement Priorities in Applying Article 82 of the EC Treaty to Abusive Exclusionary Conduct by Dominant Undertakings [2009] OJ C45/2

9. The assessment of whether an undertaking is in a dominant position and of the degree of market power it holds is a first step in the application of Article [102]. According to the case-law, holding a dominant position confers a special responsibility on the undertaking concerned, the scope of which must be considered in the light of the specific circumstances of each case…

---

[16] The market share of the leading firms, variability of market shares, existence of substitute products, barriers to entry, barriers to expansion, existence of spare capacity, and the nature of competitive interaction in the market.

[17] Azevedo and Walker cite as an example the licensing of sports rights: for the action by the Commission over the licensing of Premier League football to BSkyB, see Chap. 10.

[18] L. Ortiz Blanco, *Market Power in EU Antitrust Law* (Hart Publishing, 2012), 47. See also Geradin et al., *EU Competition Law and Economics* (cited in n. 7), 4.52.

[19] Case T-321/05, *AstraZeneca* v. *Commission* [2010] ECR II-2805, para. 267. On appeal the CJ affirmed the passage which includes para. 267 without commenting on it directly, Case C-457/10 P, *AstraZeneca* v. *Commission*, 6 December 2012, paras. 177–181.

[20] Guidance on the Commission's Enforcement Priorities in Applying Article 82 of the EC Treaty to Abusive Exclusionary Conduct by Dominant Undertakings [2009] OJ C45/2 (the Guidance Paper), paras. 9–15.

10. Dominance has been defined under Community law as a position of economic strength enjoyed by an undertaking, which enables it to prevent effective competition being maintained on a relevant market, by affording it the power to behave to an appreciable extent independently of its competitors, its customers and ultimately of consumers…This notion of independence is related to the degree of competitive constraint exerted on the undertaking in question. Dominance entails that these competitive constraints are not sufficiently effective and hence that the undertaking in question enjoys substantial market power over a period of time. This means that the undertaking's decisions are largely insensitive to the actions and reactions of competitors, customers and, ultimately, consumers. The Commission may consider that effective competitive constraints are absent even if some actual or potential competition remains…In general, a dominant position derives from a combination of several factors which, taken separately, are not necessarily determinative…

11. The Commission considers that an undertaking which is capable of profitably increasing prices above the competitive level for a significant period of time does not face sufficiently effective competitive constraints and can thus generally be regarded as dominant…In this Communication, the expression 'increase prices' includes the power to maintain prices above the competitive level and is used as short-hand for the various ways in which the parameters of competition—such as prices, output, innovation, the variety or quality of goods or services—can be influenced to the advantage of the dominant undertaking and to the detriment of consumers…

C. EFFECTS-BASED ANALYSIS AND THE CONCEPT OF DOMINANCE

We explained in Chapter 5 how the debate about the reform, or 'modernisation', of Article 102 centres on the widely accepted idea that an effects-based analysis of Article 102 concerned only with consumer welfare should be adopted. It can be argued from this that if a rigorous economic approach is taken to determining whether the conduct of an undertaking harms consumers the preliminary question of whether an undertaking is in a dominant position need not be separately answered.[21] This approach was urged by a report prepared for the Commission, during the internal review which led to the Discussion Paper, by the Economic Advisory Group on Competition Policy (EAGCP).[22] It should be noted that this was not a suggestion of 'abuse, *ergo* dominance' but a plea for an *integrated* examination of the issues as a whole.[23]

Report by the EAGCP, 'An Economic Approach to Article 102', Brussels, 14–15 July 2005, available at <http://ec.europa.eu/dgs/competition/economist/eagcp_july_21_05.pdf>

In proposing to reduce the role of separate assessments of dominance and to integrate the substantive assessment of dominance with the procedure for establishing competitive harm itself, we depart from the tradition of case law concerning Art. [102], but *not*, we believe, from the legal norm itself. Art. [102] is concerned not just with dominance as such, but with abuses of dominance. The case law tradition of having separate assessments of dominance and of abusiveness of behaviour simplifies procedures, but this simplification involves a loss of precision in the implementation of the legal norm. The structural indicators which traditionally serve as proxies for 'dominance' provide an appropriate measure of power in some markets, but not in others. In a market in which these indicators do not properly measure the firm's ability

---

[21] See *Eastman Kodak Co v. Image Technical Services Inc* 504 US 451, 112 S.Ct 2072 (1992) for this approach in the US.

[22] For EAGCP, see Chap. 2.

[23] J. Vickers, 'Market Power in Competition Cases' (2006) 2 *Competition Law Journal* 3, 11.

to impose abusive behaviour on others, the competition authority's intervention under traditional modes of procedure is likely to be inappropriate, too harsh in some cases and too lenient in others. Given that the Treaty itself does not provide a separate definition of dominance, let alone call for any of the traditionally used indicators as such, it seems more appropriate to have the implementation of the Treaty itself focus on the abuses and to treat the assessment of dominance in this context.

Lawyers are likely to have more trouble than economists with the inconvenient fact that for 40 years since *Continental Can* in 1974[24] the EU Courts have said that, in applying Article 102, first dominance must be established and then the conduct under review judged abusive or not. However, commentators also disagreed with EAGCP's suggestion for other reasons, particularly arguing that it is possible for anti-competitive effects to be caused by the conduct of non-dominant undertakings,[25] that a dominance 'screen' is desirable for administrative reasons to avoid Type 1 'false positive errors', and that a requirement of a preliminary finding of dominance frees the vast majority of undertakings from the need to worry about accusations of abuse.[26]

4. ESTABLISHING DOMINANCE

We now consider how the existence of a 'dominant position' is actually established, that is, how it is decided whether or not a particular undertaking is dominant.

In *Continental Can* the CJ stressed that dominance exists only in relation to a particular market and not in the abstract. It held that 'the definition of the relevant market is of essential significance'[27] to the determination of whether or not an undertaking is dominant. Commission decisions applying Article 102 will be quashed if the market is not properly defined.[28] In accordance with this judgment the practice of the Commission in ascertaining dominance is to follow a two-stage procedure by first identifying the relevant market and, secondly, examining the undertaking's position on that market and analysing the competitive constraints which the undertaking faces.[29] It does this by looking at the market share of the undertaking concerned and at 'other factors indicating dominance' including barriers to entry and expansion.

The two-stage procedure can be problematic. Not only are markets notoriously difficult to define,[30] but the process of market definition may be hard to separate from what is supposed to be the second step, assessing the undertaking's power on that market. It can be difficult to determine

---

[24] See Case 6/72, *Europemballage Corp and Continental Can Co Inc v. Commission* [1973] ECR 215.

[25] See, e.g., G. Monti, 'The Concept of Dominance in Article 82' (2006) 2 *European Competition Journal* 31, 45–46, discussing in particular predatory pricing; I. Kokkoris, *A Gap in the Enforcement of Article 82* (BIICL, 2009).

[26] J. Vickers, 'Market Power in Competition Cases' (2006) 2 *Competition Law Journal* 3, 11–12; G. J. Werden, 'Competition Policy on Exclusionary Conduct: Towards an Effects-based Analysis' (2006) 2 *European Competition Journal* 53, 55–57.

[27] Case 6/72, *Europemballage Corp and Continental Can Co Inc v. Commission* [1973] ECR 215, para. 32. See also Case C-7/97, *Oscar Bronner GmbH & Co KG v. Mediaprint* [1998] ECR I-7791, para. 32; Case C-52/07, *Kanal 5 Ltd and TV 4 AB* [2008] ECR I-9275, para. 19.

[28] In *Continental Can*, the CJ quashed the Commission's decision on account of its failure to define adequately the market from the supply side.

[29] In COMP/C-3/37.990 *Intel*, on appeal Case T-286/09, *Intel v. Commission*, judgment pending, however, the Commission left open the question of whether there was one relevant market, CPUs for all computers, or three separate markets (CPUs for respectively desktops, laptops, and servers). It made no difference to the finding of dominance either way.

[30] See Chap. 1.

which factors should be taken into account when defining markets and which factors should be taken into account when considering the undertaking's position on the market. For example, it may not be easy to decide whether account should be taken of the presence of a producer which can switch its production to making a particular product when defining the market (supply side substitutability) or when assessing the competitive constraints that the allegedly dominant undertaking faces on a particular market. In addition, the question whether a particular undertaking is dominant can be hard to disentangle from the question whether or not it has committed an abuse of its dominant position.[31]

The criteria the Commission employs, and the way it applies them, have not always met with the approval of commentators or the approbation of economists. On the contrary, the Commission has often been criticised for finding that an undertaking occupies a 'dominant position' where, in reality, it has little market power. In particular the Commission has been criticised for defining markets too narrowly[32] and for being too ready to find that an undertaking is dominant on a particular market by relying heavily on market shares, finding dominance to exist at comparatively low market shares and/or not taking a sufficiently rigorous view of what amounts to a barrier to entry. This approach, coupled with the wide interpretation given to the term 'abuse',[33] means that the Commission has played a notably interventionist role in the market through the application of Article 102. If a more stringent approach was taken to identifying abusive conduct, easy findings of dominance would not be so significant.

5. MARKET DEFINITION IN ARTICLE 102 CASES

A. GENERAL

Chapter 1 explained that the purpose of defining the relevant market is to identify those products and services that are such close substitutes for the product or service under consideration that they operate as a competitive constraint on the behaviour of the suppliers of the latter. In this chapter we focus on market definition in Article 102 cases. It is always important to remember that market definition is not an end in itself. Rather, it is a preliminary step and a tool necessary to answer the real question: does this firm occupy a dominant position for the purposes of Article 102?

It should be noted that the market must be defined anew, and a fresh analysis of the conditions of competition made, each time Article 102 is applied. The Commission cannot rely on findings of dominance in previous cases.[34]

In most Article 102 cases the undertaking concerned will argue that the market is a wide one (for example, all fruit, rather than just bananas). The broader the market, the less likely the finding of dominance.[35] The assessment of the relevant market is therefore crucial. If it is defined too

---

[31] In some cases it has been indicated that the undertaking must be dominant, since if it was not it could not possibly have engaged in the conduct concerned: see Section 6.C.(v)k, p. 358.

[32] In Art. 102 cases where the Commission is investigating what it suspects to be a breach of Art. 102 it may begin its case with a predisposition to a finding of dominance. This may encourage a narrow market definition. In merger cases the Commission may be more objective in its definition of the market.

[33] See Chap. 7.

[34] Cases T-125/97, etc. *Coca-Cola* v. *Commission* [2000] ECR II-1733, para. 82.

[35] Occasionally the undertaking argues for a narrow definition: e.g., in Case C-62/86, *AKZO Chemie BV* v. *Commission* [1991] ECR I-3359, the undertaking argued for a narrow market definition as in the narrow niche market it was relatively weak, but in the wider market as a whole it had a large market share.

narrowly, an undertaking's position will be exaggerated and a finding of dominance made more likely. Furthermore, there may be a question as to whether a 'market' exists at all.[36]

It was seen in Chapter 1 that in the Notice on market definition the Commission identifies three main competitive constraints to which firms are subject: demand substitutability, supply substitutability, and potential competition.[37] Demand and, to a more limited extent, supply substitutability are relevant to the determination of the market. Although potential competition may be relevant when considering supply substitutability it will more usually be relevant when considering the allegedly dominant undertaking's position on the relevant market once defined.

B. THE PRODUCT MARKET

(i) Demand Substitution

a. Substitutability

As we saw in Chapter 1, the Commission's Notice on market definition prefers quantitative methods for measuring substitutability rather than qualitative methods which look at characteristics, price, and intended use. It particular it adopts the SSNIP test which essentially asks whether a small (5–10 per cent) but non-transitory increase in price of one product (product A) will cause purchasers to purchase sufficient of another product instead (product B) to make the price increase unsustainable.[38] However, as explained in Chapter 1[39] the use of the SSNIP test in Article 102 cases is complicated by the 'cellophane fallacy'.

The problems of identification using characteristics, price, and intended use are illustrated in Sections 5.B.i.b and 5.B.i.c by two leading Article 102 cases, United Brands and Michelin.[40] These are followed in Section 5.B.i.d by a case in the new economy, Wanadoo (France Télécom) which employed both a qualitative assessment of characteristics and use and also the SSNIP test.

b. The United Brands case

In United Brands (UBC) the CJ had to consider why people eat bananas and whether or not they are treated by consumers as reasonably interchangeable with other kinds of fresh fruit.[41] It decided that there was only a small degree of substitutability between bananas and other fruit, partly because of the unique appearance, taste, softness, seedlessness, and easy handling nature of the banana. The judgment does not make it clear why these distinctive characteristics should impact on the determination of the product market.

---

[36] See the discussion on 'input' markets in Section 5.B.i.i, p. 321 and Case T-219/99, British Airways plc v. Commission [2003] ECR II-5917, aff'd Case C-95/04 P, British Airways v. Commission [2007] ECR I-2331.

[37] Commission Notice on the definition of the relevant market for the purposes of Community competition law [1997] OJ C372/5, para. 13.

[38] See Chap. 1, Section 10.B, p. 67.

[39] See Chap. 1, Section 10.B.(v)d, p. 71.

[40] Case 27/76, United Brands v. Commission [1978] ECR 207; Case 322/81, NV Nederlandsche Banden-Industrie Michelin v. Commission [1983] ECR 3461.

[41] Mayras AG confidently declared: 'As far as eating habits are concerned there is no doubt that a mother who gives her young child a fruit yoghurt will not give him a banana as well...' [1978] ECR 207, 312.

Case 27/76, *United Brands* v. *Commission* [1978] ECR 207

United Brands Company was a US company which produced bananas. Its European subsidiary was United Brands Continental BV. The Commission found that United Brands had abused its dominant position on the banana market in a number of different ways, in particular by engaging in excessive and discriminatory pricing and refusal to supply. United Brands challenged the Commission's decision. One of the arguments raised was that the Commission had been wrong to find that there was a separate market for bananas. It claimed that, on the contrary, bananas formed part of a wider fresh fruit market. Bananas were reasonably interchangeable with other kinds of fresh fruit such as apples, oranges, grapes, peaches, and strawberries. The Commission contended that bananas were a separate market because of their unique physical, functional, and economic characteristics and because Food and Agriculture Organization studies had demonstrated only low cross-elasticity between bananas and other fruit.

Court of Justice

12. As far as the product market is concerned it is first of all necessary to ascertain whether, as the applicant maintains, bananas are an integral part of the fresh fruit market, because they are reasonably interchangeable by consumers with other kinds of fresh fruit such as apples, oranges, grapes, peaches, strawberries, etc. or whether the relevant market consists solely of the banana and is a market sufficiently homogeneous and distinct from the market of other fresh fruit.

13. The applicant submits in support of its argument that bananas compete with other fresh fruit in the same shops, on the same shelves, at prices which can be compared, satisfying the same needs: consumption as a dessert or between meals.

14. The statistics produced show that consumer expenditure on the purchase of bananas is at its lowest between June and December when there is a plentiful supply of domestic fresh fruit on the market.

15. Studies carried out by the Food and Agriculture Organization (FAO) (especially in 1975) confirm that banana prices are relatively weak during the summer months and that the price of apples for example has a statistically appreciable impact on the consumption of bananas in the Federal Republic of Germany.

16. Again according to these studies some easing of prices is noticeable at the end of the year during the 'orange season'.

17. The seasonal peak periods when there is a plentiful supply of other fresh fruit exert an influence not only on the prices but also on the volume of sales of bananas and consequently on the volume of imports thereof.

18. The applicant concludes from these findings that bananas and other fresh fruit form only one market and that UBC's operations should have been examined in this context for the purpose of any application of Article [102 TFEU].

19. The Commission maintains that there is a demand for bananas which is distinct from the demand for other fresh fruit especially as the banana is a very important part of the diet of certain sections of the community.

20. The specific qualities of the banana influence customer preference and induce him not to readily accept other fruits as a substitute.

21. The Commission draws the conclusion from the studies quoted by the applicant that the influence of the prices and availability of other types of fruit on the prices and availability of bananas on the relevant market is very ineffective and that these effects are too brief and too spasmodic for such other fruit to be regarded as forming part of the same market as bananas or as a substitute therefor.

22. For the banana to be regarded as forming a market which is sufficiently differentiated from other fruit markets it must be possible for it to be singled out by such special features distinguishing it from other fruits that it is only to a limited extent interchangeable with them and is only exposed to their competition in a way that is hardly perceptible.

23. The ripening of bananas takes place the whole year round without any season having to be taken into account.

24. Throughout the year production exceeds demand and can satisfy it at any time.

25. Owing to this particular feature the banana is a privileged fruit and its production and marketing can be adapted to the seasonal fluctuations of other fresh fruit which are known and can be computed.

26. There is no unavoidable seasonal substitution since the consumer can obtain this fruit all the year round.

27. Since the banana is a fruit which is always available in sufficient quantities the question whether it can be replaced by other fruits must be determined over the whole of the year for the purpose of ascertaining the degree of competition between it and other fresh fruit.

28. The studies of the banana market on the Court's file show that on the latter market there is no significant long term cross-elasticity any more than—as has been mentioned—there is any seasonal substitutability in general between the banana and all the seasonal fruits, as this only exists between the banana and two fruits (peaches and table grapes) in one of the countries (West Germany) of the relevant geographic market.

29. As far as concerns the two fruits available throughout the year (oranges and apples) the first are not interchangeable and in the case of the second there is only a relative degree of substitutability.

30. This small degree of substitutability is accounted for by the specific features of the banana and all the factors which influence consumer choice.

31. The banana has certain characteristics, appearance, taste, softness, seedlessness, easy handling, a constant level of production which enable it to satisfy the constant needs of an important section of the population consisting of the very young, the old and the sick.

32. As far as prices are concerned two FAO studies show that the banana is only affected by the prices—falling prices—of other fruits (and only of peaches and table grapes) during the summer months and mainly in July and then by an amount not exceeding 20 per cent.

33. Although it cannot be denied that during these months and some weeks at the end of the year this product is exposed to competition from other fruits, the flexible way in which the volume of imports and their marketing on the relevant geographic market is adjusted means that the conditions of competition are extremely limited and that its price adapts without any serious difficulties to this situation where supplies of fruit are plentiful.

34. It follows from all these considerations that a very large number of consumers having a constant need for bananas are not noticeably or even appreciably enticed away from the consumption of this product by the arrival of other fresh fruit on the market and that even the personal peak periods only affect it for a limited period of time and to a very limited extent from the point of view of substitutability.

35. Consequently, the banana market is a market which is sufficiently distinct from the other fresh fruit markets.

It will be noted from this extract that the CJ was concerned with the question of whether the banana could be 'singled out by such special features distinguishing it from other fruits that it is only to a limited extent interchangeable with them and is only exposed to their competition in a way that is hardly perceptible' (paragraph 22). The 'special features' identified were first that the banana was a 'privileged fruit' (paragraph 25) in that it was not seasonal, and secondly that it had 'certain characteristics' making it suitable for the very young, the old, and the sick (paragraph 31). These characteristics, apart from constant availability, were appearance, taste, softness, seedlessness, and easy handling.

This is a strange list. Softness, seedlessness, and easy handling may make bananas suitable for the young, old, and sick but it is difficult to see why their appearance does and it is never explained what is so special about their taste. Moreover, as we saw in Chapter 1,[42] it is unsatisfactory to conclude from the dependence of one group of customers that a product forms a separate market unless it is possible to price discriminate at the point of sale and to prevent arbitrage. This is now recognised in the Commission's Notice.[43] It may be that if the question arose again bananas would still be held to constitute a separate market, but it is most unlikely that this would be on the basis of their 'special suitability' for certain customers.[44] Rather, evidence would be sought from technology such as supermarket scanners, which would enable own-price and cross-price elasticities to be measured.[45]

c. The *Michelin* case

In *Michelin I* the Commission found that Michelin had committed an abuse of a dominant position on the market for new replacement tyres for lorries, buses, and similar vehicles. Michelin claimed, inter alia, that the Commission's definition of the market was narrow and arbitrary and that Michelin did not hold a dominant position on the wider tyre market.[46] The CJ had to determine whether or not the Commission had correctly defined the market. In considering this question a number of facts had to be taken into account: that lorries and buses need larger tyres than cars and vans; that there are different sizes of lorry and bus tyres; that tyre manufacturers supply their tyres separately to new lorry and bus manufacturers *and* to dealers who fit tyres on lorries and buses as replacements; and that tyre dealers also fit retreaded or remoulded tyres to vehicles whose owners do not want new replacement tyres. Which, if any, of these tyres were substitutes for each other so that they formed part of the same product market?

Case 322/81, *Nederlandsche Banden-Industrie Michelin* v. *Commission* [1983] ECR 3461

Court of Justice

(aa) The market in replacement tyres for heavy vehicles

(37. As the Court has repeatedly emphasized, most recently in its judgment of 11 December 1980 in Case 31/90 *NV L'Oreal and SA L'Oreal* v. *PVBA De Nieuwe AMCK*… for the purposes of investigating the possibly dominant position of an undertaking on a given market, the possibilities of competition must be judged in the context of the market comprising the totality of the products which, with respect to their characteristics, are particularly suitable for satisfying constant needs and are only to a limited extent interchangeable with other products. However, it must be noted that the determination of the relevant market is useful in assessing whether the undertaking concerned is in a position to prevent effective competition from being maintained and behave to an appreciable extent independently of its competitors and customers and consumers. For this purpose, therefore, an examination limited to the objective characteristics only of the relevant products cannot be sufficient: the competitive conditions and the structure of supply and demand on the market must also be taken into consideration.

---

[42] See Chap. 1, Section 10.B.(vii)b, p. 77.

[43] Para. 43.

[44] Moreover, changes in market conditions would affect the conclusion: many more fruits, e.g., are now available in Europe all year round, and kitchen technology is such that few fruits cannot be pulped (although blenders were in fact readily available in the mid-1970s!).

[45] See R. O'Donoghue and A. J. Padilla, *The Law and Economics of Article 102* (2nd edn, Hart Publishing, 2013), 98.

[46] Michelin also challenged the definition of the geographic market as being the Netherlands. See Section 5.C, p. 326.

38. Moreover, it was for that reason that the Commission and Michelin NV agreed that new, original-equipment tyres should not be taken into consideration in the assessment of market shares. Owing to the particular structure of demand for such tyres characterized by direct orders from car manufacturers, competition in this sphere is in fact governed by completely different factors and rules.

39. As far as replacement tyres are concerned, the first point which must be made is that at the user level there is no interchangeability between car and van tyres on the one hand and heavy-vehicle tyres on the other. Car and van tyres therefore have no influence at all on competition on the market in heavy-vehicle tyres.

40. Furthermore, the structure of demand for each of those groups of products is different. Most buyers of heavy-vehicle tyres are trade users, particularly haulage undertakings, for whom, as the Commission explained, the purchase of replacement tyres represents an item of considerable expenditure and who constantly ask their tyre dealers for advice and long-term specialized services adapted to their specific needs. On the other hand, for the average buyer of car or van tyres the purchase of tyres is an occasional event and even if the buyer operates a business he does not expect such specialized advice and service adapted to specific needs. Hence the sale of heavy-vehicle tyres requires a particularly specialized distribution network which is not the case with the distribution of car and van tyres.

...

42. The Commission rightly examined the structure of the market and demand primarily at the level of dealers to whom Michelin NV applied the practice in question. Michelin NV has itself stated, although in another context, that it was compelled to change its discount system to take account of the tendency towards specialization amongst its dealers, some of whom, such as garage owners, no longer sold tyres for heavy vehicles and vans. This confirms the differences existing in the structure of demand between different groups of dealers. Nor has Michelin NV disputed that the distinction drawn between tyres for heavy vehicles, vans and cars is also applied by all its competitors, especially as regards discount terms, even if in the case of certain types of tyre the distinctions drawn by different manufacturers may vary in detail.

43. Nevertheless, it cannot be deduced from the fact that the conduct to which exception is taken in this case affects dealers that Michelin NV's position ought to be assessed on the basis of the proportion of Michelin heavy-vehicle tyres in the dealers' total turnover. Since it is a question of investigating whether Michelin NV holds a dominant position in the case of certain products, it is unimportant that the dealers also deal in other products if there is no competition between those products and the products in question.

44. On the other hand, in deciding whether a dominant position exists, neither the absence of elasticity of supply between different types and dimensions of tyres for heavy vehicles, which is due to differences in the conditions of production, nor the absence of interchangeability and elasticity of demand between those types and dimensions of tyre from the point of view of the specific needs of the user allow a number of smaller markets, reflecting those types and dimensions, to be distinguished, as Michelin NV suggests. Those differences between different types and dimensions of tyre are not vitally important for dealers, who must meet demand from customers for the whole range of heavy-vehicle tyres. Furthermore, in the absence of any specialization on the part of the undertakings concerned, such differences in the type and dimensions of a product are not a crucial factor in the assessment of an undertaking's market position because in view of their similarity and the manner in which they complement one another at the technical level, the conditions of competition on the market are the same for all the types and dimensions of the product.

45. In establishing that Michelin NV has a dominant position the Commission was therefore right to assess its market share with reference to replacement tyres for lorries, buses and similar vehicles and to exclude consideration of car and van tyres.

(bb) The taking into consideration of competition from retreads

...

48. ... it must first be recalled that although the existence of a competitive relationship between two products does not presuppose complete interchangeability for a specific purpose, it is not a pre-condition

for a finding that a dominant position exists in the case of a given product that there should be a complete absence of competition from other partially interchangeable products as long as such competition does not affect the undertaking's ability to influence appreciably the conditions in which that competition may be exerted or at any rate to conduct itself to a large extent without having to take account of that competition and without suffering any adverse effects as a result of its attitude.

49. It is clear from the facts, as established from the parties' statements and those made by the witnesses examined at the hearing during the administrative procedure, that it cannot be denied that new tyres and retreads are interchangeable to some degree but only to a limited extent and not for all purposes. Although Michelin NV has produced calculations to show that the price and quality of retreads are comparable to those of new tyres and that a number of users do in fact consider the two groups of products interchangeable for their purposes; it has nevertheless admitted that in terms of safety and reliability a retread's value may be less than that of new tyre and, what is more, the Commission has shown that a number of users have certain reservations, which may or may not be justified, regarding the use of a retread, particularly on a vehicle's front axle.

50. In order to assess the effect of this limited competition from retreads on Michelin NV's market position it must be borne in mind that at least some retreads are not put on sale but are produced to order for the user as some transport undertakings attach importance to having their own tyre carcasses retreaded in order to be sure of not receiving damaged carcasses. It must be acknowledged that there has been no agreement between the parties as regards the percentage of tyres retreaded in this way as a form of service; the Commission has estimated it at 80 per cent to 95 per cent of retreads whereas Michelin NV maintains that it is only 15 to 20 per cent and that in most cases the order is placed in the name of the dealer and not that of the user. Despite that disagreement between the parties it may [be] said that a proportion of retreads reaching the consumer stage are not in competition with new tyres because they involve a service provided directly by the retreading firms to the users.

51. Furthermore, in assessing the size of Michelin NV's market share in relation to its competitors' it must not be overlooked that the market in renovated tyres is a secondary market which depends on supply and prices on the market in new tyres since every retread is made from a tyre which was originally a new tyre and there is a limit to the number of occasions on which a tyre may be retreaded. Consequently a considerable proportion of demand will inevitably always be satisfied by new tyres. In such circumstances the possession by an undertaking of a dominant position in new tyres gives it a privileged position as regards competition from retreading undertakings and this enables it to conduct itself with greater independence on the market than would be possible for a retreading undertaking.

52. It is clear from the considerations set out above that the partial competition to which manufacturers of new tyres are exposed from retreading undertakings is not sufficient to deprive a manufacturer of new tyres of the economic power which he possesses by virtue of his dominant position on the market in new tyres. In assessing Michelin NV's position in relation to the strength and number of its competitors the Commission was therefore right to take into consideration a market share [of] 57 to 65 per cent on the market in new replacement tyres for heavy vehicles. Compared with the market shares of Michelin NV's main competitors amounting to 4 to 8 per cent, that market share constitutes a valid indication of Michelin NV's preponderant strength in relation to its competitors, even when allowance is made for some competition from retreads.

The CJ thus upheld the Commission's decision in *Michelin*.[47] It will be noted that in paragraph 48 the CJ considers that in the context of finding a dominant position it is not necessary that products be completely interchangeable—partial interchangeability is enough. The issue is whether the other product exerts a competitive restraint.[48]

---

[47] [1981] OJ L353/33, [1982] 1 CMLR 643.

[48] See also Case T-301/04, *Clearstream Banking v. Commission* [2009] ECR II-3155, para. 64.

The definition of the replacement tyre market was revisited 20 years later in a second Commission decision finding that Michelin's discount and rebate system was an abuse of its dominant position.[49] The Commission concluded that new replacement tyres for trucks and buses in France and retreaded tyres for trucks and buses in France were two separate markets and that Michelin had a dominant position on both of them.[50] The Commission's reasons for separating new tyres and retreads were essentially the same as they had been in 1981:[51] the supply and demand for the two types of tyre were different;[52] retreaders were skilled *service* providers who did not necessarily have any links to tyre dealers, whereas new tyres were supplied to dealers; the retread market was a secondary 'after-sales' market, in which new tyres were the raw material and the purpose was to prolong the life of the tyre to avoid purchasing another new one; and, finally, there was still a safety issue in that many final (haulier) customers perceived retreads as less safe ('the situation that prevailed in 1981 has thus not changed significantly').[53] The Commission did not employ the SSNIP test in *Michelin II*.

d. The *France Télécom* case

In *Wanadoo*[54] the Commission defined the relevant market as the French market for high-speed internet access for residential customers (the products with which the infringement of predatory pricing was concerned were internet access services based on ADSL technology).[55] The Commission examined the differences in performance between high- and low-speed internet access and concluded that the differences were clearly perceived by consumers, and that an analysis of price differences between them showed that consumers were prepared to pay a premium for the extra performance and convenience of high speed.[56] On appeal, France Télécom pleaded, inter alia, that the Commission should have considered the market as comprising both high-speed and low-speed access.[57]

Case T-340/03, *France Télécom SA* v. *Commission* [2007] ECR II-107

General Court

78. According to settled case-law (Case 322/81 *Michelin* v *Commission*.... paragraph 37; Case T-65/96 *Kish Glass* v *Commission*.... paragraph 62; and Case T-219/99 *British Airways* v *Commission*...paragraph 91), for the purposes of investigating the possibly dominant position of an undertaking on a given product market, the possibilities of competition must be judged in the context of the market comprising the totality of the products or services which, with respect to their characteristics, are particularly suitable for

---

[49] *Michelin* [2001] OJ L143/1 (*Michelin II*). The abuse aspect of the case is discussed in Chap. 7.

[50] On appeal to the GC, Case T-203/01, *Manufacture Française des Pneumatiques Michelin* v. *Commission* [2003] ECR II-4071, Michelin did not challenge the market definition or the finding of dominance.

[51] *Michelin II* decision, paras. 109–118, despite the heavy criticism of the market definition in *Michelin I*, see e.g., V. Korah, 'The Michelin Decision of the Commission' (1982) 7 *ELRev* 130.

[52] See Section 5.B.f, p. 316.

[53] *Michelin II* decision, para. 116.

[54] COMP/38.233, [2005] 5 CMLR 120.

[55] Asynchronous Digital Subscriber Line. It allows broadband services to be provided over the traditional telephone copper wire.

[56] COMP/38.233, para. 187.

[57] France Télécom had succeeded to the rights of Wanadoo Interactive (WIN) following a merger. On appeal to the CJ, Case C-202/07P, *France Télécom SA* v. *Commission* [2009] ECR I-2369 the market definition was not challenged.

satisfying constant needs and are only to a limited extent interchangeable with other products or services. Moreover, since the determination of the relevant market is useful in assessing whether the undertaking concerned is in a position to prevent effective competition from being maintained and to behave to an appreciable extent independently of its competitors and, in this case, of its service providers, an examination to that end cannot be limited solely to the objective characteristics of the relevant services, but the competitive conditions and the structure of supply and demand on the market must also be taken into consideration.

79. If a product could be used for different purposes and if these different uses are in accordance with economic needs, which are themselves also different, there are good grounds for accepting that this product may, according to the circumstances, belong to separate markets which may present specific features which differ from the standpoint both of the structure and of the conditions of competition. However, this finding does not justify the conclusion that such a product, together with all the other products which can replace it as far as concerns the various uses to which it may be put and with which it may compete, forms one single market.

80. The concept of the relevant market in fact implies that there can be effective competition between the products which form part of it and this presupposes that there is a sufficient degree of interchangeability between all the products forming part of the same market in so far as a specific use of such products is concerned (Case 85/76 *Hoffmann-La Roche* v *Commission*...paragraph 28).

81. It is also apparent from the Commission Notice on the definition of the relevant market for the purposes of Community competition law...that '[a] relevant product market comprises all those products and/or services which are regarded as interchangeable or substitutable by the consumer, by reason of the products' characteristics, their prices and their intended use'.

82. It must be stated that there is not a mere difference in comfort or quality between high- and low-speed access. It is clear from the evidence provided by the Commission (recital 175 of the decision), which was not contradicted by WIN, that some applications available with high-speed access are simply not feasible with low-speed access, including, for example, the downloading of very voluminous video files or interactive network games. WIN also confirmed, in its reply of 4 March 2002 to the first statement of objections, that there are 'audiovisual/multimedia activities...more specific to ADSL'. In addition, the study undertaken by the Centre de recherche pour l'étude et l'observation des conditions de vie (Research Centre for the Study and Monitoring of Living Standards) (Crédoc) on behalf of WIN which it presented in an annex to its application also describes new uses developed on the internet by the extense service and which are specific to high-speed access, that is, playing network games, listening to radio online, watching a video online and shopping online. According to that study, moreover, the subscriber with high-speed access goes online far more often and, on average, for considerably longer than the low-speed access user.

83. As regards the differences in technical features and performances, it is clear from the Commission's contentions (recitals 181 to 187 of the decision), which have not been denied by the applicant, that an important technical feature of high-speed internet access is the specific nature of the modems used. A high-speed internet access modem cannot be used for low-speed internet access and vice versa (recital 181 of the decision). In addition, in the case of high-speed access, the connection is always on and the telephone line always available for making calls.

84. In addition, in the case of the French market, it should be pointed out that, for the period investigated, the offers of high-speed access involved download speeds in the region of 512 kbits/s (recital 185 of the decision). The offers of traditional low-speed access (limited to 56 kbits/s) and of ISDN (integrated services digital network) (64 or 128 kbits/s) only allowed speeds of 4 to 10 times less. The ADSL offers with download speeds of 128 kbits/s, which, according to the applicant, bear witness to the continuity between low-speed and high-speed, only became available at the end of the period covered by the decision. In addition, even in the case of an offer of 128 kbits/s, the difference between low-speed and high-speed access is considerable. The difference in performance was therefore considerable during the period investigated.

85. In addition to the differences in use, features and performances, there is a significant price differential between low-speed and high-speed access (recitals 188 to 192 of the decision).

86. As regards the degree of substitutability, it is appropriate to recall, in addition to the case-law cited in paragraph 78 above, the criteria laid down by the Commission in its Notice on the definition of the relevant market for the purposes of Community competition law (see paragraph 81 above).

87. According to that notice, the assessment of demand substitution entails a determination of the range of products which are viewed as substitutes by the consumer. One way of making this determination can be viewed as a speculative experiment, postulating a hypothetical small but lasting change in relative prices and evaluating the likely reactions of customers to that increase. In paragraph 17 of the notice, the Commission states '[t]he question to be answered is whether the parties' customers would switch to readily available substitutes…in response to a hypothetical small (in the range 5 to 10%) but permanent relative price increase in the products and areas being considered'.

88. In recital 193 of the decision, the Commission admits that low-speed and high-speed access indeed present some degree of substitutability. It adds in recital 194, however, that the operation of such substitutability is extremely asymmetrical, the migrations of customers from offers of high-speed to low-speed access being negligible compared with the migrations in the other direction. However, according to the Commission, if the products were perfectly substitutable from the point of view of demand, the rates of migration should be identical or at least comparable.

89. It should be pointed out, in this respect, that, first of all, it is clear from the information gathered by WIN and reproduced in Table 7 of the decision that the migration rates of high-speed subscribers to integral low-speed offers were very low during the period covered, in spite of the difference in price between those services, which should have prompted numerous internet users to turn to low-speed access. This large discrepancy in the rates of migration between low-speed and high-speed access and between high-speed and low-speed access does not lend credence to the argument that those services are interchangeable in the eyes of consumers. In the application, WIN also failed to adduce any evidence to cast doubt on that analysis.

90. Secondly, it transpires that, according to a survey carried out on behalf of the Commission and presented by WIN in an annex to its application, 80% of subscribers would maintain their subscription in response to a price increase in the range 5 to 10%. According to paragraph 17 of the Notice on the definition of the relevant market for the purposes of Community competition law (see paragraph 87 above), this high percentage of subscribers who would not abandon high-speed access in response to a price increase of 5 to 10% provides a strong indication of the absence of demand-side substitution.

91. Consequently, on the basis of all the foregoing, it should be held that the Commission was right to find that a sufficient degree of substitutability between high-speed and low-speed access did not exist and to define the market in question as that of high-speed internet access for residential customers.

It will be noted that in this judgment the GC cited the case law of the CJ on identifying substitute products by reference to characteristics and use. However, it also referred to the Commission Notice and to the SSNIP test (paragraph 87) and to a survey showing that 80 per cent of subscribers to the high-speed service would be impervious to a 5–10 per cent price increase. The GC concluded that this 'provides a strong indication' of the absence of demand-side substitution.[58]

e. Chains of Substitution and Products with Multiple Applications

Hoffmann-La Roche demonstrates the chain of substitution problem discussed in Chapter 1.[59] Hoffmann-La Roche (HLR) challenged the Commission's finding that it had committed a number

---

[58] Given that everyone in the case must have been familiar with the product at issue it may not have needed SSNIP tests to convince the Court that low-speed internet access is no substitute for high-speed.

[59] Chap. 1, Section 10.B.(vii)a, p. 76.

of abuses of dominant positions held on several separate vitamin markets. Two of the vitamins concerned, C and E, had two distinct uses. In each case the vitamin had a bio-nutritive use for which there were no substitutes, and an antioxidant use. Both vitamins C and E and other products could be used for the antioxidant use. Hoffmann-La Roche claimed that the two vitamins were in the same market for antioxidants together with these other products. The CJ, concentrating on the bio-nutritive use, upheld the Commission's finding that the vitamins each constituted a separate market. The reasoning was not, however, entirely satisfactory. In particular, the judgment can be criticised for the Court's failure to take account of the two distinct uses. If HLR could not profitably increase the price to customers in the bio-nutritive market without also losing customers in the antioxidant market, then arguably they should have been found to form part of the same market.

Case 85/76, *Hoffmann-La Roche & Co AG* v. *Commission* [1979] ECR 461

Court of Justice

28. If a product could be used for different purposes and if these different uses are in accordance with economic needs, which are themselves also different, there are good grounds for accepting that this product may, according to the circumstances, belong to separate markets which may present specific features which differ from the standpoint both of the structure and of the conditions of competition. However this finding does not justify the conclusion that such a product together with all the other products which can replace it as far as concerns the various uses to which it may be put and with which it may compete, forms one single market. The concept of the relevant market in fact implies that there can be effective competition between the products which form part of it and this presupposes that there is a sufficient degree of interchangeability between all the products forming part of the same market in so far as a specific use of such products is concerned. There was no such interchangeability, at any rate during the period under consideration, between all the vitamins of each of the groups C and E and all the products which, according to the circumstances, may be substituted for one or other of these groups of vitamins for technological uses which are themselves extremely varied.

29. On the other hand there may be some doubt whether, for the purpose of delimiting the respective markets of the C and E groups of vitamins, it is necessary to include all the vitamins of each of these groups in a market corresponding to that group, or whether, on the contrary, each of these groups must be placed in a separate market, one comprising vitamins for bio-nutritive use and the other vitamins for technological purposes.

30. However, in order to calculate the market shares of Roche and its competitors correctly this question did not have to be answered because, as the Commission has rightly pointed out, if it had been necessary to draw this distinction, it would have to be drawn for Roche's competitors as well as for Roche itself, and—in the absence of any indication to the contrary by the applicant—in similar proportions with the result that the market shares in percentages would remain unchanged. Finally Roche, in answer to a question put to it by the Court, has stated that all the vitamins of each group, irrespective of the ultimate intended use of the product, were subject to the same price system so that they could not be split up into specific markets. It follows from the foregoing that the Commission has correctly delimited the relevant markets in its contested decision.

In one sense the narrow definition in *Hoffmann-La Roche* is of no concern if it is remembered that market definition is not an end in itself, but a step towards assessing market power. What matters is the recognition that markets are not impermeable and may be subject to competitive pressures from *outside* the market.[60] The problem, however, is that a narrow market definition may be more likely to result in a finding of dominance because of the importance accorded to market share in making that finding, as discussed in Section 6. The Commission Notice on market definition, paragraph 57, which is set out in Chapter 1,[61] recognises that where chains of substitution are present practical problems may arise in determining both the geographic and the product market. It will be recalled that the Commission's conclusion is that the crucial question is the extent to which the existence of substitutes constrains an undertaking's pricing policy.[62]

AKZO[63] shows how the particular circumstances of the case can influence the definition of the market where there are chains of substitution. AKZO produced organic peroxides, which had multiple uses. They were used in polymer manufacture, where in some fields of application they had limited substitutes but the main organic peroxide, benzoyl peroxide, could also be used as a bleaching agent in flour-milling in the UK and Ireland. AKZO argued that the relevant market should be considered as that for flour additives (where its market share was low). The Commission found that the relevant market was the organic peroxides market as a whole. AKZO's share of the whole peroxides market was 50 per cent. The CJ upheld the Commission's definition of the market because AKZO's conduct—lowering its prices in the flour-milling sector in order to protect its position in the polymer sector—as well as its internal documentation, showed that the undertaking itself treated the market as a single one.

In the extract from *France Télécom*[64] it can be seen at paragraph 79 that the GC explained that a product used for separate purposes may belong to separate markets and that this does not mean that the product, along with all its replacements for the different uses, can be placed in one single market.

f. The Structure of Supply and Demand

The importance of the structure of supply and demand in market definition was first stated in *Michelin I*, paragraph 37, which is set out in the extract from the judgment.[65]

Michelin shows that the structure of supply and demand may even cause identical products to fall into different markets. It is seen in the extract that the CJ upheld the Commission finding that identical new heavy vehicle tyres and retreads formed two separate product markets and that the market for the supply of heavy vehicle tyres to vehicle manufacturers as original equipment was distinct from the market for the supply to dealers to be fitted as replacements. In both cases the Court stressed the difference in the dynamics of the transactions.[66] Conversely, the Court accepted (in paragraph 44) that different types of heavy vehicle tyres, although not substitutes for each other, were in the same market. This was because dealers[67] had to stock all tyres and the conditions of competition were the same for all types and dimensions.

Similarly, in *Van den Bergh Foods* the Commission placed emphasis on the structure of supply and demand in finding that the markets for single wrapped individual ice cream and individual portions of soft ice cream were distinct. Although the consumer might perceive the two types of ice cream to be reasonably interchangeable, the competitive conditions under which they were offered to the retail trade were different and distinct. Soft ice cream had, for example, to be processed by the retailer

---

[60] See, e.g., C. W. Baden Fuller, 'Article 86: Economic Analysis of the Existence of a Dominant Position' (1979) 4 *ELRev* 423; and V. Korah, 'Concept of a Dominant Position within the Meaning of Art 86' (1980) 17 *CMLRev* 395.

[61] Chapter 1, Section 10.B.(vii)a, p. 77.

[62] As it has demonstrated in a number of merger cases, such as *AstraZeneca/Novartis* COMP/M.1806.

[63] Case C-62/86, *AKZO Chemie BV v. Commission* [1991] ECR I-3359.

[64] Section 5.B.d., p. 313.

[65] In Section 5.B.i.c, p. 309.

[66] See also Case C-333/94 P, *Tetra Pak International SA v. Commission* [1996] ECR I-5951, para. 13.

[67] For the abuse issues in *Michelin* see Chap. 7.

and so required the installation of special processing and dispensing machines; it was not self-service and was not normally branded. Similarly, single wrapped ice cream was distinct from multiple packs of ice cream sold in supermarkets.

> The consumer's point of view is…not in every instance the sole criterion in the determination of a product market; nor is an examination limited only to the objective characteristics of the products in question sufficient. The competitive conditions and the structure of supply and demand on the market must also be taken into consideration.[68]

The importance of considering the structure of supply and demand on the market was stressed in *France Télécom*[69] and in *Clearstream* where primary clearing and settlement services to intermediaries in respect of securities issued under German law was held to be a relevant market.[70]

g. One Product or Market or Two

The question of whether a product is to be considered a single whole or as a number of separate products[71] is illustrated by *Microsoft*.[72] There the Commission took action against Microsoft for infringing Article 102 by 'tying' in that it supplied its Windows desktop operating system with the Windows Media Player (WMP) ready installed. As the issue of whether products are distinct is inextricably bound up with that of the abuse of tying, it is discussed in Chapter 7.

h. Primary and Secondary Markets (Aftermarkets)

Microsoft concerned complementary products. An 'aftermarket' is a particular instance of complementary products. As explained in Chapter 1, an aftermarket is a product or service which is complementary to, and follows on from, another, such as spare parts,[73] consumables, or maintenance services. Competition issues can arise when the supplier of the original (primary) product or equipment also supplies the product or service in the secondary market, the aftermarket (in some markets the producer makes more money from the sale of consumables than from the original product). There are two possible scenarios.

First, the supplier may not be the only source of products or services in the aftermarket as the primary product may be compatible with different brands.[74] In this situation the supplier may try to ensure that its customers obtain the aftermarket goods or services from itself rather the competitors. Where the supplier is in a dominant position on the market for the primary product the steps it takes to this end may constitute the abuse of 'tying' or 'bundling'.[75] This was so in *Hilti*[76] and *Tetra Pak II*.[77]

---

[68] [1998] OJ L246/1, [1998] 5 CMLR 530, para. 133. The decision was upheld by the GC on appeal, Case T-65/98, *Van den Bergh Foods Ltd* v. *Commission* [2003] ECR II-4653 (aff'd Case C-552/03 P, *Unilever Bestfoods (Ireland) Ltd* v. *Commission* [2006] ECR I-9091), where the definition of the market was not challenged.

[69] Para. 78.

[70] Case T-301/04, *Clearstream Banking* v. *Commission* [2009] ECR II-3155, para. 65. It was in fact a 'sub-market' but the GC said that a sub-market 'which has specific characteristics from the point of view of demand and supply and which offers products which occupy an essential and non-interchangeable place in the more general market of which it forms part must be considered to be a distinct product market'.

[71] See Chap. 1, Section 10.B(vii)f, p. 79.

[72] COMP/C-3/37.792, [2005] 4 CMLR 965, on appeal Case T-201/04, *Microsoft* v. *Commission* [2007] ECR II-3601.

[73] A replacement for an integral part of the original product, produced by the supplier of that product and/or by independent manufacturers. Motor vehicle tyres have never been considered 'spare parts' in this sense.

[74] This means that the primary product producer does not have intellectual property rights (IPR) which prevent competitors making compatible spare parts or consumables. For the possibility of a refusal to license others to make compatible products constituting an abuse under Art. 102, see Chap. 7.

[75] Effected through various pricing mechanisms, promises of favourable treatment, or threats of unfavourable treatment: see further Chap. 7.

[76] Case T-30/89, *Hilti AG* v. *Commission* [1991] ECR II-439, discussed in text at n. 84.

[77] Case C-333/94 P, *Tetra Pak International SA* v. *Commission* [1996] ECR I-5951 (*Tetra Pak II*), discussed in text at n. 86.

The dominant manufacturer of the primary product may therefore seek to present itself as supplying an indivisible 'system' consisting of the durable primary product and, for example, an ongoing supply of the consumable and a maintenance and repair service. If there is found to be only one product, consisting of the 'system', then tying or bundling is not an issue.

Secondly, the supplier may be the only source of products or services in the aftermarket which are compatible with the primary product. The one brand of spare parts, complements, etc. has no substitutes. In this scenario there are two further possibilities:

• The supplier is dominant on the market for the primary product; or

• The supplier is not dominant on the market for the primary product.

In the first case on spare parts and aftermarkets, *Hugin*,[78] the undertaking was not dominant on the primary market. The Commission defined the market narrowly, finding that the spare parts were a separate market from the original equipment supplied. The justification for this approach is that the original equipment and its spare parts or consumables are not substitutes for one another. The result is that where only the supplier's brand in the aftermarket is compatible with the primary product an undertaking with a small share of the original equipment market may be found to be dominant in the aftermarket and find its behaviour constrained by Article 102. This was what happened in *Hugin* itself.

Hugin was a Swedish producer of cash registers and their spare parts. It had approximately 12 per cent of the Community cash register market. After-sales, maintenance, and repair services of Hugin machines were conducted by local subsidiaries, agents, and distributors in, inter alia, all the Member States. Hugin decided no longer to supply machines or their spare parts to Liptons, a small firm in south-east England which sold, leased, repaired, serviced, and reconditioned cash registers, including Hugin machines. Without the spare parts Liptons could not continue servicing and repairing Hugin machines. The Commission held that the relevant product market consisted of Hugin spare parts required by the independent undertakings which maintained and repaired Hugin cash registers and since Hugin was the sole supplier of those spare parts it was dominant on that market (and had abused its dominance by refusing to continue to supply). The CJ upheld the finding on the relevant market and dominance.[79]

The CJ's finding that the market was defined not as the market for spare parts needed by the owners of Hugin machines, but by general repairers and servicers of the machines, is problematic.[80] For example, if the focus of the case was the independent repairer, an analysis was needed of the feasibility of their shifting their business to dealing with other brands of machine. Moreover, the interests of the ultimate consumer—the owners of Hugin machines—seem not to have been considered. Nevertheless, the principle established in *Hugin*, that one brand of spare parts can constitute a separate product market for the purposes of Article 102, has been applied in a number of cases, including the motor industry cases, *Volvo*[81] and *Renault*.[82] There it was held that spare parts for cars constitute a separate market from the cars themselves.

The *Hugin* principle was applied to consumables in *Hilti*. Hilti was dominant in the market for nail guns for the construction industry. The guns were used together with cartridge strips and nails. Nails compatible with Hilti guns were made not only by Hilti but by a number of independent firms,

---

[78] [1978] OJ L22/23, [1978] CMLR D19, on appeal Case 22/78, *Hugin Kassaregister AB and Hugin Cash Registers Ltd v. Commission* [1979] ECR 1869.

[79] The CJ quashed the Commission finding of abuse on the grounds that it had not been established that there was an effect on inter-Member State trade.

[80] Baden Fuller, 'Article 86: Economic Analysis of the Existence of a Dominant Position' (cited in n. 60), 423.

[81] Case 238/87, *AB Volvo v. Erik Veng* [1988] ECR 6211.

[82] Case 53/87, *CICCRA v. Renault* [1988] ECR 6039.

who complained that Hilti was indulging in practices designed to ensure that purchasers of the guns bought only Hilti's own nails. The Commission held that these practices constituted an abuse.[83] Hilti argued that the consumables were useless without the nail guns and that the guns and consumables formed a 'powder–actuated fastening system' which was in competition with, and in the same market as, other forms of construction fastening systems. Since the nail guns, cartridges, and nails were not distinct but formed one indivisible product, its conduct in 'tying' the sales together could not constitute an abuse. These arguments were rejected the GC.[84]

Case T-30/89, *Hilti AG v. Commission* [1991] ECR II-439

General Court

66. The Court takes the view that nail guns, cartridge strips and nails constitute three specific markets. Since cartridge strips and nails are specifically manufactured, and purchased by users, for a single brand of gun, it must be concluded that there are separate markets for Hilti-compatible cartridge strips and nails, as the Commission found in its decision (paragraph 55).

67. With particular regard to the nails whose use in Hilti tools is an essential element of the dispute, it is common ground that since the 1960s there have been independent producers, including the interveners, making nails intended for use in nail guns. Some of those producers are specialized and produce only nails, and indeed some make only nails specifically designed for Hilti tools. That fact in itself is sound evidence that there is a specific market for Hilti-compatible nails.

68. Hilti's contention that guns, cartridge strips and nails should be regarded as forming an indivisible whole, 'a powder-actuated fastening system' is in practice tantamount to permitting producers of nail guns to exclude the use of consumables other than their own branded products in their tools. However, in the absence of general and binding statements or rules, any independent producer is quite free, as far as Community competition law is concerned, to manufacture consumables intended for use in equipment manufactured by others, unless in doing so it infringes a patent or some other industrial or intellectual property right. Even on the assumption that, as the applicant has argued, components of different makes cannot be interchanged without the system characteristics being influenced, the solution should lie in the adoption of appropriate laws and regulations, not in unilateral measures taken by nail gun producers which have the effect of preventing independent producers from pursuing the bulk of their business.

In paragraph 68 the GC states that independent producers are free, as far as competition law is concerned, to manufacture consumables. This statement is revealing of the policy behind the narrow market definition adopted in some of the cases. It is not, as the wording suggests, that competition law *allows* independents to manufacture but that Article 102 may preclude the producer of the original equipment from excluding others' access to the market.[85]

In *Tetra Pak II*[86] the Commission refused to accept that Tetra Pak supplied 'systems' and held rather that it operated on four separate product markets. The following extract is from the judgment of the GC, which was confirmed by the CJ.

---

[83] *Eurofix-Bauco v. Hilti* [1988] OJ L65/19, [1989] 4 CMLR 677. For the abuse issue, see Chap. 7.

[84] Aff'd by the CJ, Case C-53/92 P, *Hilti AG v. Commission* [1994] ECR I-667.

[85] See Chap. 7.

[86] *Elopak Italia/Tetra Pak* [1991] OJ L72/1, aff'd Case T-83/91, *Tetra Pak International SA v. Commission* [1994] ECR II-755, aff'd Case C-333/94 P, *Tetra Pak International SA v. Commission* [1996] ECR I-5951.

Case T-83/91, *Tetra Pak Rausing* v. *Commission* [1994] ECR II-755

Tetra Pak produced aseptic cartons for packaging ultra-heat treated milk and the machines for processing the milk and filling the cartons. It also produced non-aseptic cartons for pasteurized (non-aseptic) milk and the machines for pasteurizing the milk and filling those cartons. The Courts confirmed the Commission's finding that there were four product markets concerned: aseptic packaging machines, aseptic cartons, non-aseptic machines, and non-aseptic cartons.

General Court

82. First, and contrary to the arguments of the applicant, consideration of commercial usage does not support the conclusion that the machinery for packaging a product is indivisible from the cartons. For a considerable time there have been independent manufacturers who specialize in the manufacture of non-aseptic cartons designed for use in machines manufactured by other concerns and who do not manufacture machinery themselves. It is apparent in particular from the Decision... and not disputed by the applicant, that, until 1987, Elopak, which was set up in 1957, manufactured only cartons and accessory equipment, for example handling equipment. Moreover, also according to the Decision... and not contested by the applicant, approximately 12 per cent of the non-aseptic carton sector was shared in 1985 between three companies manufacturing their own cartons, generally under licence and acting, for machinery, only as distributors. In those circumstances, tied sales of machinery and cartons cannot be considered to be in accordance with commercial usage, given that such sales were not the general rule of the non-aseptic sector and that there were only two manufacturers in the aseptic sector, Tetra Pak and PKL.

83. Furthermore, the applicant's argument as to the requirements for the protection of public health and its interests and those of its customers cannot be accepted. It is not for the manufacturers of complete systems to decide that, in order to satisfy requirements in the public interest, consumable products such as cartons constitute, with the machines with which they are intended to be used, an inseparable integrated system. According to settled case-law, in the absence of general and binding standards or rules, any independent producer is quite free, as far as Community competition law is concerned, to manufacture consumables intended for use in equipment manufactured by others, unless in doing so it infringes a competitor's intellectual property right: see Case T-30/89, *Hilti* v. *EC Commission*... and Case C-53/92P, *Hilti* v. *EC Commission*...

84. In those circumstances, whatever the complexity in this case of aseptic filling processes, the protection of public health may be guaranteed by other means, in particular by notifying machine users of the technical specifications with which cartons must comply in order to be compatible with those machines, without infringing manufacturers' intellectual property rights. Moreover, even on the assumption, shared by the applicant, that machinery and cartons from various sources cannot be used together without the characteristics of the system being affected thereby, the remedy must lie in appropriate legislation or regulations, and not in rules adopted unilaterally by manufacturers, which would amount to prohibiting independent manufacturers from conducting the essential part of their business.

85. It follows that the applicant's argument that the markets in machinery for packaging a product and those in packaging cartons are inseparable cannot be accepted.

In *Info-Lab/Ricoh*,[87] however, the Commission held there was no separate market for empty toner cartridges compatible with a specific (Ricoh) photocopy machine. No producer or dealer produced or sold empty toner cartridges. There was no consumer demand for such a product. Rather, cartridge and powder were always sold together as a single product.

---

[87] Case IV/36431, rejection of a complaint by decision: see *Competition Policy Newsletter* 1999, No. 1, 35.

As explained in Chapter 1 it may be that the interaction between the primary market and the aftermarket is such that the primary and secondary products form one single 'system' market and the competition is between the 'systems' as a whole. Whether this is so mainly depends on the likely reactions of customers to moderate price increases in the aftermarket, so that a separate aftermarket consisting of the secondary products or services of one brand of primary product will be a relevant market only if, (i) switching to other brands of secondary products is not possible and (ii) there are high switching costs in the market for the primary product.[88] In the *Pelikan/Kyocera* decision[89] the Commission held that Kyocera was not dominant in the aftermarket for its own brand of printer cartridges because customers made purchasing decisions based on whole-life costs and commonly used the 'total cost per page' criterion when choosing a printer. Printers are a product where the long-term costs in the aftermarket significantly exceed those for the primary product.[90] The Commission did not expressly state that this was a 'systems' market, but did find that the intense competition on the primary market so restrained Kyocera's behaviour on the aftermarket that it could not be dominant on the latter. This, in effect, amounted to the same thing.[91] The Commission applied the principles in *Pelikan/Kyocera* to another printers-and-cartridges case, *EFIM*, in which it rejected a complaint alleging that the conduct of four manufacturers of inkjet printers illegally excluded competitors from the aftermarket. It held that purchasers of printers were well informed about the prices for consumables and that such was the balance between the capital cost of the printer and the total cost of consumables over the printer's lifetime that consumers had a strong incentive to switch printer brand were the price of consumables for that brand to rise. The primary market was intensely competitive and therefore, 'even if' each of the various markets for cartridges constituted separate relevant markets, the manufacturers were not dominant on their respective aftermarkets.[92]

The Commission found a different situation on the mainframe computer market in its *IBM Maintenance Services* Commitments Decision where it held that the conditions as to the lack of ability of customers to switch to other brands of secondary products, and, the presence of high switching costs in the primary product market were fulfilled. There was therefore a separate aftermarket on which IBM was dominant.[93]

i. Markets for Raw Materials and Inputs

In *Commercial Solvents* it was held that a raw material, aminobutanol, used to produce ethambutol, an anti-TB drug, constituted a product market of its own.[94] Zoja manufactured ethambutol from aminobutanol which had been manufactured by Commercial Solvents. Other, non-ethambutol-based, anti-TB drugs were on the market. The CJ held that the relevant market was not the market for the derivatives (the drugs) but the market for the raw material. There may have been substitute drugs which could be used to combat TB but a manufacturer of ethambutol, such as Zoja, could not operate without aminobutanol.[95]

---

[88] See Case T-427/08, *CEAHR v. Commission* [2010] ECR II-5865; F. Domanico and M. Angeli, 'An Analysis of the IBM Commitment Decision concerning the aftermarket for IBM mainframe computers' (2012) 1 *Competition Policy Newsletter*.

[89] *Pelikan /Kyocera*, see Commission's *XXVth Report on Competition Policy* (Commission, 1995), pp. 41–42.

[90] Apparently, volume for volume, ink in toner cartridges is more expensive than the finest champagne.

[91] See also *Info-Lab/Ricoh*, in n. 87.

[92] COMP/C-3/39.391 *EFIM*, rejection decision 20 May 2009; upheld by the GC, Case T-296/09, *European Federation of Ink and Ink Cartridge Manufacturers (EFIM)* v. *Commission* [2011] ECR II-425, on appeal Case C-59/12 P, judgment pending.

[93] The aftermarket consisted of inputs needed to provide maintenance services for IBM mainframes which could not be sourced outside IBM, and for maintenance services for the mainframes.

[94] Cases 6 and 7/73, *Istituto Chemioterapico Italiano SpA and Commercial Solvents Corp v. Commission* [1974] ECR 223.

[95] Other possible ways of producing ethambutol, using thiophenol or butatone, were dismissed by the CJ as they were uncertain and experimental and had not been used on an industrial scale.

Commercial Solvents was the first case to deal with the problems posed by derivative or ancillary markets. The concept developed in this case, that such markets can be distinguished from those for the primary product, has proved of great importance in the Article 102 jurisprudence. The raw material in *Commercial Solvents* was an input into a production process and had been previously sold by Commercial Solvents to Zoja. The question has arisen, however, as to whether there can be a market in an 'input' which the producer of the 'input' does not offer for sale but uses only for its own purposes. In *Magill*[96] the CJ upheld the Commission's definition of a market in 'television listings' although the broadcasting companies did not sell them for publication.[97] In *Bronner*[98] the CJ accepted that there could be a market in schemes for the home delivery of newspapers even though the undertaking concerned had developed its scheme solely to distribute its own newspapers and did not 'sell' it independently. In *IMS*[99] the CJ said that there could be a 'potential' or 'hypothetical' market in inputs which a dominant undertaking decided not to market independently. In that case the 'input' was a system for representing pharmaceutical sales data over which the undertaking claimed copyright. The undertaking used it to produce the sales reports it sold to pharmaceutical companies. There was no suggestion that the undertaking had ever contemplated 'selling' (licensing) the scheme to others. Nevertheless, the CJ found that there could be a 'market' for it. All that is needed is that two stages of production can be identified. In *Microsoft* the 'input' was the IPRs over its Windows technology.[100] The point can be of great importance in cases (such as *Magill*, *Bronner*, *IMS*, and *Microsoft*) where the alleged abuse is a refusal to supply, because there can be such an abuse only where two markets are involved.

j. Markets in the Pharmaceutical Sector

The general principles of market definition in the pharmaceutical sector are explained in Chapter 1. The *AstraZeneca* case[101] demonstrated the complexities of market definition in this sector in practice. There the Commission defined the relevant market as consisting of proton pump inhibitors (PPIs) used for the treatment of acid-related gastrointestinal conditions. PPIs act by operating directly on the proton pump (PP) which pumps acid into the stomach. From the early 1990s it was accepted by the scientific community that PPIs are superior to the previous treatment by antihistamines (H2 blockers) which block only one of the stimulants of the PP (the histamine receptors in the parietal cells). From then on sales of PPIs gradually increased at the expense of sales of H2 blockers. In *AstraZeneca* the issue was whether H2 blockers and other ulcer medicines exert such competitive pressure on PPIs that they should be considered part of the same market. They treat the same condition but with different therapeutic effects (although only PPIs are effective in respect of some of the most serious conditions). The Commission concluded that the market should be defined as that for PPIs. The fact that the replacement of H2 blockers by PPIs as the treatment of choice was only gradual was not caused by competitive constraints from the former but by the conservative caution of prescribing doctors. Doctors and patients were not sensitive to relative price changes. The GC, affirmed by the CJ, therefore held that the Commission was entitled to take the view that, in principle, the gradual nature of the increase in sales of a new product substituting for an existing product cannot in itself suffice to conclude that the existing product exercises a significant competitive constraint over

---

[96]   Cases C-241–242/91 P, *RTE & ITP v. Commission (Television Listings/Magill)* [1995] ECR I-743.

[97]   Their refusal to license them to publishers of independent 'composite' television magazines was the subject of the case, see Chap. 7.

[98]   Case C-7/97, *Oscar Bronner GmbH & Co KG v. Mediaprint* [1998] ECR I-7791.

[99]   Case C-418/01, *IMS Health GmbH & Co OHG v. NDC Health GmbH & Co KG* [2004] ECR I-503, paras. 43–44. The case is discussed in Chap. 7.

[100]   Case T-201/04, *Microsoft v. Commission* [2007] ECR II-3601, para. 335.

[101]   COMP/A.37.507/F3, [2006] 5 CMLR 287, upheld Case T-321/05, *AstraZeneca v. Commission* [2010] ECR II-2805, aff'd Case C-457/10 P, *AstraZeneca AB and AstraZeneca plc v. Commission*, 6 December 2012.

the new one.[102] The GC pointed out that the issue in the case was concerned only with whether PPIs were subject to competitive constraints, and not with any competitive constraints that PPIs might have exercised over other products.[103]

k. Markets on the Buying Side (Procurement Markets)

It is possible for a buyer to be in a dominant position.[104] The complications of market definition in such situations are illustrated by a case which concerned BA's system of rewards to travel agents for selling BA tickets. BA is a supplier of services—air travel. However, like any other supplier it must also *purchase* goods and services as inputs into its business. The issue in the case was BA's relationship with travel agents. The Commission held that the travel agents supplied a service to BA by selling tickets for BA flights.[105] That service, 'air travel agency services' in the UK, was a relevant market. The Commission found that BA was the dominant buyer in this market and that it had abused its dominance. It concentrated not on BA as a provider of air transport services to persons wanting to fly, but on BA as a buyer of services from numerous travel agents. BA argued that the market identified by the Commission did not really exist and that even if it did it was not the relevant market to consider here. It claimed that the Commission should have looked instead at its position on the air transport market. The GC upheld the Commission's definition of the market.[106]

Case T-219/99, *British Airways plc* v. *Commission* [2003] ECR II-5917

General Court

89. The Commission took the view in the contested decision that the product market to be taken into consideration, for the purposes of establishing the dominant position of BA, is comprised by the services which airlines purchase from travel agents for the purposes of marketing and distributing their airline tickets (recital 72). In the Commission's view, that practice by airlines has the effect of creating a market for air travel agency services distinct from the air transport markets.

90. The Commission has also taken the view that the relevant geographic market in this case was the territory of the United Kingdom, given the national dimension of travel agents' business.

91. According to settled case-law (Case 322/81 *Michelin* v. *Commission*...paragraph 37; Case T-65/96 *Kish Glass* v. *Commission*...paragraph 62, confirmed on appeal by order of the Court of Justice in Case C-241/00 P *Kish Glass* v. *Commission*...), for the purposes of investigating the possibly dominant position of an undertaking on a given product market, the possibilities of competition must be judged in the context of the market comprising the totality of the products or services which, with respect to their characteristics, are particularly suitable for satisfying constant needs and are only to a limited extent interchangeable with other products or services. Moreover, since the determination of the relevant market is useful in assessing whether the undertaking concerned is in a position to prevent effective competition from being maintained and behave to an appreciable extent independently of its competitors and, in this case, its service providers, an examination to that end cannot be limited to the objective characteristics only of the relevant services, but the competitive conditions and the structure of supply and demand on the market must also be taken into consideration.

---

[102] *AstraZeneca*, GC, para. 90.

[103] *AstraZeneca*, GC, para. 97.

[104] See Section 3.A, p. 300.

[105] *Virgin/BA* [2000] OJ L30/1, [2000] 4 CMLR 999.

[106] And also the finding of a dominant position, see Section 6.B.(vi), p. 341, and the Commission's controversial finding of abuse: see Chap. 7. The GC's judgment was affirmed by the CJ, Case C-95/04 P, *British Airways* v. *Commission* [2007] ECR I-2331, where the market definition point was not appealed.

92. It is clear from BA's pleadings that it itself acknowledges the existence of an independent market for air travel agency services, since it states in paragraph 11.34 of its application that travel agents themselves operate in a competitive market, competing with each other to provide the best possible service to their customers.

93. In that regard, although travel agents act on behalf of the airlines, which assume all the risks and advantages connected with the transport service itself and which conclude contracts for transport directly with travellers, they nevertheless constitute independent intermediaries carrying on an independent business of providing services (see, to that effect, the judgment in *VVR*...[107] at paragraph 20).

94. As the Commission states in recital 31 of the contested decision, that specific business of travel agents consists, on the one hand, in advising potential travellers, reserving and issuing airline tickets, (and) collecting the price of the transport and remitting it to the airlines, and, on the other hand, in providing those airlines with advertising and commercial promotion services.

95. In that regard, BA itself states that travel agents are and will remain, in the short term at least, a vital distribution channel for airlines, allowing them efficiently to sell seats on the flights they offer, and that there is a mutual dependence between travel agents and airlines which are not in themselves in a position to market their air transport services effectively.

96. As BA has also stated, travel agents offer a wider range of air routes, departure times and arrival times than any airline could. Travel agents filter information concerning various flights for the benefit of travellers faced with the proliferation of different air transport fare structures, which arise from the real-time pricing systems operated by airlines.

97. BA has further recognised that the role which travel agents play in the distribution of airline tickets explains why airlines seek to offer them advantages so that they sell seats on their flights. The irreplaceable nature of the services which travel agents provide to airlines is thus borne out by all the payments which the airlines make to them.

98. Finally, BA has itself emphasised that major travel agents individually negotiate agreements for the distribution of air tickets and that they are thus in a position to set the airlines in competition.

99. That specific nature of the services provided to airlines by travel agents, without any serious possibility of the airlines substituting themselves for the agents in order to carry out the same services themselves, is corroborated by the fact that, at the time of the events of which complaint is made, 85 per cent of air tickets sold in the territory of the United Kingdom were sold through the intermediary of travel agents.

100. The Court therefore considers that the services of air travel agencies represent an economic activity for which, at the time of the contested decision, airlines could not substitute another form of distribution of their tickets, and that they therefore constitute a market for services distinct from the air transport market.

101. With regard to the fact that the restrictions on competition which the Commission imputes to BA's performance reward schemes arise from the position which BA holds in its capacity not as supplier but as purchaser of air travel agency services, this is irrelevant having regard to the definition of the market in question. Article [102] applies both to undertakings whose possible dominant position is established, as in this case, in relation to their suppliers and to those which are capable of being in the same position in relation to their customers.

102. BA itself acknowledged at the hearing, moreover, that it is possible both for a seller and for a purchaser to hold a dominant position within the meaning of Article [102].

103. BA cannot therefore validly argue that, in order to define the product market in question, with a view to assessing the effects on competition of the financial advantages which it allows to travel agents established in the United Kingdom, it is necessary to determine whether a single supplier of air transportation services on a particular route can profitably increase its prices.

---

[107] This is a reference to Case 311/87, *VZW Vereniging van Vlaamse Reisbureaus v. VZW Sociale Dienst van de Plaatselijke en Gewestelijke Overheidsdiensten* [1987] ECR 3801, which concerned price-fixing amongst Belgian travel agents.

104. Such a parameter, which might be relevant in relation to each airline, is not of such a kind as to enable measurement of BA's economic strength in its capacity not as provider of air transport services but as purchaser of travel agency services, on all routes to and from United Kingdom airports, either in relation to all other airlines regarded in the same capacity as purchasers of air travel agency services or in relation to travel agents established in the United Kingdom.

105. BA's objections to the relevance of the product market adopted by the Commission, based on the possible marginalisation of the distribution of airline tickets through the intermediary of travel agents, on the exclusive specialisation of airlines by geographical destinations, and on the independent behaviour of an airline in a monopoly situation on certain routes, therefore have no bearing.

106. Those arguments are based on situations which are either hypothetical or foreign to the conditions of competition operating in the product market in question constituted by air travel agency services, both between the agents providing those services and between the airlines using them.

107. The Commission did not therefore make any error of assessment in defining the relevant product market as that for services provided by travel agents in favour of airlines, for the purposes of establishing whether BA holds a dominant position on that market in its capacity as bidder for those services.

(ii) Supply Substitution

In *Continental Can* the CJ held that the market must be defined from the supply side as well as the demand side. In that case the Commission found three separate markets consisting of different types of metal containers for food packaging. The Court found that the Commission had not explained why these products were in separate markets and were not all part of a larger light metal container market. In particular, it had not set out why competitors could not enter the identified markets by a simple adaptation of their production facilities.

Case 6/72, *Europemballage Corp & Continental Can Co Inc v. Commission* [1973] ECR 215

Court of Justice

32. For the appraisal of SLW's dominant position and the consequences of the disputed merger, the definition of the relevant market is of essential significance, for the possibilities of competition can only be judged in relation to those characteristics of the products in question by virtue of which those products are particularly apt to satisfy an inelastic need and are only to a limited extent interchangeable with other products.

33. In this context recitals Nos 5 to 7 of the second part of the decision deal in turn with a 'market for light containers for canned meat products', a 'market for light containers for canned seafood', and a 'market for metal closures for the food packing industry, other than crown corks', all allegedly dominated by SLW and in which the disputed merger threatens to eliminate competition. The decision does not, however, give any details of how these three markets differ from each other, and must therefore be considered separately. Similarly, nothing is said about how these three markets differ from the general market for light metal containers, namely the market for metal containers for fruit and vegetables, condensed milk, olive oil, fruit juices and chemico-technical products. In order to be regarded as constituting a distinct market, the products in question must be individualized, not only by the mere fact that they are used for packing certain products, but by particular characteristics of production which make them specifically suitable for this purpose. Consequently, a dominant position on the market for light metal containers for meat and fish cannot be decisive, as long as it has not been proved that competitors from other sectors of the market for light metal containers are not in a position to enter this market, by a simple adaptation, with sufficient strength to create a serious counterweight.

The CJ also held that the Commission should not have dismissed the possibility of the customers themselves commencing manufacture of their own cans.[108]

Subsequent to *Continental Can* it is common for supply-side substitution to be considered. For example, in *Michelin*[109] the CJ held that there was no elasticity of supply between tyres for heavy vehicles and car tyres 'owing to significant differences in production techniques and in the plant and tools needed for their manufacture. The fact that time and considerable investment are required in order to modify production plant for the manufacture of light-vehicle tyres instead of heavy-vehicle tyres or vice versa means that there is no discernible relationship between the two categories of tyre enabling production to be adapted to demand on the market.' Similarly, in *Tetra Pak I*[110] the Commission dismissed the feasibility of supply-side substitution. Manufacturers of other types of milk-packaging machinery were not readily able to switch to producing aseptic packaging machinery and cartons. In *Clearstream* the GC said the Commission was correct in finding that no other institution could provide in the near future the full clearing and settlement services for securities issued under German law, given that the undertaking concerned was the final depository for 90 per cent of all existing German securities.[111]

The difficulty when considering supply-side substitution is to distinguish undertakings that are able easily to switch production (including also necessary adjustments to marketing and distribution) to produce another product, from potential competitors. When is a potential competitor, capable of switching production, to be considered at the stage of market definition and when at the stage of assessing market power on the defined market?[112] In Chapter 1 it was seen that the Commission stipulates in its Notice on market definition, at paragraphs 20–23, that potential competition is relevant to market definition only when a supplier is able to switch production in the short term without incurring significant additional costs or risks. Only where the impact is effective and immediate is it equivalent to the demand substitution effect. The GC said in *Atlantic Container Line*:

> Although potential competition and supply-side substitution are conceptually different issues…those issues overlap in part, as the distinction lies primarily in whether the restriction of competition is immediate or not.[113]

These difficulties illustrate once more how problematic it may be to divide market definition from the assessment of market power. Although it could be argued that it does not matter *when* the possibility of other producers switching is considered so long as it *is* considered, the reliance EU law places on market shares makes the proper definition of the market crucial.

C. THE GEOGRAPHIC MARKET

We saw in Chapter 1 that the relevant market has a geographic as well as a product dimension and that the Commission Notice on market definition explains at length how the geographic market is determined.[114]

---

[108] Case 6/72, *Europemballage Corp & Continental Can Co Inc* v. *Commission* [1973] ECR 215, para. 36.

[109] Case 322/81, *NV Nederlandsche Banden-Industrie Michelin* v. *Commission* [1983] ECR 3461, para. 41. The issue of supply substitutability was not addressed by the Commission in its decision, *Bandengroothandel Frieschebebrug BV/ Nederlandsche Banden-Michelin NV* [1981] OJ L353/33.

[110] Commission Decision in *TetraPak (BTG Licence)* [1988] OJ L272/27, [1990] 4 CMLR 47, paras. 36–38, upheld by the GC, Case T-51/89, *Tetra Pak Rausing SA* v. *Commission* [1990] ECR II-309 where the market definition was not challenged.

[111] Case T-301/04, *Clearstream Banking* v. *Commission* [2009] ECR II-3155, paras. 58–63.

[112] The approach in the US is to take no account of supply-side substitutability at the market definition stage but to consider other undertakings switching production only in calculating market shares at the next stage.

[113] Cases T-191 and 212–214/98, *Atlantic Container Line* v. *EC Commission* [2003] ECR II-3275, para. 834.

[114] See Chap. 1, Section 10.B (viii), p. 82 ff.

It is clear from the case law that legal regulation may create national markets, as in the type-approval certificate cases.[115] Similarly, in *British Telecommunications*[116] BT was found to have a statutory monopoly and in *AKZO*[117] the geographic market was confined by the fact that the UK and Ireland were the only Member States which permitted the use of bleaching agents in flour. Narrow geographic markets may be created through factors such as EU regulation (as was the case with sugar),[118] high transport costs, language, marketing infrastructures, consumer preference,[119] or national or local regulations.[120] The market may then be confined to a number of Member States,[121] to a single Member State, or to part of a Member State.

In cases involving the transport sector narrow geographic markets have been defined (in these cases the geographic and product markets may in effect be the same). The Commission has, for example, defined as separate markets the air route between Dublin and Heathrow,[122] the air route between Brussels and Luton,[123] and in *Sealink/B&I Holyhead: Interim Measures* the ferry route between Holyhead and Dun Laoghaire.[124] In the latter decision the Commission distinguished the 'northern', 'southern', and 'central' corridor routes between Great Britain and Ireland. Further, within the 'central corridor' it distinguished the Liverpool and Holyhead routes, concluding that 'potential competition from Liverpool does not constrain the market power of Sealink at Holyhead'.

One of the most notorious cases on the geographic market is *Michelin*.[125] In this case the CJ upheld the Commission's finding that there was a separate market for heavy vehicle new replacement tyres in the Netherlands.

Case 322/81, *Nederlandsche Banden-Industrie Michelin v. Commission* [1983] ECR 3461

Court of Justice

23. The applicant's first submission under this head challenges the Commission's finding that the substantial part of the common market on which it holds a dominant position is the Netherlands. Michelin NV maintains that this geographical definition of the market is too narrow. It is contradicted by the fact that the Commission itself based its decision on factors concerning the Michelin group as a whole such as its technological lead and financial strength which, in the applicant's view, relate to a much wider market or even the world market. The activities of Michelin NV's main competitors are world-wide too.

---

[115] Case 26/75, *General Motors v. EC Commission* [1975] ECR 1367; Case 226/84, *British Leyland v. Commission* [1986] ECR 3263.

[116] [1982] OJ L360/36, [1983] 1 CMLR 457.

[117] Case C-62/86, *AKZO Chemie BV v. Commission* [1991] ECR I-3359.

[118] See *Napier Brown-British Sugar* [1988] OJ L284/41, [1990] 4 CMLR 196; *Irish Sugar* [1997] OJ L258/1, [1997] 5 CMLR 666.

[119] In the merger case *Nestlé/Perrier* [1992] OJ L356/1 (see Chap. 15), for example, the Commission found that the relevant geographic market for mineral water was limited to France. Irrespective of European integration, French consumers obstinately continued to choose local products.

[120] As in *DSD*, Case C-385/07 P, *Der Grüne Punkt—Duales System Deutschland GmbH v. Commission* [2009] ECR I-6155, which concerned the German recycling regime.

[121] Case 27/76, *United Brands v. Commission* [1978] ECR 207.

[122] *British Midland v. Aer Lingus* [1992] OJ L96/34, [1993] 4 CMLR 596.

[123] *London European-Sabena* [1988] OJ L317/47, [1989] 4 CMLR 662.

[124] [1992] 5 CMLR 255.

[125] Case 322/81, *NV Nederlandsche Banden-Industrie Michelin v. Commission* [1983] ECR 3461.

24. The Commission maintains that this objection concerns less the definition of the market than the criteria used to establish the existence of a dominant position. Since tyre manufacturers have on the whole chosen to sell their products on the various national markets through the intermediary of national subsidiaries, the competition faced by Michelin NV is on the Netherlands market.

25. The point to be made in this regard is that the Commission addressed its decision not to the Michelin group as a whole but only to its Netherlands subsidiary whose activities are concentrated on the Netherlands market. It has not been disputed that Michelin NV's main competitors also carry on their activities in the Netherlands through Netherlands subsidiaries of their respective groups.

26. The Commission's allegation concerns Michelin NV's conduct towards tyre dealers and more particularly its discount policy. In this regard the commercial policy of the various subsidiaries of the groups competing at the European or even the world level is generally adapted to the specific conditions existing on each market. In practice dealers established in the Netherlands obtain their supplies only from suppliers operating in the Netherlands. The Commission was therefore right to take the view that the competition facing Michelin NV is mainly on the Netherlands market and that it is at that level that the objective conditions of competition are alike for traders.

27. This finding is not related to the question whether in such circumstances factors relating to the position of the Michelin group and its competitors as a whole and to a much wider market may enter into consideration in the adoption of a decision as to whether a dominant position exists on the relevant product market.

28. Hence the relevant substantial part of the common market in this case is the Netherlands and it is at the level of the Netherlands market that Michelin NV's position must be assessed.

In this case it was not asked whether or not customers could easily have bought Michelin or other tyres outside the Netherlands. Rather, the geographic market appears to have been confined to the area in which the Commission found that the abuse had been committed.[126]

In some cases the EU Courts have been more sceptical about narrowly drawn markets. In *Alsatel v. Novasam*,[127] for example, it did not accept that the evidence established that a particular region of France, rather than the country as a whole, was the geographic market for telephonic installations. In *BPB*,[128] however, a national market was found despite the existence of pressure from imports from elsewhere. The market was defined as being just the UK and Ireland.

In its 2001 *Michelin II* decision[129] the Commission was careful to devote considerable attention to the delineation of the geographic market. Taking into account the CJ's judgment of 1983 the company argued that the new replacement tyre market was no longer national but had become international in the intervening years. The Commission refuted this claim. It said that what mattered was 'to assess the real capacity of dealers to obtain supplies from outside their national territory and the similarities or differences in the supply structure'.[130] Michelin argued that 'the structure of competition on the replacement tyre market is worldwide: the main

---

[126] Bishop and Walker, *The Economics of EC Competition Law* (cited in n. 8), para. 4.70. See also the criticism in V. Korah, 'The Michelin Decision of the Commission' (1982) 7 *ELRev* 130.

[127] Case 247/86 [1988] ECR 5987.

[128] *BPB Industries* [1989] OJ L10/50, [1990] 4 CMLR 464, upheld in Case T-65/89, *BPB Industries and British Gypsum Ltd v. Commission* [1993] ECR II-389, and Case C-310/93 P, *BPB Industries plc and British Gypsum Ltd v. Commission* [1995] ECR I-865.

[129] *Michelin* [2001] OJ L143/1.

[130] *Michelin* [2001] OJ L143/1, para. 124.

players...compete on a world scale'.[131] The Commission denied that this situation implied that there were not national markets:

123. The argument that the largest international tyre producers compete in numerous countries and across the European Union in no way means that it can be supposed that the relevant geographic market is the world market. This situation is perfectly compatible with the existence of conditions of competition that are appreciably different in each of the relevant countries. This was already the situation in the tyre industry at the time, when the Court of Justice found that the Dutch new replacement tyre market was a national market.

The Commission took into account the fact that the large manufacturers still organised their distribution and sales along national lines;[132] that there were considerable differences in the large manufacturers' market shares from country to country which 'are hardly compatible with the theory of a European market characterised by homogeneous competition';[133] and that there were appreciable price differences from country to country.[134] It also rejected the argument that the hauliers could easily purchase their tyres from abroad if they wished: among the reasons for this was the structure of the road haulage industry in France which was composed in the main of small firms[135] which meant, inter alia, that they were unlikely to have the resources to surmount the linguistic obstacles to intra-Community trade.[136] As far as the retread market was concerned the Commission held that since the retread market was a market for the provision of *services* rather than goods 'it is a national market and therefore at most of national dimension'. Moreover there were differences in the structure of demand within the Community which helped to set the French market apart, including the fact that in France the predominant method of retreading was 'mould-cure' and custom retreading, rather than 'precure' treading.[137]

In *British Airways* geographic market definition arose in a case involving the dominance of a buyer, not a supplier. As we have seen, the GC upheld the Commission's definition of the product market as being air travel agency services. The geographic market was defined as the UK.[138]

Case T-219/99, *British Airways plc* v. *Commission* [2003] ECR II-5917

General Court

108. As for the geographic market to be taken into consideration, consistent case-law shows that it may be defined as the territory in which all traders operate in the same or sufficiently homogeneous conditions of competition in so far as concerns specifically the relevant products or services, without it being necessary for those conditions to be perfectly homogeneous (Case T-83/91 *Tetra*

---

[131] *Michelin* [2001] OJ L143/1, para. 121.

[132] *Michelin* [2001] OJ L143/1, paras. 125–131.

[133] *Michelin* [2001] OJ L143/1, para. 133.

[134] *Michelin* [2001] OJ L143/1, paras. 134–141.

[135] 'Micro-enterprises' in EU-speak, see *Michelin* [2001] OJ L143/1, para. 144.

[136] *Michelin* [2001] OJ L143/1, para. 144.

[137] *Michelin* [2001] OJ L143/1, para. 157. Mould-cure involves industrial retreading plants and, unlike the precure method, usually requires an intermediary between the retreader and the haulier.

[138] Note (para. 110 of the judgment quoted) that under IATA rules tickets bought outside the UK could not be used to depart from non-UK airports.

Pak v. *Commission*...paragraph 91, confirmed on appeal by judgment in Case C-333/94 P *Tetra Pak* v. *Commission (Tetra Pak II)*...).

109. It can hardly be denied that, in the overwhelming majority of cases, travellers reserve airline tickets in their country of residence. Although BA has argued that not all tickets sold by travel agents in the United Kingdom are necessarily sold to residents of that country, it has acknowledged that transactions taking place outside the United Kingdom could not be quantified.

110. Moreover, as the Commission has stated in recital 83 of the contested decision, without challenge from BA, IATA's rules on the order of using the coupons in airline tickets prevent tickets sold outside the territory of the United Kingdom from being used for flights departing from United Kingdom airports.

111. Since the distribution of airline tickets takes place at national level, it follows that airlines normally purchase the services for distributing those tickets on a national basis, as is shown by the agreements signed to that end by BA with travel agents established in the United Kingdom.

112. Nor has any doubt been cast on the fact that airlines structure their commercial services at the national level, that travel agents' handling of air tickets is carried out in the context of IATA's national plans for bank settlement and, in this case, through the Billing and Settlement Plan for the United Kingdom (BSPUK).

113. Nor has BA challenged the Commission's statement that BA applies its performance reward schemes to travel agents established in the United Kingdom in a uniform manner over the whole of the territory of that Member State.

114. Nor has BA denied that the disputed financial incentives apply only to sales of BA tickets carried out in the United Kingdom, even if those incentives form part of agreements concluded with travel agents whose activities extend to more than one Member State.

115. Contrary to what BA maintains, the fact that BA concludes global agreements with certain travel agents is not capable of establishing that the latter increasingly deal with airlines on the international level. As is shown in recital 20 of the contested decision, which BA has not challenged, those global agreements were signed with only three travel agents and only for the winter season 1992/1993. Moreover, those agreements were merely added to local agreements made in the countries concerned.

116. It does not therefore appear that the Commission erred in defining the relevant geographic market as the United Kingdom market, for the purposes of demonstrating that BA held a dominant position on that market in its capacity as the purchaser of air travel agency services provided by agents established in the United Kingdom.

117. The plea alleging incorrect definition of the relevant product and geographic market cannot therefore be accepted.

Again the difficulty involved in defining the geographic market, as when defining product markets, can be tempered if competition from outside the market is taken into account when assessing market power. If that is done, over-narrow market definitions and the rather artificial distinction between market definition and market power assessment are not so misleading. However, the size, financial strength, and degree of diversification of competitors at world level does not necessarily deprive an undertaking of dominance in the relevant geographical market.

D. THE TEMPORAL MARKET

The temporal dimension of the market is often ignored and the Commission Notice does not refer to it. Many markets do not have a temporal dimension.[139] It can, however, be relevant when considering

[139] Case 322/81, *Nederlandsche Banden-Industrie Michelin v. Commission* [1983] ECR 3461, para. 59.

transport markets, for example.[140] In such markets the temporal dimension may in fact be an inherent part of the definition of the product market.

In *United Brands*[141] there was evidence that the demand for bananas fluctuated from season to season depending on the availability of other fruits. This suggested that there were different seasonal markets and that in the summer at least bananas were part of a wider fruit market. The Commission disregarded this evidence and defined a single year-round market consisting only of bananas. The CJ did not pursue the issue. In *ABG Oil*[142] the Commission looked at the oil market just in the period of the OPEC crisis in the 1970s.

E. THE TETRA PAK II CASE

Tetra Pak II[143] is a good illustration of the complexities of market definition and of the application of the principles of demand substitution. The section of the GC judgment on the aftermarket aspect of the case has already been discussed.[144] The following extract deals with the issue of the interchangeability of different forms of packaging. The GC judgment was affirmed by the CJ.[145]

Case T-83/91, *Tetra Pak Rausing* v. *Commission* [1994] ECR II-755

Tetra Pak produced aseptic cartons for packaging ultra-heat treated milk and the machines for processing the milk and filling the cartons. It also produced non-aseptic cartons for pasteurized (non-aseptic) milk and the machines for pasteurizing the milk and filling those cartons. The Court confirmed the Commission's finding that there were four product markets concerned: aseptic packaging machines, aseptic cartons, non-aseptic machines, and non-aseptic cartons.

General Court

63. A preliminary point to note is that, according to settled case law, the definition of the market in the relevant products must take account of the overall economic context, so as to be able to assess the actual economic power of the undertaking in question. In order to assess whether an undertaking is in a position to behave to an appreciable extent independently of its competitors and customers and consumers, it is necessary first to define the products which, although not capable of being substituted for other products, are sufficiently interchangeable with its products, not only in terms of the objective characteristics of those products, by virtue of which they are particularly suitable for satisfying constant needs, but also in terms of the competitive conditions and the structure of supply and demand on the market: see Case 322/81, *Michelin* v. *EC Commission*...

64. In this case, the 'interchangeability' of aseptic packaging systems with non-aseptic systems and of systems using cartons with those using other materials must be assessed in the light of all the competitive conditions on the general market in systems for packaging liquid food products. Accordingly, in the

---

[140] In Cases T-374–375, 384, and 388/94, *European Night Services* v. *Commission* [1998] ECR II-3141, where the GC annulled an Art. 101 Commission decision on a joint venture, the Commission raised during the appeal the matter of confining the business transport market to early morning and late evening rather than all round the clock.

[141] Case 27/76, *United Brands* v. *Commission* [1978] ECR 207.

[142] [1977] OJ L117/1, [1977] 2 CMLR D1 (the decision was annulled on appeal but on abuse, not dominance, grounds: Case 77/77, *Benzine Petroleum Handelsmaatschappij BV* v. *Commission* [1978] ECR 1513, see Chap. 7).

[143] *Elopak Italia/Tetra Pak* [1992] OJ L72/1, upheld by the GC, Case T-83/91, *Tetra Pak International SA* v. *Commission* [1994] ECR II-755, *aff'd* Case C-333/94 P, *Tetra Pak International SA* v. *Commission* [1996] ECR I-5951. See V. Korah, 'The Paucity of Economic Analysis in the EEC Decisions on Competition—Tetra Pak II' [1993] *Current Legal Problems* 148.

[144] See Section 5.B.i.h. p. 320.

[145] The abuse issues in the case are dealt with in Chap. 7.

specific context of this case, the applicant's approach of dividing that general market into differentiated sub-markets depending on whether the packaging systems are used for packaging milk, dairy products other than milk or non-dairy products by virtue of the specific characteristics of the packaging of those different categories of products, in which the possibility exists that various kinds of substitutable equipment may be used, would lead to a compartmentalization of the market which would not reflect economic reality. There is a comparable structure of supply and demand for both aseptic and non-aseptic machinery and cartons, however they are used, since all belong to one sector, the packaging of liquid food products. Whether they are used for packaging milk or other products, aseptic and non-aseptic machinery and cartons not only share the same characteristics of production but also satisfy identical economic needs. In addition, a not insignificant proportion of Tetra's Pak's customers operate in both the milk sector and the fruit juice sector, as the applicant has admitted. In all those respects, therefore, this case is distinguishable from the situation contemplated in Case 85/76, *Hoffmann-La Roche* v. *EC Commission*...relied on by the applicant, in which the Court of Justice had first considered the possibility of finding that there were two separate markets for one product which, unlike in this case, was used in two ways in wholly distinct sectors, one 'bio-nutritive' and the other 'technological'...Furthermore, as both parties have submitted, Tetra Pak machinery and cartons of the same type were uniformly priced whether they were intended for packaging milk or other products, which confirms that they belong to a single product market. There is accordingly no need, contrary to the applicant's arguments, to find that there are differentiated sub-markets for packaging systems of the same type depending on whether they are used for packaging a particular category of products.

65. Accordingly, in order to ascertain whether the four markets defined in the Decision were indeed separate markets during the period in question, it is necessary—as the Commission submits—to determine in particular which products were sufficiently interchangeable with aseptic and non-aseptic machinery and cartons in the predominant milk sector. To the extent that the carton-packaging systems were used primarily for packaging milk, a dominant position in that sector was sufficient evidence, if relevant, of a dominant position on the market as a whole. Any such dominant position could not be called in question by the existence of substitutable equipment, alleged by the applicant, in the non-milk product packaging sector, since such equipment accounted for only a very small proportion of all products packaged in cartons during the period covered by the Decision. The predominance of the milk-packaging sector is clearly demonstrated by data given in the Decision (recital 6) and not disputed by the applicant...Those figures indicate that, notwithstanding a decrease, the majority of Tetra Pak aseptic cartons were used for packaging milk during the period in question. As for non-aseptic cartons, 100 per cent were used for packaging milk until 1980 and 99 per cent thereafter, according to the same source. For all those reasons, the Commission was entitled to take the view that it was not necessary to carry out a separate analysis of the non-milk-packaging sector.

66. In the milk-packaging sector, the Commission correctly based itself, in this case, on the test of sufficient substitutability of the different systems for packaging liquid foods, as laid down by the Court of Justice: see in particular Case 6/72, *Europemballage and Continental Can* v. *EC Commission*...and Case 85/76 *Hoffmann La Roche* v. *EC Commission*...It is also in accordance with case-law (see Joined Cases 6 & 7/73, *Commercial Solvents* v. *EC Commission*) that the Commission applied the test of sufficient substitutability of products at the stage of the packaging systems themselves, which constitute the market in intermediate products on which Tetra Pak's position must be assessed, and not at the stage of the finished products, in this case the packaged liquid food products.

67. In order to assess the interchangeability for packers of the packaging systems, the Commission necessarily had to take account of the repercussions of the final consumers' demand on the packers' intermediate demand. It found that the packers could influence consumer habits in the choice of types of product packaging only by promotion and publicity in a long and costly process, extending over several years, as Tetra Pak had expressly acknowledged in its reply to the statement of objections. In those circumstances, the various types of packaging could not be considered to be sufficiently interchangeable for packers, whatever their bargaining power, referred to by the applicant.

68. It is therefore exclusively to assess the effect of final demand on the packers' intermediate demand that the Commission referred to the lack of perfect substitutability, which concerned only the packaged products and not the packaging systems. In particular, the Commission correctly considered that, because of the small proportion of the retail price of milk accounted for by the cost of its packaging, 'small but significant changes in the relative price of the different packages would not be sufficient to trigger off shifts between the different types of milk with which they are associated because the substitution of different milks is less than perfect' (decision in *Tetra Pak I*...). The applicant's complaints that the Commission based itself on the model of perfect competition and defined the relevant markets solely by reference to consumer demand must accordingly be rejected.

69. The [General Court] therefore holds first that the Commission was entitled to find that during the period in question there was not sufficient interchangeability between machinery for aseptic packaging in cartons and machinery for non-aseptic packaging whatever the material used. At the level of demand, aseptic systems are distinguished by their inherent characteristics, satisfying specific consumer needs and preferences in relation to the duration and quality of conservation and to taste. Moreover, to move from packaging UHT milk to packaging fresh milk requires the setting up of a distribution system which ensures that the milk is continuously kept in a refrigerated environment. Furthermore, at the level of supply, the manufacture of machinery for the aseptic packaging of UHT milk in cartons requires complex technology, which only Tetra Pak and its competitor PKL have succeeded in developing and making operational during the period considered in the Decision. Manufacturers of non-aseptic machinery using cartons, operating on the market closest to the market in the aseptic machinery in question, were therefore not in a position to enter the latter market by modifying their machinery in certain respects for the market in aseptic machinery.

70. As for aseptic cartons, they also constituted a market distinct from that in non-aseptic packaging. At the level of the packers' intermediate demand, aseptic cartons were not sufficiently interchangeable with non-aseptic packages, including cartons, for the same reasons as those already set out in the preceding paragraph in relation to machinery. At the level of supply, the documents before the Court indicate that notwithstanding the absence of insurmountable technical problems, manufacturers of non-aseptic cartons were not in a position in the circumstances in question to adapt to the manufacture of aseptic cartons. The fact that on that market there was only one competitor of Tetra Pak, namely PKL, with only 10 per cent of the market in aseptic cartons during the period in question, demonstrates that the conditions of competition were such that in practice there was no possibility for manufacturers of non-aseptic cartons to enter the market in aseptic cartons, in particular given the lack of aseptic filling machines.

71. Secondly, the Court holds that, during the period in question, aseptic machinery and cartons were not sufficiently interchangeable with aseptic packaging systems using other materials. According to the data provided in the documents before the Court, which are not disputed by the applicant, no such substitutable equipment existed, with the exception of the arrival on the market towards the end of the relevant period of systems for aseptic packaging in plastic bottles, returnable glass bottles and pouches in France, Germany and Spain respectively. However, each of those new products was introduced in only one country and, what is more, accounted for only a marginal share of the UHT-milk-packaging market. According to information provided by the applicant, that share has been only 5 per cent of the market in France since 1987. In the Community as a whole, in 1976, all UHT milk was packaged in cartons. The observations submitted by the applicant in response to the statement of objections indicate that in 1987 approximately 97.7 per cent of UHT milk was packaged in cartons. At the end of the period in question, that is 1991, cartons still accounted for 97 per cent of the UHT-milk-packaging market, the remaining 3 per cent being held by plastic containers, as the applicant indicated in answer to a written question from the Court. The marginal share of the market thus held by aseptic containers made out of other materials demonstrates that those containers cannot be considered, even during the last years of the period covered by the Decision, as products which are sufficiently interchangeable with aseptic systems using cartons (see *Commercial Solvents* v. *EC Commission*...).

72. Thirdly, the Court finds that non-aseptic machinery and cartons constituted markets which were distinct from those in non-aseptic packaging systems using materials other than cartons. It has already been shown…that, because of the marginal proportion of the price of milk attributable to packaging costs, packers would have been led to consider that containers—in this case cartons, glass or plastic bottles and non-aseptic pouches—were easily interchangeable only if there had been an almost perfect substitutability of final consumer demand. In the light of their very different physical characteristics and the system of doorstep delivery of pasteurized milk in glass bottles in the UK, that form of packaging was not interchangeable for consumers with packaging in cartons. Moreover, the fact that environmental factors led some consumers to prefer certain types of packaging, such as returnable glass bottles, did not promote the substitutability of those containers with cartons. Consumers who were aware of those factors did not consider those containers to be interchangeable with cartons. The same applies to consumers who, conversely, were attracted to a certain convenience in using products packaged in cartons. As for plastic bottles and plastic pouches, they were on the market only in countries where consumers accepted that type of packaging, in particular, according to information in the Decision which is not disputed by the applicant, Germany or France. Furthermore, according to the same source, that packaging was used for only approximately one-third of pasteurised milk in France and 20 per cent in Germany. It follows that those products were not in practice sufficiently interchangeable with non-aseptic cartons throughout the Community during the period covered by the Decision.

73. Analysis of the markets in the milk-packaging sector thus shows that the four markets concerned, defined in the Decision, were indeed separate markets.

74. Moreover and in any event, the Court finds that an examination of the substitutability of the various packaging systems in the fruit-juice sector, fruit juices being the largest category of liquid foods other than milk, shows that in that sector also there was no sufficient interchangeability either between aseptic and non-aseptic systems or between systems using cartons and systems using other materials.

75. The market in the carton packaging of fruit juices was held mainly by aseptic systems during the period in question. In 1987, 91 per cent of cartons used for packaging fruit juice were aseptic. That proportion remained stable until 1991, when 93 per cent of all cartons were aseptic according to Tetra Pak's reply to a written question from the Court. The marginal share held by non-aseptic cartons for packaging fruit juice, which continued for several years as has been shown, demonstrates that in practice they were barely interchangeable with aseptic cartons.

76. Nor were aseptic machinery and cartons sufficiently interchangeable with equipment using other materials for packaging fruit juice. The tables provided by Tetra Pak in answer to a written question from the Court show that during the period in question the two major rival types of packaging in the fruit-juice sector were glass bottles and cartons. In particular, the tables indicate that in 1976 in the Community more than 76 per cent of fruit-juice (by volume) was packaged in glass bottles, 9 per cent in cartons and 6 per cent in plastic bottles. The share held by cartons reached approximately 50 per cent of the market in 1987 and 46 per cent in 1991. The share held by glass bottles increased from 30 to 39 per cent between those dates and the share held by plastic bottles remained negligible, decreasing from approximately 13 per cent to 11 per cent.

77. Taking into account their very different characteristics, concerning both price and presentation, weight and the way in which they are stored, cartons and glass bottles could not be considered to be sufficiently interchangeable. In relation particularly to comparative prices, both parties' answers to a written question from the Court show that the total cost to the packer of packaging fruit juice in non-returnable glass bottles is significantly higher by approximately 75 per cent than that of packaging in aseptic cartons.

78. It follows from all the above considerations that the Commission has established to the requisite legal standard that the markets in aseptic machinery and cartons and those in non-aseptic machinery and cartons were insulated from the general market in systems for packaging liquid foods.

6. ASSESSING MARKET POWER

A. GENERAL

Once the market has been defined the power which the undertaking has on that market must be assessed in order to determine whether the undertaking is 'dominant'.

If legal regulation causes the undertaking concerned to have 100 per cent of the market and no competitors can enter the market, for example where a statutory monopoly over the market has been conferred upon it, then it may be a true monopoly. In other situations the matter will not be so clear.[146]

It is possible, although rare in the absence of a statutory monopoly, for an undertaking to have 100 per cent of a market[147] (although transitory very high market shares are frequently found in high technology markets). It was seen in Chapter 1, however, that even an undertaking with a 100 per cent share of the market does not, in the theory of industrial economics, necessarily occupy a dominant position or possess market power. Market shares do not indicate why the undertaking has 100 per cent of the market or tell us about potential competition. They do not explain, for example, whether the undertaking has a high market share because it produces the best products most efficiently, or because the minimum efficient scale of production means that it is a 'natural' monopoly. Nor do they indicate whether or not the undertaking is vulnerable to market entry. The vulnerability of an undertaking to market entry will be dependent upon whether or not there are 'barriers to entry' to the market. This is why barriers to entry, discussed in Chapter 1, is such a central concept.

We saw in Chapter 1 that there is an ongoing debate about what constitutes a barrier to entry or expansion (hereafter, unless the context otherwise requires 'barriers to entry')[148] and even about how the term should be defined. It should also be noted that there is an argument that the disciplining effect of potential, as distinct from existing, competitors can be exaggerated.[149]

EU law on barriers to entry certainly does not follow Stigler's view. In the past at least, a very wide variety of factors have been found to be barriers to entry or, in the terminology often used by the EU Courts, 'other factors indicating dominance'.[150] The use of the term 'other factors indicating dominance' may be a recognition that not all the difficulties facing competitors entering a market can really be described as barriers to entry under any definition. This eclectic approach means that in trying to ascertain whether an undertaking is likely to be held dominant for the purposes of Article 102 it is necessary carefully to study the case law of the EU Courts and the decisional practice of the Commission.

Sections 6.B to 6.E set out the approach of the EU Courts and the Commission to date when determining whether or not an undertaking is dominant on a particular market. It will be seen that reliance is placed first on the market shares of the undertakings concerned and then on barriers to entry

---

[146] See D. Landes and R. A. Posner, 'Market Power in Antitrust Cases' (1981) 94 *Harvard LR* 937; R. Schmalensee, 'Another Look at Market Power' (1982) 95 *Harvard LR* 1789.

[147] See Chap. 1. *GVL* [1981] OJ L370/49 is an example of a monopoly which was not in that category (a collecting society in Germany).

[148] Most barriers to entry are barriers to expansion as well, although Faull and Nikpay, *The EC Law of Competition* (cited in n. 1), 4.99, point out that barriers to expansion tend to be high in sectors where an increase in capacity would require a large investment.

[149] See E. M. Fox and L. A. Sullivan, 'Antitrust—Retrospective and Prospective: Where Are We Coming From? Where Are we Going?' (1987) 62 *New York Univ LR* 936, 975: 'Potential competition is not an existing alternative source of supply; it does not satisfy buyers' desires for choice or the opportunity for buyers to play one seller against another; and it is normally an inconsequential source of pressure to innovate.'

[150] 'Other' meaning factors other than market share. The Commission now uses the term 'barriers to entry': see, e.g., Commission Guidelines on the assessment of horizontal mergers under the Council Regulation on the control of concentrations between undertakings [2004] OJ C31/5 and the Guidance Paper. For Stigler, see G. J. Stigler, *The Organization of Industry* (Irwin, 1968), discussed in Chap. 1, Section 10.C, p. 86.

and other factors indicating dominance. Throughout these sections it will be seen that one criticism of the case law and decisions taken under Article 102 has been their tendency to place too great an emphasis on market shares and the failure, at least in the past, to display rigorous economic analysis when dealing with barriers to entry. On the contrary, barriers to entry have often been seen as pervasive. When combined with the tendency to define markets narrowly, the importance attached to market shares and the broad approach to barriers to entry mean that an undertaking's market power may be considerably exaggerated. Undertakings which do not in reality have market power may, therefore, be precluded or deterred from engaging in conduct which is pro-competitive or at least neutral from a competition perspective (Type 1 errors). Competition law may then have the perverse effect of inhibiting the competitive process on the market.

Hitherto the Commission has not issued a general Notice on market power analogous to that on market definition although it has issued Guidelines on market analysis and the assessment of significant market power under the regulatory framework for electronic communications and services.[151] However, the matter is considered in the Guidance Paper, paragraphs 9–18. In paragraph 12 the Commission says that the assessment of dominance will take into account the competitive structure of the market and in particular:

- The market position of the dominant undertaking and its competitors (i.e. current market shares);
- Constraints imposed by credible threats of expansion or entry (barriers to expansion or entry); and
- Countervailing buyer power.

B. MARKET SHARES

(i) General

Market share relates to the first indent in paragraph 12 of the Guidance Paper. Market shares indicate the *present* state of the market.

If an undertaking has a statutory monopoly over a relevant market, that is the end of the matter. It is in a dominant position. In the absence of statutory monopoly it has been settled case law since *Hoffmann-La Roche*[152] that the starting point for the assessment of dominance is market share.

The EU Courts have placed great reliance on market shares although, as already explained, economic theory holds that in the absence of barriers to entry high market shares are not themselves indicative of dominance. Critics of this reliance point, inter alia, to the fact that it depends on the uncertain art of market definition and that market definition is an 'in or out' (zero-one fallacy) game, whereas in reality products are often imperfect substitutes for one another and undertakings may be constrained by the existence of products which are outside the defined market. One economist has suggested that it may be possible to devise a 'weighted market share' approach 'to take account of the fact that substitutability is a matter of degree in market power assessment'. This would involve taking into account imperfect substitutes when calculating the market share of a product but with a lesser weight than if it were a more perfect substitute.[153] Another problem with reliance on market share is that market share analysis is 'static' and not suited for application to dynamically competitive markets such as those in the new economy.[154]

---

[151] [2002] OJ C165/6. See also the Guidelines on horizontal mergers and on non-horizontal mergers, discussed in Chap. 15.

[152] Case 85/76, *Hoffmann-La Roche & Co AG v. Commission* [1979] ECR 461.

[153] J. Vickers, 'Market Power in Competition Case' (2006) 2 *European Law Journal* 3, 8–10.

[154] See Section 6.E, p. 361.

(ii) The Calculation of Market Shares

The calculation of market shares is dealt with in the Commission's Notice on market definition which explains that in some industries sales figures may not be the most appropriate basis for the calculation.

Commission Notice on the Definition of the Relevant Market for the Purposes of Community Competition Law [1997] OJ C372/5

53. The definition of the relevant market in both its product and geographic dimensions allows the identification of the suppliers and the customers/consumers active on that market. On that basis, a total market size and market shares for each supplier can be calculated on the basis of their sales of the relevant products in the relevant area. In practice, the total market size and market shares are often available from market sources, i.e., companies' estimates, studies commissioned from industry consultants and/or trade associations. When this is not the case, or when available estimates are not reliable, the Commission will usually ask each supplier in the relevant market to provide its own sales in order to calculate total market size and market shares.

54. If sales are usually the reference to calculate market shares, there are nevertheless other indications that, depending on the specific products or industry in question, can offer useful information such as, in particular, capacity, the number of players in bidding markets, units of fleet in aerospace, or the reserves held in the case of sectors such as mining.

55. As a rule of thumb, both volume sales and value sales provide useful information. In cases of differentiated products, sales in value and their associated market share will usually be considered to better reflect the relative position and strength of each supplier...

Pursuant to this approach market share has, for example, been calculated using the number of subscribers signed up to a high-speed internet service;[155] the number of units shipped;[156] the units sold and the shares of the installed base (i.e. the number of the relevant machines installed in a given market at a particular point in time);[157] and by the number of retail telecommunications lines and by revenues.[158]

(iii) High Market Shares and the Presumption of Dominance

The case law establishes that the higher the market share the more likely a finding of dominance. In *Hoffmann-La Roche*[159] the CJ, although recognising that the significance of market shares may vary from market to market, and acknowledging the relevance of other factors, held that 'very large shares' held over 'some time' are in themselves indicative of dominance unless there are 'exceptional

---

[155] *Wanadoo*, COMP/38.233, [2005] 5 CMLR 120, upheld Case T-340/03, *France Télécom SA v. Commission* [2007] ECR II-107.

[156] Case T-201/04, *Microsoft v. Commission* [2007] ECR II-3601, p aras. 555–85 and 1038.

[157] COMP/E-1.38.113 *Prokent/Tomra* [2009] 4 CMLR 101, para. 59. The Commission said that this favoured Tomra, the undertaking under investigation, as a calculation on sales *value* would have given Tomra a greater market share (the point was not taken on appeal to the GC, Case T-155/06, *Tomra Systems v. Commission* [2010] ECR II-4361).

[158] COMP/39.525, *Telekomunikacja Polska* 22 June 2011, on appeal Case T-486/11, judgment pending.

[159] Case 85/76, [1979] ECR 461, para. 41.

circumstances'.[160] The 'exceptional circumstances' referred to in *Hoffmann-La Roche* includes the absence of barriers to entry.

Case 85/76, *Hoffmann-La Roche & Co AG* v. *Commission* [1979] ECR 461

39. ..., The existence of a dominant position may derive from several factors which, taken separately, are not necessarily determinative but among these factors a highly important one is the existence of very large market shares.

40. A substantial market share as evidence of the existence of a dominant position is not a constant factor and its importance varies from market to market according to the structure of these markets, especially as far as production, supply and demand are concerned...

41. Furthermore although the importance of the market shares may vary from one market to another the view may legitimately be taken that very large shares are in themselves, and save in exceptional circumstances, evidence of the existence of a dominant position. An undertaking which has a very large market share and holds it for some time, by means of the volume of production and the scale of the supply which it stands for—without those having much smaller market shares being able to meet rapidly the demand from those who would like to break away from the undertaking which has the largest market share—is by virtue of that share in a position of strength which makes it an unavoidable trading partner and which, already because of this secures for it, at the very least during relatively long periods, that freedom of action which is the special feature of a dominant position.

The approach indicated in the *Hoffmann-La Roche* case, therefore, is that where an undertaking has 'very high market shares' there is a *presumption* of dominance. In *Hilti*[161] and *Tetra Pak II*[162] the GC held, citing *Hoffmann-La Roche*, that market shares respectively of 70–80 per cent and 90 per cent were in themselves evidence of a dominant position. In both cases, however, the GC also stated briefly that barriers to entry were high.

In *AKZO* the CJ explained what was meant by a 'very high market share' within the meaning of the test set out in *Hoffmann-La Roche*. It interpreted it as 50 per cent of the market:

With regard to market shares the Court has held that very large shares are in themselves, and save in exceptional circumstances, evidence of the existence of a dominant position: Case 85/76 *Hoffmann-La Roche* v. *EC Commission*. That is the situation where there is a market share of 50 per cent such as that found to exist in this case.[163]

In *AKZO* the Court added that the Commission had 'rightly pointed out that other factors confirmed AKZO's predominance in the market'. Nonetheless the significance of this case is enormous: once the market share is at 50 per cent there is, essentially, a presumption of dominance.[164] An undertaking is, of course, free to adduce evidence establishing that despite its high market share it has no market power. However, this will be a heavy burden to discharge. The fact that there is a presumption of dominance at a 50 per cent market share is a striking and important feature of EU competition law. Many commentators consider it to be far too low. It stands in stark contrast to the US where in applying

---

[160] See also e.g., Case C-457/10 P, *AstraZeneca* v. *Commission*, 6 December 2012, para. 176.

[161] Case T-30/89, *Hilti AG* v. *Commission* [1991] ECR II-1439, paras. 91–94, upheld by the CJ, Case C-53/92 P, *Hilti AG* v. *Commission* [1994] ECR I-667.

[162] Case T-83/91, *Tetra Pak International SA* v. *Commission* [1994] ECR II-755, paras. 109–110, upheld by the CJ, Case C-333/94 P, *Tetra Pak International SA* v. *Commission* [1996] ECR I-5951.

[163] Case C-62/86, *AKZO Chemie BV* v. *Commission* [1991] ECR I-3359, para. 60.

[164] See also Case T-395/94, *Atlantic Container Line AB and others* v. *Commission* [2002] ECR II-875, para. 328.

section 2 of the Sherman Act the courts rarely find an offence of 'monopolization' to have been committed where an undertaking has less than 70 per cent of the market, let alone apply a presumption at 50 per cent.

Hoffmann-La Roche refers to high market shares held for 'some time'. The CJ in *AstraZeneca* rendered this as 'a long period'.[165] What this means has never been precisely spelt out, but Bellamy and Child suggest that a high and stable market share for 'a period of five years would probably afford sufficient evidence while any period of less than three years, especially in a dynamic market, might be considered too short for a high market share to be an indicator of dominance'.[166]

(iv) Relative Market Shares

Market shares must be looked at in relative as well as absolute terms, as recognised in paragraph 13 of the Guidance Paper. This means that when considering the market shares of the undertaking under scrutiny it is also necessary to consider the market shares of its competitors. The CJ said in *Hoffmann-La Roche* that 'the relationship between the market shares of the undertaking concerned and of its competitors, especially those of the next largest' was a relevant factor.[167] The market power of an undertaking with a market share of 51 per cent will be considerably different depending on whether, for example, it simply has one competitor with a 49 per cent share of the market, three competitors which have 16, 16, and 17 per cent of the market respectively or 49 competitors each with 1 per cent of the market. The differentials in market share are extremely significant. A market where there are two undertakings, A with 51 per cent and B with 49 per cent, is an oligopoly. It is not dominated by A alone, although there may be a position of collective dominance with B.[168]

In *United Brands*[169] UBC was held to be dominant even though it had a market share of only 45 per cent. That was however almost twice as large as the share of its nearest competitor. In *Michelin*[170] Michelin was found to hold a share of 57–65 per cent of the relevant market but the remainder was fragmented, the competitors each having only 4–8 per cent. In *Michelin II* there was some uncertainty about Michelin's exact market share in France but it was taken as being over 50 per cent and thus over five times greater than that of its nearest competitor,[171] and in *British Airways*[172] BA's share was seven times greater. In *AstraZeneca* the CJ agreed with the GC that the 'generally very large' market shares of AstraZeneca (AZ) indicated that its market power was 'out of all comparison to those of the other market players'.[173] Once an undertaking has a market share as large as 70 per cent it is bound to have at least twice the share of its nearest competitor.[174] In these circumstances it will be very difficult indeed for the undertaking to

---

[165] Case C-457/10 P, *AstraZeneca v. Commission*, see n. 161, para. 176.

[166] Bellamy and Child (V. Rose and D. Bailey, eds.), *European Law of Competition* (7th edn, Oxford University Press, 2013), 10.026. In 'bidding markets' where contracts are awarded by a competitive tendering process and the 'winner takes all', market shares are not necessarily a useful indicator of dominance, Bellamy and Child, 10.027, although see the merger case, Case T-210/01, *General Electric v. Commission* [2005] ECR II-5575, paras. 148 ff. where the GC agreed with the Commission that it was an indicator of market strength for an undertaking to maintain or increase its market share over a number of years on a bidding market.

[167] Case 85/76, *Hoffmann-La Roche & Co AG v. Commission* [1979] ECR 461, para. 48.

[168] For collective dominance in respect of Art. 102 see Chap. 5, Section 5.A.iii, p. 276 ff.

[169] Case 27/76, *United Brands v. Commission* [1978] ECR 207.

[170] Case 322/81, *Nederlandsche Banden-Industrie Michelin v. Commission* [1983] ECR 3461.

[171] *Michelin* [2001] OJ L143/1, [2002] 5 CMLR 388.

[172] Case T-219/99, *British Airways v. Commission* [2003] ECR II-5917.

[173] Case C-457/10 P, *AstraZeneca v. Commission*, 6 December 2012, para. 177, affirming para. 253 of Case T-321/05, *AstraZeneca v. Commission* [2010] ECR II-2805. AZ's market shares in different Member States are set out in paras 246–252 of the GC judgment.

[174] See also COMP/E-1.38.113 *Prokent Tomra* [2009] 4 CMLR 101, paras. 84–85, on appeal Case T-155/06, *Tomra Systems v. Commission* [2010] ECR II-4361 *aff'd* Case C-549/10 P, *Tomra Systems ASA v. European Commission*, 19 April 2012.

preclude a finding of dominance. There is no case where an undertaking with such a high market share has not been held dominant. It will therefore be appreciated why narrow market definitions may be fatal for undertakings and how important it is to make a realistic determination of the market.

(v) Market Share and the Commission Guidance Paper

In the Guidance Paper the Commission says that market shares provide it with a *useful first indication* of market structure[175] and downplays the reliance on market share.

Guidance on the Commission's Enforcement Priorities in Applying Article 82 of the EC Treaty to Abusive Exclusionary Conduct by Dominant Undertakings [2009] OJ C45/2

13. Market shares provide a useful first indication for the Commission of the market structure and of the relative importance of the various undertakings active on the market…However, the Commission will interpret market shares in the light of the relevant market conditions, and in particular of the dynamics of the market and of the extent to which products are differentiated. The trend or development of market shares over time may also be taken into account in volatile or bidding markets.

…

15. Experience suggests that the higher the market share and the longer the period of time over which it is held, the more likely it is that it constitutes an important preliminary indication of the existence of a dominant position and, in certain circumstances, of possible serious effects of abusive conduct, justifying an intervention by the Commission under Article [102].[176] However, as a general rule, the Commission will not come to a final conclusion as to whether or not a case should be pursued without examining all the factors which may be sufficient to constrain the behaviour of the undertaking.

It will be noted here that in the last sentence the Commission does not completely preclude reaching a finding of dominance without looking at 'all the factors'. Nevertheless, in recent cases the Commission has been at pains to consider whether there are barriers to entry i.e. 'exceptional circumstances' even when dealing with undertakings with extremely high market shares. This was so in *Microsoft*, for example, where it examined barriers to entry (in particular network effects) even though Microsoft had a market share of over 90 per cent,[177] in *AstraZeneca*, and in *Intel* where there were market shares of over 70 and 80 per cent in the various relevant markets.[178]

(vi) Low Market Shares and Dominance

It is important to know the minimum market share at which an undertaking is likely to be found to be dominant. The crucial range is 40–50 per cent for above that there is a presumption of dominance and below that dominance is unlikely though possible. The lower the market share of the undertaking the greater the significance which attaches to the other factors indicating dominance. The lowest

---

[175] The same phrase appears in the Horizontal Merger Guidelines [2004] OJ C31/3, para. 14.

[176] The Commission has a footnote here referring to the relationship between degrees of dominance and the finding of abuse. See further Chap. 7, Section 3.C.iv, p. 375.

[177] COMP/C-3/37.792 *Microsoft*, paras. 448–464 and 515–540.

[178] Case COMP/C-3/37.990 *Intel*, on appeal Case T-286/09, *Intel v. Commission*, judgment pending, para. 852.

share at which an undertaking has been found dominant for the purposes of Article 102[179] is 39.7 per cent in *British Airways*. The market definition aspect of *British Airways* has been dealt with already.[180] As is apparent from the extract from the GC judgment, there were a number of special circumstances which led the GC to uphold the Commission's finding that BA was dominant with such a low market share.

BA argued, inter alia, that the Commission should not have found it dominant as a buyer without taking into account the intense competition it faced as a supplier of air transport services; that the Commission had not explained how its dominance as a buyer of air travel agency services arose from its successful position in air transport; that its market share did not establish a position of dominance; that its market share was falling; that it was not an 'obligatory business partner' of the travel agents; and finally, that if it *were* dominant it would not have had to spend substantial sums on improving its services.

Case T-219/99, *British Airways* v. *Commission* [2003] ECR II-5917

General Court

195… BA cannot profitably disregard the total number of air routes it operates in order to deny its capacity to act with an appreciable degree of independence in relation to its competitors on each of those routes, to travel agents, and to travellers, who have the ability to choose their airline.

196. Nor can BA validly accuse the Commission of failing to explain how its dominant position in the United Kingdom market for air travel agency services arises from its successes in air transport.

197. For the purposes of establishing whether BA holds a dominant position on the United Kingdom market for air travel agency services, there is no need to assess its economic strength on that market by reference to the competition between airlines providing services on each of the routes served by BA and its competitors to and from United Kingdom airports.

198….those various United Kingdom markets in air transport services are distinct from air travel agency services, including the distribution of air tickets in particular.

….

208. The same applies to ticket sales by other companies using BA as an agent and not participating in the performance reward schemes at issue. As the Commission has stated, without being contradicted by BA, the latter merely stated that the amount of those sales might represent a percentage of 5 per cent or less.

209. The Court still needs to examine whether the reasoning followed by the Commission in order to establish BA's dominant position, on the basis of the evidence which it thus lawfully used, might not be vitiated by errors of assessment.

210. In that respect, account must be taken of the highly significant indicator which is the fact that the undertaking in question holds large shares of the market and of the ratio between the market share held by the undertaking concerned and that of its nearest rivals (*Hoffmann-La Roche*…at paragraphs 39 and 48), particularly since the nearest rivals hold only marginal market shares (see, to that effect, Case 27/76 *United Brands* v. *Commission*…paragraph 111).

211. As is shown by the table reproduced below, which is taken from recital 41 of the contested decision and the factual accuracy which BA has not been able to disprove…not only is BA's market share in the total of air ticket sales handled by BSPUK[181] to be regarded as large, but it invariably constitutes a

---

[179] Mergers are a different matter, see Chap. 15.

[180] See Section 5.B.i.k, p. 323.

[181] The Billing and Settlement Plan for the United Kingdom.

multiple of the market shares of each of its five main competitors on the United Kingdom market for air travel agency services.

	1992	1993	1994	1995	1996	1997	1998
British Airways	46.3	45.6	43.5	42.7	40.3	42.0	39.7
American Airlines	–	5.4	7.3	7.7	7.6	3.6	3.8
Virgin	2.8	3.0	3.7	4.0	4.0	5.8	5.5
British Midland	3.6	3.4	3.2	3.0	2.7	–	–
Quantas	3.0	2.7	3.0	2.6	6.4	3.0	3.3
KLM	2.5	–	–	–	–	3.8	5.3

212. The economic strength which BA derives from its market share is further reinforced by the world rank it occupies in terms of international scheduled passenger-kilometres flown, the extent of the range of its transport services and its hub network.

213. According to BA's own statements, its network operations allow it, in comparison with its five competitors, to offer a wider choice of routes and more frequent flights.

214. It is further shown by recital 38 of the contested decision, not challenged by BA, that, in 1995, it operated 92 of the 151 international routes from Heathrow Airport and 43 of the 92 routes in service at Gatwick, that is to say several times the number of routes served by each of its three or four nearest rivals (operating) from those two airports.

215. As a whole, the services operated by BA on routes to and from United Kingdom airports have the cumulative effect of generating the purchase by travellers of a preponderant number of BA air tickets through travel agents established in the United Kingdom, and, correspondingly, at least as many transactions between BA and those agents for the purposes of supplying air travel agency services, particularly in the distribution of BA air tickets.

216. It necessarily follows that those agents substantially depend on the income they receive from BA in consideration for their air travel agency services.

217. BA is therefore wrong to deny that it is an obligatory business partner of travel agents established in the United Kingdom and to maintain that those agents have no actual need to sell BA tickets. BA's arguments are not capable of calling into question the finding, in recital 93 of the contested decision, that BA enjoys a particularly powerful position in relation to its nearest rivals and the largest travel agents.

218. The facts of this case therefore show that BA was in a position, unilaterally by circular of 17 November 1997, to impose a reduction as from 1 January 1998 of its rates of commission in force up to that date and to extend its new performance reward scheme to all travel agents established in the United Kingdom.

219. In those circumstances, neither the possibly modest size of the share of BA ticket sales in the business of some of the main agencies, which has moreover merely been alleged, nor the alleged fluctuations of BA's share in the total figure of air ticket sales by travel agents established in the United Kingdom can call into question the Commission's finding that BA holds a dominant position on the United Kingdom market for air travel agency services.

220. Nor are the great dependence of United Kingdom travel agents upon BA and BA's corresponding freedom of manoeuvre in relation to other companies using the services of air travel agencies capable of being called into question by the fact that those agents do not normally hold stocks of air tickets.

221. Such a purely logistical circumstance is not of such a kind as to affect the dominant position which BA derives from its preponderant weight on the United Kingdom market for air travel agency services.

222. The argument that, as an undertaking in a dominant position, BA would have no interest in spending considerable sums improving its services so as to compete more effectively with its rivals is irrelevant in that it concerns the United Kingdom air transport markets and not the United Kingdom market for air travel agency services which the Commission took to establish the dominant position of BA.

223. Finally, for the same reason, neither the decline in the percentage of BA air ticket sales nor the advance in market share of certain rival companies is sufficiently large to call into question the existence of BA's dominant position on the United Kingdom market for air travel agency services.

224. In this case, the reduction in BA's market share cannot, in itself, constitute proof that there is no dominant position. The position which BA still occupies on the United Kingdom market for air travel agency services remains very largely preponderant. As the table in paragraph 211 above shows, a substantial gap remained, during the whole of the period of the infringement found by the Commission, between, on the one hand, BA's market share and, on the other, both the market share of its closest rival and the cumulative shares of its five main competitors on the United Kingdom market for air travel agency services.

225. The Commission was therefore right to hold that BA held a dominant position on the United Kingdom market for air travel agency services.

It should also be noted that in *Gøttrup Klim* the CJ did not dismiss the possibility of an undertaking with 36 and 32 per cent of two relevant markets being in a dominant position:

While an undertaking which holds market shares of that size may, depending on the strength and number of its competitors, be considered to be in a dominant position, those market shares cannot on their own constitute conclusive evidence of the existence of a dominant position.[182]

As with the presumption of dominance at 50 per cent of the market, the fact that it is possible to have a dominant position, and thus be subject to Article 102, at a market share even lower than 40 per cent is a striking and much criticised feature of EU competition law. It is frequently argued[183] that there should be a 'safe harbour' in respect of Article 102, similar to that provided by the block exemptions in respect of Article 101, whereby a finding of dominance would be ruled out at, say, below a 40 per cent market share. Such a 'dominance screen' could possibly allow some firms with market power to escape Article 102 but would, it is argued, generate legal certainty for undertakings and avoid Type 1 errors (generally considered to be more damaging in respect of unilateral behaviour than Type 2 errors). The Commission, which had never ruled out the possibility of finding dominance at a market share of 20–40 per cent[184] sets out a *qualified* safe harbour in the Guidance Paper.

Guidance on the Commission's Enforcement Priorities in Applying Article 82 of the EC Treaty to Abusive Exclusionary Conduct by Dominant Undertakings [2009] OJ C45/2

14. The Commission considers that low market shares are generally a good proxy for the absence of substantial market power. The Commission's experience suggests that dominance is not likely if the

---

[182] Case C-250/92, *Gøttrup Klim v. KLG* [1994] ECR I-5641.

[183] See the comments received on the Commission Staff Discussion Paper, <http://ec.europa.eu/competition/antitrust/art82/contributions.html>. The Discussion Paper, para. 31, did not merely fail to rule out dominance below 40%, it expressly said that undertakings with market share below 25% were merely 'not likely' to enjoy a dominant position.

[184] See Commission's *Xth Report on Competition Policy* (Commission, 1981), point 150. The EU Merger Reg., Council Reg. 139/2004 [2004] OJ L24/1, recital 32, states a presumption that a concentration will not be liable to impede effective

undertaking's market share is below 40 % in the relevant market. However, there may be specific cases below that threshold where competitors are not in a position to constrain effectively the conduct of a dominant undertaking, for example where they face serious capacity limitations. Such cases may also deserve attention on the part of the Commission.

The Guidance Paper is therefore a disappointment to those who argue for a real safe harbour. Dominance below 40 per cent is 'not likely' but the Commission reserves its position over certain 'specific cases'. In this, paragraph 14 is like many other places in the Guidance Paper where the Commission sets out a general position and then qualifies it.

(vii) Market Shares in the Case of Collective Dominance

Most of the existing Article 102 cases finding a collective dominant position concern situations involving undertakings with combined market shares above 90 per cent in a 'quasi-monopoly'.[185] However, in *Atlantic Container Line*[186] a liner conference with a market shares of 60–70 per cent on various markets was held to be in a collective dominant position and the GC rejected the argument that a market share in excess of 50 per cent could not suffice to found a presumption of a collective dominant position. In cases of 'oligopolistic' collective dominance, where the undertakings can coordinate their behaviour without express collusion or structural links,[187] the situation may well be different because the significance of high market shares is not the same.[188]

C. OTHER FACTORS INDICATING DOMINANCE AND BARRIERS TO ENTRY

(i) General

A wide range of matters have been held by the EU Courts and the Commission to constitute 'other factors indicating dominance'. In *United Brands* and *Hoffmann-La Roche* the CJ held that a dominant position derives from a combination of several factors which, taken separately, are not necessarily determinative.[189] It should be noted, however, that carrying out a full economic analysis before a

competition where the merging undertakings' aggregate market share is less than 25%. The Commission Guidelines on the assessment of significant market power under the regulatory framework for electronic communications, networks, and services (Guidelines on the assessment of significant market power under the Community regulatory framework for electronic communications, networks and services [2002] OJ C165/15) says: 'Although a high market share alone is not sufficient to establish the possession of significant market power (dominance), it is unlikely that a firm without a significant share of the relevant market would be in a dominant position. Thus, undertakings with market shares of no more than 25 per cent are not likely to enjoy a (single) dominant position on the market concerned…In the Commission's decision-making practice, single dominance concerns normally arise in the case of undertakings with market shares of over 40 per cent, although the Commission may in some cases have concerns about dominance even with lower market shares…as dominance may occur without the existence of a large market share' (para. 75).

[185] Case T-228/97, *Irish Sugar plc* v. *Commission* [1999] ECR II-2969, *aff'd*, Case C-497/99 P, *Irish Sugar plc* v. *Commission* [2001] ECR I-5333; Cases C-395 and 396/96P, *Compagnie Maritime Belge Transports SA* v. *EC Commission* [2000] ECR I-1365, discussed in Chap. 9. Case T-193/02, *Laurent Piau* v. *Commission* [2005] ECR II-209 concerned the position of FIFA.

[186] Cases T-191/98, 212/98, and 214/98, *Atlantic Container Line* v. *Commission* [2003] ECR II-3275, paras. 931–935.

[187] See Chap. 5, Section 5.A.iii, p. 276.

[188] G. Monti, 'The Scope of Collective Dominance Under Article 82 EC' (2001) 38 *CMLRev* 131, 136–138; Ortiz Blanco, *Market Power in EU Antitrust Law* (cited in n. 18), 168–172. For oligopolistic collective dominance see Chap. 9.

[189] Case 27/76, *United Brands* v. *Commission* [1978] ECR 207, para. 66; Case 85/76, *Hoffmann-La Roche & Co AG* v. *Commission* [1979] ECR 461, para. 39.

finding of dominance is made would preclude any one factor (including market share) being determinative, so the inclusion of the word 'necessary' in this famous sentence is unfortunate. The 'other factors indicating dominance' comprise both matters to do with the undertaking itself and barriers to entry and expansion.

(ii) Indications from the Undertaking

a. The Undertaking's Own Assessment of its Position

The EU Courts and the Commission have sometimes relied on an undertaking's own internal documentation as indicating its dominance. Such evidence was referred to in *BBI/Boosey & Hawkes* ('"automatic first choice" of all the top brass bands')[190] and *AKZO* ('AKZO regards itself as the world leader in the peroxides market').[191] In *Prokent/Tomra* several company documents found during the Commission's dawn raid referred to its dominant position.[192] The opinions of managers, however, are not incontrovertible evidence of their truth. Managers may try to 'talk up' the undertaking's position to convince themselves, others, or both.[193]

b. Profits

Since a monopolist can reap the benefits of its market power by earning monopoly profits, it is possible that these profits can be used as a means of identifying market power. However, it may be difficult to determine whether or not an undertaking is in fact earning monopoly profits. Perhaps for this reason profitability assessment has not hitherto been much used in EU cases as a tool to assist in the assessment of dominance, although in *Microsoft* the Commission was impressed by the fact that Microsoft was operating on a profit margin of approximately 81 per cent.[194] In EU cases it has been held that the fact that an undertaking is not earning profits at all, or a lack of profits, is not necessarily a contra-indication of dominance. In *United Brands*[195] and *Michelin*[196] the CJ held that an undertaking's economic strength is not measured by profitability alone. On the contrary, losses, at least if temporary, may demonstrate the economic strength of the undertaking which has the ability to absorb them.

c. Performance Indicators and Price Levels

The undertaking's economic performance can be an indicator of dominance. In *Hoffmann-La Roche*[197] the CJ took spare manufacturing capacity into account as a factor indicating dominance, although

[190] *BBI/Boosey & Hawkes* [1987] OJ L286/36, [1988] 4 CMLR 67, para. 18.

[191] Case C-62/86, *AKZO Chemie BV v. Commission* [1991] ECR I-3359, para. 61.

[192] COMP/E-1.38.113 *Prokent Tomra* [2009] 4 CMLR 101, upheld on appeal Case T-155/06, *Tomra Systems v. Commission* [2010] ECR II-4361, *aff'd* Case C-549/10 P, *Tomra Systems ASA v. European Commission*, 19 April 2012.

[193] The same problem of taking account of internal documentation arises when it is used to show that an abuse has been committed: see Chap. 7.

[194] As a percentage of revenues in the year ending 30 June 2003, COMP/C-3/37.792, [2005] 4 CMLR 965, para. 464. In UK domestic law, however, it has been employed more often. In July 2003 a report prepared by an economics consultancy for the UK competition authority, the Office of Fair Trading, discussed ways of assessing profitability, inter alia, for the purpose of identifying a firm's market power (OFT 657, 'Assessing profitability in competition policy analysis', prepared for the OFT by OXERA Consulting Ltd (Economic Discussion Paper 6). The report concluded that useful results *could* be achieved if the methodology used the measures of internal rate of return (IRR) and net present value (NPV). The other uses for profitability analysis are to assess whether a dominant undertaking has been charging excessive prices, or whether *low* profits suggest, e.g., predatory pricing or a margin squeeze.

[195] Case 27/76, *United Brands v. Commission* [1978] ECR 207, paras. 126–128.

[196] Case 322/81, *NV Nederlandsche Banden-Industrie Michelin v. Commission* [1983] ECR 3461, para. 59.

[197] Case 85/76, *Hoffmann-La Roche & Co AG v. Commission* [1979] ECR 461, para. 48.

it did not distinguish between idle and excess capacity. Capacity is idle when its use would not be profitable because the market price is less than the cost of its use. It is found on both competitive and non-competitive markets. Excess capacity means that the undertaking is producing less output than the optimal output the plant is designed to produce, so that it could increase its output without its unit costs increasing.[198]

The ability of an undertaking to obtain premium prices was relevant in *United Brands*[199] and in *BBI/Boosey & Hawkes*.[200] In *AstraZeneca* it was relevant that AZ was able to maintain its prices at a higher level than those of its competitors while retaining a much higher share. This was a consequence of the way in which public health systems operate in covering the cost of medicines and the resulting insensitivity of prescribing doctors and patients.[201]

d. Overall Size and Strength and Range of Products (Portfolio Power)

In its decision in *Hoffmann-La Roche* the Commission took into account the undertaking's position as the world's largest vitamin producer and leading pharmaceuticals producer and the wide range of vitamins it manufactured. The CJ rejected the assertion that these factors were indicators of dominance, saying:[202]

45. The fact that Roche produces a far wider range of vitamins than its competitors must similarly be rejected as being immaterial. The Commission regards this as a factor establishing a dominant position and asserts that 'since the requirements of many users extend to several groups of vitamins, Roche is able to employ a sales and pricing strategy which is far less dependent than that of the other manufacturers on the conditions of competition in each market.'

46. However, the Commission has itself found that each group of vitamins constitutes a specific market and is not, or at least not to any significant extent, interchangeable with any other group or with any other products (Recital 20 to the decision) so that the vitamins belonging to the various groups are as between themselves products just as different as the vitamins compared with other products of the pharmaceutical and food sector. Moreover, it is not disputed that Roche's competitors, in particular those in the chemical industry, market besides the vitamins which they manufacture themselves, other products which purchasers of vitamins also want, so that the fact that Roche is in a position to offer several groups of vitamins does not in itself give it any advantage over its competitors, who can offer, in addition to a less or much less wide range of vitamins, other products which are also required by the purchasers of these vitamins.

47. Similar considerations lead also to the rejection as a relevant factor of the circumstance that Roche is the world's largest vitamin manufacturer, that its turnover exceeds that of all the other manufacturers and that it is at the head of the largest pharmaceuticals group in the world. In the view of the Commission these three considerations together are a factor showing that there is a dominant position, because 'it follows that the applicant occupies a preponderant position not only within the Common Market but also on the world market; it therefore enjoys very considerable freedom of action, since its position enables it to adapt itself easily to the developments of the different regional markets. An undertaking operating throughout the markets of the world and having a market share which leaves all its competitors far behind it does not have to concern itself unduly about any competitors within the Common Market.' Such reasoning based on the benefits reaped from economics of scale and on the possibility of adopting a strategy which varies according to different regional markets is not conclusive, seeing that it is accepted that each group of vitamins constitutes a group of separate products which require their own particular plant and form a separate market, in that the volume of the overall production of products which are different as between themselves does not give Roche a competitive

---

[198] Excess capacity can be used against potential competitors as a form of strategic entry deterrence.

[199] Case 27/76, *United Brands* v. *Commission* [1978] ECR 207, para. 91.

[200] *BBI/Boosey & Hawkes* [1987] OJ L286/36, [1988] 4 CMLR 67, para. 18.

[201] Case T-321/05, *AstraZeneca* v. *Commission* [2010] ECR II-2805, paras 256–268, *aff'd* Case C-457/10 P, *AstraZeneca* v. *Commission*, 6 December 2012, paras 178–180.

[202] [1976] OJ L223/27, [1976] 2 CMLR D25 at recitals 5, 6, and 21. On appeal Case 85/76, *Hoffmann La Roche & Co AG* v. *Commission* [1979] ECR 461.

advantage over its competitors, especially over those in the chemical industry, who manufacture on a world scale other products as well as vitamins and have in principle the same opportunities to set off one market against the other as are offered by a large overall production of products which differ from each other as much as the various groups of vitamins do.

Although size is not therefore per se an indicator of dominance on a particular market, it has been found relevant in some situations. In *Michelin* the CJ took into account the advantages Michelin NV derived from belonging to a group of undertakings which operated throughout Europe and the world.[203] In *Soda Ash–Solvay*[204] the Commission considered Solvay's manufacturing strength with plant in six other Member States to be part of the 'relevant economic evidence' to be taken into account in assessing dominance. The geographical spread of an undertaking's operations has also been held to be an advantage where it makes it less vulnerable to natural disasters[205] and/or other fluctuations.[206] In *AstraZeneca* the GC approved the Commission's taking into account as 'relevant indicia' (although not as in themselves sufficient to warrant a finding of dominance) the fact that AZ's resources and performances outclassed those of its competitors, inter alia, as regards its general financial solidity, R & D resources and marketing resources. AZ's turnover, unlike its competitors', was derived almost exclusively from the sale of pharmaceutical products and these superior resources were devoted to its pharmaceutical business.[207]

It can be seen from the previous discussion that in *Hoffmann-La Roche* the CJ overturned the Commission's finding that the wide range of vitamins produced by the undertaking was an indication of dominance because each vitamin was a separate market. It is otherwise if the undertaking benefits from the diversity of products. In *Tetra Pak II*[208] the Commission held that the diversity 'allows it, if necessary, to make financial sacrifices on one or other of its products without affecting the overall profitability of its operations'. This is a polite way of saying that a 'deep pocket' can facilitate practices such as predatory pricing.[209]

(iii) Barriers to Entry and Expansion

The second indent in paragraph 12 of the Guidance Paper refers to the constraints imposed on an undertaking by credible threats of future entry or expansion. Barriers to entry and expansion are important because where they exist competitors cannot enter or expand on the market and erode the incumbent's existing market share. The Commission explains the importance of potential expansion by existing competitors or potential entry by new ones in paragraph 16 of the Guidance Paper. It will only consider that such entry or expansion is a curb on the putatively dominant undertaking if it is 'likely, timely and significant'. Small-scale or niche entry is not enough, for example. In paragraph 17 the Commission sets out a number of forms that barrier to entry or expansion can take. This section is less detailed than that in the Discussion Paper.[210] It will be noted that in the last sentence the Commission says that persistent high market shares may indicate the existence of barriers to entry and expansion.

---

[203] Although without specifying what these were: Case 322/81, *Nederlandsche Banden-Industrie Michelin v. Commission* [1983] ECR 346, para. 55.

[204] [2003] OJ L10/10, para. 138.

[205] As with the banana plantations in *United Brands* [1978] ECR 207, para. 75.

[206] See *Elopak Italia/Tetra Pak* [1991] OJ L72/1, [1992] 4 CMLR 551, para. 101.

[207] Case T-321/05, *AstraZeneca v. Commission* [2010] ECR II-2805, paras 284–286; the CJ dismissed the appeal against this finding as inadmissible as the cross-appellant did not indicate how it was vitiated by legal error, Case C-457/10 P, *AstraZeneca v. Commission*, 6 December 2012, para. 185.

[208] *Elopak Italia/Tetra Pak* [1991] OJ L72/1, [1992] 4 CMLR 551, para. 101.

[209] One of the abuses which was found in *Tetra Pak II* : see Chap. 7.

[210] Discussion Paper, paras. 34–40.

Guidance on the Commission's Enforcement Priorities in Applying Article 82 of the EC Treaty to Abusive Exclusionary Conduct by Dominant Undertakings [2009] OJC 45/2

16. Competition is a dynamic process and an assessment of the competitive constraints on an undertaking cannot be based solely on the existing market situation. The potential impact of expansion by actual competitors or entry by potential competitors, including the threat of such expansion or entry, is also relevant. An undertaking can be deterred from increasing prices if expansion or entry is likely, timely and sufficient. For the Commission to consider expansion or entry likely it must be sufficiently profitable for the competitor or entrant, taking into account factors such as the barriers to expansion or entry, the likely reactions of the allegedly dominant undertaking and other competitors, and the risks and costs of failure. For expansion or entry to be considered timely, it must be sufficiently swift to deter or defeat the exercise of substantial market power. For expansion or entry to be considered sufficient, it cannot be simply small-scale entry, for example into some market niche, but must be of such a magnitude as to be able to deter any attempt to increase prices by the putatively dominant undertaking in the relevant market.

17. Barriers to expansion or entry can take various forms. They may be legal barriers, such as tariffs or quotas, or they may take the form of advantages specifically enjoyed by the dominant undertaking, such as economies of scale and scope, privileged access to essential inputs or natural resources, important technologies... or an established distribution and sales network... They may also include costs and other impediments, for instance resulting from network effects, faced by customers in switching to a new supplier. The dominant undertaking's own conduct may also create barriers to entry, for example where it has made significant investments which entrants or competitors would have to match... or where it has concluded long-term contracts with its customers that have appreciable foreclosing effects. Persistently high market shares may be indicative of the existence of barriers to entry and expansion.

The way in which dominance is derived from a combination of factors in addition to market share is illustrated by some of the leading cases on Article 102.

(iv) Some Leading Cases on Barriers to Entry

a. *United Brands*

Case 27/76, *United Brands* v. *Commission* [1978] ECR 207

The issues in *United Brands* were firstly whether bananas were a separate relevant market from other fruit (see Section 5.B in the discussion on market definition) and if so whether, secondly, United Brands was dominant on it.

Court of Justice

67. In order to find out whether UBC is an undertaking in a dominant position on the relevant market it is necessary first of all to examine its structure and then the situation on the said market as far as competition is concerned.

68. In doing so it may be advisable to take account if need be of the facts put forward as acts amounting to abuses without necessarily having to acknowledge that they are abuses.

...The structure of UBC

69. It is advisable to examine in turn UBC's resources for and methods of producing, packaging, transporting, selling and displaying its product.

70. UBC is an undertaking vertically integrated to a high degree.

71. This integration is evident at each of the stages from the plantation to the loading on wagons or lorries in the ports of delivery and after those stages, as far as ripening and sale prices are concerned, UBC even extends its control to ripener/distributors and wholesalers by setting up a complete network of agents.

72. At the production stage UBC owns large plantations in Central and South America.

73. In so far as UBC's own production does not meet its requirements it can obtain supplies without any difficulty from independent planters since it is an established fact that unless circumstances are exceptional there is a production surplus.

74. Furthermore several independent producers have links with UBC through contracts for the growing of bananas which have caused them to grow the varieties of bananas which UBC has advised them to adopt.

75. The effects of natural disasters which could jeopardize supplies are greatly reduced by the fact that the plantations are spread over a wide geographic area and by the selection of varieties not very susceptible to diseases.

76. This situation was born out by the way in which UBC was able to react to the consequences of hurricane 'Fifi' in 1974.

77. At the production stage UBC therefore knows that it can comply with all the requests which it receives.

78. At the stage of packaging and presentation on its premises UBC has at its disposal factories, manpower, plant and material which enable it to handle the goods independently.

79. The bananas are carried from the place of production to the port of shipment by its own means of transport including railways.

80. At the carriage by sea stage it has been acknowledged that UBC is the only undertaking of its kind which is capable of carrying two thirds of its exports by means of its own banana fleet.

81. Thus UBC knows that it is able to transport regularly, without running the risk of its own ships not being used and whatever the market situation may be, two thirds of its average volume of sales and is alone able to ensure that three regular consignments reach Europe each week, and all this guarantees it commercial stability and well being.

82. In the field of technical knowledge and as a result of continual research UBC keeps on improving the productivity and yield of its plantations by improving the draining system, making good soil deficiencies and combating effectively plant disease.

83. It has perfected new ripening methods in which its technicians instruct the distributor/ripeners of the Chiquita banana.

84. That is another factor to be borne in mind when considering UBC's position since competing firms cannot develop research at a comparable level and are in this respect at a disadvantage compared with the applicant.

85. It is acknowledged that at the stage where the goods are given the final finish and undergo quality control UBC not only controls the distributor/ripeners which are direct customers but also those who work for the account of its important customers such as the Scipio group.

86. Even if the object of the clause prohibiting the sale of green bananas was only strict quality control, it in fact gives UBC absolute control of all trade in its goods so long as they are marketable wholesale, that is to say before the ripening process begins which makes an immediate sale unavoidable.

87. This general quality control of a homogeneous product makes the advertising of the brand name effective.

88. Since 1967 UBC has based its general policy in the relevant market on the quality of its Chiquita brand banana.

89. There is no doubt that this policy gives UBC control over the transformation of the product into bananas for consumption even though most of this product no longer belongs to it.

90. This policy has been based on a thorough reorganization of the arrangements for production, packaging, carriage, ripening (new plant with ventilation and a cooling system) and sale (a network of agents).

91. UBC has made this product distinctive by large-scale repeated advertising and promotion campaigns which have induced the consumer to show a preference for it in spite of the difference between the price of labelled and unlabelled bananas (in the region of 30 to 40 per cent) and also of Chiquita bananas and those which have been labelled with another brand name (in the region of 7 to 10 per cent).

92. It was the first to take full advantage of the opportunities presented by labelling in the tropics for the purpose of large-scale advertising and this, to use UBC's own words, has 'revolutionized the commercial exploitation of the banana' (Annex II to the application, p. 10).

93. It has thus attained a privileged position by making Chiquita the premier banana brand name on the relevant market with the result that the distributor cannot afford not to offer it to the consumer.

94. At the selling stage this distinguishing factor—justified by the unchanging quality of the banana bearing this label—ensures that it has regular customers and consolidates its economic strength.

95. The effect of its sales networks only covering a limited number of customers, large groups or distributor/ripeners, is a simplification of its supply policy and economies of scale.

96. Since UBC's supply policy consists—in spite of the production surplus—in only meeting the requests for Chiquita bananas parsimoniously and sometimes incompletely UBC is in a position of strength at the selling stage.

...

121. UBC's economic strength has thus enabled it to adopt a flexible overall strategy directed against new competitors establishing themselves on the whole of the relevant market.

122. The particular barriers to competitors entering the market are the exceptionally large capital investments required for the creation and running of banana plantations, the need to increase sources of supply in order to avoid the effects of fruit diseases and bad weather (hurricanes, floods), the introduction of an essential system of logistics which the distribution of a very perishable product makes necessary, economies of scale from which newcomers to the market cannot derive any immediate benefit and the actual cost of entry made up, *inter alia*, of all the general expenses incurred in penetrating the market such as the setting up of an adequate commercial network, the mounting of very large-scale advertising campaigns, all those financial risks, the costs of which are irrecoverable if the attempt fails.

123. Thus, although, as UBC has pointed out, it is true that competitors are able to use the same methods of production and distribution as the applicant, they come up against almost insuperable practical and financial obstacles.

124. This is another factor peculiar to a dominant position.

125. However UBC takes into account the losses which its banana division made from 1971 to 1976—whereas during this period its competitors made profits—for the purpose of inferring that, since dominance is in essence the power to fix prices, making losses is inconsistent with the existence of a dominant position.

126. An undertaking's economic strength is not measured by its profitability; a reduced profit margin or even losses for a time are not incompatible with a dominant position, just as large profits may be compatible with a situation where there is effective competition.

127. The fact that UBC's profitability is for a time moderate or non-existent must be considered in the light of the whole of its operations.

128. The finding that, whatever losses UBC may make, the customers continue to buy more goods from UBC which is the dearest vendor, is more significant and this fact is a particular feature of the dominant position and its verification is determinative in this case.

129. The cumulative effect of all the advantages enjoyed by UBC thus ensures that is has a dominant position on the relevant market.

b. *Hoffmann-La Roche*

Case 85/76, *Hoffmann-La Roche & Co AG* v. *Commission* [1979] ECR 461

The case concerned Hoffmann-La Roche's practices on various vitamin markets.

Court of Justice

48. . . .the relationship between the market shares of the undertaking concerned and of its competitors, especially those of the next largest, the technological lead of an undertaking over its competitors, the existence of a highly developed sales network and the absence of potential competition are relevant factors, the first because it enables the competitive strength of the undertaking in question to be assessed, the second and third because they represent in themselves technical and commercial advantages and the fourth because it is the consequence of the existence of obstacles preventing new competitors from having access to the market. As far as the existence or non-existence of potential competition is concerned it must, however, be observed that, although it is true—and this applies to all the groups of vitamins in question—that because of the amount of capital investment required the capacity of the factories is determined according to the anticipated growth over a long period so that access to the market by new producers is not easy, account must also be taken of the fact that the existence of considerable unused manufacturing capacity creates potential competition between established manufacturers. Nevertheless Roche is in this respect in a privileged position because, as it admits itself, its own manufacturing capacity was, during the period covered by the contested decision, in itself sufficient to meet world demand without this surplus manufacturing capacity placing it in a difficult economic or financial situation.

49. It is in the light of the preceding considerations that Roche's shares of each of the relevant markets, complemented by those factors which in conjunction with the market shares make it possible to show that there may be a dominant position, must be evaluated. Finally, it will also be necessary to consider whether Roche's submissions relating to the implication of its conduct on the market, mainly as far as concerns prices, are of such a kind as to alter the findings to which the examination of the market shares and the other factors taken into account might lead.

c. Michelin

Case 322/81, *Nederlandsche Banden-Industrie Michelin* v. *Commission* [1983] ECR 3461

As discussed in Section 5.B.i., p. 309 in relation to market definition, this case concerned Michelin's position on the tyre market. The Commission's definition of the market as being that for new replacement lorry and bus tyres was upheld. The alleged abuse concerned the terms Michelin offered its dealers. This part of the judgment deals with the assessment of dominance.

Court of Justice

53. The applicant challenges next the relevance of the other criteria and evidence used by the Commission to prove that a dominant position exists. It claims that it is not the only undertaking to have commercial representatives, that the numbers employed by its main competitors are even larger in relative terms and that its wide range of products is not a competitive advantage because the different types of tyre are not interchangeable and it does not require dealers to purchase its whole range of tyres.

54. It also claims that the Commission took no account of a number of evidential factors which were incompatible with the existence of a dominant position. For instance, dealers' net margins on Michelin tyres and competing tyres are comparable and the cost per mile of Michelin tyres is the most favourable for users. Since 1979 Michelin NV has made a loss. As its production capacity is insufficient, its competitors, which are also financially stronger and more diversified than the Michelin group, can at any moment replace the quantities which it supplies. Lastly, because users of heavy-vehicle tyres are experienced trade buyers they have the ability to act as a counterpoise to the tyre manufacturers.

55. In reply to those arguments it should first be observed that in order to assess the relative economic strength of Michelin NV and its competitors on the Netherlands market the advantages which those undertakings may derive from belonging to groups of undertakings operating throughout Europe or even the world must be taken into consideration. Amongst those advantages, the lead which the Michelin group has over its competitors in the matters of investment and research and the special extent of its range of products, to which the Commission referred in its decision, have not been denied. In fact in the case of certain types of tyres the Michelin group is the only supplier on the market to offer them in its range.

56. That situation ensures that on the Netherlands market a large number of users of heavy-vehicle tyres have a strong preference for Michelin tyres. As the purchase of tyres represents a considerable investment for a transport undertaking and since much time is required in order to ascertain in practice the cost-effectiveness of a type or brand of tyre, Michelin NV therefore enjoys a position which renders it largely immune to competition. As a result, a dealer established in the Netherlands normally cannot afford not to sell Michelin tyres.

57. It is not possible to uphold the objections made against those arguments by Michelin NV, supported on this point by the French Government, that Michelin NV is thus penalized for the quality of its products and services. A finding that an undertaking has a dominant position is not in itself a recrimination but simply means that, irrespective of the reasons for which it has such a dominant position, the undertaking concerned has a special responsibility not to allow its conduct to impair genuine undistorted competition on the common market.

58. Due weight must also be attached to the importance of Michelin NV's network of commercial representatives, which gives it direct access to tyre users at all times. Michelin NV has not disputed the fact that in absolute terms its network is considerably larger than those of its competitors or challenged the description, in the decision at issue, of the services performed by its network whose efficiency and quality of service are unquestioned. The direct access to users and the standard of service which the network can

give them enables Michelin NV to maintain and strengthen its position on the market and to protect itself more effectively against competition.

59. As regards the additional criteria and evidence to which Michelin NV refers in order to disprove the existence of a dominant position, it must be observed that temporary unprofitability or even losses are not inconsistent with the existence of a dominant position. By the same token, the fact that the prices charged by Michelin NV do not constitute an abuse and are not even particularly high does not justify the conclusion that a dominant position does not exist. Finally, neither the size, financial strength and degree of diversification of Michelin NV's competitors at the world level nor the counterpoise arising from the fact that buyers of heavy-vehicle tyres are experienced trade users are such as to deprive Michelin NV of its privileged position on the Netherlands market.

60. It must therefore be concluded that the other criteria and evidence relevant in this case in determining whether a dominant position exists confirm that Michelin NV has such a position.

61. Michelin NV's submissions disputing that it has a dominant position on a substantial part of the common market are therefore unfounded.

d. *Eurofix-Bauco* v. *Hilti*

For the market definition aspects of this case see the discussion of market definition in Section 5.[211] The case concerned the consumables (nails and cartridges) for Hilti's nail guns.

Eurofix-Bauco v. *Hilti* [1988] OJ L65/19[212]

Commission

69. In addition to the strength derived from its market share and the relative weakness of its competitors, Hilti has other advantages that help reinforce and maintain its position in the nail gun market:

— its biggest selling nail gun, the DX 450, has certain novel technically advantageous features which are still protected by patents,

— Hilti has an extremely strong research and development position and is one of the leading companies worldwide not only in nail guns but also other fastening technologies,

— Hilti has a strong and well-organised distribution system—in the EEC it has subsidiaries and independent dealers integrated into its selling network who deal mostly direct with customers, and

— the market for nail guns is relatively mature, which may discourage new entrants since sales or market shares can only be obtained at the expense of existing competitors in the market for replacements.

70. The foregoing considerations lead to the conclusion that Hilti holds a dominant position in the EEC for nail guns, as well as the markets for Hilti-compatible nails and cartridge strips. These are the relevant markets for the purposes of this Decision. It should be stressed that, in this particular case, the relevant markets for Hilti compatible nails and cartridge strips are important because of Hilti's large share of sales of nail guns. Because of this large share, independent manufacturers of nails and cartridge strips must manufacture nails and/or cartridge strips which can be used in Hilti tools if they are to produce for more than a small segment of the market thus achieving the economies of scale necessary to be both competitive and profitable.

71. Hilti's market power and dominance stem principally from its large share of the sales of nail guns coupled with the patent protection for its cartridge strips. The economic position it enjoys is such that it

[211] Section 5.B.i.h, p. 319.
[212] The appeals, Case T-30/89, *Hilti AG v. Commission* [1991] ECR II-1439 and Case C-53/92 P, *Hilti v. Commission* [1994] ECR I-667, confirmed the Commission's decision.

enables it to prevent effective competition being maintained on the relevant markets for Hilti-compatible nails and cartridge strips. In fact Hilti's commercial behaviour, which has been described above and is analysed below, is witness to its ability to act independently of, and without due regard to, either competitors or customers on the relevant markets in question. In addition, Hilti's pricing policy also described above reflects its ability to determine, or at least to have an appreciable influence on the conditions under which competition will develop. This behaviour and its economic consequences would not normally be seen where a company was facing real competitive pressure. Therefore the Commission considers that Hilti holds a dominant position in the two separate relevant markets for Hilti-compatible nails and cartridge strips.

(v) Summary of 'Other Factors Indicating Dominance'

It is possible from looking at the cases set out in Section 6.C.iv and other cases to describe the main factors which have been held to indicate dominance. These are summed up in paragraph 17 of the Guidance Paper.[213] This section should also be read in the light of the section on barriers to entry in Chapter 1.

a. Economies of Scale and Scope and Sunk Costs

In *United Brands* (paragraph 122) the CJ recognised that economies of scale can operate as a barrier to entry. It also referred to sunk costs when it spoke of 'costs which are irrecoverable if the attempt fails'.[214] Whether or not competitors can enter a market on a small scale depends on the characteristics of the market. In *Intel*, the Commission found that in respect of the x86CPU market there were (i) significant sunk costs in R & D, (ii) significant sunk costs in plant production, and (iii) resulting significant economies of sale which meant that the minimum efficient scale was high relative to overall market demand, so that there were significant barriers to entry. Furthermore, once entry had taken place expanding output would have required additional sunk investment into new property, plant, and equipment and several years' lead time.[215] The Commission explained the link between economies of scale, sunk investments, and high fixed costs:[216]

In general, a high share of fixed costs is indicative of significant barriers to entry and expansion. These barriers to entry give rise to market power, which in turn enables a firm to set prices above marginal costs. In the presence of fixed costs, pricing above marginal cost is necessary for a firm to generate profits and thus remain viable. As long as barriers to entry remain moderate, new entrants could be expected to compete away any supra-competitive profits, leading to more or less comparable levels of net profits across companies (after accounting for risk). The higher the proportion of fixed costs in a given industry, the more concentrated it is likely to be, because higher mark-ups are necessary for firms to remain profitable.

In *Telefónica* the Commission also noted the significant sunk costs for new operators and the fact that the incumbent benefited from economies of scale and scope whereas new operators would have to secure a sufficient number of customers while facing higher unit costs.[217]

---

[213] See Section 6.C.iii, p. 348.

[214] Case 27/76, *United Brands* v. *Commission* [1978] ECR 207, para. 122.

[215] COMP/C-3/37.990 *Intel*, para. 866, on appeal Case T-286/09, *Intel* v. *Commission*, judgment pending.

[216] COMP/C-3/37.990 *Intel*, para. 878, on appeal Case T-286/09, *Intel* v. *Commission*, judgment pending.

[217] COMP/38.784 *Wanadoo España* v. *Telefónica*, 4 July 2007, [2011] 4 CMLR 414, paras. 224–226, upheld Case T-336/07, *Telefónica and Telefónica de España* v. *Commission*, 29 March 2012 (on appeal Case C-295/12 P, judgment pending), para. 154.

b. Access to Key Inputs or Facilities

New entrants may be unable to enter the market because of lack of access to key inputs. This can cover items such as airport slots or things which are covered by IPRs (see Section 6.C.(v)d) or mean there is no access to raw materials. In BPB[218] a new entrant to the market would have needed access to the raw material, gypsum. There was no access to this in the UK without opening new mines. The only alternative was thus to import it. This would incur cost and risk and therefore relates to access to financial resources as discussed in Section 6.C.(v)c. Where key inputs are unavailable to new entrants, refusals to supply can amount to strategic entry-deterring behaviour by the incumbent undertaking and may in certain circumstances amount to an abuse of a dominant position: see Commercial Solvents and the case law on refusal to supply and the essential facilities doctrine discussed in Chapter 7. Access to facilities is a particular problem in network industries, where it may be dealt with by sector regulation.

c. Access to Financial Resources and the Need for Investment

In United Brands[219] and Hoffmann-La Roche[220] the CJ considered that the need for large-scale capital investment constituted a barrier to entry. In Continental Can[221] the Commission also appeared to consider that the undertaking's access to international capital markets was an indicator of its dominance.

d. Legal and Regulatory Barriers and Intellectual Property Rights

State or regulatory measures which subject a market to licensing requirements, or grant to a particular undertaking a statutory monopoly, an exclusive concession (such as in the provision of undertaking services in Bodson v. Pompes Funèbres[222]), or exclusive access to finite resources (such as radio frequencies in Decca Navigator[223] or airport slots in British Midland–Aer Lingus[224]) are obvious barriers to entry. Even economists of the Chicago School recognise that governmental restrictions may operate as a barrier to entry. Most legal and regulatory barriers to entry can be classified as of absolute costs advantages.[225] They are structural factors: characteristics inherent in the relevant market.[226] The EU Courts and the Commission have frequently held such measures to be factors indicating dominance and many cases on Article 102 concern statutory monopolists.[227]

Although not legal regulation as such, the organisation and dynamics of the health and social security systems in the Member States made it more difficult for competitors to gain market share in AstraZeneca.[228] This gave AZ first mover advantages.

IPRs are a particular type of legal right granted by national (or European) law. The CJ has consistently held that the mere possession of IPRs does not necessarily confer a dominant position.[229]

---

[218] BPB Industries [1989] OJ L10/50, [1990] 4 CMLR 464, para. 120.

[219] Case 27/76, United Brands v. Commission [1978] ECR 207, para. 122.

[220] Case 85/76, Hoffmann-La Roche v. EC Commission [1979] ECR 461, para. 49.

[221] Re Continental Can Co Inc [1972] JO L7/25, [1972] CMLR D11, para. 13.

[222] Case 30/87, Bodson v. Pompes Funèbres des Régions Libérées [1988] ECR 2479.

[223] [1989] OJ L43/7, [1990] 4 CMLR 627.

[224] [1992] OJ L96/34, [1993] 4 CMLR 596.

[225] See D. Harbord and T. Hoehn, 'Barriers to Entry and Exit in European Competition Policy' (1994) 14 International Review of Law and Economics 411.

[226] Faull and Nikpay, The EC Law of Competition (cited in n. 1), 4.62.

[227] e.g. Case 311/84, Centre Belge d'Etudes du Marché-Télémarketing v. Compagnie Luxembourgeoise de Télédiffusion SA and Information Publicité Benelux SA [1985] ECR 3261; Cases C241–242/91 P, RTE & ITP v. Commission (Magill) [1995] ECR I-743; Case 226/84, British Leyland v. Commission [1986] ECR 3263; Sealink/B&I Holyhead: Interim Measures [1992] 5 CMLR 255, and other transport cases.

[228] Case C-457/10 P, AstraZeneca v. Commission, 6 December 2012.

[229] Case 24/67, Parke Davis v. Probel [1968] ECR 55; Cases C-241–242/91 P, RTE & ITP v. Commission (Magill) [1995] ECR I-743.

The legal monopoly may not equate to an economic monopoly if the relevant market is wider than the protected product. The issue is how far the possession of the IPRs enables the holder to prevent effective competition. The fact that access to a market is protected by IPRs may therefore be relevant as a barrier to entry.[230] This was found to be the case in *Hugin*,[231] (where the CJ seemed to accept the argument that the spare parts were protected by the UK's Design Copyright Act 1968), *Eurofix-Baucov. Hilti*,[232] and *Tetra Pak II*.[233] In *Intel* the Commission remarked on the 'significant intellectual property-related barriers that any new entrant would have to overcome'[234] and the strength of the patent protection enjoyed by AZ, and its rigorous enforcement of its rights, were major factors contributing to the finding of dominance in *AstraZeneca*.[235] Cases on refusal to license copyrights have arisen because without access to the copyright-protected material the competitor is unable to enter the market.[236] The Commission is also concerned with standard-essential patents (SEPs), where an undertaking has a patent which is necessary to the technical standard adopted by an industry for a particular product or process, although the ownership of a SEP does not necessarily confer dominance.[237]

Economists classify IPRs as absolute cost advantages. They are also first-mover advantages.

e. Superior Technology

The superior technology of an undertaking has been found to be a factor indicating dominance. This can be seen from the extracts set out from *United Brands, Hoffmann-La Roche, Michelin, Eurofix-Bauco v. Hilti,* and *Tetra Pak* in Section 6.C.iv. It is, however, questionable from an economic point of view to hold that an undertaking's technological superiority operates as a barrier to entry per se. It is true that expenditure on technological development can be a sunk cost of entry but it is also true that a new entrant on to the market may not have to spend the same resources on R&D as the incumbent on the market: there is no need to reinvent the wheel.[238] Superior technology could not operate as a barrier to entry according to Stigler[239] since it does not represent a cost to the new entrant which was not borne by the incumbent.

f. Established Distribution and Sales Networks

The overall efficacy of the undertaking's commercial arrangements have been held to contribute to its dominant position in several cases. This is particularly marked in *United Brands* (paragraphs 75–95 of the judgment), which was also a case of vertical integration, in *Michelin* (paragraph 58), and

---

[230] The issue here is with patents, copyrights, and designs: it is unlikely that the holding of a trade mark alone would confer dominance although the ownership of a popular brand name may constitute a barrier to entry.

[231] Case 22/78, *Hugin Kassaregister AB and Hugin Cash Registers Ltd v. EC Commission* [1979] ECR 1869, [1979] 3 CMLR 345.

[232] [1988] OJ L65/19, [1989] 4 CMLR 677.

[233] Case C-333/94 P, *Tetra Pak International SA v. Commission* [1996] ECR I-5951, [1997] 4 CMLR 662.

[234] COMP/C-3/37.990, *Intel* (on appeal Case T-286/09, *Intel v. Commission*, judgment pending), para. 858.

[235] Case T-321/05, *AstraZeneca v. Commission* [2010] ECR II-2805, paras. 270–275, *aff'd* Case C-457/10 P, *AstraZeneca v. Commission*, 6 December 2012, paras 186–188.

[236] Case C-418/01, *IMS Health GmbII & Co. OHG v. NDC Health GmbH & Co. KG* [2004] ECR I-5039; Cases C-241–242/91 P, *RTE & ITP v. Commission (Magill)* [1995] ECR I-743 (although unlike the GC (Cases T-69/70, 76/89 *RTE, ITP, BBC v. EC Commission* [1991] ECR II-485) the CJ treated the lack of the *information* as being the barrier to entry and interpreted the undertakings' behaviour as a refusal to supply the *information* rather than a refusal to license: see Chap. 7).

[237] For SEPs, see further Chap. 7, Section 13.C.ii, p. 563 and Chap. 10, Section 11.A, p. 758.

[238] See V. Korah, 'Concept of a Dominant Position Within The Meaning of Art. 86' (1980) 17 *CMLRev* 395, 408, and 410; Harbord and Hoehn, 'Barriers to Entry and Exit in European Competition Policy' (cited in n. 225), 411, 419; Baden Fuller, 'Article 86 EEC: Economic Analysis of the Existence of a Dominant Position' (cited in n. 60), 423, 437.

[239] See Chap. 1, Section 10.C.

in *Eurofix-Bauco* (paragraph 69) where the CJ and the Commission took into account the effectiveness of the undertakings' distribution networks. These judgments may be criticised for failing to explain sufficiently *why* a new entrant could not replicate these arrangements. Otherwise, the authorities appear simply to be penalising the undertaking in respect of its efficiency.[240] In the Discussion Paper the Commission listed 'a highly developed distribution and sales network' as barriers to entry and expansion and simply stated that 'the allegedly dominant undertaking may have its own dense outlet network, established distribution logistics or wide geographical coverage that would be difficult for rivals to replicate'.[241] In the Guidance Paper, paragraph 17, they are simply listed without comment, with a reference to *Hoffmann-La Roche*.

g. Vertical Integration

Vertical integration has been considered a barrier to entry. In some contexts this appears to condemn an undertaking in respect of its efficiency. Further, it can be argued that when vertical integration takes place the barriers to entry are only added up and are not multiplied. Vertical integration may therefore accompany monopoly but is not an indicator of it.[242] Nonetheless in *United Brands* UBC's vertical integration was an important factor for the CJ in the finding of dominance. Clearly in the context of the growing and marketing of bananas, a highly perishable product, this vertical integration played an important part in UBC's ability to get its bananas across the world and into the hands of European distributors as quickly as possible. It is quite another thing, however, to hold that this vertical integration constituted a barrier to entry. There was no explanation in the case of why, or even if, the vertical integration was to be regarded as a barrier to entry.[243] However, in a number of telecommunication cases it has been found that the benefits to a vertically integrated undertaking of operating on both upstream and downstream markets gave it a competitive advantage over competitors operating at only one level of the market.[244] The discrimination of a vertically integrated undertaking in favour of its own downstream operations may constitute a strategic barrier to entry and amount to an abuse.[245]

h. Advertising, Reputation, Product Differentiation

In *United Brands* the CJ considered that advertising and promotion had enhanced United Brands' large market share, because it had 'induced the customer to show a preference for' branded Chiquita bananas despite a large price differential with unlabelled and differently labelled bananas.[246] United Brands had 'thus attained a privileged position by making Chiquita the premier banana brand name'.[247] The Court did not appear to contemplate the possibility that consumers might have been swayed by the quality of the product rather than by advertising. The CJ concluded that among the barriers faced by new competitors would be 'the mounting of very large-scale advertising campaigns'.[248] Similarly, in the merger

---

[240] Despite the CJ's protestations in, inter alia, *Michelin* (para. 57) that finding an undertaking has a dominant position is not a reproach, the consequences are such that it is invariably to the undertaking's disadvantage.

[241] Discussion Paper, para. 40.

[242] See Baden Fuller, 'Article 86 EEC: Economic Analysis of the Existence of a Dominant Position' (cited in n. 60), 423, 440 and the economic literature cited there; Harbord and Hoehn, 'Barriers to Entry and Exit in European Competition Policy' (cited in n. 225), 411, 419; V. Korah, 'Concept of a Dominant Position Within The Meaning of Art. 86' (1980) 17 *CMLRev* 395, 408.

[243] See also *Soda Ash-Solvay* [2003] OJ L10/10, where the Commission gave Solvay's production of the raw material (salt) as a factor indicating its dominance.

[244] See Case T-340/03, *France Télécom SA v. Commission* [2007] ECR II-107; *Wanadoo España v. Telefónica*, cited in n. 217; COMP/39.525, *Telekomunikacja Polska*, 22 June 2011, on appeal Case T-486/11, judgment pending.

[245] As in the margin squeeze cases, and in *Google*, see Chap. 7, Sections 9 and 13.E respectively.

[246] Case 27/76, *United Brands v. Commission* [1978] ECR 207, para. 91.

[247] Case 27/76, *United Brands v. Commission* [1978] ECR 207, para. 93.

[248] Case 27/76, *United Brands v. Commission* [1978] ECR 207, para. 122.

case of *Nestlé/Perrier*[249] the Commission considered it relevant to the existence of a dominant position that any new entrant to the market would face formidable advertising and promotion requirements. The Commission considered the difficulty of access to distribution outlets in a brand-crowded market and referred to the problem of shelf-space in retail stores. In *BBI/Boosey & Hawkes*[250] the Commission relied on the goodwill and reputation enjoyed by Boosey & Hawkes, listing among 'other factors which tend…to support a preliminary finding of dominance' the 'strong buyer preference for B&H instruments' and 'its close identification with the brass band movement'. In *Intel* the Commission found that Intel's extensive advertising campaigns and product differentiation constituted barriers.[251]

i. Opportunity Costs

Opportunity costs are the value of something which must be given up in order to achieve or acquire something else and can be classified as an absolute cost advantage for the incumbent undertaking. In *British Midland–Aer Lingus*[252] the Commission considered as a barrier to entry to the Heathrow–Dublin air route the opportunity costs involved in an airline having to divert its Heathrow airport slots, currently employed for other (profitable) routes, to service the less profitable Irish destination.

j. Switching Costs

Switching costs are costs which a customer would have to bear were it to move its custom to a competitor. They can include having to invest in new infrastructure, staff training or procedures, or having to sacrifice advantages obtained from the existing supplier (such as frequent flyer programmes).[253] Network effects may make it unattractive to change supplier.[254] The costs to the customers in switching supplier were taken into account in, inter alia, *Tetra Pak I*,[255] *IMS/NDC*,[256] and *Microsoft*.[257] Switching costs arising from, for example, the loss of rebates or the privileges attached to long-term or exclusive supply contracts may be strategic behaviour on the part of a dominant firm which constitutes an abuse. Switching costs are first mover advantages.

k. Conduct

An undertaking's ability to act in a certain way may indicate that it is dominant but moreover its conduct may constitute a barrier to entry.

In *United Brands* the Commission considered that the undertaking's geographical price discrimination and export bans were evidence of its dominance and the CJ said that its economic strength had 'enabled it to adopt a flexible overall strategy directed against new competitors'.[258] In *Eurofix-Bauco* the Commission said that the undertaking's behaviour was 'witness to its ability to act independently of, and without due regard to, either competitors or customers…This behaviour and its economic consequences would not normally be seen where a company was facing real competitive pressure'.[259]

---

[249] [1992] OJ L356/1, [1993] 4 CMLR M17 at recital 97. See Chap. 15.

[250] *BBI/Boosey & Hawkes* [1987] OJ L286/36, [1988] 4 CMLR 67, para. 18, where the product concerned was brass band instruments.

[251] COMP/C-3/37.990 *Intel*, paras. 867–870, on appeal Case T-286/09, *Intel v. Commission*, judgment pending. Between 1997 and 2007 Intel had spent 14–17% of its annual turnover on advertising and marketing the relevant product, CPUs.

[252] *British Midland–Aer Lingus* [1992] OJ L96/34, [1993] 4 CMLR 596.

[253] See R. J. Van den Bergh and P. D. Camesasca, *European Competition Law and Economics: A Comparative Perspective* (2nd edn, Sweet & Maxwell, 2006), 146.

[254] Network effects are particularly significant in new economy industries, see Section 6.E.

[255] [1988] OJ L272/37, [1990] 4 CMLR 97.

[256] *NDC Health/IMS: Interim Measures* [2002] OJ L59/18, [2002] 4 CMLR 111.

[257] COMP/C-3/37.792, [2005] 4 CMLR 965.

[258] Case 27/76, *United Brands v. Commission* [1978] ECR 207, para. 121.

[259] [1988] OJ L65/19, [1989] 4 CMLR 677 at recital 71. See similarly *ECS/AKZO* [1985] OJ L374/1, [1986] 3 CMLR 273 at recital 56, upheld in Case C-62/86, *AKZO Chemie BV v. Commission* [1991] ECR I-3359, para. 61.

This reasoning causes some concern on account of its circularity: the conduct leads to finding dominance which leads to finding the conduct is an abuse because the undertaking is dominant. It is justified, however, in some circumstances so long as caution is exercised. First, some conduct is impossible without market power. Secondly, some conduct may operate as a strategic entry barrier.[260] If the conditions of post-entry competition are an important factor in undertakings' decisions about entering markets, predatory behaviour may deter entry, and practices such as exclusive dealing, tying, and refusals to supply may foreclose markets to new entrants.[261] Modern industrial organisation theory, by emphasising the analysis of strategic competition, makes the incumbent undertakings' conduct a major consideration in assessing dominance. Giving a prime place to conduct in the assessment of market power is a major reason why the issue of ascertaining whether an undertaking is dominant, and the issue of deciding whether it has abused that position, cannot be neatly separated. The Guidance Paper states that the fact that the undertaking has made significant investments which entrants or competitors would have to match can constitute a barrier (citing in a footnote *United Brands* for this).[262]

l. An Unavoidable Trading Partner

In *Hoffmann-La Roche* the CJ described the undertaking as being in a position vis-à-vis its customers where it was an 'unavoidable trading' partner.[263] The railway operators were described as being in a position of 'economic dependence' on the supplier of rail services in *Deutsche Bahn*.[264] In *British Airways* the GC confirmed the Commission's finding that BA was an 'obligatory business partner' for travel agents.[265] In view of BA's leading position on the UK air transport market it was imperative that travel agents could offer their customers BA tickets. In these situations there is no countervailing buyer (or, in the BA situation, supplier) power to dilute the power of the undertaking in question. An undertaking can therefore be an unavoidable trading partner not because there is no other source of the undertaking's product or service but because it has become a 'must-stock' product, perhaps as the result of advertising, marketing, and/or product differentiation, as was found to be the case in *Intel*.[266] Such a situation can both indicate that the undertaking is dominant and act as a barrier to entry.

D. COUNTERVAILING BUYER POWER

Countervailing buyer power is mentioned in the third indent of paragraph 12 of the Guidance Paper. As the essence of dominance is defined as the independence of an undertaking from, inter alia, its customers,[267] it follows that an undertaking constrained by a powerful buyer may not be in a dominant position.[268] However, it is not enough that powerful buyers extract favourable terms from the supplier *for themselves*: in order to counter a finding of dominance they must be able to protect *the market itself* by defeating any price increase through paving the way for new entry or leading existing competitors to expand production. This is possible, for example, where the buying side is highly concentrated.[269] It is possible that powerful buyers able to get a good deal for themselves could

---

[260] See Chap. 1.

[261] For a discussion of these practices as abuses see Chap. 7.

[262] Guidance Paper, para. 17.

[263] Case 85/76, *Hoffmann-La Roche & Co AG v. Commission* [1979] ECR 461, para. 41, reproduced in Section 6.B.iii, p. 338.

[264] Case T-229/94, *Deutsche Bahn v. Commission* [1997] ECR II-1689, [1998] 4 CMLR 220, para. 57.

[265] Case T-219/99, [2003] ECR II-5917, para. 217, confirming *Virgin/BA* [2000] OJ L30/1, [2000] 4 CMLR 999, para. 92.

[266] COMP/C-3/37.990 *Intel* .

[267] Case 85/76, *Hoffmann-La Roche & Co AG v. Commission* [1979] ECR 461, para. 38.

[268] See Case T-228/97, *Irish Sugar plc v. Commission* [1999] ECR II-2969, paras. 97–104 where such a situation was considered (although held not to apply on the facts).

[269] As, e.g., in the merger cases, *Enso/Stora*, COMP.M/1225; *Behringwerke/Armour Pharmaceutical*, Case. No. IV/M.495.

constitute a market for market definition purposes separate from that of other customers.[270] The Guidance Paper says of countervailing buyer power:

18. Competitive constraints may be exerted not only by actual or potential competitors but also by customers. Even an undertaking with a high market share may not be able to act to an appreciable extent independently of customers with sufficient bargaining strength....Such countervailing buying power may result from the customers' size or their commercial significance for the dominant undertaking, and their ability to switch quickly to competing suppliers, to promote new entry or to vertically integrate, and to credibly threaten to do so. If countervailing power is of a sufficient magnitude, it may deter or defeat an attempt by the undertaking to profitably increase prices. Buyer power may not, however, be considered a sufficiently effective constraint if it only ensures that a particular or limited segment of customers is shielded from the market power of the dominant undertaking.

In *Prokent/Tomra*[271] a supplier of reverse vending machines with over 70 per cent of the relevant markets argued that it was constrained by the power of its customers, the supermarkets, and other retail outlets. The Commission said that the concentration on the demand side was much lower than that on the supply side.

COMP/E-1.38.113 *Prokent Tomra*, 29 March 2006, [2009] 4 CMLR 101

89. The existence of buyer power on the demand side requires that there are either credible alternative suppliers to which the customers could turn, or that customers are able to sponsor new entrants. However, in the absence of established competitors which achieve significant and stable market shares, there cannot be a credible threat of even the largest customers moving all or a very large proportion of their requirements away from Tomra, by way of a bidding process or otherwise. Procurement of reverse vending equipment is not part of the core activities of retail groups. The circumstances of the case do not suggest that they are likely to act in a strategic manner in order to subsidise and actively build up competing suppliers to which large parts of the demand could be diverted. There is no evidence for any such behaviour of sponsoring new entry in the period under investigation. Moreover, such behaviour would have been prone to free riding, as building up a competitor would have resulted in a public good. Therefore, there was no substantial countervailing buyer power which would have been able to challenge Tomra's dominance in any of the markets concerned.

Even a monopoly buyer (monopsonist) may be unable to constrain the behaviour of a dominant firm to a significant extent. This is notably so in respect of pharmaceutical companies and national health services. In the UK case *Genzyme* where there was only one drug efficacious in treating a rare disease, the Competition Appeal Tribunal (CAT) described the monopoly buyer, the NHS, as being in a 'relatively weak' bargaining position.[272] In *AstraZeneca* the argument that AZ was constrained by the public authorities which paid for the drugs was dismissed after an analysis of the way in which AZ's first mover advantages enabled it to maintain both high prices and high market share.[273]

---

[270] Discussion Paper, para. 42; the Notice on the definition of the relevant market, para. 43, acknowledges that the ability of an undertaking to price discriminate may put customers in different markets. For the technique of market definition where there is market power on the demand side, see I. Kokkoris, 'Buyer Power Assessment in Competition Law: A Boon or A Menace?' (2006) 29(1) *World Competition* 139.

[271] On appeal, Case T-155/06, *Tomra Systems v. Commission* [2010] ECR II-4361, the dominance point was not argued.

[272] *Genzyme Ltd v. OFT* [2004] CAT 4, [2004] CompAR 358 (Competition Appeal Tribunal, upholding *Genzyme* CA 98/03/03, [2003] UKCLR 950), para. 250. There was no alternative to Cerezyme for treating Gaucher's Disease patients, and without it they would die.

[273] COMP/A.37.507/F3, *AstraZeneca* [2006] 5 CMLR 287, 15 June 2005, upheld Case T-321/05, *AstraZeneca v. Commission* [2010] ECR II-2805, paras 256–268, *aff'd* Case C-457/10 P, *AstraZeneca v. Commission*, 6 December 2012,

E. DOMINANT POSITIONS IN THE NEW ECONOMY

As we have seen[274] competition in the new economy tends to be on innovation. Dominant positions are often temporary and fragile. In the next extract the authors (a lawyer and two economists) argue that market share is not a good basis from which to find dominance in new economy industries.

C. Ahlborn, D. Evans, and A. Padilla, 'Competition Policy in the New Economy: Is Competition Law Up To The Challenge?' [2001] *ECLR* 156, 162

…[I]n new economy industries, the incumbent typically has a large market share since competition is often a matter of 'winner-takes-most'. Their large market share, however, is under permanent threat from innovating competitors and they are only able to retain their position if they continue to innovate…

Equating high market shares with dominance in the case of these 'fragile monopolists' of the new economy is potentially very damaging to innovation and competition, as E.C. competition law imposes a 'special responsibility' to the market upon dominant firms…Apart from the fact that this special responsibility often prohibits welfare-enhancing action where it has a negative effect on rivals' profits, in the new economy it prevents companies with high market shares (which nevertheless are under competitive threat and do not have the power to act independently of competitors and customers) to compete vigorously on an equal footing with their rivals.

A better test of market power is contestability. If the market is contestable, as new economy markets often are…a firm with a high market share does not enjoy a position of dominance because potential entry imposes an effective competitive constraint on its conduct; i.e., it cannot act independently of its (potential) competitors.[275]

The argument is therefore that in dynamically competitive markets in the new economy the *immediate* competitive constraints facing the undertaking are far less important than the *potential* competition.[276]

It has been suggested[277] that a multi-attribute SSNIP could be used to avoid the dangers of reaching over-narrow market definitions. This would involve asking whether a change in the *performance attributes* of one product, as well as in price, would induce substitution to or from another. Such a test is difficult to apply because of the problems in quantifying performance changes.[278]

'Network effects' (or 'network externalities') are a feature of many new economy markets as mentioned in Chapter 1.[279] The more users a network has, the more valuable it becomes to an individual user.

---

paras. 178–180. In the UK, for example, the answer to the monopoly pricing of a pharmaceutical company would be for the relevant authority, the National Institute for Health and Clinical Excellence (NICE) to refuse to license it for use in the NHS on financial grounds in the first place. This is sometimes done in respect of, e.g., new cancer drugs whose only effect would be to prolong life expectancy. However, the drug in issue in *AstraZeneca*, Losec (Omneprazole), is a very widely prescribed first-line treatment for gastro-intestinal disorders.

[274] In Chap. 1, Section 7.E, p. 54.

[275] See also C. Ahlborn, V. Denicolò, D. Deradin, and A. J. Padilla, 'DG Comp's Discussion Paper on Article 102: Implications of the Proposed Framework and Antitrust Rules for Dynamically Competitive Industries', in B. Allan, C. Ahlborn, and D. Bailey, eds., *Rethinking Article 102* (Linklaters, 2006), 6, and available at <http://papers.ssrn.com/sol3/papers.cfm?abstract_id=894466>, 22, where the authors conclude that '[g]iven these problems, market definition should perhaps play a less significant role in the competitive assessment of unilateral behaviour in dynamically competitive industries. Market shares should not be blindly used as relevant indicators of market power in those industries, and supply-side constraints should be carefully considered at the assessment stage'.

[276] Ahlborn et al., 'DG Comp's Discussion Paper on Article 102' (cited in n. 275), 25.

[277] See, e.g., D. Teece and M. Coleman, 'The meaning of Monopoly: Antitrust Analysis in High–technology Industries' [1998] *Ant Bull* 801, 853–857.

[278] Economists have, however, devised tests for doing this: see R. Hartman, D. Teece, W. Mitchell, and T. Jorde, 'Assessing Market Power in Regimes of Rapid Technological Change' (1993) 2 *Indus. & Corp Change* 317.

[279] Chapter 1, Section 7.E, p. 54.

Once a network has a certain number of users, therefore, the market may 'tip' towards that network. That is why it is said that competition may be *for* rather than *in* the market ('the winner takes all'). The winner may be aided by the behaviour of the producers of complementary products, who will want to design products (such as software) which are compatible with the dominant network. More customers will be attracted to the dominant network because of the large number of complementary products which can be used with it. So it becomes a vicious circle. The prime example of this effect is Microsoft, and its ubiquitous Windows operating system.[280] In the *Microsoft* decision the Commission noted that:

In industries exhibiting strong network effects, consumer demand depends critically on expectations about future purchases. If consumers expect a firm with a strong reputation in the current (product) generation to succeed in the next generation, this will tend to be self-fulfilling as the consumers direct their purchases to the product that they believe will yield the greatest network gains.[281]

Network effects played a very important part in the *Microsoft* case. Network effects are a feature of two-sided (or multi-sided) markets,[282] including those in the digital economy. In these markets not only does the product become more attractive to customers the more users it has, but there are ('indirect') externalities from the relationship between the two sides of the market.

It can be argued that the presence of network effects leads to the conclusion that competition authorities should intervene at an earlier moment, and not wait until one undertaking becomes dominant. On the other hand consumers may be better served by one network. Furthermore, some economists consider that the implications of network effects can be exaggerated.[283] There is often room for several networks and one important question is whether they connect to each other. Mobile telephone networks, for example, connect with each other.[284] Moreover, the argument that once a network has 'won' it cannot be dislodged is not convincing. If a new product (or network) offers clearly superior benefits, consumers will be prepared to bear the switching costs, and there are always *new* consumers coming on stream. Vinyl was replaced first by tapes and then by CDs because consumers appreciated their greater convenience[285] despite having in many cases acquired large record collections on vinyl and expensive turntable equipment. The next generation of consumers turned straight to CDs, which are now being replaced by downloads and other ways of 'consuming' music. There is a general consensus, however, that competition authorities need to be sensitive to special characteristics of new economy markets and refrain from moving against dominant positions which are ephemeral.[286]

The Commission and the EU Courts have been quite robust in their treatment of new economy markets, as shown by *Microsoft*.[287] In *France Télécom*[288] the applicant claimed that market shares were not a reliable indicator in the context of an emerging market. The GC said that the fact that this was

---

[280] See COMP/C-3/37.792, *Microsoft*, 24 Mar. 2004, in Chap. 7.

[281] *Microsoft*, COMP/C-3/37.792, [2005] 4 CMLR 965, para. 438, upheld by the General Court, Case T-210/04, *Microsoft v. Commission* [2007] ECR II-3601. The Commission also noted (para. 520) that the easier it is to find technicians to service the product (*in casu* Microsoft *work* group server operating systems) the more customers will buy it, and the more customers buy it, the more technicians will learn to service it, thus making it even more popular with customers, and so on.

[282] See Chap. 1, Section 10.B.(vii)j, p. 81.

[283] See, e.g., C. Veljanovski, 'Antitrust in the New Economy: Is the European Commission's View of the Network Economy Right?' [2001] *ECLR* 115.

[284] There is also a distinction between 'single-homing' (the customer can have access only to one network/platform/facility) and 'multi-homing' (e.g., the internet user is connected to a number of networks or able to use a number of search engines).

[285] Although there are many aficionados who believe in the matchless superiority of the vinyl sound.

[286] Teece and Coleman, 'The meaning of Monopoly' (cited in n. 277), 801; C. Ahlborn, D. S. Evans, and A. J. Padilla, 'Competition Policy in the New Economy: Is European Competition Law up to the Challenge?' [2001] *ECLR* 156; R. Lind and P. Muysert, 'Innovation and Competition Policy: Challenges for the New Millennium' [2003] *ECLR* 87.

[287] COMP/C-3/37.792, [2005] 4 CMLR 965, discussed in Chap. 7.

[288] Case T-340/03, *France Télécom SA v. Commission* [2007] ECR II-107, *aff'd*, Case C-202/07 P, *France Télécom v. Commission* [2009] ECR I-2963.

a fast-growing market could not preclude application of the competition rules.[289] But it did examine the claimant's contention that the market should be looked at from a dynamic perspective by assessing potential as well as actual competition, and found that the Commission had taken proper account of this.[290] The recent tendency of the Commission is to deal with cases in the digital economy by way of Commitments Decisions, a strategy which leaves many questions untested, including those of the finding of a dominant position.[291]

7. CONCLUSIONS

1. The definition in the case law of what constitutes a 'dominant position' is now usually interpreted as substantial market power which enables the undertaking concerned to profitably raise prices above the competitive level over a significant period of time.

2. The way that dominance is assessed for the purposes of Article 102 puts great emphasis on market shares. However, market definition is an inexact science which places products either in a market or outside it, whereas in reality there are degrees of substitution. Further, market shares are a static measurement that does not reflect dynamic developments in the market and potential competition. There is a presumption of dominance at 50 per cent of the market laid down in the case law.

3. The situation is exacerbated by the broad approach taken to barriers to entry and expansion.

4. The danger is that undertakings may be found to be in a dominant position when in reality they do not have significant market power.

5. Dominance has been found in EU law at market shares of 40 per cent. Moreover, the EU Courts and the Commission have not ruled out finding dominance below that point. There are good arguments for a dominance 'screen' or 'safe harbour' whereby undertakings with shares of the market below a certain point would have the legal certainty of knowing they were not subject to Article 102. The Commission did not include a definite safe harbour in the Guidance Paper. The danger with Article 102 is generally considered to be its over-, rather than under-, inclusiveness (i.e. the danger is of Type I 'false positive' errors).

8. FURTHER READING

A. BOOKS

BAIN, J. S., *Barriers to New Competition* (Harvard University Press, 1956)

BISHOP, S., and WALKER, M., *The Economics of EC Competition Law: Concepts, Application and Measurement* (3rd edn, Sweet & Maxwell, 2010), Chap. 6, 6.001–6.013

FAULL, J., and NIKPAY, A., *The EC Law of Competition* (2nd edn, Oxford University Press, 2007), Chap. 4

GERADIN, D., LAYNE-FARRAR, A., and PETIT, N., *EU Competition Law and Economics* (Oxford University Press, 2012), Chap. 4, 4.01–4.130

MOTTA, M., *Competition Policy* (Cambridge University Press, 2004), Chap. 3

O'DONOGHUE, R., and PADILLA, A. J., *The Law and Economics of Article 102* (2nd edn, Hart Publishing, 2013), Chaps. 3 and 4

ORTIZ BLANCO, L., *Market Power in EU Antitrust Law* (Hart Publishing, 2012), Chap. 3

SCHERER, F. M., and ROSS, D., *Industrial Market Structure and Economic Performance* (3rd edn, Houghton Mifflin, 1990), Chaps. 4 and 16

[289] Case T-340/03, *France Télécom SA v. Commission* [2007] ECR II-107, aff'd, Case C-202/07 P, *France Télécom v. Commission* [2009] ECR I-2963, para.10

[290] Case T-340/03, *France Télécom SA v. Commission* [2007] ECR II-107, aff'd, Case C-202/07 P, *France Télécom v. Commission* [2009] ECR I-2963, paras. 110–113.

[291] e.g., the *Google* case, see further Chap. 7, Section 13.E., p. 565.

SUTTON, J., *Sunk Costs and Market Structure: Price Competition, Advertising, and the Evolution of Concentration* (MIT Press, 1991)

B. ARTICLES

AHLBORN, C., EVANS, D. S., and PADILLA, A. J., 'Competition Policy in the New Economy: Is European Competition Law up to the Challenge?' [2001] *ECLR* 156

AZEVEDO, J. P., and WALKER, M. 'Dominance: Meaning and Measurement' [2002] *ECLR* 363

BADEN FULLER, C. W., 'Article 86 EEC: Economic Analysis of the Existence of a Dominant Position' (1979) 4 *ELRev* 423

BISHOP, W., 'Editorial: The Modernisation of DGIV' [1997] *ECLR* 481

—— and CAFFARRA, C., 'Editorial, Dynamic Competition and Aftermarkets' [1998] *ECLR* 265

EILSMANSBERGER, T., 'Dominance—The Lost Child? How the Effects-Based Rules Could and Should Change Dominance Analysis' (2006) 2 *European Law Journal* 15

FJELL, K., and SØRGARD, L., 'How to Test for Abuse of Dominance?' (2006) 2 *European Law Journal* 69

FOX, E. M., and SULLIVAN, L. A., 'Antitrust—Retrospective and Prospective: Where Are We Coming From? Where Are We Going?' (1987) 62 *New York Univ LR* 936

HARBORD, D., and HOEHN, T., 'Barriers to Entry and Exit in European Competition Policy' (1994) 14 *International Review of Law and Economics* 411

HARTMAN, R., TEECE, D., MITCHELL, W., and JORDE, T., 'Assessing Market Power in Regimes of Rapid Technological Change' (1993) 2 *Indus & Corp Change* 317

KOKKORIS, I., 'Buyer Power Assessment in Competition Law: A Boon or A Menace?' (2006) 29(1) *World Competition* 139

—— *A Gap in the Enforcement of Article 82* (BIICL, 2009)

KORAH, V., 'Concept of a Dominant Position within the Meaning of Article 86' (1980) 17 *CMLRev* 395

—— 'The Michelin Decision of the Commission' (1982) 7 *ELRev* 13

—— 'The Paucity of Economic Analysis in the EEC Decisions on Competition—Tetra Pak II' [1993] *Current Legal Problems* 148

LANDES, D., and POSNER, R. A., 'Market Power in Antitrust Cases' (1981) 94 *Harvard LR* 937

LIND, R., and MUYSERT, P., 'Innovation and Competition Policy: Challenges for the New Millennium' [2003] *ECLR* 87

MONTI, G., 'The Concept of Dominance in Article 82' (2006) 2 *European Competition Journal* 31

MULDOOM, D., 'The Kodak Case: Power in Aftermarkets' [1996] *ECLR* 473

MURPHY, F., and LIBERATORE, F., 'Abuse of Regulatory Procedures—the *Astra-Zeneca Case*' [2009] *ECLR* 223

SCHMALENSEE, R., 'Entry Deterrence in the Ready–to–eat Breakfast Cereal Industry' (1978) 9 *Bell J Econ* 305

—— 'Product Differentiation Advantages of Pioneering Brands' (1981) 72 *American Economics Review* 349

—— 'Another Look at Market Power' (1981–1982) 95 *Harvard LR* 1789

—— 'Ease of Entry: Has the Concept Been Applied too Readily?' (1987) 56 *Antitrust LJ* 41

SHAPIRO, C., 'Aftermarkets and Consumer Welfare: Making Sense of Kodak' (1995) 63 *Antitrust LJ* 483

SPENCE, M., 'Notes on Advertising, Economies of Scale and Entry Barriers' (1980) 95 *Quart. J of Econ* 493

TEECE, D., and COLEMAN, M., 'The meaning of Monopoly: Antitrust Analysis in High-technology Industries' [1998] *Ant Bull* 801

TEMPLE LANG, J., 'Monopolisation and the Definition of "Abuse" of a Dominant Position under Article 86 EEC Treaty' (1979) 16 *CMLRev* 345

VELJANOVSKI, C., 'Antitrust in the New Economy: Is the European Commission's View of the Network Economy Right?' [2001] *ECLR* 115

VICKERS, J., 'Market Power in Competition Case' (2006) 2 *European Law Journal* 3

WESTIN, J., 'Defining Relevant Market in the Pharmaceutical Sector in the Light of the Losec Case—Just How Different is the Pharmaceutical Market?' [2011] *ECLR* 57

VAN DEN BERGH, R. J., and CAMESASCA, P. D., *European Competition Law and Economics: A Comparative Perspective* (2nd edn, Sweet & Maxwell, 2006), Chap. 4

7

ARTICLE 102 TFEU: CONDUCT WHICH CAN BE AN ABUSE

1. CENTRAL ISSUES

1. The definition of (exclusionary) abuse was laid down by the Court of Justice (CJ) in *Hoffmann-La Roche* in 1979. This leads to a difficult distinction between 'competition on the merits' and conduct which is an abuse.

2. The main concern of the Commission in applying Article 102 has been with what are called 'exclusionary' rather than 'exploitative' abuses.

3. The EU Courts have held that dominant undertakings have a 'special responsibility' to the competitive process. That principle has had a major effect on the type of conduct which has been held to be abusive.

4. The Guidance on the Commission's Enforcement Priorities in Applying Article 82 (2009) deals only with exclusionary abuses and covers in detail only the main exclusionary abuses: predatory pricing, exclusive dealing (single branding), discounts and rebates, tying, and refusal to supply.

5. The Guidance Paper adopts a concept of *anti-competitive foreclosure* to identify those cases which are an enforcement priority for the Commission. This has two elements, exclusion of competitors and harm to consumers.

6. The Guidance Paper adopts the 'as efficient competitor' test in respect of pricing abuses. The CJ has adopted the 'as efficient competitor' in respect of predatory pricing and margin squeeze but not in respect of rebates and discounts.

7. The EU predatory pricing rules centre on a costs-based test. The Guidance Paper adopts a 'sacrifice' test for predatory pricing.

8. The conduct of dominant undertakings may infringe Article 102 even where it has been approved by national sector regulators. This has

been shown in cases on 'margin squeezes' in the telecommunications sector.

9. The application of Article 102 to exclusive dealing, discounts, and rebates has hitherto treated some of these practices as virtually per se abuses and others as requiring only a capability of restricting competition. The Guidance Paper considers their effects rather than their form. However, there is still a question of how the effects are to be measured, and how far presumptions should be used to assess them.

10. Some forms of tying have also been treated as akin to per se abuses. The *Microsoft* decision involved a 'technological tie' whereby two elements are integrated into the product sold to the consumer.

11. The idea that it can be an abuse for a dominant undertaking to refuse to supply another party is contrary to fundamental notions of freedom of contract. There is also a danger that it may be harmful to consumer welfare as it may discourage innovation and investment. Nevertheless, the case law establishes that in certain situations it can be an abuse for a dominant undertaking to refuse to supply. This is particularly so in the case of vertically integrated undertakings. There is a special problem over dominant undertakings being forced to license their intellectual property rights (IPRs).

12. The Commission has paid less attention to exploitative abuses. One exploitative abuse is the charging of unfair prices. There is great difficulty in assessing whether a price is excessive. It is a question of assessing whether the price is excessive in relation to the 'economic value' of the product or service in issue.

13. Article 102(c) specifically prohibits discrimination which puts the other parties at a competitive

disadvantage with one another. In general, price discrimination may be welfare enhancing or otherwise depending on the circumstances of the case.

14. Refusals to supply may be abusive simply on the grounds that they prevent or hinder parallel trade between Member States.

2. INTRODUCTION

In this chapter we consider the meaning of 'abuse' in Article 102 and examine the types of conduct which may constitute an abuse. This has to be seen in the context of the objectives of EU competition law in general and of Article 102 in particular, as discussed in Chapter 1 and Chapter 5.

In Chapter 5 we explained that in 2003 the Commission embarked upon a review of Article 102 aimed at 'modernising' its application. The reason for this was the growing belief that Article 102 should be applied with the objective of protecting competition as a means of enhancing consumer welfare rather than, as often in the past, protecting competition and competitors for their own sakes. Further, the Commission wished to take an effects-based, rather than a form-based, approach to the application of Article 102. The practice of judging the conduct of dominant firms by its form, considering some conduct abusive per se, and looking at effects on competitors rather than consumers will be seen from the cases and decisions discussed in this chapter. The extent to which this approach has changed, or not changed, over the years will be observed. This chapter looks at the Commission Guidance Paper on exclusionary abuses.[1]

3. THE MEANING OF ABUSE

A. GENERAL

Article 102 does not forbid the holding of a dominant position but only the abuse thereof.[2] The meaning of 'abuse' is of vital importance. Although the term is not defined, Article 102 sets out what abuse 'may, in particular, consist in':

(a) directly or indirectly imposing unfair purchase or selling prices or other unfair trading conditions;

(b) limiting production, markets or technical development to the prejudice of consumers;

(c) applying dissimilar conditions to equivalent transactions with other trading parties, thereby placing them at a competitive disadvantage;

(d) making the conclusion of contracts subject to acceptance by the other parties of supplementary obligations which, by their nature or according to commercial usage, have no connection with the subject of such contracts.

---

[1] Guidance on the Commission's Enforcement Priorities in Applying Article 82 of the EC Treaty to Abusive Exclusionary Conduct by Dominant Undertakings [2009] OJ C45/2 (Guidance Paper).

[2] Reiterated in Case C-209/10, *Post Danmark A/S v. Konkurrencerådet*, 27 March 2012, para. 21; cf. the rather strange statement by the GC in Case T-201/04, *Microsoft v. Commission* [2007] ECR II-3601, para. 664, see Section 12.D.vi, p. 546. In Case C-52/09, *Konkurrensverket v. TeliaSonera Sverige AB* [2011] ECR I-527, para. 24, the CJ said, 'Whilst Article 102 TFEU does not prohibit an undertaking from acquiring, *on its own merits*, [emphasis added] the dominant position in a market', which could suggest that where the dominant position has been acquired otherwise, such as by the past conferment of a legal monopoly, special considerations might apply, and see E. Rousseva and M. Marquis, 'Hell Freezes Over: A Climate Change for Assessing Exclusionary Conduct under Article 102 TFEU' (2012) 4 *J'nl of European Competition Law and Practice* 32.

Unlike Article 101 there is no reference to 'object or effect the restriction of competition' which could help to clarify why particular conduct might be an abuse. Article 102 does not indicate what 'theory of harm' it embodies.

B. TYPES OF ABUSE

(i) Exploitative and Exclusionary Abuses

The two most important terms for describing abuses are 'exploitative' and 'exclusionary'. An exploitative abuse is conduct whereby the dominant undertaking takes advantage of its market power to exploit its trading partners (customers). An exclusionary abuse is conduct whereby it prevents or hinders competition on the market. The CJ understood 'exclusionary abuse' in *Post Danmark* to refer to 'practices that cause consumers harm through their impact on competition'.[3] The distinction between exploitative and exclusionary (or 'anti-competitive') abuses stems from the *Continental Can* case in 1973[4] although the terminology did not become current until later.[5]

The obvious objection to an undertaking with market power is its ability to 'exploit' its position in a way which would be impossible for an undertaking operating on a competitive market.[6] It is clearly the purpose of Article 102 to prevent such conduct as the provision refers specifically to ways in which market power may be exploited (Article 102(a) prohibits the imposition of unfair prices or trading conditions). It was questioned initially whether or not Article 102 went any further than this. In particular, the text of Article 102 in some language versions suggested that the Article was intended to forbid *only* the exploitation and use of the dominant position in certain ways. For example the French and German texts state that there should be an 'abusive exploitation'.[7]

Some scholars in the early days of EC competition law therefore argued that Article 102 should be interpreted to catch only exploitative behaviour which harms consumers directly and should not prohibit conduct which has structural effects by excluding or disadvantaging other competitors.[8] Recent research in the *travaux préparatoires* has tended to confirm that the drafters of the Treaty were indeed concerned with protecting the dominant firm's trading partners from exploitation, rather than with the exclusion of competitors.[9]

The Commission, however, considered that Article 102 *could* be applied to prohibit conduct affecting the structure of the market.[10] In 1972 it issued its decision in *Continental Can*, finding that an undertaking which had merged with another had committed an abuse of a dominant position.[11] In the subsequent appeal the CJ confirmed this broad view of what may constitute an abuse for the purposes of Article 102.[12] In the following extract from *Continental Can* the references to what are now Articles 101 and 102 TFEU have been left as references to Articles 85 and 86 of the EEC Treaty as

---

[3] *Post Danmark*, 27 March 2012, para. 20.

[4] Case 6/72, *Europemballage Corp and Continental Can Co Inc* v. *Commission* [1973] ECR 215.

[5] See J. Temple Lang, 'Monopolisation and the Definition of "Abuse" of a Dominant Position under Article 86 EEC Treaty' (1979) 16 *CMLRev* 345.

[6] See Chap. 1.

[7] '...d'exploiter de façon abusive' in French; '*mibbräuchliche Ausnutzung*' in German.

[8] In particular, René Joliet, later a judge at the CJ, argued that the prohibition of conduct because of its structural effects would be tantamount to the prohibition of the dominant position itself, which was not the purpose of Art. 102, see R. Joliet, *Monopolization and Abuse of Dominant Position* (Nijhoff, 1970).

[9] P. Akman, 'Searching for the Long-Lost Soul of Article 82EC' (2009) 29 *Oxford Journal of Legal Studies* 267; P. Akman, *The Concept of Abuse in EU Competition Law* (Hart Publishing, 2012).

[10] *Le Problème de la Concentration dans le Marché Commun*, Etudes CEE, Série Concurrence No. 3, 1966, particularly paras. 25–27.

[11] *Re Continental Can Co Inc* [1972] OJ L7/25, [1972] CMLR D11. There has never been a Treaty provision expressly dealing with merger control; for the current position in respect of EU merger control, see Chap. 15.

[12] Case 6/72, *Europemballage Corp and Continental Can Co Inc* v. *Commission* [1973] ECR 215.

they were then, because the extract deals with those Articles in the context of their relationship with Articles 2 and 3(f) (later Article 3(1)(g)).

Case 6/72, *Europemballage Corp and Continental Can Co Inc v. Commission* [1973] ECR 215

Continental Can Co Inc, a US company, manufactured metal packaging. It acquired an 85.8 per cent share in a German metal can manufacturer, SLW. Through SLW it formed a wholly owned subsidiary under Belgian law, Europemballage, through which it acquired TDV, another can manufacturer. The Commission adopted a decision holding that this was contrary to Article 86 (now Article 102 TFEU) on the grounds that through SLW Continental Can held a dominant position in a substantial part of the common market in the markets for light packaging for preserved meat, fish and crustacea and for metal caps for glass jars, and that by Europemballage's purchase of a majority shareholding in TDV Continental Can had abused this dominant position by practically eliminating competition in the relevant market.

On appeal the Court of Justice annulled the decision on the grounds that the Commission had wrongly defined the relevant market because it had failed properly to take into account supply side substitutability.[13] Nevertheless, and contrary to the Opinion of Advocate General Roemer, the Court held that where there *was* a dominant position it was possible for a merger to amount to an abuse within what was then Article 86 EEC.

Court of Justice

19. The applicants maintain that the Commission by its decision, based on an erroneous interpretation of Article 86 of the EEC Treaty, is trying to introduce a control of mergers of undertakings, thus exceeding its powers. Such an attempt runs contrary to the intention of the authors of the Treaty, which is clearly seen not only from a literal interpretation of Article 86, but also from a comparison of the EEC Treaty and the national legal provisions of the Member States. The examples given in Article 86 of abuse of a dominant position confirm this conclusion, for they show that the Treaty refers only to practices which have effects on the market and are to the detriment of consumers or trade partners. Further, Article 86 reveals that the use of economic power linked with a dominant position can be regarded as an abuse of this position only if it constitutes the means through which the abuse is effected. But structural measures of undertakings—such as strengthening a dominant position by way of merger—do not amount to abuse of this position within the meaning of Article 86 of the Treaty. The decision contested is, therefore, said to be void as lacking the required legal basis.

20. Article 86 (1) of the Treaty says 'Any abuse by one or more undertakings of a dominant position within the common market or in a substantial part of it shall be prohibited as incompatible with the common market in so far as it may affect trade between Member States'. The question is whether the word 'abuse' in Article 86 refers only to practices of undertakings which may directly affect the market and are detrimental to production or sales, to purchasers or consumers, or whether this word refers also to changes in the structure of an undertaking, which lead to competition being seriously disturbed in a substantial part of the Common Market.

21. The distinction between measures which concern the structure of the undertaking and practices which affect the market cannot be decisive, for any structural measure may influence market conditions, if it increases the size and the economic power of the undertaking.

22. In order to answer this question, one has to go back to the spirit, general scheme and wording of Article 86, as well as to the system and objectives of the Treaty. These problems thus cannot be solved by comparing this Article with certain provisions of the ECSC Treaty.

---

[13] See Chap. 6, Section 5.B.ii, p. 325.

e question of the link of
ominant position and its
ng may be an abuse and
by which it is achieved,

mission since it had no
ntal Can was the seminal

hibited conduct.[15] This
the GC said that Article
within one paragraph
British Airways,[17] and in

ect consumers directly
luct which through its
n other words, Article
ouses. Paragraph 26 of
portant when looking
rn with the impact on
e Court accepted that
ition by taking over a

t undertaking had not
. Thus conduct which
petition on the market
this.

letermining the scope
and construed Article
an early indication of

lated in that way by the
ction to the prejudice of
la, *The Law and Economics*

ll exclusionary abuses: J.
Be Resolved?' (2012) 37

ases C-395 and 396/96P,
se C-333/94 P, *Tetra Pak*

on 10.D.iii.f, p. 469.

it was established that

adequately to define the

Commission [1974] ECR
. 2 of the Merger Reg.,
/1, to encompass a col-
375 and Case T-102/96,

n the Community's policy in the field
ccording to which the Community's
tition in the Common Market is not
iins a general programme devoid of
e objectives which it lays down to be
ards in particular the aim mentioned
ations for the interpretation of which

ring that competition in the Common
must not be eliminated. This require-
y would be pointless. Moreover, it cor-
ch one of the tasks of the Community
ient of economic activities'. Thus the
onditions because of the need to har-
quirements of Articles 2 and 3. Going
on would conflict with the aims of the

objectives set out in Articles 2 and 3 of
le to undertakings. Article 85 concerns
undertakings and concerted practices,
dertakings. Articles 85 and 86 seek to
ffective competition within the Common
result of behaviour falling under Article
ceeds under the influence of a dominant
ned. In the absence of explicit provisions
ertain decisions of ordinary associations
mits in Article 86 that undertakings, after
ition that any serious chance of competi-
tment would make a breach in the entire
of the Common Market. If, in order to
close connections between the undertaking within the scope of that of Article 86,
arket, the partitioning of a substantial part
s of the Treaty to maintain in the market
competition are permitted, was explicitly
ontain the same explicit provisions, but this
ninant positions, unlike Article 85(3), does
system the obligation to observe the basic
s from the obligatory force of these objec-
such a way that they contradict each other,

n imposed by Article 86 is to be interpreted
position must have been abused. The provi-
ohibits. The list merely gives examples, not
nt position prohibited by the Treaty. As may
rovision is not only aimed at practices which
which are detrimental to them through their
ioned in Article 3(f) of the Treaty. Abuse may
ngthens such position in such a way that the
ion, i.e., that only undertakings remain in the

> 27. Such being the meaning and the scope of Article 86, of the EEC Treaty th[
> causality raised by the applicants which in their opinion has to exist between the d[
> abuse, is of no consequence, for the strengthening of the position of an undertaki[
> prohibited under Article 86 of the Treaty, regardless of the means and procedure[
> if it has the effects mentioned above.

The finding that Article 102 could prohibit mergers was crucial to the Com[
tailor-made system of merger control until 17 years later.[14] Moreover, Contine[
judgment on Article 102.

First, it clarified that Article 102 does not set out an exhaustive list of pro[
important principle has been repeated many times. In *Microsoft*, for example,
102 must be interpreted as a whole and that conduct does not have to fit neatl[
to constitute an abuse.[16] The CJ relied upon the principle in the rebates case[
respect of margin squeeze as a stand-alone abuse in *Deutsche Telekom*.[18]

Secondly, the CJ established that the object of Article 102 is not just to prot[
from the exploitation of market power, but also to protect them from cond[
impact on the structure of competition is detrimental to them indirectly. I[
102 applies to what are now called exclusionary, as well as to exploitative, a[
Continental Can is one of the important passages in EU competition law. It is in[
at the subsequent application of Article 102 to remember that the CJ's conce[
the competitive structure was because of its effect on *consumers*. In this case t[
a dominant undertaking could strengthen its position and eliminate compe[
competitor.[19]

Thirdly, the merger was prohibited irrespective of the fact that the dominan[
exploited, or otherwise used, its market power in concluding the transaction[
excludes competitors, strengthens the dominant position, and weakens comp[
can fall within the prohibition even if the market power is not used to achieve[

Fourthly, the *way* in which the CJ interpreted Article 102 was significant. In [
of the provision the Court looked to the basic objectives of the Community [
102 as a specific application of Article 3(f).[20] This 'teleological' reasoning was[
how the competition rules would be interpreted.[21]

---

[14] See Chap.15. Article 102(b) covers a wide range of conduct and, although not artic[
CJ, the merger in *Continental Can* can be interpreted as a type of conduct which limits prod[
consumers and so is implicitly covered by paragraph (b), see R. O'Donoghue and A. J. Padi[
of Article 102 (2nd edn, Hart Publishing, 2013), 257.

[15] It has been argued that the width of Article 102(b) means that it should be the test for [
Temple Lang, 'How Can the Problems of Exclusionary Abuses under Article 102 TFEU[
ELRev 136.

[16] Case T-201/04, *Microsoft* v. *Commission* [2007] ECR II-3601, paras. 860–861. See also [
Compagnie Maritime Belge Transports SA v. *Commission* [2000] ECR I-1365, para. 112, and [
International SA v. *Commission* [1996] ECR I-5951, para. 37 (*Tetra Pak II*).

[17] Case C-95/04 P, *British Airways* v. *Commission* [2007] ECR I-2331, paras. 57–58, see Sect[

[18] Case C-280/08 P, *Deutsche Telekom* v. *Commission* [2010] ECR I-9555, para. 173, wher[
margin squeeze is a stand-alone abuse, see Section 9.B.i, p. 427 ff.

[19] On the facts, however, the CJ quashed the Commission's decision because it had failed[
market and, consequently, to show that the undertaking was dominant.

[20] Later Article 3(1)(g), now Protocol 27, see Chap. 1, Section 7.B, p. 37 ff.

[21] e.g. Cases 6 and 7/73, *Istituto Chemioterapico Italiano SpA and Commercial Solvents Corp* v[
223, para. 32. For a striking example see the interpretation of 'dominant position' in Ar[
Council Reg. 4064/89 [1989] OJ L395/1, as amended by Council Reg. 1310/97 [1997] OJ L18[
lective dominant position in Cases C-68/94 and C-30/95, *France* v. *Commission* [1998] ECR I-1[
Gencor v. *Commission* [2000] ECR II-753.

23. Article 86 is part of the chapter devoted to the common rules on the Community's policy in the field of competition. This policy is based on Article 3 (f) of the Treaty according to which the Community's activity shall include the institution of a system ensuring that competition in the Common Market is not distorted. The applicants' argument that this provision merely contains a general programme devoid of legal effect, ignores the fact that Article 3 considers the pursuit of the objectives which it lays down to be indispensable for the achievement of the Community's tasks. As regards in particular the aim mentioned in 3(f), the Treaty in several provisions contains more detailed regulations for the interpretation of which this aim is decisive.

24. But if Article 3(f) provides for the institution of a system ensuring that competition in the Common Market is not distorted, then it requires a fortiori that competition must not be eliminated. This requirement is so essential that without it numerous provisions of the Treaty would be pointless. Moreover, it corresponds to the precept of Article 2 of the Treaty according to which one of the tasks of the Community is 'to promote throughout the Community a harmonious development of economic activities'. Thus the restraints on competition which the Treaty allows under certain conditions because of the need to harmonize the various objectives of the Treaty, are limited by the requirements of Articles 2 and 3. Going beyond this limit involves the risk that the weakening of competition would conflict with the aims of the Common Market.

25. With a view to safeguarding the principles and attaining the objectives set out in Articles 2 and 3 of the Treaty, Articles 85 to 90 have laid down general rules applicable to undertakings. Article 85 concerns agreements between undertakings, decisions of associations of undertakings and concerted practices, while Article 86 concerns unilateral activity of one or more undertakings. Articles 85 and 86 seek to achieve the same aim on different levels, *viz.* the maintenance of effective competition within the Common Market. The restraint of competition which is prohibited if it is the result of behaviour falling under Article 85, cannot become permissible by the fact that such behaviour succeeds under the influence of a dominant undertaking and results in the merger of the undertakings concerned. In the absence of explicit provisions one cannot assume that the Treaty, which prohibits in Article 85 certain decisions of ordinary associations of undertakings restricting competition without eliminating it, permits in Article 86 that undertakings, after merging into an organic unity, should reach such a dominant position that any serious chance of competition is practically rendered impossible. Such a diverse legal treatment would make a breach in the entire competition law which could jeopardize the proper functioning of the Common Market. If, in order to avoid the prohibitions in Article 85, it sufficed to establish such close connections between the undertakings that they escaped the prohibition of Article 85 without coming within the scope of that of Article 86, then, in contradiction to the basic principles of the Common Market, the partitioning of a substantial part of this market would be allowed. The endeavour of the authors of the Treaty to maintain in the market real or potential competition even in cases in which restraints on competition are permitted, was explicitly laid down in Article 85(3)(b) of the Treaty. Article 86 does not contain the same explicit provisions, but this can be explained by the fact that the system fixed there for dominant positions, unlike Article 85(3), does not recognize any exemption from the prohibition. With such a system the obligation to observe the basic objectives of the Treaty, in particular that of Article 3 (f), results from the obligatory force of these objectives. In any case Articles 85 and 86 cannot be interpreted in such a way that they contradict each other, because they serve to achieve the same aim.

26. It is in the light of these considerations that the condition imposed by Article 86 is to be interpreted whereby in order to come within the prohibition a dominant position must have been abused. The provision states a certain number of abusive practices which it prohibits. The list merely gives examples, not an exhaustive enumeration of the sort of abuses of a dominant position prohibited by the Treaty. As may further be seen from letters (c) and (d) of Article 86 (2), the provision is not only aimed at practices which may cause damage to consumers directly, but also at those which are detrimental to them through their impact on an effective competition structure, such as is mentioned in Article 3(f) of the Treaty. Abuse may therefore occur if an undertaking in a dominant position strengthens such position in such a way that the degree of dominance reached substantially fetters competition, i.e., that only undertakings remain in the market whose behaviour depends on the dominant one.

27. Such being the meaning and the scope of Article 86, of the EEC Treaty the question of the link of causality raised by the applicants which in their opinion has to exist between the dominant position and its abuse, is of no consequence, for the strengthening of the position of an undertaking may be an abuse and prohibited under Article 86 of the Treaty, regardless of the means and procedure by which it is achieved, if it has the effects mentioned above.

The finding that Article 102 could prohibit mergers was crucial to the Commission since it had no tailor-made system of merger control until 17 years later.[14] Moreover, *Continental Can* was the seminal judgment on Article 102.

First, it clarified that Article 102 does not set out an exhaustive list of prohibited conduct.[15] This important principle has been repeated many times. In *Microsoft*, for example, the GC said that Article 102 must be interpreted as a whole and that conduct does not have to fit neatly within one paragraph to constitute an abuse.[16] The CJ relied upon the principle in the rebates case *British Airways*,[17] and in respect of margin squeeze as a stand-alone abuse in *Deutsche Telekom*.[18]

Secondly, the CJ established that the object of Article 102 is not just to protect consumers directly from the exploitation of market power, but also to protect them from conduct which through its impact on the structure of competition is detrimental to them indirectly. In other words, Article 102 applies to what are now called exclusionary, as well as to exploitative, abuses. Paragraph 26 of *Continental Can* is one of the important passages in EU competition law. It is important when looking at the subsequent application of Article 102 to remember that the CJ's concern with the impact on the competitive structure was because of its effect on *consumers*. In this case the Court accepted that a dominant undertaking could strengthen its position and eliminate competition by taking over a competitor.[19]

Thirdly, the merger was prohibited irrespective of the fact that the dominant undertaking had not exploited, or otherwise used, its market power in concluding the transaction. Thus conduct which excludes competitors, strengthens the dominant position, and weakens competition on the market can fall within the prohibition even if the market power is not used to achieve this.

Fourthly, the *way* in which the CJ interpreted Article 102 was significant. In determining the scope of the provision the Court looked to the basic objectives of the Community and construed Article 102 as a specific application of Article 3(f).[20] This 'teleological' reasoning was an early indication of how the competition rules would be interpreted.[21]

[14] See Chap.15. Article 102(b) covers a wide range of conduct and, although not articulated in that way by the CJ, the merger in *Continental Can* can be interpreted as a type of conduct which limits production to the prejudice of consumers and so is implicitly covered by paragraph (b), see R. O'Donoghue and A. J. Padilla, *The Law and Economics of Article 102* (2nd edn, Hart Publishing, 2013), 257.

[15] It has been argued that the width of Article 102(b) means that it should be the test for all exclusionary abuses: J. Temple Lang, 'How Can the Problems of Exclusionary Abuses under Article 102 TFEU Be Resolved?' (2012) 37 *ELRev* 136.

[16] Case T-201/04, *Microsoft v. Commission* [2007] ECR II-3601, paras. 860–861. See also Cases C-395 and 396/96P, *Compagnie Maritime Belge Transports SA v. Commission* [2000] ECR I-1365, para. 112, and Case C-333/94 P, *Tetra Pak International SA v. Commission* [1996] ECR I-5951, para. 37 (*Tetra Pak II*).

[17] Case C-95/04 P, *British Airways v. Commission* [2007] ECR I-2331, paras. 57–58, see Section 10.D.iii.f, p. 469.

[18] Case C-280/08 P, *Deutsche Telekom v. Commission* [2010] ECR I-9555, para. 173, where it was established that margin squeeze is a stand-alone abuse, see Section 9.B.i, p. 427 ff.

[19] On the facts, however, the CJ quashed the Commission's decision because it had failed adequately to define the market and, consequently, to show that the undertaking was dominant.

[20] Later Article 3(1)(g), now Protocol 27, see Chap. 1, Section 7.B, p. 37 ff.

[21] e.g. Cases 6 and 7/73, *Istituto Chemioterapico Italiano SpA and Commercial Solvents Corp v. Commission* [1974] ECR 223, para. 32. For a striking example see the interpretation of 'dominant position' in Art. 2 of the Merger Reg., Council Reg. 4064/89 [1989] OJ L395/1, as amended by Council Reg. 1310/97 [1997] OJ L180/1, to encompass a collective dominant position in Cases C-68/94 and C-30/95, *France v. Commission* [1998] ECR I-1375 and Case T-102/96, *Gencor v. Commission* [2000] ECR II-753.

(ii) The Position since *Continental Can*

Since *Continental Can* the story of Article 102 has predominantly been one of action against exclusionary abuses. There have been few cases in which an undertaking's exploitation of its dominant position has been prohibited, as we see later.[22] This is partly because a dominant undertaking's ability to exploit its customers for a significant period of time indicates that there is something wrong with the market. For example, the ability to reap supra-competitive profits by charging excessive prices should in theory act as a spur to attract new competitors on to the market. In some markets in which this cannot happen, such as those with high barriers to entry because of network effects or high minimum efficient scale, the solution may be to impose price controls through sector regulation. In situations other than this competition authorities such as the Commission may prefer to take action against anti-competitive practices which are preventing entry and causing the market failure, rather than tackle the high prices directly. Tackling high prices directly is an unattractive option for competition authorities. First, there are problems in identifying what is an excessive price and secondly there is the matter of the remedy. Competition authorities do not like acting as price regulators. However, the Commission has made it clear that there is no question of Article 102 being applied *only* to exclusionary abuses. 'Article 102 can properly be applied, where appropriate, to situations in which a dominant undertaking's behaviour directly prejudices the interests of consumers, notwithstanding the absence of any effect on the structure of competition.'[23] Moreover, as the imposition of 'unfair prices' is expressly listed as an abuse in Article 102(a) the Commission could not pursue a policy of never prosecuting excessive pricing and it will take action where the circumstances warrant it.[24] As a Commission official put it: 'the [EEC] Founding Fathers' faith in competition as a process of rivalry between competitors was not strong enough to tolerate customer/consumer exploitation in the short run'.[25]

The prohibition of exclusionary behaviour may benefit consumers by protecting the competitive structure. The view that consumer welfare is the objective of competition law holds that consumer benefit is the *only* reason for this prohibition. However, such a prohibition also *directly* benefits competitors. It prevents their exclusion from the market. The prohibition of exclusionary behaviour may, therefore, encourage the competition authorities to go beyond the objective of protecting competition as a way of benefiting consumers. Indeed, this chapter is full of examples (some of them recent) where Article 102 has been applied to protect *competitors* and not *competition* and where it is questionable whether preventing the exclusion of the competitors did, in fact, benefit consumers.[26] This raises again the question of the objectives of competition law.

(iii) Categories of Abuse

In addition to 'exploitative' and 'exclusionary' abuses it has been suggested that there is a type of abuse which can be called 'reprisal' abuses. These are abuses which are specifically aimed at another

---

[22] See Section 15.

[23] *1998 World Cup* [2000] OJ L5/55, [2000] 4 CMLR 963, para. 100.

[24] See the (then) Competition Commissioner, Mario Monti, at the 8th EU Competition Law and Policy Workshop, EUI, June 2003, published in C. D. Ehlermann and I. Atanasiu (eds.), 'European Competition Law Annual 2003: What is an Abuse of a Dominant Position?' (Hart Publishing, 2006), 3, 6–7; Director General of DG Comp, Philip Lowe, at Fordham Corporate Law Institute 30th Annual Conference on International Antitrust Law and Policy, 23 Oct. 2003, published in 2003 *Fordham Corp L Inst* (B. Hawk (ed.), 2004), 163, 169–170. The cases on excessive pricing are discussed in Section 15, A.p. 575.

[25] L. Gyselen, 'Rebates: Competition on the Merits or Exclusionary Practice?', in Ehlermann and Atanasiu (eds.), *European Competition Law Annual 2003* (cited in n. 24) 287, 290. This contrasts with the US Sherman Act, s. 2, which is not applied to exploitative conduct.

[26] See, e.g., Cases 6 and 7/73, *Istituto Chemioterapico Italiano SpA and Commercial Solvents Corp* v. *Commission* [1974] ECR 223; Case 22/78, *Hugin Kassaregister AB and Hugin Cash Registers Ltd* v. *Commission* [1979] ECR 1869; Case T-201/04, *Microsoft* v. *Commission* [2007] ECR II-3601. In Case C-280/08 P, *Deutsche Telekom* v. *Commission* [2010] ECR I-9555, Article 102 was applied to the short-term *detriment* to consumers in the form of higher prices.

undertaking and encompass steps taken to discipline or punish it. Reprisal abuses are normally a form of exclusionary abuse.[27] Discrimination between those trading with the dominant undertaking, who are its customers but not its competitors on any relevant market, is another form of abuse. There is also a category of abuse which consists of conduct which divides the single market.[28]

(iv) Categories of Abuse are Not Mutually Exclusive

It must be emphasised that these categories of abuse—exploitative, exclusionary, discrimination, single market—are not mutually exclusive. The same conduct may be exploitative *and* may make it more difficult for a competitor to gain access to the market, or may be both exclusionary and discriminatory. For example, discriminatory prices offered to customers (prohibited by Article 102(c)) may also exclude competitors by charging lower prices to customers who might otherwise purchase from the competitor.[29] Limiting production and tying can also simultaneously exploit customers and exclude competitors. Similarly, conduct aimed at dividing the single market may be also exclusionary in that it excludes a competitor distributor from the territory the dominant undertaking is trying to protect[30] or exploitative in that the object is to charge consumers higher prices.[31]

The line between exploitative and exclusionary abuses becomes increasingly blurred with the concentration on consumer welfare in Article 102 analysis:

The explicit introduction of a consumer harm element for exclusionary abuses further weakens the importance of the distinction between exclusionary and exploitative abuses, the only difference being that for exploitative abuses there is already evidence of actual consumer detriment, which could, for example, be 'excessive' pricing (as compared to a competitive level).[32]

One scholar has argued that in order to be an abuse conduct should both exploit trading partners or final consumers *and* exclude competitors (as well as not increasing efficiency).[33]

Nevertheless, the terminology of exploitative and exclusionary remains current and is employed by the Commission.[34]

C. THE BROAD NATURE OF THE CONCEPT OF ABUSE

(i) The Definition of 'Abuse'

In *Hoffmann La-Roche* the CJ gave a definition of the concept of an (exclusionary) abuse which has been the foundation of the jurisprudence ever since.[35]

---

[27] See J. Temple Lang, 'Monopolisation and the Definition of "Abuse" of a Dominant Position under Article 86 EEC Treaty' (1979) 16 *CMLRev* 345, 363–364 and J. Temple Lang, 'Reprisals and Overreaction by Dominant Companies as an Anti-competitive Abuse under Article 82(b)' [2008] *ECLR* 11. The best example of a 'reprisal' abuse is the termination of supply in Case 2/76, *United Brands* v. *Commission* [1978] ECR 207, discussed in Section 12.E, p. 549, which was also exclusionary. Dr Temple Lang suggests in the 2008 article that it should be an abuse for a dominant undertaking to take reprisals against those complaining about its conduct to a competition authority: for complaints, see Chap. 13.

[28] Cases C-468–478/06, *Sot. Lélos kai Sia and others EE* v. *GlaxoSmithKline AEVE Farmakeftikon Proionton* [2008] ECR I-7139.

[29] See Case C-95/04 P, *British Airways* v. *Commission*, [2007] ECR I-2331, where this was held to be so.

[30] As in *Sot. Lélos*, see n. 28.

[31] Case 226/84 *British Leyland* v. *Commission* [1986] ECR 3323.

[32] I. Lianos, 'Categorical Thinking in Competition Law and the "Effects-based" Approach in Article 82', in A. Ezrachi (ed.), *Article 82 EC: Reflections on its Recent Evolution* (Hart Publishing, 2009), 19, 44.

[33] Akman, *The Concept of Abuse in EU Competition Law* (cited in n. 9).

[34] e.g., its Guidance Paper on enforcement priorities [2009] OJ C45/2 applies only to 'exclusionary abuses'.

[35] Repeated in numerous cases, such as Case C-62/86 AKZO Chemie BV v. *Commission* [1991] ECR I-3359, para. 69; Case C-202/07 P, *France Télécom* v. *Commission* [2009] ECR I-2369, para. 104; Case C-280/08 P, *Deutsche Telekom*

> **Case 85/76, *Hoffmann-La Roche & Co AG* v. *Commission* [1979] ECR 461, para. 91**
>
> **Court of Justice**
>
> For the purpose of rejecting the finding that there has been an abuse of a dominant position the interpretation suggested by the applicant that an abuse implies that the use of the economic power bestowed by a dominant position is the means whereby the abuse has been brought about cannot be accepted. The concept of abuse is an objective concept relating to the behaviour of an undertaking in a dominant position which is such as to influence the structure of a market where, as a result of the very presence of the undertaking in question, the degree of competition is weakened and which, through recourse to methods different from those which condition normal competition in products or services on the basis of the transactions of commercial operators, has the effect of hindering the maintenance of the degree of competition still existing in the market or the growth of that competition.[36]

In 2012 the CJ (Grand Chamber) added a consumer detriment element to the *Hoffmann-La Roche* definition.

> **Case C-209/10, *Post Danmark A/S* v. *Konkurrencerådet*, 27 March 2012**
>
> **Court of Justice**
>
> In that regard, it is also to be borne in mind that Article [102] applies, *in particular*, [emphasis added] to the conduct of a dominant undertaking that, through recourse to methods different from those governing normal competition on the basis of the performance of commercial operators, has the effect, *to the detriment of consumers*, [emphasis added] of hindering the maintenance of the degree of competition existing in the market or the growth of that competition (see, to that effect, *AKZO* v *Commission*, paragraph 69; *France Télécom* v *Commission*…paragraphs 104 and 105; and Case C-280/08 P *Deutsche Telekom* v *Commission*…paras 174, 176 and 180 and case-law cited).

However, in *Tomra*, three weeks later, the CJ (Third Chamber) reverted to the old *Hoffmann-La Roche* wording, with no mention of consumers,[37] as did the First Chamber in *AstraZeneca*.[38]

(ii) The Market Power Does Not Need to be Used for an Abuse to be Committed

As already noted, *Continental Can* established that the dominant undertaking does not need to be *using* its dominance to commit the abuse.[39] However, it is the fact that the undertaking is dominant

v. *Commission* [2010] ECR I-9555, para. 174; Case C-52/09, *Konkurrensverket* v. *TeliaSonera Sverige AB* [2011] ECR I-527, para. 27.

[36] See also Case 322/81, *NV Nederlandsche Banden-Industrie Michelin* v. *Commission* [1983] ECR 3461, para. 70, where the CJ repeated this in slightly different wording.

[37] Case C-549/10 P, *Tomra Systems ASA* v. *European Commission*, 19 April 2012, para. 17.

[38] Case C-457/10 P, *AstraZeneca* v. *Commission*, 6 December 2012, para. 74.

[39] Case 6/72, *Europemballage Corp and Continental Can Co Inc* v. *Commission* [1973] ECR 215, [1973] CMLR 199, particularly paras. 26–27. O'Donoghue and Padilla, *The Law and Economics of Article 102* (cited in n. 14), 263 suggest that the comments of the CJ in *Continental Can* should be seen in the context of that case, where the Court was supporting

that renders its behaviour abusive. The dominance means that the behaviour has effects which the behaviour of a non-dominant undertaking would not have. Since a dominant undertaking may be prohibited from some conduct even though it is not actually *using* its market power, some strategies possible for, and permitted to, non-dominant firms will be prohibited. This is because the EU Courts hold that a dominant undertaking has a special responsibility. It may abuse its position by engaging in conduct which is acceptable when carried out by its competitors and irrespective of any intention to commit an abuse.[40]

(iii) The Special Responsibility of Dominant Undertakings

The EU Courts have consistently stressed that although the finding that an undertaking is in a dominant position is not a reproach, dominant firms have a 'special responsibility' towards the competitive process. This idea was first expressed by the CJ in *Michelin*:

A finding that an undertaking has a dominant position is not in itself a recrimination but simply means that, irrespective of the reasons for which it has such a dominant position, the undertaking concerned has a special responsibility not to allow its conduct to impair genuine undistorted competition on the common market.[41]

Although hitherto, as one scholar says, 'once the Courts mention this responsibility in their reasoning, one may not expect anything other than a finding of abuse'[42] the CJ did, in *Post Danmark* in 2012, recite the 'special responsibility' as usual but nevertheless ruled that certain pricing practices were not, after all, abusive.[43] The special responsibility arises irrespective of the reasons for which the undertaking has a dominant position but in *Post Danmark* the CJ accorded particular importance to the origin of the dominant position in a legal monopoly:

According to equally settled case-law, a dominant undertaking has a special responsibility not to allow its behaviour to impair genuine, undistorted competition on the internal market (Case C-202/07 P *France Telecom* v *Commission*...paragraph 105 and case-law cited). When the existence of a dominant position has its origins in a former legal monopoly, that fact has to be taken into account.[44]

This is highly significant in respect of dominant undertakings in liberalised markets where the incumbents are still reaping the advantages of their previous legal monopoly.[45]

The principle that dominant firms have a 'special responsibility' towards the competitive process is a key element in the application of Article 102.[46] It imposes what is in effect a *positive*, or affirmative,

---

the Commission's move to plug part of the gap in its armoury left, at the time, by the absence of a regime for merger control.

[40] Case T-111/96, *ITT Promedia* v. *Commission* [1998] ECR II-2937, para. 139, and see the case law in the rest of this chapter. For a recent application of the principle, see Case C-202/07 P, *France Télécom* v. *Commission* [2009] ECR I-2369.

[41] Case 322/81, *NV Nederlandsche Banden-Industrie Michelin* v. *Commission* [1983] ECR 3461, para. 57. See also, e.g., Case T-228/97, *Irish Sugar plc* v. *Commission* [1999] ECR II-2969, para. 112; Case T-201/04, *Microsoft* v. *Commission* [2007] ECR II-3601, para. 229; Case C-202/07 P, *France Télécom* v. *Commission* [2009] ECR I-2369, para. 105; Case C-52/09, *Konkurrensverket* v. *TeliaSonera Sverige AB* [2011] ECR I-527, para. 24; Case C-457/10 P, *AstraZeneca* v. *Commission*, 6 December 2012, para. 134.

[42] E. Rousseva, *Rethinking Exclusionary Abuses in EU Competition Law* (Hart Publishing, 2010), 71. See also K. McMahon, 'A Reformed Approach to Article 82 and the Special Responsibility Not to Distort Competition' in Ezrachi (ed.), *Article 82 EC: Reflections on Its Recent Evolution* (cited in n. 32), 121.

[43] Case C-209/10, *Post Danmark A/S* v. *Konkurrencerådet*, 27 March 2012

[44] Case C-209/10, *Post Danmark A/S* v. *Konkurrencerådet*, 27 March 2012, para. 23.

[45] See further Rousseva and Marquis, 'Hell Freezes Over: A Climate Change for Assessing Exclusionary Conduct under Article 102 TFEU' (cited in n. 2), 32; and see the discussion of the exceptions the Commission makes to its position on refusal to supply in the Guidance Paper, para. 82, in Section 12.G, p. 552.

[46] See, e.g., COMP/A.37.507.F3, *Generics/AstraZeneca*, 15 June 2005, IP/05/737 upheld Case T-321/05, *AstraZeneca* v. *Commission* [2010] ECR II-2805, *aff'd* Case C-457/10 P, *AstraZeneca* v. *Commission*, 6 December 2012, paras 134 and

duty on the dominant undertaking to act in certain ways. The consequences of the imposition of special responsibility will be seen in the discussion throughout this chapter. It is a fundamental principle governing Article 102.

(iv) Super-dominance

A line of case law has suggested that the dominant undertaking's special responsibility increases with its degree of dominance. The idea first appeared in *Tetra Pak II*[47] where the CJ approved the GC's's statement that '[t]he actual scope of the special responsibility imposed on an undertaking in a dominant position must therefore be considered in the light of the specific circumstances of the case'.[48] The 'special circumstances' there included the undertaking's 'quasi-monopoly'.[49] In *Compagnie Maritime Belge* Advocate General Fennelly spoke of the 'super-dominance' of monopolists and quasi-monopolists and of the 'particularly onerous special responsibility' upon undertakings enjoying 'a position of dominance approaching a monopoly'.[50] Although the CJ did not expressly endorse this it did state that the scope of the special responsibility was affected by the circumstances of the case and the competition existing on the market. It indicated that an undertaking with a very large market share and only one competitor would be more likely to be found to have abused its dominant position than a dominant undertaking with a lesser degree of market power.[51] In *Deutsche Post AG: Interception of Cross-Border Mail* the Commission said that the 'actual scope of the dominant firm's special responsibility must be considered in relation to the degree of dominance held by the firm and to the special characteristics of the market which may affect the competitive situation'. The GC made much of the undertaking's 'quasi-monopoly' in *Microsoft*.[52]

The concept of super-dominance has long been criticised as lacking economic or legal foundation.[53] In *TeliaSonera* the referring court asked, inter alia, whether the degree of market dominance held by the undertaking was relevant to establishing whether the impugned pricing practice was abusive. Advocate General Mazák recommended that the answer was 'no', saying that Article 102 'makes no reference to a "super-dominant" position'.[54] The CJ agreed.

Case C-52/09, *Konkurrensverket* v. *TeliaSonera Sverige AB* [2011] ECR I-527

Court of Justice

79 As stated in paragraph 23 of this judgment, the dominant position referred to in Article 102 TFEU relates to a position of economic strength enjoyed by an undertaking which enables it to prevent effective competition being maintained on the relevant market by affording it the power to behave to an appreciable extent independently of its competitors, its customers and ultimately of consumers.

149, where it was used to justify as an abuse the failure to maintain in force a regulatory authorisation, see Section 13.C.i, p. 560.

[47] Case C-333/94 P, *Tetra Pak International SA v. Commission* [1996] ECR I-5951, [1997] 4 CMLR 662 *(Tetra Pak II)*, para. 24.

[48] Case T-83/91, *Tetra Pak International SA v. Commission* [1994] ECR II-755, para. 115.

[49] CJ, Case C-333/94 P, *Tetra Pak International SA v. Commission* [1996] ECR I-5951, [1997] 4 CMLR 662, para. 31.

[50] Cases C-395 and 396/96 P, *Compagnie Maritime Belge Transports SA v. Commission* [2000] ECR I-1365, Opinion of Fennelly AG, para. 137. This is the source of the term 'super-dominance'.

[51] Cases C-395 and 396/96 P, *Compagnie Maritime Belge Transports SA v. Commission* [2000] ECR I-1365, paras. 112–119.

[52] Case T-201/04, *Microsoft v. Commission* [2007] ECR II-3601, for example at paras 435 and 775.

[53] See L. Ortiz Blanco, *Market Power in EU Antitrust Law* (Hart Publishing, 2012), 49–50 and the literature there cited.

[54] *TeliaSonera*, para. 41 of the Opinion.

80 Accordingly, that provision, as stated by the Advocate General in point 41 of his Opinion, does not envisage any variation in form or degree in the concept of a dominant position. Where an undertaking has an economic strength such as that required by Article 102 TFEU to establish that it holds a dominant position in a particular market, its conduct must be assessed in the light of that provision.

81 Of course, that does not mean that an undertaking's strength is not relevant to the assessment of the lawfulness of the conduct in the market of such an undertaking in the light of Article 102 TFEU. The Court itself has based its analyses on the fact that an undertaking enjoyed a position of super-dominance or a quasi-monopoly (see, to that effect, Case C-333/94 P Tetra Pak v Commission ... paragraph 31, and Compagnie maritime belge transports and Others v Commission, paragraph 119). Nonetheless the degree of market strength is, as a general rule, significant in relation to the extent of the effects of the conduct of the undertaking concerned rather than in relation to the question of whether the abuse as such exists.

82 It follows that the application of a pricing practice resulting in margin squeeze by an undertaking may constitute an abuse of a dominant position where that undertaking has such a position, and, as a general rule, the degree of dominance in the market concerned is not relevant in that regard.

The CJ confirmed paragraphs 80 and 81 in Tomra.[55]

The CJ thus considers that as a general rule the degree of market power held by a dominant undertaking is irrelevant to whether its conduct constitutes an abuse. Rather, it is relevant only to the *extent of the effects* of the conduct. It may therefore affect the lawfulness of the conduct because effects play a part in Article 102 analysis. As usual, the CJ enters the caveat 'as a general rule'. One cannot therefore say that super-dominance as a determinant of what conduct can constitute an abuse is completely dead. Moreover, the CJ said in *Post Danmark*, apropos the special responsibility, that the fact that the existence of a dominant position has its origins in a legal monopoly has to be taken into account.[56] It may be, therefore, that previous legal monopoly is in some cases substituting for 'super-dominance' as a relevant factor.

(v) Abuse is an Objective Concept

In *Hoffmann-La Roche*[57] the CJ said that the notion of an abuse is an 'objective concept'. This reinforces the fact that it is not essential to a finding of an abuse that the dominant undertaking has used its dominant position.[58] Further, it means that the characterisation of a dominant undertaking's conduct as abusive does not imply fault and does not depend on the undertaking's subjective intent to exclude competitors or weaken competition. For example, in *Clearstream* the GC stated that the undertaking's argument that it had not pursued an anti-competitive objective was irrelevant to the legal characterisation of the facts.[59] In *Michelin II* the GC stated that establishing the anti-competitive object and the anti-competitive effect are the same thing for the purposes of Article 102 and that if it is shown that the object pursued by the conduct of an undertaking in a dominant position is to limit competition, that conduct will also be liable to have such an effect.[60]

---

[55] Case C-549/10 P, *Tomra Systems ASA v. European Commission*, 19 April 2012, para. 39.

[56] Case C-209/10, *Post Danmark A/S v. Konkurrencerådet*, 27 March 2012, para. 23.

[57] Case 85/76, *Hoffmann-La Roche & Co AG v. Commission* [1979] ECR 461.

[58] See Kirschner AG in Case T-51/89, *Tetra Pak Rausing SA v. Commission* [1990] ECR II-309, para. 64.

[59] Case T-301/04, *Clearstream Banking v. Commission* [2009] ECR II-3155, paras. 142–144, citing Case T-65/89, *BPB Industries Plc and British Gypsum Ltd v. Commission* [1993] ECR II-389, para. 70.

[60] Case T-203/01, *Manufacture Française des Pneumatiques Michelin v. Commission* [2003] ECR II- 4071, para. 241, echoing what the GC had said in Case T-228/97, *Irish Sugar plc v. Commission* [1999] ECR II-2969, para. 170, albeit not so clearly.

However, the presence of an anti-competitive objective may 'reinforce' the conclusion that there is an abuse of a dominant position even though it is not a condition for such a finding.[61] Anti-competitive intent is one of the factors which may be taken into account in establishing abuse, but an intent to compete on the merits does not save conduct from being abusive, as the CJ stated in *Tomra*.

Case C-549/10 P, *Tomra Systems ASA* v. *European Commission*, 19 April 2012

Court of Justice

16 By their first ground of appeal, the appellants seek, in essence, to establish that the General Court was wrong to endorse an alleged finding by the Commission of anti-competitive intent on the part of the Tomra group, in particular by failing to take into account internal documents proving that the Tomra group was intent on competing on the merits.

17 In order to assess whether this ground of appeal is well founded, it must be recalled that the concept of abuse of a dominant position prohibited by Article 102 TFEU is an objective concept relating to the conduct of a dominant undertaking which, on a market where the degree of competition is already weakened precisely because of the presence of the undertaking concerned, through recourse to methods different from those governing normal competition in products or services on the basis of the transactions of commercial operators, has the effect of hindering the maintenance of the degree of competition still existing in the market or the growth of that competition (see Case C-52/09 *TeliaSonera*...paragraph 27 and case-law cited).

18 None the less, the Commission, as part of its examination of the conduct of a dominant undertaking and for the purposes of identifying any abuse of a dominant position, is obliged to consider all of the relevant facts surrounding that conduct (see, to that effect, C-95/04 P *British Airways* v *Commission*...paragraph 67).

19 It must be observed in that regard that where the Commission undertakes an assessment of the conduct of an undertaking in a dominant position, that assessment being an essential prerequisite of a finding that there is an abuse of such a position, the Commission is necessarily required to assess the business strategy pursued by that undertaking. For that purpose, it is clearly legitimate for the Commission to refer to subjective factors, namely the motives underlying the business strategy in question.

20 Accordingly, the existence of any anti-competitive intent constitutes only one of a number of facts which may be taken into account in order to determine that a dominant position has been abused.

21 However, the Commission is under no obligation to establish the existence of such intent on the part of the dominant undertaking in order to render Article [102] applicable.

22 In that regard, the General Court correctly stated, in paragraph 36 of the judgment under appeal, that it was perfectly legitimate for the contested decision to concentrate primarily on Tomra's anti-competitive conduct, since it was precisely that conduct which it was the Commission's task to establish. The existence of an intention to compete on the merits, even if it were established, could not prove the absence of abuse.

As seen later in this chapter there are some types of conduct where the undertaking's intent is of particular relevance in establishing an abuse, for example predatory pricing,[62] and 'vexatious litigation'.[63]

---

[61] *Clearstream*, para. 142; Case T-321/05, *AstraZeneca* v. *Commission* [2010] ECR II-2805, para. 359.

[62] See Case C-62/86, *AKZO Chemie BV* v. *Commission* [1991] ECR I-3359.

[63] Case T-111/96, *ITT Promedia NV* v. *Commission* [1998] ECR II-2937.

It should be noted that it appears that conduct may be abusive even if the dominant undertaking obtains no advantage, either financial or competitive, for itself. The behaviour of the French body which organised the 1998 World Cup was condemned as abusive in that it distributed tickets in a way which discriminated against fans who were not resident in France. It was accepted that the body had not gained any commercial or other advantage from its actions.[64]

D. EXCLUSIONARY ABUSES: DISTINGUISHING ILLEGITIMATE FROM LEGITIMATE CONDUCT

(i) The Problem of Applying the *Hoffmann-La Roche* Definition

The finding that a dominant undertaking has a special responsibility to the competitive process and that any conduct which strengthens the dominant position or further weakens the competitive structure may be an abuse potentially brings within the prohibition an indefinite spectrum of conduct. The parameters of that spectrum are the subject of judgments by the EU Courts, decisions of the Commission, and an enormous body of literature. The difficulty is that anything done by a dominant undertaking may improve its market position in comparison to those of its competitors. New and attractive products, better quality, better service, good advertising, and low prices may all attract custom from the competitors. Should improving market share as a result of the dominant undertaking's increased efficiency and unbeatable products be forbidden? Obviously such a finding would be absurd.

The key to distinguishing between illegitimate and legitimate conduct lies in the judgments in *Hoffmann-La Roche* and *Michelin*.[65] In these cases the CJ spoke respectively of 'recourse to methods different from those which condition normal competition in products or services on the basis of the transactions of commercial operators' and 'recourse to methods different from those governing normal competition in products or services based on traders' performance'.[66] The Court thus distinguished between anti-competitive behaviour and 'competition on the basis of performance'. A dominant undertaking providing a superior product at a low price which reflects its costs is competing on performance. Its conduct is not prohibited even though its competitors, producing inferior products at less attractive prices, lose customers. This is the natural operation of the market. In contrast, a dominant undertaking which almost gives away its products, below cost, in order to attract customers from its competitors and drive them out of business, is acting anti-competitively. The term most often used (in English) to denote what *Hoffmann-La Roche* refers to 'as normal competition in products or services on the basis of the transactions of commercial operators' is 'competition on the merits'.[67] The enduring difficulty with Article 102 is where and how the line is drawn between anti-competitive conduct and competition on the merits. Prohibiting conduct that is in fact pro-competitive (making Type I errors) may be detrimental to consumers and to social welfare, stifling innovation and hindering dynamic competition. Moreover, companies need to be able to pursue business strategies in the knowledge that they are behaving legally, in other words there needs to be a sufficient degree of legal certainty in the interpretation and application of Article 102. In the discussion in this chapter of the types of conduct which may constitute an abuse we see over and over

---

[64] *1998 World Cup* [2000] OJ L5/55, [2000] 4 CMLR 963, para. 102; cf. Case T-155/04, *SELEX Sistemi Integrati Spa v. Commission* [2006] ECR II-4797, para. 108 (where, however, the context was the issue of whether an entity (Eurocontrol) was carrying out an economic activity).

[65] See Section 3.C.i, p. 373.

[66] The phraseology in English of *Hoffmann-La Roche* and *Michelin* is ungainly and unhelpful. For an explanation of the source of the original German in *Hoffmann-La Roche* and its translation see J. Kallaugher and B. Sher, 'Rebates Revisited: Anti-Competitive Effects and Exclusionary Abuse Under Article 82' [2004] *ECLR* 263.

[67] e.g. Case C-202/07 P, *France Télécom v. Commission*, 2 April 2009 [2009] ECR I-2369, para. 106; Case C-549/10 P, *Tomra Systems ASA v. European Commission*, 19 April 2012, para. 42; Case C-209/10, *Post Danmark A/S v. Konkurrencerådet*, 27 March 2012, para. 22; Case C-457/10 P, *AstraZeneca v. Commission*, 6 December 2012, paras. 93 and 134; Guidance Paper, paras. 1 and 6.

again the conflict between applying Article 102 in a way which is economically literate and rational and formulating workable rules in the light of which undertakings can plan commercial strategies.

Temple Lang and O'Donoghue, writing in 2002, deplored the lack of clarification about what kind of conduct constitutes an abuse.

J. Temple Lang and R. O'Donoghue, 'Defining Legitimate Competition: How to Clarify Pricing Abuses under Article 82EC' (2002) 26 *Fordham Int'l LJ* 83, 83–84

Although a now universally-accepted distinction is drawn in the European Community ('Community') competition law between exploitative and exclusionary (or anti-competitive) abuses...very little effort has been made to clarify the general principles about the kinds of behavior that are contrary to Article [102]...which prohibits abuse of a dominant position. The case law and practice has arisen pragmatically, and largely in response to complaints to the European Commission and appeals to the Community Courts against Commission decisions adopted on the basis of such complaints. With the exception of specialized Notices and guidance in the telecommunications and postal sectors, the Commission has not attempted to develop any kind of general or comprehensive statement on abusive behavior. There have been several consequences of this unplanned growth. First, the Commission and the Community Courts have dealt with individual cases that were said to raise questions of abuse by reference to the facts of the individual case, seemingly without having any clear general analytical or intellectual framework for doing so. Second, a number of basic questions have not been answered or even discussed, because due to the accidents of litigation or otherwise, they did not arise in any of the cases that have been decided. Finally, the influence that economic thinking has had on the Community rules on distribution, horizontal agreements, and mergers has not been felt, to the same extent or at all, in the interpretation and application of Article [102].

The Commission's initiative to 'modernise' the application of Article 102 to exclusionary abuses, described in Chapter 5, was an attempt to inject the missing intellectual coherence and interpret the vague and unscientific language of the EU Courts in terms of rigorous economic principle.

(ii) The Implications of Competition on the Merits: It is Not the Role of Article 102 to Keep Less Efficient Competitors on the Market

Modernisation put the interests of consumers at the centre of the application of Article 102. Ironically, almost all exclusionary abuse cases arise not from action by customers or consumers (who may be very happy with the predatory (low) prices, low prices arising from a margin squeeze, or bundled products) but from complaints or legal action by competitors. However, competition on the merits may hurt competitors. The CJ made an important statement in *Post Danmark*, making it clear that it is not the function of Article 102 to protect less efficient competitors and that excluding competitors is not necessarily detrimental to competition.

Case C-209/10, *Post Danmark A/S v. Konkurrencerådet*, 27 March 2012

Court of Justice

21 It is settled case-law that a finding that an undertaking has such a dominant position is not in itself a ground of criticism of the undertaking concerned (Case 322/81 *Nederlandsche Banden-Industrie-Michelin*

> v *Commission*…paragraph 57, and Joined Cases C-395/96 P and C-396/96 P *Compagnie maritime belge transports and Others* v *Commission*…paragraph 37). It is in no way the purpose of Article [102] to prevent an undertaking from acquiring, on its own merits, the dominant position on a market (see, inter alia, *TeliaSonera Sverige*, paragraph 24). Nor does that provision seek to ensure that competitors less efficient than the undertaking with the dominant position should remain on the market.
>
> 22 Thus, not every exclusionary effect is necessarily detrimental to competition (see, by analogy, *TeliaSonera Sverige*, paragraph 43). Competition on the merits may, by definition, lead to the departure from the market or the marginalisation of competitors that are less efficient and so less attractive to consumers from the point of view of, among other things, price, choice, quality or innovation.[68]

(iii) Tests for Determining what is 'Competition on the Merits'

While it may be comparatively easy to identify conduct at the extremes of the spectrum as being competition on the merits or an exclusionary abuse,[69] the concept does not provide a tool for objectively drawing a line between 'good' and 'bad' conduct in the middle. In *Microsoft*,[70] for example, the GC confined the 'merits' of a product, on which competition should be based, to its 'intrinsic merits' separate from the way that it was distributed or to the way it worked with other products (*in casu*, interoperability).

There are a number of economic tests which can aid identification of competition on the merits. Each of these has its drawbacks, and they all have their advocates and critics, but nevertheless they can be useful as analytical tools.[71] The best known tests are:

- The 'as efficient competitor' (or 'equally efficient') test. The 'as efficient competitor' is a 'hypothetical competitor having the same costs as the dominant company'.[72] The idea behind this test is that conduct should be unlawful only if it is capable of excluding such a competitor, because only some kind of anti-competitive conduct can exclude equally efficient rivals. It has drawbacks if it is interpreted as allowing the exclusion of less efficient new competitors which could in time have become as efficient. Furthermore, conduct caught by the as efficient competitor test might nevertheless enhance consumer welfare (the test may not have the necessary correlation to consumer welfare), and the test is not useful in situations where the efficiency of competitors is not an issue.[73] The CJ has endorsed the as efficient competitor test in respect of predatory pricing[74] and margin squeeze[75] and the Guidance Paper adopts the 'as efficient

---

[68] See also the then Commissioner Neelie Kroes on the review of Article 102 in 2005, 'I like aggressive competition—including by dominant companies—and I don't care if it may hurt competitors—as long as it ultimately benefits consumers. That is because the main and ultimate objective of Article 102 is to protect consumers, and this does, of course, require the protection of an undistorted competitive process on the market', 'Preliminary Thoughts on Policy Review of Article 102', Fordham Corporate Law Institute, SPEECH/05/537, 23 September 2005.

[69] See the Guidance Paper, para. 22, for the Commission's examples of per se 'bad' conduct.

[70] Case T-201/04, *Microsoft* v. *Commission* [2007] ECR II-3601, para. 1046.

[71] See, e.g., OECD *Policy Brief* (2006) 'What is Competition on the Merits?' Available at <http://78.41.128.130/dataoecd/10/27/37082099.pdf>; J. Vickers, 'Abuse of Market Power' (2005) 115 *Economic Journal* F244; K. Fjell and L. Sørgard, 'How to Test for Abuse of Dominance?' (2006) 2 *European Law Journal* 69; O'Donoghue and Padilla, *The Law and Economics of Article 102* (cited in n. 14) 227–237.

[72] OECD *Policy Brief* (2006), 4.

[73] e.g., *Astra/Zeneca*, IP/05/737, upheld Case T-321/05, *AstraZeneca* v. *Commission* [2010] ECR II-2805, [2010] 5 CMLR 1575 and *aff'd* Case C-457/10 P, *AstraZeneca* v. *Commission*, 6 December 2012, where the undertaking was held to have misused the patent system to exclude competitors.

[74] Case C-62/86 *AKZO Chemie* [1991] ECRI-3359, para. 72, and see further Section 8, p. 401 ff.

[75] Case C-280/08 P, *Deutsche Telekom* v. *Commission* [2010] ECR I-9555, paras. 177 and 183; Case C-52/09, *Konkurrensverket* v. *TeliaSonera Sverige AB* [2011] ECR I-527, paras. 61–77.

competitor' test as the standard by which pricing policies are normally assessed but allows for exceptions.[76]

- The 'profit sacrifice' test. This examines the dominant undertaking's conduct to see if it involves sacrificing profits in circumstances where it would only be rational to do so if the undertaking was thereby able to exclude competitors. The obvious example is predatory pricing (when an undertaking prices below cost to drive competitors from the market). It does not, however, capture other types of anti-competitive exclusionary conduct and can catch welfare-enhancing conduct such as investing in research and development (R&D) (which if successful might result in an innovation so successful that competitors are eliminated).[77] The Guidance Paper adopts a profit-sacrifice test as the usual test for predatory pricing.[78]

- The 'no economic sense' test. This is similar to the profit sacrifice test, but more inclusive as it does not depend on the one element of sacrificing profits. It states that conduct should be considered abusive only if it makes no economic sense except for its tendency to lessen or exclude competition. The test has been in favour with the US Department of Justice (DOJ) when arguing cases under section 2 of the Sherman Act.[79] Like the other tests it has its proponents and detractors.[80] The Guidance Paper, para. 22, adopts what is in effect a no economic sense test when it says that where conduct can only raise obstacles to competition and create no efficiencies anti-competitive effect may be inferred.

- The consumer welfare balancing test. The various versions of this test involve balancing the positive and negative effects of the conduct on consumer welfare. As the OECD says, '[t]hey all have a degree of intuitive appeal because they attempt to use consumer welfare effects themselves, rather than indirect factors such as profit sacrifice, as the gauge of dominant firm conduct'.[81] O'Donoghue and Padilla conclude:

  Although proponents of the consumer harm test have made its operational features as useful as possible, complex and precarious balancing acts are still likely to be necessary in marginal cases where the cost of error is likely to be high. Moreover, if issues of proportionality come into play, economics contributes very little by way of predictability and the outcomes will represent matters of policy rather than precision.[82]

- The 'own efficiency' test.[83] This asks whether the monopolist has improved its own efficiency by the conduct under review, or whether it has impaired a competitor's efficiency (regardless of whether it has impaired its own efficiency). The former would be permitted and the latter would be prohibited. This test seems to be most suitable where the alleged exclusionary conduct is of the 'refusal to deal' kind,[84] and it still requires a determination of whether the conduct is efficient or not.

[76] Guidance Paper, paras. 23 and 24, see Section 7.D, p. 399 ff.

[77] See S. Salop, 'Exclusionary Conduct, Effect on Consumers, and the Flawed Profit-Sacrifice Standard' (2005–2006) 73 Antitrust LJ 311; E. Elhauge, 'Defining Better Monopolisation Standards' (2003–2004) 56 Stan LR 253, 271 ('Sacrificing profits is neither sufficient nor necessary to show that conduct that excludes rivals is undesirable, nor does it even correlate well with the desirability of such conduct').

[78] Guidance Paper, paras. 64–65.

[79] e.g., in its briefs in Microsoft, available at<http://www.doj.gov/atr/cases/f7200/7230.htm>; United States v. AMR Corp 335 F.3d 1109 (American Airlines); United States v. Dentsply International Inc 399 F. 3d 181.

[80] The criticisms are summed up in O'Donoghue and Padilla, The Law and Economics of Article 102 (cited in n. 14), 230; cf. G. J. Werden, 'Competition Policy on Exclusionary Conduct: Towards an Effects-based Analysis' (2006) 2 European Competition Journal 53, who suggests that the 'no economic sense' test should generally be applied (note that, although writing in a personal capacity, Werden was at the time Senior Economic Counsel at the US DOJ).

[81] OECD Policy Brief (2006), 5.

[82] O'Donoghue and Padilla, The Law and Economics of Article 102 (cited in n. 14), 237.

[83] Put forward in a leading article in 2003, see E. Elhauge, 'Defining Better Monopolisation Standards' (2003–2004) 56 Stan LR 253.

[84] See Section 12, p. 510 ff.

E. FORM- AND EFFECTS-BASED ANALYSIS

One of the most criticised aspects of the application of Article 102 over the years has been the use of 'form' rather than 'effects' based analysis. This has meant that the EU Courts and the Commission have condemned conduct as being an exclusionary abuse because it has taken a certain form, rather than examining its effects. So, for example, exclusive requirements contracts entered into by dominant undertakings have been akin to per se abuses.[85] There is now, however, a much greater emphasis on whether the impugned conduct has anti-competitive effects.[86] These do not necessarily have to be actual or concrete effects, it can suffice if they are 'potential'.[87] This is understandable as although there are some cases in which the effects of the conduct are already apparent[88] it is essential to the effectiveness of Article 102 that where possible anti-competitive effects are prevented before they take hold. Once potential or 'likely' anti-competitive effects suffice, however, it becomes a question of how 'likely' these have to be. The EU Courts have accepted in some cases that it is enough if a practice is 'capable' of anti-competitive effects or 'tends to' restrict competition,[89] or is 'such as' to do so.[90] This can look very much like condemning conduct for its form again. We see this issue played out in many of the cases discussed in this chapter.

Even if competitors are shown to be (potentially) excluded by the conduct, should it be assumed that consumers are thereby harmed as a result? This is one of the most contentious issues of all and goes back to the reason for prohibiting exclusionary abuses. If the competition rules really do only protect competition as a means of protecting consumers, then exclusion which does not harm consumers should be permitted. Much of the criticism of the decisional practice of the Commission and the case law of the EU Courts centres around the tendency to assume detrimental effects on consumers from the exclusion of competitors.[91]

4. THE COMMISSION'S APPROACH TO EXCLUSIONARY ABUSES IN THE GUIDANCE PAPER: THE ADOPTION OF THE 'ANTI-COMPETITIVE FORECLOSURE' CONCEPT

The publication of the Commission's Guidance Paper is discussed in Chapter 5.[92] In the Guidance Paper the Commission adopts the concept of 'anti-competitive foreclosure' as the normal standard for intervention.[93] It is important to note that this is not just 'foreclosure' but '*anti-competitive*

---

[85] See Section 10, p. 450 ff.

[86] See e.g. Case C-280/08 P, *Deutsche Telekom v. Commission* [2010] ECR I-9555 where the CJ ruled out the possibility that the very existence of a certain pricing practice could constitute an abuse (a margin squeeze) without it being necessary to demonstrate an anti-competitive effect, see Section 9.B.i, p. 427 ff.

[87] Case C-52/09, *Konkurrensverket v. TeliaSonera Sverige AB* [2011] ECR I-527, para. 64.

[88] As in Case C-209/10, *Post Danmark A/S v. Konkurrencerådet*, 27 March 2012.

[89] See e.g. Case C-95/04 *British Airways v. Commission* [2007] ECR I-2331, para. 293; Case C-549/10 P, *Tomra Systems ASA v. European Commission*, 19 April 2012, para. 213.

[90] Case C-457/10 P, *AstraZeneca v. Commission*, 6 December 2012, para. 153,

[91] For a full discussion of the effects issue, see Akman, *The Concept of Abuse in EU Competition Law* (cited in n. 9), 130–143.

[92] See Chapter 5, Section 6.C, p. 289.

[93] For a general commentary on the Guidance Paper, see N. Petit, 'From Formalism to Effects? The Commission's Communication on Enforcement Priorities in Applying Article 82' (2009) 32(4) *World Competition* 485; P. Akman,

foreclosure'. This is explained in paragraph 19 as a situation where the exclusion of competitors is likely to result in the dominant undertaking being in a position where it can profitably increase prices to the detriment of consumers.[94] In paragraph 20 the Commission explains how it will generally assess this. Anti-competitive foreclosure therefore comprises two elements:

- Foreclosure (the hindrance, exclusion, or elimination of actual or potential competitors); and

- Consumer harm.

Guidance on the Commission's Enforcement Priorities in Applying Article 82 of the EC Treaty to Abusive Exclusionary Conduct by Dominant Undertakings [2009] OJ C45/2

19. The aim of the Commission's enforcement activity in relation to exclusionary conduct is to ensure that dominant undertakings do not impair effective competition by foreclosing their competitors in an anti-competitive way, thus having an adverse impact on consumer welfare, whether in the form of higher price levels than would have otherwise prevailed or in some other form such as limiting quality or reducing consumer choice. In this document the term 'anti-competitive foreclosure' is used to describe a situation where effective access of actual or potential competitors to supplies or markets is hampered or eliminated as a result of the conduct of the dominant undertaking whereby the dominant undertaking is likely to be in a position to profitably increase prices...to the detriment of consumers. The identification of likely consumer harm can rely on qualitative and, where possible and appropriate, quantitative evidence. The Commission will address such anti-competitive foreclosure either at the intermediate level or at the level of final consumers, or at both levels. [95]

20. The Commission will normally intervene under Article [102] where, on the basis of cogent and convincing evidence, the allegedly abusive conduct is likely to lead to anti-competitive foreclosure. The Commission considers the following factors to be generally relevant to such an assessment:

   - the position of the dominant undertaking: in general, the stronger the dominant position, the higher the likelihood that conduct protecting that position leads to anti-competitive foreclosure,

   - the conditions on the relevant market: this includes the conditions of entry and expansion, such as the existence of economies of scale and/or scope and network effects. Economies of scale mean that competitors are less likely to enter or stay in the market if the dominant undertaking forecloses a significant part of the relevant market. Similarly, the conduct may allow the dominant undertaking to 'tip' a market characterised by network effects in its favour or to further entrench its position on such a market. Likewise, if entry barriers in the upstream and/or downstream market are significant, this means that it may be costly for competitors to overcome possible foreclosure through vertical integration,

   - the position of the dominant undertaking's competitors: this includes the importance of competitors for the maintenance of effective competition. A specific competitor may play a significant competitive role even if it only holds a small market share compared to other competitors. It may, for example, be the closest competitor to the dominant undertaking, be a particularly innovative competitor, or have the reputation of systematically cutting prices. In its assessment, the Commission may also consider in appropriate cases, on the basis of information available, whether there are realistic, effective and timely counterstrategies that competitors would be likely to deploy,

---

'The European Commission's Guidance on Article 102 TFEU: From *Inferno* to *Paradiso*?' (2010) 73 *MLR* 605; L. Lovdahl Gormesen, 'Why the European Commission's Enforcement Priorities on Article 82 Should Be Withdrawn' (2010) *ECLR* 45.

[94] 'Increase prices', as usual, is used as shorthand for the other parameters of competition as well: influencing output, innovation, variety, and quality, Guidance Paper, para. 11.

[95] For the footnote at this point of the Guidance, see text accompanying n. 97.

- the position of the customers or input suppliers: this may include consideration of the possible selectivity of the conduct in question. The dominant undertaking may apply the practice only to selected customers or input suppliers who may be of particular importance for the entry or expansion of competitors, thereby enhancing the likelihood of anti-competitive foreclosure...In the case of customers, they may, for example, be the ones most likely to respond to offers from alternative suppliers, they may represent a particular means of distributing the product that would be suitable for a new entrant, they may be situated in a geographic area well suited to new entry or they may be likely to influence the behaviour of other customers. In the case of input suppliers, those with whom the dominant undertaking has concluded exclusive supply arrangements may be the ones most likely to respond to requests by customers who are competitors of the dominant undertaking in a downstream market, or may produce a grade of the product—or produce at a location—particularly suitable for a new entrant. Any strategies at the disposal of the customers or input suppliers which could help to counter the conduct of the dominant undertaking will also be considered,

- the extent of the allegedly abusive conduct: in general, the higher the percentage of total sales in the relevant market affected by the conduct, the longer its duration, and the more regularly it has been applied, the greater is the likely foreclosure effect,

- possible evidence of actual foreclosure: if the conduct has been in place for a sufficient period of time, the market performance of the dominant undertaking and its competitors may provide direct evidence of anti-competitive foreclosure. For reasons attributable to the allegedly abusive conduct, the market share of the dominant undertaking may have risen or a decline in market share may have been slowed. For similar reasons, actual competitors may have been marginalised or may have exited, or potential competitors may have tried to enter and failed,

- direct evidence of any exclusionary strategy: this includes internal documents which contain direct evidence of a strategy to exclude competitors, such as a detailed plan to engage in certain conduct in order to exclude a competitor, to prevent entry or to pre-empt the emergence of a market, or evidence of concrete threats of exclusionary action. Such direct evidence may be helpful in interpreting the dominant undertaking's conduct.

21. When pursuing a case the Commission will develop the analysis of the general factors mentioned in paragraph 20, together with the more specific factors described in the sections dealing with certain types of exclusionary conduct, and any other factors which it may consider to be appropriate. This assessment will usually be made by comparing the actual or likely future situation in the relevant market (with the dominant undertaking's conduct in place) with an appropriate counterfactual, such as the simple absence of the conduct in question or with another realistic alternative scenario, having regard to established business practices.

Many of the factors listed in paragraph 20 of the Guidance concern the structure of the market and are factors the Commission customarily takes into account in both antitrust and merger analysis. These relate to the 'foreclosure' part of the test. The Commission will also take any other appropriate factors into account, including those that are conduct-specific. Paragraph 21 also states that the Commission will base its assessment on an appropriate 'counterfactual' (meaning a 'but for' analysis in which it tries to determine what would be the situation in the absence of the impugned conduct). The assessment of consumer harm is mainly contained in the last sentence of paragraph 19. The Guidance Paper is open to the criticism that although 'anti-competitive foreclosure' has consumer harm as one of its elements the treatment of many of the specific abuses in the Guidance Paper assumes such harm far too readily.[96]

---

[96] See e.g. P. Marsden, 'Some Outstanding Issues from the European Commission's Guidance on Article 102 TFEU: Not-So-Faint Echoes of Ordoliberalism', in F. Etro and I. Kokkoris (eds.), *Competition Law and the Enforcement of Article 102* (Oxford University Press, 2010), Chap. 3.

Paragraph 19 has an important footnote[97] which says that '"consumers" encompasses all direct and indirect users, including intermediate producers'. That is the established interpretation of 'consumer' in EU competition law.[98] However here the footnote also states that 'where intermediate users are actual or potential competitors of the dominant undertaking, the assessment focuses on the effects of the conduct on users further downstream'. This is significant in the 'competitors or consumer welfare' debate because in some abuses (such as refusals to supply and margin squeezes) the intermediate customers may be downstream competitors of the dominant undertaking. In such a situation emphasis on the effects on those competitor-customers may distort the analysis of the effects on the final consumers.

Paragraph 22 turns away from an effects-based analysis and says that there may be conduct which is so egregious that its anti-competitive effect can be inferred.[99] This can be seen as an application of the 'no economic sense' test.

22. There may be circumstances where it is not necessary for the Commission to carry out a detailed assessment before concluding that the conduct in question is likely to result in consumer harm. If it appears that the conduct can only raise obstacles to competition and that it creates no efficiencies, its anti-competitive effect may be inferred. This could be the case, for instance, if the dominant undertaking prevents its customers from testing the products of competitors or provides financial incentives to its customers on condition that they do not test such products, or pays a distributor or a customer to delay the introduction of a competitor's product.

5. OBJECTIVE JUSTIFICATION, EFFICIENCY, AND OTHER DEFENCES

A. GENERAL

Although Article 102 does not contain an exemption provision similar to Article 101(3), the EU Courts have developed the concept of 'objective justification' by which otherwise abusive conduct may escape infringing Article 102, and the analysis in Article 102 cases now invariably contains a reference to objective justification. The concept of objective justification has been problematic because the EU Courts failed to formulate a theoretical framework for it. The main debate has been in regard to whether, and in what circumstances, efficiencies can provide objective justification. It was not until *Post Danmark* in 2012 that the CJ clearly set out that conduct with anti-competitive effects may be justified as objectively necessary or as producing efficiencies. Whether *Post Danmark* means that 'objective necessity' is a synonym for 'objective justification' and that 'efficiency' is a separate defence, is a moot point.[100]

In this section we look first at objective justification in the case law; secondly at the treatment of objective justification in the Guidance Paper; thirdly at the question of which party bears the burden of proof; and fourthly at difficulties which remain in respect of the formulation and application of the concept. We then look at the 'protecting its own commercial interests' defence which may be conceptualised as a type of objective justification, and at the 'meeting competition' defence.

---

[97] n. 2, indicated by n. 95.

[98] See Chap. 1, Section 7.C.ii.b, p. 45.

[99] Instances of the examples given can be seen in Case T–228/97, *Irish Sugar plc* v. *Commission* [1999] ECR II-2969, and Case COMP/C-3/37.990, *Intel* [2010] 4 CMLR 314.

[100] Rousseva and Marquis, 'Hell Freezes Over: A Climate Change for Assessing Exclusionary Conduct under Article 102 TFEU' (cited in n. 2), 32 consider that they are separate. In COMP/39.525, *Telekomunikacja Polska*, 22 June 2011, on appeal Case T-486/11, judgment pending the Commission referred to a dominant undertaking providing an objective justification *or* demonstrating that its conduct produces efficiencies (paras. 873–874).

B. OBJECTIVE JUSTIFICATION IN THE CASE LAW

In *Télémarketing* the CJ said that an abuse would be committed where the dominant undertaking engaged in certain conduct 'without any objective necessity'.[101] It referred to the possibility of the refusal to supply in that case being justified by technical or commercial requirements relating to the nature of television.[102] Conduct necessary to protect legitimate public interest objectives could in principle be objectively justified[103] and this could include the health and safety of consumers. However, in both *Hilti*[104] and *Tetra Pak II*[105] claims that tie-ins were justified in order to ensure public safety were rejected on the grounds that safety is ensured by public authorities enforcing safety regulations and not by private undertakings indulging in exclusionary practices.[106] In *Kanal*[107] the CJ said that objective justification could arise from the task and method of financing public service undertakings and left it to the referring court to decide whether that was so in this case. It should be noted, however, that undertakings entrusted with services of general economic interest have a derogation from the competition rules under Article 106(2) TFEU.[108] In *FAG-Flughafen-Frankfurt/Main*[109] the undertaking argued that the refusal to allow independent ramp-handling and self-handling services at an airport was objectively justified by space and capacity restraints and the Commission only rejected this after carefully considering technical reports.[110]

The question of objective justification on the grounds of efficiency gains was raised in *British Airways* where the CJ said it was necessary to examine whether there was an 'objective economic justification' for the bonus system. It accepted that the dominant undertaking's conduct *could* be justified by efficiencies:[111]

It has to be determined whether the exclusionary effect arising from such a system, which is disadvantageous for competition, may be counterbalanced, or outweighed, by advantages in terms of efficiency which also benefit the consumer. If the exclusionary effect of that system bears no relation to advantages for the market and consumers, or if it goes beyond what is necessary in order to attain those advantages, that system must be regarded as an abuse.

In *Microsoft*, six months later, the GC considered Microsoft's arguments that its conduct in respect of tying and refusal to supply was objectively justified.[112] It rejected Microsoft's arguments but did not find it necessary to explain what constituted grounds for objective justification. In *TeliaSonera* the CJ

---

[101] Case 311/84, *Centre Belge d'Etudes du Marché-Télémarketing v. Compagnie Luxembourgeoise de Télédiffusion SA and Information Publicité Benelux SA* [1985] ECR 3261, para. 27. The conduct in question was the reservation of an ancillary activity on a separate market.

[102] Case 311/84, *Centre Belge d'Etudes du Marché-Télémarketing v. Compagnie Luxembourgeoise de Télédiffusion SA and Information Publicité Benelux SA* [1985] ECR 3261, para. 26. The case was an Article 267 reference.

[103] See P. Lowe, 'DG Competition's Review of the Policy on Abuse of Dominance', in B. Hawk (ed.), [2004] *Fordham Corp L Inst*, 163 (the author was then Director-General of DG Comp).

[104] Case T-30/89, *Hilti AG v. Commission* [1991] ECR II-1439, para. 118.

[105] Case C-333/94P, *Tetra Pak International SA v. Commission* [1996] ECR I-5951.

[106] See also the Guidance Paper, see Section 5.D.i. p. 389; R. Nazzini, *The Foundations of European Union Competition Law, The Objectives and Principles of Article 102* (Oxford University Press, 2011), 317–320, categorises this as a 'social welfare' defence.

[107] Case C-52/07, *Kanal 5 Ltd v. Föreningen Svenska Tonsättares Internationella Musikbyrå (STIM) upa* [2008] ECR I-9275, para. 47. The case concerned different royalty fees paid to public and commercial undertakings.

[108] See Chap. 8.

[109] [1998] L72/30.

[110] But note COMP/39, ENI, Commitments Decision, 29 September 2010, where capacity constraints did not prevent the view of the Commission that there was an abuse.

[111] Case C-95/04, *British Airways v. Commission* [2007] ECR I-2331, para. 69.

[112] Case T-201/04, *Microsoft v. Commission* [2007] ECR II-3601, paras. 666–712 and 1090–1167.

repeated exactly what it had said in *British Airways*.[113] In *Post Danmark,* however, the CJ gave the fullest yet account of justification (it did not preface it with the word 'objective').

Case C-209/10, *Post Danmark A/S* v. *Konkurrencerådet,* 27 March 2012

The facts of the case, an Article 267 reference, are given later in this chapter.[114] The CJ ruled on the application of Article 102 to certain types of pricing and then said that it was for the referring court to decide whether there were anti-competitive effects. Even if there were, however, it was open to the dominant undertaking to provide justification for its conduct.

Court of Justice

40 If the court making the reference, after carrying out that assessment, should nevertheless make a finding of anti-competitive effects due to Post Danmark's actions, it should be recalled that it is open to a dominant undertaking to provide justification for behaviour that is liable to be caught by the prohibition under Article [102] (see, to this effect, Case 27/76 *United Brands and United Brands Continentaal* v *Commission*...paragraph 184; Joined Cases C-241/91 P and C-242/91 P *RTE and ITP* v *Commission*...paragraphs 54 and 55; and *TeliaSonera Sverige,* paragraphs 31 and 75).

41 In particular, such an undertaking may demonstrate, for that purpose, either that its conduct is objectively necessary (see, to that effect, Case 311/84 *CBEM*...paragraph 27), or that the exclusionary effect produced may be counterbalanced, outweighed even, by advantages in terms of efficiency that also benefit consumers (Case C-95/04 P *British Airways* v *Commission*...paragraph 86, and *TeliaSonera Sverige,* paragraph 76).

42 In that last regard, it is for the dominant undertaking to show that the efficiency gains likely to result from the conduct under consideration counteract any likely negative effects on competition and consumer welfare in the affected markets, that those gains have been, or are likely to be, brought about as a result of that conduct, that such conduct is necessary for the achievement of those gains in efficiency and that it does not eliminate effective competition, by removing all or most existing sources of actual or potential competition.

43 In the present case, it is enough to state, with regard to the considerations set out at paragraph 11 above, that the mere fact that a criterion explicitly based on gains in efficiency was not one of the factors appearing in the schedules of prices charged by Post Danmark cannot justify a refusal to take into account, where necessary, such gains in efficiency, provided that their actual existence and their extent have been established in accordance with the requirements set out in paragraph 42 above.

In paragraphs 41 and 42 the CJ identifies two particular grounds of justification.

(i) Objective necessity. On this the CJ refers to the judgment in *Télémarketing* (CBEM). *Post Danmark* does not elaborate on what this means. The Guidance Paper conceptualises objective necessity as relating to factors external to the dominant undertaking. This is also the view of the Commission in its decisional practice. In *Telekomunikacja Polska*[115] the Commission referred to 'allegedly abusive conduct that is actually necessary on the basis of factors external to the dominant undertaking and is proportionate'.

---

[113] Case C-52/09, *Konkurrensverket* v. *TeliaSonera Sverige AB* [2011] ECR I-527, para. 76.

[114] Section 8.D, p. 408 ff.

[115] COMP/39.525, *Telekomunikacja Polska* 22 June 2011, para. 874, on appeal Case T-486/11, judgment pending.

(ii) Efficiencies. The CJ's conditions for a successful 'efficiency defence' are in effect those the Commission had set out (in more detail) in the Guidance Paper, which is discussed in Section 5.D.ii. The *Post Danmark* conditions are:

- The efficiency gains counteract any likely negative effects on competition and consumer welfare;
- The gains have been, or are likely to be, brought about as a result of the conduct;
- The conduct is necessary for the achievement of the efficiency gains; and
- The conduct does not eliminate effective competition.

By prefacing the two grounds of objective necessity and efficiencies with 'in particular' the CJ does not rule out there being other grounds of justification. The reference in paragraph 40 of the judgment to *United Brands*, where the undertaking tried to justify its conduct on the ground that it was merely protecting its own commercial interests, suggests that the CJ considers that this is another type of justification rather than a separate defence. In *AstraZeneca*, however, the CJ referred to 'the absence…of the defence of legitimate interests…*or* in the absence of objective justification' [emphasis added].[116] Also, in *AstraZeneca* the CJ said that the imposition of pharmacovigilance obligations on a dominant undertaking could constitute objective justification for deregistering a marketing authorisation, although it was not proved to be so in that case.[117]

C. THE BURDEN OF PROOF

In *Microsoft* the GC explained where the burden of proof lies in claims of objective justification.

Case T-201/04, *Microsoft* v. *Commission* [2007] ECR II-3601

688 [and 1114].[118] The Court notes, as a preliminary point, that although the burden of proof of the existence of the circumstances that constitute an infringement of Article [102] is borne by the Commission, it is for the dominant undertaking concerned, and not for the Commission, before the end of the administrative procedure, to raise any plea of objective justification and to support it with arguments and evidence. It then falls to the Commission, where it proposes to make a finding of an abuse of a dominant position, to show that the arguments and evidence relied on by the undertaking cannot prevail and, accordingly, that the justification put forward cannot be accepted.

It appears from this that the evidential burden in respect of objective justification is on the dominant undertaking, in that once an abuse has been *prima facie* established it is up to the undertaking to adduce evidence and arguments that its conduct was justified. However, as the party alleging the infringement (the Commission in *Microsoft* itself) bears the ultimate burden of proof under Regulation 1/2003, Article 2, it is for that party to show that the conduct was not objectively justified in the light of the evidence put forward.[119] If this is so objective justification differs in a vital respect from Article 101(3), as Regulation 1/2003, Article 2 expressly provides that although the burden of proof as

---

[116] Case C-457/10 P, *AstraZeneca v. Commission*, 6 December 2012, para. 134.

[117] *AstraZeneca*, para. 135. The argument was raised for the first time before the GC.

[118] *Microsoft* covered two separate abuses. The identical passage appears in both halves of the judgment. The passage was repeated in Case T-301/04, *Clearstream Banking v. Commission*, [2009] ECR II-3155, para. 185.

[119] See also R. Nazzini, 'The Wood Began to Move: An Essay on Consumer Welfare, Evidence and Burden of Proof in Article 102 EC Cases' (2006) 31 *ELRev* 518, 535: 'The analysis of the jurisprudence on objective justification demonstrates that this concept is not technically a defence. Rather it is used to explain the shifting of the evidential burden to the dominant undertaking once a prima facie case of abuse has been established', and further, Nazzini,

regards Article 101(1) is on the Commission it is on the undertaking concerned as regards Article 101(3). The wording of paragraphs 41 and 42 of *Post Danmark* suggests that in effect the CJ is placing the legal as well as the evidential burden in respect of efficiencies on the undertaking under Article 102 too, which would produce congruence with Article 101. However, the matter is not beyond doubt.

D. JUSTIFICATION IN THE GUIDANCE PAPER

The words 'objective justification' do not appear in the Guidance Paper. Rather, the Guidance Paper states that the Commission will examine claims from a dominant undertaking that 'its conduct is justified'.[120] The undertaking may do this by demonstrating that its conduct is 'objectively necessary' or that it produces substantial efficiencies which outweigh any anti-competitive effects on consumers. The Commission will assess the indispensability and proportionality of the conduct to the alleged goal of the dominant undertaking.

(i) Objective Necessity

The Commission relates conduct that is 'objectively necessary' to 'factors external to the undertaking'. The only examples it gives are health and safety reasons, and it repeats the proviso given in *Hilti* and *Tetra Pak II*.[121]

Guidance on the Commission's Enforcement Priorities in Applying Article 82 of the EC Treaty to Abusive Exclusionary Conduct by Dominant Undertakings [2009] OJ C45/2

29. The question of whether conduct is objectively necessary and proportionate must be determined on the basis of factors external to the dominant undertaking. Exclusionary conduct may, for example, be considered objectively necessary for health or safety reasons related to the nature of the product in question. However, proof of whether conduct of this kind is objectively necessary must take into account that it is normally the task of public authorities to set and enforce public health and safety standards. It is not the task of a dominant undertaking to take steps on its own initiative to exclude products which it regards, rightly or wrongly, as dangerous or inferior to its own product...

(ii) Efficiencies

The Guidance Paper provides for an 'efficiency defence'. Four cumulative conditions must be fulfilled. The efficiencies must relate to the conduct in issue;[122] the conduct must be indispensable to their realisation; the efficiencies must outweigh any negative effects on competition and consumer welfare; and the conduct must not eliminate effective competition.

The Foundations of European Union Competition Law (cited in n. 106), 289–294. See also the Opinion of AG Jacobs in Case C-53/03, *Synetairismos Farmakopoion Aitolias & Akarnanias (Syfait)* v. *GlaxoSmithKline* [2005] ECR I-4609, para. 72.

[120] Guidance Paper, para. 28.

[121] See Section 5.B, p. 386.

[122] This is similar to 'merger specificity' in the 'Efficiencies' section of the Horizontal Merger Guidelines, [2004] OJ C31/3, para. 85, see Chap. 15. The Guidance Paper conditions are similar overall to those in the Horizontal Merger Guidelines.

Guidance on the Commission's Enforcement Priorities in Applying Article 82 of the EC Treaty to Abusive Exclusionary Conduct by Dominant Undertakings [2009] OJ C45/2

30. The Commission considers that a dominant undertaking may also justify conduct leading to fore-closure of competitors on the ground of efficiencies that are sufficient to guarantee that no net harm to consumers is likely to arise. In this context, the dominant undertaking will generally be expected to dem-onstrate, with a sufficient degree of probability, and on the basis of verifiable evidence, that the following cumulative conditions are fulfilled [123]:

- the efficiencies have been, or are likely to be, realised as a result of the conduct. They may, for exam-ple, include technical improvements in the quality of goods, or a reduction in the cost of production or distribution,

- the conduct is indispensable to the realisation of those efficiencies: there must be no less anti-competitive alternatives to the conduct that are capable of producing the same efficiencies,

- the likely efficiencies brought about by the conduct outweigh any likely negative effects on competi-tion and consumer welfare in the affected markets,

- the conduct does not eliminate effective competition, by removing all or most existing sources of actual or potential competition. Rivalry between undertakings is an essential driver of economic efficiency, including dynamic efficiencies in the form of innovation. In its absence the dominant undertaking will lack adequate incentives to continue to create and pass on efficiency gains. Where there is no residual competition and no foreseeable threat of entry, the protection of rivalry and the competitive process outweighs possible efficiency gains. In the Commission's view, exclusionary conduct which maintains, cre-ates or strengthens a market position approaching that of a monopoly can normally not be justified on the grounds that it also creates efficiency gains.

31. It is incumbent upon the dominant undertaking to provide all the evidence necessary to demon-strate that the conduct concerned is objectively justified. It then falls to the Commission to make the ultimate assessment of whether the conduct concerned is not objectively necessary and, based on a weighing-up of any apparent anti-competitive effects against any advanced and substantiated efficiencies, is likely to result in consumer harm.

Paragraph 31 reflects the relevant paragraphs of *Microsoft*, reproduced in Section 5.C, p. 388.

E. COMMENTS

The conditions regarding efficiencies laid down in paragraph 30 of the Guidance Paper were adopted by the CJ in paragraph 42 of *Post Danmark* but with the substitution of 'counteract' for 'outweigh' in the third indent. In paragraph 41 of *Post Danmark*, however, the CJ couches the requirement of the relation-ship between the efficiencies and the exclusionary effect in terms of the *British Airways* judgment, i.e. that the exclusion 'may be counterbalanced, outweighed even, by advantages in terms of efficiency that also benefit consumers'. One commentator has argued that the Guidance Paper, in demanding that the net effect on consumer welfare must at least be neutral, is incompatible with the *British Airways* judgment which required only that the efficiencies '*also* benefit' consumers.[124]

The Guidance Paper is fuller than *Post Danmark* in explaining the four conditions. Nothing in either the Guidance Paper or *Post Danmark*, however, suggests that the conditions are easy to satisfy. There is yet to be any Article 102 case in which the conduct or practices have been saved from infringing

---

[123] The Commission's footnote here refers to the Guidelines on Article 101(3).

[124] Nazzini, *The Foundations of European Union Competition Law* (cited in n. 106), 306–309.

Article 102 because they are justified on efficiency grounds (nor has any undertaking been saved by 'necessity'). Paragraph 30 of the Guidance Paper demands that the efficiencies must guarantee no net harm to consumers is likely to arise. The undertaking must demonstrate the satisfaction of the conditions 'with a sufficient degree of probability, and on the basis of verifiable evidence'. This is a high standard of proof and is in sharp contrast to the case law which requires the Commission merely to demonstrate 'likely' anti-competitive effects. Moreover, there is an inherent problem in applying the 'no elimination of effective competition' condition in refusal to supply cases where the refusal would not be a *prima facie* abuse in the first place without the (likely) elimination of effective competition in the downstream market.[125] The 'elimination of competition' condition means that consumers are deprived of the benefits of efficiencies because of the degree of dominance of the supplier.

Post Danmark and the Guidance Paper in effect import Article 101(3) into Article 102. However, there are cogent reasons for arguing that a provision designed as an exemption for negotiated agreements between independent undertakings which restrict competition is not suitable for application *ex post* to the unilateral actions of dominant undertakings where the theory of harm is far more difficult to prove.[126] It is not a matter of the desirability of taking efficiencies into account before finding an infringement of Article 102 but rather of at what stage of the analysis they should be taken into account and the conditions that they need to fulfil.

F. PROTECTING THE UNDERTAKING'S OWN COMMERCIAL INTERESTS

'Protection of the undertaking's own commercial interests' as a defence was first accepted in *United Brands* where the undertaking cut off supplies to a distributor to discipline it for participating in a rival's promotion. A 'commercial interest' in this context has been described as 'an interest consistent with the rational profit-maximizing behaviour of a non-dominant undertaking'.[127] The CJ said in *United Brands*:[128]

189. Although it is true, as the applicant points out, that the fact that an undertaking is in a dominant position cannot disentitle it from protecting its own commercial interests if they are attacked, and that such an undertaking must be conceded the right to take such reasonable steps as it deems appropriate to protect its said interests, such behaviour cannot be countenanced if its actual purpose is to strengthen this dominant position and abuse it.

190. Even if the possibility of a counter-attack is acceptable that attack must still be proportionate to the threat taking into account the economic strength of the undertakings confronting each other.

The CJ thus established the principle that Article 102 does not prevent an undertaking from protecting its own commercial interests when they are attacked. However, the principle does not apply if the undertaking's 'actual purpose is to strengthen this dominant position and abuse it', i.e. if the undertaking has an anti-competitive intent. Furthermore, the undertaking's response must be 'reasonable' and 'proportionate'.

The EU Courts and the Commission have relied on *United Brands* many times when considering an undertaking's claim that the allegedly abusive conduct was merely the protection of its own

---

[125] See e.g. Case C-7/97 *Oscar Bronner GmbH & Co KG v. Mediaprint* [1998] ECR I-7791; Case C-418/01 *IMS Health GmbH & Co. OHG v. NDC Health GmbH & Co. KG* [2004] ECR I-5039; Case T-201/04, *Microsoft v. EC Commission* [2007] ECR II-3601.

[126] See further Akman, *The Concept of Abuse in EU Competition Law* (cited in n. 9), 280–284; Nazzini, *The Foundations of European Union Competition Law* (cited in n. 106), 304–309; D. Walbroeck, 'The Assessment of Efficiencies under Article 102 TFEU and the Commission's Guidance Paper' in Etro and Kokkoris (eds.), *Competition Law and the Enforcement of Article 102* (cited in n. 96), 115.

[127] Nazzini, *The Foundations of European Union Competition Law* (cited in n. 106), 300.

[128] Case 27/76, *United Brands v. Commission* [1978] ECR 207.

commercial interests.[129] The question of what is 'reasonable and proportional' arose in *BBI/Boosey & Hawkes*, another case in which a dominant undertaking cut off an existing customer, this time because the customer went into competition with it.[130] In this case it seems to have been the undertaking's *immediate* withdrawal of supplies which was unacceptable. It was not proportional to the threat it faced. As in *United Brands* the dominant undertaking was held to have gone too far in the defence of its interests. In *Tetra Pak I* Advocate General Kirschner said of proportionality:

> Applied to the conduct of an undertaking in a dominant position, that principle has the following meaning: the undertaking in a dominant position may act in a profit-oriented way, strive through its efforts to improve its market position and pursue its legitimate interests. But in so doing it may employ only such methods as are necessary to pursue those legitimate aims. In particular it may not act in a way which, foreseeably, will limit competition more than is necessary.[131]

As will be seen later in this chapter, the protecting legitimate commercial interests defence has particularly been raised in cases of refusal to supply.[132] It played an important part in *Sot. Lélos*.[133] The pharmaceutical company's arguments were in effect an efficiency defence, but the CJ's judgment treated the matter as protection of its legitimate commercial interests.[134] However it is worth noting here that the CJ said that the competition rules are incapable of being interpreted in such a way that in order to defend its own commercial interests the undertaking has no choice but to leave a particular market altogether.[135] There is little doubt that conduct protecting the dominant undertaking's interests would be justified if it consisted of legitimate business practices such as cutting off supplies to a bad debtor.[136]

G. THE 'MEETING COMPETITION' DEFENCE

The 'meeting competition defence' is the plea that the dominant undertaking is merely reacting to competition in a proportionate and reasonable way. It is an aspect of the 'protecting legitimate commercial interests' defence,[137] often pleaded in pricing cases where the dominant undertaking's prices are alleged to be predatory[138] and/or exclusionary of equally efficient competitors.[139] The 'meeting competition' defence cannot save predatory pricing from constituting an abuse: in *France Télécom*,[140]

---

[129] See e.g. Case T-65/89, *BPB Industries and British Gypsum v. Commission* [1993] ECR II-389, para. 69; Cases T-24/93 to T-26/93 and T-28/93, *Compagnie Maritime Belge Transports v. Commission* [1996] ECR II-1201, para. 107; Case T-228/97, *Irish Sugar plc v. Commission* [1999] ECR II-2969, para. 112; Cases T-191 and 212–214/98, *Atlantic Container Line v. Commission* [2003] ECR II- 3275, paras. 1113–1114 (the GC said that according to the case law objective justification applied only to practices reasonably taken to protect the undertaking's commercial interests); Case T-203/01, *Manufacture Française des Pneumatiques Michelin v. Commission* [2003] ECR II-407, para. 55; Case C-468–478/06, *Sot. Lélos kai Sia and others EE v. GlaxoSmithKline AEVE Farmakeftikon Proionton* [2008] ECR I-7139, para. 39; Case T-301/04, *Clearstream Banking v. Commission* [2009] ECR II-3155, para. 132.

[130] *BBI/Boosey & Hawkes: Interim Measures* [1987] OJ L282/36, para. 19.

[131] Case T-51/89, *Tetra Pak Rausing SA v. Commission* [1990] ECR II-309, para. 68 of the Opinion.

[132] As in *United Brands* and *BBI/Boosey & Hawkes*.

[133] Cases C-468–478/06, *Sot. Lélos kai Sia and others EE v. GlaxoSmithKline AEVE Farmakeftikon Proionton* [2008] ECR I-7139.

[134] See Section 16, p. 586 ff.

[135] *Sot. Lélos*, para. 68.

[136] See *BBI/Boosey & Hawkes: Interim Measures* [1987] OJ L286/36, [1988] 4 CMLR 67.

[137] See COMP/38.784 *Wanadoo España v. Telefónica*, 4 July 2007, [2008] 4 CMLR 414 (*Telefónica*), para. 638.

[138] The problems of applying a meeting competition defence to predatory pricing are discussed in Section 8.E, p. 414.

[139] As in margin squeeze cases, see the plea of 'meeting competition' in *Telefónica*, para. 639, cited in n. 137.

[140] Case C-202/07 P, *France Télécom SA v. Commission* [2009] ECR I-2369, paras. 47–48, affirming Case T-340/03, *France Télécom SA v. Commission* [2007] ECR II-107. And see the unsuccessful 'meeting competition' plea in the selective pricing case, Cases C-395 and 396/96P *Compagnie Maritime Belge Transports SA v. EC Commission* [2000] ECR I-1365, and Case T-228/97, *Irish Sugar plc v. Commission* [1999] ECR II-2969.

the CJ confirmed that there is no absolute right for a dominant undertaking to align its prices with those of its competitors.

6. DOMINANCE AND ABUSE ON DIFFERENT MARKETS

The dominant position may be held on a different market from that where the effects of the abuse are felt.

The earliest cases involved dominant undertakings which abused their position on one market in order to gain advantages on downstream, or ancillary, markets. The prevention of such 'leverage' has been a major theme in the application of Article 102, as the rest of this chapter reveals. In the leading case of *Commercial Solvents*[141] the dominant undertaking was held to have abused its position on a raw material market when it refused to supply it to a producer of a derivative drug because the dominant undertaking wished to enter the market in the derivative drug itself.

In *Télémarketing* (CBEM or *Centre Belge*)[142] Luxembourg television stopped accepting tele-sales advertisements on its television station unless the sales agent phone number used was that of its own subsidiary. This could be seen both as a refusal to supply and as contractual tying. Either way the statutory monopolist's purpose was to exclude other undertakings from competing with its own subsidiary on the ancillary market. The CJ considered the conduct an abuse:[143]

an abuse within the meaning of Article [102] is committed where, without any objective necessity, an undertaking holding a dominant position on a particular market reserves to itself or to an undertaking belonging to the same group an ancillary activity which might be carried out by another undertaking as part of its activities on a neighbouring but separate market, with the possibility of eliminating all competition from such undertaking.

The notion of a dominant undertaking reserving to itself an activity on another market case has frequently been relied on by the EU Courts and the Commission in subsequent cases and in particular has featured in the development of the law on refusals to supply.[144]

Tying, where the firm dominant in one market uses its position to encourage or force customers also to buy from it products which fall into other markets, is a clear instance of a situation where the dominant position on one market is used to affect competition on another, second market. The markets concerned do not necessarily have to be up- or downstream, or ancillary to one another.[145] As we see in Section 11, tying may sometimes be 'defensive' in that it is aimed not at preventing competition on the second market but at protecting the dominant position on the first.[146] In *BPB Industries*[147] too, the undertaking tried to protect its dominant position on one market by conduct on another. In

---

[141] Cases 6 and 7/73, *Istituto Chemioterapico Italiano Spa & Commercial Solvents v. Commission* [1974] ECR 223, [1974] 1 CMLR 309.

[142] Case 311/84, *Centre Belge d'Etudes du Marché-Télémarketing v. Compagnie Luxembourgeoise de Télédiffusion SA and Information Publicité Benelux SA* [1985] ECR 3261. See also Case C-260/89, *Elliniki Radiophonia Tileorasi (ERT) v. DEP* [1991] ECR I-2925, paras. 37–38 where the CJ held that it was contrary to Art. 102 for a television monopoly to pursue a discriminatory broadcasting policy which favoured its own programmes (the case also raised Art. 106 issues which are discussed in Chap. 8).

[143] Case 311/84, *Centre Belge d'Etudes du Marché-Télémarketing v. Compagnie Luxembourgeoise de Télédiffusion SA and Information Publicité Benelux SA* [1985] ECR 3261, para. 27.

[144] See Section 12, p. 510 ff.

[145] For tying generally, see Section 11, p. 485 ff. See, e.g., *De Poste-La Poste* [2002] OJ L61/32, [2002] 4 CMLR 1426 where the statutory monopolist in the basic letter service tried to exclude competition on the business-to-business market.

[146] See Section 11.C, p. 488.

[147] Case T-65/89, *BPB Industries and British Gypsum v. Commission* [1993] ECR II-389.

that case British Gypsum, which was dominant in the *plasterboard* market, promised priority delivery of *plaster* to plasterboard customers who stayed loyal to it and did not buy plasterboard from importers. This was held to be an abuse.[148]

In *British Airways*[149] the impugned conduct was the way in which BA paid commission to travel agents selling its tickets, which was said to put pressure on the agents to push BA tickets, rather than those of rival airlines (particularly Virgin), to those intending to fly. The Commission did not try to prove that BA was dominant on any air route. Instead, it defined a market consisting of UK air travel agency services in which BA was dominant (as a *buyer*)[150] and held that it had abused this dominant position in order to gain anti-competitive advantages in the air transport market. To this extent *British Airways* is an application of the original principle in *Commercial Solvents*. However, the reality was rather different. The case stemmed from the intense rivalry in air transport. The Commission found an abuse on one (arguably rather artificial) market, assessing BA as dominant (with an unprecedentedly low market share), and identifying the effects of the abuse on another market where the powerful position of the undertaking was in effect the source of the dominance on the first market.[151] The GC upheld the Commission.[152]

In *Tetra Pak II* an undertaking was held to have infringed Article 102 by predatory (i.e. below cost) pricing where it was dominant on one market and the predatory pricing took place on another. Unlike tying or refusal to supply cases the dominant undertaking was not directly *using* its dominance to commit the abuse.[153] Unlike *BPB Industries* the dominant undertaking was not trying to protect its dominant position. The case involved two carton markets: aseptic and non-aseptic. They were held to be separate, distinct markets. Neither was ancillary to the other or upstream or downstream of the other.[154] The Commission held that Tetra Pak was dominant on the aseptic market but made no finding of dominance with regard to the non-aseptic market. It held, however, that Tetra Pak had abused its dominant position on the aseptic market by its conduct on the non-aseptic market which was designed to obtain a competitive advantage on the latter. The Commission's decision was upheld by the GC,[155] which was affirmed by the Court of Justice.

Case C-333/94 P, *Tetra Pak International SA* v. *Commission* [1996] ECR I-5951

Court of Justice

27. It is true that application of Article [102] presupposes a link between the dominant position and the alleged abusive conduct, which is normally not present where conduct on a market distinct from the dominated market produces effects on that distinct market. In the case of distinct, but associated, markets, as in the present case, application of Article [102] to conduct found on the associated, non-dominated, market and having effects on that associated market can only be justified by special circumstances.

28. In that regard, the [General Court] first considered, at paragraph 118 of its judgment, that it was relevant that Tetra Pak held 78 per cent of the overall market in packaging in both aseptic and non-aseptic

---

[148] See also *De Poste-La Poste* [2002] OJ L61/32, [2002] 4 CMLR 1426.

[149] *Virgin/British Airways* [2000] OJ L30/1, [2000] 4 CMLR 999.

[150] See Chap. 6.

[151] It also found that the abuse affected the air travel agency services market itself because it involved discrimination between travel agents: see Section 14, p. 573.

[152] BA did not appeal the point to the CJ in Case C-95/04 P, *British Airways* v. *Commission* [2007] ECR I-2331.

[153] Although the fact that it was dominant in another market facilitated cross-subsidisation.

[154] For market definition in *Tetra Pak II*, see Chap. 6.

[155] Case T-83/91, *Tetra Pak Rausing* v. *Commission* [1994] ECR II-755.

cartons, that is to say seven times more than its closest competitor. At paragraph 119, it stressed Tetra Pak's leading position in the non-aseptic sector. Then, in paragraph 121, it found that Tetra Pak's position on the aseptic markets, of which it held nearly a 90 per cent share, was quasi-monopolistic. It noted that that position also made Tetra Pak a favoured supplier of non-aseptic systems. Finally, at paragraph 122, it concluded that, in the circumstances of the case, application of Article [102] was justified by the situation on the different markets and the close associative links between them.

29. The relevance of the associative links which the [General Court] thus took into account cannot be denied. The fact that the various materials involved are used for packaging the same basic liquid products shows that Tetra Pak's customers in one sector are also potential customers in the other. That possibility is borne out by statistics showing that in 1987 approximately 35 per cent of Tetra Pak's customers bought both aseptic and non-aseptic systems. It is also relevant to note that Tetra Pak and its most important competitor, PKL, were present on all four markets. Given its almost complete domination of the aseptic markets, Tetra Pak could also count on a favoured status on the non-aseptic markets. Thanks to its position on the former markets, it could concentrate its efforts on the latter by acting independently of the other economic operators.

30. The circumstances thus described, taken together and not separately, justified the [General Court], without any need to show that the undertaking was dominant on the non-aseptic markets, in finding that Tetra Pak enjoyed freedom of conduct compared with the other economic operators on those markets.

31. Accordingly, the [General Court] was right to accept the application of Article [102] of the Treaty in this case, given that the quasi-monopoly enjoyed by Tetra Pak on the aseptic markets and its leading position on the distinct, though closely associated, non-aseptic markets placed it in a situation comparable to that of holding a dominant position on the markets in question as a whole.

The reference to *AKZO* in paragraph 25 is strange since ultimately only one relevant market was held to exist in that case, so the dominant position and the abuse were actually on the same market.[156] *Tetra Pak II* extended the previous law because the abuse was committed on a non-dominated market, unrelated vertically to the dominated one, in order to gain an advantage in the former. The Court stated in paragraph 27 that Article 102 can be applied to conduct by a dominant undertaking on a distinct, non-dominated market only where it is justified by 'special circumstances'. The special circumstances in this case were the 'close associative links' between the two markets, the quasi-monopolistic position held by Tetra Pak on the dominated market (where it had a 90 per cent market share), and the leading position on the non-dominated market. Both types of carton were used for packaging the same basic liquid, and many customers bought on both markets. Its powerful position on the dominated market therefore meant that Tetra Pak could concentrate its efforts on the associated market where it enjoyed a greater freedom of action than its competitors. It was thus in a position *comparable to that of holding a dominant position on the two markets as a whole* (paragraph 31). *Tetra Pak II* does not mean that dominance on one market can always be abused by conduct on another, distinct market, but that it is a possibility where particular circumstances mean that the undertaking's dominance gives it significant advantages on the second market. In *TeliaSonera*,[157] the CJ stressed that Article 102 gives no explicit guidance about requirements as to where on the product markets the abuse took place. So 'while Article 102 TFEU presupposes a link between the dominant position and the alleged abusive conduct, which is normally not present where conduct on a market distinct

---

[156] Case C-62/86, *AKZO Chemie* [1991] ECR I-3359. Organic peroxides had various uses but the Court accepted that it was all one market: see Chap. 6.

[157] Case C-52/09, *Konkurrensverket v. TeliaSonera Sverige AB* [2011] ECR I-527, paras 84–86.

from the dominated market produces effects on that distinct market, the application of Article 102 TFEU to conduct found on the associated, non-dominated, market and having effects on that associated market can nonetheless be justified by special circumstances...'.[158]

7. GENERAL ISSUES IN RESPECT OF ABUSES CONCERNING PRICES

A. EXPLOITATIVE AND EXCLUSIONARY PRICING POLICIES

Many cases and decisions on Article 102 concern the pricing policies of dominant firms. One of the most serious consequences of a firm being found to be in a dominant position is that its pricing policies may be condemned as abusive. Although some pricing practices, such as excessive pricing, are impossible or at least unlikely in the absence of market power, others, such as discriminatory pricing in the form of discount and rebate schemes, can be practised by any firm, and in non-dominated markets may be applauded as lively competition. Abusive pricing policies cannot be completely separated from other forms of abuse, such as tying policies or exclusive contracts, since, as becomes apparent later in this chapter, the former are often pursued in furtherance of the latter.

For the convenience of the reader this chapter deals with pricing abuses under various headings. Again for the sake of convenience the sections on exclusionary price-based abuses, with the exception of margin squeeze, follow the categorisation used in the Commission Guidance Paper.[159] However, it must be appreciated that many of these abuses are interrelated and that pricing policies may be characterised under more than one head and may arise in combination. Exploitative pricing abuses are discussed in Section 15.

B. PRICE DISCRIMINATION

(i) What is Price Discrimination?

Price discrimination[160] occurs where the same commodity is sold at different prices to different customers despite identical costs, i.e. the sales have different ratios of price to marginal cost. It also covers sales at the same price despite different costs. Price discrimination covers a wide range of practices. As seen below predatory pricing and rebate policies, for example, may involve price discrimination.

Price discrimination is described as persistent when a supplier maintains a policy of obtaining a higher rate of return from some customers than from others. The ability to practise persistent price discrimination is a characteristic of market power. In a competitive market the customers who are 'disfavoured', i.e. charged the higher price, are able to take their custom elsewhere. Persistent discrimination against some customers shows that it is difficult or impossible for them to change suppliers.

---

[158] The markets in *TeliaSonera* were vertically related.

[159] The Guidance Paper, unlike the CJ more recently (Case C-52/09, *Konkurrensverket v. TeliaSonera Sverige AB* [2011] ECR I-527), deals with margin squeeze as a type of refusal to supply, see Section 9.D, p. 445.

[160] See F. M. Scherer and D. Ross, *Industrial Market Structure and Economic Performance* (3rd edn, Houghton & Mifflin, 1993), Chap. 13; L. Philips, *The Economics of Price Discrimination* (Cambridge University Press, 1983); H. Varian, 'Price Discrimination', in R. Schmalensee and R. Willig (eds.), *Handbook of Industrial Organisation, Volume 1* (North Holland, 1989), Chap. 10; D. Geradin, A. Layne-Farrar, and N. Petit, *EU Competition Law and Economics* (Oxford University Press, 2012), 4.452–4.452; O'Donoghue and Padilla, *The Law and Economics of Article 102* (cited in n. 14) Chap. 15.

Price discrimination occurs in competitive markets too but it tends to be sporadic, i.e. it changes frequently and customers may be in a favoured group today and a disfavoured one tomorrow.

All customers have a 'reservation price', the maximum price they will pay for the product.[161] In *perfect price discrimination* (first-degree discrimination) the dominant supplier charges each customer his reservation price. In the real world this is often impossible and the supplier can only practise *imperfect* price discrimination whereby he identifies different groups of customers with similar reservation prices and charges each group differently. In second-degree discrimination he does this by offering different 'deals' in the form of goods or services in different packages and lets the customer 'self-select' by choosing the one he wants. In third-degree discrimination the supplier identifies different groups of customers by some easily observable or ascertainable characteristic, such as old-age pensioners, students, residents of a particular country.[162] Information technology has made price discrimination easier in some markets because suppliers may have detailed data on individual buyers because of the information which users of social media sites reveal and the footprint they leave online or from their use of loyalty cards or similar schemes.

Price discrimination works only if arbitrage is not feasible. Arbitrage is where the customers trade amongst themselves, which means the customers charged the lowest prices sell on to those charged more. There is no incentive to do this if the difference in prices charged is not sufficient to recompense the selling customer for the transport, administrative, or other costs involved in selling on. Arbitrage is often not possible. In *United Brands*,[163] for example, it was difficult to transport bananas, a highly delicate and perishable product, between Member States. Price discrimination is easier in respect of services consumed on the spot than in respect of goods because of the lack of opportunities for arbitrage.[164]

The general consensus among economists is that price discrimination is welfare enhancing if it increases output.[165] Price discrimination may be pro-competitive in industries with high fixed (or sunk) costs and low marginal costs if an undertaking can charge above marginal cost to customers willing to pay in order to recover some fixed costs, while charging lower, marginal cost prices, to others.[166] This may in particular be a feature of high technology markets in the new economy. However, it is also possible for price discrimination to be anti-competitive and produce adverse effects on efficiency. It depends on the facts of the case. The problem for competition law is to develop the tools for distinguishing the situations in which price discrimination is welfare enhancing from those in which it is not.

(ii) Primary Line and Secondary Line Injury

Price discrimination may involve primary line or secondary line injury. Primary line injury prejudices the supplier's competitors. Price discrimination can cause primary line injury by having exclusionary (foreclosure) effects on competitors. For example, in *Irish Sugar*[167] and *Compagnie Maritime Belge*[168] the dominant undertakings were held to have pursued selective (and therefore discriminatory) low

---

[161] See Chap. 1.

[162] M. Motta, *Competition Policy* (Cambridge University Press, 2004), 492.

[163] Case 27/76, *United Brands v. Commission* [1978] ECR 207.

[164] D. Begg, G. Vernasca, S. Fischer, and R. Dornbusch, *Economics* (10th edn, McGraw-Hill, 2011), 190.

[165] There is a large literature on the economics of price discrimination, but see in particular R. Schmalensee, 'Output and Welfare Implications of Third Degree Price Discrimination' (1981) 71 *American Economic Review* 242; H. R. Varian, 'Price Discrimination and Social Welfare' (1985) 75 *Am Economic Review* 870.

[166] See D. Ridyard, 'Exclusionary Pricing and Price Discrimination Abuses under Article 102—An Economic Analysis' [2002] *ECLR* 286, 287–278; J. Temple Lang and R. O'Donoghue, 'Defining Legitimate Competition: How to Clarify Pricing Abuses under Article 102EC' (2002) 26 *Fordham Int'l LJ* 83, 89–90.

[167] Case T-228/97, *Irish Sugar plc v. Commission* [1999] ECR II-2969.

[168] Cases C-395 and 396/96 P, *Compagnie Maritime Belge and Others v. Commission* [2000] ECR I-1365.

pricing policies in order to exclude their competitors. Secondary line injury is where the impact is in downstream markets, between the supplier's customers or third parties *inter se*. If a supplier sells a product to X more cheaply than to Y, and X and Y are competing manufacturers who need the product as an input, then X's costs will be lower than Y's. The supplier *may* have distorted competition between them as a result.

Primary and secondary line injury may arise from the same scenario. In *Virgin/BA*[169] the differential rebates given to travel agents for selling BA tickets were held to have both an excluding effect on BA's competitor airlines (primary line), and to cause distortions to competition between the agents (secondary line).

Primary line injury through price discrimination is a major target of the Commission, as it can be exclusionary. However, in *Post Danmark* the CJ clarified that the fact that the practice of a dominant undertaking may be described as 'price discrimination' cannot of itself suggest that an exclusionary abuse exists.[170] Secondary line injury through discriminatory pricing is expressly listed as an abuse in Article 102(c)[171] although in several cases discussed in this chapter the Commission has also used Article 102(c) in respect of primary line discrimination.[172]

C. COSTS LEVELS

Before looking at abuses which involve pricing, it is necessary to understand the terminology of costs.[173]

1. *Total cost* The total costs of production.

2. *Average Total Cost (ATC)* The total costs involved in the production of one unit of output (i.e. total cost divided by the number of units produced).

3. *Total costs are of two kinds*:

   (a) Fixed costs. Those which do not change with output over a given time period.

   (b) Variable costs. Those which do change with output.

4. *Average Variable Cost (AVC)* The variable costs involved in the production of one unit (i.e. the variable costs added up and divided by the number of units produced).

5. *Marginal Cost* The increase in total costs of a firm caused by increasing its output by one extra unit.

6. *Short-run Marginal Cost (SRMC)* The marginal cost based on a firm's existing plant and equipment, not on that which would be the most efficient.

7. *Avoidable Costs* The costs that will not be incurred if an undertaking ceases a particular operation. They are variable costs plus any fixed costs that are incurred during the period under examination (they cannot include sunk costs because sunk costs have already been spent and cannot be recovered).

8. *Average avoidable cost (AAC)* The average of the costs that could have been avoided if the undertaking had not produced a discrete amount of extra output.[174]

---

[169] [2000] OJ L30/1, [2000] 4 CMLR 999, upheld on appeal, Case T-219/99, *British Airways v. Commission* [2003] ECR II-5917 and Case C-95/04 P, *British Airways v. Commission* [2007] ECR I-2331.

[170] Case C-209/10, *Post Danmark A/S v. Konkurrencerådet*, 27 March 2012, para. 30; see further Sections 8.D and 8.I, pp. 408 and 420.

[171] See Section 14, p. 567.

[172] See Geradin et al., *EU Competition Law and Economics* (cited in n. 160), 4.999–4.

[173] See also Chap. 1.

[174] The definition of average avoidable cost given in the Guidance Paper, para. 26, n. 2.

9. *(Long run) average incremental cost ((LR)AIC)* The average of all the (variable and fixed) costs that an undertaking incurs to produce a particular product.[175] The standard is useful in industries where there are large fixed costs but low, or even negligible, variable costs (because the main cost is the provision of a network for example, as is the case with telecommunications). LRAIC includes product-specific fixed costs made before the period under examination and is useful in the case of multi-product undertakings where there are fixed costs common to a number of different activities carried on by an undertaking resulting in economies of scope. LRAIC does not include true common costs.[176] The Guidance Paper says that LRAIC and ATC are good proxies for one another and are the same in respect of a single product undertaking.[177] It also explains that in the case of multiple products, any costs that could have been avoided by not producing a particular product or range are not considered to be common costs.[178]

10. *Stand-alone costs* The costs which are involved in producing a product without taking into account that some of those costs are shared with the production of other products (i.e. that there are common costs).

The following should be noted:

- Average variable cost is always lower than average total cost.
- Long run means a period of time long enough for all the factors of production to be costlessly varied (i.e. the period needed for complete adjustment).
- Short run means a period of time so short that the factors of production cannot be costlessly varied (i.e. a period too short for complete adjustment).

D. THE GENERAL APPROACH IN THE GUIDANCE PAPER TO PRICE-BASED EXCLUSIONARY CONDUCT: THE 'AS EFFICIENT COMPETITOR' STANDARD

The Guidance Paper contains a preliminary section, paragraphs 23 to 27, setting out the general principles the Commission will apply when deciding whether to intervene in respect of a dominant undertaking's pricing conduct. It will act with a view to preventing anti-competitive foreclosure and will *normally* intervene where the conduct has been, or is capable of, hampering competition from competitors who are as efficient as the dominant undertaking. The Commission thus adopts the 'as efficient competitor' test. However, the Commission lodges a proviso (paragraph 24) saying that 'in certain circumstances' competitive constraints may be exerted by *less* efficient competitors which should be taken into account when assessing foreclosure. The example given is of a competitor which, in the absence of abusive conduct might benefit from demand-led advantages such as network and learning effects which could enhance its efficiency.[179] The proviso is an example of the Commission's strategy throughout the Guidance Paper which was noted in Chapter 5, of setting out the normal rule but expressly reserving some freedom to depart from it in certain circumstances. In this instance it means that the Commission can take account of dynamic efficiencies. However, the result is that undertakings can never be sure that their case will not be one of those where the

---

[175] The definition of LRAIC given in the Guidance Paper, para. 26, n. 2.

[176] See however Case C-209/10, *Post Danmark A/S v. Konkurrencerådet*, 27 March 2012, where the national competition authority (NCA) had included some common costs in its calculation of LRAIC.

[177] See Guidance Paper, para. 26, n. 2.

[178] Guidance Paper, para. 26, n. 2.

[179] Guidance Paper, para. 24.

Commission is concerned with the exclusion of less efficient competitors.[180] The Commission will assess whether a competitor is 'as efficient' by examining the costs and sales price data of the dominant undertaking itself, but if this information is unavailable the Commission is prepared to use that of the competitor. The problem here is that the use of the competitor's data alone cannot tell the Commission whether the competitor is 'as efficient'. One practitioner has made the point that given the Commission's extensive powers of investigation and of sanctioning non-cooperation[181] it may merely be issuing a warning to dominant undertakings to produce the data it requires.[182]

Guidance on the Commission's Enforcement Priorities in Applying Article 82 of the EC Treaty to Abusive Exclusionary Conduct by Dominant Undertakings [2009] OJ C45/2

C. Price-based Exclusionary Conduct

23. The considerations in paragraphs 23 to 27 apply to price-based exclusionary conduct. Vigorous price competition is generally beneficial to consumers. With a view to preventing anti-competitive foreclosure, the Commission will normally only intervene where the conduct concerned has already been or is capable of hampering competition from competitors which are considered to be as efficient as the dominant undertaking…

24. However, the Commission recognises that in certain circumstances a less efficient competitor may also exert a constraint which should be taken into account when considering whether particular price-based conduct leads to anti-competitive foreclosure. The Commission will take a dynamic view of that constraint, given that in the absence of an abusive practice such a competitor may benefit from demand-related advantages, such as network and learning effects, which will tend to enhance its efficiency.

25. In order to determine whether even a hypothetical competitor as efficient as the dominant undertaking would be likely to be foreclosed by the conduct in question, the Commission will examine economic data relating to cost and sales prices, and in particular whether the dominant undertaking is engaging in below-cost pricing. This will require that sufficiently reliable data be available. Where available, the Commission will use information on the costs of the dominant undertaking itself. If reliable information on those costs is not available, the Commission may decide to use the cost data of competitors or other comparable reliable data.

26. The cost benchmarks that the Commission is likely to use are average avoidable cost (AAC) and long-run average incremental cost (LRAIC)… Failure to cover AAC indicates that the dominant undertaking is sacrificing profits in the short term and that an equally efficient competitor cannot serve the targeted customers without incurring a loss. LRAIC is usually above AAC because, in contrast to AAC (which only includes fixed costs if incurred during the period under examination), LRAIC includes product specific fixed costs made before the period in which allegedly abusive conduct took place. Failure to cover LRAIC indicates that the dominant undertaking is not recovering all the (attributable) fixed costs of producing the good or service in question and that an equally efficient competitor could be foreclosed from the market…

27. If the data clearly suggest that an equally efficient competitor can compete effectively with the pricing conduct of the dominant undertaking, the Commission will, in principle, infer that the dominant

---

[180] Less efficient competitors can provide consumers with choice that some may value. See Case T-201/04, *Microsoft* v. *Commission* [2007] ECR II-3601, para. 652; N. Petit, 'From Formalism to Effects? The Commission's Communication on Enforcement Priorities in Applying Article 82' (2009) 32(4) *World Competition* 485, 491.

[181] See Chap. 13.

[182] L.Kjølbe, 'Rebates Under Article 82EC: Navigating Uncertain Waters' [2010] *ECLR* 66, 74. Undertakings will know their own costs but competition law can hardly require them to know those of their competitors!

undertaking's pricing conduct is not likely to have an adverse impact on effective competition, and thus on consumers, and will therefore be unlikely to intervene. If, on the contrary, the data suggest that the price charged by the dominant undertaking has the potential to foreclose equally efficient competitors, then the Commission will integrate this in the general assessment of anti-competitive foreclosure (see Section B [of the Guidance] above), taking into account other relevant quantitative and/or qualitative evidence.

The Commission therefore favours using AAC and LRAIC as its benchmarks. As it points out in a footnote, in most cases AAC and AVC are the same, as are LRAIC and ATC in the case of single product undertakings.

E. THE GENERAL APPROACH OF THE EU COURTS TO PRICING ABUSES

The CJ in effect applied the 'as efficient competitor' principle in the 1991 predatory pricing case of *AKZO* where it established that whether or not low prices amounted to an abuse depended on their relationship to the dominant undertaking's own costs.[183] Since then it has firmly established that the as efficient competitor test is the standard to be used in predatory pricing and margin squeeze cases.[184] Its application of the as efficient competitor test to margin squeeze post-dated the Guidance Paper which applied refusal to supply principles to margin squeeze and did not treat margin squeeze as a form of pricing abuse. However, the EU Courts have not applied the as efficient competitor test to discount and rebate cases and the current approach of the Courts therefore differs from the methodology set out in respect of rebates in the Guidance Paper.[185]

In *Michelin I* the CJ said that in deciding whether the undertaking's discount system was abusive it was necessary to consider all the circumstances and decide whether the practice tended to remove or restrict the buyer's freedom to choose his sources of supply, to bar competitors from access to the market, to apply dissimilar conditions to equivalent transactions with other trading parties, or to strengthen the dominant position by distorting competition. This principle now invariably appears in all judgments on pricing abuses.[186]

8. PREDATORY PRICING

A. GENERAL

Predatory pricing is the practice whereby an undertaking prices its product so low that competitors cannot live with the price and are driven from the market.[187] Once the competitors are excluded from

---

[183] Case C-62/86 *AKZO Chemie BV* v. *Commission* [1991] ECR I-3359.

[184] Case C-209/10, *Post Danmark A/S* v. *Konkurrencerådet*, 27 March 2012; Case C-280/08 P, *Deutsche Telekom* v. *Commission* [2010] ECR I-9555; Case C-52/09, *Konkurrensverket* v. *TeliaSonera Sverige AB* [2011] ECR I-527.

[185] Case T-203/01, *Manufacture Française des Pneumatiques Michelin* v. *Commission* [2003] ECR II-4071; Case C-95/04 P, *British Airways* v. *Commission* [2007] ECR I-2331; Case C-549/10 P, *Tomra Systems ASA* v. *European Commission*, 19 April 2012; see Section 10.D, p. 454 ff.

[186] Case C-280/08 P, *Deutsche Telekom* v. *Commission* [2010] ECR I-9555, para. 175; Case C-52/09, *Konkurrensverket* v. *TeliaSonera Sverige AB* [2011] ECR I-527, para. 28; Case C-209/10, *Post Danmark A/S* v. *Konkurrencerådet*, 27 March 2012, para. 26; Case C-549/10 P, *Tomra Systems ASA* v. *European Commission*, 19 April 2012, para. 71 (which omits the 'applying dissimilar conditions' phrase); Case T-336/07, *Telefónica and Telefónica de España* v. *European Commission*, 29 March 2012, para. 175. In some cases 'thereby placing them at a competitive disadvantage' is added to the phrase about applying dissimilar conditions; for the significance of these words see Section 14, p. 572.

[187] See generally P. L. Joskow and A. K. Klevorick, 'A Framework for Analyzing Predatory Pricing Policy (1979) 89 *Yale LJ* 213; S. Bishop and M. Walker, *The Economics of EC Competition Law* (3rd edn, Sweet & Maxwell, 2010), paras. 6-084–6.112; O'Donoghue and Padilla, *The Law and Economics of Article 102* (cited in n. 14), Chap. 6. Conduct, other than low pricing, designed to drive competitors out of the market can also be described as 'predatory'.

the market the undertaking hopes to increase prices to monopoly levels and recoup its losses. It is anti-competitive because, although it means low prices in the short term, its effects are to strengthen the power of the dominant undertaking to the prejudice of consumers. It is generally thought, as reflected in the Guidance Paper, that competition policy should not be concerned with the exclusion of *less* efficient competitors from the market but the problem with predatory pricing is that it can exclude firms which are *equally as efficient* as the predator.[188]

The intractable problem for competition authorities is to identify where robust price competition ends and predatory pricing begins. As one American commentator has stated: '[p]redatory pricing is one of the most daunting subjects confronting nations with competition policies'.[189] False positives (Type 1 errors, wrongfully identifying robust price competition as predatory pricing) and false negatives (Type 2 errors, wrongfully failing to identify predatory pricing when it occurs) are both prejudicial to consumer welfare, but many commentators argue that in respect of predatory pricing the avoidance of Type 1 errors should be the priority.

There are different opinions about how often predatory pricing actually occurs. The strategy of the predator is to sacrifice profit-maximisation in the short term in order to reap monopoly profits in the long term. Some economists have argued that it is hardly ever a rational business strategy and that it is very rare. This view was famously adopted by Bork: '[i]t seems unwise…to construct rules about a phenomenon that probably does not exist or which, should it exist in very rare cases, the courts would have grave difficulty in distinguishing from competitive price behavior'.[190] The mainstream view now is that predatory pricing can be a rational strategy where the conditions are right. In particular, predatory pricing may be rational in new economy markets.[191]

One obvious condition for the rationality of predatory pricing generally is the existence of barriers to entry. Otherwise, after one competitor is knocked out by the low prices others will enter when the incumbent raises them again. The incumbent will never be able to enjoy the fruits of its predation. However, it is important to appreciate that predatory pricing may itself *constitute* a barrier to entry. Industrial organisation theory suggests that the conditions of post-entry competition are a major factor in decisions about market entry and that the presence of a known predator on the market is a disincentive to entry. In this way predatory pricing not only drives out existing competitors, but also repels potential competition. It may be easier to deter potential competitors through predatory pricing than to expel existing ones, as incumbents may have incurred sunk costs and have an incentive to remain on the market. Further, it is unlikely that all the actors on the market have perfect information. It is also argued that a predatory price may give the potential entrant erroneous signals about price levels in the market, which will deter entry as it will not appear worthwhile.

---

[188] Although some economists argue that the efficiency of the entrant is irrelevant: what matters is whether there is room for another player in a non-cooperative Nash equilibrium (a market where all the participants are pursuing their best possible strategy given the strategies of all the others, see Chap. 9); see, e.g., L. Philips, *Competition Policy: A Game-Theoretic Perspective* (Cambridge University Press, 1995), 233.

[189] E. Fox, 'Price Predation—US and EEC: Economics and Values' [1989] *Fordham Corp L Inst* 687, 687.

[190] R. Bork, *The Antitrust Paradox* (Basic Books, 1978, reprinted with new introduction and epilogue, Free Press, Macmillan, 1993), 154. This conclusion was based, inter alia, on a study in the US by J. McGee, 'Predatory Price Cutting; The Standard Oil (New Jersey) Case' (1958) 1 *Journal of Law and Economics* 137, described by R. T. Rapp, 'Predatory Pricing and Entry Deterring Strategies: the Economics of *AKZO*' [1986] *ECLR* 233, n. 1 as 'a work combining exceptionally bad economics and equally bad history' and its influence on US courts as showing 'that bad economic history can have a long, happy life'. For the influence on US courts see *Matsushita Elec. Indust. Co Ltd v. Zenith Radio Corp*, 475 US 574 (1986), where the Supreme Court, having quoted Bork, McGee, and others said, 'for this reason, there is a consensus among commentators that predatory pricing schemes are rarely tried, and even more rarely successful', before rejecting claims of predatory pricing by a cartel.

[191] Bork's thesis was formulated before the explosion of the new economy.

Predatory pricing is often considered to be feasible only where firms operate multi-market because if the firm operates in only one market it is more rational for it to absorb the new entrant (by merger or take-over, insofar as that is permitted by the competition authorities), or to accommodate it, rather than incur greater losses by undercutting. Losses suffered by the predator are suffered *today*, and may be heavy: the profits above the competitive level are *tomorrow* if and when the predation strategy works, and are inherently uncertain. There is also the problem that in exiting the entrant may dispose of its assets to other competitors still on the market. Where a firm is multi-market, however, it may be able to offset the losses on one market from the profits on another. Moreover, a firm which establishes a reputation for aggressive reaction to competition in one market may deter entrants into others, so predation in one market may protect several others. The firm may be multi-market in a geographical rather than a product sense, so that a reputation for predation in one geographic market may deter entrants elsewhere.[192]

It is also said that predation can be a rational strategy only for a firm which is very dominant, in the sense that it has a very high market share:

> Mere market power is not enough. The predator's sales must account for a sizeable fraction of market sales. If not, loss-making prices attract sales from the entire market which makes the strategy unworkably expensive. What is more, eliminating only one of many rivals leads to insufficient gains. All the incumbents stand to bene-fit from that turn of events and the prior investment by any one of them in loss-making prices never pays off.[193]

In short, there is great controversy about predatory pricing. Mainstream opinion can be summed up as saying that it can occur, but only in certain conditions. The Commission and the EU Courts consider that it can and does occur and that it infringes Article 102 when it does.

If it is accepted that predatory pricing *does* occur the problem is to identify it. Most predatory pricing theory centres around costs levels. The basic concept of predatory pricing is that a dominant firm prices below cost. The difficulty with this is that a firm's costs are usually difficult to compute and so is the relationship between its costs and prices. Particular problems arise where a firm uses the same production capacity to make different products.

B. THE AREEDA–TURNER TEST

In a seminal *Harvard Law Review* article Areeda and Turner put forward a test for identifying predatory pricing.[194] Under this test a price lower than reasonably anticipated short-run marginal cost (SRMC) is predatory, whilst a price equal to or higher than reasonably anticipated SRMC is not predatory. 'Reasonably anticipated' means that a firm's conduct is not judged *ex post facto*. The marginal cost is judged by what seemed reasonable at the time. If the SRMC turned out to be higher than anticipated the firm should not be condemned for predatory pricing.

SRMC is, however, almost impossible to compute in practice, as it is a question of looking back to determine what the firm's marginal cost was during a past period of time. The Areeda–Turner test therefore uses average variable cost (AVC) as a surrogate for SRMC. The test is stated as follows:

- A price at or above reasonably anticipated AVC should be conclusively presumed lawful.

- A price below reasonably anticipated AVC should be conclusively presumed unlawful.

---

[192] But see R. Selten, 'The Chain Store Paradox' (1978), *Theory and Decision* 9, 127–159 for a model of how predation in a series of geographic markets would be impossible.

[193] R. T. Rapp, 'Predatory Pricing and Entry Deterring Strategies: the Economics of *AKZO*' [1986] *ECLR* 233, 234; see also H. Hovenkamp, *Federal Antitrust Policy* (4th edn, West, 2011), 381–382.

[194] P. Areeda and D. Turner, 'Predatory Pricing and Related Practices Under Section 2 of the Sherman Act' (1975) 88 *Harvard LR* 697.

Despite criticisms of the shortcomings in the Areeda–Turner test it has been highly influential in antitrust thinking and some version of it is commonly used in US antitrust cases.[195] It formed the basis for the argument in the AKZO case.

C. THE TEST LAID DOWN IN AKZO

(i) The AKZO Case

The Commission first considered predatory pricing in AKZO.[196]

ECS was a small UK firm which produced benzoyl peroxide, a catalyst used in plastics production and also (in the UK and Ireland) as a bleaching agent in flour-milling. ECS concentrated on the flour sector, where its major customer was Allied Mills. AKZO, a multinational chemicals company, produced benzoyl peroxide but concentrated on the plastics sector. The Commission found that when ECS decided to expand its operations in the plastics sector (capturing one of AKZO's largest customers) AKZO retaliated by threatening to attack ECS's business in the UK flour sector by reducing prices. It then supplied benzoyl peroxide to the UK flour sector at low prices, offering large discounts to ECS's best customers. ECS complained to the Commission which adopted a decision holding that AKZO had abused a dominant position contrary to Article 102.[197]

The Commission found that AKZO was dominant in the organic peroxides market as a whole[198] and had infringed Article 102 by pursuing a course of predation against ECS designed to drive it from the plastics sector. It fined AKZO ECU 10 million and ordered it to terminate the infringement. It required AKZO to refrain from offering or applying prices which would result in customers in respect of whose business it was competing with ECS paying prices dissimilar to those applied to comparable customers. The Commission decision finding predation focused on AKZO's threats[199] and its eliminatory intent. The decision did not adopt the Areeda–Turner rule or lay down specific rules about the point at which low prices become predatory, and abusive. It suggested that even prices above ATC could be predatory.[200]

AKZO appealed to the CJ. It argued that it could not be guilty of an abuse since it had not reduced its prices below AVC, and that under the Areeda–Turner test its prices were therefore not predatory. The CJ confirmed the Commission's definition of the market and the finding of dominance. It did accept AKZO's arguments that some costs which the Commission had classified as variable were, in this case, fixed. The CJ confirmed that AKZO had been guilty of predatory pricing,[201] but set out a more structured, costs-based test for identifying it.

---

[195] See J. Brodley and D. Hay, 'Predatory Pricing: Competing Economic Theories and the Evolution of Legal Standards' (1981) 66 *Cornell LR* 738; J. Hurwitz and W. Kovacic, 'Judicial Analysis of Predation: the Emerging Trends' (1982) 35 *Vand LR* 63; E. Elhauge and D. Geradin, *Global Competition Law and Economics* (2nd edn, Hart Publishing, 2011), 353–368; Hovenkamp, *Federal Antitrust Policy* (cited in n. 193), 372-379.

[196] *ECS/AKZO* [1985] OJ L374/1, [1986] 3 CMLR 273; on appeal Case C-62/86, *AKZO Chemie BV v. Commission* [1991] ECR I-3359.

[197] [1985] OJ L374/1, [1986] 3 CMLR 273. ECS had originally obtained an interim injunction in the High Court in London to prevent AKZO from implementing its threats, and those proceedings were terminated by agreement.

[198] See Chap. 6 for the market definition aspects of the case.

[199] It uncovered the evidence of these to support ECS's contentions when it conducted a Reg. 17, Art. 14(3) investigation on AKZO's premises (see Chap. 13).

[200] *ECS/AKZO* [1985] OJ L374/1, [1986] 3 CMLR 273, para. 79.

[201] It annulled the Commission's decision in respect of offers made to one particular customer and reduced the fine to ECU 7.5 million.

Case C-62/86, *AKZO Chemie BV* v. *Commission* [1991] ECR I-3359

Court of Justice

66. AKZO disputes the relevance of the criterion of lawfulness adopted by the Commission, which it regards as nebulous or at least inapplicable. It maintains that the Commission should have adopted an objective criterion based on its costs.

67. In that respect, it states that the question of the lawfulness of a particular level of prices cannot be separated from the specific market situation in which the prices were fixed. There is no abuse if the dominant undertaking endeavours to obtain [an] optimum selling-price and a positive coverage margin. A price is optimum if the undertaking may reasonably expect that the offer of another price or the absence of a price would produce a less favourable operating profit in the short term. Furthermore, coverage margin is positive if the value of the order exceeds the sum of the variable costs.

68. According to AKZO, a criterion based on an endeavour to obtain an optimal price in the short term cannot be rejected on the grounds that it would jeopardise the viability of the undertaking in the long term. It is only after a certain time that the undertaking in ... question could take measures to eliminate the losses or withdraw from a loss-making branch of business. In the meantime the undertaking would have to accept 'optimum orders' in order to reduce its deficit and to ensure continuity of operation.

69. It should be observed that, as the Court held in Case 85/76, *Hoffmann-La Roche* v. *E.C. Commission* ... paragraph 91, the concept of abuse is an objective concept relating to the behaviour of an undertaking in a dominant position which is such as to influence the structure of a market where, as a result of the very presence of the undertaking in question, the degree of competition is weakened and through recourse to methods which, different from those which condition normal competition in products or services on the basis of the transactions of commercial operations, has the effect of hindering the maintenance of the degree of competition still existing in the market or the growth of that competition.

70. It follows that Article [102] prohibits a dominant undertaking from eliminating a competitor and thereby strengthening its position by using methods other than those which come within the scope of competition on the basis of quality. From that point of view, however, not all competition by means of price can be regarded as legitimate.

71. Prices below average variable costs (that is to say, those which vary depending on the quantities produced) by means of which a dominant undertaking seeks to eliminate a competitor must be regarded as abusive. A dominant undertaking has no interest in applying such prices except that of eliminating competitors so as to enable it subsequently to raise its prices by taking advantage of its monopolistic position, since each sale generates a loss, namely the total amount of the fixed costs (that is to say, those which remain constant regardless of the quantities produced) and, at least, part of the variable costs relating to the unit produced.

72. Moreover, prices below average total costs, that is to say, fixed costs plus variable costs, but above average variable costs, must be regarded as abusive if they are determined as part of a plan for eliminating a competitor. Such prices can drive from the market undertakings which are perhaps as efficient as the dominant undertakings but which, because of their smaller financial resources, are incapable of withstanding the competition waged against them.

73. These are the criteria that must be applied to the situation in the present case.

74. Since the criterion of legitimacy to be adopted is a criterion based on the costs and strategy of the dominant undertaking itself, AKZO's allegation concerning the inadequacy of the Commission's investigation with regard to the cost structure and the pricing policy of its competitors must be rejected at the outset.

The costs-based test in *AKZO* differs significantly from the Areeda–Turner test. The *AKZO* test states that prices below AVC 'must be regarded as abusive' because there is no profit-maximising reason for them. The only explanation for them is that they are intended to eliminate competitors. This sets out a strong presumption that pricing below AVC is abusive. It presumes eliminatory intent. The Court went on to hold that above AVC but below ATC prices can also be abusive if they are part of a plan to eliminate competitors (under the Areeda–Turner test there is no predation where prices are above AVC). There is no presumption as to the undertaking's intention, so the onus is on the Commission, or other party alleging abuse. Eliminatory intent was found in *AKZO* from the direct threats and from the price cuts the dominant firm introduced.

The CJ did not expressly deal with the situation where prices are at or above ATC. Nor did it say anything *expressly* about the dominant undertaking's possibility of recouping its losses, although it can be argued that it is implicit in paragraph 71.[202]

The test in *AKZO* is therefore:

- Prices below AVC are presumed to be predatory.
- Prices above AVC but below ATC (the 'grey' area) are not *presumed* predatory but are predatory if they are proved to be part of a plan to eliminate a competitor.

The *AKZO* test was reaffirmed in *Tetra Pak II*[203] and *France Télécom*.[204] It was further developed in *Post Danmark*.[205]

(ii) The Criteria Laid Down in AKZO

a. Problems with Costs-based Tests

Costs-based criteria for predatory pricing are inherently problematic. The problems include:

- AVC is an unsatisfactory substitute for SRMC, because the AVC cost curve tends to be U-shaped and gives the undertaking a lot of room for manoeuvre. Marginal cost rises and falls more dramatically than AVC because AVC averages out the cost of one additional unit over the entire output being produced. The assumption that SRMC and AVC are equivalent holds good only in the long run;[206]

- It is difficult to draw a rigid demarcation line between fixed and variable categories. Classification is dependent upon the industry and the time period in issue. The longer the time period, the more costs become variable. In *AKZO* the parties submitted to the Court very different calculations of AKZO's costs. The Court stated that 'an item of cost is not fixed or variable by nature' and overruled the Commission's classification of the labour costs as variable rather than fixed as in this case there was no direct correlation between labour costs and quantities produced.[207] In *Wanadoo*[208] the Commission classified the advertising of the undertaking's residential broadband services as a variable rather than a fixed cost, which the undertaking disputed.[209] Areeda and Turner recognised the problem of classification and proposed that certain costs

---

[202] Fennelly AG argued this in his opinion in Cases C-395 and 396/96P *Compagnie Maritime Belge* [2000] ECR I-1365. For the question of recoupment generally, see Section 8.F, p. 412.

[203] Case C-333/94 P, *Tetra Pak International SA v. Commission* [1996] ECR I-5951 (*Tetra Pak II*).

[204] Case C-202/07 P, *France Télécom v. Commission* [2009] ECR I-2369.

[205] Case C-209/10, *Post Danmark A/S v. Konkurrencerådet*, 27 March 2012.

[206] Bishop and Walker, *The Economics of EC Competition Law* (cited in n. 187), para. 6.097.

[207] *ECS/AKZO* [1985] OJ L374/1, [1986] 3 CMLR 273, para. 95.

[208] COMP/38.233, [2005] 5 CMLR 120.

[209] The GC dismissed the appeal on this point in *France Télécom*, on procedural grounds. The undertaking's arguments that the Commission had calculated its recovery of costs incorrectly were likewise dismissed.

should always be considered fixed (interest on debt, depreciation, taxes which do not vary with output);[210]

- They are unsatisfactory in markets in which AVC (or SRMC) is minimal (such as markets in the new economy, or software for example).[211]

In *AKZO* the CJ gave no guidance as to the allocation of costs in multi-product/service firms. This was, however, addressed by the Commission in its *Deutsche Post* decision where it applied the (LR)AIC standard when dealing with a statutory monopolist (DPAG) which was also active on a competitive market.[212] In *Post Danmark*,[213] the CJ dealt with the application of AIC to a multi-service undertaking, which also involved a universal service obligation (USO).

b. Rational Reasons for Below AVC Pricing

There can be rational, non-predatory reasons for pricing under AVC: for example the launch of new lines, obsolete stock clearance, and using continuous production facilities. It may be better for an undertaking to sell temporarily at a loss and make *some* return, than to make none at all. As paragraph 71 of *AKZO* only sets out a presumption, circumstances such as these could be recognised and the presumption rebutted. Two-sided markets[214] present a particular problem, as undertakings may choose to price by charging only one side of the market or charging very low prices on one side. Such a charging strategy may be perfectly rational, and not anti-competitive:

> As a result, the proper assessment of allegations of predatory pricing within a two-sided market must take into account the prices and costs on both sides of the market to ensure that undertakings are not incorrectly accused simply on the basis of following a widespread, and generally welfare-enhancing, pricing strategy that sets prices on one side at or near zero.[215]

In the Guidance Paper the Commission recognises that in two-sided markets it may be necessary to look at revenues and costs of both sides at the same time.[216]

c. Ascertaining Intention between AVC and ATC

Under the *AKZO* test the intention of the undertaking becomes the crucial factor when prices are in the 'grey' area between AVC and ATC. The test accepts that pricing at that level can be a rational, non-predatory strategy in certain circumstances because the undertaking will be covering the variable costs and at least some part of the fixed costs on every unit sold. However, all undertakings might be said to intend to eliminate their competitors by the very fact that they are participating in the struggle for custom in the marketplace. The Court presumably means intending to eliminate competitors by competition which is not on the merits (a better widget, better service, etc.), and

---

[210] P. Areeda and D. Turner, *Antitrust Law* (Little Brown, 1978), para. 715c.

[211] But cf. E. Elhauge, 'Why Above-Cost Price Cuts to Drive Out Entrants are not Predatory—And the Implications for Defining Costs and Market Power' (2003)112 *Yale LJ* 681, 710–711 ('The fact that marginal or variable costs are uniformly low in an industry thus raises no difficulty if one is careful to consider all (and only) costs that are variable during the period of alleged predation. Different problems might be raised, however, if the equally efficient rival has a different ratio of fixed to variable costs than the alleged predator, or if the alleged predatory price is timed after the predator has incurred a fixed or sunk cost that the rival must decide whether to incur in the future').

[212] *Deutsche Post* [2001] OJ L125/27. The Commission looked at the cost of providing the mail-order parcels service (which was open to competition) and deducted from it the costs of which it shared with the services in respect of which it had a USO. The incremental cost was the additional cost which DPAG incurred solely as a result of the mail-order service. The Commission disregarded the common fixed costs shared with the universal service, apparently because of the extra costs arising from the USO, see J. Temple Lang and R. O'Donoghue, 'Defining Legitimate Competition: How to Clarify Pricing Abuses under Article 82EC' (2002) 26 *Fordham Int'l LJ* 83, 156.

[213] See Section 8.D, p. 409.

[214] See Chap. 1, Section 10.B.vii.j, p. 81.

[215] Geradin et al., *EU Competition Law and Economics* (cited in n. 160), 4.527.

[216] Guidance Paper, para. 26, n.3.

therefore not, in the words of *Hoffmann-La Roche*, 'normal' competition, but the distinction between 'normal' price competition and predatory pricing is the very thing this test is trying to identify. 'Determined as part of a plan' seems to denote some degree of systematic and deliberate strategy and the EU Courts treat 'plan' to eliminate and 'intent' to eliminate as synonymous.[217]

A finding of intention to eliminate must be established 'on the basis of sound and consistent evidence'[218] which may be 'direct' or 'indirect'.[219] Documentary evidence from the allegedly predating undertaking is 'direct evidence' of an intention to predate. In *AKZO* eliminatory intention was derived partly from company documentation. However, words may be open to different interpretations and what seemed like an exhortationary address to the troops in the sales department at the time may read like threats of ruthless predatory intent months or years afterwards.[220] *AKZO* itself may have made proving intent more difficult as undertakings are now advised to be more careful in what they record. Nevertheless, in *Wanadoo* (*France Télécom*) the Commission relied, inter alia, upon internal documents to show that the undertaking (WIN) had dropped its price for residential high-speed broadband access in order to 'pre-empt' the developing market. WIN disputed the scope and significance of the documents, alleging that some were merely informal or impromptu. The GC pointed out that some of the incriminating words and phrases came from management level staff and were expressed in the context of formal presentations for the taking of a decision or of a very detailed framework letter[221] and did not consider the phrase 'our pre-emption of the ASDL market is imperative' could be read as anything other than a strategy to 'pre-empt'.[222] WIN claimed on appeal that this amounted to the GC finding a plan of predation on 'subjective' instead of 'objective' factors. The CJ rejected this, holding that the GC had deduced a 'strategy to pre-empt' from 'objective factors such as that of the undertaking's internal documents'.[223] It has been said that despite the GC's suggestions in *France Télécom* about the sufficiency of direct evidence such as internal documents in practice the Commission always relies on 'indirect' corroborative evidence as well.[224] The type of indirect evidence used is illustrated by *Tetra Pak II* where factors such as the duration and scale of the losses, and the tactics of specially importing the products into Italy in order to sell them at a loss there, were taken into account in identifying a predatory strategy.

The Commission indicates the evidence it will consider in identifying a predatory strategy in paragraphs 20, 65, and 66 of the Guidance Paper.[225]

D. THE *POST DANMARK* CASE

Post Danmark[226] was a ruling in a preliminary reference from a Danish court hearing an appeal from a decision of the competition authority (Konkurrencerådet)[227] in respect of the pricing practices

---

[217] Case T-83/91, *Tetra Pak International SA v. Commission* [1994] ECR II-755 (*Tetra Pak II*), para. 151; *France Télécom* (GC), para.197.

[218] *Tetra Pak II* (GC), para. 151.

[219] For a discussion of the required evidence generally see Geradin et al., *EU Competition Law and Economics* (cited in n. 160), 4.272–4.278.

[220] See, e.g., *Napier Brown/British Sugar* [1988] OJ L284/41, [1990] 4 CMLR 196 where an internal memo which said '[i]f we are to succeed in seeing off the Whitworths threat, we MUST attack on all fronts. It is time to get nasty!' did not go down well with the Commission.

[221] Case T-340/03, *France Télécom SA v. Commission* [2007] ECR II-107, para. 202.

[222] Case T-340/03, *France Télécom SA v. Commission* [2007] ECR II-107, para. 206.

[223] Case C-202/07 P, *France Télécom v. Commission* [2009] ECR I-2369, para. 98.

[224] Rousseva and Marquis, 'Hell Freezes Over' (cited in n. 2), 32, and available at <http://ssrn.com/abstract=2171693>.

[225] See Section 8.G, p. 417.

[226] Case C-209/10, *Post Danmark A/S v. Konkurrencerådet*, 27 March 2012.

[227] Confirmed by the appeals tribunal, Konkurrenceankenævnet.

of Post Danmark (PD) on the liberalised market for unaddressed mail in Denmark. PD had a statutory monopoly and USO in respect of normal addressed mail under a certain weight. For this purpose it had an infrastructure, a network covering the whole national territory, which it also used for its unaddressed mail business. A competitor on the unaddressed mail market claimed that PD was enticing away its three biggest customers through selective price reductions. The Konkurrencerådet could not establish that PD had intentionally sought to eliminate competition. Examining its costs by reference to the concept of average incremental cost (AIC) in order to take account of the shared infrastructure, the Konkurrencerådet found that in two cases (Spar and SuperBest) PD's prices were above ATC and in one (the Coop) they were below ATC but above AIC. As it found no intention to eliminate the Konkurrencerådet, following the *AKZO* criteria, held that PD had not abused its dominant position by predatory pricing. However, it found that PD had abused it by practising a policy of selective price reductions which amounted to price discrimination, in that it had pursued a pricing policy for the competitor's former customers which was different from its policy for its pre-existing customers, without being able to justify the difference on cost-related grounds.

The referring court defined 'incremental costs' in the case as those 'destined to disappear in the short and medium term (three to five years), if PD were to give up its business activity of distributing unaddressed mail' and the ATC as 'average incremental costs to which were added a portion, determined by estimation, of Post Danmark's common costs connected to activities other than those covered by the universal service obligation'.[228] As there were common costs arising from the use of the network infrastructure for both the USO obligations and the unaddressed mail, the costs of the USO could be reduced over three to five years if PD were to give up the unaddressed mail business. The Konkurrencerådet therefore included in its estimation of the average incremental costs (AIC) not only the fixed and variable costs attributable solely to distributing unaddressed mail but also a certain proportion of the common costs.[229] The CJ commented on this method of assessment that 'in the specific circumstances of the case...such a method of attribution would seem to seek to identify the great bulk of the costs attributable to the activity of unaddressed mail' (the CJ was not asked in the reference about the *correctness* of the assessment methodology).[230] As we have already seen[231] incremental cost normally includes only the fixed and variable costs incurred in providing the particular product or service, and none of the common costs.

On the abuse issue the CJ said that price discrimination cannot of itself suggest that there is an exclusionary abuse; that the prices above ATC could not be considered to have anti-competitive effects; and that selective low prices may not be considered to amount to an exclusionary abuse merely because the price is lower than ATC but higher than AIC.

Case C-209/10, *Post Danmark A/S* v. *Konkurrencerådet*, 27 March 2012

Court of Justice

35 ...it was found, among other things, that the price offered to the Coop group did not enable Post Danmark to cover the average total costs attributed to the activity of unaddressed mail distribution taken as a whole, but did enable it to cover the average incremental costs pertaining to that activity, as estimated by the Danish competition authorities.

---

[228] *Post Danmark*, para. 31.

[229] 75% of the attributable common costs of logistical capacity and 25% of non-attributable common costs, *Post Danmark*, paras 32–33.

[230] *Post Danmark*, para. 34. Mengozzi AG was very firmly in favour of using AIC rather than AVC, Opinion, paras. 33–37.

[231] See Section 7.C, p. 398.

36 Moreover, it is common ground that, in the present case, the prices offered to the Spar and SuperBest groups were assessed as being at a higher level than those average total costs, as estimated by those authorities. In those circumstances, it cannot be considered that such prices have anti-competitive effects.

37 As regards the prices charged the Coop group, a pricing policy such as that in issue in the main proceedings cannot be considered to amount to an exclusionary abuse simply because the price charged to a single customer by a dominant undertaking is lower than the average total costs attributed to the activity concerned, but higher than the average incremental costs pertaining to the latter, as respectively estimated in the case in the main proceedings.

38 Indeed, to the extent that a dominant undertaking sets its prices at a level covering the great bulk of the costs attributable to the supply of the goods or services in question, it will, as a general rule, be possible for a competitor as efficient as that undertaking to compete with those prices without suffering losses that are unsustainable in the long term.

39 It is for the court making the reference to assess the relevant circumstances of the case in the main proceedings in the light of the finding made in the previous paragraph. In any event, it is worth noting that it appears from the documents before the Court that Forbruger-Kontakt managed to maintain its distribution network despite losing the volume of mail related to the three customers involved and managed, in 2007, to win back the Coop group's custom and, since then, that of the Spar group.

40 If the court making the reference, after carrying out that assessment, should nevertheless make a finding of anti-competitive effects due to Post Danmark's actions, it should be recalled that it is open to a dominant undertaking to provide justification for behaviour that is liable to be caught by the prohibition under Article [102] (see, to this effect, Case 27/76 *United Brands and United Brands Continentaal* v *Commission*... paragraph 184; Joined Cases C-241/91 P and C-242/91 P *RTE and ITP* v *Commission*... paragraphs 54 and 55; and *TeliaSonera Sverige*, paragraphs 31 and 75).

...

45 ...On those grounds, the Court (Grand Chamber) hereby rules:

Article [102] must be interpreted as meaning that a policy by which a dominant undertaking charges low prices to certain major customers of a competitor may not be considered to amount to an exclusionary abuse merely because the price that undertaking charges one of those customers is lower than the average total costs attributed to the activity concerned, but higher than the average incremental costs pertaining to that activity, as estimated in the procedure giving rise to the case in the main proceedings. In order to assess the existence of anti-competitive effects in circumstances such as those of that case, it is necessary to consider whether that pricing policy, without objective justification, produces an actual or likely exclusionary effect, to the detriment of competition and, thereby, of consumers' interests.

The *Post Danmark* judgment is significant for the way it develops *AKZO* in respect both of the costs benchmarks which can be used and of the position where prices are between ATC and AVC but no intent to eliminate competitors has been shown.

The CJ noted that the Konkurrencerådet had recourse to incremental costs rather than the variable costs concept used in the *AKZO* case law[232] but accepted for the purposes of the ruling the Konkurrencerådet's use of the ATC and AIC benchmarks, whatever the peculiarities of their calculation (adding only the non-USO common costs to ATC and adding some common costs to AIC). AIC is lower than ATC but always higher than AVC,[233] so some of the prices in the case fell within the 'grey' area identified in *AKZO* between ATC and AVC where intent to eliminate is necessary for an abuse. PD's intention to eliminate had not been proved, so applying *AKZO* without further ado

---

[232] *Post Danmark*, para. 31.

[233] See the explanation of costs level, in Section 7.C, p. 398.

would have rendered these prices not abusive. However, the CJ still left it open to the national court to find that the pricing was abusive *if it made a finding of anti-competitive effects*.[234] The CJ clearly thought this would be unlikely because if, as here, the dominant undertaking is setting its prices at a level covering the bulk of its attributable costs, *as a general rule* an equally efficient competitor would be able to compete without suffering long-term unsustainable losses,[235] and in this case the competitor had actually remained on the market and won back some of the customers.[236] Although in paragraph 37 the CJ specifically talked about below ATC prices charged to a *single customer*, paragraph 38, to which paragraphs 39 and 40 refer ('it is for the court making the reference to assesses the relevant circumstances…in the light of the finding made in the previous paragraph') makes a general point about the ability of equally efficient competitors to compete. It is clear from paragraph 37 that mere selectivity alone does not make a below ATC price abusive.

It is reasonable to conclude from this that the CJ has added to the *AKZO* test in providing for anti-competitive effects as an alternative to intent where prices are between ATC and AIC. The question then arises whether effects could also be an alternative where prices are between AIC and AVC. It is illogical that effects should be relevant when prices are above AIC but not when they are below it, but it has been argued that given the 'indirect' evidence admissible to show intent, an intent-based test and an effects-based test may actually converge.[237]

E. THE 'MEETING COMPETITION' DEFENCE AND PREDATORY PRICING

In *France Télécom* the dominant undertaking, WIN, claimed that in pricing below cost it was only meeting competition and that it had an absolute right to 'align' its prices with its competitors. The CJ upheld the GC[238] in saying that it did not.

> ### Case C-202/07 P, *France Télécom* v. Commission [2009] ECR I-2369
>
> #### Court of Justice
>
> 43 Accordingly, in paragraph 176 of the judgment under appeal, the [General Court] noted, first, that recital 315 of the contested decision contests WIN's right to align its prices on those charged by its competitors only in so far as the exercise of that option 'would result in its not recovering the costs of the service in question'.
>
> 44 Next, the Court explained, in paragraphs 178 to 182 of the judgment under appeal, the reasons why such a right to align could be based neither on Commission Decision 83/462/EEC of 29 July 1983 relating to a proceeding under Article [102] (IV/30.698—ECS/AKZO: interim measures)…nor the judgment in *AKZO v Commission*, upon which the appellant relies.
>
> 45 Lastly, the Court determined whether limiting WIN's right to align its prices on those of its competitors, inasmuch as it 'would result in its not recovering the costs of the service in question', was compatible with Community law.

[234] *Post Danmark A/S v. Konkurrencerådet*, 27 March 2012, para. 40.

[235] *Post Danmark A/S v. Konkurrencerådet*, 27 March 2012, para. 38.

[236] On 13 February 2013 the Danish Supreme Court, applying this ruling, overturned the Konkurrencerådet's decision.

[237] Rousseva and Marquis, 'Hell Freezes Over: A Climate Change for Assessing Exclusionary Conduct under Article 102 TFEU' (cited in n. 2). For general comments on *Post Danmark*, see S. Barazza, 'Post Danmark: the CJEU Calls for an Effect-based Assessment of Pricing Policies' (2012) 3 *Journal of European Competition Law and Practice* 466; R. Subiotto and D. Little, 'The Application of Article 102 TFEU by the European Commission and the European Courts' (2012) 3 *Journal of European Competition Law and Practice* 175.

[238] Case T-340/03, *France Télécom SA v. Commission* [2007] ECR II-107.

46 To that end, the Court refers in paragraphs 185 and 186 of the judgment under appeal to the Community case-law according to which Article [102] imposes specific obligations on undertakings in a dominant position. In particular, the Court recalled that, although the fact that an undertaking is in a dominant position cannot deprive it of the right to protect its own commercial interests if they are attacked and such an undertaking must be allowed the right to take such reasonable steps as it deems appropriate to protect those interests, it is not possible, however, to countenance such behaviour if its actual purpose is to strengthen that dominant position and abuse it.

47 It was on the basis of that case-law that the [General Court] thus found, in paragraph 187 of the judgment under appeal, that WIN cannot rely on any absolute right to align its prices on those of its competitors in order to justify its conduct where that conduct constitutes an abuse of its dominant position.

48 Nor can the appellant object that the Court merely made such a finding without ascertaining whether, in the present case, WIN's conduct was abusive. The Court specifically rejected, inter alia in paragraphs 195 to 218 and 224 to 230 of the judgment under appeal, all the appellant's arguments seeking to question whether that abusive conduct existed, as found in the contested decision.

It should be noted that the CJ said that a dominant undertaking does not have an *absolute* right to align. The problem for a dominant undertaking pleading a meeting competition defence in predatory pricing cases is that the *AKZO* test is formulated in intent terms. If the undertaking is pricing below cost and the intent is presumed (below AVC), or has been proved (in the 'grey area') then that is the end of the matter. The 'right to align' has been taken away by the fact of the undertaking's dominance, which imposes on it 'specific obligations' (paragraph 46) which, as the GC said, deprives it 'of the right to adopt a course of conduct or take measures which are not in themselves abuses and which would even be unobjectionable if adopted or taken by non-dominant undertakings'.[239] The GC rejected the plea that below-cost pricing could be justified by the efficiencies to be garnered through economies of scale.[240]

F. RECOUPMENT

(i) The Issue of the Possibility of Recoupment

The concept of predatory pricing rests on the assumption that the predator sacrifices short-term profits for future gains. It hinges on the possibility that the predator can recoup its losses, i.e. that short-term loss of profitability is more than compensated for by long-run profitability when, after the competitor's exit, the undertaking can raise prices to monopoly level. If there are no barriers to entry to the market the undertaking will not be able to recoup if it continually has to price low in order to fight off new competitors (although predation may constitute a barrier to entry). The economics literature emphasises that the ability to recoup is central to recognising predatory pricing as a rational strategy in certain conditions. It is another matter, however, to say that it should be *necessary* for the party alleging predation to show that recoupment is possible or likely[241] before predatory pricing can be found.

The present position in the US is that the courts do not find predatory pricing to have occurred unless the plaintiff demonstrates that the alleged predator had a dangerous probability of recouping its investment in below-cost prices. This stems from the Supreme Court ruling in *Brooke Group Ltd* v. *Brown & Williamson Tobacco Corp* in 1993.[242] It means in effect that even if the plaintiff can show

---

[239] Case T-340/03, *France Télécom SA* v. *Commission* [2007] ECR II-107, para. 186.

[240] Case T-340/03, *France Télécom SA* v. *Commission* [2007] ECR II-107, para. 217.

[241] Depending on the standard of proof which is applied.

[242] 509 US 209, 113 S.Ct 2578.

below-cost prices[243] and an anti-competitive intent, there will be no antitrust violation.[244] The result of this, especially when wedded to the sceptical judicial attitude to predatory pricing shown in the *Matsushita* case,[245] is that it is very hard for predatory pricing actions to succeed in the US courts.[246]

There are good arguments against making feasibility of recoupment part of the legal test. There are problems wherever the burden of proof is placed, predicting recoupment is difficult, and the 'recoupment' gained by the firm may, for example, consist of deterring entrants in other markets, which is impossible to measure. Temple Lang and O'Donoghue approve of the present position of EU law in not having a strict recoupment requirement.

J. Temple Lang and R. O'Donoghue, 'Defining Legitimate Competition: How to Clarify Pricing Abuses under Article 82EC' (2002) 26 *Fordham Int'l LJ* 83, 144–145

There are, however, reasons to treat a strict recoupment requirement with caution. First, it is often difficult to prove what the dominant company could do successfully at an unspecified time in the future. It would be necessary to show that there would be no entry by more competitive or more determined rivals, and that when the dominant company increased its price, it would not attract new entry. It would also be necessary to show that the price elasticity of the product was such that, although buyers were accustomed to low prices, they would be willing to pay significantly higher ones in the future. All of this suggests that the burden of proof is crucial. If the burden of proof was on the party alleging illegal low prices, it would make it difficult to bring a successful case. If the burden of proof was on the dominant company, it would be obliged to prove a negative, that is, to prove that it would be unable to recoup its losses if it tried to do so.

Second, predatory pricing by a dominant company may have anti-competitive effects even if the dominant company does not or could not recoup its losses. The most effective form of predatory pricing is one where a company discourages market entry, or causes exit, by signaling to actual or potential competitors that their profitability in the market in question will be low as long as the dominant company is price leader in that market. This signaling would be more effective, and the effects of it would last longer, if the dominant company did not have to recover its losses, but held its prices only a little above competitive levels. This discouraging or signaling effect is particularly likely to be important if the dominant company is active on several markets, because predatory pricing on one market may discourage market entry on the others. This is particularly important in air transport, where predatory pricing, if it occurred on one route, would discourage entry on the other routes on which the dominant airline was operating.

Finally, predatory pricing may have anti-competitive effects even if the rival is not forced out of the market, but instead decides to raise its prices to approximately the prices of the dominant company. In particular, in a concentrated market predatory pricing may demonstrate the dominant company's ability and willingness to retaliate against aggressive pricing by a competitor, and so may give rise to oligopolistic pricing. In such circumstances it would be extremely difficult to prove that recoupment had occurred, even if it had.

---

[243] They were below AVC in *Brooke Group*.

[244] *Brooke Group* was an action brought under the Robinson–Patman Act, 15 U.S.C. § 13(a) on price discrimination but the analysis applies equally to section 2 of the Sherman Act. See J. B. Baker, 'Predatory Pricing after *Brooke Group*: An Economic Perspective' (1994) 62 *Antitrust LJ* 585.

[245] *Matsushita Elec. Indust. Co Ltd v. Zenith Radio Corp*, 475 US 574 (1986), see n. 190.

[246] It is not difficult for a properly advised defendant to raise sufficient doubts as to the possibility of recoupment. The question of how courts can judge the possibility of recoupment is discussed in C. Scott Hemphill, 'The Role of Recoupment in Predatory Pricing Analyses' (2001) *Stan LR* 1581.

(ii) The EU Case Law

EU law differs from the US law. The CJ did not expressly consider whether predation was a plausible strategy for AKZO although it is argued that it is implicit in paragraph 71.[247] The question of whether a possibility or likelihood of recoupment is part of the test for predatory pricing was raised in *Tetra Pak II* and answered in the negative—at least in the circumstances of that case, where the principles laid down in *AKZO* were confirmed and developed.[248] Tetra Pak's share of the dominated market (aseptic cartons) was over 90 per cent although, as already discussed, the impugned pricing conduct took place on the unrelated non-dominated market.

One of the abuses found in *Tetra Pak II* was that the undertaking had engaged in predatory pricing in the non-aseptic carton market. This included selling at below AVC in Italy. On appeal Tetra Pak argued that economic theory found predatory pricing to be plausible only if losses can be recouped after the competitor's exit. The Commission had not found that it did have a reasonable chance of recoupment: ergo it could not be guilty of predation. The CJ held that the Commission did not have to prove that Tetra Pak could recoup.

Case C-333/94 P, *Tetra Pak International SA* v. *Commission* [1996] ECR I-5951

Court of Justice

39. In its fourth plea, Tetra Pak submits that the [General Court] erred in law when, at paragraph 150 of the judgment under appeal, it characterised Tetra Pak's prices in the non-aseptic sector as predatory without accepting that it was necessary for that purpose to establish that it had a reasonable prospect of recouping the losses so incurred.

40. Tetra Pak considers that the possibility of recouping the losses incurred as a result of predatory sales is a constitutive element in the notion of predatory pricing. That is clear, it claims, from paragraph 71 of the *AKZO* judgment. Since, however, both the Commission and the [General Court] accept that sales below cost took place only on the non-aseptic markets, on which Tetra Pak was not found to hold a dominant position, it had no realistic chance of recouping its losses later.

41. In *AKZO* this Court did indeed sanction the existence of two different methods of analysis for determining whether an undertaking has practised predatory pricing. First, prices below average variable costs must always be considered abusive. In such a case, there is no conceivable economic purpose other than the elimination of a competitor, since each item produced and sold entails a loss for the undertaking. Secondly, prices below average total costs but above average variable costs are only to be considered abusive if an intention to eliminate can be shown.

42. At paragraph 150 of the judgment under appeal, the [General Court] carried out the same examination as did this Court in *AKZO*. For sales of non-aseptic cartons in Italy between 1976 and 1981, it found that prices were considerably lower than average variable costs. Proof of intention to eliminate competitors was therefore not necessary. In 1982, prices for those cartons lay between average variable costs and average total costs. For that reason, in paragraph 151 of its judgment, the [General Court] was at pains to establish—and the appellant has not criticized it in that regard—that Tetra Pak intended to eliminate a competitor.

43. The [General Court] was also right, at paragraphs 189 to 191 of the judgment under appeal, to apply exactly the same reasoning to sales of non-aseptic machines in the United Kingdom between 1981 and 1984.

---

[247] See para. 136 of the Opinion of Fennelly AG in Cases C-395 and 396/96 P, *Compagnie Maritime Belge and others* v. *Commission* [2000] ECR I-1365.

[248] Case C-333/94 P, *Tetra Pak International SA* v. *Commission* [1996] ECR I-5951, affirming Case T-83/91, *Tetra Pak Rausing* v. *Commission* [1994] ECR II-755, and Commission decision [1992] OJ L72/1.

44. Furthermore, it would not be appropriate, in the circumstances of the present case, to require in addition proof that Tetra Pak had a realistic chance of recouping its losses. It must be possible to penalize predatory pricing whenever there is a risk that competitors will be eliminated. The [General Court] found, at paragraphs 151 and 191 of its judgment, that there was such a risk in this case. The aim pursued, which is to maintain undistorted competition, rules out waiting until such a strategy leads to the actual elimination of competitors.

In paragraph 44 the CJ stressed that the important factor in the determination of predation is the risk that competitors will be eliminated. This could be shorthand for saying that once that happened Tetra Pak would be able to raise prices. Economic theory, however, suggests that the possibility of recoupment can only be judged after a thorough analysis of the structure of the market and other factors. The CJ did not say in paragraph 44 that it would *never* be necessary to show the feasibility of recoupment, but only that it would not be appropriate *in the circumstances of the present case*. Those circumstances included the fact that Tetra Pak had a quasi-monopoly and that the alleged predation was on a market distinct from the dominated one (so that Tetra Pak could cross-subsidise). Further, there was clear evidence from the data uncovered by the Commission that Tetra Pak was pursuing a deliberate strategy of eliminating competitors.

In *Compagnie Maritime Belge* Advocate General Fennelly considered that the possibility of recoupment should be an essential part of the test for predatory pricing[249] but the CJ did not address the point. The GC, however, did deal with the issue in *France Télécom*.[250] It held that proof of recoupment was not a precondition to a finding of predatory pricing.[251] On appeal to the CJ Advocate General Mazák considered that in the light of paragraph 44 of *Tetra Pak II* (no need '*in the circumstances of the present case*') proof of the possibility of recoupment should be required as without that possibility 'consumers and their interests should, in principle not be harmed'.[252] However, the CJ upheld the GC in the most trenchant terms. It recited the *AKZO* and *Tetra Pak II* case law and said that EU law does not require proof of the possibility of recoupment. Such proof might, nevertheless, be a relevant factor in excluding economic justification for below AVC pricing or assist in establishing an eliminatory plan (paragraph 111). The CJ also considers in paragraph 107 that the abuse arises from the objective of elimination of competitors—there is no mention of effects.

Case C-202/07P, *France Télécom SA* v. *Commission* [2009] ECR I-2369

Court of Justice

103 In considering the merits of the first part of this ground of appeal, it is necessary to note at the outset that, according to settled case-law, Article [102] is an application of the general objective of European Community action laid down by Article 3(1)(g) EC, namely, the institution of a system ensuring that competition in the common market is not distorted. Thus, the dominant position referred to in Article [102] relates to a position of economic strength enjoyed by an undertaking which enables it to prevent effective competition being maintained on the relevant market by affording it the power to behave to an appreciable extent independently of its competitors, its customers and ultimately of the consumers (Case 85/76 *Hoffmann-La Roche v Commission*...paragraph 38).

---

[249] Para. 136 of his Opinion in Cases C-395 and 396/96 P, *Compagnie Maritime Belge and others v. Commission* [2000] ECR I-1365.

[250] Case T-340/03, *France Télécom SA v. Commission* [2007] ECR II-107.

[251] Both above and below AVC pricing was involved.

[252] Case C-202/07P, *France Télécom SA v. Commission*, paras. 73–74 of the Opinion.

104 In that context, in prohibiting the abuse of a dominant market position in so far as trade between Member States is capable of being affected, Article [102] refers to conduct which is such as to influence the structure of a market where the degree of competition is already weakened and which, through recourse to methods different from those governing normal competition in products or services on the basis of the transactions of commercial operators, has the effect of hindering the maintenance of the degree of competition still existing in the market or the growth of that competition (*Hoffman-La Roche v Commission*, paragraph 91; Case 322/81 *Nederlandsche Banden-Industrie-Michelin v Commission*...paragraph 70; *AKZO v Commission*, paragraph 69; and Case C-95/04 P *British Airways v Commission*...paragraph 66).

105 Therefore, since Article [102] refers not only to practices which may cause damage to consumers directly, but also to those which are detrimental to them through their impact on an effective competition structure (Case 6/72 *Europemballage and Continental Can v Commission*...paragraph 26), an undertaking which holds a dominant position has a special responsibility not to allow its behaviour to impair genuine undistorted competition on the common market (*Nederlandsche Banden-Industrie-Michelin v Commission*, paragraph 57).

106 As the Court has already stated, it follows that Article [102] prohibits a dominant undertaking from eliminating a competitor and thereby strengthening its position by using methods other than those which come within the scope of competition on the basis of quality. From that point of view, not all competition by means of price can be regarded as legitimate (*AKZO v Commission*, paragraph 70).

107 In particular, it must be found that an undertaking abuses its dominant position where, in a market the competition structure of which is already weakened by reason precisely of the presence of that undertaking, it operates a pricing policy the sole economic objective of which is to eliminate its competitors with a view, subsequently, to profiting from the reduction of the degree of competition still existing in the market.

108 In order to assess the lawfulness of the pricing policy applied by a dominant undertaking, the Court, in paragraph 74 of *AKZO v Commission*, relied on pricing criteria based on the costs incurred by the dominant undertaking and on its strategy.

109 Thus, the Court of Justice has held, first, that prices below average variable costs must be considered prima facie abusive inasmuch as, in applying such prices, an undertaking in a dominant position is presumed to pursue no other economic objective save that of eliminating its competitors. Secondly, prices below average total costs but above average variable costs are to be considered abusive only where they are fixed in the context of a plan having the purpose of eliminating a competitor (see *AKZO v Commission*, paragraphs 70 and 71, and *Tetra Pak v Commission*, paragraph 41).

110 Accordingly, contrary to what the appellant claims, it does not follow from the case-law of the Court that proof of the possibility of recoupment of losses suffered by the application, by an undertaking in a dominant position, of prices lower than a certain level of costs constitutes a necessary precondition to establishing that such a pricing policy is abusive. In particular, the Court has taken the opportunity to dispense with such proof in circumstances where the eliminatory intent of the undertaking at issue could be presumed in view of that undertaking's application of prices lower than average variable costs (see, to that effect, *Tetra Pak v Commission*, paragraph 44).

111 That interpretation does not, of course, preclude the Commission from finding such a possibility of recoupment of losses to be a relevant factor in assessing whether or not the practice concerned is abusive, in that it may, for example where prices lower than average variable costs are applied, assist in excluding economic justifications other than the elimination of a competitor, or, where prices below average total costs but above average variable costs are applied, assist in establishing that a plan to eliminate a competitor exists.

112 Moreover, the lack of any possibility of recoupment of losses is not sufficient to prevent the undertaking concerned reinforcing its dominant position, in particular, following the withdrawal from the market of one or a number of its competitors, so that the degree of competition existing on the market, already

weakened precisely because of the presence of the undertaking concerned, is further reduced and customers suffer loss as a result of the limitation of the choices available to them.

113 The [General Court] was right therefore to hold, in paragraph 228 of the judgment under appeal, that demonstrating that it is possible to recoup losses is not a necessary precondition for a finding of predatory pricing.

(iii) Recoupment in the Guidance Paper

The Guidance Paper does not mention the word 'recoupment'. The Commission, indicating when it will intervene, nevertheless says that consumers are most likely to be harmed if the dominant undertaking can reasonably expect an increase in market power after its conduct has ended.[253] An increase in market power, however, does not necessarily denote an ability to recoup, which will depend on the specific circumstances.[254] The Commission will intervene not only if prices can be increased again, but also if the conduct could prevent or delay a lowering of prices.

Guidance on the Commission's Enforcement Priorities in Applying Article 82 of the EC Treaty to Abusive Exclusionary Conduct by Dominant Undertakings [2009] OJ C45/2

70. Generally speaking, consumers are likely to be harmed if the dominant undertaking can reasonably expect its market power after the predatory conduct comes to an end to be greater than it would have been had the undertaking not engaged in that conduct in the first place, that is to say, if the undertaking is likely to be in a position to benefit from the sacrifice.

71. This does not mean that the Commission will only intervene if the dominant undertaking would be likely to be able to increase its prices above the level persisting in the market before the conduct. It is sufficient, for instance, that the conduct would be likely to prevent or delay a decline in prices that would otherwise have occurred. Identifying consumer harm is not a mechanical calculation of profits and losses, and proof of overall profits is not required. Likely consumer harm may be demonstrated by assessing the likely foreclosure effect of the conduct, combined with consideration of other factors, such as entry barriers.... In this context, the Commission will also consider possibilities of re-entry.

G. PREDATORY PRICING IN THE GUIDANCE PAPER AND THE SACRIFICE PRINCIPLE

The Guidance Paper states that the principle that the Commission will employ in deciding whether to intervene in a possible predatory pricing case (in pursuance of the general as efficient competitor analysis) is whether the undertaking deliberately incurs losses or foregoes profits in the short term ('sacrifice') so as to foreclose actual or potential competitors with a view to maintaining or strengthening market power thereby causing consumer harm. The Guidance Paper reflects the *AKZO* test but the Commission will use AAC and LRAIC rather than AVC and ATC in assessing the 'sacrifice'.[255]

---

[253] The reference in para. 70 of the Guidance Paper to sacrifice is to the 'profit sacrifice' principle in the Guidance Paper noted in Section 8.G.

[254] See E. Rousseva, *Rethinking Exclusionary Abuses in EU Competition Law* (Hart Publishing, 2010), 408.

[255] The Commission had already used the LRAIC standard in the *Deutsche Post AG* decision in 2001, [2001] OJ L125/27. See also the Notice on the Application of the Competition Rules to Access Agreements in the Telecommunications Sector, [1998] OJ C265/2, paras. 114 and 115.

Pricing below AAC (which is usually the same as AVC[256]) is clear evidence of sacrifice. LRAIC and ATC are the same in single-product undertakings but LRAIC may be lower in the case of multi-product undertakings. Subsequent to the Guidance Paper the CJ accepted the use of LRAIC in *Post Danmark*, as already discussed. In paragraph 74 the Commission expressly does not rule out justification by efficiencies but considers that the conditions in the Guidance Paper[257] are unlikely to be satisfied in cases of predatory pricing.

Guidance on the Commission's Enforcement Priorities in Applying Article 82 of the EC Treaty to Abusive Exclusionary Conduct by Dominant Undertakings [2009] OJ C45/2

63. In line with its enforcement priorities, the Commission will generally intervene where there is evidence showing that a dominant undertaking engages in predatory conduct by deliberately incurring losses or foregoing profits in the short term (referred to hereafter as 'sacrifice'), so as to foreclose or be likely to foreclose one or more of its actual or potential competitors with a view to strengthening or maintaining its market power, thereby causing consumer harm…

(a) Sacrifice

64. Conduct will be viewed by the Commission as entailing a sacrifice if, by charging a lower price for all or a particular part of its output over the relevant time period, or by expanding its output over the relevant time period, the dominant undertaking incurred or is incurring losses that could have been avoided. The Commission will take AAC as the appropriate starting point for assessing whether the dominant undertaking incurred or is incurring avoidable losses. If a dominant undertaking charges a price below AAC for all or part of its output, it is not recovering the costs that could have been avoided by not producing that output: it is incurring a loss that could have been avoided [40]. Pricing below AAC will thus in most cases be viewed by the Commission as a clear indication of sacrifice…

65. However, the concept of sacrifice does not only include pricing below AAC…In order to show a predatory strategy, the Commission may also investigate whether the allegedly predatory conduct led in the short term to net revenues lower than could have been expected from a reasonable alternative conduct, that is to say, whether the dominant undertaking incurred a loss that it could have avoided…The Commission will not compare the actual conduct with hypothetical or theoretical alternatives that might have been more profitable. Only economically rational and practicable alternatives will be considered which, taking into account the market conditions and business realities facing the dominant undertaking, can realistically be expected to be more profitable.

66. In some cases it will be possible to rely upon direct evidence consisting of documents from the dominant undertaking which clearly show a predatory strategy…such as a detailed plan to sacrifice in order to exclude a competitor, to prevent entry or to pre-empt the emergence of a market, or evidence of concrete threats of predatory action…

(b) Anti-competitive foreclosure

67. If sufficient reliable data are available, the Commission will apply the equally efficient competitor analysis, described in paragraphs 25 to 27, to determine whether the conduct is capable of harming consumers. Normally only pricing below LRAIC is capable of foreclosing as efficient competitors from the market.

68. In addition to the factors already mentioned in paragraph 20, the Commission will generally investigate whether and how the suspected conduct reduces the likelihood that competitors will compete. For instance, if the dominant undertaking is better informed about cost or other market conditions, or can distort market signals about profitability, it may engage in predatory conduct so as to influence the

---

[256] Guidance Paper, para. 26, n.2.
[257] Guidance Paper, para. 30, see Section 5.D, p. 390.

expectations of potential entrants and thereby deter entry. If the conduct and its likely effects are felt on multiple markets and/or in successive periods of possible entry, the dominant undertaking may be shown to be seeking a reputation for predatory conduct. If the targeted competitor is dependent on external financing, substantial price decreases or other predatory conduct by the dominant undertaking could adversely affect the competitor's performance so that its access to further financing may be seriously undermined.

69. The Commission does not consider that it is necessary to show that competitors have exited the market in order to show that there has been anti-competitive foreclosure. The possibility cannot be excluded that the dominant undertaking may prefer to prevent the competitor from competing vigorously and have it follow the dominant undertaking's pricing, rather than eliminate it from the market altogether. Such disciplining avoids the risk inherent in eliminating competitors, in particular the risk that the assets of the competitor are sold at a low price and stay in the market, creating a new low cost entrant.

...

72. It may be easier for the dominant undertaking to engage in predatory conduct if it selectively targets specific customers with low prices, as this will limit the losses incurred by the dominant undertaking.

73. It is less likely that the dominant undertaking engages in predatory conduct if the conduct concerns a low price applied generally for a long period of time.

(c) Efficiencies

74. In general it is considered unlikely that predatory conduct will create efficiencies. However, provided that the conditions set out in Section III D are fulfilled, the Commission will consider claims by a dominant undertaking that the low pricing enables it to achieve economies of scale or efficiencies related to expanding the market.

In a footnote to paragraph 63 of the Guidance Paper the Commission specifically says that it may pursue predatory practices by dominant undertakings on secondary markets on which they are not yet dominant. This may particularly be so where a dominant undertaking on a market protected by a legal monopoly uses its profits there to cross-subsidise its activities in another market. Cross-subsidisation has never been held to be an abuse *in itself*. It is the below-cost prices on the subsidised market, or other abusive practices, which may infringe Article 102.[258]

H. PREDATORY PRICING AND NEW ECONOMY MARKETS

We have noted previously the particular characteristics of markets in the new economy.[259] One of these is the 'tipping' effect, whereby the competitor who wins takes most (or all) of the market because its product or service becomes the standard. Predatory pricing may therefore be a highly rational strategy in such markets: low pricing may achieve the critical mass of customers which results in the undertaking winning the competition 'for' the market. Further, high technology markets commonly have very high fixed costs and very low variable costs (it costs Microsoft a great deal to develop a new software product and very little to reproduce another copy of it once it is on the market) which may confuse predatory pricing tests based on average variable cost.

---

[258] See *Deutsche Post* [2001] OJ L125/27; Case C-333/94 P, *Tetra Pak International SA v. Commission* [1996] ECR I-5951.

[259] See Chap. 1, Section 7.E, p. 54 and Chap. 6.

France Télécom, discussed in Section 8.E, concerned a new economy market, the pricing of WIN's ADSL services.[260] WIN was a 72 per cent owned subsidiary of France Télécom which at the relevant time had almost 100 per cent of the wholesale ADSL services for internet service providers. The Commission found that in one period WIN's prices were below AVC and thereafter they were above AVC but still below ATC.[261] It also found that the undertaking deliberately pursued a pricing policy which made losses but 'was designed to take the lion's share of a booming market at the expense of other competitors'.[262] Indeed, one competitor went out of business. WIN claimed that its conduct was perfectly rational, in that its pricing attracted new customers who would be profitable in the end (in less than five years). It said that this was a rational way of developing a new market and reaching profitability in the medium term. The Commission, however, saw this reasoning as demonstrating that the pricing *was* predatory, '[i]ndeed, the recoupment of initial losses over a certain period of time is in the most common settings the very objective of a predatory pricing behaviour... Admitting WIN's reasoning in this respect would have led to the conclusion that by essence predatory pricing can simply not exist.'[263] The Commission also rejected the argument that it was inappropriate for it to intervene in a market at a nascent stage.[264] The Commission fined WIN €10.35 million and later placed WIN's accounts under review until the end of 2006, to ensure month by month that its prices were not anti-competitive.

The decision demonstrated the Commission's disinclination to alter the fundamentals of the predatory pricing rules to take account of the peculiar characteristics of a new economy market. The Commission stood firm against the argument that it should adopt a 'hands off' approach while the ADSL market developed. The decision was upheld by the GC and the CJ.[265] Nevertheless, it is doubtful that normal predatory pricing rules can be applied to some markets in the new economy without Type I errors. We have already mentioned the problems of two-sided markets.[266] As Rato and Petit say of the ICT sector 'the fact that no price is charged to consumers does not mean that no price is charged at all, or that none of the dominant firm's costs are recouped'. They point out that the fact that no charge is made for a particular service does not mean that no price is charged to all customers, as often customers can use the basic service for free and then are charged when they move on to premium services with added features.[267]

It is worth noting that the situation in *France Télécom* was in effect a type of margin squeeze but because of the relationship between WIN and France Télécom at the relevant time it was not analysed as such. It was therefore dealt with as predatory pricing rather than a margin squeeze.[268]

I. SELECTIVE ABOVE-COST PRICING

As can be seen from *AKZO*, predatory pricing may involve not just low prices to all customers but price discrimination[269]— selectively targeting the low prices on certain customers so that they are

---

[260] *Wanadoo* COMP/38.233, [2005] 5 CMLR 120, IP/03/1025. See also R. Klotz and J. Fehrenbach, (2003) 3 *Competition Policy Newsletter* (Autumn 2003), 10.

[261] The Commission calculated the costs in a way which it claimed was highly favourable to Wanadoo, e.g., treating customer acquisition costs as capital expenditures. This lowered Wanadoo's AVC (and therefore the significant cost level for the *AKZO* test).

[262] *Wanadoo* COMP/38.233, [2005] 5 CMLR 120, IP/03/1025; Klotz and Fehrenbach (cited in n. 260), 11.

[263] Klotz and Fehrenbach (cited in n. 260), 12.

[264] See Chap. 1, Section 7.E, p. 54.

[265] Case T-340/03, [2007] ECR II-107 and Case C-202/07 P, *France Télécom v. Commission* [2007] ECR I-2369.

[266] In Section 8.C.ii.b, p. 407.

[267] M. Rato and N. Petit, 'Abuse of Dominance in Technology-Enabled Markets: Established Standards Reconsidered?' (2013) 9 *European Competition Journal* 1, 50–51.

[268] For margin squeeze, see Section 9, p. 426 ff.

[269] For price discrimination generally, see Section 7.B, p. 396.

charged less than others for the same product. The Guidance Paper recognises this practice in paragraph 72. There are cases, however, in which prices which were *not* below costs, and did not involve the dominant undertakings in making losses (although they may have made less profit than previously), have also been held to infringe Article 102. Such selective low pricing can be seen as a species of predatory pricing, although if predatory pricing is defined as below-cost pricing to eliminate competitors, it is *not* properly described as such. The cases where selective above-cost prices have been held to be abusive—*Compagnie Maritime Belge*[270] and *Irish Sugar*[271]— both had special features, and in the later case of *Post Danmark*[272] the CJ clarified that prices above average incremental cost are presumed to be legal.

In *Compagnie Maritime Belge* the Commission found that undertakings in a collective dominant position had engaged in predatory conduct through selective low pricing targeted at a competitor's customers.[273] The undertakings were parties to a liner conference[274] (CEWAL) which faced competition from an independent shipping line (G & C). Among the practices it adopted to counter this threat was the use of so-called 'fighting ships', specially designated CEWAL vessels whose sailing dates were close to those of G & C ships. CEWAL dropped the rates on fighting ships to match those of G & C. The Commission condemned this conduct as an abuse of CEWAL's collective dominant position[275] without an analysis of CEWAL's costs. The prices caused the members of CEWAL some revenue losses, but did not appear to have been below their total costs. The shipping lines appealed, inter alia, on the grounds that as their prices were not predatory within the *AKZO* test they were not an abuse.

The GC upheld the Commission, focusing on CEWAL's intent to eliminate G & C and the possible effect of its actions.[276] The GC rejected the argument that CEWAL was merely trying to *meet* rather than *beat* the competition and said that its response to the threat from G & C was not reasonable and proportionate.[277] The Commission was therefore justified in holding that the response by CEWAL's members was an abuse of their collective dominant position. Advocate General Fennelly took the view that this was a case of a 'super-dominant' entity setting out to exclude a competitor. In such a situation targeted, selective price cuts designed to eliminate would be an abuse regardless of the relationship of the prices to costs.[278]

The CJ held that the prices charged were abusive,[279] but its judgment was couched in narrower terms than the wide sweep of the Advocate General's Opinion. It concentrated on the specifics of the case.

---

[270] Cases C-395 and 396/96 P, *Compagnie Maritime Belge and Others v. Commission* [2000] ECR I-1365.

[271] Case T–228/97, *Irish Sugar plc v. Commission* [1999] ECR II-2969, *aff'd* Case C-497/99P, *Irish Sugar plc v. Commission* [2001] ECR I-5333.

[272] Case C-209/10, *Post Danmark A/S v. Konkurrencerådet*, 27 March 2012.

[273] *CEWAL* [1993] OJ L34/20, [1995] 5 CMLR 198. An earlier Commission decision which condemned low prices without regard to costs, *Eurofix–Bauco* [1988] OJ L65/19, was a tying case.

[274] A 'liner conference', according to the UNCTAD Liner Code, is a group of two or more vessel-operators providing international liner services for carrying cargo on a particular route or routes within specified geographical limits, which has an agreement or arrangement within the framework of which they operate under uniform or common freight rates and other agreed conditions. At the time of the case Council Reg. 4056/86, [1986] OJ L378/4, provided a (generous) block exemption for liner conferences which, inter alia, allowed horizontal price-fixing between the members of the conference. Art. 8 of Reg. 4056/86 provided that an abuse of a dominant position within Art. 102 was prohibited and that the Commission had power to withdraw the benefit of the exemption if the exemption brought about effects incompatible with Art. 102. This provision was referred to by the GC in Cases T-68/89, etc. *Società Italiana Vetro Spa v. Commission* [1992] ECR II-1403, para. 359, as support for interpreting Art. 102 as applying to collective dominance. Reg. 4056/86 was repealed by Council Reg. 1419/2006, [2006] OJ L269/1.

[275] For the collective dominance aspects of the case, see Chap. 6.

[276] Case T-24/93, etc. *Compagnie Maritime Belge Transports v. Commission* [1996] ECR II-1201.

[277] Case T-24/93, etc. *Compagnie Maritime Belge Transports v. Commission* [1996] ECR II-1201, para. 148.

[278] Cases C-395 and 396/96P *Compagnie Maritime Belge Transports SA v. EC Commission* [2000] ECR I-1365, Opinion of AG Fennelly, para 137.

[279] The fines on the shipping lines were, however, annulled for procedural reasons as the Commission had not stated in its Statement of Objections that it intended to impose fines on the individual members. They were

Cases C-395 and 396/96 P, *Compagnie Maritime Belge and Others* v. *Commission* [2000] ECR-1365

Court of Justice

111. The third ground of appeal concerns the question whether the alleged abuse, as defined in the contested decision and the defence, can properly be so characterised.

112. It is settled case-law that the list of abusive practices contained in Article [102] of the Treaty is not an exhaustive enumeration of the abuses of a dominant position prohibited by the Treaty (Case 6/72 *Europemballage and Continental Can* v. *Commission*...paragraph 26).

113. It is, moreover, established that, in certain circumstances, abuse may occur if an undertaking in a dominant position strengthens that position in such a way that the degree of dominance reached substantially fetters competition (*Europemballage and Continental Can*, paragraph 26).

114. Furthermore, the actual scope of the special responsibility imposed on a dominant undertaking must be considered in the light of the specific circumstances of each case which show that competition has been weakened (Case C-333/94 P *Tetra Pak* v. *Commission*..., paragraph 24).

115. The maritime transport market is a very specialised sector. It is because of the specificity of that market that the Council established, in Regulation No. 4056/86, a set of competition rules different from that which applies to other economic sectors. The authorisation granted for an unlimited period to liner conferences to co-operate in fixing rates for maritime transport is exceptional in light of the relevant regulations and competition policy.

116. It is clear from the eighth recital in the preamble to Regulation No. 4056/86 that the authorisation to fix rates was granted to liner conferences because of their stabilising effect and their contribution to providing adequate efficient scheduled maritime transport services. The result may be that, where a single liner conference has a dominant position on a particular market, the user of those services would have little interest in resorting to an independent competitor, unless the competitor were able to offer prices lower than those of the liner conference.

117. It follows that, where a liner conference in a dominant position selectively cuts its prices in order deliberately to match those of a competitor, it derives a dual benefit. First, it eliminates the principal, and possibly the only, means of competition open to the competing undertaking. Second, it can continue to require its users to pay higher prices for the services which are not threatened by that competition.

118. It is not necessary, in the present case, to rule generally on the circumstances in which a liner conference may legitimately, on a case by case basis, adopt lower prices than those of its advertised tariff in order to compete with a competitor who quotes lower prices, or to decide on the exact scope of the expression 'uniform or common freight rates' in Article 1(3)(b) of Regulation No. 4056/86.

119. It is sufficient to recall that the conduct at issue here is that of a conference having a share of over 90 per cent of the market in question and only one competitor. The appellants have, moreover, never seriously disputed, and indeed admitted at the hearing, that the purpose of the conduct complained of was to eliminate G & C from the market.

120. The [GC] did not, therefore, err in law, in holding that the Commission's objections to the effect that the practice known as 'fighting ships', as applied against G & C, constituted an abuse of a dominant position were justified. It should also be noted that there is no question at all in this case of there having been a new definition of an abusive practice.

121. The grounds of appeal concerning fighting ships must therefore be rejected as inadmissible or unfounded.

re-imposed, *Compagnie Maritime Belge* [2005] OJ L171/28, appeal dismissed Case T-276/04, *Compagnie Maritime Belge* [2008] ECR II-1277.

The CJ stated that the 'special responsibility' of dominant undertakings has to be considered in the light of the circumstances in each case (paragraph 114), citing *Tetra Pak II*. However, it confined its remarks thereafter to the facts of the case and stressed the specialised nature of the maritime transport sector (paragraph 115).[280] It considered that a competitor to a liner conference in a dominant position would have to offer *lower* prices than the conference (paragraph 116). In that context selective price-cutting deliberately made in order to meet the prices of the only competitor was an abuse. The CJ declined to say (paragraph 118) when a liner conference *could* legitimately drop its prices from its advertised tariff in order to compete with a competitor. The general question of when above-cost price competition designed to eliminate a new competitor is illegitimate, remained unanswered. However, in paragraph 119 the CJ noted that the conference had over 90 per cent of the market, and its comments about liner conferences in paragraphs 116–117, read with the reference to *Tetra Pak II*, suggested that undertakings in a monopolistic or quasi–monopolistic position have a particularly heavy responsibility towards the competitive process. Nazzini sees the CJ in *Compagnie Maritime Belge* as applying the dynamic as efficient competitor test.[281]

In *Irish Sugar*,[282] Irish Sugar was the sole producer of sugar beet in Ireland and Northern Ireland. It reacted to increasing imports from other Member States by a variety of practices,[283] inter alia, dropping its prices to customers identified as most vulnerable to the imports, although the reductions do not seem to have taken prices below total cost. As in *CEWAL* the Commission held that the conduct was abusive because of the intent to exclude competition (shown by company documents) and the selective, targeted nature of the price cuts. Again, the appeal to the GC on the grounds that it was only defending its position as it was entitled to do, and that its pricing policy could not be considered an abuse, was rejected.

Case T-228/97, *Irish Sugar plc* v. *Commission* [1999] ECR II-2969

General Court

111. The case law shows that an 'abuse' is an objective concept referring to the behaviour of an undertaking in a dominant position which is such as to influence the structure of a market where, as a result of the very presence of the undertaking in question, the degree of competition is already weakened and which, through recourse to methods different from those governing normal competition in products or services on the basis of the transactions of commercial operators, has the effect of hindering the maintenance of the degree of competition still existing in the market or the growth of that competition (*Hoffmann-La Roche*, paragraph 91 …). It follows that Article [102] of the Treaty prohibits a dominant undertaking from eliminating a competitor and thereby reinforcing its position by having recourse to means other than those within the scope of competition on the merits. From that point of view, not all competition on price can be regarded as legitimate (*AKZO*, paragraph 70 …). The prohibition laid down in Article [102] is also justified by the consideration that harm should not be caused to consumers (*Continental Can*, paragraph 26; *Suiker Unie*, paragraphs 526 and 527 …).

112. Therefore, whilst the finding that a dominant position exists does not in itself imply any reproach to the undertaking concerned, it has a special responsibility, irrespective of the causes of that position, not to allow its conduct to impair genuine undistorted competition on the Common Market (*Michelin* paragraph 57 …). Similarly, whilst the fact that an undertaking is in a dominant position cannot deprive it of its entitlement to protect its own commercial interests when they are attacked, and whilst such an undertaking must

---

[280] And thus the liner conference had already been given a lot of leeway by the competition rules in the shape of Reg. 4056/86, [1986] OJ L378/4.

[281] Nazzini, *The Foundations of European Union Competition Law* (cited in n. 106), 242–243.

[282] [1997] OJ L258/1, [1997] 5 CMLR 666.

[283] Such as target rebates, export rebates, and product swaps.

> be allowed the right to take such reasonable steps as it deems appropriate to protect those interests, such behaviour cannot be allowed if its purpose is to strengthen that dominant position and thereby abuse it (*United Brands*, paragraph 189; *BPB Industries*, paragraph 69; Case 83/91 *Tetra Pak II*, paragraph 147; Case T-24/93 *CMB*, paragraph 107 ...).
>
> ...
>
> 189. Thus, even if the existence of a dominant position does not deprive an undertaking placed in that position of the right to protect its own commercial interests when they are threatened (see paragraph 112 above), the protection of the commercial position of an undertaking in a dominant position with the characteristics of that of the applicant at the time in question must, at the very least, in order to be lawful, be based on criteria of economic efficiency and consistent with the interests of consumers. In this case, the applicant has not shown that those conditions were fulfilled.

Again, this case concerned an undertaking with a very high market share. In paragraph 189 the GC refers to an undertaking 'with the characteristics of that of the applicant at the time in question' and relates the abuse to that. According to this judgment the ability of such undertakings to react to encroachments on their market position is limited, as they have to act in a way 'based on criteria of economic efficiency' and consistent with consumers' interests.

Compagnie Maritime Belge and *Irish Sugar* had a number of features in common:

- the infringing undertakings were in collective dominant positions;
- the collectively dominant undertakings had a market position which gave them a position of 'super-dominance' or quasi-monopoly (although the implications of 'super-dominance' must now be read in the light of the CJ's remarks in *TeliaSonera*[284]);
- an exclusionary intent was clearly identified (which is similar to the second part of the *AKZO* test, where eliminatory intent is relevant in the 'grey' area between AVC and ATC);
- in both cases the undertakings were engaged in a range of exclusionary practices and there were cumulative effects from a number of abuses.

In addition, *Compagnie Maritime Belge* concerned a liner conference in the maritime transport sector created by horizontal agreements, and as such already benefited from favourable treatment by the competition rules, as the CJ stressed in its judgment.

A US commentator, engaging in a debate as to whether above-cost price cuts can be predatory because they can exclude new entrants who would, in time, become as efficient as the incumbent dominant undertaking,[285] concludes that above-cost price cuts should never be held predatory, but that care should be taken in measuring costs.

E. Elhauge, 'Why Above-Cost Price Cuts to Drive Out Entrants are not Predatory—And the Implications for Defining Costs and Market Power' (2003) 112 *Yale LJ* 681, 682–687

> Even when incumbents do have market power, restrictions on their ability to adopt reactive above-cost price cuts are unlikely to achieve the objective of encouraging and protecting entry because less efficient entrants cannot survive in the long run, and entrants who are (or will predictably become) more efficient

---

[284] Case C-52/09, *Konkurrensverket v. TeliaSonera Sverige AB* [2011] ECR I-527, paras. 78–82, see Section 3.C.iv, p. 375.

[285] See also A. Edlin, 'Stopping Above-Cost Predatory Pricing' (2002) 111 *Yale LJ* 952; Geradin et al., *EU Competition Law and Economics* (cited in n. 160), 4.284–4.291; Rousseva and Marquis, 'Hell Freezes Over: A Climate Change for Assessing Exclusionary Conduct under Article 102 TFEU' (cited in n. 2).

need no encouragement or protection. Further, such restrictions will have harmful effects by raising prices and lowering productive efficiency during any period of price restriction, inflicting wasteful transition and entry costs, as well as distorting innovation and price flexibility in response to changing market conditions. And the restrictions will discourage the creation of more efficient incumbents and entrants, which is ultimately far more important.

This analysis reaffirms the wisdom of the position that antitrust law should not recognize any claim of above-cost predatory pricing. It also helps specify just what should count as costs. Costs should be defined in whatever way assures that an incumbent pricing at cost could not deter or drive out an equally efficient entrant. This test should be met by a cost measure that includes all costs that are varied by the allegedly predatory increase in output, since short-term threats or pricing strategies that exceed short-term costs should not be able to deter long-term investments or entry. Alternatively, if short-term pricing could deter such long-term decisions, this test would be met by a cost measure that reflected the magnitude of predator costs for the sorts of costs that are variable to the rival during the period of entry or investment decisions influenced by the short-term existence or threat of such pricing.

The case of *Post Danmark* has already been discussed.[286] We have seen that in the judgment the CJ ruled that discriminatory pricing was not of itself abusive, and that that selective low prices cannot be considered to amount to an exclusionary abuse merely because the price is lower than ATC but higher than AIC. However, PD had offered prices which were above its own ATC to two customers. The CJ said in respect of this:

In those circumstances, it cannot be considered that such prices have anti-competitive effects.[287]

This is a highly significant statement. In the judgment the CJ mentioned *Compagnie Maritime Belge* only in support of the principle of the special responsibility of dominant undertakings, and did not mention *Irish Sugar* at all. However, Advocate General Mengozzi discussed both cases, and concluded that they were only 'marginally relevant' to *Post Danmark* for three reasons: first, in those cases there was documentary evidence of intention to exclude; secondly, they concerned undertakings in near monopoly positions; and thirdly the pricing was one of a series of other practices which constituted abuses.[288] Given the words '[i]n those circumstances' it cannot be concluded, therefore, that above-ATC pricing could *never* be an abuse, although normally it will not be so as it will not exclude equally efficient competitors.

The Guidance Paper does not rule out intervention in cases of above-cost selective pricing.[289] It does not specifically deal with the issue, although it says in paragraph 72 that it is easier to engage in predatory conduct if the dominant undertaking selectively targets specific customers. However, paragraph 63 defines 'sacrifice' to include '*foregoing profits*' as well as incurring losses and in paragraph 24 the Commission contemplates intervening to protect less efficient competitors in some situations. Article 102 might therefore still be enforced against such pricing in exceptional circumstances.

---

[286] Case C-209/10, *Post Danmark A/S v. Konkurrencerådet*, 27 March 2012, see Section 8.D, p. 408.

[287] *Post Danmark*, para. 37.

[288] *Post Danmark*, Opinion of Mengozzi AG, paras. 91–94.

[289] The Discussion Paper treated the idea of above-ATC selective pricing as an abuse with circumspection (para. 127). It would be an abuse only in exceptional situations. An example was where 'companies in a collective dominant situation apply a clear strategy to collectively exclude or discipline a competitor by selectively undercutting the competitor and thereby putting pressure on its margins, while collectively sharing the loss of revenues' (para. 128), i.e. the situation in *Compagnie Maritime Belge* itself.

9. MARGIN SQUEEZE

A. GENERAL

A margin squeeze occurs where a vertically integrated undertaking which is dominant on the upstream market for an input sets its prices at such a level that its competitors on the downstream market cannot compete with it for the supply of products or services to customers.[290] The dominant undertaking can apply a margin squeeze by setting a high price for the input, charging low prices on the downstream market, or by a combination of the two. Margin squeeze can occur in both regulated and non-regulated sectors but it has proved a particular issue in the EU following the liberalisation of the telecommunications sector which is intended to bring about competition in retail services. Despite liberalisation the previous state-owned monopoly may have retained control of the network or infrastructure whilst also being in competition on the downstream retail market.

The first Commission decision on margin squeeze was an interim measure under the ECSC Treaty. In *National Carbonizing* the Commission stated that an 'enterprise in a dominant position may have an obligation to arrange its prices so as to allow a *reasonably efficient* manufacturer of the derivatives a margin sufficient to enable it to survive in the long term' [emphasis added].[291] The second decision was *Napier Brown/British Sugar*[292] where the Commission found that British Sugar (BS) had abused its dominant position in the industrial sugar market by maintaining a price for its own retail sugar which did not reflect its repackaging and selling costs. Napier Brown (NB), which was dependent on BS for supplies of industrial sugar, could not therefore viably compete on the retail market. The Commission said that if BS maintained its reduced margin NB, or any company *equally efficient* in repackaging as BS but without a self-produced source of industrial sugar, would have to leave the market.[293] The GC recognised the concept of price or margin squeezing in *Industrie des poudres sphériques*:

178 .... Price squeezing may be said to take place when an undertaking which is in a dominant position on the market for an unprocessed product and itself uses part of its production for the manufacture of a more processed product, while at the same time selling off surplus unprocessed product on the market, sets the price at which it sells the unprocessed product at such a level that those who purchase it do not have a sufficient profit margin on the processing to remain competitive on the market for the processed product.[294]

The Commission referred to margin squeeze in its 1998 Telecommunications Notice.[295]

---

[290] See e.g., R. Downing and A. Jones, 'Margin Squeezes in Telecommunications Markets', in S. Anderman and A. Ezrachi (eds.), *Intellectual Property and Competition Law: New Frontiers* (Oxford University Press, 2011); N. Dunne, 'Margin Squeeze: From Broken Regulation to Legal Uncertainty' (2011) 70 *CLJ* 34; N. Dunne, 'Margin Squeeze: Theory, Practice, Policy', Parts I and II, [2012] *ECLR* 29 and 61; D. W. Carlton, 'Should "Price Squeeze" be a Recognized Form of Anti-competitive Conduct?' (2008) 4 *Journal of Competition Law and Economics* 271; J. G. Sidak, 'Abolishing the Price Squeeze as a Theory of Antitrust Liability' (2008) 4 *Journal of Competition Law and Economics* 279; A. M. Panner, 'Are Price Squeezes Anti-competitive?' (2009) April (1) *Global Competition Policy*; H. Hovenkamp and E. Hovenkamp, 'The Viability of Antitrust Price Squeeze Claims', available at <http://ssrn.com/abstract=1156974>; O'Donoghue and Padilla, *The Law and Economics of Article 102* (cited in n. 14), Chap. 7; Bishop and Walker, *The Economics of EC Competition Law* (cited in n. 187), 6.119–6.139; G. Faella and R. Pardolesi 'Squeezing Price Squeeze under EC Antitrust Law' (2010) 6 *European Competition Journal* 255; Geradin et al., *EU Competition Law and Economics* (cited in n. 160), 4.340–4.370.

[291] *National Coal Board, National Smokeless Fuels Ltd and the National Carbonizing Company Ltd*, 79/185/ECSC, [1976] OJ L35/6 at 7.

[292] [1988] OJ L284/41, [1990] 4 CMLR 196.

[293] *Napier Brown*, para. 66.

[294] Case T-5/97, *Industrie des poudres sphériques SA v. Commission of the European Communities* [2000] ECR II-3755; the GC upheld the Commission's rejection of the downstream competitor's complaint about the dominant undertaking's pricing.

[295] Notice on the Application of the Competition Rules to Access Agreements in the Telecommunications Sector [1998] OJ C265/12, paras. 117–119.

The current EU law on margin squeeze is set out in a series of cases in the telecommunications sector, *Deutsche Telekom*,[296] *TeliaSonera*,[297] and *Telefónica*.[298]

B. THE CASE LAW

(i) *Deutsche Telekom*

The Commission decision in *Deutsche Telekom*[299] was taken before the inauguration of the review of Article 102. In *Deutsche Telekom* the Commission held that Deutsche Telekom (DT) had effected a margin squeeze by charging its competitors on the retail market in Germany a higher price for access to the 'local loop',[300] to which it was obliged to offer access under German law pursuant to the EU telecommunications regime,[301] than it was charging its own retail end-user customers. Therefore the competitors could not offer retail prices which were competitive with DT's unless they could find additional efficiency gains elsewhere. The Commission found that even when DT raised its own retail prices (from 2002) the margin between the wholesale access price and its retail prices was insufficient to cover its own downstream costs. DT's prices had been approved by the German telecommunications regulator (RegTP) and the Commission refused to take into account that losses on the access charges were still subsidised by higher telephone charges as Germany had not yet implemented the relevant Directive.[302]

The Commission held that there was a margin squeeze where:[303]

…the difference between the retail prices charged by a dominant undertaking and the wholesale prices it charges its competitors for comparable services is negative, or insufficient to cover the product-specific costs to the dominant operator of providing its own retail services on the downstream market.

Although the Commission did in fact proceed to analyse the likely exclusionary effects of DT's prices, it stated that once a margin squeeze was shown it was not necessary to assess the effects on competition, as by proving the existence of a margin squeeze the Commission had done enough to establish the existence of an abuse.[304]

The GC upheld the Commission's decision. It dismissed DT's argument that it could not have infringed Article 102 as its prices had been approved by RegTP.[305] It also dismissed the argument that DT had not been left enough scope by the regulator to adjust its retail prices to avoid the margin squeeze (the GC proceeded on the basis that the wholesale access price was fixed and that DT did

[296] Case C-280/08 P, *Deutsche Telekom v. Commission* [2010] ECR I-955, affirming Case T-271/03, *Deutsche Telekom v. Commission* [2008] ECR II-477.

[297] Case C-52/09, *Konkurrensverket v. TeliaSonera Sverige AB* [2011] ECR I-527; Case note, W. Wurmnest, (2012) 49 *CMLRev* 721.

[298] Case T-336/07, *Telefónica SA and Telefónica de España v. European Commission*, 29 March 2012, the appeal from COMP/38.784 *Wanadoo España/Telefónica*; on appeal Case C-295/12 P, judgment pending.

[299] Case COMP/C-1/37.451, 37.578, 37.579 *Deutsche Telekom AG* [2003] OJ L263/9, [2004] 4 CMLR 790.

[300] The local loop is the physical circuit connecting the network termination point at a subscriber's premises to the main distribution frame or equivalent facility in the fixed public telephone network: Case T-271/03, *Deutsche Telekom v. Commission* [2008] ECR II-477, para. 3.

[301] Decision No 223a of the Federal Ministry of Post and Telecommunications of 28 May 1997, pursuant to the EU legislative regime for the telecommunications sector (since amended).

[302] Directive 90/388/EEC [1990] OJ L192/10, which required Member States to rebalance historic charging structures. In *Deutsche Telekom* the Commission used what was in effect AAC as the cost measure. The GC accepted that the calculation was a matter of complex economic assessment (Case T-271/03, *Deutsche Telekom v. Commission*, para. 185) and that the Commission had not made a manifest error.

[303] [2003] OJ L263/9, para.107.

[304] [2003] OJ L263/9, paras. 179–180.

[305] Case T-271/03, *Deutsche Telekom v. Commission* [2008] ECR II-477, paras. 106–120; For the distinction between regulation and competition law see further Chap. 1, Section 7.D, p. 52.

not have scope to adjust it).[306] The GC said the Commission was correct in identifying the abuse as consisting of the unfair 'spread' between the wholesale and resale prices[307] and that the wholesale and retail prices did not have to be abusive taken individually in themselves. The GC thus considered a margin squeeze as a separate abuse, independent from predatory pricing. The GC also upheld the Commission's finding that the correct test was that of the 'as efficient competitor' in that the relevant costs benchmark for calculating the spread was DT's own costs and not those of the competing undertakings.[308] This was required on grounds of legal certainty as a dominant undertaking cannot be expected to make commercial decisions on the basis of the costs of a competitor about which it cannot have proper information and also on the basis of the principle of 'equality of opportunity'. The GC did not, however, agree with the Commission's statement that proof of a margin squeeze was alone sufficient to establish an abuse. Rather, the Commission had to demonstrate anti-competitive effects related to the barriers to entry that the pricing practices *could have created* for the growth of competition.[309] The small market shares gained by the competitors could be evidence of the anti-competitive effects of DT's pricing despite the worse development of competition in the telecommunications markets in other Member States.[310] DT appealed to the CJ, which upheld the GC's judgment.

Case C-208/08 P, *Deutsche Telekom* v. *Commission* [2010] ECR I-955

Court of Justice

80 According to the case-law of the Court of Justice, it is only if anti-competitive conduct is required of undertakings by national legislation, or if the latter creates a legal framework which itself eliminates any possibility of competitive activity on their part, that Articles [101] and [102] [do] not apply. In such a situation, the restriction of competition is not attributable, as those provisions implicitly require, to the autonomous conduct of the undertakings. Articles [101] and [102] may apply, however, if it is found that the national legislation leaves open the possibility of competition which may be prevented, restricted or distorted by the autonomous conduct of undertakings (Joined Cases C-359/95 P and C-379/95 P *Commission and France* v *Ladbroke Racing*…paragraphs 33 and 34 and the case-law cited).

81 The possibility of excluding anti-competitive conduct from the scope of Articles [101] and [102] on the ground that it has been required of the undertakings in question by existing national legislation or that the legislation has precluded all scope for any competitive conduct on their part has thus been accepted only to a limited extent by the Court of Justice (see Case 41/83 *Italy* v *Commission*…paragraph 19; Joined Cases 240/82 to 242/82, 261/82, 262/82, 268/82 and 269/82 *Stichting Sigarettenindustrie and Others* v *Commission*…paragraphs 27 to 29; and Case C-198/01 *CIF*…paragraph 67).

82 Thus, the Court has held that if a national law merely encourages or makes it easier for undertakings to engage in autonomous anti-competitive conduct, those undertakings remain subject to Articles [101] and [102] (Joined Cases 40/73 to 48/73, 50/73, 54/73 to 56/73, 111/73, 113/73 and 114/73 *Suiker Unie and Others* v *Commission*…paragraphs 36 to 73, and *CIF*, paragraph 56).

83 According to the case-law of the Court, dominant undertakings have a special responsibility not to allow their conduct to impair genuine undistorted competition on the common market (Case 322/81 *Nederlandsche Banden-Industrie-Michelin* v *Commission*…paragraph 57).

---

[306] Case T-271/03, *Deutsche Telekom*, paras. 121–151.

[307] Case T-271/03, *Deutsche Telekom*, para. 167. The GC dismissed the plea that the Commission had wrongly calculated DT's prices, paras. 195–212.

[308] Case T-271/03, *Deutsche Telekom*, paras 194 and 237.

[309] Case T-271/03, *Deutsche Telekom*, para. 235.

[310] Case T-271/03, *Deutsche Telekom*, paras. 242–243.

84 It follows from this that the mere fact that the appellant was encouraged by the intervention of a national regulatory authority such as RegTP to maintain the pricing practices which led to the margin squeeze of competitors who are at least as efficient as the appellant cannot, as such, in any way absolve the appellant from responsibility under Article [102] (see, to that effect, Case 123/83 *Clair*...paragraphs 21 to 23).

85 Since, notwithstanding such interventions, the appellant had scope to adjust its retail prices for end-user access services, the General Court was entitled to find, on that ground alone, that the margin squeeze at issue was attributable to the appellant.

86 In the present case, it must be noted that the appellant does not deny the existence of such scope in the arguments put forward in the first part of the first ground of appeal. In particular, the appellant does not challenge the General Court's findings in paragraphs 97 to 105 and 121 to 151 of the judgment under appeal that, in essence, the appellant was able to make applications to RegTP for authorisation to adjust its retail prices for end-user access services, specifically retail prices for narrowband access services for the period between 1 January 1998 and 31 December 2001, and retail prices for broadband access services for the period from 1 January 2002.

87 Instead, in its various complaints and arguments the appellant merely underlines the encouragement provided by RegTP's intervention, and states, in particular, that RegTP itself considered and approved the margin squeeze at issue in the light both of national and European Union telecommunications law and of Article [102] and, moreover, that the Bundesgerichtshof held in a judgment of 10 February 2004 that the appellant cannot take the place of RegTP in assessing whether a pricing practice is contrary to Article [102].

88 For the reasons set out in paragraphs 80 to 85 of the present judgment, such arguments cannot, however, in any way alter the fact that that pricing practice is attributable to the appellant, since it is common ground that the appellant had scope to adjust its retail prices for end-user access services, and, therefore, such arguments are ineffective as a means of challenging the General Court's findings on that point.

89 In particular, the appellant cannot complain that the General Court did not consider whether there was 'fault' on its part by failing to use the scope which it had to apply to RegTP for authorisation to adjust its retail prices for end-user access services. The existence or otherwise of any 'fault' in such conduct cannot alter the finding that the appellant had scope to adopt that conduct, and can be taken into account only in determining whether that conduct was an infringement and at the stage of setting the level of the fines.

90 Moreover, as the General Court held in paragraph 120 of the judgment under appeal, the Commission cannot, in any event, be bound by a decision taken by a national body pursuant to Article [102] EC (see, to that effect, Case C-344/98 *Masterfoods and HB*...paragraph 48). In the present case, the appellant does not, indeed, deny that RegTP's decisions are not binding on the Commission.

...

124 As regards, in the first place, the complaints as to whether the General Court's findings are well founded, it must be borne in mind, in relation to the question whether the infringements were committed intentionally or negligently and are, therefore, liable to be punished by a fine in accordance with the first subparagraph of Article 15(2) of Regulation No 17, that it follows from the case-law of the Court that that condition is satisfied where the undertaking concerned cannot be unaware of the anti-competitive nature of its conduct, whether or not it is aware that it is infringing the competition rules of the Treaty (see Joined Cases 96/82 to 102/82, 104/82, 105/82, 108/82 and 110/82 *IAZ International Belgium and Others* v *Commission*...paragraph 45, and *Nederlandsche Banden-Industrie-Michelin* v *Commission*, paragraph 107).

125 In the present case, the General Court took the view in paragraphs 296 and 297 of the judgment under appeal that that condition was satisfied, since the appellant could not have been unaware that, notwithstanding the authorisation decisions of RegTP, it had genuine scope to set its retail prices for

end-user access services and, moreover, the margin squeeze entailed serious restrictions on competition, particularly in view of its monopoly on the wholesale market in local loop access services and its virtual monopoly on the retail market in end-user access services.

126 It must be held that such reasoning, which is based on findings of fact which, in the absence of any allegation of distortion, are for the General Court alone to assess, is not vitiated by any error of law.

127 In so far as the appellant complains that the General Court did not take RegTP's decisions or the lack of any precedent in the European Union into account, it is sufficient to note that such arguments are merely intended to show that the appellant was unaware that the conduct complained of in the decision at issue was unlawful in the light of Article [102]. Such arguments must, therefore, in accordance with the case-law cited in paragraph 124 of the present judgment, be rejected as unfounded.

. . .

169 . . . in order to consider whether the present complaint is well founded, the Court must consider whether the General Court was right, in particular in paragraphs 166 and 168 of the judgment under appeal, to find that, even if the appellant does not have scope to adjust its wholesale prices for local loop access services, its pricing practices can nevertheless be categorised as an abuse within the meaning of Article [102] where, irrespective of whether those wholesale prices and the retail prices for end-user access services are, in themselves, abusive, the spread between them is unfair, namely, according to that judgment, where that spread is either negative or insufficient to cover the appellant's product-specific costs of providing its own services, so that a competitor who is as efficient as the appellant is prevented from entering into competition with the appellant for the provision of end-user access services.

170 In that regard, it has consistently been held that Article [102] is an application of the general objective of European Community action, namely the institution of a system ensuring that competition in the common market is not distorted. Thus, the dominant position referred to in Article [102] relates to a position of economic strength enjoyed by an undertaking which enables it to prevent effective competition being maintained on the relevant market by affording it the power to behave to an appreciable extent independently of its competitors, its customers and ultimately of consumers (see Case 85/76 *Hoffmann-La Roche* v *Commission* . . . paragraph 38, and Case C-202/07 P *France Télécom* v *Commission* . . . paragraph 103).

171 In the present case, it must be borne in mind that, as is apparent from paragraphs 50 to 52 of the present judgment, the appellant does not deny that it enjoys a dominant position on all the relevant service markets, namely both on the wholesale market in local loop access services and on the retail market in end-user access services.

172 As regards the abusive nature of the appellant's pricing practices, it must be noted that subparagraph (a) of the second paragraph of Article [102] expressly prohibits a dominant undertaking from directly or indirectly imposing unfair prices.

173 Furthermore, the list of abusive practices contained in Article [102] is not exhaustive, so that the practices there mentioned are merely examples of abuses of a dominant position. The list of abusive practices contained in that provision does not exhaust the methods of abusing a dominant position prohibited by the Treaty (see *British Airways* v *Commission*, paragraph 57 and the case-law cited).

174 In that regard, it must be borne in mind that, in prohibiting the abuse of a dominant position in so far as trade between Member States is capable of being affected, Article [102] refers to the conduct of a dominant undertaking which, on a market where the degree of competition is already weakened precisely because of the presence of the undertaking concerned, through recourse to methods different from those governing normal competition in products or services on the basis of the transactions of commercial operators, has the effect of hindering the maintenance of the degree of competition still existing in the market or the growth of that competition (see, to that effect, *Hoffman-La Roche* v *Commission*, paragraph 91; *Nederlandsche Banden-Industrie-Michelin* v *Commission*, paragraph 70; Case C-62/86 *AKZO* v *Commission* . . . paragraph 69; *British Airways* v *Commission*, paragraph 66; and *France Télécom* v *Commission*, paragraph 104).

175 It is apparent from the case-law of the Court that, in order to determine whether the undertaking in a dominant position has abused such a position by its pricing practices, it is necessary to consider all the circumstances and to investigate whether the practice tends to remove or restrict the buyer's freedom to choose his sources of supply, to bar competitors from access to the market, to apply dissimilar conditions to equivalent transactions with other trading parties, thereby placing them at a competitive disadvantage, or to strengthen the dominant position by distorting competition (see, to that effect, *Nederlandsche Banden-Industrie-Michelin* v *Commission*, paragraph 73, and *British Airways* v *Commission*, paragraph 67).

176 Since Article [102] thus refers not only to practices which may cause damage to consumers directly, but also to those which are detrimental to them through their impact on competition, a dominant undertaking, as has already been observed in paragraph 83 of the present judgment, has a special responsibility not to allow its conduct to impair genuine undistorted competition on the common market (see, to that effect, *France Télécom* v *Commission*, paragraph 105 and the case-law cited).

177 It follows from this that Article [102] prohibits a dominant undertaking from, inter alia, adopting pricing practices which have an exclusionary effect on its equally efficient actual or potential competitors, that is to say practices which are capable of making market entry very difficult or impossible for such competitors, and of making it more difficult or impossible for its co-contractors to choose between various sources of supply or commercial partners, thereby strengthening its dominant position by using methods other than those which come within the scope of competition on the merits. From that point of view, therefore, not all competition by means of price can be regarded as legitimate (see, to that effect, *Nederlandsche Banden-Industrie-Michelin* v *Commission*, paragraph 73; *AKZO* v *Commission*, paragraph 70; and *British Airways* v *Commission*, paragraph 68).

178 In the present case, it must be noted that the appellant does not deny that, even on the assumption that it does not have the scope to adjust its wholesale prices for local loop access services, the spread between those prices and its retail prices for end-user access services is capable of having an exclusionary effect on its equally efficient actual or potential competitors, since their access to the relevant service markets is, at the very least, made more difficult as a result of the margin squeeze which such a spread can entail for them.

179 At the hearing the appellant submitted, however, that the test applied in the judgment under appeal for the purpose of establishing an abuse within the meaning of Article [102] required it, in the circumstances of the case, to increase its retail prices for end-user access services to the detriment of its own end-users, given the national regulatory authorities' regulation of its wholesale prices for local loop access services.

180 It is true, as paragraphs 175 to 177 of the present judgment have already shown, that Article [102] aims, in particular, to protect consumers by means of undistorted competition (see Joined Cases C-468/06 to C-478/06 *Sot. Lélos kai Sia and Others*...paragraph 68).

181 However, the mere fact that the appellant would have to increase its retail prices for end-user access services in order to avoid the margin squeeze of its competitors who are as efficient as the appellant cannot in any way, in itself, render irrelevant the test which the General Court applied in the present case for the purpose of establishing an abuse under Article [102].

182 By further reducing the degree of competition existing on a market—the end-user access services market—already weakened precisely because of the presence of the appellant, thereby strengthening its dominant position on that market, the margin squeeze also has the effect that consumers suffer detriment as a result of the limitation of the choices available to them and, therefore, of the prospect of a longer-term reduction of retail prices as a result of competition exerted by competitors who are at least as efficient in that market (see, to that effect, *France Télécom* v *Commission*, paragraph 112).

183 In those circumstances, in so far as the appellant has scope to reduce or end such a margin squeeze, as observed in paragraphs 77 to 86 of the present judgment, by increasing its retail prices for end-user access services, the General Court correctly held in paragraphs 166 to 168 of the judgment under appeal that that margin squeeze is capable, in itself, of constituting an abuse within the meaning of Article [102]

in view of the exclusionary effect that it can create for competitors who are at least as efficient as the appellant. The General Court was not, therefore, obliged to establish, additionally, that the wholesale prices for local loop access services or retail prices for end-user access services were in themselves abusive on account of their excessive or predatory nature, as the case may be.

...195 As a preliminary point, it must be noted that, contrary to Vodafone's contention, the present complaint is admissible even though it partly reiterates the arguments put forward at first instance, since, in accordance with the case-law cited in paragraph 25 of the present judgment, the complaint is that, by resorting to the as-efficient-competitor test notwithstanding the fact that the appellant is not subject to the same legal and material conditions as its competitors, the General Court applied an incorrect legal test to the application of Article [102] to the pricing practices at issue and, therefore, committed an error of law on that point.

196 As to whether that complaint is well founded, as is apparent from paragraph 186 of the judgment under appeal and from paragraphs 4 and 12 of the present judgment, the as-efficient-competitor test used by the General Court in the judgment under appeal consists in considering whether the pricing practices of a dominant undertaking could drive an equally efficient economic operator from the market, relying solely on the dominant undertaking's charges and costs, instead of on the particular situation of its actual or potential competitors.

197 In the present case, as is apparent from paragraph 169 of the present judgment, the appellant's costs were taken into account by the General Court in order to establish the abusive nature of the appellant's pricing practices where the spread between its wholesale prices for local loop access services and its retail prices for end-user access services was positive. In such circumstances, the General Court considered that the Commission was entitled to regard those pricing practices as unfair within the meaning of Article [102], where that spread was insufficient to cover the appellant's product-specific costs of providing its own services.

198 In that regard, it must be borne in mind that the Court has already held that, in order to assess whether the pricing practices of a dominant undertaking are likely to eliminate a competitor contrary to Article [102], it is necessary to adopt a test based on the costs and the strategy of the dominant undertaking itself (see *AKZO* v *Commission*, paragraph 74, and *France Télécom* v *Commission*, paragraph 108).

199 The Court pointed out, inter alia, in that regard that a dominant undertaking cannot drive from the market undertakings which are perhaps as efficient as the dominant undertaking but which, because of their smaller financial resources, are incapable of withstanding the competition waged against them (see *AKZO* v *Commission*, paragraph 72).

200 In the present case, since, as is apparent from paragraphs 178 and 183 of the present judgment, the abusive nature of the pricing practices at issue in the judgment under appeal stems in the same way from their exclusionary effect on the appellant's competitors, the General Court did not err in law when it held, in paragraph 193 of the judgment under appeal, that the Commission had been correct to analyse the abusive nature of the appellant's pricing practices solely on the basis of the appellant's charges and costs.

201 As the General Court found, in essence, in paragraphs 187 and 194 of the judgment under appeal, since such a test can establish whether the appellant would itself have been able to offer its retail services to end-users otherwise than at a loss if it had first been obliged to pay its own wholesale prices for local loop access services, it was suitable for determining whether the appellant's pricing practices had an exclusionary effect on competitors by squeezing their margins.

202 Such an approach is particularly justified because, as the General Court indicated, in essence, in paragraph 192 of the judgment under appeal, it is also consistent with the general principle of legal certainty in so far as the account taken of the costs of the dominant undertaking allows that undertaking, in the light of its special responsibility under Article [102], to assess the lawfulness of its own conduct. While a dominant undertaking knows what its own costs and charges are, it does not, as a general rule, know what its competitors' costs and charges are.

203 Those findings are not affected by what the appellant claims are the less onerous legal and material conditions to which its competitors are subject in the provision of their telecommunications services to end-users. Even if that assertion were proved, it would not alter either the fact that a dominant undertaking, such as the appellant, cannot adopt pricing practices which are capable of driving equally efficient competitors from the relevant market, or the fact that such an undertaking must, in view of its special responsibility under Article [102], be in a position itself to determine whether its pricing practices are compatible with that provision.

204 The appellant's complaint concerning the misapplication of the as-efficient-competitor test must, therefore, be rejected.

…

251 It should be borne in mind that, in accordance with the case-law cited in paragraph 174 of the present judgment, by prohibiting the abuse of a dominant position in so far as trade between Member States is capable of being affected, Article [102] refers to the conduct of a dominant undertaking which, through recourse to methods different from those governing normal competition in products or services on the basis of the transactions of commercial operators, has the effect of hindering the maintenance of the degree of competition still existing in the market or the growth of that competition.

252 The General Court therefore held in paragraph 235 of the judgment under appeal, without any error of law, that the anti-competitive effect which the Commission is required to demonstrate, as regards pricing practices of a dominant undertaking resulting in a margin squeeze of its equally efficient competitors, relates to the possible barriers which the appellant's pricing practices could have created for the growth of products on the retail market in end-user access services and, therefore, on the degree of competition in that market.

253 As is already apparent from paragraphs 177 and 178 of the present judgment, a pricing practice such as that at issue in the judgment under appeal that is adopted by a dominant undertaking such as the appellant constitutes an abuse within the meaning of Article [102] if it has an exclusionary effect on competitors who are at least as efficient as the dominant undertaking itself by squeezing their margins and is capable of making market entry more difficult or impossible for those competitors, and thus of strengthening its dominant position on that market to the detriment of consumers' interests.

254 Admittedly, where a dominant undertaking actually implements a pricing practice resulting in a margin squeeze of its equally efficient competitors, with the purpose of driving them from the relevant market, the fact that the desired result is not ultimately achieved does not alter its categorisation as abuse within the meaning of Article [102]. However, in the absence of any effect on the competitive situation of competitors, a pricing practice such as that at issue cannot be classified as exclusionary if it does not make their market penetration any more difficult.

255 In the present case, since, as has already been noted in paragraph 231 of the present judgment, the wholesale local loop access services provided by the appellant are indispensable to its competitors' effective penetration of the retail markets for the provision of services to end-users, the General Court was entitled to hold in paragraph 237 of the judgment under appeal, as paragraphs 233 to 236 of the present judgment have already shown, that a margin squeeze resulting from the spread between wholesale prices for local loop access services and retail prices for end-user access services, in principle, hinders the growth of competition in the retail markets in services to end-users, since a competitor who is as efficient as the appellant cannot carry on his business in the retail market for end-user access services without incurring losses.

256 The appellant has not challenged that finding. For the reasons already set out in paragraphs 233 to 236 of the present judgment, the complaint concerning the failure to take into account revenues from any provision of other telecommunications services to end-users must be rejected as unfounded. The argument relating to paragraph 238 of the judgment under appeal concerning the possibility of cross-subsidisation must be rejected as ineffective for the reasons stated in paragraphs 238 to 241 of the present judgment.

257 In addition, in paragraph 239 of the judgment under appeal, the General Court found—as, in the absence of an allegation of distortion, it is for the General Court alone to do—that 'the small market

shares acquired by ... competitors in the retail ... market [in end-user access services] since the market was liberalised by the entry into force of the TKG on 1 August 1996 are evidence of the restrictions which the applicant's pricing practices have imposed on the growth of competition in those markets'. In that regard, contrary to what is claimed by the appellant, it is clear from the expression 'have imposed' that the General Court did find a causal connection between the appellant's pricing practices and the small market shares acquired by competitors. The appellant's complaint on that point is, therefore, unfounded.

258 Furthermore, the General Court concluded in paragraph 244 of its judgment, which also remained unchallenged in the present appeal, that the appellant had not produced any evidence to rebut the findings in the decision at issue that its pricing practices actually restricted competition in the retail market in end-user access services.

259 In those circumstances, it must be concluded that the General Court was correct to hold that the Commission had established that the particular pricing practices of the appellant gave rise to actual exclusionary effects on competitors who were at least as efficient as the appellant itself.

The Court of Justice in *Deutsche Telekom* thus established the following main points:

- the approval by a national sector regulator of a dominant undertaking's prices does not mean that those prices cannot constitute an abuse under Article 102 as it is not possible for the actions of a national sector regulator to immunise a dominant undertaking's conduct from the application of the EU competition rules; a dominant undertaking escapes liability for infringement of the competition rules only if the anti-competitive conduct is required of it by national legislation or if the national framework eliminates any possibility of competitive activity— mere encouragement is not enough;[311]

- margin squeeze is a stand-alone abuse, independent of excessive pricing of the input or predatory pricing downstream; the essence of a margin squeeze is the unfairness of the spread between the wholesale and retail prices;[312]

- the test for identifying a margin squeeze abuse is the 'as efficient competitor' test, i.e. whether the dominant undertaking's downstream operation could trade profitably if it was subject to the same pricing regime as the downstream competitors;[313]

- in order for a margin squeeze to constitute an abuse there must be anti-competitive effects in the form of exclusionary effects on as efficient competitors; however it is a question of whether the pricing is *capable* of making market entry more difficult or impossible, and thus of strengthening the dominant position to the detriment of consumers' interests;[314]

- DT should have avoided the margin squeeze even if it meant raising its prices to consumers on the downstream market.[315]

(ii) *TeliaSonera*

In *TeliaSonera* the Court of Justice clarified and elaborated upon the principles it set out in *Deutsche Telekom*. *TeliaSonera* was an Article 267 reference from a Swedish court, the Stockholms tingsrätt,

---

[311] Case C-280/08 P, *Deutsche Telekom*, paras. 80–90.
[312] Case C-280/08 P, *Deutsche Telekom*, paras 157, 159, and 183.
[313] Case C-280/08 P, *Deutsche Telekom*, paras. 198–203.
[314] Case C-280/08 P, *Deutsche Telekom*, paras. 252–255.
[315] Case C-280/08 P, *Deutsche Telekom*, para. 181.

made in the course of proceedings between TeliaSonera and the Konkurrensverket, the national competition authority. TeliaSonera was in an analogous position to Deutsche Telekom—a vertically integrated former State monopolist which retained ownership, inter alia, of the local loop. TeliaSonera offered access to the local loop to operators supplying broadband to end users. It also offered broadband connection services via the local loop directly to end users. It had no statutory obligation to grant access on the wholesale market to the downstream competitors in the retail market,[316] which distinguished the case from the situation in *Deutsche Telekom*. Moreover, it appears that there were a number of alternative technologies available to provide users with broadband services.[317] Nevertheless, the Konkurrensverket alleged that TeliaSonera had abused its dominant position by applying a margin squeeze in that the spread between its wholesale and retail prices was not sufficient to cover the costs which TeliaSonera itself had to incur in order to supply its services to end users.

Case C-52/09, *Konkurrensverket* v. *TeliaSonera Sverige AB* [2011] ECR I-527

Court of Justice

25 As regards the abusive nature of pricing practices such as those in the main proceedings, it must be noted that subparagraph (a) of the second paragraph of Article 102 TFEU expressly prohibits a dominant undertaking from directly or indirectly imposing unfair prices.

26 Furthermore, the list of abusive practices contained in Article 102 TFEU is not exhaustive, so that the list of abusive practices contained in that provision does not exhaust the methods of abusing a dominant position prohibited by EU law (*Deutsche Telekom* v *Commission*, paragraph 173 and case-law cited).

...

28 In order to determine whether the dominant undertaking has abused its position by the pricing practices it applies, it is necessary to consider all the circumstances and to investigate whether the practice tends to remove or restrict the buyer's freedom to choose his sources of supply, to bar competitors from access to the market, to apply dissimilar conditions to equivalent transactions with other trading parties, or to strengthen the dominant position by distorting competition (*Deutsche Telekom* v *Commission*, paragraph 175 and case-law cited).

29 Those are the principles in the light of which the referring court must examine the pricing practice at issue in the main proceedings in order to establish whether it constitutes an abuse of any dominant position that may be held by TeliaSonera.

30 In particular, after ascertaining whether the other conditions for the applicability of Article 102 TFEU are satisfied in the present case—including whether TeliaSonera holds a dominant position and whether trade between Member States was affected by its conduct—it is for the referring court to examine, in essence, whether the pricing practice introduced by TeliaSonera is unfair in so far as it squeezes the margins of its competitors on the retail market for broadband connection services to end users.

31 A margin squeeze, in view of the exclusionary effect which it may create for competitors who are at least as efficient as the dominant undertaking, in the absence of any objective justification, is in itself

---

[316] The access subject to the dispute was not covered by the obligations laid down in Regulation 2887/2000 [2000] OJ L336/4 on unbundled access to the local loop.

[317] *Deutsche Telekom*, Opinion of Mazák AG, para. 20; this was why the referring court specifically asked the CJ (Question 7 of the reference) whether the input had to be indispensable for there to be an abuse.

capable of constituting an abuse within the meaning of Article 102 TFEU (see, to that effect, *Deutsche Telekom* v *Commission*, paragraph 183).

32 In the present case, there would be such a margin squeeze if, inter alia, the spread between the wholesale prices for ADSL input services and the retail prices for broadband connection services to end users were either negative or insufficient to cover the specific costs of the ADSL input services which TeliaSonera has to incur in order to supply its own retail services to end users, so that that spread does not allow a competitor which is as efficient as that undertaking to compete for the supply of those services to end users.

33 In such circumstances, although the competitors may be as efficient as the dominant undertaking, they may be able to operate on the retail market only at a loss or at artificially reduced levels of profitability.

34 It must moreover be made clear that since the unfairness, within the meaning of Article 102 TFEU, of such a pricing practice is linked to the very existence of the margin squeeze and not to its precise spread, it is in no way necessary to establish that the wholesale prices for ADSL input services to operators or the retail prices for broadband connection services to end users are in themselves abusive on account of their excessive or predatory nature, as the case may be (*Deutsche Telekom* v *Commission*, paragraphs 167 and 183).

35 In addition, as maintained by TeliaSonera, before the spread between the prices of those services can be regarded as squeezing the margins of competitors of the dominant undertaking, account must be taken not only of the prices of services supplied to competitors which are comparable to the services which TeliaSonera itself must obtain to have entry to the retail market, but also of the prices of comparable services supplied to end users on the retail market by TeliaSonera and its competitors. Similarly, a comparison must be made between the prices actually applied by TeliaSonera and its competitors over the same period of time.

...

The prices to be taken into account

38 The Stockholms tingsrätt seeks to ascertain, first, whether, for that purpose, account should be taken not only of the retail prices applied by the dominant undertaking for services to end users, but also those applied by competitors for those services.

39 t must be recalled, in that regard, that the Court has already made clear that Article 102 TFEU prohibits a dominant undertaking from, inter alia, adopting pricing practices which have an exclusionary effect on its equally efficient actual or potential competitors (see, to that effect, *Deutsche Telekom* v *Commission*, paragraph 177 and case-law cited).

40 Where an undertaking introduces a pricing policy intended to drive from the market competitors who are perhaps as efficient as that dominant undertaking but who, because of their smaller financial resources, are incapable of withstanding the competition waged against them, that undertaking is, accordingly, abusing its dominant position (see, to that effect, *Deutsche Telekom* v *Commission*, paragraph 199).

41 In order to assess the lawfulness of the pricing policy applied by a dominant undertaking, reference should be made, as a general rule, to pricing criteria based on the costs incurred by the dominant undertaking itself and on its strategy (see, to that effect, Case C-62/86 *AKZO* v *Commission*...paragraph 74, and *France Télécom* v *Commission*, paragraph 108).

42 In particular, as regards a pricing practice which causes margin squeeze, the use of such analytical criteria can establish whether that undertaking would have been sufficiently efficient to offer its retail services to end users otherwise than at a loss if it had first been obliged to pay its own wholesale prices for the intermediary services (see, to that effect, *Deutsche Telekom* v *Commission*, paragraph 201).

43 If that undertaking would have been unable to offer its retail services otherwise than at a loss, that would mean that competitors who might be excluded by the application of the pricing practice in question

could not be considered to be less efficient than the dominant undertaking and, consequently, that the risk of their exclusion was due to distorted competition. Such competition would not be based solely on the respective merits of the undertakings concerned.

44 Furthermore, the validity of such an approach is reinforced by the fact that it conforms to the general principle of legal certainty, since taking into account the costs and prices of the dominant undertaking enables that undertaking to assess the lawfulness of its own conduct, which is consistent with its special responsibility under Article 102 TFEU, as stated in paragraph 24 of this judgment. While a dominant undertaking knows its own costs and prices, it does not as a general rule know those of its competitors (*Deutsche Telekom* v *Commission*, paragraph 202).

45 That said, it cannot be ruled out that the costs and prices of competitors may be relevant to the examination of the pricing practice at issue in the main proceedings. That might in particular be the case where the cost structure of the dominant undertaking is not precisely identifiable for objective reasons, or where the service supplied to competitors consists in the mere use of an infrastructure the production cost of which has already been written off, so that access to such an infrastructure no longer represents a cost for the dominant undertaking which is economically comparable to the cost which its competitors have to incur to have access to it, or again where the particular market conditions of competition dictate it, by reason, for example, of the fact that the level of the dominant undertaking's costs is specifically attributable to the competitively advantageous situation in which its dominant position places it.

46 It must therefore be concluded that, when assessing whether a pricing practice which causes a margin squeeze is abusive, account should as a general rule be taken primarily of the prices and costs of the undertaking concerned on the retail services market. Only where it is not possible, in particular circumstances, to refer to those prices and costs should those of its competitors on the same market be examined.

The absence of any regulatory obligation to supply

47 It is apparent from the order for reference that, contrary to the case which gave rise to *Deutsche Telekom* v *Commission*, TeliaSonera, as stated in paragraph 6 of this judgment, was not under any regulatory obligation to supply ADSL input services to operators.

...

53 The special responsibility which a dominant undertaking has not to allow its conduct to impair genuine undistorted competition in the internal market concerns specifically the conduct, by commission or omission, which that undertaking decides on its own initiative to adopt (see, to that effect, the order in Case C-552/03 P *Unilever Bestfoods* v *Commission*...paragraph 137).

54 TeliaSonera maintains, in that regard, that, in order specifically to protect the economic initiative of dominant undertakings, they should remain free to fix their terms of trade, unless those terms are so disadvantageous for those entering into contracts with them that those terms may be regarded, in the light of the relevant criteria set out in Case C-7/97 *Bronner*...as entailing a refusal to supply.

55 Such an interpretation is based on a misunderstanding of that judgment. In particular, it cannot be inferred from paragraphs 48 and 49 of that judgment that the conditions to be met in order to establish that a refusal to supply is abusive must necessarily also apply when assessing the abusive nature of conduct which consists in supplying services or selling goods on conditions which are disadvantageous or on which there might be no purchaser.

56 Such conduct may, in itself, constitute an independent form of abuse distinct from that of refusal to supply.

57 Moreover, it must be observed that since the Court was, in the said paragraphs of *Bronner*, called upon, in essence, only to interpret Article [102] with regard to the conditions under which a refusal to supply may be abusive, the Court did not make any ruling on whether the fact that an undertaking refuses access to its home-delivery scheme to the publisher of a rival newspaper where the latter does not at the same time entrust to it the carrying out of other services, such as sales in kiosks or printing, constitutes some other form of abuse of a dominant position, such as tied sales.

58 Moreover, if *Bronner* were to be interpreted otherwise, in the way advocated by TeliaSonera, that would, as submitted by the European Commission, amount to a requirement that before any conduct of a dominant undertaking in relation to its terms of trade could be regarded as abusive the conditions to be met to establish that there was a refusal to supply would in every case have to be satisfied, and that would unduly reduce the effectiveness of Article 102 TFEU.

59 It follows that the absence of any regulatory obligation to supply the ADSL input services on the wholesale market has no effect on the question of whether the pricing practice at issue in the main proceedings is abusive.

Whether an anti-competitive effect is required and whether the product offered by the undertaking must be indispensable

60 The referring court seeks to ascertain, thirdly, whether the abusive nature of the pricing practice in question depends on whether there actually is an anti-competitive effect and, if so, how that effect can be determined. Moreover, it seeks to ascertain whether the product offered by TeliaSonera on the wholesale market must be indispensable for entry onto the retail market.

61 It must be observed in that regard that, bearing in mind the concept of abuse of a dominant position explained in paragraph 27 of this judgment, the Court has ruled out the possibility that the very existence of a pricing practice of a dominant undertaking which leads to the margin squeeze of its equally efficient competitors can constitute an abuse within the meaning of Article 102 TFEU without it being necessary to demonstrate an anti-competitive effect (see, to that effect, *Deutsche Telekom* v *Commission*, paragraphs 250 and 251).

62 The case-law has furthermore made clear that the anti-competitive effect must relate to the possible barriers which such a pricing practice may create to the growth on the retail market of the services offered to end users and, therefore, on the degree of competition in that market (*Deutsche Telekom* v *Commission*, paragraph 252).

63 Accordingly, the practice in question, adopted by a dominant undertaking, constitutes an abuse within the meaning of Article 102 TFEU, where, given its effect of excluding competitors who are at least as efficient as itself by squeezing their margins, it is capable of making more difficult, or impossible, the entry of those competitors onto the market concerned (see, to that effect, *Deutsche Telekom* v *Commission*, paragraph 253).

64 It follows that, in order to establish whether such a practice is abusive, that practice must have an anti-competitive effect on the market, but the effect does not necessarily have to be concrete, and it is sufficient to demonstrate that there is an anti-competitive effect which may potentially exclude competitors who are at least as efficient as the dominant undertaking.

65 Where a dominant undertaking actually implements a pricing practice resulting in a margin squeeze on its equally efficient competitors, with the purpose of driving them from the relevant market, the fact that the desired result, namely the exclusion of those competitors, is not ultimately achieved does not alter its categorisation as abuse within the meaning of Article 102 TFEU.

66 However, in the absence of any effect on the competitive situation of competitors, a pricing practice such as that at issue in the main proceedings cannot be classified as an exclusionary practice where the penetration of those competitors in the market concerned is not made any more difficult by that practice (see, to that effect, *Deutsche Telekom* v *Commission*, paragraph 254).

67 In the present case, it is for the referring court to examine whether the effect of TeliaSonera's pricing practice was likely to hinder the ability of competitors at least as efficient as itself to trade on the retail market for broadband connection services to end users.

68 In that examination that court must take into consideration all the specific circumstances of the case.

69 In particular, the first matter to be analysed must be the functional relationship of the wholesale products to the retail products. Accordingly, when assessing the effects of the margin squeeze, the question whether the wholesale product is indispensable may be relevant.

70 Where access to the supply of the wholesale product is indispensable for the sale of the retail product, competitors who are at least as efficient as the undertaking which dominates the wholesale market and who are unable to operate on the retail market other than at a loss or, in any event, with reduced profitability suffer a competitive disadvantage on that market which is such as to prevent or restrict their access to it or the growth of their activities on it (see, to that effect, *Deutsche Telekom* v *Commission*, paragraph 234).

71 In such circumstances, the at least potentially anti-competitive effect of a margin squeeze is probable.

72 However, taking into account the dominant position of the undertaking concerned in the wholesale market, the possibility cannot be ruled out that, by reason simply of the fact that the wholesale product is not indispensable for the supply of the retail product, a pricing practice which causes margin squeeze may not be able to produce any anti-competitive effect, even potentially. Accordingly, it is again for the referring court to satisfy itself that, even where the wholesale product is not indispensable, the practice may be capable of having anti-competitive effects on the markets concerned.

73 Secondly, it is necessary to determine the level of margin squeeze of competitors at least as efficient as the dominant undertaking. If the margin is negative, in other words if, in the present case, the wholesale price for the ADSL input services is higher than the retail price for services to end users, an effect which is at least potentially exclusionary is probable, taking into account the fact that, in such a situation, the competitors of the dominant undertaking, even if they are as efficient, or even more efficient, compared with it, would be compelled to sell at a loss.

74 If, on the other hand, such a margin remains positive, it must then be demonstrated that the application of that pricing practice was, by reason, for example, of reduced profitability, likely to have the consequence that it would be at least more difficult for the operators concerned to trade on the market concerned.

75 That said, it must be borne in mind that an undertaking remains at liberty to demonstrate that its pricing practice, albeit producing an exclusionary effect, is economically justified (see, to that effect, Case C-95/04 P *British Airways* v *Commission*...paragraph 69, and *France Télécom* v *Commission*, paragraph 111).

76 The assessment of the economic justification for a pricing practice established by an undertaking in a dominant position which is capable of producing an exclusionary effect is to be made on the basis of all the circumstances of the case (see, to that effect, *Nederlandsche Banden-Industrie-Michelin* v *Commission*, paragraph 73). In that regard, it has to be determined whether the exclusionary effect arising from such a practice, which is disadvantageous for competition, may be counterbalanced, or outweighed, by advantages in terms of efficiency which also benefit the consumer. If the exclusionary effect of that practice bears no relation to advantages for the market and consumers, or if it goes beyond what is necessary in order to attain those advantages, that practice must be regarded as an abuse (*British Airways* v *Commission*, paragraph 86).

77 It must then be concluded that, in order to establish that a pricing practice resulting in margin squeeze is abusive, it is necessary to demonstrate that, taking into account, in particular, the fact that the wholesale product is indispensable, that practice produces, at least potentially, an anti-competitive effect on the retail market which is not in any way economically justified.

...

The relevance of the fact that the supply concerned is to a new customer

94 The point must be made that the abusiveness of a pricing practice such as that at issue in the main proceedings must be assessed not only with regard to the possibility that the effect of that practice may be that equally efficient operators who are already active in the relevant market may be driven from it, but

also by taking into account any barriers which the practice is capable of creating in the way of operators who are potentially equally efficient and who are not yet present on the market (see, to that effect, *Deutsche Telekom* v *Commission*, paragraph 178).

95 Consequently, whether the pricing practice at issue is liable to drive out from the market concerned existing clients of the dominant undertaking or rather new clients of that undertaking is not, as a general rule, relevant to the assessment of whether the practice is abusive.

The opportunity to recoup losses

...

98 However, a margin squeeze is the result of the spread between the prices for wholesale services and those for retail services and not of the level of those prices as such. In particular, that squeeze may be the result not only of an abnormally low price in the retail market, but also of an abnormally high price in the wholesale market.

99 Consequently, an undertaking which engages in a pricing practice which results in a margin squeeze on its competitors does not necessarily suffer losses.

100 In any event, even if the dominant undertaking suffers losses in order to squeeze the margins of its competitors, there can be no requirement that, in order to establish the existence of an abuse, evidence must be produced of the capacity to recoup any such losses.

101 The possibility that competitors may be driven from the market does not depend on either the fact that the dominant undertaking suffers losses or the fact that that undertaking may be capable of recouping its losses, but depends solely on the spread between the prices applied by the dominant undertaking on the markets concerned, the result of which may be that it is not the dominant undertaking itself which suffer losses but its competitors.

102 Lastly, in the event that the dominant undertaking were nonetheless to apply a price on the retail market which was so low that sales would engender losses, beyond the fact that such conduct is likely to constitute an autonomous form of abuse, namely the application of predatory prices, the Court has in any event already rejected the argument that, even in such a case, proof of the possibility of recoupment of losses suffered by the application, by an undertaking in a dominant position, of prices lower than a certain level of costs constitutes a necessary precondition to establishing that such a pricing policy is abusive (see, to that effect, *France Télécom* v *Commission*, paragraph 110).

103 It follows that whether the dominant undertaking is able to recoup any losses suffered as a result of applying the pricing practice at issue has no relevance to the matter of establishing whether that pricing practice is abusive.

In *TeliaSonera* the CJ therefore confirmed and developed its judgment in *Deutsche Telekom* to establish:

- A margin squeeze may constitute an abuse if the spread between the wholesale and retail prices is either negative or insufficient to cover the costs which the dominant undertaking has to incur to supply its own retail services to end users;[318]

- The unfairness of the pricing practice relates to the very existence of the margin squeeze and not to the excessive or predatory nature of the wholesale or retail prices (following *Deutsche Telekom*, paragraphs 167 and 183);[319]

- The question is whether there are exclusionary effects on as efficient competitors; in ascertaining this the relevant costs and prices are normally those of the undertaking itself (following *Deutsche Telekom*, paragraph 202).[320] However, *TeliaSonera* added the proviso that in some

[318] *TeliaSonera*, paras. 32–33.
[319] *TeliaSonera*, para. 34.
[320] *TeliaSonera*, para. 44.

circumstances the prices and costs of the competitors on the retail market should be used instead;[321]

- Margin squeeze is an independent form of abuse distinct from that of refusal to supply. In the absence of any regulatory duty to supply there may be a margin squeeze abuse even if there is no duty to supply according to the *Bronner* criteria.[322] There may be a margin squeeze even if the wholesale product is not indispensable to the supply of the retail product (indispensability is one of the criteria for a duty to supply according to *Bronner*);[323]

- Although it is necessary to demonstrate anti-competitive effects, as the CJ held in *Deutsche Telekom* (paragraphs 250 and 251), those effects need not be concrete but need only to potentially exclude competitors;[324] where the input is indispensable at least potentially anti-competitive effects are probable;[325] where it is not indispensable, pricing which causes a margin squeeze may still be capable of having anti-competitive effects;[326]

- An effect which is at least potentially exclusive is probable where the pricing is negative, i.e., the input price is higher than the dominant undertaking's retail price to end users but there may be anti-competitive effects even where it remains positive;[327]

- It is normally irrelevant whether the affected competitors on the downstream market are existing or new customers of the dominant undertaking;[328]

- As in the case of predatory pricing, the ability to recoup is irrelevant;[329]

- A margin squeeze can be objectively justified; it is possible to justify it on the basis of efficiencies.[330]

Furthermore, the CJ also held that the degree of dominance held by TeliaSonera on the upstream wholesale market was irrelevant;[331] the finding of a margin squeeze abuse does not depend on the undertaking dominant on the upstream market also being dominant on the downstream retail market;[332] and 'the fact that the markets concerned are growing rapidly and involve new technology, requiring high levels of investment, is not, as a general rule, relevant to establishing whether the pricing practice at issue constitutes an abuse'.[333]

(iii) *Telefónica*

The Commission adopted a decision in 2007 imposing a fine of nearly €152 million on Telefónica for abusing a dominant positions for wholesale ADSL broadband in Spain at both national and regional level between 2001 and 2006.[334] Before the liberalisation of the telecommunications markets in Spain in 1998 Telefónica had a statutory monopoly over the retail provision of landline

---

[321] *TeliaSonera*, paras. 45–46.

[322] *TeliaSonera*, paras. 54–59. For the criteria in Case C-7/97 *Oscar Bronner GmbH & Co KG v. Mediaprint* [1998] ECR I-7791 see the discussion of refusal to supply as an abuse, in Section 12.C.v, p. 518 ff.

[323] *TeliaSonera*, para. 72

[324] *TeliaSonera*, para. 65.

[325] *TeliaSonera*, para. 71.

[326] *TeliaSonera*, para. 72.

[327] *TeliaSonera*, paras. 73–74.

[328] *TeliaSonera*, paras. 92–95.

[329] *TeliaSonera*, paras. 96–103.

[330] *TeliaSonera*, paras. 31 and 75–76.

[331] *TeliaSonera*, paras. 78–82; see the discussion of 'super-dominance', see Section 3.C.iv, p. 375.

[332] *TeliaSonera*, paras. 83–89; see the discussion of abuses committed on a market on which the undertaking is not dominant, in Section 6.

[333] *TeliaSonera*, para. 104.

[334] COMP/38.784 *Wanadoo España v. Telefónica*, 4 July 2007 [2008] 4 CMLR 414, Telefónica was fined €151,875,000.

telecommunications services and it continued to be the only Spanish telecommunications operator with a nationwide fixed telephone network. It used that network both to provide wholesale broadband services to other telecommunications operators to enable them to supply retail broadband services to end users and to provide its own retail broadband services directly to end users. The decision is notable for the Commission's careful analysis of Telefónica's costs and of the possible prejudicial effects on consumers, including the finding that retail broadband prices were too high.[335] The Commission found that Telefónica had imposed unfair prices in the form of a margin squeeze between its wholesale and retail prices in that the margin between its wholesale and retail prices was insufficient to cover the costs that an operator equally as efficient as Telefónica would have to incur. It assessed this on the basis of Telefónica's downstream costs, using LRAIC as the appropriate standard.

Under Spanish law[336] Telefónica was under a regulatory duty to supply the wholesale product to the downstream competitors. There were price controls at the wholesale level but the Commission found that these were maximum prices and that Telefónica had scope to reduce them itself or to apply to the regulator to reduce them. The retail prices were not controlled during the relevant period and Telefónica was free to increase them.[337] Telefónica claimed that margin squeeze was a type of constructive refusal to supply and that the Commission could not deduce from the *regulatory* duty to supply that there was a duty to supply under Article 102, as that would depend on the fulfilment of the *Bronner* criteria,[338] which it submitted were not satisfied here.[339] The Commission, without stating that it agreed that margin squeeze was a type of refusal to supply,[340] did say that this case was fundamentally different from the situation in *Bronner* in two particular ways which meant that the legal test laid down by the CJ in *Bronner* was not applicable. First, the dominant undertaking had a regulatory duty to supply which resulted from the balancing by the public authorities of the incentives of Telefónica and its competitors to invest and innovate. Secondly, Telefónica's *ex ante* incentives to invest were not at stake because the infrastructure had been built up before the advent of broadband and at a time when Telefónica benefited from special or exclusive rights.[341] These two circumstances, which have been called the 'Telefónica exceptions',[342] were later repeated in the section on refusal to supply in the Guidance Paper.[343]

By the time the GC delivered judgment in Telefónica's appeal[344] the CJ had pronounced on margin squeeze in *Deutsche Telekom* and *TeliaSonera*. In upholding the Commission decision the GC followed those judgments. It therefore held that in order to establish that a margin squeeze constituted an abuse there was no need to show excessive or predatory prices as the abuse lay in the spread; that the applicable test is that of the equally efficient competitor, normally based on the dominant undertaking's own costs but in exceptional circumstances using those of the competitors (the GC held that the Commission had not manifestly erred in its calculation of Telefónica's costs);[345] and that the

---

[335] *Wanadoo España*, in particular Section E and paras. 543–544.

[336] Pursuant to the Community telecoms regime as it then was.

[337] *Wanadoo España*, paras. 665–675.

[338] Case C-7/97 *Oscar Bronner GmbH & Co KG v. Mediaprint* [1998] ECR I-7791, see Section 12.C.v, p. 518.

[339] *Wanadoo España*, paras. 299–301.

[340] A view which it did, nevertheless, set out 18 months later in the Guidance Paper, para. 80.

[341] *Wanadoo España*, paras. 303–304.

[342] D. Geradin, 'Refusal to Supply and Margin Squeeze: A Discussion of Why the "Telefonica Exceptions" are Wrong', *TILEC Discussion Paper* No 2011-009, available at <http://papers.ssrn.com/sol3/papers.cfm?abstract_id=1762687>.

[343] Guidance Paper, para. 82, see Section 12.G, p. 552.

[344] Case T-336/07, *Telefónica and Telefónica de España v. European Commission*, 29 March 2012, on appeal Case C-295/12 P, judgment pending; Spain brought a parallel appeal against the decision, Case T-398/07, *Spain v. European Commission*, 29 March 2012.

[345] The Commission examined whether the dominant undertaking's downstream arm could operate profitably on the basis of the charges applied by its upstream arm using LRAIC as the cost measure (*Wanadoo España*, paras.

applicability of the competition provisions was not excluded by *ex ante* regulatory approval. On the refusal to supply issue the GC did not consider the 'Telefónica exceptions' as, following *TeliaSonera*, it held that margin squeeze is a distinct type of abuse from refusal to supply and that the indispensability criterion in *Bronner* is relevant only to an assessment of the *effects* of the margin squeeze. The GC was careful to point out that the Commission had not, in the decision, analysed the margin squeeze as a refusal to supply.

Case T-336/07, *Telefónica and Telefónica de España* v. *European Commission*, 29 March 2012, [2012] 5 CMLR 931

General Court

173 As regards the abusive nature of pricing practices such as those in the main proceedings, it must be noted that subparagraph (a) of the second paragraph of Article [102] EC expressly prohibits a dominant undertaking from directly or indirectly imposing unfair prices (*TeliaSonera*, paragraph 146 above, paragraph 25).

174 Furthermore, the list of abusive practices contained in Article [102] is not exhaustive, so that the list of abusive practices contained in that provision does not exhaust the methods of abusing a dominant position prohibited by EU law (see *TeliaSonera*, paragraph 146 above, paragraph 26 and the case-law cited).

175 In order to determine whether the dominant undertaking has abused its position by the pricing practices it applies, it is necessary to consider all the circumstances and to investigate whether the practice tends to remove or restrict the buyer's freedom to choose his sources of supply, to bar competitors from access to the market, to apply dissimilar conditions to equivalent transactions with other trading parties, or to strengthen the dominant position by distorting competition (see *TeliaSonera*, paragraph 146 above, paragraph 28 and the case-law cited).

176 In the first place, the applicants maintain that it is clear from the contested decision that the Commission analyses the alleged margin squeeze as an abuse whose exclusionary effects are analogous to the effects of the de facto refusal to enter into a contract. Yet the Commission did not apply the legal criterion corresponding to that type of conduct, established by the Court of Justice in Case C-7/97 *Bronner*... In particular, the Commission has not demonstrated that the wholesale products concerned constituted essential inputs or infrastructures, or that the refusal to supply is capable of eliminating all competition on the retail market.

177 Such an argument cannot be upheld.

178 Contrary to the applicants' contention, the Commission, in the contested decision, did not analyse the margin squeeze as a de facto refusal to contract. The Commission referred in the contested decision to the concept of abuse within the meaning of Article [102] and the resulting obligations (recitals 279 and 280). It also defined the practice of a margin squeeze, relying in particular on the case-law of the EU judicature and on its own practice in taking decisions (recitals 281 to 284). In that regard, the Commission emphasised, at recital 285 to the contested decision, that from September 2001 to December 2006 Telefónica had abused its dominant position on the Spanish broadband access markets in the form of a margin squeeze generated by disproportion between its wholesale and retail charges for broadband access, with the consequence that competition on the retail market was likely to be restricted. The Commission also considered, at recitals 299 to 309 to the contested decision, that the criteria defined in *Bronner*, paragraph 176 above, were not applicable in the present case.

179 In particular, it must be observed that, in the contested decision, the Commission did not require Telefónica to give access to the wholesale products to its competitors, as the obligation to do so arises under the Spanish regulatory framework. Thus, Telefónica had been required to provide the regional wholesale product since March 1999 and the national wholesale product (ADSL-IP) since April 2002, that

obligation being the result of the intention of the public authorities to encourage Telefónica and its competitors to invest and innovate (recitals 88, 111, 287 and 303 to the contested decision).

180 Furthermore, the Court of Justice observed in *TeliaSonera*, paragraph 146 above, that it cannot be inferred from *Bronner*, paragraph 176 above, that the conditions to be met in order to establish that a refusal to supply is abusive must necessarily also apply when assessing the abusive nature of conduct which consists in supplying services or selling goods on conditions which are disadvantageous or on which there might be no purchaser. Such conduct may, in itself, constitute an independent form of abuse distinct from that of refusal to supply (*TeliaSonera*, paragraph 146 above, paragraphs 55 and 56).

181 If *Bronner*, paragraph 176 above, were to be interpreted otherwise, that would amount to a requirement that before any conduct of a dominant undertaking in relation to its terms of trade could be regarded as abusive the conditions to be met to establish that there was a refusal to supply would in every case have to be satisfied, and that would unduly reduce the effectiveness of Article [102] (see, to that effect, *TeliaSonera*, paragraph 146 above, paragraph 58).

182 In that regard, although in *TeliaSonera*, paragraph 146 above, paragraph 69, the Court of Justice did indeed observe that the indispensable nature of the wholesale product may be relevant in the context of the assessment of the effects of the margin squeeze, it must be emphasised that the applicants have relied on the indispensable nature of the wholesale products only in support of their assertion that the Commission did not apply the appropriate legal criterion to the alleged de facto refusal to contract penalised in the contested decision. Their argument must therefore be rejected.

. . .

204 According to the case-law, a system of undistorted competition, as laid down in the Treaty, can be guaranteed only if equality of opportunity is secured as between the various economic operators. Equality of opportunity means that Telefónica and its at least equally efficient competitors are placed on an equal footing on the retail market. That is not the case, first, if the prices of national and regional wholesale products paid to Telefónica by the alternative operators could not be reflected in their retail prices and, second, if the alternative operators, given the prices of Telefónica's national and regional wholesale products, could offer those products only at a loss, which they would have to offset by revenues coming from other markets (see, to that effect, *Deutsche Telekom* v *Commission*, paragraph 170 above, paragraph 230, and *Deutsche Telekom* v *Commission*, paragraph 69 above, paragraphs 198 and 199 and the case-law cited).

Telefónica appealed to the CJ.[346]

C. CASES AND DECISIONS OUTSIDE THE TELECOMMUNICATIONS SECTOR

The earlier cases and decisions of *National Carbonising*, *Napier Brown*, and *Industrie des poudres sphériques* have been noted.[347] In 2007 the Commission initiated proceedings against the German energy undertaking, RWE, in respect of the gas transmission market.[348] The Commission came to the preliminary view that RWE, which controlled the gas transmission network in North-Rhine Westphalia, had intentionally set its transmission tariffs at an artificially high level in order to squeeze the margins of

310 and 397) and by two methods of analysing profitability, the period-by-period method and the discounted cash flow method (paras. 310–542). The former measured Telefónica's profitability year by year and the latter allowed for below-cost pricing in the initial period. Both led to the conclusion that the downstream arm could not cover its costs. The GC subjected the Commission decision to detailed scrutiny but concluded that there was no manifest error of assessment with the choice of methodology or the details of the calculations (*Telefónica*, paras. 198–265). See also Nazzini, *The Foundations of European Union Competition Law* (cited in n. 106), 230–232.

[346] Case C-295/12 P, judgment pending.
[347] See Section 9.A, p. 426.
[348] MEMO/07/186.

its competitors on the downstream gas supply markets.[349] It had done this by maintaining elevated network tariffs and an asymmetric cost structure. The Commission also considered that other conduct of RWE amounted to a refusal to supply. RWE offered commitments to divest itself of its transmission network which the Commission accepted and made binding by a commitments decision under Regulation 1/2003, Art 9.[350]

D. MARGIN SQUEEZE IN THE GUIDANCE PAPER

In the Guidance Paper on Article 102, the Commission considers margin squeezes as a type of refusal to supply (paragraphs 75–90). It explains why:

> 80. Finally, instead of refusing to supply, a dominant undertaking may charge a price for the product on the upstream market which, compared to the price it charges on the downstream market...does not allow even an equally efficient competitor to trade profitably in the downstream market on a lasting basis (a so-called 'margin squeeze'). In margin squeeze cases the benchmark which the Commission will generally rely on to determine the costs of an equally efficient competitor are the LRAIC of the downstream division of the integrated dominant undertaking...[351]

This is contrary to the position reached more recently by the CJ in *TeliaSonera* and followed by the GC in *Telefónica*. The Guidance Paper sets out some special circumstances where the Commission considers the normal criteria on refusal to supply do not apply.[352] These correspond to the 'Telefónica exceptions' already mentioned,[353] and are dealt with in Section 12 on refusal to supply.

E. US LAW ON MARGIN SQUEEZE

The law stated by the EU Courts in *Deutsche Telekom*, *TeliaSonera*, and *Telefónica* differs significantly from US law. The Supreme Court held in *linkLine*[354] that prices which 'squeeze' the margin for as efficient competitors downstream are not an antitrust offence contrary to the Sherman Act s.2 unless there is an antitrust duty to deal on the upstream wholesale market (which, following *Verizon v. Trinko*[355] is highly unlikely) or the downstream retail price is predatory according to the normal principles on predatory pricing (as laid down in *Brooke Group*).[356] The Supreme Court rejected the idea later accepted by the CJ that the 'spread' itself can be illegal. It can only be a matter of refusal to supply or predatory pricing ('excessive' pricing is not in practice an issue for s. 2[357] and the US test concentrates solely on the downstream price). Moreover, in *Verizon v. Trinko* the Supreme Court had already declined to apply s.2 to a refusal to supply in the telecommunications sector where the regulatory authority had jurisdiction over questions of access.[358]

---

[349] COMP/39.402 *RWE—Gas Foreclosure* Commitments Decision 18 March 2009, [2009] OJ C133/10, IP/09/410.

[350] For the conclusion of Article 102 proceedings by adopting commitments decisions, see Chap. 13, Section 8.D.iii, p. 982.

[351] The Guidance Paper states, in fnn. 8 and 9 to para. 80, that it includes in this situation a scenario where an integrated supplier of a system of complementary products refuses to sell one of the products on an unbundled basis to a competitor that produces the other complementary product. It also states that it might in some cases use the LRAIC of the downstream competitor as the benchmark when the dominant undertaking's costs cannot be allocated clearly between up- and downstream operations.

[352] Guidance Paper, para. 82.

[353] In Section 9.C, p. 442.

[354] *Pacific Bell Telephone Company* v. *linkLine Communications Inc.* 129 S.Ct. 1109; see F. Enrique González Díaz and J. Padilla, 'The *linkLine* judgment—a European Perspective' (2009) 1 *GCP*.

[355] *Verizon Communications Inc* v. *Trinko LLP* 540 US 398, 124 S Ct 872 (2004); see Section 12.H, p. 554.

[356] *Brooke Group Ltd* v. *Brown & Williamson Tobacco Corp* 509 US 209 (1993).

[357] The Sherman Act s.2 is not applied to situations of excessive pricing.

[358] *Verizon Communications Inc* v. *Trinko LLP* 540 US 398, 124 S Ct 872 (2004).

F. COMMENT

The CJ judgments in *Deutsche Telekom* and *TeliaSonera* repeat the familiar principle that the list of abusive practices in Article 102 is not exhaustive before concluding that margin squeeze is a distinct abuse from predatory and excessive pricing and (in the case of *TeliaSonera*) from refusal to supply.[359] The conclusion on refusal to supply, which was contrary to the opinion of the Advocate General in *TeliaSonera*,[360] is particularly difficult to rationalise. Logic suggests that if one has no duty to supply one can have no duty to supply at a particular price. However, EU law has reached the position that an undertaking which does not infringe Article 102 by refusing to supply (because the conditions laid down in the case law for a duty to supply are not fulfilled)[361] can nevertheless infringe if it *does* supply at a price deemed to give rise to an abusive margin squeeze. A vertically integrated dominant undertaking which has no regulatory duty to supply may therefore decide not to supply at all, which may be more anti-competitive and have detrimental welfare implications. The CJ's rationale for this seemingly bizarre state of affairs is that were the established refusal to supply conditions required to be fulfilled before a dominant undertaking's terms of trade could be abusive it 'would unduly reduce the effectiveness of Article 102'.[362] The CJ does not clearly explain why this is so. However, although the divorce of margin squeeze from refusal to supply means that the indispensability of the input to the downstream competitor is not a necessary condition for the pricing to constitute an abuse, it may be relevant to the issue of whether there are anti-competitive effects as indispensability renders at least potential anti-competitive effects 'probable'.[363] In other words the CJ's concern is with anti-competitive effects, not the indispensability of the input. The judgments in *TeliaSonera* and *Telefónica* in respect of the independence of margin squeeze from refusal to supply differ both from US law and from the position of the Commission in the Guidance Paper.[364] It has been suggested that the CJ's stance stems from a failure to distinguish between horizontal and vertical foreclosure.

> **Renato Nazzini, *The Foundations of European Union Competition Law, The Objectives and Principles of Article 102* (Oxford University Press, 2011), 274–275**
>
> The Court might have been induced in error because margin squeeze consists in the modulation of upstream and downstream prices. The refusal to supply test must, therefore, necessarily be complemented by the as efficient competitor test. This does not mean, however, that margin squeeze is a form of customer foreclosure analogous to predation, rebates, or exclusivity. But, regrettably, an analogy with non-vertical foreclosure is what the Court probably had in mind when it said that it would be absurd to hold that all abuses relating to the dominant undertaking's prices or trading terms presuppose a duty to deal. Thus the Court failed to distinguish horizontal foreclosure practices in which the dominant undertaking only deals with customers and vertical foreclosure practices in which the issue is whether and, if so, on what terms, the dominant undertaking must deal with its competitors so as to allow them to compete effectively. It is only in relation to vertical foreclosure that Article 102 requires the conditions for a duty to deal to be established as a safeguard against over-deterrence of market-wide investments.

---

[359] Case C-280/08 P, *Deutsche Telekom* v. *Commission* [2010] ECR I-9555, para. 173; Case C-52/09, *Konkurrensverket* v. *TeliaSonera Sverige AB* [2011] ECR I-527, para. 26.

[360] *TeliaSonera*, Opinion of Mazák AG, paras. 21–23.

[361] See Case C-7/97 *Oscar Bronner GmbH & Co KG* v. *Mediaprint* [1998] ECR I-7791 and Section 12.C.

[362] *TeliaSonera*, para. 58, followed by the GC in *Telefónica*, para. 181.

[363] *TeliaSonera*, paras. 69–72.

[364] As already noted, the Commission in the *Deutsche Telekom* decision took the view that the *Bronner* refusal to supply conditions did not apply because the situation fell within what it considers exceptions to those conditions, not because it expressly rejected the classification of a margin squeeze as a refusal to supply.

In all three telecommunications cases the EU Courts state the principle originally enunciated in *Michelin I*, and now appearing in some form in all the pricing cases, that it is necessary to consider all the circumstances and decide whether the practice tends to remove or restrict the buyer's freedom to choose his sources of supply, bar competitors from access to the market, apply dissimilar conditions, or strengthen the dominant position by distorting competition.[365] The fact that in EU law it is the unfair 'spread' which identifies a margin squeeze abuse means that both upstream and downstream prices are taken into account, whereas if the issue is whether prices downstream are predatory only the one market is relevant. Although the dismissal of the predatory pricing standard can be criticised as protecting competitors and risking consumer welfare[366] the conceptualisation of a margin squeeze as a stand-alone abuse independent of predatory (and excessive) pricing has the advantage of being better able to reflect the realities of the situation and behaviour of a vertically integrated undertaking, in particular internal transfer pricing, cross-subsidies, and the leveraging of market power.[367]

In *Deutsche Telekom* and *TeliaSonera* the CJ endorsed the 'as efficient competitor' test as applicable to margin squeeze cases. This aligns margin squeeze with predatory pricing. The as efficient competitor test, by using the dominant undertaking's own costs as the benchmark, should ensure that the competition rules are applied only to prevent the anti-competitive foreclosure of those whose exclusion from the market would be detrimental to welfare. The test also has the advantage spelt out in the cases of complying with the principle of legal certainty and enabling the dominant undertaking to assess the lawfulness or otherwise of its own conduct. Moreover, in *Deutsche Telekom* the CJ (followed by the GC in *Telefónica*) approved the GC's finding that the as efficient competitor test chimed with principle of 'equality of opportunity' between economic operators, referring to the CJ having consistently held that this was necessary to guarantee a system of undistorted competition. This is an interesting importation from the case law on Article 106, on which the GC has since delivered a further judgment.[368] However, the CJ left the door open to the use of the downstream competitors' own costs (the 'reasonably efficient competitor test') in *TeliaSonera* (paragraph 45) holding that the costs and prices of competitors could be relevant in certain circumstances. The CJ summed these up as situations where 'it not possible' to use those of the dominant undertaking.[369] This reasonably efficient competitor test deprives dominant undertakings of the legal certainty the CJ thinks important and makes life more difficult for dominant undertakings. The actual application of the as efficient competitor test can be extremely problematic as is seen in the arguments about the methodology used to calculate the margin squeeze in *Deutsche Telekom* and *Telefónica*: in particular the very fact of the vertical integration and the complications of regulated prices make carrying out the test difficult. It is important that opportunity costs are taken into account.[370]

---

[365] *Deutsche Telekom*, para. 175; *TeliaSonera*, para. 28, *Telefónica*, para. 175. And see also Case C-209/10, *Post Danmark A/S v. Konkurrencerådet*, 27 March 2012, para. 26; Case C-549/10 P, *Tomra Systems ASA v. European Commission*, 19 April 2012, para. 71 where the phrase about dissimilar conditions is omitted).

[366] See J. G. Sidak, 'Abolishing the Price Squeeze as a Theory of Antitrust Liability' (2008) 4 *Journal of Competition Law and Economics* 279.

[367] See further G. Faella and R. Pardolesi, 'Squeezing Price Squeeze under EC Antitrust Law' (2010) 6 *European Competition Journal* 255, 256–259; J. Meisel, 'The Law and Economics of Margin Squeezes in the US versus the EU' (2012) 8 *European Competition Journal* 383, 397–398.

[368] Case T-169/08, *Dimosia Epicheirisi Ilektrismou AE (DEI) v. Commission*, 12 September 2012 (*Greek Lignite*), see Chap. 8, Section 5.B, p. 619.

[369] Only the first example in paragraph 45, the non-identification of the dominant undertaking's own costs, can strictly be described as 'not possible'. The other examples are situations where the CJ does not consider it *acceptable* to use those costs and presumably it in this sense that 'possible' must be construed.

[370] See further S. C. Salop, 'Refusals to Deal and Price Squeezes by an Unregulated Vertically Integrated Monopolist' (2010) 76 *Antitrust Law Journal* 709; J. Meisel, 'The Law and Economics of Margin Squeezes in the US versus the EU' (2012) 8 *European Competition Journal* 383, 396–397; L. Colley and S. Burnside, 'Margin Squeeze Abuse' (2006) 2 *European Competition Journal*, Special Issue, 185, 193–195.

The EU Courts have made it clear that it cannot be assumed that a margin squeeze will always cause harm to consumers. Rather, it is necessary to consider the likely anti-competitive effects of the pricing in either the upstream or downstream markets, and the impact of any ruling on innovation upstream. However, it is not necessary to show *concrete effects* as it is sufficient to demonstrate an anti-competitive effect which *may potentially* exclude competitors.[371] There is therefore a need to demonstrate a coherent theory of harm[372] relating to entry barriers to the retail market and thus to the degree of competition on that market. It is notable, however, that in *Telefónica* the GC upheld the Commission's reliance on 'probable' anti-competitive effects despite the fact that the decision was taken six years after the start of the abuse. The Commission was not required to show that the effects had materialised (and the GC expressly rejected the argument that the higher degree of probability of 'in all likelihood' required under the EUMR in *Tetra Laval*[373] concerning assessment of a conglomerate merger, should apply here).

The CJ accepted in *Deutsche Telekom* (where the upstream prices were regulated) that it may be that the only way a dominant undertaking can avoid the margin squeeze is to increase its retail prices to consumers. This seems a regrettable outcome to the application of the competition rules, and can only be justified by the longer-term benefits to consumers in the future which can be expected to arise through the maintenance of competition. Today's consumers have to make sacrifices for tomorrow's.[374] However, it should be recalled that at the beginning of the *TeliaSonera* judgment the CJ stated the function of the competition rules as being 'to prevent competition from being distorted to the detriment of the public interest, individual undertakings and consumers, thereby ensuring the well-being of the European Union'[375] and this denotes a longer-term view than the immediate short-term interests of consumers.[376]

The margin squeeze cases provide the fullest treatment yet of the relationship between regulation and Article 102 and the resulting situation for dominant undertakings is not a happy one.[377] The main reasons for finding that *ex ante* sector regulation does not preclude the application of the competition rules to the same conduct—that EU competition law cannot be prevented from applying by decisions of national regulators and that regulation and competition law may pursue different objectives[378]—are perfectly understandable, but the result leaves dominant undertakings in a difficult position and produces unsatisfactory outcomes. The undertakings are subject to two separate sets of rules and can infringe Article 102 even though they have done everything required of them by the sector regulator.[379] Moreover, the situation in which a vertically integrated dominant undertaking finds itself may have been largely created by the regulator. In *Deutsche Telekom* the wholesale price was taken as having been fixed by the regulator and so in respect of an abuse which was founded on the spread between two prices, the dominant undertaking had no power over one of them. DT was held to have 'scope' for remedying the margin squeeze because the 'state compulsion'

---

[371] *TeliaSonera*, para. 64.

[372] W. Wurmnest, Case note on *TeliaSonera* (2012) 49 *CMLRev* 721.

[373] Case T-5/02, *Tetra Laval BV v. Commission* [2002] ECR II-4381, para. 153, *aff'd* on appeal Case C-12/03P *Commission v. Tetra Laval* [2005] ECR I-987.

[374] Cf. the discussion of benefits to consumers arising from the application of Article 101(3), see Chap. 4, Section 4.D, p. 258 ff.

[375] *TeliaSonera*, para. 22.

[376] See the discussion in Chap. 1, Section 7.C.ii., p. 46.

[377] See in particular D. Geradin and R. O'Donoghue, 'The Concurrent Application of Competition Law and Regulation: the Case of Margin Squeeze Abuses in the Telecommunications Sector' (2005) *Journal of Competition Law and Economics* 355, GCLC Working Paper 04/05; N. Dunne, 'Margin Squeeze: Theory, Practice, Policy', Part II [2012] *ECLR* 61.

[378] See Chap. 1, Section 7.D, p. 52.

[379] The GC dismissed claims that the principle of legitimate expectation had been breached, Case T-271/03, paras. 267–269; the CJ held the appeal against this was inadmissible, *Deutsche Telekom*, paras. 105–110.

defence was attenuated to the narrowest of circumstances and it therefore infringed Article 102 by failing to take the initiative and request an alteration to the second (retail) price. In *TeliaSonera* the CJ said that a dominant undertaking may infringe by omission as well as commission,[380] and DT was liable for having failed to apply to the regulator to change the retail price in favour of its competitors. In effect the dominant undertaking in this situation is put under a duty to help its competitor by taking positive action in a situation in which regulation has failed to achieve the best competitive outcome. There has been not just a market failure but a regulatory failure. It is doubtful, however, whether competition authorities should attempt to remedy defects in regulation by application of the competition rules or use competition law to achieve what are regulatory rather than competition objectives.[381] In both *Deutsche Telekom* and *Telefónica* the argument that the Commission should have brought proceedings against the Member State under Article 258 for failure to properly implement the telecommunications Directives, instead of against the undertakings under Article 102, was dismissed.[382]

G. SUMMARY

The EU Courts have established that margin squeeze is a stand-alone abuse, independent from predatory and excessive pricing, and based on the unfair spread between the vertically integrated dominant undertaking's wholesale and retail prices. The test is normally the 'as efficient competitor' which asks whether the difference between the wholesale and retail prices is either negative or insufficient to cover the undertaking's own downstream costs, i.e. whether the undertaking could survive on the downstream market if it were subject to the pricing policy it imposed on its downstream competitors. However, in some situations the competitors' own costs will be used as the benchmark instead. A number of factors are normally irrelevant to the existence of an abuse: the degree of dominance of the vertically integrated undertaking on the upstream market; whether it is dominant on the downstream market; whether the market involves new technology; whether the vertically integrated undertaking can recoup losses; and whether the downstream competitors are new or existing customers. Margin squeeze is a separate form of abuse from refusal to supply and it is not necessary that the input is indispensable. A margin squeeze will infringe Article 102 only if it has anti-competitive effects, but the effect need not be concrete and it is enough that competitors are potentially excluded. Anti-competitive effects are considered 'probable' if the input is indispensable or the margin is negative. A dominant undertaking's prices may infringe Article 102 even if they have been approved by a sector regulator and the undertaking will escape liability only if it had no room for manoeuvre whatsoever. A margin squeeze that produces exclusionary effects may nevertheless be objectively justified.

The conceptualisation of margin squeeze as a separate abuse from excessive and predatory pricing more readily captures the anti-competitive effects of vertical integration. However, the application of Article 102 to situations approved by regulators raises many difficulties and the separation of margin squeeze from refusal to supply and from the requirement of indispensability of the input (contrary to the view of the Commission in the Guidance Paper) is problematic. Dominant undertakings in the EU are left widely exposed to margin squeeze claims and this may impact prejudicially on their incentives to invest and innovate.

[380] *TeliaSonera*, para. 53.

[381] Geradin and O'Donoghue, 'The Concurrent Application of Competition Law and Regulation' (cited in n. 377), sections IV and V; Dunne, 'Margin Squeeze: Theory, Practice, Policy' (cited in n. 377), 63–66.

[382] *Deutsche Telekom*, paras. 46–47; *Telefónica*, para. 307; and see Dunne, 'Margin Squeeze: Theory, Practice, Policy' (cited in n. 377), 66.

10. EXCLUSIVE PURCHASING (SINGLE BRANDING) CONTRACTS AND DISCOUNT AND REBATE SCHEMES

A. GENERAL

Exclusive purchasing contracts (also called requirements contracts and, more recently, single branding or non-compete obligations) are arrangements by which a customer is obliged to obtain all or most of its requirements for the relevant product from one supplier.[383] It should be noted that in the past the term 'exclusive dealing' has often been used interchangeably with 'exclusive purchasing'. However, in the Guidance Paper[384] the Commission adopts the term 'exclusive dealing' to encompass both exclusive purchasing and conditional rebates because, as we shall see, they may have the same effects.[385] For that reason this chapter uses 'exclusive purchasing' when referring to single-branding contracts.

B. THE CASE LAW ON EXCLUSIVE PURCHASING

In *Hoffmann-La Roche* the CJ spoke in terms which suggest that exclusive purchasing is per se abusive when entered into by dominant suppliers:

> An undertaking which is in a dominant position on the market and ties purchasers—even if it does so at their request—by an obligation or promise on their part to obtain all or most of their requirements exclusively from the said undertaking abuses its dominant position within the meaning of Article [102]…[386]

The objection to exclusive purchasing commitments involving dominant suppliers is that they may be exclusionary and foreclose competitors from the market. The argument against having a per se rule against them is that they should be judged by their effects in the specific context of the case. Moreover, what should matter is whether they harm *consumers*. They should not be condemned per se.

The 2000 Guidelines on Vertical Restraints stated that 'Dominant companies may not impose non-compete obligations on their buyers unless they can objectively justify such commercial practice within the context of Article [102]'.[387] However, in line with the Commission's current effects-based analysis the 2010 Vertical Restraint Guidelines state:[388]

> Single branding obligations are more likely to result in anticompetitive foreclosure when entered into by dominant companies.

In *Hoffmann-La Roche* the Court referred to an exclusive purchasing obligation covering 'all or most' of the customer's requirements.[389] Guidance as to what this means can be derived from the Verticals

---

[383] See P. Lugard, 'Eternal Sunshine on a Spotless Policy? Exclusive Dealing under Article 82 EC' (2006) 2 *European Competition Journal* 163.

[384] Guidance Paper, paras. 32–46.

[385] Guidance Paper, para. 32.

[386] Case 85/76, *Hoffmann-La Roche v. Commission* [1979] ECR 461, para. 89.

[387] [2000] OJ C291/1, para. 141.

[388] Guidelines on Vertical Restraints [2010] OJ C130/1, para. 133.

[389] In *Soda-Ash–ICI* [2003] OJ L10/33, para. 142, the Commission said that an obligation or promise on the part of customers to 'obtain the whole or substantially the whole of their requirements' exclusively from the dominant undertaking will constitute an infringement of Art. 102.

Regulation where a non-compete obligation is defined as including an obligation on a buyer to purchase 80 per cent of its requirements from one source.[390]

The abusive nature of exclusive contracts (and loyalty rebates) is not removed by the presence of an 'English clause'. This is a clause in a supply contract whereby the customer is allowed to switch suppliers without penalty if the dominant undertaking cannot or will not match more favourable terms offered by another supplier. In *Hoffmann-La Roche*[391] the dominant firm argued that the English clause denuded the loyalty rebate provision of its anti-competitive effect so that there was no abuse. The Court held that, on the contrary, the clause exacerbated the abuse by enabling Hoffmann-La Roche to learn of its competitors' offers.[392] In *Hoffmann-La Roche*[393] Article 102 was infringed by exclusive purchasing induced by loyalty rebates. In *BPB Industries* the incentives to exclusivity were not only loyalty rebates[394] but also priority deliveries at times of shortage. The Commission's condemnation of this as an abuse was upheld by the GC.[395]

Article 102 can be infringed where the supply arrangements do not stipulate exclusivity, or offer rewards in exchange for exclusivity, but the nature of the arrangements is such that exclusivity results, i.e. there is *de facto* exclusivity. *Van Den Bergh*[396] is the paradigm case of this, as recognised in the Guidance Paper.[397] It concerned freezer exclusivity, the practice whereby frozen goods suppliers (*in casu*, ice cream manufacturers) provide retail outlets with freezers but stipulate that no other supplier's brand can be stored there.[398] It is argued that this creates a strategic barrier to the entry of new competition and reduces the intensity of competition between incumbent firms, because in practice it is impractical for a retailer to make room for a second freezer and he has no incentive to do so.[399] In *Van den Bergh* HB entered into distribution agreements for its impulse ice cream with retailers in Ireland under which freezer cabinets were made available to the retailers for the storage and display of HB's ice cream at the point of sale. The cabinet was either loaned with no direct charge or leased for a nominal sum which was not collected, and the maintenance and repair of the cabinet was done by HB. The cabinet had to be used exclusively for HB's products. These agreements were found by the Commission to infringe Article 101 and not to satisfy the criteria for exemption in Article 101(3).[400] The Commission also found that HB held a dominant position in the Irish impulse ice cream market (its market share was 75 per cent) and that its inducement of the retailers to accept the distribution arrangements infringed Article 102.[401]

---

[390] Previously Reg. 2790/99 [1999] OJ L336/21, Art. 1(b), now Reg. 330/2010 [2010] OJ L102/1, Art.1(b); for the Verticals Regulation, see Chap. 11.

[391] Case 85/76, *Hoffmann-La Roche v. Commission* [1979] ECR 461.

[392] Case 85/76, *Hoffmann-La Roche v. Commission* [1979] ECR 461, paras. 107–108. The Commission objected to an English clause in IRI/Nielsen, *XXXVIth Report on Competition Policy* (1996), part 64. The 2000 Guidelines on Vertical Restraints, [2000] OJ C291/1, para.152 stated that Art. 102 specifically prevented dominant companies from applying English clauses. That sentence does not appear in the 2010 Guidelines.

[393] Case 85/76, *Hoffmann-La Roche v. Commission* [1979] ECR 461.

[394] See Section 10.D, p. 454 ff.

[395] *BPB Industries* [1989] OJ L10/50, [1990] 4 CMLR 464, paras. 141–147, upheld Case T-65/89. *BPB Industries Plc and British Gypsum Ltd v. Commission* [1993] ECR II-389.

[396] [1998] OJ L246/1, [1998] 5 CMLR 530.

[397] Guidance Paper, para. 33.

[398] The issue relates to 'impulse ice cream', i.e. ice cream sold in individually wrapped portions for immediate consumption, not ice cream bought in multi-packs from supermarkets.

[399] The practice was also considered in the UK under the Fair Trade Act 1973 by the Mergers and Monopolies Commission (MMC) in its report, *Ice Cream: A report on the Supply in the UK of Ice Cream for Immediate Consumption*, Cm. 2524 (TSO, 1994), and by the Competition Commission in its report, *The Supply of Impulse Ice Cream* Cm. 4510 (TSO, 2000).

[400] See paras. 130–254 of the decision in *Van Den Bergh* [1998] OJ L246/1, [1998] 5 CMLR 530.

[401] See I. Lianos, 'Categorical Thinking in Competition Law and the Effects-based Approach in Article 82', in Ezrachi (ed.), *Article 82EC: Reflections on its Recent Evolution* (cited in n. 32), 19, 24–25, who makes the often overlooked point that what was condemned under Art. 102 was the inducement of retailers who had not yet concluded the agreements, rather than the agreements themselves.

HB put forward certain arguments which were equally relevant to both Article 101 and Article 102. It argued, inter alia, that the application of the competition rules to the exclusivity provisions in the freezer agreements would be tantamount to interference with its property rights, contrary to Article 345 TFEU,[402] in that it would permit other manufacturers' products to be stored in its property. The Commission rejected these arguments. On appeal the GC upheld the decision.[403]

Van den Bergh was a (rare) case of an effects approach to the application of Article 102 to exclusive purchasing. The Commission had held that the agreements also infringed Article 101, and the GC considered their effects on the market very carefully, applying the principle in *Delimitis*,[404] before upholding that finding. When it came to Article 102 the GC did not simply view the inducements to enter the arrangements as per se abusive but held that they breached Article 102 because of their effects in preventing competitors gaining access to the market.[405] The GC considered it significant that 40 per cent of the retail outlets were foreclosed by HB's freezer policy. It is clearly rational that where Articles 101 and 102 are both applied to the same scenario the same approach is taken.[406] In this way the economic effects approach under Article 101 leads to a more economic approach under Article 102.[407] Although some cases in which only Article 102 was in issue have continued to take a more absolute view of exclusivity,[408] an indication of a more effects-based approach in the GC is discernible in an interesting statement of the GC in *Tomra*, a case on rebates:[409]

It may be concluded from that line of cases [i.e. *Hoffmann-La Roche* and *Michelin II*[410]], as the applicants indeed maintain, that in order to determine *whether exclusivity agreements*, individualised quantity commitments and individualised retroactive rebate schemes are compatible with Article [102], it is necessary to ascertain whether, following an assessment of all the circumstances and, thus, also of the context in which those agreements operate, those practices are intended to restrict or foreclose competition on the relevant market or are capable of doing so [emphasis added].

This was despite the GC having just cited paragraph 89 of *Hoffmann-La Roche*. It is more in line with the Guidance Paper which applies an effects analysis to exclusive purchasing.[411]

Exclusive contracts can also have anti-competitive effects where they limit customers' avenues of supply. This is illustrated by *DeBeers/Alrosa*.[412] The Commission objected to an agreement between De Beers, the world's leading diamond mining company,[413] and Alrosa, a Russian company which was the world's second largest diamond producer, accounting for over 98 per cent of Russian diamond production, whereby, in effect, Alrosa would distribute almost all its diamonds sold outside

---

[402] Then Art. 295 EC.

[403] Case T-65/98 *Van den Bergh Foods Ltd* v. *EC Commission* [2003] ECR II-4653; the appeal to the CJ was shortly dismissed by Order, Case C-552/03 P, *Unilever Bestfoods (Ireland) Ltd* v. *Commission* [2006] ECR I-9091.

[404] Case C-234/89 *Stergios Delimitis* v. *Henniger Bräu* [1991] ECR I-9350, see Chap. 4.

[405] Para. 160 of the GC judgment: Case T-65/98 *Van den Bergh Foods Ltd* v. *EC Commission* [2003] ECR II-4653.

[406] For the argument that agreements entered into by dominant undertakings would be better dealt with entirely under Art. 101 see E. Rousseva, 'Modernising by Eradicating: How the Commission's New Approach to Article 81 EC Dispenses with the Need to Apply Article 82 to Vertical Restraints' (2005) 42 *CMLRev* 587 and Rousseva, *Rethinking Exclusionary Abuses in EU Competition Law* (cited in n. 42), 431–456.

[407] O'Donoghue and Padilla, *The Law and Economics of Article 102* (cited in n. 14), 431–432.

[408] See Case T-57 and 58/01, *Solvay* v. *Commission* [2009] ECR II-4621, para. 365 (judgment overruled on the procedural pleas, Case C-109/10 P, *Solvay SA* v. *European Commission* [2011] ECR I-10329 where the substantive arguments were not considered), and, Case T-66/01, *ICI* v. *Commission* [2009] ECR II-2631, para. 315.

[409] Case T-155/06, *Tomra Systems* v. *Commission* [2010] ECR II-4361, para. 215. The point did not arise in the appeal, Case C-549/10 P, *Tomra Systems ASA* v. *European Commission*, 19 April 2012.

[410] Case T-203/01, *Manufacture Française des Pneumatiques Michelin* v. *Commission* [2003] ECR II- 407, also a case on rebates.

[411] Guidance Paper, paras. 33–36.

[412] Case COMP/B-2/38.381, 22 February 2006.

[413] Its current market share is omitted from the decision, but for much of the 20th century it controlled over 80% of the world supply of rough diamonds.

the former USSR through De Beers. The Commission viewed it as the outcome of a long relationship between De Beers and Alrosa aimed at jointly regulating the volume, assortment, and prices of rough diamonds on the world market and considered that the agreement would lead to *de facto* distribution exclusivity for De Beers. De Beers gave commitments[414] to phase out its purchases from Alrosa, and ultimately to cease purchasing altogether. The GC annulled the decision as the remedy infringed the principles of proportionality and freedom of contract but that judgment was set aside by the CJ.[415]

The Commission's major push to liberalise the European energy market led to a number of Article 102 proceedings in the wake of the energy sector enquiry.[416] These include cases in which the Commission has adopted commitments decisions whereby vertically integrated suppliers have agreed to abandon long-term exclusive supply agreements, see *Distrigaz*[417] and *EDF—Long Term Electricity Contracts in France*.[418]

C. EXCLUSIVE PURCHASING IN THE GUIDANCE PAPER

The Guidance Paper deals with exclusive purchasing along with rebates in a section on 'exclusive dealing'. The Commission, applying its general effects-based approach, sets out the factors it considers relevant in determining whether to intervene in exclusive purchasing arrangements. It makes the preliminary point that it is not concerned just with the effect on the customer who is party to the agreement. After all, the particular customer may be perfectly happy with the deal he has negotiated with the dominant supplier and the *quid pro quo* for his agreement to purchase exclusively. Rather, the Commission is concerned with other customers and with the final consumers. It will be particularly concerned where consumers as a whole will not benefit, which is likely to be the case where the dominant firm has exclusive contracts with many customers so that competing undertakings are prevented from entering or expanding.[419] In paragraph 36 the Commission explains that it will treat as an enforcement priority those cases where anti-competitive foreclosure is likely as the dominant undertaking is an 'unavoidable trading partner' because, for example, its brand is a 'must stock item' or the competitors are unable for reasons of capacity constraints to satisfy the entire demand of each individual customer. The Commission considers that if competitors can compete on equal terms for each individual customer's entire demand, exclusive purchasing obligations are generally unlikely to hamper effective competition unless the switching of supplier by customers is rendered difficult due to the duration of the exclusive purchasing obligation, and that in general, the longer the duration of the obligation, the greater the likely foreclosure effect.[420] However, it says that if the dominant undertaking is an unavoidable trading partner for all or most customers, even an exclusive purchasing obligation of short duration can lead to anti-competitive foreclosure.[421]

---

[414] For commitments decisions under Reg. 1/2003, Art. 9, see Chap. 13, Section 8.D.iii, p. 982.

[415] Case T-170/06, *Alrosa v. Commission* [2007] ECR II-2601, set aside Case C-441/07P, *European Commission v. Alrosa* [2010] ECR I-5949.

[416] COM(2006)851 final.

[417] Commitments Decision 11 October 2007, COMP/B-1/200337.966. Pre-liberalisation, Distrigaz was the only gas supplier on the wholesale Belgian gas market. Two problems identified by the Commission were the duration of the contracts and the volume of gas tied. The commitments decision limits the ability of Distrigaz to enter into long-term supply contracts: for gas, an average of 70% of the market is to be open to competitors each year.

[418] Commitments Decision 17 March 2010, COMP/39.386 IP/10/290. The Commission was concerned that EDF's supply contracts could prevent other electricity suppliers entering and expanding on the French electricity market. EDF will now ensure that every year a significant number of customers are free to contract with other suppliers.

[419] Guidance Paper, para. 34.

[420] Guidance Paper, para. 36.

[421] Guidance Paper, para. 36. Marsden, 'Some Outstanding Issues from the European Commission's Guidance on Article 102 TFEU' (cited in n. 96), Chap. 3, 62–63 criticises the Commission for appearing inherently suspicious of the customer's desire for the dominant undertaking's product, which simply reflects past consumer demand and future expectations of that demand. The Commission thus casts 'normal business operations' in a 'pejorative light'. He concludes that 'a policy document that supposedly prioritizes abuses that most harms consumers should

The Guidance Paper accepts that exclusive purchasing contracts could be justified by efficiencies: this possibility will be considered alongside its application to conditional rebates.[422]

D. DISCOUNT AND REBATE SCHEMES

(i) General

Granting discounts and rebates is a common commercial practice and a major way in which suppliers compete on price but the case law on Article 102 establishes that where undertakings are dominant their discounting and rebating policies are severely constrained.

The concern of the Commission and the EU Courts over rebates has centred on the exclusionary primary line injury they may cause although, puzzlingly, Article 102(c) which should be applied to discrimination affecting downstream markets has been expressly relied upon in some cases.[423] Exclusionary effects are better conceptualised as 'limiting production, markets or technical development to the prejudice of consumers' within Article 102(b).[424] Discounts and rebates are a highly contentious area in which the stance taken by EU law has been widely criticised. In brief, the criticisms are that the law has distinguished between different types of discounts and rebates in a way that makes no economic sense; that it has condemned certain types of rebates as an abuse per se, or because they have exclusionary capabilities, without sufficient analysis of the effects on the market; that it has assumed that an exclusionary effect on competitors means consumer harm; and that it has taken no account of the reasons why undertakings adopt certain discounting and rebating practices and the fact that these might be pro-competitive.[425] In 1999 and 2001 the Commission adopted two decisions, *Virgin/British Airways*[426] and *Michelin II*,[427] which were as controversial as ever. It was widely thought that on appeal the EU Courts might take the opportunity to review the law, placing it on a more economically rigorous footing. In the event both decisions were upheld and the previous trends in the case law confirmed, and even extended.[428] Furthermore, nearly four years after the Guidance Paper had adopted a new approach to rebates the CJ in *Tomra* maintained the established position, at least in respect of target rebates.[429]

actually set out and apply some test for consumer harm, rather than assume that such harm is likely when retailers and their largest suppliers agree exclusive deals'.

[422] Guidance Paper, para. 46.

[423] See Geradin et al., *EU Competition Law and Economics* (cited in n. 160), 4.499–4.505. Article 102(c) is discussed in Section 14, p. 567 ff.

[424] See J. Temple Lang and R. O'Donoghue, 'Defining Legitimate Competition: How to Clarify Pricing Abuses under Article 82EC' (2002) 26 *Fordham Int'l LJ* 83; J. Temple Lang, 'How Can the Problems of Exclusionary Abuses under Article 102 TFEU be Resolved?' (2012) 37 *ELRev* 136.

[425] See, e.g., J. Temple Lang and R. O'Donoghue, 'Defining Legitimate Competition: How to Clarify Pricing Abuses under Article 82EC' (2002) 26 *Fordham Int'l LJ* 83; J. Kallaugher and B. Sher, 'Rebates Revisited: Anti-competitive Effects and Exclusionary Abuse under Article 82' [2004] *ECLR* 263; C. Ahlborn and D. Bailey, 'Discounts, Rebates and Selective Pricing by Dominant Firms: A Trans-Atlantic Comparison' (2006) 2 *European Competition Journal* 101; D. Spector, 'Loyalty Rebates: An Assessment of Competition Concerns and a Proposed Structured Rule of Reason' (2005) 1(2) *Competition Policy International* 89; Geradin et al., *EU Competition Law and Economics* (cited in n. 160), 4.159–4.219; J. Temple Lang, 'How Can the Problems of Exclusionary Abuses under Article 102 TFEU be Resolved?' (2012) 37 *ELRev* 136; H. Zenger, 'Loyalty Rebates and the Competitive Process' (2012) 8 *Journal of Competition Law and Economics* 717.

[426] [2000] OJ L30/1, [2000] 4 CMLR 999.

[427] [2002] OJ L143/1, [2002] 5 CMLR 388.

[428] Case T-203/01, *Manufacture Française des Pneumatiques Michelin* [2003] ECR II-4071; Case T-219/99, *British Airways v. Commission* [2003] ECR II-5917 *aff'd* Case C-95/04 P, *British Airways v. Commission* [2007] ECR I-2331.

[429] Case T-155/06, *Tomra Systems v. Commission* [2010] ECR II-4361, *aff'd* Case C-549/10 P, *Tomra Systems ASA v. European Commission*, 19 April 2012.

(ii) Types of Discounts and Rebates and the Policy of the EU Courts and the Commission

Before turning to the policy of the EU Courts and the Commission it is useful to understand what kinds of discount and/or rebate an undertaking may give.[430] Technically a discount is a deduction from a price list and a rebate is refund granted retrospectively, but the terms are often used synonymously, particularly in the earlier case law. In this chapter the term 'rebate' is used to encompass both discounts and rebates, unless the context otherwise requires.

a. *Quantity* (or *volume*) discounts or rebates are reductions given to a purchaser who buys a certain objective amount (such as ten widgets for the price of nine).

b. *Loyalty* (or *fidelity*) rebates are rebates given in return for exclusivity, whereby the supplier gives a rebate to a customer who purchases all (or nearly all)[431] of its requirements for the product from that supplier.

c. *Target* rebates are rebates given to customers who buy more than a target (threshold) amount in a certain period (the reference period). The target may be set according to the customer's perceived capacity to absorb the goods, and is often set according to its previous purchases, i.e. the customer is required to buy a certain amount in excess of its purchases in the past. Target rebates can be retroactive (rolled back) or incremental, and standardised or individualised:

  • *Rolled-back* (*retroactive*) target rebates are those awarded on *all* purchases once the customer has hit the target. If the target is 100 widgets, once the customer hits the target it gets a rebate on the first 100 as well as the 101st onwards;

  • *Incremental* target rebates are those awarded only on purchases *above* the target;

  • *Standardised* target rebates are schemes where all customers are set the same target and get the same rebates;

  • *Individualised* target rebates are where customers are set different targets and/or different rebates.

d. *Loyalty-inducing* rebates are not a separate category of rebates but a concept developed in EU law to describe rebates which, while not strictly loyalty rebates given in return for exclusivity as such, are perceived by the EU Courts to have analogous effects. The term is usually used in respect of target rebate schemes.

e. *Aggregated* (or *multi-product* or *bundled*) rebates are schemes whereby discounts are given on aggregated purchases of products belonging to different product markets. If the dominant supplier of widgets also supplies blodgets, and offers a discount scheme whereby purchases of blodgets (for which the customer is not dependent on the supplier) are aggregated with those of widgets for discount purposes, the customer will have an incentive to buy the blodgets from the dominant widget supplier.[432] This can have the effects of a tie.[433]

f. *Selective* or '*targeted*' rebates (not to be confused with the target rebates described previously) are discounts or rebates offered only to certain customers or classes of customers who the supplier

---

[430] D. Ridyard, 'Exclusionary Pricing and Price Discrimination Abuses Under Article 102—An Economic Analysis' (2002) *ECLR* 286; Bishop and Walker, *The Economics of EC Competition Law* (cited in n. 187), 6.037–6.062.

[431] This is generally taken as meaning more than 80%, by analogy with the non-compete obligation definition in the Verticals Regulation, Commission Regulation 330/2010 on the application of Article 101(3) to categories of vertical agreements and concerted practices [2010] OJ L102/1, Art. 1(1)(d).

[432] See 85/76, *Hoffmann-La Roche v. Commission* [1979] ECR 461 and *Elopak Italia/Tetra Pak* [1991] OJ L72/1, [1992] 4 CMLR 551.

[433] And is treated as such in the Guidance Paper, paras. 59–61.

identifies to be likely to switch to or from a competitor. Whether selective, targeted low prices can be an abuse has already been discussed.[434]

Originally, the basic distinction made in the cases was between quantity discounts relating to objective amounts offered on equal terms to all customers without discrimination, and loyalty rebates.

Loyalty rebates may have the same effects as exclusive purchasing. As we have seen, provisions whereby a customer contractually commits itself to buying all its requirements of a product from a dominant supplier have been treated as virtually per se abuses.[435] However, a supplier may offer a customer a rebate if it buys all its requirements for the product from that supplier, or a rebate system may be set up so that it rewards customers who *do* buy exclusively. Other rebate schemes, while not expressly rewarding exclusivity as such, may strongly encourage the customer to stay with the supplier. Target rebates, for example, may encourage a customer to buy exclusively or almost exclusively from the dominant undertaking. This is why the EU Courts use the much-criticised description 'loyalty-inducing' (or 'fidelity-inducing'). The Commission currently calls rebates which reward customers for a particular form of purchasing behaviour 'conditional rebates'.[436] Loyalty-inducing rebates, like loyalty rebates, are seen in the Article 102 cases as going beyond competition on the merits. Rather, they are considered to enmesh the customer into deals with the dominant supplier with which equally efficient competitors cannot compete thereby having an exclusionary effect and foreclosing the market. The Commission and the EU Courts are particularly concerned with the so-called 'suction effect' (the 'effect at the margin') in rolled-back rebates, whereby the nearer the customer gets to the target the more difficult it is for a competitor to entice it away as by switching even a small portion of its demand from the dominant undertaking the customer would lose all the retroactive rebate.[437]

A fundamental question about the application of Article 102 to rebates is whether some practices have such a pernicious effect when adopted by dominant firms that they are per se abuses or at least subject to a strong presumption of illegality, or whether every case should be judged individually to identify any exclusionary effects. As the 2000 Commission Guidelines on Vertical Restraints[438] baldly stated, reflecting the case law, 'Article 102 specifically prevents dominant companies from applying...fidelity rebate schemes'. However, current emphasis on economic analysis and on consumer harm as the test for whether the behaviour of the dominant firm amounts to an abuse suggests two things: first, that the actual or likely exclusionary effects in a particular case should be assessed, rather than presumed and, secondly, that it should not be presumed that the exclusion of *competitors* harms *consumers*.

The starting point in the cases has traditionally been that a dominant firm can give quantity discounts without infringing Article 102. However, that simple proposition must be treated with caution. It is established that to be non-abusive a quantity discount must be non-discriminatory, not just on paper but in fact.[439] It also appears that quantity discounts are legal only to the extent that they reflect efficiencies, economies of scale, or costs savings.[440]

The distinction between quantity rebates and conditional rebates is blurred. In *Michelin II*, a quantity rebate scheme was based on standardised targets and was held to be an abuse as it was

---

[434] See Section 8.D, p. 408 ff.

[435] Case 85/76, *Hoffmann-La Roche v. Commission* [1979] ECR 461.

[436] See, e.g., *Intel*, Case COMP/C-3/37.990 [2010] 4 CMLR 314, section 4.2; Guidance Paper, paras. 37–46.

[437] See particularly Case T-219/99, *British Airways v. Commission* [2003] ECR II-5917, paras. 272–273; Case C-95/04 P, *British Airways v. Commission* [2007] ECR I-2331, para. 74; Case C-549/10 P, *Tomra Systems ASA v. European Commission*, 19 April 2012, paras. 78–79; Guidance Paper, para. 40.

[438] [2000] OJ C291/1, para. 152.

[439] Case C-163/99, *Portugal v. EC Commission* [2001] ECR I-2613 (*Portuguese Airports*).

[440] *Portuguese Airports*, para. 52, see Section 14.C, p. 569); Case T-203/01, *Manufacture Française des Pneumatiques Michelin v. Commission* [2003] ECR II- 4071, paras 58 and 59.

loyalty-inducing. In Section 10.D.iii we look at the major cases and decisions on discounts and rebates and consider what principles are discernible therefrom. We then look at the approach of the Commission as set out in the Guidance Paper and (in Section 10.D.v) at the post-Guidance Paper case law and decisional practice.

(iii) The Case Law Prior to the Guidance Paper

a. The *European Sugar Cartel* Case: Rebates in Return for Exclusive Purchasing

The *European Sugar Cartel* case[441] was mainly concerned with a cartel between the European sugar producers but the Commission also found the rebate scheme of one dominant producer to be an abuse. The scheme gave an 'annual quantity rebate' to customers who purchased their annual requirements only from that producer. If the customer purchased elsewhere at all it lost the rebate on the entire year's purchases. The CJ upheld the decision, and for the first time made a distinction between true quantity rebates and loyalty rebates and classified this as the latter:

> ... the rebate at issue is not to be treated as a quantity rebate exclusively linked with the volume of purchases from the producer concerned but has rightly been classified by the Commission as a loyalty rebate designed, through the grant of a financial advantage, to prevent customers obtaining their supplies from competing producers.[442]

The loyalty rebate was an abuse for two reasons. It discriminated against purchasers who did not buy exclusively from the dominant firm (the main thrust of the Commission's objections and an application of Article 102(c)) and it excluded competitors (who would have to offer a low enough price to compensate the customer for the loss of its whole year's rebate).

b. *Hoffmann-La Roche*: The Abusive Nature of Loyalty Rebates

In the seminal case of *Hoffmann-La Roche* the CJ laid down the basis for the treatment of loyalty rebates which remains the foundation of the law.

Case 85/76, *Hoffmann-La Roche* v. *Commission* [1979] ECR 461

Hoffmann-La Roche (HLR) supplied a number of vitamins. The Commission held that it was in a dominant position[443] and had abused its position by giving loyalty rebates to 22 large customers. HLR appealed. The Court dealt with three arguments on the question of the loyalty rebates: whether such rebates are an abuse, what was the nature of the rebates in this case, and whether they were saved from infringing Article 102 by the presence in the contracts of an 'English clause'.[444]

Court of Justice

89. An undertaking which is in a dominant position on the market and ties purchasers—even if it does so at their request—by an obligation or promise on their part to obtain all or most of their requirements exclusively from the said undertaking abuses its dominant position within the meaning of Article [102], whether the obligation in question is stipulated without further qualification or whether it is undertaken in consideration of the grant of a rebate. The same applies if the said undertaking, without tying the

---

[441] Cases 40/73, etc. *Suiker Unie* v. *EC Commission* [1975] ECR 1663.

[442] Cases 40/73, etc. *Suiker Unie* v. *EC Commission* [1975] ECR 1663, para. 513.

[443] For the dominance aspects of this case see Chap. 6.

[444] For 'English clauses' see Section 10.B, p. 451.

purchasers by a formal obligation, applies, either under the terms of agreements concluded with these purchasers or unilaterally, a system of fidelity rebates, that is to say discounts conditional on the customer's obtaining all or most of its requirements—whether the quantity of its purchases be large or small—from the undertaking in a dominant position.

90. Obligations of this kind to obtain supplies exclusively from a particular undertaking, whether or not they are in consideration of rebates or of the granting of fidelity rebates intended to give the purchaser an incentive to obtain his supplies exclusively from the undertaking in a dominant position, are incompatible with the objective of undistorted competition within the Common Market, because—unless there are exceptional circumstances which may make an agreement between undertakings in the context of Article [101] and in particular of paragraph (3) of that Article, permissible—they are not based on an economic transaction which justifies this burden or benefit but are designed to deprive the purchaser of or restrict his possible choice of sources of supply and to deny other producers access to the market. The fidelity rebate, unlike quantity rebates exclusively linked with the volume of purchases from the producer concerned, is designed through the grant of a financial advantage to prevent customers from obtaining their supplies from competing producers. Furthermore, the effect of fidelity rebates is to apply dissimilar conditions to equivalent transactions with other trading parties in that two purchasers pay a different price for the same quantity of the same product depending on whether they obtain their supplies exclusively from the undertaking in a dominant position or have several sources of supply. Finally, these practices by an undertaking in a dominant position and especially on an expanding market tend to consolidate this position by means of a form of competition which is not based on the transactions effected and is therefore distorted.

The most controversial issue in this famous passage is that it seems to say that dominant firms cannot enter into exclusive purchasing agreements and cannot operate rebate schemes which have the same effect as an exclusive purchasing agreements: in other words, they are per se abusive. It does not depend on assessing the effect of the rebate in the particular case, as it is assumed that if a dominant firm rewards customers for not buying elsewhere it is bound to have an exclusionary effect on competitors. This may have been justifiable in *Hoffmann-La Roche* itself, where on the facts the dominant supplier had designed a system intended to have the same effect as an exclusive (or near-exclusive) purchasing obligation.[445] However, the statements in *Hoffmann-La Roche* have been heavily relied upon in subsequent cases where the factual situation and the form of the rebates were different. Moreover, it will be noted that the effect of the assumed exclusion of competitors on *consumers* is not mentioned at all.

The hostility to loyalty rebates can lead undertakings to present their rebates as quantity discounts related to objective volumes. In *Hoffmann-La Roche* itself the CJ detected that what appeared at first sight to be quantity discounts were in fact disguised loyalty rebates.[446] The obvious tactic is to calculate the anticipated requirements of the customer for the product and to offer the customer a discount based on that quantity. This failed to get past the Commission in *Deutsche Post*, for example, where the Commission once again stressed that quantity rebates are fixed objectively and applicable to all possible purchasers and that rebates linked to an estimate of each customer's presumed capacity of absorption are loyalty rebates.[447]

---

[445] See J. Temple Lang and R. O'Donoghue, 'Defining Legitimate Competition: How to Clarify Pricing Abuses under Article 102EC' (2002) 26 *Fordham Int'l LJ* 83, 94, 110–111.

[446] Case 85/76, *Hoffmann-La Roche v. Commission* [1979] ECR 4611, paras. 95–101.

[447] [2001] OJ L125/27, [2001] 5 CMLR 99, para. 33, see also Case T–228/97, *Irish Sugar plc v. Commission* [1999] ECR II-2969, paras. 213 and 218.

c. The Case Law on Loyalty Rebates Post *Hoffmann-La Roche*

In *BPB Industries and British Gypsum*, BPB, through its subsidiary British Gypsum (BG), was held to be the dominant supplier of plasterboard in the UK and Ireland. It faced increasing competition from imports from France and Spain. It inaugurated a system of payments for promotional and advertising expenses to customers (builders' merchants) in Great Britain who bought exclusively from it,[448] and in Northern Ireland it offered rebates to those buying exclusively from BG and not dealing with the importers.[449] Both schemes were condemned as abuses on the grounds that a dominant undertaking may not give rebates or other advantages conditional upon exclusivity.[450] The plea that the promotional payments were normal commercial practice, and that BG was entitled to take steps to protect its legitimate commercial interests, were rejected on the basis of the *United Brands* judgment that such behaviour could not be countenanced if its 'actual purpose is to strengthen this dominant position and abuse it'.[451]

In the *Soda Ash* cases[452] the Commission condemned a pricing structure based on 'top slice' rebates, whereby customers got the basic tonnage, which would have been bought from the dominant undertaking anyway, at the normal price, but were offered substantial discounts on extra amounts above that. These were held to be exclusionary loyalty rebates and were also held to be discriminatory contrary to Article 102(c) in that the basic tonnage was set at a different figure for each customer, so giving them different costs.[453] Although the second GC judgment in respect of Solvay was overturned by the CJ on the procedural questions and therefore the decision was annulled without addressing the substantive law on rebates it is worth noting the comments in the Opinion of Advocate General Kokott in *Solvay* on the loyalty rebate case law:

80. I would add merely for the sake of completeness that Solvay's (ill-substantiated) complaint to the effect that the case-law of the Court of Justice concerning fidelity rebates is formalistic and has no economic basis is also unfounded. As has already been said, when assessing rebate schemes, the Court of Justice takes into account all the circumstances of the individual case and expressly recognises the possibility of an objective economic justification... This is anything but formalistic.[454]

In 2012, in *Tomra*, a case concerning retroactive target rebates (a longer extract from which appears later in this chapter)[455] the CJ made the following statement.

---

[448] According to the Commission's decision these were devised after the managing director asked the marketing director how the company could 'reward the loyalty of merchants who remained exclusively with us', *BPB Industries plc* [1989] OJ L10/50, [1990] 4 CMLR 464, para. 58.

[449] The company also put in place a system of priority deliveries for loyal customers.

[450] Case T-65/89, *BPB Industries and British Gypsum Ltd v. Commission* [1993] ECR II-389, aff'd on appeal Case C-310/93P *BPB Industries PLC and British Gypsum Ltd v. Commission* [1995] ECR I-865.

[451] Case T-65/89, para. 69, citing Case 2/76 *United Brands v. EC Commission* [1978] ECR 207, para. 189.

[452] *Soda Ash–ICI* and *Soda Ash–Solvay* [1991] OJ L152/40 and 152/21, [1994] 4 CMLR 645, annulled for procedural reasons, Cases T-30/91, etc. *Solvay v. Commission* [1995] ECR II-1775, aff'd Cases C-286–288/96 P, *Commission v. Solvay* [2000] ECR I-2391; replaced by *Soda Ash–Solvay* [2003] OJ L10/10 and *Soda Ash–ICI* [2003] OJ L10/33, upheld in respect of *Solvay*, Case T-57 and 58/ 01, *Solvay v. Commission* [2009] ECR II-4621, annulled for procedural reasons Case C-109/10 P, *Solvay SA v. European Commission* [2011] ECR I-10329, upheld in respect of ICI, Case T-66/01, *ICI v. Commission* [2009] ECR II-2631.

[453] [1991] OJ L152/40, [2003] OJ L10/10, paras. 181–182.

[454] Opinion of AG Kokott of 14 April 2011 in Case C-109/10 P, *Solvay SA v. European Commission*, para. 80. In *Solvay* the GC found that 'even where it is moderate, the amount of a fidelity rebate has an impact on the conditions of competition', Case T-57/01, para. 355, a statement which the Advocate General described as 'beyond legal reproach in the light of the circumstances of the present case. It is based on reasonable economic considerations', Opinion of AG Kokott of 14 April 2011, para. 86, basing herself on the commission payments found to be abusive in Case C-95/04 P, *British Airways v. Commission* [2007] ECR I-2331, discussed in Section 10.D.iii.f, p. 469.

[455] See Section 10.D.v.a, p. 479.

C-549/10 P, *Tomra Systems ASA* v. *European Commission*, 19 April 2012

Court of Justice

70 In the event that an undertaking in a dominant position makes use of a system of rebates, the Court has ruled that that undertaking abuses that position where, without tying the purchasers by a formal obligation, it applies, either under the terms of agreements concluded with these purchasers or unilaterally, a system of loyalty rebates, that is to say, discounts conditional on the customer's obtaining—whether the quantity of its purchases is large or small—all or most of its requirements from the undertaking in a dominant position (see Case 85/76 *Hoffman-La Roche*...paragraph 89, and Case 322/81 *Nederlandsche Banden-Industrie-Michelin* v *Commission*...paragraph 71).

71 In that regard, it is necessary to consider all the circumstances, particularly the criteria and rules governing the grant of the rebate, and to investigate whether, in providing an advantage not based on any economic service justifying it, the rebates tend to remove or restrict the buyer's freedom to choose his sources of supply, to bar competitors from access to the market, or to strengthen the dominant position by distorting competition (see *Nederlandsche Banden-Industrie-Michelin* v *Commission*, paragraph 73).

In paragraph 70, despite years of relentless criticism of the EU Courts' position on loyalty rebates, the CJ restated the law laid down in *Hoffmann-La Roche*, i.e. that a dominant undertaking abuses its position by applying a system of loyalty rebates. However, in paragraph 71 it says, quoting *Michelin I*,[456] that it is necessary to consider all the circumstances. That would be unremarkable if paragraph 71 applies only to retroactive target rebates of the kind at issue both in *Michelin I* (and to which paragraph 73 of that judgment applies) and in *Tomra* itself. The interesting point is the words '[i]n that regard' (in the French version 'à cet égard') which introduce the paragraph, which appear to refer back to paragraph 70 and suggest that loyalty rebates are not always abusive but must also be considered in the light of the circumstances. If the CJ did indeed intend to change its stance on loyalty rebates it is a strange way in which to do it, but welcome nonetheless.

d. *Michelin I*: The Abusive Nature of Target Rebates

Target rebates were first considered, and held to be an abuse, on account of their exclusionary effect, in the first *Michelin* case. Significantly, the CJ described the rebates (paragraph 73) as removing or restricting the buyer's 'freedom to choose his sources of supply' in line with paragraph 90 of *Hoffmann-La Roche* in relation to loyalty rebates.

Case 322/81, *Nederlandsche Banden-Industrie Michelin* v. *Commission* [1983] ECR 3461

Michelin supplied heavy vehicle new replacement tyres to tyre dealers who sold both Michelin tyres and competing brands. It ran a fixed invoice discount and a cash discount for early payment, which were the same for all dealers. These were not found to infringe Article 102. Michelin also offered a discount linked to an annual sales target which was personal to each dealer. A proportion of this variable discount was paid in advance, initially every month and then every four months as an advance on the annual sum. The full sum became payable only if the dealer attained a pre-determined sales target. The target was fixed for

---

[456] Case 322/81, NV *Nederlandsche Banden-Industrie Michelin* v. *Commission* [1983] ECR 3461.

each dealer by a Michelin sales representative at the beginning of each year. The discount was basically geared to turnover and to the proportion of Michelin tyres sold and the aim was to ensure that the dealer sold more Michelin tyres than he had in the year before although if times were hard it might be sufficient to equal the previous year. Towards the end of each sales year Michelin's sales representative would urge the dealer to place an order big enough to obtain the full discount. The Commission held that the scheme infringed Article 102. This finding was upheld by the Court of Justice.

Court of Justice

71. In the case more particularly of the grant by an undertaking in a dominant position of discounts to its customers the court has held in its judgments of 16 December 1975 in Joined Cases 40 to 48, 50, 54, to 56, 111, 113 and 114/73 *Cooperatieve Vereniging 'Suiker Unie' UA and others* v. *Commission*...and of 13 February 1979 in Case 85/76 *Hoffmann-La Roche* v. *Commission*...that in contrast to a quantity discount, which is linked solely to the volume of purchases from the manufacturer concerned, a loyalty rebate, which by offering customers financial advantages tends to prevent them from obtaining their supplies from competing manufacturers, amounts to an abuse within the meaning of Article [102].

72. As regards the system at issue in this case, which is characterized by the use of sales targets, it must be observed that this system does not amount to a mere quantity discount linked solely to the volume of goods purchased since the progressive scale of the previous year's turnover indicates only the limits within which the system applies. Michelin NV has moreover itself pointed out that the majority of dealers who bought more than 3 000 tyres a year were in any case in the group receiving the highest rebates. On the other hand the system in question did not require dealers to enter into any exclusive dealing agreements or to obtain a specific proportion of their supplies from Michelin NV, and that this point distinguishes it from loyalty rebates of the type which the court had to consider in its judgment of 13 February 1979 in *Hoffmann-La Roche*.

73. In deciding whether Michelin NV abused its dominant position in applying its discount system it is therefore necessary to consider all the circumstances, particularly the criteria and rules for the grant of the discount, and to investigate whether, in providing an advantage not based on any economic service justifying it, the discount tends to remove or restrict the buyer's freedom to choose his sources of supply, to bar competitors from access to the market, to apply dissimilar conditions to equivalent transactions with other trading parties or to strengthen the dominant position by distorting competition.

74. It is in the light of those considerations that the submissions put forward by the applicant in answer to the two objections raised in the contested decision to the discounted system in general, namely that Michelin NV bound tyre dealers in the Netherlands to itself and that it applied to them dissimilar conditions in respect of equivalent transactions, must be examined.

...

81. The discount system in question was based on an annual reference period. However, any system under which discounts are granted according to the quantities sold during a relatively long reference period has the inherent effect, at the end of that period, of increasing pressure on the buyer to reach the purchase figure needed to obtain the discount or to avoid suffering the expected loss for the entire period. In this case the variations in the rate of discount over a year as a result of one last order, even a small one, affected the dealer's margin of profit on the whole year's sales of Michelin heavy-vehicle tyres. In such circumstances, even quite slight variations might put dealers under appreciable pressure.

82. That effect was accentuated still further by the wide divergence between Michelin NV's market share and those of its main competitors. If a competitor wished to offer a dealer a competitive inducement for placing an order, especially at the end of the year, it had to take into account the absolute value of Michelin NV's annual target discount and fix its own discount at a percentage which, when related to the dealer's lesser quantity of purchases from that competitor, was very high. Despite the apparently low percentage of Michelin NV's discount, it was therefore very difficult for its competitors to offset the benefits or losses resulting for dealers from attaining or failing to attain Michelin NV's targets, as the case might be.

83. Furthermore, the lack of transparency of Michelin NV's entire discount system, whose rules moreover changed on several occasions during the relevant period, together with the fact that neither the scale of discounts nor the sales targets or discounts relating to them were communicated in writing to dealers meant that they were left in uncertainty and on the whole could not predict with any confidence the effect of attaining their targets or failing to do so.

84. All those factors were instrumental in creating for dealers a situation in which they were under considerable pressure, especially towards the end of a year, to attain Michelin NV's sales targets if they did not wish to run the risk of losses which its competitors could not easily make good by means of the discounts which they themselves were able to offer. Its network of commercial representatives enabled Michelin NV to remind dealers of this situation at any time so as to induce them to place orders with it.

85. Such a situation is calculated to prevent dealers from being able to select freely at any time in the light of the market situation the most favourable of the offers made by the various competitors and to change supplier without suffering any appreciable economic disadvantage. It thus limits the dealers' choice of supplier and makes access to the market more difficult for competitors. Neither the wish to sell more nor the wish to spread production more evenly can justify such a restriction of the customer's freedom of choice and independence. The position of dependence in which dealers find themselves and which is created by the discount system in question, is not therefore based on any countervailing advantage which may be economically justified.

86. It must therefore be concluded that by binding dealers in the Netherlands to itself by means of the discount system described above Michelin NV committed an abuse, within the meaning of Article [102], of its dominant position in the market for new replacement tyres for heavy vehicles. The submission put forward by the applicant to refute that finding in the contested decision must therefore be rejected.

The particular objections to the *Michelin* scheme were therefore that it required the customer to purchase more than in the preceding period, it set a different target for each customer based on exceeding the previous purchases (i.e. it was individualised), it had a long reference period (a year), and it was not transparent. On this basis it could be argued that a more transparent scheme, with a short reference period and less discriminatory targets, would be less likely to infringe Article 102. However, in *Irish Sugar*[457] the Commission unequivocally condemned rebate schemes which are conditional on the customer buying more than in a previous period because they tie the customers to the supplier and foreclose the market to competitors. Although it found that the lack of transparency in Irish Sugar's entire rebate scheme was in itself an abuse[458] it was clear from *Irish Sugar* that the Commission had fundamental objections to this type of target. The Commission rejected the contention that they are a species of quantity discount. The GC upheld the Commission's decision:

the Commission has not committed an error of assessment in taking the view that a rebate granted by an undertaking in a dominant position by reference to an increase in purchases made over a certain period, without that rebate being capable of being regarded as a normal quantity discount (point 153), as the applicant does not deny, constitutes an abuse of that dominant position, since such a practice can only be intended to tie the customers to which it is granted and place competitors in an unfavourable competitive position.[459]

Target rebates are seen as loyalty-inducing in that they put pressure on the customer to stay with the supplier in order to ensure that the discount at the end of the reference period is obtained. In *Coca-Cola*,[460] the Commission settled the proceedings against Coca-Cola by taking undertakings by

[457] [1997] OJ L258/1, [1997] 5 CMLR 666.
[458] *Irish Sugar* [1997] OJ L258/1, [1997] 5 CMLR 666, para. 150.
[459] Case T-228/97, *Irish Sugar plc v. Commission* [1999] ECR II-2969, para. 213.
[460] *XIXth Report on Competition Policy* (Commission, 1989), para. 50.

which the company undertook not to include in agreements concluded with distributors in Member States 'clauses which make the granting of rebates subject to the joint contracting party's purchasing quantities of "Coca-Cola" set individually during a period of more than three consecutive months'. Individually set targets of less than three months were accepted because the Commission considered that the new scheme did not substantially impede the customers from switching suppliers.[461]

In 1999, in *Virgin/British Airways*,[462] the Commission for the first time condemned a target scheme in the services sector and on the buying side. As the GC judgment in the appeal from this decision was not given until four years later the case is dealt with in Section 10.D.iii.g, after the *Michelin II* judgment.

e. *Michelin II*

In 2001 the Commission adopted another decision holding Michelin to have infringed Article 102, *Michelin II*.[463] This time Michelin was operating a wide range of pricing schemes in respect of the supply of replacement tyres for heavy vehicles in France. The schemes were complex. One involved a 'progress bonus'[464] in which the tyre dealer was rewarded if he increased his purchases of Michelin tyres compared to the previous year. The 'target' at which the dealer had to aim was therefore individualised, varying from dealer to dealer, as in *Michelin I*. The Commission roundly condemned it:

263. This individualised bonus corresponds exactly to that the Court ruled against in the…*Michelin* judgment…An undertaking in a dominant position cannot require dealers to exceed, each year, their figures for the previous years and thus automatically increase its market shares by taking advantage of its dominant position.

264. Here again, the bonus was unfair, because of the requirement imposed by Michelin to increase purchases and because of the insecurity brought about by the individualised determination of the minimum base. The bonus was also loyalty-inducing and market-partitioning since it applied only to purchases made from Michelin France.[465]

Other forms of discounts, rebates, and payments at issue in *Michelin II* were primarily quantity rebates based on standardised volume targets (*rappels quantitatifs*); a 'service bonus' scheme; and arrangements known as the 'Michelin Friends Club'.

The quantity rebates were given according to a grid. Rebates were a percentage of the tyre dealers' annual turnover and increased with the volumes purchased during the reference period (a year) but the target volumes were not based on estimates of each dealer's purchase requirements. The grid had a large number of 'steps'. When a dealer went up a step by hitting a particular target the extra discount was 'rolled back'. *Michelin II* was the first time that the Commission had made a decision on a *standardised* target scheme. The Commission held that it infringed Article 102.

The Commission also objected to the 'service bonus' whereby the dealer earned 'points' for compliance with various commitments entered into with Michelin. The operation of the scheme left considerable discretion to Michelin. The Commission said the service bonus scheme was unfair, loyalty-inducing, and (in some parts) equivalent to tied sales.

The 'Michelin Friends Club' was an arrangement by which, in return for additional payments, larger dealers could enter into a closer relationship with Michelin thus maintaining the

---

[461] The Commission's clearance in 1997 of the *Coca-Cola/Amalgamated Beverages* merger [1997] OJ L218/15 was on the basis that Coca-Cola undertook to adopt the 1989 undertakings (para. 212 of the decision).

[462] [2000] OJ L30/1, [2000] 4 CMLR 999.

[463] [2002] OJ L143/1, [2002] 5 CMLR 388.

[464] Some of the schemes changed in their detail during the period under review. The 'progress bonus' became an 'achieved-target' bonus in 1997–1998 but essentially it worked in the same way.

[465] The finding against the individualised target scheme was not specifically appealed to the GC. Michelin did, however, contend in respect of *all* its impugned practices that the Commission should have carried out a specific analysis of their effects. This plea was dismissed.

dealer's 'température Michelin'. The Commission found the Club terms to be abusive as they were loyalty-inducing and left the dealers completely dependent on Michelin.[466]

Michelin appealed, primarily in respect of the quantity rebates, the service bonus, and the Friends Club. It appealed against the progress bonus only insofar as it claimed that the Commission was wrong to find that the combination of all the discount systems together had a further impact, and that it had wrongfully failed to carry out an analysis of the *effects* of the discounting practices.[467] The GC upheld the Commission's decision in its entirety, despite holding that the Commission was wrong to suggest that the CJ had expressly held that a reference period could not exceed three months.[468]

The GC (paragraphs 54 and 55 of the judgment) rehearsed again the definition of abuse from *Hoffmann-La Roche*, and the special responsibility of dominant undertakings laid down in *Michelin I*. It said again that dominant undertakings may protect their own commercial interests when they are attacked but cannot abuse their dominant position in so doing.[469] It then continued as set out in the following extract. The judgment was the first time the EU Courts employed the concept of 'loyalty-inducing', which the Commission had used in its decision. As in *Michelin I*, the exclusionary effect was linked to the removal or restriction of the buyer's freedom to choose sources of supply (paragraph 60).

Case T-203/01, *Manufacture Française Des Pneumatiques Michelin* v. *Commission* [2003] ECR II-4071

General Court

56. With more particular regard to the granting of rebates by an undertaking in a dominant position, it is apparent from a consistent line of decisions that a loyalty rebate, which is granted in return for an undertaking by the customer to obtain his stock exclusively or almost exclusively from an undertaking in a dominant position, is contrary to Article [102]. Such a rebate is designed through the grant of financial advantage, to prevent customers from obtaining their supplies from competing producers (Joined Cases 40/73 to 48/73, 50/73, 54/73 to 56/73, 111/73, 113/73 and 114/73 *Suiker Unie and Others* v. *Commission*...paragraph 518; *Hoffmann-La Roche* v. *Commission*...paragraphs 89 and 90; *Michelin* v. *Commission*...paragraph 71; and Case T-65/89 *BPB Industries and British Gypsum* v. *Commission*...paragraph 120).

57. More generally, as the applicant submits, a rebate system which has a foreclosure effect on the market will be regarded as contrary to Article [102] if it is applied by an undertaking in a dominant position. For that reason, the Court has held that a rebate which depended on a purchasing target being achieved also infringed Article [102] (*Michelin* v. *Commission*...).

58. Quantity rebate systems linked solely to the volume of purchases made from an undertaking occupying a dominant position are generally considered not to have the foreclosure effect prohibited by Article [102] (see *Michelin* v. *Commission*...paragraph 71, and Case C-163/99 *Portugal* v. *Commission*...paragraph 50). If increasing the quantity supplied results in lower costs for the supplier, the latter is entitled to pass on that reduction to the customer in the form of a more favourable tariff (Opinion of Advocate General Mischo in *Portugal* v. *Commission*...at point 106). Quantity rebates are therefore deemed to reflect gains in efficiency and economies of scale made by the undertaking in a dominant position.

59. It follows that a rebate system in which the rate of the discount increases according to the volume purchased will not infringe Article [102] unless the criteria and rules for granting the rebate reveal that the system is not based on an economically justified countervailing advantage but tends,

---

[466] 'Certainly the members of the Club all shared the feeling that there could be no turning back...The commitment they had all entered into could fairly be described as a lifetime one', *Michelin II*, para. 326.

[467] Michelin also appealed against the amount of the fine.

[468] *Michelin II*, para. 85, referring to para. 216 of the decision.

[469] Citing *United Brands*, *BPB Industries*, *Compagnie Maritime Belge*, and *Irish Sugar*.

following the example of a loyalty and target rebate, to prevent customers from obtaining their supplies from competitors (see *Hoffmann-La Roche* v. *Commission*, cited at paragraph 54 above, paragraph 90; *Michelin* v. *Commission*…paragraph 85; *Irish Sugar* v. *Commission*…paragraph 114; and *Portugal* v. *Commission*…paragraph 52).

60. In determining whether a quantity rebate system is abusive, it will therefore be necessary to consider all the circumstances, particularly the criteria and rules governing the grant of the rebate, and to investigate whether, in providing an advantage not based on any economic service justifying it, the rebates tend to remove or restrict the buyer's freedom to choose his sources of supply, to bar competitors from access to the market, to apply dissimilar conditions to equivalent transactions with other trading parties or to strengthen the dominant position by distorting competition (see *Hoffmann-La Roche* v. *Commission*…paragraph 90; *Michelin* v. *Commission*…paragraph 73; and *Irish Sugar* v. *Commission*…paragraph 114).

…

62.… the Court points out that the mere fact of characterising a discount system as quantity rebates does not mean that the grant of such discounts is compatible with Article [102]. It is necessary to consider all the circumstances, particularly the criteria and rules governing the grant of the discounts, and to investigate whether, in providing an advantage not based on any economic service justifying it, the quantity rebates tend to remove or restrict the buyer's freedom to choose his sources of supply, to bar competitors from access to the market, to apply dissimilar conditions to equivalent transactions with other trading parties or to strengthen the dominant position by distorting competition (see the case-law cited at paragraph 60 above).

…

64. It is apparent from the contested decision that the Commission considers that the quantity rebate system applied by the applicant constitutes an infringement of Article [102] because it is unfair, it is loyalty-inducing and it has a partitioning effect…

65. However, it may be inferred generally from the case-law that any loyalty-inducing rebate system applied by an undertaking in a dominant position has foreclosure effects prohibited by Article [102] (see paragraphs 56 to 60 above), irrespective of whether or not the rebate system is discriminatory. In *Michelin* v. *Commission*…the Court, when considering the lawfulness of Commission Decision 81/969/EEC of 7 October 1981 …(…*Bandengroothandel Frieschebrug BV/NV Nederlandsche Banden-Industrie Michelin*) (OJ 1981 L 353, p. 33, the NBIM Decision), did not uphold the Commission's claim that the rebate system applied by Michelin was discriminatory but nevertheless held that it infringed Article [102] because it placed dealers in a position of dependence in relation to Michelin.

66. This Court considers that it is necessary, first, to consider whether the Commission had good reason to conclude, in the contested decision, that the quantity rebate system was loyalty-inducing or, in other words, that it sought to tie dealers to the applicant and to prevent them from obtaining supplies from the applicant's competitors. As the Commission acknowledges in its defence, moreover, the alleged unfairness of the system was closely linked to its loyalty-inducing effect. Furthermore, it must be held that a loyalty-inducing rebate system is, by its very nature, also partitioning, since it is designed to prevent the customer from obtaining supplies from other manufacturers.

…

95. It follows from all of the foregoing that a quantity rebate system in which there is a significant variation in the discount rates between the lower and higher steps, which has a reference period of one year and in which the discount is fixed on the basis of total turnover achieved during the reference period, has the characteristics of a loyalty-inducing discount system.

96. Admittedly, as the applicant points out, the aim of any competition on price and any discount system is to encourage the customer to purchase more from the same supplier.

97. However, an undertaking in a dominant position has a special responsibility not to allow its conduct to impair genuine undistorted competition on the common market (*Michelin* v. *Commission*...paragraph 57). Not all competition on price can be regarded as legitimate (*AKZO* v. *Commission*...paragraph 70, and *Irish Sugar* v. *Commission*...paragraph 111). An undertaking in a dominant position cannot have recourse to means other than those within the scope of competition on the merits (*Irish Sugar* v. *Commission*...paragraph 111).

98. In those circumstances, it is necessary to consider whether, in spite of appearances, the quantity rebate system applied by the applicant is based on a countervailing advantage which may be economically justified (see, in that regard, *Michelin* v. *Commission*...paragraph 73; *Irish Sugar* v. *Commission* paragraph 114; and *Portugal* v. *Commission*...paragraph 52) or, in other words, if it rewards an economy of scale made by the applicant because of orders for large quantities. If increasing the quantity supplied results in lower costs for the supplier, the latter is entitled to pass on that reduction to the customer in the form of a more favourable tariff (Opinion of Advocate General Mischo in *Portugal* v. *Commission*...point 106).

...

100. It must be borne in mind that, according to settled case-law, discounts granted by an undertaking in a dominant position must be based on a countervailing advantage which may be economically justified (*Michelin* v. *Commission*...paragraph 85; *Irish Sugar* v. *Commission*...paragraph 114; and *Portugal* v. *Commission*...paragraph 52). A quantity rebate system is therefore compatible with Article [102] if the advantage conferred on dealers is justified by the volume of business they bring or by any economies of scale they allow the supplier to make (*Portugal* v. *Commission*, paragraph 52).

...

107. It is then necessary to examine whether the applicant has established that the quantity rebate system, which presents the characteristics of a loyalty-inducing rebate system, was based on objective economic reasons (see, in that regard, *Irish Sugar* v. *Commission*...paragraph 188, and *Portugal* v. *Commission*...paragraph 56).

108. It must be stated that the applicant provides no specific information in that regard. It merely states that orders for large amounts involve economies and that the customer is entitled to have those economies passed on to him in the price that he pays (point 57 of the application). It also refers to its reply to the statement of objections and to the transcript of the hearing (reply, point 91). Far from establishing that the quantity rebates were based on actual cost savings (Opinion of Advocate General Mischo in *Portugal* v. *Commission*...point 118), the applicant merely states generally that the quantity rebates were justified by economies of scale in the areas of production costs and distribution (transcript of the hearing, p. 62).

109. However, such a line of argument is too general and is insufficient to provide economic reasons to explain specifically the discount rates chosen for the various steps in the rebate system in question (see, in that regard, *Portugal* v. *Commission*...paragraph 56).

110. It follows from all of the foregoing that the Commission was entitled to conclude, in the contested decision, that the quantity rebate system at issue was designed to tie truck tyre dealers in France to the applicant by granting advantages which were not based on any economic justification. Because it was loyalty-inducing, the quantity rebate system tended to prevent dealers from being able to select freely at any time, in the light of the market situation, the most advantageous of the offers made by various competitors and to change supplier without suffering any appreciable economic disadvantage. The rebate system thus limited the dealers' choice of supplier and made access to the market more difficult for competitors, while the position of dependence in which the dealers found themselves, and which was created by the discount system in question, was not therefore based on any countervailing advantage which might be economically justified (see *Michelin* v. *Commission*...paragraph 85).

111. The applicant cannot find support in the transparent nature of the quantity rebate system. A loyalty-inducing rebate system is contrary to Article [102], whether it is transparent or not. Furthermore,

the quantity rebates formed part of a complex system of discounts, some of which on the applicant's own admission constituted an abuse...The simultaneous application of various discount systems—namely, the quantity rebates, the service bonus, the progress bonus, and the bonuses linked to the PRO Agreement and the Michelin Friends Club—which were not obtained on invoice, made it impossible for the dealer to calculate the exact purchase price of Michelin tyres at the time of purchase. That situation inevitably put dealers in a position of uncertainty and dependence on the applicant.

...

113. It follows from the foregoing that the Commission was correct to find that the quantity rebate system applied by the applicant infringed Article [102], *inter alia*, because it was loyalty-inducing.

...

140. The granting of a discount by an undertaking in a dominant position to a dealer must be based on an objective economic justification (*Irish Sugar* v. *Commission*...paragraph 218). It cannot depend on a subjective assessment by the undertaking in a dominant position of the extent to which the dealer has met his commitments and is thus entitled to a discount. As the Commission points out in the contested decision (recital 251), such an assessment of the extent to which the dealer has met his commitments enables the undertaking in a dominant position to put strong pressure on the dealer...and allow[s] it, if necessary, to use the arrangement in a discriminatory manner.

141. It follows that a discount system which is applied by an undertaking in a dominant position and which leaves that undertaking a considerable margin of discretion as to whether the dealer may obtain the discount must be considered unfair and constitutes an abuse by an undertaking of its dominant position on the market within the meaning of Article [102] (see, in that regard, *Hoffmann-La Roche* v. *Commission*...paragraph 105). Because of the subjective assessment of the criteria giving entitlement to the service bonus, dealers were left in uncertainty and on the whole could not predict with any confidence the rate of discount which they would receive by way of service bonus (see, in that regard, *Michelin* v. *Commission*...paragraph 83).

...

219. The fact remains that, by its arguments, the applicant merely accepts the conclusion which the Commission reached in the contested decision, namely that the obligations imposed on dealers to provide information and the obligation to accept the list of areas suggested by Michelin only reflect Michelin's desire to supervise distribution in detail (recital 322 of the contested decision). Although some of that information (the balance-sheet and income statement) is public, most of it is not. The applicant's sole aim in imposing on dealers obligations to communicate detailed information on turnover, statistics and sales forecasts, future strategies and the development of Michelin market shares is to obtain information about the market which is not public and which is of value for the carrying out of its own marketing strategy (see, in that regard, *Hoffmann-La Roche* v. *Commission*...paragraph 107). Furthermore, the applicant's right, by way of exception, to examine in detail the activities of the Club members must inevitably increase the dependence on Michelin of the Club members, who, in exchange for fulfilling those obligations, receive financial advantages (recitals 104 to 106 of the contested decision). Dealers are no longer able to increase the market share of products of rival brands without Michelin being aware of the fact.

220. The obligations referred to at paragraph 215 above are therefore designed to monitor the Club members, to tie them to the applicant and to eliminate competition from other manufacturers. The Commission was therefore correct to characterise those obligations as abusive in the contested decision.

...

232. The applicant points out that, in recital 274 of the contested decision, the Commission states that the combination and interaction of the various conditions helped to reinforce their impact and thus the abusive nature of the system considered as a whole. The applicant contends that lawful discounts cannot become unlawful as a result of the cumulative or contagious effect produced by the coexistence of several

parallel discount systems. In any event, the Commission has failed to state the reasons why a lawful discount becomes unlawful solely because another discount exists alongside it.

233. The premise on which the applicant bases its argument is misconceived. In the contested decision, the Commission established that the various discount systems applied by the applicant were unlawful. The Commission did not therefore, in the contested decision, infer the unlawful nature of the system applied by Michelin from the combination of discount systems which were lawful in themselves.

...

237. The Court points out that Article [102] prohibits, in so far as it may affect trade between Member States, any abuse of a dominant position within the common market or in a substantial part thereof. Unlike Article [101(1)], Article [102] contains no reference to the anti-competitive aim or anti-competitive effect of the practice referred to. However, in the light of the context of Article [101], conduct will be regarded as abusive only if it restricts competition.

238. In support of its argument, the applicant refers to the consistent line of decisions which show that an abuse is an objective concept referring to the behaviour of an undertaking in a dominant position which is such as to influence the structure of a market where, as a result of the very presence of the undertaking in question, the degree of competition is already weakened and which, through recourse to methods different from those governing normal competition in products or services on the basis of the transactions of commercial operators, has the *effect* of hindering the maintenance of the degree of competition still existing in the market or the growth of that competition (*Hoffmann-La Roche* v. *Commission*...paragraph 91; *Michelin* v. *Commission*...paragraph 70; *AKZO* v. *Commission*...paragraph 69; and *Irish Sugar* v. *Commission*...paragraph 111; emphasis added).

239. The effect referred to in the case-law cited in the preceding paragraph does not necessarily relate to the actual effect of the abusive conduct complained of. For the purposes of establishing an infringement of Article [102], it is sufficient to show that the abusive conduct of the undertaking in a dominant position tends to restrict competition or, in other words, that the conduct is capable of having that effect.

240. Thus, in *Michelin* v *Commission* (cited at paragraph 54 above), the Court of Justice, after referring to the principle reproduced at paragraph 238 above, stated that it is necessary to consider all the circumstances, particularly the criteria and rules for the grant of the discount, and to investigate whether, in providing an advantage not based on any economic service justifying it, the discount tends to remove or restrict the buyer's freedom to choose his sources of supply, to bar competitors from access to the market, to apply dissimilar conditions to equivalent transactions with other trading parties or to strengthen the dominant position by distorting competition (paragraph 73). It concluded that Michelin had infringed Article [102], since its discount system [was] calculated to prevent dealers from being able to select freely at any time in the light of the market situation the most favourable of the offers made by the various competitors and to change supplier without suffering any appreciable economic disadvantage (paragraph 85).

241. It follows that, for the purposes of applying Article [102], establishing the anti-competitive object and the anti-competitive effect are one and the same thing (see, in that regard, *Irish Sugar* v *Commission*, cited at paragraph 54 above, paragraph 170). If it is shown that the object pursued by the conduct of an undertaking in a dominant position is to limit competition, that conduct will also be liable to have such an effect.

The judgment firmly linked the legality of quantity rebates to efficiencies. At paragraph 58 the GC stated that quantity rebates are 'deemed' to lower suppliers' costs, and in paragraph 59 that quantity rebates are not an abuse unless the system is not based on an economically justified countervailing advantage. When this was applied to Michelin's system, however, Michelin was found to have infringed Article 102 because it did not establish what exactly were the costs savings (paragraphs 108–109) and the Commission was entitled to find it loyalty-inducing (paragraph 110).

According to *Michelin II* loyalty rebates are per se abuses on the basis of the case law stemming from *Hoffmann-La Roche*. Quantity rebates which are not linked to a demonstrable economic justification may be loyalty-inducing.

In respect to loyalty-inducing rebates the 'effect' of hindering the maintenance of the degree of competition still existing on the market, referred to in the definition of the abuse concept in *Hoffmann-La Roche* and *Michelin I*,[470] does not have to relate to an *actual* effect (*Michelin II*, paragraph 239). It can be presumed by showing that the conduct is *capable* of it.

Moreover, anti-competitive object and anti-competitive effect are the same thing for the purposes of Article 102 (paragraph 241).

f. *British Airways*

The *Virgin/British Airways* decision[471] resulted from a complaint from rival airline Virgin about the incentives which British Airways (BA) gave travel agents to push its tickets to their customers. As explained in Chapter 6,[472] the Commission found BA to be in a dominant position as a buyer in the market for air travel agency services. BA was fined €6.8 million for offering travel agents commission schemes which included extra payments in return for meeting or exceeding their previous year's sales of BA tickets. The Commission particularly noted that the schemes all had one feature in common: meeting its target meant that the agent received an increase in commission not just on the tickets sold thereafter, but on *all* the tickets it had sold in the reference period (i.e. the rebates were retroactive). This meant that 'when a travel agent is close to one of the thresholds for an increase in commission rate selling relatively few extra BA tickets can have a large effect on his commission income. Conversely a competitor of BA who wishes to give a travel agent an incentive to divert some sales from BA to the competing airline will have to pay a much higher rate of commission than BA on all of the tickets sold by it to overcome this effect'.[473] The Commission held that the schemes were exclusionary as 'they represent loyalty discounts as condemned in the *Michelin* ... and *Hoffmann-La Roche* cases'.[474] It said that the fact that BA's competitors had nevertheless been able to gain market share from BA could not indicate that the schemes had had no effect as 'it can only be assumed that competitors would have had more success in the absence of these abusive commission schemes'.[475] The Commission decision also condemned the schemes for being discriminatory, contrary to Article 102(c), in that the different levels of commission the travel agents received distorted competition between them.[476]

The GC upheld the decision.[477] In the part of the judgment concerning the exclusionary effect on competitors the GC followed *Michelin II* very closely.[478] The GC agreed with the Commission that concrete effects on the market did not have to be proved and that it was sufficient to demonstrate that the conduct *tends* to restrict competition i.e. that it is *capable* of having such an effect.[479] The GC was satisfied that the BA scheme had this capability, in particular because of its 'very noticeable

---

[470] At paras. 91 and 70 respectively. See Section 3.C.i, p. 373.

[471] [2000] OJ L30/1, [2000] 4 CMLR 999 (*Virgin/BA*).

[472] Chap. 6, p. 341.

[473] *Virgin/BA*, para. 29.

[474] *Virgin/BA*, para. 96. At the time of the decision the Commission issued a statement setting out the principles it considered applied to such practices by airlines: target discounts (or commissions) and indeed any discounts not reflecting costs savings or differences in value, were not allowed: Principles concerning travel agents' commissions: Press Release IP/99/504, 14 July 1999.

[475] *Virgin/BA*, para. 107.

[476] *Virgin/BA*, paras. 108–111.

[477] Case T-219/99, *British Airways v. Commission* [2003] ECR II-5917 (*British Airways*).

[478] In particular, paras. 241–247 are almost identical to paras. 54–59 of *Michelin II*.

[479] *British Airways*, para. 293.

effect at the margin'[480] and the inability of the competitors to make competitive counter-offers to the agents.[481] In a striking passage the GC agreed with the Commission that the fact that the market shares of some of BA's competitors had actually increased during the relevant period did not disprove the exclusionary effect of the commission payments.[482] Furthermore, it stated that Article 102 is aimed at the protection of the competitive structure and so dismissed the argument that there was no proof of consumer harm.[483] However, the GC was prepared to accept that the rebates could be objectively justified. It said that it needed to be determined whether the schemes were based on 'economically justified considerations'.[484] In this case it found that they were not, dismissing arguments about the relevance of the high fixed costs in the air transport industry.[485]

BA appealed. As already noted, there had in the intervening three years been an ever more intensive debate about the correct approach to rebates, and a general consensus had emerged that the law needed to be realigned towards a concern with effects on consumers rather than with formalistic analysis and presumptions.[486] In the seven years since its original decision the Commission had become convinced of the need to apply an effects-based, consumer welfare analysis to rebates and it had set out an innovative way of assessing the exclusionary effects of rebates in the 2005 Staff Discussion Paper.[487] Nevertheless, the British Airways judgment was upheld by the CJ, building on its previous case law.

Case C-95/04 P, *British Airways* v. *Commission* [2007] ECR I-2331

British Airways began by arguing that: 'in order to distinguish between legitimate competition on price and unlawful anti-competitive or exclusionary conduct, the [General Court] should have applied subparagraph (b) of the second paragraph of Article [102], according to which practices constituting an abuse of a dominant position may, in particular, consist in limiting production, markets or technical development to the prejudice of consumers. It should therefore have verified whether BA had actually limited the markets of rival airlines and whether a prejudice to consumers had resulted.'[488]

Court of Justice

57. Concerning, first, the plea that the [General Court] wrongly failed to base its argument on the criteria in subparagraph (b) of the second paragraph of Article [102] in assessing whether the bonus schemes at issue were abusive, the list of abusive practices contained in Article [102] is not exhaustive, so that the

---

[480] *British Airways*, para. 272.

[481] *British Airways*, para. 276.

[482] *British Airways*, para. 298. The GC cited its own judgment in Cases T-24/93 to T-26/93 and T-28/93, *Compagnie Maritime Belge Transports and Others* v. *Commission* [1996] ECR II-1201, para. 149 for this approach.

[483] *British Airways*, para. 311.

[484] *British Airways*, para. 271.

[485] *British Airways*, paras. 284–285.

[486] For the arguments for a new approach to rebates see, e.g., B. Sher, 'Price Discounts and *Michelin II*; What Goes Around, Comes Around' [2002] *ECLR* 482; J. Temple Lang and R. O'Donoghue, 'Defining Legitimate Competition: How to Clarify Pricing Abuses under Article 82EC' (2002) 26 *Fordham Int'l LJ* 83; J. Kallaugher and B. Sher, 'Rebates Revisited: Anti-competitive Effects and Exclusionary Abuse under Article 102' (2004) 25(5) *European Competition Law Journal* 263; D. Spector, 'Loyalty Rebates: An Assessment of Competition Concerns and a Proposed Structured Rule of Reason' (2005) 1(2) *Competition Policy International*, 89; C. Ahlborn and D. Bailey, 'Discounts, Rebates and Selective Pricing by Dominant Firms' (2006) 2 *European Competition Journal* 101. For a defence of the more traditional position, see L. Gyselen, in Ehlermann and Atanasiu (eds.), *European Competition Law Annual 2003* (cited in n. 24), 287. See also J Temple Lang, 'How Can the Problems of Exclusionary Abuses under Article 102 TFEU be Resolved?' (2012) 37 *ELRev* 136.

[487] DG Comp Discussion Paper on the application of Article 82 of the Treaty to exclusionary abuses, paras. 151–176.

[488] Case C-95/04 P, para. 46.

practices there mentioned are merely examples of abuses of a dominant position (see, to that effect, Case C-333/94 P *Tetra Pak* v *Commission*...paragraph 37). According to consistent case-law, the list of abusive practices contained in that provision does not exhaust the methods of abusing a dominant position prohibited by the EC Treaty (Case 6/72 *Europemballage and Continental Can* v *Commission*...paragraph 26; Joined Cases C-395/96 P and C-396/96 P *Compagnie maritime belge transports a.o.* v *Commission*...paragraph 112).

58. It follows that discounts and bonuses granted by undertakings in a dominant position may be contrary to Article [102] even where they do not correspond to any of the examples mentioned in the second paragraph of that article. Thus, in determining that fidelity discounts had an exclusionary effect, the Court based its argument in *Hoffmann-La Roche* and *Michelin* on Article [102]...in its entirety, and not just on subparagraph (b) of its second paragraph. Moreover, in its judgment in Joined Cases 40/73 to 48/73, 50/73, 54/73 to 56/73, 111/73, 113/73 and 114/73 *Suiker Unie and Others* v *Commission*...paragraph 523, concerning fidelity rebates, the Court expressly referred to subparagraph (c) of the second paragraph of Article [102], according to which practices constituting abuse of a dominant position may consist, for example, in applying dissimilar conditions to equivalent transactions with other trading parties, thereby placing them at a competitive disadvantage.

59. The plea that the [General Court] erred in law by not basing its argument on the criteria in subparagraph (b) of the second paragraph of Article [102] is therefore unfounded.

60. Nor does it appear that the Court's assessment of the exclusionary effect of the bonus schemes in question was based on a misapplication of the case-law of the Court of Justice.

61. In the *Hoffmann-La Roche* and *Michelin* judgments, the Court of Justice found that certain discounts granted by two undertakings in a dominant position were abusive in character.

62. The first of those two judgments concerned discounts granted to undertakings whose business was the production or sale of vitamins, and the grant of which was, for most of the time, expressly linked to the condition that the co-contractor obtained its supplies over a given period entirely or mainly from Hoffmann-La Roche. The Court found such a discount system an abuse of a dominant position and stated that the granting of fidelity discounts in order to give the buyer an incentive to obtain its supplies exclusively from the undertaking in a dominant position was incompatible with the objective of undistorted competition within the common market (*Hoffmann-La Roche*, paragraph 90).

63. In *Michelin*, unlike in *Hoffmann-La Roche*, Michelin's co-contractors were not obliged to obtain their supplies wholly or partially from Michelin. However, the variable annual discounts granted by that undertaking were linked to objectives in the sense that, in order to benefit from them, its co-contractors had to attain individualised sales results. In that case, the Court found a series of factors which led it to regard the discount system in question as an abuse of a dominant position. In particular, the system was based on a relatively long reference period, namely a year, its functioning was non-transparent for co-contractors, and the differences in market share between Michelin and its main competitors were significant (see, to that effect, *Michelin*, paragraphs 81 to 83).

64. Contrary to BA's argument, it cannot be inferred from those two judgments that bonuses and discounts granted by undertakings in a dominant position are abusive only in the circumstances there described. As the Advocate General has stated in point 41 of her Opinion, the decisive factor is rather the underlying factors which have guided the previous case-law of the Court of Justice and which can also be transposed to a case such as the present.

65. In that respect, *Michelin* is particularly relevant to the present case, since it concerns a discount system depending on the attainment of individual sales objectives which constituted neither discounts for quantity, linked exclusively to the volume of purchases, nor fidelity discounts within the meaning of the judgment in *Hoffmann-La Roche*, since the system established by Michelin did not contain any obligation on the part of resellers to obtain all or a given proportion of its supplies from the dominant undertaking.

66. Concerning the application of Article [102] to a system of discounts dependent on sales objectives, paragraph 70 of the *Michelin* judgment shows that, in prohibiting the abuse of a dominant market position

in so far as trade between Member States is capable of being affected, that article refers to conduct which is such as to influence the structure of a market where, as a result of the very presence of the undertaking in question, the degree of competition is already weakened and which, through recourse to methods different from those governing normal competition in products or services on the basis of the transactions of commercial operators, has the effect of hindering the maintenance of the degree of competition still existing in the market or the growth of that competition.

67. In order to determine whether the undertaking in a dominant position has abused such a position by applying a system of discounts such as that described in paragraph 65 of this judgment, the Court has held that it is necessary to consider all the circumstances, particularly the criteria and rules governing the grant of the discount, and to investigate whether, in providing an advantage not based on any economic service justifying it, the discount tends to remove or restrict the buyer's freedom to choose his sources of supply, to bar competitors from access to the market, to apply dissimilar conditions to equivalent transactions with other trading parties or to strengthen the dominant position by distorting competition (*Michelin*, paragraph 73).

68. It follows that in determining whether, on the part of an undertaking in a dominant position, a system of discounts or bonuses which constitute neither quantity discounts or bonuses nor fidelity discounts or bonuses within the meaning of the judgment in *Hoffmann-La Roche* constitutes an abuse, it first has to be determined whether those discounts or bonuses can produce an exclusionary effect, that is to say whether they are capable, first, of making market entry very difficult or impossible for competitors of the undertaking in a dominant position and, secondly, of making it more difficult or impossible for its co-contractors to choose between various sources of supply or commercial partners.

69. It then needs to be examined whether there is an objective economic justification for the discounts and bonuses granted. In accordance with the analysis carried out by the [General Court] in paragraphs 279 to 291 of the judgment under appeal, an undertaking is at liberty to demonstrate that its bonus system producing an exclusionary effect is economically justified.

70. With regard to the first aspect, the case-law gives indications as to the cases in which discount or bonus schemes of an undertaking in a dominant position are not merely the expression of a particularly favourable offer on the market, but give rise to an exclusionary effect.

71. First, an exclusionary effect may arise from goal-related discounts or bonuses, that is to say those the granting of which is linked to the attainment of sales objectives defined individually (*Michelin*, paragraphs 70 to 86).

72. It is clear from the findings of the [General Court] in paragraphs 10 and 15 to 17 of the judgment under appeal that the bonus schemes at issue were drawn up by reference to individual sales objectives, since the rate of the bonuses depended on the evolution of the turnover arising from BA ticket sales by each travel agent during a given period.

73. It is also apparent from the case-law that the commitment of co-contractors towards the undertaking in a dominant position and the pressure exerted upon them may be particularly strong where a discount or bonus does not relate solely to the growth in turnover in relation to purchases or sales of products of that undertaking made by those co-contractors during the period under consideration, but extends also to the whole of the turnover relating to those purchases or sales. In that way, relatively modest variations—whether upwards or downwards—in the turnover figures relating to the products of the dominant undertaking have disproportionate effects on co-contractors (see, to that effect, *Michelin*, paragraph 81).

74. The [General Court] found that the bonus schemes at issue gave rise to a similar situation. Attainment of the sales progression objectives gave rise to an increase in the commission paid on all BA tickets sold by the travel agent concerned, and not just on those sold after those objectives had been attained (paragraph 23 of the judgment under appeal). It could therefore be of decisive importance for the commission income of a travel agent as a whole whether or not he sold a few extra BA tickets after achieving a certain turnover (paragraphs 29 and 30 of the grounds for the Commission's decision,

reproduced in paragraph 23 of the judgment under appeal). The [General Court], which describes that characteristic and its consequences in paragraphs 272 and 273 of the judgment under appeal, states that the progressive nature of the increased commission rates had a 'very noticeable effect at the margin' and emphasises the radical effects which a small reduction in sales of BA tickets could have on the rates of performance-related bonus.

75. Finally, the Court took the view that the pressure exerted on resellers by an undertaking in a dominant position which granted bonuses with those characteristics is further strengthened where that undertaking holds a very much larger market share than its competitors (see, to that effect, *Michelin*, paragraph 82). It held that, in those circumstances, it is particularly difficult for competitors of that undertaking to outbid it in the face of discounts or bonuses based on overall sales volume. By reason of its significantly higher market share, the undertaking in a dominant position generally constitutes an unavoidable business partner in the market. Most often, discounts or bonuses granted by such an undertaking on the basis of overall turnover largely take precedence in absolute terms, even over more generous offers of its competitors. In order to attract the co-contractors of the undertaking in a dominant position, or to receive a sufficient volume of orders from them, those competitors would have to offer them significantly higher rates of discount or bonus.

76. In the present case, the [General Court] held in paragraph 277 of the judgment under appeal that BA's market share was significantly higher than that of its five main competitors in the United Kingdom. It concluded, in paragraph 278 of that judgment, that the rival airlines were not in a position to grant travel agents the same advantages as BA, since they were not capable of attaining in the United Kingdom a level of revenue capable of constituting a sufficiently broad financial base to allow them effectively to establish a reward scheme similar to BA's (paragraph 278 of the judgment under appeal).

77. Therefore, the [General Court] was right to examine, in paragraphs 270 to 278 of the judgment under appeal, whether the bonus schemes at issue had a fidelity-building effect capable of producing an exclusionary effect.

At this point the CJ refused BA's plea that it review the GC's finding that the bonus scheme was capable of an exclusionary effect in particular because of the strong effect at the margin and the competitors' inability to make competitive counter-offers. The CJ would not review the GC's findings in respect of facts. This plea was therefore inadmissible. It continued by examining the GC's assessment of the objective justification for the scheme.

84. Discounts or bonuses granted to its co-contractors by an undertaking in a dominant position are not necessarily an abuse and therefore prohibited by Article [102]. According to consistent case-law, only discounts or bonuses which are not based on any economic counterpart to justify them must be regarded as an abuse (see, to that effect, *Hoffmann-La Roche*, paragraph 90, and *Michelin*, paragraph 73).

85. As has been held in paragraph 69 of this judgment, the [General Court] was right, after holding that the bonus schemes at issue produced an exclusionary effect, to examine whether those schemes had an objective economic justification.

86. Assessment of the economic justification for a system of discounts or bonuses established by an undertaking in a dominant position is to be made on the basis of the whole of the circumstances of the case (see, to that effect, *Michelin*, paragraph 73). It has to be determined whether the exclusionary effect arising from such a system, which is disadvantageous for competition, may be counterbalanced, or outweighed, by advantages in terms of efficiency which also benefit the consumer. If the exclusionary effect of that system bears no relation to advantages for the market and consumers, or if it goes beyond what is necessary in order to attain those advantages, that system must be regarded as an abuse.

87. In this case, correctly basing its examination upon the criteria thus inferred from the case-law, the [General Court] examined whether there was an economic justification for the bonus schemes at issue. In paragraphs 284 and 285 of the judgment under appeal, it adopted a position in relation to the arguments submitted by BA, which concerned, in particular, the high level of fixed costs in air transport and the importance of aircraft occupancy rates. On the basis of its assessment of the circumstances of the case, the [General Court] came to the conclusion that those systems were not based on any objective economic justification.

Again, the CJ refused to review the GC's findings of fact on this issue, stating that the plea was to that extent inadmissible. It confined itself to stating that the GC had not committed an error of *law*. Unfortunately this meant that BA's arguments about the fixed costs were again not reviewed.

90. The [General Court] did not therefore make any error of law in holding that the bonus schemes at issue had a fidelity-building effect, that they therefore produced an exclusionary effect, and that they were not justified from an economic standpoint.

96. Concerning BA's argument that the [General Court] did not examine the probable effects of the bonus schemes at issue, it is sufficient to note that, in paragraphs 272 and 273 of the judgment under appeal, the [General Court] explained the mechanism of those schemes.

97. Having emphasised the very noticeable effect at the margin, linked to the progressive nature of the increased commission rates, it described the exponential effect on those rates of an increase in the number of BA tickets sold during successive periods, and, conversely, the disproportionate reduction in those rates in the event of even a slight decrease in sales of BA tickets in comparison with the previous period.

98. On that basis, the [General Court] was able to conclude, without committing any error of law, that the bonus schemes at issue had a fidelity-building effect. It follows that BA's plea accusing the Court of not examining the probable effects of those schemes is unfounded.

99. Moreover, in paragraph 99 of its appeal, BA acknowledges that, in its judgment, the [General Court] rightly held that travel agents were given an incentive to increase their sales of BA tickets. In addition, in paragraph 113 of its appeal, it states that, if the [General Court] had examined the actual or probable impact of the bonus schemes at issue on competition between travel agents, it would have concluded that that impact was negligible.

100. It follows that BA is not seriously denying that those schemes had a fidelity-building effect on travel agents and thus tended to affect the situation of competitor airlines.

101 Concerning BA's allegations of evidence showing that no exclusionary effect arose from the bonus schemes at issue, of which evidence the [General Court] is alleged to have taken insufficient account, it is sufficient to note that this part of the second plea is inadmissible on an appeal for the reasons already set out in paragraph 78 of this judgment.

Again, the ECJ rejected as inadmissible the plea that the GC had taken insufficient account of BA's evidence of the lack of exclusionary effects. It then dealt with BA's plea that the GC should have examined whether BA's conduct involved a 'prejudice [to] consumers' within Article 102(b).

105. It should be noted first that, as explained in paragraphs 57 and 58 of this judgment, discounts or bonuses granted by an undertaking in a dominant position may be contrary to Article [102] even where they do not correspond to any of the examples mentioned in the second paragraph of that article.

> 106. Moreover, as the Court has already held in paragraph 26 of its judgment in *Europemballage and Continental Can*, Article [102] is aimed not only at practices which may cause prejudice to consumers directly, but also at those which are detrimental to them through their impact on an effective competition structure, such as is mentioned in Article 3(1)(g) EC.
>
> 107. The [General Court] was therefore entitled, without committing any error of law, not to examine whether BA's conduct had caused prejudice to consumers within the meaning of subparagraph (b) of the second paragraph of Article [102], but to examine, in paragraphs 294 and 295 of the judgment under appeal, whether the bonus schemes at issue had a restrictive effect on competition and to conclude that the existence of such an effect had been demonstrated by the Commission in the contested decision.
>
> 108. Having regard to those considerations, the third plea must be dismissed as unfounded.

In this judgment the CJ confirmed that a system whereby the rebate is conditional on purchasing mainly or exclusively from the dominant undertaking is abusive, on the basis of *Hoffmann-La Roche* (paragraph 62); and that other types of discount or rebate such as that in *Michelin I* (paragraph 65) must be judged in the light of the circumstances, but in particular in the light of two criteria (paragraph 67). These are:

(i) whether the discounts or bonuses are *capable* of producing an exclusionary effect (see also paragraph 77) in that they make market entry very difficult or impossible for competitors and make it more difficult or impossible for the other party to choose other sources of supply (paragraph 68); and

(ii) whether there is objective economic justification for the system (paragraph 69).

In assessing the *capability* of a scheme to cause exclusion (paragraph 73) the CJ particularly stressed the effect of a 'roll-back' provision, whereby the bonus applies not only to the sales or purchases above the target, but extends backwards to all the previous sales or purchases during the reference period once the target is hit. The CJ referred here to the 'very noticeable effect at the margin' which the roll-back feature of the BA schemes produced. It did not demand that concrete effects should be shown. It said that the GC had explained the mechanism of the schemes, their effect at the margin, and so on (paragraph 97), and so had been able to conclude that they did have a 'fidelity-building effect'. The CJ refused to review the GC's actual assessment of whether the schemes were exclusionary on the basis of lack of jurisdiction.

The CJ's second criterion recognises that loyalty-inducing rebates could be objectively justified. Paragraph 86 describes this in terms of countervailing efficiencies which produce benefits for consumers.

The CJ rejected the plea that the GC should have examined whether the schemes infringed Article 102(b) which refers to 'prejudice to consumers' on the grounds that the list of abuses in Article 102 is not exhaustive (paragraphs 57 and 58), the decisive factor being rather the (unspecified and unexplained) 'underlying factors' which have guided the previous case law,[489] and that in order to show a detrimental effect on consumers it is only necessary to conclude that there is a restrictive effect on *competition* (paragraphs 106 and 107). Paragraphs 106 and 107 are highly significant. The CJ took a form- rather than effects-based approach to Article 102 and ignored any consideration of economic notions of consumer welfare or proof of consumer harm.[490] This case was a major reason for the Commission abandoning any idea of 'Guidelines' on Article 102 embodying a 'modernised' approach to Article 102 and settling instead for Guidance on 'enforcement priorities'.

---

[489] For criticism of this statement, see J Temple Lang, 'How Can the Problems of Exclusionary Abuses under Article 102 TFEU Be Resolved?' (2012) 37 *ELRev* 136.

[490] For a critical analysis of the law on rebates after the CJ's *British Airways* judgment see Rousseva, *Rethinking Exclusionary Abuses in EU Competition Law* (cited in n. 42), 173–218.

(iv) Rebates in the Guidance Paper

The Commission's Staff Discussion Paper[491] proposed a complex new methodology for dealing with single branding, rebates and discounts. As well as the concepts of contestable and non-contestable shares, which also appear in the Guidance Paper, the terms 'required share', and the 'commercially viable share' were employed.[492] The general reception of this part of the Discussion Paper was favourable in principle, but there was much criticism, inter alia, of the extensive use still made of presumptions, and of the complexity of the framework for assessing conditional rebates. The latter, although grounded in economic theory, was thought to be almost impossible to implement in practice, particularly in respect of the assessment of the 'commercially viable share' concept. The Guidance Paper follows the Discussion Paper in setting out the importance the Commission attaches to assessing whether there is anti-competitive foreclosure and the method the Commission will use in doing this, but it is less complex. However, it still presents problems.[493] Unlike the rest of the Guidance Paper, which is rooted in the case law, the rebates section presents a different approach entirely.

Paragraphs 37–45 of the Guidance Paper deal with what the Commission calls 'conditional rebates', defined as 'rebates granted to customers to reward them for a particular form of purchasing behaviour'. It states that:[494]

…The usual nature of a conditional rebate is that the customer is given a rebate if its purchases over a defined reference period exceed a certain threshold, the rebate being granted either on all purchases (retroactive rebates) or only on those made in excess of those required to achieve the threshold (incremental rebates).

The Commission accepts that such rebates may stimulate demand and benefit consumers. However, they can also have foreclosure effects.[495]

The section on rebates has to be read in conjunction with the general section on price-based exclusionary conduct, paragraphs 23–27.[496] The Commission is therefore concerned with the anti-competitive foreclosure of as efficient competitors. However, the Commission notes that conditional rebates can have such foreclosure effects without necessarily entailing a sacrifice for the dominant undertaking (and the assessment of conditional rebates is therefore different from that for predation which, according to paragraphs 64–66, always entails a sacrifice).[497] The question the Commission asks is what price a competitor would need to offer to compensate customers for the loss of the conditional rebate if the customer switched part of its demand away from the dominant undertaking.

The concepts used in the assessments are 'contestable' and 'non-contestable' portions of a customer's demand and the 'relevant range'. The 'non-contestable portion' is the amount the customer would buy from the dominant undertaking in any event. This could be, for example, because the dominant undertaking supplies a 'must-stock' product (to which consumers have brand loyalty) or because the competitors have capacity constraints and could not satisfy all the customer's demand. The 'contestable' portion is the amount for which the customer may prefer, and be able to find,

---

[491] Discussion Paper, paras. 151–169.

[492] Respectively, the share of the customer's requirements which a competitor needed to capture so that the effective price resulting from the application of the rebate equalled the dominant undertaking's ATC and the share of the customer's requirements which an efficient entrant could reasonably be expected to capture. The 'required share' and the 'commercially viable share' had to be compared. The Discussion Paper stated that if the 'required share' was greater than the 'commercially viable share' the rebate system was likely to have a foreclosure effect.

[493] See Marsden, 'Outstanding Issues from the European Commission's Guidance on Article 102 TFEU' (cited in n. 96), Chap. 3, 64–66.

[494] Guidance Paper, para. 37.

[495] Guidance Paper, para. 37.

[496] See Section 7.D.

[497] Guidance Paper, para. 37, n. 3.

substitutes. The Commission's concern is that the dominant undertaking may grant conditional rebates in order to use the non-contestable portion as leverage to decrease the price for the contestable portion.[498] The market may be significantly foreclosed if retroactive rebates make it less attractive for customers to switch small amounts of contestable demand. Therefore the Commission will try to estimate the price which a competitor would have to offer to compensate for the loss of the rebate if the customer were to switch part of its demand (the 'relevant range'). The effective price the competitor has to match is the normal list price less the rebate lost by switching.[499] The Commission, using a method similar to the tests for predatory pricing, will apply costs levels to assess whether an as efficient competitor could compete profitably notwithstanding the rebate. If the effective price remains above the dominant undertaking's LRAIC the rebate is not 'normally' capable of anti-competitive foreclosure.[500] If it is below AAC 'as a general rule' it *is* capable of foreclosing as efficient competitors whereas if it is between LRAIC and AAC the Commission 'will investigate whether other factors point to the conclusion that entry or expansion even by equally efficient competitors is likely to be affected'.[501] One important matter to consider is whether the rebate is retroactive or incremental.[502] The Commission will consider efficiencies in respect of exclusive dealing in line with the principles laid out in the section of the Guidance Paper on objective necessities and efficiencies.[503] The Commission considers that transaction-related costs advantages (which are passed on to consumers) are more likely with standardised volume targets than with individualised ones.[504]

Although the section on rebates in the Guidance Paper is less complex than that in the Discussion Paper it may still be difficult to operate in practice. One must always bear in mind that undertakings need to be able to assess with some confidence whether their business strategies are lawful or not. In the following extract a practitioner describes some of the problems with the 'contestable share' element of the assessment.

L.Kjølbe, 'Rebates Under Article 82EC: Navigating Uncertain Waters' [2010] *ECLR* 66, 73 and 80

Superficially, the model developed by the Commission looks both theoretically persuasive and simple. However, the theoretical simplicity of an approach based on calculating the contestable share hides its practical complexity. Leaving aside the difficulty of determining costs, which arises in any predation cases, calculating the contestable share of demand with any degree of accuracy is fraught with difficulty … The Commission does not explain in any detail how to determine the contestable share in practice and there does not appear to be consensus amongst economists on how to do so. Legally, this is a very substantial problem if the model is to be used as the primary screen for determining the legality of rebate schemes. Companies must be in a position to determine with a reasonable degree of certainty whether their conduct is legal or not … If the law is unclear it will unduly discourage conduct which on balance is pro-competitive, and deprive customers of the benefits of rebates. An unworkable test also lends itself to arbitrary application according to the 'needs' of individual cases and exposes the competition authority that uses it to judicial review.…

The analysis of the contestable share must therefore be complemented by several additional elements, including a careful analysis of the counterstrategies available to rivals. Even if the counterstrategies

---

[498] Guidance Paper, para. 39.

[499] Guidance Paper, paras. 41–42.

[500] Guidance Paper, para. 43. For LRAIC (long run average incremental cost), see Section 7.C., pp. 398–399.

[501] Guidance Paper, para. 44.

[502] Guidance Paper, para. 45.

[503] Guidance Paper, para. 46, referring to paras. 28–31.

[504] Guidance Paper, para. 46.

available to rivals are not such that they would lead to the conclusion that the dominant firm's products are not 'must-stock', they may still allow the rival to compete effectively for the contestable share. It must thus be carefully analysed whether there are any objective and substantial barriers to equally efficient rivals expanding their sales which cannot be overcome by adopting counterstrategies. In the absence of such barriers there is no anti-competitive foreclosure, as equally efficient rivals can compete effectively with the dominant firm in spite of the rebate scheme...

... In the Commission's framework the calculation of the contestable share of demand plays a central role. However, as in practice it is very difficult to do so accurately, this part of the Commission's framework should rather be seen as a thought experiment that is used to frame the analysis of likely effects based on a variety of factors...

(v) The Case Law and Decisional Practice After the Guidance Paper

a. *Tomra*

In *Tomra* in 2006[505] the Commission applied Article 102 to the exclusive dealing and rebate schemes of Tomra, a firm holding market shares of more than 80 per cent in various national markets in the supply of reverse vending machines (RVM) used by supermarkets to collect empty drink containers from consumers and return the deposit to them. Tomra's agreements with the supermarket customers variously featured exclusivity clauses, individualised quantity commitments, and retroactive rebate schemes the thresholds of which usually corresponded to total or almost total machine requirements of its customers. The decision was adopted during the Commission's review of Article 102, three months after the publication of the Staff Discussion Paper which contained the extensive section on assessing the foreclosure effects of rebate schemes previously noted. The decision set out the law on rebates according to the case law of the EU Courts as already described but then went on to examine the likely and actual effects along the lines suggested in the Discussion Paper. In particular the Commission found that the nature of the market was such that customers would at first buy only a small number of machines from a new competitor and that these would have to be supplied at very low, or even negative prices, in order to match the effect of Tomra's rebates.[506]

One of Tomra's grounds of appeal to the GC was that the Commission had wrongfully applied a per se test to its rebates. The GC rejected this and held that the Commission had properly considered all the circumstances of the case, as required by *Michelin II*.[507] In doing this it confirmed that target rebates are not per se abusive, but despite citing paragraph 89 of *Hoffmann-La Roche* it also, confusingly, appeared to suggest that exclusivity agreements are not per se abusive either.[508] As already mentioned,[509] this point was also confused in the judgment of the CJ on appeal.[510] Further, before Tomra's appeal to the GC was heard the Commission had published the Guidance Paper. Tomra argued, inter alia, along the lines of the Guidance Paper, (i) that in order to prove that the market was foreclosed the Commission should have determined the minimum viability threshold necessary to operate on the market and then have determined whether the part of the demand tied by Tomra's practices was sufficiently large to have exclusionary effects on competitors and (ii) that the

---

[505] *Prokent/Tomra*, COMP/38.113 [2009] 4 CMLR 101. Tomra was fined €24 million. See F. Maier-Rigaud and D. Vaigauskaite, 'Prokent/Tomra, a Textbook Case? Abuse of Dominance under Perfect Information' (2006) 2 *EC Competition Policy Newsletter*, 19.

[506] *Prokent/Tomra*, paras. 165–166.

[507] Case T-155/06, *Tomra Systems v. Commission* [2010] ECR II-4361, paras 208–218 (*Tomra Systems*).

[508] *Tomra Systems*, para. 215.

[509] See Section 10.D.iii.c, p. 460.

[510] Case C-549/10 P, *Tomra Systems ASA v. European Commission*, 19 April 2012, paras. 70–72. For comments on what the GC seemed to mean by 'all the circumstances' in *Tomra*, see L. Peeperkorn and E. Rousseva, 'Article 102 TFEU: Exclusive Dealing and Rebates' (2011) 2 *J'nl of European Competition Law and Practice*, 36, 36.

Commission should have examined whether Tomra's prices were below its costs. The GC dismissed the appeal and the case went to the CJ.

The *Tomra* appeal to the CJ was the first case it had heard on rebates since *British Airways* five years before and the first since the Guidance Paper. Commentators saw *Tomra* as the opportunity for the CJ to reshape the law and take it in a 'modern' direction, moving away from form-based rules and presumptions and towards effects-based analysis, in particular renouncing the peculiarities of *British Airways*, and adopting the kind of approach set out in the Guidance Paper. In the event they were disappointed. In confirming the GC's judgment the CJ arguably went in the opposite direction. However, paragraph 81 of the judgment contains an interesting statement about the effect of the Guidance Paper.

Case C-549/10 P, *Tomra Systems ASA* v. *European Commission*, 19 April 2012

Court of Justice

40 It is true that, as is stated in paragraph 239 of the judgment under appeal, the Commission did not establish a precise threshold beyond which the practices of the Tomra group would be capable of excluding its competitors from the market in question.

41 However, in paragraph 240 of the judgment under appeal, the General Court properly approved the Commission's reasoning that, by foreclosing a significant part of the market, the Tomra group had restricted entry to one or a few competitors and thus limited the intensity of competition on the market as a whole.

42 In fact, and as stated by the General Court in paragraph 241 of the judgment under appeal, the foreclosure by a dominant undertaking of a substantial part of the market cannot be justified by showing that the contestable part of the market is still sufficient to accommodate a limited number of competitors. First, the customers on the foreclosed part of the market should have the opportunity to benefit from whatever degree of competition is possible on the market and competitors should be able to compete on the merits for the entire market and not just for a part of it. Second, it is not the role of the dominant undertaking to dictate how many viable competitors will be allowed to compete for the remaining contestable portion of demand.

43 Further, the General Court stated, in paragraph 242 of the judgment under appeal, that only an analysis of the circumstances of the case, such as the analysis carried out by the Commission in the contested decision, may make it possible to establish whether the practices of an undertaking in a dominant position are capable of excluding competition. It would, however, be artificial to establish without prior analysis the portion of the tied market beyond which the practices of a dominant undertaking may have an exclusionary effect on competitors.

44 The General Court accordingly determined, following that analysis of the circumstances of this case, in paragraph 243 of the judgment under appeal, that a considerable proportion (two fifths) of total demand during the period and in the countries under consideration was foreclosed to competition.

45 That conclusion of the General Court cannot be regarded as containing any error of law.

46 As regards the appellants' argument that the Commission should have applied the 'minimum viable scale' test, suffice it to observe that, first, the General Court was correct to hold that the determination of a precise threshold of foreclosure of the market beyond which the practices at issue had to be regarded as abusive was not required for the purposes of applying Article 102 TFEU and, secondly, in the light of the findings made in paragraph 243 of the judgment under appeal, it was, in any event, in the present case, proved to the requisite legal standard that the market had been closed to competition by the practices at issue.

...

68 The General Court was correct to observe, in paragraph 289 of the judgment under appeal, that, for the purposes of proving an abuse of a dominant position within the meaning of Article 102 TFEU, it is sufficient to show that the abusive conduct of the undertaking in a dominant position tends to restrict competition or that the conduct is capable of having that effect.

69 As regards rebates granted by a dominant undertaking to its customers, the Court has stated that those may infringe Article 102 TFEU, even where they do not correspond to any of the examples mentioned in the second paragraph of that Article 102 (see, to that effect, *British Airways* v *Commission*, paragraph 58 and case-law cited).

70 In the event that an undertaking in a dominant position makes use of a system of rebates, the Court has ruled that that undertaking abuses that position where, without tying the purchasers by a formal obligation, it applies, either under the terms of agreements concluded with these purchasers or unilaterally, a system of loyalty rebates, that is to say, discounts conditional on the customer's obtaining—whether the quantity of its purchases is large or small—all or most of its requirements from the undertaking in a dominant position (see Case 85/76 *Hoffman-La Roche*...paragraph 89, and Case 322/81 *Nederlandsche Banden-Industrie-Michelin* v *Commission*...paragraph 71).

71 In that regard, it is necessary to consider all the circumstances, particularly the criteria and rules governing the grant of the rebate, and to investigate whether, in providing an advantage not based on any economic service justifying it, the rebates tend to remove or restrict the buyer's freedom to choose his sources of supply, to bar competitors from access to the market, or to strengthen the dominant position by distorting competition (see *Nederlandsche Banden-Industrie-Michelin* v *Commission*, paragraph 73).

72 As regards the present case, it is clear from paragraph 213 of the judgment under appeal that a rebate system must be regarded as infringing Article 102 TFEU if it tends to prevent customers of the dominant undertaking from obtaining their supplies from competing producers.

73 Contrary to what is claimed by the appellants, the invoicing of 'negative prices', in other words prices below cost prices, to customers is not a prerequisite of a finding that a retroactive rebates scheme operated by a dominant undertaking is abusive.

74 As the General Court was fully entitled to observe, in paragraph 258 of the judgment under appeal, the third part of the second and fourth pleas in law submitted at first instance was based on an incorrect premiss. The fact that the retroactive rebate schemes oblige competitors to ask negative prices from Tomra's customers benefiting from rebates cannot be regarded as one of the fundamental bases of the contested decision in showing that the retroactive rebate schemes are capable of having anti-competitive effects. Further, the General Court correctly stated, in paragraph 259 of the judgment under appeal, that a whole series of other considerations relating to the retroactive rebates operated by Tomra underpinned the contested decision as regards its conclusion that those types of practices were capable of excluding competitors in breach of Article 102 TFEU.

75 In that regard, the General Court observed, more particularly, that, according to the contested decision, in the first place, the incentive to obtain supplies exclusively or almost exclusively from Tomra was particularly strong when thresholds, such as those applied by Tomra, were combined with a system whereby the achievement of the bonus threshold or, as the case may be, a more advantageous threshold benefited all the purchases made by the customer during the reference period and not exclusively the purchasing volume exceeding the threshold concerned (paragraph 260 of the judgment under appeal). Secondly, the rebate schemes were individual to each customer and the thresholds were established on the basis of the customer's estimated requirements and/or past purchasing volumes and represented a strong incentive for buying all or almost all the equipment needed from Tomra and artificially raised the costs of switching to a different supplier, even for a small number of units (paragraphs 261 and 262 of the judgment under appeal). Third, the retroactive rebates often applied to some of the largest customers of the Tomra group with the aim of ensuring their loyalty (paragraph 263 of the judgment under appeal). Lastly, Tomra failed to show that their conduct was objectively justified or that it generated significant efficiency gains which outweighed the anti-competitive effects on consumers (paragraph 264 of the judgment under appeal).

76 Accordingly, it is apparent from all the reasoning set out in paragraphs 260 to 264 of the judgment under appeal, referred to above, that the General Court came to the conclusion that the third part of the second and fourth pleas in law submitted at first instance was based on an incorrect premiss as regards the evidential value, in respect of whether the rebates scheme at issue was anti-competitive, of the specific characteristics of that scheme, irrespective of the precise level of prices charged.

77 The General Court took its reasoning further by stating, in paragraph 266 of the judgment under appeal, that the Commission, in the contested decision, first, did not state that the rebate schemes automatically resulted in negative prices and, second, did not maintain that showing that is a prerequisite to finding those rebate schemes to be abusive.

78 The General Court added, in that regard, in paragraph 267 of the judgment under appeal, that the exclusionary mechanism represented by retroactive rebates does not require the dominant undertaking to sacrifice profits, since the cost of the rebate is spread across a large number of units. If retroactive rebates are given, the average price obtained by the dominant undertaking may well be far above costs and ensure a high average profit margin. However, retroactive rebate schemes ensure that, from the point of view of the customer, the effective price for the last units is very low because of the 'suction effect'. The General Court therefore rejected as ineffective the claims made by Tomra that there were errors of fact in the analysis within the contested decision of the level of prices charged by them.

79 The General Court was therefore justified in ruling, in essence, in paragraphs 269 to 271 of the judgment under appeal, that the loyalty mechanism was inherent in the supplier's ability to drive out its competitors by means of the suction to itself of the contestable part of demand. When such a trading instrument exists, it is therefore unnecessary to undertake an [analysis] of the actual effects of the rebates on competition given that, for the purposes of establishing an infringement of Article 102 TFEU, it is sufficient to demonstrate that the conduct at issue is capable of having an effect on competition, as recalled in paragraph 68 of this judgment.

80 That being the case, the alleged absence, in the judgment under appeal, of an examination of the arguments raised by the applicants at first instance, on the need to compare the prices charged by them with their costs, which underlies both the complaint of a procedural irregularity and that of an error of law, cannot mean that the judgment under appeal is vitiated by an error of law. The Commission established the existence of an abuse of a dominant position by relying on the other considerations set out in paragraphs 260 to 264 of the judgment under appeal, and the General Court correctly found that that analysis was adequate and sufficient to establish the existence of that abuse. Accordingly, neither the Commission nor the General Court was obliged to examine the question of whether the prices charged by the Tomra group were or were not lower than their long-run average incremental costs, and accordingly this ground of appeal must fail in the context of the present appeal.

81 The appellants' arguments that the Commission's Guidance (see paragraph 52 of this judgment) provides for a comparative analysis of prices and costs cannot invalidate that conclusion. As the Advocate General observes in point 37 of his Opinion, the Guidance, published in 2009, has no relevance to the legal assessment of a decision, such as the contested decision, which was adopted in 2006.

The most problematic aspects of the judgment are as follows:

- First, the question of how much of the market must be foreclosed before there can be anti-competitive effects. In paragraph 42 the CJ set out the principle that 'competitors should be able to compete on the merits for the entire market and not just for a part of it'. The paragraph of the GC judgment (241) which paragraph 42 approved and repeated has been described as 'one of the most extraordinary statements ever made in a competition law judgment'. The authors of that comment explain why:

  That position is entirely untenable as, taken literally, it suggests that if a dominant firm grants loyalty rebates to customers whose combined purchases amount to 10 per cent of the market (hence, leaving the other 90 per cent up for grabs by new entrants), that firm would nevertheless have committed an abuse...[511]

In fact, the GC had satisfied itself that in this case 40 per cent of the market was foreclosed and the CJ affirmed the judgment on this basis. Nevertheless, the general statements as to what competitors should be able to do, the lack of a requirement to determine the threshold of foreclosure, and the irrelevance of the fact that the contestable part of the market is sufficient to accommodate a limited number of competitors sits uneasily with the methodology set out in the Guidance Paper.

- Secondly, the CJ rejected the argument that a costs-based test should be applied to rebates (as to predatory pricing and margin squeeze) and said that it did not matter whether or not the dominant undertaking was sacrificing profits or charging negative prices (paragraphs 73–78).[512] The CJ took the 'suction effect' very seriously.

- Thirdly, the considerations which the GC took into account in concluding that the target rebates were capable of excluding competitors (paragraphs 260–264, summed up by the CJ, paragraph 75 quoted in the *Tomra Systems ASA v. European Commission* case extract, see p. 480) are matters which are likely to be present in the majority of such schemes, i.e. the rebates were retroactive (rolled-back); they were individualised and based on the customer's estimated requirements; the thresholds corresponded to the customer's total requirements or a large proportion thereof; and they were offered to the largest customers.

- Fourthly, the CJ was content that the rebates are 'capable' of excluding competition. It did not require the demonstration of actual or likely effects. There is no theory of harm in respect of effects on consumers. This is a good example of the assumption that the foreclosure of competitors harms consumers without demonstrating why that is so.[513]

The implications in the judgment for the per se or otherwise nature of loyalty rebates have been discussed earlier.[514]

In paragraph 81 of the judgment there is a cryptic comment about the Guidance Paper. The undertaking argued that the Commission's lack of reliance on a cost-price analysis was contrary to the Guidance Paper. The CJ agreed with its Advocate General that the Guidance Paper was irrelevant as the decision was adopted before its publication. What is unclear, of course, is whether the CJ can be construed as saying that it *would* have been relevant had the decision been after publication. Post the Guidance Paper there would be a question about the Commission having to follow its own published methodology,[515] whereas in *Tomra* the CJ was deciding whether the GC had committed an error of law in upholding a decision which complied with the case law extant at the time of its adoption. The issue then arises as to the effect of the Guidance Paper, particularly in the light of the fact that cases may come to the CJ by way of preliminary reference rather than on appeal.[516]

b. The Commission's *Intel* Decision

In *Intel*[517] the Commission fined the undertaking €1.06 billion for a number of practices it found foreclosed the market against its competitor, AMD, to the detriment of consumers. The practices

---

[511] Geradin et al., *EU Competition Law and Economics* (cited in n. 160), 4.217.

[512] But see Rousseva and Marquis, 'Hell Freezes Over: A Climate Change for Assessing Exclusionary Conduct under Article 102 TFEU' (cited in n. 2) for a generous interpretation of *Tomra*, suggesting that the CJ could have been saying that a cost-price analysis is not the *only* way of assessing whether rebates exclude equally efficient competitors.

[513] See further Marsden, 'Outstanding Issues from the European Commission's Guidance on Article 102 TFEU' (cited in n. 96), Chap. 3, 64–66.

[514] See Section 10.D.iii.c, p. 460.

[515] See Chap. 2, Section 5, p. 118 for the status of Commission 'soft law' instruments.

[516] See Chap. 5, Section 6.C.iii, p. 291 for the effects of the Guidance Paper.

[517] *Intel* COMP/C-3/37.990 [2010] 4 CMLR 314, Summary decision [2010] OJ C227/13, on appeal Case T-286/09, *Intel* v. *Commission*, judgment pending.

included giving rebates (wholly or partially hidden) on its x86 central processing units (CPUs) to computer manufacturers (OEMs) such as Dell and HP.[518] The rebates were conditional on the OEMs purchasing 80–100 per cent of their requirements from Intel.[519] The Commission stated in the decision that the Guidance Paper was not applicable since it did not apply to existing proceedings[520] but was a 'document intended to set out priorities for cases that the Commission will focus upon in the future'. Nevertheless, it took the view that 'this Decision is in line with the orientations set out in the Guidance Paper'.[521] Given that the Guidance Paper, as already discussed, takes an effects-based approach to rebates, Intel was likely to benefit from the application of Guidance Paper principles. In the decision the Commission, as in *Prokent/Tomra*, set out its understanding of the existing case law. It therefore quoted paragraph 89 of *Hoffmann-La Roche*[522] and cited *Michelin I, Michelin II*, and *British Airways* as establishing that no evidence of actual foreclosure was required.[523] The Commission then went on to demonstrate that Intel's conditional rebates *were* 'capable of causing or likely to cause anti-competitive foreclosure (which is likely to result in consumer harm)'[524] even though the case law did not require it to do so. In particular, it carried out an as efficient competitor analysis[525] which entailed it examining the size of the conditional rebates, the 'contestable share',[526] the time horizon (the time on which the OEMs base their decisions about changing suppliers—some factors may be less constraining over a longer rather than shorter time), and the viable costs (the Commission took AAC as the benchmark).

The decision has been subjected to considerable criticism, inter alia, on the grounds that the theory of harm the Commission puts forward in respect of the effect of the rebates on the OEM's purchasing strategy is highly speculative, that the analysis of the evidence is flawed, and that the analysis of 'harm to competition and consumers'[527] is entirely theoretical.[528]

(vi) US Law on Discounts and Rebates under Section 2 of the Sherman Act

The US courts applying section 2 of the Sherman Act have taken a different attitude to discounts and rebates than have the EU Courts.[529] US law generally sees any price reduction by a leading firm as pro-competitive (at least so long as prices are not predatory),[530] and rebates are normally not held

[518] The other practices were making direct payments to OEMs to halt or delay launching certain products incorporating the competitors, x86 CPUs and making direct payments to a major retailer for only stocking computers incorporating Intel x86 CPUs.

[519] In Dell's case, for example, the rebate was conditional on 100% exclusivity. In HP's case it was 95%: when AMD offered HP one million CPUs *free* it took only 160,000 of them in order to stay within Intel's limit (*Intel*, paras. 956–957).

[520] The decision was adopted on 13 May 2009, after the publication of the Guidance Paper [2009] OJ C45/9. The case originated in a complaint made by Intel's competitor, AMD, in 2000, the investigation commenced with dawn raids in 2005 (which brought forth a number of interesting emails reproduced in the decision), and the initial statement of objections was sent in 2007.

[521] *Intel*, para. 916.

[522] See Section 10.D.iii.b.

[523] *Intel*, paras. 920–923. It also cited Case T-201/04, *Microsoft v. Commission* [2007] ECR II-3601, as showing that the EU Courts do not look at the actual impact of the alleged anti-competitive conduct on the market.

[524] *Intel*, para. 925.

[525] *Intel*, paras. 1002–1576.

[526] See the discussion of the Guidance Paper in Section 10.D.iv, p. 476.

[527] *Intel*, paras. 1597–1616.

[528] D. Geradin, 'The Decision of the Commission of 13 May 2009 in the *Intel* case: Where is the Foreclosure and Consumer Harm?' (2009) 2 J'nl of European Competition Law and Practice 9.

[529] See Elhauge and Geradin, *Global Competition Law and Economics* (cited in n. 195), 640–664.

[530] Which in US law means proving that the prices were below an appropriate measure of cost and that there was a reasonable prospect of the firm recouping its losses.

to infringe section 2.[531] The contrast was dramatically illustrated by the fact that Virgin brought an action in the US against BA's commission scheme at the same time as its complaint to the European Commission. The trial court in the US granted summary judgment in favour of BA and this was upheld by the Second Circuit Court of Appeals. The US courts said that Virgin had failed to show that BA's incentive scheme harmed consumers.[532]

(vii) Conclusions

The application of Article 102 to discounts and rebates is one of the most contentious areas of EU competition law. It is to be hoped that the law will be put on a more satisfactory footing in the *Intel* appeal.[533] In the meantime the present situation is summed up by two critics, the first a lawyer and the second an economist.

J. Temple Lang, 'How Can the Problems of Exclusionary Abuses under Article 102 TFEU be Resolved?' (2012) 37 *ELRev* 136, 141–142

No clear economic rationale has been suggested by either the Commission or the Court. This is not an academic comment: the law is so unclear that it is difficult to give advice with confidence to a dominant company on the basis of these judgments.

- The Commission's argument that the discount on the total quantity when the threshold is reached might exceed the competitor's minimum price *for the last few units needed to reach the threshold* is artificial and unjustifiable. Competitors never compete only for those units. A dominant company's prices should be considered exclusionary only if they are conditional on exclusivity or below its production costs overall, not because a discount is notionally applied to a small number of units...

- Both the Commission and the Court have used language that seemed to say, in effect, that discounts that competitors could not match were anti-competitive. This disregards the fact that low prices, when they are the result of legitimate competition, may squeeze competitors entirely out of the market. (The Commission recognised this in the Guidance Notice.) The law needs a test to distinguish anti-competitive prices or conduct from pro-competitive low prices, however inconvenient the latter may be for competitors. The judgments do not provide such a test. It also fails to recognise that a dominant company may legitimately have competitive advantages which its competitors have not got, and from which consumers should be able to benefit.

- The language saying that customers were 'prevented' from choosing competitors' products...merely because the dominant company charged low prices, was made more unfortunate and liable to misunderstanding by the use of the phrases 'fidelity-inducing' ('loyalty-inducing' means the same thing) as a test of anti-competitive pricing. This phrase is ambiguous. If the dominant company offers the best value or the lowest price, the result may be that customers buy only from it. This is 'fidelity', but it is pro-competitive, and entirely legitimate. It is only when the pricing conditions cause a customer which buys even a small quantity from a competitor to suffer a loss or penalty (as distinct from possibly losing a chance to get a bigger discount), or where the uncertainty of the criteria is likely to lead

---

[531] For US law, see Hovenkamp, *Federal Antitrust Policy: The Law of Competition and its Practice* (cited in n. 193), 401–407; C. Ahlborn and D. Bailey, 'Discounts, Rebates and Selective Pricing by Dominant Firms: A Transatlantic Comparison' (2006) 2 *European Competition Journal, Special Issue*, 101, 125.

[532] *Virgin Atl. Airways Ltd* v. *British Airways plc*, 257 F.3d 256 (2d Cir. 2001).

[533] Case T-286/09, *Intel* v. *Commission*, judgment pending, and/or any appeal therefrom to the CJ.

to that result, that the conditions are illegal. It should be the condition of exclusivity, not the low price or high discount, that is or may be illegal. It cannot be illegal to offer a buyer such favourable prices that it is likely to buy only from the dominant company.

- The Court has used language that suggests that quantity rebates and other rebates may be lawful *only* if they are based on cost savings to the dominant company...But price reductions for quantity are given in almost every industry. The Guidance Notice does not suggest that rebates must be based on cost savings.

- The Court has said that the Commission need not consider whether the conduct in fact had anti-competitive effects...

- The Court seems to assume that if there is harm to competitors, there is no need to prove harm to consumers. The judgments concentrated on exclusion of competitors rather than harm to consumers...

H. Zenger, 'Loyalty Rebates and the Competitive Process' (2012) 8 *Journal of Competition Law and Economics*, 717, 763–765

There is no benefit in continuing to adhere to a delusive and antiquated theory of anticompetitive rebates that had no counterpart in economic reality even at the time when it was written down. The costs of adherence, however, are particularly large in the case of loyalty rebates. The competitive harm caused by the prevailing legal doctrine not only draws from the handful of cases over which the Court has actually presided. It accumulates over the thousands of products in the economy that could potentially be considered dominant, whose producers are today advised by their legal counsels to avoid competing aggressively in rebates...It is not consistent with the spirit of the Treaty to penalize the successful innovations of these firms and to restrain their ability to compete on price, lest the application of Article 102 be turned against the motive forces of the competitive process itself.

...

But not only are loyalty rebates pervasively used in competitive markets; they are also efficient...[T]he use of loyalty rebates of different forms and shapes is the natural outcome of the competitive process. Consequently, competitive firms naturally employ retroactive rebates, individualized rebates and market share contracts across intermediate goods markets. Loyalty rebates enable firms that have created an enhanced product or a more efficient production technology to earn a higher reward for their creative efforts, which encourages firms to provide those efforts in the first place. But rebates also yield a particularly fierce form of competition between a dominant incumbent and rivals once competing manufacturers have entered the market to a significant extent. Ultimately, allowing firms to compete at the margin is the most effective way of bringing market prices down, because competition for marginal purchases determines the level of demand each supplier can attract.

11. TYING AND BUNDLING

A. GENERAL

Tying and bundling are closely connected practices. For convenience they are dealt with together in this section. They encompass practices whereby an undertaking supplies a product[534] (the tying product) on condition that the customer obtains something else (the tied product) from the supplier as well (or provides them more cheaply if he does), or the undertaking only supplies the two things

---

[534] Or service. Throughout this section 'product' includes 'service' unless otherwise stated.

together or ensures that the two things only work properly together and do not work at all or as well with competitors' products.

Tying and bundling can be practised by non-dominant undertakings[535] but in this chapter we are concerned with the possibility that it can constitute an abuse under Article 102 when pursued by an undertaking in a dominant position.

The concepts of tying and bundling for the purposes of Article 102 are described in the Guidance Paper.[536]

48. 'Tying' usually refers to situations where customers that purchase one product (the tying product) are required also to purchase another product from the dominant undertaking (the tied product). Tying can take place on a technical or contractual basis... 'Bundling' usually refers to the way products are offered and priced by the dominant undertaking. In the case of pure bundling the products are only sold jointly in fixed propor tions. In the case of mixed bundling, often referred to as a multi-product rebate, the products are also made available separately, but the sum of the prices when sold separately is higher than the bundled price.

Technical tying occurs 'when the tying product is designed in such a way that it only works properly with the tied product (and not with the alternatives offered by competitors)'[537] or where the two products are physically integrated so that they are only sold together. The latter type of technical tying is a form of *pure bundling*, and sometimes called *technical bundling*. The integration of Microsoft's Windows Operating System (Windows) with the Windows Media Player (WMP) in *Microsoft*,[538] was such a situation.

Contractual tying 'occurs when the customer who purchases the tying product undertakes also to purchase the tied product (and not the alternatives offered by competitors)'.[539] Suppose X makes both widgets and blodgets. X is the monopoly supplier of widgets but the blodget market is competitive. Customers for widgets need to buy blodgets as well. If X refuses to supply widgets unless the customers buy its blodgets rather than those of its competitors that is a contractual tie. Contractual tying can also be effected through offering non-financial inducements, such as refusing to honour guarantees on the tying product if the tied product is not bought[540] or offering priority delivery to customers who take both products.[541]

Pure bundling means that the products are only sold together, in fixed proportions, as stated in paragraph 48 of the Guidance Paper. It means that the elements of a package are not supplied separately. For example, where services are tied to products the supplier may quote a price for the product which includes the service (such as repair and maintenance). If the customer does not want the service he will normally still have to pay the full price (or be offered only a reduction which does not reflect the true cost of the service element). Pure bundling includes, as already mentioned, technical tying as in *Microsoft*.

Mixed bundling is also known as a multi-product rebate or economic tying. Instead of providing that the customer must obtain the tied product from itself in order to be supplied with the tying product, or technically tying them together, the supplier offers a financially advantageous deal if the customer buys both. For example, if the normal unit price for widgets is £10 and the competitive unit price for blodgets is £5 the dominant widget supplier may offer both together for £13.

---

[535] In distribution arrangements, for example (see Chap. 11) and in technology transfer agreements, such as patent licensing (see Chap. 12).

[536] See also the Horizontal Merger Guidelines [2008] OJ C265/6, paras. 96–97; see also Case T-210/01, *General Electric* v. *Commission* [2005] ECR II-5575, para. 406.

[537] Guidance Paper, para. 48, n. 2.

[538] Case T-201/04, *Microsoft* v. *Commission* [2007] ECR II-3601.

[539] Guidance Paper, para. 48, n. 2.

[540] See *Eurofix-Bauco* v. *Hilti* [1988] OJ L65/19, para. 44.

[541] See Case T-65/89, *BPB Industries and British Gypsum Ltd* v. *Commission* [1993] ECR II-389.

As the Commission explains in the Guidance Paper,[542] for Article 102 to apply the undertaking should be dominant in the tying product market but not necessarily in the tied product market. In bundling cases the undertaking needs to be dominant in one of the bundled markets. In the case of aftermarkets (see *Hilti* and *Tetra Pak II* discussed in Section 11.E.i) the undertaking must be dominant in the tying and/or the tied market.

B. THE COMMERCIAL RATIONALE FOR TYING AND BUNDLING

Tying and bundling may make good commercial and economic sense for reasons which are not necessarily anti-competitive. They can be used as methods for obtaining royalties or fees for the use of a process or product, i.e. as a metering device.[543] They can enable a supplier to 'spread the risk' when trying to penetrate a new market. Tying and bundling can also allow the supplier to achieve economies of scale which are then reflected in the price reduction offered to customers, or to offer a 'bundle' which is more attractive (and of greater value) to consumers than the sum of its separate parts. They can therefore have beneficial effects on consumer welfare. Suppliers may also tie products or services together in order to ensure their optimal performance and maintain the supplier's reputation, or to ensure safety, although the EU Courts have not proved receptive to the latter justification for tying.[544]

C. THE ECONOMIC ARGUMENTS OVER TYING AND BUNDLING

The basic objection to tying and bundling by dominant undertakings is that it enables 'monopoly leveraging' of market power—the projection of dominance from one market to another. In other words, the dominant undertaking uses its position on the market where it is dominant to foreclose competition on another market and acquire substantial market power there too ('offensive leveraging'). The fear is that the dominant supplier can extract two monopoly prices, one from the tying and one from the tied product. This may lead to competition laws proscribing the practice as per se illegal.[545] The Chicago School argues that the extraction of two profits is not possible and advanced the 'single monopoly profit theorem' which was a powerful riposte to the per se illegality position. An explanation of this is set out in the judgment of Judge Easterbrook in a US case.[546]

> ### *Schor* v. *Abbott Laboratoires* No. 05-3344 (US Court of Appeals, 7th Circuit, 2006)
>
> The basic point is that a firm that monopolizes some essential component of a treatment (or product or service) can extract the whole monopoly profit by charging a suitable price for the component alone. If

---

[542] Para. 50, n. 3.

[543] A good example is the patent licensing case *Vaassen/Moris* [1979] OJ L19/32, [1979] 1 CMLR 511 where the inventor of a device for filling *saucissons de Boulogne* supplied it royalty free but on the condition that customers bought their sausage skins from him. This was an easy way of monitoring, and charging for, the use of the device. The tie was condemned by the Commission as contrary to Art. 101(1).

[544] See the *Hilti* and *Tetra Pak II* cases (in Section 11.E.i), p. 490.

[545] The US modified its previous absolute per se illegality rule in *Jefferson Parish Hospital District No 2* v. *Hyde* 466 US 2 (1984).

[546] See the discussion in J. Vickers, 'Some Economics of Abuse of Dominance' in X. Vives (ed.), *Competition Policy in the EU: Fifty Years on from the Treaty of Rome* (Oxford University Press, 2009), 71, 79. R. A. Posner, *Antitrust Law* (2nd edn, University of Chicago Press, 2001), 197–209 also sets out the Chicago position.

the monopolist gets control of another component as well and tries to jack up the price of that item, the effect is the same as setting an excessive price for the monopolized component. The monopolist can take its profit just once; an effort to do more makes it worse off and is self-deterring...

The monopolist's profit-maximizing strategy is not to take over the market in related products...But to promote competition among the other producers. The less the complements cost, the more the monopolist can charge for its own product...

We appreciate the potential reply that it is impossible to say that a given practice 'never' could injure consumers. A creative economist could imagine unusual combinations of costs, elasticities, and barriers to entry that would cause injury in the rate situation...But just as rules of per se illegality condemn practice[s] that almost always injure consumers, so antitrust law applies rules of per se legality to practices that almost never injure consumers.

Lower prices almost always benefit consumers. Subjecting all low prices to litigation, and the inevitable risk of error in a search for the rate instances in which consumers could be made worse off in the long run by low prices today, would make it more risky for firms to reduce prices, and they would be less inclined to do so—to consumers' considerable detriment. That's why in Matsushita and Brooke Group the Supreme Court held that low prices are lawful, even if the seller has considerable market power, unless rivals have been driven out of the market and recoupment is either ongoing or imminent. It is why any firm's unilateral conduct is almost always deemed lawful unless it creates a dangerous probability of success in monopolizing...

Just so with arguments that low prices are designed to 'leverage' a firm from one monopoly to another. As long as rivals continue to sell, and no second monopoly is in prospect, the search for the rare situation in which that second monopoly just might allow the firm to gain a profit by injuring consumers is not worth the candle. The search itself (and the risk of error in the judicial process) has much more chance of condemning a beneficial practice than of catching a detrimental one. A price high enough to avoid condemnation under predatory-pricing rules cannot be condemned under a 'monopoly leveraging' theory that is just a predatory pricing variant without the intellectual discipline of that doctrine.

Post-Chicagoans, however, have argued that it is possible for tying to serve as a mechanism for leveraging market power because the single monopoly profit theorem depends on certain assumptions. One of these is that the two products are used in fixed proportions, another is that the market for the tied good has a competitive, constant, returns-to-scale structure. The complex economics of tying and bundling[547] have generated a large and lively literature.[548] Ultimately this shows that these practices may have both pro- and anti-competitive effects. Everything will depend on the facts of each case.

It is possible for leveraging to be 'defensive'. The theory of defensive leveraging concentrates on the prolongation of power in the tying market. In this model the dominant undertaking eliminates competitors on the tied market in order to prevent entry on to the tying market, or make it more

---

[547] For the economics, see Bishop and Walker, *The Economics of EC Competition Law* (cited in n. 187), paras. 6-063–6-083; M. Motta, *Competition Policy* (Cambridge University Press, 2004), 7.3; R. J. Van den Bergh and P. D. Camesasca, *European Competition Law and Economics: A Comparative Perspective* (2nd edn, Sweet & Maxwell, 2006), 265–270; O'Donoghue and Padilla, *The Law and Economics of Article 102* (cited in n. 14), 599–609; Rousseva, *Rethinking Exclusionary Abuses in EU Competition Law* (cited in n. 42), 239–245; Elhauge and Geradin, *Global Competition Law and Economics* (cited in n. 195), 562–571.

[548] The seminal article setting out the arguments against the Chicago position is M. Whinston, 'Tying, Foreclosure and Exclusion' (1990) 80(4) *American Economic Review* 837; see also J. Choi and C. Stefanadis, 'Tying, Investment and Dynamic Leverage Theory' (2001) 32 *RAND Journal of Economics* 52; K.-U. Kuhn, R. Stillman, and C. Caffarra, 'Economic Theories of Bundling and their Policy Implications in Abuse Cases' (2005) 1 *European Competition Journal* 85; D. Crane and J. Wright, 'Can Bundled Discounting Increase Consumer Prices Without Excluding Rivals?' (2009) 5 *Competition Policy Int'l* 209; D. S. Evans and M. Salinger, 'Why Do Firms Bundle and Tie? Evidence from Competitive Markets and Implications for Tying Law' (2005) 22 *Yale J Reg.* 37; B. Nabeluff, 'Exclusionary Bundling' (2005) 50 *Ant Bull* 321. An article published by in 2009, E. Elhauge, 'Tying, Bundled Discounts, and the Death of the Single Monopoly Profit Theory' (2009) 123(2) *Harvard LR* 399 attracted much debate, see particularly P. Seabright, 'The

difficult, by depriving the entrant of access to the consumable. It may also be that the dominant undertaking wishes to exclude the competitor in the tied market where there is a possibility that the tied product may in time become a substitute for the tying product.[549]

D. TYING AND BUNDLING AND ARTICLE 102

The Guidance Paper says:

49 Tying and bundling are common practices intended to provide customers with better products or offerings in more cost effective ways. However, an undertaking which is dominant in one product market (or more) of a tie or bundle (referred to as the tying market) can harm consumers through tying or bundling by foreclosing the market for the other products that are part of the tie or bundle (referred to as the tied market) and, indirectly, the tying market.

EU competition law is concerned with tying because of the leverage problem already discussed which may result in the foreclosure of competitors from the market.[550] Tying can do this because the supplier is dominant in the market for the *tying* product, so the customer has difficulty going elsewhere for it and therefore cannot or does not shop around for the *tied* product; mixed bundling can have a foreclosure effect because it offers a price the competitors on the tied market cannot match. Mixed bundling is a type of pricing policy. Contractual tying can be seen as a *refusal to supply* as well as a tie,[551] although as we will see, the competition rules apply differently to tying and refusal to supply.[552]

Article 102(d) specifically lists tying as a type of abuse:

making the conclusion of contracts subject to acceptance by the other parties of supplementary obligations which, by their nature or according to commercial usage, have no connection with the subject of such contracts.

However, the case law shows that tying and bundling may infringe Article 102 even if it does not fit within that provision. The list of abusive practices in Article 102 is not exhaustive.

E. THE CASE LAW

(i) Contractual Tying and Aftermarkets

Two leading cases which concerned consumables in an aftermarket tied to a primary product, *Hilti* and *Tetra Pak II*, established tying as virtually a per se abuse. In both cases the Commission found an abuse after very little analysis of the market. Once it had found dominance, separate

---

Undead? A Comment on Professor Elhauge's Paper' (2009) 5 *Competition Policy Int'l* 243; H. First, 'No Single Monopoly Profit, No Single Policy Prescription?' (2009) 5 *Competition Policy Int'l* 199; and Elhauge's response, E. Elhauge, 'The Failed Resurrection of the Single Monopoly Profit Theory', *Harvard Discussion Paper No. 664*, (2010) 6 *Competition Policy Int'l* 155.

[549] D. Carlton and M. Waldman, 'The Strategic Use of Tying to Preserve and Create Market Power in Evolving Industries' (2002) 33 *RAND Journal of Economics* 194; see generally P. Këllezi, 'Rhetoric or Reform: Does the Law of Tying and Bundling Reflect the Economic Theory', in Ezrachi (ed.), *Article 82 EC: Reflections on Its Recent Evolution* (cited in n. 32), 148, 152 ff.

[550] In the *cause célèbre* merger case *GE/Honeywell*, Case T-210/01, *General Electric v. Commission* [2005] ECR II-5575 the fear (inter alia), that the merged entity might bundle its products in the future and thereby exclude competitors caused the Commission, unlike the US authorities, to prohibit the transaction, see Chap. 15.

[551] See, e.g., Case 311/84, *Centre Belge v. CLT (Télémarketing)* [1985] ECR 3261; *Napier Brown/British Sugar* [1988] OJ L284/41(delivered pricing).

[552] See Section 12 for Refusal to Supply and see Rousseva, *Rethinking Exclusionary Abuses in EU Competition Law* (cited in n. 42), 228–230.

products, and no objective justification, the finding of abuse followed almost automatically. In both cases the appeals to the EU Courts concentrated on the issues of market definition and objective justification.

Eurofix-Bauco/Hilti [1988] OJ L65/19

Hilti was dominant in the supply of nail guns for the construction industry which were protected by patents. The cartridge strips... were also protected by Hilti's patents. The nails fired out of the cartridge strips were not, however, so protected and there were small, independent manufacturers of Hilti-compatible nails. Hilti followed a number of practices to ensure that customers for its cartridges also bought its nails and did not buy nails from the independent suppliers: i) making the sale of patented cartridge strips conditional upon taking a corresponding complement of nails; ii) reducing discounts on cartridges where the customer did not order nails as well; iii) inducing its distributors not to supply certain customers so that the independent nail producers could not get hold of Hilti cartridges; iv) refusing supplies of cartridges to long-standing customers who might resell to independent nail producers; v) frustrating or delaying applications for licences of right of the cartridge strip technology; vi) refusing to honour guarantees on nail-guns if non-Hilti nails had been used with them.

The Commission held that the nail-guns, cartridges, and nails each constituted a separate relevant product market and that Hilti was dominant in the EEC in all of them. It held that Hilti had infringed Article 102 by the practices above which were designed to tie the nails to the cartridges and thus to prevent or limit the entry of independent producers of Hilti-compatible consumables into the markets. Hilti claimed that the practices were objectively justified in that safety required that Hilti guns were only used with Hilti consumables and it claimed that the nails produced by the independents were sub-standard. The Commission rejected this, pointing out that Hilti had never communicated its safety concerns to the independents or taken steps to alert the UK authorities about any danger and that there had never been any report of safety difficulties from the use of non-Hilti nails. Hilti appealed to the General Court both on the issue of market definition[553] and on the finding of abuse.

Commission

74. Hilti has abused its dominant position in the EEC in the relevant market for nail guns and most importantly the markets for Hilti-compatible cartridge strips and nails. It has done this principally through its attempts to prevent or limit the entry of independent producers of Hilti-compatible consumables into these markets. Hilti's attempts to block or limit such entry went beyond the means legitimately available to a dominant company. The different aspects of Hilti's commercial behaviour were designed to this effect and were aimed at preventing Hilti-compatible cartridge strips from being freely available. Without such availability of Hilti-compatible cartridge strips, for which in the EEC Hilti until recently enjoyed protection afforded by patents, independent producers of Hilti-compatible nails have been severely restricted in their penetration of the market. Furthermore, customers have been obliged to rely on Hilti for both cartridges and nails for their Hilti nail guns. By limiting the effective competition from new entrants Hilti has been able to preserve its dominant position. The ability to carry out its illegal policies stems from its power on the markets for Hilti-compatible cartridge strips and nail guns (where its market position is strongest and the barriers to entry are highest) and aims at reinforcing its dominance on the Hilti-compatible nail market (where it is potentially more vulnerable to new competition)... Most of the abuses took place in or were centred on the UK which constitutes a substantial part of the common market. However, at least one of these abuses had direct effects in another Member State and in addition the strategy of Hilti was aimed indirectly at the whole EEC in its attempt both to stop new entrants into the market (who might start exporting) and to prevent otherwise profitable arbitrage.

---

[553] See Chap. 6, Section 5.B.i.h, p. 319.

75. Making the sale of patented cartridge strips conditional upon taking a corresponding complement of nails constitutes an abuse of a dominant position, as do reduced discounts and other discriminatory policies described above on cartridge-only orders. These policies leave the consumer with no choice over the source of his nails and as such abusively exploit him. In addition, these policies all have the object or effect of excluding independent nail makers who may threaten the dominant position Hilti holds. The tying and reduction of discounts were not isolated incidents but a generally applied policy.

The GC upheld the decision, dismissing pleas about the products forming a 'system' and refusing to accept that Hilti's conduct was justified by safety concerns.[554] The judgment was affirmed by the CJ.[555]

The facts of *Tetra Pak II* have already been set out.[556] The Commission held that aseptic packaging machines, aseptic cartons, non-aseptic machines, and non-aseptic cartons were four separate relevant markets, and that Tetra Pak was dominant on the markets for aseptic machines and cartons and had committed abuses on the associated non-aseptic markets.[557] One of the abuses found by the Commission was that Tetra Pak had tied the supply of its non-aseptic packaging machines to the supply of cartons which the machines filled. Customers had to obtain the cartons only from Tetra Pak itself[558] and were obliged to obtain all maintenance and repair services and the supplies of spare parts from Tetra Pak. Tetra Pak claimed that the machines and the cartons formed 'integrated distribution systems' and that in any event the tie was justified for technical reasons, considerations of public liability and health, and by the need to protect its reputation. The Commission rejected these arguments and said that the system of tied sales, 'which again limits outlets and makes contracts subject to acceptance of conditions (the purchase of cartons) which have no connection with their purpose (the sale of machines), constitutes a serious infringement of Article [102]'.[559] The GC upheld this, referring to the tied-sales clause intending to 'strengthen Tetra Pak's dominant position by reinforcing its customers' economic dependence on it'.[560]

On appeal to the CJ Tetra Pak claimed in particular that Article 102(d) prohibited tying only where the supplementary obligations imposed had by their nature, or according to commercial usage, no connection with the subject of the contract. The CJ confirmed the GC's judgment. It held that the reasoning of the GC, holding that there was no natural link, was correct. It also held that, as the examples in Article 102 are not exhaustive, a tie may constitute an abuse even if there is a natural link or the tied sale is in accordance with commercial usage.

Case C-333/94 P, *Tetra Pak International SA* v. *Commission* [1996] ECR I-5951

Court of Justice

34. In its third plea, Tetra Pak submits that the [General Court] erred in law in holding that the tied sales of cartons and filling machines were contrary to Article [102] in circumstances where there was a natural link between the two and tied sales were in accordance with commercial usage.

---

[554] Case T-30/89, *Hilti v. Commission* [1991] ECR II-1439.

[555] Case C-53/92, P *Hilti AG v. EC Commission* [1994] ECR I-667.

[556] See Section 8.F, p. 414 and Chap. 6, Section 5.B.i.h, p. 320.

[557] *Elopak Italia/Tetra Pak* [1991] OJ L72/1. For the issue of the dominant position and the abuse being on different markets, see Section 6, p. 393.

[558] Or from a company it designated. As there were no independent distributors the Commission pointed out that this clause was superfluous.

[559] *Elopak Italia/Tetra Pak*, para. 117.

[560] Case T-83/91, *Tetra Pak v. Commission* [1994] ECR II-755, para. 140.

35. Tetra Pak interprets Article [102 (d)] as prohibiting only the practice of making the conclusion of contracts dependent on acceptance of additional services which, by nature or according to commercial usage, have no link with the subject-matter of the contracts.

36. It must be noted, first, that the [General Court] explicitly rejected the argument put forward by Tetra Pak to show the existence of a natural link between the machines and the cartons. In paragraph 82 of the judgment under appeal, it found: 'consideration of commercial usage does not support the conclusion that the machinery for packaging a product is indivisible from the cartons. For a considerable time there have been independent manufacturers who specialise in the manufacture of non-aseptic cartons designed for use in machines manufactured by other concerns and who do not manufacture machinery themselves'. That assessment, itself based on commercial usage, rules out the existence of the natural link claimed by Tetra Pak by stating that other manufacturers can produce cartons for use in Tetra Pak's machines. With regard to aseptic cartons, the [General Court] found, at paragraph 83 of its judgment, that 'any independent producer is quite free, as far as Community competition law is concerned, to manufacture consumables intended for use in equipment manufactured by others, unless in doing so it infringes a competitor's intellectual property right'. It also noted, at paragraph 138, rejecting the argument based on the alleged natural link, that it was not for Tetra Pak to impose certain measures on its own initiative on the basis of technical considerations or considerations relating to product liability, protection of public health and protection of its reputation. Those factors, taken as a whole, show that the [General Court] considered that Tetra Pak was not alone in being able to manufacture cartons for use in its machines.

37. It must, moreover, be stressed that the list of abusive practices set out in the second paragraph of Article [102] is not exhaustive. Consequently, even where tied sales of two products are in accordance with commercial usage or there is a natural link between the two products in question, such sales may still constitute abuse within the meaning of Article [102] unless they are objectively justified. The reasoning of the [General Court] in paragraph 137 of its judgment is not therefore in any way defective.

It is clear from *Tetra Pak II* that, once it is shown that the products or services tied together are distinct, a dominant undertaking cannot rely on the words about nature and commercial usage in Article 102(d). 'Commercial usage' may merely have been established by the dominant undertaking itself[561] and the Court stressed the non-exhaustive character of the particular examples listed in the Article, thereby emasculating the conditions in that sub-paragraph. *Hilti* and *Tetra Pak II* were both driven by concerns about the structure of the market, not about the extraction of monopoly profits or the protection of consumers. In *Tetra Pak II* the monopoly profit could have been extracted from the tying product (the machines), had Tetra Pak wished.[562] The concern was with the ability of smaller firms to compete. This was a matter of policy and is summed up in paragraph 36 of the *Tetra Pak II* judgment, quoting the GC, where the CJ said 'any independent producer is quite free, as far as Community competition law is concerned, to manufacture consumables intended for use in equipment manufactured by others'.[563]

(ii) Mixed Bundling

There have been a number of cases and settlements concerning mixed bundling. Two of these involved Coca-Cola. In *Coca-Cola Italia Undertaking* (1989)[564] the Commission's Statement of

---

[561] See V. Korah, 'The Paucity of Economic Analysis in the EEC Decisions on Competition: Tetra Pak II' [1993] *CLP* 150; see also *Microsoft*, para. 940.

[562] See V. Korah, 'The Paucity of Economic Analysis in the EEC Decisions on Competition: Tetra Pak II' [1993] *CLP* 150.

[563] This passage also appeared in the GC judgment in *Hilti*, Case T-30/89, *Hilti v. Commission* [1991] ECR II-1439, para. 68, where it dealt with the definition of the market, see Chap. 6, Section 5.B.i.h, p. 319.

[564] Commission's *XIXth Report on Competition Policy* (Commission, 1989), para. 50.

Objections alleged that Coca-Cola's practice of offering discounts to retailers based on a package of cola and non-cola was an abuse. Coca-Cola agreed not to make discounts on cola conditional on the retailers buying non-cola, and the case was settled on that basis. In *Coca-Cola Undertaking* (2005)[565] Coca-Cola agreed, inter alia, to no longer offer a rebate to its customers if the customer agreed to buy other products together with its best-selling products or to reserve shelf space for the entire group of products.

In the aftermarket case, *Digital Undertaking*,[566] Digital, a computer supplier, offered a package of hardware maintenance services and software support services for its systems. The primary product market of computer systems was competitive but the Commission alleged that by offering customers the package in the aftermarket Digital abused its dominant position on the software support market for Digital systems as it made it uneconomic for customers to buy the hardware maintenance from a third party. Competitors in the hardware maintenance market were therefore excluded from servicing Digital systems. The Commission settled the proceedings when Digital undertook, inter alia, to offer hardware maintenance services on a stand-alone basis and to price its package in a way which fell below the list prices of the individual component services only insofar as the reduction reflected the passing on to customers of costs savings or other benefits stemming from the efficient packaging together of the different elements.

(iii) Technical Bundling and the *Microsoft* Case

In 1984 the Commission came to a settlement with IBM[567] after it had alleged that IBM had infringed Article 102 by, inter alia, tying various computer products together.[568]

In *Microsoft*[569] the Commission returned to the issue of tying in software markets. The Commission adopted a decision finding that Microsoft had abused its dominant position on the client PC operating systems market, where Microsoft's Windows system had over 90 per cent of the market, by supplying Windows to the computer manufacturers (OEMs) with its Windows Media Player (WMP) pre-installed. The Commission's conclusions were based on the finding that the Windows operating system and the WMP were two distinct products and that by bundling them together Microsoft was leveraging its monopoly power on to the media player market where it faced more competition. The Commission held that for tying to infringe Article 102 four elements must be present (see paragraph 794 in the extract from the Commission's decision): two separate products; dominance in the tying market; the customers are given no choice to obtain the tying product alone; and the tying forecloses competition. The Commission held all four conditions were present in this case. In this extract the Commission explains the detrimental effects of Microsoft's practices.

---

[565] [2005] OJ L253/21.

[566] Commission Press Release IP/97/868. Cf. the *Pelikan/Kyocera* case, *XXVth Report on Competition Policy* (Commission, 1995) part 87: see Chap. 6. See also D. Maldoom, 'The Kodak Case: Power in Aftermarkets' [1996] *ECLR* 473; M. Dolmans and V. Pickering, 'The 1997 Digital Undertaking' [1998] 2 *ECLR* 108; P. Andrews, 'Aftermarket Power in the Computer Services Market: The Digital Undertaking' (1998) 3 *ECLR* 176.

[567] See *XIVth Report on Competition Policy* (Commission, 1984) paras. 94–95.

[568] This involved not offering central processing units (CPUs) without a capacity of main memory included in the price (memory bundling); and not offering CPUs without the basic software included in the price (software bundling). IBM did not admit it had a dominant position or that it had committed an abuse but nevertheless undertook to offer its CPUs in the EEC either without main memory or with only such capacity as was strictly required for testing. IBM was also alleged to have committed an abuse by failing to disclose interface information, see Section 12.D.vi, p. 537, and by discriminating between users of IBM software, i.e. refusing to supply certain software installation services to users of non-IBM CPUs. In 2010 the Commission examined complaints (from rival software suppliers) that IBM had tied its mainframe hardware with its operating system. The Commission closed the proceedings on 20 September 2011 and the complaints were withdrawn.

[569] COMP/C-3/37.792, 24 March 2004, [2005] 4 CMLR 965. The case also concerned a refusal to supply, discussed in Section 12.D.vi, p. 536.

Microsoft, Commission Decision COMP/C-3/37.792

Commission

(794) Tying prohibited under [Article 102] of the Treaty requires the presence of the following elements: (i) the tying and tied goods are two separate products; (ii) the undertaking concerned is dominant in the tying product market; (iii) the undertaking concerned does not give customers a choice to obtain the tying product without the tied product; and (iv) tying forecloses competition.

...

(979) Through tying WMP with Windows, Microsoft uses Windows as a distribution channel to anti-competitively ensure for itself a significant competition advantage in the media player market. Competitors, due to Microsoft's tying, are *a priori* at a disadvantage irrespective of whether their products are potentially more attractive on the merits.

(980) Microsoft thus interferes with the normal competitive process which would benefit users in terms of quicker cycles of innovation due to unfettered competition on the merits. Tying of WMP increases the content and applications barrier to entry which protects Windows and it will facilitate the erection of such a barrier for WMP. A position of market strength achieved in a market characterised by network effects—such as the media player market—is sustainable, as once the network effects work in favour of a company which has gained a decisive momentum, they will amount to entry barriers for potential competitors...

(981) This shields Microsoft from effective competition from potentially more efficient media player vendors which could challenge its position. Microsoft thus reduces the talent and capital invested in innovation of media players, not least its own...and anti-competitively raises barriers to market entry. Microsoft's conduct affects a market which could be a hotbed for new and exciting products springing forth in a climate of undistorted competition.

(982) Moreover, tying of WMP allows Microsoft to anti-competitively expand its position in adjacent media-related software markets and weaken effective competition to the eventual detriment of consumers.

It is notable that the Commission took a more 'effects-based' approach in *Microsoft* than it had done in the past, in *Hilti* and *Tetra Pak II*. It did not assume foreclosure of competitors. Instead it said:[570]

There are indeed circumstances relating to the tying of WMP which warrant a closer examination of the effects that tying has on competition in this case. While in classical tying cases, the Commission and the Courts considered the foreclosure effect for competing vendors to be demonstrated by the bundling of a separate product with the dominant product, in the case at issue, users can and do to a certain extent obtain third party media players through the internet, sometimes for free. There are therefore indeed good reasons not to assume without further analysis that tying WMP constitutes conduct which by its very nature is liable to foreclosure competition.

It carefully set out the effects of Microsoft's tying practice. First, installing WMP on Windows provided a more efficient distribution system than was available to the competitors and led to the 'ubiquity' of WMP.[571] That meant, secondly, that content providers and software developers increasingly used the WMP format to the detriment of the main competitors and their technologies.[572] That led, thirdly, to network effects which in the end would result in the market 'tipping' to WMP: it is not

---

[570] *Microsoft* decision, para. 841.

[571] *Microsoft* decision, paras. 843–878.

[572] *Microsoft* decision, paras. 879–944.

necessary for a competition authority to wait until the tipping has actually occurred, by which time meaningful intervention would be too late.[573]

Microsoft was fined €497,196,304.[574] More seriously for Microsoft the Commission ordered it to offer the OEMs a version of Windows without the WMP. The OEMs must be able to choose between Windows alone and a 'package' of Windows plus the WMP. If they choose the former they can install a rival media player. Consumers therefore have a choice of media player when they buy their PC. Microsoft is not allowed to offer any technological, commercial, or contractual term or inducement to make the bundled version the more attractive, and the unbundled version of Windows must work as well as the bundled version.

The Commission's decision raised a number of difficult and controversial issues. Among these was how far even dominant suppliers should be free to develop new versions of their products with 'built in' features. Microsoft appealed to the GC.[575]

Meanwhile, in the US the competition authorities charged Microsoft with an illegal tie by bundling its own Internet Explorer browser (IE) with its Windows operating system. The District Court held that they were two products and that the browser/operating system package constituted a per se illegal tie-in.[576] However, the Court of Appeals reversed and remanded this finding.[577] It sent it back to be tried under a rule of reason analysis. The US DOJ then withdrew the tying claim, so it was not retried.[578] The Court of Appeals was concerned that the bundling of the system and browser served consumer welfare, in that consumers welcome being able to buy a computer with a browser ready installed, rather than having to shop around for one. The attitude of the DOJ to tying was manifest in a public statement by the US Assistant Attorney General for Antitrust which was highly critical of the EU *Microsoft* decision.

Assistant Attorney General for Antitrust, R. Hewitt Pate, Issues Statement on the EC's Decision in its Microsoft Investigation, 24 March 2004[579]

The EC has today pursued a different enforcement approach by imposing a 'code removal' remedy to resolve its media player concerns. The U.S. experience tells us that the best antitrust remedies eliminate impediments to the healthy functioning of competitive markets without hindering successful competitors or imposing burdens on third parties, which may result from the EC's remedy. A requirement of 'code removal' was not at any time—including during the period when the U.S. was seeking a breakup of Microsoft prior to the rejection of that remedy by the court of appeals—part of the United States' proposed remedy.

Imposing antitrust liability on the basis of product enhancements and imposing 'code removal' remedies may produce unintended consequences. Sound antitrust policy must avoid chilling innovation and competition even by 'dominant' companies. A contrary approach risks protecting competitors, not

[573] *Microsoft* decision, para. 946.

[574] The fine included that for the other abuse investigated, refusal to supply interface information. This was not a case where the Commission refrained from imposing a fine because of the novelty of the case: it said that as regards the tying/bundling abuse it was not applying a new rule but that *Hilti* and *Tetra Pak II* should been sufficient guidance to Microsoft in making it clear that its conduct infringed Art. 102: 'the software industry is not exempted from the application of competition law' (*Microsoft* decision, para. 1057).

[575] Case T-201/04, *Microsoft v. Commission* [2007] ECR II-3601; there was no further appeal to the CJ.

[576] Judge Jackson, 87 F. Supp. 2d 30 (DDC 2000).

[577] (DC Circuit), 253 F.3d 34. A number of other practices *were* held illegal, including co-mingling the browser and operating system codes.

[578] The States which were also plaintiffs followed the DOJ and withdrew their claims.

[579] Available on the DOJ website,<http://www.usdoj.gov/atr/public/press_releases/2004/202976.htm>.

competition, in ways that may ultimately harm innovation and the consumers that benefit from it. It is significant that the U.S. district court considered and rejected a similar remedy in the U.S. litigation.

While the imposition of a civil fine is a customary and accepted aspect of EC antitrust enforcement, it is unfortunate that the largest antitrust fine ever levied will now be imposed in a case of unilateral competitive conduct, the most ambiguous and controversial area of antitrust enforcement. For this fine to surpass even the fines levied against members of the most notorious price fixing cartels may send an unfortunate message about the appropriate hierarchy of enforcement priorities.

In the *Microsoft* appeal the GC, having stated at the outset the limited nature of its judicial function where complex economic and technical appraisals are concerned,[580] stuck closely to its brief of establishing that the Commission had provided adequate reasoning based on factually accurate, reliable, and consistent evidence capable of substantiating its conclusions. It confirmed (in paragraph 859) that the four factors set out in the Commission's decision,[581] i.e. two products, dominance in the tying market, no choice, and foreclosure, were correct.

The Commission's conclusions were based on the premiss that there were two products, desktop operating systems and media players. Microsoft therefore claimed, first, that it did not supply two distinct products but one integrated one and that therefore it could not commit the abuse of tying or bundling. It argued that it was relevant to ask whether there was consumer demand for the tying product (Windows) without the tied product (WMP). The GC upheld the Commission's decision that there were two products.

Case T-201/04, *Microsoft* v. *Commission* [2007] ECR II-3601

General Court

917 First of all, it must be observed that, as the Commission correctly states at recital 803 to the contested decision, the distinctness of products for the purpose of an analysis under Article [102] has to be assessed by reference to customer demand. Furthermore, Microsoft clearly shares that opinion…

918 The Commission was also correct to state, at the same recital, that in the absence of independent demand for the allegedly tied product, there can be no question of separate products and no abusive tying.

919 Microsoft's argument that the Commission thus applied the wrong test and that it ought in reality to have ascertained whether what was alleged to be the tying product was regularly offered without the tied product or whether customers 'want[ed] Windows without media functionality' cannot be accepted.

920 In the first place, the Commission's argument finds support in the case-law (see, to that effect, Case C-333/94 P *Tetra Pak II*…paragraph 36; Case T-30/89 *Hilti*…paragraph 67; and Case T-83/91 *Tetra Pak II*…paragraph 82).

921 In the second place, as the Commission correctly observes in its pleadings, Microsoft's argument, based on the concept that there is no demand for a Windows client PC operating system without a streaming media player, amounts to contending that complementary products cannot constitute separate products for the purposes of Article [102], which is contrary to the Community case-law on bundling. To take Hilti, for example, it may be assumed that there was no demand for a nail gun magazine without nails, since a magazine without nails is useless. However, that did not prevent the Community Courts from concluding that those two products belonged to separate markets.

[580] *Microsoft*, paras. 85–89, see Chap. 13.
[581] *Microsoft* decision, para. 794.

922 In the case of complementary products, such as client PC operating systems and application software, it is quite possible that customers will wish to obtain the products together, but from different sources. For example, the fact that most client PC users want their client PC operating system to come with word-processing software does not transform those separate products into a single product for the purposes of Article [102].

923 Microsoft's argument ignores the particular intermediary role played by OEMs, who combine hardware and software from different sources in order to offer a ready-to-use PC to the end user. As the Commission very correctly observes at recital 809 to the contested decision, if OEMs and consumers were able to obtain Windows without Windows Media Player, that would not mean that they would choose to obtain Windows without a streaming media player. OEMs follow consumer demand for a pre-installed media player on the operating system and offer a software package including a streaming media player that works with Windows, the difference being that that player would not necessarily be Windows Media Player.

924 In the third place, and in any event, Microsoft's argument cannot succeed because, as the Commission observes at recital 807 to the contested decision, there exists a demand for client PC operating systems without streaming media players, for example by companies afraid that their staff might use them for non-work-related purposes. That fact is not disputed by Microsoft.

925 Next, the Court finds that a series of factors based on the nature and technical features of the products concerned, the facts observed on the market, the history of the development of the products concerned and also Microsoft's commercial practice demonstrate the existence of separate consumer demand for streaming media players.

926 In the first place, it must be borne in mind that the Windows client PC operating system is system software while Windows Media Player is application software. As the Commission explains at recital 37 to the contested decision, '"[s]ystem software" controls the hardware of the computer, to which it sends instructions on behalf of "applications" fulfilling a specific user need, such as word processing', and '[o]perating systems are system software products that control the basic functions of a computer and enable the user to make use of such a computer and run application software on it'. More generally, it is clear from the description of those products at recitals 324 to 342 and 402 to 425 to the contested decision that client PC operating systems and streaming media players clearly differ in terms of functionalities.

927 In the second place, there are distributors who develop and supply streaming media players on an autonomous basis, independently of client PC operating systems. Thus, Apple supplies its QuickTime player separately from its client PC operating systems. A further particularly convincing example is that of RealNetworks, Microsoft's main competitor on the streaming media players market, which neither develops nor sells client PC operating systems. It must be pointed out, in that regard, that according to the case-law the fact that there are on the market independent companies specialising in the manufacture and sale of the tied product constitutes serious evidence of the existence of a separate market for that product (see, to that effect, Case C-333/94 P *Tetra Pak II*...paragraph 36; Case T-30/89 *Hilti*...paragraph 67; and Case T-83/91 *Tetra Pak II*...paragraph 82).

928 Likewise, in the third place, Microsoft, as it confirmed in answer to a written question put by the Court, develops and markets versions of Windows Media Player which are designed to work with its competitors' client PC operating systems, namely Apple's Mac OS X and Sun's Solaris. Similarly, RealNetworks' RealPlayer works with, inter alia, the Windows, Mac OS X, Solaris and some UNIX operating systems.

929 In the fourth place, Windows Media Player can be downloaded, independently of the Windows client PC operating system, from Microsoft's Internet site. Likewise, Microsoft releases upgrades of Windows Media Player, independently of releases or upgrades of its Windows client PC operating system.

930 In the fifth place, Microsoft engages in promotions specifically dedicated to Windows Media Player (see recital 810 to the contested decision).

931 In the sixth place, as the Commission pertinently observes at recital 813 to the contested decision, Microsoft offers SDK licences which differ according to whether they relate to the Windows client PC operating system or to Windows Media technologies. There is thus a specific SDK licence for Windows Media Player.

932 Last, and in the seventh place, in spite of the bundling applied by Microsoft, a not insignificant number of customers continue to acquire media players from Microsoft's competitors, separately from their client PC operating system, which shows that they regard the two products as separate.

933 The foregoing facts demonstrate to the requisite legal standard that the Commission was correct to conclude that client PC operating systems and streaming media players constituted two separate products for the purposes of Article [102].

934 That conclusion is not undermined by Microsoft's other arguments.

935 In the first place, as regards Microsoft's argument that the integration of Windows Media Player in the Windows operating system from May 1999 constitutes a normal and necessary step in the evolution of that system and is in keeping with the constant improvement of its media functionality, it is sufficient to observe that the fact that tying takes the form of the technical integration of one product in another does not have the consequence that, for the purpose of assessing its impact on the market, that integration cannot be qualified as the bundling of two separate products.

936 As Microsoft itself acknowledged in answer to a question put to it by the Court at the hearing, its decision to supply WMP 6 as a functionality integrated in the Windows operating system from May 1999 was not the consequence of a technical constraint. At that time there was nothing to prevent Microsoft from distributing WMP 6 in the same way as it had distributed its previous player, NetShow, which since June 1998 had been included on the Windows 98 installation CD: and none of the four Windows 98 default installations provided for the installation of NetShow, which had to be installed by users if they wished to use it.

937 Furthermore, Microsoft's argument that the integration of Windows Media Player in the Windows operating system was dictated by technical reasons is scarcely credible in the light of the content of certain of its own internal communications. Thus, it follows from Mr Bay's email of 3 January 1999 to Mr Gates (see paragraph 911 above) that the integration of Windows Media Player in Windows was primarily designed to make Windows Media Player more competitive with RealPlayer by presenting it as a constituent part of Windows and not as application software that might be compared with RealPlayer.

938 In the second place, Microsoft cannot claim that the Commission fails to show that media functionality is not linked, by nature or according to commercial usage, to client PC operating systems.

939 First, it follows from the considerations set out at paragraphs 925 to 932 above that client PC operating systems and streaming media players do not, by their nature, constitute indissociable products. While it is true that there is a link between a client PC operating system such as Windows and application software such as Windows Media Player, in the sense that both products are on the same computer from the user's perspective and that a media player will only work when an operating system is present, that does not mean that the two products are not dissociable in economic and commercial terms for the purpose of competition rules.

940 Second, as the Commission rightly observes, it is difficult to speak of commercial usage in an industry that is 95% controlled by Microsoft.

941 Third, Microsoft cannot rely on the fact that vendors of competing client PC operating systems also bundle those systems with a streaming media player. On the one hand, Microsoft has not adduced any evidence that such bundling was already carried out by its competitors at the time when the abusive bundling commenced. On the other hand, moreover, it is clear that the commercial conduct of those competitors, far from invalidating the Commission's argument, corroborates it. As may be seen from recitals 822 and 823 to the contested decision and as the Commission observes in its pleadings, some vendors of non-Microsoft operating systems who supply their operating systems with a media player make the

installation of the media player optional, or allow it to be uninstalled, or offer a selection of different media players.

942 Fourth, and in any event, it is settled case-law that even when the tying of two products is consistent with commercial usage or when there is a natural link between the two products in question, it may none the less constitute abuse within the meaning of Article [102], unless it is objectively justified (Case C-333/94 P *Tetra Pak II* . . . paragraph 37).

943 Finally, in the third place, the argument which Microsoft put forward at the hearing, that the unbundled version of Windows which it placed on the market pursuant to the remedy had met with no success, must also be rejected. As already stated at paragraph 260 above, the lawfulness of a Community measure must be assessed on the basis of the matters of fact and of law existing at the time when the measure was adopted. Furthermore, any doubts as to the effectiveness of the remedy ordered by the Commission do not in themselves prove that its finding as to the existence of two separate products is wrong.

944 The Court concludes from all of the foregoing considerations that the Commission was correct to find that client PC operating systems and streaming media players constituted separate products.

The test for determining whether products are distinct for the purposes of Article 102 is thus 'consumer demand' (paragraphs 917–918). One relevant issue was not whether consumers wanted Windows without media functionality but whether they necessarily wanted them from the same source (paragraphs 921–922); a second was the important role of the OEMs (paragraph 923); and a third was that some operating systems users (e.g. kill-joy employers) did not want built-in media players (paragraph 924). The GC also looked at features of the market and at aspects of Microsoft's commercial practice. It noted that operating systems and streaming media players have different functionality (paragraph 926); distributors supply media players separately from any supply of a PC client operating system (paragraph 927); Microsoft distributed versions of the WMP designed to work with its competitors' operating systems (paragraph 928); WMP could be downloaded independently from Microsoft's internet site (paragraph 929); Microsoft engaged in WMP-specific promotion (paragraph 930); Microsoft applied different licensing arrangements to Windows and to WMP (paragraph 931); and some consumers obtained media players from the competitors, separately from their PC operating system (paragraph 932).

Secondly, Microsoft argued that the situation did not fall within Article 102(d) and that the Commission had added a foreclosure element not expressly provided for in Article 102(d).[582] The GC confirmed that the second paragraph of Article 102 is not exhaustive and that the Commission's 'four factors' could be deduced from the very concept of bundling and from the case law.

Case T-201/04, *Microsoft* v. *Commission* [2007] ECR II-3601

General Court

850 The Court finds that Microsoft's arguments are purely semantic and cannot be accepted.

851 It is appropriate to recall the way in which the Commission structures its argument relating to bundling in the contested decision.

852 At recital 794 to the contested decision, the Commission states that tying prohibited under Article [102] requires the presence of the four factors set out at paragraph 842 above.

853 Next, it examines Microsoft's conduct in the light of those four factors (recitals 799 to 954 to the contested decision).

---

[582] *Microsoft* decision, paras. 845–847.

854 So, the Commission first observes that Microsoft has a dominant position on the client PC operating systems market (recital 799 to the contested decision). The Court notes that Microsoft does not dispute that fact.

855 Second, the Commission says that streaming media players and client PC operating systems are two separate products (recitals 800 to 825 to the contested decision).

856 Third, the Commission states that Microsoft does not give customers the choice of obtaining Windows without Windows Media Player (recitals 826 to 834 to the contested decision).

857 Fourth, the Commission claims that the tying of Windows Media Player forecloses competition in the media players market (recitals 835 to 954 to the contested decision). It observes, in particular, that in classical tying cases both it and the Community Courts 'considered the foreclosure effect for competing vendors to be demonstrated by the bundling of a separate product with the dominant product' (recital 841 to the contested decision). The Commission states, however, that in the present case there are good reasons not to assume without further analysis that tying Windows Media Player constitutes conduct which by its very nature is liable to foreclose competition (ibid.). The Commission considers, in essence, that 'tying [Windows Media Player] with the dominant Windows makes [Windows Media Player] the platform of choice for complementary content and applications which in turn [creates a risk of] foreclosing competition in the market for media players' (recital 842 to the contested decision). Furthermore, '[t]his has spillover effects on competition in related products such as media encoding and management software (often server-side), but also in client PC operating systems for which media players compatible with quality content are an important application' (ibid.).

858 Last, the Commission examines the basis on which Microsoft relies in its attempt to demonstrate that the abusive conduct imputed to it is objectively justified (recitals 955 to 970 to the contested decision).

859 The Court considers that the Commission's analysis of the constituent elements of bundling is correct and that it is consistent both with Article [102] and with the case-law. The Commission was correct to rely on the factors set out at recital 794 to the contested decision and on the fact that the tying was without objective justification in deciding whether Microsoft's conduct constituted abusive tying. Those factors can be deduced both from the very concept of bundling and from the case-law (see, in particular, Case T-30/89 *Hilti v Commission*...upheld in Case C-53/92 P *Hilti v Commission*...(both cases being referred to below as 'Hilti') and judgments of the [General Court] and the Court of Justice in *Tetra Pak II*, paragraph 293 above).

860 It must be borne in mind that the list of abusive practices set out in the second paragraph of Article [102] is not exhaustive and that the practices mentioned there are merely examples of abuse of a dominant position (see, to that effect, Case C-333/94 P *Tetra Pak II*, paragraph 293 above, paragraph 37). It is settled case-law that the list of practices contained in that provision is not an exhaustive enumeration of the abuses of a dominant position prohibited by the EC Treaty (Case 6/72 *Europemballage and Continental Can v Commission*...paragraph 26, and *Compagnie maritime belge transports and Others v Commission*, paragraph 229 above, paragraph 112).

861 It follows that bundling by an undertaking in a dominant position may also infringe Article [102] where it does not correspond to the example given in Article [102(d)]. Accordingly, in order to establish the existence of abusive bundling, the Commission was correct to rely in the contested decision on Article [102] in its entirety and not exclusively on Article [102 (d)].

862 In any event, the Court holds that the constituent elements of abusive tying identified by the Commission at recital 794 to the contested decision coincide effectively with the conditions laid down in Article[102 (d)].

863 The Court thus rejects Microsoft's argument that in the present case the Commission applied conditions which differ, from two perspectives, from those laid down in Article [102(d)].

864 In the first place, when the Commission states that it is necessary to examine whether the dominant undertaking 'does not give customers a choice to obtain the tying product without the tied product',

it is merely expressing in different words the concept that bundling assumes that consumers are compelled, directly or indirectly, to accept 'supplementary obligations', such as those referred to in Article [102(d)].

865 In the present case, as the Court will explain in greater detail at paragraphs 962 and 965 below, that coercion is mainly applied first of all to OEMs, who then pass it on to the end user. The end user is directly exposed to that coercion in the less frequent situation in which, rather than deal through an OEM, he acquires a Windows client PC operating system directly from a retailer.

866 In the second place, it cannot be claimed that the Commission introduced a new condition relating to the foreclosure of competitors from the market in order to establish the existence of abusive bundling within the meaning of Article [102(d)].

867 In that regard, the Court observes that, while it is true that neither that provision nor, more generally, Article [102] as a whole contains any reference to the anti-competitive effect of bundling, the fact remains that, in principle, conduct will be regarded as abusive only if it is capable of restricting competition (see, to that effect, Case T-203/01 *Michelin v Commission*...('Michelin II'), paragraph 237).

868 Furthermore, as will be made explicit at paragraphs 1031 to 1058 below, the applicant cannot claim that the Commission relied on a new and highly speculative theory to reach the conclusion that a foreclosure effect exists in the present case. As indicated at recital 841 to the contested decision, the Commission considered that, in light of the specific circumstances of the present case, it could not merely assume, as it normally does in cases of abusive tying, that the tying of a specific product and a dominant product has by its nature a foreclosure effect. The Commission therefore examined more closely the actual effects which the bundling had already had on the streaming media player market and also the way in which that market was likely to evolve.

869 In light of the foregoing, the Court considers that the question of the bundling must be assessed by reference to the four conditions set out at recital 794 to the contested decision (see paragraph 842 above) and to the condition relating to the absence of objective justification.

870 The second condition set out at recital 794 to the contested decision must be considered to be met, because it is common ground that Microsoft has a dominant position on the market for what is alleged to be the tying product, namely client PC operating systems. The arguments which Microsoft puts forward in relation to the first three parts of the first plea (see paragraph 839 above) will be examined in conjunction with the four other conditions which must be satisfied to substantiate the finding of abusive tying. In carrying out that examination, the Court will proceed as follows. First, it will examine the condition relating to the existence of two separate products in the light of the arguments advanced by Microsoft on the second and third parts of the plea. Second, it will examine the condition to the effect that the conclusion of contracts is made subject to supplementary obligations, in the light of the arguments which Microsoft puts forward in support of the third part of the plea. Third, the Court will analyse the condition relating to the restriction of competition on the market in the light of the submissions made by Microsoft in connection with the first part of the plea. Fourth, it will examine the objective justifications on which the applicant relies, taking into account the arguments which it puts forward in connection with the second part of the plea.

Thirdly, Microsoft said that there was no restriction of *actual* (rather than *hypothetical*) customer choice. It argued that there was no 'coercion' or supplementary obligation involved. Consumers did not pay more for the WMP functionality of Windows. They did not have to use it. They could install and use third-party media players. The GC held that none of this mattered. It was not necessarily true that the WMP was free just because there was no separate charge for it and, anyway, it was not required that consumers had to pay a certain price for the tied product.[583] Nor did Article 102(d), as could be seen from *Hilti*, demand that the consumers had to use the tied product.[584] Although both

[583] *Microsoft* decision, paras. 968–969.
[584] *Microsoft* decision, para. 970.

OEMs and consumers *could* install and/or use other media players, they had little incentive to do so.[585] This last point was vital for the issue of foreclosure.

Fourthly, Microsoft claimed that the Commission had failed to prove that the integration of WMP with Windows involved foreclosure of competition. It argued that the Commission, recognising that it was not dealing with a 'classical tying case', had applied a 'highly speculative theory, relying on a prospective analysis of the possible reactions of third parties, in order to reach the conclusion that the tying at issue was likely to foreclose competition'.[586] The GC rejected this too.

Case T-201/04, *Microsoft* v. *Commission* [2007] ECR II-3601

General Court

1046 Thus, the release of the bundled version of Windows and Windows Media Player as the only version of the Windows operating system capable of being pre-installed by OEMs on new client PCs had the direct and immediate consequence of depriving OEMs of the possibility previously open to them of assembling the products which they deemed most attractive for consumers and, more particularly, of preventing them from choosing one of Windows Media Player's competitors as the only media player. On this last point, it must be borne in mind that at the time RealPlayer had a significant commercial advantage as market leader. As Microsoft itself acknowledges, it was only in 1999 that it succeeded in developing a streaming media player that performed well enough, given that its previous player, NetShow, 'was unpopular with customers because it did not work very well' (recital 819 to the contested decision). It must also be borne in mind that between August 1995 and July 1998 it was RealNetworks' products—first RealAudio Player, then RealPlayer—that were distributed with Windows. There is therefore good reason to conclude that if Microsoft had not adopted the impugned conduct competition between RealPlayer and Windows Media Player would have been decided on the basis of the intrinsic merits of the two products.

1054 It follows from the foregoing that in the analysis set out at recitals 843 to 878 to the contested decision, which is the first stage of its reasoning, the Commission demonstrated to the requisite legal standard that the bundling of Windows and Windows Media Player from May 1999 inevitably had significant consequences for the structure of competition. That practice allowed Microsoft to obtain an unparalleled advantage with respect to the distribution of its product and to ensure the ubiquity of Windows Media Player on client PCs throughout the world, thus providing a disincentive for users to make use of third-party media players and for OEMs to pre-install such players on client PCs.

1052 As the Commission asserts at recital 870 to the contested decision, while downloading is in itself a technically inexpensive way of distributing media players, vendors must deploy major resources to 'overcome end-users' inertia and persuade them to ignore the pre-installation of [Windows Media Player]'.

1053 Second, Microsoft has put forward no argument capable of calling in question the Commission's finding that the other methods of distributing streaming media players mentioned in the contested decision, namely bundling the media player with other software or Internet access services, and retail sale, are only a 'second-best solution and [do] not rival the efficiency and effectiveness of distributing software pre-installed on [Windows] PCs' (recitals 872 to 876 to the contested decision).

1054 It follows from the foregoing that in the analysis set out at recitals 843 to 878 to the contested decision, which is the first stage of its reasoning, the Commission demonstrated to the requisite legal standard that the bundling of Windows and Windows Media Player from May 1999 inevitably had significant consequences for the structure of competition. That practice allowed Microsoft to obtain an unparalleled advantage with respect to the distribution of its product and to ensure the ubiquity of Windows Media

---

[585] *Microsoft* decision, para. 971.
[586] *Microsoft* decision, para. 1032.

Player on client PCs throughout the world, thus providing a disincentive for users to make use of third-party media players and for OEMs to pre-install such players on client PCs.

1055 Admittedly, as Microsoft contends, a number of OEMs continue to add third-party media players to the packages which they offer to their customers. It is also common ground that the number of media players and the extent of the use of multiple players are continually increasing. However, those factors do not invalidate the Commission's conclusion that the impugned conduct was likely to weaken competition within the meaning of the case-law. Since May 1999 vendors of third-party media players have no longer been able to compete through OEMs to have their own products placed instead of Windows Media Player as the only media player on the client PCs assembled and sold by OEMs.

1056 It should further be noted that the merits of the findings made above are borne out by data examined by the Commission in the third stage of its reasoning. More particularly, as will be explained at paragraphs 1080 to 1084 below, the data mentioned at recitals 905 to 926 to the contested decision show a clear tendency in favour of using Windows Media Player to the detriment of competing media players.

1057 It follows from information communicated by Microsoft itself during the administrative procedure and referred to at recitals 948 to 951 to the contested decision that the significant growth in the use of Windows Media Player has not come about because that player is of better quality than competing players or because those media players, and particularly RealPlayer, have certain defects.

1058 In the light of all the foregoing considerations, the Court concludes that the Commission's findings in the first stage of its reasoning are in themselves sufficient to establish that the fourth constituent element of abusive bundling is present in this case. Those findings are not based on any new or speculative theory, but on the nature of the impugned conduct, on the conditions of the market and on the essential features of the relevant products. They are based on accurate, reliable and consistent evidence which Microsoft, by merely contending that it is pure conjecture, has not succeeded in showing to be incorrect.

1059 It follows from the foregoing that it is not necessary to examine the arguments which Microsoft puts forward against the findings made by the Commission in the other two stages of its reasoning. None the less, the Court considers that it should examine them briefly.

1060 In the second stage of its reasoning, the Commission seeks to establish that the ubiquity of Windows Media Player as a result of its bundling with Windows is capable of having an appreciable impact on content providers and software designers.

1061 The Commission's theory is based on the fact that the market for streaming media players is characterised by significant indirect network effects or, to use the expression employed by Mr Gates, on the existence of a 'positive feedback loop' (recital 882 to the contested decision). That expression describes the phenomenon where, the greater the number of users of a given software platform, the more there will be invested in developing products compatible with that platform, which, in turn reinforces the popularity of that platform with users.

1062 The Court considers that the Commission was correct to find that such a phenomenon existed in the present case and to find that it was on the basis of the percentages of installation and use of media players that content providers and software developers chose the technology for which they would develop their own products (recital 879 to the contested decision). The Commission correctly stated, first, that those operators tended primarily to use Windows Media Player as that allowed them to reach the very large majority of client PC users in the world and, second, that the transmission of content and applications compatible with a given media player was in itself a significant competitive factor, since it increased the popularity of that media player, and, in turn, favoured the use of the underlying media technology, including codecs, formats (including DRM) and server software (recitals 880 and 881 to the contested decision).

...

1078 In the third stage of its reasoning, the Commission examines the evolution of the market in light of market surveys carried out by Media Metrix, Synovate and Nielsen/NetRatings and concludes that the data in those surveys 'consistently point to a trend in favour of usage of [Windows Media Player] and Windows Media formats to the detriment of the main competing media players (and media player technologies)' (recital 944 to the contested decision).

1079 The Court finds that the conclusion referred to in the preceding paragraph is correct.

…

1088 It follows from the foregoing considerations that the final conclusion which the Commission sets out at recitals 978 to 984 to the contested decision concerning the anti-competitive effects of the bundling is well founded. The Commission is correct to make the following findings:

– Microsoft uses Windows as a distribution channel to ensure for itself a significant competitive advantage on the media players market (recital 979 to the contested decision);

– because of the bundling, Microsoft's competitors are a priori at a disadvantage even if their products are inherently better than Windows Media Player (ibid.);

– Microsoft interferes with the normal competitive process which would benefit users by ensuring quicker cycles of innovation as a consequence of unfettered competition on the merits (recital 980 to the contested decision);

– the bundling increases the content and applications barriers to entry, which protect Windows, and facilitates the erection of such barriers for Windows Media Player (ibid.);

– Microsoft shields itself from effective competition from vendors of potentially more efficient media players who could challenge its position, and thus reduces the talent and capital invested in innovation of media players (recital 981 to the contested decision);

– by means of the bundling, Microsoft may expand its position in adjacent media-related software markets and weaken effective competition, to the detriment of consumers (recital 982 to the contested decision);

– by means of the bundling, Microsoft sends signals which deter innovation in any technologies in which it might conceivably take an interest and which it might tie with Windows in the future (recital 983 to the contested decision).

1089 The Commission therefore had ground to state, at recital 984 to the contested decision, that there was a reasonable likelihood that tying Windows and Windows Media Player would lead to a lessening of competition so that the maintenance of an effective competition structure would not be ensured in the foreseeable future. It must be made clear that the Commission did not state that the tying would lead to the elimination of all competition on the market for streaming media players. Microsoft's argument that, several years after the beginning of the abuse at issue, a number of third-party media players are still present on the market therefore does not invalidate the Commission's argument.

1090 It follows from all of the foregoing considerations that Microsoft has put forward no argument capable of vitiating the merits of the findings made by the Commission in the contested decision concerning the condition relating to the foreclosure of competition. The Court must therefore conclude that the Commission has demonstrated to the requisite legal standard that the condition was satisfied in the present case.

The section on foreclosure is the most interesting part of the judgment. The GC took a far more formalistic approach to foreclosure than did the Commission with its carefully constructed effects analysis.[587] The GC concerned itself with the threat to the structure of competition. In paragraph 1034 it talked of 'appreciably altering the balance of competition in favour of Microsoft', and in paragraph

---

[587] For comment on this see, e.g., C. Ahlborn and D. S. Evans, 'The *Microsoft* Judgment and its Implications for Competition Policy Towards Dominant Firms in Europe' (2008–2009) 75 *Antitrust LJ* 887; Rousseva, *Rethinking Exclusionary Abuses in EU Competition Law* (cited in n. 42), 252–255; L. Lovdahl Gormsen, 'Why the European Commission's Enforcement Priorities on Article 82 EC Should be Withdrawn' [2010] *ECLR* 45, 48; D. Howarth and K. McMahon, '"Windows has performed an illegal operation": the Court of First Instance's judgment in Microsoft v Commission' [2008] *ECLR* 117.

1054 it deduced from the *first stage of the Commission's reasoning*, i.e. just its findings as to the ubiquity of WMP, that the Commission had demonstrated to the requisite legal standard that the bundling 'inevitably had significant consequences for the structure of competition'.[588] It was assumed that this advantage led to foreclosure.[589] The GC did not think it necessary to examine the further stages of the Commission's reasoning, i.e. the impact on the software developers and the evolution of the market,[590] although it did so for the sake of completeness. The emphasis of the judgment is on the market structure, on the fact that the ubiquity of WMP gave it an advantage unrelated to its 'intrinsic merits'[591] (which means its qualities rather than its advantages in distribution).[592]

Microsoft argued that its behaviour was objectively justified.[593] It defended its 'business model' as having benefits for software developers, OEMs, and consumers. The GC pointed out, however, that some of the benefits could be achieved without integration and the fact that software developers and site creators were convenienced by knowing that WMP was present on nearly all client PCs in the world was exactly why the integration led to foreclosure.[594] The GC dismissed the claim that the removal of WMP from Windows would lead to a degradation of the latter.[595] Above all the GC stressed that the Commission had not ordered Microsoft to cease supplying Windows with WMP, but only to also supply Windows without it.

The Commission's remedy in *Microsoft*, the supply of an alternative 'naked' version of Windows without WMP installed, was not a success. OEMs had no interest in such a product.[596] It would have been different had the Commission ordered Microsoft *not* to supply Windows with WMP.

In January 2009 the Commission sent a statement of objections to Microsoft saying that Microsoft might have infringed Article 102 by tying its Internet Explorer (IE) browser to Windows in that Windows was only supplied with IE ready installed.[597] The matter was concluded with a commitments decision whereby Microsoft undertook to provide users of Windows PCs who have Internet Explorer set as a default web browser with a browser 'Choice Screen' and to allow OEMs to choose which browser to install.[598] The 'Choice Screen' was made operational on 1 March 2010 and the outcome of Microsoft's commitments was explained in a Commission press release.

---

[588] The point at para.1055 where the GC in effect speculates that an increase in the use of the competitors' products might have been greater in the absence of the impugned conduct recalls the finding about the rise in Virgin's market share in *British Airways*: see Section 10.D.iii.f, p. 469 ff.

[589] *Microsoft* decision, para. 1058.

[590] *Microsoft* decision, para. 1059.

[591] *Microsoft* decision, para. 1046.

[592] Ahlborn and Evans, 'The *Microsoft* Judgment and its Implications for Competition Policy Towards Dominant Firms in Europe' (cited in n. 587), 887.

[593] At this point in the judgment the GC clarified where the burden of proof lies when objective justification is raised. See Section 5.C, p. 388.

[594] *Microsoft* decision, para. 1151.

[595] *Microsoft* decision, paras. 1164–1166.

[596] The GC said that the lawfulness of the Commission decision had to be judged at the time of its adoption. The fact that the remedy had not worked was irrelevant and could not be taken into account by the GC looking at the separate product issue with hindsight (para. 943). According to Ahlborn and Evans, 'The *Microsoft* Judgment and its Implications for Competition Policy Towards Dominant Firms in Europe' (cited in n. 587) (who acted for or on behalf of Microsoft), between the date of the naked Windows being made available and the date of the oral hearing in the case no OEM in the world chose to install it. Retailers bought 11,787 copies of the naked Windows XP, less than 0.005% of those sold in Europe. For the argument that the lack of demand for a naked version of Windows should have led to the adoption of a different separate product test, see Section 11.D.iv.a, p. 507.

[597] MEMO/09/15. The tying of Windows and IE was the subject of the DOJ proceedings in the US discussed in the text at n. 576, p. 495.

[598] IP/09/1941; [2010] OJ C36/7. In a speech on 21 October 2009 in Brussels, 'Competition and Consumers in the 21st Century' SPEECH/09/486, available at <http://europa.eu/rapid/press-release_SPEECH-09-486_en.htm>, Neelie Kroes said, 'In IT we have stopped dominant companies abusing their position to restrict consumer choice. No matter how big those infringers are—we have consistently said that no company is above the law. Our message to these

> ## Antitrust: Commission welcomes Microsoft's roll-out of web browser choice IP/10/216, 2 March 2010
>
> Since the beginning of March, Internet users in the European Economic Area...who receive automatic updates for Windows and have Microsoft's browser set as default are being invited to choose from several browsers. In addition to Microsoft's web browser, the user will have the opportunity to choose between eleven additional web browsers...
>
> It is expected that the browser Choice Screen will be displayed on over 100 million personal computers (PCs) in Europe between now and mid-May. The central page of the choice screen is also available to any internet user at <http://www.browserchoice.eu>.
>
> In compliance with the December commitments, computer manufacturers are now able to install competing browsers on Windows PCs instead of, or in addition to, Internet Explorer. Microsoft further committed not to retaliate against PC manufacturers who pre-install a non-Microsoft web browser on the PCs they ship and make it the default web browser.

Microsoft's agreement to give commitments in this case meant that the Commission did not have to produce a fully reasoned decision and the possibility of the technical tying issue being re-examined in the GC did not arise. However, on 6 March 2013 the Commission fined Microsoft €561 million for failing to comply with its commitments.[599]

(iv) The EU Position on Tying and Bundling after *Microsoft* and in the Guidance Paper

We have seen that in *Microsoft* the GC agreed with the Commission that tying prohibited under Article 102 requires the presence of the following elements:

  (i)   the tying and the tied goods are two separate products;

  (ii) the undertaking concerned is dominant in the tying product market;

  (iii) the undertaking concerned does not give customers a choice to obtain the tying product without the tied product; and

  (iv) the tying forecloses competition.

The Commission deals with tying and bundling in paragraphs 47–74 of the Guidance Paper. In paragraph 50 the Commission states that it will normally take action under Article 102 where an undertaking is dominant in the tying market and (i) the tying and tied products are distinct products; and (ii) the tying practice is likely to lead to anti-competitive foreclosure. The Guidance Paper says nothing about the lack of choice/coercion condition. The matter of dominance (ii) is discussed in Chapter 6.

a. The Tying and the Tied Goods are Two Separate Products

Both the case law and the Guidance Paper recognise that there must be distinct products involved. The problem is that almost any product can be broken down into smaller parts:

---

companies is: You can't run away or spend your way around Europe's rules. Speaking of this—promising news on Microsoft, don't you think? In the New Year we hope that hundreds of millions of consumers in Europe will get a choice of which web browser to use on their computers.'

[599] IP/13/2013. The Commission found that Microsoft failed to roll out the browser choice screen with its Windows 7 Service Pack 1 from May 2011 to July 2012, so that 15 million Windows users in the EU did not see the choice screen during that period.

A coat can be sold without its buttons, a desk without its drawers…The market would come to a standstill, however, if the antitrust laws gave every customer a legal right to atomize his purchases as much as he chose.[600]

In some cases the separation is clear. This was so in the *Télémarketing* case,[601] for example, where the television company tied the use of its own sales agents to the sale of its advertising slots and in *Napier Brown/British Sugar*[602] where the undertaking adopted a delivered pricing policy which, by only providing the product and the delivery together, excluded competition on the separate although ancillary transport market. However, it is more difficult when there is a possibility that the undertaking is supplying a 'system' consisting of several components, as in *Hilti* and *Tetra Pak II*.[603] The issue is even more difficult where IT markets are concerned.

The test for whether there are distinct products is 'consumer demand'—is there actual or potential consumer demand for the products separately? However, there may be demand for only one of them on a stand-alone basis. In *Microsoft* the GC approved the Commission's statement that there can be no abusive tying in the absence of independent demand for the allegedly *tied* product.[604] It rejected the relevance of Microsoft's arguments that there was no demand for the tying product separately. Nevertheless, the inconvenient fact in *Microsoft* was that there was no longer any such demand and so it proved once the remedy was implemented. Once consumers had tasted operating systems with media functionality a 'naked' system was unwanted and the OEMs saw no point in purchasing it.

The Guidance Paper states:

51. Whether the products will be considered by the Commission to be distinct depends on customer demand. Two products are distinct if, in the absence of tying or bundling, a substantial number of customers would purchase or would have purchased the tying product without also buying the tied product from the same supplier, thereby allowing stand-alone production for both the tying and the tied product [citing paragraphs 917, 921, and 922 of Microsoft]. Evidence that two products are distinct could include direct evidence that, when given a choice, customers purchase the tying and the tied products separately from different sources of supply, or indirect evidence, such as the presence on the market of undertakings specialised in the manufacture or sale of the tied product without the tying product [citing paragraph 67 of Hilti] or of each of the products bundled by the dominant undertaking, or evidence indicating that undertakings with little market power, particularly in competitive markets, tend not to tie or not to bundle such products.

It is clear from the second sentence that the test is whether, without the tie, a substantial number of customers would purchase the tied product *from the same supplier*. That is not the same as asking whether there would be a demand for the tying product *if the tied product did not exist*. In *Hilti* and *Tetra Pak II* the answer to that would be 'no' because the machinery was useless without the consumables.[605]

The Guidance Paper does not specifically mention the 'commercial usage' test in Article 102(d) which, as we have seen, the CJ dismissed as not decisive in *Tetra Pak II*[606] and which is unhelpful where the dominant undertaking has a quasi-monopoly. Nevertheless, the last sentence of paragraph 51 contemplates using evidence of the practices of undertakings with little market power in competitive markets, if relevant.

---

[600] Hovenkamp, *Federal Antitrust Policy: The Law of Competition and its Practice* (cited in n. 193), 436–437.

[601] The CJ treated this as a refusal to supply scenario: see Section 12.

[602] [1988] OJ L284/41, [1990] 4 CMLR 196.

[603] See also Case T-427/08, *Confédération européenne des associations d'horlogers-réparateurs v. Commission (CEAHR)* [2010] ECR II-5865, see Chap. 1, Section 10.B.vii.g, p. 80.

[604] *Microsoft* decision, para. 918.

[605] The GC relied on *Hilti* and *Tetra Pak II* in paras. 920–921 of the *Microsoft* judgment. See Ahlborn and Evans, 'The *Microsoft* Judgment and its Implications for Competition Policy Towards Dominant Firms in Europe' (cited in n. 587).

[606] *Tetra Pak II*, para. 37.

Consumer demand can change, sometimes very quickly, and nowhere more so than in the new economy.[607] New products are brought on to the market but may become commonly integrated into others, or products may be introduced which in time are broken down and the elements sold separately. Where new products are concerned, the 'commercial usage' test is again unhelpful. If the purpose of the rules on tying is the welfare of consumers, rather than the welfare of competitors, then the enquiry about distinct products is just part of the overall assessment of whether 'the efficiencies of tying outweighs the inherent reduction in choice for the consumer'.[608] Although there are usually consumers whose wants are different from those of the majority the consumer welfare test has to ensure that *most* consumers are better off and that consumer gains exceed consumer losses.

The Discussion Paper contained a statement that two products may be sufficiently differentiated to be distinct for the purposes of a tying abuse but still be part of the same relevant product market.[609] This does not appear in the Guidance Paper. If the objection to tying is leveraging monopoly power from one market to another it is difficult to see how that applies where both products are part of the same market.

b. Lack of Customer Choice/Coercion

The lack of customer choice referred to as an element of the abuse in *Microsoft*[610] is sometimes described as 'coercion'.[611] According to Faull and Nikpay it can arise from the refusal of the dominant undertaking to sell the tying product without the tied one, either as a contractual clause or *de facto*; from the unavailability of the products separately; from pressure exerted on the customer through the promise of favourable treatment to customers who take both products or threats to those who do not; or from pricing incentives which may be 'so powerful that no rational customer would choose to buy the products separately'.[612] However, the complications of using 'coercion' and 'lack of choice' as conditions for identifying abusive tying and bundling are graphically demonstrated by *Microsoft* and the Guidance Paper does not mention this criterion. The choices open to customers can be satisfactorily subsumed into the analysis of foreclosure.

c. Anti-competitive Foreclosure

The Guidance Paper adopts an effects-based approach to tying. There is no suggestion that tying and bundling by a dominant undertaking is per se illegal. Instead the Commission sets out the matters that it will take into account when deciding whether to pursue dominant undertakings for such practices. Given that this specific section of the Guidance Paper, like the others, must be read in the light of the overall principle that the Commission's enforcement activity is focused on foreclosure which is 'anti-competitive' in that it operates to the detriment of consumers, this means that it is the effects on consumers which is the issue. This contrasts with the concern of the GC in *Microsoft* for the impact on competitors and the lack of attention to consumers. The factors for identifying anti-competitive foreclosure set out in paragraphs 53–58 have to be read in conjunction with those in paragraph 20.[613]

The Commission will take into account whether the dominant undertaking's strategy is a lasting one, for example through technical tying;[614] whether the undertaking is dominant in respect

---

[607] The Court has to consider the position at the date of the adoption of the decision, *Microsoft* decision, para. 943.

[608] See the comments of Linklaters on the Discussion Paper, <http://ec.europa.eu/competition/antitrust/art82/127.pdf>, p. 17.

[609] Discussion Paper, para. 185.

[610] See, e.g., *Microsoft* decision, paras. 865 and 963.

[611] See J. Faull and A. Nikpay (eds.), *The EC Law of Competition* (2nd edn, Oxford University Press, 2007), paras. 4.247–4.250.

[612] Faull and Nikpay (eds.), *The EC Law of Competition* (cited in n. 611), 4.250.

[613] See Section 4, p. 383.

[614] Guidance Paper, para. 53.

of more than one product in the bundle;[615] and whether there are insufficient customers who buy the tied product alone to sustain competitors, in which case the customers who *are* there may face higher prices.[616] The Commission is also concerned with inputs to a production process where a dominant undertaking may use tying to prevent customers avoiding a rise in the price of the tying product:[617]

56. If the tying and the tied product can be used in variable proportions as inputs to a production process, customers may react to an increase in price for the tying product by increasing their demand for the tied product while decreasing their demand for the tying product. By tying the two products the dominant undertaking may seek to avoid this substitution and as a result be able to raise its prices.

The Commission also highlights the situation where the tying product market is regulated so that, constrained in its pricing freedom in the tying market, the undertaking may use tying to raise prices in the tied market instead.[618]

The Guidance Paper recognises both 'offensive and 'defensive' leverage[619] and one of the factors the Commission will consider is the effect of tying in reducing the number of alternative tied product suppliers to the prejudice of those trying to enter the tying market alone.[620]

d. Multi-product Rebates (Mixed Bundling)

The Guidance Paper deals specifically with multi-product rebates.[621] The Commission's approach to multi-product rebates is similar to its approach to rebates generally.[622] It would prefer to examine whether the incremental revenue covers the incremental costs for each product in the discounted bundle but, since that is not usually possible, the Commission will normally use the incremental price as a proxy. It will normally intervene only if the price of each product in the dominant undertaking's bundle falls below LRAIC.[623] This is the application of the 'as efficient competitor' test to what is in essence a pricing issue. Where both the dominant undertaking and its competitors are selling identical bundles[624] the Commission will examine whether the price of the *bundle* is predatory.[625]

e. Efficiencies

If the conditions laid down in paragraph 30 of the Guidance Paper for the 'efficiency defence' are fulfilled the Commission will consider efficiency claims.[626] It will look at claims of savings in production or distribution, reduced transaction costs for customers and suppliers, and enabling pass-on of efficiencies stemming from the supplier producing or purchasing large quantities of the tied product. Notably, it will also examine the possibility that combining two products into a single new one might 'enhance the ability to bring such a product to the market to the benefit of consumers'.

---

[615] Guidance Paper, para. 54.

[616] Guidance Paper, para. 55.

[617] Guidance Paper, para. 56.

[618] Guidance Paper, para. 57.

[619] Guidance Paper, para. 52. For offensive and defensive leverage see Section 11.C, p. 488.

[620] Guidance Paper, para. 58.

[621] Guidance Paper, paras. 59–61.

[622] See Section 10.D.iv, p. 476 ff.

[623] Long-run average incremental cost.

[624] Or could do so in a timely way without being deterred by possible additional costs.

[625] Guidance Paper, para. 61.

[626] Guidance Paper, para.62.

12. REFUSAL TO SUPPLY

A. GENERAL

It is possible for a dominant undertaking to infringe Article 102 by refusing to supply its products or services or grant access to its facilities. Refusal to supply as an abuse also encompasses 'constructive' refusals, where the offer is such that the supplier knows it is unacceptable, or the terms are unreasonable or supply is unduly delayed, (there may be an obligation to supply on 'FRAND' terms, i.e. fair, reasonable, and non-discriminatory).[627] Unilateral refusals to supply by non-dominant firms are not caught by the competition rules, as seen in *Bayer*.[628] This is an example of conduct being prohibited only because of the dominant position

Dominant undertakings do not have an absolute duty to supply all those who request them to do so. However, in certain situations a refusal to supply is an abuse. Refusals to supply are normally exclusionary abuses, in that the dominant undertaking's behaviour denies the other party the tools it needs to compete on the market. Most of the cases have concerned vertically integrated undertakings dominant in an upstream market refusing to supply competitors in the downstream market. This is the only refusal to supply scenario that is dealt with in the Guidance Paper. However, there are some cases that do not fall into this category.[629]

The idea that a dominant undertaking has a duty to supply, and that a refusal to do so will be an abuse, is contrary to deep-seated notions of freedom of contract which decree that one should be free to deal with whom one chooses. It also threatens the dominant undertaking's incentives to invest and innovate, which is harmful to dynamic efficiency and welfare. The EU position on when and why in the name of competition a duty to supply should be imposed has been developed in stream of decisions and judgments beginning with *Commercial Solvents*[630] in 1973.

Conduct which can be classified under some other heading of abuse, such as tying, can also be seen as a refusal to supply. In *Télémarketing*[631] the condition that advertisers could buy advertising time on television only if they used the television company's own telesales agency was both a refusal to supply and a tie, as was the delivered pricing policy in *Napier Brown/British Sugar*.[632] The difficulty with this is that the law has developed different principles in respect of tying and refusal to supply.[633]

---

[627] e.g., in *Napier Brown/British Sugar* [1988] OJ L284/41, [1990] 4 CMLR 196 the downstream competitor asked for industrial sugar, but British Sugar was prepared to offer only 'special grain' sugar and at so high a price that the competitor could not use it; see also *Sealink/B&I Holyhead: Interim Measures* [1992] 5 CMLR 255; *Deutsche Post AG: Interception of cross-border mail* [2001] OJ L331/40, [2002] 4 CMLR 558; Case T-301/04, *Clearstream Banking v. Commission* [2009] ECR II-3155; COMP/39.525, *Telekomunikacja Polska*, 22 June 2011, on appeal Case T-486/11, judgment pending; COMP/39.692, *IBM Maintenance Services*, Commitments Decision, 13 December 2011.

[628] Case T-41/96, *Bayer AG v. Commission* [2000] ECR II-3383, confirmed Cases C-2 and 3/01, *Bundesverband der Arzneimittel-Importeure EV and the Commission v. Bayer AG* [2004] ECR I-23.

[629] Such as Case 2/76, *United Brands v. EC Commission* [1978] ECR 207; and Case 7/82, *GVL v. Commission* [1983] ECR 483, which concerned the German collecting society's refusal to offer its services to artists established outside Germany unless they were of German nationality. In Case 77/77, *BP v. Commission* [1978] ECR 1513 the CJ held there was no duty to supply where during the OPEC oil boycott in 1973 an oil supplier dealt with the shortage by supplying its regular, long-term rather than occasional customers. The Commission found that the refusal to deal with occasional customers on the basis of what they ordered in a previous period was an abuse (*ABG Oil* [1977] OJ L117/1, [1977] 2 CMLR D1). However, the CJ held that the supply strategy was reasonable in the circumstances and that the refusal to supply ABG was justified. The Commission had held that for the duration of the crisis each supplier was in a dominant position in respect of its former customers, which was upheld by the Court. *BP* is a rare example of the Commission losing an Article 102 case on the substance.

[630] Cases 6, 7/73, *Istituto Chemioterapico Italiano SpA and Commercial Solvents Corp v. Commission* [1974] ECR 223.

[631] Case 311/84, *Centre Belge d'Etudes du Marché-Télémarketing v. Compagnie Luxembourgeoise de Télédiffusion SA and Information Publicité Benelux SA* [1985] ECR 3261.

[632] *Napier Brown/British Sugar* [1988] OJ L284/41, [1990] 4 CMLR 196.

[633] As can be seen by comparing the discussion in Section 11 with that in this section. In J.-Y. Art and G. S. McCurdy, 'The European Commission's Media Player Remedy in its Microsoft Decision: Compulsory Code Removal Despite

In the Guidance Paper the Commission states that it will deal with refusals to supply customers who do not agree to tying arrangements in accordance with the principles set out in Section 11 on tying and bundling.[634]

Refusal to supply as an abuse raises the question of the appropriate remedy. Article 3 of Regulation 17 provided that where the Commission finds an infringement of Article 102 'it may by decision require the undertakings…concerned to bring such infringement to an end'. In *Commercial Solvents* the CJ established that the Commission was not restricted to prohibiting infringing conduct but could also order an undertaking positively to do certain acts or to provide certain advantages which had been wrongfully withheld, including making specific orders about what exactly the dominant undertaking should supply to whom. This continues to be the position under Article 7 of Regulation 1/2003.[635] Some proceedings in the energy sector have been resolved by the dominant undertaking agreeing to divest itself of assets.[636]

The issue of refusal to supply as a way of hindering parallel trade is dealt with in Section 16.

B. THE *COMMERCIAL SOLVENTS* CASE: REFUSAL TO SUPPLY EXISTING CUSTOMERS IN ORDER TO EXCLUDE COMPETITORS FROM DOWNSTREAM MARKETS

Commercial Solvents was the first case in which a refusal to supply was held to be capable of infringing Article 102.

Cases 6 and 7/73, *Istituto Chemioterapico Italiano Spa and Commercial Solvents Corp* v. *Commission* [1974] ECR 223

Commercial Solvents (CSC) supplied aminobutanol, a raw material from which a derivative, ethambutol, could be produced. CSC's Italian subsidiary, Istituto, resold aminobutanol in Italy to Zoja, an Italian pharmaceutical company which made ethambutol based anti-TB drugs from it. In 1970 Zoja cancelled its orders for aminobutanol from Istituto as independent distributors were supplying it cheaper. When this proved unsatisfactory Zoja placed new orders with Istituto. However, CSC had decided no longer to supply aminobutanol to the EEC but only an upgraded product, dextroaminobutanol, which Istituto would convert into ethambutol itself, manufacturing its own ethambutol based drugs. Zoja was therefore refused supplies. Zoja could not obtain supplies on the world market as all its searches led back to CSC. Zoja complained to the Commission which held that CSC was dominant in the market for aminobutanol and had abused its position by refusing to supply it to Zoja, a refusal which would lead to the elimination of one of the principal manufacturers of ethambutol in the common market. CSC appealed to the CJ, which upheld the finding of dominance on the raw material market[637] and the finding of abuse.[638]

---

the Absence of Tying or Foreclosure' [2004] *ECLR* 694, Microsoft's lawyers argued that the WMP part of *Microsoft* should have been judged under refusal to supply rather than tying principles.

[634] Guidance Paper, para. 77.

[635] [2003] OJ L1/1.

[636] COMP/39.402 *RWE—Gas Foreclosure* Commitments Decision, 18 March 2009, see Section 12.C.v, p. 522.

[637] See Chap. 6.

[638] It also upheld the finding that there was an effect on inter-Member State trade on the basis that although few of Zoja's ethambutol-based drugs were exported to other Member States the elimination of Zoja as a competitor would affect the competitive structure of the common market: see Chap. 5.

Court of Justice

23. The applicants state that they ought not to be held responsible for stopping supplies of aminobutanol to Zoja for this was due to the fact that in the spring of 1970 Zoja itself informed Istituto that it was cancelling the purchase of large quantities of aminobutanol which had been provided for in a contract then in force between Istituto and Zoja. When at the end of 1970 Zoja again contacted Istituto to obtain this product, the latter was obliged to reply, after consulting CSC, that in the meantime CSC had changed its commercial policy and that the product was no longer available. The change of policy by CSC was, they claim, inspired by a legitimate consideration of the advantage that would accrue to it of expanding its production to include the manufacture of finished products and not limiting itself to that of raw material or intermediate products. In pursuance of this policy it decided to improve its product and no longer to supply aminobutanol save in respect of commitments already entered into by its distributors.

24. It appears from the documents and from the hearing that the suppliers of raw material are limited, as regards the EEC, to Istituto, which, as stated in the claim by CSC, started in 1968 to develop its own specialities based on ethambutol, and in November 1969 obtained the approval of the Italian government necessary for the manufacture and in 1970 started manufacturing its own specialities. When Zoja sought to obtain further supplies of aminobutanol, it received a negative reply. CSC had decided to limit, if not completely to cease, the supply of nitropropane and aminobutanol to certain parties in order to facilitate its own access to the market for the derivatives.

25. However, an undertaking being in a dominant position as regards the production of raw material and therefore able to control the supply to manufacturers of derivatives, cannot, just because it decides to start manufacturing these derivatives (in competition with its former customers) act in such a way as to eliminate their competition which in the case in question, would amount to eliminating one of the principal manufacturers of ethambutol in the Common Market. Since such conduct is contrary to the objectives expressed in Article [3(1)(g)] of the Treaty and set out in greater detail in Articles [101 and 102], it follows that an undertaking which has a dominant position in the market in raw materials and which, with the object of reserving such raw materials for manufacturing its own derivatives, refuses to supply a customer, which is itself a manufacturer of these derivatives, and therefore risks eliminating all competition on the part of this customer, is abusing its dominant position within the meaning of Article [102]. In this context it does not matter that the undertaking ceased to supply in the spring of 1970 because of the cancellation of the purchases by Zoja, because it appears from the applicants' own statement that, when the supplies provided for in the contract had been completed, the sale of aminobutanol would have stopped in any case.

26. It is also unnecessary to examine, as the applicants have asked, whether Zoja had an urgent need for aminobutanol in 1970 and 1971 or whether this company still had large quantities of this product which would enable it to reorganize its production in good time, since that question is not relevant to the consideration of the conduct of the applicants.

27. Finally CSC states that its production of nitropropane and aminobutanol ought to be considered in the context of nitration of paraffin, of which nitropropane is only one of the derivatives, and that similarly aminobutanol is only one of the derivatives of nitropropane. Therefore the possibilities of producing the two products in question are not unlimited but depend in part on the possible sales outlets of the other derivatives.

28. However the applicants do not seriously dispute the statement in the Decision in question to the effect that 'in view of the production capacity of the CSC plant it can be confirmed that CSC can satisfy Zoja's needs, since Zoja represents a very small percentage (approximately 5–6 per cent) of CSC's global production of nitropropane'. It must be concluded that the Commission was justified in considering that such statements could not be taken into account.

29. These submissions must therefore be rejected.

According to paragraph 25 of the judgment, the factors leading to the finding of abuse were that CSC was using its dominant position on the raw material market to affect competition on the derivatives market, that it refused to supply an existing customer[639] because it wanted to compete with it downstream, and that the refusal risked eliminating the customer from the downstream market.

CSC had, in effect, decided to integrate vertically. The CJ did not consider whether this strategy might produce efficiencies, and there is no discussion in the judgment about the possible benefits to the end user, the consumer. This was an instance of Article 102 being applied to protect the situation of the 'small' competitor with no consideration of consumer welfare.

The *Commercial Solvents* principle was applied to a deliberate move to remove a competitor from a downstream market in *Napier Brown/British Sugar*,[640] where the dominant supplier of industrial sugar, which itself produced the derivative retail sugar, refused to supply industrial sugar to a competitor on the downstream market who was an existing customer.

C. REFUSAL TO SUPPLY ON A DOWNSTREAM MARKET AND THE 'ESSENTIAL FACILITIES' CONCEPT

(i) General

In *Commercial Solvents* and in *Télémarketing* it was found that an outright refusal to supply, or a refusal to supply unless tied products or services were accepted, constituted an abuse. In both cases the refusal interfered with competition on a downstream market. *Commercial Solvents* concerned a refusal to supply existing customers but *Télémarketing* concerned a refusal to supply new customers as well (with a service). The principle in those cases has been expanded upon since and given rise to the issue of the concept of 'essential facilities' in EU law.

The definition of an 'essential facility' is fraught with difficulty. However, the basic idea is that it is something owned or controlled by a vertically integrated dominant undertaking to which other undertakings need access in order to provide products or services to customers. This is sometimes called a 'bottleneck monopoly'. A refusal to grant access to an essential facility may be a breach of the special responsibility that the holder of the facility has as a dominant undertaking.

The essential facilities doctrine originated in US law, where it has proved to be highly contentious. When the Commission started using the expression in 1992 it was therefore employing a concept which was familiar to competition lawyers and the subject of much debate in the US context. The present position in US law is described in Section 12.H.[641] The CJ has never used the expression 'essential facility'. Indeed, it has carefully avoided doing so. However, much of the discourse on refusal to supply has been couched in terms of essential facilities or, as one scholar has called it, 'the epithet that dares not speak its name'.[642]

Two points about the essential facilities concept should be noted at the outset. First, there may be an obligation to supply new as well as existing customers.[643] Secondly, it has been widely employed in the context of liberalised sectors of the economy, in forcing access to transport and network infrastructures. It is its use outside those sectors which is the most problematic.

---

[639] It was not material that Zoja had previously cancelled its purchases from Istituto (see para. 25, last sentence).

[640] *Napier Brown/British Sugar* [1988] OJ L284/41, [1990] 4 CMLR 196.

[641] Section 12.H, p. 553.

[642] S. Anderman, 'The Epithet That dares Not Speak Its Name: The Essential Facilities Concept in Article 82 EC and IPRs After the *Microsoft* Case', in Ezrachi (ed.), *Article 82EC: Reflections on its Recent Evolution* (cited in n. 32), 87.

[643] Where IPRs are concerned the conditions governing the duty to supply may vary as regards existing and new customers, see *Microsoft* and the discussion in Section 12.D.vi, p. 536 ff.

(ii) The Commission Decisions Developing the 'Essential Facilities' Doctrine in EU Law

A number of Commission decisions on access to resources and infrastructure developed the essential facilities doctrine in EU law. The Commission did not use the expression 'essential facility' until 1992[644] but it is possible, particularly with hindsight, to see the essential facilities rationale in the earlier cases, even *Commercial Solvents* itself.[645] This is also true of the Commission decision *London-European Sabena*[646] and *British-Midland/Aer Lingus*.[647] In *London-European/Sabena* the Belgian airline Sabena was dominant in Belgium in the computer reservation services market. It refused to give London-European, a competing airline, access to the system (although it had spare capacity). The Commission found that the refusal, which was to pressurise London-European either to withdraw from the London–Brussels route or to raise prices, and also to punish London-European for its failure to use Sabena's ground-handling services, was an abuse. In *Aer Lingus* Aer Lingus refused to interline the tickets of another airline (British Midland) when the latter began competing on the London (Heathrow)–Dublin air-route.[648] The Commission held that Aer Lingus was in a dominant position on that route, which was found to be a relevant market, and that the refusal was an abuse. It did not condemn refusals to interline per se but only where they have significant effects on competition and are not objectively justified.[649] Moreover, although the mode of reasoning is similar to the Commission decisions which succeeded it, here the refusal to supply affected competition on the market on which the dominant position existed, and not on a downstream market.[650] The decision is best seen in context as part of the Commission's drive to liberalise the European air transport sector.[651]

The first express reference to essential facilities in EU law was made in *B&I/Sealink*.

Sealink/B&I Holyhead: Interim Measures [1992] 5 CMLR 255

Sealink Harbours was the owner and operator of the port at Holyhead, in Wales, and as such was held by the Commission to be in a dominant position on the market on the British side for port facilities for ferry services on the 'central corridor' route between Wales and Ireland (i.e., Holyhead to Dublin and Dun Laoghaire). It ran ferries on that route. B&I also ran ferries from the port. B&I used a particular berth, the Admiralty Pier, and the limitations of the harbour were such that whenever Sealink's ferries passed the berth the drawing away of water and turbulence meant that B&I had to cease all loading and unloading activity. B&I complained that Sealink intended to introduce a new timetable which would cause greater disruption to B&I's schedules in this way. The Commission adopted a decision providing

---

[644] *Sealink/B&I Holyhead: Interim Measures* [1992] 5 CMLR 255.

[645] See J. Temple Lang, 'Defining Legitimate Competition: Companies' Duties to Supply Competitors and Access to Essential Facilities' (1994) 18 *Fordham Int'l LJ* 437 and the Commission's citation of cases in *Sealink/B&I*.

[646] [1988] OJ L317/47, [1989] 4 CMLR 662.

[647] [1992] OJ L96/34.

[648] Interlining is a standard practice in the air transport industry, operated by IATA through a multilateral agreement to which interested airlines become parties, whereby airlines are authorised to sell each other's services. As a result a single ticket can be issued which comprises segments to be performed by different airlines. The issuing airline collects the price for all segments from the passenger and pays the fare due to the carrying line.

[649] Para. 26 of the decision. Aer Lingus's strategy was merely a delaying and hindering tactic. It did not result in British Midland's departure from the route.

[650] For the significance of there being two markets rather than one, see Section 12.G, p. 550 ff.

[651] See the Commission's *XXIInd Report on Competition Policy* (Commission, 1992), point 218. Aer Lingus, however, was dominant only because of the narrowly defined market and no more than a minnow in the wider European airline market, a point which was made in a question about the decision put to the Competition Commissioner by an Irish MEP: E.P. Deb. 3-418/222 (13 May 1992), question No. H-0464/92, [1992] 5 CMLR 209.

for interim measures, ordering Sealink to return to its previous timetable. The matter never went to a final decision as the dispute was settled.

Commission

41. A dominant undertaking which both owns or controls and itself uses an essential facility, i.e., a facility or infrastructure without access to which competitors cannot provide services to their customers, and which refuses its competitors access to that facility or grants access to competitors only on terms less favourable than those which it gives its own services, thereby placing the competitors at a competitive disadvantage, infringes Article [102], if the other conditions of that Article are met…[652] A company in a dominant position may not discriminate in favour of its own activities in a related market (Case C-260/89 *Elliniki Radiophonia*, paragraphs 37–38)…The owner of an essential facility which uses its power in one market in order to strengthen its position in another related market, in particular, by granting its competitor access to that related market on less favourable terms than those of its own services, infringes Article [102] where a competitive disadvantage is imposed upon its competitor without objective justification.

…

42. The owner of the essential facility, which also uses the essential facility, may not impose a competitive disadvantage on its competitor, also a user of the essential facility, by altering its own schedule to the detriment of the competitor's service, where, as in this case, the construction or the features of the facility are such that it is not possible to alter one competitor's service in the way chosen without harming the other's. Specifically, where, as in this case, the competitor is already subject to a certain level of disruption from the dominant undertaking's activities, there is a duty to the dominant undertaking not to take any action which will result in further disruption. That is so even if the latter's actions make, or are primarily intended to make its operations more efficient. Subject to any objective elements outside its control, such an undertaking is under a duty not to impose a competitive disadvantage upon its competitor in the use of the shared facility without objective justification, as seemed to be accepted by SHL in 1989.

In the first sentence of paragraph 41 of its judgment the Commission laid down the basic principle that an owner of an essential facility may have to provide non-discriminatory access to a competitor. The Commission developed the theme in three further decisions concerning ports, *Sea Containers Ltd/Stena*,[653] *Port of Rødby (Euro-port) v. Denmark*,[654] and *Morlaix (Port of Roscoff)*.[655] In *Sea Containers* Stena Sealink (previously Sealink, the port authority and ferry operator involved in *Sealink/B I Holyhead*), refused to give the requested access to a company wanting to operate a new fast ferry service on the Wales–Ireland central corridor route by lightweight catamaran. The Commission, repeating the *B&I* decision, held this was an abuse.

The *Sea Containers/Stena* decision made it clear that the duty to supply essential facilities set out in *Sealink/B&I* applies to *new* as well as to existing customers. This was also shown in another decision taken on the same day, *Port of Rødby*, in which the Commission held that Denmark had infringed

---

652 The Commission here cited Cases 6 and 7/73, *Istituto Chemioterapico Italiano Spa and Commercial Solvents Corp v. Commission* [1974] ECR 223; Case 311/84, *Centre Belge d'Etudes du Marché-Télémarketing v. Compagnie Luxembourgeoise de Télédiffusion SA and Information Publicité Benelux SA* [1985] ECR 3261; Case 53/87, *CICCRA v. Renault* [1988] ECR 6039; Case 238/87, *AB Volvo v. Erik Veng* [1988] ECR 6211; Case C-260/89, *Elliniki Radiophonia Tileorasi (ERT) v. DEP* [1991] ECR I-2925; Cases T-69–70/89, *RTE, ITP, BBC v. EC Commission (Magill)* [1991] ECR II-485 (the CJ judgment had not yet been given); Case C-18/88, *LRTT v. GB-INNO-BM SA* [1991] ECR I-5941; and the Commission decisions *National Carbonising* [1976] OJ L35/6, [1976] 1 CMLR D82; *London-European/Sabena* [1988] OJ L317/47; *British Midland/Aer Lingus* [1992] OJ L 96/34.

653 *Sea Containers Ltd/Stena Sealink* [1994] OJ L15/8, [1995] 4 CMLR 84.

654 [1994] OJ L55/52, [1994] 5 CMLR 457.

655 [1995] 5 CMLR 177.

Article 106(1) in conjunction with Article 102.[656] *Morlaix (Port of Roscoff)*[657] dealt with a significantly different situation. Irish Continental Group (ICG) wanted to run a ferry service from Ireland to Brittany and needed access to the port of Roscoff, which was managed by CCI Morlaix, a French administrative body granted a concession by the State for that purpose. CCI Morlaix did *not* run ferries itself, although it did have a shareholding of about five per cent in Brittany Ferries, which at the time operated the only ferry running from Ireland to Brittany. The Commission found that CCI Morlaix's difficult behaviour over the negotiations for access amounted to a refusal to supply and that the refusal would have been an abuse even if the authority had had no interest in Brittany Ferries.

(iii) Issues in the Essential Facilities Doctrine

The recognition of the concept of essential facilities is just the beginning. Even if the doctrine is accepted many questions follow: What exactly constitutes an essential facility? When does access have to be given? To whom does it have to be given? On what terms must it be given?

In *B&I/Sealink* essential facilities were defined as 'a facility or infrastructure without access to which competitors cannot provide services to their customers'. This definition provides only a starting point. 'Essential facilities' should be narrowly confined since a finding that an undertaking's resources or assets fall within that concept may result in that undertaking being forced to share them with its competitors. This represents a severe interference with an undertaking's rights which can only be justified where there would otherwise be a serious effect on competition which cannot be remedied by less intrusive measures.

There has to be some way of identifying assets to which access by competitors is truly 'essential' rather than merely desirable. Even when these are identified there may be practical problems about access or sharing. Some facilities (ports for example) have limited physical capacity, and the question arises *which* competitors should be given access. There is also the matter of the terms on which access is given. If the parties are left to settle their own terms the owner of the facility may be able to impose a price which is prohibitively high.[658] If the terms are to be set by an authority such as the Commission, however, the authority ends up acting as a price regulator.[659]

Outside the area of access to facilities in liberalised sectors where existing facilities, such as networks, were built with public money the essential facilities concept needs to be treated with great caution.[660] An over-enthusiastic approach may result in undertakings having to share with competitors assets which they have developed over many years at great expense. Robbing firms of the fruits of their endeavours may be injurious to the public interest and consumer welfare as it removes

---

[656] *Port of Rødby* [1994] OJ L55/52, [1994] 5 CMLR 457. The port of Rødby in Denmark was owned and managed by a publicly owned port authority (DSB) which operated the only ferry between there and Puttgarden in Germany jointly with German national railways (DB). Two other companies, Euro-Port and Scan-Port, wanted to run a ferry on the same route. The Danish Government refused either to grant them access to the port or to grant permission to build another terminal in the immediate vicinity. The Commission held that DSB was a public undertaking in a dominant position on the market for the organisation of port services in Denmark for ferries on the Rødby–Puttgarden route and that the double refusal had the effect of eliminating a potential competitor and infringed Art. 102. '... [A]n undertaking that owns or manages an essential port facility from which it provides a maritime transport service may not, without objective justification, refuse to grant a shipowner wishing to operate on the same maritime route access to that facility without infringing Article [102]' (*Port of Rødby*, para. 12). For Art. 106, which deals with the application of the competition rules to public undertakings, see Chap. 8.

[657] [1995] 5 CMLR 177.

[658] See Case C-242/95, *GT–Link A/S v. De Danske Statsbaner (DSB)* [1997] ECR I-4449, where the CJ held that excessive duties levied by a public undertaking on a ferry company in breach of Art. 106, in conjunction with Art. 102, must be repaid.

[659] The order in the *Microsoft* case that Microsoft should supply interoperability information to its competitors downstream led to a further Commission decision finding that it had not supplied this on 'reasonable' terms, COMP/37.792, *aff'd* on appeal Case T-167/08, *Microsoft v. Commission*, 27 June 2012.

[660] But for the problems of identifying assets acquired with public money, and of treating them differently, see Section 12.G, p. 553.

incentives to innovation. The following extract is the conclusion from Areeda's critical survey of the essential facilities doctrine in US law. He considers that it should be treated with the greatest circumspection, in particular because of the dangerous disincentive to innovation. Obviously, his remarks relate to the doctrine in US law at the time of writing, but the first two sentences of paragraph 6 were cited with approval by the US Supreme Court in *Verizon v. Trinko*.[661]

P. Areeda, 'Essential Facilities: An Epithet in Need of Limiting Principles' (1990) 58 *Antitrust LJ*, 841, 852–853

I conclude by offering six principles that should limit application of the essential facilities concept.

(1)   There is no general duty to share. Compulsory access, if it exists at all, is and should be very exceptional...

(2)   A single firm's facility, as distinct from that of a combination, is 'essential' only when it is both critical to the plaintiff's competitive vitality and the plaintiff is essential for competition in the marketplace. 'Critical to the plaintiff's competitive vitality' means that the plaintiff cannot compete effectively without it and that duplication or practical alternatives are not available.

(3)   No one should be forced to deal unless doing so is likely substantially to improve competition in the marketplace by reducing price or by increasing output or innovation. Such an improvement is unlikely (a) when it would chill desirable activity; (b) [when] the plaintiff is not an actual or potential competitor; (c) when the plaintiff merely substitutes itself for the monopolist or shares the monopolist's gains; or (d) when the monopolist already has the usual privilege of charging the monopoly price for its resources...

(4)   Even when all these conditions are satisfied, denial of access is never per se unlawful; legitimate business purpose always saves the defendant. What constitutes legitimacy is a question of law for the courts. Although the defendant bears the burden of coming forward with a legitimate business purpose, the plaintiff bears the burden of persuading the tribunal that any such claim is unjustified.

(5)   The defendant's intention is seldom illuminating, because every firm that denies its facilities to rivals does so to limit competition with itself and increase its profits. Any instruction on intention must ask whether the defendant had an intention to exclude by *improper* means. To get ahead in the marketplace is not, itself the kind of intention that contaminates conduct...

(6)   No court should impose a duty to deal that it cannot explain or adequately and reasonably supervise. The problem should be deemed [irremediable] by antitrust law when compulsory access requires the court to assume the day-to-day controls characteristic of a regulatory agency. Remedies may be practical (a) when admission to a consortium is at stake, especially at the outset, (b) when divestiture is otherwise appropriate and effective, or (c) when, as in *Otter Tail*, a regulatory agency already exists to control the terms of dealing. However, the availability of a remedy is not reason to grant one. Compulsory sharing should remain exceptional.

(iv) The *European Night Services* Case

The Commission decision in *European Night Services*,[662] was taken under Article 101 of the Treaty. It raised similar issues to the Article 102 cases although the Commission did not actually use the expression 'essential facilities'. Railway undertakings in the UK, France, Germany, and the Netherlands formed a joint venture (ENS) to provide overnight passenger rail services between the UK and the Continent via the Channel Tunnel. The Commission granted an exemption conditional on the parent companies providing locomotives, train crews, and train paths to any other undertaking wishing to

---

[661]   540 US 398, 124 S.Ct. 872 (2004).

[662]   [1994] OJ L259/20, [1995] 5 CMLR 76.

compete in the running of a similar service, on the same terms as they gave to the joint venture. The GC annulled the decision, inter alia,[663] in respect of the condition as regards the locomotives and train crews. It held that the Commission had not properly analysed why the requirement to supply was appropriate and had not supplied adequate reasoning for imposing this condition. In this case the GC expressly referred to essential facilities. It stressed that a facility can be essential only if there are no substitutes. Mere advantage to the competitor is not enough. This judgment showed a disinclination to apply the essential facilities concept too widely.

(v) The *Oscar Bronner* Case

Bronner was an Article 267 reference.[664] It is a leading judgment in which the CJ set out the limited circumstances in which access to a facility will be ordered. Before looking at the case it is important to note that both the Advocate General and the CJ refer to the 1995 judgment of the latter in the *Magill* case,[665] which concerned IPRs. Refusals to supply which involve IPRs raise particular problems, and the IPRs cases are dealt with together in Section 12.D.[666] However, in order to understand the *Magill* reference points in *Bronner*, a brief outline of the case is given here.

Magill concerned an Irish publisher who wanted to publish a composite television listings magazine. However, the broadcasters whose programmes could be received in Ireland at the time refused to allow him to publish their schedules, which were protected by copyright under Irish and UK law. The CJ found that in exceptional cases a refusal to supply material protected by an intellectual property right could be an abuse. The exceptional circumstances in *Magill* were that there was no substitute for a weekly television guide, the refusal to supply was preventing the appearance of a new product for which there was consumer demand, there was no justification for the refusal, and the refusal was excluding competition on a secondary market by denying access to the indispensable raw material.

Bronner was notable for the Opinion of Advocate General Jacobs urging the necessity of confining the essential facilities concept within strict limits. He reminded the Court that the primary purpose of Article 102 was to protect consumers, not competitors.

Case C-7/97, *Oscar Bronner GmbH & Co KG* v. *Mediaprint* [1998] ECR I-7791

Bronner published a newspaper, *Der Standard* which had approximately 3.6 per cent of the daily newspaper market in Austria in terms of circulation and 6 per cent in terms of advertising revenue. Mediaprint published two daily newspapers in Austria, which together had a combined market share of 46.8 per cent of circulation and 42 per cent of advertising revenues. For the distribution of its newspapers Mediaprint had established a nationwide home-delivery scheme. Bronner wanted Mediaprint to include *Der Standard* in its delivery scheme but Mediaprint refused. Mediaprint did include another newspaper it did not publish in its scheme but it did the whole of the printing and distribution in respect of that paper. Bronner sought an order from the Austrian courts requiring Mediaprint to cease abusing its alleged dominant position on the home-delivery market and requiring it to include *Der Standard* in its home-delivery service in return for

---

[663] Cases T-374–375, 384, and 388/94, *European Night Services v. Commission* [1998] ECR II-3141. Other aspects of this case are dealt with in Chap. 4. The requirement that train paths should be provided was quashed because it was based on false premisses to do with the relevant transport directive (91/440 [1991] OJ L237/25).

[664] The case actually involved a question of Austrian law (there was no appreciable effect on inter-Member State trade) but the referring court was concerned not to apply the law in a way which conflicted with Community law. It therefore asked for an interpretation of Art. 102. The CJ held the reference to be admissible, see paras. 12–22 of the judgment.

[665] Cases C-241–242/91 P, *RTE & ITP v. Commission* [1995] ECR I-743.

[666] Section 12.D, p. 526 ff.

reasonable remuneration. It claimed that other methods of sale, such as postal delivery, were less advantageous than home-delivery and that given the small circulation of *Der Standard* it would be entirely unprofitable for it to organise its own home-delivery service. The Austrian court referred to the CJ two questions as to whether the conduct in issue amounted to an abuse of a dominant position.

Advocate General Jacobs

56. First, it is apparent that the right to choose one's trading partners and freely to dispose of one's property are generally recognized principles in the laws of the Member States, in some cases with constitutional status. Incursions on those rights require careful justification.

57. Secondly, the justification in terms of competition policy for interfering with a dominant undertaking's freedom to contract often requires a careful balancing of conflicting considerations. In the long term it is generally pro-competitive and in the interest of consumers to allow a company to retain for its own use facilities which it has developed for the purpose of its business. For example, if access to a production, purchasing or distribution facility were allowed too easily there would be no incentive for a competitor to develop competing facilities. Thus while competition was increased in the short term it would be reduced in the long term. Moreover, the incentive for a dominant undertaking to invest in efficient facilities would be reduced if its competitors were, upon request, able to share the benefits. Thus the mere fact that by retaining a facility for its own use a dominant undertaking retains an advantage over a competitor cannot justify requiring access to it.

58. Thirdly, in assessing this issue it is important not to lose sight of the fact that the primary purpose of Article [102] is to prevent distortion of competition—and in particular to safeguard the interests of consumers—rather than to protect the position of particular competitors. It may therefore, for example, be unsatisfactory, in a case in which a competitor demands access to a raw material in order to be able to compete with the dominant undertaking on a downstream market in a final product, to focus solely on the latter's market power on the upstream market and conclude that its conduct in reserving to itself the downstream market is automatically an abuse. Such conduct will not have an adverse impact on consumers unless the dominant undertaking's final product is sufficiently insulated from competition to give it market power.

Court of Justice

38. Although in *Commercial Solvents* v. *Commission and CBEM*, cited above, the Court of Justice held the refusal by an undertaking holding a dominant position in a given market to supply an undertaking with which it was in competition in a neighbouring market with raw materials (*Commercial Solvents* v. *Commission*, paragraph 25) and services (*CBEM*, paragraph 26) respectively, which were indispensable to carrying on the rival's business, to constitute an abuse, it should be noted, first, that the Court did so to the extent that the conduct in question was likely to eliminate all competition on the part of that undertaking.

39. Secondly, in *Magill*, at paragraphs 49 and 50, the Court held that refusal by the owner of an intellectual property right to grant a licence, even if it is the act of an undertaking holding a dominant position, cannot in itself constitute abuse of a dominant position, but that the exercise of an exclusive right by the proprietor may, in exceptional circumstances, involve an abuse.

40. In *Magill*, the Court found such exceptional circumstances in the fact that the refusal in question concerned a product (information on the weekly schedules of certain television channels) the supply of which was indispensable for carrying on the business in question (the publishing of a general television guide), in that, without that information, the person wishing to produce such a guide would find it impossible to publish it and offer it for sale (paragraph 53), the fact that such refusal prevented the appearance of a new product for which there was a potential consumer demand (paragraph 54), the fact that it was not justified by objective considerations (paragraph 55), and that it was likely to exclude all competition in the secondary market of television guides (paragraph 56).

41. Therefore, even if that case-law on the exercise of an intellectual property right were applicable to the exercise of any property right whatever, it would still be necessary, for the *Magill* judgment to be effectively relied upon in order to plead the existence of an abuse within the meaning of Article [102] in a situation such as that which forms the subject-matter of the first question, not only that the refusal of the service comprised in home delivery be likely to eliminate all competition in the daily newspaper market on the part of the person requesting the service and that such refusal be incapable of being objectively justified, but also that the service in itself be indispensable to carrying on that person's business, inasmuch as there is no actual or potential substitute in existence for that home-delivery scheme.

42. That is certainly not the case even if, as in the case which is the subject of the main proceedings, there is only one nationwide home-delivery scheme in the territory of a Member State and, moreover, the owner of that scheme holds a dominant position in the market for services constituted by that scheme or of which it forms part.

43. In the first place, it is undisputed that other methods of distributing daily newspapers, such as by post and through sale in shops and at kiosks, even though they may be less advantageous for the distribution of certain newspapers, exist and are used by the publishers of those daily newspapers.

44. Moreover, it does not appear that there are any technical, legal or even economic obstacles capable of making it impossible, or even unreasonably difficult, for any other publisher of daily newspapers to establish, alone or in co-operation with other publishers, its own nationwide home-delivery scheme and use it to distribute its own daily newspapers.

45. It should be emphasised in that respect that, in order to demonstrate that the creation of such a system is not a realistic potential alternative and that access to the existing system is therefore indispensable, it is not enough to argue that it is not economically viable by reason of the small circulation of the daily newspaper or newspapers to be distributed.

46. For such access to be capable of being regarded as indispensable, it would be necessary at the very least to establish, as the Advocate General has pointed out at point 68 of his Opinion, that it is not economically viable to create a second home-delivery scheme for the distribution of daily newspapers with a circulation comparable to that of the daily newspapers distributed by the existing scheme.

47. In the light of the foregoing considerations, the answer to the first question must be that the refusal by a press undertaking which holds a very large share of the daily newspaper market in a Member State and operates the only nationwide newspaper home-delivery scheme in that Member State to allow the publisher of a rival newspaper, which by reason of its small circulation is unable either alone or in co-operation with other publishers to set up and operate its own home-delivery scheme in economically reasonable conditions, to have access to that scheme for appropriate remuneration does not constitute abuse of a dominant position within the meaning of Article [102].

It is significant that in this judgment the CJ continued to avoid using the term 'essential facilities'. It referred back again to *Commercial Solvents*. In paragraph 41 the CJ listed four factors which would have to be present before the refusal could be an abuse:

- First, the refusal would have to be likely to eliminate all competition in the downstream market *from the person requesting access*;
- Secondly, the refusal must be incapable of objective justification;
- Thirdly, the access must be indispensable to carrying on the other person's business; and
- Fourthly, there must be no actual or potential substitute for it.

These criteria were patently not fulfilled in *Bronner*.

In *Bronner* the CJ took a restrictive view of the obligation to grant access to facilities. It stressed that the refusal must be likely to *eliminate* all competition from the undertaking requesting access. It was not sufficient that the refusal would just make it harder for it to compete. Access must also be *indispensable*, not desirable or convenient, since there must be no actual or potential substitute for the requesting undertaking. Moreover, in paragraphs 45–46 the CJ held that in the case before it access could have been indispensable only if it was not economically viable to create a home-delivery system for a newspaper *with a comparable circulation to the dominant firm's*. It was not enough to show it was not viable for a small-circulation paper.[667] *Bronner* left many questions unanswered. It did not address the problems about pricing, for example, or how the facility owner should deal with competing claims for access, or the role of competition authorities in essential facilities scenarios. The judgment side-stepped the question whether the case law on IPRs (i.e. *Magill*), is applicable to other property rights. It did, however, make quite clear that an obligation to grant access to a facility will arise only in exceptional circumstances. *Bronner*, of course, was an easy case for the CJ. It concerned a facility built up by a private undertaking with its own resources and a situation in which the other undertaking was operating satisfactorily on the downstream market without access to it. If the CJ had considered that it was a situation suitable for the application of the essential facilities doctrine then all dominant firms owning or controlling a facility someone else might have found useful should have been worried, and incentives to innovation would have been seriously undermined. However, it was made apparent that facilities are not lightly to be termed 'essential' or access lightly required. The essential facilities doctrine was 'reined in' by the CJ[668] and shows that it was alive to the harm to competition which can arise from an over-broad application of a duty to deal.

In some decisions since *Bronner* the Commission appears to have relaxed the requirement about the elimination of competition. In *Telekomunikacja Polska*, where the Commission found that the dominant telecommunications incumbent (TP) had proposed unreasonable conditions for wholesale access and delayed negotiations over access to its network the Commission said:

The establishment of likely effects of a refusal to supply does not mean that rivals were actually forced to exit the market. It is sufficient that rivals are disadvantaged and consequently compete less aggressively.[669]

The Commission considered that it was of crucial importance to the competitors to obtain a minimum critical network size. TP's delaying tactics had prevented the competitors from reaching the critical customer size rapidly and so prevented them from climbing the 'investment ladder' earlier.[670] In *ENI*, the Commission's preliminary view was that the *Bronner* test was satisfied if the refusal was 'likely to lead either to the elimination or the prevention of the development of effective competition on the downstream market resulting in consumer harm'.[671] The 'effective competition' standard echoes the *Microsoft* judgment.[672]

In *TeliaSonera*, the margin squeeze case, it will be recalled that the CJ said that the *Bronner* conditions do not necessarily apply when assessing the abusive nature of conduct which consists in supplying services or selling goods on conditions which are disadvantageous or on which there might be no purchaser.[673] The Commission cited this in its *IBM Mainframe Services* commitments decision.[674] In

---

[667] See M. A. Bergman, 'Editorial: The Bronner Case—A Turning Point for the Essential Facilities Doctrine?' [2000] *ECLR* 59.

[668] As the Commission recognised in *Info-Lab* Case IV/36431, see (1999) 1 *Competition Policy Newsletter* 35 where Ricoh, a photocopier manufacturer, refused to supply a toner producer with empty cartridges compatible with Ricoh machines. The Commission held that Ricoh did not have a dominant position on a relevant market (see Chap. 6) but that, even if it had, in the light of *Bronner* such forced cooperation could be envisaged only under exceptional circumstances which did not pertain there.

[669] COMP/39.525, 22 June 2011, para. 815, on appeal Case T-486/11, *Telekomunikacja Polska* v. *Commission*, judgment pending.

[670] *Telekomunikacja Polska*, para. 818, see D. Kamiński, A. Rogozińska, and B.Sasinowska, 'Telekomunikacja Polska Decision: competition law enforcement in regulated markets' (2011) 3 *Competition Policy Newsletter* 3; see also Case T-301/04, *Clearstream Banking* v. *Commission* [2009] ECR II-3155.

[671] COMP/39, *ENI*, Commitments Decision, 29 September 2010, para. 40.

[672] See Section 12.D.vi, p. 536 ff.

[673] Case C-52/09, *Konkurrensverket* v. *TeliaSonera Sverige AB* [2011] ECR I-527, para. 55; see Section 9.B, p. 434 ff.

[674] COMP/39.692, *IBM Maintenance Services*, 13 December 2011, para. 37.

its *Telefónica* margin squeeze decision[675] the Commission considered that the *Bronner* conditions did not have to be satisfied in the circumstances of the case which fundamentally differed from those in *Bronner*.[676] The point was not discussed on appeal because the GC, following *TeliaSonera*, considered margin squeeze to be an abuse independent of refusal to supply but the 'Telefónica exceptions', as they have been called[677] appear in the Guidance Paper and are therefore discussed in the context of the Guidance Paper.[678]

As already seen, the markets most ripe for the application of the essential facilities doctrine in the EU are those concerning transport infrastructures and/or network infrastructures originally developed with public money. Where competition is being brought on to markets which have previously been statutory monopolies, duplication of facilities such as networks may not be feasible. Liberalisation therefore cannot be fully realised unless the new competitors are given access to the incumbent's established facilities. The Commission decisions discussed in this section demonstrate how the essential facilities concept can be used to open up transport markets.[679] It can be applied both through, and alongside, sector regulation. The Commission has also been active in using Article 102 in the energy sector. In *RWE* the Commission was concerned that RWE was restricting its downstream competitors' access to its gas transmission network. It adopted a commitments decision whereby RWE undertook to divest itself of part of its network.[680] In *ENI* one of the Commission's objections was the dominant gas company's strategic limitation of investment ('strategic under-investment in its international transmission pipeline system') which limited the access of competitors.[681] According to the commitments decision ENI had embarked on a strategy of deliberately avoiding capacity expansions in order to limit third party access.[682] The Commission considered that the mere fact that current capacities are fully used does not suffice to exclude an abuse, and that a 'dominant essential facility holder' is under an obligation to take all possible measures to remove the capacity constraints and organise its business to maximise the capacity available.[683] Like RWE, ENI undertook to divest itself of some of its assets and businesses. *ENI* raises the question of the existence of a 'duty to invest' as well as a 'duty to supply', at least in the case of incumbents in liberalised sectors and it will be recalled that the CJ in *Post Danmark* said in respect of the special responsibility of dominant undertakings that the origin of the dominant position in a former legal monopoly was a fact to be taken into account. Unfortunately where cases are terminated by commitments decisions the principles therein do not come before the EU Courts.

The Commission has dealt specifically with access agreements in the telecommunications sector.[684]

---

[675] Case COMP/38.784 *Wanadoo España v. Telefónica*, 4 July 2007, [2008] 4 CMLR 414; upheld Case T-336/07, *Telefónica and Telefónica de España v. European Commission*, 29 March 2012, on appeal Case C-295/12 P, judgment pending.

[676] As explained in Section 12.G., p. 550 ff.

[677] D. Geradin, 'Refusal to Supply and Margin Squeeze: A Discussion of Why the "Telefonica Exceptions" are Wrong', *TILEC Discussion Paper* No 2011-009, available at <http://papers.ssrn.com/sol3/papers.cfm?abstract_id=1762687>.

[678] In Section 12.G.

[679] And see also *GVG/FS* [2004] OJ L11/17, [2004] 4 CMLR 1446 where the Italian state-owned railway company (FS) abused its dominant position on the Italian passenger rail market by refusing to enter into an international grouping with a German railway company. FS gave undertakings to grant access.

[680] COMP/39.402 *RWE—Gas Foreclosure*, Commitments Decision, 18 March 2009 (for commitments decisions, see Chap. 13); the Competition Commissioner's press release said this, along with the other remedies, would result in more customer choice and that she was satisfied 'that RWE will no longer be able to use the control of its network to favour its own gas supply affiliate over its competitors', IP/09/410. See also, e.g., COMP/39.316 *Gaz de France*, Commitments Decision, 3 December 2009 and COMP/39.389 *German Electricity Wholesale Markets* and *German Electricity Balancing Markets (E.ON)*, Commitments Decision, 26 November 2008, [2009] OJ C36/8.

[681] COMP B-1/39.351, *ENI*, Market Test Notice, 5 March 2010, [2010] OJ C55/13.

[682] COMP/39.315, *ENI*, Commitments Decision, 29 September 2010, paras. 57–60.

[683] COMP/39.315, *ENI*, Commitments Decision, 29 September 2010, paras. 57–60, n. 43.

[684] Commission Notice on access agreements in the telecommunications sector [1998] OJ C265/2.

(vi) Refusal to Supply in the Financial Industry

The Commission intervened in the financial services sector when it issued a notice on cross-border credit transfers, because it considered that access to payment systems is vital if banks are to compete on relevant markets.[685] It took its first decision on a refusal to supply in the financial sector in *Clearstream*.[686] Clearstream (CBF) was the Central Securities Depository (CSD) for securities issued under German Law and kept in collective safe custody. At the time it was the only recognised bank securities depository in Germany. The Commission found it was in a dominant position in the market for the provision of primary clearing and settlement services for securities issued according to German law to CSDs in other Member States and to international CSDs (ICSDs). It held that CBF and its parent had infringed Article 102 in denying Euroclear Bank (EB) clearing and settlement services for two years (and, for a period, in charging it discriminatory prices which were higher than those charged to other security depositories outside Germany). ED was a direct competitor of CBF's sister company, CBL. Although the infringement had ceased the Commission adopted the decision (without imposing a fine) 'to make it clear that the competition rules are being applied in the financial industry'.[687] The Commission said that CBF's behaviour qualified as a refusal to supply contrary to Article 102 because it was an unavoidable trading partner, new entry into its activity being unrealistic for the foreseeable future; EB could not duplicate the requested services; and CBF's behaviour had the effect of impairing EB's ability to provide efficient cross-border clearing and settlement services to clients. The Commission referred to EB's 'legitimate expectation' that it would be supplied with services within a reasonable period of time. The Commission stated that anti-competitive practices committed by market players in the area of cross-border clearing and settlement 'are a major source of inefficiencies that harm consumers', thereby emphasising that the application of Article 102 in this case was for the protection of consumer welfare, not of competitors.[688] The GC upheld the Commission decision. The judgment contains several references to the *Microsoft* judgment.[689]

Case T-301/04, *Clearstream Banking* v. *Commission* [2009] ECR II-3155

General Court

140 According to settled case-law, the concept of abuse is an objective concept relating to the behaviour of an undertaking in a dominant position which is such as to influence the structure of a market where, as a result of the very presence of the undertaking in question, the degree of competition is weakened and which, through recourse to methods different from those which condition normal competition in products or services on the basis of the transactions of commercial operators, has the effect of hindering the maintenance of the degree of competition still existing on the market or the growth of that competition (*Hoffmann-La Roche v Commission*, paragraph 49 above, paragraph 91; see also Case T-203/01 *Michelin v Commission*, paragraph 132 above, paragraph 54, and the case-law cited).

141 Accordingly, the conduct of an undertaking in a dominant position may be regarded as an abuse within the meaning of Article [102] even in the absence of any fault (Case T-65/89 *BPB Industries and British Gypsum v Commission* … paragraph 70).

---

[685] Commission Notice on the application of the competition rules to cross-border credit transfers [1995] OJ C251/3; see also *SWIFT, XXVIIth Report on Competition Policy* (Commission, 1997), 143.

[686] Case COMP/38.096, *Clearstream Banking AG and Clearstream International SA*, IP/04/705, 2 June 2004; and see *Clearstream: Questions and Answers on Commission Decision*, MEMO/04/705.

[687] Commissioner Monti, IP/04/705.

[688] MEMO/04/705, n. 686.

[689] Case T-201/04, *Microsoft v. Commission* [2007] ECR II-3601, see Section 12.D.vi, p. 536 ff.

142 Consequently, the applicants' argument that they did not pursue an anti-competitive objective is irrelevant to the legal characterisation of the facts. In that context, proving that it was the applicants' objective to postpone the grant of access in order to prevent a customer and competitor of the Clearstream group from providing its services effectively may reinforce the conclusion that there is an abuse of a dominant position but is not a condition for such a finding.

143 It should also be noted that, in the present case, access was refused to EB which was, at the same time, a customer of CBF on the German market for securities in collective custody, but also a direct competitor of CBL—a sister company of CBF and the only other ICSD in the European Union—on the downstream market for clearing and settlement of cross-border securities transactions. While the contested decision does not establish that the applicants intended to cause EB a competitive disadvantage, it assesses on the other hand the reasoning for and consequences of that refusal to provide services in the context of EB's position and that of the entire Clearstream group on the relevant market. Thus, the Commission puts forward various indicia to suggest that the applicants' intention was to exclude EB from the provision of their services and, therefore, to hinder competition in the provision of cross-border secondary clearing and settlement services (recitals 234 and 300 of the contested decision). However, given that the abuse of a dominant position is an objective concept, it is not necessary to rule on that point.

144 The effect referred to in the case-law cited in paragraph 140 above does not necessarily relate to the actual effect of the abusive conduct complained of. For the purposes of establishing an infringement of Article [102], it is sufficient to show that the abusive conduct of the undertaking in a dominant position tends to restrict competition or, in other words, that the conduct is capable of having that effect (Case T-203/01 *Michelin v Commission*, paragraph 132 above, paragraph 239).

145 It must therefore be examined whether the Commission has proved in the present case that the applicants' conduct tended to restrict competition on the market in secondary clearing and settlement services.

146 As explained in relation to the examination of the first plea in law, the contested decision shows that the Commission carried out a full analysis of the market in services. On that basis, the Commission was entitled to conclude that CBF held a de facto monopoly and was therefore an indispensable trading partner in the provision of primary clearing and settlement services on the market in question. In addition, it found that the barriers to entry on that market, in terms of regulations, technical requirements, interest by market participants, cost of entry, cost for consumers and likelihood of being able to provide competitive products, were so significant that the possibility of new market entries exercising a competitive constraint on CBF in the foreseeable future could be excluded (recitals 205 to 215 of the contested decision).

147 In that regard, it follows from the case-law of the Court of Justice that, in order to find the existence of an abuse within the meaning of Article [102], the refusal of the service in question must be likely to eliminate all competition on the market on the part of the person requesting the service, such refusal must not be capable of being objectively justified, and the service must in itself be indispensable to carrying on that person's business (Case C-7/97 *Bronner*...paragraph 41). According to settled case-law, a product or service is considered necessary or essential if there is no real or potential substitute (see Joined Cases T-374/94, T-375/94, T-384/94 and T-388/94 *European Night Services and Others v Commission*... paragraph 208, and the case-law cited).

148 With regard to the condition of elimination of all competition, it is not necessary, in order to establish an infringement of Article [102], to demonstrate that all competition on the market would be eliminated, but what matters is that the refusal at issue is liable to, or is likely to, eliminate all effective competition on the market. It is for the Commission to establish such a risk of the elimination of all effective competition (*Microsoft v Commission*, paragraph 47 above, paragraphs 563 and 564).

It should be noted that in paragraph 144 the GC says that in establishing an abuse it is sufficient to show that the conduct 'tends to' or 'is capable of' restricting competition. Although the Court also cited the *Bronner* 'likely elimination of all competition on the market on the part of the person requesting the service' test (paragraph 147) and the *Microsoft* 'elimination of all effective competition' test (paragraph 148) it was content with the Commission's conclusion that the refusal had merely 'hindered' EB:

the applicants' refusal to provide it with primary clearing and settlement services for registered shares hindered EB's capacity to provide comprehensive, pan-European and innovative services. That harmed innovation and competition in the provision of cross-border secondary clearing and settlement services and ultimately the consumers within the single market.[690]

It has been suggested that this standard can be explained by the fact that the case concerned the emergence of a pan-European settlement and clearing market and that it is therefore of limited precedential value.[691]

(vii) Refusal to Supply Spare Parts and Services in Aftermarkets

A firm which refuses to supply spare parts and services for its product may infringe Article 102 even though it is not dominant in the primary product market, but only in the market for its own spare parts. This was established in *Hugin*, the facts of which were given in Chapter 6.[692] In *Hugin* the undertaking stopped supplying the customer, Liptons, which repaired and serviced its machines, because it wanted to carry out those operations itself. Like Commercial Solvents, it wanted to integrate vertically. The Commission rejected its claim of objective justification and said that the refusal to supply was an abuse because it would lead to an existing customer being unable to carry out a particular line of business. As in *Commercial Solvents* the Commission did not consider questions of efficiencies or the advantages of the vertical integration to consumers (here the owners of the machines) but looked at the situation from the perspective of Liptons. The Commission's objective was Lipton's continued presence on the market: the protection of competitors rather than competition. The CJ annulled the decision because it found no effect on inter-Member State trade, but it confirmed the finding of dominance. As discussed in Chapter 6, however, the spare parts of a particular brand do not always constitute a separate relevant market.[693] In *CHEAR*[694] the Commission's rejection of a complaint from independent watch repairers about the refusal of luxury watch manufacturers to continue to supply them with spare parts was annulled, partly on the grounds that the Commission had wrongly defined the market.

The CJ dealt obliquely with refusal to supply spare parts in two Article 267 references concerning the licensing of IPRs covering car parts, *Renault*[695] and *Volvo*.[696] In *Renault* the Court held that a refusal by the car manufacturer to license did not necessarily constitute an abuse, but would do so if it gave rise to 'certain abusive conduct...such as the arbitrary refusal to deliver spare parts to independent repairers'.[697] The Commission cited *Volvo* in its 2012 commitments decision *IBM Maintenance Services*.[698] There maintenance services for IBM mainframe computers were offered both by IBM

[690] *Clearstream*, para. 149.

[691] Nazzini, *The Foundations of European Union Competition Law* (cited in n. 106), 268–269.

[692] Case 22/78 *Hugin v. EC Commission* [1979] ECR 1869.

[693] See Chap. 6, Section 5.B.i.h.

[694] Case T-427/08, *Confédération européenne des associations d'horlogers-réparateurs (CEAHR) v. Commission* [2010] ECR II-5865, see Chap. 1, Section 10.B.vii.g.

[695] Case 53/87, *CICCRA v. Renault* [1988] ECR 6039.

[696] Case 238/87, *AB Volvo v. Erik Veng* [1988] ECR 6211.

[697] Case 53/87, *CICCRA v. Renault*, para 16..

[698] COM/39.692, *IBM Maintenance Services*, 13 December 2011.

itself and by third parties (TPMs). The Commission was concerned with aspects of IBM's dealings with TPMs in respect of the supply of spare parts and other resources which TPMs needed. These included restricted access to spare parts, unreasonable terms for the supply of some parts, unreasonably delayed access, and withheld information. The Commission considered the cumulative effect might amount to a constructive refusal to supply that could raise concerns under Article 102(b) as the conduct had the potential to lead to the exclusion of the few existing rival firms that competed with IBM on the downstream market which might limit markets to the prejudice of consumers. IBM gave commitments as to its future practices and contractual conditions.[699]

D. REFUSAL TO SUPPLY AND INTELLECTUAL PROPERTY RIGHTS

(i) General

The question whether it is an abuse to refuse to supply others with IPRs has become intertwined with the question of essential facilities and the debate about the interaction of competition law and intellectual property is one of the most hotly disputed in competition law. Neither the EU Courts nor the Commission has applied the phrase 'essential facilities' to IPRs but the leading case on IPRs, *Magill*,[700] featured significantly in *Bronner*,[701] and, in turn, *Bronner* was relied upon in the intellectual property case *IMS*.[702] The arguments on this matter centre around the fact that the law has already put in place a regime to deal with intellectual property; that compulsory licensing of IPRs is a dangerous disincentive to innovation; and that the law to date has not properly explained why some situations are so 'exceptional' that the normal rights of an intellectual property right owner to exclude others should be eroded.

It is obvious that the existence of IPRs will prevent undertakings competing on certain markets. Although the EU Courts have held that the ownership of IPRs does not necessarily mean that an undertaking holds a dominant position,[703] some rights can nonetheless constitute a barrier to entry under any conception of that term.[704] An undertaking cannot usually produce or use something protected by IPRs without the consent of the rights holder. IPRs owners often *do* license their rights to others and Chapter 12 deals with the application of Article 101 to such agreements. Article 102 may be relevant, however, when the rights holder is in a dominant position and refuses to give licences to those wanting them.

(ii) The *Car Parts* Cases

The matter first came before the CJ in two Article 267 references, *AB Volvo v. Erik Veng* and *CICCRA v. Renault*.[705] In essence the CJ was asked the same thing: is it an abuse for a car manufacturer to refuse to license the design rights on its car parts to third parties wishing to manufacture and sell

---

[699] See F. Domanico and M. Angeli, 'An Analysis of the IBM Commitment Decision concerning the aftermarket for IBM mainframe computers' (2012) 1 *Competition Policy Newsletter*.

[700] Cases C-241–242/91 P, *RTE & ITP v. Commission* [1995] ECR I-743, on appeal from Cases T-69–70/89, 76/89, *RTE, ITP, BBC v. Commission* [1991] ECR II-485.

[701] Case C-7/97, *Oscar Bronner GmbH & Co KG v. Mediaprint* [1998] ECR I-7791.

[702] Case C-418/01, *IMS Health GmbH & Co OHG v. NDC Health GmbH & Co KG* [2004] ECR I-5039.

[703] See Chap. 6.

[704] See Chap. 1.

[705] Case 238/87, *AB Volvo v. Erik Veng* [1988] ECR 6211 and Case 53/87, *CICCRA and Maxicar v. Renault* [1988] ECR 6039, decided on the same day.

such parts?[706] The CJ held that a refusal to license was not per se an abuse, but might become so in certain circumstances.

Case 238/87, *AB Volvo* v. *Erik Veng* [1988] ECR 6211

Court of Justice

8. It must also be emphasized that the right of the proprietor of a protected design to prevent third parties from manufacturing and selling or importing, without its consent, products incorporating the design constitutes the very subject-matter of his exclusive right. It follows that an obligation imposed upon the proprietor of a protected design to grant to third parties, even in return for a reasonable royalty, a licence for the supply of products incorporating the design would lead to the proprietor thereof being deprived of the substance of his exclusive right, and that a refusal to grant such a licence cannot in itself constitute an abuse of a dominant position.

9.[707] It must however be noted that the exercise of an exclusive right by the proprietor of a registered design in respect of car body panels may be prohibited by Article [102] if it involves, on the part of an undertaking holding a dominant position, certain abusive conduct such as the arbitrary refusal to supply spare parts to independent repairers, the fixing of prices for spare parts at an unfair level or a decision no longer to produce spare parts for a particular model even though many cars of that model are still in circulation, provided that such conduct is liable to affect trade between Member States.

The references in the judgments to the 'very subject-matter of the exclusive right' and the 'exercise of an exclusive right' are to concepts which the Court had already developed to deal with the tension between IPRs and Community law, mainly in the area of the free movement of goods and services. The outcome of their application in *Volvo* and *Renault* was that the CJ held that a refusal to grant licences would be an abuse only if it involved or gave rise to 'certain abusive conduct'. In effect the car makers were given a choice: either they could license third parties, or they could retain their monopoly and ensure, inter alia, that they did not arbitrarily refuse to supply independent repairers, did not charge unfairly and continued to supply parts for old models. One way of looking at this is to see an order to license as a *remedy* for other abuses.[708] The examples of abusive conduct given are not unproblematic, however, including the issue of what is an 'unfair' price.[709] The refusal to supply spare parts to independent repairers was classed as an abuse even though it involved the supply of products to new, rather than existing, customers, albeit within a very particular context.[710]

---

[706] The cases arose after the CJ had confirmed in Case 22/78, *Hugin Kassaregister AB* v. *EC Commission* [1979] ECR 1869 that an undertaking may be dominant on the market for its own spare parts even if the primary product market is competitive.; see Chap. 6.

[707] Para. 9, with only insignificant changes in wording, was repeated in the *Renault* judgment at para. 16.

[708] See the discussion in J. Temple Lang, 'Anti-competitive Non-Pricing Abuses under European and National Antitrust Law' in B. Hawk (ed.) [2003] *Fordham Corp L Inst* 235, 292–301.

[709] See Section 15.A, p. 575. And see generally V. Korah, 'No Duty to License Independent Repairers to Made Spare Parts: The Renault, Volvo and Bayer and Hennecke Cases' [1988] *EIPR* 381 who argues that if the car maker itself is not interested in further production it will not object to a third party manufacturing the parts and may be happy to profit through licensing, although on the other hand the car maker may have an interest in obsolescence and not want old models to be repairable; see also I. Govaere, *The Use and Abuse of Intellectual Property Rights in EC Law* (Sweet & Maxwell, 1996), paras. 8.55–8.56. The extent to which a car manufacturer has power to charge excessively in the aftermarket for spare parts without affecting sales in the competitive foremarket is questionable, see Chap. 6, Section 5.B.i.h, p. 317 ff.

[710] EU competition law has for some time had special provisions covering motor vehicle distribution, see Chap. 11.

(iii) The *Magill* Case

Magill[711] concerned copyright in 'television listings' (television programme schedules). Under UK and Irish law copyright protects not only literary works which result from creative or intellectual endeavour but also compilations of information resulting from 'skill, judgment and labour' or the 'sweat of the brow', including listings of programmes to be broadcast.[712] Such compilations were not protected by intellectual property laws in the other Member States of the EU, where copyright covered only the fruits of creative or intellectual effort. The EU Courts have said on several occasions that where intellectual property laws are not harmonised EU law recognises the *existence* of rights granted by the Member States.

In 1985 RTE had a statutory monopoly over television broadcasting in Ireland and the BBC and IBA had a statutory duopoly in the UK (including Northern Ireland). Most television viewers in Ireland and Northern Ireland could receive the channels of all three television authorities. RTE and the BBC owned the copyright in the programme listings for their respective channels and ITP owned the copyright in the listings of the IBA franchised channels. RTE, the BBC, and ITP each published a weekly TV guide containing only their own individual weekly programme listings. They also gave listings information to the press to be published according to strictly enforced licensing conditions. An Irish publisher, Magill, started to publish a comprehensive weekly TV guide giving details of all programmes available to viewers in Ireland and Northern Ireland, but the television companies obtained injunctions against it in national legal proceedings. Magill complained to the Commission that the television companies, by refusing to give out reliable advance listings information and protecting their listings by enforcing their copyright, were infringing Article 102.

The EU Courts and the Commission appear to have been influenced by the fact that the UK and Ireland were alone among the Member States in affording copyright protection to TV listings, and comprehensive composite TV guides could therefore be published in the other Member States, where they were popular and common.[713] The case became perceived as a battle between the protection of national IPRs and competition law, for if the TV companies' refusal to deal with Magill *was* an abuse the only remedy was, in effect, to order them to give the publisher a licence of their copyrights.

The Commission found that the television companies had infringed Article 102. It held that the companies were each dominant in the market for their weekly listings and that their policies in restricting the availability of the information were driven by a desire to protect their own individual weekly guides in the downstream market. The GC upheld the Commission's decision. The GC related its discussion of Article 102 to the case law on IPRs in the context of the free movement of goods and services.[714] RTE and ITP appealed. The CJ confirmed the finding of abuse but its judgment was strikingly narrow. It concentrated on the specific scenario in issue and eschewed extended discussion about the nature of IPRs and their relationship to the competition rules.[715] The CJ treated the

---

[711] Cases C-241–242/91 P, *RTE & ITP* v. *Commission* [1995] ECR I-743 on appeal from Cases T-69–70/89, 76/89, *RTE, ITP, BBC* v. *EC Commission* [1991] ECR II-485, on appeal from *Magill TV Guide* [1989] OJ L78/43, [1989] 4 CMLR 757.

[712] The relevant UK law is now the Copyright Designs and Patents Act 1988, although at the time of the *Magill* decision it was still the Copyright Act 1956. The protection of programme listings by copyright in the UK was confirmed by *Independent Television Publications* v. *Time Out* [1984] FSR 64. The Broadcasting Act 1990, s. 176 specifically provides that persons broadcasting television and radio programmes in the UK have to make information about the programme schedules available to any person in the UK who wants to publish it: the actual dispute in *Magill* therefore became a dead issue as regards the UK during the course of the case, which is why the BBC was not party to the appeal to the CJ.

[713] See particularly the Commission's submissions to the GC, [1991] ECR II-485, summarised in paras. 43–59 of the judgment, culminating in the Commission's statement in para. 59 that 'copyright should not subsist in compilations of banal information'.

[714] There were three separate judgments, but the crucial paras. are the same in all three: see *RTE* v. *Commission*, para. 71, *BBC* v. *Commission*, para. 58, *ITP* v. *Commission*, para. 56.

[715] See particularly para. 58 of the judgment. The CJ did not follow the opinion of Gulmann AG, who recommended setting aside the GC judgment, primarily to uphold the inviolability of intellectual property rights.

matter as a straightforward refusal to supply and applied the principles laid down in previous Article 102 case law.

Cases C-241–242/91 P, *RTE & ITP* v. *Commission* [1995] ECR I-743

Court of Justice

(a) Existence of a dominant position

46. So far as dominant position is concerned, it is to be remembered at the outset that mere ownership of an intellectual property right cannot confer such a position.

47. However, the basic information as to the channel, day, time and title of programmes is the necessary result of programming by television stations, which are thus the only source of such information for an undertaking, like Magill, which wishes to publish it together with commentaries or pictures. By force of circumstance, RTE and ITP, as the agent of ITV, enjoy, along with the BBC, a *de facto* monopoly over the information used to compile listings for the television programmes received in most households in Ireland and 30–40 per cent. of households in Northern Ireland. The appellants are thus in a position to prevent effective competition on the market in weekly television magazines. The [General Court] was therefore right in confirming the Commission's assessment that the appellants occupied a dominant position (*Michelin, paragraph 30*)

(b) Existence of an abuse

48. With regard to the issue of abuse, the arguments of the appellants and IPO wrongly presuppose that where the conduct of an undertaking in a dominant position consists of the exercise of a right classified by national law as 'copyright', such conduct can never be reviewed in relation to Article [102].

49. Admittedly, in the absence of Community standardization or harmonization of laws, determination of the conditions and procedures for granting protection of an intellectual property right is a matter for national rules. Further, the exclusive right of reproduction forms part of the author's rights, so that refusal to grant a licence, even if it is the act of an undertaking holding a dominant position, cannot in itself constitute abuse of a dominant position (*Volvo* v. *Veng*, paragraphs 7 and 8).

50. However, it is also clear from that judgment (paragraph 9) that the exercise of an exclusive right by the proprietor may, in exceptional circumstances, involve abusive conduct.

51. In the present case, the conduct objected to is the appellants' reliance on copyright conferred by national legislation so as to prevent Magill—or any other undertaking having the same intention—from publishing on a weekly basis information (channel, day, time and title of programmes) together with commentaries and pictures obtained independently of the appellants.

52. Among the circumstances taken into account by the [General Court] in concluding that such conduct was abusive was, first, the fact that there was, according to the findings of the [General Court], no actual or potential substitute for a weekly television guide offering information on the programmes for the week ahead. On this point, the [General Court] confirmed the Commission's finding that the complete lists of programmes for a 24-hour period—and for a 48-hour period at weekends and before public holidays—published in certain daily and Sunday newspapers, and the television sections of certain magazines covering, in addition, 'highlights' of the week's programmes, were only to a limited extent substitutable for advance information to viewers on all the week's programmes. Only weekly television guides containing comprehensive listings for the week ahead would enable users to decide in advance which programmes they wished to follow and arrange their leisure activities for the week accordingly. The [General Court] also established that there was a specific, constant and regular potential demand on the part of consumers (see the *RTE* judgment, paragraph 62, and the *ITP* judgment, paragraph 48).

53. Thus the appellants—who were, by force of circumstance, the only sources of the basic information on programme scheduling which is the indispensable raw material for compiling a weekly television

guide—gave viewers wishing to obtain information on the choice of programmes for the week ahead no choice but to buy the weekly guides for each station and draw from each of them the information they needed to make comparisons.

54. The appellants' refusal to provide basic information by relying on national copyright provisions thus prevented the appearance of a new product, a comprehensive weekly guide to television programmes, which the appellants did not offer and for which there was a potential consumer demand. Such refusal constitutes an abuse under heading (b) of the second paragraph of Article [102].

55. Second, there was no justification for such refusal either in the activity of television broadcasting or in that of publishing television magazines (RTE judgment, paragraph 73, and ITP judgment, paragraph 58).

56. Third, and finally, as the [General Court] also held, the appellants, by their conduct, reserved to themselves the secondary market of weekly television guides by excluding competition on that market (Commercial Solvents, paragraph 25) since they denied access to the basic information which is the raw material indispensable for the compilation of such a guide.

57. In the light of all those circumstances, the [General Court] did not err in law in holding that the appellants' conduct was an abuse of a dominant position within the meaning of Article [102].

58. It follows that the plea in law alleging misapplication by the [General Court] of the concept of abuse of a dominant position must be dismissed as unfounded. It is therefore unnecessary to examine the reasoning of the contested judgments in so far as it is based on Article [36 TFEU].

It can be seen that in this judgment the CJ said (paragraph 48) that while it is not true that the exercise of IPRs can *never* be reviewed under Article 102, a refusal to grant a licence to reproduce cannot *in itself* constitute an abuse of a dominant position (paragraph 49). It cited *Volvo* as establishing that a refusal might constitute an abuse *in exceptional circumstances*. In this case the exceptional circumstances were:

— there was no substitute for a composite weekly television guide, for which there was a specific, constant, and regular potential demand on the part of consumers;

— the appellants' refusal to supply prevented the appearance of a new product for which there was a potential consumer demand[716] (this constituted an abuse under Article 102 (b), in 'limiting production, markets or technical development to the prejudice of consumers');

— there was no justification for such refusal;

— the appellants were reserving to themselves the secondary market of weekly television guides by excluding all competition on the market.

The 'list' of exceptional circumstances in *Magill* acquired great significance. It was not clear whether the circumstances were cumulative. In particular it was not clear whether the hindrance of a new product is a necessary or a separate and sufficient ground for holding the refusal to supply to be abusive. If the television companies had already produced their *own* composite guides by cross-licensing each other, the composite guide of a third party would not have been a new product, but the undertakings would still have reserved for themselves a special position on the secondary market. Whether or not the hindrance or prevention of a new product is a necessary condition for finding a refusal to supply abusive in cases involving IPRs became a major issue, as is seen from the subsequent case law.

The following points about the *Magill* judgment should also be noted:

• The CJ based its finding of dominance on the fact that the TV companies had a *de facto* monopoly over the listings, i.e. they were responsible for producing the TV schedules and were the

---

[716] The AG on the other hand (paras. 93–102 of the Opinion) thought that the fact that the product Magill wanted to produce was new and would compete with the right holders' own products was a reason to find that the refusal to supply was *not* abusive.

only source of advance information about them (paragraph 47). The Commission (paragraph 22) based the finding of dominance on both the *de facto* monopoly and the legal monopoly stemming from the copyright. The GC based it on the legal monopoly (paragraph 63 of the *RTE* judgment). The CJ did not even mention the existence of the IPRs in its discussion of dominance in paragraph 47.

- The CJ (paragraphs 53 and 56) described the companies' conduct in terms of refusal to supply a raw material. It did not use essential facilities terminology.

- The CJ referred back to the early case of *Commercial Solvents* (paragraph 56), seeing the present case as an example of the established abuse of an undertaking dominant on one market trying to exclude competition on a downstream market.

- Unlike the car makers in *Volvo* and *Renault* the television companies were not given a choice of how they could avoid committing an abuse. Although the judgment did not mention compulsory licensing there was only one way in which the abuse could be remedied.[717]

- The judgment established that the norm is that refusal to license is *not* generally an abuse. The judgment was less of an assault on IPRs than it was on the exploitation of compilations of information gained as a by-product of an undertaking's main business. The case was thus of a piece with all the previous cases on interference with ancillary markets: a significant difference between *Magill* and the car parts cases is that in the latter the would-be licensee wished to compete with the dominant undertaking in the core area of its business. In contrast, the television companies were not set up to publish magazines.[718]

It is possible to see *Magill* as a limitation of the power wielded by statutory monopolists. The power of the television companies in respect of the TV guides arose as a result of their privileged position on the broadcasting market. In a market which had more numerous television channels they would probably have been glad to provide their programme details to composite magazines: although consumers may buy two or three guides, they will not buy 50, and television companies *need* to advertise their programme schedules.

(iv) The *Ladbroke* Case

In the next case concerning a refusal to license IPRs, *Tiercé Ladbroke*,[719] the GC dismissed an appeal from Ladbrokes against the Commission's rejection of its complaint that the French race course societies (*sociétés de courses*) and their associated companies refused to supply broadcasts of French horse races to Ladbroke's betting shops in Belgium. The *sociétés de courses* and the associated companies had exclusive responsibility for organising off-course betting in France, taking bets abroad on French races, taking bets in France on races run abroad, and exploiting outside France televised pictures of, and information about, French horse races.

The GC distinguished the situation before it from that in *Magill*. The *sociétés de courses* did not operate betting shops in Belgium, so the downstream market issue did not arise. Showing films of the races was not essential to providing services in betting shops. The copyright owners were not discriminating (contrary to Article 102(c)) in that they did not supply anybody with licences in the relevant market (Belgium). The GC said that the refusal to supply could constitute an abuse only if *either* the product or service was essential to the activity in question *or* the introduction of a new product demanded by consumers was being prevented.[720] The GC thus suggested that a refusal to

---

[717] The existence of the Copyright Tribunal in the UK meant that the Commission itself did not have to become involved in price-setting.

[718] It is true that *British Midland* also concerned competition with the dominant undertaking's core business, but that case did not involve IPRs and was bound up with the liberalisation of the air transport market.

[719] Case T-504/93, *Tiercé Ladbroke SA v. EC Commission* [1997] ECR-II 923.

[720] Case T-504/93, *Tiercé Ladbroke SA v. EC Commission* [1997] ECR-II 923, para. 131.

supply which precluded the introduction of a new product might constitute an abuse for that reason alone, even if the access demanded was not 'essential'. In other words, the GC read the 'exceptional circumstances' in *Magill* as severable, not cumulative.

(v) The *IMS* Case

a. The Facts and Sequence of Events in *IMS*

The *IMS* case concerned the '1860 brick structure', a system for representing regional pharmaceutical sales data in Germany. In effect it consisted of a grid superimposed on the map of Germany, breaking down the country into small geographical areas (bricks) based on factors including postcodes, administrative and political boundaries, and the location of doctors and pharmacies.[721] IMS collected pharmaceutical sales information from wholesalers, formatted it in accordance with the brick structure so enabling it to be analysed in various ways, and then provided sales reports to its customers, the pharmaceutical companies. The brick structure had been developed over many years, in collaboration by IMS with the pharmaceutical industry[722] and the Commission found that it had become the *de facto* industry standard. IMS's competitors[723] attempted to develop similar brick structures but IMS claimed that these infringed its copyright and obtained interim injunctions in the German courts to restrain their use. The competitors complained to the Commission that IMS's refusal to license the brick structure meant that it was impossible for them to provide pharmaceutical data services to customers as they could not present data in a way acceptable to the customers without infringing IMS's copyright and there was no prospect of the customers changing to a radically different structure. The Commission found that the brick structure was indispensable to carrying on business in the relevant market as there was no actual or potential substitute for it; there was no objective justification for IMS's refusal to license; and that there were 'exceptional circumstances' in the *Magill* sense. It ordered interim measure by which *IMS* was to give a licence on request and on a non-discriminatory basis to all undertakings currently on the German regional sales data services market.[724] The execution of the decision was suspended pending the appeal.[725]

In the meantime, litigation between IMS and NDC was ongoing in Germany and a preliminary reference was made to the CJ asking about the interpretation of Article 102 in the context of IMS's refusal to license. Before judgment was given, however, the Oberlandesgericht Frankfurt am Main gave judgment on the issue of IMS's claim to copyright in the brick structure, holding that the brick structure was protected by copyright but that this did not prevent other parties from developing a similar structure. Moreover, NDC began to compete more successfully with IMS. The Commission therefore did not proceed to a final decision and withdrew the interim measures.[726] The CJ however proceeded to give its ruling on the preliminary reference.

b. The CJ judgment

The judgment of the CJ, which largely followed the Opinion of Advocate General Tizzano, set out the conditions in which a refusal to supply a copyright is an abuse, and left the German court to decide whether the conditions were satisfied in the situation before it.

---

[721] There are around 21,500 pharmacies and 287,000 doctors in Germany (*IMS/NDC* [2002] OJ L59/18, para. 14). German privacy laws prevent the production of data which can identify sales in individual pharmacies.

[722] There was considerable dispute about the extent of this collaboration.

[723] One of the competitors, PII, was founded by a former director of IMS, and later taken over by NDC.

[724] *NDC Health/IMS: Interim Measures* [2004] OJ L59/18, [2002] 4 CMLR 111. The Commission ordered the royalties to be fixed by agreement between the parties within two weeks, failing which recourse was to be had to independent expert(s) appointed by the parties. If the parties could not agree on the expert(s) within a further week the Commission would make the appointment (Art. 2).

[725] Case T-184/01 R, *IMS Health v. Commission* [2001] ECR II-3193, para. 125, *aff'd* Case C-481/01 P(R), *IMS Health v. Commission* [2002] ECR I-3401.

[726] Commission Decision 2003/741/EC, 13 Aug. 2003, [2003] OJ L268/69; IP 03/1159.

Case C-418/01, *IMS Health GmbH & Co OHG* v. *NDC Health GmbH & Co KG* [2004] ECR I-5039

The Landgericht Frankfurt am Main asked three questions:

- first, whether it was an abuse not to grant a licence in a situation where the competitor was seeking access to the same geographical and product market and the customers would only accept a product based on material protected by the copyright;
- secondly, was the participation of the customers in developing the copyright material relevant;
- thirdly, were the costs which the customers would occur in switching to a product protected by a different data bank relevant.

The Court held that the second and third questions both concerned factors which had to be taken into consideration in determining whether the protected structure was indispensable for the relevant marketing studies. The following extract is the part of the judgment dealing with the first question.

Court of Justice

34. According to settled case-law, the exclusive right of reproduction forms part of the owner's rights, so that refusal to grant a licence, even if it is the act of an undertaking holding a dominant position, cannot in itself constitute abuse of a dominant position (judgment in Case 238/87 *Volvo*...paragraph 8, and *Magill*, paragraph 49).

35. Nevertheless, as is clear from that case-law, exercise of an exclusive right by the owner may, in exceptional circumstances, involve abusive conduct (*Volvo*, paragraph 9, and *Magill*, paragraph 50).

36. The Court held that such exceptional circumstances were present in the case giving rise to the judgment in *Magill*, in which the conduct complained of by the television channels in a dominant position involved invoking the copyright conferred by national legislation on the weekly listings of their programmes in order to prevent another undertaking from publishing information on those programmes together with commentaries, on a weekly basis.

37. According to the summary of the *Magill* judgment made by the Court at paragraph 40 of the judgment in *Bronner*, the exceptional circumstances were constituted by the fact that the refusal in question concerned a product (information on the weekly schedules of certain television channels), the supply of which was indispensable for carrying on the business in question, (the publishing of a general television guide), in that, without that information, the person wishing to produce such a guide would find it impossible to publish it and offer it for sale (paragraph 53), the fact that such refusal prevented the emergence of a new product for which there was a potential consumer demand (paragraph 54), the fact that it was not justified by objective considerations (paragraph 55), and was likely to exclude all competition in the secondary market (paragraph 56).

38. It is clear from that case-law that, in order for the refusal by an undertaking which owns a copyright to give access to a product or service indispensable for carrying on a particular business to be treated as abusive, it is sufficient that three cumulative conditions be satisfied, namely, that that refusal is preventing the emergence of a new product for which there is a potential consumers demand, that it is unjustified and such as to exclude any competition on a secondary market.

39. In light of the order for reference and the observations submitted to the Court, which reveal a major dispute as regards the interpretation of the third condition, it is appropriate to consider that question first.

The third condition, relating to the likelihood of excluding all competition on a secondary market

40. In that regard, it is appropriate to recall the approach followed by the Court in the *Bronner* judgment, in which it was asked whether the fact that a press undertaking with a very large share of the daily newspaper

market in a Member State which operates the only nationwide newspaper home-delivery scheme in that Member State refuses paid access to that scheme by the publisher of a rival newspaper, which by reason of its small circulation is unable either alone or in cooperation with other publishers to set up and operate its own home-delivery scheme under economically reasonable conditions, constitutes the abuse of a dominant position.

41. The Court, first of all, invited the national court to determine whether the home delivery schemes constituted a separate market (*Bronner*, paragraph 34), on which, in light of the circumstances of the case, the press undertaking held a de facto monopoly position and, thus, a dominant position (paragraph 35). It then invited the national court to determine whether the refusal by the owner of the only nationwide home-delivery scheme in a Member State, which used that scheme to distribute its own daily newspapers, to allow the publisher of a rival daily newspaper access to it deprived that competitor of a means of distribution judged essential for the sale of its newspaper (paragraph 37).

42. Therefore, the Court held that it was relevant, in order to assess whether the refusal to grant access to a product or a service indispensable for carrying on a particular business activity was an abuse, to distinguish an upstream market, constituted by the product or service, in that case the market for home delivery of daily newspapers, and a (secondary) downstream market, on which the product or service in question is used for the production of another product or the supply of another service, in that case the market for daily newspapers themselves.

43. The fact that the delivery service was not marketed separately was not regarded as precluding, from the outset, the possibility of identifying a separate market.

44. It appears, therefore, as the Advocate General set out in points 56 to 59 of his Opinion, that, for the purposes of the application of the earlier case-law, it is sufficient that a potential market or even hypothetical market can be identified. Such is the case where the products or services are indispensable in order to carry on a particular business and where there is an actual demand for them on the part of undertakings which seek to carry on the business for which they are indispensable.

45. Accordingly, it is determinative that two different stages of production may be identified and that they are interconnected, the upstream product is indispensable in as much as for supply of the downstream product.

46. Transposed to the facts of the case in the main proceedings, that approach prompts consideration as to whether the 1860 brick structure constitutes, upstream, an indispensable factor in the downstream supply of German regional sales data for pharmaceutical products.

47. It is for the national court to establish whether that is in fact the position, and, if so be the case, to examine whether the refusal by IMS to grant a licence to use the structure at issue is capable of excluding all competition on the market for the supply of German regional sales data on pharmaceutical products.

The first condition, relating to the emergence of a new product

48. As the Advocate General stated in point 62 of his Opinion, that condition relates to the consideration that, in the balancing of the interest in protection of copyright and the economic freedom of its owner, against the interest in protection of free competition the latter can prevail only where refusal to grant a licence prevents the development of the secondary market to the detriment of consumers.

49. Therefore, the refusal by an undertaking in a dominant position to allow access to a product protected by copyright, where that product is indispensable for operating on a secondary market, may be regarded as abusive only where the undertaking which requested the licence does not intend to limit itself essentially to duplicating the goods or services already offered on the secondary market by the owner of the copyright, but intends to produce new goods or services not offered by the owner of the right and for which there is a potential consumer demand.

50. It is for the national court to determine whether such is the case in the dispute in the main proceedings.

The second condition, relating to whether the refusal was unjustified

51. As to that condition, on whose interpretation no specific observations have been made, it is for the national court to examine, if appropriate, in light of the facts before it, whether the refusal of the request for a licence is justified by objective considerations.

52. Accordingly, the answer to the first question must be that the refusal by an undertaking which holds a dominant position and is the owner of an intellectual property right over a brick structure which is indispensable for the presentation of data on regional sales of pharmaceutical products in a Member State, to grant a licence to use that structure to another undertaking which also wishes to supply such data in the same Member State, constitutes an abuse of a dominant position within the meaning of Article [102] where the following conditions are fulfilled:

— the undertaking which requested the licence intends to offer, on the market for the supply of the data in question, new products or services not offered by the copyright owner and for which there is a potential consumer demand;

— the refusal is not justified by objective considerations;

— the refusal is such as to reserve to the copyright owner the market for the supply of data on sales of pharmaceutical products in the Member State concerned by eliminating all competition on that market.

In this judgment the CJ laid down (paragraphs 38 and 52) that three *cumulative* conditions made the refusal to license a copyright an abuse. First, a 'new product' was involved. Secondly, access to the protected material was 'indispensable' so that the refusal would exclude *any* (paragraph 38) or *all* (paragraph 52) competition on a secondary market (not, as in *Bronner*, all competition from the person requesting access). Thirdly, the refusal was unjustified.

One view of the judgment is that the CJ came down firmly on the 'side' of the IPR holder, in that there is a presumption against the licence (see paragraph 48). The CJ repeated that a refusal to grant a licence cannot in itself constitute an abuse (paragraph 34). It allowed for the possibility of compulsory licences but only in 'exceptional circumstances' (paragraph 35). It incorporated into the exceptional circumstances the requirement of 'indispensability' in the *Bronner* sense, which as we have seen,[727] put the bar at a high level, and demanded that the party requiring the licence intends to offer new goods and services for which there is a potential consumer demand. On the other hand, the 'indispensable' and 'new product' requirements are such that everything will turn on the application of these conditions to the facts of the case. In *IMS* the CJ referred everything back to the national court without giving any indication as to whether the requirements were in fact satisfied in the case. In *IMS* there was room for argument about whether NDC was providing a 'new product'.[728] The Commission stated in its Decision that the sales reports of the firms 'differ markedly'.[729] It came down to a matter of whether this would fulfil the condition of not 'essentially duplicating' the right holder's product. The key to this is the interests of consumers. In paragraph 48 the Court said that the only situation in which free competition can override the rights of the copyright holder is where the refusal prevents the development of the secondary market to the detriment of consumers (in other words limiting production to the detriment of consumers as provided for in Article 102(b)). The licence is not ordered to protect the competitor but to protect consumers.

The CJ did require that the development of a *secondary* market be affected. As the Commission had done it spelt two markets out of the situation in *IMS*. The Court said (paragraph 44) that it is enough

[727] See Section 12.C.v, p. 518 ff.

[728] Unlike *Bronner*, where the CJ made it clear that that the conditions laid down there were not satisfied.

[729] According to the customers the coverage of parts of Germany was more complete and they provided more detail on types of information, Commission Decision [2002] OJ L59/18, para. 15.

if a 'potential or even hypothetical' market can be identified upstream. It only required that 'two different stages of production' can be identified.[730] The question here of course is how hypothetical can the market for the input be. The upstream market in *IMS* was a very artificial one: IMS only developed the brick structure in order to produce its own sales reports. It was different in *Magill* where the television listings existed as a by-product of the broadcasting activities and would have existed whether or not the broadcasters had published their own magazines. As one commentator said (critically) of the Commission decision in *IMS*, it was enough 'even if the input is a competitive advantage of a kind which has never previously been marketed or licensed by any company, and which it would not be economically rational to license to a direct competitor'.[731] There are few production processes that cannot be divided as in *IMS* if one thinks hard enough and anything protected by an IPR can on this basis form an upstream market. One can compare *IMS* on this point with the judgment of the US Supreme Court in *Verizon v. Trinko*,[732] set out in Section 12.H, where the fact that 'the services allegedly withheld are not otherwise marketed or available to the public' and existed 'only deep in the bowels of Verizon' was a factor in holding the refusal to deal lawful.[733]

The *IMS* judgment gave little flavour of the underlying factual situation. It is necessary to read the Commission decision to fully appreciate that *IMS*, like *Magill*, involved a 'weak' copyright. Indeed, the Commission seemed to consider that IMS had more or less hijacked the industry standard.[734] If *IMS* could be taken as turning on the particular facts of how the brick structure had been developed and the copyright acquired it could be viewed as a response to a quirk of national law. Some commentators considered that the cases should be viewed in this light—as exceptional responses to unsatisfactory copyright laws—and argued that there was no reason to suppose that the same approach would be taken to strong patent rights, for example.[735] However, *Magill* and *IMS* were relied upon by the GC in the *Microsoft* case, where any IPRs concerned were certainly not the product of quirks of copyright laws. As far as the indispensability requirement is concerned it should be noted that the Commission withdrew its interim decision in August 2003 because the situation had changed, in that NDC had succeeded in concluding contracts with some larger pharmaceutical companies and there was no longer a threat that it might be eliminated from the market. The Commission stated that its decision was without prejudice to whether the improvement in NDC's position had been caused by the judgment of the Oberlandesgericht on the copyright.[736] If it was not caused by this it throws doubt on how indispensable the 1860 brick structure was in the first place.

(vi) The *Microsoft* Case

A particular kind of refusal to supply arises in the IT sector in respect of 'interface information'. Providers of software need to be able to make products which operate with other systems and programs. This is known as 'interoperability'. For this they require interface information, i.e.

---

[730] It can be argued that by saying that it was a matter of whether two *stages of production* can be identified the Court was abandoning the requirement of two *markets*: it is enough that there are two *products*. See J. Venit, 'The IP/Antitrust Interface After *IMS Health*', in Ehlermann and Atanasiu (eds.), *European Competition Law Annual 2005* (cited in n. 24), 609, 625.

[731] J. Temple Lang, 'Anti-competitive Non-Pricing Abuses under European and National Antitrust Law' in B. Hawk (ed.) [2003] *Fordham Corp L Inst* 235, 307.

[732] 540 US 398, 124 S.Ct 872.

[733] Moreover *IMS* did not involve leveraging. IMS was not leveraging its dominance from the upstream to the downstream market: see J. Venit, 'The IP/Antitrust Interface After *IMS Health*', in Ehlermann and Atanasiu (eds.), *European Competition Law Annual 2005* (cited in n. 24).

[734] And see F. Fine, '*NDC/IMS*: A Logical Application of the Essential Facilities Doctrine' [2002] *ECLR* 457; F. Fine, '*NDC/IMS*: In Response to Professor Korah' (2002) 70 *Antitrust LJ* 247.

[735] See, e.g., M. Delrahim, 'Forcing Firms to Share the Sandbox: Compulsory Licensing of Intellectual Property Rights and Antitrust', BIICL conference, 10 May 2004, available at <http://www.usdoj.gov/atr/public/speeches/203627.htm> (Delrahim was at the time US Deputy Assistant Attorney General, DOJ Antitrust Division).

[736] See Section 12.C.v.a, p. 532.

information about the systems and programs of other producers with which they want their products to be compatible and usable. This information may be protected by IPRs (copyright). It may be obtainable by decompilation (reverse engineering) but this can be impossible or not practically or economically feasible.[737] Where there is a dominant undertaking on a software market it may be essential to the competitive viability of other providers that their products are compatible with those of that undertaking.

The Commission first addressed this issue in 1984 when it dealt with a number of IBM's practices.[738] It alleged that IBM had abused its dominant position by failing to supply other manufacturers with interface information needed to make competitive products work with IBM's System/370. The Commission and IBM reached a settlement by which IBM, while not admitting the existence of a dominant position or any abuse thereof, undertook to disclose sufficient interface information to enable competitors in the EEC to attach hardware and software products of their own design to System/370.[739]

The Commission began investigating Microsoft in 1998 after Sun Microsystems lodged a complaint. Microsoft had over 90 per cent of the PC operating systems market and the Commission described this as approaching a near monopoly and Microsoft as being in an 'overwhelmingly dominant position'.[740] Sun complained that Microsoft refused to disclose to Sun (and others) who provided server operating systems sufficient interface information to enable them to create 'workgroup server operating systems' (WGOS) that would operate satisfactorily with Microsoft's Windows desktop and server operating systems. Microsoft had previously supplied full interoperability information to producers of servers but cut it back after it entered that market itself. Five years and three statements of objections after the investigation began the Commission held that Microsoft held a dominant position on both the client PC operating systems market and the WGOS market and that it had committed an abuse by refusing to supply the interface information. The Commission fined Microsoft €497,196,304[741] and ordered that within 120 days it should make the relevant information available to undertakings on the WGOS market and should ensure that the information was kept updated on an ongoing basis and in a timely manner.[742]

In the decision the Commission examined whether the *Bronner* and *Magill*[743] criteria were fulfilled, although it noted that it was 'of interest' that this was a case (unlike *Bronner* and *Magill*) of the disruption of previous levels of supply.[744] It held that the criteria were fulfilled. In doing so the Commission followed the 'effects-based' approach to the application of Article 102 which it set out the following year in the Discussion Paper. It examined the facts closely, identified effects on consumers, and considered the issues of incentives to innovation.

The Commission found that the information was indispensable by adopting a two-stage approach. First, it considered what degree of interoperability with Windows non-Microsoft WGOS required in order for the competitors to be able to remain viably on the market and secondly it appraised whether the information that Microsoft refused to disclose was indispensable to attaining that. On

---

[737] For the arguments about the possibilities of reverse engineering in *Microsoft*, see text at n. 745.

[738] For the tying aspects, see Section 11.E.iii, p. 493.

[739] See *XIVth Report on Competition Policy* (Commission, 1984) parts. 94–95.

[740] *Microsoft*, Commission Decision COMP/C-3/37.792, [2005] 4 CMLR 965, para. 435.

[741] The fine was also in respect of the abuse Microsoft had committed in tying its media player to Windows, see Section 11.E.iii, p. 493.

[742] To be enforced by the appointment of a 'monitoring trustee' to ensure that the disclosures are complete and accurate. For the issue of the monitoring trustee see Chap. 13, Section 8.D.ii.b, p. 981. The dispute between the Commission and Microsoft as to whether Microsoft was complying with the obligation to supply the information on fair and reasonable terms led to a further decision imposing a periodic penalty payment on Microsoft, upheld by the GC, Case T-167/08, *Microsoft* v. *Commission*, 27 June 2012, see Section 15.A, p. 580.

[743] The decision was adopted a month before the judgment of the CJ in Case C-418/01, *IMS* v. *NDC* [2004] ECR I-5039.

[744] i.e. like *Commercial Solvents* and *Télémarketing*: *Microsoft Decision*, para. 556.

the basis of customer surveys the Commission found that although the competitors' systems had features and functionalities which customers preferred to those of Microsoft's this was trumped by the attraction of full interoperability with Windows. It concluded that the competitors' systems had to be able to interoperate with Windows on an equal footing with Microsoft's own systems if they were to compete viably with them and that this was not possible without the information Microsoft refused to disclose. There were no substitutes for disclosure by Microsoft. Microsoft argued, inter alia, that reverse engineering was a means of its competitors accessing the information but the Commission held that reverse engineering programs such as Windows required 'considerable efforts with uncertain chances of success'[745] and that the viability of products produced by reverse engineering depended on Microsoft not breaking the compatibility (for instance by upgrading the operating system): '[r]everse engineering is therefore an unstable basis for a business model'.[746] The Commission held, with regard to the criteria of the elimination of competition, that the refusal to supply put Microsoft's competitors 'at a strong competitive disadvantage...to an extent where there is a *risk* of elimination of competition' (emphasis added).[747] This would impact on technical development to the prejudice of consumers contrary to Article 102(b)[748] because the competitors would, at best, be confined to niche existences and there would be little scope for innovation,[749] while Microsoft's incentives to innovate would be diminished by the disappearance of its competitors.[750] The Commission rejected Microsoft's plea that the refusal to supply was justified by the fact that the information was protected by IPRs and that forced disclosure would lessen its incentives to innovate. Even if there was such a disincentive the Commission held that 'the possible negative impact of an order to supply on Microsoft's incentives to innovate is outweighed by its positive impact on the level on innovation of the whole industry (including Microsoft)'.[751]

The *Microsoft* decision stretched the *Magill* criteria. For example, the Commission held not that the refusal prevented the appearance of a specific new product but rather that 'technical development' would be limited. The Commission therefore hedged its bets. In case the Microsoft situation did not satisfy the principles laid down in the previous cases it argued that there was no 'exhaustive check-list' of exceptional circumstances and that it could have regard to other circumstances that deserved to be taken into account, i.e. a refusal to supply should be examined on a case-by-case basis so that refusal that did not fit exactly within the *Bronner* or *Magill* criteria could still be an abuse.[752]

Before the GC the Commission argued that it was entitled to take account of all the particular circumstances surrounding the refusal and identified three particular characteristics in this case: i) the information related to interoperability, 'a matter to which the Community legislature attaches particular importance'; ii) Microsoft was using its 'extraordinary power' on one market to eliminate competition on an adjacent market; and iii) the case involved the disruption of previous levels of supply.[753] The GC examined first whether the Commission was justified in finding that the highest standard—the *Magill/IMS* exceptional circumstances test—was satisfied and, having decided that it was, upheld the Commission decision without expressly considering the position had it not

---

[745] *Microsoft* decision, para. 685.

[746] *Microsoft* decision, para. 686.

[747] *Microsoft* decision, para. 589.

[748] *Microsoft* decision, paras. 693–701.

[749] *Microsoft* decision, para. 700.

[750] *Microsoft* decision, para. 725.

[751] *Microsoft* decision, para. 783.

[752] *Microsoft* decision, para. 555. In the Staff Discussion Paper of 2005 the Commission reinforced this argument by placing interoperability in a separate category of refusal to supply. It said that 'it may not be appropriate to apply to such refusals to supply information the same high standards for intervention as those described in the previous subsections' (which set out the principles derived from the previous cases, by that time including *IMS*): Discussion Paper, paras. 271–272.

[753] Case T-201/04, *Microsoft v. Commission* [2007] ECR II-3601, paras. 316–317.

been.[754] However, the GC had to give an expansive interpretation of the criteria in the case law in order to do this and it might have been preferable had it seized the opportunity to consider the other relevant special circumstances put forward by the Commission.[755]

It is necessary, when looking at the GC's judgment, to note the standard of review it adopted.[756] The GC said that the 'review of complex economic appraisals made by the Commission is necessarily limited to checking whether the relevant rules on procedure and on stating reasons have been complied with, whether the facts have been accurately stated and whether there has been any manifest error of assessment or a misuse of powers…'. The 'manifest error' standard is particularly relevant in *Microsoft* where the Commission was making predictions about the elimination of competition and the effects on innovation rather than judging past events.

In respect of the *Magill/IMS* criteria the GC reiterated what was said in *IMS*, i.e. that in order for a refusal to supply to be abusive on the grounds that it denies access to an indispensable product or service two markets must be involved but the upstream market may merely be 'hypothetical'.[757] It examined the Commission decision in the light of the four conditions established in the case law: indispensability; elimination of competition; new product; no objective justification, and upheld it.

Case T-201/04 *Microsoft* v. *Commission* [2007] ECR II-3601

General Court

332 It also follows from that case-law that the following circumstances, in particular, must be considered to be exceptional:

- in the first place, the refusal relates to a product or service indispensable to the exercise of a particular activity on a neighbouring market;

- in the second place, the refusal is of such a kind as to exclude any effective competition on that neighbouring market;

- in the third place, the refusal prevents the appearance of a new product for which there is potential consumer demand.

333 Once it is established that such circumstances are present, the refusal by the holder of a dominant position to grant a licence may infringe Article [102] unless the refusal is objectively justified.

334 The Court notes that the circumstance that the refusal prevents the appearance of a new product for which there is potential consumer demand is found only in the case-law on the exercise of an intellectual property right.

335 Finally, it is appropriate to add that, in order that a refusal to give access to a product or service indispensable to the exercise of a particular activity may be considered abusive, it is necessary to distinguish two markets, namely, a market constituted by that product or service and on which the undertaking refusing to supply holds a dominant position and a neighbouring market on which the product or service is used in the manufacture of another product or for the supply of another service. The fact that the indispensable product or service is not marketed separately does not exclude from the outset the possibility of identifying a separate market (see, to that effect, *IMS Health*…paragraph 43). Thus, the Court of Justice

---

[754] Case T-201/04, *Microsoft* v. *Commission* [2007] ECR II-3601, para. 712.

[755] See P. Larouche, 'The European Microsoft Case at the Crossroads of Competition Policy and Innovation: Comment on Ahlborn and Evans' (2008–2009) 75 *Antitrust LJ* 933, 959.

[756] For the standard of review and the standard of proof generally, see Chap. 5, Section 4.B.v, p. 274.

[757] *IMS*, paras. 43–44.

held, at paragraph 44 of *IMS Health*…that it was sufficient that a potential market or even a hypothetical market could be identified and that such was the case where the products or services were indispensable to the conduct of a particular business activity and where there was an actual demand for them on the part of undertakings which sought to carry on that business. The Court of Justice concluded at the following paragraph of the judgment that it was decisive that two different stages of production were identified and that they were interconnected in that the upstream product was indispensable for supply of the down-stream product.

336 In the light of the foregoing factors, the Court considers that it is appropriate, first of all, to decide whether the circumstances identified in *Magill* and *IMS Health*…as described at paragraphs 332 and 333 above, are also present in this case. Only if it finds that one or more of those circumstances are absent will the Court proceed to assess the particular circumstances invoked by the Commission…

On the indispensability condition the GC confirmed the Commission's approach to finding indispensability through the two-fold test described, and its conclusion was that the test was satisfied.[758] On the other conditions it concluded as follows.

Case T-201/04 *Microsoft* v. *Commission* [2007] ECR II-3601

General Court

Elimination of competition

– The applicable criterion

560 In the contested decision, the Commission considered whether the refusal at issue gave rise to a 'risk' of the elimination of competition on the work group server operating systems market (recitals 585, 589, 610, 622, 626, 631, 636, 653, 691, 692, 712, 725, 781, 992 and 1070 to the contested decision). Microsoft contends that that criterion is not sufficiently strict, since according to the case-law on the exercise of an intellectual property right the Commission must demonstrate that the refusal to license an intellectual property right to a third party is 'likely to eliminate all competition', or, in other words, that there is a 'high probability' that the conduct in question will have such a result.

561 The Court finds that Microsoft's complaint is purely one of terminology and is wholly irrelevant. The expressions 'risk of elimination of competition' and 'likely to eliminate competition' are used without distinction by the Community judicature to reflect the same idea, namely that Article [102] does not apply only from the time when there is no more, or practically no more, competition on the market. If the Commission were required to wait until competitors were eliminated from the market, or until their elimination was sufficiently imminent, before being able to take action under Article [102], that would clearly run counter to the objective of that provision, which is to maintain undistorted competition in the common market and, in particular, to safeguard the competition that still exists on the relevant market.

562 In this case, the Commission had all the more reason to apply Article [102] before the elimination of competition on the work group server operating systems market had become a reality because that market is characterised by significant network effects and because the elimination of competition would therefore be difficult to reverse (see recitals 515 to 522 and 533 to the contested decision).

563 Nor is it necessary to demonstrate that all competition on the market would be eliminated. What matters, for the purpose of establishing an infringement of Article [102], is that the refusal at issue is liable to, or is likely to, eliminate all effective competition on the market. It must be made clear that the fact that the competitors of the dominant undertaking retain a marginal presence in certain niches on the market cannot suffice to substantiate the existence of such competition.

[758] Case T-210/04, *Microsoft*, paras. 369–436.

564 Last, it must be borne in mind that it is for the Commission to establish that the refusal to supply gives rise to a risk of the elimination of all effective competition. As already stated at paragraph 482 above, the Commission must base its assessment on accurate, reliable and coherent evidence which comprises all the relevant data that must be taken into consideration in order to assess a complex situation and which are capable of substantiating the conclusions drawn from them.

...The new product

643 It must be emphasised that the fact that the applicant's conduct prevents the appearance of a new product on the market falls to be considered under Article [102(b)]...which prohibits abusive practices which consist in 'limiting production, markets or technical developments to the...prejudice of consumers'.

644 Thus, at paragraph 54 of *Magill*...the Court of Justice held that the refusal by the broadcasting companies concerned had to be characterised as abusive within the meaning of that provision because it prevented the appearance of a new product which the broadcasting companies did not offer and for which there was a potential consumer demand.

645 It is apparent from the decision at issue in that case that the Commission had, more specifically, considered that by their refusal, the broadcasting companies limited production or markets to the prejudice of consumers (see the first paragraph of recital 23 to Commission Decision 89/205/EEC...*Magill TV Guide/ITP, BBC and RTE*...). The Commission had found that that refusal prevented publishers from producing and publishing a weekly television guide for consumers in Ireland and Northern Ireland, a type of guide not then available on that geographic market. Although each of the broadcasting companies concerned published a weekly television guide, each guide was devoted to that particular broadcaster's own programmes. In finding an abuse of a dominant position by those broadcasting companies, the Commission had emphasised the harm which the absence of a general weekly television guide on the market in Ireland and in Northern Ireland caused to consumers, who, if they wished to know what programmes were being offered in the coming week, had no alternative to buying the weekly guides of each channel and themselves extracting the relevant information in order to make comparisons.

646 In *IMS Health*...the Court of Justice, when assessing the circumstance relating to the appearance of a new product, also placed that circumstance in the context of the damage to the interests of consumers. Thus, at paragraph 48 of that judgment, the Court emphasised, with reference to the Opinion of Advocate General Tizzano in that case...that that circumstance related to the consideration that, in the balancing of the interest in protection of the intellectual property right and the economic freedom of its owner against the interest in protection of free competition, the latter can prevail only where refusal to grant a licence prevents the development of the secondary market, to the detriment of consumers.

647 The circumstance relating to the appearance of a new product, as envisaged in *Magill* and *IMS Health*...cannot be the only parameter which determines whether a refusal to license an intellectual property right is capable of causing prejudice to consumers within the meaning of Article [102(b)]...As that provision states, such prejudice may arise where there is a limitation not only of production or markets, but also of technical development.

648 It was on that last hypothesis that the Commission based its finding in the contested decision. Thus, the Commission considered that Microsoft's refusal to supply the relevant information limited technical development to the prejudice of consumers within the meaning of Article [102(b)]...(recitals 693 to 701 and 782 to the contested decision) and it rejected Microsoft's assertion that it had not been demonstrated that its refusal caused prejudice to consumers (recitals 702 to 708 to the contested decision).

649 The Court finds that the Commission's findings at the recitals referred to in the preceding paragraph are not manifestly incorrect.

650 Thus, in the first place, the Commission was correct to observe, at recital 694 to the contested decision, that '[owing] to the lack of interoperability that competing work group server operating system

products can achieve with the Windows domain architecture, an increasing number of consumers are locked into a homogeneous Windows solution at the level of work group server operating systems'.

651 It must be borne in mind that it has already been stated at paragraphs 371 to 422 above that Microsoft's refusal prevented its competitors from developing work group server operating systems capable of attaining a sufficient degree of interoperability with the Windows domain architecture, with the consequence that consumers' purchasing decisions in respect of work group server operating systems were channelled towards Microsoft's products...

652 The limitation thus placed on consumer choice is all the more damaging to consumers because, as already observed at paragraphs 407 to 412 above, they consider that non-Microsoft work group server operating systems are better than Windows work group server operating systems with respect to a series of features to which they attach great importance, such as 'reliability/availability of the...system' and 'security included with the server operating system'.

653 In the second place, the Commission was correct to consider that the artificial advantage in terms of interoperability that Microsoft retained by its refusal discouraged its competitors from developing and marketing work group server operating systems with innovative features, to the prejudice, notably, of consumers (see, to that effect, recital 694 to the contested decision). That refusal has the consequence that those competitors are placed at a disadvantage by comparison with Microsoft so far as the merits of their products are concerned, particularly with regard to parameters such as security, reliability, ease of use or operating performance speed (recital 699 to the contested decision).

654 The Commission's finding that '[i]f Microsoft's competitors had access to the interoperability information that Microsoft refuses to supply, they could use the disclosures to make the advanced features of their own products available in the framework of the web of interoperability relationships that underpin the Windows domain architecture' (recital 695 to the contested decision) is corroborated by the conduct which those competitors had adopted in the past, when they had access to certain information concerning Microsoft's products...

655 The Commission was careful to emphasise, in that context, that there was 'ample scope for differentiation and innovation beyond the design of interface specifications' (recital 698 to the contested decision). In other words, the same specification can be implemented in numerous different and innovative ways by software designers.

656 Thus, the contested decision rests on the concept that, once the obstacle represented for Microsoft's competitors by the insufficient degree of interoperability with the Windows domain architecture has been removed, those competitors will be able to offer work group server operating systems which, far from merely reproducing the Windows systems already on the market, will be distinguished from those systems with respect to parameters which consumers consider important (see, to that effect, recital 699 to the contested decision).

...

658 Nor would Microsoft's competitors have any interest in merely reproducing Windows work group server operating systems. Once they are able to use the information communicated to them to develop systems that are sufficiently interoperable with the Windows domain architecture, they will have no other choice, if they wish to take advantage of a competitive advantage over Microsoft and maintain a profitable presence on the market, than to differentiate their products from Microsoft's products with respect to certain parameters and certain features. It must be borne in mind that, as the Commission explains at recitals 719 to 721 to the contested decision, the implementation of specifications is a difficult task which requires significant investment in money and time

659 Last, Microsoft's argument that it will have less incentive to develop a given technology if it is required to make that technology available to its competitors (see paragraph 627 above) is of no relevance to the examination of the circumstance relating to the new product, where the issue to be decided is the impact of the refusal to supply on the incentive for Microsoft's competitors to innovate and not on

Microsoft's incentives to innovate. That is an issue which will be decided when the Court examines the circumstance relating to the absence of objective justification.

660 In the third place, the Commission is also correct to reject as unfounded Microsoft's assertion during the administrative procedure that it was not demonstrated that its refusal caused prejudice to consumers (recitals 702 to 708 to the contested decision).

661 First of all, as has already been observed at paragraphs 407 to 412 above... contrary to Microsoft's contention, consumers consider non-Microsoft work group server operating systems to be better than Windows work group server operating systems on a number of features to which they attach great importance.

662 Next, Microsoft cannot rely on the fact that consumers never claimed at any time during the administrative procedure that they had been forced to adopt a Windows work group server operating system as a consequence of its refusal to disclose interoperability information to its competitors. In that connection, it is sufficient to point out that Microsoft does not dispute the Commission's findings at recitals 705 and 706 to the contested decision. Thus, at recital 705 to the contested decision, the Commission observes that it is developers of complementary software required to interoperate with Microsoft's systems who 'depend on the interface information' and that '[c]ustomers will not always exactly know what is disclosed by Microsoft to other work group operating system vendors and what is not'. At recital 706 to the contested decision, the Commission states '[w]hen confronted with a "choice" between putting up with interoperability problems that render their business processes cumbersome, inefficient and costly, and embracing a homogeneous Windows solution for their work group network, customers will tend to opt for the latter proposition' and that '[o]nce they have standardised on Windows, they are unlikely to report interoperability problems between their client PCs and the work group servers'.

663 Furthermore, Microsoft's own statements concerning the disclosures made under the United States settlement show that those disclosures had the consequence of offering greater choice to consumers (see recital 703 to the contested decision).

664 Last, it must be borne in mind that it is settled case-law that Article [102]... covers not only practices which may prejudice consumers directly but also those which indirectly prejudice them by impairing an effective competitive structure (Case 85/76 *Hoffmann-La Roche v Commission*... paragraph 125, and *Irish Sugar v Commission*... paragraph 232). In this case, Microsoft impaired the effective competitive structure on the work group server operating systems market by acquiring a significant market share on that market.

665 The Court concludes from all of the foregoing considerations that the Commission's finding to the effect that Microsoft's refusal limits technical development to the prejudice of consumers within the meaning of Article [102(b)]... is not manifestly incorrect. The Court therefore finds that the circumstance relating to the appearance of a new product is present in this case.

... The absence of objective justification

688 The Court notes, as a preliminary point, that although the burden of proof of the existence of the circumstances that constitute an infringement of Article [102]... is borne by the Commission, it is for the dominant undertaking concerned, and not for the Commission, before the end of the administrative procedure, to raise any plea of objective justification and to support it with arguments and evidence. It then falls to the Commission, where it proposes to make a finding of an abuse of a dominant position, to show that the arguments and evidence relied on by the undertaking cannot prevail and, accordingly, that the justification put forward cannot be accepted.

689 In the present case, as the Commission found at recital 709 to the contested decision and as Microsoft expressly confirmed in the application, Microsoft relied as justification for its conduct solely on the fact that the technology concerned was covered by intellectual property rights. It made clear that if it were required to grant third parties access to that technology, that 'would... eliminate future incentives to invest in the creation of more intellectual property' (recital 709 to the contested decision). In the reply,

the applicant also relied on that fact that the technology was secret and valuable and that it contained important innovations.

690 The Court considers that, even on the assumption that it is correct, the fact that the communication protocols covered by the contested decision, or the specifications for those protocols, are covered by intellectual property rights cannot constitute objective justification within the meaning of *Magill* and *IMS Health*…Microsoft's argument is inconsistent with the raison d'être of the exception which that case-law thus recognises in favour of free competition, since if the mere fact of holding intellectual property rights could in itself constitute objective justification for the refusal to grant a licence, the exception established by the case-law could never apply. In other words, a refusal to license an intellectual property right could never be considered to constitute an infringement of Article [102] even though in *Magill* and *IMS Health*…above, the Court of Justice specifically stated the contrary.

691 It must be borne in mind that, as stated at paragraphs 321, 323, 327 and 330 above, the Community judicature considers that the fact that the holder of an intellectual property right can exploit that right solely for his own benefit constitutes the very substance of his exclusive right. Accordingly, a simple refusal, even on the part of an undertaking in a dominant position, to grant a licence to a third party cannot in itself constitute an abuse of a dominant position within the meaning of Article [102]…It is only when it is accompanied by exceptional circumstances such as those hitherto envisaged in the case-law that such a refusal can be characterised as abusive and that, accordingly, it is permissible, in the public interest in maintaining effective competition on the market, to encroach upon the exclusive right of the holder of the intellectual property right by requiring him to grant licences to third parties seeking to enter or remain on that market. It must be borne in mind that it has been established above that such exceptional circumstances were present in this case.

692 The argument which Microsoft puts forward in the reply, namely that the technology concerned is secret and of great value to the licensees and contains important innovations, cannot succeed either.

693 First, the fact that the technology concerned is secret is the consequence of a unilateral business decision on Microsoft's part. Furthermore, Microsoft cannot rely on the argument that the interoperability information is secret as a ground for not being required to disclose it unless the exceptional circumstances identified by the Court of Justice in *Magill* and *IMS Health*, above, are present, and at the same time justify its refusal by what it alleges to be the secret nature of the information. Last, there is no reason why secret technology should enjoy a higher level of protection than, for example, technology which has necessarily been disclosed to the public by its inventor in a patent-application procedure.

694 Second, from the moment at which it is established that—as in this case—the interoperability information is indispensable, that information is necessarily of great value to the competitors who wish to have access to it.

695 Third, it is inherent in the fact that the undertaking concerned holds an intellectual property right that the subject-matter of that right is innovative or original. There can be no patent without an invention and no copyright without an original work.

696 The Court further observes that in the contested decision the Commission did not simply reject Microsoft's assertion that the fact that the technology concerned was covered by intellectual property rights justified its refusal to disclose the relevant information. The Commission also examined the applicant's argument that if it were required to give third parties access to that technology there would be a negative impact on its incentives to innovate (recitals 709 and 712 to the contested decision).

697 The Court finds that, as the Commission correctly submits, Microsoft, which bore the initial burden of proof (see paragraph 688 above), did not sufficiently establish that if it were required to disclose the interoperability information that would have a significant negative impact on its incentives to innovate.

698 Microsoft merely put forward vague, general and theoretical arguments on that point. Thus, as the Commission observes at recital 709 to the contested decision, in its response of 17 October 2003 to the third statement of objections Microsoft merely stated that '[d]isclosure would…eliminate future incentives

to invest in the creation of more intellectual property', without specifying the technologies or products to which it thus referred.

699 In certain passages in the response referred to in the preceding paragraph, Microsoft envisages a negative impact on its incentives to innovate by reference to its operating systems in general, namely both those for client PCs and those for servers.

700 In that regard, it is sufficient to note that, at recitals 713 to 729 to the contested decision, the Commission quite correctly refuted Microsoft's arguments relating to the fear that its products would be cloned. It must be borne in mind, in particular, that the remedy prescribed in Article 5 of the contested decision does not, and is not designed to, allow Microsoft's competitors to copy its products (see paragraphs 198 to 206, 240 to 242 and 656 to 658 above).

701 It follows that it has not been demonstrated that the disclosure of the information to which that remedy relates will significantly reduce—still less eliminate—Microsoft's incentives to innovate.

702 In that context, the Court observes that, as the Commission correctly finds at recitals 730 to 734 to the contested decision, it is normal practice for operators in the industry to disclose to third parties the information which will facilitate interoperability with their products and Microsoft itself had followed that practice until it was sufficiently established on the work group server operating systems market. Such disclosure allows the operators concerned to make their own products more attractive and therefore more valuable. In fact, none of the parties has claimed in the present case that such disclosure had had any negative impact on those operators' incentives to innovate.

...

704 Last, the Court finds that Microsoft's assertion that in the contested decision the Commission applied a new evaluation test when rejecting the objective justification which Microsoft had submitted is based on a misreading of that decision.

705 That assertion is based on a single sentence in recital 783 to the contested decision, which is in a part of that decision containing the findings of the Commission's analysis, at recitals 560 to 778, of the refusal at issue.

706 That sentence reads as follows:

'[A] detailed examination of the scope of the disclosure at stake leads to the conclusion that, on balance, the possible negative impact of an order to supply on Microsoft's incentives to innovate is outweighed by its positive impact on the level of innovation of the whole industry (including Microsoft)'.

707 However, that sentence must be read in conjunction with the one coming immediately afterwards in the same recital, which states that '...the need to protect Microsoft's incentives to innovate cannot constitute an objective justification that would offset the exceptional circumstances identified'.

708 It must also be compared with recital 712 to the contested decision, where the Commission sets out the following considerations:

'It has been established above...that Microsoft's refusal to supply [creates a risk of elimination of] competition in the relevant market for work group server operating systems, that this is due to the fact that the refused input is indispensable to carry on business in that market and that Microsoft's refusal has a negative impact on technical development to the prejudice of consumers. In view of these exceptional circumstances, Microsoft's refusal cannot be objectively justified merely by the fact that it constitutes a refusal to license intellectual property. It is therefore necessary to assess whether Microsoft's arguments regarding its incentives to innovate outweigh these exceptional circumstances.'

709 In other words, in accordance with the principles laid down in the case-law...the Commission, after establishing that the exceptional circumstances identified by the Court of Justice in *Magill* and *IMS Health*...were present in this case, then proceeded to consider whether the justification put forward by Microsoft, on the basis of the alleged impact on its incentives to innovate, might prevail over those exceptional circumstances, including the circumstance that the refusal at issue limited technical development to the prejudice of consumers within the meaning of Article [102(b)]...

710 The Commission came to a negative conclusion but not by balancing the negative impact which the imposition of a requirement to supply the information at issue might have on Microsoft's incentives to innovate against the positive impact of that obligation on innovation in the industry as a whole, but after refuting Microsoft's arguments relating to the fear that its products might be cloned (recitals 713 to 729 to the contested decision), establishing that the disclosure of interoperability was widespread in the industry concerned (recitals 730 to 735 to the contested decision) and showing that IBM's commitment to the Commission in 1984 was not substantially different from what Microsoft was ordered to do in the contested decision (recitals 736 to 742 to the contested decision) and that its approach was consistent with Directive 91/250 (recitals 743 to 763 to the contested decision).

711 It follows from all of the foregoing considerations that Microsoft has not demonstrated the existence of any objective justification for its refusal to disclose the interoperability at issue.

712 As the exceptional circumstances identified by the Court of Justice in *Magill* and *IMS Health*... were also present in this case, the first part of the plea must be rejected as wholly unfounded.

Before looking at any other aspects of this part of the *Microsoft* judgment it is worth noting the strange statement in paragraph 664 where the GC says, when repeating yet again that Article 102 covers practices that impair the 'competitive structure', that Microsoft 'impaired the effective competitive structure on the work group server operating systems market by acquiring a significant market share on that market'. This comes dangerously near to suggesting that it is an abuse simply to acquire the dominant position.

As seen from the preceding extracts of the judgment, the GC upheld the Commission decision on the basis that the *Magill/IMS* exceptional circumstances were present. In doing so the GC gave an elastic interpretation to those exceptional circumstances. It should also be noted that the GC did not confine its statements to copyrights.

- *Indispensability*. The GC upheld the Commission's finding that it was indispensable for the competitors' systems to work as seamlessly with Windows as Microsoft's own products[759] even though a fringe of competitors unable to do so were operating on the market. The interface information might have been greatly more convenient for the competitors, but they *were* functioning without it. Indispensability in *Microsoft* did not mean exclusion from the market.[760]

- *Elimination of competition*. First, the GC interpreted this requirement as meaning the elimination of *effective* competition on the downstream market (paragraph 563). The continued existence of fringe competitors in niche markets was irrelevant. Secondly, the GC was content that the Commission should demonstrate merely a 'risk' of the elimination of effective competition and accepted that the Commission did not have to wait for the elimination of competition before it could act. It dismissed as semantics all Microsoft's arguments about a difference between 'risk', 'likely to', and 'high probability' (paragraphs 560–561) despite the oft-quoted plea of a Microsoft lawyer at the hearing that there is a world of difference between a risk of getting bird flu and the likelihood of getting it.[761] Unlike *Magill* where the potential entrant was entirely excluded from the market because of the refusal to supply, the competitors in *Microsoft* were on the market but might leave it, or become marginalised, at some future time as a result of Microsoft's conduct. This all involved speculation as to how the (constantly evolving, high technology) market

---

[759] The Commission explained further at the hearing that this included a non-Windows WGOS being able to 'talk' to a Microsoft WGOS just as if it were itself a Microsoft WGOS: *Microsoft* decision, para. 237.

[760] See D. Ridyard, 'Compulsory Access under EC Competition Law—A New Doctrine of –"Convenient Facilities" and the Case for Price Regulation' [2004] *ECLR* 670.

[761] Said on Day Three of the *Microsoft* hearing, 26 April 2009, Ahlborn and Evans, 'The *Microsoft* Judgment and its Implications for Competition Policy Towards Dominant Firms in Europe' (cited in n. 587), 927; D. Beard, '*Microsoft*: What Sort of Landmark' (2008) 4 *Competition Policy Int'l* 39.

would develop in the future. As has been pointed out, this is akin to the kind of prediction that is undertaken in merger cases, where the EU Courts have held the Commission to a rigorous standard of proof.[762] In *Microsoft*, however, the GC was happy that the Commission had established a 'risk' based on accurate, reliable, and coherent evidence.[763] Furthermore, it has been pointed out that in Article 102 cases which may take years to reach the GC (over three in *Microsoft*) any 'risk' foreseen by the Commission at the time of the decision may or may not have materialised to a greater or lesser extent. The problem is then how far the Court could employ the benefit of hindsight, given the limitations of its judicial review jurisdiction.[764]

- A '*new product*'. The GC said that the Commission had not made a manifest error in failing to identify a specific new product for which there was actual or potential consumer demand whose emergence was prevented by the refusal to supply. It was enough that the refusal limited 'technical developments to the prejudice of consumers' within Article 102(b). After *IMS* there had been much discussion about what constituted a product 'new' enough to satisfy that limb of the test. However, having noted that in *IMS* itself the CJ was concerned about refusals which prevented the development of the secondary market to the detriment of consumers,[765] the GC said that the appearance of a 'new product' was not the only relevant parameter (paragraphs 646–647). It noted that Article 102(b) applies to the limitation of technical development as well as production and markets. Accordingly the Commission was correct in considering that the test included (as yet unspecified and unknown) products emerging from innovation by the competitors which would not occur if the competitors left the market and/or were unable to develop products fully compatible with Windows. The lack of interoperability meant that consumers were increasingly locked into Windows WGOS (paragraph 650). The GC also agreed with the Commission's view that the competitors would not have any interest in just 'cloning' Microsoft's products but had every reason to develop differentiated products (paragraph 658). However, it has been argued that mere cloning could be profitable for competitors if they could compete with Microsoft on price.[766] Notably (paragraph 659), Microsoft's argument that it would have less incentive to develop new technology if it were required to divulge it to competitors was held by the GC to be irrelevant to the 'new product' circumstance which was concerned only with the *competitors'* incentives to innovate (Microsoft's incentives were considered an objective justification issue).

It is important to remember that *Microsoft* was a case of the disruption of previous supply. Given that the competitors were already on the market the limitation of technical development stemming from the refusal to supply could be seen. The change of 'new product' to 'limitation of technical development' in a case where a new entrant is asking for access would be a step further.[767]

In dealing with Microsoft's plea of objective justification the GC provided clarification of how the defence actually works (paragraph 688). The case itself, however, demonstrates how difficult it is to separate out objective justification from the initial finding of abuse (see paragraph 659 of the judgment). The GC rejected Microsoft's plea that the fact that the information was covered by IPRs justified its refusal to disclose, on the grounds that it would lead to the conclusion that a refusal to license could never be an abuse. It also rejected Microsoft's pleas that disclosure would have a negative impact on its incentives to innovate, dismissing them as 'vague and theoretical arguments'

---

[762] See Beard, '*Microsoft*: What Sort of Landmark' (cited in n. 761), 42–43; for mergers, see Chap. 15.

[763] *Microsoft* decision, paras. 564, 620.

[764] See further on this, Beard, '*Microsoft*: What Sort of Landmark' (2008) 4 *Competition Policy Int'l* (cited in n. 761) 47.

[765] *IMS*, para. 48.

[766] D. Howarth and K. McMahon, '"Windows has performed an Illegal Operation": The Court of First Instance's Judgment in Microsoft v Commission' [2008] *ECLR* 117 at 124.

[767] See S. Anderman, 'The Epithet That Dares Not Speak its Name: The Essential Facilities Concept in Article 82 EC and IPRs after the *Microsoft* Case' in Ezrachi (ed.), *Article 82 EC: Reflections on its Recent Evolution* (cited in n. 32), 87, 94–96.

which did not specify the technologies or products concerned (paragraph 698). The judgment suggests, therefore, that the defence might succeed if a greater level of detail were given. However, in paragraph 696 the GC puts the burden of proof on the dominant undertaking to demonstrate that its incentives would be harmed by compulsory licensing and, especially where (as here) the evolution of high technology markets is involved, it is questionable whether it would ever be possible to discharge that burden. The GC's judgment on this point should also be contrasted to its willingness to accept, without similar specificity, the claims about 'technical development' being limited and assuming that the refusal to deal will lead to consumer harm. One curious point on objective justification is the GC's treatment of the Commission's statement that that the positive impact on the industry as a whole outweighed the negative impact on Microsoft's incentives.[768] Microsoft argued before the GC that this introduced a whole new test into the application of Article 102,[769] and the GC's attempt to try to explain away what the Commission was saying is unconvincing (paragraphs 705–710).[770] From the efficiencies point of view it can be argued that the Commission was correct[771] although it is also said that balancing tests are 'an inherently unreliable and unpredictable method to address mandatory access cases'.[772]

As with the tying part of the judgment,[773] *Microsoft* is significant not only in respect of the substantive law on refusal to supply and IPRs but also in the context of the 'modernisation' of Article 102 and the Commission's review. There are a number of interesting aspects of the GC's reasoning, and the judgment has been criticised for following a 'form-based' analysis, although this is less pronounced here than in respect of the tying issue. First, the GC concentrated on looking at the position of the competitors and stressed the fall in their market share and the rise in Microsoft's (for example, paragraph 428). Secondly, it emphasised the disadvantage to the competitors and deduced consumer prejudice from that. Thirdly, as already noted, the GC in paragraph 664 repeated that Article 102 is concerned with the impairment of the competitive structure, but said that Microsoft had done that by acquiring a significant market share on the market and did not explain how it led to consumer detriment in this case.

The GC is also criticised for failing to engage sufficiently with the implications of networks effects. One American commentator has suggested that the GC, instead of straining to apply the existing rules, could instead have asked the 'important questions', i.e. i) are consumers and the market seriously disadvantaged by denial of full access to interoperability information and if 'yes', ii) would the respondent and the market be seriously disadvantaged by a duty to grant access?[774]

E. REFUSAL TO SUPPLY IN RESPONSE TO AN ATTACK ON THE DOMINANT UNDERTAKING'S COMMERCIAL INTERESTS

A dominant undertaking may infringe Article 102 by refusing to supply as a disciplinary measure in response to a perceived threat to its commercial interests. In *United Brands* the Commission held

---

[768] *Microsoft* decision, para. 783.

[769] Case T-102/04, *Microsoft v. Commission*, paras. 669–670.

[770] i.e. that if the sentence was read in conjunction with other passages of the decision it was clear that the Commission was considering whether the alleged impact on Microsoft's innovation incentives might prevail over the presence of the exceptional circumstances laid down in *Magill* and *IMS*.

[771] C. Ritter, 'Refusal to Deal and Essential Facilities: Does Intellectual Property Require Special Deference compared to Tangible Property?' (2005) 3 *World Competition* 281, 298.

[772] D. Geradin, 'Limiting the Scope of Article 82 EC: What Can the EU Learn from the Supreme Court's Judgment in *Trinko*, in the Wake of *Microsoft*, *IMS* and *Deutsche Telekom*?' (2004) 41 *CMLRev* 1526, 1542.

[773] See Section 11.E.iii, p. 496 ff.

[774] E. Fox, '*Microsoft* (EC) and Duty to Deal: Exceptionality and the Transatlantic Divide' (2008) 4 *Competition Policy Int'l* 25, 29. The Commission initiated a further investigation in January 2008 for refusing 'to disclose interoperability

that UBC had abused its dominant position on the banana market by refusing to continue supplying its Chiquita bananas to its Danish ripener/distributor, Oelsen, in response to Oelsen taking part in an advertising and promotion campaign for Standard Fruit's 'Dole' bananas. Oelsen was not under an exclusive purchasing obligation but UBC argued that Oelsen had sold fewer and fewer Chiquitas in comparison to Doles, and had taken less trouble in ripening them. Without gainsaying UBC's allegations, the CJ upheld the Commission's finding that the refusal to supply infringed Article 102.

Case 27/76, *United Brands* v. *Commission* [1978] ECR 207

Court of Justice

182. … [i]t is advisable to assert positively from the outset that an undertaking in a dominant position for the purpose of marketing a product—which cashes in on the reputation of a brand name known to and valued by the consumers—cannot stop supplying a long standing customer who abides by regular commercial practice, if the orders placed by that customer are in no way out of the ordinary.

183. Such conduct is inconsistent with the objectives laid down in Article [3(1)(g)] of the Treaty, which are set out in detail in Article [102], especially in paragraphs (b) and (c), since the refusal to sell would limit markets to the prejudice of consumers and would amount to discrimination which might in the end eliminate a trading party from the relevant market.

…

189. Although it is true, as the applicant points out, that the fact that an undertaking is in a dominant position cannot disentitle it from protecting its own commercial interests if they are attacked, and that such an undertaking must be conceded the right to take such reasonable steps as it deems appropriate to protect its said interests, such behaviour cannot be countenanced if its actual purpose is to strengthen this dominant position and abuse it.

190. Even if the possibility of a counter-attack is acceptable that attack must still be proportionate to the threat taking into account the economic strength of the undertakings confronting each other.

191. The sanction consisting of a refusal to supply by an undertaking in a dominant position was in excess of what might, if such a situation were to arise, reasonably be contemplated as a sanction for conduct similar to that for which UBC blamed Oelsen.

192. In fact UBC could not be unaware of that fact that by acting in this way it would discourage its other ripener/distributors from supporting the advertising of other brand names and that the deterrent effect of the sanction imposed upon one of them would make its position of strength on the relevant market that much more effective.

193. Such a course of conduct amounts therefore to a serious interference with the independence of small and medium sized firms in their commercial relations with the undertaking in a dominant position and this independence implies the right to give preference to competitors' goods.

194. In this case the adoption of such a course of conduct is designed to have a serious adverse effect on competition on the relevant banana market by only allowing firms dependant upon the dominant undertaking to stay in business.

195. The applicant's argument that in its view the 40 per cent fall in the price of bananas on the Danish market shows that competition has not been affected by the refusal to supply Oelsen cannot be upheld.

196. In fact this fall in prices was only due to the very lively competition—called at the time the 'banana war'—in which the two transnational companies UBC and Castle and Cooke engaged.

---

information across a broad range of products, including information related to its Office suite, a number of its server products, and also in relation to the so called.NET Framework': MEMO/08/19. In July 2009, the Commission announced that Microsoft had 'made proposals in relation to disclosures of interoperability information that would improve interoperability' between third party products and several Microsoft products: MEMO/09/352.

Whilst affirming that dominant undertakings are justified in acting to prevent attacks on their commercial interests, the CJ nevertheless judged UBC's response to be disproportionate. This was despite recognising that UBC was in the midst of a 'banana war'.[775] It is not clear, given Oelsen's conduct, what the CJ meant when it stated, in paragraph 182, that a dominant undertaking could not stop supplying a regular customer who 'abides by regular commercial practice'[776] but that statement was relied upon by the CJ in its 2008 judgment *Sot. Lélos* on a refusal to supply to prevent parallel trade.[777] The Guidance Paper does not deal with the 'punishment' situation in the refusal to supply section but says that it will apply the exclusive dealing principles to it.[778]

In *Boosey & Hawkes*[779] B&H, which the Commission held to be dominant in the narrowly defined British-style brass band instrument market, refused to have further dealings with two firms, one a distributor of its instruments and the other a repairer, who formed a company to manufacture and market instruments which competed with B&H's. The Commission took interim measures, ordering B&H to recommence supplies to its two customers. Again, the Commission recognised the right of dominant undertakings to protect their interests when attacked but refused to accept that B&H's conduct was justified and proportionate. B&H took the measures to retaliate against its customers for entering into competition with it. Had the new company been successful it could have seriously threatened B&H's position in a highly specialised market. The Commission saw a dominant undertaking trying to exclude others from the market and seemed only reluctantly to admit that in the circumstances 'even a dominant producer is entitled to review its commercial relations'. It shows, like *United Brands*, how seriously a finding of dominance limits an undertaking's conduct. The case is an instance of 'horizontal foreclosure' not involving an upstream/downstream situation and so is not covered by the refusal to supply section in the Guidance Paper.

F. REFUSAL TO SUPPLY AND PARALLEL TRADE

Refusals to supply in order to limit parallel trade are discussed in Section 16 along with other abuses hindering the single market.

G. REFUSAL TO SUPPLY IN THE GUIDANCE PAPER

The Guidance Paper deals with refusals to supply in paragraphs 75–90. It is limited to the situation in which a vertically integrated dominant undertaking competes downstream with a buyer it refuses to supply (see paragraph 77). No other refusal to supply scenarios are dealt with.

The refusal to supply section starts with a statement of the basic principle of freedom to contract with whom one chooses and then sets out the reasons why great care needs to be taken before competition law intervenes.

75. When setting its enforcement priorities, the Commission starts from the position that, generally speaking, any undertaking, whether dominant or not, should have the right to choose its trading partners and to

---

[775] In para. 196. As discussed in Chap. 6, UBC was found dominant with 45% of a narrowly drawn market (bananas rather than fruit) despite evidence of what the Court itself called 'very lively competition'.

[776] It has been argued that 'the Court of Justice inferred an anti-competitive motive on United Brands' part, without, as far as one can see, a scintilla of evidence, and then condemned United Brands for having had this improper motive', resulting in the CJ effectively precluding dominant undertakings 'from refusing to supply customers who either directly or indirectly wage an assault on their businesses': P. Jebsen and R. Stevens, 'Assumptions, Goals, and Dominant Undertakings: The Regulation of Competition Under Art. 86 of the European Union' (1996) 64 *Antitrust LJ* 443, 510–511.

[777] Cases C-468–478/06, *Sot. Lélos kai Sia and others EE v. GlaxoSmithKline AEVE Farmakeftikon Proionton* [2008] ECR I-7139, see Section 12.F, p. 586.

[778] Guidance Paper, para. 77.

[779] *BBI/Boosey & Hawkes* [1987] OJ L286/36, [1988] 4 CMLR 67. There were other alleged abuses by B&H, such as engaging in vexatious litigation (see Section 13.D, p. 564).

dispose freely of its property. The Commission therefore considers that intervention on competition law grounds requires careful consideration where the application of Article [102] would lead to the imposition of an obligation to supply on the dominant undertaking…The existence of such an obligation—even for a fair remuneration—may undermine undertakings' incentives to invest and innovate and, thereby, possibly harm consumers. The knowledge that they may have a duty to supply against their will may lead dominant under-takings—or undertakings who anticipate that they may become dominant—not to invest, or to invest less, in the activity in question. Also, competitors may be tempted to free ride on investments made by the dominant undertaking instead of investing themselves. Neither of these consequences would, in the long run, be in the interest of consumers.

The Guidance Paper makes no distinction between refusal to license IPRs and other refusals. It says that the concept of refusal to supply includes 'a broad range of practices' such as refusing to supply products to existing or new customers, refusal to license IPRs, including for purposes of interface information, or refusal to grant access to an essential facility or network.[780] It covers 'constructive refusals' such as undue delay, degradation of supply, or imposing unreasonable conditions.[781] The Guidance Paper also considers margin squeeze as a type of refusal to supply[782] but this has been overtaken by the judgment of the CJ in *TeliaSonera*, which held that margin squeeze was a distinct abuse from refusal to supply, as discussed earlier.[783]

The Guidance Paper sets out a test (paragraph 81) for when the Commission will consider it a pri-ority to intervene. It comprises three cumulative conditions, reflecting the case law:

(i)   the refusal relates to a product or service that is objectively necessary to be able to compete on a downstream market;

(ii) the refusal is likely to lead to the elimination of effective competition in the downstream market;

(iii) the refusal is likely to lead to consumer harm.

On condition (i), the objective necessity of the input, the Commission relies on *Microsoft* for saying that this does not mean that without it no competitor could enter or survive on the downstream market.[784] The test is whether an alternative source of supply is capable of allowing competitors to exert a competitive constraint.

On condition (ii) the Commission states that if the objective necessity of the input is shown the refusal to supply is generally liable to eliminate, immediately or over time, effective competition in the downstream market.[785] The requirement for the elimination of *effective competition* comes from *Microsoft* and the Commission has preferred this to the standard in the non-IPR cases, *Commercial Solvents* and *Bronner*, which, as we have seen, requires the elimination of competition from the person requesting access.[786]

---

[780]   Guidance Paper, para. 78.

[781]   Guidance Paper, para. 79.

[782]   Guidance Paper, para. 80.

[783]   See Section 9.B, p. 434 ff.

[784]   Guidance Paper, para. 83.

[785]   Guidance Paper, para. 85. Nazzini, *The Foundations of European Union Competition Law* (cited in n. 106), 267 takes issue with this, saying that proof of the effect of the refusal on downstream competition is a free-standing element of the test, and pointing out that the Commission itself in para. 85 sets out a number of factors which affect the likeli-hood of effective competition being eliminated. These include a high market share in the downstream market, the extent to which the dominant undertaking is comparatively capacity constrained downstream, the substitutability between the dominant undertaking's output and that of its downstream competitors, and the proportion of down-stream competitors that are affected by the refusal. Marsden, 'Outstanding Issues from the European Commission's Guidance on Article 102 TFEU' (cited in n. 96), 68 considers that the list of factors in para. 85 shows the Commission's concern with dominance per se rather than with the conduct.

[786]   Nazzini, *The Foundations of European Union Competition Law* (cited in n. 106), 267, argues that elimination of all competition and elimination of competition from the person requiring access amount in reality to the same

On condition (iii), the impact on consumer harm, the Commission says it will normally pursue the case if the likely negative effects of the refusal outweigh over time the negative effects of ordering supply. It then continues:[787]

The Commission considers that consumer harm may, for instance, arise where the competitors that the dominant undertaking forecloses are, as a result of the refusal, prevented from bringing innovative goods or services to market and/or where follow-on innovation is likely to be stifled… This may be particularly the case if the undertaking which requests supply does not intend to limit itself essentially to duplicating the goods or services already offered by the dominant undertaking on the downstream market, but intends to produce new or improved goods or services for which there is a potential consumer demand or is likely to contribute to technical development…

The reference to innovation is not confined to IPR situations, although the footnotes cite *Microsoft* (after the word 'stifled') and *IMS* and *Microsoft* at the end. Rather than distinguish between IPR and non-IPR cases on the basis that IPR refusals require prevention of a new product/technical development, therefore, the Commission has applied the need for 'consumer harm' to all cases.

The Commission says it will apply the paragraph 81 criteria to both new and existing customers. However, the termination of existing supply is more likely to be found abusive. This is because:

…For example, if the dominant undertaking had previously been supplying the requesting undertaking, and the latter had made relationship-specific investments in order to use the subsequently refused input, the Commission may be more likely to regard the input in question as indispensable. Similarly, the fact that the owner of the essential input in the past has found it in its interest to supply is an indication that supplying the input does not imply any risk that the owner receives inadequate compensation for the original investment. It would therefore be up to the dominant company to demonstrate why circumstances have actually changed in such a way that the continuation of its existing supply relationship would put in danger its adequate compensation.[788]

The three conditions laid down in paragraph 81 for enforcement priority are subject to a proviso (paragraph 82). In certain situations, such as (i) where sector regulation has already provided for supply obligations or (ii) the upstream position of the dominant undertaking has been developed through state protection or state financing, the Commission's normal wariness about the intervention having negative effects on investment and innovation incentives is eased. In such cases the Commission will not be concerned if the three paragraph 81 conditions are not fulfilled and will revert to its general enforcement standard set out in the Guidance Paper, i.e. likely anti-competitive foreclosure.

82. In certain specific cases, it may be clear that imposing an obligation to supply is manifestly not capable of having negative effects on the input owner's and/or other operators' incentives to invest and innovate upstream, whether ex ante or ex post. The Commission considers that this is particularly likely to be the case where regulation compatible with Community law already imposes an obligation to supply on the dominant undertaking and it is clear, from the considerations underlying such regulation, that the necessary balancing of incentives has already been made by the public authority when imposing such an obligation to supply. This could also be the case where the upstream market position of the dominant undertaking has been developed under the protection of special or exclusive rights or has been financed by state resources. In such specific cases there is no reason for the Commission to deviate from its general enforcement standard of showing likely anti-competitive foreclosure, without considering whether the three circumstances referred to in paragraph 81 are present.

thing as indispensability is an objective concept so a refusal capable of excluding one competitor must be capable of excluding all.

[787] Guidance Paper, para. 87.

[788] Guidance Paper, para. 84. There is no case law cited in support of this paragraph.

The exceptional situations in this paragraph are the 'Telefónica exceptions' which appeared in the Commission's margin squeeze decision *Telefónica*, discussed earlier.[789] They were considered by Advocate General Mazák in *TeliaSonera*[790] who accepted the first (regulatory obligations) but had reservations about the second (State resources or special or exclusive rights). They have both been trenchantly criticised[791] by those who argue in respect of the first that regulation pursues broader objectives than competition law and that national regulators may impose an obligation to supply in circumstances where the Commission is not entitled to impose one; and in respect of the second that 'it is difficult to apply in practice and is likely to lead to unpredictable and erroneous results'[792] because how far the dominant undertaking's position has been developed in that way may not be clear-cut and in particular which parts of the assets were paid for pre- rather than post-liberalisation may be difficult to determine.[793]

The Guidance Paper states that the Commission will consider efficiencies claims. Paragraph 89 reflects the kinds of arguments that were raised in *Microsoft*:

The Commission will consider claims by the dominant undertaking that a refusal to supply is necessary to allow the dominant undertaking to realise an adequate return on the investments required to develop its input business, thus generating incentives to continue to invest in the future, taking the risk of failed projects into account. The Commission will also consider claims by the dominant undertaking that its own innovation will be negatively affected by the obligation to supply, or by the structural changes in the market conditions that imposing such an obligation will bring about, including the development of follow-on innovation by competitors.

Citing *Microsoft* the Guidance Paper says that it is for the dominant undertaking to demonstrate the negative impact of an obligation to supply on its own level of innovation.[794]

H. REFUSAL TO SUPPLY AND THE 'ESSENTIAL FACILITIES' DOCTRINE IN US LAW

We noted earlier[795] that the essential facilities doctrine originated in US law. Section 2 of the Sherman Act prohibits the acquisition or maintenance of monopoly power. In *United States v. Colgate & Co*[796] the Supreme Court said that in the absence of any purpose to create or maintain a monopoly a private trader may freely 'exercise his own independent discretion as to parties with whom he may deal' and the US courts have consequently been generally reluctant to condemn refusals to deal. However, they have held that such refusals do come within section 2, by way of exception to the *Colgate* principle, in certain limited circumstances, and some courts have applied an 'essential facilities'

---

[789] Case T-336/07, *Telefónica and Telefónica de España v. European Commission*, 29 March 2012, see Section 9.B, p. 442.

[790] Case C-52/09, *Konkurrensverket v. TeliaSonera Sverige AB* [2011] ECR I-527. The CJ did not refer to them because once it had separated margin squeeze from refusal to supply they were not relevant.

[791] See D. Geradin, 'Refusal to Supply and Margin Squeeze: A Discussion of Why the "Telefonica Exceptions" are Wrong', *TILEC Discussion Paper* No 2011-009, available at <http://papers.ssrn.com/sol3/papers.cfm?abstract_id=1762687>; Geradin et al., *EU Competition Law and Economics* (cited in n. 160), 4.351–4.354, 4.366–4.367; G. Faella and R. Pardolesi 'Squeezing Price Squeeze under EC Antitrust Law' (2010) 6 *European Competition Journal* 255, 271–273.

[792] Geradin et al., *EU Competition Law and Economics* (cited in n. 160), 4.354.

[793] See also Mazák AG in *TeliaSonera*, para. 27 of the Opinion. The Commission is also criticised for ignoring the dominant undertaking's future incentives to invest, D. Geradin, 'Refusal to Supply and Margin Squeeze: A Discussion of Why the "Telefonica Exceptions" are Wrong', *TILEC Discussion Paper* No 2011-009, available at <http://papers.ssrn.com/sol3/papers.cfm?abstract_id=1762687>.

[794] Guidance Paper, para. 90, citing para. 659 of *Microsoft*.

[795] See Section 12.C.i, p. 513.

[796] 250 US 300, 39 S.Ct 465 (1919).

doctrine.[797] There has been controversy in US antitrust law as to whether the doctrine is really part of the recognised exceptions to the *Colgate* principle, or whether it is a separate principle.[798] In any event, many American commentators are highly critical of the doctrine. We have already seen that Areeda expressed caution about it[799] and Hovenkamp says the 'so-called essential facilities doctrine is one of the most troublesome, incoherent and unmanageable bases for Sherman section 2 liability. The antitrust world would almost certainly be a better place if it were jettisoned, with a little fine tuning of the general doctrine of the monopolist's refusal to deal to fill in the resulting gaps'.[800] In 2004 a case concerning a refusal to supply where the essential facilities doctrine was raised finally came before the Supreme Court. The case concerned the telecommunications sector, which is regulated under federal law. The Supreme Court dismissed the claim that there was a refusal to deal under section 2 and was less than enthusiastic about the essential facilities doctrine. The extracts from the case rehearse again (albeit in the context of the US provisions) the dangers of forcing undertakings to share with or supply competitors and should be compared with the similar arguments of Advocate General Jacobs in *Bronner*.

Verizon Communications Inc v. *Trinko LLP* 540 US 398 124 S.Ct. 872

Customers who received local telephone services from competing local exchange carriers (LEC) brought an action against the incumbent LEC alleging that it had breached its duty to share under the Telecommunications Act 1996 and that its failure to share violated section 2 of the Sherman Act. The Supreme Court held that the duties under the 1996 Act could not be enforced through a section 2 claim, but the Act did not affect any liability which the LEC had under general antitrust law. It therefore examined the customers' claims under antitrust law. The Court held (paragraph 6) that even if the essential facilities doctrine existed it served no purpose here as the question of access was taken care of by the 1996 Act.

Supreme Court of the United States (Justice Scalia delivered the opinion of the Court)

III

[2] ... The mere possession of monopoly power, and the concomitant charging of monopoly prices, is not only not unlawful; it is an important element of the free-market system. The opportunity to charge monopoly prices—at least for a short period—is what attracts 'business acumen' in the first place; it induces risk taking that produces innovation and economic growth. To safeguard the incentive to innovate, the possession of monopoly power will not be found unlawful unless it is accompanied by an element of anti-competitive *conduct*.

[3] Firms may acquire monopoly power by establishing an infrastructure that renders them uniquely suited to serve their customers. Compelling such firms to share the source of their advantage is in some tension with the underlying purpose of antitrust law, since it may lessen the incentive for the monopolist,

---

[797] The leading cases are discussed by the Supreme Court in *Verizon v. Trinko*, 540 US 398, 124 S.Ct. 872; see also Elhauge and Geradin, *Global Competition Law and Economics* (cited in n. 195). 425-449.

[798] See L. Hancher, 'Case note on *Oscar Bronner*' (1999) 36 *CMLRev* 1289.

[799] P. Areeda, 'Essential Facilities: An Epithet in Need of Limiting Principles' [1990] *Antitrust LJ* 841, extracted in Section 12.C.iii.p. 517.

[800] Hovenkamp, *Federal Antitrust Policy* (cited in n. 193), 336, and Chap. 7 generally. Jacobs AG, reviewing the US position in Case C-7/97, *Oscar Bronner GmbH & Co KG v. Mediaprint* [1998] ECR I-7791, para. 46 of his Opinion, pointed out that s. 2 of the Sherman Act and Art. 102 protect competition in different ways. The Sherman Act prohibits the acquisition or maintenance of monopoly power, whereas Art. 102 regulates the actions of companies in dominant positions.

the rival, or both to invest in those economically beneficial facilities. Enforced sharing also requires anti-trust courts to act as central planners, identifying the proper price, quantity, and other terms of dealing—a role for which they are ill-suited. Moreover, compelling negotiation between competitors may facilitate the supreme evil of antitrust: collusion. Thus, as a general matter, the Sherman Act 'does not restrict the long recognized right of [a] trader or manufacturer engaged in an entirely private business, freely to exercise his own independent discretion as to parties with whom he will deal.' *United States* v. *Colgate & Co*, 250 U.S. 300, 307…(1919).

[4] However, '[t]he high value that we have placed on the right to refuse to deal with other firms does not mean that the right is unqualified.' *Aspen Skiing Co* v. *Aspen Highlands Skiing Corp*, 472 U.S. 585, 601…(1985). Under certain circumstances, a refusal to cooperate with rivals can constitute anti-competitive conduct and violate § 2. We have been very cautious in recognizing such exceptions, because of the uncertain virtue of forced sharing and the difficulty of identifying and remedying anti-competitive conduct by a single firm. The question before us today is whether the allegations of respondent's complaint fit within existing exceptions or provide a basis, under traditional antitrust principles, for recognizing a new one.

Justice Scalia then reviewed the case law and continued:

[6] We conclude that Verizon's alleged insufficient assistance in the provision of service to rivals is not a recognized antitrust claim under this Court's existing refusal-to-deal precedents. This conclusion would be unchanged even if we considered to be established law the 'essential facilities' doctrine crafted by some lower courts, under which the Court of Appeals concluded respondent's allegations might state a claim. See generally Areeda, Essential Facilities: An Epithet in Need of Limiting Principles, 58 Antitrust L.J. 841 (1989). We have never recognized such a doctrine, see *Aspen Skiing Co*, 472 U.S., at 611, n. 44, 105 S.Ct. 2847; *AT & T Corp* v. *Iowa Utilities Bd.*, 525 U.S., at 428, 119…(opinion of BREYER, J.), and we find no need either to recognize it or to repudiate it here. It suffices for present purposes to note that the indispensable requirement for invoking the doctrine is the unavailability of access to the 'essential facilities'; where access exists, the doctrine serves no purpose. Thus, it is said that 'essential facility claims should…be denied where a state or federal agency has effective power to compel sharing and to regulate its scope and terms.' P. Areeda & H. Hovenkamp, Antitrust Law, p. 150, 773e (2003 Supp.). Respondent believes that the existence of sharing duties under the 1996 Act supports its case. We think the opposite: The 1996 Act's extensive provision for access makes it unnecessary to impose a judicial doctrine of forced access. To the extent respondent's 'essential facilities' argument is distinct from its general § 2 argument, we reject it.

IV

[7] Finally, we do not believe that traditional antitrust principles justify adding the present case to the few existing exceptions from the proposition that there is no duty to aid competitors. Antitrust analysis must always be attuned to the particular structure and circumstances of the industry at issue. Part of that attention to economic context is an awareness of the significance of regulation…

Against the slight benefits of antitrust intervention here, we must weigh a realistic assessment of its costs. Under the best of circumstances, applying the requirements of § 2 'can be difficult' because 'the means of illicit exclusion, like the means of legitimate competition, are myriad.' *United States* v. *Microsoft Corp*, 253 F.3d 34, 58 (C.A.D.C.2001)…Mistaken inferences and the resulting false condemnations 'are especially costly, because they chill the very conduct the antitrust laws are designed to protect.' *Matsushita Elec. Industrial Co* v. *Zenith Radio Corp*, 475 U.S. 574, 594…(1986). The cost of false positives counsels against an undue expansion of § 2 liability…

Even if the problem of false positives did not exist, conduct consisting of anti-competitive violations of § 251 may be, as we have concluded with respect to above-cost predatory pricing schemes, 'beyond the practical ability of a judicial tribunal to control.' *Brooke Group Ltd* v. *Brown & Williamson Tobacco Corp*, 509 U.S. 209, 223 … (1993). Effective remediation of violations of regulatory sharing requirements will ordinarily require continuing supervision of a highly detailed decree. We think that Professor Areeda got it exactly right: 'No court should impose a duty to deal that it cannot explain or adequately and reasonably supervise. The problem should be deemed irremedia[ble] by antitrust law when compulsory access requires the court to assume the day-to-day controls characteristic of a regulatory agency.' Areeda, 58 Antitrust L.J., at 853. In this case, respondent has requested an equitable decree to '[p]reliminarily and permanently enjoi[n] [Verizon] from providing access to the local loop market…to [rivals] on terms and conditions that are not as favorable' as those that Verizon enjoys. App. 49–50. An antitrust court is unlikely to be an effective day-to-day enforcer of these detailed sharing obligations.

In paragraph 6 Justice Scalia points out that the Supreme Court has never recognised the essential facilities doctrine, which has been 'crafted by some lower courts'. Given that it could not apply in this case he states that there is 'no need either to recognize or repudiate it here'.[801] However, the tenor of the judgment is not sympathetic towards it. Earlier he is careful to confine the Court's existing refusal to deal precedents to their own facts. Even taking into account the CJ's conservative approach in *Bronner*, refusals to deal and essential facilities are an area of divergence between US and EU law. Some commentators argue strongly that the EU should take the same robust approach to demands for access to the facilities of others as the Supreme Court has taken.[802] The divergence on refusal to supply demonstrates the difference between US law's concern with incentives to innovate—and the assumption in the case of refusal to supply that a requirement to deal will chill incentives—and the requirement in EU law that it is for the dominant undertaking to demonstrate negative impact on innovation.[803] Also, it should be remembered when reading *Trinko* that the relationship between regulation and competition law is different in the EU and the US. In the US regulation law is federal, whereas in the EU there are only national regimes.[804]

13. OTHER EXCLUSIONARY PRACTICES

A. GENERAL

It is clear that any conduct which excludes competitors from the market may be capable of constituting an exclusionary abuse, whatever form it takes. The extent to which actual or likely foreclosure effects on consumers have to be demonstrated or measured is discussed throughout the preceding sections of this chapter. Miscellaneous exclusionary conduct which has come before the EU Courts or Commission includes alleging to third parties that a competitor is a bad debtor,[805] buying up a competitor's machines,[806] and monopolising the specialist advertising media.[807] In *Irish Sugar*[808] the dominant undertaking in the Irish sugar market persuaded certain wholesalers and retailers to swap

---

[801] Thus disappointing many people. The Supreme Court's pronouncement on the essential facilities doctrine had been eagerly awaited.

[802] See in particular D. Geradin, 'Limiting the Scope of Article 82 EC: What Can the EU Learn from the Supreme Court's Judgment in *Trinko*, in the Wake of *Microsoft, IMS* and *Deutsche Telekom*?' (2004) 41 *CMLRev* 1526.

[803] See further Marsden, 'Outstanding Issues from the European Commission's Guidance on Article 102 TFEU' (cited in n. 96), 68–72.

[804] See Chap. 1 and the *Deutsche Telekom* margin squeeze case, Case C-280/08 P, *Deutsche Telekom* v. *Commission* [2010] ECR I-9555, for the interaction between EU competition rules and national sector regulators.

[805] *BBI/Boosey & Hawkes* [1987] OJ L286/36, [1988] 4 CMLR 67.

[806] *Elopak Italia/Tetra Pak* [1991] OJ L72/1, [1992] 4 CMLR 551, para. 165.

[807] *Elopak Italia/Tetra Pak* [1991] OJ L72/1, [1992] 4 CMLR 551, para. 165.

[808] Case T-228/97, *Irish Sugar plc* v. *Commission* [1999] ECR II-2969.

the sugar they had bought from a competitor for its own. This conduct was found to be an abuse. One of the abuses found in the 2009 *Intel* decision was the payment of grants to computer manufacturers (OEMs) to delay, cancel, or otherwise restrict the launch of the competitors' products. The Commission stressed the effects of this on consumers.

Case COMP/C-3/37.990 *Intel* [2010] 4 CMLR 314

1679 As a consequence, AMD-based products for which there was a customer demand did not reach the market, or did not reach it at the time or in the way they would have in the absence of Intel's conduct. As a result, customers were deprived of a choice which they would have otherwise had and competition on the merits was harmed…

1680 Furthermore, there is no link between the conducts and any criterion which could potentially be a legitimate objective justification, and the Commission cannot therefore discern any economic justification in the conducts.

Irish Sugar also put pressure on a shipping line to stop carrying the competitor's product by threatening to withdraw its own custom if this continued. The Commission said that '[p]utting pressure on a carrier to prevent him from transporting competing goods cannot be considered to constitute a normal business practice'.[809] In *TACA*[810] the Commission held that a liner conference had committed an abuse by 'inducing' a competitor shipping line to join it. This in effect neutralised the competition by turning the competitor into one of the club. On appeal the GC held that the Commission had not proved that there had been the alleged 'inducement' and overturned the decision.[811] In *Compagnie Maritime Belge* it was an abuse for the dominant liner conference to pressurise the Zaïrean government to observe the exclusive dealing provisions in their agreements and exclude rival carriers.[812]

In Sections 13.B to 13.F we discuss specific exclusionary practices which have been held to infringe Article 102.

B. THE ACQUISITION OF INTELLECTUAL PROPERTY RIGHTS

It was seen in Chapter 5 that in *Tetra Pak*[813] the acquisition by a dominant undertaking of an exclusive patent licence was held to be an abuse even though the licence agreement did not infringe Article 101 as it fell within the block exemption regulation.[814] The GC said that although the acquisition of an exclusive licence by a dominant undertaking is not an abuse per se, it may be so, and was on the facts of this case. The principle in *Tetra Pak I* is a striking example of the onerous nature of the 'special responsibility' towards the competitive process imposed on dominant firms.[815]

---

[809] Commission Decision, [1997] OJ L258/1, [1997] 5 CMLR 666, paras. 120–122.

[810] *Transatlantic Con2ference Agreement (TACA)* [1999] OJ L95/1, [1999] 4 CMLR 1415.

[811] Cases T-191/98 and T-212–14/98, *Atlantic Container Line AB v. Commission* [2003] ECR II-3275.

[812] Cases C-395 and 396/96P *Compagnie Maritime Belge Transports SA v. Commission* [2000] ECR I-1365, paras. 80–88.

[813] Case T-51/89, *Tetra Pak Rausing v. Commission* [1990] ECR II-309.

[814] Reg. 2349/84, [1984] OJ L219/15, on patent licensing agreements (replaced by Reg. 240/96, [1996] OJ L31/2, on Technology Transfer Agreements and subsequently by Reg. 772/2004 [2004] OJ L123/11 (see Chap. 12)).

[815] The principle has been applied subsequently in cases which were settled informally to the Commission's satisfaction: *Carlsberg/Interbrew*, XXIVth Report on Competition Policy (Commission, 1994), paras. 209 and 213; *Svenska Tobaks*, XXVIIth Report on Competition Policy (Commission, 1997), para. 66. See Faull and Nikpay (eds.), *The EC Law of Competition* (cited in n. 611), paras. 4.355–4.356.

C. THE MISUSE OF INTELLECTUAL PROPERTY RIGHTS OR OTHER REGULATORY PROCEDURES

(i) The *AstraZeneca* Case

The CJ confirmed in *AstraZeneca*[816] that it can be an abuse for a dominant undertaking to make misrepresentations to regulatory authorities or to take steps with regard to regulatory procedures in order to exclude competitors.

The Commission had fined AstraZeneca (AZ) €60 million[817] for (a) misrepresenting certain dates to national patent offices and national courts in order to obtain extra patent protection for Losec (an anti-ulcer medicine which is the main oral proton pump inhibitor[818]) in the form of supplementary protection certificates (SPCs) to which it would otherwise not have been entitled; and (b) misusing marketing authorisation procedures by switching Losec from capsule to tablet form in order to hinder generic versions of the drugs coming on to the market, and also to hinder parallel imports. By deregistering the capsule marketing authorisation AZ prevented generic drug manufacturers from making use of simplified marketing authorisation procedures which, at the time, were only open to generic producers if the authorisation for the original product was still in force. The Commission found that depriving the generic manufacturers of the ability to use the faster and simpler procedure delayed the entry on to the market of the generic product.

The Commission took the decision at a time when it was increasingly concerned with what it perceived as delays in generic medicines coming on to the market and with delays in the development of new medicines to compete with those already available.[819]

a. Misrepresentations to National Patent Offices and National Courts

The GC upheld the Commission's finding that the presentation of the relevant dates which AZ made to the national patent offices and courts amounted to the giving of misleading information.[820] The GC cited the case law establishing that an abuse of a dominant position does not necessarily have to involve the dominant undertaking using its economic power in order to engage in the infringing conduct. It said that giving public authorities misleading information making possible the grant of an exclusive right to which the undertaking was not entitled constituted a practice falling outside the scope of competition on the merits which may be particularly restrictive of competition. In this case the public authorities had a limited discretion to verify the information provided to them which was a relevant factor in assessing whether the misrepresentations were liable to raise regulatory obstacles to competition. The GC referred to the special responsibility of a dominant undertaking which required it, in this situation, at least to inform the public authorities of any error it had made so that the matter could be rectified. As far as intention is concerned, the GC said that although abuse is an objective concept and so does not require deliberation and bad faith, nevertheless intention can constitute a relevant factor to be taken into account to support the conclusion that an undertaking has abused its dominant position.

The GC held that it was irrelevant whether or not the public authorities to whom misrepresentations were made were actually misled or not, and whether the exclusive rights obtained were afterwards revoked as the abusive nature of the behaviour could not depend on the contingencies of third parties' reactions. Nor was it relevant whether or not the exclusive right obtained had actually been enforced as the mere possession of an IPR normally keeps competitors away. To make the

---

[816] Case C-457/10 P, *AstraZeneca v. Commission*, 6 December 2012.

[817] COMP/A.37.507/F3, *AstraZeneca* [2006] 5 CMLR 287, 15 June 2005.

[818] For the market definition and dominance aspects of the case, see Chap. 6, Section 5.B.i.j, p. 322 and Section C.

[819] See the Commission inquiry into the pharmaceutical sector, 8 July 2009, and press release IP/09/1098.

[820] The GC did, however, hold that the abuse started later than the Commission had found.

application of Article 102 dependent on whether or not the dominant undertaking had exercised its right in legal proceedings would render it conditional on the competitors having contravened public regulations. The GC rejected the plea that the criteria used by the Commission in *ITT Promedia*[821] should be applied to the situation.

In respect of the elimination of competition the GC held that finding that the unlawful acquisition of an exclusive right constituted an abuse did not depend on it having the effect of eliminating all competition. It distinguished the situation before it from that in *Tetra Pak I* but doubted that the judgment in *Tetra Pak I* did in fact require elimination. It rejected the argument that for the misrepresentations to constitute an abuse there must have been a direct effect on competition. It was only necessary that they were *capable* of restricting competition. The ability of the practice to restrict competition could be *indirect* provided that it could be shown that it was *actually liable* to do so. The existence of specific remedies within the patent system did not mean that in this situation proof of anti-competitive effect was required.

On appeal the CJ affirmed the judgment of the GC.

Case C-457/10 P, *AstraZeneca AB and AstraZeneca plc* v. *Commission*, 6 December 2012

Court of Justice

[The third ground of appeal, that the GC had taken a legally flawed approach to competition on the merits]

98 Regarded in the light of the facts found by the General Court, which the appellants have expressly stated that they are not calling into question, the third ground of appeal raised by them is tantamount to an argument that where an undertaking in a dominant position considers that it can, in accordance with a legally defensible interpretation, lay claim to a right, it may use any means to obtain that right, and even have recourse to highly misleading representations with the aim of leading public authorities into error. Such an approach is manifestly not consistent with competition on the merits and the specific responsibility on such an undertaking not to prejudice, by its conduct, effective and undistorted competition within the European Union.

99 Lastly, contrary to what the EFPIA submits, the General Court did not hold that undertakings in a dominant position had to be infallible in their dealings with regulatory authorities and that each objectively wrong representation made by such an undertaking constituted an abuse of that position, even where the error was made unintentionally and immediately rectified. It is sufficient to note in this connection that, first, that example is radically different from AZ's conduct in the present case, and that, secondly, the General Court pointed out, at paragraphs 357 and 361 of the judgment under appeal, that the assessment of whether representations made to public authorities for the purposes of improperly obtaining exclusive rights are misleading must be made *in concreto* and may vary according to the specific circumstances of each case. It thus cannot be inferred from that judgment that any patent application made by such an undertaking which is rejected on the ground that it does not satisfy the patentability criteria automatically gives rise to liability under Article [102].

[The fourth ground of appeal, that the GC erred in holding that the mere fact of applying for an SPC was sufficient to constitute an abuse]

...

105 As is apparent, inter alia, from paragraph 357 of the judgment under appeal, the General Court examined in the present case whether, in the light of the context in which the practice in question had been implemented, that practice was such as to lead the public authorities wrongly to create regulatory obstacles to competition, for example by the unlawful grant of exclusive rights to the dominant undertaking. It

---

[821] Case T-111/96 *ITT Promedia NV v. European Commission* [1998] ECR II-2937, see Section 13.D, p. 564.

held in this connection that the limited discretion of public authorities or the absence of any obligation on their part to verify the accuracy or veracity of the information provided could be relevant factors to be taken into consideration for the purposes of determining whether the practice in question was liable to raise regulatory obstacles to competition.

106 Contrary to what the appellants submit, that examination by the General Court is not in any way based on the assumption that the practice in question constitutes an 'abuse in itself', regardless of its anti-competitive effect. On the contrary, the General Court expressly pointed out, at paragraph 377 of the judgment under appeal, that representations designed to obtain exclusive rights unlawfully constitute an abuse only if it is established that, in view of the objective context in which they are made, those representations are actually liable to lead the public authorities to grant the exclusive right applied for.

...

111 So far as concerns the fact that the misleading representations did not enable AZ to obtain SPCs in Denmark and that in Ireland and the United Kingdom the SPCs were ultimately issued on the basis of the correct date, it must be stated that the General Court did not err in law in holding, at paragraphs 602 to 604 of the judgment under appeal, that that fact does not mean that AZ's conduct in those countries was not abusive, since it is established that those representations were very likely to result in the issue of unlawful SPCs. In addition, as the Commission has pointed out, in so far as the impugned conduct forms part of an overall strategy seeking to unlawfully exclude manufacturers of generic products from the market by means of obtaining SPCs in breach of the regulatory framework which established them, the existence of an abuse is not affected by the fact that that strategy did not succeed in some countries.

112 Lastly, as regards the circumstances which, according to the appellants, must be present in order to be able to find that the misleading representations were such as to restrict competition, it is sufficient to note that in actual fact they amount to a requirement that current and certain anti-competitive effects be shown. However, it follows from the Court's case-law that, although the practice of an undertaking in a dominant position cannot be characterised as abusive in the absence of any anti-competitive effect on the market, such an effect does not necessarily have to be concrete, and it is sufficient to demonstrate that there is a potential anti-competitive effect (see, to that effect, *TeliaSonera Sverige*, paragraph 64).

b. Withdrawal of the Marketing Authorisations

In respect of the misuse of marketing authorisation procedures the GC distinguished the situation before it from that in the case law on what it described as 'essential facilities', referring to *Bronner* and *Microsoft*. It observed that as a result of the scheme for marketing authorisations for generic products established by Directive 65/65[822] AZ could not prevent national authorities from using the relevant data when giving authorisations under the abridged procedure. So this was not a 'refusal to supply' scenario.[823] The GC rejected the argument that, as the undertaking was entitled under the relevant rules to request the withdrawal of its marketing authorisations for Losec capsules, the deregistration could not constitute an abuse because 'the illegality of abusive conduct under [Article 102] is unrelated to its compliance or non-compliance with other legal rules'.[824] The GC held that in cases of conduct by which regulatory procedures are used without any basis in competition on the merits, evidence that the conduct is *capable* of restricting competition is sufficient to classify it as an abuse of a dominant position.[825]

---

[822] [1965–1966] OJ Special Edition 24, as amended.

[823] *AstraZeneca*, GC, paras. 678–684.

[824] *AstraZeneca*, GC, para. 677.

[825] *AstraZeneca*, GC, para. 824.

In this case the Commission had established that the deregistration was not based on the legitimate protection of an investment that was part of competition on the merits.[826] The Court admitted that a dominant undertaking is under no obligation to protect the interests of its competitors but held that nonetheless that does not make practices implemented solely to exclude competitors compatible with Article 102: the desire of a dominant undertaking to protect its own commercial interests does not justify recourse to practices falling outside the scope of competition on the merits.[827] Therefore, in the absence of objective justification a dominant undertaking 'cannot use regulatory procedures solely in such a way as to prevent or make more difficult the entry of competitors on the market'.[828] The GC did, however, annul the decision to the extent that it found that the deregistration was capable of restricting parallel imports in Denmark and Norway on the grounds that the Commission had not established this.

The CJ affirmed the judgment of the GC.

Case C-457/10 P, *AstraZeneca AB and AstraZeneca plc* v. *Commission*, Court of Justice, 6 December 2012

[The fifth ground of appeal, that the GC had misinterpreted the concept of 'competition on the merits']

129 As a preliminary point it must be stated that, as the General Court observed at paragraph 804 of the judgment under appeal, the preparation by an undertaking, even in a dominant position, of a strategy whose object it is to minimise the erosion of its sales and to enable it to deal with competition from generic products is legitimate and is part of the normal competitive process, provided that the conduct envisaged does not depart from practices coming within the scope of competition on the merits, which is such as to benefit consumers.

130 However, contrary to what the appellants submit, conduct like that impugned in the context of the second abuse—consisting in the deregistration, without objective justification and after the expiry of the exclusive right to make use of the results of the pharmacological and toxicological tests and clinical trials granted by Directive 65/65, of the MAs for Losec capsules in Denmark, Sweden and Norway, by which AZ intended, as the General Court held at paragraph 814 of the judgment under appeal, to hinder the introduction of generic products and parallel imports—does not come within the scope of competition on the merits.

131 In this connection, it must in particular be stated that, as the General Court observed at paragraph 675 of that judgment, after the expiry of the period of exclusivity referred to above, conduct designed, inter alia, to prevent manufacturers of generic products from making use of their right to benefit from those results was not based in any way on the legitimate protection of an investment which came within the scope of competition on the merits, precisely because, under Directive 65/65, AZ no longer had the exclusive right to make use of those results.

132 Furthermore, the General Court was correct to hold, at paragraph 677 of that judgment, that the fact, relied on by the appellants, that under Directive 65/65 AZ was entitled to request the withdrawal of its MAs for Losec capsules in no way causes that conduct to escape the prohibition laid down in Article 82 EC. As that court pointed out, the illegality of abusive conduct under Article 82 EC is unrelated to its compliance or non-compliance with other legal rules and, in the majority of cases, abuses of dominant positions consist of behaviour which is otherwise lawful under branches of law other than competition law.

133 Moreover, as the Advocate General observes in point 78 of his Opinion, the primary purpose of Directive 65/65 is to safeguard public health while eliminating disparities between certain national

---

[826] *AstraZeneca*, GC, paras. 675, 812.

[827] *AstraZeneca*, GC, para. 816.

[828] *AstraZeneca*, GC, para. 817.

provisions which hinder trade in medicinal products within the Union, and it therefore does not, as claimed by the appellants, pursue the same objectives as Article 82 EC in such a way that the application of the latter is no longer required for the purposes of ensuring effective and undistorted competition within the internal market.

134 It is important to point out, in this context, that an undertaking which holds a dominant position has a special responsibility in that latter regard (see Case C-202/07 P *France Télécom* v *Commission* [2009] ECR I-2369, paragraph 105) and that, as the General Court held at paragraphs 672 and 817 of the judgment under appeal, it cannot therefore use regulatory procedures in such a way as to prevent or make more difficult the entry of competitors on the market, in the absence of grounds relating to the defence of the legitimate interests of an undertaking engaged in competition on the merits or in the absence of objective justification.

....

[The sixth ground of appeal, that the GC erred in law in considering that the impugned conduct tended to restrict competition]

148 ...The situation which characterises the second abuse is not in any way comparable to a compulsory licence or to the situation which gave rise to the judgment in *IMS Health*, relied upon by the appellants, which concerned the refusal by an undertaking in a dominant position, which was the owner of an intellectual property right in a 'brick structure', to grant its competitors a licence for the use of that structure.

149 In fact, the possibility provided for in Directive 65/65 of deregistering a MA is not equivalent to a property right. Consequently, the fact that, in the light of its special responsibility, an undertaking in a dominant position cannot make use of such a possibility in such a way as to prevent or render more difficult the entry of competitors on the market, unless it can, as an undertaking engaged in competition on the merits, rely on grounds relating to the defence of its legitimate interests or on objective justifications, does not constitute either an 'effective expropriation' of such a right or an obligation to grant a licence, but a straightforward restriction of the options available under European Union law.

150 The fact that the exercise of such options by an undertaking in a dominant position is limited or made subject to conditions in order to ensure that competition already weakened by the presence of that undertaking is not subsequently undermined is in no way an exceptional case and does not justify a derogation from Article [102], unlike a situation in which the unfettered exercise of an exclusive right awarded for the realisation of an investment or creation is limited.

...

153 The General Court therefore did not commit any error of law in rejecting, at paragraphs 678 to 684 of the judgment under appeal, the appellants' argument that the compatibility with Article [102] of the conduct impugned in the context of the second abuse should be assessed in accordance with the criteria applied, inter alia, in *IMS Health*, or in holding, at paragraphs 824 and 826 of the judgment under appeal, that, for the purposes of characterising that conduct as an abuse of a dominant position, it is sufficient to demonstrate that it is such as to restrict competition and, in particular, to constitute an impediment to generic products entering the market and to parallel imports.

154 The General Court was also fully entitled, in ascertaining whether the Commission had actually proved this in respect of generic products, to hold, at paragraphs 829 to 835 of the judgment under appeal, that the fact that the regulatory framework offers alternative means, which are longer and more costly, to obtain a MA did not prevent the conduct of an undertaking in a dominant position from being abusive where that conduct, considered objectively, has the sole purpose of rendering the abridged procedure provided for by the legislator in point 8(a)(iii) of the third paragraph of Article 4 of Directive 65/65 unavailable and therefore of excluding the producers of generic products from the market for as long as possible and of increasing the costs incurred by them in overcoming barriers to entry to the market, thereby delaying the significant competitive pressure exerted by those products.

In this highly significant judgment the CJ concurred with the GC in widening the reach of Article 102. A dominant undertaking may commit an abuse even if it is exercising legal rights. The marketing authorisation part of the *AstraZeneca* judgment places severe limitations on the strategies adopted by dominant pharmaceutical companies for managing the life-cycle of their products and extracting the maximum return from their investments in innovation. Despite accepting that a dominant undertaking has no duty to protect its competitors the EU Courts in effect imposed an obligation on AZ to maintain in force its marketing authorisations in order to assist its competitors to enter the market. This was on the basis of the 'special responsibility' and a particular interpretation of 'competition on the merits'. Moreover, the requirement is only that there is sufficient evidence that the conduct is 'capable' of anti-competitive effects rather than that it produces actual or likely effects. AZ's intentions were accorded more importance than such effects and there is no emphasis on consumers.

AstraZeneca has to be seen in the context of the Commission's whole policy over generic drugs and the position of 'blockbuster' medicines,[829] and it is highly fact-specific. It leaves pharmaceutical companies, at least, in a difficult and uncertain position in respect of what positive obligations can be imposed upon them and the extent of their freedom to pursue their own commercial interests.[830]

(ii) Standard-essential Patents and Patent Ambushes

Standardisation agreements, whereby undertakings in a particular industry or market define technical or quality requirements with which current or future products, production processes, services, or methods may comply, are discussed in Chapter 10. Patents which are essential to the technology incorporated in such standards are known as standard-essential patents (SEPs).[831] Negotiations before the standard is adopted usually cover the use of SEPs and the owners of such patents are normally required to commit themselves to licensing their rights to third parties on FRAND terms.[832] The owner of an SEP may be in a dominant position but this is not necessarily so. There are an increasing number of disputes concerning SEPs, particularly in the high-technology sector. Where a party to the agreement conceals that it has patents and patent technology relevant to the technology incorporated in the standard and then attempts to enforce its rights the action is known as a 'patent ambush'. Where an undertaking is in a dominant position on the relevant market a patent ambush can be an exclusionary abuse in that the undertaking concerned may gain control over the standard, thereby excluding potentially competing technologies and raising barriers to entry.[833] In *Rambus*[834] the Commission was concerned with the conduct of an undertaking which it considered had engaged in a 'patent ambush' in respect of the DRAM standard.[835] Because Rambus was not in a dominant position during the standard-setting procedure, the Commission dealt with the matter as one of excessive pricing for the royalties it claimed for the use of the patents and adopted a

---

[829] See e.g., the Competition Commissioner's Press Release at the time of the decision, IP/05/737.

[830] For a lengthy consideration of the issues, see F. Murphy and F. Liberatore, 'Abuse of Regulatory Procedures—the *Astra-Zeneca Case*' [2009] ECLR 223, 289, and 314 (the article, in three parts, was written before the GC judgment).

[831] See P. Chappatte, 'FRAND Commitments—the Case for Antitrust Intervention' (2009) 5 *European Competition Journal* 320; D. Geradin, 'Ten Years of DG Competition Effort to Provide Guidance on the Application of Competition Rules to the Licensing of Standard-Essential Patents: Where Do We Stand?', available at <http://ssrn.com/abstract=2204359>.

[832] Fair, reasonable, and non-discriminatory. See Guidelines on horizontal co-operation agreements [2011] OJ C11/1, paras. 283–287.

[833] See Commission MEMO/09/544, issued at the time of the *Rambus* Commitments decision.

[834] COMP/38.636; Commitments decision, 9 December 2009, Summary [2010] OJ C30/17; IP/09/1867; MEMO/09/544. For commitments decisions, see Chap. 13.

[835] Dynamic Random Access Memory chips. They are used to temporarily store data, particularly on PCs. At the time of the decision DRAMs compliant with the standard (the JEDEC standard) had approximately 95% of the (world) market and were used in nearly all PCs, see IP/09/1867.

Commitments Decision whereby Rambus agreed to cap the royalties.[836] In two subsequent cases, both arising out of the intensive battles on the mobile phone market, the Commission has sent Statements of Objections to two undertakings, Samsung and Motorola Mobility, stating that it considers that their attempts to enforce their SEPs against Apple by seeking injunctions in various national courts amounts to an abuse of a dominant position contrary to Article 102.[837]

D. PURSUIT OF LEGAL PROCEEDINGS, VEXATIOUS LITIGATION, AND ENFORCING LEGAL RIGHTS

It may be an abuse for a dominant undertaking to pursue legal proceedings against a competitor. This was suggested by *BBI/Boosey & Hawkes*[838] but the Commission did not pursue the point, concentrating rather on the refusal to supply aspect.[839] In *ITT Promedia*.[840] Belgacom, the dominant supplier of voice telephony services in Belgium was engaged in a dispute with Promedia about the publication of telephone directories. Promedia complained to the Commission that Belgacom was abusing its dominant position by conducting national litigation against it. The Commission rejected the complaint on the grounds that the conduct of litigation by a dominant firm could be abusive only if two cumulative criteria were met: (i) that the action could not reasonably be considered as an attempt to establish its rights and could therefore serve only to harass the opposite party and (ii) it was conceived in the framework of a plan whose goal was to eliminate competition. The Commission considered the case did not fulfil the criteria. Promedia appealed, alleging that the Commission had applied the criteria incorrectly. The GC expressly said that it was not necessary for it to rule on the correctness of the criteria[841] and confined itself to holding that they had been properly applied. The implication of the GC judgment, however, is that the criteria themselves are correct. The following extract deals with the first criterion.

Case T-111/96, *ITT Promedia* v. *EC Commission* [1998] ECR II-2937

General Court

60.... [a]s the Commission has rightly emphasised, the ability to assert one's rights through the courts and the judicial control which that entails, constitute the expression of a general principle of law which underlies the constitutional traditions common to the Member States and which is also laid down in Articles 6 and 13 of the European Convention for the Protection of Human Rights and Fundamental Freedoms of 4 November 1950 (see Case 222/84, *Johnson* v. *Chief Constable of the Royal Ulster Constabulary*...). As access to the Court is a fundamental right and a general principle ensuring the rule of law, it is only in wholly exceptional circumstances that the fact that legal proceedings are brought is capable of constituting an abuse of a dominant position within the meaning of Article [102].

61. Second, since the two cumulative criteria constitute an exception to the general principle of access to the courts, which ensures the rule of law, they must be construed and applied strictly, in the manner which does not defeat the application of the general rule (see, *inter alia*, Case T-105/95, *WWF UK* v. *E.C.Commission*...).

...

---

[836] See Section 15.A.i, p. 581. See also *Qualcomm* MEMO/09/516, see Section 15,A.i, n. 931.

[837] *Samsung*, IP/12/1448, 21 December 2012; *Motorola Mobility*, IP/13/406, 6 May 2013.

[838] *BBI/Boosey & Hawkes* [1987] OJ L286/36, [1988] 4 CMLR 67.

[839] See Section 12.E, p. 550.

[840] Case T-111/96, *ITT Promedia NV* v. *Commission* [1998] ECR II-2937.

[841] *ITT Promedia NV* v. *Commission* [1998] ECR II-2937, para. 57.

72. According to the first of the two cumulative criteria set out by the Commission in the contested decision, legal proceedings can be characterised as an abuse, within the meaning of Article [102], only if they cannot reasonably be considered to be an attempt to assert the rights of the undertaking concerned and can therefore only serve to harass the opposing party. It is therefore the situation existing when the action in question is brought which must be taken into account in order to determine whether that criterion is satisfied.

73. Furthermore, when applying that criterion, it is not a question of determining whether the rights which the undertaking concerned was asserting when it brought its action actually existed or whether that action was well founded, but rather of determining whether such an action was intended to assert what that undertaking could, at that moment, reasonably consider to be its rights. According to the second part of that criterion, as worded, it is satisfied solely when the action did not have that aim, that being the sole case in which it may be assumed that such action could only serve to harass the opposing party.

The Commission based its criteria on human rights—the rights of access to the courts. The test is not whether the right claimed exists, but whether the dominant undertaking may reasonably consider that it does. The GC judgment therefore confirms that vexatious litigation *can* be an abuse, but only in limited circumstances. Moreover, the GC held that Belgacom was entitled to rely on its rights under national law unless and until it was ruled that the national law had been invalidated.[842]

In *AstraZeneca* the Commission considered the question of whether a patent holder's defence to an action for a declaration of invalidity could be an abuse. The Commission differentiated between *defending* an action and *initiating* an action, but as it viewed the costs and delays at issue as having arisen from AZ's misrepresentations to the patent authorities rather than from its defence of legal proceedings, the question was not pursued.[843] It has been seen that the Commission has taken the view that it may be an abuse for the owner of a SEP to bring an injunction to enforce its rights.[844]

The GC also held in *ITT* v. *Promedia* that a dominant undertaking which sought performance of a contract would commit an abuse only if the claim went beyond what it could reasonably expect from the contract.[845] However, the CJ held that it was an abuse for the dominant liner conference in *Compagnie Maritime Belge*[846] to insist on the Zaïrean authorities keeping strictly to the terms of the exclusive contract they had signed. This meant that Zaïre could not continue giving a small amount of trade to a new competitor.

E. SEARCH ENGINE PRACTICES

In November 2010 the Commission opened an investigation into alleged anti-competitive practices by Google after receipt of complaints from 17 undertakings including Microsoft and Oracle.[847] After protracted negotiations[848] Google proposed commitments in April 2013.[849] The *Google* case

---

[842] *ITT Promedia NV v. Commission* [1998] ECR II-2937, paras. 93–95.

[843] COMP/A.37.507/F3, *AstraZeneca* [2006] 5 CMLR 287, 15 June 2005, paras. 736–739.

[844] *Samsung* and *Motorola*, see n, 837. See generally M. Rato and N. Petit, 'Abuse of Dominance in Technology-Enabled Markets: Established Standards Reconsidered?' (2013) 9 *European Competition Journal* 1, 58–64.

[845] *ITT Promedia NV v. Commission* [1998] ECR II-2937, para. 129.

[846] Cases C-395 and 396/96 P, *Compagnie Maritime Belge Transports SA v. EC Commission* [2000] ECR I-1365, paras. 72–88.

[847] IP/10/1624.

[848] See the statement by Commissioner Almunia, Speech/12/967, 18 December 2012.

[849] These were put out for a market test on 25 April 2013, pursuant to the procedure for taking a commitments decision under Reg. 1/2003, Art. 9. See further Chap. 13, Section 8.D.iii, p. 982.

is described here as a whole although it raises specific issues such as discrimination and unfair practices which are dealt with elsewhere.

The Commission found that Google had a 90 per cent share of the market for general web search services (horizontal searches) in the EEA. It also operated specialised 'vertical' search services, which are search engines focusing on specific product or service areas, such as Google Shopping and Google Flights. These competed with the vertical search services of other undertakings. Google also had a strong position in the market for online search advertising. The Commission had four concerns:[850]

(i) The favourable treatment, within Google's web search results, of links to Google's own specialised web search services as compared to links to competing specialised web search services (i.e. services allowing users to search for specific categories of information such as restaurants, hotels or products);

(ii) The use by Google without consent of original content from third party web sites in its own specialised web search services;

(iii) Agreements that oblige third party web sites ('publishers') to obtain all or most of their online search advertisements from Google; and

(iv) Contractual restrictions on the transferability of online search advertising campaigns to rival search advertising platforms and the management of such campaigns across Google's Adwords and rival search advertising platforms.

The Commission considered that these practices could harm consumers by reducing choice and stifling innovation in the fields of specialised search services and online search advertising. To remedy these the Commission proposed accepting Google's commitments that for five years it would:

(i) - label promoted links to its own specialised search services so that users can distinguish them from natural web search results,

- clearly separate these promoted links from other web search results by clear graphical features (such as a frame), and

- display links to three rival specialised search services close to its own services, in a place that is clearly visible to users,

(ii) - offer all websites the option to opt-out from the use of all their content in Google's specialised search services, while ensuring that any opt-out does not unduly affect the ranking of those web sites in Google's general web search results,

- offer all specialised search web sites that focus on product search or local search the option to mark certain categories of information in such a way that such information is not indexed or used by Google,

- provide newspaper publishers with a mechanism allowing them to control on a web page per web page basis the display of their content in Google News,

(iii) no longer include in its agreements with publishers any written or unwritten obligations that would require them to source online search advertisements exclusively from Google,

and

(iv) no longer impose obligations that would prevent advertisers from managing search advertising campaigns across competing advertising platforms.

These commitment proposals followed a settlement between Google and the FTC in the US in respect of Google's search-related practices.[851]

The proposed commitments in respect of the alleged unfair practices of using third party content without consent and of employing exclusivity clauses are less controversial than those pertaining to

---

[850] IP/13/371, 25 April 2013; see also MEMO/13/383 (Questions and Answers).

[851] FTC Press Release 3 January 2013, available at <http://ftc.gov/opa/2013/01/google.shtm>.

the alleged 'search bias'. Many questions have been raised about what theory of harm underlies the issue of what is called 'search neutrality'.[852] In the press release following the FTC settlement the FTC said that it had concluded that 'the introduction of Universal Search, as well as additional changes made to Google's search algorithms—even those that may have had the effect of harming individual competitors—could plausibly be justified as innovations that improved Google's product and the experience of users'. If the EU *Google* case is indeed settled by commitments then these issues will not be tested further at present. The commitments may, however, benefit rather than disadvantage Google in ensuring that its own specialist services are prominently labelled as such, which, given the strength of the Google brand, could make them more attractive to searchers.[853]

F. VERTICAL AND HORIZONTAL INTEGRATION

Although it is not an infringement of Article 102 for a dominant undertaking to integrate vertically, it has been seen that actions taken in pursuit of a policy of vertical integration may infringe. Many cases finding a refusal to supply[854] or tying[855] to infringe Article 102 involved actions taken by a dominant undertaking which would enable it to integrate vertically.

In *Continental Can*[856] it was established that Article 102 could apply to mergers whereby an undertaking strengthened its dominant position. Since the EU Merger Regulation regime has been in force, however, the general rule is that the Regulation alone applies to mergers falling within its scope.[857]

14. DISCRIMINATION CONTRARY TO ARTICLE 102(C)

A. GENERAL

Article 102(c) states that an abuse may, in particular, consist in:

applying dissimilar conditions to equivalent transactions with other trading parties, thereby placing them at a competitive disadvantage.

This is a clear reference to secondary line injury, i.e. between the customers of the dominant undertaking. 'Dissimilar conditions' obviously includes dissimilar prices. There are a number of problems in the application of Article 102(c). First, in some cases, particularly older ones, Article 102(c) has been applied to situations of primary line injury. Secondly, 'equivalent transactions' refers to the fact that discrimination involves different prices or conditions for transactions entailing the same costs.[858] However, the elements which make up a transaction are complex and identifying equivalence is difficult, and the EU Courts and the Commission have often assumed that transactions are equivalent without a sufficient analysis.[859] Thirdly, an infringement of Article 102(c) has sometimes been found without identifying

---

[852] See in particular, G. A. Manne and J. D. Wright, 'If Search Neutrality is the Answer, What's the Question?', available at <http://papers.ssrn.com/sol3/papers.cfm?abstract_id=1807951>; D. Crane, 'Search Neutrality as an Antitrust Principle', available at <http://papers.ssrn.com/sol3/papers.cfm?abstract_id=1961742>.

[853] A spokesman for one of the complainants, Foundem, was quoted in the *Daily Telegraph* on 26 April 2013 as saying that any settlement should stop Google abusing its monopoly, not require it change the way it does so.

[854] Such as Cases 6 and 7/73, *Istituto Chemioterapico Italiano Spa and Commercial Solvents Corp* v. *Commission* [1974] ECR 223 and Case 22/78, *Hugin Kassaregister AB* v. *EC Commission* [1979] ECR 1869.

[855] e.g., the *Digital Undertaking*, Commission Press Release IP/97/868.

[856] Case 6/72, *Europemballage Corp & Continental Can Co Inc* v. *Commission* [1973] ECR 215; see Chaps. 5 and 15.

[857] Council Regulation Reg. 139/2004 [2004] OJ L24/1, see Chap. 15.

[858] For price discrimination generally, see Section 7.B.

[859] e.g., railway traffic via German ports and via Belgian and Dutch ones (Case T-229/94, *Deutsche Bahn AG* v. *Commission* [1997] ECR II-1689), and transactions with exclusive and non-exclusive customers (in the loyalty rebate cases).

any competitive disadvantage and furthermore financial disadvantage has been too easily equated with competitive disadvantage.

Where a vertically integrated dominant undertaking price discriminates between its own downstream operation and its downstream competitors it may be committing an exclusionary abuse such as a margin squeeze and it should be a matter of Article 102(b) rather than Article 102(c). A non-vertically integrated undertaking will normally only have an interest in discriminating between its customers if it can thereby take account of factors such as their different elasticities of demand (in which case the question of whether the transactions are 'equivalent' arises), or possibly if it is preparing to enter the downstream market. However, in some cases, particularly in the transport sector and/or where statutory monopolists are concerned, a non-vertically integrated dominant undertaking has discriminated to favour certain customers on nationality, or similar, grounds. Furthermore, Article 102(c) has been applied to geographical price discrimination.

B. THE APPLICATION OF ARTICLE 102(C) TO PRIMARY LINE INJURY AND EXCLUSIONARY CONDUCT

The enforcement of Article 102 law has more often been concerned with the exclusionary effects on competitors of the pricing policies of dominant undertakings i.e. primary line injury,[860] than with secondary line injury. However, Article 102 (c) has sometimes been applied in cases of exclusionary abuses, particularly those concerning discounts and rebates, without a proper analysis of whether the conditions in Article 102(c) were satisfied. This can be traced back to *Hoffmann-La Roche* itself[861] and was a feature of *Michelin I*[862] and *Irish Sugar*.[863] In *British Airways*,[864] *Clearstream*,[865] and *Solvay*[866] conduct which was held to be exclusionary was also condemned as price discrimination contrary to Article 102(c). The tendency to use Article 102(c) in exclusionary situations has been widely criticised.[867]

C. ARTICLE 102(C) AND NON-VERTICALLY INTEGRATED UNDERTAKINGS

The Commission has taken a number of decisions finding the operators of transport infrastructures guilty of abusive conduct by charging discriminatory prices contrary to Article 102(c), often on nationality grounds. In the first *Corsica Ferries* case[868] the port operator in Genoa charged different

---

[860] See Sections 8, 9, and 10.D.

[861] Case 85/76, *Hoffmann-La Roche & Co AG v. Commission* [1979] ECR 461, para. 90, which does not actually mention Article 102(c) but says that '…the effect of fidelity rebates is to apply dissimilar conditions to equivalent transactions with other trading parties …'. The Commission had characterised the rebates as contrary to Article 102(c).

[862] Case 322/81, *NV Nederlandsche Banden-Industrie Michelin v. Commission* [1983] ECR 3461, where, nevertheless, the CJ annulled the Commission's finding of discrimination contrary to Article 102(c) on the facts (paras. 90–91).

[863] Case T–228/97, *Irish Sugar plc v. Commission* [1999] ECR II-2969, aff'd, Case C-497/99P, *Irish Sugar plc v. Commission* [2001] ECR I-5333. See also Case T-65/89, *BPB Industries and British Gypsum Ltd v. Commission* [1993] ECR II-389, aff'd Case C-310/93P, *BPB Industries PLC and British Gypsum Ltd v. Commission* [1995] ECR I-865.

[864] Case C-95/04 *British Airways v. EC Commission* [2007] ECR I-2331; see Section 10.D.iii.f, p. 470.

[865] Case T-301/04, *Clearstream Banking v. Commission* [2009] ECR II-3155.

[866] Cases T-57 and 58/01, *Solvay v. Commission* [2009] ECR II-4621; the Commission decision was annulled for procedural reasons, Case C-109/10 P, *Solvay SA v. European Commission*, 25 October 2011, without the substance of the Article 102 issues being discussed.

[867] See e.g. J. Temple Lang and R. O'Donoghue, 'Defining Legitimate Competition: How to Clarify Pricing Abuses under Article 102EC' (2002) 26 *Fordham Int'l LJ* 83; E. Rousseva, *Rethinking Exclusionary Abuses in EU Competition Law* (Hart Publishing, 2010), 215–217; Nazzini, *The Foundations of European Union Competition Law* (cited in n. 106), 249–250; Geradin et al., *EU Competition Law and Economics* (cited in n. 160), 4.475–4.505; Rousseva and Marquis, 'Hell Freezes Over: A Climate Change for Assessing Exclusionary Conduct under Article 102 TFEU' (cited in n. 2), 32.

[868] Case C-18/93, *Corsica Ferries Italia Srl v. Corporazione dei Piloti del Porto di Genova* [1994] ECR I–1783.

prices for pilotage services depending on whether the vessels were sailing between two domestic (Italian) ports[869] or were on an international route; in *Deutsche Bahn*[870] a national rail operator applied different prices in respect of railway traffic via German ports and traffic via Belgian and Dutch ones; and in *Aeroports de Paris*[871] the airport authority at Orly and Charles de Gaulle in Paris charged different levels of fees to companies it licensed to provide ground-handling services. In none of these cases was there found to be any objective justification for the differentials.[872] In *Portuguese Airports*[873] the airport authority applied a seemingly uniform system of quantity discounts which was so constructed that it gave larger discounts to Portuguese airlines than to others. This was found to infringe Article 102(c) and the CJ took the opportunity to discuss the application of Article 102(c) to quantity discounts. The airport operator, inter alia, gave discounts on landing fees to airlines depending on the number of planes they landed. There were a number of discount bands and the highest rate of discount could be earned only by airlines with a very large number of landings. The only airlines to qualify for this high rate were the two Portuguese carriers, TAP and Portugalia. The CJ said that while it was inherent in any quantity discount system that the largest buyers obtained the highest reductions, nevertheless it could be discriminatory if the system included thresholds that only a few very large users could reach and which gave them disproportionate rewards.[874] The relevant passage from *Portuguese Airports* was cited in *Solvay* where the CJ applied Article 102(c) to 'quantity' rebates in an exclusionary situation.[875]

D. VERTICALLY INTEGRATED UNDERTAKINGS

Findings of Article 102(c) discrimination where there was an element of vertical integration include *Deutsche Post: Interception of Cross-Border Mail*,[876] where the German postal authority was held to have discriminated without objective justification between different types of mail coming into Germany;[877] *Deutsche Bahn*[878] where a national rail operator applied different prices in respect of railway traffic via German ports and traffic via Belgian and Dutch ones; and *Clearstream*, the facts of which are given earlier,[879] where for a period the undertaking had charged higher prices to a competitor of its sister company.

The *Google* proceedings discussed previously[880] involve the claim that Google manipulates the results of its general search engine to discriminate in favour of its own vertical search engines at the expense of those of its competitors. This would appear to be a matter of possible application of Article 102(c).

---

[869] This is known as maritime cabotage.

[870] Case T-229/94, *Deutsche Bahn AG v. Commission* [1997] ECR II–1689, aff'd Case C-436/97, *Deutsche Bahn AG v. Commission* [1999] ECR I-2387.

[871] Case T-128/98, *Aeroports de Paris v. Commission* [2000] ECR II–3929, upheld by the CJ, Case C-82/01, [2002] ECR I-9297.

[872] See also *Brussels National Airport (Zaventem)* [1995] OJ L216/8, [1996] 4 CMLR 232; *Ilmailulaitos/Luftsfartverket (Finnish Airports)* [1999] OJ L69/24, [1999] 5 CMLR 90; *Spanish Airports* [2000] OJ L208/36.

[873] Case C-163/99, *Portugal v. Commission* [2001] ECR I-2613 (*Portuguese Airports*).

[874] *Portuguese Airports*, paras. 50–53.

[875] Case T-57, *Solvay v. Commission* [2009] ECR II-4621, para. 396.

[876] [2002] OJ L331/40, [2002] 4 CMLR 598.

[877] Statutory monopolists entrusted with a 'service of general economic interest' have a limited exemption from the competition rules under Article 106(2) of the Treaty. This is discussed in Chap. 8.

[878] Case T-229/94, *Deutsche Bahn AG v. Commission* [1997] ECR II–1689, aff'd Case C-436/97, *Deutsche Bahn AG v. Commission* [1999] ECR I-2387.

[879] Case T-301/04, *Clearstream Banking v. Commission* [2009] ECR II-3155, see Section 12.C.vi, p. 523.

[880] IP/13/371, 25 April 2013, see Section 13.E, p. 565.

E. GEOGRAPHICAL PRICE DISCRIMINATION

Geographical price discrimination means charging different prices for the same products or services in different geographical territories. It is more of an issue in EU competition law than in national systems because its most obvious form—different prices in different Member States—may be contrary to the single market objective. Artificial price differences across the EU should be eliminated or reduced by arbitrage and parallel trade (and indeed the price differences should encourage parallel trade) but this may be impeded by other factors. If those factors are measures taken by the dominant undertaking to buttress the pricing policy the prices will be an abuse in themselves and the buttressing measures are also likely to infringe Article 102. In both leading cases on geographical price discrimination, *United Brands*[881] and *Tetra Pak II*,[882] Article 102(c) was applied and the dominant undertaking was found to have taken measures to prevent parallel trade.

Case 27/76, *United Brands* v. *Commission* [1978] ECR 207

United Brands shipped its bananas across the Atlantic and unloaded them at Rotterdam and Bremerhaven. At those ports it sold them to its approved ripener/distributors from various Member States at different prices. The prices reflected the different prices in the retail markets in the Member States. The contractual conditions under which the bananas were sold contained a prohibition on the distributors reselling the bananas while they were still green (the 'green banana clause'). The Commission concluded that this clause was simply a tactic to reinforce the price differences because once the bananas had started to turn yellow they were so perishable that it was not possible to export them to other Member States. The Commission also found that United Brands' practice of supplying the distributors with less than they ordered made them sell locally instead of in other markets. The Commission held that these practices infringed Article 102. United Brands appealed, inter alia on this issue.

Court of Justice

...

227. Although the responsibility for establishing the single banana market does not lie with the applicant, it can only endeavour to take 'what the market can bear' provided that it complies with the rules for the regulation and co-ordination of the market laid down by the Treaty.

228. Once it can be grasped that differences in transport costs, taxation, customs duties, the wages of the labour force, the conditions of marketing, the differences in the parity of currencies, the density of competition may eventually culminate in different retail selling price levels according to the Member States, then it follows those differences are factors which UBC only has to take into account to a limited extent since it sells a product which is always the same and at the same place to ripener/distributors who—alone—bear the risks of the consumer's market.

229. The interplay of supply and demand should, owing to its nature, only be applied to each stage where it is really manifest.

230. The mechanisms of the market are adversely affected if the price is calculated by leaving out one stage of the market and taking into account the law of supply and demand as between the vendor and the ultimate consumer and not as between the vendor (UBC) and the purchaser (the ripener/distributor).

231. Thus, by reason of its dominant position UBC, fed with information by its local representatives, was in fact able to impose its selling price on the intermediate purchaser. This price and also the 'weekly

---

[881] Case 27/76, *United Brands* v. *Commission* [1978] ECR 207.

[882] Case C-333/94 P, *Tetra Pak International SA* v. *Commission* [1996] ECR I-5951.

quota allocated' is only fixed and notified to the customer four days before the vessel carrying the bananas berths.

232. These discriminatory prices, which varied according to the circumstances of the Member States, were just so many obstacles to the free movement of goods and their effect was intensified by the clause forbidding the resale of bananas while still green and by reducing the deliveries of the quantities ordered.

233. A rigid partitioning of national markets was thus created at price levels, which were artificially different, placing certain distributor/ripeners at a competitive disadvantage, since compared with what it should have been competition had thereby been distorted.

234. Consequently the policy of differing prices enabling UBC to apply dissimilar conditions to equivalent transactions with other trading parties, thereby placing them at a competitive disadvantage, was an abuse of a dominant position.

This part of the *United Brands* judgment contains some unconvincing reasoning which has been savagely criticised.[883] For example, treating the law of supply and demand as normative or prescriptive ('to be applied', paragraph 229) rather than descriptive; allowing an undertaking to take into account different retail conditions and taking what the market can bear only if it bears the risks of the consumer market, thus giving undertakings an incentive to vertically integrate; describing the discriminatory prices as 'just so many obstacles to the free movement of goods' (paragraph 232) whereas differential pricing would normally stimulate parallel trade;[884] and favouring profits going to distributors rather than producers. The real objection to the price discrimination in *United Brands* was of course that it offended against the concept of the single market.

In *Tetra Pak II* the Commission found wide disparities in the prices that Tetra Pak charged for its milk packaging machinery and cartons in different Member States despite the fact that the geographical market was Community-wide. It held these prices differences to be due to artificial partitioning of the market and not to objective market conditions.[885] The decision was upheld by the GC, which found that 'those disparities in price could not be attributed to objective market conditions'.[886]

In *Irish Sugar*[887] the dominant undertaking operated a system of 'sugar export rebates', granted on sales of industrial sugar to companies exporting to other Member States. The Commission found that this practice discriminated against customers of industrial sugar supplying the domestic Irish market. The GC upheld the Commission's finding that this was an abuse, holding that market mechanisms were distorted by pricing according to the location of the customers' buyers.

Whether or not geographical price discrimination is an abuse in the absence of measures taken by the dominant undertaking to partition the market is unclear. In *Tetra Pak II* the GC reiterated that setting different prices could be justified by local conditions. In *United Brands*, however, local conditions did not justify variations in retail prices. This suggests that once the Member States are held to be in the same geographic market and costs are the same, objective justification for price discrimination between them will be hard to prove. However, in the absence of buttressing measures (such as the

[883] W. Bishop, 'Price Discrimination under Article 86: Political Economy in the European Court' (1981) 44 *MLR* 282; L. Zanon, 'Price Discrimination under Article 102 of the EEC Treaty: A Comment on the UBC Case' (1982) 31 *ICLQ* 36; M. Siragusa, 'The Application of Article 86 to the Pricing Policy of Dominant Companies: Discriminatory and Unfair Prices' (1979) 16 *CMLRev* 179.

[884] The problem in *United Brands* was rather the buttressing 'green banana' clause which did not intensify the effect of the differing prices but neutralised it.

[885] e.g., customers for the machines could purchase cartons only from Tetra Pak itself or a company designated by it, and so customers in high-price countries were not free to purchase from third parties in lower-price areas.

[886] Case T-83/91, *Tetra Pak Rausing v. Commission* [1994] ECR II-755, para. 170. See also Case T-168/01, *GlaxoSmithKline Services Unlimited v. Commission* [2006] ECR II-2969, para. 177.

[887] [1997] OJ L258/1, [1997] 5 CMLR 666.

'green banana clause') the ability to maintain different prices in different geographical areas suggests that there are *different* geographic markets, and so Article 102(c) should not apply.[888]

F. COMPETITIVE DISADVANTAGE AND ARTICLE 102(C)

The abuse set out in Article 102(c) is the application of dissimilar conditions to equivalent transactions with other trading parties 'thereby placing them at a competitive disadvantage'. In respect of the export rebates in *Irish Sugar*, the GC did not accept that the non-export customers suffered no competitive disadvantage.[889] However, in *United Brands* the CJ applied Article 102(c) even though the ripener/distributors from different Member States were not in competition with one another (partly because of the measures United Brands had taken to prevent parallel trade, such as the 'green banana clause') and greengrocers in Ireland certainly did not compete with those in Germany. Likewise, in *Corsica Ferries I* the CJ applied Article 102(c) regardless of the fact that the domestic and international shipping lines were not competing with each other.[890] In *Deutsche Post—Interception of Cross-Border Mail*, the Commission answered the argument that customers were not put at a competitive disadvantage by having to pay more than others for their cross-border mail: the Commission pointed out that the list in Article 102 is not exhaustive:

> In any event, the Court of Justice has stated that the list of abuses mentioned in Article [102] itself is not exhaustive and thus only serves as examples of possible ways for a dominant firm to abuse its market power…Article [102] may be applied even in the absence of a direct effect on competition between undertakings on any given market. This provision may…also be applied in situations where a dominant undertaking's behaviour causes damage directly to consumers…The senders of the disputed mailings are consumers of postal services. Due to the behaviour of DPAG, these consumers are affected negatively by having to pay prices for these services which are higher than those charged to other senders and by having their mailings delayed significantly. Likewise, the German addressees are to be regarded as consumers who are affected in a negative manner by the behaviour of DPAG. Having their incoming mail delayed may prevent the addressees from benefiting from commercial offers made by the senders.[891]

The Commission here was saying that directly damaging consumers may infringe Article 102, although of course consumers will usually not be 'in competition' with one another. Since Deutsche Post was a statutory monopolist the consumers had no alternative supplier: nor indeed did the shipping lines in *Corsica Ferries*. Moreover, both *Deutsche Post* and *Corsica Ferries* involved discrimination in the context of inter-Member State transactions, while *United Brands*, as we have seen, involved compartmentalising the common market. In such situations one can expect that EU law will disapprove of discriminatory behaviour, but it is difficult to reconcile this with the wording of Article 102(c).

In *British Airways* the bonus/commission scheme operated by British Airways was found by the Commission to infringe Article 102 because of its capability to exclude competitors.[892] It was also held to specifically infringe Article 102(c) because it discriminated between the travel agents in giving different rewards to different agents for selling the same number of tickets. This was upheld by the GC[893] and the CJ.

---

[888]   See further Geradin et al., *EU Competition Law and Economics* (cited in n. 160), 4.525–4.541.

[889]   Case T-228/97, *Irish Sugar plc v. Commission* [1999] ECR II-2969, paras. 140–9.

[890]   Case C-18/93, *Corsica Ferries Italia Srl v. Corporazione dei Piloti del Porto di Genova* [1994] ECR I-1783. The CJ did not mention the issue at all: the AG did, but stated that it did not matter, para. 34 of the Opinion of Van Gerven AG.

[891]   [2002] OJ L331/40, [2002] 4 CMLR 598, para. 133.

[892]   *Virgin/British Airways* [2000] OJ L30/1, [2000] 4 CMLR 999, see Section 10.D.iii.f., p. 469 ff.

[893]   Case T-219/99, *British Airways v. Commission* [2003] ECR II-5917.

Case C-95/04 P, *British Airways* v. *Commission* [2007] ECR I-2331

Court of Justice

133. Subparagraph (c) of the second paragraph of Article [102] prohibits any discrimination on the part of an undertaking in a dominant position which consists in the application of dissimilar conditions to equivalent transactions with other trading parties, thereby placing them at a competitive disadvantage (Case C-163/99 *Portugal* v *Commission*...paragraph 46).

134. In the present case, it is undisputed that BA applied different commission rates to travel agents operating in the United Kingdom according to whether or not they had achieved their sales objectives by comparison with the reference period.

135. It remains to be examined, first, whether the [General Court] was right to rely on the equivalence of the travel agents' services in order to conclude that the bonus schemes at issue, being capable of entailing the application of different rates of commission to agents who had sold the same number of BA tickets, were discriminatory, and, secondly, whether, without committing an error of law, that Court could dispense with detailed findings concerning the existence of a competitive disadvantage.

136. In the first part of its fifth plea, BA criticises the analysis by the [General Court] of the comparability of the services carried out by travel agents who attained their objectives in BA ticket sales and those carried out by agents who did not attain those objectives. In particular, BA accuses the [General Court] of failing to take account of the greater economic usefulness from the airline's point of view of the services of travel agents who attained their sales objectives or increased their turnover.

137. On that latter point, which concerns the assessment by the [General Court] of the circumstances of this case from which it might be possible to deduce the comparability or otherwise of travel agents' services for an airline such as BA, it is sufficient to point out that the assessment of facts and evidence is a matter for the [General Court] alone. It is thus not for the Court of Justice, on an appeal, to substitute its own assessment of market data and the competitive position for that of the [General Court]. This claim is therefore inadmissible.

138. As for the second claim, that the [General Court] erred in law in relation to subparagraph (c) of the second paragraph of Article [102], by holding that transactions involving a travel agent who had increased his sales of BA tickets and transactions involving an agent who had not increased them constituted 'equivalent transactions' within the meaning of that provision, it should be noted that, in paragraph 234 of the judgment under appeal, the [General Court] pointed out that attainment by United Kingdom travel agents of their BA ticket sales growth targets led to an increase in the rate of commission paid to them by BA not only on BA tickets sold after the target was reached but also on all BA tickets handled by the agents during the period in question.

139. The [General Court] logically inferred therefrom that the bonus schemes at issue led to the sale of an identical number of BA tickets by United Kingdom travel agents being remunerated at different levels according to whether or not those agents had attained their sales growth targets by comparison with the reference period.

140. The [General Court] does not therefore appear to have erred in law by regarding as equivalent the services of travel agents whose sales of BA tickets had, in absolute terms, been at the same level during a given period. This second claim is therefore unfounded.

141. Therefore, the first part of the fifth plea must be dismissed as in part inadmissible and in part unfounded.

142. In the second part of its fifth plea, BA argues that, for the purposes of correctly applying subparagraph (c) of the second paragraph of Article [102], the mere finding of the [General Court], in paragraph 238 of the judgment under appeal, that travel agents, in their capacity to compete with each other, are 'naturally affected by the discriminatory conditions of remuneration inherent in BA's performance reward schemes' is not sufficient, since concrete evidence of a competitive disadvantage was required.

143. The specific prohibition of discrimination in subparagraph (c) of the second paragraph of Article [102] forms part of the system for ensuring, in accordance with Article 3(1)(g) EC, that competition is not distorted in the internal market. The commercial behaviour of the undertaking in a dominant position may not distort competition on an upstream or a downstream market, in other words between suppliers or customers of that undertaking. Co-contractors of that undertaking must not be favoured or disfavoured in the area of the competition which they practise amongst themselves.

144. Therefore, in order for the conditions for applying subparagraph (c) of the second paragraph of Article [102] to be met, there must be a finding not only that the behaviour of an undertaking in a dominant market position is discriminatory, but also that it tends to distort that competitive relationship, in other words to hinder the competitive position of some of the business partners of that undertaking in relation to the others (see, to that effect, *Suiker Unie*, paragraphs 523 and 524).

145. In that respect, there is nothing to prevent discrimination between business partners who are in a relationship of competition from being regarded as being abusive as soon as the behaviour of the undertaking in a dominant position tends, having regard to the whole of the circumstances of the case, to lead to a distortion of competition between those business partners. In such a situation, it cannot be required in addition that proof be adduced of an actual quantifiable deterioration in the competitive position of the business partners taken individually.

146. In paragraphs 237 and 238 of the judgment under appeal, the [General Court] found that travel agents in the United Kingdom compete intensely with each other, and that that ability to compete depended on two factors, namely 'their ability to provide seats on flights suited to travellers' wishes, at a reasonable cost' and, secondly, their individual financial resources.

147. Moreover, in the part of the judgment under appeal relating to the examination of the fidelity-building effect of the bonus schemes at issue, the [General Court] found that the latter could lead to exponential changes in the revenue of travel agents.

148. Given that factual situation, the [General Court] could, in the context of its examination of the bonus schemes at issue having regard to subparagraph (c) of the second paragraph of Article [102], move directly, without any detailed intermediate stage, to the conclusion that the possibilities for those agents to compete with each other had been affected by the discriminatory conditions for remuneration implemented by BA.

149. The [General Court] cannot therefore be accused of an error of law in not verifying, or in verifying only briefly, whether and to what extent those conditions had affected the competitive position of BA's commercial partners. The [General Court] was therefore entitled to take the view that the bonus schemes at issue gave rise to a discriminatory effect for the purposes of subparagraph (c) of the second paragraph of Article [102]. The second part of the fifth plea is therefore unfounded.

Paragraph 144 therefore restates that requirement that for discrimination to be an abuse under Article 102(c) there must be competitive disadvantage. However, the Court assumed that the different financial arrangements the agents had with BA because of the different rebates they received automatically meant that some were at a competitive disadvantage compared to others. Paragraphs 144 and 145 only require that the behaviour of the dominant undertaking 'tends' to distort competition and expressly do not require proof of an actual quantifiable deterioration in the individual's competitive position. The standard of proof, therefore, is very low.

In *Kanal*[894] the CJ was asked in effect whether the fact that a copyright management organisation calculates the royalties paid with respect to remuneration due for the television broadcast of musical works protected by copyright differently according to whether the broadcasting companies are commercial or public constituted an abuse of a dominant position. The CJ said that it could, if it put the companies at a competitive disadvantage. However, the practice was capable of being objectively

---

[894] Case C-52/07, *Kanal 5 Ltd v. Föreningen Svenska Tonsättares Internationella Musikbyrå (STIM) upa* [2008] ECR I-9275.

justified because of the task and method by which public services were financed. The matter was referred back to the national court:

> 47 Finally, in order to determine whether the fact that a copyright management organisation calculates royalties paid with respect to remuneration due for the broadcast of musical works protected by copyright in a different manner according to whether they are commercial companies or public service undertakings constitutes an abuse within the meaning of Article [102], the referring court must consider whether such a practice may be objectively justified (see, to that effect, *United Brands and United Brands Continental v Commission*, paragraph 184; *Tournier*, paragraphs 38 and 46; Case C-95/04P *British Airways v Commission* [...paragraph 69; and *Sot. Lélos kai Sia and Others*, paragraph 39). Such justification may arise, in particular, from the task and method of financing of public service undertakings.
>
> 48 ...Article [102] is to be interpreted as meaning that, by calculating the royalties with respect to remuneration paid for the broadcast of musical works protected by copyright in a different manner according to whether the companies concerned are commercial companies or public service undertakings, a copyright management organisation is likely to exploit in an abusive manner its dominant position within the meaning of that article if it applies with respect to those companies dissimilar conditions to equivalent services and if it places them as a result at a competitive disadvantage, unless such a practice may be objectively justified.

15. EXPLOITATIVE ABUSES

A. UNFAIRLY HIGH OR LOW PRICING

(i) Unfairly High Prices

a. General

Article 102(a) specifically provides that an abuse may consist in 'directly or indirectly imposing 'unfair purchase or selling prices or other unfair trading conditions'.[895] We have discussed unfairly *low* prices on the selling side in the sections on predatory pricing and other exclusionary pricing abuses earlier.[896] Here we look at unfairly *high* prices. Excessive pricing is the most obvious way in which a monopolist can exploit its position. We saw in Chapter 1 that monopoly prices are likely to be higher than those in competitive markets and excessive prices match the popular conception of the evils of monopoly. However, it is argued that the free market economy needs the lure of monopoly pricing: '[t]he opportunity to charge monopoly prices—at least for a short period—is what attracts "business acumen" in the first place; it induces risk taking that produces innovation and economic growth'.[897] Excessive prices may therefore be pro- rather than anti-competitive because high prices and profits may act as a signal to attract new competitors on to the market.[898] Where this cannot happen because barriers to entry are high the spectre of competition authorities acting as price regulators arises. Price regulation, however, is the antithesis of the free market and competition

---

[895] See generally A. Svetlicinii and M. Botta, 'Article 102 TFEU as a Tool for Market Regulation' (2012) 8 *European Law Journal* 473; T. Ackermann, 'Excessive Pricing and the Goals of Competition Law' and J. P. Terhechte, 'Excessive Pricing and the Goals of Competition Law: an Enforcement Perspective—Comment on Ackermann', in D. Zimmer (ed.), *The Goals of Competition Law* (Edward Elgar, 2012), Chaps. 18 and 19 respectively; M. Furse, 'Excessive Prices, Unfair Prices and Economic Value' (2008) *European Competition Journal* 59; Geradin et al., *EU Competition Law and Economics* (cited in n. 160), 4.475–4.542.

[896] Sections 8 and 13 respectively.

[897] *Verizon Communications Ltd v. Trinko* 540 US 398, 124 S.Ct 872 (2004), para. 2 (Scalia J).

[898] But against this view, see A. Ezrachi and D. Gilo, 'Are Excessive Prices Really Self-Correcting?' (2009) 5 *Journal of Competition Law and Economics* 249 who argue that high prices alone are not sufficient reason to persuade a new entrant to compete with the incumbent.

authorities are rarely equipped to act as price regulators. They should not be called upon to arbitrate how profits ought to be shared out amongst the players on the market where there is no issue on anti-competitive exclusion (the error the CJ fell into in *United Brands*[899]).

The European Commission has not much concerned itself with high prices,[900] agreeing with the view that in many circumstances interference with high prices and profits per se is a disincentive to innovation and investment and considering it preferable to solve problems of unfair pricing by taking action against exclusionary conduct whereby dominant firms seek to preserve their dominance, as the Commission said in its 1994 Competition Report.[901] The former Director General of DG Comp has said of high prices:[902]

High prices certainly harm consumers in the short run. But is that a sufficient case for intervention by a competition authority? What if high prices would in the medium term attract entry and spur competition? If there are no high or insurmountable barriers to entry, it might well be that high prices are actually likely to be, on balance and with a longer term perspective, good for consumers. There is much more for consumers to gain through increased competition than a mere decrease in prices: competition brings more choice, scope for differentiation in quality, innovation, etc.

Price regulation is better restricted to situations of natural or legal monopoly, where it can be applied within a system of *ex ante* sector regulation.[903] Outside that regulatory context, it has been argued that exploitative high prices which do not have exclusionary potential should be dealt with by contract or consumer protection laws rather than being seen as a matter for competition law.[904] There are, however, cases on the application of Article 102 to high prices in situations not involving exclusion, and we look at those in later sections. It will be noted that many of these cases have come to the CJ from national courts by way of Article 267 references and did not involve enforcement by the Commission.

b. Ascertaining What Constitutes an Unfairly High Price

A major problem in applying Article 102(a) is to decide what constitutes an unfair price. Ascertaining what the price might have been in a more competitive market is rarely possible in practice, so what other yardstick can be used? In *United Brands* the Commission condemned UBC for charging excessive prices for Chiquita bananas in Germany, Denmark, and Benelux. It compared the prices with those for unbranded bananas, competitors' bananas, and with the price of Chiquitas in Ireland, and it said that the prices were 'excessive in relation to the economic value of the product supplied'. The CJ, however, annulled the Commission's decision that unfair prices had been charged.

---

[899] Where the CJ preferred the distributors over the producers, see Section 14.E, p. 571.

[900] Although note the special sector of telecommunications, e.g., the investigation into prices in mobile telephone services in the EC (Press Releases IP/98/141, IP 98/707, IP (98) 1036). The Commission found 14 cases of discrimination and high prices but closed its files when prices were reduced or there was action by the domestic regulator.

[901] *XXIVth Report on Competition Policy* (Commission, 1994), point. 207: 'The existence of a dominant position is not itself against the rules of competition. Consumers can suffer from a dominant company exploiting this position, the most likely way being through prices higher than would be found if the market were subject to effective competition. However, the Commission in its decision-making practice does not normally control or condemn the high level of prices as such. Rather it examines the behaviour of the dominant company designed to preserve its dominance, usually directed against competitors or new entrants who would normally bring about effective competition and the price level associated with it.'

[902] P. Lowe, 'Consumer Welfare and Efficiency—New Guiding Principles of Competition Policy?' 13th International Conference on Competition and 14th European Competition Day, 27 March 2007.

[903] For the interaction of price regulation by sector regulators and Article 102 see the margin squeeze cases, Section 9.B, p. 426 ff.

[904] Akman, *The Concept of Abuse in EU Competition Law* (cited in n. 9), Chap. 5.

Case 27/76, *United Brands* v. *Commission* [1978] ECR 207

Court of Justice

248. The imposition by an undertaking in a dominant position directly or indirectly of unfair purchase or selling prices is an abuse to which exception can be taken under Article [102].

249. It is advisable therefore to ascertain whether the dominant undertaking has made use of the opportunities arising out of its dominant position in such a way as to reap trading benefits which it would not have reaped if there had been normal and sufficiently effective competition.

250. In this case charging a price which is excessive because it has no reasonable relation to the economic value of the product supplied would be such an abuse.

251. This excess could, *inter alia*, be determined objectively if it were possible for it to be calculated by making a comparison between the selling price of the product in question and its cost of production, which would disclose the amount of the profit margin; however the Commission has not done this since it has not analysed UBC's costs structure.

252. The questions therefore to be determined are whether the difference between the costs actually incurred and the price actually charged is excessive, and, if the answer to this question is in the affirmative, whether a price has been imposed which is either unfair in itself or when compared to competing products.

253. Other ways may be devised—and economic theorists have not failed to think up several—of selecting the rules for determining whether the price of a product is unfair.

254. While appreciating the considerable and at times very great difficulties in working out production costs which may sometimes include a discretionary apportionment of indirect costs and general expenditure and which may vary significantly according to the size of the undertaking, its object, the complex nature of its set up, its territorial area of operations, whether it manufactures one or several products, the number of its subsidiaries and their relationship with each other, the production costs of the banana do not seem to present any insuperable problems.

...

258. The Commission bases its view that prices are excessive on an analysis of the differences—in its view excessive—between the prices charged in the different Member States and on the policy of discriminatory prices which has been considered above.

...

260. Having found that the prices charged to ripeners of the other Member States were considerably higher, sometimes by as much as 100 per cent, than the prices charged to customers in Ireland it concluded that UBC was making a very substantial profit.

...

264. However unreliable the particulars supplied by UBC may be...the fact remains that it is for the Commission to prove that the applicant charged unfair prices.

265. UBC's retraction, which the Commission has not effectively refuted, establishes beyond doubt that the basis for the calculation adopted by the latter to prove the UBC's prices are excessive is open to criticism and on this particular point there is doubt which must benefit the applicant, especially as for nearly 20 years banana prices, in real terms, have not risen on the relevant market.

266. Although it is also true that the price of Chiquita bananas and those of its principal competitors is different, that difference is about 7 per cent, a percentage which has not been challenged and which cannot automatically be regarded as excessive and consequently unfair.

267. In these circumstances it appears that the Commission has not adduced adequate legal proof of the facts and evaluations which formed the foundation of its finding that UBC had infringed Article [102] of the Treaty by directly and indirectly imposing unfair selling prices for bananas.

The Commission's decision on excessive pricing was thus quashed because it had failed to do its homework properly. It had not presented sufficient evidence and had not analysed UBC's costs.

In *United Brands* the CJ accepted that 'excessive' prices can constitute an abuse and that charging a price which has no relation to the product's 'economic value' would be excessive (paragraph 250). But what is the economic value of a banana other than what a customer is prepared to pay for it? The Court thought the excess might be determined by comparing the selling and production costs (the 'cost+ standard'), which would disclose the profit margin (paragraph 251), but it did not suggest the level at which the profit would become excessive. In paragraph 252 the Court said that finding the price is 'excessive' by these means is not the end of the matter: it must then be determined whether the excessive price is *unfair*. So a finding that prices are high in relation to the costs of production is not a sufficient condition for an infringement of Article 102.

The notion that the price charged should relate to the 'economic value' of the product or service was first discussed by the CJ in *General Motors*.[905] There a car company was charging a high price for the production of documentation without which car owners could not bring their cars into Belgium. The documentation was obviously cheap to produce, but in fact the 'value' to the customers was great since without the certificate the car could not be imported. On the facts the Court accepted that no abuse had been committed[906] and so the meaning of 'economic value' or excessive prices did not need to be more specifically defined. After *United Brands*, a similar case arose in *British Leyland*[907] where the manufacturer demanded a high price for type-approval certificates as a way of discouraging individuals from importing cars into the UK from Member States where they were cheaper. The price was condemned as 'excessive and discriminatory' but viewed by the CJ as a part of a policy of maintaining price differentials and compartmentalising the common market rather than as a simple garnering of monopoly profits.

In *United Brands* the CJ referred to 'other ways' devised by economists for identifying unfair prices (paragraph 253) but did not identify them. It did however consider that a comparison with the price of other products (paragraph 252) was valid. In *Deutsche Post: Interception of Cross-Border Mail*[908] DPAG had a statutory monopoly which encompassed, inter alia, the forwarding and delivery of cross-border mail in Germany. It (wrongfully) classified certain categories of incoming mail from the UK as unauthorised remail[909] and levied a charge which the British Post Office had to pay before the mail was released for delivery. The Commission said that when judging whether a price is excessive in a market which is open to competition, the normal test is to compare the prices of the dominant operator with those charged by competitors. Given the undertaking's wide-ranging monopoly in this case such a comparison was impossible, and in the absence of 'reliable cost accounting' the Commission compared the cross-border tariff with the domestic tariff and held the former to be excessive as it had 'no sufficient or reasonable relationship to real costs or to the real value of the service provided'.[910]

The CJ also said in *United Brands* that a comparison could be made with prices in other areas. It dismissed the comparison with Ireland for lack of proper analysis, not because it rejected the comparison as a technique. In *Bodson v. Pompes Funèbres des Régions Libérées*,[911] which concerned funeral services in areas of France where there were monopoly concessions granted by local authorities,

---

[905] Case 26/75, *General Motors v. Commission* [1975] ECR 1367.

[906] Because the high price had been a temporary blip while national procedures were changed.

[907] Case 226/84, *British Leyland v. EC Commission* [1986] ECR 3263.

[908] [2002] OJ L331/40, [2002] 4 CMLR 598. The case raised issues in respect of competition rules and undertakings granted monopoly rights by the State, and the application of Art. 106(2): see Chap. 8.

[909] DPAG's policy towards remailing was also the subject of a preliminary reference to the CJ, Cases C-147–148/97, *Deutsche Post AG v. Gesellschaft für Zahlungssysteme mbH (GZS) and Citicorp Kartenservice GmbH* [2000] ECR I-825 (*Deutsche Post*), discussed in Chap. 8.

[910] *Deutsche Post*, paras. 159–167.

[911] Case 30/87, [1988] ECR 2479, para. 31.

the CJ talked of whether the price was 'fair' in comparison with prices in areas where there were no such concessions. In *Ministère Public* v. *Tournier*[912] it said in the context of a complaint about the high charges imposed by the French copyright collecting society, SACEM, that:

38. When an undertaking holding a dominant position imposes scales of fees for its services which are appreciably higher than those charged in other member-States and where a comparison of the fee levels has been made on a consistent basis, that difference must be regarded as indicative of an abuse of a dominant position. In such a case it is for the undertaking in question to justify the difference by reference to objective dissimilarities between the situation in the member-State concerned and the situation prevailing in all the other member-States.

In *Deutsche Grammophon*[913] the CJ said that the fact that the price of the product in one Member State was different from that when re-imported from another did not necessarily constitute an abuse, but it would be a determining factor if the difference was very marked and unjustified by any objective criteria. In *Alsatel* v. *Novasam* the CJ said that a rental increase of 25 per cent for telephone installations might 'constitute unfair trading conditions'.[914] The CJ has also considered excessive pricing in references concerning IPRs. In *Parke, Davis*[915] it said that the higher price of a patented compared with a non-patented product did not necessarily mean that an abuse had been committed. In *Renault*,[916] however, it suggested that a car manufacturer which refused to license its IPRs in respect of its spare parts to other manufacturers might commit an abuse if it charged 'unfair prices' for its own parts. The idea that IPR owners are not entitled to extract the maximum return from their monopoly position, however, raises serious questions about the value of such rights. If cost-price comparisons are used to detect excessive pricing the undertaking's past research costs, including research costs which do not result in commercially exploitable products, need to be considered. This is particularly true in high technology markets in the new economy. Large resources may be devoted to the development of new products by a number of competitors and the undertaking which 'wins' the market may reap huge rewards (for a time at least). The incentive of that level of profit is, it is argued, necessary to persuade undertakings to incur R&D costs which may never be recovered.[917]

The Commission's reluctance to bring excessive pricing cases has led to a dearth of decisional practice on this issue, but in 2004 it adopted the *Scandlines* decision,[918] rejecting complaints of such pricing, in which it took the opportunity to systematically analyse the *United Brands* judgment and explain when a price is 'unfair' and constitutes an abuse within the meaning of Article 102. The complaints were lodged by two ferry operators and related to the port fees charged by the Port authority at Helsingborg, Sweden, in respect of the services provided to ferry operators active on the Helsingborg–Elsinore route between Sweden and Denmark. The Commission saw the central question, derived from *United Brands*, as being the relation between the price and the economic value of the product or service provided. Although *United Brands* referred to several ways of determining whether prices are excessive and/or unfair, the Commission adopted the methodology set out in paragraph 252 of the case: the first question to be determined is whether the difference between cost and price is excessive and *if it is*, then the second question is whether the price is unfair in itself or when compared to competing products. The Commission rejected the contention that it was just a question of 'cost+', i.e. of determining the supplier's costs, adding a profit margin and considering

[912] Case 395/87, [1989] ECR 2521, para. 38.

[913] Case 78/70, *Deutsche Grammophon* v. *Metro* [1971] ECR 487.

[914] Case 247/86, *Alsatel* v. *Novasam* [1988] ECR 5987.

[915] Case 24/67, *Parke, Davis & Co* v. *Probel* [1968] ECR 55.

[916] Case 53/87, *CICCRA* v. *Renault* [1988] ECR 6039, para. 16.

[917] This is particularly true also of the pharmaceutical industry, and the cost of R&D played a major part in e.g Cases C-468–478/06, *Sot. Lélos kai Sia and others EE* v. *GlaxoSmithKline AEVE Farmakeftikon Proionton* [2008] ECR I-7139 and Case C-501/06 P, *GlaxoSmithKline Services Unlimited* v. *Commission* [2009] ECR I-9291.

[918] COMP/36.568, *Scandlines Sverige* v. *Port of Helsingborg* [2006] 4 CMLR 1298 (*Scandlines*).

any price above this excessive. Rather, the economic value had to be determined with regard to the particular circumstances of the case and taking into account non-cost-related factors, particularly demand-side aspects of the product or service concerned. The demand side was relevant because 'customers are notably willing to pay more for something specific attached to the product/service that they consider valuable. This specific feature does not necessarily imply higher production costs for the provider. However it is valuable for the customer and also for the provider, and thereby increases the economic value of the product/service'.[919]

The *Scandlines* approach was followed in the UK case *Attheraces Ltd* v. *The British Horseracing Board Ltd*, which was a perfect example of the problem of ascertaining 'economic value'.[920]

In *Microsoft*[921] the Commission was concerned with the implementation of the remedies imposed on Microsoft in its decision in 2004.[922] These involved providing interoperability information to competitors on a downstream market on 'reasonable and non-discriminatory terms'. There was an ongoing dispute about whether Microsoft was providing access to the information in a satisfactory manner and about the rates of remuneration it was charging, culminating in a further decision in which the Commission imposed periodic penalty payments. In coming to the conclusion that the rates were unreasonable the Commission had to determine the 'economic value' of the information. It took into account the necessity of allowing competitors to compete viably with Microsoft while representing fair compensation for the value of the technology transferred. However, it excluded the value that derived from Microsoft's market power. The GC upheld the Commission.[923] In particular it said:[924]

...allowing Microsoft to charge remuneration rates reflecting the value resulting from the mere ability to inter-operate with Microsoft's operating systems—in other words the strategic value stemming from Microsoft's power in the client PC operating systems market or the work group server operating systems market—would in effect allow it to transform the benefits of the abuse into remuneration for the grant of licences.

In *Duales System Deutschland* DSD charged a fee for all the packaging bearing its 'Green Dot' logo even where customers showed that they did not use DSD's system for taking back and recovering packaging. The CJ upheld the GC's finding that this amounted to an abuse under Article 102(a) on the basis of the case law about 'economic value.'[925]

---

[919] *Scandlines*, para. 227. See also the comment on this decision in (2004) 3 *EC Competition Policy Newsletter*, 40 (M. Lamalle, L. Lindström-Rossi, and A. C. Teixara). The complainants withdrew their appeal to the GC against the decision.

[920] [2005] EWHC 3015 (Ch), on appeal [2007] EWCA Civ 38. The case concerned the supply of 'pre-race data' amassed by the British horse-racing authorities pursuant to running horse racing, which was valuable to an undertaking (ATR) which operated online and television gambling sites and channels. The Court of Appeal said the object of Art. 102 was the protection of consumers and that if ATR succeeded in obtaining the pre-race data at a lower price there was no suggestion that it would have charged the customers less. Any 'unfairness' to ATR was not a concern of competition law: 'Despite its elaborate legal and economic arguments and the high levels of moral indignation, the case is about who is going to get their hands on ATR's revenues from overseas bookmakers' (para. 214). The case was cited by Mazák AG in Case C-52/09, *Konkurrensverket* v. *TeliaSonera Sverige AB* [2011] ECR I-527, para. 30 of his Opinion.

[921] COMP/C-3/37.792, C9 (2008) 764 final, 27 February 2008.

[922] Upheld by the GC, Case T-201/04, *Microsoft* v. *Commission* [2007] ECR II-3601.

[923] Case T-167/08, *Microsoft* v. *Commission*, 27 June 2012.

[924] *Microsoft* v. *Commission*, para. 142.

[925] Case T-289/01, *Der Grüne Punkt–Duales System Deutschland GmbH* v. *Commission* [2007] ECR II-1691, *aff'd* Case C-385/07 P, *Der Grüne Punkt Duales System Deutschland GmbH* v. *Commission* [2009] ECR I-6155. The Commission had said (*DSD* [2001] OJ L166/1, para. 111) that an infringement of Art. 102(a) exists where the price charged for a service is 'clearly disproportionate to the cost of supplying it'. The case concerned Germany's highly developed system for making users responsible for disposing of packaging.

Kanal[926] concerned the royalties for broadcast music set by a copyright association (STIM, a *de facto* monopolist). It calculated these on the basis of the revenue of companies broadcasting those works and the amount of music broadcast. The CJ said that the royalties had to be analysed with respect to the value of their use. The method adopted by STIM was in principle reasonable and would not constitute an abuse unless there was some more accurate method available for identifying the music with the audience which did not involve a disproportionate increase in costs.

In the Commitments decision *Standard and Poor's*[927] the Commission was able to use an international standard, the ISO costs-recovery principle, as its benchmark in coming to the view that the charges of the ratings agency, S&P, for distributing US International Securities Identification Numbers (ISINs) were unfairly high.[928] The ISO standard 6166 was developed at international level as a public service to the financial services industry.

In another commitments decision, *Rambus*,[929] the undertaking undertook to cap (worldwide) for five years the royalty rates it charged for licences of its DRAM chips. This was in the context of the Commission's concerns that the standard-setting procedure which had led to the adoption of the relevant standard in the DRAM market had been subject to a patent ambush by Rambus.[930] Rambus could not be shown to be in a dominant position at the time of the standard setting, so the Commission pursued it for infringing Article 102 by unfair prices rather than for its conduct during the procedure. As with *Microsoft*, this was a case of unfair prices in the context of an exclusionary abuse. There is great difficulty in applying the principles laid down in *United Brands* to royalty rates charged by holders of SEPs.[931]

(ii) Low Prices on the Buying Side

Although there is little case law on it, it is possible that unfairly low purchase prices may constitute an abuse where the dominant position is on the buying side. *CICCE v. Commission*[932] concerned a complaint about the allegedly low prices paid as licence fees for the showing of films on French television. The Commission dismissed the complaint on the ground that the complainant had produced insufficient evidence but did not deny that low prices could constitute an abuse. This may become more of an issue in future, as in several Member States there is disquiet about the power of large retail groups.[933]

---

[926] Case C-52/07, *Kanal 5 Ltd, TV 4 AB v. Föreningen Svenska Tonsättares Internationella Musikbyrå (STIM) upa* [2008] ECR I-9275.

[927] COMP/39.592, Commitments decision 15 November 2011, C (2011) 8209 final; IP/11/1354.

[928] COMP/39.592, Commitments decision 15 November 2011, C (2011) 8209 final; IP/11/1354, paras. 26–30 of the decision. S&P undertook not to impose any licensing charges on 'indirect' users and to charge 'direct' users no more than the amounts set out in the decision, which were set by reference to S&P's costs data.

[929] COMP/38.636; Commitments decision 9 December 2009, Summary [2010] OJ C30/17; IP/09/1867; MEMO/09/544.

[930] See Section 13.C.ii, p. 563.

[931] See the discussion of SEPs in Section 13.C.ii, p. 563, and D. Geradin, 'Ten Years of DG Competition Effort to Provide Guidance on the Application of Competition Rules to the Licensing of Standard-Essential Patents: Where Do We Stand?', available at <http://ssrn.com/abstract=2204359>. For the issue of 'fair and reasonable' (FRAND) terms in respect of SEPs, see Chap. 10, Section 11.A, p. 757 ff. Another case, *Qualcomm*, in which the Commission had received complaints about the royalties being charged for an SEP, ended with the Commission closing its formal proceedings without taking commitments: MEMO/09/516.

[932] Case 298/83, *CICCE v. Commission* [1985] ECR 1105, upholding the Commission.

[933] The Commission noted the matter in its *XVIth Report on Competition Policy* (Commission, 1986), points 345–348. In the UK the prices and conditions offered to suppliers by supermarkets was raised in the market investigation reference under the Enterprise Act 2002, *Groceries*.

B. IMPOSING UNFAIR TRADING CONDITIONS AND ENTERING INTO RESTRICTIVE AGREEMENTS

Article 102(a) expressly condemns unfair conditions as well as prices, and Article 102(c) condemns discriminatory conditions as well as prices. A number of conditions imposed by dominant undertakings on their customers have been condemned as abuses because they were unfair, and some of these have been dealt with under other heads of abuse. In many cases the unfair or discriminatory trading conditions are imposed in pursuit of a policy to exclude competitors. For example, in 1994 the Commission launched an investigation into Microsoft's licensing practices. In particular it was concerned that Microsoft's standard agreements for licensing software to PC manufacturers excluded competitors from selling their products. For example, Microsoft: (a) used 'per processor' 'per system' licences which required payment of royalties on every computer made by a PC manufacturer either containing a particular processor type or belonging to a particular model series, whether or not the computer was shipped with Microsoft software pre-installed; (b) used 'minimum commitment' clauses which required licensees to pay for a minimum number of copies of a product regardless of actual use; and (c) had excessively long licence agreements. The Commission (and the US DOJ) reached a settlement with Microsoft.[934] Microsoft undertook not to enter licence contracts of more than one year's duration, not to impose minimum commitments, and not to use per processor clauses: per system clauses would be allowed if the licensees were given flexibility not to buy Microsoft products and not to have to pay for what they did not buy.[935]

In *Tetra Pak II*[936] the terms on which the dominant undertaking dealt with its customers (in pursuance of a marketing policy which aimed to restrict supply and compartmentalise national markets) were found by the Commission to be unfairly onerous. The conditions included placing limitations on the purchasers' use of the machines, binding purchasers to Tetra Pak's repair and maintenance services, and reserving to Tetra Pak the right to make surprise inspections. The Commission held that these conditions deprived the purchaser of certain aspects of its property rights. Although it accepted that stipulations in the terms upon which the supplier *leased* machines, such as prohibitions on modifying or moving the equipment, were not in themselves abusive, it held they were in this case. The rental payments were so high in comparison to sale prices that the supplier had to be taken to have relinquished its property rights to the hirer. Lease terms which exceeded the technological (though not the physical) life of the machine were abusive. Further, clauses imposing penalties for breach of any of the terms of the agreements at Tetra Pak's discretion also infringed Article 102, as these were aimed at ensuring that the customers complied with terms of the agreements which were in themselves abuses.

The terms on which DSD did business in respect of its 'Green Dot' logo in Germany were considered unfair in *Duales System Deutschland* as DSD charged licence fees in circumstances where the trade mark was not actually being used. This was an infringement of Article 102(a) as '[u]nfair commercial terms exist where an undertaking in a dominant position fails to comply with the principle of proportionality'.[937] The CJ rejected DSD's argument that the Commission's decision had amounted to an obligation to grant a licence to use the logo.[938]

---

[934] *Microsoft*, IP (94) 653 of 17 July 1994, [1994] 5 CMLR 143. The US FTC was investigating similar concerns over Microsoft at the same time.

[935] See also Case T-65/89, *BPB Industries and British Gypsum Ltd* v. *Commission* [1993] ECR II-389, *aff'd* Case C-310/93 P, *BPB Industries plc and British Gypsum Ltd* v. *Commission* [1995] ECR I-865, The company had applied dissimilar conditions to equivalent transactions on one market in order to strengthen its dominance on the other. Another example of customers (allegedly) suffering unfair conditions in pursuit of an exclusionary policy was the conditions imposed by IBM in COMP/39.692, *IBM Maintenance Services*, Commitments decision, 13 December 2011.

[936] Case C-333/94 P, *Tetra Pak International SA* v. *Commission* [1996] ECR I-595.

[937] [2001] OJ 1166/1, para. 112, *aff'd* on appeal, see also Section 15.A.i.b., p. 580 on the excessive pricing finding.

[938] Case C-385/07 P, *Der Grüne Punkt–Duales System Deutschland GmbH* v. *Commission* [2009] ECR I-6155.

In *AAMS* v. *Commission*[939] the terms of the distribution agreements which the dominant wholesale distributor of cigarettes in Italy imposed on foreign producers were held to be unfair. They were also objectionable in that they limited the foreign producers' access to the Italian market, contrary to the imperative of the single market.[940]

In a number of cases concerning performing rights societies the Commission has found the society to have committed abuses by virtue of the terms on which the society did business. For example, in *GEMA*[941] the society wished to prevent members leaving it and entering into direct relationships with undertakings such as record companies. Its rules took the rights to works even after the member's resignation, provided for long periods of withdrawal, and made payments to the social fund payable only to members of 20 years' standing.

GEMA also discriminated on grounds of nationality, always a heinous offence in EU law.[942] Discriminatory treatment of other trading parties on any grounds without objective justification is expressly prohibited by Article 102(c) and is a policy which the dominant undertaking is likely to have adopted in pursuance of some other abusive practice.

When a dominant undertaking enters into restrictive agreements it may be caught by both Article 101 and Article 102. In *Ahmed Saeed*[943] the CJ, in the context of an agreement fixing air tariffs, said that what appeared to be an agreement could really be the imposition on the other party of the dominant undertaking's will, the agreement simply constituting 'the formal measure setting the seal on an economic reality characterised by the fact that an undertaking in a dominant position has succeeded in having the tariffs in question applied by other undertakings'.

In *FENIN*[944] a group of suppliers to the bodies which run the Spanish national health service (SNS) complained to the Commission that SNS was abusing its position as a dominant buyer by persistently paying its debts late (an average of 300 days). The suppliers said that the bodies took advantage of the fact that the suppliers could exert no commercial pressure on them. The GC and the CJ upheld the Commission's view that the SNS organisations were not 'undertakings' for the purpose of Article 102[945] and therefore the question of whether a practice such as late payment could constitute an abuse was not addressed.

The fact that there are not more cases and decisions on the imposition of unfair trading conditions can be explained by the prevalence of other legislative regimes, such as consumer protection and unfair competition and general contract and tort laws. Some of rules have been enacted at EU level.[946]

C. INEFFICIENCY AND LIMITING PRODUCTION

The Article 102(b) prohibition of 'limiting production, markets, or technical development to the prejudice of consumers' has been applied to dominant undertakings operating inefficiently and unable to meet demand, particularly public undertakings with statutory monopolies where Article 102

---

[939] Case T-139/98, *Amministrazione Autonoma dei Monopoli di Stato (AAMS)* v. *Commission* [2001] ECR II-3413.

[940] See Section 16, p. 584.

[941] [1971] OJ L134/15, [1971] CMLR D35.

[942] Which is contrary to Art. 18 TFEU where it relates to citizens of the Union; see also Case 7/82, *GVL* v. *Commission* [1983] ECR 483. See also *1998 Football World Cup* [2000] OJ L5/55, [2000] 4 CMLR 963.

[943] Case 66/86, *Ahmed Saeed Flugreisen and Silver Line Reiseburo GmbH* v. *Zentrale zur Bëkämpfung Unlauteren Wettwerbs eV* [1989] ECR 803.

[944] Case T-319/99, *Federación Nacional de Empresas de Instrumentación Científica, Médica, Técnica y Dental (FENIN)* v. *Commission* [2003] ECR II-357 and Case C-205/03 P, *Federación Española de Empresas de Tecnología Sanitaria (FENIN)* v. *Commission* [2006] ECR I-6295.

[945] See the discussion of the concept of an undertaking for the purposes of Arts 101 and 102 in Chap. 3.

[946] Such as Council Directive 93/13/EEC [1993] OJ L95/29 on unfair contract terms.

has applied in conjunction with Article 106.[947] In *Port of Genoa*[948] the Court held that an undertaking with the exclusive right to organise dock work at Genoa, which refused to use modern technology and thus raised costs and caused delays, was in breach of Article 102. In *Höfner* v. *Macrotron* the Court held that a state employment agency which was unable to meet the demand for its services would infringe Article 102.[949] This type of abuse can, however, also be committed by private undertakings. In *P and I Clubs*,[950] which concerned associations providing marine insurance, the Commission stated that it would intervene in situations only where there is 'clear and uncontroversial evidence that a very substantial share of the demand is being deprived of a service that it manifestly needs'.[951] In the E.ON electricity case, where the Commission accepted commitments, one of the charges was that E.ON had limited its production of electricity in order to raise prices in the wholesale market.[952]

16. REFUSAL TO SUPPLY, EXPORT BANS, AND OTHER CONDUCT HINDERING INTER-MEMBER STATE TRADE

Practices dividing markets or hindering trade between Member States in the EU may be abusive as contrary to single market integration.[953] The excessive prices charged for the type approval certificates in *British Leyland*[954] were held to be an abuse because they both hindered parallel imports and exploited consumers. In *United Brands*[955] the 'green banana clause' UBC imposed on its ripener/distributors, prohibiting them from reselling the bananas while they were still green, was treated by the CJ and the Commission as tantamount to an export ban (bananas once yellow were so perishable that exporting them was not feasible) which reinforced UBC's policy of geographical price discrimination.[956] UBC claimed throughout that the necessary measure of quality control had never been understood, applied, or enforced as an export ban, but it was nevertheless held to infringe Article 102. The unfair distribution terms imposed by the dominant undertaking in *AAMS*[957] hindered the trade in cigarettes between Member States.

The issue of whether a refusal to supply in order to restrict parallel imports between Member States is an abuse on that ground alone has arisen in respect of the pharmaceutical sector.[958] Greek

---

[947] See further Chap. 8. The issue often arises in cases in which the special or exclusive rights given to the undertaking are being challenged by a would-be entrant.

[948] Case C-179/90, *Merci Convenzionali Porto di Genova* v. *Siderurigica Gabrielle* [1991] ECR I-5889.

[949] Case C-41/90, *Höfner* v. *Macrotron* [1991] ECR I-1979; Case C-55/96, *Job Centre Co-op. arl* [1997] ECR I-7119 was a similar case from Italy. See also, for example, *Dutch Express Delivery Services* [1994] OJ L10/47; Case C-475/99; *Ambulanz Glöckner* v. *Landkreis Südwestpfalz* [2001] ECR I-8089; COMP/39.562 *Slovakian Hybrid Mail* [2009] 4 CMLR 663.

[950] [1999] OJ L125/12.

[951] *P and I Clubs* [1999] OJ L125/12, para. 128. The Commission's Statement of Objections stated that the undertaking had abused its (collective) dominant position by offering only a single insurance product. The undertaking amended its arrangements and the Decision found that there was no longer any question of an infringement of Art. 102.

[952] COMP/39.388 *German Electricity Balancing Markets (E.ON)* Commitments Decision [2009] OJ C36/8.

[953] See, e.g., Case 40/73, *Suiker Unie* v. *EC Commission* [1975] ECR 1663; *Eurofix–Bauco* [1988] OJ L65/19, [1989] 4 CMLR 677; Case C-333/94 P, *Tetra Pak International SA* v. *Commission* [1996] ECR I-5951; Case C-310/93 P, *BPB Industries PLC and British Gypsum Ltd* v. *Commission* [1995] ECR I-865; Case T-228/97, *Irish Sugar plc* v. *Commission* [1999] ECR II-2969.

[954] Case 226/84, *British Leyland* v. *EC Commission* [1986] ECR 3263.

[955] Case 27/76, *United Brands* v. *Commission* [1978] ECR 207.

[956] See Section 14.E, p. 570.

[957] Case T-139/98, *Amministrazione Autonoma dei Monopoli di Stato (AAMS)* v. *Commission* [2001] ECR II-3413.

[958] Outside the pharmaceutical sector the issue arose previously in the context of the *Polaroid/SSI* investigation where Polaroid was alleged to have refused to supply a customer with the quantities ordered because of concerns

pharmaceutical wholesalers have been in dispute with GlaxoSmithKline who they claimed refused to fulfil all their orders in respect of certain pharmaceuticals in order to prevent them exporting to other Member States in which prices were higher. The efforts of pharmaceutical companies to prevent such parallel trade had resulted in Article 101 proceedings, as seen in Chapters 3 and 4.[959] The first case to reach the CJ on the application of Article 102 to this was *Syfait*,[960] an Article 267 reference from the Greek Competition Commission. Advocate General Jacobs considered that in the context of the European pharmaceutical sector it was not necessarily an abuse to refuse to supply to prevent parallel trade.[961] He recognised special circumstances pertaining to trade in pharmaceuticals. First, the price differentials between Member States were due to pervasive and diverse State intervention; secondly, Community and Member State regulation imposed obligations on pharmaceutical undertakings and wholesalers to ensure adequate stocks; thirdly, parallel trade could have potentially negative consequences on R&D incentives; and fourthly, end consumers could not be assumed to benefit from parallel trade, given that the Member States' public authorities are the main purchasers and that parallel trade does not necessarily result in any price competition discernible to the end consumers. In the circumstances, therefore, a refusal to supply that aimed thereby to limit parallel trade was capable of objective justification and thus of not constituting an abuse. The Advocate General was careful to say that his conclusion was 'highly specific' to the peculiarities of the European pharmaceutical market and did not generalise about refusals to supply and parallel trade.[962] The CJ refused to give judgment on the issue as it held the reference inadmissible on the grounds that the Greek Competition Commission is not a 'court or tribunal of a Member State' within Article 267 from which the CJ can accept a reference. The Advocate General's Opinion, however, showed both a reluctance to widen the ambit of refusal to supply abuses simply on single market grounds, and a sympathetic stance towards the pharmaceutical industry.

The same matter involving the same parties came before the CJ again on a reference from a Greek court in *Sot. Lélos* (often known as *Glaxo Greece*).[963] In the meantime the GC had delivered the Article 101 judgment, *GlaxoSmithKline* (or *Glaxo Spain*) in which Advocate General Jacob's arguments in *Syfait* were largely accepted. The GC said that an agreement restricting parallel trade in the pharmaceutical sector was not restrictive by object because it could not be assumed that it reduced consumer welfare.[964]

In *Sot. Lélos* the ECJ reframed the questions it was asked as:

- whether there is an abuse of a dominant position contrary to Article 102 if a pharmaceuticals company occupying such a position on the national market for certain medicinal products refuses to meet orders sent to it by wholesalers on account of the fact that those wholesalers are involved in parallel exports of those products to other Member States (paragraph 28); and

- the relevance of a series of factors such as the degree of regulation to which the pharmaceuticals sector is subject in Member States, the impact of parallel trade on the pharmaceuticals

---

that SSI intended to export some of the products. Polaroid agreed to supply the full amount and the Commission closed its file: see *XIIIth Report on Competition Policy* (Commission, 1983), point 157.

[959] See Cases C-2 and 3/01P, *Bundesverband der Arzneimittel-Importeure eV and the Commission v. Bayer AG* [2004] ECR I-23, discussed in Chap. 3 (where it was held that there was no breach of Art. 101(1) as the refusal was a unilateral act and did not constitute an agreement: it was not claimed that Bayer was dominant) and Case C-501/06 P, *GlaxoSmithKline Services Unlimited v. Commission* [2009] ECR I-9291.

[960] Case C-53/03, *Synetairismos Farmakopoion Aitolias & Akarnanias (Syfait) v. GlaxoSmithKline plc and GlaxoSmithKline AEVE* [2005] ECR I-4609.

[961] *Syfait*, Opinion, paras. 77–104.

[962] *Syfait*, paras. 101–102.

[963] See R. O'Donoghue and L. Macnab, 'Dominant Firms' Duties to Deal with Pharmaceutical Parallel Traders Following *Glaxo Greece*' (2009) 5(1) *Competition Policy Int'l* 153; S. Kingston, 'Casenote on *Sot. Lélos*' (2009) 46 *CMLRev* 683.

[964] Case T-168/01, *GlaxoSmithKlineServices Unlimited* [2006] ECR II-2969, see Chap. 4. A year after the *Sot. Lélos* judgment the CJ overruled the GC on that point, Case C-501/06 P, *GlaxoSmithKline Services Unlimited v. Commission* [2009] ECR I-9291.

companies' revenues, and the question whether parallel trade is capable of generating financial benefits for the ultimate consumers of the medicinal products (paragraph 29).

The CJ ruled that 'there can be no escape' from Article 102 for the practices of an undertaking in a dominant position which are aimed at avoiding all parallel exports between Member States (paragraph 66). The peculiarities of the EU pharmaceutical sector did not alter this. However, the CJ was prepared to accept that the practices could be objectively justified by the undertaking's need to protect its own commercial interests and so it could refuse to meet orders which are out of the ordinary.

This means that there is a different rule for refusals to supply to prevent parallel trade than for others. As the Commission recognises in the Guidance Paper, EU law normally starts from the position that 'any undertaking, whether dominant or not, should have the right to choose its trading partners'.[965] That is why the 'exceptional circumstances' in the case law already discussed,[966] which impose a duty to supply in derogation from this principle, are so important. In respect of parallel trade refusals, however, the position is that they are *prima* facie abusive, and can escape Article 102 only by objective justification.

Cases C-468/06 to C-478/06, *Sot. Lélos kai Sia EE* v. *GlaxoSmithKline AEVE Farmakeftikon Proionton* [2008] ECR I-7139

Court of Justice

The existence of a refusal to supply liable to eliminate competition

33 Article [102] prohibits any abuse by one or more undertakings of a dominant position within the common market or in a substantial part of it as incompatible with the common market in so far as it may affect trade between Member States. According to point (b) of the second paragraph of that article, such abuse may, in particular, consist in limiting production, markets or technical development to the prejudice of consumers.

34 The established case-law of the Court shows that the refusal by an undertaking occupying a dominant position on the market of a given product to meet the orders of an existing customer constitutes abuse of that dominant position under Article [102] where, without any objective justification, that conduct is liable to eliminate a trading party as a competitor (see, to that effect, Joined Cases 6/73 and 7/73 *Istituto Chemioterapico Italiano and Commercial Solvents v Commission*...paragraph 25, and Case 27/76 *United Brands and United Brands Continentaal v Commission*...paragraph 183).

35 With regard to a refusal by an undertaking to deliver its products in one Member State to wholesalers which export those products to other Member States, such an effect on competition may exist not only if the refusal impedes the activities of those wholesalers in that first Member State, but equally if it leads to the elimination of effective competition from them in the distribution of the products on the markets of the other Member States.

36 In this case it is common ground between the parties in the main proceedings that, by refusing to meet the Greek wholesalers' orders, GSK AEVE aims to limit parallel exports by those wholesalers to the markets of other Member States in which the selling prices of the medicinal products in dispute are higher.

37 In respect of sectors other than that of pharmaceutical products, the Court has held that a practice by which an undertaking in a dominant position aims to restrict parallel trade in the products that it puts on the market constitutes abuse of that dominant position, particularly when such a practice has the effect of curbing parallel imports by neutralising the more favourable level of prices which may apply in other sales

---

[965] Guidance Paper, para.75.
[966] See Sections 12.C and 12.D.

areas in the Community (see, to that effect, Case 26/75 *General Motors Continental v Commission*...paragraph 12) or when it aims to create barriers to re-importations which come into competition with the distribution network of that undertaking (Case 226/84 *British Leyland v Commission*, paragraph 24). Indeed, parallel imports enjoy a certain amount of protection in Community law because they encourage trade and help reinforce competition (Case C-373/90 *X* [1992] ECR I-131, paragraph 12).

...

39 In order to determine whether the refusal by a pharmaceuticals company to supply medicinal products to such wholesalers indeed falls within the prohibition laid down in Article [102], in particular at point (b) of the second paragraph of that article, it must be examined whether, as GSK AEVE maintains, there are objective considerations based on which such a practice cannot be regarded as an abuse of the dominant position occupied by that undertaking (see, to that effect, *United Brands and United Brands Continentaal v Commission*, paragraph 184, and Case C-95/04 P *British Airways v Commission*...paragraph 69).

The abusive nature of the refusal to supply

...

49 It should be recalled that in paragraph 182 of its judgment in United Brands and *United Brands Continentaal v Commission* the Court held that an undertaking in a dominant position for the purpose of marketing a product—which cashes in on the reputation of a brand name known to and valued by consumers—cannot stop supplying a long-standing customer who abides by regular commercial practice, if the orders placed by that customer are in no way out of the ordinary. In paragraph 183 of the same judgment, the Court held that such conduct is inconsistent with the objectives laid down in [Article 3(1)(g) EC], which are set out in detail in Article [102], particularly in points (b) and (c) of the second paragraph of that article, since the refusal to sell would limit the markets to the prejudice of consumers and would amount to discrimination which might in the end eliminate a trading party from the relevant market.

50 In paragraph 189 of the judgment in *United Brands and United Brands Continentaal v Commission*, the Court stated that, although the fact that an undertaking is in a dominant position cannot deprive it of its right to protect its own commercial interests if they are attacked, and that such an undertaking must be conceded the right to take such reasonable steps as it deems appropriate to protect those interests, such behaviour cannot be accepted if its purpose is specifically to strengthen that dominant position and abuse it.

51 It must be examined in this context whether, as GSK AEVE claims, particular circumstances are present in the pharmaceuticals sector, by reason of which the refusal by an undertaking in a dominant position to supply clients in a given Member State who engage in parallel exports to other Member States where prices for medicines are higher does not, generally speaking, constitute an abuse.

The consequences of parallel trade for the ultimate consumers

52 The first thing to consider is GSK AEVE's argument that parallel trade in any event brings only few financial benefits to the ultimate consumers.

53 In that connection, it should be noted that parallel exports of medicinal products from a Member State where the prices are low to other Member States in which the prices are higher open up in principle an alternative source of supply to buyers of the medicinal products in those latter States, which necessarily brings some benefits to the final consumer of those products.

54 It is true, as GSK AEVE has pointed out, that, for medicines subject to parallel exports, the existence of price differences between the exporting and the importing Member States does not necessarily imply that the final consumer in the importing Member State will benefit from a price corresponding to the one prevailing in the exporting Member State, inasmuch as the wholesalers carrying out the exports will themselves make a profit from that parallel trade.

55 Nevertheless, the attraction of the other source of supply which arises from parallel trade in the importing Member State lies precisely in the fact that that trade is capable of offering the same products on the market of that Member State at lower prices than those applied on the same market by the pharmaceuticals companies.

56 As a result, even in the Member States where the prices of medicines are subject to State regulation, parallel trade is liable to exert pressure on prices and, consequently, to create financial benefits not only for the social health insurance funds, but equally for the patients concerned, for whom the proportion of the price of medicines for which they are responsible will be lower. At the same time, as the Commission notes, parallel trade in medicines from one Member State to another is likely to increase the choice available to entities in the latter Member State which obtain supplies of medicines by means of a public procurement procedure, in which the parallel importers can offer medicines at lower prices.

57 Accordingly, without it being necessary for the Court to rule on the question whether it is for an undertaking in a dominant position to assess whether its conduct vis-à-vis a trading party constitutes abuse in the light of the degree to which that party's activities offer advantages to the final consumers, it is clear that, in the circumstances of the main proceedings, such an undertaking cannot base its arguments on the premise that the parallel exports which it seeks to limit are of only minimal benefit to the final consumers.

The impact of State price and supply regulation in the pharmaceutical sector

...

64 On the other hand, it should be recalled that, where a medicine is protected by a patent which confers a temporary monopoly on its holder, the price competition which may exist between a producer and its distributors, or between parallel traders and national distributors, is, until the expiry of that patent, the only form of competition which can be envisaged.

65 In relation to the application of Article [101] the Court has held that an agreement between producer and distributor which might tend to restore the national divisions in trade between Member States might be such as to frustrate the objective of the Treaty to achieve the integration of national markets through the establishment of a single market. Thus on a number of occasions the Court has held agreements aimed at partitioning national markets according to national borders or making the interpenetration of national markets more difficult, in particular those aimed at preventing or restricting parallel exports, to be agreements whose object is to restrict competition within the meaning of that Treaty article (see, for example, Joined Cases 96/82 to 102/82, 104/82, 105/82, 108/82 and 110/82 *IAZ International Belgium and Others v Commission*...paragraphs 23 to 27; Case C-306/96 *Javico*...paragraphs 13 and 14; and Case C-551/03 P *General Motors v Commission*...paragraphs 67 to 69).

66 In the light of the abovementioned Treaty objective as well as that of ensuring that competition in the internal market is not distorted, there can be no escape from the prohibition laid down in Article [102] for the practices of an undertaking in a dominant position which are aimed at avoiding all parallel exports from a Member State to other Member States, practices which, by partitioning the national markets, neutralise the benefits of effective competition in terms of the supply and the prices that those exports would obtain for final consumers in the other Member States.

67 Although the degree of price regulation in the pharmaceuticals sector cannot therefore preclude the Community rules on competition from applying, the fact none the less remains that, when assessing, in the case of Member States with a system of price regulation, whether the refusal of a pharmaceuticals company to supply medicines to wholesalers involved in parallel exports constitutes abuse, it cannot be ignored that such State intervention is one of the factors liable to create opportunities for parallel trade.

68 Furthermore, in the light of the Treaty objectives to protect consumers by means of undistorted competition and the integration of national markets, the Community rules on competition are also incapable of being interpreted in such a way that, in order to defend its own commercial interests, the only choice

left for a pharmaceuticals company in a dominant position is not to place its medicines on the market at all in a Member State where the prices of those products are set at a relatively low level.

69 It follows that, even if the degree of regulation regarding the price of medicines cannot prevent any refusal by a pharmaceuticals company in a dominant position to meet orders sent to it by wholesalers involved in parallel exports from constituting an abuse, such a company must nevertheless be in a position to take steps that are reasonable and in proportion to the need to protect its own commercial interests.

70 In that respect, and without it being necessary to examine the argument raised by GSK AEVE that it is necessary for pharmaceuticals companies to limit parallel exports in order to avoid the risk of a reduction in their investments in the research and development of medicines, it is sufficient to state that, in order to appraise whether the refusal by a pharmaceuticals company to supply wholesalers involved in parallel exports constitutes a reasonable and proportionate measure in relation to the threat that those exports represent to its legitimate commercial interests, it must be ascertained whether the orders of the wholesalers are out of the ordinary (see, to that effect, *United Brands and United Brands Continentaal v Commission*, paragraph 182).

71 Thus, although a pharmaceuticals company in a dominant position, in a Member State where prices are relatively low, cannot be allowed to cease to honour the ordinary orders of an existing customer for the sole reason that that customer, in addition to supplying the market in that Member State, exports part of the quantities ordered to other Member States with higher prices, it is none the less permissible for that company to counter in a reasonable and proportionate way the threat to its own commercial interests potentially posed by the activities of an undertaking which wishes to be supplied in the first Member State with significant quantities of products that are essentially destined for parallel export.

72 In the present cases, the orders for reference show that, in the disputes which gave rise to those orders, the appellants in the main proceedings have demanded not that GSK AEVE should fulfil the orders sent to it in their entirety, but that it should deliver them quantities of medicines corresponding to the monthly average sold during the first 10 months of 2000. In 6 of the 11 actions in the main proceedings, the appellants asked for those quantities to be increased by a certain percentage, which was fixed by some of them at 20%.

73 In those circumstances, it is for the referring court to ascertain whether the abovementioned orders are ordinary in the light of both the previous business relations between the pharmaceuticals company holding a dominant position and the wholesalers concerned and the size of the orders in relation to the requirements of the market in the Member State concerned (see, to that effect, *United Brands and United Brands Continentaal v Commission*, paragraph 182, and Case 77/77 *Benzine en Petroleum Handelsmaatschappij and Others v Commission*, paragraphs 30 to 32).

74 Those considerations equally deal with the argument raised by GSK AEVE, namely the impact of State regulation on the supply of medicinal products, and more particularly the argument that undertakings that engage in parallel exports are not subject to the same obligations regarding distribution and warehousing as the pharmaceuticals companies and are therefore liable to disrupt the planning of production and distribution of medicines.

75 It is true that in Greece, as is apparent from paragraph 8 of this judgment, national legislation places pharmaceuticals wholesalers under an obligation to supply the needs of a defined geographical area with a range of pharmaceutical products. It is equally true that, in cases where parallel trade would effectively lead to a shortage of medicines on a given national market, it would not be for the undertakings holding a dominant position but for the national authorities to resolve the situation, by taking appropriate and proportionate steps that were consistent with national legislation as well as with the obligations flowing from Article 81 of Directive 2001/83.

76 However, a producer of pharmaceutical products must be in a position to protect its own commercial interests if it is confronted with orders that are out of the ordinary in terms of quantity. Such could be the case, in a given Member State, if certain wholesalers order from that producer medicines in quantities

which are out of all proportion to those previously sold by the same wholesalers to meet the needs of the market in that Member State.

77 In view of the foregoing, the answer to the questions referred should be that Article [102] must be interpreted as meaning that an undertaking occupying a dominant position on the relevant market for medicinal products which, in order to put a stop to parallel exports carried out by certain wholesalers from one Member State to other Member States, refuses to meet ordinary orders from those wholesalers is abusing its dominant position. It is for the national court to ascertain whether the orders are ordinary in the light of both the size of those orders in relation to the requirements of the market in the first Member State and the previous business relations between that undertaking and the wholesalers concerned.

The CJ (paragraphs 52–57) considered that final consumers and social security systems did derive some benefit from parallel trade and that an undertaking in GSK's position could not argue from the basis that the benefit to final consumers was only minimal (paragraph 57). It considered the effect of price controls by Member States but stressed that for patented pharmaceuticals it is only parallel trade which can provide any competition (paragraph 64). Although the features of the pharmaceutical sector did not remove it from the normal competition rules against restrictions on parallel trade the Court did, however, recognise the effect of national intervention on the opportunities for parallel trade (paragraph 67). It accepted that the undertaking had a right to protect its own commercial interests and said (paragraph 68) that the competition rules could not be interpreted in such a way that it left an undertaking in Glaxo's position with no way to do this but to leave the market (which here would have meant ceasing to supply in Greece). The CJ therefore made the very important concession that although Glaxo could not, without infringing Article 102, cease honouring the 'ordinary orders of an existing customer' it *could* refuse orders which were 'out of the ordinary'. It was left to the national court to draw the difficult line between 'ordinary' and 'out of the ordinary' orders.[967] The method for this assessment is to examine the orders in the light of the previous business relations between the distributor and the supplier and the size of the order in relation to the market requirements in the Member State concerned to see if they are 'out of all proportion' (paragraphs 73 and 76).

The judgment is notable for the way in which it treated Glaxo's arguments about the need to limit parallel trade in order to maintain profits for investment in R&D (also the argument in *GlaxoSmithKline*). In its formulation of the questions referred to it (paragraph 29) the CJ referred to 'the pharmaceutical companies revenues' and in paragraph 70 it simply treated their protection as a 'legitimate commercial interests' matter. It does not engage in any discussion at all about justifying the hindrance of parallel trade on 'efficiency' grounds and indeed specifically states that it is not necessary to examine the R&D question.

The judgment only dealt with the position of *existing* customers, because that was the subject matter of the case. This does not mean that there is not also a duty to supply new customers, particularly given the *prima facie* nature of the abuse. Obviously different criteria for assessing the reasonable and proportionate nature of the refusal to protect legitimate commercial interests would need to be devised since there would be no 'ordinary' orders for comparison. The size of the market in the Member State would still be germane however.

17. ABUSE AND COLLECTIVE DOMINANCE

It was explained in Chapter 5 that a 'dominant position' may be held by a single undertaking or by one or more independent undertakings which hold a collective dominant position. This concept and

---

[967] This concept of 'ordinary' orders is found in *United Brands* which the CJ cites. *United Brands* was, however, a totally different scenario, a reprisal abuse against customers who dealt with a competitor, see Section 12.E, p. 549.

its application are explored in Chapter 9, in the context of cartels and oligopolies and the question of what can amount to the abuse of a collective dominance position is discussed there.[968] In some of the cases discussed in this chapter, the dominant position being abused was a collective one.[969] It should be noted here, however, that in *Irish Sugar* the GC said that it was not necessary for the collective dominant position to be *abused* collectively. It is possible therefore that an undertaking may individually commit an abuse of a dominant position held collectively with other undertakings, at least insofar as the abuse is committed to protect the collective dominant position.[970]

18. CONCLUSIONS

1. The matter of what conduct on the part of a dominant undertaking can constitute an infringement of Article 102 should be put on a sound and consistent economic footing. Conduct should be judged by its effects on the market, not on its form. However, theoretically sound, effects-based rules that are too complex or impractical are not a good basis on which to build a sound competition policy. Undertakings need legal certainty and they should be able to adopt commercial policies in the knowledge that their conduct is legal.

2. An abuse of a dominant position should only be found on the basis of a clearly articulated theory of harm.

3. The Guidance Paper is a welcome move which helps to clarify when certain types of conduct merit intervention by the Commission. The effect of the Guidance Paper on the EU Courts is not yet clear.

4. The increasing use of Commitments decisions is injurious to the development of the law. Commitments negotiated between undertakings and the Commission do not result in a finding that (perhaps novel) conduct does indeed constitute an abuse and the questions at issue do not come before the EU Courts. If this continues the development of the jurisprudence on Article 102 will become more dependent on cases which go straight from national courts to the CJ under the preliminary reference procedure, but in such cases the Court is not called upon to apply the law to the facts.

5. Another growing trend is the use by undertakings in the digital economy, of Article 102 as a major weapon in their commercial battles, particularly since Article 102 is applied in a more interventionist way than section 2 of the US Sherman Act.

19. FURTHER READING

A. BOOKS

AKMAN, P., *The Concept of Abuse in EU Competition Law* (Hart Publishing, 2012)

BELLAMY, G., and CHILD, G. (V. Rose and D. Bailey, eds.), *European Law of Competition* (7th edn, Oxford University Press, 2013), Chap. 9, 9.049–9.064, Chap. 10, 10.053–10.152

BISHOP, S., and WALKER, M., *The Economics of EC Competition Law: Concepts, Application and Measurement* (3rd edn, Sweet & Maxwell, 2010), Chap. 6

BORK, R., *The Antitrust Paradox* (Basic Books, 1978, reprinted with a new Introduction and Epilogue, 1993), Chap. 7

EHLERMANN, C. D., and ATANASIU, I. (eds.), *European Competition Law Annual 2003: What is Abuse of a Dominant Position?* (Hart Publishing, 2006)

——, —— (eds.), *European Competition Law Annual 2005: The Interaction Between Competition Law and Intellectual Property Law* (Hart Publishing, 2007)

---

[968] See Chap. 9, Section B.ii, p. 723.

[969] See, for example, Cases C-395 and 396/96 P, *Compagnie Maritime Belge and others v. Commission* [2000] ECR I-1365 and Case T-193/02, *Laurent Piau v. Commission* [2005] ECR II-209.

[970] Case T-228/97, *Irish Sugar plc v. Commission* [1999] ECR II-2969, para. 66.

—— and MARQUIS, M., *European Competition Law Annual 2007: A Reformed Approach to Article 82 EC* (Hart Publishing, 2008)

ETRO, F., and KOKKORIS, I. (eds), *Competition Law and the Enforcement of Article 102* (Oxford University Press, 2010)

EZRACHI, A. (ed.), *Article 82 EC: Reflections on its Recent Evolution* (Hart Publishing, 2009)

GERADIN, D., LAYNE-FARRAR, A., and PETIT, N., *EU Competition Law and Economics* (Oxford University Press, 2012), 4.131–4.542

HOVENKAMP, H., *Federal Antitrust Policy* (4th edn, West, 2011), Chaps. 6, 7, 8, and 10

JOLIET R., *Monopolization and Abuse of Dominant Position* (Nijhoff, 1970)

LANGER, J., *Tying And Bundling As A Leveraging Concern Under EC Competition Law* (Kluwer Law International, 2008)

LOVDHAL GORMSEN, L., *A Principled Approach to Abuse of Dominance in European Competition Law* (Cambridge University Press, 2010)

MOTTA, M., *Competition Policy* (Cambridge University Press, 2004), Chaps. 2 and 7

NAZZINI, R., *The Foundations of European Union Competition Law, The Objectives and Principles of Article 102* (Oxford University Press, 2011)

O'DONOGHUE, R., and PADILLA, A. J., *The Law and Economics of Article 102* (2nd edn, Hart Publishing, 2013)

PACE, L. F. (ed), *European Competition Law: The Impact of the Commission's Guidance on Article 102* (Edward Elgar, 2011)

PHILIPS, L., *The Economics of Price Discrimination* (Cambridge University Press, 1983)

POSNER, R. A., *Antitrust Law* (2nd edn, University of Chicago Press, 2001), Chaps. 7 and 8

ROUSSEVA, E., *Rethinking Exclusionary Abuses in EU Competition Law* (Hart Publishing, 2010)

SCHERER, F. M., and ROSS, D., *Industrial Market Structure and Economic Performance* (3rd edn, Houghton Mifflin, 1990), Chaps. 13 and 16

SCHMIDT, H., *Competition Law, Innovation and Antitrust* (Edward Elgar, 2009)

VAN DEN BERGH, R. J., and CAMESASCA, P. D., *European Competition Law and Economics: A Comparative Perspective* (2nd edn, Sweet & Maxwell, 2006), Chap. 7

B. CHAPTERS IN BOOKS

ACKERMANN, T., 'Excessive Pricing and the Goals of Competition Law' in D. Zimmer (ed.), *The Goals of Competition Law* (Edward Elgar, 2012), Chap. 18

DOWNING, R., and JONES, A., 'Margin Squeezes in Telecommunications Markets', in S. Anderman and A. Ezrachi (eds.), *Intellectual Property and Competition Law: New Frontiers* (Oxford University Press, 2011)

FOX, E., 'Abuse of Dominance and Monopolisation: How to Protect Competition Without Protecting Competitors', in C. D. Ehlermann and I. Atanasiu (eds.), *European Competition Law Annual 2003: What is Abuse of a Dominant Position?* (Hart Publishing, 2006), 69

HATZOPOULOS, V., 'The EC Essential Facilities Doctrine' in G. Amato and C.-D. Ehlermann (eds.), *EC Competition Law: A Critical Assessment* (Hart Publishing, 2007), 333

HOWARTH, D., 'Unfair and Predatory Pricing under Article 82 EC: From Cost-Price Comparisons to the Search for Strategic Standards' in G. Amato and C.-D. Ehlermann (eds.), *EC Competition Law: A Critical Assessment* (Hart Publishing, 2007), 249

JONES, A., 'Refusal to Deal—EC and US Law Compared', in Marsden, P. (ed.), *Handbook of Research in Trans-Atlantic Antitrust* (Edward Elgar Publishing, 2006), Chap. 8, 236–286

LANGER, J., 'A Four-step Test to Assess the Exclusionary Effects of Bundling under Article 82 EC' in G. Amato and C.-D. Ehlermann (eds.), *EC Competition Law: A Critical Assessment* (Hart Publishing, 2007), 297

MARSDEN, P., 'Some Outstanding Issues from the European Commission's Guidance on Article 102 TFEU: Not-So-Faint Echoes of Ordoliberalism' in F. Etro and I. Kokkoris, *Competition Law and the Enforcement of Article 102* (Oxford University Press, 2010), Chap. 3

ROELLER, L.-H., 'Exploitative Abuses' in C.-D. Ehlermann and M. Marquis (eds.), *European Competition Law Annual 2007: A Reformed Approach to Article 82* (Hart Publishing, 2008)

ROUSSEVA, E., 'Objective Justification and Article 82 EC in the Era of Modernisation', in G. Amato and C.-D. Ehlermann, (eds.), *EC Competition Law: A Critical Assessment* (Hart Publishing, 2007), 377

TERHECHTE, J. P., 'Excessive Pricing and the Goals of Competition Law: an Enforcement Perspective— Comment on Ackermann' in D. Zimmer (ed.), *The Goals of Competition Law* (Edward Elgar, 2012), Chap. 19

VICKERS, J., 'How Does the Prohibition of Abuse of Dominance Fit with the Rest of Competition Policy?', in C.-D. Ehlermann and I. Atanasiu (eds.), *European Competition Law Annual 2003: What is Abuse of a Dominant Position* (Hart Publishing, 2006), 147

—— 'Some Economics of Abuse of Dominance', in X. Vives (ed.), *Competition Policy in the EU: Fifty Years on from the Treaty of Rome* (Oxford University Press, 2009) 71

C. ARTICLES

AHLBORN, C., and BAILEY, D., 'Discounts, Rebates and Selective Pricing by Dominant Firms: A Trans-Atlantic Comparison' (2006) 2 *European Competition Journal* 101

—— and EVANS, D. S., 'The *Microsoft* Judgment and its Implications for Competition Policy Towards Dominant Firms in Europe' (2008–2009) 75 *Antitrust LJ* 887

—— —— and PADILLA, J., 'The Logic and Limits of Exceptional Circumstances Test in *Magill* and *IMS Health*' (2005) *Fordham Int'l LJ* 1062

AKMAN, P. ' "Consumer Welfare" and Article 82: Practice and Rhetoric' (2009) 32 *World Competition* 71

—— 'Searching for the Long-Lost Soul of Article 82EC' (2009) 29 *Oxford Journal of Legal Studies* 267

ALLAN, B., 'Article 102: A Commentary on DG Competition's Discussion Paper' [2006] *Competition Policy International* 43

ANDREANGELI, A., 'Interoperability as an "Essential Facility" in the Microsoft Case—Encouraging Competition or Stifling Innovation' (2009) 34 *ELRev* 584

ANDREWS, P., 'Aftermarket Power in the Computer Services Market: The Digital Undertaking' [1998] *ECLR* 176

AREEDA, P., 'Essential Facilities: An Epithet in Need of Limiting Principles' (1990) 58 *Antitrust LJ* 841

—— and TURNER, D., 'Predatory Pricing and Related Practices under Section 2 of the Sherman Act' (1975) 88 *Harvard LR* 697

BARAZZA, S., 'Post Danmark: the CJEU Calls for an Effect-based Assessment of Pricing Policies' (2012) 3 *Journal of European Competition Law and Practice* 466

BEARD, D., '*Microsoft*: What Sort of Landmark?' (2008) 4 *Competition Policy Int'l* 33

BISHOP, W., 'Price Discrimination under Article 86: Political Economy in the European Court' (1981) 66 *MLR* 282

BORLINI, L., 'Methodological Issues of the "More Economic Approach" to Unilateral Exclusionary Conduct' (2009) *European Competition Journal* 409

BRODLEY, J., and HAY, D., 'Predatory Pricing: Competing Economic Theories and the Evolution of Legal Standards' (1981) 66 *Cornell LR* 738

BUNDESKARTELLAMT, 'Competition Law Forum Debate on Reform of Article 102: A "Dialectic" on Competing Approaches' (2006) 2 *European Competition Journal*, 211

CAPOBIANCO, A., 'The Essential Facility Doctrine: Similarities and Differences between the American and European Approaches' (2001) 26 *ELRev* 548

CARLTON, D., 'Should "Price Squeeze" be a Recognized Form of Anticompetitive Conduct?' (2008) 4 *Journal of Competition Law and Economics* 271

—— and Waldman, W., 'The Strategic Use of Tying to Preserve and Create Market Power in Evolving Industries' (2002) 33 *Rand Journal of Economics* 194

CHOI, J., and STEFANADIS, C., 'Tying, Investment and Dynamic Leverage Theory' (2001) 32 *Rand Journal of Economics* 52

COLLEY, L., and BURNSIDE, S., 'Margin Squeeze Abuse' (2006) 2 *European Competition Journal* 185

CRANE, D., and WRIGHT, J., 'Can Bundled Discounting Increase Consumer Prices Without Excluding Rivals?' (2009) 5 *Competition Policy Int'l* 209

DOHERTY, B., 'Just What Are Essential Facilities?' (2001) 38 *CMLRev* 397

DUNNE, N., 'Margin Squeeze: From Broken Regulation to Legal Uncertainty' (2011) 70 *CLJ* 34

—— 'Margin Squeeze: Theory, Practice, Policy', Parts I and II [2012] *ECLR* 29 and 61

EILSMANSBERGER, T., 'How to Distinguish Good from Bad Competition under Article 102 EC: In Search of Clearer and More Coherent Standards for Anti-competitive Abuses' (2005) *CMLRev* 129

ELHAUGE, E., 'Defining Better Monopolisation Standards' (2003–2004) 56 *Stan LR* 253

—— 'Tying, Bundled Discounts, and the Death of the Single Monopoly Profit Theory' (2009) 123(2) *Harvard LR* 399

EVANS, D. S., and SALINGER, M., 'Why Do Firms Bundle and Tie? Evidence from Competitive Markets and Implications for Tying Law' (2005) 22 *Yale J Reg.* 37

EZRACHI, A., and GILO, D., 'Are Excessive Prices Really Self-Correcting?' (2009) 5 *Journal of Competition Law and Economics* 249

FAELLA, G. and PARDOLESI, R., 'Squeezing Price Squeeze under EC Antitrust Law' (2010) 6 *European Competition Journal* 255

FINE, F., 'NDC/IMS: A Logical Application of the Essential Facilities Doctrine' [2002] *ECLR* 457

—— 'NDC/IMS: In Response to Professor Korah' (2002) 70 *Antitrust LJ* 247

FIRST, H., 'No Single Monopoly Profit, No Single Policy Prescription?' (2009) 5 *Competition Policy Int'l* 199

FJELL, K., and SØRGARD, L., 'How to Test for Abuse of Dominance?' (2006) 2 *European Competition Journal*, 69

FOX, E., 'Price Predation—US and EEC: Economics and Values' [1989] Fordham Corp L Inst 687

—— 'What is Harm to Competition? Exclusionary Practices and Anti-competitive Effect' (2002) 70 *Antitrust LJ* 371

—— 'We Protect Competition, You Protect Competitors' (2003) 26(2) *World Competition* 149

FURSE, M., 'Excessive Prices, Unfair Prices and Economic Value' (2008) 4 *European Competition Journal* 59

GERADIN, D., 'Limiting the Scope of Article 82 EC: What Can the EU Learn from the Supreme Court's Judgment in *Trinko*, in the Wake of *Microsoft*, *IMS* and *Deutsche Telekom*?' (2004) 41 *CMLRev* 1526

—— 'Is the Guidance Paper on the Commission's Enforcement Priorities in Applying Article 102 TFEU to Abusive Exclusionary Conduct Useful?' <http://ssrn.com/abstract=1569502>

—— 'The Decision of the Commission of 13 May 2009 in the *Intel* case: Where is the Foreclosure and Consumer Harm?' (2009) 2 *J'nl of European Competition Law and Practice* 9

—— 'Refusal to Supply and Margin Squeeze: A Discussion of Why the "Telefonica Exceptions" are Wrong', *TILEC Discussion Paper* No 2011-009, http://ssrn.com/abstract=1750226

—— 'Ten Years of DG Competition Effort to Provide Guidance on the Application of Competition Rules to the Licensing of Standard-Essential Patents: Where Do We Stand?', <http://ssrn.com/abstract=2204359>

—— and O'DONOGHUE, R., 'The Concurrent Application of Competition Law and Regulation: the Case of Margin Squeeze Abuses in the Telecommunications Sector' (2005) I *Journal of Competition Law and Economics* 355

GOHARI, R. S., 'Margin Squeeze in the Telecommunications Sector: A More Economics-Based Approach' (2012) 2 *World Comp* 205

GRIMES, W. S., 'The Antitrust Tying Law Schism: 'A Critique of *Microsoft III* and a Response to Hylton and Salinger' (2002) 70 *Antitrust LJ* 199

HANCHER, P., 'Case Note on Oscar Bronner' (1999) 36 *CMLRev* 1289

HOPPNER, T., 'Competition Law in Intellectual Property Litigation: The Case for a Compulsory Licence Defence under Article 102 TFEU' (2011) *European Competition Journal* 297

HOWARTH, D., and MCMAHON, K., '"Windows has performed an Illegal Operation": The Court of First Instance's Judgment in *Microsoft v Commission*' [2008] *ECLR* 117

INCARDONA, R., 'Modernization of Article 82 EC and Refusal to Supply' (2006) 2 *European Competition Journal* 337

JEBSEN, P., and STEVENS, R., 'Assumptions, Goals and Dominant Undertakings: The Regulation of Competition Under Article 86 of the European Union' (1996) 64 *Antitrust LJ* 443

JONES, A., 'Distinguishing Predatory Prices from Competitive Ones' [1995] *EIPR* 252

KALLAUGHER, J., and SHER, B., 'Rebates Revisited: Anti-Competitive Effects and Exclusionary Abuse Under Article 82' [2004] *ECLR* 263

KATE, A., and NIELS, G., 'On the Rationality of Predatory Pricing: The Debate between Chicago and Post-Chicago' (2002) *Antitrust Bull* 1

KELLERBAUER, M., 'The Commission's New Enforcement Priorities in Applying Article 82EC to Dominant Companies' Exclusionary Conduct: A Shift Towards a More Economic Approach?' (2010) *ECLR* 175, 185

KINGSTON, S., 'Casenote on *Sot. Lélos* (2009) 46 *CMLRev* 683

KJØLBE, L., 'Rebates Under Article 82 EC: Navigating Uncertain Waters' [2010] *ECLR* 66

—— 'Article 82 EC as Remedy to Patent System Imperfections: Fighting Fire with Fire?' (2009) 32 *World Competition* 163

KLEIN, B., and SHEPARD WILEY, J., 'Competitive Price Discrimination as an Antitrust Justification for IP Refusals to Deal' (2003) 70 *Antitrust LJ* 599

KORAH, V., 'The Paucity of Economic Analysis in the EEC Decisions on Competition: Tetra Pak II' [1993] *Current Legal Problems* 150

—— 'The Interface between Intellectual Property and Antitrust: the European Experience' (2002) 69 *Antitrust LJ* 801

KROES, N., 'Tackling Exclusionary Practices to Avoid Exploitation of Market Power: Some Preliminary Thoughts on the Policy Review of Article 82', in (2005) Fordham Corp L Inst (B. Hawk (ed.), 2006), 381

KUHN, K.-U., STILLMAN, R., and CAFFARRA, C., 'Economic Theories of Bundling and their Policy Implications in Abuse Cases' (2005) 1 *European Competition Journal* 85

LAROUCHE, P., 'The European Microsoft Case at the Crossroads of Competition Policy and Innovation: Comment on Ahlborn and Evans' 75 *Antitrust LJ* 933

LIANOS, I., 'Competition Law and Intellectual Property Rights: Is the Property Rights Approach Right?' (2005–2006) 8 *Cambridge Yearbook of European Legal Studies*

LOVDAHL GORMESEN, L., 'The Conflict between Economic Freedom and Consumer Welfare in the Modernisation of Article 82' (2007) 3 *European Competition Journal* 329

—— 'Why the European Commission's Enforcement Priorities on Article 82 Should Be Withdrawn' [2010] *ECLR* 45

LUGARD, P., 'Eternal Sunshine on a Spotless Policy? Exclusive Dealing under Article 82 EC' (2006) 2 *European Competition Journal* 163

MCGEE, J., 'Predatory Price Cutting: The Standard Oil (New Jersey) Case' (1958) 1 *Journal Law and Economy* 137

MAIER-RIGAUD, F., 'Article 82 Rebates: Four Common Fallacies' (2006) 2 *European Competition Journal* 85

MATEUS, A., 'Predatory Pricing: A Proposed Structured Rule of Reason (2011) 7 *European Competition Law* 243

MEISEL, J., 'The Law and Economics of Margin Squeezes in the US versus the EU' (2012) 8 *European Competition Journal* 383

MOURADE SILVA, M., 'Predatory Pricing and the Recoupment Test: Do Not Go Gentle Into That Good Night' [2009] *ECLR* 61

MÜLLER, U., and RODENHAUSEN, A., 'The Rise and Fall of the Essential Facilities Doctrine' [2008] *ECLR* 310

MURPHY, F., and LIBERATORE, F., 'Abuse of Regulatory Procedures—the *Astra-Zeneca Case*' [2009] *ECLR* 289 and 314

NABELUFF, B., 'Exclusionary Bundling' (2005) 50 *Antitrust Bulletin* 321

NAZZINI, R., 'The Wood Began to Move: An Essay on Consumer Welfare, Evidence and Burden of Proof in Article 82 EC Cases' (2006) 31 *ELRev* 518

O'DONOGHUE, R., and MACNAB, L., 'Dominant Firms' Duties to Deal with Pharmaceutical Parallel Traders Following *Glaxo Greece*' (2009) 5(1) *Competition Policy Int'l* 153

PANNER, A. M., 'Are Price Squeezes Anticompetitive?' (2009) April (1) *Global Competition Policy*

PEEPERKORN, L., and ROUSSEVA, E., 'Article 102 TFEU: Exclusive Dealing and Rebates' (2011) 2 *J'nl of European Competition Law and Practice* 36

PETIT, N., 'From Formalism to Effects? The Commission's Communication on Enforcement Priorities in Applying Article 82' (2009) 32(4) *World Competition* 485

PITOFSKY, R., PATTERSON, D., and HOOKS, J., 'The Essential Facilities Doctrine under US Antitrust Law' (2002) 70 *Antitrust LJ* 443

RAPP, R. T., 'Predatory Pricing and Entry Deterring Strategies: The Economics of AKZO' [1986] *ECLR* 233

RATO, M., and PETIT, N., 'Abuse of Dominance in Technology-Enabled Markets: Established Standards Reconsidered?' (2013) 9 *European Competition Journal* 1

RIDYARD, D., 'Essential Facilities and the Obligation to Supply Competitors' [1996] *ECLR* 438

—— 'Exclusionary Pricing and Price Discrimination Abuses under Article 102—An Economic Analysis' [2002] *ECLR* 286

—— 'Compulsory Access under EC Competition Law—A New Doctrine of "Convenient Facilities" and the Case for Price Regulation' [2004] *ECLR* 670

—— 'The Commission's Article 82 Guidelines: some Reflections on the Economic Issues' [2009] *ECLR* 230

RITTER, C., 'Refusal to Deal and Essential Facilities: Does Intellectual Property Require Special Deference compared to Tangible Property?' (2005) 3 *World Competition* 281

ROUSSEVA, E., 'Modernizing by Eradicating: How the Commission's New Approach to Article 81 EC Dispenses with the Need to Apply Article 82 EC to Vertical Restraints' (2005) 42 *CMLRev* 587

—— and Marquis, M., 'Hell Freezes Over: A Climate Change for Assessing Exclusionary Conduct under Article 102 TFEU' (2012) 4 *J'nl of European Competition Law and Practice* 32

SCHMALENSEE, R., 'Output and Welfare Implications of Third Degree Price Discrimination' (1981) 71 *American Economic Review* 242

SCOTT HEMPHILL, C., 'The Role of Recoupment in Predatory Pricing Analyses' (2001) *Stan LR* 1581

SEABRIGHT, P., 'The Undead? A Comment on Professor Elhauge's Paper' (2009) 5 *Competition Policy Int'l* 243

SHER, B., 'Price Discounts And *Michelin II*; What Goes Around, Comes Around' [2002] *ECLR* 482

—— 'The Last of the Steam-Powered Trains: Modernising Article 82' [2004] *ECLR* 243

SIDAK, J. G, 'Abolishing the Price Squeeze as a Theory of Antitrust Liability' (2008) 4 *Journal of Competition Law and Economics* 279

—— and TEECE, D. J., 'Dynamic Competition in Antitrust Law' (2009) 5 *Journal of Competition Law and Economics* 581

SPECTOR, D., 'Loyalty Rebates: An Assessment of Competition Concerns and a Proposed Structured Rule of Reason' (2005) 1(2) *Competition Policy International* 89

—— 'From Harm to Competitors to Harm to Competition: One More Effort, Please!' (2006) 2 *European Competition Journal* 145

SUBIOTTO, R., and LITTLE, D., 'The Application of Article 102 TFEU by the European Commission and the European Courts' (2012) 3 *Journal of European Competition Law and Practice* 175

SVETLICINII, A., and BOTTA, M., 'Article 102 TFEU as a Tool for Market Regulation' (2012) 8 *European Law Journal* 473

TEMPLE LANG, J., 'Defining Legitimate Competition: Companies' Duties to Supply Competitors and Access to Essential Facilities' (1994) 18 *Fordham Int'l LJ* 437

—— 'The Principle of Essential Facilities in European Community Competition Law—The Position since *Bronner*' (2000) 1 *Journal of Network Industries*, 375

—— 'Anti-competitive Non-Pricing Abuses under European and National Antitrust Law' in B. Hawk (ed.) [2003] *Fordham Corp L Inst* 235

—— 'Reprisals and Overreaction by Dominant Companies as an Anti-competitive Abuse under Article 82(b)' [2008] *ECLR* 11

—— 'How Can the Problems of Exclusionary Abuses under Article 102 TFEU be Resolved?' (2012) 37 *ELRev* 136

—— and O'DONOGHUE, R., 'Defining Legitimate Competition: How to Clarify Pricing Abuses under Article 102 EC' (2002) 26 *Fordham Int'l LJ* 83

VICKERS, J., 'Abuse of Market Power' (2005) 115 *Economic Journal* F244

WERDEN, G., 'Competition Policy on Exclusionary Analysis: Towards an Effects-based Analysis?' (2006) 2 *European Competition Journal* 53

WHINSTON, M., 'Tying, Foreclosure and Exclusion' (1990) 80(4) *American Economic Review* 837

ZENGER, H., 'Loyalty Rebates and the Competitive Process' (2012) 8 *Journal of Competition Law and Economics*, 717

8

COMPETITION, THE STATE, AND PUBLIC UNDERTAKINGS: ARTICLE 106 TFEU

1. CENTRAL ISSUES

1. Article 4(3) TEU contains the principle of Union loyalty. Member States are required to take any appropriate measures to ensure fulfilment of their Union obligations, facilitate the achievement of the Union's tasks, and refrain from any measure that could jeopardise the attainment of the Union's objectives.

2. Article 106 TFEU addresses the application of the competition rules (and other rules of the Treaties) to State measures in respect of public undertakings and to undertakings granted special or exclusive rights, and to undertakings entrusted with services of general economic interest (SGEIs).

3. Article 106(1) is a prohibition addressed to Member States. Its object is to prevent Member States from depriving Treaty rules of their effectiveness by the measures they adopt in respect of public undertakings and those to which they grant special or exclusive rights.

4. The cases show that Article 106(1) is infringed if, in merely exercising the special or exclusive rights, the undertaking cannot avoid abusing its dominant position or if it is thereby led to abuse its dominant position. Some cases, however, have suggested that the very granting of special or exclusive rights is contrary to Article 106(1).

5. Services of general interest may be economic or non-economic. Non-economic services are not subject to the competition rules. Economic services are subject to the competition rules. However, Article 106(2) provides a derogation from, inter alia, the competition rules for undertakings entrusted with SGEIs if otherwise they would be obstructed in the performance of their tasks. However, in some cases entities are removed from the ambit of the competition rules because they are not undertakings engaged in an economic activity for the purposes of Article 101 or Article 102 in the first place. This may be because the entity is found to operate on the basis of 'solidarity'.

6. It may be a crucial factor in the application of Article 106(2) that the undertaking has 'universal service' obligations (USO). Further, it may be important to shield an undertaking from competition so that it can cross-subsidise from profitable sectors to uneconomic ones and competitors cannot come in and 'cherry pick' the profitable parts of the operation.

7. Article 106(3) provides the Commission with special supervisory and policing powers to ensure the application of the Article. It can adopt directives as well as issue decisions.

8. Article 14 TFEU specifically deals with SGEIs. They are also the subject of an article in the Charter of Fundamental Rights and services of general interest are dealt with in a Protocol attached to the TEU and TFEU.

2. INTRODUCTION

A. GENERAL

In this chapter we consider how competition law applies to the actions of the State when it intervenes in the market through undertakings which it controls or owns or which it places in a privileged position.[1] We do not deal specifically with the subject of State aid, which is outside the scope of the printed edition of this book, but it is important to note that Article 106 TFEU has significant links to State aid.

A competition policy which did not deal with the State in the market place would be incomplete. The State plays some part in the marketplace, directly or indirectly, in all the Member States, although the means and extent of this vary. The means and extent have also changed over time since the inception of the EEC. In 1957 there was still a fashion for nationalisation, and it will be remembered that the leading case on the supremacy of EU law, *Costa v. ENEL*,[2] concerned the nationalisation of the Italian electricity industry. Since then there has been a move in Europe away from public ownership, and indeed a revolution in the way that public services are delivered. There has been increasing 'marketisation', whereby Member States have turned to the market to provide services to the public, and an erosion of the distinction between public and private providers. This is due not only to shifts in ideology but also to technological and economic advances which have meant that the arguments for publicly owned monopolies in sectors such as telecommunications and electricity generation have been transformed.[3] The EU has pursued a programme of liberalisation whereby sectors in which there were formerly State-owned monopolies have been opened up to competition and competition law is employed alongside the liberalising measures to make this effective. Liberalisation, which has been described as inspired as much by the desire to increase the integration of the market as by increasing competition (national monopolies tend to maintain the compartmentalisation of the internal market),[4] has been accompanied by the imposition of public service obligations (PSOs) such as universal service (USO) on undertakings operating on the liberalised market and the strengthening of consumer and user rights.[5]

E. Szyszczak, 'Public Service Provision in Competitive Markets' (2001) 20 *YEL* 35, 36

The economic, political, and social world has been shaped by a number of processes in recent years: most significantly by rapid technological change, globalization of economic activity, the development of capital markets, the liberalization and restructuring of product and service markets and deregulation of markets. Governments and private companies alike have persuaded their electorates and consumers of the

---

[1] For an analysis of the development of the law in this area, see L. Hancher, 'Community, State and Market', in P. Craig and G. de Búrca (eds.), *The Evolution of EU Law* (Oxford University Press, 1999), 721 and E. Szyszczak, *The Regulation of the State in Competitive Markets in the EU* (Hart Publishing, 2007). And see generally J. Faull and A. Nikpay (eds.), *The EC Law of Competition* (2nd edn, Oxford University Press, 2007), Chap. 6; J. L. Buenida Sierra, *Exclusive Rights and State Monopolies in EC Law* (Oxford University Press, 1999, 2nd edn forthcoming, 2014); T. Prosser, *The Limits of Competition Law* (Oxford University Press, 2005).

[2] Case 6/64, *Flaminio Costa v. ENEL* [1964] ECR 585.

[3] See G. Amato, *Antitrust and the Bounds of Power: The Dilemma of Liberal Democracy in the History of the Market* (Hart Publishing, 1997), 88–89; E. Szyszczak, 'Public Service Provision in Competitive Markets' (2001) 20 *YEL* 35.

[4] See Hancher, 'Community, State and Market', in Craig and de Búrca (eds.), *The Evolution of EU Law* (cited in n. 1), 722.

[5] See the Commission's comments on this in the 2007 Communication, para. 2.2 (cited in n. 16).

capacity of markets to provide not only private goods and services, but also what have traditionally been viewed as publicly provided services...The belief in free markets is premised on the view not only that private enterprise is more efficient than state provision but that it may also be more responsive to consumer wishes. This change in attitude towards free markets has complemented other goals being pursued by governments, particularly the exercise of tighter fiscal discipline on public spending and the embracing of new forms of public management by neo-liberal governments seeking to provide a climate in which markets can develop and flourish...Such beliefs are particularly prevalent in the EU, indeed liberalization of the public sector has been viewed by one Commissioner responsible for competition, Van Miert, as an *unavoidable* consequence of the establishment of the Internal Market:

'It is obvious that a market based on competition and free circulation of goods, services, people and capital is at odds with systems based on national monopolies. Our liberalisation policy was therefore conceived as an indispensable instrument for the establishment of the internal market'.[6]

...

The result has been a radical restructuring of the relationship between the State and the market.

The original version of the Treaty of Rome was neutral as between public and private ownership. Article 295 EC[7] stated that the Treaty in no way prejudiced the rules in Member States governing the system of property ownership. That Article, now Article 345 TFEU, is unchanged but it is arguable that the insertion by the Treaty of European Union (Maastricht) of what is now Article 119 TFEU,[8] represented a shift in policy which favours private over public ownership. Article 119 says that the activities of the Member States and the Union shall be conducted 'in accordance with the principle of an open market economy with free competition'. Article 119 is elaborated upon in Article 173[9] which provides that the 'Union and Member States shall ensure that the conditions necessary for the competitiveness of the Union's industry exist' and that their action in this respect which should be aimed, inter alia, at encouraging an environment favourable to initiative and the development of small and medium-sized undertakings, should be in accordance 'with a system of open and competitive markets'.

The answer to the question as to which, if any, areas of activity the normal principles of competition law should not apply, belongs in the political rather than the legal realm. However, the original Treaty of Rome contained nothing about the limits to competition law and the provision of public services, save for a provision about State aid in the inland transport sector in respect of 'certain obligations inherent in the concept of a public service' being permitted,[10] and a derogation in what is now Article 106(2)[11] pertaining to 'services of general economic interest' (SGEIs). The 'services of general economic interest' concept was not defined and appeared nowhere else in the Treaty or in secondary legislation. Before 1990[12] the application of competition law to State-owned, State-controlled, or

---

[6] K. Van Miert, 'Liberalization of the Economy of the European Union: The Game is not (yet) Over' in D. Geradin (ed.), *The Liberalization of State Monopolies in the European Union and Beyond* (Kluwer, 2000), 1.1.

[7] Ex Art. 222.

[8] Ex Art. 4 EC.

[9] Ex Art. 157 EC.

[10] Art. 73 EC, ex Art. 77. The Article was at issue in Case C-280/00, *Altmark Trans GmbH, Regierungspräsidium Magdeburg v. Nahverkehrsgesellschaft Altmark GmbH* [2003] ECR I-7747 on whether compensation for services of general economic interest is a State aid: see Section 9, p. 656.

[11] Ex Art. 86(2) EC, ex Art. 90(2).

[12] The early 1990s saw the four major Art. 267 rulings, Case C-41/90, *Höfner v. Macrotron* [1991] ECR I-1979; Case C-179/90, *Merci Convenzionali v. Porto di Genova* [1991] ECR I-5889; Case C-260/89, *Elliniki Radiophonia Tileorasi (ERT)*

State-privileged undertakings was not a significant issue. It has become so because of technological, ideological, social, and economic changes, the increasing sophistication and reach of EU competition law, and the more aggressive enforcement of the law.

As will be seen in this chapter, the case law of the EU Courts has sometimes been inconsistent and confusing. The debate about the relationship between competition law and public services, conducted in the shadow of that case law, resulted in the introduction into the Treaty of Rome by the Treaty of Amsterdam of what is now (with some modification) Article 14 TFEU,[13] and the inclusion in the Charter of Fundamental Rights of the European Union of Article 36, both of which proclaim the value and importance of 'services of general economic interest'.[14] A Protocol (No. 26) on 'services of general interest' is attached to the TEU and the TFEU by the Treaty of Lisbon.[15] The Commission has complemented these provisions with 'soft law' in a series of Communications on services of general interest,[16] the latest one being 'A Quality Framework for Services of General Interest in Europe' in December 2011 ('the 2011 Communication')[17] which is accompanied by a Commission Staff Working Document[18] (the Staff Working Document).

B. THE LIMITS OF COMPETITION LAW

There are two ways in which the application of EU competition law to public services can be limited. First, the activity can be found not to be 'economic', and therefore not subject to Articles 101 and 102 in the first place. Secondly, it can be found to be economic but allowed to take advantage of a derogation from the rules (in particular, the derogation provided in Article 106(2)).

Whether or not an activity is economic in the first place goes back to the definition of 'undertaking' which was discussed in Chapter 3. Articles 101 and 102 apply only to 'undertakings', and denying a body the status of an undertaking removes it from the ambit of the competition rules. It will be recalled that 'undertaking' is a concept of EU law and that it is immaterial how the entity is regarded in national law. The fundamental question is whether it carries out commercial activities and not whether it is governed by public law or is non-profit-making. The CJ held in *Höfner* v. *Macrotron* that in regard to competition law 'the concept of an undertaking encompasses every entity engaged in an economic activity, regardless of the legal status of the entity and the way it is financed'.[19] In that case the fact that employment procurement was normally entrusted to public agencies could not affect the economic nature of the activity the entity carried out. It was not always an activity carried out by public entities and it followed that a public employment agency could be classified as an undertaking.[20]

---

v. *DEP* [1991] ECR I-2925; and Case C-18/88, *RTT* v. *GB-Inno-BM SA* [1991] ECR I-5973; and the telecommunications cases between the Commission and Member States, Case C-202/88, *France* v. *Commission* [1991] ECR I-1223 and Cases C-271, 281, and 289/90, *Spain, Belgium & Italy* v. *Commission* [1992] ECR I-5833.

[13] Ex Art. 16 EC, ex Art.7d EC. For the Article and the way in was modified see Section 6.A.i, p. 630 ff.

[14] See Section 6.A.i p. 630 ff.

[15] See Section 6.A.i, p. 631.

[16] Communication on Services of General Interest in Europe [1996] OJ C281/03; Communication on Services of General Interest [2001] OJ C17/4; Communication on 'Services of General Interest, including Social Services of General Interest: a New European Commitment' accompanying the Communication on 'A Single Market for 21st Century Europe', COM(2007) 725 final. The 2007 Communication followed the Commission's Green and White Papers of 2003 and 2004, COM(2003) 270 final and COM(2004) 374, 12 May 2004 respectively.

[17] Communication from the Commission to the European Parliament, the Council, the European Economic and Social Committee and the Committee of the Regions, COM(2011) 900 final.

[18] SEC(2010) 1545 final.

[19] Case C-41/90, *Höfner* v. *Macrotron* [1991] ECR I-1979, para. 21.

[20] Case C-41/90, *Höfner* v. *Macrotron* [1991] ECR I-1979, paras. 22–23.

It was also seen in Chapter 3 that bodies which exercise powers which can be seen as part of the prerogatives of the State, such as the air traffic control in *Eurocontrol*[21] and the anti-pollution surveillance in *Diego Cali*,[22] are not engaging in activities of an economic nature.

Particular problems, however, have arisen in determining the status of various types of social security and health insurance funds. Here the EU Courts have considered not whether the services are such that they may potentially be provided on the market (health insurance can undoubtedly be provided on the market and is therefore 'economic' in nature), but whether the details of the schemes demonstrate 'solidarity'. The principle of solidarity, the 'inherently uncommercial act of involuntary subsidisation of one social group by another'[23] has been used by the EU Courts to distinguish economic from non-economic activities.[24] The social aim of an insurance scheme is not sufficient in itself to preclude it from being an economic activity: it must also apply the principle of solidarity.[25] Solidarity can take various forms, depending on the type of scheme in issue. Inter alia, it can involve low-risk persons subsidising high-risk persons, the richer subsidising the poorer, one generation subsidising another, or more profitable schemes subsidising less profitable ones.[26] A number of cases have involved the issue of whether or not, using the criterion of solidarity, an entity should be classified as an entity.[27]

3. ARTICLE 4 TEU

Article 4(3) TEU contains the principle of Union loyalty which previously appeared as Article 10 EC. It requires Member States to take any appropriate measures to ensure fulfilment of their obligations under the Treaties or resulting from acts of the institutions; to facilitate the achievement of the Union's tasks, and to refrain from measures which could jeopardise the attainment of the Union's objectives. The CJ held in *Inno* v. *ATAB*, and has consistently stated ever since, that Member States are under a duty not to adopt or maintain in force measures which could deprive the competition provisions of their effectiveness. It is an infringement of Articles 4(3) and 101, for example, for a Member State to require or favour the adoption of agreements, decisions, or concerted practices contrary to Article 101, or to reinforce their effect.[28]

---

[21] Case C-364/92, *SAT Fluggesellschaft* v. *Eurocontrol* [1994] ECR I-43, and Case C-113/07, *SELEX Systemi Integrati SpA* v. *Commission*, [2009] ECR I-2207.

[22] Case C-343/95, *Diego Cali* v. *SEPG* [1997] ECR I-1547.

[23] Case C-70/95, *Sodemare* v. *Regione Lombardia* [1997] ECR I-3395, Opinion of Fennelly AG, para. 29.

[24] See N. Boeger, 'Solidarity and EC Competition Law' (2007) 32 *ELRev*319.

[25] Case C-350/07, *Kattner Stahlbau GmbH* v. *Maschinenbau-und Metall-Berufsgenossenschaft* [2009] ECR I-1513; Case C-437/09, *AG2R Prévoyance* v. *Beaudout* [2011] ECR I-973.

[26] See A. Winterstein, 'Nailing the Jellyfish: Social Security and Competition Law' [1999] *ECLR* 324.

[27] See Cases C-159–160/91 *Poucet and Pistre* v. *Assurances Générales de France* [1993] ECR I-637; Case C-244/94, *Fédération Française des Sociétés d'Assurance and Others* v. *Ministère de l'Agriculture et de la Pêche* [1995] ECR I-4013; Case C-67/96, *Albany International BV* v. *Stichting Bedrijfspensioenfonds Textielindustrie* [1999] ECR I-5751; Cases C-180–184/98, *Pavlov* v. *Stichting Pensioenfonds Medische Specialisten* [2000] ECR I-6451; Case C-218/00, *Cisal di Battistello Venanzio & Co* v. *Istituto Nazionale per L'Assicurazione Contro Gli Infortuni Sul Lavoro (INAIL)* [2002] ECR I-691; Cases C-264/01, C-306/01, C-354/01, and C-355/01, *AOK Bundesverband and others* v. *Ichthyol-Gesellschaft Cordes, Hermani & Co* [2004] ECR I-2493 discussed in Chap. 3.

[28] Case 267/86, *Van Eycke* v. *ASPA NV* [1988] ECR 4769, para. 16; Cases C-140–142/94, *DIP and Others* v. *Commune di Bassano del Grappa and Commune di Chioggia* [1995] ECR I-3257, para. 15; Case C-266/96, *Corsica Ferries France SA* v. *Gruppo Antichi Ormeggiatori del Porto di Genova* [1998] ECR I-3949, paras. 35, 36, 49; Cases C-67/96, 115–117/97 and 219/97, *Albany International BV* v. *Stichting Bedrijfspensioenfonds Textielindustrie* [1999] ECR I-5751, para. 65; Case C-437/09, *AG2R Prévoyance* v. *Beaudout* [2011] ECR I-973, paras. 24 and 37.

Case 13/77, *NV GB-Inno-BM SA* v. *ATAB* [1977] ECR 2115

The CJ was asked by the Belgian Court of Cassation about the compatibility with Community law of Belgian rules prohibiting the sale of tobacco at less than the price fixed by the manufacturers or importers.

Court of Justice

28. First, the single market system which the Treaty seeks to create excludes any national system of regulation hindering directly or indirectly, actually or potentially, trade within the Community.

29. Secondly, the general objective set out in Article [3(1)(g) EC] is made specific in several Treaty provisions concerning the rules on competition, including Article [102], which states that any abuse by one of more undertakings of a dominant position shall be prohibited as incompatible with the Common Market in so far as it may affect trade between Member States.

30. [Article 4(3) TEU] provides that Member States shall abstain from any measure which could jeopardize the attainment of the objectives of the Treaty.

31. Accordingly, while it is true that Article [102] is directed at undertakings, nonetheless it is also true that the Treaty imposes a duty on Member States not to adopt or maintain in force any measure which could deprive that provision of its effectiveness.

32. Thus Article [106] provides that, in the case of public undertakings and undertakings to which Member States grant special or exclusive rights, Member States shall neither enact nor maintain in force any measure contrary, *inter alia*, to the rules provided for in Articles [101 to 109 TFEU].

33. Likewise, Member States may not enact measures enabling private undertakings to escape from the constraints imposed by Articles [101 to 109 TFEU].

34. At all events, Article [102] prohibits any abuse by one or more undertakings of a dominant position, even if such abuse is encouraged by a national legislative provision.

35. In any case, a national measure which has the effect of facilitating the abuse of a dominant position capable of affecting trade between Member States will generally be incompatible with Articles [34] and [35], which prohibits quantitative restrictions on imports and exports and all measures having equivalent effect.

4. ARTICLE 106

The application of EU rules to public undertakings and those granted special or exclusive rights is dealt with in Article 106 (ex Article 86 EC).[29]

Article 106 states:

1. In the case of public undertakings and undertakings to which Member States grant special or exclusive rights, Member States shall neither enact nor maintain in force any measure contrary to the rules contained in the Treaties, in particular to those rules provided for in Article 18 and Articles 101 to 109.

2. Undertakings entrusted with the operation of services of general economic interest or having the character of a revenue-producing monopoly shall be subject to the rules contained in the Treaties, in particular to the rules on competition, in so far as the application of such rules does not obstruct the performance, in law or in fact, of the particular tasks assigned to them. The development of trade must not be affected to such an extent as would be contrary to the interests of the Union.

[29] Previously Art. 90.

3. The Commission shall ensure the application of the provisions of this Article and shall, where necessary, address appropriate directives or decisions to Member States.

A. THE OBJECTIVES OF ARTICLE 106

As will be appreciated from its wording, Article 106 is applied in conjunction with another Article, since its function is to limit the ways in which State measures protecting certain undertakings hinder the operation of the Treaties. Thus Article 106 does not deal only with competition, despite its position in the TFEU. It deals rather with the application of *all* the rules in the Treaties (hereafter called 'the Treaty rules'), although it mentions in particular the competition rules (Articles 101–109 TFEU) and the prohibition on discrimination on the grounds of nationality (Article 18 TFEU). Article 106 does, however, have particular relevance to the competition provisions and especially Article 102, because public undertakings and undertakings granted special or exclusive rights frequently hold a dominant position.[30]

Article 106 is a specific manifestation of the duty of Union loyalty contained in Article 4 TEU.

B. THE FORMAT OF ARTICLE 106

Article 106 contains three interrelated provisions.

(i) Article 106(1): Prohibition Addressed to Member States

The prohibition in Article 106(1) is addressed to Member States, not to undertakings. It prohibits Member States from enacting or maintaining in force any measures in relation to public undertakings and undertakings to which they have granted special or exclusive rights which are contrary to the Treaty rules. It is designed to prevent Member States from depriving the Treaty rules of their effectiveness through the measures they adopt in respect of public undertakings or through measures which enable private undertakings to escape the constraints of the competition provisions.

(ii) Article 106(2): Provision Addressed to Undertakings Providing for Limited Immunity from the Treaty Rules

Article 106(2) is addressed to the undertakings themselves. It gives a limited derogation from the Treaty rules to 'undertakings entrusted with the operation of services of general economic interest or having the character of a revenue producing monopoly' insofar as that is necessary for the carrying out of their tasks. Despite being addressed to undertakings, Article 106(2) can be invoked by Member States in relation to exclusive rights they have granted.[31]

(iii) Article 106(3): Policing and Legislative Powers of the Commission

Article 106(3) provides that the Commission may address decisions to Member States to ensure the observance of Article 106. This is an expedited enforcement mechanism which does not have to comply with the procedures of the general enforcement provision, Article 258 TFEU, which provides for infraction proceedings brought by the Commission against Member States.

---

[30] But not inevitably: the usual criteria of dominance apply, and the exclusive right has to be over a relevant market: see Case 30/87, *Bodson v. Pompes Funèbres des Régions Libérées* [1988] ECR 2479, paras. 26–29.

[31] See Section 6.C, p. 634.

It also gives the Commission power to issue directives to Member States to ensure the application of the Article. The power does not have to be exercised within the detailed procedural framework ordinarily applicable to the adoption of directives, which involves other Union institutions and is set down in Articles 289 to 297 TFEU.

The Commission's exercise of these special powers under Article 106(3) has led to challenges by Member States claiming that the situation concerned was not one to which Article 106(3) applied, that the Commission was acting ultra vires, and/or that some other legislative base should have been used.[32]

5. ARTICLE 106(1)

A. DEFINITIONS

When considering Article 106(1) it is first necessary to determine the meaning of the concepts it employs, in particular the terms 'public undertakings', 'granted special or exclusive rights', and 'measures'.

(i) 'Public Undertakings'

Determining the meaning of 'public undertakings' is a two-step procedure. First, one must ask whether a particular body is an 'undertaking' and secondly, if it is, whether it is a 'public undertaking'.

The answer to the first question, what constitutes an undertaking, has already been considered in the context of Articles 101 and 102[33] and mentioned in Section 2.B. The second question is whether an undertaking is a 'public' undertaking. Again, this is a Union concept[34] because Article 106(1) would be deprived of its effect if Member States were free to choose their own conception of 'public undertaking'. State participation in the ownership or running of undertakings comes in an almost indefinite range of guises and the Union concept must embrace them all.

The concept of a 'public undertaking' is defined Article 2(b) of the Transparency Directive:[35]

'public undertakings' means any undertaking over which the public authorities may exercise, directly or indirectly, a dominant influence by virtue of their ownership of it, their financial participation therein or the rules which govern it. A dominant influence on the part of the public authorities shall be presumed when these authorities, directly or indirectly, in relation to an undertaking:

(i) hold the major part of the undertaking's subscribed capital: or

(ii) control the majority of votes attached to the shares issued by the undertakings; or

(iii) can appoint more than half of the members of the undertaking's administrative, managerial or supervisory body.

The key to the concept is therefore control by the State. This can be through ownership or through some contractual, financial, or structural connection between the State and the undertaking. In *Greek*

---

[32] Cases 188-90/88, *France, Italy and the UK v. Commission* [1982] ECR 2545 (the *Transparency Directive* case); Cases C-271, 281, and 289/90, *Spain, Belgium & Italy v. Commission* [1992] ECR I-5833 (the *Telecommunications Services* case); Case C-202/88, *France v. Commission* [1991] ECR I-1223 (the *Telecommunications Equipment* case).

[33] Chaps. 3 and 5; and see Case 82/71, *Pubblico Ministero della Repubblica Italiana v. Società Agricola Industria Latte (SAIL)* [1972] ECR 119; Case 155/73, *Sacchi* [1974] ECR 409; Case 52/76, *Benedetti v. Munari* [1977] ECR 163; Case 123/83, *BNIC v. Clair* [1985] ECR 391; *European Broadcasting Union* [1993] OJ L179/23; Case C-364/92, *SAT Fluggesellschaft v. Eurocontrol* [1994] ECR I-43; Case C-159/91, etc. *Poucet* [1993] ECR I-637; Case C-343/95, *Diego Cali v. Servizi Ecologici Porto di Genova* [1997] ECR I-1547.

[34] See the Opinion of Reischl AG in Cases 188–190/88, *France, Italy and the UK v. Commission* [1982] ECR 2545, para. 9 (the *Transparency Directive* case).

[35] Commission Directive on the transparency of financial relations between Member States and public undertakings as well as on financial transparency within certain undertakings [2006] OJ L 318/17; (formerly Commission Dir. 80/723 [1980] OJ L195/35, amended by Commission Dir. 85/413) [1985] OJ L229/20; see Cases 188–190/88, *France, Italy and the UK v. Commission* [1982] ECR 2545).

Lignite, for example, the Commission held that the former legal electricity monopoly company in Greece was a public undertaking as 51 per cent of the voting stock was held by the State.[36]

(ii) Undertakings Granted Special or Exclusive Rights

Special or exclusive rights may be granted in the whole of a national territory or in only part of it.[37] Difficulties have arisen over the definition of 'special and exclusive rights'. Two categories are involved here: 'special' and 'exclusive' are not synonymous. Entities with such rights may or may not be public undertakings.

Exclusive rights are the most easily identified. They exist where a monopoly has been granted by the State to one entity to engage in a particular economic activity on an exclusive basis. They have been held to have been conferred, for example, upon broadcasting monopolies,[38] and upon undertakings granted the sole right to operate employment recruitment services,[39] the sole right to operate on a particular air route,[40] the sole right to supply unloading services at a port,[41] the sole right to provide bovine insemination services,[42] and the exclusive right to receive and manage the contributions made under a compulsory social insurance scheme.[43] The rights granted to the television duopoly in the Greek television case, *ERT*,[44] were designated as 'special or exclusive'. Rather strangely, however, the CJ described the three firms who were entitled to collect waste for recycling in Copenhagen, as holding 'exclusive' rights.[45] It is important to note that the grant of intellectual property rights does not entail the granting of exclusive rights for the purposes of Article 106(1) because it involves laws which lay down criteria which any undertaking is free to satisfy: there is no question of a closed class.

What amounts to 'special rights' has been determined by the CJ as a result of a series of challenges brought by Member States to directives issued by the Commission under Article 106(3) in pursuance of its objective to liberalise the telecommunications market. This liberalisation inevitably meant ensuring the removal of the protection hitherto given by Member States to national telecommunications operators.

France v. *Commission*, the *Telecommunications Equipment* case[46] concerned the challenge by France to Directive 88/301 on competition in the markets in telecommunications terminal equipment.[47] According to Article 2, Member States which had granted special or exclusive rights to undertakings

---

[36] COMP/38.700 *Greek Lignite and Electricity Markets*[2009] 4 CMLR 495, 5 March 2008, para. 5, decision annulled on other grounds; Case T-169/08, *Dimosia Epicheirisi Ilektrismou AE (DEI)* v. *Commission*, 12 September 2012, on appeal Case C-554/12 P, *Commission* v. *DEI*, judgment pending. The State's holding could never fall below 51 per cent.

[37] e.g., Case 30/87, *Bodson* v. *Pompes Funèbres des Régions Libérées* [1988] ECR 2479 (funeral services in particular French communes); Case C-179/90, *Merci Convenzionali* v. *Porto di Genova* [1991] ECR I-5889 (unloading services in the port of Genoa); Case C-323/93, *Société Civile Agricole du Centre d'Insémination de la Crespelle* v. *Coopérative d'Elevage et d'Insémination Artificielle du Département de la Mayenne* [1994] ECR I-5077 (exclusive rights to provide bovine insemination services in defined areas of France).

[38] Case 155/73, *Sacchi* [1974] ECR 409.

[39] Case C-41/90, *Höfner* v. *Macrotron* [1991] ECR I-1979.

[40] Case 66/86, *Ahmed Saeed Flugreisen and Silver Line Reiseburo GmbH* v. *Zentrale zur Bëkampfung Unlauteren Wettwerbs eV* [1989] ECR 803; *Sterling Airways/SAS Denmark*, Commission's Xth Report on Competition Policy (Commission, 1980), paras. 136–138.

[41] Case C-179/90, *Merci Convenzionali* v. *Porto di Genova* [1991] ECR I-5889.

[42] Case C-323/93, *Société Civile Agricole du Centre d'Insémination de la Crespelle* [1994] ECR I-5077.

[43] Case C-437/09, *AG2R Prévoyance* v. *Beaudout* [2011] ECR I-973.

[44] Case C-260/89, *Elliniki Radiophonia Tileorasi (ERT)* v. *DEP* [1991] ECR I-2925.

[45] Case C-209/98, *Entreprenørforeningens Affalds (FFAD)* v. *Københavns Kommune* [2000] ECR I-3743.

[46] Case C-202/88, *France* v. *Commission* [1991] ECR I-1223.

[47] [1988] OJ L131/73.

for the importation, marketing, connection, bringing into service of telecommunications terminal equipment, and/or maintenance of such equipment were to ensure that those rights were withdrawn. The CJ held that Article 2 was void insofar as it concerned the withdrawal of *special* rights because:

45 ....neither the provisions of the directive nor the preamble thereto specify the type of rights which are actually involved and in what respect the existence of such rights is contrary to the various provisions of the Treaty.

46. It follows that the Commission has failed to justify the obligation to withdraw special rights regarding the importation, marketing, connection, bringing into service and/or maintenance of telecommunications terminal equipment.

The *Telecommunications Services*[48] case concerned a similar challenge by Spain, Belgium, and Italy to Directive 90/388 on competition in the markets for telecommunications services.[49] Again the CJ annulled the provisions concerning the requirement to withdraw all special rights. In this directive the Commission had defined 'special or exclusive rights' in Article 1 as being 'rights granted by a Member State or a public authority to one or more private or public bodies through any legal, regulatory or administrative instrument reserving them the right to provide a service or undertake an activity'. The CJ held that this was inadequate as it did not make it possible 'to determine the type of special rights with which the directive is concerned or in what respect the existence of those rights is contrary to the various provisions of the Treaty'.[50]

As a result of these cases, the Commission set out an extended definition of the meaning of 'special rights' in the field of telecommunications in the Preamble to Directive 94/46[51] stating that a special right (in the field of telecommunication services) was one that was:

granted by a Member State to a limited number of undertakings through any legislative, regulatory or administrative instruments which, within a given geographical area, limits to two or more, otherwise than according to objective, proportional and non-discriminatory criteria, the number of undertakings which are authorised to provide any such service, or designates, otherwise than according to such criteria, several competing undertakings, as those which are authorised to provide any such service, or confers on any undertaking or undertakings otherwise than according to such criteria, legal or regulatory advantages which substantially affect the ability of any other undertaking to provide that same telecommunications service in the same geographical area under substantially equivalent conditions.

Although this definition was set out in a directive relating to telecommunications there is no reason to suppose that it is not also applicable in other fields. What it does is to identify as 'special rights' those which are given by the State to a limited number of undertakings chosen in a subjective and discretionary manner.[52] In *Ambulanz Glöckner* the CJ referred to a special or exclusive right existing where 'protection is conferred by a legislative measure on a limited number of undertakings which may substantially affect the ability of other undertakings to exercise the economic activity in question in the same geographical area under substantially equivalent conditions'.[53]

In *NV-GB-Inno-BM SA* v. *ATAB* the CJ doubted whether special or exclusive rights could result from allowing manufacturers and importers of a particular product to impose resale price maintenance.[54] In

---

[48] Cases C-271, 281, and 289/90, *Spain, Belgium & Italy* v. *Commission* [1992] ECR I-5833.

[49] [1990] OJ L192/10.

[50] [1992] ECR I-5833, para. 31.

[51] Directive amending Dir. 88/301 and 90/388 in particular with regard to satellite communications [1994] OJ L268/15.

[52] See also the Commission's statement at the hearing in the *Telecommunications Services* case, Cases C-271, 281, and 289/90, *Spain, Belgium & Italy* v. *Commission* [1992] ECR I-5833, quoted by Jacobs AG at para. 50 of his Opinion.

[53] Case C-475/99, *Ambulanz Glöckner* v. *Landkreis Südwestpfalz* [2001] ECR I-8089, para. 24.

[54] Case 13/77, [1977] ECR 2115: the point did not actually have to be answered because of the reply given to an earlier question.

Banchero[55] it held that Italian laws on the distribution of tobacco did not entail special or exclusive rights as, although they governed access to the market, all undertakings were treated in the same way. Further, in *GEMA*[56] the Commission held that an authors' rights society did not enjoy special or exclusive rights even though legislation required authors to exercise their rights through such a society, because there was no limit on the number of rights societies which could exist. As with exclusive rights, special rights involve the creation of some sort of limited, closed class.

(iii) 'Measures'

The word 'measures' also appears in Article 4 TEU which obliges Member States to fulfil their Treaty obligations and not to jeopardise the objectives of the Treaties, and in Article 34 TFEU which prohibits, inter alia, measures having an equivalent effect to quantitative restrictions on imports between Member States. In Directive 70/50[57] the Commission defined measures as 'laws, regulations, administrative provisions, administrative practices, and all instruments issued from a public authority, including recommendations' and both Articles 4 TEU and 34 TFEU are widely interpreted. Recommendations do not have to be binding. The best illustration of this point is provided by the *Buy Irish* case[58] in which a number of steps taken by the Irish Government to encourage the public to buy home-produced goods were condemned as contrary to Article 34. The CJ held that 'measures' do not have to have a binding effect.[59] 'Measures' does not, however, cover the actions of private undertakings rather than the State actions which allow or authorise them, so that anti-competitive conduct engaged in by undertakings on their own initiative must be dealt with by Articles 101 and 102.[60]

B. MEASURES WHICH ARE FORBIDDEN BY ARTICLE 106(1)

There is some uncertainty about what measures violate Article 106(1). In some cases there is clearly a violation in that some aspect of the State's arrangements inherently infringes a Treaty rule in itself. A good example, which does not involve the competition rules, is *Merci Convenzionali*,[61] where Italian laws reserved the loading and unloading of ships at an Italian port to certain dock-work companies whose worker-members had to be of Italian nationality. This infringed what was then Article 48 EC[62] on the free movement of workers, which specifically applied the prohibition of nationality discrimination in situations governed by Union law.[63] In other cases the measures taken by the Member State *result in* violations of the Treaties. The problem is that where the measures result in violations of the competition rules there are suggestions in some cases that the very fact of granting monopoly rights may itself be a violation. If this is so, the neutrality as to the organisation of economic activities within the Member States discussed at the beginning of the chapter is seriously eroded and the right of Member States to make certain economic choices is limited.

---

[55] Case C-387/93, *Banchero* [1995] ECR I-4663.

[56] [1971] OJ L134/15, [1971] CMLR D35.

[57] On the abolition of measures which have an effect equivalent to quantitative restrictions on imports and are not covered by other provisions [1970] OJ Spec. Ed. 17.

[58] Case 249/81, *Commission v. Ireland* [1982] ECR 4005.

[59] Case 249/81, *Commission v. Ireland* [1982] ECR 4005, para. 28.

[60] Case C-202/88, *France v. Commission* [1991] ECR I-1223, para. 55.

[61] Case C-179/90, *Merci Convenzionali Porto di Genova v. Siderurgica Gabrielli SpA* [1991] ECR I-5889.

[62] Now Article 45 TFEU.

[63] Then Art 7 EC, now Art. 18 TFEU; *Merci Convenzionali Porto di Genova v. Siderurgica Gabrielli SpA* [1991] ECR I-5889, paras. 10–13.

It has been clear since the *France v. Commission, Telecommunications Equipment* case in 1991 that Member States do not have unassailable rights to create legal monopolies under any conditions they choose.

Case C-202/88, *France* v. *Commission* [1991] ECR I-1223

France challenged the Telecommunications Terminal Equipment Directive, 88/301, *inter alia*, on the grounds that the Commission had no competence to adopt it on the basis of Article 106(3). France claimed that Article 106 did not allow the Commission to interfere with the granting of special or exclusive rights by Member States because Article 106(1) presupposed the existence of special or exclusive rights so the granting of such rights could not itself constitute a 'measure' within the Article.

Court of Justice

21 .... it must be held in the first place that the supervisory power conferred on the Commission includes the possibility of specifying, pursuant to Article [106(3)], obligations arising under the Treaty. The extent of that power therefore depends on the scope of the rules with which compliance is to be ensured.

22. Next, it should be noted that even though that article presupposes the existence of undertakings which have certain special or exclusive rights, it does not follow that all the special or exclusive rights are necessarily compatible with the Treaty. That depends on different rules, to which Article [106(1)] refers.

...

51 It should be observed that a system of undistorted competition, as laid down in the Treaty, can be guaranteed only if equality of opportunity is secured as between the various economic operators. To entrust an undertaking which markets terminal equipment with the task of drawing up the specifications for such equipment, monitoring their application and granting type-approval in respect thereof is tantamount to conferring upon it the power to determine at will which terminal equipment may be connected to the public network, and thereby placing that undertaking at an obvious advantage over its competitors.

52 Consequently, the Commission was justified in seeking to entrust responsibility for drawing up technical specifications, monitoring their application and granting type-approval to a body independent of public or private undertakings offering competing goods and/or services in the telecommunications sector.

In this judgment the CJ mentioned the concept of 'equality of opportunity', which has featured in subsequent cases, as we see at p. 618. This could not be guaranteed if the undertaking given the task of controlling specifications and issuing type approval certificates in respect of telecommunications equipment also marketed that equipment itself, in competition with the other suppliers it was overseeing.

As Edward and Hoskins[64] say:

It follows from *France v. Commission* that Member States have not retained complete sovereignty in relation to the creation of legal monopolies. Rather, the creation of such monopolies must be balanced with the principle of free competition.

It is therefore a question of examining the cases to determine how that balance is struck.

---

[64] D. Edward and M. Hoskins, 'Art. 90: Deregulation and EC Law. Reflections Arising from the XVI FIDE Conference' (1995) 32 *CMLRev* 157, 160.

Case C-41/90, *Höfner* v. *Macrotron* [1991] ECR I-1979

A dispute arose in a German court, the Oberlandesgericht München, between a company and the recruitment consultants it had employed to find it a sales director. In a dispute about fees the company claimed that the contract between the parties was void as it infringed the German law on the promotion of employment, the Arbeitsförderungsgesetz (the AFG). The AFG conferred on the Bundesanstalt, the Federal Office for Employment, the exclusive right to put prospective employees and employers in contact with one another. Nevertheless, to some extent the Bundesanstalt tolerated the existence and activities of independent recruitment consultants and it appeared that the Bundesanstalt was unable, on its own, to meet the demand for executive recruitment. The questions referred by the Oberlandesgericht raised the issue of whether there was an abuse of a dominant position involved and whether Article 106(1) was infringed by the exclusive rights. The Court first held that the Bundesanstalt was an undertaking for the purposes of Articles 102 and 106.[65] It then considered the possible infringements.

Court of Justice

24. It must be pointed out that a public employment agency which is entrusted, under the legislation of a Member State, with the operation of services of general economic interest, such as those envisaged in Article 3 of the AFG, remains subject to the competition rules pursuant to Article [106(2)] unless and to the extent to which it is shown that their application is incompatible with the discharge of its duties (see judgment in Case 155/73 *Sacchi*...).

25. As regards the manner in which a public employment agency enjoying an exclusive right of employment procurement conducts itself in relation to executive recruitment undertaken by private recruitment consultancy companies, it must be stated that the application of Article [102] cannot obstruct the performance of the particular task assigned to that agency in so far as the latter is manifestly not in a position to satisfy demand in that area of the market and in fact allows its exclusive rights to be encroached on by those companies.

26. Whilst it is true that Article [102] concerns undertakings and may be applied within the limits laid down by Article [106(2)] to public undertakings or undertakings vested with exclusive rights, or specific rights, the fact nevertheless remains that the Treaty requires the Member States not to take or maintain in force measures which could destroy the effectiveness of that provision (see judgment in Case 13/77 *GB-Inno-BM*...paragraphs 31 and 32). Article [106(1)] in fact provides that the Member States are not to enact or maintain in force, in the case of public undertakings and the undertakings to which they grant special or exclusive rights, any measure contrary to the rules contained in the Treaty, in particular those provided for in Articles [101] to [109].

27. Consequently, any measure adopted by a Member State which maintains in force a statutory provision that creates a situation in which a public employment agency cannot avoid infringing Article [102] is incompatible with the rules of the Treaty.

28. It must be remembered, first, that an undertaking vested with a legal monopoly may be regarded as occupying a dominant position within the meaning of Article [102] of the Treaty (see judgment in Case 311/84 *CBEM*, [1985] ECR 3261) and that the territory of a Member State, to which that monopoly extends, may constitute a substantial part of the common market (judgment in Case C 322/81 *Michelin*....paragraph 28).

29. Secondly, the simple fact of creating a dominant position of that kind by granting an exclusive right within the meaning of Article [106(1)] is not as such incompatible with Article [102] (see Case 311/84 *CBEM*, above, paragraph 17). A Member State is in breach of the prohibition contained in those two provisions only if the undertaking in question, merely by exercising the exclusive right granted to it, cannot avoid abusing its dominant position.

---

[65] See Chap. 3.

30. Pursuant to Article [102(b)], such an abuse may in particular consist in limiting the provision of a service, to the prejudice of those seeking to avail themselves of it.

31. A Member State creates a situation in which the provision of a service is limited when the undertaking to which it grants an exclusive right extending to executive recruitment activities is manifestly not in a position to satisfy the demand prevailing on the market for activities of that kind and when the effective pursuit of such activities by private companies is rendered impossible by the maintenance in force of a statutory provision under which such activities are prohibited and non-observance of that prohibition renders the contracts concerned void.

32. It must be observed, thirdly, that the responsibility imposed on a Member State by virtue of Articles [102 and [106(1)] is engaged only if the abusive conduct on the part of the agency concerned is liable to affect trade between Member States. That does not mean that the abusive conduct in question must actually have affected such trade. It is sufficient to establish that the conduct is capable of having such an effect (see Case 322/81 *Michelin*, above, paragraph 104).

33. A potential effect of that kind on trade between Member States arises in particular where executive recruitment by private companies may extend to the nationals or to the territory of other Member States.

34. In view of the foregoing considerations, it must be stated in reply to the fourth question that a public employment agency engaged in employment procurement activities is subject to the prohibition contained in Article [102], so long as the application of that provision does not obstruct the performance of the particular task assigned to it. A Member State which has conferred an exclusive right to carry on that activity upon the public employment agency is in breach of Article [106(1)] where it creates a situation in which that agency cannot avoid infringing Article [102]. That is the case, in particular, where the following conditions are satisfied.

— the exclusive right extends to executive recruitment activities;

— the public employment agency is manifestly incapable of satisfying demand prevailing on the market for such activities;

— the actual pursuit of those activities by private recruitment consultants is rendered impossible by the maintenance in force of a statutory provision under which such activities are prohibited and non-observance of that prohibition renders the contracts concerned void;

— the activities in question may extend to the nationals or to the territory of other Member States.

In *Höfner v. Macrotron* the CJ said (at paragraph 29) that the fact of creating a dominant position by granting exclusive rights is not as such incompatible with the Treaties. However, a Member State will infringe if the undertaking in question, merely by exercising the exclusive right granted to it, cannot avoid abusing its dominant position. In this case the criterion was fulfilled as German law had given the undertaking a monopoly over executive recruitment services, the demand for which it was incapable of satisfying. Such limitation of the service offered to customers constituted an abuse under Article 102(b), and so the Member State had created a situation in which the agency could not avoid infringing the Article.[66] This was reiterated in *Job Centre* where Italian law gave public placement offices a monopoly to act as employment intermediaries. Again, the statutory monopolist was unlikely to be able to satisfy the demand on the employment market for recruitment services. The Member State had therefore created a situation in which the provision of a service was limited, contrary to Article 102(b).[67]

The principle in *Höfner v. Macroton* was applied by the Commission in the *Slovakian Hybrid Mail Services* decision, where it cited paragraphs 30–31 of the judgment.[68] In Slovakia the delivery of hybrid

[66] See para. 27 of the judgment.

[67] Case C-55/96, *Job Centre Coop. arl* [1997] ECR I-7119. The Commission came to a similar conclusion in *Spanish Courier Services* [1990] OJ L233/19 (courier services reserved to Post Office which could not offer complete services). For inefficiency and the limitation of production and services as an abuse, see Chap. 7.

[68] COMP/39.562, [2009] 4 CMLR 663, on appeal Case T-556/08, *Slovenská Poštă v. Commission*, judgment pending.

mail[69] had been open to competition but by legislation in 2008 it was in effect 're-monopolised' and reserved to Slovenská Pošta, an undertaking wholly owned by the Slovak State. The service offered by Slovenská Pošta did not include many of the added features which the private operators had been offering and which customers valued.[70] The Commission held that granting an exclusive right to an undertaking manifestly unable to satisfy the demand infringed Article 106 in conjunction with Article 102 on the basis of *Höfner*.[71]

In *ERT*, the Court took a slightly different approach to that in *Höfner*.

Case C-260/89, *Elliniki Radiophonia Tileorassi Anonimi Etaira (ERT)* v. *Dimotiki Etairia Pliroforissis (DEP)* [1991] ECR I-2925

The Thessaloniki Regional Court referred to the CJ under Article 267 various questions concerning the position of the Greek radio and television undertaking (ERT) to which the Greek government had granted exclusive rights in regard to the original broadcasting and retransmitting of programmes in Greece. Greek law prohibited any person from engaging in activities for which ERT had an exclusive right without ERT's authorisation. The Mayor of Thessaloniki and a municipal company, DEP, set up a television station and began to broadcast television programmes. ERT sought an injunction and the seizure of the new station's technical equipment.

Court of Justice

10. In Case C-155/73 *Sacchi*...paragraph 14, the Court held that nothing in the Treaty prevents Member States, for considerations of a non-economic nature relating to the public interest, from removing radio and television broadcasts from the field of competition by conferring on one or more establishments an exclusive right to carry them out.

11. Nevertheless, it follows from Article [106(1) and (2)] that the manner in which the monopoly is organized or exercised may infringe the rules of the Treaty, in particular those relating to the free movement of goods, the freedom to provide services and the rules on competition.

12. The reply to the national court must therefore be that Community law does not prevent the granting of a television monopoly for considerations of a non-economic nature relating to the public interest. However, the manner in which such a monopoly is organized and exercised must not infringe the provisions of the Treaty on the free movement of goods and services or the rules on competition.

...

27. As a preliminary point, it should be observed that Article [3(1)(g)] of the Treaty states only one objective for the Community which is given specific expression in several provisions of the Treaty relating to the rules on competition, including in particular Articles [101], [102] and [106].

28. The independent conduct of an undertaking must be considered with regard to the provisions of the Treaty applicable to undertakings, such as, in particular, Articles [101], [102] and [106(2)].

29. As regards Article [101], it is sufficient to observe that it applies, according to its own terms, to agreements 'between undertakings'. There is nothing in the judgment making the reference to suggest the existence of any agreement between undertakings. There is therefore no need to interpret that provision.

---

[69] Hybrid mail is that where the content is transferred electronically from the sender to the postal service operator who prints it out, puts it in envelopes, sorts and delivers it.

[70] Such as tracking services and seven days a week delivery.

[71] See also Case C-437/09, *AG2R Prévoyance v. Beaudout* [2011] ECR I-973.

30. Article [102] declares that any abuse of a dominant position within the common market or in any substantial part of it is prohibited as incompatible with the common market in so far as it may affect trade between Member States.

31. In that respect it should be borne in mind that an undertaking which has a statutory monopoly may be regarded as having a dominant position within the meaning of Article [102] (see the judgment in Case C-311/84 *CBEM* v. *CLT and IBP*... paragraph 16) and that the territory of a Member State over which the monopoly extends may constitute a substantial part of the common market (see the judgment in Case C-322/81 *Michelin* v. *Commission*... paragraph 28).

32. Although Article [102] does not prohibit monopolies as such, it nevertheless prohibits their abuse. For that purpose Article [102] lists a number of abusive practices by way of example.

33. In that regard it should be observed that, according to Article [106(2)], undertakings entrusted with the operation of services of general economic interest are subject to the rules on competition so long as it is not shown that the application of those rules is incompatible with the performance of their particular task (see in particular, the judgment in *Sacchi*, cited above, paragraph 15).

34. Accordingly it is for the national court to determine whether the practices of such an undertaking are compatible with Article [102] and to verify whether those practices, if they are contrary to that provision, may be justified by the needs of the particular task with which the undertaking may have been entrusted.

35. As regards State measures, and more specifically the grant of exclusive rights, it should be pointed out that while Articles [101] and [102] are directed exclusively to undertakings, the Treaty none the less requires the Member States not to adopt or maintain in force any measure which could deprive those provisions of their effectiveness (see the judgment in Case C-13/77 *Inno* v. *ATAB*... paragraphs 31 and 32).

36. Article [106(1)] thus provides that, in the case of undertakings to which Member States grant special or exclusive rights, Member States are neither to enact nor to maintain in force any measure contrary to the rules contained in the Treaty.

37. In that respect it should be observed that Article [106(1)] prohibits the granting of an exclusive right to retransmit television broadcasts to an undertaking which has an exclusive right to transmit broadcasts, where those rights are liable to create a situation in which that undertaking is led to infringe Article [102] by virtue of a discriminatory broadcasting policy which favours its own programmes.

38. The reply to the national court must therefore be that Article [106(1)] prohibits the granting of an exclusive right to transmit and an exclusive right to retransmit television broadcasts to a single undertaking, where those rights are liable to create a situation in which that undertaking is led to infringe Article [102] by virtue of a discriminatory broadcasting policy which favours its own programmes, unless the application of Article [102] obstructs the performance of the particular tasks entrusted to it.

In this case the CJ said that the Treaty did not prevent the granting of a monopoly (*in casu* a television monopoly) but stressed, as it had in *Inno* v. *ATAB*, that Member States are prohibited from adopting measures which deprive the competition rules of their effectiveness. This means that the manner in which the monopoly is organised may infringe the competition rules (paragraph 11). The Court therefore concluded that the rules did prohibit the granting of an exclusive right to retransmit TV broadcasts to an undertaking which has exclusive rights to transmit broadcasts where those rights are liable to create a situation in which that undertaking is led to infringe Article 102 by virtue of a discriminatory broadcasting policy which favours its own programmes (paragraphs 37 and 38). This is different from the situation in *Höfner*, where the infringement was unavoidable because the State had given monopoly rights to a body manifestly unable to deal with the demand for its services. In *ERT* the cumulation of rights in the hands of the monopolist did not result in an unavoidable infringement of Article 102 but did result in a situation where the monopolist was *led to* infringe the Article because it would inevitably discriminate in favour of retransmitting its own programmes rather than those of anyone else.

The theme of the monopolist being led to an infringement was taken up in the next case, *Merci Convenzionali*.

Case C-179/90, *Merci Convenzionali Porto di Genova* v. *Siderurgica Gabrielli SpA* [1991] ECR I-5889

By Italian law Merci had the exclusive right to organise the loading, unloading, and other handling of goods within the Port of Genoa through a dock-work company.[72] There was a delay in unloading Siderurgica's ship, caused in particular by the dock-work company's workers being on strike. The exclusive rights meant that the vessel's crew were not able to do the work themselves. Siderurgica demanded compensation for the damage it suffered due to the delay and the reimbursement of the charges it had paid to Merci, which it claimed were unfair given the service it had received, or rather, not received. The Tribunale di Genoa made an Article 267 reference, asking, *inter alia*,[73] whether Article 106(1) in conjunction with Article 102 precluded the Italian rules. The CJ confirmed in paragraph 14 that an undertaking with a statutory monopoly over a substantial part of the common market[74] could be regarded as having a dominant position within Article 102.

Court of Justice

16. It should next be stated that the simple fact of creating a dominant position by granting exclusive rights within the meaning of Article [106(1)] is not as such incompatible with Article [102].

17. However, the Court has had occasion to state, in this respect, that a Member State is in breach of the prohibitions contained in those two provisions if the undertaking in question, merely by exercising the exclusive rights granted to it, cannot avoid abusing its dominant position (see the judgment in Case C-41/90 *Höfner*, cited above, paragraph 29) or when such rights are liable to create a situation in which that undertaking is induced to commit such abuses (see the judgment in Case C-260/89 *ERT*, cited above, paragraph 37).

18. According to subparagraphs (a), (b) and (c) of the second paragraph of Article [102], such abuse may in particular consist in imposing on the persons requiring the services in question unfair purchase prices or other unfair trading conditions, in limiting technical development, to the prejudice of consumers, or in the application of dissimilar conditions to equivalent transactions with other trading parties.

19. In that respect it appears from the circumstances described by the national court and discussed before the Court of Justice that the undertakings enjoying exclusive rights in accordance with the procedures laid down by the national rules in question are, as a result, induced either to demand payment for services which have not been requested, to charge disproportionate prices, to refuse to have recourse to modern technology, which involves an increase in the cost of the operations and a prolongation of the time required for their performance, or to grant price reductions to certain consumers and at the same time to offset such reductions by an increase in the charges to other consumers.

20. In these circumstances it must be held that a Member State creates a situation contrary to Article [102] where it adopts rules of such a kind as those at issue before the national court, which are capable of affecting trade between Member States as in the case of the main proceedings, regard being had to the factors mentioned in paragraph 15 of this judgment relating to the importance of traffic in the Port of Genoa.

---

[72] For another case involving Italian law on dock-work companies, see Case C-163/96, *Silvano Raso* [1998] ECR I-533.

[73] For the nationality discrimination issue, see Section 5.B, p. 607.

[74] The CJ held (para. 15) that the Port of Genoa was a substantial part: for this aspect of Art. 102 see Chap. 5.

In this judgment the CJ quoted *Höfner* and *ERT* and cited the latter for the proposition that a Member State infringes Article 102 where it grants rights which are liable to *induce* the undertaking to commit abuses (paragraphs 17 and 19). The abuses were unfair payment demands and prices (Article 102(a)), inefficiency (Article 102(b)), and discrimination between customers (Article 102(c)). So we reach the position that although, as the Court said in *Merci* (paragraph 16), the simple fact of creating a dominant position by granting exclusive rights is not incompatible with Article 106(1), the granting of rights which induce or lead to the undertakings committing abuses is incompatible.[75]

ERT was less to do with the fact of abusive conduct than with the possibility of it. This is also shown in *GB-Inno-BM SA*. Both *ERT* and *GB-Inno-BM SA* involved the cumulation of rights, a matter of particular concern.[76]

Case C-18/88, *RTT* v. *GB-Inno-BM SA* [1991] ECR I-5973

Under Belgian law RRT held a monopoly over the establishment and operation of the public telephone system. The law also provided that only equipment supplied by RTT or approved by it could be connected to its network. GB-Inno sold in its shops telephones which had not been approved by RTT. RTT brought proceedings in the Commercial Court for an order that GB-Inno should not sell telephones without informing the purchasers that they were not approved. The Commercial Court asked the Court, *inter alia*, whether a Member State was precluded from granting to the company operating the public telephone network the power to lay down the standards for telephone equipment and to check that economic operators meet those standards when it is competing with those operators on the market for terminals.

Court of Justice

15. Under Belgian law, the RTT holds a monopoly for the establishment and operation of the public telecommunications network. Moreover, only equipment supplied by the RTT or approved by it can be connected to the network. The RTT thus has the power to grant or withhold authorization to connect telephone equipment to the network, the power to lay down the technical standards to be met by that equipment, and the power to check whether the equipment not produced by it is in conformity with the specifications that it has laid down.

16. At the present stage of development of the Community, that monopoly, which is intended to make a public telephone network available to users, constitutes a service of general economic interest within the meaning of Article [106(2)].

17. The Court has consistently held that an undertaking vested with a legal monopoly may be regarded as occupying a dominant position within the meaning of Article [102] and that the territory of a Member State to which that monopoly extends may constitute a substantial part of the common market (judgments in Case C-41/90 *Höfner*...paragraph 28, and in Case C-260/89 *ERT*...paragraph 31).

18. The Court has also held that an abuse within the meaning of Article [102] is committed where, without any objective necessity, an undertaking holding a dominant position on a particular market reserves to itself an ancillary activity which might be carried out by another undertaking as part of its activities on a neighbouring but separate market, with the possibility of eliminating all competition from such undertaking (judgment in Case 311/84 *CBEM*...).

19. Therefore the fact that an undertaking holding a monopoly in the market for the establishment and operation of the network, without any objective necessity, reserves to itself a neighbouring but separate market, in this case the market for the importation, marketing, connection, commissioning and

---

[75] See also Case C-18/93, *Corsica Ferries Italia Srl* v. *Corpo dei Piloti del Porto di Genovo* [1994] ECR I-1783.

[76] Although note that in Cases C-67/96, 115–117/97, and 219/97, *Albany International BV* v. *Stichting Bedrijfspensioenfonds Textielindustrie* [1999] ECR I-5751, paras. 112–121, the CJ, unlike Jacobs AG in his Opinion (paras. 441–468), was not concerned that the pension funds with the exclusive rights were also the authority able to grant exemptions from compulsory participation in the pension schemes.

maintenance of equipment for connection to the said network, thereby eliminating all competition from other undertakings, constitutes an infringement of Article [102].

20. However, Article [102] applies only to anti-competitive conduct engaged in by undertakings on their own initiative (see judgment in Case C-202/88 *France v. Commission* 'Telecommunications terminals'…), not to measures adopted by States. As regards measures adopted by States, it is Article [106(1)] that applies. Under that provision, Member States must not, by laws, regulations or administrative measures, put public undertakings and undertakings to which they grant special or exclusive rights in a position which the said undertakings could not themselves attain by their own conduct without infringing Article [102].

21. Accordingly, where the extension of the dominant position of a public undertaking or undertaking to which the State has granted special or exclusive rights results from a State measure, such a measure constitutes an infringement of Article [106] in conjunction with Article [102].

22. The exclusion or the restriction of competition on the market in telephone equipment cannot be regarded as justified by a task of a public service of general economic interest within the meaning of Article [106(2)]. The production and sale of terminals, and in particular of telephones, is an activity that should be open to any undertaking. In order to ensure that the equipment meets the essential requirements of, in particular, the safety of users, the safety of those operating the network and the protection of public telecommunications networks against damage of any kind, it is sufficient to lay down specifications which the said equipment must meet and to establish a procedure for type-approval to check whether those specifications are met.

23. According to the RTT, there could be a finding of an infringement of Article [106(1)] only if the Member State had favoured an abuse that the RTT itself had in fact committed, for example by applying the provisions on type-approval in a discriminatory manner. It emphasizes, however, that the order for reference does not state that any abuse has actually taken place, and that the mere possibility of discriminatory application of those provisions by reason of the fact that the RTT is designated as the authority for granting approval and is competing with the undertakings that apply for approval cannot in itself amount to an abuse within the meaning of Article [102].

24. That argument cannot be accepted. It is sufficient to point out in this regard that it is the extension of the monopoly in the establishment and operation of the telephone network to the market in telephone equipment, without any objective justification, which is prohibited as such by Article [102], or by Article [106(1)] in conjunction with Article [102], where that extension results from a measure adopted by a State. As competition may not be eliminated in that manner, it may not be distorted either.

25. A system of undistorted competition, as laid down in the Treaty, can be guaranteed only if equality of opportunity is secured as between the various economic operators. To entrust an undertaking which markets terminal equipment with the task of drawing up the specifications for such equipment, monitoring their application and granting type-approval in respect thereof is tantamount to conferring upon it the power to determine at will which terminal equipment may be connected to the public network, and thereby placing that undertaking at an obvious advantage over its competitors (judgment in Case C-202/88, paragraph 51).

26. In those circumstances, the maintenance of effective competition and the guaranteeing of transparency require that the drawing up of technical specifications, the monitoring of their application, and the granting of type-approval must be carried out by a body which is independent of public or private undertakings offering competing goods or services in the telecommunications sector (judgment in Case C-202/88, paragraph 52).

27. Moreover, the provisions of the national regulations at issue in the main action may influence the imports of telephone equipment from other Member States, and hence may affect trade between Member States within the meaning of Article [102].

28. Accordingly, it must first be stated, in reply to the national court's questions, that Articles [3(1)(g) EC], [106] and [102] preclude a Member State from granting to the undertaking which operates the public telecommunications network the power to lay down standards for telephone equipment and to check that economic operators meet those standards when it is itself competing with those operators on the market for that equipment.

It will be noticed here that there was no allegation that RTT had actually behaved improperly in its authorisation of equipment. The objection was that the State measures in effect extended the monopoly position from one market to another, by giving the undertaking the authorisation power over its competitors, a situation which if brought about by the conduct of an undertaking rather than by State measures would have constituted an abuse, as the Court pointed out at paragraphs 18–20.[77] In paragraph 25 the Court said that a system of undistorted competition needs 'equality of opportunity' between the economic operators. The *Slovakian Mail Services* decision also contained the element of extending the public undertaking's monopoly, there from ordinary mail to hybrid mail. It that case it led to an infringement of Article 102 by inability to meet demand.[78]

The rights conferred on the undertakings in both *ERT* and *GB-Inno-BM SA* were also contrary to Article 106 since they created a conflict of interest. This was also so in *Silvano Raso*[79] where an Italian law, which gave the exclusive right to supply temporary labour to other dock-work companies operating in a port to an undertaking which was also authorised to carry out dock-work itself. Again the CJ said that the company would have a conflict of interest:[80]

29. That is because merely exercising its monopoly will enable it to distort in its favour the equal conditions of competition between the various operators on the market in dock-work services (Case C-260/89, *ERT v. DRP*...and Case C-18/88, *GB-Inno-BM SA*).

30. The result is that the company in question is led to abuse its monopoly by imposing on its competitors in the dock-work market unduly high costs for the supply of labour or by supplying them with labour less suited to the work to be done.

The conflict of interest in *ERT* and *GB-Inno-BM SA* arose from the bundling together of regulatory functions and commercial activities. It was again shown in *MOTOE* that State measures must not do this.[81]

Case C-49/07, *Motosykletistiki Omospondia Ellados NPID (MOTOE)* v. *Ellinkio Dimosi* [2008] ECR I-4863

Greek legislation (Road Traffic Code, Article 49) requires authorisation from the Minister for Public Order for motorcycling competitions on public or private roads and spaces. The Code provides that authorisation can only be given following the consent of ELPA (Automobile and Touring Club of Greece), the official Greek representative of FIM (International Motorcycling Federation). ELPA, a non-profit making association, organised motorcycling events in Greece and entered into sponsorship, advertising and insurance contracts in that connection. MOTOE, another non-profit making association, also organised motor-cycling events in Greece. ELPA failed to give its consent to various events MOTOE wanted to hold. MOTOE sued for damages. On an Article 267 reference one of the questions asked by the Greek court concerned the authorisation power granted to ELPA in the situation where it also competed on the market with those it authorised.

---

[77] See Case 311/84, *Centre Belge d'Etudes du Marché-Télémarketing* v. *Compagnie Luxembourgeoise de Télédiffusion SA and Information Publicité Benelux SA* [1985] ECR 3261 (quoted in para. 18 of the *GB-Inno-BM* judgment) and the cases discussed in Chap. 7.

[78] COMP/39.562, [2009] 4 CMLR 663, see Section 5.B, p. 610.

[79] Case C-163/96, *Silvano Raso* [1998] ECR I-533.

[80] Case C-163/96, *Silvano Raso* [1998] ECR I-533, para. 28.

[81] See A. Veermersch, 'Casenote on Case C-49/07' (2009) 46 CMLRev 1327.

Court of Justice

48 As regards, third, the question whether Articles [102 and 106(1)] preclude a national rule, such as Article 49 of the Greek Road Traffic Code, which confers on a legal person like ELPA, which can itself take on the organisation of motorcycling events and their commercial exploitation, the power to give consent to applications for authorisation to organise those events, without that power being made subject to restrictions, obligations and review, it should be recalled that the mere creation or reinforcement of a dominant position through the grant of special or exclusive rights within the meaning of Article [106(1)] is not in itself incompatible with Article [102].

49 On the other hand, a Member State will be in breach of the prohibitions laid down by those two provisions if the undertaking in question, merely by exercising the special or exclusive rights conferred upon it, is led to abuse its dominant position or where such rights are liable to create a situation in which that undertaking is led to commit such abuses (*Höfner and Elser*, cited above, paragraph 29; *ERT*, cited above, paragraph 37; Case C-179/90 *Merci convenzionali porto di Genova*…paragraphs 16 and 17; and Case C-323/93 *Centre d'insémination de la Crespelle*…paragraph 18). In this respect, it is not necessary that any abuse should actually occur (see, to that effect, Case C-55/96 *Job Centre*…paragraph 36).

50 In any event, Articles [102 and 106(1)] are infringed where a measure imputable to a Member State, and in particular a measure by which a Member State confers special or exclusive rights within the meaning of Article [106(1)], gives rise to a risk of an abuse of a dominant position (see, to that effect, *ERT*, cited above, paragraph 37; *Merci convenzionali porto di Genova*, cited above, paragraph 17; and Case C-380/05 *Centro Europa 7*…paragraph 60).

51 A system of undistorted competition, such as that provided for by the Treaty, can be guaranteed only if equality of opportunity is secured as between the various economic operators. To entrust a legal person such as ELPA, which itself organises and commercially exploits motorcycling events, the task of giving the competent administration its consent to applications for authorisation to organise such events, is tantamount *de facto* to conferring upon it the power to designate the persons authorised to organise those events and to set the conditions in which those events are organised, thereby placing that entity at an obvious advantage over its competitors (see, by analogy, Case C-202/88 *France* v *Commission*…paragraph 51, and Case C-18/88 *GB Inno BM*… paragraph 25). Such a right may therefore lead the undertaking which possesses it to deny other operators access to the relevant market. That situation of unequal conditions of competition is also highlighted by the fact, confirmed at the hearing before the Court, that, when ELPA organises or participates in the organisation of motorcycling events, it is not required to obtain any consent in order that the competent administration grant it the required authorisation.

52 Furthermore, such a rule, which gives a legal person such as ELPA the power to give consent to applications for authorisation to organise motorcycling events without that power being made subject by that rule to restrictions, obligations and review, could lead the legal person entrusted with giving that consent to distort competition by favouring events which it organises or those in whose organisation it participates.

53 In the light of the foregoing, the answer to the questions referred must be that a legal person whose activities consist not only in taking part in administrative decisions authorising the organisation of motorcycling events, but also in organising such events itself and in entering, in that connection, into sponsorship, advertising and insurance contracts, falls within the scope of Articles [102 and 106]. Those articles preclude a national rule which confers on a legal person, which organises motorcycling events and enters, in that connection, into sponsorship, advertising and insurance contracts, the power to give consent to applications for authorisation to organise such competitions, without that power being made subject to restrictions, obligations and review.

One of the reasons the CJ gave in *MOTOE* for finding that the national rule infringed Article 106(1) was that it created inequality of opportunity (paragraph 51), a concept already seen in *GB-Inno-BM SA*. That was also so in the earlier case of *Connect Austria*[82] where the Austrian regulatory agency charged an applicant for new standard digital mobile telecommunications licence fees that were greatly in excess of those it charged the incumbent public undertaking. This was likely to lead to the public undertaking extending or strengthening its dominant position, and the distorted competition 'would therefore result from a State measure which creates a situation where equality of opportunity for the various economic operators concerned cannot be ensured'.[83]

The Commission condemned the arrangements in *Greek Lignite* as contrary to Article 106(2) in conjunction with Article 102 on the grounds that they created inequality of opportunity.[84] Lignite is coal ore from which electricity can be produced. It is the cheapest combustible for producing electricity in Greece, where the extensive lignite deposits are State-owned. The Greek government gave PCC, the former monopoly generator of electricity in Greece prior to liberalisation (and now a limited liability company in which the State had a controlling shareholding), rights to explore and exploit approximately half of the lignite deposits. No exploitation rights over the remaining deposits were granted to anyone. The Commission concluded that by granting and maintaining quasi-monopolistic lignite exploration rights in favour of PCC Greece had created inequality of opportunity between economic operators on the wholesale electricity market and thus distorted competition, thereby reinforcing the PCC's dominant position on that market.[85] On appeal the GC annulled the decision.[86] It held that it was not enough to establish that a State measure simply distorted competition by creating equality of opportunity. Rather, a breach of Article 106(1) in combination with Article 102 required an abuse to be identified. The GC distinguished the case from *France v. Commission, MOTOE, Raso, Job Centre, GB-Inno-BM SA, Connect Austria*, and the other cases discussed in previous paragraphs (referred to in paragraph 103 of the judgment set out in the next extract) because it considered that in all of those the way in which the undertaking was led, or would or could be led, to abuse its rights was identified. It this case the Commission had held it was an infringement just to maintain PCC in a dominant position. However, the mere exercise of its licence could not amount to the undertaking extending its dominant position.

Case T-169/08, *Dimosia Epicheirisi Ilektrismou AE(DEI)* v. *Commission*, 12 September 2012

General Court

103 It is apparent from those judgments, referred to in paragraphs 96 to 102 above, that the abuse of a dominant position by the undertaking enjoying an exclusive or special right may either result from the possibility of exercising that right in an abusive way or be a direct consequence of that right. However, it does not follow from that case-law that the mere fact that the undertaking in question finds itself in an

---

[82] Case C-462/99, *Connect Austria Gesellschaft für Telekommunikation GmbH* v. *Telekom-Control-Kommission* [2003] ECR I-5147.

[83] Case C-462/99, *Connect Austria Gesellschaft für Telekommunikation GmbH* v. *Telekom-Control-Kommission* [2003] ECR I-5147, para. 87.

[84] COMP/38.700 *Greek Lignite and Electricity Markets* [2009] 4 CMLR 495.

[85] COMP/38.700 *Greek Lignite and Electricity Markets* [2009] 4 CMLR 495, paras. 190 and 238.

[86] Case T-169/08, *Dimosia Epicheirisi Ilektrismou AE (DEI)* v. *Commission*, 12 September 2012.

advantageous situation in comparison with its competitors, by reason of a State measure, in itself constitutes an abuse of a dominant position.

104 Basing its argument in particular on the judgments in *France* v *Commission*, *GB-Inno-BM*, and *Connect Austria*, the Commission nevertheless argues that it based its conclusion finding infringement of the combined provisions of Article [106(1)] and Article [102] more precisely on the case-law according to which a system of undistorted competition such as that required by the Treaty cannot be guaranteed unless equality of opportunities between the various economic operators is assured. If the inequality of opportunities between economic operators and thus distorted competition, is the result of a State measure, such a measure constitutes an infringement of Article [106(1)] EC read in combination with Article [102].

105 However, it does not follow from those judgments that, for it to be concluded that an infringement of Article [106(1)] applied in combination with Article [102] has been committed, it is sufficient to establish that a State measure distorts competition by creating inequality of opportunities between economic operators, without it being necessary to identify an abuse of the dominant position of the undertaking.

The GC also rejected the Commission's argument that its decision was supported by the judgment in *Dusseldorp*,[87] in which the CJ found that the Dutch prohibition on an undertaking from exporting its waste oil filters for treatment in Germany amounted, in practice, to imposing an obligation on it to deliver the filters to the Dutch undertaking which held the exclusive right to incinerate dangerous waste. The GC said that in *Dusseldorp* the obligation to use the undertaking with the exclusive right resulted in a restriction of outlets, which was contrary to Article 102 and that the infringement did not arise simply from the creation of inequality of opportunity between economic operators.[88]

Greek Lignite was an unusual case in that it originated in a Commission infringement decision. The great majority of the cases on Article 106(1), as is apparent from this chapter, are preliminary references. The real problem that the Commission had in *Greek Lignite* was with what it considered the unsatisfactory situation in the Greek electricity market even after liberalisation. Unable to attack directly the Greek Government's failure to grant exploitation licences for the remaining deposits to PCC's competitors it turned to the 'equality of opportunity' concept but omitted to identify what even *potential* abuse PCC was being led to commit. The Commission has appealed to the CJ.[89] The CJ said that a system of undistorted competition can be guaranteed only if equality of opportunity is secured between the various economic operators in *OTOC*,[90] a preliminary ruling subsequent to the GC judgment in *Greek Lignite* which concerned the rules for a compulsory training system for chartered accountants in Portugal. The Court referred to equality of opportunity in the part of the judgment dealing with the application of Article 101 and before it proceeded to deal (briefly) with the Article 106 arguments. The Court related inequality of opportunity to the power which the undertaking (the Order of Chartered Accountants (OTOC)) had been given over its competitors (other training bodies), which could lead it to distort competition by favouring its own operation.[91]

---

[87] Case C-203/96, *Chemische Afvalstoffen Dusseldorp BV* v. *Minister van Volkshuisvesting, Ruimtelijke Ordening en Milieubeheer* [1998] ECR I-4075.

[88] *DEI*, paras. 117–118.

[89] Case C-554/12 P, *Commission* v. *DEI*, judgment pending.

[90] Case C-1/2012, *Ordem dos Técnicos Oficiais de Contas (OTOC)* v. *Autoridade da Concorrência*, 28 February 2013.

[91] Case C-1/2012, *Ordem dos Técnicos Oficiais de Contas (OTOC)* v. *Autoridade da Concorrência*, 28 February 2013, paras. 88–91.

The appeal to the CJ in *Greek Lignite* may be the opportunity for a review of the case law on Article 106(1), which in many respects is confused and inconsistent. In the case of *Corbeau*, for instance, the CJ appeared to suggest that the very granting of special or exclusive rights, even where the elements in the cases previously discussed are not present, might be contrary to Article 106(1). Subsequent cases in effect retreated from this position and, notably, *Corbeau* was not cited by the GC in *Greek Lignite* or relied upon by the Commission in the decision.

Case C-320/91, *Corbeau* [1993] ECR I-2533

Belgian law conferred a monopoly on the Belgian Post Office, the Regie des Postes, in respect of the collection, transporting, and delivery throughout the Kingdom of various forms of correspondence. Criminal sanctions were imposed for infringing the monopoly. Corbeau set up his own postal service in the Liège area, whereby personal collection would be made from the sender's premises and delivery made before noon next day in the same area, although deliveries outside the area were made by putting the items in the ordinary post. Corbeau was prosecuted for infringing the Post Office's monopoly. The Liège court referred questions to the Court concerning the compatibility of the post office monopoly with Articles 101, 102 and 106, whether the monopoly should be modified to comply with Article 106(1), the application of Article 106(2) and whether the post office was in a dominant position. (The part of the judgment concerning Article 106(2) is reproduced in Section 6.E.iii).

Court of Justice

7. With regard to the facts in the main proceedings, the questions referred to the Court must be understood as meaning that the national court is substantially concerned with the question whether Article [106] must be interpreted as meaning that it is contrary to that Article for the legislation of a Member State which confers on a body such as the Régie des Postes the exclusive right to collect, carry and distribute mail to prohibit an economic operator established in that State from offering, under threat of criminal penalties, certain specific services on that market.

8. To reply to that question, as thus reformulated, it should first be pointed out that a body such as the Régie des Postes, which has been granted exclusive rights as regards the collection, carriage and distribution of mail, must be regarded as an undertaking to which the Member State concerned has granted exclusive rights within the meaning of Article [106(1)].

9. Next it should be recalled that the Court has consistently held that an undertaking having a statutory monopoly over a substantial part of the Common Market may be regarded as having a dominant position within the meaning of Article [102] (see the judgments in Case C-179/90 *Merci Convenzionali Porto di Genova*.... paragraph 14 and in Case C-18/88 *RTT* v. *GB-Inno-BM*.... paragraph 17).

10. However, Article [102] applies only to anti-competitive conduct engaged in by undertakings on their own initiative, not to measures adopted by States (see the *RTT* v. *GB-Inno-BM* judgment, cited above, paragraph 20).

11. The Court has had occasion to state in this respect that although the mere fact that a Member State has created a dominant position by the grant of exclusive rights is not as such incompatible with Article [102], the Treaty none the less requires the Member States not to adopt or maintain in force any measure which might deprive those provisions of their effectiveness (see the judgment in Case C-260/89 *ERT*.... paragraph 35).

12. Thus Article [106(1)] provides that in the case of public undertakings to which Member States grant special or exclusive rights, they are neither to enact nor to maintain in force any measure contrary to the rules contained in the Treaty with regard to competition.

13. That provision must be read in conjunction with Article [106(2)] which provides that undertakings entrusted with the operation of services of general economic interest are to be subject to the rules on competition in so far as the application of such rules does not obstruct the performance, in law or in fact, of the particular tasks assigned to them.

14. That latter provision thus permits the Member States to confer on undertakings to which they entrust the operation of services of general economic interest, exclusive rights which may hinder the application of the rules of the Treaty on competition in so far as restrictions on competition, or even the exclusion of all competition, by other economic operators are necessary to ensure the performance of the particular tasks assigned to the undertakings possessed of the exclusive rights.

There was no suggestion in *Corbeau* that the Régie des Postes had acted abusively. The challenge raised by Corbeau's defence to the criminal charges was to the monopoly itself.[92] The CJ answered this in paragraphs 7–12 of the judgment. It repeated there (paragraph 11) its usual mantra about the mere grant of exclusive rights not in itself being incompatible with the Treaty but said that Member States are not to adopt or maintain provisions which may deprive the provisions of their effectiveness. It then quoted Article 106(1). It never clearly identified which, if any, features of the Belgian legislation were contrary to Article 106(1) and Article 102.[93] This case did not concern an undertaking accused of acting abusively, the extension of the monopoly into a neighbouring market, a conflict of interest, or the bundling of regulatory functions with entrepreneurial activities. It did however, as Hancher notes,[94] appear to suggest that, in order to ensure the *effet utile* or effectiveness of Articles 106(1) and 102 and, despite the Court's statement to the contrary at paragraph 11, the very existence of national rules conferring a dominant position on an undertaking is unacceptable unless the rights at issue can be justified under Article 106(2) (see paragraphs 13 and 14). In effect, it reversed the burden of proof: exclusive rights are not *prima facie* legal, but *prima facie* illegal unless they are objectively justified or fulfil the Article 106(2) criteria.[95]

As already noted, the CJ has not subsequently pursued the line it took in *Corbeau*. In *La Crespelle* it again held that a Member State contravenes the Treaty only if, in merely exercising the exclusive right granted to it, the undertaking cannot avoid abusing its dominant position:[96] it is not possible automatically to impute the abuse to the existence of the right. In this case, where the exclusive right concerned bovine insemination centres, there was nothing in the grant of exclusive rights which made an abuse (excessive pricing) unavoidable.

Case C-323/93, *Société Civile Agricole du Centre d'Insémination de la Crespelle* v. *Coopérative d'Elevage et d'Insémination Artificielle du Département de la Mayenne* [1994] ECR I-5077

French law conferred on certain bovine insemination centres the exclusive right to provide insemination services over a particular geographical area. It was alleged that the centres charged excessively for their services.

---

[92] It should be noted that since *Corbeau* the postal sector has been liberalised.

[93] As Jacobs AG pointed out in his Opinion in Cases C-67/96, 115–117/97, and 219/97, *Albany International BV* v. *Stichting Bedrijfspensioenfonds Textielindustrie* [1999] ECR I-5751, para. 417.

[94] See L. Hancher, 'Casenote on *Corbeau*' (1994) 31 *CMLRev* 105, 111.

[95] See Faull Nikpay (eds.), *The EC Law of Competition* (cited in n. 1), para. 6.80.

[96] See also Case C-387/93, *Banchero* [1995] ECR I-4663.

Court of Justice

15. So far as concerns the relevant provisions of the Treaty, Article [4 TEU] requires Member States to carry out their Community obligations in good faith. However, the Court has consistently held that that provision cannot be applied independently when the situation concerned is governed by a specific provision of the Treaty, as in the present case (see the judgment in Joined Cases C-78/90 to C-83/90 *Compagnie Commerciale de l'Ouest and Others*...paragraph 19). The question must therefore be considered in the light of Articles [106(1) and 102].

16. Article [106(1)] provides that, in the case of public undertakings and undertakings to which Member States grant special or exclusive rights, Member States may neither enact nor maintain in force any measure contrary to the rules contained in the Treaty, in particular to those rules provided for in Article [18] and Articles [101] to [109].

17. In this case, by making the operation of the insemination centres subject to authorization and providing that each centre should have the exclusive rights to serve a defined area, the national legislation granted those centres exclusive rights. By thus establishing, in favour of those undertakings, a contiguous series of monopolies territorially limited but together covering the entire territory of a Member State, those national provisions create a dominant position, within the meaning of Article [102], in a substantial part of the common market.

18. The mere creation of such a dominant position by the granting of an exclusive right within the meaning of Article [106(1)] is not as such incompatible with Article [102]. A Member State contravenes the prohibitions contained in those two provisions only if, in merely exercising the exclusive right granted to it, the undertaking in question cannot avoid abusing its dominant position (see the judgments in Case C-41/90 *Höfner and Elser*...paragraph 29, and most recently, in Case C-179/90 *Merci Convenzionali Porto di Genova*...paragraph 17).

19. The alleged abuse in the present case consists in the charging of exorbitant prices by the insemination centres.

20. The question to be examined is therefore whether such a practice constituting the alleged abuse is the direct consequence of the national Law. It should be noted in this regard that the Law merely allows insemination centres to require breeders who request the centres to provide them with semen from other production centres to pay the additional costs entailed by that choice.

21. Although it leaves to the insemination centres the task of calculating those costs, such a provision does not lead the centres to charge disproportionate costs and thereby abuse their dominant position.

22. The answer to this part of the question must therefore be that Articles [106(1) and 102] do not preclude a Member State from granting to approved bovine insemination centres certain exclusive rights within the defined area.

The same approach can be seen in *Corsica Ferries*,[97] where the CJ held that the grant of the exclusive right to offer compulsory piloting services in a port was not in itself an infringement of Article 106(1) but the approval of the discriminatory tariffs, which were contrary to Article 102(c), *was* an infringement.

Albany, which concerned the Dutch regime of compulsory affiliation to sectoral pension funds is another interesting case taking the same approach.[98]

---

[97] Case C-18/93, *Corsica Ferries Italia Srl v. Corpo dei Piloti del Porto di Genova* [1994] ECR I-1783.

[98] See L. Gyselen, 'Case note on *Albany, Brentjens'* and *Drijvende Bokken*' (2000) 37 CMLRev 425.

Case C-67/96, *Albany International BV v. Stichting Bedrijfspensioenfonds Textielindustrie* [1999] ECR I-5751

Under Dutch law pension provision included a system whereby, at the request of the representatives of employers and employees in a particular sector of the economy, affiliation to a sectoral pension fund was made compulsory for all undertakings in that sector. This was to provide a pension supplementary to the basic State pension. Various undertakings brought proceedings in the Dutch courts challenging the compulsory affiliation regime on the grounds that they provided equivalent supplementary pension schemes themselves. The Dutch courts referred to the CJ the question, *inter alia*, whether the exclusive rights conferred on the sectoral pension funds infringed the Treaty.[99]

Court of Justice

90. It must be observed at the outset that the decision of the public authorities to make affiliation to a sectoral pension fund compulsory, as in this case, necessarily implies granting to that fund an exclusive right to collect and administer the contributions paid with a view to accruing pension rights. Such a fund must therefore be regarded as an undertaking to which exclusive rights have been granted by the public authorities, of the kind referred to in Article [106(1)].

91. Next, it should be noted that according to settled case-law an undertaking which has a legal monopoly in a substantial part of the common market may be regarded as occupying a dominant position within the meaning of Article [102] (see Case C-179/90 *Merci Convenzional Porto di Genova*...paragraph 14, and Case C-18/88 *GB-Inno-BM*...paragraph 17).

92. A sectoral pension fund of the kind at issue in the main proceedings, which has an exclusive right to manage a supplementary pension scheme in an industrial sector in a Member State and, therefore, in a substantial part of the common market, may therefore be regarded as occupying a dominant position within the meaning of Article [102].

93. It must not be forgotten, however, that merely creating a dominant position by granting exclusive rights within the meaning of Article [106(1)] is not in itself incompatible with Article [102]. A Member State is in breach of the prohibitions contained in those two provisions only if the undertaking in question, merely by exercising the exclusive rights granted to it, is led to abuse its dominant position or when such rights are liable to create a situation in which that undertaking is led to commit such abuses (*Höfner and Elser*, cited above, paragraph 29; Case C-260/89 *ERT*...paragraph 37; *Merci Convenzionali Porto di Genova*, cited above, paragraphs 16 and 17; Case C-323/93 *Centre d'Insémination de la Crespelle*...paragraph 18; and Case C-163/96 *Raso and Others*...paragraph 27).

94. Albany contends in that connection that the system of compulsory affiliation to the supplementary pension scheme managed by the Fund is contrary to the combined provisions of Articles [102 and 106]. The pension benefits available from the Fund do not, or no longer, match the needs of the undertakings. The benefits are too low, are not linked to wages and, consequently, are generally inadequate. Employers have therefore to make other pension arrangements. The system of compulsory affiliation deprives those employers of any opportunity of arranging for comprehensive pension cover from an insurance company. Pension arrangements spread over a number of insurers would increase administrative costs and reduce efficiency.

95. It should be remembered that, in *Höfner and Elser*, cited above, paragraph 34, the Court held that a Member State which conferred on a public employment agency an exclusive right of recruitment was in breach of Article [106(1)] where it created a situation in which that office could not avoid infringing Article

---

[99] See also Cases C-115–117/97, *Brentjens' Handelsonderneming BV v. Stichting Bedrijfspensioenfonds voor de Handel in Bouwmaterialen* [1999] ECR I-6025 and Case C-219/97, *Maatschappij Drijvende Bokken BV v. Stichting Pensioenfonds voor de Vervoer-en Havenbedrijven* [1999] ECR I-6121, which raised the same issue. The cases also raised questions about the application of the competition rules to collective agreements between employers and employees. For these aspects, see Chap. 3.

[102], in particular because it was manifestly incapable of satisfying the demand prevailing on the market for such activities.

96. In the present case, it is important to note that the supplementary pension scheme offered by the Fund is based on the present norm in the Netherlands, namely that every worker who has paid contributions to that scheme for the maximum period of affiliation receives a pension, including the State pension under the AOW, equal to 70 per cent of his final salary.

97. Doubtless, some undertakings in the sector might wish to provide their workers with a pension scheme superior to the one offered by the Fund. However, the fact that such undertakings are unable to entrust the management of such a pension scheme to a single insurer and the resulting restriction of competition derive directly from the exclusive right conferred on the sectoral pension fund.

98. It is therefore necessary to consider whether, as contended by the Fund, the Netherlands Government and the Commission, the exclusive right of the sectoral pension fund to manage supplementary pensions in a given sector and the resultant restriction of competition may be justified under Article [106(2)] as a measure necessary for the performance of a particular social task of general interest with which that fund has been charged.

The CJ then proceeded to consider whether the exclusive right and the restriction of competition could indeed be justified under Article 106(2). This part of the judgment is reproduced in Section 6.E.[100]

It can be seen from the previous extract that the CJ said once again that the granting of exclusive rights is not contrary to the Treaty unless merely by exercising the right the undertaking is led to commit an abuse (paragraph 93) or unless an abuse is unavoidable (paragraph 95). However, the Court did not proceed to consider whether the undertaking here *was* put in such a position, but instead turned to see whether the justification under Article 106(2) applied.[101]

Deutsche Post was another case in which Article 106(1) was held to apply and the CJ then turned to consider whether or not the situation was justified under Article 106(2). The undertaking concerned was a State monopoly with the exclusive right to collect, carry, and deliver certain categories of mail in Germany, and carried out the obligations flowing from the Universal Postal Convention (UPC).

Cases C-147–148/97, *Deutsche Post AG v. Gesellschaft für Zahlungssysteme mbH (GZS) and Citicorp Kartenservice GmbH* [2000] ECR I-825

Under the Universal Postal Convention 1989 the contracting states are obliged to forward and deliver international mail addressed to persons resident in their country which is passed to them by the postal services of other contracting parties. The Convention provides for the receiving state to charge a fixed fee for the costs of delivering the mail (terminal dues). The Convention also provides, *inter alia*, that where senders resident in country A cause mail addressed to addressees in country A to be posted in bulk in country B, country A is entitled to either charge its full internal rate for the items or to return them to their origin (Article 25). Various credit-card companies based in Germany electronically transmitted the data for their

---

[100] See Section 6.E.iii, p. 647.

[101] See L. Gyselen, 'Case note on *Albany, Brentjens'* and *Drijvende Bokken*' (2000) 37 *CMLRev* 425. In other cases too the Court has expressly left open the question of the position brought about by the exclusive right before considering whether or not Art. 106(2) applied: see, e.g., Case C-209/98, *Entreprenørforeningens Affalds (FFAD) v. Københavns Kommune* [2000] ECR-3743.

customers' bills to processing centres outside Germany which prepared the German customers' bills and posted them back to Germany. In one case this resulted in the bills being posted in Denmark, where the rate for international mail is lower than the internal rate in Germany. Deutsche Post was merely paid the terminal dues. It demanded the full internal rate. The credit companies refused to pay. In the course of the subsequent litigation the German courts referred to the Court questions about whether it was contrary to Article 106 and Article 102 (and Article 56, which was also relevant since the situation involved the freedom to provide services) for Deutsche Post to exercise its rights under Article 25 of the Convention to charge the internal postage rate.

Court of Justice

37 …. it should first be noted that a body such as Deutsche Post, which has been granted exclusive rights as regards the collection, carriage and delivery of mail, must be regarded as an undertaking to which the Member State concerned has granted exclusive rights within the meaning of Article [106(1)] (Case C-320/91 *Corbeau*…paragraph 8).

38. Also, it is settled case-law that an undertaking having a statutory monopoly over a substantial part of the common market may be regarded as holding a dominant position within the meaning of Article [102] (see Case C-179/90 *Merci Convenzionali Porto di Genova* v. *Siderurgica Gabrielli*…paragraph 14, Case C-18/88 *RTT* v. *GB-Inno-BM*…paragraph 17, and *Corbeau*, cited above, paragraph 9).

39. The Court has had occasion to state in this respect that although the mere fact that a Member State has created a dominant position by the grant of exclusive rights is not as such incompatible with Article [102], the Treaty none the less requires the Member States not to adopt or maintain in force any measure which might deprive that provision of its effectiveness (see Case C-260/89 *ERT*…paragraph 35, and *Corbeau*, cited above, paragraph 11).

40. Article [106(1)] thus provides that in the case of undertakings to which Member States grant special or exclusive rights, they are neither to enact nor to maintain in force any measure contrary, in particular, to the rules contained in the Treaty with regard to competition (see *Corbeau*, paragraph 12).

41. That provision must be read in conjunction with Article [106(2)] which provides that undertakings entrusted with the operation of services of general economic interest are to be subject to the rules contained in the Treaty in so far as the application of such rules does not obstruct the performance, in law or in fact, of the particular tasks assigned to them.

42. A final point to note is that the UPC proceeds on the basis of a market in letter-post where the postal services of the various Contracting States of the Universal Postal Union are not in competition.

43. In that context, the UPC is designed to establish rules ensuring that international items of mail addressed to residents of a Contracting State and passed on by the fundamental principles of the UPC, set out in Article 1 thereof, is the obligation of the postal administration of the Contracting State to which international mail is sent to forward and deliver it to addressees resident in its territory using the most rapid means of its letter post. In that regard, the States which have adopted the Convention of the Universal Postal Union constitute a single postal territory, in which the freedom of transit of reciprocal international mail is in principle guaranteed.

44. For the postal services of the Member States, performance of the obligations flowing from the UPC is thus in itself a service of general economic interest within the meaning of Article [106(2)].

45. In the present case, German legislation assigns the operation of that service to Deutsche Post.

46. As has been noted in paragraph 5 of this judgment, postal services initially delivered international mail without being paid for that task. However, when it became apparent that the flows of postal traffic between two Contracting States frequently did not balance out, so that the postal services of the various Contracting States had to process quantities of international mail which differed greatly, specific provisions were laid down in that regard, one of which is Article 25 of the UPC.

47. Under Article 25(3) of the UPC, the postal services of the Contracting States may in particular, in the cases referred to in Article 25(1) and (2), charge postage on items of mail at their internal rates.

48. The grant to a body such as Deutsche Post of the right to treat international items of mail as internal post in such cases creates a situation where that body may be led, to the detriment of users of postal services, to abuse its dominant position resulting from the exclusive right granted to it to forward and deliver those items to the relevant addressees.

49. It is accordingly necessary to examine the extent to which exercise of such a right is necessary to enable a body of that kind to perform its task of general interest pursuant to the obligations flowing from the UPC and, in particular, to operate under economically acceptable conditions.

50. If a body such as Deutsche Post were obliged to forward and deliver to addressees resident in Germany mail posted in large quantities by senders resident in Germany using postal services of other Member States, without any provision allowing it to be financially compensated for all the costs occasioned by that obligation, the performance, in economically balanced conditions, of that task of general interest would be jeopardised.

51. The postal services of a Member State cannot simultaneously bear the costs entailed in the performance of the service of general economic interest of forwarding and delivering international items of mail, which is their responsibility by virtue of the UPC, and the loss of income resulting from the fact that bulk mailings are no longer posted with the postal services of the Member State in which the addressees are resident but with those of other Member States.

52. In such a case, it must be regarded as justified, for the purposes of the performance, in economically balanced conditions, of the task of general interest entrusted to Deutsche Post by the UPC, to treat cross-border mail as internal mail and, consequently, to charge internal postage.

...

54. Article [106(2)] therefore justifies, in the absence of an agreement between the postal services of the Member States concerned fixing terminal dues in relation to the actual costs of processing and delivering incoming trans-border mail, the grant by a Member State to its postal services of the statutory right to charge internal postage on items of mail where senders resident in that State post items, or cause them to be posted, in large quantities with the postal services of another Member State in order to send them to the first Member State.

...

56. On the other hand, in so far as part of the forwarding and delivery costs is offset by terminal dues paid by the postal services of other Member States, it is not necessary, in order for a body such as Deutsche Post to fulfil the obligations flowing from the UPC, that postage be charged at the full internal rate on items posted in large quantities with those services.

57. It is to be remembered that a body such as Deutsche Post which has a statutory monopoly over a substantial part of the common market may be regarded as holding a dominant position within the meaning of Article [102].

58. Thus, the exercise by such a body of the right to demand the full amount of the internal postage, where the costs relating to the forwarding and delivery of mail posted in large quantities with the postal services of a Member State other than the State in which both the senders and the addressees of that mail are resident are not offset by the terminal dues paid by those services, may be regarded as an abuse of a dominant position within the meaning of Article [102].

59. In order to prevent a body such as Deutsche Post from exercising its right, provided for by Article 25(3) of the UPC, to return items of mail to origin, the senders of those items have no choice but to pay the full amount of the internal postage.

60. As the Court has stated in relation to a refusal to sell on the part of an undertaking holding a dominant position within the meaning of Article [102], such action would be inconsistent with the objective laid down by Article [3(1)(g)] of the EC Treaty...as explained in Article [102], in particular in subparagraphs (b) and (c) of its second paragraph (Case 27/76 *United Brands* v. *Commission*...paragraph 183).

In this judgment the CJ said that Deutsche Post had been granted exclusive rights within the meaning of Article 106(1), and that Article 106(1) had to be read in conjunction with Article 106(2). In saying this (paragraphs 40–41), the Court repeated the wording in paragraphs 12–13 of the *Corbeau* judgment. The performance of the obligations of the UPC was a service of general economic interest within the meaning of Article 106(2) (paragraph 44). The Court held that granting Deutsche Post the right under the UPC to treat international mail as internal mail *did* create a situation where 'it may be led, to the detriment of users of postal services, to abuse its dominant position' (paragraph 48). It therefore said it must examine whether the exercise of the right was necessary to perform its task of general interest 'under economically acceptable conditions' (paragraph 49). It concluded that it *was* necessary, because of the financial loss Deutsche Post would otherwise incur.[102] However, it would be an abuse of a dominant position if Deutsche Post were to charge the full internal postage without offsetting the terminal dues against the money demanded from the senders.

A similar approach to the application of Article 106(1) was taken in *Ambulanz Glöckner*.

Case C-475/99, *Ambulanz Glöckner* v. *Landkreis Südwestpfalz* [2001] ECR I-8089

The provision of the public ambulance service in Germany was governed by legislation referred to in the judgment below as the 'RettDG 1991'. This distinguished between 'emergency transport' and 'patient transport' (non-emergency). Emergency transport in the *Land* of Rheinland-Pfalz was entrusted to two medical aid organizations which also ran a non-emergency service. Ambulanz Glöckner had previously also provided a non-emergency service. However, when it applied to the relevant public authority for a renewal of its permit, the two medical aid organizations objected, claiming that competition on the non-emergency market would affect their ability to provide the emergency service. As a result the public authority refused Ambulanz Glöckner a permit.

Court of Justice

39. It must be borne in mind that the mere creation of a dominant position through the grant of special or exclusive rights within the meaning of Article [106(1)] is not in itself incompatible with Article [102]. A Member State will be in breach of the prohibitions laid down by those two provisions only if the undertaking in question, merely by exercising the special or exclusive rights conferred upon it, is led to abuse its dominant position or where such rights are liable to create a situation in which that undertaking is led to commit such abuses (see *Pavlov*, cited above, paragraph 127).

40. It is settled case-law that an abuse within the meaning of Article [102] is committed where, without any objective necessity, an undertaking holding a dominant position on a particular market reserves to itself an ancillary activity which could be carried out by another undertaking as part of its activities on a neighbouring but separate market, with the possibility of eliminating all competition from that undertaking (judgment in Case C-18/88 *GB-Inno-BM*...paragraph 18). Where the extension of the dominant position of an undertaking to which the State has granted special or exclusive rights results from a State measure, such a measure constitutes an infringement of Article [106] in conjunction with Article [102] (*GB-Inno-BM*, paragraph 21, and Case C-203/96 *Dusseldorp and Others*...paragraph 61).

41. In the present case, the argument put forward by Ambulanz Glöckner is indeed that it is excluded from the market for patient transport as a result of the application of Paragraph 18(3) of the RettDG 1991, which, in its submission, enables the medical aid organisations, acting in concertation with the public authorities, to restrict access to that market.

42. The Commission also contends that the extension of the dominant position on the urgent transport market to the related, but separate, market for patient transport is due to the changes made in the federal

---

[102] See Section 6.E.iii, p. 649.

legislation governing the latter type of transport, then in the legislation of the Land of Rheinland-Pfalz and, in particular, to the adoption of Paragraph 18(3) of the RettDG 1991. Such a restriction of competition, it contends, constitutes a breach of Article [106] in conjunction with Article [102] thereof.

43. As far as those arguments are concerned, it must be concluded that, in enacting Paragraph 18(3) of the RettDG 1991, the application of which involves prior consultation of the medical aid organisations in respect of any application for authorisation to provide non-emergency patient transport services submitted by an independent operator, the legislature of the Land of Rheinland-Pfalz gave an advantage to those organisations, which already had an exclusive right on the urgent transport market, by also allowing them to provide such services exclusively. The application of Paragraph 18(3) of the RettDG 1991 therefore has the effect of limiting markets...to the prejudice of consumers within the meaning of Article [102(b)], by reserving to those medical aid organisations an ancillary transport activity which could be carried on by independent operators.

The CJ then went on to consider whether Article 106(2) applied.[103]

C. SUMMARY OF THE MEASURES WHICH MAKE ABUSE UNAVOIDABLE OR CREATE A SITUATION IN WHICH THE UNDERTAKING IS LED TO ABUSE ITS DOMINANT POSITION

It is not possible to neatly categorise the types of measure whose results infringe Article 106(1). Furthermore, it must be stressed that even if it were, the categories would not be closed. However, looking at the case law discussed previously, one can identify the following.

(i) Inability to Meet Demand

It is clear from *Höfner* v. *Macroton*[104] that Article 106(1) is infringed where a statutory monopoly is set up in such a way that it is incapable of meeting the demand in the reserved sector. This was also the case in *Job Centre Coop. arl*[105] and *AG2R Prévoyance* v. *Beaudout*.[106] *Merci Convenzionali* showed that Article 106(1) is infringed where the monopolist is enabled to behave inefficiently, exploit customers, and not modernise.[107] In *Amblanz Glöckner* the Advocate General discussed the possible causes for inefficiency or inability to meet demand. He considered that a Member State is only liable under Article 106(1) if the fault is in the system it has set up, and not where the only reason that an organisation is 'manifestly not able to satisfy demand' is inefficient management.[108] The CJ did not address this point in its judgment. There are a number of cases in the postal[109] and telecommunications[110] sectors which were the subject of Article 106(3) decisions[111] because of an inability to meet demand, a recent

---

[103] See Section 6.E.iii, p. 650.
[104] See Section 5.B, p. 609.
[105] Case C-55/96, [1997] ECR I-7119.
[106] Case C-437/09, [2011] ECR I-973.
[107] See Section 5.B, p. 613.
[108] Case C-475/99, *Ambulanz Glöckner* v. *Landkreis Südwestpfalz* [2001] ECR I-8089, Opinion of Jacobs AG, para. 148.
[109] See *Dutch Express Delivery Services* [1994] OJ L10/47; *Spanish Express Courier Services* [1990] OJ L233/19.
[110] See *Italian GSM* [1995] OJ L280/49; *Spanish GSM* [1997] OJ L79/19.
[111] See Section 8.B, p. 653.

example being *Slovakian Hybrid Mail*.[112] The abuses at issue under this head are violations of Article 102(b), 'limiting production, markets or technical development to the prejudice of consumers'.

(ii) The Cumulation of Rights Conferred on an Undertaking Create a Conflict of Interest

Cumulation of rights was an issue in *France* v. *Commission*, *GB-Inno-BM SA*,[113] *ERT*,[114] *Raso*,[115] and *MOTOE*[116] where some type of 'regulatory' function given to the monopoly would enable it to disadvantage competitors in a downstream market.

The CJ did not appear to find the dual role of the pension funds in *Albany* (as both managers of the scheme and the authority with power to grant exemptions whereby companies could be allowed to insure with other undertakings) to constitute a conflict of interest. The Court held the situation justified because '[e]xercise of that power of exemption involves an evaluation of complex data relating to the pension schemes involved and the financial equilibrium of the fund, which necessarily implies a wide margin of appreciation'.[117] In that case, however, the Court concentrated on the application of Article 106(2) rather than Article 106(1) and, as we have seen,[118] passed rather quickly over the issue of Article 106(1) altogether. It is therefore unclear whether there was no infringement of Article 106(1) or whether the Court was applying Article 106(2) at this point.

(iii) The Extension of Exclusive Rights

Cases where Article 106(1) has been infringed by measures enabling an undertaking to extend its monopoly into neighbouring markets include *GB-Inno-BM SA* which can be classified under this head as well as head (ii) (cumulation of rights), as can *ERT*. The telecommunications case *France* v. *Commission*[119] was also a matter of extension of rights. In *Ambulanz Glöckner* the CJ said that the fact that the medical aid organisations providing emergency transport were consulted by the authorities about the permit applications of other undertakings wishing to operate in the non-emergency market gave the aid organisations an advantage in the latter. The 'essential facilities' case, *Port of Rødby*,[120] concerned an infringement of Article 106(1) as the port authority was able to refuse access to the port it controlled, thus eliminating competition from a competitor ferry company.

(iv) Pricing Abuses

Undertakings with exclusive rights may be enabled to commit pricing abuses. Indeed, price discrimination has featured in a number of cases concerning the conduct of undertakings given control over transport infrastructures.[121] *GT-Link*, where the port authority was guilty of price discrimination

---

[112] COMP/39.562 *Slovakian Hybrid Mail*, [2009] 4 CMLR 663, on appeal Case T-556/08, *Slovenská Posta*, judgment pending.

[113] Case C-18/88, *RTT* v. *GB-Inno-BM SA* [1991] ECR I-5973.

[114] Case C-260/89, *Elliniki Radiophonia Tileorasi (ERT)* v. *DEP* [1991] ECR I-2925.

[115] Case C-163/96, *Silvano Raso* [1998] ECR I-533, see Section 5.B, p. 616.

[116] Case C-49/07, *MOTOE* [2008] ECR I-4863.

[117] Case C-67/96, *Albany International BV* v. *Stichting Bedrijfspensioenfonds Textielindustrie* [1999] ECR I-5751, para. 119. Jacobs AG was not so sanguine and considered that Art. 106(1) was infringed, see paras. 441–468 of the Opinion.

[118] Section 5.B, p. 623.

[119] Case C-202/88, *France* v. *Commission* [1991] ECR I-1223.

[120] [1994] OJ L55/52, [1994] 5 CMLR 457, see a Chap. 7.

[121] See, e.g., Case C-266/96, *Corsica Ferries France SA* v. *Gruppo Antichi Ormeggiatori del Porto di Genova* [1998] ECR I-3949 (discussed in Section 6.E.iii, p. 645); Case C-163/99, *Portugal* v. *Commission* [2002] ECR I-2613 (concerning the landing fees at Portuguese airports, and discussed in Chap. 7).

in waiving harbour duties in respect of its own ferry services and those of its partners but charging them to its competitors on the ferry market, is also a case where there was a cumulation of rights and where the undertaking was extending its monopoly into a downstream market.[122]

(v) Refusal to Supply

There may be refusal to supply in cases involving 'essential facilities', as in *Port of Rødby*. The refusal to deliver incoming cross-border mail in *Deutsche Post*[123] unless extra payments were made was treated as a refusal to supply.

(vi) Inequality of Opportunity and Distortion of Competition

Inequality of opportunity was an issue cases in a number of cases such as *France v. Commission, GB-Inno-BM SA, Connect Austria,* and *MOTOE*. However, according to the GC in *Greek Lignite,*[124] a measure which creates inequality of opportunity and distorts competition does not thereby infringe Article 102 unless it leads to at least the potential for an identifiable abuse on the part of the undertaking given the special or exclusive right.

There are some cases in which the nature of the abusive conduct was not altogether clear. This is true, for instance, of *Albany*, where the CJ concentrated on the application of Article 106(2). The most striking case, however, is *Corbeau*, where, as discussed,[125] the Court appeared to consider that a monopoly which was too wide infringed Article 106(1) for that reason alone and did not identify any abuse.

6. ARTICLE 106(2)

A. THE INSTITUTIONAL SETTING OF SERVICES OF GENERAL ECONOMIC INTEREST

(i) Article 14 TFEU and Protocol 26

In the period leading up to the Intergovernmental Conference of 1996 there was a lively debate in the European Union about liberalisation, how public services should be delivered, and how far competition principles should be modified as regards public services. The Commission suggested that a new paragraph should be inserted into Article 3 of the EC Treaty, adding 'a contribution to the promotion of services of general interest' to the activities of the Community. That suggestion was not taken up. Instead, the Treaty of Amsterdam which came into force in 1999 added a new 'Principle', latterly Article 16, to the EC Treaty.[126] Article 16 was expanded by the Treaty of Lisbon and now appears as Article 14 TFEU.

---

[122] Case C-242/95, *GT-Link A/S v. Danske Staatsbaner (DSB)* [1997] ECR I-4449. In this case the Court in effect imposed on undertakings in this position an obligation to maintain a transparent accounting system demonstrating that they did not favour their own operations. Otherwise they will not be able to avoid a finding of abuse.

[123] Cases C-147–148/97, *Deutsche Post AG v. Gesellschaft für Zahlungssysteme mbH (GZS) and Citicorp Kartenservice GmbH* [2000] ECR I-825. See Section 5.B, p. 624 and Section 6.E.iii, p. 649.

[124] Case T-169/08, *DEI v. Commission,* 20 September 2012, on appeal Case C-553/12 P, *Commission v. DEI* (judgment pending).

[125] See Section 5.B, p. 620.

[126] It was Article 16 after the renumbering. It was accompanied by a Declaration. For a discussion of the problems in the interpretation and application of Art. 16, see M. Ross, 'Article 16 EC and Services of General Interest: From Derogation to Obligation' (2000) 25 *ELRev* 22; L. Flynn, 'Competition Policy and Public Services in EC Law after the

a. Article 14 TFEU

Without prejudice to Article 4 of the Treaty on European Union or to Articles 93[127], 106 and 107[128]of this Treaty, and given the place occupied by services of general economic interest in the shared values of the Union as well as their role in promoting social and territorial cohesion, the Union and the Member States, each within their respective powers and within the scope of application of the Treaties, shall take care that such services operate on the basis of principles and conditions, particularly economic and financial conditions, which enable them to fulfil their missions. The European Parliament and the Council, acting by means of regulations in accordance with the ordinary legislative procedure, shall establish these principles and set these conditions without prejudice to the competence of Member States, in compliance with the Treaties, to provide, to commission and to fund such services.

The two additions which did not appear in Article 16 EC are the phrase 'particularly economic and financial conditions' towards the end of the first sentence, and the whole second sentence which gives the EU power to legislate to establish the principles and conditions under which SGEIs operate.

Article 14 needs to be read in the context of the post-Lisbon Treaties as a whole. The 'shared values of the Union' is an important feature of the TEU. According to Article 2 the Union is founded on values common to the Member States, which are 'respect for human dignity, freedom, democracy, equality, the rule of law and respect for human rights, including the rights of persons belonging to minorities'. As noted in Chapter 1[129] Article 3 TEU states that the Union is working for the sustainable development of Europe based on a highly competitive social market economy.

Furthermore, a Protocol on *services of general interest* (rather than just SGEIs) was attached to the TEU and TFEU by the Treaty of Lisbon.

b. Protocol (No 26) on Services of General Interest

The High Contracting Parties,
 Wishing to emphasise the importance of services of general interest,
 Have Agreed Upon the following interpretative provisions, which shall be annexed to the Treaty on European Union and to the Treaty on the Functioning of the European Union:

Article 1
 The shared values of the Union in respect of services of general economic interest within the meaning of Article 14 of the Treaty on the Functioning of the European Union include in particular:
 the essential role and the wide discretion of national, regional and local authorities in providing, commissioning and organising services of general economic interest as closely as possible to the needs of the users;
 the diversity between various services of general economic interest and the differences in the needs and preferences of users that may result from different geographical, social or cultural situations;
 a high level of quality, safety and affordability, equal treatment and the promotion of universal access and of user rights.

Article 2
 The provisions of the Treaties do not affect in any way the competence of Member States to provide, commission and organise non-economic services of general interest.

Maastricht and Amsterdam Treaties', in D. O'Keefe and P. Twomey (eds.), *Legal Issues of the Amsterdam Treaty* (Hart, 1999), 185. The Treaty of Amsterdam also added a Protocol dealing with public service broadcasting to the EC Treaty.

[127] Art. 93 TFEU (ex Art. 73 EC) is a specific provision dealing with State aid in the transport sector.

[128] Art. 107 TFEU is the general provision on State aid.

[129] See Chap. 1, Section 7.B, p. 36.

The Protocol therefore contains two Articles, one expanding on the meaning of Article 14 TFEU which refers only to services of general economic interest, and one which states that the Treaties do not in any way affect the competence of Member States in respect to services of *general interest*.

(ii) Article 36 of the Charter of Fundamental Rights

Article 36 of the Charter of Fundamental Rights of the European Union is entitled 'Access to Services of General Economic Interest'. It states:

The Union recognises and respects access to services of general economic interest as provided for in national laws and practices, in accordance with the Treaties, in order to promote the social and territorial cohesion of the Union.

This provision is about *access to* SGEIs rather than to their content or establishment because this is a Charter about *rights*. It appears in Chapter IV of the Charter, 'Solidarity', and elevates access to services of general economic interest to the status of a fundamental right.

(iii) Commission Communications on Services of General Economic Interest and Services of General Interest

The Commission has issued a number of Communications and other documents on services of general economic interest and services of general interest.[130] These attempt to grapple with the problem of what services are, and are not, subject to the internal market and competition rules. The Communication of December 2011, entitled 'A Quality Framework for Services of General Interest in Europe'[131] (the 2011 Communication) was adopted at the same time as a package of measures on SGEIs and State aid[132] to deal, inter alia, with the issues in the *Altmark* case,[133] and on SGEIs and public procurement.

B. THE CONCEPTS AND TERMINOLOGY OF 'SERVICES OF GENERAL ECONOMIC INTEREST' AND 'SERVICES OF GENERAL INTEREST'

The phrase '*services of general economic interest*' (SGEIs) has appeared in a Treaty Article, in what is now Article 106(2) TFEU, since the inception of the EEC. It has appeared in what is now Article 16 TFEU since 1999, as already explained. It now appears in Protocol 26 and Article 36 of the Charter as well. Article 106(2) gives a limited derogation from (inter alia) the competition rules to undertakings entrusted with such services, in certain circumstances. What amounts to an SGEI is the subject of a considerable body of case law. The phrase is an unhappy one because of the placing of the word 'economic'. It is the service to which the word 'economic' really applies, rather than the 'interest'. It also overlaps with the concept of a service of *general interest*. The words *service of general interest* appear only in Protocol 26.

---

[130] See Section 2.A, p. 600.

[131] COM(2011) 900 final.

[132] Consisting of a Decision ([2012] OJ L73), two Communications ([2012] OJ C8/4 and [2012] OJ C8/15) and a de minimis Regulation (Reg. 360/12 [2012] OJ L114/8). The Commission also issued a Staff Working Document on the application of the State aid rules to SGEIs and social services of general interest, SWD(2013) 53/final/2.

[133] Case C-280/00, *Altmark Trans GmbH, Regierungspräsidium Magdeburg v. Nahverkehrsgesellschaft Altmark GmbH* [2003] ECR I-7747.

In the 2011 Communication the Commission admits that 'the debate on services of general interest suffers from a lack of clarity on terminology. The concepts are used interchangeably and inaccurately.' The Commission therefore sets out what it understands by the various concepts,[134] which it describes as 'dynamic and evolving'. It also says that in doing this it is bound by EU primary law and by the case law of the Court (which is discussed in later sections of this chapter). The Commission describes the types of services and explains the terminology follows:[135]

Service of general interest (SGI): SGI are services that public authorities of the Member States classify as being of general interest and, therefore, subject to specific public service obligations (PSO). The term covers both economic activities (see the definition of SGEI below) and non-economic services. The latter are not subject to specific EU legislation and are not covered by the internal market and competition rules of the Treaty. Some aspects of how these services are organised may be subject to other general Treaty rules, such as the principle of non-discrimination.

Service of general economic interest (SGEI): SGEI are economic activities which deliver outcomes in the overall public good that would not be supplied (or would be supplied under different conditions in terms of quality, safety, affordability, equal treatment or universal access) by the market without public intervention. The PSO is imposed on the provider by way of an entrustment and on the basis of a general interest criterion which ensures that the service is provided under conditions allowing it to fulfil its mission.

Social services of general interest (SSGI): these include social security schemes covering the main risks of life and a range of other essential services provided directly to the person that play a preventive and socially cohesive/inclusive role... While some social services (such as statutory social security schemes) are not considered by the European Court as being economic activities, the jurisprudence of the Court makes clear that the social nature of a service is not sufficient in itself to classify it as non-economic... The term social service of general interest consequently covers both economic and non-economic activities.

Universal service obligation (USO): USO are a type of PSO which sets the requirements designed to ensure that certain services are made available to all consumers and users in a Member State, regardless of their geographical location, at a specified quality and, taking account of specific national circumstances, at an affordable price. The definition of specific USO are set at European level as an essential component of market liberalization of service sectors, such as electronic communications, post and transport.

Public service: Public service is used in article 93 TFEU in the field of transport. However, outside this area, the term is sometimes used in an ambiguous way: it can relate to the fact that a service is offered to the general public and/or in the public interest, or it can be used for the activity of entities in public ownership. To avoid ambiguity, this Communication does not use the term but follows the terminology 'service of general interest' and 'service of general economic interest'.

The Commission therefore makes it clear that 'services of general economic interest'(SGEIs) are a sub-set of services of general interest (SGIs). SGIs comprise:

- non-economic (i.e. non-market) services, to which the competition and internal market rules[136] do not apply in the first place. They are services of general interest but not services of general economic interest;

- services of general *economic* interest (i.e. market services) which are subject to the competition rules and the internal market rules since their activities are *economic* in nature.

Whether a service falls into the category of 'economic' or 'non-economic' services depends on the application of the concept of an 'economic activity'. Services provided as part of the

---

[134] It had previously explained the terminology in the 2007 Communication, see n. 16.

[135] 2011 Communication, pp. 3–4.

[136] Other EU rules, such as the principle of non-discrimination may, however, apply.

prerogatives of the State are non-economic.[137] It is 'economic' services, SGEIs, which are the subject of Article 106(2).

C. THE PURPOSE OF ARTICLE 106(2)

Article 106(2) provides a limited derogation from the Treaty rules in order to deal with the activities of undertakings entrusted by the State with certain tasks. It provides that the Treaty rules shall apply to two sorts of undertaking—revenue-producing monopolies and those entrusted with services of general economic interest—only insofar as that does not obstruct the performance of their tasks. It is subject to the proviso that the exception should not affect trade to an extent contrary to the interests of the Union. Unlike Article 106(1), Article 106(2) is addressed to undertakings themselves and not to Member States, although Member States may rely on Article 106(2)[138] and, as we have seen, the two provisions may be applied together. As with Article 106(1), the competition rules are singled out for special mention and Article 106(2) is particularly important in relation to the application of Article 102.

Article 106(2) does not state what value is to be accorded to services of general economic interest and in particular does not say that 'universal service' (USO) should be protected or promoted.[139] In the past the provision has tended to be construed narrowly (as have other derogations from the Treaty), an interpretation which has preserved the widest possible application of the competition rules.[140] Nevertheless, from the case of *Corbeau* in 1993 onwards the Court has been more willing to accept that providers of public services may need to be protected from the full rigours of competition and has become more flexible in the way in which the criteria in Article 106(2) are applied.

D. UNDERTAKINGS HAVING THE CHARACTER OF A REVENUE-PRODUCING MONOPOLY

This is a reference to undertakings which exploit their exclusive rights to raise revenue for the State. They may constitute commercial monopolies and so be subject to the rules laid down in Article 37 TFEU. Article 37 applies to 'any body through which a Member State, in law or in fact, either directly or indirectly supervises, determines or appreciably influences imports or exports between Member States'. Article 37 appears among the free movement provisions, but the CJ has said that it aims to eliminate distortions in competition in the internal market as well as discrimination against the products and trade of other Member States.[141]

E. UNDERTAKINGS ENTRUSTED WITH THE OPERATION OF SERVICES OF GENERAL ECONOMIC INTEREST

(i) 'Undertakings Entrusted With ....'

'Undertaking' has the meaning previously discussed.[142] The legal status of the undertaking in national law is immaterial. It can be a public or private undertaking, but the important thing is that the State has assigned it certain tasks by a positive act conferring on it certain functions or

---

[137] Such as the police and the justice system.

[138] See, e.g., Case C-203/96, *Chemische Afvalstoffen Dusseldorp BV v. Minister van Volkshuisvesting, Ruimtelijke Ordening en Milieubeheer* [1998] ECR I-4075.

[139] See M. Ross, 'Art. 16 EC and Services of General Interest: From Derogation to Obligation?' (2000) 25 *ELRev* 22, 24; see further Case T-289/03, *BUPA v. Commission* [2008] ECR II-18, see Section 6.E.i, p. 635.

[140] See Case 127/73, *BRT v. SABAM* [1974] ECR 313.

[141] For a discussion of Art. 37 see Bellamy and Child (V. Rose and D. Bailey, eds.), *European Law of Competition* (7th edn, Oxford University Press, 2013), 11.036–11.045.

[142] See Chaps. 3 and 5.

by granting it a concession. Merely tolerating, approving, or endorsing its activities is insufficient. So, according to the Commission, the Member States' approval of the Eurocheque system did not mean that Article 106(2) applied to the banks concerned.[143] The CJ held that an author's rights society was not within the provision merely because it was subject to obligations imposed on all monopolies by national law[144] but the Commission has left open the question of whether a rights society might be 'entrusted' if the Member State's legislation described the functions and status of the society in an appropriate way.[145] In *Dusseldorp* the Advocate General said that an undertaking is 'entrusted' with a service where 'certain obligations are imposed on it by the State in the general economic interest'.[146]

In *BUPA* the Irish Government introduced a risk equalisation scheme in respect of private medical insurance (PMI) following the liberalisation of the sector. Under the scheme, insurers with a risk profile below the average were liable to pay a levy and those with a profile above the average were entitled to receive payments. The result of this was in effect to transfer funds from the private insurer, BUPA, to other operators. BUPA claimed that this amounted to illegal State aid. The question arose as to whether or not the PMI scheme adopted by Ireland had an SGEI mission. The question was relevant as there is an important link between SGEIs and State aid because compensation paid for the supply of SGEIs may not, in certain conditions, constitute State aid.[147] In an appeal from the Commission decision holding that the scheme did not constitute State aid on these grounds, BUPA claimed that the insurers had not been 'entrusted' with an SGEI mission as required by Article 106(2).

Case T-289/03, *BUPA* v. *Commission* [2008] ECR II-18

General Court

178 ...[A]s the case-law shows, the provision of the service in question must, by definition, assume a general or public interest. Thus, SGEIs are distinguished in particular from services in the private interest, even though that interest may be more or less collective or be recognised by the State as legitimate or beneficial (see, to that effect, *Züchner*, paragraph 97 above, paragraph 7, and *GVL v Commission*, paragraph 98 above, paragraphs 31 and 32). In addition, as the applicants claim, the general or public interest on which the Member State relies must not be reduced to the need to subject the market concerned to certain rules or the commercial activity of the operators concerned to authorisation by the State. The mere fact that the national legislature, acting in the general interest in the broad sense, imposes certain rules of authorisation, of functioning or of control on all the operators in a particular sector does not in principle mean that there is an SGEI mission (see, to that effect, *GVL v Commission*, paragraph 98 above, paragraph 32, and *GB-Inno-BM*, paragraph 98 above, paragraph 22).

179 On the other hand, the recognition of an SGEI mission does not necessarily presume that the operator entrusted with that mission will be given an exclusive or special right to carry it out. It follows from a reading of paragraph 1 together with paragraph 2 of Article [106 TFEU] that a distinction must be drawn between a special or exclusive right conferred on an operator and the SGEI mission which, where appropriate, is attached to that right (see, in that regard, *Merci Convenzionali Porto di Genova*, paragraph 97

[143] *Uniform Eurocheques* [1985] OJ L35/43, [1985] 3 CMLR 434.

[144] *GEMA* [1971] OJ L134/15.

[145] COMP/38.698 *CISAC Agreement* [2009] 4 CMLR 577, on appeal decisions partially annulled on other grounds, Cases T-442/08 etc., *CISAC* v. *Commission*, 12 April 2012.

[146] Opinion of Jacobs AG, para. 103, in Case C-203/96, *Chemische Afvalstoffen Dusseldorp BV* v. *Minister van Volkshuisvesting, Ruimtelijke Ordening en Milieubeheer* [1998] ECR I-4075.

[147] Case C-280/00, *Altmark Trans GmbH, Regierungspräsidium Magdeburg* v. *Nahverkehrsgesellschaft Altmark GmbH* [2003] ECR I-7747, see Section 9, p. 656.

above, paragraphs 9 and 27; *Almelo*, paragraph 97 above, paragraphs 46 to 50; and *Albany*, paragraph 101 above, paragraphs 98 and 104 to 111). The grant of a special or exclusive right to an operator is merely the instrument, possibly justified, which allows that operator to perform an SGEI mission. Therefore...the Commission's finding at recital 47 to the contested decision, which refers to paragraphs 14 and 15 of the communication on services of general interest, that the attribution of an SGEI mission may also consist in an obligation imposed on a large number of, or indeed on all, the operators active on the same market, is not vitiated by an error (see, with respect to an SGEI mission entrusted in the context of a non-exclusive concession governed by public law, *Almelo*, paragraph 97 above, paragraph 47).

180 Consequently, the applicants' argument that the existence of an SGEI mission is precluded because all PMI insurers are subject to certain obligations cannot succeed.

181 In the second place, it must be borne in mind that, in essence...the wording of Article [106(2)], as such, require[s] that the operator in question be entrusted with an SGEI mission by an act of a public authority and that the act clearly define the SGEI obligations in question (see, to that effect, *Züchner*, paragraph 97 above, paragraph 7; Case 66/86 *Ahmed Saeed Flugreisen*...paragraph 55; *GT-Link*, paragraph 97 above, paragraph 51; *Altmark*, paragraph 89; and *Olsen v Commission*, paragraph 166 above, paragraph 186).

182 In the present case, contrary to the theory put forward by the applicants, the relevant Irish legislation does not involve any regulation or authorisation whatsoever relating to the activity of PMI insurers, but must be characterised as an act of a public authority creating and defining a specific mission consisting in the provision of PMI services in compliance with the PMI obligations...Furthermore, with the stated object of serving the general interest by allowing what is at present approximately half of the Irish population to benefit from alternative cover for certain health care, in particular hospital care, the above mentioned PMI obligations restrict the commercial freedom of the PMI insurers to an extent going considerably beyond ordinary conditions of authorisation to exercise an activity in a specific sector (see paragraph 191 et seq. below).

183 ...Furthermore, since the system chosen by Ireland does not provide for the grant of exclusive or special rights, but for the achievement of the mission by all operators active on the Irish PMI market, which is a choice open to the Member State (see paragraph 179 above), it follows that, contrary to what the applicants appear to claim, there can be no requirement that each of the operators subject to the PMI obligations be separately entrusted with that mission by an individual act or mandate.

184 Accordingly, the complaint that the activity of the PMI insurers is governed by 'normal' regulatory obligations and that there is no act of a public authority creating and entrusting an SGEI mission must be rejected.

In this case, therefore, the GC drew a distinction between a State imposing general regulatory rules on a sector and entrusting undertakings with an SGEI mission. It did not matter that the SGEI was entrusted to a number of undertakings and not to just one. Being entrusted with an SGEI did not necessarily mean that an undertaking had to be granted a special or exclusive right. It was therefore not required that each undertaking concerned had to be individually entrusted with the SGEI rather than just being subject to the scheme laid down by the State.

(ii) Operation of Services of General Economic Interest

The word 'services' is construed to cover the widest spectrum of activities and is not limited to the meaning of the term as used in the free movement provisions. 'Services of general economic interest' denotes activities that need to be carried out in the public interest. As the Advocate General said in *Dusseldorp*:[148]

---

[148] Opinion of Jacobs AG in Case C-203/96, *Chemische Afvalstoffen Dusseldorp BV v. Minister van Volkshuisvesting, Ruimtelijke Ordening en Milieubeheer* [1998] ECR I-4075, para. 105.

The reason for the assignment of particular tasks to undertakings is often that the tasks need to be undertaken in the public interest but might not be undertaken, usually for economic reasons, if the service were to be left to the private sector.

In the *Telecommunications Equipment* case the CJ explained that Article 106(2) reconciles the interests of Member States and the Union:[149]

In allowing derogations to be made from the general rules of the Treaty in certain circumstances, that provision seeks to reconcile the Member States' interest in using certain undertakings, in particular in the public sector, as an instrument of economic or fiscal policy with the Community's interest in ensuring compliance with the rules on competition and the preservation of the unity of the common market.

Further, this passage refers to undertakings which are used as instruments of economic or fiscal policy. In *Albany International* the CJ applied the same principle to social policy.[150]

In *BUPA*, as seen in the extract on p. 639 (paragraph 172), the GC stated that an SGEI has to satisfy certain minimum criteria derived from the case law. These are, in addition to the act of entrusting, that the mission has to be 'universal' and 'compulsory'. Within those criteria the Member States have a wide discretion.

The most obvious candidates for recognition as services of general economic interest on this basis are the utilities, as the Commission stated in its *XXth Report on Competition Policy*.[151] The EU Courts have accepted as services of general economic interest the administration of major waterways;[152] the operation of non-economically viable air routes;[153] the operation of the electricity supply network;[154] the operation of the basic, as distinct from extra 'added-value', postal service;[155] mooring services in ports;[156] the treatment of waste;[157] sectoral supplementary pension funds;[158] the performance of obligations flowing from the Universal Postal Convention;[159] the provision of emergency ambulance services;[160] and the provision of private medical insurance.[161] The Commission held that in principle the provision of banking services to people who have difficulty in accessing basic banking services could be an SGEI (although it was not in the case concerned).[162] It will be seen from this

---

[149] Case C-202/88, *France v. Commission* [1991] ECR I-1223 (the *Telecommunications Equipment* case), para. 12; see also Case C-157/94, *Commission v. Netherlands (Re Electricity Imports)* [1997] ECR I-5699, para. 39.

[150] Case C-67/96, *Albany International BV v. Stichting Bedrijfspensioenfonds Textielindustrie* [1999] ECR I-5751, paras. 103–105.

[151] (Commission, 1990), Introduction, 12.

[152] Case 10/71, *Ministère Public of Luxembourg v. Muller* [1971] ECR 723.

[153] Case 66/86, *Ahmed Saeed Flugreisen and Silver Line Reiseburo GmbH v. Zentrale zur Bëkampfung Unlauteren Wettwerbs eV* [1989] ECR 803.

[154] Case C-393/92, *Gemeente Almelo* [1994] ECR I-1477; in Case C-157/94, *Commission v. Netherlands (Re Electricity Imports)* [1997] ECR I-5699 the Commission did not contest that the monopoly electricity distributor in the Netherlands provided a service of general economic interest.

[155] *Dutch Courier Services* [1990] OJ L10/47, [1990] 4 CMLR 947; *Spanish Courier Services* [1990] OJ L233/19, [1991] 4 CMLR 560; Case C-320/91, *Corbeau* [1993] ECR I-2533.

[156] Case C-266/96, *Corsica Ferries France SA v. Gruppo Antichi Ormeggiatori del Porto di Genova* [1998] ECR I-3949.

[157] Case C-209/98, *Entreprenørforeningens Affalds (FFAD) v. Københavns Kommune* [2000] ECR I-3743.

[158] Case C-67/96, *Albany International BV v. Stichting Bedrijfspensioenfonds Textielindustrie* [1999] ECR-5751.

[159] Joined Cases C-147–148/97, *Deutsche Post AG v. Gesellschaft für Zahlungssysteme mbH (GZS) and Citicorp Kartenservice GmbH* [2000] ECR I-825.

[160] Case C-475/99, *Ambulanz Glöckner v. Landkreis Südwestpfalz* [2001] ECR I-8089. Jacobs AG considered that non-emergency ambulance services were also services of general economic interest, see Opinion, para. 175.

[161] Case T-289/03, *BUPA v. Commission* [2008] ECR II-18; see M. G. Ross, 'A healthy approach to services of general economic interest? The BUPA judgment of the Court of First Instance' (2009) 34 *ELRev* 127.

[162] *La Banque Postale, les Caisses d'Épargne et de Prévoyance and the Crédit Mutuel, for the distribution of the Livret A and Livret Bleu Commission Decision* C(2007) 2110 Final of 10 May 2007; the appeal, Cases T-279 and 289/07, was withdrawn on 23 March 2010.

list that the application of the concept of services of general economic interest has been expanded significantly beyond the basic utilities. The CJ did not, however, accept that commercial port operations are services of general economic interest[163] and it has sometimes left open the status of the services provided, and said that even if they were of general economic interest the other criteria in Article 106(2) were not fulfilled.[164]

Extracts from the judgments in the leading cases on what amounts to a service of general economic interest are set out in Section 6.E.iii as they usually deal also with the question of whether non-compliance with the Treaty rules is essential to the fulfilment of the entrusted tasks. However, the following extract from *BUPA*, the facts of which have already been given, deals with the width of the Member States' discretion to define SGEIs and with what is meant by 'universal service'. In paragraph 167 the GC stresses that in an area such as health, which is within the competence of the Member States, the Commission (in taking the decision on State aid) was limited to examining whether there had been a manifest error of assessment.

Case T-289/03, *BUPA* v. *Commission* [2008] ECR II-18

GC

166 As regards competence to determine the nature and scope of an SGEI mission within the meaning of the Treaty, and also the degree of control that the Community institutions must exercise in that context, it follows from paragraph 22 of the Communication on SGEIs…. [2000] and from the case-law of the [General Court] that Member States have a wide discretion to define what they regard as SGEIs and that the definition of such services by a Member State can be questioned by the Commission only in the event of manifest error (see Case T-17/02 *Fred Olsen v Commission*…. paragraph 216 and the case-law there cited).

167 That prerogative of the Member State concerning the definition of SGEIs is confirmed by the absence of any competence specially attributed to the Commission and by the absence of a precise and complete definition of the concept of SGEI in Community law. The determination of the nature and scope of an SGEI mission in specific spheres of action which either do not fall within the powers of the Community, within the meaning of the first paragraph of Article [5 TEU], or are based on only limited or shared Community competence, within the meaning of the second paragraph of that article,[165]remains, in principle, within the competence of the Member States. As the defendant and Ireland maintain, the health sector falls almost exclusively within the competence of the Member States. In that sector, the Community can engage, under Article [168 TFEU] and [5 TEU], only in action which is not legally binding, while fully respecting the responsibilities of the Member States for the organisation and provision of health services and medical care. It follows that the determination of SGEI obligations in this context also falls primarily within the competence of the Member States. That division of powers is also reflected, generally, in Article [14 TFEU], which provides that, given the place occupied by SGEIs in the shared values of the Union as well as their role in promoting social and territorial cohesion, the Community and the Member States, each within their respective powers and within the scope of application of the Treaty, are to take

---

[163] Case C-179/90, *Merci Convenzionali Porto di Genova* v. *Siderurigica Gabrielle* [1991] ECR I-5889; Case C-242/95, *GT-Link* v. *De Danske Statsbaner (DSB)* [1997] ECR I-4449.

[164] e.g., Case C-203/96, *Chemische Afvalstoffen Dusseldorp BV* v. *Minister van Volkshuisvesting, Ruimtelijke Ordening en Milieubeheer* [1998] ECR I-4075.

[165] Art. 5 TEU replaced Art. 5 EC to which this judgment actually refers. Both Articles deal with the competence of respectively the EU and the EC. Art. 5 TEU is more detailed and specific but does not alter the principle upon which the GC relied here.

care that such services operate on the basis of principles and conditions which enable them to fulfil their missions.

168 In that regard, the applicants cannot validly rely on Case 41/83 *Italy v Commission*, paragraph 100 above (paragraph 30), to demonstrate the need for full and unrestricted control by the Community institutions of the existence of an SGEI mission in the health sector....

169 Consequently, the control which the Community institutions are authorised to exercise over the use of the discretion of the Member State in determining SGEIs is limited to ascertaining whether there is a manifest error of assessment. In the contested decision (recital 44), the Commission did in fact exercise that control by considering whether Ireland's assessment of the presence of an SGEI mission and of the characterisation of the PMI obligations as SGEI obligations was vitiated by a manifest error.

170 Accordingly, the complaint that the Commission unlawfully delegated to the Irish authorities the definition of the SGEIs in question and that it failed to exercise full and unrestricted control of the assessment made by those authorities with respect to a strict and objective definition of the SGEIs in Community law cannot be upheld.

iii) The existence of an SGEI mission in the present case

...

172 ... In that regard, the Court notes at the outset that even though the Member State has a wide discretion when determining what it regards as an SGEI, that does not mean that it is not required, when it relies on the existence of and the need to protect an SGEI mission, to ensure that that mission satisfies certain minimum criteria common to every SGEI mission within the meaning of the EC Treaty, as explained in the case-law, and to demonstrate that those criteria are indeed satisfied in the particular case. These are, notably, the presence of an act of the public authority entrusting the operators in question with an SGEI mission and the universal and compulsory nature of that mission. Conversely, the lack of proof by the Member State that those criteria are satisfied, or failure on its part to observe them, may constitute a manifest error of assessment, in which case the Commission is required to make a finding to that effect, failing which the Commission itself makes a manifest error. Furthermore, it follows from the case-law on Article [106(2)] that the Member State must indicate the reasons why it considers that the service in question, because of its specific nature, deserves to be characterised as an SGEI and to be distinguished from other economic activities (see, to that effect, *Merci Convenzionali Porto di Genova*, paragraph 97 above, paragraph 27, and *Enirisorse*, paragraph 131 above, paragraphs 33 and 34). In the absence of such reasons, even a marginal review by the Community institutions ....with respect to the existence of a manifest error by the Member State in the context of its discretion would not be possible.

173 It is in the light of those considerations that the Court will examine the complaints whereby the applicants seek to demonstrate that in this case the Commission was wrong to accept the existence of an SGEI mission.

...

4) The universal and compulsory nature of the services coming within the SGEI mission

185 The applicants submit that the fact that the PMI services are not universal and compulsory by nature supports their conclusion that there is no SGEI mission in this case.

General observations

186 As regards the universal nature of the PMI services, it must be noted at the outset that, contrary to the theory put forward by the applicants, it does not follow from Community law that, in order to be capable of being characterised as an SGEI, the service in question must constitute a universal service in the strict sense, such as the public social security scheme. In effect, the concept of universal service, within the meaning of Community law, does not mean that the service in question must respond to a need common to the whole population or be supplied throughout a territory (see, in that regard, *Ahmed Saeed Flugreisen*, paragraph 181 above, paragraph 55; *Corsica Ferries France*, paragraph 97 above,

paragraph 45; and *Olsen v Commission*, paragraph 166 above, paragraph 186 et seq.). As stated at recital 47 to the contested decision, with reference to paragraph 14 of the communication on SGEIs, although those characteristics correspond to the classical type of SGEI, and the one most widely encountered in Member States, that does not preclude the existence of other, equally lawful, types of SGEIs which the Member States may validly choose to create in the exercise of their discretion.

187 Accordingly, the fact that the SGEI obligations in question have only a limited territorial or material application or that the services concerned are enjoyed by only a relatively limited group of users does not necessarily call in question the universal nature of an SGEI mission within the meaning of Community law. It follows that the applicants' restrictive understanding of the universal nature of an SGEI, based on certain Commission reports or documents, the content of which, moreover, is not legally binding, is not compatible with the scope of the discretion which Member States have when defining an SGEI mission. Consequently, that argument must be rejected as unfounded.

188 As regards the argument that the PMI services represent only optional, indeed 'luxury', financial services, intended to provide complementary or supplementary cover by reference to the compulsory universal services provided for by the public health insurance system, the Court observes that the compulsory nature of the service in question is an essential condition of the existence of an SGEI mission within the meaning of Community law. That compulsory nature must be understood as meaning that the operators entrusted with the SGEI mission by an act of a public authority are, in principle, required to offer the service in question on the market in compliance with the SGEI obligations which govern the supply of that service. From the point of view of the operator entrusted with an SGEI mission, that compulsory nature—which in itself is contrary to business freedom and the principle of free competition—may consist, inter alia, particularly in the case of the grant of an exclusive or special right, in an obligation to exercise a certain commercial activity independently of the costs associated with that activity (see also, to that effect, paragraph 14 of the communication on SGEIs). In such a case, that obligation constitutes the counterpart of the protection of the SGEI mission and of the associated market position by the act which entrusted the mission. In the absence of an exclusive or special right, the compulsory nature of an SGEI mission may lie in the obligation borne by the operator in question, and provided for by an act of a public authority, to offer certain services to every citizen requesting them (see also, to that effect, paragraph 15 of the communication on SGEIs).

189 Contrary to the applicants' opinion, however, the binding nature of the SGEI mission does not pre-suppose that the public authorities impose on the operator concerned an obligation to provide a service having a clearly predetermined content . . . In effect, the compulsory nature of the SGEI mission does not preclude a certain latitude being left to the operator on the market, including in relation to the content and pricing of the services which it proposes to provide. In those circumstances, a minimum of freedom of action on the part of operators and, accordingly, of competition on the quality and content of the services in question is ensured, which is apt to limit, in the community interest, the scope of the restriction of competition which generally results from the attribution of an SGEI mission, without any effect on the objectives of that mission.

190 It follows that, in the absence of an exclusive or special right, it is sufficient, in order to conclude that a service is compulsory, that the operator entrusted with a particular mission is under an obligation to provide that service to any user requesting it. In other words, the compulsory nature of the service and, accordingly, the existence of an SGEI mission are established if the service-provider is obliged to contract, on consistent conditions, without being able to reject the other contracting party. That element makes it possible to distinguish a service forming part of an SGEI mission from any other service provided on the market and, accordingly, from any other activity carried out in complete freedom (see, to that effect, *GT-Link*, paragraph 97 above, paragraph 53, and *Merci Convenzionali Porto di Genova*, paragraph 97 above, paragraph 27).

The GC therefore held that Ireland's PMI scheme did have an SGEI mission. This was despite the fact that it was not 'a universal service in the strict sense' of responding to a need common to the entire population or being supplied throughout a territory. It did not matter that there was a limited territorial or material application or that the services concerned were enjoyed by only a relatively limited group of users (paragraph 187). Thus the GC had a wider conception of 'universal service' than that set out in some Commission documents. The important thing was the compulsory nature of the service and the fact that the service-provider was obliged to contract, on consistent conditions, and could not refuse the other contracting party (paragraph 190). It is these features which define an SGEI.

(iii) Obstruct the Performance of the Particular Tasks Assigned to Them

Even if an activity is accepted as a service of general economic interest it still has to be shown that compliance with the Treaty rules would 'obstruct the performance' of the particular tasks assigned to the undertaking. As Article 106(2) is a derogation from the normal rules it is for those claiming its benefit to show that its terms are satisfied.

Until 1993 the CJ took a very strict view of the 'obstruct the performance' test. Thus, in *Höfner v. Macrotron* the CJ accepted that the Bundesanstalt had been entrusted with services of general economic interest but said that such an undertaking remained subject to the competition rules 'unless and to the extent to which it is shown that their application is *incompatible* [emphasis added] with the discharge of its duties';[166] in *Merci Convenzionali*[167] it said that even if services of general economic interest had been involved it would not have been necessary for the undertaking to infringe the Treaty rules; in *British Telecom*[168] it said that Italy had failed to establish that compliance by BT with the competition rules would obstruct it in carrying out its tasks; and in *GB-Inno-BM SA*[169] it did not accept that the undertaking entrusted with the public telephone network also needed power to lay down the standards for telephone equipment and to check rival equipment suppliers' compliance with them.[170]

The CJ changed its approach in *Corbeau*,[171] and recognised that Article 106(2) contains what is in effect a proportionality requirement. The facts of *Corbeau* have already been given. It will be recalled that the CJ considered both Article 106(1) and Article 106(2) and seemed to say that Member States may grant special or exclusive rights only insofar as they entrust undertakings with services of general economic interest and the criteria in Article 106(2) are fulfilled.[172] The Court went on to consider the application of Article 106(2).

---

[166] Case C-41/90, *Höfner v. Macroton* [1991] ECR I-1979, para. 24.

[167] Case C-179/90, *Merci Convenzionali Porto di Genova v. Siderurigica Gabrielle* [1991] ECR I-5009.

[168] Case 41/83, *Italy v. Commission* [1985] ECR 873.

[169] Case C-18/88, *RTT v. GB-Inno-BM SA* [1991] ECR I-5973.

[170] See also Case 66/86, *Ahmed Saeed Flugreisen and Silver Line Reiseburo GmbH v. Zentrale zur Bёkampf Unlauteren Wettwerbs eV* [1989] ECR 803; Commission Decision, *Dutch Courier Services* [1990] OJ L10/47, [1990] 4 CMLR 947.

[171] Case C-320/91, *Corbeau* [1993] ECR I-2533.

[172] Case C-320/91, *Corbeau* [1993] ECR I-2533, para. 14.

Case C-320/91, *Corbeau* [1993] ECR I-2533

Court of Justice

15. As regards the services at issue in the main proceedings, it cannot be disputed that the Régie des Postes is entrusted with a service of general economic interest consisting in the obligation to collect, carry and distribute mail on behalf of all users throughout the territory of the Member State concerned, at uniform tariffs and on similar quality conditions, irrespective of the specific situations or the degree of economic profitability of each individual operation.

16. The question which falls to be considered is therefore the extent to which a restriction on competition or even the exclusion of all competition from other economic operators is necessary in order to allow the holder of the exclusive right to perform its task of general interest and in particular to have the benefit of economically acceptable conditions.

17. The starting point of such an examination must be the premise that the obligation on the part of the undertaking entrusted with that task to perform its services in conditions of economic equilibrium presupposes that it will be possible to offset less profitable sectors against the profitable sectors and hence justifies a restriction of competition from individual undertakings where the economically profitable sectors are concerned.

18. Indeed, to authorize individual undertakings to compete with the holder of the exclusive rights in the sectors of their choice corresponding to those rights would make it possible for them to concentrate on the economically profitable operations and to offer more advantageous tariffs than those adopted by the holders of the exclusive rights since, unlike the latter, they are not bound for economic reasons to offset losses in the unprofitable sectors against profits in the more profitable sectors.

19. However, the exclusion of competition is not justified as regards specific services dissociable from the service of general interest which meet special needs of economic operators and which call for certain additional services not offered by the traditional postal service, such as collection from the senders' address, greater speed or reliability of distribution or the possibility of changing the destination in the course of transit, in so far as such specific services, by their nature and the conditions in which they are offered, such as the geographical area in which they are provided, do not compromise the economic equilibrium of the service of general economic interest performed by the holder of the exclusive right.

20. It is for the national court to consider whether the services at issue in the dispute before it meet those criteria.

21. The answer to the questions referred to the Court by the Tribunal Correctionnel de Liége should therefore be that it is contrary to Article [106] for legislation of a Member State which confers on a body such as the Régie des Postes the exclusive right to collect, carry and distribute mail, to prohibit, under threat of criminal penalties, an economic operator established in that State from offering certain specific services dissociable from the service of general interest which meet the special needs of economic operators and call for certain additional services not offered by the traditional postal service, in so far as those services do not compromise the economic equilibrium of the service of general economic interest performed by the holder of the exclusive right. It is for the national court to consider whether the services in question in the main proceedings meet those criteria.

In this judgment the Court accepted that the operation of a basic postal system providing a universal service is a service of general economic interest and that the normal principles of competition law will not apply to the extent necessary to preserve it through cross-subsidy. The undertaking must have 'economically acceptable conditions' (paragraph 16) and be able to perform its task in 'conditions of economic equilibrium' (paragraph 17). If competitors are allowed to come in and 'cherry-pick' or 'cream-skim' the most profitable parts of the system the holder of the exclusive right required to operate the universal service cannot operate under economically acceptable conditions. The Court said, however, in paragraph 19 that this does not justify the exclusion of competition from additional services, separable from the basic public service, if these could be offered by other undertakings without compromising the economic viability of the latter. *Corbeau* is a paradoxical case: it is the high-water mark of hostility by the Court to the very existence of statutory monopoly in the context of Article 106(1) but the dawn of a much more flexible and generous (to incumbents) interpretation of Article 106(2).

The CJ elaborated on the *Corbeau* ruling in *Commission* v. *Netherlands*. It said again that the entrusted undertaking must be allowed 'economically acceptable conditions'. It also said that the undertaking does not have to prove that there is no other way but the impugned measure whereby it could carry out its task.[173]

Case 157/94, *Commission* v. *Netherlands* (Re Electricity Imports) [1997] ECR I-5699

Court of Justice

52. ... it is not necessary, in order for the conditions for the application of Article [106(2)] to be fulfilled, that the financial balance or economic viability of the undertaking entrusted with the operation of a service of general economic interest should be threatened. It is sufficient that, in the absence of the rights at issue, it would not be possible for the undertaking to perform the particular tasks entrusted to it, defined by reference to the obligations and constraints to which it is subject.

53. Moreover, it follows from the *Corbeau* judgment.... that the conditions for the application of Article [106(2)] are fulfilled in particular if maintenance of those rights is necessary to enable the holder of them to perform the tasks of general economic interest assigned to it under economically acceptable conditions.

...

58. Whilst it is true that it is incumbent upon a Member State which invokes Article [106(2)] to demonstrate that the conditions laid down by that provision are met, that burden of proof cannot be so extensive as to require the Member State, when setting out in detail the reasons for which, in the event of elimination of the contested measures, the performance, under economically acceptable conditions, of the tasks of general economic interest which it has entrusted to an undertaking would, in its view, be jeopardized, to go even further and prove, positively, that no other conceivable measure, which by definition would be hypothetical, could enable those tasks to be performed under the same conditions.

In *Corbeau* the Court did not consider whether the universal service provision could be achieved by a less extreme measure than granting a monopoly. Universal service and cross-subsidisation are not inseparable: it is possible for the State to subsidise the universal service, for example. It will be noted that it was left (paragraph 21) to the national court actually to determine whether or not the additional services *were* severable and able to be operated by other undertakings without prejudicing the economic equilibrium of the traditional postal service. This left the national court with a difficult task involving extensive economic analysis. It had to decide the extent of the cross-subsidisation, and how far this was necessary to maintain the 'economic equilibrium'.[174] Cross-subsidisation is a problematic issue, particularly in respect of network monopolies.

---

[173] Cf. the Opinion of Darmon AG in Case C-393/92, *Gemeente Almelo and others* v. *Energiebedrijf Ijsselmij NV* [1994] ECR I-1477, on this point.

[174] See L. Hancher, 'Casenote on *Corbeau*' (1994) 31 CMLRev 105 at 119–120. For the issue of the direct effect of Art.106, see Section 7, p. 652.

Issues similar to those in *Corbeau* arose in *Almelo* where the Court dealt with a preliminary reference from a Dutch court seised of litigation between regional and local electricity distributors concerning, inter alia, the legality of an exclusive purchasing clause.

Case C-393/92, *Gemeente Almelo and Others* v. *Energiebedrijf Ijsselmij NV* [1994] ECR I-1477

Court of Justice

46. Article [106(2)] provides that undertakings entrusted with the operation of services of general economic interest may be exempted from the application of the competition rules contained in the Treaty in so far as it is necessary to impose restrictions on competition, or even to exclude all competition, from other economic operators in order to ensure the performance of the particular tasks assigned to them (see the judgment in Case C-320/91 *Corbeau*…. paragraph 14).

47. As regards the question whether an undertaking such as IJM has been entrusted with the operation of services of general interest, it should be borne in mind that it has been given the task, through the grant of a non-exclusive concession governed by public law, of ensuring the supply of electricity in part of the national territory.

48. Such an undertaking must ensure that throughout the territory in respect of which the concession is granted, all consumers, whether local distributors or end-users, receive uninterrupted supplies of electricity in sufficient quantities to meet demand at any given time, at uniform tariff rates and on terms which may not vary save in accordance with objective criteria applicable to all customers.

49. Restrictions on competition from other economic operators must be allowed so far as they are necessary in order to enable the undertaking entrusted with such a task of general interest to perform it. In that regard, it is necessary to take into consideration the economic conditions in which the undertaking operates, in particular the costs which it has to bear and the legislation, particularly concerning the environment, to which it is subject.

50. It is for the national court to consider whether an exclusive purchasing clause prohibiting local distributors from importing electricity is necessary in order to enable the regional distributor to perform its task of general interest.

Here again, the CJ accepted that the undertaking provided a service of general economic interest and that Article 106(2) allows the restrictions of competition necessary for the performance of its universal service obligations (although it was for the national court to make the decision whether the actual restriction at issue in the case was necessary for that purpose). Ross comments that *Almelo*, reinforcing *Corbeau*, was a movement towards recognising the value of public service independently of its economic viability because 'it clearly indicated that the availability of the derogation was to be measured by a balancing exercise based upon competing priorities rather than inhibiting that choice by insisting upon narrow economic tests to be satisfied before the normal market rules can be disapplied'.[175]

In *Dusseldorp*,[176] however, where the Court was dealing with an undertaking with a monopoly over certain waste incineration, it was less flexible and reverted to a previous, more stringent approach. It said that even if the task could constitute a task of general economic interest it was for the Dutch Government to show to the satisfaction of the national court that the objective could not be equally

---

[175] M. Ross, 'Art. 16 EC and Services of General Interest: From Derogation to Obligation' (2000) 25 *ELRev* 22, 25.

[176] Case C-203/96, *Chemische Afvalstoffen Dusseldorp BV* v. *Minister van Volkshuisvesting, Ruimtelijke Ordening en Milieubeheer* [1998] ECR I-4075.

achieved by other means, and that Article 106(2) could apply only if it was shown that without the contested measure the undertaking could not carry out its entrusted task.[177]

In some cases, unlike *Corbeau* and *Almelo*, the Court has not left the decision to the national court but has actually decided that the conditions in Article 106(2) were satisfied. This can be seen in *Corsica Ferries France*, *Albany*, and *Deutsche Post*.

Case C-266/96, *Corsica Ferries France SA v. Gruppo Antichi Ormeggiatori del Poro di Genovo Coop. and Others* [1998] ECR I-3949

Under Italian law ships from other Member States were required to use the services of local mooring companies who held exclusive concessions in each port. Corsica Ferries claimed that the Genoa and La Spezia mooring groups were abusing their dominant positions by preventing shipping companies using their own staff to carry out mooring operations, in the excessive nature of the price of the service which bore no relation to the actual cost of the service provided, and in fixing tariffs that varied from port to port for equivalent services. The Italian court asked, inter alia, whether the Treaty prohibited national measures which put the mooring companies in the position to act in this way.

Court of Justice

36. The national court asks whether there is an abuse, on the part of the Genoa and La Spezia mooring groups, of their dominant position on a substantial part of the Common Market by virtue of the exclusive rights conferred upon them by the Italian public authorities.

37. There are three aspects of the abuse alleged in this case. It is said to reside in the grant of exclusive rights to local mooring groups, preventing shipping companies from using their own staff to carry out mooring operations, in the excessive nature of the price of the service, which bears no relation to the actual cost of the service provided, and in the fixing of tariffs that vary from port to port for equivalent services.

38. As regards the definition of the market in question, it appears from the order for reference that it consists in the performance on behalf of third persons of mooring services relating to container freight in the ports of Genoa and La Spezia. Having regard, *inter alia*, to the volume of traffic in those ports and their importance in intra-Community trade, those markets may be regarded as constituting a substantial part of the Common Market (Case C-179/90, *Merci Convenzionali Porto di Genova*... and Case C-163/96, *Raso and Others*...

39. As far as the existence of exclusive rights is concerned, it is settled law that an undertaking having a statutory monopoly in a substantial part of the Common Market may be regarded as having a dominant position within the meaning of Article [102] of the Treaty (Case C-41/90, *Höfner and Elser* v. *Macrotron*.... Case C-260/89, *ERT* v. *DEP*.... *Merci Convenzionali Porto di Genova*....and *Raso and Others*...

40. Next, it should be pointed out that although merely creating a dominant position by granting exclusive rights within the meaning of Article [106 (1)] is not in itself incompatible with Article [102], a Member State is in breach of the prohibitions contained in those two provisions if the undertaking in question, merely by exercising the exclusive rights granted to it, is led to abuse its dominant position or if such rights are liable to create a situation in which that undertaking is led to commit such abuses (Case C-41/90, *Höfner and Elser* v. *Macrotron*...Case C-260/89, *ERT* v. *DEP*...*Merci Convenzionali Porto di Genova*...Case C-323/93, *Centre d'Insemination de la Crespelle*...*Raso and others*...).

---

[177] Case C-203/96, *Chemische Afvalstoffen Dusseldorp BV* v. *Minister van Volkshuisvesting, Ruimtelijke Ordening en Milieubeheer* [1998] ECR I-4075, para. 67.

41. It follows that a Member State may, without infringing Article [102], grant exclusive rights for the supply of mooring services in its ports to local mooring groups provided those groups do not abuse their dominant position or are not led necessarily to commit such an abuse.

42. In order to rebut the existence of such abuse, the Genoa and La Spezia mooring groups rely on Article [106(2)], which provides that undertakings entrusted with the operation of services of general economic interest are to be subject to the competition rules contained in the Treaty only in so far as their application does not obstruct the performance, in law or in fact, of the particular tasks assigned to them. Article [106(2)] further provides that, in order for it to apply, the development of trade must not be affected to such an extent as would be contrary to the interests of the Community.

43. They maintain that the tariffs applied are indispensable if a universal mooring service is to be maintained. On the one hand, the tariffs include a component corresponding to the additional cost of providing a universal mooring service. On the other hand, the difference in the tariffs from one port to another, which, according to the file, result from account being taken, when the tariffs are calculated, of corrective factors reflecting the influence of local circumstances—which would tend to indicate that the services provided are not equivalent—are justified by the characteristics of the service and the need to ensure universal coverage.

44. It must therefore be considered whether the derogation from the rules of the Treaty provided for in Article [106(2)] may fall to be applied. To that end, it must be determined whether the mooring service can be regarded as a service of general economic interest within the meaning of that provision and, if so, first, whether performance of the particular tasks assigned to it can be achieved only through services for which the charge is higher than their actual cost and for which the tariff varies from one port to another, and secondly, whether the development of trade is not affected to such an extent as would be contrary to the interests of the Community (see, to that effect, Case C-157/94, *E.C. Commission* v. *Netherlands...*).

45. It is evident from the file on the case in the main proceedings that mooring operations are of general economic interest, such interest having special characteristics, in relation to those of other economic activities, which is capable of bringing them within the scope of Article [106(2)] Mooring groups are obliged to provide at any time and to any user a universal mooring service, for reasons of safety in port waters. At all events, Italy could properly have considered that it was necessary, on grounds of public security, to confer on local groups of operators the exclusive right to provide a universal mooring service.

46. In those circumstances it is not incompatible with Articles [102] and [106(1)] to include in the price of the service a component designed to cover the cost of maintaining the universal mooring service, inasmuch as it corresponds to the supplementary cost occasioned by the special characteristics of that service, and to lay down for that service different tariffs on the basis of the particular characteristics of each port.

47. Consequently, since the mooring groups have in fact been entrusted by the Member State with managing a service of general economic interest within the meaning of Article [106(2)], and the other conditions for applying the derogation from application of the Treaty rules which is laid down in that provision are satisfied, legislation such as that at issue does not constitute an infringement of Article [102], read in conjunction with Article [106(1)].

As in *Corbeau*, the CJ considered that the exclusive rights could escape the prohibition in Article 106(1) if they satisfied Article 106(2). However, the Court did not leave this determination to the national court, but said that the mooring operations were services of general economic interest provided on a universal basis and that it was, in the circumstances, not incompatible with the Treaty to include supplementary costs related to the running of that service and to charge varying tariffs (paragraph 46). Therefore there was no infringement of Article 106(1). There is no explanation of how the Court reached its conclusions in paragraph 46, or of how the supplementary costs arose or what cross-subsidisation was taking place.

The CJ also made a clear decision on the application of Article 106(2) in *Albany*. It will be remembered from the earlier discussion of Article 106(1)[178] that the case concerned the Dutch regime of compulsory affiliation to sectoral pension schemes. The Court considered whether the derogation in Article 106(2) applied, and held that it did because the scheme involved a service of general economic interest which had to operate under 'economically acceptable conditions'.

Case C-67/96, *Albany International BV* v. *Stichting Bedrijfspensioenfonds Textielindustrie* [1999] ECR I-5751

Court of Justice

102. It is important to bear in mind first of all that, under Article [106(2)], undertakings entrusted with the operation of services of general economic interest are subject to the rules on competition in so far as the application of such rules does not obstruct the performance, in law or in fact, of the particular tasks assigned to them.

103. In allowing, in certain circumstances, derogations from the general rules of the Treaty, Article [106(2)] seeks to reconcile the Member States' interest in using certain undertakings, in particular in the public sector, as an instrument of economic or fiscal policy with the Community's interest in ensuring compliance with the rules on competition and preservation of the unity of the common market (Case C-202/88 *France* v. *Commission*... paragraph 12, and Case C-157/94 *Commission* v. *Netherlands*... paragraph 39).

104. In view of the interest of the Member States thus defined they cannot be precluded, when determining what services of general economic interest they entrust to certain undertakings, from taking account of objectives pertaining to their national policy or from endeavouring to attain them by means of obligations and constraints which they impose on such undertakings (*Commission* v. *Netherlands*, cited above, paragraph 40).

105. The supplementary pension scheme at issue in the main proceedings fulfils an essential social function within the Netherlands pensions system by reason of the limited amount of the statutory pension, which is calculated on the basis of the minimum statutory wage.

106. Moreover, the importance of the social function attributed to supplementary pensions has recently been recognised by the Community legislature's adoption of Council Directive 98/49/EC of 29 June 1998 on safeguarding the supplementary pension rights of employed and self-employed persons moving within the Community (OJ 1998 L209, p. 46).

107. Next, it is not necessary, in order for the conditions for the application of Article [106(2)] to be fulfilled, that the financial balance or economic viability of the undertaking entrusted with the operation of a service of general economic interest should be threatened. It is sufficient that, in the absence of the rights at issue, it would not be possible for the undertaking to perform the particular tasks entrusted to it, defined by reference to the obligations and constraints to which it is subject (*Commission* v. *Netherlands*, cited above, paragraph 52) or that maintenance of those rights is necessary to enable the holder of them to perform tasks of general economic interest which have been assigned to it under economically acceptable conditions (Case C-320/91 *Corbeau*...paragraphs 14 to 16, and *Commission* v. *Netherlands*, cited above, paragraph 53).

108. If the exclusive right of the fund to manage the supplementary pension scheme for all workers in a given sector were removed, undertakings with young employees in good health engaged in non-dangerous activities would seek more advantageous insurance terms from private insurers. The progressive departure of 'good' risks would leave the sectoral pension fund with responsibility for an increasing share of 'bad'

---

[178] See Section 5.B, p. 623.

risks, thereby increasing the cost of pensions for workers, particularly those in small and medium-sized undertakings with older employees engaged in dangerous activities, to which the fund could no longer offer pensions at an acceptable cost.

109. Such a situation would arise particularly in a case where, as in the main proceedings, the supplementary pension scheme managed exclusively by the Fund displays a high level of solidarity resulting, in particular, from the fact that contributions do not reflect the risk, from the obligation to accept all workers without a prior medical examination, the continuing accrual of pension rights despite exemption from the payment of contributions in the event of incapacity for work, the discharge by the Fund of arrears of contributions due from an employer in the event of insolvency and the indexing of the amount of pensions in order to maintain their value.

110. Such constraints, which render the service provided by the Fund less competitive than a comparable service provided by insurance companies, go towards justifying the exclusive right of the Fund to manage the supplementary pension scheme.

111. It follows that the removal of the exclusive right conferred on the Fund might make it impossible for it to perform the tasks of general economic interest entrusted to it under economically acceptable conditions and threaten its financial equilibrium.

...

123. The answer to the third question must therefore be that Articles [102] and [106] do not preclude the public authorities from conferring on a pension fund the exclusive right to manage a supplementary pension scheme in a given sector.

It is important to note that, again, the Court (paragraph 107) did not demand that the economic viability of the entrusted undertaking should be threatened without the exclusive right. Article 106(2) can apply where it is necessary to provide economically acceptable conditions. Here again this meant preventing 'cherry-picking': without the exclusive rights other insurers would be able to offer a better deal to companies with predominantly young, healthy workforces. Paragraph 107 was repeated by the CJ in *AG2R Prévoyance*.[179]

The cross-subsidy argument did not succeed, however, in *Air Inter* where the proportionality requirement was not satisfied. There the Commission challenged the granting of exclusive rights on two internal French air routes to Air Inter. The undertaking claimed that domestic air transport in France was based on cross-subsidy between profitable and unprofitable routes, but the Commission and the GC were not convinced.

Case T-260/94, *Air Inter* v. *Commission* [1997] ECR II-997

General Court

138. The application of those articles could, however, be excluded only in as much as they 'obstructed' performance of the tasks entrusted to the applicant. Since that condition must be interpreted strictly, it was not sufficient for such performance to be simply hindered or made more difficult. Furthermore, it was for the applicant to establish any obstruction of its task (see, to that effect, Case 155/73, *Sacchi*...).

139. In that regard, the applicant merely asserts that the organization of domestic air transport was based on a system of cross-subsidy between profitable routes and unprofitable routes and that the exclusivity which had been granted to it on the Orly–Marseille and Orly–Toulouse routes was justified by its obligation

---

[179] Case C-437/09, *AG2R Prévoyance v. Beaudout* [2011] ECR I-973, para. 76.

to operate the unprofitable routes regularly and at tariffs that were not prohibitive, in order to contribute to regional development. It does not put a figure on the probable loss of revenue if other air carriers are allowed to compete with it on the two routes in question. Nor has it shown that that loss of income will be so great that it will be forced to abandon certain routes forming part of its network.

140. In any event, the domestic air network system combined with the internal cross-subsidy system to which the applicant refers in support of its case did not constitute an aim in themselves, but were the means chosen by the French public authorities for developing the French regions. The applicant has not argued and still less established that, following the entry into force of Regulation 2408/92, there was no appropriate alternative system capable of ensuring that regional development and in particular of ensuring that loss-making routes continue to be financed (see also the order of the President of the Court in Case C-174/94 R, *France* v. *E.C.Commission*. . .).

141. Consequently, the applicant has not shown that the contested decision would obstruct the performance in law or in fact of the particular task assigned to it. It follows that the plea of infringement of Article [106(2)] cannot be accepted either.

In *Deutsche Post*,[180] the facts of which are given in a previous section,[181] the CJ had to consider a statutory monopolist's exercise of a right (charging for international mail as though it were internal mail) stemming from an international convention. It held that the German Post Office was justified in doing this. Fulfilling the obligations under the UPC was a service of general economic interest and the Court simply stated without further explanation that levying the charges in issue was necessary to the performance of the task in economically balanced conditions. Otherwise the task would be jeopardised.[182] Bartosch points out that this was very favourable treatment of Deutsche Post. He argues that the need for cross-subsidisation should have been more closely examined.

A. Bartosch, 'Casenote on Cases C-147–148/97, *Deutsche Post AG v. Gesellschaft für Zahlungssysteme mbH (GZS) and Citicorp Kartenservice GmbH*' (2001) 38 *CMLRev* 195, 207–208

. . .a postal administration cannot be regarded as entitled to ask for the derogation provided for in Article [106(2)] for each individual element of such a universal service. Deutsche Post AG can consequently on the one hand not be asked to use revenues generated from services dissociable from the universal service concept to cross-subsidize the burdens associated with such universal service, the burden of which has been entrusted to it by the Federal Republic of Germany. . .On the other hand, it has to use revenues from activities that do fall under this universal service to cross-subsidize other less profitable parts of the same. If it were permitted to split up the whole of the universal service into its different elements for the purposes of applying Article [106(2)], it would become possible for the entrusted undertaking to compete effectively with regard to those elements that can be operated profitably and to ask for a derogation from the application of the Treaty's competition rules wherever this is not feasible. Article [106(2)] could therefore be relied on for each individual operation within the universal service that can be shown to operate at a loss. This is exactly why the Court in the. . .*Corbeau* case distinguished between universal services and those which are clearly dissociable from them.

[180] Cases C-147–148/97, *Deutsche Post AG v. Gesellschaft für Zahlungssysteme mbH (GZS) and Citicorp Kartenservice GmbH* [2000] ECR I-825.

[181] Section 5.B, p. 624.

[182] Cases C-147–148/97, *Deutsche Post AG v. Gesellschaft für Zahlungssysteme mbH (GZS) and Citicorp Kartenservice GmbH* [2000] ECR I-825, para. 50.

In *Ambulanz Glöckner*, however, the CJ again took an approach to the cross-subsidisation issue which greatly favoured the incumbent. It identified the emergency ambulance service as being a service of general economic interest subject to universal service but held the extension of provider's exclusive rights to the non-emergency market was justified so that it could subsidise the emergency from the non-emergency service.

Case C-475/99, *Ambulanz Glöckner* v. *Landkreis Südwestpfalz* [2001] ECR I-8089

Court of Justice

55. With regard to those arguments, the medical aid organisations are incontestably entrusted with a task of general economic interest, consisting in the obligation to provide a permanent standby service of transporting sick or injured persons in emergencies throughout the territory concerned, at uniform rates and on similar quality conditions, without regard to the particular situations or to the degree of economic profitability of each individual operation.

56. However, Article [106(2)], read in conjunction with paragraph (1) of that provision, allows Member States to confer, on undertakings to which they entrust the operation of services of general economic interest, exclusive rights which may hinder the application of the rules of the Treaty on competition in so far as restrictions on competition, or even the exclusion of all competition, by other economic operators are necessary to ensure the performance of the particular tasks assigned to the undertakings holding the exclusive rights (Case C-320/91 *Corbeau*... paragraph 14).

57. The question to be determined, therefore, is whether the restriction of competition is necessary to enable the holder of an exclusive right to perform its task of general interest in economically acceptable conditions. The Court has held that the starting point in making that determination must be the premise that the obligation, on the part of the undertaking entrusted with such a task, to perform its services in conditions of economic equilibrium presupposes that it will be possible to offset less profitable sectors against the profitable sectors and hence justifies a restriction of competition from individual undertakings in economically profitable sectors (*Corbeau*, paragraphs 16 and 17).

58. In the case before the national court, for the reasons advanced by the Landkreis, the ASB, the Vertreter des öffentlichen Interesses, Mainz, and the Austrian Government, which are set forth in paragraph 53 above and which are for the national court to assess, it appears that the system put in place by the RettDG 1991 is such as to enable the medical aid organisations to perform their task in economically acceptable conditions. In particular, the evidence placed before the Court shows that the revenue from non-emergency transport helps to cover the costs of providing the emergency transport service.

59. It is true that, in paragraph 19 of *Corbeau*, the Court held that the exclusion of competition is not justified in certain cases involving specific services, severable from the service of general interest in question, if those services do not compromise the economic equilibrium of the service of general economic interest performed by the holder of the exclusive rights.

60. However, that is not the case with the two services now under consideration, for two reasons in particular. First, unlike the situation in *Corbeau*, the two types of service in question, traditionally assumed by the medical aid organisations, are so closely linked that it is difficult to sever the non-emergency transport services from the task of general economic interest constituted by the provision of the public ambulance service, with which they also have characteristics in common.

61. Second, the extension of the medical aid organisations' exclusive rights to the non-emergency transport sector does indeed enable them to discharge their general-interest task of providing emergency transport in conditions of economic equilibrium. The possibility which would be open to private operators to concentrate, in the non-emergency sector, on more profitable journeys could affect the degree of

economic viability of the service provided by the medical aid organisations and, consequently, jeopardise the quality and reliability of that service.

62. However, as the Advocate General explains in point 188 of his Opinion, it is only if it were established that the medical aid organisations entrusted with the operation of the public ambulance service were manifestly unable to satisfy demand for emergency ambulance services and for patient transport at all times that the justification for extending their exclusive rights, based on the task of general interest, could not be accepted.

63. In this regard, Ambulanz Glöckner contends that Paragraph 18(3) of the RettDG 1991 does indeed promote the creation of a situation in which the medical aid organisations are not always able to satisfy all demand for patient transport services at acceptable prices (see, by analogy, Case C-41/90 *Höfner and Elser...* paragraph 31, and Case C-55/96 *Job Centre...* paragraph 35). On the other hand, the Landkreis and the ASB maintain that the public ambulance service is incontestably able to satisfy both demand for emergency transport and that for patient transport, even without private undertakings.

64. It is for [the] national court to determine whether the medical aid organisations which occupy a dominant position on the markets in question are in fact able to satisfy demand and to fulfil not only their statutory obligation to provide the public emergency ambulance services in all situations and 24 hours a day but also to offer efficient patient transport services.

65. Consequently, a provision such as Paragraph 18(3) of the RettDG 1991 is justified under Article [106(2)] provided that it does not bar the grant of an authorisation to independent operators where it is established that the medical aid organisations entrusted with the operation of the public ambulance service are manifestly unable to satisfy demand in the area of emergency transport and patient transport services.

In *Slovakian Hybrid Mail Services*[183] the Commission stated that the presumption in the Postal Directive[184] of *prima facie* justification under Article 106(2) for services covered by the 'reserved area' as defined in that directive did not apply in that case because the hybrid service had previously been liberalised without endangering the public service. Therefore, extending the monopoly to cover hybrid mail again needed specific justification. Under the Postal Directive it is only possible to subsidise the universal service through extending or maintaining the reserved areas. It was not possible to finance any other type of service.[185]

In OTOC[186] there was no cross-subsidisation issue. The case concerned the rules for the training of chartered accountants in Portugal. The CJ doubted, on the documents before it, whether 'compulsory training of chartered accountants is of general economic interest exhibiting special characteristics as compared with that of other economic activities' but even if it was the CJ was doubtful that the restrictions on competition were necessary to the performance of OTOC's tasks and therefore the application of the competition rules would not obstruct it.[187]

---

[183] COMP/39.562, [2009] 4 CMLR 663, on appeal Case T-556/08, *Slovenská Poštá* v. *Commission*, judgment pending.

[184] Dir. 97/67 [1998] OJ L15/14 as amended.

[185] *Slovakian Hyrid Mail*, paras. 165–167. For the sectoral regime in the postal sector, see Bellamy and Child *European Law of Competition* (cited in n. 141), 12.135–12.147.

[186] Case C-1/2012, *Ordem dos Técnicos Oficiais de Contas (OTOC)* v. *Autoridade da Concorrência*, 28 February 2013.

[187] Case C-1/2012, *Ordem dos Técnicos Oficiais de Contas (OTOC)* v. *Autoridade da Concorrência*, 28 February 2013, paras 104–107. OTOC is the Portuguese Order of Chartered Accountants, empowered by statute to plan, organise, and provide compulsory training schemes for members. OTOC adopted a regulation the effect of which was to impose stricter conditions on independent providers than on its own training operation.

F. NO EFFECT ON TRADE CONTRARY TO THE INTERESTS OF THE UNION

Article 106(2) contains the proviso that 'the development of trade must not be affected to such an extent as would be contrary to the interests of the Union'. This is similar to the proviso in Article 36 TFEU that the derogation from the free movement provisions should not be 'a means of arbitrary discrimination or a disguised restriction on trade between Member States', but unlike that proviso the tailpiece to Article 106(2) has not so far been of importance. It was pleaded by the Commission in the electricity cases[188] but the CJ held that the Commission had provided no explanation to demonstrate such an effect on trade. The proviso must denote something different from the phrase 'affect trade between Member States' in Articles 101 and 102 because without such an effect on trade those Articles cannot apply at all. It may, however, simply be a further proportionality requirement. In *De Post-La Poste*[189] the Commission held that the undertaking with a statutory monopoly over the general letter mail in Belgium had infringed Article 102 by operating a tying policy in order to exclude competitors from the neighbouring business-to-business (B2B) market. The undertaking did not rely on Article 106(2) in its defence, but the Commission went out of its way to say that, if it had, the sealing off of a national market would have impeded trade to an extent contrary to the Community interest.

7. THE DIRECT EFFECT OF ARTICLE 106(1) AND (2)

A. ARTICLE 106(1)

As Article 106(1) prohibits Member States from enacting or maintaining measures contrary to rules contained in the Treaties it applies, as we have seen, only in conjunction with some other rule. Whether or not individuals may invoke Article 106(1) before a national court, i.e. whether Article 106(1) is directly effective, therefore depends on whether the rule infringed by the Member State is itself directly effective. In *Höfner v. Macrotron*, for example, the litigant was able to claim in the German court that the German laws breached Article 106(1) because they led to an infringement of Article 102, which is directly effective. The litigant was therefore able to rely on the Articles in conjunction with one another.

B. ARTICLE 106(2)

There are four questions raised by Article 106(2): is the undertaking 'entrusted' with a task; is that task a 'service of general economic interest'; would the task be obstructed by complying with the Treaty rules; and would a derogation from the Treaty rules have an effect on trade contrary to the interests of the Union?

As far as the first two questions are concerned, the Court confirmed long ago that Article 106(2) is directly effective in that a national court may decide whether or not an undertaking has been entrusted with a service of general economic interest.[190]

---

[188] Case 157/94, *Commission v. Netherlands (Re Electricity Imports)* [1997] ECR I-5699, paras. 66–72; Case C-159/94, *Commission v. France (Re Electricity and Gas Imports)* [1997] ECR I-5815, paras. 109–116.

[189] [2002] OJ L61/32.

[190] Case 127/73, *BRT v. SABAM* [1974] ECR 313.

As for the third question, whether the task would be obstructed, for a long time it appeared from the judgment in *Muller*[191] that the national courts were not competent to answer it and that only the Community institutions could decide the point in favour of the undertaking. However, the position has changed and the CJ expressly said at paragraph 34 of the *ERT* judgment[192] that it is for the national court to verify whether the application of the competition rules would obstruct the undertaking's task. The CJ also left this determination to the national court in *Corbeau* and *Almelo*.

The fourth question is more problematic as it requires an assessment of whether the *interests of the Union* would be adversely affected. At first sight the issue seems more suited to a decision by the Commission than to a judgment by a national court. However, it may be that this is not an additional requirement at all, but part of the overall proportionality requirement to which the first sentence is subject.[193] If this is so Article 106(2) as a whole has direct effect. On the other hand, it can also be argued that only the first sentence of Article 106(2) has direct effect and that the Commission alone has competence to declare that the interest of the Union is being infringed.[194] There is as yet no definitive ruling of the EU Courts on the point.

8. ARTICLE 106(3)

A. THE AMBIT OF THE PROVISION

Article 106(3) provides that the Commission shall ensure the application of the Article[195] and gives it the supervisory and policing powers with which to do this. These powers are in addition to the general powers conferred upon the Commission elsewhere in the Treaties. Under Article 106(3) the Commission can adopt two types of measure, decisions addressed to Member States (not to the undertakings themselves, in respect of whom the Commission must use its powers under Regulation 1/2003) and directives. The Commission may use these powers either to deal with some existing infringement of the Treaty rules or to take steps to prevent future infringements. The adoption of directives to deal with the latter has proved particularly contentious.

B. DECISIONS

The power to issue decisions addressed to Member States provides the Commission with an enforcement mechanism in respect of infringements of the Treaty in addition to the general power in Article 258 TFEU.[196] However, the Commission still has to comply with the general principles of Union law, such as giving reasons and allowing the addressee to be heard, and failure to do so means that the decision can be quashed.[197] In *max.mobil*[198] the GC held that the Commission was under an obligation to examine complaints based on Article 106 diligently and objectively. However, the CJ overruled the GC and held that the Commission's refusal to act under Article 106(3) is not susceptible to judicial review.[199] The Commission has adopted Article 106(3) decisions in several of the cases

---

[191] Case 10/71, *Ministère Public of Luxembourg v. Muller* [1971] ECR 723; see also Case 155/73, *Sacchi* [1974] ECR 409; Case 172/82, *Syndicat National des Fabricants Raffineurs d'Huile de Graissage v. Inter Huiles* [1983] ECR 555.

[192] Case C-260/89, *Elliniki Radiophonia Tileorasi (ERT) v. DEP* [1991] ECR I-2925; see Section 5.B, p. 611; see also Case 66/86, *Ahmed Saeed Flugreisen and Silver Line Reiseburo GmbH v. Zentrale zur Běkampf Unlauteren Wettwerbs eV* [1989] ECR 803, paras. 55–57.

[193] See Faull and Nikpay (eds.), *The EC Law of Competition* (cited in n. 1), para. 6.205.

[194] See Faull and Nikpay (eds.), *The EC Law of Competition* (cited in n. 1), 6.206.

[195] This is a specific manifestation of the Commission's general duty of enforcement and supervision under Art. 17 TEU.

[196] Cases C-48 and 66/90, *Netherlands and Koninklijke PTT Netherland v. Commission* [1992] ECR I-565.

[197] Cases C-48 and 66/90, *Netherlands and Koninklijke PTT Netherland v. Commission* [1992] ECR I-565.

[198] Case T-54/99, *max.mobil* [2002] ECR II-313.

[199] Case C-141/02 P, *max.mobil* [2005] ECR I-1283.

mentioned in this chapter and in Chapter 7, such as *Spanish Courier Services*,[200] *ANA*,[201] and the essential facilities case, *Port of Rødby*.[202] Following the *Altmark* judgment the Commission issued a decision, now replaced with another, on State aid and public service compensation.[203]

C. DIRECTIVES

The reason that the adoption of directives under Article 106(3) is contentious is that the Commission can thereby legislate alone, without going through any of the usual legislative procedures laid down in Articles 289 to 297 involving other Union institutions. The Member States therefore do not have any opportunity to vote against the measures in the Council, the Parliament is not involved, and the Commission can act where there is no political consensus. This became an issue with regard to liberalisation where there is a thin line to be drawn between harmonisation under Articles 114 and 115 TFEU[204] and what is 'appropriate' under Article 106(3). Directives adopted under Article 106(3) have been challenged by Member States claiming that the wrong legal base was used for their adoption. The Commission used its Article 106(3) powers for the first time in adopting the Transparency Directive[205] which was challenged by France, Italy, and the UK. The CJ confirmed that the Commission was entitled to proceed under Article 106(3) in adopting the Directive, a preventive measure which was aimed at creating greater transparency in the financial relationship between Member States and public undertakings, as it was necessary to its duty of surveillance under the Article.[206]

The Commission used Article 106(3) as the legal basis for two directives in the telecommunications sector, on telecommunications equipment[207] and telecommunications services,[208] both of which were challenged by Member States.[209] In the *Telecommunications Equipment* case the CJ held that Article 106(3) does not give the Commission a general legislative power, but a specific one to deal with State measures concerning legal monopolies.

Case C-202/88, *France* v. *Commission (Telecommunications Equipment)* [1991] ECR I-1223

Court of Justice

23. As regards the allegation that the Commission has encroached on the powers conferred on the Council by Articles [103 and 114 TFEU], those provisions have to be compared with Article [106], taking into account their respective subject-matter and purpose.

---

[200] [1990] OJ L233/19.

[201] [1999] OJ L69/31, [1999] 5 CMLR 103, confirmed on appeal, Case C-163/99, *Portugal v. Commission* [2001] ECR I-2613, concerning discriminatory landing charges at Portuguese airports, discussed in Chap. 7.

[202] [1994] 5 CMLR 457, discussed in Chap. 7.

[203] See Section 9, p. 656.

[204] Ex Arts 94 and 95 EC.

[205] 80/723/EEC [1980] OJ L195/35 as amended [1985] OJ L229/20.

[206] Cases 188–190/80, *France, Italy and the UK v. Commission* [1982] ECR 2545.

[207] Dir. 88/301/EEC [1988] OJ L131/73.

[208] Dir. 90/388 [1990] OJ L192/10.

[209] For other aspects of the litigation, see Section 5.B, p. 608.

24. Article [114] is concerned with the adoption of measures for the approximation of the provisions laid down by law, regulation or administrative action in Member States which have as their object the establishment and functioning of the internal market. Article [103] is concerned with the adoption of any appropriate regulations or directives to give effect to the principles set out in Articles [101] and [102], that is to say the competition rules applicable to all undertakings. As for Article [106], it is concerned with measures adopted by the Member States in relation to undertakings with which they have specific links referred to in the provisions of that article. It is only with regard to such measures that Article [106] imposes on the Commission a duty of supervision which may, where necessary, be exercised through the adoption of directives and decisions addressed to the Member States.

25. It must therefore be held that the subject-matter of the power conferred on the Commission by Article [106(3)] is different from, and more specific than, that of the powers conferred on the Council by either Article [114] or Article [103].

26. It should also be noted that, as the Court held in Joined Cases 188 to 190/80 (*France, Italy and United Kingdom* v. *Commission*... paragraph 14), the possibility that rules containing provisions which impinge upon the specific sphere of Article [106] might be laid down by the Council by virtue of its general power under other articles of the Treaty does not preclude the exercise of the power which Article [106] confers on the Commission.

27. The plea in law alleging lack of powers on the part of the Commission must therefore be rejected.

In this case, although the CJ upheld the Commission's power to legislate over telecommunications equipment it did annul Article 7 of the directive, which required Member States to ensure the telecommunications monopolies did not enter into certain types of long-term contracts. The Court said that 'anti-competitive conduct engaged in by undertakings on their own initiative' could be dealt with only by individual decisions adopted under Articles 101 and 102 and that Article 106(3) was not an appropriate basis. Likewise in the *Telecommunications Services* case[210] the CJ upheld the Commission's right to use Article 106(3) for measures which were necessary for its surveillance function.[211]

The Member States look jealously at the Commission's use of its Article 106(3) powers and the Commission strives to distinguish its surveillance and supervisory powers from other measures. The Open Network Provision Directive,[212] to which the Services Directive was an accompaniment, was adopted under Article 114 because it was a harmonisation measure, dealing with the conditions for access to, and use of, public networks and services.

The Constitutional Treaty of 2004, which never came into force,[213] would have amended Article 106(3) to read:

The Commission shall ensure the application of this Article and shall, where necessary, adopt appropriate European regulations or decisions.

This would, in effect, have enacted the case law discussed earlier and clarified the limited extent of the Commission's powers. In the event the Treaty of Lisbon left Article 106(3) unchanged.

---

[210] Cases C-271, 281, and 289/90, *Spain, Belgium & Italy v. Commission* [1992] ECR I-5833.

[211] Although Art. 8 was annulled on the same grounds as Art. 7 of the Equipment Directive, Dir. 88/301/EEC [1988] OJ L131/73 and the provisions on special rights were annulled for inadequacy of reasons.

[212] Council Dir. 90/387/EEC [1990] OJ L192/1.

[213] See Chap. 2.

9. SERVICES OF GENERAL ECONOMIC INTEREST AND STATE AID

The printed edition of this book does not cover State aid, but it should be noted here that there is a major issue over the financing of services of general economic interest and State aid. In particular the question is whether, or in what circumstances, compensation for services of general economic interest is to be considered a State Aid under Article 107. A series of cases[214] culminated in the ruling in *Altmark*,[215] where the CJ established that compensation that does not exceed what is necessary to cover the minimum possible costs incurred in the discharge of public service obligations is not a State aid.[216] Following the judgment the Commission adopted a decision, 2005/842, now replaced by 2012/21 specifying that certain types of compensation paid by Member States to undertakings dealing with services of general economic interest are compatible with Article 106(2) and exempt from the State aid notification obligation under Article 108.[217]

10. CONCLUSION ON SERVICES OF GENERAL ECONOMIC INTEREST

The significance of SGEIs in the Union is summed up in the following passage.

E. Szyszczak, *The Regulation of the State in Competitive Markets in the EU* (Hart Publishing, 2007), 215–216

The creation of a European idea of services of general economic interest has largely been as a result of negative integration processes. In particular the use of Article [106(1)] to attack public monopolies through the national courts and the use of Article [106(2)] to defend services of general interest from the full rigour of the competition and free market rules. Within this process the European Courts have created ideas of how services of general economic interest should be regulated and how they should perform in competitive markets. The EC Commission, through soft law processes, has built up a concept of a European idea of services of general economic interest, attempting a balance between national and EU competence. Legislative intervention has been through the use of concepts such as public service obligations in the liberalisation processes, and more recently in finding ways in which the state may fund services of general economic interest that are compatible with the new attitudes towards state aid in the EU.

Thus we have only a partial concept of services of general economic interest at the EU level, complemented by national models. However, the litigation and debate over the role of services of general economic interest form part of a wider debate over the future economic and social constitution of Europe and the political battle over competing visions of the European Social Model...

---

[214] Case 240/83, *ADBHU* [1985] ECR 531; Case T-106/95, *Fédération Française des Sociétés d'assurances (FFSA)* [1997] ECR II-0229; Case C-53/00, *Ferring* [2001] ECR I-9067.

[215] Case C-280/00, *Altmark Trans GmbH, Regierungspräsidium Magdeburg v. Nahverkehrsgesellschaft Altmark GmbH* [2003] ECR I-7747.

[216] See S. Santamato and N. Pesaresi, 'Compensation for Services of General Economic Interest: Some Thoughts on the *Altmark* Ruling' (2004) 1 *Competition Policy Newsletter* 1.

[217] [2012] OJ L7/3 (adopted under Art. 106(3)).

11. CONCLUSIONS

1. Since 1990 the question of the relationship between competition law and public services has gone from being a side issue to a matter of central concern.

2. Liberalisation has been a major element of EU activity during the last 20 years. This has given Article 106 great significance.

3. Article 106(1) has been used to attack national monopolies.

4. Union policy on the role of services of general economic interest has developed to the point where they are seen as a core unifying factor in the enlarged Union.

5. The case law on Article 106 is not always consistent. It reflects the tensions that exist within the EU and between Member States on the different choices that can be made in respect of the delivery of public services and to what extent they can be fully marketised.

12. FURTHER READING

A. BOOKS

BELLAMY, G., and CHILD, G. (V. Rose and D. Bailey, eds.), *European Law of Competition* (7th edn, Oxford University Press, 2013), Chap. 11

BUENIDA SIERRA, J. L., *Exclusive Rights and State Monopolies in EC Law* (Oxford University Press, 1999, 2nd edn forthcoming, 2014)

CREMONA, M. (ed.), *Market Integration and Public Service in the EU* (Oxford University Press, 2011)

FAULL, J., and NIKPAY, A., *The EC Law of Competition* (2nd edn, Oxford University Press, 2007), Chap. 6 (J. L. Buenida Sierra)

HANCHER, L., and SAUTER, W., *EU Competition and Internal Market Law in the Healthcare Sector* (Oxford University Press, 2012)

PROSSER, T., *The Limits of Competition Law* (Oxford University Press, 2005)

SZYSZCZAK, E., *The Regulation of the State in Competitive Markets in the European Union* (Hart Publishing, 2007)

B. CHAPTERS IN BOOKS

BARNARD, C., 'EU Citizenship and the Principle of Solidarity', in M. Dougan and E. Spaventa (eds.), *Social Welfare and the Law* (Hart Publishing, 2005)

BOEGER, N., '"New" Social Democracy before the Court of Justice', in J. Bell and C. Kilpatrick (eds.), *Cambridge Yearbook of European Legal Studies* 8 (2005–2006), Chap. 5

FLYNN, L. 'Competition Policy and Public Services in EC Law after the Maastricht and Amsterdam Treaties', in D. O'Keefe and P. Twomey (eds.), *Legal Issues of the Amsterdam Treaty* (Hart Publishing, 1999)

GARCIA, E. M., 'Public Service, Public Services, Public Functions, and Guarantees of the Rights of Citizens: Unchanging Needs in a Changed Context', in M. Freedland and S. Sciarra (eds.), *Public Services and Citizenship in European Law* (Clarendon Press, 1998)

HANCHER, L., 'Community, State and Market', in P. Craig and G. de Búrca (eds.), *The Evolution of EU Law* (Oxford University Press, 1999)

SAUTER, W., 'Universal Service Obligations and the Emergence of Citizens' Rights in European Telecommunications Liberalisation', in M. Freedland and S. Sciarra (eds.), *Public Services and Citizenship in European Law* (Clarendon Press, 1998)

SZYSZCZAK, E., 'Public Service Provision in Competitive Markets' (2001) 20 *YEL* 35 (Oxford University Press)

—— 'Public Service and the Limits to Competition Law', in C. Graham and F. Smith (eds.), *Competition, Regulation and the New Economy* (Hart Publishing, 2004)

VAN MIERT, K., 'Liberalization of the Economy of the European Union: The Game is not (yet) Over', in D. Geradin (ed.), *The Liberalization of State Monopolies in the European Union and Beyond* (Kluwer, 2000)

C. ARTICLES

BARTOSCH, A., 'Casenote on Cases C-147–8/97, *Deutsche Post AG v. Gesellschaft für Zahlungssysteme mbH (GZS) and Citicorp Kartenservice GmbH*' (2001) 38 *CMLRev* 195

BOEGER, N., 'Solidarity and EC Competition Law' (2007) 32 *ELRev* 319

EDWARD, D., and HOSKINS, M., 'Article 90: Deregulation and EC Law. Reflections Arising from the XVI FIDE Conference' (1995) 32 *CMLRev* 157

GYSELEN, L., 'Case note on *Albany, Brentjens'* and *Drijvende Bokken*' (2000) 37 *CMLRev* 425

HANCHER, L., 'Casenote on *Corbeau*' (1994) 31 *CMLRev* 105

—— and BUENIDA SIERRA, J. L., 'Cross-Subsidization and EC Law' (1998) 35 *CMLRev* 901

ROSS, M. G., 'Article 16 EC and Services of General Interest: From Derogation to Obligation?' (2000) 25 *ELRev* 22

—— 'Promoting Solidarity: From Public Services to a European Model of Competition?' (2007) 44 *CMLRev* 1057

—— 'A healthy approach to services of general economic interest? The BUPA judgment of the Court of First Instance' (2009) 34 *ELRev* 127

SANTAMATO, A., and PESARESI, N., 'Compensation for Services of General Economic Interest: Some Thoughts on the Altmark Ruling' (2004) 1 *Competition Policy Newsletter* 1

SAUTER, W., 'Casenote on Case T-289/03, BUPA v. Commission' (2009) 46 *CMLRev* 269

SLOT, P. J., 'Applying the Competition Rules in the Healthcare Sector' [2003] *ECLR* 580

TESAURO, G. 'The Community's Internal Market in the Light of the Recent Case-law of the Court of Justice' (1995) 15 *YEL* 1

VAN DE GRONDEN, J. W., 'Purchasing Care: Economic Activity or Service of General Economic Interest?' [2004] *ECLR* 87

VEERMERSCH, A., 'Casenote on Case C-49/07, *Motosykletistiki Omospondia Ellados NPID v. Ellinkio Dimosi*' (2009) 46 *CMLRev* 1327

9
CARTELS AND OLIGOPOLY

1. CENTRAL ISSUES

1. This chapter deals with explicit and tacit collusion. Explicit and tacit collusion is most likely to occur on oligopolistic markets, that is markets on which there are only a few suppliers.

2. Firms may explicitly collude by concluding naked agreements to fix prices, restrict output, share markets, or rig bids (hardcore cartels).

3. Hardcore cartel activity leads to higher prices, deadweight loss, and reduced incentives for firms to keep costs low and to innovate. They 'diminish social welfare, create allocative inefficiency and transfer wealth from consumers to the participants in the cartel'.

4. Since the 1990s, the Commission has increasingly focused its resources on detecting cartels and fining undertakings involved. The number of cartel decisions adopted each year and the fines imposed have increased dramatically since 2000. In some Member States, as in the US, cartel activity constitutes a criminal offence.

5. Another problem for consumer welfare is tacit collusion (or tacit coordination). Economic theory predicts that, on some oligopolistic markets, the players will recognise that the profitability of what they do is dependent on the behaviour of other firms operating on the market, and that they are all better off if they charge higher prices and earn greater profits. They are thus able to coordinate their behaviour in a similar way to those operating a cartel, without explicitly colluding or agreeing to do so. Such coordination is known as tacit collusion or tacit coordination.

6. A significant problem for competition law is how to deal with tacit collusion. This chapter explores the tools that the EU competition rules offer. In particular, whether, and if so when, Article 101 or Article 102 can be used *ex post* to condemn the behaviour of firms engaged in tacit collusion or behaviour that may be facilitating tacit collusion on a market. Further, whether the EU Merger Regulation can be used *ex ante* to prevent mergers likely to create conditions conducive to tacit collusion (see also Chapter 15).

2. INTRODUCTION

A. CARTELS AND OLIGOPOLY

This chapter examines explicit collusion and tacit collusion (or tacit coordination). Both explicit and tacit collusion may result in a reduction of social welfare, mainly through the raising of prices and the restriction of output. These practices may also damage variety and innovation on a market.

Explicit collusion occurs where undertakings agree, collectively, to exploit their joint economic power and to improve their profitability by raising prices, restricting output, sharing markets or rigging bids. Successful cartels raise the joint profits of all the firms in the industry, maintain the parties' respective position on the market, and achieve pricing stability or an increase in prices. They thus enable the member firms to enjoy market power and profits over and beyond what would otherwise result and to reproduce artificially the market outcomes and welfare loss arising on a monopolised market. Cartel activity is most likely to be successful on oligopolistic markets (markets having only a small number of or a 'few' producers or sellers).

Tacit collusion occurs where undertakings operating on some oligopolistic markets, set their prices 'as if' there had been some explicit collusion between them. Oligopolists may recognise their interdependence and, without explicitly agreeing to do so, align their conduct and charge supra-competitive prices as a rational response to market circumstances. Market conditions may therefore dictate that, without any communication between the undertakings, they align their behaviour in a manner which maximises the profits of the players involved.

This chapter considers how EU competition law applies both to undertakings operating cartels and to undertakings that tacitly coordinate their behaviour on an oligopolistic market. We start by looking in more detail at the difference between 'explicit' and 'tacit' collusion. Section 3 then deals with cartels and other agreements which may be used to bolster cartels or which may facilitate explicit or tacit collusion on a market. Section 4 considers the problem of tacit collusion and whether, in particular, Articles 101 and 102 operate as effective mechanisms for dealing with the problem. It also considers other options that EU competition law might offer to deal with tacit collusion, either *ex ante* or *ex post*.

B. EXPLICIT AND TACIT COLLUSION

(i) Cartels and Explicit Collusion

a. Introduction

In Chapter 10, it will be seen that some horizontal cooperation between undertakings operating at the same level of the market may be highly beneficial to the competitive structure of that market. A joint venture agreement may, for example, seek to improve the parties' competitive position on a market by pooling resources and know-how and sharing the financial risk necessary to launch a new, better, cheaper, and/or more innovative product on that market. In this chapter, however, we focus on cooperation between producers which is purely intended to maximise the joint profits of the parties to the agreement. The objective of a cartel is to maintain the parties' respective positions on the market and to achieve pricing stability or an increase in prices. The parties thus deliberately set out to interfere with free competition (the best environment for ensuring the optimum allocation of resources and continuous economic progress) and to act instead to protect the prosperity of the industrial group as a whole. Such cartels 'diminish social welfare, create allocative inefficiency and transfer wealth from consumers to the participants in the cartel'.[1] The formation and successful operation of a cartel is easier for firms operating in an oligopolistic market, where each firm's profits are strongly dependent upon the course of action chosen by its competitors.

b. Oligopolistic Interdependence, the Prisoner's Dilemma, and Theory of Games

Where only a few players operate on a market firms recognise that the price and output decisions they take are affected by the choices made by their rivals—i.e. that they are interdependent. Further, as it seems clear that 'virtually anything can happen'[2] on oligopolistic markets economic pricing theories seeking to explain the behaviour are numerous:[3]

[1] Commission *XXXIInd Report on Competition Policy* (2002), part 26.

[2] F. M. Sherer and D. Ross, *Industrial Market Structure and Economic Performance* (3rd edn, Houghton Mifflin, 1990), 199.

[3] See e.g., Cournot's and Bertrand's oligopoly pricing model, discussed in S. Bishop and M. Walker, *The Economics of EC Competition Law: Concepts Application and Measurement* (3rd edn, Sweet & Maxwell, 2010), 2.23–2.28.

Some industries—cigarettes and breakfast cereals come readily to mind—succeed in maintaining prices well above production costs for years. Others, despite conditions that would appear at first glance to encourage cooperative behavior, gravitate towards price warfare.[4]

In some oligopolistic markets, therefore, firms may recognise their mutual interdependence and that price cutting by one will lead to price cutting by the others which only leads to decreased profits, so that monopoly (supra-competitive) pricing occurs. In others, however, complications may prevent monopoly pricing from ensuing and competition may be intense.

Because firms in an oligopolistic market recognise that their profits are dependent on the strategies of others on the market, pricing decisions resemble a game or contest between them. In the 1940s the pioneering work of von Neumann and Morgenstern[5] laid the foundation for the development of a new branch of economics, 'game theory', which deals with the strategic interaction of firms and which is now highly developed. Game theory is a helpful tool used to explain and predict the behaviour of firms on an oligopolistic market.

The basic model applied to illustrate decision-making on such a market is the 'prisoners' dilemma'. It demonstrates how both cooperative and non-cooperative outcomes may result on an oligopolistic market. It explains the incentives that exist for firms operating on a market to agree to coordinate their behaviour and to charge prices which are higher than those which would occur on a competitive market. It also illustrates, through the Nash non-cooperative equilibrium, the practical difficulties involved in operating such an agreement. The Nash non-cooperative equilibrium arises 'when, given the behaviour of all other firms in the market, no firm wishes to change its behaviour (i.e. each firm maximises profit, given the behaviour of all the other firms).'[6] The theory thus helps to predict which market conditions are likely to result in price levels above the competitive price. In the extract, Bishop and Walker explain insights from game theory and how it is relevant to the study of oligopoly.

S. Bishop and M. Walker *The Economics of EC Competition Law: Concepts Application and Measurement* (3rd edn, Sweet & Maxwell, 2010), 2.020–2.022

Oligopoly Models

2.020 Neither the paradigm of perfect competition nor that of monopoly provide adequate descriptions of competition in most industries. While the models of perfect competition and monopoly provide a good basis for understanding the basic economic principles, particularly in illustrating the detrimental welfare consequences of monopoly, neither model provides a solid framework on which to base policy prescriptions. These models ignore the interaction between firms and how this interaction may affect the outcomes of the competitive process. In the model of perfect competition, each firm is so small that it can put as much or as little for sale on the market without affecting the market price. For this reason, a firm in a competitive market has no reason to worry about what other firms will do when it makes its own plans. For example, a farmer selling his product in an international market does not consider whether his output will affect the market price but instead takes the market price as a given that he cannot affect. At the other extreme, the monopolist can directly set the market price as it has no rivals to worry about.

But in most markets, firms do need to take into account the commercial decisions of rivals when formulating their own commercial strategy. In most markets, firms recognise that changes in their own plans—*e.g.* prices, planned production and additions to capacity—may affect the decisions of other

[4] Sherer and Ross, *Industrial Market Structure and Economic Performance* (cited in n. 2), 199.

[5] J. von Neumann and O. Morgenstern, *The Theory of Games and Economic Behaviour* (Princeton University Press, 1944). See e.g. J. Tirole, *The Theory of Industrial Organization* (MIT Press, 1988) and Chap. 1.

[6] Bishop and Walker, *The Economics of EC Competition Law: Concepts, Application and Measurement* (cited in n. 3), 2.020.

firms in the industry and will take this into account when making commercial decisions. When addressing what constitutes effective competition, these interactions between firms must be taken into account. This requires one to examine more realistic models of competition: models of oligopolistic behaviour. It is the outcomes produced by these models which should underpin our understanding of effective competition.

With advances in game theory, economic models of competition have become much more sophisticated and have started to take explicit account of the interactions between competing firms. Until the 1970s, the examination of oligopoly received little attention, reflecting the lack of analytical tools available in this area. But since that time, a new branch of economics—non-co-operative game theory—has grown up which addresses directly the strategic interactions between firms. Non-co-operative game theory sees competition between firms as each firm trying to do the best it can subject to the actions of its competitors. A key concept in this analysis is that of the Nash non-co-operative equilibrium. An equilibrium is a Nash non-co-operative equilibrium when, given the behaviour of all other firms in the market, no firm wishes to change its behaviour (*i.e.* each firm maximises profit given the behaviour of all the other firms).

2.021 The concept of a non-co-operative Nash equilibrium can be illustrated by reference to the following game, commonly known as the Prisoners' Dilemma. There are two firms, A and B, who must each decide whether to charge a high price or to charge a low price. There are therefore four possible outcomes: they could both charge high prices, both charge low prices, or one or other could charge a low price whilst the other charges a high price. The numbers in each box in Figure 2.4 denote the profits resulting from the outcome of the decisions of the two firms. The first number in each box shows the profits firm A makes whilst the second number shows the profits firm B makes. For example, if both firms choose a low price, each firm makes profits of 4 (see bottom right quadrant).

Figure 2.4 Illustrating a Nash Equilibrium

2.022 Considering the various outcomes, both firms would prefer an outcome in which both charged a high price to that in which they both charged a low price. In this case, both firms would earn profits of 10 (top left quadrant). But if firm A chooses a high price, what is the best action that firm B can take? With firm A choosing a high price, if firm B also chooses a high price it earns profits of 10 (top left). But if firm B chooses a low price, it earns profits of 30 as a result of undercutting firm A (top right). Hence, given that firm A chooses a high price, firm B's best strategy is to charge a low price.

But if firm B charges a low price, what is the best course of action for firm A? With firm B charging a low price, if firm A charges a high price, it earns zero profits (top right) but if it charges a low price, firm A earns profits of 4 (bottom right quadrant). Hence, firm A will charge a low price if firm B charges a low price. This outcome (the shaded area) represents a Nash equilibrium: the best firm A can do if firm B charges a low price is also to choose a low price and vice versa. In this example, it is also the only Nash equilibrium. In each of the other three quadrants, at least one of the firms wishes to change its behaviour given the behaviour of the other firm. So in the top left quadrant both firms wish to change their behaviour, in the bottom left Firm B wants to change and in the top right Firm A wants to change.

> This simple model shows that while both firms prefer a situation in which both firms charge a high price, the incentive to charge a low price while the rival firm charges a high price results in both firms charging a low price.

The model thus illustrates that firms operating on a market realise that the profitability of what they do is dependent on the behaviour of other firms operating on the market. If firms compete vigorously with one another and charge low prices their overall profits will be considerably less than if they increase prices and increase profits. They are all better off if they coordinate their behaviour and charge higher prices—there is therefore a strong *incentive* to collude explicitly on such markets. As Adam Smith noted in *The Wealth of Nations*:

people of the same trade seldom meet together, even for merriment and diversion, but the conversation ends in a conspiracy against the public, or in some contrivance to raise prices.

A player on the market nevertheless knows that if its competitor charges a high price, it will be better off if it charges a low price (and cheats on any cartel agreement). The Nash equilibrium for a one-shot game is, therefore, for the two firms to lower prices: it is better for both firms to charge a low price, whatever the other one does. Where, however, the game is repeated, it may be possible through recurring market interaction for collusion at the high price to be sustained.

It can be seen from this theory that achieving and sustaining a cartel and coordinated behaviour is not easy. The success of a cartel is dependent upon the parties being able to interact over a period of time and to:

(i) align their behaviour (the competitors must reach an understanding on prices, output, or another factor of competition);

(ii) monitor the market so that deviations from the collusive strategy can quickly be detected (it is the fear of retaliation and punishment that makes the collusion sustainable); and

(iii) punish those that cheat on the cartel agreement.

It is also important that any alignment of behaviour and increase in price is not counteracted by buyer power or new entry into the market.

c. Alignment, Detection, and Punishment of Deviation

Clearly it will be easier to align behaviour on some markets than others: for example, alignment is more feasible where there are fewer players on the market; the players are of similar sizes; their products are very similar (there is little non-price competition for the product); and their cost structures are similar (there will then be less disagreement as to the collusive price to be charged).

Further, the cartel members will need to be able to monitor the market and detect cheating on the collusive arrangement, and to find a mechanism for punishing those that cheat so that cheating becomes unprofitable. Cheating on a cartel is obviously easier the less transparent the markets, the greater the number of firms, where products are differentiated, and where demand is unpredictable. The incentive to cheat is also affected by the 'punishment' that can be levied on a firm that cheats. Punishment usually takes the form of a promise of loss of profits once the collusion is uncovered: i.e. the other firms lower price and expand output so that prices revert to the non-collusive or competitive price.

The operation of internal enforcement mechanisms is inevitably time-consuming and expensive and on some markets may be impossible. These difficulties will become more acute the larger the number of participants and the greater the differentiation in their products. The more elaborate the monitoring and enforcement devices, the more vulnerable the cartel is to detection by competition authorities.

d. Markets Prone to Explicit Collusion

The previous discussion indicates that markets with the following characteristics are more likely to support the successful operation of a cartel.

Fewer Firms and Higher Market Concentration

The fewer the number of operators on the market, or controlling the market, the simpler it is to coordinate actions, the cheaper the costs of collusion, the easier it is to detect cheating, and the easier it is to keep the arrangement secret. Further, the larger the market share that each undertaking has the greater the potential profits to be earned from successful collusion (the bigger the share that each will receive of the collusive pie!). The greater the anticipated rewards the more likely they are to outweigh the risks of detection. Oligopolistic markets are therefore particularly prone to cartelisation.

Barriers to Entry

Barriers to entry are important to the successful operation of a cartel. In the absence of barriers, an increase in price will attract new competitors into the market.

Homogeneous Goods

It will be much easier for firms to collude where products are similar and where the main dimension of competition is price competition (competition is not multidimensional). Where goods are homogeneous the costs of collusion are reduced and the likelihood of successful collusion increased. The possibility for non-price competition through product differentiation is, of course, reduced. Many of the Commission's decisions prohibiting the operation of a cartel have been taken against undertakings whose products offer little scope for differentiation, for example, steel tubes, vitamins, sugar, cement, cartonboard, pvc, soda ash, polypropylene. In *BELASCO*[7] cartel members actually took steps, for example through standardisation and joint advertising, to foster an impression in consumers that their products were homogeneous in order to limit the scope of competition by means of product differentiation.

Firms with Similar Cost Structures or Operating Efficiencies and Market Shares

The more similar the cost structures, the easier it is for the firms to cooperate on prices to be charged. Where costs are not similar, lower-cost firms are likely to want lower prices than other cartel members.

Market Transparency

The more transparent the market, the easier it will be for firms to monitor what their competitors are doing and to detect cheating on, or deviation from, any cartel arrangement.

Mechanisms for Coordination

To be successful cartels may need considerable coordination—to allow alignment of behaviour and to ensure the stability of the cartel. Cartel members thus often, in addition to price-fixing, agree to share markets and/or to adhere to quotas (restriction of output is ordinarily essential to sustain a price rise). The allocation of markets, customers, and quotas may be easier to implement and police than price increases. It may be easier to detect if firms are not complying with quotas or are selling outside their allotted territory. Cartels may use buyback or other schemes to ensure that those selling more than their allocated quotas are punished. In *BELASCO*,[8] for example, a trade association of which the parties to the cartel were members took steps to monitor compliance with a price- and

[7] [1986] OJ L232/15 *aff'd* on appeal, Case 246/86, *Re Roofing Felt Cartel: BELASCO* v. *Commission* [1989] ECR 2117.

[8] [1986] OJ L232/15 *aff'd* on appeal, Case 246/86, *Re Roofing Felt Cartel: BELASCO* v. *Commission* [1989] ECR 2117. See also discussion of the global lysine cartel uncovered in the US, S. Hammond, 'Caught in the Act: Inside an

quota-fixing cartel. Indeed, it employed an accountant which fined undertakings who exceeded the quota allocated to them under the terms of the cartel agreement. Other agreements between firms may also facilitate collusion between them, for example by rendering the market more transparent through agreements to exchange information or vertical agreements containing provisions such as meeting competition clauses or resale price maintenance.[9]

Dispersed Buyers with No Controlling Purchasing Power

Where buyers are numerous and dispersed it is almost impossible to advertise price-cuts or reductions and, consequently, to cheat on the cartel without it being brought to the attention of the other members. Further, it will be easier to operate a cartel where individual buyers do not have controlling purchasing power.

Demand Patterns

Cyclical changes in demand may lead to the breakdown of a cartel. In these circumstances undertakings may find it difficult to determine whether the decline in demand for their products is due to a reduction in demand as a whole or to another member cheating on the cartel. This uncertainty may cause the members to deviate from the terms of the cartel. Further, where large orders are put in for a product occasionally (rather than on a regular basis) there may be a greater temptation for cheating since the gains from cheating in each case will obviously be greater.

Depressed Conditions or Low Innovation Rate

Firms operating in industries in recession or suffering from declining demand may be tempted to adopt price-fixing or other collusive agreements to maintain profits.

In a speech, the then Competition Commissioner Mario Monti referred to these types of factors as those likely to lead to collusive arrangements between market operators. He stated his belief, however, that cartel agreements might also operate outside industries with these traditional characteristics, and a number of the cartels unearthed bear this statement out.

M. Monti, 'Fighting Cartels Why and How? Why Should we be Concerned with Cartels and Collusive Behaviour?' 3rd Nordic Competition Policy Conference, Stockholm, 11–12 September 2000

As we all know, cartels do not occur with the same frequency in all sectors. Indeed, some sectors have been particularly prone to cartelisation. These sectors are generally characterised by a relatively high degree of concentration, significant barriers to entry, homogeneous products, similar cost structures and mature technologies. In such stable sectors it is easier to reach consensus on the collusive outcome and to maintain it. The steel, cement and chemical industries can be mentioned as examples of sectors that fit this description and in which the Commission has in the past uncovered cartels.

However, our experience shows that cartel behaviour is not limited to such traditional industries. Recent investigations concerning the banking sector and the liberal professions demonstrate that we should certainly not lose sight of other sectors. In the case of the liberal professions collusion has generally involved

---

International Cartel', Speech at OECD Competition Committee Working Party No. 3 Public Prosecutors Program, Paris, 18 October 2005.

[9] How provisions requiring buyers to sell at minimum resale prices and other provisions, e.g., meeting competition clauses (a clause providing that a seller will meet any lower price offered to the buyer by a competing seller) and/or most favoured nation clauses (requiring a supplier to offer any price reduction offered to one buyer to all buyers), might facilitate collusion is discussed further in Chap. 11.

the fixing of tariffs. In these sectors it is often quite difficult to assess with precision the level of quality. Price competition is therefore quite an important aspect of competition. It is also interesting to note that in these cases the cartels have virtually always been operated by a trade association. The involvement of an association is necessary due to the large number of operators. One study has found that trade associations were involved in most of the cases that involved more than 10 undertakings. Moreover, in the case of the liberal professions the rules of the association can be a very effective weapon in maintaining discipline.

e. The Desire to Combat and Eliminate Cartels

It is arguable that in the long run most cartels will break down without the intervention of any competition authority. The Commission has, however, uncovered a number of cartels that have been operated successfully over long periods of time: for example, the market-sharing agreement in *Soda Ash*[10] was thought to have been in operation since the nineteenth century and the cartel in *Peroxygen Products*[11] for a period of at least 20 years.[12] In *Sorbates*[13] the Commission found that the investigation had established, beyond any doubt, that the cartel operated 'between the end of December 1978 and 31 October 1996'[14] and in *Organic Peroxides*[15] the cartel was found to have lasted 29 years. In the meantime loss to society as a whole is suffered. It is thus widely accepted that cartels should be deterred.[16] Of all agreements, cartels most contradict the principles of the free market economy as the operators specifically attempt to eliminate or limit the free play of competition. Further, they differ from other agreements considered in this book,[17] in that they are 'naked'. 'They seek to restrict competition without producing any objective countervailing benefits.'[18] They lead to higher prices (transferring wealth from consumers to the cartel), deadweight loss (allocative ineffiency), and, ordinarily, productive inefficiency and dynamic harm resulting from reduced incentives to innovate and to strive for efficiency. The costs of forming and enforcing the cartel are also welfare-reducing,[19]

Cartels harm consumers and have pernicious effects on economic efficiency. A successful cartel raises price above the competitive level and reduces output. Consumers (which include businesses and governments) choose either not to pay the higher price for some or all of the cartelised product that they desire thus forgoing the product, or they pay the cartel price and thereby unknowingly transfer wealth to the cartel operators.

---

[10] [1991] OJ L152/1 annulled on procedural grounds Case T-30/91, *Solvay SA v. Commission* [1995] ECR II-1775 (see Chap. 13) but readopted [2003] OJ L10/1, see Case T-57/01, *Solvay v. Commission* [2009] ECR II-4621.

[11] [1985] OJ L35/1.

[12] In the US a series of cases were taken between 1988 and 1997 against bid-rigging on school milk markets. In some cases, it was thought that the bid-rigging had occurred since the late 1960s, see, e.g., Department of Justice Press Release, 25 April 1997 'Minnesota, Iowa Dairies agreed to plead guilty and will each pay $1 million for participating in milk price fixing conspiracy'.

[13] IP/03/1330.

[14] IP/03/1330.

[15] [2005] OJ L110/44, *aff'd*, Case T-120/04, *Peróxidos Orgánicos SA v. Commission* [2006] ECR II-4441.

[16] See e.g., R. H. Bork, *The Antitrust Paradox* (Basic Books, 1978, reprinted with a new Introduction and Epilogue, 1993), 67.

[17] See especially Chaps. 10–12.

[18] M. Monti, 'Fighting Cartels Why and How? Why should we be concerned with cartels and collusive behaviour?', 3rd Nordic Competition Policy Conference Stockholm, 11–12 Sept. 2000. As they are intrinsically detrimental to the competitive process and are not reasonably related to the lawful realisation of cost-reducing or output-enhancing efficiencies they cannot be held lawful under competition law, see J. Faull and A. Nikpay, *The EC Law of Competition* (2nd edn, Oxford University Press, 2007), para. 8.02.

[19] R. Van den Bergh and P. Camesasca, *European Competition Law and Economics: A Comparative Perspective* (2nd edn, Sweet & Maxwell, 2006), 5.2.1.2. See OFT 386, 'The development of targets for consumer savings arising from competition policy', Chap. 5.

Further, a cartel shelters its members from full exposure to market forces, reducing pressures on them to control costs and to innovate. All of these effects harm efficiency in a market economy.[20]

Cartels have, therefore, provoked strong and hostile reactions from competition enforcement authorities and are generally considered to constitute 'the supreme evil of antitrust'[21] and to be 'the most egregious violations of competition law'.[22] In the EU, the (then) Competition Commissioner Mario Monti has described them as 'cancers on the open market economy'.[23]

It is clear today that most competition authorities agree that one of the, if not the, most important objective of the competition rules is to detect, punish, prevent, and eliminate the operation of 'hard-core cartels'. In a Recommendation of the OECD Council Concerning Effective Action Against Hard Core Cartels, a hardcore cartel was defined as:

an anti-competitive agreement, anti-competitive concerted practice, or anti-competitive arrangement by competitors to fix prices, make rigged bids (collusive tenders), establish output restrictions or quotas, or share or divide markets by allocating customers, suppliers, territories or lines of commerce.[24]

In a subsequent report prepared by the OECD in 2000, *Hard Core Cartels*, urging an OECD anti-cartel programme,[25] it was estimated that cartels cost society billions and thwart the gains sought to be achieved through global market liberalisation.[26] 'The average increase from price fixing is estimated to amount to 10% of the selling price and the corresponding reduction of output to be as high as 20 %. In some recent big cases prices have been increased by the cartel participants 30% (graphite electrodes) and 50 % (citric acid).'[27] At the EU level, cartels also thwart attempts to liberalise and integrate European markets.

It is essential to ensure that the removal of State measures that have shielded companies from competition is not replaced by collusion, having the same effect. Companies that have been used to the absence of effective competition, may have a particularly strong incentive to collude rather than to compete. Indeed, liberalisation of markets and removal of other regulatory obstacles to effective competition increases competition and thereby the payoffs from successful collusion. The higher the degree of competition in a market, the greater the incentive to form a cartel and the greater the harm to the economy and consumers.[28]

Cartels thus pose a serious threat to economies and consumers and there is now 'a global trend toward enhanced sanctions combined with common enforcement techniques'.[29] Many competition authorities now work together through formal and informal bilateral and multilateral

---

[20] *Fighting Hard Core Cartels, Recent Progress and Challenges Ahead* (OECD, 2003), and 'Hard Core Cartels—Harm and Effective Sanctions' (OECD Policy Brief, May 2002), both available at <http://www.oecd.org>.

[21] *Verizon Communications* v. *Law Offices of Curtis V. Trinko*, (2004) 540 U.S. 398, 408.

[22] 'Recommendation of the Council Concerning Effective action Against Hard Core Cartels' OECD Publication C(98)35/FINAL, of May 1998, available on the OECD's website, <http://www.oecd.org>.

[23] Monti, 'Fighting Cartels Why and How?' (cited in n. 18).

[24] OECD Publication C(98)35/FINAL, May 1998, available on the OECD's website, <http://www.oecd.org>. The ICN Cartel Working Group has also prepared Reports on Cartel Settlements (2008) and Cooperation between Competition Agencies in Cartel Investigations (2006).

[25] The findings of this programme were published in OECD, *Fighting Hard Core Cartels* (cited in n. 20), available on the OECD's website.

[26] OECD estimated, for example, that the Graphite electrodes cartel affected $6 billion in commerce worldwide and that the harm of such cartel was up to 65% of this sum, in *Fighting Hard Core Cartels* (cited in n. 20), 97. See also OFT 386, 'The development of targets for consumer savings arising from competition policy', *Economic Discussion Paper* 4, June 2002. In conclusion this report suggests that bid-rigging cartels lead to price increases of 10–20%, whilst price-fixing cartels did not lead so consistently to higher prices, but when they did, the price rises were often well in excess of 10%.

[27] Monti, 'Fighting Cartels Why and How?' (cited in n. 18).

[28] Monti, 'Fighting Cartels Why and How?' (cited in n. 18).

[29] See e.g. G. C. Shaffer and N. H. Nesbitt, 'Criminalizing Cartels: A Global Trend?' (2011) University of Minnesota Law School Legal Studies Research Paper Series, Research Paper No. 11–26, 3.

arrangements to combat such cartels,[30] are prepared to coordinate searches and investigations across jurisdictions, and are increasingly allocating their scarce resources towards the detection and elimination of cartels. Sanctions for those involved in cartels are mounting and leniency regimes are playing a central role in cartel enforcement. Many competition law regimes provide for hefty sanctions for the undertakings or corporations found to be in breach. Although Regulation 1/2003 specifically provides that decisions adopted by the Commission following its administrative procedure 'shall not be of a criminal law nature',[31] a number of the Member States, following the success of the US criminal enforcement programme, have criminalised cartel activity or certain types of it,[32] and the view that individuals responsible for violation of cartel rules should be punished is gaining some traction.[33] In the UK, a criminal cartel offence was introduced in 2003 which applies to individuals who dishonestly agree with others to engage in specified cartel arrangements.[34] Although the offence to date has not led to many convictions, only three individuals (former employees of Dunlop Oil & Marine Ltd involved in the international marine hose cartel[35]) have been found guilty and imprisoned under it, the UK Government has amended the offence (in particular by removing the 'dishonesty' requirement from it) in order to try and make it more effective.[36] In the UK it is also possible for directors of companies in breach of the competition rules to be disqualified from acting as directors for a period of up to 15 years where they contributed to a breach or knew, or should have known, of the breach.[37]

In the US, Richard Posner has commented that '[t]he elimination of the formal cartel from…industries is an impressive, and remains the major, achievement of American antitrust law'.[38] Hardcore cartel activity is prosecuted criminally in the US and, since the mid-1990s, the

---

[30] An International Anti-Cartel Enforcement Workshop has been held each year since 1999 for cartel investigators and prosecutors, see, e.g., 'Status Report: An Overview of Recent Developments in the Antitrust Division's Criminal Enforcement Program', Department of Justice Antitrust Division, 25 February 2004. International cooperation is discussed in Chap. 16. See also, e.g., n. 33.

[31] [2003] OJ L1/1, Art 23(5).

[32] The more states that have criminal regimes the harder it will be for an individual to avoid extradition to a jurisdiction in which a criminal cartel offence was committed. In the UK the criminal cartel offence is an extraditable offence: Enterprise Act 2002, s. 191.

[33] See, e.g., C. Beaton-Wells and A. Ezrachi (eds.), *Criminalising Cartels: Critical Studies of an International Regulatory Movement* (Hart Publishing, 2011), The EU legislature could, possibly, require Member States to impose criminal penalties for European cartel offences. For a discussion of this issue see, e.g., Faull and Nikpay (eds.), *The EC Law of Competition* (cited in n. 18), paras. 8.868–8.874 and W. Wils, 'Does the Effective Enforcement of Articles 81 and 82 Require Not Only Fines on Undertakings But Also Individual Penalties, In Particular Imprisonment?' in C.-D. Ehlermann (ed.), *European Competition Law Annual 2001: Effective Private Enforcement of EC Antitrust Law* (Hart Publishing, 2002); P. H. Roshowicz, 'The Appropriateness of Criminal Sanctions in the Enforcement of Competition Law' [2004] ECLR 12 and G. J Werden and M. J. Simon, 'Why Price Fixers should go to Prison' (1987) 32 *Ant Bull* 917. Some form of criminal regime exists in more than 30 jurisdictions including, e.g., Canada, US, Japan, France, Austria, Norway, South Korea, Iceland, Slovakia, Slovenia, Ireland, Romania, Denmark, Germany, UK, Estonia, Hungary, Czech Republic, South Africa, Mexico and Australia.

[34] Enterprise Act 2002, Part 6. The offence applies to agreements concluded outside the UK if implemented within it.

[35] In this case the defendants had been prosecuted in the US but were returned to the UK under a plea bargain agreement—they pleaded guilty in the UK and were sentenced to terms of imprisonment that exceeded the minimum terms agreed with the US prosecutors. On appeal the Court of Appeal reduced the sentences to the minimum terms agreed with the US authorities (30, 24, and 20 months), see *R v. Whittle and ors* [2008] EWCA Crim 2560. Although no fines were imposed on them, they were disqualified from acting as directors for periods of between five and seven years. In this case, the OFT worked closely with both the Commission (see 'Commission fines marine hose producers € 131 million for market sharing and price-fixing cartel', IP/09/137) and the US Department of Justice, S. D. Hammond, 'Recent Developments, Trends, and Milestones in the Antitrust Division's Criminal Enforcement Program', 26 March 2008, and A. Nikpay, 'Cartel Enforcement: Past, Present and Future', Speech, 11 December 2012.

[36] See Enterprise and Regulatory Reform Act 2013 and e.g., Nikpay, 'Cartel Enforcement: Past, Present and Future' (cited in n. 35).

[37] Enterprise Act 2002, s. 204.

[38] R. A. Posner, *Antitrust Law* (University of Chicago Press, 1976), 39.

Department of Justice (DOJ) has concentrated its enforcement resources on international cartels that victimise American consumers and businesses. Huge fines are now imposed on corporations and executives, and executives are sent to prison for long periods. The DOJ takes the view that individual jail sentences are the most effective deterrent to cartel activity.[39] Further, firms in breach may be liable to treble damages to persons injured by the violation.[40] Damages paid may exceed any fine imposed.[41]

If the Commission once felt inhibited about acting against national champions and industrial giants engaged in the operation of cartels, this can no longer be said to be the case. It is determined to take vigorous action against cartels, believing that their effect is to deprive consumers of the benefits of undistorted competition. The fight against cartels has, since the end of the 1990s, been one of the principal concerns of the Commission[42] and it deploys all the resources necessary to take effective action against them despite the major effort in terms of manpower and lengthy procedure that their identification and combating involves.[43] This policy was not softened following the financial and economic crisis in 2008 in order to allow firms to weather the crisis and to prevent ruinous competition between them.

If we create the impression that it is OK to 'turn a blind eye' to cartels or for an executive to fail to ask questions about suspicious behaviour, then we create only more trouble—not only in competition, but across all our markets. This sort of misbehaviour is infectious. They breed the sorts of complacent cultures that have generated our current financial and economic situation.[44]

The hardening attitude towards cartels has been reflected by a number of factors, for example:

- increasing numbers of decisions have been adopted prohibiting cartels (10 in 2001, nine in 2002, five in 2003, seven in 2004, five in 2005, seven in 2006, eight in 2007, seven in 2008, six in 2009, seven in 2010, four in 2011, and five in 2012);[45]

- increasing fines are imposed on cartel members (see Figure 9.1 and Table 9.1).[46]

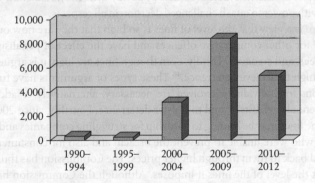

Figure 9.1 Levels of Fines (in € Millions, Adjusted for Court Judgments) 1999–2012

---

[39] See e.g., Hammond, 'Recent Developments, Trends, and Milestones' (cited in n. 35).

[40] Clayton Act, s. 4.

[41] In the *Vitamins* cartel case, e.g., the defendants agreed to pay US customers more than $1 billion in damages, see 'Status Report: An Overview of Recent Developments in the Antitrust Division's Criminal Enforcement Program' DOJ Antitrust Division, 25 February 2004.

[42] See Monti, 'Fighting Cartels Why and How?' (cited in n. 18).

[43] See, e.g., *XXIIIrd Report on Competition Policy* (Commission, 1993), part 209.

[44] N. Kroes, 'Private and public enforcement of EU competition law—5 years on', Brussels, 12 March 2009.

[45] See cartel statistics, available on DGComp's website at: <http://ec.europa.eu/competition/cartels/statistics/statistics.pdf>.

[46] <http://ec.europa.eu/competition/cartels/statistics/statistics.pdf>.

Table 9.1 Fines Imposed (Adjusted for Court Judgments) 2008–2012

Year	Amount in Euros
2008	2,263,279,900
2009	1,074,651,400
2010	2,868,459,674
2011	614,053,000
2012	1,875,694,000
Total	8,696,137,974

The recent spike in the level of fines has partly resulted from the Commission's revision, in 2006, of its fining guidelines with the specific objective of providing more effective sanctions and deterrents for cartels and multiplying the level of fines in cases of infringements of long duration and recidivism. Fining policy is discussed in detail in Chapter 13 but a few issues discussed there are also introduced here.

First, the level of the fines, combined with the more aggressive policy towards cartels, has led to a growing number of complaints that the administrative procedure is 'quasi-criminal' in nature and so is incompatible with due process principles set out in the European Convention for the Protection of Human Rights and Fundamental Freedoms 1950. Although it has even been argued that the *entire* procedure, under which the Commission performs investigative, enforcement, and adjudicative functions, is inappropriate and incompatible with those fundamental rights, case law now indicates[47] that it is legitimate for an administrative agency to determine whether a competition law infringement has been committed by an undertaking, and to impose fines on it as a preliminary matter, so long as its proceedings are governed by sufficiently strong procedural guarantees and its decisions are subject to sufficient judicial control by a body with 'full jurisdiction' on questions of fact and of law and with power to quash challenged decision in all respects.

Secondly, there is a view that the level of fines is so high that they are now out of proportion to those applicable for other comparative offences and have the effect of penalising innocent shareholders, employees, and creditors. Thirdly, even though fines are high, it is argued that they are still not sufficiently high to achieve deterrence.[48] These types of arguments have fuelled the view that criminal sanctions for individuals involved are necessary, alternatively or additionally, to 'focus the mind of potential cartelists',[49] and to bolster deterrence. Fourthly, since 2008, fears have been expressed that the fines may be leading to hardship for struggling companies and their shareholders and employees (who were unable to prevent the breach) and also for consumers as fines are indirectly channelled back to them through higher prices. The Commission has thus been facing some pressure to limit the level of the fines it imposes. Although the Commission has sometimes been willing to reduce fines for firms suffering financial hardship or which have acted during an industry crisis, perhaps with governmental support, it has not generally been sympathetic to these types of arguments, believing that the level of EU fines still represents a fraction of the harm caused each

---

[47] *A Menarini Diagnostics SRL v. Italy*, 43509/08, ECtHR, 21 September 2011.

[48] In its 2002 report the OECD looked at a number of cartels in a number of different States and in some considered how much the fines were in proportion to the estimated harm of the cartel, OECD, 'Fighting Cartels (cited in n. 20), 96–98. In only four cases of those where fines were assessed as a percentage of the estimated harm, did it appear that the fine exceeded the gains made by the cartel members. See also J. Connor, 'Optimal Deterrence and Private International Cartels', Purdue Working Paper, 2006, E. Combe and C. Monnier, 'Fines against hard core cartels in Europe: The myth of over enforcement' (2011) *Ant Bull* 235 (finding that EU fines regularly fall below the minimum illegal profit realised by the cartel and consequently are too low to confiscate the illegal gain and deter cartel formation).

[49] Joint Treasury/DTI Report, 'The UK's Competition Regime', 2001 and OFT365, 'Proposed criminalisation of cartels in the UK', A report prepared for the OFT by Sir Anthony Hammond KCB QC and Roy Penrose OBE QPM (November 2001), 1.4.

year by cartel behaviour. Neelie Kroes, when Competition Commissioner thus set out an alternative proposal: 'if a company thinks fines are too high, I have an excellent suggestion... *don't engage in cartels*'.[50] Even though Neelie Kroes recognised that it might be an own goal for competition law were a competition agency to levy such a large fine on a firm that it goes out of business, she considered that such a result should generally be precluded in the EU as fines levied may not exceed 10 per cent of the infringing firm's turnover in the preceding year of business.

The Commission's efforts to increase sanctions on cartelists have broadly been supported by the EU courts, which have confirmed that the Commission has authority to set its own guidelines and a wide fining discretion so long as it does not exceed the 10 per cent annual turnover ceiling. Although an appeal to the GC is generally perceived to be worthwhile (as it will frequently result in the court's reducing the level of the applicant's fine), in *BASF v. Commission*[51] the GC provided a reminder that it has power to increase, as well as to decrease, fines in appeals (increasing the level of fine imposed on BASF). Table 9.2 sets out the 10 largest fines imposed by the Commission in its cartel cases between 1969 and the end of May 2013.

Table 9.2 Highest Cartel Fines per Case, 1969–May 2013[52]

Commission Decision	Total Fines (in €)
TV and Computer Monitor Tubes	1,470,515,000 (including a fine of over 705 million on Philips)
Car Glass	1,383,896,000 (including a fine of 896 million on Saint Gobain)
Lifts and Escalators	832,422,250 (including a fine of 320 million on ThyssenKrupp)
Airfreight	799,445,000
Vitamins	790,515,000 (including a fine of 462 million on Hoffman La-Roche)
Paraffin Candle Wax	676,011,400
LCD	648,925,000
Gas	640,000,000 (including fines of 320 million for both E.ON and GDF Suez)
Bathroom Fittings	622,250,782 (including a fine of over 326 million for Ideal Standard)
Gas Insulated Switchgear	539,185,000 (including a fine of over 396 million on Siemens)

Other factors that reflect the hardening attitude towards cartels include:

- increased international cooperation focused on the elimination of international hardcore cartel activity;

- the introduction in 1996 of a successful leniency programme encouraging parties to blow the whistle and to confess to their participation in an illegal cartel. The Commission thus adopts a 'carrot and stick' policy: imposing large fines on those found to violate the rules but rewarding those who come forward with information on cartels. The programme was revised in 2002 to address defects in the original system and again in 2006 with the objective of strengthening, clarifying, and improving it;[53]

- the abolition of the notification and authorisation system set up in Regulation 17. The changes introduced by Regulation 1/2003 on 1 May 2004 enable the Commission to refocus its activities and to divert resources from scrutinising (mainly innocuous) notified agreements to

---

[50] N. Kroes, 'Private and Public Enforcement of EU Competition Law—5 years on', Brussels, 12 March 2009.

[51] Case T-101/05, [2007] ECR II-4949.

[52] See <http://ec.europa.eu/competition/cartels/cases/cases.html> and <http://ec.europa.eu/competition/cartels/statistics/statistics.pdf>.

[53] The leniency rules are discussed in Section 3.B.ii (in outline), pp. 676–678 and in Chap. 13.

uncovering the most serious infringements of competition law, especially the detection and prevention of cross-border cartels. It has also acquired broader powers to investigate breaches of the rules;

- the Commission's initiative to encourage greater private enforcement of the competition rules, see further Chapter 14. Each Commission press release announcing fines in a cartel case now contains a reminder that any person or firm affected by the anti-competitive behaviour described can seek damages submitting elements of the published decision as evidence that the behaviour took place and was illegal;

- the creation of an entire cartel directorate (Directorate F) within DG Comp to focus on cartel activity; and

- the Commission's introduction of a procedure for the settlement of cartel cases. The purpose of the procedure is to speed up investigations and to free up Commission resources, enabling it to handle more cartel cases and leading to a reduction in the number of infringement decisions appealed to the GC. This new procedure offers those involved in Commission cartel investigations the possibility of settling early with the Commission in return for a 10 per cent discount on their fines.[54]

(ii) Tacit Collusion, Coordinated Effects on an Oligopolistic Market

In Chapter 1 it was seen that in the 1930s and 1940s an ascendant view was that the structure of a market affected outcome on that market and that concentrated markets delivered poorer outcomes for consumers and higher profitability for firms. Many of the assumptions of the 'structuralists' have, however, been challenged. Indeed, game theory, for example, indicates that although in some oligopolistic markets players may coordinate their behaviour, coordination will not always occur.[55] On the contrary, there are oligopolistic markets where price and/or non-price competition is intense. Although, therefore, undertakings operating on a market on which there are only a few players *may* align their conduct and charge supra-competitive prices as a rational response to market circumstances, this is by no means an inevitable outcome. The prisoners' dilemma provides a framework for understanding when an oligopolistic market may be conducive to collusion and when it may not.

The prisoners' dilemma, set out in Section B.i.b, illustrates how, even without contractual arrangements or other explicit collusion between the parties, collusion (tacit collusion) may occur on an oligopolistic market. A and B know, even without conferring, that if they both choose a high price they will, collectively, maximise their profits (by raising their prices and restricting their output). However, A is aware that if B charges a high price, A can increase its profits, at B's expense, by reducing its price and attracting away B's customers. B is also aware that it can achieve substantial profits by reducing its price and soliciting A's customers. In the event that both A and B end up lowering their prices or having a price war, prices will be driven down to a lower level. In the first game, therefore, A and B may reduce prices and achieve a result that is disadvantageous for both parties. Where, however, the game is played continually, A and B may reconsider their situation independently, without meeting and agreeing, and realise that they are both much better off if they decide to charge a high price. Oligopolists thus have heightened awareness of other firms' presence on the market. They are likely to monitor the behaviour of their competitors (a reduction in one's price will swiftly attract away the others' customers) and to recognise their interdependence. They may realise, without the need for communication, that the most efficient course of conduct is for them all to set their prices at a profit-maximising level and to behave 'as if' they have agreed to act in a manner

---

[54] See <http://ec.europa.eu/comm/competition/cartels/legislation/settlements.html> and IP/08/1056 and the UK settlement of the investigation of price fixing by independent schools, available at: <http://www.oft.gov.uk/news-and-updates/press/2006/88–06#.UelH275wbiw> . This issue is discussed further in Chap. 13.

[55] G. Stigler, 'A Theory of Oligopoly' (1964) 72 *Journal of Political Economy* 44.

which maximises the profits of the market players and 'tacitly' to coordinate their behaviour. Tacit collusion thus occurs where, without any arrangement or explicit cooperation between them, firms simply understand that if they compete less vigorously they will be able to earn higher profits and that conversely, cutting prices will simply lead to their rivals following suit. Because economists consider the outcome or effects to be similar to explicit collusion, they generally describe this behaviour as tacit collusion. Because, however, collusion is the evil against which Article 101 acts, lawyers may feel uncomfortable with this terminology as it is not neutral and suggests the existence of a joint conduct (targeted by Article 101) between the parties.[56] In this chapter, the terms tacit collusion and tacit coordination are used interchangeably.

To be conducive to such tacit collusion, tacit coordination, or oligopolistic interdependence, the market must possess features which make tacit collusion feasible or likely. Thus, it is necessary for the firms to have the incentive to avoid competing, to realise their mutual interdependence, to be able successfully to engage in a common form of behaviour, i.e. to align their conduct (this is of course more difficult to achieve without explicit collusion), to monitor what their competitors are doing on the market, and to realise that if they deviate from the common behaviour they will be punished or disciplined (with low prices and low profits). These markets are likely to have similar characteristics to those in which explicit collusion is possible. For example, the market is likely to be transparent and characterised by high concentration, barriers to entry, homogenous products, firms with similar cost and demand structures, and a common high valuation of future profits, some mechanism for alignment (through either signalling[57] or a focal point[58]), and a mechanism for punishing those deviating from parallelism (perhaps through costly price wars or expansion of output). In contrast, markets characterised by differentiated products, volatile demand or demand booms, the existence of large and sophisticated buyers, and ease of entry or cost asymmetries are likely to make coordination more unlikely.[59]

C. COMPETITION LAW AND COLLUSION (EXPLICIT AND TACIT)

Where undertakings agree to fix or otherwise *explicitly collude* in fixing prices, restricting output, and/ or sharing markets, there will be sufficient cooperation between the undertakings to constitute an agreement, decision, or concerted practice and so to trigger the operation of Article 101(1) (assuming of course that the other requirements of Article 101 are satisfied).

The difficulty with *tacit* collusion is that although the impact of such coordination on the market is the same as, or at least similar to, where it is explicit (consumer welfare is harmed), the parties have not in fact *agreed* or otherwise explicitly cooperated with each other to coordinate their behaviour. How then should the competition rules deal with tacit collusion?

In the EU, the European Commission has utilised the merger rules to try and prevent mergers between firms, which are likely to *create* a market situation in which tacit collusion between the parties is likely, or more likely.[60] Further, Article 101 may be used to prevent practices which may facilitate tacit or explicit collusion on a market, for example by rendering the market more transparent

---

[56] See, e.g., R. Whish and D. Bailey, *Competition Law* (7th edn, Oxford University Press, 2012), 562.

[57] By signalling, e.g., making price announcements in advance, firms may be able to indicate what their future pricing policy will be. It will be a question of degree whether or not this type of conduct can be characterised as concerted behaviour contrary to Art. 101(1), see Section 4.A.iii.

[58] A practice of recommending prices can operate as a focal point and facilitate alignment of behaviour, see Chap. 11. So too can historical price leadership.

[59] See, e.g., Van den Bergh and Camesasca, *European Competition Law and Economics: A Comparative Perspective* (cited in n. 19), 5.2.3.

[60] It has the power to prevent mergers that will significantly impede effective competition by leading to coordinated and unilateral or non-coordinated effects, see Chap. 15.

through the exchange of information or the incorporation of meeting competition clauses into sales agreements. But what can be done about markets which are already concentrated and on which tacit collusion is, or may be, occurring? What action can be taken *ex post* as opposed to *ex ante*? As the tacit collusion stems from the *structure* of the market, should the Commission adopt a structural solution and try to deconcentrate the market, perhaps by ordering the firms operating on the market to sell off parts of their business?[61] In the US, in the 1960s there was significant support for the view that unreasonable market power should be condemned and that there should be power to dissolve firms found to possess it.[62] Indeed, in 1968 a White House Task Force on Antitrust Policy proposed legislation that would permit deconcentration of markets where four or fewer firms had a combined market share of 70 per cent or more *unless* the defendant could establish that such a step would reduce efficiency.[63] Support for this kind of legislation was, however, abandoned following 'post-1970s scepticism about ambitious governmental interventions in the economy'.[64]

Alternatively, should tacit collusion be seen as a problem stemming from the anti-competitive *behaviour* of the oligopolists?[65] Since the effects of tacit collusion are similar to cases in which there is explicit collusion and the firms' decisions could be seen as not having been taken truly unilaterally (but rather taking into account the anticipated reaction of their competitors), could parallel behaviour or conscious parallelism, without any proof of actual collusion between the undertakings, be prohibited as an illegal concerted practice under Article 101? In the US, Richard Posner was a proponent of the view that the concepts of contract, combination, or conspiracy in section 1 of the Sherman Act 1890 were capable of reaching, and an appropriate mechanism for dealing with, tacit collusion.[66] This view has not, however, been accepted by the US Supreme Court[67] and such an approach has also been rejected by the CJ. Alternatively, could Article 102, which applies to firms that 'collectively' hold a dominant position, be used to condemn tacit collusion (or other behaviour of tacitly colluding oligopolists) as an abuse of a collective dominant position? Or is it inappropriate to characterise tacit collusion, which is a consequence of the structure of the market (and not, as the term collusion perhaps suggests, a consequence of a conspiracy between the firms), as illegal under either Article 101 or Article 102? Section 3 considers the extent to which Article 101 or Article 102 may be applied as an effective tool against tacit collusion on a market. It also considers the extent to which those Articles can be used to prevent *other* behaviour of oligopolistic firms operating on the market, for example practices which might lead to or encourage tacit collusion. The extent to which the EU Merger Regulation (EUMR) can be used to prevent mergers that will increase concentration on an oligopolistic market and lead to coordinated or unilateral (non-coordinated) effects is considered in Chapter 15.

---

[61] Such an outcome is, since 1 May 2004, now theoretically possible but only so long as a breach of Art. 101 or Art. 102 is established, see Reg. 1/2003, Art. 7 and the discussion in Chap. 13. See discussion of UK's market investigation powers in Section 45. p. 730.

[62] See, e.g., C. Kaysen and D. Turner, *Antitrust Policy* (Harvard University Press, 1959), 110–119 and 266–272 and criticisms of these 'startling' conclusions set out in Bork, *The Antitrust Paradox* (cited in n. 16), 176.

[63] The White House Task Force Report on Antitrust Policy (the Neal Report), 1968 recommended adoption of this Concentrated Industries Act (it was endorsed by 11 of its 13 members) but the views set out in this Report reflected the beliefs of the Harvard School which subsequently were challenged and criticised, particularly by members of the Chicago School, see e.g. H. Hovenkamp, 'The Neal Report and the Crisis in Antitrust', *University of Iowa Legal Studies Research Paper, No. 09 09*, March 2009.

[64] Posner, *Antitrust Law* (cited in n. 38), 102. The author takes the view that deconcentration would confer few benefits and even if it were effective its social costs would exceed its social benefits.

[65] Other approaches might be regulatory or investigatory ones, see e.g., Whish and Bailey, *Competition Law* (cited in n. 56), 567 and discussion of market investigations later in this chapter.

[66] See R. Posner, 'Oligopoly and the Antitrust Laws: A Suggested Approach' (1969) 21 *Stan LR* 1562 (but see now Posner *Antitrust Law* (cited in n. 38)). But contrast, e.g., D. F. Turner, 'The Definition of Agreement under the Sherman Act: Conscious Parallelism and Refusals to Deal' [1962] 75 *Harv LR* 655.

[67] See, in particular, *Theatre Enterprises v. Paramount Film Distributing Corp.* 346 US 537 (1954).

3. CARTELS

A. INTRODUCTION

It is Article 101, of course, which prohibits the creation and operation of cartels.

B. SCOPE OF ARTICLE 101

(i) Article 101(1)

In order to ensure that detrimental collusion between undertakings does not escape the ambit of the competition rules, the requirements of Article 101(1) have been interpreted broadly.

In Chapters 3 and 4 it is seen that the terms agreement, decision, and concerted practice have been interpreted generously to catch all illicit cooperation (agreements whatever their form, complex arrangements, the activities of trade associations,[68] and other conduct of firms designed to substitute cooperation for the risks of competition) between firms.[69] Further, that cartel activities, price-fixing and market-sharing agreements or agreements to restrict output or capacity or to rig bids, and agreements to exchange price information are likely to have as their *object* the restriction of competition[70] and that such a characterisation is not generally affected by the fact that: the agreement has proved difficult to apply in practice (and may not, therefore, have had the effect of restricting competition);[71] a participant always intended to ignore the terms of the agreement and that it did, in fact, cheat on the cartel (when cheating the undertaking inevitably relies on the existence of the agreement or concerted practice and will not gain unless the others adhere to its terms);[72] price control is in place;[73] the subjective motive of the parties to any such agreement may have been to deal with an industry crisis or overcapacity[74] and/or the parties had acted with the knowledge, or with support from, a national government.[75] In most such cases the effect of the agreement will, therefore, be relevant only when

---

[68] In a number of cartels uncovered by the Commission, a significant role has been played by a trade association or a fiduciary company. Where this is the case the trade association or fiduciary company may be held responsible for the breach and fined, see, e.g., Case 246/86, *Re Roofing Felt Cartel: BELASCO v. Commission* [1989] ECR 2117 and *Organic Peroxides* [2005] OJ L110/44, *aff'd* Case T-120/04, *Peróxidos Orgánicos SA v. Commission*, [2006] ECR II-4441 and Case T-99/04, *AC-Treuhand AG v. Commission* [2008] ECR II-1501.

[69] The fact that the parties have cheated on the cartel agreement during its course cannot be used to demonstrate that there is no agreement or concerted practice because the parties were not committed to the scheme. On the contrary, cheating is seen as part and parcel of ordinary cartel activity which may sometimes be characterised by sporadic price wars or outbreaks of conflict, see, e.g., *Pre-Insulated Pipes* [1999] OJ L24/1, para. 132 and J. Joshua, 'Single Continuous Infringement of Article 81 EU: Has the Commission Stretched the Concept Beyond the Limit of its Logic?' (2009) 5 *European Competition Journal* 451, 460.

[70] See, e.g., *BELASCO* [1986] OJ L232/15, *aff'd* on appeal, Case 246/86, *Re Roofing Felt Cartel: BELASCO v. Commission* [1989] ECR 2117; Case 96/82, *IAZ International Belgium NV v. Commission* [1983] ECR 3369; Case T-7/89, *SA Hercules NV v. Commission* [1991] ECR II-1711; and Cases T-374, 375, 384, and 388/94, *European Night Services v. Commission* [1998] ECR II-3141. Only where a horizontal agreement is not naked will it be necessary to determine whether or not its effect is to restrict competition.

[71] *Ferry Operators* [1997] OJ L26/23.

[72] See *BELASCO* [1986] OJ L232/15, *aff'd* on appeal, Case 246/86, *Re Roofing Felt Cartel: BELASCO v. Commission* [1989] ECR 2117.

[73] See *Belgian Brewers* [2003] OJ L200/1, para. 247, *aff'd* Case T-38/02, *Groupe Danone v. Commission* [2005] ECR II-4407 (small reduction in fine) *aff'd* Case C-3/06 P, *Groupe Danone v. Commission* [2007] ECR I-1331.

[74] See, e.g., Case C-209/07, *Competition Authority v. Beef Industry Development Society Ltd and Barry Brothers (Carrigmore) Meals Ltd (BIDS)* [2008] ECR I-8637 and Cases C-101 and 110/07 P *Coop de France bétail et viande v. Commission* [2008] ECR I-10193.

[75] See, e.g., Case C-209/07, *Competition Authority v. Beef Industry Development Society Ltd and Barry Brothers (Carrigmore) Meals Ltd (BIDS)* [2008] ECR I-8637 and Cases C-101 and 110/07 P *Coop de France bétail et viande v. Commission* [2008] ECR I-10193.

determining whether its impact on competition or trade is appreciable,[76] whether it meets the criteria set out in Article 101(3), or, where a breach of the rules is established, to the determination of the fine, if any, imposed or the damages to be awarded.[77]

The core issue to be determined in cartel cases is, therefore, ordinarily whether an agreement or concerted practice between undertakings or a decision by an association of undertakings to fix prices, etc. exists.

(ii) Establishing a Breach of Article 101(1)

a. General

In cartel cases it is normally the detection of cartels, rather than the legal intricacies of Article 101, which presents the main difficulty. Because of the serious nature of such infringements, proof of collusion is likely to prove the breach. Even though, therefore, the terms agreement, decision, and concerted practice have been interpreted broadly parties are likely to operate any arrangements covertly in order to make detection difficult. A competition authority's task of proving the existence of the cartel is an onerous one.

M. Monti, 'Fighting Cartels Why and How? Why Should we be Concerned with Cartels and Collusive Behaviour?' 3rd Nordic Competition Policy Conference, Stockholm, 11–12 September 2000

Fighting cartels is not an easy business to be in. Companies operating cartels are of course very much aware of the illegality of their conduct under the antitrust laws. For that reason, cartels are typically operated in secrecy and considerable efforts are devoted by the participants to avoiding detection by the authorities. Meetings are held in exotic places around the globe. Incriminating documents are destroyed or stored outside the premises of the companies. Practices are arranged so as to simulate normal market behaviour and so on.

In order to be successful a competition authority must be able to play a number of different cards. In particular, a successful fight against cartels presupposes an effective leniency programme, effective enforcement powers and sanctions, and close cooperation amongst competition authorities.

In 1996 the Commission adopted for the first time a Leniency Programme. The first experience shows that it has led to a substantial increase in the number of cartels that have been uncovered and punished.

The programme provides a strong incentive for companies to come forward and to co-operate. Companies which provide information on a secret cartel before the Commission has opened an investigation can benefit even from total immunity from fines. Moreover, companies which cooperate with the Commission in the course of a pending investigation can benefit from a substantial reduction of their fines... Such substantial reductions of the fines are based on the premise that the public interest in detection and prohibition of cartels is higher than the interest in fining colluding companies.

---

b. Proof, Powers, and Leniency

Because the burden of proof is on the Commission, or other person alleging a breach, to prove that Article 101(1) has been infringed, Regulation 1/2003 confers broad powers of enforcement and

---

[76] These types of agreement are not covered by the Commission's Notice on Agreements of Minor Importance, discussed in Chap. 4.

[77] Case 246/86, *Re Roofing Felt Cartel: BELASCO v. Commission* [1989] ECR 2117.

investigation on the Commission to aid it in the task of gathering the evidence it requires to establish a breach. Despite the existence of these powers, difficulties remain in uncovering covertly operated cartels. Many competition authorities now encourage undertakings to cooperate with them prior to or during cartel investigations and to destabilise the nervous and unstable existence of cartels through the operation of 'leniency' regimes.[78] Leniency regimes have become a key part of policy in the fight against cartels. Authorities operating such regimes believe that the public interest in terminating and eradicating cartels outweighs the public interest in punishing those involved in the operation of cartels.[79] The leniency regime in the US, for example, seems to have been particularly successful for three reasons:[80] (i) it makes a genuinely good offer—complete immunity from a big penalty (fines and/or imprisonment) for the first to come forward; (ii) it generates and exploits a nervousness that other cartel members may well be tempted by the same offer and win the race to obtain it; and (iii) 'the ploy is reinforced by the general knowledge that only the first whistle-blower gets the big prize. It is thus reminiscent of the classical "Prisoner's Dilemma"—whether to play ball now, and quickly, or risk losing altogether. The strategy thus promotes within the cartel the sense of a higher risk, first, that somebody will blow the whistle and, secondly and consequently, of the other members being convicted. This serves to outweigh the previous benefits of solidarity, that is, of big profit from the offence plus a low risk of detection and conviction.'[81]

The Commission has operated a leniency regime since 1996, amending and improving it in 2002 and 2006.[82] Central to both the 2002 and 2006 Notices is the provision that total immunity is available but only to the *first* undertaking to submit evidence to the Commission (subject to other conditions also being satisfied). This provides a strong incentive for a cartel member to blow the whistle prior to its co-collaborators and destabilises the game of collusion set up by the members.[83] The leniency regime is generally perceived to have operated extremely successfully and firms have cooperated with the Commission in a high proportion of the cases occurring since 1996.[84]

Although total immunity from fines has now been granted in a number of cases, the Commission, like most competition authorities, aims to ensure that its policy is not dependent upon the leniency programme—the Commission has made it clear that it will search for and find out about cartels whether or not one of the members blows the whistle.[85] Nonetheless, the existence of the leniency regime has had an effect on the nature of cartel decisions and appeals: in many cases the dispute now revolves around the nature and duration of the infringement, which firms should be given what credit for cooperation under the relevant Leniency Notice, and other factors (such as the principle of equal treatment) which affect the level of the fine. The leniency regime is dealt with fully in Chapter 13 but two other points are stressed here. First, the Notice cannot give whistle-blowers immunity

---

[78] See, e.g., C. Harding and J. Joshua, *Regulating Cartels in Europe* (2nd edn, Oxford University Press, 2010), Chap. 8.

[79] Harding and Joshua, *Regulating Cartels in Europe* (cited in n. 78), Chap. 8 See 'Report on Leniency Programs to Fight Hard Core Cartels' (OECD, 2001), and the 'Anti-Cartel Enforcement Manual' of the ICN's Cartel Working Group, April 2006, available at <http://www.internationalcompetitionnetwork.org/media/library/conference_5th_capetown_2006/FINALFormattedChapter2-modres.pdf>. See also the ECN Model Leniency Programme explained in Chaps. 13 and 14.

[80] Harding and Joshua, *Regulating Cartels in Europe* (cited in n. 78), 235.

[81] Harding and Joshua, *Regulating Cartels in Europe* (cited in n. 78), 235

[82] Commission Notice on immunity from fines and reduction of fines in cartel cases [2006] OJ C298/17, see also 1996 and 2002 notices, [1996] OJ C207/4 and [2002] OJ C45/3.

[83] Reductions in fines are also available to those who are not eligible for total immunity but who nevertheless provide the Commission with evidence that represents significant added value. Essentially, greater reductions are offered to those that provide evidence first, see Chap. 13.

[84] But see, e.g., A. Stephan, 'An Empirical Assessment of the European Leniency Notice' (2009) 5 *Journal of Competition Law & Economics* 537.

[85] 'Companies that engage in cartels will be found out, whether or not one of their members blows the whistle. And when such cartels are found out, the punishment will be severe because the Commission will not tolerate companies cheating consumers and business customers by fixing prices and depriving them of the benefits of the Single Market.' N. Kroes, 'Flat Glass Cartel and Non-Horizontal Mergers' 28 November 2007.

from the civil law consequences of their participation in an illegal agreement. A third party injured by the cartel's actions may, therefore, commence private civil proceedings for damages. This was perceived to be a particular problem in the US where, generally, treble damages are available to those who can establish that they have suffered loss in consequence of another's breach of the competition rules. In 2004 a new Act was adopted which reduces damages to 'single' damages from corporations that participate in the 'amnesty' programme and cooperate with the claimants in their damages actions.[86] The Commission has now proposed that leniency statements and settlement submissions should not be disclosed in damages actions (see Chapter 14). In some jurisdictions, the fact that an *individual* might gain immunity from criminal prosecution may encourage leniency applications to be brought, irrespective of the possibility of civil damages.

Secondly, a leniency application to the Commission does not constitute an application to any other competition authority within the European Competition Network (ECN) or elsewhere. An undertaking applying for leniency will, therefore, need to consider simultaneous applications in all States where leniency programmes are operated and where a breach of the rules may have been committed.

(iii) Article 101(3)

Where an infringement of Article 101(1) is established, the parties to the agreement may seek to show that the agreement meets the criteria of Article 101(3). It is very unlikely, however, that hardcore cartel activity will satisfy all, or any, of the four criteria set out therein. Occasionally, however, it will be relevant, for example, to instances where price-fixing is argued to be indispensable to achieve a pro-competitive objective.

C. PRICE-FIXING, RESTRICTIONS ON OUTPUT, MARKET-SHARING, AND COLLUSIVE TENDERING

(i) General

It has been seen that classic 'hardcore cartels' are operated by fixing prices and/or by imposing quotas on the members and/or by sharing markets between them. In some situations, cartel members may limit price competition and share the market between them by engaging in collusive tendering.

(ii) Article 101(1)

a. Price-fixing Agreements

Selling prices

Article 101(1) specifically provides that agreements 'directly or indirectly fixing purchase or selling prices or any other trading conditions' may infringe Article 101(1) of the Treaty. In *Dyestuffs*,[87] the CJ stressed that:

The function of price competition is to keep prices down to the lowest possible level…Although every producer is free to change his prices, taking into account in so doing the present or foreseeable conduct of his competitors, nevertheless it is contrary to the rules on competition contained in the Treaty for a producer to co-operate with his competitors, in any way whatsoever, in order to determine a co-ordinated course of action relating to a price increase and to ensure its success by prior elimination of all uncertainty as to each

---

[86] The Antitrust Criminal Penalty Enhancement and Reform Act 2004. The Act also increases the maximum Sherman Act corporate and individual fines, and maximum jail term. The 'detrebling' provision is designed to remove the disincentive to submitting amnesty applications.

[87] Cases 48, 49, and 51–57/69, *ICI v. Commission (Dyestuffs)* [1972] ECR 619.

other's conduct regarding the essential elements of that action, such as the amount, subject-matter, date and place of the increases.[88]

In many cartel cases investigated by the Commission, and discussed here, it has uncovered and condemned price-fixing arrangements between cartel members. Often the price-fixing is accompanied by other provisions which strengthen the operation of the cartel, such as market-sharing or information-sharing provisions or the imposition of quotas or output restraints.

Target Prices and Indirect Price-Fixing

Not only are agreements to fix prices prohibited, but the discussion and implementation of target prices will be condemned:

[I]f a system of imposed selling prices is clearly in conflict with that provision [Article 101], the system of [target prices] is equally so. It cannot in fact be supposed that the clauses of the agreement concerning the determination of target prices are meaningless. In fact the fixing of a price, even one which merely constitutes a target, affects competition because it enables all the participants to predict with a reasonable degree of certainty what the pricing policy pursued by their competitors will be.[89]

Other agreements which may directly or indirectly facilitate level pricing will also be condemned, for example, agreements fixing or prohibiting discounts, rebates,[90] or other financial concessions,[91] agreements to consult on price lists,[92] to restrict advertising,[93] to exchange information and give warning of price increases to provide reassurance that a price war will not break out,[94] to pursue a collaborative strategy of higher pricing,[95] or to exchange price information.[96]

It is contrary to the provisions of Article [101(1)]…for a producer to communicate to his competitors the essential elements of his price policy such as price lists, the discounts and terms of trade he applies, the rates and date of any change to them and the special exceptions he grants to specific customers.[97]

Obviously there is little incentive to make a price cut to attract business from a competitor if that information must be disclosed to the competitor.

In *Polypropylene*[98] the Commission fined producers of polypropylene approximately €57 million for their participation in an agreement and/or concerted practice to implement price initiatives, to set target prices, and to operate production and sales quotas.[99] In a series of cases both the GC and

---

[88] Cases 48, 49, and 51–57/69, *ICI v. Commission (Dyestuffs)* [1972] ECR 619, paras. 115 and 118.

[89] Case C-8/72, *Vereeniging van Cementhandelaren v. Commission* [1972] ECR 977, para. 21.

[90] Case 311/85, *ASBL Vereniging van Vlaamse Reisbureaus v. ASBL Sociale Dienst van de Plaatselijke en Gewestelijke Overheidsdiensten* [1987] ECR 3801. See also *Dutch Beer*, IP/07/309.

[91] e.g., *IFTRA Rules on Glass Containers* [1974] OJ L160/1.

[92] *Cast Iron Steel Rolls* [1983] OJ L137/1.

[93] See Section 3.D.

[94] See *Plasterboard* [2005] OJ L166/8, see Case T-50/03, *Saint-Gobain Gyproc Belgium NV v. Commission* [2008] ECR II-114

[95] *British Sugar plc, Tate & Lyle plc, Napier Brown & Company Ltd, James Budgett Sugars Ltd (British Sugar)* [1999] OJ L76/1, substantially upheld by the GC, Case T-202/98, *Tate & Lyle v. Commission* [2001] ECR II-2035, on appeal Case C-359/01 P, [2004] ECR I-4933.

[96] Cases T-25, etc./95, *Cimenteries CBR SA v. Commission* [2000] ECR II-491, para. 1531 (at least where it underpins another anti-competitive agreement), broadly *aff'd* Cases C-204, etc./00 P, *Aalborg Portland A/S v. Commission* [2004] ECR I-123. See also *IFTRA Rules on Glass Containers* [1974] OJ L160/1. See also discussion of *T-Mobile* in Section 3.D.

[97] *IFTRA Rules on Glass Containers* [1974] OJ L160/1.

[98] *Polypropylene* [1986] OJ L230/1, appeals substantially dismissed by both the GC and the CJ, see, e.g., Case C-51/92 P, *SA Hercules NV v. Commission* [1999] ECR I-4235 and Case C-199/92 P, *Hüls AG v. Commission (Polypropylene)* [1999] ECR I-4287.

[99] *Polypropylene* [1986] OJ L230/1, appeals substantially dismissed both by the GC and the CJ: see Case T-7/89, etc., *SA Hercules NV v. Commission* [1991] ECR II-1711 and Case C-51/92 P, etc., *SA Hercules/Hüls/ICI/Shell v. Commission* [1999] ECR I-4235.

the CJ broadly dismissed the appeals.[100] However, in a few cases, where the Court found that the Commission had not sufficiently proved the period of time during which an undertaking had participated in the collusion, the amount of the fine was reduced.[101]

In *FENEX*,[102] the Commission held that tariffs recommended by a Dutch association to its members constituted a decision by an association of undertakings.

Buying Prices

Price-fixing amongst buyers can have quite different effects to price-fixing by sellers. Whilst the latter is clearly likely to be designed to maximise sellers' profits and to extract higher prices from purchasers, the former may be designed to achieve lower prices for members which may then be passed on to their customers.[103] Nonetheless, horizontal agreements restricting the parties' freedom to negotiate buying prices might be prohibited by Article 101. For example, agreement by cartel members on the purchase price of a key raw material may facilitate the operation of the cartel at the downstream level.[104] In both the Spanish and Italian raw tobacco cases,[105] the Commission imposed fines on companies active in raw tobacco processing for colluding on the prices paid to (as well as the quantities bought from) tobacco growers.

Joint Selling

Joint selling is likely to be condemned under Article 101(1) although in certain circumstances the Commission has been prepared to accept that joint selling may meet the criteria of Article 101(3).[106]

Agreements between Distributors and Resale Price Maintenance

It is, of course, also an infringement of Article 101(1) for distributors of a product to agree to fix prices. Collusion between distributors as to selling prices achieved indirectly, through the intermediary of a supplier, is also prohibited.[107] The Commission has also condemned horizontal agreements by suppliers to impose resale prices insofar as they have an impact on inter-State trade. In particular, it has been unsympathetic to the arguments in favour of collective resale price maintenance in the book industry.[108] Both the Commission and the Court have also found that agreements directly or indirectly imposing individual resale price maintenance infringe Article 101(1). Individual resale price maintenance is discussed in Chapter 11, which deals generally with vertical restraints.

---

[100]   See, e.g., Case T-7/89, *SA Hercules NV v. Commission* [1991] ECR II-1711; Case T-11/89, *Shell International Chemical Co Ltd v. Commission* [1992] ECR II-757; Case T-13/89, *Imperial Chemical Industries plc v. Commission* [1992] ECR II-1021; Case C-51/92 P, *SA Hercules NV v. Commission* [1999] ECR I-4235; Case C-199/92 P, *Hüls AG v. Commission* [1999] ECR I-4287; Case C-200/92 P, *Imperial Chemical Industries plc v. Commission* [1999] ECR I-4399; Case C-234/92 P, *Shell International Chemical Co Ltd v. Commission* [1999] ECR I-4501.

[101]   e.g., Case T-2/89, *Petrofina v. Commission* [1991] ECR II-1087 and Case T-11/89, *Shell v. Commission* [1991] ECR II-757.

[102]   [1996] OJ L181/28.

[103]   See Research Paper prepared by RBB for the OFT on cooperation by purchasers, 'The Competitive Effects of Buyer Groups', Jan. 2007.

[104]   See, e.g., *Zinc Producer Group* [1984] OJ L220/7. It may also harm welfare by causing the input suppliers to reduce output.

[105]   IP/04/1256 *Spanish Raw Tobacco*, Cases T-37/05, etc., *World Wide Tobacco España v. Commission*, 8 March 2011. IP/05/1315 *Italian Raw Tobacco*, Cases T-11–12/06, *Romana Tabacchi v. Commission*. 5 October 2011.

[106]   See Chap. 11.

[107]   See e.g. discussion of UK Case 1022/1/1/03, *JJB Sports Plc v. Office of Fair Trading* [2004] CAT 17, *aff'd* [2006] EWCA Civ 1318, discussed in Chap. 3.

[108]   *VBVB/VBBB* [1982] OJ L54/36, *aff'd* Cases 43 and 63/82, *VBVB and VBBB v. Commission* [1984] ECR 19. See *Publishers' Association—Net Book Agreement* [1989] OJ L22/12 (Commission), on appeal Case T-66/89, [1992] ECR II-1995, and Case C-360/92 P, [1995] ECR I-23.

Supplementary Provisions

Other devices, such as information exchanges, or meeting competition clauses aimed at strengthening the operation of the cartel, frequently supplement price-fixing agreements.

Some Examples of Price-fixing Agreements

It has already been explained that in more recent years the Commission has adopted numerous cartel decisions, adopting between 5 and 10 decisions per year since 2001. Most of these have involved some element of price-fixing, either alone or together with other anti-competitive practices. In *Cartonboard*[109] the Commission fined 19 producers of cartonboard (used primarily for the manufacture of folding cartons for packaging food and non-food consumer goods) for their participation in a price-fixing cartel. The producers had met secretly but regularly in order to plan and implement uniform and regular price increases within the Union, to plan and coordinate price initiatives in advance, to freeze market shares, to control output, and to organise the exchange of confidential information.

The Commission found incriminating documentation that disclosed evidence of collusion at the premises of a number of the participants. The collusion was complex and long, having lasted since at least mid-1986 (although one of the undertakings, Stora, had informed the Commission that the parties had been cooperating since 1975, the Commission had no documentary evidence to corroborate Stora's statements). The documents established that implementation of uniform price increases for each grade of cartonboard was closely monitored. Failure to cooperate would be the subject of discussion and laggards would be strongly urged to support the increases. Although not entirely watertight, the agreement caused considerable harm to competition.

Further, the Commission has found price-fixing, for example by French federations in the beef sector[110] and by undertakings selling: aluminium fluoride; sodium chlorate; synthetic rubber; calcium carbide; magnesium-based reagents; concrete reinforcing bars; stainless steel, synthetic rubber, bleaching chemicals, acrylic glass, road bitumen, copper fittings, methylglucamine; Dutch industrial gases; zinc phosphates; carbonless paper; vitamin products; graphite electrodes; lysine; plasterboard; airfreight; LCD panels; washing powder; bananas; glass for cathode ray tubes; refrigeration compressors; mounting for windows and window doors; freight forwarders; water management products; and TV and computer monitor tubes.[111] In many of the cases, the price-fixing was supplemented by other restrictive operations such as measures designed: to limit imports;[112] to allocate sales quotas;[113] to share markets;[114] to share customers;[115] to fix other trading conditions (such as transport costs);[116] and to share customers.[117] Some of these cartels have been global ones where European proceedings followed high-profile criminal proceedings and private litigation in the US.

---

[109] [1994] OJ L243/1, in a series of appeals, see e.g., Case T-334/94, *Sarrió SA v. Commission* [1998] ECR II-1439, the GC broadly upheld the fines imposed but the CJ reduced three fines, referred two cases back to the GC for reassessment, and dismissed the remainder of the appeals: see, e.g., Case C-286/98 P, *Stora Kopparbergs Bergslags AB v. Commission* [2000] ECR I-9925.

[110] *French Beef* [2003] OJ L209/12, *aff'd* (but fines reduced) in Cases T-217 and 245/03, *FNCBV v. Commission* [2004] ECR II-239, Cases C-101 and 110/07, *Coop de France Bétail, FNSEA and others v. Commission* [2008] ECR I-10193.

[111] See <http://ec.europa.eu/competition/cartels/cases/cases.html>.

[112] *French Beef* (cited in n. 110).

[113] *Zinc Phosphate* [2003] OJ L153/1.

[114] See, e.g., *Graphite Electrodes* [2002] OJ L100/1, on appeal Cases T-236/01, *Tokai Carbon v. Commission* [2004] ECR II-1181 (some of the fines reduced on appeal), Cases C-301/04 P and 308/04 P, *SGL v. Commission* [2006] ECR I-5915 (fine increased on SGL).

[115] *Synthetic Rubber* IP/06/1851, Cases T-44 and 45/07 Kaučuk v. Commission, 13 July 2011.

[116] *Dutch Industrial Gases* [2003] OJ L84/1, *aff'd* Case T-303, *Westfalen Gassen Nederland v. Commission* [2006] II-4567 and Case T-304/02, *Hoek Loos NV v. Commission* [2006] ECR II-1887.

[117] *Dutch Industrial Gases* [2003] OJ L84/1, *aff'd* Case T-303, *Westfalen Gassen Nederland v. Commission* [2006] II-4567 and Case T-304/02, *Hoek Loos NV v. Commission* [2006] ECR II-1887.

For example, Hoffman-la Roche and BASF were fined $500 million and $225 million respectively in the US in 1999 for their participation in the *Vitamins* cartel.[118] Subsequently, in *Vitamins*[119] the Commission imposed fines on the companies involved totalling €855.2 million. The parties agreed target and minimum prices, agreed quotas (agreeing to maintain the status quo in respect of market shares), and provided for compensation payments to be paid in case quotas were exceeded. Elaborate provisions for monitoring and enforcing the agreements were also established and a formal structure and management was involved in the operation of the agreements, including most senior levels of management. In the case of Hoffmann-La Roche the Commission considered that the arrangements were part of a strategic plan to control the world market in vitamins by illegal means.

Price-Fixing in the Services Sector

Article 101(1) also applies to agreements operated in the services sector. In *Eurocheque: Helsinki Agreement*[120] the Commission imposed heavy fines on French banks and Eurocheque for operating a scheme under which the same commission was charged for both Eurocheque transactions and the use of Carte Bleu. The Commission considered that the scheme eliminated the positive features of the Eurocheque system (that it was free to the payee). Further, it eliminated competition between Eurocheques and Carte Bleu. Fines have also been imposed on banks in *German Banks*[121] and *Austrian Banks ('Lombard Club')*.[122] In the latter case, the Commission found that the Austrian banks had concluded agreements about interest rates and charges/fees and by meeting regularly had 'coordinated their conduct with respect to every essential factor of competition'.[123] The Commission is also currently investigating the setting of LIBOR rates and the conduct of firms involved in financial derivative products linked to the Euro Interbank Offered Rate (EURIBOR).[124]

In *Fine Art Auction Houses*[125] the Commission found that Christie's and Sotheby's had fixed commission fees and other trading conditions between 1993 and 2000. A significant fine was imposed on Sotheby's, although Christie's escaped a fine in consequence of its cooperation with the Commission.

Price-Fixing and Liberal Professions

The Commission has been concerned that high levels of regulation (including State or self-regulation) within the sphere of professional services in Europe serve to restrict competition. Although the Commission accepts that some carefully targeted regulation may be necessary to deal with specific issues arising in this sphere, such as asymmetry of information between customers and service providers, externalities, and to ensure adequate and sufficient supply of these services, it has paid close attention to the professions and has adopted two reports on the subject, a 'Report on Competition in

---

[118] The defendants also agreed to pay US customers more than $1 billion in damages, see 'Status Report: An Overview of Recent Developments in the Antitrust Division's Criminal Enforcement Program' DOJ Antitrust Division, 25 February 2004. High fines were also imposed on companies such as SGL Carbon and Archer Daniels Midland for their participation in the graphite electrode and lysine cartels respectively.

[119] [2003] OJ L6/1, see Case T-15 and 26/02, [2006] ECR II-497 (reducing some of the fines).

[120] [1992] OJ L95/50, partially annulled and fines reduced on appeal, see Case T-39/92, *Groupement des Cartes Bancaires* v. *Commission* [1994] ECR II-49. But see *Uniform Eurocheques* [1985] OJ L35/43.

[121] [2003] OJ L15/1, annulled Case T-44/02, *Dresdner Bank* v. *Commission* [2006] ECR II-0356.

[122] [2004] OJ L56/1, *aff'd* (but fine reduced on Osterrechische Postssparkasse AG) see Cases T-259–264 and 271/02, *Raiffeisen Zentralbank Österreich* v. *Commission* [2006] ECR II-5169, Case C-125/07 *Raiffeisen Zentralbank Österreich* v. *Commission* [2009] I-8681.

[123] [2004] OJ L56/1, *aff'd* (but fine reduced on Osterrechische Postssparkasse AG) see Cases T-259–264 and 271/02, *Raiffeisen Zentralbank Österreich* v. *Commission* [2006] ECR II-5169, Case C-125/07 *Raiffeisen Zentralbank Österreich* v. *Commission* [2009] I-8681, para. 1.

[124] A number of other agencies in Europe, the US, and Japan are also investigating.

[125] IP/02/1585.

Professional Services'[126] and 'Professional Services—Scope for more reform'.[127] These reports focus on the question of whether the regulatory regimes existing for lawyers, notaries, accountants, architects, engineers, and pharmacies can be adapted or modernised to spur economic growth and value to consumers. The Commission is particularly concerned about regulation, involving the fixing of prices or recommended prices,[128] and believes that such practices, which may infringe Article 101, are widespread in the liberal professions.[129] In the first report the Commission states that 'within an otherwise competitive market, price regulation is unlikely to ensure prices that are lower than competitive levels'.[130] Further, that price recommendations 'like fixed prices, may have a significant negative effect on competition. First, recommended prices may facilitate the coordination of prices between service providers. Secondly, they can mislead consumers about reasonable price levels'.[131] It believes that competition in this sphere is often additionally, or alternatively, restricted by advertising restrictions, entry restrictions and reserved tasks, and business structure regulation (for example, the scope for collaboration with other professions).[132] Recognising the complex issues involved in this area, however, the Commission called, at first instance, for these restrictions to be reviewed and, where not objectively justified, removed or replaced by less restrictive rules.[133] Further, it considers that, since in most cases the professional rules have their origin and effect in a single Member State, they should be dealt with at the national level, with progress being monitored and coordinated through the ECN.[134] The 2005 report comments on the progress that has been made at the national level.

The Commission will itself also consider infringement procedures. In particular, it takes the view that rules relating to price are likely to constitute automatic violations of Article 101(1), even though in practice an increase in price may be very difficult to sustain in this sphere.[135] In *Belgian Architects*,[136] the Commission sent out a clear message that restrictive practices operated by members of the liberal professions should be eliminated and reform promoted. The Commission fined the Belgian Architects' Association in respect of its operation of a recom-

---

[126] Communication from the Commission, 'Report on Competition in Professional Services' COM(2004) 83 final (Brussels, 9 February 2004), available on DG Comp's website. Table 1 indicates that professions with fixed, minimum, or maximum prices exist in Austria, Belgium, France, Germany, Greece, Italy, Luxembourg, Netherlands, and Spain.

[127] 'Professional Services—Scope for More Reform. Follow-up on Competition in Professional Services', SEC (2005) 1064.

[128] Communication from the Commission, 'Report on Competition in Professional Services' (cited in n. 126), Table 2 indicating that recommended prices existed in Austria, Belgium, Denmark, Greece, Ireland, Luxembourg, Portugal, and Spain.

[129] Occupations requiring special training in the liberal arts or sciences, for example lawyers, notaries, accountants, architects, engineers, and pharmacists, see Communication from the Commission, 'Report on Competition in Professional Services' (cited in n. 126), para. 1.

[130] Communication from the Commission, 'Report on Competition in Professional Services' (cited in n. 126), para. 32.

[131] Communication from the Commission, 'Report on Competition in Professional Services' (cited in n. 126), para. 37.

[132] Communication from the Commission, 'Report on Competition in Professional Services' (cited in n. 126), paras. 42–64.

[133] Communication from the Commission, 'Report on Competition in Professional Services' (cited in n. 126), para. 90.

[134] Communication from the Commission, 'Report on Competition in Professional Services' (cited in n. 126), paras. 93–102.

[135] 'Since the number of practitioners in these markets is high, cartel discipline is difficult to maintain and cheating very attractive. The non-sustainability of price cartels under such circumstances is also confirmed by empirical evidence...Current European competition law, however allows the relevant economic evidence to be pushed aside if the objective to fix prices or control output can be proven, and the (lack of) economic impact on the market will only be taken into account when determining the ultimate fine.' Van den Bergh and Camesasca, *European Competition Law and Economics: A Comparative Perspective* (cited in n. 19), 5.3.1.1.

[136] [2005] OJ L004/10.

mended minimum fee scale. The fee scale recommended the laying down of fees as a percentage of the value of work realised. The Commission considered that this practice infringed Article 101 and had as its object the restriction of competition since it sought to coordinate the pricing behaviour of architects which was unnecessary for the proper practice of the profession. Rather, the architects should have been free to charge a fee commensurate with their skills, efficiency, costs, and reputation.

Some commentators are critical of the Commission's approach, believing that specific problems will result from trying to introduce competition in markets for professional services in the ordinary way.[137]

b. Output Restrictions and Restrictions Limiting or Controlling Production

Beneficial collaboration between competitors or potential competitors may involve restrictions on production.[138] Where, however, restrictions on output are 'naked', competition law is likely to be hostile. A restriction of output automatically creates an imbalance between supply and demand and causes an increase in market prices. Indeed, volume control is an indispensable condition and inevitable consequence of any price initiative adopted. Article 101(1)(b) specifically provides that agreements which 'limit or control production…or investment' may restrict competition within the meaning of that provision.

A number of the cases discussed in Section 3.C.ii.a, dealing with price-fixing, involved collusion to fix both prices and sales quotas. In many cases the implementation of quotas is easier to operate than adherence to a pricing policy: no undertaking can benefit from price-cutting if it is obliged to adhere to sales restrictions, and the adherence to quotas may be easier to monitor. Further, a decision to adhere to quotas may facilitate collusion where participants with different cost structures cannot agree on the prices to be charged for their products. Organisation of Petroleum Exporting Countries (OPEC), for example, operated simply by the members voluntarily restricting their outputs following the negotiation of quotas in 1973. As a result of the output restrictions, the world price of oil nearly quadrupled within a year. The increase in wealth to the participants was so enormous that, initially at least, there was little temptation to cheat on the cartel.

The *Quinine Cartel*[139] was the first case in which the Commission fined undertakings for the operation of a cartel which raised prices by means of the restriction of output. In particular, certain French companies had agreed not to manufacture synthetic quinidine. The parties contended that, in any event, the companies did not have either the expertise or the resources to manufacture quinidine. The Court dismissed those arguments:

The fact relied upon that, when the gentlemen's agreement was concluded, the French undertakings were not in a position to manufacture synthetic quinidine does not render lawful such a restriction which entirely precluded them from taking up this activity.[140]

In BELASCO,[141] an accountant appointed by BELASCO monitored compliance with quotas at the end of each year. Undertakings which had exceeded these quotas were required to pay penalties.

---

[137] See Van den Bergh and Camesasca, *European Competition Law and Economics: A Comparative Perspective* (cited in n. 19), Box 5.3.

[138] See Chap. 10.

[139] *Quinine Cartel* [1969] OJ L192/5.

[140] Case 41/69, *ACF Chemiefarma NV v. Commission* [1970] ECR 661.

[141] [1986] OJ L232/15, on appeal, Case 246/86, *Re Roofing Felt Cartel: BELASCO v. Commission* [1989] ECR 2117.

The *Polypropylene*[142] cartel not only operated price initiatives and set target prices but operated production and sales quotas. The GC in *Hercules* v. *Commission* had no hesitation in holding that the object of meetings to fix target prices and sale volume targets was anti-competitive.[143]

In *Zinc Producer Group*[144] the Commission held that an agreement to fix prices, to adhere to production quotas, and to refrain from the building of new production capacity without the consent of the Group infringed Article 101(1). The purpose of the agreement was to substitute its common zinc producer price for the London Metal Exchange (LME) price. Production controls precluded producers from supplying surplus zinc to the LME or zinc producers at lower prices. The fact that the practices had been tolerated/approved by Member States could not be used as a defence to the operation of the EU competition rules (the position might be different, however, if the conduct is required of the undertakings by national law).[145]

Allocation of market share quotas was also the central plank of the *Zinc Phosphate* cartel.[146] The parties calculated initial market shares. Each cartel member then had to adhere to its allotted market share, and sales quotas were allocated at the European level. A monitoring system was set up to ensure that the parties adhered to the terms of the agreement. Pressure was brought to bear on those that did not, and customer allocation was used as a form of compensation for a company which had not achieved its quota. On an annual basis the market shares of the producers did in fact closely follow their specified shares.[147] The parties also agreed on 'bottom' prices, and on some occasions, the allocation of customers. The cartel in this case, in operation from 1994, appeared to have been concluded in response to a prior period of low prices, aggressive price-cutting, and targeting of mutual customers.

A practice in the professions which can cause significant reductions in competition in the spectrum of services offered is the use of business structure regulations. It will be remembered that in *Wouters* v. *Algemene Raad van de Nederlandse Orde van Advocaten*[148] the CJ had to deal with a professional rule that prevented lawyers from working in partnership with accountants. In Chapter 4 it was seen that the CJ did not treat this agreement as one that had as its object the restriction of competition. Further, that the CJ held that such a provision, despite constituting a restriction on production and technical development within the meaning of Article 101(1)(b), did not have as its *effect* the restriction of competition. Rather, it held that restrictions required to ensure the proper practice of the profession as organised in a Member State, and which did not go beyond what was necessary to ensure the proper practice of the legal profession, did not infringe Article 101(1). In Section 3.C.ii.a it was seen that the Commission has issued a report on competition in professional services. The view set out in that report does not seem to support such a robust view as that set out by the CJ in *Wouters*. Rather, the Commission clearly takes the view that such restrictions 'may have a negative economic impact',[149] particularly where collaboration is prevented between members of the same

[142] *Polypropylene* [1986] OJ 1230/1, appeals substantially dismissed by both the GC and the CJ: see, e.g., Case C-51/92 P, *SA Hercules NV* v. *Commission* [1999] ECR I-4235 and Case C-199/92 P, *Hüls AG* v. *Commission (Polypropylene)* [1999] ECR I-4287. See also, e.g., *Cartonboard* [1994] OJ L243/1.

[143] Case C-51/92 P, *SA Hercules NV* v. *Commission* [1999] ECR I-4235 and Case C-199/92 P, *Hüls AG* v. *Commission (Polypropylene)* [1999] ECR I-4287.

[144] [1984] OJ L220/27. See also, e.g., *Amino Acid* [2001] OJ L152/24, appeal dismissed in part, Case T-224/00, *Archer Daniels Midlands Company and Archer Daniels Ingredients Ltd* v. *Commission* [2003] ECR II-2597, aff'd Case C-397/03 P, *Archer Daniels Midlands Company and Archer Daniels Ingredients Ltd* v. *Commission* [2006] ECR I-4429.

[145] *Zinc Producer Group* [1984] OJ L220/27. See also, e.g., *Amino Acid* [2001] OJ L152/24, appeal dismissed in part, Case T-224/00, *Archer Daniels Midlands Company and Archer Daniels Ingredients Ltd* v. *Commission* [2003] ECR II-2597, aff'd Case C-397/03 P, *Archer Daniels Midlands Company and Archer Daniels Ingredients Ltd* v. *Commission* [2006] ECR I-4429.

[146] [2003] OJ L153/1, para. 66.

[147] *Zinc Phosphate* [2003] OJ L153/1, paras. 65–72.

[148] Case C-309/99, [2002] ECR I-1577 (discussed in Chap. 4).

[149] Communication from the Commission, 'Report on Competition in Professional Services' (cited in n. 126), para. 60.

profession or between professions where there is no overriding need to protect independence or ethical standards.

Communication from the Commission, 'Report on Competition in Professional Services' COM(2004) 83 final (Brussels, 9 February 2004)

4.5 Business structure regulations

59. A number of professions are subject to sector-specific regulations on business structure. These regulations can restrict the ownership structure of professional services companies, the scope for collaboration with other professions and, in some cases, the opening of branches, franchises or chains.

60. Business structure regulations may have a negative economic impact if they inhibit providers from developing new services or cost-efficient business models. For example, these regulations might inhibit lawyers and accountants from providing integrated legal and accountancy advice for tax issues or prevent the development of one-stop shops for professional services in rural areas. Certain ownership regulations such as prohibition of incorporation can also reduce access to capital in professional services markets, hindering new entry and expansion.

61. On the other hand, it is argued that business structure and ownership regulation may be necessary to ensure practitioner's personal responsibility and liability towards clients and avoid conflicts of interest. It has also been suggested that these regulations may be necessary to ensure practitioners' independence. If professional service companies were controlled or influenced by non-professionals, this might compromise practitioners' judgement or respect for professional value.

62. In the Commission's view business structure regulations appear to be least justifiable in cases where they restrict the scope for collaboration between members of the same profession. Collaboration between members of the same profession would appear less likely to reduce the profession's independence or ethical standards

63. Business structure regulations appear likewise to be less justifiable in professions where there is no overriding need to protect practitioners' independence. The architectural and engineering professions, for example, function effectively without these regulations in most Member States. It therefore appears unlikely that business structure regulations are essential to protect consumers of these services.

64. Business structure regulations appear to be more justifiable in markets where there is a strong need to protect practitioners' independence or personal liability. There might however be alternative mechanisms for protecting independence and ethical standards which are less restrictive of competition. In some markets, stringent ownership restrictions might therefore be replaced or partially replaced by less restrictive rules.

c. Market or Customer Sharing

Market-sharing agreements also have restrictive effects on competition and Article 101(1)(b) and (c) specifically prohibit collusive practices which 'limit or control…markets' or 'share markets and sources of supply'. Like sales quotas, market-sharing agreements may provide an extremely effective means of operating a cartel. Exclusivity in a particular geographical area, or over a particular customer group, obviously grants an undertaking a monopoly within that area or over that group which it is free to exploit. No price or non-price competition between the parties to the agreement thus operates at all. From the perspective of the Commission, geographical market-sharing agreements are viewed particularly seriously. In addition to restricting competition, such agreements thwart the objective of integrating the single market by dividing up the common market. The Commission is likely to punish such infringements particularly severely. The Commission has stated:

Market sharing agreements are particularly restrictive of competition and contrary to the achievement of a single market. Agreements or concerted practices for the purpose of market-sharing are generally based on the principle of mutual respect of the national markets of each Member State for the benefit of producers resident there. The direct object and result of their implementation is to eliminate the exchange of goods between the Member States concerned. The protection of their home market allows producers to pursue a commercial policy—particularly a pricing policy—in that market which is insulated from the competition of other parties to the agreement in other Member States, and which can sometimes only be maintained because they have no fear of competition from that direction.[150]

The Commission and Court have acted against all forms of geographical market-sharing: whether through agreements to refrain from exporting from home markets; agreements to make sales only through the home manufacturer; agreements to limit sales to home markets; or agreements between EU and non-EU undertakings to protect the EU market from low-priced imports.[151]

In *Cement*[152] the Commission found that EU cement producers had operated a systematic and well-policed policy of, amongst other things, dividing markets on the basis of the 'home market principle' (refraining from exporting to other Member States). The agreements showed that the parties made concerted efforts to stem cross-frontier flows and to reduce trade between Member States. A number of bilateral and multilateral agreements were concluded in order to back up the main agreement, for example to exchange sensitive price information. The agreement, which aimed to ensure the non-trans-shipment of products to home markets of Member States and the regulation of sales to other Member States' markets, was clearly prohibited by Article 101(1), market-sharing being expressly referred to in Article 101(1).

In *Peroxygen Products*[153] the Commission fined producers of hydrogen peroxide a total of €9 million for operating agreements which included a 'home market' rule. The agreement provided that undertakings would confine their activities to their traditional home markets. It had eliminated all competition between the competitors and excluded virtually all trade between Member States (prices varied enormously between States).

In *Soda Ash*[154] the Commission imposed large fines (of approximately €7 million) on ICI and Solvay, the two largest producers of synthetic soda ash in the Union, for the operation of an agreement under which ICI was exclusively to supply the UK and Ireland and Solvay was exclusively to supply continental Europe. Although the formal written agreement had been abandoned in 1972 (on the UK's accession to the EU) the Commission found that the agreement/concerted practice in fact continued unaltered. This decision was annulled on procedural grounds[155] but the Commission subsequently readopted it.[156]

In *SAS/Maersk*[157] the Commission imposed fines of €52.5 million for market-sharing in the air transport sector. In this case, the parties had notified a cooperation agreement to the Commission.

---

[150] Commission's *1st Report on Competition Policy* (Commission, 1971), para. 2.

[151] See, e.g., *Seamless Steel Tubes* [2003] OJ L140/1, on appeal Case T-44/00, *Mannesmannröhren-Werke AG v. Commission* [2004] ECR II-2223 (fine reduced), Cases C-403, etc./04, *Sumitomo Metal Industries Ltd v. Commission* [2007] ECR I-729.

[152] [1994] OJ L343/1, *aff'd* Case T-25/95, etc., *Cimenteries CBR SA v. Commission*, [2000] ECR II-491, broadly *aff'd* Cases C-204, etc/00 P, *Aalborg Portland v. Commission* [2004] ECR I-123.

[153] [1985] OJ L35/1.

[154] [1991] OJ L152/1, annulled on procedural grounds Case T-30/91, *Solvay SA v. Commission* [1995] ECR II-1775 (see Chap. 13) but readopted [2003] OJ L10/1, see Case T-57/01, *Solvay v. Commission* [2009] ECR II-4621.

[155] Case T-30/91, *Solvay SA v. Commission* [1995] ECR II-1775; see further Chap. 13.

[156] [2003] OJ L10/1, see Case T-57/01, *Solvay v. Commission* [2009] ECR II-4621.

[157] [2001] OJ L265/15, *aff'd* Case T-241/01, *Scandinavian Airlines System AB v. Commission* [2005] ECR II-2917.

The Commission became suspicious that the agreements were more far-reaching than the notified agreements made out. Following investigations at the parties' premises, the Commission discovered that the parties had omitted to provide information relating to a broad market-sharing agreement under which, essentially, the parties would withdraw from each other's routes and would share out domestic routes.

In *Gas*,[158] the Commission imposed very significant fines[159] on E.ON AG and GDF Suez SA (two of the largest players in the EU gas industry) for an agreement which had been in place since 1975 not to sell gas, transported through a jointly built and owned MEGAL pipeline, into each other's home markets. The market-sharing arrangement was maintained after the EU gas market was liberalised in 2000 and was only definitively abandoned in 2005. The agreement had helped the parties to maintain their strong positions in the German and French gas markets respectively when they were being liberalised, and had thwarted the liberalisation process. Through adopting this decision the Commission sought to send a strong message to energy incumbents that it would not tolerate anti-competitive behaviour, especially market-sharing which had in this case deprived customers in two of the largest EU gas markets of choice of supplier. On appeal, the GC confirmed that an agreement between actual or potential competitors not to penetrate each other's home market was restrictive by object and upheld the Commission's decision for the periods in which it had established that the parties had been potential competitors.[160] Market-sharing, through customer allocation, is also prohibited. In *Methylglucamine*,[161] for example, the parties sought to maintain the status quo of 50 per cent market share for both companies operating on the market. In particular, they tried to prevent switching by their respective customers from one to the other supplier and agreed not to compete for each other's customers.

A more unusual case of market-sharing was that condemned by the Commission in both *Luxembourg Brewers*[162] and *Belgian Brewers*.[163] It is seen in Chapters 3, 4, and 11 that it is common in beer markets for brewers to require publicans or café proprietors to purchase beer exclusively from them (beer ties). In *Luxembourg Brewers*, four Luxembourg brewers had agreed in 1985 (in signed writing!)[164] not to supply beer, for an unlimited duration, to any customer tied to another by an exclusive purchasing commitment or beer tie. When taking on a new customer, each would consult one another to check that a beer tie did not bind the customer to another. Further, the parties had measures in place that impeded trade from other Member States, and which were designed to keep foreign brewers out of the market. The Commission held that this agreement had as its object the restriction of competition. In *Belgian Brewers* Interbrew and Danone also shared out their distribution channels and pursued a policy of non-aggression.

---

[158] *Gas* [2009] OJ C248/5.

[159] See Table 9.2.

[160] Case T-360/09, *E.ON Ruhrgas AG v. Commission* 29 June 2012 (it annulled the Commission's finding insofar as it had not done so and consequently reduced the level of the fines).

[161] [2004] OJ L38/18. See also, e.g. *Synthetic Rubber* IP/06/1851, Cases T-44 and 45/07, *Kaučuk v. Commission* 13 July 2011.

[162] [2002] OJ L253/21, *aff'd* Case T-49/02, *Brasserie nationale SA v. Commission* [2005] ECR II-3033.

[163] [2003] OJ L200/1, para. 247, *aff'd* Case T-38/02, *Groupe Danone v. Commission* [2005] ECR II-4407 (small reduction in fine) *aff'd* Case C-3/06 P [2007] ECR I-1331. 'After the Commission, on its own initiative, uncovered a cartel on the Belgian beer market, InBev provided information under the auspices of the Commission's leniency policy that it was also involved in cartels in other European countries. This led to surprise inspections on brewers in France, Luxembourg, Italy, and the Netherlands. These investigations led to decisions condemning cartels in Belgium (see IP/01/1739 upheld by the CFI and ECJ, see CJE/07/13), France (see IP/04/1153, not appealed) and Luxembourg (see IP/01/1740, upheld by the CFI). The Italian investigation was closed without charges being brought' (IP/07/309). The Netherlands cartel decision was adopted on 18 April 2007 (IP/07/309).

[164] The agreement was subject to a 12-month notice period. No party had given notice when Interbrew disclosed details of the cartel to the Commission in 2000, following an investigation into its practices on the Belgian beer market, see n. 163.

d. Collusive Tendering or Bid-Rigging

Collusive tendering occurs where undertakings collaborate on responses to invitations to tender for the supply of goods and services. The practice limits price competition between the parties and amounts to an attempt by the tenderers to share markets between themselves. Instead of competing to submit the lowest possible tender at the tightest possible margin, the parties may agree on the lowest offer to be submitted or agree amongst themselves who should be the most successful bidder. The practice will automatically infringe Article 101(1).

In a system of tendering, competition is of the essence. If the tenders submitted by those taking part are not the result of individual economic calculation, but of knowledge of the tenders by other participants or of concertation with them competition is prevented, or at least distorted and restricted.[165]

Despite the relative paucity of EU bid-rigging cases, evidence suggests that bid-rigging, at least in some countries, may be rather widespread, in particular in government procurement cases.[166] Further, that they may lead to greater price increases than ordinary price-fixing. The extract from OFT 368, a UK discussion paper, makes this point.

OFT 386, 'The Development of Targets for Consumer Savings Arising from Competition Policy', Economic Discussion Paper 4, June 2002, chapter 5, paras. 5.3–5.8

Evidence from US bid rigging cases

5.3 Froeb, Koyak and Werden (1993) noted that in the five years to 1993, 70 per cent of the cartel cases investigated by the US Department of Justice (DoJ) involved bid rigging rather than price fixing, bid rigging in government procurement being typical. Perhaps for this reason, much of the empirical literature on the effect of cartels concentrates on bid rigging. While there are exceptions, in general, the evidence suggests that cartels lead to prices well in excess of 10 per cent, and sometimes in excess of 20 per cent, of competitive levels.

School milk markets

5.4 Some recent papers refer to bid rigging cartels in school milk markets. These markets lend themselves to collusion for several reasons set out in Porter and Zona (1999):

- Price competition is the only dimension of competition,
- Demand is inelastic and stable,
- Firms face similar costs of production,
- Building a new plant would be unattractive solely on the basis of higher margins made on school milk contracts, and this reduces the scope for new entry,
- Markets tend to be concentrated and localised (transport costs reduce the scope of supply side substitution) which facilitates market sharing,
- The 'game' is repeated year by year and multi-market contact is enhanced by disaggregated contracts staggered throughout the year,
- Although tendering is by sealed bid auctions, immediately after contracts are won, bids and bidders are made public so cheating can be observed,

---

[165] *Re The European Sugar Cartel* [1973] OJ L140/17, para. 42.

[166] In Germany, e.g., bid-rigging is a specific criminal offence, which can be punished by imprisonment for up to 5 years and/or by the imposition of a fine, see s. 298 of the Criminal Code. The UK's OFT has uncovered a number of instances of collusive tendering in the construction and roofing industries.

> • Competitors can obtain each other's list prices for sales of milk to retail customers which may facilitate signalling, and
>
> • Parties often meet through trade associations or by being customers of each other.
>
> …
>
> ### Bid rigging cases in Europe
>
> 5.8 The European Commission imposed record fines for bid rigging in the Pre-Insulated Pipe cartel. The Commission does not provide a formal analysis of how much higher prices were during the periods when the conspiracy had effect. However, there is a suggestion that the cartel inflated prices in Denmark by 15–20 per cent or more, whilst information from one of the cartel meetings suggests that prices in most other markets were inflated by about the same amount. Given the US evidence of bid rigging against the public sector, price rises of 15–20 per cent would certainly seem plausible.

In the *Pre-Insulated Pipe Cartel*[167] the Commission imposed fines in excess of €92 million on 10 undertakings it had found to be engaged in market-sharing, price-fixing, and bid-rigging in the market for pipes used for district heating systems (contracts for the supply of pipes were almost all awarded on the basis of competitive tendering procedures). The parties had also tried to squeeze out of the market the only competitor that had refused to participate in the cartel and had deliberately flouted the EU Public Procurement Rules. The large fines imposed reflected the deliberate nature, the gravity, and duration of the infringement (in particular, the fact that the parties had continued to operate the cartel after the Commission investigation had commenced). Further, in *Lifts and Escalators*[168] the Commission imposed record fines of €992 million on four firms for operating a number of bid-rigging cartels for the installation and maintenance of lifts and escalators in Belgium, Germany, Luxembourg, and the Netherlands. The Commission was particularly outraged by this cartel since it affected a vast market for the sale, installation, maintenance, and modernisation of lifts and escalators, the cartel would have long-term effects because of the maintenance contracts which lasted decades, and because the cartel had effected the installation of lifts and escalators in the buildings of the Commission itself and the courts in Luxembourg!

e. Bolstering Provisions

Provisions designed to reinforce or bolster the operation of a hardcore cartel, such as: measures designed to block imports;[169] refusals to supply or boycott customers who purchase from sellers outside the cartel; boycotts of competitors refusing to participate in the cartel arrangements,[170]

---

[167] *Pre-Insulated Pipe* [1999] OJ L24/1; decision substantially upheld on appeal (although some fines reduced) Case T-9/99, etc., *HFB Holdings* v. *Commission* [2002] ECR II-1487 *aff'd* Cases C-189/02 P *Dansk Rørindustri A/S* [2005] ECR I-5425. See also *Building and Construction Industry in the Netherlands* [1992] OJ L92/1, *aff'd* Case T-29/92, *SPO* v. *Commission* [1995] ECR II-289.

[168] IP/07/209, Cases T-138/07, etc., *Schindler Holding* v. *Commission* 13 July 2011. See also *Gas Insulated Switchgear* IP/07/80.

[169] See, e.g., *Meldoc* [1986] OJ L348/50, *Luxembourg Brewers* [2002] OJ L253/21, *aff'd* Case T-49/02, *Brasserie nationale SA* v. *Commission* [2005] ECR II-3033.

[170] *Pre-Insulated Pipe* [1999] OJ L24/1; decision substantially upheld on appeal (although some fines reduced) Case T-9/99, etc., *HFB Holdings* v. *Commission* [2002] ECR II-1487 *aff'd* Case C-189/02 P, *Dansk Rørindustri A/S* [2005] ECR I-5425. See also *Building and Construction Industry in the Netherlands* [1992] OJ L92/1, *aff'd* Case T-29/92, *SPO* v. *Commission* [1995] ECR II-289.

collective exclusive dealing;[171] or information-sharing arrangements, especially agreements to exchange price information,[172] are likely to infringe Article 101(1).

(iii) Article 101(3)

a. The Possibility of Meeting the Article 101(3) Criteria

All agreements may, in theory, meet the criteria of Article 101(3).[173] In practice, however, agreements to fix prices, share markets, restrict output, or rig bids are the sorts of agreement which are explicitly prohibited under Article 101(1) and are frequently examples of 'naked' cartels which do not produce efficiencies or benefits and are therefore incapable of satisfying the conditions of Article 101(3).

b. Price-fixing Agreements

Price-fixing agreements generally fall into 'the category of manifest infringements under Article [101(1)] which it is always impossible to exempt under Article [101(3)] because of the total lack of benefit to the consumer'.[174] Even in cases concerning 'crisis cartels'[175] the Commission would not extend its benevolent approach to terms fixing prices.

Some restrictions on pricing have, however, on rare occasions been accepted. For example, the Commission has been prepared in the past to grant an exemption to agreements incorporating terms which limit price competition where the agreements are not 'naked', but pursue some efficiency-enhancing objective. A key issue in these types of case (see Chapter 4) is also whether such agreements have as their 'object' the restriction of competition (and so are prohibited unless the parties establish that they satisfy the Article 101(3) criteria) or whether a recognition that the agreement is not naked means that the agreement falls outside the object category, requiring the Commission, or other person seeking to demonstrate the same, to establish that the 'effect' of the agreement is to restrict competition.[176]

In *Uniform Eurocheques*,[177] the Commission was prepared to exempt for a limited period an agreement which fixed commissions for the cashing of Eurocheques. Although the uniformity of prices and conditions for Eurocheque services led to a restriction of competition between banks in different countries in cashing Eurocheques, the Commission found that the agreement (i) improved payment methods and (ii) benefited users (all currencies were available and interest-free credit was available whilst the cheques were being cleared). The restrictions were essential in the circumstances and did not lead to an elimination of competition. Customers using the facilities knew that they would be charged a uniform amount throughout the EU. Further, it was seen in Chapter 4 that although in *Visa International-Multilateral Interchange Fee*[178] the Commission held that an agreement containing a provision to fix the 'Multilateral interchange fee (MIF)' paid by issuing banks to acquiring banks within the Visa system, which had as its effect the restriction of competition, met the Article 101(3) criteria,[179] in *MasterCard* the Commission rejected such an argument—finding that the arrangements infringed

---

[171] See, e.g., *Nederlandse Federative Vereniging voor de Grootlandel op Elektrotechnisch Gebied and Tecnhische Unie (FEG and TU)* [2000] OJ L39/1.

[172] Cases T-25, 26, 30–32, 34–9, 42–46, 48, 50–71, 87, 88, 103, and 104/95, *Cimenteries CBR SA v. Commission* [2000] ECR II-491, para. 1531, broadly aff'd Cases C-204, 205, 211, 213, 217, and 219/00 P, *Aalborg Portland A/S v. Commission* [2004] ECR I-123, *IFTRA Rules on Glass Containers* [1974] OJ L160/1.

[173] Case T-17/93, *Matra Hachette v. Commission* [1994] ECR II-595, see Chap. 4.

[174] Commission's *Xth Report on Competition Policy* (Commission, 1980), 115.

[175] See Chap. 4 and the text accompanying n. 196.

[176] See Chap. 4 and also Chap. 11.

[177] [1985] OJ L35/43. But see *Eurocheque: Helsinki Agreement* [1992] OJ L95/50, partially annulled and fines reduced on appeal, see Case T-39/92, *Groupement des Cartes Bancaires v. Commission* [1994] ECR II-49.

[178] [2002] OJ L318/17.

[179] See also discussion of the case in Chap. 4.

Article 101(1) and that no objective advantages under Article 101(3) had been demonstrated—and its decision to do so was upheld by the GC.[180] In particular, the GC stated that even if it could be inferred from the evidence that the MIF contributed to increasing the output of the MasterCard system, that was not sufficient to establish that the first condition of Article 101(3) was satisfied: the primary beneficiaries of such an increase were the MasterCard payment organisation and participating banks. Case law specified that the improvement demanded in Article 101(3) could not be identified with all the advantages which the parties obtain from the agreement in their production or distribution activities. The improvements had to displace appreciable objective advantages so as to compensate for the disadvantages which they cause in the field of competition.

The Commission has subsequently opened further proceedings against MasterCard[181] and Visa Europe. In the latter, it has set out its preliminary view that the MIF set by Visa restricted competition between banks without benefiting consumers by contributing to technical and economic progress. The proceedings, in relation to MIFs concerning Visa immediate debit card transactions, were resolved by commitments under Article 9 of Regulation 1/2003 and the Commission is testing commitments to reduce the MIF for credit card payments and to reform its rules in order to facilitate cross-border competition.[182] A number of NCAs around the network are also concerned about the compatibility of MIFs with the competition rules.[183]

In *Reims II*[184] the Commission exempted price-fixing with 'unusual characteristics'. The Commission held that the fixing of terminal dues,[185] payable by post offices for the delivery of letters in other Member States, would lead to an improvement in efficiency[186] and eliminate cross-subsidy. In none of the cases were the price restraints exempted 'naked'.

On a number of occasions, the Commission has also granted exemption to joint distribution, joint selling, or collective licensing arrangements. The Commission is ordinarily hostile to joint selling or sales joint ventures as they restrict competition between the parents on the supply-side and limit purchaser's choice. They effectively operate as horizontal price-fixing agreements. Particularly when dealing with copyright, or other neighbouring rights, however, the Commission has been persuaded that joint selling or licensing may be beneficial and meet the criteria of Article 101(3).

In *UIP*,[187] for example, the Commission granted an exemption to agreements creating United International Pictures BV (UIP) a joint film distribution company established by Paramount Pictures Corporation, Universal Studios Inc, and Metro-Goldwyn Mayer Inc. UIP distributed and licensed on an exclusive basis feature motion pictures, short subjects, and trailers produced by the parties for showing in cinemas. Following modifications to the agreement, in particular by limiting the effect of the exclusivity provisions by allowing UIP only a right of first refusal to the parent companies'

---

[180] Case T-111/08, 24 May 2012.

[181] IP/13/314, 9 April 2013.

[182] See IP/10/1684 (Visa, however is seeking to have the 2010 settlement in relation to debit cards annulled, see Case T-447/12 *Visa Europe v. European Commission*), MEMO/13/431, and <http://ec.europa.eu/competition/elojade/isef/case_details.cfm?proc_code=1_39398>.

[183] A number of complaints have been lodged before, or investigations launched and/or concluded by, NCAs such as France, Germany, and Hungary (where fines of €1.75 million were imposed on both Visa and MasterCard), Italy, Poland, and the UK (MasterCard, 6 September 2005 (OFT decision), set aside on appeal, *Mastercard UK Members Forum Ltd v. OFT* [2006] CAT 14). The heads of Europe's antitrust authorities met to discuss their investigative powers and actions against payment-card fees at a meeting in Brussels on 25 June 2013.

[184] [1999] OJ L275/17 and [2004] OJ L56/76 (effective until 31 December 2006).

[185] The remuneration that public postal operators (PPO) pay each other for the delivery of incoming cross-border mail. The receiving PPO is remunerated by the sending PPO for the delivery of the latter's mail.

[186] The agreement would lead to a correlation between the terminal dues paid and cost and improve the quality of service for cross-border mail.

[187] [1989] OJ L226/35.

films,[188] the Commission was prepared to accept that the Article 101(3) requirements were met. The Commission accepted that the cooperation produced economic benefits for the production and distribution of motion pictures and for consumers, which could not be achieved in the absence of the joint venture and which outweighed its disadvantages. In particular, the creation of UIP made possible a more effective and rationalised distribution of the parents' products, avoiding duplication of distribution organisations, and creating an economically viable distribution network in a deteriorating market where high financial risks were present. When the parties applied for an extension of the exemption the Commission required further amendments to the agreements before issuing a comfort letter.[189]

In *IFPI*[190] the International Federation of the Phonic Industry notified a reciprocal agreement in the name of national collecting societies of music record companies. The main objective of the agreement was to facilitate the grant of a multi-territorial licence[191] which broadcasters could exploit *globally*, and not just nationally, by simulcasting sound recordings on to the global digital network of the internet. The agreement would therefore facilitate the creation of a new type of licence and ensure effective administration and protection of producers' rights in the face of global internet exploitation and provide broadcasters with an alternative to obtaining a licence from the local society in every country in which their internet transmissions could be accessed. Although the agreement did involve some prices restrictions between the parties, the Commission concluded that the restrictions were indispensable to the agreement, would lead to substantial economic benefits, and would improve the distribution of music, which would benefit consumers.

Broadcasting rights to sports matches or competitions are frequently sold collectively on behalf of clubs or participants by sports associations. The agreements in the sporting sector also frequently involve exclusivity, which leads to concern as it distorts competition between broadcasters, encourages media concentration, and stifles the development of new products and services such as internet sports services and new generation mobile phones.[192] The Commission has therefore taken a keen interest in such cases.[193]

In *Joint Selling of commercial rights to the UEFA Champions League*[194] the Commission, following revision of their terms, exempted regulations concerning the joint selling of the commercial rights to the UEFA Champions League on behalf of the clubs participating in the league. The Commission accepted that the new joint selling arrangements would improve production and distribution of the League by the creation of a quality branded content product and creating a single point of sale for the acquisition of a packaged League product.

c. Output Restrictions and Restrictions Limiting or Controlling Production

The Commission has been prepared to accept that agreements which restrict output meet the Article 101(3) criteria. For example, where a restriction of output is ancillary to a beneficial R&D or specialisation agreement the terms in such agreements may, in certain circumstances, satisfy the

---

[188] This meant that the parent company concerned had first to offer its product for distribution in the EU to UIP but if UIP elected not to distribute a picture, the parent company could impose its distribution on UIP or distribute the film independently, either itself or through a third party.

[189] IP/99/681.

[190] [2003] OJ C107/58.

[191] Ordinarily, collecting societies have the right to grant licences for exploitation of sound recordings in their territory only.

[192] The Commission is concerned that exclusivity agreements do not lead to other broadcasters being excluded from the market altogether. Thus a long duration of exclusivity may be prohibited if there is a risk that a broadcaster might prevent its competitors gaining access.

[193] See Chap. 13.

[194] [2003] OJ L291/25.

terms of Article 101(3).[195] Further, in the past, where there has been serious over-capacity in an industry, the Commission has occasionally been sympathetic to parties that notified 'crisis cartels' (for example, restructuring agreements) for exemption (see Chapter 4).[196] It permitted undertakings operating in industries suffering severe difficulties to conclude cooperation agreements providing, for example, for an orderly reduction in over-capacity where the economic effect of the improved rationalisation outweighs the disadvantages of the reduced competition in the short term. However, it would not allow the restructuring to be achieved by unacceptable means such as price-fixing or market-sharing. Further, it would regard the restrictions as indispensable only if the agreement was concerned solely with the reduction of capacity and was limited from the outset to a period necessary for its setting up and implementation. It permitted several agreements in the petrochemical and thermoplastics sector.[197] Arguably, such agreements may achieve efficiencies through the removal of inefficient capacity from the industry and by enabling remaining players on the market to achieve benefits through increased capacity utilisation rate.

These crisis cartel decisions are old ones, however, and more recently the Commission has not seemed to be willing to tolerate crisis cartels, at least where it could be expected that market forces would be able to remedy structural over-capacity. Indeed, in a speech on 8 October 2009, Neelie Kroes made it clear that a benevolent approach to these types of agreements should not be taken during the financial and economic crisis. Not only did she indicate that the Commission would not turn a blind eye to cartels but she also warned that the Commission would be vigilant for them, recognising that anti-competitive collaboration is a hugely tempting mechanism for firms to employ to shield themselves from ruinous competition in a climate of rising competition for a shrinking demand. In a speech in October 2009, Neelie Kroes stated:

If I may quickly mention the issue of so-called 'crisis-cartels'... There may be many temptations in 2009 to cut corners, but encouraging cartelists and others would be guaranteeing disaster. It would drag down recovery, increase consumer harm and create more cartel and cartel cases into the future. No-one wins—today's softness is tomorrow's nightmare.

This hard-line stance has, however, raised some concern, especially in cases where, for example, governments may have endorsed or encouraged industry-wide measures to permit the weathering of an industry storm or even pressured industry members to adopt voluntary measures to achieve broader public policy objectives. This type of disquiet was perhaps reflected by the Irish courts in the *BIDS* case, which had to adjudicate on the compatibility of a crisis cartel (made with the knowledge of the Irish Government) with Article 101(3). In Chapter 3 it is seen that the CJ in *BIDS* held, following a reference to it from the Irish Supreme Court, that because an agreement to reduce capacity had as its object the restriction of competition, the fact that the parties did not intend to harm consumers but to benefit them through rationalisation of the industry was not relevant under Article 101(1). The objective pursued might, however, be relevant under Article 101(3). When the matter returned to the Irish Supreme Court, the only matter remaining to be resolved, therefore, was whether or not the arrangements could benefit from Article 101(3). The Irish Supreme Court[198] felt that this issue should be remitted to the Irish High Court for decision, but nonetheless expressed a view on some general legal points that would be relevant to the Article 101(3) assessment. In particular, it stressed that the case was far removed from a cartel scheme hatched in a smoke-filled room,[199] indicated

---

[195] See Chap. 10.

[196] One of the Commission's objectives was to ensure the elimination of over-capacity in an industry and to enable the industry to recover its profitability, *XX1st Report on Competition Policy* (Commission, 1991), 207 ff.

[197] e.g., in *ENI/Montedison* [1987] OJ L5/13, for 15 years there was an agreement between two large petrochemical groups for rationalisation of their production capacities and transfer of certain businesses, leading to a *de facto* specialisation by each party.

[198] *Competition Authority v. Beef Industry Development Society Ltd* [2009] IESC 72.

[199] Not only had the agreement been concluded with the knowledge of the Irish Government but it had been notified to the Irish competition authority. The latter felt it was anticompetitive, however, and for this reason brought proceedings before the Irish courts to have the agreement struck down.

(having regard to the Commission's previous decisions in *Synthetic Fibres* and *Dutch Bricks (Stichting Baksteen)*) that the agreement was likely to realise substantial efficiencies (even if the value of those efficiencies could not be demonstrated), and pointed out that no consumers had complained and that powerful buyers (such as Tesco) were unlikely to tolerate the passing on of any price increases. The Court noted further that restraints designed to prevent players who had been paid to leave the industry from re-entering and acquiring capacity seemed indispensable to the success of the arrangements. When the matter reverted to the Irish High Court the Commission intervened in the case to submit observations to the Court on the application of Article 101(3). The opinion indicates that the Commission considers that it will only be in relatively rare circumstances that parties to an agreement involving a reduction in capacity will be able to demonstrate efficiencies, that the restrictive agreement is indispensable to achieve those efficiencies (and that they cannot be achieved by market forces), and that any benefits would be passed on to consumers.[200] Before the High Court had an opportunity to reach its decision on the application of Article 101(3), however, BIDS withdrew its claim for exemption and agreed to pay a substantial proportion of the competition authority's costs. The authority has now published a guidance note on agreements to reduce capacity which is based on its experience in the *BIDS* case.[201]

In another case the Commission granted an exemption to an agreement which did not restrict output but which restricted the type of goods that the parties to the agreement could produce or import. In *European Council of Manufacturers of Domestic Appliances*[202] the Commission exempted an agreement concluded between 95 per cent of the producers and importers of washing machines operating on the EU market that restricted their freedom to manufacture or import the least energy-efficient washing machines. The agreement was found to restrict competition within the meaning of Article 101(1).[203] Nonetheless the Commission considered that the agreement met the criteria set out in Article 101(3) since it would reduce the potential energy consumption of new machines and consequently lessen pollution, create more technically efficient machines, and focus future R&D on furthering energy efficiency. Such economic and technical progress would benefit society and consumers. The Commission considered that the restrictions were indispensable to the agreement, which would not substantially eliminate competition.

d. Market-Sharing Agreements

It is particularly unlikely that market-sharing agreements will meet the Article 101(3) criteria. The Commission has stated its opinion that:

in principle, exemption from the prohibition cannot be considered for market-sharing agreements. The elimination of a competitor from a market—either in whole or in part—cannot be justified objectively on economic or technical grounds or in the interests of the consumer.[204]

e. Collusive Tendering

As with other hardcore cartel activity it is unlikely that bid-rigging would meet the Article 101(3) criteria.[205] In *FIEC/CEETB*,[206] however, the Commission indicated that it would take a favourable view of an agreement designed to standardise and reduce the cost of the tendering process between build-

---

[200] Available at, <http://ec.europa.eu/competition/court/antitrust_amicus_curiae.html>.

[201] Notice on Agreements to Reduce Capacity, 16 June 2011, available at <http://www.tca.ie/images/uploaded/documents/N-11–001%20Notice%20on%20Agreements%20to%20Reduce%20Capacity.pdf>.

[202] [2000] OJ L187/47.

[203] See Chap. 4, IP/01/1659 (where the Commission indicated its intention to take a similar approach to environmental agreements for water heaters and dishwashers) and contrast e.g., *Consumer Detergents*, 13 April 2011.

[204] *1st Report on Competition Policy* (Commission, 1971), 3.

[205] See, e.g., *Cast Iron and Steel Rolls* [1983] OJ L317/1.

[206] [1998] OJ C52/2.

ing contractors and sub-contractors but which would not in any way limit either the firms who could tender or the prices at which they could tender.

D. RESTRICTIONS ON NON-PRICE TRADING CONDITIONS, ADVERTISING, AND PROMOTION AND INFORMATION-SHARING AGREEMENTS

(i) General

Agreements relating to non-price trading conditions or relating to advertising or promotion may not have such a serious impact on competition as the agreements discussed in Section 3.C. They may, nonetheless, restrict important methods of competition between undertakings operating on the market. Further, such restraints may chill competition between firms operating on the market and may, in some circumstances, be used to complement and facilitate the operation of a hardcore cartel agreement or may have the effect of facilitating tacit collusion between firms operating on the market. Although these types of restraints do not generally have as their object the restriction of competition, they may have to be carefully scrutinised to consider whether or not they have that effect and, if so, whether or not they meet the criteria of Article 101(3).

(ii) Restrictions on Non-price Trading Conditions

a. Introduction

Because non-price competition may also be an important part of competition between undertakings, Article 101(1)(a) prohibits—as incompatible with the common market—collusive practices which 'directly or indirectly fix…any other trading conditions'. Restraints on such trading conditions may also bolster other hardcore cartel activities. In *Fine Art Auction Houses*,[207] for example, Christie's and Sotheby's fixed not only the commissions that they charged but other conditions as well, such as payment conditions, guarantees, and advances. In some cases, however, it may be advantageous for undertakings to have access to suitably drafted terms and conditions and/or to adopt common quality or technical standards. In such cases, it is possible that the agreements will not infringe Article 101(1) at all or that they will meet the criteria of Article 101(3).[208]

b. Uniform Terms and Conditions

The use of printed forms setting out standard terms and conditions to be applied by undertakings will not necessarily infringe Article 101(1). However, where the terms and conditions relate to 'important secondary aspects of competition',[209] that is, to any aspect of a supplier's offer which has economic value in the eyes of the customer, they may infringe Article 101(1).

In *Fabricants de Papiers Peints de Belgique*,[210] the Commission found that general conditions of sale concluded by Belgian manufacturers of wallpaper, which related to terms of delivery, returns policy, lengths of rolls, etc. infringed Article 101(1) and did not satisfy the conditions of Article 101(3).

---

[207] IP/02/1585.

[208] *Concordato Incendio* [1990] OJ L15/27.

[209] *Vimpoltu* [1983] OJ L200/44.

[210] [1974] OJ L237/3.

c. Customer Services

Prohibitions on parties to an agreement offering customers special services such as the loan of products or special delivery arrangements are likely to cause an infringement of Article 101(1).[211]

d. Product Quality

The adoption of a common quality label (establishing that products meet a minimum quality standard) will not necessarily infringe Article 101(1). However, a provision restricting suppliers from producing products of a different, inferior standard (and limiting the quality of products supplied) is likely to infringe Article 101(1).[212]

e. Technical Development

Similarly, the adoption of a label identifying products that achieve a certain common technical standard will not infringe Article 101(1) where the quality mark is freely available and the parties are free to market products of a different or inferior standard.[213] There may, however, be an infringement of Article 101(1) where the agreement limits technical development[214] or is used to hinder imports, as in *IAZ*.[215]

In *IAZ* a Belgian trade association agreed with Belgian manufacturers and sole importers for washing machines and dishwashers that only appliances with a 'conformity' label could be connected to the mains. To receive a conformity label the appliances had to comply with technical standards laid down by Belgian law. In fact, the label was available only to Belgian manufacturers or sole importers of products. Thus parallel imports of the appliances were made impossible in practice.

(iii) Restrictions on Advertising and Promotion

The advertising and promotion of a product may be an extremely important aspect of competition between undertakings. It may be a vital means of distinguishing the products, in the eyes of the consumer, from those of competitors and may draw attention to the different characteristics, prices, and qualities of the relevant products. It can also provide an important mechanism for entering a new market.

Restrictions on the ability of parties to an agreement to advertise is likely to be seen as a restriction on their competitive freedom and competition.[216] The Commission is concerned about restrictions on advertising in the liberal professions.

Communication from the Commission, 'Report on Competition in Professional Services' Com(2004) 83 final (Brussels, 9 February 2004)

42. A large number of the EU professions are subject to sector-specific advertising regulation...in some cases advertising as such is prohibited. In others, specific media or advertising methods such as radio

---

[211] See, e.g., *VCH* [1972] OJ L13/34.

[212] *Belgian Association of Pharmacists* [1990] OJ L160/1. But see also *European Council of Manufacturers of Domestic Appliances* [2000] OJ L187/47, Chap. 4 and Case C-309/99, *Wouters v. Algemene Raad van de Nederlandse Order van Advocaten* [2002] ECR I-1577.

[213] Notice on Cooperation Agreements [1968] JO C75/3, para. II(8).

[214] See, e.g., *Video Cassette Recorders* [1978] OJ L47/42.

[215] *Anseau* [1982] OJ L167/39; on appeal Case 96/82, *IAZ International Belgium NV v. Commission* [1983] ECR 3369.

[216] See, e.g., *Consumer Detergents*, 13 April 2011 (the Commission treated restrictions on promotional activity as a form of price collusion in the context of the case).

advertising, televisions advertising or 'cold calling' or specific types of advertising content are proscribed. In certain cases, there is a lack of clarity in existing advertising regulations which, in itself, may deter professions from employing certain advertising methods.

43. According to economic theory, advertising may facilitate competition by informing consumers about different products and allowing them to make better informed purchasing decisions. Advertising restrictions may thus reduce competition by increasing the costs of gaining information about different products, making it more difficult for consumers to search for the quality and price that best meets their needs. It is also widely recognised that advertising, and in particular comparative advertising, can be a crucial competitive tool for new firms entering the market and for existing firms to launch new products.

44. The proponents of advertising restrictions emphasise the asymmetry of information between practitioners and consumers of professional services. According to this argument, consumers find it difficult to assess information about professional services and therefore need particular protection from misleading or manipulative claims.

45. There is, however, an increasing body of empirical evidence which highlights the potentially negative effects of some advertising restrictions. This research suggests that restrictions may under certain circumstances increase the fees for professional services without having a positive effect on the quality of those services. The implication of these findings is that advertising restrictions as such do not, necessarily, provide an appropriate response to asymmetry of information in professional services. Conversely, truthful and objective advertising may actually help consumers to overcome the asymmetry and to make more informed purchasing decisions.

In general, where parties agree jointly to advertise industry products or products of a common brand, there is no infringement of Article 101(1) so long as the parties are also free to advertise individually. However, different rules may apply in an oligopolistic market where product differentiation and advertising may play a more vital role.

In *Milchförderúngsfonds*,[217] the German dairy industry established a milk promotion fund. The fund was financed by a voluntary levy on milk delivered to dairies. The purpose of the fund was to promote the export of milk products. Brand-advertising campaigns and subsidised sales were conducted abroad. The Commission considered that the campaign distorted competition within the meaning of Article 101(1) and artificially strengthened the position of German exporters abroad. Although generic advertising, which did not commend the products solely on the ground of their national origin and did not disparage foreign products, would have benefited all exporters, brand-oriented advertising appreciably reduced the possibility of sales for competing brands. Individual manufacturers benefited from the campaign without having to suffer a corresponding cost which otherwise would have been reflected in the sales price.

In *BELASCO*,[218] Belgian manufacturers jointly advertised and promoted their products, which were sold under a common trade mark, through the association, BELASCO. The Commission considered that the purpose of the standardisation of the products and the joint advertising was to reinforce the other provisions of the agreement which provided for a common price list and sales quotas. The fostering of an impression in consumers that their products were homogeneous limited the scope of competition by means of product differentiation.

The Commission has, on occasion, accepted that it may be advantageous for undertakings to rationalise and coordinate their advertising efforts, particularly in the context of trade fairs.[219]

---

[217] [1985] OJ L35/35.

[218] [1986] OJ L232/15.

[219] See, e.g., *UNIDI* [1984] OJ L322/10.

(iv) Information-Sharing Agreements

a. Exchange of Information between Competitors

The dissemination and exchange of information between competitors and the creation of a transparent market may be harmless or even highly beneficial to the competitive structure of the market.[220] In particular, the transparency created in a market by information exchanges can produce significant efficiencies and benefits to both suppliers and customers. 'Many sectors of our economies now depend upon ready access to detailed information'.[221] For example, it may allow suppliers to improve commercial strategies, to improve allocative efficiency, to increase internal efficiency (for example by benchmarking their processes and performance against other industry performance), to promote innovation, and/or to improve product positioning, it may reduce search costs and may increase transparency for consumers. Trade associations thus frequently collect industry data on prices, outputs, capacity, and investment and circulate information to their members which may make it easier for undertakings to plan their own business strategies. Further, the theory of perfect competition rests upon the assumption that there is perfect freedom of information. A market characterised by many buyers and sellers should, therefore, positively benefit from such transparency. Where information is available generally, consumers with complete knowledge of what is on offer may fully utilise their power of choice.

However, information exchanges may also present the opportunity for competitors to coordinate their behaviour and to achieve and maintain a collusive equilibrium over time. They may be used to bolster or facilitate the operation of a cartel. Where the information is exchanged to support price-fixing or other hardcore cartel activity the Commission or other enforcing authority will obviously take a dim view.[222] In *Methylglucamine*,[223] for example, cartel meetings (where price increases and customer allocation were agreed) normally started with an exchange of information and views on the worldwide demand for the product, referring to the volumes sold to the respective main clients during the previous year. In this case, however, the Commission concluded that this practice had not materialised into a full systematic exchange of sales data.[224]

Information exchange may also form part of a horizontal cooperation agreement, for example a standardisation or a R&D agreement,[225] or be operated as a standalone practice which is not dependent on a cartel or another arrangement between the parties. Standalone agreements, involving the exchange of strategic information may, '[b]y artificially increasing transparency in the market, ... can facilitate coordination (that is to say, alignment) of companies' competitive behaviour and result in restrictive effects on competition.'[226] In particular, information exchanged about firms' past, current, or future behaviour may provide a focal point facilitating competitors' coordination of price or output levels on a market. It may also allow firms operating on a market to determine quickly whether competitors are deviating from a coordinated strategy (it may contribute to the internal stability of the coordinated strategy) or whether new entrants may be threatening a collusive strategy (it may contribute to the external stability of the coordinated strategy). Information-sharing

---

[220] See Commission's Guidelines on the applicability of Article 101 of the Treaty on the Functioning of the European Union to horizontal co-operation agreements [2011] OJ C11/1 ('Horizontal Cooperation Guidelines'), especially paras. 57–58 and 64–71 and, e.g., M. Bennett and P. Collins, 'The Law and Economics of information sharing: the good, the bad and the ugly' [2010] *European Competition Law Journal* 311, K. U. Kühn and X. Vives, 'Information exchanges among firms and their impact on competition' (Office for Official Publications of the European Community, Luxembourg, 1995) and OECD Roundtable on Information Exchange DAF/COMP(2010)37.

[221] Bennett and Collins, 'The Law and Economics of information sharing' (cited in n. 220), 311.

[222] See, e.g., *Building and Construction Industry in the Netherlands* [1992] OJ L92/1, *aff'd* Case T-29/92, *SPO v. Commission* [1995] ECR II-289.

[223] [2004] OJ L38/18.

[224] [2004] OJ L38/18, paras. 76–82.

[225] See Chap. 10.

[226] Horizontal Cooperation Guidelines, para. 65.

arrangements may also present opportunities to foreclose competitors from a market, for example where the information exchange provides the recipients with a significant competitive advantage over rivals in the relevant market or in a downstream market.[227] A standalone information exchange may therefore in *itself* be sufficient to establish a violation of Article 101(1).[228]

As information exchanges ancillary to a cartel or a horizontal cooperation agreement are assessed in the broader context of, and in combination with, the cartel or cooperation arrangements in which they are operated, this section focuses on the question of how 'standalone' information exchanges are analysed under the EU competition law rules. In addition to the case law, the Commission's Guidelines on the applicability of Article 101 of the Treaty on the Functioning of the European Union to horizontal cooperation agreements (Horizontal Cooperation Guidelines)[229] provide guidance on how the Commission applies the competition law rules to standalone agreements.

b. Agreement, Concerted Practice, or Decision Essential: Direct and Indirect Sharing of Data and Hub and Spoke Arrangements

Information exchange can result from some form of direct sharing of data between competitors or through sharing of that data indirectly 'through a common agency (for example, a trade association) or a third party such as a market research organisation or through the companies' suppliers or retailers'.[230] Sharing of data can, however, of course 'only be addressed under Article 101 if it establishes or is part of an agreement, a concerted practice or a decision by an association of undertakings'[231] (see further Chapter 3). It is essential, therefore, that, for Article 101 to apply, it be established that the sharing of information results from joint not unilateral conduct, for example a direct exchange of data through:

- reciprocal exchanges of strategic information between competitors (even if only on a single occasion, see *T-Mobile Netherlands BV v. Raad van bestuur van de Nederlandse Mededingingsautoriteit*);[232] or

- a disclosure of strategic information by one undertaking to a competitor (whether by, for example, mail, email, phone call, or orally at a meeting) where the recipient requests the information or accepts it.[233]

In *Bananas*,[234] for example, the Commission held that three banana importers, Chiquita, Dole, and Weichert, which had engaged in direct bilateral pre-pricing communications in relation to price-setting factors (prior to setting their weekly quotation prices), had taken part in a concerted practice to coordinate quotation prices for bananas.

More difficult to categorise are situations where undertakings do not directly pass information to each other but disclose information which is nonetheless received by competitors, for example, because the information was published publicly by an undertaking (perhaps on a website or to

---

[227] Horizontal Cooperation Guidelines, paras. 69–71.

[228] See, e.g. Case T-141/94, *Thyssen Stahl v. Commission* [1999] ECR II-347, paras. 379–392.

[229] [2011] OJ C11/01. The Commission's Guidelines on the application of Article 101 to maritime transport services also provide guidance on the compatibility of information agreements with Article 101.

[230] [2011] OJ C11/01, para. 55.

[231] [2011] OJ C11/01, para. 60.

[232] Case C-8/08 *T-Mobile Netherlands BV v. Raad van bestuur van de Nederlandse Mededingingsautoriteit* [2009] ECR I-4529(see Chap. 3), paras. 54–62.

[233] See, e.g., Cases 40–48, 50, 54–56, 111, and 113–114/73, *Re the European Sugar Cartel: Coöperatieve Vereniging 'Suiker Unie' UA v. Commission* [1975] ECR 1663, Cases T-25/95, etc., *Cimenteries CBR SA v. Commission* [2000] ECR II-491, Cases T-202/98, etc., *Tate & Lyle, Napier Brown and British Sugar* [2001] ECR II-2035 *aff'd* Case C-359/01P *British Sugar* [2004] ECR I-4933.

[234] Case COMP/39188 *Bananas* 15 October 2008, *aff'd* Cases T-587/08 *Fresh Del Monte Produce v. Commission* and T-588/08 P *Dole Food and Dole Germany v. Commission* 14 March 2013, on appeal Cases C-293 and 294/13 P (judgments pending). The appeal by Weichart, Case T-2/09, was dismissed as manifestly inadmissible as it was lodged out of time, *aff'd* Case C-73/10 P.

investors[235]) or because the information was received and published or transferred by an intermediary (such as a newspaper or trade journal, an independent consultant, a trade association, or a mutual customer or supplier). In such situations it is necessary to assess carefully on the facts whether or not the firm and its competitors can be proved to have agreed or concerted (see further Chapter 3 and discussion of *Wood Pulp*[236] in Section 4.A.ii–4.A.iii).

c. Assessing the Competitive Effects of an Information-Sharing Arrangement

Although a category of information exchange may be considered to be restrictive by object in principle, the majority of information agreements are assessed individually in their market context to determine their actual or likely effects on competition. Apart from the de minimis principle,[237] no safe harbour applies for standalone information exchanges and there are relatively few bright lines or clear rules for business to adhere to in this area.

An approach closely in tune with economic effects might suggest that only a relatively narrow category of information-sharing agreements should potentially be considered to be restrictive by object—for example, the private sharing of disaggregated, confidential information on future pricing or output intentions between competitors should be held to restrict competition by object.[238] Indeed the Commission provides only one example, in its Horizontal Cooperation Guidelines, of information exchanges that restrict competition by object, that is information exchanges 'on companies' individualised intentions concerning future conduct regarding prices or quantities'.[239] The Commission states that such exchanges are likely to allow competitors to arrive at a common higher price level and are less likely to be made for pro-competitive reasons than exchanges of actual data. Further, that 'private exchanges between competitors on their individualised intentions regarding future prices or quantities would normally be considered and fined as cartels because they generally have the object of fixing prices or quantities'.[240] In *Bananas*[241] the Commission fined three banana importers for engaging in a concerted practice which had as its object the restriction of competition, as the Commission found that it concerned the fixing, development, and evolution of prices; the parties' regular pattern of communications relating to price-setting factors (such as the sales situation, supply and demand conditions liable to affect price levels for the coming weeks, and price trends and/or indications of quotation prices for the coming week), all of which were ultimately aimed at reducing or eliminating uncertainty as to the future pricing behaviour of the parties (the setting of quotation prices) and to maximise the price that they could individually and/or collectively obtain. The arguments that the exchanges should not be considered to be restrictive by object were rejected by the GC.[242] The GC found that the frequent and regular discussion of price-setting factors relevant to the setting of quotation prices was sufficient basis for a finding of anti-competitive object. Further,

---

[235] e.g., earnings calls with industry analysts are often monitored by competitors.

[236] Cases C-89, 104, 114, 116–117, and 125–129/85, *Re Wood Pulp Cartel: Ahlström Osakeyhtiö (Wood Pulp II)* v. *Commission (Wood Pulp II)* [1993] ECR I-1307.

[237] See Chap 4, Sections 3.D.v and 3.E.v.

[238] See, e.g., Bennett and Collins, 'The Law and Economics of information sharing' (cited in n. 220), 329–331 and Swedish Competition Authority, *The Pros and Cons of Information Sharing* (2006) and B. Meyring, 'T-Mobile: Further confusion on information exchanges between competitors' (2010) 1 *Journal of European Competition Law & Practice* 31 (and extract set out in Chap. 4, Section 3.D.iii).

[239] Horizontal Cooperation Guidelines, para. 73. It does, however, also state that in assessing whether any specific exchange is restrictive by object, the Commission will pay particular attention to the legal and economic context in which the information exchange takes place and whether by its very nature the exchange may possibly lead to a restriction of competition,

[240] Horizontal Cooperation Guidelines, paras. 72–74.

[241] Case COMP/39188 *Bananas* 15 October 2008, *aff'd* Cases T-587/08 *Fresh Del Monte Produce* v. *Commission*, and T-588/08 P *Dole Food and Dole Germany* v. *Commission* 14 March 2013.

[242] Case COMP/39188 *Bananas* 15 October 2008, *aff'd* Cases T-587/08 *Fresh Del Monte Produce* v. *Commission*, and T-588/08 P *Dole Food and Dole Germany* v. *Commission* 14 March 2013.

it examined in detail, and rejected, all arguments against a finding of anti-competitive object, including those relating to the legal and economic context of the case and the specific characteristics of the banana market (for example, the regulatory framework and market supply, the nature of the product, and the structure of the market).

Although the CJ's judgment in *T-Mobile Netherlands BV v. Raad van bestuur van de Nederlandse Mededingingsautoriteit*[243] reinforces the view that a private[244] information exchange designed to remove uncertainties concerning the intended conduct of the participating firms and facilitating, directly or indirectly, the fixing of purchase or selling prices falls within the category of restraints which are restrictive by object,[245] it was seen in Chapter 4 that the CJ went further in its ruling than perhaps was required for the national court to decide the case. It stated that 'an exchange of information which is capable of removing uncertainty between participants as regard the timing, extent and details of the modifications to be adopted by the undertakings concerned must be regarded as pursuing an anti-competitive object' and:

in order for a concerted practice to be regarded as having an anti-competitive object, it is sufficient that it has the potential to have a negative impact on competition. In other words, the concerted practice must simply be capable in an individual case, having regard to the specific legal and economic context, of resulting in the prevention, restriction or distortion of competition...Whether and to what extent, in fact, such anti-competitive effects result can only be of relevance for determining the amount of any fine and assessing any claim for damages.[246]

This statement, which was repeated and reaffirmed by the GC in *Fresh Del Monte Produce Inc* v. *Commission*, seems potentially to extend the category of object restraints to an overly broad and somewhat uncertain group of information-exchange agreements.

Where an agreement is not found to have as its object the restriction of competition, it will need to be assessed individually in its market context to determine its actual or likely effect. 'For an information exchange to have restrictive effects on competition within the meaning of Article 101(1), it must be likely to have an appreciable adverse impact on one (or several) of the parameters of competition such as price, output, product quality, product variety or innovation.'[247] The CJ in *Asnef-Equifax, Servicios de Información sobre Solvencia y Crédito, SL* v. *Asociación de Usuarios de Servicios Bancarios (Ausbanc)* stated:[248]

the appraisal of the effects of agreements or practices...entails the need to take into consideration the actual context to which they belong, in particular the economic and legal context in which the undertakings concerned operate, the nature of the goods or services affected, as well as the real conditions of the functioning and the structure of the market or markets in question...

Accordingly...the compatibility of an information exchange system...with the [EU] competition rules cannot be assessed in the abstract. It depends on the economic conditions on the relevant markets and on the specific characteristics of the system concerned, such as, in particular, its purpose and the conditions of

---

[243] Case C-8/08 *T-Mobile Netherlands BV* v. *Raad van bestuur van de Nederlandse Mededingingsautoriteit* [2009] ECR I-4529, paras. 36–43.

[244] For the view that public information exchanges relating to future (or current) prices are less likely to produce anti-competitive effects than private exchanges, see Bennett and Collins, 'The Law and Economics of information sharing'(cited in n. 220), 334 and discussion of public announcements in Section 4.A.iii.

[245] The same principles apply to the exchange of price information between distributors, see *Hasselblad* OJ 1982 L161/18, [1982] 2 CMLR 233, on appeal Case 86/82 *Hasselblad v. Commission* [1984] ECR 883, [1984] 1 CMLR 559: where a market is not oligopolistic, the Commission has been prepared to accept that even the exchange of individual and confidential information concerning costs, sales volumes, and market shares may not infringe Article 101: *Eudim* [1996] OJ C111/8.

[246] Case C-8/08 *T-Mobile Netherlands BV* v. *Raad van bestuur van de Nederlandse Mededingingsautoriteit* [2009] ECR I-4529, para. 31.

[247] Horizontal Cooperation Guidelines, para. 75.

[248] Case C-238/05, [2006] ECR I-11125, para. 54.

access to it and participation in it, as well as the type of information exchanged—be that, for example, public or confidential, aggregated or detailed, historical or current—the periodicity of such information and its importance for the fixing of prices, volumes or conditions of service.

Two factors are, therefore, particularly relevant in the marking of the assessment: (1) the specific characteristics of the system—its purpose, conditions of access and participation, and the type of information exchanged; and (2) the nature and economic conditions of the relevant market.

(1) When determining the likely effect of the information exchange on competition it is necessary to assess a number of factors including the type of information exchange and the nature of the data, in the context of the facts of the case and the market in which the information exchange is operated.[249] Statistical information which enables undertakings to assess the level of demand and output in the market or the costs of its competitors may be beneficial and is not of itself objectionable.[250] Similarly, exchange of technical or other information that does not restrict the parties' freedom to determine their market behaviour independently should not be objectionable. However, exchange of strategic data (that reduces strategic uncertainty in the market), such as information relating to prices, individual output or sales figures,[251] capacity increases,[252] costs,[253] demand, investment plans,[254] new technology and research projects, or other business secrets, is liable to decrease the parties' incentive to compete and increase opportunities for coordinated activity. It has been seen that the exchange of particularly sensitive, confidential data may be sufficient to establish a restriction by object. In *Cobelpa/VNP*,[255] for example, the Commission held that although there was nothing wrong in a trade association exchanging information on industry output and sales, in this case, where the information exchanged identified the output and sales of individual undertakings, the practice was prohibited. By exchanging information about matters normally regarded as confidential (especially where the information was not available to consumers) the parties were replacing practical cooperation for the normal risks of competition. It made no difference that the information could have been obtained from elsewhere.

The nature of the data (whether it is individualised or aggregated) and its age is also important. The exchange of aggregated industry-wide data (which does not identify the performance of individual competitors), even if it relates to output or price, is less likely to enable firms to coordinate their behaviour or to detect deviations from a coordinated strategy. Similarly, if the information exchanged is 'historic'[256] rather than current it is unlikely to facilitate the future coordination of conduct on a market in the future.[257] In contrast, exchanges are more likely to facilitate 'a common understanding on the market and punishment strategies by allowing the coordinating companies to single out a deviator or entrant'[258] when the data exchanged is individualised and/or when it relates

---

[249] Horizontal Cooperation Guidelines, paras. 86–94.

[250] Case T-334/94, *Sarrió SA v. Commission* [1998] ECR II-1439.

[251] See *UK Agricultural Tractor Registration Exchange* [1992] OJ L68/19.

[252] See e.g., *Re Cimbell* [1972] OJ L303/24.

[253] See, e.g., *IFTRA Glass Containers* [1974] OJ L160/1; *IFTRA Aluminium* OJ 1975 L228/3.

[254] See, e.g., *Zinc Producer Group* [1984] OJ L220/27.

[255] [1977] OJ L242/10.

[256] There may be no objection under Art. 101(1) if information as to the production or sales of particular undertakings is made publicly available under the auspices of a trade association provided the information is sufficiently historical that it no longer has any real impact on future behaviour, *UK Agricultural Tractor Registration Exchange* [1992] OJ L68/19.

[257] 'Aggregated information at the industry level is unlikely to be useful for coordination. It is difficult to come to a focal point or monitor and understanding when firms cannot see from the information how their individual competitors are performing. Likewise, information which is significantly historic in nature is unlikely to be useful for present or future coordination...Of course, what qualifies as "historic" will depend upon the nature of the market and the competitive interaction within the sector', Bennett and Collins, 'The Law and Economics of information sharing' (cited in n. 220), 331.

[258] Horizontal Cooperation Guidelines, para. 89.

to future or current conduct. Other factors, such as the frequency of the exchange, whether the information exchanged is in the public domain,[259] and whether the information is actually exchanged in public or is a private exchange,[260] may also to be relevant to the assessment. 'The fact that information is exchanged in public may decrease the likelihood of a collusive outcome on the market to the extent that non-coordinating companies, potential competitors, as well as customers may be able to constrain potential restrictive effect on competition.'[261] The purpose of the exchange and conditions of access may also be important to the assessment.

(2) In assessing information agreements close attention also needs to be paid to the structure of the market. The tendency for firms to fall in line with the behaviour of their competitors is particularly strong in oligopolistic markets. The improved knowledge of market conditions aimed at by information agreements strengthens the connection between the undertakings, in that they are enabled to react very efficiently to one another's actions, and thus lessens the intensity of competition.[262] Information exchanges are therefore more likely to be problematic on oligopolistic markets which are conducive to interdependent coordinated behaviour, in particular, markets with a few players which are sufficiently transparent, concentrated, complex, stable, and symmetric: 'In those types of markets companies can reach a common understanding on the terms of coordination and successfully monitor and punish deviations.'[263]

Information exchanges can also facilitate interdependent behaviour by creating the conditions for it—by increasing transparency, reducing complexity, buffering instability, or compensating for asymmetry.[264] For example, exchange of individualised market data on a concentrated market may facilitate the identification of those cheating on a cartel. Alternatively, it may facilitate conscious parallel behaviour by enabling undertakings to react rapidly to one another's actions. The effect of information exchanges is likely to be less serious (a) where consumers also have access to the information, and (b) where the agreement provides for post-notification of historic information rather than pre-notification of information.

In *UK Agricultural Tractor Registration Exchange*,[265] the Commission condemned the exchange of information relating to past transactions. In this case eight UK manufacturers and importers of agricultural tractors operated, through the Agricultural Engineers Association, an information-exchange agreement called the UK Agricultural Tractor Registration Exchange. The information identified the volume of retail sales and market shares of each of the eight manufacturers individually. In condemning the agreement under Article 101(1) and refusing to exempt it under Article 101(3), the Commission took account of the facts that:

(i) the market was highly concentrated, (the eight manufacturers/importers had approximately 87–88 per cent of the relevant market);

(ii) there were high barriers to entry into the market;

---

[259] Art. 101(1) may be infringed even if the information could have been obtained from other, less convenient, sources, see, e.g. Case C-238/05, *Asnef-Equifax v. Asociación Usuarios de Servicios Bancarios (Ausbanc)* [2006] ECR I-11125, para. 58.

[260] Any 'market transparency' attained may be offset by the fact that the information remains private to the undertakings concerned, see, e.g., *UK Agricultural Tractor Registration Exchange* [1992] OJ L68/19.

[261] Horizontal Cooperation Guidelines, para. 94. The public information exchanges will, of course, be caught by Art. 101(1) only if it can be established that the parties have engaged in an agreement to exchange the information or concerted to do so.

[262] Commission's VIIth Report on Competition Policy (Commission, 1977), part 7(2).

[263] Horizontal Cooperation Guidelines, para. 77. See also, e.g., *Agricultural Tractor* (discussed in text accompanying n. 265) and Case T-141/94, *Thyssen Stahl AG v. Commission* [1999] ECR II-347.

[264] Horizontal Cooperation Guidelines, para. 77.

[265] [1992] OJ L68/19; on appeal Case T-34/92, *Fiatagri & Ford New Holland v. Commission* [1994] ECR II-905 and Case T-35/92, *John Deere Ltd v. Commission* [1994] ECR II-957; on appeal to the ECJ, Case C-7/95 P, *John Deere Ltd v. Commission* [1998] ECR I-3111.

(iii) there were insignificant extra-Union imports;

(iv) the information exchanged was detailed and identified the exact retail sales and shares of the undertakings which were generally trade secrets between competitors; and

(v) the members met regularly.

First, the Commission held that the exchange of information prevented hidden competition by creating transparency on a market which was already highly concentrated and largely shielded from outside competition. Where demand was stable, a forecast of a competitor's future actions could be largely determined on the basis of past transactions. The forecast would be more effective the more accurate and recent the information was. The exchange of information could, however, truly be categorised as historic from a certain period of time (for example, if it was more than one year old).[266] Although the Commission recognised that there were benefits of transparency in a competitive market, in this case the concentration of the market was not low and the market transparency was not in any way directed towards the benefit of consumers. The information in this case enabled each participant accurately to establish its rivals' market position and to see immediately if a rival increased its market share (for example, by price reductions or other marketing incentives). It limited price competition since competitors would be able to react quickly to changes in market positions (this would, of course, mean that there was little incentive for a potential initiator to take steps to improve its position). Information would thus limit the possibility of surprise or secrecy if a rival received information disclosing sensitive information about its competitors. It would then be able to react quickly and eliminate any possible advantage to be gained by the initiator.

Secondly, the information would also be likely to increase barriers to entry since participants would know immediately of new market entrants and would be able to react accordingly.

The Commission's analysis was upheld by the GC in *John Deere Ltd* v. *Commission*.[267] The Court accepted that a truly competitive market would benefit from transparency but that exchanges of precise information at short intervals on a highly concentrated market would be likely to impair the competition which existed between the traders.

Case T-35/92, *John Deere Ltd* v. *Commission* [1994] ECR II-957

General Court

51. The Court observes that, as the applicant points out, the Decision is the first in which the Commission has prohibited an information exchange system concerning sufficiently homogeneous products which does not directly concern the prices of those products, but which does not underpin any other anti-competitive arrangement either. As the applicants correctly argue, on a truly competitive market transparency between traders is in principle likely to lead to the intensification of competition between suppliers, since in such a situation, the fact that a trader takes into account information made available to him in order to adjust his conduct on the market is not likely, having regard to the atomized nature of the supply, to reduce or remove for the other traders any uncertainty about the foreseeable nature of its competitors' conduct. On the other hand, the Court considers that, as the Commission argues this time, general use, as between main suppliers and, contrary to the applicant's contention, to their sole benefit and consequently to the exclusion of the other suppliers and of consumers, of exchanges of precise information at short intervals, identifying registered vehicles and the place of their registration is, on a highly concentrated oligopolistic market such as the market in question and on which competition is as a result already greatly reduced and

---

[266] See also *CEPI/Cartonboard* [1996] OJ C310/3.

[267] Case T-35/92 [1994] ECR II-957.

exchange of information facilitated, likely to impair substantially the competition which exists between traders (see paragraph 81). In such circumstances, the sharing, on a regular and frequent basis, of information concerning the operation of the market has the effect of periodically revealing to all the competitors the market positions and strategies of the various individual competitors.

52. Furthermore, provision of the information in question to all suppliers presupposes an agreement, or at any rate a tacit agreement, between the traders to define the boundaries of dealer sales territories by reference to the United Kingdom postcode system, as well as an institutional framework enabling information to be exchanged between the traders through the trade association to which they belong and, secondly, having regard to the frequency of such information and its systematic nature, it also enables a given trader to forecast more precisely the conduct of its competitors, so reducing or removing the degree of uncertainty about the operation of the market which would have existed in the absence of such an exchange of information. Furthermore, the Commission correctly contends, at points 44 to 48 of the Decision, that whatever decision is adopted by a trader wishing to penetrate the United Kingdom agricultural tractor market, and whether or not it becomes a member of the agreement, that agreement is necessarily disadvantageous for it. Either the trader concerned does not become a member of the information exchange agreement and, unlike its competitors, then forgoes the information exchanged and the market knowledge which it provides; or it becomes a member of the agreement and its business strategy is then immediately revealed to all its competitors by means of the information which they receive.

53. It follows that the pleas that the information exchange agreement at issue is not of such a nature as to infringe the [EU] competition rules must be dismissed.

...

81. Secondly, with regard to the type of information exchanged, the Court considers that, contrary to the applicant's contention, the information concerned, which relates in particular to sales made in the territory of each of the dealerships in the distribution network, is in the nature of business secrets. Indeed, this is admitted by the members of the agreement themselves, who strictly defined the conditions under which the information received could be disseminated to third parties, especially to members of their distribution network. The Court also observes that, as stated above (in paragraph 51), having regard to its frequency and systematic nature the exchange of information in question makes the conduct of a given trader's competitors all the more foreseeable for it in view of the characteristics of the relevant market as analyzed above, since it reduces, or even removes, the degree of uncertainty regarding the operation of the market, which would have existed in the absence of such an exchange of information, and in this regard the applicant cannot profitably rely on the fact that the information exchanged does not concern prices or relate to past sales. Accordingly, the first part of the plea, to the effect that there is no restriction of competition as a result of alleged 'prevention of hidden competition', must be dismissed.

An appeal before the CJ against the judgment of the GC was unsuccessful.[268]

The Commission in *Wirtschaftsvereinigung Stahl*[269] also condemned, under Article 65 ECSC, information sharing in a market that was concentrated and had high barriers to entry. This decision was, however, annulled by the GC essentially on the grounds that the Commission's decision was marred by errors of fact.[270] In contrast to these cases the Commission considered in *Eudim*[271] that information sharing in a market that was competitive on both the purchasing and selling side did not infringe Article 101(1).

[268] See Case C-7/95 P, *John Deere Ltd v. Commission* [1998] ECR I-3111.

[269] [1998] OJ L1/10.

[270] Case T-16/98, [2000] ECR II-1217.

[271] [1996] OJ C111/8.

d. *Asnef-Equifax, Servicios De Información sobre Solvencia Y Crédito, SL v. Asociación de Usuarios de Servicios Bancarios (Ausbanc)*[272]

In this case Ausbanc had challenged the exchange of information between financial institutions on the solvency of customers and borrower default. Following an Article 267 reference to it the CJ set out guidance for the referring court to determine the compatibility of the provisions for exchange with Article 101(1). With regard to the question of whether the agreement had as its effect the restriction of competition the CJ stressed the importance of considering whether supply on the market was highly concentrated, whether information identified competitors individually, and whether access to the information was available in a non-discriminatory manner to all operators.

Case C-238/05, *Asnef-Equifax, Servicios de Información sobre Solvencia y Crédito, SL v. Asociación de Usuarios de Servicios Bancarios (Ausbanc)* [2006] ECR I-11125

55. As indicated at paragraph 47 of this judgment, registers such as the one at issue in the main proceedings, by reducing the rate of borrower default, are in principle capable of improving the functioning of the supply of credit. As the Advocate General observed, in substance, at point 54 of his Opinion, if, owing to a lack of information on the risk of borrower default, financial institutions are unable to distinguish those borrowers who are more likely to default, the risk thereby borne by such institutions will necessarily be increased and they will tend to factor it in when calculating the cost of credit for all borrowers, including those less likely to default, who will then have to bear a higher cost than they would if the institutions were in a position to evaluate the probability of repayment more precisely. In principle, registers such as that mentioned above are capable of reducing such a tendency.

56. Furthermore, by reducing the significance of the information held by financial institutions regarding their own customers, such registers appear, in principle, to be capable of increasing the mobility of consumers of credit. In addition, those registers are apt to make it easier for new competitors to enter the market.

57. None the less, whether or not there is in the main proceedings a restriction of competition within the meaning of Article [101(1) TFEU] depends on the economic and legal context in which the register exists, and in particular on the economic conditions of the market as well as the particular characteristics of the register.

58. In that regard, first of all, if supply on a market is highly concentrated, the exchange of certain information may, according in particular to the type of information exchanged, be liable to enable undertakings to be aware of the market position and commercial strategy of their competitors, thus distorting rivalry on the market and increasing the probability of collusion, or even facilitating it. On the other hand, if supply is fragmented, the dissemination and exchange of information between competitors may be neutral, or even positive, for the competitive nature of the market (see, to that effect, *Thyssen Stahl v Commission*, paragraphs 84 and 86). In the present case, it is common ground, as may be seen from paragraph 10 of this judgment, that the referring court premi[s]ed its reference for a preliminary ruling on the existence of 'a fragmented market', which it is for that court to verify.

59. Secondly, in order that registers such as that at issue in the main proceedings are not capable of revealing the market position or the commercial strategy of competitors, it is important that the identity of lenders is not revealed, directly or indirectly. In the present case, it is apparent from the decision for referral that the Tribunal de Defensa de la Competencia imposed on Asnef-Equifax, which accepted it, a condition that the information relating to lenders contained in the register not be disclosed.

---

[272] Case C-238/05 [2006] ECR I-11125.

60. Thirdly, it is also important that such registers be accessible in a non-discriminatory manner, in law and in fact, to all operators active in the relevant sphere. If such accessibility were not guaranteed, some of those operators would be placed at a disadvantage, since they would have less information for the purpose of risk assessment, which would also not facilitate the entry of new operators on to the market.

61. It follows that, provided that the relevant market or markets are not highly concentrated, that the system does not permit lenders to be identified and that the conditions of access and use by financial institutions are not discriminatory, an information exchange system such as the register is not, in principle, liable to have the effect of restricting competition within the meaning of Article [101(1) TFEU].

62. While in those conditions such systems are capable of reducing uncertainty as to the risk that applicants for credit will default, they are not, however, liable to reduce uncertainty as to the risks of competition. Thus, each operator could be expected to act independently and autonomously when adopting a given course of conduct, regard being had to the risks presented by applicants. Contrary to Ausbanc's contention, it cannot be inferred solely from the existence of such a credit information exchange that it might lead to collective anti-competitive conduct, such as a boycott of certain potential borrowers.

63. Furthermore, since, as the Advocate General observed, in substance, at point 56 of his Opinion, any possible issues relating to the sensitivity of personal data are not, as such, a matter for competition law, they may be resolved on the basis of the relevant provisions governing data protection. In the main proceedings, it is apparent from the documents before the Court that, under the rules applicable to the register, affected consumers may, in accordance with the Spanish legislation, check the information concerning them and, where necessary, have it corrected, or indeed deleted.

The CJ in *Asnef-Equifax* also recognised that the referring court might need to carry out an Article 101(3) assessment in order to resolve the dispute at issue.[273] For example, the court might be required to determine whether objective economic advantages, such as helping to prevent over-indebtedness for consumers of credit and leading to a greater overall availability of credit, might be such as to offset the disadvantages of any restriction of competition identified. The CJ stressed that in making the Article 101(3) determination, it was not necessary that all consumers should benefit from the system. Rather, it was not inconceivable that some applicants for credit would be faced with increased interest rates or refused credit. This circumstance was not in itself sufficient to prevent the condition that consumers be allowed a fair share of the benefit from being satisfied since 'it is the beneficial nature of the effect on all consumers in the relevant markets that must be taken into consideration, not the effect on each member of that category of consumers'.[274] Indeed, the exchange in this situation might be capable of leading to a greater overall availability of credit, including for applicants for whom interest rates might be excessive if lenders did not have appropriate knowledge of their personal system.

e. Business-to-Business (B-2-B) Exchanges

B-2-B e-marketplaces, which allow industrial buyers and sellers to transact business online over the internet, have become common.[275] Although such marketplaces may create huge efficiency gains in purchasing and supply chain management there has also been a concern that such markets would create an ideal climate for collusion, due to increased communication and transparency in the market,[276] exchange of confidential information, and foreclosure. The Commission, however,

---

[273] But see, e.g., *International Energy Program* [1983] OJ L376/30.

[274] Case C-238/05, *Asnef-Equifax v. Asociación Usuarios de Servicios Bancarios (Ausbanc)* [2006] ECR I-11125, para. 70.

[275] J. Lüking, 'B2B e-marketplaces and EU competition law: where do we stand?' (2001) *Competition Policy Newsletter* 14 (October). See also S. Stroux, 'B2B E-market-places: The Emerging Competition Law Issues' [2001] 24 *World Competition* 125 and D. Lancefield, 'The regulatory Hurdles Ahead in B2B' [2001] *ECLR* 9.

[276] *E-Commerce and Its Implications for Competition Policy*, OFT 308, para. 6.54.

recognises the clear advantages that may result from such marketplaces and has sought to develop a coherent approach to their assessment and has in many cases accepted that such agreements do not infringe Article 101(1) at all.[277] In *Covisint*,[278] for example, the Commission sent a comfort letter clearing the creation of the Covisint Automotive Internet Marketplace (the agreement did not infringe Article 101(1)). Six car manufacturers notified to the Commission a joint venture to serve the procurement needs of major car makers and suppliers and to reduce costs and improve efficiency in the supply chain. The Commission noted in its press release that in general B-2-B marketplaces should have pro-competitive effects by creating more transparency, integrating markets, and creating marketing efficiencies by reducing search and information costs and improving inventory management, leading ultimately to lower prices for the end consumer. In this case the Commission was satisfied that potential competition concerns had been eliminated:

> Covisint is open to all firms in the industry on a non-discriminatory basis, is based on open standards, allows both shareholders and other users to participate in other B-2-B exchanges, does not allow joint purchasing between car manufacturers or for automotive-specific products, and provides for adequate data protection, including firewalls and security rules.

It has also sent negative clearance comfort letters in relation to B-2-B electronic marketplaces set up in other sectors.[279] In an article by a Commission official in the competition policy newsletter several guidelines are set out for companies considering setting up e-marketplaces.[280]

4. OLIGOPOLY

A. OLIGOPOLY AND ARTICLE 101

(i) The Oligopoly Problem

It has been explained that in some oligopolistic markets the players may, without explicit communication, 'tacitly' coordinate their behaviour, aligning their conduct and setting their prices at supra-competitive levels This section and Section B consider whether tacit collusion is, or may be, prohibited by either Article 101 or Article 102.

(ii) Tacit Collusion, Concerted Practices, and Parallel Conduct

a. The Problem

A question which has arisen is whether the concept of a concerted practice in Article 101 is broad enough to catch tacit collusion since the firms do not behave totally unilaterally, but determine their strategy by taking account of the likely response of their competitors. It will be remembered that the term concerted practice has been construed broadly to catch all:

---

[277] See, e.g., M. Monti, 'European Competition Policy for the 21st century' [2000] Fordham Corp L Inst (B. E. Hawk (ed.)), chap. 15 and 'Competition in the New Economy' 10th International Conference on Competition of the Bundeskartellamt, Berlin, 21 May 2001.

[278] IP/01/1155 (a negative clearance comfort letter).

[279] See *Eutilia/Endorsia* IP/01/1775, *Eurex* IP/02/4, *Inreon* IP/02/761, *Centradia* IP 02/943, *Water Portal* IP/02/956, and J. Lüking, 'B2B e-marketplaces and EC competition law: where do we stand?' (2001) *Competition Policy Newsletter* (October).

[280] J. Lüking, 'B2B e-marketplaces and EC competition law: where do we stand?' (2001) *Competition Policy Newsletter* 15–16 (October).

co-ordination between undertakings which, without having reached the stage where an agreement, properly so called, has been concluded, knowingly substitutes practical co-operation between them for the risks of competition.[281]

The purpose is to catch undertakings which have not agreed but which determine their market policy in cooperation with other undertakings, for example through direct or indirect conduct, and not *independently*. A key issue is, therefore, whether tacit collusion constitutes practical cooperation between undertakings or independent behaviour outside the scope of Article 101(1). In addition, if tacit collusion cannot be *equated* with a concerted practice a further question arising is whether parallel conduct by firms operating on an oligopolistic market can ever be used as circumstantial evidence to justify a finding that an agreement or concerted practice existed between the undertakings.

The answer to these questions appears to have been provided in the CJ's judgment in *Wood Pulp*.[282] First, it makes clear that parallel conduct or tacit collusion is not in itself prohibited by Article 101(1). Secondly, that although parallel behaviour may furnish circumstantial proof of explicit collusion it will not do so if the behaviour can be explained by the conditions of competition on the market, for example that the conditions have led to tacit collusion of the undertaking's behaviour (there is a plausible explanation for the conduct other than collusions). Before looking at the Court's judgment in *Wood Pulp* it is, however, useful to consider some of the Court's previous rulings, in particular in *Dyestuffs*,[283] *Suiker Unie*,[284] and *Züchner*.[285]

b. The *Dyestuffs* Case

In *Dyestuffs*,[286] three general and uniform increases in the prices of dyestuffs had taken place within the common market over a period of years. The first, in 1964, took place on the markets in Italy, Holland, Belgium, and Luxembourg, the second in 1965 on the market in Germany, and in 1967 uniform increases took place in Germany, Holland, Belgium, Luxembourg, and France (the latter at a different rate, since prices had previously been frozen by the Government there).

In this case the Commission concluded that the increases had occurred as a result of a concerted practice operating between 10 producers (it had discovered significant evidence of actual direct/indirect contact between the parties).[287]

The CJ upheld the decision. The behaviour constituted a concerted practice prohibited by Article 101(1) of the Treaty. In particular, the Court relied upon the fact that price increases had been announced in advance (the announcements eliminating all uncertainty between them as regards their future conduct and the risk inherent in any independent change in conduct) and that the announcements rendered the market transparent as regards the rates of increases. Further, given the number of producers on the European dyestuffs market, it did not consider that it was possible to say, as the applicants had alleged, that the market was an oligopolistic one. Price competition should have been able to play a substantial role. It was not plausible, therefore, that the parallel conduct could have been brought into effect within a period of two to three days without prior concertation. The Court concluded that, taking into account the nature of the market in the products in question, the conduct of the undertakings was designed to replace both the risks of competition and the hazards of competitors' spontaneous reactions with cooperation.

---

[281] Cases 48, 49, and 51–57/69, *ICI v. Commission* [1972] ECR 619, paras. 64 and 65.

[282] Cases C-89, 104, 114, 116–117, and 125–129/85, [1993] ECR I-1307.

[283] Case 48/69, *ICI v. Commission* [1972] ECR 619.

[284] Joined Cases 40, etc./73 *Re the European Sugar Cartel: Coöperatieve Vereniging 'Suiker Unie' UA v. Commission* [1975] ECR 1663.

[285] Case 172/80, *Züchner v. Bayerische Vereinsbank* [1981] ECR 2021.

[286] Case 48/69, *ICI v. Commission* [1972] ECR 619.

[287] *Re Cartel in Aniline Dyes* [1969] OJ L195/11.

There were suggestions and concern after the Court's judgment that its interpretation of the term 'concerted practice' would be used broadly to catch rational, and purely parallel, market behaviour.[288] The Court had relied mainly on market data to support its finding that the parties had cooperated, without conducting a thorough study of the market. In particular, the Court characterised behaviour as apparently innocuous as making price announcements in advance as an impermissible means of indirect communication.[289]

However, the Commission had, in fact, discovered significant evidence of actual direct/indirect contact between the parties. It had not relied on economic evidence of parallel behaviour alone. Apart from the similarity in rates and dates of increases, the Commission found proof of concertation from the similarity of the content of the orders sent by the producers to their subsidiaries or representatives on the various markets, to make the increases. The orders were on occasion sent on the same day (at the same hour), were couched in similar terms, and showed a very great similarity in drafting. Some messages contained exactly identical phrases which, the Commission concluded, could not be explained in the absence of prior concertation between the undertakings involved. The Commission also discovered records of meetings of the producers in Basel and London. The records disclosed that not only was the question of prices discussed but on occasion the dates and timings of intended price increases were announced.

Further, the CJ specifically stated that 'parallel behaviour may not by itself be identified with a concerted practice' although it could provide 'strong evidence of such a practice if it leads to conditions of competition which do not correspond to the normal conditions of the market, having regard to the nature of the products, the size and number of the undertakings, and the volume of the said market'.[290] This would be the case where prices were stabilised at a level different from that to which competition would otherwise have led. A producer was thus 'free to charge his prices, taking into account in so doing the present or foreseeable conduct of his competitors'. In contrast, he was precluded from cooperating 'with his competitors, in any way whatsoever, in order to determine a coordinated course of action relating to a price increase to ensure its success by prior elimination of all uncertainty as to each other's conduct'.[291] However,

[a]s Professor Joliet pointed out, the judgment was not so much worrying because of its definition of a concerted practice but more because it so easily assumed, without a detailed study of the market characteristics and without evidence of concertation, that parties had cooperated. Although the Court recognised the need to consider the specific features of the market in weighing the evidence, ... it only did so superficially.[292]

c. *Suiker Unie* and *Züchner*

In both *Suiker Unie*[293] and *Züchner*[294] the CJ stressed that Article 101(1) did not prevent an undertaking from adapting its behaviour intelligently to the existing or anticipated conduct of competitors. In accordance with these judgments the Commission, in *Zinc Producer Group*,[295] accepted the legitimacy of parallel/oligopolistic behaviour. It held that:

---

[288] See, e.g., V. Korah, 'Concerted Practices' (1973) 36 MLR 260; R. Joliet, 'La notion de pratique concertée et l'arrêt I.C.I. dans une perspective comparative' [1974] CDE 251.

[289] See Section 4.A.iii.

[290] Cases 48, 49, and 51–57/69 [1972] ECR 619, para. 66.

[291] Cases 48, 49, and 51–57/69 [1972] ECR 619, para. 118.

[292] G. van Gerven and E. N. Varona, 'The Wood Pulp Case and the Future of Concerted Practices' (1994) 31 CMLRev 575, 590.

[293] Cases 40, etc./73, *Re the European Sugar Cartel: Coöperatieve Vereniging 'Suiker Unie' UA v. Commission* [1975] ECR 1663.

[294] Case 172/80, *Züchner v. Bayerische Vereinsbank* [1981] ECR 2021.

[295] [1984] OJ L220/27.

parallel pricing behaviour in an oligopoly producing homogeneous goods [would] not in itself be sufficient evidence of a concerted practice.[296]

Thus, parallel action explicable in terms of barometric price leadership (that is to say, linked to a change in the market conditions, for example, an increase in the price of the main raw material) would not be sufficient evidence of a concerted practice.

d. *Wood Pulp*

The CJ in *Re Wood Pulp Cartel: Ahlström Oy v. Commission (Wood Pulp II)*[297] delivered the clearest judgment on the relationship between conscious parallelism (or tacit collusion) and concerted practices. The Commission had investigated alleged restrictive practices and agreements between pulp producers operating on the bleached sulphate wood pulp market. The Commission found several breaches of Article 101(1) and levied fines on 43 wood pulp producers.[298] In particular, it found that concertation between many of the Finnish, US, and Canadian undertakings with regard to both announced and transaction prices in the pulp market had led to prices which were both artificially high and rigid. The Commission considered that the parallel behaviour was not explicable as rational behaviour.[299] It could not be explained as independently chosen parallel conduct in a narrow oligopolistic market (the market was characterised by a large number of producers, customers, and products; the market was not inherently transparent, but was only so as a result of the producers' deliberately chosen strategy of making price announcements in advance and there was no clear price leader, etc.). The parties sought annulment of the Commission's decision before the CJ.

The Court annulled much of the Commission's decision and many of the fines on substantive grounds. It considered two separate points: first whether or not the price announcements were in themselves prohibited by Article 101(1) and secondly whether they provided evidence of a concerted practice and concertation in advanced prices.

The Court reiterated its previous statements that parallel conduct could not be used to establish the existence of a concerted practice unless, taking account of the nature of the products, the size and the number of undertakings, and the volume of the market in question, it could not be explained otherwise than by concertation. Parallel behaviour would furnish proof of concertation only where it constituted the only plausible explanation for such conduct. Every producer was free to react intelligently to market forces and to alter its course of action, taking into account in so doing the present or foreseeable conduct of its competitors.

The Court was not prepared to reject, as the Commission had done, the protestations that the undertakings' behaviour was a consequence, not of a concerted practice, but of non-collusive interdependence or conscious parallelism. It commissioned two independent reports from economic experts to analyse the wood pulp market and the evidence involved. The reports were extremely damaging to the Commission's case. On the facts and relying on experts' reports, the Court found that the system of quarterly price announcements did not, of itself, amount to an infringement of Article 101(1)[300] and that this system and the parallelism of announced prices were not evidence of concertation. Further, it could not be said that the system of advance price announcements and parallel behaviour was not explicable otherwise than by concertation. The Commission had failed sufficiently to appreciate that the wood pulp market had oligopolistic tendencies, being characterised by oligopolies and oligopsonies (on the buying side) in particular pulp types. Also the market was inherently transparent. Paper manufacturers were in constant touch with a number of pulp

[296] [1984] OJ L220/27, paras. 75–76.

[297] Cases C-89, 104, 114, 116–117, and 125–129/85, [1993] ECR I-1307.

[298] [1985] OJ L85/1.

[299] Although the Commission relied on some documentary evidence to supplement its finding, this was excluded by the Court.

[300] Cases C-89, 104, 114, 116–117, and 125–129/85, [1993] ECR I-1307.

suppliers and exchanged price information amongst themselves and the transparency was reinforced both by a number of common agents that operated throughout the market and an active trade press.

The system of advanced announced prices was, therefore, explicable as a rational response to the fact that the pulp market was a long-term one and met a legitimate business concern of customers.

Cases C-89, 104, 114, 116–117 and 125–129/85, *Re Wood Pulp Cartel: Ahlström Oy v. Commission (Wood Pulp II)* [1993] ECR I-1307

Court of Justice

70. Since the Commission has no documents which directly establish the existence of concertation between the producers concerned, it is necessary to ascertain whether the system of quarterly price announcements, the simultaneity or near-simultaneity of the price announcements and the parallelism of price announcements as found during the period from 1975 to 1985 constitute a firm, precise and consistent body of evidence of prior concertation.

71. In determining the probative value of those different factors, it must be noted that parallel conduct cannot be regarded as furnishing proof of concertation unless concertation constitutes the only plausible explanation for such conduct. It is necessary to bear in mind that, although Article [101]…prohibits any form of collusion which distorts competition, it does not deprive economic operators of the right to adapt themselves intelligently to the existing and anticipated conduct of their competitors (see *Suiker Unie,*…paragraph 174).

72. Accordingly, it is necessary in this case to ascertain whether the parallel conduct alleged by the Commission cannot, taking account of the nature of the products, the size and the number of the undertakings and the volume of the market in question, be explained otherwise than by concertation.

…

126. Following that analysis, it must be stated that, in this case, concertation is not the only plausible explanation for the parallel conduct. To begin with, the system of price announcements may be regarded as constituting a rational response to the fact that the pulp market constituted a long-term market and to the need felt by both buyers and sellers to limit commercial risks. Further, the similarity in the dates of price announcements may be regarded as a direct result of the high degree of market transparency, which does not have to be described as artificial. Finally, the parallelism of prices and the price trends may be satisfactorily explained by the oligopolistic tendencies of the market and by the specific circumstances prevailing in certain periods. Accordingly, the parallel conduct established by the Commission does not constitute evidence of concertation.

127. In the absence of a firm, precise and consistent body of evidence, it must be held that concertation regarding announced prices has not been established by the Commission. Article 1(1) of the contested decision must therefore be annulled.

e. Conclusions on Article 101 and Parallel Behaviour

It is clear that purely parallel behaviour on a market is not prohibited by Article 101. Rather, the concept of a concerted practice appears to demand *reciprocal* cooperation, through direct or indirect contact, designed to influence the conduct of an actual or potential competitor or to disclose to them the course of conduct that will or may be adopted on the market.[301]

---

[301] See also Chap. 3 and, e.g., A. Albors-Lorens, 'Horizontal Agreements and Concerted Practices in EC Competition Law: Unlawful and Legitimate Contacts between Competitors' [2006] 51 *Ant Bull* 837 and A. Jones, 'Wood Pulp: Concerted Practice and/or Conscious Parallelism' [1993] *ECLR* 273, 275–276.

Where direct evidence of reciprocal cooperation is not available, parallel behaviour may, however, furnish circumstantial proof of an agreement or concerted practice if it is not the kind of behaviour which would be anticipated on the market involved (whether the parallel conduct alleged by the Commission cannot, taking into account the nature of the products, the size and number of the undertakings, and the volume of the market in question, be explained otherwise than by concertation) and if there is no other plausible explanation for the conduct. In *Wood Pulp* the CJ's judgment describes the market characteristics in meticulous detail. In particular, it seems clear that the number of undertakings on the market, the homogeneity of the product, and the transparency of the market will be relevant to the analysis. The market structure may, therefore, provide a plausible explanation for the behaviour. It can be seen from *Wood Pulp* itself that explanations may well be available outside a tight oligopoly situation.

It is unclear whether, on the proof of parallel behaviour, the burden shifts onto the accused to establish that there *is* a plausible explanation for the conduct. In *Wood Pulp*, the Advocate-General appeared to consider that '[t]he burden of proof cannot be shifted simply by a finding of parallel conduct. Unless the Court can be satisfied by a set of presumptions having a solid basis, concertation is not established.'[302] If, as seems correct, the onus does not shift it is impossible to imagine how the Commission (or any other) could establish that there is no other plausible explanation for the parallel conduct. It would thus seem inadvisable to rely solely on economic evidence to establish the existence of a cartel. Rather, other evidence is required to corroborate a case. Indeed, in *Cartonboard*[303] the Commission stated:

Had they been challenged, the producers could as a result of this elaborate scheme of deception have attributed the series of uniform, regular and industry-wide price increases in the cartonboard sector to the phenomenon of 'oligopoly behaviour'. They could argue that it made sense for all the producers to decide of their own volition to copy an increase initiated by one or other of the market leaders as soon as it became publicly known; unlawful collusion as such would not necessarily be indicated. Customers might well suspect and even accuse them of operating a cartel; and given the relatively large number of producers, economic theory would be stretched to its limits and beyond, but unless direct proof of collusion were forthcoming— and they went to some lengths to ensure it was not—the producers must have had hopes of defeating any investigation into their pricing conduct by the competition authorities by invoking the defence of oligopolistic interdependence.[304]

It is clear, however, that where plausible explanations are raised each of those must be ruled out by the Commission. In *CISAC*,[305] for example, the GC, once it found that the Commission had not proven the existence of a concerted practice by factors other than parallel conduct, went on to consider whether the Commission had provided sufficient evidence to render implausible explanations of the undertakings for their parallel conduct. It annulled the Commission's decision when it found it had not.

(iii) Concerted Practices and Unilateral Price Announcements in Advance

Price announcements in advance on a market may signal to other players on the market what a firm's future price policy will be and may facilitate alignment of their behaviour and tacit collusion on an oligopolistic market. Could price announcements in advance constitute indirect contact with a

---

[302] [1993] ECR I-1307, Darmon AG, para. 195. This conclusion seems to be necessitated by the presumption of innocence that applies in competition law cases, see further Chap. 13.

[303] *Cartonboard* [1994] OJ L243/1.

[304] *Cartonboard* [1994] OJ L243/1, para. 73.

[305] 16 July 2008, IP/08/1165

competitor sufficient to establish a concerted practice to fix prices? In *Dyestuffs*,[306] the CJ considered that advance price communications provided, in the circumstances, proof of a concerted practice. It held that the announcements rendered the market artificially transparent and eliminated all uncertainty between the operators as regards the rates of increase, future conduct, and the risks inherent in an independent change of conduct. The Court commented:

> …the undertakings taking the initiative…announced their intentions of making an increase some time in advance, which allowed the undertakings to observe each other's reactions on the different markets, and to adapt themselves accordingly. By means of these advance announcements the various undertakings eliminated all uncertainty between them as to their future conduct and, in doing so, also eliminated a large part of the risk usually inherent in any independent change of conduct on one or several markets. This was all the more the case since these announcements, which led to the fixing of general and equal increases in prices for the markets in dyestuffs, rendered the market transparent as regard the percentage rates of increase. Therefore, by the way in which they acted, the undertakings in question temporarily eliminated with respect to prices some of the preconditions for competition on the market which stood in the way of the achievement of parallel uniformity of conduct.[307]

This case must now be assessed in the light of its own particular facts and the judgment of the CJ in *Wood Pulp*.[308] In the latter case the Commission found concertation in respect of both announced and actual transaction prices. The CJ, however, held that price announcements in advance did not, per se, constitute an infringement of Article 101(1).

> 64. In this case, the communications arise from the price announcements made to users. They constitute in themselves market behaviour which does not lessen each undertaking's uncertainty as to the future attitude of its competitors. At the same time when each undertaking engages in such behaviour, it cannot be sure of the future conduct of the others.
>
> 65. Accordingly, the system of quarterly price announcements on the pulp market is not to be regarded as constituting in itself an infringement of Article [101](1).

Further, the Court held that it had not been established that the system amounted to a means of indirect communication between the competitors. The announcements served the need of customers desiring the information to plan the cost of their paper products. This provided a plausible or alternative explanation for the parallel behaviour (see the discussion on parallel behaviour in Section 4.A.ii.d).

In the light of these two cases it is conceivable that, where advanced price announcements or other price signalling do not have a legitimate business justification, the conduct might amount to indirect contact between the undertakings and an illegitimate concerted practice prohibited by Article 101.[309]

G. van Gerven and E. N. Varona, 'The Wood Pulp Case and the Future of Concerted Practices' (1994) 31 *CMLRev* 575, 595

It is clear that in deciding whether price signalling is illegal, one should not overlook the circumstances. In the *Wood Pulp* case, it was established that (i) there was a clear lawful business justification for advance

---

[306] Cases 48, 49, and 51–57/69, *ICI v. Commission (Dyestuffs)* [1972] ECR 619.

[307] Cases 48, 49, and 51–57/69, *ICI v. Commission (Dyestuffs)* [1972] ECR 619, paras. 100–103.

[308] Cases C-89, 104, 114, 116–117 and 125–129/85, *Re Wood Pulp Cartel: Ahlström Oy v. Commission (Wood Pulp II)* [1993] ECR I-1307.

[309] See the Opinion of Darmon AG in Cases C-89, 104, 114, 116–117, and 125–129/85, *Re Wood Pulp Cartel: Ahlström Oy v. Commission (Wood Pulp II)* [1993] ECR I-1307, para. 251. For greater discussion, see G. van Gerven and E. N. Varona, 'The Wood Pulp Case and the Future of Concerted Practices' (1994) 31 *CMLRev* 575.

price communications, since the price of wood pulp constituted a major proportion of the cost of paper and it was the paper producers themselves which had requested prior announcement; (ii) the announcements were made to customers. If, given the high transparency of the market, firms become aware of the prospective pricing of their competitors, so be it. If a rival adapts its pricing to the information it has obtained, it merely 'adapts intelligently to existing or anticipated conduct of its competitors' as allowed by the *Dyestuffs* and *Suiker Unie* judgments.

Firstly, as Advocate Darmon pointed out in his opinion, if price signalling does not correspond to a legitimate business justification, such advance announcements may very well be considered as an illegal exchange of information. In the end, as so often in antitrust law, the decisive question in practice may be whether there is a valid business reason for the particular market conduct. In the *Wood pulp* judgment, the Court had no difficulty finding such a valid business reason for the price announcements and, therefore, it was easy and correct to conclude that the system of price announcements did not give rise to a concerted practice. However, price signalling, if not warranted by any legitimate explanation and clearly not in the individual (non-collusive) self-interest of the individual companies may constitute sufficient evidence of concertation.

Secondly, in *Wood Pulp*, it appeared that the trade press was also very rapidly informed of the advance price announcements but the Court went out of its way to state that most of the wood pulp producers did not send as a matter of course their announced prices to the trade press and that if, sporadically, this was done, such communications were made at the request of the press. Thus the Court implicitly rejected the Commission's claim that wood pulp producers had deliberately made the market transparent or increased transparency by talking to the press.

In the *Cartonboard*[310] case, where the producers, twice a year, announced price increases several months in advance, the Commission took care to produce documentary evidence establishing that the undertakings had agreed the date and sequence of advance price increases.

The Commission will inevitably be sensitive to attempts by oligopolists to make the market artificially more transparent than it otherwise would be. The present discussion indicates that agreements which have this effect may violate Article 101(1).

B. OLIGOPOLY AND ARTICLE 102

(i) 'One or More Undertakings'

a. Introduction

It was seen in Chapter 5 that Article 102 prohibits as incompatible with the internal market, insofar as trade between Member States is affected, '[a]ny abuse by one or more undertakings of a dominant position'. It was further seen there that Article 102 has been interpreted to apply to 'collective' dominant positions as well as those held by single undertakings and that collective dominance has been held to include situations where undertakings operating in a tight oligopoly tacitly collude.

b. The Acceptance of a Concept of Collective Dominance[311]—the Judgment in Flat Glass

Chapter 5 explains that although, initially at least, it was believed that the term 'one or more undertakings' referred only to bodies which were within the same corporate group or which formed part

---

[310] *Cartonboard* OJ [1994] L243/1. The decision was broadly upheld by the GC. On appeal, the CJ reduced three fines, referred two cases back to the GC for reassessment, and dismissed the remainder of the appeals, see, e.g., Case C-286/98 P, [2000] ECR I-9925.

[311] The terms collective, joint, and oligopolistic dominance have sometimes been used interchangeably. See generally on this subject R. Whish, 'Collective Dominance' in D. O'Keefe and M. Andenas (eds.), *Liber Amicorum for Lord*

of the same economic entity (in *Hoffmann La-Roche* v. *Commission*, the CJ stated that '[a] dominant position must also be distinguished from parallel courses of conduct which are peculiar to oligopolies in that in an oligopoly the courses of conduct interact, while in the case of an undertaking occupying a dominant position the conduct of the undertaking which derives profits from that position is to a great extent determined unilaterally'[312]), such an interpretation would have been inconsistent with the interpretation of the term 'undertaking' adopted for the purposes of Article 101.[313] In *Flat Glass*[314], the GC thus confirmed that Article 102 could apply where a dominant position was held collectively by one or more *economically independent* undertakings. Article 102 was not confined to the activities of one or more undertakings within the same corporate group.

Cases T-68, 77, and 78/89, *Società Italiana Vetro SpA* v. *Commission ('Flat Glass')* [1992] ECR II-1403

General Court

357. The Court notes that the very words of the first paragraph of Article [102] provide that 'one or more undertakings' may abuse a dominant position. It has consistently been held, as indeed all the parties acknowledge, that the concept of agreement or concerted practice between undertakings does not cover agreements or concerted practices among undertakings belonging to the same group if the undertakings form an economic unit…It follows that when Article [101] refers to agreements or concerted practices between 'undertakings', it is referring to relations between two or more economic entities which are capable of competing with one another.

358. The Court considers that there is no legal or economic reason to suppose that the term 'undertaking' in Article [102] has a different meaning from the one given to it in the context of Article [101]. There is nothing in principle, to prevent two or more independent economic entities from being, on a specific market, united by such economic links that, by virtue of that fact, together they hold a dominant position *vis-à-vis* the other operators on the same market. This could be the case, for example, where two or more independent undertakings jointly have, through agreements or licences, a technological lead affording them the power to behave to an appreciable extent independently of their competitors, their customers and ultimately of their consumers (judgment of the Court in *Hoffmann-La Roche*…., paragraphs 38 and 48).

359. The Court finds support for that interpretation in the wording of Article 8 of Council Regulation 4065/86…laying down detailed rules for the application of Articles [101] and [102] to maritime transport. Article 8(2) provides that the conduct of a liner conference benefiting from an exemption from a prohibition laid down by Article [101(1)] may have effects which are incompatible with Article [102]. A request by a conference to be exempted from the prohibition laid down by Article [101(1)] necessarily presupposes an agreement between two or more independent economic undertakings.

The crucial paragraph in this judgment is 358 where the GC states that there is nothing, in principle, to prevent two or more independent economic entities from being, on a specific market, united by such economic links that, by virtue of that fact, together they hold a dominant position vis-à-vis the other operators on the same market. The Court gave examples of when such economic links would exist, for example where two or more independent undertakings jointly have, through agreements

---

Slynn (Kluwer, 2000) and J. Temple-Lang, 'Oligopolies and Joint dominance in Community Antitrust Law' [2002] Fordham Corp L Inst (ed. B. E. Hawk), chap. 12.

[312] 85/76, *Hoffmann-La Roche* v. *Commission* [1979] ECR 461, para. 39.

[313] See discussion in Chap. 3.

[314] Cases T-68, 77–78/89, *Società Italiana Vetro SpA* v. *Commission* [1992] ECR II-1403, paras. 357–358.

or licences, a technological lead affording them the power to behave to an appreciable extent independently of their competitors, of their customers, and ultimately of their consumers.

The judgment was not as helpful as it might have been. The requirement that the entities be united by '*economic links*' arguably supports a wide view of collective dominance whereby such links might be derived from the structure of a market which dictates that the undertakings operating upon it may tacitly collude (as already explained in this chapter). However, the Court, by subsequently referring to 'agreements or licences' operating between independent undertakings as an example of economic links, cast doubt on this interpretation. The reference to such contractual, structural, or more tangible links between the parties caused speculation that Article 102 would not apply unless something *more* than mutual interdependence existed between the undertakings, perhaps an agreement or some other special relationship between the parties. This latter narrower view of the concept was supported by the Court's reliance on Article 8(2) of Council Regulation 4056/86[315] which provided that Article 102 could be applied to agreements between undertakings even though they have been exempted under the Regulation.

If this latter position had been the correct one it is hard to see how much the concept of an abuse of a collective dominant position could usefully have added to the Commission's armoury. Agreements between undertakings could, in any event, be controlled under Article 101 (the concept would be useful only to act against agreements between the undertakings which fall outside Article 101(1) or which meet the Article 101(3) criteria). It seemed unlikely, therefore, that the GC intended to confine the term 'economic links' to circumstances in which an agreement existed between the undertakings. Nonetheless, the judgment left the matter far from clear. Although the Commission decisions and Court judgments delivered soon after *Flat Glass* did not add much clarity to the picture, subsequent case law now confirms that both Article 102 and the EUMR will apply where the only link between the parties is the 'economic interdependence' which independent undertakings have with each other on an oligopolistic market.

c. The Development of the Concept of Collective Dominance under Article 102

As explained in Chapter 5 the early decisions of the Commission subsequent to *Flat Glass* concerned cases where the undertakings were linked by express agreements.[316] However, in *Almelo*,[317] an Article 267 reference, the CJ stated that 'in order for such a collective dominant position to exist, the undertakings in the group must be linked in such a way that they adopt the same conduct on the market'.[318] This interpretation lent support to the view that the purpose of requiring links between the undertakings is simply to determine whether the parties are likely to engage in a coordinated course of conduct on the market (such as tacit collusion). Nevertheless, again the judgment did not elaborate on what links were necessary between undertakings before they could be found, collectively, to hold a dominant position on the market, and so did not clarify the position.

Since *Almelo*, judgments given in the context of both the EUMR and Article 102 have developed the concept of collective dominance. The developments that have occurred within the sphere of the EUMR are thus outlined here as they are also relevant to the interpretation of Article 102.[319]

---

[315] [1986] OJ L378/1.

[316] *French-West African Shipowners' Committees* [1992] OJ L134/1, *CEWAL* [1993] OJ L34/20, *Trans-Atlantic Conference Agreement (TACA)* [1999] OJ L95/1, *Irish Sugar* [1997] OJ L258/1.

[317] Case C-393/92, *Almelo v. NV Energiebedrijf Ijsselmij* [1994] ECR I-1477.

[318] Case C-393/92, *Almelo v. NV Energiebedrijf Ijsselmij* [1994] ECR I-1477, paras. 42–43 ('It is for the national court to consider whether there exist between the regional electricity distributors in the Netherlands links which are sufficiently strong for there to be a collective dominant position in a substantial part of the common market'), see also, e.g., Case C-96/94, *Centro Servizi Spediporto Srl v. Spedizioni Marittima de Golfo Srl* [1995] ECR I-2883, Case C-70/95, *Sodemare SA v. Regione Lombardia* [1997] ECR I-3395, and Cases T-24/93, etc., *Compagnie Maritime Belge Transports SA v. Commission* [1996] ECR II-1201.

[319] The EUMR developments are also discussed in greater detail in Chap. 15.

d. Collective Dominance and the EU Merger Regulation (EUMR)

The question of whether the EUMR authorises the Commission to prevent mergers which might result in coordinated effects on oligopolistic markets, through tacit collusion[320] or non-coordinated effects (such as increased prices and restricted output in response to a merger which makes the market more concentrated) has been of critical importance.

Although the wording of the EUMR, as originally drafted and prior to substantive changes introduced to the EUMR in 2004,[321] made it unclear whether or not it authorised the prohibition of mergers leading to the creation or strengthening of a collective dominant position, the Commission, undeterred by this ambiguity, took the view that it did so apply and applied it to such situations almost from the outset.[322] This view was upheld by the CJ in *France v. Commission*[323] and in *Gencor*[324] the GC confirmed that a 'relationship of interdependence existing between the parties to a tight oligopoly' which would make alignment of conduct likely constituted an economic link sufficient for a finding of collective dominance. In *Airtours*[325] the GC built on *Gencor* stating that a collective dominant position would exist where each member of a dominant oligopoly would 'consider it possible, economically rational, and hence preferable, to adopt on a lasting basis a common policy on the market with the aim of selling at above competitive prices, without having to enter into an agreement or resort to a concerted practice within the meaning of Article 101 ...'. It considered that a finding of collective dominance could be established if:

first, each firm knew how other members were behaving (they could monitor the market to see if they were adopting the common policy);

secondly, tacit co-ordination was sustainable over time, (i.e., there was not an incentive to depart from the common policy on the market); and

thirdly, the foreseeable reactions of competitors (actual and potential) and customers would not jeopardize the results expected from the common policy.

In *Impala*,[326] the GC confirmed that these three conditions are necessary for establishing the strengthening or creation of a collective dominant position and that the characteristics of the market must provide evidence of those conditions. Although, on appeal from this judgment, the CJ in *Bertelsmann and Sony Corp v. Commission*[327] expressed the test in a slightly different way, the criteria it set out for establishing collective dominance and coordinated effects are similar to and compatible with those set out by the GC.[328] In the context of the EUMR therefore, it became clear that it applied to collective dominance and that a collective dominant position will be created where the market structure provokes the undertakings *to align their conduct* on the market; and where the links between the undertakings are such that tacit coordination on the market could be expected. Nonetheless, it seemed possible that the EUMR could not prevent mergers which would result in non-coordinated effects (but not the creation or strengthening of a dominant position).[329]

---

[320] These markets are also easy to cartelise and may make explicit collusion more likely.

[321] Reg. 4064/89 [1989] OJ L395/1, as amended by Reg. 1310/97 [1997] OJ L180/1. This has been replaced by Reg. 139/2004, [2004] OJ L24/1.

[322] Case IV/M190, *Nestlé/Perrier* [1992] OJ L356/1 discussed in Chap. 15.

[323] Cases C-68/94 and C-30/95, *France v. Commission, Société Commerciale des Potasses et de l'Azote v. Commission* [1998] ECR I-1375, para. 178 (Commission decision, Case IV/M308 [1994] OJ L186/30).

[324] Case T-102/96, *Gencor Ltd v. Commission* [1999] ECR II-753.

[325] Case T-342/99, *Airtours v. Commission* [2002] ECR II-2585. See also Case T-464/04, *Independent Music Publishers and Labels Association (Impala) v. Commission* [2006] ECR II-2289.

[326] Case T-464/04, *Independent Music Publishers and Labels Association (Impala) v. Commission* [2006] ECR II-2289.

[327] Case C-413/06 P, [2008] ECR I-4951.

[328] See Chap. 15.

[329] See Chap. 15.

e. Alignment of the Tests: The Judgments in *Irish Sugar, Compagnie Maritime Belge, TACA,* and *Laurent Piau*

It now seems clear that the concept of collective dominance is interpreted in the same way for the purposes of both the EUMR and Article 102. In *Gencor* the GC based its ruling upon the interpretation of the concept of collective dominance set out in its judgment in *Flat Glass* (an Article 102 case).[330] Similarly, in *Irish Sugar*[331] (an Article 102 case) the GC relied on the CJ's ruling in *France* v. *Commission*[332] for its finding that:

a joint dominant position consists in a number of undertakings being able together, in particular because of factors giving rise to a connection between them, to adopt a common policy on the market and act to a considerable extent independently of their competitors, their customers, and ultimately consumers (Joined Cases C-68/94 and C-30/95 *France and Others* v. *Commission . . .*, paragraph 221).[333]

In both *CEWAL*, known on appeal as *Compagnie Maritime Belge,* and *TACA* the CJ and the GC respectively relied on the CJ's EUMR ruling in *France* v. *Commission* when defining collective dominance for the purposes of Article 102. The *Compagnie Maritime Belge* judgment devotes a number of paragraphs to the meaning and means of establishing the existence of collective dominance.

Cases C-395 and 396/96 P, *Compagnie Maritime Belge Transports SA* v. *Commission* [2000] ECR I-1365

Court of Justice

35. In terms of Article [102], a dominant position may be held by several 'undertakings'. The Court of Justice has held, on many occasions, that the concept of 'undertaking' in the chapter of the Treaty devoted to the rules on competition presupposes the economic independence of the entity concerned (see, in particular, Case 22/71 *Béguelin Import* v. *G.L. Import Export . . .*

36. It follows that the expression 'one or more undertakings', in Article [102] implies that a dominant position may be held by two or more economic entities legally independent of each other, provided that from an economic point of view they present themselves or act together on a particular market as a collective entity. That is how the expression 'collective dominant position', as used in the remainder of this judgment, should be understood.

37. However, a finding that an undertaking has a dominant position is not in itself a ground of criticism but simply means that, irrespective of the reasons for which it has such a dominant position, the undertaking concerned has a special responsibility not to allow its conduct to impair genuine undistorted competition on the common market (see *Michelin*, paragraph 57).

38. The same applies as regards undertakings which hold a collective dominant position. A finding that two or more undertakings hold a collective dominant position must, in principle, proceed upon an economic assessment of the position on the relevant market of the undertakings concerned, prior to any examination of the question whether those undertakings have abused their position on the market.

39. So, for the purposes of analysis under Article [102], it is necessary to consider whether the undertakings concerned together constitute a collective entity *vis-à-vis* their competitors, their trading partners and consumers on a particular market. It is only where that question is answered in the affirmative that it is

---

[330] Case T-102/96, *Gencor Ltd* v. *Commission* [1999] ECR II-753, para. 273.

[331] In *Irish Sugar* [1997] OJ L258/1, the Commission fined Irish Sugar €8,800,000 for a number of breaches of Art. 102, see Chap. 7, finding of collective dominance *aff'd* Case T-228/97, *Irish Sugar plc* v. *Commission* [1999] ECR II-2969.

[332] Cases C-68/94 and C-30/95, [1998] ECR I-1375.

[333] Case T-228/97, *Irish Sugar plc* v. *Commission* [1999] ECR II-2969, para. 46.

appropriate to consider whether that collective entity actually holds a dominant position and whether its conduct constitutes abuse.

40. In the contested judgment, the [GC] was careful to examine separately those three elements, namely the collective position, the dominant position and the abuse of such a position.

41. In order to establish the existence of a collective entity as defined above, it is necessary to examine the economic links or factors which give rise to a connection between the undertakings concerned (see, *inter alia*, Case C-393/92 *Almelo* [1994] ECR I-1477, paragraph 43, and Joined Cases C-68/94 and C-30/95 *France and Others* v. *Commission*...paragraph 221).

42. In particular, it must be ascertained whether economic links exist between the undertakings concerned which enable them to act together independently of their competitors, their customers and consumers (see *Michelin*).

43. The mere fact that two or more undertakings are linked by an agreement, a decision of associations of undertakings or a concerted practice within the meaning of Article [101(1)] of the Treaty does not, of itself, constitute a sufficient basis for such a finding.

44. On the other hand, an agreement, decision or concerted practice (whether or not covered by an exemption under Article [101(3)]) may undoubtedly, where it is implemented, result in the undertakings concerned being so linked as to their conduct on a particular market that they present themselves on that market as a collective entity *vis-à-vis* their competitors, their trading partners and consumers.

45. The existence of a collective dominant position may therefore flow from the nature and terms of an agreement, from the way in which it is implemented and, consequently, from the links or factors which give rise to a connection between undertakings which result from it. Nevertheless, the existence of an agreement or of other links in law is not indispensable to a finding of a collective dominant position; such a finding may be based on other connecting factors and would depend on an economic assessment and, in particular, on an assessment of the structure of the market in question.

Not only does this judgment follow the pattern of earlier cases of not distinguishing between cases on collective dominance decided under Article 102 and those decided under the EUMR, but it supports the view that, as in EUMR cases, formal links (for example, contractual links) between the parties will be unnecessary to a finding of collective dominance.

The CJ starts by spelling out that a dominant position within the meaning of Article 102 can be held by two or more undertakings provided that they *present themselves or act together on a particular market as a collective entity*. It then states that the proof of the existence of a collective dominant position involves a two-stage process: it is necessary first to establish the existence of a collective entity and then, where the position is established, to establish that the collective entity holds a dominant position.

It was when discussing the means of establishing the existence of a collective entity that the Court relied on the ruling in *Almelo* and its own ruling in the merger case, *France* v. *Commission*. These cases establish the necessity of 'economic links or factors which give rise to a connection between the undertakings concerned'. The Court held that such links could, but would not necessarily, be established by an agreement, decision, or concerted practice within the meaning of Article 101 concluded by the undertakings (even if exempted from the prohibition in Article 101(1) by Article 101(3)). The *CEWAL* agreement[334] did in fact provide the requisite links. The Court stressed, however, in paragraph 45 that 'the existence of an agreement or of other links in law is not indispensable to a finding of a collective dominant position; such a finding may be based on other connecting factors and would depend on an economic assessment and, in particular, on an assessment of the structure of the market in question'. This indicates that, as the GC held in both *Gencor* and *Airtours*, undertakings

---

[334] *CEWAL* [1993] OJ L34/20.

which are able to engage in a parallel manner on a market by tacitly coordinating their behaviour may be found collectively to hold a dominant position on a market.

This view receives support from the GC judgments in *Atlantic Container Lines AB (TACA)*[335] and *Laurent Piau*.[336] In the *TACA* case there were again contractual links in place between the parties,[337] but the GC gave support to a broad view of the links required to establish a finding of collective dominance by relying on both EUMR and Article 102 cases. It concluded that for a collective dominant position to exist:[338]

the undertakings concerned must…be sufficiently linked between themselves to adopt the same line of action on the market (*Centro Servizi Spediporto*…, paragraph 33; *DIP and Others*, paragraph 26; Joined Cases C-68/94 and C-30/95 *France and Others* v. *Commission* (*Kali und Salz*)…, paragraph 221; Case C-309/99 *Wouters and Others*…, paragraph 113; and *CEWAL I*…, paragraph 62). In that regard, it is necessary to examine the links or factors of economic correlation between the undertakings concerned and to ascertain whether those links or factors allow them to act together independently of their competitors, their customers and consumers (*Almelo*, cited at paragraph 594, paragraph 43; *Kali und Salz*, cited earlier, paragraph 221; Joined Cases C-395/96 P and C-396/96 P *Compagnie maritime belge transports and Others* v. *Commission* (*CEWAL II*)…, paragraphs 41 and 42; and *Wouters*…, paragraph 114).

More clearly, the GC in *Laurent Piau*[339] stated, relying on *Airtours*,[340] that:

[t]hree cumulative conditions must be met for a finding of collective dominance: first, each member of the dominant oligopoly must have the ability to know how the other members are behaving in order to monitor whether or not they are adopting the common policy; second, the situation of tacit coordination must be sustainable over time, that is to say, there must be an incentive not to depart from the common policy on the market; thirdly, the foreseeable reaction of current and future competitors, as well as of consumers, must not jeopardise the results expected from the common policy.

f. Summary

The concept of a collective dominant position is of importance to Article 102 and has been of critical importance to the EUMR. It now seems clear from the case law that:

(1) The concept of a collective dominant position is defined in the same way for the purposes of both the EUMR and Article 102.[341]

(2) An important difference between the provisions is, of course, that in Article 102 cases a collective dominant position must exist as a threshold matter (it prohibits only abuses of a dominant or collective dominant position not abuses that may lead to the creation of a collective dominant position), whilst in merger cases the Commission may act to prevent mergers which lead either to the creation of a collective dominant position *or* to the strengthening of a pre-existing collective dominant position. This may affect the question of how proof of collective dominance is established.[342]

---

[335] Cases T-191 and 214–216/98, *Atlantic Container Line AB* v. *Commission* [2003] ECR II-3275, para. 602.

[336] Case T-193/02, *Laurent Piau* v. *Commission* [2005] ECR II-209.

[337] See Chap 5.

[338] Cases T-191 and 214–216/98, *Atlantic Container Line AB* v. *Commission* [2003] ECR II-3275, para. 595. The Court also considered that the fact that the parties had not always adopted the same policy on the market did not negate the finding of collective dominance. There was 'no need to show that those undertakings have in fact all adopted that common policy in all circumstances', para. 631 relying on Case C-30/95, *France and others* v. *Commission* (*Kali und Salz*) [1998] ECR I-1375, para. 221.

[339] Case T-193/02, *Laurent Piau* v. *Commission* [2005] ECR II-209, para. 111.

[340] Case T-342/99, *Airtours plc* v. *Commission* [2002] ECR II-2585.

[341] Obviously the assessments in each case will be different: in the case of Art. 102 the examination determines whether or not there has been an abuse of an existing collective dominant position; in contrast an EUMR assessment is prospective in nature, to determine whether or not the merger (or concentration for the purposes of the Regulation) *will* lead to the creation of a collective dominant position or the strengthening of a pre-existing collective dominant position.

[342] See Chap. 15.

(3) Independent economic entities may hold a collective dominant position provided that they are united by economic links which enable them to present themselves as a collective entity and to adopt the same conduct on the market.

(4) The economic links may be contractual, structural (such as cross shareholdings or common directorships), or provided by the structure of the market which ensures parallelism of behaviour between firms on an oligopolistic market.[343]

(ii) Abuse of a Collective Dominant Position

The development of the concept of collective dominance was of enormous importance in the context of the EUMR as it was important that the Commission should have the power to prevent mergers which will later lead to tacit collusion on a market.[344] A more difficult issue is what should be done if firms *are* already tacitly coordinating their behaviour on a market. Even if it is settled that Article 102 applies to undertakings which hold a collective dominant position, what conduct may amount to an abuse of a collective dominant position?[345]

a. Flat Glass

In *Flat Glass*,[346] the Commission had concluded that the undertakings' communication of, for example, identical prices to customers and granting of identical discounts constituted abuses within the meaning of Article 102. However, the GC criticised the Commission for simply having recycled the facts of the Article 101 infringement to present an infringement of Article 102. Since then the Commission has sought to spell out the relevant market for the purposes of Article 102, the position of the undertakings on the market, and the abuses in the context of the express provisions of Article 102.

The conduct alleged to be abusive in *French-West African Shipowners' Committee*, *CEWAL*, and *TACA* was nonetheless broadly the same as that which the Commission had already held to infringe Article 101 (the attempt by the members of the committee to eliminate effective competition from non-committee shipowners).[347]

b. Collective Abuses

In Chapter 7 it was seen that Article 102 has been used to condemn a range of conduct. It prohibits both exploitative practices (such as excessive pricing or inertia) and anti-competitive practices (such as predatory or discriminatory pricing, tying, refusals to supply, etc.). It is a crucial question whether or not these notions of abuse will be useful to control the behaviour of oligopolists that are not united by virtue of contractual or other formal links.

In this chapter we have seen that where there is no explicit collusion, the key cause for concern in an oligopolistic market is that undertakings may engage in tacit collusion rather than price competition, setting their prices at a level which produces supra-competitive profits and restricts output.[348]

---

[343] See, e.g., Faull and Nikpay, *The EC Law of Competition* (cited in n. 18), paras. 4.109–4.126.

[344] The fear that a merger might alternatively result in 'non-coordinated' effects but not dominance or collective dominance on the market led to the decision to alter the substantive test set out in the original Merger Regulation, Reg. 4064/89 [1989] OJ L395/1, as amended by Reg. 1310/97 [1997] OJ L180/1, see Reg. 139/2004 [2004] OJ L24/1, Art. 2(2) and (3).

[345] See, e.g., P. Fernandez, 'Increasing Powers and increasing Uncertainty: Collective Dominance and Pricing Abuses' [2000] 5 *ELRev* 645 and G. Monti, 'The scope of collective dominance under Article 82' (2001) 38 *CMLRev* 131.

[346] Cases T-68, 77, and 78/89, *Società Italiana Vetro SpA v. Commission ('Flat Glass')* [1992] ECR II-1403.

[347] Although the Commission couched its analysis in terms of Art. 102 and was careful not to recycle the facts, the fact remains that much of the conduct was anyway condemned under Art. 101.

[348] Case IV/M524, *Airtours/First Choice* [2000] OJ L93/1, annulled on appeal Case T-342/99, *Airtours plc v. Commission* [2002] ECR II-2585, discussed in Chap. 15.

A question which arises, therefore, is could this behaviour be caught by Article 102, which expressly provides that an abuse may consist of directly or indirectly imposing 'unfair selling prices'?

Exploitative Behaviour and Excessive Pricing

It is seen in Chapter 7 that Article 102 has, in fact, rarely been used to condemn exploitative, unfair, or excessive prices. In practice it is very hard to establish that prices charged are excessive and the Commission has not sought to do so, preferring to avoid acting as price regulator.[349] Although therefore it might seem possible, in principle, for the Commission to condemn oligopolists that have engaged in parallel pricing at a level that the Commission considers to be 'excessive' it seems extremely unlikely that it would attempt to do so. In addition, it is arguably perverse to prohibit conduct which is 'natural' in some oligopolies as abusive and, consequently, to render the relevant undertakings open to large fines by way of penalties and/or to actions in national courts.[350] As the collusion is not such that it is capable of being addressed under Article 101, it would not be appropriate to do so 'through the back door' under Article 102. It is only when the tacit collusion results in the commission of an abuse that Article 102 can be applied.[351]

Collective Exclusionary Abuses

In the liner conference cases already discussed the Commission condemned behaviour that was targeted at eliminating competitors seeking to compete outside the liner conference. In *Compagnie Maritime Belge*[352] the CJ upheld the Commission's finding of abuse in *CEWAL*, including the finding that the putting on of fighting ships by the undertakings was an abuse for the purposes of Article 102. In *TACA*[353] the Commission found that the members had abused their dominant position by (1) agreeing to place restrictions on the availability and content of service contracts[354] and (2) altering the competitive structure of the market so as to reinforce TACA's dominant position (in particular, by trying to ensure that any potential competitor wishing to enter the market would do so only after it had become a party to the TACA). Although the existence of the first abuse was upheld on the appeal, the GC found that on the facts the Commission had failed to demonstrate that the members had induced potential competitors to join the TACA by the measures referred to in the decision.[355]

It is hard to envisage what other abuses may be committed by undertakings indulging in non-collusive parallel behaviour. It would be difficult to explain collective decisions refusing to supply an undertaking, or targeting a new entrant to the market, on the grounds of mutual interdependence. However, it could be argued, for example, that an abuse will have been committed by collectively dominant undertakings which are inefficient or which refuse to innovate[356] or perhaps which all impose exclusive purchasing commitments on their distributors.[357]

[349] See Chap. 7. See also, e.g., *Attheraces Ltd v. British Horseracing Board Ltd* [2007] EWCA Civ 38.

[350] See R. Whish and B. Sufrin, 'Oligopolistic Markets and EC Competition Law' [1992] YEL 59, 74–75. In condemning excessive prices of a monopolist, however, Art. 102 in the same sense also condemns natural or rational behaviour by a monopolist.

[351] J. Faull and A. Nikpay, *The EC Law of Competition* (2nd edn, Oxford University Press, 2007), para. 4.125.

[352] Cases C-395 and 396/96 P, *Compagnie Maritime Belge Transports SA v. Commission* [2000] ECR I-1365.

[353] [1999] OJ L95/1, on appeal, Case T-191/98, *Atlantic Container Line AB and Others v. Commission* [2003] ECR II-3275.

[354] Contracts by which a shipper undertakes to provide a minimum quantity of cargo to be transported by the conference (conference service contracts) or by an individual carrier (individual service contracts) over a fixed period of time and the carrier or the conference commits to a certain rate or rate schedule as well as a defined service level.

[355] Cases T-191 and 212–214/98, *Atlantic Container Line v. Commission* [2003] ECR II-3275.

[356] See Chap. 7.

[357] Such conduct would be likely to be caught by Art. 101(1) in any event, see Chap. 4.

c. Abuse by One of the Collectively Dominant Undertakings

In *Irish Sugar plc v. Commission*[358] the GC held that an *individual* undertaking could engage in conduct which constitutes an abuse of its dominant position held collectively with one or more undertakings:

> Whilst the existence of a joint dominant position may be deduced from the position which the economic entities concerned together hold on the market in question, the abuse does not necessarily have to be the action of all the undertakings in question. It only has to be capable of being identified as one of the manifestations of such a joint dominant position being held. Therefore, undertakings occupying a joint dominant position may engage in joint or individual abusive conduct.[359]

This finding was made in the context of a dominant position held jointly by a dominant undertaking and its distributor (on a vertical level). In this case Irish Sugar had such a close relationship with its distributor that it only narrowly failed to qualify as a single economic unit.[360] Had the Commission been able to make such a finding, it would of course have been unnecessary to invoke the concept of collective dominance. Further, the parties were clearly acting to safeguard their collective dominant position on the market.[361]

In contrast, it is less easy to envisage what conduct which is traditionally seen as anti-competitive when indulged in by an individual dominant undertaking may also be found to be abusive when engaged in by one of a group of oligopolists. The granting of loyalty rebates, discriminatory pricing, or selective price-cutting by single dominant undertakings may be condemned as exclusionary abuses.[362] On an oligopolistic market, however, the granting of rebates to customers, discriminatory pricing, or selective price-cutting by one of the undertakings may mean that price competition is in fact operating between the oligopolists.[363] Nonetheless it seems that the concept of an individual abuse of a dominant position could, perhaps, be useful to preclude behaviour targeted by one of the members at a new entrant with the objective of protecting the oligopoly generally or to prevent signalling an oligopolist's pricing preferences to other members of the oligopoly.[364] In addition, it could be used to prevent price cuts targeted at a price-cutter that is destabilising tacit collusion on a tight oligopolistic market.[365]

The implications of the *Irish Sugar* judgment are explored by G. Monti in an extract from his article.

G. Monti, 'The Scope of Collective Dominance under Article 82 EC' [2001] 38 *CMLRev* 131, 143

This is an important conclusion, which could apply to a variety of situations, horizontal and vertical. On a horizontal level, it may be deployed to catch a scenario like this: say there are three companies that enjoy collective dominance (e.g. because of membership in an export cartel). Let us now say that a fourth

---

[358] Case T-228/97, [1999] ECR II-2969.

[359] Case T-228/97, [1999] ECR II-2969, para. 66. In the case these included seven individual abuses on the market in granulated sugar intended for retail sale and for industry in Ireland and some abuses of a collective dominant position held with a distributor.

[360] Case T-228/97, *Irish Sugar plc v. Commission* [1999] ECR II-2969, para. 28.

[361] G. Monti, 'The Scope of Collective Dominance under Article 82' (2001) 38 *CMLRev* 131.

[362] See, e.g., Case 85/76, *Hoffmann-La Roche v. Commission* [1979] ECR 461, and Chap. 7. It should be noted that in the light of Case C-209/10, *Post Danmark A/S v. Konkurrencerådet*, 27 March 2012, selective price cutting which is not predatory is more likely to be an abuse if the dominant position is a collective one, see Chap.7, Section 8.D.

[363] See TACA [1999] OJ L95/6.

[364] G. Monti, 'The Scope of Collective Dominance under Article 82' (2001) 38 *CMLRev* 131, 146–149.

[365] In this case the predation may represent the 'punishment' mechanism which means that tacit collusion subsequently follows, see, e.g., the facts that arose in *Brooke Group Ltd v. Brown & Williamson Tobacco Corp.*, 509 US 209 (1993).

competitor attempts to penetrate the market and one of the three engages in predatory pricing or other exclusionary tactics not forbidden by Article [101]. In this scenario, the Commission is now empowered to find that undertaking liable under Article [102] for abusing the collective dominant position. It does not need to fine the other two undertakings. Moreover, and potentially more significantly, the *Irish Sugar* decision states that collective dominance can be held by undertakings in a vertical relationship, which entails that a non-dominant distributor who has sufficiently strong links with a dominant manufacturer has the same degree of responsibility not to hinder competition that the manufacturer has, thus any attempt to protect his market position (e.g. terminating a retailer who sells competing goods) may be found to be an abuse.

This vastly extends the jurisdiction of the Commission under Article [102]. While it is obviously a ruling which could be overturned by the CJ, it is submitted that the reasoning of the [GC] can be supported as consistent with well-established principles. Specifically, there is no need for a causal link between the dominant position and the abuse: the dominant position does not have to be used, so long as the conduct of a dominant firm has anti-competitive effects. This was established in *Continental Can* where the ECJ said that 'the strengthening of the position of an undertaking may be an abuse and prohibited under Article [102], regardless of the means and procedure by which it is achieved' if it has anti-competitive effects. On this basis a contract clause that has an anti-competitive effects (e.g. SDL's product swap)[366] is a breach of Article [102] even if SDL is not individually dominant, because its effect was to consolidate the collective dominance by excluding potential competitors. This broad, effects-based application of Article [102] is in line with the 'special responsibility' imposed on dominant firms not to distort competition.

(iii) Remedies and Fines

In considering the appropriateness of Article 102 as a mechanism for dealing with oligopolistic markets it is also important to bear in mind the remedies available for a breach of Article 102. Under Regulation 1/2003, the Commission has power to require an undertaking to bring an infringement to an end (Article 7), and to impose fines on undertakings for any infringements committed (Article 15).[367] Article 7 is broad, enabling, for example, the Commission to order both behavioural and structural remedies where necessary to bring the infringement to an end. In theory the Commission could, therefore, in exceptional circumstances, order 'divestiture' where essential to improve the competitive structure of the market.[368] Although the Commission might be able to order price reductions were it to find abusive unfairly high pricing, it could not engage in price control or look pragmatically for other problems causing price rigidity in the market and suggest solutions for resolving them.

(iv) Conclusions

It appears that Article 102 may be applicable to independent undertakings that are not linked together by some agreement or other special relationship. Even if Article 102 is applied to oligopolists linked only by their mutual interdependence, it has been seen that the concept of abuse, developed in relation to individually dominant firms, is not a mechanism ideally equipped to control the behaviour of oligopolists. The idea that an 'individual' undertaking may commit an abuse of a

---

[366] One of the abuses of a collective dominant position found by the Commission was that SDL, the distributor, had agreed with one retailer and one wholesaler to exchange its sugar for the sugar that the wholesaler and retailer had purchased from France.

[367] [2003] OJ L1/1. See Chap. 13.

[368] Structural remedies can, however, only be imposed where there is no equally effective behavioural remedy or where the behavioural remedy would be more burdensome, see Reg. 1/2003, recital 12. Further, the recital states that structural remedies will only be proportionate where there is a risk of lasting or repeated infringement which derives from the very structure of the undertaking, see Chap. 13.

collective dominant position may, however, render Article 102 more effective. Further, the action that the Commission may take under Regulation 1/2003 on the finding of an infringement may not be the most appropriate means of dealing with the problems posed. It is far from clear that imposing fines on undertakings for behaving in an economically rational way is logical. In addition, the power to order an undertaking to bring its infringement to an end may be an ineffective means of dealing with the oligopoly problem.

It is, however, perhaps the lack of any other effective method of dealing with oligopolies rather than the appropriateness of Article 102 itself that has led the Commission to persist in the development of the concept of an abuse of a collective dominant position.

C. ALTERNATIVE METHODS FOR DEALING WITH OLIGOPOLISTIC MARKETS UNDER EU LAW

(i) Merger Regulation

Given that oligopolistic markets often do not function as effectively as ones in which free competition operates, and given the difficulties involved in applying either Article 101 or Article 102 to the conduct of undertakings operating on such markets, it may be that the Merger Regulation holds the key. It seems sensible to ensure that the EUMR is utilised to prevent mergers which create or strengthen a collective dominant position or which will lead to non-coordinated effects on an oligopolistic market. Prevention is better than a cure. If the Commission prohibits mergers causing market imperfections it will have to worry less frequently about corrective measures. This objective was extremely influential in the debate leading up to the eventual decision to change the substantive test for appraisal under the EUMR.

A strict merger policy may, therefore, reduce some of the difficulties that arise in attempting to control oligopolistic markets and markets on which one undertaking only is found to be dominant. Where a market is already an oligopolistic one the EUMR can obviously only be of use to ensure that the undertakings' positions on the market are not strengthened through merger. Other solutions may need to be found to deal with an oligopolistic market which already exists.

(ii) Sector Inquiries

Article 12(1) of Regulation 17 gave the Commission a wide discretion to conduct sector inquiries and to decide whether or not to investigate markets that it considers to be malfunctioning. To conduct such an investigation the Commission did not have to have any evidence of, or even suspect, an infringement of either Article 101 or Article 102. Unfortunately the provision conferred no power on the Commission to take action to remedy any defects identified in an investigation and was therefore, initially at least, rarely used.

Whish and Sufrin argued that 'given the political will' the provision could form:[369]

[the] basis of a proper investigative system. Although there may be understandable concern about giving the Commission such large elements of discretion in respect of oligopolistic markets it is doubtful whether it is more worrying than the prospect of the Article [102] prohibition applied wholesale to the complex behaviour of oligopolies.

Article 17 Regulation 1/2003 amended the Commission's powers but does not give it the broad basis called for by Whish and Sufrin.

---

[369] R. Whish and B. Sufrin, 'Oligopolistic Markets and EC Competition Law' [1992] YEL 59, 83.

Regulation 1/2003, Article 17

Investigations into sectors of the economy and into types of agreement

1. Where the trend of trade between Member States, the rigidity of prices or other circumstances suggest that competition may be restricted or distorted within the common market, the Commission may conduct its inquiry into a particular sector of the economy or into a particular type of [agreement] across various sectors. In the course of that inquiry, the Commission may request undertakings or associations of undertakings concerned to supply the information necessary for giving effect to Articles [101] and [102] of the Treaty.

The Commission may in particular request the undertakings or associations of undertakings concerned to communicate to it all agreements, decisions and concerted practices.

The Commission may publish a report on the results of its inquiry into particular sectors of the economy or of particular types of agreements across various sectors and invite comments from interested parties.

Article 17(2) provides the Commission with the powers to collect such information. The provision still does not, however, confer power on the Commission to adopt remedies following such a report. Through such an inquiry the Commission can obtain a broader view of the sector and examine more sector-wide practices than it would when concentrating on individual agreements concluded by firms operating on those markets. Having done this it could then take further action, perhaps under the competition, or other Treaty, rules. The powers may be particularly useful for investigating suspicious pricing or other practices in oligopolistic markets where the presence of a small number of players may incite concerted practices or for scrutinising agreements being used on the market that may shape the future competitive environment.

Since 2004 the Commission has used Article 12 of Regulation 17 on a number of occasions concluding inquiries into: the sale of sports rights to internet companies and to providers of the third generation (3G) of mobile phones services; roaming; leased lines; local loop; and the energy, financial services, and pharmaceutical sectors.[370] The energy report, published in January 2007, identified a number of barriers to competition in the sector. The Commission stated that it would pursue Article 101 and 102 proceedings, where appropriate to remedy anti-competitive practices identified (such as long-term downstream contracts, collusion between incumbents to share markets, and lack of access to infrastructure), will consider competition and regulatory remedies to deal with other identified problems, will use the State Aid rules where State subsidies contribute to maintenance of concentrated markets and prevent liberalisation from taking root, and will use the Merger Regulation to prevent increasing market concentration in this area. A number of Article 102 proceedings have now been brought in the energy sector.[371]

The pharmaceutical sector inquiry, concluded in July 2009,[372] found 'a number of structural shortcomings and problems in the companies' practices that potentially led to distortions of competition and delays to entry of new, innovative as well as cheaper generic medicines to the EU market'.[373] It made a number of recommendations, including stronger enforcement of the competition rules, particularly in respect of patent settlements.[374] As a result of matters discovered during the inquiry the

---

[370] See <http://ec.europa.eu/competition/antitrust/sector_inquiries.html>.

[371] See Chap.7

[372] <http//:ec.europa.eu/competition/sectors/pharmaceuticals/inquiry/communication_en.pdf>.

[373] IP/09/1098; see also MEMO/09/321.

[374] The Report recommended continuing monitoring of patent settlements in the pharmaceutical sector. The Commission published its third report on such settlements in July 2012.

Commission opened a number of proceedings against pharmaceutical companies in 2011.[375] In July 2012 the Commission sent Statements of Objections to two further companies alleging that each had entered into anti-competitive agreements with generic competitors which may have hindered the entry of generic drugs on to the market contrary to Article 101 and, in one case (Les Laboratoires Servier), had adopted practices to shut out competitors from the market, contrary to Article 102.[376]

(iii) Cartels and Other Agreements

Many oligopolistic markets have characteristics which make them particularly prone to cartelisation. The Commission is vigilant in these markets in case cartels are being operated. Further, it has been seen that other agreements, such as information-sharing agreements, agreements on advertising or relating to trading terms and conditions and meeting competition provisions, may exacerbate the problems arising on oligopolistic markets, in particular by increasing transparency. Further, horizontal cooperation and vertical agreements concluded between and by players on oligopolistic markets may facilitate tacit collusion on markets.[377] EU block exemptions do not, therefore, generally apply to agreements concluded between or by undertakings with large market shares and their benefit may be withdrawn where a market is affected by networks of agreements. In such cases, agreements need to be examined individually to ensure that they are not unduly restrictive of competition.

5. CONCLUSIONS

1. The Commission has wide investigative powers which it can use to unearth covertly operated cartels.

2. Where hardcore cartel activity (agreements to fix prices, restrict output, share markets, and/or rig bids) is uncovered, heavy fines will be imposed by the Commission on the undertakings involved.

3. A number of Member States have criminalised cartel activity and set out sanctions for individuals involved in the conclusion of cartels.

4. The fight against cartels is now one of the, if not the, major priorities of the Commission. Whistle-blowers are encouraged and repeat offenders are punished particularly severely.

5. The Commission is trying to encourage consumers to seek compensation in the national courts from those engaged in hardcore cartel activity.

6. Article 101 also prohibits provisions designed to supplement and facilitate the operation of a cartel agreement.

7. Tacit collusion engaged in by firms operating on an oligopolistic market is not prohibited by Article 101(1). An agreement or some reciprocal direct or indirect contact between the undertakings operating on the market must be established. Article 101 may, however, prohibit practices such as exchange of information, meeting competition clauses or other clauses in vertical agreements which facilitate tacit collusion on a market. Further, the EUMR prohibits mergers which may lead to an increase in price through unilateral or coordinated effects on an oligopolistic market.

8. Article 102 may apply to oligopolists which collectively hold a dominant position on the market. Collective or individual actions designed to exclude new entrants into the market or to punish those deviating from the cooperative structure might constitute abuses of a collective dominant position.

9. Article 17 of Regulation 1/2003 is becoming an important mechanism for investigating concentrated markets or markets on which competition does not appear to be working well. The Commission is using it to identify problems on a market which can later be addressed through use of its powers under Articles 101, 102, 106, the EUMR, and/or the State Aid rules.

---

[375] IP/11/511, IP/11/1228.

[376] IP/12/834 and IP/12/835. See also Case C-457/10 P, *AstraZeneca AB and AstraZeneca plc v. Commission*, 6 December 2012, discussed in Chap 7.

[377] See Chaps. 10 and 11.

10. In the UK, for example, the Enterprise Act[378] provides for the investigation of markets where a feature or features of it appear to prevent, restrict, or distort competition in the UK. Where adverse effects on competition are identified following an investigation, remedies to deal with the problem may be imposed or recommended: for example, the total or partial termination of an agreement; that the prices to be charged for any specified goods or services on a market should be regulated; or that any business, or part of a business, be disposed of (by the sale of any part of an undertaking or assets or otherwise). It may also be suggested, or ordered, that measures should be taken by or against bodies other than the market players (for example, where it considers that the market rigidity has been caused, partly at least, by advertising restrictions or other legal or regulatory barriers).

11. Resort to such draconian remedies as price control and divestiture may not always be a suitable means of dealing with the problems arising on oligopolistic markets. However, it can also be seen that a more flexible system may have advantages over one focusing exclusively on the abusive conduct, or the behaviour, of the undertakings on the market. Significant changes in the EU rules would need to be made before such a system could be operated by the Commission.

6. FURTHER READING

A. BOOKS

BISHOP, S., and WALKER, M., *The Economics of EC Competition Law: Concepts, Application and Measurement* (3rd edn, Sweet & Maxwell, 2009)

HARDING, C., and JOSHUA, J., *Regulating Cartels in Europe* (2nd edn, Oxford University Press, 2010)

JEPHCOTT, M., *Law of Cartels* (2nd edn, Jordans, 2011)

SCHERER, F. M., and MOSS, D., *Industrial Market Structure and Economic Performance* (3rd edn, Houghton Mifflin, 1990), Chaps. 7 and 8

CHAPTERS IN BOOKS

WILS, W., 'Does the Effective Enforcement of Articles 81 and 82 Require Not Only Fines on Undertakings But Also Individual Penalties, In Particular Imprisonment?' in C.-D. Ehlermann (ed.), *European Competition Law Annual 2001: Effective Private Enforcement of EC Antitrust Law* (Hart Publishing, 2002)

C. ARTICLES

ALBORS-LLORENS, A., 'Horizontal Agreements and Concerted Practices in EC Competition Law: Unlawful and Legitimate Contacts between Competitors' [2006] 51 *Ant Bull* 837

CASTILLO DE LA TORRE, F., 'Evidence, Proof and Judicial Review in Cartel Cases' (2009) *World Competition* 505

FRANZOSI, M., 'Oligopoly and the Prisoners' Dilemma: Concerted Practices and As If Behaviour' [1988] *ECLR* 385

JONES, A., 'Wood Pulp: Concerted Practice and/or Conscious Parallelism' [1993] *ECLR* 273

KORAH, V., 'Concerted Practices' (1973) 36 *MLR* 260

—— 'Gencor v. Commission: Collective Dominance' [1999] *ECLR* 337

MONTI, G., 'The Scope of Collective Dominance under Article 82' (2001) 38 *CMLRev* 131

ROSHOWICZ, P. H., 'The Appropriateness of Criminal Sanctions in the Enforcement of Competition Law' [2004] *ECLR* 12

VAN GERVEN, G., and VARONA, E. N., 'The Wood Pulp Case and the Future of Concerted Practices' (1994) 31 *CMLRev* 575

VEECHI, T., 'Unilateral Conduct in an Oligopoly according to the Discussion Paper on Art. 82: Conscious Parallelism or Abuse of Collective Dominance?' (2008) *World Competition* 385

WERDEN, G. J., 'Sanctioning Cartel Activity: Let the Punishment Fit the Crime' (2009) *European Competition Journal* 19

—— and SIMON, M. J., 'Why Price Fixers should go to Prison' (1987) 32 *Ant Bull* 917

WHISH, R., and SUFRIN, B., 'Oligopolistic Markets and EC Competition Law' [1992] *YEL* 59

WILS, W., 'Is Criminalisation of EU Competition Law the Answer?' [2005] 28(2) *World Competition* 117

10

HORIZONTAL COOPERATION AGREEMENTS

1. CENTRAL ISSUES

1. Horizontal cooperation agreements are often pro-competitive and bring benefits to consumers.

2. A joint venture is an arrangement by which two or more firms come together, pool their resources, and integrate part of their operations to achieve particular commercial goals. Joint ventures which amount to a concentration are dealt with under the regime established by the Merger Regulation, currently Regulation 139/2004.

3. The Commission's policy towards horizontal cooperation agreements which fall to be assessed under Article 101 has evolved, from a time when a wide range of essentially pro-competitive agreements were held to be caught by Article 101(1) but then exempted under Article 101(3) to the present position when a more effects-based assessment is made of whether the agreement is within Article 101(1) in the first place.

4. New block exemptions and Guidelines were adopted and issued in 2010. Since 2004 undertakings have had to self-assess as it is no longer possible to individually notify and gain an individual exemption.

5. Two of the block exemptions cover research and development (R&D) agreements, and specialisation agreements. They are 'new generation' type block exemptions, containing black clauses covering hardcore restrictions and market share thresholds. The block exemption regulations adopted in 2010 expire at the end of December 2022. A third block exemption is on joint compilations, tables, and studies in the insurance industry.

6. The 2010 Guidelines, after a general section, deal with six particular types of agreement: information exchanges, R&D, production (including specialisation), purchasing, commercialisation (including joint selling), and standardisation. Unlike the 2000 Guidelines there is no separate section on environmental agreements.

2. INTRODUCTION

Cooperation between firms at the same level of the market is not necessarily anti-competitive. Outside the realm of hardcore cartel arrangements involving price-fixing, market-sharing, and quotas, discussed in Chapter 9, horizontal agreements may promote economic efficiency and integration. Cooperation may enable economies of scale to be achieved, new products or services to be brought on to the market, and/or new markets to be penetrated. Competition authorities will wish to allow and even encourage such beneficial arrangements while remaining steadfast against agreements and concerted practices which rig prices and markets.

Non-cartel-type cooperation between undertakings can take a wide variety of forms. It ranges from temporary arrangements at one level of activity, such as the research and development (R&D) stage, to what is in effect a merger uniting the undertakings' entire operations in a particular area of interest. Sometimes the parties to the arrangements are actual or potential competitors in the field in which they are cooperating, but sometimes they bring to the collaborative enterprise skills or resources which are complementary rather than parallel. Competition authorities, in judging whether the arrangements restrict competition, and if so whether they should be permitted, will be concerned not only with reductions of competition between the parties themselves but also with effects on third parties, spill-over effects on to other markets, and network effects.

These types of cooperative arrangements are very common. Firms frequently look for 'partners' for particular operations, either in the short or long term. They often seek to form what are sometimes called 'strategic alliances'. Notably, modern technological developments (and the liberalisation of previously regulated markets) have led to an increase in collaborative arrangements as companies active in rapidly developing markets such as telecommunications, information technology, and the media decide to pool their resources and expertise in order to make the next leap forward feasible.

EU competition policy towards horizontal cooperation between undertakings has changed over the years, and one cannot assume that the same attitude towards a particular arrangement would be taken now as in the past. The Commission's thinking about what amounts to a 'restriction of competition' in this context has developed, and there have also been changes in the procedures dealing with cooperation between undertakings. In 1997[1] the Commission announced the launch of a review of its policy towards horizontal arrangements with the object of clarifying the instruments, such as regulations and notices, in this field. In 2000 the review culminated in a set of Guidelines on horizontal cooperation and new block exemptions for R&D agreements and specialisation agreements. The block exemptions expired at the end of 2010 and were replaced, and the Commission adopted a new set of Guidelines. This chapter considers first some general issues in respect of horizontal cooperation and then, in the light of the Guidelines and the block exemptions, how Article 101 applies to particular types of cooperation. It then looks briefly at cases in various sectors. It will be seen that in this area of competition law there are comparatively few judgments of the EU Courts. This is because, on the whole, in the pre-2004 system of notification and exemption the Commission permitted cooperation in R&D and production to take place, although sometimes after requiring that the plans be amended. Undertakings given the go-ahead therefore did not challenge the Commission in the EU Courts, preferring to comply with the Commission's requirements if necessary and get on with the project. The result is that in some parts of this area of competition law the Commission has had an even freer hand than usual. There have been more cases, however, in respect of purchasing and commercialisation. Since 2004 the Commission has been able to deal with concerns in horizontal cooperation by way of commitments decisions.[2]

During the process of modernisation questions were raised about the loss of certainty for undertakings that would no longer be able to notify complex horizontal arrangements involving very large sums of money. The Commission's White Paper on Modernisation[3] conceded that the new system might result in too much uncertainty for partial-function production joint ventures as 'operations of this kind generally require substantial investment and far reaching integration of operations, which makes it difficult to unravel them afterwards at the behest of a competition authority'.[4] It therefore proposed that such joint ventures should be subject to the Merger Regulation (EUMR)[5] as full-function production joint ventures are,[6] if there was no applicable block exemption.[7]

---

[1] Commission, *XXVIIth Report on Competition Policy* (Commission, 1997) paras. 46 and 47. The review was provoked by the imminent expiry of the relevant block exemptions: see Section 3.D.i, p. 735.

[2] Regulation 1/2003, Art. 9, see Chap. 13, Section 8.D.iii, p. 1019. The Star airline alliance between Air Canada, United, and Lufthansa was dealt with by a commitments decision in April 2013, IP/13/456. In the field of standard setting the Commission took commitments decisions in COMP/38.636, *Rambus*, Commitments decision, 9 December 2009; *Samsung*, IP/12/1448, 21 December 2012; and *Motorola Mobility*, IP/13/406, 6 May 2013, see Section 11.A, p. 758.

[3] White Paper on modernisation of the rules implementing Articles 85 and 86 [now 101 and 82] of the EC Treaty [1999] OJ C132/1 (White Paper).

[4] White Paper, para. 79.

[5] Reg. 1309/2004 [2004] OJ L24/1, replacing Reg. 4064/89 [1989] OJ L395/1.

[6] For the distinction between partial and full-function joint ventures and the significance of this, see Section 3.C, p. 734 and Chap. 15.

[7] White Paper, para. 80.

Partial-function production joint ventures would be subject to both the Merger Regulation dominance/effective competition test under Article 2(3) and the Article 101 test under Article 2(4).[8] In the event this proposal was dropped, and there is no special treatment for partial-function joint ventures in the modernised system. Undertakings may, however, seek a 'Guidance Letter' in accordance with the Commission's Notice on informal guidance.[9] One of the elements the Commission may take into account when deciding whether it is appropriate to issue a letter is 'the extent of the investments linked to the transaction in relation to the size of the companies concerned and the extent to which the transaction relates to a structural operation such as the creation of a non-full function joint venture'.[10] Furthermore, under Regulation 1/2003, Article 10, the Commission, acting on its own initiative, may adopt a decision finding that Article 101 is inapplicable to a particular agreement. This will only be done where 'the Community public interest…so requires'.[11] As at 1 July 2013 neither procedure had ever been used.

3. JOINT VENTURES

A. WHAT IS A JOINT VENTURE?

The term 'joint venture' could be used to describe virtually any commercial arrangement involving two or more firms.[12] It is normally used in competition law, however, to describe an arrangement by which two or more undertakings (the 'parents'), in order to achieve a particular commercial goal, integrate part of their operations, and put them under joint control.

According to the Commission's 1993 Notice on cooperative joint ventures[13] joint ventures 'embody a special, institutionally fixed form of cooperation between undertakings. They are versatile instruments at the disposal of the parents, with the help of which different goals can be pursued and attained.' In the Notice on the concept of a full-function joint venture[14] the Commission said that joint ventures encompass a broad range of operations from merger-like operations to cooperation for particular functions such as R&D, production, and distribution. However, it identified the essential feature as joint control by two or more other undertakings. The entity set up by the parents may take the form of a jointly controlled subsidiary company, but it may only be a joint committee or a partnership. In every case, however, the parents each put resources into the enterprise: finance, intellectual property rights (IPRs), know-how, personnel, premises, or equipment, for example.

B. COMPETITION CONCERNS IN RESPECT OF JOINT VENTURES

The competition concerns over joint ventures are in respect of, first, the relations between the parents. A joint venture, unlike a full-scale merger, leaves the parents as economically independent undertakings. Their common links to the joint venture, however, may lead them to engage in collusion in matters outside the ambit of the joint venture, so-called 'spill-over effects'. If this happens the efficiency gains and other advantages derived from the activities of the joint venture may be offset by restrictions of competition in other respects. Secondly, there is the matter of a reduction of actual or

---

[8] White Paper, para. 101. For the application of the tests under Reg. 139/2004 [2004] OJ L24/1, see Chap. 15.

[9] Commission Notice on informal guidance relating to novel questions concerning Articles 81 and 82 of the EC Treaty that arise in individual cases (guidance letters) [2004] OJ C101/78, see Chap. 13 (Notice on informal guidance).

[10] Notice on informal guidance, para. 8(b).

[11] See Chap. 13, Section 8.D.iv, p. 990.

[12] See J. Faull and A. Nikpay (eds.), *The EC Law of Competition* (2nd edn, Oxford University Press, 2007), para. 7.15.

[13] [1993] OJ C43/2, para. 1.

[14] [1998] OJ C66/1 (replaced by the Consolidated Jurisdictional Notice [2008] OJ C95/1), para. 3.

potential competition between the parents or between the parents and the joint venture within the ambit of the joint venture. This needs to be weighed against the competitive gains from the new presence on the market. Thirdly, a joint venture may have the effect of foreclosing the market to competition. As in other areas of competition law, the question whether the undertakings concerned have market power plays an important part.

C. JOINT VENTURES AND THE MERGER REGULATION

As explained in Chapter 15, since the system of EU merger control came into force in 1990 some joint ventures have been dealt with under the Merger Regulation rather than under Article 101. The criteria for deciding which joint ventures fall within the ambit of the Merger Regulation have changed since 1990, but the current position is that under Article 3(4) the Merger Regulation applies to joint ventures 'performing on a lasting basis all the functions of an autonomous economic entity', i.e. 'full-function' joint ventures. This concept is now elaborated upon in the Consolidated Jurisdictional Notice.[15] Article 2(4) of the Merger Regulation subjects the matter of the coordination of the competitive behaviour of the parents to appraisal in accordance with Article 101(1) and Article 101(3) but this is done within the Merger Regulation procedure. The application of the Merger Regulation to full-function joint ventures is discussed in Chapter 15. The Commission recognises in the 2010 Guidelines the thin line between full-function and non-full-function joint ventures:

21. The analysis of horizontal co-operation agreements has certain common elements with the analysis of horizontal mergers pertaining to the potential restrictive effects, in particular as regards joint ventures. There is often only a fine line between full-function joint ventures that fall under the Merger Regulation and non-full-function joint ventures that are assessed under Article 101. Hence, their effects can be quite similar.

D. THE DEVELOPMENT OF THE COMMISSION'S APPROACH TO THE ASSESSMENT OF JOINT VENTURES UNDER ARTICLE 101

(i) General

Despite more transactions being drawn within the scope of the Merger Regulation there nevertheless remain many joint ventures which are not full-function. In respect of these the question is still whether they fall within Article 101(1) and, if so, whether they fulfil the Article 101(3) criteria. It must always be remembered that any restriction of competition arising from the joint venture must be *appreciable* under the normal criteria for the application of Article 101(1), and it was partly on this point that the GC annulled the Commission decision in *European Night Services*.[16]

The Commission previously took a very interventionist approach to joint ventures based on a fear of coordination between the parents and on the loss of potential competition. However, the *XIIIth Competition Policy Report* signalled a change of policy which was applied in subsequent cases.

An early Notice on cooperation agreements in 1968[17] stated that there were certain forms of cooperation between undertakings which would not normally fall within Article 101(1). This was in effect incorporated into the Notice which the Commission issued in 1993. This Notice concerned the assessment of cooperative joint ventures pursuant to Article 101[18] and summarised

---

[15] Consolidated Jurisdictional Notice, paras. 91–109; see Chap. 15, Section 3.A.ii, p. 1144 ff.

[16] Cases T-374–375, 384, and 388/94, *European Night Services* v. *Commission* [1998] ECR II–3141.

[17] [1968] OJ C75/3, rectified [1968] OJ C84/14.

[18] [1993] OJ C43/2 (notice on cooperative joint ventures).

the Commission's administrative practice to date in order to inform undertakings 'about both the legal, and economic criteria which will guide the Commission in the future application of Article [101(1)] and Article [101(3)] to cooperative joint ventures'.[19] In 1985 the Commission adopted two block exemption regulations relevant, inter alia, to joint ventures. These were Regulation 417/85 on specialisation agreements,[20] and Regulation 418/85 on R&D agreements.[21] Both regulations were of limited use because of their limited provisions. They were replaced in 2000 by Regulation 2658/2000 on specialisation agreements[22] and Regulation 2659/2000 on research and development agreements[23] and in 2010 by Regulations 1218/2010[24] and 1217/2010 respectively.[25] The 2010 Commission Guidelines on horizontal cooperation agreements, like the 2000 Guidelines, do not deal with joint ventures as a separate species of agreement, but consider them according to their provisions and effects in the light of the principles set out therein. The general Article 101(3) Guidelines also apply.[26]

(ii) The Development of a More Economic Approach Towards the Application of Article 101 to Joint Ventures

Until the early 1980s the practice of the Commission was to hold that joint ventures were caught by Article 101(1), but then to exempt them under Article 101(3). It was invariably impressed by the benefits the joint venture offered, but considered that there was a restriction of competition involved which brought the joint venture within the prohibition. The concern about the loss of potential competition was vividly illustrated by the *Vacuum Interrupters* decision where the Commission found that the formation of a joint venture infringed Article 101(1) on the basis of the hypothetical possibility that despite all the evidence to the contrary the parents *might* each have proceeded alone, and *might* each have ultimately produced a commercial product which they could have sold in other Member States in competition with each other if a market had developed for it there.

AEI/Reyrolle Parsons re Vacuum Interrupters [1977] OJ L48/32

Two UK companies, AEI and Reyrolle Parsons, formed a jointly owned subsidiary company, Vacuum Interrupters Ltd, to develop, produce, and sell a particular type of vacuum interrupter, a product to be incorporated into circuit-breakers in switchgear apparatus. Both parents had been researching the product for ten years, but its construction and operation were complex and difficult and neither had been able to bring the product to the market. The agreement provided for the parents to cease independent work on the interrupter. As the Commission said (paragraph 10): 'Each of the companies found the cost of development was very substantial and each recognised that if vacuum interrupters were to be brought to commercial use at a price which would make them competitive with the conventional forms of switchgear, a collaboration and pooling of the resources available was essential in order that the heavy expenditure involved by the individual companies would be reduced'.

---

[19] [1993] OJ C43/2, para. 7.

[20] [1985] OJ L53/1 as amended by Commission Reg. 151/93 [1993] OJ L21/8 and extended by Commission Reg. 2236/97 [1997] OJ L306/12.

[21] [1985] OJ L53/5.

[22] [2000] OJ L304/3.

[23] [2000] OJ L304/7.

[24] [2010] OJ L335/43

[25] [2010] OJ L335/36.

[26] Guidelines on the application of Article 81(3) of the Treaty [2004] C101/97, see Chap. 4.

Commission

15. Prior to the signing of the agreement of 25 March 1970 neither Associated Electrical Industries Ltd nor Reyrolle Parsons Ltd were manufacturing vacuum interrupters. However, their experience in the field of heavy electrical equipment and their ability to manufacture components therefor, the extent and quality of their R&D work, some of which was concentrated in the field of vacuum interrupters, their skill in producing electrical equipment generally and the natural growth of their activities in the field of manufacture of electrical equipment might well have led them to extend their range of products to include vacuum interrupters, thereby making them direct competitors in the relevant product market. They must therefore be assumed to be potential competitors and the agreement of 25 March 1970 to have been concluded between potentially competing manufacturers.

16. The object and effect of the agreement is to restrict competition within the common market. There is not at present even one manufacturer of components for electrical equipment within the area of the common market which makes and sells vacuum interrupters. When two companies, each of which is a potential manufacturer and which are each within the common market, merge their activity in the fields of research, development, manufacture and sale by establishing a joint venture concerned with this one product on such terms that they deprive themselves of the possibility of developing and selling that product independently of and in competition with each other, there is a restriction of competition.

However, the joint venture scheme had obvious advantages and the Commission exempted it under Article [101(3)]:

22 ...

(1) The availability of vacuum interrupters enables switchgear manufacturers to design, develop and manufacture electric circuit breakers which have technical advantages over existing air and liquid apparatus.

(2) The agreement makes provision for the financial resources and technical support necessary to enable the R&D of vacuum interrupters to be carried out in depth.

(3) The users of switchgear incorporating vacuum interrupters receive benefits therefrom.

(4) The agreement enables the vacuum type interrupter to be developed, manufactured, and sold to consumers within the EEC on a competitive basis with those which will be available for import into the EEC from the United States and Japan when a market for the vacuum interrupter is established within the Member States of the EEC.

(5) The technical and financial effort required to produce the vacuum interrupter as a commercially viable product within a useful period of time would not have been achieved if both of the parties had relied solely on their own resources.

Decisions of this kind were subject to considerable criticism for finding restrictions of potential competition based on unrealistic assumptions. Further, exempting transactions like *Vacuum Interrupters* under Article 101(3) was theoretically inconsistent with their coming within Article 101(1) in the first place. One of the criteria for the application of Article 101(3) is that the agreement does not impose on undertakings restrictions which are not indispensable to the attainment of the agreement's (beneficial) objectives. Yet if the parents *were* able to enter the market independently, how could their coming together be indispensable?

The Commission re-evaluated its attitude towards the potential competition issue and in its *XIIIth Report on Competition Policy* (Commission, 1983) signalled a new approach. It set out a checklist of questions it would ask in future in gauging whether there really was a restriction of potential competition.

The result of this change of heart was seen in a number of subsequent decisions. *Optical Fibres* is considered to be the first manifestation of the new policy in practice.

Optical Fibres [1986] OJ L236/30

This concerned three joint ventures set up between a US company, Corning Glass Works, on the one hand and respectively BICC in the UK (a 50/50 unlimited partnership), Siemens in Germany (a joint venture company owned 50/50), and COFOCO in France (a joint venture company owned 40/60). The joint ventures were set up to develop, produce, and sell optical fibres and optical cables for use in the European telecommunications market. Corning had experience in optical fibre manufacture but none in cables and the European partners had no experience in optical fibres. There were no clauses restricting competition between Corning and the other parties and they were all free to do independent research and development in optical fibres although in reality there was no prospect of the European companies doing this.

Commission

46. The individual joint venture agreements do not as such restrict competition between Corning and its partners. When the agreements were concluded, the parties were not actual or potential competitors in the market for optical fibres or optical cables. The production of optical fibres and optical cables are different activities. Corning had no experience in cable manufacture, while Corning's partners had no experience in glass manufacture which could have led to an invention competitive with Corning's. In spite of the parties' considerable financial resources, the entry by Corning into the optical cables market or by Corning's partners into the optical fibres market was not a natural and reasonably foreseeable extension of their respective business activities. The cooperation between Corning and its partners is rather of a complementary nature which does not give rise to restriction or distortion of competition at the level of the cooperating parties. Moreover, the agreements do not foreclose market access by third parties or have any other foreseeable anti-competitive impact on their activities. The various amendments made to the original agreements ensure that competition is maintained and that third parties do not suffer from discrimination or market partitioning. In addition, by virtue of the conditions and obligations attached to this Decision, competition is safe-guarded and the Commission is in a position to monitor future developments.

47. There is neither restriction nor distortion of competition between the parents and the joint venture. The agreements provide that the parents are free to engage in independent R&D of optical fibres. Furthermore, the individual joint venture agreements do not contain obligations which go beyond what would be admitted in simple licensing agreements between non-competitors. Thus the parties are free to engage in independent R&D of optical fibres, although in practice they depend on a continuous transfer of technology from Corning. In addition, there is no obligation on the joint ventures to grant exclusive licenses to Corning in respect of improvements or innovations.

48. The principal restrictions and distortions of competition in this case are to be found rather in the relationship between the joint ventures. The joint ventures have substantially the same business activity, namely the production and marketing of optical fibres. These joint ventures are therefore directly competing companies. The agreements taken together give rise to the creation of a network of inter-related joint ventures with a common technology provider in an oligopolistic market. Corning is one of the major producers and distributors of optical fibres in the world. Its partners are cable makers with large market shares in their respective home countries. The joint ventures therefore bring together companies with strong positions in the optical fibres and cables markets. Although the joint ventures are free to make active and passive sales into each other's territories, only passive sales are permitted in territories where Corning has an exclusive licensee. Corning has interests, whether through joint ventures, subsidiaries or licensees, in several Member States. Its financial stake and key technical and financial personnel representation in the joint ventures, the success of which depends on rapid access to Corning's technology, ensure that Corning is in a position to influence and coordinate the joint venture's conduct.

It can be seen from paragraphs 46 and 47 that the Commission did not consider that there was a restriction of competition between Corning and its partners. Neither side was able to develop and put on to the market the joint venture product without the collaboration of the other, and the individual joint venture agreements were therefore outside Article 101(1). What concerned the Commission was the setting up of the network of three joint ventures. This aspect of the operation *was* within Article 101(1) and needed exemption under Article 101(3). Exemption was given (for 15 years) after modifications were made to the agreements to ensure competition between the joint ventures and to reduce Corning's control over them.[27]

In *ODIN*[28] however, the liberal policy led to a negative clearance. Metal Box (UK) and Elopak (Norway) set up a 50/50 jointly owned company called ODIN. Metal Box manufactured a range of metal, plastic, and polythene containers, bottles and other packaging, and various closures and seals. Elopak's expertise was in cartons for the dairy and food industries. The joint venture was to develop a new form of paperboard-based package with a separate laminated metal lid to be used for UHT-treated foods with a long shelf-life. The parties were not existing competitors and neither of them had all the technology required for the new product or the technical knowledge to develop it separately. The agreement did not contain ancillary restrictions[29] beyond those necessary to make the joint venture work. *Konsortium ECR 900*[30] concerned a cooperative joint venture between three undertakings for the development, manufacture, and distribution of a telecommunications system. It was held not to be caught by Article 101(1) because the undertakings could not have done it individually in the time required by the relevant tender deadline, the financial expenditure and staff resources required were too great for individual action, and as there were only 15 potential customers the parties could not have borne the financial risk individually.

The Commission adopted its 1993 Notice on cooperative joint ventures[31] in order to aid undertakings and their advisers by setting out its then current approach to the application of Article 101 to the assessment of joint ventures. It set out its policy of making a realistic economic analysis before finding that the joint venture restricted competition within Article 101(1). Nevertheless, despite the policy reflected in the 1993 Notice, the Commission sometimes still engaged in economic analysis under Article 101(3) rather than under Article 101(1). The judgment of the GC in *European Night Services*,[32] however, showed that the Commission could not rely on granting exemption under Article 101(3) as a substitute for analysis under Article 101(1).

The Commission found that a joint venture between four railway companies to provide overnight passenger rail services between the UK and the Continent through the Channel Tunnel restricted competition between the parents, between the parents and the joint venture, and vis-à-vis third parties and that these effects were exacerbated by a network of joint ventures set up by the parents. The joint venture was exempted, however, although subject to conditions unacceptable to the parties. The GC found that the Commission had not shown why Article 101(1) applied. It had not identified the relevant market properly, had not applied the appreciability criteria properly, and had demonstrated insufficient economic reasoning: for example, the holding that potential competition was restricted was based on 'a hypothesis unsupported by any evidence or any analysis of the structures of the relevant market from which it might be concluded that it represented a real, concrete possibility'.[33] The exemption conditions were flawed as well, as the Commission had applied the essential

---

[27] See also *Mitchell Cotts/Solfitra* [1987] OJ L41/31, [1988] 4 CMLR 111 (parents neither actual nor potential competitors, but the distribution arrangements brought it within Article 101(1) because they raised barriers to entry).

[28] *Metal Box/Elopak (ODIN)* [1990] OJ L209/15, [1991] 4 CMLR 832.

[29] For ancillary restraints in mergers, see Chap. 15, Section 5.F, p. 1244.

[30] [1990] OJ L228/31, [1992] 4 CMLR 54.

[31] [1993] OJ C43/2.

[32] Cases T-374–375, 384, and 388/94, *European Night Services* v. *Commission* [1998] ECR II-3141; see further Chap. 4.

[33] *European Night Services* v. *Commission* [1998] ECR II-3141, para. 142.

facilities concept inappropriately[34] and had given the exemption for too short a time in view of the long-term investment required.

The Commission subsequently refined its policy, as shown in the 2000 Guidelines, and its latest thinking is now set out in the 2010 Guidelines.

(iii) Joint Ventures and the Single Economic Entity Doctrine

Once the joint venture has been formed the Commission in the past treated the parents and the joint venture as separate undertakings so arrangements between them would be caught by Article 101. However, more recently the cases have suggested that the parents and the joint venture could be part of the same single economic entity. The matter is discussed in Chapter 3.[35]

4. THE CONTENTS OF THE GUIDELINES

After a general section, the 2010 Guidelines (the Guidelines) deal with six particular types of agreement: information exchanges, R&D, production (including specialisation), purchasing, commercialisation (including joint selling), and standardisation. Unlike the 2000 Guidelines there is no separate section on environmental agreements. In practice an agreement may span two or more of the categories. The Guidelines explain that it may be necessary to identify the 'centre of gravity' of an agreement.[36] This is particularly necessary because of the different 'safe harbours' that apply to different types of agreement and the fact that there are block exemptions in respect of R&D and specialisation agreements.

5. THE GENERAL APPROACH TO HORIZONTAL COOPERATION AGREEMENTS IN THE GUIDELINES

The Guidelines apply to cooperation of a 'horizontal' nature, that is, an agreement entered into between actual or potential competitors.[37] A company is treated as a potential competitor of another company if

10 ... in the absence of the agreement, in case of a small but permanent increase in relative prices it is likely that the former, within a short period of time ... would undertake the necessary additional investments or other necessary switching costs to enter the relevant market on which the latter is active. This assessment has to be based on realistic grounds, the mere theoretical possibility to enter a market is not sufficient (see Commission Notice on the definition of the relevant market for the purposes of Community competition law). ...

In a footnote the Commission explains that 'short period of time' depends on the facts of the case in hand, its legal and economic context and, in particular, whether the company in question is a party to the agreement or a third party.

---

[34] See Chap. 7.

[35] And see A. Jones, 'The Boundaries of an Undertaking in EU Competition Law' (2012) 8 *European Competition Journal* 301.

[36] Guidelines, paras. 13–14.

[37] Guidelines, para. 1.

The general de minimis Notice, by which agreements between actual or potential competitors which do not contain hardcore restrictions will not normally give rise to an appreciable restriction of competition where the parties' aggregate market share does not exceed 10 per cent, is discussed in Chapter 3. The Guidelines provide that agreements in the specific categories are unlikely to infringe Article 101 (because the parties are unlikely to be able to exercise and maintain market power) if the parties have aggregate market shares less than certain levels. These are R&D, 25 per cent;[38] production and specialisation, 20 per cent;[39] purchasing, 15 per cent;[40] and commercialisation and joint selling, 15 per cent.[41]

The Commission explains its basic principles for the assessment under Article 101 in paras 20–53. It explains restrictions by object and restrictions by effect.[42] In paragraphs 28–29 it explains when anti-competitive effects are likely to occur and how it will determine whether a particular agreement is likely to have those effects:

28. Restrictive effects on competition within the relevant market are likely to occur where it can be expected with a reasonable degree of probability that, due to the agreement, the parties would be able to profitably raise prices or reduce output, product quality, product variety or innovation. This will depend on several factors such as the nature and content of the agreement, the extent to which the parties individually or jointly have or obtain some degree of market power, and the extent to which the agreement contributes to the creation, maintenance or strengthening of that market power or allows the parties to exploit such market power.

29. The assessment of whether a horizontal co-operation agreement has restrictive effects on competition within the meaning of Article 101(1) must be made in comparison to the actual legal and economic context in which competition would occur in the absence of the agreement with all of its alleged restrictions (that is to say, in the absence of the agreement as it stands (if already implemented) or as envisaged (if not yet implemented) at the time of assessment). Hence, in order to prove actual or potential restrictive effects on competition, it is necessary to take into account competition between the parties and competition from third parties, in particular actual or potential competition that would have existed in the absence of the agreement. This comparison does not take into account any potential efficiency gains generated by the agreement as these will only be assessed under Article 101(3).

30. Consequently, horizontal co-operation agreements between competitors that, on the basis of objective factors, would not be able to independently carry out the project or activity covered by the co-operation, for instance, due to the limited technical capabilities of the parties, will normally not give rise to restrictive effects on competition within the meaning of Article 101(1) unless the parties could have carried out the project with less stringent restrictions....

A footnote to paragraph 30 refers to paragraph 18 of the general Article 101(3) guidelines.

The Guidelines then discuss how the 'nature and content of the agreement'[43] may limit competition. The Commission is concerned with possible price increases,[44] the facilitation of coordination,[45] and anti-competitive foreclosure.[46] Then there is a section on 'market power and other

---

[38] Guidelines, para. 134.

[39] Guidelines, para. 169.

[40] Guidelines, para. 208.

[41] Guidelines, para. 240.

[42] Guidelines, paras. 23–31.

[43] Guidelines, paras. 32–38.

[44] Guidelines, para. 34.

[45] Guidelines, paras 35–37.

[46] Guidelines, para. 38. For the concept of anticompetitive foreclosure in the Guidance on the Commission's Enforcement Priorities in Applying Article 102 to Abusive Exclusionary Conduct by Dominant Undertakings [2009] OJ C 45/2, see Chap. 7.

market characteristics'[47] Finally, the Guidelines say that even where there are restrictions by object or effect under Article 101(1), Article 101(3) may apply. Again, they refer to the general Article 101(3) guidelines.[48]

6. INFORMATION AGREEMENTS

The Guidelines contain a section on stand-alone information exchanges.[49] Information may be exchanged as part of another type of horizontal cooperation agreement, such as a production agreement, and where that is so the information exchange will be assessed along with the assessment of the agreement as a whole. The Commission accepts that other exchanges of information between competitors in other contexts may generate efficiencies.[50] However, it is also concerned that:

59..... communication of information among competitors may constitute an agreement, a concerted practice, or a decision by an association of undertakings with the object of fixing, in particular, prices or quantities. Those types of information exchanges will normally be considered and fined as cartels. Information exchange may also facilitate the implementation of a cartel by enabling companies to monitor whether the participants comply with the agreed terms. Those types of exchanges of information will be assessed as part of the cartel.

The question of when information exchanges infringe Article 101 is a complex one and we deal with the issue as a whole in Chapter 9.

7. RESEARCH AND DEVELOPMENT AGREEMENTS

A. THE APPLICATION OF ARTICLE 101(1)

Research and development (R&D) agreements are one of three types of horizontal cooperation agreements in respect of which the Commission has adopted a block exemption. The current one is Regulation 1217/2010.[51]

R&D is crucial to the competitiveness of the EU.[52] However, R&D agreements may have anti-competitive effects. R&D can take many forms, as the Guidelines say:

111. R&D agreements vary in form and scope. They range from outsourcing certain R&D activities to the joint improvement of existing technologies and co-operation concerning the research, development and marketing of completely new products. They may take the form of a co-operation agreement or of a jointly controlled company. This chapter applies to all forms of R&D agreements, including related agreements concerning the production or commercialisation of the R&D results.

In assessing the compatibility of an R&D agreement with Article 101 it is first necessary to define the market. That will involve identifying 'those products, technologies or R&D efforts that will act as the main competitive constraints on the parties'.[53] An R&D agreement may be aimed at a change to existing products but may also be aimed at creating new products which may form an entirely new

---

[47] Guidelines, paras. 39-47. For the concept of market power, see Chap. 1.

[48] Guidelines, para. 48.

[49] Guidelines, paras. 55–110.

[50] Guidelines, para. 58.

[51] [2010] OJ L335/36.

[52] Recital 2 of the block exemption, Reg. 1217/2010, mentions Art. 179(2) TFEU which provides for the EU to encourage undertakings, including SMEs, in R&D and to support their cooperation efforts.

[53] Guidelines, para. 112.

market and paragraphs 114–126 explain how relevant markets are defined in those circumstances. It may be necessary to define relevant upstream markets for technologies[54] or for innovation.[55] The calculation of market shares is particularly difficult where the agreement aims to develop a product which will create an entirely new demand, and this issue is dealt with in the block exemption.

As far as assessment under Article 101 is concerned the Guidelines say that R&D agreements restrict competition by object only if they are really a tool for a disguised cartel. As far as effects are concerned, agreements which relate to cooperation in R&D at an early stage, far removed from exploitation of the results, will fall outside Article 101(1).[56] Agreements between non-competitors generally do not have restrictive effects.[57] R&D cooperation which does not go as far as joint exploitation of possible results rarely falls within Article 101(1). It will do so only if the parties have market power on the existing markets and/or competition with respect to innovation is appreciably reduced.[58] The Guidelines do not explain what 'market power' is for this purpose but it will be seen that the block exemption applies only if the parties' aggregate market share is below 25 per cent.

B. THE APPLICATION OF ARTICLE 101(3)

(i) The Block Exemption for R&D Agreements, Regulation 1217/2010

Where the agreement does fall within Article 101(1) the block exemption Regulation 1217/2010 may apply. The Regulation defines R&D agreements (Article 1), and provides an exemption for such agreements provided they meet certain conditions (Article 2). Article 3 sets out the conditions for exemption and Article 4 contains the market share threshold and the duration of the exemption. Article 4 makes a distinction between agreements between competitors and agreements between non-competitors. The exemption is more generous as regards the latter. Article 5 contains a list of 'hardcore' restrictions, the inclusion of which prevents the exemption applying, and Article 6 contains two 'excluded restrictions' which are not block exempted but do not take the rest of the agreement outside the protection of the Regulation.

Article 1 defines the scope of the exemption.

Article 1

Definitions

1. For the purposes of this Regulation, the following definitions shall apply:

   (a) 'research and development agreement' means an agreement entered into between two or more parties which relate to the conditions under which those parties pursue:

      (i) joint research and development of contract products or contract technologies and joint exploitation of the results of that research and development;

      (ii) joint exploitation of the results of research and development of contract products or contract technologies jointly carried out pursuant to a prior agreement between the same parties;

      (iii) joint research and development of contract products or contract technologies excluding joint exploitation of the results;

---

[54] Guidelines, paras. 116–118.
[55] Guidelines, paras. 119–122.
[56] Guidelines, para. 129.
[57] Guidelines, para. 130.
[58] Guidelines, paras. 132–133.

(iv) paid-for research and development of contract products or contract technologies and joint exploitation of the results of that research and development;

(v) joint exploitation of the results of paid-for research and development of contract products or contract technologies pursuant to a prior agreement between the same parties; or

(vi) paid-for research and development of contract products or contract technologies excluding joint exploitation of the results...

Paragraph 1(1)(a). Note that paragraph 1(g) defines 'exploitation of the results' as 'the production or distribution of the contract products or the application of the contract technologies or the assignment or licensing of intellectual property rights or the communication of know-how required for such manufacture or application'.

In order to be covered by the block exemption an agreement within Article 1 must fulfil the conditions in Article 3.

Article 3

Conditions for exemption

1. The exemption provided for in Article 2 shall apply subject to the conditions set out in paragraphs 2 to 5.

2. The research and development agreement must stipulate that all the parties have full access to the final results of the joint research and development or paid-for research and development, including any resulting intellectual property rights and know-how, for the purposes of further research and development and exploitation, as soon as they become available. Where the parties limit their rights of exploitation in accordance with this Regulation, in particular where they specialise in the context of exploitation, access to the results for the purposes of exploitation may be limited accordingly. Moreover, research institutes, academic bodies, or undertakings which supply research and development as a commercial service without normally being active in the exploitation of results may agree to confine their use of the results for the purposes of further research. The research and development agreement may foresee that the parties compensate each other for giving access to the results for the purposes of further research or exploitation, but the compensation must not be so high as to effectively impede such access.

3. Without prejudice to paragraph 2, where the research and development agreement provides only for joint research and development or paid-for research and development, the research and development agreement must stipulate that each party must be granted access to any pre-existing know-how of the other parties, if this know-how is indispensable for the purposes of its exploitation of the results. The research and development agreement may foresee that the parties compensate each other for giving access to their pre-existing know-how, but the compensation must not be so high as to effectively impede such access.

4. Any joint exploitation may only pertain to results which are protected by intellectual property rights or constitute know-how and which are indispensable for the manufacture of the contract products or the application of the contract technologies.

5. Parties charged with the manufacture of the contract products by way of specialisation in the context of exploitation must be required to fulfil orders for supplies of the contract products from the other parties, except where the research and development agreement also provides for joint distribution within the meaning of point (m)(i) or (ii) of Article 1(1) or where the parties have agreed that only the party manufacturing the contract products may distribute them.

The basic position is therefore that all parties must have full access to the final results, including any IP rights and know-how. There are two exceptions to this, one of which is to cover the position of universities, research bodies, and commercial research entities which are not in the business of exploitation. It should be noted that joint exploitation can cover only results which are protected by IPRs or constitute know-how and are indispensable for the manufacture of the contract products or application of the contract technologies.

Article 4

Market share threshold and duration of exemption

1. Where the parties are not competing undertakings, the exemption provided for in Article 2 shall apply for the duration of the research and development. Where the results are jointly exploited, the exemption shall continue to apply for 7 years from the time the contract products or contract technologies are first put on the market within the internal market.

2. Where two or more of the parties are competing undertakings, the exemption provided for in Article 2 shall apply for the period referred to in paragraph 1 of this Article only if, at the time the research and development agreement is entered into:
   (a) in the case of research and development agreements referred to in point (a)(i), (ii) or (iii) of Article 1(1), the combined market share of the parties to a research and development agreement does not exceed 25 % on the relevant product and technology markets; or
   (b) in the case of research and agreements referred to in point (a)(iv), (v) or (vi) of Article 1(1), the combined market share of the financing party and all the parties with which the financing party has entered into research and development agreements with regard to the same contract products or contract technologies, does not exceed 25 % on the relevant product and technology markets.

3. After the end of the period referred to in paragraph 1, the exemption shall continue to apply as long as the combined market share of the parties does not exceed 25 % on the relevant product and technology markets.

Article 4(1) applies to agreements between non-competitors. It distinguishes between R&D agreements that extend into the exploitation stage and those which do not. The former are limited to seven years. Article 4(2) applies to agreements between competing undertakings. The effect of the provision is that where the parties' market shares exceed 25 per cent the exemption is not available. Further provisions about the calculation of market shares are set out in Article 7.

Article 5

Hardcore restrictions

The exemption provided for in Article 2 shall not apply to research and development agreements which, directly or indirectly, in isolation or in combination with other factors under the control of the parties, have as their object any of the following:

(a) the restriction of the freedom of the parties to carry out research and development independently or in cooperation with third parties in a field unconnected with that to which the research and development agreement relates or, after the completion of the joint research and development or the paid-for research and development, in the field to which it relates or in a connected field;

(b) the limitation of output or sales, with the exception of:
   (i) the setting of production targets where the joint exploitation of the results includes the joint production of the contract products;
   (ii) the setting of sales targets where the joint exploitation of the results includes the joint distribution of the contract products or the joint licensing of the contract technologies within the meaning of point (m)(i) or (ii) of Article 1(1);
   (iii) practices constituting specialisation in the context of exploitation; and

(iv) the restriction of the freedom of the parties to manufacture, sell, assign or license products, technologies or processes which compete with the contract products or contract technologies during the period for which the parties have agreed to jointly exploit the results;

(c) the fixing of prices when selling the contract product or licensing the contract technologies to third parties, with the exception of the fixing of prices charged to immediate customers or the fixing of licence fees charged to immediate licensees where the joint exploitation of the results includes the joint distribution of the contract products or the joint licensing of the contract technologies within the meaning of point (m)(i) or (ii) of Article 1(1);

(d) the restriction of the territory in which, or of the customers to whom, the parties may passively sell the contract products or license the contract technologies, with the exception of the requirement to exclusively license the results to another party;

(e) the requirement not to make any, or to limit, active sales of the contract products or contract technologies in territories or to customers which have not been exclusively allocated to one of the parties by way of specialisation in the context of exploitation;

(f) the requirement to refuse to meet demand from customers in the parties' respective territories, or from customers otherwise allocated between the parties by way of specialisation in the context of exploitation, who would market the contract products in other territories within the internal market;

(g) the requirement to make it difficult for users or resellers to obtain the contract products from other resellers within the internal market.

Article 5 is a long list of hardcore restrictions. Paragraphs 5(a) and 5(b) deal with the freedom of the parties to carry out independent R&D in unconnected areas or after the completion of the joint R&D, and limiting output or sales (subject to exceptions). Paragraph 5(c) is the usual prohibition against price-fixing. Paragraphs 5(d) to 5(g) are a prohibition of territorial restrictions, of a type familiar from the Verticals Regulations.[59] Article 6 sets out 'Excluded Restrictions'.

Article 6

Excluded restrictions

The exemption provided for in Article 2 shall not apply to the following obligations contained in research and development agreements:

(a) the obligation not to challenge after completion of the research and development the validity of intellectual property rights which the parties hold in the internal market and which are relevant to the research and development or, after the expiry of the research and development agreement, the validity of intellectual property rights which the parties hold in the internal market and which protect the results of the research and development, without prejudice to the possibility to provide for termination of the research and development agreement in the event of one of the parties challenging the validity of such intellectual property rights;

(b) the obligation not to grant licences to third parties to manufacture the contract products or to apply the contract technologies unless the agreement provides for the exploitation of the results of the joint research and development or paid-for research and development by at least one of the parties and such exploitation takes place in the internal market vis-à-vis third parties.

The first of these restrictions which cannot be block exempted but do not affect the exemption of the remaining provisions of the agreement are two kinds of no-challenge clause (although it is acceptable

---

[59] Currently Reg. 330/2010.

to provide for termination in the event of a challenge), and the second covers licensing third parties. Both these provision were in the hardcore list in the previous block exemption, Regulation 2659/2000.

(ii) The Individual Application of Article 101(3)

The Guidelines discuss the individual application of Article 101(3) in paragraphs 141–149 (giving worked examples in paragraphs 147–149). In theory Article 101(3) could be applied individually to agreements that do not fulfil the conditions in Article 3 or contain hardcore Article 5 restrictions, or where the parties are above the market share thresholds. However, the Commission says in paragraph 142 that it is unlikely that the Article 5 restrictions would fulfil the 'indispensable' criterion in Article 101(3). Many R&D agreements will lead to efficiency gains by improvements to production or distribution or economic or technical progress, but the Commission will look closely at whether a fair share of the benefits is passed on to consumers.[60] The Guidelines consider the time element. Although Article 101(3) ceases to apply if the criteria were once fulfilled but no longer are, the Commission will take into account the need for the parties to recoup sunk investments.[61] The Commission accepts that some R&D agreements are irreversible events in that once the agreement has been implemented the *ex ante* situation cannot be restored. In such a case the assessment is made on the basis of the facts at the time of implementation.[62]

8. PRODUCTION AGREEMENTS

A. GENERAL

Production agreements cover a number of scenarios. Undertakings may wish to jointly produce certain goods (joint production) or one party may wish to entrust the other with production of certain goods (sub-contracting). Specialisation is a particular form of sub-contracting, whereby the parties agree to specialise in manufacture by allocating the manufacture of certain products amongst themselves. In unilateral specialisation one party ceases production altogether, whereas in reciprocal specialisation each agrees to give up manufacturing certain products and leave it to the other.[63] If sub-contracting is between parties at different stages of the market it is not covered by the Horizontal Guidelines but may be covered by the Verticals Guidelines[64] or by the Notice on sub-contracting agreements.[65]

B. THE APPLICATION OF ARTICLE 101(1)

In paragraphs 157–159 of the Guidelines the Commission identifies the 'main competition concerns' in respect of production agreements, These are the direct limitation of competition between the parties; the coordination of the parties' competitive behaviour; and the anticompetitive foreclosure of third parties in a related market. The normal rule that an agreement involving price-fixing, limiting production, or sharing markets or customers is restrictive by object does not, however, apply where (i) the parties agree on the output directly concerned by the production agreement and do not

---

[60] Guidelines, para. 143.

[61] Guidelines, para. 145.

[62] Guidelines, para. 146.

[63] The classic example is *Jaz/Peter* [1969] OJ L195/5, [1970] CMLR 129. Both parties manufactured clocks. Under the agreement Jaz in France was to continue making only electric clocks and domestic alarm clocks and Peter in Germany was to make large mechanical alarm clocks. They agreed that they would each supply the other with their products and spare parts, that they could both sell the whole range of the products in their respective territories, and that they would not buy the products covered by the agreement from third parties.

[64] [2010] OJ C130/1; and possibly by the Verticals Regulation, see Chap. 11.

[65] [1979] OJ C1/2.

eliminate the other parameters of competition or (ii) a production agreement providing for joint distribution of the jointly manufactured products envisages setting the sale price just for those products provided that the parties would not have had an incentive to enter the agreement otherwise.

The Guidelines consider in paragraphs 162–182 when a production agreement is likely to be restrictive by effects. It is necessary to consider the situation that would prevail in the absence of the agreement[66] (i.e. the 'counter-factual). Production agreements which also involve commercialisation functions, such as joint distribution or marketing carry a higher risk of restrictive effects than pure production agreements. i.e. the closer to the consumer the agreement goes the more problematic it becomes.[67] The Guidelines conclude that restrictive effects are unlikely if the parties do not have market power,[68] but even where market power is present restrictive effects may still be low if the market is dynamic.[69] However, the Commission is concerned that there may be a collusive outcome if a production agreement between parties with market power increases their commonality of costs to a level which enables them to collude.[70]

C. THE APPLICATION OF ARTICLE 101(3)

(i) The Block Exemption for Specialisation Agreements, Regulation 1218/2010

The block exemption, Regulation 1218/2010, applies to three types of specialisation agreement, as set out in Article 1. It is a less complex block exemption than 1217/2010 on R&D. It does not contain 'conditions' as 1217/2010 does in Article 3, or 'excluded restrictions' as in Article 6. Instead, Article 2 states the exemption, Article 3 the market share threshold, Article 4 lists three hardcore provisions which prevent the exemption applying, and Article 5 explains the calculation of the market share threshold.

Article 1

Definitions

1. For the purposes of this Regulation, the following definitions shall apply:

    (a) 'specialisation agreement' means a unilateral specialisation agreement, a reciprocal specialisation agreement or a joint production agreement;

    (b) 'unilateral specialisation agreement' means an agreement between two parties which are active on the same product market by virtue of which one party agrees to fully or partly cease production of certain products or to refrain from producing those products and to purchase them from the other party, who agrees to produce and supply those products;

    (c) 'reciprocal specialisation agreement' means an agreement between two or more parties which are active on the same product market, by virtue of which two or more parties on a reciprocal basis agree to fully or partly cease or refrain from producing certain but different products and to purchase these products from the other parties, who agree to produce and supply them;

    (d) 'joint production agreement' means an agreement by virtue of which two or more parties agree to produce certain products jointly. ...

---

[66] Guidelines, para. 163.

[67] Guidelines, para. 167.

[68] Guidelines, paras. 168–169.

[69] Guidelines, para. 170.

[70] Guidelines, paras. 175–176.

The block exemption therefore covers not only unilateral and reciprocal specialisation but also joint production, which is not really 'specialisation' in the normal sense of that word, but defined as such for the purposes of the Regulation. It will be noted that the definitions of unilateral and reciprocal specialisation agreements include obligations on the non-producing party to purchase the products from the other (unilateral) and on both parties to purchase from each other (reciprocal). Without those obligations an agreement is not one to which the block exemption applies.

Article 2

Exemption

1. Pursuant to Article 101(3) of the Treaty and subject to the provisions of this Regulation, it is hereby declared that Article 101(1) of the Treaty shall not apply to specialisation agreements.

    This exemption shall apply to the extent that such agreements contain restrictions of competition falling within the scope of Article 101(1) of the Treaty.

2. The exemption provided for in paragraph 1 shall apply to specialisation agreements containing provisions which relate to the assignment or licensing of intellectual property rights to one or more of the parties, provided that those provisions do not constitute the primary object of such agreements, but are directly related to and necessary for their implementation.

3. The exemption provided for in paragraph 1 shall apply to specialisation agreements whereby:

    (a) the parties accept an exclusive purchase or exclusive supply obligation; or

    (b) the parties do not independently sell the specialisation products but jointly distribute those products.

By Article 2(2) IP licensing and assignment provisions are covered by the exemption but only to the extent that they are ancillary to a specialisation agreement. If they were really the primary object of the agreement they would need to come within the Technology Transfer Regulation in order to be block exempted.[71] Article 2(3)(a) allows the purchase or supply obligations mentioned in Article 1 to be exclusive and Article 2(3)(b) allows for joint distribution of the specialisation products.

Article 3

Market share threshold

The exemption provided for in Article 2 shall apply on condition that the combined market share of the parties does not exceed 20 % on any relevant market.

Article 4

Hardcore restrictions

The exemption provided for in Article 2 shall not apply to specialisation agreements which, directly or indirectly, in isolation or in combination with other factors under the control of the parties, have as their object any of the following:

(a) the fixing of prices when selling the products to third parties with the exception of the fixing of prices charged to immediate customers in the context of joint distribution;

(b) the limitation of output or sales with the exception of:

---

[71] See Chap. 12.

(i) provisions on the agreed amount of products in the context of unilateral or reciprocal specialisation agreements or the setting of the capacity and production volume in the context of a joint
production agreement; and

(ii) the setting of sales targets in the context of joint distribution;

(c) the allocation of markets or customers.

Article 4 does not allow three basic hardcore provisions: price-fixing, limiting sales or output, and
market or customer allocation. With the first two there are exceptions related to the particular nature
of specialisation agreements.

(ii) The Individual Application of Article 101(3)

Production agreements can provide efficiency gains in the form of costs savings or better production technologies.[72] As far as indispensability is concerned, restrictions on the parties' competitive
conduct outside the cooperation and joint setting of prices where the production agreement does
not involve joint commercialisation, are not normally considered indispensable.[73] The Commission
considers parties to a production agreement are more likely to pass on variable costs saving to consumers than fixed costs savings.[74] The elimination of competition must be considered in relation to
any possible spill-over markets and not just to the market on which the cooperation is occurring.[75]
The Guidelines illustrate the possible application of Article 101(3) to production agreements in a
series of examples.[76] High market shares are not necessarily a bar to Article 101(3) exemption. It will
depend on the circumstances of the case. When individual exemptions were available, before 2004,
the Commission gave exemptions with conditions attached to parties with high market shares in
BPCL/ICI,[77] *Philips/Osram*,[78] and *GEAE/P&W*,[79] for example.[80]

9. PURCHASING AGREEMENTS

A. THE NATURE OF JOINT PURCHASING AND ITS
TREATMENT IN THE GUIDELINES

The purchasing concerned here is *joint* purchasing. Usually, as the Guidelines say, joint purchasing
agreements are aimed at creating buying power.[81] That can lead to lower prices or better quality
products or services for consumers.

Joint buying can be carried out by a jointly controlled company, by a company in which many
firms hold a non-controlling stakes, by contractual arrangements or by even looser forms of

---

[72] Guidelines, para. 183.

[73] Guidelines, para. 184.

[74] Guidelines, para. 185.

[75] Guidelines, para. 186.

[76] Guidelines, paras. 187–193.

[77] [1984] OJ L212/1 (petroleum plastics).

[78] [1994] OJ l378/37 (lead glass).

[79] [2000] OJ L58/16 (aircraft engines).

[80] See further Bellamy and Child (V. Rose and D. Bailey, eds), *European Law of Competition* (7th edn, Oxford
University Press, 2013), 6.060-6.061.

[81] Guidelines, para. 194.

cooperation.[82] The Guidelines recognise that a common form of joint purchasing arrangement is an 'alliance' whereby a group of retailers form a group for the joint purchasing of products.[83]

Both horizontal and vertical agreements may be involved in joint purchasing and have to be analysed in turn. First, there will be horizontal agreements (assessed in accordance with the Horizontal Cooperation Guidelines) between the joint purchasers. If that is acceptable the vertical agreements between the joint purchasers and their suppliers and between the joint purchasers (the alliance) and individual members must be assessed in accordance with the Guidelines on Vertical Restraints[84] and the Verticals Regulation.[85]

Moreover, joint purchasing agreements may affect two markets. First, the market(s) on which the joint purchasers buy (the purchasing, or procurement, market) and secondly, the downstream market(s) on which they sell. The purchasing market will have to be defined from the supply side and it is the alternatives for suppliers which are relevant. The downstream selling market will be relevant if the joint purchasers are competitors there.[86]

The Commission considers that joint purchasing arrangements are less likely to give rise to competition concerns when the parties do not have market power on the selling market(s).[87] Joint purchasing arrangements only restrict competition by object if they are really a disguised cartel. The normal position as to the fixing of prices being restrictive by object does not apply in the joint purchasing context. Rather the actual or likely effects must be assessed. The Guidelines say:[88]

206. Agreements which involve the fixing of purchase prices can have the object of restricting competition within the meaning of Article 101(1)…However, this does not apply where the parties to a joint purchasing arrangement agree on the purchasing prices the joint purchasing arrangement may pay to its suppliers for the products subject to the supply contract. In that case an assessment is required as to whether the agreement is likely to give rise to restrictive effects on competition within the meaning of Article 101(1). In both scenarios the agreement on purchase prices will not be assessed separately, but in the light of the overall effects of the purchasing agreement on the market.

5.3.3. Restrictive effects on competition

207. Joint purchasing arrangements which do not have as their object the restriction of competition must be analysed in their legal and economic context with regard to their actual and likely effects on competition. The analysis of the restrictive effects on competition generated by a joint purchasing arrangement must cover the negative effects on both the purchasing and the selling markets.

The suggested market power threshold below which joint purchasing arrangements are unlikely to give rise to competition concerns is a combined 15 per cent market share on the purchasing market(s) *and* a combined market share of 15 per cent on the selling market(s), but this is not an absolute threshold and market shares above that do not automatically indicate that there are likely restrictive effects. In any event, where the combined market shares are below these figures it is likely that the Article 101(3) conditions are fulfilled.[89] The concern of the Commission is that buying power can have restrictive effects if it forecloses access to the market. Moreover, 'a high degree of buying power may indirectly affect the output, quality and variety of products on the selling market'.[90] However:

---

[82] Guidelines, para. 194.

[83] Guidelines, para. 196.

[84] [2010] OJ C130/1.

[85] Regulation 330/2010 [2010] OJ L102/1. See Guidelines, para. 196.

[86] Guidelines, paras. 197–199.

[87] Guidelines, para. 204.

[88] Case C-250/92 *Gøttrup Klim* v. *KLG* [1994] ECR I-5641, where a joint purchasing arrangement was held not restrictive by object, is not mentioned in the Guidelines, but is discussed in Chap. 4.

[89] Guidelines, paras. 208–209.

[90] Guidelines, para. 210.

212. If ...competing purchasers co-operate who are not active on the same relevant selling market (for example, retailers which are active in different geographic markets and cannot be regarded as potential competitors), the joint purchasing arrangement is unlikely to have restrictive effects on competition unless the parties have a position in the purchasing markets that is likely to be used to harm the competitive position of other players in their respective selling markets.

In fact, retailers forming a joint purchasing association to give themselves a better bargaining position vis-à-vis their suppliers may well be active in different geographic markets.

There will be concerns about joint purchasing arrangements if they facilitate the coordination of the parties' behaviour on the selling market so that they lead to collusive outcomes.[91] This may arise from the exchange of commercially sensitive information. However:

216 ...If the information exchange does not exceed the sharing of data necessary for the joint purchasing of the products by the parties to the joint purchasing arrangement, then even if the information exchange has restrictive effects on competition within the meaning of Article 101(1), the agreement is more likely to meet the criteria of Article 101(3) than if the exchange goes beyond what was necessary for the joint purchasing.

There is no block exemption in respect of joint purchasing. The Guidelines explain the assessment of joint purchasing arrangements under Article 101(3) as follows (and then give a number of examples).

5.4. Assessment under Article 101(3)

5.4.1. Efficiency gains

217. Joint purchasing arrangements can give rise to significant efficiency gains. In particular, they can lead to cost savings such as lower purchase prices or reduced transaction, transportation and storage costs, thereby facilitating economies of scale. Moreover, joint purchasing arrangements may give rise to qualitative efficiency gains by leading suppliers to innovate and introduce new or improved products on the markets.

5.4.2. Indispensability

218. Restrictions that go beyond what is necessary to achieve the efficiency gains generated by a purchasing agreement do not meet the criteria of Article 101(3). An obligation to purchase exclusively through the co-operation may, in certain cases, be indispensable to achieve the necessary volume for the realisation of economies of scale. However, such an obligation has to be assessed in the context of the individual case.

5.4.3. Pass-on to consumers

219. Efficiency gains, such as cost efficiencies or qualitative efficiencies in the form of the introduction of new or improved products on the market, attained by indispensable restrictions must be passed on to consumers to an extent that outweighs the restrictive effects of competition caused by the joint purchasing arrangement. Hence, cost savings or other efficiencies that only benefit the parties to the joint purchasing arrangement will not suffice. Cost savings need to be passed on to consumers, that is to say, the parties' customers. To take a notable example, this pass-on may occur through lower prices on the selling markets. Lower purchasing prices resulting from the mere exercise of buying power are not likely to be passed on to consumers if the purchasers together have market power on the selling markets, and thus do not meet the criteria of Article 101(3). Moreover, the higher the market power of the parties on the selling market or markets the less likely they will pass on the efficiency gains to consumers to an extent that would outweigh the restrictive effects on competition.

---

[91] Guidelines, para. 213.

5.4.4. No elimination of competition

220. The criteria of Article 101(3) cannot be fulfilled if the parties are afforded the possibility of eliminating competition in respect of a substantial part of the products in question. That assessment has to cover both purchasing and selling markets.

B. CASES ON JOINT PURCHASING

Gøttrup-Klim,[92] which is discussed in Chapter 4,[93] was a major case on joint purchasing. It will be recalled that there was a Danish cooperative association (DLG) which purchased farming supplies such as fertilisers on behalf of its members. The case arose because of a challenge to DLG's rules, which precluded its members from belonging to any competing cooperative. The CJ held that the rules were not caught by Article 101(1) insofar as they were necessary to ensure the proper functioning of the cooperative. The Court recognised that the whole point of the cooperative was to present a significant counterweight to the large multinational suppliers.

In *Métropole Télévision*[94] the Commission dealt with a joint purchasing agreement in respect of television rights to sporting events. The European Broadcasting Union (EBU) is an association of radio and television organisations established in 1950. The main framework of the exchange of programmes amongst EBU members is Eurovision. To become an active member a broadcasting organisation must satisfy certain conditions, inter alia, as to its national coverage and the nature and financing of programmes. Métropole tried six times since 1987 to join the EBU but was rejected each time. This led to an ongoing battle between Métropole and the EBU which has surfaced several times in the EU Courts. In the present case Métropole had complained about EBU practices concerning the acquisition of TV rights to sporting events. The original EBU rules on this were exempted by the Commission[95] but the decision was annulled on appeal by Métropole.[96] The Commission adopted a decision in May 2000 exempting revised rules.[97] This too was challenged by Métropole in the GC.

Cases T-185/00, T-216/00, T-299/00, and T-300/00, *Métropole Télévision SA (M6) and others* v. *Commission* [2002] ECR II-3805

The rules in question concerned granting access to Eurovision rights for pay-TV. The rules provided a 'sub-licensing scheme' which granted access to Eurovision rights to major sporting events to third parties who were competitors of EBU members. The Commission exempted EBU's rules for the sharing of jointly acquired sports TV rights on the grounds that the sub-licensing scheme guaranteed access to the competitors and therefore avoided the elimination of competition in the market. The condition in Article 101(3) was therefore satisfied. Métropole claimed this was not so. The Commission did not settle on an exact definition of the market but contended that even on the basis of the narrowest possible definition (the acquisition of rights for a specific event such as the Football World Cup or the Summer Olympics) there was no elimination of competition. The GC accepted that the Commission's assertion that the market

---

[92] Case C-250/92, *Gøttrup-Klim Grovvareforeninger v. Dansk Landburgs Grovvareselskab AmbA* [1994] ECR I-5641.

[93] Chap. 4, Section 3.F.iii, p. 244.

[94] Cases T-185/00, T-216/00, T-299/00, and T-300/00, *Métropole Télévision SA (M6) and others v. Commission* [2002] ECR II-3805.

[95] [1993] OJ L179/23, [1995] 4 CMLR 56.

[96] Cases T-528, 542, 543, and 546/93, *Métropole Télévision SA v. Commission* [1996] ECR II-649.

[97] [2000] OJ L151/18, [2000] 5 CMLR 650.

could consist entirely of major sporting events did not affect the analysis of whether Article 101(3) was satisfied. It then turned to consider whether in making that analysis the Commission had made a manifest error of assessment.

General Court

63. As regards the effects of the Eurovision system on competition, the contested decision shows (paragraphs 71 to 80) that there are two types of restrictions. First, the joint acquisition of television rights to sporting events, their sharing and the exchange of signal restricts or even eliminates competition among EBU members which are competitors on both the upstream market, for the acquisition of rights, and for the downstream market, for televised transmission of sporting events. In addition, that system gives rise to restrictions on competition as regards third parties since those rights, as set out in paragraph 75 of the contested decision, are generally sold on an exclusive basis, so that EBU non-members would not in principle have access to them.

64. While it is true that the purchase of televised transmission rights for an event is not in itself a restriction on competition likely to fall under Article [101(1)] and may be justified by particular characteristics of the product and the market in question, the exercise of those rights in a specific legal and economic context may none the less lead to such a restriction (see, by analogy, Case 262/101 *Coditel v. Ciné-Vog Films*...paragraphs 15 to 17).

65. In that vein, the Commission states, in paragraph 45 of the contested decision, that 'the acquisition of exclusive TV rights to certain major sporting events has a strong impact on the downstream television markets in which the sporting events are broadcast'.

66. In addition, it appears from the analysis of the documents in the case and the arguments of the parties that the acquisition of transmission rights to a major international sporting event such as the Olympics or the football World Cup cannot fail to affect strongly the market in sponsorship and advertising, which is the main source of revenue for television channels which broadcast free-to-air, since those programmes attract a very wide audience.

67. Moreover, as pointed out by SIC, the effects which restrict competition for third parties as a result of the Eurovision system are accentuated, first, by the level of vertical integration of the EBU and its members, which are not merely purchasers of rights but also television operators which broadcast the rights purchased, and second, by the geographic extent of the EBU, whose members broadcast in all the countries of the European Union. As a result, when the EBU acquires transmission rights for an international sporting event, the access to that event is in principle automatically precluded for all non-member operators. By contrast, the situation appears to be different when the transmission rights for sporting events are acquired by an agency which buys those rights in order to resell them, or when they are bought by a media group which only has operators in certain Member States, since that group will tend to enter into negotiations with operators in other Member States in order to sell those rights. In that case, despite the exclusive purchase of the rights, other operators still have the opportunity to negotiate their acquisition for their respective markets.

68. In light of those facts—that is, the structure of the market, the position of the EBU in the market for certain international sporting events and the level of vertical integration of the EBU and its members—there is reason to determine whether the scheme for third-party access to the Eurovision system makes it possible to counterbalance the restrictions on competition affecting those third parties and thus to avoid their exclusion from competition.

73. However, even if it proves necessary, for reasons linked to exclusive transmission rights for sporting events and the guarantee of their economic value (see paragraph 60 above), for EBU members to reserve for themselves live transmission of the programmes acquired by the EBU, none of these reasons justifies their being able to extend that right to all the competitions which are part of the same event, even when they do not intend to broadcast all those competitions live.

...

83. All the information provided to the [General Court] thus goes to show that, contrary to what the Commission concludes in the contested decision, the sub-licensing scheme does not guarantee competitors

> of EBU members sufficient access to rights to transmit sporting events held by the latter on the basis of their participation in that purchasing association. Apart from a few exceptions, nothing in the rules or mode of implementation of the scheme enables competitors of EBU members to obtain sub-licences for the live broadcast of unused Eurovision rights. In reality, the scheme merely permits the acquisition of sub-licences to transmit roundups of competitions under extremely restrictive conditions.

The GC therefore annulled the decision on the ground that the condition about no elimination of competition in Article 101(3) was not satisfied.[98]

10. COMMERCIALISATION AGREEMENTS

A. GENERAL

Commercialisation agreements are dealt with in paragraphs 225–256 of the Guidelines. They are agreements which involve cooperation between competitors in the selling, distribution, or promotion of their substitute products. This covers a wide spectrum of agreements.

225. ...At one end of the spectrum, joint selling agreements may lead to a joint determination of all commercial aspects related to the sale of the product, including price. At the other end, there are more limited agreements that only address one specific commercialisation function, such as distribution, after-sales service, or advertising.

Where the commercialisation is in the context of another form of cooperation upstream, e.g., joint production or purchasing, the centre of gravity of the agreement should be determined and the analysis conducted accordingly.[99] That may involve another section of the Guidelines.

Where the commercialisation agreement deals solely with joint distribution, the Guidelines point out that (as will be recalled from Chapter 11) the Verticals Regulation[100] only covers non-reciprocal agreements between competitors and then only if the conditions in Article 2(4) are met. Reciprocal and non-reciprocal agreements between competitors must first be analysed in accordance with the Horizontal Cooperation Guidelines and if the horizontal aspects are acceptable the vertical aspects will be assessed under the Verticals Guidelines.[101]

B. THE APPLICATION OF ARTICLE 101(1)

Commercialisation agreements between non-competitors do not infringe Article 101(1) in relation to their *horizontal* aspects, but may fall within Article 101(1) in respect of their *vertical* aspects. The Guidelines specifically say that there is no restriction of competition where undertakings submit a joint tender for projects for which they could not bid individually. The Commission states that in this situation the undertakings are not potential competitors for the tender.[102]

The Commission's main concern about commercialisation agreements between competitors is price-fixing, but it has other concerns too.

---

[98] Other cases and decisions on joint purchasing include *National Sulphuric Acid Association* [1980] OJ L260/24 (Art. 101(3) applied after agreement amended) and *National Sulphuric Acid Association* [1989] OJ L190/22; Case 61/80, *Coöperatieve Stremsel-en Kleursfabriek v. Commission* [1981] ECR 851 (the appeal from *Rennet* [1980] OJ L51/19) where the obligation of a group of over 90 per cent of Dutch dairy producers to buy rennet exclusively from a cooperative was held to infringe Art. 101(1) and not satisfy Art. 101(3).

[99] Guidelines, para. 228. For 'centre of gravity' see Section 4, p. 739.

[100] Reg. 330/2010 [2010] OJ L102/1.

[101] Guidelines, para. 227.

[102] Guidelines, para. 143.

6.3. Assessment under Article 101(1)

6.3.1. Main competition concerns

230. Commercialisation agreements can lead to restrictions of competition in several ways. First, and most obviously, commercialisation agreements may lead to price fixing.

231. Secondly, commercialisation agreements may also facilitate output limitation, because the parties may decide on the volume of products to be put on the market, therefore restricting supply.

232. Thirdly, commercialisation agreements may become a means for the parties to divide the markets or to allocate orders or customers, for example in cases where t he parties' production plants are located in different geographic markets or when the agreements are reciprocal.

233. Finally, commercialisation agreements may also lead to an exchange of strategic information relating to aspects within or outside the scope of the co-operation or to commonality of costs—in particular with regard to agreements not encompassing price fixing—which may result in a collusive outcome.

Agreements limited to joint selling generally have the aim of coordinating the parties' pricing policies and so are likely to be restrictive by object even if the agreement is non-exclusive (so that the parties can sell outside the agreement).[103] Distribution arrangements between parties active in different geographic markets can be an instrument of market partitioning or customer allocation. Where restrictions by effect are concerned the Commission's view is that commercialisation agreements are normally unlikely to raise competition concerns if they are the only way that a party can enter the market.

6.3.3. Restrictive effects on competition

237. A commercialisation agreement is normally not likely to give rise to competition concerns if it is objectively necessary to allow one party to enter a market it could not have entered individually or with a more limited number of parties than are effectively taking part in the co-operation, for example, because of the costs involved. A specific application of this principle would be consortia arrangements that allow the companies involved to participate in projects that they would not be able to undertake individually. As the parties to the consortia arrangement are therefore not potential competitors for implementing the project, there is no restriction of competition within the meaning of Article 101(1).

238. Similarly, not all reciprocal distribution agreements have as their object a restriction of competition. Depending on the facts of the case at hand, some reciprocal distribution agreements may, nevertheless, have restrictive effects on competition. The key issue in assessing an agreement of this type is whether the agreement in question is objectively necessary for the parties to enter each other's markets. If it is, the agreement does not create competition problems of a horizontal nature. However, if the agreement reduces the decision-making independence of one of the parties with regard to entering the other parties' market or markets by limiting its incentives to do so, it is likely to give rise to restrictive effects on competition. The same reasoning applies to non-reciprocal agreements, where the risk of restrictive effects on competition is, however, less pronounced.

239. Moreover, a distribution agreement can have restrictive effects on competition if it contains vertical restraints, such as restrictions on passive sales, resale price maintenance, etc.

Once again, the Commission considers that there will be restrictive effects on competition only if the parties have some degree of market power. As with joint purchasing agreements it sets this

---

[103] Guidelines, paras. 234–235.

'safe harbour' at a combined market share of 15 per cent.[104] The Commission does have some concerns that, even if the agreement does not involve price-fixing there may be collusive outcomes if it increases the parties' commonality of variable costs.[105] As with joint purchasing agreements there are also concerns about the exchange of sensitive commercial information, particularly on marketing strategy and pricing and where there is joint advertising.[106]

C. THE APPLICATION OF ARTICLE 101(3)

As with joint purchasing, there is no block exemption on commercialisation. The Guidelines say of the individual application of Article 101(3):

6.4. Assessment under Article 101(3)

6.4.1. Efficiency gains

246. Commercialisation agreements can give rise to significant efficiency gains. The efficiencies to be taken into account when assessing whether a commercialisation agreement fulfils the criteria of Article 101(3) will depend on the nature of the activity and the parties to the co-operation. Price fixing can generally not be justified, unless it is indispensable for the integration of other marketing functions, and this integration will generate substantial efficiencies. Joint distribution can generate significant efficiencies, stemming from economies of scale or scope, especially for smaller producers.

247. In addition, the efficiency gains must not be savings which result only from the elimination of costs that are inherently part of competition, but must result from the integration of economic activities. A reduction of transport cost which is only a result of customer allocation without any integration of the logistical system can therefore not be regarded as an efficiency gain within the meaning of Article 101(3).

248. Efficiency gains must be demonstrated by the parties to the agreement. An important element in this respect would be the contribution by the parties of significant capital, technology, or other assets. Cost savings through reduced duplication of resources and facilities can also be accepted. However, if the joint commercialisation represents no more than a sales agency without any investment, it is likely to be a disguised cartel and as such unlikely to fulfil the conditions of Article 101(3).

6.4.2. Indispensability

249. Restrictions that go beyond what is necessary to achieve the efficiency gains generated by a commercialisation agreement do not fulfil the criteria of Article 101(3). The question of indispensability is especially important for those agreements involving price fixing or market allocation, which can only under exceptional circumstances be considered indispensable.

6.4.3. Pass-on to consumers

250. Efficiency gains attained by indispensable restrictions must be passed on to consumers to an extent that outweighs the restrictive effects on competition caused by the commercialisation agreement. This can happen in the form of lower prices or better product quality or variety. The higher the market power of the parties, however, the less likely it is that efficiency gains will be passed on to consumers to an extent that outweighs the restrictive effects on competition. Where the parties have a combined market share

---

[104] Guidelines, paras. 240–241. In para. 240 the Guidelines actually use the expression 'safe harbour' to describe this threshold.

[105] Guidelines, paras. 242–243.

[106] Guidelines, paras. 244–245.

of below 15 %, it is likely that any demonstrated efficiency gains generated by the agreement will be sufficiently passed on to consumers.

6.4.4. No elimination of competition

251. The criteria of Article 101(3) cannot be fulfilled if the parties are afforded the possibility of eliminating competition in respect of a substantial part of the products in question. This has to be analysed in the relevant market to which the products subject to the co-operation belong and in possible spill-over markets.

Joint selling is a particular issue in respect of media rights to sporting events, and this is dealt with later in this chapter.[107] It is also an issue in respect of the collective selling of rights to music and films.[108]

11. STANDARDISATION AGREEMENTS

A. STANDARDISATION AND STANDARD-SETTING

Standardisation agreements are those which 'have as their primary objective the definition of technical or quality requirements with which current or future products, production processes, services or methods may comply'.[109] The Guidelines do not apply to the provision of professional services[110] but do cover agreements on the environmental performance of products or production processes.[111]

Four relevant markets may be affected by a standardisation agreement: (i) that for the product(s) or service(s) to which the standard(s) relate; (ii) the relevant technology market, if the standard-setting involves the selection of technology and IPRs are marketed separately from the products to which they relate; (iii) the market for standard-setting (if a number of standard-setting bodies or agreements exist); and (iv) a distinct market for testing and certification.[112]

Standardisation agreements usually have positive economic effects. However, they will be restrictive by object if used as part of a broader restrictive agreement aimed at excluding actual or potential competitors,[113] or directly influence prices charged to customers.[114] Further, the Commission is concerned that in specific circumstances there may be restrictive effects through a reduction in price competition, foreclosure of innovative technologies, and exclusion of, or discrimination against, certain companies by preventing effective access to the standard.[115]

---

[107] See Section 12.D.

[108] e.g UIP [1989] OJ L226/25. In COMP/38.698 CISAC, 16 July 2008, the Commission took a prohibition decision against an international federation of copyright collecting societies. The decision was largely annulled, Case T-442/08, *International Confederation of Societies of Authors and Composers (CISAC) v.Commission*, 13 April 2013, see Chap. 12, Section 8.C.

[109] Guidelines, para. 257. Standardisation can range from the adoption of consensus standards by the recognised European or national standards bodies, through consortia or fora, to agreements between independent companies (Guidelines, para. 257, n. 1).

[110] Guidelines, para. 258.

[111] Guidelines, para. 257.

[112] Guidelines, para. 261.

[113] As in COMP/35.691, *Pre-Insulated Pipe Cartel* [1999] OJ L24/1, para. 147. In Case 96/82 etc., *IAZ v. Commission* [1983] 3369 it was held that the agreement between Belgian water companies and Belgian washing machine and dishwasher manufacturers in respect of conformity standards partitioned the market in excluding imports.

[114] Guidelines, paras. 273–276.

[115] Guidelines, paras. 264–268.

In respect of standardisation agreements there is a particular concern over IPRs, in particular where a participant in the standard-setting which holds IPRs essential to the standard could obtain control over the standard:[116]

269. Intellectual property laws and competition laws share the same objectives…of promoting innovation and enhancing consumer welfare. IPR promote dynamic competition by encouraging undertakings to invest in developing new or improved products and processes. IPR are therefore in general pro-competitive. However, by virtue of its IPR, a participant holding IPR essential for implementing the standard, could, in the specific context of standard-setting, also acquire control over the use of a standard. When the standard constitutes a barrier to entry, the company could thereby control the product or service market to which the standard relates. This in turn could allow companies to behave in anti-competitive ways, for example by 'holding-up' users after the adoption of the standard either by refusing to license the necessary IPR or by extracting excess rents by way of excessive…royalty fees thereby preventing effective access to the standard. However, even if the establishment of a standard can create or increase the market power of IPR holders possessing IPR essential to the standard, there is no presumption that holding or exercising IPR essential to a standard equates to the possession or exercise of market power. The question of market power can only be assessed on a case by case basis.

Here the Commission is concerned with what are known as 'patent ambushes', which occur when an undertaking taking part in the standard-setting process hides the fact that it holds essential IPRs over aspects of the standard being developed. After the standard has been agreed and other competitors are locked in to using it, the undertaking starts asserting its rights. The Commission considers that patent ambushes represent a 'system failure of the standard-setting process' as they may enable the undertaking to gain control over the standard and thereby exclude competing technologies.[117] We see in Chapter 7 a number of cases of the application of Article 102 where it is alleged that an undertaking holding an IPR essential to a standard may have been involved in a 'patent ambush' or in which an undertaking is bringing procedures to enforce standard-essential IPRs (SEPs).[118]

In *EMC v. Commission*[119] an undertaking appealed against a Commission decision rejecting a complaint in respect of the adoption of a standard in the cement industry. The GC rejected the appeal holding that the Commission had been correct to apply the criteria set out in the 2001 Guidelines, which in effect said that standard-setting agreements would not infringe Article 101(1) if the standard-setting was non-discriminatory, open, and transparent. The 2010 Guidelines build on these criteria, but the relevant paragraphs are far more detailed.[120] They lay down four conditions to be fulfilled if a standard-setting agreement which risks creating market power is to fall outside Article 101(1). Agreements which do not comply with these principles are not presumed to fall within Article 101(1) but will necessitate a self-assessment to establish whether they do fall within Article 101(1) and if so, whether Article 101(3) is satisfied.[121] The four conditions are unrestricted participation in the standard-setting; transparent procedure; no obligation to comply with the standard; and effective access to the standard on FRAND (fair, reasonable and non-discriminatory) terms.

---

[116] See e.g. P. Chappatte, 'FRAND Commitments—the Case for Antitrust Intervention' (2009) 5 *European Competition Journal* 320; D. Geradin, 'Ten Years of DG Competition Effort to Provide Guidance on the Application of Competition Rules to the Licensing of Standard-Essential Patents: Where Do We Stand', available at <http://ssrn.com/abstract=2204359>.

[117] FAQ Press Release on the *Rambus* commitments decision, MEMO IP/09/544; see also G. Piesiewicz and R. Schellingerhour, 'Intellectual Property Rights in Standard Setting from a Competition Law Perspective' (2007) 3 *Competition Policy Newsletter* 36.

[118] COMP/38.636, *Rambus*, Commitments decision 9 December 2009; *Samsung*, IP/12/1448, 21 December 2012; *Motorola Mobility*, IP/13/406, 6 May 2013.

[119] Case T-432/05, *EMC v. Commission* [2010] ECR II-1629, appeal dismissed by Order, Case C-367/10, [2011] ECR I-46.

[120] Guidelines, paras. 280–291.

[121] Guidelines, para. 279.

280. Where participation in standard-setting is unrestricted and the procedure for adopting the standard in question is transparent, standardisation agreements which contain no obligation to comply ... with the standard and provide access to the standard on fair, reasonable and non-discriminatory terms will normally not restrict competition within the meaning of Article 101(1).

281. In particular, to ensure unrestricted participation the rules of the standard-setting organisation would need to guarantee that all competitors in the market or markets affected by the standard can participate in the process leading to the selection of the standard. The standard-setting organisations would also need to have objective and non-discriminatory procedures for allocating voting rights as well as, if relevant, objective criteria for selecting the technology to be included in the standard.

282. With respect to transparency, the relevant standard-setting organisation would need to have procedures which allow stakeholders to effectively inform themselves of upcoming, on-going and finalised standardisation work in good time at each stage of the development of the standard.

283. Furthermore, the standard-setting organisation's rules would need to ensure effective access to the standard on fair, reasonable and non discriminatory terms....

284. In the case of a standard involving IPR, a clear and balanced IPR policy ... adapted to the particular industry and the needs of the standard-setting organisation in question, increases the likelihood that the implementers of the standard will be granted effective access to the standards elaborated by that standard-setting organisation.

285. In order to ensure effective access to the standard, the IPR policy would need to require participants wishing to have their IPR included in the standard to provide an irrevocable commitment in writing to offer to license their essential IPR to all third parties on fair, reasonable and non-discriminatory terms ('FRAND commitment') ... That commitment should be given prior to the adoption of the standard. At the same time, the IPR policy should allow IPR holders to exclude specified technology from the standard-setting process and thereby from the commitment to offer to license, providing that exclusion takes place at an early stage in the development of the standard. To ensure the effectiveness of the FRAND commitment, there would also need to be a requirement on all participating IPR holders who provide such a commitment to ensure that any company to which the IPR owner transfers its IPR (including the right to license that IPR) is bound by that commitment, for example through a contractual clause between buyer and seller.

286. Moreover, the IPR policy would need to require good faith disclosure, by participants, of their IPR that might be essential for the implementation of the standard under development. This would enable the industry to make an informed choice of technology and thereby assist in achieving the goal of effective access to the standard. Such a disclosure obligation could be based on ongoing disclosure as the standard develops and on reasonable endeavours to identify IPR reading on the potential standard ... It is also sufficient if the participant declares that it is likely to have IPR claims over a particular technology (without identifying specific IPR claims or applications for IPR). Since the risks with regard to effective access are not the same in the case of a standard-setting organisation with a royalty-free standards policy, IPR disclosure would not be relevant in that context.

FRAND Commitments

287. FRAND commitments are designed to ensure that essential IPR protected technology incorporated in a standard is accessible to the users of that standard on fair, reasonable and non-discriminatory terms and conditions. In particular, FRAND commitments can prevent IPR holders from making the implementation of a standard difficult by refusing to license or by requesting unfair or unreasonable fees (in other words excessive fees) after the industry has been locked-in to the standard or by charging discriminatory royalty fees.

Where these principles are not fulfilled paragraphs 292–299 of the Guidelines set out the considerations which must be taken into account in assessing whether Article 101(1) applies. These are whether (i) the members of the standard-setting organisation remain free to develop alternative standards or procedures; (ii) the terms and conditions on which access to the standard is given; (iii) whether participation in the standard-setting process is open; and (iv) what are the market shares of the goods or services based on the standard ('although high market shares will not necessarily lead to the conclusion that the standard is likely to give rise to restrictive effects on competition').

If a standardisation agreement does fall within Article 101(1) there is no block exemption, but it may satisfy the Article 101(3) conditions.[122] It will be noted in paragraph 318 of the Guidelines that the Commission does not consider that a provision making the standard binding and obligatory is indispensable.

7.4. Assessment under Article 101(3)

7.4.1. Efficiency gains

Standardisation agreements

308. Standardisation agreements frequently give rise to significant efficiency gains. For example, Union wide standards may facilitate market integration and allow companies to market their goods and services in all Member States, leading to increased consumer choice and decreasing prices. Standards which establish technical interoperability and compatibility often encourage competition on the merits between technologies from different companies and help prevent lock-in to one particular supplier. Furthermore, standards may reduce transaction costs for sellers and buyers. Standards on, for instance, quality, safety and environmental aspects of a product may also facilitate consumer choice and can lead to increased product quality. Standards also play an important role for innovation. They can reduce the time it takes to bring a new technology to the market and facilitate innovation by allowing companies to build on top of agreed solutions.

309. To achieve those efficiency gains in the case of standardisation agreements, the information necessary to apply the standard must be effectively available to those wishing to enter the market…

310. Dissemination of a standard can be enhanced by marks or logos certifying compliance thereby providing certainty to customers. Agreements for testing and certification go beyond the primary objective of defining the standard and would normally constitute a distinct agreement and market.

311. While the effects on innovation must be analysed on a case-by-case basis, standards creating compatibility on a horizontal level between different technology platforms are considered to be likely to give rise to efficiency gains.

…

7.4.2. Indispensability

…

314. Restrictions that go beyond what is necessary to achieve the efficiency gains that can be generated by a standardisation agreement or standard terms do not fulfil the criteria of Article 101(3).

Standardisation agreements

315. The assessment of each standardisation agreement must take into account its likely effect on the markets concerned, on the one hand, and the scope of restrictions that possibly go beyond the objective of achieving efficiencies, on the other…

316. Participation in standard-setting should normally be open to all competitors in the market or markets affected by the standard unless the parties demonstrate significant inefficiencies of such participation or recognised procedures are foreseen for the collective representation of interests…

317. As a general rule standardisation agreements should cover no more than what is necessary to ensure their aims, whether this is technical interoperability and compatibility or a certain level of quality. In cases where having only one technological solution would benefit consumers or the economy at large

---

[122] See e.g., Case IV/29/151, *Philips VCR*; Case IV/31.458, *X/Open Group*; Cases IV/34.179 etc., *Dutch Cranes* [1995] OJ L 312/79; COMP/39.416, *Ship Classification*, Commitments decision, 14 October 2009.

that standard should be set on a non-discriminatory basis. Technology neutral standards can, in certain circumstances, lead to larger efficiency gains. Including substitute IPR...as essential parts of a standard while at the same time forcing the users of the standard to pay for more IPR than technically necessary would go beyond what is necessary to achieve any identified efficiency gains. In the same vein, including substitute IPR as essential parts of a standard and limiting the use of that technology to that particular standard (that is to say, exclusive use) could limit inter-technology competition and would not be necessary to achieve the efficiencies identified.

318. Restrictions in a standardisation agreement making a standard binding and obligatory for the industry are in principle not indispensable.

319. In a similar vein, standardisation agreements that entrust certain bodies with the exclusive right to test compliance with the standard go beyond the primary objective of defining the standard and may also restrict competition. The exclusivity can, however, be justified for a certain period of time, for example by the need to recoup significant start-up costs...The standardisation agreement should in that case include adequate safeguards to mitigate possible risks to competition resulting from exclusivity. This concerns, inter alia, the certification fee which needs to be reasonable and proportionate to the cost of the compliance testing.

....

7.4.3. Pass-on to consumers

Standardisation agreements

321. Efficiency gains attained by indispensable restrictions must be passed on to consumers to an extent that outweighs the restrictive effects on competition caused by a standardisation agreement or by standard terms. A relevant part of the analysis of likely pass-on to consumers is which procedures are used to guarantee that the interests of the users of standards and end consumers are protected. Where standards facilitate technical interoperability and compatibility or competition between new and already existing products, services and processes, it can be presumed that the standard will benefit consumers.

...

7.4.4. No elimination of competition

324. Whether a standardisation agreement affords the parties the possibility of eliminating competition depends on the various sources of competition in the market, the level of competitive constraint that they impose on the parties and the impact of the agreement on that competitive constraint. While market shares are relevant for that analysis, the magnitude of remaining sources of actual competition cannot be assessed exclusively on the basis of market share except in cases where a standard becomes a de facto industry standard...In the latter case competition may be eliminated if third parties are foreclosed from effective access to the standard. Standard terms used by a majority of the industry might create a de facto industry standard and thus raise the same concerns. However, if the standard or the standard terms only concern a limited part of the product or service, competition is not likely to be eliminated.

Environmental agreements are no longer a separate section in the Guidelines but there are cases in which the Commission has allowed standardisation agreements with environmental benefits, either because they fell outside Article 101(1) or because they satisfied Article 101(3). The *CECED* decision[123] gave an exemption to an agreement between washing machine manufacturers to cease production and importation of less efficient machines despite such agreement being restrictive by object under

---

[123] [2000] OJ L187/47. See Chap. 4, Section 4.D.i.c, p. 257. It was followed by approval of a similar agreement concerning dishwashers: see Commission Press Release IP/01/1659.

Article 101(1). Its benefits were mainly collective environmental ones. The Commission also gave an individual exemption in *DSD*[124] in respect of exclusive service agreements which facilitated the collection and disposal of waste packaging. The *CECED* decision is not mentioned expressly in the Guidelines, but Example 5 in paragraph 329 is clearly based upon it.

B. STANDARD TERMS

The Guidelines also deal with standard terms. The standard terms may cover only a small part of the final contract or a very large part. When standard terms are used by most of the industry and/or for most parts of the product or service it leads to a limitation or lack of consumer choice.[125] The effects of standard terms are felt on the downstream market where the companies using them compete for customers.[126] It is possible for standard terms to have restrictive effects on competition by limiting product choice and innovation and restricting price competition.[127] Standard terms which directly influence prices charged to customers are restrictive by object.[128] However, anti-competitive foreclosure is unlikely if the standard terms are open for anyone to use.[129] When considering restrictive effects, therefore, the question is whether participation in the establishment of standard terms is unrestricted for competitors in the relvant market, and whether the established standard terms are non-binding and effectively accessible.[130]

As far as the application of Article 101(3) is concerned, the Commission view is as follows.

Standard terms

312. The use of standard terms can entail economic benefits such as making it easier for customers to compare the conditions offered and thus facilitate switching between companies. Standard terms might also lead to efficiency gains in the form of savings in transaction costs and, in certain sectors (in particular where the contracts are of a complex legal structure), facilitate entry. Standard terms may also increase legal certainty for the contract parties.

313. The higher the number of competitors on the market, the greater the efficiency gain of facilitating the comparison of conditions offered.

...

320. It is generally not justified to make standard terms binding and obligatory for the industry or the members of the trade association that established them. The possibility cannot, however, be ruled out that making standard terms binding may, in a specific case, be indispensable to the attainment of the efficiency gains generated by them.

...

322. Both the risk of restrictive effects on competition and the likelihood of efficiency gains increase with the companies' market shares and the extent to which the standard terms are used. Hence, it is not

---

[124] [2001] OJ L319/1. An appeal by the undertaking against the obligations to which the exemption was subject was dismissed: Case T-289/01, *Der Grüne Punkt-Duales System Deutschland* v. *Commission* [2007] ECR II-1691. Negative clearance was given to a waste disposal scheme in France in *Eco-Emballages* [2001] OJ L233/37.

[125] Guidelines, para. 259 and footnotes thereto. As the Commission says, standard terms play an important role in the banking and insurance sectors.

[126] Guidelines, para. 262.

[127] Guidelines, paras. 270–271.

[128] Guidelines, para. 276.

[129] Guidelines, para. 272.

[130] Guidelines, paras. 300–307.

possible to provide any general 'safe harbour' within which there is no risk of restrictive effects on competition or which would allow the presumption that efficiency gains will be passed on to consumers to an extent that outweighs the restrictive effects on competition.

323. However, certain efficiency gains generated by standard terms, such as increased comparability of the offers on the market, facilitated switching between providers, and legal certainty of the clauses set out in the standard terms, are necessarily beneficial for the consumers. As regards other possible efficiency gains, such as lower transaction costs, it is necessary to make an assessment on a case-by-case basis and in the relevant economic context whether these are likely to be passed on to consumers.

In respect of the elimination of competition, standard terms raise the same concerns explained in paragraph 324 (reproduced in the extract from the Guidelines in Section 11.A, p. 761) as do standardisation agreements.

12. AGREEMENTS IN PARTICULAR SECTORS

A. GENERAL

Horizontal cooperation agreements can take many forms, apart from the six major ones discussed in Sections 3 and 6–11. In this section we look briefly at agreements in some particular sectors.

B. INSURANCE

The Commission has in the past cleared horizontal cooperation agreements in the insurance sector. For example, exemption under Article 101(3) was given in *Concordato Incendio* (fire insurance premiums),[131] and *Nuovo CEGAM* (basic premiums of engineering insurers[132] but exemption was refused in *Fire Insurance* to recommendations by German property insurers about an increase in fire insurance rates.[133] The Commission issued a block exemption, Regulation 358/2003, in the insurance sector to deal with, inter alia, common risk premium tariffs, non-binding standard policy conditions, and the common coverage of certain risks.[134] This was replaced in 2010 by Regulation 267/2010.[135] The exemption covers the joint compilation and distribution of information necessary for calculating the average cost of covering a specified risk in the past, constructing tables on matters such as mortality and illness, and the joint carrying out of studies on the probable impact of general circumstances external to the interested undertakings.[136] The exemption is subject to conditions (Article 3). The Regulation also exempts agreements for setting up and operating pools of insurance undertakings or reinsurance undertakings for the common coverage of a specific category of risks. The exemption is subject to market share thresholds (20 per cent combined market share for insurance pools and 25 per cent for reinsurance pools).[137]

---

[131] [1990] OJ L15/25, [1991] 4 CMLR 199.
[132] [1984] OJ L99/29, [1984] 2 CMLR 484.
[133] [1985] OJ L35/20, upheld by the CJ, Case 45/85, *VdS v. Commission* [1987] ECR 405.
[134] [2003] OJ L53/8, replacing Reg. 3932/92.
[135] [2010] OJ L83/1.
[136] [2010] OJ L83/1, Art.2.
[137] [2010] OJ L83/1, Art. 6.

C. PAYMENT SERVICES

In *MasterCardMIF Charges*[138] the Commission found MasterCard's multilateral interchange fees (MIF) for cross-border payment card transactions infringed Article 101. The Commission rejected the argument that the MIF led to objective efficiencies which would balance the negative effects on price competition between its member banks. Pending the appeal MasterCard was given six months to remove the fee from consumer debit and credit cards. It temporarily repealed them and then adjusted them to the satisfaction of the Commission.[139] The GC rejected MasterCard's appeal and upheld the decision in May 2012[140] and MasterCard appealed to the CJ.[141]

A former exemption given to Visa[142] in respect of its MIF expired in 2007 but in 2012 the Commission adopted a Commitments decision under Regulation 1/2003, Article 9 in respect of the MIF on consumer debit cards.[143] The Commission then turned its attention to the MIF on Visa's credit cards. It sent a supplementary SO to Visa in April 2009. Visa offered commitments under Article 9 in May 2013 and these were market tested on 6 June.[144]

In 2008 Visa was fined €10.2 million for infringing Article 101 by refusing to admit Morgan Stanley as a member of the Visa network.[145] In *Groupement des Cartes Bancaires* the GC upheld the Commission decision finding that measures agreed by the French banks which increased the cost of issuing cards infringed Article 101(1) (by object and effect) and did not satisfy the conditions of Article 101(3).

D. SPORT

(i) General

Cases involving sport occur throughout this book and can involve infringements of Article 102 as well as Article 101.[146] However, for the sake of convenience, an outline of the issues is given here as rules of sporting organisations often stem from horizontal agreements between their members or constituent bodies.

Annex 1 to the Staff Working Document accompanying the Commission White Paper on Sport of July 2007[147] sets out examples of sporting rules which are likely and unlikely to comply with the competition rules. According to the Annex, rules that are more likely to comply include the selection criteria for competitions; 'home and away' rules; transfer periods; nationality requirements in

---

[138] COMP/34.579, *MasterCard MIF charges*, 19 December 2007. See L. Repa, A. Malczewska, A. C. Teixeira, and E. Martinez Rivero, 'Commission Prohibits MasterCard's Multilateral Interchange Fees for Cross-Border Card Payments in the EEA' (2008) 1 *Competition Policy Newsletter* 1.

[139] See MEMO/08/397. It repealed them in June 2008. It reimposed them in October 2008 and the Commission commenced proceedings for non-compliance with the decision. MasterCard undertook to reduce them and the Commission announced it was dropping the non-compliance proceedings, IP/09/515.

[140] Case T-111/08, *MasterCard Inc, MasterCard International Inc, and MasterCard Europe SPRL v. Commission*, 24 May 2012.

[141] Case C-382/12 P, judgment pending.

[142] [2002] OJ L318/17.

[143] COMP/39.398, decision 8 December 2010, IP/10/1684.

[144] COMP/39.398, Market Test Notice, 6 June 2013, MEMO/13/554.

[145] COMP/37.860, upheld on appeal Case T-461/07, *Visa Europe and Visa International Service Association v. Commission* [2011] ECR II-1729; see also COMP/38.606 *Groupement des Cartes Bancaires*, upheld on appeal Case T-491/07 *CB v. Commission*, 24 November 2012, on appeal Case C-67/13P.

[146] See, e.g., Case C-519/04 P, *Meca-Medina and Majcen v. Commission* [2006] ECR I-699; Case C-49/07, *Motosykletistiki Omospondia Ellados NPID (MOTOE) v. Ellinkio Dimosi*, [2008] ECR I-4863. For a summary of the application of the competition rules to sport, see Chap. 2, Section 4.A.iii.f, p. 111.

[147] 'The EU and Sport: Background and Context (SEC(2007) 935, accompanying the White Paper, COM(2007) 391 final. For a full discussion of Annex 1 see P. Kienapfel and A. Stein, 'The Application of Articles 81 and 82 EC in the Sports Sector' (2007) 3 *Competition Policy Newsletter* 6.

respect of national teams; prohibitions on multiple club or team ownership; anti-doping rules; and the basic rules of the game (such as duration, the off-side rule, the number of players, etc.). Rules less likely to comply include rules shielding sports associations from competition for commercial reasons; rules regarding professions ancillary to the sport itself (for example, football agents); and rules excluding legal challenges to sport associations' decisions before the ordinary courts. The Annex expressly does not take a view on the questions of UEFA's home-grown players rule, salary caps in professional football, and the release for national teams rule.[148]

(ii) Joint Buying

Joint buying of sports media rights was considered in Annex 1 to the Staff Working Document. The Commission explained its concerns:

> 3.1.4 In the downstream markets joint buying arrangements may also be caught under Article [101(1)], in particular when the exclusive acquisition of sports media rights leads to foreclosure and output restrictions as a result of vertical restraints in agreements between seller and buyer or by horizontal agreements between different buyers. In cases where *ex ante* (single or collective) dominance exists at the acquisition market, under certain circumstances the acquisition and use of exclusive sports media rights could constitute an abuse of dominance by the buyer within the meaning of Article [102].
>
> Foreclosure issues are especially relevant whenever exclusive rights constitute 'premium' content. In such situations (mostly concerning broadcasting rights for live football matches), competition may be adversely affected through the monopolisation of the acquisition of this premium content, if this content is an essential input for effective competition in the downstream market…In addition, because of insecurity about technological developments, the existence of some substitution between different platforms and asymmetric value of rights, powerful operators on one retail market may seek to prevent players in neighbouring markets from acquiring meaningful rights. The acquisition of exclusive audiovisual rights for all platforms by a powerful retail operator in one downstream market (e.g., a pay-TV operator) may create additional anti-competitive *foreclosure effects in neighbouring markets* (e.g., 3G mobile telephony), thereby hampering the development of new services.
>
> Output restrictions may occur when exclusive rights, which are either bought collectively by different operators or bought by a dominant firm for one or more downstream markets, are subsequently not exploited by the buyers.

The Commission may consider structural or behavioural remedies to address these concerns.[149]

(iii) The Joint Selling of Media Rights to Sporting Events

The Commission has been much concerned with the joint selling of commercial rights[150] to sporting events, particularly the media rights to football. The Commission's position on this is explained in Annex 1 to the Staff Working Document. As the Commission said in its *UEFA* decision, the rights to screen football matches, particularly live, are immensely valuable.

In most countries football is not only the driving force for the development of pay-TV services but is also an essential programme item for free-TV broadcasters. Joint selling of free-TV and pay-TV rights combined with wide exclusive terms therefore has significant effects on the structure of the TV broadcasting markets as it can

---

[148] Annex 1, 2.3. The rule requiring football teams to release players required for national teams in international competition was before the CJ in a preliminary reference, Case C-243/06, *SA Sporting du Pays de Charleroi and Groupement des clubs de football européens v. FIFA* but was removed from the register, [2009] OJ C69/30.

[149] Annex 1, 3.1.4.2.

[150] Media rights (radio, television, internet, and UMTS), sponsorship, suppliership, licensing, and IPRs.

enhance media concentration and hamper competition between broadcasters. If one broadcaster holds all or most of the relevant football TV rights in a Member State, it is extremely difficult for competing broadcasters to establish themselves successfully in that market.[151]

The selling arrangements amount to joint selling in as much as the media rights are not sold by the individual clubs, but collectively, through the league or association to which they belong. The Commission stated its basic position in the Helsinki Report on Sport in 1999:

Any exemptions granted in the case of the joint sale of broadcasting rights must take account of the benefits for consumers and of the proportional nature of the restriction on competition in relation to the legitimate objective pursued. In this context, there is also a need to examine the extent to which a link can be established between the joint sale of rights and financial solidarity between professional and amateur sport, the objectives of the training of young sportsmen and women and those of promoting sporting activities among the population. However, with regard to the sale of exclusive rights to broadcast sporting events, it is likely that any exclusivity which, by its duration and/or scope, resulted in the closing of the market, would be prohibited.[152]

The consequences of football media rights being sold by individual clubs can be seen by looking at the position in Spain, where the rights are not sold collectively, and *La Liga* is dominated by two clubs.[153]

A declaration on sport, based on the Helsinki Report, was pronounced at the European Council in Nice in December 2000. This proclaimed the Community's recognition of the social, educational, and cultural functions of sport and laid down principles with a view to preserving, inter alia, 'the cohesion and ties of solidarity that exist in sport at all levels' and fair competition. Of the sale of television rights it said:

As the sale of television broadcasting rights is one of the greatest sources of income for certain sports, the sharing of part of the corresponding revenue among the appropriate levels may be beneficial in order to preserve the principle of solidarity in sport.

In July 2003 the Commission granted an Article 101(3) exemption to the arrangements for selling the media rights to the UEFA Champions League.[154] UEFA is an association of national football associations and the regulatory authority of European football. The exemption was the outcome of a lengthy negotiation. UEFA finally agreed to amend the selling arrangements.

The Commission adopted a commitments decision in respect of the German Bundesliga's joint selling of broadcasting rights.[155] It accepted commitments which were essentially similar to those in the UEFA case. The Bundesliga was to make several packages available to broadcasters and exclusivity was not to last longer than three years at a time. This was the first commitments decision taken under Regulation 1/2003, Article 9.[156]

The Commission adopted another commitments decision in 2006, *FA Premier League*,[157] which governed the selling of the rights to the English Premier League until 2013. The major leagues across the EU which have collective selling now know that it is the norm for the Commission to be interested in their negotiations, as do the international authorities such as UEFA.

[151] *Joint selling of the commercial rights of the UEFA Champions League* [2003] OJ L291/25, [2004] 4 CMLR 9 (UEFA), para. 20.

[152] Report from the Commission to the European Council with a view to safeguarding current sports structures and maintaining the social function of sport within the Community framework—*The Helsinki Report on Sport*, 10 December 1999, para. 4.2.1.3.

[153] This is not to suggest that money is the only reason for Barcelona's success.

[154] *Joint selling of the commercial rights of the UEFA Champions League* [2003] OJ L291/25, [2004] 4 CMLR 549; Commission Press Release, IP/03/2003.

[155] *DFB* [2005] OJ L134/46.

[156] See Chap. 13, Section 8.D.iii, p. 982.

[157] COMP/38.173, *Joint Selling of the Media Rights to the FA Premier League*, 26 March 2006.

13. CONCLUSIONS

1. The Commission's current policy towards horizontal cooperation agreements, as set out in the Guidelines, is to take a realistic view, based on economic analysis, of whether an agreement really does restrict competition in the first place, and to focus on market power as the main concern for the competition authorities.

2. The abolition of individual notification under Regulation 1/2003 poses considerable problems for parties entering into cooperation arrangements in that outside the scope of the R&D and Production block exemptions they must 'self-assess' in respect of operations where the scale of the overall cooperation and the resources involved may be very large. The 2010 Guidelines are an attempt to give as much detailed guidance as possible, but all depends on the specific facts of the individual case.

3. There are increasing problems with standard-setting, particularly in the area of the digital economy, and the 2010 Guidelines are an important development in the Commission's policy towards them.

14. FURTHER READING

BOOKS

BELLAMY, G., and CHILD, G. (V. Rose and D. Bailey, eds.), *European Law of Competition* (7th edn, Oxford University Press, 2013), Chap. 6

GERADIN, D., LAYNE-FARRAR, A., and PETIT, N., *EU Competition Law and Economics* (Oxford University Press, 2012), Chap. 7

ARTICLES

BJÖRKROTH, T., 'Joint Purchasing Agreements in the Food Supply Chain: Who's in the Sheep's Clothing?' (2013) 9 *European Competition Journal* 175

BRODLEY, J., 'Joint Ventures and Antitrust Policy' (1982) 95 *Harvard LR* 1521

BROOKS, R., and GERADIN, D., 'Interpreting and Enforcing the Voluntary FRAND Commitment' (2011) 9 *International J IT Standards and Standardization Research* 1

CAMESASCA, P., and SCHMIDT, A., 'New EC Horizontal Guidelines: Providing Helpful Guidance in the Highly Diverse and Complex Field of Competitor Cooperation and Information Exchange' (2011) 2 *J European Competition Law and Practice* 227

CHAPPATTE, P., 'FRAND Commitments—the Case for Antitrust Intervention' (2009) 5 *European Competition Journal* 320

GERADIN, D., LAYNE-FARRAR, A., and PADILLA, A. J., 'Competing Away Market Power? An Economic Assessment of *Ex Ante* Auctions in Standard Setting' (2008) 4 *European Competition Journal* 443

KATTAN, J., 'Antitrust Analysis of Technology Joint Ventures: Allocative Efficiency and the Rewards of Innovation' (1993) 61 *Antitrust LJ* 937

KIENAPFEL, P., and STEIN, A., 'The Application of Articles 81 and 82 EC in the Sports Sector' (2007) 3 *Competition Policy Newsletter* 6

KITCH, E., 'The Antitrust Economics of Joint Ventures' (1987) 54 *Antitrust LJ* 957

MCAULEY, D., 'Exclusively for All and Collectively for None: Refereeing Broadcasting Rights Between the Premier League, the European Commission and BskyB' [2004] *ECLR* 370

NITSCHE, I., 'Collective Marketing of Broadcasting by Sports Associations in Europe' [2000] *ECLR* 208

PIESIEWICZ, G., and SCHELLINGERHOUR, R., 'Intellectual Property Rights in Standard Setting from a Competition Law Perspective' (2007) 3 *Competition Policy Newsletter* 36

WILBERT, S., 'Joint Selling of Bundesliga Media Rights—First Commission Decision Pursuant to Article 9 of Regulation 1/2003' (2005) 2 *EC Competition Policy Newsletter* 44

11

VERTICAL AGREEMENTS

1. CENTRAL ISSUES

1. Vertical agreements are agreements concluded between firms which operate at different levels of the production and supply chain. Vertical agreements provide the links in the distribution chain from raw material to the final consumer.

2. Parties to vertical agreements generally produce complementary products or services, not competing products or services.

3. Initially, the Commission took an extremely formalistic approach when determining whether vertical agreements infringed Article 101. This led to treatment of agreement by category and form, rather than by economic effect. This approach may have deterred the conclusion of pro-competitive agreements and innovative distribution methods and may have encouraged firms to integrate forward.

4. The recognition that restraints in distribution agreements are frequently pro-competitive has, however, provoked the Commission to take a more economic approach to Article 101.

The Commission overhauled and modernised its approach to vertical agreements in 1999 adopting a broad block exemption for vertical agreements and publishing accompanying guidelines. The block exemption and guidelines were reviewed and replaced in May 2010.

5. Many vertical agreements are now compatible with Article 101, either because their impact on competition is de minimis or because they satisfy the conditions of the overarching block exemption which provides a safe harbour for many vertical agreements: in particular, where the 30 per cent market share threshold is met and where the agreement does not contain any 'hardcore' restraints.

6. Only if the block exemption does not apply is individual assessment of the vertical agreement required to determine whether or not it infringes Article 101(1) and, if it does, whether it satisfies the conditions of Article 101(3).

2. INTRODUCTION

A. GENERAL

A manufacturer of a product (or a supplier of a service) is not solely concerned with manufacturing. If it does not itself use that product as an input, it must also plan for its distribution. Generally, the manufacturer will wish to minimise the costs of distribution and to ensure that its products are distributed to customers in the most efficient manner. Broadly, this may be achieved either by distributing the product itself or by delegating the task to a third party (for example, an independent distributor or an agent). Similarly, a supplier of a service will need to decide how best to distribute its services.

This chapter starts by outlining the choices available to a supplier when deciding how best to market and sell its products or services to customers and the impact that the competition rules may have on a supplier's choice. The discussion focuses, however, on distribution agreements concluded between vertically related firms, for example, a manufacturer and an independent wholesaler or retailer[1] (the terms supplier and distributor or dealer will generally be used to describe the upstream and downstream parties respectively in this chapter), and the competition law problems that such agreements raise.[2] These problems differ significantly from those raised in relation to horizontal agreements since the agreements are not usually concluded by competitors (actual or potential), but by suppliers of complementary products or services. This first section outlines the main pro- and anti-competitive effects that may result from vertical restraints and the consequences that the debate about these competing effects has for antitrust analysis. In Section 3, the EU approach to vertical restraints is summarised, stressing the impact that the single market project and the Regulation 17 notification and exemption system has had on Article 101 analysis. Further, it charts the evolution in policy which has occurred, in particular the move from a more formalistic to a more effects-based approach to vertical agreements heralded by the adoption in 1999 of a new block exemption on vertical restraints, Regulation 2790/1999[3] together with accompanying Guidelines on Vertical Restraints,[4] and the review and subsequent amendment, following consultation,[5] of these documents. The new Verticals block exemption, Regulation 330/2010 (the Verticals Regulation)[6] and new Guidelines on Vertical Restraints (the Guidelines)[7] were published in April 2010. In Sections 4 and 5 the application of Article 101(1) and Article 101(3) (including the Verticals Regulation) to vertical agreements is critically assessed. In Sections 6 and 7 sub-contracting agreements and the possible application of Article 102 to distribution agreements are outlined. Section 8 concludes that although a more effects-based approach is now adopted, some problems still remain. For example, not only does the existence of a broad block exemption regulation somewhat cloud the relationship between Article 101(1) and Article 101(3), but the rigid approach to 'hardcore' restraints may be deterring the conclusion and operation of vertical agreements with efficiency-enhancing effects.

B. METHODS OF DISTRIBUTION

(i) Factors Affecting Choice

Essentially a supplier has the choice of distributing its product itself (through employees or a subsidiary), through the market using an independent distributor, or through a hybrid model using an agent. The method of distribution selected by a supplier is likely to be determined after consideration of a wide range of factors. In particular, the relative costs of organising distribution internally compared with the costs of using the market or an agent, the nature of the product or service, the nature of the market, the size and resources of the supplier, and any tax or legal implications will be relevant to the assessment.

(ii) Vertical Integration

A supplier who wishes to retain maximum control over distribution may take charge of this itself. This may be appealing to a supplier with considerable resources seeking to sell a highly complex product or to a supplier seeking to sell a high volume of low-margin products. This has perhaps

---

[1] An agreement between a manufacturer of a component and a producer of a product that uses that component is also a vertical agreement.

[2] It will focus on the way Art. 101 applies to such agreements. Although clauses inserted into a distribution agreement by a dominant supplier may infringe Art. 102, this issue is not discussed in detail in this chapter but is dealt with in Chap. 7.

[3] [1999] OJ L336/21.

[4] [2000] OJ C291/1.

[5] The Commission published a draft regulation and guidelines for consultation in 2009. Those documents and the responses filed are available on DGComp's website.

[6] [2010] OJ L102/1.

[7] [2010] OJ C130/10.

become more popular since the internet has taken off as a mode of distribution. The supplier may set up a distribution arm (internal growth) or may acquire an undertaking that is already in the distribution business (external growth).

A decision to move into distribution may, however, be impractical and/or an inefficient use of a firm's resources. There may not be a close fit between the supplier's product and the retailer's scope, the firm may become less efficient, and management may find it harder to keep track of what the firm's employees are doing as it grows, or the firm may simply not have the resources to move into retailing.

Retailers commonly secure economies of scope by offering the consumer under one roof dozens or even thousands of products, often gathered together from a diversity of manufacturers. It would be prohibitively costly for the manufacturer of paper towels, crescent wrenches, or anti-biotics to establish its own retail distribution facilities in order to control the conditions under which its product is resold to consumers. And even when there is a reasonably close fit between manufacturer product line and retail outlets' scope, as in automobiles, major appliances, or photo supplies, the two stages require quite different skills, attitudes, and spans of managerial focus, and the advantages of specialization typically require that retailers be kept separate organizationally from their primary suppliers.[8]

In many cases a supplier may, therefore, consider it preferable to leave distribution to entities that are experienced in retailing and who know more about the markets and customers to be targeted. In particular, local distributors may be able to penetrate new markets more quickly and effectively.

(iii) Agency

Whether or not a supplier decides to appoint a commercial agent or an independent distributor is likely to be dependent mainly on the independence it wishes the third party to be given, the risk it wishes to bear, and the responsibilities of the supplier on the termination of the relationship. Ordinarily, the functions of an agent are restricted and limited to negotiating sales or purchasing agreements on behalf of a principal. Indeed, the Commission defines agency agreements in the Guidelines as 'the situation in which a legal or physical person (the agent) is vested with the power to negotiate and/or conclude contracts on behalf of another person (the principal), either in the agent's own name or in the name of the principal, for the: purchase of goods or services by the principal, or sale of goods or services supplied by the principal'.[9] It thus typically operates as a marketing resource for the principal and bears little responsibility for the products it negotiates to sell. Agents usually receive either a commission based on the sales they make or a fixed salary.

If any agent appointed satisfies the definition of a 'commercial agent', Directive 86/653 may provide the agent with some protection,[10] for example, as to the remuneration payable to it during the term of the agreement and as to indemnification or compensation on the termination or expiration of the agency contract.[11] This could, of course, act as a disincentive to appointing an agent. Another drawback may be that agents are 'often less entrepreneurial, and may use less initiative in marketing than an independent dealer'.[12]

---

[8] F. M. Scherer and D. Ross, *Industrial Market Structure and Economic Performance* (3rd edn, Houghton Mifflin, 1990), 542.

[9] Guidelines, para. 12.

[10] A commercial agent is defined as a self-employed intermediary who has continuing authority to negotiate the sale or purchase of goods on behalf of another person (his principal) or to negotiate and conclude such transactions on behalf of and in the name of the principal, Council Dir. 86/653 on the coordination of the laws of the Member States relating to self-employed commercial agents [1986] OJ L382/17, Art. 1(2). See, e.g., J. Goyder, *EU Distribution Law* (4th edn, Hart Publishing, 2005), para. 6.4.

[11] Council Dir. 86/653 [1986] OJ L382/17, Art. 19.

[12] V. Korah and D. O'Sullivan, *Distribution Agreements under the EC Competition Rules* (Hart Publishing, 2002), para. 2.8.4.

(iv) Distribution through Independent Distributors

Alternatively, distribution may be left to an independent distributor that will itself sell, or use, the goods or supply the services.[13] Where an independent undertaking is chosen, a distribution agreement will be necessary. A supplier may simply wish to ensure that its products or services are distributed through as many outlets as possible. Alternatively or additionally restrictions and obligations limiting the number or type of distributors or restricting the conduct of the distributors may be considered necessary to make the distribution agreement commercially viable and/or acceptable. Although restraints in vertical agreements were at one time treated with extreme suspicion in both the US and the EU, it is now recognised that they are frequently imposed for pro-competitive purposes and with the objective of minimising distribution costs, of ensuring efficient and effective distribution arrangements, and of enhancing sales of the supplier's product. In short, they aim to bring a product or service to market in the most efficient manner. A supplier may, for example, wish to encourage consumers to purchase its product by requiring its distributors to provide specific services, to contribute to the creation of a specific brand image for the contract product or service, and/or to concentrate their selling efforts on the supplier's products. Additionally, the supplier may wish to conclude an agreement which allows it to exploit economies of scale in distribution.

A distributor may not be willing to incur the costs involved in providing such services unless other distributors, who are not subject to similar promotional, servicing, and/or stocking obligation, are prevented from taking a free-ride on its promotional or other efforts (*free-riders*). The supplier may, therefore, only be able to influence the level of services furnished by its distributors by selecting or limiting the number of dealers it appoints and/or by limiting competition between them. The supplier may achieve this, for example, by:

- granting each dealer an exclusive sales territory (*exclusive distribution*) or allocating it an exclusive customer group (*exclusive customer allocation*). This may be reinforced by imposing restraints on the territories into which, or the customers to whom, the dealers, and the supplier itself, may sell the contract products or services (*territorial or customer restraints*). Where the supplier is obliged or induced to sell the contract products only or mainly to one single buyer, there is an *exclusive supply agreement*. *Upfront access payments*, fixed fees that suppliers pay to distributors in order to get access to their distribution networks or to remunerate services provided to the suppliers by the retailers (such as slotting allowances and 'pay to stay' fees to ensure access to shelf space), may induce a supplier to sell through only one distributor, or a limited number of distributors and so may operate like an exclusive supply agreement;

- specifying the price at which the products may be resold, for example a fixed or a minimum resale price (*resale price maintenance* (RPM)) or a maximum resale price (*maximum RPM*);

- selecting the type or number of outlets in which the supplier's products are sold and precluding dealers from selling to unauthorised distributors outside the network (*selective distribution*). 'Selective distribution is almost always used to distribute branded final products.'[14]

These types of restriction limit *intra-brand* competition (competition between distributors of the supplier's product or service). They do not, *directly*[15] at least, limit *inter-brand* competition (competition between the supplier and producers of competing products). On the contrary, their main purpose may be to encourage distributors to concentrate their selling efforts on the suppliers' products and so to increase inter-brand competition.

---

[13] In some cases the distributor will not just resell the product supplied but may use a raw material or component to produce another product.

[14] Guidelines, para. 174.

[15] See Section 2.C.iii, pp. 777–784.

In addition, and in order to ensure security of supply, purchase price and/or focused selling efforts, a vertical agreement may incorporate restraints which limit competition between the supplier and producers of competing goods and services and hence *inter-brand competition*. It may preclude or deter dealers from manufacturing, buying, marketing, or selling products which compete with the contract goods or services (through *non-competition provisions*, *quantity forcing*, or *requirements contracts*). For example:

- the distributor may be obliged or have incentives to purchase a specific brand of product exclusively from the supplier (in the Guidelines the Commission describes this kind of obligation as *exclusive sourcing*. Exclusive sourcing does not preclude the distributor from purchasing or selling competing goods or services from another supplier);[16]

- the distributor may be precluded from manufacturing, buying, marketing, and/or selling competing products or services (*non-compete* or *non-competition obligations*) or required to purchase a specific percentage or a specific amount of its requirements of a type of product from the supplier (*quantity forcing* or *requirements contracts*). The Commission describes agreements in which a buyer is induced to concentrate orders for a type of product with one supplier as *single-branding* agreements.[17] Upfront access payments may operate like single branding provisions if widespread use of such payments create barriers to entry for small entrants. Further *category management agreements*, by which the distributors entrust the supplier (the category captain) with the marketing of a category of products (including the suppliers' and its competitors' products), may foreclose other suppliers and operate like single branding agreements if the category captain is able to disadvantage the distribution of products of competing suppliers;[18]

- the distributor may be required to purchase a second distinct (tied) product as a condition of purchasing the first (tying) product (*tying*);

- distributors may be required not to open a competing business for a certain period after the distribution agreement has been terminated. Such an obligation may be of particular importance in, for example, a *franchising agreement* where a supplier, a franchisor, grants the right to a distributor, a franchisee, to exploit a franchise and to set up a business marketing specified goods or services as part of a uniform business network established by the franchisor. The franchising agreement will ordinarily authorise the use of intellectual and industrial property rights, such as trade marks and know-how, to enable and to aid the franchisee to resell the goods and services. In addition, the franchisor usually provides the franchisee with commercial or technical assistance during the life of the agreement and requires a franchise fee for the use of the business method.

It is seen in Chapter 7 that single branding and tying provisions may create significant competition law problems where the firm imposing the provision is dominant.

---

[16] The Commission describes exclusive sourcing as 'requiring the exclusive distributors to buy their supplies for the particular brand directly from the manufacturer'. This eliminates arbitrage between distributors who are prevented from buying from other distributors in the system, Guidelines, para. 162. Exclusive sourcing leaves the buyer free to purchase and sell competing products, for instance competing brands of beer. In practice, however, exclusive sourcing is frequently backed by a non-compete obligation, a prohibition on selling competing products: see, e.g., Case C-234/89, *Delimitis v. Henninger Bräu* [1991] ECR I-935, para. 10.

[17] Guidelines, para. 129.

[18] Guidelines, paras. 129, 205, 209–210.

C. COMPETITION RULES AND DISTRIBUTION

(i) The Impact of the Competition Rules on Methods of Distribution

It will be seen that a decision to distribute products through an independent distributor raises most problems from an EU competition law perspective and has raised significant difficulties in the past. This may therefore mean that competition law is a relevant factor when a business is deciding how to distribute its products or services. Arguably, this should not be the case. Rather, '[u]nless there is a good reason, businessmen should be left to select the most cost effective method with as little distortion as possible induced by the competition rules and other kinds of legal measure'.[19] In particular, if the competition rules on distribution are too severe when compared with the treatment of vertical integration there is a danger that this policy might sharply accelerate the trend towards vertical integration of the distribution process.[20]

(ii) Intra-undertaking Arrangements: Vertical Integration and Agency Agreements

a. Parent-Subsidiary Arrangements

In Chapter 3 it is seen that Article 101(1) does not apply to agreements concluded between entities forming part of the same economic unit (such as a parent supplier and its subsidiary distributor, where the conduct is considered to be the unilateral workings of an economic unit and not joint conduct).[21] A supplier that sets up its own distribution arm is therefore unlikely to encounter difficulties with EU competition law unless (i) the integration is through external growth and the acquisition transaction is problematic under the EU merger rules (which is relatively rare);[22] and/or (ii) Article 102 applies, because the undertaking is dominant on a relevant market.

b. Agency Agreements

The CJ has also held that the close economic links existing in an agency relationship may mean that an agent is so closely interrelated with its principal that, as with the relationship between a parent and its subsidiary, the agent forms an integral part of the principal's business and the relationship is characterised by 'economic unity'.[23] Thus under EU law:

- some agents operate as an 'auxiliary organ' 'forming an integral part of the principal's undertaking'[24] (an agent);

- whilst others operate as an independent economic operator assuming financial and commercial risks linked to sale or the performance of contracts entered into with third parties so that the agreement concluded between them and a supplier is, like other vertical agreements, subject to Article 101(1)).[25]

---

[19] Korah and O'Sullivan, *Distribution Agreements under the EC Competition Rules* (cited in n. 12) para. 1.1. See also discussion of transaction cost economics and Coase Theory in Chap. 1.

[20] In the US, the Supreme Court recognised that 'the *per se* illegality of vertical restraints would create a perverse incentive for manufacturers to integrate vertically into distribution', *Business Electronics Corp* v. *Sharp Electronics Corp*, 485 US 717, 725, per Scalia J.

[21] See Chap. 3.

[22] See Chap. 15.

[23] See Chap. 3, Section 5.A.vi, pp. 137–147 for a discussion of the economic unit principle.

[24] See Case 311/85, *ASBL Vereniging van Vlaamse Reisbureaus* v. *ASBL Sociale Dienst van de Plaatselijke en Gewestelijke Overheidsdiensten* [1987] ECR 3801, paras. 19–20 and Case C-266/93, *Bundeskartellamt* v. *Volkswagen AG and VAG Leasing GmbH* [1995] ECR I-3477, para. 19.

[25] Guidelines, para. 21.

The jurisprudence makes it clear that it is not the parties' characterisation of the arrangement (the form) which is determinative to the question of whether the agent is to be treated as independent undertaking or not but the 'economic reality'. Indeed, in a number of cases no 'genuine' agency agreement (as the Commission used to describe those falling outside Article 101(1)) has been found to exist, even though the parties had characterised it as one of agency.[26] It is for the Commission, or other person trying to prove a violation of Article 101(1), however, to establish whether an entity is in fact acting as an independent operator.[27]

In *Confederación Española de Empresarios de Estaciones de Servicio v. Compañía Española de Petróleos (CEES)*[28] and *CEPSA Estaciones de Servicio SA v. LV Tobar e Hojos SL (CEPSA)*,[29] the CJ provided guidance to national courts on the factors relevant to the assessment of whether 'agency' contracts fall within the ambit of Article 101(1). In both cases the compatibility with Article 101(1) of motor fuel agreements concluded with operators of Spanish service-stations had arisen before the Spanish courts. In each case the CJ held that:[30]

- Vertical agreements are covered by Article 101 only where the operator is regarded as an independent economic operator and there is, consequently, an agreement between two undertakings.

- 'The decisive factor for the purposes of determining whether [an entity] is an independent economic operator is to be found in the agreement concluded with the principal and, in particular, in the clauses of that agreement, implied or express, relating to the assumption of the financial and commercial risks linked to sales of goods to third parties. The question of risk must be analysed on a case-by-case basis, taking account of the real economic situation rather than the legal categorisation of the contractual relationship in national law.'[31]

- Article 101 is not applicable where the operator bears only a negligible proportion of the risk.[32]

Somewhat surprisingly perhaps, the appraisal does not appear to be affected by the question of whether the agent acts only for one or for several principals.[33] Thus it appears that the same agent

---

[26] See e.g., *Pittsburgh Corning* (where the Commission found that although an agreement in the form of an agency had been selected for tax purposes the parties were not in a relationship of economic dependency, see Commission Decision (72/403/EEC) OJ [1972] L272/35); Case 40/73, *Suiker Unie v. Commission* [1975] ECR 1663, paras. 539–542 (where the CJ held that parties, although technically commercial agents under German law, were in fact powerful intermediaries which accepted the financial risks of the sales or of the performance of the contracts and operated at arm's length from their notional principals, and worked simultaneously as independent dealers for several undertakings); Case C-266/93, *Bundeskartellamt v. Volkswagen AG and VAG Leasing GmbH* [1995] ECR I-3477, paras. 18–19 (where Volkswagen AG and VAG Leasing argued that the German VAG dealers, as intermediaries of VAG Leasing, constituted exclusive agency agreements which were not caught by Art. 101(1). The CJ rejected this argument, holding that, 'Representatives can lose their character as independent traders only if they do not bear any of the risks resulting from the contracts negotiated on behalf of the principal and they operate as auxiliary organs forming an integral part of the principal's undertaking'. On the facts, the German VAG dealers bore some of the risks of leasing the contract vehicles by repurchasing them at the end of the leasing contract and by providing their own independent sales and after-sales services. Thus, the dealers could not be regarded as forming one economic unit with Volkswagen AG and VAG Leasing.)

[27] Case T-325/01, *DaimlerChrysler v. Commission* [2005] ECR II-3319.

[28] Case C-217/05, [2006] ECR I-11987. See also Guidelines, paras. 12-21.

[29] Case C-279/06, [2008] ECR I-6681.

[30] Case C-279/06, *CEPSA Estaciones de Servicio SA v. LV Tobar e Hojos SL* ('CEPSA') [2008] ECR I-6681, paras. 33–44, Case C-217/05, *Confederación Española de Empresarios de Estaciones de Servicio (CEES) v. Compañía Española de Petróleos SA* [2006] ECR I-11987, paras. 38–63.

[31] Case C-279/06, *CEPSA* [2008] ECR I-6681, para. 36, relying on Case C-217/05, *CEES* [2006] ECR I-11987, para. 46.

[32] Case C-279/06, *CEPSA* [2008] ECR I-6681,, para. 40, relying on Case C-217/05, *CEES* [2006] ECR I-11987, para. 61.

[33] Guidelines, para. 13 and see n. 46 and accompanying text. Although some older cases indicate that genuine agents should not act for more than one principal (see e.g. Case 40/73, *Suiker Unie v. Commission* [1975] ECR 1663 and Case 311/85, *VZW Vereniging van Vlaamse Reisbureaus v. VZW Sociale Dienst van de Plaatselijke en Gewestelijke*

may form part of the same undertaking of one or more principals. In determining whether an 'agent' accepts more than a 'negligible share' of the financial or commercial risks the following 'risks' are relevant:

- risks which are directly related to the contracts concluded and/or negotiated by the agent on behalf of the principal. It may be important therefore whether, for example, the 'agent' takes possession of goods prior to selling them to a third party, assumes costs linked to distribution of goods, such as transport costs, maintains stocks at his own expense, assumes responsibility for any damage caused to the goods or by the goods to third parties or bears the financial risk linked to the goods;[34]

- risks related to market-specific investments. These are investments specifically required for the type of activity for which the agent has been appointed by the principal and so to enable the agent to conclude and/or negotiate this type of contract. These include investments in premises, equipment, or advertising. Such investments are frequently sunk.[35]

The Commission states in its Guidelines that risks related to other activities required by the principal to be undertaken in the same product market are also relevant.[36]

In contrast, it seems that the following risks will not affect an entity's characterisation as a genuine agent: risks regarded as part and parcel of providing agency services (such as an agent's dependence on sales success for its income, an agent's investments in premises or personnel (which are not specific market investments),[37] and the ability of an agent to grant discounts from its commission); and risks accepted by the agent on another market (separate from the goods sold on behalf of the principal).[38] In *Mercedes Benz*,[39] for example, the Commission had rejected the argument that restrictions on the export of new Mercedes-Benz vehicles agreed between a supplier and German 'commercial agents' fell outside Article 101(1) on the basis that the relevant agreements were agency agreements. It concluded that the Mercedes-Benz agents bore a number of risks, which went beyond the scope of a genuine commercial agent contract.[40] On appeal, however, the GC annulled this aspect of the decision, holding that the German agents were agents so that an agreement between undertakings had not been substantiated and that the Commission had wrongly assessed the legal relationship between the supplier and its commercial agents.[41] The GC stressed that, in considering whether an entity constituted an independent distributor or an agent, it had to be determined whether the entity bore any of the risks resulting from the contracts negotiated on behalf of the principal. On the facts, it found that Mercedes-Benz did in fact bear the risk associated with the contract and the purchase of new cars, not the commercial agents which operated, acting on the instructions of the principal,

---

Overheidsdiensten [1987] ECR 3801 (Flemish travel agents observed travel prices set by tour operators. The travel agents, which acted on behalf of a large number of tour operators, could not be regarded as an auxiliary part of the tour operator even though they contracted in the name of and on behalf of the tour operators). Later cases stress that the key factor in the determination is the risk borne by the agent and that clauses preventing agents from acting for other principals may have to be assessed for their compatibility with Art. 101(1).

[34] Case 279/06, *CEPSA* [2008] ECR I-6681, para. 38, Case C-217/05, *CEES* [2006] ECR I-11987, paras. 50–61.

[35] Which means that upon leaving that particular field of activity the investment cannot be used for other activities or sold other than at a significant loss, Guidelines, para. 14.

[36] Guidelines, para. 14.

[37] Guidelines, para. 15.

[38] Case T-325/01, *DaimlerChrysler v. Commission* [2005] ECR II-3319, paras. 99 and 113.

[39] [2002] OJ L257/1.

[40] It did not consider this view to be affected by the fact that the agents formed an integral part of the Mercedes-Benz organisation. 'The criterion of integration is, unlike risk allocation, not a separate criterion for distinguishing a commercial agent from a dealer', *Mercedes-Benz* [2002] OJ L257/1, para. 163, relying on Case C–266/93, *Bundeskartellamt v. Volkswagen AG and VAG Leasing GmbH* [1995] ECR I–3477, paras. 4 and 9.

[41] Case T-325/01, *DaimlerChrysler v. Commission* [2005] ECR II-3319.

as an auxiliary organ integrated into the principal's business. Title in the cars passed direct from Mercedes-Benz to the customer and the agent had no authority to negotiate rebates except out of its own commission.[42] The fact that the agents bore responsibility for some activities and financial obligations on separate markets (such as transportation of the cars, purchase of demonstration cars, and provision of after-sales guarantee services) did not detract from this conclusion.

Although the Commission states in the Guidelines that the question of risk must be assessed on a case-by-case basis, it also states that Article 101(1) is unlikely to apply where the property in the contract goods bought or sold on behalf of the principal does not vest in the agent or the contract services are not supplied by the agent and where a number of other conditions are satisfied. Even if a relationship between a supplier and its distributor is characterised as one of agency, it will be remembered that a functional approach is taken to the concept of an undertaking. It is therefore only with regard to the market on which the agent offers its principal's goods or services to potential customers and obligations delineating the scope of that relationship that the principal and agent are considered to be acting unilaterally:[43] in particular, limitations of the territory into which, customers to whom, or prices and conditions at which the agent sells the goods or services and, possibly, exclusive agency provisions (provision preventing the principal from appointing other agents in respect of a given type of transaction, customer, or territory).

In contrast, the agent is normally regarded as an independent operator with regard to the market on which the agent offers its agency services to potential principals.[44] Thus even terms within a 'genuine' agency agreement may infringe Article 101(1) if they prevent the agent from acting as an agent or distributor of undertakings which compete with the principal (non-compete provisions) and so foreclose or lock up the relevant market,[45] or where they facilitate collusion.[46] In *Confederación Española de Empresarios de Estaciones de Servicio v. Compañia Española de Petróleos* the CJ held that:[47]

only the obligations imposed on the intermediary in the context of the sale of the goods to third parties on behalf of the principal fall outside the scope of that article. As the Commission submitted, an agency contract may contain clauses concerning the relationship between the agent and the principal to which that article applies, such as exclusivity and non-competition clauses. In that connection it must be considered that, in the context of such relationships, agents are, in principle, independent economic operators and such clauses are capable of infringing the competition rules in so far as they entail locking up the market concerned.

The requirements set out in EU competition law are complex and stringent and are not easy to navigate in practice. This has led some to call for a more realistic approach to be taken which does not obscure the economic nature of agency relationships and is more in tune with it. If not, 'parties who wish to enter into benign agency agreements will likely renegotiate and choose alternative but less efficient contractual arrangements. Such contractual changes imposed solely on account of the law could lead to unintended consequences that could harm social welfare'.[48]

---

[42] Case T-325/01, *DaimlerChrysler v. Commission* [2005] ECR II-3319, paras. 93 and 94.

[43] Guidelines, paras. 18–19.

[44] See Case C-279/06, *CEPSA* [2008] ECR I-6681, para. 41; Case C-217/05, *CEES* [2006] ECR I-11987, paras. 62–63; Guidelines, paras. 18–21.

[45] Such provisions may, however, meet the conditions of the Verticals Regulation.

[46] This could for instance be the case when a number of principals use the same agents while collectively excluding others from using these agents, or when they use the agents to collude on marketing strategy or to exchange sensitive market information between the principals, Guidelines, para. 20.

[47] Case C-217/05, *CEES* [2006] ECR I-11987, para. 62.

[48] See A. H. Zhang, 'Toward an Economic Approach to Agency Agreements' (2013) 9(3) *Journal of Competition Law and Economics* 553.

(iii) Distribution Agreements

a. Restraints on Conduct and Restrictions of Competition—The Problem

It has already been seen that vertical agreements concluded between suppliers and independent distributors operating at different levels of the supply chain generally contain restraints on the conduct or commercial freedom of one or more of the parties. A key question arising is whether or not these restraints restrict competition for the purposes of Article 101(1) and/or generate efficiencies cognisable under Article 101(3).[49] Although economic theory supports a suspicion of horizontal agreements, '[e]conomists are much more equivocal about vertical agreements, between firms at different stages of the value-added chain'.[50]

b. The Positive Effects of Vertical Restraints

In the 1960s many commentators, especially members of the Chicago School, argued that competition law should rarely, if at all, be troubled by vertical restraints which lead to increased sales and to the minimisation of distribution costs. In particular, they propounded the view that a supplier will impose vertical restraints on intra-brand competition only where necessary to enhance sales of its product and to encourage inter-brand competition.

One of the main arguments is that vertical restraints on intra-brand competition are frequently necessary to enable a supplier to protect its distributors from free-riders. For example, vertical agreements imposing RPM, awarding a distributor an exclusive distribution territory, or restricting supplies to selected retailers may be essential to encourage distributors to provide additional services necessary to boost sales and to persuade consumers to purchase more of the supplier's product. In the absence of such restraints, distributors might be unwilling to incur the cost of providing additional services since other distributors would be able to take a 'free-ride' on their investment.[51]

Bork went further, arguing that not only was the rationale for the imposition of such vertical restraints[52] obvious, but their implication for economic efficiency were clear. A supplier would only ever impose vertical restraints in order to achieve distributive efficiency and to increase its output. If the supplier wrongly required distributors to provide services that customers did not want, or did not consider to be worth the increase in price, those consumers would purchase rival products instead. The market itself would provide retribution for a supplier's mistaken belief that a vertical restraint was desirable. Where it did not, the problem would be the monopoly power of the supplier, not the vertical restraint. This led to a greater focus on the positive effects that may result from vertical restraints on intra-brand competition, even price restraints imposing RPM, which might be necessary to encourage retailers to compete on non-price criteria, such as service and promotion, to protect a retailer's reputation for providing high-quality services and stocking high-quality products, to facilitate market entry by a new competitor or an undertaking producing a new product, and to protect the retailer from free-riding.

Comanor explains these free-rider and distributive efficiency arguments more fully.

---

[49] Or, indeed, whether or not vertical agreements should fall within that provision at all, see Chap. 3.

[50] F. Fishwick, *Making Sense of Competition Policy* (Kogan Page, 1993), 56.

[51] See especially L. Telser, 'Why Should Manufacturers Want Fair Trade?' (1960) 3 *JL & Econ* 86; L. Telser, 'Why Should Manufacturers Want Fair Trade II?' (1990) 33 *JL & Econ* 409; R. A. Posner, 'The Next Step in the Antitrust Treatment of Restricted Distribution: Per Se Legality', (1981) 48 *Univ Chic LR* 1; F. H. Easterbrook, 'Vertical Arrangements and the Rule of Reason' (1984) 53 *Antitrust LJ* 135.

[52] See, e.g., R. H. Bork, 'The Rule of Reason and the Per Se Concept: Price Fixing and Market Division Part I' (1965) 74 *Yale LJ* 775; R. H. Bork, 'The Rule of Reason and the Per Se Concept: Price Fixing and Market Division Part II' (1966) 5 *Yale LJ* 373 (1966); R. H. Bork, *The Antitrust Paradox: A Policy at War with Itself* (Basic Books, 1978, reprinted with a new Introduction and Epilogue, 1993).

W. S. Comanor, 'Vertical Price-fixing, Vertical Market Restrictions, and the New Antitrust Policy' (1985) 98 *Harvard LR* 983, 986–90

Building on earlier studies...Lester Telser offered a detailed explanation of why manufacturers benefit from resale price maintenance [L. Telser, 'Why Should Manufacturers Want Fair Trade?, (1960) 3 *J.L. & E.* 86] As he observed, because the quantity sold of a manufacturer's product depends on the final price paid by consumers, the manufacturer normally stands to gain from competition among dealers that limits the distribution margin. Only if other factors intervene can the manufacturer benefit from restraints on competition among his dealers...

Telser's primary explanation centered on the distributor's role in furnishing 'services' along with the manufactured product. By 'services,' Telser referred not only to delivery, credit, and repair, but also to selling, advertising, and promotional activities...In short...all factors supplied by the distributor that may influence demand for the manufacturer's product. The provision of these services benefits the manufacturer as long as the positive effect on demand outweighs the depressing effect of the accompanying rise in price.

The manufacturer, however, can influence the level of services furnished only by limiting competition among his distributors. He cannot simply lower his price in the hope that distributors will use their increased revenues to finance the appropriate services. Even if some distributors will do so—recognizing that greater sales result from providing services jointly with the product—others will not, and might compete by setting a lower price. The result is the classic 'free rider' problem:

> Sales are diverted from the retailers who do provide the special services at the higher price to the retailers who do not provide the special services and offer to sell the product at the lower price. The mechanism is simple. A customer, because of the special services provided by one retailer, is persuaded to buy the product. But he purchases the product from another paying the latter a lower price. In this way the retailers who do not provide the special services get a free ride at the expense of those who have convinced consumers to buy the product...

In order to remain competitive with free riders, other distributors will cease to provide the requisite services...Thus, fewer services will be offered and total sales of the product will be lower than they would be otherwise...The solution, according to Telser, is for manufacturers to establish minimum retail prices, forcing retailers 'to compete by providing special services,'...and thereby eliminating the free-rider problem...

Telser's analysis explains why manufacturers would wish to impose vertical restraints. What it does not do, nor claim to do, is answer the question whether dealers' provision of additional services is efficient—that is, whether the additional services justify the higher price charged for the product...

Judge Bork wrote the first article directly addressing the implications of vertical restraints for economic efficiency [R. H. Bork, 'The Rule of Reason and the per se Concept: Price Fixing and Market Division (pt. 2)' (1966) 75 *Yale LJ* 373]. His test was simple: restrictions on output are anti-competitive, and increases in output are pro-competitive. Using this criterion, Bork concluded that all restraints imposed by manufacturers *must* be efficiency-enhancing and pro-competitive...

According to Bork, because a manufacturer will impose vertical restraints only if they lead to increased output and, in turn, to increased profits, such restraints must be pro-competitive...his position assumes that the interests of manufacturers and consumers fully coincide.

The reasoning behind Bork's theory, which appears to have gained acceptance among both lawyers and economists, is that manufacturers will not find it profitable to impose vertical restraints when customers do not find the value of the new services exceeds their incremental cost. Otherwise a rival manufacturer would surely offer the product without the additional services and lure customers away.

The government's…brief in *Spray-Rite* adopts precisely this position. Monsanto, the manufacturer whose products were distributed by Spray-Rite, believed that demand for its products was unnecessarily low because many potential customers understood neither which Monsanto herbicides were appropriate for particular farming needs, nor the proper method of applying the products. To spur the dissemination of information and avoid free-rider problems, the company initiated a policy of vertical restraints. The government argued that the restraints were pro-competitive:

> [A]lthough vertical restrictions increase both dealer costs and price, such restrictions will be unprofitable for the manufacturer unless they also increase the quantities of product that dealers sell. This is the critical, pro-competitive respect in which such vertical restrictions differ from a mere widening of dealer margins, which would increase price but *reduce* quantities of product sold. Indeed, the manufacturer usually will anticipate that its marketing program will enable its dealers to increase their prices, precisely so that they can recover their added costs. That is true whether the manufacturer uses restricted sales territories, location clauses, exclusive dealing arrangements, or some other vertical restriction. [Brief for the United States as Amicus Curiae in Support of Petitioner, *Spray-Rite* (No. 102-914)]

In addition, inter-brand restraints limiting a purchaser's freedom to buy products from sources other than the seller or another specified supplier, such as exclusive dealing obligations, quantity forcing provisions, requirements contracts, and tying arrangements, are also common practices, often with pro-competitive effect.[53] Single-branding obligations, for example, may induce the dealer to concentrate its selling efforts on the promotion of the supplier's products, allow the seller to overcome free-rider issues (and give the seller an incentive to give dealers more support), reduce transaction costs, afford protection to the parties against price fluctuations, enable both parties to engage in long-term planning, and ensure a steady supply for the buyer and steady sales for the seller. Similarly, it has been argued that tying may achieve pro-competitive objectives through assurance of product quality,[54] achieving cost saving on the production or consumption side, the prevention of excessive charges for the tied product (avoiding the double marginalisation problem),[55] innovation, by incorporating new features into products, or enabling beneficial price discrimination between buyers by, for example, metering.

The Commission in its Guidelines shows that it is fully aware of the benefits that vertical restraints may bring, recognising that, '[f]or most vertical restraints, competition concerns can only arise if there is insufficient competition at one or more levels of trade, i.e. if there is some degree of market power at the level of the supplier or the buyer or at both levels. Vertical restraints are generally less harmful than horizontal restraints and may provide substantial scope for efficiencies.'[56] 'When a company has no market power, it can only try to increase its profits by optimising its manufacturing or distribution processes'.[57] Consequently, it accepts that vertical restraints may be essential to the realisation of efficiencies and the development of new markets and to ensure the optimal level of investment and sales. In paragraphs 106–109 it summarises the positive effects that vertical restraints on both intra- and inter-brand competition may bring, especially the promotion of non-price competition and the improved quality of service.

---

[53] See further Chap. 7.

[54] Ensuring that its product is not used with another which will impair its performance and/or quality.

[55] See e.g., B. Nalebuff, *Bundling, Tying, and Portfolio Effects* (DTI Economics Paper No. 1, 2003).

[56] Guidelines, para. 6.

[57] Guidelines, para. 106.

In paragraph 107 a number of justifications for the imposition of certain vertical restraints are listed (a listing which does not purport to be complete or exhaustive). In particular, the following justifications are recognised:

(i) to 'solve a "free-rider" problem', to prevent free riding on pre-sales services, for example by the allocation of an exclusive territory to a distributor, or the imposition of a non-compete obligation;[58]

(ii) to 'open up or enter new markets', to induce a distributor to engage in sufficient investment to enable a manufacturer to enter a new geographic market, for example, by the allocation of an exclusive territory to a distributor;

(iii) the 'certification free-rider issue', to introduce a new product on a market particularly by selling through retailers that have a reputation for selling only 'quality' products, for example, by appointing an exclusive distributor or establishing a selective distribution system;

(iv) to deal with the 'hold-up problem' and encourage client-specific investment and innovation, for example, a distributor may require exclusivity in distribution if it is to contribute to the cost of developing a manufacturer's new product;

(v) to deal with the 'specific hold-up problem that may arise in the case of transfer of substantial know-how', to protect know-how transferred under a distribution agreement, for example, by the imposition of non-compete restrictions;

(vi) the 'vertical externality' issue. The manufacturer may wish to ensure that retailers are not pricing too high or making too little sales efforts as increased sales also benefits manufacturers by bestowing a positive externality on it (if its wholesale price exceeds its marginal production costs). The negative externality of too high pricing by the retailer is sometimes called the 'double marginalisation problem' and it can be avoided by imposing a maximum resale price on the retailer. To increase retailer's sales efforts selective distribution, exclusive distribution or similar restrictions may also be used;

(vii) to enable a manufacturer to exploit 'economies of scale in distribution' and to realize lower prices, for example, by using exclusive or selective distribution systems or quantity forcing provisions;[59]

(viii) to deal with 'capital imperfections', to provide security in respect of loans made in the terms of the agreement, for example, through the use of exclusivity provisions; and/ or

(ix) to achieve 'uniformity and quality standardization', to increase sales by creating a brand image and increasing the attractiveness of a product to the final consumer, for example, through the use of selective distribution or franchising agreements.

The Commission states in its Guidelines that these nine identified situations 'make clear that under certain conditions vertical agreement are likely to help realise efficiencies and the development of new markets and that these may offset possible negative effects'.[60] Importantly, however, the Commission states that:

[t]here is a large measure of substitutability between the different vertical restraints. For instance, economies of scale in distribution may possibly be achieved by using exclusive distribution, selective distribution, quantity forcing or exclusive sourcing. This is important as the negative effects on competition may differ between the various vertical restraints. This plays a role when indispensability is discussed under Article 101(3).[61]

c. The Negative Effects of Vertical Restraints

The fact that vertical restraints might provide positive effects does not, however, mean that the imposition of vertical restraints is always justified and that such restraints will inevitably result in

---

[58] A supplier who funds a distributor's promotional expenses may also demand that the distributor purchase exclusively from it in order to prevent other suppliers free-riding or benefiting from its promotional effort.

[59] The limitation of the number of distributors within the system will reduce the costs of distribution and of monitoring any promotional efforts required of distributors.

[60] Guidelines, para. 104.

[61] Guidelines, para. 105.

distributive efficiency.[62] Rather, economists are generally 'cautious in their assessment of vertical restraints' and are unwilling 'to make sweeping generalisations' and to regard them 'as *per se* beneficial for competition'.[63]

Comanor, for example, criticised Bork's assumption that restraints would always lead to the most efficient result. The theory failed to attach sufficient importance to the different preferences of consumers for extra dealer-provided services and to distinguish between marginal and infra-marginal consumers.

The 'marginal consumer' is one whose valuation of the product approximates to its current price. This consumer is, therefore, sensitive to improvements leading to an increase in the market price of a product. He or she will purchase more of the product only if he considers that the improvement in service or quality of the product is worth the increase in its price. If he does not he will generally purchase less. In contrast 'infra-marginal consumers' are consumers that place a value on the product substantially higher than the original price. Such consumers are relatively insensitive to increases in price. They will, therefore, not refrain from purchasing the product on an increase in price even if, in their view, the improvement in the quality of the products did not merit that increase in price.[64]

In the view of Comanor 'societal gains or losses from changes in the product depend on the preferences of *all* consumers, not merely those at the margin. To the extent that such alterations fail to reflect the preferences of infra-marginal consumers, the interests of consumers in general may not be served.'[65] He thus takes the view that vertical restraints which are profitable to a manufacturer may not always achieve economic efficiency. They may lead to a reduction in consumer welfare as a whole. In particular, vertical restraints imposed to promote the sale of established products may induce distributors to supply an excessive level of information services. In contrast, where consumers must be persuaded to purchase new products vertical restraints are less likely to harm consumer welfare. Consumers will require more information to entice them to purchase the products.

W. S. Comanor, Vertical Price-fixing, Vertical Market Restrictions, and the New Antitrust Policy (1984–1985) 98 *Harvard LR* 983, 992–9

Suppose, for example, that the service in question is the provision of information about how to use a product. Consumers who are 'ignorant' about the product value this information and are willing to pay more for it. For 'knowledgeable' consumers—those already familiar with the product—the opposite is true: this class of consumers is unwilling to pay the increased price for the product necessary to fund the information services.

Assume further that a large number of infra-marginal consumers are 'knowledgeable.' Many of the consumers in this class may be previous customers who originally learned about the product from outside

---

[62] 'As on several other fronts, the debate over vertical restraints can be characterized with only mild imprecision as a contest between the University of Chicago…and the rest of the world. And as in other areas, the "Chicago school" has through superior organization, fervor…and timing, if not superior access to revealed truth, sent the rest of the world reeling. But as competing in the marketplace of ideas continued, serious weaknesses in the Chicago position materialized': Scherer and Ross, *Industrial Market Structure and Economic Performance* (cited in n. 8) 541.

[63] European Commission, Green Paper on Vertical Restraints in EC Competition Policy, COM(96) 721, para. 54. See, e.g., W. S. Comanor, 'Vertical Price-Fixing, Vertical Market Restrictions, and the New Antitrust Policy' (1984–1985) 98 *Harvard LR* 983 and J. J. Flynn, 'The "Is" and "Ought" of Vertical Restraints After Monsanto Co v. Spray-Rite Service Corp' (1985–1986) 71 *Cornell LR* 1095.

[64] Comanor, 'Vertical Price-Fixing, Vertical Market Restrictions, and the New Antitrust Policy' (cited in n. 63) 991.

[65] Comanor, 'Vertical Price-Fixing, Vertical Market Restrictions, and the New Antitrust Policy' (cited in n. 63) 991.

sources or from advertising provided directly by the manufacturer. The 'ignorant' consumers, we may assume, are largely marginal. Perhaps they value the product less than 'knowledgeable' consumers do simply because they are uncertain of its merits.

Because marginal consumers desire the information services, the manufacturer will impose vertical restraints. But this action may not lead to an efficient result: the interests of 'knowledgeable' infra-marginal consumers must also be taken into account. If they are great in number, the harm caused by making them pay for unwanted services may exceed the benefit derived by marginal consumers. Thus, the mere fact that the services are profitable for the manufacturer is not sufficient evidence that all—or even most—consumers benefit from their supply... In short, these services may be oversupplied in relation to the consumer optimum...

Economic theory alone cannot predict whether the imposition of vertical restraints—and dealers' provision of additional services—will benefit consumers and enhance efficiency. Whether consumers benefit depends on whether gains to marginal consumers outweigh losses to their infra-marginal counterparts. Because such losses may predominate—particularly when the restraints are used to support services for established products—consumer harm may result.

Several other concerns also cause scepticism about the necessity or legitimacy in all cases of vertical restraints, even those that limit only intra-brand competition. In the EU, there is a particular concern that agreements which impose territorial restrictions on dealers whilst restricting only intra-brand competition lead to the division of markets on national lines in contravention of the single market objective.[66] The extract from the Commission's Green Paper on Vertical Restraints[67] reinforces the importance of the 'wider objective of achieving an integrated internal market. Market integration enhances competition in the EU. Companies should not be allowed to recreate private barriers between Member States where State barriers have been successfully abolished.'[68]

Green Paper on Vertical Restraints in Competition Policy, COM(96) 721

70. The ongoing integration process of the Single Market adds an extra dimension to the analysis of vertical restraints. The 1992 programme was the result of a widely held conviction that the failure to achieve a single market has been costing European industry millions in unnecessary costs and lost opportunities. The exact title of the Cecchini Report, 'The cost of Non-Europe'... is a clear reflection of this. The efforts made since the entry into force of the EEC Treaty in 1958 had not exhausted by the mid-1980's all the potential gains to be expected from the full economic integration of the economies of the Member States. Now that more steps have been taken to eliminate the remaining obstacles to the free movement of goods, services and factors of production, it is still apparent that further efforts are necessary to achieve the maximum possible level of integration...

78. The EC experience shows that the removal of non-tariff barriers is not sufficient for the full development of parallel trade, arbitrage and changes in distribution across Europe. For the complete success of economic integration it is necessary that producers, distributors and consumers, find it profitable to move towards the new market situation and do not take actions to avoid or counteract the effects of the Single Market measures. The elimination of barriers to trade may not achieve its objectives if producers and/or distributors introduce practices contrary to integration. Unfortunately in many cases it is likely that they have strong incentives to do so.

---

[66] See Chaps. 1, 4, and 7.

[67] European Commission, Green Paper on Vertical Restraints in EC Competition Policy, COM(96) 721.

[68] Guidelines, para. 7.

Further, and more generally, it is now generally accepted that restrictions on intra-brand competition may, in certain circumstances, reinforce horizontal agreements, push up prices, and weaken inter-brand competition or that restraints, particularly single branding and tying obligations, may affect and stifle inter-brand competition more directly through foreclosure.[69]

The Commission indicates in the Guidelines that its anxieties about vertical restraints are relatively broad. In particular, it fears that vertical restraints may foreclose the market, reduce rivalry and facilitate collusion between undertakings operating on the market, reduce intra-brand competition, and create obstacles to the single market.

Guidelines on Vertical Restraints

100. The negative effects on the market that may result from vertical restraints which EU competition law aims at preventing are the following:

(i) anticompetitive foreclosure of other suppliers or other buyers by raising barriers to entry or expansion;

(ii) softening of competition between the supplier and its competitors and/or facilitation of collusion amongst these suppliers, often referred to as reduction of inter-brand competition;

(iii) softening of competition between the buyer and its competitors and/or facilitation of collusion amongst these competitors, often referred to as reduction of intra-brand competition if it concerns distributors' competition on the basis of the brand or product of the same supplier;

(iv) the creation of obstacles to market integration, including, above all, limitations on the possibilities for consumers to purchase goods or services in any Member State they may choose.

101. Foreclosure, softening of competition and collusion at the manufacturer's level may harm consumers in particular by increasing the wholesale prices of the products, limiting the choice of products, lowering their quality or reducing the level of product innovation. Foreclosure, softening of competition and collusion at the distributors' level may harm consumers in particular by increasing the retail prices of the products, limiting the choice of price-service combinations and distribution formats, lowering the availability and quality of retail services and reducing the level of innovation of distribution.

102. In a market where individual distributors distribute the brand(s) of only one supplier, a reduction of competition between the distributors of the same brand will lead to a reduction of intra-brand competition between these distributors, but may not have a negative effect on competition between distributors in general. In such a case, if inter-brand competition is fierce, it is unlikely that a reduction of intra-brand competition will have negative effects for consumers.

103. Exclusive arrangements are generally worse for competition than non-exclusive arrangements. Exclusive dealing makes, by the express language of the contract or its practical effects, one party fulfil all or practically all its requirements from another party. For instance, under a non-compete obligation the buyer purchases only one brand. Quantity forcing, on the other hand, leaves the buyer some scope to purchase competing goods. The degree of foreclosure may therefore be less with quantity forcing.

104. Vertical restraints agreed for non-branded goods and services are in general less harmful than restraints affecting the distribution of branded goods and services. Branding tends to increase product differentiation and reduce substitutability of the product, leading to a reduced elasticity of demand and an increased possibility to raise price. The distinction between branded and non-branded goods or services will often coincide with the distinction between intermediate goods and services and final goods and services.

---

[69] See e.g., London Economics, *Competition in Retailing* (OFT Research Paper No. 13, 1997).

105. In general, a combination of vertical restraints aggravates their negative effects. However, certain combinations of vertical restraints are better for competition than their use in isolation from each other. For instance, in an exclusive distribution system, the distributor may be tempted to increase the price of the products as intra-brand competition has been reduced. The use of quantity forcing or the setting of a maximum resale price may limit such price increases. Possible negative effects of vertical restraints are reinforced when several suppliers and their buyers organise their trade in a similar way, leading to so-called cumulative effects.[70]

3. THE EU APPROACH—AN OVERVIEW

A. THE BACKGROUND: THE SINGLE MARKET PROJECT AND RESTRICTIONS ON ECONOMIC FREEDOM

In Section 2.C it has been seen that vertical restraints enable efficiencies to be achieved but that they can also result in an anti-competitive outcome. These pro- and anti-competitive effects have caused many competition lawyers and economists to disagree vigorously about when and/or how often the different types of vertical restraint cause anti-competitive harm, how any such harm should be reconciled with the efficiencies that vertical restraints may generate, and how legal rules should be constructed to identify and weigh the competing effects.

The Commission's historical approach to Article 101(1), and in particular to vertical distribution agreements, sparked huge controversy and intense debate. For many years the Commission appeared unwilling to recognise the distribution efficiencies resulting from vertical restraints. Rather, it adopted a strict, extremely interventionist, and over-inclusive approach when dealing with them. One of the key causes of the Commission's preoccupation with vertical restraints has been that they often demarcate territories between distributors, isolate national markets, erect barriers to trade, and maintain price differences between Member States.[71] Even where a distribution agreement did not impact on the single market project the Commission was concerned about agreements that restrained the parties' 'economic freedom'.[72] It sought to encourage and to nurture the process of rivalry between undertakings and to foster the freedom and right of initiative of the individual economic operator and the spirit of enterprise.[73] It took the view, often without serious analysis of the effect of the agreement on the competitive process, that restrictions on parties' freedom of action, such as price or non-price restraints or non-compete clauses, amounted to restrictions of competition.[74] It thus took a broad view of what constituted a restriction of competition within the meaning of Article 101(1). In addition, it adopted a strict and formalistic approach when applying the Article 101(3) criteria.

B. CRITICISMS OF THIS APPROACH

The Commission received significant criticism for its failure to take a sufficiently realistic view of whether an agreement restricted competition for the purposes of Article 101(1). Not only was this

---

[70] In later sections, the Commission identifies more specific possible competition risks that arise from different types of restraints.

[71] See n. 66 and accompanying text and D. Deacon, 'Vertical Restraints under EU Competition Law: New Directions' [1995] Fordham Corp L Inst 307, para. 8.

[72] See, e.g., B. E. Hawk, 'System Failure: Vertical Restraints and EC Competition Law' (1995) 32 *CMLRev* 973.

[73] See Chap. 4.

[74] Deacon, 'Vertical Restraints under EU Competition Law' (cited in n. 71) 307, para. 9.

approach considered difficult conceptually, the main objective of an agreement being to bind the parties and to restrict their freedom of action,[75] but it caused the Commission to deal with agreements by category, applying certain rules to one type of agreement and different rules to others. It also meant, with the host of accompanying drawbacks, that businesses felt the need to secure exemptions for their distribution agreements.[76] At the time, and partly because the block exemptions preceding Regulation 2790/1999 were rigid and more difficult to satisfy, this policy imposed an enormous, and, arguably, unnecessary, burden on firms wishing to conclude distribution agreements. It meant that in practice firms would often have to seek an individual exemption for their agreement, or more realistically since exemptions were rarely granted, rely on a comfort letter.[77] This may have deterred the conclusion and operation of many pro-competitive distribution arrangements.

Although the Commission introduced devices to try and deal with the problems experienced[78] the approach was widely criticised by practitioners and academic commentators. In 1995, Hawk, in a seminal article,[79] fiercely criticised the Commission, for: its over-broad application of Article 101(1) (based on an incoherent rationale—notably the economic freedom notion, the market integration objective, and the desire to protect small and medium-sized enterprises—and the consequent anaemic economic analysis which was inconsistent with Court judgments); which generated extraordinary legal uncertainty; and led to a proliferation of block exemption and legal formalisms and analysis of agreements by categories and a de-emphasis on or lack of substantive economic analysis. The approach, he contended, ultimately eliminated 'what should be the heart of the matter: and antitrust (i.e. economics/law) substantive analysis of a particular agreement or practice, i.e. its competitive harms and benefits'.[80] In short he claimed that there was system failure: the whole notification system had failed. This article is perceived to have been the straw (or at least one of the straws) which finally broke the camel's back and convinced the Commission that its approach to vertical restraints would have to change.[81]

C. THE MORE ECONOMIC APPROACH: THE BLOCK EXEMPTION AND REFORM

The relentless stream of criticism that the Commission's approach to vertical restraints provoked, charging it with a failure to take a sufficiently economic approach and stultifying innovation in the distribution process, eventually led the Commission to heed of the criticisms and introduce changes. In 1996 it issued a Green Paper on Vertical Restraints in which it discussed possible ways for developing and ameliorating its approach to vertical restraints. The Paper sought opinion upon possible options for reform. An additional option, to adopt a more realistic approach when assessing

[75] See Chap. 4, Section 2.C, pp. 194–195.

[76] 'A broad definition of restriction of competition under Art. [101(1)] shifts most of the inquiry over to Art. [101(3)] where only the Commission has the power to grant exemptions, thus requiring notification and excluding the national courts from the more important part of the antitrust analysis': B. E. Hawk, 'The American (Anti-Trust) Revolution: Lessons for the EEC' [1988] ECLR 53, 65.

[77] 'Only a limited number of formal decisions can be rendered each year for cases under Articles [101] and [102]....In most cases of application for negative clearance or individual exemption, the Commission declares by simple letter known as a "comfort letter"': European Commission Green Paper on Vertical Restraints COM(96) 721, 30.

[78] e.g., the Commission developed the doctrine of appreciability within the context of Art. 101(1), and introduced block exemptions to exempt distribution agreements from the prohibition of Art. 101(3).

[79] Hawk, 'System Failure' (cited in n. 72) 973. A long extract from the article is set out in previous editions of this book.

[80] Hawk, 'System Failure' (cited in n. 72) 2.5.

[81] See also Deakin, 'Vertical Restraints under EU Competition Law' (cited in n. 71) 307.

the agreement's compatibility with Article 101(1), was not discussed within the Paper but attracted much attention in the debate that followed.

Following the introduction of the Green Paper a follow-up document was published and several significant changes were introduced to the way in which vertical restraints are dealt with under Article 101 of the Treaty. On 22 December 1999, the Commission adopted a new block exemption regulation, for all vertical agreements that may fall within Article 101(1)[82] and published accompanying Guidelines on the appraisal of vertical agreements. The block exemption and Guidelines were revised and replaced following consultation in 2010 with some (not fundamental) modifications to deal, principally, with market changes, including increased retailer power and the growth of internet selling. The Verticals Regulation adopts a flexible approach applying to *all* vertical agreements that satisfy the requirements set out in the Regulation. Essentially this depends upon the parties not exceeding a specified market share threshold (of 30 per cent) and on the agreement not containing any hardcore vertical restraints.

Where a vertical agreement is not exempted by the Verticals Regulation, or another block exemption, the parties to the agreement will have to make their own determination whether or not the agreement infringes Article 101(1) at all and, if it does, whether or not it meets the criteria set out in Article 101(3). The Guidelines explain the operation of the block exemption and set out the Commission's analysis of agency agreements and vertical agreements falling outside the block exemption.[83] The Guidelines have to be read alongside the Guidelines on the application of Article 81(3) [now Article 101(3)] of the Treaty (the Article 101(3) Guidelines)[84] which set out general guidance on how the Commission interprets Article 101(1) and Article 101(3)[85] and the Commission's Notice on agreements of minor importance. The Guidelines recognise that vertical restraints are generally less harmful than horizontal restraints as in vertical relationships the exercise of market power 'by either the upstream or downstream company would normally hurt the demand for the product of the other. The companies involved in the agreement therefore usually have an incentive to prevent the exercise of market power by the other.'[86] The Guidelines clarify that even agreements concluded between undertakings with more than 30 per cent of the relevant market (and hence falling outside the block exemptions safe harbour) may not fall within Article 101(1).[87] It has also issued a number of decisions adopting a more economically realistic approach.[88]

D. METHODOLOGY

The Commission's modernised approach to vertical agreements signals, in line with the case law of the Court, that many such agreements will not infringe Article 101(1) at all. Further, that even if they do, or may, the Article 101(3) criteria are to be applied more flexibly.

Logically, the first question that should be addressed in a verticals case is, does this agreement infringe Article 101(1) at all?[89] Many vertical agreements will fall outside Article 101(1) on account of

---

[82] [1999] OJ L336/21.

[83] [2000] OJ C291/1.

[84] See Guidelines on the application of Article 81(3) of the Treaty [2004] OJ C101/97.

[85] See generally Chap. 4.

[86] Guidelines, para. 98.

[87] Where the parties to the agreement do not have more than 15% of the relevant market, the agreement is likely to be de minimis so long as there are no network effects and it does not contain hardcore restraints, see Chap. 4.

[88] See, e.g., *Spring* [2000] OJ L195/49; *Whitbread* [1999] OJ L88/26, upheld on appeal Case T-131/99, *Shaw v. Commission* [2002] ECR II-2023 and *Bass* [1999] OJ L186/1 upheld on appeal Case T-231/99, *Joynson v. Commission* [2002] ECR II-2085.

[89] Assuming that there is an agreement between two or more undertakings (and not, e.g., an agreement between a parent and subsidiary) and that the agreement is not a genuine agency agreement.

their minor importance, because they do not appreciably affect trade between Member States, and/or because they do have as their object or effect an appreciable restriction of competition. Practically, however, where an agreement appears to affect trade and competition appreciably, the parties may prefer to rely on the 'safe haven' of the block exemption rather than going through the full economic analysis required to determine whether or not the agreement has as its effect the restriction of competition. It is for this reason perhaps that the Commission states, in its Guidelines at paragraph 110, that the first question for undertakings to ask is whether the agreement falls within the block exemption, *not* whether the agreement actually falls within Article 101(1) and so requires scrutiny under Article 101(3).

(1) First, the undertakings involved need to establish the market shares of the supplier and the buyer on the markets where they [purchase] the contract products.

(2) If the relevant market share of the supplier and the buyer each do not exceed the 30 % threshold, the vertical agreement is covered by the Block Exemption Regulation, subject to the hardcore restrictions and conditions set out in that regulation.

(3) If the relevant market share is above the 30 % threshold for supplier and/or buyer, it is necessary to assess whether the vertical agreement falls within Article 101(1).

(4) If the vertical agreement falls within Article 101(1), it is necessary to examine whether it fulfils the conditions for exemption under Article 101(3).[90]

Although this approach clearly represents sensible, pragmatic advice, this methodology turns Article 101 on its head as undertakings should not need to comply with the block exemption or Article 101(3) criteria if the agreement does not infringe Article 101(1). In this chapter we thus start with the question of whether the agreement infringes Article 101(1) before going on to consider the terms of the block exemption and how Article 101(3) applies to vertical agreements which may violate Article 101(1) but do not benefit from the block exemption. It should be remembered, however, that in many cases it will, in practice, be preferable when determining the compatibility of an existing or proposed distribution arrangement with Article 101, to side-step the more complex Article 101(1) analysis and to start as the Commission suggests with the question: is this agreement covered by the block exemption and so exempted from Article 101(1) if within it? It should also be remembered from Chapter 4 (see also Figure 11.1) that a fundamentally different approach applies depending upon whether the agreement contains object restraints or restraints identified as hardcore restraints in the Verticals Regulation. Agreements which incorporate object restraints are *presumed to be incompatible* with Article 101, to infringe Article 101(1), and the Commission's view is that they come within its list of hardcore restraints which are presumed not to satisfy the conditions of Article 101(3) (for which reason the block exemption does not apply). The parties to the agreement containing such restraints will have an uphill struggle to demonstrate that this presumption should be rebutted. In contrast, a large number of vertical agreements which do not incorporate such restraints are presumed to be compatible with Article 101, either because they fall outside Article 101(1) altogether on de minimis grounds or because they satisfy the conditions of the Verticals Regulation (or the Motor Vehicle Block Exemption). Only when they do not do so is a full individual assessment under Article 101(1) and 101(3) required.

Because of these critical differences an important issue to be determined initially is whether an agreement incorporates a restraint which is likely to result in the agreement being characterised as a restriction of competition by object.

---

[90] Guidelines, para. 110.

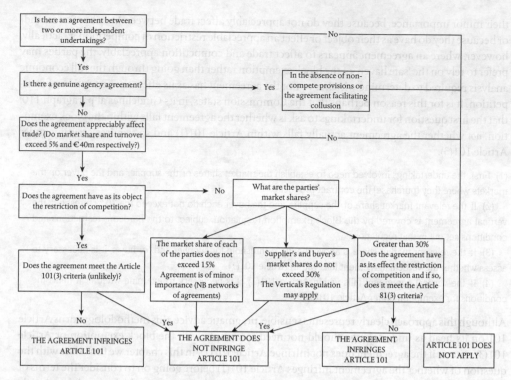

Figure 11.1 Analysis of Vertical Agreements under Article 101

4. DISTRIBUTION AGREEMENTS AND ARTICLE 101(1) OF THE TREATY

A. VERTICAL AGREEMENTS WHICH RESTRICT COMPETITION BY OBJECT

(i) Types of Restraints which are Likely to be Characterised as Restrictive by Object

It was seen in Chapter 4 that in order to determine whether restraints are restrictive by object, 'regard must be had inter alia to the content of its provisions, the objectives it seeks to ascertain and the economic and legal context of which it forms part'.[91] Further, that unless the objectives, or context, of the agreement suggests otherwise, vertical agreements containing the following restraints are highly likely to be found to be restrictive by object:

- RPM provisions (requiring buyers to observe fixed or minimum resale prices);
- Restraints conferring ATP on a distributor or otherwise limiting parallel trade or partitioning national markets.

---

[91] Case C-501/06 P, *GlaxoSmithKline Services Unlimited v. Commission* [2009] ECR I-9291, para. 58.

(ii) Resale Price Maintenance

A number of cases establish that, where an agreement between the supplier and distributor can be established,[92] a provision fixing minimum resale prices to be charged by distributors (or indirectly operating as an RPM provision) will be found to be by its very nature injurious to competition. In *Pronuptia de Paris v. Schillgallis* the CJ, in setting out guidelines on the compatibility of distribution franchises with Article 101(1), held that 'provisions which impair the franchisee's freedom to determine his own prices are restrictive of competition'.[93] In *Metro v. Commission (No. 1)*, the CJ stated that 'price competition is so important that it can never be eliminated',[94] and in *SA Binon & Cie v. SA Agence et Messageries de la Presse* it held that 'provisions which fix the prices to be observed in contracts with third parties constitute, of themselves, a restriction on competition within the meaning of Article [101(1)]'.[95] The Commission's Guidelines indicate, however, that it is acceptable for a supplier to provide dealers 'with price-guidelines, so long as there is no concerted practice between the [parties] for the actual application of the prices'.[96] Further, a producer may operate a selective distribution system in which 'price competition is not generally emphasized either as an exclusive or indeed as a principal factor'. In *Metro v. Commission* the Court accepted that price competition 'does not constitute the only effective form of competition or that to which absolute priority must in all circumstances be afforded'.[97] Thus the provision of price guidelines or the operation of a selective distribution system may be compatible with Article 101(1) so long as it is not operated in a way which precludes price discounting.[98] Further, it seems that maximum prices may not infringe Article 101(1) so long as they do not operate as a 'focal point for the resellers' and which will be followed by them.[99] Recommended and maximum RPM and selective distribution may also be covered by the Verticals Regulation.[100]

The Commission has taken[101] enforcement against RPM seriously and imposed significant fines on those found to have participated in such a practice. For example: in *Yamaha*[102] the Commission imposed fines for practices designed to partition the single market and for fixing resale prices of its products in certain EU countries; and in *JCB*[103] the Commission found that JCB had imposed resale prices on Community distributors of its construction and earthmoving equipment. This aspect of its finding was, however, annulled by the GC on appeal on the grounds that the manufacturer's suggested retail prices 'although strongly indicative, were nonetheless not binding'.[104] Similarly in

---

[92] Case T-208/01, *Volkswagen v. Commission* [2003] ECR II-5141, *aff'd* Case C-74/04 P, [2006] ECR I-6585, the GC quashed a Commission decision condemning RPM on the grounds that the Commission had failed to establish that the distributors had agreed to or acquiesced in the supplier's policy of RPM.

[93] Case 161/84, [1986] ECR 353, para. 25.

[94] Case 26/76, [1977] ECR 1875, para. 21.

[95] Case 243/83, [1985] ECR 2015, para. 44.

[96] Case 161/84, *Pronuptia de Paris GmbH v. Pronuptia de Paris Irmgard Schillgallis* [1986] ECR 353, para. 25.

[97] Case 26/76, *Metro-SB-Grossmärkte GmbH v. Commission (No. 1)* [1977] ECR 1875, para. 21.

[98] Case 107/82, *AEG-Telefunken v. Commission* [1983] ECR 3151. See also *Pierre Fabre*, para. 40, discussed in Section 4.B.iv.d.

[99] Guidelines, para. 227.

[100] See Section 5.C.

[101] The Commission has not, however adopted a RPM decision since 2003. This could be an indication that it no longer considers this to be an enforcement priority or, more likely, that it prefers to leave enforcement to the national level (NCAs or to private litigants and the national courts), see e.g., A. Jones and J. Goyder, 'Vertical Agreements and competition law: An overview of EU and national case law', 21 March 2013, e-Competitions, N°51217, available at <http://www.concurrences.com>.

[102] *Yamaha* IP/03/1028, 16 July 2003.

[103] [2002] OJ L691.

[104] Case T-67/01, *JCB Service v. Commission* [2004] ECR II-49, para. 130. This finding was not challenged before the CJ, which broadly upheld the judgment of the GC, Case C-167/04 P, *JCB Service v. Commission* [2006] ECR I-8935. Note that the agreement in *JCB* was originally notified to the Commission in June 1973!

Volkswagen,[105] the Commission imposed fines of €30.96 million on VW for RPM in Germany but the decision was annulled by the GC on the grounds that the Commission had failed to establish that the distributors had agreed to, or acquiesced in, the manufacturer's policy of RPM.[106] The CJ[107] upheld the annulment ruling that a call by a manufacturer would only be prohibited by Article 101(1) if the Commission established concurrence of wills on the part of the parties to the dealership agreement.[108] These cases establish that the Commission has a heavy burden to discharge before it can establish that an actual agreement to fix minimum resale prices exists. Article 101 does not prevent a supplier from pursuing a policy of minimum resale prices if that policy is not accepted by its distributors.[109]

Although the Commission now rarely dedicates its resources to enforcement in this area a number of NCAs regularly impose fines on undertakings involved in RPM or other practices.[110]

(iii) ATP and Export Bans

In Chapter 4 it was seen that ever since *STM* and *Consten and Grundig*[111] it has been clear that although appointing an exclusive distributor for a specific sales territory might not infringe Article 101(1), clauses in a distribution agreement which go beyond this and result in the isolation of a national market, and/or in maintaining separate national markets, have as their object the restriction of competition since they shelter the distributor from all intra-brand competition and lead to the division of national markets. *Consten and Grundig* provides a clear example of the Court struggling to balance the EU policy of market integration against competition and efficiency.

G. Monti, 'Article 81 EC and Public Policy' (2002) *CMLRev* 1057–1099, 1065–1066

The more complex question is how to balance market integration with competition and efficiency, especially in the context of distribution agreement. The problem manifests itself because it has been argued (contrary to the Commission's position) that territorial protection is a means to increase competition in the market. This well-known argument can be summarized by reference to the decision in *Consten and Grundig*: Grundig's attempt to isolate the French market so as to give its exclusive distributor in France the opportunity to devote resources to market a new product was held unlawful, the ECJ being deaf to the argument that without territorial protection, no reasonable distributor would have taken the risk of sinking costs into a new and uncertain market if he knew that a free rider would later enter and sell goods taking advantage of its marketing efforts.

---

[105] [2001] OJ L162/14. It imposed a fine of €30.96 million on Volkswagen in respect of the infringement, the decision was annulled on appeal, Case T-208/01, *Volkswagen* v. *Commission* [2003] ECR II-5141, *aff'd* Case C-74/04 P, [2006] ECR I-6585.

[106] Case T-208/01, *Volkswagen* v. *Commission* [2003] ECR II-5141, *aff'd* Case C-74/04 P, [2006] ECR I-6585, see Chap. 3.

[107] *Volkswagen* v. *Commission* [2003] ECR II-5141, *aff'd* Case C-74/04 P, [2006] ECR I-6585.

[108] Case C-74/04 P, [2006] ECR I-6585, paras. 39–56. In this case the Commission had not attempted to show that the dealers had tacitly acquiesced in the manufacturer's call but had found that the concurrence was part of the dealership agreement.

[109] For a discussion of unilateral conduct and agreements, see Chap. 3, Section 5.B.ii.

[110] See, e.g., Jones and Goyder, 'Vertical Agreements and competition law' (cited in n. 101).

[111] Cases 56 and 58/64, *Établissements Consten S.à.R.L. & Grundig-Verkaufs-GmbH* v. *Commission* (*Consten and Grundig*) [1966] ECR 299 (see extract set out in Chap. 4). See also, e.g., Case T-77/92, *Parker Pen* v. *Commission* [1994] ECR II-549, Case C-501/06 P, *GlaxoSmithKline Services Unlimited* v. *Commission* [2009] ECR I-9291, para. 61 and Case T-360/09, *E.ON Ruhrgas AG* v. *Commission* 29 June 2012.

Some economists would argue that in this situation, territorial protection is a necessary incentive to convince a distributor to market goods to remove the free-rider effect. Instead, under EC competition law, as Gyselen once memorably put it, the free rider is a 'hero' because he integrates markets by selling across borders. Paradoxically, this hard line may result in less competition and less integration: there would be less competition because firms might decide to integrate vertically, thus reducing the number of distributors in a Member State, to the possible disadvantage of new manufacturers who might find it harder to distribute their products; alternatively firms might decide not to export at all if they fear that commercial success will not materialize with an unprotected distributor, diminishing both competition and integration; or they might waste resources trying to find other means to prevent free riding without infringing competition provisions. These considerations suggest that territorial restrictions should be looked upon generously and that preference for market integration is counterproductive. However, economic learning and evidence from the United States suggests that absolute territorial protection does not *always* yield an efficient outcome. Comanor for example has argued that while with resale price maintenance agreements distributors are still able to compete against each other on things other than price, with territorial segregation all competition among rival distributors is lost, meaning that the increased prices set by distributors are not necessarily designed to recoup the costs of additional services provided to consumers, but are evidence of a welfare loss. Even in an integrated market like the United States, there is evidence that a lack of intra-brand competition can lead to anti-competitive results.

Therefore, economic evidence shows that it is impossible to state either that all territorial restraints by firms which lack market power are efficiency-enhancing (as some Chicago School lawyers would contend) nor that they are all inefficient (as *Consten and Grundig* suggests). This ambiguity poses a difficulty for competition authorities: the best approach would be to analyse territorial restrictions on a case-by-case basis to determine what the right amount of territorial protection is: however, this would lead to undesirable delay and uncertainty. The second-best solution is to devise some rule of thumb which draws a clear distinction between those territorial restrictions that are lawful and those that are unlawful which is a close as possible to the economic evidence but which allows parties to implement agreements speedily and with certainty. The rules of thumb deployed in the EC are stricter than those in the U.S. but, as will be demonstrated below, the Commission has become increasingly willing to relax its tough stance against market partitioning agreement when this results in greater efficiencies.

In Chapter 12 it is seen that in 2011, the Grand Chamber of CJ adopted, in *Premier League Ltd* v. *QC Leisure* and *Murphy* v. *Media Protection Services Ltd*,[112] a similar approach to that which it had adopted in *Consten and Grundig* 45 years earlier, when it distinguished between the situation where a sole licensee was given an exclusive right to broadcast protected subject matter in a specified territory and agreements which went further, and partitioned national markets according to national borders (through clauses prohibiting broadcasters from effecting any cross-border provision of services).[113] The CJ confirmed that the former, the mere grant of a sole licence, is not sufficient to justify the finding that such an agreement has an anti-competitive object but that the latter, an agreement which tends to restore divisions between national markets, is liable to frustrate the Treaty's objective of achieving the integration of those markets through the establishment of a single market and must be regarded, in principle, as an agreement whose object is to restrict competition.[114]

---

[112] Cases C-403 and 429/08, 4 October 2011.

[113] *Premier League Ltd* v. *QC Leisure* and *Murphy* v. *Media Protection Services Ltd*, Cases C-403 and 429/08, 4 October 2011, paras 137–139.

[114] *Premier League Ltd* v. *QC Leisure* and *Murphy* v. *Media Protection Services Ltd*, Cases C-403 and 429/08, 4 October 2011, para. 139. See also *GSK*.

The Commission, supported by the EU Courts, has generally maintained a strict policy against any measure inserted in an agreement, or imposed unilaterally by the supplier and explicitly or tacitly accepted by the distributor,[115] which directly, or indirectly, divides the EU market on territorial lines and *totally* prevents parallel imports or otherwise limits parallel trade (passive selling to customers in other territories as well as active selling efforts). Even an agreement which does not explicitly contain an export ban or confer ATP on a distributor will be found to restrict competition if this is its purpose,[116] for example:[117] where circulars are sent discouraging[118] or prohibiting[119] export; where export is permitted but only if the consent of the producer is obtained;[120] where the producer must be contacted before exporting via the internet;[121] where goods are supplied to distributors but the invoice for supply bears the words 'export prohibited';[122] where insufficient quantities of goods are supplied with the objective of precluding export;[123] where performance bonuses are dependent upon dealers not exporting;[124] where exported products are bought back by the manufacturer;[125] where products supplied are marked so that parallel importers can be identified;[126] where guarantees are limited to the Member State in which the product was purchased;[127] where dual pricing is utilised to discourage export;[128] where an agreement requires a distributor to pass on any customer enquiries coming from outside the contract territory to the producer;[129] where a producer threatens to terminate or actually terminates contractual arrangements with distributors or dealers which sell outside their allotted territory;[130] where financial support is contingent on products supplied to distributors being used only within a distributor's allotted territory;[131]

---

[115] See Chap. 3. But see, in particular, Case T-41/96, *Bayer AG v. Commission* [2000] ECR II-3383, *aff'd* Cases C-2 and 3/01 P, [2004] ECR I-23. See also Case T-208/01, *Volkswagen v. Commission* [2003] ECR II-5141, *aff'd* Case C-74/04 P, [2006] ECR I-6585.

[116] An export ban will be prohibited even if it is stipulated to be applicable only 'unless prohibited by law', *Novalliance/Systemform* [1997] OJ L47/11.

[117] See also the discussion of hardcore restraints prohibited by the Verticals Reg., in Section 5.C.vi.

[118] *Konica* [1988] OJ L78/34.

[119] *Mercedes-Benz* [2002] OJ L257/1. This aspect of the case was annulled on appeal, Case T-325/01, *DaimlerChrysler v. Commission* [2005] ECR II-3319, on the grounds that the agreements were of agency, see Section 2.C.ii, pp. 773–776.

[120] Case T-77/92, *Parker Pen v. Commission* [1994] ECR II-549; Case 19/77, *Miller v. Commission* [1978] ECR 131.

[121] *Yamaha* IP/03/1028.

[122] Case C-277/87, *Sandoz Prodotti Farmaceutici SpA v. Commission* [1990] ECR I-45.

[123] See *Volkswagen* [1998] OJ L124/60, on appeal Case T-62/98, *Volkswagen AG v. Commission* [2000] ECR II-2707, the appeal to the CJ was dismissed, see Case C-338/00 P, *Volkswagen AG v. Commission* [2003] ECR I-9189, and, e.g., *Peugeot* IP/05/1227, *aff'd* (but fine reduced) Case T-450/05, *Peugeot v. Commission* [2009] ECR II-2533.

[124] *Peugeot* IP/05/1227, *aff'd* (but fine reduced) Case T-450/05, *Peugeot v. Commission* [2009] ECR II-2533. In this case the discriminatory bonus system was backed up by a threat to reduce supplies to exporting dealers.

[125] Case T-38/92, *All Weather Sports Benelux v. Commission* [1994] II-211 and Case T-43/92, *Dunlop Slazenger v. Commission* [1994] ECR II-441.

[126] *Tretorn* [1994] OJ L378/45, *Hasselblad AG* [1982] OJ L161/18.

[127] *Zanussi* [1978] OJ L322/26; Case 31/85, *ETA Fabriques d'Ébauches v. DK Investments SA* [1985] ECR 3933. Guarantees can be limited to products sold by an authorised distributor of a selective distribution system, however, see Case C-376/92, *Metro v. Cartier* [1994] ECR I-15, paras. 32–34.

[128] *The Distillers Company Ltd* [1978] OJ L50/16, on appeal Case 30/78, *Distillers Company v. Commission* [1980] ECR 2229; and see *Distillers Company plc (Red Label)* [1983] OJ C245/3; *Newitt/Dunlop Slazenger International* [1992] OJ L131/32, on appeal Case T-38/92, *All Weather Sports Benelux v. Commission* [1994] ECR II-211 and Case T-43/92, *Dunlop Slazenger v. Commission* [1994] ECR II-441; and Case C-501/06 P, *GlaxoSmithKline Services Unlimited v. Commission* [2009] I-9291, see Chap. 4.

[129] Case T-175/95, *BASF Coating AG v. Commission* [1999] ECR II-1581.

[130] *Volkswagen* [1998] OJ L124/60, on appeal Case T-62/98, *Volkswagen AG v. Commission* [2000] ECR II-2707, and Case C-338/00 P, *Volkswagen AG v. Commission* [2003] ECR I-9189.

[131] *JCB* [2002] OJ L69/1. This aspect of the decision was upheld on appeal, Case T-67/01, *JCB Service v. Commission* [2004] ECR II-49, *aff'd* Case C-167/04 P, *JCB Service v. Commission* [2006] ECR I-8935.

where foreign customers are required to pay a deposit to the producer not required of national consumers.[132]

The Commission has taken these kinds of practices very seriously in the past and, where it can establish that the practice is a result of an agreement or concerted practice and is not simply a policy unilaterally pursued by one of the parties,[133] undertakings in breach can expect high fines. For example: in VW[134] the Commission imposed fines of €102 million (reduced to €90 million on appeal)[135] in respect of a wide range of contractual practices designed to prevent distributors selling outside their contractual territory; and in Nintendo,[136] the Commission imposed a fine of €167.8 million on Nintendo and seven of its European distributors for colluding through agreements and/or concerted practices to prevent exports from low-priced to high-priced countries. The Commission stated:

Contrary to the Commission's policy in respect of exclusive distribution that passive sales are always to be allowed, the territorial protection awarded to exclusive distributors was thereby enhanced to a state of absolute territorial protection and in each territory all competition facing the distributor of the products in that territory was eliminated. As a result, intra-brand competition was severely restricted and the single market partitioned...Because their object is to restrict competition, it is not necessary to consider the actual effects upon competition.[137]

In Pierre Fabre v. Président de l'Autorité de la concurrence[138] the CJ held that an agreement incorporating a ban, or de facto ban, on internet selling considerably reduces the ability of a distributor to sell the contractual products outside its area of activity and is 'liable to restrict competition'.[139] As the CJ did not consider that the ban on internet selling in that case constituted a proportionate measure to achieve a legitimate aim it considered it to constitute a restriction 'by object'.[140]

(iv) Other Object Restraints and *Pierre Fabre* and *Allianz Hungária*

In Chapter 4 it is seen that there is no list or finite list of object restraints and that the category may be expanded to cover all restraints capable, taking account of the objectives and context of the case, of having a sufficiently harmful impact on competition. The Commission takes the view that all of the 'hardcore' restraints set out in Article 4 of the Verticals Regulation (which also include prohibitions on active or passive selling and on cross-selling by members of a selective distribution system[141] and certain restrictions on components suppliers) are restrictive of competition by object, but the determination is of course for the EU courts to make. Further, some wording in recent judgments of the CJ

---

[132] Mercedes-Benz [2002] OJ L257/1. This aspect of the case was annulled on appeal, Case T-325/01, DaimlerChrysler v. Commission [2005] ECR II-3319.

[133] See Case T-41/96, Bayer AG v. Commission, [2000] ECR II-3383, aff'd Cases C-2 and 3/01 P, [2004] ECR I-23, see Chap. 3.

[134] Volkswagen [1998] OJ L124/60.

[135] Case T-62/98, Volkswagen AG v. Commission [2000] ECR II-2707 (essentially the fine was reduced because the GC did not consider that the breach had been established for the full period found by the Commission), the appeal to the CJ was dismissed, see Case C-338/00 P, Volkswagen AG v. Commission [2003] ECR I-9189.

[136] [2003] OJ L255/33, aff'd (but fines reduced), Case T-12/03, Itochu v. Commission [2009] ECR II-909 and Case T-13/03, Nintendo and Nintendo of Europe v. Commission [2009] ECR II-975, Case C-260/09 P, Activision Blizzard Germany GmbH v. Commission, 10 February 2011.

[137] Case T-13/03, Nintendo and Nintendo of Europe v. Commission [2009] ECR II-975, para. 331. See also Apple/iTunes IP/08/22, where the Commission welcomed Apple's announcement to equalise prices for music downloads from iTunes in Europe.

[138] Case C-439/09, 13 October 2011.

[139] Pierre Fabre v. Président de l'Autorité de la concurrence, Case C-439/09, 13 October 2011, para. 38.

[140] Pierre Fabre v. Président de l'Autorité de la concurrence, Case C-439/09, 13 October 2011, para. 39.

[141] See Case 86/62, Hasselblad v. Commission [1984] ECR 883, para. 46 ('As the Commission rightly points out, a prohibition of sales between authorized dealers constitutes a restriction of their economic freedom and, consequently, a restriction of competition').

indicate that the category may be more expansive than has generally been thought and, in particular, may encompass all selective distribution systems which are not objectively justified—that is necessary to achieve a legitimate aim. If this is correct a series of structured steps must be taken before it can be determined whether a selective distribution system automatically violates Article 101(1) or falls outside it altogether (see the discussion of *Pierre Fabre* v. *Président de l'Autorité de la concurrence* in Section 4.B.iv.d).[142]

In *Allianz Hungária Biztosító Zrt, Generali-Providencia Biztosító Zrt v. Gazdasági Versenyhivatal*,[143] the CJ also made it clear that as vertical restrictions could have particularly significant restrictive potential, the agreements, their objectives, and context had to be examined before the national court could determine whether a national court should classify it as restrictive by object or not.[144] This case involved proceedings which had been brought by the Hungarian competition authority, GVH, in relation to a series of bilateral vertical agreements concluded annually between Hungarian insurance companies and car dealer/repairers. Under the terms of the agreement hourly fees for repair work were agreed but this rate was increased if the dealers (which also acted as agents selling different insurance products) sold a specific percentage of insurance products of the given insurance company. The individual rates charged by repairers were based on prices for hourly repair rates recommended by the trade association for car repairers, GÉMOSZ. The GVH concluded that the arrangements had as their object the restriction of competition and imposed significant fines.

Following judicial proceedings in the Hungarian courts the Hungarian Supreme Court referred to the CJ the question of whether:

bilateral agreements between an insurance company and individual car repairers, or between an insurance company and a car repairers' association, under which the hourly repair charge paid by the insurance company to the repairer for the repair of vehicles insured by the insurance company depends, among other things, on the number and percentage of insurance policies taken out with the insurance company through the repairer, acting as the insurance broker for the insurance company in question, qualify as agreements which have as their object the prevention, restriction or distortion of competition, and thus contravene Article 101(1) TFEU?'

The CJ held that in considering whether the agreements at issue were restrictive by object account had to be taken of a number of facts, including that the agreements: linked the dealers' remuneration and the insurance broker function, were designed to increase the market shares of Generali and Allianz, and were concluded on the basis of 'recommended prices' established in decisions taken by GÉMOSZ. In particular, the CJ held that the insurance companies by concluding agreements with GÉMOSZ could be treated as confirming the decision of GÉMOSZ to recommend prices, which had as its object the restriction of competition, and rendering those agreements as restrictive by object.

Case C-32/11, *Allianz Hungária Biztosító Zrt, Generali-Providencia Biztosító Zrt* v. *Gazdasági Versenyhivatal*, 14 March 2013

36 In order to determine whether an agreement involves a restriction of competition 'by object', regard must be had to the content of its provisions, its objectives and the economic and legal context of which it forms a part (see *GlaxoSmithKline Services and Others* v *Commission and Others*, paragraph 58; *Football*

---

[142] See also the discussion of Case C-8/08, *T-Mobile Netherlands BV* v. *Raad van bestuur van de Nederlandse Mededingingsautoriteit* [2009] ECR I-4529 in Chaps 4 and 9.

[143] Case C-32/11, 14 March 2013.

[144] *Allianz Hungária Biztosító Zrt, Generali-Providencia Biztosító Zrt* v. *Gazdasági Versenyhivatal*, Case C-32/11, 14 March 2013, para. 48.

Association Premier League and Others, paragraph 136; and *Pierre Fabre Dermo-Cosmétique*, paragraph 35). When determining that context, it is also appropriate to take into consideration the nature of the goods or services affected, as well as the real conditions of the functioning and structure of the market or markets in question (see *Expedia*, paragraph 21 and the case-law cited).

37 In addition, although the parties' intention is not a necessary factor in determining whether an agreement is restrictive, there is nothing prohibiting the competition authorities, the national courts or the Courts of the European Union from taking that factor into account (see, to that effect, *GlaxoSmithKline Services and Others* v *Commission and Others*, paragraph 58 and the case-law cited).

38 The Court has, moreover, already held that, in order for the agreement to be regarded as having an anti-competitive object, it is sufficient that it has the potential to have a negative impact on competition, that is to say, that it be capable in an individual case of resulting in the prevention, restriction or distortion of competition within the internal market. Whether and to what extent, in fact, such an effect results can only be of relevance for determining the amount of any fine and assessing any claim for damages (see *T-Mobile Netherlands and Others*, paragraph 31).

39 Concerning the agreements referred to in the question submitted, it should be noted that they relate to the hourly charge to be paid by the insurance company to car dealers, acting as repair shops, for the repair of cars in the event of accidents. They provide that that charge is increased in accordance with the number and percentage of insurance contracts that the dealer sells for that company.

40 Such agreements therefore link the remuneration for the car repair service to that for the car insurance brokerage. The linkage of those two different services is possible because of the fact that the dealers act in relation to the insurers in a dual capacity, namely as intermediaries or brokers, offering car insurance to their customers at the time of sale or repair of vehicles, and as repair shops, repairing vehicles after accidents on behalf of the insurers.

41 However, while the establishment of such a link between two activities which are in principle independent does not automatically mean that the agreement concerned has as its object the restriction of competition, it can nevertheless constitute an important factor in determining whether that agreement is by its nature injurious to the proper functioning of normal competition, which is the case, in particular, where the independence of those activities is necessary for that functioning.

42 Moreover, it is necessary to take account of the fact that such an agreement is likely to affect not only one, but two markets, in this case those of car insurance and car repair services, and that its object must be determined with respect to the two markets concerned.

43 In that regard, it must, first, be noted that, in contrast to the view apparently held by Allianz and Generali, the fact that both cases concern vertical relationships in no way excludes the possibility that the agreement at issue in the main proceedings constitutes a restriction of competition 'by object'. While vertical agreements are, by their nature, often less damaging to competition than horizontal agreements, they can, nevertheless, in some cases, also have a particularly significant restrictive potential. The Court has thus already held on several occasions that a vertical agreement had as its object the restriction of competition (see Joined Cases 56/64 and 58/64 *Consten and Grundig* v *Commission* [1966] ECR 429; Case 19/77 *Miller International Schallplatten* v *Commission* [1978] ECR 131; Case 243/83 *Binon* [1985] ECR 2015; and *Pierre Fabre Dermo-Cosmétique*).

44 Next, with regard to determining the object of the agreements at issue in the main proceedings with respect to the car insurance market, it should be noted that, by such agreements, insurance companies such as Allianz and Generali aim to maintain or increase their market shares.

45 It is not disputed that, if there was a horizontal agreement or a concerted practice between those two companies designed to partition the market, such an agreement or practice would have to be treated as a restriction by object and would also result in the unlawfulness of the vertical agreements concluded in order to implement that agreement or practice. Allianz and Generali dispute however that they acted in agreement or concert and claim that the contested decision found that there was no such agreement or practice. It is for the referring court to check the accuracy of those claims and, to the extent that it is

enabled under domestic law, to determine whether there is enough evidence to establish the existence of an agreement or concerted practice between Allianz and Generali.

46 Nevertheless, even if there is no agreement or concerted practice between those insurance companies, it will still be necessary to determine whether, taking account of the economic and legal context of which they form a part, the vertical agreements at issue in the main proceedings are sufficiently injurious to competition on the car insurance market as to amount to a restriction of competition by object.

47 That could in particular be the case where, as is claimed by the Hungarian Government, domestic law requires that dealers acting as intermediaries or insurance brokers must be independent from the insurance companies. That government claims, in that regard, that those dealers do not act on behalf of an insurer, but on behalf of the policyholder and it is their job to offer the policyholder the insurance which is the most suitable for him amongst the offers of various insurance companies. It is for the referring court to determine whether, in those circumstances and in light of the expectations of those policyholders, the proper functioning of the car insurance market is likely to be significantly disrupted by the agreements at issue in the main proceedings.

48 Furthermore, those agreements would also amount to a restriction of competition by object in the event that the referring court found that it is likely that, having regard to the economic context, competition on that market would be eliminated or seriously weakened following the conclusion of those agreements. In order to determine the likelihood of such a result, that court should in particular take into consideration the structure of that market, the existence of alternative distribution channels and their respective importance and the market power of the companies concerned.

49 Finally, with regard to determining the object of the agreements at issue in the main proceedings with respect to the car repair service market, it is necessary to take account of the fact that those agreements appear to have been concluded on the basis of 'recommended prices' established in the three decisions taken by GÉMOSZ from 2003 to 2005. In that context, it is for the referring court to determine the exact nature and scope of those decisions (see, to that effect, Case C-260/07 *Pedro IV Servicios* [2009] ECR I-2437, paragraphs 78 and 79).

50 In the event that that court holds that the decisions taken by GÉMOSZ during that period in fact had as their object the restriction of competition by harmonising hourly charges for car repairs and that, by the agreements at issue, the insurance companies voluntarily confirmed those decisions, which can be assumed where the insurance company concluded an agreement directly with GÉMOSZ, the unlawfulness of those decisions would vitiate those agreements, which would then also be considered a restriction of competition by object.

51 In the light of all of the foregoing considerations, the answer to the question submitted is that Article 101(1) TFEU must be interpreted as meaning that agreements whereby car insurance companies come to bilateral arrangements, either with car dealers acting as car repair shops or with an association representing those dealers, concerning the hourly charge to be paid by the insurance company for repairs to vehicles insured by it, stipulating that that charge depends, inter alia, on the number and percentage of insurance contracts that the dealer has sold as intermediary for that company, can be considered a restriction of competition 'by object' within the meaning of that provision, where, following a concrete and individual examination of the wording and aim of those agreements and of the economic and legal context of which they form a part, it is apparent that they are, by their very nature, injurious to the proper functioning of normal competition on one of the two markets concerned.

In addition, an issue that is beginning to arise before the Commission and NCAs is how certain practices which resemble RPM, in particular price relationship agreements or contracts that reference rivals, are to be characterised and/or analysed under Article 101 generally and, specifically, under Article 101(1). Indeed, in September 2012 the UK's Office of Fair Trading (OFT) published a report prepared by Laboratorio di Economia, Antitrust, Regolamentazione (LEAR) on the competition implications of price relationship agreements.[145] Further, in a case concerning *Tobacco*[146] the OFT had examined and held that bilateral vertical agreements concluded between two tobacco manufacturers and their retailers, under which retailers agreed to set retail prices for cigarettes and other tobacco products in accordance with set 'parity and differential requirements' relating to competing linked brands, restricted competition by object (for the purposes of the Competition Act 1998, the UK equivalent of Article 101). In so ruling, the OFT relied on its finding that the arrangements had a restrictive nature in the legal and economic context in which they operated and stated that the scope of object infringements should not be interpreted narrowly. It also imposed huge fines, totalling £225 million, on the parties involved. As, during appeal proceedings, the OFT significantly refined its case, the Competition Appeal Tribunal annulled the decision of the OFT, insofar as it related to the applicants, and did not have to rule on the important question of whether the OFT had been correct to categorise the restraints as restrictive by object.[147] In *e-books*[148] the Commission also investigated whether five international publishers and Apple had engaged in anti-competitive practices—by switching distribution arrangements from the wholesale model to agency contracts containing a retail price most favoured nation (MFN) clause—which had an impact on the sale of e-books. The Commission was concerned in this case that the undertakings had contrived to limit retail price competition for e-books as under the arrangements the publishers set retail prices but had to lower prices for an e-book to match a lower retail price charged by any retailer. In the end the Commission accepted commitments from four of the publishers and Apple to terminate existing agency agreements and refrain from adopting price MFN clauses. The decision did not, however, take a position on the compatibility of the vertical agency agreements themselves with Article 101, as it focused on a suspected concerted practice between the publishers, with the help of Apple. The arrangements thus had a horizontal aspect as well as a vertical one.

(v) Object Restrictions—A Need for a Rethink?

Given a greater acceptance that vertical restraints on intra-brand competition (including ATP and RPM provisions) may be imposed for pro-competitive reasons, it has been questioned whether it is right to continue to treat these (or any) vertical restraints as object restraints, which are presumed to restrict competition. Rather, in light of the potential of these restraints to enhance efficiency, should it not be for the Commission, or other person trying to prove the same, to demonstrate the anti-competitive effects of the provisions before they are found to infringe Article 101(1)?

In the US, challenges in the 1960s and the 1970s to the Supreme Court's rulings that many vertical intra-brand restraints, including minimum RPM,[149] maximum RPM,[150] and customer and territorial restraints,[151] were illegal per se under section 1 of the Sherman Act of 1890 led the Court to rethink and review the rules and, eventually, to disband each of the per se prohibitions. In 1977, in its landmark opinion in *Continental TV, Inc. v. GTE Sylvania*,[152] the Supreme Court overruled the per se rule against non-price intra-brand restraints and instated the rule of reason as the prevailing and presumptive standard of antitrust analysis. In so doing the Court accepted that the market impact of a vertical *non-price* intra-brand restriction (in that case, a location clause) was complex because of its

---

[145] See, OFT1438, 'Can "Fair" Prices be Unfair? A Review of Price Relationship Agreements' September 2012, <http://www.oft.gov.uk/shared_oft/research/OFT1438.pdf>.

[146] Case CE/2596–03, *Tobacco*, 15 April 2010.

[147] Cases 1160–1165/1/1/10 [2011] CAT 41, see A. Jones and A. Turati, 'The UK Tobacco Case: Identifying Restrictions by Object in Vertical Agreements' (2012) *JECLAP* 287.

[148] MEMO/12/983, see also Chap. 13.

[149] *Dr Miles Medical Co* v. *John D Park & Sons Co* 220 US 373 (1911).

[150] See *Keifer-Stewart Co* v. *Joseph E Seagram & Sons Inc* 340 US 211 (1951) and *Albrecht* v. *Herald Co* 390 US 145 (1968).

[151] *United States* v. *Arnold, Schwinn & Co* 388 US 365, 376 (1967).

[152] 433 US 36 (1977).

ability simultaneously to reduce intra-brand competition and to stimulate inter-brand competition. The Court held that inter-brand competition was the primary concern of antitrust law,[153] emphasised the distribution efficiencies brought about by vertical restraints,[154] and concluded that any anti-competitive effects resulting from vertical non-price intra-brand restraints could adequately be identified and judged under the rule of reason.[155] Subsequently, in *State Oil v. Khan*,[156] the Court overruled the per se rule against maximum RPM and in *Leegin Creative Leather Products Inc. v. PSKS, Inc., DBA Kay's Kloset… Kay's Shoes*[157] the Supreme Court held that fixed and minimum RPM should also be analysed under the rule of reason. Very broadly, the majority[158] accepted that as the economics literature was 'replete' with pro-competitive justifications for a manufacturer's use of RPM (in particular, where necessary to stimulate inter-brand competition by, for example, preventing free-riding on a dealer's services or reputation, to allow suppliers to open up and enter new markets, to achieve a desired level of investment in retail services, to deal with demand uncertainty at the retail level, and/or to ensure high prices where such prices constitute part of a product's allure (to encourage higher prices for branded, luxury goods))[159] the impact of RPM should be analysed under the rule of reason (the accepted standard for testing whether a practice restrains trade in violation of section 1) even though it might sometimes be anti-competitive.[160] In stark contrast to the position that existed in 1976, therefore, minimum RPM, maximum RPM, and all non-price intra-brand restraints are illegal in the US only if proved to be in unreasonable restraint of trade under a rule of reason analysis.

The dramatic evolution of US law in this area has fuelled the debate about the strict approach against ATP and, especially RPM, in the EU. Indeed, the view could be taken that the economic arguments accepted by the majority in *Leegin* also suggest that these types of restraints are inappropriate for categorisation as restrictive by object. Rather, a fuller analysis should be required in each case to determine whether the effect of such conduct is in fact restrictive of competition (a theory of harm should be demonstrated). Even if normatively this were considered to be correct, it seems most unlikely in reality that the CJ could be persuaded that such a change in approach would be desirable. Not only have vertical agreements containing ATP or RPM provisions been characterised time after time as restraints which have as their object the restriction of competition, but the CJ has consistently been reluctant to hold that the characterisation can be contradicted by an argument that the parties pursued a legitimate object or on the basis that legal and economic context implies that it may not in fact restrict competition.[161] Indeed, in *GlaxoSmithKline Services Unlimited v. Commission*[162] the CJ denied that an agreement limiting parallel trade could only be found to have had as its object the restriction of competition, insofar as it could be presumed to deprive final consumers of the advantages of effective competition.

---

[153] 433 US 36, fn. 19 (1977).

[154] It thus indicated that non-competition factors, such as the protection of property rights and the autonomy of independent dealers, should not be relevant to the appraisal

[155] On remand, the location clauses were found to be reasonable. The Ninth Circuit affirmed, stating that the plaintiff had to prove the unreasonableness of the restraint given its overall effect on intra- and inter-brand competition (simply proving a lessening of intra-brand competition does not shift the burden of justification to the defendant), *Continental TV Inc v. GTE Sylvania Inc.*, 694 F.2d 1132 (9th Cir. 1982), and see E. M. Fox, L. A. Sullivan, and R. J. R. Peritz, *Cases and Materials on US Antitrust in Global Context* (Thomson West, 2004), 517.

[156] 522 US 3 (1997).

[157] 551 US 887 (2007). For a fuller analysis of the case, see, e.g., A. Jones, 'Completion of the Revolution in Antitrust Doctrine on Restricted Distribution—*Leegin* and its Implications for EC Competition Law' (2008) *Ant Bull* 903.

[158] Roberts C. J. and Scalia, Thomas, and Alito, JJ joined in the Opinion.

[159] B. Orbach, 'Antitrust Vertical Myopia: The Allure of High Prices' (2008) 50 *Arizona Law Review* 261–287, Arizona Legal Studies, Discussion Paper No. 07-25.

[160] And not the per se rule which was confined to restraints that always or almost always tend to restrict competition, have manifestly anti-competitive effects, and lack any redeeming virtue.

[161] See Chap. 4, especially Section 3.D, pp. 205–232.

[162] Case C-501/06 P, [2009] I-9291, discussed in Chap. 4.

Further, it seems most unlikely that the CJ could, more radically, be persuaded, as *Leegin* persuaded the US Supreme Court, that either restraint is no longer a suitable candidate for 'object' analysis. It only rarely reverses previous rulings[163] and it seems doubtful that it would see fit to do so in relation to either of these situations. Not only do the objectives of the EU competition rules run more broadly than those of the US antitrust laws[164] (in the EU, cases on vertical restraints have been influenced not only by concerns about the welfare of consumers but also by the single market objective and a concern about protecting the process of rivalry between firms on a market, including at the distribution level),[165] but it has been questioned whether or not the Supreme Court in *Leegin* was right to have dismantled the per se rule against RPM.[166] In particular, proponents of the per se rule (or at least a (rebuttable) presumption of illegality for RPM) have pointed to evidence that RPM may be used to facilitate, encourage, and/or allow collusion (explicit or tacit) between retailers or manufacturers,[167] leads to a rise in consumer prices,[168] eliminates innovative and dynamic competition from discounting retailers,[169] might be used to 'appease dealer interests in excess profits or the quiet life',[170] and/or may even produce anti-competitive effects in markets where there is competition upstream and downstream.[171] They have also raised concern that the free-rider argument, used to justify many vertical restraints on intra-brand competition, is frequently exaggerated and in fact applies only to relatively few products.[172] Indeed, concerns that RPM might cause anti-competitive effects with some regularity led four justices in *Leegin* to dissent. Justice Breyer, writing for the minority, noted

[163] See Chap. 4.

[164] Which focus on restraints on inter-brand competition.

[165] The EU institutions thus appear to 'continue to see merit in protecting, albeit to a significantly lesser degree than in the past, the process ... of competition rather than focusing exclusively on the direct or probable economic effects of agreements. This means that in certain circumstances agreements which have a neutral or even *net positive* effect consumer welfare and allocative efficiency can fall within the scope of Article 81(1)', J. Faull and A. Nikpay (eds.), *The EC Law of Competition* (2nd edn, Oxford University Press, 2007), para 3.142.

[166] See, e.g., W. S. Comanor, 'Vertical Price-Fixing, Vertical Market Restrictions, and the New Antitrust Policy' (1984–1985) 98 *Harv LR* 983; R. Pitofsky, 'In Defense of Discounters: The No-Frills Case for a Per Se Rule Against Vertical Price Fixing' (1983) 71 *Geo LJ* 1487; M. L. Lao, 'Free Riding: An Overstated, and Unconvincing, Explanation for Resale Price Maintenance', Seton Hall Law School, Public Law and Legal Theory Research Paper Series. Available at SSRN: <http://ssrn.com/abstract=1024221>; and amici curiae brief filed by 37 states supporting the respondent before the Supreme Court in *Leegin*.

[167] See, e.g., D. O'Brien and G. Shaffer, 'Vertical Control with Bilateral Contracts' (1992) *RAND Journal of Economics* 299; B. Jullien and P. Rey, 'Resale Price Maintenance and Collusion' (2007) 38(4) *RAND Journal of Economics* 983; Patrick Rey and Thibaud Vergé, 'Resale Price Maintenance and Horizontal Cartel', CMPO Discussion Paper 02/047, 2004, and L. Peeperkorn, 'RPM and its Alleged Efficiencies' (2008) 4 *European Competition Journal* 1.

[168] M. Allain and C. Chambolle, *Anti-Competitive Effects of Resale-Below Cost Laws* (Working Papers hal-00367492_vl, 2007).

[169] If RPM is widespread, retailers engaging in significant price discounts will be eliminated from the market, consumers may be deprived of innovative retailing and price discounting so that prices may increase, price competition between suppliers may be softened, and tacit collusion between suppliers may result. See, e.g., T. R. Overstreet, *Resale Price Maintenance: Economic Theories and Empirical Evidence* (Federal Trade Commission Bureau of Economics staff report, November 1983). This report indicated that the more widespread practice of RPM in Europe delayed the arrival of supermarkets. For a detailed discussion of the pro- and anti-competitive effects of RPM, see the majority and dissenting opinions of Kennedy and Breyer JJ respectively in *Leegin Creative Leather Products Inc v. PSKS Inc., DBA Kay's Kloset ... Kay's Shoes*, 551 US 877 (2007).

[170] P. Areeda and H. Hovenkamp, *Antitrust Law: An Analysis of Antitrust Principles and Their Applications* (3rd edn, Aspen Publishers, 2004), 35. See also Scherer and Ross, *Industrial Market Structure and Economic Performance* (cited in n. 8) 550 and Guidelines, para. 224.

[171] See G. Shaffer, 'Anti-Competitive Effects of RPM (Resale Price Maintenance) Agreements in Fragmented Markets), OFT report, February 2013.

[172] It applies only to pre-sales services (not post-sales services). Pre-sales services are unnecessary where consumers know what they want to buy (see the extract from Comanor, 'Vertical Price-Fixing, Vertical Market Restrictions, and the New Antitrust Policy' (cited in n. 63) and set out in Section 2.C.iii.c) and the free rider argument is justified only in purchases of relatively high value. 'The consumer who secures from her friendly local hardware store a ten-minute demonstration of a $1.79 potato peeler's merits and then makes a special trip to the discount house to buy one is a candidate for something other than center stage in the economic theory of shopping behaviour', Scherer and Ross, *Industrial Market Structure and Economic Performance* (cited in n. 8) 552.

that US history provided empirical support for the view that RPM led to considerably higher retail prices[173] and that economists generally concurred on this point.[174] In contrast, he found no satisfactory answer to the question as to when and how often benefits, such as the prevention of free-riding, were likely to occur[175] and considered that courts would have extreme difficulty in identifying instances in which benefits were likely to outweigh harm. As antitrust law should be informed by economics but could not always replicate economists' (sometimes conflicting) views, he concluded that it would sometimes be acceptable to provide a rule of per se unlawfulness to a business practice which could at times produce benefits. The Commission, although recognising that RPM may sometimes lead to efficiencies which can be considered under Article 101(3), echoes these concerns about anti-competitive effects in its Guidelines and supports the view that RPM should be presumed to infringe Article 101(1). This view seems to be supported by other competition EU authorities.[176] The Guidelines set out the Commission's core concerns about RPM.

224. RPM may restrict competition in a number of ways. Firstly, RPM may facilitate collusion between suppliers by enhancing price transparency in the market, thereby making it easier to detect whether a supplier deviates from the collusive equilibrium by cutting its price. RPM also undermines the incentive for the supplier to cut its price to its distributors, as the fixed resale price will prevent it from benefiting from expanded sales. This negative effect is in particular plausible if the market is prone to collusive outcomes, for instance if the manufacturers form a tight oligopoly, and a significant part of the market is covered by RPM agreements. Secondly, by eliminating intra-brand price competition, RPM may also facilitate collusion between the buyers, i.e. at the distribution level. Strong or well organised distributors may be able to force/convince one or more suppliers to fix their resale price above the competitive level and thereby help them to reach or stabilize a collusive equilibrium. This loss of price competition seems especially problematic when the RPM is inspired by the buyers, whose collective horizontal interests can be expected to work out negatively for consumers. Thirdly, RPM may more in general soften competition between manufacturers and/or between retailers, in particular when manufacturers use the same distributors to distribute their products and RPM is applied by all or many of them. Fourthly, the immediate effect of RPM will be that all or certain distributors are prevented from lowering their sales price for that particular brand. In other words, the direct effect of RPM is a price increase. Fifthly, RPM may lower the pressure on the margin of the manufacturer, in particular where the manufacturer has a commitment problem, i.e. where he has an interest in lowering the price charged to subsequent distributors. In such a situation, the manufacturer may prefer to agree to RPM, so as to help it to commit not to lower the price for subsequent distributors and to reduce the pressure on its own margin. Sixthly, RPM may be implemented by a manufacturer with market power to foreclose smaller rivals. The increased margin that RPM may offer distributors, may entice the latter to favour the particular brand over rival brands when advising customers, even where such advice is not in the interest of these customers, or not to sell these rival brands at all. Lastly, RPM may reduce dynamism and innovation at the distribution level. By preventing price competition between different distributors, RPM may prevent more efficient retailers from entering the market and/or acquiring sufficient scale with low prices. It also may prevent or hinder the entry and expansion of distribution formats based on low prices, such as price discounters.

[173] Breyer J stated that after the repeal of the Fair Trade Acts in the US (permitting RPM in many states), FTC staff, after studying numerous price surveys, wrote that the surveys indicated that RPM in most cases increased the prices of products sold with RPM, Bureau of Economic Staff Report to the FTC, T. Overstreet, 'Resale Price Maintenance: Economic Theories and Empirical Evidence', 169 (1983), 551 US 877, 127 S.Ct. 2705, 2727 (2007).

[174] See, e.g., F. H. Easterbrook, 'Vertical Arrangements and the Rule of Reason' (1984) 53 *Antitrust Law Journal* 135 ('There is no such thing as a free lunch; the manufacturers can't get the dealer to do more without increasing the dealer's margin'); Pamela Jones Harbour's Open Letter to the Supreme Court, 26 February 2007 ('Vertical minimum price fixing is almost always harmful to consumers. It creates no incentive for distributors and retailers to become more cost-effective in the delivery of goods and services to consumers. Indeed, it transfers to consumers the consequences of inefficient business practices: it typically leads to higher prices without bestowing countervailing benefits'); and amici curiae brief filed by 37 states supporting the respondent before the Supreme Court in *Leegin*.

[175] 'All this is to say that the ultimate question is not whether, but how much, "free riding" of this sort take place. And, after reading the briefs, I must answer that question with an uncertain "sometimes"', Breyer J 551 US 877, 127 S.Ct. 2705, 2730 (2007).

[176] See n. 101.

In addition, arguably, there is not such a pressing need for such a dramatic change in EU approach at the Article 101(1) stage, as a classification of a restraint as an 'object' restraint obviously has different consequences from a finding of per se illegality in the US. A finding of per se illegality does not allow any justifications for the conduct to be raised and considered (there is a conclusive presumption of unreasonableness). In the EU, however, even if an agreement has as its object the restriction of competition it is still in theory feasible to argue that the objectives or context of the case makes the presumption inappropriate on the facts of the case. Further, even where the presumption applies it will only violate Article 101(1) if the restriction of competition is 'appreciable' (but see the CJ's judgment in *Expedia*) and if it does not satisfy the conditions of Article 101(3).[177] It is not therefore technically illegal per se but in most cases shifts the burden to the parties to justify it under Article 101(3). Nonetheless, the Commission has been extremely unwilling in the past to accept that an object or hardcore restraint can escape the Article 101(1) prohibition on the grounds that it does not appreciably restrict competition or satisfies the conditions of Article 101(3) (so that, in practice, the restraints are perceived to be illegal per se). Rather, the Commission has equated object restraints with a list of hardcore restraints which it considers are both presumed to violate Article 101(1) and presumed *not* to satisfy the conditions of Article 101(3).[178] In the run-up to the adoption of the new Verticals Regulation and Guidelines, one of the critical issues that arose was whether the Commission should relax its approach to hardcore restraints under Article 101(3) and, if so, how that change could be manifested.[179]

B. ANALYSING THE RESTRICTIVE 'EFFECT' OF VERTICAL RESTRAINTS

(i) Introduction

Where an agreement does not have as its object the restriction of competition, it is necessary to look at the *effect* of the agreement. Only then can it be determined whether or not competition has in fact been restricted. Despite the strict approach taken by the Commission initially, more recent decisions, the Guidelines, and the Article 101(3) Guidelines demonstrate that, in line with case law, a more principled economic approach is adopted when applying Article 101(1). In particular, the Article 101(3) Guidelines indicate that in effect cases it must be established that the agreement affects inter-brand or intra-brand competition, i.e. that it affects 'actual or potential competition to such an extent that on the relevant market negative effects on prices, output, innovation or the variety or quality of goods and services can be expected with a reasonable degree of probability'[180] or it restricts, without objective justification, distributors from competing with each other.[181] Further that if, following these principles, the transaction is not restrictive of competition, restraints 'ancillary' to the main non-restrictive transaction also fall outside Article 101(1).[182]

In paragraphs 96–230 of the Guidelines the Commission sets out its enforcement policy in relation to vertical restraints in individual cases (i.e. in relation to those agreements which will not benefit from the new Verticals Regulation). The Commission explicitly recognises that '[v]ertical

---

[177] See Section 5 and discussion of appreciability and Article 101(3) in Chap. 4.

[178] See Chap. 4 and Section 5, pp. 817–841.

[179] See also discussion in Section 5, pp. 817–841.

[180] Article 101(3) Guidelines, para. 24. This could be because the agreement restricts actual or potential competition between the parties or between any one of the parties and third parties that could have existed absent the agreement, paras. 25–6.

[181] Thus according to the Commission two counterfactuals may need to be used—one to determine whether the agreement restricts inter-brand competition (whether the agreement restricts actual or potential competition that would have existed without the agreement) and one to determine whether it restricts intra-brand competition (whether the agreement restricts actual or potential competition that would have existed in the absence of the contractual restraints), see Chap. 4.

[182] Article 101(3) Guidelines, paras. 28–31 and see Chap. 4.

restraints are generally less harmful than horizontal restraints'[183] and states that it will adopt an economic approach in its application of Article 101. In paragraphs 111–121 the Commission sets out the factors it considers to be most important when assessing whether or not an agreement appreciably restricts competition under Article 101(1). The central enquiry focuses on the *market power* of the undertakings concerned:

111 ... The following factors are in particular relevant to establish whether a vertical agreement brings about an appreciable restriction of competition under Article 101(1):

    a) nature of the agreement;

    b) market position of the parties;

    c) market position of competitors;

    d) market position of buyers of the contract products;

    e) entry barriers;

    f) maturity of the market;

    g) level of trade;

    h) nature of the product;

    i) other factors.

112. The importance of individual factors may vary from cases to case and depends on all other factors. For instance, a high market share of the parties is usually a good indicator of market power, but in the case of low entry barriers it may not be indicative of market power. It is therefore not possible to provide firm rules on the importance of the individual factors...

The importance of these factors on individual assessment is fleshed out in further detail in paragraphs 113–121.

Subsequent sections consider the case law, decisional practice, and guidance on the question of how Article 101(1) applies to specific types of vertical agreements and restraint. It is stressed again, however, that the complex analysis demanded in effect cases will ordinarily be circumvented where the parties' market shares do not exceed 30 per cent, since in nearly all cases the block exemption should apply.

(ii) Single Branding Agreements and *Delimitis*

One of the most important of all of the Court's judgments in the context of distribution agreements is *Delimitis* v. *Henninger Bräu*.[184] In this case the Court had to give guidance to a national court asked to rule on the compatibility of a beer supply agreement with Article 101(1). It will be remembered (from Chapter 4) that the contract obliged the café proprietor to obtain his beer requirements from the brewer, Henninger Bräu (although once a fixed quantity had been bought, Delimitis was free to purchase beer from other Member States). Agreements such as this which oblige a buyer to obtain all, most, or a certain percentage or amount of its requirements from a named supplier frequently lead to efficiencies in distribution. A supplier is enabled to plan the number of sales it will make with greater precision, and distributors are encouraged actively to promote the supplier's product. Further, suppliers often confer reciprocal benefits (such as loans at below market rates, training, business and financial advice) on distributors who agree not to purchase a competitor's products. Obviously the supplier will wish to ensure that these benefits are not used to assist sales of competitors' products.

---

[183] Guidelines, para. 100.

[184] Case C-234/89, *Delimitis* v. *Henninger Bräu* [1991] ECR I-935 and see also discussion and extract set out in Chap. 4, Section 5.E.iii.

Since, however, these non-compete or quantity-forcing agreements prohibit or deter distributors from handling competitors' products, there is a concern that these agreements, or networks of similar agreements, might tie up outlets and preclude competitors (actual and potential) from gaining access to distributors (they have a direct impact on inter-brand competition by foreclosing the market to competing and potential suppliers). This worry is particularly acute in markets where access to the market is not easy on account of the existence of barriers to entry, such as planning restrictions or licensing requirements. Further, there is a concern that such agreements may restrict inter-brand competition by softening competition and facilitating collusion between suppliers (especially in case of cumulative use) or through a loss of in-store inter-brand competition.[185]

In *Delimitis*[186] the CJ recognised that an obligation imposed on the café proprietor to purchase most of its beer requirements from the brewer entailed advantages for both the supplier and the reseller. It set out guidelines for the national court to determine whether or not the effect of such an agreement foreclosed access to the market and so prevented, restricted, or distorted competition. This could be determined by, first, defining the relevant market and considering whether or not that market was foreclosed to other competitors or precluded expansion by existing competitors. If it was, secondly, it had to be determined whether or not the agreement in question restricted competition. It would only do so if the agreements concluded by that producer appreciably contributed to the foreclosure effect.

This case clearly demonstrates that in the absence of territorial exclusivity or RPM a careful analysis of the impact of the agreement on the market should be made. The Court focused its enquiry on the important question whether or not the agreement, alone or in conjunction with a network of similar agreements, would lead to a restriction of inter-brand competition. The Court considered that only where the agreement contributed to the foreclosure of the market and to a restriction of inter-brand competition would it be found to restrict competition within the meaning of Article 101(1).

The GC has adopted a similar approach in respect of agreements affecting the market for ice creams for impulse purchase. In *Langnese-Iglo GmbH v. Commission*,[187] the GC upheld a finding of the Commission that an agreement providing for the exclusive sale of ice creams for impulse purchase in retail outlets infringed Article 101(1) and could not be exempted under Article 101(3).[188] Similarly, in *Van den Bergh Foods v. Commission*[189] the GC upheld a finding that freezer exclusivity operated by HB in Ireland infringed Article 101(1) and did not meet the criteria of Article 101(3). The freezer exclusivity had the same effect as outlet exclusivity. In respect to the analysis required under Article 101(1) the GC reiterated that a *Delimitis*-type analysis was required.[190]

83. In order to determine whether HB's exclusive distribution agreements fall within the prohibition contained in Article [101(1)] of the Treaty, it is appropriate, in accordance with the case-law, to consider whether all the similar agreements entered into in the relevant market and the other features of the economic and legal context of the agreements at issue, show that those agreements cumulatively have the effect of denying access to that market to new competitors. If, on examination, that is found not to be the case, the individual agreements making up the bundle of agreements cannot impair competition within the meaning of Article [101(1)] of the Treaty. If, on the other hand, such examination reveals that it is difficult to gain access to the market, it is then necessary to assess the extent to which the agreements at issue contribute to the cumulative

---

[185] See Guidelines, para. 130.

[186] Case C-234/89, *Delimitis v. Henninger Bräu* [1991] ECR I-935. The relevant paragraphs of the judgment are set out in Chap. 4, Section 5.E.iii.

[187] Case T-7/93, [1995] ECR II-1533.

[188] *Langnese-Iglo GmbH* [1993] OJ L183/19, see especially paras. 94–95 and 101. See also *Schöller Lebensmittel GmbH & Co KG* [1993] OJ L183/1.

[189] Case T-65/98, [2003] ECR II-4653, aff'd Case C-552/03 P, *Unilever Bestfoods v. Commission* [2006] ECR I-9091.

[190] *Van den Bergh Foods v. Commission*, Case T-65/98, [2003] ECR II-4653, aff'd Case C-552/03 P, *Unilever Bestfoods v. Commission* [2006] ECR I-9091, paras. 84–85.

effect produced, on the basis that only those agreements which make a significant contribution to any partitioning of the market are prohibited (*Delimitis*, paragraphs 23 and 24, and *Langnese-Iglo* v. *Commission*, paragraph 99).

On the facts the Court considered that the Commission had proved to the required legal standard that there was evidence of demand for ice creams of other manufacturers but that freezer exclusivity had prevented retailers from stocking such competing ice creams. The network of HB's agreements and their supply of exclusive freezer cabinets had 'a considerable dissuasive effect on retailers with regard to the installation of their own cabinet or that of another manufacturer and operate de facto as a tie on sales outlets that have only HB freezer cabinets'.[191] It thus concluded that it was 'clear from an examination of the entirety of the similar distribution agreements concluded on the relevant market, and other evidence of the economic and legal context of which those agreements form part, that the distribution agreements concluded by HB are liable to have an appreciable effect on competition for the purposes of Article [101(1)] of the Treaty and contribute significantly to a foreclosure of the market'.[192]

The Commission's approach in the Guidelines is consistent with the Court's case law.[193] In particular, the Commission stresses the central importance in the appraisal of single branding agreements of examining: the capacity of the obligation to result in anti-competitive foreclosure of competitors and the market position of the supplier (considering the market power of the supplier and the market position of its competitors and their ability to compete on equal terms for each individual customer's entire demand); and the extent to, and the duration for, which the supplier applies a non-compete obligation. The foreclosure will be more significant the greater the tied market share and the longer the duration of the non-compete obligation.[194] The Commission takes the view that non-compete obligations for under one year by non-dominant companies are in general not considered to give rise to appreciable anti-competitive effects, non-compete clauses in excess of five years are generally unnecessary and will outweigh claimed efficiencies, and clauses imposing non-compete obligations of between one and five years will require a proper balancing of the pro- and anti-competitive effects.[195]

The Commission states that it does not anticipate a single or cumulative anti-competitive effect where the market share of the largest supplier is below 30 per cent and the market share of the five largest suppliers is below 50 per cent.[196] The Commission states that it will also take into account entry barriers, countervailing buyer power and the level of trade.[197]

In a series of cases subsequent to *Delimitis*, the Commission dealt with single branding agreements notified to it for exemption. In some decisions it found that single branding agreements infringed Article 101(1) and did not meet the Article 101(3) criteria,[198] in some cases it found that the agreements infringed Article 101(1) but met the Article 101(3) criteria,[199] and in some cases it found that

---

[191] Case T-65/98, [2003] ECR II-4653, *aff'd* Case C-552/03 P, *Unilever Bestfoods* v. *Commission* [2006] ECR I-9091, para. 98.

[192] *Van den Bergh Foods* v. *Commission*, Case T-65/98, [2003] ECR II-4653, *aff'd* Case C-552/03 P, *Unilever Bestfoods* v. *Commission* [2006] ECR I-9091, para. 118.

[193] See also Case C-214/99, *Neste Markkinointi Oy* v. *Yötuuli* [2000] ECR I-11121.

[194] Guidelines, paras. 132–133.

[195] Guidelines, para. 133. The Commission states that '[s]ingle branding obligations are more likely to result in anti-competitive foreclosure when entered into by dominant companies'.

[196] Guidelines, para. 143.

[197] Guidelines, para. 141.

[198] See, e.g., the Commission's decision in *Langnese-Iglo GmbH* [1993] OJ L183/19 and *Schöller Lebensmittel GmbH & Co KG* [1993] OJ L183/1, in which the Commission appeared to adopt an extremely narrow construction of the Court's judgment in Case C-234/89, *Delimitis* v. *Henninger Bräu* [1991] ECR I-935.

[199] See, e.g., *Bass* [1999] OJ L186/1 and *Whitbread* [1999] OJ L88/26. But see the discussion of *Inntrepreneur Pub Company* v. *Crehan* [2006] UKHL 38, in Chap. 14.

such agreements did not infringe Article 101(1) at all.[200] A fairly remarkable example of the latter is *Interbrew*[201] where the Commission found that beer supply agreements concluded by Interbrew, which had 56 per cent of the Belgian horeca market[202] did not, as amended following negotiations with the Commission, infringe Article 101(1). Essentially the amended agreements gave Belgian horeca outlets extended freedom to carry other beers not brewed by Interbrew. Although the agreements did incorporate non-compete obligations (clauses forcing the outlets to serve exclusively Interbrew's beer) these were essentially limited to draught pils and, in the case of loan-tie agreements, the agreements could be terminated quite easily.

(iii) Exclusive Distribution Agreements and STM

Exclusive distribution agreements, in which a manufacturer appoints a sole distributor for a particular area, have a number of positive effects and may consequently stimulate the competitive process. For example: efficiencies flow from the manufacturer's decision to deal only with one distributor in a particular territory; transaction costs are saved; customer feedback may be more easily obtained; and such an agreement may be essential to solve a free-rider problem. If the distributor is sheltered from intra-brand competition it will be encouraged to incur expenditure promoting and advertising the product, safe in the knowledge that other distributors will not be able to 'free-ride' on that expenditure.

In drawing up an exclusive distribution agreement varying degrees of immunity from intra-brand competition can be granted. The manufacturer may agree only to refrain from distributing the product itself within the distributor's territory. Additionally or alternatively, protection may be given from the selling efforts of other distributors. Distributors may be prohibited from actively seeking sales outside their own territory (qualified territorial protection) or from making any sales outside their territories at all (ATP).[203] Although it is clear that where the territorial protection granted to the distributor is absolute the agreement will be found to have as its object the restriction of competition, the case law clearly recognises that benefits for the competitive process potentially flow from exclusive distribution agreements so that, in the absence of ATP, such agreements do not automatically infringe Article 101(1). In *Société Technique Minière* v. *Maschinenbau Ulm GmbH*[204] the CJ held that exclusive distribution agreements will not restrict competition if the appointment of the exclusive distributor is necessary to enable the manufacturer to penetrate a new market. The Court accepted that a restraint necessary to persuade the distributor to take on the commercial risk inherent in the agreement would not constitute a restriction of competition within the meaning of Article 101(1).

The Commission's approach to exclusive distribution agreements is summarised in paragraphs 151–167 of its Guidelines. The Commission expresses concerns that these agreements, especially where accompanied by limits on selling into other exclusively allocated territories, may reduce intra-brand competition and cause market partitioning, which may facilitate price discrimination. Further, when most or all of the suppliers apply exclusive distribution, this may soften competition and facilitate collusion, both at the suppliers' and distributors' level and/or foreclose other distributors and reduce competition and the distribution level.[205] When considering the effect of these

---

[200] See *Roberts/Greene King* IP/98/967 where the Commission concluded that Greene King's network of agreements did not make a significant contribution to the foreclosure of the market of the distribution on beer in establishments selling alcoholic beverages for consumption on the premises in the UK. The decision was upheld on appeal Case T-25/99, *Roberts* v. *Commission* [2001] ECR II-1881.

[201] IP/03/545.

[202] Horeca (hotel/restaurant/catering) outlets are those that have concluded loan agreements or lease/sublease agreements with a brewer.

[203] ATP may be reinforced by the grant of IPRs: see, e.g., Cases 56 and 58, *Consten and Grundig* [1966] ECR 299.

[204] Case 56/65, [1966] ECR 235 (STM). See extract set out in Chap. 4, Section 3.E.iv, p. 239.

[205] Guidelines, para. 151.

agreements on competition, the Commission looks at the market position of the supplier, the position of its competitors, barriers to trade, buying power, the maturity of the market, and the level of trade. The Commission states that 'the loss of intra-brand competition can only be problematic if inter-brand competition is limited. The stronger the "position of the supplier", the more serious is the loss of intra-brand competition.'[206] In its Article 101(3) Guidelines, however, the Commission appears to display a stricter approach to these types of restraint, stating that territorial or customer intra-brand restraints are caught by Article 101(1) unless 'objectively necessary' for the existence of an agreement of that type or nature.[207] This approach potentially brings many vertical agreements containing territorial or customer restraints within Article 101(1) whether or not the parties have market power and/or the ability to affect prices or output on the market, for example by foreclosing access to supply or distribution channels to competitors.

To encourage concentration of selling efforts exclusive distribution agreements are often combined with a single branding commitment. Single branding provisions can of course foreclose other suppliers. The Commission deals with the combination of exclusive distribution and single branding in its Guidelines.

161.... foreclosure of other suppliers does not arise as long as exclusive distribution is not combined with single branding. But even when exclusive distribution is combined with single branding anticompetitive foreclosure of other suppliers is unlikely, except possibly when the single branding is applied to a dense network of exclusive distributors with small territories or in case of a cumulative effect. In such a case it may be necessary to apply the principles on single branding set out in section 2.1. However, when the combination does not lead to significant foreclosure, the combination of exclusive distribution and single branding may be pro-competitive by increasing the incentive for the exclusive distributor to focus its efforts on the particular brand. Therefore, in the absence of such a foreclosure effect, the combination of exclusive distribution with non-compete may very well fulfil the conditions of Article 101(3) for the whole duration of the agreement, particularly at the wholesale level.

(iv) Selective Distribution Agreements and the *Metro* Criteria

A supplier wishing to project an image for its goods and/or to ensure that sales are accompanied by the provision of specific services may decide to establish a selective distribution system. Under such a system the supplier will select its retailers, perhaps by number or by reference to quality or location of the distributor. Where the supplier wishes to portray and enhance a luxury image and to capitalise on consumers' desires to purchase a luxury product it may restrict supplies to retailers selling from a high-quality location. Alternatively, a supplier may agree only to supply retailers that will comply with certain obligations as to service, sales promotion, or regular ordering. It may wish to ensure that consumers purchasing its product receive a minimum level of pre-sales services and are fully informed about the product's qualities and capabilities. If such a system is to be effective both the supplier and the distributors will wish to ensure that non-authorised retailers, who will detract from the image they are attempting to create or which will free-ride on the pre-sales services provided, are not supplied.

A prohibition on the supply of retailers that have not been authorised to sell the products impacts on *intra-brand* competition and may be aimed at promoting inter-brand competition. In an ideal world a consumer who does not value the luxury image or the additional services imposed will purchase other competing products instead. Nonetheless, in some cases it may be arguable that the justifications for a selective distribution system are not as strong as the supplier suggests and that, especially where networks of similar agreements are operated (in cases of cumulative effect), the

---

[206] Guidelines, para. 153. The Commission notes, however, that if the number of competitors becomes small and their market position is rather similar, there is a risk of collusion, para. 154.

[207] Article 101(3) Guidelines, para. 18(2) and see Chap. 4.

practice may foreclose certain types of distributors, soften competition, and facilitate collusion between suppliers or buyers.[208]

For many years the CJ has recognised that certain qualitative selective distribution systems may escape the Article 101(1) prohibition but has been less willing than it has in the context of franchising agreements to accept that clauses do not fall within Article 101(1).[209] The leading case on the compatibility of selective distribution systems with Article 101(1) is *Metro-SB-Grossmarkte GmbH v. Commission (No. 1)*.[210] The principles set out in this case (and built on in subsequent jurisprudence) relating to the compatibility of selective distribution networks with Article 101(1) are different from those adopted in relation to other vertical agreements. The Court has developed a particular jurisprudence on this type of distribution which is at times hard to comprehend or rationalise fully.[211] Although relatively clear, it is overly formalistic and has been criticised for ignoring the economic realities and effects of the arrangements. Nonetheless, the *Metro* judgment throws interesting light on the Court's thinking. It indicates that certain restrictions in the selective distribution network are not caught by Article 101(1) because they are necessary in pursuance of a desirable end.

Case 26/76, *Metro-SB-Grossmärkte GmbH* v. *Commission (No. 1)* [1977] ECR 1875

SABA manufactured televisions, radios, and tape-recorders, which it distributed through a selective distribution system, whereby only specialist dealers who met certain criteria sold the products.[212] The Commission held that some aspects of the selective distribution network (SDN) were outside Article 101(1). Other provisions it held to be within Article 101(1) but it granted an exemption. Metro was a self-service dealer who SABA refused to admit to the network because it did not fulfil all the criteria. It appealed to the Court of Justice under Article 263 against the grant of the exemption to SABA.

Court of Justice

19. The applicant maintains that Article 2 of the contested decision is vitiated by misuse of powers inasmuch as the Commission has failed to recognise 'what is protected under Article [101] [namely] freedom of competition for the benefit of the consumer, not the coincident interests of a manufacturer and a given group of traders who wish to secure selling prices which are considered to be satisfactory by the latter'. Furthermore, if it were to be considered that an exemption from the prohibition might be granted in respect of the distribution system in dispute pursuant to Article [101(3)], the applicant maintains that the Commission has misapplied that provision by granting an exemption in respect of restrictions on competition which are not indispensable to the attainment of the objectives of improving production or distribution or promoting technical or economic progress and which lead to the elimination of competition from self-service wholesale traders.

---

[208] Guidelines, para. 175.

[209] 'The Commission (and the Court) generally accord more favourable treatment to restrictive clauses in franchising agreements as compared to distributions agreements ... For example, dealer location clauses, minimum purchasing obligations and stocking requirements in franchise agreement do not even fall within Art. [101(1)], while in selective distribution agreements the same clauses not only fall within Art. [101(1)] but might also be denied an exemption under Art. [101(3)]. This is problematic: many distribution agreements have elements that are characteristic of franchises, ... i.e., the transfer of commercial know-how to independent parties operating under the supplier's trade mark and not dealing in certain competing goods', B. E. Hawk, 'System Failure: Vertical Restraints and EC Competition Law' [1995] 32 *CMLRev* 973, 985.

[210] Case 26/76, [1977] ECR 1875. The Court's judgment was given soon after the US Supreme Court's judgment in *Sylvania* which overruled *Schwinn*: see Section 4.A.v, pp. 797–801.

[211] See Case 75/84, *Metro-SB-Grossmärkte GmbH* v. *Commission (No. 2)* [1986] ECR 3021; Case T-19/92, *Groupement d'Achat Édouard Leclerc (Leclerc)* v. *Commission* [1996] ECR II-1851.

[212] Selective distribution system is defined in the Verticals Reg., see Section 5.C.iii, pp. 818–820.

A Misuse of Powers

20. The requirement contained in…[Art. 101] that competition shall not be distorted implies the existence on the market of workable competition, that is to say the degree of competition necessary to ensure the observance of the basic requirements and the attainment of the objectives of the Treaty, in particular the creation of a single market achieving conditions similar to those of a domestic market. In accordance with this requirement the nature and intensiveness of competition may vary to an extent dictated by the products or services in question and the economic structure of the relevant market sectors. In the sector covering the production of high quality and technically advanced consumer durables, where a relatively small number of large- and medium-scale producers offer a varied range of items which, or so consumers may consider, are readily interchangeable, the structure of the market does not preclude the existence of a variety of channels of distribution adapted to the peculiar characteristics of the various producers and to the requirements of the various categories of consumers. On this view the Commission was justified in recognising that selective distribution systems constituted, together with others, an aspect of competition which accords with Article [101(1)], provided that resellers are chosen on the basis of objective criteria of a qualitative nature relating to the technical qualifications of the reseller and his staff and the suitability of his trading premises and that such conditions are laid down uniformly for all potential resellers and are not applied in a discriminatory fashion.

21. It is true that in such systems of distribution price competition is not generally emphasised either as an exclusive or indeed as a principal factor. This is particularly so when, as in the present case, access to the distribution network is subject to conditions exceeding the requirements of an appropriate distribution of the products. However, although price competition is so important that it can never be eliminated, it does not constitute the only effective form of competition or that to which absolute priority must in all circumstances be accorded. The powers conferred upon the Commission under Article [101(3)] show that the requirements for the maintenance of workable competition may be reconciled with the safeguarding of objectives of a different nature and that to this end certain restrictions on competition are permissible, provided that they are essential to the attainment of those objectives and that they do not result in the elimination of competition for a substantial part of the Common Market. For specialist wholesalers and retailers the desire to maintain a certain price level, which corresponds to the desire to preserve, in the interests of consumers, the possibility of the continued existence of this channel of distribution in conjunction with new methods of distribution based on a different type of competition policy, forms one of the objectives which may be pursued without necessarily falling under the prohibition contained in Article [101(1)], and, if it does fall thereunder, either wholly or in part, coming within the framework of Article [101(3)]. This argument is strengthened if, in addition, such conditions promote improved competition inasmuch as it relates to factors other than prices.

In this case the CJ thus recognised that a simple, purely qualitative, selective distribution system is compatible with Article 101(1). Although recognising that selective distribution limits price competition it accepted that price competition does not necessarily constitute the only form of competition.[213] It is clear, however, from the Court's judgments,[214] reiterated in the Commission's Guidelines,[215] that Article 101(1) is only inapplicable if certain conditions are satisfied:

(i) the characteristics or nature of the product in question necessitate a selective distribution system;

---

[213] Case 26/76, *Metro-SB-Grossmärkte GmbH v. Commission (No. 1)* [1977] ECR 1875, para. 21.

[214] Case 26/76, *Metro-SB-Grossmärkte GmbH v. Commission (No. 1)* [1977] ECR 1875, paras. 20, 33–34 and Case T-19/92, *Leclerc v. Commission* [1996] ECR II-1851, para. 112.

[215] Guidelines, para. 175.

(ii) the distributors are chosen by reference to objective criteria of a qualitative nature which are set out uniformly and are not used arbitrarily to discriminate against certain retailers; and

(iii) the criteria set out do not go beyond what is necessary for the product in question.[216]

Further, that even a simple selective distribution system complying with these requirements may infringe Article 101(1) if the market is tied up with a network of similar agreements, leading to excessive rigidity and no room for other methods of distribution.[217]

Although this approach represents a welcome recognition that selective distribution systems may enhance inter-brand competition, the discussion of the principles set out in this section establish that they are limiting and frustrating. The requirement that the product should fall within one of two categories that the Court has ruled should be able to benefit from such a system may not always be appropriate or relevant. Although it may be true that the need for a selective distribution system has sometimes been exaggerated, a producer operating on a competitive market will be punished by consumers if they do not believe that the product in question merits the system. Further, the requirement that retailers should be selected by reference only to *qualitative* criteria makes no economic sense. If a retailer has to comply with stringent qualitative criteria this may involve considerable expense which may demand that a quantitative limit on distributors is imposed. Apart from being economically indefensible, the requirement has also proved difficult to apply in practice and identical restrictions have sometimes been labelled as qualitative and in other cases as quantitative.

The net outcome has been that selective distribution systems have not, in the context of Article 101(1), adequately been assessed to determine whether or not they have led to an anti-competitive outcome on the market.[218] This problem was rectified in the past by the Commission accepting that many quantitative restrictions, for example an obligation to engage in sales promotions, met the criteria of Article 101(3).[219] Now most selective distribution systems, even quantitative systems where the criteria are not objectively justified by reference to the nature of product or service and which are not applied in a uniform and non-discriminatory manner, may benefit from the Verticals Regulation.[220] Where the Verticals Regulation does not apply, however, guidance on the application of Article 101(1) and 101(3) is still of importance.[221]

a. The Characteristics or the Nature of the Product

In Metro[222] the Court stated that the operation of a selective distribution system was justified in 'the sector covering the production of high quality and technically advanced consumer durables'. It is accepted that two categories of products justify a selective distribution system in order to protect the quality of the product and ensure its proper use: technically complex products and luxury or branded products.

In the context of technically complex products it is necessary to determine whether or not the technology involved is so complex as to justify a distribution network involving specialised wholesalers and retailers.[223] In the case of luxury products it is necessary to assess the need for the producer to preserve its brand image and the need to safeguard, in the mind of the consumer, the aura

---

[216] Case 31/80, *L'Oréal NV aud L'Oréal SA* v. *PVBA 'De Nieuwe AMCK'* [1980] ECR 3775 and Case T-19/91, *Société d'Hygiène Dermatologique de Vichy* v. *Commission* [1992] ECR II-415. The restrictions must be objectively necessary to protect the quality of the products in question: see, e.g., *Grohe* [1985] OJ L19/17.

[217] See Case 75/84, *Metro* v. *Commission (No. 2)* [1986] ECR 3021.

[218] But see Case 75/84, *Metro* v. *Commission (No. 2)* [1986] ECR 3021.

[219] See Case 26/76, *Metro-SB-Grossmärkte GmbH* v. *Commission (No. 1)* [1977] ECR 1875; *Grundig* [1985] OJ L233/1, renewed [1994] OJ L20/15; *Parfums Givenchy* [1992] OJ L236/11.

[220] See Case C-158/11, *Auto24 SARL* v. *Jaguar Land Rover France SAS*, 14 June 2012.

[221] Guidelines, paras. 174–188.

[222] Case 26/76, *Metro-SB-Grossmärkte GmbH* v. *Commission (No. 1)* [1977] ECR 1875.

[223] Case 75/84, *Metro* v. *Commission (No. 2)* [1986] ECR 3021.

of exclusivity and prestige of the product. In such cases appropriate marketing and a setting and presentation in line with the luxurious and exclusive nature and brand image of the product is essential.[224]

It has been found that the following products justify such a system: televisions,[225] hi-fis,[226] cameras,[227] personal computers,[228] clocks and watches,[229] high-quality gold and silver products,[230] luxury cosmetics/perfumes,[231] dinner services,[232] and cars.[233] It has been doubted whether plumbing fittings are technically advanced products that necessitate a selective distribution system.[234] It also seems that 'selective distribution systems which are justified by the specific nature of the products or the requirements for their distribution may be established in other economic sectors'.[235] In *SA Binon & Cie v. SA Agence et Messageries de la Presse*,[236] for example, it was accepted that newspapers and periodicals would constitute a suitable product for selective distribution, partly because of the limited shelf life which each had.

Such a system may be established for the distribution of newspapers and periodicals, without infringing the prohibition in Article [101(1)], given the special nature of those products as regards their distribution. As AMP rightly pointed out, newspapers and periodicals can, as a general rule, only be sold by retailers during an extremely limited period of time whereas the public expects each distributor to be able to offer a representative selection of press publications, in particular those of the national press. For their part, publishers undertake to take back unsold copies and this gives rise to a continuous exchange of products between publishers and distributors.

It may be hard to persuade the Commission or a court that a product merits a selective distribution system if such a system is not operated in all jurisdictions in which the product is sold.

b. Qualitative not Quantitative Criteria Applied Uniformly, and in a Non-discriminatory Manner

The Court in *Metro* stated clearly that a selective distribution system in which 'resellers are chosen on the basis of objective criteria of a qualitative nature relating to the technical qualifications of the reseller and his staff and the suitability of his trading premises and that such conditions are laid down uniformly for all potential resellers and are not applied in a discriminatory fashion'[237] would accord with Article 101. Any distributor satisfying the qualitative criteria should be supplied.

An immediate problem is to determine whether or not criteria are qualitative or quantitative in nature. The distinction is a difficult one since qualitative restrictions inevitably lead to restrictions on the number of resellers selected. It seems however that the distinction is between criteria designed to

---

[224] Case T-19/92, *Leclerc v. Commission* [1996] ECR II-1851, para. 116.

[225] Case 75/84, *Metro v. Commission (No. 2)* [1986] ECR 3021.

[226] *Grundig* [1985] OJ L233/1, renewed [1994] OJ L20/15.

[227] *Hasselblad* [1982] OJ L161/18, Case 86/62, *Hasselblad v. Commission* [1984] ECR 883.

[228] *IBM* [1984] OJ L118/24.

[229] *Junghans* [1977] OJ L30/10; cf. Case 31/85, *ETA Fabriques d'Ébauches v. DK Investments SA* [1985] ECR 3933.

[230] *Murat* [1983] OJ L348/20.

[231] *Parfums Givenchy* [1992] OJ L236/11, partially annulled Case T-88/92, *Groupement d'Achat Édouard Leclerc v. Commission* [1996] ECR II-1961; *Yves Saint Laurent* [1992] OJ L12/24, partially annulled Case T-19/92, *Leclerc v. Commission* [1996] ECR II-1851. The *Yves Saint Laurent* selective distribution system now satisfies the terms of the Verticals Reg., see IP/01/713.

[232] *Villeroy & Bosch* [1985] OJ L376/15.

[233] *BMW* [1975] OJ L29/1.

[234] *Grohe* [1985] OJ L19/17.

[235] Case T-19/92, *Leclerc v. Commission* [1996] ECR II-1851, para. 113.

[236] Case 243/83, [1985] ECR 2015, para. 32.

[237] Case 26/76, *Metro-SB-Grossmärkte GmbH v. Commission (No. 1)* [1977] ECR 1875, para. 20.

select dealers on the basis of their objective suitability to distribute a particular kind of good (qualitative criteria) and criteria which 'more directly limit the potential number of dealers by, for instance, requiring minimum or maximum sales, by fixing the number of dealers, etc'[238] (quantitative criteria). The Court's judgments and the Commission's decisions indicate the types of restrictions likely to be held to be qualitative and the types of restrictions likely to be found to be quantitative. Unfortunately, the cases are not always entirely consistent.

It is clear from *Metro* itself that criteria relating to the technical qualification of the reseller and its staff and the suitability of trading premises are of a qualitative nature. Further, it seems that obligations precluding the sale of goods that would detract from the product's brand image[239] and requiring dealers to provide after-sales services[240] are qualitative and compatible with Article 101(1). In some cases the Commission has found an obligation requiring a dealer to stock a wide or an entire range of products to be qualitative and in others it has found it to be quantitative. It seems that the classification of the obligation as qualitative or quantitative may turn upon the nature of the product involved.[241]

An obligation precluding members of the system from supplying unauthorised retailers does not infringe Article 101(1) since it is the corollary of the essential system of selective distribution.[242] Further, a provision precluding wholesalers from supplying private customers does not infringe Article 101(1).[243] In contrast, quantitative restrictions will infringe Article 101(1). Although the exact meaning of the term quantitative is elusive, the purpose appears to be to catch all provisions that protect approved network members from the competition of other retailers meeting the qualitative criteria. It is thus broader than where a simple numerical limit is placed on the number of distributors in a particular area, although a clause fixing the number of distributors for a specific area[244] is of course prohibited. The following have also been held to be quantitative restrictions which infringe Article 101(1):[245] clauses restricting sales to specific types of stores;[246] or clauses requiring distributors to maintain specific amounts of stocks,[247] to promote the manufacturer's product, to stock an entire range of products,[248] or to have a minimum annual turnover.[249]

---

[238] Guidelines, para. 175.

[239] *Parfums Givenchy* [1992] OJ L236/11, Case T-88/92, *Leclerc v. Commission* [1996] ECR II-1961.

[240] *Grundig* [1985] OJ L233/1, renewed [1994] OJ L20/15; *Villeroy & Bosch* [1985] OJ L376/15.

[241] Contrast *Grundig* OJ [1985] L 233/1, renewed [1994] OJ L20/15 (requirement that retailers had to carry and stock a whole range of products went beyond what was necessary for the distribution of products and was an impediment to competition (the agreement was, however, granted an exemption under Art. 101(3)) and *Villeroy & Bosch* [1985] OJ L376/15 (the requirement that the retailer had to display and stock a sufficiently wide and varied range of products did not infringe Art. 101(1)—sales targets were not imposed, the requirement did not prevent retailers stocking competing products, and inter-brand competition was high). In the Guidelines, para. 187, the Commission states that an obligation requiring distributors to sell a certain range of the products is purely of a qualitative nature.

[242] Case 26/76, *Metro-SB-Grossmärkte GmbH v. Commission (No. 1)* [1977] ECR 1875, para. 27.

[243] Case 26/76, *Metro-SB-Grossmärkte GmbH v. Commission (No. 1)* [1977] ECR 1875, para. 27.

[244] In, e.g., *Hasselblad* [1982] OJ L161/18, Case 86/62, *Hasselblad v. Commission* [1984] ECR 883, the supplier supplied only a few of those distributors which satisfied the criteria set out.

[245] Such clauses may also limit the freedom of a distributor to purchase other suppliers' products.

[246] Case T-19/92, *Leclerc v. Commission* [1996] ECR II-1851 (it is not justifiable to have a provision precluding supermarkets or hypermarkets from becoming part of the network). See also Case T-19/91, *Société d'Hygiène Dermatologique de Vichy v. Commission* [1992] ECR II-415.

[247] Case 26/76, *Metro-SB-Grossmärkte GmbH v. Commission (No. 1)* [1977] ECR 1875.

[248] *Grundig* [1994] OJ L20/15.

[249] See, e.g., *Parfums Givenchy* [1992] OJ L236/11, partially annulled Case T-88/92, *Leclerc v. Commission* [1996] ECR II-1961 and *Yves Saint Laurent* [1992] OJ L12/24, Case T-19/92, *Leclerc v. Commission* [1996] ECR II-1851 (the GC annulled part of the decision which raised indirect obstacles to sale in supermarkets. The system was then modified to permit sales of perfume in multi-product sales points).

Further, provisions directly or indirectly aimed at RPM[250] or preventing approved retailers from selling to each other (bans on cross-suppliers)[251] or to consumers in other Member States (see further *Pierre Fabre* in Section 4.B.iv.d)[252] will infringe Article 101(1).

Provisions setting out a difficult or lengthy procedure for retailers to join the network may also infringe Article 101(1).[253]

Article 101(1) will apply if the supplier precludes network members from supplying other members of the system[254] or if the supplier itself, acting in agreement with its distributors (and not unilaterally), refuses to supply those that meet its requirements. A breach of Article 101 may therefore be committed if a supplier refuses to supply distributors known, for example, to sell at prices below those recommended by the supplier or outside their territory. This will only be the case, however, if an 'agreement' is established. Distributors who are part of the network but who understand that they will not be supplied if they do not adhere to the manufacturer's policy may be taken to have agreed, explicitly or implicitly, to these terms.[255]

Where a supplier is found to be operating a selective distribution system in a discriminatory manner in breach of Article 101(1) it appears that the Commission may *not* make an order for supply.[256] In *Automec v. Commission (No. 2)* the GC indicated that the Commission did not have power to order supply and to insist on contractual arrangements when other suitable means were available to ensure that the infringement was terminated.[257] The Commission[258] may declare that the relevant agreement infringes Article 101(1), consider whether or not the agreement meets the conditions of Article 101(3) (where the system is being operated so as to deter distributors from selling outside their territory or to interfere with their freedom to set resale prices the Article 101(3) criteria will also almost certainly not be met) and, where appropriate, fine the parties in breach.[259]

c. The Criteria Must Not Go beyond what is Necessary for the Product in Question

In *Metro (No. 1)*[260] the CJ held that there must be a relationship between the goods protected by the selective distribution system and the restrictions imposed on distributors: the restrictions are permissible provided that they are essential to protect the 'quality' of the relevant product. Restrictions that go beyond this will infringe Article 101(1). In *Vichy v. Commission*,[261] for example, the GC held that 'the requirement of the status of dispensing chemist, which is a pre-condition for admission to the distribution network for Vichy products, is certainly not necessary for the proper distribution of those [cosmetic] products'. Rather such a requirement in relation to cosmetic products was 'entirely unnecessary' and 'disproportionate'.[262]

---

[250] Case 243/83, *SA Binon & Cie v. SA Agence et Messageries de la Presse* [1985] ECR 2015 and Case 107/82, *AEG-Telefunken v. Commission* [1983] ECR 3151.

[251] *Hasselblad* [1982] OJ L161/18, Case 86/62, *Hasselblad v. Commission* [1984] ECR 883.

[252] See Cases 228 and 229/82, *Ford-Werke AG and Ford of Europe Inc v. Commission* [1984] ECR 1129; Case 32/78, *BMW v. Commission* [1979] ECR 2435; *Kodak* [1970] JO L142/24. Guarantees granted on sale in one Member State must be honoured by distributors in other Member States: Case 31/85, *ETA Fabriques d'Ebauches v. DK Investments SA* [1985] ECR 3933.

[253] *Parfums Givenchy* [1992] OJ L236/11, partially annulled Case T-88/92, *Leclerc v. Commission* [1996] ECR II-1961 and *Yves Saint Laurent* [1992] OJ L12/24, Case T-19/92, *Leclerc v. Commission* [1996] ECR II-1851.

[254] See n. 251.

[255] See Chap. 3.

[256] But see discussion of refusal to deal in Chap. 7.

[257] Case T-24/90, [1992] ECR II-2223, para. 51. This aspect of *Automec II* is discussed in Chap. 13.

[258] NCAs and national courts also, of course, have power to enforce the rules, see Chaps. 13 and 14.

[259] See Chap. 13.

[260] Case 26/76, [1977] ECR 1875.

[261] Case T-19/91, [1992] ECR II-415.

[262] *Vichy v. Commission*, Case T-19/91 [1992] ECR II-415, para. 69.

d. Impact of the *Pierre Fabre* Judgment

To date, the case law dealing with selective distribution has been interpreted as requiring a *sui juris* type of analysis to determine whether such agreements are restrictive by effect within the meaning of Article 101(1). In *Pierre Fabre* v. *Président de l'Autorité de la concurrence*,[263] however, the CJ casts doubt on this view.

Case C-439/09, *Pierre Fabre* v. *Président de l'Autorité de la concurrence*, 13 October 2011

Court of Justice

The classification of the restriction in the contested contractual clause as a restriction of competition by object

34 It must first of all be recalled that, to come within the prohibition laid down in Article 101(1) TFEU, an agreement must have 'as [its] object or effect the prevention, restriction or distortion of competition within the internal market'. It has, since the judgment in Case 56/65 LTM...been settled case-law that the alternative nature of that requirement, indicated by the conjunction 'or', leads, first, to the need to consider the precise purpose of the agreement, in the economic context in which it is to be applied. Where the anti-competitive object of the agreement is established it is not necessary to examine its effects on competition (see Joined Cases C-501/06 P, C-513/06 P, C-516/06 P and C-519/06 P *GlaxoSmithKline Services and Others* v. *Commission and Others*...paragraph 55 and the case-law cited).

35 For the purposes of assessing whether the contractual clause at issue involves a restriction of competition 'by object', regard must be had to the content of the clause, the objectives it seeks to attain and the economic and legal context of which it forms a part (see *GlaxoSmithKline and Others* v. *Commission and Others*, paragraph 58 and the case-law cited).

36 The selective distribution contracts at issue stipulate that sales of cosmetics and personal care products by the Avène, Klorane, Galénic and Ducray brands must be made in a physical space, the requirements for which are set out in detail, and that a qualified pharmacist must be present.

37 According to the referring court, the requirement that a qualified pharmacist must be present at a physical sales point de facto prohibits the authorised distributors from any form of internet selling.

38 As the Commission points out, by excluding de facto a method of marketing products that does not require the physical movement of the customer, the contractual clause considerably reduces the ability of an authorised distributor to sell the contractual products to customers outside its contractual territory or area of activity. It is therefore liable to restrict competition in that sector.

39 As regards agreements constituting a selective distribution system, the Court has already stated that such agreements necessarily affect competition in the common market (Case 107/82 *AEG-Telefunken* v. *Commission*...paragraph 33). Such agreements are to be considered, in the absence of objective justification, as 'restrictions by object'.

40 However, it has always been recognised in the case-law of the Court that there are legitimate requirements, such as the maintenance of a specialist trade capable of providing specific services as regards high-quality and high-technology products, which may justify a reduction of price competition in favour of competition relating to factors other than price. Systems of selective distribution, in so far as they aim at the attainment of a legitimate goal capable of improving competition in relation to factors other than price, therefore constitute an element of competition which is in conformity with Article 101(1) TFEU (*AEG-Telefunken* v. *Commission*, paragraph 33).

---

[263] Case C-439/09, 13 October 2011.

41 In that regard, the Court has already pointed out that the organisation of such a network is not prohibited by Article 101(1) TFEU, to the extent that resellers are chosen on the basis of objective criteria of a qualitative nature, laid down uniformly for all potential resellers and not applied in a discriminatory fashion, that the characteristics of the product in question necessitate such a network in order to preserve its quality and ensure its proper use and, finally, that the criteria laid down do not go beyond what is necessary (Case 26/76 *Metro SB-Grossmärkte* v. *Commission*... paragraph 20, and Case 31/80 *L'Oréal*... paragraphs 15 and 16).

42 Although it is for the referring court to examine whether the contractual clause at issue prohibiting de facto all forms of internet selling can be justified by a legitimate aim, it is for the Court of Justice to provide it for this purpose with the points of interpretation of European Union law which enable it to reach a decision (see *L'Oréal*, paragraph 14).

43 It is undisputed that, under Pierre Fabre Dermo-Cosmétique's selective distribution system, resellers are chosen on the basis of objective criteria of a qualitative nature, which are laid down uniformly for all potential resellers. However, it must still be determined whether the restrictions of competition pursue legitimate aims in a proportionate manner in accordance with the considerations set out at paragraph 41 of the present judgment.

44 In that regard, it should be noted that the Court, in the light of the freedoms of movement, has not accepted arguments relating to the need to provide individual advice to the customer and to ensure his protection against the incorrect use of products, in the context of non-prescription medicines and contact lenses, to justify a ban on internet sales (see, to that effect, Deutscher Apothekerverband, paragraphs 106, 107 and 112, and Case C-108/09 *Ker-Optika*... paragraph 76).

45 Pierre Fabre Dermo-Cosmétique also refers to the need to maintain the prestigious image of the products at issue.

46 The aim of maintaining a prestigious image is not a legitimate aim for restricting competition and cannot therefore justify a finding that a contractual clause pursuing such an aim does not fall within Article 101(1) TFEU.

47 In the light of the foregoing considerations, the answer to the first part of the question referred for a preliminary ruling is that Article 101(1) TFEU must be interpreted as meaning that, in the context of a selective distribution system, a contractual clause requiring sales of cosmetics and personal care products to be made in a physical space where a qualified pharmacist must be present, resulting in a ban on the use of the internet for those sales, amounts to a restriction by object within the meaning of that provision where, following an individual and specific examination of the content and objective of that contractual clause and the legal and economic context of which it forms a part, it is apparent that, having regard to the properties of the products at issue, that clause is not objectively justified.

The CJ thus clearly states (i) that selective distribution systems necessarily affect competition and 'are to be considered, in the absence of objective justification, as "restrictions by object"'; but (ii) that they may in conformity with Article 101 and justified insofar as they aim at the attainment of legitimate goals (such as the maintenance of a specialist trade capable of providing specific services as regards high-quality or high-technology products[264]) where 'resellers are chosen on the basis of objective criteria of a qualitative nature, laid down uniformly for all potential resellers and not applied in a discriminatory fashion, that the characteristics of the product in question necessitate such a network in order to preserve its quality and ensure its proper use and, finally, that the criteria laid down do not go beyond what is necessary'.[265]

---

[264] Case C-439/09, *Pierre Fabre* v. *Président de l'Autorité de la concurrence*, 13 October 2011, para 40.

[265] Case C-439/09, *Pierre Fabre* v. *Président de l'Autorité de la concurrence*, 13 October 2011, para 41.

Although the narrow finding of the CJ—that the contractual clause at issue (prohibiting all forms of internet selling) was incompatible with Article 101(1)—is consistent with earlier precedent dealing with object restraints, the broader wording suggesting that *all* selective distribution systems are restrictive by object unless 'objectively justified' is more surprising (and does not seem to have been strictly necessary for the ruling in question). Nonetheless, the CJ treats the *Metro* criteria as a mechanism for distinguishing between selective distribution systems which are restrictive by object and those which are objectively justified as they are necessary to achieve a legitimate aim and so outside Article 101 altogether (rather than a mechanism for conducting effects analysis). Not only is such an approach perhaps more reminiscent of free movement[266] and Article 102 cases, than Article 101 cases, but the CJ does not clearly link its approach with that adopted in other case law traditionally dealing with object restraints (and discussed in Chapter 4) which establishes that restrictions of competition essential to, or inherent in, the pursuit of a legitimate objective or objectively necessary for the existence of the agreement fall outside Article 101(1).[267] Further, although authority might support a statement that the aim of maintaining a prestigious brand is not a legitimate justification for an outright ban on passive sales, the broader suggestion of the Court that it is not a legitimate aim for restricting competition within selective distribution systems is inconsistent with previous case law holding that such systems based on qualitative criteria in the luxury cosmetics sector may be compatible in principle with Article 101(1).[268]

(v) Franchising Agreements and *Pronuptia De Paris*

The Commission describes franchise agreements in its Guidelines:

189. Franchise agreements contain licences of intellectual property rights relating in particular to trade marks or signs and know-how for the use and distribution of goods or services. In addition to the licence of IPRs, the franchisor usually provides the franchisee during the life of the agreement with commercial or technical assistance. The licence and the assistance are integral components of the business method being franchised. The franchisor is in general paid a franchise fee by the franchisee for the use of the particular business method. Franchising may enable the franchisor to establish, with limited investments a uniform network for the distribution of his products. In addition to the provision of the business method, franchise agreements usually contain a combination of different vertical restraints concerning the products being distributed, in particular selective distribution and/or non-compete and/or exclusive distribution or weaker forms thereof.

Franchising arrangements in which a franchisee, or franchisees, is appointed and established as part of a uniform business network, may have a positive impact on competition on a market. Franchise arrangements assist the entry of new competitors to a market and lead to an increase in inter-brand competition. They enable a franchisor to expand its reputation and network without engaging in substantial investment. A franchisee is also enabled to set up and to enter a market with the assistance of an entrepreneur whose business has already been tried and tested on the market.

In *Pronuptia de Paris GmbH v. Pronuptia de Paris Irmgard Schillgallis*[269] the CJ held that two categories of clauses essential to the successful operation of distribution *franchise agreements* did not constitute

---

[266] The CJ relies on free movement cases (holding that the need to provide individual advice to a customer and to protect against incorrect use of products cannot justify a ban on internet sales of non-prescription medicines and contact lenses, in support of its conclusion that the aim of maintaining a prestigious brand is not a legitimate aim for restricting internet selling, Case C-108/09 *Ker-Optika* [2010] ECR I-12213, paras. 44–46.

[267] See the opinion of Mazák AG who relies on *Wouters* (Case C-309/99, *Wouters v. Algemene Raad van de Nederlandse Order van Advocaten* [2002] ECR I-1577) for the view that the ban on internet selling would fall outside Article 101(1) provided the limitations imposed were appropriate in the light of the legitimate objective (of a public law nature) sought and did not go beyond what was necessary, see para. 35.

[268] See, e.g., Case T-88/92, *Groupement d'Achat Édouard Leclerc v. Commission* [1996] ECR II-1961 paras. 105–117.

[269] Case 161/84, *Pronuptia de Paris GmbH v. Pronuptia de Paris Irmgard Schillgallis* [1986] ECR 353.

restrictions of competition for the purposes of Article 101(1): first, the franchisor had to be able to communicate its know-how to franchisees and to protect it from use by competitors and secondly, the franchisor had to be able to maintain the identity and reputation of its network.[270] The Court thus held that a restriction on the ability of a franchisee:

(1) to open a shop of a similar nature during the period of the contract and for a reasonable period thereafter; and

(2) to sell the shop without the franchisor's consent will not restrict competition where essential to protect the know-how and assistance provided under the terms of the contract. Similarly, clauses requiring the franchisee:

- to apply and to use the franchisor's business methods and know how;

- to locate, lay out and decorate the sales premises according to the franchisor's instructions;

- to gain the franchisor's approval prior to an assignment of the franchise;

- to sell only products supplied by the franchisor; and

- to gain the franchisor's approval for all advertising

may also be essential to preserve the identity and the reputation of the network and so fall outside Article 101(1).

The Court did not, however, totally embrace an economic approach to franchise agreements.[271] It would not accept that: (1) clauses effecting a division of territories between the franchisor and franchisees or between the franchisees *inter se*,[272] or that (2) clauses preventing price competition between them were essential to the operation of the franchise agreement. These are the types of clauses which automatically restrict competition. Arguments raised justifying their imposition can be considered only when determining their compatibility with Article 101(3).

The Commission has scrutinised a number of franchise agreements in the past and frequently takes a favourable view of such agreements. Ordinarily, however, following the approach of the CJ in *Pronuptia*, the Commission has taken the view that certain clauses in the agreement (generally clauses involving market-sharing between the franchisor and franchisees or the franchisees *inter se*) infringe Article 101(1). It has therefore completed its assessment under Article 101(3).[273] The Guidelines recognise however that franchising agreements may fall outside Article 101(1) altogether.[274]

(vi) Tying

Although there have been relatively few cases which have dealt with tying under Article 101 (but see the discussion of the circumstances in which tying may constitute an abuse of a dominant position in Chapter 7), paragraphs 214–222 of the Guidelines deal with tying under Article 101. In particular, the Commission is concerned that tying may result in anti-competitive foreclosure on the tying and/or tied product markets. The Guidelines state that the main criteria for determining the effects of tying under Article 101 are: the market power of the supplier on the tying market; entry barriers; and the power of buyers on the market.

---

[270] Case 161/84, *Pronuptia de Paris GmbH v. Pronuptia de Paris Irmgard Schillgallis* [1986] ECR 353, paras. 16–17.

[271] See also Chap. 4.

[272] This has created difficulties since many franchisees are not willing to make the requisite investment without such protection.

[273] See, e.g., *Pronuptia* [1987] OJ L13/39, *Yves Rocher* [1987] OJ L8/49, *ServiceMaster* [1988] OJ L332/38 and *Charles Jourdan* [1989] OJ L35/31.

[274] Guidelines, paras. 189–191.

(vii) Other Restraints

The Commission's Guidelines also provide specific guidance on the compatibility of exclusive customer allocation (treated in a similar, but not identical, way to exclusive distribution), exclusive supply (i.e. where one distributor only is appointed within the European Union and where the main competition risk of such agreement is foreclosure of other buyers), upfront access payments, and category management agreements with Article 101(1) and Article 101(3).[275]

5. ARTICLE 101(3)

A. GENERAL

The broad view taken of Article 101(1) in the past has meant that many vertical agreements have been dealt with under Article 101(3). Indeed, the procedural difficulties that were involved in gaining an individual exemption (or comfort letter)[276] meant that the block exemptions, which provide automatic exemption from Article 101(1), were of utmost importance. The complex assessment required to determine whether or not an agreement infringes Article 101(1) or meets the Article 101(3) criteria, means that block exemptions are still of enormous importance in practice.

B. THE OLD BLOCK EXEMPTIONS

Regulation 2790/1999, the first overarching block exemption for vertical agreements, replaced three block exemptions which applied to different categories of distribution agreement: Regulation 1983/83[277] applied to exclusive distribution agreements; Regulation 1984/83 applied to exclusive purchasing agreements (the regulation contained special provisions for beer supply and petrol agreements);[278] and Regulation 4087/88[279] applied to franchising agreements.

Regulation 2790/1999 did not replace the separate block exemption for motor vehicles (considered in Section 5.D). The Commission had been able through the exclusive distribution, exclusive purchasing, and franchising block exemptions (the 'old block exemptions') to mould and influence the content of distribution agreements and policy towards them. This came at a cost, however, as agreements did not always fit neatly within one of these categories which the Commission, not business, had identified. The limited types identified did not cater for the variety of distribution arrangements that suppliers sought to use (including selective distribution) so that diversity of distribution arrangements was stultified. Further, even within those confines, the parties' freedom of contract was significantly curtailed. Each block exemption applied only if it related to goods for resale and set out categories of clauses that were permissible (a white list)[280] and categories of clauses that were not (a black list of hardcore restraints). Any restriction on conduct not specifically exempted by the Regulation would compromise and risk the validity of the agreement.[281] The bargaining ability of

---

[275] Guidelines, paras. 168–173, 192–202, 203–208 and 209–213 respectively.

[276] See Chaps. 4 and 13.

[277] [1988] OJ L173/1.

[278] Regs. 1983/83 [1983] OJ L173/1 and 1984/83 [1983] OJ L173/7 were the successors to Reg. 67/67 [1967] OJ Spec. Ed. 10.

[279] [1988] OJ L359/46.

[280] These block exemptions applied only where one party agreed to supply the other with 'goods for resale'. They did not therefore apply to agreements relating to services or to intermediate goods that the distributor had to finish or prepare for resale. This obviously severely limited the scope of application of the block exemptions. The Verticals Reg. applies to goods (whether for resale or use by the distributor) and services.

[281] The impact of having a white list (of clauses that were exempted insofar as they infringed Art. 101(1)) was that if the agreement contained any other clause that constituted a restriction of competition within the meaning of

the parties was thus constrained and, instead, distribution agreements tended to be drafted in similar, if not identical, ways.

The Commission sought to address these problems and criticisms of the old regimes in the 1999 Verticals Regulation. The new 2010 Verticals Regulation has not made dramatic changes to the 1999 regime, although the block exemption no longer applies where the buyer exceeds market share thresholds in the market on which it purchases the contract goods or services.

C. THE VERTICALS REGULATION—REGULATION 330/2010

(i) The Background

The Verticals Regulation[282] provides an umbrella block exemption which applies to vertical agreements generally (but see discussion of motor vehicle distribution agreements in Section 5.D). Regulation 330/2010 came into force on 1 June 2010, replacing Regulation 2790/1999. It operates as a safe harbour, setting out a presumption of legality for distribution agreements, whether for goods or services, which satisfy its provisions. It will be remembered that in *Pierre Fabre* v. *Président de l'Autorité de la concurrence*,[283] the CJ held that, because of the possibility of Article 101(3) applying individually to an agreement, the block exemption provisions are not to be interpreted broadly.

The flowchart in Figure 11.2 explains the principal provisions of the block exemption. The subsequent commentary sets out and explains the main provisions of the block exemption, drawing on the explanation set out in the Commission's Guidelines.

(ii) The Recitals

The block exemption contains recitals that set out background to the Regulation. Of particular importance is the Commission's recognition in the recitals that vertical agreements 'can improve economic efficiency within a chain of production or distribution' and that the 'likelihood that such efficiency-enhancing effects will outweigh any anti-competitive effects due to restrictions contained in vertical agreement depends on the degree of market power of the parties to the agreement'.[284] It thus operates on the presumption that where the market-share thresholds are not exceeded, vertical agreements which do not contain certain severe restrictions will generally lead to an improvement in production or distribution and allow consumers a fair share of the benefit.[285]

(iii) Article 1—Definitions

Article 1 defines concepts relevant to the remainder of the block exemption: competing undertakings, non-compete obligation, exclusive supply obligation, selective distribution system, intellectual property rights, know-how, and buyer.

Art. 101(1) the benefit of the block exemption would be lost. Thus the insertion of a restriction, even one which was not specifically prohibited by the black list, would lead to a risk that the block exemption did not apply. In practice, therefore, parties to an agreement would attempt to limit the restrictions on conduct and obligations imposed to the clauses explicitly permitted by the white list.

[282] Guidelines, paras. 23–73 deal with the application of the block exemption.

[283] Case C-439/09 13 October 2011.

[284] Verticals Reg., recitals 6 and 7.

[285] Verticals Reg., recital 8.

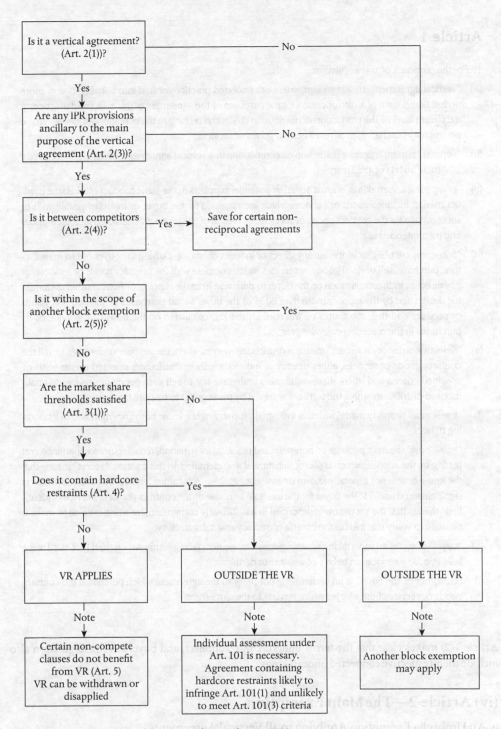

Figure 11.2 Application of the Verticals Regulation (VR)

Article 1

1. For the purposes of this Regulation:

(a) "vertical agreement" means an agreement or concerted practice entered into between two or more undertakings each of which operates, for the purposes of the agreement or the concerted practice, at a different level of the production or distribution chain, and relating to the conditions under which the parties may purchase, sell or resell certain goods or services;

(b) "vertical restraint" means a restriction of competition in a vertical agreement falling within the scope of Article 101(1) of the Treaty;

(c) "competing undertakings" means actual or potential suppliers in the same product market; the product market includes goods or services which are regarded by the buyer as interchangeable with or substitutable for the contract goods or services, by reason of the products' characteristics, their prices and their intended use;

(d) "non-compete obligation" means any direct or indirect obligation causing the buyer not to manufacture, purchase, sell or resell goods or services which compete with the contract goods or services, or any direct or indirect obligation on the buyer to purchase from the supplier or from another undertaking designated by the supplier more than 80 % of the buyer's total purchases of the contract goods or services and their substitutes on the relevant market, calculated on the basis of the value of its purchases in the preceding calendar year;

(e) "Selective distribution system" means a distribution system where the supplier undertakes to sell the contract goods or services, either directly or indirectly, only to distributors selected on the basis of specified criteria and where these distributors undertake not to sell such goods or services to unauthorised distributors within the territory reserved by the supplier to operate that system;

(f) "intellectual property rights" includes industrial property rights, know how, copyright and neighbouring rights;

(g) "know-how" means a package of non-patented practical information, resulting from experience and testing by the supplier, which is secret, substantial and identified: in this context, "secret" means that the know-how is not generally known or easily accessible; "substantial" means that the know-how is significant and useful to the buyer for the use, sale or resale of the contract goods or services; "identified" means that the know-how is described in a sufficiently comprehensive manner so as to make it possible to verify that it fulfils the criteria of secrecy and substantiality;

(h) "buyer" includes an undertaking which, under an agreement falling within Article 101(1) of the Treaty, sells goods or services on behalf of another undertaking;

(i) "customer of the buyer" is an undertaking not party to the agreement which purchases the contract goods or services from a buyer which is party to the agreement.

Article 1(2) makes clear that the terms undertakings, suppliers, and buyers in the Regulation also include their respective connected undertakings.

(iv) Article 2—The Main Exemption

a. An Umbrella Exemption Applying to all Vertical Agreements

Vertical Agreements

The Regulation exempts *all* vertical agreements (as defined in Article 1(1)(a), set out in Section 5.C.iii) which meet its requirements, whether they relate to goods or services,[286] and whatever their main

---

[286] Many of the old block exemptions, e.g. Reg. 1983/83, applied only where the agreements related to goods for resale, see n. 280.

objective (exclusive distribution, exclusive purchasing, franchising, selective distribution, or some other). The focus of the Regulation is thus more on the restrictive nature of the clause (substantive effect) than the type or form of the agreement involved.

Agreements between Two or More Undertakings

The exemption applies to agreements and concerted practices concluded between two or more undertakings so long as each undertaking operates, for the purposes of the agreement, at different levels of the production or distribution chain (for example, supplier, wholesaler, and retailer or a supplier of a raw material which the other uses as an input).[287]

Agreements Relating to the Conditions under which the Parties may Purchase, Sell, or Resell Certain Goods or Services

The block exemption covers purchase and distribution agreements. These are agreements which:

[r]elate to the conditions under which the parties to the agreement, the supplier and the buyer, 'may purchase, sell or resell certain goods or services'. This reflects the purpose of the Block Exemption Regulation to cover purchase and distribution agreements. These are agreements which concern the conditions for the purchase, sale or resale of the goods or services supplied by the supplier and/or which concern the conditions for the sale by the buyer of the goods or services which incorporate these goods or services. For the application of the Block Exemption Regulation both the goods or services supplied by the supplier and the resulting goods or services are considered to be contract goods or services. Vertical agreements relating to all final and intermediate goods and services are covered. The only exception is the automobile sector, as long as this sector remains covered by a specific block exemption…The goods or services provided by the supplier may be resold by the buyer or may be used as an input by the buyer to produce his own goods or services.[288]

The Regulation does not exempt agreements or restrictions or obligations that do not relate to the purchase, sale, or resale of goods or services, such as rent or leasing agreements or clauses preventing parties from carrying out independent research and development.[289]

b. Agreements between Competing Undertakings

Although the term vertical agreements encompasses agreements concluded between undertakings which for the purposes of the agreement operate at different levels of the production or distribution chain, Article 2(4) of the Verticals Regulation prevents the block exemption from applying to agreements concluded between competing undertakings[290] (even if operating for the purposes of the agreement at different levels of the production or distribution chain), except:

it shall apply where competing undertakings enter into a non-reciprocal vertical agreement and:

(a) the supplier is a manufacturer and a distributor of goods, while the buyer is a distributor and not a competing undertaking at the manufacturing level,[291] or

(b) the supplier is a provider of services at several levels of trade, while the buyer provides its goods or services at the retail level and is not a competing undertaking at the level of trade where it purchase the contract services.

A potential supplier is a supplier who could and would be likely to produce a competing product or service in response to a small and permanent increase in relative prices. A theoretical possibility of

---

[287] It does not, therefore, apply to an agreement between a supplier and two wholesalers.

[288] Guidelines, para. 25.

[289] Guidelines, para. 26.

[290] See definition of competing undertaking in Art. 1 and set out in Section 5.C.iii (it includes actual or potential suppliers in the same product market, irrespective of whether or not they operate in the same geographic market).

[291] Dual distribution occurs where 'the manufacturer of particular goods also acts as a distributor of the goods in competition with independent distributors of his goods': Guidelines, para. 28.

entering a market is not enough. The supplier should be able to make the necessary investments and enter the market within a period of one year.[292]

c. Association of Retailers of Goods

Article 2(2) provides that the block exemption applies to vertical agreements concluded between an association of retailers[293] (no member of which, together with its connected undertakings, has a total turnover of more than €50 million) and its members or its supplier—i.e. cooperation between retailers in the area of purchasing and selling. Any horizontal agreement concluded between the members (such as an obligation on members to purchase from the association) must however be assessed first and separately for its compatibility with Article 101.

d. Provisions Relating to the Assignment of Intellectual Property Rights

The assignment of IPRs, such as trade marks, copyright, or know-how, may be essential or extremely useful to the effective performance of a vertical agreement. Article 2(3) provides that the block exemption applies to vertical agreements containing provisions relating to the assignment to, or use by, the buyer of IPRs but only if they are ancillary (the provisions do not constitute the primary object of the agreement) and are directly related to the use, sale, or resale of goods or services by the buyer or its customers. This provision is of importance to all vertical agreements, but is particularly relevant to franchise agreements that ordinarily involve the assignment or licensing of IPRs. Five conditions have to be fulfilled before the block exemption applies,[294] so it will not apply unless:

(i) the agreement is a vertical one and not, for example, an assignment of IPRs for the manufacture of goods or licensing agreements;[295]

(ii) the assignment or the licence of the IPRs must be made by the supplier to the buyer and not vice versa;

(iii) the IPR provisions are ancillary to the implementation of the vertical agreement and not its primary object;

(iv) the IPR provisions are directly related to the use, sale, or resale of goods or services by the buyer or its customers, for example, where the licensing of a trade mark or know how is necessary for the marketing of a good.

It is also essential that:

(v) the clauses relating to the IPRs must not have the same object or effect as restrictions that are not exempted under the regulation. For example, territorial exclusivity, which is prohibited by Article 4, cannot be circumvented by arrangements involving licensing or assignment of IPRs.[296]

Franchise Agreements Franchise agreements, which no longer benefit from their own independent regime, are dealt with in some detail in paragraphs 43–45 of the Guidelines. In particular, the Guidelines indicate that franchise agreements will ordinarily meet all five of the conditions set out in Article 2(3) as:

the franchisor provides goods and/or services, in particular commercial or technical assistance services, to the franchisee. The IPRs help the franchisee to resell the products supplied by the franchisor or by a supplier designated by the franchisor or to use these products and sell the resulting goods or services.[297]

---

[292] Guidelines, para. 27.

[293] Retailers 'are distributors reselling goods to final consumers', Guidelines, para. 29.

[294] Guidelines, para. 31.

[295] Reg. 772/2004 [2004] OJ L123/11, which applies to technology transfer agreements, may apply to such agreements; see Chap. 12. Paragraph 33 of the Guidelines sets out some examples of agreements which would not benefit from the Verticals Regulation.

[296] See also Cases 56 and 58/64, *Consten and Grundig* [1966] ECR 299, para. 48.

[297] Guidelines, para. 44.

Franchise agreements that do not fall within the block exemption on the ground that they principally concern the licensing of IPRs will be treated in a similar way to those dealt with under the block exemption.

Paragraph 45 of the Guidelines sets out the types of obligations related to IPRs which are likely to benefit from the block exemption:

45. The following IPR-related obligations are generally considered to be necessary to protect the franchisor's intellectual property rights and are, if these obligations fall under Article 101(1), also covered by the Block Exemption Regulation:

(a) an obligation on the franchisee not to engage, directly or indirectly, in any similar business;

(b) an obligation on the franchisee not to acquire financial interests in the capital of a competing undertaking such as would give the franchisee the power to influence the economic conduct of such undertaking;

(c) an obligation on the franchisee not to disclose to third parties the know-how provided by the franchisor as long as this know-how is not in the public domain;

(d) an obligation on the franchisee to communicate to the franchisor any experience gained in exploiting the franchise and to grant it, and other franchisees, a nonexclusive licence for the know-how resulting from that experience;

(e) an obligation on the franchisee to inform the franchisor of infringements of licensed intellectual property rights, to take legal action against infringers or to assist the franchisor in any legal actions against infringers;

(f) an obligation on the franchisee not to use know-how licensed by the franchisor for purposes other than the exploitation of the franchise;

(g) an obligation on the franchisee not to assign the rights and obligations under the franchise agreement without the franchisor's consent.

e. Agreements Falling within the Scope of Another Block Exemption

Article 2(5) states that the Verticals Regulation does not apply to vertical agreements the subject matter of which falls within the scope of another block exemption, unless otherwise provided for in such a regulation. Agreements potentially falling within the Technology Transfer Regulation[298] or the Motor Vehicle Distribution Regulation[299] and vertical agreements concluded in connection with horizontal agreements that may potentially benefit from a block exemption[300] are, therefore, excluded. The exclusion is for types of agreements so, for example, a technology transfer agreement which does not meet the criteria of the technology transfer block exemption cannot be exempted by virtue of the Verticals Regulation.[301] As it is of a different type it falls within the scope of the technology transfer regime, not the verticals regime.

(v) Article 3—The Market Share Cap

a. The 30 Per Cent Threshold

A new feature introduced by Regulation 2790/1999, which was not used in previous block exemptions (which applied, unless withdrawn, whatever the market shares of the parties), was the introduction of a market share cap of 30 per cent. Essentially, Regulation 2790/1999 applied where the supplier's market did not exceed 30 per cent. This reflected the Commission's view that vertical

---

[298] Reg. 772/2004 [2004] OJ L123/11, see Chap. 12.

[299] See Section 5.D, p. 834.

[300] See Chap. 10.

[301] Broadly, patent, know-how, or software copyright licensing agreements or a mixed patent, know-how, or software copyright licensing agreement: Reg. 772/2004 [2004] OJ L128/11.

restraints were unlikely to pose competition problems, where inter-brand competition is strong[302] and where imposed by a firm without significant market power.[303] The buyer's market share was relevant only where there was an exclusive supply obligation (where a supplier agrees to supply only one buyer inside the Community).[304] When the block exemption was reviewed, however, the Commission decided to amend this provision to deal with potential competition problems arising from an increase in retailers' market power. Under Regulation 330/2010, therefore, the market share of both the supplier (on the market on which it sells the contract goods or services) and the buyer (on the market on which it purchases them) are now taken into account. In a multi-party situation (for example, an agreement between a supplier, wholesaler, and retailer), the market shares of the supplier and the wholesaler (on the markets on which they sell the contract goods or services) and the market shares of the wholesaler and the retailer (on the market on which they purchase the goods or services) are relevant.

In practice, the additional requirement to take account of buyers' market shares is likely to cause suppliers seeking to comply with the block exemption some difficulty—the uncertainty surrounding buyers' market shares on the purchasing market may make it hard to be certain that the block exemption applies. Article 3 provides:

1. The exemption provided for in Article 2 shall apply on condition that the market share held by the supplier does not exceed 30 % of the relevant market on which it sells the contract goods or services and the market share held by the buyer does not exceed 30 % of the relevant market on which it purchases the contract goods or services.

2. For the purposes of paragraph 1, where in a multi party agreement an undertaking buys the contract goods or services from one undertaking party to the agreement and sells the contract goods or services to another undertaking party to the agreement, the market share of the first undertaking must respect the market share threshold provided for in that paragraph both as a buyer and a supplier in order for the exemption provided for in Article 2 to apply.

b. Defining the Market

In addition to the Commission's Notice on definition of the relevant market, which provides general guidance on market definition[305] and jurisprudence, the Guidelines set out guidance on market definition and market share calculation issues, focused on distribution cases. Nonetheless, use of a market share test inevitably introduces an element of uncertainty into the block exemption which, arguably, is principally intended to provide legal certainty. Given the call for greater economic analysis in the approach to vertical restraints it is difficult, however, to be critical of the imposition of the market share cap. However, many commentators would perhaps have preferred to see the more economic approach manifested at the Article 101(1) stage of assessment, rather than when exempting the agreement under Article 101(3).

c. Exceeding the Market Shares

Because of the inherent uncertainty which the market share test brings, it is important that the Guidelines recognise that even if the market share thresholds are (or may be) exceeded there is no presumption that the agreement either infringes Article 101(1) or does not satisfy the Article 101(3) criteria (unless the agreement contains object or hardcore restraints). The Regulation provides for the situation where the agreement satisfies the market share thresholds initially but subsequently exceeds them.[306]

---

[302] So long as the agreement does not contain hardcore restraints, see Section 5.C.vi, pp. 825–834.

[303] The Commission recognises that firms that do not hold a dominant position may, nonetheless, have significant market power, see Chap. 1.

[304] See Section 5.C.iii, pp. 818–820.

[305] See Chap. 1.

[306] Verticals Reg., Art. 7, discussed in Section 5.C.x, p. 833.

d. Portfolio of Products Distributed through the Same Distribution System

Where the supplier uses the same distribution system to distribute several goods or services some of which are, and some of which are not, in view of the market share thresholds, covered by the block exemption the block exemption exempts only the former.[307]

(vi) Article 4—Hardcore Restrictions[308]

a. The Block Exemption is not Applicable to Vertical Agreements Containing Hardcore Restraints

Vertical agreements are exempted from the Article 101(1) prohibition whatever restrictions or obligations they contain so long as they are not hardcore restraints prohibited by Article 4.[309] The insertion of just one of these clauses precludes the entire vertical agreement from benefiting from the block exemption.[310] Article 4 focuses on clauses, such as those imposing price or territorial restraints, which restrict intra-brand competition. It will be remembered that there has been concern that EU competition law has treated these types of restraint too harshly (especially when compared to the position that exists in the US). Nonetheless, in the review of the Verticals Regulation and Guidelines the Commission never proposed removing these restraints from the list of hardcore restraints. Indeed, such a step would have resulted in a presumption of legality—which can only be withdrawn prospectively—for such restraints where incorporated in an agreement satisfying the market share thresholds. Arguably, this would be inappropriate, given their clear potential for serious anti-competitive effects.[311] Although the Verticals Regulation does not apply to these restraints, however, the Commission does accept that hardcore restraints may satisfy the Article 101(3) criteria in exceptional circumstances.[312]

Article 4 prohibits all clauses which, directly or indirectly, have as their object certain restrictions specified in paragraphs (a)–(e) of the Article.

Article 4

Restrictions that remove the benefit of the block exemption—hardcore restrictions

The exemption provided for in Article 2 shall not apply to vertical agreements which, directly or indirectly, in isolation or in combination with other factors under the control of the parties, have as their object:

(a) the restriction of the buyer's ability to determine its sale price, without prejudice to the possibility of the supplier to impose a maximum sale price or recommend a sale price, provided that they do not amount to a fixed or minimum sale price as a result of pressure from, or incentives offered by, any of the parties;

(b) the restriction of the territory into which, or of the customers to whom, a buyer party to the agreement, without prejudice to a restriction on its place of establishment, may sell the contract goods or services, except:

---

[307] Guidelines, para. 72.

[308] Guidelines, paras. 47–59.

[309] But see also the discussion of Art. 5 in Section 5.C.vii, pp. 830–832.

[310] In contrast, clauses infringing Art. 5 do not benefit from the block exemption, but the remainder of the agreement may benefit.

[311] RPM could, however, possibly have been classified as a non-exempted restraint rather than a hardcore one.

[312] See Section 5.E.ii, pp. 834–837.

(i) the restriction of active sales into the exclusive territory or to an exclusive customer group reserved to the supplier or allocated by the supplier to another buyer, where such a restriction does not limit sales by the customers of the buyer,

(ii) the restriction of sales to end users by a buyer operating at the wholesale level of trade,

(iii) the restriction of sales by the members of a selective distribution system to unauthorised distributors within the territory reserved by the supplier to operate that system, and

(iv) the restriction of the buyer's ability to sell components, supplied for the purposes of incorporation, to customers who would use them to manufacture the same type of goods as those produced by the supplier;

(c) the restriction of active or passive sales to end users by members of a selective distribution system operating at the retail level of trade, without prejudice to the possibility of prohibiting a member of the system from operating out of an unauthorised place of establishment;

(d) the restriction of cross-supplies between distributors within a selective distribution system, including between distributors operating at different level of trade;

(e) the restriction, agreed between a supplier of components and a buyer who incorporates those components, of the supplier's ability to sell the components as spare parts to end-users or to repairers or other service providers not entrusted by the buyer with the repair or servicing of its goods.

b. Article 4(a): Fixed or Minimum Sales Prices

Article 4(a) prohibits clauses resulting in the establishment of a fixed or minimum resale price or a fixed or minimum price level to be observed by the buyer. Recommended or maximum prices may be imposed so long as they do not amount to indirect means of achieving RPM.[313] Examples of price fixing through indirect means and measures facilitating direct or indirect price fixing are set out in paragraph 48 of the Guidelines:

an agreement fixing the distribution margin, fixing the maximum level of discount the distributor can grant from a prescribed price level, making the grant of rebates or reimbursement of promotional costs by the supplier subject to the observance of a given price level, linking the prescribed resale price to the resale prices of competitors, threats, intimidation, warnings, penalties, delay or suspension of deliveries or contract terminations in relation to observance of a given price level. Direct or indirect means of achieving price fixing can be made more effective when combined with measures to identify price-cutting distributors, such as the implementation of a price monitoring system, or the obligation on retailers to report other members of the distribution network that deviate from the standard price level. Similarly, direct or indirect price fixing can be made more effective when combined with measures which may reduce the buyer's incentive to lower the resale price, such as the supplier printing a recommended resale price on the product or the supplier obliging the buyer to apply a most-favoured-customer clause. The same indirect means and the same 'supportive' measures can be used to make maximum or recommended prices work as RPM. However, the use of a particular supportive measure or the provision of a list of recommended prices or maximum prices by the supplier to the buyer is not considered in itself as leading to RPM.

In paragraph 49 the Commission also objects, where agency agreements do fall within Article 101(1), to contractual provisions preventing or restricting the agent from sharing commission with the customer. As the principal sets the price, the agent should be 'free to lower the effective price paid by the customer without reducing the income for the principal'.

---

[313] Guidelines, para. 226. The Commission provides further guidance for the assessment of maximum and fixed resale prices where not covered by the Verticals Reg. in paras 227–229.

c. Article 4(b): Restrictions of the Territory or the Customers to whom the Buyer may Sell

Article 4(b) prohibits clauses that directly or indirectly restrict the territory into which, or the customers to whom, the buyer party to the agreement or its customers may sell the contract goods or services. The provision prohibits both direct restrictions and indirect provisions that, in practice, prevent or deter a buyer or its customers from making sales outside specific territories or customer groups.

The hardcore restriction set out in Article 4(b)…concerns agreements or concerted practices that have as their direct or indirect object the restriction of sales by a buyer party to the agreement or its customers, in as far as those restrictions relate to the territory into which or the customers to whom the buyer or its customers may sell the contract goods or services. This hardcore restriction relates to market partitioning by territory or by customer group. That may be the result of direct obligations, such as the obligation not to sell to certain customers or to customers in certain territories or the obligation to refer orders from these customers to other distributors. It may also result from indirect measures aimed at inducing the distributor not to sell to such customers, such as refusal or reduction of bonuses or discounts, termination of supply, reduction of supplied volumes or limitation of supplied volumes to the demand within the allocated territory or customer group, threat of contract termination, requiring a higher price for products to be exported, limiting the proportion of sales that can be exported or profit pass-over obligations. It may further result from the supplier not providing a Union-wide guarantee service under which normally all distributors are obliged to provide the guarantee service and are reimbursed for this service by the supplier, even in relation to products sold by other distributors into their territory (4). Such practices are even more likely to be viewed as a restriction of the buyer's sales when used in conjunction with the implementation by the supplier of a monitoring system aimed at verifying the effective destination of the supplied goods, such as the use of differentiated labels or serial numbers. However, obligations on the reseller relating to the display of the supplier's brand name are not classified as hardcore. As Article 4(b) only concerns restrictions of sales by the buyer or its customers, this implies that restrictions of the supplier's sales are also not a hardcore restriction, subject to what is stated in paragraph (59) regarding sales of spare parts in the context of Article 4(e)…. Article 4(b) applies without prejudice to a restriction on the buyer's place of establishment. Thus, the benefit of the Block Exemption Regulation is not lost if it is agreed that the buyer will restrict its distribution outlet(s) and warehouse(s) to a particular address, place or territory.[314]

Article 4 itself sets out four exceptions to the prohibition:

(1) Restrictions on Active Sales into Exclusive Territories or to an Exclusive Customer Group Reserved to Another

The first exception allows a supplier to restrict active sales by a buyer into an exclusive territory or to an exclusive consumer group reserved either to itself or to another buyer. It thus allows a supplier to reserve both exclusive territories and/or exclusive customer groups to a buyer. A buyer can be appointed to supply a certain customer group in a certain territory and can be precluded from actively selling both into other territories reserved to another and to a customer group reserved to another within its territory.

The Regulation only permits the supplier to prohibit the buyer from making 'active' sales to another's customers or customers in another's territory. The Commission makes the corollary clear in the Guidelines, a prohibition on the making of 'passive' sales into another's territory or to another's customer group is not permitted in the context of exclusive distribution and exclusive customer allocation. The agreement must admit the possibility of some parallel trade in the goods or services. The distinction between active and passive sales is thus critically important, since it defines the border between what is and what is not permissible, so the issue is dealt with in some detail in

---

[314] Guidelines, para. 50, but see Case T-67/01, *JCB Service v. Commission* [2004] ECR II-49 (where distributors pay for the guarantee service it can be agreed that a distributor which sells outside its allotted territory must reimburse the distributor providing the service for the cost of the services plus a reasonable profit margin).

the Guidelines. They explain that the prohibition on active sales is intended to prohibit a distributor from individually approaching customers, for example, by mailing, emailing, visiting, or targeting advertising on other customer groups or customers within another's territory.[315] No prohibition is permitted, however, on sales made in response to unsolicited requests from customers.

In the debate which led up to the adoption of the new Verticals Regulation in 2010 one of the core issues which arose for discussion, apart from the treatment of RPM, was the extent to which suppliers (especially those operating selective distribution systems—see also discussion of Article 4(c) in Section 5.C.vi.d) should be allowed to control or prevent sales by buyers over the internet (whether by 'click and brick'—brick and mortar stores which also sell over the internet—or 'pure players'— which sell only over the internet). Selling over the internet has grown exponentially since the last block exemption and Guidelines were drafted and finalised. Internet selling clearly offers enormous potential benefits for both sellers and consumers. It enables a distributor to target a broader range of customers than is possible through traditional sales methods as well as allowing it to provide 24-hour, and other, services not offered by traditional retailers. It may also intensify price competition,[316] allowing internet sellers to pass on their lower costs to customers, to overcome geographic barriers and provide customers with a broader range of outlets. A point which became of acute importance, therefore, during the drafting of, and consultation on,[317] the new Verticals Regulation and Guidelines was whether or not a requirement especially in the context of selective distribution, that dealers should have a brick and mortar shop, could be block exempted and/or whether exclusive dealers could be prohibited from selling or advertising on the internet—i.e. whether this amounts to active selling.

With regard to exclusive distribution, the Commission's starting point is that use of the internet constitutes passive selling so that a restriction on such sales and parallel trade is prohibited:

> The internet is a powerful tool to reach a greater number and variety of customers than by more traditional sales methods, which explains why certain restrictions on the use of the internet are dealt with as (re)sales restrictions. In principle, every distributor must be allowed to use the internet to sell products. In general, where a distributor uses a website to sell products that is considered a form of passive selling, since it is a reasonable way to allow customers to reach the distributor. The use of a website may have effects that extend beyond the distributor's own territory and customer group; however, such effects result from the technology allowing easy access from everywhere. If a customer visits the web site of a distributor and contacts the distributor and if such contact leads to a sale, including delivery, then that is considered passive selling. The same is true if a customer opts to be kept (automatically) informed by the distributor and it leads to a sale. Offering different language options on the website does not, of itself, change the passive character of such selling.[318]

Thus, agreeing that an exclusive distributor shall: prevent customers located in another exclusive territory from viewing its website; reroute customers to other distributors' websites; terminate consumers' transactions once their credit card data reveal an address that is not within the distributor's exclusive territory; limit the proportion of its overall internet sales; pay a higher price for products intended to be resold online are generally regarded by the Commission as hardcore restrictions on passive selling in view of their capability to limit the distributor's ability to reach more and different

[315] Guidelines, para. 51.

[316] The French competition authority has brought a number of cases involving bans on internet selling within a selective distribution system (including *Pierre Fabre* itself) and in September 2012 published a report on an inquiry into online commerce which focused on the distribution of domestic appliances, luxury perfumes, and cosmetic and personal care products. The report concludes that as e-commerce often puts significant pressure on prices, offering consumers lower prices and more choice, vertical agreements should not generally curb the development of on-line sales. It has thus committed to keep a close eye on developments in this sector.

[317] See the Commission's initiatives in relation to online retailing,<http://ec.europa.eu/competition/sectors/media/online_commerce.html>.

[318] Guidelines, para. 52.

customers.[319] The Commission does recognise, however, that some internet selling might constitute active selling which may be restricted, for example, online advertising specifically addressed to certain customers, territory-based banners on third party websites, or paying a search engine to have its website found more easily in a particular territory or by a particular customer group.[320]

(2) Restrictions on Wholesalers

The second exception permits a prohibition on a buyer at the wholesale level of trade from making active or passive sales to end users.

(3) The Restriction on Sales to Unauthorised Distributors by the Members of a Select Distribution System

This provision reiterates that where a selective distribution system is operated it is possible to prohibit members of the system from selling (actively or passively) to unauthorised distributors. In the absence of such a provision the system would obviously break down. The way in which the Verticals Regulation applies to selective distribution systems is discussed further in Section 5.C.vi.d.

(4) Buyers of Components

A supplier may preclude a buyer of components for incorporation into another product from selling (actively or passively) to a customer who would use them to manufacture a product which competes with that produced by the supplier.

d. Articles 4(c) and 4(d): Restrictions in Selective Distribution Systems

It has been seen that as an exception to the rule that suppliers may not restrict the customers to whom, or the territories in which, the buyers sell the contract goods, Article 4(b) provides that members of a selective distribution system can be precluded from making sales to unauthorised distributors outside the system and wholesalers can be prohibited from making sales to end users. Articles 4(c) and 4(d) also deal with the compatibility with Article 101 of sales restraints imposed on authorised members of the network. Article 4(c) prohibits restrictions on active or passive selling by retailers to end users, but permits the prohibition of retailers operating out of an authorised place of establishment. In *Pierre Fabre* v. *Président de l'Autorité de la concurrence*,[321] the CJ held that a requirement that cosmetic products could be sold only at a premises with a pharmacist present operated as a ban on passive selling for the purposes of Article 4(c): the contractual clauses prohibited *de facto* internet selling which had as its object the restriction of passive sales to end users wishing to purchase online and located outside the physical trading area of the retailer. The Court rejected Pierre Fabre's argument that the ban on internet selling was simply equivalent to a prohibition on the retailer operating out of an authorised establishment. Article 4(d) provides that members of a system may not be precluded from making cross-supplies *inter se*.

It appears therefore that, insofar as a selective distribution system is caught by Article 101(1) at all, the main constraints on the operation of a selective distribution system under the block exemption are that:

- the supplier and buyer do not exceed the 30 per cent market share threshold set out;
- RPM is not directly or indirectly imposed;

---

[319] Guidelines, para. 52, subject to some exceptions (e.g., a supplier may require, without limiting the online sales of the distributor, that the buyer sells at least a certain absolute amount of products offline to ensure an efficient operation of its bricks and mortar shop).

[320] Guidelines, para. 53.

[321] Case C-439/09, 13 October 2011.

- retail members are not restrained from making sales to any end user (whether or not with the help of the internet);[322] and

- members are not restrained from making sales to another member of the network.[323] The members may not, therefore, be required to purchase products only from the supplier (exclusive sourcing).[324] Article 5 makes it clear, however, that non-compete obligations are permissible so long as they are not excessive in time and are not targeted at specific suppliers (see Section 5.C.vii.a).

Restraints can be imposed on the location and nature of the distributors' premises[325] and on sales being made to unauthorised distributors.[326] Further, the supplier may require distributors to adhere to quality standards for the use of an internet site to resell goods and to have one or more bricks and mortar shops or showrooms before engaging in online distribution.[327] Obligations going beyond this, however, and designed to dissuade appointed dealers from using the internet to reach more and different customers will constitute hardcore restrictions.[328]

In contrast to the position under Article 101(1) it is not necessary to establish that the products concerned merit a selective distribution system nor that the members of the system are chosen only by reference to qualitative criteria. Quantitative criteria may be used to select distributors.[329] The Guidelines provide that a selective distribution system cannot be combined with exclusive distribution in the territory within which the supplier operates a selective distribution system, as this would lead to a restriction of active or passive selling by dealers (although selected dealers can be prevented from running their business from different premises or from opening a new outlet in a different location).[330]

e. Article 4(e): Restrictions on Suppliers of Components

Where a supplier supplies a buyer with components which the latter incorporates into its goods, a restriction may not be imposed which prevents the supplier from selling the components to customers or repairers which have not been authorised by the buyer to repair or service its goods.

(vii) Article 5—Excluded Restraints: Severable, Non-exempted Obligations

a. Obligations which are Excluded (not Exempted) but which may be Severable

Article 5, in comparison with Article 4, focuses on non-compete clauses[331] that are capable of foreclosing the market and restricting inter-brand competition directly. In contrast to the provision in Article 4, Article 5 provides that where an agreement contains a non-compete obligation which goes beyond its provisions, that *clause* does not benefit from the block exemption. The insertion of such a clause does not, therefore, necessarily prevent the possibility of the remaining provisions of

---

[322] They should be free to advertise and sell with the help of the internet, Guidelines, para. 53.

[323] In *B&W Loudspeakers* IP/00/1418 (opening of proceedings) and IP/02/916 (comfort letter), the Commission objected to price restraints, restraints on cross-supplies between dealers, and restraints on distant selling via the internet in a selective distribution system notified to it under the old notification system. Eventually, however, it granted a comfort letter after the parties agreed to remove the hardcore restraints.

[324] Guidelines, para. 58.

[325] Verticals Reg., Art. 4(c).

[326] Verticals Reg., Art. 4(b).

[327] Guidelines, para. 54.

[328] Guidelines, para. 56

[329] See Section 4.B.iv.b., pp. 810–812

[330] Guidelines, para. 57.

[331] See the definition of non-compete obligations in the Verticals Reg., see Section 5.C.iii, p. 820.

the agreement benefiting from the Regulation. It will only do so where the offensive clauses violate Article 101 and are *not* severable from the remaining provisions of the agreement.[332]

Article 5

Excluded restrictions

1. The exemption provided for in Article 2 shall not apply to the following obligations contained in vertical agreements:

   (a) any direct or indirect non-compete obligation, the duration of which is indefinite or exceeds five years;

   (b) any direct or indirect obligation causing the buyer, after termination of the agreement, not to manufacture, purchase, sell or resell goods or services;

   (c) any direct or indirect obligation causing the members of a selective distribution system not to sell the brands of particular competing suppliers.

   For the purposes of point (a) of the first subparagraph, a non-compete obligation which is tacitly renewable beyond a period of five years shall be deemed to have been concluded for an indefinite duration.

2. By way of derogation from paragraph 1(a), the time limitation of five years shall not apply where the contract goods or services are sold by the buyer from premises and land owned by the supplier or leased by the supplier from third parties not connected with the buyer, provided that the duration of the non-compete obligation does not exceed the period of occupancy of the premises and land by the buyer.

3. By way of derogation from paragraph 1(b), the exemption provided for in Article 2 shall apply to any direct or indirect obligation causing the buyer, after termination of the agreement, not to manufacture, purchase, sell or resell goods or services where the following conditions are fulfilled:

   (a) the obligation relates to goods or services which compete with the contract goods or services;

   (b) the obligation is limited to the premises and land from which the buyer has operated during the contract period;

   (c) the obligation is indispensable to protect know-how transferred by the supplier to the buyer;

   (d) the duration of the obligation is limited to a period of one year after termination of the agreement.

   Paragraph 1(b) is without prejudice to the possibility of imposing a restriction which is unlimited in time on the use and disclosure of know-how which has not entered the public domain.

b. Article 5(1): Non-compete Obligations

Article 5(1) provides that the exemption does not apply to non-compete obligations imposed (or tacitly renewable) in excess of five years. An exception applies, however, where the buyer of the goods or services operates from premises owned by the supplier or leased by it from a third party not connected with the buyer. In this case the non-compete obligation can be imposed for the duration of the buyer's occupancy of the land. It thus seems, for example, that brewers leasing premises to a publican will be able to impose a non-compete obligation for the entire duration of the lease. The reason for this latter exception is that 'it is normally unreasonable to expect a supplier to allow competing products to be sold from premises and land owned by the supplier without its permission'. But

---

[332] It seems that whether or not the offending clauses can be severed is a question of national, not EU, law. See Chaps. 3 and 14.

'[a]rtificial ownership constructions...intended to avoid the five-year duration limit cannot benefit from this exception'.[333]

c. Article 5(3): Non-compete Obligations after the Termination of the Agreement

Article 5(3) states that the exemption does not apply to obligations imposed on the buyer which prevent it from manufacturing, purchasing, or selling or reselling goods or services after the termination of the agreement *unless* the prohibition: relates to competing goods or services; is limited to the premises and land from which the buyer has operated during the agreement; is indispensable to protect know-how[334] transferred by the supplier under the agreement; and is limited to a period of one year. A restriction which is unlimited in time may be possible, however, where essential to prevent the use or disclosure of know-how which has not entered the public domain.

d. Article 5(1)(c): Non-compete Obligations and Selective Distribution Systems

The block exemption covers 'the combination of selective distribution with a non-compete obligation, obliging the distributor not to resell competing brands in general'. Article 5(1)(c) provides, however, that the exemption will not apply where the supplier prevents distributors from buying products for resale from *specific* competing suppliers.

The objective of the exclusion of this obligation is to avoid a situation whereby a number of suppliers using the same selective distribution outlets prevent one specific competitor or certain specific competitors from using these outlets to distribute their products (foreclosure of a competing supplier which would be a form of collective boycott).[335]

(viii) Withdrawal of the Block Exemption by the Commission or the National Competition Authorities

The benefit of the block exemption can be withdrawn in relation to an agreement which, either in isolation or in conjunction with similar agreements, infringes Article 101(1) and does not in fact satisfy the conditions of Article 101(3).[336] The Commission has the exclusive power to withdraw the benefit of the block exemption in respect of vertical agreements restricting competition on a relevant geographic market which is wider than the territory of a single Member, but concurrent jurisdiction with the NCAs where the relevant geographic market constitutes the territory of a single Member State, or a part thereof.[337] Where the Commission wishes to so withdraw the benefit of the Verticals Regulation it will have to prove that the agreement infringes Article 101(1) and does not fulfil one or several of the four conditions set out in Article 101(3).[338] The Commission may, for example, wish to do so where foreclosure occurs as a result of parallel networks of vertical agreements. Responsibility for anti-competitive effects identified will be attributed to the undertakings which make an appreciable contribution to them.[339] A withdrawal does not apply retrospectively, it only has *ex nunc* effect, 'which means that the exempted status of the agreements concerned will not be affected until the date at which the withdrawal becomes effective'.[340]

---

[333] Guidelines, para. 67.
[334] Verticals Reg., Art. 1(1)(g).
[335] Guidelines, para. 69 providing the example of *Parfums Givenchy* [1992] OJ L236/11.
[336] Reg. 1/2003, Art. 29(1)(2). See also Chap. 4.
[337] Guidelines, para. 78.
[338] Guidelines, para. 77.
[339] Guidelines, paras. 75–76.
[340] Guidelines, para. 77.

(ix) Article 6—Non-application of the Regulation—Networks of Agreements

This provision also allows (but does not require) the Commission to declare by regulation (applicable not to an individual undertaking but to all undertakings addressed) that the block exemption should not apply to agreements containing specified restraints in cases where more than 50 per cent of a relevant market is covered by networks of similar vertical restraints.[341] Any such regulation, fully restoring the application of Article 101 to the restraints and markets concerned,[342] could not take effect earlier than six months following its adoption[343] and does not affect the exempted status of the agreements concerned for the period preceding its coming into force.[344] When deciding whether to adopt a regulation the Commission will also consider whether withdrawal of the block exemption would be more appropriate. This will depend on the number of competing undertakings contributing to the cumulative effects and the number of affected geographic markets.[345]

Because the regulation must specify the scope of the regulation in relation both to the relevant product and geographic markets to which it applies and to the vertical restraints in respect of which the Verticals Regulation will not apply, the regulation may not apply to all agreements concluded on an affected market. Rather:

the Commission may modulate the scope of its regulation according to the competition concern which it intends to address. For instance, while all parallel networks of single-branding type arrangements shall be taken into account in view of establishing the 50 % market coverage ratio, the Commission may nevertheless restrict the scope of the disapplication regulation only to non-compete obligations exceeding a certain duration. Thus, agreements of a shorter duration or of a less restrictive nature might be left unaffected, in consideration of the lesser degree of foreclosure attributable to such restraints. Similarly, when on a particular market selective distribution is practised in combination with additional restraints such as non-compete or quantity-forcing on the buyer, the disapplication regulation may concern only such additional restraints. Where appropriate, the Commission may also provide guidance by specifying the market share level which, in the specific market context, may be regarded as insufficient to bring about a significant contribution by an individual undertaking to the cumulative effect.[346]

(x) Articles 7, 8, and 9—Market Share, Turnover, and Transitional Provisions

Articles 7 and 8 contain provisions relating to the calculation of market share and turnover for the purposes of the Regulation. In particular, Article 7(d) makes provision to exempt agreements for a period of two consecutive calendar years which satisfy the 30 per cent threshold initially but subsequently rise above it (without exceeding 35 per cent). Article 9 provides that agreements already in force on 31 May 2010 and satisfying the provisions of Regulation 2790/1999, but not Regulation 330/2010, shall not be prohibited from 1 June 2010 to 31 May 2011.

---

[341] Guidelines, para. 80, e.g., when parallel networks of selective distribution covering more than 50% of a market are liable to foreclose the market by using selection criteria which are not required by the nature of relevant goods or which discriminate against certain forms of distribution capable of selling such goods, Guidelines, para. 81.

[342] Guidelines,, para. 101.

[343] Art. 6(2).

[344] Guidelines, paras. 84–85.

[345] Guidelines, para. 82.

[346] Guidelines, para. 83.

(xi) Article 10—Commencement and Expiry

Article 10 provides that the block exemption entered into force on 1 June 2010,[347] and expires on 31 May 2022.

D. THE MOTOR VEHICLE DISTRIBUTION BLOCK EXEMPTION

Until the end of May 2010, motor vehicle distribution agreements and agreements relating to repair, maintenance, and the supply of spare parts were not governed by the ordinary regime for vertical agreements but by a specific block exemption, Regulation 1400/02[348] which recognised the special features of the motor vehicle sector. Before the block exemption was due to expire on 31 May 2010, the Commission, in 2008, evaluated its working. Following consultation on a future framework for motor vehicle agreements, the Commission concluded that motor vehicle manufacturers and dealers did not continue to require different treatment as compared to agreements in any other sector. In 2010, the Commission published a regulation, Regulation 461/2010, and Guidelines to replace Regulation 1400/2002.[349] This provided that from 31 May 2013, motor vehicle distribution agreements were brought within the ordinary regime for vertical agreements (subject to a three-year adaptation period). Repair and maintenance agreements, however, continue to be dealt with by a separate block exemption.[350]

E. ARTICLE 101(3)—INDIVIDUAL ASSESSMENT

(i) Introduction

Where the parties cannot ensure that their agreement benefits from either the Verticals Regulation or the motor vehicle distribution block exemption, and the risk of infringing Article 101(1) is real, it may still be important to consider the application of Article 101(3) to an agreement. It will be remembered that any restrictive agreement is, in theory, capable of satisfying the criteria[351] but all four criteria must be satisfied.[352]

(ii) 'Hardcore' Restraints

A supplier or distributor may perceive territorial and/or price restraints to be essential to the operation of a distribution agreement. Prior to the 2010 Guidelines, the Commission appeared unwilling in both its decisional practice and the Guidelines to accept that agreements which confer RPM[353] or confer ATP on a distributor or which otherwise operate to prevent parallel imports meet the requirements of Article 101(3).[354] Rather, it generally took the view that such restraints are unlikely

---

[347] Except for the provision extending the application of the block exemption which has applied since 1 January 2000.

[348] [2002] OJ L203/30. It entered into force in October 2002. In C-158/11, *Auto24 SARL* v. *Jaguar Land Rover France SAS* 14 June 2012, the CJ gave a judgment which focused on the interpretation of specific provisions of Regulation 1400/2002 and the distinction set out therein between quantitative and qualitative selective distribution systems.

[349] See <http://ec.europa.eu/competition/sectors/motor_vehicles/legislation/legislation.html>.

[350] See <http://ec.europa.eu/competition/sectors/motor_vehicles/legislation/legislation.html>.

[351] Case T-17/93, *Matra Hachette* v. *Commission* [1994] ECR II-595, para. 85, see Chap. 4.

[352] The requirements are cumulative, Case T-528/93, *Métropole Télévision S A* v. *Commission* [1996] ECR II-649, para. 86.

[353] See, e.g., *B&W Loudspeakers* n. 323.

[354] See, e.g., *Volkswagen* [1998] OJ L124/60, on appeal Case T-62/98, *Volkswagen AG* v. *Commission* [2000] ECR II-2707, the appeal to the CJ was dismissed, see Case C-338/00 P, *Volkswagen AG* v. *Commission* [2003] ECR I-9189.

to benefit consumers or to be indispensable to achieve the efficiencies specific to the agreement (which are likely to be achievable by other practicable and less restrictive means).[355] In *Grundig*,[356] for example, it was the clauses resulting in Consten being granted the exclusive right to sell Grundig's products in France which caused the Commission to find that the agreement both infringed Article 101(1) and did not meet the Article 101(3) criteria (it refused an exemption). The result was that Grundig acquired Consten. Subsequently, the Commission has not proved receptive to any argument that these types of clauses may be essential to prevent free riding on the distributors' services or to ensure that a product is successfully launched in a new market.[357] Further, in 2003 in *Nintendo*,[358] the Commission relied on *Grundig* when it stated that agreements conferring ATP, would not meet the criteria of Article 101(3) (the provisions were not indispensable to realise the potential benefits of the exclusive distribution system).[359]

Nonetheless, the EU Courts have always made it clear that even object restraints are capable of meeting the Article 101(3) criteria. In Chapter 4 it was seen that in *GlaxoSmithKline Services Unlimited v. Commission*,[360] the GC held that: the Commission's decision to refuse an exemption to a dual pricing system operated by Glaxo which prevented parallel trade was fundamentally flawed; and the Commission had not adequately discharged its duty under Article 101(3). Similarly, in *Binon*, the CJ indicated that the Commission might have to consider whether or not an agreement, where a publisher fixed the prices of its newspapers and periodicals, fulfilled the requirements of Article 101(3).[361]

Case 243/85, *SA Binon & Cie* v. *SA Agence et Messageries de la Presse* [1985] ECR 2015

44. It should be observed in the first place that provisions which fix the prices to be observed in contracts with third parties constitute, of themselves, a restriction on competition within the meaning of Article [101(1)]…

45. In those circumstances, where an agreement which establishes a selective distribution system and which affects trade between Member States includes such a provision, an exemption from the prohibition contained in Article [101(1) of the [EU] Treaty may only be granted by means of a decision adopted by the Commission in the conditions laid down by Article [101(3)].

46. If, in so far as the distribution of newspapers and periodicals is concerned, the fixing of the retail price by publishers constitutes the sole means of supporting the financial burden resulting from the taking back of unsold copies and if the latter practice constitutes the sole method by which a wide selection of newspapers and periodicals can be made available to readers, the Commission must take account of those factors when examining an agreement for the purposes of Article [101(3)].

---

[355] See Chap. 4.

[356] [1964] CMLR 489. See also, e.g., *The Distillers Company Limited* [1978] OJ L50/16, Case 30/78, *Distillers Company v. Commission* [1980] ECR 2229 and *Transocean Marine Paint Associations* [1967] OJ L/10.

[357] See Chap. 4.

[358] [2003] OJ L255/33, aff'd Case T-12/03, *Itochu v. Commission* [2009] ECR II-909 and, Case T-13/03, *Nintendo and Nintendo of Europe v. Commission* [2009] ECR II-975.

[359] 'Instead, in regard to the goods in question territories are hermetically sealed off, making interpenetrating of national markets impossible, thereby bringing to nought economic integration' [2003] OJ L255/33, para. 338.

[360] Case T-168/01, [2006] ECR II-2969 aff'd Cases C-501, 513, 515, 519/06, 6 October 2009. But see further discussion of the case in Chap. 4, especially Section 3.D., 205–232.

[361] In neither case did the Court hold that the Art. 101(3) criteria were satisfied, however.

In accordance with the case law and more modern economic thinking, the Commission was, therefore, when drafting the 2010 Guidelines, urged to ensure that the Guidelines reflected this position, that even hardcore restraints may in certain circumstances be indispensable to achieve efficiencies that would be passed on to consumers. The Commission has attempted to meet these calls, making it clear that although the block exemption does not apply to hardcore restrictions and that there is a presumption of negative effects under Article 101(1), individual satisfaction of the Article 101(3) criteria is not excluded where there is convincing evidence of likely efficiencies. In particular the Guidelines state:[362]

Including such a hardcore restriction in an agreement gives rise to the presumption that the agreement falls within Article 101(1). It also gives rise to the presumption that the agreement is unlikely to fulfil the conditions of Article 101(3), for which reason the block exemption does not apply. However, undertakings may demonstrate pro-competitive effects under Article 101(3) in an individual case. Where the undertakings substantiate that likely efficiencies result from including the hardcore restriction in the agreement and demonstrate that in general all the conditions of Article 101(3) are fulfilled, the Commission will be required to effectively assess the likely negative impact on competition before making an ultimate assessment of whether the conditions of Article 101(3) are fulfilled.

More specifically in paragraphs 60–64 and 223–229 the Commission recognises that in certain circumstances parties may be able to plead 'an efficiency defence'[363] to justify territorial and price restraints.

For example, the Commission recognises that ATP may be necessary for a period of time to protect a distributor which must incur significant expenses (often sunk) to start up and/or develop a new brand or an existing brand on a new market. Indeed, the Commission considers that these restraints may not even violate Article 101(1). It thus states in the Guidelines:

61 ... Where substantial investments by the distributor to start up and/or develop the new market are necessary, restrictions of passive sales by other distributors into such a territory or to such a customer group which are necessary for the distributor to recoup those investments generally fall outside the scope of Article 101(1) during the first two years that the distributor is selling the contract goods or services in that territory or to that customer group, even though such hardcore restrictions are in general presumed to fall within the scope of Article 101(1).

62. In the case of genuine testing of a new product in a limited territory or with a limited customer group and in the case of a staggered introduction of a new product, the distributors appointed to sell the new product on the test market or to participate in the first round(s) of the staggered introduction may be restricted in their active selling outside the test market or the market(s) where the product is first introduced without falling within the scope of Article 101(1) for the period necessary for the testing or introduction of the product.

The Commission also recognises that restraints on active sales by wholesalers in a selective distribution system may be necessary to protect promotional activities which must be conducted in wholesalers' own territories and that dual pricing arrangements (for example, where the supplier charges higher prices for products to be sold online) may be justified where sales online lead to substantially higher costs for the manufacturer.[364]

In addition, the Commission states that efficiencies raised to justify RPM will be assessed under Article 101(3), for example:[365]

---

[362] Guideline, para. 47. See also para. 223.

[363] In addition, the Guidelines state at para. 60 that hardcore restrictions may be objectively necessary 'to align on a public ban on selling dangerous substances to certain customers for reasons of safety or health', see Chap. 4.

[364] Guidelines, paras. 63–64.

[365] Guidelines, para. 225.

where a manufacturer introduces a new product, RPM may be helpful during the introductory period of expanding demand to induce distributors to better take into account the manufacturer's interest to promote the product. RPM may provide the distributors with the means to increase sales efforts and if the distributors on this market are under competitive pressure this may induce them to expand overall demand for the product and make the launch of the product a success, also for the benefit of consumers. Similarly, fixed resale prices, and not just maximum resale prices, may be necessary to organise in a franchise system or similar distribution system applying a uniform distribution format a coordinated short term low price campaign (2 to 6 weeks in most cases) which will also benefit the consumers. In some situations, the extra margin provided by RPM may allow retailers to provide (additional) pre-sales services, in particular in case of experience or complex products. If enough customers take advantage from such services to make their choice but then purchase at a lower price with retailers that do not provide such services (and hence do not incur these costs), high-service retailers may reduce or eliminate these services that enhance the demand for the supplier's product. RPM may help to prevent such free-riding at the distribution level. The parties will have to convincingly demonstrate that the RPM agreement can be expected to not only provide the means but also the incentive to overcome possible free riding between retailers on these services and that the pre-sales services overall benefit consumers as part of the demonstration that all the conditions of Article 101(3) are fulfilled.

The Commission does therefore now recognise, in line with the case law of the Court, that even hardcore restraints may sometimes satisfy the conditions of Article 101(3). Nonetheless, an extremely onerous burden remains on the parties who seek to demonstrate that efficiencies will result from including ATP or RPM in their agreement and to demonstrate also that the other conditions of Article 101(3) are fulfilled. The tendency of the Commission and NCAs to fine undertakings which incorporate these restraints in their contracts, combined with the very limited and narrow examples provided in the Guidelines of the situations where the Article 101(3) conditions might be satisfied (and the lack of jurisprudence on this issue), is, however, likely to make firms wary about incorporating these restraints into their agreements. Indeed, it is not clear that the Commission has moved so far from the view expounded in the Article 101(3) Guidelines that hardcore restraints are unlikely to create objective economic benefits, to benefit consumers, or to be indispensable to the attainment of any efficiencies created by the agreement.[366] In particular, the 2010 Guidelines suggest that indispensability is likely to continue to present a problem to those seeking to rely on Article 101(3) to justify hardcore restraints as they will need to demonstrate that no other restraint would be sufficient to achieve the efficiencies alleged. Paragraph 109 makes this point clearly:

> [a] large measure of substitutability exists between the different vertical restraints. As a result, the same inefficiency problem can be solved by different vertical restraints. For instance, economies of scale in distribution may possibly be achieved by using exclusive distribution, selective distribution, quantity forcing or exclusive sourcing. However, the negative effects on competition may differ between the various vertical restraints, which play a role when indispensability is discussed under Article 101(3).

(iii) Non-compete Provisions and Other Restraints

In other cases, it is extremely important when drafting agreements to look both generally at the Article 101(3) Guidelines and,[367] more specifically, at the Guidelines which set out how the Commission will enforce Article 101 in respect of individual agreements not covered by the block exemption and containing specified restraints (such as: single branding; exclusive distribution and customer allocation; selective distribution; franchising; exclusive supply; and/or recommended and maximum prices).[368] Past decisional practice of the Commission when granting or refusing

---

[366] See Chap. 4.

[367] [2004] OJ C101/97.

[368] See, especially, paras. 131–136 and 139–226.

individual exemptions should also be examined. Article 5 of the Verticals Regulation also gives an indication of how Article 101(3) will apply to non-compete provisions. On occasion, however, it may be possible to argue that a non-compete provision for longer than that permitted in Article 5 is indispensable to the operation of the agreement.[369] When deciding whether or not an agreement meets the criteria of Article 101(3), in particular whether a restriction is indispensable to the operation of the agreement, the Guidelines make it clear that the determination must be made with regard to the *justification* for the vertical restraints (for example, whether or not it is necessary to help solve a free-rider problem, to create brand image, or to deal with a hold-up problem).

An example of a case in which a non-compete provision was found not to meet the criteria of Article 101(3) is *Van den Bergh Foods*.[370] In this case the GC rejected the applicants' assertion that the Commission had erred in law in applying Article 101(3), in particular by wrongly concluding that the restrictive effects of its freezer exclusivity agreements outweighed the advantages flowing from the distribution efficiency they produced. The GC held that as the agreement did not satisfy the first condition of Article 101(3), the Commission was entitled to refuse an exemption.[371] The advantages produced by the agreement were not objective ones but ensued to the parties to the agreement.[372]

Case T-65/98, *Van den Bergh Foods Ltd* v. *Commission* [2003] ECR II-4653[373]

General Court

138. The Court finds that, contrary to HB's submission in paragraph 123 above, it is clear from the contested decision that the Commission carried out a detailed analysis of the HB distribution agreement in the light of each of the four conditions laid down by Article [101(3)] of the Treaty (see recitals 221 to 254 of the contested decision).

139. As regards the first of those conditions, the agreements capable of being exempted are those which contribute to improving the production or distribution of goods or to promoting technical or economic progress. The Court would point out in that regard that it is settled law of the Court of Justice and of the [General Court] that the improvement cannot be identified with all the advantages which the parties obtain from the agreement in their production or distribution activities. The improvement must in particular display appreciable objective advantages of such a character as to compensate for the disadvantages which they cause in the field of competition (Joined Cases 56/64 and 58/64 *Consten and Grundig* v. *Commission*...at 348, and *Langnese-Iglo*, paragraph 180).

---

[369] See, e.g., Guidelines, paras. 155 (longer periods may be possible where significant investment is required), and 158 and 171 (a non-compete provision may be permitted for the duration of an exclusive distribution agreement).

[370] Case T-65/98, *Van den Bergh Foods* v. *Commission* [2003] ECR II-4653, aff'd Case C-552/03 P, *Unilever Bestfoods* v. *Commission* [2006] ECR I-9091.

[371] Under the old notification and exemption system the Court reiterated that 'the review carried out...of the complex economic assessments undertaken by the Commission in the exercise of the discretion conferred on it by Article [101(3)] of the Treaty in relation to each of the four conditions laid down therein, must be limited to ascertaining whether the procedural rules have been complied with, whether proper reasons have been provided, whether the facts have been accurately stated and whether there has been any manifest error of appraisal or misuse of powers (see, to that effect, Joined Cases T-39/92 and T-40/92, *CB and Europay* v. *Commission* [1994] ECR II-49, para. 109; Case T-17/93, *Matra Hachette* v. *Commission* [1994] ECR II-595, para. 104; and Case T-29/92, *SPO and others* v. *Commission* [1995] ECR II-289, para. 288). It is not for the [General Court] to substitute its own assessment for that of the Commission', Case T-65/98, *Van den Bergh Foods* v. *Commission* [2003] ECR II-4653, para. 135, aff'd Case C-552/03 P, *Unilever Bestfoods* v. *Commission* [2006] ECR I-9091.

[372] The GC held that rather than improving distribution or promoting progress, the effect of the agreements was to strengthen the strong position of HB on the market.

[373] Aff'd Case C-552/03 P, *Unilever Bestfoods* v. *Commission* [2006] ECR I-9091.

140. The first condition is examined in recitals 222 to 238 of the contested decision. The Commission acknowledged in particular that the agreements whereby freezer cabinets are made available might secure some or all of the benefits described in the fifth recital to Regulation No. 1984/83 for HB itself and for the retailers who are the other parties to the agreements, and that the distribution method currently used by HB might offer it and its retailers certain advantages in terms of efficiency of planning, organisation and distribution. Therefore, the Commission held that those arrangements did not present appreciable objective advantages of such a character as to compensate for the disadvantages caused to competition. In support of that assertion, it pointed out that the freezer cabinet agreements in question considerably strengthened HB's position in the relevant market, especially vis-à-vis potential competitors. It rightly observed in that regard that the strengthening of an undertaking which is as important on the market as HB leads not to more but to less competition because the network of that undertaking's agreements constitutes a major barrier to the entry of others into the market, as well as to expansion within the market by its existing competitors (see in particular recitals 225 and 236 of the contested decision, and, by analogy, *Langnese-Iglo* v. *Commission*, paragraph 182). It must also be pointed out that the level of foreclosure of the relevant market is in the order of 40 per cent (see paragraph 98 above) and not 6 per cent as HB submits ...

141. Consequently, the Court finds that, contrary to HB's contention ... the Commission rightly took into consideration the barriers to entry to the relevant market resulting from the exclusivity clause, and the consequent weakening of competition, when it assessed HB's distribution agreement in the light of the first condition laid down by Article [101(3)] of the Treaty (see, by analogy, *Consten and Grundig* v. *Commission* at p. 348, and *Langnese-Iglo* v. *Commission*, paragraph 180). It follows that the Court cannot accept HB's argument ... to the effect that recitals 222 to 225 of the contested decision contain a fundamental logical flaw with regard to the relationship between Article [101(1)] and Article [101(3)] of the Treaty, as the Commission was obliged, pursuant to settled case-law on the subject, to ascertain whether there were objective advantages of such a character as to compensate for the disadvantages which an agreement creates for competition.

142. The Court also notes that HB's distribution agreements have two particular aspects, namely, first, they make freezer cabinets available without charge to retailers and, second, the retailers undertake to use those cabinets to stock HB ice creams only. The benefits ensured by the agreements in question are the result of the first aspect and can therefore be achieved even without the exclusivity clause.

143. The Court also accepts the Commission's argument in recital 227 of the contested decision that although the wide availability in outlets of freezer cabinets intended for the sale of impulse ice-creams, covering the entire geographic market and consisting mainly of HB's cabinets, could be considered an objective advantage in the distribution of those products in the public interest, it is nevertheless unlikely that HB would definitely cease to supply freezer cabinets to retailers, whatever the conditions, except in small number of cases, if its power to impose an obligation of exclusivity in respect of those freezers were to be restricted. HB has not shown that the Commission committed a manifest error in taking the view that business reality for a company such as HB, which wishes to maintain its position on the relevant market, is to be present in the maximum number of outlets possible (see recital 228 and paragraph 125 above). Contrary to HB's submission, the Commission did not merely assume continuity of provision by HB of freezer cabinets on the relevant market, but carried out a prospective analysis of the operation of the market after the adoption of the contested decision. Furthermore, contrary to HB's argument (see paragraph 125 above), the Commission could validly rely on the argument that manufacturers competing with HB might adopt a policy of supplying freezer cabinets to sales outlets whose turnover in impulse ice-creams is too low to be of interest to HB, and do so upon more advantageous conditions than those which the retailers might expect to obtain themselves if HB ceased to supply freezer cabinets to certain sales outlets. Similarly, the Commission could validly point to the possibility that cabinets would be installed by independent resellers who would obtain supplies from various sources and satisfy demand from all the sales outlets from which HB had withdrawn its equipment or to which it decided not to supply equipment. HB cannot claim that the Commission's prospective analysis is vitiated by a manifest error of assessment unless it does so on the basis of concrete evidence, which HB has failed to adduce in the present case.

144. As HB's distribution agreements do not satisfy the first of the conditions laid down by Article [101(3)], the third plea must therefore be rejected and it is not necessary to consider whether the Commission committed a manifest error in regard to its assessment of the other conditions laid down by that provision. If any one of the four conditions is not satisfied, the exemption must be refused.

In *Telenor/Canal+/Canal Digital*,[374] the European Commission granted negative clearance, in combination with an exemption, to complex contractual arrangements providing for the exclusive distribution by Canal Digital of pay-TV premium content channels and pay-per-view and near-video-on demand (PPV/NVOD) channels in the Nordic region.[375] The agreements also imposed non-compete obligations which, broadly, prohibited Canal Digital from owning, operating, or retailing any other pay-TV premium content or PPV/NVOD channels.

In order to gain approval for the agreements the parties agreed to modify the agreements and: to mitigate foreclosure of potential entrants in the downstream DTH pay-TV market by reducing the duration and scope of Canal Digital's exclusivity; to alleviate foreclosure of potential entrants on the supply side in the upstream market for the wholesale supply of pay-TV by reducing the duration of the pay-TV non-compete obligations on Canal Digital; and to alleviate foreclosure of potential entrants on the supply side in the upstream market for the provision of transponder capacity for TV broadcasting by reducing non-compete obligations on Canal+.[376]

The Commission took the view that most of the clauses, even in their revised form, appreciably restricted competition within the meaning of Article 101(1).[377] Further, the Commission noted that the Verticals block exemption was not available to the parties, both because the primary purpose of the exclusivity and non-compete arrangement was the use by the buyer of IPRs and because of Canal+'s strong market position, which exceeded the 30 per cent threshold. The Commission stressed, however, that this did not mean that there was a presumption that the vertical agreement was illegal. 'Rather the agreements need individual examination by the Commission in the application of Article 101(3) of the Treaty.'[378]

The Commission found that the modified exclusivity and non-compete provisions generated efficiencies and contributed to the improvement in distribution and the promotion of economic progress within the meaning of Article 101(3) and that consumers received a fair share of the benefits. Although the Commission accepted that the provisions were indispensable to attain the efficiencies, this was only so subject to a strict limitation period, for example: of four years' duration for the pay-TV channel exclusivity provisions; and of three years in respect of the obligation on Telenor/Canal Digital not to own, operate, or distribute via DTH any other pay-TV premium content channels. The Commission concluded that the various contractual arrangements did not eliminate competition in the affected markets during the term of their validity. The cooperation for a limited period

[374] 29 December 2003.

[375] The notified agreements also related to the divestiture by Canal+ of its 50% shareholding in Canal Digital, previously jointly run with Telenor Broadband Services (TBS), and its acquisition by TBS. The distribution agreements related to the distribution by Canal Digital of Canal+ Nordic's pay-TV premium content channels and PPV/NVOD channels via Direct to home (DTH) satellite platform, satellite master antenna television system networks (SMATV), and small cable networks in the Nordic region. Essentially, the agreements aimed to ensure continuity of the pay-TV content supply and distribution that had previously been secured within the vertically integrated company structure. Under the new arrangements there was a vertical relationship between the independent upstream supplier of pay-TV premium content, Canal+ Nordic, and an independent downstream DTH platform for the distribution of pay-TV to end consumers, Canal Digital.

[376] The parties also took steps to address horizontal cooperation concerns and to avoid foreclosure in related market segments.

[377] It granted negative clearance, however, to the clauses governing exclusive distribution by Canal Digital of Canal+ Nordic's PPV/NVOD channels, 29 December 2003, paras. 170–178.

[378] 29 December 2003, para. 196.

would maintain competition with the second satellite pay-TV distributor in the Nordic region, MTV/ VIASAT and preserve the possibility of market entry in the Nordic pay-TV segments in the mid- to long-term. It thus granted an exemption to the provisions found to infringe Article 101(1) for a five-year period.[379]

6. SUB-CONTRACTING AGREEMENTS

Sub-contracting agreements, under which a contractor entrusts the manufacture of goods or the supply of services to a sub-contractor, are vertical in nature.[380] Goods or services in sub-contracting agreements are provided, on the instructions of the contractor, to that contractor or, on its behalf, to a third party. The arrangement may also involve a licence of IPRs from the contractor to the sub-contractor.

A Commission Notice concerning the assessment of certain sub-contracting agreements in relation to Article 101(1) of the Treaty (the 'Subcontracting Notice') recognises that these agreements are frequently pro-competitive. It thus indicates that certain clauses in sub-contracting agreements are unlikely to restrict competition and infringe Article 101(1). For example, a requirement that: (1) technology or equipment provided by the contractor (a) may not be used except for the purposes of the sub-contracting agreement and (b) may not be made available to third parties; and (2) goods or services resulting from such technology or equipment may be supplied only to the contractor or performed on his behalf, will fall outside Article 101(1) on condition that the technology or equipment provided is necessary to enable the sub-contractor to manufacture the goods or supply the services or to carry out the work in accordance with the contractor's instructions.[381] Further, paragraph 3 provides that the following provisions are unlikely to violate Article 101(1): (1) an obligation that a specified 'trade mark, trade name or get-up' provided under the contract be used by the sub-contractor only as a means of identification in relation to the contract goods, services, or work; (2) an undertaking by either party not to reveal secret know-how (which has not become public knowledge) given by the other party during the negotiation and performance of the agreement; (3) an undertaking by the sub-contractor not to make use, even after expiry of the agreement, of secret know-how (which has not become public knowledge) received during the currency of the agreement; and (4) an undertaking by the sub-contractor to pass on to the contractor on a non-exclusive basis technical improvements or patentable inventions relating to improvements and/or new applications of the original invention, discovered during the currency of the agreement.

Where there is concern that the sub-contracting agreements may violate Article 101(1), the agreement may be able to benefit from the Verticals Regulation.[382] It has been seen in the previous discussion, however, that this block exemption is not generally applicable if the agreement is between competitors[383] or if the subject matter of the agreement falls within the scope of another block exemption.[384] Further, it does not cover the licensing or assignment of IPRs unless they are assigned to the buyer, in this case, the *contractor*. In practice, therefore, although some sub-contracting agreements may benefit from the Verticals Regulation, such as agreements between non-competitors whereby the contractor provides only specifications to the sub-contractor describing the goods or services

---

[379] The Commission took due account of Telenor's/Canal Digital's and Canal+ Nordic's legitimate interest in achieving a reasonable return on their investment in their pay-TV business so far.

[380] See Notice of 18 December 1978 concerning its assessment of certain sub-contracting agreements in relation to Article [101(1)] (the 'Subcontracting Notice'), [1979] OJ C1/2, para. 1.

[381] The Subcontracting Notice, para. 2.

[382] Since the agreement is between undertakings which operate, for the purposes of the agreement, at different levels of the production or distribution chain, and the agreement relates to the conditions under which the parties may purchase, sell or resell certain goods or services.

[383] See Section 5.C.iv.b, p. 821.

[384] See Section 5.C.iv.e, p. 823.

to be supplied, many will in fact fall outside its scope. Nonetheless, where the primary object of the agreement is to enable the sub-contractor to use licensed technology exclusively for the production of products for the contractor, the technology transfer block exemption may apply. Technology transfer agreements are discussed in Chapter 12. Alternatively, if the agreement is between competitors, and if any provisions concerning the assignment or use of IPRs do not constitute the primary object of the agreement, the sub-contracting agreement might constitute a specialisation agreement (capable of benefiting from the specialisation block exemption) or a production agreement, dealt with in the Commission's Guidelines on horizontal cooperation agreements. Horizontal cooperation agreements are discussed in Chapter 10.

7. ARTICLE 102 AND DISTRIBUTION

Where the supplier has a market share approaching 40 per cent a finding of dominance within the meaning of Article 102 is possible. In such cases, it should be considered whether provisions within a vertical agreement, such as clauses imposing unfair or discriminatory selling prices, single branding provisions, or tying provisions, or granting discounts and rebates to purchasers,[385] may infringe Article 102 as well as Article 101.[386] Conduct that amounts to an abuse of a dominant position is unlikely to meet the criteria of Article 101(3).[387]

8. CONCLUSIONS

1. Figure 11.3 seeks to provide a broad summary of how vertical agreements are analysed under Article 101.

2. The Verticals Regulation and Guidelines indicate that the Commission adopts an economic approach to vertical agreements. An actual assessment of the effects of a vertical agreement occurs, however, only when a presumption of legality or a presumption of illegality does not apply.

3. The Verticals Regulation sets out a presumption that vertical agreements between undertakings whose market shares do not exceed the 30 per cent market share threshold and satisfy the conditions of the Regulation are compatible with Article 101.

4. In contrast, agreements containing hardcore restraints are presumed to infringe Article 101. Experience indicates that that presumption is extremely hard to rebut in practice. Indeed the lack of clarity on the question of exactly when Article 101 does not apply to such practices is likely to result in businesses continuing to be wary about incorporating such provisions in their agreements, even if they perceive them to be helpful, or even indispensable, to the efficient distribution of their products or services. This uncertainty is compounded by the fact that (i) NCAs continue to fine firms that incorporate vertical price restraints within their distribution agreements; but, in contrast, (ii) there is little concrete jurisprudence dealing with the application of Article 101(3) to these types of restraints.

5. The centrality of the Verticals Regulation and the Commission's recommended methodology of approach means that the main focus of attention remains on a rather more mechanical application of clear presumptions of legality and illegality rather than a detailed assessment of whether the agreement in question restricts competition in the context in which it operates. Although this affords business with clarity and some legal certainty, it might at times be at the expense of accuracy and result in false negatives and/or positives.

---

[385] See Chap. 7.
[386] See Chap. 7.
[387] See Chap. 4.

Restraints	Market shares			
	</=5%	5–15% (deminimis)	15–30% (within Verticals Regulation)	>30% (individual assessment necessary)
Agreements containing object restraints (for example RPM provisions, or conferring ATP on dealers or preventing cross-supplies between them)	Yes, if no appreciable effect on trade. Possible that may not have an appreciable effect on competition?	Presumption that infringes Article 101(1) The Verticals Regulation does not apply and it will be difficult to establish that the criteria of Article 101(3) are met		
Agreement with non-compete provision	Yes, if no object restraints agreement unlikely to restrict competition or trade appreciably	Yes, if no object restraint unlikely to appreciably restrict competition so long as market not restricted by cumulative effect of agreements	Yes, except if certain non-compete provisions incorporated, only if compatible with Article 101 (Art. 5)	Individual application of Art 101(1) and 101(3). If market shares over 40% may need to consider the application of Art 102—especially for single-branding, tying, and rebates
Exclusive Distribution (including restrictions on passive selling to groups reserved to other)			Yes, but can only restrict active selling into territories/customer groups reserved to another (Art. 4(b), exception 1)	
Selective distribution			Yes, subject to a number of conditions set out in the block exemption (Arts 4 and 5)	

Figure 11.3 Compatibility of Vertical Agreements with Article 101

6. Although the Guidelines acknowledge that Article 101(1) may not apply even where the 30 per cent market share threshold set out in the Verticals Regulation is exceeded, no explanation is offered as to why such a broad overarching block exemption is necessary if a more economic approach is required at the Article 101(1) stage. Such an approach would suggest that most vertical agreements do not require block exemption at all.

7. Even though the Verticals Regulation provides legal certainty and is intended to operate as a safe harbour, its existence muddies the water when trying to rationalise and understand the analysis required under Article 101(1) and Article 101(3) respectively. Inevitably, businesses will seek to comply, where possible, with the terms of the block exemption.

8. The review of the Verticals Regulation and Guidelines before 2010 provided the opportunity for the Commission to evaluate the working and operation of the block exemption and Guidelines. The Commission narrowed the scope of the Verticals Regulation by also requiring that the market share threshold be satisfied by the buyer. It has also amended the Guidelines to deal with internet selling in greater detail and to clarify the Commission's position in relation to hardcore restraints. Although the Guidelines do acknowledge that these restraints might create efficiencies which can be raised under Article 101(3), they may not have done enough to persuade firms that the strong presumption against such restraints satisfying the Article 101(3) conditions no longer exists. Rather, the Commission still seems to adhere to the view that in most situations less severe restraints will be able to achieve the efficiencies pursued.

9. The Commission now rarely enforces Article 101 in relation to purely vertical agreements. The last infringement decisions it adopted in this sphere was in 2005[388] and in October 2012 it rejected a complaint brought against Oxford University Press, Burlington Books, and Pearson PLC alleging that restrictions had been imposed on their distributors' ability to sell English Language Teaching (ELT) books across borders and setting resale prices.[389] Even though the allegations related to 'hardcore' restrictions of competition, the Commission considered that an investigation would be disproportionate in light of the limited impact that the conduct was likely to have on the functioning of the internal market, the complexity of the investigation required, and the limited likelihood of establishing proof of a violation. Further, the Commission noted that the alleged infringement had ceased. This fact could be taken as evidence of a more measured approach to hardcore restraints at EU level. On the other hand, the Commission's inactivity in this area could plausibly be attributed to a decision by it to focus resources elsewhere, combined with confidence that there is a healthy level of enforcement at the national level. Indeed, an important reason for rejecting the complaint relating to the distribution of ELT books was that the Greek competition authority had already dealt with the matter and would be well placed to deal with the alleged infringements.

10. Although NCAs vary widely as to the level of their enforcement activity against vertical restraints, many of them do regularly bring cases, in particular in relation to RPM and bans on internet selling. NCAs and national courts are therefore beginning to play an important role in the development of EU competition policy towards and the application of Article 101 to vertical restraints. So far, national courts and authorities do not seem to have been particularly willing to accept, in accordance with the Court's case law, that an agreement does not infringe Article 101(1) at all or that, in exceptional circumstances, agreements containing price or territorial restraints satisfy the requirements of Article 101(3). Rather, most NCAs seem to support a strict policy against such restraints.

---

[388] See *Peugeot* IP/05/1227.

[389] Case COMP/39771, 10 October 2012.

9. FURTHER READING

A. BOOKS

BORK, R. H., *The Antitrust Paradox: A Policy at War with Itself* (Basic Books, 1978, reprinted with a new Introduction and Epilogue, 1993), chap. 14

GOYDER, J., *EU Distribution Law* (5th edn, Hart Publishing, 2011)

SCHERER, F. M., and ROSS, D., *Industrial Market Structure and Economic Performance* (3rd edn, Houghton Mifflin, 1990), chap. 15

B. ARTICLES

COMANOR, W. S., 'Vertical Price-Fixing, Vertical Market Restraints, and the New Antitrust Policy' (1984–1985) 98 *Harvard LR* 983

EASTERBROOK, F. H., 'Vertical Arrangements and the Rule of Reason' (1984) 53 *Antitrust LJ* 135

GOEBEL, R. J., 'Metro II's Confirmation of the Selective Distribution Rules: Is this the End of the Road?' (1987) 24 *CMLRev* 605

GYSELEN, L., 'Vertical Restraints in the Distribution Process: Strengths and Weaknesses of the Free Rider Rationale under EEC Competition Law' (1984) 21 *CMLRev* 647

HAWK, B. E., 'System Failure: "Vertical Restraints and EC Competition Law"' (1995) 32 *CMLRev* 973

JONES A., 'Resale Price Maintenance: A Debate About Competition Policy in Europe' (2009) *European Competition Journal* 425

KORAH, V., 'Goodbye Red Label: Condemnation of Dual Pricing by Distillers' (1978) *ELRev* 62

PITOFSKY, R., 'In Defense of Discounters: The No-Frills Case for a Per Se Rule against Vertical Price Fixing' (1983) 71 *Geo LJ* 1487

VENIT, J., 'Pronuptia: Ancillary Restraints or Unholy Alliances?' (1986) 11 *ELRev* 213

WHISH, R., and BAILEY, D., 'Regulation 330/201: the Commission's New Block Exemption for Vertical Agreements' (2010) 47(6) *CMLRev* 1757

ZHANG, A., 'Toward an Economic Approach to Agency Agreements' [2013] 9(3) *Journal of Competition Law and Economics* 553

12

LICENSING AGREEMENTS AND OTHER AGREEMENTS INVOLVING INTELLECTUAL PROPERTY RIGHTS

1. CENTRAL ISSUES

1. Intellectual property rights (IPRs), such as patents, trade marks, copyrights, and designs, grant the holder of the right an exclusionary, and sometimes exclusive, right to the exploitation of an emanation of the human intellect. They are designed to provide an incentive for innovation and invention.

2. IPRs are still generally granted at the national level (although there are some EU rights).

3. The existence and exercise of IPRs (especially national rights) has sometimes created tension with the EU rules both on free movement and competition.

4. This chapter focuses on the compatibility of intellectual property (IP) licensing agreements with Article 101.

5. As with vertical agreements, the Commission's policy towards IP licensing agreements has been a tumultuous one. The policy has evolved from a permissive approach, to a more interventionist and formalistic one, to the current more economic approach reflected in a 2004 block exemption for technology transfer agreements (the TTBER) and accompanying guidelines.

6. The 2004 TTBER (which is currently under review) provides a safe harbour for bilateral technology transfer agreements concluded between parties who do not exceed specified market shares and which do not contain specified hardcore restraints. Certain other specified provisions in the contract are excluded and not covered by the block exemption.

7. The market share thresholds set out in the TTBER mean that, in practice, it provides less legal certainty than previous block exemptions governing licensing of IPRs.

8. The framework for Article 101 analysis set out in the Technology Transfer Guidelines is thus of utmost importance. These guidelines set out general principles concerning Article 101 and IPRs, explain the provisions and application of the TTBER, and explain the application of Article 101(1) and Article 101(3) to technology transfer agreements outside the scope of the TTBER.

9. Trade mark and copyright (except software copyright) licensing agreements are not technology transfer agreements and are not covered by the technology transfer block exemption or guidelines.

2. INTRODUCTION

A. GENERAL

Intellectual property rights (IPRs) grant the holder of the right an exclusionary, and sometimes exclusive, right to the exploitation of the product of the human intellect. They are recognised and protected in some way in all developed countries and encompass a broad spectrum of different rights. For example, they safeguard the creators of aesthetic and artistic works from having their creations distorted and purloined by others, they provide an incentive for invention and innovation by enabling those who develop new products and processes to reap the financial rewards of their efforts, and they allow those who develop brand names to exploit the reputation attached to the brand. The importance of IPRs in the modern commercial world is incontrovertible, but their interaction with EU law is complex. They raise problems not only for competition law but also for the free movement of goods and services and the operation of the single market. This is because:

(a) Despite the introduction of some EU-wide rights[1] IPRs are still typically granted by national laws and enforced on a national basis, conferring protection within national territories. This inevitably leads to a conflict with the EU provisions governing the free movement of goods and services since simple reliance on a national right could be used as a mechanism to prevent importation of a good or service from another Member State.

(b) IPRs may erect barriers to entry to a market and thus affect the determination of whether an undertaking is in a dominant position for the purposes of Article 102.[2] In addition, the use by a dominant undertaking of its IPRs may constitute an abuse.

(c) Transactions involving IPRs may be agreements falling within Article 101. Holders of IPRs often exploit them not by producing products or services exclusively themselves but, additionally or alternatively, by licensing others to use them (or assigning rights to them). The terms of such licences may involve restrictions of competition, including territorial restrictions which divide the internal market.

This chapter starts by looking at some of the different types of IPRs before outlining the relationship between intellectual property and both EU competition law and the EU free movement rules. The chapter focuses, however, on IP licensing agreements and their treatment under Article 101. The application of Article 101 to IP licensing agreements has changed dramatically over the years and especially since modernisation in 2004. In particular, on 1 May 2004 a new Technology Transfer Block Exemption, Regulation 772/2004 (the TTBER), came into force exempting certain 'technology transfer agreements' (patent, design, know-how, and/or software copyright licensing agreements) from Article 101(1).[3] The TTBER is accompanied by Technology Transfer Guidelines (the Guidelines)

---

[1] See, e.g., harmonising measures enabling companies to obtain unitary trade mark protection effective throughout the EU (Council Directive 89/104/EEC) to approximate the laws of the Member States relating to Trade Marks, [1989] OJ L40/1 (implemented in the UK by the Trade Marks Act 1994), which was repealed and codified by Directive 2008/95/EC, OJ [2008] L299/25, COM(2006)812; Council Regulation 40/94/EEC on the Community trade mark, [1994] OJ L11/1 was replaced by Regulation 207/2009/EC, OJ [2009] L78/1—the Commission is proposing to modernise and streamline these provisions); the European Patent Convention of 1973 (the EPC) allows companies to obtain multiple national (rather than EU) patents from the European Patent Office on a single application; attempts to introduce a unitary EU patent are also now progressing, see regulations establishing enhanced cooperation for unitary patent protection and its translation arrangements and the Agreement on a Unified Patent Court which will provide the legal basis for the future European Unitary Patent System, see EU Council Press Releases 17824/12 and 6590/13 (24 Member States have now signed the Unified Patent Court agreement) and, e.g., W. Allan, M. Furse, and B. Sufrin (eds.), *Butterworths Competition Law* (Butterworths, looseleaf), Div V, chap. 1.

[2] See Chap. 6.

[3] Reg. 772/2004 on technology transfer agreements (the TTBER) [2004] OJ L123/11.

which explain in detail the Commission's approach to technology transfer agreements.[4] Although the TTBER is due to expire on 30 April 2014 and the Commission is consulting on the provisions of a new Regulation and Guidelines (likely to be published at the end of 2013 or early in 2014),[5] significant changes to the current regime are not anticipated. Section 3 of this chapter traces the development of EU competition policy to IP licensing agreements whilst Sections 4 and 5 examine the current TTBER and the Guidelines in close detail (noting where significant changes might occur in 2014). Sections 6, 7, and 8 deal with trade mark licences, trade mark delimitation agreements, and copyright (other than software) licences not covered by the TTBER and Guidelines. Section 9 outlines issues arising in cases involving IPRs under Article 102. In Section 10 some conclusions are drawn.

B. TYPES OF INTELLECTUAL PROPERTY RIGHTS

(i) The Nature of Intellectual Property Rights

IPRs give the holder an exclusionary, and sometimes exclusive, right to the exploitation of an emanation of the intellect. The nature of the right varies from one type of intellectual property to another. IPRs vary in duration. Some arise only upon registration, while others arise from the act of creation itself. In the absence of harmonisation, EU law does not regulate the conditions upon which national law grants IPRs,[6] although it may curtail the exercise of them.[7] This section briefly describes the main types of IPRs.[8]

(ii) Patents

Patents relate to inventions. The grant of a patent confers on the holder (the patentee), normally for a maximum period of 20 years,[9] a monopoly over a new and inventive product or process, and the right to prevent others from making, disposing of, using, or importing a product which is the subject of the patent or derived from it, or from using the patented process itself. Patents protect applied technology, not abstract ideas. Patents are granted in respect of the product or process disclosed in the specification when the patent is applied for, and on the expiry of the patent anyone else in the world may use the information contained in the specification.

(iii) Trade Marks

A trade mark is a mark or sign used to identify and differentiate a product or service. Registration of a trade mark gives the holder an exclusive right to use it as such, although if it is a non-invented word it does not take the word out of general use, but only prevents its use by others as a trade mark.[10] Other parties remain free to offer competing goods and services under other marks and brand names. If

---

[4] Guidelines on the application of Article 81 of the EC Treaty to technology transfer agreements [2004] OJ C101/2.

[5] See <http://ec.europa.eu/competition/consultations/2013_technology_transfer/index_en.html> and, e.g., P. Regibeau and K. Rockett, 'Revising the Technology Transfer Guidelines' (2012) 4 *Antitrust Chronicle, Competition Policy International*.

[6] See, e.g., Case 144/81, *Keurkoop v. Nancy Kean Gifts* [1982] ECR 2853; Cases C-241–242/91 P, *RTE & ITP v. Commission* [1995] ECR I-743, para. 49.

[7] Through, e.g., the application of the free movement and competition laws.

[8] See further W. Cornish, D. Llewelyn, and T. Aplin, *Intellectual Property: Patents, Copyright, Trade Marks and Allied Rights* (7th edn, Sweet & Maxwell, 2010).

[9] The maximum 20-year term is common throughout the EU because of the European Patent Convention (see n. 1). Council Reg. 1768/92, [1992] OJ L182/1, on the creation of supplementary protection certificates for medicinal products, enables a period not exceeding five years to be added to this in respect of delays in regulatory approval.

[10] And the use of a similar mark or sign on identical or similar goods or services where there is a likelihood of confusion, Directive 2008/95/EC OJ [2008] L299/25 (Directive to approximate the laws of the Member States relating to Trade Marks), Art. 4(1)(b).

renewal procedures are complied with trade mark registration can continue indefinitely. Trade mark law in the EU was harmonised by the First Trade Marks Directive of 21 December 1988.[11]

Marks and brand names which are not registered may also be protected by other means. In the UK this is by the law on passing-off, and in many other EU countries by laws on unfair competition.

(iv) Copyright

Copyright protects 'works' such as literary, dramatic, musical and artistic works, films, sound recordings, and broadcasts from unauthorised exploitation by third parties. Unlike a patent, copyright does not confer a monopoly because it prevents only *copying*: if a third party independently comes up with the same melody or words, he will not be liable for breach of copyright. Copyright does not depend on registration or formal procedures but arises automatically when the work is set down or recorded in some form. Copyright in the EU lasts for the lifetime of the author plus 70 years.[12]

There are greater differences between the laws of EU Member States in respect of copyright than there are with other forms of intellectual property. Common law notions of copyright emphasise the right of the author to prevent others exploiting its work for commercial gain whereas the civil law emphasises the right of the creator of a work to be recognised as such and to be morally entitled to protect its integrity.[13] UK copyright law covers performers' rights and similar rights, but in most EU countries there is a distinction drawn between 'author's right' and 'neighbouring rights' (those accorded to sound recordings, broadcasts, and performers). Under UK law works created by the 'sweat of the brow', such as compilations of information, are accorded copyright protection, whereas civil law systems require a greater degree of creativity: this difference seemed to be a material issue in the Article 102 case on television listings, *Magill*.[14] The Information Society Directive has harmonised national laws on certain aspects of the protection of copyright owners' rights to control reproduction, distribution, and communication (primarily on the internet).[15]

(v) Designs

Under the Berne Convention[16] countries are free to choose the way in which they protect industrial designs. In the UK a design which has features which in the finished article are 'new and [have] individual character' can be registered.[17] Registration gives the proprietor a monopoly over the use of a design for a maximum of 25 years, in respect of articles for which it has been registered. UK law also recognises unregistered design rights in respect of the original design of any aspect of the shape or

[11] Council Dir. 89/104/EEC to approximate the laws of the Member States relating to Trade Marks [1989] OJ L40/1 implemented in the UK by the Trade Marks Act 1994. The directive leaves to Member States the procedural details for applying for or revoking a mark or bringing infringement proceedings. See also Council Reg. 40/94 on the Community trade mark [1994] OJ L11/1, replaced by Regulation 207/2009/EC, OJ [2009] L78/1, see n. 1.

[12] Under Dir. 2006/116/EC [2006] OJ L372/12, on the term of protection of copyright and certain related rights.

[13] The Copyright Designs and Patents Act 1988, ss. 77–85, introduced express 'moral rights' into UK law, partly to come into line with the Berne Convention for the Protection of Literary and Artistic Works, 1886.

[14] Cases C-241–242/91 P, *RTE & ITP* v. *Commission* [1995] ECR I-743; see Chap. 7. Specific protection is now accorded to databases under Dir. 96/9/EC [1996] OJ L77/20.

[15] Dir. 2001/29/EC on Copyright and Related Rights in the Information Society [2001] OJ L167/10. The directive was adopted to fulfil the EU's obligations under the WIPO (World Intellectual Property Organization) Copyright Treaty 1996 and the WIPO Performances and Phonograms Treaty 1996. It has been implemented in the UK by the Copyright and Related Rights Regulations 2003 (SI 2003/2498).

[16] Berne Convention for the Protection of Literary and Artistic Works, 1886 (as subsequently revised).

[17] Registered Designs Act 1949, s. 1B(1), as amended by the Copyright Designs and Patents Act 1988, s. 265 and the Registered Designs Regulations 2001 (SI 2001/3949), and the Registered Designs Regulations 2003 (SI 2003/550).

configuration of an article.[18] The right is analogous to copyright in that it arises automatically when the design is created, but it lasts for a maximum of 15 years. Like copyright it protects the holder against *copying*, not against independent creation, whereas a registered design right is like a patent in protecting against independent creation. The 1998 Directive on the legal protection of designs[19] dealt only with registered designs and is a partial harmonisation measure only. Under the directive, protection is for 25 years and entitles the holder to prevent the making, offering, putting on the market, importing, exporting, and stocking of a product incorporating the design.

(vi) Know-how

Strictly speaking, know-how is not an IPR, but it often features in commercial transactions such as licensing arrangements to which Article 101 applies. Know-how is confidential, technical, commercially valuable information which is not patented or registered in any way.[20] Know-how is defined in the TTBER[21] and is protected by contractual provisions and breach of confidence laws.

(vii) Miscellaneous

a. Plant Breeders' Rights

Plant breeders' rights are given in respect of the creation of new plant varieties. They are similar to patents in that they confer a monopoly. Council Regulation 2100/94 on plant variety rights created an EU plant variety right which coexists with national regimes.[22]

b. Semiconductor Topographies The protection of the topography of semiconductor chips was the subject of harmonisation in Directive 87/54.[23]

c. Databases

Databases were the subject of specific harmonisation in the 1996 Database Directive[24] which creates a *sui generis* right for their protection. Previously, Member States' copyright laws differed according to the extent of the protection that was afforded to databases.

d. Computer Software

Before the implementation of the Software Directive[25] Member States varied in their ways of protecting software. The directive requires them to do it by way of copyright as a literary work within the meaning of the Berne Convention. However, the Commission proposed that software programs

---

[18] Copyright Designs and Patents Act 1988, s. 213. There are a number of exceptions: e.g., a design right does not subsist in surface decoration, or features which enable the article to fit with or match another article.

[19] Dir. 98/71/EC [1998] OJ L289/28. There is a proposal to amend the directive to harmonise design protection for spare parts, see Proposal for a Directive amending Directive 98/71 on the legal protection of designs (COM/2004/582). See also Council Reg. 6/2002 on Community designs [2002] OJ L3/1.

[20] Usually because it does not fulfil the necessary criteria for patentability, but sometimes the creator chooses not to patent in order to keep the information out of the public domain.

[21] Commission Reg. 772/2004 [2004] OJ L123/11, Art. 1(1)(i), further explained in Commission Guidelines on the application of Art. 81 to technology transfer agreements, [2004] OJ C101/2, para. 47.

[22] [1994] OJ L227/1.

[23] [1987] OJ L24/36. In the UK semiconductor topography is protected as an unregistered design. See the Design Right (Semi-conductor Topographies) Regulations 1989 (SI 1989/1100).

[24] Dir. 96/9/EC on the legal protection of databases [1996] OJ L77/20.

[25] Council Dir. 91/250/EEC on the legal protection of computer programs [1991] OJ L122/42, replaced by Directive 2009/24/EC [2009] OJ L111/16.

should also qualify for patent protection in all Member States.[26] In May 2004 the Council agreed on a common position on a proposed directive to extend patent protection to computer-implemented inventions.[27]

C. THE RELATIONSHIP BETWEEN INTELLECTUAL PROPERTY RIGHTS AND COMPETITION LAW

The relationship between IPRs and competition law has sometimes been an uneasy one. In the EU, this has particularly been the case in the (rather rare) instances where competition law has required unwilling dominant firms to license their rights to others.[28] The underlying issue, however, is whether IPRs and competition law are fundamentally in conflict or whether they are different routes to the same goals. It appears to be generally accepted at present that IPRs and competition law do not have conflicting aims but that, on the contrary, both pursue the promotion of consumer welfare. This view is set out in two extracts, one written by a Commission official, Luc Peeperkorn,[29] and the other by Anderman and Kallaugher in their book on technology transfer agreements.

L. Peeperkorn, 'IP Licences and Competition Rules: Striking the Right Balance' (2003) 26 *World Competition* 527, 527–528

II. Do IP and competition law have conflicting aims?

Recognising that early copying of an innovation and free riding on an innovator's efforts undermine the incentive to innovate, IP laws (intellectual property laws) grant the innovator a legal monopoly. They provide the innovator the right to exclusively exploit the innovation and exclude others from exploiting it. This legal monopoly may, depending on the availability of substitutes in the relevant market, in turn lead to market power and even monopoly as defined under competition law. This has given rise to the alleged source of conflict often mentioned: that competition law would take away what IP law is providing.

However, in principle this is only an apparent source of conflict. At the highest level of analysis IP and competition law are complementary because they both aim at promoting consumer welfare. The objective of IP laws is to promote technical progress to the ultimate benefit of consumers. This is done by striking a balance, hopefully the right one, between over- and under-protection of innovators' efforts. The aim is not to promote the individual innovator's welfare. The property right provided by IP laws is awarded to try to ensure a sufficient reward for the innovator to elicit its creative or inventive effort while not delaying follow-on innovation or leading to unnecessary long periods of high prices for consumers. A delay in follow-on innovation may result when the innovation consists of an improvement on earlier ideas that have been granted patent protection already. Unnecessary long periods of high prices will result when the innovation allows the IPR holder to obtain market power in the antitrust market(s) where the IPR is exploited and where the IPR protects this monopoly position longer than is required to elicit the innovative effort.

In order to correctly strike the balance between under- and over-protecting innovators' efforts, IPRs differ from and are usually less absolute than 'normal' property rights: they are often limited in duration

---

[26] See Commission Communication 'Promoting Innovation through Patents: the Follow-up to the Green Paper on the Community Patent System in Europe' COM(1999)42.

[27] 19 May 2004, IP/04/659.

[28] See Chap. 7.

[29] L. Peeperkorn is an official in DG Comp who was responsible for conducting the review of the EU IP licensing regime which resulted in the adoption of a new block exemption on technology transfer agreements in April 2004, Reg. 772/2004 on technology transfer agreements [2004] OJ L123/11.

(patents, copyright), not protected against parallel creation by others (copyright, know how) or lose their value once they become public (know how).

Competition policy aims at promoting consumer welfare by protecting competition as the driving force of efficient markets, providing the best quality products at the lowest prices. Companies under competitive pressure will be less complacent and will have more incentive to innovate and gain market share. Product market competition and a strict competition policy work as an effective stick to promote innovative effort. The relevant question is therefore not one of conflict but of complementarity and possibly adjustment in the individual case.

S. D. Anderman and J. Kallaugher, *Technology Transfer and the New EU Competition Rules: IP Licensing after Modernisation* (Oxford University Press, 2006)

B. Background—the Relationship between Competition Law and IP

1.11 The introduction of the new [EU] paradigm comes at a time when advocates of competition policy and proponents of intellectual property have reached an accommodation that recognises that both competition law and IPRs legislation constitute complementary components of a modern industrial policy. Although both policies pursue the common aim of improving innovation and consumer welfare each does so using rather different means. Intellectual property rights legislation such as patent, copyright and design rights laws offer intellectual property right holders a period of exclusive rights to exploit their property right as both a reward to the individual and as an incentive to the wider process of innovation and R&D investment. Trademarks perform a different function. Their exclusivity is meant to protect the consumer as well as to reward the originator. Modern competition policy attempts to keep markets innovative and competitive by maintaining effective competition. The means it uses to pursue this aim include maintaining access to markets and preventing 'foreclosure' or monopolisation of markets.

1.12 At first sight there may seem to be a potential clash in the methods used by the two systems of legal regulation to achieve their common aim. The concern to maintain access to markets appears to be implacably opposed to the concept of exclusive rights to make, use and sell a product. And indeed, there was a period when the misunderstanding of the economic effects of IPRs led EC competition law and policy to attempt to place overly strict limits on the exercise of IPRs, particularly in the field of patent licensing. Today, however, the interrelationship between the two systems of law is characterised more by its accommodations than by its conflict. These accommodations tend to occur most often as an incidental result of the ordinary doctrines of each system. Thus, intellectual property laws make a contribution to effective competition and maintaining access to market by devices within their own internal doctrine that strive to maintain a balance between 'initial' inventors and creators and 'follow-on' invention and creation. Good examples are the 'fair use' doctrine in copyright laws, the doctrine of 'non-obviousness' and the provision of compulsory licensing in patent law and interoperability imperatives and decompilation rights in the computer program directive. On rare occasions, as in the [EU] database directive, the accommodation will be explicitly spelt out in the intellectual property law itself.

1.13 Within EC competition law the accommodation also tends to occur more owing to the incidental effect of the logic of the general doctrines of competition law rather that in the form of special treatment. When one looks at EC competition law the most obvious example of special treatment is the 'exceptional circumstances' test embedded within the abuse of refusal to supply under Article [102]…

1.14 This observation offers a good perspective for viewing the relationship between Article [101] and IP licensing under the new post-modernised legal framework. The accommodation with IPRs in the new Technology Transfer Block Exemption Regulation (TTBER) and Guidelines occurs almost entirely within the logic of the doctrines of competition law. Most of the accommodation takes place as an incidental benefit of the ordinary interpretation of Article [101] under the modernisation programme. In the Guidelines and Recitals there is evidence that the competition authorities have made a considerable effort to understand the nature of IPRs and their licensing. Thus, they acknowledge that the creation of IPRs often entails substantial investment and that it is often a risky endeavour. They state plainly that '[I]n order not to reduce dynamic competition and to maintain the incentive to innovate the innovator must not be unduly restricted in the exploitation of the IPR that turn out to be valuable'. In particular, they must be able to seek compensation for successful projects that takes failed projects into account. The Commission also acknowledges that technology licensing may require the licensee to make considerable sunk investment in the licensed technology and production assets necessary to exploit it. Moreover, the Guidelines have accepted that the great majority of licensing agreements are pro-competitive and compatible with Article [101].

1.15 This approach represents a conscious rejection of the argument that a special self-contained regime (like the old block exemptions) is necessary to satisfy the special requirements of IP licensing. As the Guidelines confidently proclaim '[in] assessing licensing agreements under Article [101], the existing analytical framework is sufficiently flexible to take due account of the dynamic aspects of technology licensing'. The new framework clearly harmonises the treatment of licensing agreements with that of other commercial agreements under Article [101] and, on the whole, this results in a reasonable treatment of IP licensing. However, as we shall see, the process of harmonisation has not been complete; the analytical framework has had to make certain adjustments to take due account of the special features of technology licensing.

D. THE RELATIONSHIP BETWEEN INTELLECTUAL PROPERTY RIGHTS AND THE FREE MOVEMENT RULES

Perhaps surprisingly for a document purporting to lay down the foundations for a single market, the TFEU itself contains very little about intellectual property. Article 345 TFEU (ex Article 295 EC), however, contains a general rule about property rights:

The Treaties shall in no way prejudice the rules in Member States governing the system of property ownership.

EU law therefore recognises the existence and ownership of rights given by national law. Nevertheless, there is a fundamental conflict between this and the principle of the free movement of goods. Article 34 TFEU (ex Article 28 EC), the basic provision on the free movement of goods, states:

Quantitative restrictions on imports and all measures having equivalent effect shall, without prejudice to the following provisions, be prohibited between Member States.

However, if widgets made in France by F cannot be imported into Germany because they would infringe G's German patent, the market is divided along national lines. Not only that, but G may wish to use its German patent to prevent its *own* widgets, which it has manufactured in the UK, from being imported into Germany by a parallel importer. In both these examples national IPRs can seriously impede the free circulation of goods.

IPRs are specifically dealt with in Article 36 TFEU, which provides a derogation from Article 34. Article 36 provides:

The provisions of Articles 34 and 35 shall not preclude prohibitions or restrictions on imports, exports or goods in transit justified on grounds of public morality, public policy or public security; the protection of health and life of humans, animals or plants; the protection of national treasures possessing artistic, historic or archaeological value; or the protection of industrial and commercial property.[30] Such prohibitions or

---

[30] It could be argued that the phrase 'industrial and commercial' property does not cover copyright, but the CJ has held that it does: see Case 78/70, *Deutsche Grammophon* v. *Metro* [1971] ECR 487, and Cases 55 and 57/80, *Musik-Vertrieb Membran* v. *GEMA* [1981] ECR 147. 'Intellectual property' is the generic phrase now used both at EU and international level.

restrictions shall not, however, constitute a means of arbitrary discrimination or a disguised restriction on trade between Member States.

EU law therefore accepts that restrictions on free movement may be justified to protect national IPRs. However, Article 36 contains a final proviso in the last sentence. The restrictions are not to constitute 'a means of arbitrary discrimination or a disguised restriction' on inter-Member State trade. This proviso has been used to justify many of the limitations which the CJ has placed on the exercise of national IPRs.[31] Indeed, in a long line of cases, a series of rulings have interpreted when a national measure can be so justified. That case law is not dealt with further in this book,[32] but very broadly, it has developed a number of interlinking concepts by which the Court has sought to reconcile the conflicting demands of the economic integration of the single market and the protection of IPRs. In particular:

(a) It has drawn a dichotomy between the *existence* of IPRs and their *exercise*: the existence of rights is unaffected by the TFEU but their exercise may be.[33]

(b) It developed the idea that there is a 'specific subject matter' of each kind of IPR, the protection of which is justified even if it leads to restrictions on inter-Member State trade: the exercise of IPRs which partitions the market will be allowed insofar as it is necessary to protect the 'specific subject matter' of that right.

(c) It has built up a jurisprudence on the 'exhaustion of rights'. Once a rights holder has consented to the marketing of the protected product within the EU,[34] the rights encompassed in the 'specific subject matter' are exhausted and the holder cannot rely on national rights to prevent the movement of the goods between Member States.

3. EXPLOITING INTELLECTUAL PROPERTY RIGHTS BY LICENSING

A. GENERAL

The owner of an IPR has a choice of ways in which to benefit from the right commercially. He may exploit it himself, assign it to a third party, or license it. The method chosen will depend on a number of factors. These include the resources available to the owner, the type of right concerned, the nature of the product and its life cycle, manufacturing costs and complexity, the overall commercial

---

[31] Art. 56 is the basic provision which governs free movement of services. The CJ has held that the principle in Art. 36 should be applied to it by analogy. Restrictions on the movement of services may therefore be justified by the need to protect IPRs in the same way as they are justified in respect of the movement of goods, see Case 62/79, *Coditel v. Ciné Vog Films* [1980] ECR 881 (*Coditel I*); Case 262/81, *Coditel v. Ciné Vog Films* [1982] ECR 3381 (*Coditel II*) and Cases C-403 and 429/08, *Premier League Ltd v. QC Leisure* and *Murphy v. Media Protection Services Ltd*, 4 October 2011.

[32] But see, e.g., Bellamy & Child, *European Community Law of Competition* (7th. edn, Oxford University Press, 2013), chap. 9 and *Butterworths Competition Law* (cited in n. 1), Div V, chap. 2.

[33] The distinction between the existence and exercise of rights (first introduced in Cases 56 and 58/64, *Consten & Grundig v. Commission* [1966] ECR 299) is not convincing. A property right which cannot be exercised has no value, see the Opinion of Fennelly AG, para. 95 in Cases C-267 and 268/95, *Merck and Co Inc v. Primecrown Ltd (Merck II)* [1996] ECR I-6285. IPRs are valuable because they enable the holder to exercise rights which prevent third parties from committing infringing acts. If EU law limits the holder's ability to control third parties then the value of the right is diminished, and the fact that the 'existence' of the right is untouched is of little comfort. Arguably the existence/exercise dichotomy has simply provided a flexible tool to enable the Court to develop policy in this area.

[34] 'The EU' should be interpreted in this context to mean the whole EEA. The EEA (see Chap. 2) is the relevant area by virtue of Protocol 28 of the EEA Agreement, which provides for exhaustion throughout the EEA in accordance with the case law of the Court.

strategy of the owner, local conditions in the territory in which the right is held, and taxation considerations. Some rights may be able to be carved up: for example the owner of copyright in a book may deal separately with the rights to make a television programme of it, the rights to film it, the rights to serialise it in a newspaper, and the rights to make an audio tape or other recordings of it.

An *assignment* involves the outright transfer of the right to a third party. After transfer the original owner is excluded from using it without a licence from the new owner. An assignment may be gratuitous or by way of sale or swap. It may be made pursuant to a contract of employment when an employee assigns to the employer rights which he acquires in the course of employment. Rights are commonly sold on the transfer or take-over of a business, when they pass to the new owner along with the other assets. In contrast, a *licence* involves the owner of an IPR conferring permission upon another party to exploit the owner's legally protected exclusive right. The advantages of licensing include:

(i) the owner (the licensor) has continuing control of the use of the rights (insofar as this is not limited by competition law);

(ii) the ability to carve up the rights is normally greater with licensing than assignment;

(iii) the owner can obtain a continuing revenue stream from the exploitation and can benefit from the licensee's success;

(iv) the owner can continue to exploit the right himself.

The TTBER treats certain assignments of patents, designs, know-how, and software copyright as licences where part of the risk associated with their exploitation remains with the assignor. This is particularly so where the consideration is related to the turnover the assignee obtains from the products produced with the assigned technology or the quantity of the products the assignee produces (or the number of operations he carries out) with the licensed technology.[35]

B. COMMERCIAL CONSIDERATIONS IN LICENCES

(i) General

A number of IPRs may be licensed together, for example patents, know-how, and trade marks. Whatever the licence consists of, the licensor will normally be concerned with maximising the financial return. The licensor may also wish to incorporate provisions in a licence agreement relating to, for example: safeguarding confidential information; ensuring quality control; supplying essential components or other goods to the licensee; ensuring (in the case of patents and know-how) that the licensor benefits from improvements made by the licensee; safeguarding the licensor from challenges by the licensee to the validity of the rights;[36] limiting what the licensee may do with the goods or services produced under the licence; ensuring that the licensee does not compete with the licensor; and providing for termination. Licensees will be concerned with the same issues but from the other side. How far such commercial requirements can be met will depend, in part, on competition law. In this section we look briefly at some of the terms commonly found in licensing agreements that may raise competition law concerns.

(ii) Royalties

Payment by the licensee for the licence will be by way of royalty obligations which may, for instance, take the form of lump sum payments, a percentage of the selling price, or a fixed amount for each

---

[35] TTBER, Art. 1(1)(b), see Section 4, pp. 874–894.

[36] With a patent, a licensee working it will be in the best position to identify the weaknesses in it.

product incorporating the licensed technology.[37] 'Running royalties' means royalties calculated on the basis of individual product sales. Where royalties are calculated on the basis of the licensee's products which incorporate the licensed technology the licensor may wish to stipulate that a minimum number are produced.

(iii) Territorial Restrictions on Production: Exclusive and Sole Licences

Licences can be exclusive, sole or non-exclusive.

A licence is *exclusive* as regards a particular territory where it provides that the licensor will not grant further licences for that territory to other parties and will not itself exploit the licensed IPRs in the territory. It means that only the licensee can exercise the licensed rights in the territory covered by the licence.

A *sole* licence is where the licensor undertakes not to grant other licences for the territory but remains free to exploit the rights there itself. The rights can therefore be exploited in the territory by the licensor, the licensee, and no one else.

A *non-exclusive* licence is where the licensor remains free to grant other licences if it wishes and to exploit the licence in the territory itself.

Exclusive and sole licences are common phenomena. Licensees will often be interested in taking a licence only if they are assured of exclusivity. An undertaking may be interested in taking a licence of X's French patent, for example, only if it can be certain that having invested large resources in tooling up to exploit the patented process it will not face competition from other licensees in France or from the licensor itself operating in France. In the EU, however, clauses conferring such protection may raise serious concerns on account of the fact that they compartmentalise the single market. The concern will be particularly acute where they are coupled (as they frequently are) with territorial sales restrictions, whereby the licensor and/or the licensee are limited as to where they may *sell* the products produced with or incorporating the licensed technology. Sales restrictions are dealt with in Section 3.B.iv.

In EU law the term 'exclusive licence' has often been used in the past to cover both exclusive and sole licences, without distinction. The correct use of the terminology is now set out in the Guidelines on technology transfer agreements.[38]

(iv) Sales Restrictions

A licence may include restrictions as to where the licensor and/or licensee may sell (territorial restrictions) or to whom they may sell (customer allocation).

a. Territorial Sales Restrictions

A licensee may be unwilling to take a licence unless he can be protected not only from the licensor and/or other licensees *producing* in the same territory as him, but also from them *selling* there. This is similar to the wish of a distributor to be protected from intra-brand competition which we discussed in Chapter 11. Indeed, the reasons for a licensee requiring such protection may be stronger than in the case of a mere distributor because the licensee may have to invest very heavily in order to tool up to exploit the licensed technology. A licensee may therefore want protection from sales by the licensor and other licensees and for the licensor to impose export bans on other licensees. On the other side, the licensor may not be willing to disseminate its technology through licensing unless it can stop the

---

[37] See Commission Notice, Guidelines on the application of Article 81 of the EC Treaty to technology transfer agreements [2004] OJ C101/2 (hereinafter 'Guidelines'), para. 156.

[38] Guidelines, para. 162.

licensees selling their production in territories where it sells itself. As with distribution agreements, sales bans can be of two kinds, active or passive (soliciting sales and responding to unsolicited sales respectively).[39] Moreover, provisions such as quantity restrictions on output can amount to indirect sales bans. EU competition law, not surprisingly, takes a strict view of territorial sales restrictions, particularly those which attempt to give the parties absolute territorial protection (ATP).

b. Customer Allocation

Provisions limiting the customers or customer groups to which parties can sell are another form of sales restriction. The licensor may wish to keep certain customers as its own preserve, or grant a licence to a licensee to service only particular customers. Again, these restrictions may be in respect of active and passive sales, or only active sales.

(v) Field of Use Restrictions

Field of use restrictions confine the licensee to exploitation of the technology within certain technical fields of application. Technology may be exploited in different ways, for example, a patented chemical may be used to produce both fertilisers and pesticides. A licensor may wish to grant a licence to exploit only one or some of the uses, or to grant licences for different uses to different licensees.[40]

Field of use restrictions may be difficult to distinguish from, and have the same effect as, customer allocation as different customers may require the technology for different purposes. Thus in *French State/Suralmo*,[41] the Commission objected to provisions dividing the exploitation of engine technology for use in military equipment and use in civilian equipment respectively. The Commission explains the distinction in the Guidelines on technology transfer agreements.[42]

(vi) Tying and Bundling

Tying and bundling on the part of dominant undertakings was discussed in Chapter 7. In the context of the licensing of IPRs it is described in the Guidelines on technology transfer agreements as follows:

In the context of technology licensing tying occurs when the licensor makes the licensing of one technology (the tying product) conditional upon the licensee taking a licence for another technology or purchasing a product from the licensor or someone designated by him (the tied product). Bundling occurs where two technologies or a technology and a product are only sold together as a bundle. In both cases, however, it is a condition that the products and technologies involved are distinct in the sense that there is distinct demand for each of the products and technologies forming part of the tie or the bundle. This is normally not the case where the technologies or products are by necessity linked in such a way that the licensed technology cannot be exploited without the tied product or both parts of the bundle cannot be exploited without the other...[43]

The licensor may use tying and bundling in order to exercise quality control over the licensee's output and maintain standards by ensuring that the licensee uses only certain inputs in its production process. It may be necessary for the licensee to use these inputs to ensure the proper exploitation of the IPR. On the other hand it may also be a means of giving the licensor a guaranteed outlet for products not covered by IPRs and foreclosing competitors from the licensee's custom.

---

[39] See Chap. 11.

[40] Guidelines, para. 179.

[41] Commission's *IXth Report on Competition Policy* (Commission, 1979), part 114.

[42] Guidelines, para. 180.

[43] Guidelines, para. 191.

(vii) Non-compete Obligations

The licensor may wish to ensure that the licensee does not also use its own (or a third party's) technology to produce goods in competition with those produced under the licence. Limiting the licensee's ability to do this is one way of ensuring that the licensee produces a minimum amount under the licence and generates adequate royalties.

(viii) No-challenge Clauses

The owner of a valid IPR is able to sue anyone who infringes its right. What amounts to an infringing act depends on the nature of the IPR. As already explained, a licence entitles another party to use the technology or other matter protected by the IPR without infringing. However, he can only use it in accordance with the terms of the licence and these will normally entail the payment of royalties. Were the IPR not valid he would be able to produce without payment and be free from the terms of the licence. A licensee exploiting licensed technology is in a good position to detect anything which might render the IPR invalid (for example, that the subject matter of a patent is obvious in the light of prior art and therefore not novel). Licensors, knowing this, often wish to insert 'no-challenge clauses' into licences which make it a breach of contract (and therefore actionable by damages) for the licensee to challenge the validity of the licensed IPR or even to challenge the validity of *any* of the licensor's IPRs. It should be noted, however, that it is not necessarily in the licensee's interest to establish the invalidity of the right because then anyone else may freely use the hitherto protected subject matter (although the licensee may have a great advantage on the market in being already tooled up and producing).

(ix) Improvements

While exploiting the licensed technology the licensee may well develop improvements or further know-how. These may be severable or non-severable. A severable improvement is one which can be exploited without infringing the licensed technology. Unless prevented by the terms of the licence therefore the licensee could continue using it after the licence has expired and/or could license or assign it to third parties. Licensors, however, frequently want exclusive access to the improvements and want terms in the licence which oblige the licensee to 'grant back' severable improvements. This enables them to improve their own technology, prevent third parties gaining access to the improvements, and, perhaps, prevent the licensee from becoming a stronger competitor. They may also want to 'feed-on' improvements made by one licensee to the others.[44] Competition law may be concerned to limit the terms of severable improvements clauses. Non-severable improvements do not raise the same issues as they can be used only with the licensor's technology.

C. DEVELOPMENT OF COMPETITION POLICY TOWARDS LICENSING OF INTELLECTUAL PROPERTY RIGHTS

(i) General

The licensing of IPRs helps to disseminate new technology, brings new competitors on to the market, and increases the rewards for innovation. Its effects are generally pro-competitive and beneficial

---

[44] The dynamics of this are complex. Feed-on arrangements disseminate technology but licensees will only be happy with the arrangements if they are getting as much out of them as they put in. If one licensee does all the innovation and the others get the benefits while contributing little to the common knowledge the first licensee may lose the incentive to innovate and will certainly not be keen to reveal its improvements, see, e.g., W. Cornish, D. Llewelyn, and T. Aplin, *Intellectual Property: Patents, Copyright, Trade Marks and Allied Rights* (7th edn, Sweet & Maxwell, 2010).

to consumer welfare. It can be argued that since a licence of IPRs allows a third party to exploit the rights, allowing it to do what would otherwise be unlawful, the grant of a licence opens up markets and does not restrict competition. It should not therefore infringe Article 101(1). However, it has been seen that licence agreements commonly contain provisions which go beyond a bare permission for the licensee to exploit the right.[45] Competition law has to decide whether, and in what circumstances, these further obligations have the effect of restricting competition.

The Commission's policy to IP licensing agreements has developed and varied significantly over the years. Initially, a fairly permissive approach was adopted but, gradually, the Commission's attitude hardened and a more formalistic and interventionist approach was taken. The TTBER and Technology Transfer Guidelines, however, have heralded a more economic and effects-based approach to these types of agreements. The Commission has played an extremely influential role in the development of policy in this area, especially as there have been comparatively few Court decisions on licensing. This is due to a number of factors, in particular that: parties granted an Article 101(3) exemption had little incentive to challenge the decision (even if they had to change the agreement to obtain the exemption); and because from 1984 onwards block exemptions covered patent licences (and mixed patent/know-how licences and later pure know-how licences too). Therefore after 1984 the name of the game was for the parties to enter into licensing arrangements which were covered by the block exemptions wherever possible. The importance of the block exemptions has meant that an enormous amount of lobbying and discussion has gone on whenever new block exemptions have been drawn up, as exemplified by the activity which preceded the adoption of the latest TTBER, Regulation 772/2004.[46] The judgments of the Court which have been given, however, are of great importance. This is particularly true of the judgment of the CJ in *Nungesser* (the *Maize Seeds* case)[47] which was significant in the development not only of the law on licensing but also on the question of what amounts to a restriction of competition for the purposes of Article 101(1) generally.[48]

(ii) The Evolution of the Commission's Policy towards Licensing Agreements

The Commission's early attitude, illustrated by its 1962 Notice on patent licensing agreements (the so-called Christmas Message)[49] was that even exclusive patent licensing agreements did not fall within Article 101(1) so long as the restrictions did not go beyond the 'scope of the patent'.[50]

Later, however, the Commission's attitude began to change and it moved towards the position that exclusive licences, unless de minimis, always fell within Article 101 and that many common non-territorial restraints also went beyond the scope of the patent and violated Article 101(1). This essentially led to the position that a patent (or other) licence which went beyond a simple right to exploit a patented invention against payment of royalties would violate Article 101(1) and require exemption.[51] The Commission's sharp change in attitude was triggered by the development of the exhaustion of rights doctrine and the elaboration of the existence/exercise dichotomy as more IPRs issues came before the Court and were notified to the Commission. Significant to this change, was

---

[45] See discussion of such clauses in Section 3.B, pp. 855–858.

[46] [2004] OJ L123/11.

[47] Case 258/78, *Nungesser* v. *Commission* [1982] ECR 2015.

[48] See Chap. 4.

[49] 24 December 1962 [1962–1963] JO 2922/62, finally withdrawn in 1984 [1984] OJ C220/14. The same approach could be seen in Art. 4(2)(b) of Reg. 17, [1959–1962] OJ Spec.Ed.87, as amended by Council Reg. 1216/1999 [1999] OJ L148/5, which classed a narrow category of licensing agreements as non-notifiable.

[50] See further S. Anderman, *EC Competition Law and Intellectual Property Rights* (Clarendon Press, 1998), 53–54.

[51] See, e.g., the Commission's *Fourth Report on Competition Policy* (1974), point 20.

the CJ's judgment in *Consten & Grundig*[52] in which it dealt with a trade mark licence which had been used as a mechanism to create ATP for the distributor/licensee and to seal off the French market. The Commission became acutely conscious of the potential of exclusive licensing agreements for isolating markets. It was haunted by the idea that if the licensor had not given an *exclusive* licence he might have given a *non-exclusive* one, which would have led to competition between the different licensees in the same territory.

In the real world, however, licensees will frequently not entertain any licence but an exclusive (or at least a sole) one. The commercial risk is too great. The choice is often therefore between an exclusive licence and no licence, not between an exclusive and a non-exclusive one. The Commission was frequently criticised for considering matters with hindsight, *ex post*, rather than *ex ante*, as the parties would have done, when the transaction might well have looked risky.[53] Nevertheless, throughout the 1970s the Commission held in a series of decisions that exclusive licences were restrictive of competition and so came within Article 101(1). However, so long as the parties were willing to modify the exclusivity clauses and other provisions held to be restrictions (such as tie-ins, no-challenge clauses, and grant-backs of improvements), the Commission would exempt them under Article 101(3).[54]

The broad interpretation of Article 101(1) of course created a pressing need for some form of block exemption.[55] With the experience it gained from handling notified licensing agreements, the Commission set about constructing a block exemption regulation on patent licences. The first draft was produced in 1979 but there were lengthy negotiations with Member States, businesses, and other interested parties. The Commission also waited to take account of the CJ's judgment in *Nungesser*, the appeal from its 1978 decision in *Maize Seeds*.[56] The first IP licensing block exemption was finally adopted in 1984.[57]

(iii) Exclusivity and Territorial Restrictions in the Case Law of the Court

The CJ never endorsed such a strict approach to exclusivity as that adopted by the Commission. This is shown by its judgment in *Nungesser (Maize Seeds)*, the first judgment after *Consten & Grundig* in which it had to deal with an exclusive licence. The case concerned plant breeders' rights but the principles set out in the judgment are not limited to this type of right.[58]

Case 258/78, *Nungesser* v. *EC Commission* [1982] ECR 2015

INRA, a French State research institute, developed new strains of hybrid maize seed of great importance in European agriculture. Acting through FRASEMA, a French company set up to deal with INRA's seed varieties, it gave Kurt Eisele (later Nungesser KG) the exclusive right to produce and distribute INRA varieties in Germany. INRA agreed with Eisele not to import its seed into Germany itself and to prevent

---

[52] Cases 56 and 58/64, *Consten & Grundig* v. *Commission* [1966] ECR 299.

[53] See discussion of Cases 56 and 58/64, *Établissements Consten SA & Grundig-Verkaufs-GmbH* v. *Commission* [1966] ECR 299 in Chap. 4.

[54] See, e.g., *Re the Agreements of Davidson Rubber Co* [1972] OJ L143/31; *Burroughs/Deplanque* [1972] OJ L13/50; *Raymond/Nagoya* [1972] OJ L143/39; *Bronbemaling* v. *Heidemaatschappij* [1975] OJ L249/27; *AOIP* v. *Beyrard* [1976] OJ L6/8.

[55] See Chaps. 2–4.

[56] [1978] OJ L286/23.

[57] Commission Reg. 2349/84 on patent licences, [1984] OJ L219/15.

[58] Plant breeders' rights were excluded from the scope of block exemption Reg. 2349/84 [1984] OJ L219/15 on patent licensing but were covered by the block exemption on technology transfer agreements, Commission Reg. 240/96: [1996] OJ L31/2, and are now covered by Reg. 772/2004 (the TTBER).

others from doing so. Eisele relied on the rights in Germany to prevent parallel importers from importing seed obtained from another source in France. One importer settled the action, but another complained to the Commission.

The Commission held that the exclusivity and territorial protection provisions were caught by Article 101(1) and could not be exempted. Eisele/Nungesser appealed.

Court of Justice

41. Th[e] synopsis of the German legislation shows that seeds certified and approved for marketing are subject to quality control on the part of the public authorities and that that control extends to the stability of the variety. However, breeders' rights are not intended to substitute for controls carried out by the competent authorities, controls carried out by the owner of those rights, but to confer on the owner a kind of protection, the nature and effects of which all derive from private law. From that point of view the legal position of a breeder of seeds is not different from that of the owner of patent or trade mark rights over a product subject to strict control by the public authorities, as is the case with pharmaceutical products.

...

43. It is therefore not correct to consider that breeder's rights are a species of commercial or industrial property right with characteristics of so special a nature as to require, in relation to the competition rules, a different treatment from other commercial or industrial property rights. That conclusion does not affect the need to take into consideration, for the purposes of the rules on competition, the specific nature of the products which form the subject-matter of breeders' rights.

...

48. The statement of reasons on which the decision is based refers to two sets of circumstances in order to justify the application of Article [101(1)] to the exclusive licence in question (II, No. 3). The accuracy of the facts thus stated has not been challenged.

49. The first set of circumstances is described as follows...

By licensing a single undertaking to exploit his breeders' rights in a given territory, the licensor deprives himself for the entire duration of the contract of the ability to issue licences to other undertakings in the same territory...

By undertaking not to produce or market the product himself in the territory covered by the contract the licensor likewise eliminates himself, as well as FRASEMA and its members, as suppliers in that territory.

50. Corresponding to that part of the statement of reasons is Article 1(b) of the decision, which in its first and second indents declares the exclusive nature of the licence granted by the 1965 contract to be contrary to Article [101(1) TFEU] in so far as it imposes:An obligation upon INRA or those deriving rights through INRA to refrain from having the relevant seeds produced or sold by other licensees in Germany, and an obligation upon INRA or those deriving rights through INRA to refrain from producing or selling the relevant seeds in Germany themselves.

51. The second set of circumstances referred to in the decision is described as follows:

The fact that third parties may not import the same seed [namely the seed under licence] from other [EU] countries into Germany, or export from Germany to other [EU] countries, leads to market sharing and deprives German farmers of any real room for negotiation since seed is supplied by one supplier and one supplier only.

52. That part of the statement of reasons is also reflected in Article 1 (b) of the decision, which in its third and fourth indents declares the exclusive nature of the licence granted by the 1965 contract to be contrary to Article [101(1) TFEU] in so far as it imposes:

An obligation upon INRA or those deriving rights through INRA to prevent third parties from exporting the relevant seeds to Germany without the licensee's authorization for use or sale there, and

Mr Eisele's concurrent use of his exclusive contractual rights and his own breeder's rights to prevent all imports into Germany or exports to other Member States of the relevant seeds.

53. It should be observed that those two sets of considerations relate to two legal situations which are not necessarily identical. The first case concerns a so-called open exclusive licence or assignment and the exclusivity of the licence relates solely to the contractual relationship between the owner of the right and the licensee, whereby the owner merely undertakes not to grant other licences in respect of the same territory and not to compete himself with the licensee on that territory. On the other hand, the second case involves an exclusive licence or assignment with absolute territorial protection, under which the parties to the contact propose, as regards the products and the territory in question, to eliminate all competition from third parties, such as parallel importers or licensees for other territories.

54. That point having been clarified, it is necessary to examine whether, in the present case, the exclusive nature of the licence, in so far as it is an open licence, has the effect of preventing or distorting competition with the meaning of Article [101(1) TFEU].

55. In that respect the Government of the Federal Republic of Germany emphasized that the protection of agricultural innovations by means of breeders' rights constitutes a means of encouraging such innovations and the grant of exclusive rights for a limited period, is capable of providing a further incentive to innovative efforts.

From that it infers that a total prohibition of every exclusive licence, even an open one, would cause the interest of undertakings in licences to fall away, which would be prejudicial to the dissemination of knowledge and techniques in the Community.

56. The exclusive licence which forms the subject-matter of the contested decision concerns the cultivation and marketing of hybrid maize seeds which were developed by INRA after years of research and experimentation and were unknown to German farmers at the time when the co-operation between INRA and the applicants was taking shape. For that reason the concern shown by the interveners as regards the protection of new technology is justified.

57. In fact, in the case of a licence of breeders' rights over hybrid maize seeds newly developed in one Member State, an undertaking established in another Member State which was not certain that it would not encounter competition from other licensees for the territory granted to it, or from the owner of the right himself, might be deterred from accepting the risk of cultivating and marketing that product; such a result would be damaging to the dissemination of a new technology and would prejudice competition in the Community between the new product and similar existing products.

58. Having regard to the specific nature of the products in question, the Court concludes that in a case such as the present, the grant of an open exclusive licence, that is to say a licence which does not affect the position of third parties such as parallel importers and licensees for other territories, is not in itself incompatible with Article [101(1) TFEU].

59. Part B of the third submission is thus justified to the extent to which it concerns that aspect of the exclusive nature of the licence.

…

76. It must be remembered that under the terms of Article [101(3) TFEU] an exemption from the prohibition contained in Article [101(1) TFEU] may be granted in the case of any agreement between undertakings which contributes to improving the production or distribution of goods or to promoting technical progress, and which does not impose on the undertakings concerned restrictions which are not indispensable to the attainment of those objectives.

77. As it is a question of seeds intended to be used by a large number of farmers for the production of maize, which is an important product for human and animal foodstuffs, absolute territorial protection manifestly goes beyond what is indispensable for the improvement of production or distribution or the promotion of technical progress, as is demonstrated in particular in the present case by the prohibition, agreed to by both parties to the agreement of any parallel imports of INRA maize seeds into Germany even if those seeds were bred by INRA itself and marketed in France.

> 78. It follows that the absolute territorial protection conferred on the licensee, as established to exist by the contested decision, constituted a sufficient reason for refusing to grant an exemption under Article [101(3) TFEU]. It is therefore no longer necessary to examine the other grounds set out in the decision for refusing to grant such an exemption.

In this judgment the CJ distinguished between 'open' and 'closed' exclusive licences (paragraph 53). On the one hand there is an 'open' licence which pertains only to the position between licensor and licensee. The licensor agrees not to grant further licences in the same territory and not to operate there itself. On the other hand there is a licence containing provisions which affect third parties and which create ATP.[59]

The distinction between 'open' licences and others is not completely clear as the Court did not expressly deal with a situation where the provisions fall short of granting ATP, for example where restrictions on the licensee's activities outside the licensed territory are imposed. Presumably a provision whereby the licensee undertakes not to compete with the licensor in the latter's territory is covered by the 'open' designation, as it 'relates solely to the contractual relationship between the owner of the right and the licensee'. However, it appears that any further limitation on the licensee, other than an obligation not to produce outside its allocated territory, renders the licence closed rather than open.[60] As far as open licences are concerned, the Court did not conclude in *Nungesser* that the exclusivity provisions automatically infringed Article 101(1), as the Commission had done. Instead the Court looked at the licence in its economic context: if the exclusivity provisions were necessary to induce the licensee to enter the transaction then competition was not restricted. It should be noted that the Court's realistic approach was limited. In paragraphs 77 and 78 the Court condemned outright the clauses leading to the imposition of ATP without considering their possible economic justifications.[61] Not only were these provisions automatically caught by Article 101(1), they did not qualify for exemption under Article 101(3).

The principles in *Nungesser* apply to other kinds of 'manufacturing' licences involving the licensing of patents and know-how, and not just to plant breeders' rights. The general applicability of *Nungesser* to such transactions is manifest from the Court's rationale for holding the open exclusive licence outside Article 101(1) (i.e. the need to provide incentives for investment by the licensee). This can apply equally to other kinds of rights. However, it can be seen from paragraph 58 of *Nungesser* that, in deciding whether or not Article 101(1) applies, regard has to be had to the specific nature of the *products* in question. In the subsequent case of *Erauw-Jacquéry*[62] the nature of the products concerned was crucial to the Court's finding that even an export ban could fall outside Article 101(1). *Erauw-Jacquéry* concerned basic seed, which is seed which can lawfully be used to propagate further seed, as distinct from the certified seed sold to produce crops. Plant breeders' rights in basic seeds are particularly vulnerable as they can easily be lost.[63]

Case 27/87, *Erauw-Jacquéry* v. *La Hesbignonne* [1988] ECR 1919

The owner of plant breeders' rights licensed them to a co-operative on the terms that the co-operative could propagate basic seed and sell seed of the first or second generation but could not sell or export basic

---

[59] See the discussion of exclusive and sole licences and sales restrictions in Section 3.B.iii.

[60] See M. Siragusa, 'EEC Technology Transfers—A Private View' [1982] Fordham Corp L Inst 95, 116–118 and, e.g., *Boussois/Interpane* [1987] OJ L50/30.

[61] See further the discussion of the application of Art. 101(3) generally, in Chap. 4.

[62] Case 27/87, *Erauw-Jacquéry* v. *La Hesbignonne* [1988] ECR 1919.

[63] They are subject to cancellation if they cease to be stable or uniform. See in the UK the Plant Varieties and Seeds Act 1997, ss. 4(2) and 22 and, in respect of EU plant variety, Arts 8, 9, and 21 of Reg. 2100/94 [1994] OJ L227/1.

seed. The Court of Justice recognized the need for quality control and for assuring the proper handling of the basic seed by those allowed to propagate it. Advocate General Mischo likened the situation to one of a franchise, where the franchisor is justified in preventing its know-how benefiting competitors.

Court of Justice

8. In the first place the national court seeks to ascertain whether the provision prohibiting the holder of the licence for propagating basic seed from selling, assigning or exporting that seed falls within Article [101 (1)].

9. The Commission and the breeder maintain that the provision prohibiting the sale and exportation of E2 basic seed, which is placed at the disposal of the growers only for the purposes of propagation, is not contrary to Article [101(1) TFEU]. Such a provision falls within the ambit of the plant breeder's rights.

10. In this respect, it must be pointed out that, as the Court acknowledged in its judgment of 8 June 1982 (in Case 258/78 *Nungesser v. Commission...*), the development of the basic lines may involve considerable financial commitment. Consequently, a person who has made considerable efforts to develop varieties of basic seed which may be the subject-matter of plant breeders' rights must be allowed to protect himself against any improper handling of those varieties of seed. To that end, the breeder must be entitled to restrict propagation to the growers which he has selected as licensees. To that extent, the provision prohibiting the licensee from selling and exporting basic seed falls outside the prohibition contained in Article [101(1)].

11. Therefore, the answer to the first part of the question referred by the national court must be that a provision of an agreement concerning the propagation and sale of seed, in respect of which one of the parties is the holder or the agent of the holder of certain plant breeders' rights, which prohibits the licensee from selling and exporting the basic seed is compatible with Article [101(1) TFEU] in so far as it is necessary in order to enable the breeder to select the growers who are to be licensees.

The Court in this case stressed the need to protect the licensor's investment. The Court recognised the particularly fragile nature of basic seed and was prepared to hold that in these special circumstances ATP was not within Article 101(1). The Court referred to *Nungesser*, but in that case, where certified rather than basic seed was concerned, the ATP caused the agreement both to infringe Article 101(1) and to be denied exemption pursuant to Article 101(3).[64]

The compatibility of exclusive licences also arose in *Premier League Ltd* v. *QC Leisure* and *Murphy* v. *Media Protection Services Ltd*[65] in the context of copyright licensing. Although the CJ had held in *Coditel II*[66] that an exclusive licence (amounting in effect to ATP) was not *of itself* prohibited by Article 101(1) in the context of the case (given the nature of the protected work and the characteristics of the film industry), in this case the Grand Chamber of the CJ indicated that it would rarely be willing to accept that exclusive licences conferring ATP would not be restrictive by object. Rather, it drew an important distinction between the situation where:

- a sole licensee was granted an exclusive right to broadcast protected subject matter from a Member State—which would not justify a finding that an agreement had an anti-competitive objective; and

- the agreement went further and was aimed at partitioning national markets according to national borders—which was liable to frustrate the Treaty's objective of achieving the

---

[64] The Commission emphasised the special nature of basic seeds in its comment on the case in its *XVIIIth Report on Competition Policy* (1989), part 103; in *Sicasov* [1999] OJ L4/27, the Commission applied *Erauw-Jacquéry* to another licence of basic seed.

[65] Cases C-403 and 429/08, 4 October 2011.

[66] Case 262/81, *Coditel v. SA Ciné Vog Films (Coditel II)* [1982] ECR 3381.

integration of those markets through the establishment of a single market and had to be regarded, in principle, as an agreement whose object is to restrict competition.[67]

The case, which concerned the broadcasting of Premier League football matches in the UK through the unauthorised use of Greek satellite decoder cards, is discussed in further detail in Section 8.

(iv) Non-territorial Restraints

The Commission also took the view that many non-territorial restraints in licences restricted competition within the meaning of Article 101(1). Its approach is exemplified by the *Windsurfing* case.[68]

Windsurfing International (WI), an American company founded by Hoyle Schweitzer, granted a number of non-exclusive licences of its German patent for windsurfing equipment to firms within the EU. Litigation was current in Germany over whether or not the patent covered both the rig and the board, but the Commission proceeded on the basis that it covered only the rig. The Commission found that the following provisions concerning quality control, tying, licensed-by notices, no-challenge clauses, and royalty calculation infringed Article 101(1):

- an obligation on the licensee to mount the patented rig only on boards approved by the licensor; the Commission rejected WI's contention that this was a permissible measure of quality control, as the controls did not relate to a product covered by the patent and were not laid down in advance on the basis of objectively verifiable criteria;

- an obligation on the licensee to sell the rigs only as part of a complete sailboard, and not separately; the Commission held that an obligation arbitrarily placed on a licensee to sell the patented product only in conjunction with a product outside the scope of the patent was not indispensable to the exploitation of the patent;

- an obligation on the licensee to pay royalties calculated on the net selling price of the whole sailboard and not just the rig; the Commission held that this method of calculation could be justified only where 'the number of items manufactured or consumed or their value are difficult to establish separately in a complex production process or... there is for the patented item on its own no separate demand which the licensee would be prevented from satisfying through such a method of calculation';

- an obligation on the licensee to affix to boards manufactured and marketed in Germany a notice saying 'licensed by Hoyle Schweitzer' or 'licensed by Windsurfing International'; the Commission said that this created the false impression that the board as well as the rig was covered by the patent;

- an obligation on the licensees to acknowledge the word marks 'Windsurfer' and 'Windsurfing' as well as a design mark or logo as valid trade marks; the Commission considered this tantamount to a no-challenge clause to the validity of the trade mark, while WI claimed it was part of an attempt to stop its trade mark being used as a generic designation;

- an obligation on the licensees to restrict production of the licensed product to a specific manufacturing plant in Germany; the Commission rejected the plea that this was a measure of quality control and held that it limited freedom of competition by means of a clause which had

---

[67] Case 262/81, *Coditel v. SA Ciné Vog Films (Coditel II)* [1982] ECR 3381, para. 139. See also Case C-403 and 428/08 4 October 2011, para. 139.

[68] *Windsurfing International* OJ [1982] L229/1; Case 193/83, *Windsurfing International v. Commission* [1986] ECR 611. Note that, despite a very different approach post-modernisation, the Commission cites *Windsurfing* in the Guidelines, para. 81, when explaining that price-fixing within the hardcore restriction list in Art. 4(1)(a) includes agreements whereby royalties are calculated on the basis of all product sales irrespective of whether the licensed technology is being used.

nothing to do with the patent; neither the Commission nor the Court dealt with the position of a prohibition relating only to territories where there was patent protection;

- an obligation on the licensees not to challenge the validity of the licensed patents; the Commission had long held that no-challenge clauses restrict competition and that it is in the public interest that invalid patents should be challenged.

The CJ, which agreed that the Commission was justified in treating the patent as covering only the rig, upheld all of the Commission's findings except for (c), on royalties, where it held that the global calculation of royalties on the complete sailboard was not a restriction of competition on the sale of separate *rigs*, although it was on the sale of *boards*. Like the Commission, the CJ took a highly formalistic approach and condemned the other provisions for going beyond the 'scope of the patent' and the 'specific subject matter of the patent' without engaging in any economic analysis. As one critical commentator put it, the judgment as a whole is 'based on the assumptions that there is something inherently anti-competitive in the patent monopoly and that patent licenses [*sic*], even when arguably vertical in nature, differ fundamentally from distribution arrangements and warrant stricter treatment'.[69]

As the agreements had not been notified to the Commission, the CJ did not have to rule on the compatibility of the agreement with Article 101(3) and whether the Commission had been correct to hold that the agreement could not have been exempted. Between the date of the decision in *Windsurfing* and the judgment the Commission had adopted the block exemption regulation on patent licensing agreements, 2349/84.[70] Both the decision and the judgment reflected the approach taken by the Commission in the block exemption.

(v) The Block Exemptions on Patent Licensing and Know-how Licensing Prior to 1 May 2004

Despite the urgent need for block exemptions caused by the broad interpretation of Article 101(1) in the field of IP licensing agreements, the first block exemption was not adopted until 1984. Regulation 2349/84[71] applied to pure patent licensing agreements or to mixed patent and know-how licensing agreements where the patent was the predominant element. The second block exemption, Regulation 556/89,[72] applied to pure know-how licensing agreements and to mixed know-how and patent licensing agreements where know-how was the predominant element. Both exemptions applied only to bilateral agreements. The two regulations were very similar: specifying the type of agreement covered and exempted and containing 'white lists' and 'black lists'.[73] Both regulations were replaced in 1996 by a single block exemption, Regulation 240/96 on technology transfer agreements,[74] which encompassed any transaction in which the predominant element was the licensing of patents or know-how. Compared to the previous Regulations it had a shortened 'black list' of prohibited clauses and a longer 'white list'. It was replaced on 1 May 2004 by Regulation 772/2004 on technology transfer agreements (the TTBER).[75]

---

[69] J. Venit, 'In the Wake of Windsurfing: Patent Licensing in the Common Market' [1986] Fordham Corp L Inst 517, 560–561.
[70] [1984] OJ L219/15.
[71] [1984] OJ L219/15.
[72] [1989] OJ L61/1.
[73] See Chap. 4.
[74] [1996] OJ L31/2.
[75] [2004] OJ L123/11.

D. THE ADOPTION OF THE 2004 TTBER AND THE TECHNOLOGY TRANSFER GUIDELINES

(i) The Commission's Review Process and the Adoption of the New Measures

In December 2001 the Commission adopted a mid-term review Report on the application of Regulation 240/96, pursuant to Article 12 of that Regulation.[76] The report concluded that the regulation was too formalistic, narrow, and 'straitjacketing', catching some pro-competitive agreements while missing anti-competitive ones, and that it was out of line with the approach of newer block exemptions—then the Verticals Regulation (1999)[77] and the block exemptions for specialisation agreements[78] and for research and development (R&D) agreements (2000).[79] Less than four years separated Regulation 240/96 from the Verticals Regulation but in that period the Commission had adopted a new pattern of block exemptions and a more economic approach to the assessment of agreements. The new regulations had moved away from a legalistic approach based on form, to a more economic one, focused on the effects of the agreement. Moreover, it had become apparent by 2001 that the Commission's proposals for modernising the system for the enforcement of the competition rules[80] were likely to be adopted. Although Regulation 240/96 was not due to expire until 2006 the Commission thus considered that it would be desirable for a more 'modern' block exemption on technology transfer to be put in place.[81] The Commission invited (and received) comments on the Evaluation Report[82] and produced a draft for a new block exemption and accompanying guidelines on 1 October 2003. There followed a period of heated debate and much lobbying.[83]

The critics were most concerned that the draft proposed a 'safe harbour' only for undertakings whose market shares were below certain thresholds. The block exemption would not apply where these thresholds were exceeded. Although a market share cap was in line with the other new block exemptions it caused particular consternation in respect of IP licences. Market share is notoriously difficult to assess in many IP licensing situations because, primarily, of the market definition problems. Further, use of a market share threshold is, arguably, an inappropriate and arbitrary indicator of the real competitive situation in technology markets.[84] Moreover, the draft proposed a different threshold depending on whether the agreement was between 'competitors' or 'non-competitors'.[85] The narrower reach of the proposed block exemption combined with the proposed removal of the notification system meant that companies would face less legal certainty, and greater *ex post* control of the agreements

---

[76] *Evaluation Report on the Transfer of Technology Block Exemption Regulation No. 240/96*, available at <http://www.ftc.gov/opp/intellect/020522chin.doc2.pdf>.

[77] Reg. 2790/99 [1999] OJ L336/21 (now replaced by Reg. 330/2010 [2010] OJ L336/21), discussed in Chap. 11.

[78] Reg. 2658/2000 [2000] OJ L304/3 (now replaced by Reg. 1218/2010 [2010] OJ L335/43), discussed in Chap. 10.

[79] Reg. 2659/2000 [2000] OJ L304/7 (now replaced by Reg. 1217/2010 [2010] OJ L335/36), discussed in Chap. 10.

[80] Commission's White Paper on modernisation of the rules implementing Articles 85 and 86 of the EC Treaty [now Articles 101 and 102 TFEU] [1999] OJ C132/1.

[81] Reg. 240/96 contained provisions (e.g., an opposition procedure) which would not have worked in a system without provision for the notification of agreements. The abolition of notification and exemption also meant that guidelines were desirable to assist undertakings make their own assessment of agreements outside the block exemption.

[82] Published on the Commission's website on 19 July 2002.

[83] Over 70 submissions were received from industry, trade associations, law and IP societies, individual law firms, national authorities, individual companies, universities, and consultants.. And see also the speech by Commissioner Mario Monti, 'The New EU Policy on Technology Transfer Agreements', Ecole des Mines, Paris, 16 January 2004, available at <http://europa.eu/rapid/press-release_SPEECH-04-19_en.htm?locale=en>.

[84] See, e.g., the submission of the International Chamber of Commerce to the Commission, available on the Commission's website, but cf. M. Monti, speech of 16 January 2004 (cited in n. 83).

[85] There was also concern that parties might start life as non-competitors but move into the competitor category during the lifetime of the agreement, with serious consequences for its validity.

by the Commission, NCAs or (much more likely in respect of licensing agreements) national courts if the validity of the licence was challenged. Furthermore, there was concern about other provisions in the draft. For example, although the Commission proposed a more flexible block exemption than Regulation 240/96 the draft contained both a list of hardcore restrictions which in some respects was more severe than the black list in Regulation 240/96, and a list of 'excluded' restrictions.[86] The Guidelines were also criticised, in particular for their approach to incentives to innovation.[87]

The Commission accepted some, but by no means all, of these criticisms.[88] Above all, it adhered to its decision to impose market share thresholds despite pressure to drop them:

> The use of market share thresholds is mainly opposed because it is considered that market shares are of no relevance in high tech sectors, that the assessment of market shares throughout the life of the agreement decreases legal certainty and is costly and furthermore that relevant product and geographic markets are often difficult to define.
>
> Let me first recall that the TTBER applies to all sectors not just high tech ones. It is fair to state that most sectors are mature and that even sectors that are in such a state of flux are so usually only for a limited period. Therefore in most sectors, and that also means in most sectors where licensing takes place, market shares do matter. In addition, usually licensing concerns products that either will continue to compete with existing products or that will replace existing products. There are not many products which cater to a human need for which nothing existed before. Therefore market definition in case of licensing will not be markedly more difficult than market definition for most other agreements.[89]

In any event, time was limited as the Commission wished to introduce the new rules by 1 May 2004, as part of the modernisation package, if possible. The new block exemption, Regulation 772/2004 on the application of Article 81(3) [now 101(3)] to categories of technology transfer agreements (hereafter the TTBER), was adopted, and accompanying technology transfer Guidelines published, on 7 April 2004 (the Guidelines).[90] Regulation 772/2004 came into force on 1 May 2004.

(ii) Methodology

The TTBER and the Guidelines must be considered as a whole. The TTBER obviously provides the key block exemption for technology transfer agreements but the Guidelines go further, doing three things. First, they set out a framework of general principles concerning Article 101 and IPRs. Secondly, they explain the provisions and application of the TTBER. Thirdly, they explain the application of Article 101(1) and Article 101(3) to agreements outside the scope of the TTBER. This latter role is of utmost importance in the regime post-modernisation as the new TTBER now plays a reduced role than that played by the previous IP licensing block exemptions. The introduction of market share thresholds into the TTBER means that it provides less legal certainty than its predecessors and operates more as a 'safe harbour' providing, along with the Guidelines, a framework for analysis.[91] Where individual analysis is required, further insight into the Commission's thinking

---

[86] e.g., the territorial and customer restrictions were stricter.

[87] See, e.g., Charles River Associates Ltd, *Competition Policy Discussion Papers 8* (Nov. 2003), available at <http://www.crai.co.uk> and on the Commission's website as a submission to the Commission's consultation on the draft. Charles Rivers Associates was the firm of consultants responsible for the preparation of the Commission report, *Multiparty Licensing* (April 2003), available at <http://www.crai.uk> and at <http://ec.europa.eu/competition/antitrust/legislation/multiparty_licensing.pdf>.

[88] See speech by Mario Monti, 16 January 2004 (cited in n. 83).

[89] Speech by Mario Monti, 16 January 2004 (cited in n. 83).

[90] Reg. 772/2004 [2004] OJ L123/11, Commission Guidelines on the application of Article 81 of the EC Treaty to technology transfer agreements [2004] OJ C101/2.

[91] 'Previous BERS in the IP licensing field conferred an exemption on parties without market share and subject only to a formal power of withdrawal by the Commission or a national competition authority. If there was a blacklisted provision in the agreement, the agreement was unexemptable and unenforceable. In the current group

can be found in the Article 101(3) Guidelines[92] which set out general guidance on Article 101(1), Article 101(3), and their interrelationship. Anderman and Kallaugher explain the central importance of the Guidelines in the 2004 framework.

S. D. Anderman and J. Kallaugher, *Technology Transfer and the New EU Competition Rules: IP Licensing after Modernisation* (Oxford University Press, 2006)

1.19 The Guidelines are the real centrepiece of the reformed treatment of technology transfer under Article [101]. The Guidelines commence with a summary of the general principles applicable under the new paradigm. The Guidelines continue with a detailed and useful summary of the TTBER and the conditions for its application. They then lay out a 'general framework for analysis'—applying the general principles set out in the first section to IP licensing. They conclude by applying this analytical framework to a host of specific restrictions commonly found in IP licences. The central theme of the Guidelines is the need to identify competitive harm and to identify economic benefits that might outweigh those competitive harms in order to determine whether a licence agreement raised Article [101] issues.

1.20 The system of assessment created by the Guidelines entails a fundamental change in the way that practitioners must address competition law issues in the intellectual property context. In place of a purely legalistic evaluation of the contents of licensing agreements, the new system demands a new type of legal and economic assessment of individual agreements. The old system offered legal certainty and this was important for technology transfer agreement because of the ever present risk that licensees might go into competition with their licensors once they mastered the problems of efficient manufacture of the new technology. However, it also created a tight corset or legal straitjacket. The parties had to adjust their commercial arrangements to fit the legal rules or forgo the benefits of legally certain enforceability of the commercial agreement throughout its duration. For those commercial agreements whose curves could fit within the corset of the BER, there were considerable benefits. However, for those commercial agreements whose contours were either too angular or too plump to fit within the golden corset, there was a form of legal limbo.

1.21 The new reform entails some benefits to intellectual property owners. First, the Commission has finally recognised that 'vertical' licensing agreements, or agreements between non-competitors should systematically be treated more leniently than 'horizontal' licensing agreements, agreements between competitors. A lighter regulatory burden on purely vertical licensing agreements is entirely appropriate because such agreements present fewer risks to competition. Secondly, there are benefits for the parties to licensing in the reduced list of hard core restrictions in the new TTBER. These changes have meant that the new framework offers considerably greater flexibility to the parties to draft IP licensing agreements to reflect their preferred underlying commercial bargain. No longer is it so necessary to distort commercial arrangements to fit the strictly defined categories offered by the existing BERs. The Guidelines to the interpretation of the TTBER as well as to the more general application of Article [101] to licensing agreements outside the scope of the TTBER are also an improvement in the regulatory framework.

1.22 However, these improvements in the regulatory structure are accompanied by serious costs. First, and most obvious, has been the loss of legal certainty in the applicability of the safe harbour of the TTBER owing to its market share limits. Under the previous TTBER an agreement normally retained its exemption for its entire duration. This allowed lawyers to enjoy the authority to determine the lawfulness

---

of BERs, including the TTBER, the BER takes a reduced role within the legal framework', S. D. Anderman and J. Kallaugher, *Technology Transfer and the New EU Competition Rules: IP Licensing after Modernisation* (Oxford University Press, 2006), 1.16.

[92] Guidelines on the application of Article 81(3) of the Treaty [now Article 101(3) TFEU] [2004] OJ C101/2 (the Article 101(3) Guidelines).

of the licensing agreement with some finality. That type of legal certainty has disappeared to be replaced by a legal structure requiring a methodology to ensure continued legal enforceability for IP licensing agreements.

1.23 Second, the new legal methodology itself requires a considerable adjustment by lawyers to a new methodology for assessing licensing agreements for the purposes of exemption. Since the TTBER has practically no value other than as a reference for identifying hard core restraints, effective counselling requires lawyers to learn the new skills required by the new paradigm as applied in the Guidelines. This in turn requires lawyers to accept the need to combine legal and economic analysis in vetting licensing agreements under Article [101].

Despite the limitations of the new TTBER, as with vertical agreements[93] the mere existence of the TTBER turns the appraisal of the agreement under Article 101 on its head. It encourages undertakings to consider first whether their agreement falls (or can be made to fall) within the safe harbour of the TTBER:

many licence agreements fall outside Article [101](1), either because they do not restrict competition at all or because the restriction of competition is not appreciable…To the extent that such agreements would anyhow fall within the scope of the TTBER, there is no need to determine whether they are caught by Article [101(1)] .[94]

Only if a technology transfer agreement does not fall within the TTBER (because, for instance, the market share threshold is exceeded) is it necessary to consider the application of Article 101(1) and 101(3).

In the next sections the general principles applicable to IPRs and the general principles and framework for the assessment of technology transfer agreements set out in the Guidelines are considered. The provisions of the TTBER are then analysed prior to looking at how Article 101 applies to technology transfer agreements falling outside the safe harbour of the TTBER.

It is important to remember that the Guidelines are not binding but might influence interpretation by a national competition authority (NCA) or court insofar as they are consistent with the judgments of the CJ.[95]

(iii) General Principles: Application of Article 101 to Intellectual Property Rights

The Commission sets out the general principles by which it approaches the application of Article 101 to IPRs at the beginning of the Guidelines.[96] This section of the Guidelines considers the value of IPRs and the relationship of IPRs and competition law.

Guidelines on the Application of Article 81 of the EC Treaty [now Article 101 TFEU] to Technology Transfer Agreements

1. Article [101] and intellectual property rights

5. The aim of Article [101] as a whole is to protect competition on the market with a view to promoting consumer welfare and an efficient allocation of resources. Article [101(1)] prohibits all agreements and

---

[93] See Chap. 11.

[94] Guidelines, para. 36.

[95] As the Commission recognises in the Guidelines, para. 4. See also discussion of the nature of Commission Notices and Guidance in Chaps. 2 and 3.

[96] [2004] OJ C101/2.

concerted practices between undertakings and decisions by associations of undertakings…which may affect trade between Member States…and which have as their object or effect the prevention, restriction or distortion of competition…As an exception to this rule Article [101(3)] provides that the prohibition contained in Article [101(1)] may be declared inapplicable in the case of agreements between undertakings which contribute to improving the production or distribution of products or to promoting technical or economic progress, while allowing consumers a fair share of the resulting benefits and which do not impose restrictions which are not indispensable to the attainment of these objectives and do not afford such undertakings the possibility of eliminating competition in respect of a substantial part of the products concerned.

6. Intellectual property laws confer exclusive rights on holders of patents, copyright, design rights, trademarks and other legally protected rights. The owner of intellectual property is entitled under intellectual property laws to prevent unauthorised use of his intellectual property and to exploit it, *inter alia*, by licensing it to third parties. Once a product incorporating an intellectual property right has been put on the market inside the EEA by the holder or with his consent, the intellectual property right is exhausted in the sense that the holder can no longer use it to control the sale of the product…(principle of Community exhaustion). The right holder has no right under intellectual property laws to prevent sales by licensees or buyers of such products incorporating the licensed technology…The principle of Community exhaustion is in line with the essential function of intellectual property rights, which is to grant the holder the right to exclude others from exploiting his intellectual property without his consent.

7. The fact that intellectual property laws grant exclusive rights of exploitation does not imply that intellectual property rights are immune from competition law intervention. Articles [101] and [102] are in particular applicable to agreements whereby the holder licenses another undertaking to exploit his intellectual property rights. (See, e.g., Joined Cases 56/64 and 58/64, *Consten and Grundig* [1966] ECR 429.) Nor does it imply that there is an inherent conflict between intellectual property rights and the Community competition rules. Indeed, both bodies of law share the same basic objective of promoting consumer welfare and an efficient allocation of resources. Innovation constitutes an essential and dynamic component of an open and competitive market economy. Intellectual property rights promote dynamic competition by encouraging undertakings to invest in developing new or improved products and processes. So does competition by putting pressure on undertakings to innovate. Therefore, both intellectual property rights and competition are necessary to promote innovation and ensure a competitive exploitation thereof.

8. In the assessment of licence agreements under Article [101] it must be kept in mind that the creation of intellectual property rights often entails substantial investment and that it is often a risky endeavour. In order not to reduce dynamic competition and to maintain the incentive to innovate, the innovator must not be unduly restricted in the exploitation of intellectual property rights that turn out to be valuable. For these reasons the innovator should normally be free to seek compensation for successful projects that is sufficient to maintain investment incentives, taking failed projects into account. Technology licensing may also require the licensee to make significant sunk investments in the licensed technology and production assets necessary to exploit it. Article [101] cannot be applied without considering such *ex ante* investments made by the parties and the risks relating thereto. The risk facing the parties and the sunk investment that must be committed may thus lead to the agreement falling outside Article [101(1)] or fulfilling the conditions of Article [101(3)], as the case may be, for the period of time required to recoup the investment.

9. In assessing licensing agreements under Article [101], the existing analytical framework is sufficiently flexible to take due account of the dynamic aspects of technology licensing. There is no presumption that intellectual property rights and licence agreements as such give rise to competition concerns. Most licence agreements do not restrict competition and create pro-competitive efficiencies. Indeed, licensing as such is pro-competitive as it leads to dissemination of technology and promotes innovation. In addition, even licence agreements that do restrict competition may often give rise to pro-competitive efficiencies, which must be considered under Article [101(3)] and balanced against the negative effects on competition. The great majority of licence agreements are therefore compatible with Article [101].

(iv) Points of General Importance in the Application of Article 101 to Technology Transfer Agreements

The appraisal of agreements falling outside the TTBER are discussed in Section 5. However, it is useful at the outset to note a few points of general importance stressed in the Guidelines.

First, there is no presumption of illegality for a technology transfer agreement falling outside the TTBER so long as it does not contain hardcore restrictions on competition.

Secondly, there is a negative presumption that a technology transfer agreement, which does not contain hardcore restraints, will be compatible with Article 101 where four or more independently controlled substitutable technologies exist in addition to those controlled by the parties.

Thirdly, in paragraphs 10 to 18 of the Guidelines the Commission states, in line with its approach set out in the Article 101(3) Guidelines, that in applying Article 101 to technology transfer agreements it is concerned both with restrictions on inter-technology competition (competition between undertakings using different technologies) and restrictions on intra-technology competition (competition between undertakings using the same technology). This underpins the reliance upon *two* different 'counterfactuals' i.e. benchmarks against which the restriction of competition is measured.[97] The tests are set out paragraphs 12(a) and (b) of the Guidelines. Both may be applied to the same restraint.

Paragraph 12(a) asks:

Does the licence agreement restrict actual or potential competition that would have existed *without the contemplated agreement?* If so, the agreement may be caught by Article [101(1)]. In making this assessment it is necessary to take into account competition between the parties and competition from third parties. For instance, where two undertakings established in different Member States cross licence competing technologies and undertake not to sell products in each other's home markets, (potential) competition that existed prior to the agreement is restricted. Similarly, where a licensor imposes obligations on his licensees not to use competing technologies and these obligations foreclose third party technologies, actual or potential competition that would have existed in the absence of the agreement is restricted [emphasis added].

It can be seen that this paragraph is dealing with inter-technology competition, by asking whether the agreement restricts competition between existing technologies by, for example, sales bans in cross-licensing agreements between undertakings holding competing technologies or non-compete obligations.

Paragraph 12(b) asks:

Does the agreement restrict actual or potential competition that would have existed *in the absence of the contractual restraint(s)?* If so, the agreement may be caught by Article [101(1)]. For instance, where a licensor restricts its licensees from competing with each other, (potential) competition that could have existed between the licensees absent the restraints is restricted. Such restrictions include vertical price fixing and territorial or customer sales restrictions between licensees. However, certain restraints may in certain cases not be caught by Article [101(1)] when the restraint is objectively necessary for the existence of an agreement of that type or that nature (see in this respect the judgment in *Société Technique Minière* ... and Case 258/78, *Nungesser* [1982] ECR 2015). Such exclusion of the application of Article [101(1)] can only be made on the basis of objective factors external to the parties themselves and not the subjective views and characteristics of the parties. The question is not whether the parties in their particular situation would not have accepted to conclude a less restrictive agreement, but whether, given the nature of the agreement and the characteristics of the market, a less restrictive agreement would not have been concluded by undertakings in a similar setting. For instance, territorial restraints in an agreement between non-competitors may fall outside Article [101(1)] for a certain duration if the restraints are objectively necessary for a licensee to penetrate a new market. Similarly, a prohibition imposed on all licensees not to sell to certain categories of end users may not be restrictive of

---

[97] See L. Peeperkorn, 'IP Licences and Competition Rules: Striking the Right Balance' (2003) 26 *World Competition* 527.

competition if such a restraint is objectively necessary for reasons of safety or health related to the dangerous nature of the product in question. Claims that in the absence of a restraint the supplier would have resorted to vertical integration are not sufficient. Decisions on whether or not to vertically integrate depend on a broad range of complex economic factors, a number of which are internal to the undertaking concerned [emphasis added].

Paragraph 12(b) focuses on restrictions on intra-technology competition. It looks at the competitive situation arising from the agreement and compares it with less restrictive alternatives. It is seen in Chapter 4 that the Article 101(3) Guidelines also state that Article 101(1) is applied to restraints on intra-brand competition unless 'objectively necessary' for the existence of an agreement of that type or nature (as in *Nungesser* itself). It does not ask, however, as paragraph 12(b) makes clear, whether these particular parties would have concluded a less restrictive agreement, but whether undertakings 'in a similar setting' would have done so. This is because the issue is what is *objectively necessary*.

This concern with intra-technology restrictions (and intra-brand competition more generally) distinguishes EU from US law.[98] This concern still supports a relatively interventionist approach to technology transfer agreements under Article 101 and influences the interpretation of both Article 101(1) and Article 101(3). The Commission appears unapologetic about this.[99]

L. Peeperkorn, 'IP Licences and Competition Rules: Striking the Right Balance' (2003) 26 *World Competition* 527, 538–539

The proposed new block exemption regulation and guidelines maintain a stricter EU approach, stricter than the United States, towards intra-technology restrictions contained in agreements between non-competitors. The reasons for this divergence with the United States are threefold:

First, territorial restrictions are paid more attention in particular because of the additional market integration objective which EC competition policy has. Secondly, it reflects the higher importance EC competition policy attaches to intra-brand and intra-technology competition in general. It is considered important to protect intra-brand and intra-technology competition as a useful and sometimes essential complement to inter-brand competition. For instance, production costs of licensees and distribution costs of distributors make up a good deal of the end price of most products and competition between licensees or distributors may help to reduce these costs. It is also recognition of the fact that restraints are almost never only affecting intra-brand competition. There is no neat distinction between intra-brand and inter-brand restrictions. Reduced intra-brand competition may facilitate collusion and restrict inter-brand competition, especially in cases of cumulative use.

Thirdly, sales restrictions may be used to prevent arbitrage and support price discrimination between different markets, what economists call third degree price discrimination. This will in general lead to a loss of consumer welfare. While some consumers will pay a higher price and others will pay a lower price, collectively consumers will have to pay more to finance the extra profits obtained by the supplier (its motive to do price discrimination) and to cover the extra costs of supporting the price discrimination scheme and prevent arbitrage. Consumer welfare will also decline because of the loss of allocative efficiency because the marginal consumer in the high price market is willing to pay more than the marginal consumer in the

---

[98] See M. Delrahim (US Deputy Assistant Attorney General), 'US and EU Approaches to the Antitrust Analysis of IP licensing: Observations from the Enforcement Perspective', ABA Antitrust Section Meeting, Washington, 1 April 2004, available on the DOJ website, <http://www.usdoj.gov/atr/public/speeches>, and 1995 Department of Justice and Federal Trade Commission Antitrust Guidelines for the Licensing of Intellectual Property (the Intellectual Property Guidelines).

[99] The following extract is from Peeperkorn's paper and contains the usual disclaimer that the views expressed are the author's and do not necessarily represent those of the Commission or DG Comp.

low price market. Therefore consumer welfare will in general decline unless it can be clearly shown that otherwise the lower priced market would not be served at all and that therefore the price discrimination will lead to an undisputable increase of output. It is only in the latter case that consumer welfare may actually increase.

(v) Review of the 2004 Regime

As the TTBER is due to expire on 30 April 2014, the Commission started, in 2011, to collect views from stakeholders about their experience with the regime. In 2013, it published a draft replacement TTBER and Guidelines for consultation.[100] Although the new regime looks set to contain a number of changes in the details, it appears that the 2004 regime will not be fundamentally overhauled.

4. REGULATION 772/2004, THE TECHNOLOGY TRANSFER BLOCK EXEMPTION

A. GENERAL

As already explained, the TTBER was born in controversy. It is at once both more flexible and more strict than Regulation 240/96. It is more flexible as, like the other 'new' block exemptions, it does not contain lists of 'white' or 'grey' clauses. All provisions which are not in the list of hardcore restrictions or the list of excluded restrictions are permitted. Therefore it does not force parties into such a straitjacket as did its predecessor, Regulation 240/96. Recital 4 of the TTBER explains:

It is appropriate to move away from the approach of listing exempted clauses and to place greater emphasis on defining the categories of agreements which are exempted up to certain levels of market power and on specifying the restrictions or clauses which are not to be contained in such agreements.

The TTBER also covers a wider range of agreements and draws an important distinction between agreements between competitors and agreements between non-competitors. On the other hand, the lists of hardcore and excluded restrictions decrease, in some respects, the parties' contractual freedom in comparison to the previous position. In addition, and most importantly, it has been seen that the decision to introduce market share thresholds into the TTBER renders it far less useful to many undertakings.[101] As there is no possibility of notification of an agreement to the Commission, parties to technology transfer agreements face greater uncertainty and greater risk of litigation and other allegations that their licensing agreements violate Article 101.

The Commission is currently consulting on a number of changes to be incorporated into the replacement block exemptions which are referred to further in Sections 4.B, 4.C, and 4.D. In particular, some fairly significant changes are proposed for agreements incorporating exclusive 'grant back' provisions, termination clauses, passive sales restrictions protecting exclusive licensees, and/ or agreements between non-competitors, but where the licensee owns a technology substitutable for the licensed technology in-house.

---

[100] See IP/13/120; the documents are available at <http://ec.europa.eu/competition/consultations/2013_technology_transfer/index_en.html>.

[101] See extract from Anderman and Kallaugher, *Technology Transfer and the New EU Competition Rules* (cited in n. 91), paras. 1.19–1.23 set out in boxed text in Section 3.D.ii.

B. THE SCHEME OF THE TTBER

The TTBER comprises 20 recitals and 11 Articles.

Article 1 contains definitions of the most important terms in the Regulation.

Article 2 contains the exemption for bilateral technology transfer agreements which fall within it.

Article 3 contains the market share thresholds which limit the application of the Regulation. Thus technology transfer agreements can only benefit from the 'safe harbour' of the block exemption if the relevant market shares (of 20 per cent, for agreements between competitors, and 30 per cent, for agreements between non-competitors) are satisfied.

Article 4 contains the list of hardcore restrictions. The presence in the agreement of any of these restrictions removes the entire agreement from the protection of the block exemption, including provisions which would otherwise have been exempted.[102]

Article 5 contains the list of excluded restrictions. These restrictions are not exempted by the TTBER but their presence in an agreement does not remove the remainder of the agreement from the protection of the block exemption. The effect of including an excluded restraint is, therefore, as in the application of the Verticals Regulation, quite different from including a hardcore restraint.

Article 6 provides that the Commission and NCAs may withdraw the benefit of the TTBER from a particular agreement in certain circumstances.

Article 7 provides that the Commission may by regulation declare the TTBER inapplicable in situations where parallel networks of similar technology transfer agreements cover more than 50 per cent of a market.

Article 8 contains provisions about the calculation of the market share thresholds and provides for some marginal relief where market share increases during the lifetime of the agreement.

Article 9 repeals Regulation 240/96.

Article 10 contains the transitional provisions. Agreements in force on 30 April 2004 which satisfied the conditions for exemption in Regulation 240/96 remained exempt from Article 101(1) until 31 March 2006. Otherwise agreements are not block exempted unless they comply with the TTBER. Undertakings were therefore given two years in which to examine existing licensing agreements.

Article 11 provides that the TTBER enters into force on 1 May 2004 and expires on 30 April 2014.

C. PRINCIPAL FEATURES OF THE TTBER

Certain features of the TTBER should be noted at the outset:

- The category of agreements covered by the TTBER is wider than that covered by Regulation 240/96 in that the TTBER covers not only patents and know-how licensing but also licences of computer software and of designs;[103]

- As already mentioned, the TTBER applies only where certain market share thresholds are not exceeded;[104]

- Throughout the TTBER a distinction is drawn between agreements between competitors and agreements between non-competitors. The market share thresholds, the hardcore restrictions,[105] and the excluded restrictions[106] differ depending on whether the agreement is between competitors or non-competitors;

---

[102] Pursuant to the judgment of the Court in Case C-234/89, *Delimitis* [1991] ECR I-935.

[103] Reg. 772/2004, Art. 1(1)(b) and 1(1)(h). Designs are brought into the scope by the definition of 'patent' in Art. 1(h).

[104] TTBER, Art. 3.

[105] TTBER, Art. 4.

[106] TTBER, Art. 5.

- In respect of some types of provisions the TTBER draws a distinction between reciprocal and non-reciprocal obligations;[107]
- In applying the TTBER two markets need to be taken into account: the *technology* market (consisting of the licensed technology and its substitutes) and the *product or service* market (consisting of the market for the product or service incorporating the licensed technology).[108]

D. SCOPE OF THE TTBER

(i) Agreements to which the TTBER May Apply

a. Bilateral Technology Transfer Agreements

Article 2 of the TTBER exempts from Article 101(1) bilateral technology transfer agreements permitting the production of contract products. It states:

Pursuant to Article [101(3) TFEU] and subject to the provisions of this Regulation, it is hereby declared that Article [101(1) TFEU] shall not apply to technology transfer agreements entered into between two undertakings permitting the production of contract products.

This exemption shall apply to the extent that such agreements contain restrictions of competition falling within the scope of Article [101(1)]. The exemption shall apply for as long as the intellectual property right in the licensed technology has not expired, lapsed or been declared invalid or, in the case of know-how, for as long as the know-how remains secret, except in the event where the know-how becomes publicly known as a result of action by the licensee, in which case the exemption shall apply for the duration of the agreement.

b. The Number of Parties

The TTBER is limited to bilateral agreements, i.e. agreements between *two* undertakings. It does not therefore cover agreements between three or more undertakings.[109] When counting the parties to an agreement, however, each group of 'connected undertakings' are counted as a single party.[110] The TTBER itself defines 'connected undertaking'.[111] The two-party limitation does not prevent an agreement which affects third parties from falling within the TTBER however. For example, an agreement may require the licensee to impose obligations on resellers of the product produced under the licence.[112]

c. Definition of Technology Transfer Agreement

The definition of a technology transfer agreement is set out in the TTBER, Article 1(1)(b):

'technology transfer agreement' means a patent licensing agreement, a know-how licensing agreement, a software copyright licensing agreement or a mixed patent, know-how or software copyright licensing agreement, including any such agreement containing provisions which relate to the sale and purchase of products or which relate to the licensing of other intellectual property rights or the assignment of intellectual property rights, provided that those provisions do not constitute the primary object of the agreement and are directly related to the production of the contract products; assignments of patents, know-how, software copyright

---

[107] e.g., in the active and/or passive sales provisions in Art. 4.

[108] Guidelines, paras. 19–22.

[109] Council Reg. 19/65 [1965–1966] OJ Spec. Ed. Series I, p. 35, the relevant enabling Regulation, only empowers the Commission to block exempt technology transfer agreements between two undertakings.

[110] See also the discussion of the single economic entity doctrine in Chap. 3.

[111] TTBER, Art. 1(2).

[112] Guidelines, para. 39.

or a combination thereof where part of the risk associated with the exploitation of the technology remains with the assignor, in particular where the sum payable in consideration of the assignment is dependent on the turnover obtained by the assignee in respect of products produced with the assigned technology, the quantity of such products produced or the number of operations carried out employing the technology, shall also be deemed to be technology transfer agreements...

Article 1(1)(b) thus makes it clear that a technology transfer agreement can comprise:

- A pure patent licensing agreement. 'Patent' is defined in Article 1(1)(h) to cover patents, patent applications, utility models, applications for registration of utility models, designs, topographies of semiconductor products, supplementary protection certificates for medicinal products or other products for which such supplementary protection certificates may be obtained, and plant breeder's certificates;

- A pure know-how licensing agreement. Know-how is defined in Article 1(1)(i) as: a package of non-patented practical information, resulting from experience and testing, which is:

  (i) secret, that is to say, not generally known or easily accessible,

  (ii) substantial, that is to say, significant and useful for the production of the contract products, and

  (iii) identified, that is to say, described in a sufficiently comprehensive manner so as to make it possible to verify that it fulfils the criteria of secrecy and substantiality.

  The meaning of 'secret', 'substantial' and 'identified' is further elaborated upon in paragraph 47 of the Guidelines.

- A pure software copyright licence. Such licences are brought within a block exemption for the first time. Other forms of copyright are not covered by the TTBER;[113]

- A pure design licence (as already noted, the definition of 'patent' means that design licences are for the first time covered by a block exemption);

- A 'mixed' agreement, by which two or more rights (patents, know-how, software copyright, designs) are licensed together (it is very common, for example, to license know-how together with a patent);

- An agreement which comprises a licence of one of thesee rights and *other* IPRs not covered by the TTBER, provided that the licence of the other right(s) is only ancillary to the licence of the covered rights and not the 'primary object' of the agreement.[114] The TTBER also covers licences which contain provisions about the sale and purchase of goods provided the sale and purchase is not the 'primary object'.[115]

The TTBER only covers agreements whereby technology is *transferred*, meaning that technology 'flows from one undertaking to another', i.e. normally where the licensor grants a licensee the right to use its technology against the payment of royalties. It also covers a sub-licence by the licensee for the exploitation of the technology,[116] assignments where the licensor retains the risk, and

---

[113] But the provisions apply by analogy to some other copyright licensing: see Guidelines, paras. 50–52, and Section 8.

[114] This point is well illustrated by the *Moosehead/Whitbread* decision, [1990] OJ L100/32, in which a Canadian brewer granted to Whitbread an exclusive know-how and trade mark licence to produce, promote, market, and sell in the UK beer under the name 'Moosehead' using Moosehead's know-how. The Commission held that the agreement was not covered by Reg. 556/89 on know-how agreements because the exploitation of the *trade mark* was the crucial element in the deal and it was not ancillary to the know-how licence. See further n. 307 and accompanying text.

[115] As explained in Guidelines, paras. 49–50.

[116] Guidelines, para. 48.

sub-contracting, where the licensee uses the licensed technology exclusively to produce products for the licensor or where the licensor supplies equipment to be used in the production of goods and services covered by the agreement.[117]

d. The Agreement Must Concern the Production of Contract Products

Article 2 provides that the TTBER exempts technology transfer agreements 'permitting the production of contract products'. The point of the licence must be to allow the licensee to use the licensed technology to produce goods or services (the word 'goods' is hereafter used in this chapter to denote both goods and services unless the context otherwise requires). The TTBER does not therefore cover:

- 'Technology pools' whereby two or more parties agree to pool their respective technologies and license them as a package;[118]

- Agreements which are in effect 'master licensing' agreements of which the primary object is sub-licensing;[119]

- Agreements whose object is to enable the licensee to carry out R&D rather than produce goods or services. For an agreement to be covered by the TTBER there must be 'a direct link between the licensed technology and an identified contract product'.[120] The TTBER does not cover R&D sub-contracting whereby the licensee carries out R&D for the licensor and returns the improved technology package to the licensor;

- Agreements whose primary object is the sale and purchase of products (rather than their production).[121]

- On the other hand the TTBER *does* cover agreements:

- which *permit* the licensee to sub-license as distinct from where sub-licensing is the purpose of the agreement;[122]

- which are entered into to settle disputes over IPRs within the scope of the TTBER (called 'settlement' or 'non-assertion' agreements), including cross-licensing;[123]

- which are sub-contracting agreements whereby the technology is licensed in order for the licensee to produce certain products exclusively for the licensor;[124]

- whereby the licensee has to carry out development work before obtaining a product or process that can be commercially exploited, provided that a contract product has been identified and the primary purpose of the agreement is not R&D.[125]

---

[117] For a fuller discussion of sub-contracting agreements, see Chap. 11.

[118] Guidelines, para. 31. There is a lengthy section of the Guidelines (paras. 210–235) on technology pools: see Section 5. In any event such agreements are unlikely to be 'bilateral' and the parties are unlikely to meet the market share thresholds of the TTBER.

[119] Guidelines, para. 42.

[120] Guidelines, para. 45.

[121] Guidelines, para. 49.

[122] Guidelines, para. 42.

[123] Guidelines, para. 43.

[124] Guidelines, para. 44. If the licensor supplies the licensee with equipment for this purpose the TTBER will not apply if the supply of the equipment rather than the supply of the technology is the primary purpose of the agreement. According to the 1979 Notice on sub-contracting agreements, [1979] OJ C1/20032, sub-contracting agreements whereby the sub-contractor only undertakes to produce certain products exclusively for the contractor generally fall outside Art. 101(1), see Chap. 11.

[125] Guidelines, para. 45.

(ii) Relationship with other Block Exemptions

Specialisation, R&D, and vertical agreements may involve the transfer of technology between the contracting parties. In such cases it is important to know whether a particular agreement is in essence a technology transfer agreement potentially covered by the TTBER and the Guidelines or a horizontal cooperation or vertical agreement potentially covered by one of the other block exemptions and guidelines.[126] Broadly:

- Licensing of technology used in the production of products produced by a joint venture is normally subject to Regulation 2658/2000,[127] the specialisation block exemption, and not the TTBER. Regulation 2658/2000 does not, however, apply to the situation where the joint venture engages in licensing technology to a third party. That amounts to a technology pool.[128]

- Licensing between parties for joint R&D and joint exploitation of results of such activities will normally be covered by Regulation 2659/2000, the R&D block exemption, and not the TTBER;[129] and

- The umbrella block exemption on vertical restraints, Regulation 339/2010,[130] applies to vertical agreements involving licences of intellectual property so long as the licence is ancillary to the vertical agreement and IPRs are assigned to the buyer for the purpose of using or selling the goods or services supplied under the agreement.[131] Regulation 339/2010 is of particular relevance to franchise agreements.[132] Further, the Verticals Regulation may apply where a licensee sells products incorporating licensed technology to a buyer. Thus even though the TTBER will block exempt (within the safe harbour) a technology transfer agreement requiring a licensee to distribute the products in a particular way, e.g., through an exclusive or selective distribution system, such agreements will be vertical and subject to Regulation 339/2010 and the Guidelines on Vertical Restraints.[133] Paragraph 64 of the Guidelines addresses the situation where the licensees sell under a common brand name:

Furthermore, distributors must in principle be free to sell both actively and passively into territories covered by the distribution systems of other licensees producing their own products on the basis of the licensed technology. This is because for the purposes of Regulation 2790/1999 each licensee is a separate supplier. However, the reasons underlying the block exemption contained in that Regulation may also apply where the products incorporating the licensed technology are sold by the licensees under a common brand belonging to the licensor. When the products incorporating the licensed technology are sold under a common brand identity there may be the same efficiency reasons for applying the same types of restraints between licensees' distribution systems as within a single vertical distribution system. In such cases the Commission would be unlikely to challenge restraints where by analogy the requirements of Regulation 2790/1999 are fulfilled. For a common brand identity to exist the products must be sold and marketed under a common brand, which is predominant in terms of conveying quality and other relevant information to the consumer. It does not suffice that in addition to the licensees' brands the product carries the licensor's brand, which identifies him as the source of the licensed technology.

---

[126] Guidelines, paras. 56–64.

[127] [2000] OJ L304/3. See Chap. 10.

[128] In para. 131 of the Guidelines the Commission states that there is unlikely to be a violation of Art. 101 where there are a number of other independently controlled competing technologies, see Section 5.C, pp. 906–908.

[129] Guidelines, paras. 59–60.

[130] [2010] OJ L102/1. See Chap. 11.

[131] See [1999] OJ L336/21, Art. 2(3) and (5).

[132] Franchise agreements are intended to be covered by Reg. 339/2010 despite the view of the CJ in Case 161/84, *Pronuptia de Paris GmbH v. Pronuptia de Paris Irmgard Schillgallis* [1986] ECR 353, that the essence of a franchise is that it is a transaction concerning IPRs.

[133] Guidelines, paras. 62–63.

E. SAFE HARBOUR: THE MARKET SHARE THRESHOLDS

(i) The Market Share Thresholds

Article 3 provides that the block exemption applies on condition that specified market share thresholds are not exceeded on affected technology and product markets. Where the parties are competitors the relevant market share is 20 per cent. Where the parties are non-competitors the relevant market is 30 per cent. The Commission has proposed that in the new BER the 20 per cent threshold should also apply where the undertakings are not competing but the licensee owns a technology, substitutable for the licensed technology, which it uses only for in-house production. For non-competitors, therefore, the new BER may make a distinction between the scenario where the licensee does not own a substitute technology and the scenario where the licensee already owns a substitute technology but that technology is not licensed out and is only used captively. The market share thresholds set out in Article 3 provide the 'safe harbour'.[134]

Article 3

Market-share thresholds

1. Where the undertakings party to the agreement are competing undertakings, the exemption provided for in Article 2 shall apply on condition that the combined market share of the parties does not exceed 20 per cent on the affected relevant technology and product market.

2. Where the undertakings party to the agreement are not competing undertakings, the exemption provided for in Article 2 shall apply on condition that the market share of each of the parties does not exceed 30 per cent on the affected relevant technology and product market.

The Commission explains Article 3(1) and (2) in paragraph 69 of the Guidelines:

69. In the case of agreements between competitors the market share threshold is 20 per cent and in the case of agreements between non-competitors it is 30 per cent (cf. Article 3(1) and (2) of the TTBER). Where the undertakings party to the licensing agreement are not competitors the agreement is covered if the market share of neither party exceeds 30 per cent on the affected relevant technology and product markets. Where the undertakings party to the licensing agreement are competitors the agreement is covered if the combined market shares of the parties do not exceed 20 per cent on the relevant technology and product markets. The market share thresholds apply both to technology markets and markets for products incorporating the licensed technology. If the applicable market share threshold is exceeded on an affected relevant market, the block exemption does not apply to the agreement for that relevant market. For instance, if the licence agreement concerns two separate product markets or two separate geographic markets, the block exemption may apply to one of the markets and not to the other.

It should be noted that with regard to competitors it is the *combined* market share which is relevant, but in the case of non-competitors it is the market share of *each* of the parties that is relevant.

Where the thresholds are exceeded the TTBER does not apply. If the parties' market shares are below the thresholds at the time the agreement is entered into, but subsequently increase so that

---

[134] In para. 131 of the Guidelines the Commission states that Art. 101 is unlikely to be infringed where there are a number of other independently controlled competing technologies, see Section 5.A.iii. Although this is referred to as a 'second safe harbour' it is important to remember that in the TTBER itself there is only *one* safe harbour and that it is expressed in terms of market share.

they exceed it, the agreement will cease to be covered by the TTBER. The matter is not settled once and for all at the outset. This means that the parties (and their lawyers) need to keep the agreement under review. Article 8 provides for some marginal relief, providing that the TTBER will continue to apply for two consecutive calendar years following the year in which the relevant threshold is first exceeded.

In order to determine whether the market share thresholds are exceeded it is therefore ordinarily necessary to determine the relevant markets, to calculate market shares, and to determine whether or not the parties are competitors.

(ii) Market Definition

The normal principles of market definition as set out in the Commission Notice on market definition apply.[135] However, the Guidelines provide guidance on specific issues which arise in the technology transfer context.[136] For technology transfer agreements, both the technology market and the product market need to be considered. It has already been explained that market definition raises acute difficulties in this area.[137]

a. The Technology Market

The technology market is the licensed technology and any other technology that the licensees consider to be interchangeable with, or substitutable for, the technology by reason of the technologies' characteristics, their royalties, and their intended use. Paragraph 22 of the Guidelines states that the objective is therefore to identify competing technologies to which licensees could switch in response to a small but permanent increase in prices (which in this context means the royalties). This is an application of the SSNIP test.[138] Paragraph 22 of the Guidelines also provides 'an alternative approach' to defining the technology market, which looks to the market for products incorporating the licensed technology.[139] This method is discussed in Section 4.E.iii dealing with the calculation of market shares.

b. The Product Market

The term 'product' market in the TTBER is shorthand for the product *and* geographical dimensions of goods and services markets. The term is used in contradistinction to the technology market. The relevant product market comprises products regarded as interchangeable with or substitutable for the contract products incorporating the licensed technology by reason of the products' characteristics, price, and intended use.[140] Occasionally, it may be necessary to define an innovation market, in particular where the agreement affects innovation aimed at creating new products and R&D poles can be identified.[141]

---

[135] Commission Notice on the definition of the relevant market [1997] OJ C372/5, see Chap. 1.

[136] Guidelines, para. 19.

[137] See Section 3.D.i, pp. 867–868.

[138] See Chap. 1.

[139] It refers to para. 23 of the Guidelines which discusses the method adopted by the Art. 3(3) TTBER, for calculating shares on the technology market, which 'is defined in terms of the presence of the licensed technology on the relevant product market'.

[140] TTBER, Art. 1(1)(j)(ii) and Guidelines, para. 21.

[141] Guidelines, para. 25.

(iii) Market Shares

a. Means of Calculation

Where it is available, market share is to be calculated on the basis of market sales value data. Otherwise 'other reliable market information' including market sales volume data may be used.[142]

b. The Technology Market

The Guidelines suggest more than one method of calculating market shares on the technology market. One solution is to calculate the market shares by reference to the licensed technology and its substitutes. Market share can then be calculated on the basis of each technology's share of total licensing income from royalties. In practice, however, this test is hard to apply—especially as companies are unlikely to know the level of royalty income derived by their competitors. Article 3(3) thus provides that the market share can be defined with regard to the presence of the licensed technology on the relevant product market. This means looking at the sales on the downstream market of products incorporating the licensed technology produced by the licensor and licensee, and calculating what share of the product market they have, taking into account products which use substitute technologies.[143] The advantages of this method are:

- it takes account of 'captive use', which means undertakings producing products using their own technology which they do not license out at present (but could start licensing if there was a small but significant increase in licence prices);

- it takes account of the fact that a licensor's market power may be constrained if the downstream product market is competitive, because what the licensee can be made to pay will be limited if an increase in its costs would make the licensee less able to compete on that downstream market.

The licensor's market share of the relevant technology market is the combined market share of the contract products produced by the licensor and all its licensees.[144] Where the parties are competitors on the technology market, sales of products incorporating the licensee's own technology are added to the sales of products incorporating the licensed technology.[145] The Commission states that it may use both methods when assessing agreements falling outside the safe harbour thresholds of the TTBER.[146]

c. The Product Market

Market shares on the product market are assessed in the usual way, using sales data value if available.[147] The licensee's market share is the total sales of the licensee on the product market, i.e. products incorporating the licensor's technology and competing products. The licensor's sales (if any) on the product market must be included, but not those of other licensees.[148]

---

[142] TTBER, Art. 8(1). The calculation is on the basis of the preceding year.

[143] Explained in Guidelines, para. 23, which is not clearly written.

[144] TTBER, Art. 3(3) and Guidelines, para. 70.

[145] TTBER, Art. 3(3) and Guidelines, para. 70. The market share will be zero where no products have yet been made incorporating the technology.

[146] TTBER, Art. 3(3) and Guidelines, paras. 23 and 70.

[147] TTBER, Art. 3(3) and Guidelines, para. 71.

[148] Guidelines, para. 71.

(iv) The Distinction between Competitors and Non-competitors (Competing and Non-competing Undertakings)

The provisions of the TTBER are based on the premise that agreements between competitors are likely to be more dangerous to the competitive process than agreements between non-competitors.[149] Thus not only are the market share thresholds lower for agreements between competitors but a different, stricter set of hardcore restraints applies. Paragraph 27 of the Guidelines explains:

In order to determine the competitive relationship between the parties it is necessary to examine whether the parties would have been actual or potential competitors in the absence of the agreement. If without the agreement the parties would not have been actual or potential competitors in any relevant market affected by the agreement they are deemed to be non-competitors.

Article 1(1)(j) of the TTBER defines competing undertakings as undertakings that compete on the relevant technology market and/or the relevant product market.

(i) competing undertakings on the relevant technology market, being undertakings which license out competing technologies without infringing each others' intellectual property rights (actual competitors on the technology market);...

(ii) competing undertakings on the relevant product market, being undertakings which, in the absence of the technology transfer agreement, are both active on the relevant product and geographic market(s) on which the contract products are sold without infringing each others' intellectual property rights (actual competitors on the product market) or would, on realistic grounds, undertake the necessary additional investments or other necessary switching costs so that they could timely enter, without infringing each others' intellectual property rights, the(se) relevant product and geographic market(s) in response to a small and permanent increase in relative prices (potential competitors on the product market)...

It can be seen from this definition that as far as product markets are concerned, both actual and potential competitors are treated as competitors. As far as technology markets are concerned, however, only actual competitors are relevant. If the licensor and licensee are both active on the same technology or product market, without infringing each other's IPRs, they are actual competitors on the market. They are potential competitors on the product market if, in the absence of the agreement and without infringing IPRs, they would be likely to undertake the necessary investments required to enter the market within a short period (one to two years) in response to a small but permanent increase in price.[150] On technology markets the parties will be considered actual competitors if the licensee is already licensing out its technology and the licensor enters the technology market by granting a licence for a competing technology to the licensee.[151] Outside the safe harbour of the TTBER potential competitors on the technology market are taken into account.[152]

The reference in Article 1(1)(j) to parties being competing undertakings only where they are both active on the technology market or product market 'without infringing each other's [IPRs]' means that if there is a one-way (one party cannot exploit its technology without infringing the other's IPRs) or two-way (neither party can exploit its technology without infringing the other's IPRs) blocking situation, the parties will *not* be characterised as competitors. The Commission is, however, alive to the fact that the parties will usually prefer to be classified as non-competitors and will examine blocking claims carefully.[153] In addition, the parties will not be competitors where the licensor is

---

[149] Guidelines, para. 26.

[150] Guidelines, para. 26.

[151] Guidelines, para. 28.

[152] See Guidelines, para. 66. This does not lead to the application of the hardcore list of restrictions relating to agreements between competitors.

[153] Guidelines, para. 32. Where opinions of independent experts are relied upon the Commission will 'closely examine how the expert has been selected'!

neither an actual nor a potential supplier of products on the product market and the licensee does not license out a competing technology.[154]

The Guidelines state that in cases of 'drastic innovation' parties should be classed as non-competitors even though they produce competing products. This will be the case where the licensed technology represents such a technological breakthrough that the licensee's technology becomes obsolete or uncompetitive (for example, the replacement of LP vinyl technology with CD technology).[155] Often, however, it will not be possible to draw this conclusion at the time the agreement is concluded. If it is *not* obvious at this time the parties will be classified as competitors initially but can be recognised as non-competitors later.[156]

It is extremely important when deciding whether the parties are competitors or non-competitors to remember that activities of their 'connected undertakings' must be taken into account.[157]

(v) Non-competitors who Subsequently Become Competitors

What is the position if the parties are not competitors at the time the agreement is concluded but subsequently become competitors? Article 4(3) of the TTBER provides that the more liberal black list of hardcore restrictions for agreements between non-competitors will apply during the lifetime of the agreement even if the parties later become competitors *unless* the agreement is amended 'in any material respect' (in which case restraints previously block exempted may become hardcore restraints).[158] Neither Article 4(3) nor the Guidelines comment, however, on the position if the 20 per cent market share threshold is exceeded (i.e. whether or not the TTBER ceases to apply if the parties' combined market shares exceed 20 per cent). This suggests that subject to the two-year transitional relief provided by Article 8(2), the benefit of the TTBER will be lost where parties become competitors and their combined market shares exceed the 20 per cent threshold.

F. HARDCORE RESTRICTIONS

(i) General

The hardcore restraints are set out in Article 4 of the TTBER.[159] As is the case in the context of vertical agreements, a restraint will be hardcore whether achieved directly or indirectly. The presence in the agreement of any one of the hardcore restrictions takes the entire agreement out of the safe harbour of the block exemptions. Indeed, the Commission's view is that hardcore restraints are restrictive of competition by object and are most unlikely even *individually* to satisfy the Article 101(3) conditions.[160] As already noted, there are two separate lists of hardcore restrictions: those applying to agreements between competitors (Article 4(1)) and those applying to agreements between non-competitors (Article 4(2)). In addition, the list of hardcore restraints in agreements between competitors may differ depending upon whether the agreement is reciprocal or non-reciprocal. These

---

[154] Guidelines, paras. 30 and 68.

[155] Guidelines, para. 33.

[156] Guidelines, para. 33. This was a major concession by the Commission, which had originally intended that the agreement would have to be reassessed if the relationship of the parties subsequently changed to that of competitors. It was persuaded to change its mind on this point.

[157] See text accompanying n. 110.

[158] As would be the case if the licensee developed and began to exploit a competing technology, or if the licensor subsequently entered the product market on which the licensee was active. See Guidelines, para. 31.

[159] The TTBER, with the objective of minimising the straitjacketing effect of the block exemption, does not contain a list of permissible restrictions. As is the case for the Verticals Regulation, the idea is that if it is not prohibited, the restraint is exempted by the block exemption.

[160] Guidelines, paras. 74–76. See generally on this point Chap. 4.

terms are defined in TTBER, Article 1(1)(c) and (d). Essentially, an agreement is reciprocal where the parties cross-license competing technologies or technologies which can be used for the production of competing products.

(ii) Agreements between Competing Undertakings

The list of hardcore restraints applicable to agreements between competitors is set out in Article 4(1). It focuses, subject to specified exceptions, on: price-fixing; limitations of output; allocation of markets or customers; restrictions on the licensee's ability to exploit its own technology; and provisions restraining either party from carrying out R&D unless indispensable to prevent disclosure of the licensed technology.

Article 4(1)

1. Where the undertakings party to the agreement are competing undertakings, the exemption provided for in Article 2 shall not apply to agreements which, directly or indirectly, in isolation or in combination with other factors under the control of the parties, have as their object:

    (a) the restriction of a party's ability to determine its prices when selling products to third parties;

    (b) the limitation of output, except limitations on the output of contract products imposed on the licensee in a non-reciprocal agreement or imposed on only one of the licensees in a reciprocal agreement;

    (c) the allocation of markets or customers except:

        (i) the obligation on the licensee(s) to produce with the licensed technology only within one or more technical fields of use or one or more product markets,

        (ii) the obligation on the licensor and/or the licensee, in a non-reciprocal agreement, not to produce with the licensed technology within one or more technical fields of use or one or more product markets or one or more exclusive territories reserved for the other party,

        (iii) the obligation on the licensor not to license the technology to another licensee in a particular territory,

        (iv) the restriction, in a non-reciprocal agreement, of active and/or passive sales by the licensee and/or the licensor into the exclusive territory or to the exclusive customer group reserved for the other party,

        (v) the restriction, in a non-reciprocal agreement, of active sales by the licensee into the exclusive territory or to the exclusive customer group allocated by the licensor to another licensee provided the latter was not a competing undertaking of the licensor at the time of the conclusion of its own licence,

        (vi) the obligation on the licensee to produce the contract products only for its own use provided that the licensee is not restricted in selling the contract products actively and passively as spare parts for its own products,

        (vii) the obligation on the licensee, in a non-reciprocal agreement, to produce the contract products only for a particular customer, where the licence was granted in order to create an alternative source of supply for that customer;

    (d) the restriction of the licensee's ability to exploit its own technology or the restriction of the ability of any of the parties to the agreement to carry out research and development, unless such latter restriction is indispensable to prevent the disclosure of the licensed know-how to third parties.

a. Article 4(1)(a)—Price Restrictions

Price-fixing between competitors is treated more strictly than price-fixing in agreements between non-competitors. Article 4(1)(a) prohibits agreements 'that have as their object the fixing of prices' whether in the form of fixed, minimum, maximum, or recommended prices.[161] An obligation on the licensee to pay a certain minimum royalty does not in itself amount to price-fixing.[162] However, indirect price restraints, for example through disincentives to deviate from a certain price level or through provisions for the royalty rate to increase if prices are reduced below a certain level, are prohibited.[163]

b. Article 4(1)(b)—Output Limitations

An output restriction is a limitation on how much a party may produce and sell. Article 4(1)(b) permits output limitations on the licensee in a non-reciprocal agreement or on only one licensee in a reciprocal agreement. This means, in effect, that reciprocal output restrictions and output restrictions on the licensor in respect of its own technology constitute hardcore restrictions.[164] Provisions which have the effect of output restrictions, such as disincentives to produce more than a certain amount, are also caught by Article 4(1)(b).[165]

c. Article 4(1)(c)—Market or Customer Allocation

Article 4(1)(c) seeks to reconcile the need to ensure that competitors are not able to share markets between themselves with an acceptance that in certain circumstances a licensee will require an exclusive or sole licence and protection from sales into its territory.[166] It prohibits agreements between competitors that share markets or customers unless they fall within one of seven very important exceptions.

Article 4(1)(c)(i)

Field of use and product market restrictions may be imposed on the licensee in a reciprocal or non-reciprocal agreement. This means that a licensee can be restricted to using the technology for a specific purpose.

Article 4(1)(c)(ii)

In a non-reciprocal agreement only, the licensor and/or the licensee can agree not to produce within one or more fields of use, product markets, or exclusive territories reserved to the other party.[167] This provides a licensee with an incentive to invest in and develop the technology. Note that this exception relates to production and not to sales.

Article 4(1)(c)(iii)

The licensor may agree not to grant another licence of the same technology in the same territory. This permits the grant of a sole licence and protects the licensee from competition from other licensees *producing* in the same territory. The exception applies to both reciprocal and non-reciprocal agreements but must not affect the parties' ability to exploit their own technology in their respective territories.[168]

---

[161] Guidelines, para. 79.

[162] A licensor is entitled to ensure that it obtains a certain minimum return for the licence.

[163] Guidelines, paras. 79–81.

[164] Guidelines, para. 102.

[165] Guidelines, para. 102.

[166] It considers that agreements between competitors sharing markets or customers have as their object the restriction of competition, Guidelines, para. 84.

[167] See Guidelines, para. 86.

[168] Guidelines, para. 88.

Article 4(1)(c)(iv)

In a *non-reciprocal* licence both licensor and licensee can be restricted from making both *active* and *passive* sales into an exclusive territory or to the exclusive customer groups reserved to the other.

Article 4(1)(c)(v)

In a *non-reciprocal* licence the licensee can be prohibited from making *active* sales (but *not* passive sales) into exclusive territories or to customer groups allocated to another licensee (so long as that other licensee was not a competitor of the licensor when it was given its licence). If the licensees agree among themselves not to actively or passively sell into each other's territories or to customers this clearly goes beyond what is permitted and indeed amounts to market-sharing, which is clearly prohibited by Article 101.[169]

Article 4(1)(c)(vi)

This exception permits licensing where the licensee takes a licence in order to make products for its own use (known as captive use restrictions).[170] It enables the licensor to limit the licensee to making components to be incorporated into the licensee's own products and to prohibit it from selling them to others. The licensee must, however, not be restricted from selling the components as spare parts.

Article 4(1)(c)(vii)

A non-reciprocal licence granted specifically to create a source of supply for a customer may restrict the licensee to producing the contract products only for that customer. This is called a 'second source' provision. The restriction is permitted as the whole point of the agreement is to provide a particular customer with an alternative source of the products. It is possible, however, for more than one licensee to be given a licence in respect of the same customer (so the latter gets a third or even fourth source of supply).[171]

A list of permissible market or customer restraints in agreements between competitors is summarised in a table in *Butterworths Competition Law*.

W. Allan, M. Furse, and B. Sufrin (eds.), *Butterworths Competition Law* (Butterworths, looseleaf), Division V, Chapter 3, para. 575

Table of Permissible Market or Customer Restraints in Agreements between Competitors under the TTBER

RESTRAINT	PERMITTED IN A RECIPROCAL AGREEMENT?	PERMITTED IN A NON-RECIPROCAL AGREEMENT?
Obligation on the licensee to produce with licensed technology within one or more technical fields	Yes, so long as restriction does not go beyond scope of licensed technology and does not limit use of licensee's own technology	Yes, so long as restriction does not go beyond scope of licensed technology and does not limit use of licensee's own technology

---

[169] Guidelines, para. 89. 'Active' and 'passive' sales have the same meaning as in respect of vertical agreements (see Chap. 11).

[170] Guidelines, para. 92.

[171] Guidelines, para. 93.

RESTRAINT	PERMITTED IN A RECIPROCAL AGREEMENT?	PERMITTED IN A NON-RECIPROCAL AGREEMENT?
Obligation on the licensor and/or licensee not to use technology to produce within one or more technical fields of use, product markets, or exclusive territories reserved to the other	No	Yes, licensor can grant exclusive licence to product and agree not to produce itself
An obligation on the licensor not to license the technology to another licensee in a particular territory	Yes	Yes
Ban on active or passive selling into territory or exclusive customer group reserved to other (licensor or licensee)	No	Yes
Ban on active selling into territory of, or to the exclusive customer group reserved to, another licensee	No	Yes, as long as other licensee was not a competitor of the licensor at time the agreement was concluded
Ban on passive selling into territory of, or to exclusive customer group reserved to, another licensee	No	No
Captive use restriction	Yes, so long as can sell as spare parts	Yes, so long as can sell as spare parts
Second source provision (obligation on licensee to produce for a single customer)	No	Yes, if the licence was granted specifically to create a source of supply for that customer

d. Article 4(1)(d)—Limitations on Technology Exploitation or R&D

Whether the agreement is reciprocal or non-reciprocal, neither party to the agreement can be restricted from carrying out R&D unless it is to prevent the licensed know-how from being disclosed to third parties (in which case the restriction must be proportionate and necessary).[172] In addition, the licensee must not be prevented from exploiting its own technology.

(iii) Agreements between Non-competing Undertakings

Where the parties are non-competitors they are allowed more leeway. The list of hardcore restraints is briefer and less limiting. To some extent, it resembles the list contained in Article 4 of the Verticals Regulation, focusing on fixed or minimum resale price maintenance and, subject to specified exceptions, restrictions on the territory into which, or the customers to whom, the licensee may sell the contract product.

Article 4(2)

Where the undertakings party to the agreement are not competing undertakings, the exemption provided for in Article 2 shall not apply to agreements which, directly or indirectly, in isolation or in combination with other factors under the control of the parties, have as their object:

(a) the restriction of a party's ability to determine its prices when selling products to third parties, without prejudice to the possibility of imposing a maximum sale price or recommending a sale price, provided

---

[172] Guidelines, para. 94.

that it does not amount to a fixed or minimum sale price as a result of pressure from, or incentives offered by, any of the parties;

(b) the restriction of the territory into which, or of the customers to whom, the licensee may passively sell the contract products, except:

    (i) the restriction of passive sales into an exclusive territory or to an exclusive customer group reserved for the licensor,

    (ii) the restriction of passive sales into an exclusive territory or to an exclusive customer group allocated by the licensor to another licensee during the first two years that this other licensee is selling the contract products in that territory or to that customer group,

    (iii) the obligation to produce the contract products only for its own use provided that the licensee is not restricted in selling the contract products actively and passively as spare parts for its own products,

    (iv) the obligation to produce the contract products only for a particular customer, where the licence was granted in order to create an alternative source of supply for that customer,

    (v) the restriction of sales to end-users by a licensee operating at the wholesale level of trade,

    (vi) the restriction of sales to unauthorised distributors by the members of a selective distribution system;

(c) the restriction of active or passive sales to end-users by a licensee which is a member of a selective distribution system and which operates at the retail level, without prejudice to the possibility of prohibiting a member of the system from operating out of an unauthorised place of establishment.

a. Article 4(2)(a)—Price Restrictions

It will be noted that the prohibition of resale price maintenance (RPM) does not, unlike the hardcore competitor list, cover maximum or recommended prices so long as they do not really amount to fixed or minimum prices. This clause is the same as that in the Verticals Regulation. Like that clause it covers indirect means of fixing selling prices.[173]

b. Article 4(2)(b)—Passive Sales Restrictions Imposed on the Licensee

The point of this clause is to identify as hardcore restrictions 'agreements or concerted practices that have as their direct or indirect object the restriction of passive sales by licensees of products incorporating the licensed technology'.[174] It therefore includes provisions in agreements which are a disincentive to make unsolicited sales, such as financial measures and monitoring systems. The Commission does not assume that quantity limitations are imposed as passive sales restrictions but indications that they are being used as such will be examined.[175] It is important to note that Article 4(2)(b) does not black list any sales restrictions on the *licensor* or *active* sales restrictions on the *licensee*. Therefore sales restrictions on the licensor and active sales restrictions on the licensee (except those falling within Article 4(2)(b)(vi), discussed in the text at n. 179) are block exempted.[176] There are, moreover, a number of major exceptions to the ban on licensees making passive sales outside their allocated territory or customer group. These are listed in Article 4(2)(b).

Article 4(2)(b)(i)

The licensee can be prevented from making passive sales into an exclusive territory or to a customer group which the licensor has reserved for itself. If the licensor could not prevent this it might not disseminate the technology through licensing in the first place.[177]

---

  [173] See Guidelines, para. 97.

  [174] Guidelines, para. 98.

  [175] Guidelines, para. 98.

  [176] Guidelines, para. 99.

  [177] Guidelines, para. 100.

Article 4(2)(b)(ii)

The licensee can be restricted from making passive sales into the exclusive territory, or to a customer group, allocated by the licensor to another licensee. However, this restriction is only block exempted for the first two years in which the other licensee is serving that territory or customer group. Indeed, paragraph 101 of the Guidelines indicates that such a clause will often fall outside Article 101(1) for the first two years because the licensee needs the protection the clause affords to persuade it to take the licence. This passive sales exemption for licensees is less generous than in Regulation 240/96, which allowed five years. Further, the Commission has now proposed removing this exception entirely from the new block exemption. If this principle is eventually incorporated into the new block exemption, such restraints would in the future be likely to be found to infringe Article 101 unless established to be objectively necessary for the licensee to penetrate a new market.

Article 4(2)(b)(iii)

This clause exempts captive use restrictions. The licensee can, therefore, be required to produce the product only for its own use provided it is not restricted from selling the products as spare parts.

Article 4(2)(b)(iv)

This clause exempts second source provisions. The licensee can therefore be required to produce only as an alternative source for a specified customer.

Article 4(2)(b)(v)

The block exemption permits the maintenance of a distinction between wholesale and retail levels of trade. The licensor can give the wholesale distribution function to a licensee and prohibit it from serving the end customers.[178]

Article 4(2)(b)(vi)

As under the Verticals Regulation[179] this provision allows members of a selective distribution system to be restricted from selling to unauthorised distributors, thereby preserving the integrity of the system.

The table reproduced from *Butterworths Competition Law,* provides in tabular form the passive sales restraints that may be imposed on licensees in a licence agreement between non-competitors.

W. Allan, M. Furse, and B. Sufrin (eds.), *Butterworths Competition Law* (Butterworths, looseleaf), Division V, Chapter 3, para. 591

Table of Permissible Restraints in the Context of Agreements between Non-competitors on the Territory into which or the Customer to whom the Licensee can Passively Sell the Contract Products

RESTRAINT	PERMISSIBLE?
Passive sales into an exclusive territory or to an exclusive customer group reserved to the licensor	Yes

---

[178] Guidelines, para. 104.
[179] Reg. 2790/99, Art. 4(b).

RESTRAINT	PERMISSIBLE?
Restriction on passive sales into an exclusive territory or to an exclusive customer group reserved to another licensee	Yes, for a period of 2 years after the licensee first starts selling the contract products
Captive use restriction	Yes, the licensee can be required to produce the product only for its own use provided he can sell as spare parts to customers or third parties performing after sales services
Second source provision	Yes, an obligation on the licensee to produce the products only for a specified customer is permissible where the licence was granted to create an alternative source of supply
Sales to end users	Yes, where the licensee operates at the wholesale level
Sales to unauthorised distributors within a selective distribution system	Yes, but unless the licensee operates at the wholesale level, the licensee must be able to make sales (actively or passive) to end users

c. Article 4(2)(c)—Active or Passive Sales Bans to End Users within Selective Distribution Systems

A licensee which operates at the retail level of a selective distribution system cannot be prevented from active or passive selling to any end users. Again, this is similar to the Verticals Regulation.[180]

G. EXCLUDED RESTRICTIONS

(i) Introduction

Article 5 sets out the 'excluded restrictions'. These are restrictions which are not exempted by the TTBER but the inclusion of which does not remove the protection of the TTBER from the remainder of the agreement. Individual assessment is required to determine whether the excluded restraints infringe Article 101 and, if they do, whether they can be severed from the rest of the agreement.[181]

Article 5

Excluded restrictions

1. The exemption provided for in Article 2 shall not apply to any of the following obligations contained in technology transfer agreements:

    (a) any direct or indirect obligation on the licensee to grant an exclusive licence to the licensor or to a third party designated by the licensor in respect of its own severable improvements to or its own new applications of the licensed technology;

---

[180] Reg. 2790/99, Art. 4(b).

[181] See also the discussion of excluded but severable restraints in Chap. 11 in the context of the Verticals Regulation.

(b) any direct or indirect obligation on the licensee to assign, in whole or in part, to the licensor or to a third party designated by the licensor, rights to its own severable improvements to or its own new applications of the licensed technology;

(c) any direct or indirect obligation on the licensee not to challenge the validity of intellectual property rights which the licensor holds in the common market, without prejudice to the possibility of providing for termination of the technology transfer agreement in the event that the licensee challenges the validity of one or more of the licensed intellectual property rights.

2. Where the undertakings party to the agreement are not competing undertakings, the exemption provided for in Article 2 shall not apply to any direct or indirect obligation limiting the licensee's ability to exploit its own technology or limiting the ability of any of the parties to the agreement to carry out research and development, unless such latter restriction is indispensable to prevent the disclosure of the licensed know-how to third parties.

(ii) Improvements

Article 5(1)(a) and (b) deals with improvements made by the licensee to the licensed technology. Article 5(1)(a) and (b) exclude from the ambit of the block exemption a provision by which the licensee is obliged to give an exclusive licence (grant back) over, or to assign to, the licensor (or a designated third party) any severable improvements it has made to the licensed technology or any new applications that it has developed (even if the grant or assignment is compensated). The reason for excluding these restrictions is to preserve the licensee's incentives to innovate.[182] Such an incentive might be undermined if the licensee is prevented from exploiting its own innovation.

It should be noted that Article 5 does not cover (so that the block exemption does cover) *non-exclusive* grant back provisions even if they are non-reciprocal (i.e. the licensor does not have to license its improvements to the licensee).[183] Further, it does not prevent provisions allowing the licensor to feed the severable improvements on to other licensees.[184] It does not, therefore, prevent a licence from providing for an exclusive grant back of non-severable improvements, a non-exclusive grant back of severable improvements, and a feed-on of any such improvements by the licensor to other licensees. The Commission has, however, proposed expanding Article 5 so as to remove the benefit of the block exemption for all exclusive grant backs, severable or non-severable. Non-exclusive grant back obligations will remain covered however (even if non-reciprocal).

(iii) Non-challenge and Termination Clauses

Article 5(1)(c) excludes no-challenge clauses, whereby the licensee is prohibited from challenging the validity of any IPRs which the licensor holds in the common market, from the coverage of the TTBER, but without prejudice to the licensor being able to reserve the right to terminate the licence in the event of a challenge to the licensed rights. The licensor is therefore not obliged to carry on dealing with a party which is trying to challenge the very subject matter of the agreement. The Commission has proposed, however, that this provision be extended to all clauses obligating a party not to challenge the validity of IPRs held by the other party in the EU (even if it relates to the licensed technology). This proposal is likely to provoke some animated discussion during the consultation process.

---

[182] Guidelines, para. 108.
[183] Guidelines, para. 109.
[184] Guidelines, paras. 110–111.

(iv) Limitations on Technology Exploitation or R&D

Although restrictions on the licensee's ability to exploit its own technology or on either party's ability to carry out R&D are not hardcore restraints in agreements between non-competitors, Article 5(2) provides that such restraints are excluded restraints and are not exempted by the TTBER.[185]

H. WITHDRAWAL AND DISAPPLICATION OF THE BLOCK EXEMPTION

(i) Withdrawal

Regulation 1/2003, Article 29(1) provides that the Commission has a general right to withdraw the benefit of a block exemption from any agreement which has effects which are incompatible with Article 101(3). Article 29(2) of Regulation 1/2003 also confers power on the national authorities of the Member States to withdraw the benefit of the TTBER where the agreement has restrictive effects incompatible with Article 101(3) in the territory of their Member State. The TTBER, Article 6(1) and (2) indicate that withdrawal may be appropriate in respect of technology transfer agreements where foreclosure effects result from networks of similar agreements[186] or where the parties do not exploit the licensed technology so that no efficiency-enhancing activity takes place and the rationale of the block exemption disappears.[187] Thus withdrawal may be proper where:

(a) access of third parties' technologies to the market is restricted, for instance by the cumulative effect of parallel networks of similar restrictive agreements prohibiting licensees from using third parties' technologies;

(b) access of potential licensees to the market is restricted, for instance by the cumulative effect of parallel networks of similar restrictive agreements prohibiting licensors from licensing to other licensees;

(c) without any objectively valid reason, the parties do not exploit the licensed technology.

Withdrawal may only be made prospectively (it has *ex nunc* effect and does not affect prior validity). Further, where the Commission or a national authority wishes to withdraw the benefit of the block exemption, it must issue an infringement decision (finding that the agreement infringes Article 101(1) *and* that it does not meet the conditions of Article 101(3)[188]) or a decision making commitments binding on the undertakings concerned.[189]

(ii) Disapplication

As is the case for the Verticals Regulation, the TTBER, Article 7, provides that the Commission may, by regulation, exclude from the scope of the TTBER parallel networks of similar agreements containing specified restraints, which cover more than 50 per cent of a relevant market. Whereas withdrawal under Article 6 is by decision addressed to specific undertakings, disapplication under Article 7 is by a regulation describing a certain type of agreement to which it applies. Disapplication does not therefore operate as an infringement decision but simply restores the possibility of Article 101(1) applying to the affected agreements. The circumstances in which the Commission would consider exercising this power are discussed in paragraphs 123–129 of the Guidelines.

---

[185] TTBER, Art. 5(2).

[186] Guidelines, para. 121.

[187] And where this happens in the context of an agreement between competitors the Commission may suspect that the arrangement is really a disguised cartel, see Guidelines, para. 122.

[188] The burden of proving that the agreement satisfies the conditions is not then, as it usually is, on the persons seeking to rely on Art. 101(3), see Guidelines, para. 19 (cf. Reg. 1/2003, Art. 2).

[189] See Chap. 13.

I. DURATION OF THE EXEMPTION

Article 2(1) sets out the length of time for which the TTBER exemption applies:

This exemption shall apply to the extent that such agreements contain restrictions of competition falling within the scope of Article [101(1)]. The exemption shall apply for as long as the intellectual property right in the licensed technology has not expired, lapsed or been declared invalid or, in the case of know-how, for as long as the know-how remains secret, except in the event where the know-how becomes publicly known as a result of action by the licensee, in which case the exemption shall apply for the duration of the agreement.

This is different from Regulation 240/96 which exempted some provisions in pure know-how agreements for a maximum of 10 years.

5. THE APPLICATION OF ARTICLE 101 TO LICENSING AGREEMENTS FALLING OUTSIDE THE TTBER

A. GENERAL PRINCIPLES

(i) Technology Transfer Agreements Outside the TTBER

Agreements may fall outside the TTBER because:

- they are not bilateral technology transfer agreements under Article 1(1)(b);
- they exceed the market share thresholds;
- they contain hardcore restrictions.

In addition, individual provisions may be outside the TTBER because they are excluded restrictions under Article 5.

The Guidelines provide guidance as to how Article 101 applies to agreements falling outside the TTBER because they exceed the market share thresholds or contain hardcore restraints and to agreements containing excluded restraints. Although the principles applied in the TTBER and the Guidelines do not apply to agreements that do not constitute technology transfer agreements, the Guidelines indicate that these principles will apply by analogy to: technology transfer agreements to which more than two undertakings are party;[190] 'master licensing agreements';[191] and the licensing of copyright for the purposes of the reproduction and distribution of the protected work.[192] In the case of other licensing agreements that do not constitute technology transfer agreements, however, such as: R&D sub-contracting;[193] licensing of rights in performance and other rights related to copyright (other than software licensing and licensing of copyright for the purposes of the reproduction and distribution of the protected work),[194] and trade mark licences,[195] guidance must be sought from other sources: the case law of the Court; the Commission's decisional practice; and the Commission's Article 101(3) Guidelines.

---

[190] Guidelines, para. 40.
[191] Guidelines, para. 42.
[192] Guidelines, para. 51.
[193] Guidelines, para. 45.
[194] Guidelines, para. 52.
[195] Guidelines, para. 53.

(ii) No Presumption of Illegality

The general framework for analysis of technology transfer agreements falling outside the TTBER is set out in paragraphs 130–132 of the Guidelines. The basic principle is that there is no presumption of illegality for agreements that fall outside the TTBER provided they do not contain hardcore restrictions. In particular, there is no presumption that Article 101(1) applies just because the market share thresholds are exceeded.

(iii) The Second Safe Harbour

The Commission sets out in Guideline paragraph 131 the 'second safe harbour':

Article [101] is unlikely to be infringed in the absence of hardcore restrictions where there are four or more independently controlled technologies in addition to the technologies controlled by the parties to the agreement that may be substitutable for the licensed technology at a comparable cost to the users.

The fact that the agreement falls outside the second safe harbour does not imply that the agreement is caught by Article 101(1) and, if so, that Article 101(3) is not satisfied. The safe harbour merely creates a negative presumption that, in the stipulated circumstances, the agreement is not prohibited. The basis for determining whether the technologies are sufficiently substitutable is discussed in paragraph 131 of the Guidelines.

(iv) The Approach to the Analysis of Individual Agreements

a. Article 101(1)

The general approach to the application of Article 101 to technology transfer agreements is described in paragraphs 10–18 of the Guidelines.

The first question to be asked is, of course, whether or not the agreement has as its object or effect the prevention, restriction, or distortion of competition.[196] In making this determination the relevant case law of the Court is of utmost importance. Guidance can also be sought from the Commission's decision and Guidelines. The Technology Transfer Guidelines seek to bring together the principles derived from these sources and to provide a coherent structure for the appraisal.

It has already been seen that in determining what constitutes a restriction of competition for the purposes of Article 101(1), restraints on both inter-technology and intra-technology competition are relevant. The Commission is concerned that a licensing agreement will lead to negative effects from:

1. reduction of inter-technology competition between companies operating on a technology market or on a market for products incorporating the technologies in question, including facilitation of collusion, both explicit and tacit;

2. foreclosure of competitors by raising their costs, restricting their access to essential inputs or otherwise raising barriers to entry; and

3. reduction of intra-technology competition between undertakings that produce products on the basis of the same technology.[197]

Guidance on what constitutes a restraint by object can be found in the list of hardcore restrictions set out in the TTBER, Article 4.[198] Where the object of the agreement is not to restrict competition,

---

[196] Art. 101(1) also only applies if the agreement appreciably restricts competition and appreciably affects trade between Member States, see Chap. 3.

[197] Guidelines, para. 141.

[198] See also, e.g., Cases T-374, 375, 384, and 388/94, *European Night Services v. Commission* [1998] ECR II-3141; Case 243/83, *SA Binon & Cie v. S.A. Agence et Messageries de la Presse* [1985] ECR 2015; Case C-501/06 P, *GlaxoSmithKline Services*

it must be established that this is its effect. Essentially, this will require proof that the licence agreement: affects competition to such an extent that a negative effect on prices, output, innovation, or variety of quality of goods or services has occurred or is likely; forecloses competitors; and/or restricts competition between licensees where not objectively necessary to the existence of an agreement of that type or nature.

b. Article 101(3)

Agreements that restrict competition will be excepted from the Article 101(1) prohibition if they satisfy the Article 101(3) criteria. Thus, restrictions of competition identified under Article 101(1) must be balanced against pro-competitive effects in the context of Article 101(3).[199] The Commission recognises in the Guidelines that restrictive licence agreements will frequently produce pro-competitive effects in the form of efficiencies.[200]

Licence agreements thus have substantial pro-competitive potential. Indeed, the vast majority of licence agreements are pro-competitive. Licence agreements may promote innovation by allowing innovators to earn returns to cover at least part of their R&D costs. Licence agreements also lead to a dissemination of technologies, which may create value by reducing the production costs of the licensee or by enabling it to produce new or improved products. Efficiencies at the level of the licensee often stem from a combination of the licensor's technology with the assets and technologies of the licensee. Such integration of complementary assets and technologies may lead to a cost/output configuration that would not otherwise be possible. For instance, the combination of an improved technology of the licensor with more efficient production or distribution assets of the licensee may reduce production costs or lead to the production of a higher-quality product. Licensing may also serve the pro-competitive purpose of removing obstacles to the development and exploitation of the licensee's own technology. In particular, in sectors where large numbers of patents are prevalent, licensing often occurs in order to create design freedom by removing the risk of infringement claims by the licensor. When the licensor agrees not to invoke its IPRs to prevent the sale of the licensee's products, the agreement removes an obstacle to the sale of the licensee's product and thus generally promotes competition.[201]

The burden of Article 101(3) is on those seeking its benefit. The Guidelines provide that hardcore restraints will rarely satisfy the conditions of Article 101(3). It will be remembered, however, that all agreements are, theoretically, capable of satisfying the Article 101(3) conditions and that in exceptional circumstances even hardcore restraints may do so.[202] The burden of satisfying the Article 101(3) conditions is an onerous one requiring proof that: efficiency gains (such as the creation of new and improved products or production at lower cost) will result from the activity that forms the object of the agreement;[203] that the restrictions are indispensable to the attainment of the efficiencies (in particular 'whether individual restrictions make it possible to perform the activity in question more efficiently than would have been the case in the absence of the restriction concerned');[204] that consumers receive a fair share of benefit through off-setting the likely negative impact of the agreement on prices, output, and other relevant matters;[205] and that the agreement does not afford the parties the possibility of eliminating competition in respect of a substantial part of the products concerned. The remaining competitive pressures on the market must therefore be

---

Unlimited v. Commission [2009] ECR I-9291, (discussed in Chap. 4); Case 27/87, *Erauw-Jacquéry Sprl v. La Hesbignonne Société Coopérative* [1988] ECR 1919; and Case 258/78, *Nungesser and Eisele v. Commission* [1982] ECR 2015 and Chap. 4.

[199] Guidelines, para. 18.

[200] Guidelines, para. 146.

[201] Guidelines, para. 17.

[202] See Chap. 4.

[203] Guidelines, para. 148. For the conditions of Art. 101(3) generally see Chap. 4.

[204] Guidelines, para. 149.

[205] Guidelines, para. 150.

analysed to ensure that the parties are not afforded the possibility of eliminating competition.[206] An *ex ante* approach is taken, assessing the position at the time the contract was concluded.[207] The Article 101(3) exception lasts for as long as its conditions are fulfilled.[208]

(v) Relevant Factors

The Guidelines discuss factors which are particularly relevant to the application of Article 101 in individual cases.[209]

a. The Nature of the Agreement

The agreement must be analysed in terms of the competitive relationship between the parties and the analysis must go beyond the express terms of the agreement.[210]

b. The Market Position of the Parties

The higher the market share of the parties the greater their market power is likely to be. They may also enjoy first mover advantages, hold essential patents, or have superior technology.[211] Even where the parties are not competitors it is relevant whether or not the licensee owns a competing technology.[212]

c. The Market Position of Competitors

The stronger the actual competitors are, and the more numerous they are, the less risk there is of the parties individually exercising market power.[213]

d. The Market Position of the Buyers of the Licensed Product

Buyer power may prevent the licensor and/or licensee from exercising market power, thereby solving a competition problem which might otherwise have existed, but whether this is so will depend on the conduct of the buyers in question.[214] A good indicator of buyer power is the buyer's market share of the purchasing market.

e. Entry Barriers

Entry barriers will be relevant to an assessment of the parties' market power but the Commission states that 'actual competition is in general more effective and will weigh more heavily in the assessment of a case than potential competition'.[215]

f. The Maturity of the Market

A market is said to be mature when it has existed for some time, the technology used is well known, widespread and not changing very much, and demand is relatively stable or declining. In mature markets restrictions on competition are more likely to have negative effects.[216]

---

[206] Guidelines, para. 151, and see the general discussion of Art. 101(3) in Chap. 4.

[207] Guidelines, para. 147.

[208] See Chap. 4.

[209] Guidelines, para. 132.

[210] Guidelines, para. 133.

[211] Guidelines, para. 134.

[212] Guidelines, para. 135.

[213] Guidelines, para. 136.

[214] Guidelines, para. 137.

[215] Guidelines, para. 138.

[216] Guidelines, para. 139.

g. Other Factors

Other factors which may be taken into account include the coverage of the market by similar agreements (cumulative effects), the duration of the agreement, the regulatory environment, and behaviour that may indicate or facilitate collusion.[217]

B. THE APPLICATION OF THE TTBER AND THE GUIDELINES TO SPECIFIC PROVISIONS

It is essential to remember that within the safe harbour of the TTBER any restriction not in the list of hardcore or excluded restrictions is permitted. The Guidelines provide guidance on the compatibility of specific restraints in technology transfer agreements which do *not* benefit from the safe harbour of the block exemption. The Guidelines do not, however, provide further guidance on hardcore restraints as the Commission considers that such restraints automatically infringe Article 101(1) and are most unlikely to satisfy the Article 101(3) conditions (see further Chapters 4 and 11).

(i) Provisions not Generally Restrictive of Article 101(1)

Paragraph 155 of the Guidelines sets out a list of obligations in licence agreements which are generally not restrictive of competition within the meaning of Article 101(1). These are:

- confidentiality obligations;
- obligations on licensees not to sub-license;
- obligations not to use the licensed technology after the expiry of the agreement, provided that the licensed technology remains valid and in force;
- obligations to assist the licensor in enforcing the licensed IPRs;
- obligations to pay minimum royalties or to produce a minimum quantity of products incorporating the licensed technology;
- obligations to use the licensor's trade mark or indicate the name of the licensor on the product.

(ii) Royalty Obligations

a. Agreements between Competitors

Provisions relating to royalty payments are not normally caught by Article 101(1)[218] even if the royalty obligations extend beyond the validity of the licensed IPR.[219]

In agreements between competitors, the Guidelines state[220] that occasionally royalty clauses could amount to price-fixing arrangements, which constitute a hardcore restriction (under TTBER, Article 4(1)(a)). This will be so, for example, if the competitors provide for reciprocal running royalties in circumstances in which the licence is a sham to disguise price-fixing or if royalties have to be paid on products produced solely with the licensee's own technology (see Article 4(1)(a) and Article 4(1)(d)).[221] If the royalty provisions do not amount to hardcore restraints, they will of course be block exempted if the parties' market shares do not exceed the 20 per cent threshold. Outside the safe harbour, however, the Guidelines indicate that Article 101 may be infringed where competitors

---

[217] Guidelines, *para.* 140.

[218] Guidelines, paras. 155 and 156.

[219] Guidelines, para. 159. Once the IPR has expired third parties can legally compete with the parties to the agreement so such a provision is unlikely to have appreciable anti-competitive effects.

[220] Guidelines, para. 157.

[221] Guidelines, para. 81, citing Case 193/83, *Windsurfing International v. Commission* [1986] ECR 611.

cross-license and the running royalties are 'clearly disproportionate' to the market value of the licence or where running royalties per unit increase as output increases.[222]

b. Agreements between Non-competitors

In agreements between non-competitors the TTBER covers agreements whereby royalties are calculated on the basis of both products produced with the licensed technology and those produced with technology licensed from third parties. Outside the 30 per cent safe harbour, however, such a provision must be analysed for appreciable foreclosure effects (similar to a non-compete provision) which would bring the agreement within Article 101(1) and make the fulfilment of Article 101(3) unlikely.[223]

(iii) Exclusive and Sole Licences

The grant of exclusive and sole licences is often accompanied by sales restrictions (discussed in Section 5.B.iv).

a. Agreements between Competitors

The effect of the TTBER is that sole licensing and *non-reciprocal* exclusive licensing are exempted up to the 20 per cent market share threshold. The effect of Article 4(1)(c), however, is to make reciprocal exclusive licensing between competitors a hardcore restriction as it amounts to market-sharing.[224]

Outside the safe harbour, a non-reciprocal exclusive licence must be analysed for likely anti-competitive effect. The licence will result in either the licensor leaving the market altogether (if the licence is worldwide), or ceasing to produce inside a particular territory (if the licence is limited to a territory). The key issue, therefore, is the competitive significance of the licensor leaving the market in question. It may be that where the licensor is insignificant (e.g., a small research undertaking active only on the technology market), Article 101(1) may not be infringed in the first place.[225] Reciprocal sole licensing may facilitate collusion where the parties have market power.[226]

b. Agreements between Non-competitors

To the extent that exclusive or sole licensing between non-competitors is caught by Article 101(1) at all[227] it is exempted by the TTBER up to the 30 per cent threshold. Outside the safe harbour, the Guidelines accept that exclusive licensing agreements between non-competitors may not infringe Article 101(1) and will usually fulfil the Article 101(3) conditions because of the need to give the licensee sufficient incentive to invest. The Commission 'will therefore only exceptionally intervene' irrespective of the territorial scope of the licence. A reason for intervention might be that there is a foreclosure problem because the licensee obtains an exclusive licence to crucial competing technologies.[228]

c. Cross-licences

The Commission is also concerned that where parties cross-license each other and undertake not to license third parties it could lead to the creation of a closed *de facto* industry standard. Such arrangements are treated according to the same principles as technology pools discussed

---

[222] Guidelines, para. 158.
[223] Guidelines, para. 160.
[224] Guidelines, para. 163.
[225] Guidelines, para. 164.
[226] Guidelines, para. 164.
[227] See Case 258/78, *Nungesser v. Commission* [1982] ECR 2015.
[228] Guidelines, paras. 165 and 166.

in Section 5.C. Normally, to satisfy the conditions of Article 101(3) it will be necessary for technology supporting such a standard to be licensed to third parties on fair, reasonable, and non-discriminatory terms.[229]

(iv) Sales Restrictions

a. Agreements between Competitors

In a reciprocal agreement between competitors, restrictions on active or passive sales of products incorporating the licensed technology into another territory or to another customer group are hard-core restrictions.[230] As such provisions amount to market-sharing, they are unlikely to fulfil the Article 101(3) conditions when they are individually assessed.[231]

In non-reciprocal agreements, restrictions on active or passive sales by either party to customer groups or territories of the other are block exempted by the TTBER.[232] Restrictions on active (but not passive) sales by the licensee into another licensee's territory or to its customer group are exempted too, but only if the latter licensee was not a competitor of the licensor at the time its own licence agreement was concluded.[233]

Outside the safe harbour active and passive sales restrictions are likely to fall within Article 101(1) where either party has a significant degree of market power. However, the conditions of Article 101(3) could be fulfilled if the restrictions are indispensable to protect substantial investments made by the licensee and the dissemination of the technology.[234]

b. Agreements between Non-competitors

The TTBER exempts all restrictions on active sales in agreements between non-competitors.

The TTBER also exempts passive sales restrictions on the licensor and passive sales restrictions which protect the licensor from the licensee.[235] Outside the safe harbour, restrictions on the licensee selling into the territory of the licensor are unlikely to fall within Article 101(1) if without them the licensing would not occur.[236] Sales restrictions on the licensor are likely, if they do fall within Article 101(1), to satisfy the Article 101(3) criteria unless no real alternatives to the licensor's technology exist.[237]

The TTBER exempts restrictions on passive sales by a licensee into the territory, or to the customers, of another licensee only for the first two years that the other licensee is selling the contract products.[238] Restrictions lasting for more than two years are hardcore restraints and are likely to be caught by Article 101(1) and are unlikely to satisfy Article 101(3).[239]

Above the 30 per cent threshold active sales restrictions are likely to be caught by Article 101(1) if the licensee has significant market power (because they limit intra-technology competition) but may satisfy the Article 101(3) conditions where necessary to prevent free riding and to induce investment by the licensee.[240]

---

[229] Guidelines, para. 167.
[230] TTBER, Art. 4(1)(c).
[231] Guidelines, paras. 12(b), 77, and 169.
[232] TTBER, Art. 4(1)(c)(iv).
[233] TTBER, Art. 4(1)(c)(v).
[234] Guidelines, paras. 170–171.
[235] TTBER, Art. 4(2)(b)(i) (ii).
[236] Guidelines, para. 172.
[237] Guidelines, para. 173.
[238] TTBER, Art. 4(2)(b)(ii).
[239] Guidelines, para. 174.
[240] Guidelines, para. 174.

(v) Output Restrictions

a. Agreements between Competitors

Output limitations in agreements between competitors are hardcore restrictions under the TTBER, Article 4(1)(b) but this is subject to two exceptions. They are exempted up to the 20 per cent threshold, first, where they are imposed on the licensee in a non-reciprocal agreement and, secondly, where they are imposed on only one of parties in a reciprocal agreement. Above the thresholds, restrictions on the licensee may restrict competition where the parties have significant market power. Article 101(3) may apply, however, where the licensor's technology is substantially better than the licensee's and the licensee's output under the agreement substantially exceeds its previous output. The key issue in the application of Article 101(3) is whether the licensor would be willing to disseminate its technology to licensees in the absence of output limitations on the licensee (including site licences).[241]

b. Agreements between Non-competitors

Output restrictions in agreements between non-competitors are exempted by the TTBER up to the 30 per cent threshold (they do not appear in the hardcore list at all). Above the threshold the Commission is concerned that restraints on quantities will restrain intra-technology competition between licensees.[242] However, again it is recognised that the licensor may only be prepared to licence its technology if output restrictions are possible.[243] The Commission nevertheless considers that output restrictions combined with exclusive territory or customer group provisions increase the likelihood of the agreement partitioning markets.[244]

(vi) Field of Use Restrictions

a. General

The distinction between field of use restrictions and customer allocation provision is explained in Section 3.B.v.[245] The Guidelines stress the importance of this distinction and that field of use restrictions are frequently pro-competitive.

Given that field of use restrictions are block exempted and that certain customer restrictions are hardcore restrictions under Articles 4(1)(c) and 4(2)(b) of the TTBER, it is important to distinguish the two categories of restraints. A customer restriction presupposes that specific customer groups are identified and that the parties are restricted in selling to such identified groups. The fact that a technical field of use restriction may correspond to certain groups of customers within a product market does not imply that the restraint is to be classified as a customer restriction. For instance, the fact that certain customers buy predominantly or exclusively chipsets with more than four CPUs does not imply that a licence which is limited to chipsets with up to four CPUs constitutes a customer restriction. However, the field of use must be defined objectively by reference to identified and meaningful technical characteristics of the licensed product.[246]

b. Agreements between Competitors

Field of use restrictions constitute a form of 'allocation of markets and customers' within the meaning of Article 4(1)(c) of the TTBER. Thus, field of use restrictions imposed on licensors in reciprocal

---

[241] Guidelines, para. 175. A site licence is one that may be exploited only on one site.
[242] Guidelines, para. 176.
[243] Guidelines, para. 178.
[244] Guidelines, para. 177.
[245] Also see Guidelines, para. 179.
[246] Guidelines, para. 180.

agreements between competitors are hardcore restrictions. Article 4(1)(c)(i), however, exempts field of use restrictions on licensees up to the 20 per cent threshold, so long as the restrictions do not go beyond the scope of the licensed technology and the licensee is not limited in the use of its own technology.[247] Field of use restrictions on licensors are block exempted below the threshold only in non-reciprocal agreements where the field of use is reserved to the licensee. Outside the safe harbour, the Commission's main concern is that the licensee may cease to be a competitive force outside the licensed field of use; the Commission considers the risk of this greatest where the parties cross-license and the restrictions are asymmetrical (the parties are licensed for different fields of use). The agreement is likely to be caught by Article 101(1) if it is likely to lead to the licensee reducing output outside the licensed field of use. Where there are symmetrical restrictions (the parties each license the other to use their technology in the same field of use) the agreement is unlikely to be caught by Article 101(1).[248]

c. Agreements between Non-competitors

Field of use restrictions imposed on the licensor and licensee are block exempted by the TTBER up to the 30 per cent threshold. Outside the safe harbour the Guidelines indicate that allowing the licensor to limit the licensee to certain fields of use will generally be pro-competitive since it enables the licensor to license exploitation of the technology in fields which it does not want to exploit itself.[249] In agreements between non-competitors the licensor may normally grant sole or exclusive licences to different licensees for different fields of use.[250]

(vii) Captive Use Restrictions

a. Agreements between Competitors

Captive use restrictions are block exempted in agreements between competitors up to the 20 per cent threshold. Outside the safe harbour there is concern that the provision will prevent the licensee from supplying components to third party producers. The Article 101 analysis is thus affected by the question of whether or not the licensee was an actual or potential supplier of components to third parties. If it was not, the captive use restriction does not change anything. If it was a supplier, the impact of the restriction must be examined, as competition which existed prior to the agreement is restricted.[251]

b. Agreements between Non-competitors

Captive use restrictions in agreements between non-competitors are block exempted up to the 30 per cent threshold. Outside the block exemption, two main competitive risks arise: first, the provision may restrict intra-technology competition on the market for inputs; and secondly, the provision may exclude arbitrage between licensees, which may enable the licensor to impose discriminatory royalties on the licensees.[252] If the licensor is itself a component supplier the restriction may be pro-competitive as otherwise it would not give the licence, being unwilling to create competition for its own components. In that case the restriction may not be caught by Article 101(1), and, if it is, it may satisfy the conditions of Article 101(3).[253] Where, however the licensor is not a supplier of

---

[247] Guidelines, paras. 77 and 90.

[248] Guidelines, para. 183.

[249] While retaining for itself fields in which it does want to operate. Guidelines, para. 184.

[250] Guidelines, para. 185.

[251] Guidelines, para. 187.

[252] Guidelines, para. 188.

[253] Guidelines, para. 189.

components a captive use restriction normally infringes Article 101 since it is not necessary for the dissemination of the technology.[254]

(viii) Tying and Bundling

Tying (the expression is used in the Guidelines to cover both tying and bundling) is block exempted by the TTBER in agreements between both competitors and non-competitors where the market share thresholds are satisfied. The market share thresholds apply to any relevant technology or product market affected by the agreement including that for the tied product. Outside the thresholds the pro- and anti-competitive effects have to be balanced.

The key concern with tying is the foreclosure of competing suppliers from the tied market. It may also enable a licensor to maintain market power in the tying market.

The main restrictive effect of tying is foreclosure of competing suppliers of the tied product. Tying may also allow the licensor to maintain market power in the market for the tying product by raising barriers to entry since it may force new entrants to enter several markets at the same time. Moreover, tying may allow the licensor to increase royalties, in particular when the tying product and the tied product are partly substitutable and the two products are not used in fixed proportion. Tying prevents the licensee from switching to substitute inputs in the face of increased royalties for the tying product. These competition concerns are independent of whether the parties to the agreement are competitors or not. For tying to produce likely anti-competitive effects the licensor must have a significant degree of market power in the tying product so as to restrict competition in the tied product. In the absence of market power in the tying product the licensor cannot use his technology for the anti-competitive purpose of foreclosing suppliers of the tied product. Furthermore, as in the case of non-compete obligations, the tie must cover a certain proportion of the market for the tied product for appreciable foreclosure effects to occur. In cases where the licensor has market power on the market for the tied product rather than on the market for the tying product, the restraint is analysed as non-compete or quantity forcing, reflecting the fact that any competition problem has its origin on the market for the 'tied' product and not on the market for the 'tying' product…[255]

On the other hand, tying may be a source of efficiency gains and may be necessary to protect the reputation of the licensor and the products produced with the licensed technology.[256] This will particularly be so when it is necessary for the licensee to use the tied product in order to exploit the technology in a technically satisfactory way, in order to ensure conformity to quality standards or to exploit the licensed technology more efficiently. In these cases tying will not normally infringe Article 101.

(ix) Non-compete Obligations

Non-compete obligations are obligations on the licensee not to use third party technologies which compete with the licensed technology. Obligations covering products, or additional technologies supplied by the licensor, are dealt with under Tying (Section 5.B.viii).

Non-compete obligations do not constitute hardcore restraints and are block exempted by the TTBER up to the relevant thresholds. Outside the thresholds the Commission's main concern, in regard to both agreements between competitors and non-competitors, is the risk of foreclosure of third parties who may not be able to find outlets for their technology and/or, in cases of cumulative use, that the agreements may facilitate collusion between licensors. Foreclosure may arise where a single licensor has a significant degree of market power or a number of licensors conclude similar agreements that cumulatively have the effect of foreclosing the market to competitors (which is

---

[254] Guidelines, para. 190.
[255] Guidelines, para. 193.
[256] Guidelines, para. 194.

unlikely if less than 50 per cent of the market is tied) and where barriers to entry for new licensees are relatively high.[257] Even if a substantial part of the market is not covered by non-compete obligations the risk may be high if the non-compete obligations are targeted at those undertakings most likely to license competing technologies.[258]

On the other hand, non-compete obligations may have pro-competitive effects. The Guidelines accept that they: may promote the dissemination of technology by reducing the misappropriation of licensed technology (particularly know-how); may ensure that the licensee has an incentive to invest in and exploit the licensed technology effectively (possibly in combination with an exclusive territory); and may induce the licensor to make specific investments (such as training the licensee or tailoring the technology to its needs). However, the Commission considers that this can often be achieved by less restrictive means (such as charging directly by way of a lump sum).[259]

(x) No-challenge Clauses

No-challenge clauses, which prohibit a challenge to the licensor's technology, are 'excluded restrictions' within the meaning of Article 5 since it is generally considered to be in the interests of undistorted competition, and of the IPRs system, that invalid IPRs should be eliminated. 'Invalid intellectual property stifles innovation rather than promoting it.'[260] The licensee is normally in the best position to spot the invalidity of the rights because it is actually working with the technology. The Guidelines state that no-challenge clauses are likely to violate Article 101 where the licensed technology is valuable. However, with regard to know-how, a more favourable attitude to these clauses is adopted, as once know-how has been disclosed it is often impossible or difficult to recover it (the genie cannot be put back in the bottle). A no-challenge clause may therefore in these circumstances promote the dissemination of new technology, for example, by preventing stronger licensees from absorbing the know-how of weaker licensors and then challenging it.[261]

It will be recalled, however, that the TTBER does not exclude clauses permitting the licensor to terminate the licence if the licensee challenges *the licensed technology*.[262] The licensor is not forced to continue to deal with a licensee that challenges the subject matter of the licence and, following termination of the agreement, the use of the technology will be at the licensee's own risk.

No-challenge clauses in settlement and non-assertion agreements will normally fall outside Article 101(1).[263]

(xi) Improvements

Article 5 also excludes from the benefit of the TTBER exclusive grant backs or assignments of severable improvements to the licensor.[264] When such provisions are individually assessed under Article 101 the existence and level of consideration given for the improvements may be relevant. If the licensee is to obtain compensation he will have greater incentive to innovate. The market position of the licensor will also be relevant, as the stronger the licensor's position the more likely it is that that exclusive grant backs will have restrictive effects on competition in innovation. In addition, there

---

[257] Guidelines, para. 199.

[258] Guidelines, para. 200.

[259] Guidelines, paras. 201–203.

[260] Guidelines, para. 112.

[261] Guidelines, para. 112.

[262] TTBER, Art. 5(2) and Guidelines, para. 113.

[263] Guidelines, para. 209, see n. 280 and accompanying text.

[264] Art. 5 does not cover *non-exclusive* grant back obligations, even if the grant back is not reciprocal (i.e. only imposed on the licensee) and where the licensor is entitled to feed-on the severable improvements to other licensees. Non-reciprocal grant back may be pro-competitive because of its effect on the licensor, Guidelines, para. 109.

may be negative effects on competition where there are parallel networks of licence agreements containing such obligations.[265]

The Commission is concerned that where competitors cross-license each other with grant back obligations neither can gain a competitive advantage over the other because they will be sharing improvements.[266]

Grant backs of non-severable improvements are not restrictive of competition within Article 101(1) since the licensee cannot exploit them without the licensor's permission as they cannot be separated from the licensed technology.[267]

(xii) Settlement and Non-assertion Agreements

The TTBER covers settlement and non-assertion agreements[268] insofar as they do not contain hard-core restrictions. Outside the safe harbour, the approach of the Commission is set out in paragraph 204 of the Guidelines:

Licensing may serve as a means of settling disputes or avoiding that one party exercises his intellectual property rights to prevent the other party from exploiting his own technology. Licensing including cross licensing in the context of settlement agreements and non-assertion agreements is not as such restrictive of competition since it allows the parties to exploit their technologies post agreement. However, the individual terms and conditions of such agreements may be caught by Article 101(1). Licensing in the context of settlement agreements is treated like other licence agreements. In the case of technologies that from a technical point of view are substitutes, it is therefore necessary to assess to what extent it is likely that the technologies in question are in a one-way or two-way blocking position...If so, the parties are not deemed to be competitors.

If the parties cross-licensing under the agreement have a significant degree of market power, and the restrictions clearly go beyond what is required to unblock, the arrangement is likely to be caught by Article 101(1).[269] Where the agreement entitles the parties to use each other's technology and extends to future developments the Commission will be concerned with the impact of the agreement on the parties' incentives to innovate. If they have a significant degree of market power and the agreement prevents them from gaining a competitive lead over one another the agreement is likely to be caught by Article 101(1) and not satisfy Article 101(3).[270] In its Preliminary and Final Reports into the pharmaceuticals sector[271] the Commission indicated concern that patent settlement agreements concluded between originator and generic pharmaceutical companies might be restricting the ability of generic companies to market medicines or delaying entry into the markets.[272] The Report noted that just under half of the patent settlement agreements concluded in the EU, between January 2007 and July 2008, involved a limitation on generic entry and that just under half of those agreements involved a value transfer to the generic company (in the form of a direct payment, a licence, a distribution agreement, or a side deal). The Commission noted that of 207 settlement

---

[265] Guidelines, para. 110.

[266] This is also a concern over clauses in settlement or non-assertion agreements, where the parties settle disputes by, *inter alia*, agreeing to share future technological developments: see Guidelines, para. 208.

[267] Guidelines, para. 109.

[268] As settlements are designed to enable the parties to settle disputes or to prevent one party exercising its intellectual property rights to preclude the other from exploiting its own technology and to enable the parties to exploit their technologies, the agreements are not in themselves restrictive of competition although individual terms and conditions may be.

[269] Guidelines, para. 207.

[270] Guidelines, para. 208.

[271] Pharmaceutical Sector Inquiry, Preliminary Report, 28 November. 2008, Final Report, 8 July 2009. The Inquiry was launched under Reg. 1/2003, Art. 17, see <http://ec.europa.eu/comm/competition/sectors/pharmaceuticals/inquiry/index.html>.

[272] See Pharmaceutical Sector Inquiry, Preliminary Report, 28 November 2008 (cited in n. 271), 2.4.

agreements concluded in at least one EU27 Member State between January 2007 and June 2008, 99 contained limitation on generic entry and 45 of those involved a value transfer from the originator company. The Commission has since then been monitoring patent settlements[273] and has concluded two reports on the issue. It believes that this process has increased awareness of antitrust issues and led to a decline in the conclusion of anti-competitive settlement agreements and is investigating a number of agreements. Indeed, the Commission has conducted investigations in relation to Cephalon and Teva;[274] Johnson & Johnson and Novartis,[275] Les Laboratoires Servier and five generic pharmaceutical companies;[276] and AstraZeneca and Nycomed.[277] Although the Commission closed an investigation into the question of whether Laboratoires Servier provided misleading and incorrect information during the pharmaceutical sector inquiry, the investigation into possible breaches of Arts 101 and 102 is ongoing. Further in *Lundbeck* the Commission fined both Lundbeck and producers of generic medicines for agreements designed to delay market entry.[278] In the US, the Federal Trade Commission (FTC) has also been concerned that potentially anti-competitive settlement agreements are prevalent in the US pharmaceuticals sector. A split in the circuits as to how such agreements should be analysed under the US antitrust laws led the Supreme Court in December 2012 to take certiorari of a case involving the drug, Androgel. The Supreme Court held that pay-for-delay settlements are subject to, and are not immune from, antitrust laws.[279]

No-challenge clauses will generally be outside Article 101(1) in settlement and non-assertion agreements since the whole point of the agreement is to settle disputes and avoid future ones.[280]

The Commission's draft replacement guidelines expand this section on settlement agreements, presumably in the light with its experience in this area since 2004. For example, the draft Guidelines clarify that settlement agreements involving a licence may run counter to Article 101, in particular where it involves a 'pay-for-delay' agreement or 'reverse payment patent settlement'. The draft Guidelines also stress that no-challenge clauses may be problematic in patent settlement agreements, particularly where the licensor knows or could reasonably be expected to know that the licensed technology does not meet the criteria for IP protection.

C. TECHNOLOGY POOLS

Agreements setting up technology pools, where two or more parties come together to assemble a 'package' of technology that is then licensed to the contributors to the pool and possibly third parties,[281] are not covered by the TTBER (although it may cover a licence granted by a technology pool to a third party). However, they are specifically dealt with in the Guidelines.[282] The Commission has indicated that it will closely monitor existing or new technology pools, in particular those that support or establish a *de facto* or *de jure* industry standard.[283]

---

[273] IP/11/40.

[274] IP/11/511

[275] IP/11/1228 (to consider whether their action may have had the object or effect of hindering the entry on to the market of generic products).

[276] Memo/08/734, IP/12/210 and N. Kroes, 'Five years of sector and antitrust inquiries' 3 December 2009.

[277] But in 2012 the Commission closed the investigation into the question of whether the undertakings had engaged in individual or joint action to delay new market entry, see IP/12/210.

[278] Case COMP/39226, IP/13/563 and IP/12/834.

[279] See *Federal Trade Commission v. Actavis, Inc*, 17 June 2013.

[280] The Guidelines, para. 209.

[281] Technology pools can be simple arrangements but may also be very elaborate, with the pooled technology entrusted to a separate entity, Guidelines, para. 210.

[282] Particularly Guidelines, paras. 210–235.

[283] See, e.g., IP/06/139. In this press release the Commission announced that it had closed an investigation into the practices of Philips Electronics which had offered European manufacturers of CD-Recordable disks a joint

The competitive risks of technology pools, resulting from collusion (price-fixing or market-sharing) and/or exclusion (foreclosure of competing technologies), have to be balanced against their efficiency-enhancing potential, for example the ability to facilitate dissemination of technology, to reduce costs, to clear blocking positions, and to provide one-stop licensing of technologies. In assessing the competing risks and efficiency potentials account must taken of: the nature of the pooled technologies, and whether they are (a) complementary[284] or substitutes[285] and (b) essential[286] or non-essential;[287] and the institutional framework of the pool.[288] The way in which this assessment is carried out is explained in paragraphs 217–222 of the Guidelines. In assessing individual restraints commonly found in technology pools the current Guidelines state that the Commission applies three guiding principles:

- The stronger the market position of the pool the greater the risk of anti-competitive effects;
- Pools that hold a strong position on the market should be open and non-discriminatory;
- Pools should not unduly foreclose third party technologies or limit the creation of alternative pools.[289]

Where a technology pool compatible with Article 101 is created, all provisions ancillary to the establishment of the standard or pool, such as royalty provisions, also fall outside Article 101. Where, however, the pool has a dominant position, the Guidelines indicate that closer scrutiny of the licensing provisions will be necessary and, for example, that the licensing and royalty provisions should be fair, non-discriminatory, and non-exclusive.[290]

The Commission's draft Guidelines provide more extensive discussion of technology pools than the current ones. They provide further clarification on when technology is 'essential' and clarify that licensing agreements between a pool and third parties in principle fall outside the scope of the TTBER as this is normally considered to be a multi-party agreement. Importantly, however, they also provide a safe harbour for the creation of certain technology pools and subsequent licensing out by it, with the objective of encouraging the conclusion of pro-competitive pools. For example, paragraph 224 provides:

(244) The creation and operation of the pool generally falls outside Article 101(1) irrespective of the market position of the parties if all the following conditions are fulfilled:

(a) participation in the standard and pool creation process is open to all interested parties;

(b) sufficient safeguards are adopted to ensure that only essential technologies (which therefore by necessity are also complements) are pooled;

(c) sufficient safeguards are adopted to ensure that exchange of sensitive information is restricted to what is necessary for the creation and operation of the pool;

---

portfolio licence which included both its own CD-Recordable disc patents and those of Sony and Taiyo Yuden. The Commission closed the investigation once Philips undertook to discontinue the joint patent portfolio licence in Europe and to offer revised individual licences limited to its own patents.

[284] Both technologies are required to produce the product or carry out the process in question.

[285] Either technology allows the holder to produce the product or carry out the process.

[286] There are no substitutes for the technology inside or outside the pool and the technology in question constitutes a necessary part of the package of technologies for the purposes of producing the product(s) or carrying out the process(es) to which the pool relates. The draft Guidelines provide greater clarity on this issue.

[287] Guidelines, paras. 215–216. Broadly, the creation of a pool composed of only essential complementary technologies is likely to fall outside Art. 101(1). In contrast, a pool of substitute technologies will constitute a price-fixing arrangement which violates Art. 101(1) and is unlikely to satisfy the conditions of Art. 101(3). A pool comprising non-essential substitute technologies may foreclose third party competing technologies, Guidelines paras. 219–222.

[288] Factors such as whether participation in the pool is open, whether experts are involved, how information exchange is dealt with and how disputes should be resolved are relevant, Guidelines, paras. 230–235.

[289] Guidelines, para. 224.

[290] Guidelines, paras. 225–229.

(d) the pooled technologies are licensed into the pool on a non-exclusive basis;

(e) the pooled technologies are licensed out to all potential licensees on FRAND terms

(f) the parties contributing technology to the pool and the licensees are free to challenge the validity and the essentiality of the pooled technologies, and;

(g) the parties contributing technology to the pool and the licensee remain free to develop competing products and technology.

Pooling arrangements may sometimes involve IPRs being used in the establishment of an industry standard. The Horizontal Co-operation Guidelines[291] contain additional guidance on the question of whether the agreement to establish an industry standard is compatible with Article 101—i.e. on standardisation agreements (agreements which 'have as their primary objective the definition of technical or quality requirements' for 'current or future products, production processes, services or methods'[292]) and on the licensing of IPRs essential for technology used to implement a standard on fair, reasonable, and non-discriminatory (FRAND) terms, see Chapter 10. Neither set of Guidelines provides guidance on patent ambushes or other post-standardisation practices by patentees which might hold-up and foreclose competitors. A patent ambush may occur where, during the course of a standard-setting procedure, an undertaking withholds or does not reveal information but later, once the standard is adopted, asserts patent claims against the undertakings which have asserted and are using the standard. The Commission has been concerned about anti-competitive use of standards and abuse of the IP system in a standard-setting context. In 2007, it brought proceedings against Rambus alleging breach of Article 102 for claiming unreasonable royalties for use of certain patents for Dynamic Random Access Memory (DRAM) chips not disclosed in the context of a standard-setting process. In the end, the proceedings were ended by the Commission adopting an Article 9 commitments decision, rendering agreed commitments binding on Rambus. It is also investigating possible infringements of Article 102 by Samsung and Motorola.[293]

6. TRADE MARK LICENCES

A. GENERAL

There is no block exemption which specifically covers trade mark licences. In the discussion of the TTBER in Section 4 and Section 5, however, it is seen that where the licence of a trade mark is ancillary to a licence of patents, know-how, designs, or software the TTBER may apply.[294] In this situation the trade mark licence may enable the licensee to exploit the licensed technology better. The licence may authorise the licensee to use its trade mark on products incorporating the licensed technology. This will help consumers make the link between the licensee's products and the licensed technology and may promote the dissemination of the licensed technology by allowing the licensor to identify itself as its source.[295] In other situations the TTBER does not cover trade mark licensing and, because

---

[291] Guidelines on the applicability of Article 101 of the Treaty on the Functioning of the European Union to horizontal co-operation agreements [2011] OJ C11/1 (Horizontal Co-operation Guidelines).

[292] Horizontal Co-operation Guidelines, para. 257.

[293] See Chap. 7, IP/09/1897, and IP/13/406. See also the rejection of complaint by Hynix, *Rambus*, 15 January 2010, on appeal Case T-149/10, *Hynix v. Commission* (judgment pending) and N. Kroes, '*Being open about standards*', Speech to Open Forum Europe, Brussels, 10 June 2008 (Speech/08/317). In November 2009 the Commission closed an investigation against Qualcomm (Memo/09/516) in respect of unreasonably high pricing of royalties for technology which had become part of an industry standard, see also Chap. 10. The Commission has also opened proceedings against both Samsung (IP/12/89) and Motorola (IP/12/345) for abusively using essential patents in standard-setting procedures and failing to license on FRAND terms. It is urging ETSI, Europe's telecommunications standards body, to find a solution to the technology-licensing disputes arising in this area.

[294] Reg. 772/2004, [2004] OJ L123/11, Art. 1(1)(b).

[295] Guidelines on technology transfer agreements [2004] OJ C101/2, para. 50.

the trade mark licences are not sufficiently linked to the dissemination of technology, the principles developed in the TTBER and the Guidelines do *not* apply by analogy.[296]

Trade mark licences may also be ancillary to a vertical agreement, such as a franchising agreement.[297] The Verticals Regulation, Regulation 339/2010, which applies to agreements between two or more undertakings each of which operates at a different level of the production or distribution chain and which relates to the conditions under which the parties may purchase, sell, or resell certain goods or services,[298] covers agreements containing provisions relating to the assignment to the buyer or use by the buyer of trade marks where these provisions do not constitute the primary object of the agreement and where they are directly related to the use, sale, or resale of the goods by the buyer or its customers.[299]

Where the block exemptions are not applicable, however, it will be necessary to seek guidance from the case law of the CJ, Commission decisions, the Article 101(3) Guidelines and, where appropriate, the Technology Transfer and Vertical Guidelines. The paucity (and age) of the case law and decisional practice mean that frequently, principles to be applied in the Article 101 analysis may have to be derived more broadly from the case law and the relevant Commission Guidelines.

In *Consten & Grundig*[300] it was held that an agreement seeking to confer ATP on the licensee of a trade mark would infringe Article 101(1). Further, the Commission's two formal decisions relating to trade mark licences, *Campari*[301] and *Moosehead/Whitbread*,[302] demonstrate that the Commission took a strict approach to exclusivity provisions[303] and applied broadly the same principles to trade mark licences as it did at the time in its decisions to patent and know-how licences. As the Commission's thinking has evolved considerably since this time, the reasoning in these cases, which support a formalistic approach to restraints on economic freedom, should be treated with some caution.

B. THE *CAMPARI* DECISION

The *Campari* transaction[304] is difficult to classify but the trade mark licence was a predominant element. The aperitifs Bitter Campari and Cordial Campari were made by mixing alcohol with a secret herbal concentrate. Campari-Milano set up a network of licensees to manufacture and sell its products in all EU countries except the UK and Ireland.[305] Under the agreements the licensees purchased the secret concentrate and colouring matter from the licensor and manufactured the drink in compliance with the licensor's instructions. The resulting bottles of aperitif were then sold under the licensor's Campari trade mark. The licences were exclusive, prevented the licensees from manufacturing or handling competing products or pursuing an active sales policy outside their territory, banned exports outside the common market, and provided that only the original Italian product could be supplied to certain customers/outlets. There were also provisions about manufac-

---

[296] Guidelines, para. 53.

[297] As the Guidelines recognise, see para. 53.

[298] Franchising agreements were formerly dealt with in a specific block exemption, Reg. 4087/88 [1988] OJ L359/46: see Chap. 11.

[299] Reg. 339/2010 [2010] OJ L102/1, Art. 2(3): see Chap. 11.

[300] Cases 56 and 58/64, *Établissements Consten SA & Grundig-Verkaufs-GmbH* v. *Commission* [1966] ECR 299.

[301] *Re the Agreement of Davide Campari-Milano SpA* [1978] OJ L70/69.

[302] [1990] OJ L100/32.

[303] Even though this approach bore 'no relation to the reality that no lager brewer would contemplate developing and marketing a new brand in competition with one of its rivals', N. Green and A. Robertson, *Commercial Agreements and Competition Law* (2nd edn, Kluwer, 1997), 931.

[304] *Re the Agreement of Davide-Campari-Milano SpA* [1978] OJ L70/69.

[305] The UK and Ireland were covered by a straightforward distribution agreement which fell within the block exemption then in force, Reg. 67/67 [1967] OJ Spec. Ed. 10.

ture only at approved sites, confidentiality, advertising, and non-assignment. The Commission held that the following provisions were outside Article 101(1): the ban on exports outside the common market, as in the circumstances there was little chance of this indirectly affecting inter-Member State trade; the restriction of the licence to those plants capable of guaranteeing the quality of the product; the obligation to follow the licensor's manufacturing instructions and to buy secret raw materials from the licensor, as this was central to the product being of proper 'Campari' quality;[306] the confidentiality of the know-how; the minimum advertising commitments; and the prohibition on assignment. Other clauses, including the exclusivity and the active sales ban, were held to infringe Article 101(1).

The Commission granted an exemption however. This part of the decision is a particularly good illustration of how the four criteria in Article 101(3) are, or were, applied. Note that in paragraph 71 the Commission distinguishes between the effects of a non-competition clause in a trade mark licence and one in a patent licence.

Re the Agreement of Davide-Campari-Milano SpA [1978] OJ L70/69

Commission

III APPLICABILITY OF ARTICLE [101(3)]...

...

A. The restrictions of competition mentioned at points 1 to 4 of item II A satisfy the tests of Article [101(3)].

1. The exclusivity granted by Campari-Milano contributes to improving the production and distribution of the products. By giving each licensee a guarantee that no other undertaking will obtain a licence within its allocated territory, and that in this territory neither Campari-Milano nor any other licensee may manufacture products bearing the licensor's trade mark this commitment confers upon each licensee an advantage in its allotted territory. This territorial advantage is such as to permit a sufficient return on the investment made by each licensee for the purpose of manufacturing the product bearing the trade mark under conditions acceptable to the licensor and holder of the trade mark, and it enables the licensee to increase its production capacity and constantly to improve the already long-established distribution network. In practice the exclusivity granted has allowed each licensee to improve its existing plant and to build new plant. It has also enabled each licensee to strengthen its efforts to promote the brand, doubling the total volume of sales in the Benelux countries and Germany over the last six years, and, by establishing a multistage distribution network, to secure a constantly increasing number of customers and thus to ensure supplies throughout the allotted territory.

2. The ban on dealing in competing products also contributes to improving distribution of the licensed products by concentrating sales efforts, encouraging the build-up of stocks and shortening delivery times.

The restriction on the licensees' freedom to deal in other products at the same time as the products here in question prevents the licensees from neglecting Campari in the event of conflict between the promotion of Campari sales and possible interest in another product. Although a non-competition clause in a licensing agreement concerning industrial property rights based on the result of a creative activity, such as a patent, would constitute a barrier to technical and economic progress by preventing the licensees from taking an interest in other techniques and products, this is not the case with the licensing agreements under consideration here. The aim pursued by the parties, as is clear from the agreements taken as a whole, is to decentralise manufacture within the EEC and to rationalise the distribution system linked to it, and thus

---

[306] Certain other ingredients did not necessarily have to be bought from the licensor but had to be sourced on the basis of objective quality considerations.

to promote the sale of Campari-Milano's Bitter, manufactured from the same concentrates provided by Campari-Milano, according to the same mixing process and using the same ingredients, and bearing the same trade mark, as that of the licensor.

The prohibition on dealing in competing products, therefore, makes for improved distribution of the relevant product in the same way as do exclusive dealing agreements containing a similar clause, which are automatically exempted by Regulation 67/67/EEC; a declaration that the prohibition in Article [101(1)] is inapplicable to this clause is accordingly justified.

3. Distribution will also be improved by the prohibition against the parties engaging in an active sales policy outside their respective territories. This restriction on the licensees will help to concentrate their sales efforts, and provide a better supply to consumers in their territories for which they have particular responsibility, without preventing buyers elsewhere in the Community from securing supplies freely from any of the licensees. Application of the same restriction to Campari-Milano encourages the efforts made by... each territory allotted; the licensees thus have the benefit of a certain protection relative to Campari-Milano's strong market position.

4. The obligation on licensees to supply the original Italian product rather than that which they themselves manufacture, when selling to diplomatic corps, ships' victuallers, foreign armed forces and generally speaking all organisations with duty-free facilities, also helps to promote sales of Campari-Milano's Bitter. By restricting licensees' freedom to supply the products they manufacture themselves it makes sure that particular categories of consumers, who are deemed to be outside the licensee's territory and are usually required to move frequently from one territory to another, can always purchase the same original product with all its traditional features as regards both composition and outward appearance. Even though quality standards are observed, it is impossible in particular to avoid differences in taste between the products of the various manufacturers. This obligation is thus designed to prevent these consumers from turning to other competing products and to ensure that they continue to buy Bitter Campari, with the facility of being able to obtain stocks from their local dealer. Further, such consumers are not prevented from freely obtaining the licensees' own products even though any such purchase would be on the normal trading conditions applicable to non-duty free purchasers. B. The licensing agreements have increased the quantities of Bitter Campari available to consumers and improved distribution, so that consumers benefit directly. There are other producers of bitter on the market, and effective competition will be strengthened by the growing quantities produced by Campari-Milano's licensees, so that it can be assumed that the improvements resulting from the agreements and the benefits which the licensees obtain from them are shared by consumers.

As buyers may secure supplies of Bitter from other territories through unsolicited orders, they are in a position to exert pressure on the prices charged by the exclusive licensee in their territory if these should be too high.

C. The restrictions of competition imposed on the parties must be considered indispensable to the attainment of the benefits set out above. None of the restrictions could be omitted without endangering the parties' object of promoting sales of Bitter Campari by concentrating the activities of the licensees on this product and offering the same original product to certain customers. In particular, none of the licensees and in all probability no other undertaking in the spirituous liquors industry would have been prepared to make the investment necessary for a significant increase in sales of Bitter if it were not sure of being protected from competition from other licensees or Campari-Milano itself.

D. The licensing agreements which are the subject of this Decision do not give Campari-Milano or its licensees the possibility of eliminating competition in respect of a substantial part of the Bitter products in question. In the EEC there exists a fairly large number of other well-known brands of bitter, which are all able to compete against Bitter Campari. Campari-Milano's licensees and Campari-Milano itself are also free to sell the Campari products in question within the Common Market but outside their territory for which they have particular responsibility.

C. THE MOOSEHEAD/WHITBREAD DECISION

This case concerned the manufacture in the UK of a lager produced by the Canadian brewer Moosehead.[307] According to the Commission, it had a taste typical of Canadian lagers.[308] Under the agreement Moosehead granted to the British brewer, Whitbread, the sole and exclusive right to produce and promote, market, and sell beer manufactured for sale under the name 'Moosehead' in the UK using Moosehead's secret know-how. Moosehead gave Whitbread an exclusive licence of its UK trade mark rights and agreed to provide it with all the relevant know-how (the know-how licence was non-exclusive) and to supply it with the necessary yeast. Whitbread agreed not to make active sales outside its territory, not to produce or promote any other beer identified as a Canadian beer, not to contest the ownership or validity of the trade mark, to comply with Moosehead's directions in relation to the know-how, and to buy the yeast only from Moosehead or a designated third party.

The Commission held that the exclusivity provisions and the active sales ban in the trade mark licence were caught by Article 101(1). It did not consider the no-challenge clause to the *ownership* of the mark was caught because no matter whose name it was registered in, other parties would be prevented from using it. A no-challenge clause in respect of validity, however, was another matter. The Commission held that whether such clauses may infringe Article 101(1) would depend on the circumstances, but in this case it did not:

15.4. In relation to the trade mark non-challenge clause:

(a) in general terms, a trade mark non-challenge clause can refer to the ownership and/or the validity of the trade mark:

— The ownership of a trade mark may, in particular, be challenged on grounds of the prior use or prior registration of an identical trade mark.

— A clause in an exclusive trade mark licence agreement obliging the licensee not to challenge the ownership of a trade mark, as specified in the above paragraph, does not constitute a restriction of competition within the meaning of Article [101(1)]. Whether or not the licensor or licensee has the ownership of the trade mark, the use of it by any other party is prevented in any event, and competition would thus not be affected.

— The validity of a trade mark may be contested on any ground under national law, and in particular on the grounds that it is generic or descriptive in nature. In such an event, should the challenge be upheld, the trade mark may fall within the public domain and may thereafter be used without restriction by the licensee and any other party.

Such a clause may constitute a restriction of competition within the meaning of Article [101(1)], because it may contribute to the maintenance of a trade mark that would be an unjustified barrier to entry into a given market.

Moreover in order for any restriction of competition to fall under Article [101(1)], it must be appreciable. The ownership of a trade mark only gives the holder the exclusive right to sell products under that name. Other parties are free to sell the product in question under a different trade mark or trade name. Only where the use of a well-known trade mark would be an important advantage to any company entering or competing in any given market and the absence of which therefore constitutes a significant barrier to entry, would this clause which impedes the licensee to challenge the validity of the trade mark, constitute an appreciable restriction of competition within the meaning of Article [101(1)].

(b) In the present case Whitbread is unable to challenge both the ownership and the validity of the trade mark.

[307] *Moosehead/Whitbread* [1990] OJ L100/32.
[308] *Moosehead/Whitbread* [1990] OJ L100/32, para. 3.

As far as the validity of the trade mark is concerned it must be noted that the trade mark is comparatively new to the lager market in the territory. The maintenance of the 'Moosehead' trade mark will thus not constitute an appreciable barrier to entry for any other company entering or competing in the beer market in the United Kingdom. Accordingly, the Commission considers that the trade mark non-challenge clause included in the agreement, in so far as it concerns its validity...does not constitute an appreciable restriction of competition and does not fall under Article [101(1)].

The Commission granted an exemption to the agreement, holding that the exclusivity provisions, active sales ban, and non-competition clauses met the Article 101(3) criteria, particularly in view of the amount of inter-brand competition on the UK beer market.

D. THE CURRENT POSITION

Although the Commission's decisions in *Campari* and *Moosehead* reflect the more formalistic approach to Article 101(1) it pursued prior to modernisation, they are useful in: (1) confirming that some types of clauses, such as non-challenge clauses, confidentiality provisions, and provisions dealing with quality control and manufacturing standards, may fall outside Article 101(1): and (2) setting out when provisions that may infringe Article 101(1) (such as exclusive licences, sales restraints, and non-compete provisions) are likely to satisfy the conditions of Article 101(3). It must not be forgotten, however, that the Commission (or a national court or NCA) analysing a case today would now be likely to adopt a more economic approach, in particular when applying Article 101(1). Although case law could be interpreted to support the Commission's view that exclusive licences, especially if accompanied by sales restraints, violate Article 101(1), it is likely that fuller analysis would now be required before it could be determined whether other provisions such as non-compete clauses restrict competition within the meaning of Article 101(1).

7. TRADE MARK DELIMITATION AGREEMENTS

Trade mark delimitation agreements are entered into in order to settle disputes.[309] They usually occur where one party opposes the other's application for, or use of, a mark on the ground that it is confusingly similar to one owned by the first party for similar products. The trade mark delimitation agreement may be adopted to settle protracted litigation. The CJ and Commission have made it clear that the provisions in such agreements may infringe Article 101(1)[310] in the same way as they might in any other agreement. The context in which the agreement is made does not therefore mean that it is immune from the application of Article 101(1). Delimitation agreements may restrict the class of products for which a party may use the mark, or the territories in which it may use the mark, or a party may accept a no-challenge obligation in relation to certain products or territories. In *BAT v. Commission*[311] the Court took a more liberal attitude to delimitation agreements than the Commission had done previously. The position now appears to be that an agreement will be outside Article 101(1) if there is a genuine risk of confusion between the parties, and it is not just a ploy for market-sharing, and if the agreement does not divide markets within the EU (at least if there is no less restrictive means of dealing with the dispute).[312]

---

[309] See n. 268 and accompanying text for non-assertion and settlement agreements in respect of IPRs potentially within the scope of the TTBER.

[310] See Case 65/86, *Bayer AG and Maschinenfabrik Hennecke v. Heinz Süllhöfer* [1988] ECR 5249, concerning a no-challenge clause.

[311] Case 35/83, *BAT v. Commission* [1985] ECR 363, the appeal from *Toltecs/Dorcet* [1982] OJ L379/19.

[312] See also *Sirdar/Phildar* [1975] OJ L125/27; *Hershey/Schiffers*, Commission Press Release IP/90/87; *Chiquita/Fyffes* IP(92)461. See also Allan et al. (eds.), *Butterworths Competition Law* (cited in n. 1), Div V, chap. 4.

8. COPYRIGHT (OTHER THAN SOFTWARE) LICENCES

A. GENERAL

Software licences are 'technology transfer agreements' and are thus governed by the TTBER and the accompanying Guidelines. Licences of other types of copyright, however, do not benefit from the TTBER or the Verticals Regulation, unless the licence is ancillary to a technology transfer or vertical agreement.[313] In discussing copyright licensing the Technology Transfer Guidelines distinguish between the licensing of copyright for the purpose of reproduction and distribution of the protected work, i.e. the production of copies for resale on the one hand, and the licensing of rights in performances (such as film, television, and radio broadcasts) and other rights related to copyright on the other. The principles set out in the TTBER and the Guidelines will, as a general rule, be applied to licensing for the purpose of reproduction and distribution.[314] Because the licences in this situation relate to the production and sale of a physical product embodying the work (such as a book or audio CD), the view is taken that such licensing is of a similar nature to technology transfer. The principles set out in the TTBER and Guidelines will not be applied, however, to licences involving 'performance' and other rights,[315] which raise particular issues.

B. PERFORMANCE COPYRIGHT

In the case of exploitation through performance, the CJ held in *Coditel II*[316] that an exclusive licence (amounting in effect to ATP) did not in itself infringe Article 101(1). The Court recognised the special nature of the product and rights concerned. In *Coditel I*[317] the Court considered the application of the exhaustion of rights doctrine to copyright in films and concluded that the owner's rights were not exhausted by the first showing of the film because the specific subject matter was the entitlement of the owner to charge each time the film was shown. The same facts (a Belgian cable company relaying in Belgium the transmission of a film (Chabrol's *Le Boucher*) shown in Germany for which Ciné Vog had exclusive distribution rights in Belgium) gave rise to a second case in which the cable company claimed that the exclusive licence granted to Ciné Vog infringed Article 101(1).

Case 262/81, *Coditel* v. *SA Ciné Vog Films (Coditel II)* [1982] ECR 3381

Court of Justice

10. It should be noted, by way of a preliminary observation, that Article [36] permits prohibitions or restrictions on trade between Member States provided that they are justified on grounds, *inter alia*, of the protection of industrial and commercial property, a term which covers literary and artistic property, including copyright, whereas the main proceedings are concerned with the question of prohibitions or restrictions placed upon the free movement of services.

---

[313] TTBER, Art. 1(1)(b).

[314] Guidelines, para. 51.

[315] Guidelines, para. 52.

[316] Case 262/81, *Coditel v. SA Ciné Vog Films (Coditel II)* [1982] ECR 3381.

[317] Case 62/79, *SA Compagnie Générale pour la Diffusion de la Télévision, Coditel v. Ciné Vog Films (Coditel I)* [1980] ECR 881.

11. In this regard, as the Court held in its judgment of 18 March 1980 (*Coditel v. Ciné-Vog Films* [1980] ECR 881), the problems involved in the observance of a film producer's rights in relation to the requirements of the Treaty are not the same as those of which arise in connection with literary and artistic works the placing of which at the disposal of the public is inseparable from the circulation of the material form of the works, as in the case of books or records, whereas the film belongs to the category of literary and artistic works made available to the public by performances which may be infinitely repeated and the commercial exploitation of which comes under the movement of services, no matter whether the means whereby it is shown to the public be the cinema or television.

12. In the same judgment the Court further held that the right of the owner of the copyright in a film and his assigns to require fees for any showing of that film is part of the essential function of copyright.

13. The distinction, implicit in Article [36], between the existence of a right conferred by the legislation of a Member State in regard to the protection of artistic and intellectual property, which cannot be affected by the provisions of the Treaty, and the exercise of such right, which might constitute a disguised restriction on trade between Member States, also applies where that right is exercised in the context of the movement of services.

14. Just as it is conceivable that certain aspects of the manner in which the right is exercised may prove to be incompatible with Articles [56] and [57] it is equally conceivable that some aspects may prove to be incompatible with Article [101] where they serve to give effect to an agreement, decision or concerted practice which may have as its object or effect the prevention, restriction or distortion of competition within the common market.

15. However, the mere fact that the owner of the copyright in a film has granted to a sole licensee the exclusive right to exhibit that film in the territory of a Member State and, consequently, to prohibit, during a specified period, its showing by others, is not sufficient to justify the finding that such a contract must be regarded as the purpose, the means or the result of an agreement, decision or concerted practice prohibited by the Treaty.

16. The characteristics of the cinematographic industry and of its markets in the [EU], especially those relating to dubbing and subtitling for the benefit of different language groups, to the possibilities of television broadcasts, and to the system of financing cinematographic production in Europe serve to show that an exclusive exhibition licence is not, in itself, such as to prevent, restrict or distort competition.

17. Although copyright in a film and the right deriving from it, namely that of exhibiting the film, are not, therefore, as such subject to the prohibitions contained in Article [101], the exercise of those rights may, none the less, come within the said prohibitions where there are economic or legal circumstances the effect of which is to restrict film distribution to an appreciable degree or to distort competition on the cinematographic market, regard being had to the specific characteristics of that market.

18. Since neither the question referred to the Court nor the file on the case provides any information in this respect, it is for the national court to make such inquiries as may be necessary.

19. It must therefore be stated that it is for national courts, where appropriate, to make such inquiries and in particular to establish whether or not the exercise of the exclusive right to exhibit a cinematographic film creates barriers which are artificial and unjustifiable in terms of the needs of the cinematographic industry, or the possibility of charging fees which exceed a fair return on investment, or an exclusivity the duration of which is disproportionate to those requirements, and whether or not, from a general point of view, such exercise within a given geographic area is such as to prevent, restrict or distort competition within the common market.

20. Accordingly, the answer to be given to the question referred to the Court must be that a contract whereby the owner of the copyright in a film grants an exclusive right to exhibit that film for a specific period in the territory of a Member State is not, as such, subject to the prohibitions contained in Article [101 TFEU]. It is, however, where appropriate, for the national court to ascertain whether, in a given case, the manner in which the exclusive right conferred by that contract is exercised is subject to a situation in the economic or legal sphere the object or effect of which is to prevent or restrict the distribution of films or to distort competition within the cinematographic market, regard being had to the specific characteristics of the market.

The Court therefore accepted that the exclusive right, which in this case precluded showing of the film by others during a specified period, was not *of itself* prohibited by Article 101(1), given the nature of the protected work and the characteristics of the film industry. It did not, nevertheless, rule out the possibility that in certain circumstances the exercise of the exclusive right might fall within Article 101(1). However, the criteria in the qualifications in paragraphs 17 and 19 of the judgment as to when exclusivity *will* infringe the prohibition (the exclusivity might create artificial and unjustifiable barriers to trade, lead to excessive prices, or be for an excessive duration) are imprecise and uncertain.[318] Some indication of how the Commission will apply them was given in its decision in *Film Purchases by German Television Stations*.[319] In this case an exclusive broadcasting licence of MGM/UA films was granted to a group of German TV stations for 15 years with a further 'selection period' which preceded this.[320] The Commission held that the agreement was within Article 101(1) because of the number of films covered by the transaction[321] and the long duration of the arrangements which excluded third parties for a length of time which was described as 'disproportionate within the *Coditel II* judgment of the Court of Justice' and 'an artificial barrier to other undertakings'.[322] The agreement was exempted after provision was made for third-party broadcasters in Germany to apply for licences to show the films at times which did not clash with those of the licensees. The Commission held that Article 101(3) was satisfied because the arrangements as a whole allowed more films to be shown to German audiences and to be dubbed into German.

In the Guidelines the Commission cites *Coditel II* and recognises the special factors that arise in connection with this type of copyright:

...In the case of the various rights related to performances value is created not by the reproduction and sale of copies of a product but by each individual performance of the protected work. Such exploitation can take various forms including the performance, showing or the renting of protected material such as films, music or sporting events. In the application of Article [101] the specificities of the work and the way in which it is exploited must be taken into account (See in this respect Case 262/81, *Coditel (II)*...). For instance, resale restrictions may give rise to less competition concerns whereas particular concerns may arise where licensors impose on their licensees to extend to each of the licensors more favourable conditions obtained by one of them. The Commission will therefore not apply the TTBER and the present guidelines by way of analogy to the licensing of these other rights.[323]

The compatibility of exclusive copyright licences with Article 101 was, however, raised in cases arising before the English courts. For example, *The Football Association Premier League Ltd v. QC Leisure*[324] concerned the broadcasting of Premier League (PL) football matches in the UK through the unau-

---

[318] Para. 19 provides that a relevant factor is whether the rewards are excessive, although no indication is given of how the national court is to make such judgments in the context of the film industry.

[319] [1989] OJ L284/36.

[320] In fact the Commission left open whether the transaction amounted to a licence 'in the legal and technical sense' or an assignment of rights for a limited period and to a limited extent. In either case the Commission considered that there was a restriction of competition: *Film Purchases by German Television Stations* [1989] OJ L284/36, para. 41.

[321] And the fact that many of the films were important or noteworthy or had 'particular mass appeal such as the James Bond films': [1989] OJ L284/36, para. 43.

[322] [1989] OJ L284/36, para. 44.

[323] Guidelines, para. 52.

[324] [2008] EWHC 44 (Ch), [2008] EWHC 1411. The cases also raised the compatibility of the licences with the free movement rules. See also, e.g., *Murphy v. Media Protection Services Ltd* [2008] EWHC 1666 (Admin) (similar issues were raised in the context of criminal proceedings against the defendant for violation of the Copyright, Designs and Patents Act 1988, s. 297(1) (dishonestly receiving a programme included in a broadcasting service provided from a place in the UK with intent to avoid payment of any charge applicable to the reception of the programme). The defendant was convicted in the magistrates court but the High Court held that a reference should be made to the CJ in case the conviction had been based upon a misunderstanding of EU law, including the question of whether an exclusive licence, requiring broadcasters to prevent satellite decoders from being used outside the licensed territory, contravened Art. 101(1).

thorised use of a non-UK decoder. In this case, the Football Association Premier League Ltd (FAPL) had licensed to foreign broadcasters the right to broadcast live Premier League football matches in their licensed territory. Broadcasts are made by encrypted signals via satellite, and paying customers receive the broadcasts by use of a decoder card. Under the terms of the arrangements foreign broadcasters were prohibited from supplying non-UK decoder cards for use in the UK. The proceedings in this case were brought by the FAPL against defendants alleged either to have supplied non-UK decoders or to have broadcast live PL football matches using a non-UK decoder. One of the defences raised was that the territorial restraints preventing supply for use in the UK were in breach of Article 101. The FAPL argued that the Article 101 defence had no real prospect of success on the basis that the CJ had held in *Coditel* that exclusive territorial licences of copyright in broadcasts did not offend Article 101, However, FAPL's application for summary judgment was rejected[325] as the judge considered that *Coditel II* did not necessarily provide the answer in this case. Rather, the issue was something for the trial judge to decide in the light of fuller argument and, conceivably, following a reference to the CJ. Subsequent to a full trial, a number of questions were referred to the CJ under Article 267 including the compatibility of the licensing arrangements with Article 101. It has been seen that the CJ[326] drew an important distinction in its ruling between sole exclusive licences and licences which went further and restored divisions between national markets. The CJ went on to conclude that the FAPL licensing arrangements were restrictive by object (the FAPL had not put forward any circumstances falling within the economic and legal context to justify a finding otherwise) and that the clauses of the licence did not meet the Article 101(3) conditions. In so ruling the Court followed and entrenched the traditional stance adopted in the jurisprudence for nearly fifty years, and cursorily dismissed arguments relating to the cultural and economic aspects of the IPRs underlying the broadcast rights. The rigidity of the approach adopted in this case may mean that in the future licensors grant pan-European rights or simply do not license in countries where the rights have lower cultural or economic appeal for fear that they could be exported to countries where the appeal is higher.

Cases C-403 and 429/08, *Premier League Ltd* v. *QC Leisure* and *Murphy* v. *Media Protection Services Ltd*, 4 October 2011

Court of Justice

134 By Question 10 in Case C-403/08 and Question 8 in Case C-429/08, the referring courts ask, in essence, whether the clauses of an exclusive licence agreement concluded between a holder of intellectual property rights and a broadcaster constitute a restriction on competition prohibited by Article 101 TFEU where they oblige the broadcaster not to supply decoding devices giving access to that right holder's protected subject-matter outside the territory covered by the licence agreement concerned.

135 First of all, it should be recalled that an agreement falls within the prohibition laid down in Article 101(1) TFEU when it has as its object or effect the prevention, restriction or distortion of competition. The fact that the two criteria are alternatives means that it is appropriate, first and foremost, to determine whether just one of them is satisfied, here the criterion concerning the object of the agreement. It is only secondarily, when the analysis of the content of the agreement does not reveal a sufficient degree of impairment of competition, that the consequences of the agreement should be considered, and for it to be open to prohibition it is necessary to find that those factors are present which show that competition has in fact been prevented, restricted or distorted to an appreciable extent (see, to this effect, Case C-8/08

---

[325] [2008] EWHC 44 (Ch).

[326] Cases C-403 and 429/08, *Premier League Ltd* v. *QC Leisure* and *Murphy* v. *Media Protection Services Ltd*, 4 October 2011, see n. 65 and accompanying text.

T-Mobile Netherlands and Others...paragraph 28, and Joined Cases C-501/06 P, C-513/06 P, C-515/06 P and C-519/06 P *GlaxoSmithKline Services and Others v Commission and Others*...paragraph 55).

136 In order to assess whether the object of an agreement is anti-competitive, regard must be had inter alia to the content of its provisions, the objectives it seeks to attain and the economic and legal context of which it forms a part (see, to this effect, *GlaxoSmithKline Services and Others v Commission and Others*, paragraph 58 and the case-law cited).

137 As regards licence agreements in respect of intellectual property rights, it is apparent from the Court's case-law that the mere fact that the right holder has granted to a sole licensee the exclusive right to broadcast protected subject-matter from a Member State, and consequently to prohibit its transmission by others, during a specified period is not sufficient to justify the finding that such an agreement has an anti-competitive object (see, to this effect, Case 262/81 *Coditel and Others ('Coditel II')*...paragraph 15).

138 That being so, and in accordance with Article 1(2)(b) of the Satellite Broadcasting Directive, a right holder may in principle grant to a sole licensee the exclusive right to broadcast protected subject-matter by satellite, during a specified period, from a single Member State of broadcast or from a number of Member States.

139 None the less, regarding the territorial limitations upon exercise of such a right, it is to be pointed out that, in accordance with the Court's case-law, an agreement which might tend to restore the divisions between national markets is liable to frustrate the Treaty's objective of achieving the integration of those markets through the establishment of a single market. Thus, agreements which are aimed at partitioning national markets according to national borders or make the interpenetration of national markets more difficult must be regarded, in principle, as agreements whose object is to restrict competition within the meaning of Article 101(1) TFEU (see, by analogy, in the field of medicinal products, Joined Cases C-468/06 to C-478/06 *Sot. Lélos kai Sia and Others* [2008] ECR I-7139, paragraph 65, and *GlaxoSmithKline Services and Others v Commission and Others*, paragraphs 59 and 61).

140 Since that case-law is fully applicable to the field of the cross-border provision of broadcasting services, as follows inter alia from paragraphs 118 to 121 of the present judgment, it must be held that, where a licence agreement is designed to prohibit or limit the cross-border provision of broadcasting services, it is deemed to have as its object the restriction of competition, unless other circumstances falling within its economic and legal context justify the finding that such an agreement is not liable to impair competition.

141 In the main proceedings, the actual grant of exclusive licences for the broadcasting of Premier League matches is not called into question. Those proceedings concern only the additional obligations designed to ensure compliance with the territorial limitations upon exploitation of those licences that are contained in the clauses of the contracts concluded between the right holders and the broadcasters concerned, namely the obligation on the broadcasters not to supply decoding devices enabling access to the protected subject-matter with a view to their use outside the territory covered by the licence agreement.

142 Such clauses prohibit the broadcasters from effecting any cross-border provision of services that relates to those matches, which enables each broadcaster to be granted absolute territorial exclusivity in the area covered by its licence and, thus, all competition between broadcasters in the field of those services to be eliminated.

143 Also, FAPL and others and MPS have not put forward any circumstance falling within the economic and legal context of such clauses that would justify the finding that, despite the considerations set out in the preceding paragraph, those clauses are not liable to impair competition and therefore do not have an anticompetitive object.

144 Accordingly, given that those clauses of exclusive licence agreements have an anticompetitive object, it is to be concluded that they constitute a prohibited restriction on competition for the purposes of Article 101(1) TFEU.

145 It should be added that while, in principle, Article 101(1) TFEU does not apply to agreements which fall within the categories specified in Article 101(3) TFEU, clauses of licence agreements such as the clauses at issue in the main proceedings do not meet the requirements laid down by the latter provision for reasons stated in paragraphs 105 to 124 of the present judgment and therefore the possibility of Article 101(1) TFEU being inapplicable does not arise.

146 In light of the foregoing, the answer to the questions referred is that the clauses of an exclusive licence agreement concluded between a holder of intellectual property rights and a broadcaster constitute a restriction on competition prohibited by Article 101 TFEU where they oblige the broadcaster not to supply decoding devices enabling access to that right holder's protected subject-matter with a view to their use outside the territory covered by that licence agreement.

There is almost no other precedent which indicates how *other* provisions in performance copyright licences will be appraised under Article 101. Further, as the Commission has not expanded the Guidance in the Technology Transfer Guidelines and Guidelines on Vertical Restraints to include these agreements, caution must be exercised in determining whether they are helpful in assessing the compatibility of provisions in performance copyright licences with Article 101.[327] In 2004, the Commission indicated that it might be suspicious of favoured nation clauses incorporated in such contracts. In a press release, it reported that it had closed an investigation into contracts concluded by certain of the major Hollywood studios. These contracts, providing for the sale of their entire film production to European pay-TV broadcasters, had originally included most favoured nation clauses, giving the studios the right to enjoy the most favourable terms agreed between a pay-TV company and any one of them. The Commission considered that the cumulative effect of these clauses was an alignment of prices paid to the studios for the broadcasting rights. It closed its investigation into the contracts of six of the studios after they withdrew the clauses.[328]

C. COLLECTIVE LICENSING OF COPYRIGHT

As with technology pooling, the collective licensing of copyright may frequently be pro-competitive and necessary to the operation of an agreement.[329] Generally a benign approach has been taken (under Article 102 and Article 101) to the conduct of collecting societies which manage authors' rights in the musical works which they have created, in particular by licensing categories of rights to commercial users on behalf of the societies' members.[330] Collecting societies exist because of the impracticality of performers, musicians, etc. individually giving permission for their work to be performed or collecting royalties. Performers' rights societies are usually organised on a national basis and often have a *de facto* monopoly. Their activities have often given rise to competition law problems under Article 102. The Commission is concerned to address the issue of collecting societies as a whole and published a Communication on this in 2004.[331] Further, in *Kanal 5 v. STIM*[332] the CJ set out guidance on the question of when a copyright management organisation holding a dominant

---

[327] For a fuller discussion of how individual clauses may be appraised under Art. 101 see Allan et al. (eds.), *Butterworths Competition Law* (cited in n. 1), Div V, chap. 5.

[328] IP/04/1314.

[329] See, e.g., *Joint Selling of commercial rights to the UEFA Champions League* [2003] OJ L291/25.

[330] See, e.g., T-224/95, *Tremblay v. Commission* [1997] ECR II-2215, Case 195/87, *Ministère Public v. Tournier* [1989] ECT 2521.

[331] Communication from the Commission to the Council, European Parliament and ESC on the Management of Copyright and Related Rights in the Internal Market COM(2004) 261 final. See also, e.g., the commitments adopted in relation to the Cannes Agreement, see IP/06/1311.

[332] Case C-52/07, *Kanal 5 v. STIM* [2008] ECR I-9275, judgment of 11 December 2008.

position might abuse that dominant position by engaging in excessive or discriminatory pricing practices.

Further, in *CISAC*,[333] the Commission became concerned about clauses in model contracts drawn up by the International Confederation of Societies of Authors and Composers (CISAC) and to be completed by contracting collecting societies. It declined, following market testing, to accept commitments offered by CISAC[334] and held that a number of clauses infringed Article 101(1) and that national territorial limitations (limiting the ability of each collecting society to offer services outside its domestic territory) resulted from a concerted practice which restricted competition between the collecting societies. On appeal, however, the GC[335] held that the Commission had not established, to the requisite legal standard, the existence of a concerted practice between the collecting societies to fix the national territorial limitations and had not put forward sufficient evidence to render implausible the collecting societies' explanation for their parallel conduct, based on the need to ensure the effectiveness of the fight against the unauthorised use of musical works. As no concerted practice was established the GC did not have to examine the argument put forward by CISAC that the national territorial limitations were not restrictive of competition but were necessary 'in order to avoid a race to the bottom with regard to royalties and to maintaining the existence of national one-stop-shops'.[336]

9. THE APPLICATION OF ARTICLE 102 TO INTELLECTUAL PROPERTY RIGHTS

There are two facets to the relationship between Article 102 and IPRs. First, there is the extent to which the ownership of IPRs puts the holder in a dominant position. Secondly, there is the question whether the holding, acquisition, or exploitation of IPRs can constitute an abuse of a dominant position, and if so in what circumstances.

The application of Article 102 to IPRs is dealt with in Chapters 6 and 7 because it is impossible to divorce these questions about IPRs from the operation of Article 102 as a whole. Looking at them in isolation from other developments in Article 102 jurisprudence can lead to an incomplete and distorted picture. Reference should therefore be made to those chapters.

10. CONCLUSIONS

1. The TTBER and Guidelines adopt a more economic approach to IP licensing agreements. The TTBER sets out a presumption that technology transfer agreements which do not incorporate hardcore restraints and which are concluded between undertakings which do not exceed the market share thresholds are compatible with Article 101.

2. As with the approach to vertical agreements, the centrality of the TTBER means that the main focus of attention is still on whether or not a technology transfer agreement is compatible with Article 101(3), not whether it is compatible with Article 101(1), i.e. whether it actually restricts competition.

---

[333] COMP/38.698 *CISAC*, 16 July 2008.

[334] [2007] OJ C128/12.

[335] Case T-442/08, *International Confederation of Societies of Authors and Composers (CISAC) v. Commission*, 12 April 2013.

[336] Case T-442/08, para. 183.

3. In contrast with the position for vertical agreements, however, in practice it is likely to be much harder for firms to be sure about compliance with the provisions of the TTBER. Not only is it inherently more difficult to define technology markets but the hardcore and excluded restraints are more complex than those set out in the Verticals Regulation.

4. The practical reality is, therefore, that in many situations parties to IP licensing agreements will have to rely on self-assessment to determine their agreement's compatibility with Article 101. As there is relatively little decisional practice and case law dealing with IP licensing agreements, reliance on the Technology Transfer Guidelines and Article 101(3) Guidelines will be essential. As trade mark and copyright licences are generally not covered by the TTBER and Guidelines, recourse to general Article 101 principles will be necessary in such cases.

11. FURTHER READING

A. BOOKS

ANDERMAN, S. D., *EC Competition Law and Intellectual Property Rights* (Clarendon Press, 1988)

—— and KALLAUGHER, J., *Technology Transfer and the New EU Competition Rules: IP Licensing after Modernisation* (Oxford University Press, 2006)

GOVAERE, I., *The Use and Abuse of Intellectual Property Rights in EC Law* (Sweet & Maxwell, 1996)

KORAH, V., *Intellectual Property Rights and the EC Competition Rules* (Hart Publishing, 2006)

B. CHAPTERS IN BOOKS

ANDERMAN, S. D., 'Substantial Convergence: the US influence on the development of the regulatory framework for IP licensing in the EC' in P. Marsden

(ed.), *Handbook of Research In Trans-Atlantic Antitrust* (Edward Elgar Publishing, 2007)

C. ARTICLES

AITMAN, D., and JONES A., 'Competition and Copyright: has the copyright owner lost control?' [2003] *EIPR* 137

ANDERMAN, S. D., 'EC Competition Law and Intellectual Property Rights in the New Economy' [2002] *Ant Bull* 285

COTTER, T. F., 'Intellectual Property and the Essential Facilities Doctrine' [1999] *Ant Bull* 211

DOLMANS, M., and PIILOLA, A., 'The New Technology Transfer Block Exemption, A Welcome Reform After All' (2004) 27(3) *World Competition* 351

PEEPERKORN, L., 'IP Licences and Competition Rules: Striking the Right Balance' (2003) 26 *World Competition* 527

VENIT, J., 'In the Wake of Windsurfing: Patent Licensing in the Common Market' [1986] Fordham Corp L Inst 517

13

PUBLIC ENFORCEMENT BY THE COMMISSION AND THE NATIONAL COMPETITION AUTHORITIES OF THE ANTITRUST PROVISIONS

1. CENTRAL ISSUES

1. The EU's method for enforcing the competition rules is primarily by a public enforcement system.

2. The system for enforcing Articles 101 and 102 was fundamentally changed on 1 May 2004 when Regulation 1/2003 replaced Regulation 17 of 1962. Regulation 1/2003 rendered Article 101(3) directly applicable and 'decentralised' the enforcement of the antitrust provisions so that the Commission and the national competition authorities (NCAs) have parallel competence to apply the rules. The European Competition Network (ECN) is the network of national competition authorities and the Commission working in close cooperation with one another.

3. The Commission's own powers of enforcement, previously contained in Regulation 17, are now set out in Regulation 1/2003. The Commission combines investigative, prosecutorial, and adjudicative functions in one body.

4. In investigating suspected breaches of the competition rules the Commission may require information and may carry out, inter alia, unannounced inspections at the premises of undertakings, and at private homes.

5. There are questions about the compatibility of some aspects of the Commission's procedures with fundamental rights as provided for in the European Convention on Human Rights and the EU Charter.

6. The Commission may take a number of decisions, including decisions ordering terminations of infringements, imposing fines, or accepting commitments. It can impose behavioural or structural remedies. Commitments decisions were introduced by Regulation 1/2003 and are an increasingly important instrument in the hands of the Commission.

7. The Commission pursues an aggressive policy towards the detection and punishment of cartels. It operates a 'leniency policy' whereby participants in cartels are given immunity or a reduced penalty in exchange for providing the Commission with information about the cartel and their co-conspirators. The Commission imposes heavy fines on undertakings found to have committed serious breaches of the competition rules. In 2008 it adopted a new direct settlement procedure to enable it to dispose more quickly of cartel cases where the undertakings admit liability.

8. Commission decisions in competition cases are subject to judicial review by the EU Court. The extent of the compatibility of the judicial review with the European Convention on Human Rights and the EU Charter is a matter of controversy.

9 Decentralisation and the parallel enforcement competence of the NCAs mean that there are complex procedures and arrangements within the ECN formatters such as allocating cases and sharing information.

10. Complaints about breaches of the competition rules play an important role. The Commission has no duty to pursue complaints but is obliged to make a formal rejection of them—and this can be challenged before the EU Courts.

2. INTRODUCTION

The primary method of enforcement of the EU antitrust rules is by way of public enforcement by the Commission and the competition authorities of the Member States (NCAs). A fundamental change in the enforcement system was made in 2004. The powers to enable the Commission to carry out its task of enforcing the competition rules are now contained in Council Regulation 1/2003,[1] which also confers enforcement powers on the NCAs.

In Section 3 of this chapter we explain the change in the enforcement regime which took place on 1 May 2004. In Section 4 we describe briefly the system under Regulation 17 which applied before then. In Section 5 the reasons for, and salient features of, the 'modernisation' in Regulation 1/2003 are considered. In Sections 6, 7, and 8 the powers of the Commission are examined. In Section 9 we look at role of the EU Courts. In Sections 10 and 11 we deal with enforcement by NCAs and the relationship between EU and national law. In Section 12 we consider the possibility of sanctions against individuals and in Section 13 the position of those who make complaints about alleged infringements of the competition rules. Some conclusions are set out in Section 14.[2]

3. THE CHANGE TO THE ENFORCEMENT REGIME IN MAY 2004

Regulation 1/2003[3] is the linchpin of the 'modernised' enforcement regime. We have already seen that the modernisation of EU competition law has included a more 'economic' approach to the substantive law[4] and a revised Merger Regulation (EUMR).[5] Regulation 1/2003 introduced fundamental changes to the way in which Articles 101 and 102 are enforced.

The previous implementing legislation, Regulation 17,[6] conferred the central role in the application and enforcement of EC competition law upon the Commission and the role of the NCAs and national courts was peripheral. Regulation 1/2003 'decentralised' application and enforcement and gave the NCAs a greater role. Furthermore, the reforms were designed to encourage more 'private' enforcement of competition law through litigation in the national courts of the Member States. 'Decentralisation' therefore means decentralisation to the national courts as well as to the NCAs. Private enforcement through civil litigation in the national courts is discussed in Chapter 14.

The post-modernisation enforcement of Articles 101 and 102 by the Commission has in practice become notable for a heavy reliance on negotiated procedures. This was not an (express) aim of the modernisation, but Regulation 1/2003 contains a new procedure for 'commitments decisions'[7] of which the Commission makes great use in non-cartel cases.[8] In respect of cartels the Commission introduced a 'settlement procedure' in 2008. These developments have changed Commission enforcement more radically than might have been anticipated in 2004.

---

[1] [2003] OJ L1/1.

[2] For a detailed account of enforcement procedure, reference should be had to practitioners' books. See e.g. C. Kerse and N. Khan (Khan ed.), *EU Antitrust Procedure* (6th edn, Sweet and Maxwell, 2012); L. Ortiz Blanco, *EU Competition Procedure* (3rd edn, Oxford University Press, 2013); Bellamy and Child (V. Rose and D. Bailey, eds.), *European Law of Competition* (7th edn, Oxford University Press, 2013), Chaps. 13–16.

[3] [2003] OJ L1/1.

[4] See in particular Chaps. 4, 10, 11, and 12 in respect of Article 101, and Chaps. 5–7 in respect of Art. 102.

[5] Reg. 139/2004, [2004] OJ L24/1, see Chap. 15.

[6] [1959–1962] OJ Spec. Ed. 87.

[7] Regulation 1/2003, Art. 9, see Section 8.D.iii, p. 982.

[8] Commission Notice on the conduct of settlement procedures [2008] OJ C167/1, see Section 8.E, p. 992.

A significant number of the Articles of Regulation 1/2003 are identical in effect (if not in exact wording) to Articles in Regulation 17. In respect of these the previous case law applies to the new provisions as to the old. In 40 years of pronouncing on the Commission's powers under Regulation 17 the EU Courts laid down and developed many important principles governing the exercise of the Commission's powers which also apply in the modernised system.

Some extracts in this chapter contain references to Articles in Regulation 17. The original numbers have been left intact and the corresponding Articles in Regulation 1/2003 indicated where necessary.

4. THE OLD ENFORCEMENT REGIME SET UP BY REGULATION 17

Regulation 17[9] set up a system whereby an agreement falling within Article 101(1) could only escape via Article 101(3) if it was 'exempted'. The granting of an exemption was a 'constitutive act'. There were two ways of obtaining exemption. First, the parties could bring their agreement within a 'block exemption' regulation. It is still possible to do this. Block exemptions are an important part of the current system and are examined in various chapters of this book.[10] Secondly, the parties could obtain an individual exemption from the Commission. Article 9(1) of Regulation 17 conferred 'sole power' on the Commission 'to declare Article [101(1)] inapplicable pursuant to Article [101(3)]'. From this simple monopoly enormous consequences flowed.[11] Article 4(1) of Regulation 17 provided that parties to an agreement seeking an exemption had to notify it to the Commission. Until they did so, no decision pursuant to Article 101(3) could be taken. Only notification gave the possibility of exemption.[12] Agreements could also be notified for 'negative clearance', i.e. a decision finding that an agreement did not infringe Article 101(1) at all.[13] Article 15(5) of Regulation 17 provided those that notified with immunity from fines.[14]

When notifying an agreement it was necessary for the parties and the Commission to comply with the requisite procedure.[15] Notification had to be made in the prescribed format.[16] Following notification there were no time limits within which the Commission had to give a decision.[17]

Decisions granting individual exemption could be issued only for a specified period and could be made subject to conditions and obligations.[18] The decisions had to specify the date from which they

---

[9] [1959–1962] OJ Spec. Ed. 87.

[10] For block exemptions generally, see Chap. 4.

[11] For an account of the workings of the system under Reg. 17, see J. Goyder and A. Albors-Llorens, *Goyder's EC Competition Law* (5th edn, Oxford University Press, 2009), Chaps. 4 and 5.

[12] Certain agreements could be exempted retrospectively to the date that the agreement was concluded irrespective of whether they had or had not been notified. Non-notifiable agreements were defined in Reg. 17, Art. 4(2), as amended by Reg. 1216/99 [1999] OJ L148/5, to cover all vertical agreements.

[13] Reg. 17, Art. 2. Negative clearance could also be sought in respect of Art. 102.

[14] The immunity could be lifted under Reg. 17, Art. 15(6) following a preliminary examination of the agreement by the Commission.

[15] Antitrust Procedure (Applications and Notifications) Reg. 3385/94 [1994] OJ L377/28, replacing Reg. 27/62 [1959–1962] OJ Spec. Ed. 132 as amended, in respect of notifications under Reg. 17; Reg. 2843/98 [1998] OJ L354/22 adopted a single form for notification of agreements within the transport sector.

[16] Form A/B, set out in Reg. 3385/94, which required extensive information. Some block exemptions contained an 'opposition procedure' whereby agreements not falling precisely within the terms of the block exemption could be notified to the Commission and allowed to benefit from the block exemption unless 'opposed' by the Commission within a specified time limit. e.g., Reg. 240/96 on technology transfer agreements [1996] OJ L31/2.

[17] Except that in 1993 a 'fast-track' was introduced for the treatment of structural joint ventures: Reg. 3385/94, Form A/B, Introduction, Section D.

[18] Reg. 17, Art. 8(1). The parties could apply for it to be renewed (Reg. 17, Art. 8(2)). In certain circumstances they could be revoked or amended (Reg. 17, Art. 8(3)).

ran and the general rule was that this could not be earlier than the date of notification.[19] This meant that a non-notified agreement which infringed Article 101(1) was void pursuant to Article 101(2) even if, had it been notified, it would have merited exemption pursuant to Article 101(3).[20] Such an agreement was not, therefore, enforceable in a national court in respect of the period between the agreement coming into force and its notification. This was one reason for the large number of notifications the Commission received. In practice the Commission could not issue decisions granting exemption or negative clearance to all notified agreements. It granted a formal decision to a very small percentage of the notifications that it received.[21] The remainder were dealt with informally by administrative letter, a 'comfort letter'. The comfort letter enabled the Commission to deal with notifications whilst giving priority to cases which raised greater concern from the Community perspective. The system was far from satisfactory however.[22]

The use of comfort letters rather than formal decisions meant that for many years prior to 1 May 2004 the notification-and-exemption procedure did not operate in real life as had been intended by Regulation 17.

5. MODERNISATION

A. THE MODERNISATION WHITE PAPER

In 1999 the Commission adopted a White Paper on modernisation of the rules implementing Articles 101 and 102.[23] The Commission wanted to promote greater decentralisation of enforcement through the national courts and NCAs.[24] However, the Commission's exclusive right to grant individual exemptions under Article 101(3) made it difficult for national courts and NCAs to participate fully in the enforcement process.[25] Further, the widespread perception that the Commission alone enforced the competition rules meant that undertakings preferred to complain to the Commission rather than bring private proceedings before the national courts. The net result was that the Commission's limited resources were spent dealing with exemptions for essentially innocuous agreements leaving less available for the detection and prohibition of more serious violations of the rules. Moreover, the problem was about to worsen in view of the imminent further expansion of the European Union.[26]

The obvious way of reforming the system was to confer power on the NCAs to grant individual exemptions. The Commission had consistently resisted this idea. The White Paper proposed a far more radical and fundamental change, namely complete abolition of the notification-and-exemption system. Article 101(3) should become a 'directly applicable exception'. The decision on whether or not an agreement fulfilled the criteria in Article 101(3) would no longer be taken by the Commission after notification. Rather, the decision would be made by a national court if the matter were relevant to litigation before it, or by an NCA or the Commission itself if the matter became of concern. In

---

[19] Reg. 17, Art. 6(1). There was an exception to this in respect of 'non-notifiable' agreements under Art. 4(2): see n. 12.

[20] Reg. 17, Art. 6(1), art 4(2).

[21] The Commission stated in its White Paper on modernisation of the rules implementing Articles 85 and 86 [1999] OJ C132/1, para. 34, that 91% of cases (150–200 letters per year) were settled informally.

[22] For example, although assuring the parties that the Commission would not pursue the matter further, the letter was not a decision which could be applied by the national courts and consequently did not give the parties the same degree of legal certainty as that which resulted from a decision.

[23] White Paper on modernisation of the rules implementing Articles 85 and 86 of the EU Treaty [1999] OJ C132/1.

[24] The problems of the private enforcement of EU competition law are discussed in Chap. 14, where it will be seen that modernisation has by no means solved them all.

[25] Indeed, at the time of the White Paper only half of the NCAs had power under their domestic law to enforce the EC competition rules.

[26] Ten new Member States acceded on 1 May 2004 and two more (Bulgaria and Romania) in January 2007.

other words, *ex ante* control would be replaced by *ex post* control.[27] Undertakings would, therefore, be deprived of the comfort of being able to notify and receive assurance of the compatibility of their agreement with Article 101. Instead they would be left to judge for themselves the legitimacy of their arrangements.[28] The White Paper called for 'intensified *ex post* control' in which the Commission's powers of enquiry would be strengthened and it would be easier to lodge complaints.[29]

The proposals generated much debate.[30] One issue was whether Article 101(3) could be directly applied as an exception to the Article 101(1) prohibition (the doctrine '*de l'exception légale*') or whether the wording of Article 101(3) 'may...be declared inapplicable' required a constitutive act of a public authority to lift the Article 101(1) prohibition.[31] Another was whether Article 101(3) was suitable for direct application in national courts. This point was bound up with the debate about whether in the application of Article 101(3) other 'non-competition' factors, such as social, cultural, industrial, and environmental considerations, can be taken into account.[32]

The Commission recognised in the White Paper the critical importance of ensuring that the consistent and uniform application of the competition rules was maintained and not jeopardised. The great advantage of the system set up by Regulation 17 was that it had left the application and enforcement of the competition rules in the hands of one body (subject only to review by the Court) which, by maintaining its iron grip, had directed the development of competition policy and ensured that the law was applied uniformly across the Community. The limited private litigation in national courts at least meant that this uniformity was not significantly compromised. The Commission was determined that its proposal for decentralisation should not be accompanied by divergent application among the various Member States. The White Paper thus proposed mechanisms and procedures to ensure continuing coherence and consistency.[33]

The Commission recognised that the abolition of the notification and authorisation system would entail greater responsibility on undertakings in ensuring that they complied with the competition rules. The Commission's official view was that 'undertakings are generally well placed to assess the legality of their actions in such a way as to enable them to take an informed decision on whether to go ahead with an agreement or practice and in what form'.[34]

---

[27] In fact *ex post* control was already exercised in respect of cartel-type arrangements where the parties knew they were infringing the competition rules. They were most unlikely to notify and would be striving to keep their agreements secret.

[28] Unless the transaction was a partial-function production joint venture; see the White Paper, para. 79, see n. 23. This suggestion was ultimately abandoned.

[29] White Paper on modernisation, para. 108.

[30] See R. Whish and B. Sufrin, 'Community Competition Law: Notification and Individual Exemption: Goodbye to All that', in D. Hayton (ed.), *Law's Future(s)* (Hart Publishing, 2000); C. D. Ehlermann and I. Atanasiu (eds.), *European Competition Law Annual 2000: The Modernisation of EC Antitrust Policy* (Hart Publishing, 2001); C. D. Ehlermann and I. Atanasiu (eds.), *European Competition Law Annual 2001: Effective Enforcement of EC Antitrust Law* (Hart Publishing, 2003); W. Wils, *The Optimal Enforcement of EC Antitrust Law* (Kluwer Law International, 2002); [2000] Fordham Corp L Inst (B. Hawk (ed.)); B. Rodger, 'The Commission White Paper on Modernisation of the Rules Implementing Articles 101 and 102 of the EC Treaty' (1999) 24 *ELRev* 653; R. Wesseling, 'The Commission White Paper on Modernisation of EC Antitrust: Unspoken Consequences and Incomplete Treatment of Alternative Options' [1999] *ECLR* 420; R. Wesseling, 'The Draft Regulation Modernising the Competition Rules: the Commission is Married to One Idea' (2001) 26 *ELRev* 357; D. Gerber, 'Modernising European Competition Law: A Developmental Perspective' [2001] *ECLR* 122.

[31] In the White Paper the Commission stated that the delegations from the original six future Member States who drafted the EC Treaty could not decide between a directly applicable system and an authorisation system, as some favoured one and some the other. Art. 101(3) was therefore deliberately drafted to allow for either possibility. It was only on the adoption of Reg. 17 that the Community legislator finally chose an authorisation system. The main proponent of the view that Art. 101(3) did not allow for a directly applicable exception was the German Government: see summary of observations on the White Paper, DG Comp. Doc. 29 February 2000, para. 3.2. The arguments were set out in the submissions of the German Monopolkommission.

[32] See Chap. 4.

[33] Coherence and consistency are not necessarily the same thing, see C. Townley 'Which Goals Count in Article 101 TFEU?: Public Policy and its Discontents' (2011) *ECLR* 441, 446.

[34] Commission Notice on informal guidance relating to novel questions concerning Articles 81 and 82 that arise in individual cases (guidance letters) [2004] OJ C101/78, para. 3.

The changes made in 2004 shifted the focus of the Commission's enforcement. The Commission now expends more of its resources on cartels and abuses of dominance rather than on vertical agreements (unless they involve price-fixing and market-sharing) and horizontal cooperation agreements.

B. THE MODERNISATION 'PACKAGE'

(i) Regulation 1/2003, the Implementing Regulation, and the Modernisation Notices

After an extensive consultation exercise the Commission's proposal to abolish notification, render Article 101(3) a directly applicable exception, and decentralise the application and enforcement of the competition rules was accepted. The Council adopted Regulation 1/2003 on 16 December 2002[35] and it replaced Regulation 17 on 1 May 2004. The adoption of Regulation 1/2003 was accompanied by a number of Notices which flesh out the bare bones of the Regulation. A major concern was to establish mechanisms and procedures for the cooperation between the Commission and the NCAs, without which the new decentralisation could not work. The creation of the European Competition Network (ECN) has been of great importance in this respect. The 'modernisation package' thus consisted of the following:

(i)   Council Regulation 1/2003;

(ii)   Commission Regulation 773/2004 on the conduct of proceedings by the Commission pursuant to Articles 81 and 82 (the Implementing Regulation);[36]

(iii)   Commission Notice on cooperation within the network of competition authorities;[37]

(iv)   Commission Notice on cooperation between the Commission and the courts of the EU Member States in the application of Articles 81 and 82;[38]

(v)   Commission Notice on the handling of complaints;[39]

(vi)   Commission Notice on informal guidance relating to novel questions concerning Articles 81 and 82 that arise in individual cases (guidance letters);[40]

(vii)   Guidelines on the effect on trade concept contained in Articles 81 and 82;[41]

(viii) Guidelines on the application of Article 81(3).[42]

(ii) Informal Guidance

Regulation 1/2003 abolished the notification and exemption procedure but recital 38 states:

Legal certainty for undertakings operating under the Community competition rules contributes to the promotion of innovation and investment. Where cases give rise to genuine uncertainty because they present novel or unresolved questions for the application of these rules, individual undertakings may wish to seek informal guidance from the Commission. This Regulation is without prejudice to the ability of the Commission to issue such informal guidance.

---

[35] [2003] OJ L1/1.
[36] [2004] OJ L123/18.
[37] [2004] OJ C101/43.
[38] [2004] OJ C101/54.
[39] [2004] OJ C101/65.
[40] [2004] OJ C101/78.
[41] [2004] OJ C101/101.
[42] [2004] OJ C101/96.

The Commission set out in a Notice[43] the circumstances in which it may consider it appropriate to issue such informal guidance. This states that the new enforcement system 'is designed to restore the focus on the primary task of effective enforcement' by rendering Article 101(3) directly applicable and doing away with notification[44] and that undertakings are best placed to assess the legality of their actions, given the block exemptions, notices, case law, and case practice which are available to assist them.[45] Nevertheless, it recognises that in some situations this may not be adequate. It will therefore provide informal guidance to individual undertakings 'in so far as this is compatible with its enforcement priorities'.[46]

Commission Notice on Informal Guidance Relating to Novel Questions Concerning Articles 81 and 82 that Arise in Individual Cases (Guidance Letters) [2004] OJ C101/78

5. Where cases, despite the above elements, give rise to genuine uncertainty because they present novel or unresolved questions for the application of Articles [101 and 102], individual undertakings may wish to seek informal guidance from the Commission…Where it considers it appropriate and subject to its enforcement priorities, the Commission may provide such guidance on novel questions concerning the interpretation of Articles [101 and/or 102] in a written statement (guidance letter). The present Notice sets out details of this instrument.

…

8. Subject to point 7, [the enforcement priorities of the Commission] the Commission, seized of a request for a guidance letter, will consider whether it is appropriate to process it. Issuing a guidance letter may only be considered if the following cumulative conditions are fulfilled:

(a) The substantive assessment of an agreement or practice with regard to Articles [101 and/or 102], poses a question of application of the law for which there is no clarification in the existing [EU] legal framework including the case law of the [Union judicature], nor publicly available general guidance or precedent in decision-making practice or previous guidance letters.

(b) A prima facie evaluation of the specificities and background of the case suggests that the clarification of the novel question through a guidance letter is useful, taking into account the following elements:
— the economic importance from the point of view of the consumer of the goods or services concerned by the agreement or practice, and/or
— the extent to which the agreement or practice corresponds or is liable to correspond to more widely spread economic usage in the marketplace and/or
— the extent of the investments linked to the transaction in relation to the size of the companies concerned and the extent to which the transaction relates to a structural operation such as the creation of a non-full function joint venture.

(c) It is possible to issue a guidance letter on the basis of the information provided, i.e., no further fact-finding is required.

---

[43] Commission Notice on informal guidance relating to novel questions concerning Articles 81 and 82 that arise in individual cases (guidance letters) [2004] OJ C101/78.

[44] Commission Notice on informal guidance, para. 1.

[45] Commission Notice on informal guidance, paras. 3 and 4.

[46] Commission Notice on informal guidance, para. 7.

The condition in paragraph 8(a) emphasises that guidance will be given only in respect of 'novel' questions. The Commission is the judge of the novelty. In respect of the second condition, the 'usefulness' of the guidance, the first two indents in 8(b) show that an element of 'public interest' is relevant. The third indent specifically indicates that guidance letters may be forthcoming in certain cases involving non-full function joint ventures.[47] The Commission will not issue a guidance letter if it would entail further fact-finding. It is entirely up to parties to provide the necessary information.[48]

Guidance letters will not be issued if the questions (identical or similar) are raised in a case pending before the EU Courts, or the agreement or practice in issue is subject to proceedings before the Commission, an NCA, or a national court in a Member State.[49] They will not be issued in respect of hypothetical questions or agreements or practices that are no longer being implemented. They will, however, be considered in respect of an agreement or practice which is envisaged but not yet implemented, so long as it has reached a sufficiently advanced stage.[50] Guidance letters do not prevent the Commission opening proceedings under Regulation 1/2003 with regard to the same facts (although it will take the letter into account),[51] do not prejudge any assessment by the EU Courts,[52] and do not bind the NCAs or national courts, although NCAs and national courts are entitled to take the Commission's views in the guidance letters into account 'in the context of a case'.[53] The letters are to be posted on the Commission's website.[54]

As at 1 July 2013 no Guidance Letters had been posted on the Commission's website. In the Staff Working Paper[55] in April 2009 the Commission said that it had issued no letters up to then because very few approaches had been made to it, and none of those that had been made came near to fulfilling the conditions set out in the Notice.[56] Nevertheless the Commission 'remains firmly committed' to giving guidance on new or unresolved policy issues of general application which *do* fulfil the conditions.[57]

(iii) Council Regulation 1/2003

Broadly, Regulation 1/2003 deals with two matters. First, it renders Article 101(3) directly applicable and lays down the basic framework for the Commission, the NCAs, and the national courts to cooperate in the decentralised system. Secondly, it provides for the powers and procedures of the Commission in the investigation of competition matters. It accomplishes the shift from *ex ante* to *ex post* control.

Regulation 1/2003 contains 11 Chapters and 45 Articles, as follows:

- **Chapter I Principles**

  - Article 1 The application of Articles 101 and 102.

  - Article 2 Burden of proof.

  - Article 3 The relationship between Articles 101 and 102 and national competition laws.

---

[47] In respect of which the abolition of notification was recognised in the White Paper as being particularly serious.

[48] Commission Notice on informal guidance, para. 8(c). There is no form or format on or in which the information must be provided, but para. 14 lists the matters which the memorandum accompanying a request for a guidance letter should contain.

[49] Commission Notice on informal guidance, para. 9.

[50] Commission Notice on informal guidance, para. 10.

[51] Commission Notice on informal guidance, paras. 11 and 24.

[52] Commission Notice on informal guidance, para. 23.

[53] Commission Notice on informal guidance, para. 24.

[54] Commission Notice on informal guidance, para. 21.

[55] Commission Staff Working paper on the functioning of Regulation 1/2003, SEC (2009) 574 final.

[56] Commission Notice on informal guidance, para. 45.

[57] Commission Staff Working Paper (see n. 55), para. 48.

- **Chapter II Powers**
  - Article 4 Statement that in applying Articles 101 and 102 the Commission has the powers provided for in this Regulation.
  - Article 5 Powers of the NCAs.
  - Article 6 Powers of the national courts.

- **Chapter III Commission Decisions**
  - Article 7 The Commission's power to order the termination of infringements and the types of remedy it can impose. Article 7(2) explains who can lodge a complaint with the Commission.
  - Article 8 The Commission's power to order interim measures.
  - Article 9 The Commission's power to make binding the commitments offered by undertakings.
  - Article 10 The Commission's power to make findings of inapplicability.

- **Chapter IV Cooperation**
  - Article 11 Procedures for cooperation between the Commission and the NCAs.
  - Article 12 Exchanges of information between the Commission and the NCAs and between the NCAs *inter se* .
  - Article 13 The suspension or termination of proceedings.
  - Article 14 The Advisory Committee on Restrictive Practices and Dominant Positions.
  - Article 15 Cooperation with national courts.
  - Article 16 The uniform application of EU competition law (Commission decisions are binding on national courts).

- **Chapter V Powers of Investigation**
  - Article 17 Investigations into sectors of the economy and into types of agreement.
  - Article 18 Requests for information.
  - Article 19 Power of the Commission to interview and take statements.
  - Article 20 The Commission's powers of inspection of undertakings.
  - Article 21 Commission power to inspect other premises, including the homes of the directors, managers, and staff of undertakings.
  - Article 22 Investigations (inspections) by NCAs.

- **Chapter VI Penalties**
  - Article 23 The Commission's power to fine.
  - Article 24 The Commission's power to impose periodic penalty payments.

- **Chapter VII Limitation Periods**
  - Article 25 Limitation periods for the imposition of penalties.
  - Article 26 Limitation periods for the enforcement of penalties.

- **Chapter VIII Hearings and Professional Secrecy**
  - Article 27 Hearings before the Commission takes decisions. Article 27(2) gives a right of access to the file.
  - Article 28 Professional secrecy.

- **Chapter IX Exemption Regulations**
  - Article 29 General power of withdrawal of block exemptions in individual cases.

- **Chapter X General Provisions**
  - Article 30 The publication of decisions.

- **Chapter XI Transitional, Amending and Final Provisions**
  - Article 31 Unlimited jurisdiction of the CJEU to review Commission decisions imposing fines or periodic penalty payments.
  - Article 32 Matters excluded from the scope of the Regulation.
  - Article 33 Power of the Commission to take implementing measures.
  - Article 34 Transitional provisions.
  - Article 35 Designation by the Member States of the responsible competition authorities.
  - Articles 36–42 Amendment of other Regulations.
  - Article 43 Repeal of Regulation 17 (except for Article 8(3), which means that the Commission may revoke or amend an existing individual exemption decision until it expires) and Regulation 141.
  - Article 44 Commission shall report to the European Parliament and the Council on the application of Regulation 1/2003 after five years.
  - Article 45 Regulation 1/2003 to apply from 1 May 2004.

Regulation 1/2003, Article 44 provides that five years from the application of the Regulation the Commission should report on its functioning to the Council and the European Parliament. On the basis of the Report the Commission must assess whether to propose any revisions. Pursuant to this the Commission launched a public consultation exercise in July 2008[58] and adopted the Report on 29 April 2009. The Report[59] (hereafter the Report) was accompanied by a more extensive Commission Staff Working Paper (hereafter the Working Paper).[60] The Commission's overall conclusion was that Regulation 1/2003 works well:[61]

Regulation 1/2003 has brought about a landmark change in the way the European competition law is enforced. The Regulation has significantly improved the Commission's enforcement of Articles [101 and 102 TFEU]. The Commission has been able to become more proactive, tackling weaknesses in the competitiveness of key sectors of the economy in a focused way.

There were a few matters which the Commission highlighted as meriting further evaluation but it left open the question as to whether any amendments were required.[62] The views of the Commission on specific matters in Regulation 1/2003 are dealt with in this chapter in the appropriate sections.

(iv) Commission Regulation 773/2004

Regulation 773/2004[63] deals with the conduct of Commission proceedings in its application of the competition rules. It covers in more detail some of the matters provided for in Regulation 1/2003

---

[58] IP/08/1203.

[59] Communication from the Commission to the European Parliament and the Council, Report on the Functioning of Regulation 1/2003 COM(2009) 206 final; Press Release IP/09/683.

[60] Commission Staff Working Paper accompanying the Communication from the Commission to the European Parliament and the Council, Report on the Functioning of Regulation 1/2003 SEC(2009) 574 final. The Report and the Working Paper are available on the Commission website, <http://ec.europa.eu/competition/antitrust/legislation/regulations.html>.

[61] Report, para. 41.

[62] Report, para. 43.

[63] [2004] OJ L123/18, as amended by Commission Reg. 622/2008 [2008] OJ L171/3 on the conduct of settlement procedures in cartel cases.

(such as power to take statements, the handling of complaints, the exercise of the right of the parties and others to be heard[64] and the right of 'access to the file'). The provisions of Regulation 773/2004 are discussed in this chapter in the context of the matters to which they relate.

(v) The Modernisation Notices

The Commission's Modernisation Notices are discussed and referred to throughout this book. The Commission Notice on cooperation within the network of competition authorities,[65] the Commission Notice on cooperation between the Commission and the courts of the EU Member States,[66] and the Commission Notice on the handling of complaints are of particular relevance to this chapter and Chapter 14.[67]

6. THE EUROPEAN COMPETITION NETWORK

The European Competition Network (ECN) is the network of NCAs and the Commission who under Regulation 1/2003 share parallel competence to apply and enforce Articles 101 and 102. The close cooperation of the authorities is crucial to the effective operation of the decentralised system. This is dealt with further in Section 10.

7. THE BEST PRACTICES NOTICE AND THE MANUAL OF PROCEDURES

In 2011 the Commission published a Notice on 'Best Practices for the Conduct of Proceedings' (hereafter Best Practices) to give practical guidance on the Commission's procedure in respect of the enforcement of Articles 101 and 102.[68] The Notice seeks to 'increase understanding of the Commission's investigation process…and thereby enhance the efficiency of investigations and ensure a high degree of transparency and predictability in the process'. The Notice apples only to cases that were ongoing at the date of its publication, and to future ones.[69] The Commission has also issued a Staff Working Paper on 'Best Practices for the Submission of Economic Evidence'.[70]

In 2012 the Commission published for the first time its internal manual on procedures (the 'Antitrust ManProc').[71]

---

[64] Reg. 773/2004 replaced Reg. 2842/98 [1998] OJ L354/18.

[65] [2004] OJ C101/43.

[66] [2004] OJ C101/54.

[67] [2004] OJ C101/65.

[68] [2011] OJ C308/6.

[69] Best Practices, para. 6 and Case T-299/08, *Elf Aquitaine SA v. Commission* (sodium chlorate), [2011] ECR II-2149, 17 May 2011, para. 148.

[70] <http://ec.europa.eu/competition/antitrust/legislation/best_practices_submission_en.pdf>. This covers Articles 101 and 102, and mergers.

[71] Available on theDGComp website, <http://ec.europa.eu/competition/antitrust/information_en.html>. This followed a complaint to the European Ombudsman about its previous non-disclosure, invoking the Transparency Regulation, 1049/2001 (see Section 8.C.v.f, p. 976): Complaint 297/2010/(ELB)GG, decision 26 September 2011. The Commission stresses that the ManProc only constitutes internal guidance to staff and does not in any way create or alter any rights or obligations under the competition rules. For a critique of the usefulness of publication of the ManProc, see J. Temple Lang, 'The Strengths and Weaknesses of the DG Competition Manual of Procedure' (2013) 1(1) *J Antitrust Enforcement* 132.

8. ENFORCEMENT BY THE COMMISSION

A. GENERAL

(i) The Broad Powers of the Commission

In *Dansk Rørindustri* the CJ said:[72]

The supervisory task conferred on the Commission by Articles [101(1)] and [102]…not only includes the duty to investigate and punish individual infringements but also encompasses the duty to pursue a general policy designed to apply, in competition matters, the principles laid down by the Treaty and to guide the conduct of undertakings in the light of those principles.

The Commission may commence an investigation into alleged infringements of the competition rules on its own initiative or acting on a complaint.[73] Complaints and the position of complainants are dealt with in Section 13 of this chapter. In competition cases the Commission plays the parts of law-maker, policeman, investigator, prosecutor, judge, and jury, subject only to review by the EU Courts. It is notable that this situation, which has been widely criticised but fiercely defended by the Commission, was not changed by modernisation.[74] The accumulation of functions in the Commission and the limited role of the EU Courts have human rights implications. The Commission has a margin of discretion to set priorities in enforcing the competition rules.[75] It has certain obligations when dealing with complaints[76] but otherwise can choose against whom, and when, to bring proceedings. In *British Airways* the GC dismissed the airline's plea that the Commission had infringed the principle of non-discrimination by bringing an Article 102 action against it but not against other airlines.[77]

Although Regulation 1/2003 abolished the notification procedure, it is recognised that in some novel cases guidance as to the compatibility of an agreement or practice with the rules may be necessary, perhaps to provide legal certainty to the parties[78] and/or to aid the consistent application of the competition rules in the decentralised system.[79] Regulation 1/2003 thus allows the Commission to adopt decisions of 'inapplicability'[80] and, as already mentioned, envisages that 'guidance letters' may be issued.[81] As at 1 July 2013 neither of these procedures had ever been used.

---

[72] Cases C-189/02 P, 202/02 P, 208/02 P, and 213/02 P, *Dansk Rørindustri A/S and others* v. *Commission* [2005] ECR I-5425, para. 170, referring to Cases 100–103/80, *Musique Diffusion Française SA* v. *Commission (Pioneer)* [1983] ECR 1825, para. 105; see also Case T-99/04, *AC-Treuhand AG* v. *Commission* [2008] ECR II-1501, para. 163.

[73] This is clear from Reg. 1/2003, Art. 7 which gives the Commission power to take decisions when it has found an infringement; see also Best Practices, paras. 9–11. Many investigations in cartel cases are triggered by a leniency application.

[74] See A. Pera and M. Todino, 'Enforcement of EC Competition Rules: Need for a Reform?' [1996] Fordham Corp Law Inst 125, 144; F. Montag, 'The Case for Radical Reform of the Infringement Procedure under Regulation' [1998] *ECLR* 428; W. Wils, 'The Combination of the Investigative and Prosecutorial Function and the Adjudicative Function in EC Antitrust Enforcement: A Legal and Economic Analysis' (2004) 27(2) *World Competition* 201; I. Forrester, 'Due Process in EC Competition Case: A Distinguished Institution with Flawed Procedures' (2009) 34 *ELRev* 817; D. Slater, S. Thomas, and D. Waelbroeck, 'Competition Law Proceedings before the European Commission and the Right to a Fair Trial: No Need for Reform?' (2009) *European Competition Journal* 97.

[75] Case T-24/90, *Automec Srl* v. *Commission (Automec II)* [1992] ECR II-2223.

[76] See Section 13.

[77] Case T-219/99, *British Airways* v. *Commission* [2003] ECR II-5917.

[78] See Reg. 1/2003, recital 38.

[79] See Reg. 1/2003, recital 14 and Commission Notice on informal guidance, para. 2.

[80] Reg. 1/2003, Art. 10, see Section 8.D.iv, p. 990.

[81] Reg. 1/2003, recital 38 and Commission Notice on informal guidance relating to novel questions that arise in individual cases (guidance letters) [2004] OJ C101/78, see Chap. 2, Section 5.B.ii, p. 927.

(ii) Human Rights

a. General

The general position of human rights in EU law is described in Chapter 2.[82] The relevance and application of human rights provisions in respect of the enforcement of EU competition law are dealt with in context throughout this chapter. In this section, however, we make some general points.

Recital 37 to Regulation 1/2003 states:

This Regulation respects the fundamental rights and observes the principles recognised in particular by the Charter of Fundamental Rights of the European Union. Accordingly, this Regulation should be interpreted and applied with respect to those rights and principles.

Article 52 of the Charter provides that where it contains rights corresponding to those in the ECHR their meaning and scope shall be the same as the latter (as a minimum).

The EU Courts have frequently emphasised the importance of ensuring that Commission enforcement proceedings respect the rights of the defence as a fundamental principle. For example, in *Archer Daniels Midland*:[83]

It should be recalled that in all proceedings in which sanctions, especially fines or penalty payments, may be imposed, observance of the rights of the defence is a fundamental principle of Community law which must be complied with even if the proceedings in question are administrative proceedings (see, in particular, Case C-328/05 P *SGL Carbon v Commission*...paragraph 70).

The principle of effective judicial protection, a general principle of EU law, is enshrined in the European Convention on Human Rights (ECHR) and in Article 47 of the Charter.[84]

b. The Relevant Articles of the ECHR and the Charter

The European Court of Human Rights (ECtHR) has held that certain Articles of the ECHR, including two that are particularly relevant to the enforcement of competition law, Article 8 and Article 6, can apply to both natural and legal persons (such as undertakings).[85]

Article 8 ECHR states:

1. Everyone has the right to respect for his private and family life, his home and his correspondence.
2. There shall be no interference by a public authority with the exercise of this right except such as is in accordance with the law and is necessary in a democratic society in the interests of national security, public safety or the economic well-being of the country, for the prevention of disorder or crime, for the protection of health or morals, or for the protection of the rights and freedoms of others.

This guarantee is relevant to the Commission's powers to carry out inspections at premises (particularly unannounced 'dawn raids') under Regulation 1/2003, Articles 20 and 21.[86]

The corresponding provision of the Charter is Article 7:

Everyone has the right to respect for his or her private and family life, home and communications.

---

[82] Chap. 2, Section 3.B, p. 100 and Section 3.F, p. 107. For the ECHR, see Harris, O'Boyle and Warbrick (D. J. Harris, M. O'Boyle, E. P. Bates, and C. M. Buckley, eds.), *Law of the European Convention on Human Rights* (2nd edn, Oxford University Press, 2009).

[83] Case C-511/06 P, *Archer Daniels Midland v. Commission* [2009] ECR I-5843, para. 84.

[84] Case C-389/10 P, *KME Germany AG v. Commission*, 8 December 2011. For the EU Charter of Fundamental Rights, see Chapter 2, Section 3.B, p. 100.

[85] See, e.g., *Niemitz v. Germany*, Series A, No. 251–B, (1992) 16 EHRR 97. For the reasons why fundamental human rights are extended to corporate bodies see, e.g., A. Andreangeli, *EU Competition Enforcement and Human Rights* (Edward Elgar, 2008), 17–18.

[86] See Section 8.B.ii, p. 941 ff.

Article 7 enshrines the general principle of EU law that there should be no arbitrary or disproportionate intervention by public authorities in the private sphere of any natural or legal person.[87]

Article 6 ECHR provides the right to a fair trial and due process. It states:

1. In the determination of his civil rights and obligations or of any criminal charge against him, everyone is entitled to a fair and public hearing within a reasonable time by an independent and impartial tribunal established by law. Judgment shall be pronounced publicly but the press and public may be excluded from all or part of the trial in the interest of morals, public order or national security in a democratic society, where the interests of juveniles or the protection of the private life of the parties so require, or the extent strictly necessary in the opinion of the court in special circumstances where publicity would prejudice the interests of justice.

2. Everyone charged with a criminal offence shall be presumed innocent until proved guilty according to law.

3. Everyone charged with a criminal offence has the following minimum rights:

  (a) to be informed promptly, in a language which he understands and in detail, of the nature and cause of the accusation against him;

  (b) to have adequate time and the facilities for the preparation of his defence;

  (c) to defend himself in person or through legal assistance of his own choosing or, if he has not sufficient means to pay for legal assistance, to be given it free when the interests of justice so require;

  (d) to examine or have examined witnesses against him and to obtain the attendance and examination of witnesses on his behalf under the same conditions as witnesses against him.

The right to a fair trial includes the right to give evidence in one's own defence, hear the evidence against one and be able to examine and cross-examine witnesses,[88] and other matters of due process such as the right against self-incrimination.[89]

The corresponding provision of the Charter is Article 47:

Everyone whose rights and freedoms guaranteed by the law of the Union are violated has the right to an effective remedy before a tribunal in compliance with the conditions laid down in this Article.

Everyone is entitled to a fair and public hearing within a reasonable time by a fair and impartial tribunal previously established by law. Everyone shall have the possibility of being advised, defended and represented.

Legal aid shall be made available to those who lack sufficient resources in so far as such aid is necessary to ensure effective access to justice.

However Article 47, unlike Article 6 ECHR, contains no reference to civil and criminal matters, which may be significant in respect of the application of these Articles to the EU enforcement system.[90]

The presumption of innocence in Article 6(2) appears as Article 48(1) of the Charter and the rights of defence in Article 6(3) are guaranteed by Article 48(2).

c. The Requirements of Article 6 ECHR

The first sentence of Article 6(1), providing for a hearing before an independent and impartial tribunal, applies to civil as well as criminal proceedings. Article 6(2) and (3) provides further rights in criminal proceedings.

In respect of the distinction in Article 6 between civil and criminal proceedings, it is well established in the case law of the ECtHR that the notion of a 'criminal charge' is an autonomous concept

---

[87] Case T-135/09, *Nexans France SAS v. Commission*, 14 November 2012, para. 40.

[88] *Jussila v. Finland* 2006-XIV, (2007) 45 EHRR 39.

[89] *Saunders v. UK* [1997] 23 EHRR 313.

[90] See A-L. Sibony, 'Casenote on *KME v. Commission*' (2012) 49 *CMLRev* 1977.

which is a matter of Convention law. The principles laid down by the ECtHR for identifying a criminal charge are known as the 'Engel criteria'.[91] They are:

- The classification of the offence under national law;[92]
- The nature of the offence;[93] and
- The nature and severity of the potential penalty.[94]

The second and third Engel criteria are alternatives but a cumulative approach is taken when a conclusion cannot be drawn on one of them alone.[95]

'Criminal' does not imply any particular degree of seriousness but the case law draws a distinction between the 'hardcore' of criminal law and more minor offences not strictly belonging to the traditional categories of criminal law, such as traffic offences and tax surcharges.[96] The criminal-head guarantees do not necessarily apply with their full stringency to these 'minor offences'.[97]

Where civil proceedings are concerned ECtHR case law establishes that the right to a hearing before an impartial and independent tribunal does not preclude some matters of an administrative or professional disciplinary nature from being decided by administrative organs at the initial stage so long as they are subject ultimately to judicial control.[98] Similarly, 'later' judicial control is also possible in the case of minor 'non-core' criminal offences.[99] However, both civil and minor criminal offences must be able to come at some point to a public hearing before an independent and impartial judicial body with full jurisdiction.[100] In respect of 'core' criminal offences the right to the hearing in Article 6(1) applies to first instance proceedings. An initial decision by an administrative body is not sufficient.

d. The Application of Article 6 to the Enforcement of EU Competition Law

The issues arising in respect of the enforcement of EU competition law by the Commission in the light of the criteria in Section 8.A.ii.c are (i) whether the proceedings are civil or criminal; (ii) if they are criminal are they 'core' or 'minor' offences; and (iii) do the procedures for making decisions in competition cases comply with the relevant requirements of the ECHR pertaining to the type of proceedings concerned. There has been a long-standing controversy as to these matters, in particular whether EU competition procedure satisfies Article 6 and, if it does not, how the system could be reformed.[101]

---

[91] Engel v. Netherlands Series A, No. 22, (1976) 1 EHRR 647.

[92] The classification of the offence as not criminal is not decisive, whereas the classification of it as being criminal is decisive, see Öztürk v. Germany Series A, No 73, (1984) 6 EHRR 409.

[93] The case law clarifies that matters to be taken into account in judging the 'nature of the offence' include whether the legal norm is generally applicable (Bendenoun v. France Series A, No. 284, (1994) 18 EHRR 54); whether the sanctions have a deterrent and/or punitive character (Bendenoun, para. 47, Öztürk, cited in n. 92); whether the proceedings are instituted by a public body with statutory powers of enforcement (Benham v. UK 1996-III No. 10, (1996) 22 EHRR 293); whether the penalty is dependent on a finding of guilt (Benham, para. 56); and how other Council of Europe States classify comparable offences (Öztürk, para. 53).

[94] This takes into account the maximum penalty for the offence and the stigma attaching to it, see Öztürk, para. 54.

[95] Bendenoun, para. 47.

[96] Jussila v. Finland (cited in n. 88), para. 43.

[97] Jussila v. Finland (cited in n. 88), para. 43.

[98] Le Compte, Van Leuven, and De Meyere v. Belgium Series A, No. 54, (1983) 5 EHRR 183.

[99] Bendenoun v. France; Jussila v. Finland, para. 43.

[100] Le Compte, para. 29.

[101] See e.g., A. Andreangeli, 'Towards an EU Competition Court: "Article-6-Proofing" Antitrust Proceedings before the Commission?' (2007) 4 World Competition 595; I. Forrester, 'Due Process in EC Competition Case: A Distinguished Institution with Flawed Procedures' (2009) 34 ELRev 817; D. Slater, S. Thomas, and D. Waelbroeck, 'Competition Law Proceedings before the European Commission and the Right to a Fair Trial: No Need for Reform?' (2009) European Competition Journal 97 and GCLC Working Paper 04/08; F. Castillo de la Torre, 'Evidence, Proof and Judicial review in Cartel Cases' in C.-D. Ehlermann and M. Marquis (eds.), European Competition Law Annual 2009: Evaluation of Evidence

Regulation 1/2003, Article 23(5)[102] expressly states that decisions imposing fines (for either substantive or procedural offences) 'shall not be of a criminal law nature'. However, it is clear from the *Engel* criteria that such a statement cannot be conclusive of the matter for the purposes of the ECHR.[103] Moreover, even if the *fine* is not 'criminal' that does not mean that the *proceedings* concerned are not criminal.[104] In *Menarini*[105] in 2011 the ECtHR held, in the context of a challenge to a sanction imposed by the Italian competition authority, that Italian competition law fines are of a criminal nature for the purposes of Article 6.[106] It is reasonable to assume that EU fines are likewise.

In the EU it had already been generally accepted that the Commission's fining procedures were 'criminal' within Article 6 ECHR[107] and in *Hüls* the CJ accepted that the presumption of innocence in Article 6(2) applies to Commission proceedings that may result in fines.[108] A dispute still rages around whether the extent of the judicial review provided by the Treaty satisfies the requirements of the ECHR Article 6(1) for a public hearing before an impartial and independent tribunal, given that the administrative proceedings before the Commission cannot possibly do so.[109] In *Menarini* in 2011 the ECtHR held that decisions imposing fines could be taken by administrative, non-judicial competition authorities provided that the decisions were subject to full judicial review on matters of law and fact by independent courts with full jurisdiction. The Italian system at issue in the case was held to satisfy these criteria, although there was a powerful dissenting opinion.[110] The nature and

---

and its Judicial Review in Competition Cases (Hart Publishing, 2011), 319; I. Forrester, 'A Bush in Need of Pruning: the Luxuriant Growth of "Light Judicial Review"', in C.-D. Ehlermann and M. Marquis (cited earlier in this note), 407; W. Wils, 'The Increased Level of Antitrust Fines, Judicial Review, and the European Convention on Human Rights' (2010) 33(1) *World Competition* 5; Editorial, 'Towards a More Judicial Approach? EU Antitrust Fines Under the Scrutiny of Fundamental Rights' (2011) 48 *CMLRev* 1405; W. Wils,'EU Antitrust Enforcement Powers and Procedural Rights and Guarantees: The Interplay between EU Law, National Law, the Charter of Fundamental Rights of the EU and the European Convention of Human Rights' (2011) 2 *World Competition* 189; R. Nazzini, 'Administrative Enforcement, Judicial Review and Fundamental Rights in EU Competition Law: A Comparative Contextual-Functionalist Perspective' (2012) 49 *CMLRev* 971.

[102] Formerly Reg. 17, Art. 15(4).

[103] The fines imposed by the Commission for substantive offences can be up to 10% of the undertaking's turnover in the previous year (Reg. 1/2003, Art. 23(2)), can run into billions of Euros, and serve as both sanction and deterrent. Fines for procedural offences (Reg. 1/2003, Art. 23(1)) and periodic penalty payments for non-compliance (Reg. 1/2003, Art. 24) can also be very heavy. Infringements of the competition rules, especially hardcore cartels, are excoriated in Commission press releases and speeches. All these factors are relevant to the second and third *Engel* criteria. See Section 8.G.

[104] Slater et al., 'Competition Law Proceedings before the European Commission and the Right to a Fair Trial' (cited in n. 101).

[105] *Menarini Diagnostics S.R.L v. Italy*, App 43509/08, judgment 27 September 2011, and see also *Société Bouygues Telecom v. France*, Applicant 2324/08.

[106] In *Société Stenuit v. France* (1992) 14 EHRR 509 the European Commission on Human Rights had held in its Opinion that a fine imposed on undertakings by the French competition authorities was criminal in nature. *Stenuit* did not proceed to a judgment by the ECtHR as the applicant and the French authorities settled the matter, but the ECtHR referred approvingly to this finding in *Jussila v. Finland* (cited in n. 88).

[107] Either expressly or impliedly. See Judge Vesterdorf, acting as AG in Cases T-1–4/89 and 6–15/89, *Rhône-Poulenc and others v. Commission* [1991] ECR II-867, 885; Léger AG in Case C-185/95 P, *Baustahlgewebe v. Commission* [1998] ECR I-8417, para. 31 of the Opinion; Cases C-189/02P, 202/02P, 208/02P, and 213/02P, *Dansk Rørindustri A/S and others v. Commission* [2005] ECR I-5425, para. 202; Sharpston AG in Case C-272/09 P, *KME Germany AG v. Commission*, para. 64 of the Opinion, 10 February 2011 (the judgment, post *Menarini*, cited Art. 47 rather than Art. 6(1) itself, see Section 9.A.viii, p. 1041).

[108] Case C-199/92 P, *Hüls v. Commission* [1999] ECR I-4287, para. 150.

[109] See e.g. Slater et al., 'Competition Law Proceedings before the European Commission and the Right to a Fair Trial' (cited in n. 101); W. Wils, 'The Increased Level of Antitrust Fines, Judicial Review, and the European Convention on Human Rights' (2010) 33(1) *World Competition* 5; I. Forrester, 'Due Process in EC Competition Case: A Distinguished Institution with Flawed Procedures' (2009) 34 *ELRev* 817; A. Andreangeli, 'Towards an EU Competition Court: "Article-6-Proofing" Antitrust Proceedings before the Commission?' (2007) 4 *World Competition* 595.

[110] By Judge Pinto de Albuquerque. For comments on *Menarini*, see P. Oliver, 'Diagnostics—a Judgment Applying the European Convention of Human Rights to the Field of Competition' (2012) 3 *Journal of European Competition Law and Practice* 163.

intensity of judicial review of Commission decisions and the application to it of Article 6(1) ECHR and Article 47 of the Charter are discussed further later in this chapter,[111] as are other issues such the compatibility with Article 6 of the EU position on self-incrimination.[112]

e. The Application of the Charter

Since 2010 the EU Courts have referred to the Charter in a number of cases, for example:[113]

- Articles 20 and 21 (equality before the law and non-discrimination);[114]

- Article 41(1) (the right to good administration: the right to have one's affairs handled by EU bodies in a reasonable time);[115]

- Article 41(2) (the right to good administration: the right to be heard and the right of every person to have access to his or her file);[116]

- Article 47 (right to an effective remedy/fair trial);[117]

- Article 48(1) (presumption of innocence);[118]

- Article 49(1) (legality and proportionality of criminal offences and penalties);[119]

- Article 50 (*ne bis in idem*, the right not to be tried or punished in criminal proceedings twice for the same offence).[120]

(iii) The Two Stages of the Commission's Administrative Procedure and the Initiation of Proceedings

As the GC explained in *Treuhand*, there are two distinct stages to the Commission's administrative procedure. The first is the preliminary investigation stage, covering the period up until the notification of the statement of objections (SO), which is a period of fact-finding intended 'to enable the Commission to gather all the relevant information confirming or not the existence of an infringement of the competition rules and to adopt an initial position on the course of the procedure and how it is to proceed'.[121] The second, 'inter partes' stage, covers the period from the notification of the SO to the adoption of the final Decision. The move from one stage to the other entails the 'initiation of proceedings'. The initiation of proceedings by the Commission is a formal act[122] by which the Commission indicates its intention to adopt a decision under Regulation 1/2003.[123] Under Regulation 1/2003, Article 11(6) the initiation of proceedings by the Commission relieves the NCAs

---

[111] Section 9.A.vi, p. 1029 ff.

[112] See Section 8.B.vi, p. 953 ff.

[113] See Bellamy and Child, *European Law of Competition* (cited in n. 2), 13.007.

[114] Case C-550/07 P, *Akzo Nobel Chemicals Ltd v. Commission* [2010] ECR I-8301.

[115] Case T-461/07, *Visa Europe v. Commission* [2011] ECR II-1729.

[116] Case C-109/10 P, *Solvay v. Commission* [2011] ECR I-10329.

[117] C-407/08P, *Knauf Gips v. Commission* [2010] ECR I-6375, Cases T-117/07 and 121/07 *Areva and Alstom v. Commission* [2011] ECR II-633, Case T-132/07, *Fuji Electric Co Ltd v. Commission* [2011] ECR II-4091, 12 July 2011.

[118] Case T-141/07, etc., *General Technic-Otis Sàrl v. Commission* [2011], 13 July 2011.

[119] Case C-352/09 P, *ThyssenKrup Nirosta v. Commision* [2011] ECR I-2359.

[120] Case T-343/08, *Arkema France v. Commission* [2011] ECR II-2287.

[121] See Case T-99/04, *AC-Treuhand AG v. Commission* [2008] ECR II-1501, para. 47; see also Cases C-238, 244–245, 247, 250, 251–252 and 254/99, *Limburgse Vinyl Maatschappij NV v. Commission* [2002] ECR I-8375, paras. 181–183; Case C-105/04 P, *Nederlandse Federatieve Vereniging voor de Groothandel op Elektrotechnisch Gebied v. Commission* [2006] ECR I-8725, paras. 37–38.

[122] See Case 48/72, *SA Brasserie de Haecht v. Wilkin-Janssen* [1973] ECR 77 para. 16: 'the initiation of a procedure...obviously concerns an authoritative act of the Commission, evidencing its intention to take a decision'.

[123] Notice on cooperation within the Network of Competition Authorities [2004] OJ C101/54, para. 52.

of their competence to apply Articles 101 and 102 in the case. National courts are not relieved of their competence, but they may not take a decision running counter to one adopted by the Commission.[124] Moreover, they must also avoid giving decisions which would conflict with a decision contemplated by the Commission.[125]

Regulation 773/2004, Article 2 provides that the Commission may publicise the initiation of proceedings, in any appropriate way,[126] having previously informed the parties. Article 2(1) states:

The Commission may decide to initiate proceedings with a view to adopting a decision pursuant to Chapter III of Regulation (EC) No 1/2003 at any point in time, but no later than the date on which it issues a preliminary assessment as referred to in Article 9(1) of that Regulation, a statement of objections or a request for the parties to express their interest in engaging in settlement discussions, or the date on which a notice pursuant to Article 27(4) of that Regulation is published, whichever is the earlier.[127]

It is not necessary for the Commission to initiate proceedings before rejecting a complaint.[128]

Regulation 773/2004, Article 2(3) expressly states that the Commission may exercise its powers of investigation before initiating proceedings. This is vital as until the Commission has carried out an investigation it may not be in a position to issue an SO.

B. THE INVESTIGATION STAGE OF THE ADMINISTRATIVE PROCEDURE: FACT-FINDING BY THE COMMISSION

(i) General

The Commission has extensive fact-finding powers under Regulation 1/2003, Articles 18 and 20 (which correspond respectively to Articles 11 and 14 of Regulation 17). These formal powers are crucial for obtaining information when undertakings do not provide it voluntarily. The exercise of the powers is often hotly contested by the undertakings subjected to them. The rights of the parties have been spelt out in the case law of the EU Courts when the Commission's actions have been challenged, often on the grounds that the Commission has acted in breach of the general principles of law or fundamental rights.

Under Regulation 1/2003, Article 18, the Commission may request undertakings to supply it with information.[129] However, where the Commission investigates suspected infringements of the competition rules, either following a complaint or on its own initiative, it is frequently looking for information which the parties would rather not give it and which they may have taken active steps

---

[124] Regulation 1/2003, Art. 16(1).

[125] See Chap. 14.

[126] See N. Petit and M. Rato, 'From Hard to Soft Enforcement of EC Competition Law—A Bestiary of "Sunshine" Enforcement Instruments', available at <http://ssrn.com/abstract=1270109>. Best Practices, para. 24, says that in cartel cases the opening of proceedings and the SO are normally simultaneous.

[127] The preliminary assessment in Reg. 1/2003, Art. 9(1) is the initial view of the Commission that an infringement has occurred, although it may accept from the undertakings commitments which meet its concerns and therefore decide to take no further action (see Section 8.D.iii, p. 982). A statement of objections (SO) is the serving on the undertakings concerned of a notice setting out the Commission's case against them (see Section 8.C.iii, p. 968 ff). An interest in engaging in settlement discussions is a reference to the settlement procedure in cartel cases (see Section 8.E, p. 992; Art. 2(1) was amended in 2008 to take account of the introduction of that procedure). An Art. 27(4) notice is the publication of a summary of the case and other details which must take place where the Commission intends to adopt a decision pursuant to Art. 9 (decisions making commitments binding) or Art. 10 (finding of applicability decision).

[128] Reg. 773/2004, Art. 2(4).

[129] In the case of complaints complainants should provide the Commission with any relevant information they possess. See Form C (Annex to Reg. 773/2004) and Section 13.D, p. 1071.

to conceal. Under Article 18 the Commission may turn to the undertakings under investigation and to other undertakings such as customers, competitors, or suppliers of the allegedly infringing firms and request them, and ultimately require them, to supply information.

Article 20 enables the Commission to conduct inspections on the undertakings' premises. It can proceed directly to Article 20, and need not make a prior request for information under Article 18. Undertakings have an obligation to cooperate actively with the investigative measures.[130]

Regulation 1/2003, Article 19 gave the Commission a new power to interview any natural or legal person who consents to be interviewed. Article 21 gave it a new power to carry out inspections at non-business premises.

(ii) Article 18 Requests for Information

Article 18 provides that the Commission 'may, by simple request or by decision, require undertakings and associations of undertakings to provide all necessary information'.[131] This includes requests for the disclosure of documents.[132] Under Regulation 1/2003, Article 18, the Commission can choose to demand information from undertakings by decision from the outset, unlike under Article 11 of Regulation 17 where it had first to simply 'request' it. By Article 18(6) the governments of the Member States and the NCAs have to supply the Commission with all necessary information it requests.

The meaning of 'necessary information' was considered by the Court in *SEP*. [133] The GC stated that the term 'necessary information' must be interpreted by reference to the purposes for which the powers of investigation in question were conferred upon the Commission. The requirement for a correlation between the request for information and the presumed infringement is met if, at this stage of the procedure, the request can be legitimately considered to be related to the presumed infringement.[134] The CJ upheld this.[135] Although it is not easy, therefore, to show that the information requested is outside the leeway allowed to the Commission, it does mean that the Commission cannot go on a complete 'fishing expedition' and that the Court would be prepared to hold in an appropriate case that the request was excessive.[136]

Article 18(2) states what must be contained in a simple request for information:

When sending a simple request for information to an undertaking or association of undertakings, the Commission shall state the legal basis and the purpose of the request, specify what information is required and fix the time-limit within which the information is to be provided, and the penalties provided for in Article 23 for supplying incorrect or misleading information.

There is no *duty* to comply with the request, although the intentional or negligent provision of *incorrect* or *misleading* information can be penalised with a fine under Regulation 1/2003, Article 23(1)(a), and, as will be noted from Article 18(2), the undertakings must be warned of this. The level of fine for providing incorrect or misleading information was raised by Regulation 1/2003, Article 23(1) to a maximum of one per cent of the undertaking's total turnover in the preceding business year.[137] A desire to cooperate with the Commission and not to make the situation worse also tends to be a

---

[130] Case 374/87, *Orkem SA v. Commission* [1989] ECR 3283, paras. 22 and 27.

[131] Reg. 1/2003, Art. 18(1); see Kerse and Khan, *EU Antitrust Procedure* (cited in n. 2), 3.013–3.030.

[132] Case 374/87, *Orkem SA v. Commission* [1989] ECR 3283, para. 14.

[133] Case T-39/90, *SEP v. Commission* [1991] ECR II-1497.

[134] Case T-39/90, *SEP v. Commission* [1991] ECR II-1497, para. 29.

[135] Case C-36/92 P, *SEP v. Commission* [1994] ECR I-1911.

[136] See also Case 155/79, *AM&S Ltd v. Commission* [1982] ECR 1575 and Case 374/87, *Orkem SA v. Commission* [1989] ECR 3283; and see now by analogy Case T-135/09, *Nexans France SAS v. Commission*, 14 November 2012 on Art. 20(4) inspections, see Section 8.B.iii.b.

[137] For fines, generally see Section 8.G, p. 994 ff. Under Reg. 17, Art. 15(1)(b) the fine was only €100 to €5,000 (which was worth rather more in 1962, when it was set, than in 2004).

spur to accuracy. The fact that ultimately the Commission can demand the information by adopting a decision under Article 18(3) is another reason for complying with the Article 18(2) request.[138]

An Article 18 request is not precluded by the fact that the Commission has already carried out an Article 20 inspection and is using Article 18 to obtain documents which it failed to obtain during the inspection.[139]

A decision under Article 18(3) has to state, like a request, its legal basis and purpose, the information required and the time limit. In addition to warning of Article 23 fines, it must also indicate or impose the periodic penalties under Article 24, whereby the Commission may impose periodic penalty payments of up to five per cent of the average daily turnover[140] in order to compel the production of complete and correct information.[141] Further, the decision must indicate that it can be reviewed by the Court.

Article 18(4) of Regulation 1/2003 provides that lawyers may supply the information on behalf of their clients, although the client remains fully responsible if the information is incorrect, incomplete, or misleading. The Commission's Staff Working Paper on 'Best Practices for the Submission of Economic Evidence'[142] sets out the way in which the Commission prefers undertakings to present economic and econometric evidence in reply to requests for quantitative data.

The Commission has to send a copy of the request or decision to the NCA of the Member State in whose territory the seat of the undertaking concerned is situated and to the NCA of the Member State whose territory is affected.[143]

The questions of when undertakings may withhold documents from the Commission on the ground that they are legally privileged, and to what extent they can refuse to supply information on grounds of self-incrimination, are dealt with in later sections.[144]

(iii) Article 20 Inspections

a. General

Article 20(1) gives the Commission powers to carry out 'all necessary inspections' of undertakings and associations of undertakings. This means investigations at the undertaking's premises. Inspections are carried out by officials and 'other accompanying persons authorised by the Commission'[145] such as IT experts. By Article 20(2) inspections involve the power:[146]

(a) to enter any premises, land and means of transport of undertakings and associations of undertakings;

(b) to examine the books and other records related to the business, irrespective of the medium on which they are stored;

(c) to take or obtain in any form copies of or extracts from such books or records;

(d) to seal any business premises and books or records for the period and to the extent necessary for the inspection;

(e) to ask any representative or member of staff of the undertaking or association of undertakings for explanations on facts or documents relating to the subject-matter and purpose of the inspection and to record the answers.

---

[138] See Case T-46/92, *The Scottish Football Association v. Commission* [1994] ECR II-1039 for a case in which a reaction to a request for information which consisted of pained surprise, an explanation of the undertaking's policy, and a statement that the undertaking was 'happy' to meet the Commission at any time to explain its views was treated by the GC as a 'polite but explicit refusal to co-operate' (para. 33).

[139] Case 374/87, *Orkem SA v. Commission* [1989] ECR 3283, [1991] 4 CMLR 502, para. 14.

[140] See Section 8.G.iii, p. 995.

[141] Art. 24(1)(d).

[142] See n. 70.

[143] Reg. 1/2003, Art. 18(5).

[144] See Section 8.B.vii and Section 8.B.vi.

[145] Reg. 1/2003, Art. 20(3), (5), and (6).

[146] See generally Kerse and Khan, *EU Antitrust Procedure* (cited in n. 2), 3.072–3.138.

Under Article 20(3) the Commission can carry out the inspection at the premises simply on production of a 'written authorisation'.[147] The officials may either give advance notice of their arrival or come without warning (although they have to give notice 'in good time before the inspection' to the NCA of the Member State in whose territory the inspection is conducted). So long as they carry only the Article 20(3) 'authorisation' an undertaking is under no legal obligation to submit to the inspection. Under Article 20(4), however, undertakings *must* submit to procedures ordered by a decision of the Commission.[148] Article 20(4) decisions can be taken by the Commissioner responsible for competition. The delegation by the College of Commissioners is valid as it does not involve a matter of principle.[149] The Commission cannot carry out inspections if it suspects that there is an agreement or a concerted practice which produces effects exclusively outside the internal market as Articles 101 and 102 apply only to effects on inter-Member State trade.[150]

The most notorious form of inspection is that where the officials arrive without warning, armed with a decision.[151] The CJ held in *National Panasonic*[152] that they were entitled to do this under what is now Article 20(4), without going through the 'voluntary' (now Article 20(3)) procedure first. Although popularly known as 'dawn raids' unannounced inspections take place during normal business hours. There may, however, be simultaneous surprise arrivals at undertakings across the EU where, for example, the Commission suspects the existence of a hardcore cartel or abuses of a dominant position. The *Polypropylene* cartel investigation,[153] for example, involved 10 simultaneous raids. Julian Joshua, at one time Deputy Head of the Cartel Unit in DG Comp, explained in 1983 why the apparently draconian powers of the Commission are necessary:[154]

More often, the most serious cartels are not modified at all. They are operated in conditions of strict secrecy. Communication between participants is kept to a minimum and knowledge of the arrangements confined to certain key employees. Meetings take place in safe countries or under the cover of a seemingly innocent trade association. There may even be emergency arrangements to shred documents and warn other participants by coded telex messages in the event of an investigation. Sometimes the cartel rules provide for members to deny all knowledge of documents or their contents even when these are found in the safe. In such circumstances resort to surprise must be a legitimate and essential precaution.[155]

---

[147] This must contain the same or equivalent matters as required in respect of requests for information under Art. 18(2).

[148] Case 5/85, *AKZO v. Commission* [1986] ECR 2585; Cases 46/87 and 227/88, *Hoechst AG v. Commission* [1989] ECR 2859. The decision must contain the same or equivalent matters as required in respect of decisions under Art. 18(3). The form of authorisation carried by the inspectors executing a Decision is on DG Comp's website, see <http://ec.europa.eu/competition/antitrust/legislation/inspection_authorisation.pdf>

[149] Case 53/85, *AKZO v. Commission* [1986] ECR 2585.

[150] Case T-135/09, *Nexans France SAS v. Commission*, 14 November 2012, para. 99. It can, however, examine documents relating to markets outside the EU in order to detect anti-competitive conduct which is liable to affect trade between Member States.

[151] The Commission may confirm by press release that dawn raids have taken place. The Commission issued a Press Release, MEMO/13/435, on 14 May 2013 about the dawn raids in the oil and biofuel sectors. These featured on the BBC News at Ten the same night, were headlines on the front pages of many newspapers the following morning, and the possibility of price-fixing in the sector soon became a major news story.

[152] Case 136/79, *National Panasonic v. Commission* [1980] ECR 2033.

[153] *Polypropylene Cartel* [1986] OJ L230/1, [1988] 4 CMLR 347.

[154] J. M. Joshua, 'The Element of Surprise' (1983) 8 *ELRev* 3, 5.

[155] For a most instructive (and amusing) look at the inner workings of a cartel, see James M. Griffin, 'An Inside Look at a Cartel at Work: Common Characteristics of International Cartels', Speech 6 April 2000, available on the US DOJ website,<http://www.justice.gov/atr/public/speeches/4489-7.htm>. This includes transcripts of cartel meetings caught on hidden microphones (obtaining which involved, inter alia, FBI agents disguised as hotel employees). The cartel concerned, the lysine (amino acids) cartel, also became the subject of an EC decision, [2001] OJ L152/24, [2001] 5 CMLR 322, on appeal to the GC, Case T-224/00, *Archer Daniels Midland v. Commission* [2003] ECR II-2597, *aff'd* by the CJ, Case C-397/03 P, *Archer Daniels Midland v. Commission* [2006] ECR I-4429 and was the subject of the 2009 Stephen Soderbergh film, *The Informant!* starring Matt Damon as the whistle-blower.

An Explanatory Note on the conduct of Article 20(4) inspections, setting out the Commission's view of its Article 20(4) powers, is published on DG Comp's website.[156]

In *National Panasonic* an undertaking subjected to the first unannounced dawn raid, under Regulation 17, Article 14(3), claimed that the procedure infringed its fundamental rights. It relied in particular on Article 8 of the ECHR. It also claimed that in this case the principle of proportionality was infringed.

Case 136/79, *National Panasonic* v. *Commission* [1980] ECR 2033

Commission officials arrived at Panasonic's offices in Slough at 10.00 a.m. The directors asked if the inspection could be delayed to await the arrival of their solicitor, who was in Norwich. The officials waited until 10.45 a.m. and then began. The solicitor did not arrive until 1.45 p.m. and the inspection finished at 5.30 p.m. Panasonic subsequently challenged the validity of the decision ordering the inspection in the CJ and asked that all the documents taken by the Commission should be returned or destroyed.

Court of Justice

17. The applicant then claims that by failing previously to communicate to it beforehand the decision ordering an investigation in question, the Commission has in this instance infringed fundamental rights of the applicant, in particular the right to receive advance notification of the intention to apply a decision regarding it, the right to be heard before a decision adversely affecting it is taken and the right to use the opportunity given to it under Article [278 TFEU] to request a stay of execution of such a decision. The applicant relies in particular on Article 8 of the European Convention for the Protection of Human Rights and Fundamental Freedoms of 4 November 1950 whereby 'everyone has the right to respect for his private and family life, his home and his correspondence'. It considers that those guarantees must be provided *mutatis mutandis* also to legal persons.

18. As the Court stated in its judgment of 14 May 1974 in Case 4/73, *J. Nold, Kohlen-und Baustoffgrosshandlung* v. *Commission of the European Communities*...at p. 507, fundamental rights form an integral part of the general principles of law, the observance of which the Court of Justice ensures, in accordance with constitutional traditions common to the Member States and with international treaties on which the Member States have collaborated or of which they are signatories.

19. In this respect it is necessary to point out that Article 8(2) of the European Convention, in so far as it applies to legal persons, whilst stating the principle that public authorities should not interfere with the exercise of the rights referred to in Article 8(1), acknowledges that such interference is permissible to the extent to which it 'is in accordance with the law and is necessary in a democratic society in the interests of national security, public safety or the economic well-being of the country, for the prevention of disorder or crime, for the protection of health or morals, or for the protection of the rights and freedom of others.'

20. In this instance, as follows from the seventh and eighth recitals of the preamble to Regulation No 17, the aim of the powers given to the Commission by Article 14 of that regulation is to enable it to carry out its duty under the EEC Treaty of ensuring that the rules on competition are applied in the common market. The function of these rules is, as follows from the fourth recital of the preamble of the Treaty, Article 3[(1) (g) EC] and Articles [101 and 102 TFEU], to prevent competition from being distorted to the detriment of the public interest, individual undertakings and consumers. The exercise of the powers given to the Commission by Regulation No 17 contributes to the maintenance of the system of competition intended by the Treaty which undertakings are absolutely bound to comply with. In these circumstances, it does not therefore appear that Regulation No 17, by giving the Commission powers to carry out investigations without previous notification, infringes the right invoked by the applicant.

---

[156] <http://ec.europa.eu/competition/antitrust/legislation/explanatory_note.pdf>, last revised 18 March 2013 in the light of developments such as the *Nexans* judgment, and the *EPH* decision, discussed in Section 8.B.iii.b, p. 945.

21. Moreover, as regard more particularly the argument that the application was in this instance denied the right to be heard before a decision was taken regarding it, it is necessary to state that the exercise of such a right of defence is chiefly incorporated in legal or administrative procedures for the termination of an infringement or for a declaration that an agreement, decision or concerted practice is incompatible with Article [101], such as the procedures referred to by Regulation No 99/63/EEC. On the other hand, the investigation procedure referred to in Article 14 of Regulation No 17 does not aim at terminating an infringement or declaring that an agreement, decision or concerted practice is incompatible with Article [101]; its sole objective is to enable the Commission to gather the necessary information to check…the actual existence and scope of a given factual and legal situation. Only if the Commission considers that the data for the appraisal thereof collected in this way justify the initiation of a procedure under Regulation No 99/63/EEC must the undertaking or association of undertakings concerned be heard before such a decision is taken pursuant to Article 19(1) of Regulation No 17 and to the provisions of Regulation No 99/63/EEC. Precisely this substantive difference between the decisions taken at the end of such a procedure and decisions ordering an investigation explains the wording of Article 19(1) which, in listing the decisions which the Commission cannot take before giving those concerned the opportunity of exercising their right of defence, does not mention that laid down in Article 14(3) of the same regulation.

22. Finally, the argument that the absence of previous information deprived the applicant of the opportunity of exercising its rights under Article [278 TFEU] to request the Court for a stay of execution of the decision in question is contradicted by the very provisions of Article [278]. That article presupposes in fact that a decision has been adopted and that it is effective whereas the previous notification, which the applicant complains that the Commission did not send it, should have preceded the adoption of the contested decision and could not have been binding.

23. In view of these considerations, the second submission is not well founded.

(D) The violation of the principle of proportionality

28. The applicant points out in addition that the principle of proportionality, as established by the case-law of the Court of Justice, implies that a decision ordering an investigation adopted without the preliminary procedure may only be justified if the situation is very grave and where there is the greatest urgency and the need for complete secrecy before the investigation is carried out. It points out, finally, that the contested decision violates such a principle by not indicating in the statement of the reasons upon which it is based that any of those facts exists.

29. The Commission's choice between an investigation by straightforward authorization and an investigation ordered by a decision does not depend on the facts relied upon by the applicant but on the need for an appropriate inquiry, having regard to the special features of the case.

30. Considering that the contested decision aimed solely at enabling the Commission to collect the necessary information to appraise whether there was any infringement of the Treaty, it does not therefore appear that the Commission's action in this instance was disproportionate to the objective pursued and therefore violated the principle of proportionality.

The CJ therefore rejected National Panasonic's claims and held that an unannounced inspection authorised by a decision did not infringe the inspected undertaking's fundamental rights.

Inspections must be precise in scope. The Commission cannot use its Article 20(4) powers to go on 'fishing expeditions' and must have reasonable grounds for adopting an inspection decision. This was confirmed and clarified by the GC in *Nexans*,[157] an appeal against an inspection decision adopted

---

[157] Case T-135/09, *Nexans France SAS v. Commission*, 14 November 2012, on appeal Case C-37/13 P, judgment pending, and Case T-140/09, *Prysmian SpA v. Commission*, 14 November 2012; see A. Laghezza, 'From the Nexans judgement to the "next" improvements of the EU dawn raid procedure?' (2013) *ECLR* 214.

in the Commission's investigation into a suspected electric cables cartel, in which for the first time the GC (partially) annulled a decision authorising a dawn raid. The GC stressed that, as the CJ had established,[158] inspections are intended to enable the Commission to gather documentary evidence to check the actual existence and scope of a given factual and legal situation about which it *already possesses certain information*. There must be facts capable of justifying an inspection and if reviewing an Article 20(4) decision the Court must satisfy itself that reasonable grounds for suspecting an infringement by the undertaking concerned exist.[159] Therefore the Commission has to describe the sectors covered by the alleged infringement with sufficient precision to enable the undertaking to limit its cooperation with the Commission's inspectors to its activities in the sector where the infringement is reasonably suspected.[160] In *Nexans* the GC reviewed in detail the evidence upon which the Commission took the decision to mount the dawn raid, which had mainly come from a leniency applicant.[161] The GC's readiness to check that the Commission has reasonable grounds to justify an Article 20(4) inspection is of particular importance given that the Commission does not have to obtain any kind of warrant[162] and that the consequences of a dawn raid are so serious, not least in terms of bad publicity.

b. The Powers of the Inspectors

The undertaking must actively and fully cooperate with the inspection. However this duty exists only in connection with its activities in the sectors in respect of which the Commission has reasonable grounds for suspecting an infringement, as discussed earlier. In *Nexans* the GC held that although the broad terms of the inspection decision did not invalidate it, the Commission had reasonable grounds to suspect an infringement only in respect of high voltage underwater and underground high voltage cables and not all electric cables. The inspectors should therefore have limited themselves to material relevant to those two kinds of cable only. They should not have gone on a 'fishing expedition' during the inspection.

Case T-135/09, *Nexans France SAS* v. *Commission*, General Court, 14 November 2012

62 In the first place, it should be observed in that regard that, as the Commission contends, its powers of investigation would serve no useful purpose if it could do no more than ask for documents which it was able to identify with precision in advance. On the contrary, its right to investigate implies the power to search for various items of information which are not already known or fully identified. Without such a power, it would be impossible for the Commission to obtain the information necessary to carry out the inspection if the undertakings concerned refused to cooperate or adopted an obstructive attitude (*Hoechst* v *Commission*, paragraph 41 above, paragraph 27; Case T-59/99 *Ventouris* v *Commission*... paragraph 122).

63 In the second place, the exercise of that power to search for various items of information which are not already known or fully identified makes it possible for the Commission to examine certain business

---

[158] Case C-94/00, *Roquette Frères SA* v. *Directeur Général de la Concurrence, de la Consommation et de la Répression des Fraudes* [2002] ECR I-9011, paras. 54–55.

[159] *Nexans France SAS* v. *Commission*, para. 43.

[160] *Nexans France SAS* v. *Commission*, para. 45. In *Nexans* the inspection decision described the subject matter as 'the supply of electric cables and material associated with such supply, including, amongst others, high voltage underwater electric cables, and, in certain cases, high voltage underground electric cables'. The Commission was really concerned about the high voltage cables and meant 'in particular' rather than 'including'. The GC accepted that the wording could have been 'less ambiguous' (para. 54) but nonetheless upheld the decision on this point.

[161] *Nexans*, paras. 74–92; for the Commission's leniency policy for participants in cartels, see Section 8.G.v, p. 1019.

[162] Cf. the position in respect of private homes under Article 21, see Section 8.B.iv, p. 952.

records of the undertaking which is the recipient of a decision under Article 20(4) of Regulation No 1/2003, even if it does not know whether they relate to activities covered by that decision, in order to ascertain whether that is so and to prevent the undertaking from hiding from it evidence which is relevant to the investigation, on the pretext that that evidence is not covered by the investigation.

64 Nevertheless, notwithstanding the above, when the Commission carries out an inspection at the premises of an undertaking under Article 20(4) of Regulation No 1/2003, it is required to restrict its searches to the activities of that undertaking relating to the sectors indicated in the decision ordering the inspection and accordingly, once it has found, after examination, that a document or other item of information does not relate to those activities, to refrain from using that document or item of information for the purposes of its investigation.

65 First of all, if the Commission were not subject to that restriction, it would in practice be able, every time it has indicia suggesting that an undertaking has infringed the competition rules in a specific field of its activities, to carry out an inspection covering all those activities, with the ultimate aim of detecting any infringement of those rules which might have been committed by that undertaking. That is incompatible with the protection of the sphere of private activity of legal persons, guaranteed as a fundamental right in a democratic society.

66 Next, the obligation on the Commission to indicate the purpose and the subject-matter of the inspection in decisions taken under Article 20(4) of Regulation No 1/2003 would be a mere technicality if it were defined in the manner suggested by the Commission. The case-law according to which the purpose of that obligation is, in particular, to enable the undertakings concerned to assess the scope of their duty to cooperate would not be complied with, inasmuch as that obligation would be systematically extended to all the activities of the undertakings at issue.

67 It must therefore be held that, in the present case, the Commission was under an obligation, in order to adopt the inspection decision, to have reasonable grounds to justify an inspection at the applicants' premises covering all the applicants' activities in relation to electric cables and the material associated with those cables.

68 In the application initiating proceedings, the applicants rely on two grounds to substantiate their assertion that the high voltage underwater cable sector was the only sector in relation to which the Commission had at its disposal information concerning potential anti-competitive conduct. First, they claim that, in a press release dated 3 February 2009, the Commission had declared that it had carried out inspections at the premises of undertakings engaged exclusively in the manufacture of those cables. Secondly, they claim that, during the inspection, the Commission showed interest in certain employees of Nexans France working in that sector.

69 It must be noted that, when the application was filed at the Court Registry, the applicants had not had access to the evidence in the possession of the Commission at the time of the inspection decision and on which its suspicions were based. Moreover, the Commission was not required to communicate that evidence to them (see, to that effect, *Dow Chemical Ibérica and Others* v *Commission*, paragraph 39 above, paragraphs 45 and 51).

70 Accordingly, the applicants cannot be required to provide, in addition to the grounds mentioned in paragraph 68 above, evidence in support of their assertion that the high voltage underwater cable sector is the only sector in relation to which the Commission had information concerning potential anti-competitive conduct.

71 Such a requirement would have the consequence in practice that an undertaking which was the recipient of a decision taken under Article 20(4) of Regulation No 1/2003 would not be able to call into question the reasonable nature of the grounds on which the Commission had adopted that decision. That would prevent the Court from checking that the decision was in no way arbitrary.

72 It must therefore be concluded that, at least when undertakings which are the recipients of a decision taken under Article 20(4) of Regulation No 1/2003 produce, as in the present case, some evidence casting doubt on whether the Commission had reasonable grounds for adopting such a decision, the Court of the European Union must examine those grounds and determine whether they are reasonable.

The GC therefore annulled the inspection decision insofar as it concerned electric cables other than high voltage underwater and underground.[163] However, it did not specify what the consequences were for the Commission's continuing investigation. Furthermore, as demonstrated by *Nexans*, the EU Courts may review disputes over procedural issues arising in the course of an inspection only as part of the review of the Commission's final decision in the case and not in a separate action, because they are only 'measures implementing the inspection decision'.[164] This can leave investigated undertakings in a difficult position. If they refuse to cooperate with the disputed measures during the inspection they are liable to be fined for obstruction under Article 23(1) (which at least they could challenge immediately) although the Commission may instead wait and punish the obstruction by increasing any fine imposed in the final infringement decision.[165]

Of the five powers listed in Article 20(2), the power to seal any business premises or records did not appear in Regulation 17, and the power to ask for explanations on facts or documents is wider than the power to ask for 'oral explanations on the spot' in Regulation 17, Article 14(1). It is standard procedure at the start of an inspection for the inspectors to request to block email accounts of key personnel, and set a new password known only to the inspectors. In *EPH* the Commission fined two Czech companies for modifying the password to one account during the inspection and for diverting all emails away from some blocked accounts.[166]

The Power to Enter any Premises, Land and Means of Transport (Article 20(2)(a))

The extent of this power was set out by the CJ in *Hoechst*.[167] If the undertakings are willing to cooperate, the Commission officials have power to have shown to them the documents they request, and to enter such premises they choose and have shown to them the contents of particular furniture they indicate. They are *not* entitled forcibly to enter premises or furniture or carry out searches without the undertaking's consent. If the undertaking does not submit to the investigation Article 20(6) comes into play and the Commission has to rely on the assistance of the Member State.[168]

The Power to Examine Books and Other Records (Article 20(2)(b))

Article 20(2)(b) says that the Commission may examine records 'irrespective of the medium on which they are stored'. This encompasses all forms of information technology. The Explanatory Note elaborates on this and details what IT tools the inspectors can use. In *EPH* the Commission noted 'that over the last decade paper-based evidence has become less important and most of the documents collected nowadays during inspections are extracted from e-mail accounts and electronic files and that data stored in electronic format are much easier and quicker to destroy than paper files'.[169]

The Power to Take or Obtain in any Form Copies of or Extracts from such Books or Records (Article 20(2)(c))

The details of the Commission's practice in dealing with copies and extracts (which now will usually be mainly in electronic format) are provided in the Explanatory Note. The Note was amended in March 2013 after the *Nexans* case, in which the undertaking challenged the Commission's action in taking copies of computer hard drives back to Brussels for examination (a much disputed practice).[170] The GC refused to consider this matter until a challenge to any final decision in the case is

---

163 *Nexans*, para. 137.

164 *Nexans*, para. 125. See also Case T-340/03, *France Télécom SA v. Commission* [2007] ECR II-107.

165 There is, however, a trend towards pursuing procedural offences by stand-alone proceedings.

166 COMP/39.793, *EPH*, IP/12/319. The companies were fined €2.5 million under Regulation 1/2003, Art. 23(1)(c). The decision has been appealed, Case T-272/12, *Energetický a průmyslový holding v. Commission*, judgment pending.

167 Cases 46/87 and 227/88, *Hoechst v. EC Commission* [1989] ECR 2859, paras. 31–32.

168 See Section 8.B.iii.c, p. 949.

169 *EPH*, Summary of decision [2012] OJ C316/8, para. 17.

170 Instead of assessing each separate document on the undertaking's premises the Commission takes a copy of data still to be searched (e.g. the hard drive), places it in a sealed envelope, and invites the undertaking's representatives to its opening in Brussels. See Ortiz Blanco (cited in n. 1), p. 341.

made, as taking copies or extracts under Article 2(2)(c) merely constitute measures 'implementing' the inspection decision.[171] In the meantime the Explanatory Note makes it clear that the Commission intends to carry on with the practice.

The Power to Seal any Business Premises and Books or Records for the Period and to the Extent Necessary for the Inspection (Article 20(2)(d))

This power was expressly conferred on the Commission in Regulation 1/2003, although previously the Commission affixed seals when it thought it necessary. Recital 25 says that seals should not normally be affixed for more than 72 hours. Undertakings can be fined under Article 23(1)(e) for breaching seals. In 2008 the Commission imposed a fine of €38 million on E.ON for breaching a seal during an inspection. The seal had been affixed overnight to the door of a room in which the inspectors had placed documents.[172]

The Power to Ask any Representative or Member of Staff of the Undertaking or Association of Undertakings for Explanations on Facts or Documents Relating to the Subject Matter and Purpose of the Inspection and to Record the Answers

Under Article 20(2)(e)[173] the inspectors may ask 'any representative or member of staff' for explanations on *facts and documents* relating to *the subject matter and purpose* of the inspection. The answers can be recorded.[174] Article 23(1)(d) provides that the Commission may fine the undertaking up to one per cent of total turnover of the previous business year if:

in response to a question asked in accordance with Article 20(2)(e),

— they give an incorrect or misleading answer,
— they fail to rectify within a time-limit set by the Commission an incorrect, incomplete or misleading answer given by a member of staff, or
— they fail or refuse to provide a complete answer on facts relating to the subject-matter and purpose of an inspection ordered by a decision adopted pursuant to Article 20(4).

The 'they' in this paragraph refers to the undertaking, not to the individual member of staff. There are no powers under Regulation 1/2003 to impose fines on individuals.[175] The imposition of a fine for failure or refusal to rectify incomplete, incorrect, or misleading answers is elaborated upon in Regulation 773/2004, Article 4(3) which provides:

In cases where a member of staff of an undertaking or of an association of undertakings who is not or was not authorised by the undertaking or by the association of undertakings to provide explanations on behalf of the undertaking or association of undertakings has been asked for explanations, the Commission shall set a time-limit within which the undertaking or the association of undertakings may communicate to the Commission any rectification, amendment or supplement to the explanations given by such member of staff. The rectification, amendment or supplement shall be added to the explanations as recorded pursuant to paragraph 1.[176]

---

[171] *Nexans* (cited in n. 164), paras. 120–121.

[172] Commission Decision 30.1.2008, COMP/B-1/39.326, Press Release IP/08/2008. The decision was upheld by the GC, Case T-141/08, *E.ON Energie AG v. Commission* [2010] ECR II-5761, *aff'd* Case C-89/11 P, *E.ON Energie AG v. Commission*, 22 November 2012. Among E.ON's explanations for the damage to the seal was that it had been damaged by aggressive cleaning products and the cleaning lady wiping it with a damp cloth (see para. 84 of the decision). See also COMP/39.796 *Suez Environnement*, IP/11/632, where a fine of €8 million was imposed for breaching a seal, see C. Gauer, K. Bansard and F. Christ, 'The Suez Environnement Case—Eur 8 million fine for breaching a Commission seal during an inspection' (2011) 3 *Competition Policy Newsletter* 8.

[173] Which has expanded the power to ask questions from what was the position under Reg. 17, Art. 14(1)(c).

[174] Under Reg. 773/2004, Art. 4(2) a copy of any recording made has to be made available to the undertaking after the inspection.

[175] The absence under EU law of liability on individuals is in contrast to the position in some Member States, including the UK.

[176] Under Reg. 773/2004, Art. 17(3) the time limit has to be at least two weeks.

This provision appears to relate only to staff 'not authorised by the undertaking to provide explanations'. Undertakings might also wish, however, to rectify or supplement answers given by staff who *are* 'authorised'.

It is clear from *Nexans* that questioning employees is an 'implementing measure'; it is not a separately reviewable act that can be challenged earlier than any challenge to the final infringement decision. It should be noted that in addition to this wider power to ask for explanations during an inspection the Commission has a new power of interview under Regulation 1/2003, Article 19. This is discussed later.[177]

c. The Role of the NCAs, the Member States, and the National Courts in Article 20 Inspections

Regulation 1/2003, Article 20(5) provides that officials from the NCA on whose territory the inspection is conducted may actively assist the Commission officials (and have the Article 20(2) powers) if either the NCA or the Commission requests it. The role of the Member State becomes more important, however, if the undertaking does not submit to the investigation. The duty to submit to an Article 14(3) investigation was a continuing one, entailing both allowing the inspection to begin and cooperating thereafter, but the limited nature of the Commission officials' powers, and their reliance on national authorities and national procedures, was sharply demonstrated in the case of *Hoechst*.[178] Article 20(6), replacing Regulation 17, Article 14(6), provides:

Where the officials and other accompanying persons authorised by the Commission find that an undertaking opposes an inspection ordered pursuant to this Article, the Member State concerned shall afford them the necessary assistance, requesting where appropriate the assistance of the police or of an equivalent enforcement authority, so as to enable them to conduct their inspection.

If the 'assistance' requires authorisation, under national law, from a judicial authority (e.g., because national law requires a court to sanction coercive measures such as forcible entry) that must be applied for.[179]

Regulation 1/2003, Article 20(8) now sets out the role of the national court. The provision enacts, in effect, the judgment of the CJ in *Roquette Frères SA*.[180]

Regulation 1/2003, Article 20(8)

Where authorisation as referred to in paragraph 7 is applied for, the national judicial authority shall control that the Commission decision is authentic and that the coercive measures envisaged are neither arbitrary nor excessive having regard to the subject matter of the inspection. In its control of the proportionality of the coercive measures, the national judicial authority may ask the Commission, directly or through the Member State competition authority, for detailed explanations in particular on the grounds the Commission has for suspecting infringement of [Articles 101 and 102 TFEU], as well as on the seriousness of the suspected infringement and on the nature of the involvement of the undertaking concerned. However, the national judicial authority may not call into question the necessity for the inspection nor demand that it be provided with the information in the Commission's file. The lawfulness of the Commission decision shall be subject to review only by the Court of Justice.

---

[177] Section 8.B.v.

[178] Cases 46/87 and 227/88, *Hoechst AG v. Commission* [1989] ECR 2859, in which Hoechst simply refused to admit the Commission inspectors when they arrived for a dawn raid in the course of the Commission's investigations into the PVC and polyethylene cartels, and the local district court initially refused to issue a search warrant.

[179] Reg. 1/2003, Art. 20(7). Under the Competition Act 1998, the OFT (from 2014 the Competition and Markets Authority (CMA)) has power to enter premises with a warrant from the High Court in England and Wales or a Court of Session in Scotland using reasonable force as necessary.

[180] Case C-94/00, *Roquette Frères SA v. Directeur Général de la Concurrence, de la Consommation et de la Répression des Fraudes* [2002] ECR I-9011. The powers and duties of the national court in this situation, which were not expressly mentioned under Regulation 17, were initially spelt out in *Hoechst*; and in *Roquette Frères* the CJ looked at the issue in the context of the general principles of Community law and the ECHR as developed since *Hoechst*.

Furthermore, the role of the national courts in the context of Commission inspections is spelt out again in the Notice on cooperation between the Commission and the courts of the EU Member States.[181]

d. The Application of Article 8 of the ECHR

In *Hoechst* [182] the CJ stated that the principle of the inviolability of the home in Article 8(1) of the ECHR[183] does not apply to commercial premises. However, the ECtHR subsequently said in *Niemitz* [184] that the words 'private life' and 'home' in Article 8(1) included certain professional or business activities or premises. In that case a lawyer's office was protected. The ECtHR said this interpretation was necessary because otherwise unequal treatment could arise, in that self-employed persons may carry on professional activities at home and private activities at their place of work. In *PVC Cartel II* [185] the GC said that the fact that the case law of the ECtHR had evolved since *Hoechst* had no direct impact on the merits of the solutions adopted in that case.[186] On appeal the CJ did not find it necessary to rule on the matter.[187] However, in *Roquette Frères SA*,[188] the CJ was again concerned with compatibility with the principle of Community law that protected the private activities of natural or legal persons against the arbitrary or disproportionate intervention by public authorities. It was prepared to depart from *Hoechst*:

29. For the purposes of determining the scope of that principle in relation to the protection of business premises, regard must be had to the case-law of the European Court of Human Rights subsequent to the judgment in *Hoechst*. According to that case-law, first, the protection of the home provided for in Article 8 of the ECHR may in certain circumstances be extended to cover such premises (see, in particular, the judgment of 16 April 2002 in *Colas Est and Others v. France*, not yet published in the *Reports of Judgments and Decisions*, § 41) and, second, the right of interference established by Article 8(2) of the ECHR might well be more far-reaching where professional or business activities or premises were involved than would otherwise be the case (Niemietz v. Germany, cited above, § 31).[189]

The case referred to by the CJ, *Colas Est*,[190] involved the French competition authority simultaneously raiding 56 undertakings in the course of investigating suspected bid-rigging. Three of the undertakings challenged the legality of the raids on the grounds that the investigating officers had no warrant and were not accompanied by a police officer with judicial investigation powers. The ECtHR held that the rights guaranteed by Article 8 can apply to a company's head office, branch office, or place of business and that the inspections were disproportionate to the legitimate objectives being pursued. The French law at the time did not contain enough guarantees against abuse and Article 8 was violated. Although it was suggested at the time that in the light of this case Commission inspections do

---

[181] [2004] OJ C101/54, paras. 38–41.

[182] Cases 46/87 and 227/88, *Hoechst AG v. Commission* [1989] ECR 2859, para. 18.

[183] To which Art. 7 of the Charter corresponds.

[184] *Niemitz v. Germany*, Series A, No. 251–B, (1993) 16 EHRR 97, para. 31.

[185] Cases T-305–307, 313–316, 318, 325, 328–329, and 335/94, *Limburgse Vinyl Maatschappij NV v. Commission* [1999] ECR II-931.

[186] Cases T-305–307, 313–316, 318, 325, 328–329, and 335/94, *Limburgse Vinyl Maatschappij NV v. Commission* [1999] ECR II-931, para. 420.

[187] Cases C-238, 244–245, 247, 250, 251–252, and 254/99 P, *Limburgse Vinyl Maatschappij NV v. Commission* [2002] ECR I-8375, para. 251.

[188] Cited in n. 180.

[189] The Advocate General considered the application of the ECHR at length, see in particular paras. 28–48 of his Opinion.

[190] Case No. 37971/97, Reports of Judgments and Decisions 2002-III.

not comply with Article 8,[191] Commission officials (speaking personally) have strongly argued that, particularly in the light of Article 20 of Regulation 1/2003, they do comply:[192]

When the Commission carries out an inspection, it cannot seize documents; nor is it empowered to copy the documents if the undertaking opposes such copying. It must in that event…turn to the NCA and ask for assistance. The opposition is noted in the minutes and triggers the assistance: …the undertakings know precisely when the coercion, if any, starts. The assistance is regulated by national law and most laws foresee a judicial authorisation beforehand. When national powers are used to overcome the opposition, national law provides for safeguards of the rights of defence and for legal means to challenge the use of coercion before a judge…Finally, and most importantly, the undertakings are able to contest the legality of the Commission decision before the Community Courts. Contrary to the French authority in the *Colas* case, the Commission is therefore not in a position to determine alone '*the expediency, number, length and scale of inspections*' (see point 49 of *Colas*). It acts under effective judicial control.

As will be seen,[193] the Commission has power under Regulation 1/2003, Article 21 to carry out inspections at 'other premises' including the homes of directors, managers, and other members of staff of undertakings and associations of undertakings.

e. Legal Advice

Article 20, like Regulation 17, Article 14 before it, says nothing about an undertaking's right to have legal advisers present during the investigation. When conducting the unannounced investigation in *National Panasonic* the Commission was prepared to wait for some time for the undertakings' legal advisers to arrive, but after a while proceeded in their absence. The CJ held that Panasonic's fundamental rights had not been infringed in the investigation, although it did not expressly avert to the legal adviser point. The Explanatory Note on inspections[194] says that the officials may enter the premises and occupy offices without waiting for the undertaking to consult its lawyer and will only accept a short delay before proceeding with the inspection. During any wait the undertaking's management has to ensure that business records remain as they were on the officials' arrival and the officials have to be allowed to enter and remain in the offices of their choice. In *Koninklijke Wegenbouw Stevin* an undertaking's refusal to allow the inspection to begin before the arrival of its external lawyer was held by the GC to constitute a refusal to submit to the inspection.[195]

f. Legal Privilege

The issue of the withholding of documents on the grounds of legal privilege is considered separately.[196]

g. Self-incrimination

The issue of self-incrimination is considered later.[197]

[191] J. Temple Lang and C. Rizza, 'The *Ste Colas Est and Others v. France* case: European Court of Human Rights Case of 16 April 2002' [2002] *ECLR* 417.

[192] K. Dekeyser and C. Gauer, 'The New Enforcement System for Articles 101 and 102 and the Rights of Defence' [2004] Fordham Corp L Inst (B. Hawk (ed.), 2005), 549, 556–557.

[193] See Section 8.B.iv, p. 952.

[194] See n. 156, para. 6.

[195] Case 357/06, *Koninklijke Wegenbouw Stevin BV v. Commission*, 27 September 2012. When the lawyer arrived he refused to permit the inspectors to enter one particular office, which was also held to be a refusal to submit.

[196] See Section 8.B.vii, p. 957.

[197] See Section 8.B.vi, p. 953.

(iv) Inspections on Private Premises Under Article 21

Regulation 1/2003 gave the Commission a new power to conduct inspections at private premises. In other words, dawn raids may be conducted at the homes (and on the private vehicles) of directors and employees. Article 21(1) states:

If a reasonable suspicion exists that books or other records related to the business and to the subject-matter of the inspection, which may be relevant to prove a serious violation of Article [101] or Article [102]... are being kept in any other premises, land and means of transport, including the homes of directors, managers and other members of staff of the undertakings and associations of undertakings concerned, the Commission can by decision order an inspection to be conducted in such other premises, land and means of transport.

Recital 26 explains that the provision was introduced because '[e]xperience has shown that there are cases where business records are kept in the homes of directors or other people working for an undertaking'. In particular, the Commission is determined that its efforts to crack hardcore cartels are not frustrated by individuals keeping the incriminating evidence at home.[198] Obviously, the safeguards provided by Article 8 of the ECHR,[199] apply par excellence to Article 21. Moreover, the inspection may only take place with prior authorisation from the national judicial authority of the Member State concerned. The right of the national court to query the necessity for the inspection, however, is limited as in Article 20(8) so that the national judicial authority may not call into question the necessity for the inspection nor demand that it be provided with information in the Commission's file. In controlling that the Commission decision is authentic and that the coercive measures envisaged are neither arbitrary nor excessive, however, the national court should have regard to 'the importance of the evidence sought' and 'the reasonable likelihood that business books and records relating to the subject matter of the inspection are kept in the premises for which the authorisation is requested'.[200] In the light of the jurisprudence of the ECtHR there is some doubt as to whether the limited functions of the national courts in respect of Article 21 inspections do fully comply with the ECHR.[201]

There is no provision in Article 21 for sealing private premises, or for questioning the person whose premises are being searched. Regulation 1/2003 does not impose penalties for opposing the inspection: there is no provision in Article 23 for fining the undertaking concerned and nothing in Regulation 1/2003 puts any liability on individuals. The position as regards forcible entry if provided for in national law is the same as in respect of Article 20.[202] The first 'dawn raid' on a private home under Article 21 was carried out on 2 May 2007 in the UK in connection with the investigation of the Marine Hoses cartel.[203]

---

[198] See *SAS/Maersk* [2001] OJ L265/15, for a case in which documents relating to a market-sharing agreement were kept at home, although they were voluntarily surrendered a few days after the Reg. 17, Art. 14(3) inspection. A note of one meeting recorded a Maersk representative as saying that 'all material on price agreements, market-sharing agreements and the like *had* to be destroyed before going home today. Anything that might be needed *had* to be taken home...' (*SAS/Maersk*, para. 89).

[199] See Section 8.Biii.d, p. 950.

[200] Art. 21(3). See also Notice on cooperation between the Commission and the courts of the EU Member States, [2004] OJ C101/54, para. 40.

[201] See Bellamy and Child, *European Law of Competition* (cited in n. 2), para. 13.029, and Case 29613/08, *Primagaz v. France*, judgment 26 August 2011.

[202] See Section 8.B.iii.b, p. 947.

[203] Case COMP/39.406, 28 January 2009, [2010] 4 CMLR 148; Press Release IP/09/137; on appeal Cases T-146/09, etc., *Parker ITR and Parker-Hannifin* v. *Commission*, 17 May 2013. The cartel was also prosecuted in the US. The individual concerned in the Art. 21 inspection and two others were prosecuted in the US but under a plea bargain with the DOJ they were returned to the UK after agreement with the UK authorities that they would be prosecuted under the Enterprise Act 2002. They were arrested at Heathrow, pleaded guilty, and were sentenced to terms of imprisonment that exceeded the minimum terms agreed with the US prosecutors. They appealed their sentences and the Court of Appeal reduced them to the agreed minimum terms (30, 24, and 20 months): *R* v. *Whittle and others* [2008] EWCA Crim 2560; see Chap. 9.

(v) The Power to Take Statements

Regulation 1/2003, Article 19 gave the Commission a new power to 'take statements' by which it can conduct formal interviews with natural or legal persons. It can be exercised only with the consent of the person concerned, and only to collect information in relation to the subject matter of an investigation. Article 19 states:

1. In order to carry out the duties assigned to it by this Regulation, the Commission may interview any natural or legal person who consents to be interviewed for the purpose of collecting information relating to the subject-matter of an investigation.

2. Where an interview pursuant to paragraph 1 is conducted in the premises of an undertaking, the Commission shall inform the competition authority of the Member State in whose territory the interview takes place. If so requested by the competition authority of that Member State, its officials may assist the officials and other accompanying persons authorised by the Commission to conduct the interview.

Regulation 773/2004, Article 3 further provides:

1. Where the Commission interviews a person with his consent in accordance with Article 19 of Regulation (EC) No 1/2003, it shall, at the beginning of the interview, state the legal basis and the purpose of the interview, and recall its voluntary nature. It shall also inform the person interviewed of its intention to make a record of the interview.

2. The interview may be conducted by any means including by telephone or electronic means.

3. The Commission may record the statements made by the persons interviewed in any form. A copy of any recording shall be made available to the person interviewed for approval. Where necessary, the Commission shall set a time-limit within which the person interviewed may communicate to it any correction to be made to the statement.[204]

The interviewee is free not to accept the Commission's invitation to be interviewed, and there is no sanction for refusing. During the interview the person concerned can refuse to answer questions, refuse to give reasons for the refusal, and need not find documents, etc. There are no penalties for giving incorrect or misleading information under Article 19. This is in sharp contrast to Article 20(2)(e) (explanations on facts). In the Report the Commission says it has used Article 19 regularly but that 'experience has shown that the absence of penalties for misleading or false replies may be a disincentive to provide correct and complete statements'.[205] Interviewees are entitled to be accompanied by lawyers and interviews may take place on or away from business premises. The Antitrust ManProc says that nobody can be prevented by their current or former employer from giving an interview, unless he/she acts on behalf of the undertaking.[206]

(vi) The Right not to Incriminate Oneself

The fact that the Commission has such wide powers to carry out inspections and ask for information under Regulation 1/2003, Articles 18, 20, and 21 raises the issue of whether EU law recognises as part of the rights of the defence a privilege against self-incrimination.

Orkem established that the duty actively to cooperate with the Commission does not mean that the undertaking has to incriminate itself by admitting to infringements of the competition rules. However, the Commission may ask questions, or demand the production of documents, by means of which it can establish an infringement.

---

[204] The time limit is at least two weeks, Reg. 773/2004, Art. 17(3).

[205] Report on the Functioning of Reg. 1/2003, see n. 59, para.12.

[206] Antitrust ManProc (cited in n. 71), Module 8, para. 14.

Case 374/87, *Orkem SA* v. *Commission* [1989] ECR 3283

The Commission was investigating alleged cartels in the thermoplastics industry. The questions it required to be answered asked for (1) factual information about a meeting, (2) clarification on 'every step or concerted measure which may have been envisaged or adopted to support such price initiatives', (3) the 'details of any system or method which made it possible to attribute sales or targets or quotas to the participants', and (4) 'details of any methods facilitating annual monitoring of compliance with any system of targets in terms of volumes or quotas'. The undertaking challenged the decision claiming that the Commission had infringed the general principle that no-one may be compelled to give evidence against himself, a principle which was part of Community law as it was recognised by the Member States, by Article 6 of the ECHR and by paragraph 3(g) of the International Covenant on Civil and Political Rights, 1966.

Court of Justice

28. In the absence of any right to remain silent expressly embodied in Regulation 17, it is appropriate to consider whether and to what extent the general principles of Community law, of which fundamental rights form an integral part and in the light of which all Community legislation must be interpreted, require, as the applicant claims, recognition of the right not to supply information capable of being used in order to establish against the person supplying it, the existence of an infringement of the competition rules.

29. In general, the laws of the Member-States grant the right not to give evidence against oneself only to a natural person charged with an offence in criminal proceedings. A comparative analysis of national law does not therefore indicate the existence of such a principle, common to the laws of the Member-States, which may be relied upon by legal persons in relation to infringements in the economic sphere, in particular infringements of competition law.

30. As far as Article 6 of the European Convention is concerned, although it may be relied upon by an undertaking subject to an investigation relating to competition law, it must be observed that neither the wording of that Article nor the decisions of [the] European Court of Human Rights indicate that it upholds the right not to give evidence against oneself.

31. Article 14 of the International Covenant, which upholds, in addition to the presumption of innocence, the right (in paragraph 3(g)) not to give evidence against oneself or to confess guilt, relates only to persons accused of a criminal offence in court proceedings and thus has no bearing on investigations in the field of competition law.

32. It is necessary, however, to consider whether certain limitations on the Commission's powers of investigation are implied by the need to safeguard the rights of the defence which the Court has held to be [a] fundamental principle of the Community order (Case 322/102, *Michelin* v. *E.C. Commission* .

33. In that connection, the court observed recently in its judgment in Joined Cases 46/87 and 227/88 *Hoechst* v. *E.C. Commission* . . . that whilst it is true that the rights of the defence must be observed in administrative procedures which may lead to the imposition of penalties, it is necessary to prevent those rights from being irremediably impaired during preliminary inquiry procedures which may be decisive in providing evidence of the unlawful nature of conduct engaged in by undertakings and for which they may be liable. Consequently, although certain rights of the defence relate only to contentious proceedings which follow the delivery of the statement of objections, other rights must be respected even during the preliminary inquiry.

34. Accordingly, whilst the Commission is entitled, in order to preserve the useful effect of Article 11(2) and (5) of Regulation 17, to compel an undertaking to provide all necessary information concerning such facts as may be known to it and to disclose to it, if necessary, such documents relating thereto as are in its possession, even if the latter may be used to establish, against it or another undertaking, the existence of anti-competitive conduct, it may not, by means of a decision calling for information, undermine the rights of defence of the undertaking concerned.

35. Thus, the Commission may not compel an undertaking to provide it with answers which might involve an admission on its part of the existence of an infringement which it is incumbent upon the Commission to prove.

On this basis, the CJ annulled the decision in respect of all the questions listed except the first one. The Court drew a distinction (paragraphs 34 and 35) between a right to compel the undertaking to provide factual information which can be used to establish a breach of the rules, and a right to compel it to admit to the breach. The Commission has the former but not the latter right.

The problem is that this may not be in line with the interpretation by the ECtHR of Article 6 of the ECHR, which guarantees the right to a fair trial.[207] The Court denied in *Orkem* (in paragraph 30 of the extract) that Article 6 included the right not to provide evidence against oneself. In *Funke* four years later, however, the ECtHR held that as a result of Article 6(1) a person charged with a criminal offence within the meaning of that Article had the right 'to remain silent and not…contribute to incriminating himself'.[208] This was held to include the production of documents and meant in *Funke* that the French authorities had infringed Article 6(1) by fining the applicant for failing to produce bank statements, evidence of whose existence they had uncovered when searching his house under a warrant. In *Saunders* v. *United Kingdom* [209] the ECtHR considered the use against Ernest Saunders in a subsequent criminal fraud trial[210] of incriminating statements compulsorily obtained from him by the Department of Trade and Industry in the course of an administrative company law investigation. The penalty for not answering the inspectors' questions was a fine or imprisonment for contempt of court. The ECtHR held that this had impaired his ability to defend himself in the criminal trial and infringed Article 6(1). However, it went on to say that the right not to incriminate oneself did not extend to 'material which may be obtained from the accused through the use of compulsory powers but which has an existence independent of the will of the suspect such as, inter alia, *documents acquired pursuant to a warrant*, breath, blood and urine samples and bodily tissue for the purpose of DNA testing'[211] (emphasis added). The concept of 'independent existence' is a difficult one and following *Funke*, *Saunders*, and further case law of the ECtHR[212] the position as regards self-incrimination and Article 6(1) can best be described as confused.[213]

As far as EU law is concerned, the GC reviewed the matter in *Mannesmannröhren-Werke AG* in 2001[214] and restated the *Orkem* position. In that case the Commission was conducting an investigating into an alleged cartel in the seamless tube industry.[215] The undertaking refused to reply to some requests for information under Regulation 17, Article 11(4) relating to three sets of meetings. In respect of each of them the Commission asked for dates, places, names of participants, copies of all agendas, minutes, and records relating to them and (each time) 'in the case of meetings for which you are unable to find the relevant documents, please describe the purpose of the meeting, the decisions adopted and the type of documents received before and after the meeting'. The undertaking refused to answer, claiming it was being asked to incriminate itself. Another set of questions related to four agreements. The undertaking was asked, inter alia, about the relationship of the agreements to

---

[207] See Section 8.A.iii, p. 935 and see, on the self-incrimination point, A. Riley, 'Saunders and the Power to Obtain Information in Community and United Kingdom Competition Law' (2000) 25 *ELRev* 264.

[208] *Funke* v. *France*, Series A, No. 256–A, (1993) 16 EHRR 297, para. 44.

[209] *Saunders* v. *United Kingdom* (1997) 23 EHRR 313.

[210] He was convicted of conspiracy to contravene s. 13(1)(a)(i) of the Prevention of Fraud (Investments) Act 1958, false accounting, and theft, in relation to dishonest conduct in a share support operation in connection with the take-over of Distillers by Guinness.

[211] *Saunders*, para. 69.

[212] Such as *JB* v. *Switzerland* [2001] *Crim LR* 748 and *Heaney and McGuinness* v. *Ireland* (2001) 33 EHRR 12.

[213] See further Harris, O'Boyle, and Warbrick, *Law of the European Convention on Human Rights* (cited in n. 82), 259–264; M. Berger, 'Self-Incrimination and the European Court of Human Rights: Procedural Issues in the Enforcement of the Right to Silence' (2007) 5 *EHRLR* 514; M. Redmayne, 'Rethinking the Privilege Against Self-Incrimination' (2007) 27 *Oxford JLS* 209; N. Andrews, 'Privilege Against Self-Incrimination in the Human Rights Era' [2007] *CLJ* 47; A. Ashworth, 'Self-Incrimination in European Human Rights Law—A Pregnant Pragmatism?' (2008–2009) 30 *Cardozo LR* 751.

[214] Case T-112/98, *Mannesmannröhren-Werke AG* v. *Commission* [2001] ECR II-729.

[215] This culminated in the *Seamless Steel Tubes* decision in 1999, [2003] OJ L14/1.

another arrangement, and to what extent 'did the existence and implementation of these agreements influence the decisions adopted within the Europe-Japan Club and/or within the Special Circle?' On the undertaking's refusal the Commission adopted a decision under Regulation 17, Article 11(5), demanding answers on pain of periodic penalty payments. The undertaking appealed against the decision. On the basis of *Orkem* the GC held that the last question in respect of each of the three sets of meetings asked the undertaking about the 'purpose' of meetings, and the 'decisions' adopted. This went beyond mere factual information: 'it follows that requests of this kind are such that they may compel the applicant to admit its participation in an unlawful agreement...'.[216] The decision was therefore annulled in respect of the three last questions. The decision was also annulled in respect of the whole question about the agreements as '[a]nswering this question would require the applicant to give its assessment of the nature of those decisions'.[217] The rest of the decision was upheld. In *PVC Cartel II* [218] the CJ held that the developments in the ECtHR jurisprudence since *Orkem* did not alter the established position.

In *Tokai Carbon* in 2004[219] the GC, although appearing to consider that it was following settled case law, nonetheless held that the Commission's request for documents in respect of meetings such as the protocols, working documents, preparatory documents, hand-written notes, planning and discussion documents, etc. was tantamount to requiring that the undertaking admit its participation. The GC reasoned that since, therefore, the undertaking concerned was not required to produce such documents on grounds of self-incrimination, if it *did* do so it must be regarded as doing so voluntarily and was thereby eligible for leniency under the Commission's leniency policy.[220] On appeal by the Commission the CJ held that the GC had erred in law, and that its judgment had weakened the principle that undertakings subject to an investigation have a duty to cooperate. The CJ re-established the position that undertakings cannot refuse to produce documents on grounds of self-incrimination.

Case C-301/04 P, *Commission* v. *SGL Carbon* [2006] ECR I-5915

Court of Justice

39. It must be recalled first that, under Article 11(1) of Regulation No 17, in carrying out the duties assigned to it in the matter, the Commission may obtain all necessary information from the governments and competent authorities of the Member States and from undertakings and associations of undertakings. As set out in Article 11(4) thereof, the owners of the undertakings or their representatives and, in the case of legal persons, companies or firms, or of associations having no legal personality, the persons authorised to represent them by law or by their constitution are to supply the information requested.

40. As regards the Commission's powers to make such requests, it is important to note that, in paragraph 27 of the judgment in *Orkem* v *Commission*, the Court pointed out that Regulation No 17 does not give an undertaking which is being investigated under that regulation any right to evade the investigation and that, on the contrary, the undertaking in question is subject to an obligation to cooperate actively, which implies that it must make available to the Commission all information relating to the subject-matter of the investigation.

---

[216] *Mannesmannröhren-Werke AG*, para. 71.

[217] *Mannesmannröhren-Werke AG*, para. 74.

[218] Cases C-238, 244–245, 247, 250, 251–252, and 254/99 P, *Limburgse Vinyl Maatschappij NV and others* v. *Commission* [2002] ECR I-8375.

[219] Cases T-236/01, T-239/01, T-244/01 to T-246/01, T-251/01, and T-252/01, *Tokai Carbon Co. Ltd and others* v. *Commission* [2004] ECR II-1181 (the appeal from the *Graphite Electrodes* cartel, [2002] OJ L100/1).

[220] *Tokai Carbon*, paras. 408–409. For the leniency policy, see Section 8.G.v, p. 1019.

41. So far as concerns the question whether that obligation also applies to requests for information which could be used to establish, against the undertaking which provides the information, an infringement of the competition rules, the Court held, in paragraph 34 of that judgment that in order to ensure the effectiveness of Article 11(2) and (5) of Regulation No 17 the Commission is entitled to compel an undertaking, if necessary by adopting a decision, to provide all necessary information concerning such facts as may be known to it and to disclose to it, if necessary, such documents relating thereto as are in that undertaking's possession, even if the latter may be used to establish, against it or another undertaking, the existence of anti-competitive conduct.

42. By contrast, the situation is completely different where the Commission seeks to obtain answers from an undertaking which is being investigated by which that undertaking would be led to admit an infringement which it is incumbent upon the Commission to prove (see *Orkem* v *Commission*, paragraph 35).

43. It must be added that the Court of Justice, in paragraphs 274 to 276 of the judgment in *Limburgse Vinyl Maatschappij and Others* v *Commission*, observed that since the judgment in *Orkem* v *Commission* there have been further developments in the case-law of the European Court of Human Rights which the Community judicature must take into account when interpreting the fundamental rights. The Court of Justice stated however in that regard that those developments were not such as to put in question the statements of principle in *Orkem* v *Commission*.

44. It does not follow from that case-law that the Commission's powers of investigation have been limited as regards the production of documents in the possession of an undertaking which is subject to investigation. The undertaking concerned must therefore, if the Commission requests it, provide the Commission with documents which relate to the subject-matter of the investigation, even if those documents could be used by the Commission in order to establish the existence of an infringement.

45. It is important to point out also that the [General Court] itself, in paragraph 405 of the judgment under appeal, expressly referred to the principles stated in *Orkem* v *Commission* and to the fact that the Court of Justice has not reversed its previous case-law on the point.

46. The [General Court] found, however, in the course of its reasoning, that the Commission's request for information of 31 March 1999 was such as to require SGL Carbon to admit its participation in infringements of the Community competition rules.

47. That finding of the [General Court] misconstrues the scope of Article 11 of Regulation No 17, as interpreted by the Court of Justice, and therefore weakens the principle that undertakings subject to a Commission investigation must cooperate.

48. That obligation to cooperate means that the undertaking may not evade requests for production of documents on the ground that by complying with them it would be required to give evidence against itself.

49. In addition, as the Advocate General correctly observed in point 67 of his Opinion, while it is evident that the rights of the defence should be respected, the undertaking concerned is still able, either during the administrative procedure or in the proceedings before the Community Courts, to contend that the documents produced have a different meaning from that ascribed to them by the Commission.

50. Thus, the [General Court] made an error of law in holding that the conditions for a reduction in the fine by virtue of the Leniency Notice were fulfilled.

(vii) Legal Professional Privilege

a. The Extent of Legal Professional Privilege

The situation as regards legal professional privilege (LPP) has been developed in the case law. Regulation 1/2003, like Regulation 17, does not deal with the issue. In English law LPP means that confidential communications passing between lawyer and client with a view to giving or securing legal advice are privileged so far as the client is concerned, and protected from disclosure. In *AM&S* a UK undertaking argued that it was entitled to keep from the Commission correspondence with its legal advisers that would have been privileged under English law. There were two main issues: first, whether LPP applied in EC competition cases, and if so, whether it was a *Community* principle or a matter of recognising the rule in the Member State concerned; secondly, if legal privilege was recognised, how procedurally should it be dealt with? It is not attractive to the investigated undertakings for the Commission inspectors to look at documents and then decide they are to be disregarded, whatever 'Chinese walls' the Commission erects internally between the inspectors and those deciding on the existence or otherwise of an infringement.

Case 155/79, *AM&S Ltd* v. *Commission* [1982] ECR 1575

On 20 February 1979 Commission officials arrived at the offices of AM&S in Bristol for an unannounced Article 14(2) investigation. The investigation proceeded for two days and at the end the Commission inspectors left with copies of about thirty-five documents, leaving behind a written request for certain other documents to be supplied. In response to this the Managing Director sent a further seven files of documents on 26 March with a letter saying that certain of the requested documents were not being produced because the undertaking's lawyers considered they were covered by LPP. Without any further communication the Commission adopted a decision on 6 July under Article 14(3) demanding that the undertaking submit to an inspection and in particular produce the excluded documents. In the preamble to the decision the Commission stated that although Community competition law did not provide for protection for legal papers nonetheless it was willing not to use certain communications between the undertaking and its lawyers as evidence and that '[w]hen the Commission comes across such papers it does not copy them'. It was for the Commission, subject to review by the Court, to decide whether a given document should be used or not. The Commission inspectors arrived in Bristol and served the decision on 25 July and carried out a further investigation. The undertaking still refused to disclose all the disputed documents but finally, after a meeting with the Commission in Brussels, it disclosed all except one. On 4 October the undertaking commenced an action under Article 263 claiming that the decision of 6 July was void insofar as it required the disclosure of legally privileged documents.

The CJ received evidence from several Member States and from the Consultative Committee of the Bars and Law Societies of the European Community. Advocate General Warner presented in his Opinion a survey of the position on legal privilege in all Member States.

Court of Justice

15. The purpose of Regulation No 17 of the Council which was adopted pursuant to the first subparagraph of Article [103(1) TFEU] is, according to paragraph (2)(a) and (b) of that article, 'to ensure compliance with the prohibitions laid down in Article [101(1)] and in Article [102]' and 'to lay down detailed rules for the application of Article [101(3)]'. The regulation is thus intended to ensure that the aim stated in Article [3(1) (g) EC] is achieved. To that end it confers on the Commission wide powers of investigation and of obtaining information by providing in the eighth recital in its preamble that the Commission must be empowered, throughout the Common Market, to require such information to be supplied and to undertake such investigations 'as are necessary' to bring to light infringements of Articles [101] and [102].

16. In Articles 11 and 14 of the regulation, therefore, it is provided that the Commission may obtain 'information' and undertake the 'necessary' investigations, for the purpose of proceedings in respect of infringements of the rules governing competition. Article 14(1) in particular empowers the Commission to require production of business records, that is to say, documents concerning the market activities of the undertaking, in particular as regards compliance with those rules. Written communications between lawyer and client fall, in so far as they have a bearing on such activities, within the category of documents referred to in Articles 11 and 14.

17. Furthermore since the documents which the Commission may demand are, as Article 14(1) confirms, those whose disclosure it considers 'necessary' in order that it may bring to light an infringement of the Treaty rules on competition, it is in principle for the Commission itself, and not the undertaking

concerned or a third party, whether an expert or an arbitrator, to decide whether or not a document must be produced to it.

(b) Applicability of the protection of confidentiality in Community law

18. However, the above rules do not exclude the possibility of recognizing, subject to certain conditions, that certain business records are of a confidential nature. Community law, which derives from not only the economic but also the legal interpenetration of the Member States, must take into account the principles and concepts common to the laws of those States concerning the observance of confidentiality, in particular, as regards certain communications between lawyer and client. That confidentiality serves the requirements, the importance of which is recognized in all of the Member States, that any person must be able, without constraint, to consult a lawyer whose profession entails the giving of independent legal advice to all those in need of it.

19. As far as the protection of written communications between lawyer and client is concerned, it is apparent from the legal systems of the Member States that, although the principle of such protection is generally recognized, its scope and the criteria for applying it vary, as has, indeed, been conceded both by the application and by the parties who have intervened in support of its conclusions.

20. Whilst in some of the Member States the protection against disclosure afforded to written communications between lawyer and client is based principally on a recognition of the very nature of the legal profession, inasmuch as it contributes towards the maintenance of the rule of law, in other Member States the same protection is justified by the more specific requirement (which, moreover, is also recognized in the first-mentioned States) that the rights of the defence must be respected.

21. Apart from these differences, however, there are to be found in the national laws of the Member States common criteria inasmuch as those law protect, in similar circumstances, the confidentiality of written communications between lawyer and client provided that, on the one hand, such communications are made for the purposes and in the interests of the client's rights of defence and, on the other hand, they emanate from independent lawyers, that is to say, lawyers who are not bound to the client by a relationship of employment.

22. Viewed in that context Regulation No 17 must be interpreted as protecting, in its turn, the confidentiality of written communications between lawyer and client subject to those two conditions, and thus incorporating such elements of that protection as are common to the laws of the Member States.

23. As far as the first of those two conditions is concerned, in Regulation No 17 itself, in particular in the eleventh recital in its preamble and in the provisions contained in Article 19, care is taken to ensure that the rights of the defence may be exercised to the full, and the protection of the confidentiality of written communications between lawyer and client is an essential corollary to those rights. In those circumstances, such protection must, if it is to be effective, be recognized as covering all written communications exchanged after the initiation of the administrative procedure under Regulation No 17 which may lead to a decision on the application of Articles [101] and [102] of the Treaty or to a decision imposing a pecuniary sanction on the undertaking. It must also be possible to extend it to earlier written communications which have a relationship to the subject-matter of that procedure.

24. As regards the second condition, it should be stated that the requirement as to the position and status as an independent lawyer, which must be fulfilled by the legal adviser from whom the written communications which may be protected emanate, is based on a conception of the lawyer's role as collaborating in the administration of justice by the courts and as being required to provide, in full independence, and in the overriding interests of that cause, such legal assistance as the client needs. The counterpart of that protection lies in the rules of professional ethics and discipline which are laid down and enforced in the general interest by institutions endowed with the requisite powers for that purpose. Such a conception reflects the legal traditions common to the Member States and is also to be found in [the] legal order of the Community, as is demonstrated by Article 17 of the Protocols on the Statutes of the Court of Justice of the EEC and the EAEC, and also by Article 20 of the Protocol on the Statute of the Court of Justice of the ECSC.

25. Having regard to the principles of the Treaty concerning freedom of establishment and the free-dom to provide services the protection thus afforded by Community law, in particular in the context of Regulation No 17, to written communications between lawyer and client must apply without distinction to any lawyer entitled to practice his profession in one of the Member States, regardless of the Member State in which the client lives.

26. Such protection may be not be extended beyond those limits which are determined by the scope of the common rules on the exercise of the legal profession as laid down in Council Directive 77/249/EEC of 22 March 1977 (OJ L 78, p. 17), which is based in its turn on the mutual recognition by all the Member States of the national legal concepts of each of them on this subject.

27. In view of all these factors it must therefore be concluded that although Regulation No 17, and in particular Article 14 thereof, interpreted in the light of its wording, structure and aims, and having regard to the laws of the Member States, empowers the Commission to require, in the course of an investigation within the meaning of that article, production of the business documents the disclosure of which it considers necessary including written communications between lawyer and client, for proceedings in respect of any infringements of Articles [101] and [102], that power is, however, subject to a restriction imposed by the need to protect confidentiality, on the conditions defined above, and provided that the communications in question are exchanged between an independent lawyer, that is to say one who is not bound to his client by a relationship of employment, and his client.

28. Finally, it should be remarked that the principle of confidentiality does not prevent a lawyer's client from disclosing the written communications between them if he considers that it is in his interests to do so.

(c) The procedures relating to the application of the principle of confidentiality

29. If an undertaking which is the subject of an investigation under Article 14 of Regulation No 17 refuses, on the ground that it is entitled to protection of the confidentiality of information, to produce, among the business records demanded by the Commission, written communications between itself and its lawyer, it must nevertheless provide the Commission's authorised agents with relevant material of such a nature as to demonstrate that the communications fulfil the conditions for being granted legal protection as defined above, although it is not bound to reveal the contents of the communications in question.

30. Where the Commission is not satisfied that such evidence has been supplied, the appraisal of those conditions is not a matter which may be left to an arbitrator or to a national authority. Since this is a matter involving an appraisal and a decision which affect the conditions under which the Commission may act in a field as vital to the functioning of the common market as that of compliance with the rules on competition, the solution of disputes as to the application of the protection of the confidentiality of written communications between lawyer and client may be sought only at Community level.

31. In that case it is for the Commission to order, pursuant to Article 14(3) of Regulation No 17, production of the communications in question and, if necessary, to impose on the undertaking fines or periodic penalty payments under that regulation as a penalty for the undertaking's refusal either to supply such additional evidence as the Commission considers necessary or to produce the communications in question whose confidentiality, in the Commission's view, is not protected in law.

32. The fact that by virtue of Article [278 TFEU] any action brought by the undertaking concerned against such decisions does not have suspensory effect provides an answer to the Commission's concern as to the effect of the time taken by the procedure before the Court on the efficacy of the supervision which the Commission is called upon to exercise in regard to compliance with the Treaty rules on competition, whilst on the other hand the interests of the undertaking concerned are safeguarded by the possibility which exists under Articles [278 and 279 TFEU], as well as under Article 83 of the Rules and Procedure of the Court, of obtaining an order suspending the application of the decision which has been taken, or any other interim measure.

The Court thus held that EU law does recognise LPP. This judgment, holding that the Community (now Union) legal order should recognise a principle contained in some form in nearly every Member State, is a famous example of the development of the jurisprudence on the general principles of law.[221] LPP in EU law is, however, a *Union* concept subject to two conditions. The first is that the protected communications must be made for the purposes and in the interests of the clients' rights of defence (paragraphs 21 and 23). The Court interpreted this broadly in *AM&S* itself, and in practice it has not caused difficulty, as the Commission accepts that communications, earlier than the initiation of proceedings but with a relationship to the subject matter of the proceedings, are covered. The second condition is that the communication must be with[222] an independent lawyer entitled to practise in one of the Member States, not an (in-house) lawyer bound to the undertaking by an employment relationship.

The limitation of privilege to 'independent' lawyers (paragraph 24) is grounded in the role of the lawyer as a collaborator in the administration of justice and the fact that in some Member States different rules of professional discipline apply once a lawyer is operating in an in-house employment relationship. Representations were made by in-house lawyers in submissions on the White Paper strongly arguing that privilege should be extended to them. In the system of non-notification brought in by Regulation 1/2003 undertakings are more heavily reliant on legal advice, and the lawyers said that such an extension would promote effective compliance with the competition rules. They argued that all lawyers must act ethically as defined in the rules of professional ethics and discipline.[223] Regulation 1/2003, however, contained no provision changing the position.

In *Akzo Nobel* in 2007[224] the GC revisited the issue. The undertaking concerned[225] argued first, that the CJ in *AM&S* did not mean to attribute the notion of 'independent' only to external lawyers and that in-house lawyers could also be 'independent' and secondly, in the alternative, that if it did mean to equate 'independent' with 'external' then both the evolution of EU competition law since 1982 (particularly the principle of equality and the reforms contained in Regulation 1/2003) and the evolution of the national legal systems required the solution in *AM&S* to be reconsidered. The GC refused to depart from the law laid down in *AM&S* and continued to equate 'independent' with 'external'. It expressly rejected the argument that the abolition of the notification system was relevant to the question of LPP.[226] The undertaking appealed. The CJ upheld the GC.

Case C-550/07 P, *Akzo Nobel Chemicals Ltd* v. *Commission* [2010] ECR I-8301

Court of Justice

40 It must be recalled that, in *AM & S Europe* v *Commission*, the Court, taking account of the common criteria and similar circumstances existing at the time in the national laws of the Member States, held, in paragraph 21 of that judgment, that the confidentiality of written communications between lawyers and

---

[221] J. Temple Lang, 'The *AM & S* Judgment' in M. Hoskins and W. Robinson, *A True European—Essays for Judge David Edward* (Hart Publishing, 2004), Chap. 12. See generally, T. Tridimas, *The General Principles of EC Law* (2nd edn, Oxford University Press, 2006).

[222] The judgment is worded with reference to communications *from* the lawyer, but the right does encompass communications in both directions.

[223] Summary of observations on the White Paper on reform of Reg. 17, published by the Commission, 29 February 2000, para. 7.7.

[224] Cases T-125/03 and T-253/03, *Akzo Nobel Chemicals Ltd* v. *Commission* [2007] ECR II-3523.

[225] Supported by various international and national Bar Associations including the Council of the Bars and Law Societies of the EU and the International Bar Association.

[226] *Akzo Nobel*, GC, para. 172.

clients should be protected at Community level. However, the Court stated that that protection was subject to two cumulative conditions.

41 In that connection, the Court stated, first, that the exchange with the lawyer must be connected to 'the client's rights of defence' and, second, that the exchange must emanate from 'independent lawyers', that is to say 'lawyers who are not bound to the client by a relationship of employment'.

42 As to the second condition, the Court observed, in paragraph 24 of the judgment in *AM & S Europe v Commission*, that the requirement as to the position and status as an independent lawyer, which must be fulfilled by the legal adviser from whom the written communications which may be protected emanate, is based on a conception of the lawyer's role as collaborating in the administration of justice and as being required to provide, in full independence and in the overriding interests of that cause, such legal assistance as the client needs. The counterpart to that protection lies in the rules of professional ethics and discipline which are laid down and enforced in the general interest. The Court also held, in paragraph 24, that such a conception reflects the legal traditions common to the Member States and is also to be found in the legal order of the European Union, as is demonstrated by the provisions of Article 19 of the Statute of the Court of Justice.

43 The Court repeated those findings in paragraph 27 of that judgment, according to which written communications which may be protected by legal professional privilege must be exchanged with 'an independent lawyer, that is to say one who is not bound to his client by a relationship of employment'.

44 It follows that the requirement of independence means the absence of any employment relationship between the lawyer and his client, so that legal professional privilege does not cover exchanges within a company or group with in-house lawyers.

45 As the Advocate General observed in points 60 and 61 of her Opinion, the concept of the independence of lawyers is determined not only positively, that is by reference to professional ethical obligations, but also negatively, by the absence of an employment relationship. An in-house lawyer, despite his enrolment with a Bar or Law Society and the professional ethical obligations to which he is, as a result, subject, does not enjoy the same degree of independence from his employer as a lawyer working in an external law firm does in relation to his client. Consequently, an in-house lawyer is less able to deal effectively with any conflicts between his professional obligations and the aims of his client.

46 As regards the professional ethical obligations relied on by the appellants in order to demonstrate Mr S.'s independence, it must be observed that, while the rules of professional organisation in Dutch law mentioned by Akzo and Akcros may strengthen the position of an in-house lawyer within the company, the fact remains that they are not able to ensure a degree of independence comparable to that of an external lawyer.

47 Notwithstanding the professional regime applicable in the present case in accordance with the specific provisions of Dutch law, an in-house lawyer cannot, whatever guarantees he has in the exercise of his profession, be treated in the same way as an external lawyer, because he occupies the position of an employee which, by its very nature, does not allow him to ignore the commercial strategies pursued by his employer, and thereby affects his ability to exercise professional independence.

48 It must be added that, under the terms of his contract of employment, an in-house lawyer may be required to carry out other tasks, namely, as in the present case, the task of competition law coordinator, which may have an effect on the commercial policy of the undertaking. Such functions cannot but reinforce the close ties between the lawyer and his employer.

49 It follows, both from the in-house lawyer's economic dependence and the close ties with his employer, that he does not enjoy a level of professional independence comparable to that of an external lawyer.

50 Therefore, the General Court correctly applied the second condition for legal professional privilege laid down in the judgment in *AM & S Europe v Commission* .

...

54 It must be recalled that the principle of equal treatment is a general principle of European Union law, enshrined in Articles 20 and 21 of the Charter of Fundamental Rights of the European Union.

55 According to settled case-law, that principle requires that comparable situations must not be treated differently and that different situations must not be treated in the same way unless such treatment is objectively justified (see Case C-344/04 *IATA and ELFAA*. paragraph 95; Case C-303/05 *Advocaten voor de Wereld*. paragraph 56; and Case C-127/07 *Arcelor Atlantique et Lorraine and Others*. paragraph 23).

56 As to the essential charactcristics of those two categories of lawyer, namely their respective professional status, it is clear from paragraphs 45 to 49 of this judgment that, despite the fact that he may be enrolled with a Bar or Law Society and that he is subject to a certain number of professional ethical obligations, an in-house lawyer does not enjoy a level of professional independence equal to that of external lawyers.

57 As the Advocate General stated, in point 83 of her Opinion, that difference in terms of independence is still significant, even though the national legislature, the Netherlands legislature in this case, seeks to treat in-house lawyers in the same way as external lawyers. After all, such equal treatment relates only to the formal act of admitting an in-house lawyer to a Bar or Law Society and the professional ethical obligations incumbent on him as a result of such admission. On the other hand, that legislative framework does not alter the economic dependence and personal identification of a lawyer in an employment relationship with his undertaking.

58 It follows from those considerations that in-house lawyers are in a fundamentally different position from external lawyers, so that their respective circumstances are not comparable for the purposes of the case-law set out in paragraph 55 of this judgment.

59 Therefore, the General Court rightly held that there was no breach of the principle of equal treatment.

...

69 It must be recalled that the Court stated, in its reasoning in the judgment in *AM & S Europe* v *Commission* relating to legal professional privilege in investigation procedures in matters of competition law, that that area of European Union law must take into account the principles and concepts common to the laws of the Member States concerning the observance of confidentiality, in particular, as regards certain communications between lawyer and client (see paragraph 18 of that judgment). For that purpose, the Court compared various national laws.

70 The Court observed, in paragraphs 19 and 20 of the judgment in *AM & S Europe* v *Commission* that, although the protection of written communications between lawyer and client is generally recognised, its scope and the criteria for applying it vary in accordance with the different national rules. However, the Court acknowledged, on the basis of that comparison, that legal professional privilege should be protected under European Union law, as long as the two conditions laid down in paragraph 21 of that judgment are fulfilled.

71 As the General Court held, in paragraph 170 of the judgment under appeal, even though it is true that specific recognition of the role of in-house lawyers and the protection of communications with such lawyers under legal professional privilege was relatively more common in 2004 than when the judgment in *AM & S Europe* v *Commission* was handed down, it was nevertheless not possible to identify tendencies which were uniform or had clear majority support in the laws of the Member States.

72 Furthermore, it is clear from paragraph 171 of the judgment under appeal that a comparative examination conducted by the General Court shows that a large number of Member States still exclude correspondence with in-house lawyers from protection under legal professional privilege. Additionally, a considerable number of Member States do not allow in-house lawyers to be admitted to a Bar or Law Society and, accordingly, do not recognise them as having the same status as lawyers established in private practice.

73 In that connection, Akzo and Akcros themselves accept that no uniform tendency can be established in the legal systems of the Member States towards the assimilation of in-house lawyers and lawyers in private practice.

74 Therefore no predominant trend towards protection under legal professional privilege of communications within a company or group with in-house lawyers may be discerned in the legal systems of the 27 Member States of the European Union.

75 In those circumstances, and contrary to the appellants' assertions, the legal regime in the Netherlands cannot be regarded as signalling a developing trend in the Member States, or as a relevant factor for determining the scope of legal professional privilege.

76 The Court therefore considers that the legal situation in the Member States of the European Union has not evolved, since the judgment in *AM & S Europe* v *Commission* was delivered, to an extent which would justify a change in the case-law and recognition for in-house lawyers of the benefit of legal professional privilege.

...

83 Although it is true that Regulation 1/2003 has introduced a large number of amendments to the rules of procedure relating to European Union competition law, it is also the case that those rules do not suggest that they require lawyers in independent practice and in-house lawyers to be treated in the same way with respect to legal professional privilege, since that principle is not at all the subject-matter of the regulation.

84 It is clear from the provisions of Article 20 of Regulation No 1/2003 that the Commission may conduct all necessary inspections of undertakings and associations of undertakings, and in that context, examine the books and other records related to the business, irrespective of the medium on which they are stored, and also take or obtain in any form copies or extracts of such books or records.

85 That regulation, like Article 14(1)(a) and (b) of Regulation No 17, has therefore defined the powers of the Commission broadly. As it is clear from Recitals 25 and 26 in the preamble to Regulation No 1/2003, the detection of infringements of the competition rules is growing ever more difficult, and, in order to protect competition effectively and safeguard the effectiveness of inspections, the Commission should be empowered to enter any premises where business records may be kept, including private homes.

86 Thus, Regulation No 1/2003, contrary to the appellants' assertions, does not aim to require in-house and external lawyers to be treated in the same way as far as concerns legal professional privilege, but aims to reinforce the extent of the Commission's powers of inspection, in particular as regards documents which may be the subject of such measures.

87 Therefore, the amendment of the rules of procedure for competition law, resulting in particular from Regulation No 1/2003, is also unable to justify a change in the case-law established by the judgment in *AM & S Europe* v *Commission*.

...

92 It must be recalled that in all proceedings in which sanctions, especially fines or penalty payments, may be imposed observance of the rights of the defence is a fundamental principle of European Union law which has been emphasised on numerous occasions in the case-law of the Court (see Case C-194/99 P *Thyssen Stahl* v *Commission*...paragraph 30; Case C-289/04 P *Showa Denko* v *Commission*...paragraph 68; Case C-3/06 P *Groupe Danone* v *Commission*...paragraph 68), and which has been enshrined in Article 48(2) of the Charter of Fundamental Rights of the European Union.

93 By this ground of appeal, the appellants seek to establish that the rights of the defence must include the right of freedom of choice as to the lawyer who will provide legal advice and representation and that legal professional privilege forms part of those rights, regardless of the professional status of the lawyer concerned.

94 In that connection, it must be observed that, when an undertaking seeks advice from its in-house lawyer, it is not dealing with an independent third party, but with one of its employees, notwithstanding any professional obligations resulting from enrolment at a Bar or Law Society.

95 It should be added that, even assuming that the consultation of in-house lawyers employed by the undertaking or group were to be covered by the right to obtain legal advice and representation, that

would not exclude the application, where in-house lawyers are involved, of certain restrictions and rules relating to the exercise of the profession without that being regarded as adversely affecting the rights of the defence. Thus, in-house lawyers are not always able to represent their employer before all the national courts, although such rules restrict the possibilities open to potential clients in their choice of the most appropriate legal counsel.

96 It follows from those considerations that any individual who seeks advice from a lawyer must accept the restrictions and conditions applicable to the exercise of that profession. The rules on legal professional privilege form part of those restrictions and conditions.

97 Therefore, the argument alleging breach of the rights of the defence is unfounded.

The CJ also held that the GC's findings undermined neither the principle of legal certainty (paragraphs 100–108) nor the principle of national procedural autonomy (paragraphs 113–122).

The exclusion of in-house lawyers from LPP is a matter of great practical importance and remains a highly contentious issue.[227] Neither the GC nor the CJ in *Akzo Nobel* dealt with the further limitation of LPP to lawyers entitled to practise in one of the Member States.[228]

b. Procedure in Claims of LPP

In *AM&S* the CJ reserved to itself the determination of whether any particular document is protected. The procedure is for the undertaking claiming that documents are privileged to provide the inspectors with proof of that fact without revealing their contents. If the inspectors are not convinced the Commission may take a decision under Regulation 1/2003, Article 20(4), requiring the production of the document or further evidence of its status. Such a decision may be challenged by the undertaking under Article 263 TFEU (with an application for interim measures under Articles 278 and 279 if appropriate) and so the Court will ultimately decide the matter. In *Akzo Nobel* the GC considered the mechanics of how claims of LPP are dealt with in practice.[229] If the Commission officials cannot tell from a 'mere cursory look at the general layout, heading, title or other superficial features which would not reveal its content,' whether a document is protected by LPP and there is a genuine doubt about its classification, the officials place the document in a sealed envelope and take it back to Brussels to await the outcome of any proceedings.[230] The details of how LPP claims are handled are explained in Best Practices.[231] Disputes about whether documents are covered by LPP can be referred by the undertaking concerned to the Hearing Officer.[232] If the matter remains unresolved even after the Hearing Officer's recommendation the Commission can take a decision ordering the production of the document or the opening of the sealed envelope which the undertaking can then challenge before the GC.

The categorisation of particular documents into those protected by LPP and those not protected may be difficult. In *Hilti*[233] a report made and circulated within the undertaking of the legal advice received from an external legal adviser was held privileged. On the other hand, in *John Deere*[234] the

---

[227] See M. Frese, 'The Development of General Principles for EU Competition Law Enforcement—the Protection of Legal Professional Privilege' (2011) *ECLR* 196; G. di Frederico, 'Casenote' (2011) 48 *CMLRev* 581.

[228] Although it was touched upon by Kokott AG, in para. 190 of her Opinion.

[229] *Akzo Nobel*, paras. 79–90. This issue was not appealed to the CJ.

[230] *Akzo Nobel*, GC, paras. 81–83; see also the Working Paper, see n. 60, paras. 76–78. Best Practices, paras. 47–52.

[231] Best Practices, paras. 51–58.

[232] Decision on the function and terms of reference of the hearing officer [2011] OJ L275/29, Art. 4(2)(a); W. Wils, 'The Role of the Hearing Officer in Competition Proceedings before the European Commission' (2012) 35(3) *World Comp* 431, 448–450; for the functions of the Hearing Officer generally, see Section 8.C.iv, p. 969.

[233] Case T-30/89, *Hilti AG v. Commission* [1990] ECR II-163.

[234] [1985] OJ L35/58.

Commission examined advice from in-house lawyers and concluded therefrom that the undertaking was aware that it was infringing Article 101. It took this into account when imposing the fine. In *AKZO Nobel* the GC stated that a preparatory document drawn up exclusively for the purpose of seeking advice from a lawyer in exercise of the rights of the defence may be covered by LPP.[235]

C. THE SECOND, 'INTER PARTES', STAGE OF THE PROCEDURE

(i) General: The Rights of the Defence and the Right to be Heard

At the end of the investigative phase the Commission may decide to close the case. It may also decide to proceed to a commitments decision if the parties are offering commitments at that stage.[236] If the Commission finds evidence of an infringement and no commitments are being offered, it opens a formal procedure.

Before taking Regulation 1/2003 decisions finding an infringement, taking interim measures, or imposing fines or periodic payments the Commission must, by Article 27(1), grant the undertakings which are the subject of proceedings 'the opportunity of being heard on the matters to which the Commission has taken objection'.[237] Article 27(2) provides that 'the rights of defence of the parties concerned shall be fully respected in the proceedings' and they 'shall be entitled to have access to the Commission's file'.[238] The Commission may also hear other natural or legal persons. Article 27(4) provides for the hearing of interested third parties during the commitments decision procedure.[239]

The right to be heard in all proceedings initiated against a person which are liable to culminate in a measure adversely affecting that person is part of the rights of the defence and a fundamental principle of EU law which must be guaranteed even in the absence of any rules governing the proceedings in question.[240] The CJ has held that the right to a hearing means in the first place that parties must be told the case against them. It said in *Transocean Marine Paint*[241] that this is an application of the general rule that a person whose interests are perceptibly affected by a decision made by a public authority must be given the opportunity to make his views known, and to make his views known he must know the case against him. This case law is now embedded in Article 27(1) which provides that '[t]he Commission shall base its decisions only on objections on which the parties concerned have been able to comment'. The Commission satisfies this requirement by sending the

---

[235] *Akzo Nobel*, GC, para. 123. The GC refused to accept that the disputed document in issue met this description.

[236] For commitments decisions, see Section 8.D.iii, p. 982.

[237] The corresponding provision in Reg. 17 was Art. 19(1). Under that provision there was a right to a hearing before the Commission took a decision granting, refusing, or revoking an exemption, which was one reason those decisions took such a long time. Note that there is no duty to give parties a hearing where the Commission is simply replacing a decision ruled invalid for procedural defects at the final, authentication stage with another which relies on the same evidence as that which was annulled: see Cases C-238, 244–245, 247, 250, 251–252, and 254/99 P, *Limburgse Vinyl Maatschappij NV and others v. Commission* [2002] ECR I-8375; Case C-109/10 P, *Solvay v. Commission* [2011] ECR I-10329, para. 67. It is otherwise where the defects involved a failure to hear the parties in respect of the first decision, *Solvay*, paras. 68–71; the Commission's actions in readopting the decision in COMP/F/38.638—*Butadiene Rubber and Emulsion Styrene Butadiene Rubber*—which was partially annulled by the GC in Case T-39/07, *ENI v. Commission*, 13 July 2011 are being challenged before the GC, Case T-240/12, *ENI v. Commission*, judgment pending.

[238] For the application of this in the Article 9 commitments decision, see Case C-441/07P, *European Commission v. Alrosa* [2010] ECR I-5949, see Section 8.D.iii, p. 982.

[239] see Section 8.D.iii, p. 982.

[240] Case C-32/95 P, *Commission v. Lisrestal* [1996] ECR I-5373, para. 121 (a case on the European Social Fund).

[241] Case 17/74, *Transocean Marine Paint Association v. Commission (No. 2)* [1974] ECR 1063, where the decision concerned was an Art. 101(3) exemption which was subject to conditions to which the addressee objected. See also Cases C-68/94 and 30/95, *France & SCPA v. Commission* [1998] ECR I-1375, para. 174.

undertakings a document called the statement of objections (SO). The undertakings may then make submissions in reply and are offered the opportunity of an oral hearing. The procedures are now set out in Commission Regulation 773/2004.[242] If at the end of the proceedings the Commission finds that the competition rules have been infringed it may adopt a decision under Regulation 1/2003, Articles 7 or 8, and may impose a penalty under Article 23.

Considerable problems arise over the content of the rights of defence during these procedures, particularly where the rights of undertakings to know the case against them conflict with the Commission's duty to preserve the confidentiality of business secrets.

(ii) State of Play and Other Meetings

The Commission offers undertakings who are subject to proceedings the opportunity to attend 'State of Play' meetings with officials of DG Comp.[243] The meetings are not provided for in Regulation 1/2003 or in Regulation 773/2004 but have become an important part of Commission procedure. Best Practices says:[244]

Throughout the procedure the Directorate-General for Competition endeavours to give, on its own initiative or upon request, parties subject to the proceedings ample opportunity for open and frank discussions—taking into account the stage of the investigation—and to make their points of view known.

In this respect the Commission will offer State of Play meetings.

The meetings take place at the Commission's premises or, if appropriate, by telephone or video-conferencing and are normally chaired by senior DG Competition management.[245] Where several parties are being investigated the Commission offers separate bilateral meeting to each one. The meetings are not offered to complainants except in certain circumstances[246] or to third parties. Normally, State of Play meetings are offered (i) shortly after the opening of proceedings, (ii) at 'a sufficiently advanced stage in the investigation' where the parties can be given the opportunity to understand the Commission's preliminary views, and, (iii) if a statement of objections (SO) is issued, after the addressees have replied or after the Oral Hearing. The timing of State of Play meetings is different under the commitments decision procedure[247] and in cartel cases the undertakings are offered just one meeting, after the oral hearing.[248] The formalisation of 'State of Play' meetings does not exclude the parties having discussions with the Commission on other occasions throughout the procedure.[249]

'Exceptionally' DG Comp may invite *all* the parties (and possibly the complainant and/or third parties too) to a 'triangular' meeting.[250] Triangular meetings are held before any SO is issued. Senior officers of parties subject to proceedings can ask for a discussion of the case with the Director-General or Deputy Director-General of DG Comp, or even the Commissioner.[251]

---

[242] [2004] OJ L123/18, which replaced Reg. 2842/98 [1998] OJ L354/18, which in turn replaced Reg. 99/63 [1963–1964] OJ Spec. Ed. 47.

[243] Best Practices, paras. 60–66; Antitrust ManProc, Module 10, paras. 21–27.

[244] Best Practices, paras. 60–61.

[245] Best Practices, para. 61.

[246] Best Practices, para. 65.

[247] Best Practices, para. 65.

[248] Best Practices, para. 65.

[249] Best Practices, para. 66.

[250] Best Practices, paras. 67–69. Antitrust ManProc, Module 10, paras 28–30. If DG Comp believes it is desirable to hear the views of all of them in a single meeting (e.g. if two or more opposing views on key data or evidence have been advanced).

[251] Best Practices, para. 70.

(iii) The Statement of Objections

By Regulation 773/2004, Article 10(1),[252] 'the Commission shall inform the parties in writing of the objections raised against them'. By Article 11(2) Commission decisions can deal only with objections in respect of which the parties have been able to comment. The SO sets out the facts as understood by the Commission, a legal analysis explaining why it considers Article 101 or 102 to be infringed and any proposed remedy the Commission is contemplating adopting.[253] The SO also indicates what remedies, if any, the Commission envisages imposing, in sufficient detail to allow the addressees to defend themselves on the necessity and proportionality of the remedies[254] and this detail includes the factors in the case which may affect the amount of the fine.[255] The SO must state the duration of the infringement.[256] The parties are invited to reply to the SO within a set time limit.[257] The Commission can send the parties fresh documents on which it intends to rely, after the initial SO[258] so long as it gives the necessary time for the parties to comment on them.[259] The Commission cannot fine parties in the ultimate decision unless it has expressed an intention to do so in the SO.[260] It cannot fine an undertaking for its direct and personal involvement in an infringement if the SO has referred only to its liability as a parent company for the conduct of its subsidiary as, if the undertaking does not know the capacity in which it is alleged to have committed an infringement, its ability to defend itself is compromised.[261] An undertaking which does not challenge a matter of law or fact in the SO during the administrative procedure is not barred from later challenging it before the GC.[262]

In order for the parties to make their views known, the Commission must reveal the documents on which it intends to rely. The SO therefore indicates the addressee's right of access to the file, so that the addressee can see the evidence on which the Commission has based its case.[263] However, it is not sufficient for the Commission to rely on items of evidence annexed to the SO which are not expressly referred to in the body of the SO as that infringes the rights of the defence.[264] The addressees may

---

[252] [2004] OJ L123/18. See Best Practices, paras. 81–91; Kerse and Khan, *EU Antitrust Procedure* (cited in n. 2), paras 4-011–4.027.

[253] See Antitrust ManProc, Module 11, 'Drafting of Statement of Objections'.

[254] Best Practices, para. 83.

[255] Best Practices, para. 84.

[256] Cases 100–103/80, *Musique Diffusion Française v. Commission (Pioneer)* [1983] ECR 1825.

[257] Reg. 773/2004, Art. 10(2). The minimum time set down in Reg. 773/2004 is four weeks, but the period is usually two months and may be longer, see Best Practices, para.100, Antitrust ManProc, Module 11, paras. 48–56.

[258] A supplementary SO or 'letter of facts'. See Best Practices, paras. 109–111. A 'letter of facts' is sent where the new evidence merely corroborates previous evidence, rather than raising new objections.

[259] Case 107/82, *AEG-Telefunken v. Commission* [1983] ECR 3151; Cases T-305–307, 313–316, 318, 328–329, and 335/94, *Re the PVC Cartel II: Limburgse Vinyl Maatschappij NV and others v. Commission* [1999] ECR II-931, para. 497.

[260] In Cases T-25/95, etc., *Cimenteries CBR SA v. Commission* [2000] ECR II-491 the GC annulled the fines on associations of undertakings where the Commission had not announced in the SO its intention to fine the associations as distinct from their individual members. On the other hand, the CJ annulled the fines on the individual members of a liner conference in Cases C-395 and 396/96 P, *Compagnie Maritime Belge and others v. Commission* [2000] ECR I-1365, because the Commission had announced an intention to fine only the conference, not the individual shipping lines.

[261] Cases C-322/07 P, C-327/07 P, and C-338/07 P, *Papierfabrik August Koehler AG v. Commission* [2009] ECR I-7191, paras. 34–48. The CJ annulled the fine. The GC had made the same finding about the SO but had not annulled the fine as it did not consider the error serious enough to vitiate the decision, Cases T-109/02 etc., *Bolloré and others v. Commission* [2007] ECR II-947.

[262] Case C-407/08P, *Knauf Gips v. Commission* [2010] ECR I-6375, paras. 88–92. The CJ overruled the GC on this point, citing the fundamental principles of the rule of law, the rights of the defence, and the right to an effective remedy and of access to an impartial tribunal guaranteed by Article 47 of the Charter.

[263] If the addressee accompanies its reply to the SO with other documents the Commission can subsequently rely on them even though they were not referred to in the SO, Case T-11/89, *Shell v. Commission* [1992] ECR II-757.

[264] Case C-511/06 P, *Archer Daniels Midland* [2009] ECR I-5843, paras. 74–96. The Commission relied on documents annexed to the SO but not referred to in it in order to establish that ADM was a leader of the cartel. This increased the fine (as an 'aggravating factor', see Section 8.G.iv.h, p. 1015). The CJ reduced the fine on this basis (from €39.6 million to €29.4 million).

then exercise their rights to inspect the file, at least insofar as the documents are 'accessible'.[265] The current practical arrangements for this are contained in the Commission's 2005 Notice on access to the file.[266]

The SO is not a reviewable act against which an action for annulment can be brought, as it is only a preparatory act and can be challenged in an action brought against the act concluding the proceedings.[267] However, an *inadequate* SO amounts to a breach of an essential procedural requirement and so is a ground for annulment under Article 263.

The views set out by the Commission in the SO are not binding upon it and it is 'inherent in the nature of the statement of objections that it is provisional'.[268] The Commission is free to depart from the standpoint it has taken in the SO.[269] Findings of fact set out in the SO are not to be treated as established and so the Commission is free to depart from them in the final decision.[270]

(iv) The Hearing Officer

In 1982 the Commission decided to meet some of the criticisms of its position as investigator, prosecutor, and judge, and of the lack of objectivity in its decision-making process, by establishing the position of Hearing Officer.[271] Originally, his or her role was to preside over the oral hearing, but in 1994 it was extended to cover the whole of the Commission's administrative procedure. The role and functions are now governed by Commission Decision 2011/695[272] and are explained in this chapter at the relevant points. Since 1994 the Hearing Officer also has jurisdiction in relation to hearings provided for in the Merger Regulation.[273]

The rationale for creating the post in 1982 was to inject an element of disinterested objectivity into the Commission's decision-making process. He or she is attached, for administrative purposes, to the Competition Commissioner but the principle is that he or she is 'independent'.[274]

---

[265] See Section 8.C.v, p. 975.

[266] [2005] OJ C325/7.

[267] Case 60/81, *IBM v. Commission* [1981] ECR 2639.

[268] Case C-328/05 P, *SGL Carbon AG v. Commission* [2007] ECR I-3921, para. 62.

[269] Cases 142 and 156/84, *British American Tobacco Company Ltd and R. J. Reynolds Industries Inc. v. Commission* [1986] ECR 1899, para. 13.

[270] C-413/06 P, *Bertelsmann AG and Sony Corporation of America v. Commission (Impala)* [2008] ECR I-4951, paras. 63–67, holding that the GC had committed an error of law in finding otherwise, see Case T-464/04, *Independent Music Publishers and Labels Association (Impala) v. Commission* [2006] ECR II-2289. For the substantive issues in the case, see Chap. 15.

[271] See Commission's *XIth Report on Competition Policy* (Commission, 1981), paras. 26 and 27 and the *XIIth Report* (Commission, 1982), paras. 36 and 37. The original terms of reference of the Hearing Officer, [1982] OJ C215/2, were reformulated in 1990 because of the need to take on board hearings in transport cases: see EC Commission, *XXth Report on Competition Policy* (Commission, 1990), 312–314, and revised in 1994: Commission Decision 94/810 on the terms of reference of hearing officers in competition procedures before the Commission, [1994] OJ L330/67. See generally M. van der Woude, 'Hearing Officers and EC Antitrust Procedures; The Art of Making Subjective Procedures More Objective' (1996) 33 *CMLRev* 531; M. Albers and J. Jourdan, 'The Role of the Hearing Officers in EU Competition Proceedings: A Historical and Practical Perspective' (2011) 2 *Journal of European Competition Law and Practice* 185; W. Wils, 'The Role of the Hearing Officer in Competition Proceedings before the European Commission' (2012) 35(3) *World Competition* 431 (Wouter Wils has been a Hearing Officer since 2010).

[272] Decision of the President of the European Commission of 13 October 2011 on the function and terms of reference of the hearing officer in certain competition proceedings [2011] OJ L275/29 (the 'HO Terms of Reference'), replacing Commission December 2001/462/EC on the terms of reference of hearing officers in certain competition proceedings [2001] OJ L162/21.

[273] Reg. 4064/89 [1989] OJ L395/1, now Reg. 139/2004 [2004] OJ L24/1. See the HO Terms of Reference, Art. 1(2).

[274] HO Terms of Reference, Recitals 3–8 and Art. 2(2); 2001 Terms of Reference, recital 6 and Art. 2(2). It should be noted that the Hearing Officer does not appear on the chart of the organisation of DG Comp on its website. There are currently two Hearing Officers.

(v) Access to the File

a. General

Article 27(2) gives 'the parties concerned' a right of access to the Commission's file. There is a problem about how far the parties are entitled to examine all the evidence in the Commission's file on which the SO is based so that they may know the case against them. It appears from the judgment in *Hercules* [275] that 'access to the file' is an integral part of the right to be heard and not a right in itself:

75. ... access to the file in competition cases is intended in particular to enable the addressees of Statements of Objections to acquaint themselves with the evidence in the Commission's file so that on the basis of that evidence they can express their views effectively on the conclusions reached by the Commission in its Statement of Objections.

76. Thus the general principles of Community law governing the right of access to the Commission's file are designed to ensure effective exercise of the rights of the defence, including the right to be heard provided for in Article 19(1) of Regulation 17 and Articles 3 and 7 to 9 of Commission Regulation 99/63 of 25 July 1963[276] on the hearings provided for in Article 19(1) and (2) of Regulation 17.

b. The Right of Parties to Know the Case Against Them

The extent of the right of access to the file has changed over the years. Initially the CJ expressed the right of the parties quite conservatively[277] but then began to insist on the parties being properly apprised of the details of the case against them.[278] In the *XXIInd Report* the Commission said it intended to 'go beyond the requirements laid down by the Court of Justice and improve the exercise of the rights of defence in the course of administrative procedures' and lay down a procedure for organising the file and allowing undertakings to inspect it at the Commission's offices.[279] The GC held in *Hercules* [280] that, although the Commission had imposed on itself rules exceeding the requirements laid down by the CJ, it now had to follow them. Accordingly:

54. It follows that the Commission has an obligation to make available to the undertakings involved in Article [101(1)] proceedings all documents, whether in their favour or otherwise, which it has obtained in the course of the investigation, save where the business secrets of other undertakings, the internal documents of the Commission or other confidential information are involved.[281]

The right of access to the file is now set out in Regulation 1/2003, Article 27(2) and expanded upon in Regulation 773/2004.[282] The practical arrangements for access to the file are currently contained in the 2005 Notice on access to the file.[283]

---

[275] Case C-51/92 P, *Hercules Chemicals NV v. Commission (Polypropylene)* [1999] ECR I-4235, paras. 75–76; see also Case C-185/95 P, *Baustahlgewebe GmbH v. Commission* [1998] ECR I-8471, para. 89 and Cases T-10–12, 14–15/92, *Cimenteries CBR SA v. Commission* [1992] ECR II-2667, para. 38; note that the principles governing access to the Commission's file do not, as such, apply to Court proceedings, which are governed by the Rules of Procedure of the CJ and the Rules of Procedure of the GC: see C-185/95 P, *Baustahlgewebe* at para. 90.

[276] Now Arts 10–14 of Reg. 773/2004 [2004] OJ L123/18.

[277] See Cases 56 and 58/64, *Établissements Consten SA & Grundig-Verkaufs-GmbH v. Commission* [1966] ECR 299; Cases 43 and 63/82, *VBVB and VBBB v. Commission* [1984] ECR 19.

[278] See, e.g., Case C-185/95 P, *Baustahlgewebe GmbH v. Commission* [1998] ECR I-8471, paras. 89–90, Case C-51/92 P, *Hercules Chemicals NV v. Commission (Polypropylene)* [1999] ECR I-4235, paras. 75–79.

[279] Commission's *XXIInd Report on Competition Policy* (Commission, 1982) pts. 34 and 35.

[280] Case T-7/89, *Hercules v. Commission* [1991] ECR II-1711.

[281] Case T-7/89, *Hercules v. Commission* [1991] ECR II-1711, para. 54.

[282] Arts 15 and 16.

[283] Commission Notice on the rules for access to the Commission file [2005] OJ C325/07; and see the Antitrust ManProc, Module 12. Access to the file can be granted in one or more of several ways: electronically, paper copies sent by mail, or examination of the accessible file at the Commission's premises: the choice is the Commission's. See 2005 Notice, para. 44. The parties are usually informed that they may have a CD–ROM/DVD of the non-confidential versions of the accessible documents, detailing all the documents in the file. See Kerse and Khan, *EU Antitrust Procedure* (cited in n. 2), 4-059.

The rules for allowing the parties access to the file reflect the principles laid down in *Solvay*.[284] In that case, involving rebates in the soda-ash sector, the GC annulled the Commission's decision because of the Commission's failure properly to disclose to the parties documents which might have been useful in their defence. The GC said that it is important that the undertakings have disclosed to them documents which tend to exonerate them (exculpatory documents) as well as those which tend to incriminate them (inculpatory documents). It is not for the Commission alone to decide what documents are useful to the defence. In *Solvay* the GC relied on the 'general principle of equality of arms' between the Commission and the undertakings being investigated. This means that the undertakings' knowledge of the file used in the proceedings is the same as that of the Commission:[285]

81. In that context the Commission observes that although its officials themselves examined and re-examined all the documents in its possession, they found no evidence which might exculpate the applicant, so that there was no point in disclosing them. In that regard, it should be stated that in the defended proceedings for which Regulation 17 provides it cannot be for the Commission alone to decide which documents are of use for the defence. Where, as in the present case, difficult and complex economic appraisals are to be made, the Commission must give the advisers of the undertaking concerned the opportunity to examine documents which may be relevant so that their probative value for the defence can be assessed.

...

83. Having regard to the general principle of equality of arms, which presupposes that in a competition case the knowledge which the undertaking concerned has of the file used in the proceeding is the same as that of the Commission, the Commission's view cannot be upheld. The Court considers that it is not acceptable for the Commission alone to have had available to it, when taking a decision on the infringement, the documents marked 'V', and for it therefore to be able to decide on its own whether or not to use them against the applicant, when the applicant had no access to them and was therefore unable likewise to decide whether or not it would use them in its defence. In such a situation, the rights of defence which the applicant enjoys during the administrative procedure would be excessively restricted in relation to the powers of the Commission, which would then act as both the authority notifying the objections and the deciding authority, while having more detailed knowledge of the case-file than the defence.

It is clear, however, that breach of the principle laid down in *Solvay* will not always lead to annulment of the decision. It will depend on whether, in the Court's view, the undertaking's ability to defend itself was prejudiced.[286]

The law on access to the file was restated by the CJ in the final *Cement Cartel* appeals.

Cases C-204/00 P, C-205/00 P, C-211/00 P, C-213/00 P, C-217/00 P, and C-219/00 P, *Aalborg Portland A/S and Others v. Commission* [2004] ECR I-123

Court of Justice

68. A corollary of the principle of respect for the rights of the defence, the right of access to the file means that the Commission must give the undertaking concerned the opportunity to examine all the documents in the investigation file which may be relevant for its defence (see, to that effect, Case T-30/91,

---

[284] Case T-30/91, *Solvay SA v. Commission* [1995] ECR II-1775 and Case T-36/91, *ICI v. Commission* [1995] ECR II-1847, *aff'd* Cases C-288/95 P and 287/95 P, *Commission v. Solvay* [2000] ECR I-2391, applied in Cases T-305–307, 313–316, 318, 328–329, and 335/94, *Re the PVC Cartel II: Limburgse Vinyl Maatschappij NV and others v. Commission* [1999] ECR II-931.

[285] For an interesting insight into the actual circumstances in *Solvay* see C. D. Ehlermann and B. J. Drijber, 'Legal Protection of Enterprises: Administrative Procedure, in Particular Access to the File and Confidentiality' [1996] 7 *ECLR* 375.

[286] See Cases T-305–307, 313–316, 318, 328–329, and 335/94, *Re the PVC Cartel II: Limburgse Vinyl Maatschappij NV and others v. Commission* [1999] ECR II-931, paras. 1011–1022, confirmed by the CJ Cases C-238, 244–245, 247, 250, 251–252, and 254/99 P, *Limburgse Vinyl Maatschappij NV and others v. Commission* [2002] ECR I-8375, paras. 315–328; Case C-51/92 P, *Hercules Chemicals NV v. Commission* [1999] ECR I-4235, paras. 75–101.

Solvay v. *Commission*...paragraph 101, and Case C-199/99 P *Corus UK* v. *Commission*...paragraphs 125 to 128). Those documents include both incriminating evidence and exculpatory evidence, save where the business secrets of other undertakings, the internal documents of the Commission or other confidential information are involved (see Case 85/76, *Hoffmann-La Roche* v. *Commission*...paragraphs 9 and 11; Case C-51/92 P, *Hercules Chemicals* v. *Commission*...paragraph 75; and Joined Cases C-238/99 P, C-244/99 P, C-245/99 P, C-247/99 P, C-250/99 P to C-252/99 P and C-254/99 P, *Limburgse Vinyl Maatschappij and Others* v. *Commission*...paragraph 315).

69. It may be that the undertaking draws the Commission's attention to documents capable of providing a different economic explanation for the overall economic assessment carried out by the Commission, in particular those describing the relevant market and the importance and the conduct of the undertakings acting on that market (see, to that effect, *Solvay* v. *Commission*, cited above, paragraphs 76 and 77).

70. The European Court of Human Rights has none the less held that, just like observance of the other procedural safeguards enshrined in Article 6(1) of the ECHR, compliance with the adversarial principle relates only to judicial proceedings before a tribunal and that there is no general, abstract principle that the parties must in all instances have the opportunity to attend the interviews carried out or to receive copies of all the documents taken into account in the case of other persons (see, to that effect, Euro. Court H.R., the *Kerojärvi* v. *Finland* judgment of 19 July 1995, Series A No 322, § 42, and the *Mantovanelli* v. *France* judgment of 18 March 1997, Reports of Judgments and Decisions 1997-II, § 33).

71. The failure to communicate a document constitutes a breach of the rights of the defence only if the undertaking concerned shows, first, that the Commission relied on that document to support its objection concerning the existence of an infringement (see, to that effect, Case 322/101, *Michelin* v. *Commission*...paragraphs 7 and 9) and, second, that the objection could be proved only by reference to that document (see Case 107/102 *AEG* v. *Commission*...paragraphs 24 to 30, and *Solvay* v. *Commission*, cited above, paragraph 58).

72. If there were other documentary evidence of which the parties were aware during the administrative procedure that specifically supported the Commission's findings, the fact that an incriminating document not communicated to the person concerned was inadmissible as evidence would not affect the validity of the objections upheld in the contested decision (see, to that effect, *Musique Diffusion française and Others* v. *Commission*, cited above, paragraph 30, and *Solvay* v. *Commission*, cited above, paragraph 58).

73. It is thus for the undertaking concerned to show that the result at which the Commission arrived in its decision would have been different if a document which was not communicated to that undertaking and on which the Commission relied to make a finding of infringement against it had to be disallowed as evidence.

74. On the other hand, where an exculpatory document has not been communicated, the undertaking concerned must only establish that its non-disclosure was able to influence, to its disadvantage, the course of the proceedings and the content of the decision of the Commission (see *Solvay* v. *Commission*, paragraph 68).

75. It is sufficient for the undertaking to show that it would have been able to use the exculpatory documents in its defence (see *Hercules Chemicals* v. *Commission*, paragraph 101, and *Limburgse Vinyl Maatschappij and Others* v. *Commission*, paragraph 318), in the sense that, had it been able to rely on them during the administrative procedure, it would have been able to put forward evidence which did not agree with the findings made by the Commission at that stage and would therefore have been able to have some influence on the Commission's assessment in any decision it adopted, at least as regards the gravity and duration of the conduct of which it was accused and, accordingly, the level of the fine (see, to that effect, *Solvay* v. *Commission*, paragraph 98).

76. The possibility that a document which was not disclosed might have influenced the course of the proceedings and the content of the Commission's decision can be established only if a provisional examination of certain evidence shows that the documents not disclosed might—in the light of that

evidence—have had a significance which ought not to have been disregarded (see *Solvay v. Commission*, paragraph 68).

77. In the context of that provisional analysis, it is for the [General Court] alone to assess the value which should be attached to the evidence produced to it (see order of 17 September 1996 in Case C-19/95 P *San Marco* v *Commission*…paragraph 40). As stated at paragraph 49 of this judgment, its assessment of the facts does not, provided the evidence is not distorted, constitute a question of law which is subject, as such, to review by the Court of Justice.

The principles laid down *Aalborg* were followed and applied by the CJ in the appeal against the re-adopted *Solvay* soda-ash decisions.[287] The GC upheld the decisions despite the Commission still not having given the undertaking access to all the documents, including those likely to be useful to its defence (five binders had gone missing).[288] The CJ set the judgment aside, saying that the rights of the defence, as explained in *Aalborg*, were now referred to in Article 41(2)(a) and (b) of the Charter.[289]

c. Confidentiality

There is a fundamental tension between the rights of the parties to know the case against them and the Commission's obligation to preserve confidentiality. A general duty of confidentiality is laid down in the Treaty itself. Article 339 TFEU says:

The members of the institutions of the Union, the members of committees, and the officials and other servants of the Union shall be required, even after their duties have ceased, not to disclose information of the kind covered by the obligation of professional secrecy, in particular information about undertakings, their business relations or their cost components.

Regulation 1/2003, Article 28 on 'Professional Secrecy' states that information collected pursuant to Articles 17–22 shall only be used for the purposes for which it is acquired. Article 28(2) addresses the matter of exchange of information within the network of competition authorities.[290] Article 30 says that the publication of decisions shall 'have regard to the legitimate interest of undertakings in the protection of their business secrets'.[291]

Regulation 1/2003, Article 27(2) says that the parties' right to have access to the Commission's file is 'subject to the legitimate interest of undertakings in the protection of their business secrets'. This is repeated in Regulation 773/2004, Article 15(2), which says that the right of access does not extend to 'business secrets or other confidential information'.[292] Further, Article 16(1) states:

Information, including documents, shall not be communicated or made accessible by the Commission in so far as it contains business secrets or other confidential information of any person.

Confidentiality is a significant issue in the context of competition proceedings because of the highly sensitive information which the Commission may obtain during an investigation. 'Business secrets'

---

[287] Case C-109/10 P, *Solvay* v. *Commission*, [2011] ECR I-10329, judgment 25 October 2011. See also Case T-161/05, *Hoechst GmbH* v. *Commission*, [2009] ECR II-3555, paras. 160–166, and Case T-53/03, *BPB plc v. Commission* [2008] ECR II-1333, paras. 43–45.

[288] Case T-57/01, etc., *Solvay SA* v. *Commission* [2009] ECR II-4621.

[289] Case C-109/10 P, *Solvay* v. *Commission*, para. 53. Art. 41, the right to good administration, includes the right to be heard and the right of every person to have access to his or her file.

[290] See Notice on cooperation within the Network of Competition Authorities [2004] OJ C101/54. The Notice (para. 28(a)) states that 'professional secrecy' is a Community law concept.

[291] The GC held in Case T-474/04, *Pergan Hilfsstoffe für Industrielle Prozesse GmbH* v. *Commission* [2007] ECR II-4225 that this should have prevented the Commission stating in a published decision (*Organic Peroxides* [2005] OJ L110/44) that an undertaking had been involved in the organic peroxides cartel but that it did not have sufficient evidence of its involvement (at a time that was not subject to the limitation period bar) to bring proceedings against it (the Hearing Officer had allowed it).

[292] Reg. 1/2003, Art. 27(2), and Reg. 773/2004, Art. 15(2) also exclude from the right of access certain Commission and NCA documents.

comprises information about an undertaking's business activity disclosure of which could result in serious harm to the undertaking.[293] 'Other confidential information' is information other than business secrets whose disclosure would significantly harm a person or undertaking.[294] This includes matters which would identify 'whistle-blowers',[295] complainants, or other third parties who have a justified wish to remain anonymous. The 2005 Notice recognises that the EU Courts have acknowledged that it is legitimate to refuse to reveal letters from an undertaking's customers which might expose the writers to retaliatory measures.[296]

The basic principle, laid down in *Hoffmann-La Roche*, is that the Commission cannot use to an undertaking's detriment facts or documents which it cannot disclose to it, where the absence of disclosure adversely affects the undertaking's opportunity to be heard.

Case 85/76, *Hoffmann-La Roche* v. *Commission* [1979] ECR 461

Court of Justice

14. The said Article 20 [of Regulation 17] by providing undertakings from whom information has been obtained with a guarantee that their interests which are closely connected with observance of professional secrecy, are not jeopardized enables the Commission to collect on the widest possible scale the requisite data for the fulfilment of the task conferred upon it by Articles [101 and 102 TFEU] without the undertakings being able to prevent it from doing so, but it does not nevertheless allow it to use, to the detriment of the undertakings involved in a proceeding referred to in Regulation 17, facts, circumstances or documents which it cannot in its view disclose if such a refusal of disclosure adversely affects that undertaking's opportunity to make known effectively its views on the truth or implications of those circumstances on those documents or again on the conclusions drawn by the Commission from them.

Regulation 773/2004, Article 16, puts the onus on the parties to identify confidential material which they do not want disclosed.

Regulation 773/2004, Article 16

2. Any person which makes known its views pursuant to Article 6(1), Article 7(1), Article 10(2) and Article 13(1) and (3) or subsequently submits further information to the Commission in the course of the same procedure, shall clearly identify any material which it considers to be confidential, giving reasons, and provide a separate non-confidential version by the date set by the Commission for making its views known.

---

[293] 2005 Access to the file Notice, para. 18; Case T-353/94, *Postbank NV* v. *Commission* [1996] ECR II-921, para. 87. Examples given in the 2005 Notice are technical and/or financial information relating to an undertaking's know-how, methods of assessing costs, production secrets and processes, supply sources, quantities produced and sold, market shares, customer and distributor lists, marketing plans, cost and price structure, and sales strategy.

[294] 2005 Notice, para. 19.

[295] The Commission's notorious failure to conceal the identity of the whistle-blower Stanley Adams from Hoffmann-La Roche rendered the Commission liable to him in damages under Art. 340 (ex Art. 288(2), ex Art. 215(2)): Case 145/83, *Adams* v. *Commission* [1985] ECR 3539.

[296] 2005 Notice, para. 19. In Case C-310/93 P, *BPB Industries and British Gypsum Ltd* [1995] ECR I-865 the CJ accepted that the Commission was entitled to keep such correspondence confidential because of the fear of retaliation from the dominant firm in an Article 102 case. It has been argued (see M. Levitt, 'Commission Notice on Internal Rules of Procedure for Access to the File' [1997] *ECLR* 187) that whether the undertaking is in fact dominant may be one of the things which is in dispute and that the so-called 'economic or commercial pressure' may be no more than an unrealised fear of potential retaliation unrelated to the actual abuse allegation. In *Michelin II* (Case T-203/01, *Manufacture Française des Pneumatiques Michelin* v. *Commission* [2003] ECR II-4071) the GC held that the Commission was justified, on account of the risk of retaliation, in withholding from Michelin the identity of the dealers who had answered its requests for information. Refusal by the Commission to reveal the identity of third parties has also been held justified in merger cases, see Case T-221/95, *Endemol* v. *Commission* [1999] ECR II-1299; Case T-5/02, *Tetra Laval* v. *Commission* [2002] ECR II-4381.

The 2005 Notice sets out the practical arrangements for giving access to the Commission's file while preserving confidentiality. The Notice clarifies that access to the file is granted only to addressees of SOs, and that other parties (complainants and other parties involved in merger cases) have a separate, more limited, right of access to specific documents.

A distinction is made in the Notice between 'accessible' and 'non-accessible' documents. The Hearing Officer has jurisdiction to determine whether or not particular documents fall within the protected 'non-accessible' category. We have seen that Article 16(2) and (3) provides for undertakings providing information to the Commission (voluntarily or not), and persons making their views known, to detail what they regard as confidential or business secrets and supply a non-confidential version.[297] Both business secrets and confidential information are 'non-accessible'. The Commission's internal documents are also 'non-accessible', as are those of the NCAs, correspondence between the Commission and the NCAs, and correspondence between the NCAs inter se (insofar as this is in the Commission's file).[298] The Commission's rationale for the protection of internal documents is that they are not, by their nature, either incriminating or exculpatory and are not the sort of evidence on which the Commission can rely in its assessment of a case.[299] The 2005 Notice sets out the procedure for resolving confidentiality and access to non-accessible information claims. In essence, if the Commission and the undertakings or other parties cannot agree, the matter is dealt with by the Hearing Officer.[300] In Best Practices the Commission sets out two practical possibilities for handling situations where otherwise undertakings would need to redact their submissions in relation to confidential information: a 'negotiated disclosure procedure'[301] and the 'data room' procedure.[302]

[297] 2005 Notice, paras. 35–38. The non-confidential version and the description of the deleted information have to be such that any party with access to the file would be able to determine whether the deleted information is likely to be relevant for its defence and therefore to determine whether there are sufficient grounds for requesting access to the confidential information. DG Comp publishes informal guidance on making confidentiality claims, and the standard Annex on business secrets and other confidential information which is enclosed in all requests for information, on its website, <http://ec.europa.eu/competition/antitrust/information_en.html>.

[298] Reg. 1/2003, Art. 27(2), and Reg. 773/2004, Art. 15(2). For the exchange of information within the European Competition Network (ECN) of the Commission and the NCAs, see Section 10.B.ii, p. 1055.

[299] 2005 Notice, para. 12. Examples of internal documents given in the Notice are drafts, opinions, memos, or notes from the Commission departments or other public authorities concerned. The Commission's correspondence with other public authorities (including, inter alia, with the NCAs and with competition authorities of non-Member States) are non-accessible (para. 15), although there are provisions for releasing non-confidential versions of some of these in exceptional circumstances (para. 16). The Commission is under no obligation to take any minutes of any meetings with any person or undertaking. The Ombudsman made a finding of maladministration (1935/2008/FOR) against the Commission for failing during its investigation in the Intel case (Case COMP/C-3/37.990) to take minutes of a meeting it had held with Dell, the computer manufacturer. Since it had taken no minutes they were not on the file. The Commission's view (Antitrust ManProc, Module 12, para. 20) is that the case law (Cases T-191 and 212–214/98 Atlantic Container Line v. Commission [2003] ECR II-3275) does not require Commission departments to draft minutes of meetings with another person or undertaking. If, however, the Commission does take minutes and they are agreed with the other parties, they may be made accessible (after deletion of confidential information and business secrets: see Notice, para. 13). Another complaint to the Ombudsman about access to the file, by an investigated undertaking, was rejected in 1881/2006/JF.

[300] 2005 Notice, paras. 42 and 47; HO Terms of Reference, Arts 7 and 8. In Case T-345/12 R, Akzo Nobel v. Commission, 16 November 2012, the President of the GC granted interim measures suspending a Commission decision which would have published a second, fuller version of the non-confidential version of the Hydrogen and Perborate cartel decision (2007). The Hearing Officer had rejected Akzo Nobel's claim for continued confidential treatment on the grounds, inter alia, that he could determine only whether the information might be disclosed because it contained business secrets or confidential information whereas the applicants were objecting to the second version solely because it contained information provided pursuant to the Leniency Notice (for Leniency, see Section 8.G.v, p. 1019).

[301] Whereby the party being granted access agrees bilaterally with interested parties to receive the entirety of the information they have provided to the Commission, including the confidential information rather than the redacted version. This involves the party granted access restricting its right to have access to the full file and the other party waiving confidentiality; Best Practices, para. 96.

[302] By which part of the file, including confidential information, is gathered in a room at the Commission's premises. Access to the room is given to a limited group of persons (normally the party's external lawyers or economic

In the Leniency Notice there is special provision for the protection of 'corporate statements' made by applicants for leniency. Access is granted only to the addressees of statements of objections, and then only under strict conditions which include being prohibited from making electronic or mechanical copies.[303]

d. Confidentiality and Complainants

It was held in *AKZO*,[304] that business secrets are accorded 'very special protection' and cannot be disclosed to third parties who have lodged complaints.[305] Otherwise, as the CJ said, competitors could obtain access to other undertakings' secrets simply by lodging a complaint. In *AKZO* the Commission had sent a copy of the SO and a number of documents in the annexes to the complainant, and the CJ's order to the Commission to recover the documents meant that ECS was unable to rely on them in national proceedings.

It is clear from *AKZO* therefore that complainants cannot have the same access to the file as alleged infringers. The rights of third parties (now laid down in Regulation 1/2003, Article 27) are limited to the right to participate in the administrative procedure.[306] This is embodied in paragraphs 30–31 of the 2005 Notice. A complainant who has been told of the intention to reject his complaint[307] may request access to the documents on which the Commission based the rejection but cannot have access to the confidential information or business secrets of the firm complained about, or those of any third parties, which the Commission has acquired in the course of its investigations.

e. Confidentiality, NCAs, and National Proceedings

The issue of exchanges of information and confidentiality with regard to NCAs and national courts in the decentralised system of enforcement under Regulation 1/2003 is dealt with later[308] and in Chapter 14.

f. The Relevance of the Transparency Regulation

The Transparency Regulation of 2001[309] was adopted to implement what is now Article 15(2) TFEU.[310] Article 2 provides that any citizen of the Union, and any natural or legal person residing or having its registered office in a Member State, has a right of access to documents of the institutions, subject to the principles, conditions and limits defined in the Regulation.[311] This applies to all documents held by an institution, that is, documents drawn up or received by it and in its possession, in all areas of activity of the EU.[312] Exceptions to the right of access are set out in Article 4. Article 4(1) provides an absolute exception to disclosure and Article 4(2) and (3) provides for discretionary, or relative, exceptions where access to a document shall be refused unless there is an overriding public interest in disclosure.

---

advisers) under the Commission's supervision. The external lawyers may record information contained in the data room but not disclose any confidential information to their client; Best Practices, paras. 97–98.

[303] Commission Notice on Immunity from Fines and Reduction of Fines in Cartel Cases [2006] OJ C298/17, paras. 33–34, see Section 8.G.v, p. 1019.

[304] Case 53/85, *AKZO v. Commission* [1986] ECR 1965.

[305] For complaints generally, see Section 13, p. 1066 ff.

[306] Case T-17/93, *Matra Hachette SA v. Commission* [1994] ECR II-595.

[307] See Section 13.F, p. 1071.

[308] In Section 10.B.ii.

[309] Regulation 1049/2001 [2001] OJ L145/43. For the application of the Transparency Regulation in competition law, see Bellamy and Child, *European Law of Competition* (cited in n. 2), 16-045–16.048; Kerse and Khan, *EU Antitrust Procedure* (cited in n. 2), 4-096–4-105; R. Hempel, 'Access to DG Competition's Files: An Analysis of Recent EU Court Case Law' (2012) *ECLR* 195.

[310] Previously Art. 255 EC. The right is pursuant to the principle in Art. 15(1) that Union institutions and bodies, etc. shall conduct their work as openly as possible.

[311] Transparency Regulation, Art.2(1)

[312] Transparency Regulation, Art. 2(3).

Regulation 1049/2001 [2001] OJ L145/43, Article 4

Exceptions

1. The institutions shall refuse access to a document where disclosure would undermine the protection of:

   (a) the public interest as regards:
   - public security,
   - defence and military matters,
   - international relations,
   - the financial, monetary or economic policy of the Community or a Member State;

   (b) privacy and the integrity of the individual, in particular in accordance with Community legislation regarding the protection of personal data.

2. The institutions shall refuse access to a document where disclosure would undermine the protection of:
   - commercial interests of a natural or legal person, including intellectual property,
   - court proceedings and legal advice,
   - the purpose of inspections, investigations and audits,

   unless there is an overriding public interest in disclosure.

3. Access to a document, drawn up by an institution for internal use or received by an institution, which relates to a matter where the decision has not been taken by the institution, shall be refused if disclosure of the document would seriously undermine the institution's decision-making process, unless there is an overriding public interest in disclosure.

   Access to a document containing opinions for internal use as part of deliberations and preliminary consultations within the institution concerned shall be refused even after the decision has been taken if disclosure of the document would seriously undermine the institution's decision-making process, unless there is an overriding public interest in disclosure.

4. As regards third-party documents, the institution shall consult the third party with a view to assessing whether an exception in paragraph 1 or 2 is applicable, unless it is clear that the document shall or shall not be disclosed.

The Article 4 derogations from the general principle are strictly construed.[313]

The Transparency Regulation has an effect not only on access to the file in the antitrust context, but also on access to documents in merger cases,[314] and in State aid.[315] The relationship between the Transparency Regulation and the rules governing disclosure in the specific context of the Merger Regulation (EUMR)[316] was considered by the CJ in *Éditions Odile Jacob*, where it said:[317]

Those regulations do not contain a provision expressly giving one regulation primacy over the other. Accordingly, it is appropriate to ensure that each of those regulations is applied in a manner compatible with the other and which enables a coherent application of them.

---

[313] Case C506/08P, *Kingdom of Sweden v. Commission* [2011] ECR I-75, para. 75.

[314] Case T-403/05, *MyTravel v. Commission* [2008] ECR II-2027, on appeal Case C506/08P, *Kingdom of Sweden v. Commission*; Case C-404/10 P, *Commission v. Éditions Odile Jacob*, 28 June 2012; Case C-477/10 P, *Commission v. Agrofert Holding a.s.*, 28 June 2012.

[315] Case C-139/07P, *Commission v. Technische Glaswerke Ilmenau* [2010] ECR I-5885 (*TGI*).

[316] Regulation 139/2004, see Chap. 15.

[317] Case C-404/10 P, *Commission v. Éditions Odile Jacob*, see n. 314, paras. 109–110.

It appears that this would also apply to the *lex specialis* of Regulation 1/2003. The GC had already said, in *EnBW Energie Baden-Württemberg* (*EnBW*), that nothing in the Regulation 'gives any grounds for assuming that EU competition policy should enjoy, in the application of that Regulation, treatment different from other EU policies'.[318] An attempt to circumvent the access to the file rules in antitrust cases while the case is ongoing would be likely to fail on the reasoning set out in *Technische Glaswerke Ilmenau* [319] and *Éditions Odile Jacob*, that the Commission can rely on a general presumption that disclosure would undermine the purpose of the inspection or investigation (Article 4(3), first paragraph), unless there is an overriding public interest in disclosure.[320] Rather, the Transparency Regulation is of most significance in respect of damages claims brought in national courts in the wake of infringement decisions, particularly Article 101 cartel decisions, where the undermining of an ongoing investigation is no longer an issue, and access is wanted to statements made in leniency applications.[321]

(vi) The Oral Hearing

The right to be heard is primarily exercised in writing, but Regulation 773/2004, Article 12 gives the parties to whom an SO has been addressed the right to an oral hearing, if they request it in their written submissions.[322] The oral hearing is controlled and supervised by the Hearing Officer.[323] Third parties such as complainants may be heard in addition to the parties.[324] The oral hearing is not a formal 'trial'. It may last anything from a day to two or three weeks, depending on the complexity of the case. It is not heard in public.[325] Regulation 773/2004, Article 14(5) provides that the persons being heard may be 'assisted by' their lawyers. It does not say 'represented by' because it is considered necessary that someone from the undertaking itself (although that can be an in-house lawyer) is present to provide relevant information about the organisation.[326]

Regulation 773/2004, Article 14(8) provides that the statements made at the hearing shall be recorded and the record made available to the persons who attended the hearing, regard being had to the protection of business secrets and confidential information. Business secrets and other confidential information are deleted.

The Hearing Officer is not a judge. It is not his or her function to come to a decision, but to make an interim report to the Competition Commissioner on the hearing and the conclusions to be drawn from it in respect of the right to be heard.[327] This report is not made available to the parties, who have no right to see it or comment on it. The Hearing Officer makes a final report which is attached to the draft decision submitted to the College of Commissioners[328] which is made known to the addressees

---

[318] Case T-344/08, *EnBW Energie Baden-Württemberg* v. *Commission*, 22 May 2012, para. 127, on appeal Case C-365/12 P, *Commission* v. *EnBW Energie Baden-Württemberg*, judgment pending.

[319] Cited in n. 315.

[320] In *Éditions Odile Jacob* the CJ applied this to *closed* merger procedures as well.

[321] Chap. 14, Section 2.D., p. 1090. The Commission's refusals to disclose have mainly been overturned for lack of sufficient reasoning, a failure to demonstrate how exactly disclosure would undermine the interest protected by Art. 4(2) or (3) and/or insufficient analysis of each document; see Case T-2/03, *Verein für Konsumenteninformation* [2005] ECR II-1121; Case T-437/08, *CDC Hydrogen Peroxide* v. *Commission*, 15 December 2011; Case T-344/08, *EnBW*, (cited in n. 318). The Ombudsman dealt with a Transparency Regulation request by a private claimant in Case 3699/2006/ELB. For access to Leniency statements, see Section 8.G.v, p. 1025.

[322] See Best Practices, paras. 106–108; Antitrust ManProc, Module 3.3.

[323] HO Terms of Reference, Art. 10. See S. Durande and K. Williams, 'The Practical Impact of the Exercise of the Right to be Heard: A Special Focus on the Effect of Oral Hearings and the Role of the Hearing Officers' (2005) 2 *Competition Policy Newsletter* 22; W. Wils, 'The Oral Hearing in Competition Proceedings Before the European Commission' (2012) 35(3) *World Competition* 397.

[324] Reg. 773/2004, Art. 13.

[325] Reg. 773/2004, Art. 14(6).

[326] See Case 49/69, *BASF* v. *Commission* (*Dyestuffs*) [1972] ECR 713. Persons 'invited to attend' may be represented by legal representatives, Reg. 773/2004, Art. 14(4).

[327] HO Terms of Reference, Art. 13(1).

[328] HO Terms of Reference, Art. 14(1).

of the decision and is published in the Official Journal together with the decision.[329] The limited nature of the Hearing Officer's role is relevant to the question of whether competition procedure complies with Article 6(1) of the ECHR.[330]

D. COMMISSION DECISIONS

(i) General

The Commission may take a final decision ordering the termination of infringements of the competition rules and may take procedural decisions during the course of its investigation, as we have seen. It may also take interim measures in order to prevent irreparable damage occurring before it can come to a final decision. It was given two new powers under Regulation 1/2003: to take a decision making commitments binding but without making an infringement finding, and to take a 'positive' decision finding Article 101 or Article 102 inapplicable. It is usual to speak of 'the Commission' when discussing the conduct of EU competition policy, meaning the policy and actions of the Competition Directorate General, DG Comp. However, it is important to remember that unless the taking of particular acts of management or administration has been delegated to a single Commissioner, decisions are collegiate acts of the whole Commission.[331] When the Commission adopts an infringement decision, therefore, the Commissioner responsible for competition lays the draft before the whole College and the measure is adopted by the College.[332]

This section deals with the content of decisions other than the imposition of fines: fines are dealt with in Section 8.G.

(ii) Final Decisions: Infringement Decisions under Regulation 1/2003, Article 7

a. Finding and Termination of Infringements

Regulation 1/2003, Article 7[333] states:

Finding and termination of infringement

1. Where the Commission, acting on a complaint or on its own initiative, finds that there is an infringement of Article [101] or of Article [102], it may by decision require the undertakings and associations of undertakings concerned to bring such infringement to an end. For this purpose, it may impose on them any behavioural or structural remedies which are proportionate to the infringement committed and necessary to bring the infringement effectively to an end. Structural remedies can only be imposed either where there is no equally effective behavioural remedy or where any equally effective behavioural remedy would be more burdensome for the undertaking concerned than the structural remedy. If the Commission has a legitimate interest in doing so, it may also find that an infringement has been committed in the past.

2. Those entitled to lodge a complaint for the purposes of paragraph 1 are natural or legal persons who can show a legitimate interest and Member States.

---

[329] HO Terms of Reference, Art. 16..

[330] In Section 8.I, p. 1028.

[331] This aspect of decisions was stressed by the GC in the *Cement* appeal. Two of the applicants claimed a breach of the principle of impartiality, in that the same Commission official had carried out the investigation, acted as rapporteur, drawn up the SO, and prepared the draft decision. The GC held that the principle was not breached because the contested decision was actually taken by the College of Commissioners, not by the official: Joined Cases T-25/95, etc., *Cimenteries CBR SA v. Commission* [2000] ECR II-491, para. 721.

[332] The failure of the College to adopt an authenticated version of the decision was one reason for the annulment of the *PVC* decision in Case C-137/92 P, *Commission v. BASF and others* [1994] ECR I-2555: see Section 9.A.v, p. 1035.

[333] Reg. 1/2003 [2003] OJ L1/1.

A decision finding an infringement may therefore order undertakings to bring the infringement to an end where it has not definitely been terminated already. These are called 'cease and desist orders'. The decision may also contain a 'like effects order' whereby the parties are prohibited from entering into similar arrangements.[334]

On the other hand, in *Langnese-Iglo* [335] the GC held that the Commission was not entitled to withdraw the benefit of the exclusive purchasing block exemption then in force[336] from future agreements and prohibit the undertakings from entering into such agreements in the future. This was an Article 101 proceeding, and whether or not an exclusive purchasing agreement is restrictive of competition and satisfies the Article 101(3) conditions depends on the circumstances and context. The Court established in *Cementhandelaren* that the Commission is justified in taking a decision after an infringement has terminated so that the decision is in effect only a declaration that the past conduct did infringe.[337]

b. Behavioural and Structural Remedies

The corresponding provision to Article 7 in Regulation 17 was Article 3, which did not state whether the Commission could take decisions ordering the parties to take *positive* steps (i.e. adopt positive behavioural remedies) in order to bring the infringement to an end. The CJ, however, held in *Commercial Solvents* that it could:[338]

[Article 3] must be applied in relation to the infringement which has been established and may include an order to do certain acts or provide certain advantages which have been wrongfully withheld as well as prohibiting the continuation of certain actions, practices or situations which are contrary to the Treaty.

In *Commercial Solvents* the dominant undertaking was ordered to supply a certain amount of raw material to the complainant, which involved the parties entering into contractual relations. Many subsequent Article 102 cases on refusal to supply have involved ordering a dominant undertaking to supply or to share facilities.[339] The Commission may also order an undertaking to amend its contractual terms or its pricing policies.[340] Regulation 1/2003, Article 7(1) now expressly gives the Commission power to make positive orders by stating that it may impose 'any behavioural ... remedies which are proportionate to the infringement committed and necessary to bring the infringement effectively to an end'. The overriding principle is proportionality. In *Automec*, an Article 101 case, the GC said that the Commission does not have the power to order a party to enter into a contractual relationship where there are other ways of making the party end the infringement.

In *Atlantic Container Line AB* [341] the Commission found that shipping companies had infringed Article 101(1) by an agreement which fixed prices and capacity. The decision, inter alia, required the parties to inform customers that they were entitled to renegotiate the terms of contracts concluded

---

[334] See Case T-410/03, *Hoechst GmbH v. Commission* [2008] ECR II-881, where the Commission decision prohibited future similar conduct although Hoechst had already left the market on which the infringement had been committed (sorbates). The GC upheld the decision, stating that the prohibition was preventive and did not depend on the undertaking's position at the time of the decision (the decision referred only to conduct on the sorbates market).

[335] Cases T-7 and 9/93, *Langnese-Iglo & Schöller Lebensmittel v. Commission* [1995] ECR II-1533, upheld by the CJ in Case C-279/95 P, *Langnese-Iglo v. Commission* [1998] ECR I-5609.

[336] Reg. 1984/83.

[337] Case 8/72, *Cementhandelaren v. Commission* [1972] ECR 977; see also COMP/37.860 *Morgan Stanley/Visa International and Visa Europe*, on appeal Case T-461/07, *Visa Europe and Visa International Service Association v. Commission* [2011] ECR II-1729.

[338] Cases 6, 7/73, *Istituto Chemioterapico Italiano Spa and Commercial Solvents Corp v. EC Commission* [1974] ECR 223, para. 45.

[339] See Chap. 7.

[340] As in, e.g., Case C-333/94 P, *Tetra Pak International SA v. Commission* [1996] ECR I-5951. See generally Chap. 7.

[341] Case T-395/94, *Atlantic Container Line AB v. Commission* [2002] ECR II-875.

within the context of the agreement or to terminate them.[342] The GC annulled that part of the decision as it went beyond what was required to terminate the infringement:

...the Commission may specify the scope of the obligations imposed on the undertakings concerned in order to bring an end to the infringements identified. That power must however be implemented according to the nature of the infringement declared (see, by analogy, *Istituto Chemioterapico Iitaliano and Commercial Solvents v. Commission*, paragraph 45; *RTE and ITP v. Commission*, paragraph 90; and Case C-279/95 P *Langnese-Iglo v. Commission...*paragraph 74) and the obligations imposed must not exceed what is appropriate and necessary to attain the objective sought, namely re-establishment of compliance with the rules infringed (see *RTE and ITP v. Commission*, paragraph 93).[343]

The problems of ensuring compliance with positive behavioural remedies are shown by *Microsoft*, in which the Commission, inter alia, ordered Microsoft to make available certain interoperability information (to remedy its refusal to supply) on fair and reasonable terms.[344] Part of the Commission's decision in respect of the remedy was, however, annulled by the GC. The decision provided for Microsoft to submit a proposal for the establishment of a mechanism, including the appointment of an independent monitoring trustee (IMT), to oversee Microsoft's compliance with the decision. The IMT was to be empowered to access Microsoft's information, documents, premises, and employees and also the source code of its relevant products. It provided for Microsoft to bear all the costs of the appointment of the IMT, including his remuneration. The GC said that in effect the Commission was compelling Microsoft to grant to the IMT powers which the Commission was not itself authorised to confer on a third party. Moreover the continuing intervention of the IMT was without time limit. There was nothing in Regulation 17 (under which the decision was taken) to authorise such a remedy. The requirement for Microsoft to supply the interoperability information was left standing, however, and the outcome of the battle over that is noted in Section 8.G.[345]

The power to order positive measures in appropriate cases in Regulation 17, Article 3(1) did not appear to include a general power to order divestiture. Article 102 is infringed by an abuse, not by the dominant position per se and Regulation 17, Article 3 provided only for the Commission to order the termination of the *infringement*. It did not give a power to restructure the market to prevent future abuses. However, in *Continental Can*[346] the Commission decision held that an undertaking had committed an abuse by acquiring another company and required the undertaking to dispose of it. The decision was annulled on substantive grounds, and so the order was never enforced. In this case, however, the order to divest related to the very subject matter of the abuse. Regulation 1/2003, Article 7(1) now expressly provides for the Commission to take any structural remedies 'which are proportionate to the infringement committed and necessary to bring the infringement to an end'. The structural remedy can only be imposed where no behavioural remedy would be equally effective or where the behavioural remedy would be more burdensome for the undertaking concerned. Recital 12 of Regulation 1/2003 further states that changes to the structure of an undertaking as it existed prior to the infringement would only be proportionate 'where there is a substantial risk of a lasting or repeated infringement that derives from the very structure of the undertaking'.

The ability to impose a structural remedy, i.e. to order divestment or break up companies is a powerful weapon in the hands of a competition authority and not one to be used lightly.[347] Since 2007 the Commission has turned to structural remedies with increasing frequency (because of its

---

[342] *Trans-Atlantic Agreement* [1994] OJ L376/1, Art. 5.

[343] Case T-395/94, para. 410.

[344] *Microsoft*, COMP/C-3/37.792, [2005] 4 CMLR 965, on appeal Case T-201/04, *Microsoft v. Commission* [2007] ECR II-3601.

[345] See Section 8.G.iii, p. 996.

[346] Case 6/72, *Europemballage Corp & Continental Can Co Inc v. EC Commission* [1973] ECR 215; see Chaps. 6, 7, and 15.

[347] The consequences of a competition authority deciding to restructure an industry can be seen in the saga of the UK beer sector following the Monopolies and Mergers Commission Report, *The Supply of Beer*, Cm. 651 (1989).

enforcement of the competition rules in the energy sector) but these have been obtained through commitments decisions (see Section 8.D.iii) rather than in prohibition decisions.[348]

(iii) Final Decisions: Commitments Decisions under Regulation 1/2003, Article 9

a. General

A new power was introduced by Regulation 1/2003, Article 9 whereby the Commission, without taking a final decision finding an infringement, may nevertheless render binding undertakings given by the parties.[349] The Commission may wish to do this where it has identified competition concerns but the parties are willing to give binding undertakings about their future conduct in order to avoid a finding of infringement. Recital 13 of Regulation 1/2003 states that Commitment decisions are not suitable where the Commission intends to impose a fine and Best Practices says that consequently the Commission does not apply the Article 9 procedure to secret cartels that fall under the Leniency Notice.[350] However, Article 9 has been used in respect of what, if proved, would have been serious infringements of Article 102 where a heavy fine might have been expected to be imposed,[351] and in *Ebooks* commitments were taken in a case which in effect involved price-fixing and resale maintenance.[352]

Regulation 1/2003, Article 9

1. Where the Commission intends to adopt a decision requiring that an infringement be brought to an end and the undertakings concerned offer commitments to meet the concerns expressed to them by the Commission in its preliminary assessment, the Commission may by decision make those commitments binding on the undertakings. Such a decision may be adopted for a specified period and shall conclude that there are no longer grounds for action by the Commission.

   2. The Commission may, upon request or on its own initiative, reopen the proceedings:

     (a) where there has been a material change in any of the facts on which the decision was based;

     (b) where the undertakings concerned act contrary to their commitments; or

     (c) where the decision was based on incomplete, incorrect or misleading information provided by the parties.

It will be noted that the power to take a commitments decision arises only where the Commission otherwise intends to adopt a termination decision under Article 7. This does not mean that it has to have sent a statement of objections (SO) before taking an Article 9 decision. The requirement is

---

[348] The Competition Commissioner stressed the powers of the Commission to impose structural remedies for breaches of Arts 101 and 102 when the Commission presented its report on its Regulation 1/2003, Art. 17 enquiry into the European gas and energy sectors, Communication from the Commission COM(2006)851, 10 January 2007.

[349] See generally J. Temple Lang, 'Commitment Decisions and Settlements with Antitrust Authorities and Private Parties Under European Antitrust Law' [2005] Fordham Corp L Inst 265 (B. Hawk (ed.), 2006); C. Cook, 'Commitment Decisions: The Law and Practice under Article 9' (2006) 29(2) *World Competition* 209; W. Wils, 'Settlements of EU Antitrust Investigations; Commitment Decisions under Article 9 of Regulation 1/2003' (2006) *World Competition* 345; W. Wils, 'The Use of Settlements in Public Antitrust Enforcement: Objectives and Principles' (2008) 31 *World Competition* 335; W. Wils, 'Discretion and Prioritisation in Public Antitrust Enforcement' (2011) 34(3) *World Competition* 353.

[350] Best Practices, para. 116. For the Leniency Notice see Section 8.G.v, p. 1019.

[351] For example, COMP/38.636, *Rambus*, IP/09/1897; COMP/39.530, *Microsoft* (tying), IP/13/2013; COM/39.692, *IBM Maintenance Services*, IP/11/1539; see Chap. 7.

[352] Case 39.847, IP/12/1367. Commitments from four publishers plus Apple were made binding on 12 December 2012; proposed commitments from Penguin were market tested on 19 April 2013.

that the Commission has made a 'preliminary assessment'. The procedure the Commission follows before taking commitments decisions is explained in Best Practices.[353] If the parties wish to avoid the issue of an SO they have to offer commitments early on, and then the Commission may issue a preliminary assessment rather than an SO.[354] A vital step in the proceedings is the 'market test' of the commitments whereby in accordance with Regulation 1/2003, Article 27(4) the Commission publishes the proposed commitments in the Official Journal and invites third party comments.[355] If the parties do not agree to any amendments the Commission requires that as a result the Commission reverts to the normal Article 7 procedure. It will be noted that Article 9(2) gives the Commission power to reopen the proceedings in certain circumstances. A breach of an Article 9 decision may result in the Commission taking a decision imposing a fine under Regulation 1/2003, Article 23(2)(c). The Commission did this for the first time in March 2013 when it fined Microsoft €561 million[356] for breaching its commitments in respect of the browser choice screen.[357]

It quickly became apparent after Regulation 1/2003 came into operation that commitments decisions would play a major role in the Commission's application of the competition rules. First of all the Commission used the procedure to dispose of a number of cases in which investigations had been opened before May 2004.[358] A wide-ranging initiative against exclusionary practices in the energy sector has seen a number of commitments decisions since 2007.[359] These have been described as the Commission using Article 9 to pursue regulatory goals in furtherance of its liberalisation agenda,[360] and this has included securing structural remedies in some cases.[361] A number of other high-profile and sometimes controversial cases under Article 102 have been settled by commitments decisions, as discussed in Chapter 7.[362] By April 2013 the Commission had taken 30 commitments decisions since the procedure became available.[363] Outside hardcore cartels, commitments decisions have become the most common way the Commission deals with cases it wishes to pursue. This has, as discussed in Section 8.D.iii.b, shifted public enforcement from imposed infringement decisions to negotiated outcomes.

b. The *Alrosa* Case

The extent of the Commission's discretion and freedom of action under Article 9 was established in the *Alrosa* case, in which the CJ overturned the GC's annulment of the Commission decision.

De Beers and Alrosa had entered into an exclusive purchasing agreement whereby Alrosa, which had sold diamonds to De Beers for years, undertook to sell a large proportion of its rough diamonds

---

[353] Best Practices, paras. 115–133; Antitrust ManProc, Module 16.

[354] Although if an SO has already been sent the SO fulfils the requirements of the Preliminary Assessment.

[355] Best Practices, paras. 129–133.

[356] COMP/39.530, *Microsoft*, IP/13/196

[357] COMP/39.530, *Microsoft*, IP/10/216.

[358] Two of them, *Deutsche Bundesliga* [2005] OJ L134/46 and COMP/C-2/38.173 *FA Premier League* [2006] 5 CMLR 1430, concerned the collective selling of media rights to football matches. The *Cannes Extension Agreement* IP/06/1311 concerned online music. *Repsol*, [2006] OJ L176/104, was a move to open up the fuel distribution system in Spain, and involved a structural remedy.

[359] Such as Case 39.386 *EDF—Long Term Electricity Contracts in France*; COMP/B-1/337.966 *Distrigaz* [2008] OJ C9/8; COMP/39.316 *GDF, Gas market in France* OJ C57/13, IP/09/1872, 3 December 2009; COMP/39.388 *German Electricity Wholesale Markets* and COMP/39.389 *German Electricity Balancing Markets* (E.ON) [2009] OJ C36/8; Case COMP/39.402 *RWE—Gas Foreclosure*, [2009] OJ C133/9; COMP 39.317 *E.ON (Gas)*, [2010] OJ C278/9, 4 May 2010; COMP/39.727, *CEZ*, IP/13/320, 10 April 2013. See further Chap. 7.

[360] F. Cengiz, 'Judicial Review and the Rule of Law in the EU Competition Law Regime after *Alrosa*' (2011) 7 *European Competition Journal* 127, 138.

[361] See *Distrigaz, RWE, E.ON (Gas), CEZ*, cited in n. 359.

[362] Including *Rambus, Microsoft* (tying), and *IBM Maintenance Services*, cited in n. 351; proposed commitments from Google in respect, inter alia, of search engine neutrality were put out to market test on 25 April 2013 (COMP/39.740).

[363] The Commission recorded this statistic in the 'Questions and Answers' Memo that accompanied the Google market test Notice on 25 April 2013, MEMO/13/838 (in answering in the negative the 'question' of 'Is Google benefitting from special treatment from the Commission?').

exclusively to De Beers. De Beers was the world's largest diamond producer and Alrosa the second. The agreement was notified to the Commission in 2001. The Commission considered Articles 101 and 102 might both apply to the agreement. In 2005 De Beers and Alrosa jointly offered commitments which provided for a 'cap' on Alrosa's sales to De Beers. The commitments were not pursued by the Commission after the market test produced negative responses.[364] De Beers (alone, as the dominant undertaking) then gave commitments to phase out between 2006 and 2008, and to cease completely from 2009, all direct and indirect purchases of rough diamonds from Alrosa. The Commission accepted these commitments and adopted an Article 9(1) decision.[365]

Alrosa, which felt it would be seriously affected by the termination of its arrangements with De Beers, appealed. The GC, in a highly critical judgment, annulled the decision on the grounds that it infringed the principle of proportionality and Article 9.[366] Moreover, Alrosa's right to be heard as a 'party concerned' under Article 27(2) had been infringed. The GC held that, (i) although commitments arise from an offer made by the parties and accepted by the Commission that does not mean that the Commission is not the 'sole author' of the decision, which is binding *erga omnes*, and (ii) the Commission cannot take a decision under Article 9(1) that it could not take as a final decision under Article 7(1). Only the most exceptional circumstances[367] could justify an Article 9(1) decision indefinitely prohibiting parties from entering into any contractual arrangements whatsoever. The principle of proportionality would have been infringed if this had been an Article 7(1) decision, as there were less onerous options open to the Commission than the one it had adopted, so the principle of proportionality was equally infringed by the Article 9(1) decision. The Commission was not entitled to cast upon Alrosa responsibility, in effect, for restructuring the diamond market (paragraphs 147–149).

The GC also held that Alrosa's right to be heard had been infringed as it had not been able to comment fully on De Beers' proposed commitments (its access to the file was insufficient). Although it was not 'an undertaking concerned' under Article 9(1) in respect of the Article 102 proceedings because it was not in a dominant position (paragraphs 89 and 90) it was more than a mere 'interested third party'. Until the Commission dropped the Article 101 proceedings and relied solely on Article 102 it *had* been' an undertaking concerned' and these circumstances should have led to its being accorded the rights given to an undertaking concerned even though 'strictly speaking, it did not fall to be so classified' in the Article 102 proceedings. The right to be heard was a fundamental right, enshrined in Article 41(2) of the Charter.[368]

The Commission appealed. The CJ set aside the GC judgment.[369] The CJ clarified that the principle of proportionality applies to commitment decisions under Article 9 differently from the way in which it applies to infringement decisions under Article 7. In particular, it held that Article 9 is a new mechanism intended to provide a more rapid solution to competition problems identified by the Commission. Although the Commission is bound to respect the principle of proportionality in adopting commitment decisions, its task under Article 9 is confined to examining and possibly accepting commitments offered by the undertakings concerned in the light of problems identified by the Commission in its preliminary assessment. In contrast, Article 7 expressly provides that the Commission can only impose remedies on undertakings which are proportionate to the infringement committed and necessary to bring it effectively to an end. Undertakings offering commitments in Article 9 cases consciously accept that the concessions they make may go beyond what

---

[364] The third parties responding to the Art. 27(4) market test notice, [2005] OJ C136/32, thought the cap inadequate to meet the competition concerns.

[365] Case T-170/06, *Alrosa v. Commission* [2007] ECR II-2601.

[366] COMP/38.381, *DeBeers/Alrosa*, decision 22 February 2006, [2006] OJ L205/24.

[367] Such as possibly a collective dominance situation, which had not been established here.

[368] And appeared in Recital 37 and Art. 27(2).

[369] See M. Kellerbauer, 'Playground Instead of Playpen: The Court of Justice of the European Union's Alrosa Judgment on Article 9 of Regulation 1/2003' (2011) *ECLR* 1.

the Commission could impose on them in an Article 7 decision. In Article 9 cases the application of the principle of proportionality is therefore confined to verifying that the commitments offered addressed the concerns expressed, taking into consideration the interests of third parties.

The CJ also held that in holding that alternative solutions, which were less onerous than a complete ban on dealing, existed in this case, the GC had gone beyond considering whether the Commission had committed a manifest error of assessment and had wrongly substituted its own assessment for that of the Commission. Further, the GC had misinterpreted the extent of Alrosa's 'right to be heard' in the Commission proceedings. As far as the Article 102 proceedings were concerned, Alrosa was not an 'undertaking concerned' as it was not the dominant undertaking. Its rights were limited to those of an interested third party only.

Case C-441/07 P, *Commission* v. *Alrosa* [2010] ECR I-5949

Court of Justice

34 Under Article 9 of Regulation No 1/2003, where the Commission intends to adopt a decision requiring an infringement to be brought to an end, it may make the commitments offered by the undertakings concerned binding if they meet the competition concerns expressed in its preliminary assessment.

35 This is a new mechanism introduced by Regulation No 1/2003 which is intended to ensure that the competition rules laid down in the EC Treaty are applied effectively, by means of the adoption of decisions making commitments, proposed by the parties and considered appropriate by the Commission, binding in order to provide a more rapid solution to the competition problems identified by the Commission, instead of proceeding by making a formal finding of an infringement. More particularly, Article 9 of the regulation is based on considerations of procedural economy, and enables undertakings to participate fully in the procedure, by putting forward the solutions which appear to them to be the most appropriate and capable of addressing the Commission's concerns.

36 As observed by the parties and by the Advocate General in point 42 of her Opinion, although Article 9, unlike Article 7 of Regulation No 1/2003, does not expressly refer to proportionality, the principle of proportionality, as a general principle of European Union law, is none the less a criterion for the lawfulness of any act of the institutions of the Union, including decisions taken by the Commission in its capacity of competition authority.

37 That being so, in the examination of acts of the Commission, whether in the context of Article 7 or of Article 9 of Regulation No 1/2003, the questions always arise, first, of the precise extent and limits of the obligations which flow from the observance of that principle and, second, of the limits of judicial review.

38 The specific characteristics of the mechanisms provided for in Articles 7 and 9 of Regulation No 1/2003 and the means of action available under each of those provisions are different, which means that the obligation on the Commission to ensure that the principle of proportionality is observed has a different extent and content, depending on whether it is considered in relation to the former or the latter article.

39 Article 7 of Regulation No 1/2003 expressly indicates the extent to which the principle of proportionality applies in situations covered by that article. In accordance with Article 7(1) of the regulation, the Commission may impose on the undertakings concerned any behavioural or structural remedies which are proportionate to the infringement committed and necessary to bring the infringement effectively to an end.

40 Article 9 of that regulation, by contrast, provides merely that in proceedings under that provision, as follows from recital 13 in the preamble to the regulation, the Commission is not required to make a finding of an infringement, its task being confined to examining, and possibly accepting, the commitments offered by the undertakings concerned in the light of the problems identified by it in its preliminary assessment and having regard to the aims pursued.

41 Application of the principle of proportionality by the Commission in the context of Article 9 of Regulation No 1/2003 is confined to verifying that the commitments in question address the concerns it expressed to the undertakings concerned and that they have not offered less onerous commitments that also address those concerns adequately. When carrying out that assessment, the Commission must, however, take into consideration the interests of third parties.

42 Judicial review for its part relates solely to whether the Commission's assessment is manifestly incorrect.

43 In the judgment under appeal, the General Court proceeded from the proposition that the application of the principle of proportionality has the same effect in relation to decisions taken under Article 7 of Regulation No 1/2003 as in relation to those taken under Article 9 of that regulation.

44 In paragraph 101 of the judgment under appeal, the General Court held that it would be contrary to the scheme of Regulation No 1/2003 for a decision which would, under Article 7(1) of the regulation, have to be regarded as disproportionate to the infringement that had been established to be taken by having recourse to the procedure laid down under Article 9(1) in the form of a commitment that is made binding.

45 That conclusion is not correct.

46 Those two provisions of Regulation No 1/2003, as noted in paragraph 38 above, pursue different objectives, one of them aiming to put an end to the infringement that has been found to exist and the other aiming to address the Commission's concerns following its preliminary assessment.

47 There is therefore no reason why the measure which could possibly be imposed in the context of Article 7 of Regulation No 1/2003 should have to serve as a reference for the purpose of assessing the extent of the commitments accepted under Article 9 of the regulation, or why anything going beyond that measure should automatically be regarded as disproportionate. Even though decisions adopted under each of those provisions are in either case subject to the principle of proportionality, the application of that principle none the less differs according to which of those provisions is concerned.

48 Undertakings which offer commitments on the basis of Article 9 of Regulation No 1/2003 consciously accept that the concessions they make may go beyond what the Commission could itself impose on them in a decision adopted under Article 7 of the regulation after a thorough examination. On the other hand, the closure of the infringement proceedings brought against those undertakings allows them to avoid a finding of an infringement of competition law and a possible fine.

49 Moreover, the fact that the individual commitments offered by an undertaking have been made binding by the Commission does not mean that other undertakings are deprived of the possibility of protecting the rights they may have in connection with their relations with that undertaking.

50 It must therefore be concluded that the Commission is right to submit that in the judgment under appeal the General Court wrongly considered that the application of the principle of proportionality must be assessed, in the case of decisions taken under Article 9 of Regulation No 1/2003, by reference to the way in which it is assessed in connection with decisions taken under Article 7 of that regulation despite the different concepts underlying those two provisions.

...

59 It should be recalled that the Commission examined the joint commitments after inviting third parties to submit observations and finding that the results of that public consultation were negative. From that it concluded that those commitments were not sufficient.

60 To answer the Commission's complaint and ascertain whether the General Court really did, as the Commission submits, infringe the discretion it has in connection with accepting commitments under Article 9 of Regulation No 1/2003, the extent of that discretion should first be defined.

61 Since the Commission is not required itself to seek out less onerous or more moderate solutions than the commitments offered to it, as was observed in paragraphs 40 and 41 above, its only obligation in the present case in relation to the proportionality of the commitments was to ascertain whether the joint

commitments offered in the proceedings initiated under Article [101] were sufficient to address the concerns it had identified in the proceedings initiated under Article [102].

62 As the Advocate General observes in point 80 et seq. of her Opinion, the Commission concluded, after taking note of the results of the market test it had conducted, that the joint commitments were not appropriate for resolving the competition problems it had identified.

63 The General Court could have held that the Commission had committed a manifest error of assessment only if it had found that the Commission's conclusion was obviously unfounded, having regard to the facts established by it.

64 However, the General Court made no such finding.

65 Instead it examined other less onerous solutions for the purpose of applying the principle of proportionality, including possible adjustments of the joint commitments, in paragraphs 128, 129 and 137 to 153 of the judgment under appeal.

66 In paragraphs 129 to 136 of the judgment under appeal, the General Court expressed its own differing assessment of the capability of the joint commitments to eliminate the competition problems identified by the Commission, before concluding in paragraph 154 that alternative solutions that were less onerous for the undertakings than a complete ban on dealings existed in the present case.

67 By so doing, the General Court put forward its own assessment of complex economic circumstances and thus substituted its own assessment for that of the Commission, thereby encroaching on the discretion enjoyed by the Commission instead of reviewing the lawfulness of its assessment.

68 That error of the General Court in itself justifies setting aside the judgment under appeal.

85 In the judgment under appeal the General Court proceeds from the assumption that, in the circumstances of the case, having regard especially to the fact that the proceedings brought by the Commission under Articles [101] and [102] were always *de facto* regarded both by the Commission and by De Beers and Alrosa as forming a single set of proceedings, Alrosa should have been allowed the rights accorded to an 'undertaking concerned' within the meaning of Regulation No 1/2003, even though it did not strictly have the status of 'undertaking concerned' in the proceedings brought under Article [102].

86 After acknowledging in paragraph 195 of the judgment under appeal that the Commission was entitled to take the view, after receipt of the observations from the third parties, that the joint commitments did not address the concerns expressed in its preliminary assessment, the General Court none the less held in paragraph 196 of the judgment that, in a case of this kind, compliance with the right to be heard requires, first, that undertakings which propose commitments should be informed of the essential factual elements on the basis of which the Commission has required new commitments and, second, that those undertakings can express their views on the matter. In the present case, Alrosa was provided only with a summary of the conclusions which the Commission drew from the third parties' observations. At the meeting of 27 October 2005, Alrosa received a summary of the third parties' observations and was informed of the nature of the commitments which the Commission expected the parties to give following the negative result of the consultation with third parties, namely cessation of all relations with effect from 2009 and a new offer of commitments on that basis.

87 The General Court concluded, in paragraph 201 of the judgment under appeal, that Alrosa had not had an opportunity to exercise fully its right to be heard on the individual commitments proposed by De Beers, because the third parties' observations had been supplied to it at the same time as the copy of the individual commitments of De Beers, so that it was impossible for it to make an effective reply and to propose new joint commitments with De Beers.

88 It must be observed here that in the present case two sets of proceedings were started by the Commission, one under Article [101] concerning the conduct of De Beers and Alrosa on the market in rough diamonds, and the other under Article [102] concerning the unilateral practices of De Beers. In those two sets of proceedings, separate statements of objections were addressed to De Beers and Alrosa. It follows that Alrosa could have had the status of 'undertaking concerned' only in the context of the

proceedings brought under Article [101], in which no decision was taken. In that context, Alrosa could not therefore claim the procedural rights reserved to the parties to the proceedings concerning the individual commitments, since those commitments were offered by De Beers in the administrative proceedings relating to the application of Article [102] EC under reference COMP/E-2/38.381, which were terminated by the contested decision.

89 As the Advocate General observes in points 176 and 177 of her Opinion, only if it transpired that the Commission without an objective reason made a single factual situation the subject of two separate sets of proceedings would Alrosa have to be accorded the rights enjoyed by an undertaking concerned in relation to the proceedings brought under Article [102]. However, the General Court did not find that the Commission misused its powers in that way in the present case, nor indeed was there any evidence in support of that view. It was objectively justified for the Commission to conduct two separate sets of administrative proceedings in view of their different material legal bases, Article [101] on the one hand and Article [102] on the other. With regard to the proceedings under Article [102], only De Beers as the presumed dominant undertaking could be the addressee of the statement of objections and the Commission's final decision in those proceedings.

90 That being so, it is permissible for a third-party undertaking which considers itself to be affected by a decision taken under Article 7 or Article 9 of Regulation No 1/2003 to protect its rights by bringing an action against that decision. It does not follow, however, that such an undertaking, in the present case Alrosa, acquires the status of a 'party concerned' within the meaning of Article 27(2) of Regulation No 1/2003.

91 As the Advocate General observes in point 175 of her Opinion, in the proceedings under Article [102] which were concluded by the contested decision, Alrosa therefore enjoyed only the less extensive rights of an interested third party.

92 It should be noted, moreover, that the General Court based its reasoning on the incorrect proposition that the Commission was obliged to provide Alrosa with a reasoned explanation of why the observations of the third parties had changed its position on the appropriateness of the joint commitments, in order to enable it to offer new joint commitments with De Beers.

93 In this respect the General Court, first, held in paragraph 196 of the judgment under appeal that Alrosa had been provided only with a summary of the conclusions which the Commission drew from the third parties' observations and, second, stated in paragraph 201 of the judgment that the non-confidential version of the third parties' observations had been supplied to Alrosa late, at the same time as the copy of the individual commitments of De Beers, thus making it impossible for it to make an effective reply and propose new joint commitments with De Beers.

94 However, the Commission's acceptance of the individual commitments offered by De Beers did not depend on the position of Alrosa or any other undertaking in this respect. It follows from Article 9(1) of Regulation No 1/2003 that the Commission has a wide discretion to make a proposed commitment binding or to reject it.

95 It follows from the foregoing that the second ground of appeal is also well founded in that, first, the General Court misinterpreted the concept of 'undertaking concerned' within the meaning of Regulation No 1/2003 by comparing the legal position of Alrosa in the proceedings relating to the individual commitments with that of De Beers and, second, the General Court based its reasoning on the incorrect proposition that the Commission was required to give reasons for rejecting the joint commitments and to suggest to Alrosa that it offer new joint commitments with De Beers.

c. The Position after *Alrosa*

Alrosa showed the different conceptions which the GC and the CJ hold of the nature of commitments decisions. The GC took what has been called a more 'public-law paradigm' view, whereby commitments decisions are part of an enforcement process 'epitomized by an authoritative, unilateral, top-down hierarchical command by the "State".[370] The CJ however, saw them as having more of a 'contract-law' character, where they are the outcome of a negotiation and agreement between parties of similar bargaining power able to safeguard their own interests.[371] The result of the CJ's conception of commitments decisions is the marginalisation of judicial review and the sidelining of the principle of proportionality.[372] The CJ's judgment was an extreme example of the Court's willingness to defer to the Commission's discretion.[373]

Commitments decisions are an extremely attractive procedure for the Commission. They enable it to terminate cases quickly while retaining control (it has no obligation to accept the undertakings' commitments and can proceed to a final Article 7(1) decision if it wishes). The Commission can try out the application of Article 102 in novel situations without having to prove its case with extensive economic and legal analysis. There are advantages for undertakings too. Once they have suffered the misfortune of their business practices attracting the attention of the Commission Article 9 at least offers the benefits of not being embroiled for years and years in expensive, time-consuming, and uncertain proceedings which may end (particularly in Article 102 cases) in a finding of infringement, bad publicity, large fines, and the further possibility of 'follow-on' private actions.[374] They may be willing to compromise with the Commission at least so long as the commitments required do not go to the heart of their business model.[375] Undertakings in Article 9(1) proceedings do not have to admit guilt—in *Rambus* for example, the undertaking strongly disagreed with the Commission's assessment as regards both the factual and legal elements and denied the allegations against it.[376]

The effect on the development and certainty of the law is another matter. Outside the area of cartels there have been few Article 7(1) decisions in Article 101 cases since the abolition of notification in 2004 and it has been suggested that in effect Article 9(1) decisions are becoming a replacement for the decisions which used to follow notification (such as in the airline alliance cases).[377] We noted in Chapter 7 that the use of commitments decisions is already showing that it will lead to a lack of development in the jurisprudence of the EU Courts on Article 102. The Commission proclaimed the Microsoft internet browser commitments,[378] for example, as a great victory but its case was never put to the test. The 'public interest' does not appear to be well served by the extensive use of commitments.[379]

Third parties are disadvantaged by Article 9 decisions, as shown in *Alrosa*, despite their ability to comment in the market test phase. Although Alrosa was able to mount a challenge under Article 263 TFEU the wide discretion left to the Commission by the CJ's judgment ensured that Alrosa was unable to overturn the decision. A major problem for third parties—which is one of the great advantages for the dominant undertaking—is that Article 9 does not result in a finding of infringement and they do not have an Article 7 decision on which to base a follow-on action.[380] Although complainants

---

[370] F. Wagner-Von Papp, 'Best and Even Better Practices in Commitment Procedures after Alrosa: The Dangers of Abandoning the "Struggle for Competition Law"' (2012) 49 *CMLRev* 929, 933.

[371] Wagner-Von Papp, 'Best and Even Better Practices in Commitment Procedures after Alrosa' (cited in n. 370), 929, 933.

[372] See also Cengiz, 'Judicial Review and the Rule of Law in the EU Competition Law Regime after *Alrosa*' (cited in n. 360).

[373] For this, see further Section 9.A.vi, p. 1036.

[374] See Chap. 14.

[375] See I. Forrester, 'Creating New Rules or Closing Easy Cases' in C-D. Ehlermann and M. Marquis (eds.), *European Competition Law Annual 2008* (Hart Publishing, 2009), 637.

[376] COMP/38.636, *Rambus*, IP/09/1897.

[377] I. Forrester, 'Creating New Rules or Closing Easy Cases' (cited in n. 375).

[378] COMP/39.530, *Microsoft*, IP/10/216.

[379] See Cengiz, 'Judicial Review and the Rule of Law in the EU Competition Law Regime after Alrosa' (cited in n. 360); and Wagner-Von Papp, 'Best and Even Better Practices in Commitment Procedures after Alrosa' (cited in n. 370).

[380] See Chap. 14.

have a right to a decision[381] the wide discretion given to the Commission again makes this of doubtful use. The position as to the effect on NCAs of Article 9 decisions is unclear.[382]

(iv) Final Decisions: Findings of Inapplicability

Under Regulation 1/2003, Article 10 the Commission is able to take 'positive' decisions finding that Articles 101 and 102 are inapplicable to particular agreements or practices.

Regulation 1/2003, Article 10, Finding of Inapplicability

Where the Community public interest relating to the application of Articles [101] and [102] so requires, the Commission, acting on its own initiative, may by decision find that Article [101] is not applicable to an agreement, a decision by an association of undertakings or a concerted practice, either because the conditions of Article [101(1)] are not fulfilled, or because the conditions of Article [101(3)] are satisfied.

The Commission may likewise make such a finding with reference to Article [102] of the Treaty.

Article 10 provides that a finding of inapplicability will be made by decision and, as far as Article 101 is concerned, the finding may be that the conditions in Article 101(1) are not fulfilled or that the conditions in Article 101(3) are satisfied. The information required by the Commission could be acquired through the fact-finding procedures previously discussed or through the parties supplying it voluntarily. Article 10 states that these declaratory decisions will be made when the *[Union] public interest* so requires and that the Commission will act *on its own initiative*, making it clear that the decisions are not intended (at least primarily) to be for the benefit of the parties. Regulation 1/2003, recital 14, says that Article 10 decisions will be adopted *in exceptional cases* 'with a view to clarifying the law and ensuring its consistent application throughout the [Union], in particular with regard to new types of agreements or practices that have not been settled in the existing case-law and administrative practice'. Nevertheless, Article 10 decisions are clearly advantageous to the parties as they are enforceable in national courts and give complete legal certainty. Further, Article 10 may be used by the Commission to pre-empt a decision by an NCA since Article 11(6) of Regulation 1/2003 provides that if the Commission initiates proceedings NCAs are relieved of their competence to act 'under the same legal basis against the same agreement(s) or practice(s) by the same undertaking(s) on the same relevant geographic and product market'.[383] As of 1 July 2013 no Article 10 decisions had been adopted. In the Working Paper[384] the Commission said of the (then) lack of such decisions that it was because Article 10 was designed to avoid being used as a replacement for the old exemption decisions and intended for truly exceptional cases only, and that the success of the ECN in promoting the coherent application of the competition rules has made its use to remove matters from the NCAs unnecessary to date.

(v) Procedural Decisions

As we have seen, the Commission, in the course of its investigations, may take decisions about procedural matters. Thus, information may be demanded by decision under Regulation 1/2003, Article 18(3), and an inspection may be ordered under Regulation 1/2003, Article 20(4). Failure to comply

---

[381] See Section 13.F.iv, p. 1075.

[382] See Bellamy and Child, *European Law of Competition* (cited in n. 2), 13.102.

[383] Notice on cooperation within the Network of Competition Authorities [2004] OJ C101/43, para. 51. And see also para. 54(d).

[384] Working Paper, paras. 112–114.

with such decisions may be penalised by fines.[385] The question of the confidentiality of documents is settled by decision under Article 8 of Decision 2011/695.[386]

(vi) Interim Measures

Regulation 1/2003, Article 8 gives the Commission power to take decisions ordering interim measures.

Regulation 1/2003, Article 8

1. In cases of urgency due to the risk of serious and irreparable damage to competition, the Commission, acting on its own initiative may by decision, on the basis of a prima facie finding of infringement, order interim measures.

2. A decision under paragraph 1 shall apply for a specified period of time and may be renewed in so far this is necessary and appropriate.

This was a new provision in Regulation 1/2003, given that Regulation 17 did not expressly provide powers for the Commission to take interim measures in relation to possible infringements of Articles 101 and 102. However, case law established that the Commission *did* have such powers. The CJ recognised that otherwise there would be a serious lacuna, as Commission proceedings can be protracted and irreparable damage might occur before it could take a final decision under Regulation 17, Article 3. The power to take interim measures was first established in *Camera Care*,[387] in a striking example of the Court's teleological interpretative technique, and developed in subsequent cases, in particular *La Cinq*[388] and *IMS*.[389] The cases establish that certain conditions must be fulfilled before interim measures are taken:

- There must be a *prima facie* infringement of the competition rules;
- It must be a situation of proven urgency where there would otherwise be serious and irreparable damage to competition. Financial damage cannot, save in exceptional circumstances, be regarded as irreparable if it can ultimately be the subject of financial compensation unless the applicant can adduce evidence that would justify a *prima facie* finding that without the measures sought it would suffer losses that would threaten its survival.[390] Damage may also be irreparable if without the measures there are likely to be developments on the market which will be very difficult, or impossible, to reverse.[391]

---

[385] See Section 8.G.ii, p. 995.

[386] The Hearing Officer terms of reference [2010] OJ L275/29. The jurisdiction of the Hearing Officer to take decisions in this respect means that the power to adopt a challengeable act has been delegated by the Commission to a single official. Such delegation is permitted where it does not involve a matter of principle: see Case T-450/93, *Lisrestal* [1994] ECR II-1177; M. van der Woude, 'Hearing Officers and EC Antitrust Procedures; The Art of Making Subjective Procedures More Objective' (1996) 33 *CMLRev* 531. Cf. the delegation of Reg. 1/2003, Art. 20(4) decisions to a single *Commissioner*: the validity of this in respect of Reg. 17, Art. 14(3) was confirmed in Case 53/85, *AKZO v. Commission* [1986] ECR 1965.

[387] [1980] ECR 119.

[388] Case T-44/90, *La Cinq SA v. Commission* [1992] ECR II-1; see also Cases 228–229/82 R, *Ford Werke AG v. Commission* [1982] ECR 3091.

[389] Case T-184/01 R, *IMS Health v. Commission* [2001] ECR II-3193, upheld Case C-481/01 P (R), *NDC v. IMS and Commission* [2002] ECR I-3401, the appeals against the interim decision, *NDC Health/IMS: Interim Measures* [2002] OJ L59/18, adopted by the Commission because it considered that the competitors refused permission to use the dominant undertaking's copyright might otherwise not survive on the market. For interim measures generally, see Antitrust ManProc, Module 17.

[390] Case T-184/01 R, *IMS Health*, paras. 119–121.

[391] Case T-184/01 R, *IMS Health*, paras. 128–129.

- The measures must be of a temporary and conservatory nature only and restricted to what is required in the particular situation to preserve the status quo; the measures have to accord with the principle of proportionality;

- The legitimate rights of the party on which the measures are being imposed must be observed and the 'essential guarantees' provided for by Regulation 1/2003, especially Article 27 on the right to be heard, must be maintained;

- The measures must be in a form which is subject to review by the EU Courts, i.e. in the form of a reasoned decision.

A number of Commission decisions on refusal to supply as an abuse of a dominant position under Article 102 involved interim decisions. In *Boosey & Hawkes*[392] the interim measures ordered the dominant undertaking to maintain supplies to the complainant on the terms and conditions on which the parties had previously done business and in *Sealink/B&I*[393] the port authority was ordered to return to its previous published timetable. In *Sea Containers/Stena*[394] the Commission held that there was a *prima facie* case of abuse, but refused interim measures on the ground that there was not sufficient urgency as since the initial application the complainant had been offered and had accepted an offer of access so there was no danger of serious and irreparable harm occurring. The most notorious case of interim measures was the decision ordering an undertaking to license its copyright in *NDC Health/IMS: Interim Measures*.[395] The decision was suspended and ultimately withdrawn without a final decision being taken.[396] *NDC Health/IMS* was the last interim measures decision to be taken. As at 1 July 2013 none had been adopted under Article 8.

E. THE SETTLEMENT PROCEDURE IN CARTEL CASES

In 2008 the Commission adopted a Notice on a new 'direct settlement' procedure for cartel cases.[397] The object is to dispose more quickly of cartel cases in which undertakings are prepared to admit liability, by rewarding cooperation. On the conclusion of the Commission's investigation it decides whether the case is suitable for settlement and, if it is, it invites the parties concerned to reach an agreement with it. It informs them of the evidence and tells them its conclusions as to duration, seriousness, liability, and the likely fine. Officially the Commission does not negotiate with the undertakings. Rather, the parties have to agree with the Commission's assessment. They have to make (orally or in writing) a final settlement submission in which (Notice, paragraph 20) they acknowledge their liability 'in clear and unequivocal terms'; indicate the maximum fine they would accept in the

---

[392] *BBI/Boosey & Hawkes* [1987] OJ L286/36.

[393] *Sealink/B&I Holyhead: Interim Measures* [1992] 5 CMLR 255, where the decision ordering the interim measures contained the Commission's first explicit statement of the essential facilities doctrine in Community law (see Chap. 7): as in *Boosey & Hawkes* the case did not go to a final decision.

[394] [1994] OJ L15/8.

[395] [2002] OJ L59/18.

[396] Case T-184/01 R, and Case C-481/01 P (R), *IMS Health v. Commission*, cited in n. 389. For the substantive issues in this case see Chap. 7. The Presidents of the GC and CJ were concerned that, as IMS claimed, the decision went beyond the existing case law. The decision was therefore suspended on the ground that the status quo should be maintained pending the GC's judgment in the appeal. It was held that the balance of interests favoured preserving the copyright unimpaired during the appeal proceedings: there was potentially serious and irreparable harm to IMS in having to license its copyright and the copyright should not be devalued by reducing it to a purely economic right to receive financial compensation: the conditions for granting interim relief were therefore fulfilled.

[397] Commission Notice on the conduct of settlement procedures [2008] OJ C167/1. The adoption of the settlement procedure required the amendment of Commission Reg. 773/2004 by Reg. 622/2008 [2008] OJ L171/3. See M. L. Tierno Centella, 'The New Settlement Procedure in Selected Cartel Cases' (2008) 3 *Competition Policy Newsletter* 30; J. Tyler, 'Act of Settlement' (2008) 3 CLI 79; J. Joshua, K. Hugmark, and I. Daems, 'What's the Deal? Navigating the European Commission's 2008 Settlement Notice' (2009) *The European Antitrust Review* 2; R. Gamble, '"Speaking (formally) with the Enemy"—Cartel Settlements Evolve' [2011] *ECLR* 449.

framework of the settlement procedure; confirm that they have been informed of the case against them and that they have been given sufficient opportunity to make their views known; confirm that they do not envisage requesting access to the file or requesting to be heard orally again, and agree to accept an SO. The SO reflects the settlement submissions. The Commission then proceeds, without any further procedural steps, to adopt an Article 7 decision.

The advantages to the Commission are obvious. It saves time and resources, and reduces appeals to the EU Courts. One advantage to the parties is that they receive a 10 per cent reduction (but only 10 per cent) on the fine that would otherwise have been imposed on them. Also, they are saved all the trouble of full-scale protracted cartel proceedings and may confine themselves to purely oral submissions. However, there are disadvantages for them. The procedure is totally in the control of the Commission, which offers the settlement on a 'take it or leave it' basis. They lose some rights of defence (the oral hearing and access to the file) and have to assess what fine they think the Commission will accept (albeit in the light of the Commission's indication). The admission of liability may form the basis for future third party actions.[398] What is more, the Commission can decide right up to the end to revert to the normal procedure.

The first settlement decision, in May 2010, was in respect of a cartel involving 10 producers of DRAM memory chips (the investigation had commenced in 2002).[399] The fines, totalling €331,273,800 million included a reduction of 10 per cent for the companies' acknowledgement of the facts. The second was *Animal Feed Phosphates Producers*,[400] which was a 'hybrid' decision in which five undertakings followed the settlement route and one undertaking withdrew from the procedure and, having been found liable, did not get the 10 per cent reduction.

Leniency[401] and settlement can both be applied in the same case.

F. INFORMAL SETTLEMENTS

The Commission has sometimes not proceeded to a formal decision but terminated the matter informally. As we have seen, under the 'old' Regulation 17 regime notified agreements were often, and indeed usually, dealt with by way of comfort letter rather than by formal decision.[402] Cases have also been terminated informally because the Commission and the parties have come to a settlement, usually because the companies had made enough concessions to satisfy the Commission, and the latter considered that nothing would be gained by pursuing a formal proceeding any further. The settlements were reached both before and after the SO. Settlements often included the parties giving undertakings to the Commission. Several important cases were terminated in this way, such as *IBM*,[403] *Microsoft*,[404] *Digital*,[405] and *Deutsche Telekom Tariffs*.[406] Settlements were frequently publicised, in Commission press releases, in law reports, and in the Commission's annual reports, and inevitably they could attain the status of precedent. Clearly they were valuable guidance to other companies on what was acceptable to the Commission but by their nature they involved compromise and concession. Under Regulation 1/2003, Article 9 the Commission acquired a new power to take decisions which make commitments offered by companies binding upon them and it has made extensive use

---

[398] See Chap. 14.

[399] COMP/38.511, *DRAMS*, IP/10/586

[400] COMP/38.866, 20 July 2010, IP/10/985, OJ C111/19.

[401] See Section 8.G.v, p. 1019.

[402] see Section 4, p. 924.

[403] [1984] 3 CMLR 147.

[404] Commission Press Release IP(94)653 [1994] 5 CMLR 143.

[405] Commission Press Release IP/97/868.

[406] Commission's *XXVIIth Report on Competition Policy* (Commission, 1997), pt. 77.

of this.[407] There is nothing in Regulation 1/2003 to prevent informal settlements but given the existence of Article 9 they are likely to be rare.[408]

G. FINES AND PERIODIC PENALTY PAYMENTS

(i) General

Regulation 1/2003 empowers the Commission to take decisions to impose fines on undertakings and associations of undertakings both for substantive infringements of the competition rules (Article 23(2)) and for procedural infringements (Article 23(1)). The Commission may also impose periodic penalty payments, in order to compel undertakings to do what the Commission requires by penalising defiance (Article 24). Regulation 1/2003 provides for fines and penalties to be levied only on *undertakings* : it does not impose liability on natural persons such as company directors and executives, unlike, for example, UK competition law and US antitrust law.

The Commission's multiplicity of roles in the enforcement regime means that the prosecutor determines guilt and fixes the fine. However, Article 261 TFEU[409] provides that regulations 'may give the Court of Justice of the European Union unlimited jurisdiction with regard to the penalties provided for in such regulations'. Pursuant to this Regulation 1/2003, Article 31 states:

The Court of Justice shall have unlimited jurisdiction to review decisions whereby the Commission has fixed a fine or periodic penalty payment. It may cancel, reduce or increase the fine or periodic penalty payment imposed.

This jurisdiction is dealt with later in this chapter.[410]

The limitation periods for the imposition of penalties is provided for in Regulation 1/2003, Article 25. It is three years in respect of procedural infringements (in connection with requests for information and inspections) and five years in respect of all other infringements. Time runs from the day the infringement was committed or on the day it ended in the case of a repeated or continuous infringement. Under Article 26 the time limit for the enforcement of penalties is five years from the date of the decision.[411]

Note, in looking at past cases and decisions, that the units of account and ECUs in which the fines and penalties were expressed can be taken as equivalent to the sum in Euros.[412] Regulation 1/2003 uses turnover percentages rather than objective monetary amounts in setting maximum fines.[413]

---

[407] See Section 8.D.iii.

[408] J. Temple Lang, 'Commitment Decisions and Settlements with Antitrust Authorities and Private Parties under European Antitrust Law' [2005] Fordham Corp L Inst (B. Hawk (ed.), 2006), 265 (he suggests that informal settlements may still be used in 'small unimportant cases'); Kerse and Khan (cited in n. 2), 6-091. There were informal settlements in *OMV/Gazprom*, IP/05/195 in 2005, *E.ON Ruhrgas/Gazprom*, IP/05/710 in 2005 and *Philips CD-Recordable Discrimination Patent Licensing*, IP/06/139 in 2006. The Commission reached an informal settlement with Apple over iTunes in 2008, IP/08/22.

[409] Ex Art. 229.

[410] See Section 9.A. vii, p. 1039.

[411] In Case T-153/04, *Ferriere Nord SpA v. Commission* [2006] ECR II-3889, the Commission had failed to pursue payment of the outstanding balance of one of the fines imposed in the *Welded Steel Mesh Cartel* [1989] OJ L260/1, after the decision was finally upheld by the CJ, Case C-219/95 P, *Ferriere Nord v. Commission* [1997] ECR I-4411. The undertaking had written to the Commission twice soon after the judgment asking it to reconsider the amount of the fine because of, inter alia, the severe devaluation of the lira. The Commission did not reply until 2004. The GC held that the enforcement of the balance was time-barred since 2002, despite the existence of a bank guarantee which could have been called in at any time. The GC judgment was overruled by the CJ, Case C-516/06 P, *Commission v. Ferriere Nord SpA* [2007] ECR I-10685 (the provision concerned in the case was Reg. 2988/74 on limitation periods, now replaced as regards competition proceedings, by Reg. 1/2003, Art. 26).

[412] Regulation 17 expressed the monetary amounts of fines and penalties in units of account but these were read as referring to Euros after the introduction of the single currency (having previously become ECUs), pursuant to Art. 2(1) of Council Reg. 1103/97 [1997] OJ L162/1 on certain provisions relating to the introduction of the Euro. For the problems of expressing fines in ECUs, where the exchange rate with national currency fluctuated, see, e.g., Cases T-305–307, 313–316, 318, 328–329, and 335/94, *Re the PVC Cartel II: Limburgse Vinyl Maatschappij NV and others v. Commission* [1999] ECR II-931 at paras. 1225–1235.

[413] In respect of procedural and substantive fines, see Sections 8.G.ii and 8.G.iii respectively.

(ii) Fines for Procedural Infringements

Regulation 1/2003, Article 23(1) states:

The Commission may by decision impose on undertakings and associations of undertakings fines not exceeding 1 per cent of the total turnover in the preceding business year where, intentionally or negligently:

(a) they supply incorrect or misleading information in response to a request made pursuant to Article 17 or Article 18(2);

(b) in response to a request made by decision adopted pursuant to Article 17 or Article 18(3), they supply incorrect, incomplete or misleading information or do not supply information within the required time-limit;

(c) they produce the required books or other records related to the business in incomplete form during inspections under Article 20 or refuse to submit to inspections ordered by a decision adopted pursuant to Article 20(4);

(d) in response to a question asked in accordance with Article 20(2)(e),

— they give an incorrect or misleading answer,

— they fail to rectify within a time-limit set by the Commission an incorrect, incomplete or misleading answer given by a member of staff, or

— they fail or refuse to provide a complete answer on facts relating to the subject-matter and purpose of an inspection ordered by a decision adopted pursuant to Article 20(4);

(e) seals affixed in accordance with Article 20(2)(d) by officials or other accompanying persons authorised by the Commission have been broken.

Under this provision the Commission imposes fines for failure to cooperate with, or obstructing, its investigations under Regulation 1/2003, Articles 17,[414] 18, and 20 or for supplying incorrect, incomplete, or misleading information.[415] The maximum amount, one per cent of turnover, is a large increase on the maximum in Regulation 17, Article 15(1), which was €5,000.[416]

(iii) Periodic Penalty Payments

Periodic penalty payments may be imposed at a daily rate for defiance of the Commission. Regulation 1/2003, Article 24, states:

1. The Commission may, by decision, impose on undertakings or associations of undertakings periodic penalty payments not exceeding 5 per cent of the average daily turnover in the preceding business year per day and calculated from the date appointed by the decision, in order to compel them:

(a) to put an end to an infringement of Article [101] or Article [102], in accordance with a decision taken pursuant to Article 7;

(b) to comply with a decision ordering interim measures taken pursuant to Article 8;

(c) to comply with a commitment made binding by a decision pursuant to Article 9;

(d) to supply complete and correct information which it has requested by decision taken pursuant to Article 17 or Article 18(3);

(e) to submit to an inspection which it has ordered by decision taken pursuant to Article 20(4).

2. Where the undertakings or associations of undertakings have satisfied the obligation which the periodic penalty payment was intended to enforce, the Commission may fix the definitive amount of the periodic penalty payment at a figure lower than that which would arise under the original decision. Article 23(4) shall apply correspondingly.

[414] The provision which provides for investigations into sectors of the economy and types of agreements: see Chap. 9, Section 4.C.ii, p. 727.

[415] See Section 8.B.ii and Section 8.B.iii, pp. 940–949.

[416] Not a large amount in 1962, and derisory by 2004. The maximum procedural fines in the new EUMR, Council Reg. 139/2004 [2004] OJ L24/1, Art. 14 are the same as in Reg. 1/2003. This is also true with regard to the maximum amounts of periodic penalties.

The maximum amount (five per cent of average daily turnover) was an even bigger increase from Regulation 17 (Article 16(1) (a maximum of €1,000)) than that in respect of procedural fines.

Microsoft was the first undertaking to be fined under these provisions for failing to comply with a decision. A long battle over its compliance with the 2004 decision requiring it to disclose interoperability information on 'fair and reasonable terms'[417] ended in two decisions imposing penalty payments. The first, in July 2006, was €280.5 million (€1.5 million per day for the period from 16 December 2005 to 20 June 2006) for failing to disclose the required level of information.[418] The second was on 27 February 2008 for failing to make the information available on 'fair and reasonable terms' but instead charging royalties until 22 October 2007 that were unreasonable. The amount was €899 million.[419] The GC approved the imposition of a fine but reduced it to €860 million.[420] Microsoft then became the first undertaking to be fined (€561 million) under Article 24(1)(c) for failing to comply with a commitments decision under Article 9.[421]

(iv) Fines for Substantive Infringements

a. Regulation 1/2003, Article 23(2)

Regulation 1/2003, Article 23(2), formerly Regulation 17, Article 15(2), provides for the imposition of fines for substantive infringements:

2. The Commission may by decision impose fines on undertakings and associations of undertakings where, either intentionally or negligently:

(a) they infringe Article [101] or Article [102]; or

(b) they contravene a decision ordering interim measures under Article 8; or

(c) they fail to comply with a commitment made binding by a decision pursuant to Article 9.

For each undertaking and association of undertakings participating in the infringement, the fine shall not exceed 10 per cent of its total turnover in the preceding business year.[422]

Where the infringement of an association relates to the activities of its members, the fine shall not exceed 10 per cent of the sum of the total turnover of each member active on the market affected by the infringement of the association.

3. In fixing the amount of the fine, regard shall be had both to the gravity and to the duration of the infringement.

4. When a fine is imposed on an association of undertakings taking account of the turnover of its members and the association is not solvent, the association is obliged to call for contributions from its members to cover the amount of the fine. Where such contributions have not been made to the association within a time-limit fixed by the Commission, the Commission may require payment of the fine directly by any of the undertakings whose representatives were members of the decision-making bodies concerned of the association.

---

[417] COMP/C-3/37.792, *Microsoft*, upheld on appeal Case T-201/04, *Microsoft v. Commission* [2007] ECR II-3601, see Chap. 7.

[418] Commission Decision of 12 July 2006, C(2006)4420, IP/06/076.

[419] C(2008) 764. The Competition Commissioner said in the Press Release (IP/08/318): 'Microsoft was the first company in fifty years of EU competition policy that the Commission has had to fine for failure to comply with an antitrust decision. I hope that today's Decision closes a dark chapter in Microsoft's record of non-compliance with the Commission's March 2004 Decision and that the principles confirmed by the General Court ruling of September 2007 will govern Microsoft's future conduct.'

[420] Case T-167/08, *Microsoft v. Commission*, 27 June 2012.

[421] COMP/39.530, *Microsoft*, see Chap. 7, and Section 8.D.iii.a, p. 983, IP/13/196, 6 March 2013.

[422] The 'preceding business year' to which the turnover relates means the last full business year of each of the undertakings concerned at the date of adoption of the decision. Cases T-25/95, etc., *Cimenteries CBR SA v. Commission* [2000] ECR II-491, para. 5009.

After the Commission has required payment under the second subparagraph, where necessary to ensure full payment of the fine, the Commission may require payment of the balance by any of the members of the association which were active on the market on which the infringement occurred.

However, the Commission shall not require payment under the second or the third subparagraph from undertakings which show that they have not implemented the infringing decision of the association and either were not aware of its existence or have actively distanced themselves from it before the Commission started investigating the case.

The financial liability of each undertaking in respect of the payment of the fine shall not exceed 10 per cent of its total turnover in the preceding business year.

5. Decisions taken pursuant to paragraphs 1 and 2 shall not be of a criminal law nature.

This crucial provision, which confers upon the Commission its power to punish violations of the competition rules, says four things (apart from the provisions about fining associations of undertakings in Article 23(4)):

- Fines can only be imposed for intentional or negligent infringements;
- The maximum fine is 10 per cent of turnover in the preceding business year[423] (although it does not specify what turnover is to be taken into account);
- In fixing the fine regard is to be had both to the gravity of the infringement and to its duration;
- Fines are not criminal penalties.[424]

b. The Position of Trade Associations

Regulation 1/2003, Article 23 contains new provisions in respect of fines imposed on associations of undertakings. Regulation 17, Article 15 did not provide that the members are jointly and severally liable, and this could prevent the collection of fines.[425] Article 23(4) provides that if the association is insolvent it must call upon its members for contributions to the fine. If that does not produce the fine within the time limit imposed the Commission may fine the members directly (up to 10 per cent of that undertaking's turnover) but only those which were implicated in the infringement. The first fine on a professional body under this provision was imposed in ONP.[426]

c. Intentional or Negligent Infringement

Article 23(2) provides that the Commission may impose a fine only where the infringement was intentional or negligent. An undertaking, however, can act only through human agency and the intentions and negligence in issue are in effect those of its human directors and employees. EU competition law has not concerned itself with theories of vicarious liability or agonised over the imputation of the employees' conduct to the company. The position is that an undertaking is responsible for the conduct of its directors and employees and it should have in place, and enforce, a compliance programme to prevent infractions of the rules.[427]

---

[423] In Case T-33/02, *Britannia Alloys and Chemicals Ltd v. Commission* [2005] ECR II-4973, para. 50, the GC confirmed that the Commission was correct to use the undertaking's last 'full' business year.

[424] But see the discussion as to the position in respect to the ECHR, in Section 8.A.ii.

[425] Commission's White Paper on Modernisation [1999] OJ C132/1, paras. 127–128, and see Cases T-213/95 and T-18/96, *SCK and FNK v. Commission* [1997] ECR I-1739.

[426] COMP/39.510, on appeal Case T-90/11, *Ordre National des Pharmaciens en France (ONP) v. Commission*, judgment pending.

[427] See W. Wils, 'The Undertaking as Subject of EC Competition Law and the Imputation of Infringements to Natural or Legal Persons' (2000) 25 *ELRev* 99, 109–111. In Case C-338/00 P, *Volkswagen AG v. Commission* [2004] ECR I-9189, paras. 94–98, the appellant argued that the Commission and GC should have identified the persons who acted improperly and were therefore to be treated as responsible for the infringement. The CJ held that this was unnecessary.

'Intentional' means an intention to restrict competition, not an intention to infringe the rules. In *PVC Cartel II* the GC said:[428]

For an infringement of the competition rules of the Treaty to be regarded as having been committed intentionally, it is not necessary for an undertaking to have been aware that it was infringing those rules; it is sufficient that it could not have been unaware that its conduct was aimed at restricting competition.

In *Miller International* [429] the undertaking claimed that it had not intentionally infringed Article 101(1) by prohibiting exports and that its lawyers had not pointed out the infringement. The CJ dismissed this:[430]

17. The applicant has requested in the alternative that the fine of 70 000 u.a. [units of account] should be annulled or reduced.

It has maintained that it did not intentionally commit the infringements of which it is accused and furthermore that those infringements were not serious. It claims that in adopting the clauses prohibiting exports it did not intentionally infringe the prohibitions contained in Article [101(1)].

This lack of awareness is said to be demonstrated by the opinion of a legal adviser consulted by the applicant concerning the drafting of its terms and conditions of sale, which opinion, produced as an annex to its reply, does not mention the fact that a clause prohibiting exports might be incompatible with Community law.

18. As is clear from the foregoing as a whole, the clauses in question were adopted or accepted by the applicant and the latter could not have been unaware that they had as their object the restriction of competition between its customers. Consequently, it is of little relevance to establish whether the applicant knew that it was infringing the prohibition contained in Article [101].

In this connection, the opinion of a legal adviser, on which it relies, is not a mitigating factor.

It must thus be held that the acts prohibited by the Treaty were undertaken intentionally and in disregard of the provisions of the Treaty.

Even if the infringement is not characterised as intentional it is likely to be held negligent. The EU Courts have never defined negligence for this purpose but the Commission and the Courts expect experienced commercial entities to understand what they are doing. Their attitude to claims of ignorance or inadvertence can be illustrated by *United Brands* and *Sandoz*. In *United Brands* the undertaking claimed that it did not know it was in a dominant position for the purposes of Article 102 and did not know its conduct constituted an abuse. The CJ held:[431]

298. The applicant submits that it did not know that it was in a dominant position, still less that it had abused it, especially as, according to the case-law of the Court to date, only undertakings which were pure monopolies or controlled an overwhelming share of the market have been held to be in a dominant position.

299. UBC is an undertaking which, having engaged for a very long time in international and national trade, has special knowledge of antitrust laws and has already experienced their severity.

300. UBC, by setting up a commercial system combining the prohibition of the sale of bananas while still green, discriminatory prices, deliveries less than the amounts ordered, all of which was to end in strict partitioning of national markets, adopted measures which it knew or ought to have known contravened the prohibition set out in Article [102].

301. The Commission therefore had good reason to find that UBC's infringements were at the very least negligent.

---

[428] Cases T-305–307, 313–316, 318, 328–329, and 335/94, *Re the PVC Cartel II: Limburgse Vinyl Maatschappij NV and others v. Commission* [1999] ECR II-931, para. 1111; see also Cases 100–103/80, *Musique Diffusion Française SA v. Commission (Pioneer)* [1983] ECR 1825, para. 221; Case T-65/89, *BPB Industries and British Gypsum Ltd v. Commission* [1993] ECR II-389, paras. 165–166; Case T-143/89, *Ferriere Nord v. Commission* [1995] ECR II-917, para. 41.

[429] Case 19/77, *Miller International Schallplatten GmbH v. Commission* [1978] ECR 131.

[430] Case 19/77, *Miller International Schallplatten GmbH v. Commission* [1978] ECR 131. And see C-681/11, *Bundeswettbewerbsbehörde and Bundeskartellanwalt v. Schenker*, 18 June 2013, where the CJ ruled that acting on the erroneous advice of an NCA does not exempt an undertaking from the liability to be fined.

[431] Case 27/76, *United Brands v. Commission* [1978] ECR 207, paras. 298–301.

In *Sandoz* the undertaking, a major pharmaceutical producer, sent invoices to its customers with 'export prohibited' printed on them. The company said it had used these invoices for many years, since before the inception of the Community, and had simply omitted to amend them. The Commission did not absolve it of liability:[432]

34. … the invoices in question were adopted by Sandoz PF which could not have been unaware that the export ban had as its object the restriction of competition on trade between member-States. Consequently, it is of little relevance to establish whether or not Sandoz PF knew that it was infringing the prohibition contained in Article [101]. Therefore it can only be concluded that the acts prohibited by that Article were undertaken intentionally. However, even if Sandoz PF's thesis of a 'mere oversight' were to be accepted, this would not exclude its liability and would represent a grave form of negligence.

Since both intention and negligence produce liability to fines it may be unnecessary to decide into which category the infringement falls, except that intentional infringements tend to attract heavier fines.[433]

There are rare instances where ignorance has led to non-imposition of a fine[434] and the Commission has sometimes considered that an undertaking has not been negligent where it condemned a practice as an infringement of the competition rules for the first time.[435] No fine was imposed in *Clearstream* [436] for abuse of a dominant position in the clearing and settlement markets, as the infringement had come to an end and there had been no previous case law or decisional practice dealing with the competition analysis of clearing and settlement, which was a novel economic activity. The Commission therefore adopted the decision in order to clarify the legal situation 'at a moment when cross-border trade in securities is becoming more important within the EU'.[437] It refused the same latitude in *Intel*, however, where it said that the economic activity concerned did not raise similar controversial issues or novel or specific circumstances.[438] No fine was imposed for an Article 102 infringement in *DSD*. No reason was given for this, but it is to be noted that the matter had originated in a notification to the Commission.[439] In the *Organic Peroxide Cartel* decision the Commission imposed a fine of only €1,000 on a company which was the first it had ever fined for acting as a secretariat and facilitator while not being active itself on the market in question.[440]

---

[432] *Sandoz* [1987] OJ L222/28, upheld by the CJ, Case C-277/87, *Sandoz Prodotti Farmaceutici SpA v. Commission* [1990] ECR I-45.

[433] It has been pointed out that the type of conduct which attracts fines rarely appears to be 'negligent', see H. de Broca, 'The Commission revises its Guidelines for setting fines in antitrust cases' (2006) 3 *EC Competition Policy Newsletter* 1. Committing an infringement negligently is an attenuating circumstance under both the 1998 and 2006 Fining Guidelines.

[434] See *Bayer Dental* [1990] OJ L351/46; *Stainless Steel* [1990] OJ L220/28 and the other cases discussed by L. Gyselen in 'The Commission's Fining Policy in Competition Cases— "Questo è il catalogo"', in P. Slot and A. McDonnell (eds.), *Procedure and Enforcement in EC and US Competition Law* (Sweet & Maxwell, 1993), 63–75.

[435] See, e.g., *Vegetable Parchment* [1978] OJ L70/54. On the other hand, the arguable novelty of the developments in Art. 102 did not save United Brands, (see text at n. 431) or Hoffmann-La Roche in Case 85/76, *Hoffmann-La Roche v. Commission* [1979] ECR 461; nor did it save Tetra Pak in Case C-333/94 P, *Tetra Pak International SA v. Commission* [1996] ECR I-5951. The Commission did not, however, impose a fine on Van den Bergh Foods when it held for the first time that freezer exclusivity was contrary to Art. 101 and an abuse under Art. 102: *Van den Bergh Foods Ltd* [1998] OJ L246/1, [1998] 5 CMLR 530, discussed in Chap. 7, and Chap. 11.

[436] COMP/38.096, *Clearstream* [2009] OJ C165/7, on appeal Case T-301/04, *Clearstream Banking v. Commission* [2009] ECR II-3155.

[437] Commission Press Release IP/04/705.

[438] Case COMP/C-3/37.990, *Intel* [2010] 4 CMLR 314, para. 1768, on appeal Case T-286/09, *Intel v. Commission*, judgment pending; on the contrary, Intel was fined €1.6 billion.

[439] [2001] OJ L166/1, upheld Case T-151/01, *Der Grüne Punkt—Duales System Deutschland GmbH v. Commission* [2007] ECR II-1607, and Case C-385/07 P, [2009] ECR I-6155.

[440] COMP/37.857, on appeal Case T-99/04, *AC-Treuhand AG v. Commission* [2008] ECR II-1501.

d. Development of the Commission's Fining Policy

It can be seen from the text of Article 23(2) set out in Section 8.G.iv, which does not depart in any major respect from Regulation 17, Article 15(2), that there is remarkably little guidance in the legislation about the level at which the Commission should set fines. There is just the ceiling and the references to gravity and duration. There is no indication in the regulation whether the purpose of the fines is deterrence, punishment, ensuring that the offence does not pay,[441] or some combination of these and perhaps other factors. In 1983, however, the Commission said that the purpose was twofold: 'to impose a pecuniary sanction on the undertaking for the infringement and prevent a repetition of the offence, and to make the prohibition in the Treaty more effective'.[442] The Commission's fining policy has developed over the years in its decisional practice and in two sets of Guidelines, the first in 1998[443] and the second in 2006 (currently in force).[444]

The CJ has consistently held that the Commission is entitled to change its fining policy at any time.[445] Undertakings do not have any legitimate expectation that infringing behaviour will only attract a certain level of fines. However, as we shall see, the Commission must comply with the other general principles of Union law.

The Commission first imposed a fine in 1969 in the *Quinine Cartel*.[446] The amount was 500,000 units of account. For the next 10 years the level of fines was 'relatively light'.[447] Change came in 1979 when the Commission indicated in *Pioneer* that it intended to reinforce the deterrent effect of fines by raising their general level in cases of serious infringements. It fined one culprit over four million units of account.[448] The undertakings appealed and the CJ confirmed the legality of the Commission's policy and strategy.

Cases 100–103/80, *Musique Diffusion Française SA* v. *Commission* (*Pioneer*) [1983] ECR 1825

Court of Justice

106. It follows that, in assessing the gravity of an infringement for the purpose of fixing the amount of the fine, the Commission must take into consideration not only the particular circumstances of the case but also the context in which the infringement occurs and must ensure that its action has the necessary deterrent effect, especially as regards those types of infringement which are particularly harmful to the attainment of the objectives of the Community.

---

[441] But note that the former President of the GC considers that Reg. 1/2003 does not provide any basis for confiscating the possible illegal gains made by the infringement, and that for the Commission to use it as a means to confiscate would amount to an abuse of power, Bo Vesterdorf, 'The Court of Justice and Unlimited Jurisdiction: What Does It Mean in Practice?' (2009) 2 *Global Competition Policy* n. 16. In *Devenish Nutrition Ltd* v. *Sanofi-Aventis* [2008] EWCA Civ 1086, the UK Court of Appeal considered that the fines imposed by the Commission in the *Vitamins Cartel* [2003] OJ L6/1 decision might have included an account of the profits but, not having heard argument on this, left the point open, see para. 112 (Arden LJ).

[442] *XIIIth Report on Competition Policy* (Commission, 1983), para. 62.

[443] Guidelines on the method of setting fines imposed pursuant to Reg. No. 17, Art. 15(2) and Art. 65(5) of the ECSC treaty [1998] OJ C9/3.

[444] Guidelines on the method of setting fines imposed pursuant to Art. 23(2)(a) of Reg. No. 1/2003 [2006] OJ C210/2.

[445] See Cases 100–103/80, *Musique Diffusion Française SA* v. *Commission (Pioneer)* [1983] ECR 1825; Cases C-189/02 P, 202/02 P, 208/02 P, and 213/02 P, *Dansk Rørindustri A/S and others* v. *Commission* [2005] ECR I-5425.

[446] [1969] OJ L192/5.

[447] According to the Commission in the *XIIIth Report on Competition Policy* (Commission, 1983), para. 63.

[448] *Pioneer* [1980] OJ L60/21.

107. From that point of view, the Commission was right to classify as very serious infringements prohibitions on exports and imports seeking artificially to maintain price differences between the markets of the various member-States. Such prohibitions jeopardize the freedom of intra-Community trade, which is a fundamental principle of the Treaty, and they prevent the attainment of one of its objectives, namely the creation of a single market.

108. It was also open to the Commission to have regard to the fact that practices of this nature, although they were established as being unlawful at the outset of Community competition policy, are still relatively frequent on account of the profit that certain of the undertakings concerned are able to derive from them and, consequently, it was open to the Commission to consider that it was appropriate to raise the level of fines so as to reinforce their deterrent effect.

109. For the same reasons, the fact that the Commission, in the past, imposed fines of a certain level for certain types of infringement does not mean that it is estopped from raising that level within the limits indicated in Regulation 17 if that is necessary to ensure the implementation of Community competition policy. On the contrary, the proper application of the Community competition rules requires that the Commission may at any time adjust the level of fines to the needs of that policy.

...

119. Thus the only express reference to the turnover of the undertaking concerns the upper limit of a fine exceeding 1 000 000 units of account. In such a case the limit seeks to prevent fines from being disproportionate in relation to the size of the undertaking and, since only the total turnover can effectively give an approximate indication of that size, the aforementioned percentage must, as the Commission has argued, be understood as referring to the total turnover. It follows that the Commission did not exceed the limit laid down in Article 15 of the Regulation.

120. In assessing the gravity of an infringement regard must be had to a large number of factors, the nature and importance of which vary according to the type of infringement in question and the particular circumstances of the case. Those factors may, depending on the circumstances, include the volume and value of the goods in respect of which the infringement was committed and the size and economic power of the undertaking and, consequently, the influence which the undertaking was able to exert on the market.

121. It follows that, on the one hand, it is permissible, for the purpose of fixing the fine, to have regard both to the total turnover of the undertaking, which gives an indication, albeit approximate and imperfect, of the size of the undertaking and of its economic power, and to the proportion of that turnover accounted for by the goods in respect of which the infringement was committed, which gives an indication of the scale of the infringement. On the other hand, it follows that it is important not to confer on one or the other of those figures an importance disproportionate in relation to the other factors and, consequently, that the fixing of an appropriate fine cannot be the result of a simple calculation based on the total turnover. That is particularly the case where the goods concerned account for only a small part of the figure. It is appropriate for the Court to bear in mind those considerations in its assessment, by virtue of its powers of unlimited jurisdiction, of the gravity of the infringements in question.

This confirmed that the Commission was justified in suddenly raising the level of fines and in using fines to deter other undertakings from infringing.

It will be seen from paragraphs 120 and 121 of *Pioneer* that the Commission must take into account a number of factors, depending on the nature of the infringement and the circumstances of the case. In paragraph 119 the Court said that 'turnover' in Article 15(2) meant the *total* turnover of the undertaking or group, and not just that of the products in respect of which the infringement was committed.[449] On the other hand, the Commission should have regard to the latter turnover when fixing the

---

[449] See also Case T-327/94, *SCA Holding v. Commission* [1998] ECR II-1373, para. 176; Case T-23/99, *LR AF 1998 A/S v. Commission* [2002] ECR II-1705, paras. 278–280.

fine, because it gives an indication of the scale of the infringement.[450] This remains the position even after the adoption of fining guidelines. The total turnover means total *worldwide* turnover, not just that in the EU.[451]

The Commission explained its fining policy in the light of its 'vindication' by the *Pioneer* case.

The Commission has discretion in fixing the size of fines, subject to the general power of judicial review by the Court of Justice. In assessing the fine, the Commission takes into account all relevant facts of the case as to the gravity and duration of the infringement and whether it was deliberate or merely negligent. It also endeavours to observe the principle of proportionality in its fining policy, i.e., to relate the fine to the infringement, the size of the undertaking concerned and its responsibility for the infringement.

The complexity of the factors to be weighed means that the assessment of fines, rather than being a mathematical exercise based on an abstract formula, involves a legal and economic appraisal of each case on the basis of the above principles.

It will be appreciated that this policy gave the Commission a very wide discretion, allowing it to 'individualise' the fine to each infringing undertaking.[452] The Commission increasingly took into account the Community turnover in the product concerned in the infringement and stated the importance of this factor in the *Cement Cartel* press release, where it said 'calculation is normally based on the Community turnover in the product concerned'.[453] In addition it took into account a number of other factors, either in mitigation or as aggravation, such as profits from the infringement insofar as these were calculable,[454] the economic circumstances faced by the undertakings,[455] the degree of cooperation with the Commission,[456] the knowledge and intention of the parties, the nature and gravity of the infringement,[457] the duration of the infringement,[458] the responsibility of each of the undertakings concerned where they are acting in concert, the actual effect of the infringement, uncertainty about the illegality of the conduct concerned, the adoption of a compliance programme,[459] and the willingness of the infringer to undertake to remedy the situation.

In 1992 the Commission said that in future it would continue to move closer to the maximum fine laid down in Regulation 17[460] and that whenever it could ascertain the level of the ill-gotten gains from the infringement the calculation of the fine would take this as its starting point.[461] From the mid-1980s onwards the size of fines increased markedly. In 1992 a fine of 75 million ECUs,

---

[450] *Pioneer* [1980] OJ L60/21.

[451] The GC confirmed in Cases T-25/95, etc., *Cimenteries CBR SA v. Commission* [2000] ECR II-491, paras. 5022–5023, that only total turnover gives an approximate indication of the undertaking's size and influence on the market and that Reg. 17, 15(2) (now Reg. 1/2003 Art. 23(2)) contained no territorial limit, so that the Commission could choose which turnover to take in terms of territory and products in order to determine the fine. See also Case C-289/04 P, *Showa Denko v. Commission* [2006] ECR I-5859, paras. 16–18, and the 2006 Fining Guidelines, para. 18.

[452] The GC said in Case T-150/89, *Martinelli v. Commission* [1995] ECR II-1165, para. 69, that the Commission could not be expected to apply a precise mathematical formula to fining calculations. And see also Case 322/81, *Nederlandsche Banden-Industrie Michelin v. Commission* [1983] ECR 3461, paras. 17–21, Case T-53/03, *BPB plc v. Commission* [2008] ECR II-1333.

[453] Press Release IP/1108 of 30 Nov. 1994.

[454] See, e.g., *Eurocheque: Helsinki Agreement* [1992] OJ L95/50.

[455] e.g. in *Polypropylene Cartel* [1986] OJ L230/1.

[456] *Polypropylene Cartel* [1986] OJ L230/1, in regard to ICI.

[457] Art. 15(2), like Reg. 1/2003, Art. 23(2), obliged the Commission to take gravity into account.

[458] Also stipulated in Art. 15(2), now Reg. 1/2003, Art. 23(2).

[459] See Section 8.G.iv.h, p. 1014 ff.

[460] *XXIst Competition Policy Report* (Commission, 1992) at para. 139.

[461] In Cases T-25/95, etc., *Cimenteries CBR SA v. Commission* [2000] ECR II-491, paras. 4884–4885 the GC explained that this did not mean that the Commission had taken it upon itself to establish in every case the financial advantage obtained, but merely that it would take it more into account where it could be assessed, albeit not precisely. But see the comments of Vesterdorf, cited in n. 441.

approximately 2.5 per cent of its overall turnover, was imposed on Tetra Pak for abuse of a dominant position[462] and 41 participants in the *Cement Cartel* were fined a total of 248 million ECUs (including one fine of over 32 million ECUs) in 1994.[463] In 1996 the Commission, in pursuance of its desire to obtain hard evidence of the existence of cartels, introduced a Notice offering leniency over fines to cartel participants which informed on the cartel to the Commission.[464]

The fining policy was criticised for its lack of transparency. It was said that the Commission appeared to pluck figures from the air in what could only be described as a lottery[465] and that the increasingly swingeing fines (particularly on cartelists) were based on no discernible methodology. The absence of a proper 'tariff', or to put it in the Commission's words, the rejection of 'a mathematical exercise based on an abstract formula' was contrasted unfavourably with the normal position in most national legal systems in relation to both civil damages and criminal sanctions. In the US, the federal sentencing guidelines apply to criminal antitrust. The debate about the desirability of more certainty in fining practice involves, inter alia, assessing which is the best deterrent, certainty or uncertainty. If undertakings know what infringements will cost them, will they engage in a cost–benefit analysis and, deciding that they will on balance gain or lose, then act accordingly? Will they be deterred only if they face unknown amounts? Such questions are not, of course, unique to competition law and there is a large literature on deterrence in criminal law and the economics of crime deterrence including work specifically on deterrence in competition law.[466]

Decisions levying fines can be challenged before the GC. As the Commission has to observe the normal general principles of Union law these decisions can be challenged on grounds, inter alia, of lack of adequate reasoning, lack of proportionality, and discrimination (the last is particularly relevant to the different treatment of cartel participants). A good example of the judicial attitude to fining policy was *Tréfilunion* in 1995[467] where one of the participants in the *Welded Steel Mesh Cartel*[468] claimed that the reasoning which led to the calculation of its fine was inadequate. The GC accepted that it should not be necessary for an undertaking to have to bring court proceedings in order to ascertain how the fine was calculated, but still upheld the decision. It also upheld the Commission's decision in *PVC Cartel II*, where some undertakings argued that the decision contained no specific information explaining the level of fines imposed on each of them and that the Commission had failed to specify the objective standards used to assess the liability of the undertakings and their respective importance. The GC held that in the light of the detailed account in the decision of the factual allegations made against the undertakings the decision did contain sufficient and relevant indications of the factors the Commission had taken into account.[469]

---

[462] *Tetra Pak II* [1992] OJ L/72/1,551, upheld on appeal Case T-83/91, *Tetra Pak International SA v. Commission* [1994] ECR II-755 and Case C-333/94 P, *Tetra Pak International SA v. Commission* [1996] ECR I-5951: the fact that it was the first time that the Commission had held that an undertaking dominant on one market could abuse it by its conduct on the other did not reduce the size of the fine.

[463] Some of these fines were reduced on appeal where the Commission had not proved the length of the infringement it alleged: Cases T-25/95, etc., *Cimenteries CBR SA v. Commission* [2000] ECR II-491.

[464] See Section 8.G.v, p. 1019.

[465] See I. Van Bael, 'Fining à la Carte: The Lottery of EU Competition Law' [1995] 4 *ECLR* 237.

[466] See W. P. J. Wils, 'EC Competition Fines: To Deter or Not to Deter' [1995] *YEL* 17 and the literature cited there; G. Becker, 'Crime and Punishment: An Economic Approach' (1968) 76 *Journal of Political Economy*; W. Landes, 'Optimal Sanctions for Antitrust Violations' (1983) 50 *University of Chic LR* 652; R. Hardy, 'Casenote on Case C-510/06 P, *Archer Daniel Midlands*' (2009) 46 *CMLRev* 2095. The GC has held that too much predictability in the fine is undesirable, see Case T-53/03, *BPB plc v. Commission* [2008] ECR II-1333, para. 336.

[467] Case T-148/89, etc., *Tréfilunion v. Commission* [1995] ECR II-1063.

[468] [1989] OJ L260/1.

[469] Cases T-305–307, 313–316, 318, 328–329, and 335/94, *Re the PVC Cartel II: Limburgse Vinyl Maatschappij NV and others v. Commission* [1999] ECR II-931, para. 1179.

e. The Adoption of the Commission's 1998 Guidelines and 2006 Guidelines on the Method of Setting Fines

Conscious of the problems surrounding its fining policy the Commission published a Notice in January 1998, the Guidelines on the method of setting fines.[470] The Commission did not thereby surrender its discretion. Rather it set out a methodology which still allowed a very wide margin of discretion. The Notice did not mean that fines could henceforth be precisely calculated with mathematical accuracy and much of it, in particular as regards aggravating and attenuating (mitigating) circumstances, reflected the previous practice of the Commission and the rulings of the Court.

The Guidelines built on the two criteria stipulated in Regulation 17, gravity and duration, and based the calculation of fines on these. The Guidelines divided the gravity of infringements into 'minor',[471] 'serious',[472] and 'very serious'.[473] The fines for these were in the ranges €1,000 to €1 million, €1 million to €20 million, and above €20 million respectively. The starting figure was then increased according to the duration of the infringement: short (generally less than a year), no increase; medium (generally one to five years), up to 50 per cent increase; long (generally more than five years), up to 10 per cent per year increase. The gravity plus duration calculation gave the basic amount of the fine, which could then be increased where there were 'aggravating circumstances'[474] or decreased where there were 'attenuating circumstances'.[475] The Commission confirmed its freedom to apply different fines to undertakings involved in the same infringing conduct to take into account the 'real impact' of each undertaking's behaviour. This was particularly relevant to cartels. The Commission also stressed the necessity of producing a sufficient deterrent effect[476] and of taking account of an undertaking's capacity to cause damage to others.

Although the Guidelines brought a more systematic approach to the calculation of fines it was still impossible for undertakings to compute their liability exactly. The Notice contained many variables and many matters which were a matter of discretionary assessment by the Commission,[477] and the language of the Notice was imprecise—full of 'might be', 'generally speaking', 'in general', 'particularly'. Above all, the base figure from which the calculation flowed was in the discretion of the

---

[470] Guidelines on the method of setting fines [1998] OJ C9/3.

[471] Trade restrictions, usually of a vertical nature, with a limited market impact and affecting only a substantial but relatively limited part of the Community market: 1998 Guidelines, para. 1.

[472] Horizontal or vertical restrictions of the same type as 'minor' infringements, but more rigorously applied, with a wider market impact, and with effects in extensive areas of the common market; and some abuses of a dominant position: 1998 Guidelines, para. 1.

[473] Horizontal restrictions such as price cartels and market-sharing quotas, or other practices jeopardising the proper functioning of the single market, such as the partitioning of national markets and clear-cut abuse of a dominant position by undertakings holding a virtual monopoly: 1998 Guidelines, para. 1. In Cases T-49/02 and 51/02, *Brasserie Nationale SA and others* v. *Commission* [2005] ECR II-3033 (the *Luxembourg Brewers* cartel), para. 178, the GC appeared to consider that all horizontal cartels should be classified as 'very serious'.

[474] Repeated infringements, refusal to cooperate with or obstruction of the Commission, being the leader or instigator, taking retaliatory enforcement measures against other undertakings, a need to increase the penalty in order to exceed the ill-gotten gains (1998 Guidelines, section 2). The CJ confirmed this in Case C-3/06 P, *Group Danone* v. *Commission* [2007] ECR I-1331, para. 47.

[475] Playing only a passive role, not implementing the infringing agreements or practices, terminating the infringement as soon as the Commission intervened, the undertaking reasonably doubting that its conduct constituted an infringement, negligence or lack of intention, cooperation outside the scope of the Leniency Notice (1998 Guidelines, section 3. For the Leniency Notices, see Section 8.G.v, p. 1019).

[476] The CJ recognises that the imposition of a 'deterrence multiplier' is justified, see e.g., Case C-289/04 P, *Showa Denko* v. *Commission* [2006] ECR I-5859 (one of the *Graphite Electrodes Cartel* appeals), paras. 28–39. The deterrent effect means that the fact that an undertaking did not benefit from an infringement cannot preclude the imposition of fines, so the Commission is not required to establish that the undertaking concerned profited from the infringement: Case T-143/89, *Ferriere Nord* v. *Commission* [1995] ECR II-917; Cases T-25/95 etc., *Cimenteries CBR SA* v. *Commission* [2000] ECR II-491, para. 4881.

[477] See, e.g., the decision to add 20% for aggravating circumstances in *Volkswagen* [1998] OJ L124/60.

Commission. The result of this uncertainty was a flood of appeals to the Community Courts against the calculation of the fines imposed in infringement decisions, particularly in cartel cases.

The 1998 Guidelines were replaced by the 2006 Guidelines[478] in respect of cases where a statement of objections was notified after 1 September 2006.[479]

f. The Legality and Legal Effect of Fining Guidelines

In *Dansk Rørindustri*[480] the CJ confirmed that the Commission was legally empowered to adopt fining Guidelines and had not exceeded its discretion in so doing. The criteria of gravity and duration used in the Guidelines were those referred to in Article 15(2) of Regulation 17 (now Regulation 1/2003, Article 23(2)) and the Guidelines were therefore in conformity with the legal framework of penalties set out there. The Commission was not required by Article 15(2) to calculate the fines on the basis of the turnover of the undertakings concerned, although it was permissible to take turnover into account in order to assess the gravity of the infringement. However, disproportionate importance should not be attributed to turnover in comparison with other relevant factors.[481]

In a number of cases the Commission imposed fines calculated in accordance with the principles in the 1998 Guidelines in respect of conduct that took place before they were adopted. In *Dansk Rørindustri* the CJ held that the principles of legitimate expectation and non-retroactivity were not thereby infringed. Echoing the *Pioneer (Musique Diffusion)* judgment, it said that the Commission could at any time adjust fining levels in the light of the needs of competition policy.[482] The Commission had wide discretionary powers in the field of competition policy and the changes in fining policy were reasonably foreseeable at the time of the infringements.[483] In considering the principle of non-retroactivity the CJ referred to the ECHR. It also made the point that although the legal basis of the fines was Article 15(2) rather than the Guidelines, the latter *were* relevant to the issue of retroactivity.

Cases C-189/02 P, 202/02 P, 208/02 P, and 213/02 P, *Dansk Rørindustri A/S and Others* v. *Commission* [2005] ECR I-5425

Court of Justice

169....the [General Court] correctly observed that the fact that the Commission, in the past, imposed fines of a certain level for certain types of infringement does not mean that it is estopped from raising that level within the limits indicated in Regulation No 17 if that is necessary to ensure the implementation of Community competition policy. On the contrary, the proper application of the Community competition rules requires that the Commission may at any time adjust the level of fines to the needs of that policy (Joined Cases 100/80 to 103/80 *Musique Diffusion française and Others* v *Commission*...paragraph 109, and *Aristrain* v *Commission*, cited above, paragraph 101).

170. The supervisory task conferred on the Commission by Articles [101 and 102] not only includes the duty to investigate and punish individual infringements but also encompasses the duty to pursue a general

---

[478] Guidelines on the method of setting fines imposed pursuant to Article 23(2)(a) of Regulation No. 1/2003 [2006] OJ C210/5.

[479] 2006 Guidelines, para. 38. The fact that the Guidelines say 'a' statement means that the Guidelines apply where a supplementary statement was notified after 1 September even if the first one was notified before, see H. de Broca, 'The Commission revises its Guidelines for setting fines in antitrust cases' (2006) 3 *EC Competition Policy Newsletter* 1, 2.

[480] Cases C-189/02 P, 202/02 P, 208/02 P, and 213/02 P, *Dansk Rørindustri A/S and others* v. *Commission* [2005] ECR I-5425, the appeal from the judgments of the GC in the *Pre-Insulated Pipes Cartel* case.

[481] Cases C-189/02 P, 202/02 P, 208/02 P, and 213/02 P, *Dansk Rørindustri A/S and others* v. *Commission* [2005] ECR I-5425, paras. 250–258.

[482] See also Case C-3/06 P, *Group Danone* v. *Commission* [2007] ECR I-1331, para. 90.

[483] This point is also relevant to the application of the 2006 Guidelines.

policy designed to apply, in competition matters, the principles laid down by the Treaty and to guide the conduct of undertakings in the light of those principles (see *Musique Diffusion française and Others* v *Commission*, paragraph 105).

171. As the [General Court] appositely observed, traders cannot have a legitimate expectation that an existing situation which is capable of being altered by the Commission in the exercise of its discretionary power will be maintained (Case C-350/88 *Delacre and Others* v *Commission*…paragraph 33 and the case-law cited).

172. That principle clearly applies in the field of competition policy, which is characterised by a wide discretion on the part of the Commission, in particular as regards the determination of the amount of fines.

173. The [General Court] was also correct to infer that undertakings involved in an administrative procedure in which fines may be imposed cannot acquire a legitimate expectation in the fact that the Commission will not exceed the level of fines previously imposed, so that in the present case the applicants could not, in particular, found a legitimate expectation on the level of fines imposed in Commission Decision 94/601/EC of 13 July 1994 relating to a proceeding under Article [101] (IV/C/33.833—*Cartonboard.*). As the Commission observes, it follows that a legitimate expectation cannot be based on a method of calculating fines either.

…

209 The Court has already held, in a judgment concerning internal measures adopted by the administration, that although those measures may not be regarded as rules of law which the administration is always bound to observe, they nevertheless form rules of practice from which the administration may not depart in an individual case without giving reasons that are compatible with the principle of equal treatment. Such measures therefore constitute a general act and the officials and other staff concerned may invoke their illegality in support of an action against the individual measures taken on the basis of the measures (see Case C-171/00 P *Libéros v Commission*…paragraph 35).

210 That case-law applies a fortiori to rules of conduct designed to produce external effects, as is the case of the Guidelines, which are aimed at traders.

211 In adopting such rules of conduct and announcing by publishing them that they will henceforth apply to the cases to which they relate, the institution in question imposes a limit on the exercise of its discretion and cannot depart from those rules under pain of being found, where appropriate, to be in breach of the general principles of law, such as equal treatment or the protection of legitimate expectations. It cannot therefore be precluded that, on certain conditions and depending on their content, such rules of conduct, which are of general application, may produce legal effects.

…

213. The [General Court] was also correct to observe, at paragraph 418 of *HFB and Others* v *Commission* and paragraph 274 of *LR AF 1998* v *Commission*, that although the Guidelines do not constitute the legal basis of the contested decision, they determine, generally and abstractly, the method which the Commission has bound itself to use in assessing the fines imposed by the decision and, consequently, ensure legal certainty on the part of the undertakings.

214. Just as the admissibility of an objection of illegality raised against rules of conduct such as the Guidelines is not subject to the requirement that those rules constitute the legal basis of the act alleged to be illegal, the relevance of the Guidelines in the light of the principle of non-retroactivity does not presuppose that the Guidelines form the legal basis for the fines.

215. In that context, it is appropriate to refer to the case-law of the European Court of Human Rights on Article 7(1) of the ECHR, which, moreover, is cited by a number of the applicants (see, in particular, Eur. Court H.R., *S.W.* v *United Kingdom* and *C.R.* v *United Kingdom*, judgments of 22 November 1995, Series A Nos 335-B and 335-C, §§ 34 to 36 and §§ 32 to 34; *Cantoni* v *France*, judgment of 15 November 1996, *Reports of Judgments and Decisions*, 1996-V, §§ 29 to 32, and *Coëme and Others* v *Belgium*, judgment of 22 June 2000, *Reports*, 2000-VII, § 145).

216. It follows from that case-law that the concept of 'law' ('*droit*') for the purposes of Article 7(1) corresponds to 'law' ('*loi*') used in other provisions of the ECHR and encompasses both law of legislative origin and that deriving from case-law.

217. Although that provision, which enshrines in particular the principle that offences and punishments are to be strictly defined by law (*nullum crimen, nulla poena sine lege*), cannot be interpreted as prohibiting the gradual clarification of the rules of criminal liability, it may, according to that case-law, preclude the retroactive application of a new interpretation of a rule establishing an offence.

218. That is particularly true, according to that case-law, of a judicial interpretation which produces a result which was not reasonably foreseeable at the time when the offence was committed, especially in the light of the interpretation put on the provision in the case-law at the material time.

219. It follows from that case-law of the European Court of Human Rights that the scope of the notion of foreseeability depends to a considerable degree on the content of the text in issue, the field it is designed to cover and the number and status of those to whom it is addressed. A law may still satisfy the requirement of foreseeability even if the person concerned has to take appropriate legal advice to assess, to a degree that is reasonable in the circumstances, the consequences which a given action may entail. This is particularly true in relation to persons carrying on a professional activity, who are used to having to proceed with a high degree of caution when pursuing their occupation. They can on this account be expected to take special care in assessing the risks that such an activity entails (see *Cantoni* v *France*, cited above, § 35).

220. Those principles are also consistently reflected in the case-law of the Court to the effect that the obligation on the national court to refer to the content of the directive when interpreting the relevant rules of its national law is limited by the general principles of law which form part of Community law and in particular the principles of legal certainty and non-retroactivity (see Case 80/86 *Kolpinghuis Nijmegen*...paragraph 13).

221. According to that case-law, such an interpretation cannot lead to the imposition on an individual of an obligation laid down by a directive which has not been transposed or, a fortiori, have the effect of determining or aggravating, on the basis of the decision and in the absence of a law enacted for its implementation, the liability in criminal law of persons who act in contravention of that directive's provisions (see, in particular, *Kolpinghuis Nijmegen*, cited above, paragraph 14, and Case C-168/95 *Arcaro*...paragraph 42).

222. Like that case-law on new developments in case-law, a change in an enforcement policy, in this instance the Commission's general competition policy in the matter of fines, especially where it comes about as a result of the adoption of rules of conduct such as the Guidelines, may have an impact from the aspect of the principle of non-retroactivity.

223. Having particular regard to their legal effects and to their general application, as indicated at paragraph 211 of this judgment, such rules of conduct come, in principle, within the principle of 'law' for the purposes of Article 7(1) of the ECHR.

224. As stated at paragraph 219 of this judgment, in order to ensure that the principle of non-retroactivity was observed, it is necessary to ascertain whether the change in question was reasonably foreseeable at the time when the infringements concerned were committed.

225. In that regard, it should be noted that, as a number of the appellants have pointed out, the main innovation in the Guidelines consisted in taking as a starting point for the calculation a basic amount, determined on the basis of brackets laid down for that purpose by the Guidelines; those brackets reflect the various degrees of gravity of the infringements but, as such, bear no relation to the relevant turnover. The essential feature of that method is thus that fines are determined on a tariff basis, albeit one that is relative and flexible.

226. It is therefore necessary to consider whether that new method of calculating fines, on the assumption that it has the effect of increasing the level of fines imposed, was reasonably foreseeable at the time when the infringements concerned were committed.

227. As already stated at paragraph 169 of this judgment in connection with the pleas alleging breach of the principle of protection of legitimate expectations, it follows from the case-law of the Court that the fact that the Commission, in the past, imposed fines of a certain level for certain types of infringement does not mean that it is estopped from raising that level within the limits indicated in Regulation No 17 if that is necessary to ensure the implementation of Community competition policy. On the contrary, the proper application of the Community competition rules requires that the Commission may at any time adjust the level of fines to the needs of that policy.

228. It follows, as already held at paragraph 173 of this judgment, that undertakings involved in an administrative procedure in which fines may be imposed cannot acquire a legitimate expectation in the fact that the Commission will not exceed the level of fines previously imposed or in a method of calculating the fines.

229. Consequently, the undertakings in question must take account of the possibility that the Commission may decide at any time to raise the level of the fines by reference to that applied in the past.

230. That is true not only where the Commission raises the level of the amount of fines in imposing fines in individual decisions but also if that increase takes effect by the application, in particular cases, of rules of conduct of general application, such as the Guidelines.

231. It must be concluded that, particularly in the light of the case-law cited at paragraph 219 of this judgment, the Guidelines and, in particular, the new method of calculating fines contained therein, on the assumption that this new method had the effect of increasing the level of the fines imposed, were reasonably foreseeable for undertakings such as the appellants at the time when the infringements concerned were committed.

232. Accordingly, in applying the Guidelines in the contested decision to infringements committed before they were adopted, the Commission did not breach the principle of non-retroactivity.

The CJ confirmed the principles in the *Dansk Rørindustri* judgment in two *Archer Daniels Midland* judgments in 2006 and 2009.[484] These cases make it clear that the principle of equality is not infringed by the Commission changing its fining policy so that the same conduct is differently sanctioned depending on when it happens to take place.

The *Dansk Rørindustri* judgment is also of crucial importance in respect of the legal effect of the Fining Guidelines, and indeed of other Notices. Although they are Notices and not binding legislation,[485] it will be noted that in paragraphs 209–211 the CJ stated that by adopting Fining Guidelines the Commission imposes limits on its discretion, departure from which may involve a breach of the principles of equal treatment and legitimate expectation. Whilst not 'rules of law' which the administration is always bound to observe 'they nevertheless form rules of practice from which the administration may not depart in an individual case without giving reasons that are compatible with the principle of equal treatment'.[486] This principle is also of great significance for other Commission Notices on competition law, such as the Guidance paper on Article 102.[487]

---

[484] Case C-397/03 P, *Archer Daniels Midland Company v. Commission* [2006] ECR I-4429 (lysine (amino acid) cartel) and Case C-510/06 P, *Archer Daniels Midland Company v. Commission* [2009] ECR I-1843 (sodium gluconate cartel).

[485] See Chap. 2.

[486] Case C-397/03 P, *Archer Daniels Midland Company v. Commission* [2006] ECR I-4429, para. 91. In that case the CJ held that the GC had erred in law in allowing the Commission to breach the 1998 Guidelines in the way in which it had dealt with the undertaking's turnover, but nevertheless upheld the judgment as the GC, in an exercise of its unlimited jurisdiction (see Section 9.A.vii, p. 1039), had ascertained that the fine would not have been different had the Commission taken account of the correct turnover, see Case T-224/00, *Archer Daniels Midland Company v. Commission* [2003] ECR II-2597.

[487] Guidance on the Commission's Enforcement Priorities in Applying Article 82 of the EC Treaty to Abusive Exclusionary Conduct by Dominant Undertakings [2009] OJ C45/2, see Chaps. 5–7.

In practice, appeals from Commission decisions imposing fines (on cartel participants in particular) now involve detailed arguments about whether the Commission correctly followed the Fining Guidelines (and the Leniency Notice)[488] more often than they involve arguments about whether or not there was an infringement in the first place.

g. The 2006 Fining Guidelines

The Commission adopted new Guidelines on the method of setting fines in June 2006 to remedy some perceived shortcomings in the 1998 methodology, to reflect the Commission's most recent practice, and to take on board recent case law.[489]

Guidelines on the Method of Setting Fines Imposed Pursuant to Article 23(2)(A) of Regulation No. 1/2003 [2006] OJ C210/2

13. In determining the basic amount of the fine to be imposed, the Commission will take the value of the undertaking's sales of goods or services to which the infringement directly or indirectly...relates in the relevant geographic area within the EEA. It will normally take the sales made by the undertaking during the last full business year of its participation in the infringement (hereafter 'value of sales').

14. Where the infringement by an association of undertakings relates to the activities of its members, the value of sales will generally correspond to the sum of the value of sales by its members.

15. In determining the value of sales by an undertaking, the Commission will take that undertaking's best available figures.

16. Where the figures made available by an undertaking are incomplete or not reliable, the Commission may determine the value of its sales on the basis of the partial figures it has obtained and/or any other information which it regards as relevant and appropriate.

17. The value of sales will be determined before VAT and other taxes directly related to the sales.

18. Where the geographic scope of an infringement extends beyond the EEA (e.g. worldwide cartels), the relevant sales of the undertakings within the EEA may not properly reflect the weight of each undertaking in the infringement. This may be the case in particular with worldwide market-sharing arrangements.[490]

In such circumstances, in order to reflect both the aggregate size of the relevant sales within the EEA and the relative weight of each undertaking in the infringement, the Commission may assess the total value of the sales of goods or services to which the infringement relates in the relevant geographic area (wider than the EEA), may determine the share of the sales of each undertaking party to the infringement on that market and may apply this share to the aggregate sales within the EEA of the undertakings concerned. The result will be taken as the value of sales for the purpose of setting the basic amount of the fine.

B. Determination of the basic amount of the fine

19. The basic amount of the fine will be related to a proportion of the value of sales, depending on the degree of gravity of the infringement, multiplied by the number of years of infringement.

---

[488] See Section 8.G.v, p. 1019.

[489] See Press Release, IP/06/857; Hubert de Broca, 'The Commission revises its Guidelines for setting fines in antitrust cases' (2006) 3 EC Competition Policy Newsletter 1; Neelie Kroes, 'Delivering the crackdown: recent developments in the European Commission's campaign against cartels, SPEECH/06/595'; W. Wils, 'The European Commission's 2006 Guidelines on Antitrust Fines: A Legal and Economic Analysis' (2007) 30(2) World Competition 197. The Guidelines refer to the EEA rather than the EU because the competition rules apply to the whole EEA area, see Chap. 2.

[490] The Commission applied para. 18 in COMP/39.406, Marine Hoses Cartel [2010] 4 CMLR 148 (approved on appeal Cases T-146/09, etc., Parker ITR and Parker-Hannifin v. Commission, 17 May 2013, paras. 205–219) where, 'given

20. The assessment of gravity will be made on a case-by-case basis for all types of infringement, taking account of all the relevant circumstances of the case.

21. As a general rule, the proportion of the value of sales taken into account will be set at a level of up to 30 % of the value of sales.

22. In order to decide whether the proportion of the value of sales to be considered in a given case should be at the lower end or at the higher end of that scale, the Commission will have regard to a number of factors, such as the nature of the infringement, the combined market share of all the undertakings concerned, the geographic scope of the infringement and whether or not the infringement has been implemented.

23. Horizontal price-fixing, market-sharing and output-limitation agreements...which are usually secret, are, by their very nature, among the most harmful restrictions of competition. As a matter of policy, they will be heavily fined. Therefore, the proportion of the value of sales taken into account for such infringements will generally be set at the higher end of the scale.

24. In order to take fully into account the duration of the participation of each undertaking in the infringement, the amount determined on the basis of the value of sales (see points 20 to 23 above) will be multiplied by the number of years of participation in the infringement. Periods of less than six months will be counted as half a year; periods longer than six months but shorter than one year will be counted as a full year.

25. In addition, irrespective of the duration of the undertaking's participation in the infringement, the Commission will include in the basic amount a sum of between 15% and 25% of the value of sales as defined in Section A above in order to deter undertakings from even entering into horizontal price-fixing, market-sharing and output-limitation agreements. The Commission may also apply such an additional amount in the case of other infringements. For the purpose of deciding the proportion of the value of sales to be considered in a given case, the Commission will have regard to a number of factors, in particular those referred in point 22.

26. Where the value of sales by undertakings participating in the infringement is similar but not identical, the Commission may set for each of them an identical basic amount. Moreover, in determining the basic amount of the fine, the Commission will use rounded figures.

2. Adjustments to the basic amount

27. In setting the fine, the Commission may take into account circumstances that result in an increase or decrease in the basic amount as determined in Section 1 above. It will do so on the basis of an overall assessment which takes account of all the relevant circumstances.

A. Aggravating circumstances

28. The basic amount may be increased where the Commission finds that there are aggravating circumstances, such as:

— where an undertaking continues or repeats the same or a similar infringement after the Commission or a national competition authority has made a finding that the undertaking infringed [Article 101 or 102]: the basic amount will be increased by up to 100 % for each such infringement established;

— refusal to cooperate with or obstruction of the Commission in carrying out its investigations;

— role of leader in, or instigator of, the infringement; the Commission will also pay particular attention to any steps taken to coerce other undertakings to participate in the infringement and/or any retaliatory measures taken against other undertakings with a view to enforcing the practices constituting the infringement.

B. Mitigating circumstances

29. The basic amount may be reduced where the Commission finds that mitigating circumstances exist, such as:

— where the undertaking concerned provides evidence that it terminated the infringement as soon as the Commission intervened: this will not apply to secret agreements or practices (in particular, cartels);

— where the undertaking provides evidence that the infringement has been committed as a result of negligence;

— where the undertaking provides evidence that its involvement in the infringement is substantially limited and thus demonstrates that, during the period in which it was party to the offending agreement, it actually avoided applying it by adopting competitive conduct in the market: the mere fact that an undertaking participated in an infringement for a shorter duration than others will not be regarded as a mitigating circumstance since this will already be reflected in the basic amount;

— where the undertaking concerned has effectively cooperated with the Commission outside the scope of the Leniency Notice and beyond its legal obligation to do so;

— where the anti-competitive conduct of the undertaking has been authorized or encouraged by public authorities or by legislation.

C. Specific increase for deterrence

30. The Commission will pay particular attention to the need to ensure that fines have a sufficiently deterrent effect; to that end, it may increase the fine to be imposed on undertakings which have a particularly large turnover beyond the sales of goods or services to which the infringement relates.

31. The Commission will also take into account the need to increase the fine in order to exceed the amount of gains improperly made as a result of the infringement where it is possible to estimate that amount.

D. Legal maximum

32. The final amount of the fine shall not, in any event, exceed 10 % of the total turnover in the preceding business year of the undertaking or association of undertakings participating in the infringement, as laid down in Article 23(2) of Regulation No 1/2003.

33. Where an infringement by an association of undertakings relates to the activities of its members, the fine shall not exceed 10% of the sum of the total turnover of each member active on the market affected by that infringement.

E. Leniency Notice

34. The Commission will apply the leniency rules in line with the conditions set out in the applicable notice.

F. Ability to pay

35. In exceptional cases, the Commission may, upon request, take account of the undertaking's inability to pay in a specific social and economic context. It will not base any reduction granted for this reason in the fine on the mere finding of an adverse or loss-making financial situation. A reduction could be granted solely on the basis of objective evidence that imposition of the fine as provided for in these Guidelines would irretrievably jeopardise the economic viability of the undertaking concerned and cause its assets to lose all their value.

The 1998 Guidelines were amended because the Commission was dissatisfied in particular with the classification of infringements into minor, serious, and very serious; recognised that the lump sum base figure provisions were widely criticised as vague and unsatisfactory; and wished to reinforce its fining policy with some more draconian elements. The 2006 Guidelines follow a similar two-step methodology to the 1998 Guidelines in providing first for a basic amount and secondly for an increase or decrease in the light of 'adjustment factors'—aggravating or attenuating circumstances. Those circumstances are much the same as under the 1998 Guidelines: repeat infringements (recidivism), non-cooperation with the Commission, and being a leader, instigator, or coercer on the one hand; and termination upon Commission intervention,[491] negligent infringement, limited involvement, cooperation with the Commission, and national authorisation of the anti-competitive conduct on the other.

The main features of the 2006 Guidelines are:

• The basic amount is calculated on a proportion of the value of sales, depending on the degree of gravity of the infringement.

• The Commission abandoned the use of categories of seriousness. Instead, the basic amount of the fine is calculated using the value of the undertaking's sales of goods or services to which the infringement directly or indirectly relates in the relevant geographic area within the EEA.[492] As a general rule the proportion of the value of the sales taken into account will be up to 30 per cent.[493] The Commission adopted the formula of value of sales multiplied by duration for the basic amount because it regards this as providing 'an appropriate proxy to reflect the economic importance of the infringement as well as the relative weight of each undertaking in the infringement'.[494] In *Intel* the Commission took five per cent of the value of the sales as the starting point.[495]

the global character of the cartel arrangements, the worldwide sales figures give the most appropriate picture of the participating undertakings' capacity to cause significant damage to other operators in the EEA' (para. 432); see also COMP/39/180, *Aluminium Fluoride*, upheld Case T-406/08, *ICF* v. *Commission*, 18 June 2013.

[491] But note that by para. 29, first indent, of the 2006 Guidelines the 'termination of an infringement as soon as the Commission intervenes' as an attenuating circumstance does not now apply to secret agreements or practices such as cartels (otherwise undertakings can carry on a cartel and just desist when found out). The GC said in Cases T-71/03, T-74/03, T-87/03, and T-91/03, *Tokai Carbon Co Ltd and others* v. *Commission* [2005] ECR II-10, para. 292 that 'the Commission is under no obligation in the exercise of its discretion...to reduce a fine for the termination of a manifest infringement, whether that termination occurred before or after its investigation'. See also Case T-53/03, *BPB plc* v. *Commission* [2008] ECR II-1333, paras. 437–438; Case C-510/06 P, *Archer Daniels Midland Company* v. *Commission* [2009] ECR I-1843, para. 149; Case C-511/06 P, *Archer Daniels Midland Company* v. *Commission* [2009] ECR I-5843, para. 105.

[492] 2006 Guidelines, para. 13. 'Indirectly' encompasses situations such as horizontal price fixing where the price of the product concerned then serves as a basis for the price of lower or higher quality products (para. 13, n. 1). In the case of worldwide cartels the Commission may take account of the value of sales in a relevant geographic area wider than the EEA (para. 18, relying on Cases T-236/01, T-239/01, T-244/01 to T-246/01, T-251/01, and T-252/01 *Tokai Carbon Co Ltd and others* v. *Commission* [2004] ECR II-1181, paras. 196–204 (aff'd by the CJ, Case C-289/04 P, *Showa Denko* v. *Commission* [2006] ECR I-5859, paras. 16–18)); Cases T-71/03, T-74/03, T-87/03, and T-91/03, *Tokai Carbon Co Ltd and others* v. *Commission* [2005] ECR II-10, para. 186).

[493] 2006 Guidelines, para. 21. In para. 37 the Commission reserves the right to depart from this limit in a particular case. The *Competition Policy Newsletter* (see n. 489) says this may be necessary, for instance, where no turnover figures are available at all.

[494] 2006 Guidelines, para. 6.

[495] Case COMP/C-3/37.990 *Intel*, [2009] OJ C 227/13, on appeal Case T-286/09, *Intel* v. *Commission*, judgment pending. The figures involved are not revealed in the published version of the decision. The Commission explained: 'the Commission took into account the factors set out above, in particular the nature, the market share and the geographic scope of the infringement. In this specific case, the Commission also took into account additional factors, namely that while Intel's conducts vis-à-vis individual OEMs constitute separate abuses, the Commission has also found Intel to have engaged in a single infringement. However, the intensity of that single infringement differs across the years. Most of the individual abuses concerned are concentrated in the period ranging from 2002 to 2005, whilst, after the end of 2005, at most two individual abuses occur simultaneously at any given point in time...The Commission also took into consideration that some of the individual abuses have a short duration. Further, the

- The amount determined by the value of sales is multiplied by the number of years of participation in the infringement.[496]

- Duration therefore plays a greater role in the determination of the basic amount than it did under the 1998 Guidelines. This provision alone would result in heavier fines than previously. The duration of the infringement in *Intel* was held to be five years and three months so the basic amount was multiplied by 5.5 to give a total fine of €1.6 billion (there being no allowance for any mitigating circumstances).

- 'Entry fees'—In the case of horizontal price-fixing, market-sharing, and output-limitation agreements (i.e. cartels) the Commission will include as part of the basic amount of the fine a further sum of between 15 per cent and 25 per cent of the value of the sales simply as a punishment for having entered into the arrangement—an 'entry fee'.[497] The purpose is to deter cartelists at the outset by making participation expensive even for a short time. The Commission may impose the entry fee in respect of other infringements too.

- Recidivism is heavily penalised—it is expensive to be a repeat offender. One of the aggravating circumstances is for an undertaking to continue or repeat the same or similar infringements after having been found by the Commission or an NCA to have infringed previously.[498] Recidivism has long been considered an aggravating feature but in the 2006 Guidelines it is specifically provided that *each* subsequent infringement will increase the basic amount of the fine by up to 100 per cent. The 2006 Guidelines were applied in the *Calcium Carbide* cartel[499] and the fine on Akzo Nobel would have been increased by 100 per cent for having been fined four times previously had it not been granted immunity for whistle-blowing.[500]

It must always be remembered that the final amount of the fine cannot exceed the 10 per cent of turnover in the preceding business year laid down in Regulation 1/2003, Article 23(2).[501] The 'entry fee' and the up to 100 per cent increase for repeat offenders also potentially make cartel participation much more expensive than previously. In paragraph 30 the Commission says that it may increase fines on undertakings which have a particularly large turnover beyond the value of sales to which the infringement relates in order to provide sufficient deterrence. This continues the 'deterrence multiplier'

---

abuses differ in their respective likely anti-competitive impact. The Commission also took account of the fact that Intel took measures to conceal the conducts established in this Decision, which made it more difficult to detect and sanction them', *Intel*, para. 1785. For the facts of *Intel*, see Chap. 7.

[496] 2006 Guidelines, para. 24. Less than six months counts as half a year, and six to twelve months counts as a full year.

[497] 2006 Guidelines, para. 25.

[498] 'Similar' means the same kind of infringement, such as price collusion in cartel cases (see e.g., COMP/F/38.638 *Butadiene Rubber and Emulsion Styrene Butadiene Rubber Cartel* [2008] OJ C7/11) or abusive loyalty-inducing discounts in the two *Michelin* cases, see Case T-203/01, *Manufacture Française des Pneumatiques Michelin v. Commission* [2003] ECR II-4071, paras. 283–288. The product or sector concerned is irrelevant. The infringements in *Michelin* were committed by two separate subsidiaries of the same parent. It does not matter that the previous infringement was under a different Treaty, see Case T-122/04, *Outokumpu Oyj v. Commission* [2009] ECR II-1135, paras 55–56 where the previous infringement was in respect of the prohibitions in the ECSC Treaty. For recidivism in the context of EU antitrust enforcement generally, see W. Wils, 'Recidivism in EU Antitrust Enforcement—A Legal and Economic Analysis' (2012) 35(1) *World Competition* 5.

[499] COMP/39.396, [2009] OJ C301/18, IP/09/1169.

[500] Under the Leniency Notice, see Section 8.G.v, p. 1019. The fine on Degussa was increased by 50% for recidivism.

[501] And previously in Reg. 17, Art. 15(2). In the course of the calculation the Commission may exceed the 10%, so long as the final sum imposed on the undertaking is below it. The 10% does not therefore apply to the intermediate calculations: Cases C-189/02 P, 202/02 P, 208/02 P, and 213/02 P, *Dansk Rørindustri A/S and others v. Commission* [2005] ECR I-5425, paras. 277–278. Where the undertaking has committed a number of infringements the ceiling applies to each one separately; in Case C-564/08 P, *SGL Carbon v. Commission* [2009] ECR I-191 the undertaking claimed that the Commission had deliberately adopted four separate decisions for four separate infringements, thus evading the 10% cap. The CJ *aff'd* the GC's dismissal of this plea (Case T-68/04, *SGL Carbon v. Commission* [2008] ECR II-2511).

practice developed in the application of the 1998 Guidelines and approved by the CJ.[502] Paragraph 31 says that the Commission may increase the fine in order to exceed the benefits of the infringement where it is possible to estimate them.[503] That provision was also in the 1998 Guidelines but among the 'aggravating factors' rather than under a separate deterrence head.[504] It is argued by economists that, in general, financial penalties should be based on the harm caused rather than the gain obtained,[505] but the practice of the Commission under the 1998 Guidelines did not appear to include any systematic attempt to gauge either the infringers' gains or the victims' losses[506] and it is not the purpose of paragraph 31 to force the Commission to make such an estimate of the gains or suggest that the Commission should systematically try to do so.[507] The Competition Commissioner considered that the effect of the 2006 Guidelines would be to increase the amount of fines by a factor of three.[508]

Arguments that the discretion of the Commission over fines infringes Article 7(1) of the ECHR[509] continue to be dismissed:[510]

…the fact that a law confers a discretion is not in itself inconsistent with the requirement of foreseeability, provided that the scope of the discretion and the manner of its exercise are indicated with sufficient clarity, having regard to the legitimate aim in question, to give the individual adequate protection against arbitrary interference.

In fact, although the thrust of the 2006 Guidelines is to increase the level of fines, the application of the leniency policy in cartel cases, discussed in Section 8.G.v, means that many infringers end up paying nothing, and others have greatly decreased fines.[511]

h. Particular Issues in the Application of the Fining Guidelines

A detailed examination of the application of the Commission's fining policy is outside the scope of this book and reference should be had to practitioner texts[512] but the following points should be noted:

---

[502] Case C-289/04 P, *Showa Denko* v. *Commission* [2006] ECR I-5859, paras. 23–29. Note also the Commission's *Methylglucamine Cartel* decision [2004] OJ L38/18, para. 329 where the fine was increased as a deterrence measure, '[I]n order to ensure that the fine has a sufficient deterrent effect and takes account of the fact that large undertakings have legal and economic knowledge and infrastructures which enable them more easily to recognize that their conduct constitutes an infringement and be aware of the consequences stemming from it under competition law …'.

[503] 2006 Guidelines, para. 31.

[504] 1998 Guidelines, para. 2, fifth indent. The CJ approved of raising the fine to exceed the improper gains in Cases C-189/02 P, 202/02 P, 208/02 P, and 213/02 P, *Dansk Rørindustri A/S and others* v. *Commission* [2005] ECR I-5425, para. 294, and see the remarks of the CJ in Cases 100–103/80, *Musique Diffusion Française SA* v. *Commission (Pioneer)* [1983] ECR 1825, set out in Section 8.G.iv.d, p. 1000.

[505] See W. Wils, 'The Commission's New Method for Calculating Fines in Antitrust Cases' (1998) 23 *ELRev* 252, 259; A. M. Polinsky and S. Shavell, 'Should Liability be Based on the Harm to the Victim or the Gain to the Injurer?' (1994) 10 *Journal of Law, Economics and Organization* 427. If the victims of competition law infringements want compensation for the harm they have suffered they have to bring private damages actions: see Chap. 14.

[506] See C. Veljanovski, 'Penalties for Price Fixers: An Analysis of Fines Imposed on 39 Cartels by the EU Commission' [2006] *ECLR* 510, and as a *Casenote* on the Case Associates website, <http://www.casecon.com>, June 2006.

[507] According to Hubert de Broca, 'The Commission revises its Guidelines for setting fines in antitrust cases' (2006) 3 *EC Competition Policy Newsletter* 1, 6.

[508] 'These innovations are likely to increase average fines, particularly for long lasting infringements in large markets, where fines could well increase by a factor of three. I think all this will make potential cartelists think twice!' Neelie Kroes, 'Delivering on the crackdown: recent developments in the European Commission's campaign against cartels', SPEECH/06/595, 13 October 2006. For an analysis of the fines imposed on cartels from 2007 to 2011 see J. M. Connor, 'Cartel Fine Severity and the European Commission 2007–2011' [2011] *ECLR* 58.

[509] 'No one shall be held guilty of any criminal offence on account of any act or omission which did not constitute a criminal offence under national or international law at the time when it was committed. Nor shall a heavier penalty be imposed than the one that was applicable at the time the criminal offence was committed.'

[510] Case T-69/04, *Schunk GmbH* v. *Commission* [2008] ECR II-2567, para. 33.

[511] See C. Veljanovski, 'Penalties for Price Fixers' (cited in n. 506).

[512] See generally, L. Ortiz Blanco, *EU Competition Procedure* (cited in n. 2), Chap. 11; Kerse and Khan, *EU Antitrust Procedure* (cited in n. 2), Chap. 7; Bellamy and Child, *European Law of Competition* (cited in n. 2), Chap. 14; see also D. Geradin and D. Henry, 'EC Fining for Competition Law Violations: An Empirical Study of the Commission's

Deterrence

The major theme of the Commission fining policy, in accordance with the duty identified back in 1983 in *Musique Diffusion*,[513] is deterrence. This encompasses not only specific deterrence (by sanctioning the undertaking concerned) but also general deterrence (deterring other undertakings).[514] Deterrence may involve imposing separate penalties for each of a number of multiple breaches.[515] The large fines imposed on cartels are part of deliberate policy of the Commission to deter undertakings from entering into such arrangements, as explained in Chapter 9.[516]

Aggravating Circumstances

The list of aggravating circumstances in Paragraph 28 of the Guidelines (recidivism, refusal to cooperate with the Commission's investigation and being the leader or instigator of the infringement, or having taken coercive or retaliatory measures) is not exhaustive. The issue of recidivism becomes a complex one where company restructuring and/or changes in ownership and control have taken place.[517] A fine may be increased for recidivism even if the previous infringement was in a different market so long as the type of infringement is similar. Aggravation in the form of non-cooperation during an inspection is illustrated by *Professional Videotape*[518] in which Sony's fine was increased by 30 per cent for failing to answer questions and shredding documents during the dawn raid. There are frequent arguments played out in appeals to the GC about whether or not an undertaking played a leadership or instigation role.[519] In *Nintendo*[520] the infringing agreement (to restrict parallel trade) was between a manufacturer and seven of its exclusive distributors. The manufacturer (Nintendo) was classified as the 'leader' and its fine increased accordingly. It argued that the leadership concept was relevant only in restrictive horizontal agreements because in vertical agreements the role of manufacturer and leader merge (in effect invariably rendering the manufacturer the 'leader' and so liable to the uplift in fine). The GC rejected this and refused to limit the leadership concept to horizontal cartels. The fact that leadership merged into the manufacturing role did not preclude it being an aggravating circumstance. It should be noted that although terminating an infringement when investigated is not a mitigating circumstance, continuing infringing conduct after the investigation has commenced is an *aggravating* circumstance.[521]

Mitigating Circumstances

Undertakings commonly plead that they were merely 'passive' participants in cartels and therefore within the third indent of the paragraph 29. It will be noted that paragraph 29 does not list as a mitigating factor the adoption of a compliance programme (that is, a set of measures put in place by an undertaking to ensure that none of its staff breach the competition rules thereby imposing

---

Decisional Practice and the Community Courts' Judgments' (2005) 1 *European Competition Journal* 401. For a detailed consideration of the application of the 2006 Guidelines see Case T-587/08, *Fresh Del Monte Produce Inc v. Commission*, 14 March 2013.

[513] See Section 8.G.iv.d, p. 1000.

[514] 2006 Guidelines, para. 4; Case C-511/11, *Versalis SpA v. Commission*, 13 June 2013.

[515] Case T-446/05 P, *Amann & Söhne GmbH & Co KG v. Commission* [2010] ECR II-1255.

[516] See Chap. 9, Section 2.B.i.e, p. 666 ff.

[517] This is similar to the problem which arises over liability for the infringement and for the fine, see Section 8.G.iv.k, p. 1018 and Chap. 3; and see e.g. *Versalis*, cited in n. 514.

[518] COMP/38.432. Sony's total fine was therefore over €47 million.

[519] See, e.g., Case T-15/02, *BASF AG v. Commission* [2006] ECR II-497 (an appeal from the *Vitamins Cartel* decision, [2003] OJ L6/1) in which the GC cancelled the 35% increase in the basic amount imposed on BASF for being a leader or instigator or leader of the cartel in respect of two vitamins (C and D3) as the Commission had not sufficiently established this. The refusal of leniency under the 1996 Notice on the ground that it was not available to the leader or instigator therefore had to be re-examined too, but the GC held that BASF still did not qualify.

[520] COMP/35.387, *PO Video Games* [2003] OJ L255/33, on appeal Case T-13/03, *Nintendo v. Commission*, [2009] ECR II-975 (the Commission had opened its investigation in 1995).

[521] See, e.g., *PO Video Games*, where Nintendo got a 25% increase for this, upheld by the GC, Case T-1/03, *Nintendo v. Commission* [2009] ECR II-975.

liability on the undertaking). Before 1992 the Commission gave some fine reductions where the infringement was carried out in contravention of the undertaking's compliance programme but its current practice is not to do so.[522] In *PO Video Games*, where Nintendo had introduced a compliance programme after the infringement the Commission said that, 'While the Commission does indeed welcome all steps taken by undertakings to raise awareness amongst their employees of existing competition rules, these initiatives cannot relieve the Commission of its duty to penalise their very serious infringement of competition rules'.[523] In *Professional Videotape* Sony claimed it was a junior employee who had shredded the documents during an inspection contrary to the company's compliance policy but the Commission still held this was an aggravating circumstance, 'it is the undertaking's responsibility to employ, instruct and control its employees, and to ensure that none of them obstructs or hampers the Commission's work during an inspection.'[524]

In the *Calcium Carbide* cartel one (Slovakian) company, NCZ, was fined an amount that nearly reached the maximum 10 per cent turnover ceiling despite pleading that its representatives at the meetings did not speak any foreign language fluently and so had on the whole to communicate through other cartel members, and that having emerged from a former Communist regime had no knowledge of competition law.[525]

Ability to Pay

Paragraph 35 of the 2006 Guidelines reflects the case law of the CJ that the Commission is not required to take into account the undertaking's ability to pay the fine, but may do so. The plea of inability to pay has become more frequent in the prevailing financial and economic crisis. However, taking difficulty in paying into account may give 'unjustified competitive advantages to undertakings least well adapted to the market conditions'.[526] 'Specific social context' in paragraph 35, according to the CJ in *SGL Carbon* [527] interpreting the 1998 Guidelines, means the consequences which payment of a fine could have, in particular, by leading to an increase in unemployment or deterioration in the economic sectors upstream and downstream of the undertakings concerned. The last sentence of paragraph 35, '. irretrievably jeopardise the economic viability and cause its assets to lose all their value...' sets 'a rather high standard'.[528] In *Novácke Chemické Závody* the GC reiterated that the case law establishes that although 'the liquidation of an undertaking in its existing legal form may adversely affect the interests of the owners, investors or shareholders, it does not mean that the personal, tangible and intangible assets of the undertaking would also lose their value'.[529] So the mere fact that the fine might give rise to bankruptcy is not sufficient as regards paragraph 35.

Nevertheless, the Commission does sometimes give reductions for inability to pay, such as in respect of one of the undertakings in the *International Removal Services Cartel* [530] and one of the

---

[522] See e.g. Case T-53/06, *UPM-Kymmene v. Commission*, 6 March 2012, paras. 123–124. For the arguments around compliance programmes, see W. Wils, 'Antitrust Compliance Programmes and Optimal Antitrust Enforcement' (2013) 1(1) *Journal of Antitrust Enforcement* 52 and D. Geradin, 'Antitrust Compliance Programmes and Optimal Antitrust Enforcement: A Reply to Wouter Wils' (2013) 1(2) *Journal of Antitrust Enforcement* 1.

[523] [2003] OJ L255/33, at para. 451.

[524] COMP/38.432, para. 226.

[525] COMP/39.396, [2009] OJ C 301/18, appeal dismissed, Case T-352/09, *Novácke Chemické Závody v. Commission*, 12 December 2012, para. 103.

[526] See Cases 96–102, 104, 105, 108, and 110/82, *IAZ International Belgium v. Commission* [1983] ECR 3369, paras. 54–55; Cases C-189/02 P, 202/02 P, 208/02 P, and 213/02 P, *Dansk Rørindustri A/S and others v. Commission* [2005] ECR I-5425, para. 327; Case C-308/04 P, *SGL Carbon AG v. Commission* [2006] ECR I-5977, paras. 105–106.

[527] *SGL Carbon AG v. Commission* [2006] ECR I-5977, para. 106.

[528] H. de Broca, 'The Commission revises its Guidelines for setting fines in antitrust cases' (2006) *EC Competition Policy Newsletter* 1, 6.

[529] Case T-352/09, *Novácke Chemické Závody v. Commission*, 12 December 2012, para. 187. When the undertaking appealed, inter alia, on the ground of its inability to pay, the GC had refused interim measures suspending the enforcement of the decision while the proceedings were pending, Case T-352/09 R, *Novácke Chemické Závody v. Commission* [2009] ECR II-208.

[530] COMP/38.543, *International Removal Services* [2008] OJ C188/16 (70% reduction).

undertakings in *Animal Feed Phosphates*. [531] In 2010 the Commission published an Information Note on Inability to Pay under Paragraph 35, explaining its policy and methodology in dealing with such claims[532] and in Best Practices sets out the information an undertaking making the claim should provide.[533]

i. General Principles of Law

In imposing fines, as in all other aspects of competition procedure, the Commission must abide by the general principles of Union law. As well as non-retroactivity and legitimate expectation the Commission must, in setting fines, particularly heed the principles of proportionality, equal treatment, and sound administration.[534] As far as proportionality is concerned, the CJ stated in *Musique Diffusion* that the upper limit on fines (10 per cent of turnover) was seeking to prevent fines from being disproportionate in relation to the size of the undertaking,[535] and the Commission recognises that in the imposition of fines it must be guided by the principle of proportionality. Equal treatment means that comparable situations must be treated in the same way and different situations treated differently, unless there is objective justification. Where a number of undertakings are involved in the same infringement—as in a cartel—the Commission applies weightings to reflect the differing impact of the undertakings' conduct. This may involve grouping the undertakings concerned.[536] The CJ confirmed in *Dansk Rørindustri* that the Commission does not have to ensure that the final amounts of the fines resulting from its calculations reflect any distinctions between them in terms of their turnover.[537]

Appeals against fines on grounds of breach of the principles of proportionality and equal treatment are common. For example, in *Hoek Loos* [538] the undertaking pointed out the fine imposed on it in the Commission *Industrial Gases Cartel* decision[539] amounted to nearly 50 per cent of the total fines imposed in that case. It claimed that this was out of all proportion to its participation in the infringement or to its market share. The GC rejected this argument, saying that the final amount of a fine is not, in principle, an appropriate factor in assessing the possible lack of proportionality of the fine as regards the importance of the participants in the cartel. That final amount was set, inter alia, on the basis of various factors linked to the individual conduct of the undertaking in question, such as the duration of the infringement, the aggravating or attenuating circumstances, and the degree to which the undertaking cooperated.[540] On the other hand, in *Degussa* [541] the GC held that the Commission was wrong in applying the same deterrence multiplier to the applicant as to another of the cartelists (Aventis) despite the difference in the size of the two undertakings. It therefore reduced the fine from €118 million to €91,125 million.

---

[531] COMP/38.866, 20 July 2010, IP/10/985, OJ C 111/19.

[532] SEC(2010)737/2.

[533] Best Practices, para. 88.

[534] For a case in which the principle of sound administration was breached, see Case T-410/03, *Hoechst GmbH v. Commission* [2008] ECR II-881, where the Commission was embroiled in negotiations with two undertakings at the same time under the Leniency Notice.

[535] Cases 100–103/80, *Musique Diffusion Française SA v. Commission (Pioneer)* [1983] ECR 1825, paras. 119–120; see Case T-33/02, *Britannia Alloys and Chemicals Ltd v. Commission* [2005] ECR II-4973, para. 43.

[536] Case T-68/04, [2008] ECR II-2511, aff'd Case C-564/08 P, *SGL Carbon AG v. Commission* [2009] ECR I-191.

[537] *Dansk Rørindustri*, para. 312.

[538] Case T-304/02, *Hoek Loos NV v. Commission* [2006] ECR II-1887.

[539] [2003] OJ L84/1.

[540] Case T-304/02, para. 85.

[541] Case T-279/02, [2006] ECR II-897. Degussa's further appeal against the fine was rejected, Case C-266/06 P, *Evonik Degussa GmbH v. Commission* [2008] ECR I-81.

j. Ne Bis in Idem

The principle of *non bis in idem* (double jeopardy) means that a party cannot be prosecuted, tried, and convicted twice for the same (criminal) behaviour.[542] It is enshrined in Article 4 of Protocol 7 of the ECHR and in Article 50 of the EU Charter of Fundamental Rights[543] and is a fundamental principle of Union law.[544] In respect of competition cases it precludes an undertaking from being found guilty or proceedings being brought against it a second time on the grounds of anti-competitive conduct in respect of which it has been penalised or declared not liable by a previous unappealable decision.[545] However, the principle did not prevent fines being imposed on four trade federations where three of them were members of the fourth.[546] Under the system for the allocation of cases within the ECN several NCAs may investigate in parallel the same matter in respect of the same undertakings.[547] However, no NCA could impose a fine on an undertaking in respect of the same matter in the same market.[548] The question has also arisen in relation to situations where fines have already been imposed outside the EU. The principle here is technically a corollary of *ne bis in idem*, as the undertakings are not pleading that the Commission had no right to take the proceedings, but only that it should have taken into account concurrent penalties concerning the same facts. The CJ held in *Archer Daniels Midland* [549] that the Commission was justified in refusing to take into account when fixing the fine that the undertaking had already been sanctioned in the US for the same cartel, at least where it had not been proved that the actions complained of were identical.[550] In *Showa Denko* the CJ explained more fully that in applying competition law the Commission is protecting specific Community (Union) interests, that the objective of deterrence which the Commission is entitled to pursue when setting the fine is to ensure compliance with the competition rules, and that consequently 'when assessing the deterrent nature of a fine to be imposed for infringement of those rules, the Commission is not required to take into account any penalties imposed on an undertaking for infringement of the competition rules of non-member States'.[551] The CJ therefore holds that in competition cases *ne bis in idem* applies only when three conditions are fulfilled: identity of the facts, unity of the offender, and unity of the legal interest protected.[552]

k. Liability for Fines

Difficulties may arise where an undertaking responsible for an infringement of the competition rules does not still exist (or does not still exist in an identical form) at the date of enforcement. This

---

[542] For the issue of whether competition proceedings are civil or criminal, see Section 8.A.ii, p. 934.

[543] See Chap. 2.

[544] Cases 18 and 35/65, *Gutmann v. Commission of the EAEC* [1966] ECR 149; Commission Green Paper, 'On Conflicts of Jurisdiction and the Principle of *ne bis in idem* in Criminal Proceedings' COM(2005) 696 final; M. Wasmeier and N. Thwaites, 'The Development of ne bis in idem into a Transnational Fundamental Right in EU Law: Comments on Recent Developments' (2006) 31 *ELRev* 565. For the ECHR implications, see A. Andreangeli, *EU Competition Enforcement and Human Rights* (Edward Elgar, 2008), 207–212.

[545] Cases C-238, 244–245, 247, 250, 251–252, and 254/99, *Limburgse Vinyl Maatschappij NV v. Commission* [2002] ECR I-8375, para. 59. In that case the CJ confirmed that the Commission could readopt a decision annulled on procedural grounds without going through all the unimpeached parts of the procedure again.

[546] Cases C-101 and 110/07 P, *Cooperate de France Bétail et Viande and FNSEA v. Commission* [2008] ECR I-10193.

[547] See Section 10.B.

[548] See W. Wils, 'Ne Bis In Idem in EC Antitrust Enforcement: A Legal and Economic Analysis' (2004) 142 *World Competition: Law and Economics Review* 131.

[549] Case C-397/03 P, *Archer Daniels Midland Company v. Commission* [2006] ECR I-4429, paras. 46–53.

[550] Archer Daniels Midland had paid US$70 million for its involvement in the lysine cartel in the US and Canadian $16 million for its involvement in lysine (amino acid) and citric acid cartels in Canada. Moreover, its executives had been jailed in the US. See also Case T-410/03, *Hoechst GmbH v. Commission* [2008] ECR II-881, paras. 597–606.

[551] Case C-289/04 P, *Showa Denko v. Commission* [2006] ECR I-5859, para. 61.

[552] Cases C-204/00 P, etc., *Aalborg Portland and others v. Commission* [2004] ECR I-123, para. 338; Case C-17/10, *Toshiba v. Úřad pro ochranu hospodářské soutěže*, 14 February 2012, para. 97.

issue of the liability of parent and successor companies is discussed in Chapter 3 along with the single economic entity concept.[553]

l. The Payment and Collection of Fines

The payment of fines is enforceable pursuant to Article 299 TFEU which provides that enforcement of decisions of the Council or Commission which impose a pecuniary obligation on persons other than States shall be governed by the rules of civil procedure in force in the State in the territory of which it is carried out. Member States must designate a relevant national authority for enforcement purposes.[554] Fines are normally expressed in euros. Decisions normally give the undertakings concerned three months in which to pay the fine and specify a bank account into which it is to be paid. They normally state that interest becomes payable after the specified time.[555] A challenge to the decision before the GC does not operate to suspend the payment of the fine but the Commission usually agrees to defer enforcing it pending the outcome of the appeal if the undertakings agree to pay interest on it and provide a bank guarantee. The question of whether fines are tax deductible arose in the Article 267 reference, *XBV*.[556] While not actually ruling on the matter the CJ clearly disapproved of deductibility, saying it might significantly reduce the effectiveness of the Commission decision.[557]

(v) The Leniency Policy in Cartel Cases

Reference has already been made in Chapter 9 to the Commission's leniency policy whereby it encourages cartel participants to come forward and 'whistle-blow' on their co-conspirators in return for immunity from fines or a reduction in the fines that would otherwise be imposed.[558]

The Commission has serious problems in detecting cartels and in proving them to the standard required by the EU Courts, particularly where oligopolistic industries are concerned and the participants plead the 'oligopoly defence'.[559] Although it has the inspection powers described previously in this chapter, obtaining direct evidence of a cartel is much easier if some of the participants can be induced to turn informer. In *Cartonboard*, in 1994, one of the ringleaders 'spontaneously admitted' the infringement and provided detailed evidence to the Commission.[560] Its fine was reduced by two-thirds to ECU 11.25 million, representing three per cent of its turnover in the Community cartonboard market for the relevant year, rather than the nine per cent suffered by the other ringleaders.[561] In 1996 the Commission published a Notice (the 'Leniency Notice' or 'Whistleblowers' Notice')[562] putting the practice on a systematic footing. It stated that in the event of participants in

---

[553] See Chap. 3, Section 5.A.vi, p. 137 ff.

[554] The UK has designated the High Court (the Court of Session in Scotland) pursuant to the European Communities (Enforcement of Community Judgments) Order 1972 (SI 1972/1590). Fines are enforced as if they were judgments of the UK courts.

[555] The payment of interest was approved by the CJ in Case 107/82, *AEG-Telefunken* v. *Commission* [1983] ECR 3151; see also the GC in Case T-275/94, *Groupement des Cartes Bancaires "CB"* v. *Commission* [1995] ECR II-2169. In Case C-564/08 P, *SGL Carbon AG* v. *Commission* [2009] ECR I-191, the CJ confirmed that the Commission could set a higher rate of interest than the market rate applicable to ordinary borrowers.

[556] Case C-429/07, *Inspecteur van de Belastingdienst* v. *Commission* [2009] ECR I-4833.

[557] Case C-429/07, *Inspecteur van de Belastingdienst* v. *Commission* [2009] ECR I-4833, para. 39. The case is important as being the first occasion on which the Commission intervened in national proceedings.

[558] Chap. 9, Section 3.B.ii.b, p. 676. See A. Stephan, 'An Empirical Assessment of the European Leniency Notice' (2009) 5(3) *Journal of Competition Law and Economics* 537.

[559] See Chap. 9.

[560] [1994] OJ L243/1, para. 171.

[561] See the discussion in the GC judgments in the appeals from the decision, e.g., Case T-319/94, *Fiskeby Board AB* v. *Commission* [1998] ECR II-1331 paras. 86–104.

[562] Commission Notice on the non-imposition or reduction of fines in cartel cases [1996] OJ C204/14.

cartels giving information to the Commission and cooperating with it in the investigation they could expect a reduction in the fine which would otherwise be imposed, or even no fine at all.[563]

The 1996 Notice was very successful. It resulted in more than 80 applications in six years.[564] Nevertheless it was unsatisfactory in several respects.[565] In particular, it provided that the first undertaking to come forward with information about the cartel before the Commission had undertaken an investigation ordered by decision 'will benefit from a reduction of at least 75 per cent of the fine or even from total exemption from the fine that would have been imposed if they had not cooperated'. It did not, however, *guarantee* full immunity (as did the US and Canadian policies).[566]

The Commission therefore amended the Notice in February 2002.[567] Amongst other improvements the 2002 Notice did guarantee immunity to the first undertaking to submit evidence which met certain criteria. Some problems remained, but the increased certainty it offered, in particular the guaranteed 100 per cent immunity, made it an outstandingly successful tool in the fight against cartels.[568] Guaranteed immunity set the scene for a race to the Commission's door.

The 2002 Notice was replaced by the current one in 2006. The 2006 Notice[569] applied from 8 December 2006 to all cases in which no undertaking had already contacted the Commission in order to claim leniency.[570] The 2006 Notice is consistent with the ECN Model Leniency Programme (MLP) published on 29 September 2006 to deal with the problems of divergences between national leniency policies.[571]

The main features of the Notice are:

• Immunity is guaranteed to the first undertaking to submit evidence sufficient for the Commission either to mount a targeted Article 20(4) inspection or to enable the Commission to find an infringement, if certain other conditions (i.e. full, continuous, and expeditious cooperation with the Commission, as set out in paragraph 12 of the Notice)[572] are fulfilled. The Notice sets out what type of information and evidence applicants need to submit to qualify for immunity: it links the threshold for immunity to what the Commission needs in order to carry out a 'targeted inspection'; it explains what applicants are and are not required to produce in their

---

[563] The Leniency Notices only apply in cartel cases, Case T-13/03, *Nintendo v. Commission* [2009] ECR II-975.

[564] *Report on Competition Policy* (Commission, 2006), para. 175.

[565] See the comments by S. Hornsby and J. Hunter, 'New Incentives for "Whistleblowing": Will the EC Commissioners Notice Bear Fruit' [1997] *ECLR* 38.

[566] The US policy only grants immunity. Reductions of fines are dealt with under a plea-bargaining process.

[567] Commission Notice on immunity from fines and reduction of fines in cartel cases [2002] OJ C45/3. For comments on the Notice, see, e.g., N. Levy and R. O'Donoghue, 'The EU Leniency Programme Comes of Age' [2004] 92 *World Competition: Law and Economics Review* 75–99.

[568] See B. van Barlingen and M. Barennes, 'The European Commission's 2002 Leniency Notice in Practice', (2005) 3 (Autumn) *Competition: Policy Newsletter* 6.

[569] Commission Notice on immunity from fines and reduction of fines in cartel cases [2006] OJ C298/11; Commission Press Release, IP/06/1705, 7 December 2006. See S. Suurnäkki and M. L. Tierno Centella, 'Commission Adopts Revised Leniency Notice to Reward Companies that Report Hardcore Cartels' (2007) 1 *EC Competition Policy Newsletter* 7.

[570] Except that the provisions on the protection of corporate statements (paras. 31–35) applied to all pending applications as well.

[571] <http://ec.europa.eu/comm/competition/ecn/model_leniency_en.pdf>; see Section 10.B.iii.

[572] In *Italian Raw Tobacco*, COMP/38.281, upheld Case T-12/06 P, *Deltafina v. Commission* [2011] ECR II-5639, on appeal Case C-578/11 P, judgment pending, one undertaking, Deltafina, applied for immunity under the 2002 Leniency Notice, only a few days after its adoption. It was the first undertaking to apply under the 2002 Notice. It was granted conditional immunity but a month later it revealed at a meeting with the other cartelists that it had confessed to the Commission and given it information about the cartel. This was before the Commission had mounted investigations under Reg. 17, Art. 14(3) at the premises of the other undertakings. The Commission withdrew the conditional immunity on the grounds that Deltafina had failed to cooperate continuously and expeditiously as such cooperation included refraining from taking any step which could undermine the Commission's ability to investigate and/or find the infringement (para. 432).

initial application; and it states explicitly that applicants need to disclose their participation in the cartel. In addition the undertaking has to end its involvement in the cartel. Immunity is not available to undertakings that have coerced others to participate in the infringement.

- Undertakings which approach the Commission later are eligible for a reduction in the fine that would otherwise have been imposed, subject to the same ongoing cooperation as for immunity applicants. However, nothing is guaranteed to them.

- A discretionary 'marker system' (first introduced in 2006) provides for an applicant for immunity to reserve its first place in the queue by initially providing only limited information.

- A procedure has been devised for protecting the corporate statements made by undertakings applying for leniency from discovery procedures in civil actions for damages.

Commission Notice on Immunity from Fines and Reduction of Fines in Cartel Cases [2006] OJ C298/17

II. Immunity from Fines

A. Requirements to qualify for immunity from fines

(8) The Commission will grant immunity from any fine which would otherwise have been imposed to an undertaking disclosing its participation in an alleged cartel affecting the Community if that undertaking is the first to submit information and evidence which in the Commission's view will enable it to:

(a) carry out a targeted inspection in connection with the alleged cartel… or

(b) find an infringement of Article [101] EC in connection with the alleged cartel.

(9) For the Commission to be able to carry out a targeted inspection within the meaning of point (8) (a), the undertaking must provide the Commission with the information and evidence listed below, to the extent that this, in the Commission's view, would not jeopardize the inspections:

(a) A corporate statement…which includes, in so far as it is known to the applicant at the time of submission:

— A detailed description of the alleged cartel arrangement, including for instance its aims, activities and functioning; the product or service concerned, the geographic scope, the duration of and the estimated market volumes affected by the alleged cartel; the specific dates, locations, content of and participants in alleged cartel contacts, and all relevant explanations in connection with the pieces of evidence provided in support of the application.

— The name and address of the legal entity submitting the immunity application as well as the names and addresses of all the other undertakings that participate(d) in the alleged cartel;

— The names, positions, office locations and, where necessary, home addresses of all individuals who, to the applicant's knowledge, are or have been involved in the alleged cartel, including those individuals which have been involved on the applicant's behalf;

— Information on which other competition authorities, inside or outside the EU, have been approached or are intended to be approached in relation to the alleged cartel; and

(b) Other evidence relating to the alleged cartel in possession of the applicant or available to it at the time of the submission, including in particular any evidence contemporaneous to the infringement.

(10) Immunity pursuant to point (8)(a) will not be granted if, at the time of the submission, the Commission had already sufficient evidence to adopt a decision to carry out an inspection in connection with the alleged cartel or had already carried out such an inspection.

(11) Immunity pursuant to point (8)(b) will only be granted on the cumulative conditions that the Commission did not have, at the time of the submission, sufficient evidence to find an infringement of Article [101] EC in connection with the alleged cartel and that no undertaking had been granted conditional

immunity from fines under point (8)(a) in connection with the alleged cartel. In order to qualify, an undertaking must be the first to provide contemporaneous, incriminating evidence of the alleged cartel as well as a corporate statement containing the kind of information specified in point (9)(a), which would enable the Commission to find an infringement of Article [101] EC.

(12) In addition to the conditions set out in points (8)(a), (9) and (10) or in points (8)(b) and 11, all the following conditions must be met in any case to qualify for any immunity from a fine:

(a) The undertaking cooperates genuinely, fully, on a continuous basis and expeditiously from the time it submits its application throughout the Commission's administrative procedure. This includes:

— providing the Commission promptly with all relevant information and evidence relating to the alleged cartel that comes into its possession or is available to it;

— remaining at the Commission's disposal to answer promptly to any request that may contribute to the establishment of the facts;

— making current (and, if possible, former) employees and directors available for interviews with the Commission;

— not destroying, falsifying or concealing relevant information or evidence relating to the alleged cartel; and

— not disclosing the fact or any of the content of its application before the Commission has issued a statement of objections in the case, unless otherwise agreed;

(b) The undertaking ended its involvement in the alleged cartel immediately following its application, except for what would, in the Commission's view, be reasonably necessary to preserve the integrity of the inspections;

(c) When contemplating making its application to the Commission, the undertaking must not have destroyed, falsified or concealed evidence of the alleged cartel nor disclosed the fact or any of the content of its contemplated application, except to other competition authorities.

(13) An undertaking which took steps to coerce other undertakings to join the cartel or to remain in it is not eligible for immunity from fines. It may still qualify for a reduction of fines if it fulfils the relevant requirements and meets all the conditions therefor.

The threshold for immunity (paragraph 8 in the extract) is information and evidence which enables the Commission to carry out a targeted inspection or to find an Article 101 infringement. 'Targeted' inspection was a new concept in the 2006 Notice and means that the Commission is able to carry out a more focused Article 20 inspection with precise 'insider' information 'as to, for instance, what to look for and where in terms of evidence'.[573] This appears to be a higher threshold than that under the 2002 Notice (which was simply that it enabled the Commission to adopt a decision to carry out 'an investigation' under Regulation 17, Article 14(3)). The greatest problem for undertakings contemplating immunity applications is still that at the time of the submission the Commission must not already have sufficient evidence to carry out the inspection or find an infringement, and the undertaking has to be the first participant to provide it. So there is no immunity if the Commission has already gathered the necessary evidence, or if the undertaking has not got to the Commission first. The threshold for evidence required under paragraph 8(a) is lower than that under 8(b) (contemporaneous and incriminating—a very high standard) in order to encourage undertakings to come forward early.

Paragraph 12 sets out (in accordance with the case law on the earlier Notices) exactly what is involved in the required ongoing cooperation. The third indent (making employees and directors

---

[573] 'Competition: revised Leniency Notice—frequently asked questions', Commission MEMO/06/469, 7 December 2006. The quality of the applicant's submission is judged *ex ante*, and not in the light of what actually happens at the inspection.

available for interview with the Commission) is a reference to Regulation 1/2003, Article 19.[574] The Commission recognises that these individuals may not be keen on being interviewed, in the light of the criminal proceedings for cartel participation under the laws of some of the Member States,[575] but has said that the provisions in Regulation 1/2003, Article 12 on the exchange of information within the ECN[576] should be a sufficient safeguard for them.[577] The information the undertaking has to provide in its corporate statement—the confession which the leniency applicant has to make to the Commission—now has to include, where necessary and as far as the applicant knows them, the home addresses of implicated individuals. This reflects the powers of the Commission under Regulation 1/2003, Article 21, to carry out inspections at private premises.

The 2006 Notice introduced a 'marker' system by which an undertaking may reserve its place in the queue for immunity (but not for fine reduction) by making an application which gives limited information. It is then given a period of time (set at the Commission's discretion)[578] to 'perfect' the application by providing the additional evidence required to reach the immunity threshold.

Commission Notice on Immunity from Fines and Reduction of Fines in Cartel Cases [2006] OJ C298/17

II. Immunity from Fines

(15) The Commission services may grant a marker protecting an immunity applicant's place in the queue for a period to be specified on a case-by-case basis in order to allow for the gathering of the necessary information and evidence. To be eligible to secure a marker, the applicant must provide the Commission with information concerning its name and address, the parties to the alleged cartel, the affected products(s) and territory(-ies), the estimated duration of the alleged cartel and the nature of the cartel conduct. The applicant should also inform the Commission on other past or possible future leniency applications to other authorities in relation to the alleged cartel and justify its request for a marker. Where a marker is granted, the Commission services determine the period within which the applicant has to perfect the marker by submitting the information and evidence required to meet the relevant threshold for immunity. Undertakings which have been granted a marker cannot perfect it by making a formal application in hypothetical terms. If the applicant perfects the marker within the period set by the Commission services, the information and evidence provided will be deemed to have been submitted on the date when the marker was granted.

(16) An undertaking making a formal immunity application to the Commission must:

(a) provide the Commission with all information and evidence relating to the alleged cartel available to it, as specified in points (8) and (9), including corporate statements; or

(b) initially present this information and evidence in hypothetical terms, in which case the undertaking must present a detailed descriptive list of the evidence it proposes to disclose at a later agreed date. This list should accurately reflect the nature and content of the evidence, whilst safeguarding the hypothetical nature of its disclosure. Copies of documents, from which sensitive parts have been removed, may be used to illustrate the nature and content of the evidence. The name of the applying

---

[574] See Section 8.B.v, p. 953.

[575] See Section 12, p. 1064.

[576] See the discussion of Art. 12, in Section 10.B.ii, p. 1055.

[577] 'Competition: revised Leniency Notice—frequently asked questions', Commission MEMO/06/469. For the problems of the exchange of information within the ECN, see Section 10.B.ii and A. Andreangeli, 'The Impact of the Modernisation Regulation on the Guarantees of Due Process in Competition Proceedings' (2006) 31 *ELRev* 342.

[578] In 'Competition: revised Leniency Notice—frequently asked questions', Commission MEMO/06/469 the Commission expressly refrained from giving any indication about the length of time; it 'will need to be decided based on the circumstances of each case'.

undertaking and of other undertakings involved in the alleged cartel need not be disclosed until the evidence described in its application is submitted. However, the product or service concerned by the alleged cartel, the geographic scope of the alleged cartel and the estimated duration must be clearly identified.

It is still possible to make a formal application in 'hypothetical terms' but a marker cannot be perfected by a hypothetical application. The difference between a marker and a formal application in hypothetical terms has been explained by the Commission as follows:[579]

A marker and a hypothetical application cannot be combined due to their different purposes and features. The hypothetical application is available to allow companies to ascertain whether the evidence in their possession would meet the immunity threshold before disclosing their identity or the infringement. In a hypothetical application, the company is supposed to actually show the evidence liable to meet the relevant immunity threshold, although it can be done by means of edited copies with the data that could identify the company and the cartel at that stage deleted.

In contrast, a marker is granted to protect the place in the queue of an applicant which has not yet gathered the evidence necessary to formalise an immunity application. In order to protect the place in the queue without obtaining the relevant evidence in exchange, the Commission must be in a position to ascertain whether it already has a previous immunity application for the same cartel and ensure that the company is seriously engaged to provide the evidence. Therefore, in order to obtain a marker, a company is expected to provide certain data listed in the Notice, which include the identity of the applicant and some details on the cartel, but not the rest of the evidence required to meet the immunity threshold. This can be submitted later within a specified timeframe.

Undertakings which do not meet the criteria for immunity can get a reduction of the fine. How much reduction depends on their position in the queue: the first gets 30–50 per cent, the second 20–30 per cent, and the subsequent ones up to 20 per cent. They are required to produce information of 'significant added value' and comply with the same cooperation stipulations as are imposed on immunity applicants by paragraph 12. Obviously, the further down the queue an undertaking is, the more difficult it is to produce information of 'significant added value' to the Commission. There is no 'marker' system in respect of reductions.

Commission Notice on Immunity from Fines and Reduction of Fines in Cartel Cases [2006] OJ C298/17

III. Reduction of a Fine

A. Requirements to qualify for reduction of a fine

(23) Undertakings disclosing their participation in an alleged cartel affecting the Community that do not meet the conditions under section II above may be eligible to benefit from a reduction of any fine that would otherwise have been imposed.

(24) In order to qualify, an undertaking must provide the Commission with evidence of the alleged infringement which represents significant added value with respect to the evidence already in the Commission's possession and must meet the cumulative conditions set out in points 12(a) to 12(c) above.

---

[579] 'Competition: revised Leniency Notice—frequently asked questions', Commission MEMO/06/469. Hypothetical applications, which were introduced by the 2002 Notice, were often popularly referred to as 'markers', although this was misleading, see B. van Barlingen, 'The European Commission's 2002 Leniency Notice after one year of operation', (2003) 2 (Summer) *Competition Policy Newsletter* 16, 18. The 2006 Notice makes it clear that putting down a marker and making a hypothetical application are different things.

(25) The concept of 'added value' refers to the extent to which the evidence provided strengthens, by its very nature and/or its level of detail, the Commission's ability to prove the alleged cartel. In this assessment, the Commission will generally consider written evidence originating from the period of time to which the facts pertain to have a greater value than evidence subsequently established. Incriminating evidence directly relevant to the facts in question will generally be considered to have a greater value than that with only indirect relevance. Similarly, the degree of corroboration from other sources required for the evidence submitted to be relied upon against undertakings involved in the case will have an impact on the value of that evidence, so that compelling evidence will be attributed a greater value than evidence such as statements which require corroboration if contested.

(26) The Commission will determine in any final decision adopted at the end of the administrative procedure the level of reduction an undertaking will benefit from, relative to the fine which would otherwise be imposed. For the:

— first undertaking to provide significant added value: a reduction of 30–50%,

— second undertaking to provide significant added value: a reduction of 20–30%,

— subsequent undertakings that provide significant added value: a reduction of up to 20%.

In order to determine the level of reduction within each of these bands, the Commission will take into account the time at which the evidence fulfilling the condition in point (24) was submitted and the extent to which it represents added value.

If the applicant for the reduction of a fine is the first to submit compelling evidence in the sense of point (25) which the Commission uses to establish additional facts increasing the gravity or the duration of the infringement, the Commission will not take such additional facts into account when setting any fine to be imposed on the undertaking which provided this evidence.

As the Commission points out in the Notice[580] nothing in the leniency programme can protect an undertaking in a civil action brought by injured third parties.[581] This is an important consideration for undertakings thinking of baring their souls to the Commission, especially as plaintiffs can rely on the Commission decisions before national courts in the EU. It is possible that an increase in private damages actions in national courts may therefore serve as a disincentive to undertakings to take advantage of the leniency programme. The Commission encourages claims for damages in national courts against cartel participants,[582] but at the same time does not want private litigation to discourage leniency applicants. There is particular concern that leniency applicants should not be deterred by the fear that the corporate statements they make to the Commission could be accessible to plaintiffs in later civil proceedings. However, in jurisdictions with generous discovery procedures, plaintiffs may try to use discovery to force access to corporate statements and this happened in a number of cases in the US courts.[583] In view of this problem the Commission had previously

---

[580] 2006 Notice, para. 31.

[581] e.g., Aventis, given immunity in *Vitamins*, was subsequently sued for compensation along with its fellow conspirators. See Chap. 14 for actions in national courts.

[582] See the Commission White Paper on damages (COM)2008 165, and the Commission's proposal for a directive on damages actions, 11 June 2013, IP/13/525, see Chap. 14.

[583] See *In re Vitamins Antitrust Litigation*, 217 F.R.D 229 (DDC 2002); *In re Methionine Antitrust Litigation*, 221 F.R.D. 1 (N.D.Cal.2002); *Intel Corp.* v. *Advanced Micro Device Inc.*, 542 U.S, S.Ct. 2466 (2004) (the Commission intervened in these cases as amicus curiae to argue against discovery); K. Nordlander, 'Discovering Discovery—US Discovery of EC Leniency Statements' [2004] *ECLR* 646; M. Reynolds and D. Anderson, 'Immunity and Leniency in EU Cartel Cases: Current Issues' [2006] *ECLR* 102; M. Bloom, *Immunity/Leniency/Financial Incentives/Plea Bargaining*, 11th EUI Competition Law and Policy Workshop, 2006.

allowed leniency applicants to make oral corporate statements[584] of which only the Commission retained a transcript and this procedure is formalised in the 2006 Notice. The Notice provides that a leniency applicant may make oral corporate statements at the Commission's premises which the Commission will record and transcribe, and which the applicant must then listen to and check.[585] The idea is that if the transcript is part of the Commission's file, and access is limited only to addressees of an SO in the same case[586] under strict conditions,[587] and the applicant itself does not retain a copy of the statement, third parties will not be able to use discovery procedures to obtain it.

However, in EnBW[588] parties who were bringing a damages action in the German courts against participants in the *Gas Insulated Switchgear* cartel[589] requested access to leniency documents under the Transparency Regulation.[590] The Commission refused. The GC annulled the Commission decision on the grounds, inter alia, that the Commission relied on the exceptions in Articles 4(2) and 4(3) of the Regulation in an abstract and general way without making a concrete, individual examination of the requested documents. Further, the GC rejected the argument that protection of investigations in the third indent of Article 4(2) did not just apply to ongoing investigations but to future ones, in the sense that future cartel investigations might be jeopardised if potential leniency applicants were discouraged from coming forward.

Case T-344/08, *EnBW Energie Baden-Württemberg* v. *Commission*, 22 May 2012

General Court

124 The Commission argues, in essence, that the concept of 'investigations' cannot be limited, in the sphere of cartels, to the proceedings leading up to a decision prohibiting the cartel but must be regarded as an integral part of the Commission's regular, ongoing task of enforcing EU competition law. The third indent of Article 4(2) of Regulation No 1049/2001 therefore applies, in the Commission's submission, after particular proceedings have been completed. Given that, in proceedings against cartels, the Commission is reliant on the cooperation of the undertakings concerned, it submits that, if the documents that those undertakings provides it with were not kept confidential, the undertakings would have less incentive to file leniency applications and would also restrict themselves to the bare minimum when providing all other information, in particular as regards requests for information and inspections. The protection of confidentiality is thus a prerequisite for the effective prosecution of infringements of competition law and, by the same token, an essential component of the Commission's competition policy.

---

[584] In the *Citric Acid Cartel* [2001] OJ L239/18 one undertaking for the first time obtained a 90 per cent reduction on the basis of an oral statement. In Cases T-236, 239, 244–246/01, *Tokai Carbon* v. *Commission* [2004] ECR II-1181 and Case T-15/02, *BASF* v. *Commission* [2006] ECR II-497, the GC held that (under the 1996 Notice) statements could be made to the Commission orally.

[585] 2006 Notice, para. 32.

[586] Because of the rights of the defence: see Commission Notice on the rules for access to the Commission file [2005] OJ C325/7 and the discussion in Section 8.C.v., p. 970.

[587] The other parties and their lawyers may not make any copy by any mechanical or electronic means and may use the information only 'for the purpose of judicial or administrative proceedings for the application of Community competition rules at issue in the related administrative proceedings' under pain of doing otherwise being counted as lack of cooperation under the Notice, and of having their fine increased (in the case of undertakings) and of being reported to their professional body (in the case of external lawyers), 2006 Notice, para. 34.

[588] Case T-344/08, *EnBW Energie Baden-Württemberg* v. *Commission*, 22 May 2012, on appeal Case C-365/12 P, *Commission* v. *EnBW Energie Baden-Württemberg*, judgment pending.

[589] COMP/3.899, 24 January 2007.

[590] Regulation 1049/2001 [2001] OJ L145/4, see Section 8.C.v.f, p. 976.

125 However, acceptance of the interpretation proposed by the Commission would amount to permitting the latter to exclude its entire activity in the area of competition from the application of Regulation No 1049/2001, without any limit in time, merely by reference to a possible future adverse impact on its leniency programme. Account should be taken, in that regard, of the fact that the consequences which the Commission fears for its leniency programme depend on a number of uncertain factors, including, in particular, the use that the parties prejudiced by a cartel will make of the documents obtained, the success of any actions which they may bring for damages, the amounts which will be awarded them by the national courts and the way in which undertakings participating in cartels will react in future.

126 Such a broad interpretation of the concept of 'investigation' is incompatible with the principle that, on account of the purpose of Regulation No 1049/2001, as stated in recital 4, namely, 'to give the fullest possible effect to the right of public access to documents', the exceptions laid down in Article 4 of that regulation must be interpreted and applied strictly (see the case-law cited in paragraph 41 above).

127 It must be stressed, in that regard, that nothing in Regulation No 1049/2001 gives grounds for assuming that EU competition policy should enjoy, in the application of that regulation, treatment different from other EU policies. There is thus no reason to interpret the concept of the 'purpose of investigations' differently in the context of competition policy than in other EU policies.

128 In addition, it must be recalled that the leniency and co-operation programmes whose effectiveness the Commission is seeking to protect are not the only means of ensuring compliance with EU competition law. Actions for damages before the national courts can make a significant contribution to the maintenance of effective competition in the European Union (Case C-453/99 *Courage and Crehan*...paragraph 27).

129 Accordingly, the Commission made an error of law in holding, in the contested decision, that the exception to the right of access to documents laid down in the third indent of Article 4(2) of Regulation No 1049/2001 was applicable in the present case. In particular, it was therefore not entitled to refuse access to the documents falling within category 3 on the basis of that exception.

The non-disclosure of the Commission's leniency documents has also been jeopardised by the judgments in *Pfleiderer* [591] and *Donau Chemie* [592] in respect of access to leniency documents held by NCAs. This is an aspect of the complications to the operation of the Commission's leniency policy caused by the decentralised enforcement system. Regulation 1/2003 did not introduce a 'one-stop shop' for leniency applicants. Leniency and NCAs are dealt with later, in the context of the workings of the ECN. [593] The proposal for a Directive on damages actions published by the Commission in June 2013 has specific provisions about disclosure. [594]

The 2006 Notice does not contain a provision for what is known as 'Amnesty Plus' (or 'Leniency Plus'), despite the urging of many consultees. [595] Amnesty Plus is a system by which an applicant for leniency in respect of one cartel is further rewarded if it reveals another cartel in the course of the proceedings. The argument for this is that undertakings which participate in cartels in one product or geographic market are likely to participate in others. [596]

---

[591] Case C-360/09, *Pfleiderer AG v. Bundeskartellamt* [2011] ECR I-5161, see Section 10.B.iii, p. 1057 and Chap. 14, Section 2.D.

[592] Case C-536/11, *Bundeswettbewerbsbehörde v. Donau Chemie AG*, 6 June 2013, see Section 10.B.iii, p. 1057 and Chap. 14, Section 2.D.

[593] See Section 10.B.iii, p. 1057.

[594] See Chap. 14.

[595] And see D. McElwee, 'Should the European Commission adopt "Amnesty Plus" in its Fight Against Hardcore Cartels?' [2004] *ECLR* 558.

[596] As any glance at the undertakings involved in EU cartel cases shows. The UK's NCA, the OFT (as from 2014 the Competition and Markets Authority (CMA)) operates an amnesty plus system, set out in OFT Guideline 423 Guidance as to the appropriate amount of a penalty, paras. 3.16–3.17, as does the US.

Leniency policies are sometimes viewed with distaste. Immunity enables wrong-doers to literally 'get away with it' in return for delivering their co-conspirators to the competition authorities,[597] and all idea of trying to recover the ill-gotten gains by a carefully formulated fining policy flies out of the window.[598] It will be recollected[599] that under the 2006 Fining Guidelines repeat offenders are heavily punished for their recidivism[600] but under the EU system recidivists are not barred from either immunity or fine reduction and can, in theory, go on infringing and obtaining immunity time after time.[601] The point of leniency programmes, however, is not to maintain a morally defensible justice system but to provide a means of deterring, destabilising, and uncovering cartels, so that in the end they may cease as a phenomenon. Leniency policies are the carrot and the fining policy the stick, and the bigger the potential fines, the more attractive is leniency. Moreover, private actions for damages are not affected by the granting of leniency. The true punishment for many of the cartel participants granted immunity from fines in Europe, however, is the class damages actions for which they are liable in the US, given the international nature of many of the most serious cartels. The Commission's proposed directive may make private actions in the EU an increasingly serious threat.

H. SECTOR INQUIRIES

As explained in Chapter 9,[602] Regulation 1/2003, Article 17 provides for the Commission to conduct general inquiries into a sector of the economy. To this end the Commission has the powers to require information and carry out inspections contained in Articles 18, 19, and 20 (but not 21)[603] and to request the NCAs to carry out investigations under Article 22. It may impose fines and penalties under Articles 23 and 24 (for example, to sanction the provision of incorrect information).

I. THE POWERS OF THE COMMISSION AND DUE PROCESS

The preceding account of the enforcement system under Regulation 1/2003 shows the extent of the Commission's powers. We have already noted[604] the requirements of the relevant human rights instruments in respect of due process. The criticisms of the EU system for enforcing its competition law centres on the multiplicity of roles played by the Commission on the one hand and the limited role of the EU Courts in reviewing Commission decisions (discussed in Section 9) on the other. The main criticisms of the present position can be summed up as follows:

- There is no division between those who investigate, draft the decision, and propose the fine or other remedy;

---

[597] In the US this can also entail delivering the individual directors and executives of the co-conspirators to the loving embrace of the US federal justice system. Some other Member States (including the UK) also have criminal liability for individuals. Jurisdictions where criminal liability attaches to individuals also have to have leniency programmes for individuals. See further Section 12, p. 1064.

[598] For an analysis of the outcome in 39 cartel cases handled by the Commission 1998–2004, see C. Veljanovski, 'Penalties for Price Fixers: An Analysis of Fines Imposed on 39 Cartels by the EU Commission' [2006] ECLR 510. Undertakings which have 'coerced' others are, not, however eligible for immunity under the EU leniency policy, see now 2006 Notice, para. 13.

[599] See Section 8.G.iv.g, p. 1013.

[600] 2006 Fining Guidelines, para. 28, provide for a 100% increase on the basic amount of the fine for repeat offenders.

[601] Not quite a matter of *never* paying, but see, e.g., Degussa AG, fined (with a reduction for cooperation, further reduced on appeal, Case T-279/02, *Degussa v. Commission* [2006] ECR II-897) in the *Methionine Cartel* [2003] OJ L255/1, and given immunity in *Bleaching Chemicals* (hydrogen peroxide and perborate), IP/06/560, 3 May 2006 and *Acrylic Glass* (methacrylates) IP/06/698, 31 May 2006.

[602] Chap. 9, Section 4.C.ii, p. 727.

[603] The power to carry out inspections on non-business premises. The first dawn raids under Article 20 in a sector inquiry were concluded when the pharmaceutical sector inquiry was launched, IP/08/49, 16 January 2008.

[604] See Section 8.A.ii, p. 934.

- There is no hearing before an independent decision-maker on matters of substance, as the Hearing Officer's role is limited to overseeing the oral hearing (which is of a limited nature) and settling questions on procedural matters such as access to the file and confidentiality of documents;

- Decisions imposing remedies and fines are ultimately taken by the entire College of Commissioners, which is political body of appointees. Severe sanctions are imposed on undertakings by people who have not heard or seen the parties or any of the evidence.

The increasing severity of the sanctions imposed with the blessing of the EU Courts has led to increased calls for reform.[605] Some proposals, such as strengthening the role of the Hearing Officer and separating the investigation, prosecution, and decision-making functions, could be achieved without any Treaty amendment. Others, such as having a separate 'competition court' as an independent first instance adjudicator, would be more radical.

9. PROCEEDINGS BEFORE THE COURT OF JUSTICE OF THE EUROPEAN UNION

A. JUDICIAL REVIEW

(i) General

Commission competition decisions can be challenged in an action for annulment under Article 263 TFEU.[606] Since 1989 annulment actions have gone first to the GC with an appeal on a point of law to the CJ. Previously, before the inception of the GC (the Court of First Instance as it then was) they went straight to the CJ. Although these actions are colloquially called 'appeals' they are in fact judicial review proceedings. They do not entail a rehearing. The question of the intensity of the review in which the GC engages when reviewing Commission competition decisions is a burning issue. As the Commission is not a tribunal for the purposes of Article 6(1) of the ECHR or Article 47 of the Charter the supervision by the GC must satisfy the requirement for a fair and public hearing before an independent and impartial tribunal if the competition proceedings are to comply with the Convention and the Charter.[607]

Under Article 261 TFEU[608] the CJEU has 'unlimited jurisdiction' in respect of fines and penalties imposed by the Commission in competition cases.

The review process before the GC is often protracted.[609] In cartel cases, for example, there may be numerous parties who appeal to the GC, all claiming slightly different defects in the details of the

---

[605] See, e.g., I. Forrester, 'Due Process in EC Competition Case: A Distinguished Institution with Flawed Procedures' (2009) 34 *ELRev* 817; B. Vesterdorf, 'Due Process Before the Commission of the European Union? Some Reflections Upon Reading the Commission Draft Paper on Best Practices in Antitrust Proceedings' (2010) 1 *CPI Antitrust Journal* April; D. Slater, S. Thomas, D. Waelbroeck, 'Competition Law Proceedings before the European Commission and the Right to a Fair Trial: No Need for Reform?' (2009) *European Competition Journal* 97, 106; *GCLC Working Paper* 04/08; A. Andreangeli, 'Towards an EU Competition Court: "Article-6-Proofing" Antitrust Proceedings before the Commission?' (2007) 4 *World Competition* 595; R. Nazzini, 'Administrative Enforcement, Judicial Review and Fundamental Rights in EU Competition Law: A Comparative Contextual-Functionalist Perspective' (2012) 49 *CMLRev* 971. For a robust defence (mainly from those within the system), see F. Castillo de la Torre, 'Evidence, Proof and Judicial Review in Cartel Cases' (2009) 3 *World Competition* 505; P. Lowe, 'Cartels, Fines and Due Process' (2009) 2 *Global Competition Policy*; W. Wils, 'The Increased Level of Antitrust Fines, Judicial Review, and the European Convention on Human Rights' (2010) 33(1) *World Competition* 5. For comments following the *KME* judgment, Case C-389/10 P, *KME Germany AG v. Commission*, 8 December 2011, see n. 698.

[606] Ex Art. 230 EC.

[607] See Section 8.A.ii.

[608] Ex Art. 229 EC.

[609] There is an expedited procedure for cases of urgency (Rules of Procedure of the General Court [1991] OJ L136/1, as amended, Art. 76a) but this is rarely applicable to this kind of appeal. For interim measures, see Section 9.A.xi, p, 1048.

Commission's procedure.[610] There is then an appeal to the CJ. By the end the argument may be about events which took place 20 years earlier.[611]

(ii) Article 263 TFEU

Article 263 states:

The Court of Justice of the European Union shall review the legality of legislative acts, of acts of the Council, of the Commission and of the European Central Bank, other than recommendations and opinions, and of acts of the European Parliament and of the European Council intended to produce legal effects vis-à-vis third parties. It shall also review the legality of acts of bodies, offices or agencies of the Union intended to produce legal effects vis-à-vis third parties.

It shall for this purpose have jurisdiction in actions brought by a Member State, the European Parliament, the Council or the Commission on grounds of lack of competence, infringement of an essential procedural requirement, infringement of the Treaties or of any rule of law relating to their application, or misuse of powers.

The Court shall have jurisdiction under the same conditions in actions brought by the Court of Auditors, by the European Central Bank and by the Committee of the Regions for the purpose of protecting their prerogatives.

Any natural or legal person may, under the conditions laid down in the first and second paragraphs, institute proceedings against an act addressed to that person or which is of direct and individual concern to them, and against a regulatory act which is of direct concern to them and does not entail implementing measures.

Acts setting up bodies, offices and agencies of the Union may lay down specific conditions and arrangements concerning actions brought by natural or legal persons against acts of these bodies, offices or agencies intended to produce legal effects in relation to them.

The proceedings provided for in this Article shall be instituted within two months of the publication of the measure, or of its notification to the plaintiff, or, in the absence thereof, of the day on which it came to the knowledge of the latter, as the case may be.

The issues which arise from this provision are:

- Is there a challengeable act?
- Does the natural or legal person wishing to make the challenge have standing to do so?
- Are there grounds for annulling the act?

There is a short time limit (two months from publication or notification) for bringing an action. The limit is strictly applied. The position of addressees who do not appeal is illustrated by that of the undertakings in *Wood Pulp* which were not party to the challenge to the Commission's decision.[612]

(iii) *Locus Standi*—Who can Bring an Action?

The Member States, the Council, Parliament, and the Commission are 'privileged applicants' who have standing to challenge any act.[613] Under Article 263(4) any other natural or legal person has

---

[610] The cases are normally joined.

[611] Although Reg. 1/2003, Art. 25 lays down limitation periods, this only runs from the day the infringement ceases in the case of continued and repeated infringements. In *Cement Cartel*, for example, the Commission commenced its investigations in April 1989, and adopted the decision in 1994 [1994] OJ L343/1. It found infringements going back to January 1983. The judgment of the GC, which ran to over 5,000 paragraphs, was delivered in 2000 (Cases T-25/95, etc., *Cimenteries CBR SA v. Commission* [2000] ECR II-491) and, on appeal, the judgment of the CJ was delivered in January 2004 (Cases C-204/00 P, C-205/00 P, C-211/00 P, C-213/00 P, C-217/00 P, and C-219/00 P, *Aalborg Portland A/S and others v. Commission* [2004] ECR I-1123).

[612] Case C-310/97 P, *Commission v. AssiDomän Kraft Products AB and Others* [1999] ECR I-5363.

[613] Art. 263(2). By para. 3 the Court of Auditors, the European Central Bank, and the Committee of the Regions may bring actions to protect their prerogatives.

limited standing, able only to challenge a decision actually addressed to them, an act which is of direct and individual concern to them, or a regulatory act of direct concern to them which does not entail implementing measures. Article 263(4) is changed from the corresponding provision in the EC Treaty, Article 230(4) whereby a non-addressee could challenge only a decision which was of 'direct and individual concern' to it although in the form of a regulation or a decision addressed to *another* person.

Article 263(4) appears not to have changed the situation under Article 230(4) EC whereby a person can only challenge an act (i.e. a decision) addressed to *another* person, if the former can show direct and individual concern. The test formulated by the CJ for judging 'direct' and 'concern' is very restrictive and generally makes it difficult for individuals to gain standing.[614] However, it has been more generously applied in competition cases. The CJ first allowed standing to a non-addressee of a decision in *Metro I*,[615] in respect of a party who had complained under Regulation 17, Article 3(2)(b),[616] objecting to the granting of an exemption under Article 101(3). In *Metro II* [617] it widened the 'complainant' category to cover a party who had not *formally* complained but who had taken part in the Commission's proceedings and been recognised by the Commission as having a 'legitimate interest'. The applicant in both *Metro* cases was a retailer who was excluded by the provisions of an exempted selective distribution system from distributing the supplier's products. In *Métropole* [618] Antena 3, a TV service, was refused admission to the EBU as an active member before the Commission adopted a decision exempting the EBU's rules. Antena 3 brought an action to have the decision annulled. The Commission argued that it was not individually and directly concerned and had not submitted observations.[619] The GC, however, held that taking part in the administrative proceedings was not a prerequisite for being accorded standing, and that its application to join the EBU distinguished Antena 3 in the same way as if it were an addressee of the decision.

On the other hand, in *Kruidvat* [620] the Commission denied standing to a retailer who wished to challenge the Article 101(3) exemption of Givenchy's selective distribution network. It had taken no part in the Commission proceedings, had not complained to the Commission, had not applied to become a member of Givenchy's network, and did not wish to be one.[621] It was simply a competitor of Givenchy's authorised distributors. The Commission said that to grant Kruidvat standing would be to 'allow a practically limitless number of actions from unforeseeable sources to be brought'. The GC agreed and said that individual concern could not be established on the basis that the legality of the decision might affect indirectly related national proceedings. Although there are no individual exemption decisions under Regulation 1/2003, it is possible that a third party might wish to challenge a 'finding of inapplicability' decision under Article 10.[622]

A non-addressee was allowed to challenge the Article 9 commitments decision in *Alrosa*.[623] The GC held that the applicant, Alrosa, was directly and individually concerned by the decision: it was adopted at the conclusion of proceedings in which Alrosa had participated; it expressly referred

---

[614] It is whether the decision 'affects them by reason of certain attributes which are peculiar to them or by reason of circumstances in which they are differentiated from all other persons and by virtue of these factors distinguishes them individually just as in the case of the person addressed', Case 25/62, *Plaumann & Co v. Commission* [1963] ECR 95.

[615] Case 26/76, *Metro SB-Grossmärkte GmbH v. Commission (No. 1)* [1977] ECR 1875.

[616] Now Reg. 1/2003, Art. 7(2).

[617] Case 75/84, *Metro SB-Grossmärkte GmbH v. Commission (No. 2)* [1986] ECR 3021.

[618] Cases T-528, 542, 543, and 546/93, *Métropole Télévision v. Commission* [1996] ECR II-649.

[619] Following the publication of the Reg. 17, Art. 19(3) notice.

[620] Case T-87/92, *BVBA Kruidvat v. Commission* [1996] ECR II-1931.

[621] Its parent company was a member of a trade association which *had* participated, although the views of the association and of Kruidvat materially differed.

[622] See Section 8.D.iv, p. 990.

[623] Case T-170/06, *Alrosa v. Commission* [2007] ECR II-2601, paras. 39–41; the judgment was set aside on appeal, Case C-441/078, *European Commission v. Alrosa* [2010] ECR I-5949, but the CJ did not deny Alrosa's right to standing (para. 90).

to Alrosa; it was aimed at ending the long-standing trading relationship between Alrosa and the addressee; it was liable to have an appreciable effect on Alrosa's competitive position; and it produced direct and immediate effects on Alrosa's legal situation.

(iv) Which Acts can be Challenged?

It is not just formal decisions which can be challenged, but also other 'acts' taken by the Commission in the course of its procedures. The basic principle, laid down in *ERTA*,[624] is that Article 263 covers 'all measures adopted by the institutions which are intended to have legal force'. This was applied in *IBM*[625] where an undertaking wished to challenge the SO. The CJ said:

> 9. Any measure the legal effects of which are binding on, and capable of affecting the interests of, the applicant by bringing about a distinct change in his legal position is an act or decision which may be the object of an action under Article [263] for a declaration that it is void.

The test here is: does the act change the applicant's legal position? The SO does not do so; it is merely a preparatory act and any irregularity can be dealt with in a challenge to the act which concludes the proceedings. Interim decisions can be challenged.[626] Where complaints are concerned, 'Article 7' letters cannot be challenged but the final rejection of the complaint can be, even if it is only in the form of a letter.[627]

(v) The Grounds of Review

a. General

Article 263 provides four grounds of challenge, although they overlap and are in a sense all really encompassed in the third one, the infringement of the Treaties or of any rule of law relating to their application, and applicants often frame their cases in general terms. However, the infringement of an essential procedural requirement is a matter of public policy and must be raised by the Court of its own motion if it is not raised by the applicant[628] and so is lack of competence.[629]

Otherwise the grounds can be considered only if they are raised by the applicant.[630] The fourth ground, misuse of powers (*détournement de pouvoir*) means that the Union institution has used its powers other than for the purpose for which they were conferred. A challenge on this ground very rarely succeeds as the burden on the applicant is a heavy one, and one has never succeeded in a competition case.[631]

---

[624] Case 22/70, *Commission v. Council, Re ERTA* [1971] ECR 263.

[625] Case 60/81, *IBM v. Commission* [1981] ECR 2639.

[626] As in the case of the *IMS* decision, Case T-184/01 R, *IMS Health v. Commission* [2001] ECR II-3193 (President of the GC), confirmed Case C-481/01 P(R), *IMS Health v. Commission* [2002] ECR I-3401 (President of the CJ).

[627] See Section 13.F.

[628] Case C-272/09 P, *KME Germany AG v. Commission*, 8 December 2011, para. 101.

[629] Cases T-79/89, etc., *BASF and others v. Commission* [1992] ECR II-315, para. 31.

[630] Case C-272/09 P, *KME Germany AG v. Commission*, 8 December 2011

[631] Although it has been pleaded: see, e.g., Case 5/85, *AKZO Chemie BV v. Commission* [1986] ECR 2585; Case T-5/93, *Roger Tremblay v. Commission* [1995] ECR II-185. In the merger case, Case T-145/06, *Omya AG v. Commission* [2009] ECR II-145, the applicant claimed that the Commission had only requested extra information in order to suspend the time running. The GC stated that even if a decision had been taken for a purpose other than that for which the powers were conferred it would only invalidate the decision if no other proper ground for taking the decision was present.

b. Lack of Competence

Lack of competence is the EU equivalent of the English concept, ultra vires. It covers: the lack of competence of the Union to act at all, because no Treaty provision has empowered it to do so; the lack of competence of the institutions to act under a particular empowering provision (incorrect legal basis); and the lack of competence of the particular institution or official to take the challenged act.

In the competition field the best example of the first situation is challenges made to the extraterritorial application of the competition rules. Undertakings outside the Union have argued that the EU rules could not be applied to them because they were outside the jurisdiction. These challenges have not hitherto succeeded.[632]

The second situation is exemplified in the challenges brought by Member States to directives adopted by the Commission on the basis of Article 106(3), where they claimed that the Commission should instead have used the harmonisation of laws provisions, which would have involved going through the Council where the States could have influenced proceedings.[633] In *British Airways*[634] the GC dismissed the undertaking's claim that the Commission had no competence to apply Regulation 17 to practices in the market for air travel agency services as it should have used Regulation 3975/87 on the air transport sector[635] instead. A number of cases arose from the expiry of the ECSC Treaty in 2002. The *Reinforcing Bars Cartel* decision[636] was annulled since the Commission had adopted it under Article 65(1) ECSC post the expiry.[637] However, the GC upheld the readopted *Alloy Surcharge* decision of 20 December 2006 in which the Commission used Regulation 1/2003 in respect of an infringement of Article 65(1).[638]

The third situation has arisen in competition cases where parties have alleged that the power to take decisions was unlawfully delegated. The delegation to the Commissioner responsible for competition of the power to take decisions ordering 'dawn raid' inspections under Regulation 17, Article 14(3) was unsuccessfully challenged in *AKZO*,[639] and the delegation of the signing of documents such as SOs has been upheld.[640] However, a challenge to the adoption of a final decision finding an infringement by a single Commissioner succeeded in the *PVC* cartel case where a challenge to a decision on both competence and infringement of an essential procedural requirement grounds spectacularly succeeded.[641] The part of the *Microsoft* decision providing for the appointment of the monitoring trustee was annulled because the Commission lacked authority to impose such measures.[642] A novel plea was made by British Airways when it claimed that the Commission had no competence to adopt the *Virgin/BA* decision of 14 July 1999[643] as, all the members of the Commission having resigned en bloc on 16 March 1999, they had authority only to deal with current

---

[632] See Chap. 16.

[633] See Case C-202/88, *France v. Commission (Telecommunications Equipment)* [1991] ECR I-1223; Cases C-271, 281, and 289/90, *Spain, Belgium & Italy v. Commission (Telecommunications Services)* [1992] ECR I-5833: see Chap. 8.

[634] Case T-219/99, *British Airways v. Commission* [2003] ECR II-5917.

[635] [1987] OJ L374/1.

[636] COMP/37.956.

[637] Cases T-27/03, etc., *SP SpA v. Commission* [2007] ECR II-4331. See Chap. 2. See also Case T-405/06, *Arcelor Mittal v. Commission* [2009] ECR II-789 aff'd Case C-201/09 P, *Arcelor Mittal v. Commission* [2011] ECR I- 2239. The Commission readopted the *Concrete Reinforcing Bars* decision under Reg.1/2003, 30 September 2009.

[638] Case T-24/07, *ThyssenKrupp Stainless AG v. Commission* [2009] ECR II-2309, on appeal Case C-352/09 P, *ThyssenKrupp Nirosta v. Commission* [2011] ECR I-2359. For the reasons for the annulment of the original *Alloy Surcharge* decision, see n. 657.

[639] Case 5/85, *AKZO Chemie BV v. Commission* [1986] ECR 2585.

[640] See Case 48/69, *ICI v. Commission (Dyestuffs)* [1972] ECR 619.

[641] Cases T-79/89, etc., *BASF and others v. Commission* [1992] ECR II-315, on appeal to the CJ, Cases C-137/92 P, etc., *Commission v. BASF and others* [1994] ECR I-2555: see Section 9.A.v.c, p. 1035.

[642] Case T-201/04, *Microsoft v. EC Commission* [2007] ECR II-3601.

[643] [2000] OJ L30/1.

business within the meaning of Article 201EC (now Article 234 TFEU) pending their replacement in September. The GC held that the Commissioners could exercise their normal powers until their resignations took effect on the date of their actual replacement.[644]

c. Infringement of an Essential Procedural Requirement

Infringement of an essential procedural requirement covers situations where a measure has been passed without complying with the legislative process laid down by the Treaties,[645] or with the rules of procedure of the relevant institution,[646] or with a general principle of law concerned with procedure,[647] or where the measure does not contain an adequate statement of reasons contrary to Article 296 TFEU.

The GC annuls acts only for breach of an *essential* procedural requirement, and what amounts to such is a matter for the Court. A requirement is essential if the failure to observe it might have affected the final outcome of the act. On this basis the wrongful revelation of confidential material to the complainant in *AKZO* [648] was not a reason for annulling the Commission decision. An adequate statement of reasons is essential because it is necessary for the review process. As the CJ said in *Germany* v. *Commission*:[649]

In imposing upon the Commission the obligation to state reasons for its decisions, Article [296] is not taking mere formal considerations into account but seeks to give an opportunity to the parties of defending their rights, to the Court of exercising its supervisory functions and to Member States and to all interested nationals of ascertaining the circumstances in which the Commission has applied the Treaty.

What amounts to adequate reasons depends on the context of the act. In an interlocking series of regulations the acts may refer to each other and the reasoning of the institutions may be deduced from them as a whole. In competition cases, where the Commission has a wide margin of appreciation and power of appraisal, the reasoning is of fundamental importance because in reviewing the decision the Court must be able to establish whether the factual and legal matters upon which the exercise of the power of appraisal depended were present. The Commission has to deal properly with the parties' arguments. In the *Net Book Agreement* case, the Publishers' Association (PA) had argued that the resale price maintenance (RPM) on books provided for in the Net Book Agreement should be allowed. It put forward as evidence the judgments of the UK Restrictive Practices Court (RPC) which permitted RPM on books in the UK and set out the benefits of such pricing. The CJ annulled the decision because the Commission had not adequately dealt with this evidence.[650]

Challenges to competition decisions frequently plead procedural defects as grounds for annulment, as seen earlier in this chapter. The GC annulled the *Soda-ash* decisions,[651] for example, on grounds that insufficient access to the Commission's file prejudiced the parties' right to be heard,

---

[644] Case T-219/99, *British Airways* v. *Commission* [2003] ECR II-5917, paras. 55–57. The resignation of the entire Santer Commission in March 1999 to avoid a motion of censure of Parliament was a situation not foreseen by the EC Treaty. Art. 215 EC, which BA claimed prevented the resigned Commission transacting 'new' business, did not fit happily with what had happened in these rather extraordinary circumstances. Art. 215 was amended by the Treaty of Nice and is now Art. 246 TFEU.

[645] As where Parliament is not consulted: Case 138/79, *Roquette Frères* v. *Council* [1980] ECR 3333.

[646] Case 68/86, *United Kingdom* v. *Council* [1988] ECR 855, and note the application of this in the *PVC cartel* case: Cases C-137/92 P, *Commission* v. *BASF and others* [1994] ECR I-2555.

[647] Such as the *audi alteram partem* rule giving parties a right to a hearing: Case 17/74, *Transocean Marine Paint* v. *Commission* [1974] ECR 1063.

[648] See Section 8.C.v.d, p. 976.

[649] Case 24/62, *Germany* v. *Commission* [1963] ECR 63.

[650] Case C-360/92 P, *Publishers' Association* v. *Commission* [1995] ECR I-23 setting aside the GC judgment, Case T-66/89, *Publishers' Association* v. *Commission* [1992] ECR II-1995.

[651] Cases T-30/91, *Solvay SA* v. *Commission (No.2)* 1995] ECR II-1775; the readopted decisions were also annulled for lack of access to the file, Case C-109/10 P, *Solvay SA* v. *European Commission* [2011] ECR I-10329.

and a significant part of the *TACA* decision[652] because the Commission had relied on an interpretation of a number of inculpatory documents upon which the undertakings had been given no opportunity to comment.[653] The most celebrated case of annulment on procedural grounds (and of lack of competence) is the *PVC* case. There the GC found differences in both the statement of reasons and the operative part of the decision between the version adopted by the College of Commissioners at its relevant meeting and the version notified to the undertakings concerned. The differences went beyond mere corrections of grammar and syntax. The Commission was unable to produce an authenticated version of the decision as adopted by the College. A draft in only three languages was available at the meeting, and the Competition Commissioner was authorised to adopt the measure in the other official Community languages, including those of undertakings to which the decision was addressed. Further, the Competition Commissioner whose signature appeared on the decision notified to all the addressees had left office some days before the notified version appeared to have been finalised. The GC considered these procedural defects, including the breach of the principle of collegiate responsibility, so serious that it did not merely annul the decision, it declared it *non-existent*.[654] On appeal the CJ held that the flaws were not so fundamental as to render the act non-existent. It put aside the judgment of the GC, held that the decision existed, but annulled it.[655]

The Commission responded to the final annulment by adopting a new decision six weeks later. The undertakings again appealed, inter alia, on the grounds that this breached the principle of double jeopardy, *ne bis in idem*, and that the Commission had denied them the right to be heard by not sending a new statement of objections and holding new hearings. The CJ held that *ne bis in idem* did not apply when the annulment was only on procedural grounds, and that given that the Court had not found any defects in the preparatory stages of the Commission's procedure, there was no need to repeat those stages. A right to be heard was necessary only in respect of matters which were not in the original decision.[656] The Commission's practice is, consequently, to readopt decisions annulled for procedural reasons.[657]

d. Infringement of the Treaties or any Rule of Law Relating to their Application

This ground is so wide that it covers the other three grounds as well. 'The Treaties' means the TEU and TFEU together with the Protocols, Treaties, and Acts of Accession, the Charter of Fundamental

---

[652] [1999] OJ L95/1.

[653] Cases T-191/98 and T-212/98–214/98, *Atlantic Container Line v. Commission* [2003] ECR II-3275.

[654] Cases T-79/89, etc., *BASF v. Commission* [1992] ECR II-315.

[655] Cases C-137/92 P, *Commission v. BASF and others* [1994] ECR I-2555. The *LdPE cartel* (low-density polyethylene) decision [1989] OJ L74/21, was annulled on similar grounds in Cases T-80/89, etc., *BASF v. Commission* [1995] ECR II-729. After the *PVC* judgment two of the undertakings concerned in the *Polypropylene Cartel*, who were challenging that decision in an action before the GC in which the oral proceedings had already been closed, asked the GC to reopen those proceedings so that they could enter pleas based on the *PVC* arguments. They claimed that the GC had wrongfully failed to raise those issues of its own motion. The GC refused and this was upheld by the CJ: see Case C-234/92 P, *Shell International Chemical Company Ltd v. Commission* [1999] ECR I-4501, at paras. 66–68. The GC did, however, annul a Commission decision in Cases T-31–32/91, *Solvay v. Commission* [1995] ECR II-1821 on non-authentication grounds. The applicants raised the plea after the close of the written procedure in the case, having read statements by Commission officials in the *Financial Times* and the *Wall Street Journal* that the Commission had been following the procedure condemned in the *PVC* case for the past 25 years. The annulment was upheld by the CJ, Cases C-286–288/95 P, *Commission v. ICI* [2000] ECR I-2341. The Commission readopted the decisions eight months after the CJ judgment, in December 2000, [2003] OJ L10/1.

[656] Cases C-238, 244–245, 247, 250, 251–252, and 254/99 P, *Limburgse Vinyl Maatschappij NV v. Commission* [2002] ECR I-8375, paras. 59–76, confirming Cases T-305–307, 313–316, 318, 328–329, and 335/94, *Re the PVC Cartel II: Limburgse Vinyl Maatschappij NV and others v. Commission* [1999] ECR II-931.

[657] For two further examples of decisions readopted after annulments for procedural reasons, see *Steel Beams* COMP/C.38/907, [2008] OJ C 235/4, undertaking fined €10 million (original decision (adopted under the ECSC Treaty) annulled in Case C-176/99 P, *Arbed SA v. Commission* [2003] ECR I-10687 as the decision had not been addressed to the same addressee as the statement of objections) and *Alloy Surcharge* COMP 39/234, 20 December 2006, undertaking fined €3,168,000 (original decision annulled in Cases C-65/02 P and C-73/02 P, *ThyssenKrupp Stainless AG v. Commission* [2005] ECR I-6773 as ThyssenKrupp was fined without being explicitly invited to give its views of the cartel behaviour of Thyssen Stahl, who had merged with another company after the infringement to form ThyssenKrupp).

Rights of the EU[658] and any future amending Treaties. 'Any rule of law relating to their application' covers all the other binding provisions of the Union legal order, including the general principles of law and human rights developed in the Court's jurisprudence (many of which are now embedded in the Charter) and provisions of international law, particularly principles of customary international law and agreements the EU itself has concluded. It also covers ensuring that the Commission has followed any Notices or other measure to which it has committed itself, such as the Fining Guidelines and the Leniency Notice. Review under Article 263 entails ensuring that the Commission has properly interpreted the law. However, the EU Courts are committed to interpreting EU law in a way which gives effect to the objectives of the Treaties. The great leaps forward which the Commission has made in the interpretation of the competition provisions have usually been confirmed: for example, the extension of the 'abuse' concept to cover mergers,[659] the development of the doctrine of collective dominance,[660] and the original finding that Article 101(1) applied equally to horizontal and vertical restraints.[661] On the other hand, the EU Courts refused to accept that what was in reality unilateral behaviour by a non-dominant firm could be caught as an agreement under Article 101(1).[662]

The GC will therefore annul a decision where the Commission has misinterpreted the law or failed to abide by general principles of law such as proportionality, non-discrimination, legitimate expectation, the presumption of innocence, or legal certainty.[663] However, this ground of annulment goes beyond misinterpreting or misapplying the law: it also covers the Court finding that the Commission committed a 'manifest error of appraisal'[664] and that the evidence relied on or the facts established by the Commission do not support the finding of law. This means that the GC does look at the facts, not to rehear the case but to see whether the factual basis of the Commission decision was correct or sufficient and that the burden of proof was discharged. It annuls decisions where it finds that the Commission drew the wrong conclusions from the facts. It can play an active role by ordering measures of inquiry such as experts' reports.[665]

(vi) Standard of Proof and Review

The EU Courts insist that the Commission produce 'sufficiently precise and coherent proof' to support its case.[666] However, there is great difficulty in the 'manifest error of appraisal' concept noted in Section 9.v.d.

Continental Can was an early case where the decision was annulled because the Commission had failed to establish why a particular type of container should be considered a relevant market. This meant there was no basis for its finding of dominance and the application of Article 102, even though

---

[658] Art. 6 TEU.

[659] And, implicitly, exclusionary as well as exploitative abuses, Case 6/72, *Europemballage Corp & Continental Can Co Inc* v. *Commission* [1973] ECR 215, although the decision was annulled because the Commission had not defined the market sufficiently, see Chaps. 6 and 7.

[660] Cases T-68/89, etc., *Società Italiana Vetro Spa* v. *Commission* [1992] ECR II-1403; Cases C-68/94 and 30/95, *France & SCPA* v. *Commission* [1998] ECR I-1375; see Chaps. 9 and 15. In the merger appeal Case T-342/99, *Airtours* v. *Commission* [2002] ECR II-2585, however, the GC narrowed the circumstances in which a collective dominant position can be held to exist, contrary to the Commission's approach in its decision, *Airtours/First Choice* [2000] OJ L93/1, [2002] 5 CMLR 494. See further Chaps. 9 and 15.

[661] Cases 56 and 58/64, *Établissements Consten SA & Grundig-Verkaufs-GmbH* v. *Commission* [1966] ECR 299; see Chap. 3.

[662] Cases C-2/01 P and 3/01 P, *Bundesverband der Arzneimittel-Importeure EV and the Commission* v. *Bayer AG* [2004] ECR I-23; Case C-74/04 P, *Commission* v. *Volkswagen* [2006] ECR I-6585.

[663] Legal certainty was cited in the *PVC* judgments (see n. 655) as being infringed when the Commission did not follow its own rules of procedure and could not produce the authenticated decision.

[664] Case 42/84, *Remia & Nutricia* v. *Commission* [1985] ECR 2545, para. 34.

[665] GC Rules of Procedure, Arts 64 to 76.

[666] See, e.g., Cases 29 and 30/83, *CRAM and Rheinzink* v. *Commission* [1984] ECR 1679, para. 20; Cases C-89/85, etc., *A. Ahlström Oy* v. *Commission* [1993] ECR I-1307, para. 127; Case T-201/04, *Microsoft* v. *Commission* [2007] ECR II-3601, para. 564.

the CJ confirmed the Commission's expansive interpretation of Article 102 to cover mergers.[667] In *Wood Pulp II* [668] the CJ appointed experts to produce a report on parallelism of prices in the wood pulp industry, whether the documents relied on by the Commission justified their conclusions on the pricing, and whether there was a distinction between the documents gathered before and after the statement of objections. A second experts' report into the structure and characteristics of the market was commissioned. These reports, particularly the finding that the market was oligopolistic, were crucial to the Court's judgment and it (largely) annulled the decision.

The GC was established largely to relieve the CJ of having to deal with complex issues of fact. One example of an assiduous examination of the factual basis of a competition decision was the wood pulp cartel already noted, and another was its treatment of the *Italian Flat Glass* decision in *Società Italiana Vetro* [669] where the GC submitted the documentary evidence to careful scrutiny and in the main found it seriously wanting. Two other examples of annulment are *Métropole* [670] and *European Night Services*.[671] In the former it annulled a decision because the Commission had not properly examined whether the fourth criterion for Article 101(3) exemption relating to the indispensability of restrictions was satisfied, and had taken into account the criteria in Article 106(2) TFEU[672] despite having decided that this Article did not apply. The latter decision was annulled because the Commission had not analysed whether there was a restriction of competition, had applied the de minimis test in too mechanistic a manner, had unsatisfactorily defined the market, and had applied the essential facilities doctrine without explaining why the resources at issue could be considered essential facilities.[673]

On the other hand, it is established that the GC does not interfere with the exercise of the Commission's powers of appraisal of what are essentially matters of economic assessment. In such cases the GC undertakes only a limited review. The CJ stated again in *Aalborg* (the *Cement Cartel*) that '[E]xamination by the Community judicature of the complex economic assessments made by the Commission must necessarily be confined to verifying whether the rules on procedure and on the statement of reasons have been complied with, whether the facts have been accurately stated and whether there has been any manifest error of appraisal or misuse of powers'.[674] The GC said the same thing in *Van den Bergh* in respect of its function in reviewing the Commission's decision as to the application of both Article 101(1) and Article 101(3).[675] It then, however, proceeded to examine

---

[667] Case 6/72, *Europemballage Corp & Continental Can Co Inc* v. *EC Commission* [1973] ECR 215.

[668] Cases C-89/85, etc., *A. Ahlström Oy* v. *Commission* [1993] ECR I-1307; see Chap. 9.

[669] Cases T-68/89, etc., *Società Italiana Vetro Spa* v. *EC Commission* [1992] ECR II-1403.

[670] Cases T-528, etc./93, *Métropole Télévision* v. *Commission* [1996] ECR II-649.

[671] Cases T-374–375, 384, and 388/94, *European Night Services* v. *Commission* [1998] ECR II–3141; see Chap. 4.

[672] Ex Art. 86(2) EC.

[673] The GC has been rigorous in its approach to Commission decisions under the Merger Regulation: see Chap. 15. So, also, was the CJ in Cases C-68/94 and 30/95, *France & SCPA* v. *Commission* [1998] ECR I-1375 (where the case went straight to the CJ because a Member State appealed against the decision: as Article 51 of the Statute of the Court has been amended by Council Decision 2004/407/EC, [2004] OJ L132/5, this would no longer be the case). The CJ took the view that the Commission's analysis of the post-merger market did not stand up to examination and that its evidence of the structural links between the parties was unconvincing. It therefore quashed the decision.

[674] Cases C-204/00 P, C-205/00 P, C-211/00 P, C-213/00 P, C-217/00 P, and C-219/00 P, *Aalborg Portland and others* v. *Commission* [2004] ECR I-123, echoing Case 42/84, *Remia* v. *Commission* [1985] ECR 2545. Reference is often made to the Commission's 'discretion' or 'margin of discretion' in this respect but it has been cogently argued that it is a 'margin of appreciation' rather than discretion (in that discretion involves choosing the standards according to which power is exercised or a decision made, while a margin of appreciation involves weighing up the evidence and assessing whether a given standard is reached, see O. Odudu, 'Article 101(3), Discretion and Direct Effect' [2002] ECLR 17; D. Bailey, 'Scope of Judicial Review Under Article 101 EC' (2004) 41 *CMLRev* 1327). In *GlaxoSmithKline* the GC again referred to the Commission's 'margin of discretion' under Article 101(3) (Case T-168/01, *GlaxoSmithKline Services Unlimited* [2006] ECR II-2696, para. 244) but in *Microsoft* (Case T-201/04, [2007] ECR II-3601, para. 89) it was 'margin of appreciation'. In Case C-389/10 P, *KME Germany AG* v. *Commission*, 8 December 2011, the appellants argued in terms of the 'margin of appreciation' while the CJ referred to the Commission's 'margin of discretion' (para. 102).

[675] Case T-65/98, *Van den Bergh Foods Ltd.* v. *Commission* [2003] ECR II-4653, paras. 80 and 135 respectively.

carefully the evidence on both matters before upholding the Commission.[676] It will be apparent from the cases discussed in other chapters of this book, however, that it comes down to what the EU Courts consider to be a 'manifest error of appraisal' and the practice has not been consistent.

Microsoft is a prime example of the GC wrestling with the inherent problems of engaging in only a limited review in an Article 102 case. It was seen in Chapter 7 that the GC explained there its role where 'complex' economic *and technical* appraisals are concerned before proceeding to examine the facts in considerable detail.[677]

87 The Court observes that it follows from consistent case law that, although as a general rule the Community Courts undertake a comprehensive review of the question as to whether or not the conditions for the application of the competition rules are met, their review of complex economic appraisals made by the Commission is necessarily limited to checking whether the relevant rules on procedure and on stating reasons have been complied with, whether the facts have been accurately stated and whether there has been any manifest error of assessment or a misuse of powers (Case T-65/96 *Kish Glass v Commission*...paragraph 64, upheld on appeal by order of the Court of Justice in Case C-241/00 *P Kish Glass v Commission*...see also, to that effect, with respect to Article [101], Case 42/84 *Remia and Others v Commission*...paragraph 34, and Joined Cases 142/84 and 156/84 BAT and *Reynolds v Commission*...paragraph 62).

88 Likewise, in so far as the Commission's decision is the result of complex technical appraisals, those appraisals are in principle subject to only limited review by the Court, which means that the Community Courts cannot substitute their own assessment of matters of fact for the Commission's (see, as regards a decision adopted following complex appraisals in the medico-pharmacological sphere, order of the President of the Court of Justice in Case C-459/00 P(R) *Commission v Trenker*...paragraphs 82 and 83; see also, to that effect, Case C-120/97 *Upjohn* [1999]...paragraph 34 and the case-law cited; Case T-179/00 *A. Menarini v Commission*...paragraphs 44 and 45; and Case T-13/99 *Pfizer Animal Health v Council*...paragraph 323).

89 However, while the Community Courts recognise that the Commission has a margin of appreciation in economic or technical matters, that does not mean that they must decline to review the Commission's interpretation of economic or technical data. The Community Courts must not only establish whether the evidence put forward is factually accurate, reliable and consistent but must also determine whether that evidence contains all the relevant data that must be taken into consideration in appraising a complex situation and whether it is capable of substantiating the conclusions drawn from it (see, to that effect, concerning merger control, Case C-12/03 P *Commission v Tetra Laval*...paragraph 39).

The reference in *Microsoft* to *Tetra Laval* is to the merger case in which the CJ set out the role of the EU Courts in dealing with complex economic assessments.[678] It will be seen in Chapter 15 that the GC has, despite its self-denying ordinance, subjected merger decisions to rigorous review and it seems ironic that recent judgments of the GC have tended to apply a lighter touch to Article 102 cases than to mergers.

Limiting the role of judicial review to 'manifest errors of appraisal' in situations of complex economic (and technical) assessments and in situations where the Commission is given a 'margin of appreciation/discretion' is problematic.[679] The pervasive problem is the Commission's multifaceted

---

[676] In respect of Art. 101(1) this meant confirming that the Commission was justified in holding that the agreements concerned were likely to significantly contribute to foreclosing the market (para. 118), and in respect of Art. 101(3) that the agreements did not produce objective advantages to compensate for its anti-competitive effect (para. 141), see Chaps. 3 and 4. The CJ upheld the GC's judgment, Case C-552/03 P, *Unilever Bestfoods (Ireland) Ltd v. Commission* [2006] ECR I-9091.

[677] Case T-201/04, *Microsoft v. Commission* [2007] ECR II-3601.

[678] Case C-12/03 P, *Commission v. Tetra Laval* [2005] ECR I-987, para. 39.

[679] Moreover, it has been pointed out that the extension of this in *Microsoft* to 'technical matters' exacerbates the matter: I. Forrester, 'A Bush in Need of Pruning: the Luxuriant Growth of "Light Judicial Review"', in C.-D. Ehlermann and M. Marquis (eds.), *European Competition Law Annual 2009: Evaluation of Evidence and its Judicial Review in Competition Cases* (Hart Publishing, 2010).

role and how far EU competition procedures are compliant with Article 6(1) of the ECHR and Article 47 of the Charter.[680] The Commission is not a tribunal within Article 6, as its decisions are those of an administrative authority[681] but the GC has held itself to be an independent and impartial court, established in order particularly to improve the judicial protection of individuals by making a close inspection of complex facts[682] and so it has been held that the requirements of Article 6(1) are satisfied by the right of the parties to challenge Commission decisions in that Court. However, the leeway given to the Commission by the limitation of judicial review to 'manifest errors of appraisal' where some of the most contentious findings of the Commission are concerned raises serious doubts as to the adequacy of the Union's procedures. Decisions emerging from a process whereby investigation, prosecution, and decision-making are rolled into one body are subjected to limited scrutiny, a system which many argue is deeply flawed.[683] The question was directly raised in a number of appeals from the GC to the CJ in respect of Commission decisions in the industrial and plumbing tube cartel, including *KME*.[684] The CJ judgments were given less than three months after the ECtHR judgment in *Menarini* had held that the Italian system did comply with the ECHR.[685] Before considering those 2011 judgments, however, we consider the other provision under which the GC can review Commission decisions, Article 261, because the *Industrial Tubes* judgments look at Articles 261 and 263 as a whole.

(vii) Appeals against Penalties: Article 261 TFEU

As already discussed[686] the Commission has a very wide discretion in setting fines under Regulation 1/2003, Article 23. Regulation 1/2003, Article 31 gives the Court 'unlimited jurisdiction to review decisions whereby the Commission has fixed a fine or periodic penalty payment'. Article 31 is pursuant to Article 261 TFEU[687] which provides that regulations may give the Court unlimited jurisdiction with regard to penalties provided for in such regulations. The action under Article 261 cannot be used to circumvent the time limits laid down in Article 263 as it not an autonomous remedy but part of the Court's Article 263 jurisdiction.[688]

The distinction between the Court's powers under Article 261 and under Article 263 is that under the former the Court has *full jurisdiction*. It may actually change the Commission's decision. It may cancel, increase, or reduce the fine (but not impose one where the Commission has not). The EU Courts are not bound by the Guidelines on Fines.[689] Under Article 263, however, the Court is limited to reviewing the legality of the decision and annulling all or part of it on the grounds laid down in the Article but cannot substitute its own judgment for that of the Commission. As with Article 263 itself, appeals against penalties go to the GC, with an appeal to the CJ.

---

[680] See Section 8.A.ii.

[681] Cases 209–215 and 218/78, *Van Landewyck v. Commission* [1980] ECR 3125, para. 101; Cases 100–103/80, *Musique Diffusion Française v. Commission* [1983] ECR 1825, para. 7; Case T-11/89, *Shell v. Commission* [1992] ECR II-757, para. 39.

[682] Case T-348/94, *Enso Española v. Commission* [1998] ECR II-1875, paras. 57–63; Cases T-25/95, etc., *Cimenteries CBR SA v. Commission* [2000] ECR II-491, paras. 718–719.

[683] For a very critical analysis of the present situation, see Forrester, 'A Bush in Need of Pruning' (cited in n. 679) and the literature cited in n. 605.

[684] Case C-272/09 P, *KME Germany AG v. Commission*, 8 December 2011.

[685] See Section 8.A.ii.d, p. 937.

[686] See Section 8.G.iv.

[687] Ex Art. 229 EC.

[688] Case T-252/03, *Fédération nationale de l'industrie et des commerces en gros des viandes (FNICGV) v. Commission* [2004] ECR II-3795.

[689] Case C-70/12 P, *Quin Barlo Ltd v. Commission*, 30 May 2013, para. 45.

The GC has been tolerant of the Commission's general approach to fining to a degree that has been criticised.[690] The CJ approved the change to higher fines for the sake of deterrence in *Pioneer* [691] and has not objected to the ever higher level of fines imposed during the last 30 years. The GC will reduce or quash the fine, however, when it takes a different view to the Commission of such matters as the duration of an infringement[692] or of an undertaking's level of involvement in an infringement.[693] The GC demands that the Commission follow the methodology laid down in the Guidelines on Fines, which creates legitimate expectations, but considers that the Commission has retained the necessary degree of discretion. In *Wieland Werke* the GC took a markedly 'hands-off' approach to reviewing fines.

Case T-116/04, *Wieland-Werke AG* v. *Commission* [2009] 1087

General Court

29 Whilst the Guidelines may not be regarded as rules of law, they nevertheless form rules of practice from which the Commission may not depart in an individual case without giving reasons (Case C-397/03 P *Archer Daniels Midland and Archer Daniels Midland Ingredients v Commission* …. paragraph 91 …).

30 It is therefore for the Court to verify, when reviewing the legality of the fines imposed by the contested decision, whether the Commission exercised its discretion in accordance with the method set out in the Guidelines and, should it be found to have departed from that method, to verify whether that departure is justified and supported by sufficient legal reasoning. In that regard, it should be noted that the Court of Justice has confirmed the validity, first, of the very principle of the Guidelines, and, secondly, the method which is there indicated (Joined Cases C-189/02 P, C-202/02 P, C-205/02 P to C-208/02 P and C-213/02 P *Dansk Rørindustri and Others v Commission*…paragraphs 252 to 255, 266, 267, 312 and 313).

31 The self-limitation on the Commission's discretion arising from the adoption of the Guidelines is not incompatible with the Commission's maintaining a substantial margin of discretion. The Guidelines display flexibility in a number of ways, enabling the Commission to exercise its discretion in accordance with the provisions of Regulation No 17, as interpreted by the Court of Justice (Dansk Rørindustri, paragraph 267).

32 Moreover, in areas such as determination of the amount of a fine imposed pursuant to Article 15(2) of Regulation No 17, where the Commission has a discretion, for example, as regards the amount of increase for the purposes of deterrence, review of the legality of those assessments is limited to determining the absence of manifest error of assessment (see, to that effect, Case T-241/01 Scandinavian *Airlines System v Commission*…paragraph 79).

33 Nor, in principle, does the discretion enjoyed by the Commission and the limits which it has imposed in that regard prejudge the exercise by the Community judicature of its unlimited jurisdiction (Joined Cases T-67/00, T-68/00, T-71/00 and T-78/00 *JFE Engineering and Others v Commission*…paragraph 538), which empowers it to annul, increase or reduce the fine imposed by the Commission (see, to that effect, Case C-3/06 P *Groupe Danone v Commission*…paragraphs 60 to 62; Case T-368/00 *General Motors Nederland and Opel Nederland v Commission*…paragraph 1101).

---

[690] See, e.g., I. Forrester, 'A Bush in Need of Pruning: the Luxuriant Growth of "Light Judicial Review"', in C.-D. Ehlermann and M. Marquis (eds.), *European Competition Law Annual 2009: Evaluation of Evidence and its Judicial Review in Competition Cases* (Hart Publishing, 2010). This is one aspect of the criticism of the intensity of the Court's judicial review of competition decisions generally.

[691] Cases 100–103/80, *Musique Diffusion Française SA* v. *Commission* (*Pioneer*) [1983] ECR 1825.

[692] See, e.g., the GC judgment in the *Cement Cartel* cases, Cases T-25/95, etc. *Cimenteries CBR SA v. Commission* [2000] ECR II-491.

[693] *Cimenteries CBR SA* v. *Commission* [2000] ECR II-491, in respect of one undertaking's involvement in the white cement market cartel.

The fact that under Article 261 the Court has 'full jurisdiction' and not merely a power of judicial review should, it is argued, enable it to subject the fines imposed by the Commission to far greater scrutiny and not just check that the Guidelines have been followed. While not curing perceived defects in the limitations of the judicial role under Article 263 such action would go some way to alleviating it in certain cases. The former President of the General Court urged a change of approach.

Bo Vesterdorf, 'The Court of Justice and Unlimited Jurisdiction: What Does It Mean in Practice?' (2009) 2 *Global Competition Policy* 6-7 (June)

Even if Article 23(3) of Regulation 1/2003 only indicates that the elements to be taken into consideration in calculating the fine are gravity and duration, it follows clearly from the case-law that the Commission, and therefore certainly also the Community Courts, must consider all relevant facts and circumstances of the case...which must include the overall general fairness of the sanction in view of all the general circumstances of any particular case. The unlimited jurisdiction granted to the Community Courts under Article 31 of Regulation 1/2003 and Article [261 TFEU] permits them to perform precisely this type of assessment. In view of the ever increasing level of fines imposed by the Commission, fines which now may amount to more than one billion Euros on a single undertaking and who knows how much more next time...it is my humble submission that it is now so much more necessary that the Community Courts fully exercise their unlimited jurisdiction and not just verify if the Guidelines have been correctly followed by the Commission.

Some of the most passionate arguments about fines before the GC are now about the amount of reduction which the Commission accords cartel participants under the Leniency Notice. In the *Graphite Electrodes* appeal the GC *increased* the fine on an undertaking which, having been granted leniency for cooperation with the Commission, then argued about the facts before the GC.[694] In *BASF* (*Choline Chloride cartel*) the applicant's successful argument that the global and European cartel arrangements in which it was implicated could not be considered a 'single and continuous infringement' of Article 101(1) resulted in its losing the benefit of the leniency policy with the result that its fine was increased by its victory.[695]

(viii) The KME judgment

The CJ's *KME* judgment was one of three given on the same day,[696] in which undertakings appealing from GC judgments in which they challenged Commission cartel decisions in the industrial/copper plumbing tubes sector argued, inter alia, that their right to effective judicial protection had been compromised by the GC's review of the decisions.[697] Because the three judgments are so similar only one is extracted here.

The applicant appealed against the GC's judgment on five grounds The first four were that the GC had made errors of law in respect of: the effect of the cartel on the relevant market, the determination

---

[694] Cases T-236/01, 244–246/01, 251/01, and 252/01, *Tokai Carbon Co Ltd v. Commission* [2004] ECR II-1181.

[695] Cases T-101/05 and T-111/05, *BASF v. Commission* [2007] ECR II-4949, paras. 212–3. BASF had been granted leniency for its cooperation over the global cartel. As there was no single continuous infringement the proceedings in respect of the global, as distinct from the European, cartel, were time-barred. It could not therefore be fined for the global cartel so leniency could not apply and the 10% reduction it had been given was removed.

[696] The other two were Case C-386/10 P, *Chalkor v. Commission* and Case C-389/10 P, *KME v. Commission (II)*.

[697] Case T-127/04, *KME v. Commission* [2009] ECR II-1167, Case T-25/05, *KME Germany AG v. Commission* [2010] ECR II-91; Case T-21/05, *Chalkor v. Commission* [2010] ECR II-1895.

of the size of the market, the infringement of the proportionality principle by the Commission, and the misapplication by the Commission of the Leniency Notice. The fifth ground was that the GC had violated its fundamental right to full and effective judicial review by failing to examine its arguments thoroughly, i.e. that the GC had deferred too much to the Commission's discretion and fallen short of the standard demanded by Article 6(1) of the ECHR. The extract from the judgment deals with the CJ's answer to the fifth plea.[698]

Case C-272/09 P, *KME Germany* v. *Commission, Court of Justice*, 8 December 2011

92 The principle of effective judicial protection is a general principle of European Union law to which expression is now given by Article 47 of the Charter (see Case C-279/09 *DEB*...paragraphs 30 and 31; order in Case C-457/09 *Chartry*...paragraph 25; and Case C-69/10 *Samba Diouf*...paragraph 49).

93 The judicial review of the decisions of the institutions was arranged by the founding Treaties. In addition to the review of legality, now provided for under Article 263 TFEU, a review with unlimited jurisdiction was envisaged in regard to the penalties laid down by regulations.

94 As regards the review of legality, the Court of Justice has held that whilst, in areas giving rise to complex economic assessments, the Commission has a margin of discretion with regard to economic matters, that does not mean that the Courts of the European Union must refrain from reviewing the Commission's interpretation of information of an economic nature. Not only must those Courts establish, among other things, whether the evidence relied on is factually accurate, reliable and consistent but also whether that evidence contains all the information which must be taken into account in order to assess a complex situation and whether it is capable of substantiating the conclusions drawn from it (see Case C-12/03 P *Commission* v *Tetra Laval*...paragraph 39, and Case C-525/04 P *Spain* v *Lenzing*...paragraphs 56 and 57).

95 With regard to the penalties for infringements of competition law, the second subparagraph of Article 15(2) of Regulation No 17 provides that in fixing the amount of the fine, regard is to be had both to the gravity and to the duration of the infringement.

96 The Court of Justice has held that, in order to determine the amount of a fine, it is necessary to take account of the duration of the infringements and of all the factors capable of affecting the assessment of their gravity, such as the conduct of each of the undertakings, the role played by each of them in the establishment of the concerted practices, the profit which they were able to derive from those practices, their size, the value of the goods concerned and the threat that infringements of that type pose to the European Community (*Musique Diffusion française and Others* v *Commission*, paragraph 129; *Dansk Rørindustri and Others* v *Commission*, paragraph 242; and Case C-534/07 P *Prym and Prym Consumer* v *Commission*...paragraph 96).

97 The Court has also stated that objective factors such as the content and duration of the anti-competitive conduct, the number of incidents and their intensity, the extent of the market affected and the damage to the economic public order must be taken into account. The analysis must also take into consideration the relative importance and market share of the undertakings responsible and also any repeated infringements (Joined Cases C-204/00 P, C-205/00 P, C-211/00 P, C-213/00 P, C-217/00 P and C-219/00 P *Aalborg Portland and Others* v *Commission*...paragraph 91).

98 This large number of factors requires that the Commission carry out a thorough examination of the circumstances of the infringement.

99 In the interests of transparency the Commission adopted the Guidelines, in which it indicates the basis on which it will take account of one or other aspect of the infringement and what this will imply as regards the amount of the fine.

---

[698] See A.-L. Sibony, 'Casenote on *KME* v. *Commission* (2012) 49 *CMLRev* 1977.

100 The Guidelines, which, the Court has held, form rules of practice from which the administration may not depart in an individual case without giving reasons compatible with the principle of equal treatment (Case C-397/03 P *Archer Daniels Midland and Archer Daniels Midland Ingredients* v *Commission*, paragraph 91), merely describe the method used by the Commission to examine infringements and the criteria that the Commission requires to be taken into account in setting the amount of a fine.

101 It is important to bear in mind the obligation to state reasons for Community acts. That is a particularly important obligation in the present case. It is for the Commission to state the reasons for its decision and, in particular, to explain the weighting and assessment of the factors taken into account (see, to that effect, *Prym and Prym Consumer* v *Commission*, paragraph 87). The Courts must establish of their own motion that there is a statement of reasons.

102 Furthermore, the Courts must carry out the review of legality incumbent upon them on the basis of the evidence adduced by the applicant in support of the pleas in law put forward. In carrying out such a review, the Courts cannot use the Commission's margin of discretion—either as regards the choice of factors taken into account in the application of the criteria mentioned in the Guidelines or as regards the assessment of those factors—as a basis for dispensing with the conduct of an in-depth review of the law and of the facts.

103 The review of legality is supplemented by the unlimited jurisdiction which the Courts of the European Union were afforded by Article 17 of Regulation No 17 and which is now recognised by Article 31 of Regulation No 1/2003, in accordance with Article 261 TFEU. That jurisdiction empowers the Courts, in addition to carrying out a mere review of the lawfulness of the penalty, to substitute their own appraisal for the Commission's and, consequently, to cancel, reduce or increase the fine or penalty payment imposed (see, to that effect, Joined Cases C-238/99 P, C-244/99 P, C-245/99 P, C-247/99 P, C-250/99 P to C-252/99 P and C-254/99 P *Limburgse Vinyl Maatschappij and Others* v *Commission*...paragraph 692).

104 It must, however, be pointed out that the exercise of unlimited jurisdiction does not amount to a review of the Court's own motion, and that proceedings before the Courts of the European Union are *inter partes*. With the exception of pleas involving matters of public policy which the Courts are required to raise of their own motion, such as the failure to state reasons for a contested decision, it is for the applicant to raise pleas in law against that decision and to adduce evidence in support of those pleas.

105 That requirement, which is procedural in nature, does not conflict with the rule that, in regard to infringements of the competition rules, it is for the Commission to prove the infringements found by it and to adduce evidence capable of demonstrating to the requisite legal standard the existence of the circumstances constituting an infringement. What the applicant is required to do in the context of a legal challenge is to identify the impugned elements of the contested decision, to formulate grounds of challenge in that regard and to adduce evidence—direct or circumstantial—to demonstrate that its objections are well founded.

106 The review provided for by the Treaties thus involves review by the Courts of the European Union of both the law and the facts, and means that they have the power to assess the evidence, to annul the contested decision and to alter the amount of a fine. The review of legality provided for under Article 263 TFEU, supplemented by the unlimited jurisdiction in respect of the amount of the fine, provided for under Article 31 of Regulation No 1/2003, is not therefore contrary to the requirements of the principle of effective judicial protection in Article 47 of the Charter.

107 It follows from this that, in so far as it relates to the rules of judicial review in the light of the principle of effective judicial protection, the fifth ground of appeal is unfounded.

It will be noticed that the CJ did not discuss Article 6 of the ECHR but rather relied solely on Article 47 of the Charter. It did not therefore consider compliance with the Article 6(1) or engage with the debate about the criminal nature of fines.[699] Rather, it concentrated on the adequacy of the intensity of the judicial review. It concluded that together Articles 261 and 263 guarantee effective judicial protection and satisfy Article 47. The judgment does suggest that 'light' judicial review is not enough and that the GC must truly engage with the Commission's 'complex economic assessments' (paragraph 94) but the effect of that will only be seen in the future practice of the GC. It is notable that the CJ lays great store by the 'unlimited jurisdiction' in Article 261, but that relates only to penalties, whereas some of the most contentious decisions of the Commission, particularly in Article 102 cases, have imposed remedies that have had far greater consequences for the undertakings concerned than the mere payment of any accompanying fine.

One commentator, Dr Temple Lang,[700] has contrasted the KME judgment (unfavourably) with the later judgment of the EFTA Court in the *Posten Norge* case.[701] The EFTA Court carefully considered Article 6 ECHR rather than Article 47 of the Charter (the Charter is not formally binding in EEA law). It had regard to *Menarini*, the *KME* judgments, and the Opinion of Advocate General Sharpston in *KME*. Dr Temple Lang considers the EFTA Court's statements in *Posten Norge* to be clearer than *KME* and broader in their implications than the Advocate General or *Menarini*.

Case E-15/10, *Posten Norge* v. *EFTA Surveillance Authority*, EFTA Court, 18 April 2012

88 Indeed, penalties such as the one at issue pursue aims of both repressive and preventive character. They are intended to act, in the interest of society in general and the good functioning of the EEA single market in particular, as a deterrent against future breaches of the competition rules both for the perpetrator and for all other undertakings that enjoy a dominant position on the market. Accordingly, having regard to the nature of the infringements in question and to the potential gravity of the ensuing penalties, it must be held that the proceedings at hand fall, as a matter of principle, within the criminal sphere for the purposes of Article 6 ECHR (compare the European Court of Human Rights *A. Menarini Diagnostics S.R.L.* v. *Italy*...see furthermore the Opinion of Advocate General Sharpston in Case C-272/09 P *KME Germany*... point 64).

89 As has been pointed out by ESA, Article 6 ECHR does not in all cases apply with its full stringency. The criminal head guarantees of Article 6 are applied in a differentiated manner, depending on the nature of the issue and the degree of stigma carried by certain criminal cases on the one hand and, on the necessity of the guarantee in question for the requirements of a fair trial on the other. Thus, to what degree these guarantees apply in a given case, must be determined with regard to the weight of the criminal charge at issue (see European Court of Human Rights *Jussila* v. *Finland*...and *Kammerer* v. *Austria*...).

90 Having regard to the nature and the severity of the charge at hand, the present case cannot be considered to concern a criminal charge of minor weight. The amount of the charge in this case is substantial and, moreover, the stigma attached to being held accountable for an abuse of a dominant position is not negligible. Thus, while the form of administrative review provided under Article 36 SCA may influence, with regard to several aspects, the way in which the guarantees provided by the criminal head of Article 6 ECHR are applied, this cannot detract from the necessity to respect these guarantees in substance (compare *A. Menarini Diagnostics S.R.L.* v. *Italy*, cited above, § 62).

---

[699] Cf. the Opinion of Sharpston AG who did discuss this and considered them criminal (she delivered her Opinion before the *Menarini* judgment).

[700] J. Temple Lang, 'Judicial Review of Competition Decisions under the European Convention on Human Rights and the Importance of the EFTA Court: the *Norway Post* Judgment' (2012) 37 *ELRev* 464.

[701] Case E-15/10, *Posten Norge* v. *EFTA Surveillance Authority*, 18 April 2012.

...

98 Also as far as past events involving complex economic features are concerned, a situation may arise in which the Court, while still considering ESA's reasoning to be capable of substantiating the conclusions drawn from the economic evidence, may come to a different assessment of a complex economic situation. However, the fact that the Court is restricted to a review of legality precludes it from annulling the contested decision if there can be no legal objection to the assessment of ESA, even if it is not the one which the Court would consider to be preferable (compare *Commission* v *Alrosa*, cited above, paragraphs 65–67; and the Opinion of Advocate General Kokott in that case, points 81–84).

99 This does not, however, mean that the Court must refrain from reviewing ESA's interpretation of information of an economic nature. Not only must the Court establish, among other things, whether the evidence relied on is factually accurate, reliable and consistent, but also whether that evidence contains all the information which must be taken into account in order to assess a complex situation and whether it is capable of substantiating the conclusions drawn from it (compare *Spain* v *Lenzing*, cited above, paragraphs 56 and 57; and, most recently, *KME* v *Commission*, cited above, paragraph 121).

100 Moreover, it must be recalled that Article 6(1) ECHR requires that subsequent control of a criminal sanction imposed by an administrative body must be undertaken by a judicial body that has full jurisdiction. Thus, the Court must be able to quash in all respects, on questions of fact and of law, the challenged decision (see, for comparison, European Court of Human Rights *Janosevic* v. *Sweden*…and *A. Menarini Diagnostics S.R.L.* v. *Italy*, cited above, § 59). Therefore, when imposing fines for infringement of the competition rules, ESA cannot be regarded to have any margin of discretion in the assessment of complex economic matters which goes beyond the leeway that necessarily flows from the limitations inherent in the system of legality review.

(ix) The Effects of Annulment

Article 264 TFEU states that if the action is well founded 'the Court of Justice of the European Union declare[s] the act concerned to be void'. However, if articles of the decision are severable, the Court can declare some void and leave others, i.e. a partial annulment. This is often done. The parts that are not annulled definitively form part of the Union legal structure and produce all their legal effects and therefore in *Compagnie Maritime Belge* annulling the fine for procedural reasons did not affect the legality of the rest of the decision finding the infringement.[702]

The EU Courts cannot substitute their own decision for that of the Commission. So, in *European Night Services* [703] the GC refused to annul the conditions which the Commission had attached to the Article 101(3) exemption and leave the applicants with an unconditional decision. It annulled the decision completely.[704]

Article 266 TFEU says:

The institution or institutions whose act has been declared void or whose failure to act has been declared contrary to the Treaties shall be required to take the necessary measures to comply with the judgment of the Court of Justice of the European Union.

---

[702] Case T-276/04, *Compagnie Maritime Belge* v. *Commission* [2008] ECR II-1277. The original fines on the shipping lines were annulled because the Commission had announced an intention to fine only the conference, not the individual shipping lines, Cases C-395 and 396/96 P, *Compagnie Maritime Belge and others* v. *Commission* [2000] ECR I-1365.

[703] Cases T-374–375, 384, and 388/94, *European Night Services* v. *Commission* [1998] ECR II-3141.

[704] In Case T-168/01, *GlaxoSmithKlineServices Unlimited* [2006] ECR II-2696, para. 320, the GC annulled the part of the decision refusing GlaxoSmithKline's request for an individual exemption under Art. 101(3) after that procedure had been abolished by Reg. 1/2003. The GC told the Commission to rule on the request for exemption insofar as GSK was still requesting it, as the annulment had retrospective effect.

This includes repaying any fine that has been paid, including default interest. Where the fine is partially reduced the relevant proportion and interest must likewise be repaid.[705]

This does not, however, mean that the Commission has to refund the fine of parties who did not challenge a decision annulled at the suit of other addressees. Twenty-eight of the 36 addressees of the *Wood Pulp* decision[706] brought an action for annulment. The CJ annulled or reduced the fines imposed on the applicants.[707] Subsequently the other addressees requested the Commission to refund to them the fines they had paid pursuant to the annulled articles. The Commission refused. The CJ upheld this: a decision finding an infringement of the competition rules addressed to each undertaking concerned individually can be annulled only as regards the addressees who have successfully challenged it. The other addressees had not challenged the decision within the two-month time limit and it continued to be valid and binding on them.[708]

(x) Appeals from the General Court to the Court of Justice

An appeal lies from the GC to the CJ on a point of law. This means that the appeal is limited to the grounds of lack of competence of the GC, a breach of procedure before it adversely affecting the interests of the applicant, or the infringement of Union law by the GC.[709] The appellant has to state the errors alleged to have been made by the GC. It is not sufficient for it simply to repeat the arguments it raised before the GC[710] and it may not adduce new arguments. The CJ cannot be asked to review the facts found by the GC, to raise matters of fact which were not found by the GC, or to consider the assessment of evidence adduced before the GC unless the GC committed a manifest error which is apparent from the documents submitted to it.[711] The CJ has explained the respective roles of the CJ and the GC on many occasions—see the following extract from the *Cement Cartel* appeal.[712]

Cases C-204/00 P, C-205/00 P, C-211/00 P, C-213/00 P, C-217/00 P, and C-219/00 P, *Aalborg Portland A/S* v. *Commission* [2004] ECR I-123

Court of Justice

The role of the Court in an appeal

47. In an appeal, the Court's task is limited to examining whether, in exercising its power of review, the [General Court] made an error of law. Under Article [256 TFEU] and Article 51, first paragraph, of the EC Statute of the Court of Justice, an appeal must be limited to points of law and must lie on grounds of lack of competence of the [General Court], a breach of procedure before it which adversely affects the interests of the applicant or infringement of Community law by the [General Court].

---

[705] Case T-53/03, *BPB* v. *Commission* [2008] ECR II-1333.

[706] [1985] OJ L85/1, [1985] 3 CMLR 474.

[707] Cases C-89/85, etc., *A. Ahlström Oy* v. *Commission* [1993] ECR I-1307.

[708] Case C-310/97 P, *Commission* v. *AssiDomän Kraft Products AB and Others* [1999] ECR I-5363.

[709] Art. 58 of the Statute of the Court of Justice.

[710] Case C-19/95 P, *San Marco* v. *Commission* [1996] ECR I-4435.

[711] Case C-53/92 P, *Hilti* v. *Commission* [1994] ECR I-667. In Case C-57/02 P, *Compañía española para la fabricación de aceros inoxidables SA (Acerinox)* v. *Commission* [2005] ECR I-6689, the CJ annulled the part of the decision relating to the Spanish market as it held that the GC had misrepresented the applicant's point of view and so the judgment contained an incorrect statement of reasons.

[712] See also, e.g., Case C-7/95 P, *John Deere* v. *Commission* [1998] ECR I-3111; Case C-185/95 P, *Baustahlgewebe GmbH* v. *Commission* [1998] ECR I-8417; Case C-199/92 P, *Hüls AG* v. *Commission (Polypropylene)* [1999] ECR II-4287; Cases

48. An appeal may therefore be based only on grounds relating to the infringement of rules of law, to the exclusion of any appraisal of the facts. The [General Court] has exclusive jurisdiction, first, to establish the facts except where the substantive inaccuracy of its findings is apparent from the documents submitted to it and, second, to assess those facts (see, *inter alia*, Case C-284/98 P *Parliament* v. *Bieber*...paragraph 31.

49. It follows that the appraisal of the facts by the [General Court] does not constitute, save where the clear sense of the evidence produced before it is distorted, a question of law which is subject, as such, to review by the Court of Justice (see, *inter alia*, Joined Cases C-280/99 P to C-2102/99 P *Moccia Irme and Others* v. *Commission*...paragraph 78).

50. Article [256 TFEU], Article 51, first paragraph, of the EC Statute of the Court of Justice and Article 112(1)(c) of the Rules of Procedure of the Court of Justice provide, in particular, that where the appellant alleges distortion of the evidence by the [General Court], he must indicate precisely the evidence alleged to have been distorted by that Court and show the errors of appraisal which, in his view, led to that distortion.

51. The requirements resulting from those provisions are not satisfied by an appeal which, without even including an argument specifically identifying the error of law allegedly vitiating the judgment of the [General Court], simply repeats or reproduces verbatim the pleas in law and arguments already put forward before that Court, including those which were based on facts expressly rejected by that Court. Such an appeal amounts in reality to no more than a request for re-examination of the application submitted to the [General Court], which the Court of Justice does not have jurisdiction to undertake (see, *inter alia*, the order in Case C-317/97 P *Smanor and Others* v. *Commission*...paragraph 21, and the judgment in Case C-352/98 P *Bergaderm and Goupil* v. *Commission*...paragraph 35).

52. It is on the basis of those considerations, in particular, that the Court rejected at the outset as manifestly inadmissible certain of the pleas in law and arguments put forward by the appellants.

The correction of a manifest error by the GC was made in *Aalborg*. The GC had included within the calculation of the fine to be imposed on one of the participants in the cement cartel the turnover of its Belgian subsidiary. However, at the time of the infringement the undertaking concerned had not yet assumed control of the Belgian company. This was apparent from the *Cement Cartel* decision itself.[713] The CJ reduced the fine by nearly €3 million as it considered it had the necessary evidence to give judgment itself. It was entitled to do this because Article 61 of the Statute of the Court of Justice provides that if an appeal is well founded the CJ must quash the GC's decision and may either refer the matter back to the GC or, 'where the state of proceedings so permits', itself give final judgment in the matter. The effect of this was nicely illustrated by CJ's judgment in *PVC Cartel II*. It held that the GC had wrongly refused to consider, on procedural grounds, Montedison's plea that its right of access to the file had been infringed, and its plea about the Commission's power to fine in the circumstances of the case.[714] The CJ therefore partially annulled the GC's decision. However, it decided that this was a case in which it could give final judgment itself. It therefore considered Montedison's pleas and rejected them, leaving Montedison in the same position as it was after the GC judgment.[715] Article 61 was also applied in *Meca-Medina* where the CJ set aside the GC's judgment on the grounds that it had committed an error of law in holding that because purely sporting rules fell outside Articles 45

C-238, 244–245, 247, 250, 251–252, and 254/99 P, *Limburgse Vinyl Maatschappij NV* v. *Commission* [2002] ECR I-8375; Case C-359/01 P, *British Sugar plc* v. *Commission* [2004] ECR I-4933; Case C-202/07 P, *France Télécom* v. *Commission* [2009] ECR I-2369, para. 41; Case C-70/12 P, *Quin Barlo Ltd* v. *Commission*, 30 May 2013, paras 25–31.

[713] [1994] OJ L343/1, [1995] 4 CMLR 327.

[714] The peculiarities of the proceedings against the PVC cartel, which resulted in a first annulled decision being replaced by a second one, are described in Section 9.A.v.c, p. 1035.

[715] Cases C-238, 244–245, 247, 250, 251–252, and 254/99, *Limburgse Vinyl Maatschappij NV* v. *Commission* [2002] ECR I-8375, [2003] 4 CMLR 397, paras. 355–379, 416–428, and 647–698.

and 56 TEU they were also excluded from the competition rules. The CJ proceeded to decide whether the IOC's doping rules were in fact subject to Articles 101 and 102.[716] Errors of law do not lead to the setting aside of a judgment where it is upheld on other grounds.[717]

In some cases applicants have claimed that proceedings before the GC were of such an excessive length that their right to a fair trial within a reasonable period under Article 6(1) of the ECHR was infringed. The CJ considers the length of the proceedings in the light of the complexity of the case.[718]

Where appeals against judgments of the GC on fines are concerned, it is also necessary to distinguish between the functions of the CJ and of the GC. The CJ holds firmly that it is for the GC to examine how the Commission assessed the gravity of the infringement and to decide whether the fine should be changed. The CJ will not substitute its own assessment for that of the GC. It stated in *Ferriere Nord*:[719]

31. As regards the allegedly unjust nature of the fine, it is important to point out that it is not for this Court, when ruling on questions of law in the context of an appeal, to substitute, on grounds of fairness, its own assessment for that of the [General Court] exercising its unlimited jurisdiction to rule on the amount of fines imposed on undertakings for infringements of Community law (Case C-310/93 P, *BPB Industries and British Gypsum* v. *E.C. Commission*...). In contrast, the Court of Justice does have jurisdiction to consider whether the [General Court] has responded to a sufficient legal standard to all the arguments raised by the appellant with a view to having the fine abolished or reduced.

(xi) Interim Measures by the Court under Article 278 TFEU

Bringing an Article 263 action for annulment does not automatically suspend the contested act. However, Article 278 TFEU states:

Actions brought before the Court of Justice of the European Union shall not have suspensory effect. The Court may, however, if it considers that circumstances so require, order that application of the contested act be suspended.

Also, Article 279 TFEU provides that in any cases before it, the Court may prescribe any necessary measures. The President of the GC normally hears applications for suspension. His or her decision may be appealed to the CJ.[720]

---

[716] Case C-519/04 P, *Meca-Medina and Majcen* v. *Commission* [2006] ECR I-6991, see Chap. 3. And see also Case C-57/02 P, *Compañía española para la fabricación de aceros inoxidables SA (Acerinox)* v. *Commission* [2005] ECR I-6689.

[717] As in, e.g., Case C-501/06 P, *GlaxoSmithKline Services Unlimited* v. *Commission* [2009] ECR I-9291; Case C-113/07 P, *SELEX Systemi Integrati SpA* v. *Commission* [2009] ECR I-2207. For instances where the GC judgment was set aside completely see, e.g., the GC upholding the Commission decision in the *Net Book Agreement* case, Case C-360/92 P, *Publishers' Association* v. *Commission* [1995] ECR II-23; replacing the GC's finding of a non-existent act in *PVC I* with a finding of an act which should be annulled: Cases C-137/92 P, *Commission* v. *BASF and others* [1994] ECR I-2555; setting aside the GC judgment against the Commission in Case C-310/97 P, *AssiDomän Kraft Products AB and others* [1999] ECR I-5363; and the overturning of the GC in Case C-441/07P, *European Commission* v. *Alrosa* [2010] ECR I-5949.

[718] e.g., Case C-185/95 P, *Baustahlgewebe GmbH* v. *Commission* [1998] ECR I-8417; Case C-194/99 P, *Thyssen Stahl AG* v. *Commission* [2003] ECR I-10821; Cases C-403 and 405/04 P, *Sumitomo Metal Industries Ltd* v. *Commission* [2007] ECR I-729. In *Baustahlgewebe* the General Court had taken 32 months between the end of the written procedure and the decision to open the oral procedure and 22 months between the oral procedure and the judgment. The CJ held the plea of excessive delay well founded but as it had not prejudiced the outcome of the proceedings, the Court merely reduced the fine of three million ECUs by 50,000 ECUs. In *Sumitomo* the case had lasted four years and three months, but it involved seven undertakings and three languages and virtually all the facts forming the basis of the contested decision were disputed at first instance and therefore had to be verified. The CJ therefore held the length of the case was justified.

[719] Case C-219/95, *Ferriere Nord* v. *Commission* [1997] ECR I-4411; see also Case C-310/93 P, *BPB Industries and British Gypsum Ltd* v. *Commission* [1995] ECR I-865, para. 34; Case C-185/95 P, *Baustahlgewebe GmbH* v. *Commission* [1998] ECR I-8417 paras. 128–129; Case C-359/01 P, *British Sugar* v. *Commission* [2004] ECR I-4933, paras. 47–48; Cases C-189/02 P, 202/02 P, 208/02 P, and 213/02 P, *Dansk Rørindustri A/S and others* v. *Commission* [2005] ECR I-5425, paras. 244–246 and 302.

[720] The Commission appealed in *Atlantic Container Line* when the President suspended its decision: Case C-149/95 P(R), *Commission* v. *Atlantic Container Line and others* [1995] ECR I-2165.

In order for a decision to be suspended the applicants must show that the main action is admissible and that suspension is urgently needed to prevent them suffering irreparable damage which could not be remedied in the event of their winning the main action. On this basis suspension was ordered, inter alia, in *United Brands*,[721] *Magill*,[722] *Net Book Agreement*,[723] *ADALAT*,[724] *Atlantic Container Line*,[725] *Van den Bergh*,[726] and *IMS*.[727] Suspension was refused in *Microsoft* on the grounds that the undertaking had failed to show the likelihood of serious and irreparable damage.[728] The Commission's intention to publish a revised 'non-confidential version' of a final decision was suspended in *Akzo Nobel*.[729]

The President has to balance the harm to the applicant from non-suspension (foreseeable with a sufficient degree of probability)[730] with any harm which will be suffered by other parties if the suspension is granted. In *Adalat*, for example, the President considered that as a result of the order the applicant, Bayer, might be obliged to lower the prices of the drug in issue, risking major and irrecoverable losses of profit, and that there was a risk that the pharmaceutical base of one subsidiary 'might be deprived of its economic basis, resulting in the dismissal of many employees'. He considered this would be disproportionate in relation to the interests of wholesalers in Spain and France in increasing their exports.[731] Moreover, he was concerned that the Commission's interpretation of the law (i.e. its view of what constitutes an 'agreement' for the purposes of Article 101) was questionable (as, indeed it proved to be).[732]

In *Van den Bergh* the Commission's decision prohibited a distribution system for impulse ice-cream which involved freezer exclusivity and which was the subject of proceedings before the Irish courts. The Irish High Court decided that the distribution system did not infringe but expressed its intention to seek an Article 267 ruling from the CJ. Meanwhile the Commission's decision was appealed to the GC. The President of the GC said that the contradiction between the decision and the judgment was 'contrary to the general principle of legal certainty' and that in the circumstances the Commission's interest in having the infringement brought to an end could not prevail over the applicant's interest in not running the risk of jeopardising its distribution system or over the interest in limiting the effects of a contradiction in the application of the provisions of the Treaty.[733] He therefore granted a suspension.[734]

The suspension in *IMS* was of an interim decision. Again, as with *Adalat*, the President of the GC was concerned about the legal basis of the Commission's decision (which concerned the compulsory licensing of a copyright). The suspension was confirmed by the President of the CJ.[735] The decision was ultimately withdrawn and a final decision not adopted.[736]

[721] Case 27/76 R, *United Brands v. Commission* [1976] ECR 425.

[722] Cases 76–77 and 91/89 R, *RTE and others v. Commission* [1989] ECR 1141.

[723] Case 56/89 R, *Publishers' Association v. Commission* [1989] ECR 1693.

[724] Case T-41/96 R, *Bayer v. Commission* [1996] ECR II-381.

[725] See n. 720.

[726] Case T-65/98 R, *Van den Bergh Foods Ltd v. Commission* [1998] ECR II-2641.

[727] Case T-184/01 R, *IMS Health v. Commission* [2001] ECR II-3193 (President of the GC), Case C-481/01 P(R), *IMS Health v. Commission* [2002] ECR I-3401 (President of the CJ).

[728] Case T-201/04 R, *Microsoft v. Commission* [2004] ECR II-4463.

[729] Case T-345/12 R, *Akzo Nobel v. Commission*, 16 November 2012.

[730] Case C-280/93 R, *Commission v. Germany* [1993] ECR I-3667.

[731] [1996] ECR II-407 at paras. 59–60.

[732] The Commission's decision was annulled in Case T-41/96, *Bayer v. Commission* [2000] ECR II-3383, confirmed by the CJ, Cases C-2/01 P and 3/01 P, *Bundesverband der Arzneimittel-Importeure EV and the Commission v. Bayer AG* [2004] ECR I-23, see Chap. 3.

[733] Case T-65/98 R, *Van den Bergh Foods Ltd v. Commission* [1998] ECR II-2641, paras. 72–33.

[734] The Commission's decision was upheld by the GC, Case T-65/98, *Van den Bergh Foods v. Commission* [2003] ECR II-4653, aff'd by the CJ, Case C-552/03 P, *Unilever Bestfoods (Ireland) Ltd v. Commission* [2006] ECR I-9091.

[735] Case C-481/01 P(R), *IMS Health v. Commission* [2002] ECR I-3401 (President of the CJ).

[736] See Chap. 7.

The GC may suspend the obligation to give a bank guarantee ensuring payment of the fine but this is done only in very exceptional circumstances.[737] The GC (and on appeal, the CJ) refused to do it in respect of one of the shipping lines fined in *TACA*.[738]

B. ACTIONS FOR DAMAGES UNDER ARTICLE 340 TFEU

Article 340 TFEU provides for damages for non-contractual liability:

In the case of non-contractual liability, the Union shall, in accordance with the general principles common to the laws of the Member States, make good any damage caused by its institutions or by its servants in the performance of their duties.

This raises the possibility that where a decision of the Commission is overturned by the EU Courts the undertakings concerned may be able to sue the Commission for any damage caused to it by the defective decision.

Actions under Article 340 are notoriously difficult for plaintiffs to win.[739] The Union institution must have committed a sufficiently serious breach of a superior rule of law intended to confer rights on individuals, and the test for 'sufficiently serious' is whether the institution manifestly and gravely disregarded the limits on its discretion.[740] These conditions were held not to be fulfilled in *Holcim* where the GC excused the Commission on the grounds, inter alia, of the difficulties it had faced in the case, which was one of the *Cement Cartel* appeals:

114. ... regard being had to the fact that *Cement* was a particularly complex case, involving a very large number of undertakings and almost the entire European cement industry, to the fact that the structure of Cembureau made the investigation difficult owing to the existence of direct and indirect members, and to the fact that it was necessary to analyse a great number of documents, including in the applicant's specific situation, it must be held that the defendant was faced with complex situations to be regulated.

115. Last, it is necessary to take account of the difficulties in applying the provisions of the EC Treaty in matters relating to cartels ... Those practical difficulties were all the greater because the factual elements of the case in question, including in the part of the decision concerning the applicant, were numerous.[741]

Stanley Adams, however, did succeed in a damages claim under Article 340 when the Commission's negligent breach of confidentiality in revealing his identity to Hoffmann-La Roche led to his imprisonment in a Swiss jail.[742] Airtours (now MyTravel) commenced proceedings against the Commission in respect of the prohibition decision of its merger with First Choice which was annulled by the GC,[743] as did Schneider Electric in respect of the *Schneider/Legrand* annulled merger decision:[744] for these, see Chapter 15.

---

[737] See Case T-295/94 R, *Buchmann* v. *Commission* [1994] ECR II-1265 (one of several applications for such interim measures by the undertakings fined in the *Cartonboard Cartel* [1994] OJ L243/1, [1994] 5 CMLR 547).

[738] Case T-191/98 R, *DSR-Senator Lines* v. *Commission* [1999] ECR II-2531, confirmed Case C-364/99 P(R), *DSR-Senator Lines* v. *Commission* [1999] ECR I-8733.

[739] See P. Craig and G. de Búrca, *EU Law: Text, Cases and Materials* (5th edn, Oxford University Press, 2011), Chap. 16.

[740] Case C-352/98 P, *Bergaderm and Goupil* v. *Commission* [2000] ECR I-5291.

[741] Case T-28/03, *Holcim* v. *Commission* [2005] ECR II-1357, aff'd by the CJ, Case C-282/05 P, *Holcim (Deutschland) AG* v. *Commission* [2007] ECR I-2941. The undertaking was claiming damages in respect of the charges it had incurred in providing for the bank guarantee for the fine pending the appeal. The GC held that the claim was, in any case, barred on limitation grounds, as it had not been brought within five years of the guarantee being provided. The five years did not run from the date that the General Court had annulled the decision.

[742] Case 53/84, *Stanley Adams* v. *Commission* [1985] ECR 3595.

[743] Case T-212/03, [2008] ECR II-1967.

[744] Case C-440/07 P, *Commission* v. *Schneider Electric* [2009] ECR I-6413, largely setting aside Case T-351/03, [2007] ECR II-2237.

10. ENFORCEMENT BY THE NATIONAL COMPETITION AUTHORITIES WITHIN THE EUROPEAN COMPETITION NETWORK

A. GENERAL

As discussed previously[745] the NCAs have, since 1 May 2004, played a much more significant role in the enforcement of the EU competition rules. Regulation 1/2003 creates a system of parallel competences in which the competition rules are enforced by a network of competition authorities (through the ECN), as well as by the national courts. Article 5 of Regulation 1/2003 provides that the 'competition authorities of the Member States shall have power to apply Articles 101 and 102' in individual cases.[746]

Regulation 1/2003, Article 5

Powers of the competition authorities of the Member States

The competition authorities for the Member States shall have the power to apply Articles [101 and 102 TFEU] in individual cases. For the purpose, acting on their own initiative or on a complaint, they may take the following decisions:

— requiring that an infringement be brought to an end,

— ordering interim measures,

— accepting commitments,

— imposing fines, periodic penalty payments or any other penalty provided for in their national law.

Where on the basis of the information in their possession the conditions for prohibition are not met they may likewise decide that there are no grounds for action on their part.

Article 5 was interpreted by the CJ in *Tele2Polska* [747] in a way which seriously limits the powers of the NCAs.[748] The CJ held that Article 5 does not permit NCAs to adopt decisions finding that Article 102 has not been infringed. An NCA may decide that Article 102 *has* been infringed and may decide that there are no grounds for action. It cannot, however, actually take a non-infringement decision. Although the preliminary reference in *Tele2Polska* concerned only Article 102, there can be little doubt, given the wording of the judgment and the Opinion of Advocate General Mazák, that it also applies to Article 101, so that NCAs are equally precluded from taking decisions holding that Article 101 is inapplicable.

Regulation 1/2003 leaves the Member State to determine which body will enforce the rules and what mechanisms for investigating infringements and enforcing decisions will apply. It does not demand any particular arrangement, so long as an NCA is designated[749] and the provisions of

---

[745] See Sections 3 and 5, and Chap. 2.

[746] The designation of the bodies responsible for the application of the rules is left to the Member States, Reg. 1/2003, Art. 35. The individual websites of each NCA are accessible through a link from the Commission's website, <http://ec.europa.eu/competition/ecn/competition_authorities.html>, some of them in more than one language. Many of them are available there in English.

[747] Case C-375/09, *Prezes Urzędu Ochrony Konkurencji i Konsumentów v. Tele2 Polska sp. z o.o., now Netia SA SA* [2011] ECR I-3055.

[748] See S. Brammer, 'Casenote on *Prezes Urzędu Ochrony Konkurencji i Konsumentów v. Tele2 Polska sp. z o.o., now Netia SA SA*' (2012) 49 *CMLRev* 1163.

[749] Reg. 1/2003, Art. 35.

the Regulation can be complied with. There is no further attempt at harmonisation. Article 35 of Regulation 1/2003 provides that the designated authorities may include courts. The Commission Report to the Council on the functioning of Regulation 1/2003[750] says that Member States' enforcement systems still diverge on matters such as fines, criminal sanctions, liability of groups of undertakings, succession of undertakings, prescription periods, the standard of proof, structural remedies, and priority setting, and that 'this aspect may merit further examination and reflection'.[751]

The creation of a network of authorities responsible for enforcing the same rules obviously creates a number of potential difficulties, in particular, how work is to be allocated between the respective authorities,[752] whether information collected by one authority can be passed on to another, where an application for leniency should be made, whether one authority can conduct inspections on behalf of another and how a uniform and consistent approach in the interpretation and application of the provisions can be maintained. These, and other matters, are dealt with in Regulation 1/2003 itself (especially Articles 11–16) and more fully in the Commission's Notice on cooperation within the Network of Competition Authorities (the Cooperation Notice). Each NCA has signed a statement acknowledging the principles set out in the Notice and agreeing to abide by the principles.[753]

In January 2010 the Commission inaugurated the publication five times a year of the 'ECN Brief', designed to keep the reader informed of the activities of the ECN and disseminate news of enforcement and other activities of the NCAs.[754]

B. DIVISION OF WORK

(i) Case Allocation—Which Authority is Well Placed to Deal with a Case?

Chapter IV of Regulation 1/2003 deals with cooperation, including cooperation between the Commission and the competition authorities of the Member States. Further, a Joint Statement of the Council and the European Commission on the Functioning of the Network of Competition Authorities (the Joint Statement)[755] sets out the main principles governing the ECN, whilst the Commission's Cooperation Notice provides fuller and more specific detail of cooperation and division of work. Under the new system Article 101 and 102 cases can be dealt with by:

- A single NCA (possibly with the assistance of others);
- Several NCAs acting in parallel;[756] or
- The Commission.[757]

The basic principles are that a case should be dealt with by the authority best placed to deal with it and able to restore or maintain competition in the market, and that cases should be allocated according to a predictable process and as soon as possible in the procedure.[758]

---

[750] See n. 59.

[751] Commission Report to the Council on the functioning of Regulation 1/2003, para. 33; see also the accompanying Staff Working Paper (cited in n. 60), paras. 200–207.

[752] The principles on work allocation set out in this Notice are of critical importance to a complainant seeking to lodge its complaint with the authority best placed to deal with the case.

[753] This gives companies a legitimate expectation that the principles set out in the Notice will be adhered to.

[754] Available on the Commission's ECN page at<http://ec.europa.eu/competition/ecn/index_en.html>.

[755] Joint Statement of the European Council and the European Commission on the functioning of the network of competition authorities, 10 December 2002, available at <http://ec.europa.eu/competition/ecn/joint_statement_en.pdf>.

[756] Cases should be dealt with by a single authority where possible.

[757] Cooperation Notice [2004] OJ C101/43, para. 5.

[758] Joint Statement, paras. 11–14.

In order for an authority to be well placed, there must be a material link between the infringement and the territory of the authority (the conduct has substantial direct actual or foreseeable effects in the territory), the authority must be able to bring the entire infringement effectively to an end (either on its own or in parallel with another authority), and the authority must be able to gather the evidence required (whether or not with the assistance of another authority). Where two or more NCAs are well placed to act, then one NCA only should act where the action of one would be sufficient to bring the entire infringement to an end. If it would not, then two or more NCAs should act. The authorities should coordinate their action and where possible designate a lead authority for the case.[759] The Cooperation Notice guidance in this respect is set out in the next extract. It can be seen from the extract that the guidance is relatively limited and does not deal with the question of what is to happen in the event of a dispute as to which NCA should act and/or which NCA should take the lead in an investigation.

The Commission is likely to be best placed to deal with an agreement or practice where: it has effects on competition in three or more Member States; the conduct is linked with other Union provisions which may be exclusively or more effectively applied by the Commission; or the Union interest requires it (to develop competition policy or to ensure effective enforcement).[760]

The determination as to which authority deals with the case may be of critical importance to the undertakings investigated, the complainant (if any), and the authorities themselves. As already noted, modernisation did not entail harmonisation of procedure, sanctions,[761] or judicial review between the Member States or between the Member States and the Commission. Even where Regulation 1/2003 did make provision for the handling of certain matters within the ECN, problems remain.[762] The allocation principles previously discussed are set out, with examples, in the Cooperation Notice.

Commission Notice on Cooperation within the Network of Competition Authorities [2004] OJ C101/43

8. An authority can be considered to be well placed to deal with a case if the following three cumulative conditions are met:

(1) the agreement or practice has substantial direct actual or foreseeable effects on competition within its territory, is implemented within or originates from its territory;

(2) the authority is able to effectively bring to an end the entire infringement, i.e., it can adopt a cease and desist order the effect of which will be sufficient to bring an end to the infringement and it can, where appropriate, sanction the infringement adequately;

(3) it can gather, possibly with the assistance of other authorities, the evidence required to prove the infringement.

9. The above criteria indicate that a material link between the infringement and the territory of a Member State must exist in order for that Member State's competition authority to be considered well placed. It can be expected that in most cases the authorities of those Member States where competition is substantially affected by an infringement will be well placed provided they are capable of effectively bringing the infringement to an end through either single or parallel action unless the Commission is better placed to act (see below paragraphs 14 and 15).

[759] Joint Statement, para. 18.

[760] Joint Statement, para. 19.

[761] In the UK, the maximum level of fine was amended and harmonised with the EU maximum, see OFT Guideline 423, 'Guidance as to the appropriate amount of a penalty'.

[762] See, e.g., R. Nazzini, *Concurrent Proceedings in Competition Law* (Oxford University Press, 2004); S. Brammer, 'Concurrent Jurisdiction under Regulation 1/2003 and the Issue of Case Allocation' (2005) 42 *CMLRev* 1383; A. Andreangeli, 'The Impact of the Modernisation Regulation on the Guarantees of Due Process in Competition Proceedings' (2006) 31 *ELRev* 342.

10. It follows that a single NCA is usually well placed to deal with agreements or practices that substantially affect competition mainly within its territory.

Example 1: Undertakings situated in Member State A are involved in a price fixing cartel on products that are mainly sold in Member State A.

The NCA in A is well placed to deal with the case.

11. Furthermore single action of an NCA might also be appropriate where, although more than one NCA can be regarded as well placed, the action of a single NCA is sufficient to bring the entire infringement to an end.

Example 2: Two undertakings have set up a joint venture in Member State A. The joint venture provides services in Member States A and B and gives rise to a competition problem. A cease and desist order is considered to be sufficient to deal with the case effectively because it can bring an end to the entire infringement. Evidence is located mainly at the offices of the joint venture in Member State A.

The NCAs in A and B are both well placed to deal with the case but single action by the NCA in A would be sufficient and more efficient than single action by [the] NCA in B or parallel action by both NCAs.

12. Parallel action by two or three NCAs may be appropriate where an agreement or practice has substantial effects on competition mainly in their respective territories and the action of only one NCA would not be sufficient to bring the entire infringement to an end and/or to sanction it adequately.

Example 3: Two undertakings agree on a market sharing agreement, restricting the activity of the company located in Member State A to Member State A and the activity of the company located in Member State B to Member State B.

The NCAs in A and B are well placed to deal with the case in parallel, each one for its respective territory.

13. The authorities dealing with a case in parallel action will endeavour to coordinate their action to the extent possible. To that effect, they may find it useful to designate one of them as a lead authority and to delegate tasks to the lead authority such as for example the coordination of investigative measures, while each authority remains responsible for conducting its own proceedings.

14. The Commission is particularly well placed if one or several agreement(s) or practice(s), including networks of similar agreements or practices, have effects on competition in more than three Member States (cross-border markets covering more than three Member or several national markets).

Example 4: Two undertakings agree to share markets or fix prices for the whole territory of the Community. The Commission is well placed to deal with the case.

Example 5: An undertaking, dominant in four different national markets, abuses its position by imposing fidelity rebates on its distributor in all these markets. The Commission is well placed to deal with the case. It could also deal with one national market so as to create a 'leading' case and other national markets could be dealt with by NCAs, particularly if each national market requires a separate assessment.

15. Moreover, the Commission is particularly well placed to deal with a case if it is closely linked to other Community provisions which may be exclusively or more effectively applied by the Commission, or if the Community interest requires the adoption of a Commission decision to develop Community competition policy when a new competition issue arises or to ensure effective enforcement.

In order to ensure that allocation takes place as quickly as possible, and normally within a period of two months,[763] Article 11(3) of Regulation 1/2003 imposes an obligation on the NCAs to inform the Commission and other NCAs 'before or without delay after commencing the first formal investigative measure'.[764] Further, the Commission is obliged to transmit copies of documents to the

[763] Cooperation Notice [2004] OJ C101/43, para. 18.

[764] In the UK this is after the use of powers of investigation set out in ss. 26–28 of the Competition Act 1998, see OFT Guideline 442, 'Guideline on Modernisation', para. 7.7.

NCAs that it has collected pursuant to its powers of investigation under Articles 18–21 of Regulation 1/2003. Once a case has been initially allocated the case should not ordinarily be reallocated unless the facts known about the case change materially during the course of the proceedings.[765] Article 13 of Regulation 1/2003 specifically provides that an authority (the Commission or an NCA) may suspend proceedings or reject a case that is being, or has been, dealt with by another competition authority.[766]

It is possible that a decision by the Commission under Article 11(6) to remove a case from an NCA and deal with it itself is a challengeable act under Article 263 TFEU[767] although decisions of NCAs to terminate or open proceedings are challengeable only under their national laws.

(ii) Transfer of Information

Where an authority does suspend national proceedings or reject a complaint on the grounds that it is being dealt with by another authority, that authority is permitted to transfer information, including confidential information, to the authority which is dealing with the case. Regulation 1/2003, Article 12(1) provides generally for the Commission and the NCAs to provide one another with and use in evidence 'any matter of fact or of law, including confidential information'.[768] In order to protect the interests of individuals and undertakings, safeguards exist against the use and exchange of this information in certain circumstances. In particular, the competition authorities are bound by an obligation of professional secrecy, the information transferred can be used only for the purposes of applying Articles 101 or 102 (and in certain circumstances national competition law) and in respect of the subject matter for which it was collected,[769] and the information can only be used to impose sanctions on *natural* persons where the law of the transmitting authority foresees sanctions of a similar kind in relation to the infringement, or the information has been collected in a way that affords the person the same level of protection of rights provided for under the rules of the receiving authorities. Thus, by Article 12(3), an NCA which may not impose sanctions on individuals, may not transfer information to an NCA which may, unless: (1) the information was collected in a way which respects the rights of defence afforded to the individuals by the rules of the receiving authority (but custodial sanctions can be imposed only where both the transmitting and the receiving authority can impose such a sanction); or (2) the receiving authority does not use the information in proceedings against an individual but only in proceedings against an undertaking. The safeguards are explained more fully in paragraph 28 of the Commission's Cooperation Notice.

Commission Notice on Cooperation within the Network of Competition Authorities [2004] OJ C101/43

28. The exchange and use of information contains in particular the following safeguards for undertakings and individuals

(a) First, Article 28 of the Council Regulation [Regulation 1/2003] states that 'the Commission and competition authorities of the Member States, their officials, servants and other persons working under the supervision of these authorities...shall not disclose information acquired or exchanged by them

---

[765] Cooperation Notice, para. 19.

[766] The Commission can also reject a complaint which lacks Union interest or which fails to substantiate an allegation, see Section 13.F, p. 1071. National provisions may also provide an alternative basis for suspending a complaint.

[767] See Section 10.C.ii, p. 1060.

[768] The information must of course have been collected in a legal manner by the transmitting authority.

[769] Reg. 1/2003, Art. 12(2).

pursuant to the' Council Regulation which is 'of the kind covered by the obligation of professional secrecy'. However, the legitimate interest of undertakings in the protection of their business secrets may not prejudice the disclosure of information necessary to prove an infringement of Articles [101 and 102]. The term 'professional secrecy' used in Article 28 of the Council Regulation is a Community law concept and includes in particular business secrets and other confidential information. This will create a common minimum level of protection throughout the Community.

(b) The second safeguard given to undertakings relate to the use of information within the network. Under Article 12(2) of the Council Regulation, information so exchanged can only be used in evidence for the application of Articles [101 and 102] and for the subject matter for which it was collected. According to Article 12(2) of the Council Regulation, the information exchanged may also be used for the purpose of applying national competition law in parallel in the same case. This is, however, only possible if the application of national law does not lead to an outcome as regards the finding of an infringement different from that under Articles [101 and 102].

(c) The third safeguard given by the Council Regulation relates to sanctions on individuals on the basis of information exchanged pursuant to Article 12(1). The Council Regulation only provides for sanctions on undertakings for violations of Articles [101 and 102]. Some national laws also provide for sanctions on individuals in connection with violations of Articles [101 and 102]. Individuals normally enjoy more extensive rights of defence (e.g., a right to remain silent compared to undertakings which may only refuse to answer questions which would lead them to admit that they have committed an infringement[770]). Article 12(3) of the Council Regulation ensures that information collected from undertakings cannot be used in a way which would circumvent the higher protection of individuals. This provision precludes sanctions being imposed on individuals on the basis of information exchanged pursuant to the Council Regulation if the laws of the transmitting and receiving authorities do not provide for sanctions of a similar kind in respect of individuals, unless the rights of the individual concerned as regards the collection of evidence have been respected by the transmitting authority to the same standard as they are guaranteed by the receiving authority. The qualification of the sanctions by national law ('administrative' or 'criminal') is not relevant for the purpose of applying Article 12(3) of the Council Regulation. The Council Regulation intends to create a distinction between sanctions which result in custody and other types of sanctions such as fines on individuals and other personal sanctions. If both the legal system of the transmitting state and that of the receiving authority provide for sanctions of similar kind (e.g., in both Member States fines can be imposed on a member of the staff of an undertaking who has been involved in the violation of Article [101 or 102]), information exchanged pursuant to Article 12 of the Council Regulation can be used by the receiving authority. In that case, procedural safeguards in both systems are considered to be equivalent. If on the other hand, both legal systems do not provide for sanctions of a similar kind, the information can only be used if the same level of protection of the rights of the individual has been respected in the case at hand (see Article 12(3) of the Council Regulation). In the latter case however, custodial sanctions can only be imposed where both the transmitting and the receiving authority have the power to impose such a sanction.

It has been argued that, despite these provisions, serious doubts remain as to how well the rights of the defence are safeguarded by the exchange of information provided for by Article 12(1).[771] There is a particular problem, for instance, in the divergence between the Member States' legal systems in the protection given to certain classes of information, such as what is covered by legal professional privilege.[772] This could result in an NCA using information it would have been unable to collect under the

---

[770] See Case 374/87, *Orkem v. Commission* [1989] ECR 3283 and Case T-112/98 *Mannesmannröhren-Werke AG v. Commission* [2001] ECR II-729 (Commission's own footnote).

[771] A. Andreangeli, 'The Impact of the Modernisation Regulation on the Guarantees of Due Process in Competition Proceedings' (2006) 31 *ELRev* 342.

[772] For the position on legal professional privilege in Union law, see Section 8.B.vii, p. 957.

rules of its own jurisdiction.[773] There are particular problems in respect of the exchange of information connected with leniency applications, as discussed in Section 10.B.iii. The Commission Report suggested that the provisions in Article12(3) about information and criminal sanctions are 'too far-reaching and an obstacle to efficient enforcement' and might appropriately be re-examined.[774]

(iii) Leniency Applications

Both in Chapter 9 and earlier in this chapter, the importance of leniency regimes in the fight against cartels has been stressed, and the Commission's leniency regime discussed.[775] According to the Commission's website, as at 22 November 2012 all the then Member States except Malta operated leniency programmes. Because, however, there is no EU-wide system 'an application for leniency to a given authority is not to be considered as an application for leniency to any other authority'.[776] An undertaking contemplating a leniency application will therefore have to consider making an application to *all* authorities which have competence to apply Article 101 in the territory affected by the infringement (which have leniency policies) and which are likely to be considered to be well placed to deal with the infringement (even if the infringement takes place in three or more Member States the applicants may not be sure that the Commission will take jurisdiction). In view of the importance of timing in leniency applications (total immunity is usually available only to the first to come forward),[777] it will usually be advisable to make simultaneous applications. An authority considering opening an investigation as a result of a leniency application has a duty to inform other members of the ECN.[778] Information submitted to the network in this way may not, however, be used by the receiving authorities as a basis for starting an investigation on their own behalf. Further, information will, generally,[779] only be transmitted pursuant to Article 12 with the consent of the leniency applicant that has submitted the information voluntarily.[780]

Given the Commission's belief that leniency plays an important part in the fight against cartels, the inability for firms to file a single 'EU' leniency application was a notable omission from the Cooperation Notice. Even though fewer Member States operated leniency programmes in 2004 it would have been possible, for example, to have established the Commission as the central recipient and coordinator of NCAs which did have such programmes or to have provided that NCAs may receive leniency applications on behalf of another NCA. The modernisation programme did not make such provision, however. The Commission was anxious that the efficacy of leniency should not be undermined by decentralisation[781] but the post-May 2004 position had clear deficiencies from the view of both the competition authorities and the (potential) applicant.

---

[773] Andreangeli, 'The Impact of the Modernisation Regulation' (cited in n. 771), 354–356; B. Vesterdof, 'Legal Professional Privilege and the Privilege against Self-Incrimination in EC Law: Recent Developments and Current Issues' [2004] Fordham Corp L Inst 19 (B. Hawk (ed.), 2005); see e.g., the UK, where legal professional privilege extends to communications with in-house lawyers (cf. the position in EU law, discussed in Section 8.B.vii) and the OFT says: 'Whilst UK privilege rules would apply to cases being investigated in the UK by the OFT on its own behalf, the OFT could be sent the communications of in-house lawyers, or lawyers qualified outside the EU, by an NCA from another Member State where the communication of such lawyers are not privileged. Under those circumstances, the OFT may use the documentation received from the other NCA in its investigation' (OFT Guideline 404, 'Powers of Investigation', 6.3).

[774] Para. 27, see also the Staff Working Paper, paras. 244–245.

[775] See Section 8.G.v, p. 1019 and Chap. 9, Section 3.B.ii.b, p. 676.

[776] Cooperation Notice [2004] OJ C101/43, para. 37.

[777] See Section 8.G.v, p. 1019.

[778] Reg. 1/2003, Art. 11.

[779] But see Cooperation Notice [2004] OJ C101/43, para. 41 for exceptions to this.

[780] Cooperation Notice [2004] OJ C101/43, paras. 39–42.

[781] S. Blake and D. Schnichels, 'Leniency Following Modernisation: Safeguarding Europe's Leniency Programmes' [2004] ECLR 765.

C. Gauer and M. Jaspers, 'Designing a European Solution for a "One Stop Leniency Shop"' (2006) *ECLR* 685, 686–687

The current system has certain deficits both from the (potential) immunity applicant's...point of view and from the Competition Authorities' perspective...

An applicant that has been involved in a cartel covering more than one jurisdiction may be faced with a number of potentially applicable leniency programmes with different rules and procedures that may even appear to be contradictory...

This fact raises two different problems. First, certain discrepancies between the existing programmes (as well as the absence of programmes in certain jurisdictions) create what can be qualified as a 'race to the top'. An applicant will only be willing to come forward under any programme if it can qualify under the most restrictive programme and if it is satisfied with the lowest degree of legal certainty provided by the least beneficial programme. If, for example, an authority does not give any assurance to applicants before the very end of its proceedings, the potential applicant will balance that uncertainty before applying to any authority. Discrepancies not only make the assessment and the decision to report illegal activities more complex but some discrepancies may even deter applicants from reporting certain conduct at all.

Secondly, multiple filing with a large number of authorities is often cumbersome, costly and difficult to organise within a very short period of time. In addition, applicants would normally be bound by a duty of co-operation vis-a-vis all these authorities, irrespective of whether the authorities would in the end investigate the case or not.

The same deficits have also some unwanted consequences from the Competition Authorities' perspective. Primarily, the absence of leniency programmes in some jurisdictions and the 'race to the top' created by the discrepancies between the existing programmes could have adverse effects on those programmes that offer a more favourable treatment to applicants and would seem to function well. It can result in potentially less applications to the authorities and to less cartel detection in the EU.

Moreover, even if the current system ensures an efficient division of work between the authorities, processing leniency applications and granting immunity in cases where the authorities know that they will not take action is unnecessarily burdensome.

Finally, the safeguards set out in the Network Notice create in a number of cases over protection of applicants...This is in particular the case when two authorities with different immunity applicants for the same cartel wish to exchange information and need to abstain from imposing any fines on the other applicant in order to do so.

In the light of these problems the Competition Commissioner announced in April 2005 that she was consulting on the idea of a 'one-stop shop' for leniency applications.[782] In the event, the ECN considered various ways of dealing with the difficulties.[783] First, a system of mutual recognition could have been established, by which immunity or a reduction of fines granted by one authority would be recognised by all other members of the ECN. This was rejected as impracticable as the authority receiving the application would have to check with all the others in order to see whether the applicant qualified (was it the first? did another authority already have sufficient information? etc.) which would inevitably cause delays in a situation where speed is vital. Also, it would be unsatisfactory without some degree of harmonisation between the policies. Secondly, a fully centralised 'one-stop shop' could have been established, by which all leniency applications would be made to the Commission: if the case was later allocated to an NCA (or NCAs) the leniency application would go

---

[782] Neelie Kroes, 'The First Hundred Days', speech, Brussels, 7 April 2005, available on DG Comp's website.

[783] C. Gauer and M. Jaspers, 'Designing a European Solution for a "One Stop Leniency Shop"' (2006) *ECLR* 685.

with the allocation. That was also rejected as being impracticable as, again, the Commission would have to ensure that no NCA had sufficient information to act before granting immunity; participants in mainly national cartels might not apply if it meant becoming embroiled with the Commission; and it would deprive the NCA of direct contact with the applicant in the crucial period when the authority is preparing for an inspection by using the information provided. Thirdly, the ECN considered a system analogous to the regime established by the Merger Regulation,[784] whereby jurisdictional criteria would be developed for allocating cases between authorities and the applicants would approach those which would be dealing with their case. This solution was rejected because of the impossibility of formulating such criteria satisfactorily, as at the time the applicant was considering a leniency application it would not necessarily be aware of the extent and effects of the cartel, and different applicants might approach different authorities. Moreover, the Commission has power to take action against any cartel under Regulation 1/2003, Article 11(6).

The ECN turned instead to further harmonisation. In September 2006 it adopted the ECN Model Leniency Programme (MLP). The aim was to produce a model setting out the minimum standards with which all ECN policies should be aligned.[785] It is without prejudice to an NCA adopting a more favourable stance towards applicants. The explanatory notes to the programme stated:

8. While it is highly desirable to ensure that all CAs operate a leniency programme, the variety of legislative frameworks, procedures and sanctions across the EU makes it difficult to adopt one uniform system. The ECN Model Programme therefore sets out the principal elements which, after the soft harmonisation process has occurred, should be common to all leniency programmes across the ECN. This would be without prejudice to the possibility for a CA to add further detailed provisions which suit its own enforcement system or to provide for a more favourable treatment of its applicants if it considers it to be necessary in order to ensure effective enforcement.

The MLP (revised in November 2012) provides for immunity (Type 1 applications: Type 1A is immunity before inspections, Type 1B is immunity after inspections, corresponding to paragraphs 8(a) and 8(b) of the Commission's 2006 Notice),[786] subject to conditions; and for a reduction in fines (Type 2 applications),[787] subject to conditions. It also contains procedural requirements, including a 'marker' system (as under the Commission's 2006 Notice)[788] and the acceptability of oral applications.[789] It provides for NCAs to accept 'summary applications' for immunity or leniency containing more limited information than normally required, where the applicant has filed, or is in the process of filing, an immunity application with the Commission.[790] The explanatory notes exhort those Member States which can impose sanctions on individuals to ensure that employees and directors of applicants for leniency are protected, in order to ensure the efficient working of the corporate programme.[791] The Commission's 2006 Notice[792] is fully in line with the MLP.

---

[784] Reg. 139/2004 [2004] OJ L24/1, see Chap. 15.

[785] Or, in the case of Member States without a leniency programme, adopted and aligned. In some Member States the adoption of, or alterations to, a leniency programme required legislation or some other form of law-making not under the control of the NCA, which meant that the wish of the NCA to have such a programme was not definitive of the matter.

[786] ECN Model Leniency Programme, paras. 5–8.

[787] ECN Model Leniency Programme, paras. 9–12.

[788] ECN Model Leniency Programme, paras. 16–18.

[789] ECN Model Leniency Programme, paras. 28–30.

[790] ECN Model Leniency Programme, paras. 22–25. This was changed in November 2012. Previously only the applicant for Type I immunity could submit a summary application to NCAs. See 'European Competition Network refines ots Model Leniency Programme' MEMO/12/887. The ECN page on the DG Comp website contains a list of NCAs which accept summary applications, see <http://ec.europa.eu/comm/competition/ecn/accepting_nca.pdf>. As at 22 November 2012 all 26 Member States with a leniency policy accepted summary applications.

[791] ECN Model Leniency Programme, Explanatory Notes, para. 15. For criminal sanctions, see Section 12, p. 1064.

[792] See Section 8.G.v, p. 1019.

In October 2009 the Commission published a report, ECN Model Leniency Programme: Report on Assessment of the State of Convergence.[793] This reported that the adoption of the MLP had encouraged Member States to introduce and/or develop their own leniency policies. It also reported on the divergences which remained and concluded that it should form the 'basis for reflections whether any further convergence is needed'.[794]

Possible problems have arisen in the operation of the MLP from the judgments of the CJ in *Pfleiderer*[795] and *Donau Chemie*.[796] In both cases litigants before national courts have sought to obtain from the NCAs in the Member States copies of leniency statements made by the defendants.[797] In *Pfleiderer* the CJ was asked, inter alia, whether Articles 11 and 12 of Regulation 1/2003 were to be interpreted as meaning that a party bringing a civil law claim could not be given access to leniency material which the NCA had received. The CJ held that it was a matter for national law and pointed out that neither the Cooperation Notice, the Leniency Notice, nor the MLP are binding on the courts and tribunals of the Member States. The judgments are discussed in Chapter 14. In the light of *Pfleiderer*, in May 2012 the ECN endorsed a Resolution in which the NCAs took the joint position that leniency materials should be protected against disclosure to the extent necessary to ensure the effectiveness of the leniency system.[798]

C. CONSISTENT APPLICATION OF ARTICLES 101 AND 102

(i) General

It has been explained that, despite the creation of a network of authorities, the Commission has sought to retain its central role 'as the guardian of the Treaty' having 'the ultimate but not the sole responsibility for developing policy and safeguarding consistency when it comes to the application of EC competition law'.[799]

(ii) Mechanism of Cooperation

Article 11 of Regulation 1/2003 deals with cooperation between the Commission and the competition authorities of the Member States, providing that the NCAs and Commission should apply the EU competition rules in 'close cooperation'.[800] It has already been seen that it provides for the Commission and NCAs respectively to inform each other when acting under Article 101 or 102,[801] and for the early allocation of cases. Article 11(4) also provides for the NCAs to inform the Commission[802] 30 days prior to the adoption of a decision applying Articles 101 or 102 and requiring that the infringement be brought to an end.[803] The Commission may then make written

---

[793] Available at <http://ec.europa.eu/competition/ecn/model_leniency_programme.pdf>, and see MEMO/09/456.

[794] Leniency Report, para. 66.

[795] Case C-360/09, *Pfleiderer AG v. Bundeskartellamt* [2011] ECR I-5161. See S. Völcker, 'Casenote on *Pfleiderer AG v. Bundeskartellamt*' (2012) 49 *CMLRev* 695; P. J. Slot, 'Does the Pfleiderer Judgment Make the Fight against International Cartels More Difficult?' [2013] *ECLR* 197.

[796] Case C-536/11, *Bundeswettbewerbsbehörde v. Donau Chemie AG*, 6 June 2013.

[797] See S. Völcker, 'Casenote on *Pfleiderer AG v. Bundeskartellamt AG v. Bundeskartellamt*' (2012) 49 *CMLRev* 695.

[798] Resolution of the Meeting of the Heads of the European Competition Authorities, 23 May 2012.

[799] Cooperation Notice, para. 43.

[800] Reg. 1/2003, Art. 11(1).

[801] NCAs informed the Commission of 180 new case investigations in 2005 (Commission's *XXXVth Report on Competition Policy* (Commission, 2006), para. 210).

[802] The information may also be shared with the NCAs, Reg. 1/2003, Art. 11(4).

[803] Art. 11(5) states that the NCAs may consult the Commission on any case involving the application of Community (now Union) law. This may be useful, e.g., where the NCA wishes to adopt a decision rejecting a complaint or closing a procedure, etc.

observations on the case before the adoption of the decision by the NCA, or may decide itself to initiate proceedings. Article 11(6) of Regulation 1/2003 provides that the initiation of proceedings by the Commission relieves the NCAs of their competence to apply Articles 101 and 102.[804] 'This means that once the Commission has opened proceedings, NCAs cannot act under the same legal basis against the same agreement(s) or practice(s) by the same undertaking(s) on the same relevant geographic and product market.'[805] The existence of Article 11(6) is thus a powerful weapon in the hands of the Commission and gives it considerable leverage over an NCA when it disapproves of the decision it is about to adopt. The Commission deals with the full consequence of its Article 11(6) power in its Cooperation Notice. The Notice indicates that it will only rarely initiate proceedings where a case has initially been allocated to another NCA.[806] At the date of the Report in April 2009 it had never done so, and attributed this to 'the commitment of national competition authorities towards coherent application, extensive horizontal exchanges in the ECN including in dedicated sectoral sub-groups, as well as informal exchanges between the Commission services and the national competition authorities in the context of the Article 11(4) submissions'.[807]

D. EU AND NATIONAL COMPETITION LAW

National competition authorities are of course entrusted with the enforcement of their own domestic competition rules as well as the EU competition rules. The question of whether and when they may or must apply national rules, EU rules, or both to anti-competitive conduct and the relationship between EU and national competition law is dealt with in Section 11.

11. THE RELATIONSHIP BETWEEN EU AND NATIONAL COMPETITION LAW

It has always been the case that Articles 101 and 102 and the domestic competition rules of the Member States can be applied concurrently. The applicability of Articles 101 and 102 has not precluded the application of the national competition provisions.[808] The fact that the rules may apply concurrently obviously leads to the possibility that their joint application may not always achieve the same outcome. Important questions which have arisen therefore are whether an NCA or national court could, for example: (1) authorise an agreement or practice prohibited by Articles 101 or 102; or (2) condemn conduct which is not prohibited by Union law (for example, because an agreement does not infringe Article 101(1) or meets the criteria of Article 101(3)).

In the context of the EUMR, the allocation of jurisdiction over mergers between the EU and national authorities has always been defined by the regulation itself.[809] In contrast, Regulation 17 did not deal with this situation. Rather, case law developed which provided, in accordance with the principle of supremacy[810] and Article 10 EC (now Article 4 TEU),[811] that national law could be applied so

---

[804] See Section 10.B.i, p. 1052.

[805] Cooperation Notice [2004] OJ C101/43, para. 51.

[806] The Commission did not open proceedings in any of the 80 cases from 18 different NCAs in which it received information under Art. 11(4) in 2005 (Commission's *XXXVth Report on Competition Policy* (Commission, 2006), paras. 216–217).

[807] Staff Working Paper, para. 264.

[808] Case 14/68, *Walt Wilhelm v. Bundeskartellamt* [1969] ECR 1.

[809] This is dealt with in Chap. 15. A Notice on referrals deals with the circumstances in which jurisdiction may be passed by the Commission to the competent national authorities and vice versa.

[810] See Chap. 2.

[811] See Chap. 8, Section 3.

long as its application did not 'prejudice the full and uniform application of Community law or the effects of measures taken or to be taken to implement it'.[812] The case law made it clear that a national authority could not authorise an agreement or conduct prohibited by Community law,[813] but was less clear on the question of whether, and if so when, national rules could be used to prohibit an agreement authorised at the Community level. The position is now more clearly dealt with in Article 3 of Regulation 1/2003.

Regulation 1/2003, Article 3

Relationship between Articles [101] and [102] of the Treaty and national competition laws

1. Where the competition authorities of the Member States or national courts apply national competition law to agreements, decisions by associations of undertakings or concerted practices within the meaning of Article [101(1) TFEU] which may affect trade between Member States within the meaning of that provision, they shall also apply Article [101 TFEU] to such agreements, decisions or concerted practices. Where the competition authorities of the Member States or national courts apply national competition law to any abuse prohibited by Article [102 TFEU], they shall also apply [Article 102 TFEU].

2. The application of national competition law may not lead to the prohibition of agreements, decisions by associations of undertakings or concerted practices which may affect trade between Member States but which do not restrict competition within the meaning of Article [101(1) TFEU], or which fulfil the conditions of Article [101(3) TFEU] or which are covered by a Regulation for the application of Article [101(3) TFEU]. Member States shall not under this Regulation be precluded from adopting and applying on their territory stricter national laws which prohibit or sanction unilateral conduct engaged in by undertakings.

3. Without prejudice to general principles and other provisions of Community law, paragraphs 1 and 2 do not apply when the competition authorities and the courts of the Member States apply national merger control laws nor do they preclude the application of provisions of national law that predominantly pursue an objective different from that pursued by Articles [101 and 102 TFEU].

It can be seen from this that Article 3(1) provides that where an NCA or national court applies national competition law to conduct which constitutes an agreement, decision, or concerted practice within the meaning of Article 101 or an abuse prohibited by Article 102, which affects trade between Member States,[814] it *shall* also apply Article 101 or Article 102.[815] National authorities are thus obliged when applying national law to agreements and abusive conduct that affect trade between Member States to also apply Union law.

In order to provide a level playing field,[816] Article 3(2) deals with the relationship between Union and national law and, specifically, with when national authorities may apply stricter national laws to agreements or conduct. The position differs depending upon whether Article 101 or Article 102 applies. If an agreement is authorised by Article 101, either because it does not restrict competition

---

[812] Case 14/68, *Walt Wilhelm* v. *Bundeskartellamt* [1969] ECR 1, para. 9.

[813] *Walt Wilhelm* v. *Bundeskartellamt* [1969] ECR 1, para. 9. The fact that an agreement had been authorised at the national level did not preclude the Commission from subsequently finding that the agreement in fact infringes Art. 101: see Case C-360/92 P, *Publishers' Association* v. *Commission* [1995] ECR I-23.

[814] For the meaning of an effect on trade between Member States, see Chap. 3.

[815] Reg. 1/2003, Art. 3(1).

[816] Reg. 1/2003, recital 8.

within the meaning of Article 101(1), it fulfils the criteria of Article 101(3), or satisfies the conditions of a block exemption, it cannot be prohibited by national law. The national authorities are, however, free to apply national competition laws which are stricter than Article 102 to unilateral conduct.[817] They may therefore prohibit or impose sanctions on unilateral conduct engaged in by undertakings which does not constitute an abuse of a dominant position.[818] The Commission would like to revisit Article 3(2) as it is swayed by complaints that 'diverging standards fragment business strategies that are typically formulated on a pan-European or global basis'.[819]

Article 3(2) does not deal with the position where conduct is prohibited by Article 101 or Article 102. However, the principle of supremacy of Community law means that such an agreement or conduct cannot be permitted under national law.

Article 3(3) makes it clear that neither Article 3(1) nor Article 3(2) applies where the authority wishes to apply national merger control rules or national provisions that predominantly pursue a different objective to agreements or conduct. An NCA applying national merger rules to an acquisition or joint venture which is not a concentration with a Community dimension (or which has a Community dimension but has been referred back to the NCA) does not have to apply Article 101 or Article 102. Further, the Regulation does not preclude the implementation of more onerous 'national legislation, which protects other legitimate interests provided that such legislation is compatible with general principles and other provisions of Community law'.[820] This means that in the UK, for example, regulators, when applying sectoral powers which pursue a predominantly different objective to Articles 101 and 102, are not obliged to apply Article 101 or Article 102. To the extent that they are applying the UK competition rules or sectoral powers pursuing the same objective, however, they are obliged to apply Articles 101 and 102 and to comply with Article 3(2).

An interesting case dealing with the principle of supremacy of EU law and the relationship between EU and national law was CIF.[821] This case concerned Italian legislation, dating from 1923, which established a consortium of domestic match manufacturers, CIF. The legislation had been altered over time but essentially conferred a monopoly on CIF over the right to manufacture and sell matches for consumption on the Italian match market. Complex rules governing the internal workings of the consortium set out production quotas for the different members of the consortium. The Italian competition authority investigated the market at the complaint of a German match manufacturer which was having trouble penetrating the Italian market. Although the Commission considered that some breaches of Article 101 had been committed by the undertakings acting 'autonomously',[822] it also declared the Italian legislation establishing and governing CIF to be contrary to Article 101, read in conjunction with what were then Articles 3(1)(g) and 10 EC.[823]

CIF challenged both the assessment of the facts and the question of whether the authority was competent to determine the validity of the national law with Community law. The Tribunale amministrativo regionale per il Lazio referred several questions to the CJ for a preliminary ruling, including the question whether Article 101 requires or permits the NCA to disapply a national measure which requires or facilitates agreements contrary to Article 101 and to penalise the anti-competitive conduct of the undertakings or, in any event, to prohibit it for the future, and if so, with what legal

---

[817] In the UK such conduct may, therefore, be examined under the market investigation provisions of the Enterprise Act 2002.

[818] In the UK, the competition authorities may investigate a market and impose remedies under the Enterprise Act 2002.

[819] Report, para. 22, Staff Working Paper, para. 181.

[820] Reg. 1/2003, recital 9.

[821] Case C-198/01, *Consorzio Industrie Fiammiferi (CIF)* v. *Autorità Garante della Concorrenza e del Mercato* [2003] ECR I-8055.

[822] See also Chap. 3.

[823] See also Chap. 8.

consequences. In its judgment the CJ stressed that the primacy of Community law required any provision of national law which contravenes a Community rule to be disapplied and that the duty applied to all organs of the State, including administrative authorities.[824] It made no difference that the undertakings themselves could not be held accountable for infringements of Articles 101 or 102 required by national law.[825] The obligations of the Member State were distinct and the NCA remained duty bound to disapply the national legislation.[826] The CJ thus gave the following answer to the first question referred by the Italian court:

58. In light of the foregoing considerations, the answer to be given to the first question referred for a preliminary ruling is that, where undertakings engage in conduct contrary to Article [101(1) TFEU] and where that conduct is required or facilitated by national legislation which legitimises or reinforces the effects of the conduct, specifically with regard to price-fixing or market-sharing arrangements, a national competition authority, one of whose responsibilities is to ensure that Article [101 TFEU] is observed:

— has a duty to disapply the national legislation;

— may not impose penalties in respect of past conduct on the undertakings concerned when the conduct was required by the national legislation;

— may impose penalties on the undertakings concerned in respect of conduct subsequent to the decision to disapply the national legislation, once the decision has become definitive in their regard;

— may impose penalties on the undertakings concerned in respect of past conduct where the conduct was merely facilitated or encouraged by the national legislation, whilst taking due account of the specific features of the legislative framework in which the undertakings acted.

Had the complaint been made to and brought before the Commission, it would not have had the power directly to disapply the national legislation that was incompatible with EU law.

12. CRIMINALISATION AND SANCTIONS AGAINST INDIVIDUALS

EU competition law does not impose criminal liability or any type of sanction on natural persons, i.e. it does not punish individuals. The conduct of employees, directors, and officers by which an undertaking infringes the competition rules results in fines for the undertaking and not in penalties for those individuals.[827]

As we saw in Chapter 9 there is, however, a global trend for criminalising some forms of 'hard-core' cartel conduct. An increasing number of jurisdictions do impose criminal liability on individuals for cartel behaviour.[828] The most notorious of these is the US, where the Sherman Act may be enforced by the DOJ through both civil and criminal processes.[829] In practice only clear, intentional

---

[824] Case C-198/01, paras. 48–50.

[825] There is a distinction between national law which requires a breach of the rules and that which merely encourages or makes it easier for undertakings to engage in autonomous anti-competitive conduct, see Chap. 3.

[826] Case C-198/01, para. 51. Generally such a step cannot expose the undertakings to sanctions in respect of actions taken before the disapplication, see Case C-198/01, paras. 52–55 and Chap. 3.

[827] See the discussion of fines, in Section 8.G.iv, p. 996 ff. Where individuals give misleading or incorrect information in the course of an inspection under Art. 20, for instance, the fine for the procedural offence is levied on the undertaking. Although the Commission now has power to conduct an inspection on the homes of individuals under Art. 21, it is still only the undertaking that is responsible for what is found there. Of course, indulging in anti-competitive practices may amount to a breach of contract meriting dismissal, particularly if the undertaking has a proper compliance programme in place. There are now instances where undertakings have commenced proceedings against employees whose unauthorised conduct has resulted in fines being imposed on the undertaking.

[828] In C. Beaton-Wells and C. Parker, 'Justifying Criminal Sanctions for Cartel Conduct: A Hard Case' (2013) 1(1) J Antitrust Enforcement 198, 199 the figure is given as more than 30. See Chap. 9, Section 2.B.i.e.

[829] The Federal Trade Commission, in contrast, has no criminal jurisdiction.

violations, mostly cases of explicit price-fixing or bid-rigging, are the subject of criminal proceedings,[830] but prosecutions in this type of case are pursued as a matter of determined and aggressive policy.[831] Individual directors and executives are imprisoned[832] and extradition sought of those who have moved out of the jurisdiction.[833] The argument in favour of criminalising competition law infringements is that it has a deterrent effect way beyond that produced by sanctions against undertakings.[834] There is evidence that the possibility of prison in the US leads some international cartels to 'carve out' the US, i.e. to collude in respect of the rest of the world but not the US.[835] However, there is also a great deal of debate about how real the deterrence actually is. In order to deter there has to be knowledge of the sanction and a likelihood of detection and punishment. These factors are not always present in the cartel context. Furthermore, in democratic societies there needs to be acceptance of cartel conduct as criminal behaviour and there are considerable practical difficulties in many jurisdictions in formulating an offence in terms which fit into the criminal law system. All these matters, and others, have produced a large body of literature on the subject of criminalisation.[836]

The problems of criminalisation in practice have been demonstrated in the UK where the Enterprise Act 2002 originally set out a statutory criminal offence for an indivdual who 'dishonestly' engages in price-fixing, market-sharing, and bid-rigging arrangements.[837] Indivduals are liable to a sentence of up to five years' imprisonment and/or a substantial fine. The standard for 'dishonesty' is the standard laid down in the normal criminal law[838] but the House of Lords held in *Norris* (in the context of rejecting the possibility of considering price-fixing as a conspiracy to defraud at common law) that a mere charge of price-fixing, without aggravating circumstances, does not show dishonesty.[839] As prosecutions under the Enterprise Act 2002, s. 188 proved very hard to bring, the UK Government decided to remove the dishonesty requirement and replace it with statutory exclusions and defences.[840]

---

[830] H. Hovenkamp, *Federal Antitrust Policy: The Law of Competition and its Practice* (4th edn, West, 2011), 643.

[831] Including pursuing individuals overseas by way of extradition proceedings, as in the *Norris* case, see n. 833 and Chap. 16.

[832] e.g., Alfred Taubman, the billionaire who invented the shopping mall concept, spent nearly a year in prison as a result of the price-fixing agreement between Sotheby's and Christie's, and in 1999 executives from Archer Daniels Midland were convicted in connection with the lysine cartel and sentenced to prison terms of 24–30 months.

[833] As in the case of Ian Norris, *Norris v. Government of the US* [2008] UKHL 16, [2008] 1 AC 920.

[834] See G. Werden, S. Hammond, and B. Barnett, 'Deterrence and Detection of Cartels: Using all the Tools and Sanctions', DOJ Speech, 1 March 2012, available at <http://www.justice.gov/atr/public/speeches/283738.pdf>.

[835] M. Bloom, *Immunity/Leniency/Financial Incentives/Plea Bargaining*, 11th EUI Competition Law and Policy Workshop, 2006; S. Hammond (Deputy Assistant Attorney General for Criminal Enforcement, Antitrust Division, US DOJ), *Charting New Waters in International Cartel Prosecutions*, 2 March 2006, available at <http://www.justice.gov/atr/public/speeches/214861.htm>. Applications for immunity under the DOJ leniency programme are usually accompanied by leniency applications from the individuals implicated.

[836] See, e.g., K. Cseres, M. Schinkel, and F. Vogelaar (eds.), *Criminalization of Competition Law Enforcement: Economic and Legal Implications for the EU Member States* (Edward Elgar, 2006); C. Beaton-Wells and C. Parker, 'Justifying Criminal Sanctions for Cartel Conduct' (cited in n. 828) (which includes the results of an empirical Australian project); C. Beaton-Wells and A. Ezrachi (eds.), *Criminalising Cartels: Critical Studies of an International Regulatory Movement* (Hart Publishing, 2011); C. Harding, 'A Pathology of Business Cartels: Original Sin or the Child of Regulation?' (2010) 1 *NJECL* 44; A. Stephan, 'Survey of Public Attitudes to Price-Fixing and Cartel Enforcement in Britain' (2008) 5 *Comp LR* 123; P. Whelan, 'A Principled Argument for Personal Criminal Sanctions as Punishment under EC Cartel Law' (2007) 30 *World Competition* 197; I. Lianos and I. Kokorris (eds.), *The Reform of Competition Law: Towards an Optimal Enforcement System* (Kluwer International, 2010). There is also a massive US literature, see, e.g., the references in the Werden, Hammond, and Barnett speech (cited in n. 834).

[837] Penalties may also be imposed on individuals for certain procedural offences under the Competition Act 1998, ss. 42–44. The OFT (from 2014 the CMA, see n. 596) has power to issue 'no-action' letters to 'whistle-blowers' confirming that an individual who meets certain stipulated conditions will not be prosecuted, Enterprise Act 2002, s. 190(4).

[838] *R v. Ghosh* [1982] 2 All ER 689.

[839] *Norris v. Government of the US* [2008] UKHL 16, [2008] 1 AC 920.

[840] See Enterprise Act 2002, s. 188 A–B, as amended by the Enterprise and Regulatory Reform Act 2014.

In the UK the OFT and sectoral regulators have power to seek a disqualification order against a director of a company that has committed a breach of the competition rules (which includes both Article 101 and Article 102 TFEU and their domestic equivalents)[841] and whose conduct makes him unfit to be concerned in the management of a company.[842] It has been cogently argued that disqualification orders may be a more effective route to securing compliance with competition rules than criminal sanctions.[843]

Liability on individuals for breach of the EU competition rules could only be imposed across the EU by a harmonisation measure which would entail each Member State making it an offence within its jurisdiction. Such a measure would need to go through the Council and EU-wide individual liability is therefore not an imminent prospect. In the meantime, the disparity between members of the ECN in matters of individual liability can lead to difficulties.[844]

13. COMPLAINTS

A. GENERAL

An entity which believes that an undertaking has committed, or is committing, a breach of EU competition law may wish to take action against that undertaking. It may wish to stop the infringement but may also hope to recover in respect of any loss suffered in consequence of the breach of the rules.

Such an entity essentially has two possibilities. It may complain to a public enforcer, the Commission, or one of the NCAs, and hope that the authority acts on the complaint, or it may commence proceedings before a national court seeking a declaration that an agreement infringes the competition rules and is unenforceable, an injunction to prevent future breaches, and/or other remedies in respect of a breach. It may both complain *and* bring an action. Both Articles 101 and 102 are directly applicable and confer rights on individuals that can be relied on before a national court. Complainants thus play an important part in the enforcement process. Not only may they draw breaches of the competition rules to the attention of the competition authorities, but they may privately enforce the rules through civil litigation.

In many cases an aggrieved person may prefer to complain to the Commission or an NCA than to commence private proceedings. Such a step is of course the cheaper and more convenient. There are great difficulties, for instance, in bringing an action against an international cartel in a national court in the absence of a prior finding of infringement by a competition authority (known as 'stand-alone' actions). The Commission and many of the NCAs are, however, trying to encourage greater private enforcement of the competition rules at the national level. The Commission wishes, in particular, to preserve its resources for cases in which a point of particular EU interest is raised. It may, therefore, decline to act on the complaint. Further, where the Commission finds an infringement of the rules it has power only to order a guilty undertaking to bring its infringement to an end[845] and to fine an undertaking in respect of any breach committed.[846] It does not have power to award damages or other compensation to those who have suffered as a result of the breach. Similarly, most NCAs only have power to impose fines, or other penalties on the undertaking in breach. It may be, therefore, that where

---

[841] Competition Act 1998, Chap. I and Chap. II prohibitions.

[842] Enterprise Act 2002, s. 204. The provisions amend the Company Directors Disqualification Act 1986.

[843] See A. Khan, 'Rethinking Sanctions for Breaching Competition Law: Is Director Disqualification the Answer?' (2012) 35(1) *World Competition* 77.

[844] See B. Perrin, 'Challenges Facing the EU Network of Competition Authorities: Insights from a Comparative Criminal Law Perspective' (2006) 31 *ELRev* 540.

[845] Reg. 1/2003, Art. 7.

[846] Reg. 1/2003, Art. 23.

an undertaking seeks compensation or another remedy a private action will be the only satisfactory option. Private enforcement of the competition rules through civil litigation is discussed in Chapter 14.

Regulation 1/2003 envisages that complaints may be made both to the Commission and to NCAs.[847] Article 7 provides that the Commission may, acting on a complaint or on its own initiative, find an infringement of Article 101 or Article 102 and that complaints may be lodged by 'natural or legal persons that can show a legitimate interest' and Member States. Further, Article 33 provides that the Commission shall be authorised to take measures as to the form, content, and other details of complaints lodged and of the procedure for rejecting complaints. In pursuit of this objective Chapter IV of the Implementing Regulation, Regulation 773/2004,[848] deals with the handling of complaints and the Commission has issued a Notice on the handling of complaints that is intended to provide guidance to those seeking relief from infringements of the competition rules. Article 5 of Regulation 1/2003 provides that an NCA, acting on a complaint or its own initiative, may take decisions ordering an undertaking to bring an infringement of Article 101 or Article 102 to an end and Article 13 provides that the Commission and NCAs may reject a claim which is being, or has been, dealt with by another competition authority.

One of the difficulties of encouraging complaints is that, in many cases, they may be lodged by disgruntled entities losing out on the competitive process rather than by entities really suffering as a result of a breach of the EU competition rules.

B. WHERE TO COMPLAIN

In Section 13.A it was seen that complaints can be made both to the Commission and to NCAs. An initial difficulty for a potential complainant is to decide who they should complain to, the Commission, one or more NCAs, or to all of these authorities?

The Commission's guidelines on the handling of complaints indicate that the complaint should be made to the 'authority most likely to be well placed to deal with their case'.[849] In determining who is best placed, guidance can be obtained from the Commission's Cooperation Notice,[850] which deals with work sharing between the Commission and NCAs inside the European Competition Network (ECN).[851] The authorities inform each other of investigations being made following a complaint, and members of the network seek to ensure that the correct authority is put in charge of the case.

Commission Notice on the Handling of Complaints by the Commission under Articles 81 and 82 of the EC Treaty [2004] OJ C101/65, paras. 23–25

23. Within the European Competition Network, information on cases that are being investigated following a complaint will be made available to the other members of the network before or without delay after

---

[847] Although Reg. 17 recognised that a complaint could be lodged with the Commission, the procedures governing complaints developed informally under this system. The Commission understood the importance of complaints which became an established part of the enforcement procedure. In its White Paper on Modernisation, the Commission considered that complaints should play a fuller part in a directly applicable system. One of the objectives of the new rules was to encourage and facilitate the lodging of complaints and to draw the competition authorities' attention to serious infringements of the rules. In the White Paper the Commission estimated that almost 30% of new cases it dealt with resulted from complaints and that many of its own-initiative investigations began with information sent to the Commission informally, White Paper on Modernisation [1999] OJ C132/1, [1999], para. 117.

[848] [2004] OJ 123/18.

[849] Commission Notice on the Handling of Complaints by the Commission under Articles 81 and 82 of the EC Treaty [2004] OJ C101/65, para. 21 (the Complaints Notice).

[850] [2004] OJ C101/54, especially points 8–15.

[851] Complaints Notice, paras. 19–25.

commencing the first formal investigative measure. Where the same complaint has been lodged with several authorities or where a case has not been lodged with an authority that is well placed, the members of the network will endeavour to determine within an indicative time-limit of two months which authority or authorities should be in charge of the case.

24. Complainants themselves have an important role to play in further reducing the potential need for reallocation of a case originating from their complaint by referring to the orientations on worksharing in the network set out in the present chapter when deciding on where to lodge their complaint. If nonetheless a case if reallocated within the network, the undertakings concerned and the complainant(s) are informed as soon as possible by the competition authorities involved.

25. The Commission may reject a complaint in accordance with Article 13 of Regulation 1/2003, on the grounds that a Member State is dealing or has dealt with the case. When doing so the Commission must, in accordance with Article 9 of Regulation 773/2004 inform the complaint without delay of the national competition authority which is dealing or has already dealt with the case.

C. STANDING

Regulation 1/2003 provides that 'natural or legal persons who can show a legitimate interest' and Member States (which are deemed to have a legitimate interest for all complaints they lodge) have standing to complain about a breach of the competition rules.[852]

Any applicant who is directly and adversely affected, or will be so affected, as a result of the infringement will have standing. It has been held, for example, that an entity which has been excluded, or threatened with exclusion, from a distribution network;[853] which believes that it was negotiating with members of a cartel;[854] or which believes itself to be a victim of abusive behaviour by a dominant undertaking,[855] has a legitimate interest within the meaning of Article 3(2). Further, in *BEMIM v. Commission* [856] the GC held that a trade association had a legitimate interest where the conduct complained of was liable to affect adversely the interests of the members that it was entitled to represent. The Commission's Complaints Notice provides further guidance on this matter, providing examples of entities which would have a legitimate interest such as consumer associations. Paragraph 38 says that those acting purely pro bono publico do not have a legitimate interest.

Commission Notice on the Handling of Complaints by the Commission under Article 101 and 102 of the EC Treaty [2004] OJ C101/65, paras. 35–40

35. The [General Court] had held that an association of undertakings may claim a legitimate interest in lodging a complaint regarding conduct concerning its members even if it not directly concerned, as an undertaking operating in the relevant market, by the conduct complained of, provided that, first, it is

---

[852] Art. 7(2). This is similar to the language previously used in Reg. 17, Art. 3.

[853] Case 210/81, *Demo-Studio Schmidt v. Commission* [1983] ECR 3045, [1984] 1 CMLR 63.

[854] See, e.g., *Building and Construction Industry in the Netherlands* [1992] OJ L92/1, [1993] 5 CMLR 135 (a complaint about collusive tendering lodged by a local authority).

[855] See, e.g., Cases 6 and 7/73, *Istituto Chemioterapico Italiano SpA and Commercial Solvents Corp v. Commission* [1974] ECR 223 (complaint by Zoja, *Zoja-CSC/ICI* [1972] OJ L299/51, [1973] CMLR D50); Case C-62/86, *AKZO Chemie BV v. Commission* [1991] ECR I-3359, complaint lodged by ECS; see Chaps. 6 and 7.

[856] Case T-114/92, [1995] ECR II-147; see in particular para. 28.

entitled to represent the interests of its members[857] and secondly, the conduct complained of is liable to adversely affect the interests of its members. Conversely, the Commission has been found to be entitled not to pursue the complaint of an association of undertakings whose members were not involved in the type of business transactions complained of.[858]

36. From this case law, it can be inferred that undertakings (themselves or through associations that are entitled to represent their interests) can claim a legitimate interest where they are operating in the relevant market or where the conduct complained of is liable to directly and adversely affect their interests. This confirms the established practice of the Commission which has accepted that a legitimate interest can, for instance, be claimed by the parties to the agreement or practice which is the subject of the complaint, by competitors whose interests have allegedly been damaged by the behaviour complained of or by undertakings excluded from a distribution system.

37. Consumer associations can equally lodge complaints with the Commission.[859] The Commission moreover holds the view that individual consumers whose economic interests are directly and adversely affected insofar as they are the buyers of goods or services that are the object of an infringement can be in a position to show a legitimate interest.[860]

38. However, the Commission does not consider as a legitimate interest within the meaning of Article 7(2) the interest of persons or organizations that wish to come forward on general interest considerations without showing that they or their members are liable to be directly and adversely affected by the infringement (*pro bono publico*).

39. Local or public authorities may be able to show a legitimate interest in their capacity as buyers or users of goods or services affected by the conduct complained of. Conversely, they cannot be considered as showing a legitimate interest within the meaning of Article 7(2) of Regulation 1/2002 to the extent that they bring to the attention of the Commission alleged infringements *pro bono publico* .

40. Complainants have to demonstrate their legitimate interest. Where a natural or legal person lodging a complaint is unable to demonstrate a legitimate interest, the Commission is entitled, without prejudice to its right to initiate proceedings of its own initiative, not to pursue the complaint. The Commission may ascertain whether this condition is met at any stage of the investigation.

In *Österreichische Postsparkasse* the GC took a broad view of those having a 'legitimate interest' under Article 3(2) of Regulation 17, the antecedent of Regulation 1/2003, Article 7(2). It extended this to any final consumer who can show that his economic interests have been harmed.

Cases T-213/01 and 214/01, *Österreichische Postsparkasse* v. *Commission* [2006] ECR II-1601

The case was an appeal against two decisions of the Hearing Officer to send to an Austrian political party (FPÖ) the non-confidential version of the statement of objections in the investigation which culminated in the *Lombard* Club decision. [861] The FPÖ complained to the Commission in June 1997 about certain practices of a group of Austrian banks. In February 1998 the Commission informed the FPÖ that it intended to reject its complaint, stating that it did not have a legitimate interest within Article 3(2) of Regulation 17. In fact, the Commission had already started an investigation on its own initiative in May 1997, before it

---

857 See, e.g., Case T-114/92, *BEMIM* v. *Commission* [1995] ECR II-147, para. 28.

858 See, e.g., Cases T-133 and 204/95, *IECC* v. *Commission* [1998] ECR II-3645, paras. 79–83.

859 See, e.g., Case T-37/92, *BEUC* v. *Commission* [1994] ECR II-285, para. 36.

860 This point was raised in Cases T-213 and 214/01 extracted later in this chapter.

861 [2004] OJ L56/1, substantially upheld by the GC in Cases T-259/02, T-264/02, and T-271/02, *Raiffeisen Zentralbank Österreich AG* v. *Commission* [2006] ECR II-5169, aff'd Case C-125/07, *Erste Bank AG (formerly Erste Bank der österreichischen Sparkassen)* v. *Commission* [2009] ECR I-8681.

had received the complaint. In due course the Commission sent the banks a statement of objections and informed them that it intended to send a non-confidential version to the FPÖ. The banks protested but the Hearing Officer overruled their objections.[862] The banks claimed that the FPÖ did not have sufficient 'legitimate interest' under Article 3(2) to merit receiving the statement of objections. The copy of the statement of objections was duly sent, and its contents [were] disclosed to the press.[863] The banks carried on with an appeal to the General Court, claiming, *inter alia*, that the FPÖ's status as a customer of banking services did not constitute a 'legitimate interest' under Article 3(2).

General Court

114. The [General Court] considers that there is nothing to prevent a final customer who purchases goods or services from being able to satisfy the notion of legitimate interest within the meaning of Article 3 of Regulation No 17. The Court considers that a final customer who shows that his economic interests have been harmed or are likely to be harmed as a result of the restriction of competition in question has a legitimate interest within the meaning of Article 3 of Regulation No 17 in making an application or a complaint in order to seek a declaration from the Commission that Articles [101 and 102] have been infringed.

115. It should be pointed out in this respect that the ultimate purpose of the rules that seek to ensure that competition is not distorted in the internal market is to increase the well-being of consumers. That purpose can be seen in particular from the wording of Article [101]. Whilst the prohibition laid down in Article [101(1)] may be declared inapplicable in the case of cartels which contribute to improving the production or distribution of the goods in question or to promoting technical or economic progress, that possibility, for which provision is made in Article [101(3)], is inter alia subject to the condition that a fair share of the resulting benefit is allowed for users of those products. Competition law and competition policy therefore have an undeniable impact on the specific economic interests of final customers who purchase goods or services. Recognition that such customers—who show that they have suffered economic damage as a result of an agreement or conduct liable to restrict or distort competition—have a legitimate interest in seeking from the Commission a declaration that Articles [101 EC and 102] have been infringed contributes to the attainment of the objectives of competition law.

116. Contrary to the claims made by the applicants, this finding does not effectively render the notion of legitimate interest meaningless by making it excessively broad or pave the way for an alleged '*actio popularis*'. Acknowledging that a consumer who can show that his economic interests have been harmed as a result of a cartel complained of by him may have a legitimate interest in this regard within the meaning of Article 3(2) of Regulation No 17 is not the same as considering that any natural or legal person has such an interest.

An individual who does not have a legitimate interest within the meaning of Article 7(2) of Regulation 1/2003 even after *Österreichische Postsparkasse*, or for some reason does not want to make an official complaint, may still draw the Commission's attention informally to market information which indicates that conduct may be in breach of the competition rules. Once the conduct has been drawn to its intention the Commission is, of course, free to commence proceedings on its own initiative if it considers it appropriate to do so.

---

[862] In Case T-213/01 R, *Österreichische Postsparkasse v. Commission* [2001] ECR II-3963, the President of the GC rejected a request to suspend the Hearing Officer's decision.

[863] By the Governor of Carinthia, Jörg Haider, the leader of the FPÖ. The FPÖ, an extreme right-wing party, joined the Austrian Government in a coalition in 2000, provoking a crisis for the EU. Article 7 of the Nice Treaty, which set out how the EU should react when 'a clear danger exists of a Member State committing a serious breach of fundamental rights' was partly in response to this.

D. THE PROCEDURE

A formal complaint must be submitted in compliance with Form C[864] which is available on DG Comp's website.[865] Form C requires the complainant to provide information regarding itself, details of the alleged infringement and evidence, an explanation of the findings sought from the Commission, the grounds on which a legitimate interest is claimed, and details of any approach made to another competition authority or lawsuits brought before a national court. In certain circumstances, the Commission may waive the need for submission of some of the comprehensive information and supporting documentation required.[866] The complainant must submit three paper copies, an electronic copy (if possible), and a non-confidential version of the complaint.

E. THE THREE-STAGE PROCEDURE

On receipt of a complaint the Commission is bound to collect information which enables it to determine whether it should reject the complaint or conduct an investigation.[867]

During the first stage of the procedure it collects information from the complainant, gives an initial reaction to the case, and allows the complainant an opportunity to expand on its allegations.[868]

During the second stage it investigates further to determine whether to initiate proceedings or to reject the complaint.[869] Before the Commission rejects a complaint, it must give the complainant an opportunity to make its views known on the Commission's provisional intention to reject, within a specified time limit.[870] This is known as sending the complainant an 'Article 7(1) letter'.[871] The complainant may also be provided with access to non-confidential documents on which the Commission has based its provisional assessment. The Article 7(1) letter is not in itself capable of being challenged before the GC.

Taking cognisance of the views of the complainant the Commission, in the third stage, either initiates proceedings or rejects the complaint.[872]

F. REJECTION OF THE COMPLAINT

(i) Introduction

The Commission may on investigation consider that no breach of the EU competition rules has occurred. Alternatively, it may consider that a breach might have occurred but that the case is of insufficient Union interest to warrant the time and resources that would be involved in investigation. It may also consider that another NCA within the ECN would be better placed to deal with the case. Although the Commission has a duty 'to examine carefully the facts and points of law brought to its notice by the complainant in order to decide whether they disclose conduct liable to distort competition in the [internal] market and affect trade between Member States'[873] it does not have a duty

---

[864] Reg. 773/2004 [2004] OJ L123/18, Art. 5.

[865] It is also set out as an annex to the Complaints Notice.

[866] Reg. 773/2004 [2004] OJ L123/18, Art. 5(1).

[867] See Section 13.F and the Complaints Notice, para. 54.

[868] Complaints Notice, para. 55.

[869] Complaints Notice, para. 56 The procedure prior to rejecting a complaint is set out in Best Practices, paras 139–141.

[870] Reg. 773/2004 [2004] OJ L123/18, Art. 7(1).

[871] i.e. Art 7(1) of Reg.773/2004.

[872] Complaints Notice, para. 57.

[873] Case T-575/93, *Koelman v. Commission* [1996] ECR II-1, para. 39.

to proceed to a final decision on the alleged breach of the rules. The Commission must, however, examine the case carefully in order to assess the Union interest in further investigation of the case.[874]

(ii) The Union Interest and the Right to Prioritise

In *Automec Srl v. Commission (Automec II)*[875] the GC held that the Commission is entitled to prioritise cases before it. As a public enforcer it has a margin of discretion to set priorities in its enforcement activity. It may reject a complaint on the ground that it does not raise a sufficient Union interest. Save where the subject matter of the complaint falls within the exclusive purview of the Commission,[876] the rights conferred upon complainants do not, therefore, include a right to obtain a decision as regards the existence or otherwise of the alleged infringement. Rather, the Commission, in fulfilling its functions, is bound to apply different degrees of priority to the cases arising before it. The Commission is therefore entitled to assess whether the complaint raises sufficient Union interest to warrant an investigation.

Case T-24/90, *Automec Srl* v. *Commission (Automec II)* [1992] ECR II-2223

A complaint was lodged by Automec Srl, in respect of the refusal by BMW to renew Automec's distributorship of BMW cars in Treviso, Italy. Automec brought proceedings before the national courts to compel BMW to continue the contractual relationship and subsequently, in 1988, lodged a complaint with the Commission. In particular, it contended that BMW was obliged to supply it with vehicles and spare parts on the terms applicable to other dealers. The Commission sent Automec a letter stating that it had no power to grant its application. Automec commenced judicial review proceedings before the GC seeking annulment of the letter and damages from the Commission in respect of loss suffered in consequence of the Commission's failure to commence proceedings against BMW (*Automec I*). Subsequently, further letters were exchanged between the Commission and Automec. In February 1990 the Commission sent Automec a letter rejecting the complaint, stating that there was not a sufficient Community interest to justify examining the facts raised by the complaint. Automec brought further proceedings before the GC seeking annulment of the February 1990 decision.

General Court

71. The Court considers that the question raised by this plea asks in substance what the Commission's obligations are when it receives an application under Article 3 of Regulation No 17 from a natural or legal person.

72. It is appropriate to point out that Regulations Nos 17 and 99/63 confer procedural rights on persons who have lodged a complaint with the Commission, such as the right to be informed of the reasons for which the Commission intends to reject their complaint and the right to submit observations in this connection. Thus the Community legislature has imposed certain specified obligations upon the Commission. However, neither Regulation No 17 nor Regulation No 99/63 contain[s] express provisions relating to the action to be taken concerning the substance of a complaint and any obligations on the part of the Commission to carry out investigations.

73. In determining the Commission's obligations in this context, the first point to note is that the Commission is responsible for the implementation and orientation of Community competition policy (see the judgment of the Court of Justice in Case C-234/89 *Delimitis* v. *Henninger Bräu AG*…at 991). For that

---

[874] Complaints Notice, para. 42.

[875] Case T-24/90, [1992] ECR II-2223.

[876] e.g., for the withdrawal of a block exemption in an individual case, see Reg. 1/2003, Art. 29.

reason, Article [101(1)] gave the Commission the task of ensuring that the principles laid down by Articles [101] and [102] were applied, and the provisions adopted pursuant to Article [103] have conferred wide powers upon it.

74. The scope of the Commission's obligations in the field of competition law must be examined in the light of Article [101(1)], which, in this area, constitutes the specific expression of the general supervisory task entrusted to the Commission by Article [17(1) TEU]. However, as the Court of Justice has held with regard to Article [258 TFEU] in Case 247/87 *Star Fruit* v. *Commission*...at 301, that task does not mean that the Commission is bound to commence proceedings seeking to establish the existence of any infringement of Community law.

75. In that regard, the Court observes that it appears from the case-law of the Court of Justice (judgment in *GEMA*...at 3189) that the rights conferred upon complainants by Regulations Nos 17 and 99/63 do not include a right to obtain a decision, within the meaning of Article [288 TFEU], as regards the existence or otherwise of the alleged infringement. It follows that the Commission cannot be required to give a decision in that connection unless the subject-matter of the complaint falls within its exclusive purview, as in the case of the withdrawal of an exemption granted under Article [101(3)].

76. As the Commission is under no obligation to rule on the existence or otherwise of an infringement it cannot be compelled to carry out an investigation, because such investigation could have no purpose other than to seek evidence of the existence or otherwise of an infringement, which it is not required to establish. In that regard, it should be noted that, unlike the provision contained in the second sentence of Article [105(1)] in relation to applications by Member States, Regulations Nos 17 and 99/63 do not expressly oblige the Commission to investigate complaints submitted to it.

77. In that connection, it should be observed that, in the case of an authority entrusted with a public service task, the power to take all the organizational measures necessary for the performance of that task, including setting priorities within the limits prescribed by the law—where those priorities have not been determined by the legislature—is an inherent feature of administrative activity. This must be the case in particular where an authority has been entrusted with a supervisory and regulatory task as extensive and general as that which has been assigned to the Commission in the field of competition. Consequently, the fact that the Commission applies different degrees of priority to the cases submitted to it in the field of competition is compatible with the obligations imposed on it by Community law.

78. That assessment does not conflict with the judgments of the Court of Justice in *Demo-Studio Schmidt*...in Case 298/83 *CICCE* v. *Commission*...and in Joined Cases 142 and 156/84 *BAT and Reynolds* v. *Commission*...In the judgment in *Demo-Studio Schmidt*, the Court of Justice held that the Commission 'was under a duty to examine the facts put forward' by the complainant, without prejudging the question whether the Commission could refrain from investigating the complaint because, in that case, the Commission had examined the facts set out in the complaint and had rejected it on the ground that there was nothing to suggest the existence of an infringement. Likewise this question did not arise in the later cases of *CICCE* (cited above) and *BAT and Reynolds* (cited above).

79. However, although the Commission cannot be compelled to conduct an investigation, the procedural safeguards provided for by Article 3 of Regulation No 17 and Article 6 of Regulation No 99/63 oblige it nevertheless to examine carefully the factual and legal particulars brought to its notice by the complainant in order to decide whether they disclose conduct of such a kind as to distort competition in the common market and affect trade between Member States (see the judgments in *Demo-Studio Schmidt*, *CICCE* and *BAT and Reynolds*, cited above).

...

84. The next point to consider is whether it is legitimate, as the Commission has argued, to refer to the Community interest in a case as a priority criterion.

85. In this connection, it should be borne in mind that, unlike the civil courts, whose task is to safeguard the individual rights of private persons in their relations *inter se*, an administrative authority must act in the public interest. Consequently, the Commission is entitled to refer to the Community interest in order

to determine the degree of priority to be applied to the various cases brought to its notice. This does not amount to removing action by the Commission from the scope of judicial review, since, in view of the requirement to provide a statement of reasons laid down by Article [296 TFEU], the Commission cannot merely refer to the Community interest in the abstract. It must set out the legal and factual considerations which led it to conclude that there was insufficient Community interest to justify investigation of the case. It is therefore by reviewing the legality of those reasons that the Court can review the Commission's action.

86. In order to assess the Community interest in further investigation of a case, the Commission must take account of the circumstances of the case, and in particular of the legal and factual particulars set out in the complaint referred to it. The Commission should in particular balance the significance of the alleged infringement as regards the functioning of the common market, the probability of establishing the existence of the infringement and the scope of the investigation required in order to fulfil, under the best possible conditions, its task of ensuring that Articles [101] and [102] are complied with.

At paragraph 44 of the Complaints Notice,[877] the Commission sets out some of the criteria, taken from the case law, which it uses to assess whether or not a particular case now has a Union interest:[878]

— The Commission can reject a complaint on the ground that the complainant can bring an action to assert its rights before national courts .

— The Commission may not regard certain situations as excluded in principle from its purview under the task entrusted to it by the Treaty but is required to assess in each case how serious the alleged infringements are and how persistent their consequences are. This means in particular that it must take into account the duration and the extent of the infringements complained of and their effect on the competition situation in the Community .

— The Commission may have to balance the significance of the alleged infringement as regards the functioning of the common market, the probability of establishing the existence of the infringement and the scope of the investigation required in order to fulfil its task of ensuring that Articles [101 and 102 TFEU] are complied with .

— While the Commission's discretion does not depend on how advanced the investigation of a case is, the stage of the investigation forms part of the circumstances of the case which the Commission may have to take into consideration .

— The Commission may decide that it is not appropriate to investigate a complaint where the practices in question have ceased. However, for this purpose, the Commission will have to ascertain whether anti-competitive effects persist and if the seriousness of the infringements or the persistence of their effects does not give the complaint a Community interest....

— The Commission may also decide that it is not appropriate to investigate a complaint where the undertakings concerned agree to change their conduct in such a way that it can consider that there is no longer a sufficient Community interest to intervene...

---

[877] [2004] OJ C101/65.

[878] After *Automec* the Commission dealt with the question of whether a particular case had a Community interest in its old 'Notice on cooperation between national courts and the Commission in applying Articles 85 and 86 [81 and 82] of the EEC [EC] Treaty' [1993] OJ C39/6, see especially paras. 13–15. In that Notice (which has now been replaced by the Commission Notice on the cooperation between the Commission and the courts of the EU Member States) the Commission stressed that it would concentrate on cases with 'particular political, economic or legal significance for the Community' (para. 14) and that it would be unwilling to take action where the Community provisions could be enforced before the national courts.

The Commission applied these principles when rejecting a complaint about Athens Airport, particularly the first and third indent, and was upheld on appeal.[879] The rejection of a complaint about the prices increases of a German electricity supplier (E.ON) resulted in a complaint to the Ombudsman about the Commission's refusal to open proceedings. The Ombudsman held that the Commission had acted within the limits of its discretion in declining to open proceedings.[880]

It is clear, however, from paragraphs 79–86 of *Automec II*, that before rejecting a complaint the Commission must carefully examine the factual and legal particulars brought to its notice; set out the legal and factual considerations which led it to the conclusion of insufficient Union interest; and take account of the circumstances of the case.[881] It must examine the complaint diligently and impartially in accordance with the principle of sound administration as confirmed in the Charter of Fundamental Rights.[882] In *CEAHR* [883] the GC held that the Commission had committed manifest errors of assessment in dealing with a complaint from luxury watch repairers about the practices of luxury watch manufacturers in that it had wrongly defined the market[884] and had given inadequate reasons for limiting the size of the relevant market and the territories it covered before concluding that there was insufficient Union interest.

The Commission said in the Report on Regulation 1/2003 that it wanted to examine further how it can streamline the handling of complaints that are not a priority case.[885] The obligations imposed by the case law (see the extract from *Guérin*) mean that non-priority cases nevertheless create an administrative burden.[886]

(iii) Investigation by Another Competition Authority

As already indicated, the Commission is entitled to reject a complaint on the grounds that an NCA is dealing, or has dealt, with the case.[887]

(iv) The Commission is Obliged to Make a Formal Rejection of the Complaint

Where the Commission decides not to act on a complaint, has communicated this to the complainant, and given it an opportunity to make its views known by the sending of an Article 7(1) letter, the Commission is bound either to initiate a procedure or to reject the complaint by decision under Regulation Reg. 773/2004, Article 7(2).[888]

---

[879] Case T-306/05, *Scippacercola and Terezakis* v. *Commission* [2008] ECR II-4 (COMP/38.469, *Athens International Airport*) upheld by order, Case C-159/08 P, [2009] ECR I-46. See also Case T-60/05, *Union Française de l'Express* v. *Commission (UFEX)* [2007] ECR II-3397 (Commission should consider seriousness of infringement even when terminated and without continuing anti-competitive effects); Case T-74/11, *Omnis* v. *Commission*, 30 May 2013 (there is no obligatory or limited list of criteria the Commission has to apply, it depends on the circumstances of the individual case).

[880] Complaint 1142/2008/(BEH)KM.

[881] Case T-432/05, *EMC Development AB* v. *Commission* [2010] ECR II-1629, paras 59–60, appeal dismissed Case C-367/10 P, [2011] ECR I-46.

[882] Case T-54/99, *max.mobil* v. *Commission* [2002] ECR II-313, paras 56–57.

[883] Case T-427/08, *Confédération européenne des associations d'horlogers-réparateurs (CEAHR)* v. *Commission* [2010] ECR II-5865.

[884] See Chap. 1, Section 10.B.vii.g, p. 80.

[885] Report on Regulation 1/2003, para. 16.

[886] See Staff Working Paper, para. 117.

[887] Reg. 1/2003, Art. 13.

[888] Reg. 773/2004 [2004] OJ L123/18, Art. 7(2). Case T-64/89, *Automec Srl* v. *Commission (Automec I)* [1990] ECR II-367.

> ### Case T-186/94, *Guérin Automobiles* v. *Commission* [1995] ECR II-1753, para. 34
>
> #### General Court
>
> [I]t should be emphasized that, having submitted within the time stipulated in the letter of 13 June 1994 comments in response to the Article [7] notification, the applicant is henceforth entitled to obtain a definitive decision from the Commission on its complaint; and that decision may, if the applicant sees fit, be challenged in an action for annulment before this court…

Although, therefore, the Commission cannot be required in every case to proceed to a final decision on the compatibility of the conduct complained of with the competition rules it must, if it is not going to investigate, formally reject the complaint by decision, stating reasons, before closing its file. This decision is subject to appeal before the GC.

G. ACTING ON A COMPLAINT

If the Commission considers it to be worthwhile to initiate proceedings, it may do so by issuing an SO. It can take an infringement decision even if the complaint has been withdrawn in the meantime.[889] The Commission's fact-finding powers and the opening of a formal procedure are discussed in Sections 8.B. and C. A few points of importance to a complainant are, however, highlighted here. First, since the Commission is bound by a general duty of confidentiality the complainant should be sure to mark any business secrets or other confidential information which it does not wish the Commission to disclose. Secondly, if the Commission initiates proceedings and issues a statement of objections (SO) relating to a matter in respect of which it has received a complaint, it must provide a non-confidential version of the SO to the complainant and give it an opportunity to make its views known in writing. This does not apply in respect of the SO in the cartel settlement procedure.[890] Where appropriate, non-confidential versions of the replies to the SO can be given to the complainant, provided that business secrets are not disclosed and the suppliers of the information have been consulted[891] and, where appropriate, non-confidential versions of the complainants' comments may be sent to the undertakings complained of.[892] Thirdly, the complainant may also be given the opportunity to make submissions at the oral hearing if it so requests.[893] Fourthly, the complainant cannot specifically request that the Commission adopt interim measures. According to Article 8 of Regulation 1/2003 the Commission may order interim measures *on its own initiative* where there is the risk of serious and irreparable damage to *competition*. The Commission takes the view that requests for interim measures should be brought before the national courts—which are better placed to decide on such measures.[894] Fifthly, if the Commission does find that an undertaking has infringed Article 101 or Article 102 it cannot compensate an entity which has suffered loss in consequence of a breach.[895] Compensation must be pursued through private action in a national court, as discussed in Chapter 14.

---

[889] COMP/37.860 *Morgan Stanley/Visa International and Visa Europe*, on appeal Case T-461/07 [2011] ECR II-1729.

[890] Introduced by Reg. 622/2008, see Section 8.E, p. 992. Nor is the complainant entitled to see the settlement submissions.

[891] Antitrust ManProc, Module 21, para. 17

[892] Antitrust ManProc, Module 21, para. 18.

[893] Reg. 773/2004 [2004] OJ L123/18, Art. 6. Complaints Notice, paras. 64–67.

[894] Complaints Notice, para. 80.

[895] The fine goes into the EU coffers.

H. JUDICIAL REVIEW PROCEEDINGS

(i) An Omission to Act

Where the Commission is in breach of an obligation to act it is possible, under Article 265, to bring proceedings in respect of its failure to act.[896] Before such proceedings can be brought it is essential that the Commission should have been called upon to act and have failed to adopt a measure in relation to the complainant which that complainant was legally entitled to claim by virtue of the rules of EU law. Since a complainant cannot insist that the Commission should commence an investigation it cannot bring proceedings under Article 265 in respect of its failure to launch such an investigation. However, the complainant can challenge the failure to issue an Article 7(1) letter within a reasonable time.[897] Because the Commission is obliged to issue a formal rejection of a complaint, a complainant can bring Article 265 proceedings where such a final decision has not been taken. Once the Commission informs a complainant that it has decided to close its file and has formally rejected a complaint that complainant may, if it so wishes, bring judicial review proceedings under Article 263 TFEU challenging the validity of that decision.

(ii) Review of Acts

a. Standing

A complainant may wish to bring proceedings to annul a Commission decision rejecting its complaint or any decision made subsequent to an investigation.[898] In the sphere of the competition rules the EU Courts have taken a broad view of when individuals are directly and individually concerned within the meaning of Article 263. If an individual has standing to complain to the Commission, it is considered that it will also have standing to institute proceedings where its complaint is rejected. In *Metro v. Commission* the CJ held that it was essential that a person with a legitimate interest 'should be able, if their request is not complied with either wholly or in part, to institute proceedings in order to protect their legitimate interests. In those circumstances, the applicant must be considered to be directly and individually concerned within the meaning of the second paragraph of Article [263], by the contested decision'.[899]

b. A Reviewable Act

The formal rejection of a complaint is a reviewable act (a legally binding measure) within the meaning of Article 263.[900] However, the Commission's initial letters (such as the Article 7(1) letter) and preliminary investigations are not reviewable, and may not be challenged. In some cases it may be difficult to determine whether or not the Commission has actually given a final decision which is susceptible to challenge under Article 263.[901]

c. Grounds for Annulment

The grounds for annulment are the ordinary grounds set out in Article 263: lack of competence, infringement of an essential procedural requirement, infringement of the Treaties, or any rule of law or misuse of power.[902]

---

[896] See Craig and de Búrca, *EU Law: Text, Cases and Materials* (cited in n. 739).

[897] See Cases T-190/95 and T-45/96, *Sodima v. Commission* [1999] ECR II-3617.

[898] See Section 9.A, p. 1029.

[899] Case 26/76, *Metro SB-Grossmärtke GmbH & Co KG v. Commission* [1977] ECR 1875, para. 13.

[900] See Section 9.A.iv, p. 1032.

[901] See, e.g., Case T-37/92, *BEUC* [1994] ECR II-285 and Case C-39/93 P, *SFEI v. Commission* [1994] ECR I-2681.

[902] see Section 9.A.ii, p. 1035.

I. COMPLAINTS AND THE MERGER REGULATION

The rights of third parties under the EU Merger Regulation are dealt with in Chapter 15.

14. CONCLUSIONS

1. Regulation 1/2003 made fundamental changes to the way that Articles 101 and 102 are enforced, with the principal objective of strengthening enforcement of those rules. The changes have had significant effects on the Commission, NCAs, and undertakings. The operation of the ECN has so far been highly successful, but the judgment in *Tele2Polska* has underlined the fact that NCAs are junior partners to the Commission.

2. The Commission gained new powers under Regulation 1/2003 to facilitate its task of detecting and punishing breaches of Articles 101 and 102. It pursues an increasingly aggressive policy, particularly towards cartels, with draconian fines. Its actions against cartels are heavily dependent on the leniency policy and the settlement procedure allows the Commission to save time and resources.

3. Outside the cartels area the Commission's extensive use of the commitments decision procedure in Article 9, and the CJ's *Alrosa* judgment, have to a large extent changed the nature of the Commission's enforcement strategy. It has replaced top-down enforcement with negotiated outcomes. This is advantageous to the Commission and may be convenient for the parties, but it is prejudicial to the development of the law as it takes what may be novel and controversial points of law away from the possibility of review by the EU Courts. The development of the law on Article 102 in particular, therefore, may come to depend more on preliminary references from the national courts.

4. The extensive powers of the Commission in competition cases and the (limited) role of the EU Courts are questionable in the light of the human rights guarantees provided in the EU's own legal order, and in the ECHR which it reflects and to which the EU is, under the Treaty of Lisbon, committed to acceding. The CJ's *KME* judgment approved the review by the Courts as compliant with the Charter, but it has not put an end to criticisms of the system. The question remains as to whether the investigation and prosecutorial functions of the Commission should be separated from adjudication.

15. FURTHER READING

A. BOOKS

AMATO, G., *Antitrust and the Bounds of Power* (Hart Publishing, 1997), Chap. 8

ANDREANGELI, A., *EU Competition Enforcement and Human Rights* (Edward Elgar, 2008)

BEATON-WELLS, C., and EZRACHI, A. (eds). *Criminalising Cartels: Critical Studies of an International Regulatory Movement* (Hart Publishing, 2011)

BELLAMY, G., and CHILD, G. (V. Rose and D. Bailey, eds.), *European Law of Competition* (7th edn, Oxford University Press, 2013), Chaps. 13–15

EHLERMANN, C. D., and ATANASIU, I. (eds.), *European Competition Law Annual 2000: The Modernisation of EC Antitrust Policy* (Hart Publishing, 2001)

——, —— (eds.), *European Competition Law Annual 2001: Effective Enforcement of EC Antitrust Law* (Hart Publishing, 2003)

—— and MARQUIS, M., (eds.), *European Competition Law Annual 2008: Antitrust Settlements Under EC Competition Law* (Hart Publishing, 2009)

——, —— (eds.), *European Competition Law Annual 2009: Evaluation of Evidence and its Judicial Review in Competition Cases* (Hart Publishing, 2010)

——, —— (eds.) *European Competition Law Annual 2009: Evaluation of Evidence and its Judicial Review in Competition Cases* (Hart Publishing, 2011)

FAULL, J., and NIKPAY, A., *The EC Law of Competition* (2nd edn, Oxford University Press, 2007), Chap. 2

KERSE, C., and KHAN, N. (Khan ed.), *EU Antitrust Procedure* (6th edn, Sweet & Maxwell, 2012)

LIANOS, I., and KOKORRIS, I. (eds), *The Reform of Competition Law: Towards an Optimal Enforcement System* (Kluwer, 2010)

MEROLA, M., and DERENNE, J., *The Role of the Court of Justice of the European Union in Competition Law Cases* (Bruylant, 2012)

NAZZINI, R., *Concurrent Proceedings in Competition Law* (Oxford University Press, 2004)

ORTIZ BLANCO, L., *EU Competition Procedure* (3rd edn, Oxford University Press, 2013)

TRIDIMAS, T., *The General Principles of EC Law* (2nd edn, Oxford University Press, 2006)

SIMONSSON, I., *Legitimacy in EU Cartel Control* (Hart Publishing, 2010)

VAN BAEL, I., *Due Process in EU Competition Proceedings* (Kluwer, 2011)

WESSELING, R., *The Modernisation of EC Antitrust Law* (Hart Publishing, 2000)

WILS, W., *The Optimal Enforcement of EC Antitrust Law: Essays in Law and Economics* (Kluwer Law International, 2002)

B. CHAPTERS IN BOOKS

FORRESTER, I., 'A Bush in Need of Pruning: the Luxuriant Growth of "Light Judicial Review"', in C.-D. Ehlermann and M. Marquis (eds.), *European Competition Law Annual 2009: Evaluation of Evidence and its Judicial Review in Competition Cases* (Hart Publishing, 2011), 407

LIANOS, I., 'Is the Availability of "Appropriate" Remedies a Limit to Competition Law Liability under Article 102 TFEU? The Mischiefs of "Discretionary Remedialism" in Competition Law', in F. Etro and I. Kokkoris (eds.), *Competition Law and the Enforcement of Article 102* (Oxford University Press, 2010), Chap. 10

C. ARTICLES

ALBERS, M., and JOURDAN, J., 'The Role of Hearing Officers in EU Competition Proceedings: A Historical and Practical Perspective' (2011) 2 *J European Competition L. & Prac.* 185

AMORY, B. E. and DESMEDT, Y. N., 'The European Ombudsman's First Scrutiny of the EC Commission in Antitrust Matters' (2009) *ECLR* 205

ANDREANGELI, A., 'The Impact of the Modernisation Regulation on the Guarantees of Due Process in Competition Proceedings' (2006) 31 *ELRev* 342

——, 'Towards an EU Competition Court: "Article-6-Proofing" Antitrust Proceedings before the Commission?' (2007) 4 *World Competition* 595

BAILEY, D., 'Scope of Judicial Review Under Article 101 EC' (2004) 41 *CMLRev* 1327

BEATON-WELLS, C., and PARKER, C., 'Justifying Criminal Sanctions for Cartel Conduct: A Hard Case' (2013) 1(1) *J Antitrust Enforcement* 198

BERGHE, P., and DAWES, A., '"Little Pig, Little Pig, Let me Come In": An Evaluation of the European Commission's Powers of Inspection in Competition Cases' (2009) *ECLR* 407

BILLIET, P., 'How Lenient is the EC Leniency Policy? A Matter of Certainty and Predictability' (2009) *ECLR* 14

BLAKE, S., and SCHNICHELS, D., 'Leniency Following Modernisation: Safeguarding Europe's Leniency Programmes' [2004] *ECLR* 765

BRAMMER, S., 'Concurrent Jurisdiction under Regulation 1/2003 and the Issue of Case Allocation' (2005) 42 *CMLRev* 1383

CASTILLO DE LA TORRE, F., 'Evidence, Proof and Judicial Review in Cartel Cases' (2009) 32(4) *World Competition* 505

CENGIZ, F., 'Multi-level Governance in Competition Policy: the European Competition Network (2010) 35 *ELRev* 660

——, 'Judicial Review and the Rule of Law in the EU Competition Law Regime after *Alrosa*' (2011) 7 *European Competition Journal* 127

CONNOR, J. M., 'Cartel Fine Severity and the European Commission 2007–2011' [2011] *ECLR* 58

DEKEYSER, K., and GAUER, C., 'The New Enforcement System for Articles 101 and 102 and the Rights of Defence' [2004] Fordham Corp L Inst (B. Hawk (ed.), 2005), 549

EHLERMANN, C.-D., 'Reflections on a European Cartel Office' (1995) 32 *CMLRev* 471

FORRESTER, I., 'Due Process in EC Competition Case: A Distinguished Institution with Flawed Procedures' (2009) 34 *ELRev* 817

——, 'A Challenge for Europe's Judges: the Review of Fines in Competition Cases' (2011) 36 *ELRev* 185

GAUER, C., and JASPERS, M., 'Designing a European Solution for a "One Stop Leniency Shop"' (2006) *ECLR* 685

GERADIN, D., 'Breaking the EU Antitrust Enforcement Deadlock: Re-Empowering the Courts?' (2011) 36 *ELRev* 457

——, 'Antitrust Compliance Programmes and Optimal Antitrust Enforcement: A Reply to Wouter Wils' (2013) 1(2) *Journal of Antitrust Enforcement* 1

—— and HENRY, D., 'EC Fining for Competition Law Violations: An Empirical Study of the Commission's Decisional Practice and the Community Courts' Judgments' (2005) 1 *European Competition Journal* 401

—— and PETIT, N., 'Judicial Remedies under EC Competition Law: Complex Issues Arising from the "Modernisation" Process' [2005] Fordham Corp L Inst 393 (B. Hawk (ed.), 2006)

GERBER, D., 'Modernising European Competition Law: A Developmental Perspective' [2001] ECLR 122

TER HAAR, M., 'Obstruction of Investigation in EU Competition Law: Issues and Developments in the European Commission's Approach' (2013) 2 World Competition 247

HARDING, C., 'A Pathology of Business Cartels: Original Sin or the Child of Regulation?' (2010) 1 NJECL 44

HEIMLER, A., and MEHTA, K., 'Violations of Antitrust Provisions: The Optimal Level of Fines for Achieving Deterrence' (2012) 35(1) World Competition 103

HEMPEL, R., 'Access to DG Competition's Files: An Analysis of Recent EU Court Case Law' (2012) ECLR 195

HOLLES, B., 'The Hearing Officer: Thirty Years Protecting the Right to Be Heard' (2013) 1 World Competition 5

JOSHUA, J., 'The Element of Surprise' (1983) 8 ELRev 3

KATSOULACOS, Y., and ULPH, D., 'Optimal Enforcement Structures for Competition Policy: Implications of Judicial Reviews and of Internal Error Correction Mechanisms (2011) European Competition Journal 71

KELLERBAUER, M., 'Playground Instead of Playpen: The Court of Justice of the European Union's Alrosa Judgment on Article 9 of Regulation 1/2003' (2011) ECLR 1

KHAN, A., 'Rethinking Sanctions for Breaching Competition Law: Is Director Disqualification the Answer?' (2012) 35(1) World Competition 77

LEVY, N. and O'DONOGHUE, R., 'The EU Leniency Programme Comes of Age' (2004) 27 World Competition 75

MELÍCIAS, M. J., 'Did They Do It ? The Interplay Between the Standard of Proof and the Presumption of Innocence in EU Cartel Investigations' (2012) 35(3) World Competition 471

MONTAG, F., 'The Case for Radical Reform of the Infringement Procedure under Regulation 17' [1996] ECLR 428

MURPHY, G., 'Is It Time to Rebrand Legal Professional Privilege in Article 82 EC Law?' (2009) ECLR 125

NAZZINI, R., 'Administrative Enforcement, Judicial Review and Fundamental Rights in EU Competition Law: A Comparative Contextual-Functionalist Perspective' (2012) 49 CMLRev 971

OLIVER, P., 'Diagnostics—a Judgment Applying the European Convention of Human Rights to the Field of Competition' (2012) 3 Journal of European Competition Law and Practice 163

PETIT, N., and RATO, M., 'From Hard to Soft Enforcement of EC Competition Law—A Bestiary of "Sunshine" Enforcement Instruments', available at <http://ssrn.com/abstract=1270109>

RILEY, A., 'Saunders and the Power to Obtain Information in Community and United Kingdom Competition Law' (2000) 25 ELRev 264

——, 'EC Antitrust Modernisation: The Commission Does Very Nicely—Thank You! Part One: Regulation 1 and the Notification Burden' [2003] ECLR 604

——, 'EC Antitrust Modernisation: The Commission Does Very Nicely—Thank You! Part Two: Between the Idea and the Reality: Decentralisation under Regulation 1' [2003] ECLR 657

——, 'The Modernisation of EU Anti-Cartel Enforcement—Will the Commission Grasp the Opportunity?' (2010) CEPS Special Report, January

RIZZA, C., 'The Duty of National Competition Authorities to Disapply Anti-Competitive Domestic Legislation and the Resulting Limitations on the Availability of the State Action Defence (Case C-198/01 CIF)' [2004] ECLR 126

RODGER, B., 'The Commission White Paper on Modernisation of the Rules Implementing Articles 101 and 102 of the EC Treaty' (1999) 24 ELRev 653

SIBONY, A.-L., 'Casenote on KME v. Commission [2012] 49 CMLRev 1977

SLATER, D., THOMAS, S., and WAELBROECK, D., 'Competition Law Proceedings before the European Commission and the Right to a Fair Trial: No Need for Reform?' (2009) European Competition Journal 97

SLOT, P. J., 'Does the Pfleiderer Judgment Make the Fight against International Cartels More Difficult?' [2013] ECLR 197

STEPHAN, A., 'An Empirical Assessment of the European Leniency Notice' (2009) 5 Journal of Competition Law and Economics 537

TEMPLE LANG, J., 'The AM &S Judgment', in M. Hoskins and W. Robinson, A True European—Essays for Judge David Edward (Hart Publishing, 2004), Chap. 12

——, 'Commitment Decisions and Settlements with Antitrust Authorities and Private Parties Under European Antitrust Law' [2005] Fordham Corp L Inst 265 (B. Hawk (ed.), 2006)

——, 'Judicial Review of Competition Decisions under the European Convention on Human Rights and the Importance of the EFTA Court: the Norway Post Judgment' (2012) 37 ELRev 464

——, 'The Strengths and Weaknesses of the DG Competition Manual of Procedure' (2013) 1(1) J Antitrust Enforcement 132

—— and RIZZA, C., 'The Ste Colas Est and Others v. France case: European Court of Human Rights Case of 16 April 2002' [2002] ECLR 417

TIERNO CENTELLA, M.L., 'The New Settlement Procedure in Selected Cartel Cases' (2008) 3 *European Policy Newsletter* 30

VARONA, E. N., 'The Undertaking as Subject of EC Competition Law and the Imputation of Infringements to Natural or Legal Persons' (2000) 25 *ELRev* 99

——, 'The Combination of the Investigative and Prosecutorial Function and the Adjudicative Function in EC Antitrust Enforcement: A Legal and Economic Analysis' (2004) 27 *World Competition* 201

—— and DURÁTEZ, H. G., 'Interim Measures in Competition Cases Before the European Commission and the Courts' [2002] *ECLR* 512

VESTERDORF, B., 'Legal Professional Privilege and the Privilege Against Self-Incrimination in EC Law: Recent Developments and Current Issues' [2004] Fordham Corp L Inst (B. Hawk, (ed.) 2005) 107

——, 'The Court of Justice and Unlimited Jurisdiction: What Does It Mean in Practice?' (2009) 2 *Global Competition Policy* (June)

VÖLCKER, S., 'Casenote on *Pfleiderer AG v. Bundeskartellamt*' (2012) 49 *CMLRev* 695

WAGNER-VON PAPP, F., 'Best and Even Better Practices in Commitment Procedures after Alrosa: The Dangers of Abandoning the "Struggle for Competition Law"' (2012) 49 *CMLRev* 929

WALSH, D. J., 'Carrots and Sticks—Leniency and Fines in EC Cartel Cases' (2009) *ECLR* 30

WASMEIER, M., and THWAITES, N., 'The Development of ne bis in idem into a transnational fundamental right in EU law: comments on recent developments' (2006) 31 *ELRev* 565

WESSELING, R., 'A Principled Argument for Personal Criminal Sanctions as Punishment under EC Cartel Law' (2007) 30 *World Competition* 197

——, 'Legal Certainty and Cartel Criminalisation within the EU Member States' [2012] *CLJ* 677

—— and VAN DER WOUDE, M., 'The Lawfulness and Acceptability of Enforcement of European Cartel Law' (2012) 35(4) *World Competition* 569

WHELAN, P., 'Cartel Criminalization and the Challenge of 'Moral Wrongfulness' [2013] 33 (3) *OJLS* 535

——, 'Cartel Criminalisation and Due Process; The Challenge Imposing Criminal Sanctions Alongside Administrative Sanctions within the EU' (2013) 64(2) Northern Ireland Legal Quarterly 143

WILS, W., 'Self-incrimination in EC Antitrust Enforcement: A Legal and Economic Analysis' (2003) 26(4) *World Competition* 567

——, 'Ne Bis In Idem in EC Antitrust Enforcement: A Legal and Economic Analysis' [2004] *World Competition: Law and Economics Review* 131

——, 'The European Commission's 2006 Guidelines on Antitrust Fines: A Legal and Economic Analysis' (2007) 30 *World Competition* 197

——, 'The Use of Settlements in Public Antitrust Enforcement: Objectives and Principles' (2008) 31(3) *World Competition* 335

——, 'The Increased Level of Antitrust Fines, Judicial Review, and the European Convention on Human Rights' (2010) 33(1) *World Competition* 5

——, 'Discretion and Prioritisation in Public Antitrust Enforcement' (2011) 34(3) *World Competition* 353

——, 'Recidivism in EU Antitrust Enforcement: A Legal and Economic Analysis' (2012) 35(1) *World Competition* 5

——, 'The Oral Hearing in Competition Proceedings Before the European Commission' (2012) 35(3) *World Competition* 397

——, 'The Role of the Hearing Officer in Competition Proceedings before the European Commission' (2012) 35(3) *World Competition* 431

——, 'Antitrust Compliance Programmes and Optimal Antitrust Enforcement' (2013) 1(1) *Journal of Antitrust Enforcement* 52

WOUDE, M., VAN DER, 'Hearing Officers and EC Antitrust Procedures: The Art of Making Subjective Procedures more Objective' (1996) *CMLRev* 531

14

PRIVATE ENFORCEMENT

1. CENTRAL ISSUES

1. In Chapter 13 it is seen that the Commission and the national competition authorities play a crucial role in detecting, punishing, and deterring violations of the EU competition law rules.

2. This chapter focuses on private civil actions which may achieve corrective justice by allowing victims to obtain compensation. Private enforcement also relieves enforcement pressure on public agencies and may help to deter violations of the rules and contribute to the development and clarification of the law. Private litigants may therefore supplement public enforcement by raising Articles 101 or 102 either as a shield, or as a sword, in civil proceedings before a national court.

3. EU law makes it clear that:

   a. National courts are bound to apply directly effective provisions of EU law, including Articles 101 and 102.

   b. Although national rules of procedure, evidence, and substance govern proceedings before the national courts, this is subject to the overriding requirement that the rules must not be less favourable than those relating to similar claims of a domestic nature and must not make it virtually impossible or excessively difficult to exercise the right that the national courts are obliged to protect (the principles of equivalence and effectiveness).

   c. Provisions in an agreement that contravene Article 101 (and it seems Article 102) are void and unenforceable. The entire agreement will be void if the prohibited provisions cannot be severed from the remainder of the agreement.

   d. Damages, entailing full compensation, must, in principle, be available to those that have suffered loss in consequence of a breach of Articles 101 or 102.

   e. National courts must not take decisions that run counter to those adopted by the Commission.

   f. Injunctions may need to be available to protect putative EU rights.

4. Until recently there has, nonetheless, been relatively little antitrust litigation brought by private individuals before national courts. Although the amount is beginning to grow in some Member States, the Commission is seeking to encourage private litigation further, particularly damages actions, in a way that will complement but not jeopardise public enforcement.

5. In 2005, the Commission published a Green Paper which identified key obstacles to damages claims in the Member States and set out possible options for overcoming these problems. A follow-up White Paper (2008) contained specific proposals to facilitate damages actions throughout the EU as a complement to public enforcement. Following consultation and debate, the Commission, in June 2013, published a range of measures designed to facilitate damage claims by victims of antitrust violations and to optimise the interaction between public and private enforcement, including:

   • a proposal for a Directive designed to remove a number of practical difficulties confronted by victims of infringements of the EU antitrust rules when instigating damages claims;

   • a recommen.dation of non-binding principles for collective redress mechanisms for Member States; and

   • a practical guide on the quantification of harm for damages to assist national courts.

2. INTRODUCTION

A. GENERAL

Without effective enforcement, the objectives of the antitrust rules will not be achieved. Chapter 13 examines public enforcement through the European competition network (the Commission and the national competition authorities (NCAs)). This chapter concentrates on private civil enforcement of the rules through claims made by private litigants in the national courts and tribunals of the individual Member States (the national courts).

The Treaty contains no specific provision governing private rights of action for damages or injunctions following a violation of the EU competition law rules.[1] Private proceedings in the national courts are, however, possible by virtue of the fact that Articles 101 and 102 have direct effect. This chapter commences by discussing the principle of direct effect and national procedural autonomy and considering why there has, nonetheless, until recently been relatively little antitrust litigation in the EU. It considers the relationship between public and private enforcement and outlines the Commission's policy towards private enforcement, the initiatives it has taken to encourage private litigation, and mechanisms for cooperation between the Commission and national courts. Section 3 and Section 4 then examine more closely the obligations on national courts when dealing with cases that raise the issue of whether a contract in violation of Article 101 or Article 102 is enforceable and whether, and if so when, damages and injunctions should be available to remedy such violations.

B. DIRECT EFFECT, THE PRINCIPLE OF NATIONAL PROCEDURAL AUTONOMY, AND 'EU' REMEDIES

EU law makes it clear that national courts are bound to apply directly effective Treaty provisions, to give them precedence over conflicting principles of national law and to protect the rights which individuals derive from them. In Chapter 2 it was seen that Articles 101 and 102 are directly effective. A litigant may, therefore, question an agreement's or other conduct's compatibility with the competition rules in proceedings before a national court. Further, he may additionally, or alternatively, seek some form of redress in respect of a breach of the rules, perhaps damages to compensate him in respect of loss, restitution, or an injunction to put an immediate end to the violation and to prevent future breaches of the rules.[2]

Where an individual seeks to vindicate or protect his EU rights before a national court, the general principle is that of 'national procedural autonomy'—national law sets out the rules governing proceedings: 'in the absence of Community rules on this subject, it is for the domestic legal system of each Member State to designate the courts having jurisdiction and to determine the procedural conditions governing actions at law intended to ensure the protection of rights which citizens have from the direct effect of Community law'.[3]

Although the protection given to EU rights and the availability of any remedy for breach of the competition rules is, in principle, dependent on the procedural, evidential, and substantive rules applicable in each particular Member State, the CJ has held that national rules:

(1) must not be less favourable than those relating to similar claims of a domestic nature (the principle of equivalence); and

---

[1] Contrast the position in the US, see Clayton Act 1914, ss. 4 and 16.

[2] For a discussion of competition law litigation in the UK Courts, see, e.g., B. Rodger, 'Competition Law Litigation in the UK Courts: A Study of All Cases to 2004'—Parts I, II and III [2006] *ECLR* 241–248, 279–292 and 341–350 and B. Rodger, 'Why not court? A study of follow-on actions in the UK' (2013) 1 *Journal of Antitrust Enforcement* 104.

[3] Case 33/76, *Rewe-Zentralfinanz eG and Rewe-Zentral AG v. Landwirtschaftskammer für das Saarland* [1976] ECR 1989.

(2) must not make it virtually impossible or excessively difficult to exercise the rights that the national courts are obliged to protect (the principle of effectiveness).[4]

The principle of effectiveness, in particular, imposes an important inhibition on the free application of the national rules. Further, the duty of sincere cooperation imposed on Member States[5] requires that remedies granted by national courts must be adequate and must guarantee real and *effective* judicial protection for EU rights.[6] Although this obligation may leave a national court freedom to determine how best to protect those rights,[7] in some cases it may require the national court to grant one of two or more possible remedies[8] or even a specific remedy to rectify a specific wrong.[9] For example, it has been held that a Member State is obliged, in specified circumstances, to compensate individuals who have been injured by its breach of EU law[10] and to repay charges it has levied in breach of EU law.[11] National courts are not required to grant *new* remedies,[12] but this obligation means that national rules may have to be adapted or extended to ensure that a remedy is available where it is required by EU law. National defences and procedural limitations to the claim apply insofar as those rules comply with the principles of equivalence and effectiveness (the *acquis communautaire*).

Section 2, 3, and 4 consider the critical question of whether and in what circumstances the principle of effectiveness requires, within the sphere of competition law, that any EU remedies should be granted. It will be seen that EU law establishes that:

(1) National courts must not take decisions that run counter to those adopted by the Commission;

(2) Provisions in an agreement that contravene Article 101 (and it seems Article 102) are void and unenforceable. The entire agreement will be void if the prohibited provisions cannot be severed from the remainder of the agreement;

(3) Full compensation, must, in principle, be available to those that have suffered loss in consequence of a breach of Article 101 or 102;

(4) Interim relief must be available where necessary to protect putative EU rights;

(5) Limitations on those rights must comply with the principles of equivalence and effectiveness.

In addition, it is seen that the Commission has proposed an EU Directive designed to facilitate damage claims by the victims of antitrust violations, which will impose further constraints on the autonomy of national systems in this sphere.[13]

---

[4] Case 33/76, *Rewe-Zentralfinanz eG and Rewe-Zentral AG v. Landwirtschaftskammer für das Saarland* [1976] ECR 1989. See discussion of Case C-360/09, *Pfleiderer AG v.Bundeskartellamt* [2011] ECR I-5161, discussed in the text accompanying n. 46.

[5] Formerly set out in Art. 10 EC but now substantially set out in Art. 4(3) TEU which provides that the Union and Member States are to assist each other in carrying out tasks flowing from the Treaties and that Member States 'shall take any appropriate measure…to ensure fulfillment of the obligations…' and 'shall facilitate the achievement of the Union's tasks and refrain from any measure which could jeopardise the attainment of the Union's objectives', see Chap. 8.

[6] See Case 14/83, *Von Colson and Kamann v. Land Nordrhein-Westfalen* [1984] ECR 1891, especially para. 23 and Case 33/76, *Rewe-Zentralfinanz eG and Rewe-Zentral AG v. Landwirtschaftskammer für das Saarland* [1976] ECR 1989, para. 5.

[7] Case 34/67, *Lück v. Hauptzollamt Köln* [1968] ECR 245.

[8] See Case C-271/91, *Marshall v. Southampton and South-West Hampshire Area Health Authority (Teaching) (No. 2)* [1993] ECR I-4367.

[9] See, e.g., Case 199/82, *Ammistrazione delle Finanze dello Stato v. San Giorgio SpA* [1983] ECR 3595 (the applicant's right to restitution is a 'consequence of and an adjunct to' the rights conferred on that individual by EU law).

[10] See Cases C-6 and 9/90, *Francovich v. Italy* [1991] ECR I-5357.

[11] See, e.g., Case C-242/95, *GT-Link A/S v. De Danske Statsbaner (DSB)* [1997] ECR I-4449.

[12] Case 158/80, *Rewe-Handelsgesellschaft Nord mbH v. Hauptzollamt Kiel* [1981] ECR 1805.

[13] See Section 4, pp. 1100–1126.

C. A PAUCITY OF ANTITRUST LITIGATION IN EUROPE?

Although it is clear that Articles 101 and 102 are directly effective and that certain remedies must be available to protect EU rights derived from the competition law provisions, until recently there has been relatively little 'antitrust litigation' brought by private individuals before national courts.[14] Indeed, the Commission notes that 'in only 25% of all antitrust infringement decisions the Commission took in the past seven years did victims seek to claim compensation'.[15] Private litigation is now beginning to grow in some Member States, such as the UK, Germany, and the Netherlands, but the EU position remains in stark contrast to that which exists in the US where there is a culture of antitrust litigation and where a large proportion of competition cases are litigated privately.[16] In the US the success of private actions has been founded on a number of factors, for example:

(1) legislative provisions which explicitly provide for damages for those injured by reason of anything forbidden in the antitrust laws and injunctive relief against threatened loss or damage by a violation;[17]

(2) the availability of treble damages;[18]

(3) the fact that defendants are jointly and severally liable for any damage caused with no right to contribution for co-defendants;

(4) the existence of wide discovery powers;

(5) the statutory right for claimants to use judgments entered against the defendant as *prima facie* evidence against that defendant;[19]

(6) the ability of the successful plaintiff (claimant), contrary to the ordinary rule in the US that each party bears its own cost, to recover costs, including reasonable attorney's fees;

(7) the ability to bring class actions;

(8) the availability of contingency fees;

(9) the fact that there is more of a 'litigation culture' in the US;

(10) the fact that most cases are tried by jury;

and

(11) the fact that the public authorities have not taken on such a central role in antitrust enforcement.

Although there is some concern in the US that the rules are too litigation friendly and have 'coercive'[20] elements which may have encouraged nuisance and unmeritorious litigation (see further Section 2.D), the prevailing view appears to be that the private enforcement has played an important contribution to the success and development of the US antitrust laws.[21]

---

[14] Collective antitrust actions have been brought in only six Member States (Austria, France, Germany, Italy, Spain, and the UK), and in none of these Member States were more than five of the actions in the last five years, see the report of the European Parliament's Economic and Monetary Affairs Committee (ECON), *Collective Redress in Antitrust* (June 2012), 39, available at <http://www.europarl.europa.eu/committees/en/studiesdownload.html?languageDocument=EN&file=74351>.

[15] IP/13/525, Commission proposes legislation to facilitate damages claims by victims of antitrust violations.

[16] In the US, 'of the 1165 antitrust cases brought in the 2006–2007 Term, 1150 were brought by private actors', O. Odudu, 'Development of Private Enforcement in the EU: Lessons from the Roberts Court' [2008] 53 *Ant Bull* 873. See also White Paper on Competition Policy, 'World Class Competition Regime', Cm. 5233 (July 2001), para. 8.1.

[17] Clayton Act 1914, ss. 4 and 16.

[18] Clayton Act 1914, s. 4.

[19] Clayton Act 1914, s. 5(a).

[20] e.g., the right to treble damages, the fact that the defendant never gets its costs, even if it wins, and the fact that liability is joint and several with no right to contribution from co-defendants.

[21] On the US, see further nn. 44 and 45 and accompanying text.

A key factor *initially* contributing to the dearth of litigation in the EU was undoubtedly the way that Articles 101 and 102 were enforced prior to modernisation. In particular, the Commission's exclusive right to grant exemptions under Article 101(3), coupled with its wide interpretation of Article 101(1), gave the Commission tight control over enforcement[22] and effectively excluded the national courts from 'what the legal system of the United States understands by antitrust analysis'[23] (the courts could apply only half of Article 101). Private litigation has also been, and is still being, deterred by a number of other obstacles which have varied over time and from jurisdiction to jurisdiction and include:[24]

- the cost and risk of litigation. This may well deter many potential claimants from acting, particularly when they have not suffered much loss individually (class or other consolidated actions and contingency fees are not widely available in Europe[25]) and/or where unsuccessful claimants may have to pay a defendant's legal costs;[26]

- uncertainty over standing issues (who may sue);

- the difficulty of gathering the requisite evidence, especially where it is situated in other Member States. Although it might be possible in certain circumstances for claimants to get access to some evidence through access to the file or by making a claim under the Transparency Regulation,[27] discovery rules and the question of when national courts can order disclosure vary considerably between Member States.[28] Further, there has been uncertainty over the question of whether, and if so when, private litigants should have access to evidence held by the Commission or other NCAs, including leniency documents;

- uncertainty over the weight to be given to decisions of the Commission or of other NCAs;

- the fact that proceedings are likely to be lengthy and protracted;

- the complex economic evidence which may have to be raised to establish a breach of the rules (most cases will require markets to be defined and may involve sophisticated economic argument);

- the need, in damages claims, to establish a causal link between the damage suffered by the applicant and the infringement of the competition rules;

- uncertainty over how national rules on damages and injunctions apply. For example, what types of damages are available in respect of a breach of the competition rules, how they should be quantified, and in what circumstances a preliminary or permanent injunction is available;

- uncertainty over issues such as how national limitation rules apply;

- the fact that national courts have an obligation to ensure that their decisions do not conflict with any decision given, or which might be given, at the EU level, so national courts may in

---

[22] See, e.g., M. Monti, 'Effective Private Enforcement of EC Antitrust Law' Sixth EU Competition Law and Policy Workshop Florence, 1–2 June 2001.

[23] C. A. Jones, *Private Enforcement of Antitrust Law in the EU, UK and USA* (Oxford University Press, 1999), 85; see also Chap. 4.

[24] See obstacles identified by the Commission in its Green Paper: Damages Actions for Breach of the EC Antitrust Rules COM/2005/0672/final, discussed in Section 4.A.i.g.

[25] See n. 14 and IP/13/524.

[26] See, e.g., J. Peysner, 'Costs and Financing in Private Third Party Competition Damages Actions' (2006) 3(1) *Competition Law Review* 97.

[27] See Chap. 13 and, e.g., Case T-2/03, *Verein für Konsumenteninformation* [2005] ECR II-1121, Case T-437/08, *CDC Hydrogen Peroxide* v. *Commission* 15 December 2011 and Ombudsman Decision 3699/2006/ELB, 2010.

[28] See Case T-5/93, *Tremblay* v. *Commission* [1995] ECR II-185 The national court may also ask the Commission to transmit to them information in its possession or its opinion on questions concerning the application of the EU competition law rules, see Regulation 1/2003, Art. 15(1) and n. 65 and accompanying text.

certain circumstances have to stay proceedings or take interim measures pending the outcome of a Commission decision or an appeal from such a decision;

and

- the fact that some national courts have limited experience dealing with antitrust arguments and may not, consequently, be the most appropriate or understanding forum for the hearing. In a case before the English Court of Appeal in 2007, for example, Mummery LJ remarked that the nature of the difficult issues arising in that case (access to essential facilities and legal curbs on excessive and discriminatory pricing) might 'be solved more satisfactorily by arbitration or by a specialist body equipped with appropriate expertise and flexible powers. The adversarial procedures of an ordinary private law action, the limited scope of expertise in the ordinary courts and the restricted scope of legal remedies available are not best suited to helping the parties out of a deadlocked negotiating position or to achieving a business-like result reflecting both their respective interests and the public interest. These are not, however, matters for decision by the court, which must do the best that it can with a complex piece of private law litigation.'[29]

The Commission hopes to tackle a number of these obstacles through harmonising and/or other measures. In particular, in June 2013 the Commission published a package of measures, discussed in Section 2.D and Section 4.A.i.g, designed to facilitate damages claims by victims of antitrust violations:

- a proposal for a Directive designed to remove a number of practical difficulties confronted by victims of infringements of the EU antitrust rules when instigating damages claims;[30]
- a recommendation of non-binding common principles for collective redress mechanisms for Member States;[31] and
- a practical guide on the quantification of harm for damages to assist national courts.[32]

D. THE RELATIONSHIP BETWEEN PRIVATE AND PUBLIC ENFORCEMENT: SHOULD PRIVATE ACTIONS BE ENCOURAGED?

Private civil actions may achieve corrective justice by allowing compensation of victims. It may, therefore, be seen as having a 'compensation function'—to compensate those harmed by the competition law infringement. Further, as private enforcement may relieve enforcement pressure on public enforcement agencies, it may also deter violations of the rules and help to develop and clarify the law. Arguably, therefore, it also serves a 'deterrent function'—to deter the violation of the competition rules and to punish the perpetrators.[33] There is a view that public enforcement is better suited

---

[29] *British Horseracing Board Limited* v. *Attheraces Limited* [2007] EWCA Civ 38, para. 7.

[30] Proposal for a directive of the European Parliament and of the Council on certain rules governing actions for damages under national law for infringements of the competition law provision of the Member States and the European Union COM(2013) 404 final, see also IP/13/205 and MEMO/13/531.

[31] Commission Recommendation on common principles for injunctive and compensatory collective redress mechanisms in the Member States concerning violations of rights granted under Union law C(2013) 3539/3, see also IP/13/524 and MEMO/13/530.

[32] Commission Staff Working Document, 'Practical Guide on Quantifying Harm in Actions for damages based on breaches of Article 101 or 102 of the Treaty on the Functioning of the European Union', SWD(2013) 205.

[33] See A. P. Komninos, 'Public and Private Antitrust Enforcement in Europe: Complement? Overlap?' (2006) 3 *Competition Law Review* 1, 9; R. Nazzini, and A. Nikpay, 'Private Actions in EC Competition Law' (2008) 4 *Competition Policy International* 107, 109.

to serve the deterrent function, whilst private enforcement is more apt to pursue the compensation function.[34] Wils describes what he calls a 'separate-tasks approach'.[35]

W. P. J. Wils, 'The Relationship between Public Antitrust Enforcement and Private Actions for Damages' [2009] 32 *World Competition* 3, 12-13

If, as argued above, public antitrust enforcement is the superior instrument to pursue the objectives of clarification and development of the law and of deterrence and punishment, whereas private actions for damages are superior for the pursuit of corrective justice through compensation, then the optimal antitrust enforcement system would appear to be a system in which public antitrust enforcement aims at clarification and development of the law and at deterrence and punishment, while private actions for damages aim at compensation. Such a separate-tasks approach, under which public antitrust enforcement and private actions for damages are each assigned the tasks they are best at, appears to be the approach adopted by the European Commission in its 2008 White Paper on Damages actions for breach of the EC antitrust rules. Indeed, the 2008 White Paper states that:

> its 'primary objective…is to improve the legal conditions for victims to exercise their right under the Treaty to reparation of all damage suffered as a result of a breach of the EC antitrust rules. Full compensation is, therefore, the first and foremost guiding principle…. Another important guiding principle of the Commission's policy is to preserve strong public enforcement of Articles [101] and [102] by the Commission and the competition authorities of the Member States. Accordingly, the measures put forward in this White Paper are designed to create an effective system of private enforcement by means of damages actions that complements, but does not replace or jeopardize, public enforcement'

Even if it is correct that the two types of enforcement primarily pursue different objectives, it is clear that that they are linked and have effects on each other.[36]

A. P. Komninos, 'Public and Private Antitrust Enforcement in Europe: Complement? Overlap?' (2006) 3 *Competition Law Review* 1, 10–13

While it is sometimes said, especially by public enforcement officials, that private enforcement cannot as such make a substantial contribution to the effectiveness of competition law enforcement, mainstream antitrust scholarship argues that the ideal antitrust enforcement model should combine both public and private elements. Each of the two systems aims at different aspects of the same phenomenon; they are complementary and both are necessary for the effectiveness of the whole competition law enforcement.

The advantages of private antitrust enforcement have long been stressed in the United States, where studies estimate its ratio to public antitrust suits at between 10 to 1 and 20 to 1. The primary function of

---

[34] Komninos, 'Public and Private Antitrust Enforcement in Europe: Complement? Overlap?' (cited in n. 33), 109; W. P. J. Wils, 'The Relationship between Public Antitrust Enforcement and Private Actions for Damages' (2009) 32 *World Competition* 3, 8–12.

[35] In its 2005 Green Paper, however, the Commission stated that damages actions and public enforcement serve the same deterrence objective, Green Paper: Damages actions for breach of the EC antitrust rules, COM/2005/0672/final, 2.7

[36] See, e.g., Wils, 'The Relationship between Public Antitrust Enforcement and Private Actions for Damages' (cited in n. 34), 3, ICN, Interaction of Public and Private Enforcement in Cartel Cases', May 2007, available at <http://www.internationalcompetitionnetwork.org/uploads/library/doc349.pdf>.

the private action is clearly compensatory. The victims of anti-competitive practices can only make up for their losses before a civil court and public enforcement cannot have any direct bearing there. At the same time, however, private action, apart from its compensatory function, furthers the overall deterrent effect of the law. Thus, economic agents themselves become instrumental in implementing the regulatory policy on competition and the general level of compliance with the law is raised. Indeed, the private litigant in US antitrust has been considered a 'private attorney-general'. A further advantage is that the weaknesses of public enforcement, most notably the 'enforcement gap' generated by the perceived inability of public enforcement to deal with all attention-worthy cases, are counter-balanced.

From a *Community* competition law perspective, however, there are additional arguments in favour of a system of antitrust enforcement that combines strong elements of private enforcement. First of all, the civil action constitutes in Europe the only complete means (complaints apart) for private parties and individuals to exercise the rights guaranteed by the Treaty competition provisions, which form part of the Community's economic constitution. Pursuant to the Court of Justice's long-standing case law, Articles [101] and [102] TFEU enjoy direct effect and grant individuals actionable rights which national courts must protect. Secondly, when citizens pursue their Community rights in the national courts, apart from serving their personal interests, they also indirectly act in the Community interest and become 'the principal "guardians" of the legal integrity of Community law within Europe'. The exercise of those rights thus becomes a question of benefiting from *general Community law*, and brings 'the application of Community competition rules closer to citizens and undertakings'…

c. The Relevance of the Goals of EC Competition Law

The question of the relationship and balance between public and private antitrust enforcement in Europe must also be seen in the context of the more substantive question of the goal of EC competition law: is it the public interest in safeguarding effective competition in the common market or the private interest in protecting one's economic freedom? This is necessary because there is a widespread misunderstanding as to the interests protected by competition law as such in the contexts of public and private antitrust enforcement. Thus some authors distinguish between public enforcement, which pursues the public interest of protecting the competition norms through administrative or criminal sanctions, and private enforcement which pursues the private interest of protecting competitors and consumers through civil 'sanctions', most notably civil claims for damages. The Commission has also at times followed a similar approach, with statements which seem to ignore the instrumental character of civil claims.

Indeed, the Commission has been reproached for insisting on distinguishing between public authorities whose acts are guided by the public interest, and national courts which decide disputes pertaining to the private interest. Such a distinction does not do justice to the role of civil courts when they enforce competition law in the context of private disputes between economic operators, since they in fact have to consider the economic public policy in their judgments when the dispute in question has a wider impact on the market. In this sense, private interest plays a complementary role to the public interest. It is correctly recognised that the courts cannot simply confine themselves to considering the interests of the litigants, but must also have regard to the general interests of economic policy.

Private and public enforcement are thus closely connected, for example: public enforcement actions have a facilitating effect on private enforcement; a public finding of infringement may be relied upon to establish the existence of a competition law infringement[37] and may provide evidence helpful in establishing causation and harm;[38] and private actions can reinforce public enforcement by increasing deterrence. Not only do they increase the resources available for the prosecution of competition

---

[37] See discussion of Reg. 1/2003, Art. 16 and Section 2.B.ii.a and Section 2.E., especially p. 1095.

[38] Wils, 'The Relationship between Public Antitrust Enforcement and Private Actions for Damages' (cited in n. 34), 3, 15–16.

law infringements[39] so filling any 'enforcement gap', but they increase the likelihood of detection and increase the cost of non-compliance.

Greater private enforcement should therefore have a significant effect on the application of the EU competition rules by enlisting those closest to violations of the competition rules in the enforcement process, relieving enforcement pressure on public enforcement agencies (freeing their resources for complex cases and preventing them from being dragged into private disputes), heightening awareness of, and respect for, the competition provisions (it creates a culture of competition), ensuring compensation for victims of breaches, and deterring violations of the rules. It may therefore contribute to social welfare by improving detection and deterrence of anti-competitive conduct and by fostering damage compensation, easier access to justice, and market competition.[40] Further, if a litigation culture does grow, the development of the competition laws would become less heavily influenced by the Commission and more heavily influenced by the courts (national and, through Article 267 references, the CJ) than has previously been the case.

The view that private enforcement should be further encouraged is not held universally, however. It has been argued, for example, that private enforcement is unnecessary either as an additional mechanism for enforcement of the rules or as a mechanism for achieving corrective justice.[41] Further, that public enforcement provides a superior and less costly mechanism for ensuring that the competition rules are not violated and that corrective justice is unlikely to be served by such proceedings. Even those supporting the view that greater private enforcement would be desirable have advocated caution against unleashing too excessive a litigation culture.[42] Indeed, in the US, there has been considerable concern that private litigation, motivated by private profit rather than public interest considerations, may sometime deter enforcement (in particular by deterring leniency applications)[43] and can be wasteful, encouraging unmeritorious or 'anaemic' claims to be brought and settled in order to avoid protracted and expensive litigation.[44] The latter concerns, in particular, may partly have led the US Supreme Court to take a series of drastic steps reducing the opportunity for successful antitrust litigation to be brought or even commenced.[45]

Difficult decisions may also have to be taken where the interaction between the two enforcement systems becomes strained. In *Pfleiderer*,[46] for example, the CJ had to give a ruling relating to the question of whether Pfleiderer, a victim of the German decor paper cartel, should be provided with access to information held on the German Federal Cartel Office's (*Bundeskartellamt*) file, including the

---

[39] Nazzini, and Nikpay, 'Private Actions in EC Competition Law' (cited in n. 33), 107, 111.

[40] See Report for the European Commission, *Making Antitrust Damages actions More Effective in the EU*, (2007), Part I, s. 2, available at <http://ec.europa.eu/competition/antitrust/actionsdamages/files_white_paper/impact_study.pdf>.

[41] See W. Wils, *Principles of European Antitrust Enforcement* (Hart Publishing, 2005), Chap. 4 and W. P. J. Wils, 'Should private antitrust enforcement be encouraged?' [2003] 26(3) *World Competition* 473 (but see now Wils, 'The Relationship between Public Antitrust Enforcement and Private Actions for Damages' (cited in n. 34), 3) and, e.g., F. G. Jacobs 'Civil Enforcement of EEC Antitrust Law' (1984) 82 *Mich LR* 1364.

[42] See, e.g., the responses to the Commission's Green Paper: Damages Actions for Breach of the EC Antitrust Rules COM/2005/0672/final and D. Wilsher, 'The Public Aspects of Private Enforcement in EC Law: some Constitutional and Administrative Challenges of a Damages Culture' (2006) 3(1) *Competition Law Review*, 27.

[43] A key plank in the DOJ's cartel policy, but see the Criminal Penalty Enhancement and Reform Act 2004 detrebling provision, discussed in Chap. 9.

[44] See, e.g., R. A. Posner, *Antitrust Law* (2nd edn, University of Chicago Press, 2001), Wils, 'The Relationship between Public Antitrust Enforcement and Private Actions for Damages' (cited in n. 34), 3.

[45] See, e.g., *Bell Atlantic Corp. v. Twombly*, 550 U.S. 544 and W. E. Kovacic, 'Private Rights of Action and the Enforcement of Public Competition Laws', in C. Baudenbacher (ed.), *Current Developments in European and International Competition Law: 17th St.Gallen International Competition Law Forum ICF 2010* (Helbing & Lichtenhahn Verlag, 2011) 421, 429–430 and O. Odudu, 'Development of Private Enforcement in the EU: Lessons from the Roberts Court' [2008] 53 *Ant Bull* 873. Indeed, the number of private civil antitrust cases commenced in US district courts has significantly dropped from 1,318 in 2008 to 702 in 2012 (see <http://www.uscourts.gov/uscourts/Statistics/JudicialBusiness/2012/appendices/C02Sep12.pdf>.

[46] Case C-360/09, *Pfleiderer AG v. Bundeskartellamt* [2011] ECR I-5161.

leniency and other documents voluntarily provided by the leniency applicant. Advocate-General Mazák took the view that an NCA should *not* grant injured parties access to self-incriminating statements voluntarily provided by leniency applicants as this could substantially reduce the attractiveness and, consequently, the effectiveness of the NCA's leniency programme and, in turn, the effective enforcement of Article 101.[47] An interference with the injured parties' right to an effective remedy and a fair trial was thus justified by the legitimate aim of ensuring the effective enforcement of Article 101 TFEU by NCAs and ultimately private litigants' possibility of obtaining an effective remedy.[48] The CJ, in contrast, in a judgment which has provoked some controversy and considerable debate, supported a more balanced approach, holding that it was necessary for the national court in each case to weigh, according to national law and taking into account all the relevant factors in the case,[49] the respective interests of the leniency applicant (to have voluntarily submitted corporate statements protected) and the claimant (to have access to documents which would facilitate the claim).[50]

Case C-360/09 *Pfleiderer AG* v. *Bundeskartellamt* [2011] ECR I-5161

Court of Justice

19 It must be recalled at the outset that the competition authorities of the Member States and their courts and tribunals are required to apply Articles 101 TFEU and 102 TFEU, where the facts come within the scope of European Union law, and to ensure that those articles are applied effectively in the general interest (see, to that effect, Case C-439/08 *VEBIC*...paragraph 56).

20 Neither the provisions of the EC Treaty on competition nor Regulation No 1/2003 lay down common rules on leniency or common rules on the right of access to documents relating to a leniency procedure which have been voluntarily submitted to a national competition authority pursuant to a national leniency programme.

...

23 ...even if the guidelines set out by the Commission may have some effect on the practice of the national competition authorities, it is, in the absence of binding regulation under European Union law on the subject, for Member States to establish and apply national rules on the right of access, by persons adversely affected by a cartel, to documents relating to leniency procedures.

24 However, while the establishment and application of those rules falls within the competence of the Member States, the latter must none the less exercise that competence in accordance with European Union law (see, to that effect, the judgment of 12 November 2009 in Case C-154/08 *Commission* v *Spain*, paragraph 121 and the case-law cited). In particular, they may not render the implementation of European Union law impossible or excessively difficult (see, to that effect, Case C-298/96 *Oelmühle and Schmidt Söhne*..., paragraphs 23 and 24 and the case-law cited) and, specifically, in the area of competition law, they must ensure that the rules which they establish or apply do not jeopardise the effective application of Articles 101 TFEU and 102 TFEU (see, to that effect, *VEBIC*, paragraph 57).

25 However, as maintained by the Commission and the Member States which have submitted observations, leniency programmes are useful tools if efforts to uncover and bring to an end infringements of competition rules are to be effective and serve, therefore, the objective of effective application of Articles 101 TFEU and 102 TFEU.

---

[47] Case C-360/09, *Pfleiderer AG* v. *Bundeskartellamt* [2011] ECR I-5161, 16 December 2010, paras. 38–42.

[48] Case C-360/09, *Pfleiderer AG* v. *Bundeskartellamt* [2011] ECR I-5161, 16 December 2010, paras. 38–42.

[49] Case C-360/09, *Pfleiderer AG* v. *Bundeskartellamt* [2011] ECR I-5161, 16 December 2010, para. 31.

[50] Case C-360/09, *Pfleiderer AG* v. *Bundeskartellamt* [2011] ECR I-5161, 16 December 2010, para. 30.

26 The effectiveness of those programmes could, however, be compromised if documents relating to a leniency procedure were disclosed to persons wishing to bring an action for damages, even if the national competition authorities were to grant to the applicant for leniency exemption, in whole or in part, from the fine which they could have imposed.

27 The view can reasonably be taken that a person involved in an infringement of competition law, faced with the possibility of such disclosure, would be deterred from taking the opportunity offered by such leniency programmes, particularly when, pursuant to Articles 11 and 12 of Regulation No 1/2003, the Commission and the national competition authorities might exchange information which that person has voluntarily provided.

28 Nevertheless, it is settled case-law that any individual has the right to claim damages for loss caused to him by conduct which is liable to restrict or distort competition (see Case C-453/99 *Courage and Crehan* [2001] ECR I-6297, paragraphs 24 and 26, and Joined Cases C-295/04 to C-298/04 *Manfredi and Others* [2006] ECR I-6619, paragraphs 59 and 61).

29 The existence of such a right strengthens the working of the Community competition rules and discourages agreements or practices, frequently covert, which are liable to restrict or distort competition. From that point of view, actions for damages before national courts can make a significant contribution to the maintenance of effective competition in the European Union (*Courage and Crehan*, paragraph 27).

30 Accordingly, in the consideration of an application for access to documents relating to a leniency programme submitted by a person who is seeking to obtain damages from another person who has taken advantage of such a leniency programme, it is necessary to ensure that the applicable national rules are not less favourable than those governing similar domestic claims and that they do not operate in such a way as to make it practically impossible or excessively difficult to obtain such compensation (see, to that effect, *Courage and Crehan*, paragraph 29) and to weigh the respective interests in favour of disclosure of the information and in favour of the protection of that information provided voluntarily by the applicant for leniency.

31 That weighing exercise can be conducted by the national courts and tribunals only on a case-by-case basis, according to national law, and taking into account all the relevant factors in the case.

32 In the light of the foregoing, the answer to the question referred is that the provisions of European Union law on cartels, and in particular Regulation No 1/2003, must be interpreted as not precluding a person who has been adversely affected by an infringement of European Union competition law and is seeking to obtain damages from being granted access to documents relating to a leniency procedure involving the perpetrator of that infringement. It is, however, for the courts and tribunals of the Member States, on the basis of their national law, to determine the conditions under which such access must be permitted or refused by weighing the interests protected by European Union law.

The Commission and NCAs have been concerned that this judgment does not allow them to guarantee the protection of whistleblower evidence and that the consequent uncertainty could result in their leniency programmes being undermined. The CJ held, however, in *Bundeswettbewerbsbehörde v. Donau Chemie*,[51] that an Austrian law which prohibited disclosure to third parties of court files on public law competition proceedings, unless all parties to the proceedings agreed, was not compatible with the principle of effectiveness and so conflicted with EU law. '[I]n competition law... any rule that is rigid, either by providing for absolute refusal to grant access... or for granting access as a matter of course... is liable to undermine the effective application of... Article 101'.[52] The CJ thus reiterated that the national court should have the opportunity to consider the issues on a case-by-case basis weighing the competing interests.

[51] Case C-536/11, 6 June 2013.
[52] Case C-536/11, *Bundeswettbewerbsbehörde v. Donau Chemie*, 6 June 2013, para. 31.

Despite the concerns and tensions between public and private enforcement the Commission has not taken the view 'that private enforcement ought to be abandoned *tout-court*'.[53] On the contrary, it has, over the years, taken a number of steps designed to try and overcome the barriers to private litigation and to encourage it,[54] recognising that it cannot bear sole responsibility for the enforcement of the EU competition laws but also that a careful balance between public and private enforcement must be maintained. 'The overall enforcement of the EU competition rules is best guaranteed through complementary public and private enforcement.'[55]

The Commission has, for example, declined to act on a complaint where the complainant can assert its rights before a national court.[56] Further, a key objective of the modernisation programme in 2004 was to decentralise the enforcement of EU competition law and to strengthen the possibility for individuals to seek and obtain effective relief before national courts.[57] In pursuit of this objective Regulation 1/2003 provides: that Articles 101 and 102 are directly effective in their entirety (Article 1); that national courts shall have the power to apply Articles 101 and 102 (Article 6) and must apply them to an agreement or abusive conduct which affects trade between Member States and to which they are applying national competition law (Article 3); for cooperation between the Commission and the national courts (Article 15); and for the uniform application of EU competition law (Article 16, see also Section 2.E). The Commission's Notice on the Co-operation between the Commission and the Courts of the EU Member States in the Application of Articles 81 and 82 EC [now Article 101 and 102 TFEU] (the 'Cooperation Notice')[58] also sets out general guidance for national courts dealing with cases which raise a point of EU competition law and addresses the cooperation between the Commission and the national courts, when the courts apply Articles 101 and 102.

In spite of these steps, the Commission has recognised that further action to stimulate private action is required as the system of damages for infringements of competition law of the Member States 'presents a picture of "total underdevelopment"'.[59] 'Despite some recent signs of improvement in a few Member States, to date most victims of infringements of the EU competition rules in practice do not obtain compensation for the harm suffered.'[60] Further, that the current legal framework does not properly regulate the interaction between public and private enforcement. The package of measures published in 2013 is, consequently, designed to ensure that victims of infringements of EU competition rules can obtain full compensation for the harm they have suffered whilst at the same time ensuring that the interaction between public and private enforcement is optimised—and,

---

[53] Report for the European Commission, *Making Antitrust Damages actions More Effective in the EU*, (2007), 57, available at <http://ec.europa.eu/competition/antitrust/actionsdamages/files_white_paper/impact_study.pdf>.

[54] See, e.g., the Commission's Thirteenth Report on Competition Policy, (1984) 147–149, Fourteenth Report on Competition Policy (1985) 59, Fifteenth Report on Competition Policy (1986), 52–55, the Commission Notice on cooperation between the national courts and the Commission in applying Articles 85 and 86 [1993] OJ C39/6.

[55] Proposal for a directive of the European Parliament and of the Council on certain rules governing actions for damages under national law for infringements of the competition law provision of the Member States and the European Union COM(2013) 404 final, Explanatory Memorandum, 1.2.

[56] Commission Notice on the handling of complaints [2004] OJ C101/65, paras. 17 and 44, and see Chap. 13. The Commission is now entitled to reject a complaint where an NCA is dealing, or has dealt, with the case, Reg. 1/2003, Art. 13. The Commission has also instituted a programme for training judges and has commissioned a study on the conditions of claims for damages in cases of infringement of EU competition rules, see <http://ec.europa.eu/competition/antitrust/actionsdamages/economic_clean_en.pdf>.

[57] See generally Chap. 13 and, e.g., Commission Notice on the handling of complaints by the Commission under Articles 81 and 82 of the EC Treaty [2004] OJ C101/65, para. 18.

[58] [2004] OJ C101/54.

[59] Green Paper: Damages actions for breach of the EC antitrust rules COM/2005/0672/final, 1.2. This view was based on a study prepared for DG Comp by Ashurst on damages actions before national courts of the then 25 Member States (cited in n. 56).

[60] Proposal for a directive of the European Parliament and of the Council on certain rules governing actions for damages under national law for infringements of the competition law provision of the Member States and the European Union COM(2013) 404 final, Explanatory Memorandum, 1.2.

in particular, that leniency programmes and settlement procedures are not compromised by private enforcement.[61] In this package the Commission makes it clear that, although it accepts that private enforcement is important to supplement public enforcement, the two enforcement mechanisms pursue different, albeit complementary, objectives. In particular, the proposed Directive on rules governing damages actions embraces the compensatory approach:[62]

Civil redress for victims obtained through private enforcement…is meant to compensate those victims for the harm they suffered.

Fines imposed by a competition authority…(public enforcement) are instead a means of sanctioning infringers for their illegal conduct, and discourage them, and other potential infringements, to commit further infringements.[63]

E. UNIFORM AND CONCURRENT APPLICATION OF ARTICLES 101 AND 102

(i) Cooperation between the Commission and National Courts

One key concern has been that decentralised enforcement of Articles 101 and 102 might lead to inconsistent interpretation and application of the rules by the Commission, the individual NCAs, and national courts respectively.

When applying Articles 101 and 102, the national courts are obviously bound to interpret those provisions in accordance with the interpretation adopted by the Court of Justice and to respect the principle of primacy of EU law. Article 267 provides an important mechanism for national courts struggling with the interpretation of EU law. Further, the CJ has held that the duty of cooperation requires the Commission to assist national courts in their application of EU law and vice versa.[64] Both Regulation 1/2003 itself and the Commission's Cooperation Notice explain how that cooperation may manifest itself.

Article 15 of Regulation 1/2003 envisages that the Commission should act as amicus curiae to the national courts. Not only does it provide that the national courts might request the Commission to provide information or an opinion on the application of the EU competition rules[65] but it provides that the Commission may, where 'the coherent application of Article [101] or Article [102] so requires', submit written observations to the national courts and also, with their permission, make oral observations.[66] Any opinion so provided is published but does not have binding effect on the courts (although it may have persuasive impact).[67] The procedural framework, dealing with how the submissions should be provided, is governed by national law.

Regulation 1/2003 also provides how the national courts must assist the Commission in the fulfilment of its tasks. In addition to providing the Commission and NCAs with the documents

---

[61] Proposal for a directive of the European Parliament and of the Council on certain rules governing actions for damages under national law for infringements of the competition law provision of the Member States and the European Union COM(2013) 404 final, Explanatory Memorandum, 1.2.

[62] Proposal for a directive of the European Parliament and of the Council on certain rules governing actions for damages under national law for infringements of the competition law provision of the Member States and the European Union COM(2013) 404 final, Explanatory Memorandum,4.1.

[63] MEMO/13/531.

[64] See, e.g., Case 234/89, *Delimitis* v. *Henninger Bräu* [1991] ECR I-935, para. 53.

[65] See also Cooperation Notice, especially para. 29.

[66] Reg. 1/2003, Art. 15(3) (NCAs are also entitled to submit written observations to the national courts of their Member State and oral observations with permission).

[67] Thesse observations are available at <http://ec.europa.eu/competition/court/antitrust_amicus_curiae.html>. See, e.g., Case C-429/07, *Inspecteur van de Belastingdienst* v. *X BV.* [2009] ECR I-4833 (the CJ upheld the Commission's ability to intercede under Art. 15(3) in national proceedings where the outcome of the dispute was capable of impairing the effectiveness of the penalty it had imposed).

necessary for preparing written or oral observations to the courts, Member States must forward to the Commission 'a copy of any written judgment of national courts deciding on the application of Articles [101] or Article [102]' without delay.[68] The Commission publishes these judgments on its website according to the Member State of origin.[69]

(ii) Judgments Contrary to Decisions of the Commission and NCAs

a. Article 16 Regulation 1/2003

The CJ has held that the duty of cooperation set out in EU law requires a national court to follow a Commission decision dealing with the same parties and the same agreement in the same Member State.[70] Further, in order to ensure a uniform application of Articles 101 and 102, Article 16 of Regulation 1/2003 provides that the national courts must not adopt decisions contrary to a previous Commission decision and must avoid giving decisions that would conflict with a decision contemplated by the Commission.[71] Although Regulation 1/2003 does not deal with the impact of decisions of NCAs within the European Competition Network on national courts, the Commission has proposed that their decisions should also be given similar effect.[72]

b. Parallel Proceedings

Where the Commission has initiated proceedings but not determined a case, a national court must not, therefore, adopt a decision which will conflict with that which will be adopted by the Commission. The Commission will provide the national court with information as to whether it has initiated proceedings, the progress of proceedings, and the likelihood of a decision. Unless the national court cannot doubt the Commission's contemplated decision or the Commission has already decided on a similar case, it should ordinarily stay the proceedings before it.[73] Where this occurs the Commission will endeavour to give the case priority.

c. Consecutive Proceedings

Where the Commission has already decided on the case, the Commission's decision is binding on the national court, without prejudice to the interpretation of EU law by the CJ.[74] If the national court does not agree with the decision of the Commission it must either await the outcome of an appeal, if any, from its decision, or refer the question to the CJ for a preliminary ruling.[75]

Where the national court does stay proceedings in the context of parallel or consecutive proceedings, it should consider whether it should impose interim measures in order to safeguard the interests of the parties involved.[76]

---

[68] Art. 15(2).

[69] See the National Court Cases Database,<http://ec.europa.eu/competition/elojade/antitrust/nationalcourts/>.

[70] See, e.g., Case C-344/98, *Masterfoods v. HB Ice Cream Ltd* [2000] ECR I-11369 and Case 234/89, *Delimitis v. Henninger Bräu* [1991] ECR I-935.

[71] See also Cooperation Notice [2004] OJ C101/54, paras. 11–13.

[72] Proposal for a directive of the European Parliament and of the Council on certain rules governing actions for damages under national law for infringements of the competition law provision of the Member States and the European Union COM(2013) 404 final, art. 9, see Section 4.A.i.g.

[73] See, e.g., Case 234/89, *Delimitis v. Henninger Bräu* [1991] ECR I-935, paras. 43–55. See *AAH Pharmaceuticals Ltd and Others v. Pfizer Ltd and UniChem Ltd* [2007] EWHC 565.

[74] Case 314/85, *Foto-Frost v. Hauptzollamt Lübeck-Ost* [1987] ECR 4199, paras. 12–20.

[75] Case 314/85, *Foto-Frost v. Hauptzollamt Lübeck-Ost* [1987] ECR 4199, para. 12.

[76] Case C-344/98, *Masterfoods v. HB Ice Cream Ltd* [2000] ECR I-11369, para. 58.

d. Consecutive Proceedings between Different Parties

In *Inntrepreneur Pub Company* v. *Crehan*[77] the House of Lords (now the Supreme Court in the UK) adopted a narrow interpretation of the national court's duty of sincere cooperation and its obligation not to adopt decisions contrary to those in a previous Commission decision.

This ruling was the last in a saga which commenced in 1993 and saw the parties endure 13 years of litigation before the High Court, the Court of Appeal, the CJ, back to the High Court, the Court of Appeal and, finally, before the House of Lords. This case is discussed in Section 4.A.i.a and Section 4.A.i.b but, essentially, its outcome eventually turned upon the question of whether an English court was bound to adopt the same approach as that which had been adopted by the Commission in similar cases, but involving different parties. The dispute centred around a beer tie agreement concluded by a UK brewer and a publican and its compatibility with Article 101(1). In a number of decisions, such as *Whitbread*, *Bass* and *Scottish & Newcastle*,[78] the Commission had held that extremely similar agreements concluded by other UK brewers foreclosed the UK market for the distribution of beer in on-licensed premises and violated Article 101(1). Further, although it did not actually adopt a decision, the Commission had indicated that the Inntrepreneur leases (the leases at issue) were also in breach of Article 101. Nonetheless, when the *Crehan* case reverted to the High Court following a ruling of the CJ that damages must in principle be available to those who have suffered loss in consequence of a violation of Article 101,[79] Park J held that the beer tie agreements did not infringe Article 101(1).[80] Applying the test set out by the CJ in *Delimitis*,[81] he considered that the UK market for the distribution of beer in on-licensed premises was not foreclosed. Although Park J accepted that he should give the Commission decisions weight, he did not consider himself to be bound by them. In so ruling, the judge departed from the approach taken not only by the Commission,[82] but also by the UK authorities,[83] and the English courts[84] in their analysis of beer tie agreements in the UK market.

On appeal, the Court of Appeal held, noting that the judge should have given greater deference to previous Commission decisional practice,[85] that the judge had been wrong on this matter: the lease incorporating the beer tie did infringe Article 101(1). The first *Delimitis* condition was satisfied and the agreements in question did contribute to the cumulative effect produced by the totality of similar contracts found on the market.

It is a striking feature of this case that, as Inntrepreneur very properly accepts, if the judge were right, the Commission has been consistently wrong for many years in its view of the foreclosure of the United Kingdom market. That view has been expressed not only in the decision and Art. 19(3) notices and comfort letters…but in other cases as well. The Commission in its XXIXth Report on Competition Policy 1999 described its decisions in *Whitbread*, *Bass* and *Scottish & Newcastle* as taken after 'an exhaustive examination by the Commission departments.[86]

As the agreement did not meet the conditions of a block exemption and had not been granted an individual exemption, the Court concluded that Article 101(1) applied and the breach was established.[87]

---

[77] [2006] UKHL 38. See, e.g., J. Temple Lang, 'Inntrepreneur and the Duties of National Courts under Article 10 EC' [2006] *Comp Law* 231.

[78] *Whitbread* [1999] OJ L88/26, *aff'd* Case T-13/99, *Shaw* v. *Commission* [2002] ECR II-2023, *Bass* [1999] OJ L186/1, and *Scottish and Newcastle* [1999] OJ L186/28.

[79] See Section 4.A.i., pp. 1100–1104.

[80] *Crehan* v. *Inntrepreneur Pub Co* [2003] EWHC 1510 (Ch).

[81] Case C-234/89, [1991] ECR I-935 discussed in Chap. 4.

[82] See the discussion in Chaps. 4 and 11.

[83] See, e.g., The Supply of Beer: a report on the supply of beer for retail sale in the United Kingdom (Cm. 651, 1989).

[84] See Section 3.A.iii, p. 1099.

[85] *Crehan* v. *Inntrepreneur Pub Company CPC* [2004] EWCA Civ 637, para. 97.

[86] *Crehan* v. *Inntrepreneur Pub Company CPC* [2004] EWCA Civ 637, para. 78.

[87] However, the Court awarded damages at a considerably lower rate than Park J would have, holding that the correct date of assessment was the date of loss (the date he lost the business on surrender of the pubs).

The House of Lords, however, disagreed with the Court of Appeal holding that the judge was not bound by the Commission's assessment. No rule of EU law required the English court in this case to follow the Commission. The duty of sincere cooperation did not require the English court to accept the factual basis of a decision reached by an EU institution when considering an issue arising between different parties in respect of a different subject matter. A conflict would only exist when agreements, decisions, or practices ruled on by the national court had been, or was about to be, the subject of a Commission decision. There was no conflict where a Commission decision related to other agreements, decisions, or practices in the same market. Lord Bingham of Cornhill thus considered that the judge was bound to consider the factual evidence presented to him and to analyse it giving particular attention to those points on which he differed from the Commission. To have done otherwise would have been an abdication of the judicial function.

Had the Court of Appeal's opinion prevailed in this case, companies might have felt compelled to intervene in and challenge decisions addressed to other parties which might have affected their interest in the future. The House of Lords opinions, however, undoubtedly leave the slightly uncomfortable and unsatisfactory position that 'because the English courts did not ask the Commission for submissions, breweries to which Commission decisions were addressed were put in a different position from Inntrepreneur, and there is no obvious way of resolving this inconsistency'.[88]

3. THE ENFORCEABILITY OF AGREEMENTS INFRINGING ARTICLES 101 OR 102

A. ARTICLE 101

(i) The Sanction of Nullity

In Chapter 3 it was seen that Article 101 itself provides that agreements or decisions prohibited by Article 101(1) are void if the agreement does not satisfy the conditions of Article 101(3) (Article 101(2)). Further, that despite the wording of Article 101, the CJ has held that the nullity provided for in Article 101(2) in fact applies only to individual clauses in the agreement affected by the Article 101(1) prohibition.[89] The agreement as a whole is thus void only where those clauses are not severable from the remaining terms of the agreement.[90] In *Manfredi* v. *Lloyd Adriatico Assicurazioni SpA* the CJ clarified that the invalidity of the agreement (or affected clauses) is absolute—the agreement has no effect as between the contracting parties and cannot be invoked against third parties.[91]

A plea that an agreement infringed Article 101 and was void caused acute difficulties under the old Regulation 17 system on account of the national courts' inability to apply Article 101(3) to individual cases.[92] Since 1 May 2004 the position is simpler since national courts may now apply Article 101 in its entirety.

The compatibility of an agreement, or clauses within it, with Article 101 has been raised in a number of cases before the English courts. Such arguments have not always been received with particular

---

[88] J. Temple Lang, 'Inntrepreneur and the Duties of National Courts under Article 10 EC' [2006] *Competition Law Journal* 231, 234.

[89] Case 56/65, *Société La Technique Minière* v. *Maschinenbau Ulm GmbH* [1966] ECR 234, 250.

[90] Case 56/65, *Société La Technique Minière* v. *Maschinenbau Ulm GmbH* [1966] ECR 234, 250; Case 319/82, *Société de Vente de Ciments et Bétons de l'Est SA* v. *Kerpen & Kerpen GmbH & Co KG* [1983] ECR 4173. See Chap. 3.

[91] See Cases C-295–298/04, [2006] ECR I-6619, para. 57.

[92] A national court could apply Art. 101(1) and (2) and the provisions of a block exemption but could not otherwise rule on the compatibility of the agreement with Art. 101(3). If the agreement had been notified to the Commission the national courts' hands were tied and ordinarily they would have to stay proceedings pending the outcome of the Commission's investigation, see Case 234/89, *Delimitis* v. *Henninger Bräu* [1991] ECR I-935 and, e.g., A. Jones and B. Sufrin, *EC Competition Law: Text, Cases and Materials* (Oxford University Press, 2001), Chap. 15, especially pp. 964–969.

sympathy. Rather, many of the cases have been marked by an air of scepticism about the merits of the 'Euro-defence' and a reluctance to accept that Article 101 should be permitted to allow a party to wriggle out of a 'bad bargain'.[93] In *Trent Taverns Ltd* v. *Sykes*, for example, Steel J stated that 'Article [101] is not concerned with furnishing a remedy for an improvident agreement'.[94] Despite this recalcitrance, it is crystal clear that should a national court find an infringement of Article 101, the sanction of nullity must be applied.[95]

(ii) Severance

Although the effect of Article 101(2) has been spelt out by the CJ, that court has held that the question of whether the prohibited clauses can actually be severed from the remaining provisions in the contract is a matter for national law.[96] Where the applicable law is English law the position is, broadly, that the courts will sever parts of a contract where sufficient consideration remains to support the agreement and it is possible to sever by running a blue pencil through that offending part. The courts will not make a new contract or rewrite the contract for the parties, for example, by adding or re-arranging words. Nor will a court strike out words of a contract if, in so doing, a contract of an entirely different scope or intention would be left.[97]

In *Chemidus Wavin Ltd* v. *TERI*[98] the Court of Appeal considered the severance rules in the context of a licence agreement containing clauses which, arguably, contravened Article 101(1). Buckley LJ stated that:

> in applying Article [101] to an English contract, one may well have to consider whether, after the excisions required by the Article of the Treaty have been made from the contract, the contract could be said to fail for lack of consideration or on any other ground, or whether the contract would be so changed in its character as not to be the sort of contract that the parties intended to enter into at all.[99]

The question of severability has arisen in a number of cases involving beer supply agreements containing a beer tie (at an exclusive commitment to purchase beer from a named supplier).[100] The courts have had to assess whether the rules allow the severance of an invalid tie from the remainder of the agreement[101] and whether the contractual provisions prohibited by Article 101(1) are not only void but *also* illegal.

---

[93] See, e.g., *Gibbs Mew plc* v. *Gemmell* [1999] 1 EGLR 43, 48 ('Mr Gemmell did receive exactly what he bargained for, and is merely complaining of what he now sees as a bad bargain. Article [101] provides no remedy for that': Peter Gibson LJ), *Panayiotou* v. *Sony Music Entertainment (UK) Ltd* [1994] ECC 395, *Society of Lloyd's* v. *Clementson* [1995] 1 CMLR 693; *Oakdale (Richmond) Ltd* v. *National Westminster Bank plc* [1997] EuLR 7, 40 *aff'd* [1997] 3 CMLR 815.

[94] [1999] EuLR 492.

[95] See *Calor Gas Ltd* v. *Express Fuels (Scotland) Ltd* [2008] ScotCS CSOH_13, 25 Jan 2008; *The Football Association Premier League Ltd* v. *QC Leisure* [2008] EWHC 44 (Ch), [2008] EWHC 1411 (discussed in Chap. 12); *Eco Swiss China Time Ltd* v. *Benetton* [1999] ECR I-3055; Case C-453/99, *Courage Ltd* v. *Crehan* [2001] ECR I-6297, para. 21. Arts 101 and 102 may also be raised as a defence in proceedings for infringement of intellectual property rights, see, e.g., *Intel Corporation* v. *VIA Technologies* [2002] EWCA Civ 1905, *Sirdar Ltd* v. *Les Fils de Louis Mulliez and Orsay Knitting Wools Ltd* [1975] FSR 309 (ChD), *British Leyland Motor Corp Ltd* v. *TI Silencers Ltd* [1981] FSR 213 (CA), *Integraph Corporation* v. *Solid Systems CAD Services Ltd* [1995] ECC 53 (ChD), *Pitney Bowes Inc.* v. *Francotyp-Postalia GmbH* [1991] FSR 72 (ChD) and *Philips Electronics NV* v. *Ingman Ltd* [1999] FSR 112 (ChD)).

[96] This means that the enforceability of a contract will vary depending on which Member State's rules are applicable and will not necessarily be uniform throughout the EU, see, e.g., R. Whish, 'The Enforceability of Agreements under EC and UK Competition Law' in F. Rose (ed.), *International Commercial Law* (LLP, 2000).

[97] See, e.g., *Goldsoll* v. *Goldman* [1914] 2 Chap. 603.

[98] [1978] 3 CMLR 514.

[99] [1978] 3 CMLR 514, 520.

[100] But see the discussion of the *Crehan* case, [2006] UKHL 38, in Section 2.E.ii.d.

[101] See *Inntrepreneur Estates Ltd* v. *Mason* [1993] 2 CMLR 293 and *Inntrepreneur Estates (GL) Ltd* v. *Boyes* [1993] 2 EGLR 112, See, in particular, *Gibbs Mew plc* v. *Gemmell* [1998] EuLR 588 and *Trent Taverns Ltd* v. *Sykes* [1998] EuLR 571, *aff'd* [1999] EuLR 492. But see also *Scottish Courage Ltd* v. *McCabe* [2006] EWHC 538.

(iii) Nullity and Illegality

In *Gibbs Mew plc v. Gemmell*[102] the Court of Appeal considered that contractual provisions offending Article 101(1) are both void and *illegal* for the purposes of the (English) *in pari delicto* rule (a principle of public policy which prevents a court from lending 'its aid to a man who founds his cause of action upon an immoral or illegal act').[103] This finding caused the defeat of many claims for damages or restitution brought by a tenant against a brewer in the beer tie cases. The impact of the plea of illegality on the claims and its compatibility with EU law is discussed in greater detail in Section 4.A.i.e.

(iv) Transient Nullity

An agreement infringes Article 101 only if all of the elements of Article 101(1) are satisfied and the four conditions of Article 101(3) are not met. It is possible that, as events change over a period of time, an agreement which does not infringe Article 101(1) will subsequently be found to infringe Article 101(1) and not to meet the Article 101(3) criteria and vice versa. Suppose, for example, a small, local undertaking concludes an agreement which does not infringe Article 101(1) on account of its minor importance (the undertaking has an extremely small share of the market). Suppose, however, that that undertaking is subsequently taken over by a larger undertaking so that the agreement now does have an appreciable effect on competition and trade, does not meet the conditions of a block exemption, and does not fulfil the conditions of Article 101(3). The agreement which previously fell outside Article 101(1) now becomes subject to its prohibition. The agreement which was valid consequently becomes void. In *Passmore v. Morland plc*[104] the reverse scenario occurred and the English Court of Appeal held that the reverse can occur: an agreement which was initially void can become valid (and possibly void again) as the agreement falls within and without the Article 101(1) prohibition.

(v) Impact of Nullity on Related Agreements

A further question which arises is whether contracts concluded in implementation, or in consequence, of an illegal agreement might be vitiated, for example, a contract for sale at prices inflated in consequence of a cartel agreement entered into by the seller or sales contracts made in consequence of an invalid beer tie. In certain circumstances EU law makes it clear that a contract confirming an illegal contract is also in violation of Article 101.[105] Otherwise, it seems it is for national law,[106] subject to the principles of equivalence and effectiveness, to determine whether or not a contract concluded with a third party on the basis of a void agreement should also be tainted by the illegality and 'regarded as springing from or founded on the agreement rendered illegal'.[107]

B. ARTICLE 102

(i) Void and Unenforceable?

Article 102 contains no declaration of nullity equivalent to that set out in Article 101. This omission is not surprising since Article 102 does not explicitly prohibit agreements but focuses on a

---

[102] [1999] 1 EGLR 43.

[103] *Holman v. Johnson* (1775) 1 Cowp 341, 343, per Lord Mansfield.

[104] [1999] 3 All ER 1005.

[105] See, e.g., discussion of Case C-32/11, *Allianz Hungária Biztosító Zrt, Generali-Providencia Biztosító Zrt v. Gazdasági Versenyhivatal*, 14 March 2013 in Chap. 11.

[106] Case 319/82, *Société de Vente de Ciments et Bétons de l'Est SA v. Kerpen & Kerpen GmbH & Co KG* [1983] ECR 4173.

[107] *Courage v. Crehan* [2004] EWCA Civ 637. See also e.g., the view of the Swedish Supreme Court in *Boliden Mineral AB v. Birka*, 23 December 2004 and C. Cauffman, 'The Impact of Voidness from Infringement of Article 101 TFEU on Related Contracts' [2012] *European Competition Journal* 95.

wider range of conduct.[108] Nevertheless, the Article implicitly prohibits many contracts and contractual terms and the effect in relation to sanctioned agreements is, despite being couched in different terms, similar to that of Article 101. It is to be expected, therefore, that Article 102 should render a contract, or severable terms of a contract, affected by its prohibition void[109] or, at the very least, unenforceable.[110] The former view was taken by the High Court of England and Wales in *English Welsh & Scottish Railway Limited* v. *E.ON UK plc*[111] where it held that the effect of finding by a UK regulator (the Office of Rail Regulation, the ORR) that a contractual provision violated Article 102,[112] is that the offending contractual provision is illegal and void and the agreement as a whole is void if the prohibited clauses cannot be severed from the remaining terms of the agreement. In this case the ORR had held that exclusionary terms incorporated within a Coal Carriage Agreement (the CCA) concluded between the claimant, EWS and E.ON infringed Article 102. On the facts, Field J held that the exclusionary aspects of the contract, being in breach of Article 102, had been illegal and void since execution. Further that, as severance of the exclusionary terms would leave a contract of a fundamentally different nature, the effect of the ORR's decision was that the entire CCA was void and unenforceable.

(ii) Illegality

The question whether a contract or contractual provision is illegal for the purposes of the English *in pari delicto* rule is more complex when dealing with Article 102, since Article 102 does not prohibit both parties from concluding the contract. However, even if the agreement is found to be illegal, that characterisation should deny only a claim brought by the dominant undertaking. The rule should not prevent recovery where the applicant can establish that the parties were not *in pari delicto* (of equal fault). Rather, the duty of observing the law is placed squarely on the shoulders of the dominant party to the contract and is, in some circumstances at least, imposed to protect the other party from exploitation. The effect of the *in pari delicto* rule on damages claims is discussed in Section 4.A.i.e.

4. REMEDIES: DAMAGES ACTIONS AND INJUNCTIONS

A. DAMAGES

(i) An EU Right to Damages

a. Introduction

The question of whether there is any EU right to damages was decided by the CJ in 2001 following a reference to it of questions by the English Court of Appeal using the Article 267 procedure.

---

[108] See Chaps. 5 and 7.

[109] See, e.g., the view of the Swedish Court of Appeal, *Scandinavian Airlines System (SAS)* v. *Swedish Board of Aviation* (unreported), T. Pettersson, and J. Aswall, 'Discriminatory Pricing: Comments on a Swedish Case' [2003] *ECLR* 295, U. Bernitz, 'The Arlanda Terminal 2 case: Substantial Damages Awarded on the Basis of Article 82 TEC' [2004] 1 *Competition Law Journal* 195, and R. Whish, *Frontiers of Competition Law*, Dr Julian Lonbay (ed.) (Wiley, 1994), Chap. 5. In many cases an agreement concluded by a dominant undertaking which incorporates a contractual clause infringing Art. 102 is likely also to infringe Art. 101(1).

[110] See, e.g., *Gibbs Mew plc* v. *Gemmell* [1999] 1 EGLR 43.

[111] [2007] EWHC 599.

[112] And the UK equivalent, Chapter II of the Competition Act 1998.

The English court made the reference in the course of hearing conjoined appeals in the case of *Courage Ltd* v. *Crehan*.[113] The case concerned two leases of public houses that had been concluded between Inntrepreneur Estates (CPC) Ltd (owned equally by Grand Metropolitan plc and Courage Ltd) and Mr Crehan and which required Mr Crehan to purchase minimum quantities of various beers for resale at the leased premises from Courage, and no other person. The proceedings involved an action brought by the brewers for the recovery of £15,266, alleged to be the price of beers sold and delivered to Mr Crehan. By way of defence Crehan alleged, amongst other things, that the beer tie in the lease was in breach of Article 101. He counterclaimed for damages and/or restitution. The case thus raised the compatibility of the beer ties and the leases with Article 101 and the impact of any such incompatibility on the claims and counter-claims made by the parties.

b. Background to the Claim

Courage Ltd v. *Crehan* was one of a series of cases that had arisen before the English courts, raising the compatibility of leases containing beer ties with Article 101 and the ability of tenants to recover in respect of their loss suffered in consequence of the void beer tie (the actions were based on the brewer's breach of statutory duty)[114] or to recover the payments made pursuant to the void contract (the restitutionary claim).[115] By the time the *Crehan* case reached the Court of Appeal, authority established that the case must fail. The English courts had given short shrift to the claims which had been rejected as 'hopeless'. Although a whole host of different reasons had been given for the rejection of the claims,[116] the most significant obstacle to the actions had been that the claims were based on an illegal act. The English courts have generally refused to assist a claimant whose action is founded on an illegal act: *ex turpi causa non oritur actio*[117] and to allow a party to a prohibited contract either to enforce that contract or to bring any other action based upon it: *in pari delicto potior est conditio defendentis*.[118] Although the Court of Appeal in *Courage Ltd* v. *Crehan*[119] agreed with the first instance judge that English law would not afford a remedy of damages to a party to an agreement prohibited by Article 101,[120] it recognised that there might be sound policy arguments in favour of accepting that a party to a prohibited agreement has a right to sue for damages.[121] Further, that a party to a prohibited agreement such as that before it, might have rights by virtue of Article 101 that were protected by EU law. If the tenant was not afforded a remedy by English law it was possible, therefore, that the principle of English law denying that right was incompatible with, and superseded by, EU law. The Court of Appeal thus made a reference to the CJ.

---

[113] The case was one in a series of cases that raised the compatibility of 'beer ties' with Art. 101 of the Treaty, see also Section 3 and discussion of the case in 2.D.ii.d, pp. 1096–1097.

[114] They therefore claimed the difference between the contract price of the beer and its market value and other consequential loss, see, e.g., *Gibbs Mew plc* v. *Gemmell* [1998] EuLR 588 and *Trent Taverns* v. *Sykes* [1999] EuLR 492

[115] In many cases the restitutionary claims were eventually abandoned, see, e.g., A. Jones, *Restitution and EC Law* (LLP, 2000), Chap. 6 and A. Jones and B. Sufrin, *EC Competition Law: Text, Cases and Materials* (Oxford University Press, 2001), Chap. 15, 991–1002.

[116] The courts questioned whether, in the context of a breach of Art. 101, any tortious action for damages for breach of statutory duty lies at all (see *Inntrepreneur Estates (CPC) plc* v. *Milne*, unreported, 30 July 1993, *Matthew Brown plc* v. *Campbell* [1998] EuLR 530).

[117] 'No court will lend its aid to a man who founds his action upon an immoral or illegal act.'

[118] 'Where both parties are equally wrongful the position of the defendant is stronger.' See *Holman* v. *Johnson* (1775) 1 Cowp 341, 343. The rule is a principle not of justice but of policy which discourages all contracts that are contrary to public policy. 'For an agreement to be illegal it need not be in breach of the criminal law': *Gibbs Mew plc* v. *Gemmell* [1999] 1 EGLR 43, 49, [1998] EuLR 588.

[119] [1999] EuLR 834.

[120] *Courage Ltd* v. *Crehan* [1999] EuLR 834.

[121] Referring to the US Supreme Court's opinion in *Perma Life Mufflers Inc* v. *International Parts Corp.* 392 US 134 (1968) (the illegality defence did not bar an action brought by a party to an anti-competitive agreement that was in an economically weaker position and not equally at fault (*in pari delicto*)—private suits important to antitrust enforcement and furthering the public policy in favour of competition).

c. The CJ's Judgments in *Courage Ltd* v. *Crehan*

> ### Case C-453/99, *Courage Ltd* v. *Crehan* [2001] ECR I-6297
>
> ### Court of Justice
>
> 19. It should be borne in mind, first of all, that the Treaty has created its own legal order, which is integrated into the legal systems of the Member States and which their courts are bound to apply. The subjects of that legal order are not only the Member States but also their nationals. Just as it imposes burdens on individuals, Community law is also intended to give rise to rights which become part of their legal assets. Those rights arise not only where they are expressly granted by the Treaty but also by virtue of obligations which the Treaty imposes in a clearly defined manner both on individuals and on the Member States and the Community institutions (see the judgments in Case 26/62 *Van Gend en Loos* [1963] ECR 1, Case 6/64 *Costa* [1964] ECR 585 and Joined Cases C-6/90 and C-9/90 *Francovich and Others* [1991] ECR I-5357, paragraph 31).
>
> 20. Secondly, according to Article 3(g) of the EC Treaty (now, after amendment, Article 3(1)(g) EC), Article [101 TFEU] constitutes a fundamental provision which is essential for the accomplishment of the tasks entrusted to the Community and, in particular, for the functioning of the internal market (judgment in Case C-126/97 *Eco Swiss* [1999] ECR I-3055, paragraph 36).
>
> 21. Indeed, the importance of such a provision led the framers of the Treaty to provide expressly, in Article [101(2) TFEU], that any agreements or decisions prohibited pursuant to that article are to be automatically void (judgment in *Eco Swiss*, cited above, paragraph 36).
>
> 22. That principle of automatic nullity can be relied on by anyone, and the courts are bound by it once the conditions for the application of Article [101(1)] are met and so long as the agreement concerned does not justify the grant of an exemption under Article [101(3) TFEU] (on the latter point, see, *inter alia*, Case 10/69 *Portelange* [1969] ECR 309, paragraph 10). Since the nullity referred to in Article [101(2)] is absolute, an agreement which is null and void by virtue of this provision has no effect as between the contracting parties and cannot be set up against third parties (see the judgment in Case 22/71 *Béguelin* [1971] ECR 949, paragraph 29). Moreover, it is capable of having a bearing on all the effects, either past or future, of the agreement or decision concerned (see the judgment in Case 48/72 *Brasserie de Haecht II* [1973] ECR 77, paragraph 26).
>
> 23. Thirdly, it should be borne in mind that the Court has held that Article [101(1) TFEU] and Article [102] produce direct effects in relations between individuals and create rights for the individuals concerned which the national courts must safeguard (judgments in Case 127/73 *BRT and SABAM* [1974] ECR 51, paragraph 16, (*BRT I*) and Case C-282/95 P *Guérin Automobiles* v. *Commission* [1997] ECR I-1503, paragraph 39).
>
> 24. It follows from the foregoing considerations that any individual can rely on a breach of Article [101(1) TFEU] before a national court even where he is a party to a contract that is liable to restrict or distort competition within the meaning of that provision.
>
> 25. As regards the possibility of seeking compensation for loss caused by a contract or by conduct liable to restrict or distort competition, it should be remembered from the outset that, in accordance with settled case-law, the national courts whose task it is to apply the provisions of Community law in areas within their jurisdiction must ensure that those rules take full effect and must protect the rights which they confer on individuals (see, *inter alia*, the judgments in Case 106/77 *Simmenthal* [1978] ECR 629, paragraph 16, and in Case C-213/89 *Factortame* [1990] ECR I-2433, paragraph 19).
>
> 26. The full effectiveness of Article [101 TFEU] and, in particular, the practical effect of the prohibition laid down in Article [101(1)] would be put at risk if it were not open to any individual to claim damages for loss caused to him by a contract or by conduct liable to restrict or distort competition.
>
> 27. Indeed, the existence of such a right strengthens the working of the Community competition rules and discourages agreements or practices, which are frequently covert, which are liable to restrict or distort

competition. From that point of view, actions for damages before the national courts can make a significant contribution to the maintenance of effective competition in the Community.

28. There should not therefore be any absolute bar to such an action being brought by a party to a contract which would be held to violate the competition rules.

29. However, in the absence of Community rules governing the matter, it is for the domestic legal system of each Member State to designate the courts and tribunals having jurisdiction and to lay down the detailed procedural rules governing actions for safeguarding rights which individuals derive directly from Community law, provided that such rules are not less favourable than those governing similar domestic actions (principle of equivalence) and that they do not render practically impossible or excessively difficult the exercise of rights conferred by Community law (principle of effectiveness) (see Case C-261/95 *Palmisani* [1997] ECR I-4025, paragraph 27).

30. In that regard, the Court has held that Community law does not prevent national courts from taking steps to ensure that the protection of the rights guaranteed by Community law does not entail the unjust enrichment of those who enjoy them (see, in particular, Case 238/78 *Ireks-Arkady* v. *Council and Commission* [1979] ECR 2955, paragraph 14, Case 68/79 *Just* [1980] ECR 501, paragraph 26, and Joined Cases C-441/98 and C-442/98 *Michaïlidis* [2000] ECR I-7145, paragraph 31).

31. Similarly, provided that the principles of equivalence and effectiveness are respected (see *Palmisani*, cited above, paragraph 27), Community law does not preclude national law from denying a party who is found to bear significant responsibility for the distortion of competition the right to obtain damages from the other contracting party. Under a principle which is recognised in most of the legal systems of the Member States and which the Court has applied in the past (see Case 39/72 *Commission* v. *Italy* [1973] ECR 101, paragraph 10), a litigant should not profit from his own unlawful conduct, where this is proven.

...

36. Having regard to all the foregoing considerations, the questions referred are to be answered as follows:

— a party to a contract liable to restrict or distort competition within the meaning of Article [101 TFEU] can rely on the breach of that article to obtain relief from the other contracting party;

— Article [101 TFEU] precludes a rule of national law under which a party to a contract liable to restrict or distort competition within the meaning of that provision is barred from claiming damages for loss caused by performance of that contract on the sole ground that the claimant is a party to that contract;

— Community law does not preclude a rule of national law barring a party to a contract liable to restrict or distort competition from relying on his own unlawful actions to obtain damages where it is established that that party bears significant responsibility for the distortion of competition.

It can be seen from this extract that the Court stresses the new legal order created by the EU, the rights the Treaty provisions confer on individuals, the centrality of the competition rules to the EU project, and the direct effect of Article 101(1). The Court did not hesitate to conclude that *any* individual is entitled to rely on a breach of Article 101(1) and the nullity set out in Article 101(2) before a national court, even a party to a prohibited contract.

The Court then goes on to underline the obligation of national courts to ensure that EU rules take full effect and to protect the EU rights those provisions conferred on individuals[122] and highlights the importance of private actions to the enforcement of the EU laws.[123] The Court thus concluded that there should be no absolute bar to a damages claim, even to one brought by a party to a contract

[122] Case C-453/99, [2001] ECR I-6297, para. 26.
[123] Case C-453/99, [2001] ECR I-6297, para. 27.

violating the competition rules. Insofar as the English principle of illegality provides an absolute bar to a claim for damages commenced under Article 101 it is therefore undoubtedly incompatible with EU law.

The Court went on to deal with the question of when an application of the English illegality rule might be compatible with EU law. The Court indicated that so long as the EU principles of equivalence and effectiveness were respected, EU law did not preclude a national court from denying a party who is found to bear *significant responsibility* for the distortion of competition the right to obtain damages from the other contracting party.[124]

The judgment thus clearly establishes that: (1) Article 101 confers rights on individuals, even parties to a contract in breach; and (2) any breach of Article 101 is sufficiently serious to trigger an EU right to damages. Individuals must be entitled to claim damages for loss caused by an agreement or conduct that restricts competition. The Court in *Crehan*[125] did not, however, specifically require that there be a direct causal link between the breach of the obligation resting on the defendant and the damage sustained by the injured party. In the absence of a ruling on this point, it seems that national rules on causation apply.[126]

d. An EU Right to Damages

The ruling in *Crehan*[127] sends out a clear message to the national courts of all Member States. Whatever the position in national law, there must, in principle, be a right to damages to compensate breaches of both Article 101 and Article 102.[128] In the absence of EU harmonising measures (but see further the Commission's proposals in Section 4.A.i.g), it is for national rules, subject to the principles of equivalence and effectiveness, to set out the rules governing recovery. The ruling in *Crehan* is of significance to all damages claims, not just those involving co-contractors.

The CJ reiterated this view in *Manfredi v. Lloyd Adriatico Assicurazioni SpA*[129] where it stated that the practical effect of the Article 101(1) prohibition would be put at risk if it were not open to any individual to claim damages for loss caused to him by a contract or by conduct liable to restrict or distort competition. 'It follows that any individual can claim compensation for the harm suffered where there is a causal relationship between that harm and an agreement or practice prohibited under Article [101].'[130] In this case, the Court was also asked whether Article 101 had to be interpreted as requiring national courts to award 'punitive' damages, greater than the advantage obtained by the offending operator, thereby deterring the adoption of prohibited agreements.[131] The CJ stressed that the right to claim damages was designed to strengthen the working of the EU competition rules and to discourage prohibited agreements but that the question of whether to award punitive damages was, in the absence of EU rules governing the matter, for the domestic legal system of each Member State to determine, provided that the principles of equivalence and effectiveness are observed. It thus stated that:

(1) it must be possible to award punitive damages if such damages may be awarded pursuant to similar actions founded on domestic law. However, EU law did not prevent national courts

---

[124] Case C-453/99, [2001] ECR I-6297, paras. 31–35. In these circumstances the principle of EU law that a litigant should not profit from his own unlawful conduct would be respected, Case 39/72, *Commission v. Italy* [1973] ECR 101, para. 10.

[125] Case C-453/99, [2001] ECR I-6297.

[126] In English law this means that the claimant will have to establish that the breach caused the loss complained of, i.e. that the damage would not have occurred but for the breach.

[127] Case C-453/99, [2001] ECR I-6297.

[128] Although the Court did not specifically deal with Art. 102 it referred to the need to compensate those who have suffered loss caused to them by a contract or by conduct liable to restrict or distort competition.

[129] Case C-295–298/04, [2006] ECR I-6619, para. 60.

[130] Case C-295–298/04, [2006] ECR I-6619, para. 61.

[131] Case C-295–298/04, [2006] ECR I-6619, paras. 83–100.

from taking steps to ensure that protection of EU rights does not entail unjust enrichment of those who enjoy them; and

(2) The right to seek compensation must include compensation not only for actual loss but also for loss of profit plus interest.[132]

The question of how national rules must be applied and developed to comply with the requirements of EU law has been a matter of some debate. In particular, the answer is likely to depend partly on how the principle of effectiveness stressed in the CJ's judgments is to be interpreted and, in particular, whether it suggests that the principal purpose of private enforcement is the attainment of corrective justice[133]—with deterrence operating merely as a socially beneficial by-product of such actions[134]— or whether private enforcement is simply a tool to increase enforcement and deter violations[135] (that is, whether the primary function of the private action is seen to be one of compensation or deterrence). Nebbia, for example, considers that uncertainty on this issue stems from an ambiguous understanding of the notion of 'effectiveness' relied on by the CJ in *Courage*. '"Effectiveness" is, in fact, the rationale, the cornerstone principle upon which the [CJ] explicitly relies in *Courage* (and in the subsequent *Manfredi*case); the problem is that the precise meaning and implications of this principle have not, as yet, been clearly spelled out. It is therefore necessary, at this stage, to step back from the nitty-gritty of the private enforcement debate and examine the broader framework of the [Union] system of remedies for the infringement of [EU] law.'[136] He thus analyses the notion of 'effectiveness' by reference to the EU's *acquis communautaire* before concluding that private enforcement should ultimately be about compensation. Nazzini, in contrast, conducts a similar exercise and concludes that the principle of effectiveness supports the deterrence approach.

P. Nebbia, 'Damages Actions for the Infringement of EC Competition Law: Compensation or Deterrence?' (2008) 33 *EL Rev*, 23, 35–36

Which principle of 'effectiveness' for Courage?

It is here submitted that the notion of 'effectiveness' on which the *Crehan* decision relies is that of 'effective judicial protection', rather than 'effective enforcement' First and foremost, *Crehan* is commonly considered as the logical extension of the same principle that generated *Francovich*and *Brasserie du Pêcheur.* As noted at the outset, the Commission acknowledges that: [T]he existence of a Community law remedy of damages against individuals for breach of Articles 81 and 82 EC follows from the same principles [as those that give rise] to such a remedy against Member States for breaches of other provisions of Community law This principle is, as discussed above, predominantly based on 'effective judicial protection'.

Secondly, the wording of the *Crehan* decision is very similar to that of *Brasserie du Pêcheur.* After highlighting that 'Community law is intended to give rise to rights which become part of [individual] legal

---

[132] The Commission recognises in its Notice on cooperation with the national courts the particular difficulties that may arise in consequence of the fact that there is no harmonisation of procedures in the Member States, see the Cooperation Notice [2004] OJ C101/54, paras. 9–10.

[133] P. Nebbia, 'Damages Actions for the Infringement of EC Competition Law: Compensation or Deterrence?' (2008) 33 *EL Rev*, 23, 28.

[134] K. Roach and M. J. Trebilcock, 'Private Enforcement of Competition Laws' (1996) 34 *Osgoode Hall Law Journal* 461, 496.

[135] F. Hoseinian, 'Passing-on Damages and Community Antitrust Policy—An Economic Background' (2005) 28 *World Competition* 3, 7.

[136] Nebbia, 'Damages Actions for the Infringement of EC Competition Law: Compensation or Deterrence?' (cited in n. 133), 23, 28.

assets', the [CJ] reaffirms the principle that: [T]he full effectiveness of Article 85 [now 101] of the Treaty would be put at risk if it were not open to any individual to claim damages for loss caused to him by a contract or conduct liable to restrict or distort competition.

The subsequent paragraph is then devoted to the 'enforcement' argument, and acknowledges the contribution that such a right would give 'to the maintenance of effective competition in the Community'. This argument, however, seems to be used to reinforce, rather than to establish, the basis of liability.

This emerges more clearly in the *Manfredi* decision. In that case, the ECJ affirmed more explicitly than in *Crehan* the existence of a Community-based right to compensation for the infringement of antitrust law but, in so doing, only echoed the part of the *Crehan* judgment that dealt with judicial protection ... :

[I]t should be recalled that the full effectiveness of Article [101] and, in particular, the practical effect of the prohibition laid down in Article [101(1)] would be put at risk if it were not open to any individual to claim damages for loss caused to him by a contract or by conduct liable to restrict or distort competition (*Courage and Crehan*...paragraph 26).

The 'enforcement' argument can only be found much later, where the [CJ] deals with the question of whether punitive damages should be awarded.

If the reasoning here developed is correct, it is clear that the [EU] context is remarkably different from that of the United States: the primary aim of private enforcement should be compensation, and any measure proposed to enhance its operation should take this priority into account. In this respect, the conclusions drawn here have significant practical implications as different views on which objective should be prioritised may imply quite different (but not necessarily conflicting) policy agendas.

R. Nazzini, 'The Objective of Private Remedies in EU Competition Law' (2011) 4 *Global Competition Litigation Review* 131, 139–140

(iii) The case law on the right to damages for breach of art. 101 or 102 TFEU

When the court was required to address the core question of whether those who have been harmed by a breach of art.101(1) TFEU have a right to damages, the enforcement rationale becomes more evident.

In *Crehan*, the Court of Justice was called upon to decide whether the English law rule *ex turpi causa non oritur actio* was incompatible with EU law in so far as it prevented a party to an agreement prohibited by art.101(1) TFEU from recovering damages from the other party. The court said that the full effectiveness of art.101 of the Treaty and, in particular, the practical effect of the prohibition laid down in art.101(1) would be put at risk if it were not open to any individual to claim damages for loss caused to him by a contract or by conduct liable to restrict or distort competition. The court added that the existence of such a right strengthens the working of the EU competition rules and discourages anti-competitive agreements or practices. Finally, the court said that actions for damages before the national courts can make a significant contribution to the maintenance of effective competition in the European Union. The enforcement rationale could not be more clearly articulated.

In the subsequent case of *Manfredi*, the court repeated almost verbatim paragraphs 26 and 27 of the *Crehan* case. The court was ruling on whether art.101 TFEU must be interpreted as requiring national courts to award punitive damages, greater than the advantage obtained by the defendant, thereby deterring agreements or concerted practices prohibited under that article. The question explicitly linked the award of punitive damages to deterrence. It was, therefore, important for the court to make it clear that the fact that EU law does not require the award of punitive damages does not mean that the right to damages for loss caused by a breach of art.101 or 102 TFEU is any less important in ensuring the effectiveness of EU competition law.

Although strictly not required to do so, the court went on to determine the content of the right in light of its function of ensuring the full effectiveness of EU competition law. The court considered that the effectiveness of EU competition law and the right to seek compensation required that the claimant be entitled to 'full compensation', including actual loss, loss of profit and interest, but leaving the award of punitive damages to national law subject to the principle of equivalence. In determining the damages recoverable, the court relied both on the principle of effectiveness and on the right to seek compensation. In doing so, the court applied a test similar to that set out in *Brasserie du Pêcheur SA and Factortame*, whereby the remedies available for the protection of the right are determined according to both the requirement of full effectiveness of EU law and the requirement of effective judicial protection.

Applying the three-stage framework proposed in this chapter, it would appear that, in the first stage, the EU right to damages for breach of art.101 or 102 TFEU is recognised based entirely upon the enforcement rationale. In the second stage, the principle of full effectiveness of EU law applies, in conjunction with the principle of effective judicial protection, to determine the content of the right. Finally, in the third stage, under the doctrine of procedural autonomy, the principles of full effectiveness of EU law and effective judicial protection apply to assess whether national rules on remedies and procedure are compatible with EU law....

Some appear to argue that the objective of the EU law right to damages for breach of the competition provisions is compensation and not the effectiveness of the regime. However, it is necessary to distinguish between the content of the right, on the one hand, and its legal basis and function, on the other. The discussion so far has demonstrated that full compensation as the content of the right is consistent with the objective of ensuring the effective enforcement of EU competition law. Furthermore, the competition law cases of *Crehan* and *Manfredi* clearly articulate in unambiguous language an enforcement rationale for the conferral of the right to damages.

The enforcement rationale which underpins the right to damages for breach of art.101 or 102 TFEU is further demonstrated by the absence of the 'protective purpose' doctrine under EU law. The protective purpose doctrine is well established under German tort law, where the claimant is only entitled to compensation if he suffers harm as a consequence of the violation of a norm the purpose of which was to protect a person in the position of the claimant from the harm in question. The concept is not alien to English tort law where the claimant, to recover damages for breach of statutory duty, must establish that he is within the category of person the statute intended to protect from the harm in question. The Court of Justice in *Manfredi* appears to have rejected, albeit implicitly, the protective purpose doctrine. The court said that art.101 TFEU must be interpreted as meaning that any individual can rely on the invalidity of an agreement or practice prohibited under that article and, where there is a causal relationship between the latter and the harm suffered, claim compensation for that harm.

The absence of the protective purpose doctrine in EU competition law is consistent with an enforcement rationale. If the legal basis of the right to damages for breach of art.101 or 102 TFEU were to protect individual interests, it would follow that the claimant would have to prove that he belongs to the category of person that art.101 or 102 TFEU intends to protect and that the harm suffered is of the type that those provisions intend to prevent....

It has already been seen that the view favoured by the Commission is that private enforcement should be about *compensation* for victims in a way that does not undermine public enforcement.[137] As it considers that the existing legal framework and national rules and procedures do not guarantee those objectives, it has proposed a Directive which seeks 'to improve the conditions under which compensation can be obtained for harm caused by (a) infringement of the EU competition rules, and (b) infringements of national competition law provisions, where the latter are applied by a national

---

[137] See n. 62 and accompanying text.

competition authority or a national court in the same case in parallel to the EU competition rules'.[138] If and when such a Directive is adopted, national rules and procedures will have to be adapted within two years to comply with its requirements. Until then, however, the rule of national procedural autonomy means that national rules will continue to govern the claims, subject, of course, to the principles of equivalence and effectiveness.

e. Claims between Co-contractors

The CJ's judgment in *Crehan* holds that although the illegality of the agreement cannot operate as a general bar to claims brought between parties to a contract concluded in breach of Article 101(1), it can do so, however, where the claimant co-contractor can be said to bear 'significant responsibility' for the breach.[139] The CJ deals with the meaning of significant responsibility in paragraphs 32–35 of its judgment.

Case C-453/99, *Courage Ltd* v. *Crehan* [2001] ECR I-6297

32. In that regard, the matters to be taken into account by the competent national court include the economic and legal context in which the parties find themselves and, as the United Kingdom Government rightly points out, the respective bargaining power and conduct of the two parties to the contract.

33. In particular, it is for the national court to ascertain whether the party who claims to have suffered loss through concluding a contract that is liable to restrict or distort competition found himself in a markedly weaker position than the other party, such as seriously to compromise or even eliminate his freedom to negotiate the terms of the contract and his capacity to avoid the loss or reduce its extent, in particular by availing himself in good time of all the legal remedies available to him.

34. Referring to the judgments in Case 23/67 *Brasserie de Haecht* [1967] ECR 127 and Case C-234/89 *Delimitis* [1991] ECR I-935, paragraphs 14 to 26, the Commission and the United Kingdom Government also rightly point out that a contract might prove to be contrary to Article [101(1) TFEU] for the sole reason that it is part of a network of similar contracts which have a cumulative effect on competition. In such a case, the party contracting with the person controlling the network cannot bear significant responsibility for the breach of Article [101], particularly where in practice the terms of the contract were imposed on him by the party controlling the network.

35. Contrary to the submission of Courage, making a distinction as to the extent of the parties' liability does not conflict with the case-law of the Court to the effect that it does not matter, for the purposes of the application of Article [101 TFEU], whether the parties to an agreement are on an equal footing as regards their economic position and function (see, *inter alia*, Joined Cases 56/64 and 58/64 *Consten and Grundig* v. *Commission* [1966] ECR 382). That case-law concerns the conditions for application of Article [101 TFEU] while the questions put before the Court in the present case concern certain consequences in civil law of a breach of that provision.

When determining whether the claimant had significant responsibility for a breach a national court should, therefore, take account of factors, including: the economic and legal context within which parties found themselves; their respective bargaining position; and the conduct of the parties. It appears that parties who encourage both the agreement and the unlawful terms will be found to have significant responsibility for the breach. In contrast, a party in a markedly weaker position than the other is unlikely to bear significant responsibility for the breach. In particular, the Court indicates

---

[138] Proposal for a directive of the European Parliament and of the Council on certain rules governing actions for damages under national law for infringements of the competition law provision of the Member States and the European Union COM(2013) 404 final, Explanatory Memorandum, 4.1.

[139] Case C-453/99, [2001] ECR I-6297, para. 31.

that a party contracting with a person controlling a network will not bear significant responsibility for the breach where the person controlling the network of agreements imposed the terms of the contract. This point was accepted and applied by the English judge when the case reverted to the English High Court.[140]

f. Limitation Rules and Other Bars to a Claim

Whether or not other national rules operating to limit or bar the claim (such as a limitation period, standing rules, or a passing-on defence) can be applied will be dependent upon their being compatible with the EU principles of equivalence and effectiveness. In *Manfredi* v. *Lloyd Adriatico Assicurazioni SpA*[141] the CJ was asked about the compatibility of a national limitation period with EU law. The relevant limitation period in that case began to run from the day on which that prohibited agreement or practice was adopted. The CJ held that such a national rule could make it practically impossible to exercise the right to seek compensation for the harm caused by that prohibited agreement or practice, particularly if that national rule also imposed a short limitation period which is not capable of being suspended. It noted that in case of continuous or repeated infringement, it was possible in these circumstances that the limitation period would expire even before the infringement is brought to an end.

Jones and Beard explore when national rules on standing and on the acceptance of a passing-on defence are likely to be compatible with EU law.

A. Jones and D. Beard, 'Co-contractors, Damages and Article 81: The ECJ Finally Speaks' [2002] *ECLR* 246, 253–255

Quantification of loss and other issues

The judgment in *Crehan* recognises that a Community right to damages should in principle be available to compensate breaches of Article [101] or Article [102] for two main reasons. First, to ensure that individuals are compensated in respect of loss caused by anti-competitive conduct ('the compensatory principle'). Secondly, to strengthen the working of the Community competition rules and to discourage anti-competitive practices—private actions contribute to the maintenance of effective competition in the Community ('the deterrence principle'). Both principles are closely linked to the need to ensure the effectiveness of the competition rules within the Community.

The recognition of a Community right to damages will mean that many national rules of procedure and substance may have to be tested for their compatibility with Community law. Two specific problems that are liable to arise in many damages actions are: who is entitled to claim? and how will loss be quantified? For example, take a cartel or monopolist that sells its goods at supra-competitive prices. A direct purchaser from the cartel or monopolist (say a wholesaler) will clearly suffer in consequence of paying a price that is in excess of the competitive price. However, the direct purchaser may be able to pass on some of the loss to the next purchaser in the chain, a retailer or a consumer. Ultimately, at least part of the inflated price may be passed on to the consumer. This leads to two related questions. First, if the direct purchaser brings a damages claim, should the national court take account...[of] the fact that some of that loss has been passed on to other purchasers along the line? Second, should indirect purchasers, further down the chain, also be entitled to bring damages actions to compensate them in respect of their loss?

In the US the courts have already had to grapple with these, and other, difficult questions. In *Hanover Shoe Inc* v. *United Shoe Machine Corp* the Supreme Court held that the possibility that a claimant might

---

[140] On remission of the case to the English Court, this factor led Park J and the Court of Appeal to hold that the tenant's claim could not be barred by the principle of illegality or significant responsibility, see Section 4.A.ii.d.

[141] Case C-295–298/04, [2006] ECR I-6619.

have recouped some of an overcharge by passing it on to its customers is *not* relevant in the assessment of damages. If such an allegation could be taken into account damages claims would become excessively complicated, private actions would be deterred and a wrongdoer in breach would be able to retain his unlawful profits and the fruits of his own illegality.

In symmetry with this conclusion, the Supreme Court in *Illinois Brick Co* v. *Illinois* stated that claims brought by *indirect* purchasers should generally be refused. If the fact that loss has been passed on by the purchaser may not be taken into account *defensively* in a claim between the seller and the purchaser, it should not be open to an indirect purchaser to use the passing on principle *offensively* in damages proceedings. This latter rule has been subjected to criticism, principally on the grounds that it precludes claims by those who have suffered loss in consequence of anti-competitive activity. However, advocates of the rule stress a number of benefits it brings: (a) it precludes a multiplicity of claims and duplicate recovery from a defendant; (b) it prevents difficult issues of remoteness and tracing of injury from arising; (c) it prevents the process costs of litigation from increasing; (d) it prevents inconsistent judgments; (e) it sits sensibly with the conclusion set out above on the passing on allegation; and (f) it increases the effectiveness of the antitrust rules by encouraging those most likely to litigate to do so.

The apportionment of recovery through the distribution chain would increase the overall costs of recovery by injecting extremely complex issues into the case; at the same time such an apportionment would reduce the benefits to each plaintiff by dividing the potential recovery among a much larger group. Added to the uncertainty of how much of an overcharge could be established at trial would be the uncertainty of how that overcharge would be apportioned among the various plaintiffs. This additional uncertainty would further reduce the incentive to sue. The combination of increasing the costs and diffusing the benefits of bringing a treble-damages action could seriously impair this important weapon of antitrust enforcement.

A national court will not of course be bound by US case law. Rather it will instead have to reach its own conclusions, ensuring that the rules it applies are compatible with the Community principles of equivalence and effectiveness.

Passing on

At first sight, it would appear that the Community rules should not prevent a national court from taking into account the fact that loss has been passed on to another purchaser further down the line. The compensatory principle would, on its face, appear to suggest that a claimant should recover only that which he has lost in consequence of an infringement. Further, the Court of Justice has consistently held that Community law does not prevent national courts from ensuring that the protection of rights guaranteed by Community law does not entail the *unjust enrichment* of those who enjoyed them and the Court specifically stated this in *Crehan*. Arguably, a claimant would be unjustly enriched if he could recover damages even though he had been able to pass some of the loss on to others.

However, the position is not quite so simple. First, even if it were accepted that theoretically the fact that losses have been passed on to customers should be taken into account, the quantification of loss then becomes fraught with difficulty. In many cases it will be difficult to determine whether or not the loss has actually been passed on. Even if this can be established, the cost of the increased price of the product can only be passed on through a price rise to customers. In most cases, this will mean a decline in sales. These types of difficulties have caused the English Court of Appeal to hold, in the context of a private claim for restitution (based on the principle of unjust enrichment), that a defence of passing on is not available.

Secondly, the possibility that such arguments might be raised by a defendant and the complications involved in the assessment might deter private actions by direct purchasers. It may, therefore, interfere with the important... Community objective of encouraging private proceedings to strengthen the working of the competition rules. In other words, if the operation of compensatory principle enunciated by the Court in *Crehan* were invoked to justify the recognition of a passing on defence in national law, it may be argued that the rule would undermine the operation of the deterrence principle and the principle of effectiveness upon which the Court also relied.

Thirdly, the acceptance of a passing on argument would frequently allow the *wrongdoer* to benefit and to retain some of the fruits of its wrong since in a great majority of cases indirect purchasers, to whom some of the higher prices have been passed on, will not sue. In a case like *Crehan*, for example, the publican-tenants may have passed some of their loss down the chain to their customers. It seems unlikely, however, that even the most hardened drinkers would contemplate their losses being sufficient to make proceedings against the brewers worthwhile. In the UK the Government's proposals to facilitate damages actions on behalf of consumers might encourage claims by indirect purchasers. Nonetheless, the Government accepts that it will be an uphill struggle to encourage actions to be brought in intractable cases such as these.

Indirect purchasers

It has already been mentioned that the rule in *Illinois Brick*, precluding claims by indirect purchasers, has been subjected to considerable criticism in the US. In some states the rule has even been reversed through legislation. The most obvious argument in support of the rule is that it precludes duplicate recovery from a defendant (full recovery from the direct purchaser and recovery in respect of the part passed on by the indirect purchaser). Coupled with the *Hanover Shoe* rule, the *Illinois Brick* rule means that wrongdoers will face damages actions from those most directly affected by their conduct and will ensure that wrongdoers are stripped of the fruits of their wrongdoing (thus deterring anti-competitive behaviour). However, it is clearly arguable that the application of such a rule by a national court would be inconsistent with [the] direct effect of Articles [101] and [102] and would undermine the operation of the principle that an individual who has suffered loss in consequence of a breach of the competition rules is entitled to compensation. In some cases, the application of the rule may allow the direct purchaser to retain at least part of the fruits of the seller's wrongdoing whilst those further down the chain, who have also suffered loss, are not compensated.

Such potential outcomes might militate against the application in national, and EC, law of the *Illinois Brick* rule. Indeed, the UK's government's proposal to foster representative claims on behalf of consumers seems to indicate that it would not be in favour of the adoption of such a rule. Arguably, the risk of double recovery is outweighed by the public interest in ensuring that anti-competitive behaviour is deterred and that those who suffer loss as a result are properly compensated. In the following extract, Clifford Jones recognises that the Court of Justice will have some difficult policy decisions to make in the future.

> The theoretical possibility of double recovery is inherent if defensive passing-on is not allowed but offensive passing-on is allowed. However, if defensive passing on is allowed and fewer than all indirect purchasers sue, then the wrongdoer retains at least some of the fruits of his violation. Both major alternatives have aspects which are unsatisfactory. At bottom, the ECJ will have to choose the approach which it considers best serves fair and effective Community law.

g. Harmonisation of National Rules? The Commission's Proposals

The previous discussion establishes that damages must in principle be available to compensate breaches of Articles 101 and 102. Further, that the principle of national procedural autonomy affords national courts some latitude in dealing with such claims and that the extent to which national rules are curtailed by the principles of equivalence and effectiveness is not always entirely clear. The principle of national procedural autonomy thus means that relevant national rules retain significant impact on the likelihood of a claim's success or failure. Because of this the Commission has been considering whether measures can or should be adopted to amend and/or harmonise national procedural and substantive rules governing damages claims, for example on costs, access to evidence, limitation periods, standing, class or representative actions, fault, and/or defences, such as the passing-on defence.

Indeed, in its 2005 Green Paper on Damages actions for breach of the EC antitrust rules[142] the Commission recognised that '[s]ignificant obstacles exist in the different Member States to the effective operation of damages actions for infringement of Community antitrust law'.[143] The Green Paper, and an accompanying Commission Staff Working Paper[144] thus sought: (1) 'to identify the main obstacles to a more efficient system of damages claims and to set out different options for further reflection and possible action to improve both follow-on actions (e.g., cases in which the civil action is brought after a competition authority has found an infringement) and stand-alone actions (that is to say actions which do not follow on from a prior finding by a competition authority of an infringement of competition law)'[145]; and (2) to invite a discussion on obstacles identified and options formulated for getting over them and allowing a competition culture to develop. In its Staff Working Paper it provided a general overview of its interpretation of the relevant *acquis communautaire* governing damages claims. Following the receipt of comments on its Green Paper, the Commission published further proposals in its White Paper on Damages actions (which has to be read together with a Commission Staff Working Document and an Impact Assessment Report)[146] which recommended a broad range of measures aimed to ensure that all victims of anti-competitive behaviour are able to obtain full compensation (but not punitive or multiple damages) for harm suffered but that unmeritorious claims are not encouraged.[147] Further that full compensation should be 'the first and foremost guiding principle' in a system that 'complements, but does not replace or jeopardize, public enforcement'. It also recognised, however, that '[i]mproving compensatory justice would…inherently also produce beneficial effects in terms of deterrence of future infringements and greater compliance with [EU] antitrust rules. Safeguarding undistorted competition is an integral part of the internal market and important for implementing the Lisbon strategy. A competition culture contributes to better allocation of resources, greater economic efficiency, increased innovation and lower prices.'[148]

In seeking to achieve its stated objectives, the Commission proposed carefully crafted, balanced measures to ensure that national rules of evidence, procedure, and remedies are modified to allow effective private enforcement of the EU competition laws to develop. In particular, it proposed that: any individual who has suffered harm—whether a direct purchaser or indirect purchaser—should have legal standing to bring an action; victims should be entitled to full compensation for actual loss (*damnum emergens*) and loss of profits (*lucrum cessans*), plus interest[149] (defendants should, however, be able to rely on a passing-on defence); national courts should not be able to take decisions counter to decisions of an NCA on Article 101 or Article 102; collective redress should be available

---

[142] COM/2005/0672/final.

[143] COM/2005/0672/final, 1.2.

[144] Commission Staff Working Paper, Annex to the Green Paper (available on DGComp's website, at <http://ec.europa.eu/comm/competition/antitrust/actionsdamages/index.html>).

[145] Green Paper: Damages actions for breach of the EC antitrust rules COM/2005/0672/final, 1.3.

[146] Com(2008) 165 final, SEC(2008)404 and SEC(2008)405, available at <http://ec.europa.eu/comm/competition/antitrust/actionsdamages/documents.html>.

[147] SEC(2008)404, paras. 2, 12, and 16.

[148] Com(2008) 165 final.

[149] The Commission states in its accompanying Staff Working Paper that it will seek to provide pragmatic, non-binding assistance on the task of quantifying antitrust damages (SEC(2008)404, 60). In 2009, an external study was prepared for the Commission on Quantifying antitrust damages: Towards non-binding guidance for courts (December 2009), available at <http://ec.europa.eu/competition/antitrust/actionsdamages/documents.html#link1>.

(through representative actions brought by designated bodies or opt-in collective actions);[150] certain minimum disclosure should be available in all jurisdictions; leniency applicants should not be required to disclose their leniency statements in damages actions, whether or not the application for leniency was accepted; EU-wide limitation periods should be adopted; there should be further consultation on the issue of costs and the possibility of limiting the civil liability of an immunity recipient to claims by his direct and indirect contractual partners (i.e. freeing immunity applications from joint and several liability for losses).

To take effect, the proposals required at least some EU legislative measures. A proposal for a Directive prepared in 2009 was not adopted. Soon afterwards, however, public consultations on quantifying harms in damages actions and how to develop a coherent European approach to collective redress were published.[151] In the latter document the Commission considered how to facilitate a fair system of collective redress without encouraging abusive or unmeritorious actions and how it should take the matter forward—that is, whether it should simply facilitate developments in Member States, enact an EU directive, or take no further action at the EU level.[152]

In June 2013 the Commission finally revealed how it would proceed in this difficult area. It has been seen that the Commission has adopted three different measures: a proposal for a Directive designed to remove some practical difficulties confronted by victims of infringements of the EU antitrust rules when instigating damages claims; a recommendation of non-binding principles for collective redress mechanisms for Member States; and a practical guide on the quantification of harm for damages to assist national courts. Neither of the latter two documents is binding on the Member States. If the Directive is adopted, however, Member States will have two years to bring into force laws to comply with it.

The Commission proposes that the Directive should set out a rebuttable presumption of harm in cartel cases (but not for other competition law infringements). The national courts will, however, even in cartel cases, have to assess the amount of damages but the idea is that the Commission's practical guide on quantifying harm will assist national courts in this respect.[153] Further that victims should obtain full compensation for actual loss suffered and loss of profits. The Commission also proposes provisions relating to: discovery (so parties will have easier access to evidence); protection of leniency and settlement documents; joint and several liability (for any participant in an infringement except for recipients of immunity); the effect of NCA decisions (which are to constitute full proof before civil courts that an infringement occurred); establishment of clear limitation periods; the legal consequences of passing on and the facilitation of settlements. These proposals are explained more fully in the Commission's Explanatory Memorandum to the proposed Directive.

---

[150] In opt-in cases, claimants must choose to be included as a member of the class. In opt-out class actions, an individual brings an action on behalf of an unidentified class of persons. An injured person is assumed to be included in the class, unless he opts out of it.

[151] See Draft Guidance Paper, Quantifying Harm in Actions for Damages based on Breaches of Article 101 or 102 of the Treaty on the Functioning of the European Union (June 2011), Public consultation, Towards a Coherent European Approach on Collective Redress (SEC(2011) 173 final),the report of ECON, *Collective Redress in Antitrust* (June 2012).

[152] See B. Hess, 'Evaluation of contributions to the public consultations and hearing: "Towards a Coherent European Approach to Collective Redress"', available on DGComp's website.Arguably, an EU-wide collective redress system would produce benefits not only for consumers and SMEs, but also for the potential defendants as well as for the EU competition law enforcement system as a whole, see report of ECON, *Collective Redress in Antitrust* (June 2012), 42.

[153] See also, e.g., an external study prepared for the Commission, Quantifying antitrust damages: Towards non-binding guidance for courts, December 2009, available at <http://ec.europa.eu/competition/antitrust/actions-damages/documents.html#link1>; and the Draft Guidance Paper, Quantifying Harm in Actions for Damages based on Breaches of Article 101 or 102 of the Treaty on the Functioning of the European Union (June 2011) available at <http://ec.europa.eu/competition/consultations/2011_actions_damages/draft_guidance_paper_en.pdf>.

4. DETAILED EXPLANATION OF THE PROPOSAL

4.1. Scope and definitions (Chapter I: Articles 1–4)

The proposed Directive seeks to improve the conditions under which compensation can be obtained for harm caused by (a) infringements of the EU competition rules, and (b) infringements of national competition law provisions, where the latter are applied by a national competition authority or a national court in the same case in parallel to the EU competition rules....

The proposed Directive sets out rules (i) ensuring that any natural or legal persons harmed by infringements of the competition rules are granted equivalent protection throughout the Union and can effectively enforce their EU right to full compensation through damages actions before national courts; and (ii) optimising the interaction between such damages actions and the public enforcement of the competition rules.

Article 2 recalls the acquis communautaire on the EU right to full compensation. The proposed Directive thus embraces a compensatory approach: its aim is to allow those who have suffered harm caused by an infringement of the competition rules to obtain compensation for that harm from the undertaking(s) that infringed the law. Article 2 also recalls the acquis communautaire on standing and on the definition of damage to be compensated. The notion of actual loss referred to in this provision is taken from the case-law of the Court of Justice, and does not exclude any type of damage (material or immaterial) that might have been caused by an infringement of the competition rules.

Article 3 recalls the principles of effectiveness and equivalence which must be complied with by national rules and procedures relating to actions for damages.

4.2. Disclosure of evidence (Chapter II: Articles 5–8)

Establishing an infringement of the competition rules, quantifying antitrust damages, and establishing causality between the infringement and the harm suffered typically require a complex factual and economic analysis. Much of the relevant evidence a claimant will need to prove his case is in the possession of the defendant or of third persons and is often not sufficiently known or accessible to the claimants ('information asymmetry'). It is widely recognised that the difficulty a claimant encounters in obtaining all necessary evidence constitutes in many Member States one of the key obstacles to damages actions in competition cases. In so far as the burden of proof falls on the (allegedly) infringing undertaking, it too may need to have access to evidence in the hands of the claimant and/or of a third party. The opportunity to ask the judge to order disclosure of information is therefore available to both parties to the proceedings.

The disclosure regime in the proposed Directive builds on the approach adopted in Directive 2004/48/EC on the enforcement of intellectual property rights. Its aim is to ensure that in all Member States there is a minimum level of effective access to the evidence needed by claimants and/or defendants to prove their antitrust damages claim and/or a related defence. At the same time, the proposed Directive avoids overly broad and costly disclosure obligations that could create undue burdens for the parties involved and risks of abuses. The Commission has also paid particular attention to ensuring that the proposal is compatible with the different legal orders of the Member States. To this end, the proposal follows the tradition of the great majority of Member States and relies on the central function of the court seized with an action for damages: disclosure of evidence held by the opposing party or a third party can only be ordered by judges and is subject to strict and active judicial control as to its necessity, scope and proportionality.

National courts should have at their disposal effective measures to protect any business secrets or otherwise confidential information disclosed during the proceedings. Furthermore, disclosure should not be allowed where it would be contrary to certain rights and obligations such as the obligation of professional secrecy. Courts must also be able to impose sanctions which are sufficiently deterrent to prevent destruction of relevant evidence or refusal to comply with a disclosure order.

To prevent that the disclosure of evidence jeopardises the public enforcement of the competition rules by a competition authority, the proposed Directive also establishes common EU-wide limits to disclosure of evidence held in the file of a competition authority:

(a) First, it provides for absolute protection for two types of documents which are considered to be crucial for the effectiveness of public enforcement tools. The documents referred to are the leniency corporate statements and settlement submissions. The disclosure of these documents risks seriously affecting the effectiveness of the leniency programme and of settlements procedures. Under the proposed Directive, a national court can never order disclosure of such documents in an action for damages.

(b) Second, it provides for temporary protection for documents that the parties have specifically prepared for the purpose of public enforcement proceedings (e.g. the party's replies to the authority's request for information) or that the competition authority has drawn up in the course of its proceedings (e.g. a statement of objections). Those documents can be disclosed for the purpose of an antitrust damages action only after the competition authority has closed its proceedings.

(c) Apart from limiting the national court's ability to order disclosure, the above protective measures should also come into play if and when the protected documents have been obtained in the context of public enforcement proceedings (e.g. in the exercise of one of the parties' right of defence). Therefore, where one of the parties in the action for damages had obtained those documents from the file of a competition authority, such documents are not admissible as evidence in an action for damages (documents of category (a) above) or are admissible only when the authority has closed its proceedings (documents of category (b) above).

(d) Documents which fall outside the above categories can be disclosed by court order at any moment in time. However, when doing so, national courts should refrain from ordering the disclosure of evidence by reference to information supplied to a competition authority for the purpose of its proceedings. While the investigation is on-going, such disclosure could hinder public enforcement proceedings, since it would reveal what information is in the file of a competition authority and could thus be used to unravel the authority's investigation strategy. However, the selection of pre-existing documents that are submitted to a competition authority for the purposes of the proceedings is in itself relevant, as undertakings are invited to supply targeted evidence in view of their cooperation. The willingness of undertakings to supply such evidence exhaustively or selectively when cooperating with competition authorities may be hindered by disclosure requests that identify a category of documents by reference to their presence in the file of a competition authority rather than their type, nature or object (e.g. requests for all documents in the file of a competition authority or all documents submitted thereto by a party). Therefore, such global disclosure requests for documents should normally be deemed by the court as disproportionate and not complying with the requesting party's duty to specify categories of evidence as precisely and narrowly as possible.

(e) Finally, to prevent documents obtained through access to a competition authority's file becoming an object of trade, only the person who obtained access to the file (or his legal successor in the rights related to the claim) should be able to use those documents as evidence in an action for damages.

To achieve coherence regarding the rules on disclosure and the use of certain documents from the file of a competition authority, it is necessary to also amend existing rules on the conduct of Commission's proceedings laid down in Commission Regulation 773/200444, notably as regards access to the Commission's file and use of documents obtained therefrom, and the explanatory Notices published by the Commission. The Commission intends doing so once the present Directive is adopted by the European Parliament and Council.

4.3. Effect of national decisions, limitation periods and joint and several liability (Chapter III: Articles 9–11)

4.3.1. Probative effect of national decisions

Pursuant to Article 16(1) of Regulation No 1/2003, a Commission decision relating to proceedings under Article 101 or 102 of the Treaty has a probative effect in subsequent actions for damages, as a national court cannot take a decision running counter to such Commission decision. It is appropriate to give final infringement decisions by national competition authorities (or by a national review court) similar effect. If an infringement decision has already been taken and has become final, the possibility for the infringing undertaking to re-litigate the same issues in subsequent damages actions would be inefficient, cause legal uncertainty and lead to unnecessary costs for all parties involved and for the judiciary. The proposed probative effect of final infringement decisions of national competition authorities does not entail any lessening of judicial protection for the undertakings concerned, as infringement decisions by national competition authorities are still subject to judicial review. Moreover, throughout the EU, undertakings enjoy a comparable level of protection of their rights of defence, as enshrined in Article 48(2) of the EU Charter on Fundamental Rights. Finally, the rights and obligations of national courts under Article 267 of the Treaty remain unaffected by this rule.

4.3.2. Limitation periods

To give victims of a competition law infringement a reasonable opportunity to bring a damages action, while ensuring an appropriate level of legal certainty for all parties involved, the Commission proposes that the national rules on limitation periods for a damages action:

- allow victims sufficient time (at least five years) to bring an action after they became aware of the infringement, the harm it caused and the identity of the infringer;
- prevent a limitation period from starting to run before the day on which a continuous or repeated infringement ceases; and
- in case a competition authority opens proceedings into a suspected infringement, the limitation period to bring an action for damages relating to such infringement is suspended until at least one year after a decision is final or proceedings are otherwise terminated.

4.3.3. Joint and several liability

Where several undertakings infringe the competition rules jointly—typically in the case of a cartel—it is appropriate that they be jointly and severally liable for the entire harm caused by the infringement. While the proposed Directive builds on this general rule, it introduces certain modifications with regard to the liability regime of immunity recipients. The objective of these modifications is to safeguard the attractiveness of the leniency programmes of the Commission and of the NCAs, which are key instruments in detecting cartels and thus of crucial importance for the effective public enforcement of the competition rules. Indeed, as leniency recipients are less likely to appeal an infringement decision, this decision often becomes final for them earlier than for other members of the same cartel. This may make leniency recipients the primary targets of damages actions. To limit the disadvantageous consequences of such exposure, while not unduly limiting the possibilities for injured parties to obtain full compensation for the loss suffered, it is proposed to limit the immunity recipient's liability, as well as his contribution owed to co-infringers under joint and several liability, to the harm he caused to his own direct or indirect purchasers or, in the case of a buying cartel, his direct or indirect providers. Where a cartel has caused harm only to others than the customers/providers of the infringing undertakings, the immunity recipient would be responsible only for his share of the harm caused by the cartel. How that share is determined (e.g. turnover, market share, role in the cartel, etc.), is left to the discretion of the Member States, as long as the principles of effectiveness and equivalence are respected.

The protection of immunity recipients cannot, however, interfere with the victims' EU right to full compensation. The proposed limitation on the immunity recipient's liability cannot therefore be absolute: the immunity recipient remains fully liable as a last-resort debtor if the injured parties are unable to obtain full compensation from the other infringers. To guarantee the effet utile of this exception, Member States have to make sure that injured parties can still claim compensation from the immunity recipient at the time they have become aware that they cannot obtain full compensation from the co-cartelists.

4.4. Passing-on of overcharges (Chapter IV: Articles 12–15)

Persons who have suffered harm caused by an infringement of the competition rules are entitled to compensation, regardless of whether they are direct or indirect purchasers. Injured parties are entitled to compensation for actual loss (overcharge harm) and for loss of profit. When an injured party has reduced his actual loss by passing it on, partly or entirely, to his own purchasers, the loss thus passed on no longer constitutes harm for which the party that passed it on has to be compensated. However, where a loss is passed on, the price increase by the direct purchaser is likely to lead to a reduction in the volume sold. That loss of profit, as well as the actual loss that was not passed on (in the case of partial passing-on) remains antitrust harm for which the injured party can claim compensation. If the harm is suffered as a result of an infringement relating to a supply to the infringing undertaking, passing-on could also take place in an upwards direction on the supply chain. This would, for example, be the case when, as a result of a buying cartel, the suppliers of the cartelists charge lower prices, and those suppliers then in turn require lower prices from their own suppliers.

To ensure that only the direct and indirect purchasers that actually suffered overcharge harm can effectively claim compensation, the proposed Directive explicitly recognises the possibility for the infringing undertaking to invoke the passing-on defence.

However, in situations where the overcharge was passed on to natural or legal persons at the next level of the supply chain for whom it is legally impossible to claim compensation, the passing-on defence cannot be invoked. Indirect purchasers may be faced with the legal impossibility of claiming compensation because of national rules on causality (including rules on foreseeability and remoteness). Allowing the passing-on defence when it is legally impossible for the party to whom the overcharge was allegedly passed on to claim compensation would be unjustified, since it would mean that the infringing undertaking is unduly freed from liability for the harm he caused. The burden of proving the passing-on always lies with the infringing undertaking. In the case of an action for damages brought by an indirect purchaser, this implies a rebuttable presumption pursuant to which, subject to certain conditions, a passing-on to that indirect purchaser occurred. As regards the quantification of the passing-on, the national court should have the power to estimate which share of the overcharge has been passed on to the level of indirect purchasers in the dispute pending before it. Where injured parties from different levels of the supply chain bring separate actions for damages that are related to the same competition law infringement, national courts should take due account, as far as allowed under applicable national or EU law, of parallel or preceding actions (or judgments resulting from such actions) in order to avoid under- and over-compensation of the harm caused by that infringement and to foster consistency between judgments resulting from such linked proceedings. Actions that are pending before the courts of different Member States may be considered as related within the meaning of Article 30 of Regulation No 1215/201247, meaning that they are so closely connected that it is expedient to hear and determine them together to avoid the risk of irreconcilable judgments resulting from separate proceedings. As a consequence, any court other than the court first seized may stay its proceedings or decline jurisdiction if the court first seized has jurisdiction over the actions in question and its law permits the consolidation of the actions.

Both Regulation No 1215/2012 and this proposed Directive thus seek to encourage consistency between judgments resulting from related actions. To achieve that, the proposed Directive has an even wider scope than Regulation No 1215/2012, as it also covers the situation of subsequent actions for damages relating to the same competition law infringement, brought by injured parties at different levels of the supply chain. These actions can be brought in the same court, in different courts in the same Member State or in different courts of different Member States. In all instances, the proposed Directive encourages the consistency of linked proceedings and judgments.

4.5. Quantification of harm (Chapter V: Article 16)

Proving and quantifying antitrust harm is generally very fact-intensive and costly, as it may require the application of complex economic models. To assist victims of a cartel in quantifying the harm caused by the competition law infringement, this proposed Directive provides for a rebuttable presumption with regard to the existence of harm resulting from a cartel. Based on the finding that more than 9 out of 10 cartels indeed cause an illegal overcharge, this alleviates the injured party's difficulties and costs related to proving that the cartel caused higher prices to be charged than if the cartel had not existed. The infringing undertaking could rebut this presumption and use the evidence at its disposal to prove that the cartel did not cause harm. The burden of proof is thus placed on the party which already has in its possession the necessary evidence to meet this burden of proof. The costs of disclosure, which would most likely be necessary for the injured parties to prove the existence of harm, are thus avoided.

Apart from the above presumption, antitrust harm is quantified on the basis of national rules and procedures. These must, however, be in line with the principles of equivalence and of effectiveness. The latter, in particular, dictates that the burden and the level of proof may not render the injured party's right to damages practically impossible or excessively difficult. In terms of quantifying antitrust harm, where the actual situation needs to be compared with a hypothetical one, this means that judges must be able to estimate the amount of harm. This increases the likelihood that victims will actually obtain an adequate amount of compensation for the harm they have suffered.

To make it easier for national courts to quantify harm, the Commission is also providing nonbinding guidance on this topic in its Communication on quantifying harm in actions for damages based on breaches of Article 101 or 102 of the Treaty on the Functioning of the European Union. The Communication is accompanied by a Commission Staff Working Paper taking the form of a Practical Guide on quantifying harm in actions for damages based on breaches of EU competition law. This Practical Guide explains the strengths and weaknesses of various methods and techniques available to quantify antitrust harm. It also presents and discusses a range of practical examples, which illustrate the typical effects that infringements of the EU competition rules tend to have and how the available methods and techniques can be applied in practice.

4.6. Consensual Dispute Resolution (Chapter VI: Articles 17–18)

One of the primary objectives of the proposed Directive is to enable victims of a competition law infringement to obtain full compensation for the harm suffered. That objective can be achieved either through a damages action in court or through a consensual out-of-court settlement between the parties. To incentivise parties to settle their dispute consensually, the proposed Directive aims at optimising the balance between out-of-court settlements and actions for damages. It therefore contains the following provisions:

(i) suspension of limitation periods for bringing actions for damages as long as the infringing undertaking and the injured party are engaged in consensual dispute resolution;

(ii) suspension of pending proceedings for the duration of consensual dispute resolution;

(iii) reduction of the settling injured party's claim by the settling infringer's share of harm. For the remainder of the claim, the settling infringer could only be required to pay damages if the non-settling co-infringers were unable to fully compensate the injured party; and

(iv) damages paid through consensual settlements to be taken into account when determining the contribution that a settling infringer needs to pay following a subsequent order to pay damages. In this context, 'contribution' refers to the situation where the settling infringer was not a defendant in the action for damages, but is asked by co-infringers who were ordered to pay damages to contribute under the rules of joint and several liability.

It has also set out a series of common, non-binding principles for collective redress mechanisms to ensure a coherent horizontal approach to it and which should be available to those wishing to rely on EU law rights.

The question of how private actions should be encouraged has also been discussed by some of the Member States. The UK Government, for example, introduced in 2013 a draft Bill designed to facilitate further private actions.[154]

---

[154] See Section 4.B.ii.a, p. 1119 and the draft Consumer Rights Bill and the OFT's Discussion Paper, OFT 916, *Private Actions in competition law: effective redress for consumers and business* (April 2007) and subsequent recommendations to the Government (OFT916resp), BIS, *A Competition Regime for Growth: A Consultation on Options for Reform* (March 2011), and BIS, *Private Actions in Competition Law: A consultation on options for reform—government response* (January 2013).

(ii) Damages Claims before the English Courts

a. A Tortious Claim

In England and Wales, competition law actions are generally brought before the Chancery Division of the High Court. Follow-on actions (where a breach of the competition laws has been established through public enforcement) can also be before the specialist Competition Appeal Tribunal (CAT, see Section 4.A.ii.b, pp. 1120–1124).[155] The UK Government is also in the process of introducing a number of other changes designed to facilitate and encourage private actions in competition law and which are expected to be in force by the end of 2014.[156] It is also promoting alternative dispute resolution, with the aim of ensuring that litigation in the courts is the option of last resort (see Section 4.B.ii.g).

One of the factors which inhibited claims before the English courts prior to the CJ's judgment in *Crehan* was that, for a long time, it was not settled that an undertaking which committed a breach of one of the directly effective competition provisions set out in the Treaty committed a wrong which was actionable in tortious proceedings. Nor was it clear, if damages were in principle available, whether the basis of the claim was breach of statutory duty or some other tort, such as unlawful interference with trade,[157] or whether a new tort should be recognised to reflect the EU nature of the claim.[158] Now that it is clear that an action must *prima facie* lie, the general consensus is that the correct basis is breach of statutory duty, the basis favoured, obiter, by Lord Diplock and three other members of the House of Lords in *Garden Cottage Foods Ltd v. Milk Marketing Board*.[159] If this is correct, then a claimant must show that:

(1) the loss suffered is within the scope of the statute, i.e. that the statute imposes a duty for the benefit of the individual harmed;

(2) the statute gives rise to a civil cause of action;

(3) there has been a breach of statutory duty (generally liability is strict once the breach of duty is established so no proof of fault is required); and

(4) the breach has caused the loss complained of.

These four requirements will of course have to be interpreted in such a way that liability is imposed where required by EU law. The action is thus to some extent *sui generis* since the substantive conditions of liability will be dictated, partially at least, by EU, not national, law. The judgment of the CJ in *Crehan*[160] establishes that the first two requirements are satisfied in cases involving Articles 101 and 102, as it highlights the rights conferred on the individuals by the competition rules. It will, therefore, be necessary only to establish a breach of the rules and that the breach has caused the loss complained of. Indeed, when the case of *Crehan*[161] reverted to the English High Court, Park J considered that the two questions of overriding importance were (1) whether the Inntrepreneur leases infringed Article 101; and if so (2) whether the failure of Mr Crehan's business was caused by the beer ties in the lease or other factors.

Defendants under English law are jointly and severally liable.[162]

---

[155] See Competition Act 1998, ss. 47A and B.

[156] These are now set out in the draft Consumer Rights Bill, see also BIS, *Private Actions in Competition Law: A consultation on options for reform—government response* (January 2013), e.g., the CAT is to be given jurisdiction over stand-alone as well as follow-on actions and cases will be able to be transferred between the CAT and High Court (and vice versa). The limitation periods applicable in each court will also be harmonised. The Government has also announced that it will introduce a limited opt-out collective actions regime for mass damages claims.

[157] See *Barretts & Baird (Wholesale) v. IPCS* [1987] IRLR 3, 6.

[158] See *Application des Gaz SA v. Falks Veritas Ltd* [1974] Ch 381.

[159] [1984] AC 130 (in this case Art. 102 was incorporated into UK law by virtue of the European Communities Act 1972, s. 2).

[160] Case C-453/99, [2001] ECR I-6297.

[161] *Crehan v. Inntrepreneur Pub Co* [2003] EWHC 1510 (Ch).

[162] As a general rule there is a right to contribution under English law so that liability is apportioned by the court between the defendants in accordance with their responsibility for the loss.

b. Proving a Breach

The burden is on the claimant to establish a breach of Article 101(1) and/or Article 102.[163] In *Shearson Lehmann v. McLaine Watson*[164] Webster J, in the English High Court, held that a breach of Article 101 would have to be established to a high degree of probability (but less than the standard required in criminal matters). As the UK CAT[165] has held that the standard of proof in cases of public enforcement of the rules, which could lead to the imposition of a penalty (a criminal charge for the purpose of the European Convention of Human Rights and Fundamental Freedoms), is the civil standard and not the criminal standard, it now seems to be accepted that the former standard, the preponderance or balance of probabilities is the test to be applied in private litigation.[166] Nonetheless, given that proof of a violation of Article 101 or Article 102 may result in severe sanctions for the defendant, the courts require strong and compelling evidence to support an allegation of breach.[167]

In *National Grid v. ABB*,[168] the question of access to evidence arose. The High Court requested that the Commission provide certain material to it under Article 15, whilst the claimants sought disclosure from the defendants of other documents which had been held on the Commission's file, including some leniency documents. In its judgment of 4 April 2012, the High Court carried out the balancing exercise required of it, in the light of *Pfleiderer*,[169] when determining whether leniency material should be disclosed (accepting that although the judgment in *Pfleiderer* related to leniency documents held by an NCA the same principles applied where they were held by the Commission). In a very important judgment the Court, having carefully reviewed the leniency documents sought, ordered disclosure of only some of them having reviewed a number of factors, including the defendants' legitimate expectations, possible prejudice to and deterrence of leniency applicants and proportionality. In particular, the Court was not prepared to accept that in serious and long-running cartels the possibility of disclosure of leniency material would be likely to deter a potential immunity applicant from blowing the whistle.

Follow-on Actions[170]

Proving a breach will, of course, generally be easier to establish where a Commission or other NCA decision establishing a breach already exists. Where the Commission has previously ruled on a decision, Article 16 of Regulation 1/2003 applies.[171] In the UK the Competition Act 1998[172] also specifically allows 'follow-on' claims to be brought before the CAT where a breach of Article 101 or Article 102 (or the UK domestic equivalent)[173] has been established in a public law decision (by the Commission or the UK's Office of Fair Trading (OFT)). Such claims may be brought both by

---

[163] Once a breach of Art. 101(1) has been established the burden shifts on to the parties, to establish that the conditions of Art. 101(3) are satisfied, see Reg. 1/2003, Art. 1, and Chap 3.

[164] [1989] 2 Lloyd's Rep 570, 619L.

[165] Case 1001/1/1/01 *Napp v. DGFT* [2002] CAT 1, especially paras. 91–113.

[166] See *Arkin v. Borchard Lines Ltd* [2000] EuLR 232 (preliminary issues), [2003] EWHC 687 (Comm Ct) (final judgment) and *Crehan v. Inntrepreneur Pub Company* [2003] EWHC 1510 (Ch) (Park J), [2004] EWCA Civ 637 (CA). In *Masterfoods v. HB Ice Cream* [1992] 3 CMLR 830 the Irish High Court took the view that the requisite standard is balance of probabilities.

[167] *Chester City Council v. Arriva plc* [2007] EWHC 1373.

[168] [2011] EWHC 1717 (Ch), [2012] EWHC 869 (Ch).

[169] See n. 46 and accompanying text.

[170] See B. Rodger, 'Why not court? A study of follow-on actions in the UK' (2013) 1 *Journal of Antitrust Enforcement* 104–131.

[171] See Section 2. It is not open to a national court to find that a decision of the Commission is invalid; that can only be done by the CJ, Case 314/85, *Foto-Frost v. Hauptzollamt Lübeck-Ost* [1987] ECR 4199.

[172] Section 47A. Claims comprising follow-on and stand-alone elements must currently be brought before the High Court (see e.g., *Cooper Tire & Rubber Co v. Shell Chemicals UK Ltd* [2010] EWCA Civ 864: *Nokia Corp v. AU Optonics Corp and Others* [2012] EWHC 732 (Ch): and *Toshiba Carrier UK Ltd and Others v. KME Yorkshire Ltd and Others* [2011] EWHC 2665 (Ch).See also, e.g., s. 33(4) of the German Competition Act which confers a binding effect on all Commission, Bundeskartellamt, and even other NCAs' decisions, in follow-on civil litigation.

[173] Competition Act 1998, Chaps. I and II (modelled on Arts 101 and 102).

individuals and by consumer organisations on behalf of wider groups of consumers (representative claims).[174] A number of follow-on claims have now been launched before both the CAT and the High Court. These have involved proceedings following on from cartel and abuse of a dominant position decisions. For example, claims have been lodged on the basis of the Commission's decisions on vitamins,[175] carbon and graphite electrodes,[176] synthetic butadiene rubber,[177] gas insulated switchgear,[178] methionine,[179] copper plumbing tubes,[180] and animal phosphates;[181] the UK OFT's decisions on Replica Football Kits,[182] Independent Schools,[183] Genzyme,[184] Albion Waters,[185] Cardiff Bus,[186] and National Grid;[187] and the UK ORR's EW&S decision.[188]

Several of these cases have raised the issues of when limitation periods begin to run and to what extent the damages actions can be lodged and processed even though appeals against the infringement decisions are still pending.

Stand-alone Actions[189]

The claimant's position is more difficult where a breach has not previously been established. It has already been seen that this proved to be a particular problem for Mr Crehan. In this case, although a number of other Commission decisions indicated that the beer tie agreements infringed Article 101(1) and the Commission had indicated that the Inntrepreneur leases were in breach of Article 101, there was no actual decision holding the leases in question to be in breach. When the matter reverted to the English courts, Mr Crehan failed to establish that the agreements in question infringed Article 101.[190]

---

[174] Competition Act 1998, ss. 47A and 47B. Representation orders may also be made by the High Court, see Civil Practice Rules, r. 19.6 (but see *Emerald Supplies Ltd v. British Airways plc* [2009] EWHC 741 (Ch).

[175] See Case 1098/5/7/08, *BCL Old Co Ltd v. BASF AG* [2008] CAT 24, [2009] EWCA 434 (claim not brought within limitation period), [2009] CAT 29 (application for extra time to make the application rejected), [2010] CAT 5 (permission to appeal refused), [2010] EWCA Civ 1258 [2012] UKSC 45 (permission to appeal to the Supreme Court dismissed); and Case 1011/5/7/08, *Grampian County Food Group v. Sanofi-Aventis SA* and *Devenish Nutrition Ltd v. Sanofi Aventis SA* [2008] EWCA Civ 10.

[176] Case 1077/5/7/07 *Emerson Electric Co v. Morgan Crucible Company plc* [2011] CAT 4 and Case 1173/5/7/10 *Deutsche Bahn AG v. Morgan Crucible plc* [2012] EWCA Civ 1055, [2012] UKSC 209 (permission to appeal granted on 21 December 2012).

[177] *Cooper Tire & Rubber Co v. Shell Chemicals UK Ltd* [2010] EWCA Civ 864.

[178] See *National Grid Electricity Transmission plc v. ABB Ltd* [2011] EWHC 1717 (Ch), [2012] EWHC 869 (Ch).

[179] See Case 1147/5/7/09 *Moy Park Ltd v. Degussa* and Case 1153/5/7/10 *Marshall Food Group Ltd v. Degussa*.

[180] See Case 1194/5/7/12 *W. H. Newson Holding Ltd and others v. IMI plc*.

[181] See Case 1202/5/7/12 *Moy Park Ltd v. Tessenderlo Chemie NV*.

[182] This was the very first representative claim by a specified consumer body. The Consumers' Association sought compensatory, exemplary, and/or restitutionary damages on behalf of some 130 customers listed in an appendix to the claim. The claim was withdrawn, however, after the proceedings were settled.

[183] The proceedings relating to independent schools were settled, Case 1108/5/7/08, *Wilson v. Lancing College*.

[184] In Case 1060/5/7/06 *Healthcare at Home Ltd v. Genzyme* [2006] CAT 29, the CAT awarded the claimant, Healthcare at Home, an interim payment of £2 million in proceedings following on from an OFT decision holding that Genzyme had engaged in an abusive margin squeeze. Following this ruling the parties settled the proceedings so the CAT did not have the opportunity to rule on the amount of total damages to award.

[185] See Case 1166/5/10 *Albion Water Ltd v. Dwr Cymru Cyfyngedig*, [2010] CAT 30, [2013] CAT 6.

[186] See Case 1178/5/7/11 *2 Travel Group plc (in liquidation) v. Cardiff City Transport Services Ltd*, 5 July 2012 (awarding damages and exemplary damages).

[187] Cases 1198/5/7/12 *Siemens plc v. National Grid plc* and 1199/5/7/12 *Capital Meters Ltd v. National Grid plc*.

[188] See also Case 1106/5/7/08, *Enron Coal Services Ltd (in liquidation) v. English Welsh & Scottish Railway Ltd* [2009] CAT 7, [2009] EWCA Civ 647 (it is only possible to rely on explicit findings in the infringement decision, so if the claimant is alleging infringement wider than those found in the decision it must claim in the High Court), [2009] CAT 36 (abuses of dominant position not proved to have caused loss to claimant), and [2011] EWCA Civ 2 (appeal dismissed); and Case 1044/2/1/04, *JJ Burgess & Sons v. OFT* [2005] CAT 25.

[189] See also n. 156. For the view that stand-alone actions have played a more important role in the US see B. Rodger, 'Why not court? A study of follow-on actions in the UK' (2013) 1 *Journal of Antitrust Enforcement* 107.

[190] See discussion of the case in Section 2.E.ii.d, pp. 1096–1097.

In *Arkin v. Borchard Lines*,[191] the claimant was also found to have failed to establish a breach of the competition rules. A claim was also rejected in *Attheraces Ltd v. British Horseracing Board*.[192]

c. Causation

Before damages can be awarded in English law it must also be proved that the breach of the competition rules 'caused' the loss. The test is satisfied where the damage would not have occurred but for the breach. The burden is on the claimant to show that the breach caused the claimed loss. In both *Crehan* and *Arkin* the judges went on to consider the issue of causation in case their finding that there had not been a breach of the rules was subsequently found to be wrong.

In *Crehan*[193] the judge took the view that if a breach of Article 101(1) were established, then, on the balance of probabilities, the beer ties did cause the failure of Mr Crehan's business. The judge thus accepted Mr Crehan's view that if he had been free of the tie, 'I would have succeeded and I would have been in my pubs today pulling beer'.[194]

In contrast, in *Arkin*,[195] Colman J took the view that even if a breach of Article 101 or Article 102 had been established, such a breach had not caused the loss suffered by the claimant. Rather the chain of causation between the breach and the losses suffered had been broken by the claimant's irrational and unjustified behaviour (reducing prices by up to 35 per cent and failing to withdraw at an earlier point from the market). Further in *Enron Coal Services Ltd (in liquidation) v. English Welsh & Scottish Railway*[196] the claimant's case failed even though it relied on the ORR's decision that EW&S had engaged in discriminatory pricing. Enron claimed that this had caused it to lose a tender for coal haulage. The CAT held, however, that the claimant had not discharged its burden of establishing that the discriminatory pricing had caused it loss.

d. Claims between Co-contractors and the Illegality Defence

In *Crehan v. Inntrepreneur Pub Co*[197] Park J, on reversion of the case to him, accepted that if a breach of Article 101 could be established in principle, Mr Crehan would be able to recover damages in respect of the loss caused by the illegal beer ties. With regard to shared responsibility, the judge accepted that the CJ's judgment had left open the possibility for a 'shared illegality defence' in holding that a claimant could be denied responsibility if he bore a significant degree of responsibility for the illegality.[198] As the leases in issue were standard form leases and Inntrepreneur was not willing to take the beer ties out of the lease or to consider any variations to it, there was no equality of bargaining power[199] and it was concluded that the defence could not apply in that case. The Court of Appeal upheld the view of the judge.

e. Standing, Quantification of Loss, and Other Issues

As damages claims emerge before the courts, difficult issues are arising and are likely to arise, such as whether a claimant must establish 'antitrust injury',[200] how damages should be

---

[191] [2003] EWHC 687 (Comm Ct).

[192] [2007] EWCA Civ 38 (allowing the appeal). The parties eventually settled the matter so Attheraces did not seek leave to appeal to the House of Lords. See also *Bookmakers Afternoon Greyhound Services Ltd v. Amalgamated Racing Ltd* [2008] EWHC 2688 (Ch), [2009] EWCA Civ 750 (joint selling arrangements by racecourses did not violate Art. 101(1)); *Chester City Council v. Arriva Plc* [2007] EWHC 1373; and *Ineos Vinyls Ltd v. Huntsman Petrochemicals (UK) Ltd* [2006] EWHC 1241 (Ch).

[193] *Crehan v. Inntrepreneur Pub Co* [2003] EWHC 1510 (Ch).

[194] *Crehan v. Inntrepreneur Pub Co* [2003] EWHC 1510 (Ch), para. 234. The Court of Appeal, [2004] EWCA Civ 637, paras. 169–171, did not interfere with this finding.

[195] [2003] EWHC 687 (Comm Ct).

[196] [2009] CAT 18; [2011] EWCA Civ 2.

[197] [2003] EWHC 1510 (Ch).

[198] Case C-453/99, [2001] ECR I-6297, para. 31.

[199] Relying on the CJ's judgment Case C-453/99, [2001] ECR I-6297 para. 34.

[200] In the US the claimant must have suffered injury of the type that the antitrust laws are designed to prevent, see, e.g., *Brunswick Corp v. Pueblo Bowl-O-Mat Inc* 429 US 477 (1977), *Atlantic Richfield Co v. USA Petroleum Co.* 495 US

quantified,[201] whether exemplary damages should be allowed (the English courts have indicated that the principle of *ne bis idem*[202] precludes punitive damages in a follow-on action involving a prior finding of infringement by the Commission or a NCA where a fine was imposed),[203] whether account should be taken of the fact that a claimant may have 'passed on' some of the injury that it has suffered to purchasers from it,[204] and whether claimants who did not purchase directly from the defendant, but who nonetheless claim to have suffered loss as a result of the infringement, should be able to bring proceedings.

f. Jurisdiction

The questions of which national court or courts have jurisdiction to hear an antitrust claim and what law is applicable are of fundamental importance. EU law provides, in the Brussels Regulation,[205] a broad choice of jurisdictions from which a claimant may choose when deciding where to launch his action. In *Provimi* v. *Aventis*[206] an important ruling was given by the English High Court. Provimi had purchased vitamins from members of the vitamin cartel across Europe. Both the European Commission and the US authorities had found the companies to have committed serious violations of the competition rules.[207] In this case the court confirmed, in the context of an interim application, that a European customer could bring a claim against a UK domiciled subsidiary (under Article 2) which had participated in the infringement—it had thus implemented the cartel and was part of the undertakings (the economic unit) to which the Commission's decision was addressed. The claimant wanted to bring a single claim in respect of all its losses in one jurisdiction. The case clearly opens the door to forum-shopping in actions against members of a Europe-wide cartel.

The question of jurisdiction was also of utmost importance in *Cooper Tire & Rubber* v. *Shell Chemicals*[208] which raised a number of points relating to the application of the Brussels Regulation. In this case tyre manufacturers have lodged proceedings in the English courts seeking to recover damages from members of the butadiene rubber cartel. Essentially, the claims in England were brought against a number of defendants, only two of which were domiciled in the UK. Although those two companies were not addressees of the Commission's cartel decision, the High Court similarly dismissed an action to strike out the claim, holding that it did have jurisdiction to hear the claim against the UK domiciled companies as they had sold the cartelised products—they had thus implemented the cartel and were part of the undertakings (the economic unit) to which the Commission's decision was addressed. It followed that the Court also had jurisdiction to hear the claim against the defendants which were not domiciled in England—Article 6(1) of the Brussels Regulation allows claims to be grouped together when they are so closely connected that it is expedient to hear and determine them together and where necessary to

---

328 (1990). The argument that there was a similar requirement in English law was raised but rejected by the Court of Appeal in the *Crehan* case, [2004] EWCA Civ 637, para. 156.

[201] But see Section 4.A.i.g, p. 1111–1118.

[202] See Chap. 13.

[203] Contrast *Devenish Nutrition Ltd* v. *Sanofi Aventis SA* [2007] EWHC 2394 (exemplary damages not available where the Commission has imposed a fine in relation to the same offence and restitutionary damages not generally available in tortious claims unless compensatory damages would be inadequate), *aff'd* [2008] EWCA Civ 10 with Case 1178/5/7/11 *2 Travel Group plc (in liquidation)* v. *Cardiff City Transport Services Ltd* [2012] CAT 19 (exemplary damages awarded) See also Case 1166/5/10 *Albion Water Ltd* v. *Dwr Cymru Cyfyngedig* [2013] CAT 6.

[204] See, e.g., Case 1147/5/7/09 *Moy Park Ltd* v. *Degussa* and Case 1153/5/7/10 *Marshall Food Group Ltd* v. *Degussa*.

[205] See Reg. 44/2001 on jurisdiction and the recognition and enforcement of judgment in civil and commercial matters [2001] OJ C189/2 (the Brussels Regulation). The Commission has published a proposal to recast the Regulation, see COM(2010) 748 final. The Lugano Convention (signed by the EU, Iceland, Norway, Denmark, and Switzerland) contains rules based on the Brussels Regulation.

[206] [2003] EWHC 961. But see also *SanDisk Corporation* v. *Koninklijke Philips Electronics N.V.* [2007] EWHC 332 (Ch).

[207] See Chap. 9.

[208] [2009] EWHC 2609 (Comm), [2010] EWCA Civ 864 (appeal dismissed). See also *Toshiba Carrier UK Ltd* v. *KME Yorkshire Ltd* [2012] EWCA Civ 1190 and *Nokia* v. *AU Optronics* [2012] EWHC 731(Ch), on appeal.

avoid the risk of irreconcilable judgments resulting from separate proceedings. The Court of Appeal affirmed, stating however that if the facts established that the UK subsidiaries had no knowledge of the anti-competitive conduct of the parent, it would have to be determined whether the claimant had jurisdiction—that is, whether it was sufficient that it formed part of the same undertaking as the parent to whom the decision was addressed or whether it had to be established that it had knowledge of the infringing conduct—and/or whether a reference to the CJ was necessary to resolve the point.

A further issue to be decided in this case was whether the English proceedings should be stayed pending the outcome of prior proceedings[209] relating to the same issue in Italy. One of the members of the cartel, Eni (which the claimants did not name as a defendant in the English proceedings), had commenced proceedings before the Italian courts seeking a declaration that the cartel did not exist or that it was not a member of the cartel or that the cartel did not cause any damage to the tyre manufacturers (the Italian torpedo).[210] The High Court declined to stay the proceedings because of these related proceedings, noting that the disputes involved different parties and that the Italian proceedings were likely to be extremely lengthy.

g. Settlement and Alternative Dispute Resolution (ADR)

Many of the uncertain issues set out in the previous sections have, perhaps, encouraged settlement of a number of the competition claims[211] arising in private proceedings before the English courts.[212] Further, procedure in the commercial courts encourages ADR as a practical means of settling claims between the parties[213] and many commercial agreements provide for disputes to be taken to arbitration. The Government is also taking measures to encourage settlement and ADR. Not only is it going to align the CAT rules governing formal settlement offers with those of the High Court but it is going to introduce a new opt-out collective settlement regime in the CAT. It is also proposing to enable competition authorities, when a company has been found to have infringed competition law, to certify a voluntary redress scheme.

h. Harmonising Rules

A number of difficult issues are arising for resolution before the English courts. Until such time as harmonising EU legislation is adopted to resolve these questions, they will have to be settled through the application of national rules. It will then be up to the CJ to determine whether or not those rules comply with the EU principles of equivalence and effectiveness. If the Commission's proposal for a Directive is transposed into legislation some of these issues will be resolved through the adoption of EU legislation. In the absence of such harmonising legislation, there may be significant incentives for undertakings to engage in national forum shopping in order to secure the most advantageous conditions for the prosecution or defence of their damages claim.

(iii) Jurisdiction in Damages Claims in the US

It has already been mentioned that private litigation, and damages actions, are more widespread in the US. A vital issue which has arisen in recent years is whether claimants that have suffered loss in consequence of a cartel operated worldwide or internationally can pursue a US class action in respect of cartelised products purchased from the companies but delivered outside the US, that is

[209] The general rule being that the first court seised of the case takes priority.

[210] Although the Milan court rejected the claim, Eni appealed the decision to the Italian Court of Appeal. See also *National Grid Electricity Transmission plc v. ABB Ltd* [2009] EWHC 1326.

[211] See Case 1105/5/7/08 *Freightliner Ltd and Freightliner Heavy Haul Ltd v. English Welsh and Scottish Railways Ltd* and Case 1008/5/7/08 *Wilson v. Lancing College Ltd.*

[212] B. Rodger, 'Private Enforcement of Competition Law, The Hidden Story: Competition Litigation Settlements in the UK 2000–2005' (2008) *ECLR* 96–116.

[213] See, e.g., The Admiralty and Commercial Courts Guide, section G (alternative dispute resolution) and the Chancery Guide, chap. 17.

encompassing claimants whose case does *not* arise from the *US effect* of the anti-competitive conduct. In *F. Hoffmann-La Roche Ltd* v. *Empagran SA*[214] the DC Court of Appeals considered that for jurisdiction to exist it was only necessary that the conduct's harmful effect on US commerce would give rise to a claim by someone, even if not the foreign plaintiff before the Court. The Court considered that this view would maximise deterrence of international cartels by forcing the conspirator to internalise the full cost of its anti-competitive conduct. The case went on appeal, however, before the Supreme Court. The US Department of Justice and Federal Trade Commission filed a brief before the Court, as amicus curiae, expressing their concern with the Court of Appeals' conclusion. In particular, they feared that the holding would substantially harm the Court's ability to uncover and break up international cartels and would undermine law enforcement relationships between the US and its trading partners. The Supreme Court[215] reined in the extent to which foreign claimants can seek damages in the US. It held that they may *not* do so in respect of injuries flowing exclusively from foreign effects of allegedly anti-competitive global conduct, where the foreign effects are independent of, and not intertwined with, the US effects.[216] This case is discussed in further detail in Chapter 16. It is also, of course, of central importance to this chapter: where a European complainant is able to join class actions in the US (where the anti-competitive conduct also has had effects on the US market which are intertwined with the foreign effects), the incentives for litigation in Europe may be reduced.

B. INJUNCTIONS

(i) General

An individual suffering in consequence of a breach of the competition rules might request an injunction to prevent the undertaking or undertakings committing a breach of the rules in future. The injunction sought might be final or interim, pending resolution of the final dispute between the parties. The availability of an interim injunction will be of particular importance to an undertaking which believes that it is being driven out of the market, for example by a dominant undertaking's predatory behaviour in breach of Article 102 or by a refusal to supply.

(ii) An EU Right to an Injunction

The CJ held in *R* v. *Secretary of State for Transport, ex parte Factortame Ltd*[217] that a national court must ensure that interim measures are available where necessary to protect putative EU rights:

19. In accordance with the case-law of the Court, it is for the national courts, in application of the principle of cooperation laid down in Article [10] of the [EC] Treaty, to ensure the legal protection which persons derive from the direct effect of provisions of Community law…

20. The Court has also held that any provision of a national legal system and any legislative, administrative or judicial practice which might impair the effectiveness of Community law by withholding from the national court having jurisdiction to apply such law the power to do everything necessary at the moment of its application to set aside national legislative provisions which might prevent, even temporarily, Community rules from having full force and effect are incompatible with those requirements, which are the very essence of Community law.

…

21.…the full effectiveness of Community law would be just as much impaired if a rule of national law could prevent a court seized of a dispute governed by Community law from granting interim relief in order

---

[214] 315 F.3d 338 (DC Cir. 2003).

[215] 542 US 155(2004) (Justice Breyer delivered the opinion of the Court).

[216] On remand, the DC Circuit ruled for the defendants, 417 F.3d 1267 (D.C. Cir., 2005). See also *In re Monosodium Glutamate Antitrust Litigation* 477 F.3d 535 (8th Cir. 2007).

[217] Case 213/89, [1990] ECR I-2433. In Case C-170/13, *Huawei Technologies* v. *ZTE* the CJ has been asked to rule on the question of whether, and if so when, the seeking of an injunction by a patentee might constitute an abuse of a dominant position, see Chap. 7.

to ensure the full effectiveness of the judgment to be given on the existence of the rights claimed under Community law. It follows that a court which in those circumstances would grant interim relief, if it were not for a rule of national law, is obliged to set aside that rule.

(iii) The Position in English Law[218]

The English High Court[219] has jurisdiction to grant both final and interim injunctions where the court considers it to be 'just and equitable' to do so.[220] Broadly, an interim injunction will be granted where the guidelines set out in *American Cyanamid Co v. Ethicon*[221] are satisfied. The guidelines require the court to take account of the following factors:

(i) Whether or not the claimant's case is frivolous or vexatious. There must be a serious issue to be tried;

(ii) Whether damages would be an adequate remedy for either party. If the injunction is granted the claimant will usually be required to give a cross-undertaking in damages to the defendant;

(iii) Whether on the balance of convenience the injunction should be granted;

(iv) Whether there are other special factors.

The injunction will not be granted if, for example, it would result in summary judgment for the claimant.[222]

These principles should enable an English court to ensure that an interim injunction is granted where necessary to give effective protection to the claimant's EU rights. Indeed, they appear to impose less stringent requirements on a claimant than those which must be satisfied by a claimant seeking interim relief from the Commission.[223]

Although the English courts have refused interim relief in competition cases on a number of occasions,[224] relief has been granted in others.[225]

5. CONCLUSIONS

1. The Commission's modernisation programme was designed to allow the Commission to refocus its scarce resources and to encourage greater enforcement of the rules at the national level. The Commission not only has sought to enlist the aid of NCAs in the enforcement of the rules, but also is eager that private actions should be used more frequently to bolster public enforcement. Both the Commission and a number of Member States are now actively taking steps to encourage private enforcement, particularly damages actions,

---

[218] See e.g., S. Peyer, *Injunctive Relief and Private Antitrust Enforcement* (2011) CCP Working Paper (11-7). (Unpublished)

[219] The CAT is also to be given jurisdiction to hear injunction cases.

[220] The principles which govern a court's decision whether or not to grant an injunction differ depending upon whether the injunction sought is final or interim.

[221] [1975] AC 396.

[222] See, e.g., *Plessey Co plc v. General Electric Co plc* [1988] ECC 384, where the award of the interim injunction would have precluded any take-over bid.

[223] See Chap. 13.

[224] See, e.g., *Garden Cottage Foods v. Milk Marketing Board* [1984] AC 130; *Claritas (UK) Ltd v. The Post Office* [2001] UKCLR 2; *Getmapping plc v. Ordnance Survey* [2002] UKCLR 410; *Suretrack Rail Services Ltd v. Infraco JNP Ltd* [2002] EWHC 316.

[225] See, e.g., *Cutsforth v. Mansfield Inns* [1986] I CMLR 1; *Network Multimedia Television Ltd v. Jobserve Ltd* Ch D (Peter Whiteman QC), judgment of 5 April 2001, appeal rejected by Court of Appeal, CA (Civ Div) 21 December 2001; *Intel Corporation v. VIA Technologies* [2002] EWCA Civ 1905; *Adidas-Salomon v. Lawn Tennis Association and Others* [2006] EWHC 1318 (Ch). See also *Software Cellular Network Limited v. T-Mobile (UK) Ltd* [2007] EWHC 1790 (Ch).

2. The abolition of the Commission's exclusive right to rule individually on the compatibility of an agreement with Article 101(3) has removed a fundamental impediment to the courts' participation in the enforcement process. Further, the CJ's ruling in *Courage Ltd* v. *Crehan* has given national courts clearer guidance on their obligations when hearing damages claims.

3. Although litigants in competition cases may continue to face a number of obstacles and hurdles to their claims, the Commission's 2013 package of measures, including its proposal for a Directive, are likely to stimulate further the private litigation which is beginning to emerge in the Member States.

4. It is to be expected, therefore, that private actions in Europe will gradually become more commonplace.

6. FURTHER READING

A. BOOKS

BASEDOW, J., TERHECHTE, J. P., and TICHÝ, L., *Private Enforcement of Competition Law* (Nomos, 2011)

FOER, A. A., and CUNEO, J. W., *The International Handbook on Private Enforcement of Competition Law* (Edward Elgar, 2012)

JONES, A., *Restitution and European Community Law* (LLP, 2000), Chap. 6

JONES, C. A., *Private Enforcement of Antitrust Law in the EU, UK and USA* (Oxford University Press, 1999)

KOMNINOS, A. P., *EC Private Antitrust Enforcement: Decentralised Application of EC Competition Law by National Courts* (Hart Publishing, 2008)

WILS, W., *Principles of European Antitrust Enforcement* (Hart Publishing, 2005), Chap. 4

B. ARTICLES

BREALEY, M., 'Adopt Perma Life but follow Hanover Shoe to Illinois? Who can sue for Damages for Breach of EC Competition Law' [2002] *Comp Law Journal* 1(2), 127

DRAKE, S., 'Scope of *Courage* and the Principle of "Individual Liability" for Damages: Further Development of the Principle of Effective Judicial Protection by the Court of Justice' (2006) 30 *ELRev* 841

HODGES, C., 'European Competition Enforcement Policy: Integrating Restitution and Behaviour Control. An Integrated Enforcement Policy, Involving Public and Private Enforcement with ADR' (2011) 34(3) *World Competition* 383

JACOBS, F. G., 'Civil Enforcement of EEC Antitrust Law' (1984) 82 *Mich LR* 1364

JONES, A., and BEARD, D., 'Co-contractors, Damages and Article 81: The ECJ finally speaks' [2002] *ECLR* 246

ODUDU, O., 'Developing private enforcement in the EU: Lessons from the Roberts Court' (2008) 53 *Ant Bull* 873

—— and EDELMAN, J., 'Compensatory damages for breach of Article 81' (2002) 27 *ELRev* 327

PARLAK, S., 'Passing-on Defence and Indirect Purchaser Standing: Should the Passing-on Defence Be Rejected Now the Indirect Purchaser Has Standing after Manfredi and the White Paper of the European Commission?' [2010] 33 *World Competition* 1

RODGER, B., 'The Interface between Competition Law and Private Law: Article 81, Illegality and Unjustified Enrichment' [2002] *Edinburgh LR* 217

—— 'Competition Law Litigation in the UK Courts: A Study of All Cases to 2004', Parts I, II, and III [2006] *ECLR* 241–248, 279–292 and 341–350

—— 'Why not court? A study of follow-on actions in the UK' (2013) 1 *Journal of Antitrust Enforcement* 104

TEMPLE LANG, J., 'Inntrepreneur and the Duties of National Courts under Article 10 EC' [2006] *Comp Law* 231

VAN GERVEN, W., 'Of Rights, Remedies and Procedures' [2000] 37 *CMLRev* 501

WILS, W. P. J., 'Should private antitrust enforcement be encouraged?' [2003] 26 *World Competition* 473

—— 'The Relationship between Public Antitrust Enforcement and Private Actions for Damages' [2009] 32 *World Competition* 3

15

MERGERS

1. CENTRAL ISSUES

1. Prior to 1990, the Commission had to rely on its power to apply Articles 102 and 101, to prevent one firm from taking over or acquiring shares in another.

2. In 1989 the Council adopted a European Merger Control Regulation (EUMR) to regulate changes in market structure in the EU. The Regulation came into force in 1990, was amended in 1997 and was amended again and consolidated into a new regulation in 2004, Regulation 139/2004.

3. The 2004 EUMR declares incompatible with the common market 'concentrations' (merger transactions) with a 'Community dimension' (or an EU dimension) which would significantly impede effective competition in the common market or a substantial part of it, in particular as a result of the creation or strengthening of a dominant position.

4. A 'concentration' occurs where two or more undertakings on a market 'merge' or where one or more undertakings acquire 'control' over another.

5. The concept of an EU dimension aims to ensure that mergers creating structural changes which impact beyond the national borders of a Member State are appraised by the Commission under the EUMR. It is a quantitative test based on the turnover of the undertakings concerned.

6. The general scheme of the EUMR is that, subject to certain limited exceptions:

   (a) concentrations with an EU dimension are appraised exclusively by the Commission under the provisions of the EUMR;

   (b) concentrations without an EU dimension are appraised exclusively at the national level.

7. Concentrations with an EU dimension must generally be notified to the Commission prior to completion and are suspended pending investigation under the tight statutory timetable set out in the EUMR.

8. Mergers are frequently motivated by the desire of the merging parties to increase efficiency. Nonetheless, mergers may significantly impede effective competition on a market. Horizontal mergers (between competitors) reduce the number of players on the market and increase the market share of the post-merger firm. They may significantly impede effective competition by enabling the post-merger firm to exercise market power either individually, or collectively, through collusion or coordination with other firms operating on the market (unilateral or coordinated effects may occur).

9. Non-horizontal mergers are less likely to cause competition concerns and provide greater scope for efficiencies. Nonetheless the Commission is concerned that where one of the parties to such a merger has market power in at least one market, vertical and conglomerate mergers may harm competition through:

   (a) foreclosure of a distinct upstream, downstream or related market; or

   (b) changing the structure of competition on a market in such a way that the firms operating on it are likely to coordinate their behaviour.

10. Merger analysis also requires assessment of factors which are likely to counteract the merged firm's ability to exercise market power, such as countervailing buyer power or new entry.

11. Efficiencies achieved by the merger may also offset any anti-competitive consequences.

12. Where one of the merging parties is failing, the merger may not be the cause of any anti-competitive harm arising on the market.

2. INTRODUCTION

A. WHAT IS A MERGER?

A merger is generally defined as occurring where two or more formerly independent entities unite. A number of different transactions and agreements concluded by undertakings could result in a unification of the independent undertakings' decision-making process. Every jurisdiction needs, therefore, to adopt a definition of what constitutes a merger for the purposes of their merger control legislation. The European Union Merger Regulation (the EUMR)[1] applies to 'concentrations'. Broadly, there is a concentration where two or more previously independent undertakings merge their businesses, where there is a change in control of an undertaking (sole or joint control of an undertaking being *acquired* by another undertaking or undertakings) or where a full-function joint venture is created.[2]

B. THE PURPOSES OF MERGER CONTROL

The purpose of merger control is to enable competition authorities to regulate changes in market structure by deciding whether two or more commercial companies may merge, combine, or consolidate their businesses into one.[3] It has been seen that the EU authorities are hostile to anti-competitive agreements concluded between independent undertakings.[4] Mergers naturally create a more permanent and lasting change on the market than agreements. It might be expected, therefore, that many mergers, especially horizontal mergers, would be forbidden. However, mergers also give the owner of a business the opportunity to sell it. Without this possibility, entrepreneurs might be reluctant to start a business. Further, mergers provide many efficiency opportunities.

The reasons for not making mergers unlawful per se or for not even coming anywhere near such a rule are plain. Widespread prohibition of mergers would impose serious, if not intolerable, burdens upon owners of businesses who wished to liquidate their holdings for irreproachable personal reasons. Moreover, economic welfare is significantly served by maintaining a good market for capital assets... Most importantly, a policy of free transferability of capital assets tends to put them in the hands of those who will use them to their utmost economic advantage, thus tending to maximize society's total output of goods and services.

Growth by merger... will often yield substantial economies of scale—in production, research, distribution, cost of capital and management. Entry by merger... may stimulate improved economic performance in an industry characterized by oligopolistic lethargy and inefficiency. Finally, acquisition of diversified lines of business, by stabilizing profits, may minimize the risk of business failure and bankruptcy.[5]

The task of the competition authorities is to identify and to prohibit those mergers which have such an adverse impact on competition or society that any benefits resulting from them are outweighed or should be ignored.

---

[1] Reg. 139/2004 [2004] OJ L24/1 (the EUMR).

[2] EUMR, Art. 3, discussed in Section 3.A, pp. 1140–1149.

[3] For merger control to be effective, it is necessary to control both amicable agreements to merge and hostile take-overs.

[4] See especially Chap. 9.

[5] D. Turner, 'Conglomerate Mergers and Section 7 of the Clayton Act' (1965) 78 *Harvard LR* 1313, 1317.

(i) The Motives for, and Advantages of, a Merger

a. Efficiency

In many cases the parties will state that the main motivation for their merger is that the merged entity will be more efficient. The entity may be able to exploit economies of scale in production (this argument will be strongest in the context of horizontal or, sometimes, vertical mergers where related operations are combined). Such economies will be of particular importance in a market in which the cost of production of a product is high in comparison to the size, or the anticipated size, of the market or where there is a minimum efficient scale of production.[6] The merger may also give rise to other operating efficiencies such as economies of scope, marketing efficiencies (arising, for example, from broader product lines, streamlining of the sales force, the use of common advertising, etc.), efficiencies arising from integration of complementary activities or the ability to pool research and development (R&D) skills (giving rise to the opportunity for greater innovation).

Mergers may, therefore, enable undertakings to increase these efficient levels of manufacture, R&D, and distribution more rapidly and more cheaply than they could by internal growth. They may also encourage management efficiency by ensuring that the most productive assets are managed by the most efficient managers (the merger may bring new and superior management to the business).[7]

b. Barriers to Exit

It has already been noted that few people would go to the trouble to set up a business if they could not sell it when they had had enough or when they wished to realise capital profits from it. In particular, many smaller business owners may wish to sell their business if no obvious successor is available.

c. Failing Undertakings, Unemployment, and/or Industry Stability

A merger may provide an escape route for a company facing an otherwise inevitable liquidation. In these circumstances the possibility of selling the business to another may mean that assets are kept in production, that creditors, owners, and employees are protected from the adverse consequences of the undertaking's failure, and that stability is preserved in a critical industry sector (for example, in the financial system).

d. Single Market Integration

Cross-border mergers may facilitate market integration. '[E]xternal growth by means of mergers and acquisitions can be a means of quickly realizing potential cost savings and integration gains offered by the internal market.'[8]

e. National or European Champions

The desire to increase the scale of national and European companies may be a goal of national, or European, industrial policy. Mergers affect the structure of a market and questions of industrial policy inevitably arise. The ability to restructure or to create national or European champions may, for example, mean that the parties can, in combination, survive and compete more effectively on international markets, contribute to technical and economic progress, and/or facilitate cross-border trade.

---

[6] See Chap. 1.

[7] The simple threat of a take-over may encourage the incumbent management of a company to strive for efficiency (rigid control of mergers will remove or greatly reduce this perceived threat).

[8] European Commission, 'Competition and Integration: Community Merger Policy' (1994) 57 *European Economy*, vii.

(ii) The Adverse Consequence of Mergers

More important perhaps than focusing on the benefits of a merger is the answer to the question: why should mergers be prohibited? When, and on what grounds, should a competition authority take steps to interfere with the market for corporate control? Failure to agree on this key issue was one of the factors which seriously delayed the introduction of any comprehensive system of merger control at the EU level. Should competition be the sole criterion relevant to a decision to clear or to prohibit a merger? Or should other wider policy issues, such as regional, industrial, or social policy, also be taken into account?

a. A Damaging Effect on the Competitive Structure of the Market

There is a danger that undertakings may wish to merge in order to achieve or to strengthen their market power.

In horizontal mergers, and especially in the massive consolidations that took place [in the US] around the turn of the [20th] century, the desire to achieve or strengthen monopoly power played a prominent role. Some 1887–1904 consolidations gained monopoly power by creating firms that dominated their industries. Others fell short of dominance, but transformed market structures sufficiently to curb the tendencies toward price competition toward which sellers gravitated in the rapidly changing market conditions of the time. As Thomas Edison remarked to a reporter concerning reasons for the formation of the General Electric Company in 1892:

> Recently there has been sharp rivalry between [Thomson-Houston and Edison General Electric], and prices have been cut so that there has been little profit in the manufacture of electrical machinery for anybody. The consolidation of the companies... will do away with competition which has become so sharp that the product of the factories has been worth little more than ordinary hardware.

> Those were days when businesspeople were not yet intimidated by the wrath of trustbusters or public opinion. Now they are more circumspect, and evidence of monopoly-creating intent is harder to find. Also, vigorous antitrust enforcement in the United States and, more recently, abroad has done much to curb competition-inhibiting mergers.[9]

Even if dominance or the acquisition of market power is not the motive for a merger, it may be its effect.

Horizontal Mergers

A horizontal merger is one which occurs between undertakings operating at the same level of the economy. As Hovenkamp points out, such mergers have two important implications for the market on which the merging firms operate:

Because the horizontal merger involves two firms in the same market, it produces two consequences that do not flow from vertical or conglomerate mergers: 1) after the merger the relevant market has one firm less than before; 2) the post-merger firm ordinarily has a larger market share than either of the partners had before the merger.[10]

The reduction in the number of firms active on the market and the increase in concentration may raise competition concerns. We have seen that markets dominated by a single undertaking may not deliver the same efficiencies as those achieved in a competitive market.[11] Further, that it is difficult

---

[9] F. M. Scherer and D. Ross, *Industrial Market Structure and Economic Performance* (3rd edn, Houghton Mifflin, 1990), 160.

[10] 'Merger policy is the most powerful weapon available in the American antitrust arsenal for combating tacit collusion or Cournot style oligopoly. Since we cannot go after oligopoly directly under [section 1 Sherman Act], we do the next best thing. We try to prevent (taking efficiencies and other factors into account) the creation of market structures that tend to facilitate Cournot or collusion-like outcomes', H. Hovenkamp, *Federal Antitrust Policy: The Law of Competition and its Practice* (4th edn, West Publishing, 2011), 12.1b, 546.

[11] See generally Chaps. 5–7.

for competition authorities to control the behaviour of a dominant undertaking and to detect abuse of market power. An active merger policy seeks to avoid these difficulties by precluding undertakings from merging where the parties will obtain or strengthen a dominant position or a position of individual market power which might be exploited at the expense of customers and protected by anti-competitive behaviour.[12]

A merger between two or more previously independent undertakings which does not lead to the creation of a dominant position may lead to a substantial increase in the concentration of a particular industry and enable the merging parties to raise prices and restrict output, whether through explicit or tacit coordination of their behaviour with other firms operating on the market (coordinated effects) or through non-coordinated, unilateral effects.[13] Many competition authorities, therefore, adopt a merger policy which is wary of mergers occurring in an already concentrated market.[14] In the EU, the extent to which the EUMR is, and has been, able to prevent mergers leading to coordinated or non-coordinated effects on oligopolistic markets has been controversial.

Vertical Mergers

A vertical merger is one concluded between firms at different levels of production in the economy. The motive for vertical mergers is frequently to achieve efficiencies and to obtain a secure supply of a raw material or to secure an outlet for the sale of products. Vertical mergers may, however, raise competition concerns. The predominant fear is that where the merging firms have market power at one or more vertical level, vertical mergers may 'foreclose' the market or a source of supply to competitors.[15] For example, a merger between a manufacturer of a product and a supplier of an essential component for that product (backward integration) may have severe implications for competing manufacturers. The foreclosure effect will be acute where there are few or no other suppliers of the essential components. Similarly, the acquisition by a manufacturer of a distributor (forward integration) may make it more difficult for competitors to distribute their products. A vertical merger may also increase price transparency or facilitate collusion between firms operating on the market. The Commission is sometimes concerned about vertical mergers and has published Guidelines on assessment on non-horizontal mergers (the Non-Horizontal Merger Guidelines) explaining how it analyses such mergers.[16]

Conglomerate Mergers

Conglomerate mergers are concentrations which have no horizontal or vertical effect. As such mergers do not result in horizontal overlaps or vertical effects, they do not obviously raise competition problems. Rather they may frequently be motivated by innocuous objectives from a competition perspective, such as the need for risk reduction. An undertaking may, for example, wish to expand into another market where it is operating in a declining or cyclical industry or where it simply wishes to spread risk. However, where post-merger a firm will have market power in one market there could be concern that it will use its power in that market to foreclose competition in a neighbouring or related market, for example by engaging in tying or by cross-subsidiing or predating in that market.[17] This may be more likely where the relevant markets are closely related and the merged undertakings will be able to offer a portfolio of products. Alternatively there may be a fear that conglomeracy

---

[12] The US antitrust authorities thus aim to prevent mergers which 'create or enhance market power or facilitate its exercise', Horizontal Merger Guidelines 2010.

[13] See Chap. 9 and Section 5.B and D, especially pp. 1182–1184.

[14] Hovenkamp, *Federal Antitrust Policy* (cited in n. 10), 12.1b, 544.

[15] See discussion of vertical mergers in Section 5.D.ix.c, pp. 1225–1230.

[16] Guidelines on the assessment of non-horizontal mergers under the Council Regulation on the control of concentrations between undertakings (the Non-Horizontal Merger Guidelines) [2008] OJ C265/6.

[17] See Chap. 7.

will lead to a loss of potential competition. A merger of firms operating in different product or geographic markets may cause a loss of potential competition. Any threat that they may enter each other's markets is eliminated. This may be of particular importance where the undertakings operate in the same product but a different geographic market or where they operate in neighbouring product markets.[18] In the EU, the elimination of a potential competitor is identified as a horizontal issue,[19] but the Commission has also displayed concerns about purely conglomerate mergers. Conglomerate mergers are also covered by the Non-Horizontal Merger Guidelines.

Efficiency and/or Other Considerations?

A further matter of controversy is whether, and if so how, account should be taken of the fact that a merger might: (1) lead to greater efficiency (the cost savings resulting from the merger outweigh the detrimental impact of the merger on consumer welfare as a whole); (2) save a firm which, otherwise, faces an inevitable failure; or (3) is supported as a matter of industrial or social or other policy. Whether or not these factors should be, or are, taken into account under the EUMR is considered in Sections 5.D.vi, 5.D.vii, and 5.D.x.

b. A Fear of Big Business

Mergers may cause other concerns, apart from competition ones. Most of the factors that will be discussed in this section and Sections 2.B.ii.c and 2.B.ii.d would not, however, cause concern on the ground of strict economic theory unless it could *also* be shown that consumer welfare was adversely affected by the merger.

Some commentators believe that conglomeracy, or mergers that would create large businesses, have implications for the freedom of society more generally. It is feared that too great an economic concentration is anti-democratic and restricts individual freedom and enterprise or that it has an adverse effect on the distribution of wealth.

[O]ur concern for the maintenance of effective competition extends beyond purely economic considerations. Competition is one of the foundations of an open society...it is therefore necessary to weigh against the gains from industrial concentration the socio-political consequences of concentrations of private power, which could discredit property owning democracy.[20]

In Chapter 1 it was seen that it has been argued that one of the goals of competition laws should be the diffusion of economic power and the protection of individual freedom.

Private power can cross economic boundaries and poses the threat of an 'extra market' power which can change the rules of the game in favour of the dominant corporations. In such a situation, where relationships between firms and their socio-economic environment constitute a mixture of market and non-market bonds, the authorities aim at the dispersion of private power. Even if this entails some loss of economic efficiency, such a choice would not necessarily be irrational, because such costs may be outweighed by social or political advantages.[21]

Further, and in particular following the 2008 financial and economic crisis, one of the questions which has arisen is whether care should be taken to ensure that any firm is not allowed to become so

---

[18] But see R. H. Bork, *The Antitrust Paradox* (Basic Books, 1978, reprinted with a new Introduction and Epilogue, 1993), 249.

[19] Guidelines on the assessment of horizontal mergers under the Council Regulation on the control of concentrations between undertakings (the Horizontal Merger Guidelines) [2004] OJ C31/5, para. 5. ('A merger with a potential competitor can generate horizontal anti-competitive effects...if the potential competitor significantly constrains the behaviour of the firms active in the market').

[20] A. Cairncross et al., *Economic Policy for the European Community* (Macmillan, 1974).

[21] A. P. Jacquemin and H. W. de Jong, *European Industrial Organisation* (Macmillan, 1997), 198–199.

large that it is 'too big to fail' and, if so, whether merger rules should play any role in enforcing such a policy.[22]

c. Special Sectors and Fear of Overseas Control

It may be believed that tighter control should be exercised over mergers which occur in particularly sensitive sectors. In these sectors it might be thought that a broader range of factors should be taken into account in determining whether or not a merger operates in the public interest. For example, interests of democracy may require the preservation of the 'plurality of the press' or national security may require that the ownership of certain industries such as oil and defence equipment does not pass overseas. In some cases States may seek more broadly to protect national industries from foreign ownership.[23]

d. Unemployment

Mergers may mean asset-stripping, profits to shareholders, rationalisation, and loss of jobs. Mergers which occur in depressed regions or in areas in which unemployment is already high may, therefore, cause concern.

C. THE HISTORY OF THE EUROPEAN MERGER CONTROL REGULATION

(i) The Initial Lacuna

The original EEC Treaty, unlike the ECSC Treaty,[24] did not contain any specific provision for controlling mergers. Articles 101 and 102 TFEU focus on the control of the behaviour of undertakings rather than mergers which effect a lasting change to the structure of the market. An explanation for the different approach set out in the ECSC and the EEC Treaties may be that the former was a *traité-loi* whilst the latter was a *traité-cadre* (a framework document, to be fleshed out by implementing legislation). However, it is more likely that other factors were responsible for the omission of merger control from the EEC Treaty. In particular, it might have been easier to agree on a rule which would affect only the specific industries dealt with by the ECSC Treaty. Indeed, the ability to control mergers in these sectors was perceived to be of vital importance given their political and military significance.[25] In contrast, it would have been more difficult to agree on rules which were to affect all firms generally. Further, at the time, it seems to have been considered that the objectives set out in Article 2 of the EEC Treaty of economic expansion might be achieved by concentrating economic power rather than prohibiting mergers.

(ii) The Drive for Merger Control at the EU Level

The drive to introduce legislation at the EU level specifically focused on merger control was led by the Commission. In 1966 it first acknowledged, in its publication of its *Memorandum on the Concentration of Enterprises in the Common Market*,[26] that some form of EU merger control was necessary.[27] The

---

[22] See, e.g., J. T. Rosch, 'Implications of the Financial Meltdown for the FTC' 29 January 2009 ('mergers should arguably be examined with an eye toward whether they are creating a merged entity that is "too big to fail"...if a merger creates a firm whose failure is likely to have a catastrophic effect on the market as a whole, because it is so integral to the market, the end result may be a substantial lessening of competition it would arguably be better to avoid the creation of such firms in the first place through merger instead of having the Treasury Department bail them out.')

[23] See the discussion in particular, Section 5.D.x, pp. 1239–1241.

[24] See Art. 66(7) of the ECSC Treaty. The ECSC Treaty expired on 23 July 2002, see Chap. 2.

[25] The French in particular were keen to have in place rules which imposed constraints on the German war industry, S. Bulmer, 'Institutions and Policy Change: The Case of Merger Control' (1994) 72 *Public Administration* 423, 427–428.

[26] EEC Competition Series Study No. 3.

[27] See C. Overbury, 'Politics or Policy? The Demystification of EC Merger Control' [1992] Fordham Corp L Inst 561.

Commission believed that its inability to control mergers inhibited its capability to operate effective competition control and it adopted its first legislative proposal for a merger control regulation in 1973.[28]

Any regulation on merger control had to be passed unanimously by the Council.[29] For a long time there was no consensus amongst the Member States that merger control was necessary at all and those that did recognise a need for it were reluctant to cede power over changes in industrial structure in their territories to the Commission. In addition, early drafts of the Merger Regulation gave the Commission a broad discretion in assessing whether or not a merger was in the EU interest. Member States were divided on what substantive criteria should be used to appraise mergers and, in particular, whether only the effects on competition should be relevant, or whether social and industrial policy considerations should also be taken into account. There were, therefore, two major sticking points:[30]

(i) *Jurisdiction*. Whether, and if so at what point, control should be relinquished by the Member States to the Commission and what the relationship between European and national law should be; and

(ii) *Appraisal criteria*. Should factors other than competition be taken into account in assessing whether a particular merger was compatible or incompatible with the common market?

(iii) The Catalyst for the EUMR

a. Articles 101 and 102 TFEU

Article 102

Frustrated by the lack of a specific provision enabling it to control mergers the Commission sought not only to persuade the Council to enact a specific merger control provision but it applied its existing tools to prevent them: it utilised Articles 102 and, subsequently, 101 TFEU to prevent take-overs and acquisitions of shareholdings in other undertakings.

In *Europemballage Corp and Continental Can Co Inc v. Commission*[31] the CJ upheld the Commission's view that Article 102 could be used to prevent a dominant undertaking from abusing its dominant position by acquiring a competitor and thereby strengthening that dominant position.[32] The CJ held that an abuse occurs 'if an undertaking in a dominant position strengthens such a position in such a way that the degree of dominance reached substantially fetters competition'.[33] Because a relatively low dominance threshold has been adopted,[34] Article 102 was a reasonably effective weapon against mergers.[35]

The use of Article 102 is, however, limited by the fact that the acquiring company must have a dominant position before Article 102 can apply (abuses can only be committed by dominant firms). It

---

[28] In the period between 1973 and 1989 a series of draft regulations was proposed and rejected by the Council: see [1973] OJ C92/1, [1982] OJ C36/3, [1984] OJ C51/8, [1988] OJ C130/4, [1989] OJ C22/141.

[29] The legal basis for the EUMR is Arts 103 (ex Art. 83) and 352 (ex Art. 308) TFEU.

[30] See B. E. Hawk and H. L. Huser, *European Community Merger Control A Practitioner's Guide* (Kluwer Law International, 1996), 2–3.

[31] Case 6/72, *Europemballage Corp and Continental Can Co Inc v. Commission* [1973] ECR 215.

[32] See Chap. 5.

[33] Case 6/72, *Europemballage Corp and Continental Can Co Inc v. Commission* [1973] ECR 215, para. 26. The abuse thus results from a limitation of competition in a market which it already dominates.

[34] See Chaps. 5–7.

[35] See e.g., C. J. Cook and C. S. Kerse, *EC Merger Control* (5th edn, Sweet & Maxwell, 2009), 1–003. The extent to which Arts 101 and 102 can now be applied to 'concentrations' is discussed in section 3.E., pp. 1171–1172.

does not, *prima facie*, apply where two or more undertakings merge to create a dominant position[36] or where a dominant undertaking is acquired by a non-dominant undertaking.

Article 101

The Commission initially appeared to accept that Article 101 would not be used to control mergers.[37] Indeed, Article 101 does not appear to be particularly suitable for the purpose. Because the Article strikes principally at *agreements* between independent undertakings it would be artificial to try and deal with many types of mergers under its provisions (for example, hostile take-overs which are opposed by the target undertaking).[38] Notwithstanding its early views, it later sought to apply Article 101 as a weapon against mergers and in *BAT and Reynolds v. Commission*[39] the CJ confirmed that Article 101 might apply to the acquisition by an undertaking of a minority shareholding in another. The difficulties raised and the ambiguities left unresolved by the judgment (in particular whether or not Article 101 might be applied more broadly to mergers) led to widespread concern in industry which 'were fully exploited by the Commission and the resulting uncertainty was used skilfully, particularly by the then Competition Commissioner, Mr Peter Sutherland, to persuade Member States to return to the negotiating table on a new draft of a merger control regulation, first proposed by the Commission in 1973'.[40] Soon after this judgment the green light was given to the Commission to put forward another proposal for a merger regulation.

The subsequent adoption of the EUMR by Peter Sutherland's successor, Sir Leon Brittan, means that the question exactly when the acquisition of shares leading to sole control is also caught by Article 101(1) is unlikely to be resolved. The judgment could still have importance, however, where direct or indirect control is not acquired so that the EUMR does not apply (although the Commission is now considering whether the EUMR should be extended to cover the acquisition of non-controlling minority stakes).[41] Article 101 also remains of relevance to 'joint ventures' which are not concentrations for the purposes of the EUMR.

The Residual Application of Articles 101 and 102

It is possible that irrespective of the existence of the EUMR the Commission itself, the national courts, and/or the national competition authorities (NCAs) may in some circumstances still be empowered to act pursuant to the Treaty provisions. This possibility is discussed in Section 3.E.

b. The Internal Market

The Commission's White Paper, *Completing the Internal Market*,[42] did not make any reference to merger control. However, business restructuring was a natural result of the programme. Commission data

---

[36] '[O]nly the strengthening of dominant positions and not their creation can be controlled under Art. [102]': Case T-102/96, *Gencor Ltd v. Commission* [1999] ECR II-753, para. 155; and see Case 6/72, *Europemballage and Continental Can v. Commission* [1973] ECR 215, para. 26.

[37] The Commission concluded in its *Memorandum on the Concentration of Enterprises in the Common Market*, EEC Competition Series Study No. 3 (published in 1966), para. 58, that Art. 101 would not be applicable to agreements 'whose purpose is the acquisition of total or partial ownership of enterprises of the reorganization of the ownership of enterprises'.

[38] Further, the sanction of nullity set out in Art. 101(2) seems an inappropriate means of controlling and authorising mergers.

[39] Cases 142 and 156/84, [1987] ECR 4487, paras. 36–39.

[40] C. J. Cook and C. S. Kerse, *EC Merger Control* (5th edn, Sweet & Maxwell, 2009), 1–003.

[41] See, e.g., *British Telecom-MCI* [1994] OJ L52/51 and. R. A. Struijlaart, 'Minority Share Acquisitions Below the Control Threshold of the EC Merger Regulation: An Economic and Legal Analysis' [2002] 25 *World Competition* 173. The Commission is reviewing whether it needs greater power to scrutinise acquisitions of minority interests, see n. 93 and accompanying text and discussion of *Ryanair/Aer Lingus*.

[42] COM(85) 310.

showed that an increasing number of mergers were completed in the lead-up to 1992,[43] many between companies in different EU countries or between EU companies and enterprises outside it. The need for some form of EU merger control thus became apparent and its absence anomalous. Industry, in particular, became keen to have a level playing field[44] and to have to comply with only *one* set of merger rules.

A combination of Commission support, pressure from industry, the single market programme, and increasing numbers of mergers led to the eventual realisation that a system of European merger control was inevitable.

(iv) The Original Merger Control Regulation—Council Regulation (EEC) 4064/89

The original Merger Control Regulation was adopted by the Council of Ministers on 21 December 1989.[45] It came into force nine months later on 21 September 1990. Its legal basis was Article 103 (ex Article 87) and Article 308 (ex Article 235) TFEU. The regulation set out jurisdictional, procedural, and substantive rules. The procedural requirements were fleshed out by Regulation 447/98, which dealt with matters such as notification, time limits, and hearings.[46] Numerous Commission notices set out guidance on how the Commission interpreted various aspects of the regulations.[47]

(v) The 1996 Green Paper and Council Regulation (EC) 1310/97

In 1996, the Commission issued its first Green Paper reviewing the EUMR.[48] In response to the Green Paper, Council Regulation 1310/97,[49] which came into force on 1 March 1998, introduced some amendments to the EUMR.[50]

(vi) The 2001 Green Paper

In 2000 the Commission had to report to the Council on the operation of the jurisdictional thresholds.[51] That Report concluded that, despite the change to the jurisdictional thresholds, an important number of transactions with significant cross-border effects remained outside the EU merger rules.[52] It considered, however, that a more in-depth analysis of the appropriate mechanisms for establishing jurisdiction was required and that other issues should be considered at the same time. It thus embarked on a further comprehensive review of the regulation. On 11 December 2001

---

[43] In 1982–1983 there were 115 mergers, by 1988–1989 the number had grown to 492 and to 622 in 1989–90: L. Tsoukalis, *The New European Economy Revisited* (2nd edn, Oxford University Press, 1993), 103.

[44] Some Member States did not have merger rules, whilst the rules in other Member States differed dramatically.

[45] Council Reg. (EEC) 4064/89 of 21 December 1989 on the control of concentrations between undertakings [1989] OJ L395/1.

[46] Commission Reg. 447/98 [1998] OJ L61/1 of 1 March 1998 on the notifications, time limits, and hearings provided for in Council Reg. 4064/89 on the control of concentrations between undertakings [1998] OJ L61/1. It replaced Reg. 2367/90 (as amended by Reg. 3666/93).

[47] The current Notices are listed *in* Section 2.C.vii, p. 1138.

[48] Community Merger Control, COM(96) 19 final.

[49] Council Reg. 1310/97 of 30 June 1997 [1997] OJ L180/1.

[50] e.g., the introduction of an additional (lower) jurisdictional threshold, and changes to the rules dealing with joint ventures and to the rules setting out when concentrations involving credit and other financial institutions have an EU dimension.

[51] The old EUMR, Art. 1(4).

[52] See the Report to the Council on the application of the Merger Regulation Thresholds, COM(2000) 399 final.

the Commission published a Green Paper[53] mooting wide-ranging changes to jurisdictional, substantive, and procedural matters set out in the EUMR. Following consultation on these issues, the Commission proposed a package of measures to reform the provisions and working of the EUMR which included a proposal for a new Council regulation on the control of concentrations between undertakings (a consolidated replacement of Regulation 4064/89 rather than an amendment).[54]

(vii) The Current Merger Control Regulation, Council Regulation (EC)139/2004

After fairly intensive negotiation and discussion, political agreement for a new recast text of the EUMR was agreed by the Competitiveness Council on 27 November 2003. The new regulation, Regulation 139/2004, was adopted and published in the Official Journal on 20 January 2004. The regulation discussed in this chapter is, of course, unless otherwise stated, the current Regulation 139/2004, which incorporates elements of the original 1989 Regulation with amendments introduced in both 1997 and 2004. In the interest of legal certainty,[55] however, the Commission decided to recast the regulation,[56] adopting a single legislative text to make the desired amendments.

The regulation is supplemented by an implementing regulation[57] and a number of Commission Notices which provide guidance as to the interpretation of various provisions of the EUMR. In particular, the following notices are of importance:[58]

(i) Commission Consolidated Jurisdictional Notice[59] (the 'Jurisdictional Notice', replacing and consolidating into a single Notice previous Notices on the concept of a concentration, undertakings concerned, the calculation of turnover, and on the concept of full function joint ventures);

(ii) Notice on simplified procedure for the treatment of certain concentrations (currently under review);[60]

(iii) Notice on remedies;[61]

(iv) Notice on restrictions directly related and necessary to concentrations;[62]

(v) Notices on the appraisal of both horizontal and non-horizontal mergers;[63]

(vi) Notice on case allocation under the referral rules of the Merger Regulation;[64]

(vii) Notice on access to the file.[65]

---

[53] 2001 Green Paper on the Review of Council Regulation (EEC) No. 4064/89, COM(2001) 745/6 final.

[54] COM(2002) 711 final, OJ [2003] C20/4.

[55] To ensure that the legislation is comprehensible and accessible, the Commission issued 'Recasting of Council Regulation (EEC) No. 4064/89 on the control of concentrations between undertakings (The EC Merger Regulation)—Some explanations regarding the formatting of the proposal for a new Council Regulation', European Commission (Brussels, 2003).

[56] In accordance with the Inter-institutional agreement of 28 November 2001 on a more structured use of recasting technique for legal acts [2002] OJ C77/1.

[57] Reg. 802/2004, [2004] OJ L133/1.

[58] The Commission's notice on market definition is also of extreme importance, see Chap. 1.

[59] [2008] OJ C95/1, replacing Notice on the concept of concentration [1998] OJ C66/5, Notice on the concept of undertakings concerned [1998] OJ C66/14, Notice on calculation of turnover [1998] OJ C66/25, and the Commission's Notice on the concept of full-function joint ventures [1998] OJ C66/1.

[60] [2005] OJ C56/32, see proposals for review in Section 3.B.i, pp. 1149–1150.

[61] [2008] OJ C267/1.

[62] [2005] OJ C56/24.

[63] [2004] OJ C31/5 and [2008] OJ C265/6.

[64] [2005] OJ C56/2.

[65] [2005] OJ C325/7. The Commission has also published a decision on the terms of reference of hearing officers [2001] L162/21, see Chap. 13.

The Commission has also published Best Practice Guidelines on the conduct of EUMR proceedings and Economic Evidence (how best to present economic and empirical evidence)[66] and model texts for divestiture commitments and trustee mandates.[67]

(viii) Subsequent Review

The EUMR provided for a mandatory review of the jurisdictional thresholds and provisions dealing with pre-notification reasoned submissions by 1 July 2009.[68] In June 2009, following a public consultation, the Commission reported to the Council.[69] Essentially, the Commission concluded that the jurisdictional thresholds and the set of corrective jurisdictional mechanisms provided for by the EUMR had provided an appropriate legal framework for allocating cases between the EU level and the Member States although there was scope for further improvements of the system. In 2013, the Commission commenced a review of the working and operation of the simplified procedure[70] and a broader review of the system of merger regulation focusing, in particular, on the question of whether to apply merger control rules to deal with the anti-competitive effects stemming from certain acquisitions of non-controlling minority interests, and the effectiveness and smoothness of the case referral system.[71]

D. SCHEME OF THE EUROPEAN UNION MERGER REGULATION

The EUMR applies to 'concentrations' with a 'Community dimension' (an EU dimension). Both terms are defined in the regulation itself. The concept of a 'Community dimension' allocates responsibility over concentrations between the Commission and the Member States and imposes an external limit of merger transactions caught within its jurisdiction. Broadly, with certain limited exceptions, concentrations that do not have an EU dimension are assessed under any applicable national competition legislation (no EU law applies), whilst concentrations with an EU dimension are assessed under the provisions of the EUMR. In the latter case, the Commission's decision under the terms of the EUMR is decisive and, as a general rule, no other rule of national or EU competition law applies. The basic scheme is, therefore, that concentrations with an EU dimension benefit from a 'one-stop shop'.

Concentrations with an EU dimension must be notified to the Commission in accordance with the requirements set out in Form CO and must, in general, be suspended until the Commission's final decision. On notification, the Commission is obliged to assess, within a period of 25–35 working days (WD), whether or not that concentration falls within the scope of the EUMR and, if so, whether it raises serious doubts about its compatibility with the common market (the Phase I investigation). Approximately 90 per cent of mergers notified to the Commission are dealt with in first-phase decisions (Phase I proceedings). Where the Commission believes that the concentration raises serious doubts about its compatibility with the common market a second-phase investigation will be launched to analyse whether or not this is the case. Phase II investigations, initiated in only about three to four per cent of notified cases,[72] must normally be concluded within a period of 90–125 WD

---

[66] 17 October 2011. See also OECD Best Practice Roundtable, *Economic Evidence in Merger Ananlysis* DAF/COMP(2011) 23.

[67] Available with the other legislation on DG Comp's website at: <http://ec.europa.eu/competition/mergers/legislation/legislation.html>.

[68] EUMR, Art. 1(4).

[69] Commission report to Council on the functioning of Regulation 139/2004, 18 June 2009, COM(2009) 281 final.

[70] See Section 3.B.i, pp. 1149–1150.

[71] See IP/13/584, Commission Staff Working Document, Towards more effective EU merger control, and n. 93 and accompanying text.

[72] See the merger statistics set out in Section 6, p. 1252.

from the initiation of the Phase II proceedings. At the end of Phase II the Commission must, unless the merger is abandoned, decide to declare the merger to be compatible with the common market (unconditionally or subject to commitments) or incompatible with it.

The procedures and tight legal time limits within which the Commission must act under the EUMR were critical to the adoption of the original EUMR.[73] There is a right of appeal from Commission decisions[74] to the GC and a further appeal, on a point of law, to the CJ. Despite the recognition of the need for speed in merger cases there is, however, only an expedited appeals procedure in straightforward cases.[75]

Section 3 sets out more fully when the Commission has jurisdiction over mergers and the procedures it adopts in appraising such mergers. Section 4 deals with procedure whilst Section 5 deals with substantive appraisal of mergers and the difficult question of how it is determined whether or not a merger is compatible with the common market. Section 6 sets out some merger statistics and appeals are dealt with in Section 7. Section 8 deals with international issues and Section 9 sets out some conclusions.

3. JURISDICTION

A. CONCENTRATIONS

(i) Definition

It has been explained that, subject to specified exceptions, the EUMR applies to concentrations with an EU dimension. The EUMR seeks to govern operations resulting in 'a lasting change in the control of the undertakings concerned and therefore in the structure of the market'.[76] The term concentration is more specifically defined in Article 3 of the EUMR. Essentially, a concentration occurs where two or more undertakings merge their businesses or where there is an acquisition of sole or joint control of the whole or part of an existing undertaking or the creation of an autonomous full-function joint venture.[77]

Article 3(1) provides:

A concentration shall be deemed to arise where a change of control on a lasting basis results from:

(a) the merger of two or more previously independent undertakings or parts of undertakings, or

(b) the acquisition, by one or more persons already controlling at least one undertaking, or by one or more undertakings whether by purchase of securities or assets, by contract or by any other means, of direct or indirect control of the whole or parts of one or more other undertakings.

Article 3(4) provides:

The creation of a joint venture performing on a lasting basis all the functions of an autonomous economic entity shall constitute a concentration within the meaning of paragraph 3(1)(b).

The Commission's Jurisdictional Notice provides guidance on how the Commission interprets the notion of a concentration.[78]

---

[73] In particular, Member States were anxious that delays should not hamper the flexibility of undertakings seeking to engage in industrial restructuring.

[74] But not a decision by the Commission to open Phase II proceedings, see n. 283.

[75] See Section 7, pp. 1253–1254.

[76] Recital 20.

[77] EUMR, Art. 3.

[78] The Commission Consolidated Jurisdictional Notice [2008] OJ C95/1 (the Jurisdictional Notice).

a. Article 3(1)(a)—Mergers between Previously Independent Undertakings

The regulation does not define what is meant by the term 'merge'. The term is merely used to describe one type of concentration which falls within the ambit of the regulation. It appears that the word is used 'narrowly'.

Were a very broad economically oriented interpretation of the term 'merge' adopted, Article 3(1)(b) would be rendered otiose. The purpose of Article 3(1)(a) appears therefore to be to catch undertakings which have fused their businesses ('legal' mergers), that is where two or more undertakings amalgamate into one business and cease to exist as separate legal entities or where one undertaking acquires and completely absorbs another undertaking (which subsequently ceases to exist), for example the merger between SmithKline Beecham and Glaxo Wellcome to create GlaxoSmithKline.[79] The distinction is relevant, to the extent that the question of whether there has been a merger, or merely a change in control, affects who must make the notification.[80]

b. Article 3(1)(b)—Acquisition of Control

Decisive Influence

Article 3(1)(b) applies where there is a change in control of an undertaking,[81] for example: where an undertaking acquires sole control of another or two or more undertakings acquire *joint* control of another. Control can therefore be acquired by one undertaking acting alone or by several undertakings acting jointly. The EUMR also applies where there is a change in the *quality* of control (see later in Section 3.A.i.b). The acquisition of control is defined in Article 3(2):

Control shall be constituted by rights, contracts or any other means which, either separately or in combination and having regard to the considerations of fact or law involved, confer the possibility of exercising decisive influence on an undertaking, in particular by:

(a) ownership or the right to use all or part of the assets of an undertaking;

(b) rights or contracts which confer decisive influence on the composition, voting or decisions of the organs of an undertaking.

The regulation is thus intended to catch transactions which lead to an undertaking or undertakings acquiring the ability to exercise *decisive influence* over another—the ability to control the strategic commercial behaviour of the undertakings concerned. This may be acquired through the acquisition of property rights, assets, through shareholders agreements or may result from economic dependence.[82]

Consolidated Jurisdictional Notice [2008] OJ C95/1

16. Control is defined by Article 3(2) of the Merger regulation as the possibility of exercising decisive influence on an undertaking. It is therefore not necessary to show that the decisive influence is or will

---

[79] See C. J. Cook and C. S. Kerse, *EC Merger Control* (5th edn, Sweet & Maxwell, 2009), 2–009 and Jurisdictional Notice, para. 9. Para. 10 of the Notice states that a merger may also occur where, in the absence of a legal merger, the combining of the activities of previously independent undertakings results in the creation of a single economic unit.

[80] See Section 4, pp. 1172–1180.

[81] It does not matter whether control is acquired in one, two, or more stages or by means of one or more transactions, provided the end result constitutes a single concentration. Thus a concentration may be deemed to arise where a number of formally distinct legal transactions are interdependent so that none of them would be carried out without the others and the result consists in conferring on one or more undertakings direct or indirect economic control over the activities of another, see Case T-282/02, *Cementbouw Handel & Industrie BV v. Commission* [2006] ECR II-319, paras. 104–109.

[82] Legal control (a controlling interest) is not therefore necessary.

be actually exercised; however, the possibility of exercising that influence must be effective. Article 3(2) further provides that the possibility of exercising decisive influence on an undertaking can exist on the basis of rights, contracts or any other means, either separately or in combination, and having regard to the considerations of fact and law involved. A concentration therefore may occur on a legal or a *de facto* basis, may take the form of sole or joint control, and extend to the whole or parts of one or more undertakings (cf. Article 3(1)(b)).

Sole Control

Sole control is acquired if one undertaking alone can exercise decisive influence on an undertaking. It can be acquired both where the one undertaking enjoys the power to determine strategic commercial decisions of the other or where a shareholder is able to veto strategic decisions in an undertaking but does not have the power to impose such decisions (negative sole control). It can be acquired on a *de jure* or *de facto* basis. Sole control, or decisive influence, is ordinarily acquired on a legal basis through an acquisition of more than 50 per cent of the share capital and with it, more than 50 per cent of the voting rights of another undertaking. However, it will always be necessary to look at other factors. Even an undertaking with more than 50 per cent of the share capital will not acquire sole control if, for example, it does not have control of a majority of the voting rights or where a super-majority of voting rights is required for strategic decisions. In such circumstances the acquisition of a simple majority may lead to a scenario of negative or joint control.[83]

Sole control may also be gained where a share of considerably less than 50 per cent is acquired (a minority shareholding).[84] For example, sole control may be acquired on a legal basis where special rights are attached to the preferential shareholding (a majority of the voting rights are nonetheless conferred on the shareholder or the shareholder has power to appoint more than half of the management team). It may be acquired on a *de facto* basis where: the remainder of the shares are widely dispersed;[85] where the shareholder is likely to get a majority of votes at a shareholders meeting;[86] or where an agreement confers an option to purchase shares in the near future.[87] The analysis in each case is very fact specific and it is important to consider a number of factors, including all share-holdings, special rights, and veto rights attached to the shareholding or set out in a management or shareholding agreement. In *Yara/Kemira GrowHow*,[88] for example, the Commission considered that the acquisition of the 30.05 per cent of the shares in GrowHow constituted an acquisition of control. In practice, based on attendance at the last three AGMs, Yara would be able to control a majority of votes at a shareholders meeting.

Negative sole control exists where a sole shareholder can veto strategic decisions in an undertaking, for example where strategic decisions require a supermajority so that one shareholder has enough voting rights to veto all strategic decisions.[89] Such a shareholder does not have joint control as although it can block strategic decisions, no other shareholder enjoys the same level of influence

---

[83] Jurisdictional Notice, para. 56. In Case M.17, *MBB/Aerospatiale* [1991] OJ C59/13 (Aerospatiale and MBB had joint control of a joint venture formed to carry out their helicopter businesses. Although Aerospatiale received 60% of equity (and MBB only 40%), all strategic decisions for the joint venture required unanimous consent of both partners).

[84] See Jurisdictional Notice, para. 57, Case M.258, *CCIE/GTE, and Case M.4994, Electrabel/CNR, aff'd Case T-332/09 Electrabel v. Commission*, 12 December 2012 (Electrabel's holding of 49.94% of CNR's capital and 47.92% of its voting right amounts to sole control), on appeal Case C-84/13P (judgment pending), see also C. Hatton and D. Cardwell, 'Minority Acquisitions: How they are treated by different merger control regimes' [2010] 1 June *Competition Law Insight* 5.

[85] See, e.g., Case M.25, *Arjomari/Wiggins Teape* [1990] OJ C321/16 (39% shareholding conferred sole control since no other entity had more than a 4% shareholding),

[86] See, e.g., Case M.343, *Société Générale de Belgique/Générale de Banque* [1993] OJ C225/2 and Case T-332/09 *Electrabel v. Commission*, 12 December 2012 on appeal Case C-84/13P (judgment pending).

[87] Case T-2/93, *Air France v. Commission* [1994] ECR II-323 and Jurisdictional Notice, paras. 59–60.

[88] Case M.4730.

[89] Jurisdictional Notice, paras. 54 and 57.

and the shareholder exercising negative control does not necessarily have to cooperate with other shareholders in determining the strategic behaviour of the controlled undertaking.[90] Decisive influence and hence control is acquired because of the ability of the shareholder to produce a deadlock situation.

In *Ryanair/Aer Lingus*,[91] the Commission concluded that Ryanair's acquisition of a 25 per cent stake in Aer Lingus did *not* constitute acquisition of control. Although the Commission prohibited the proposed merger (a hostile public bid by Ryanair for the *entire* share capital of Aer Lingus), the Commission did not therefore consider that it could require Ryanair to divest this non-controlling stake it had already acquired. The GC upheld the Commission's conclusion that Ryanair's shareholding did not confer control or amount to partial implementation of a concentration.[92]

Partly as a result of this case, the Commission considered whether its inability to review acquisitions of minority shareholdings, which do not confer control under the EUMR, constitutes a serious lacuna or gap in its powers to regulate transactions which have potential to cause significant harm to competition (through unilateral or coordinated effects). It is now consulting on a proposal that it should have the option to review such transactions—structural links—under the EUMR.[93] It is also consulting on the question of whether its powers under Article 8(4) should be amended to allow it to 'require the dissolution of partially implemented transactions declared incompatible with the internal market in line with the scope of the suspension obligation...In case COMP/M.4439 Ryanair/Aer Lingus I in 2007, Ryanair's acquisition of a non-controlling minority shareholding in Aer Lingus and Ryanair's subsequent proposal to acquire control of Aer Lingus through the acquisition of additional shares were treated as one single concentration for the purpose of EU merger control. However, although the Commission declared the proposed concentration incompatible with the internal market, the Commission could not order the divestiture of Ryanair's already acquired non-controlling minority shareholding in Aer Lingus pursuant to Article 8(4)...A modification of Article 8(4) could address such a scenario. It would need to be consistent with any new suggestion on merger control for structural links.'[94]

Joint Control

The Commission explains joint control in its Jurisdictional Notice.[95]

Consolidated Jurisdictional Notice [2008] OJ C95/1

62. Joint control exists where two or more undertakings or persons have the possibility of exercising decisive influence over another undertaking. Decisive influence in this sense normally means the power to block actions which determine the strategic commercial behaviour of an undertaking. Unlike sole control, which confers upon a specific shareholder the power to determine the strategic decisions in an

---

[90] Jurisdictional Notice, para. 54.

[91] Case M.4439.

[92] Case T-411/07, *Aer Lingus Group* v. *Commission* [2010] ECR II-3691. The UK authorities, however, are reviewing the transaction as the merger rules apply to situations where one enterprise is able to materially influence the policy of another.

[93] See IP/13/584, Commission Staff Working Document, 'Towards more effective EU merger control', Commissioner Almunia, SPEECH/11/166, Merger Regulation in the EU after 20 years, Brussels, 10 March 2011 and SPEECH/12/73, 'Merger review: Past evolution and future prospects', 12 November 2012 and, e.g., OFT1218 'Minority Interests in Competitors: A Research Report prepared by DotEcon Ltd' (March 2010). See also e.g., A. Ezrachi and D. Gilo, 'EC Competition Law and the Regulation of Passive Investments Among Competitors' (2006) 26(2) Oxford Journal of Legal Studies 327.

[94] Commission Staff Working Document, Towards more effective EU merger control, 20 June 2013, 21–22

[95] See also, in particular, the GC's judgment in Case T-282/02, *Cementbouw Handel & Industrie BV* v. *Commission* [2006] ECR II-319.

undertaking, joint control is characterized by the possibility of a deadlock situation resulting from the power of two or more parent companies to reject proposed strategic decisions. It follows, therefore, that these shareholders must reach a common understanding in determining the commercial policy of the joint venture and that they are required to cooperate.

63. As in the case of sole control, the acquisition of joint control can also be established on a *de jure* or *de facto* basis. There is joint control if the shareholders (the parent companies) must reach agreement on major decisions concerning the controlled undertaking (the joint venture).

Joint control may thus be acquired where two parents hold the voting rights equally and also in the absence of equality (for example, where minority shareholders have additional rights which allow them to veto decisions which are essential for the strategic commercial behaviour of the joint venture). It is necessary to consider not only the size of the undertakings' shareholdings but also factors such as the voting rights attached to the shareholdings and shareholder and management agreements, veto rights, and the ability of two or more undertakings to jointly exercise the majority of voting rights.[96]

Changes in the Quality of Control

Not only does the EUMR apply to transactions which lead to the acquisition of sole control, or joint control but it applies to operations leading to change in the quality of control[97] catching: transactions leading to a change from sole control to joint control; a change in joint control (by the entrance of a new shareholder, by replacement of an existing shareholder, or possibly by a reduction in the number of jointly controlling shareholders); or by a change from joint control to sole control. It thus covers two categories: (1) an entrance of one or more new controlling shareholders irrespective of whether or not they replace existing controlling shareholders; and (2) a reduction of the number of controlling shareholders.[98]

(ii) Joint Ventures

a. Introduction

The creation of a joint venture, which covers a wide spectrum of different arrangements (from an agreement to merge completely the activities of the partner companies on a particular market and to cease to operate in that market themselves, to an agreement to cooperate for particular functions such as R&D), is dealt with under the merger rules only where they amount to a 'concentration'.[99] Article 3(4) of the EUMR provides that the creation of a 'full-function' joint venture constitutes a concentration. The full-functionality criterion therefore delineates the application of the EUMR for the *creation* of joint ventures by parties and determines which joint ventures are appraised under the EUMR and which fall to be appraised under Article 101.[100]

There may be advantages to the parties if their joint venture does constitute a 'concentration' for the purposes of the EUMR. For example, it will benefit from a *'one-stop shop'* appraisal (national competition rules do not apply) where the concentration has an EU dimension and it will not generally

---

[96] Jurisdictional Notice, paras. 64–82.

[97] See Jurisdictional Notice, paras. 83–90 and, e.g., Case M.23, *ICI/Tioxide*.

[98] *Jurisdictional Notice*, para. 84. In the draft Jurisdictional Notice the Commission stated that a change from (sole) negative control to sole control would constitute a concentration. It did not adopt this position in the final Notice, however.

[99] See also Chap. 10.

[100] For the view that the Commission's guidance and decisional practice, and the relationship between Art. 3(1)(b) and 3(4) EUMR, is unclear and inconsistent see, e.g., L. Rudolf and B. Leupold, 'Joint Ventures—The Relevance of the Full Functionality Criterion under the EU Merger Regulation' (2012) 3(5) *JECLAP* 439.

be subject to EU competition law at all where it does not.[101] Further, decisions taken under the EUMR must be made within strict legal deadlines; and clearance decisions are absolute and not limited in time. In contrast, if the joint venture falls to be assessed under Article 101, the application of national law (subject to Article 3 Regulation 1/2003)[102] is not precluded. Further, an authorisation decision is most unlikely[103] and the joint venture agreement is valid only insofar as the agreement satisfies the conditions of Article 101 both at the time the agreement is concluded and in the future.

The differences in treatment of joint ventures under the EUMR and Article 101 respectively, have led the Commission to make a number of changes to its approach over the years. Not only has it sought to ameliorate the way in which it deals with joint ventures under Article 101,[104] but in 1998 the definition of joint venture set out in the EUMR was expanded.[105]

b. 'Full-Function' Joint Ventures

Article 3(4)[106] makes it clear that the creation of a joint venture constitutes a concentration only if the joint venture is jointly controlled by two or more undertakings and it is 'full-function'. The full-functionality criterion, which does *not* apply where joint control of an undertaking with market presence is *acquired* from a third party or parties,[107] requires that the joint venture is formed on a lasting basis to carry out the functions of an autonomous economic entity.

The Commission explains the concept of full-functionality in paragraphs 91–109 of the Jurisdictional Notice. It stresses the importance of the joint venture being autonomous from an operational point of view and hence having sufficient resources to operate independently on a market and being intended to operate on a lasting basis. The joint venture must therefore have 'a management dedicated to its day-to day operations and access to sufficient resources including finance, staff, and assets (tangible and intangible) in order to conduct on a lasting basis its business activities within the area provided for in the joint-venture agreement'.[108] Further, it states that a joint venture is not full-function if it simply takes over one specific function for its parents.

Consolidated Jurisdictional Notice [2008] OJ C95/1

95. A joint venture is not full-function if it only takes over one specific function within the parent companies' business activities without its own access to or presence on the market. This is the case, for example, for joint ventures limited to R&D or production. Such joint ventures are auxiliary to their parent companies' business activities. This is also the case where a joint venture is essentially limited to the distribution or sale of its parent companies' products and, therefore, acts principally as a sales agency. However, the fact that a joint venture makes use of the distribution network or outlet of one or more of its parent companies normally will not disqualify it as 'full-function' as long as the parent companies are acting only as agents of the joint venture.

---

[101]   See Section 3.D, pp. 1168–1173.

[102]   See Chap. 13.

[103]   Prior to 2004, Art. 101 negative clearance or exemption decisions were rarely granted and any such decision did not have to be adopted within a specified time period. Since modernisation, an Art. 101 decision will be possible only if the Commission is prepared to grant a non-infringement decision under Reg. 1/2003 [2004] OJ L1/1, Art. 10 (finding of inapplicability), see Chap. 13.

[104]   See Chap. 10.

[105]   There was a later suggestion that that the definition might be expanded further (see White Paper on modernisation of the rules implementing Articles 85 and 86 [now 101 and 102] of the EC Treaty [1999] OJ C132/1, paras. 79–81) but in its 2001 Green Paper the Commission decided against this.

[106]   Art. 3(2) of the old EUMR.

[107]   Jurisdictional Notice, para. 94.

[108]   Jurisdictional Notice, para. 94.

96. A frequent example where this question arises are joint ventures involved in the holding of real estate property, which are typically set up for tax and other financial reasons. As long as the purpose of the joint venture is limited to the acquisition and/or holding of certain real estate for the parents and based on financial resources provided by the parents, it will not usually be considered to be full-function as it lacks an autonomous, long term business activity on the market and will typically also lack the necessary resources to operate independently. This has to be distinguished from joint ventures that are actively managing a real estate portfolio and who act on their own behalf on the market, which typically indicates full-functionality.

Another relevant factor in the determination of full-functionality may be whether the parent companies make sales or purchases to or from the joint venture. Where sales are made to the parent companies, the main issue to be determined is whether, regardless of these sales, the joint venture can play an active role on the market and be considered economically autonomous from an operational viewpoint.[109] Further, a joint venture is unlikely to be full-function where it operates like a joint sales agency purchasing from its parents and adding little value to the products or services concerned.[110]

Consolidated Jurisdictional Notice [2008] OJ C95/1

97. The strong presence of the parent companies in upstream or downstream markets is a factor to be taken into consideration in assessing the full-function character of a joint venture where this presence results in substantial sales or purchases between the parent companies and the joint venture. The fact that for an initial start up period only, the joint venture relies almost entirely on sales to or purchases from its parent companies does not normally affect its full-function character. Such a start-up period may be necessary in order to establish the joint venture on a market. But the period will normally not exceed a period of three years, depending on the specific conditions of the market in question.

The Jurisdictional Notice also states that the fact that the agreement contains a clause providing for the dissolution of the joint venture, for example on its failure or on disagreement between the parents, does not necessarily mean that the joint venture has not been established on a lasting basis. In addition, a joint venture created for a finite period but long enough to affect the structure of the market will also be established on a lasting basis, but one established for a short finite period will not.

Consolidated Jurisdictional Notice [2008] OJ C95/1

103. Furthermore, the joint venture must be intended to operate on a lasting basis. The fact that the parent companies commit to the joint venture the resources described above normally demonstrates that this is the case. In addition, agreements setting up a joint venture often provide for certain contingencies, for example, the failure of the joint venture or fundamental disagreement as between the parent companies. This may be achieved by the incorporation of provisions for the eventual dissolution of the joint venture itself or the possibility for one or more parent companies to withdraw from the joint venture. This kind of provision does not prevent the joint venture from being considered as operating on a lasting basis. The same is normally true where the agreement specifies a period for the duration of the joint venture where

---

[109] Jurisdictional Notice, paras. 98–100.
[110] Jurisdictional Notice, para. 97.

this period is sufficiently long in order to bring about a lasting change in the structure of the undertakings concerned, or where the agreement provides for the possible continuation of the joint venture beyond this period.

104. By contrast, the joint venture will not be considered to operate on a lasting basis where it is established for a short finite duration. This would be the case, for example, where a joint venture is established in order to construct a specific project such as a power plant, but it will not be involved in the operation of the plant once its construction has been completed.

105. A joint venture also lacks the sufficient operations on a lasting basis at a stage where there are decisions of third parties outstanding that are of an essential core importance for starting the joint venture's business activity. Only decisions that go beyond mere formalities and the award of which is typically uncertain qualify for these scenarios. Examples are the award of a contract (e.g., in public tenders), licences (e.g., in the telecoms sector) or access rights to property (e.g., exploration rights for oil and gas). Pending the decision on such factors, it is unclear whether the joint venture will become operational at all. Thus, at that stage the joint venture cannot be considered to perform economic functions on a lasting basis and consequently does not qualify as full function. However, once a decision has been taken in favour of the joint venture in question, this criterion is fulfilled and a concentration arises.

The Notice deals at paragraphs 106–109 with the position if the parents enlarge the scope of the joint venture's activities in the course of its lifetime. It states that such enlargement may constitute a concentration requiring notification, in particular where the enlargement entails the acquisition of the whole or part of another undertaking from the parents that would, considered in isolation, qualify as a concentration.

Some examples of joint ventures which are not full-function and which are consequently subject to Article 101 are set out in Chapter 10.

The Relevance of Coordination of Competitive Behaviour

The original EUMR provided that a joint venture which has as its object or effect the coordination of the competitive behaviour of undertakings which remain independent could not constitute a concentration. This *negative* condition was removed in 1997 so that the complex determination required by this condition no longer has to be made at the jurisdictional stage. It is still of importance to know whether a joint venture enables the coordination of the competitive behaviour of independent undertakings, however. In particular, a different *substantive* appraisal applies. Although the basic appraisal made in the case of each joint venture will be same, the coordinative aspects of joint ventures are assessed additionally for their compatibility with the common market in accordance with the criteria set out in Article 101 TFEU.[111]

(iii) Article 3(5) and Warehousing Arrangements

Article 3(5) of the EUMR sets out several circumstances in which a concentration shall be deemed not to arise. These deal with shares held by financial institutions on a temporary basis, the acquisition of control by liquidators or other administrators, and operations carried out by financial holding companies.[112] It is unclear whether, and if so when, the exception for shares held by financial interests can apply to temporary shareholdings acquired in warehousing structures (where an ultimate purchaser seeking to acquire another does so through a third party, interim purchaser, which

---

[111] EUMR, Art. 2(4)(5), discussed in Section 5.E, pp. 1241–1244. In addition, in derogation from the general rule, the Commission is able to apply Article 101 to a joint venture which enables the coordination of the competitive behaviour of independent undertakings but which does *not* have an EU dimension, EUMR, Art. 21(1).

[112] Jurisdictional Notice, paras. 110–118.

holds the shares on a temporary basis). The Commission's view, set out in the Jurisdictional Notice, is that such structures do not benefit from the exemption if the interim transaction forms part of a broader, single concentration,[113] that is where:

an undertaking is 'parked' with an interim buyer, often a bank, on the basis of an agreement on the future onward sale of the business to an ultimate acquirer. The interim buyer generally acquires shares 'on behalf' of the ultimate acquirer, which often bears the major part of the economic risks and may also be granted specific rights. In such circumstances, the first transaction is only undertaken to facilitate the second transaction and the first buyer is directly linked to the ultimate acquirer...no other ultimate acquirer is involved, the target business remains unchanged, and the sequence of transactions is initiated alone by the sole ultimate acquirer....[T]he Commission will examine the acquisition of control by the ultimate acquirer, as provided for in the agreements entered into by the parties. The Commission will consider the transaction by which the interim buyer acquires control in such circumstances as the first step of a single concentration comprising the lasting acquisition of control by the ultimate buyer.[114]

Where the interim buyer's purchase forms part of the concentration between the ultimate acquirer, the EUMR's notification and suspensory provisions are therefore triggered.

Prior to the publication of the Jurisdictional Notice, however, in *Lagardère/ Natexis/VUP*,[115] the Commission applied Article 3(5)(a) to a scenario in which Lagardère, the ultimate buyer, agreed to take the assets out of the hands of VUP and parked the shares with a bank prior to obtaining clearance for the transaction. Had the bank's acquisition formed part of the concentration between Lagardère and VUP there would have been a breach of the stand-still obligation. Éditions Odile, one of the competing bidders for VUP, brought an appeal before the GC and CJ. Neither the GC nor the CJ had to decide the warehousing point directly as it did not affect the legality of the Commission's clearance decision (this issue affected only the question of whether the suspensory obligation had been breached and whether the parties could have been fined).[116] Although the GC[117] indicated that Lagardère had not acquired control at the time of the bank's interim acquisition, as it could not exercise control over the target at this time, the CJ made it clear that these statements had not been necessary to the ruling but had merely 'been made for the sake of completeness'.[118] If the temporary and ultimate acquisitions of the shares do not form part of the same concentration, then, unless Article 3(5) applies, the interim transaction will constitute a separate concentration.

(iv) Abandonment of a Concentration

If the Commission initiates Phase II proceedings following notification of a concentration to it, it must close the proceeding by means of a decision adopted under Article 8 of the EUMR 'unless the undertakings concerned have demonstrated to the satisfaction of the Commission that they have abandoned the concentration'.[119] In *MCI WorldCom/Sprint*,[120] for example, the Commission issued a decision prohibiting a concentration even though the parties stated that they had abandoned the merger. On appeal, however, the GC annulled the Commission's decision, holding that the Commission had exceeded its powers by adopting a prohibition decision when the notifying parties

---

[113] Jurisdictional Notice, para. 114.

[114] Jurisdictional Notice, para. 35.

[115] Case M.2978, 7 January 2004.

[116] Case C-551/10, *Éditions Odile Jacob v. Commission*, 6 November 2012, paras. 34–38.

[117] See Case T-279/04, *Éditions Odile Jacob v. Commission* [2010] ECR II-185 on appeal, Case C-551, 553, and 554/10, *Éditions Odile Jacob v. Commission*, 6 November 2012, paras. 34–38.

[118] Case C-551, 553, and 554/10, *Éditions Odile Jacob v. Commission*, 6 November 2012, para. 40.

[119] EUMR, Art. 6(1)(c).

[120] Case M.1741, on appeal Case T-310/00, *MCI v. Commission* [2004] ECR II-3253.

had formally withdrawn their notification and informed it of the abandonment of the concentration in the form envisaged in the notification.

The Commission's Jurisdictional Notice now sets out guidance as to how the parties may demonstrate that the transaction has been abandoned. General guidance, set out in paragraphs 119–120, is followed by specific guidance of the type of proof that is required depending upon whether the original concentration takes the form of a binding agreement, a good faith intention to conclude an agreement, a public announcement of a public bid or of the intention to make a public bid, or an implemented concentration.

Consolidated Jurisdictional Notice [2008] OJ C95/1

119. As a general principle, the requirements for the proof of the abandonment must correspond in terms of legal form intensity etc. to the initial act that was considered sufficient to make the concentration notifiable. In case the parties proceed from that initial act to a strengthening of their contractual links during the procedure, for example by concluding a binding agreement after the transaction was notified on the basis of a good faith intention, the requirements for the proof of the abandonment must correspond also to the nature of the latest act'.[121]

120. In line with this principle, in case of implementation of the concentration prior to a Commission decision, the re-establishment of the *status quo ante* has to be shown. The mere withdrawal of the notification is not considered as sufficient proof that the concentration has been abandoned in the sense of Article 6(1)(c). Likewise, minor modifications of a concentration which do not affect the change in control or the quality of that change, cannot be considered as an abandonment of the original concentration.

B. EU DIMENSION

(i) A Bright Line Jurisdictional Test

The EUMR aims to apply to concentrations which create significant structural changes the impact of which extend beyond the national borders of any one Member State.[122] It is concentrations with a 'Community'—an EU—dimension which fall for appraisal under the terms of the EUMR. Broadly, whether or not a merger has an EU dimension is assessed by reference to the *turnover* of the parties involved.[123] Since the notification of concentrations with an EU dimension to the Commission is compulsory, and generally means that a notification cannot be made to the competition authorities of the Member States, the jurisdictional test incorporated within the EUMR is intended to be a bright line test which can be applied relatively simply, objectively, and easily.[124] The corollary of having a simple quantitative jurisdictional test is that: some mergers between non-EU undertakings whose business is principally carried on outside the EU may be caught by the regulation; jurisdiction over EU mergers is not always allocated appropriately as between the Commission and the Member States; and concentrations between undertakings which quite obviously do not significantly impede effective competition in the common market may be brought within the regulation and subject to

---

[121] Jurisdictional Notice, para. 119.

[122] EUMR, recital 8.

[123] 'Turnover is used as a proxy for the economic resources being combined in a concentration, and is allocated geographically in order to reflect the geographic distribution of those resources', Jurisdictional Notice, para. 124.

[124] In some States, jurisdiction may be determined by reference to the market shares of parties, see, e.g., Spain, and Portugal. In these States even the question of whether the merger should be notified may be a complex one to determine.

mandatory notification. The requirement that the merger should significantly impede effective competition in the common market is relevant only to the substantive assessment. The Commission is aware of the inconvenience and cost that this imposes and has taken steps to ameliorate the situation of undertakings in the latter position. It has issued a Notice setting out a simplified procedure for the treatment of concentrations that do not raise competition concerns.[125] In such cases it may be possible to submit a short-form notification,[126] and where the Commission is satisfied that the concentration qualifies for the simplified procedure it normally adopts a short-form decision.[127] The Commission is now considering whether to improve the operation of the simplified procedure by extending its application to a greater category of 'non-problematic' mergers (with limited horizontal or vertical overlaps or where the incremental increase in market share resulting from the concentration is small) and by reducing/streamlining the information requirements.[128] The Commission hopes that these steps will encourage growth by facilitating the conclusion of efficiency-enhancing mergers with no negative effects and at the same time freeing the Commission's resources to focus on mergers raising competition concerns.

(ii) Article 1(2)

The primary test is that set out in Article 1(2). Only if this test is *not* satisfied is it necessary for an undertaking to consider whether or not the thresholds set out in Article 1(3) are satisfied.

Council Regulation (EC) No. 139/2004 of 20 January 2004 on the Control of Concentrations between Undertakings [2004] OJ L24/1, Article 1

1. Without prejudice to Article 4(5) and Article 22, this Regulation shall apply to all concentrations with a Community dimension as defined in this Article.

2. A concentration has a Community dimension where:
   (a) the combined aggregate worldwide turnover of all the undertakings concerned is more than EUR 5,000 million; and
   (b) the aggregate Community-wide turnover of each of at least two of the undertakings concerned is more than EUR 250 million

   unless each of the undertakings concerned achieves more than two-thirds of its aggregate Community-wide turnover within one and the same Member State.

This test looks to the combined worldwide turnover of the undertakings concerned and the EU-wide turnover of at least two of the undertakings involved in the concentration. Even where the thresholds are met, jurisdiction is denied if the *proviso* applies—if each of the undertakings concerned achieves more than two-thirds of its EU turnover within one and the same Member State. The purpose of the proviso is to exclude concentrations the effects of which are felt primarily in one Member State. The Commission has had some concerns about the operation of the two-thirds rule'

---

[125] [2005] OJ C56/32.

[126] See Short Form for the notification of a concentration pursuant to Regulation (EC) No. 139/2004, attached to Reg. 802/2004, [2004] OJ L133/1.

[127] Commission Notice on a simplified procedure for treatment of certain concentrations, [2005] OJ C56/32, para. 17.

[128] It launched the consultation on 27 March 2013 having conducted a review of 850 cases (2008–2010) to try to establish the market share thresholds at which concerns do not typically arise.

especially as it can mean that consolidations between large national players escape scrutiny under EU rules.[129] In its 2009 Report on the functioning of the jurisdictional thresholds provisions, however, the Commission indicated that few cases fell under the rule (only 126 out of the total Member State case load) and that it had generally appropriately distinguished between concentrations with EU relevance and those without it. Nonetheless, the Commission considered that there were 'a small number of cases with potential cross-border effects in the Community which... fall under the competence of the NCAs as a result of this rule. In a substantive respect, public interest considerations other than competition policy have been applied in a number of cases falling under this threshold to authorize mergers which could have given rise to competition concerns. More generally, it is desirable that, independently of which authority is the reviewing agency, merger control across the EU ensures the protection of undistorted competition. Against this background, the present form of the two-thirds rule merits further consideration'.[130]

(iii) Article 1(3) of the EUMR

The thresholds set in Article 1(2) are much higher than those originally proposed by the Commission[131] in the run-up to the adoption of Regulation 4064/89. This was as a result of the reluctance of many of the Member States to relinquish merger control to the Commission. The Commission's fears that it would have no work if the turnovers were set at such unrealistic levels were not realised. However, it held the view that significant mergers with cross-border effects fell outside the scope of the EUMR so the thresholds were reviewed again in the 1996 Green Paper.[132] Although the Commission (supported by much of European industry) put forward a strong case in support of its proposal to lower both the worldwide and EU-wide thresholds in Article 1(2),[133] the solution eventually reached was the addition of Article 1(3).[134] This provides that a concentration which satisfies lower worldwide and EU-wide turnovers than those set out in Article 1(2) may be caught if two additional criteria are satisfied. Broadly, these two factors aim to catch concentrations where the undertakings concerned, jointly and individually, have a minimum level of activities in three or more Member States and which are therefore likely to be subject to the merger rules of those three or more Member States.[135] Like Article 1(2), paragraph 3 contains a proviso excluding concentrations

---

[129] It can also mean that competing bids for a company are assessed under different regimes. For example: Lloyds' bid for the take-over of Midland Bank fell within the jurisdiction of the UK authorities, whilst HSBC's bid fell to be assessed under the EUMR, Case M.213; Gas Natural's (Spain's largest gas operator) bid for Spanish electricity operator, Endesa did not have an EU dimension because of the two-thirds rule (Endesa's appeal against the Commission's refusal to take jurisdiction was rejected, Case T-417/05, *Endesa v. Commission* [2006] ECR II-2533) whilst E.On's and ENEL/Acciona's bids did, see Cases M.4110 and M.4685, and see discussion of cases *in* Section 3.C.vii, p. 1167.

[130] Commission report to Council on the functioning of Regulation 139/2004 COM(2009) 281 final, para. 16 (see also Green Paper on Community Merger Control COM(96) 19 final, para. 48). The Commission had been particularly concerned about the application of the two-thirds rule in cases arising in the energy sector, see N. Kroes, Speech 06/60, Speech before the EP Economic and Monetary Affairs Committee. 31 January 2006.

[131] It recommended that the worldwide turnover should be set at ECU 1,000 million, the EU-wide turnover at ECU 100 million, and that jurisdiction should then only be denied if more than *three-quarters* of the aggregate EU-wide turnover was achieved in one and the same Member State. The thresholds were originally expressed in ECU but were read as references to Euro from 1 January 1999, Council Reg. 1103/97 [1997] OJ L162/1.

[132] The original EUMR anticipated a review, and a lowering, of the thresholds by the end of 1993. Severe opposition from a number of Member States, including Germany, the UK, and France, meant that any such review was likely to be redundant. The Commissioner for Competition at the time, Karel van Miert, thus decided not to conduct a review at that stage.

[133] For a comparison of the different regimes see, e.g., 'Getting the Deal Through, Merger Control 2013' (2013) *Global Competition Review.*

[134] On the passing of Council Reg. 1310/97.

[135] Reg. 1310/97 [1997] OJ L180/1, Art. 1(1)(a) and (b).

where two-thirds of the EU-wide turnover of all of the undertakings involved is achieved in one and the same Member State.[136]

Council Regulation (EC) No. 139/2004 of 20 January 2004 on the Control of Concentrations between Undertakings [2004] OJ L24/1, Article 1(3)

A concentration that does not meet the thresholds laid down in paragraph 2 has a Community dimension where:

(a) the combined aggregate worldwide turnover of all the undertakings concerned is more than EUR 2 500 million;

(b) in each of at least three Member States, the combined aggregate turnover of all the undertakings concerned is more than EUR 100 million;

(c) in each of at least three Member States included for the purpose of point (b), the aggregate turnover of each of at least two of the undertakings concerned is more than EUR 25 million; and

(d) the aggregate Community-wide turnover of each of at least two of the undertakings concerned is more than EUR 100 million

unless each of the undertakings concerned achieves more than two-thirds of its aggregate Community-wide turnover within one and the same Member State.

(iv) Review of the Thresholds

In 2000 and 2009 the Commission had to report to the Council on the operation of these jurisdictional thresholds.[137] The 2000 Report concluded that, despite the introduction of Article 1(3), an important number of transactions with significant cross-border effects remained outside the EUMR.[138] In its 2001 Green Paper the Commission mooted the possibility of amending the Article 1(3) thresholds to prevent inconvenience resulting from multiple filings,[139] but it ultimately recognised that these options were not feasible. It is now accepted that as Article 1 will not always allocate cases correctly as between the Commission and NCAs respectively, effective 'corrective' mechanisms should be introduced. In 2009, the Commission again reported that, although the thresholds generally operated in a satisfactory way, a number of transactions still had had to be notified in three or more Member States (100 transactions in 2007, requiring more than 360 parallel investigations).[140]

(v) Concentrations, Undertakings Concerned, and Calculation of Turnover

In order to apply the Article 1(2) and (3) tests, it is first necessary to identify the number of concentrations involved. In simple cases, such as the acquisition of B by A, there will usually be only one. In more complex cases, such as the division of an existing joint venture company between its parents,

---

[136] See n. 129 and accompanying text.

[137] The old EUMR, Art. 1(4).

[138] See the Report to the Council on the application of the Merger Regulation Thresholds, COM(2000) 399 final.

[139] Green Paper on the Review of Council Regulation (EEC) No. 4064/89 COM(2001) 745/6 Final, paras. 24–28.

[140] Commission report to Council on the functioning of Regulation 139/2004 COM(2009) 281 final.

there may however be more than one concentration.[141] Once the appropriate concentration (or concentrations) is identified it is necessary to determine (a) the undertakings concerned and (b) their turnover. Despite the aim of the regulation to provide a clear, simple jurisdictional test these steps are not always straightforward. The meaning of 'undertakings concerned' and 'turnover' is clarified in the jurisdictional notice.

The Notice seeks, guided by reference to cases previously notified to the Commission, to identify undertakings concerned in most typical situations. Paragraphs 134–153 provide detailed analysis of who the undertakings concerned are in acquisition of control cases (for example, acquisition of sole control, part or joint control change from joint to sole control or of controlling shareholders, etc.).

Consolidated Jurisdictional Notice [2008] OJ C95/1

2. MERGERS

132. In the case of a merger, the undertakings concerned are the merging undertakings.

3. ACQUISITION OF CONTROL

133. In the remaining cases, it is the concept of 'acquiring control' that will determine which are the undertakings concerned. On the acquiring side, there can be one or more undertakings acquiring sole or joint control. On the acquired side, there can be one or more undertakings as a whole or parts thereof. As a general rule, each of these undertakings will be an undertaking concerned within the meaning of the Merger Regulation.

Once the undertakings concerned have been identified their turnover must be calculated. Article 5(1) defines turnover as 'the amount derived by the undertakings concerned in the previous financial year from the sale of products and provision of services falling within the undertaking's ordinary activities' (i.e. net sales—ordinarily assessed from audited accounts from the last financial year).[142] Article 5(2) sets out rules which apply where only part of an undertaking is taken over or acquired. It provides that where the concentration consists of an acquisition of part or parts, of one or more undertakings, (such as a subsidiary or a division), only the turnover of the relevant parts which are the subject of the concentration shall be taken into account with regard to the seller or sellers.[143] Article 5(3) sets out special turnover rules which apply, for example, to credit and financial institutions and insurance undertakings. Article 5(4) provides that turnover is calculated by reference not only to those undertakings concerned but also to the turnover of all those entities which they control or by which they are controlled, and to other connected undertakings. The operation of Article 5(4) is explained in the jurisdictional notice.

[141] See, e.g., Case M.197, *Solvay/LaPorte* [1992] OJ C165/26. In this case the parties jointly notified the division of their joint venture, the Interox group of companies, between themselves. The Commission concluded that this was two separate concentrations. The Solvay concentration had an EU dimension but the Laporte concentration did not.

[142] Jurisdictional Notice, paras. 157–174.

[143] Acquisitions of parts between the same persons or undertakings in a series of transactions within a two-year period are treated as one and the same concentration, EUMR, Art. 5(2). The application of the EUMR cannot therefore be avoided through the acquisition of an undertaking in stages.

Consolidated Jurisdictional Notice [2008] OJ C95/1

175. Where an undertaking concerned by a concentration belongs to a group, not only the turnover of the undertaking concerned is considered, but the Merger Regulation requires to also take into account the turnover of those undertakings with which the undertaking concerned has links consisting in the rights or powers listed in Article 5(4) in order to determine whether the thresholds contained in Article 1 of the Merger Regulation are met. The aim is again to capture the total volume of the economic resources that are being combined through the operation irrespective of whether the economic activities are carried out directly by the undertaking concerned or whether they are undertaken indirectly via companies and undertakings with which the undertaking concerned possessed the links described in Article 5(4).

176. The Merger Regulation does not delineate the concept of a group in a single abstract definition, but sets out in Article 5(4)(b) certain rights or powers. If an undertaking concerned directly or indirectly has such links with other companies, those are to be regarded as part of its group for purposes of turnover calculation under the Merger Regulation.

177. Article 5(4) of the Merger Regulation provides the following:

Without prejudice to paragraph 2 [acquisition of parts], the aggregate turnover of an undertaking concerned within the meaning of Article 1(2) and (3) shall be calculated by adding together the respective turnovers of the following:

    (a)   the undertakings concerned;

    (b)   those undertakings in which the undertaking concerned directly or indirectly;

        (i)   owns more than half the capital of business assets, or

        (ii) has the power to exercise more than half the voting rights, or

        (iii) has the power to appoint more than half the members of the supervisory board, the administrative board or bodies legally representing the undertakings, or

        (iv) has the right to manage the undertaking's affairs;

    (c)   those undertaking which have in an undertaking concerned the rights or powers listed in (b);

    (d)   those undertakings in which an undertaking as referred to in (c) has the rights or powers listed in (b);

    (e)   those undertakings in which two or more undertakings as referred to in (a) to (d) jointly have the rights or powers listed in (b).

An undertaking which has in another undertaking the rights and powers mentioned in Article 5(4)(b) will be referred to as the 'parent' of the latter in the present section of the Notice dealing with the calculation of turnover, whereas the latter is referred to as 'subsidiary' of the former. In short, Article 5(4) therefore provides that the turnover of the undertaking concerned by the concentration (point (a)) should include its subsidiaries (point (b)), its parent companies (point (c)), the other subsidiaries of its parent undertakings (point (d)) and any other subsidiary jointly held by two or more of the undertakings identified under (a)-(d) (point (e)).

Note that with the aim of providing greater legal certainty, the definition of control in Article 5(4) is different from, and more tightly defined than, the definition of control set out in Article 3(2).[144] In general, the whole turnover of undertakings identified in Article 5 is taken into account. However, for joint ventures between two or more undertakings concerned, turnover of the joint ventures is apportioned equally amongst the undertakings concerned.[145] Further, in practice, the Commission

---

[144] Although the Commission invited comments as to whether the differences between the two meanings of control was problematic and whether it would be appropriate to harmonise the two provisions, no harmonisation of the rules was in fact made, see 2001 Green Paper on the Review of Council Regulation (EEC) No. 4064/89, COM(2001) 745/6 final.

[145] EUMR, Art. 5(5)(b).

allocates turnover for joint ventures between undertakings concerned and third parties on a per capita basis according to the number of undertakings exercising joint control.[146]

Examples

The following examples seek to clarify, through an examination of transactions carried out by entities within a larger group of companies, how Article 5 applies to identify the undertakings whose turnover is taken into account for the purposes of calculating EU dimension.

Group A

A is a wholly owned subsidiary of W. A has two wholly owned subsidiaries, X and Y. Y and a third party, TP, jointly control Z.

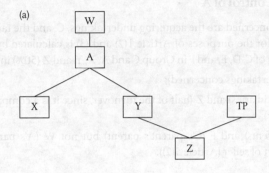

Group B

B is company jointly owned by J and K. K has a wholly owned subsidiary L. B has a wholly owned subsidiary, M.

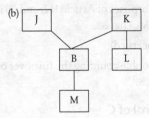

Group C

C is a company jointly controlled by D and E. E is a wholly owned subsidiary of F.

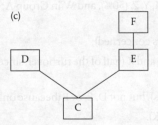

[146] Jurisdictional Notice, para. 187.

1. A Acquires B

The undertakings concerned are A and B.

The aggregate turnover for the purposes of Article 1(2) and (3) is calculated by adding together the respective turnovers of A, X, Y, Z (50%), and W in Group A and B and M (in Group B) That is:

a. A and B (the undertakings concerned);

b. X, Y, and M (subsidiaries) and Z (half of the turnover, since it is a company jointly controlled with a third party);

c. W (A's parent) but not J and K (B's parents, because only an acquisition of part of seller (Art 5(2)).

2. C Acquires Sole Control of A

The undertakings concerned are the acquiring undertakings, C, and the target company, A. The aggregate turnover for the purposes of Article 1(2) and (3) is calculated by adding together the respective turnovers of C, D, E, and F in Group C and A, X, Y, and Z (50%) in Group A. That is:

a. C and A (the undertakings concerned);

b. X and Y (the subsidiaries) and Z (half of the turnover, since it is a company jointly controlled with a third party);

c. D and E (C's parents) and F (C's parent's parent) but not W (A's parent because only an acquisition of part of seller (Article 5(2)).

3. J Acquires Sole Control of B (a Change from Joint Control with K to Sole Control by J)

The undertakings concerned are J and B. K, the existing shareholder (as seller) is not an undertaking concerned.

The aggregate turnover for the purposes of Article 1(2) and (3) is calculated by adding together the respective turnovers of J, B, and M. That is:

a. J and B (the undertakings concerned);

b. M (B's subsidiary). To avoid double counting the turnover of J has to be calculated without the turnover of the joint venture, B.[147]

4. A and B Acquire joint Control of C

The undertakings concerned are A and B (the undertakings acquiring joint control) and C (the pre-existing acquired undertaking).

The aggregate turnover for the purposes of Article 1(2) and (3) is calculated by adding together the respective turnovers of A, X, Y, Z (50%), and W in Group A; B, J, K, and L in Group B; and C in Group C. That is:

a. A, B, and C (the undertakings concerned);

b. X, Y, and M (the subsidiaries) and Z (half of the turnover, since it is a company jointly controlled with a third party);

c. W, J, and K (A and B's parents), but not D, E, or F (because only acquisition of part (Art. 5(2));

d. L (a subsidiary of B's parent K).

---

[147] The turnover of B's parents are not included. K's turnover is excluded because it is an acquisition of part and, to avoid double counting the turnover of the joint venture has to be taken without the turnover of the acquiring shareholder, J.

C. CONCENTRATIONS WITH AN EU DIMENSION: A ONE-STOP SHOP?

(i) Exclusive Competence of the Commission under the EUMR

Article 21(1)–(3) provides:

1. This Regulation alone shall apply to concentrations as defined in Article 3, and Council Regulations (EC) No 1/2003, (EEC) No 1017/68, (EEC) No 4056/86 and (EEC) No 3597/87[148] shall not apply, except in relation to joint ventures that do not have a Community dimension and which have as their object or effect the coordination of competitive behaviour of undertakings that remain independent.

2. Subject to review by the Court of Justice, the Commission shall have sole jurisdiction to take the decisions provided for in this Regulation.

3. No Member State shall apply its national legislation on competition to any concentration that has a Community dimension…

Article 21 indicates that no EU law applies to concentrations that do not have an EU dimension; the EUMR, but not national law, applies to concentrations with an EU dimension and the Commission's decision under the EUMR is decisive. The 'one-stop shop' principle held great appeal both to the Commission itself and to the business community.

(ii) Case Allocation

Notwithstanding this basic starting point, the EUMR provides for circumstances in which a concentration with an EU dimension, or aspects of it, may be referred to a national authority for assessment under its domestic law at either a pre- or post-filing stage. Further, it provides for circumstances where a concentration without an EU dimension may be referred to the Commission.[149] Several provisions in the EUMR thus provide for the transfer of cases between the competent authorities of the Member States and the Commission on the initiative or at the invitation of the Commission, the Member States, or the parties to the transaction themselves at a pre-notification stage.[150] The Commission has published a Notice on case allocation under the referral rules of the EUMR (the 'Notice on case allocation') which describes the rationale underlying the case referral system and provides practical guidance on its mechanics and best practices on cooperation between the EU NCAs.[151]

The Notice on case allocation explicitly recognises that although financial criteria relevant to the assessment of an EU dimension generally serve as effective proxies for the category of transactions for which the Commission is the most appropriate authority, the jurisdictional mechanism should be flexible in some instances so that cases may have to be reattributed by the Commission to Member States and vice versa.[152] The 2004 revisions to the EUMR were designed to facilitate re-attribution of cases, consistently with the principle of subsidiarity, so that the most appropriate authority or authorities for carrying out a particular merger investigation should, where possible, deal with the case, whilst at the same time preserving the basic principle of the one-stop shop for EU mergers.[153]

---

[148] Reg. 3597/87 has essentially been repealed by Reg. 411/2004 [2004] OJ L68/1.

[149] And/or in which Arts 101 and 102 can be applied to a concentration by the Commission itself or by a national court or NCA.

[150] See discussion of Arts 4(4), (5), and 9, and 21(4) and 22 in Sections 3.C and 3.D, pp. 1157–1171.

[151] [2005] OJ C56/2. See also P. Lowe 'The Interaction between the Commission and small Member States in Merger Review', Dublin, 10 October 2003 and 'Best Practices on Cooperation between the EU National Competition Authorities', available at <http://ec.europa.eu/competition/ecn/nca_best_practices_merger_review_en.pdf>.

[152] Commission Notice on case allocation [2005] OJ C56/2, para. 3.

[153] Commission Notice on case allocation [2005] OJ C56/2, para. 5.

The Commission describes the guiding principles for this case allocation in its Notice and also provides more specific guidance on the legal requirements of each provision.

Commission Notice on Case Allocation Under the Referral Rules of the Merger Regulation [2005] OJ C56/2

Guiding principles

8. The system of merger control established by the Merger Regulation, including the mechanism for re-attributing cases between the Commission and Member States contained therein, is consistent with the principle of subsidiarity enshrined in the EC Treaty. Decisions taken with regard to the referral of cases should accordingly take due account of all aspects of the application of the principle of subsidiarity in this context, in particular the suitability of a concentration being examined by the authority more appropriate for carrying out the investigation, the benefits inherent in a 'one-stop shop' system, and the importance of legal certainty with regard to jurisdiction. These factors are inter-linked and the respective weight placed upon each of them will depend upon the specificities of a particular case. Above all, in considering whether or not to exercise their discretion to make or accede to a referral, the Commission and Member States should bear in mind the need to ensure effective protection of competition in all markets affected by the transaction.

More appropriate authority

9. In principle, jurisdiction should only be re-attributed to another competition agency in circumstances where the latter is the more appropriate for dealing with a merger, having regard to the specific characteristics of the case as well as the tools and expertise available to the agency. Particular regard should be had to the likely locus of any impact on competition resulting from the merger. Regard may also be had to the implications, in terms of administrative effort, of any contemplated referral.

10. The case for re-attributing jurisdiction is likely to be more compelling where it appears that a particular transaction may have a significant impact on competition and thus may deserve careful scrutiny.

One-stop shop

11. Decisions on the referral of cases should also have regard to the benefits inherent in a 'one-stop-shop' system, which is at the core of the Merger Regulation. The provision of a one-stop shop is beneficial to competition authorities and businesses alike. The handling of a merger by a single competition agency normally increases administrative efficiency, avoiding duplication and fragmentation of enforcement effort as well as potentially incoherent treatment (regarding investigation, assessment and possible remedies) by multiple authorities. It normally also brings advantages to businesses, in particular to merging firms, by reducing the costs and burdens arising from multiple filing obligations and by eliminating the risk of conflicting decisions resulting from the concurrent assessment of the same transaction by a number of competition authorities under diverse legal regimes.

12. Fragmentation of cases through referral should therefore be avoided where possible, unless it appears that multiple authorities would be in a better position to ensure that competition in all markets affected by the transaction is effectively protected. Accordingly, while postal referrals are possible under Articles 4(4) and 9, it would normally be appropriate for the whole of a case (or at least all connected parts thereof) to be dealt with by a single authority.[154]

---

[154] This is consistent with the Commission's decision in Case M.2389, *Shell/DEA* and Case M.2533, *BP/E.ON* to refer to Germany all of the markets for downstream oil products. The Commission retained the parts of the cases involving upstream markets. Likewise, in Case M.2706, *P&O Princess/Carnival*, the Commission exercised its discretion not to refer a part of the case to the UK, because it wished to avoid a fragmentation of the case (see Commission press release of 11 April 2002, IP/02/552).

Legal certainty

13. Due account should also be taken of the importance of legal certainty regarding jurisdiction over a particular concentration, from the perspective of all concerned. Accordingly, referral should normally only be made when there is a compelling reason for departing from 'original jurisdiction' over the case in question, particularly at the post-notification stage. Similarly, if a referral has been made prior to notification, a post-notification referral in the same case should be avoided to the greatest extent possible.

14. The importance of legal certainty should also be borne in mind with regard to the legal criteria for referral, and particularly—given the tight deadlines—at the pre-notification stage. Accordingly, pre-filing referrals should in principle be confined to those cases where it is relatively straightforward to establish, from the outset, the scope of the geographic market and/or the existence of a possible competitive impact, so as to be able to promptly decide upon such requests.

Part III of the Notice on case allocation deals with the workings of the referral system, and cooperation within the network of competition authorities. In particular the Notice reiterates the importance of cooperation and dialogue between the Commission and NCAs and the NCAs *inter se*.[155]

Concentrations with an EU dimension, or aspects of such a concentration, may be dealt with by an NCA pursuant to Article 9 or Article 21(4) of the EUMR, Article 346 TFEU, or following a reasoned submission by a party to a concentration.

(iii) Article 9—Distinct Markets

a. Objective of Article 9

Article 21(3) paragraph 2 states that the prohibition on a Member State applying its national competition legislation to a concentration with an EU dimension under the first paragraph (set out in Section 3.C.i) is 'without prejudice to any Member State's power to carry out any enquiries necessary for the application of Articles 4(4), 9(2) or after referral, pursuant to Article 9(3) first subparagraph, indent (b), or Article 9(5), to take the measures strictly necessary for the application of Article 9(8)'.

Article 9 of the EUMR was included at the particular insistence of Germany (hence it is often known as the 'German clause'). Germany was initially opposed to the introduction of EU merger control and, in particular, it feared that the Commission's action might be less rigorous than national merger control and that local or regional issues might not be sufficiently addressed.[156] Article 9 was added at a late stage in the negotiations to meet the Germans' objections over loss of control. It provides for the referral, at the request of a national authority, of a merger, or aspects of it (i.e. total or partial referrals), to that authority where the concentration threatens competition in a 'distinct' market in that authority's State.

Although Article 9 references have always been made reasonably frequently[157] the Commission proposed, in conjunction with its review of the Article 1(3) thresholds in the 2001 Green Paper, that this provision could, along with Article 22,[158] be simplified to facilitate the exchange of cases

---

[155] See Notice on case allocation, [2005] C56/2, especially part III 13.

[156] Art. 2 of the EUMR only permits the Commission to take action against concentrations which would impede competition in 'the common market or in a substantial part of it'.

[157] Although few referrals were made in the initial years, since 1997 there have been a number of referrals each year, see statistics in Section 6, p. 1252.

[158] Which allows competent authorities of the Member States to refer concentrations without an EU dimension to the Commission for appraisal, see Section 3.D.iii, pp. 1168–1171.

between the authorities. Articles 9 and 22 thus operate as a corrective measure enabling the transfer of cases to achieve optimal allocation.

Council Regulation (EC) No. 139/2004 of 20 January 2004 on the Control of Concentrations between Undertakings [2004] OJ L24/1, Recital 11

(11) The rules governing the referral of concentrations from the Commission to Member States and from Member States to the Commission should operate as an effective corrective mechanism in the light of the principle of subsidiarity; these rules protect the competition interests of the Member States in an adequate manner and take due account of legal certainty and the 'one-stop shop' principle.

The Notice on allocation recognises that the objective of Article 9 is to ensure, subject to the principle of the one-stop shop and legal certainty, that an NCA should deal with a case when it is in the best position to do so.[159]

b. The Wording of Article 9

Council Regulation (EC) No. 139/2004 of 20 January 2004 on the Control of Concentrations between Undertakings [2004] OJ L24/1, Article 9

1. The Commission may, by means of a decision notified without delay to the undertakings concerned and the competent authorities of the other Member States, refer a notified concentration to the competent authorities of the Member State concerned in the following circumstances.

2. Within 15 working days of the date of receipt of the copy of the notification, a Member State, on its own initiative or upon the invitation of the Commission, may inform the Commission, which shall inform the undertakings concerned, that:

(a) a concentration threatens to affect significantly competition in a market within that Member State, which presents all the characteristics of a distinct market, or

(b) a concentration affects competition in a market within that Member State, which presents all the characteristics of a distinct market and which does not constitute a substantial part of the common market.

3. If the Commission considers that, having regard to the market for the products or services in question and the geographical reference market within the meaning of paragraph 7, there is such a distinct market and that such a threat exists, either:

(a) it shall itself deal with the case in accordance with this Regulation, or

(b) it shall refer the whole or part of the case to the competent authorities of the Member State concerned with a view to the application of that State's national competition law.

If, however, the Commission considers that such a distinct market or threat does not exist, it shall adopt a decision to that effect which it shall address to the Member State concerned, and shall itself deal with the case in accordance with the Regulation.

---

[159] Notice on case allocation, [2005] C56/2, paras. 9–13 and 37. See also Art. 4(4) discussed further in Section 4.B.ii.

> In cases where a Member State informs the Commission pursuant to paragraph 2(b) that a concentration affects competition in a distinct market within its territory that does not form a substantial part of the common market, the Commission shall refer the whole or part of the case relating to the distinct market concerned, if it considers that such a distinct market is affected.

c. Request

Article 9 is not triggered unless a Member State makes a request, either on its own initiative or on the invitation of the Commission, for a reference back within 15 working days of receipt of the copy of the notification from the Commission.

Where the Commission receives a request from a Member State in accordance with Article 9(2)(a), the Commission must determine whether the requesting State has *prima facie* demonstrated that (1) a distinct market exists and (2) the concentration threatens to affect significantly competition within that Member State. Even where these conditions are satisfied, the Commission has a discretion to deal with the case itself *or* to make a total or partial[160] reference of the case to the competent national authority.[161] It is only in Article 9(2)(b)[162] cases (where the Member State has provided preliminary evidence establishing that the concentration affects competition in a distinct market which does not constitute a substantial part of the common market (markets with a narrow geographic scope)[163] that the Commission *must* refer the whole or part of the case relating to the distinct market.

Article 9 thus concedes little authority to the Member States. It may express concern about the effect of a merger in its territory, but generally the Commission is the arbiter of whether or not the matter should be referred to the Member State under Article 9. In the recitals, however, the EUMR makes it clear that the Commission and competent authorities of the Member States will work together forming a 'network of public authorities' to ensure that their respective competences are applied in close cooperation, 'using efficient arrangements for information-sharing and consultation, with a view to ensuring that a case is dealt with by the most appropriate authority, in the light of the principle of subsidiarity and with a view to ensuring that multiple notifications of a given concentration are avoided to the greatest extent possible'.[164] The reality is, therefore, that in a great majority of cases a partial or full referral back is made following an Article 9 request.[165]

d. A Reference Back

The Commission's decision to refer or not to refer must generally be taken within 35 working days of notification, or 65 working days where Phase II proceedings have been initiated.[166] If the Commission does make a reference to the national authority that authority must decide the case 'without undue delay' and, in any event, must inform the undertakings concerned of the result of the preliminary competition assessment and what further action it proposes to take within 45 working days of the Commission's referral (or national notification if requested).[167]

Insofar as a reference is made, the Commission delegates power to investigate the aspects of the merger that affect competition in that distinct market. However, the Member State may only

---

[160] See Case M.180, *Steetley plc/Tarmac* discussed in n. 175 and accompanying text.

[161] EUMR, Art. 9(3). Notice on case allocation, [2005] C56/2, para. 37.

[162] Notice on case allocation, [2005] OJ C56/2, paras. 38–41.

[163] It is thus a relatively narrow provision. The first Art. 9(2)(b) reference made was Case M.2446, *Govia/Connex South Central*. See also Case COMP/M.2370, *Connex/DNVBVG* and Case COMP/M.3130, *Arla Foods/Express Dairies*.

[164] EUMR, recital 14.

[165] See the merger statistics set out in Section 6, p. 1252.

[166] EUMR Arts 9(4) and 10(1). See Case M.330, *McCormick/CPC/Ostmann*.

[167] EUMR, Art. 9(6).

take 'measures strictly necessary to safeguard or restore effective competition on the market concerned'.[168]

e. Distinct Market

Whether a distinct market exists is determined with regard to the market for the products or services in question and, in particular, the geographical reference market. The meaning of a geographical reference market is set out in Article 9(7).[169]

f. Success of Claims

Although the Commission may at first have been less willing to exercise its power to make references back under Article 9,[170] it now operates as an important corrective mechanism for reallocating appropriate cases (or aspects of them) to NCAs, for example where cases raise specific issues in a Member State[171] or regional[172] or local[173] markets. In *ProSiebenSat.1/RTL/JV*[174] the Commission made a partial reference back of aspects of the concentration to two authorities—the German and Austrian agencies—who it considered were well placed to investigate the impact of the transaction in their respective national markets.

The first case in which the Commission agreed to make a reference back was *Steetley plc/Tarmac*.[175] In this case competing bids had been made for Steetley plc by Tarmac and Redland. Only the Tarmac bid had an EU dimension and the Redland bid fell to be assessed under domestic law.[176] The concentration between Steetley and Tarmac would have pooled the building materials activities of the undertakings. In particular, the undertakings had very high market shares for bricks and clay tiles in some regions of England. The Commission agreed that the concentration would lead to particular local problems in the market for the manufacture and sale of bricks in the North East and South West of England and in relation to the manufacture of clay tiles throughout Great Britain.[177] The brick markets were regional (the cost of transporting such heavy products being high relative to the cost of the products) and trade flows in clay tiles between Great Britain and the rest of the EU were low (although the tiles were lighter and could be transported more easily throughout the country significant barriers to entry to the market remained—adequate clay reserves were necessary to manufacture the tiles). The economic implications were therefore substantially limited to the UK. The Commission issued a decision referring these aspects of the merger back to the UK to be assessed

---

[168] EUMR, Art. 9(8).

[169] It consists of an area 'in which the undertakings concerned are involved in the supply and demand of products or services, in which the conditions of competition are sufficiently homogeneous and which can be distinguished from neighbouring areas because, in particular, conditions of competition are appreciably different in those areas'.

[170] See Commission and Council Notes on the 1989 Merger Regulation, Merger Control Law in the European Union, 1998 and e.g. Case M.165, *Alcatel/AEG Kabel* [1992] OJ C6/23; Case M.12, *Varta/Bosch* [1991] OJ L320/26; Case M.222, *Mannesmann/Hoesch* [1993] OJ L114/34; and Case M.238, *Siemens/Philips* [1993] OJ C11/5 (subsequently abandoned).

[171] See, e.g., *Compass/Rail Gourmet/Gourmet Nova;* Case M.5900, *Liberty Global/Kabel Baden-Württemberg:* and Case M.5996, *Thomas Cook/CGL and Midland*.

[172] See, e.g., Case M.3373, *Accor/Barrière/Colony* [2004] OJ C196/8 and Case M.3905, *Tesco/Carrefour*.

[173] See, e.g., Case M.1388, *Total/PetroFina*, Case M.2533, *BP/E.ON*, and Case M.2730, *Connex/DNVBVG*.

[174] Case M.5881

[175] Case M.180. A number of Art. 9 referrals have involved the building or construction industries, see e.g., Case M.1030, *Redland/Lefarge;* Case M.1779, *Anglo American/Tarmac;* Case M.2495, *Haniel/Fels;* Case M.2568, *Haniel/Ytong;* and Case M.4298, *Aggregate Industries/Foster Yeoman*.

[176] Then the UK's Fair Trading Act 1973 (FTA) (the provisions have, however, now been repealed and replaced by the Enterprise Act 2002, Part 3).

[177] The Commission also considered the fact that a competing bid was being assessed at the domestic level.

under the UK merger provisions. On the same day it issued a decision finding that the remaining aspects of the concentration were compatible with the common market.[178]

In many cases a decision to make a reference to a national authority may cause concern to the notifying parties as the reference is unlikely to be requested unless the concentration is considered to pose particular risks for a distinct national market.[179]

An Article 9 case which provides an illustration of the difficulties that can result from dual scrutiny in derogation of the one-stop shop principle is *SEB/Moulinex*.[180] This case concerned a proposed concentration between two French companies. SEB put forward a proposal to purchase the small household electrical appliances business of Moulinex, which was in the midst of bankruptcy proceedings. SEB itself had a significant position in the small electrical household appliances market. The Commission appraised the concentration insofar as it affected 14 countries.[181] As the primary effects of the merger were to be felt in France, however, the Commission at the same time, exercised its discretion to make a reference to the French authorities under Article 9(2)(a). The French authorities went on to unconditionally clear the merger, applying its 'failing firm' defence, even though the combined entity would achieve an average of 60–70 per cent market share on segments of the French small electrical household appliances market. Application of the (EUMR) failing firm defence had been specifically rejected by the Commission.[182]

Two competitors of the parties, BaByliss and Royal Philips, challenged both the Commission's decisions (to clear the merger subject to commitments and to refer the French aspects of the merger back to the French authorities) and the French authorities' decision.

The challenge to the Commission's appraisal of the aspects of the transaction it considered was successful[183] but the challenge to its decision to refer the concentration to the national authority was not. The GC was not, of course, at liberty to rule on the compatibility of the French authority's decision with the Commission's approval decision (or with EU law), *only* on whether the Commission was entitled to refer the concentration to the French authorities, i.e. whether the conditions of Article 9(2)(a) were satisfied and, if so, whether the Commission had properly exercised its discretion whether or not to refer the merger back to the requesting authority. The Court held that the Commission was not entitled to make such a reference where the authority was not capable of acting so as to maintain or restore effective competition or if the reference would undermine the Commission's decision, including commitments, in respect of the parts not referred back. However, this determination had to be made at the time the reference back decision was made and not with the benefit of hindsight and the result of national proceedings. The fact that the referral fragmented the examination of the concentration and interfered with the one-stop shop principle did not affect the conclusion since

---

[178] Case M.180, [1992] OJ C50/25.

[179] See Case M.2044, *Interbrew/Bass* [2000] OJ C293/11 and Interbrew SA and Bass plc: A report on the acquisition by Interbrew SA of the brewing interests of Bass plc, Cm. 5014, 2001. But see Case M.460, *Holdercim/Cedest* [1994] OJ C211/5, (the French authorities cleared aspects of a concentration which had been referred to it under Art. 9), Case M.3130, *Express Dairies/Arla Foods* (cleared by the UK authorities: DTI Press Release, 15 October 2003), Case M.4298 *Aggregate Industries/Foster Yeoman* (the OFT accepted undertakings from the parties in lieu of a reference to the Competition Commission), and discussion of *SEB/Moulinex* in n. 180 and accompanying text.

[180] Case M.2621, IP/02/22.

[181] *SEB/Moulinex*, Case M.2621, IP/02/22. On appeal, the GC annulled the Commission's decision insofar as it had cleared the concentration without commitments in five Member States, Case T-119/02, *Royal Philips Electronics v. Commission* [2003] ECR II-1433. The Commission subsequently reopened the case and after opening Phase II proceedings it again gave unconditional approval to the merger in Spain, Finland, Ireland, Italy, and the UK having carried out a new wide-ranging survey of the five countries concerned.

[182] Case M.2621, IP/02/22. For a discussion of the failing firm defence, see Section 5.D.vii. The next application for an Art. 9 reference by the French authorities was rejected, see Case M.2978, *Lagardère/Natexis/VUP*, IP/03/808.

[183] See n. 181.

'a fragmented assessment undermining the "one-stop shop" principle is inherent in the referral procedure'.[184]

The surprising outcome in this case was, therefore, that—despite the objectives of Article 9 (to allow Member States to look at mergers where the effects are likely to be particularly acute in the national market)—'in contrast to the Commission, which approved the concentration in question only after the commitments relating to the Moulinex trade market had been offered, the French competition authorities...approved the concentration with respect to its effects on the relevant markets in France without imposing commitments relying on the "failing firm" doctrine'.[185] Eventually, however, the French administrative court (Conseil d'Etat)[186] annulled the French authorities' authorisation of the merger, holding that the failing firm conditions had not in fact been fulfilled.

g. Conclusions

The Commission has to exercise its discretion carefully, if it is not to rob the one-stop shop principle of its substance and add to the length and cost of the review unnecessarily. The Commission's Notice on case allocation[187] indicates that decisions on referral of cases will have regard to the benefits inherent in the one-stop shop system, the core of the Merger Regulation, and to the principle of legal certainty; and the GC has made it clear that such references should only be made in exceptional circumstances.[188] The statistics indicate that requests are rarely refused in practice.[189]

(iv) Article 4(4) Request for Referral to a National Competition Authority

Article 4(4) (discussed in Section 4) allows notifying parties, instead of notifying a concentration with an EU dimension to the Commission, to make a reasoned submission that a concentration may significantly affect competition in a distinct market in a Member State and should be examined in whole or in part by that Member State. In contrast, therefore, with an Article 9 request it is lodged by the parties *prior* to notification.

(v) Article 21(4)—Legitimate Interests

Article 21(4) recognises that there are some matters which are so sensitive to the national interest that the Member States should be entitled to retain control over them themselves. Under Article 21(4), a Member State may take steps to protect 'legitimate interests' which are not protected under the EUMR itself:

4. Notwithstanding paragraphs 2 and 3, Member States may take appropriate measures to protect legitimate interests other than those taken into consideration by this Regulation and compatible with the general principles and other provisions of EU law.

Public security, plurality of the media and prudential rules shall be regarded as legitimate interests within the meaning of the first subparagraph.

---

[184] Case T-119/02, *Royal Philips Electronics v. Commission* [2003] ECR II-1433, para. 355. See also Cases T-346 and 347/02, *Cableuropa v. Commission* [2005] ECR II-4251.

[185] Case T-119/02, *Royal Philips Electronics v. Commission* [2003] ECR II-1433, para. 345.

[186] No. 249627, 6 February 2004.

[187] [2005] OJ C56/2.

[188] Case T-119/02, *Royal Philips Electronics v. Commission* [2003] ECR II-1433.

[189] See <http://ec.europa.eu/competition/mergers/statistics.pdf> and Section 6, p. 1252. But see M.5549, *EDF/Segebel* where the Commission refused to refer an energy merger back to the Belgian NCA given the former's considerable expertise in the electricity sector.

Any other public interest must be communicated to the Commission by the Member State concerned and shall be recognised by the Commission after an assessment of its compatibility with the general principles and other provisions of EU law before the measures referred to above may be taken. The Commission shall inform the Member State concerned of its decision within 25 working days[190] of that communication.

So far, Article 21(4) has been used defensively—to enable a Member State to protect its legitimate interests by scrutinising, and, if necessary, prohibiting mergers which may raise concerns other than pure competition ones (even were the Commission to consider that the merger was compatible with the common market). In *Newspaper Publishing*,[191] for example, although the proposed acquisition of Newspaper Publishing plc (publisher of the *Independent*) by Promotora de Informaciones SA, Editoriale l'Espresson SpA, and Mirror Group Newspapers plc fell within the scope of the EUMR, the UK was able to take steps to protect its legitimate interests, in this case the plurality of the media. The Commission cleared the merger but noted that the UK Secretary of State would also have to grant formal consent under the UK's merger rules.[192] Any measures adopted by the UK authorities had, however, to be objectively the least restrictive to achieve the end pursued (to comply with the EU principle of proportionality). In *Thomson CSF/Racal (II)*[193] the UK authorities also stated an intention to consider the public security aspects of a concentration impacting on 'defence electronics' markets under Article 21(4) and in *Sun Alliance/Royal Insurance*[194] the Commission accepted that the UK authorities could apply UK insurance legislation to the transaction.

It is clear from the third paragraph of Article 22(4) that Member States may take steps to protect a 'public interest', other than those specifically referred to in the Article, so long as the Member State specifically notifies it to the Commission.[195] In *Lyonnaise des Eaux SA/Northumbrian Water Group*[196] the Commission accepted that the regulation of the UK water industry constituted a legitimate interest. In accepting the legitimate interests of the UK the Commission held that the UK authorities should not, in their scrutiny of the concentration, take account of factors which properly fell for assessment by the Commission.[197]

In *BSCH/A.Champalimaud*,[198] however, the Portuguese Minister of Finance opposed a concentration with an EU dimension which would give Banco Santander Central Hispano (BSCH) joint control of a group of companies, which included several insurance companies and Portuguese banks. The Portuguese authorities had not communicated any public interest to the Commission that they considered it necessary to protect. The Commission considered that it had not been established that the measure was based on prudential rules and that neither the 'protection of national interest and

---

[190] Under the old EUMR the Commission had to inform the Member State concerned within one month of its decision.

[191] Case M.423.

[192] A number of States consider that media ownership may require a different approach from that ordinarily applicable in domestic competition law. At the time the UK had special rules governing newspaper mergers: see ss. 57–62 of the Fair Trading Act 1973. Newspaper mergers are now within the general regime for mergers (see Enterprise Act 2002) although the Secretary of State can intervene in media cases on public interest grounds.

[193] Case M.1858, IP/00/628. See also, e.g., Case M.4561, *GE/Smiths Group* where the Commission approved GE's proposed acquisition of Smiths Group's aerospace division. The UK Secretary of State intervened under EUMR Art. 21(4), P/2007/60 but eventually accepted undertakings from the parties relating to the protection of sensitive information rather than referring it to the UK's Competition Commission.

[194] Case M.759, [1996] OJ C225/12.

[195] Case M.1616, *BSCH/A.Champaliaud* [1999] OJ C306/37, para. 27.

[196] Case M.567. Following the privatisation of the UK water industry, the water authority in the UK seeks to maintain competitive pressures on water suppliers (which enjoy a monopoly in the provision of local or regional services) by making comparisons of, for example, the relative operating and capital costs of the different water enterprises. In order to achieve this task a sufficient number of independent providers must be maintained. Contrast Case M.1346, *EDF/London Electricity*.

[197] Case M.567, [1996] OJ C11/3.

[198] Case M.1616, *BSCH/A.Champaliaud* [1999] OJ C306/37, para. 27. See also Case M.2054, *Secit/Holderbank/Cimpor* and discussion of breach of EUMR Art. 21, in Section 3.C.vii, p. 1167.

strategic sectors' nor the 'violation of procedural rules' could constitute a legitimate interest within the meaning of the provision. It thus required the Republic of Portugal to suspend the measures adopted.

Article 21(4) does *not* at first sight appear to enable a Member State to clear a merger which the Commission has prohibited under the EUMR and it is unclear whether it could be used in this way. For example, during the 2008 financial crisis, the UK Government stepped in to support and permit a merger which did not have an EU dimension (and so fell to be assessed under UK merger rules) between Lloyds TSB and HBOS. Controversially, the Government considered that the public interest in the stability of the UK financial system outweighed the concerns of the UK's Office of Fair Trading that the merger might substantially lessen competition in relation to banking services and the provision of mortgages in the UK. Had the merger had an EU dimension, however, and had the Commission wanted to block the transaction, it would have been interesting to see if the UK could have intervened to allow the merger relying on EUMR, Article 21(4).

(vi) Article 346 TFEU (ex Article 296 EC)—Essential Interests of Security

Article 346(1)(b) TFEU provides that the Treaties shall not preclude the application by a Member State of measures 'it considers necessary for the protection of the essential interests of its security which are connected with the production of or trade in arms, munitions and war material'. Recital 19 to the EUMR makes it clear that the regulation (and in particular Article 21(4)) does not affect a Member State's ability to act under this Article.

In the competing bids for VSEL plc (a builder of UK Trident submarines), for example, British Aerospace plc and GEC notified their competing bids (which amounted to concentrations) to the Commission only insofar as they related to the non-military activities of VSEL (only 2.5 per cent of the business). The UK, relying on Article 346(1)(b), had instructed the competitors not to notify the acquisition of the military activities. The Commission cleared the non-defence activities of the undertakings and stated that it was satisfied with the measures taken by the UK under Article 346.[199] The UK authorities also invoked Article 346 successfully in relation to the military aspects of a proposed merger between Marconi Electronic Systems (a part of GEC) and British Aerospace plc.[200]

Case No M. 1438—*British Aerospace / GEC Marconi*

III. Application of Article [346(1)(b) TFEU]

7. As already stated in paragraph 2 of this decision, the government of the United Kingdom, relying upon Article [346(1)(b) TFEU], has instructed BAe not to notify information which relates to the military aspects of the operation.

8. The Commission has considered the applicability of Article [346(1)(b) TFEU] in the present case. In this context it has noted, on the basis of the information provided by the government of the United Kingdom, that:

— the part of the concentration which has not been notified only relates to the production of or trade in arms, munitions and war material which are mentioned in the list referred to in Article [346(2)];

— the measures taken by the United Kingdom are necessary for the protection of the essential interests of its security;

---

[199] See, e.g., Case M.528, *British Aerospace/VSEL* [1994] OJ C348/6.

[200] Case M.1438, *British Aerospace/GEC Marconi* [1999] OJ C241/8, see also Case M.820, *British Aerospace/Lagardère SCA* [1997] OJ C22/6.

— the measures taken will have no spillover effects on the non-military products of BAe and MES.

9. Therefore, the Commission is satisfied that the measures taken by the United Kingdom fall within the scope of Article [346(1)b]. To the extent that these measures do not have the effect of distorting the conditions of competition in the Common Market, the Commission sees no need to invoke Article [348].

In *Saab/Celsius*,[201] however, the Commission declined to accept an invocation of Article 346.[202] In this case the Swedish Government instructed the parties only to notify aspects of the merger that related to non-military or dual-use goods. The Commission, however, requested additional information from the parties to enable it to appraise *all* aspects of the concentration, including the impact of the concentration on competition with respect to defence products.

(vii) Breach of Article 21

The Commission will launch proceedings against Member States it considers to be violating the EUMR's exclusivity provisions.[203] Indeed, the Commission has acted in a number of cases where Member States have reacted to fears over the security of strategic industries by prohibiting or imposing conditions on cross-border mergers with an EU dimension. For example, the Commission opened infringement procedures against Spain for not lifting unlawful conditions imposed by the Spanish Energy Regulator on E.ON's and ENEL/Acciona's competing bids for Spanish electricity operator, Endesa, both of which had been cleared by the Commission[204] (a third bid by Gas Natural did not have an EU dimension and was cleared by the Spanish competition authorities).[205] The CJ held that by not withdrawing conditions to the E.ON merger, Spain had failed to fulfil its Treaty obligations.[206] Similarly, the Commission adopted a preliminary conclusion that Italy had violated Article 21 of the EUMR by imposing unjustified obstacles in the way of a concentration with an EU dimension, approved by the Commission,[207] between Abertis of Spain and Autostrade of Italy.[208] This matter was resolved, however, by Italy's removal of the obstacles.[209]

---

[201] Case M.1797, IP/00/118. See also, e.g., M.1080, *Thyssen/Krupp* and M.4191, *Thales/DCN* where mergers involving the defence sector were dealt with under the ordinary EUMR procedures.

[202] It has applied the EUMR to a number of concentrations relating to 'defence' products, see, e.g., Case M.1858, *Thomson CSF/Racal (II)* (but the UK Government announced its intention to consider public security aspects of the case pursuant to Art. 21(4) of the EUMR) and Case M.2308, *Northrop Grumman/Litton Industries*, IP/01/438 (a concentration between two US companies active in the production and provision of a range of military and governmental high technology products).

[203] 'Our line is clear: if interference by any Member State—is not justified by a legitimate public interest, the Commission will continue to condemn such national measures': N. Kroes, Speech to the St Gallen International Competition Law Forum (11 May 2007) available at <http://ec.europa.eu/comm/competition/speeches>.

[204] Case M.4110, *E.On/Endesa* and Case M.4685, *ENEL/Acciona/Endesa*.

[205] Gas Natural's hostile bid for Endesa fell outside the Commission's jurisdiction as each of the firms concerned achieved more than two-thirds of its aggregate EU-wide turnover in one and the same Member State, EUMR Art. 1(2), (3), see Case M.3986, *Gas Natural/Endesa*, aff'd Case T-41/07, *Endesa SA v. Commission* [2006] ECR II-2533.

[206] Case C-196/07, *Commission v. Spain* [2008] ECR I-41; see also Case T-65/08, *Spain v. Commission*.

[207] Case M.4249, IP/06/1244.

[208] IP/06/1418. See also announcement of initiation of proceedings against Poland in relation to Case M.3894, *Unicredit/HVB*, IP/06/277.

[209] MEMO/06/414.

D. CONCENTRATIONS WITHOUT A COMMUNITY—AN EU—DIMENSION

(i) National Law Applies

Article 21(1) provides that the EUMR alone applies to 'concentrations' and disapplies Regulation 1/2003 and the other implementing regulations[210] that confer power on the Commission and NCAs to implement Articles 101 and 102. As these regulations do not apply to concentrations, and because the general rule is that the EUMR applies only to concentrations which have an EU dimension,[211] the general principle is that national law *only* applies to concentrations which do not have an EU dimension.[212]

(ii) Joint Ventures

Article 21(1) itself makes it clear that there is an exception to this general position. It will be remembered that Regulation 1310/97 amended the definition of concentration in Article 3 of the original EUMR, bringing within its scope all full-function ventures, even those which might lead to the coordination of the competitive behaviour of independent undertakings. Originally joint ventures with coordinative aspects would have been appraised under Article 101.[213] These joint ventures are now appraised under the EUMR if they have an EU dimension. If they do not, however, the Commission is still able to apply Article 101 to the joint venture using its powers under Regulation 1/2003.

(iii) Article 22, Referrals to the Commission

a. Background

Article 22 has its origins in Article 22(3)–(5) of the old EUMR, which was known as the 'Dutch clause'.[214] It also derogates from the general rule that concentrations without an EU dimension are appraised only at the national level. It provides:

1. One or more Member States may request the Commission to examine any concentration as defined in Article 3 that does not have an EU dimension within the meaning of Article 1 but affects trade between Member States and threatens to significantly affect competition within the territory of the Member State or States making the request.

Such a request shall be made at most within 15 working days of the date on which the concentration was notified, or if no notification is required, otherwise made known to the Member State concerned.

The Article provides a mechanism by which a Member State can ask the Commission to apply the provisions of the EUMR to a concentration which does not have an EU dimension but which, nonetheless, affects trade between Member States and where it has been *prima facie* established that the concentration significantly affects competition within the territory of the requesting State.[215] The original provision was included to enable Member States without merger control rules to refer particularly troublesome concentrations, from a competition perspective, to the Commission. Indeed three of the first four Article 22 references were made by Member States

---

[210] See Chap. 13.

[211] EUMR, Art. 1(1).

[212] The prohibition in Art. 21(3) on a Member State applying its national legislation on competition applies only where the concentration has an EU dimension. But see discussion in Section 3.E on the residual role of Arts 101 and 102 TFEU.

[213] See Chap. 10.

[214] The clause having been inserted at the request of the Dutch.

[215] Notice on case allocation, [2005] OJ C56/2, paras. 42–45.

which did not have merger control rules and all three of these concentrations were prohibited by the Commission.[216] In *Kesko/Tuko*,[217] for example, the Finnish Office of Free Competition requested that the Commission examine the acquisition of Tuko Oy by Kesko Oy. Although the concentration did not have an EU dimension (both undertakings achieved more than two-thirds of their respective EU-wide turnover in Finland) the Commission found that the concentration affected trade between Member States within the meaning of Article 22. It could, therefore, assess the concentration following the Member State's request. The Commission ultimately prohibited the concentration. The acquisition having already taken place, the Commission ordered Kesko to divest itself of the Tuko business.

As 26 of the 27 Member States now have merger control rules, this type of reference is unlikely in the future.[218] A Member State could, however, make an Article 22 request where, for example, a competing bid has an EU dimension which will be considered by the Commission or, critically, where the Member State considers that the case is one which is primarily of EU interest or which it could not adequately deal with under national law. In more recent years the provision has been used by Member States that do have national merger control rules but have considered that the Commission is better placed to review a particular concentration on account of its cross-border effects. *Promatech SpA/ Sulzer AG*[219] was the first case of a joint referral to the Commission made by the authorities of Spain, Italy, the United Kingdom, Germany, France, Portugal, and Austria. The Commission opened Phase II proceedings but ultimately approved the merger, subject to divestments. A number of joint referrals are made and accepted now each year, see for example, *GEES/Unison*,[220] *GE/AGFA NDT*,[221] *Omya/ Huber*,[222] *Caterpillar/MWM*,[223] and *SCJ/Sara Lee (Insecticides* and *Airfresheners)*.[224] As the Commission has cleared a number of these afterwards, there has been speculation that the Commission may be accepting these requests too readily and where the exceptional circumstances envisaged by Article 22 do not exist.[225]

The new EUMR sought to simplify and clarify the Article 22 procedure (the previous provision had both procedural and operational weaknesses),[226] and to encourage and allow Member States to join in requests where the concentration has a clear impact on intra-EU trade. It has consequently been used more regularly since 2004.[227] The Commission has power to invite Member States to make

---

[216] See Case M.553, *RTL/Veronica/Endemol* [1996] OJ L294/14 (upheld on appeal, Case T-221/95, *Endemol Entertainment Holding BV v. Commission* [1999] ECR II-1299), Case M.784, *Kesko/Tuko* [1997] OJ L174/47 (upheld on appeal Case T-22/99, *Kesko Oy v. Commission* [1999] ECR II-3775), and Case M.890, *Blokker/Toys'R'Us*. The fourth was made by Belgium which wished the Commission to intervene in the *British Airways/Dan Air* merger (Case M.278). The Belgian authorities did not have jurisdiction to preclude a merger between two UK companies. The Commission cleared the merger unconditionally.

[217] Case M.784, [1997] OJ L174/47, *aff'd*, Case T-22/97, *Kesko Oy v. Commission* [1999] ECR II-3775.

[218] The only Member State which does not have merger control rules now is Luxembourg.

[219] Case M.2698.

[220] Case M.2738, *GEES/Unison*. The was the second joint referral to the Commission, where the Commission received referral requests from the authorities of Germany, France, Spain, Italy, the UK, and Greece on 14, 15, and 27 February, and 15 March 2002 respectively. The joint referral request was published in the Official Journal on 21 March 2002 and the merger was finally cleared by the Commission on 14 April 2002.

[221] Case M.3136, *GE/AGFA NDT*, IP/03/1666 (Art. 6 clearance subject to conditions and obligations).

[222] Case M.3796, IP/06/1017.

[223] Case M.6106.

[224] Cases M.5969 and M.5895.

[225] See, e.g., G. Drauz, S. Mavroghenis, and S. Ashall, 'Recent Developments in EU Merger Control' [2012] *Journal of Competition Law & Practice* 52, 65.

[226] See 2001 Green Paper on the Review of Council Regulation (EEC) No. 4064/89, COM(2001) 745/6 final, 25–26 and EUMR, recital 12.

[227] See <http://ec.europa.eu/competition/mergers/statistics.pdf>, and Section 6, p. 1252.

an Article 22 request.[228] The Commission's Notice on case allocation recognises that nonetheless care must be exercised and that referrals should only be made where specific criteria are met:

45. As post-notification referrals to the Commission may entail additional cost and time delay for the merging parties, they should normally be limited to those cases which appear to present a real risk of negative effects on competition and trade between Member States, and where it appears that these would be best addressed at the EU level. The categories of cases normally most appropriate for referral to the Commission pursuant to Article 22 are accordingly the following:

— Cases which give rise to serious competition concerns in a market/s which is/ are wider that national in geographic scope, or where some of the potentially affected markets are wider than national, and where the main economic impact of the concentration is connected to such markets.

— Cases which give rise to serious competition concerns in a series of national or narrower than national markets located in a number of countries of the EU, in circumstances where coherent treatment (regarding possible remedies but also, in appropriate cases, the investigative efforts as such) is considered desirable, and where the main economic impact of the concentration is connected to such markets.

The Commission continues to be concerned, however, that a significant number of cross-border mergers are subject to multiple review in several Member States and has made proposals to deal with procedural and substantive shortcomings under Article 22. It is also considering whether Article 4(5) should be simplified. In particular, it has recommended that following an Article 22 reference it should have jurisdiction for the whole of the EEA.[229]

b. The Mechanics of Article 22

It can be seen from the wording of Article 22 that a Member State making an Article 22 request, on its own initiative or at the invitation of the Commission, must do so within 15 working days of the date on which the concentration was notified, or otherwise made known, to it. The procedure does not, therefore, prevent the parties from having to make national notifications (and perhaps multiple applications) prior to the request or requests being made.[230]

Where a request is made by a Member State under Article 22 the Commission must inform the competent authorities of all the Member States and the undertakings concerned of the request without delay. At this time all applicable national time limits are suspended and, to the extent that the concentration has not been implemented, the suspensory provisions in Article 7 apply.[231] Once such a notice is received the other Member States have 15 working days to decide if they would like to join the initial request. If a Member State decides not to join the request and informs the Commission the suspension of its national time limit ends.

Within 25 working days of informing the Member States and undertakings of the initial request, the Commission may decide to examine a concentration that affects trade between Member States and threatens to significantly affect competition with the territory of the requesting States (if it does not adopt a decision within this time period it is deemed to accept the request).

If the Commission accepts the request the referring Member States retain no control over the Commission's investigation[232] and they may no longer apply their national competition rules (jurisdiction ceases). The Commission may require notification from the parties. If so, the time periods

---

[228] EUMR, Art. 22(5).

[229] See IP/13/584, Commission Staff Working Document, Towards more effective EU merger control.

[230] Art. 4(5), however, enables parties to make a reasoned submission to the Commission *prior* to notification at the national level indicating that a concentration which does not have an EU dimension but which is notifiable in three or more Member States should be examined by the Commission, see Section 4.

[231] See Section 4.C, pp. 1176–1177.

[232] Case T-221/95, *Endemol Entertainment Holding BV v. Commission* [1999] ECR II-1299, para. 42.

set out in Article 10[233] run as usual from notification. Where notification is not required the time periods run from the working day after the Commission informs the undertakings that it has decided to examine the concentration.

The previous regulation provided that in Article 22 cases the Commission was empowered only to take action to maintain or restore effective competition within the territory of the Member State or States at the request of which it intervenes. Under the current regulation, however, the Commission is empowered to proceed as if the merger itself had an EU dimension. It is also theoretically possible that the transaction will be scrutinised at the national level by Member States that decided not to join in the referral. A possibility of conflicting outcomes thus arises.

(iv) Article 4(5), Request for a Referral to the Commission

Article 4(5) (discussed in Section 4) provides a mechanism for parties to a concentration which does not have an EU dimension and which is capable of being reviewed under the national competition laws of at least three Member States, to make a reasoned submission that the Commission should examine the concentration *prior* to national notification.

E. A RESIDUAL ROLE FOR ARTICLES 101 AND 102 OF THE TREATY

(i) The Relevance of Articles 101 and 102 TFEU

Prior to the enactment of the EUMR the Commission made use of both Articles 101 and 102 to prohibit transactions which would now amount to a 'concentration'.[234] Subject to the special provisions for coordinative full-function joint ventures, Article 21(1) disapplies Regulation 1/2003 and the other implementing legislation and clearly intends, subject to the provisos discussed in Section 3.C and Section 3.D, that the EUMR alone should apply to concentrations which have an EU dimension and that national law alone should apply to concentrations which do not. The purpose is to exclude the possible application of Article 101 or Article 102 to concentrations altogether.

The difficulty is that the regulation cannot disapply the application of Articles 101 and 102, which are Treaty provisions; the regulation disapplies only the implementing legislation, which delegates responsibility for the enforcement of the rules to the Commission.

A question which arises, therefore, is whether the national courts can apply Articles 101 and 102. A further question is whether the Commission, and/or an NCA, is authorised to intervene in 'concentration' cases using powers under Articles 105 and 104 TFEU respectively.[235]

(ii) Application in the National Courts

As both Articles 101 and 102 are directly effective in their entirety,[236] it is possible (unless the CJ were to find that the provisions of the EUMR somehow deprived Articles 101 and 102 of their direct effect) that a private individual might be able to challenge the compatibility of a concentration with Article 101 or Article 102 TFEU before a national court. In practice such a challenge would be most likely to occur where the concentration does not have an EU dimension (as an interested third party is able to challenge any Commission decision to clear the merger).

---

[233] See Section 4.D, pp. 1177–1178.

[234] See Section 2, pp. 1129–1140.

[235] These provisions are discussed in Chap. 2.

[236] See Chap. 2 and, e.g., Cook and Kerse, *EC Merger Control* (cited in n. 79), 1–018-21.

(iii) The Commission and National Competition Authorities

It is also possible that both the Commission and the NCAs have power to apply Articles 101 and 102 using their residual powers set out in Article 105 and Article 104 TFEU respectively.[237]

Article 105 authorises the Commission to investigate a breach of Article 101 or Article 102 on its own initiative or at the request of a Member State. Thus it could in theory investigate a breach of these provisions in respect of a concentration which does not have an EU dimension.[238] Because, however, the implementing regulations are suspended the Commission would have to operate without the powers set out therein, for example the power to request information and the power to impose fines on those found to be in breach. It may propose appropriate measures to bring an infringement to an end, and if the infringement is not brought to an end, it may issue a reasoned decision and authorise a Member State to take measures to remedy the situation. The Commission has never made use of Article 105 in this way and it seems unlikely that it would do so.[239]

Article 104 also authorises the competition authorities of the Member States to act when no implementing legislation applies.[240] Where a concentration does not have an EU dimension then neither the provisions of the EUMR nor those of Regulation 1/2003 (save in the case of joint ventures with coordinative aspects)[241] apply.[242] Where, however, a concentration has an EU dimension it seems that, since the parties are obliged to notify such concentrations to the Commission, the jurisdiction of the Member States is denied.[243]

4. PROCEDURE

A. NOTIFICATION

The EUMR requires, to ensure effective control,[244] the notification of concentrations with an EU dimension[245] within the time period set out in Article 4.

Council Regulation (EC) No. 139/2004 of 20 January 2004 on the Control of Concentrations between Undertakings [2004] OJ L24/1, Article 4

1. Concentrations with a Community dimension ... shall be notified to the Commission prior to their implementation and following the conclusion of the agreement, the announcement of the public bid, or the acquisition of a controlling interest.

Notification may also be made where the undertakings concerned demonstrate to the Commission a good faith intention to conclude an agreement or, in the case of a public bid, where they have publicly

---

[237] These provisions are discussed in Chap. 2.

[238] If the concentration does have an EU dimension it will in any event be examining the transaction under the provisions of the EUMR.

[239] See its statement at the time of the adoption of the original EUMR, [1990] 4 CMLR 314.

[240] The competent national authorities' power to apply Arts 101 and 102 TFEU by Reg. 1/2003, Art. 5 is disapplied.

[241] See Section 3.D.ii, p. 1168.

[242] Consequently it seems that both Arts 101 and 102 could be applied.

[243] See Chap. 2.

[244] EUMR, recital 17.

[245] Although the Commission is obliged to publish the fact of notification, the Commission is bound to take account of the legitimate interest of the undertakings in the protection of their business secrets and is bound by a general duty of confidentiality, see EUMR, Arts 4(2) and 17(2) and Chap. 13.

It is therefore possible to notify any time prior to the implementation of an agreement, public bid, or acquisition of a controlling interest even where an agreement or public bid has not actually been made—provided that it can be demonstrated 'that their plan for that proposed concentration is sufficiently concrete, for example on the basis of an agreement in principle, a memorandum of understanding, or a letter of intent signed by all undertakings concerned, or, in the case of a public bid, where they have publicly announced an intention to make such a bid'.[247]

Which parties to the concentration are obliged to notify is dependent on the type of transaction that occurs. Broadly, joint notification must be made by the merging parties in true merger cases or by those acquiring control in other cases.[248] The implementing regulation, Regulation 802/2004[249] and Form CO set out how notification should be made and the information and documents which must be furnished to the Commission.[250] Form CO is not a form but a pattern, divided into 11 sections, which prescribes how the information requested must be presented. A large amount of information is required (to enable the Commission to comply with the tight deadlines imposed on it). Thus the form requires a description of the concentration, information about the parties, details of the concentration, information about ownership and control, supporting documentation (which includes information bringing about the concentration and also copies of all analyses, reports, studies, surveys, and any comparable documents submitted to, or prepared by or for, any member(s) of the board of directors for the purposes of assessing or analysing the concentration with respect to market shares, competition condition, competitors, the rationale of the concentration, potential for sales growth),[251] information on market definitions and affected markets, overall market context and efficiencies, and cooperative effects of a joint venture. Section 11 requires the notification to be accompanied with a declaration signed by representatives of the undertakings.

It can be seen from this list that notification is costly and time-consuming to complete. Failure to recognise the time and effort involved in the notification could disrupt the completion of the deal between the merging undertakings. Further, if all the requisite information is not supplied the notification will be 'incomplete' and a decision from the Commission will be delayed.[252] Pre-notification discussions with the Commission are always possible and in practice are ordinarily essential and extensive and play 'an important part of the whole review process'.[253] Pre-notification discussions may minimise the possibility of an incomplete notification and may lead to a reduction in the amount of information that the parties are required to provide in a notification. The Commission's Best Practices Guidelines provide guidance on pre-notification contacts and the preparation of a

[246] Until 1 May 2004, the EUMR provided that a concentration had to be notified to the Commission 'not more than one week after the conclusion of the agreement, or the announcement of the public bid, or the acquisition of a controlling interest'. This deadline was tight and was frequently waived by the Commission. The new provision provides greater flexibility.

[247] EUMR, recital 34. As the Commission must be able to determine jurisdiction at the date of filing, the relevant date for establishing jurisdiction is the date of the conclusion of a binding legal agreement, the announcement of the public bid, the acquisition of a controlling interest, or the date of filing, whichever date is earlier. The date is crucial to the calculation of turnover, Jurisdictional Notice, paras. 154–156.

[248] EUMR, Art. 4(2).

[249] [2004] OJ L133/1.

[250] One original signed paper form must be submitted, together with five paper copies and 32 copies in CD or DVD-Rom format, see Reg. 802/2004, Art. 3(2) and Commission Communication [2006] OJ C251/2.

[251] Form CO, s. 5(4). This information can sometimes be damaging.

[252] The tight time limits do not start to run until notification is complete.

[253] DG Competition Best Practices on the conduct of EC merger control proceedings, para. 5. Section 3 of the form deals with pre-notification.

draft and final Form CO. A Short Form, also attached to the implementing regulation, applies for certain concentrations that do not raise competition concerns.[254]

In *Gencor/Lonrho*[255] the Commission took the view that the parties' notification of the concentration to it meant that they had submitted to the EU jurisdiction.[256]

B. PRE-NOTIFICATION REASONED SUBMISSIONS

(i) Background

In Section 3 it has been explained that there has been a consistent concern that the simple turnover thresholds set out in Article 1(2) and (3) do not divide jurisdiction between the Commission and NCAs in all cases. The EUMR thus provides flexible mechanisms for the transfer of such cases between the Commission and the national authorities and, since 2004, has enabled the parties to provide input into the determination of jurisdiction through the submission of reasoned submissions to the Commission *prior* to notification at the EU or national level (as relevant). Such submissions are made on Form RS, attached to the implementing regulation. The Commission's notice on case allocation[257] provides guidance on the system and practical guidance relating to the mechanics of the referral system, particularly the pre-notification referral mechanism provided for in Article 4(4) and (5).

The procedure may also enable the parties to speed up the reference procedure and may preclude the need for a notification to an authority which is simply going to refer the case to another.

(ii) Article 4(4), Request for Referral to a National Competition Authority

Article 4(4) provides that where a concentration has an EU dimension the notifying parties may, prior to notification to the Commission, make a reasoned submission that a concentration may significantly affect competition in a distinct market in a Member State and should be examined in whole or in part by that Member State. Where such a submission is made the Commission must inform the relevant Member State without delay and the relevant Member State has a period of 15 working days to express agreement or disagreement with the request to refer the case.

Unless the Member State disagrees the Commission has a period of 25 working days from receiving the reasoned submission to determine whether or not to refer the case. If it fails to adopt a decision within this time period it is deemed to have adopted a decision to refer. In deciding whether or not to make a reference the Commission, apart from verifying the legal requirements, will consider the guiding principles set out in its Notice[258] and in particular whether the authority or authorities to which it is contemplating requesting the referral of the case, is the most appropriate authority for dealing with the case. This will be dependent upon both the likely locus of the competitive effects and how appropriate the NCA would be for scrutinising the transaction.[259]

Where the Commission decides to refer the whole of the case *no* notification to the Commission is required and national competition law applies, subject to the conditions set out in Article 9.[260]

---

[254] Broadly where there are no horizontal overlaps or vertical or neighbouring market relationships or where these overlaps or relationships are small, see also the Commission notice on a simplified procedure for the treatment of certain concentrations [2005] OJ C56/32.

[255] Case M.619, [1997] OJ L11/42.

[256] See discussion in Section 8, pp. 1254–1256 and Chap. 16.

[257] [2005] OJ C56/2.

[258] [2005] OJ C56/2, paras. 8–14.

[259] [2005] OJ C56/2, paras. 19–23.

[260] See EUMR, Art. 9(6)–(9).

Article 4(4) requests may occur where, for example, the parties anticipate that an Article 9 request will be made by a Member State.

(iii) Article 4(5), Request for a Referral to the Commission

Article 4(5) provides that prior to national notifications parties to a concentration which does not have an EU dimension, and which is capable of being reviewed under the national competition laws of at least three Member States, may make a reasoned submission that the concentration should be examined by the Commission. The parties may not implement the concentration while the Commission is considering it under Article 4(5). The Commission must transmit such submissions to the Member States without delay. The Member States then have a period of 15 working days within which to express their disagreement with the procedure. The procedure is terminated if one Member State disagrees. Where, however, no Member State disagrees the concentration is deemed to have an EU dimension. It becomes notifiable to the Commission and *no* Member State is permitted to apply its national competition law to the concentration.

The advantage of the Article 4(5) procedure is apparent: if no Member State objects the parties may be saved multiple notifications and the transaction may be deemed to have an EU dimension. The risks are also obvious: if just one Member State objects the procedure is terminated. This would mean that the parties may, having already made a reasoned submission, then have to make multiple notifications to the national authorities (and still risk the possibility that some of the Member States may then make an Article 22 reference to the Commission, making a notification necessary).[261] In order to minimise this risk and to encourage the use of Article 4(5) the Commission's Notice on case allocation[262] provides guidance on the question of when a referral of the case to the Commission is likely to be considered appropriate. Again, the Commission refers to the guiding principles and provides more specific guidance as to whether the Commission is the most appropriate authority for dealing with the case.[263]

The Commission is now consulting on the question of whether Article 4(5) could be modified to facilitate its use, in particular by abolishing the need to make a reasoned submission and by allowing the parties to notify, on a modified Form CO, immediately to the Commission and for the Commission to have jurisdiction unless a Member State opposes it.[264]

(iv) Notice on Case Allocation

In order to encourage pre-filing referrals in appropriate cases it has been seen that the Commission's Notice on case allocation provides guidance on the legal requirements of Article 4(4) and (5) and provides guidance as to when a referral is likely to be appropriate. Further, the Notice stresses the dialogue and cooperation that occurs between the Commission and NCAs and the NCAs between themselves, which is aimed at ensuring that concentrations are referred in appropriate cases, that the system of pre-filing referrals operates smoothly, and that an early warning system is put in place with regard to post-notification requests. It also provides guidance for parties considering filing a Form RS. The system seems to be operating effectively as a corrective mechanism. By the end of 2012, the Commission had received 80 Article 4(4) requests (of which 75 of were referred to Member States,

---

[261] See, e.g., Case M.6502 *London Stock Exchange/LCH Clearnet Group.*

[262] [2005] OJ C56/2.

[263] [2005] OJ C56/2, paras. 25–32.

[264] See IP/13/584, Commission Staff Working Document, Towards more effective EU merger control.

two were partially referred, and none was refused) and 249 Article 4(5) requests (of which 239 were accepted and only five were refused).[265]

C. SUSPENSION

Article 7(1) provides that a concentration with an EU dimension, or to be examined by the Commission pursuant to Article 4(5), is not to be implemented 'either before its notification or until it has been declared compatible with the common market pursuant to a decision under Articles 6(1) (b), 8(1) or 8(2), or on the basis of a presumption according to Article 10(6)'. The suspensory obligation prohibits 'gun jumping', closing a transaction prior to notification or implementing a transaction which has been notified prior to obtaining clearance from the Commission. As a general rule therefore parties must take care not to take steps towards implementation of the merger *and* not to engage in information-sharing or other conduct which might infringe the competition law rules before clearance has been obtained, for example, through: coordinating their commercial activities; integrating business expertise; coordinating price, production, or research strategies; and/or engaging in joint marketing or advertising.[266]

The Commission has power to permit derogations from this suspensory effect following a request (and has occasionally used this power to allow rescue operations requiring quick closure during the financial and economic crisis)[267] and Article 7(2) provides an automatic derogation for public bids[268] 'or a series of transactions in securities including those convertible into other securities admitted to trading on a market such as a stock exchange, by which control is acquired from various sellers, provided that'[269] (1) the concentration is notified to the Commission and (2) the acquirer does not exercise its voting rights or does so only to maintain the full value of its investments (based on an express derogation by the Commission).

The Commission has power under Article 14(2)(a) of the EUMR to impose fines, not exceeding 10 per cent of the aggregate turnover of the undertakings concerned, on a party that, intentionally or negligently, fails to notify a concentration in accordance with Articles 4 and 22(3) prior to its implementation and, under Article 14(2)(b), to impose penalties not exceeding 10 per cent of the aggregate turnover on those, intentionally or negligently, breaching the suspensory provisions. The validity of any such transaction closed in breach of the notification and/or suspensory provisions is dependent upon a clearance decision of the Commission.[270]

The Commission first imposed a fine of ECU 33,000 (at this time the amount of the fine could not exceed ECU 50,000)[271] on an undertaking, Samsung, which had failed to notify a concentration in due time. Samsung had acquired control over an American firm, AST Research Inc., without the Commission's authorisation in breach of EU rules.[272] Fines have been imposed in subsequent cases and, now that the fining threshold has been significantly increased, much greater fines can be

---

[265] See merger statistics set out in Section 6, p. 1252 and up-to-date statistics available at <http://ec.europa.eu/competition/mergers/statistics.pdf>.

[266] Such actions may not only breach the EUMR but also constitute a violation of Art. 101 TFEU, see e.g., Case M.4734, *Ineos/Kerling* (suspected infringement of the standstill obligation investigated through unannounced inspections), see, e.g., F. Depoortere and S. Lelart, 'The Standstill Obligation in the ECMR' [2010] *World Competition* 103.

[267] EUMR, Art. 7(3). See, e.g., Case M.4956, *STX/Aker Yards* and Case M.5363, *Santander/Bradford & Bingley*.

[268] See, e.g., Case M.2282, *Schneider/Legrand*: Schneider make a public exchange offer in respect of the shares held in Legrand and acquired 98.7% of the shares in Legrand prior to the Commission's final decision prohibiting the merger (and ordered the separation of Schneider and Legrand (see EUMR, Art. 8(4), (5) in Section 4.E)). The Commission's decision was annulled on appeal, Case T-310/01, *Schneider Electric SA v. Commission* [2002] ECR II-4071 and Schneider subsequently brought proceedings against the Commission in respect of its loss, see Section 7.

[269] See, e.g., Case M.4730, *Yara/Kemira GrowHow*.

[270] EUMR, Art. 7(4).

[271] The fines that can be imposed were significantly increased by Reg. 139/2004.

[272] Case M.920, [1999] OJ L225/12.

anticipated.[273] Indeed, in June 2009, the Commission imposed a €20 million fine on Electrabel for acquiring control over Compagnie Nationale du Rhône (France's second largest electricity producer) in 2003 without notification.[274]

D. PHASE I INVESTIGATION

The Commission must examine notifications as soon as they are received.[275] The time limits for initiating proceedings and decisions are set out in Article 10. The implementing regulation provides further information on the operation of the EUMR time limits and compliance with them.[276]

Phase I decisions must generally be taken within 25 working days following receipt of complete notification.[277] The period is extended to 35 working days in Article 9 cases or cases where commitments designed to render the concentration compatible with the common market are offered[278] (so long as the commitments are offered within 20 working days of notification).[279] Details of notification must be published in the Official Journal in order to give third parties the opportunity to react.[280]

At the end of the 25- or 35-working day period the Commission must adopt a decision under Article 6. This may take one of several forms.

(i) Article 6(1)(a)

Where the notified transaction does not in fact fall within the EUMR at all, it does not amount to a concentration with an EU dimension, and the Commission may issue a decision to that effect.

(ii) Article 6(1)(b)

The Commission may declare the notified concentration to be compatible with the common market either unconditionally or conditionally (subject to the acceptance of commitments by the parties).[281] Clearance decisions are deemed to cover restrictions directly related and necessary to the implementation of the concentration.[282]

(iii) Article 6(1)(c)

Where the Commission has serious doubts about the concentration's compatibility with the common market it must issue a decision to that effect and initiate proceedings launching a second-phase investigation. This is in fact a relatively rare occurrence (less than five per cent of all notified cases).

Where such proceedings are launched then, without prejudice to Article 9, unless the undertakings can demonstrate to the satisfaction of the Commission that they have abandoned their

---

[273] See, e.g., Case M.969, *AP Moller* [1999] OJ L183/29.

[274] MEMO/09/267, Case T-332/09, *Electrabel v. Commission*, 12 December 2012 (dismissing Electrabel's appeal), Case C-84/13P (judgment pending).

[275] *EUMR*, Art. 6(1).

[276] Reg. 802/2004, [2004] OJ L133/1, Arts 7–10.

[277] EUMR, Art. 10(1).

[278] EUMR, Art. 10(1).

[279] Reg. 802/2004, [2004] OJ L133/1, Art. 19(1).

[280] EUMR, Art. 4(3).

[281] The Commission can also make such a finding following modifications by the undertakings concerned to the transaction, EUMR, Art. 6(2). See discussion of commitments, in Section 5.G, pp. 1245–1251.

[282] See Section 5.F, p. 1244.

concentration, the proceedings must be closed by virtue of an Article 8 decision (see Section 3.A.iv, pp. 1148–1149). An Article 6(1)(c) decision initiating proceedings is not an appealable decision.[283]

(iv) Article 10(6)

Where the Commission fails to adopt a decision within the prescribed periods the concentration 'shall be deemed to have been declared to be compatible with the common market'.

E. PHASE II

The Commission has a period of 90 working days from the day following the initiation of proceedings in which to make its assessment in Phase II proceedings.[284] This time period can be extended by 15 working days where commitments are offered by the parties *after* the 54th working day (commitments must generally be offered within 65 working days).[285] Further, it is possible that the period can be extended up to a total of 20 working days either by the parties or at the request of the Commission with the consent of the parties.[286] This means that in complex cases the time period may be extended to a maximum of 125 working days. Occasionally, however, the time periods may be expanded even beyond this statutory timetable if the Commission 'stops the clock' on account of the parties' failure to respond to requests for information by a stipulated time period.[287]

Again, if no decision is taken within the prescribed period the concentration is deemed to be compatible with the common market.[288]

At the end of the proceedings the Commission may under Article 8 of the EUMR either:

(1) declare the concentration to be compatible with the common market;

(2) declare that the concentration, following modification, is compatible with the common market. Conditions and obligations can be attached to the decision to ensure that the undertakings concerned comply with the commitments they have entered into with a view to rendering the concentration compatible with the common market (the decision can subsequently be revoked if the parties breach the commitments);[289]

(3) declare the concentration to be *incompatible* with the common market.[290]

In Article 8(1) and (2) cases the clearance decision is deemed to cover restrictions related and necessary to the concentration.[291] Where the concentration is declared incompatible with the common market and the parties have already completed the transaction the Commission has comprehensive

---

[283] See Case C-188/06 P, *Schneider Electric SA v. Commission* [2007] ECR I-35, concerning Schneider's renotification of its merger with Legrand (Case M.2283). The CJ upheld the GC's view that a challenge to a decision opening a Phase II merger investigation was inadmissible since the decision was not a challengeable act but an intermediary act, to assist the Commission in reaching a final decision. The parties had therefore to wait to contest the final decision of the Commission determining the outcome of the case (in fact the parties abandoned the merger).

[284] EUMR, Art. 10(3).

[285] Reg. 802/2004, [2004] OJ L133/1, Art. 19(2).

[286] EUMR, Art. 10(3), second paragraph.

[287] See, e.g., Case M.2282, *Schneider/Legrand* (the Commission stopped the clock on account of the failure of the parties to respond to 322 questions within 12 calendar days (five working days), *aff'd*, Case T-310/01, *Schneider Electric SA v. Commission* [2002] ECR II-4071, para. 100; the GC held that a request for information was reasonable given the circumstances of the case and the requirement for speed which characterises the overall scheme of the EUMR). See also, e.g., Case T-145/06, *Omya v. Commission* [2009] ECR II-145.

[288] EUMR, Art. 10(6).

[289] EUMR, Art. 8(6). It may also revoke decisions which are based on incorrect information.

[290] EUMR, Art. 8(2). Commitments are discussed in Section 5.G, pp. 1243–1251.

[291] See Section 5.F, pp. 1244–1245.

powers, including the power to take interim measures or to take restorative measures.[292] These powers can also be exercised where a concentration is implemented in breach of a condition or obligation.

F. CONDUCT OF MERGER INVESTIGATIONS

When making its assessment, within the short periods stipulated, the Commission has power under Articles 11 and 13 EUMR to obtain information from the parties, or third parties (such as customers, suppliers, or competitors), by means of a request, either by a simple request or decision,[293] or by an inspection (including unannounced on the spot investigations).[294] Third parties play an important role in the merger proceedings. The investigation is ordinarily conducted in the form of requests for information to customers, suppliers, or competitors but may also be addressed to the notifying parties. It may also seek the views of these parties orally. The Commission's powers of investigation were extended by the current regulation to bring them more closely into line with the Commission's corresponding powers under Regulation 1/2003.

The Commission has power under Articles 14 and 15 to impose both fines, not exceeding one per cent of the aggregate turnover of the undertakings concerned, and periodic penalty payments for a number of offences, such as intentionally or negligently failing to respond to an Article 11 letter or supplying incorrect or misleading information in a notification or following a request for information.[295] In *BP/Erdölchemie*,[296] for example, the Commission issued a decision imposing a fine of €35,000 on Deutsche BP for having omitted to identify important information in its Form CO (the maximum fine was then €50,000 but is now one per cent of the turnover of the undertaking concerned). A decision adopted on the basis of incorrect information for which one of the undertakings is responsible may be revoked.[297]

State of play meetings are generally held during the process with the objective of contributing to the quality and efficiency of the decision-making process and of ensuring transparency and communication between DG COMP and the parties. If Phase II proceedings are initiated there are usually state of play meetings at five different points in the procedure. Occasionally, voluntary 'triangular' meetings involving the parties and third parties are held.

In the course of Phase II investigations a statement of objections (SO) is served on the notifying parties. This lets the parties know the Commission's objections to the concentration.[298] Parties then have an opportunity to respond to the statement in writing by a specified date (the Commission is not obliged to take account of comments received after the expiry of the specified time limit);[299] they have a right of access to the file[300] and to attend and speak at the oral hearing, which is conducted by the Hearing Officer in full independence.[301] Further, other involved parties[302] and third parties, including customers, suppliers, competitors, members of the administrative or management bodies of the undertakings concerned or the recognised representative of their employees, and consumer associations where the proposed concentration concerns products or services used by

---

[292] EUMR, Art. 8(4) and (5), see also n. 94 and accompanying text and, e.g. Cases M.2416, *Tetra Laval/Sidel*, M.2283, *Schneider/Legrand*, M., *Blokker/Toys'R'Us* and M.784, *Kesko/Tuko*.

[293] EUMR, Art. 11.

[294] EUMR, Arts 12 and 13, see Case M.4734, *Ineos/Kerling*, and n. 266. The power to carry out dawn raids is equivalent to those set out in Reg. 1/2003 [2003] OJ L1/1, discussed in Chap. 13.

[295] EUMR, Art. 14(1), Case IV/29.895, *Telos* [1982] OJ L58/19.

[296] Case M.2624, [2004] OJ L91/40.

[297] EUMR, Arts 6(3) and 8(6).

[298] EUMR, Art. 18(1) and (2).

[299] EUMR, Art. 18(3), Reg. 802/2004, [2004] OJ L133/1, Art. 13(2)(3).

[300] EUMR, Art. 18(3), Reg. 802/2004, [2004] OJ L133/1, Art. 17(1).

[301] Reg. 802/2004, [2004] OJ L133/1, Arts 14 and 15.

[302] Parties to the transaction other than the notifying parties.

end consumers,[303] may have a right to receive the statement of objections, to respond to it, to have access to the file,[304] to attend the oral hearing, and to speak at it. If disputes arise in the course of this procedure, the issue can be raised with the Hearing Officer.

The Court takes the procedural obligations of the Commission very seriously. In *Schneider Electric SA v. Commission*[305] the GC was critical of the Commission's substantive analysis of the case but annulled the decision on account of procedural irregularities committed by the Commission, in particular denial of the rights of defence. The GC found that the SO had not adequately stated the Commission's case against the parties. In its final decision, the Commission took account of the conglomerate effects of the merger whilst the SO had identified only horizontal effects. The GC held that although the Commission was able to add to or revise its arguments identified in the SO, the SO had to state objections in a sufficiently precise way to enable the parties to rebut the case against them and/or to devise or present remedies capable of saving the merger.[306]

Concentrations are initially investigated and appraised by merger units within DG Comp. These are located both in the merger policy unit in Directorate A, and within each sectoral unit (B–E) (staff are referred to as the Merger Network). In Phase II investigations an independent 'panel' is appointed with the task of scrutinising the case team's conclusions with a fresh pair of eyes at key points of the enquiry (devil's advocate process).[307] This step was added to deal with the criticism that the case team was often convinced of its own arguments at the end of Phase I, and that this affected the outcome of the second-phase investigations. The Advisory Committee on Concentrations must be consulted before a final decision is taken.[308] The final decision is made by the College of Commissioners[309] save, where delegated,[310] where it is adopted by a single Commissioner (usually the Competition Commissioner).

5. SUBSTANTIVE APPRAISAL OF CONCENTRATIONS UNDER THE EU MERGER REGULATION

A. BACKGROUND

The correct substantive test against which concentrations with an EU dimension should be appraised was controversial both at the time of the adoption of the original EUMR and, again, at the run-up to the adoption of the recast Regulation.

At the time the original EUMR was adopted the disagreement between the Member States centred largely on the factors to be taken into account and, in particular, on whether a strict

---

[303] See, e.g., Reg. 802/2004, [2004] OJ L133/1, Art. 11(1)(b)(c). See also on the rights of third parties, Cases C-68/94 and C-30/95, *France v. Commission, Société Commerciale des Potasses et de l'Azote (SCPA) v. Commission* [1998] ECR I-1375.

[304] Third parties may also seek access to Commission documents using the Transparency Regulation, see Cases C-404/10 P, *Commission v. Éditions Odile Jacob*, and C-477/10 P, *Commission v. Agrofert Holding*, 28 June 2012.

[305] Case T-310/01, [2002] ECR II-4071.

[306] In Case T-5/02, *Tetra Laval v. Commission* [2002] ECR II-4381 (GC rejected Tetra Laval's arguments that the Commission had failed to respect Tetra's rights to access to the file).

[307] See M. Monti, 'Merger Control in the European Union: a radical reform', European Commission/International Bar Association, Brussels 7 November 2002, SPEECH/02/545. Representatives from the staff of the Chief Competition Economist participate in this panel.

[308] It must also be consulted, e.g., before a decision imposing a fine or penalty or ordering divestment is taken.

[309] In some particularly sensitive merger cases there is a fear that this factor allows political and other considerations to enter the decision-making process, see Section 5.D.x.

[310] e.g., Phase I decisions are usually delegated.

competition-based approach should be adopted.[311] The *original* EUMR[312] adopted the 'dominance' test, providing in Article 2(2) and 2(3) that:

2. A concentration which does not create or strengthen a dominant position as a result of which effective competition would be significantly impeded in the common market or in a substantial part of it shall be declared compatible with the common market.

3. A concentration which creates or strengthens a dominant position as a result of which effective competition would be significantly impeded in the common market or in a substantial part of it shall be declared incompatible with the common market.

In its 2001 Green Paper[313] the Commission discussed the merits of the dominance test, after 11 years of its application. In particular, it launched a debate as to whether there should be a move from the dominance standard to the 'substantial lessening of competition' (SLC) test. The Commission discussed both procedural and substantive arguments in favour of reform. The gist of the procedural argument was that alignment of the test with the SLC test used in a number of jurisdictions, including the US,[314] would lead to greater international convergence in the application of merger rules. The Commission was not entirely convinced by this argument, partly because of the uncertainty that switching to a new substantive test for appraisal would create, and partly because of the inconsistency it would cause in the EU where many Member and acceding States had modelled their merger rules on the dominance test.

The substantive reasons advanced hinged on the relative flexibility of the SLC test, in particular when dealing with mergers in concentrated markets. It will be seen in Section 5.D.iii.d that, despite initial doubt, it was gradually established that the old EUMR applied, not only to mergers leading to the creation or strengthening of a dominant position held by a single undertaking, but to mergers leading to the creation or strengthening of a collective dominant position (that is, a dominant position held by the merging parties and another or other undertakings operating on the market).[315] Advocates of the adoption of the SLC test[316] took the view that in spite of this development, the dominance test was not broad enough to capture and prevent all problematic mergers occurring on a concentrated market. In particular, it would not reach concentrations between undertakings on a concentrated market which would not lead to the creation or strengthening of a collective dominant position (*coordinated effects*) but which would nonetheless lead to higher prices on the market (*non-coordinated* or *unilateral effects*) without the creation of a single dominant position. For example, a merger between the second and third largest competitors on a market with only three players might not lead to the creation of a single dominant position, it might not lead to the coordination of the competitive behaviour of the two remaining firms on the market (arguably a necessary requirement for a finding of collective dominance), but it might substantially lessen competition on the market by eliminating the rivalry between the merging firms and the competitive constraint that they had exercised both on each other and on the market leader. The classic example given of this type of situation was the US 'baby food' case.[317] In this case Heinz, the third largest producer of baby food in the US,

---

[311] See Section 2.C, pp. 1134–1139.

[312] The substantive test was not amended by Reg. 1310/97 [1997] OJ L180/1.

[313] 2001 Green Paper on the Review of Council Regulation (EEC) No. 4064/89, COM(2001) 745/6 final, especially paras. 160–167.

[314] The test is also used, e.g., in Canada, Australia, the UK, and Ireland.

[315] See also the discussion of collective dominance in Chap. 9.

[316] See, e.g., J. Vickers, 'Competition Economics and Policy' [2003] *ECLR* 95, R. Whish, 'Substantive Analysis under the EC Merger Regulation: should the dominance test be replaced by "substantial lessening of competition"', in *EU Competition Law & Policy Developments & Priorities* (Hellenic Competition Commission, 2002), 45, Z. Biro and M. Parker, 'A New EC Merger Test? Dominance v. Substantial Lessening of Competition' [2002] 1 *Competition Law Journal* 157 and U. Böge and E. Müller, 'From the market dominance test to the SLC test: are there any reasons for change?' [2002] *ECLR* 495.

[317] *FTC v. HJ Heinz Co* 16 F Supp 2d 2000.

wished to acquire Milnot Holding Corporation, whose subsidiary, Beech-Nut, was the second largest producer of baby food in the US. Following the merger the parties would have acquired around 33 per cent of the relevant market, whilst Gerber would have retained 65 per cent of the prepared baby food market. The merger clearly would not have given the merging parties a 'dominant' position and it was not clear that the merger would lead to coordinated effects on the market (e.g., tacit coordination of prices by the merged entity and Gerber). Nonetheless the US Federal Trade Commission (FTC) considered that the merger would lead to a substantial lessening of competition on the market since the merging parties competed vigorously to be chosen as the number two supplier in supermarkets and in innovation in product development and differentiation. This competition also placed competitive pressure on Gerber with respect to both prices and innovation. Although the challenge to this merger led to its eventual abandonment in the US, it was argued that, had the same facts arisen in the EU, the EU authorities would have been powerless to prevent the merger under the dominance test. The EUMR was thus argued to include a 'blind spot' or gap. Indeed, this gap appeared to have contributed to the Commission's problems in the *Airtours* case.[318]

In its Green Paper the Commission indicated that it was not convinced that there was such a gap, believing it to be more hypothetical than real. Nonetheless it did open a debate which raged until the last moments before the text for the new EUMR was finally agreed. For example, the UK[319] and Irish delegations[320] were in favour of introducing the SLC test whilst the German delegation[321] favoured retention of the dominance test which it considered to be adequate to catch all problematic mergers.

B. REFORM AND THE NEW SUBSTANTIVE TEST

Given the need for unanimous agreement in the Council the end result of the reform process was a classic, yet ingenious, European 'compromise'.[322] The substantive test *was* altered but the SLC test was *not* adopted. The decision was made to utilise, but reorganise, the wording of the original EUMR. The original EUMR provided that a concentration which creates or strengthens a dominant position as a result of which effective competition would be significantly impeded in the common market or in a substantial part of it shall be declared incompatible with the common market. Article 2(3) of the current regulation states:

A concentration which would significantly impede effective competition in the common market or in a substantial part of it, in particular as a result of the creation or strengthening of a dominant position, shall be declared incompatible with the common market.

The new 'significant impediment to effective competition' (SIEC) test thus sought to meet the arguments of those in both the SLC and dominance camps. It is broader than the old test. The wording

---

[318] See Section 5.D.iii.d, pp. 1199–1208. J. Vickers, 'How to reform the EC merger test', speech at the EC/IBA merger control conference, Brussels, 9 November 2004. There was also a fear that the broadening of the concept of dominance set out in the EUMR to deal with specific problems presented in merger cases was also resulting in a broader interpretation of the concept of dominance for the purposes of Art. 102 and, consequently, curtailing the conduct of a broader category of undertakings. See also discussion of Case M.1524, *Airtours/First Choice* [2000] OJ L93/1, annulled on appeal, Case T-342/99, *Airtours v. Commission* [2002] ECR II-2585 especially in n. 433.

[319] See, e.g., submission of the DTI to the Commission's 2001 Green Paper, available on DG COMP's website. Sweden also supported a move to the SLC test.

[320] See, e.g., the submission of the Irish Competition Authorities/Industry on the Commission's 2001 Green Paper, which considered that the single most compelling argument for a switch in the test was to allow the EU agency the flexibility to examine unilateral effects mergers in an open and transparent way, rather than shrouding them under an ever-expanding concept of collective dominance. This benefit considerably outweighed the one-off cost of switching.

[321] See, e.g., the submission of the Bundeskartellamt on the Commission's 2001 Green Paper. This view was also supported by Italy, The Netherlands, and the European Parliament. Some Member States (e.g., Portugal and Denmark) favoured a retention of the dominance test, but with a clarification of how the test applied on oligopolistic markets.

[322] France and Spain had supported a dual test combining features of the SLC and dominance tests.

clearly establishes that a merger may be prohibited even if it does not create or strengthen a dominant position if a SIEC is established. By referring to the creation or strengthening of a dominant position, however, the EUMR preserves the previous decisional practice and case law of the CJ. Horizontal Merger Guidelines[323] were also adopted with the objective of clearly and comprehensively articulating the reasoning underlying the analytical approach to merger analysis.

The twin objectives, of broadening the test whilst at the same time preserving the case law on the meaning of dominance, are explained in recitals 25 and 26 of the EUMR. In particular, recital 25 makes it crystal clear that the new substantive test is designed to catch mergers that will result in non-coordinated effects on an oligopolistic market even though a position of single or collective dominance may not be established.

(25) In view of the consequences that concentrations in oligopolistic market structures may have, it is all the more necessary to maintain effective competition in such markets. Many oligopolistic markets exhibit a healthy degree of competition. However, under certain circumstances, concentrations involving the elimination of important competitive constraints that the merging parties had exerted upon each other, as well as a reduction of competitive pressure on the remaining competitors, may, even in the absence of a likelihood of coordination between the members of the oligopoly, result in a significant impediment to effective competition. The Community courts have, however, not to date expressly interpreted Regulation (EEC) No 4064/89 as requiring concentrations giving rise to such non-coordinated effects to be declared incompatible with the common market. Therefore, in the interests of legal certainty, it should be made clear that this Regulation permits effective control of all such concentrations by providing that any concentration which would significantly impede effective competition, in the common market, or in a substantial part of it, should be declared incompatible with the common market. The notion of 'significant impediment to effective competition' in Article 2(2) and (3) should be interpreted as extending, beyond the concept of dominance, only to the anti-competitive effects of a concentration resulting from the non-coordinated behaviour of undertakings which would not have a dominant position on the market concerned.

(26) A significant impediment to effective competition generally results from the creation or strengthening of a dominant position. With a view to preserving the guidance that may be drawn from past judgments of the European courts and Commission decisions pursuant to Regulation (EEC) No 4064/89, while at the same time maintaining consistency with the standards of competitive harm which have been applied by the Commission and the Community courts regarding the compatibility of a concentration with the common market, this Regulation should accordingly establish the principle that a concentration with a Community dimension which would significantly impede effective competition, in the common market or a substantial part thereof, in particular as a result of the creation or strengthening of a dominant position, is to be declared incompatible with the common market.

Article 2(1) sets out the criteria to be used in appraising whether or not the concentration is compatible with the common market. This indicates that many factors are relevant to the Commission's appraisal.

Concentrations within the scope of this Regulation shall be appraised in accordance with the objectives of this Regulation and the following provisions with a view to establishing whether or not they are compatible with the common market.

In making this appraisal, the Commission shall take into account:

(a) the need to maintain and develop effective competition within the common market in view of, among other things, the structure of all the markets concerned and the actual or potential competition from undertakings located either within or outwith the Community;

(b) the market position of the undertakings concerned and their economic and financial power, the alternatives available to suppliers and users, their access to supplies or markets, any legal or other barriers to entry, supply and demand trends for the relevant goods and services, the interests of the

---

[323] [2004] OJ C31/5, para. 5.

intermediate and ultimate consumers, and the development of technical and economic progress provided that it is to consumers' advantage and does not form an obstacle to competition.

Article 2(4) and (5) set out an additional test applying the criteria of Article 101(1) and 101(3) to the aspects of a full function joint venture that may appreciably restrict competition between undertakings that remain independent.

Section 5.D examines how the Commission applies the substantive test for assessment.

C. BURDEN AND STANDARD OF PROOF AND COUNTERFACTUAL

The burden is on the Commission to establish that the merger is either compatible or incompatible with the common market—in each case, it seems that the standard of proof is the same (there is no general presumption that the merger is either compatible or incompatible with the common market).[324] In making the determination, the merger must be assessed in the context of the position that would exist were the merger not to be completed. Thus to establish a SIEC, it is necessary to demonstrate a causal link between completion of the merger and the competitive harm.

9. In assessing the competitive effects of a merger, the Commission compares the competitive conditions that would result from the notified merger with the conditions that would have prevailed without the merger. In most cases, the competitive conditions existing at the time of the merger constitute the relevant comparison for evaluating the effects of a merger. However, in some circumstances, the Commission may take into account future changes to the market that can reasonably be predicted. It may, in particular, take account of the likely entry or exit of firms if the merger did not take place when considering what constitutes the relevant comparison.[325]

Assessing the counterfactual may thus be complex in some scenarios,[326] for example where two mergers take place close together in time in the same industry or relevant market. In this situation the Commission now seems to favour assessing the first merger without regard to the second but the second taking account of the first (giving priority to the transaction notified first).[327] It has, however, sometimes assessed both, taking into account the impact of the other on the market.[328]

It seems clear that the standard of proof is the balance of probabilities.[329] In a series of cases it has been made clear that the GC will rigorously review the Commission's decisions and, although it

---

[324]   Sec Case C-413/06 P, *Bertelsmann and Sony Corp v. Commission* [2008] ECR I-4951, paras. 46–48, Case T-87/05, *EDP v. Commission* [2005] ECR II-3745, para. 61 and Case C-12/03 P, *Commission v. Tetra Laval BV* [2005] ECR I-987. The parties, however, may need to provide evidence which may be material to the decision and, for example, to support a view that there are few barriers to entry to the market, that one of the firms is failing, or that the merger will achieve significant efficiencies, see e.g., discussion in A. Lindsay and A. Berridge, *The EC Merger Regulation: Substantive Issues* (4th edn, Sweet & Maxwell, 2012), 2.5(a) and (b).

[325]   Horizontal Merger Guidelines, para. 9. See also discussion of the failing firm defence in Section 5.D.vii. The counterfactual may be complex where the Commission has to consider two proposed mergers on a relevant market,

[326]   See also discussion of the failing firm in Section 5.D.vii, pp. 1217–1223.

[327]   See J. Almunia, SPEECH 11/561, 'Policy Objectives in Merger Control', 8 September 2011.

[328]   Compare, e.g., Cases M.2533, *BP/E.ON* and M.2389, *Shell/DEA* with Cases M.4601, *KarstadtQuelle/MyTravel* and M.4600, *TUI/First Choice* (the Commission held that it would assess the impact of these two transactions in the light of the competitive situation that prevailed at the time of the respective filings. The first filing was thus assessed independently from the second. However, any further consolidation in the tour operating business would be analysed taking into account the competitive circumstances prevailing at the time of the second filing) and see generally G. Drauz, S. Mavroghenis and S. Ashall, 'Recent Developments in EU Merger Control' [2012] *Journal of Competition Law & Practice* 52, 72–75 (setting out the view that the Commission initially favoured the combined approach—especially in coordinated effects analysis—but is now more inclined to adopt the priority rule approach).

[329]   Thus if there is appreciable uncertainty about the merger's incompatibility on the part of the Commission, it appears that the merger should be approved, Case C-12/03 P, *Commission v. Tetra Laval BV* [2005] ECR I-987, AG Tizzano, paras. 76–77. See further e.g., Cook and Kerse, *EC Merger Control* (cited in n. 79), para. 7–008 and Lindsay and Berridge, *The EC Merger Regulation: Substantive Issues* (cited in n. 324), 2.5(b).

recognises that the Commission has a margin of discretion with regard to economic matters, it will consider whether the evidence relied upon by the Commission is correct, reliable, and consistent, and is capable of substantiating the conclusions it has drawn—i.e. whether the reasoning and evidence relied upon provides a proper factual basis for the conclusions and all the information which must be taken into account in order to assess a complex situation.[330] This imposes an acute burden on the Commission which must examine how a concentration might in the future alter the factors determining the state of competition on a market in order to establish whether it would give rise to a SIEC and envisage 'various chains of cause and effect with a view to ascertaining which of them is the most likely'.[331] If the Commission does not meet the appropriate standard the GC will annul its decision (indeed, in 2002 the GC annulled three Commission decisions in a series of judgments given in close succession to one another[332]). Since then the Commission has worked hard to strengthen its decision-making processes, to improve the quality and quantity of evidence and economic analysis set out in its merger decisions, as Anne Witt notes in the following extract.[333]

5.3.3. *Burden and standards of proof*

Another central point of criticism in all three annulment judgements from 2002 was that the Commission's assessments did not meet the required stand of proof because they failed to provide convincing factual evidence in support of key assumptions. A comparison of these decisions with the Commission's decisional practice post-reform shows a dramatic improvement in the quality and quantity of evidence used by the Commission. In *Ryanair/Aer Lingus*, the Commission collated evidence to an unprecedented degree, carried out an in-depth market investigation (comprising the views of scheduled airlines, charter airlines, airports, customer, slot coordination authorities, civil aviation authorities and transport authorities) and produced several econometric studies. It used this wealth of evidence painstakingly to support its factual assumption, and published in its entirety in several annexes to the final decision.

This trend is not specific to merger review…One side effect of this commitment is that it has considerably increased the length of the Commission's prohibition decisions…

Although the complexity of the theory of competitive harm put forward does not appear to affect the standard of proof, it is an important factor which is taken into account when assessing the plausibility of the various consequences that the merger might have.[334] In *Tetra Laval BV v. Commission* the CJ stated:[335]

---

[330] But see further Chap. 13. The tight time constraints that the Commission is operating under is, however, relevant to the assessment of the appraisal conducted, see, e.g., Case T-151/05, *Nederlandse Vakbond Varkenshouders* v. *Commission* [2009] ECR II-1219 (the Commission cannot be expected to verify the accuracy to the last detail of all the information it receives in the course of Phase I proceedings).

[331] Case C-12/03 P, *Commission v. Tetra Laval* [2005] ECR I-987, para. 43 and Case C-413/06 P, *Bertelsmann and Sony Corp* v. *Commission* [2008] ECR I-4951, para. 47.

[332] See Case T-342/99, *Airtours v. Commission* [2002] ECR II-2585; Case T-310/01, *Schneider Electric SA v. Commission* [2002] ECR II-4071; and Case T-5/02, *Tetra Laval v. Commission* [2002] ECR II-4381.

[333] A. C. Witt, 'From *Airtours* to *Ryanair*: Is the more economic approach to EU merger law really about more economics?' [2012] 49 *CMLRev* 217. See also Speech by M. Monti, 'Merger Control in the European Union: A Radical Reform', 7 November 2002.

[334] C-413/06 P, *Bertelsmann and Sony Corp v. Commission* [2008] ECR I-4951, para. 51.

[335] C-12/03 P, [2005] ECR I-987.

Case T-342/99, *Airtours plc v. Commission* [2002] ECR II-2585

39. Whilst the Court recognises that the Commission has a margin of discretion with regard to economic matters that does not mean that the Community Courts must refrain from reviewing the Commission's interpretation of the information of an economic nature. Not only must the Community Courts, *inter alia*, establish whether the evidence relied on is factually accurate, reliable and consistent but also whether that evidence contains all the information which must be taken into account in order to assess a complex situation and whether it is capable of substantiating the conclusions drawn from it. Such a review is all the more necessary in the case of a prospective analysis required when examining a planned merger with conglomerate effect.

40. Thus, the [GC] was right to find…, that the Commission's analysis of a merger producing a conglomerate effect is subject to requirements similar to those defined by the Court with regard to the creation of a situation of collective dominance and that it calls for a close examination of the circumstances which are relevant for an assessment of that effect on the conditions of competition on the reference market.

41. Although the [GC] stated, in paragraph 155, that proof of anti-competitive conglomerate effects of a merger of the kind notified calls for a precise examination, supported by convincing evidence, of the circumstances which allegedly produce those effects, it by no means added a condition relating to the requisite standard of proof but merely drew attention to the essential function of evidence, which is to establish convincingly the merits of an argument or, as in the present case, of a decision on a merger.

42. A prospective analysis of the kind necessary in merger control must be carried out with great care since it does not entail the examination of past events—for which often many items of evidence are available which make it possible to understand the causes—or of current events, but rather a prediction of events which are more or less likely to occur in future if a decision prohibiting the planned concentration or laying down the conditions for it is not adopted.

43. Thus, the prospective analysis consists of an examination of how a concentration might alter the factors determining the state of competition on a given market in order to establish whether it would give rise to a serious impediment to effective competition. Such an analysis makes it necessary to envisage various chains of cause and effect with a view to ascertaining which of them are the most likely.

44. The analysis of a 'conglomerate-type' concentration is a prospective analysis in which, first, the consideration of a lengthy period of time in the future and, secondly, the leveraging necessary to give rise to a significant impediment to effective competition mean that the chains of cause and effect are dimly discernible, uncertain and difficult to establish. That being so, the quality of the evidence produced by the Commission in order to establish that it is necessary to adopt a decision declaring the concentration incompatible with the common market is particularly important, since that evidence must support the Commission's conclusion that, if such a decision were not adopted, the economic development envisaged by it would be plausible.

45. It follows from those various factors that the [GC] did not err in law when it set out the tests to be applied in the exercise of its power of judicial review or when it specified the quality of the evidence which the Commission is required to produce in order to demonstrate that the requirements of Article 2(3) of the Regulation are satisfied.

46. With respect to the particular case of judicial review exercised by the [GC] in the judgment under appeal, it is not apparent from the example given by the Commission, which relates to the growth in the use of PET packaging for sensitive products, that the [GC] exceeded the limits applicable to the review of an administrative decision by the Community Courts. Contrary to what the Commission claims, paragraph 211 of the judgment under appeal merely restates more concisely, in the form of a finding by the [GC], the admission made by the Commission at the hearing, which is summarised in paragraph 210 of the judgment, that its forecast in the contested decision with regard to the increase in the use of PET for packaging UHT milk was exaggerated. In paragraph 212 of the judgment under appeal, the [GC] gave the reasons for its finding that the evidence produced by the Commission was unfounded by stating that, of the three independent reports cited by the Commission, only the PCI report contained information on the use of PET for milk packaging. It went on, in that paragraph, to show that the evidence produced by the Commission was unconvincing by pointing out that the increase forecast in the PCI report was of little

significance and that the Commission's forecast was inconsistent with the undisputed figures on the use of HDPE contained in the other reports. In paragraph 213 of the judgment under appeal, the [GC] merely stated that the Commission's analysis was incomplete, which made it impossible to confirm its forecasts, given the differences between those forecasts and the forecasts made in the other reports.

47. Amongst the other examples given by it, the Commission challenges the [GC]'s finding, in paragraph 289 of the judgment under appeal, that 'fresh milk is not a product for which the marketing advantages offered by PET have any particular importance' and its conclusions as to the cost of PET in comparison to that of carton, which are set out in paragraphs 288 and 328 of the judgment under appeal. It should be noted that these are findings of fact, which are not subject to review by the Court in appeal proceedings. It is therefore unnecessary to give a ruling on the merits of those findings by the [GC] and it need be stated only that the [GC] was able to base those findings on various items in the contested decision.

48. It follows from these examples that the [GC] carried out its review in the manner required of it, as set out in paragraph 39 of this judgment. It explained and set out the reasons why the Commission's conclusions seemed to it to be inaccurate in that they were based on insufficient, incomplete, insignificant and inconsistent evidence.

49. In doing so, the [GC] observed the criteria to be applied in exercising the Community Courts' power of judicial review and, accordingly, complied with Article [263 TFEU].

50. Consequently, the above analyses do not show that the [GC] infringed Article 2(2) or (3) of the Regulation.

51. It follows from all of the above considerations that the first ground of appeal is unfounded.

D. A SIGNIFICANT IMPEDIMENT TO EFFECTIVE COMPETITION, IN PARTICULAR BY THE CREATION OR STRENGTHENING OF A DOMINANT POSITION

(i) General

In order to assess whether or not the merger is compatible with the common market the Commission must determine whether or not it would be a SIEC, that is whether the merger is the *cause* of the SIEC. 'The creation or the strengthening of a dominant position is a primary form of such competitive harm' and provides 'an important indication as to the standard of competitive harm that is applicable when determining whether a concentration is likely to impede effective competition to a significant degree.'[336] Decisional practice and EU case law of course clarify when mergers will lead to an SIEC. Further, the Commission has sought to clarify and explain its appraisal of when concentrations under the regulation will be a SIEC through the publication of guidance.[337] The Commission's Horizontal Merger Guidelines are, therefore, intended to provide a sound economic framework for the assessment of horizontal concentrations with a view to determining whether or not they are likely to be declared compatible with the common market. Non-Horizontal Merger Guidelines have also been published.[338] Although the Commission is bound by these guidelines (insofar as they do not depart from the TFEU or the EUMR), the guidelines describe an analytical approach to be followed and do not provide a mechanical checklist requiring application of all the mentioned factors in each and every case.[339] Rather, the Commission enjoys a degree of discretion in determining whether or not to take account of certain factors in a given case.[340]

---

[336] Horizontal Merger Guidelines [2004] OJ C31/5, paras. 1 and 4.

[337] This is provided for, EUMR, recital 28.

[338] Available on DG Comp's website. The Commission commissioned and published on its website an *ex post* review of Merger Control Decisions, prepared by LEAR.

[339] Case T-282/06, *Sun Chemical Group* v. *Commission* [2007] ECR II-2149, para. 55.

[340] Case T-282/06, *Sun Chemical Group* v. *Commission* [2007] ECR II-2149, para. 57.

(ii) Market Definition

a. The Central Role of Market Definition

[A] proper definition of the relevant market is a necessary precondition for any assessment of the effect of a concentration on competition.[341]

An economic appraisal of the impact of the merger on the competitive process in order to determine whether or not it will be a SIEC, in particular by the creation or strengthening of a dominant position, requires, as a starting point, that the relevant market be defined. The definition of the market is crucial to enable the Commission to attain meaningful information regarding the market power that the merged parties will acquire, to understand how competition operates on the market, and to make its competitive assessment. 'The main purpose of market definition is to identify in a systematic way the immediate competitive constraints facing the merged entity.'[342] It is not, therefore, 'an end in itself but a tool to identify situations where there might be competition concerns'.[343] In some Phase I clearance decisions, the Commission does not make a final determination of the relevant market, however, because the merger will not be problematic, or because it will not affect the outcome of the case,[344] whichever way the market is defined.[345]

b. The Commission's Notice on Market Definition and Previous Decisional Practice

The Commission's Notice on the definition of the relevant market[346] sets out how the Commission goes about determining the relevant market for the purposes of its merger decisions. In particular it stresses its use of the SSNIP test where possible, 'postulating a hypothetical small, non-transitory change in relative prices and evaluating the likely reaction of customers to that increase'.[347] The test has greatest utility in the application of the merger rules since the practical problem presented by the *Cellophane fallacy* does not ordinarily apply.[348] The Notice and the SSNIP test were discussed in detail in Chapter 1.

Whilst market definition must be freshly addressed in every case (market definitions may constantly change with market circumstances so a previous market definition is not binding upon the Commission),[349] there are now a significant number of Article 102[350] and merger decisions which may provide useful precedence and guidance on market definition in most spheres. In addition to being listed by case number, company name, date, and decision type, merger cases are also listed on DG Comp's website by reference to NACE code (i.e. industry sector).[351]

In many cases the parties to a merger may prefer a broad product market in which their market shares are lower. It will be much harder for the parties to persuade the Commission to clear a merger affecting a narrowly defined market in which they have, say, a 70 per cent market share than in a

---

[341] Cases C-68/94 and C-30/95, *France v. Commission, Société Commerciale des Potasses et de l'Azote (SCPA) v. Commission* [1998] ECR I-1375, para. 143.

[342] Horizontal Merger Guidelines [2004] OJ C31/5, para. 10. See also Chap. 1.

[343] M. Monti, 'Market Definition as a Cornerstone of EU Competition Policy', Speech at Workshop on Market Definition, Helsinki Fair Centre, 5 October 2001.

[344] See Case M.232, *PepsiCo/General Mills* [1992] OJ C228/6.

[345] See Case M.833, *The Coca-Cola Company/Carlsberg A/S* [1998] OJ L145/41.

[346] [1997] OJ C372/5, discussed in Chap. 1. For a comprehensive discussion of market definition in merger cases, see, e.g., Lindsay and Berridge, *The EC Merger Regulation: Substantive Issues* (cited in n. 324), Chap. 3.

[347] See Chap. 1.

[348] See Chap. 1. The Commission's practice in defining markets for the purposes of the EUMR is the inspiration behind the SSNIP test set out in the Notice.

[349] Cases T-125 and 127/97, *Coca-Cola v. Commission* [2000] ECR II-1733.

[350] In Case M.2416, *Tetra Laval/Sidel*, e.g., the market definition adopted in Case C-333/94 P, *Tetra Pak II* [1996] ECR I-5951, was followed.

[351] Nomenclature générale des Activités économiques dans les Communautés Européennes.

more broadly defined one in which they have, for example, a 30 per cent market share. On some occasions, however, a narrower product market definition may work to the parties' advantage, since this could result in a finding that there is no, or less, significant horizontal overlap in the products they produce.[352]

It will also frequently be the case that the parties will wish to argue for as wide a geographic market as possible in order to diminish their market shares. Even if, however, a more narrowly drawn geographic market will not result in horizontal overlaps the Commission may be prepared to characterise a merger between parties present on the same product market but in neighbouring geographic product markets, as having horizontal effects in consequence of their being 'potential' competitors.

A drawing of a broad 'worldwide' market is likely in the case of highly technical products involving significant R&D and large capital and manufacturing costs.[353] Further, a broad geographic market may be justified where a product is very valuable, internationally traded, and relatively cheap to transport. In *Gencor/Lonrho*,[354] for example, the Commission identified worldwide markets for various metal products, including platinum, which were traded on a global basis at publicly quoted prices and in *Aérospatiale/Alenia/de Havilland*[355] the Commission concluded that the geographic market for the commuter aircraft[356] was worldwide, excluding China and Eastern Europe. There were no tangible barriers to the importation of these aircraft into the EU and negligible costs of transportation.[357]

(iii) Competitive Assessment of Horizontal Mergers

a. Introduction and Overview

The EUMR aims to preserve effective competition on a market, and to deliver benefits to consumers in the form of low prices, high-quality products, a wide selection of goods and services, and innovation. By prohibiting mergers that will be a SIEC, the EUMR seeks to prevent mergers that would deprive customers of these benefits by significantly increasing the market power of firms.[358] 'By "increased market power" is meant the ability of one or more firms to profitably increase prices, reduce output, choice or quality of goods and services, diminish innovation, or otherwise influence the parameters of competition'.[359] Mergers between undertakings that are competitors, or potential competitors, on the same market eliminate a competitive restraint on the market, increase market concentration, and may lead to the firms' gaining or enhancing their market power. In the context of horizontal relationships, Form CO thus requires the parties to provide data in relation to affected markets where 'two or more of the parties to the concentration are engaged in business activities in the same product market and where the concentration will lead to a combined market share of 15 per cent or more'.[360]

The Commission outlines its analytical approach to the competitive assessment of a concentration with horizontal effects in its Horizontal Merger Guidelines.[361] Once it has identified the relevant market, it uses market share and concentration thresholds as a 'rule of thumb' to identify

---

[352] See, e.g., Case M.1578, *Sanitec/Sphinx* [2000] OJ L294/1.

[353] See, e.g., Case M.269, *Shell/Montecatini* [1994] OJ L332/48.

[354] Case M.619, [1997] OJ L11/30.

[355] Case M.53, [1991] OJ L334/42. See also Case M.877, *Boeing/McDonnell Douglas* [1997] OJ L336/16.

[356] The Commission relied on the evidence of customers and competitors to conclude that there was not just one market for all aircraft of between 20 and 70 seats but three separate turbo-prop commuter aircraft markets for; commuters with 20–39 seats; 40–59 seats; and 60+ seats, each of which attracted different categories of buyers.

[357] Case M.53, *Aérospatiale/Alenia/de Havilland* [1991] OJ L334/42, para. 20.

[358] This inevitably involves a comparison of the existing competitive conditions with the conditions that will exist post-merger.

[359] Horizontal Merger Guidelines [2004] OJ C31/5, para. 8.

[360] Form CO, s. 6 III.

[361] [2004] OJ C31/5, para. 5.

potentially problematic mergers.[362] It then considers the likelihood that the merger will result in anti-competitive effects on the market, through either non-coordinated or coordinated effects, in the absence of countervailing factors.[363] It then considers whether or not countervailing factors, such as buyer power, new entry, or efficiencies would counteract the potentially harmful effects identified.[364] It also considers that a concentration may be permitted where the anti-competitive effects result from the failure of a firm rather than the merger.[365]

b. Market Shares, Concentration Levels, and GUPPI

Various methods have been adopted by competition authorities to explain the principles upon which they measure market power. In 1982 the competition agencies in the US advocated use of a concentration index to make preliminary assessments of the legitimacy of a horizontal merger and the reduction in competition it will cause on a particular market. The Herfendahl–Hirschman index (the HHI) seeks to identify the concentration of a particular market by using numerical distinctions.[366] The HHI measures the concentration in a way which reflects both the concentration levels on the market generally and the degree to which larger firms are dominant in the market. It operates by adding together the squares of the market shares of each of the undertakings operating in the market.[367] The degree of concentration on the market is assessed by reference to the sum of those market shares (it thus gives greater weight proportionately to the market shares of the larger firms). The Commission's Horizontal Merger Guidelines explain that it relies on both market shares and concentration ratios to aid its *preliminary* assessment of a case. 'Market shares and concentration levels provide useful first indications of the market structure and of the competitive importance of both the merging parties and their competitors'.[368] The Commission states that where the market share of the undertakings concerned does not exceed 25 per cent the merger is not liable to impede effective competition and is presumed to be compatible with the common market. Indeed, the Commission has proposed that the simplified procedure should apply if the parties' combined market share is less than 20 per cent or if the merger leads only to a small incremental increase in market share.[369] Conversely, a market share of over 50 per cent may in itself be evidence of the existence of a dominant market position.[370]

Horizontal Merger Guidelines [2004] OJ C31/7, paras. 17–18

Market share levels

17. According to well-established case-law, very large market shares—50 per cent or more—may in themselves be evidence of the existence of a dominant position. However, smaller competitors may act

---

[362] Horizontal Merger Guidelines [2004] OJ C31/5, part III.

[363] Horizontal Merger Guidelines, part IV.

[364] Horizontal Merger Guidelines, parts V–VII.

[365] Horizontal Merger Guidelines, part VIII.

[366] The HHI has some serious limitations, see S. Bishop and M. Walker, *The Economics of EC Competition Law: Concepts, Application and Measurement* (3rd edn, Sweet & Maxwell, 2010), 3–016–3–019.

[367] 'Although it is best to include all firms in the calculation, lack of information about very small firms may not be important because such firms do not affect the HHI significantly.' Horizontal Merger Guidelines, para. 16.

[368] Horizontal Merger Guidelines, para. 14.

[369] See n. 8.

[370] Horizontal Merger Guidelines, paras. 17–18. See also later discussion of market shares and entry analysis and Case C-62/86, *AKZO Chemie BV v. Commission* [1991] ECR I-3359, para. 60 where, in the context of an Art. 102 case, the CJ reiterated that: 'very large shares are in themselves, and save in exceptional circumstances, evidence of the existence of a dominant position... That is the situation where there is a market share of 50% such as that found to exist in this case', see Chap. 6.

as a sufficient constraining influence if, for example, they have the ability and incentive to increase their supplies. A merger involving a firm whose market share will remain below 50 per cent after the merger may also raise competition concerns in view of other factors such as the strength and number of competitors, the presence of capacity constraints or the extent to which the products of the merging parties are close substitutes. The Commission has thus in several cases considered mergers resulting in firms holding market shares between 40 per cent and 50 per cent, and in some cases below 40 per cent, to lead to the creation or the strengthening of a dominant position.

18. Concentrations which, by reason of the limited market share of the undertakings concerned, are not liable to impede effective competition may be presumed to be compatible with the common market. Without prejudice to Articles 101 and 102 TFEU, an indication to this effect exists, in particular, where the market share of the undertakings concerned does not exceed 25 per cent either in the common market or in a substantial part of it.

The Commission accepts, however, that high market shares cannot necessarily be equated with market power. An adverse finding may not result, for example, where market shares are volatile,[371] or where they are met by rigorous competition from an active competitor on the market,[372] or where they will be counteracted by buyer power[373] or new entry.[374]

The Commission also looks to the overall concentration level in a market, often measured through the application of the HHI, for useful information about the competitive situation, an indication of the market structure and of the competitive importance of the merging parties and their competitors.[375] Like market shares the HHI is used as an initial indicator of the absence of competition concerns. 'However, they do not give rise to a presumption of either the existence or the absence of such concerns.'[376] The Guidelines state that the Commission is *unlikely* to identify competition concerns in a market:[377]

- with a post-merger HHI below 1,000;
- with a post-merger HHI between 1,000 and 2,000, where the change in the HHI (the delta) is below 250;
- with a post-merger HHI above 2,000, where the delta is below 150;

except where special circumstances exist, for example: one of the firms is a potential entrant or an important innovator; one of the firms is a maverick likely to disrupt coordinated conduct; one of the firms has a pre-merger market share of 50 per cent or more; cross-shareholdings exist between the market participants; or there is evidence of past coordination of facilitating practices on the market.

---

[371] In Case M.354, *American Cyanamid/Shell* [1993] OJ C273/6 the Commission considered that 'an analysis focusing on market shares alone is not particularly probative in a dynamic and R&D-intensive industry'.

[372] See, e.g., Case M.68, *Tetra Pak/Alfa Laval* [1991] OJ L290/35, 38–39; Case M.12, *Varta/Bosch* [1991] OJ L320/26 (the merged entity held 44% of the German battery market but a competitor, with only 5–10% of the market would provide strong competition on account of its reputation and resources); Case M.4, *Renault/Volvo* [1990] OJ C281/2 (Renault would acquire 54% of the French market but Mercedes, which had only 18%, had the reputation and resources to be able to exercise sufficient competitive restraint on Renault); Case M.4600, *First Choice/TUI*; Case M.4533, *SCA/P&G* (European facial tissue business) (market shares of 80–90% would not enable the merged entity to exercise market power because of vigorous competition from private labels); and Case M.4688, *Nestlé/Gerber*. However, some competitors may not provide effective competition and may be unlikely to do so in the future: Case M.190, *Nestlé/Perrier* [1992] OJ L356/1.

[373] See, e.g., Case M.1225, *Enso/Stora* [1999] OJ L254/9 and Case M.4617, *Nutreco/BASF*.

[374] Case M.42, *Alcatel/Telettra* [1991] OJ L122/48 and see Section 5.D.v.

[375] Horizontal Merger Guidelines, paras. 14–21.

[376] Horizontal Merger Guidelines, para. 21.

[377] Horizontal Merger Guidelines, paras. 19–21.

In *Sun Chemical Group* v. *Commission*[378] the GC had to consider the importance of these preliminary tools to the robustness of a Commission decision authorising a merger between Apollo and Akzo Nobel (the first and second players in the market). The appellants argued that the Commission had failed (1) to draw the right conclusions from the fact that the merger between Apollo and Akzo Nobel would result in a combined market share of 40–50 per cent (indicative of dominance) and (2) to consider concentration levels which would have indicated real concern. The GC held that the analysis of market shares did not in itself show the existence of dominance.[379] Further, that the Commission's failure to make an HHI calculation did not affect the finding on dominance (even if, as the applicants alleged, the calculation indicated that the effects of the merger exceeded the Commission's stipulated thresholds). Exceeding the HHI thresholds did not give rise to a presumption of the existence of competition concerns. On the contrary, market shares and concentration levels, whilst providing useful first indications, did not have to be assessed in every decision.

A number of competition agencies now supplement or substitute traditional analysis based on market definition, market shares, and concentration measures with other tools, such as pricing pressure indices (PPIs)—especially for mergers in differentiated product markets where the competitive effect depends more upon the closeness of competition between the merging parties than on market shares—and merger simulation,[380] based on oligopoly models.[381] 'Upward pricing pressure' seeks to measure the incentives of the merged firm to increase the price of its products post-merger and is calculated on the basis of diversion ratios and price/cost margins.[382] For example, the US Horizontal Merger Guidelines state:[383]

In some cases, where sufficient information is available, the Agencies assess the value of diverted sales, which can serve as an indicator of upward pricing pressure [UPP] on the first product resulting from the merger. Diagnosing unilateral price effects based on the value of diverted sales need not rely on market definition or the calculation of market shares and concentration. The Agencies rely much more on the value of diverted sales than on the level of the HHI for diagnosing unilateral price effects in markets with differentiated products. If the value of diverted sales is proportionately small, significant unilateral price effects are unlikely.

As, unlike UPP, this approach does not take account of efficiencies or other factors that would create downward pricing pressure, it is generally described as the 'gross upward pricing pressure index', or GUPPI. The Commission does not refer to UPP or GUPPI in its guidelines but 'apparently for the first time—made use of a gross upward pricing pressure index'[384] in *Hutchinson 3G Austria/Orange Austria*.[385]

c. Possible Non-coordinated Anti-competitive Effects

Where a merger removes important competitive constraints on the merging firms those firms may acquire greater market power. The merged entity may then be able to increase price or reduce quality, choice, or innovation irrespective of the response of its competitors.[386] Generally, such market

---

[378] Case T-282/06, [2007] ECR II-2149.

[379] Case T-282/06, [2007] ECR II-2149, paras. 133–142.

[380] See, e.g., n. 394 and accompanying text.

[381] See, e.g., OECD Roundtable on Market Definition, Discussion paper, (DAF/COMP(2012) 13) and Chap. 1.

[382] See, e.g., J. Farrell and C. Shapiro, 'Antitrust Evaluation of Horizontal Mergers: An Economic Alternative to Market Definition' (2010) 10(1) *B.E. Journal of Theoretical Economics* (Policies perspectives), Art. 9.

[383] US DOJ and FTC, Horizontal Merger Guidelines, 19 August 2010 (2010 Guidelines), 6.1.

[384] G. Drauz, P. McGeown, and B. Record, 'Recent Developments in EU Merger Control' (2013) 4(2) *JECLAP* 146, 153.

[385] Case M.6497.

[386] If other firms on the market follow, then the anti-competitive effects will be felt throughout the market. In contrast with coordinated effects cases, however, the ability of the merged entity to increase price will not be dependent upon the reaction of other undertakings in the market.

power will be acquired, and the merger will give rise to non-coordinated effects, where the merger creates or strengthens the dominant position of a single firm which, typically, acquires a larger market share than the next competitor post-merger. The Horizontal Merger Guidelines also make it clear, however, that non-coordinated effects may arise outside this classic scenario where the merger occurs on an oligopolistic market.[387]

25. Generally, a merger giving rise to such non-coordinated effects would significantly impede effective competition by creating or strengthening the dominant position of a single firm, one which, typically, would have an appreciably larger market share than the next competitor post-merger. Furthermore, mergers in oligopolistic markets involving the elimination of important competitive constraints that the merging parties previously exerted on each other together with a reduction of competitive pressure on the remaining competitors may, even where there is little likelihood of coordination between the members of the oligopoly, also result in a significant impediment to competition. The Merger Regulation clarifies that all mergers giving rise to such non-coordinated effects shall also be declared incompatible with the common market.

The Guidelines set out a non-exhaustive list of factors that the Commission considers may influence its decision as to whether significant non-coordinated anti-competitive effects are likely to result from the merger:

The Market Shares Held by the Merging Firms and the Closeness of Competition between Them

It has been seen[388] that the larger the combined market shares and the increase in market share the more likely it is that the merger will lead to a significant increase in market power.[389] The *Sun Chemical* judgment, however, provides an important reminder that market shares are just one factor in a dominance or unilateral effects assessment. Whilst being an important factor, a high market share will not constitute 'decisive proof that the merged group will hold market power'.[390] Another critical factor in non-coordinated effects cases is the closeness of competition between the merging parties.

Where products are differentiated on a market, some will be closer substitutes for each other than others. A merger between firms which produce products that are closer substitutes is more likely to produce anti-competitive consequences. The competition between firms may also be more intense the more proximately located the competitor.

S. Bishop and M. Walker, *The Economics of EC Competition Law: Concepts, Application and Measurement* (3rd edn, Sweet & Maxwell, 2010)

Mergers involving differentiated products

7.026 Potential variations in the 'closeness' of competition between competing firms that arises from product or geographical differentiation raises a number of additional complications in applying the traditional approach to assessing whether a merger gives rise to unilateral effects..., [I]t is often argued that defining the relevant market is much more problematic in industries characterized by a high degree of differentiation, But...the Hypothetical Monopolist Test is well-suited to addressing such issues.

---

[387] Horizontal Merger Guidelines, para. 25. See also the discussion of *T-Mobile/tele.ring* nn. 396–399 and accompanying text.

[388] Horizontal Merger Guidelines, paras. 27–30.

[389] See, e.g., Case M.6663, *Ryanair/Aer Lingus* (the merged entity would obtain a monopoly on 28 routes and a very high combined market share on a further 18 routes), Case M.4404, *Universal/BMG*; Case M.4523, *Travelport/Worldspan*; Case M.4381, *JCI/FIAMM*; and Case M.4734, *INEOS/Kerling*.

[390] Horizontal Merger Guidelines, para. 27. See also Case T-282/06, *Sun Chemical Group v. Commission* [2007] ECR II-2149, nn. 339 and 378 and accompanying text.

This implies that any additional complications that arise in industries with highly differentiated goods and services relate to the interpretation that can be drawn from market shares rather than the definition of the relevant market. Interpreting market shares in highly differentiated industries is rendered more difficult since the very essence of competition between differentiated products implies that consumers do not consider all products to be equally substitutable. In consequence, products do not all impose the same strength of competitive constraint on each other. Where this is the case, market shares provide a poor proxy for discriminating 'close' competitors and 'not so close' competitors.

A competitor will be said to be, loosely speaking, 'close' if following a relative price increase a significant proportion of the resulting lost sales would be gained by that competitor. The concept of 'closeness' of competition' when a merger concerns highly differentiated products can be thought of in terms of product characteristics and geographical location. For example, a premium ice cream, say, is likely to face 'closer' competition from another supplier of a premium ice cream brand than from a supplier of an own-label product. Similarly, when transportation costs are important, a supplier is likely to face 'closer' competition from suppliers located nearby than from those located far away.

The concept of 'closeness' of competition is illustrated in the following example. Suppose there are four firms, A, B, C, and D, each with sales of 100. Suppose that if A raises its price by 5 per cent, it will lose 20 per cent of its sales, which makes the price rise unprofitable. These sales would be diverted to the other three firms as shown in Table 7.2. This table shows that 15 consumers divert from A to B, three divert to C and two divert to D. In this sense, B is a closer competitor to A than either C or D; the extent to which consumers would divert from A to B is understated by B's market share. If A and B were to merge, then an increase in the post-merger price of products supplied by A would lead to the combined firm, AB, losing only five units of sales. In consequence, increasing the price of A by 5 per cent is more likely to be profitable than a merger between A and D, where the same increase in the price of products supplied by A would lead to the loss of 18 units of sale.

Table 7.2 An illustration of Unilateral Effects

Firm	Sales at current prices	Sales if A raises price 5 per cent
A	100	80
B	100	115
C	100	103
D	100	102
AB	**200**	**195**

This example illustrates that the degree to which a merger in a differentiated product market might result in a unilateral price increase depends on the relative 'closeness' of the merging firms to one another. Based on market shares alone, B, C and D all appear to be providing an equally strong competitive constraint on A. However, examination of the diversion of sales from A to these firms shows that in this hypothetical example, B provides a much stronger pre-merger competitive constraint on A than either C or D since most of A's lost sales went to B, indicating that A and B are in some sense particularly 'close' competitors.

However, it is important to understand that the concept of closeness of competition cannot be divorced entirely from an assessment of market shares. In the above example, B is said to represent a particularly close competitor because the proportion of sales lost to B exceeds that predicted by market share alone; on the basis of market shares, we would predict that six to seven units would be diverted to B whereas in reality the number of units diverted (in the hypothetical example) would be 15. Assessing whether a merger will result in a reduction in the effectiveness of competition therefore requires an assessment of whether market shares provide a good proxy for the degree of pre-merger competitive constraint or whether they understate or overstate the importance of that competitive constraint. In the case where market shares understate the competitive constraint, we can properly consider two firms to be 'close' competitors.

> When assessing closeness of competition, it is important that the source of that closeness is clearly articulated and closely examined. All too often, it is asserted that two firms are particularly close competitors without reference being made to the alleged source of that closeness. Assessing whether two firms represent particularly close competitors is an empirical question and cannot (or should not) be determined solely with reference to physical or geographical attributes of the firms concerned. For example, consider a straight road on which four petrol stations are located. On one level, it might appear intuitive that the petrol stations adjacent to one another provide 'closer' competitive constraints than no-adjacent petrol stations. But that is not necessarily the case. If all potential consumers drive past all of these four petrol stations on their way to work from home then all the petrol stations could be equally close. Similarly, the fact that two firms have more similar offerings than some other competitors cannot by itself be determinative that they represent particularly close competitors.

The Commission is thus more likely to be concerned with mergers between firms that produce products with a high degree of substitutability. In *Volvo/Scania*[391] the Commission, in assessing the effect of Volvo's acquisition of a controlling stake in Scania, was influenced by the fact that in various markets Volvo and Scania (active on the heavy trucks markets) had similar market positions and that their products were each other's closest substitutes. The loss of competition between them would significantly increase the merged entity's advantage over its competitors.[392]

In *GE/Instrumentarium*[393] the Commission was concerned about the proposed acquisition by GE Medical Equipment of a Finnish-based company, Instrumentarium, which was a leading manufacturer of hospital equipment. The merger would bring together two of the four leading players in Europe in patient monitors, markets characterised by differentiated products with competition taking place through tenders. In particular, the Commission considered that the merger would lead to the merged entity acquiring high market shares in a number of national EU markets for perioperative monitors, used by anaesthesiologists to monitor patients during operations. The Commission conducted a series of statistical analyses and relied on bidding data and win-loss analysis[394] to establish that the parties were particularly close competitors, at least on some markets, so that the merger would significantly increase their market power.[395] Analysis showed that each of the parties was likely to charge a lower price where the other took part in the bidding contest. In the end the concentration was cleared subject to a package of remedies designed to remove the horizontal overlaps in the perioperative monitoring market.

In *T-Mobile/tele.ring*[396] the Commission considered a merger between the second (T-Mobile Austria) and fourth (tele.ring) players in the Austrian mobile telephony services market. Post-merger

---

[391] Case M.1672, [2001] OJ L143/74.

[392] The scope of the market was crucial in this case, a finding as the parties alleged that the market was an EU or EEA market would have considerably diluted the parties' market shares since they did not have such a significant presence on markets outside four Nordic countries and Ireland. The Commission concluded, however, that for these five countries the relevant geographic markets were still national in scope, Case M.1672, [2001] OJ L143/74, paras. 31–70 and 107.

[393] Case M.3083.

[394] The analysis considered the closeness of competition between the merging parties by analysing the ranking of the other party in contracts won by one of them. Other mechanisms such as diversion rations, survey evidence, merger simulation, econometric techniques, shock analysis, internal documents may also be used to measure closeness of competition between the merging parties, see, e.g., Lindsay and Berridge, *The EC Merger Regulation: Substantive Issues* (cited in n. 324), 7.3 and, e.g., Case M.3765, *Amer/Salomon* and Case M.3746, *Tetra Laval/SIG Simonazzi* and Case M.3658, *Novartis/Hexal*.

[395] Case M.3083, IP/03/1193, paras. 131 ff. But contrast, e.g., M.3765, *Amer/Salomon*.

[396] Case M.3916. See also Case M.6497, *Hutchinson 3G Austria/Orange Austria* (merger that would reduce the number of players on the market for the provision of mobile telecommunication services to end consumers in Austria from four to three was cleared subject to commitments. The Commission declined to make a reference back to the Austrian authorities under Art. 9 in this case).

Mobilkom would remain the market leader so that, despite an increase in market shares, the merged entity would remain the number two player on the market. In its Phase II analysis, the Commission focused on the non-coordinated effects that would result from the merger.[397] In particular, the Commission was concerned about the removal of tele.ring from the extremely concentrated market. Although the Commission did not rely on the particular closeness of competition between the merging parties, it did consider that tele.ring had exerted significant competitive pressure on both Mobilkom and T-Mobile and that its removal from the market would significantly impede effective competition on the market. tele.ring was a relatively new entrant to the market which had quickly gained market share through vibrant competitive practices and the offering of low prices.[398] The Commission thus approved the merger only after specific remedies designed to strengthen the position of smaller players on the market were agreed.[399]

The closeness of competition between the merging parties was a critical factor in the Commission's first decision prohibiting Ryanair's hostile take-over bid for Aer Lingus.[400] This was a controversial decision, not only as it was the first merger prohibition since 2004 but also because it was the first time that the Commission has prohibited a merger between airlines.[401] The Commission defined the relevant market as point-to-point scheduled air transport services between cities (each route having its own point of origin and own point of destination). On this basis, the Commission found that the proposed transaction would lead to actual overlaps between the merging parties on 35 routes. Since then the Commission has prohibited the proposed merger between the two Greek carriers Olympic Air and Aegean Airlines[402] in 2011 and another attempt by Ryanair to take over Aer Lingus[403] in 2013.[404]

In assessing the competitive effects of the first Ryanair/Aer Lingus merger attempt, the Commission found not only that the parties would have very high combined market shares on a large number of routes as they would acquire a monopoly position on 22 of the routes and more than 60 per cent market share on 13 more routes[405] (when reviewing the merger in 2012 the Commission found these figures to have increased to 28 and 18 respectively (i.e. a total of 46 routes with very high market shares))[406] but that the merger would eliminate competition between the two closest competitors on the routes and that barriers to entry into the markets were high. Ryanair argued that it and Aer Lingus were not close competitors. On the contrary, they were very different and occupied different spaces in the markets in which they operated. In particular, Ryanair argued that it targeted customers whose alternative was not to fly with another airline but rather not to fly at all. It claimed that its

---

[397] The s. 6(1)(c) document raised concerns about both coordinated and non-coordinated effects but the former were not pursued in the final decision.

[398] The Commission described tele.ring as a 'maverick', normally an important issue in coordinated (not non-coordinated) effects cases, see Section 5.D.iii.d and Horizontal Merger Guidelines, para. 42.

[399] The merging parties agreed to divest UMTS frequencies and mobile telephony sites off to smaller players, such as Hutchison 3G. These commitments were designed to enable Hutchison 3G to expand its Austrian network without being dependent on its current national roaming agreement with Mobilkom.

[400] Case M.4439, *Ryanair/Aer Lingus*, Case T-342/07, *Ryanair v. Commission* [2010] ECR II-3457, Case T-411/07, *Aer Lingus v. Commission* [2010] ECR II-3457 (both appeals were dismissed), Case M.6663, *Ryanair/Aer Lingus*, and see C. Witt, 'From *Airtours* to *Ryanair*: Is the more economic approach to EU merger law really about more economics?' (2012) 49 *CMLRev* 217.

[401] See IP/07/893. Contrast, e.g., Case M.1328, *KLM/Martinair*, Case M.5335, *Lufthansa/SN Airholding (Brussels Airline)*, and Case M.5747, *Iberia/British Airways*.

[402] Case M.5830, on appeal, Case T-202/11 *Aeroporia Aigaiou Aeroporiki v. Commission* (pending).

[403] M.6663 (Ryanair withdrew its second attempt to take over Aer Lingus (Case M.5434) in January 2009).

[404] For a review of a number of mergers in the airlines, including a number that have been cleared under the EUMR see, e.g., G. Drauz, T. Chellingsworth, and H. Hyrkas, 'Recent Developments in EC Merger Control' [2010] *Journal of Competition Law & Practice* 12, 14–17. See also Case M.6447 *IAG/bmi* (cleared subject to commitments to give up airport slots).

[405] Case M.4439, *Ryanair/Aer Lingus*, para. 342.

[406] See IP/13/167.

low cost base was such that no other airline was capable of targeting these passengers. Accordingly, Ryanair was not constrained in its pricing by other airlines but rather by the price sensitivity of its passengers.[407] Ryanair also sought to distinguish its service from that offered by Aer Lingus, arguing that Aer Lingus was a 'mid-frills' operator offering seat allocation and flying to more centrally located airports,[408] whilst Ryanair was a 'no-frills' operator. The Commission did not find these arguments supported by its in-depth analysis and its decision was upheld by the GC. Rather, it found evidence to establish that Aer Lingus, although a former national flag carrier, had adjusted its business model to become increasingly similar to Ryanair[409] and that Aer Lingus sought to compete with the no-frills airlines rather than to differentiate itself in terms of quality.[410] In addition, both airlines flew point-to-point,[411] i.e. directly between individual airports, rather than on a hub-and-spoke model where traffic flows through a central hub.[412] Both operated out of, and were based at, Dublin airport[413] and had a combined share of about 80 per cent of all scheduled European traffic to and from Dublin.

The Commission also found evidence establishing that each party closely monitored the other's marketing campaigns and price changes and reacted to these changes. The parties constrained each other's behaviour in relation to both price and other parameters of competition (e.g. frequencies, capacity load factors, expansion of networks, advertising, and pricing of ancillary services).[414] In analysing the closeness of competition, the Commission undertook a price regression analysis, together with a specifically designed passenger survey.[415] The Commission found that the analyses established that Ryanair did constrain Aer Lingus's prices generally in a way that other carriers did not, and that customers did consider Aer Lingus or Ryanair to be closer substitutes for one another than from other carriers.[416] The Commission thus found the parties to be each other's closest actual competitor on the overlapping routes out of Ireland[417] and concluded that the merger would eliminate competition on these routes and give the merged entity significantly increased market power. The Commission's analysis predicted that, post-merger, both carriers would have an incentive to set higher fares (or reduce the number of flights) for Aer Lingus since most customers lost as a result

---

[407]   Case M.4439, *Ryanair/Aer Lingus* paras. 52, 53, 432, and 433.

[408]   Case M.4439, *Ryanair/Aer Lingus*, para. 353.

[409]   The Commission noted that there was a range of airlines offering different levels of service so that, at one end of the spectrum, would be 'full-service' airlines offering, e.g., seat reservation, online check-in, last-minute bookings, customer loyalty schemes, free baggage handling, business lounges, free drinks and food on board, etc. and at the other end of the spectrum, would be the 'no-frills' airlines offering a rudimentary level of service encompassing few, if any, of the above, Case M.4439, *Ryanair/Aer Lingus*, para. 49.

[410]   e.g., Aer Lingus had adopted its marketing slogan ('Low Fares—Way Better'). This slogan appeared to constitute a direct response to Ryanair's slogan: 'The Low Fares Airline', Case M.4439, *Ryanair/Aer Lingus*, para. 367, Case T-342/07, [2010] ECR II-3457, paras. 92–93.

[411]   Case M.4439, *Ryanair/Aer Lingus*, paras. 47–48.

[412]   In contrast to previous airline cases decided by the Commission which involved network carriers operating at different airports in different countries, see, e.g., *Lufthansa/Eurowings*, Case M.3940, *Lufthansa/Swiss*; Case M.3280, *Air France/KLM*; Case M.3280, *aff'd* Case T-177/04; and *easyJet v. Commission* [2006] ECR II-1913.

[413]   The base airport is the airport where they concentrate their operations and the point from where a majority of their flights begin and end. It is also the place of: overnighting aircraft; maintenance, customer care and ground-handling services; stand-by planes; and where staff are based. Both airlines based a large number of planes at Dublin, had best brand recognition there, and could react easily and quickly to changes in supply and demand on routes out of that base, paras. 404–407, Case T-342/07, paras. 124–125.

[414]   Case M.4439, para. 434 ff.

[415]   A price regression analysis is a specific tool for understanding the relationship between two or more variables, see e.g., M. de la Mano, E. Pesaresi, and O. Stehman, *Econometric and survey evidence in the competitive assessment of the Ryanair-Aer Lingus merger*, Competition Policy Newsletter, No. 3 (2007).

[416]   Case M.4439, paras. 79–80. *See also* Case M.4842, *Danone/Numico*.

[417]   Case M.4439, para 431.

would be captured by Ryanair. Further, the merger would take away incentives for the airlines to increase quality and to innovate.[418]

In 2012 the Commission also blocked a merger between *Deutsche Börse/NYSE Euronext*[419] which would have led to parties acquiring extremely high market shares in a number of financial derivatives markets.

The Ability of Customers to Switch

Customers unable to switch, for example because of the limited availability of alternative suppliers or because of significant switching costs, are particularly vulnerable to price rises.[420] In *Votorantim/Fischer*,[421] however, the Commission cleared a concentration between two global orange juice producers in circumstances in which a number of other suppliers existed on the market and customers could easily switch between them. The Commission thus concluded that any attempt by the merging parties to raise prices would be counteracted.

The Likelihood that Competitors will Increase Supply

If competitors cannot increase capacity[422] then it may be easier for the merging firms to restrict output themselves and to benefit from price rises.[423] The ability of competitors to increase capacity in response to such a decision might be limited by capacity constraints, the cost of increasing capacity, or 'barriers to expansion'.[424] Alternatively, the merging firms may themselves have the ability to hinder expansion by competitors,[425] for example as a result of controlling or influencing the supply of essential inputs, access to distribution channels, and access to intellectual property rights, or by giving the merged entity the ability and incentive to raise costs or decrease the quality of service to rivals in markets where interoperability between different infrastructures or platforms is important (e.g., in energy, telecommunications, and communications industries).[426]

In *MCI Worldcom/Sprint*,[427] for example, the Commission prohibited a proposed merger of two global communications companies, MCI Worldcom Inc. and Sprint Corporation. The Commission considered that the combination of the merged firms' extensive networks and customer base would lead to such a powerful force that both competitors and customers would have been dependent upon them to obtain universal internet connectivity. In particular, it would create a 'super-tier provider of global internet connectivity. It will have an inherent strong position due to its absolute and relative size compared to its competitors. Given the size of the merged entity, it will be able to control the prices of its competitors and customers. It will also be in a position to control technical developments. The combined entity will be able to sustain such behaviour due to its capacity to discipline the market notably through the threat of selective degradation of its competitors internet connectivity offering…and also through its essential ability to determine and agree any new technical

---

[418] Case M.4439, para 491. The Commission was also concerned about the impact the merger would have on potential competition. As the airlines were the main carriers operating on routes to/from Dublin, the merger would eliminate the most likely entrant on routes out of that airport currently served by only one of them.

[419] Case M.6166.

[420] Horizontal Merger Guidelines, para. 31 and see, e.g., Case M.4381, *JCI/FIAMM*.

[421] Case M.5907.

[422] Horizontal Merger Guidelines, paras. 32–35.

[423] See, e.g., Case M.3637; *Total/Sasol/JV*, Case M.4525; *Kronospan/Constantia*; and Case M.6101 *UPM.Myllykoski/Rhein Paper*.

[424] The inability of competitors to expand capacity is most likely to be problematic where products are homogenous, but it may also be important when suppliers produce differentiated products, Horizontal Merger Guidelines, para. 35.

[425] Horizontal Merger Guidelines, para. 36.

[426] The fact that such behaviour might constitute an abuse of a dominant position is one factor that must be taken into account, see nn. 563–568 and following text.

[427] Case M.1741, annulled, Case T-310/00, *MCI v. Commission* [2004] ECR II-3253.

development to enable advance internet services...'.[428] In *GE/Instrumentarium*[429] the Commission also feared that the parties would be able to foreclose other preoperative monitor suppliers from the market by making its anaesthesia machines incompatible with rival monitors. This would, of course, have made it difficult for the competitors to respond to an increase in price by increasing capacity.

The Competitive Force Eliminated by the Merger

The merger is more likely to cause concern where the merger is with a firm that is likely to change the competitive dynamics of a market more than its market share suggests, e.g., if the merger involves a new entrant or an important innovator in the market (for example, where two companies have new competing products in the pipeline).[430]

In *Boeing/McDonnell Douglas*[431] the Commission was concerned that the merger would strengthen Boeing's already dominant position in the markets for large commercial aircraft and for narrow-body and wide-body aircraft. Although McDonnell Douglas's market share had been declining, responses from airlines indicated that its competitive influence had been greater than that reflected in its market share. Its participation in the competitive process and influence on competition was of significant importance leading, it appeared, to a reduction of over seven per cent in the realised price. In the end the Commission cleared the merger subject to the parties complying with specified commitments. In *Danone/Numico*[432] the Commission was concerned about a merger between two major players on the French, Belgian, and Netherlands markets for baby milk, meals, snacks, cereals, and drinks. The merger would have resulted in the entity acquiring high market shares on many markets. In the French infant milk market, for example, the parties were close competitors and owned a high number of must-have brands. Numico had played an important role in making the market competitive, keeping prices down, and introducing innovative products. The Commission considered that the merger would lead to the removal of a strong competitive constraint on prices and would significantly impede effective competition. In the end the merger was cleared at the end of Phase I, subject to a commitment to divest the Numico baby milk business in France and a package of other remedies.

d. Possible Coordinated Anti-competitive Effects—Collective or Joint Dominance

The Horizontal Merger Guidelines deal separately with the problem of 'coordinated effects' or 'collective dominance'.

Horizontal Merger Guidelines

39. In some markets the structure may be such that firms would consider it possible, economically rational, and hence preferable, to adopt on a sustainable basis a course of action on the market aimed at selling at increased prices. A merger in a concentrated market may significantly impede effective competition, through the creation or the strengthening of a collective dominant position, because it increases the likelihood that firms are able to coordinate their behaviour in this way and raise prices, even without entering into an agreement or resorting to a concerted practice within the meaning of Article [101] TFEU. A merger may also make coordination easier, more stable or more effective for firms, that were already coordinating before the merger, either by making the coordination more robust or by permitting firms to coordinate on even higher prices.

---

[428] *MCI Worldcom/Sprint*, Case M.1741, para. 146.

[429] Case M.3083, IP/03/1193.

[430] Horizontal Merger Guidelines, paras. 37–38.

[431] Case M. 877, [1997] OJ L336/16.

[432] Case M.4842. See also Case M.4746, *Deutsche Bahn/EWS*.

40. Coordination may take various forms. In some markets, the most likely coordination may involve keeping prices above the competitive level. In other markets, coordination may aim at limiting production or the amount of new capacity brought to the market. Firms may also coordinate by dividing the market, for instance by geographic area or other customer characteristics, or by allocating contracts in bidding markets.

The Commission thus examines mergers to determine whether or not they will make coordination more likely to emerge in markets through the creation or strengthening of a collectively held dominant position. The Guidelines state that coordination is more likely to emerge in markets where it is relatively simple for the firms to reach a common understanding on terms of coordination and:

- the coordinating firms are able to monitor whether the terms of coordination are being adhered to;
- there is some form of credible deterrent mechanism to ensure discipline; and
- the reaction of outsiders, customers or competitors will not jeopardise the results expected from the coordination.[433]

These conditions derive from case law developed under the old EUMR on the meaning of a collective dominant position, and in particular the GC's judgment in *Airtours*.

Background and the Position under the Old EUMR

It was seen in Chapter 9 that tacit collusion is not prohibited by Article 101 and that Article 102 provides less than an ideal tool for controlling such behaviour. Given this lacuna, it was critical that the EUMR should be applicable to *prevent* mergers that might lead to collusion on a market. A system of merger control which did not allow it to prevent concentration, or the further concentration of an industry, would be seriously flawed.[434] The old EUMR only allowed the Commission to prohibit mergers leading to the creation or strengthening of a dominant position. A question which arose therefore was whether the concept of dominance could be interpreted in the same way as under Article 102 (see *Flat Glass*)[435] to prevent mergers which would lead to the creation or strengthening of a dominant position held collectively by two or more independent entities united together by 'economic links'.[436] Even though the old EUMR provided *no* textual support for such an approach,[437] the Commission took the view that it did.[438] It recognised the difficulties of proof that would be involved, but proceeded as a matter of expediency. In a series of judgments the EU courts affirmed the Commission's interpretation confirming in *France* v. *Commission*[439] that the EUMR did indeed apply to

---

[433] Horizontal Merger Guidelines, para. 41.

[434] See Commission's *XV1th Report on Competition Policy* (Commission, 1986), 285.

[435] Cases T-68, 77–78/89, *Società Italiana Vetro (SIV)* v. *Commission* [1992] ECR II-1403.

[436] See Chap. 9.

[437] Although Art. 102 refers to a dominant position held by 'one or more' undertakings, the old EUMR simply referred to concentrations which lead to the creation or strengthening of *a* dominant position. If it was intended that the Regulation should apply to prevent the creation or strengthening of a collective dominant position why was this not spelt out in the legislation? See the arguments raised in Case T-102/96, *Gencor Ltd* v. *Commission* [1999] ECR II-753, report for the hearing, paras. 110–127 and D. Ridyard, 'Economic Analysis of Single Firm and Oligopolistic Dominance' [1994] *ECLR* 255, 258.

[438] It introduced the concept in Case M.165, *Alcatel/AEG Kabel* [1992] OJ C6/23 but nonetheless cleared the merger. In *Nestlé/Perrier* [1992] OJ L356/1 the Commission first took commitments as a condition for clearing a concentration (between Nestlé and Perrier) which it considered would 'create a duopolistic dominant position which would significantly impede [the] effective competition position on the French bottled water market'.

[439] Cases C-68/94 and C-30/95, *France* v. *Commission, Société Commerciale des Potasses et de l'Azote (SCPA)* v. *Commission* [1998] ECR I-1375.

mergers which would create or strengthen a collective dominant position. In *Gencor v. Commission*,[440] *Airtours plc v. Commission*,[441] and in the *Sony/BMG* appeals[442] the courts also clarified that a collective dominant position could be held by members of a 'tight oligopoly'.

The CJ's judgment in *France v. Commission*[443] arose from an appeal against the Commission's clearance decision in *Kali und Salz/MdK/Treuhand*.[444] In this case the Commission had found that the concentration created or led to the creation of a market-leading duopoly on the EU (except Germany) market for potash. Two entities would enjoy a dominant position: Kali und Salz (K+S)/MdK (the merging parties) and Société Commerciale des Potasses et de l'Azote (SCPA). To prevent the Commission from declaring the concentration to be incompatible with the common market, the parties offered the Commission commitments which affected not only themselves, but also SCPA. Their aim was broadly to bring to an end the cooperation between K+S/MdK and SCPA.[445] Partly as a result of this, the affected third party (SCPA), EMC (its parent company), and France brought actions for annulment, or partial annulment, of the Commission's decision under Article 263 TFEU. On appeal, the CJ annulled the Commission's decision, finding that the Commission had not established that the concentration would in fact give rise to a collective dominant position on the market.[446] Nonetheless, the judgment was of enormous significance since the CJ held, applying an interpretation of the regulation in accordance with 'its purpose and general structure', that 'collective dominant positions do not fall outside the scope of the Regulation'.[447] The Court thus considered that a textual and historical examination of the regulation was not conclusive.[448] Rather, since the regulation was intended to apply to all concentrations insofar as they were likely to prove incompatible with the system of undistorted competition envisaged by the Treaty, it was essential that concentrations which created or strengthened a dominant position on the part of parties concerned with an entity not involved in the concentration be prohibited by the regulation.[449] Conversely, a narrow interpretation of the regulation would have meant that competition in the common market could be distorted and that the regulation would be deprived of much of its effect.

Like that in *Flat Glass*[450] this judgment did not clarify whether or not the merger provisions would apply to the creation of oligopolistic dominance in the absence of links, such as contractual links, between the members of the oligopoly. Although the Court stressed that the key to collective dominance was the parties' ability to adopt a common policy on the market and to act independently of their competitors, customers, and consumers, the Court did not expressly state what the position would have been had no contractual or other links between the parties existed.

---

[440] Case T-102/96, *Gencor Ltd v. Commission* [1999] ECR II-753.

[441] Case T-342/99 [2002] ECR II-2585.

[442] Case T-464/04 [2006] ECR II-2289, Case C-413/06 P, *Bertelsmann and Sony Corp v. Commission* [2008] ECR I-4951.

[443] Cases C-68/94 and C-30/95, *France v. Commission, Société Commerciale des Potasses et de l'Azote (SCPA) v. Commission* [1998] ECR I-1375.

[444] Case M.308, [1994] OJ L186/30; on appeal Cases C-68/94 and C-30/95, *France v. Commission, Société Commerciale des Potasses et de l'Azote (SCPA) v. Commission* [1998] ECR I-1375.

[445] e.g., the parties agreed to withdraw from an export company in which SCPA was a shareholder and to terminate cooperation with SCPA as a distribution partner in France.

[446] This was the first case in which the CJ annulled a Commission decision under the EUMR. Following the annulment, the Commission re-examined the concentration and cleared it in Phase I proceedings: see N. Hacker, 'The Kali+Salz Case—the Re-examination of a Merger after an Annulment by the Court' (1998) 3 *Competition Policy Newsletter* 46 (Commission).

[447] Cases C-68/94 and C-30/95, *France v. Commission, Société Commerciale des Potasses et de l'Azote (SCPA) v. Commission* [1998] ECR I-1375, para. 178.

[448] Cases C-68/94 and C-30/95, *France v. Commission, Société Commerciale des Potasses et de l'Azote (SCPA) v. Commission* [1998] ECR I-1375, paras. 165–167. See also especially paras. 171–178.

[449] Cases C-68/94 and C-30/95, *France v. Commission, Société Commerciale des Potasses et de l'Azote (SCPA) v. Commission* [1998] ECR I-1375, paras. 168–170.

[450] Cases T-68, 77–8/89, *Società Italiana Vetro (SIV) v. Commission* [1992] ECR II-1403.

The GC's judgment in *Gencor Ltd* v. *Commission*,[451] however, shed further light on this point. This case concerned a decision by two companies, Gencor Ltd (a South African company) and Lonrho Plc (a UK company), to merge their business activities in the platinum group metal (PGM) sector. Although the platinum businesses were both based in South Africa (and the South African Competition Board did not consider that the operation gave rise to competition policy concerns under South African law) the Commission nevertheless issued a decision prohibiting the merger. It considered that the merger would create a duopoly between the merged entity and Anglo American Corporation of South Africa Ltd (AAC), which, through its associated company, Amplats, was the remaining competitor on the market. Further, the anti-competitive effects of that duopoly would be felt on the relevant markets within the EU and EEA.[452] In this case no contractual or other structural links existed between the parties.

The applicant sought annulment of the Commission's decision. After reiterating that 'collective dominant positions do not fall outside the scope of the Regulation' the Court rejected the applicant's claim that, in order that a finding of collective dominance be made, formal 'structural' links had to exist between the undertakings involved.

Case T-102/96, *Gencor Limited v. Commission* [1999] ECR II-753

GC

273. In its judgment in the *Flat Glass* case, the Court referred to links of a structural nature only by way of example and did not lay down that such links must exist in order for a finding of collective dominance to be made.

274. It merely stated…that there is nothing, in principle to prevent two or more independent economic entities from being united by economic links in a specific market and, by virtue of that fact, from together holding a dominant position *vis-à-vis* the other operators on the same market.

…

276. Furthermore, there is no reason whatsoever in legal or economic terms to exclude from the notion of economic links the relationship of interdependence existing between the parties to a tight oligopoly within which, in a market with the appropriate characteristics, in particular in terms of market concentration, transparency and product homogeneity, those parties are in a position to anticipate one another's behaviour and are therefore strongly encouraged to align their conduct in the market, in particular in such a way as to maximise their joint profits by restricting production with a view to increasing prices. In such a context, each trader is aware that highly competitive action on its part designed to increase its market share (for example a price cut) would provoke identical action by the others, so that it would derive no benefit from its initiative. All the traders would thus be affected by the reduction in price levels.

277. That conclusion is all the more pertinent with regard to the control of concentrations, whose objective is to prevent anti-competitive market structures from arising or being strengthened. Those structures may result from the existence of economic links in the strict sense argued by the applicant or from market structures of an oligopolistic kind where each undertaking may become aware of common interests and, in particular, cause prices to increase without having to enter into an agreement or resort to a concerted practice.

278. In the [present] case, therefore, the applicant's ground of challenge alleging that the Commission failed to establish the existence of structural links is misplaced.

279. The Commission was entitled to conclude, relying on the envisaged alteration in the structure of the market and on the similarity of the costs of Amplats and [Implats/LPD], that the proposed transaction would create a collective dominant position and lead in actual fact to a duopoly constituted by those two undertakings.

---

[451] Case T-102/96, *Gencor Ltd* v. *Commission* [1999] ECR II-753.
[452] See Section 8, pp. 1254–1256 and Chap. 16.

The case is illuminating. By referring to *Flat Glass*[453] when considering the links required between undertakings before a finding of collective dominance can be made, the Court clearly envisages that collective dominance has the same meaning for the purposes of both Article 102 and the EUMR.[454]

In addition, the Court establishes that the contractual links given as examples of economic links in *Flat Glass* are not necessary to support a finding of collective dominance. Although the Court does not fully explain the difference between the 'structural' and 'economic links' it refers to in its judgment it is clear that the market structure itself (the relationship of interdependence existing between parties to a tight oligopoly) suffices to establish the economic links required for a finding of collective dominance.

The next opportunity for the GC to rule on this issue followed the Commission's decision in *Airtours/First Choice*.[455] Here the Commission adopted a controversial decision prohibiting the acquisition by Airtours of First Choice.[456] The Commission held that the concentration would lead to the creation or strengthening of a collective dominant position on the UK short-haul foreign package holiday (the FPH) market. The dominant position would be held by Airtours/First Choice (32 per cent), Thomson (27 per cent), and Thomas Cook (20 per cent). The remainder of the market was highly fragmented, and this meant that no effective restraint on the competitive conduct of the larger players would be exercised.

In reaching its decision the Commission appeared to expand the concept of collective dominance and to find its existence in circumstances beyond those which had been identified with collectively dominant positions. The Commission held at paragraph 54 of its decision that it was not necessarily essential to show that the parties would adopt a common policy on the market. Rather, it appeared to take the view that the ability to engage in explicit or tacit coordination is not essential. It was sufficient that each individual undertaking operating on the oligopolistic market had sufficient market power on that market to enable it to act independently.[457] Nonetheless the Commission did consider that tacit coordination between the parties would occur. That tacit coordination would, however, not occur in relation to price but in relation to output or capacity on the market.

On appeal the GC annulled the Commission's decision in a judgment that was highly critical of the Commission's economic reasoning. It held that the Commission's analysis had not been based on cogent evidence and that the decision was vitiated by a series of errors of assessment as to factors fundamental to any assessment of whether a collective dominant position might be created. Building upon the judgments in *France* v. *Commission and Gencor* v. *Commission* it set out the conditions necessary for a finding of a collective dominant position.

Case T-342/99, *Airtours plc v. Commission* [2002] ECR II-2585

62. As the applicant has argued and as the Commission has accepted in its pleadings, three conditions are necessary for a finding of collective dominance as defined:

— first, each member of the dominant oligopoly must have the ability to know how the other members are behaving in order to monitor whether or not they are adopting the common policy. As the Commission specifically acknowledges, it is not enough for each member of the dominant oligopoly to be aware that interdependent market conduct is profitable for all of them but each member must also have a means of knowing whether the other operators are adopting the same

---

[453] Cases T-68, 77–78/89, *Società Italiana Vetro (SIV)* v. *Commission* [1992] ECR II-1403.

[454] See Chaps. 6 and 9. See also Case T-228/97, *Irish Sugar plc* v. *Commission* [1999] ECR II-2969, para. 46.

[455] Case M.1524, *Airtours/First Choice* [2000] OJ L93/1, annulled, Case T-342/99, *Airtours* v. *Commission* [2002] ECR II-2585.

[456] See proceedings by My Travel discussed in Section 7, p. 1254.

[457] Arguably, therefore, this was a classic 'gap' case, see Section 5.B, pp. 1182–1184.

strategy and whether they are maintaining it. There must, therefore, be sufficient market transparency for all members of the dominant oligopoly to be aware, sufficiently precisely and quickly, of the way in which the other members' market conduct is evolving;

— second, the situation of tacit coordination must be sustainable over time, that is to say, there must be an incentive not to depart from the common policy on the market. As the Commission observes, it is only if all the members of the dominant oligopoly maintain the parallel conduct that all can benefit. The notion of retaliation in respect of conduct deviating from the common policy is thus inherent in this condition. In this instance, the parties concur that, for a situation of collective dominance to be viable, there must be adequate deterrents to ensure that there is a long-term incentive in not departing from the common policy, which means that each member of the dominant oligopoly must be aware that highly competitive action on its part designed to increase its market share would provoke identical action by the others, so that it would derive no benefit from its initiative (see, to that effect, *Gencor v. Commission*, paragraph 276);

— third, to prove the existence of a collective dominant position to the requisite legal standard, the Commission must also establish that the foreseeable reaction of current and future competitors, as well as of consumers, would not jeopardise the results expected from the common policy.

The GC thus requires proof of three criteria in collective dominance cases:

- Sufficient market transparency to enable each member of the dominant oligopoly to know how the other members are behaving and to monitor whether or not they are adopting a common policy;

- The ability to sustain the situation of tacit coordination over time, i.e. the existence of deterrents to ensure that there is a long-term incentive not to depart from the common policy; and

- The common policies must not be at risk from the foreseeable reaction of competitors or consumers.

These three requirements were reiterated by the GC in *Independent Music Publishers and Labels Association (Impala) v. Commission*.[458] On appeal to the CJ however, the Court had to determine whether or not the GC had misconstrued the legal criteria applicable. Although it held that it had not, it expressed the collective dominance test in slightly different terms.

Case C-413/06 *P Bertelsmann and Sony Corp v. Commission* [2008] ECR I-4951

120 In the case of an alleged creation or strengthening of a collective dominant position, the Commission is obliged to assess, using a prospective analysis of the reference market, whether the concentration which has been referred to it will lead to a situation in which effective competition in the relevant market is significantly impeded by the undertakings which are parties to the concentration and one or more other undertakings which together, in particular because of correlative factors which exist between them, are able to adopt a common policy on the market (see *Kali & Salz*, paragraph 221) in order to profit from a situation of collective economic strength, without actual or potential competitors, let alone customers or consumers, being able to react effectively.

121 Such correlative factors include, in particular, the relationship of interdependence existing between the parties to a tight oligopoly within which, on a market with the appropriate characteristics, in particular in terms of market concentration, transparency and product homogeneity, those parties are in a position to

---

[458] Case T-464/04, [2006] ECR II-2289, para. 254.

anticipate one another's behaviour and are therefore strongly encouraged to align their conduct on the market in such a way as to maximise their joint profits by increasing prices, reducing output, the choice or quality of goods and services, diminishing innovation or otherwise influencing parameters of competition. In such a context, each operator is aware that highly competitive action on its part would provoke a reaction on the part of the others, so that it would derive no benefit from its initiative.

122 A collective dominant position significantly impeding effective competition in the common market or a substantial part of it may thus arise as the result of a concentration where, in view of the actual characteristics of the relevant market and of the alteration to those characteristics that the concentration would entail, the latter would make each member of the oligopoly in question, as it becomes aware of common interests, consider it possible, economically rational, and hence preferable, to adopt on a lasting basis a common policy on the market with the aim of selling at above competitive prices, without having to enter into an agreement or resort to a concerted practice within the meaning of Article [101] and without any actual or potential competitors, let alone customers or consumers, being able to react effectively.

123 Such tacit coordination is more likely to emerge if competitors can easily arrive at a common perception as to how the coordination should work, and, in particular, of the parameters that lend themselves to being a focal point of the proposed coordination. Unless they can form a shared tacit understanding of the terms of the coordination, competitors might resort to practices that are prohibited by Article [101] in order to be able to adopt a common policy on the market. Moreover, having regard to the temptation which may exist for each participant in a tacit coordination to depart from it in order to increase its short-term profit, it is necessary to determine whether such coordination is sustainable. In that regard, the coordinating undertakings must be able to monitor to a sufficient degree whether the terms of the coordination are being adhered to. There must therefore be sufficient market transparency for each undertaking concerned to be aware, sufficiently precisely and quickly, of the way in which the market conduct of each of the other participants in the coordination is evolving. Furthermore, discipline requires that there be some form of credible deterrent mechanism that can come into play if deviation is detected. In addition, the reactions of outsiders, such as current or future competitors, and also the reactions of customers, should not be such as to jeopardise the results expected from the coordination.

124. The conditions laid down by the [GC] in paragraph 62 of its judgment in *Airtours v Commission*, which that court concluded, in paragraph 254 of the judgment under appeal, should be applied in the dispute before it, are not incompatible with the criteria set out in the preceding paragraph of this judgment.

125. In applying those criteria, it is necessary to avoid a mechanical approach involving the separate verification of each of those criteria taken in isolation, while taking no account of the overall economic mechanism of a hypothetical tacit coordination.

126. In that regard, the assessment of, for example, the transparency of a particular market should not be undertaken in an isolated and abstract manner, but should be carried out using the mechanism of a hypothetical tacit coordination as a basis. It is only if such a hypothesis is taken into account that it is possible to ascertain whether any elements of transparency that may exist on a market are, in fact, capable of facilitating the reaching of a common understanding on the terms of coordination and/or of allowing the competitors concerned to monitor sufficiently whether the terms of such a common policy are being adhered to. In that last respect, it is necessary, in order to analyse the sustainability of a purported tacit coordination, to take into account the monitoring mechanisms that may be available to the participants in the alleged tacit coordination in order to ascertain whether, as a result of those mechanisms, they are in a position to be aware, sufficiently precisely and quickly, of the way in which the market conduct of each of the other participants in that coordination is evolving.

The wording used by the CJ in this case is therefore not identical to the wording used in *Airtours* (on which the Commission relies in its Horizontal Merger Guidelines), but it is similar and not inconsistent with it. Both formulations accord with the economists' views of the conditions required for coordinated effects (i.e. the ability of firms to reach a tacit understanding as to which parameters of competition they will moderate, the ability of firms to sustain any tacit understanding (monitoring adherence to and deviations from the tacit understanding and punishing deviations) and immunity from destabilising reactions from firms outside the coordinating group)[459] but the CJ stresses that too mechanical an approach should not be adopted and a more rounded approach to the theory of harm should be taken.

Establishing Coordinated Effects or the Existence of a Collective Dominant Position

The Commission has an onerous burden to discharge to establish that a collective dominant position has been created or strengthened and that coordinated effects on a market will significantly impede effective competition. In both *France v. Commission*[460] and *Airtours plc v. Commission*[461] the CJ and GC respectively annulled the Commission's decision on the ground that this burden had not been discharged. In *France v. Commission*[462] the CJ held that the Commission had not shown to the necessary legal standard that the concentration would give rise to a collective dominant position which was liable to impede significantly effective competition in the relevant market. In particular, a market share of 60 per cent (which would be held by K+S/MdK and SCPA after the concentration, they had 23 per cent and 37 per cent shares respectively) did not of itself point conclusively to the existence of a collective dominant position on the part of the undertakings. Further, the structural links between K+S and SCPA were not in fact as tight or as binding as the Commission had sought to make out, and the Commission had not succeeded in showing that there was no effective competitive counterweight to the grouping allegedly formed by K+S/MdK and SCPA. Similarly, it has been seen that the GC in *Airtours plc v. Commission*[463] held that the Commission had not presented cogent evidence in support of its analysis and conclusion.

These cases make it clear that a finding by the Commission of collective dominance or coordinated effects will have to be rigorously supported by evidence other than that relating to market shares. Thus, where no coordination of behaviour is likely the Commission has been prepared to clear mergers, even where the number of players on the market will reduce from four to three[464] or from three to two.[465] In *Gencor/Lonrho* the Commission carefully set out the factors supporting its finding that a collective dominant position would be created on the platinum market. For example, it stated at paragraph 141 of its decision:

141. (a) on the demand side, there is moderate growth, inelastic demand and insignificant countervailing buyer power. Buyers are therefore highly vulnerable to a potential abuse;

(b) the supply side is highly concentrated with high market transparency for a homogenous product, mature production technology, high entry barriers (including high sunk costs) and suppliers with financial links and multi-market contacts. These supply side characteristics make it easy for suppliers to engage in parallel behaviour and provide them with incentives to do so, without any countervailing checks from the demand side.

---

[459] Bishop and Walker, *The Economics of EC Competition Law* (cited in n. 366), 7.049–7.053.

[460] Cases C-68/94 and C-30/95, *France v. Commission, Société Commerciale des Potasses et de l'Azote (SCPA) v. Commission* [1998] ECR I-1375. The French Government and SCPA submitted that, if the regulation did apply to collective dominant positions, the Commission's reasoning concerning the alleged creation of a dominant duopoly had been based on an assessment which was wrong in fact or law and which was inadequate. The CJ upheld this limb of the appeal, see in particular, paras. 179–250.

[461] Case T-342/99, [2002] ECR II-2585.

[462] Cases C-68/94 and C-30/95, [1998] ECR I-1375.

[463] Case T-342/99, [2002] ECR II-2585.

[464] See, e.g., Case M.4523, *Worldspan/Travelport*, Case M.4601, *KarstadtQuelle/MyTravel*.

[465] See, e.g., Case M.4753, *Antalis/MAP*, Case M.4662, *BSG/Universe*, and Case M.4600, *TUI/First Choice*.

On appeal[466] the GC affirmed that these factors had been correctly relied upon and upheld the finding of collective dominance. Obviously the relevant factors may vary from market to market. This checklist, however, seems to 'be based upon the standard "textbook" characteristics which are thought to facilitate tacit collusion in a market'.[467] In its Horizontal Merger Guidelines, the Commission devotes 13 paragraphs[468] to the market features that are likely: (1) to enable the firms to reach terms of coordination; (2) to monitor deviation; (3) to provide a deterrent mechanism; and (4) to prevent outsiders jeopardising the outcome of the expected coordination. These paragraphs obviously provide critical guidance in cases involving mergers on oligopolistic markets.

Given the difficulties involved in proving collective dominance or the likelihood of coordinated effects, an interesting twist in events was the GC's judgment in *Independent Music Publishers and Labels Association (Impala) v. Commission*[469] in which it annulled a Commission decision (taken under the old EUMR and hence the dominance test) unconditionally *clearing* a merger between two of the five music majors, Sony and BMG.[470] In its decision, the Commission, despite indicating otherwise in its statement of objections, made a dramatic U-turn, concluding that the merger would not lead either to the strengthening or the creation of a collective dominant position in the physical or digital recorded music markets.[471] With regard to the physical recorded music market, for example, the Commission found that there was no strengthening of a dominant position as the market was not characterised by features facilitating coordinated behaviour. Not only was there no evidence of parallel pricing, but the Commission considered that the market was not transparent, the heterogeneity of the products made coordination unlikely, and there was no evidence of past cheating or retaliation against deviations from a collusive strategy. Further, there was nothing to suggest that a reduction in the number of players, from five to four, would change the position such that a collective dominant position would be created.

The GC, however, annulled the Commission's decision, on the grounds that the Commission's reasoning was inadequate and contained manifest errors of assessment. The GC concluded that the Commission had failed, applying the *Airtours* criteria, to contain a sufficient statement of reasons for its finding that the market was not conducive to collective dominance. The Commission's finding that the market was not transparent was not supported and was vitiated by a failure to rely on data supporting the conclusion. Further, the reliance on the absence of previous instances of retaliation was vitiated by an error of law, or at the very least by manifest errors in the assessment.

In its assessment of whether a position of collective dominance existed, the Commission had focused on the question of whether the *Airtours* conditions existed. The GC indicated that in the case of a strengthening of an *existing* dominant position, the Commission, instead of proving the *Airtours* criteria in the traditional way through recourse to theoretical analysis, could have established satisfaction of the *Airtours* criteria by reference to 'indicia and items of evidence relating to the signs, manifestations and phenomena inherent in the presence of a collective dominant position'.[472]

---

[466] Case T-102/96, *Gencor Ltd v. Commission* [1999] ECR II-753.

[467] The Lexecon *Competition Memo* of November 1999. See Chap. 9.

[468] Horizontal Merger Guidelines, paras. 45–57.

[469] Case T-464/04 [2006] ECR II-2289 and Case C-413/06 P, *Bertelsmann and Sony Corp v. Commission* [2008] ECR I-4951.

[470] Case M.3333. The Commission therefore had to reconsider the merger and, after a very thorough investigation, again cleared the transaction in 2007. Although Impala again commenced proceedings before the GC (Case T-229/08) these proceedings were abandoned when Sony purchased Bertelsmann's share of the joint venture, which was renamed Sony Music Entertainment Inc. (notified to the Commission as it involved a change from joint to sole control, Case COMP.M/5272, *Sony/SonyBMG*).

[471] Case M.3333. See also, e.g., Case M.3692, *Reuters/Telerate*, Case M.6458, *Universal Music Group/EMI*.

[472] Case T-464/04, [2006] ECR II-2289, para. 251. The GC also quashed the Commission's finding that the merger would not lead to the *creation* of a collective dominant position on the basis that the examinations carried out by the Commission were too 'succinct' and 'superficial' to satisfy its obligation to carry out a prospective analysis and to

Case T-464/04, *Independent Music Publishers and Labels Association (Impala) v. Commission* [2006] ECR II-2289

GC

250. The determination of the existence of a collective dominant position must be supported by a series of elements of established facts, past or present, which show that there is a significant impediment of competition on the market owing to the power acquired by certain undertakings to adopt together the same course of conduct on that market, to a significant extent, independently of their competitors, their customers and consumers.

251. It follows that, in the context of the assessment of the existence of a collective dominant position, although the three conditions defined by the [GC] in [Case T-342/99] *Airtours v Commission* [[2002] ECR II-2585], which were inferred from a theoretical analysis of the concept of a collective dominant position, are indeed also necessary, they may, however, in the appropriate circumstances, be established indirectly on the basis of what may be a very mixed series of indicia and items of evidence relating to the signs, manifestations and phenomena inherent in the presence of a collective dominant position.

252. Thus, in particular, close alignment of prices over a long period, especially if they are above a competitive level, together with other factors typical of a collective dominant position, might, in the absence of an alternative reasonable explanation, suffice to demonstrate the existence of a collective dominant position, even where there is no firm direct evidence of strong market transparency, as such transparency may be presumed in such circumstances.

253. It follows that, in the present case, the alignment of prices, both gross and net, over the last six years, even though the products are not the same (each disc having a different content), and also the fact that they were maintained at such a stable level, and at a level seen as high in spite of a significant fall in demand, together with other factors (power of the undertakings in an oligopoly situation, stability of market shares, etc.), as established by the Commission in the [contested decision], might, in the absence of an alternative explanation, suggest, or constitute an indication, that the alignment of prices is not the result of the normal play of effective competition and that the market is sufficiently transparent in that it allowed tacit price coordination.

The GC thus suggested that when assessing whether a collective dominant position already exists, it may be possible, or necessary, for the Commission, instead of relying on prospective analysis of the probable development of the market or theoretical analysis, to determine, using past or present facts, that a number of undertakings have power to adopt the same course of conduct. On appeal, the CJ reversed the judgment of the GC (and remitted the case back to it)[473] but did not overrule this statement. Rather, it stated that 'the investigation of a pre-existing collective dominant position based on a series of elements normally considered to be indicative of the presence of the likelihood of tacit coordination between competitors cannot therefore be considered to be objectionable of itself. However...it is essential that such an investigation be carried out with care and, above all, that it should adopt an approach based on the analysis of such plausible coordination strategies as may exist in the circumstances.'[474] In 2012, the Commission approved, subject to commitments (to sell a number of labels), a merger between *Universal/EMI Music*[475] which would reduce the number of major players on the wholesale market for digital music by record companies from four to three.

examine carefully the circumstances which may prove relevant for the purposes of assessing the effects of the concentration on competition in the reference market, see paras. 525–528.

[473] Broadly on the grounds that the Commission's reasoning was, on the facts of the case and in the light of tight time constraints under which the Commission had to act, adequate..

[474] Case C-413/06 P, *Bertelsmann and Sony Corp v. Commission* [2008] ECR I-4951, para. 129; also see Case M.6458, *Universal Music Group/EMI.*

[475] Case M.6458. See also Case M.6459 *Sony/Mubsadala/EMI Music.*

(iv) Countervailing Buyer Power

The Horizontal Merger Guidelines stress that a competitive constraint can be exercised over possible non-coordinated or coordinated anti-competitive effects identified not only by competitors (actual and potential) but by customers with countervailing buyer power. Such a buyer may have the incentive[476] to credibly threaten to find an alternative source of supplier, perhaps by changing supplier, vertically integrating, or persuading/sponsoring new entry, were the supplier to increase price.[477] In such cases, the countervailing buyer power may neutralise the market power of the parties.[478]

In *Enso/Stora*[479] the Commission considered that even though the merging parties would acquire a market share of 60 per cent in the market for liquid packaging board the merger would not be incompatible with the common market since they would face a very concentrated buying situation. In particular, Tetra Pak purchased 60 per cent of the packaging board and would be likely to set up an alternative source of supply if the new entity sought to exploit its position of market power.

Countervailing purchaser power was also relevant in *Alcatel/Telettra*.[480] In this case the Commission cleared a merger which gave the parties market shares of 83 per cent. The Commission considered that two main factors meant that the concentration would not be able to impede competition in the common market. Telefonica, the only purchaser, would be able to exert a downward pressure on prices.[481] Further, the Commission's initiative to erode barriers to cross-border trade in this sphere meant that Telefonica would seek products elsewhere if the concentration sought to charge excessive prices (high market shares in a market are unlikely to be significant in an opening market).

(v) Entry Analysis and Barriers to Entry

a. The Importance of Entry Analysis

The Commission will not be concerned with a horizontal merger if the parties' decision to raise prices and restrict output will be met by new entry into the market. Clear evidence that a position of market strength will only be temporary and will be quickly eroded because of a high probability of strong and timely market entry will thus lead to a finding that the concentration is compatible with the common market.[482] Even mergers involving firms with extremely high market shares have been cleared where new entry will be likely, timely, and sufficient to frustrate an attempt by the merging firms to raise price or reduce quality, variety, or innovation. In *HP/Compaq*,[483] for example, the Commission cleared a merger in which the parties would gain market shares of between 85 and 95 per cent as barriers to entry were low and competitors were likely to enter the market quickly.

'For entry to be considered a sufficient competitive constraint on the merging parties, it must be shown to be likely, timely and sufficient to deter or defeat any potential anti-competitive effects of the merger.'[484] The Commission may also take account of constraining competition from manufac-

---

[476] It may not if, for example, it can pass on the price increases to its customers, see e.g. Case M.1225, *Enso/Stora* [1999] OJ L254/9, para. 91.

[477] Case M.1225, *Enso/Stora* [1999] OJ L254/9, para. 65.

[478] Case M.833, *The Coca-Cola Company/Carlsberg A/S* [1998] OJ L145/41.

[479] Case M.1225, [1999] OJ L254/9. See also, e.g., Case M.4057, *Körsnäs/AssiDomän Cartonboard*, especially paras. 57–64 (IP/06/610) and Case M. 1630, *Air Liquide/BOC* [2004] OJ L92/1.

[480] Case M.42, [1991] OJ L122/48. See also, e.g., Case M.3732, *Procter & Gamble/Gillette* and Case M.3687, *Johnson & Johnson/Guidant*.

[481] See also Case M.4, *Renault/Volvo* [1990] OJ C281/2 where the Commission found that large fleet buyers would exercise downward pressure on truck and bus prices.

[482] See, e.g., Case M.477, *Mercedes-Benz/Kässbohrer* [1995] OJ L211/1; *cf.* Case M.774, *Saint Gobain/Wacker-Chemie/NOM* [1997] OJ L247/1.

[483] Case M.2609.

[484] Horizontal Merger Guidelines, para. 68 and Chap. 1.

turers operating outside the geographic market.[485] The Commission will therefore consider a great variety of factors in its assessment of barriers to entry such as whether: legal or regulatory barriers to entry exist;[486] the ownership of patents or other intellectual property rights operate as a barrier to entry into a market, particularly in technology markets[487] (in *Tetra Pak/Alfa Laval*[488] the Commission relied on a number of factors, including Tetra Pak's ownership of patents, to conclude that new entry was not likely in the market for aseptic carton packaging machines[489]); and/or whether other technical factors will inhibit entry (in *The Coca-Cola Company/Carlsberg*[490] the Commission considered the impact of the merger on the carbonated soft drinks (CSD) markets[491] in Denmark and Sweden. The Commission concluded that new entry into the market was not likely on account of severe barriers to entry which included access to brands, access to a distribution network, access to shelf space, the need for a sales and service network, brand image, customer loyalty, and (sunk) advertising costs).[492]

Factors such as the evolution of the market (entry is less likely to be profitable in a mature market than a dynamic one), scale economies, and network effects will also impact on the likelihood of entry.[493] In making the assessment, the Commission considers only potential competitors which are likely to enter the market within a relatively short time frame (although 'timeliness' is dependent upon the characteristics or dynamics of the market, entry must generally occur within two years)[494] and whether market entry will be on a sufficient scale to deter or defeat the anti-competitive effects of the merger.[495]

In *Aérospatiale/Alenia/de Havilland*[496] the Commission held that countervailing factors would not prevent the anti-competitive effects that would result from the parties acquiring very large shares on the commuter aircraft market generally. The high risks involved in entering the market on account of the high sunk costs that would be required and the maturity of the market reduced the likelihood of new entry into the market.[497] Further that any new entry into the commuter aircraft market was likely to occur only after a period of time and too late to catch an expected period of high demand.

In *Ryanair/Aer Lingus*, the Commission concluded that significant barriers to entry meant that new entry was most unlikely. In particular, other airlines did not have a large base in Dublin, and they faced significant entry costs and capacity constraints in terms of obtaining slots at Dublin and destination airports. In addition, the Commission noted that Ryanair had a reputation of reacting aggressively against new entrants.[498] This view was reinforced by the fact that easyJet, another major low-cost carrier present in Europe, had tried and failed to enter routes in competition with

---

[485] Case M.315, *Mannesmann/Vallourec/Ilva* [1994] OJ L102/15.

[486] See, e.g., Case M.1430, *Vodafone/Airtouch* (the need for a licence to provide mobile telephony communications services).

[487] See, e.g., Case M.269, *Shell/Montecatani* [1994] OJ L332/48, para. 32.

[488] Case M.68, [1991] OJ L290/35, point 3.4.

[489] See also Chap. 6.

[490] [1998] OJ L145/41.

[491] Although the Commission considered that the market could be defined more narrowly, to include different flavours of CSDs, the exact definition did not affect the outcome of this case, *The Coca-Cola Company/Carlsberg* [1998] OJ L145/41, para. 43.

[492] *The Coca-Cola Company/Carlsberg* [1998] OJ L145/41, paras. 72–75. The Commission took the view that it was very unlikely that anyone other than the existing international brand owners would be able to launch a new international CSD.

[493] Horizontal Merger Guidelines, para. 73.

[494] Horizontal Merger Guidelines, para. 74.

[495] Horizontal Merger Guidelines, para. 75 and, e.g., Case M.1157, *Skanska/Scancem* [1999] OJ L183/1, para. 184.

[496] Case M.53, [1991] OJ L334/42, para. 53.

[497] D. Ridyard, 'Economic Analysis of Single Firm and Oligopolistic Dominance' [1994] *ECLR* 255, 256.

[498] Ryanair had a history of responding to third parties attempting to run services in competition with them by starting aggressive fare wars until the third party withdrew from the route, Case M.4439, *Ryanair/Aer Lingus*, para. 515, *aff'd* Case T-342/07, [2010] ECR II-3457, para. 286.

Ryanair.[499] In *Olympic Air/Aegean Airlines*[500] the Commission also considered that new entry was not likely, even if slots were available at Athens airport.

(vi) Efficiencies

a. An Efficiency Defence?

A merger which leads to efficiencies and thereby increases competition between the merging parties and the other undertakings on the market, may not significantly impede competition at all. A further important question that has arisen is whether the EUMR admits, or should admit, an 'efficiency defence'. Such a defence would redeem a concentration which increases concentration and market power and, *prima facie* significantly impedes effective competition, but which results in significant cost savings and economies of scale (which favour restructuring).

Horizontal mergers can create substantial efficiencies even as they facilitate collusion or enlarge market power. Courts and other policy makers have entertained three different positions concerning efficiency and the legality of mergers:

(1) mergers should be evaluated for their effect on market power or likelihood of collusion, and efficiency considerations should be largely irrelevant;

(2) mergers that create substantial efficiencies should be legal, or there should be at least a limited 'efficiency defence' in certain merger cases;

(3) mergers should be condemned because they create efficiencies, in order to protect competitors of the post-merger firm.[501]

In the US the authorities are receptive to arguments based on the efficiencies and cost savings of a merger.[502] However, the onus of proving qualifying efficiencies rests on the parties to the merger.[503] The US Merger Guidelines[504] indicate that the defence may apply where (1) efficiencies relied upon are merger-specific (they will not be achieved in the absence of the merger); (2) the efficiencies are achieved in the same market as the market in which the anti-competitive effects of the merger are likely to be felt;[505] (3) the efficiencies are cognisable—they are verifiable and measurable; and finally that (4) the efficiencies outweigh or reverse the merger's potential harm to consumers in the relevant market by, for example, preventing price increases in that market. The guidelines indicate that the more anti-competitive the merger under the concentration analysis the stronger the evidence of efficiencies must be.

Such a defence is justifiable on grounds of strict economic theory, since the costs savings give rise to an increase in consumer welfare as a whole.

b. An Increase in Consumer Welfare

The argument raised in support of such a defence is outlined by Hovenkamp.

---

[499] Case M.4439, *Ryanair/Aer Lingus*, para. 514.

[500] Case M.5830 (on appeal, Case T-202/11, *Aeroporia Aigaiou Aeroporiki v. Commission* (pending)).

[501] Hovenkamp, *Federal Antitrust Policy* (cited in n. 10), 12.2.

[502] But see the approach pursued in the 1960s, see e.g. *Brown Shoe Co v. United States* 370 US 294 (1962).

[503] Department of Justice and Federal Trade Commission, Horizontal Merger Guidelines (1992, amended 1997).

[504] 2010 Guidelines, § 10.

[505] In some cases, merger efficiencies are 'not strictly in the relevant market, but so inextricably linked with it that a partial divestiture or other remedy could not feasibly eliminate the anti-competitive effect in the relevant market without sacrificing the efficiencies in the other market(s)', 2010 Guidelines, § 10 at n. 14. If out-of-market efficiencies are not inextricably linked to the relevant market, the Agencies often find an acceptable narrowly tailored remedy that preserves the efficiencies while preventing anti-competitive effects, see DOJ/FTC Commentary on the Horizontal Merger Guidelines (2006), available at <http://www.justice.gov/atr/public/guidelines/215247.htm>.

H. Hovenkamp, *Federal Antitrust Policy: The Law of Competition and its Practice* (4th edn, West Publishing, 2011), 12.2b1

12.2b1. The Welfare 'Tradeoff' Model

Today the rule that mergers should be condemned because they create efficiency has been abandoned. The opposite position is that mergers should be legal when they create substantial efficiencies—or alternatively, that there should be an 'efficiency defense' in merger cases. Although the trail is still somewhat obscure, the courts are heading in the direction of adopting such a rule, and the government's Merger Guidelines explicitly recognize and define an 'efficiency defense.' Importantly, the rule comes into play *only* after the merger has been found presumptively anticompetitive by structural and behavioral analysis. If a merger poses no competitive threat to begin with, then analysis of possible efficiencies is unnecessary.

The argument for an 'efficiency defense' in merger cases is illustrated by the graph in Figure 1...The graph illustrates a merger that gives the post-merger firm measurably more market power than it had before the merger. As a result, the firm reduces output from Q1 to Q2 on the graph, and increases price from P1 to P2. Triangle A1 represents the monopoly 'deadweight loss' created by this increase in market power...

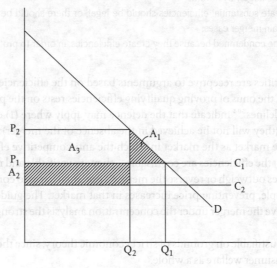

Figure 1

At the same time, the merger produces measurable economies, which show up as a reduction in the firm's costs from C1 to C2. Rectangle A2 represents efficiency gains that will result from these economies. If A2 is larger than A1 the merger produces a *net* efficiency gain, even though it permits the firm to raise its price above its marginal cost. Furthermore, A2 is often larger than A1. The efficiency gains illustrated by A2 are spread over the entire output of the post-merger firm. The deadweight losses in A1 are spread over only the reduction in output. If the post-merger firm reduced its output by 10%, each of the 90% of units still being produced would contribute to the efficiency gains; the deadweight loss, however, would accrue over only the 10% reduction.

Williamson concluded that in a market with average elasticities of demand and supply, a merger that produced 'nontrivial' economies of 1.2% would be efficient, even if it resulted in a price increase of 10%.[506]

Williamson's analysis is vulnerable to some criticism. First, his description of triangle A1 in the figure as the efficiency costs of a merger probably understates the true social cost. Rectangles A2 plus A3

506 O. Williamson, 'Economies as an Antitrust Defense: the Welfare Trade-Offs' (1968) 58 *American Economic Review* 18, 22–23 and O. Williamson, 'Economies as an Antitrust Defense: Revisited' (1977) 125 *U Pa LR* 699.

represent potential monopoly profits to the post-merger firm. A profit-maximizing firm will be willing to spend substantial resources in an effort to acquire or retain a certain amount of monopoly power…If a particular merger will give a firm $1,000,000 in additional monopoly profits, the firm will spend up to $1,000,000 in order to accomplish the merger and then retain its monopoly position. It could spend this money in highly inefficient ways, such as espionage, predatory pricing against a potential take-over target, or vexatious litigation. At the extreme, A2+A3 are not increased profits to the post-merger firm at all, but funds inefficiently spent in order to give the firm its market position. Importantly, the anticompetitive risk in the merger case is not increased likelihood of single-firm monopoly, but increased likelihood of collusion. The costs of managing a cartel or oligopoly can be quite high in relation to the profits that it produces…A cartel or oligopoly that occasions a price increase of 10% would very likely produce much smaller gains in profitability.

Another problem of the tradeoff model is that it apparently assumes a merger to monopoly. But most collusion facilitating mergers involve firms whose aggregate share is significantly less than 100%. For example, suppose a 20% firm should acquire a 10% firm, greatly increasing the extent of oligopoly performance. In that case, the increased coordination that results from the merger enables *both* the merging and the non-merging firms to increase their prices. However, gains are spread across only the output of the two merging firms, which account for only 30% of the market's output…

Broadly, Williamson establishes that in some cases mergers which enable the parties to acquire market power and, consequently, to restrict output and raise prices may nonetheless lead to an increase in consumer welfare. Although consumers lose output (and deadweight loss occurs) in some cases, where efficiency gains are large, that loss is offset by a greater gain in cost or resource savings. To determine whether or not this is the case a comparison must be made in each case of deadweight loss relative to cost savings.

Hovenkamp identifies a number of problems with the welfare trade-off model.[507] In the extract it is explained that the theory may underestimate the social costs of the merger and does not work effectively when applied to mergers occurring on oligopolistic markets. In oligopolistic markets, however, the achievement of efficiencies may provoke more aggressive competition between the players on the market by destabilising the tacit coordination. Further, Hovenkamp goes on to state that the theory can be criticised for treating all efficiency gains in the same way no matter who gets the benefit: a merger which has an overall efficient effect (increasing total welfare) may nonetheless result in an actual output reduction and still lead to an increase in price for consumers (in such case the benefits accrue to the merging parties).[508] The US Merger Guidelines require that efficiencies are sufficient to reverse the harm to consumers, by preventing price increases in the market.[509] Hovenkamp also notes that it can be difficult to determine whether or not the efficiencies pleaded could be obtained by means other than merger, and that this explains why the defence has been successful so infrequently. A final problem identified is that courts are unable to make the measurements that its analysis would require. 'Our knowledge that mergers can produce both economies and monopoly pricing is fairly secure. However, quantifying either of these in a particular merger case is impossible. Most mergers found illegal under current law probably create efficiencies. They are condemned, however, because no court is capable of balancing the increase in market power of the potential for collusion against the economies achieved.'[510] As a result he concludes that '[m]ost of the courts that have considered the efficiency defense have been skeptical. Most have rejected it although

---

[507] Hovenkamp, *Federal Antitrust Policy* (cited in n. 10), 12.2b1, 551.

[508] See the discussion of total welfare and consumer welfare in Chap. 1

[509] 2010 Guidelines, § 10.

[510] Hovenkamp, *Federal Antitrust Policy* (cited in n. 10), 12.2b4, 554.

a few have recognized the defense.'[511] Others have suggested that even if the comparison *could* be made, it *should* not. Huge cost savings would be necessary to offset any associated price increases[512] and, in contrast, a rigorous merger policy would be more likely to bring about an increase in economic welfare. Public policy should thus concentrate on preserving and fostering competition for the ultimate benefit of consumers.

c. Background—Efficiencies and the EUMR

There was doubt whether the substantive test set out in Article 2 of the EUMR left scope for the trade-off of efficiencies where a concentration significantly impedes effective competition. Although there is no express provision for an efficiency defence, however, Article 2(1)(b) allows for 'technical and economic progress' to be taken into account as part of the appraisal 'provided it is to consumers' advantage and does not form an obstacle to competition'. Some commentators have argued that although efficiency considerations may lead to an increase in consumer welfare as a whole, it is hard to see how, as required by Article 2(1)(b), the technical and economic progress could be said to be to the consumers' advantage (the consumer would have to pay monopoly prices, post-merger) or that the merger would not form an obstacle to competition.[513] As the Commission has never applied the defence to authorise a merger which would otherwise have been declared incompatible with the common market,[514] it has remained questionable as to whether the defence can be invoked under the EUMR at all.[515]

Further and conversely, some commentators have alleged that (in the past at least) the Commission's decisions have actually been reflective of an 'efficiency attack' or 'efficiency offence', a fear that mergers which would enable the parties to achieve significant economies of scale or scope may be more likely to result in a finding that the merger is incompatible with the common market as the parties will have even greater advantages over their nearest competitors.[516] For example, in some cases involving conglomerate mergers, the Commission does seem to have accepted that efficiencies would result from a merger but that these efficiencies would enable the merging parties to lower their prices and so damage competitors. In *GE/Honeywell*[517] the Commission was particularly concerned that the merged entity would be able to offer low bundled prices for those that purchased both its aircraft engines and its avionics and non-avionics systems. The focus that the Commission placed on the harm that would result to the new entity's competitors led some commentators to take

---

[511] Hovenkamp, *Federal Antitrust Policy* (cited in n. 10), 12.2b4, 505. See also Bork, *The Antitrust Paradox* (cited in n. 18).

[512] Scherer and Ross, *Industrial Market Structure and Economic Performance* (cited in n. 9), 174: statistical evidence supporting the hypotheses that profitability and efficiency increase following mergers is at best weak.

[513] See, e.g., A. Jacquemin, 'Mergers and European Policy' in P. H. Admiral (ed.), *Merger and Competition Policy in the European Community* (Blackwell, 1990), 36.

[514] 'However, commentators have often suggested that the Commission is perfectly aware of the importance of efficiency gains, and that it has taken them into account *implicitly*, for instance at the stage of determination of market dominance', M. Motta, 'E.C. Merger Policy and the Airtours Case' [2000] *ECLR* 199, 203, relying on P. D. Camesasca, 'The Explicit Efficiency Defence in Merger Control: Does it Make the Difference?' [1999] *ECLR* 26–27. For cases in which efficiencies have been relevant, see Section 5.D.vi.

[515] See Case M.1313, [2001] OJ L20/1, para. 198.

[516] In Case M.53, *Aérospatiale-Alenia/de Havilland*, e.g., the parties claim that efficiency gains that arose from the merger arguably appeared, instead of acting as an offsetting factor to mitigate the adverse competitive effects of the merger, to have 'merely strengthened the Commission's view that the merged group would enjoy benefits that would be out of the reach of its competitors. If anything, the "efficiency defence" seems in this case to have reduced the chances of clearance for the deal', D. Ridyard, 'Economic Analysis of Single Firm and Oligopolistic Dominance' [1994] *ECLR* 255, 256–257.

[517] COMP/M.2220, *aff'd* Cases T-209 and 210/01, *Honeywell* v. *Commission* and *General Electric Company* v. *Commission* [2005] ECR II-5527 and 5575. See the discussion of this case in Section 5.D.ix. Mario Monti, then Commissioner for Competition, however, refuted the assertion that the Commission when dealing with conglomerate mergers was in fact applying an 'efficiency offence', see, e.g., 'Antitrust in the US and Europe: a History of Convergence' 14 November 2001.

the view that the decision was indicative of a hostile approach to mergers that create efficiencies and as protective of competitors rather than competition.

d. The Horizontal Merger Guidelines

In view of the confusion over the part played by efficiency considerations in EU merger cases, the Commission invited discussion in its 2001 Green Paper of the proper role and scope that such considerations should play.[518] Most respondents considered that, as part of a sound economics-based merger control policy, the Commission should take account of efficiencies in its analysis of the overall effects likely to be produced by a proposed merger. Further, that guidance should be produced on the proper scope of the defence. Recital 29 of the EUMR now provides that it 'is possible that the efficiencies brought forward by the concentration counteract the effects on competition, and in particular the potential harm to consumers, that it might otherwise have and that, as a consequence, the concentration would not significantly impede effective competition, in particular as a result of the creation or strengthening of a dominant position' and the Commission deals with efficiencies in its Horizontal Merger Guidelines.[519] In the Guidelines it is recognised that in making its substantive appraisal it takes account of Article 2(1) factors including the development of technical and economic progress provided that it is to the consumers' advantage and does not form an obstacle to competition,[520] and that 'efficiencies generated by the merger are likely to enhance the ability and incentive of the merged entity to act pro-competitively for the benefit of consumers, thereby counteracting the adverse effects on competition which the merger might otherwise have'.[521] The Guidelines do not specifically state that the burden is on the parties to establish the efficiency defence. They make it clear, however, that the Commission will only take account of substantiated efficiency claims and that it is for the parties to provide the evidence to demonstrate the claimed efficiencies and that there are no less anti-competitive means of realising those efficiencies.[522] The Commission will only take account of claimed efficiencies where they:[523] (1) benefit consumers;[524] (2) are merger specific;[525] and (3) are verifiable.[526]

Benefit to Consumers

It is a requirement that consumers should not be worse off as a result of the merger. The merger must thus bring timely efficiencies that will result, for example, in lower prices (perhaps through reduction in variable or marginal costs) or in new or improved products or services (for example, from efficiency gains in the sphere of R&D). In the context of coordinated effects, efficiencies may lead to incentives to increase production and reduce output and disincentives to coordinate behaviour.

The Commission considers that the greater the market power acquired by the undertakings the more difficult it will be to show that benefits will result which will be passed on to consumers. Further, it states that the efficiencies should in principle benefit consumers in the market where the competition problems arise.[527]

---

[518] 2001 Green Paper on the Review of Council Regulation (EEC) No. 4064/89, COM(2001) 745/6 final. See also e.g. L. Roller, J. Stennek, and F. Verboven, 'Efficiency Gains from Mergers', The Research Institute of Industrial Economics, Working Paper No 543, 2000.

[519] [2004] OJ C31/5, para. 5. Form CO also has a section on efficiency gains.

[520] Horizontal Merger Guidelines, para. 76.

[521] Horizontal Merger Guidelines, para. 77.

[522] Horizontal Merger Guidelines, paras. 77, 87, and 84 respectively.

[523] Horizontal Merger Guidelines, para. 78.

[524] Horizontal Merger Guidelines, paras. 79–84.

[525] Horizontal Merger Guidelines, para. 85.

[526] Horizontal Merger Guidelines, paras. 86–88.

[527] Contrast the position in the US, see Section 5.D.vi.a.

Merger Specificity

Paragraph 85 of the Horizontal Merger Guidelines explains the requirement of merger specificity.

Efficiencies are relevant to the competitive assessment when they are a direct consequence of the notified merger and cannot be achieved to a similar extent by less anti-competitive alternatives. In these circumstances, the efficiencies are deemed to be caused by the merger and thus, merger specific. It is for the parties to provide in due time all the relevant information necessary to demonstrate that there are no less anti-competitive, realistic and attainable alternatives of a non-concentrative nature (e.g., a licensing agreement, or a cooperative joint venture) or of a concentrative nature (e.g., a concentrative joint venture, or a differently structured merger) than the notified merger which preserve the claimed efficiencies. The Commission only considers alternatives that are reasonably practical in the business situation faced by the merging parties having regard to established business practices in the industry concerned.

Verifiability

A difficult task for the parties will be to verify the efficiencies 'such that the Commission can be reasonably certain that the efficiencies are likely to materialize, and be substantial enough to counteract a merger's potential harm to consumers'.[528] The Commission states that the parties should quantify the efficiencies where possible or otherwise identify the positive impact on consumers.

Cases

Although efficiencies have not yet been given as a decisive factor for a merger clearance it was given as one of them in *Körsnäs/AssiDomän Cartonboard*.[529] In this case the Commission accepted that synergies resulting from the merger between two of the three main players active in the world-wide market for the production of liquid carton packaging board were likely to be passed on to consumers. The Commission also considered, however, that countervailing buyer power as well as competition from EnsoStora,[530] suppliers outside the EU, and suppliers of other board materials, were likely to constrain the behaviour of the merged parties.

In *Ryanair/Aer Lingus*, the Commission rejected Ryanair's argument that offsetting efficiencies would be brought about by the merger. Rather, it found that the efficiencies that would result from a reduction of Aer Lingus's operating costs constituted more of a general assertion than a verifiable claim and they were not merger specific (since it appeared that they could be generated by Aer Lingus simply applying Ryanair's business plan). Further, given that the Commission had established that the merged entity would face little, if any, competition on a number of routes and that many of the claimed efficiencies related to fixed costs, the Commission considered there to be little incentive for any cost savings made to be passed on to consumers—the efficiencies were of insufficient benefit to consumers to outweigh a merger to monopoly on some routes.[531] The GC upheld the Commission's decision and rejected Ryanair's allegation that the Commission had set the bar to establish efficiencies too high. The conclusion reached in this case lends support to the view set out in paragraph 84 of the Horizontal Merger Guidelines that it is highly unlikely that a merger leading to a market position approaching monopoly can be declared compatible with the common market on the ground that the efficiency gains would be sufficient to counteract its potential anti-competitive effects.

---

[528] Horizontal Merger Guidelines, para. 85. See, e.g., D. Gerard, 'Merger Control Policy: How to Give Meaningful Consideration to Efficiency Claims?' (2003) 40 *CMLRev* 1367.

[529] Case M.4057, especially paras. 57–64 (IP/06/610). See also e.g., Case M.4187, *Metso/Aker Kvoerner*; Case M.3732, *Procter & Gamble/Gillette*; Case M.3664, *Repsol Butano/Shell Gas*; Case M.3886, *Aster 2/Flint Ink* (efficiencies one factor in clearance), and Case M.4000, *Inco/Falconbridge* (the parties' efficiencies claims were rejected) and, e.g., P. Lowe, 'A more economic approach to competition law enforcement—making it operational', 15 December 2005.

[530] See n. 479 and accompanying text.

[531] Case No. M.4439, para. 1151, *aff'd* Case T-342/07, *Ryanair v. Commission* [2010] ECR II-3457, para. 443.

(vii) The Failing Firm Defence or Rescue Mergers

The failing firm defence is well established in US antitrust case law and referred to in the US Horizontal Merger Guidelines.[532] The defence provides an escape route for a merger involving a firm facing an otherwise inevitable liquidation. Historically, it appears to have been adopted in the US to ensure the protection of the creditors, owners, and/or employees of small businesses and it was therefore concerned not with efficiency but with distributive justice. It appears, however, that a narrowly applied failing company 'could be efficient when it (1) enables a failing firm and its creditors to avoid the high administrative costs of bankruptcy; and (2) it keeps on the market productive assets that are worth keeping in production and would likely to be taken out of production were it not for the merger. Offsetting these is the social cost of any monopoly pricing that flows from the merger itself, less the social cost that would flow from any monopoly created if the failing firm simply went out of business.'[533]

In the US the defence may be raised where an undertaking can establish that the failing company will fail to meet its financial obligations in the future, will be unable to reorganise successfully, and has unsuccessfully sought reasonable, less anti-competitive, alternative offers (i.e. an acquisition by a smaller competitor or non-competitor).[534] It has also been accepted that there is room for a failing firm defence within the scheme of the EUMR where the deterioration of the competitive structure cannot be said to be *caused* by the merger, i.e. 'where the competitive structure would deteriorate to at least the same extent in the absence of the merger'.[535]

This principle was first recognised in *Kali und Salz/MdK/Treuhand*[536] which raised the question whether or not an undertaking with large market shares could combine activities with its only, or main, failing competitor. It has already been seen that the case concerned the combination of the potash and rock-salt activities of Kali und Salz and Mitteldeutsche Kali AG (MdK, owned by Treuhand). Although the Commission found that the concentration would acquire enormous shares on the potash market in Germany and the magnesium products market of 98 per cent and 100 per cent respectively, it concluded that the concentration did not lead to the creation or strengthening of a dominant position. It was not the merger that could be said to be the cause of the deterioration in the competitive structure. Even if the merger was prohibited, the acquiring undertaking would inevitably achieve or reinforce its dominant position to the same extent. The parties established (the onus being on them to do so) that:

- the acquired undertaking would in the near future be forced out of the market if not taken over by another undertaking (MdK would inevitably have been forced out of the market as it was in a critical economic position following the collapse of the relevant markets);

- the acquiring undertaking, Kali und Salz, would inevitably acquire the market share since it was the only other relevant participator on the respective markets; and

- no less anti-competitive purchase was possible (although tenders had been invited, all other alternatives had practically been ruled out).

The Commission thus accepted that the failing company defence succeeded in that case. The French Government argued that the Commission had been wrong to use this defence to authorise

---

[532] 2010 Guidelines, § 11. See also OECD, 'Failing Firm Defence' (2009), available at <http://www.oecd.org/daf/competition/mergers/45810821.pdf>.

[533] 2010 Guidelines, para. 12.9, 545.

[534] See, e.g., *Citizen Publishing Co.* v. *United States*, 394 US 131, 138, 89 S.Ct 927, 931 (1969).

[535] Horizontal Mergers Guidelines, para. 89, relying on Case M.1578, *Sanitec/Sphinx* [2000] OJ L294/1.

[536] Case M.308, [1994] OJ L186/30; on appeal Cases C-68/94 and C-30/95, *France* v. *Commission, Société Commerciale des Potasses et de l'Azote (SCPA)* v. *Commission* [1998] ECR I-1375. The Commission had rejected the defence in Case M.53, *Aérospatiale/Alenia/de Havilland*. See G. Monti and E. Rousseva, 'Failing firms in the framework of the EC Merger Regulation' [1999] 24 *ELRev* 38.

a concentration leading to the creation of a monopoly without imposing conditions. The CJ upheld the Commission's decision, however,[537] confirming that if a concentration is not the cause of the SIEC on the market it must be declared compatible with the common market.[538] Further, that the fact that the conditions relied on for concluding that there was no causal link between the concentration and the deterioration of the competitive structure did not coincide with the conditions applied in the US was not in itself a ground for invalidating the decision. Rather, to challenge it, it would have to be shown that the conditions set by the Commission were not capable of excluding the possibility that the concentration might be the cause of the deterioration in the competitive structure.

Cases C-68/94 and C-30/95, *France v. Commission, Société Commerciale des Potasses et de l'Azote (SCPA) v. Commission* [1998] ECR I-1375

Court of Justice

111. It appears from point 71 of the contested decision that, in the Commission's opinion, a concentration which would normally be considered as leading to the creation or reinforcement of a dominant position on the part of the acquiring undertaking may be regarded as not being the cause of it if, even in the event of the concentration being prohibited, that undertaking would inevitably achieve or reinforce a dominant position. Point 71 goes on to state that, as a general matter, a concentration is not the cause of the deterioration of the competitive structure if it is clear that:

— the acquired undertaking would in the near future be forced out of the market if not taken over by another undertaking,

— the acquiring undertaking would gain the market share of the acquired undertaking if it were forced out of the market,

— there is no less anti-competitive alternative purchase.

112. It must be observed, first of all, that the fact that the conditions set by the Commission for concluding that there was no causal link between the concentration and the deterioration of the competitive structure do not entirely coincide with the conditions applied in connection with the United States 'failing company defence' is not in itself a ground of invalidity of the contested decision. Solely the fact that the conditions set by the Commission were not capable of excluding the possibility that a concentration might be the cause of the deterioration in the competitive structure of the market could constitute a ground of invalidity of the decision.

113. In the present case, the French Government disputes the relevance of the criterion that it must be verified that the acquiring undertaking would in any event obtain the acquired undertaking's share of the market if the latter were to be forced out of the market.

114. However, in the absence of that criterion, a concentration could, provided the other criteria were satisfied, be considered as not being the cause of the deterioration of the competitive structure of the market even though it appeared that, in the event of the concentration not proceeding, the acquiring undertaking would not gain the entire market share of the acquired undertaking. Thus, it would be possible to deny the existence of a causal link between the concentration and the deterioration of the competitive structure of the market even though the competitive structure of the market would deteriorate to a lesser extent if the concentration did not proceed.

---

[537] The Commission in para. 112 of its decision recognised that the conditions it set out in para. 111 were not identical to those set out in US law as it did not wish simply to imitate the US position. It has since then changed its approach, which is now broadly the same as that adopted in the US, see pp. 1219–1220.

[538] Cases C-68/94 and C-30/95, *France v. Commission, Société Commerciale des Potasses et de l'Azote (SCPA) v. Commission* [1998] ECR I-1375, para. 110.

115. The introduction of that criterion is intended to ensure that the existence of a causal link between the concentration and the deterioration of the competitive structure of the market can be excluded only if the competitive structure resulting from the concentration would deteriorate in similar fashion even if the concentration did not proceed.

116. The criterion of absorption of market shares, although not considered by the Commission as sufficient in itself to preclude any adverse effect of the concentration on competition, therefore helps to ensure the neutral effects of the concentration as regards the deterioration of the competitive structure of the market. This is consistent with the concept of causal connection set out in Article 2(2) of the Regulation.

117. As to the criticism of the Commission that it failed to show that if the concentration did not proceed MdK would inevitably have been forced out of the market, it should be observed that the Commission stated in point 73 of the contested decision that, even though MdK had been restructured by 1 January 1993, that undertaking continued to make considerable losses in the first six months of the year. According to the Commission, MdK's serious economic situation was essentially a result of its obsolete operating structure and the crisis in sales attributable primarily to the collapse of markets in eastern Europe. MdK also lacked an efficient distribution system (see points 74 and 75 of the contested decision).

118. In point 76 of the contested decision, the Commission observed that MdK had been able to continue operating until now only because Treuhand had consistently covered its losses. The Commission added, however, that Treuhand could not cover MdK's losses in the long term from public aid, since that was in any case incompatible with the Treaty provisions on State aid.

119. In the light of the foregoing, the Commission cannot be criticised for finding that MdK was no longer economically viable and for considering that it was probable that, on its own, MdK would continue to accumulate losses even if Treuhand provided the funds envisaged for restructuring purposes in the proposed concentration.

120. In those circumstances, the Commission's forecast that MdK was highly likely to close down in the near future if it were not taken over by a private undertaking cannot be regarded as unsupported by a consistent body of evidence.

121. Finally, with respect to the condition concerning the absence of an alternative, less anti-competitive method of acquiring MdK, it should be noted that the French Government's complaint is that the Commission, because of the lack of transparency in the tendering procedure, failed to show that that condition was in fact satisfied.

122. Suffice it to note that the French Government has merely observed that the MdK trade unions pointed to a lack of transparency in the tendering procedure, without providing any details as to what constituted the alleged lack of transparency.

123. In the absence of any details of that complaint, it cannot be upheld.

124. It follows from the foregoing that the absence of a causal link between the concentration and the deterioration of the competitive structure of the German market has not been effectively called into question. Accordingly, it must be held that, so far as that market is concerned, the concentration appears to satisfy the criterion referred to in Article 2(2) of the Regulation, and could thus be declared compatible with the common market without being amended. Consequently, contrary to the French Government's assertion, it is not possible without contradicting that premise to require the Commission, with respect to the German market, to attach any condition whatever to its declaration of the concentration's compatibility.

Since the *Kali and Salz* case the Commission has been prepared to apply the failing firm defence or the concept of the 'rescue merger' more broadly, and in line with the criteria set out in the US merger guidelines. The defence has been pleaded in a number of cases[539] and was successfully invoked by the parties in *BASF/Pantochim/Eurodiol*.[540] This case involved BASF's proposed acquisition of Pantochim and Eurodiol from Sisal. The concentration was likely to lead to the acquisition of high market shares on certain base chemical markets. In applying the failing firm defence in this case the Commission stressed that the approach taken by the CJ in its *Kali and Salz* judgment was wider than the criteria set out in the Commission's own decision in that case. The key requirement for a merger to be regarded as a rescue merger was that the competitive structure resulting from the concentration would deteriorate in a similar fashion even if the concentration did not proceed, i.e. even if the concentration was prohibited. Thus the essential conditions are that the undertaking to be acquired can be regarded as a 'failing firm' and that the merger will not be the *cause* of the deterioration of the competitive structure.

Case M.2314, *BASF/Pantochim/Eurodiol*

Commission

(140) In general terms, the concept of the 'rescue merger' requires that the undertakings to be acquired can be regarded as 'failing firms' and that the merger is not the cause of the deterioration of the competitive structure. Thus, for the application of the rescue merger, two conditions must be satisfied:

(a) the acquired undertaking would in the near future be forced out of the market if not taken over by another undertaking; and

(b) there is no less anti-competitive alternative purchase.

(141) However, the application of these two criteria does not completely rule out the possibility of a takeover by third parties of the assets of the undertakings concerned in the event of their bankruptcy. If such assets were taken over by competitors in the course of bankruptcy proceedings, the economic effects would be similar to a takeover of the failing firms themselves by an alternative purchaser.

Thus it needs to be established in addition to the first two criteria, that the assets to be purchased would inevitably disappear from the market in the absence of the merger.

(142) Given this general framework, the Commission regards the following criteria as relevant for the application of the concept of the 'rescue merger':

(a) the acquired undertaking would in the near future be forced out of the market if not taken over by another undertaking;

(b) there is no less anti-competitive alternative purchase; and

(c) the assets to be acquired would inevitably exit the market if not taken over by another undertaking.

(143) In any event, the application of the concept of the 'rescue merger' requires that the deterioration of the competitive structure through the merger is at least no worse than in the absence of the merger.

The Commission thus does not require that the acquiring company would inevitably acquire the entire market share of the acquired undertaking if it were forced out of the market, but only that the acquired company's assets would inevitably exit the market were the firm not taken over.[541] The

[539] It has been rejected in a number of cases, see, e.g., Case M.774, *Saint-Gobain/Wacker-Chemie-NOM* [1997] OJ L247/1; Case M.2621, *SEB/Moulinex*; Case M.2845, *Sogecable/Canalsatelite Digital/Via Digital*; and Case M.2876, *Newscorp/Telepiù*.

[540] Case COMP/M.2314, IP/01/984. See also Case M.2810, *Deloitte & Touche/Andersen (UK)*; Case M.2816, *Ernst & Young France/Andersen France*; Case M.2824, *Ernst & Young/Andersen Germany*; and Case M.3910, *Rockwood/Süd-Chemie*. See K. Joergens, 'Anderson and the "Failing Firm"' (2003) 26 *World Competition* 363 and I. Kokkoris, 'Failing Firm Defence in the European Union: A Panacea for Mergers?' [2006] *ECLR* 494.

[541] It would seem to be inherent in the defence, however, that the acquiring firm would gain much or most of the market share.

Commission explains the inevitability of the assets of the failing firm leaving the market in question as underlying, in the case of merger to monopoly, a finding that the market share of the failing firm would in any event accrue to the other merging party.[542] The approach in *BASF/Pantochim/Eurodiol* was reiterated by the Commission in *Newscorp/Telepiù*[543] and is adopted by the Commission in its Horizontal Merger Guidelines.

Guidelines on the Assessment of Horizontal Mergers under the Council Regulation on the Control of Concentrations between Undertakings [2004] OJ C31/5

VIII. Failing firm

89. The Commission may decide that an otherwise problematic merger is nevertheless compatible with the common market if one of the merging parties is a failing firm. The basic requirement is that the deterioration of the competitive structure that follows the merger cannot be said to be caused by the merger. This will arise where the competitive structure of the market would deteriorate to at least the same extent in the absence of the merger.

90. The Commission considers the following three criteria to be especially relevant for the application of a 'failing firm defence'. First, the allegedly failing firm would in the near future be forced out of the market because of financial difficulties if not taken over by another undertaking. Second, there is no less anti-competitive alternative purchase than the notified merger. Third, in the absence of a merger, the assets of the failing firm would inevitably exit the market.

91. It is for the notifying parties to provide in due time all the relevant information necessary to demonstrate that the deterioration of the competitive structure that follows the merger is not caused by the merger.

The criteria set by the Commission in the cases and guidelines are high and have, in spite of financial and economic crisis, only been met in a few cases. The Commission has not ruled out the possibility of the defence applying where only part of the firm is failing. It appears, however, that the defence, and lack of causality between the merger and the adverse effect on competition, will be much harder to establish in such cases.[544]

(viii) Assessing Mergers in Network Industries and in Two-Sided Markets

Appraisal of mergers in network markets, prone to 'tipping', or in 'two-sided' markets, may in certain circumstances require some different substantive merger assessment. The extract from Bishop and Walker explains some of the difficulties involved in appraising such mergers.

---

[542] Horizontal Merger Guidelines, n. 111.

[543] Case M.2876, IP/03/478 (in this case, involving a merger between Stream and Telepiù which would result in the parties acquiring very high shares in the Italian pay-TV market, it was the acquiring company, Stream, that was alleged to be failing. Although the Commission found that the strict legal requirements for the failing firm defence were not met it took account of the chronic financial difficulties faced by both companies in its decision and the disruption that the possible closure of Stream would cause to Italian pay-TV subscribers). See also, e.g., Case M.5332.

[544] See Case M.1221, *Rewe/Meinl* [1999] OJ L274/1 and Case M.2876, *Newscorp/Telepiù*, IP/03/478, I. Kokkoris and R. Olivares-Caminal, *Antitrust Law Amidst Financial Crises* (Cambridge University Press, 2010), p. 109, and E. F. Clark and C. E. Foss, 'When the Failing Firm Defence Fails' [2012] *JECLAP* 317.

S. Bishop and M. Walker, *The Economics of EC Competition Law: Concepts, Application and Measurement* (3rd edn, Sweet & Maxwell, 2010)

Assessing Mergers in Network Industries

7.082 In some industries, the value that consumers place on a firm's product offering depends on the number of other consumers that are using that firm's product. Where this is the case, in general, an increase in the number of consumers using the firm's product increases the value consumers place on that product and hence the more attractive the product becomes, at given prices. Such industries are termed 'network industries'.

The existence of network effects raises the possibility that a merger will give rise to *tipping* or *snowball effects*. *Tipping* refers to the phenomenon whereby network effects can sometimes lead to the market being dominated by just one product (e.g., Microsoft Windows). The basic argument of such theories is as follows. Due to the existence of network effects, if two networks were to merge, this will make that network more attractive to consumers and as a result more consumers would be attracted to the network, thereby further enhancing its competitive position. Such a virtuous circle, it is then alleged, can lead to the market tipping as all consumers drift towards the largest network operator, ultimately resulting in total monopoly.

This line of argument has been applied by the Commission in a number of cases, including *MCI/Worldcom*, *Vodafone/Mannesman* and *Microsoft Liberty Media/Telewest*....

The Commission's analysis in each of these cases can be heavily criticized for a reliance on speculative market analysis that placed too much weight on the theoretical possibility of tipping effects without subjecting those theories to empirical reality...

Finally, it is important to distinguish between the possibility that network effects are strong enough to lead to tipping and the apparent assumption that network effects inevitably lead to monopoly. To see that monopoly is not the inevitable outcome of network effects, consider the video games market. Although this market is arguably characterised by network effects it has not tipped to monopoly. There are currently three main players: Sony, Microsoft and Nintendo.

...

Assessing Mergers in Two-Sided Markets

7.084 A number of industries can be considered to be 'two-sided'. For a market to be described in economic terms as 'two-sided' two conditions must hold. First, the product at the centre of the analysis is a 'platform' that allows or facilitates the interaction of two distinct groups of customers. Secondly, the benefit that customers in one group derive from the interaction is larger the greater the number of customers on the other side of the platform (the platform creates indirect network externalities). Examples of markets with two-sided features include the media (where advertisers and audience/readership 'interact' through newspapers or television channels) and credit cards (interaction between merchants and customers).

In two-sided markets, a firm's bargaining strength with one group of customers can affect its bargaining strength with the group of consumers on the other side of the market. This raises the possibility that a change in market structure brought about by a merger could lead to adverse outcomes for one or both groups of customer. By strengthening the merged entity's position on one side of the market, it may be able to raise prices to consumers on the other side of the market.

In a traditional one-sided market, economic theory predicts that when a firm raises price this has two conflicting effects on the profits of the firm. On one side, it increases the firm's revenues on each unit sold. On the other side, higher prices induce some customers to switch to competing products, thereby reducing the firm's volume of sales. A horizontal merger may give rise to unilateral effects because, post-merger, some of the sales lost as a result of a price increase are captured by the other merging party, mitigating the loss of sales compared to the pre-merger situation and therefore creating an incentive to raise prices. In a two-sided market these conflicting incentives also exist, but the mechanism is more complicated due to the interaction between the two sides of the market. If a supplier raises its price to customers on one side of the market (call them 'downstream'), it may induce some of those customers to switch to its competitors. This would lead to a reduction in the volume of sales made through that firm and therefore reduces revenues. Moreover, the reduction in the number of downstream customers means that the firm would become less attractive to customers on the other side of the market (call them 'upstream') and this may weaken the firm's bargaining position vis-à-vis these customers. This additional feedback 'interaction' between the downstream and the upstream side of the market, which is a specific characteristic of two-sided markets, reinforces the competitive constraints existing on suppliers but may also create opportunities for suppliers to 'leverage' market power from one side of the market to the other side.

(ix) Competitive Assessment of Non-horizontal Mergers

a. The Non-Horizontal Merger Guidelines

The Commission's merger decisions have over the years reflected concerns with significant impediments to effective competition resulting from horizontal, vertical, and/or conglomerate mergers. Some of these decisions, in particular those adopted in *GE/Honeywell*[545] and *Tetra Laval/Sidel*,[546] have been extremely controversial. In 2007, however, the Commission adopted, following consultation on an earlier draft,[547] Non-Horizontal Merger Guidelines designed to provide clear and predictable guidance to companies as to how the Commission will analyse the impact of non-horizontal mergers on competition. These Guidelines aim to complement the Commission's guidance on horizontal mergers and, no doubt, to meet the challenges, standards, and demands required of it by EU courts in non-horizontal merger cases.

The Non-Horizontal Merger Guidelines accept that non-horizontal mergers are generally less likely to significantly impede effective competition than horizontal mergers. Not only do non-horizontal mergers not entail the loss of direct competition between the merging parties in the same relevant market but it is recognised that vertical and conglomerate mergers provide substantial scope for efficiencies, particularly through the integration of complementary activities and the reduction of transaction costs.[548]

Non-Horizontal Merger Guidelines

12. First, unlike horizontal mergers, vertical or conglomerate mergers do not entail the loss of direct competition between the merging firms in the same relevant market. As a result, the main source of anti-competitive effect in horizontal mergers is absent from vertical and conglomerate mergers.

13. Second, vertical and conglomerate mergers provide substantial scope for efficiencies. A characteristic of vertical mergers and certain conglomerate mergers is that the activities and/or the products of the companies involved are complementary to each other. The integration of complementary activities

---

[545] Case M.2220, *General Electric/Honeywell*, aff'd *Honeywell Intl v. Commission and General Electric v. Commission* (Cases T-209 and 210/01), [2005] ECR II-5527 and 5575 (GC).

[546] Case M.2416, annulled on appeal Case T–5/02, [2002] ECR II–4381, aff'd Case C-12/03 P, [2005] ECR I-987.

[547] On 13 February 2007, the Commission launched a public consultation on the draft guidelines (see IP/07/178). Feedback on the consultation is available on DG COMP's website, <http://ec.europa.eu/comm/competition/mergers/legislation/non_horizontal_consultation.html>. See also Report for DG Competition, European Commission prepared by Jeffrey Church (University of Calgary, Canada), September 2004, *The Impact of Vertical and Conglomerate Mergers on Competition* (available at <http://bookshop.europa.eu/is-bin/INTERSHOP.enfinity/WFS/EU-Bookshop-Site/en_GB/-/EUR/ViewPublication-Start?PublicationKey=KD7105158>.

[548] Non-Horizontal Merger Guidelines, paras. 11–13.

or products within a single firm may produce significant efficiencies and be pro-competitive. In vertical relationships for instance, as a result of the complementarity, a decrease in mark-ups downstream will lead to higher demand also upstream. A part of the benefit of this increase in demand will accrue to the upstream suppliers. An integrated firm will take this benefit into account. Vertical integration may thus provide an increased incentive to seek to decrease prices and increase output because the integrated firm can capture a larger fraction of the benefits. This is often referred to as the 'internalisation of double mark-ups'. Similarly, other efforts to increase sales at one level (e.g. improve service or stepping up innovation) may provide a greater reward for an integrated firm that will take into account the benefits accruing at other levels.

14. Integration may also decrease transaction costs and allow for a better co-ordination in terms of product design, the organisation of the production process, and the way in which the products are sold. Similarly, mergers which involve products belonging to a range or portfolio of products that are generally sold to the same set of customers (be they complementary products or not) may give rise to customer benefits such as one-stop shopping.

The Commission is nonetheless still concerned that both types of mergers may significantly impede effective competition on a market by giving rise to non-coordinated effects (principally through foreclosure) and/or coordinated effects (through changing the nature of competition so the firms are significantly more likely to coordinate and raise prices). The Commission makes it clear in its Guidelines, however, heeding perhaps the criticism it faced following its decision in *GE/Honeywell*, that it focuses on the effects of the merger on the customers to which the merged entity and its competitors are selling. 'Consequently, the fact that a merger affects competitors is not in itself a problem. It is the impact on effective competition that matters, not the mere impact on competitors at some level of the supply chain. In particular, the fact that a rival may be harmed because a merger creates efficiencies cannot in itself give rise to competition concerns.'[549]

b. Market Shares and Concentration Levels

The Commission considers that non-horizontal mergers pose no threat to effective competition unless the merged entity has a significant degree of market power in at least one of the markets affected by the merger. Thus market shares and concentration levels provide useful *first indications* of market power (a significant degree of market power is a necessary, but not sufficient, condition for competitive harm).[550] The Non-Horizontal Merger Guidelines state that the Commission is unlikely to have concerns with non-horizontal mergers where the market share post-merger of the new entity in each of the markets concerned is below 30 per cent[551] and the post-merger HHI is below 2,000.[552] Indeed, the Commission has proposed that the simplified procedure should apply where the market share of the new entity in each of the markets concerned is below 30 per cent.[553]

---

[549] Non-Horizontal Merger Guidelines, paras. 16 and 27.

[550] Indeed, Form CO only requires the parties to provide data in relation to affected markets where one or more of the parties to the concentration are engaged in business activities in a product market, which is upstream or downstream of or neighbouring and closely related to a product in which any other party to the concentration is engaged, and any of their individual or combined market shares at either level is 25% or more, see Form CO, section 6 III.

[551] This percentage accords with the market share threshold included in the Verticals Block Exemption, see Chap. 11.

[552] The Commission will extensively investigate such cases only where 'special circumstances' exist: (i) the merger involves a company that is likely to expand in the near future; (ii) there are significant cross-shareholdings or cross-directorships among market participants; (iii) one of the merging parties is a firm which is likely to disrupt coordinated conduct; or (iv) where indications of prior or ongoing facilitating practices are present, Non-Horizontal Merger Guidelines, paras. 25–26.

[553] See n. 128 and accompanying text.

c. Assessment of Vertical Mergers

A number of cases examined carefully by the Commission have raised vertical foreclosure concerns, including a number in the energy[554] and media sectors. *AOL/ Time Warner,*[555] for example, concerned a merger between Time Warner, a media and entertainment company, and AOL, the leading internet access provider in the US. The merger would create the first internet vertically integrated content provider and would be able to distribute Time Warner content (music, news, and films) through AOL's internet distribution network. AOL would also have access to Bertelsmann content in consequence of a joint venture it had with the latter in Europe. The Commission was concerned that AOL would be able to dominate the emerging market for internet music delivery online through its becoming the gatekeeper to the nascent market. In the end the Commission cleared the merger subject to a 'remedy package' which essentially required AOL to sever its links with Bertelsmann. This would leave Europe's largest media company free to compete and prevent the merged entity from dominating the market. In the Non-Horizontal Merger Guidelines the Commission states that it appraises both the possible anti-competitive effects of vertical mergers and pro-competitive effects stemming from substantiated efficiencies.

Non-coordinated Effects: Foreclosure

With regard to the danger of non-coordinated effects, the focus is on foreclosure:[556] whether actual or potential rivals' access to supplies or markets is materially hampered or eliminated as a result of the merger, thereby reducing those companies' ability to compete and so allowing the merging parties—and possibly some of its competitors as well—profitably to increase the price charged to consumers. This may result from:

    (i) input foreclosure—where the merger will restrict access to an important input raising downstream rivals' costs; and/or

    (ii) customer foreclosure—where vertical integration forecloses upstream rivals by foreclosing their access to a sufficient customer base.

In each case, the Commission assesses: the *ability* of the merging parties to foreclose access to inputs or customers;[557] the *incentive* to do so; and the overall *likely effect* on competition (taking into account efficiencies that benefit consumers, are merger-specific and verifiable where they 'are likely to enhance the ability and incentive of the merged entity to act pro-competitively for the benefit of consumers, thereby counteracting the adverse effects on competition which the merger might otherwise have').[558]

In the context of input foreclosure, it seems unlikely that these conditions will be satisfied unless the input is sufficiently important, the firm has market power in the upstream market, the foreclosure will be profitable to the merged entity, and foreclosure will be a SIEC in the downstream market (through, for example, increasing costs of downstream rivals and raising barriers to entry

---

[554] See e.g. Case M.3440, *EDP/ENI/GDP (aff'd* Case T-87/05, *EDP v. Commission* [2005] ECR II-3745) and Case M.3696, *E.ON/MOL.* See also Chap. 11.

[555] Case M.1845, *Time-Warner/AOL,* IP/00/1145. See also e.g., Case M.4504, *SFR/Télé 2 France.*

[556] The Commission is also concerned that non-coordinated effects may occur where the merged entity may, by vertically integrating, gain access to commercially sensitive information regarding the upstream or downstream activities of rivals and that the merger may also put competitors at a competitive disadvantage, thereby dissuading them from entering or expanding in the market, Non-Horizontal Merger Guidelines, para. 78.

[557] In particular, where the merger involves an important input for the downstream product and the merged firm has market power in the upstream market or where the downstream merging party is an important customer in the downstream market and there are significant economies of scale or scope in the input market.

[558] e.g., internalisation of double mark-ups; improved coordination of the production and distribution process; and alignment of incentives for investments in new products, new production processes, and marketing, Non-Horizontal Merger Guidelines, paras. 55–57.

to potential competitors). In *TomTom/Tele Atlas*,[559] for example, the Commission cleared an acquisition by TomTom, a Personal Navigation Device (PND) manufacturer with a leading position, of Tele Atlas (one of two producers of navigable digital maps, an essential input for PND manufacturers). Although the Commission had been concerned that the duopoly in the upstream market for navigable digital maps, combined with TomTom's strong position on the market for PNDs, would lead to a SIEC, following an in-depth examination it concluded that the merged entity would not have the ability to increase the costs of other PND manufacturers for navigable digital maps or to limit their access to these maps. Its ability to restrict access to digital maps for others would be limited by the presence of an upstream competitor, Navteq. Further, it found that the merged company would have no incentive to restrict access to digital maps because the sales of digital maps lost by Tele Atlas would not be compensated by additional sales of PNDs.[560]

The possibility of foreclosure was also an issue discussed in *Google/Motorola*,[561] in particular as Google's open source Android OS, one of the most popular mobile operating systems (OS), and a number of Motorola's 'standard essential' patents[562] were key inputs in smart mobile devices (Motorola, being a leading player in the development of smart phones and tablets). In the end the merger was cleared unconditionally in Phase I proceedings. With regard to the standard essential patents, the Commission did not consider that the merger would significantly change the current position and was also influenced by Google's 'legally binding' and 'irrevocable' letter to standard-setting organisations to honour Motorola's pre-existing commitment to license them on FRAND terms. Further, it did not consider that Google would have the incentive to prevent Motorola's competitors from using its OS as that would stifle the spread of its other services.

The Commission will also consider countervailing factors (such as buyer power and potential competition) and assess efficiencies resulting from the merger (such as the internalisation of double mark-ups, better coordination of the production and distribution process, and alignment of parties' incentives).

Incentives to Foreclose and Article 102 TFEU

In considering incentives to foreclose, the Commission is required, in both vertical and conglomerate effects cases, to take into account the possibility that the foreclosing conduct might be illegal (under Article 102 TFEU). The question of the extent to which the existence of Article 102 can be expected to affect the incentive of the merged entity to engage in a course of conduct in breach of it (i.e. is the merger appraisal affected by the fact that foreclosure of the downstream, upstream, or related market would, or might, constitute an abuse of a dominant position?) arose in *GE/Honeywell*[563] and *Tetra Laval/Sidel*[564] (both of which involved potential vertical *and* conglomerate effects).

In *Tetra Laval* the GC[565] stressed the importance of the Commission basing its analysis of the likelihood of engaging in anti-competitive behaviour in the future on sufficiently convincing, plausible, and cogent evidence. It held that it could not be assumed that a dominant firm would automatically

---

[559] Case M.4854.

[560] The Commission also investigated the proposed acquisition of Tele Atlas's main competitor, Navteq, by Nokia, Case M.4942 (notified shortly after TomTom/Tele Atlas.

[561] Case M.6381.

[562] For a discussion of anti-competitive conduct in the context of standard-setting organisations see also Chaps. 7 and 12.

[563] Case M.2220, *aff'd* Cases T-209 and 210/01, *Honeywell v. Commission* and *General Electric Company v. Commission* [2005] ECR II-5527 and 5575. With regard to the vertical effects, however, the GC considered that the Commission had committed a manifest error of assessment and had failed to prove that the practices would in fact create or strengthen a dominant position. In particular, the Commission had been concerned that the merged entity would have an incentive not to supply engine starters to rival manufacturers of jet engines.

[564] Case Comp/M.2416, annulled on appeal Case T-5/02, [2002] ECR II-4381, *aff'd* Case C-12/03 P, [2005] ECR I-987.

[565] Case T-5/02, [2002] ECR II-4381, especially para. 159.

commit abuses of a dominant position and that its conduct would not be constrained by the existence of the competition rules. Rather, when the Commission sought, in assessing the likely effects of the merger, to rely on foreseeable conduct which was likely to constitute such an abuse, it was also required to assess whether, despite the prohibition, it was none the less likely that the entity would act in such a way or whether the illegal nature of the conduct and/or the risk of detection would make such a strategy unlikely. Although it was right to take into account the incentives to act illegally, therefore, the Commission should also have taken into account the extent to which the incentives would be eliminated, as a result of the illegality of the conduct, the likelihood of its detection, action taken by competent authorities, and the financial penalties which could ensue.

On appeal, the Commission alleged that such a burden would be impossible to comply with in practice. The CJ[566] appeared to agree, finding that although the Commission must make some assessment of the Article 102 position, the extent of the obligation imposed by the GC was excessive. It held that although the likelihood of the merged entity engaging in a specific course had to be examined comprehensively, taking account of both the incentives to adopt such conduct and the factors liable to reduce or even eliminate those incentives, it would run counter to the purpose of the merger rules to require the Commission to examine in every merger case the extent to which the incentives to adopt anti-competitive conduct would be reduced or eliminated as a result of the unlawfulness of the conduct in question, the likelihood of its detection, the action taken by the competent authorities, both at EU and national level, and the financial penalties which could ensue.[567] Such an investigation would require too speculative an assessment about how Article 102 would apply to hypothetical future events.[568]

Case C-12/03 P, *Commission v. Tetra Laval BV* [2005] ECR I-987

Court of Justice

74. Since the view is taken in the contested decision that adoption of the conduct referred to recital 364 in that decision is an essential step in leveraging, the [GC] was right to hold that the likelihood of its adoption must be examined comprehensively, that is to say, taking account, as stated in paragraph 159 of the judgment under appeal, both of the incentives to adopt such conduct and the factors liable to reduce, or even eliminate, those incentives, including the possibility that the conduct is unlawful.

75. However, it would run counter to the Regulation's purpose of prevention to require the Commission, as was held in the last sentence in paragraph 159 of the judgment under appeal, to examine, for each proposed merger, the extent to which the incentives to adopt anti-competitive conduct would be reduced, or even eliminated, as a result of the unlawfulness of the conduct in question, the likelihood of its detection, the action taken by the competent authorities, both at Community and national level, and the financial penalties which could ensue.

76. An assessment such as that required by the [GC] would make it necessary to carry out an exhaustive and detailed examination of the rules of the various legal orders which might be applicable and of the enforcement policy practised in them. Moreover, if it is to be relevant, such an assessment calls for a high probability of the occurrence of the acts envisaged as capable of giving rise to objections on the ground that they are part of anti-competitive conduct.

77. It follows that, at the stage of assessing a proposed merger, an assessment intended to establish whether an infringement of Article [102 TFEU] is likely and to ascertain that it will be penalised in several

---

[566] Case C-12/03 P, [2005] ECR I-987.

[567] Case C-12/03 P, [2005] ECR I-987.

[568] It also held that the Commission was required to take account of behavioural undertakings that would prevent that conduct, see discussion of remedies in Section 5.G.

legal orders would be too speculative and would not allow the Commission to base its assessment on all of the relevant facts with a view to establishing whether they support an economic scenario in which a development such as leveraging will occur.

78. Consequently, the [GC] erred in law in rejecting the Commission's conclusions as to the adoption by the merged entity of anti-competitive conduct capable of resulting in leveraging on the sole ground that the Commission had, when assessing the likelihood that such conduct might be adopted, failed to take account of the unlawfulness of that conduct and, consequently, of the likelihood of its detection, of action by the competent authorities, both at Community and national level, and of the financial penalties which might ensue. Nevertheless, since the judgment under appeal is also based on the failure to take account of the commitments offered by Tetra, it is necessary to continue the examination of the second ground of appeal.

79. With respect to the argument that the [GC] departed from the approach taken by it in the Gencor judgment, it must be held that, contrary to what the Commission claims, the [GC] did not depart from the position taken by it in paragraph 94 of that judgment, namely that there will be a significant impediment to effective competition if there is a lasting alteration of the structure of the relevant markets as a result of a concentration having the direct and immediate effect of creating conditions in which abusive conduct is possible and economically rational.

80. The situation in the Gencor case was entirely different from that addressed in the contested decision. As is clear from paragraph 91 of the judgment in that case, the concentration would have led to the creation of a dominant duopoly in the platinum and rhodium markets, as a result of which effective competition would have been significantly impeded in the common market.

81. It was therefore the concentration which would have given rise to a lasting alteration of the structure of the relevant markets in that case and thus would have made abuses possible and economically rational.

82. In the present case, it is true that the notified merger was capable of slightly altering the structure of the market for carton inasmuch as the merged entity could strengthen the dominant position which Tetra had held for some time on that market and which, moreover, had been the subject of a Commission decision pursuant to Article [102 TFEU]. However, it was not effective competition on the carton market which the Commission intended to protect by prohibiting the merger but competition on the market for PET equipment, in particular that for low and high capacity SBM machines used for sensitive products.

83. The structure of that market would not have been immediately and directly affected by the notified merger but it could have been so affected only as a result of leveraging and, in particular, abusive conduct by the merged entity on the carton market.

84. It follows from the above considerations that the situation examined in the Gencor case is not sufficiently comparable to that on which the [GC] ruled by the judgment under appeal for that court to have been able to draw any useful inferences from it. The structure of the market on which the Commission intended, by the contested decision, to preserve effective competition was, in the Gencor case, directly altered by the merger whereas, in the present case, it could be altered only by leveraging.

85. With respect to consideration of the behavioural commitments offered by Tetra, the [GC] was right to hold, in paragraph 161 of the judgment under appeal, that the fact that Tetra had, in the present case, offered commitments relating to its future conduct was a factor which the Commission had to take into account when assessing the likelihood that the merged entity would act in such a way as to make it possible to create a dominant position on one or more of the relevant markets for PET equipment.

The enquiry demanded by the CJ thus appears to be a pragmatic one, proportionate to the fact that the Commission is investigating a merger under constrained time limits. Indeed, in *General Electric* v. *Commission* the GC suggests that a summary, not detailed, analysis of this issue is required. The GC does not, however, address the concern raised by the CJ in *Tetra Laval* that this issue should not have an adverse impact on the EUMR's preventative function.

Case T-210/01, *General Electric Company v. Commission* [2005] ECR II-5575569

GC

73. It follows from the foregoing that the Commission must, in principle, take into account the potentially unlawful, and thus sanctionable, nature of certain conduct as a factor which might diminish, or even eliminate, incentives for an undertaking to engage in particular conduct. That appraisal does not, however, require an exhaustive and detailed examination of the rules of the various legal orders which might be applicable and of the enforcement policy practised within them, given that an assessment intended to establish whether an infringement is likely and to ascertain that it will be penalised in several legal orders would be too speculative.

74. Thus, where the Commission, without undertaking a specific and detailed investigation into the matter, can identify the unlawful nature of the conduct in question, in the light of Article [102] or of other provisions of Community law which it is competent to enforce, it is its responsibility to make a finding to that effect and take account of it in its assessment of the likelihood that the merged entity will engage in such conduct (see, to that effect, *Commission* v *Tetra Laval*, paragraph 60 above, paragraph 74).

75. It follows that, although the Commission is entitled to take as its basis a summary analysis, based on the evidence available to it at the time when it adopts its merger-control decision, of the lawfulness of the conduct in question and of the likelihood that it will be punished, it must none the less, in the course of its appraisal, identify the conduct foreseen and, where appropriate, evaluate and take into account the possible deterrent effect represented by the fact that the conduct would be clearly, or highly probably, unlawful under Community law.

The Commission seeks to synthesise the obligations imposed on it in these cases in its Non-Horizontal Merger Guidelines when it states:

46. In addition, when the adoption of a specific course of conduct by the merged entity is an essential step in foreclosure, the Commission examines both the incentives to adopt such conduct and the factors liable to reduce, or even eliminate, those incentives, including the possibility that the conduct is unlawful. Conduct may be unlawful inter alia because of competition rules or sector-specific rules at the EU or national levels. This appraisal, however, does not require an exhaustive and detailed examination of the rules of the various legal orders which might be applicable and of the enforcement policy practised within them. Moreover, the illegality of a conduct may be likely to provide significant disincentives for the merged entity to engage in such conduct only in certain circumstances. In particular, the Commission will consider, on the basis of a summary analysis: (i) the likelihood that this conduct would be clearly, or highly probably, unlawful under EU law, (ii) the likelihood that this illegal conduct could be detected, and (iii) the penalties which could be imposed.

Other Non-coordinated Effects and Coordinated Effects in Vertical Mergers

The Commission has not ordinarily been concerned with vertical mergers which have no foreclosure effects. However the Non-Horizontal Merger Guidelines state that the vertical mergers may also cause concern where the merged entity gains access to commercially sensitive information regarding the upstream or downstream activities of rivals through vertical integration, or where vertical integration changes the nature of competition in such a way that firms that previously were not coordinating their behaviour are significantly more likely to coordinate and raise price or otherwise harm competition. A vertical merger may also make coordination easier, more stable, or more effective for firms which were coordinating prior to a merger. For example, the Non-Horizontal Merger Guidelines state that a vertical merger, by reducing the number of effective competitors in a

---

569 See also Case T-209/01, *Honeywell v. Commission* [2005] ECR II-5527.

market, may make it easier for the firms concerned to reach a common understanding on the terms of coordination. Such a merger may also increase the level of market transparency between firms (for example, through access to sensitive information on rivals or by making it easier to monitor pricing) and reduce the scope for outsiders to destabilise the coordination by increasing barriers to enter the market

In J&J/Pfizer[570] the Commission had concerns about non-coordinated effects that would result from the acquisition of Pfizer's Consumer Healthcare (PCH) division by Johnson & Johnson (J&J). Through the proposed transaction, J&J would acquire PCH's Nicorette business. As a result, J&J would own a leading Nicotine Replacement Therapy (NRT) patch brand (PCH's Nicorette) and would be the sole supplier of nicotine patches to its principal downstream competitor, GSK. The Commission considered that there was a risk that this vertical relationship would give the merged entity the ability and incentive to foreclose GSK from the market for nicotine patches/NRT products by making it harder for it to obtain supplies under similar prices and conditions as would be available absent the merger. This would advantage the merged entity's Nicorette business and lead to harm to consumers (a risk of input foreclosure). Further, there was a risk that the merged entity would gain access to confidential information about GSK which it could use post-merger to the benefit of the acquired Nicorette business. In order to resolve the vertical concerns, J&J offered to divest part of its international nicotine patch manufacturing business. It also agreed to transfer relevant supply agreements, trademarks, and technology and to provide manufacturing capacities and technical assistance to the purchaser until the latter has become fully operational. The proposed remedies would therefore structurally eliminate the vertical relationship.

d. Assessment of Conglomerate Mergers

Despite the adoption of some controversial decisions on conglomerate effects, the Commission confirms in its Non-Horizontal Merger Guidelines that the majority of conglomerate mergers will not lead to any competition problems. In certain cases, however, where the companies are active in closely related markets (for example, complementary products or products belonging to a range of products purchased by the same set of customers for the same use)[571] harm may arise. As in its assessment of vertical effects, the Commission considers both the possible anti-competitive effects arising from conglomerate mergers and the possible pro-competitive effects stemming from substantiated efficiencies.

GE/Honeywell and Tetra Laval/Sidel

The approach taken in the Guidelines is, no doubt, an attempt to meet the challenges set by the EU courts in appeals from the Commission's decisions in GE/Honeywell[572] and Tetra Laval/Sidel[573] respectively. In both of these cases the Commission prohibited mergers, principally on account of their conglomerate effects, and on the basis that the mergers would create incentives for the merged firms to leverage market power between related markets. In both cases the courts were extremely critical of the Commission's analysis. The Commission's right to intervene in mergers resulting in conglomerate effects was, however, upheld.

---

[570]   Case M.4314.

[571]   Non-Horizontal Merger Guidelines, paras. 90–91.

[572]   M.2220, aff'd Cases T-209 and 210/01, Honeywell v. Commission and General Electric Company v. Commission [2005] ECR II-5527 and 5575.

[573]   Case M.2416, annulled on appeal Case T-5/02, [2002] ECR II-4381, aff'd Case C-12/03 P, [2005] ECR I-987. See also Case M.794, Coca-Cola Enterprises/Amalgamated Beverages [1997] OJ L218/15; Case M.833, The Coca-Cola Company/Carlsberg A/S [1998] OJ L145/41; Case M.938, Guinness/Grand Metropolitan [1998] OJ L288/24.

In *GE/Honeywell*[574] the Commission prohibited the proposed acquisition of Honeywell Inc. by General Electric Co. even though it had been cleared by the US antitrust authorities.[575] Essentially, the Commission was concerned that the $42 billion merger would strengthen GE's already dominant position in the markets for jet engines for large commercial aircraft and regional aircraft and create a dominant position in avionics, non-avionics, and corporate jet engines (Honeywell was the leading supplier of these products). In particular, the Commission considered that it would allow the merged entity to leverage its market power by engaging in bundling or strategic price cuts, thereby strengthening the dominant position in the large commercial jet engine market and creating dominant positions in the corporate jet engine market and avionics/non-avionics market.[576] The anticipated outcome of the bundling or strategic price costs was that, although prices would reduce in the short term, the pricing policy would drive competitors from the market so that, eventually, prices could be expected to rise and product quality and service would reduce.[577] The speculative nature of this prediction triggered a 'firestorm of criticism', particularly in the US, 'not just from the US antitrust authorities, senior [US] administration officials, but also from the business community generally and from leading economists, antitrust legal scholars, and editorial writers'.[578]

The criticism centred on the notion that the EU authorities had prohibited a merger which was to lead to a reduction in prices and increase in output. The anti-competitive effect would only result if the other competitors could not match the merged firm's offerings. In the US, the authorities went out of their way to stress that they would not prohibit a merger which would make a firm more efficient, because of fears that it might force competitors from a market: antitrust laws 'protect competition, not competitors'.[579] In their view a competition authority should be very cautious about adopting a merger policy that sacrificed short-term efficiencies in the name of maintaining competition.[580]

W. J. Kolasky, 'Conglomerate Mergers and Range Effects: It's a long way from Chicago to Brussels', Address before George Mason University Symposium Washington, DC, 9 November 2001

At a minimum, before applying such a policy, we should make certain we have a high degree of confidence that the trade-off we are making will ultimately benefit consumers. This would require quantifying the efficiencies and determining the likely duration of the competitive round that will occur before less

---

[574] Case M.2220, *aff'd* Cases T-209 and 210/01, *Honeywell, v. Commission* and *General Electric Company v. Commission* [2005] ECR II-5527 and 5575. See, e.g., G. Drauz, 'Unbundling GE/Honeywell' [2003] *ECLR* 115.

[575] See, e.g., F. D. Platt Majoras, 'GE-Honeywell: The US Decision', 29 November 2001, Remarks before the Antitrust Law Section, State Bar of Georgia, available on the US, DOJ Antitrust Division's website. For the extraterritorial aspects of this decision see Chap. 16.

[576] It was also concerned that the aircraft financing arm of GE, GECAS, would specify Honeywell equipment in its aircraft purchases

[577] See D. Guikajis, L. Petit, G. Garnier, and P De Luyck, 'General Electric/Honeywell—An Insight into the Commission's investigation and decision' (2001) *Competition Policy Newsletter* 5 (October).

[578] See W. J. Kolasky, 'Conglomerate Mergers and Range Effects: It's a long way from Chicago to Brussels', Address before George Mason University Symposium Washington, DC, 9 November 2001. See also A. Burnside, 'GE, Honey, I sunk the merger' [2003] *ECLR* 107 and M. Pflanz and C. Caffarra, 'The Economics of GE/Honeywell' [2003] *ECLR* 115.

[579] 'The key test for assessing mergers in Europe is whether they create or strengthen a dominant position. European merger control is not about protecting competitors but about ensuring that markets remain sufficiently competitive in the long run so that consumers benefit from sufficient choice, innovation and competitive prices', IP/01/939.

[580] See Kolasky, 'Conglomerate Mergers and Range Effects: It's a long way from Chicago to Brussels' (cited in n. 578). See also the disagreement over the *Oracle/Sun Microsystems* case in which the DOJ published a press release backing the merger on the same date that the Commission launched Phase II proceedings.

efficient rivals are forced from the market. It would also require a high degree of confidence that the rivals will in fact be forced from the market—that they will not be able to develop counter-strategies that will enable them to become more efficient themselves in order to survive. Indeed, any business strategy that did not take into account competitive counter-strategies would fail the test for the Nash equilibrium...It would also require us to estimate the size of the price increases likely to occur once the merged firm gains market power to determine whether, taking into account the efficiencies, future prices to consumers are likely to be higher or lower than they would be in a market populated by several less efficient firms. Finally we would have to determine the likely duration for the monopoly period—which would be dependent on entry conditions at the time the monopoly is finally achieved.

In the United States, we have very little confidence in our ability to make these judgments which would necessarily involve predictions far out into the future. We believe...that we need to 'be humble.' We have more confidence in the self-correcting nature of the markets. This confidence is especially strong when the markets are populated by strong rivals and strong buyers, who will usually find ways to protect themselves from an aspiring monopolist. Our strong belief in markets and our humility in our predictive abilities lead us to be skeptical of claims by rivals that a merger will lead to their ultimate demise and to demand strong empirical proof before we will accept such claims.

In the appeal from the Commission's decision the GC[581] upheld the Commission's decision but *only* on the basis that its analysis of horizontal effects (the creation of a monopoly in the market for engines for large regional jets) provided a sufficient basis to prohibit the merger. With regard to the leveraging theory, the Court considered that the Commission had made a manifest error of assessment and had failed to provide evidence to substantiate its claim that bundling between engines and avionics/non-avionics was possible or feasible. The Commission had not established that the merged entity had an economic incentive to bundle and consequently it had the burden of putting forward other evidence to suggest that the merged entity would make the strategic decision to sacrifice profits in the short term with a view to reaping larger profits in the future. This could be done, for example, through economic studies or the production of internal documents showing that GE's directors had that objective on the launch of their bid for Honeywell.[582]

The GC thus carefully scrutinised the Commission's decision to determine whether it had been established that the merged entity would have the capability of engaging in the alleged bundling practices, whether it was likely to do so and if, in consequence, anti-competitive harm would occur (a dominant position would have been created or strengthened on one or more of the relevant markets in the relatively near future).[583]

Case T-210/01, *General Electric Company v. Commission* [2005] ECR II-5575[584]

General Court

399. The Commission stated in essence in the contested decision that, following the merger, the merged entity would have the ability, unlike its competitors, to offer its customers packages for large commercial aircraft, large regional aircraft and corporate aircraft, encompassing both engines and avionics

---

[581] Cases T-209 and 210/01, *Honeywell* v. *Commission* and *General Electric Company* v. *Commission* [2005] ECR II-5527 and 5575. For a good summary of the case and the issues decided on appeal, see D. Howarth, 'The Court of First Instance in *GE/Honeywell*' [2006] ECLR 485.

[582] Case T-210/01, *General Electric Company* v. *Commission* [2005] ECR II-5575, para. 466.

[583] The case was decided under the old EUMR so the dominance not the SIEC test was applicable.

[584] See also Case T-209/01, *Honeywell* v. *Commission* [2005] ECR II-5527.

and non-avionics products. It also held that such behaviour would clearly be in the commercial interests of the merged entity and would thus probably be engaged in after the merger had taken place (recitals 350 to 404, 412 to 416, 432 to 434, 443 and 444 and 445 to 458). As a consequence, a dominant position would have been created for Honeywell on the markets for avionics and non-avionics products and GE's dominant positions would have been strengthened, particularly on the market for large commercial jet aircraft engines (recital 458 of the contested decision).

400. The Commission's case is based on the fact that jet engines, on the one hand, and avionics and non-avionics products, on the other, are complementary, since all these products are indispensable in the construction of an aircraft. The final customer, the operator of the aircraft, must therefore purchase all of them, directly or indirectly, from their manufacturer. The Commission held in the contested decision that on the whole the customers are essentially the same for all those products and that the latter could therefore be bundled. The Commission also observes that the applicant's group is financially very strong, both compared with its main competitors on the engines markets and with its competitors on the markets for avionics and non-avionics products (see, as regards the latter, recitals 302 to 304, 323 and 324 of the contested decision; see also recital 398 et seq.). The merged entity would thus be in a position to reduce its profit margins on avionics and non-avionics products with a view to increasing its market share and making larger profits in the future.

401. It should be noted, as a preliminary point, that the way it is predicted that the merged entity will behave in the future is a vital aspect of the Commission's analysis of bundling in the present case. It follows from the fact that the applicant had no presence on the markets for avionics and non-avionics products prior to the merger, together with the fact that Honeywell had no presence on the market for large commercial jet aircraft engines before the merger, that the merger would have had no horizontal anti-competitive effect on those markets. Thus, the merger would, prima facie, have had no effect whatsoever on those markets.

402. Moreover, in so far as the Commission predicts, at recitals 443 and 444 of the contested decision, that bundling will have an impact on the market for engines for corporate jet aircraft, it should be noted that the applicant's pre-merger share of that market was only [10–20]%, in terms of the installed base, whilst Honeywell's was [40–50]%, and only [0–10]%, in terms of the installed base on those aircraft still in production, as compared with Honeywell's [40–50]% share (recital 88 of the contested decision). In those circumstances, even if it were shown that the merged entity would bundle those engines with avionics and non-avionics products after the merger, there would be no causal link between the merger and the bundled offers, except in the small minority of cases in which the engine was a product of the former GE. Moreover, it is not suggested in the contested decision that either of the parties to the merger manufactures engines for small regional aircraft. It follows that any bundling which might be engaged in by the merged entity on the market for regional aircraft would in any event concern only large regional aircraft.

403. The Commission held in the contested decision that each avionics product for regional and corporate aircraft constitutes a market in itself and that there is a market for each non-avionics product for all types of aircraft, including large commercial aircraft. Accordingly, its reasoning with regard to the creation, by means of bundling, of dominant positions on the markets for the different avionics products cannot be accepted in relation to the markets for each of the various avionics products for corporate and regional aircraft. Indeed, on the assumption that it actually becomes a reality after the transaction, any bundling attributable to the merger will affect only one segment of those markets, the large regional aircraft segment. In the same way, the Commission's reasoning is undermined (albeit to a lesser degree) in relation to non-avionics products, for which the Commission defined an individual market for each specific product, irrespective of the size and other features of the aircraft equipped.

404. It is therefore, in principle, in the sector for large commercial aircraft, for which the Commission has defined distinct markets both for jet engines and for each avionics product, that the Commission's case on bundling could conceivably be sustained.

405. In relation to the possible impact of the merger on (i) the markets for jet engines for large commercial aircraft and large regional aircraft, (ii) those for avionics products for large commercial aircraft and

(iii) those for non-avionics products, the Court must determine whether the Commission has established that the merged entity would not only have the capability to engage in the bundling practices described in the contested decision but also, on the basis of convincing evidence, that it would have been likely to engage in those practices after the merger and that, in consequence, a dominant position would have been created or strengthened on one or more of the relevant markets in the relatively near future (*Tetra Laval* v *Commission*, paragraph 58 above, paragraphs 146 to 162).

Notwithstanding the general controversy the Commission's decision in *GE/Honeywell* provoked, in *Tetra Laval/Sidel*[585] the Commission prohibited another merger which it considered would enable the merged entity to leverage its market power in one market into another. This case concerned a public bid by Tetra Laval SA for shares in Sidel SA. Tetra, part of the Tetra Pak company, is the world market leader in the area of liquid food carton packaging. In contrast, Sidel is involved in the production of packaging equipment and systems and is a worldwide leader for the production and supply of stretch blow moulding (SBM) machines, used in the production of polyethlylene terephthalate (PET) plastic bottles. The Commission considered that the merger would strengthen Tetra's dominant position in the market for aseptic carton packaging machines and cartons and create a dominant position in the market for PET packaging equipment. The Commission made findings of horizontal and vertical effects and held that the merger would enable the merged entity to exploit its dominant position on the carton markets by leveraging into the market for PET packaging equipment in order to dominate it. The Commission set out its reasons for concluding that the market structure was particularly conducive to leverage effects at paragraph 359 of its decision:

- There would be a common pool of customers requiring both carton and PET packaging systems to package sensitive liquids.
- Tetra has a particularly strong dominant position in aseptic carton packaging with more than [80–90 per cent] of the market and a dependent customer base.
- Tetra/Sidel would start from a strong, leading, position in PET packaging systems and in particular SBM machines with a market share in the region of [60–70 per cent].
- Tetra/Sidel would have the ability to target selectively specific customers or specific customer groups as the structure of the market enables price discrimination.
- Tetra/Sidel would have a strong economic incentive to engage in leveraging practices. As carton and PET are technical substitutes, when a customer switches to PET he/she is a lost customer on the carton side of the business either because he/she partially switched *from* carton or because he/she did not switch some of the production *to* carton from other packaging materials. This creates an added incentive to capture the customer on the PET side of the business to recover the loss. Therefore, by leveraging its current market position in carton, Tetra/Sidel would not only enhance its market share on the PET side but defend or compensate its possible loss on the carton side.
- Competitors of Tetra/Sidel in both the carton and the PET equipment markets would be much smaller, with the largest competitor having no more than [10–20 per cent] share in the market for carton packaging machines or SBM machines.

The Commission considered that the leveraging would foreclose competitors from the rest of the SBM machine market and turn Sidel's leading position on the market into a dominant one. On appeal, the GC annulled the Commission's decision, finding the pleas alleging lack of horizontal,

---

[585] Case M.2416. The Commission's decision in Case M.2283, *Schneider/Legrand* also relied on the conglomerate effects of the merger. In this case the GC annulled the Commission's decision as the Commission had not identified its conglomeracy concerns in the SO, see n. 678 and accompanying text, Case T-310/01, *Schneider Electric SA* v. *Commission* [2002] ECR II-4071.

vertical, and conglomerate anti-competitive effects were well founded.[586] The GC's judgment was upheld by the CJ on appeal.[587] The GC devoted more than half of its judgment to the plea that the Commission had failed to establish foreseeable conglomerate effects,[588] concluding that the decision did not establish that the merger would give rise to significant anti-competitive conglomerate effects to the requisite legal standard.[589]

The GC accepted that the EUMR can apply to merger transactions having horizontal, vertical, or conglomerate effects so long as the conditions set out in Article 2(3) are met[590] and drew a distinction between mergers where the conglomerate effects would be structural (arising directly from the economic structure created)[591] and those where they might be behavioural, in the sense that they arise only if the new entity created engages in certain commercial practices.[592] *Tetra Laval* was of the latter type. It was therefore necessary to determine whether the merger would have anti-competitive effects by, in all likelihood, allowing the new entity to obtain, in the relatively near future, a dominant position on a market in which one of the parties held a leading position, as a result of leveraging from a market in which the other party was already dominant.[593] In a case involving prospective analysis of conglomerate effects, the GC stated that the Commission must establish that competition will be significantly impeded in the near future:[594] the parties must have both the ability and incentive to leverage and the consequences of leveraging must be particularly plausible and must in all likelihood occur in the very near future.

The judgment stressed the importance of the Commission basing its analysis of the likelihood of leveraging, and of the consequences of such leveraging, on sufficiently convincing, plausible, and cogent evidence. Further, the GC held that it could not be assumed that a dominant firm would automatically commit abuses of a dominant position (and that its conduct would not be constrained by the existence of the competition rules).[595]

Case T-5/02, *Tetra Laval BV v. Commission* [2002] ECR II-4381

GC

146. It should be observed, first, that the Regulation, particularly at Article 2(2) and (3), does not draw any distinction between, on the one hand, merger transactions having horizontal and vertical effects and, on the other hand, those having a conglomerate effect. It follows that, without distinction between those types of transactions, a merger can be prohibited only if the two conditions laid down in Article 2(3) are met (see paragraph 120 above). Consequently, a merger having a conglomerate effect must, like any other merger (see paragraph 120 above), be authorised by the Commission if it is not established that it creates or strengthens a dominant position in the common market or in a substantial part of it and that, as a result, effective competition will be significantly impeded.

---

[586] Case T-5/02, [2002] ECR II-4381, *aff'd* Case C-12/03 P, [2005] ECR I-987. When the Commission re-examined the merger, it cleared it subject to a commitment that Tetra Laval license the new technology for making PET bottles to third parties.

[587] Case C-12/03 P, [2005] ECR I-987.

[588] Case T-5/02, [2002] ECR II-4381, paras. 142–336.

[589] Case T-5/02, [2002] ECR II-4381, para. 226.

[590] Case T-5/02, [2002] ECR II-4381, paras. 146–152.

[591] i.e. where the new entity would immediately and automatically create a second dominant position which the new entity could abuse.

[592] Case T-5/02, [2002] ECR II-4381, para. 147.

[593] Case T-5/02, [2002] ECR II-4381, para. 148.

[594] Case T-5/02, [2002] ECR II-4381, para. 153.

[595] See n. 564 and n. 565 and accompanying text.

...

> 155. The Commission's analysis of a merger producing a conglomerate effect is conditioned by require-
> ments similar to those defined by the Court with regard to the creation of a situation of collective dom-
> inance (*Kali & Salz*, paragraph 222; and *Airtours v. Commission*, paragraph 63). Thus the Commission's
> analysis of a merger transaction which is expected to have an anti-competitive conglomerate effect calls
> for a particularly close examination of the circumstances which are relevant for an assessment of that
> effect on the conditions of competition in the reference market. As the Court has already held, where
> the Commission takes the view that a merger should be prohibited because it will create or strengthen
> a dominant position within a foreseeable period, it is incumbent upon it to produce convincing evidence
> thereof (*Airtours v. Commission*, paragraph 63). Since the effects of a conglomerate-type merger are gener-
> ally considered to be neutral, or even beneficial, for competition on the markets concerned, as is recognised
> in the present case by the economic writings cited in the analyses annexed to the parties' written plead-
> ings, the proof of anti-competitive conglomerate effects of such a merger calls for a precise examination,
> supported by convincing evidence, of the circumstances which allegedly produce those effects (see, by
> analogy, *Airtours v. Commission*, paragraph 63).

The CJ rejected the Commission's appeal from this judgment in its entirety. Although it did find
that the GC had in some respects erred in the law, it held that these errors did not call into question
the judgment insofar as it annulled the Commission's decision.[596] The judgment sheds light on a
number of important issues, including the standard of proof in merger cases and the impact that the
illegality of the conduct has on the incentives of the merged entity to adopt any abusive conduct. In
particular, the CJ stressed that the prospective analysis required in merger control had to be carried
out with great care: it required an analysis not of past events but of a prediction of the future, making
it necessary to envisage various chains of cause and effect with a view to ascertaining which of them
was most likely. The quality of evidence relied upon by the Commission in such circumstances is
particularly important.[597]

Non-coordinated Effects—Foreclosure

In its Guidelines the Commission states that its analysis of non-coordinated effects focuses on the
possibility of foreclosure:[598] the possibility that the merger will confer on the merged entity the ability and incentive to leverage a strong market position from one market to another by means of tying
or bundling or other exclusionary practices.[599] The Commission will examine intertwined factors to
determine whether the merged firm would have the ability to foreclose its rivals (which is unlikely
unless, for example, one of the products is viewed by many customers as particularly important
and there is a common pool of customers for the individual products concerned), whether it would
have the economic incentive to do so (which is dependent on the profitability of the strategy and the
extent to which the incentive to adopt such conduct is reduced or eliminated by, for example, the
possibility that the conduct is unlawful), and whether a foreclosure strategy would have a significant
detrimental effect on competition causing harm to consumers.

---

[596] Case C-12/03 P, [2005] ECR I-987. The Advocate-General (Tizzano) took the view that the GC was right to have
declared that the Commission ought to have taken into consideration the various factors that might have influenced
the likelihood of the merged entity behaving in such a way as to enable it to acquire the predicted dominant position
on the PET market. '[T]he [GC] correctly found that, just as the Commission had assessed the economic incentives
for engaging in such conduct, so it ought to have taken into consideration the possible disincentives in that respect
of the unlawful nature of the conduct in question ... or of the commitments into which that company had offered to
enter', Opinion of 25 May 2004, para. 123.

[597] See Section 7.

[598] Non-Horizontal Merger Guidelines, paras. 93–118.

[599] The Commission accepts that tying and bundling as such are common practices that often have no anti-competitive consequences, Non-Horizontal Merger Guidelines, para. 92.

The Non-Horizontal Merger Guidelines indicate concern that bundling or tying may reduce sales by single-component rivals by affecting their ability or incentive to compete and allowing the merged entity subsequently to acquire market power (in the market for the tied or bundled good) and/or maintain market power (in the market for the tying or leveraging good). The effect on competition is assessed in light of substantiated efficiencies, for example, lowering margins on the sale of complementary goods[600] and costs savings in the form of economies of scope.[601] In *Google/DoubleClick*[602] the Commission investigated but ruled out various foreclosure scenarios that might result from the acquisition by Google (a leading player in search advertising and online ad intermediation services) of DoubleClick, the leading supplier of ad serving.

Portfolio Power and Foreclosure

Prior to the adoption of the Non-Horizontal Merger Guidelines, in *Guinness/Grand Metropolitan*[603] the Commission had to examine a concentration which had an impact on certain separate spirits markets. Although there was some horizontal overlap in the relevant markets in which the parties operated, the merger also led to an extension of the complementary products and range of spirits offered. The Commission displayed concern about 'portfolio power'.

Case M.938, *Guinness/Grand Metropolitan* [1998] OJ L228/24

Commission

40. The holder of a portfolio of leading spirit brands may enjoy a number of advantages. In particular, his position in relation to his customers is stronger since he is able to provide a range of products and will account for a greater proportion of their business, he will have greater flexibility to structure his prices, promotions and discounts, he will have greater potential for tying, and he will be able to realize economies of scale and scope in his sales and marketing activities, Finally, the implicit (or explicit) threat of a refusal to supply is more potent.

41. The strength of these advantages, and their potential effect on the competitive structure of the market, depends on a number of factors, including whether the holder of the portfolio has the brand leader or one or more leading brands in a particular market; the market shares of the various brands, particularly in relation to the shares of competitors; the relative importance of the individual markets in which the parties have significant shares and brands across the range of product markets in which the portfolio is held; and/or the number of markets in which the portfolio holder has a brand leader or leading brand.

The Commission concluded that the merger in that case would have portfolio effects. The effect was particularly acute on the Greek market where the merged entity would have a dominant position in the gin, brandy, and rum markets and where it would be able to supply the leading brands, with the exception of vodka. Through portfolio effects the dominant position in these markets would

---

[600] The Cournot effect, i.e. the merged firm has an incentive to lower margin on one product to boost sales of a complementary product.

[601] The Guidelines state, however, that '[s]uch economies of scope…are necessary but not sufficient to provide an efficiency justification for bundling or tying. Indeed, benefits from economies of scope frequently can be realized without any need for technical or contractual bundling', Non-Horizontal Merger Guidelines, para. 118.

[602] Case M.4371. See e.g., J. Brockhoff, B. Jehanno, V. Pozzato, C. Buhr, P. Eberl and P. Papandropoulos, 'Google/DoubleClick: The first test for the Commission's non-horizontal merger guidelines' (2008) 2 *Competition Policy Newsletter* 53.

[603] Case M.938, [1998] OJ L288/24.

be reinforced.[604] This decision received criticism not for its adoption of the concept of portfolio power but for failing to identify with sufficient clarity what is wrong with an undertaking's acquisition of a wider portfolio of products. For example, some paragraphs, including paragraph 40, of the Commission's decision indicate that the Commission objected to the economies of scale and scope offered to the parties from the increased range of products that the merger allowed.[605] Such benefits would, however, not harm but benefit consumers and intervention on these grounds would give the Commission a broad discretion. An objection to portfolio power on the ground that it would give the merged entity greater power to tie products is less controversial.[606]

The Guidelines clarify that the fact that the merged entity will have a broad range or portfolio of products does not, as such, raise competition concerns but that this factor may be relevant when determining whether the merged entity will have the ability to foreclose the market. In such circumstances, customers may have a strong incentive to save transaction costs by buying the range of products from a single source rather than from many.

In *Nestlé/Gerber*[607] the Commission unconditionally cleared Nestlé's acquisition of Novartis's Gerber baby food business. Although the activities of the parties overlapped in several segments of manufactured baby food (baby meals, drinks, and cereals) in certain Member States, the Commission found these did not give rise to competitive concerns. In the course of its investigation, the Commission considered possible portfolio effects in the context of the relative strength of competitors' brands and their portfolios. In some markets, Nestlé would become, post-merger, a full-range supplier of baby foods with strong brands in other food markets. Some respondents to the Commission's market test considered that Nestlé would be able to use its portfolio power to prevent new entry or to impede the expansion of existing 'single-brand' competitors (by, for example, limiting the access of competitors to distribution channels and reducing their shelf-space).

In assessing conglomerate effects, however, the Commission drew a distinction between a 'pure portfolio effect' (an incentive on customers to buy the range of products from a single source rather than from many suppliers because it entails efficiencies) and a strategic use of portfolio and financial leverage, such as product bundling, targeted discounts, and discriminatory across the board promotions.[608] The Commission considered that the former, although conferring a competitive advantage on suppliers, is not necessarily regarded as anti-competitive. It clarified that conglomerate effects result in a significant impediment to effective competition when the merged entity decides to condition its sales in a particular and strategic way in order to disadvantage its competitors or potential entrants. On the facts, the Commission found no evidence that Nestlé would have opportunity or incentive, post-merger, to adopt an anti-competitive bundling strategy. The Commission was also concerned about possible bundling and technical tying of security products and services (made by McAfee) with Intel's central processing units and chipsets in *Intel/McAfee*.[609] In the end, however, the merger was cleared in Phase I proceedings after commitments were offered to allay the Commission's concerns. The Commission rejected concerns about tying in *Microsoft/Skype*,[610] however.

Coordinated Effects

The Non-Horizontal Merger Guidelines also state that conglomerate mergers may, in certain circumstances, facilitate anti-competitive coordination in markets, for example by reducing the number

---

[604] Case M.938, *Guinness/Grand Metropolitan* [1998] OJ L288/24, paras. 90–118. The Commission permitted the merger only once the parties agreed to end the distribution arrangements for Bacardi rum in Greece even though the merger did not increase the parties' market shares on this market.

[605] [1998] OJ L288/24, para. 40.

[606] See, e.g., Bishop and Walker, *The Economics of EC Competition Law* (cited in n. 366), 8.030–8.032.

[607] Case M.4688.

[608] *Nestlé/Gerber*, Case M.4688, para. 35.

[609] Case M.5984.

[610] Case M.6281, Case T-79/12, *Cisco Systems and Management v. Commission* (judgment pending).

of effective competitors, where foreclosed rivals choose not to contest the situation of coordination and/or by increasing the scope and effectiveness of a disciplining mechanism by increasing the extent and importance of multi-market competition.

119. Conglomerate mergers may in certain circumstances facilitate anticompetitive co-ordination in markets, even in the absence of an agreement or a concerted practice within the meaning of Article [101 TFEU]. The framework set out in Section IV of the Notice on Horizontal Mergers also applies in this context. In particular, co-ordination is more likely to emerge in markets where it is fairly easy to identify the terms of co-ordination and where such co-ordination is sustainable.

120. One way in which a conglomerate merger may influence the likelihood of a coordinated outcome in a given market is by reducing the number of effective competitors to such an extent that tacit coordination becomes a real possibility. Also when rivals are not excluded from the market, they may find themselves in a more vulnerable situation. As a result, foreclosed rivals may choose not to contest the situation of co-ordination, but may prefer instead to live under the shelter of the increased price level.

121. Further, a conglomerate merger may increase the extent and importance of multi-market competition. Competitive interaction on several markets may increase the scope and effectiveness of disciplining mechanisms in ensuring that the terms of co-ordination are being adhered to.

(x) Industrial, Social, and other Policy

a. General

A further question which arises is whether or not non-competition factors can or should be, or are/have been taken into account when appraising mergers under Article 2. Could, for example, the fact that a merger is advantageous from an industrial or social policy point of view be used to find that an otherwise problematic merger is nonetheless compatible with the common market? Alternatively, could non-competition factors be relied upon to prohibit a merger which is otherwise unproblematic from a competition perspective?

b. Other Policies as a Countervailing Factor

Industrial policy, for example, could support industrial restructuring where it is necessary for the undertakings to compete in a global market, to encourage cross-border concentration, to encourage technical progress, to protect certain industries, or to protect employment, even where a concentration might be a SIEC. In the run-up to the adoption of the original EUMR some Member States feared that EU industrial policy, aimed at safeguarding and ensuring 'the competitiveness of European industry', might support the creation of a Euro champion in circumstances where that Euro champion would be dominant and impede effective competition within the common market.[611] Although the EUMR allows technical and economic progress to be taken into account, this is just one factor to be taken into account in the overall appraisal. Recital 23 of the EUMR does, however, state that the Commission must place its appraisal within the general framework of the fundamental objectives of the Treaties.[612] Arguably, this permits broader EU policies to be taken into account in the appraisal process. In the view of the Commissioner responsible for competition at the time the original EUMR was passed, Sir Leon Brittan, however, the wording of Article 2(1) does not open the back door to industrial policy

[611] An original draft of the EUMR gave the Commission power to exempt concentrations which led to the creation or strengthening of a dominant position but which resulted in technical and economic progress to the benefit of consumers. However, many Member States objected to the inclusion of such a defence on the ground that the Regulation would be used as an adjunct to industrial policy with the objective of supporting European winners. During the 1960s and 1970s industrial policy was applied by some Member States in a protectionist way.

[612] See Chap. 2. Recital 13 to the original EUMR also stated that the appraisal should be made within the general framework of the fundamental objectives referred to in Art. 2 of the EC Treaty, including the strengthening of the EU's economic and social cohesion, see also Case T-12/93, *Comité Central d'Enterprise de la Société Anonyme Vittel v. Commission* [1995] ECR II-1247, paras. 38–40.

considerations, especially since it permits technical and economic progress to be taken into account only 'provided that it is to the consumers' advantage and does not form an obstacle to competition'.[613] Further, the Commission has been hostile to attempts by Member States to protect or create national champions in breach of the EUMR rules.[614] Similarly, Article 2 would not appear to permit other non-competition factors such as social policy to be taken into account as part of the appraisal process.[615]

One factor that should not be overlooked, however, is that the final decision to clear or prohibit a concentration following a Phase II merger investigation is made by the College of Commissioners and not simply by the Commissioner responsible for competition.[616] This means that in controversial or politically charged cases lobbying of the Commissioners takes place. This has led to concern that, even where DG COMP concentrates exclusively on competition criteria in its assessment, these competition factors may be overridden by other policy considerations when the final decision is taken. Although some high-profile merger cases appear to have caused a clash between proponents of industrial policy and supporters of a competition policy based strictly on competition factors alone,[617] in most cases the Commission has resolutely opposed mergers which will significantly impede effective competition. In *Aérospatiale-Alenia/de Havilland*,[618] for example, controversy arose as many supported the transaction from an industrial point of view,[619] whilst others, including the then Competition Commissioner, Sir Leon Brittan, opposed it, believing that it would lead to the creation of a dominant position.[620] The Commission's decision to prohibit the merger was not a universally popular one and met with wide coverage in the media. The final decisions to block the mergers in *MSG/Media Services GmbH*[621] and *Volvo/Scania*[622] were also controversial. During the 2009 financial and economic crisis, the Commission also came under some pressure both from businesses and politicians to relax the application of the competition rules and to subordinate pro-market policies to industrial and other policies and to be supportive of struggling businesses. Nonetheless the Commission took the view that the recession was 'no time to relax the rules'. Rather it was 'business as usual in cartels, mergers and antitrust'.[623]

Although DG COMP has not therefore appeared to allow industrial or other criteria to prevail in merger policy, such criteria and other political factors could possibly arise at the final stage, the

---

[613] See, e.g., IP/04/501, 'The Commission puts industry center stage and reinforces competitiveness in an enlarged European Union'. See also, e.g., Case M.469, *MSG Media Service GmbH* [1994] OJ L364/1.

[614] Two mergers in the energy sector which would have created national energy champions were only cleared by the Commission subject to compliance with significant remedies, see Case M.3868, *DONG/Elsam/Energi E2* and Case M.4180, *Gaz de France/Suez*.

[615] Subject to a teleological interpretation being given to the provision, see Chaps. 2 and 4.

[616] See Chap. 2.

[617] In Case M.315, *Mannesmann/Vallourec/Ilva* [1994] OJ L102/1, e.g., it appears that industrial considerations may have ultimately influenced the College of Commissioners' final decision to authorise a merger which DG Comp wished to prohibit on the ground that it would lead to the creation of a collective dominant position on the Western European market for seamless steel tubes. However, the case was strongly supported by the Commissioner responsible for industry. It is believed that the College of Commissioners was deadlocked so that, since the Commission had not voted to prohibit the merger, the decision was rewritten to avoid clearance by default (which would have occurred had the Commissioners failed to deliver a formal decision in time). The fear that this type of thing could happen has led in the past to a call for an independent European Cartel Office to be created, which would be seen to operate independently and free from political constraints, see also Chap. 13.

[618] Case M.53, [1991] OJ L334/42.

[619] It seems that the French and Italian Governments, the (then) Commissioner for Industry, Martin Bangemann, and the then President of the Commission, Jacques Delors, supported the concentration.

[620] The concentration would not face effective competition from existing competitors and there was no realistic possibility of new competitors entering the market in the foreseeable future.

[621] Case M.469, 9 November 1994.

[622] Case M.1672, [2001] OJ L143/74.

[623] N. Kroes, 'Competition, the crisis and the road to recovery', 30 March 2009, available at <http://ec.europa.eu/competition/speeches/index_2009.html>.

decision of the College of Commissioners.[624] Decisions of the Commission must, of course, be taken on legitimate grounds and be adequately justified and reasoned. A decision which is not so taken may be subject to annulment in judicial review proceedings before the Court.[625]

c. Other Policy where the Concentration does not Significantly Impede Effective Competition

It is clear from the EUMR that a concentration which does not significantly impede effective competition must be declared to be compatible with the common market.[626] In such cases, however, steps may be taken by the authorities of the individual Member States to preclude the merger, or aspects of the merger, where necessary to protect their legitimate interests or essential interests of security.[627]

E. ARTICLE 2(4), (5), JOINT VENTURES

The review of joint ventures[628] under the EUMR[629] is potentially bipartite. It is first necessary to determine whether or not the joint venture significantly impedes effective competition in the common market or a substantial part of it.[630] Secondly, it is necessary to determine whether the joint venture will lead to the coordination of the competitive behaviour of undertakings which remain independent on any particular market (these joint ventures would previously have fallen for assessment not under the EUMR but under Article 101).[631] This may well occur if two or more of the parents compete in an upstream or downstream market or in the market of the joint venture itself. Where a joint venture does have such cooperative effects section 10 of Form CO requires that the parties should provide additional information about their activities in these markets.

If the object or effect of the joint venture is to coordinate the independent undertakings' behaviour Article 2(4) and (5) of the EUMR provides that these coordinative aspects of the joint venture will be appraised in accordance with criteria set out in Article 101(1) and (3):

4. To the extent that the creation of a joint venture constituting a concentration pursuant to Article 3 has as its object or effect the co-ordination of the competitive behaviour of undertakings that remain independent, such co-ordination shall be appraised in accordance with the criteria of Article [101(1)] and (3) [TFEU], with a view to establishing whether or not the operation is compatible with the common market.

    5. In making this appraisal, the Commission shall take into account in particular:

        — whether two or more parent companies retain, to a significant extent, activities in the same market as the joint venture or in a market which is downstream or upstream from that of the joint venture or in a neighbouring market closely related to this market,

---

[624] See, e.g., W. Sauter, *Competition Law and Industrial Policy in the EU* (Clarendon Press, 1997), 140.

[625] See Section 7 and Chap. 13.

[626] EUMR, Art. 2(2).

[627] See Section 3.C.v and Section 3.C.vi.

[628] From 1998 to April 2002, Art. 2(4) cases were designated as 'JV' cases and were often handled outside the then MTF. Since April 2002 they have been designated and have been handled like other merger cases within the merger network.

[629] All jointly controlled full-function joint ventures established on a lasting basis which have an EU dimension fall for assessment under the EUMR.

[630] EUMR, Art. 2(2) and (3). See G. A. Zonnekeyn, 'The treatment of joint ventures under the amended EC Merger Regulation' [1998] *ECLR* 414 and J. Temple Lang, 'International Joint Ventures under Community Law' [1999] Fordham Corporate L Inst 465.

[631] See Section 3.A.ii, pp. 1144–1147.

— whether the co-ordination which is the direct consequence of the creation of the joint venture affords the undertakings concerned the possibility of eliminating competition in respect of a substantial part of the products or services in question.

These provisions thus require the Commission to consider whether two or more parent companies retain significant activities in the same market as the joint venture or in downstream, upstream, or neighbouring markets (the identification of candidate markets), and whether any coordination which is the direct consequence of the creation of the joint venture affords the undertakings concerned the possibility of eliminating competition in respect of a substantial part of the products or services in question. There must therefore be a causal link between the setting up of the joint venture and the appreciable restriction of competition on the market.[632]

There is no Commission guidance on the application of Article 2(4) and (5) to joint venture cases. For guidance it is therefore necessary to look at previous joint venture cases decided under the EUMR and relevant guidance on the application of Article 101 to horizontal cooperation agreements.[633] The Commission's decisions under the EUMR appear, perhaps, to display a more economically realistic approach than that which has been displayed in its Article 101 decisions.[634]

In *Telia/Telenor/Schibsted*[635] the Commission considered a joint venture for the provision of various internet services. The Commission considered that the parents remained active on two markets in which coordinated behaviour might be possible. In particular both Telia and Telor remained present on the market to provide 'dial-up' internet access. Although the parents already had joint market shares of between 35 per cent and 65 per cent of the market it was concluded that coordinated behaviour between the parents was not likely. These market shares were not significant on the growing market for dial-up internet access in Sweden. The market was characterised by high growth, low barriers to entry, and low switching costs. On the other market, the website production market, the parent companies, and the joint venture had less than 10 per cent of the market. Any coordination on such a market would not amount to appreciable restriction of competition.[636]

Nonetheless the Commission has, in some cases, accepted conditions and obligations to deal with coordination concerns. In *Fujitsu/Siemens*,[637] for example, the parties' agreement to create a joint venture to develop, manufacture, distribute, market, and sell desktop computers did not have a significant impact on competition. The Commission did have concerns, however, about the effect that the merger would have on the parents' activities in a number of upstream and downstream markets. In particular, the Commission considered that the structure of the 'financial workstation'[638] market made coordination between the parents in financial workstations likely. The parties, however, proposed a remedy to resolve the problem identified and the Commission cleared the concentration subject to conditions and obligations.

---

[632] See, e.g., Case IV/JV.2, *ENEL/DT/FT* [1999] OJ C178/15. This case concerned a joint venture for fixed telephony in Italy. The Commission concluded that the likelihood of any coordination between the parents on the mobile market outside the joint venture (e.g., in France and Germany) would be due not to the joint venture at issue but to links and joint ventures previously concluded between the parties.

[633] Commission Guidelines on the application of Article 81 to horizontal cooperation agreements [2001] OJ C3/2, Commission Notice on agreements of minor importance which do not appreciably restrict competition under Article 81(1) [2001] OJ C368/13, the Commission's Guidelines on the application of Article 81(3) [2004] OJ C101/97.

[634] See Chaps. 4 and 13.

[635] Case IV/JV.2, [1999] OJ C178/15.

[636] See Chaps. 4 and 13.

[637] Case IV/JV.22, [1999] OJ C318/15.

[638] ATMs and cash dispensers.

Case IV/JV.22, *Fujitsu/Siemens*

Commission

63. For the reasons set forth below, the financial workstations market displays several structural characteristics, which make co-ordination between the parents in financial workstations likely. First, the market is highly concentrated with NCR, Siemens and Fujitsu accounting for a share of sales of approximately 70 per cent. Second, NCR and Siemens together with Fujitsu have roughly symmetrical market shares. Third, the remaining competitors all have market shares, which do not exceed 10 per cent. Fourth, the technology for financial workstations is relatively mature, as the technology needed to operate financial workstations tends to be standard personal computer-based technology.

64. Any co-ordination between the parent companies would furthermore be appreciable. Both parties will jointly hold a share of sales of [20–40] per cent and will be the second biggest competitor next to NCR, which accounts for [30–40] per cent of the financial workstations market. In light of the almost symmetrical market shares of the two major groups in the financial workstations market and the resulting relationship of interdependence existing between NCR and Siemens/Fujitsu, taken as a group, any co-ordination between the parties appears likely to cause the elimination of competition in respect of a substantial part of the financial workstations market.

65. Co-ordination between the parent companies will also have an effect on trade between Member States. Both Siemens and Fujitsu are EEA-wide operators in financial workstations with activities covering all the major Member States of the EEA. Any alteration of their competitive behaviour would have an effect on intra-Community trade in financial workstations.

66. When these concerns were communicated to the parties, Siemens offered a remedy in order to remove the competitive concerns raised by the operation with regard to the EEA-wide financial workstations market.

67. In two letters dated 15 and 23 September 1999, respectively, Siemens undertakes the following:

(i) Siemens announced, in November 1998 its intention to sell off its retail and banking systems business. This will be done through the sale of all its shares in Siemens Nixdorf Retail and Banking Systems GmbH (based in Paderborn) and the sales of all respective business activities abroad to be carved out of regional legal entities (the 'Retail and Banking System Business')...

Siemens commits itself to selling the Retail and Banking Systems Business...

...

69. The undertaking given by Siemens removes the Commission's concern that the creation of the JVC has as its effect the co-ordination of the competitive behaviour of Siemens and Fujitsu in the financial workstations market. The undertaking to divest Siemens' Retail and Banking Systems Business within... removes the incentive to co-ordinate its behaviour with that of Fujitsu.... After divestment... the financial workstation market will no longer be a candidate market for co-ordination within the meaning of Article 2(4) of the Merger Regulation.

In *BT/AT&T*[639] the coordinative aspects of a joint venture were also appraised by the Commission, this time in Phase II proceedings. Again, commitments were required to address the anti-competitive coordinative effects identified.

The methodology adopted by the Commission in these cases appears to be to consider (1) whether or not the creation of the joint venture has the object of coordinating the behaviour of the parents; and (2) if it does not, whether or not this is its effect. In making this latter determination the Commission identifies candidate markets, considers whether coordination is likely on

[639] Case IV/JV.15.

those markets, and whether the coordination would appreciably restrict competition and affect trade between Member States. The Commission did not consider Article 101(3) elements in *Fujitsu/Siemens* or *BT/AT&T* as in both cases the parties put forward remedies to deal with the Article 101(1) problems identified.

F. RESTRICTIONS DIRECTLY RELATED AND NECESSARY TO THE CONCENTRATION

Ancillary restraints are clauses the presence of which is vital to the particular concentration since the transaction, in its absence, would not take place. For example, it is usually a condition of a sale of a business that the vendor covenants not to compete with the business for a period of time. Otherwise the goodwill of the business may be rendered valueless.[640] Similarly, in joint ventures the parents may agree to license intellectual property rights to the joint venture and perhaps not to compete with the joint venture. Both the old and current EUMR have made it clear that restrictions directly related and necessary to the implementation of the concentration ('ancillary restraints') may be cleared along with the concentration.[641] To the extent that the restrictions are ancillary, the EUMR alone thus applies to them.[642] By contrast, Articles 101 and 102 remain applicable to restrictions that cannot be considered to be ancillary.

Prior to 2001 the Commission used to clear ancillary restraints concluded in agreements between undertakings in its decision to clear the concentration as a whole. It thus considered the concentration and ancillary restraints together.[643] In 2001, the Commission issued a replacement Notice regarding restrictions directly related and necessary to concentrations[644] which marked a significant change in practice by the Commission. Not only did it make it clear that the Commission did not intend to make an assessment of restrictions directly related and necessary to the concentration in its merger decisions any longer, but it adopted a narrower view of when such restrictions could be considered to be ancillary to the concentration. Although the GC held in *Lagardère SCA* and *Canal+SA v. Commission*[645] that the practice of not assessing the restraints in individual cases was not consistent with the Commission's obligations under the original EUMR, the wording of the new EUMR has been altered to legitimise this practice. It now provides that the Commission's clearance decisions (under both Phase I and Phase II) 'shall be deemed to cover' restrictions directly related and necessary to the implementation of the concentration ('ancillary restraints').[646] The 2001 Notice was replaced by a new Notice in 2004.[647]

The Commission's Notices have been of critical importance since they provide guidance as to when ancillary restraints are automatically covered by the Commission's clearance decisions. Where the restraints do not fall within that permitted by the Notice the parties risk being unable to enforce the provision if it is subsequently found to be incompatible with EU law. If the notice does not provide guidance on a particular restraint and there is no other guidance to be found in decisional practice, the parties may apply to the Commission for individual assessment. The Commission may assess

---

[640] See also, e.g., the discussion of ancillary restraints in Chap. 4.

[641] See Section 5.F.

[642] EUMR, Art. 21(1).

[643] EUMR, Art. 8(2). See also Art. 6(1).

[644] [1990] OJ C203/5.

[645] Case T-251/00, [2002] ECR II-4825. See D. Sinclair, 'Ancillary Restraints under the Merger Regulation: The Commission's approach cast into doubt by the Court of First Instance' [2003] *ECLR* 315.

[646] EUMR, Arts 6(1)(b) and 8(1) and (2) and recital 21. The Commission states that '[t]his reflects the intention of the legislator not to oblige the Commission to assess and individually address ancillary restraints', July 2004, para. 2.

[647] [2005] OJ C56/24.

the ancillary restraints if the case presents 'novel and unresolved questions giving rise to genuine uncertainty'.[648]

The Commission's 2004 Notice set out both general principles[649] and principles applicable to commonly encountered restrictions in cases of acquisition of an undertaking,[650] and joint venture cases.[651] With regard to restrictions agreed in relation to the transfer of an undertaking the Commission states, for example, that non-competition obligations on the vendor are generally justified for periods of up to two or three years (three, where both goodwill and know-how are included in the transfer).[652] Non-competition clauses are not considered necessary when the transfer is limited to physical assets or to exclusive industrial and commercial property rights.[653] Any non-competition clause should ordinarily be limited to the products and services forming the economic activity of the undertaking transferred and the geographical area in which the vendor offered them.[654] Licences of patents, similar rights, or know-how, and purchase and supply obligations may also be considered necessary to the implementation of the concentration.[655] In the context of joint venture agreements, the Commission considers that non-competition obligations between the parent undertakings and a joint venture may be directly related and necessary to the concentration for the lifetime of the joint venture where the obligations correspond to the products, services, and territories covered by the joint venture agreement or its by-laws.[656] Further, it may be legitimate for the parents to grant intellectual property right licences to the joint venture (whether granted exclusively, for a period of time, or whether a field of use restriction is incorporated), for licences to be granted by the joint venture to one of the parents, for cross-licences to be granted, or for purchase and supply agreements to be concluded by the parent undertakings and the joint venture. Licence agreements between the parents are not ancillary to the implementation of the joint venture.[657]

G. COMMITMENTS OR REMEDIES

(i) Legal Basis and Time Periods

In some cases the parties may propose modifications to the original concentration plan and offer commitments to the Commission in order to allow the Commission to declare the transaction to be compatible with the common market. It is crucial, however, that the commitments offered are full and effective and satisfy the Commission that the remedies are sufficient to restore the conditions of effective competition in the common market on a permanent basis.[658] The legal basis for

---

[648] EUMR, recital 21. See also the Commission's Notice on restrictions directly related and necessary to concentrations [2005] OJ C56/24, paras. 3–6.

[649] Commission Notice on restrictions directly related and necessary to concentrations, [2005] OJ C56/24, part II.

[650] Commission Notice on restrictions directly related and necessary to concentrations, [2005] OJ C56/24, part III.

[651] Commission Notice on restrictions directly related and necessary to concentrations, [2005] OJ C56/24, part IV.

[652] Commission Notice on restrictions directly related and necessary to concentrations, [2005] OJ C56/24, para. 20. The Commission evaluates non-solicitation and confidentiality clauses in the same way as non-competition clauses, para. 26.

[653] Commission Notice on restrictions directly related and necessary to concentrations, [2005] OJ C56/24, para. 21.

[654] Commission Notice on restrictions directly related and necessary to concentrations, [2005] OJ C56/24, paras. 22–23.

[655] Commission Notice on restrictions directly related and necessary to concentrations, [2005] OJ C56/24, paras. 27–35.

[656] Commission Notice on restrictions directly related and necessary to concentrations, [2005] OJ C56/24, para. 36.

[657] Commission Notice on restrictions directly related and necessary to concentrations, [2005] OJ C56/24, paras. 42–43.

[658] The Commission does not, otherwise, have power to authorise a concentration which has been found to be incompatible with the common market.

the acceptance of such commitments or remedies is set out in the EUMR itself. Recital 30 of the regulation provides:

Where the undertakings concerned modify a notified concentration, in particular by offering commitments with a view to rendering the concentration compatible with the common market, the Commission should be able to declare the concentration, as modified, compatible with the common market. Such commitments should be proportionate to the competition problem and entirely eliminate it. It is also appropriate to accept commitments before the initiation of proceedings where the competition problem is readily identifiable and can easily be remedied. It should be expressly provided that the Commission may attach to its decision conditions and obligations in order to ensure that the undertakings concerned comply with their commitments in a timely and effective manner so as to render the concentration compatible with the common market. Transparency and effective consultation of Member States as well as of interested third parties should be ensured throughout this procedure.

More particularly, both Articles 6(2) and 8(2) provide that the Commission may find, following modification, that the concentration is compatible with the common market and 'may attach to its decision…conditions and obligations intended to ensure that the undertakings concerned comply with the commitments they have entered into vis-à-vis the Commission with a view to rendering the concentration compatible with the common market'.

Commitments may, therefore, be submitted and accepted both at Phase I, prior to initiation of proceedings, and in Phase II proceedings (they may be submitted on Form RM). Commitments offered in Phase I will, however, have to be sufficient to clearly rule out any of the Commission's 'serious doubts' within the meaning of Article 6(1)(c). Clearly, the Commission has significant bargaining power at this first stage of the proceedings, and the parties may have to be prepared to give up more at this stage if they wish to prevent the transaction being taken through to second-phase proceedings. Nonetheless a significant number of cases are resolved through Phase I commitments each year.[659] In Phase II cases, it is for the Commission to communicate its competition concerns, for the parties to formulate appropriate remedies proposals (the Commission cannot impose them), and for the Commission, if it wants to reject the commitments, to demonstrate that the remedies offered do not resolve the competition concerns identified. It is not, therefore, for the parties to prove that their commitments eliminate the competition concerns identified (although they must provide the relevant information necessary for the assessment).[660]

Commitments must be offered within specified periods of time, 20 working days of notification in Phase I proceedings and within 65 working days of the initiation of proceedings in Phase II proceedings.[661] Where commitments are submitted within the stipulated time frame, then, if offered in Phase I, the time period for examining the concentration is extended by 10 working days and, where offered in Phase II, the time period may be extended by 15 working days.[662] In very complex cases, a further extension of up to 20 working days may be agreed in Phase II.[663] The time periods both for submitting the remedies and for the Commission to make its decision are tight, which means that the possibility of offering commitments should be considered very early on in the procedure and, generally, prior to notification.

The Commission tests the commitments submitted by taking them to the market.[664] Indeed, the regulation specifically provides that transparency must be maintained and Member States and

---

[659] Since 2001 more Phase I commitments decisions have been taken than the number of Phase II proceedings launched, see <http://ec.europa.eu/competition/mergers/statistics.pdf>.

[660] See, e.g., Case T-87/05, *EDP v. Commission* [2005] ECR II-3745, paras. 65–69.

[661] Reg. 802/2004, [2004] OJ L13/1, Art. 19(1) and (2).

[662] Only if offered after the 54th working day.

[663] See n. 286.

[664] An enforcement unit within the merger network advises on the acceptability and implementation of commitments.

interested third parties should be consulted.[665] Third parties, competitors, suppliers, and customers are, therefore, heavily involved in the process. The Commission generally prefers to find a solution along these lines than to have to prohibit the merger outright.[666] The parties' ability to influence the outcome of the decision is, therefore, significant. In cases raising serious competition problems, however, the commitments may have to substantially modify the terms and conditions of the transaction.

In *Oracle/SunMicrosystems*[667] the Commission cleared a transaction subject not to formal commitments but taking account of public announcements of a series of pledges made by Oracle to customers, users, and developers. The basis on which a breach of such a pledge could be remedied is unclear.

(ii) The Commission's Notice on Remedies Acceptable under the EUMR

In 2001, the Commission issued a Notice on remedies acceptable,[668] which set out the general principles applicable to remedies acceptable to the Commission and provided guidance on the types of commitments which may be suitable to resolve the competition concerns raised by a concentration, the procedure governing such commitments, and the main requirements for implementation of commitments. In April 2007, the Commission launched a consultation on a draft revised Commission Notice on remedies acceptable under the EUMR,[669] proposing that the 2001 Notice be modified in the light of an extensive study it published in 2005 on the implementation and effectiveness of remedies,[670] judgments of the EUMR, and the provisions of the recast EUMR adopted in 2004. Following consultation a new Remedies Notice was adopted in 2008.[671] 'The notice sets out the general principles applicable to remedies acceptable to the Commission, the main types of commitments that may be accepted... the specific requirements which proposals of commitments need to fulfil in both phases of the procedure, and the main requirements for the implementation of commitments.'[672]

(iii) Types of Commitments

Commitments concluded may relate to the *structure* of the concentration or to the *behaviour* of the parties, i.e. they may be structural or behavioural. A structural remedy ordinarily requires divestiture of the activities of an existing viable business that can operate on a stand-alone basis. Alternatively, a commitment by the parties to terminate exclusive agreements which would otherwise have foreclosure effects, post-merger, or remedies to facilitate market entry through the grant to competitors of access to infrastructure, platforms, key technology, production, or R&D facilities, or through the licensing of intellectual property rights might have a sufficient effect on the market to restore effective competition.

Although the Commission prefers structural remedies, the key requirement is that the commitments should ensure the effective competitive structure of the market and 'are capable of rendering

---

[665] EUMR, recital 30. See also Cases C-68/94 and C-30/95, *France v. Commission, Société Commerciale des Potasses et de l'Azote (SCPA) v. Commission* [1998] ECR I-1375.

[666] See the statistics set out in Section 6, p. 1252.

[667] M.5529, Case T- 292/10, *Monty Program AB* (judgment pending). See D. Zimmer, 'The Merger Between Oracle and Sun' [2010] *JECLAP* 315 and the discussion of *Google/Motorola* in n. 561 and accompanying text.

[668] [2001] OJ C6/3. See also the Commission's Merger Remedies Study, IP/05/327, available at <http://ec.europa.eu/competition/mergers/legislation/remedies_study.pdf>.

[669] See <http://ec.europa.eu/comm/competition/mergers/legislation/merger_remedies.html>.

[670] IP/05/1327.

[671] 'The Remedies Notice' [2008] OJ C267/1.

[672] 'The Remedies Notice' [2008] OJ C267/1, para. 3.

the notified transaction compatible with the common market'.[673] In practice a structural solution, such as a commitment to sell a subsidiary, may be preferable, since the commitment may prevent the impediment to effective competition arising and it does not require medium- or long-term monitoring measures.[674] Further, behavioural remedies may be difficult to control and enforce.[675] It could also be that a structural remedy will be the only possible means of solving the structural problem caused by the creation of market power, which results in the SIEC.[676]

In some situations, no remedy may be adequate to deal with the adverse effects identified or may be so complex that the Commission cannot determine with the required degree of certainty that effective competition will be restored.[677] In *Schneider/Legrand*,[678] for example, the Commission prohibited concentrations even though the parties submitted commitments. In the latter case the parties twice submitted remedies which the Commission rejected, the second time on the ground that they were too complex and did not address the Commission's concerns. On appeal, however, the GC considered that the Commission had not clearly identified its concerns in its statement of objections. Consequently, the parties had been unable to put forward proposals for divestiture capable of rendering the concentration compatible with the common market. The effect of the Commission's irregularities was particularly serious as the Commission had made it clear that remedies were the only means of preventing the concentration falling under Article 2(3) of the Regulation and being declared incompatible. The decision was thus vitiated by the infringement of the rights of defence and annulled.[679]

(iv) Structural Remedies: Divestiture

The most effective means of restoring effective competition is through divestiture of a subsidiary or production facilities and the creation of a new competitive entity or the strengthening of existing competitors.[680] The divestiture gives a new or existing competitor the possibility of gaining access to the market. In such cases the Commission will wish to ensure that the activities, consisting of a viable business which can operate on a stand-alone basis and compete effectively with the merged entity on a lasting basis, are divested to a suitable purchaser within a specified time period. Sometimes the Commission may require the parties to find a buyer prior to completion of the notified operation (an upfront buyer or fix-it-first (where a buyer is identified and a binding agreement is concluded prior to the Commission's clearance decision)).[681] The sale of the entity may itself amount to a notifiable concentration.

Usually tight deadlines are set within which the divestiture must occur and the commitments will set out specific details and procedures relating to the Commission's oversight of the divestiture, in particular, approval of the trustee and approval of the purchaser and purchase agreement.[682]

---

[673] Case T-102/96, *Gencor Ltd v. Commission* [1999] ECR II-753, para. 318. See also Case C-12/03 P, *Tetra Laval BV v. Commission* [2005] ECR I-987, paras. 85–89.

[674] Case T-102/96, *Gencor Ltd v. Commission* [1999] ECR II-753, para. 319.

[675] See Case M.490, *Nordic Satellite Distribution* [1990] OJ L53/21 where the Commission rejected the undertakings offered by the parties on these grounds.

[676] See Case M.469, *MSG Media Service GmbH* [1994] OJ L364/1, para. 99.

[677] The Remedies Notice [2001] OJ C68/3, paras. 31–32.

[678] Case M.2282.

[679] Case T-310/01, *Schneider Electric SA v. Commission* [2002] ECR II-4071, paras. 421–463.

[680] The Remedies Notice, para. 22, see, e.g., Case M.6471 *Outokumpu/Inoxum*, Case M.6503, *La Poste/Swiss Post/JV*.

[681] See the Remedies Notice, paras. 53–57, e.g., Cases M.2060, *Bosch/Rexroth, M.6410, UTC/Goodrich*, and M.6570, *UPS/TNT Express*.

[682] The Remedies Notice [2001] OJ C68/3, part IV deals with requirements for the implementation of commitments. See also the Best Practice Guidelines which provide standard model texts for divestiture commitments and for trustee mandates.

The Commission sometimes accepts alternative remedies packages, recognising that the parties' preferred divestiture option may be uncertain or difficult to complete. It may therefore accept a preferred divestiture package on condition that an alternative is available which is equally effective. The Commission explains alternative divestiture commitments and 'crown jewels' in its Remedies Notice:

1.4 Alternative Divestiture commitments: Crown Jewels

In certain cases, the implementation of the parties' preferred divestiture option (of a viable business solving the competition concerns) might be uncertain in view, for example, of third parties' pre-emption rights or uncertainty as to the transferability of key contracts, intellectual property rights, or the uncertainty of finding a suitable purchaser. Nevertheless, the parties may consider that they would be able to divest this business to a suitable purchaser within a very short time period. In such circumstances, the Commission cannot take the risk that, in the end, effective competition will not be maintained. Accordingly, the Commission will only accept such divestiture commitments under the following conditions: (a) absent the uncertainty, the first divestiture proposed in the commitments would consist of a viable business, and (b) the parties will have to propose a second alternative divestiture which the parties will be obliged to implement if they are not able to implement the first commitment within the given time frame for the first divestiture. Such an alternative commitment normally has to be a 'crown jewel', i.e. it should be as least as good as the first proposed divestiture in terms of creating a viable competitor once implemented, it should not involve any uncertainties as to its implementation and it should be capable of being implemented quickly in order to avoid that the overall implementation period exceeds what would normally be regarded as acceptable in the conditions of the market in question.[683] In order to limit the risks in the interim period, it is indispensable that interim preservation and holding separate measures apply to all assets included in both divestiture alternatives. Furthermore, the commitment has to establish clear criteria and a strict timetable as to how and when the alternative divestiture obligation will become effective and the Commission will require shorter periods for its implementation.

If there is uncertainty as to the implementation of the divestiture due to third party rights or as to finding a suitable purchaser crown jewel commitments and up-front buyers as discussed below in paragraphs 54 address the same concerns, and the parties may therefore choose between both structures.

Divestiture commitments may also be used for removing links between the parties and competitors where these links contribute to competitive concerns raised by the merger.[684]

(v) Other Remedies: Access Remedies, Behavioural Commitments, and 'Remedy Packages'

It has already been seen that divestiture is not the only remedy acceptable to the Commission.

Nevertheless, a general distinction can be made between divestitures, other structural remedies, such as granting access to key infrastructure or inputs on non-discriminatory terms, and commitments relating to the future behaviour of the merged entity. Divestiture commitments are the best way to eliminate competition concerns resulting from horizontal overlaps, and may also be the best means of resolving problems resulting from vertical or conglomerate concerns. Other structural commitments may be suitable to resolve all types of concerns if those remedies are equivalent to divestitures in their effects, as explained in more detail below in paragraphs 61 *et seq*. Commitments relating to the future behaviour of the merged entity may be acceptable only exceptionally in very specific circumstances. In particular, commitments in the form of undertakings not to raise prices, to reduce product ranges or to remove brands, etc., will generally not eliminate competition concerns resulting from horizontal overlaps. In any case, those types of remedies can only exceptionally be accepted if

---

683   See e.g., Case M.6286, *Südzucker/ED&F MAN*.

684   See, e.g., Case M.492, *VEBA/Degusa [1994] OJ C303/5*; Case M.3653; *Siemens/VA Tech*; and Case M.1845, *Time Warner/AOL*.

their workability is fully ensured by effective implementation and monitoring in line with the considerations set out in paragraphs 13–14, 66, 69, and if they do not risk leading to distorting effects on competition.

Other commitments are thus frequently offered and accepted, such as access remedies, change of long-term exclusive contracts, and other behavioural commitments.[685] The thrust of such commitments is often aimed at opening the market for competitors, for example through giving access to infrastructure[686] or key technology. The parties may also have to make commitments as to 'interoperability'. In *GE/Instrumentarium*,[687] for example, the Commission was concerned about the effect of the merger in the perioperative monitors market and also that the parties could take steps to ensure that competitors' critical care and patient monitors could not interoperate with its anaesthesia equipment. GE adopted a package of measures, the divestiture of a company, and a series of supply agreements with its acquirer, to deal with the horizontal overlaps and to ensure the emergence of an effective competitor to the merged entity on the perioperative monitors market. It also undertook to provide the electrical and mechanical interface for third parties' patient monitors to be able to interconnect with its own anaesthesia equipment.

Behavioural commitments may often be appropriate in cases involving the creation of a collective dominant position. In *Kali und Salz/MdK/Treuhand*,[688] for example, the parties to the concentration offered to sever links with its main competitor, SCPA (which were considered to facilitate anti-competitive behaviour on the oligopolistic market).[689]

In *GE/Honeywell*[690] and *Tetra Laval/Sidel*[691] the parties offered commitments to abstain from certain commercial behaviour (for example, bundling products) to deal with the Commission's concerns. The Commission rejected these on grounds that this was a pure promise and would involve excessive monitoring. In the *GE/Honeywell* appeals,[692] the GC did not need to rule on the correctness of the Commission's actions in this regard as it considered that its competition assessment of the conglomerate effects contained manifest error of assessments. In *Commission v. Tetra Laval BV*,[693] however, the CJ held that as the Commission had rejected the commitments as a matter of principle the GC had been correct to find that this was a factor that the Commission should have taken into account when assessing the likelihood that the merged entity would act in such a way as to make it possible to create a dominant position on one or more of the relevant markets for PET equipment. In *Intel/McAfee*[694] the Commission did accept a range of behavioural remedies to deal with its concerns about bundling and technical tying in a conglomerate merger case and competing security solution providers being foreclosed from the market.

In the Remedies Notice the Commission states, 'non-structural types of remedies, such as promises by the parties to abstain from certain commercial behaviour (e.g. bundling products), will generally not eliminate the competition concerns resulting from horizontal overlaps. In any case, it may be difficult to achieve the required degree of effectiveness of such a remedy due to the absence of effective monitoring of its implementation...Therefore, the Commission may

---

[685] Case M.877, *Boeing/McDonnell Douglas* [1997] OJ L336/16, [1997] 5 CMLR 270. Further, the Commission also required Boeing to make some of its intellectual property rights available, through licences, to competitors.

[686] See, e.g., IV/JV.37, *BSkyB/Kirsch*.

[687] Case M.3083, IP/03/1193.

[688] Case M.308, [1994] OJ L186/30; on appeal Cases C-68/94 and C-30/95, *France v. Commission, Société Commerciale des Potasses et de l'Azote (SCPA) v. Commission* [1998] ECR I-1375.

[689] Their imposition was one of the factors which caused SCPA and France to challenge, successfully, the legitimacy of the Commission's decision.

[690] Case M.2220.

[691] Case M.2416, annulled on appeal Case T-5/02, [2002] ECR II-4381, aff'd Case C-12/03 P, [2005] ECR I-987.

[692] Cases T-209 and 210/01, *Honeywell v. Commission* and *General Electric Company v. Commission* [2005] ECR II-5527 and 5575.

[693] Case C-12/03 P, [2005] ECR I-987, paras. 85–89.

[694] Case M.5984.

examine other types of non-divesture remedies, such as behavioural promises, only exceptionally in specific circumstances, such as in respect of competition concerns arising in conglomerate structures'.[695]

The broad range of packages accepted often requires the parties to be 'inventive' and to propose remedy packages which will resolve the competition problems identified by the Commission.

(vi) Other Cases

In some cases the Commission has accepted alternative remedies packages. For example, in *Nestlé/Ralston Purina*[696] the Commission accepted an 'alternative' remedy package. In particular, the Commission was concerned about the impact of the concentration in the Spanish markets for dry dog food, dry cat food, and snacks and treats for cats and in the Italian and Greek markets for dry cat food. With regard to Spain, the party undertook to divest itself of its 'Friskies' brand, through the grant of exclusive licences for a substantial period and to divest itself of a Spanish production plant or, if not implemented within a specified time period, alternatively, to remove the overlap in Spain by divesting itself of Ralston Purina's 50 per cent shareholding in the joint venture, Gallina Blanca Purina.

In some cases a concentration has been saved by a third party to the transaction. In *Alcatel/Telettra*,[697] for example, the Spanish telecommunications company, Telefonica, agreed to sell its interests in the parties to the concentration in order to persuade the Commission that the undertakings' potential market power would be counteracted by the countervailing exercise of monopolistic demand.

(vii) Breach of a Condition or Obligations

Commitments consist of both 'conditions' and 'obligations'. The Commission may take a decision prohibiting the concentration where it finds that it has been implemented in contravention of a condition attached to a decision.[698] Further, the Commission may revoke a decision where the undertakings concerned commit a breach of an obligation, relating to the steps necessary to implement the commitment, attached to the decision.[699] In each case, fines may be imposed on the undertakings concerned. Further, the Commission may impose fines of up to 10 per cent of the aggregate turnover of the undertakings concerned that have failed to comply with conditions or obligations imposed,[700] and periodic penalty payments on undertakings for delay caused by failure to comply with an obligation.[701]

(viii) Modification and Waiver of Commitments

In some cases the Commission has been prepared to modify or waive certain commitments which had been attached to a clearance decision.[702]

---

[695] Remedies Notice, para. 69.

[696] Case M.2337, IP/01/1136.

[697] Case M.42, *Alcatel/Telettra* [1991] OJ L122/48.

[698] EUMR, Art. 8(7).

[699] EUMR, Arts 6(3) and 8(6).

[700] EUMR, Art. 14(2)(d).

[701] EUMR, Art. 15(1)(c).

[702] See Cases M.2876, *Newscorp/Telepiù* and M.950 *Hoffmann-La Roche/Boehringer Mannheim*.

6. EUMR STATISTICS

DG COMP produces statistics, which it updates monthly,[703] setting out what happens to merger notifications. Figure 15.1 sets out the statistics up to 31 July 2013.

It can be seen from these statistics that between September 1990 and the end of August 2013 Phase II proceedings had been initiated in only 215 cases and there had, after nearly 23 years application of the EUMR, been only 24 outright prohibition decisions in total. In contrast, 4,888 concentrations were cleared under Article 6.

Table 15.1 Statistics on Merger Notifications, 21 September 1990 to 31 July 2013

I.) NOTIFICATIONS

	90	91	92	93	94	95	96	97	98	99	00	01	02	03	04	05	06	07	08	09	10	11	12	13 (August)	Total
Number of notified cases	11	64	59	59	95	110	131	168	224	276	330	335	277	211	247	318	356	402	348	259	274	309	283	171	5317
Cases withdrawn - Phase 1	0	0	3	1	6	4	5	9	5	7	8	8	3	0	3	6	7	5	10	6	4	9	4	1	114
Cases withdrawn - Phase 2	0	0	0	1	0	0	1	0	4	5	5	4	1	0	2	3	2	2	3	2	0	1	1	0	37

II.) REFERRALS

	90	91	92	93	94	95	96	97	98	99	00	01	02	03	04	05	06	07	08	09	10	11	12	13 (August)	Total
Art 4(4) request (Form RS)															2	14	13	5	9	8	6	10	13	6	86
Art 4(4) referral to Member State															2	11	13	5	9	6	7	10	12	5	80
Art 4(4) partial referral to Member State															0	0	0	1	0	0	0	1	0	1	3
Art 4(4) refusal of referral															0	0	0	0	0	0	0	0	0	0	0
Art 4(5) request (Form RS)															20	28	38	51	23	23	26	18	22	10	259
Art 4(5) referral accepted															16	24	39	50	22	25	24	17	22	8	247
Art 4(5) refusal of referral															2	0	0	2	0	0	1	0	1	0	6
Art 22 request	0	0	0	1	0	1	1	1	0	0	0	0	0	2	1	4	4	3	2	1	3	1	3	0	29
Art 22(3) referral (Art 22. 4 taken in conjunction with article 6 or 8 under Reg. 4064\89)	0	0	0	1	0	1	1	1	0	0	0	0	0	2	1	3	3	2	3	1	2	2	2	0	26
Art 22(3) refusal of referral															1	1	0	0	0	1	0	1	0	0	4
Art 9 request	0	1	1	1	1	0	3	7	4	9	4	9	8	10	4	7	6	3	5	3	11	2	2	0	101
Art 9.3 partial referral to Member State	0	0	0	1	0	1	0	0	6	3	2	3	6	7	1	1	3	1	1	2	0	3	0	1	42
Art 9.3 full referral	0	0	0	1	0	0	3	1	1	3	2	1	4	8	2	3	1	1	2	1	4	2	1	0	41
Art 9.3 refusal of referral	0	1	0	0	0	0	0	0	0	1	0	0	0	1	0	0	0	1	0	1	1	0	0	0	6

III.) FIRST PHASE DECISIONS

	90	91	92	93	94	95	96	97	98	99	00	01	02	03	04	05	06	07	08	09	10	11	12	13 (August)	Total
Art 6.1 (a) out of scope Merger Regulation	2	5	9	4	5	9	6	4	4	1	1	1	1	0	0	0	0	0	0	0	0	0	0	0	52
Art 6.1 (b) compatible	5	47	43	49	78	90	109	118	196	225	278	299	238	203	220	276	323	368	307	225	253	299	254	160	4663
Art 6.1(b) compatible, under simplified procedure (figures included in 6.1(b) compatible above)	0	0	0	0	0	0	0	0	0	0	41	141	103	110	138	169	211	238	190	143	143	191	170	101	2089
Art 6.1 (b) in conjunction with Art 6.2 (compatible w. commitments)	0	3	4	0	2	3	0	2	12	16	26	11	10	11	12	15	13	18	19	13	14	5	9	7	225

IV.) PHASE II PROCEEDINGS INITIATED

	90	91	92	93	94	95	96	97	98	99	00	01	02	03	04	05	06	07	08	09	10	11	12	13 (August)	Total
Art 6.1 (c)	0	6	4	4	6	7	6	11	11	20	18	21	7	9	8	10	13	15	10	5	4	8	10	2	215

V.) SECOND PHASE DECISIONS

	90	91	92	93	94	95	96	97	98	99	00	01	02	03	04	05	06	07	08	09	10	11	12	13 (August)	Total
Art 8.1 compatible (8.2 under Reg. 4064/89)	0	1	1	1	2	2	1	1	3	0	3	5	2	2	2	2	4	5	9	0	1	4	1	0	52
Art 8.2 compatible with commitments	0	3	3	2	2	3	3	7	4	7	12	9	5	6	4	3	6	4	5	3	2	1	6	2	102
Art 8.3 prohibition	0	1	0	0	1	2	3	1	2	1	2	5	0	0	1	0	0	1	0	0	0	1	1	2	24
Art 8.4 restore effective competition	0	0	0	0	0	0	0	2	0	0	0	0	0	2	0	0	0	0	0	0	0	0	0	0	4

VI.) OTHER DECISIONS

	90	91	92	93	94	95	96	97	98	99	00	01	02	03	04	05	06	07	08	09	10	11	12	13 (August)	Total
Art 6.3 decision revoked	0	0	0	0	0	0	0	0	0	1	0	0	0	0	0	0	0	0	0	0	0	0	0	0	1
Art 8.6 decision revoked	0	0	0	0	0	0	0	0	0	0	0	0	0	0	0	0	0	0	0	0	0	0	0	0	0
Art 14 decision imposing fines	0	0	0	0	0	0	0	0	1	4	1	0	1	0	1	0	0	0	0	1	0	0	0	0	9
Art 7.3 derogation from suspension (7.4 under Reg. 4064/89)	1	1	2	3	3	2	4	5	13	7	4	7	14	8	10	6	2	3	6	5	1	3	1	0	111
Art 21	0	0	0	0	0	0	1	0	1	0	1	1	0	0	0	2	0	1	0	0	0	0	0	0	8

Source: DG Comp. Available at <http://ec.europa.eu/competition/mergers/statistics.pdf>

---

[703] Available at <http://ec.europa.eu/competition/mergers/statistics.pdf>.

7. APPEALS

The EUMR itself provides the CJ with unlimited jurisdiction to review penalties imposed by the Commission and to cancel, reduce, or increase any such fine imposed.[704] The ordinary provisions in the TFEU also authorise the review of institutions' acts and failure to act. A party to a concentration may, therefore, institute proceedings against a Commission merger decision under Article 263 TFEU.[705] Further, third parties (such as a competitor of the merging parties[706] or a third party affected by commitments given)[707] may appeal if it can be established that that the decision although not addressed to them 'is of direct and individual concern' to them.[708] Parties[709] and third parties[710] have sometimes relied on the Transparency Regulation to gain access to documents drawn up, or held, by the Commission and which may facilitate an appeal or a decision as to whether to appeal.

Sections 1 to 5 have discussed many of the important appeals that have been brought from Commission merger decisions. It has been seen that the EU courts consistently stress that when reviewing the Commission's decisions it takes full account of the wide discretion that the regulation imposes upon the Commission and the complex economic assessments required.[711] Nonetheless, the Court has shown itself to be effective when reviewing the decisions adopted by the Commission and, where necessary, prepared to annul the Commission's decision. Where a Commission decision is annulled, in whole or in part, the Commission has to examine the concentration 'afresh' in the light of current market conditions. This means that the parties must put in a new notification or a supplement to the original notification, or, where the notification has not become incomplete, a certification stating that there are no changes. The ordinary Phase I time procedure runs from the working day following the receipt of the new notification, supplementary notification, or certification.[712]

The appeals procedure is discussed more fully in Chapters 2 and 13. An important issue which arises, especially in merger cases, however, is whether there should be a fast-track procedure for appeals. Although the Commission has to proceed within very tight time limits, under the regulation itself it may be years before a review of its decision is conducted by the Court. This, of course, puts the

---

[704] EUMR, Art. 16.

[705] Case C-188/06 P, *Schneider Electric SA* v. *Commission* [2007] ECR I-35, para. 67, see n. 283.

[706] See e.g., Case T-2/93, *Air France* v. *Commission* [1994] ECR II-323; Case T-119/02, *Royal Philips Electronics* v. *Commission* [2003] ECR II-1433; and Case T-177/04, *easyJet Airline Co. Ltd* v. *Commission* [2006] ECR II-1931.

[707] See Cases C-68/94 and C-30/95, *France* v. *Commission, Société Commerciale des Potasses et de l'Azote (SCPA)* v. *Commission* [1998] ECR I-1375, paras. 173–175. See also Case T-464/04, *Independent Music Publishers and Labels Association (Impala)* v. *Commission* [2006] ECR II-2289; Case C-413/06 P, *Bertelsmann and Sony Corp* v. *Commission* [2008] ECR I-4951; Case T-79/12, *Cisco Systems and Messagenet* v. *Commission* (pending appeal against the Commission's decision to unconditionally clear Microsoft's acquisition of Skype (Case M.6281, *Microsoft/Skype*).

[708] No direct and individual concern was established in, e.g., Case T-350/03, *Wirtschaftskammer Kärnten and best connect Ampere Strompool* v. *Commission* [2006] ECR II-68; Case T-96/92 R, *CCE de la Société générale des grandes sources and others* v. *Commission* [1995] ECR II-1213. Proceedings have also been brought by employees and shareholders of one of the undertakings concerned, see e.g. Case T-83/92, *Zunis Holding* v. *Commission* [1993] ECR II-1169.

[709] Case T-403/05, *MyTravel* v. *Commission* [2008] ECR II-2027.

[710] See cases C-404/10 P, *Commission* v. *Éditions Odile Jacob*, and C-477/10 P, *Commission* v. *Agrofert Holding*, 28 June 2012

[711] See, e.g., Cases C-68/94 and C-30/95, *France* v. *Commission, Société Commerciale des Potasses et de l'Azote (SCPA)* v. *Commission* [1998] ECR I-1375, paras. 223–224; and Case T-221/95, *Endemol Entertainment Holding BV* v. *Commission* [1999] ECR II-1299, [1999] 5 CMLR 611

[712] EUMR, Art. 10(5). In the second investigation into the *Tetra Laval/Sidel* merger, Case M.2416, the merger was eventually cleared subject to commitments. Following a launch of a further Phase II investigation in the *Schneider* case, however, the merger was eventually abandoned.

Commission in a powerful position.[713] Since 2001[714] an expedited procedure has been available for cases (not limited to competition cases) capable of being resolved by abbreviated written procedures and a full oral procedure. The procedure, which ordinarily takes between nine and 12 months, was used, for example, in the *Philips*,[715] *Schneider*,[716] *Tetra Laval*,[717] and *Impala*[718] appeals but is only available in straightforward cases.[719]

In both *My Travel* (previously *Airtours*) and *Schneider*, claimants launched damages proceedings against the Commission in respect of the loss suffered in consequence of the wrongful prohibition of their proposed acquisitions (under Article 340(2) TFEU, dealing with the non-contractual liability of the EU).[720] My Travel's claim was dismissed and although the GC in *Schneider v. Commission* awarded Schneider damages in respect of two of the categories of loss claimed (having found that some of the Commission's failures had manifestly and gravely disregarded the limit on its discretion), the CJ set aside the judgment insofar as it ordered the Commission to make good the loss claimed as a result of the reduction in the sale price of Legrand. It thus significantly reduced the sum awarded, holding that the Commission was only liable to pay compensation to Schneider to cover costs incurred in respect of the resumed merger control procedure. The sum of €50,000 eventually awarded was significantly less than the €1.6 billion originally claimed.

8. INTERNATIONAL ISSUES

A. THE LONG ARM OF THE EUMR

The quantitative jurisdictional tests incorporated within the EUMR look not to the effect of the concentration on inter-State trade or on competition but to the size of the undertakings involved. So long as the EU-wide turnovers are satisfied, mergers between non-EU undertakings will be caught even though the undertakings' business is principally carried on outside the EU, even though the merger is completed outside the EU, a joint venture set up by non-EU parents has no activities in the EU,[721] the transaction has no or little impact on competition within the EU, and even though the

---

[713] This fact may encourage the undertakings involved to give commitments to persuade the Commission to authorise the merger. Further, the parties will have to observe a prohibition or commitments imposed until the Commission's decision is suspended or annulled.

[714] [2000] OJ L322.

[715] Case T-119/02, *Royal Philips Electronics v. Commission* [2003] ECR II-1433. See also, e.g., Case T-87/05, *EDP v. Commission* [2005] ECR II-3745.

[716] Case T-310/01, [2002] ECR II-4071.

[717] Case T-5/02, [2002] ECR II-4381.

[718] Case T-464/04, *Independent Music Publishers and Labels Association (Impala) v. Commission* [2006] ECR II-2289, Case C-413/06 P, *Bertelsmann and Sony Corp v. Commission* [2008] ECR I-4951. Although this case was run under the expedited procedure, judgment was not handed down until 19 months after the Commission's decision had passed. The GC was critical of the way that Impala had handled the case, having requested the expedited procedure, and this fact was reflected in the costs order it made, see paras. 544–554.

[719] Schneider agreed to cut back its case so that the expedited procedure could be used. In both *Schneider* and *Tetra Laval* the GC gave judgment within a period of about a year from the Commission's decision. See C. Chibnall, 'Expedited Treatment of Appeals against EC competition decisions under the EC Merger Control Regulation' [2002] 1 *Competition Law Journal* 327.

[720] Case T-212/03, *MyTravel v. Commission* [2008] ECR II-1967 and Case T-351/03, *Schneider v. Commission* [2007] ECR II-2237; Case C-440/07 P, [2009] ECR I-6413, see D. Arts, '"Schneider" and the Non-Contractual Liability of the European Community in the Field of Merger Control' [2009] *JECLAP* 27. For a discussion of Art. 340 (ex Art. 288 EC) see, e.g., T. Hartley, *The Foundations of European Union Law* (7th edn, Oxford University Press, 2010), Chap. 16.

[721] If the parent companies, or other connected undertakings within the group, satisfy the worldwide and EU-wide turnover thresholds, the joint venture transaction will have an EU dimension and, accordingly, will require a notification to the Commission under the EUMR even if the joint venture created is not established in the EU, does not have activities in or make sales into the EU, and it is not foreseeable that the joint venture will produce any direct and substantial effects in the EU.

merger may have been cleared in another jurisdiction. As there is no exemption for mergers occurring outside the EU or any requirement that any of the undertakings involved is established or has substantial operations in any part of the EU,[722] the Commission's scrutiny of some mergers has been extremely politically sensitive in nature.

In 1997, for example, the Commission considered a merger announced in December 1996 between Boeing and McDonnell Douglas.[723] The merger was instigated with the encouragement of the US authorities (the Clinton administration) and was not challenged by the US FTC in July 1997.[724] The concentration had an EU dimension and was notifiable to the Commission under EU rules irrespective of the fact that neither party had any facilities or assets in the EU. The Commission was hostile to the merger, believing that it would lead to the strengthening of Boeing's dominant position on the relevant market within the EU. In the end a political storm was saved by Boeing's offer of commitments to the Commission which resolved its competition concerns. Similarly, in *Gencor/ Lonrho*[725] a concentration concluded between a South African (Gencor) and UK (Lonrho) company merging business activities based in South Africa had an EU dimension and was notifiable under the EU merger rules. In this case the Commission actually prohibited the merger even though the South African Competition Board did not consider that the operation gave rise to competition concerns under South African law. Further, in *GE/Honeywell*,[726] the Commission prohibited a merger which had been permitted by the US authorities.

It can be seen from these examples that a number of important issues arise in the application of the EUMR. The first is to what extent the Commission has *jurisdiction* to apply the EUMR extraterritorially to concentrations between foreign entities. The second relates to whether the provisions of the EUMR can be enforced against merging parties and third parties located outside the EU.[727] The third relates to comity and cooperation and what steps have been taken to cooperate with the competition authorities of other States involved in the investigation of the same case, to exchange information where possible, and to avoid conflicting decisions being taken. This has become an increasingly important issue as the number of jurisdictions around the world with merger control regimes has grown and as parties to international merger transactions more frequently have to make multi-jurisdictional filings. The Commission now often cooperates, through formal and more informal arrangements, successfully with other agencies, particularly the US ones, to coordinate their merger reviews, in so far as is possible, to ensure consistency in remedies where required. In *Deutsche Börse/NYSE Euronext* and *Intel/McAfee*,[728] for example, the Commission cooperated closely with the US DOJ and FTC respectively and in *UTC/TNT Express*[729] it cooperated closely with both the US and Canadian authorities.

---

[722] In earlier drafts of the EUMR it was a requirement that at least one of the undertakings was established in the EU and had substantial operations in one of the Member States: see Commission Proposal for a Regulation of the Council on the control of concentrations between undertakings, [1973] OJ C92/1, Art. 1(1), [1982] OJ C36/3, [1988] OJ C130/4.

[723] Case M.877, [1997] OJ L336/16. The extraterritorial aspects of this case are discussed in greater detail in Chap. 16.

[724] See US FTC Press Releases of 1 July 1997: *FTC Allows Merger of the Boeing Company and McDonnell Douglas Corporation*, 23 September 1997.

[725] Case M.619, [1997] OJ L11/30.

[726] Case M.2220, *aff'd* Cases T-209 and 210/01, *Honeywell v. Commission* and *General Electric Company v. Commission* [2005] ECR II-5527 and 5575.

[727] Neither the EUMR itself nor the implementing regulation explicitly deals with the limits of enforcement jurisdiction. Rather, the provisions apply broadly. Further, the Commission has in practice used the powers to request information from parties and even third parties located outside the EU and to prohibit, or to clear subject to compliance with conditions or obligations, transactions between non-EU firms. See Chap. 16.

[728] Cases M.6166 and M. 5984 and see revised best practices for US-EU cooperation in merger investigations (14 October 2011)

[729] Case M.6570.

In *Gencor Ltd v. Commission*[730] the GC had to deal with an argument which raised the right of the Commission to assert jurisdiction over the joint venture which Gencor alleged had no activities within the EU, was not implemented within the EU,[731] and did not have an immediate, direct, and substantial effect within the EU. The GC, however, upheld the legality of the Commission's prohibition decision, ruling that the Commission's assertion of jurisdiction was not inconsistent with the EUMR, other EU case law, or the rules of public international law.[732] Indeed, the GC made it clear that even where there is doubt about the legality of the assertion of jurisdiction under the EUMR, compulsory notification of such transactions is justifiable, as the Commission must be in a position to assess whether or not a transaction falls within its purview.[733] These issues, and this aspect of the GC's judgment in *Gencor*, are discussed in Chapter 16.

B. RECIPROCITY

Article 24 of the EUMR makes provision for the Member States to inform the Commission 'of any general difficulties encountered by their undertakings with concentrations…in a non-member country'. Further it provides for the Commission to draw up reports on this issue.

Where it appears that certain non-Member States do not permit or otherwise make it difficult for EU undertakings to carry out mergers in circumstances in which undertakings in that State would be permitted to carry out a merger in the EU, 'the Commission may submit proposals to the Council for an appropriate mandate for negotiation with a view to obtaining comparable treatment for EU undertakings'.[734]

9. CONCLUSIONS

1. In the 23-year period since the EUMR first came into force, the Commission has developed an effective and well-respected system of merger control.

2. During this period the Commission has not shied away from adopting decisions involving complex and difficult analysis within the stringent time periods prescribed by the EUMR.

3. The Commission has twice prompted a review of the operation and working of the EUMR and in 2004 a number of significant changes were made to the EUMR. The objective of these changes was to improve procedures and substantive analysis as well as tackling the complex jurisdictional problems that the EUMR provokes.

4. The challenge for the Commission remains to conduct the rigorous analysis demanded of it by the GC, within the tight time periods set out in the EUMR.

---

[730] Case T-102/96, *Gencor Ltd v. Commission* [1999] ECR II-753.

[731] The EUMR is concerned with changes in the structure of competition in the market. In contrast, an anti-competitive agreement concluded outside the EU may actually be implemented or operated within the EU. Arguably, as the structural changes in *Gencor* were not implemented within the EU, the implementation test expounded in *Wood Pulp* had not been satisfied.

[732] Further, that the principles of non-interference or proportionality did not require the Commission to refrain from exercising jurisdiction where another authority had authorised but not required the transaction.

[733] The parties may be spared the inconvenience of a full notification in this situation as the short form notification and simplified procedure is likely to apply, see nn. 125–126 and accompanying text.

[734] EUMR, Art. 24(3).

16

INTERNATIONAL ASPECTS

1. CENTRAL ISSUES

1. In a globalised marketplace, the effects of anti-competitive conduct can be felt far from where they originate and mergers frequently involve undertakings from different jurisdictions or multinational companies that operate worldwide. Very many States now have competition law regimes but although trade and competition are global, competition laws remain national (or supranational in the case of the EU).

2. It was the US which first developed concepts to deal with jurisdictional problems in competition law. The US formulated the 'effects doctrine' whereby US antitrust laws apply to conduct which has a direct, substantial, and reasonably foreseeable effect in the US.

3. The US can be an attractive jurisdiction to foreign plaintiffs. Damages actions for competition injury are more common in the US than in Europe and many aspects of US litigation are plaintiff friendly. Recent US cases, however, have limited the use of the US courts by foreign plaintiffs.

4. The EU's single economic entity doctrine has brought many foreign companies within its jurisdiction. The EU has also formulated an 'implementation' doctrine which is similar to the effects doctrine. The Merger Regulation takes jurisdiction over undertakings anywhere in the world on the basis of the amount of their turnover in the EU.

5. The EU has entered into a number of agreements, including bilateral cooperation agreements, with other States.

6. Plans for international competition regimes or rules, for instance within the WTO, have not progressed. However, there is a great deal of international cooperation in competition law matters and very successful 'soft law' developments going on stemming from cooperation between competition agencies from around the world, in particular the International Competition Network (ICN).

2. INTRODUCTION

Trade and competition are increasingly global. Restrictions on competition and anti-competitive conduct which affect trade between Member States may originate outside the EU. Firms established outside the EU may, for example, fix prices in the EU or divide the single market between them. A firm established outside the EU may hold a dominant position in the single market and may engage in behaviour which is an abuse under Article 102. Further, concentrations involving non-EU undertakings may have consequences for competition inside the EU. But how far does the jurisdiction of the EU competition authorities reach?

This issue is part of a broader debate about the rights of States to take jurisdiction outside their territory, i.e. *extraterritorially*. Extraterritoriality is a complex topic in international law. International law usually distinguishes between two types of jurisdiction. On the one hand there is what is variously called prescriptive, legislative, or subject-matter jurisdiction: the right of States to make their laws applicable to persons, territory, or situations. On the other hand there is enforcement jurisdiction, which is the capacity to take executive action to enforce compliance with those laws.

10. FURTHER READING

A. BOOKS

BRITTAN, L., *Competition Policy and Merger Control in the Single European Market* (Hersh Lauterpacht Memorial Lectures) (Grotius, 1991)

CAMESASCA, D., *European Merger Control: Getting the Efficiencies Right* (Intersentia-Hart, 2000)

COOK, C. J., and KERSE, C. S., *EC Merger Control* (5th edn, Sweet & Maxwell, 2009)

HOVENKAMP, H., *Federal Antitrust Policy: The Law of Competition and its Practice* (4th edn, West Publishing, 2011)

KOKKORIS, I., *Merger Control in Europe: The Gap in the ECMR and National Merger Regulations* (Routledge, 2010)

—— and OLIVARES-CAMINAL, R., *Antitrust Law Amidst Financial Crises* (Cambridge University Press, 2010)

LINDSAY, A., and BERRIDGE, A., *The EC Merger Regulation: Substantive Issues* (4th edn, Sweet & Maxwell, 2012)

LOWE, P., and MARQUIS, M. (eds.), *European Competition Law Annual 2010: Merger Control in European and Global Perspective* (Hart Publishing, 2013)

SAUTER, W., *Competition Law and Industrial Policy in the EU* (Oxford University Press, 1997)

SCHWALBE, U., and ZIMMER, D., *Law and Economics in European Merger Control* (Oxford University Press, 2009)

B. CHAPTERS IN BOOKS

JACQUEMIN, A., 'Mergers and European Policy' in P. H. Admiral (ed.), *Merger and Competition Policy in the European Community* (Blackwell, 1990)

C. ARTICLES

BAILEY, D., 'Standard of Proof in EC Merger Proceedings: A Common Law Perspective' (2003) 40(4) *CMLRev* 845

BAXTER, S., DETHMERS, F., and DODOO, N., 'The GE/Honeywell Judgment and the Assessment of Conglomerate Effects: What's New in Practice?' [2006] 2 *CJ* 141

BERGMAN, M. A. et al., 'Merger Control in the European Union and The United States: Just the Facts' [2011] *European Competition Journal*, 89–125.

BRITTAN, L., 'The Law and Policy of Merger Control in the EEC' (1990) 15 *ELRev* 351

COATE, M. B., 'Did the European Union's Market Dominance Policy Have a Gap? Evidence from Enforcement in the United States' (2009) *European Competition Journal* 655–676

DOWNES, T. A., and MACDOUGALL, D. S., 'Significantly Impeding Effective Competition: Substantive Appraisal under the Merger Regulation' [1994] *ELRev* 286

HACKER, N., 'The Kali+Salz Case—the Re-examination of a Merger after an Argument by the Court', (1998) 3 *Competition Policy Newsletter* 40.

HOWARTH, D., 'The Court of First Instance in GE/Honeywell' [2006] *ECLR* 485

LEVY, N., 'The EU's SIEC Test Five Years On: Has It Made a Difference?' [2010] *European Competition Journal*, 211–254

MEZZANOTTE, F. E., 'Direct versus Indirect Proof of the Airtours Criterion in Impala' (2009) *World Competition* 253

MONTI, G., and ROUSSEVA, E., 'Failing firms in the framework of the EC Merger Regulation' [1999] 24 *ELRev* 38

MOTTA, M., 'EC Merger Policy and the Airtours Case' [2000] *ECLR* 199

RÖLLER, L. H., and DE LA MANO, M., 'The Impact of the New Substantive Test in European Merger Control' [2006] *European Competition Journal* 9

SIMONS, S., AND COATE, M. B., 'UPWARD PRESSURE ON PRICE ANALYSIS: ISSUES AND IMPLICATIONS FOR MERGER POLICY' [2010] *European Competition Journal* 377

TURNER, D., 'Conglomerate Mergers and Section 7 of the Clayton Act' (1965) 78 *Harvard LR* 1313

WERDEN, G. J., 'Economic Reasoning in Merger Cases and how Courts should Evaluate it' [2009] *European Competition Journal* 701.

WHISH, R., 'Substantive analysis under the EC Merger Regulation: should the dominance test be replaced by "substantial lessening of competition"?' *EU Competition Law & Policy Developments & Priorities* (Hellenic Competition Commission, 2002)

WITT, A., 'From *Airtours* to *Ryanair*: Is the more economic approach to EU merger law really about more economics?' [2012] *CMLRev* 217

While most States agree, at least officially, that actions such as murder are criminal behaviour deserving of punishment, the belief that anti-competitive behaviour is also contrary to the public good depends on the acceptance of a certain set of economic and political beliefs.[1] Moreover, even in States with competition law regimes, the objectives of the laws may vary, or the authorities' application of them in a specific situation may differ. For example, the EU and US authorities have had different views on some transactions despite the close cooperation between the two jurisdictions in competition matters and the existence of similar laws. Moreover, if States apply their competition laws extraterritorially undertakings may find themselves subject to a number of competing and irreconcilable actions, there may be conflict between national authorities, and other States may feel that their sovereignty is infringed.

As the globalisation of the world economy advances it becomes increasingly difficult to isolate the effects of transactions which take place on that global market. A company like Microsoft has a dominant position throughout the world. Consumers anywhere can be injured by global conspiracies and one issue of current concern is in which jurisdiction(s) the victims can sue for compensation. The two most pressing matters are dealing with multinational mergers and international cartels, neither of which are confined within one jurisdiction. A number of remedies have been proposed or put in place, including the conclusion of bilateral and multilateral international arrangements and dealing with competition policy within the framework of existing international organisations (such as the World Trade Organization (WTO)). The EU has been an enthusiastic proponent of international cooperation in competition law matters, in particular of using the WTO as a vehicle.[2]

In this chapter we consider first the question of competition law and extraterritoriality, particularly in respect of the EU and the US, and then look at the 'internationalisation' of competition law and the moves which have been made towards dealing with competition issues on a global footing to match the global operations of undertakings on world markets.

3. THE POSITION IN US LAW

A. GENERAL

It is difficult to consider extraterritoriality in EU competition law without first looking at the position in US law. Because the Sherman Act dates from 1890 its extraterritorial reach inevitably became an issue before the EEC even existed.[3] The 'effects doctrine' propounded in the US courts has provided the central concept around which the discussion of extraterritoriality in competition law is conducted. The extraterritorial application of US antitrust law has long been controversial, not just as a matter of principle but because of the features of US antitrust litigation. US law provides, for example, for the recovery of 'treble damages' for breaches of the antitrust laws,[4] for far-ranging pre-trial discovery, and for 'opt-out' class actions. In recent years the attractions to litigants of pursuing in US courts competition law claims with only an indirect connection to the US have led to a lively debate about the jurisdiction of US courts in antitrust cases.[5]

Two points about US law should be noted at the outset. First, there is a multiplicity of actors in antitrust law. The two federal agencies, the Department of Justice (DOJ) and the Federal Trade Commission (FTC) are not primarily decision-makers as is the European Commission, as antitrust law is enforced in the ordinary courts. Different courts of equal authority can (and do) come to

---

[1] See Chap. 1.

[2] See, e.g., the yearly reports of the Commission on Competition Policy.

[3] See R. Y. Jennings, 'Extraterritorial Jurisdiction and the United States Antitrust Laws' (1957) 33 *BYIL*, 146.

[4] Clayton Act, 15 USC s. 15. However, see the Antitrust Criminal Penalty Enhancement and Reform Act 2004 (cited in n. 47).

[5] See *F. Hoffmann-La Roche Ltd* v. *Empagran*, see Section 3.D, p. 1265.

different conclusions on the same issues which can sometimes render it difficult to make general statements about US law.[6] Secondly, extraterritoriality in antitrust law is but one aspect of the long arm of US law.[7]

B. THE EFFECTS DOCTRINE

In the first half-century following the enactment of the Sherman Act the US courts were diffident about applying the rules extraterritorially. In the *American Banana* case[8] Justice Oliver Wendell Holmes said in the Supreme Court that 'the general and almost universal rule is that the character of an act as lawful or unlawful must be determined wholly by the law of the country where the act is done'. Later cases retreated from this self-denying ordinance,[9] and in the *Alcoa* case[10] in 1945 Judge Learned Hand laid down what is known as the 'effects doctrine'. The case concerned a cartel of aluminium producers based in Switzerland which fixed production quotas to boost prices. The Second Circuit Court of Appeals held that the Sherman Act applied to a Canadian company which had participated in the cartel. Judge Learned Hand said that the Sherman Act *did* apply to agreements concluded outside the US which were intended to affect US imports and did actually affect them.

Not surprisingly, the extraterritorial application of US antitrust laws met with hostility from other States. The US courts have not been insensitive to this. In *Timberlane*[11] the Ninth Circuit Court of Appeals considered the notion of 'international comity'. 'Comity' means living peacefully with other nations in mutual respect and accommodating their interests or, as one authority puts it, the 'rules of politeness, convenience and goodwill observed by States in their mutual intercourse without being legally bound by them'.[12] In *Timberlane* Judge Choy recognised the effects doctrine as laid down in *Alcoa*, but considered that its application had to be balanced against the interests of international comity. The case concerned an action by an American company alleging that the defendants in Honduras had conspired to exclude it from the Honduran lumber market, from where it planned to export to the US (the allegations included claims that Honduran Government officials had been bribed). Judge Choy said that three questions had to asked.

> ### *Timberlane Lumber Co* v. *Bank of America*, 549 F.2d 597 at 613 (9th Cir. 1976), Judge Choy
>
> Despite its description as 'settled law', ALCOA's assertion has been roundly disputed by many foreign commentators as being in conflict with international law, comity and good judgment. Nevertheless American courts have firmly concluded that there is some extra-territorial jurisdiction under the Sherman Act. Even among American courts and commentators, however, there is no consensus on how far the jurisdiction should extend…

---

[6] See the varying views of the different Circuits which culminated in the *Empagran* case, see Section 3.D, p. 1266.

[7] See, e.g., legislation such as the Iran–Libya Sanctions Act 1996, later the Iran Sanctions Act 2006, and most recently the Iran Freedom and Counter-Proliferation Act 2012, and the Alien Tort Statute 1789. The Alien Tort Act was considered by the Supreme Court in *Sosa* v. *Alvarez-Machain*, 542 US 2004, a case in which an arrest was effected in Mexico by US Federal agents. However, the Supreme Court has reaffirmed the principle that there is a presumption against extraterritoriality in that '[w]hen a statute gives no indication of an extraterritorial application, it has none', *Morrison* v. *National Australia Bank Ltd*, 130 S.Ct 2869 (2010) (concerning the Securities and Exchange Act 1934), *EEOC* v. *Arabian American Oil Co.*, 499 US 244.

[8] *American Banana Co* v. *United Fruit Co*, 213 US 347, 356, 29 S.Ct 511, 512 (1909).

[9] See *United States* v. *Sisal Sales Corp*, 274 US 268, 47 S.Ct 592 (1927). The *American Banana* case has been limited to its facts and read in a limited way.

[10] *United States* v. *Aluminum Co of America*, 148 F.2d 416 (2d Cir. 1945).

[11] *Timberlane Lumber Co* v. *Bank of America*, 549 F.2d 597 (9th Cir. 1976).

[12] Oppenheim's *International Law* (ed. R. Y. Jennings and A. Watts) (9th edn, Longman, 1992), i, 34 n. 1.

> There is no agreed black-letter rule articulating the Sherman Act's commerce coverage in the international context…The effects test by itself is incomplete because it fails to consider the other nation's interests; nor does it expressly take into account the full nature of the relationships between the actors and this country…
>
> A tripartite analysis seems to be indicated. As acknowledged above, the antitrust laws require in the first instance that there be *some* effect—actual or intended—on American foreign commerce before the federal courts may legitimately exercise subject-matter jurisdiction under those statutes. Second, a greater showing of burden or restraint may be necessary to demonstrate that the effect is sufficiently large to present cognizable injury to the plaintiffs and therefore a civil violation of the antitrust laws…Third, there is the additional question, which is unique to the international setting, of whether the interests of and links to the United States, including the magnitude of the effect on American commerce, are sufficiently strong, *vis-à-vis* those of other nations, to justify an assertion of extra-territorial authority…

In answering this third question, which was necessary because 'at some point the interests of the United States are too weak and the foreign harmony incentive for restraint too strong to justify an extraterritorial assertion of jurisdiction', he said that the following factors should be taken into account:

the degree of conflict with foreign law or policy, the nationality or allegiance of the parties and the locations or principal places of business of corporations, the extent to which enforcement by either state can be expected to achieve compliance, the relative significance of effects on the United States as compared with those elsewhere, the extent to which there is explicit purpose to harm or affect American commerce, the foreseeability of such effect, the relative importance to the violations charged of conduct within the United States as compared with conduct abroad.

The criteria were expanded in *Mannington Mills*,[13] where the plaintiff claimed that the defendant had infringed its export business by fraudulently obtaining foreign patents and the court added further criteria to the *Timberlane* list of factors to be brought into the balancing exercise.[14]

Timberlane and *Mannington Mills* do not deny jurisdiction to the US courts in the interests of comity, but merely hold that it should not be exercised where the interests of the US in asserting jurisdiction are outweighed by the interests of comity.[15]

In 1982 the Foreign Trade Antitrust Improvements Act (FTAIA) amended the Sherman Act. The FTAIA stipulates that as regards foreign commerce *other than import commerce* the antitrust laws will not apply unless the conduct has a *direct, substantial, and reasonably foreseeable* effect on US commerce or on US exports and such effect gives rise to a claim under the Sherman Act or FTC Acts. In other words, the FTAIA exempts export transactions from the Sherman Act unless they injure the US economy. This provision has inevitably come to be seen as a statutory formulation of the effects doctrine. The test it contains—direct, substantial, reasonably foreseeable—is very much like the

---

[13] *Accord Mannington Mills Inc* v. *Congoleum Corp*, 595 F.2D 1287 (3rd Cir. 1979).

[14] The additional criteria were: the possible effect on foreign relations if the court exercises jurisdiction; if the relief is granted, whether a party will be put in the position of being forced to perform an act illegal in either country or be under conflicting requirements by both countries; whether an order for relief would be acceptable in the US if made by a foreign nation under similar circumstances; whether a treaty with the affected nations has addressed the issue.

[15] Such a balancing act had earlier been advocated by Kingman Brewster, who called it a 'jurisdictional rule of reason' in *Antitrust and American Business Abroad* (McGraw-Hill, 1958). Note that in the *Timberlane* case itself the Court of Appeals said that, as there was no indication of a conflict with the law and policy of the Honduran Government, the trial judge could not have dismissed the action on jurisdictional grounds. Hovenkamp argues that comity should be decisive only when the conflict with the foreign government is strong (without amounting to an Act of State or foreign sovereign compulsion defence), see H. Hovenkamp, *Federal Antitrust Policy* (4th edn, West, 2011), 833.

Alcoa formula, except that it adds foreseeability.[16] It does not address any *Timberlane*-type balancing exercise.

In *Hartford Fire Insurance*[17] in 1993 the Supreme Court recognised the claims of comity, but took a robust approach to applying the effects doctrine. Re-insurers based in London were alleged to have agreed with parties in the US to boycott certain types of insurers, which meant that some types of insurance cover were not available in the US.[18] The Supreme Court, by a majority, held that the Sherman Act could be applied to the acts of the British insurers. Justice Souter, delivering the majority opinion, said that 'it is well established by now that the Sherman Act applies to foreign conduct that was meant to produce and did in fact produce some substantial effect in the United States'.[19] He looked to the FTAIA formulation as expressing the effects doctrine, and said that in the light of that the Court should first decide whether it had jurisdiction. Then it could be determined whether jurisdiction should be declined on comity grounds. In this case there was no reason to decline it. He took the view that although the UK *allowed* the conduct, it did not *compel* it.[20] There was therefore no conflict between British and American policy, and no reason for comity concerns to override the effects doctrine.

However, if international comity is only to prevent the US taking jurisdiction in such narrowly drawn conflict situations it will rarely prevail. Further, it should be noted that when dealing with internal inconsistencies between federal antitrust law and the laws of US states, it is accepted that immunity from the former may sometimes arise as a consequence of the latter, even where the individual or undertaking concerned could comply with both.[21] The disregard of another jurisdiction which merely permits rather than compels conduct which is contrary to the first State's antitrust laws also arises in EU law. It is vividly demonstrated by the merger case, *Gencor*.[22]

In *Hartford Fire Insurance* a strong dissent was voiced by Justice Scalia. His view was that comity is an integral part of determining whether the court has jurisdiction in the first place, rather than something to be taken into account when deciding whether to *exercise* jurisdiction.[23] Hovenkamp comments that antitrust law expresses the substantive economic policy of the United States and 'American "public" policy is entitled to be given as much weight by an American court as is the policy of a foreign sovereign, at least where American interests covered by the policy are substantially affected'.[24] F. A. Mann, writing in 1984,[25] disapproved of the 'balancing interests' idea. He considered that if a court has jurisdiction it must exercise it. If, on the other hand, international law says it has no jurisdiction that is the end of the matter. One cannot, however, have a court which has a discretion whether or not to exercise its own jurisdiction.

---

[16] Foreseeability indicates that the 'intent' in *Alcoa*, 274 US 268, 47 S. Ct 592 (1927) is objective rather than subjective.

[17] *Hartford Fire Insurance Co v. California*, 509 US 764, 113 S.Ct 2891 (1993).

[18] This stemmed from re-insurers' worries about certain long term risks, such as those arising from environmental pollution, where the claims could come up decades later.

[19] *Hartford Fire* at 796 (US).

[20] The 'foreign sovereign compulsion defence' (i.e. the US courts do not hold private individuals liable for acts they were compelled to perform by a foreign sovereign on that sovereign's territory) therefore did not apply. The US also recognises 'foreign sovereign immunity' (the Act of State defence) whereby foreign governments have immunity in the courts, although usually only for commercial activities (see the Foreign Sovereign Immunities Act 1976).

[21] A. Robertson and M. Demetriou, '"But That was in Another Country…": The Extraterritorial Application of US Antitrust Laws in the US Supreme Court' (1994) 43 *ICLQ* 417, 421–2.

[22] Case T-102/96, *Gencor Ltd v. Commission* [1999] ECR II-753, discussed at Section 5.D.ii, p. 1279.

[23] See also the minority opinion by Judge Adams in *Mannington Mills*, 595 F.2d. 1287 (3d Cir. 1979).

[24] Hovenkamp (cited in n. 15), 827.

[25] F. A. Mann, 'The Doctrine of International Jurisdiction Revisited After Twenty Years' (1984) 186 *RdC* 9, the sequel to the celebrated 1964 article, 'The Doctrine of Jurisdiction in International Law' (1964) 111 *RdC* 1.

In 1995 the DOJ and the FTC issued a revised set of Antitrust Enforcement Guidelines for International Operations.[26] These explain, inter alia, that the agencies will take comity into account when deciding to bring an action or seek particular remedies. The Guidelines list a number of factors[27] that will be considered when making the decision. Once the decision is made, however, this represents 'a determination by the Executive Branch that the importance of antitrust enforcement outweighs any relevant foreign policy concerns'. The Guidelines warn that the courts should not 'second-guess' its judgment 'as to the proper role of comity concerns under these circumstances'.[28]

The effects doctrine was applied in *Nippon Paper*,[29] where the Antitrust Division of the DOJ commenced criminal proceedings under the Sherman Act against a Japanese company for a cartel fixing the price at which fax paper should be sold in the US.[30] The conspirators were all Japanese and all the activities of the cartel—the meetings, monitoring, and the sales to distributors with instructions about the resale price in the US—took place in Japan. In contrast to the position in *Hartford Fire Insurance* the conduct was *illegal* under Japanese law (although the Japanese Government intervened in the case as an amicus on behalf of the defendant undertakings). The First Circuit Court of Appeals held that the US courts did have jurisdiction. The Court said that *Hartford Fire* had 'stunted' the concept of comity in antitrust cases. It considered that the Japanese undertakings should not, in these circumstances, be sheltered from prosecution by principles of comity:

> We see no tenable reason why principles of comity should shield [the Japanese undertakings] from prosecution. We live in an age of international commerce, where decisions reached in one corner of the world can reverberate around the globe in less time than it takes to tell the tale. Thus, a ruling in [the Japanese undertakings'] favor would create perverse incentives for those who would use nefarious means to influence markets in the United States, rewarding them for enacting as many territorial firewalls as possible between cause and effect.[31]

This was the first case in which extraterritorial criminal jurisdiction had been taken under the Sherman Act.

C. ENFORCEMENT AND THE REACTIONS OF OTHER STATES

Other States have tended to react unfavourably to US claims of extraterritorial jurisdiction based on the effects doctrine.[32] Particular problems have arisen where the US has wished to take antitrust enforcement action extraterritorially. As has been shown in other chapters of this book[33] competition authorities need to investigate and gather information, and may ultimately wish to levy penalties and enforce orders remedying infringements of the competition rules and litigants may wish to pursue procedural rights to discover evidence. A stark example of the conflicts that can arise is *United States* v. *ICI Ltd.*[34] There a US court ordered, on the grounds of infringement of the Sherman

---

[26] Antitrust and Trade Reg. Rep. (BNA), Special Supplement (6 April 1995).

[27] Similar to those in *Timberlane* (cited in n. 11).

[28] For the application of comity in a discovery request see *Société Nationale Industrielle Aérospatiale* v. *United States District Court for the Southern District of Iowa* 482 US 522, see n. 58.

[29] *United States* v. *Nippon Paper Industries Co.*, 109 F.3d (1st Cir. 1997).

[30] See R. M. Reynolds, J. Sicilian, and P. S. Wellman, 'The Extraterritorial Application of the US Antitrust Laws to Criminal Conspiracies' [1998] *ECLR* 151; J. Griffin, 'Reactions to US Assertions of Extraterritorial Jurisdiction' [1998] *ECLR* 64, 68.

[31] *Nippon Paper*, at 9.

[32] There has also been opposition to the extraterritorial application of measures taken in pursuit of American foreign policy, see n. 7.

[33] See particularly Chap. 13.

[34] 105 F. Supp 215 (1952).

Act, the cancellation of agreements between ICI and Du Pont, by which Du Pont assigned to ICI certain patents which were to be registered in the UK. ICI was ordered to reassign the patents to Du Pont. ICI, however, had already contracted to license the patents to British Nylon Spinners, a UK company. British Nylon Spinners sued in the English courts to enforce its rights under the contract. Danckwerts J granted a decree of specific performance, saying that the US judge 'was applying an enactment of Congress, which has no application to the United Kingdom'.[35]

US pre-trial discovery confers wide-ranging powers on US plaintiffs wishing to search abroad for evidence of antitrust violations. In the UK the House of Lords reacted with hostility in *Rio Tinto Zinc*[36] to letters rogatory requesting the High Court to require directors and employees of a British company to give oral evidence before an examiner in London and to require the company to produce the documents contained in a lengthy schedule. The request was in connection with a private antitrust suit in Virginia. The House decided that the US Court's request for assistance fell within the exceptions to the obligation to assist in requests for discovery by foreign courts contained in the Evidence (Proceedings in Other Jurisdictions) Act 1975, and consequently refused discovery.

The UK subsequently passed the Protection of Trading Interest Act 1980, to 'block' the enforcement of any foreign international trade laws, but in reality largely directed at US antitrust laws. First, the Act enables the Secretary of State to direct a person carrying on business in the UK not to comply with the orders of a foreign court or authority affecting international trade which threaten to damage the trading interests of the UK.[37] Section 2 of the Act empowers the Secretary of State to prohibit persons within the UK from complying with demands by foreign tribunals and authorities for commercial documents or information not located within the jurisdiction of the State concerned.[38] The Act also protects British defendants from the enforcement of punitive treble damages claims. Section 5 describes such awards as 'penal' and forbids their enforcement in UK courts under the usual reciprocal enforcement procedures.[39] Further, section 6 sets out a 'clawback' provision enabling British citizens or companies or persons carrying on business in the UK to bring an action in the UK courts to recover the non-compensatory part of any such damages they have paid. Other States have also passed such 'blocking' statutes.[40]

Violation of the Sherman Act, s. 1 is a criminal offence, and individuals who participate in cartel arrangements are liable to criminal prosecution, fines, and imprisonment. There is a great deal of disagreement as to whether or not the criminalisation of cartel behaviour is appropriate or useful as a way of combating hardcore cartels, but the current view of an increasing number of competition authorities is that it is.[41] However, executives can escape US jails by lurking in countries which will not extradite to the US for antitrust offences. That was true of the UK until the Enterprise Act 2002, s. 191 introduced the 'cartel offence' into UK law.[42] The offence is extraditable[43] which means a person may be extradited to another country for an equivalent offence. Section 191 is not retrospective and so does not apply to conduct prior to June 2003. An attempt by the US Government to extradite Ian Norris, the ex-Chief Executive of Morgan Crucible, to face trial in the US for violation of the

---

[35] *British Nylon Spinners Ltd v. ICI Ltd* [1955] Ch 37.

[36] *Rio Tinto Zinc Corp v. Westinghouse Electric Corp* [1978] AC 547.

[37] Protection of Trading Interest Act 1980, s. 1.

[38] Note that in the current spirit of international cooperation the UK favours the ability to exchange information in order to further the enforcement of competition laws. The Enterprise Act 2002, s. 243 sets out the circumstances in which a UK public authority could disclose information to an overseas public authority, including a competition authority. The UK/US Mutual Assistance Treaty now covers criminal infringements of competition law (UK/US Mutual Legal Assistance Treaty, 2001 (Cm. 5375)).

[39] See Chap. 14.

[40] See generally A. V. Lowe, *Extraterritorial Jurisdiction* (Grotius, 1983).

[41] See Chap. 13, Section 12, p. 1064.

[42] Enterprise Act 2002, s. 188.

[43] Enterprise Act 2002, s. 191.

Sherman Act prior to 2003 by arguing that price-fixing was an offence of conspiracy to defraud at common law, failed in the House of Lords.[44] However, the Supreme Court (as the House of Lords had become in the meantime) later held that he could be extradited on charges of obstructing justice (as that would have been an offence in the UK at the time of the alleged conduct in the US).[45]

D. FOREIGN PLAINTIFFS IN US COURTS

In Chapter 14 we saw that private litigation of antitrust cases is far more common in US courts than it is anywhere in Europe. As well as the differences in the systems of enforcement there are various features of the US legal system which make it easier or more attractive for plaintiffs in the US to bring actions. In brief, these are:

- very broad discovery rules;[46]
- class actions (in which, moreover, injured parties need not join in at the start of the case, i.e. they are 'opt-out' actions);
- contingent attorneys' fees;
- treble damages;[47]
- joint and several liability among the defendants.

Furthermore, in the US actions are heard before juries, which can be very generous in awarding damages to those they see as wronged by big corporations.

Overseas litigants often look with envy at the sight of US plaintiffs winning large damages awards in US courts. Some of these have been in respect of major international cartels which had effects in numerous countries. As explained in Chapter 14, overseas victims of international cartels recently started litigating in US courts in respect of harm suffered outside the US. At first sight these actions seemed unlikely to succeed: the FTAIA, as already mentioned,[48] states that as regards foreign commerce the antitrust laws will not apply unless the conduct has a direct, substantial, and reasonably foreseeable effect on US commerce. However, the US Court of Appeals differed in its reactions to claims over harm overseas.[49] The matter went to the Supreme Court in *F. Hoffmann-La Roche Ltd v. Empagran*.[50]

There were two strands of argument in *Empagran*. The first was a matter of statutory construction of the FTAIA in the light of international comity. The second was a matter of statutory construction in the light of its legislative history. The issue was whether the US could or should act as a kind of world policeman, welcoming litigants from all over the world who have been injured abroad by cartels which have also caused injury inside the US. *Empagran* itself was part of the saga of the worldwide vitamins cartel, punished in the US by fines of more than $800 million and jail sentences for some of the executives, and in the EC by swingeing fines, Hoffmann-La Roche alone being fined €462 million (after receiving leniency).[51] The plaintiffs were, inter alia, Ukrainian, Ecuadorean, and Panamanian

---

[44] *Norris v. Government of the United States of America* [2008] UKHL 16.

[45] *Norris v. Government of the United States of America* [2010] UKSC 9.

[46] Although, as noted in Chap. 14, the narrower discovery rules in European jurisdictions (very much narrower in some Member States) may be by-passed where the litigant is able to rely on the information laid out in a Commission decision (which may well have been uncovered by a Commission inspection under Reg. 1/2003, Art. 20).

[47] The Antitrust Criminal Penalty Enhancement and Reform Act 2004 limits the damages recoverable from a corporate amnesty applicant which also cooperates with private plaintiffs in their damages actions against remaining cartel members to the damages actually inflicted by the amnesty applicant's conduct.

[48] In Section 3.B, p. 1261.

[49] See Chap. 14.

[50] 542 US 155 (2004).

[51] *Vitamins* [2003] OJ L6/1, [2003] 4 CMLR 1030.

buyers, while the defendant sellers were German and Swiss. The District of Columbia Court of Appeals held that they could seek damages in the US, as purchasers overseas who suffer losses from a cartel could sue in US courts provided similar claims could be brought in US courts in respect of the same cartel. One argument for the US courts taking jurisdiction was that global cartels do not really 'take place' in any particular territory. When foreign purchasers contract with a multinational corporation the contract could be sourced anywhere, and there is no reason why a party's ability to recover should depend on how the multinational structures its transactions. Further it is argued that global cartels *do* harm US consumers, because in a globalised world there is no such thing as domestic price-fixing: the important thing to do is to deter cartel behaviour by making it too expensive (and allowing the victims to sue in US courts is one way to do this). The DOJ did not agree that US courts should take jurisdiction. It argued in its amicus curiae brief to the Supreme Court in *Empagran* that, in particular, the taking of jurisdiction by US courts would undermine the DOJ's leniency programme by expanding the scope of the cartellists' potential civil liability, and would undermine cooperation with other competition authorities.

The Supreme Court held that the FTAIA excluded foreign plaintiffs from seeking damages in the US where the harm flowed exclusively from the foreign effects of the conduct which infringed the Sherman Act.

F. Hoffmann-La Roche Ltd v. *Empagran SA*, 542 US 155 (2004), 14 June 2004

Opinion of the Supreme Court

Justice Breyer

IV

We turn now to the basic question presented, that of the exception's application. Because the underlying antitrust action is complex, potentially raising questions not directly at issue here, we reemphasize that we base our decision upon the following: The price-fixing conduct significantly and adversely affects both customers outside the United States and customers within the United States, but the adverse foreign effect is independent of any adverse domestic effect. In these circumstances, we find that the FTAIA exception does not apply (and thus the Sherman Act does not apply) for two main reasons. *First*, this Court ordinarily construes ambiguous statutes to avoid unreasonable interference with the sovereign authority of other nations. See, *e.g., McCulloch* v. *Sociedad Nacional de Marineros de Honduras*, 372 U.S. 10, 20–22 (1963) (application of National Labor Relations Act to foreign-flag vessels); *Romero* v. *International Terminal Operating Co.*, 358 U.S. 354, 382–383 (1959) (application of Jones Act in maritime case); *Lauritzen* v. *Larsen*, 345 U.S. 571, 578 (1953) (same). This rule of construction reflects principles of customary international law—law that (we must assume) Congress ordinarily seeks to follow. See Restatement (Third) of Foreign Relations Law of the United States §§403(1), 403(2) (1986) (hereinafter Restatement) (limiting the unreasonable exercise of prescriptive jurisdiction with respect to a person or activity having connections with another State); *Murray* v. *Schooner Charming Betsy*, 2 Cranch 64, 118 (1804) ('[A]n act of Congress ought never to be construed to violate the law of nations if any other possible construction remains'); *Hartford Fire Insurance Co.* v. *California*, 509 U.S. 764, 817 (1993) (SCALIA, J., dissenting) (identifying rule of construction as derived from the principle of 'prescriptive comity').

This rule of statutory construction cautions courts to assume that legislators take account of the legitimate sovereign interests of other nations when they write American laws. It thereby helps the potentially conflicting laws of different nations work together in harmony—a harmony particularly needed in today's highly interdependent commercial world.

No one denies that America's antitrust laws, when applied to foreign conduct, can interfere with a foreign nation's ability independently to regulate its own commercial affairs. But our courts have long held that application of our antitrust laws to foreign anti-competitive conduct is nonetheless reasonable, and hence consistent with principles of prescriptive comity, insofar as they reflect a legislative effort to redress domestic antitrust injury that foreign anti-competitive conduct has caused. See *United States* v. *Aluminum Co of America*, 148 F. 2d 416, 443–444 (CA2 1945) (L. Hand, J.); 1 P. Areeda & D. Turner, *Antitrust Law* ¶236 (1978).

But why is it reasonable to apply those laws to foreign conduct insofar as that conduct causes independent foreign harm and that foreign harm alone gives rise to the plaintiff's claim? Like the former case, application of those laws creates a serious risk of interference with a foreign nation's ability independently to regulate its own commercial affairs. But, unlike the former case, the justification for that interference seems insubstantial. See Restatement §403(2) (determining reasonableness on basis of such factors as connections with regulating nation, harm to that nation's interests, extent to which other nations regulate, and the potential for conflict). Why should American law supplant, for example, Canada's or Great Britain's or Japan's own determination about how best to protect Canadian or British or Japanese customers from anti-competitive conduct engaged in significant part by Canadian or British or Japanese or other foreign companies?

We recognize that principles of comity provide Congress greater leeway when it seeks to control through legislation the actions of American companies, see Restatement §402; and some of the anti-competitive price-fixing conduct alleged here took place in America. But the higher foreign prices of which the foreign plaintiffs here complain are not the consequence of any domestic anti-competitive conduct that Congress sought to forbid, for Congress did not seek to forbid any such conduct insofar as it is here relevant, i.e., insofar as it is intertwined with foreign conduct that causes independent foreign harm. Rather Congress sought to release domestic (and foreign) anti-competitive conduct from Sherman Act constraints when that conduct causes foreign harm. Congress, of course, did make an exception where that conduct also causes domestic harm. See House Report 13 (concerns about American firms' participation in international cartels addressed through 'domestic injury' exception). But any independent domestic harm the foreign conduct causes here has, by definition, little or nothing to do with the matter.

We thus repeat the basic question: Why is it reasonable to apply this law to conduct that is significantly foreign insofar as that conduct causes independent foreign harm and that foreign harm alone gives rise to the plaintiff's claim? We can find no good answer to the question…

…

Respondents reply that many nations have adopted antitrust laws similar to our own, to the point where the practical likelihood of interference with the relevant interests of other nations is minimal. Leaving price fixing to the side, however, this Court has found to the contrary. See, e.g., *Hartford Fire*, 509 U.S. at 797–799 (noting that the alleged conduct in the London reinsurance market, while illegal under United States antitrust laws, was assumed to be perfectly consistent with British law and policy); see also, e.g., 2 W. Fugate, Foreign Commerce and the Antitrust Laws §16.6 (5th ed. 1996) (noting differences between European Union and United States law on vertical restraints).

Regardless, even where nations agree about primary conduct, say price fixing, they disagree dramatically about appropriate remedies. The application, for example, of American private treble-damages remedies to anti-competitive conduct taking place abroad has generated considerable controversy. See, e.g., 2 ABA Section of Antitrust Law, Antitrust Law Developments 1208–1209 (5th ed. 2002). And several foreign nations have filed briefs here arguing that to apply our remedies would unjustifiably permit their citizens to bypass their own less generous remedial schemes, thereby upsetting a balance of competing considerations that their own domestic antitrust laws embody…

These briefs add that a decision permitting independently injured foreign plaintiffs to pursue private treble-damages remedies would undermine foreign nations' own antitrust enforcement policies by diminishing foreign firms' incentive to cooperate with antitrust authorities in return for prosecutorial amnesty…Respondents alternatively argue that comity does not demand an interpretation of the FTAIA that would exclude independent foreign injury cases across the board. Rather, courts can take (and sometimes have taken) account of comity considerations case by case, abstaining where comity considerations so dictate. Cf., e.g., *Hartford Fire*, supra, at 797, n. 24; *United States* v. *Nippon Paper Industries Co.*, 109 F. 3d 1, 8 (CA1 1997); *Mannington Mills, Inc* v. *Congoleum Corp*, 595 F. 2d 1287, 1294–1295 (CA3 1979).

In our view, however, this approach is too complex to prove workable. The Sherman Act covers many different kinds of anti-competitive agreements. Courts would have to examine how foreign law, compared with American law, treats not only price fixing but also, say, information-sharing agreements, patent-licensing price conditions, territorial product resale limitations, and various forms of joint venture, in respect to both primary conduct and remedy. The legally and economically technical nature of that enterprise means lengthier proceedings, appeals, and more proceedings—to the point where procedural costs and delays could themselves threaten interference with a foreign nation's ability to maintain the integrity of its own antitrust enforcement system. Even in this relatively simple price-fixing case, for example, competing briefs tell us (1) that potential treble-damage liability would help enforce widespread anti-price-fixing norms (through added deterrence) and (2) the opposite, namely that such liability would hinder antitrust enforcement (by reducing incentives to enter amnesty programs). Compare, e.g., Brief for Certain Professors of Economics as Amici Curiae 2–4 with Brief for United States as Amicus Curiae 19–21. How could a court seriously interested in resolving so empirical a matter—a matter potentially related to impact on foreign interests—do so simply and expeditiously?

We conclude that principles of prescriptive comity counsel against the Court of Appeals' interpretation of the FTAIA. Where foreign anti-competitive conduct plays a significant role and where foreign injury is independent of domestic effects, Congress might have hoped that America's antitrust laws, so fundamental a component of our own economic system, would commend themselves to other nations as well. But, if America's antitrust policies could not win their own way in the international marketplace for such ideas, Congress, we must assume, would not have tried to impose them, in an act of legal imperialism, through legislative fiat.

The Supreme Court went on to consider the legislative history of the FTAIA and concluded that 'the FTAIA's language and history suggest that Congress designed the FTAIA to clarify, perhaps to limit, but not to expand in any significant way, the Sherman Act's scope as applied to foreign commerce'.

It will be noted that in the extract from *Empagran* the Supreme Court was sensitive to the question of international comity. The effects doctrine is to 'redress domestic antitrust injury' and the Court considered there is no justification for trespassing on the preserve of foreign sovereigns by taking action against purely foreign injury. Several foreign governments (including that of the UK) submitted briefs to the Supreme Court arguing against the US courts taking jurisdiction, and the Supreme Court took these views very seriously.[52]

Nevertheless, it is important to note exactly what the Supreme Court held. Because of the way in which the case was pleaded and argued it based its judgment on the assumption that the foreign effects of the cartel were quite independent of its effects in the US. It left open the question of what would be the position if the foreign and domestic effects could be shown to be intertwined, for example if the prices abroad would have been lower had it not been for the effects in the US. However, in *Re Monosodium Glutamate Antitrust Litigation* the US Court of Appeals for the 8th Circuit upheld a ruling excluding foreign plaintiffs from bringing a class action against manufacturers involved in a cartel. The Court said that 'the domestic effects of the price fixing scheme—increased US prices—were not the direct cause of the appellants' injuries. Rather it was the foreign effects of the price fixing scheme—increased prices abroad.'[53] The Court set a high standard of proof for any effect on US

---

[52] On remand, the DC Circuit ruled for the defendants, 417 F.3d 1267 (D.C.Cir., 2005).
[53] 477 F.3d 535 (8th Cir. 2007).

commerce and rejected claims that a worldwide conspiracy in which prices must be inflated in every market (to avoid arbitrage) could satisfy the standard.

E. DISCOVERY IN US COURTS

In *Intel Corp v. Advanced Micro Devices Inc*[54] the Supreme Court delivered a judgment in a case in which a complainant to the European Commission against the microprocessor firm, Intel, wanted production of documents that had surfaced in an action against Intel in the US. Federal district courts have authority to assist in the production of evidence for use in a 'foreign or international tribunal'. The Commission refused to ask the US courts for discovery. The Supreme Court held that although the CFI (now the GC) and CJ did not themselves take proof, they did qualify as 'tribunals' which could review the decision of the Commission before which the documents could be used. This was sufficient for the Supreme Court to uphold the Court of Appeal's ruling[55] that discovery should be granted, despite the Commission's lack of support for AMD's request.

In *Re Payment Card Interchange Fee and Merchant Discount Antitrust Litigation*[56] a US District Court denied plaintiffs in a private class action the access to a Statement of Objections (SO) issued by the European Commission and to an Oral Hearing transcript which were in the possession of the defendants, after the European Commission intervened.[57] The judge decided that discovery should be precluded on the basis of international comity as explained in the Supreme Court case *Société Nationale Industrielle Aérospatiale*[58] He concluded that the Commission had strong and legitimate reasons to protect the confidentiality of the documents and that its interests in this respect were entitled to prevail.[59]

F. THE EFFECTS DOCTRINE AND FOREIGN CONDUCT AFFECTING EXPORTS

The FTAIA says that the Sherman Act only applies to export commerce where the conduct has a direct, substantial, and reasonably foreseeable effect on US commerce. It can be argued, however, that if US exports are injured by being denied access to foreign markets there may be a disadvantageous effect on commerce inside the US. Taking jurisdiction where conduct of foreign actors abroad affects the US *export* trade is true extraterritoriality. Although the US agencies consider that they do in theory have jurisdiction over conduct abroad which affects exports,[60] they do not usually take action against it.[61] Indeed, the practical enforcement problems are very great. In the *Fuji* case the US tried to use trade rather than competition law to advance the interests of its exporters. Kodak alleged that it was unable to penetrate the Japanese market because of anti-competitive activities there, in particular on the part of Fuji's distributors, despite the existence of Japanese anti-monopoly laws.

---

[54] 542 US 155 (2004).

[55] 292 F.3d 664 (2004).

[56] MDL Docket No. 1720, Master File No. 1:05 md-1720-JG-JO, District Court of the Eastern District of New York.

[57] The SO issued to Visa in April 2009 in COMP/39.398, and the Oral Hearing in COMP/34.579, *Mastercard*.

[58] 482 US 522, n. 28. Basing himself on para. 437 of the Restatement Justice Stevens said that five factors were relevant to the a comity analysis in respect of a district court's power to order foreign discovery in the face of objections from a foreign state: the importance to the litigation of the documents or other information requested; the degree of specificity of the request; whether the information originated in the United States; the availability of alternative means of securing the information; and the extent to which noncompliance with the request would undermine important interests of the US, or compliance with the request would undermine important interests of the state where the information is located.

[59] See also the note of the case in ECN Brief 4/2010 (October), 2.

[60] Antitrust Enforcement Guidelines for International Operations, para. 3.1222.

[61] But see *United States v. Pilkington* (1994-2) Trade Cases, para. 482.

Kodak brought a section 301 Trade Act 1974 petition in the US and the US Trade Representative referred the Japanese Government's conduct in tolerating the anti-competitive behaviour to the WTO. Access to the WTO dispute resolution process is limited to governments. The WTO panel held that the WTO rules apply only to governments and that it is not open to governments to attack private measures in this way.[62] This showed that the WTO rules cannot be used to force open foreign markets which are obstructed by private conduct.

4. INTERNATIONAL LAW

Given the controversy the US effects doctrine has generated, it is interesting to consider whether or not it is in conformity with international law.[63] There is no clear answer to this. The US Government considers that the effects doctrine, whereby it asserts jurisdiction based on 'direct, substantial, and reasonably foreseeable' effects within the United States, is in accordance with international law. Other governments disagree.[64]

It is generally accepted that the two undoubted bases for criminal jurisdiction[65] in international law are nationality and territory. There are two aspects to territoriality: subjective and objective. Subjective territoriality gives a State jurisdiction over acts which originated within its territory but were completed abroad. Objective territoriality gives a State jurisdiction over acts which originated abroad but were completed, at least partially, within its own territory. Objective territoriality was recognised by the Permanent Court of International Justice in the *Lotus* case.[66] However, there is continuing uncertainty about what *Lotus* actually decided. It can be argued both that the effects doctrine is validly derived from the principle of objective territoriality recognised in *Lotus* and that it is an illegitimate extension which is inconsistent with the principle of the sovereignty of nations. The US position is, of course, the former.[67]

Further possible principles of jurisdiction are the passive personality principle, by which States claim jurisdiction over aliens who have committed acts abroad harmful to their nationals, and the protective or security principle[68] by which they claim jurisdiction over aliens for acts committed

---

[62] *Japan—Measures Affecting Consumer Photographic Film and Paper* WT/DS44/R, 31 March 1998.

[63] There is an enormous literature on jurisdiction in international law, a complex issue of which the question of jurisdiction in competition law is but a small part. See, e.g., M. Akehurst, 'Jurisdiction in International Law' (1972–1973) 46 *BYIL*, 145; F. A. Mann, 'The Doctrine of International Jurisdiction Revisited After Twenty Years' (1984) 156 *RdC* 9; F. A. Mann, 'The Doctrine of Jurisdiction in International Law' (1964) 111 *RdC* 3; D. W. Bowett, 'Jurisdiction: Changing Problems of Authority over Activities and Resources' (1982) 53 *BYIL*; R. Y. Jennings and A. D. Watts (eds.), *Oppenheim's International Law* (9th edn, Longman, 1992), i, 456; O. Schachter, *International Law in Theory and Practice* (Nijhoff, 1991), Chap. XII; R. Higgins, *Problems and Process* (Oxford University Press, 1994), Chap. 4. With particular reference to antitrust law, see K. M. Meessen, 'Antitrust Jurisdiction under Customary International Law' (1984) 78 *AJIL* 783; P. J. Slot and E. Grabandt, 'Extraterritoriality and Jurisdiction' (1986) 23 *CMLRev* 545; P. M. Roth, 'Reasonable Extraterritoriality: Correcting the "Balance of Interests"' (1992) 41 *ICLQ* 245.

[64] See J. Griffin, 'Reactions to US Assertions of Extraterritorial Jurisdiction' [1998] *ECLR* 64, 68.

[65] It is not clear whether there is any significant difference between jurisdiction in criminal, civil, and monetary matters: see, e.g., I. Brownlie, *Principles of Public International Law* (7th edn, Oxford University Press, 2008), 300; M. Akehurst, 'Jurisdiction in International Law' (1972–1973) 46 *BYIL* 145, 177.

[66] (1927), PCIJ, Ser.A, No. 10, 23. The case arose from a collision on the high seas between a French ship and a Turkish ship which led to Turkey instituting criminal proceedings against the officers of the watch on the French ship when it put into a Turkish port. The PCIJ held that international law did not *prevent* Turkey instituting proceedings: it was not asked whether international law *authorised* it to do so. See J. Griffin, 'Reactions to US Assertions of Extraterritorial Jurisdiction' [1998] *ECLR* 64, 68.

[67] See the *Alcoa* case (n. 10) itself. F. A. Mann, 'The Doctrine of International Jurisdiction Revisited after Twenty Years', (1984) 186 *RdC* 9 concluded that although the effects doctrine is recognised by several countries, it does not seem to be regarded as a principle of international law.

[68] See the *Cutting* case (1886), in J. B. Moore, *Digest of International Law*, Vol. II (U.S. Government Printing Office, 1906). A further principle, not relevant here, is the universality principle, where jurisdiction is taken over aliens as a matter of international public policy for crimes such as piracy or aircraft hijacking.

abroad which harm the security of the State. The latter principle is capable of indefinite expansion and could potentially be used to justify jurisdiction over economic acts.

It should be noted that private international law (conflict of laws), as well as public international law, is relevant to jurisdiction questions in competition cases. Private international law attempts to regulate whether a particular State has jurisdiction to try an issue and which law will be applied in determining it.

The problem for States in applying competition laws extraterritorially is that merely taking legislative (prescriptive) jurisdiction is not enough. As we have seen when discussing US law, it is essential that it has enforcement jurisdiction whereby its authorities can conduct investigations, collect evidence, serve proceedings, and recover penalties abroad. The position in international law was surveyed by Advocate General Darmon in his opinion in the leading EU case, *Wood Pulp I*.[69] He recognised the distinction between prescriptive and enforcement jurisdiction and considered that the mere imposition of a pecuniary sanction is a matter of prescriptive jurisdiction, enforcement jurisdiction being involved only when steps are taken for its recovery, because only then is the State taking coercive measures in the territory of a foreign sovereign. He concluded that the effects doctrine was not contrary to international law and that it should be adopted by Community law:

57.... there is no rule of international law which is capable of being relied upon against the criterion of the direct, substantial and foreseeable effect. Nor does the concept of international comity, in view of its uncertain scope, militate against the criterion either.

58. In the absence of any such prohibitive rule and in the light of widespread State practice, I would therefore propose that in view of its appropriateness to the field of competition, it be adopted as a criterion for the jurisdiction of the Community.

As we shall see, the CJ considered that its taking of jurisdiction in *Wood Pulp* was 'covered by the territoriality principle as universally recognized in public international law'.[70]

5. THE POSITION IN EU LAW

A. GENERAL

Articles 101 and 102 are silent on the question whether or not they apply extraterritorially. At first the development of the single economic entity doctrine[71] precluded the need for resolving the issue. However, the point finally had to be dealt with in *Wood Pulp*.[72] The Merger Regulation,[73] while not expressly addressing the extraterritoriality question, contains a jurisdiction threshold which may catch concentrations between undertakings based outside the EU so long as the EU turnover thresholds set out in the regulation are satisfied.[74]

---

[69] Cases 89, 104, 114, 116, 117, and 125–9/85, *A. Ahlström Oy v. Commission* [1988] ECR 5193 (*Wood Pulp I*), paras. 19–32 and 47–58 of the Opinion.

[70] *Wood Pulp*, para. 18.

[71] See Chap. 3.

[72] Cases 89, 104, 114, 116, 117, and 125–129/85, *A. Ahlström Oy v. Commission* [1988] ECR 5193.

[73] Council Reg. 139/2004 [2004] L24/1.

[74] For the threshold generally, see Chap. 15.

B. THE *DYESTUFFS* CASE

In 1972 in *Béguelin*,[75] a case concerning a Japanese manufacturer whose distribution arrangements with its French distributor compartmentalised the common market on national lines the CJ held that the agreement infringed Article 101(1). As one of the parties to the agreement was clearly within the Community, and in the context of the case the imposition of a penalty on the Japanese undertaking did not arise, jurisdiction could be asserted without the question of an effects doctrine having to be faced.

In the *Dyestuffs* case[76] the question whether EEC law had an effects doctrine was raised for the first time. The Commission investigated an alleged cartel among the producers of aniline dyes. It found, inter alia, that ICI, a company incorporated and having its headquarters in the UK which was not at that time a member of the Community, had engaged in concerted practices contrary to Article 101(1) by virtue of the instructions it had given to its Belgian subsidiary. It imposed a fine of 50,000 units of account on ICI.[77] In paragraph 28 of the Decision the Commission said:

Under Article [101(1)]... all agreements between undertakings, all decisions by associations of undertakings and all concerted practices which may affect trade between Member States and the object or effect of which is to prevent, restrict or distort competition within the Common Market shall be prohibited as incompatible with the Common Market. The competition rules of the Treaty are, consequently, applicable to all restrictions of competition which produce within the Common Market effects set out in Article [101(1)]. There is therefore no need to examine whether the undertakings which are the cause of these restrictions of competition have their seat within or outside the Community.

It will be noted that here the Commission applied an 'effects' doctrine without any further amplification. The ICI appealed against the Commission decision, inter alia, on the jurisdiction point. It claimed that the Commission had no power to apply the competition rules to an undertaking established outside the (then) EEC. In reply the Commission relied not just on an elaboration of the effects doctrine but also on the claim that, although the subsidiaries within the Community had separate legal personality in law, the reality was that they were merely carrying out the parent's orders, so that subsidiaries appeared 'as mere extensions of ICI in the Common Market'.[78]

Advocate General Mayras recommended that the Commission's decision should be upheld on the basis of the 'effects doctrine'. He reviewed the national laws of the Member States on this issue, the international law arguments, and, of course, US law. He said that the conditions necessary for taking extraterritorial jurisdiction were that the agreement or concerted practice must create a *direct and immediate* restriction of competition, that the effect of the conduct must be *reasonably foreseeable*, and that the effect produced on the territory must be *substantial*. The Advocate General justified this adoption of what amounted to an effects doctrine not just by reference to principle, but also on grounds of pragmatism.[79]

Just as it would be quite wrong to reduce the concept of a concerted practice to so narrow a meaning that it would no longer connote anything more than a particular expression of the concept of an agreement, the obvious risk being that Article [101(1)] would not be given the effective scope intended by the authors of the Treaty, so—subject to a reservation concerning powers of enforcement—that article would be drained of a large part of its meaning and at any rate its force would be dissipated if the Community authorities were denied the use in relation to any undertaking outside the Common Market of the powers that that same Article [101] confers on them. Surely the Commission would be disarmed if, faced with a concerted practice

[75] Case 22/71, *Béguelin Import Co v. GL Import Export* [1971] ECR 949.

[76] Case 48/69, *ICI v. Commission (Dyestuffs)* [1972] ECR 619. The case was also an important early decision on concerted practices: see Chap. 9.

[77] *Re the Cartel in Aniline Dyes* [1969] OJ L195/11, [1969] CMLR D23.

[78] Case 48/69, *ICI v. Commission (Dyestuffs)* [1972] ECR 619, 627.

[79] Case 48/69, *ICI v. Commission (Dyestuffs)* [1972] ECR 619, 696.

the initiative for which was taken and the responsibility for which was assumed exclusively by undertakings outside the Common Market, it was deprived of the power to take any decision against them? This would also mean giving up a way of defending the Common Market and one necessary for bringing about the major objectives of the European Economic Community.

He drew a distinction, however, between prescriptive and enforcement jurisdiction. He considered that the *imposition* of fines is part of the legislative (prescriptive) jurisdiction, whereas their *recovery* (or other measures, such as the annulment of contracts) amounts to enforcement jurisdiction. He was prepared to accept that the decision taken by the Commission might not be capable of enforcement:[80]

the courts or administrative authorities of a State—and, *mutatis mutandis*, of the Community—are certainly not justified under international law in taking coercive measures or indeed any measure of inquiry, investigation or supervision outside their territorial jurisdiction where execution would inevitably infringe the internal sovereignty of the State on the territory of which they claimed to act.

In its judgment the CJ did not take up its Advocate General's espousal of an effects doctrine. Instead it upheld the Commission's decision on the basis of what has become known as the single economic entity doctrine. It is explained in Chapter 3 that EU law developed this doctrine by which parents and subsidiaries are considered to be one undertaking for the purposes of the application of the competition rules. In *Dyestuffs* the Court relied on this concept to impute the conduct of the subsidiary to the parent and to hold that the Commission did have jurisdiction over the UK company.

Case 48/69, *ICI* v. *Commission (Dyestuffs)* [1972] ECR 619

Court of Justice

130. By making use of its power to control its subsidiaries established in the Community, the applicant was able to ensure that its decision was implemented on that market.

131. The applicant objects that this conduct is to be imputed to its subsidiaries and not to itself.

132. The fact that a subsidiary has separate legal personality is not sufficient to exclude the possibility of imputing its conduct to the parent company.

133. Such may be the case in particular where the subsidiary, although having separate legal personality, does not decide independently upon its own conduct on the market, but carries out, in all material respects, the instructions given to it by the parent company.

134. Where a subsidiary does not enjoy real autonomy in determining its course of action in the market, the prohibitions set out in Article [101(1)] may be considered inapplicable in the relationship between it and the parent company with which it forms one economic unit.

135. In view of the unity of the group thus formed, the actions of the subsidiaries may in certain circumstances be attributed to the parent company.

136. It is well-known that at the time the applicant held all or at any rate the majority of the shares in those subsidiaries.

137. The applicant was able to exercise decisive influence over the policy of the subsidiaries as regards selling prices in the Common Market and in fact used this power upon the occasion of the three price increases in question.

138. In effect the Telex messages relating to the 1964 increase, which the applicant sent to its subsidiaries in the Common Market, gave the addressees orders as to the prices which they were to charge and the other conditions of sale which they were to apply in dealing with their customers.

---

[80] Case 48/69, *ICI* v. *Commission (Dyestuffs)* [1972] ECR 619, 695.

139. In the absence of evidence to the contrary, it must be assumed that on the occasion of the increases of 1965 and 1967 the applicant acted in a similar fashion in its relation with its subsidiaries established in the Common Market.

140. In the circumstances the formal separation between these companies, resulting from their separate legal personality, cannot outweigh the unity of their conduct on the market for the purposes of applying the rules on competition.

141. It was in fact the applicant undertaking which brought the concerted practice into being within the Common Market.

142. The submission as to lack of jurisdiction raised by the applicant must therefore be declared to be unfounded.

The CJ therefore held here that the subsidiary did not have 'real autonomy' but acted on its parent's instructions, so that the infringing conduct in the EEC could be treated as having been committed by the subsidiary as an agent of the parent.[81]

The application of the single economic entity doctrine to take what is in effect extraterritorial jurisdiction has its opponents. At the time of *Dyestuffs* the UK Government disputed the disregarding of the legal separation between parent and subsidiary.

The UK has, however, since dropped its hostility to this concept and the Competition Act 1998 received it fully into UK law, along with the other jurisprudence on the competition rules.[82] However, it is worth noting that many countries continue to have particular concerns about the application of a similar concept in US law. As Griffin explains:[83]

Nearly all nations agree that nationality can be a valid basis for asserting extraterritorial jurisdiction. However, U.S. assertions of jurisdiction based upon the control exercised by an American parent over a subsidiary incorporated and operating abroad are not accepted as valid under international law by a number of nations. These nations contend that despite the American parent's majority ownership or its possession of effective working control, under international law nationality is properly determined by the place of incorporation…Moreover, according to one knowledgeable British official,[84] 'even where nationality is a legitimate basis for extraterritorial jurisdiction it must remain subject to the primacy of the laws and policies of the territorial state.'…U.S. officials typically respond to these contentions with the assertion that they cannot permit 'technicalities' such as the place of incorporation and inconsistent policies of host states to be used by American companies to evade their obligations under U.S. law…

In *Dyestuffs* the CJ neither approved nor disapproved the views of its Advocate General on the effects doctrine. It clearly preferred to proceed on the other available ground which was less controversial. Its silence on the point, however, encouraged the Commission's belief that Community law did recognise the effects doctrine.

C. THE *WOOD PULP* CASE

Finally, a case came before the CJ in which the existence or otherwise of an effects doctrine, or something similar, in EC law was addressed. This was *Wood Pulp I*, a leading case on cartels which is discussed in Chapter 9. The Commission investigated alleged price-fixing in the wood pulp industry. It

[81] F. A. Mann argued that the facts of the case did not support this conclusion: 'Dyestuffs Case in the Court of Justice of the European Communities' (1973) 22 *ICLQ* 35 and 'Responsibility of Parent Companies for Foreign Subsidiaries' in C. Olmstead (ed.), *Extra-territorial Application of Laws and Responses Thereto* (ESC Publishing, 1984), 156.

[82] Competition Act 1998, s. 60.

[83] J. Griffin, 'Reactions to US Assertions of Extraterritorial Jurisdiction' [1998] *ECLR* 64, 69.

[84] The reference is to William M. Knighton, 'Nationality and Extraterritorial Jurisdiction: US Law Abroad', Remarks before the International Law Institute of the Georgetown University Law Center 2, 13 Aug. 1981.

found that a cartel existed, and held that 41 producers and two trade associations (Finncell and KEA) had engaged in concerted practices contrary to Article 101(1). It imposed fines on 36 of the addressees.[85] All 43 producers and trade associations concerned had their registered offices outside the EC. Most, if not all, of the producers had 'branches, subsidiaries, agencies or other establishments within the Community'.[86]

Many of the addressees appealed. There were two grounds: first that the Commission had no jurisdiction to apply its competition law to the addressees and, secondly, that they had not participated in concerted practices. The CJ heard the jurisdiction plea first.

As already noted[87] Advocate General Darmon engaged in a lengthy survey of the relevant international and US law and the scholarly literature and concluded that the Community was entitled to take, and should take, jurisdiction in this case on the basis of the effects doctrine. The CJ, however, couched its judgment in slightly different terms:

Cases 89, 104, 114, 116, 117, and 125–129/85, *A. Ahlström Oy* v. *Commission* [1988] ECR 5193

Court of Justice

11. In so far as the submission concerning the infringement of Article [101] itself is concerned, it should be recalled that that provision prohibits all agreements between undertakings and concerted practices which may affect trade between Member States and which have as their object or effect the restriction of competition within the Common Market.

12. It should be noted that the main sources of supply of wood pulp are outside the Community, in Canada, the United States, Sweden and Finland and that the market therefore has global dimensions. Where wood pulp producers established in those countries sell directly to purchasers established in the Community and engage in price competition in order to win orders from those customers, that constitutes competition within the Common Market.

13. It follows that where those producers concert on the prices to be charged to their customers in the Community and put that concertation into effect by selling at prices which are actually coordinated, they are taking part in concertation which has the object and effect of restricting competition within the Common Market within the meaning of Article [101].

14. Accordingly, it must be concluded that by applying the competition rules in the Treaty in the circumstances of this case to undertakings whose registered offices are situated outside the Community, the Commission has not made an incorrect assessment of the territorial scope of Article [101].

15. The applicants have submitted that the decision is incompatible with public international law on the grounds that the application of the competition rules in this case was founded exclusively on the economic repercussions within the Common Market of conduct restricting competition which [was] adopted outside the Community.

16. It should be observed that an infringement of Article [101], such as the conclusion of an agreement which has had the effect of restricting competition within the Common Market, consists of conduct made up of two elements, the formation of the agreement, decision or concerted practice and the implementation thereof. If the applicability of prohibitions laid down under competition law were made to depend on the place where the agreement, decision or concerted practice was formed, the result would obviously

---

[85] *Wood Pulp* [1985] OJ L85/1, [1985] 3 CMLR 474.

[86] Only some of them did according to para. 79 of the Decision, [1988] OJ L85/1, but later, in its rejoinder before the Court, the Commission stated that all of them did: see W. van Gerven, 'EC Jurisdiction in Antitrust Matters: The Wood Pulp Judgment' [1989] Fordham Corp L Inst 451, 464.

[87] See Section 4, p. 1271.

be to give undertakings an easy means of evading those prohibitions. The decisive factor is therefore the place where it is implemented.

17. The producers in this case implemented their pricing agreement within the Common Market. It is immaterial in that respect whether or not they had recourse to subsidiaries, agents, sub-agents, or branches within the Community in order to make their contacts with purchasers within the Community.

18. Accordingly the Community's jurisdiction to apply its competition rules to such conduct is covered by the territoriality principle as universally recognized in public international law.

19. As regards the argument based on the infringement of the principle of non-interference, it should be pointed out that the applicants who are members of KEA have referred to a rule according to which where two States have jurisdiction to lay down and enforce rules and the effect of those rules is that a person finds himself subject to contradictory orders as to the conduct he must adopt, each State is obliged to exercise its jurisdiction with moderation. The applicants have concluded that by disregarding that rule in applying its competition rules the Community has infringed the principle of non-interference.

20. There is no need to enquire into the existence in international law of such a rule since it suffices to observe that the conditions for its application are in any event not satisfied. There is not, in this case, any contradiction between the conduct required by the United States and that required by the Community since the Webb–Pomerene Act[88] merely exempts the conclusion of export cartels from the application of United States antitrust laws but does not require such cartels to be concluded.

21. It should further be pointed out that the United States authorities raised no objections regarding any conflict of jurisdiction when consulted by the Commission pursuant to the OECD Council Recommendation of 25 October 1979 concerning co-operation between Member Countries on Restrictive Business Practices affecting International Trade…

22. As regards the argument relating to disregard of international comity, it suffices to observe that it amounts to calling in question the Community's jurisdiction to apply its competition rules to conduct such as that found to exist in this case and that, as such, that argument has already been rejected.

23. Accordingly it must be concluded that the Commission's decision is not contrary to Article [101] or to the rules of public international law relied on by the applicants.

Significantly, this judgment avoided talking about 'effects'. Given the terms in which the Commission decision, the arguments before the Court, and the Advocate General's opinion had been couched, this avoidance of specific reference to the effects doctrine must have been deliberate. Instead, the Court talked about 'implementation' (paragraphs 16 and 17).

It will be noted that the judgment (which comprises the entirety of the section on jurisdiction) falls into distinct parts. First, paragraphs 11–14 deal with whether or not the Commission infringed *the Treaty* by applying the competition rules to the individual undertakings.[89] The CJ held that it had not, as it had correctly assessed the territorial scope of Article 101. Secondly, paragraphs 15–18 consider whether the Commission had infringed *international* law. The CJ held that it had not done this either, as the taking of jurisdiction was covered by the 'universally recognized' territoriality principle (paragraph 18). Thirdly, paragraphs 19–22 reject the argument based on a possible 'non-interference' principle by saying that the US legislation did not *require* export cartels to be entered into, but merely tolerated them. This is the same position as that reached by the Supreme Court in *Hartford Fire* in respect of the UK legislation.

---

[88] The Webb–Pomerene Act 1918 is a US statute which allows American exporters to act together in export markets in ways which would otherwise violate the Sherman Act.

[89] As far as the applicant trade association, KEA, was concerned, the CJ annulled the decision because it held that KEA had not played a separate role in the implementation of the price-fixing agreements: judgment [1988] ECR 5193, paras. 24–28 of the judgment.

In paragraph 16 the Court divided the infringing conduct into two elements, the formation of the agreement and its implementation. It did not matter where the formation of the agreement took place: the decisive factor was the place where it was 'implemented'.

The crucial question is what is meant by 'implementation' and how, if at all, this differs from the effects doctrine. The first thing to note is that the CJ said in paragraph 17 that it was immaterial whether or not the producers used subsidiaries, agents, sub-agents, or branches inside the Community. This means that 'implementation' covers direct sales to EU purchasers and does not depend on the sellers establishing some form of marketing organisation within the EU. Jurisdiction is taken simply because of sales into the EU. Some commentators believe that this is not justified in international law. Van Gerven, for example, has argued:[90]

Accepting this type of conduct [i.e., setting up a marketing organization and using it to give effect to a cartel] does not, I believe, unduly stretch the underlying strict territoriality and is, therefore, as indicated above, compatible with public international law. That cannot be said, however, of conduct which amounts to selling directly to purchasers within the Community, even when selling takes place through authorized but independent distributors or dealers that are doing business on their own behalf. Selling from abroad to purchasers and/or independent distributors or dealers within the regulating State cannot, I submit, reasonably be qualified as conduct of the 'parent' itself, or conduct imputable to it within the Common Market, because it does not constitute a sufficiently close and relevant link with the regulating State that is compelling enough to justify jurisdiction on its part. If the mere fact of selling directly in the territory (without requiring any permanent presence in the form of a sales organization, be it only a sales agent or sales representative) amounts to implementing conduct, then such a loose 'point of contact' can confer jurisdiction upon many States, thereby depriving the point of contact of its true content... The mere statement that the exercise of jurisdiction in such circumstances is permitted by the strict territoriality test, is of course, no proof of sufficient respect for that principle. It follows therefrom that I am not in a position to subscribe to the Court's statement in the *Wood Pulp* judgment that '[i]t is immaterial... whether or not [the undertakings] had recourse to subsidiaries, agents, sub-agents, or branches within the Community'...

A second point to note is that the preponderant view is that 'implementation' would not cover negative behaviour such as agreements concluded outside the EU by which undertakings agree not to sell within the EU, or agree not to purchase from EU producers.[91] However, such conduct could, it is argued, fall within the effects doctrine.[92]

In *Wood Pulp*, therefore, the Court confirmed that Article 101[93] could be applied extraterritorially, but did so by enunciating a Community (now EU) concept of extraterritorial jurisdiction based on implementation rather than by adopting the effects doctrine as developed in US law. However, it should be noted that in *Candle Waxes* the Commission said:[94]

Under the effects doctrine, as cited by MOL, jurisdiction can be established on the basis of economic effects within a territory, and MOL, as well as the other cartel participants, had sales in several Member States... When agreements and practices produce effects within the Community, they may well affect trade within the Community. The fact that the Statement of Objections does not explicitly refer to the *Gencor*

---

[90] W. van Gerven, 'EC Jurisdiction in Antitrust Matters: The Wood Pulp Judgment' [1989] Fordham Corp L Inst 451, 470.

[91] See, e.g., Griffin, 'Reactions to US Assertions of Extraterritorial Jurisdiction' (cited in n. 83); Van Gerven, 'EC Jurisdiction in Antitrust Matters', cited in n. 90. Van Gerven's view is also that any attempt to encompass such conduct within 'implementation' would be contrary to international law as there would not be a sufficiently close link to support jurisdiction.

[92] Griffin, 'Reactions to US Assertions of Extraterritorial Jurisdiction' (cited in n. 83).

[93] And presumably also Art. 102.

[94] COMP/39.181 *Candle Waxes*, 1 October 2008, [2009] 5 CMLR 2441, para. 190, on appeal Cases T-540/08 etc, *Esso v. Commission*, judgment pending. The case involves cartel activity in Hungary before Hungary's accession to the EU. The cartel had sold in the EU. The *Gencor* judgment to which the Commission refers is discussed in Section 5.D.ii, p. 1279.

judgment does not mean that the effects argument cannot be relied upon, as the relevant issue is whether the agreements produced or could produce an effect within the Community or not.

D. THE MERGER REGULATION

(i) The Terms of the Merger Regulation

As explained in Chapter 15, the EU Merger Regulation[95] provides that the Commission has sole jurisdiction[96] over concentrations with a 'Union [previously "Community"] dimension'.[97] The meaning of this is set out in Article 1. Under Article 1(2) a concentration will have a Union dimension if the worldwide (€5,000 million) and EU-wide (€250 million) turnover thresholds are met. There is a proviso which excludes concentrations in which the undertakings concerned achieve at least two-thirds of the EU-wide turnover in the same Member State. An alternative set of thresholds is provided by Article 1(3).[98] Further, it should be noted that recital 10 of the regulation states that a Union dimension exists where the thresholds are exceeded and 'that is the case irrespective of whether or not the undertakings have their seat or their principal fields of activity in the [Union] provided they have substantial operations there'.[99]

Article 1 does not, however, expressly say anything about where the undertakings concerned are incorporated, or carry on business, or whether the undertakings must have assets in the EU. Its criteria relate only to a worldwide turnover figure and a much smaller EU-wide turnover figure. Article 5, which deals with the calculation of turnover, says that '[t]urnover in the [Union] or in a Member State, shall comprise products sold and services provided to undertakings or consumers, in the [Union] or in that Member State as the case may be'.[100] The main reason that the original Merger Regulation did not directly address the jurisdiction issue seems to be that the Council Working Group was dealing with the details of the regulation at the time *Wood Pulp I* was before the CJ. In the light of the problems raised in that case express references to jurisdiction were deleted from the final version.[101]

As a result of this jurisdictional test it was inevitable that undertakings established abroad would be drawn into the net of EU merger control by involvement in transactions with EU undertakings. The way that the Union dimension threshold is formulated, however, can also catch transactions which involve *only* undertakings located outside the EU with few assets inside it, and transactions which have minimal impact inside the EU. The broad jurisdiction is unlikely to cause great problems in most cases, in that the concentration concerned will clearly not be incompatible with the internal market under the test in Article 2.[102] In a number of cases, involving, for example, Japanese banks, foreign undertakings have notified the Commission and duly received their Article 6(1) clearance within a month.[103] Even so, non-EU undertakings may object to the Commission's jurisdiction, particularly where the Commission is unhappy about a concentration.

---

[95] For the Merger Reg. 139/2004 [2004] L24/1 (replacing Reg. 4064/89 [1989] OJ L395/1) generally, see Chap. 15.

[96] Subject to certain exceptions, discussed in Chap. 15, such as Art. 9, which allows for concentrations to be referred back to national authorities.

[97] For a full analysis of the 'Union dimension' see M. Broberg, *The European Commission's Jurisdiction to Scrutinise Mergers* (4th edn, Wolters Kluwer, 2013).

[98] The object of this additional set of criteria is to provide for concentrations which do not reach the Art. 1(2) thresholds and which might otherwise fall to be dealt with by several national merger authorities in the EU.

[99] The equivalent recital (11) in the old Merger Regulation, Reg. 4064/89, was discussed in the *Gencor* judgment: see Case T-102/96, *Gencor Ltd v. Commission* [1999] ECR II-753 at paras. 83–85.

[100] Merger Reg., Art. 5(1), second para.

[101] C. J. Cook and C. S. Kerse, *EC Merger Control* (3rd edn, Sweet & Maxwell, 2000), 11–12.

[102] See Chap. 15.

[103] See, e.g., *Kyowa/Saitama Banks* [1992] 4 CMLR 1186; *Matsushita/MCA* [1992] 4 CMLR M36.

(ii) The *Gencor* Case

In *Gencor/Lonrho* the Commission prohibited a merger in the South African platinum and rhodium industry,[104] on the ground that it would create a position of oligopolistic dominance.[105] One of the parties appealed, inter alia, on the ground that the Commission had no jurisdiction over the transaction.[106]

The case concerned a proposed merger between the platinum and rhodium mining interests in South Africa of Gencor and LPD. Both were companies incorporated in South Africa, although LPD was a subsidiary of Lonrho, which was incorporated in London. LPD's sales worldwide were made through Lonrho's Belgian subsidiary. Platinum group metal (PGM) was sold throughout the world, mainly in Japan (approximately 50 per cent of world demand), and North America and Western Europe (approximately 20 per cent each).[107] Approximately 70–75 per cent of the world supply of PGM came from South Africa and 22–25 per cent from Russia[108] (although South Africa has 90 per cent of the world reserves). In South Africa the largest producer was Anglo-American, which was also incorporated there. The companies' sales figures were deleted from the published decision as business secrets, but it seems that Anglo-American probably had 35–50 per cent of world sales and LPD and Gencor 15–17 per cent each.[109]

All of Gencor's and LPD's production was in South Africa. The proposed merger was notified to the South African authorities, which found that there were no competition problems. The Deputy Foreign Minister told the Commission that he would not contest the Commission's policy, but that the South African Government considered that two equally matched competitors (as Anglo-American and Gencor/Lonrho would be) were preferable to the prevailing situation of one dominant firm (Anglo-American).[110] The merger had a Community dimension because of the worldwide and Community-wide turnover of Gencor and Lonrho. The Commission found the merger to be incompatible with the common market on account of the effect which the creation of the dominant duopoly position would have on *sales* of PGM in the Community.

Gencor contested the Commission's assumption of jurisdiction before the GC. It argued[111] that the Merger Regulation is applicable only if the activities forming the subject matter of the concentration are located within the Community. The location of the concentration was South Africa, and if the *Wood Pulp* test was applied the concentration was implemented in South Africa, not in the Community. South Africa had approved the merger. Moreover, Gencor claimed, even if the test for jurisdiction *was* whether the merger had an immediate and substantial effect on competition within the Community, that test was not satisfied either: 'the Commission cannot claim jurisdiction in respect of a concentration on the basis of future and hypothetical behaviour in which undertakings in the relevant market might engage and which might or might not fall within its purview under the Treaty'.[112] The GC, however, upheld the Commission's decision.

---

[104] Case IV/M 619, [1997] OJ L11/30, [1999] 4 CMLR 1076.

[105] For this aspect of the case see Chaps. 9 and 15.

[106] Once the Commission had blocked the merger there was no possibility of the transaction going ahead, since under the agreement between the parties it was a condition precedent that clearance from the Commission should be obtained by a certain date. The entire purchase agreement had therefore lapsed. Nevertheless, the GC held that the action for annulment was still admissible since the applicant had an interest in having the legality of the decision addressed to it examined by the Community judicature: Case T-102/96, *Gencor Ltd* v. *Commission* [1999] ECR II-753, paras. 40–46.

[107] For the exact figures from 1991 to 1995 see Table 5 in Case IV/M619, *Gencor/Lonrho* [1997] OJ L11/30, [1999] 4 CMLR 1076.

[108] *Gencor/Lonrho* [1997] OJ L11/30, [1999] 4 CMLR 1076, Table 2.

[109] See the figures extrapolated from the information in the decision in E. Fox, 'The Merger Regulation and its Territorial Reach' [1999] *ECLR* 334, 334.

[110] *Gencor Ltd* v. *Commission* [1999] ECR II-753, para. 19 of the judgment.

[111] *Gencor Ltd* v. *Commission* [1999] ECR II-753, paras. 48–63 of the judgment.

[112] *Gencor Ltd* v. *Commission* [1999] ECR II-753, para. 61.

Case T-102/96, *Gencor Ltd* v. *Commission* [1999] ECR II-753

General Court

78. The Regulation, in accordance with Article 1 thereof, applies to all concentrations with a Community dimension, that is to say to all concentrations between undertakings which do not each achieve more than two-thirds of their aggregate Community-wide turnover within one and the same Member State, where the combined aggregate worldwide turnover of those undertakings is more than ECU 5000 million and the aggregate Community-wide turnover of at least two of them is more than ECU 250 million.

79. Article 1 does not require that, in order for a concentration to be regarded as having a Community dimension, the undertakings in question must be established in the Community or that the production activities covered by the concentration must be carried out within Community territory.

80. With regard to the criterion of turnover, it must be stated that, as set out in paragraph 13 of the contested decision, the concentration at issue has a Community dimension within the meaning of Article 1(2) of the Regulation. The undertakings concerned have an aggregate worldwide turnover of more than ECU 10 000 million, above the ECU 5000 million threshold laid down by the Regulation. Gencor and Lonrho each had a Community-wide turnover of more than ECU 250 million in the latest financial year. Finally, they do not each achieve more than two-thirds of their aggregate Community-wide turnover within one and the same Member State.

81. The applicant's arguments to the effect that the legal bases for the Regulation and the wording of its preamble and substantive provisions preclude its application to the concentration at issue cannot be accepted.

82. The legal bases for the Regulation, namely Articles [103 and 352 TFEU], and more particularly the provisions to which they are intended to give effect, that is to say Articles 3(g) [EC] and [101 and 102 TFEU], as well as the first to fifth, ninth and eleventh recitals in the preamble to the Regulation, merely point to the need to ensure that competition is not distorted in the common market, in particular by concentrations which result in the creation or strengthening of a dominant position. They in no way exclude from the Regulation's field of application concentrations which, while relating to mining and/or production activities outside the Community, have the effect of creating or strengthening a dominant position as a result of which effective competition in the common market is significantly impeded.

83. In particular, the applicant's view cannot be founded on the closing words of the 11th recital in the preamble to the Regulation.

84. That recital states that 'a concentration with a Community dimension exists … where the concentrations are effected by undertakings which do not have their principal fields of activities in the Community but which have substantial operations there'.

85. By that reference, in general terms, to the concept of substantial operations, the Regulation does not, for the purpose of defining its territorial scope, ascribe greater importance to production operations than to sales operations. On the contrary, by setting quantitative thresholds in Article 1 which are based on the worldwide and Community turnover of the undertakings concerned, it rather ascribes greater importance to sales operations within the common market as a factor linking the concentration to the Community. It is common ground that Gencor and Lonrho each carry out significant sales in the Community (valued in excess of ECU 250 million).

86. Nor is it borne out by either the 30th recital in the preamble to the Regulation or Article 24 thereof that the criterion based on the location of production activities is well founded. Far from laying down a criterion for defining the territorial scope of the Regulation, Article 24 merely regulates the procedures to be followed in order to deal with situations in which non-member countries do not grant Community undertakings treatment comparable to that accorded by the Community to undertakings from those non-member countries in relation to the control of concentrations.

87. The applicant cannot, by reference to the judgment in *Wood Pulp*, rely on the criterion as to the implementation of an agreement to support its interpretation of the territorial scope of the Regulation.

Far from supporting the applicant's view, that criterion for assessing the link between an agreement and Community territory in fact precludes it. According to *Wood Pulp*, the criterion as to the implementation of an agreement is satisfied by mere sale within the Community, irrespective of the location of the sources of supply and the production plant. It is not disputed that Gencor and Lonrho carried out sales in the Community before the concentration and would have continued to do so thereafter.

88. Accordingly, the Commission did not err in its assessment of the territorial scope of the Regulation by applying it in this case to a proposed concentration notified by undertakings whose registered offices and mining and production operations are outside the Community.

2. Compatibility of the contested decision with public international law

89. Following the concentration agreement, the previously existing competitive relationship between Implats and LPD, in particular so far as concerns their sales in the Community, would have come to an end. That would have altered the competitive structure within the common market since, instead of three South African PGM suppliers, there would have remained only two. The implementation of the proposed concentration would have led to the merger not only of the parties' PGM mining and production operations in South Africa but also of their marketing operations throughout the world, particularly in the Community where Implats and LPD achieved significant sales.

90. Application of the Regulation is justified under public international law when it is foreseeable that a proposed concentration will have an immediate and substantial effect in the Community.

91. In that regard, the concentration would, according to the contested decision, have led to the creation of a dominant duopoly on the part of Amplats and Implats/LPD in the platinum and rhodium markets, as a result of which effective competition would have been significantly impeded in the common market within the meaning of Article 2(3) of the Regulation.

92. It is therefore necessary to verify whether the three criteria of immediate, substantial and foreseeable effect are satisfied in this case.

93. With regard, specifically, to the criterion of immediate effect, the words 'medium term' used in paragraphs 206 and 210 of the contested decision in relation to the creation of a dominant duopoly position are, contrary to the applicant's assertion, entirely unambiguous. They clearly refer to the time when it is envisaged that Russian stocks will be exhausted, enabling a dominant duopoly on the part of Amplats and Implats/LPD to be created on the world platinum and rhodium markets and, by the same token, in the Community as a substantial part of those world markets.

94. That dominant position would not be dependent, as the applicant asserts, on the future conduct of the undertaking arising from the concentration and of Amplats but would result, in particular, from the very characteristics of the market and the alteration of its structure. In referring to the future conduct of the parties to the duopoly, the applicant fails to distinguish between abuses of dominant position which those parties might commit in the near or more distant future, which might or might not be controlled by means of Articles [81] and/or [82] of the Treaty, and the alteration to the structure of the undertakings and of the market to which the concentration would give rise. It is true that the concentration would not necessarily lead to abuses immediately, since that depends on decisions which the parties to the duopoly may or may not take in the future. However, the concentration would have had the direct and immediate effect of creating the conditions in which abuses were not only possible but economically rational, given that the concentration would have significantly impeded effective competition in the market by giving rise to a lasting alteration to the structure of the markets concerned.

95. Accordingly, the concentration would have had an immediate effect in the Community.

96. So far as concerns the criterion of substantial effect, it should be noted that, as held in paragraph 297 below, the Commission established to the requisite legal standard that the concentration would have created a lasting dominant duopoly position in the world platinum and rhodium markets.

97. The applicant cannot maintain that the concentration would not have a substantial effect in the Community in view of the low sales and small market share of the parties to the concentration in the EEA.

While the level of sales in western Europe (20 per cent of world demand) and the Community market share of the entity arising from the concentration (…) per cent in respect of platinum) were already sufficient grounds for the Community to have jurisdiction in respect of the concentration, the potential impact of the concentration proved even higher than those figures suggested. Given that the concentration would have had the effect of creating a dominant duopoly position in the world platinum and rhodium markets, it is clear that the sales in the Community potentially affected by the concentration would have included not only those of the Implats/LPD undertaking but also those of Amplats (approximately 35 per cent to 50 per cent), which would have represented a more than substantial proportion of platinum and rhodium sales in western Europe and a much higher combined market share held by Implats/LPD and Amplats approximately (…) per cent to 65 per cent).

98. Finally, it is not possible to accept the applicant's argument that the creation of the dominant position referred to by the Commission in the contested decision is not of greater concern to the Community than to any other competent body and is even of less concern to it than to others. The fact that, in a world market, other parts of the world are affected by the concentration cannot prevent the Community from exercising its control over a concentration which substantially affects competition within the common market by creating a dominant position.

99. The arguments by which the applicant denies that the concentration would have a substantial effect in the Community must therefore be rejected.

100. As for the criterion of foreseeable effect, it follows from all of the foregoing that it was in fact foreseeable that the effect of creating a dominant duopoly position in a world market would also be to impede competition significantly in the Community, an integral part of that market.

101. It follows that the application of the Regulation to the proposed concentration was consistent with public international law.

102. It is necessary to examine next whether the Community violated a principle of non-interference or the principle of proportionality in exercising that jurisdiction.

103. The applicant's argument that, by virtue of a principle of non-interference, the Commission should have refrained from prohibiting the concentration in order to avoid a conflict of jurisdiction with the South African authorities must be rejected, without it being necessary to consider whether such a rule exists in international law. Suffice it to note that there was no conflict between the course of action required by the South African Government and that required by the Community given that, in their letter of 22 August 1995, the South African competition authorities simply concluded that the concentration agreement did not give rise to any competition policy concerns, without requiring that such an agreement be entered into (see, to that effect, *Wood Pulp*, paragraph 20).

104. In its letter of 19 April 1996 the South African Government, far from calling into question the Community's jurisdiction to rule on the concentration at issue, first simply expressed a general preference, having regard to the strategic importance of mineral exploitation in South Africa, for intervention in specific cases of collusion when they arose and did not specifically comment on the industrial or other merits of the concentration proposed by Gencor and Lonrho. It then merely expressed the view that the proposed concentration might not impede competition, having regard to the economic power of Amplats, the existence of other sources of supply of PGMs and the opportunities for other producers to enter the South African market through the grant of new mining concessions.

105. Finally, neither the applicant nor, indeed, the South African Government in its letter of 19 April 1996 have shown, beyond making mere statements of principle, in what way the proposed concentration would affect the vital economic and/or commercial interests of the Republic of South Africa.

106. As regards the argument that the Community cannot claim to have jurisdiction in respect of a concentration on the basis of future and hypothetical behaviour, namely parallel conduct on the part of the undertakings operating in the relevant market where that conduct might or might not fall within the competence of the Community under the Treaty, it must be stated, as pointed out above in connection with

the question whether the concentration has an immediate effect, that, while the elimination of the risk of future abuses may be a legitimate concern of any competent competition authority, the main objective in exercising control over concentrations at Community level is to ensure that the restructuring of undertakings does not result in the creation of positions of economic power which may significantly impede effective competition in the common market. Community jurisdiction is therefore founded, first and foremost, on the need to avoid the establishment of market structures which may create or strengthen a dominant position, and not on the need to control directly possible abuses of a dominant position.

107. Consequently, it is unnecessary to rule on the question whether the letter of 22 August 1995 from the South African Competition Board constituted a definitive position on the concentration, on whether or not the South African Government was an authority responsible for competition matters and, finally, on the scope of South African competition law. There is accordingly no need to grant the application for measures of organisation of procedure or of inquiry made by the applicant in its letter of 3 December 1996.

108. In those circumstances, the contested decision is not inconsistent with either the Regulation or the rules of public international law relied on by the applicant.

109. For the same reasons, the objection, based on Article [241] of the Treaty, that the Regulation is unlawful because it confers upon the Commission competence in respect of the concentration between Gencor and Lonrho must be rejected.

110. As regards the reasoning in the contested decision justifying Community jurisdiction to apply the Regulation to the concentration, it must be held that the explanations contained in paragraphs 4, 13 to 18, 204 to 206, 210 and 213 of the contested decision satisfy the obligations incumbent on the Commission under Article [253] of the Treaty to give reasons for its decisions so as to enable the Community judicature to exercise its power of review, the parties to defend their rights and any interested party to ascertain the conditions in which the Commission applied the Treaty and its implementing legislation.

111. Accordingly, both pleas of annulment which have been examined must be rejected, without it being necessary to grant the application for measures of organisation of procedure or of inquiry made by the applicant in its letter of 3 December 1996.

It can be seen from this extract from Case T-102/96, *Gencor Ltd* v. *Commission*, that in paragraphs 78–88 the GC looked first at the regulation itself. It concluded that it does not matter where the PGM production took place, because not only does Article 1 not require that the production should take place in the Community (now Union) (paragraph 79), it actually accords greater importance to sales. Further, in the second half of paragraph 87 it returned to the *Wood Pulp* judgment and said that the criterion of the implementation of an agreement is satisfied by *mere sale in the Community*. This point answers the doubt raised in respect of the *Wood Pulp* judgment by Van Gerven:[113] mere selling does equal implementation.

In paragraphs 89–111, the GC considered whether the decision was in accordance with public international law. It concluded that it was. In the most significant passage, paragraph 90, the GC says, in words redolent of the effects doctrine, that the Merger Regulation's application is justified in international law '*when it is foreseeable that a proposed concentration will have an immediate and substantial effect in the Community* [emphasis added]'. The GC did not expressly adopt the effects doctrine, but rather considered that the thresholds were an application of the *Wood Pulp* implementation principle. However, there is a problem[114] in that the Merger Regulation demands prior notification of mergers

[113] See n. 90.

[114] See Y. van Gerven and L. Hoet, 'Gencor: Some Notes on Transnational Competition Law Issues' (2001) 28 *LIEI* 195.

which fall within its thresholds.[115] It does not follow that all mergers which do that have foreseeable immediate and substantial effects in the EU, and yet the Merger Regulation imposes penalties for non-notification.[116]

Gencor is a striking demonstration of the implications of the effects/implementation doctrine. The EC forbade a merger involving producer undertakings in a non-member country because of the sales of the product (less than a quarter of the worldwide total) in the Community. The interests of South Africa did not come into the equation because South Africa did not *require* the transaction to take place. This raised the non-interference issue discussed in *Wood Pulp* (and in *Hartford Fire*). The GC concluded that there is no conflict of jurisdiction between a State which prohibits something and a State which allows it (rather than requires it). The difficulty with this is that merger control invariably operates only to forbid certain concentrations, not to require them, and the prohibiting jurisdiction will always trump the other. However, in *Gencor* the transaction between the mining companies was likely to have a more serious impact on the economy of South Africa than on consumers in the EC.[117]

(iii) The *Boeing/McDonnell Douglas* Case

The practical and diplomatic problems of taking jurisdiction over mergers involving undertakings established outside the EU were illustrated by *Boeing/McDonnell Douglas*.[118] Boeing and McDonnell Douglas (MDC) were both US aircraft manufacturers. In February 1997 the Commission received notification pursuant to the Merger Regulation of a concentration by which Boeing would acquire control of MDC. The merger would create the world's largest aerospace manufacturer. The transaction clearly had a Community dimension within Article 1. The Commission had serious doubts about it and opened a Phase II investigation under Article 6(1)(c).[119] It was concerned that the number of large commercial jet aircraft manufacturers would be reduced from three to two (the other one being Airbus Industrie) and that Boeing's dominant position would be strengthened. It communicated its concerns to the US Federal Trade Commission pursuant to the EC-US Cooperation Agreement.[120] On 1 July 1997 the FTC cleared the merger (it considered the deal was not anti-competitive as Boeing already had a high market share and the addition of MDC's would not be significant) and on 13 July informed the Commission that, inter alia, a decision prohibiting the proposed merger could harm important US defence interests.[121] However, the Commission continued with its objections. At the last moment the Commission cleared the merger, after Boeing had given certain undertakings.[122] The undertakings related to the cessation of existing and future exclusive supply deals, the 'ring-fencing' of MDC's commercial aircraft activities, the licensing of patents to other jet aircraft manufacturers, commitments not to abuse relationships with customers and suppliers, and a commitment to report annually to the Commission.

The Commission issued a bullish Press Release, expressing satisfaction at this outcome:[123]

These commitments are considered adequate to resolve the identified competition problems, and the Commission has therefore decided to declare the operation compatible with the common market subject to conditions and obligations. The Commission has reached its decision after a rigorous analysis based on

---

[115] Reg. 139/2004, Art. 4.

[116] In *Samsung* [1999] OJ L225/12, [1998] 4 CMLR 494 the non-EC undertaking was fined for failing to notify a merger which in the event raised no competition concerns.

[117] See E. Fox, 'The Merger Regulation and its Territorial Reach' [1999] *ECLR* 334, for a critique of *Gencor* on these grounds.

[118] The Commission's final decision in this case is at [1997] OJ L336/16.

[119] See Chap. 15 for Commission proceedings under the Merger Reg.

[120] Article VI. This agreement is discussed further, see Section 6.B, p. 1287.

[121] [1997] OJ L336/16, para. 12.

[122] [1997] OJ L336/16, paras. 115–119.

[123] IP (1997) 729 of 30 July 1997, [1997] 5 CMLR 271.

EU merger control law, and in accordance with its own past practice and the jurisprudence of the European Court. The Commission expects Boeing to comply fully with its decision, in particular as regards the commitments made by Boeing to resolve the competition problems identified by the Commission. The Commission will strictly monitor Boeing's compliance with these commitments. The EU Merger Regulation allows for appropriate measures to be taken by the Commission in the event of non-compliance by Boeing...In arriving at this decision the Commission has taken into account concerns expressed by the U.S. Government relating to important US defence interests. The Commission took the US Government's concerns into consideration to the extent consistent with EU law, and has limited the scope of its action to the civil side of the operation, including the effects of the merger on the commercial jet aircraft market resulting from the combination of Boeing's and MDC's large defence and space interests.

In fact, the commitments were widely perceived in the EU as being weak and almost impossible to enforce, while US commentators and Boeing's lawyers claimed they were merely aimed at protecting and benefiting the European Airbus.[124] The Director General for Competition, writing in the aftermath of the affair, expressed general satisfaction that in dealing with the case 'the European Commission obtained positive results for European competition policy on the one hand and for our cooperation with the US on the other' but admitted that 'diverging approaches of the competition authorities in Brussels and Washington made it impossible to reach commonly accepted solutions'.[125]

The matter showed that, despite the existence of bilateral cooperation arrangements[126] between broadly like-minded competition authorities, clashes cannot always be avoided. It should be noted that the US, the home of the effects doctrine, did not dispute the EU's assumption of extraterritorial jurisdiction, but expected that its assertions of the importance of the deal to its national interests would be deferred to by the Commission.[127]

(iv) The *GE/Honeywell* Case

In *GE/Honeywell*[128] the Commission prohibited a merger between two US companies which had been passed by the US authorities—not just *a* merger, but what would have been the biggest ever merger in US corporate history. The two corporate groups involved had a combined worldwide turnover of €180 billion. GE made aircraft engines. Honeywell made engines but, more significantly, avionics. GE had a leasing arm which was a purchaser of aircraft and therefore a downstream customer of both engines and avionics. The differences in the view of this merger lay largely in the different attitude of the Commission and the US authorities to conglomerate mergers,[129] bundling, and the possibility of leveraging. For present purposes, however, what is significant is that the prohibition happened[130] rather than why it happened. The whole affair was conducted under intense media interest and amid

---

[124] See A. Kaczorowska, 'International Competition Law in the Context of Global Capitalism' [2000] *ECLR* 117, 118. Bill Bishop, however, argued that there were very good reasons for blocking the merger, as it took the industry from three players to two, where there was evidence that the third player exerted a significant downward effect on prices. He concluded that 'the actual result was a compromise making little economic sense since customers were not protected by it at all. But by the light of international politics it was all too easy to understand the result': B. Bishop, 'Editorial, The Boeing/McDonnell Douglas Merger' [1997] *ECLR* 417.

[125] A. Schaub, 'International Co-operation in Antitrust Matters: Making the Point in the Wake of the Boeing/MDD Proceedings' (1998) 1 *Competition Policy Newsletter* 2, 3–4.

[126] See Section 6.B.i, p. 1287.

[127] See, generally, A. Bavasso, 'Boeing/McDonnell Douglas: Did the Commission Fly Too High?' [1998] *ECLR* 243.

[128] Case No. COMP/M.2220.

[129] See Chap. 15.

[130] The Commission would, it appears, have been willing to allow the merger to proceed if it had received satisfactory undertakings before its deadline. The decision was upheld by the GC, Case T-210/01, *General Electric v. Commission* [2005] ECR II-5575 because the GC agreed with the Commission about the horizontal overlaps, but it was highly critical of the Commission's treatment of the conglomerate effects and bundling. See Chap. 15, Section 5.D.ix.d, p. 1230.

much political and diplomatic activity.[131] It was a dramatic illustration of the consequences of multinational mergers being subjected to multiple jurisdictions with a slightly different 'take' on some matters. Nothing could have provided better ammunition for those who argue that the only way to deal with global transactions is through global competition mechanisms.

E. ENFORCEMENT JURISDICTION

In many cases problems of enforcement jurisdiction against non-EU undertakings may be avoided by the single economic entity doctrine.[132] Requests and demands for information under Regulation 1/2003, Article 18 may be addressed to the branch or subsidiary of a non-EU undertaking which is situated within the EU and final decisions may be served on and enforced against EU subsidiaries, as was done in *Dyestuffs*.[133]

It appears that an SO may be served on a branch or subsidiary within the EU.[134] However, it is sufficient for the purposes of EU law for the Commission to send the SO in a registered letter by post direct to the non-EU undertaking's address outside the EU. The CJ merely requires that the undertaking receives the SO in circumstances which enable it to take cognisance of the case against it.[135]

Other matters are more difficult where the Commission cannot rely on the single economic entity doctrine. There appears to be no objection to sending an Article 18(2) request for information to an undertaking outside the EU as it does not entail any element of compulsion but it is otherwise with an Article 18(3) demand by decision and the better view is that the Commission cannot do this.[136] It is generally thought inconceivable that the Commission could mount an Article 20 or 21 inspection outside the EU although it might ask the competition authorities in a non-Member State for help in its investigation. If a trade association has a presence in the EU it cannot resist an Article 20 inspection on the grounds that some of its members are outside the EU.[137] As with an SO, a final decision may be served directly on a non-EU undertaking and it is sufficient that the undertaking receives it and can take cognisance of it, even if it returns it without reading it.[138] Whilst decisions imposing fines can be sent to undertakings outside the EU[139] they cannot be enforced unless the undertaking has assets inside the EU which can be seized.

6. INTERNATIONAL COOPERATION

A. GENERAL

Faced with the globalisation of the economy and with the problems of the application and enforcement of competition laws already discussed, attention is currently focused on the desirability of

---

[131] See A. Burnside, 'GE, Honey I Sank the Merger' [2002] *ECLR* 107; D. Giotakos, L. Petit, G. Garnier, and P. De Luyck, 'GE/Honeywell—An Insight into the Commission's Investigation and Decision' (2001) 3 *Competition Policy Newsletter* 5.

[132] For enforcement in Arts 101 and 102 cases generally, see Chap. 13.

[133] Case 48/69, *ICI v. Commission* [1972] ECR 619.

[134] C. Kerse and N. Khan (Khan ed.), *EU Antitrust Procedure* (6th edn, Sweet & Maxwell, 2012), 4-023.

[135] Case 52/69, *Geigy v. Commission* [1972] ECR 787 (one of the *Dyestuffs* cases). The SO was sent to Geigy's address in Switzerland. Geigy returned it arguing that this infringed both Swiss and public international law and thus vitiated the proceedings. The CJ rejected this.

[136] Art. 18(5) provides for a copy of both an Art. 18(2) request and an Art.18(3) decision to be forwarded to the NCA of the Member State in which the undertaking's seat is situated, which would be impossible in the case of a non-EU undertaking, but this would not necessarily affect the possibility of using Art. 18(2) given the lack of coercion.

[137] *Ukwal* [1992] OJ L121/45, [1993] 5 CMLR 632.

[138] Case 6/72, *Europemballage Corp and Continental Can Co Inc v. Commission* [1973] ECR 215.

[139] As happened in, e.g., *Wood Pulp* [1985] OJ L85/1.

international agreements as at least a partial solution. Agreements in place at the moment are mainly bilateral ones between major trading partners, but there are also some multilateral regional trading arrangements which contain competition provisions.[140] The EU commonly insists on the insertion of competition law provisions in trade agreements and has particular arrangements with countries which are candidates for possible Accession. There is also significant activity at the level of international organisations and increasingly important international cooperation.

B. EU BILATERAL AGREEMENTS

(i) The EU-US Cooperation Agreements

a. The Content of the 1991 and 1998 Agreements

In 1991 the Commission concluded an agreement with the US authorities on cooperation over the enforcement of their competition laws.[141] The authority of the Commission to enter into the agreement was subsequently challenged by France, supported by Spain and the Netherlands, and the CJ found that the Commission did not have the power to conclude (as distinct from negotiate) agreements with foreign countries.[142] The agreement was finally approved by means of a joint decision of the Council and Commission in 1995.[143]

The Agreement provides for: the reciprocal notification of cases under investigation by either authority, where they may affect the important interests of the other party (Article II); exchanges of information and periodic meetings between competition officials from each country (Article III); and rendering each other assistance and coordinating their enforcement activities (Article IV). The most significant provisions, however, are Articles V and VI. Article V is the 'positive comity' Article, providing the possibility for one authority to request the other to take enforcement action, and Article VI provides for 'traditional' or 'negative' comity, i.e. for each authority to take into account the important interests of the other in the course of its enforcement activities.[144]

Agreement Between the Government of the USA and the Commission of the European Communities Regarding the Application of their Competition Laws, 1991

Article V

Cooperation regarding anti-competitive activities in the territory of one Party that adversely affect the interests of the other Party

1. The Parties note that anti-competitive activities may occur within the territory of one Party that, in addition to violating that Party's competition laws, adversely affect important interests of the other Party. The Parties agree that it is in both their interests to address anti-competitive activities of this nature.

2. If a Party believes that anti-competitive activities carried out on the territory of the other Party are adversely affecting its important interests, the first Party may notify the other Party and may request that the other Party's competition authorities initiate appropriate enforcement activities. The notification

---

[140] See C. Noonan, *The Emerging Principles of International Competition Law* (Oxford University Press, 2008), 13.2.3.

[141] Agreement between the Government of the US and the Commission of the European Communities regarding the application of their Competition Laws, 23 September 1991 [1991] 4 CMLR 823, 30 *ILM* 1487.

[142] Case C-327/91, *France v. Commission* [1994] ECR I-3641.

[143] [1995] OJ L95/45.

[144] 'Comity' was introduced earlier, in the context of the US cases, and it should be noted that Article VI seems to be less restrictive than the version which appears in *Hartford Fire Insurance*, see Section 3.B, p. 1262.

shall be as specific as possible about the nature of the anti-competitive activities and their effects on the interests of the notifying Party, and shall include an offer of such further information and other cooperation as the notifying Party is able to provide.

3. Upon receipt of a notification under paragraph 2, and after such other discussion between the Parties as may be appropriate and useful in the circumstances, the competition authorities of the notified Party will consider whether or not to initiate enforcement activities, or to expand ongoing enforcement activities, with respect to the anti-competitive activities identified in the notification. The notified Party will advise the notifying Party of its decision. If enforcement activities are initiated, the notified Party will advise the notifying Party of their outcome and, to the extent possible, of significant interim developments.

4. Nothing in this Article limits the discretion of the notified Party under its competition laws and enforcement policies as to whether or not to undertake enforcement activities with respect to the notified anti-competitive activities, or precludes the notifying Party from undertaking enforcement activities with respect to such anti-competitive activities.

Article VI

Avoidance of conflicts over enforcement activities

Within the framework of its own laws and to the extent compatible with its important interests, each Party will seek, at all stages in its enforcement activities, to take into account the important interests of the other Party. Each Party shall consider important interests of the other Party in decisions as to whether or not to initiate an investigation or proceeding, the scope of an investigation or proceeding, the nature of the remedies or penalties sought, and in other ways, as appropriate. In considering one another's important interests in the course of their enforcement activities, the Parties will take account of, but will not be limited to, the following principles:

1. While an important interest of a Party may exist in the absence of official involvement by the Party with the activity in question, it is recognized that such interests would normally be reflected in antecedent laws, decisions or statements of policy by its competent authorities.

2. A Party's important interests may be affected at any stage of enforcement activity by the other Party. The Parties recognize, however, that as a general matter the potential for adverse impact on one Party's important interests arising from enforcement activity by the other Party is less at the investigative stage and greater at the stage at which conduct is prohibited or penalized, or at which other forms of remedial orders are imposed.

3. Where it appears that one Party's enforcement activities may adversely affect important interests of the other Party, the Parties will consider the following factors, in addition to any other factors that appear relevant in the circumstances, in seeking an appropriate accommodation of the competing interests:

   (a) the relative significance to the anti-competitive activities involved of conduct within the enforcing Party's territory as compared to conduct within the other Party's territory;

   (b) the presence or absence of a purpose on the part of those engaged in the anti-competitive activities to affect consumers, suppliers, or competitors within the enforcing Party's territory;

   (c) the relative significance of the effects of the anti-competitive activities on the enforcing Party's interests as compared to the effects on the other Party's interests;

   (d) the existence or absence of reasonable expectations that would be furthered or defeated by the enforcement activities;

   (e) the degree of conflict or consistency between the enforcement activities and the other Party's laws or articulated economic policies; and

   (f) the extent to which enforcement activities of the other Party with respect to the same persons, including judgments or undertakings resulting from such activities, may be affected.

The Competition Commissioner, writing in the *XXVIIIth Report on Competition Policy* said that this amounted to 'a commitment by the EU and the USA to cooperate with respect to antitrust enforcement, and not to act unilaterally and extraterritorially unless the avenues provided by comity have been exhausted'.[145]

The successful operation of the Agreement persuaded the parties to strengthen the positive comity provisions and in 1998 they signed the EU–US Positive Comity Agreement[146] which entered into force on 4 June 1998. This spells out more clearly the circumstances in which a request for positive comity will be made and the manner in which such requests should be treated (Article III).

Positive comity

The competition authorities of a Requesting Party may request the competition authorities of a Requested Party to investigate and, if warranted, to remedy anti-competitive activities in accordance with the Requested Party's competition laws. Such a request may be made regardless of whether the activities also violate the Requesting Party's competition laws, and regardless of whether the competition authorities of the Requesting Party have commenced or contemplate taking enforcement activities under their own competition laws.

Article IV provides for investigations by the requesting party to be deferred or suspended in reliance on the requested party's enforcement. The effect of the 1998 Agreement is to create a presumption, as described by the Commission in its report on the application of the cooperation agreement for 1998.[147]

The 1998 EC/US Positive Comity Agreement, like the 1991 Agreement, does not alter existing law, nor does it require any change in existing law. However, it does create a presumption that when anti-competitive activities occur in the whole or in a substantial part of the territory of one of the parties and affect the interests of the other party, the latter 'will normally defer or suspend its enforcement activities in favour of' the former. This is expected to happen particularly when these anti-competitive activities do not have a direct, substantial and reasonably foreseeable impact on consumers in the territory of the party deferring or suspending its activities.

The presumption of deferral will only occur if the party in the territory of which the restrictive activities are occurring has jurisdiction over these activities and is prepared to deal actively and expeditiously with the matter. When dealing with the case that party will keep its counterpart closely informed of any developments in the procedure, within the limits of its internal rules protecting confidentiality.

The 1998 Agreement constituted an important development, since it represents a commitment on the part of the EU and the US to cooperate with respect to antitrust enforcement in certain situations, rather than to seek to apply their antitrust laws extraterritorially.

It is important to note that because the EU merger rules do not allow for the deferral or suspension of action which the agreement envisages the EU merger rules are not within the 1998 agreement.[148] However, the EU and US have established a merger working group which in 2002 adopted a set of 'Best Practices' on cooperation in merger investigations where the same transaction is being investigated in both jurisdictions. This was revised in 2011.[149]

---

[145] Commission's *XXVIIth Report on Competition Policy* (Commission, 1998), foreword, 5.

[146] [1998] OJ L173/28, [1999] 4 CMLR 502.

[147] At para. 3. See the *XXVIIIth Report on Competition Policy* (Commission, 1998), 315.

[148] Art. II(4)(a).

[149] Available at <http://ec.europa.eu/competition/mergers/legislation/international_cooperation.html>.

b. The Application of the Agreements

The EU and US authorities consider that their cooperation works well and has made a positive contribution to competition law enforcement. The authorities have a very close relationship. The 1991 procedures worked particularly successfully, for example, in respect of the investigation into Microsoft in 1994.[150] The US DOJ and the Commission actively cooperated. However, there is a major drawback in the operation of the agreement. Articles VII of the 1991 Agreement and V of the 1998 Agreement provide for the maintenance of the confidentiality of information acquired by the authorities in the course of their investigations. Further, Articles IX and VII, respectively, provide that nothing in the agreements is to be interpreted in a manner which is inconsistent with the parties' existing laws. This greatly limits the information which the authorities may exchange.[151] It is notable that in the 1994 investigation Microsoft, which was happy to have the US and EU investigations combined as it was easier for the company to deal with the two authorities together, agreed to waive its rights to confidentiality and to allow information exchanges between the Commission and the DOJ.[152] The EU's 2013 cooperation agreement with Switzerland[153] is innovative in enabling the competition authorities to exchange information.

The existence of the EU-US cooperation agreement did not prevent the 1997 dispute over the *Boeing/McDonnell Douglas* merger or the *GE/Honeywell* row.[154] In *Boeing/McDonnell Douglas*, for instance, the authorities did consult each other. In accordance with the provisions of the agreement the Commission and the FTC carried out the necessary notifications and consultations, and the Commission took into account the US concerns over its defence interests. In the end, however, as the Director General recognised, '[p]rocedures of notification and consultation and the principles of traditional and positive comity allow us to bring our respective approaches closer in cases of common interest but there exist[s] no mechanism for resolving conflicts in cases of substantial divergence of analysis'.[155] Nevertheless, these cases of conflict between the EU and US are rare. When adopting the 2002 Merger Best Practices the authorities recognised that 'cooperation is most effective when the investigation timetables of the reviewing agencies run more or less in parallel'. The new 2011 Best Practices state that 'cooperation between DG Competition and the US agencies is beneficial not only for the agencies, but also for merging parties and third parties, as it increases the efficiency of the respective investigations, reduces the burden on merging parties and third parties, and increases the overall transparency of the merger review process'.[156] Best Practices encourages undertakings to allow the EU and US agencies to exchange information which they have submitted during the course of an investigation and to allow joint EU/US interviews. The document identifies key points at which consultations between the agencies are likely to be particularly useful and says that consultations between senior officials in the respective agencies may be appropriate at any time.[157]

(ii) Other Dedicated Competition Cooperation Agreements

Encouraged by the success of its agreement with the US, the EU entered into a similar agreement with Canada which came into force on 29 April 1999. In particular, the Agreement contains (Articles V and VI), provisions similar to Articles V and VI of the 1991 Agreement including the principle of positive

---

[150] Although because of the case brought by France (see Section 6.B.i.a) the agreement was not officially in force.

[151] See Chap. 13 for the question of confidentiality in EU competition procedure.

[152] See further C. Cocuzza and M. Montini, 'International Antitrust Co-operation in a Global Economy' [1998] *ECLR* 156; J. Parisi, 'Enforcement Co-operation Among Antitrust Authorities' [1999] *ECLR* 133.

[153] See Section 6.B.ii, p. 1291.

[154] See Section 5.D.iii, p. 1284 and Section 5.D.iv, p. 1285.

[155] Schaub, see n. 125.

[156] Best Practices, see n. 149, para. 2.

[157] The document is available at<http://ec.europa.eu/competition/mergers/legislation/eu_us.pdf>.

comity.[158] In June 2003 it entered into an agreement with Japan. Again, the principal elements are mutual information, coordination of enforcement activities, and exchange of non-confidential information. The EU signed a similar cooperation agreement with Korea in May 2009 which came into force on 1 July 2009. It provides for the reciprocal notification of cases, the possibility of coordination by the two authorities of their enforcement activities, taking enforcement action at the request of the other and taking into account the interests of the other party during enforcement activity, the exchange of non-confidential information, 1292 and regular bilateral meetings.[159]

The cooperation agreement signed with Switzerland in May 2013[160] was hailed by Commissioner Almunia as 'unprecedented' and described as going beyond the EU's existing agreements with other third countries. In particular it contains innovative provisions on the exchange of information. The Commission's summary of the agreement says:[161]

The Agreement provides a framework for co-ordination and co-operation of enforcement activities. It enhances co-operation for an effective implementation of competition rules and provides for regular contacts in order to discuss policy issues and enforcement efforts and priorities. It also provides for the mutual notification of enforcement activities affecting each other's important interests. Under the agreement the EU and Switzerland may request the other party to start enforcement actions against anti-competitive behaviour carried out in the territory of the other party and both sides have to take into account the important interests of the other party.

Unlike other cooperation agreements the agreement with Switzerland also includes provisions on the exchange of evidence obtained by the competition authorities when they investigate the same case. The exchange of information is subject to strict conditions protecting business secrets and personal data. Such an advanced form of cooperation between competition authorities is an innovation in a bilateral cooperation agreement. The information can only be used by the receiving authority for the enforcement of its competition rules in relation to the same case and for the purpose of the initial request. In addition, no evidence can be used to impose sanctions on natural persons.

(iii) Other Bilateral Cooperation Arrangements

The EU enters into bilateral trade and development agreements with many other countries, including developing countries and/or those with economies in transition. It is usual for these to contain competition provisions and/or (where relevant) to provide for the adoption by the other party of competition rules. There are certain groups of agreements containing similar provisions: agreements with candidate countries or countries of the Western Balkans[162] (Stabilization and Association Agreements); those with other countries formerly part of the USSR (Partnership and Cooperation Agreements); and Euro-Mediterranean Agreements establishing an association with countries of the southern Mediterranean.[163] The EU also agreed to establish the EU-China competition policy dialogue in 2003 whereby the Commission and the Chinese authorities shared experience and views on competition matters and the EU provided technical and capacity-building assistance (China's Anti-Monopoly Law came into force on 1 August 2008). This culminated in a Memorandum of Understanding on Cooperation in September 2012. The EU signed a Memorandum of Understanding on Cooperation with Brazil in 2009 and one with the Russian Federation in March 2011.

---

[158] [1999] OJ L175, [1999] 5 CMLR 713.

[159] These bilateral agreements are all available at<http://ec.europa.eu/competition/international/bilateral>.

[160] 13 May 2013, IP/13/44. The agreement is subject to ratification and enters into force once it has been approved by the European Parliament and the Swiss Parliament.

[161] IP/13/44.

[162] Albania and Montenegro.

[163] Such as Algeria and Egypt.

Although not strictly bilateral, the African Caribbean and Pacific (ACP) agreement, the Cotonou Agreement, should be noted. The agreement, between the EU and a number of developing countries, replaced the Lomé Agreement. It came into force in 2003 and will last for 20 years. It contains provisions on political cooperation, trade links, and development assistance and also a provision on competition, Article 45.

C. MULTILATERAL COOPERATION

(i) General

There are now over a hundred countries in the world with some form of competition laws, many of which were adopted under pressure from or under the influence of, the EU, often as a result of the bilateral trade agreements already mentioned.[164] Needless to say, US law has been extremely influential but it is the EU 'model' which is the one most commonly adopted. This is not only because of pressure from the EU but because other countries prefer to copy the public enforcement system rather than the litigation model which is the product of a particular and singular legal system. One distinguished (American) commentator considers that the EU model has 'trumped' the US as the model for the world because it resonates with developing and transitional countries as it deals with the emergence from statism and the development of a single market while displaying qualities such as openness, transparency, and non-discrimination. Moreover, the ECN provides a model of how regional cooperation in competition policy can work.[165]

There is a continuing discourse about the suitable form and content of competition laws for developing and transitional economies and the way in which both the substantive and procedural rules need to take account of local political and cultural conditions.[166] A discussion on this is outside the scope of this book, but reference should be made to the further reading at the end of the chapter. There have been initiatives within various international fora aimed at formulating mechanisms for increasing cooperation over competition laws and avoiding conflicts. These are briefly described here. We consider the problems inherent in such multilateral international arrangements and ask whether it is possible to envisage the creation of a multilateral international competition law mechanism at present.

(ii) UNCTAD and the OECD

The United Nations' Set of Multilaterally Agreed Equitable Principles and Rules for the Control of Restrictive Business Practices were adopted in 1980 under the auspices of UNCTAD[167] but provide only a voluntary, non-binding Code. In 1967 the OECD (Organisation for Economic Cooperation and Development) adopted a Recommendation that its member countries should cooperate with each other in the enforcement of their national competition laws.[168] This provides: for one country to notify another when the latter's important interests are affected by the former's investigation or enforcement; for countries to share information and to consult; for them to coordinate parallel investigations; for countries to assist one another in obtaining information inside each other's territory; and for countries to consider dealing with anti-competitive behaviour affecting their interests but occurring in another country's territory by requesting the latter's authorities to take action

---

[164] International bodies such as the IMF have also played a role, on occasion making loans conditional on the adoption of competition rules (e.g., Indonesia).

[165] Professor Eleanor Fox speaking at the EU Competition Forum, 2 February 2012.

[166] For an interesting discussion of the relationship between Islam and competition law and policy, for example, see M. Dabbah, *Competition Law and Policy in the Middle East* (Cambridge University Press, 2007), Chap. 2.

[167] The United Nations Conference on Trade and Development.

[168] Amended, inter alia, in 1995: OECD Doc. C(95)130/FINAL.

(positive comity). The bilateral agreements described in Section 6.B reflect these provisions but the 1991 EC-US Agreement was the first to include the 'positive comity' principle. In May 1998 the OECD Committee of Competition Law and Policy adopted a recommendation on hardcore cartels, aimed at strengthening the effectiveness and efficiency of the member countries' enforcement of their competition laws against such cartels. In 2006 the OECD issued a report, 'Competition Law and Policy in the EU'.[169] The Commission cooperates closely with the competition authorities of other OECD member countries based on the 1995 OECD recommendation. There is a direct link from the Commission website to the OECD Competition Committee within the Directorate for Financial and Enterprise Affairs. The Competition Committee holds regular roundtable meetings to which the Commission contributes and its submissions to the Working Parties are available on the website.[170] Those in 2012 included the role of efficiency claims in antitrust proceedings, competition and payment systems, and market definition.

(iii) The WTO

When the WTO was being negotiated in 1993 a Draft International Antitrust Code was drawn up by a group of experts at the Max Planck Institute. This would have established an international antitrust regime.[171] The parties to the WTO did not agree to its adoption, however, and no agreement on international competition law was annexed to the WTO Charter. Promoted by the EU, the matter was later taken up at the First Ministerial Conference of the parties to the WTO in Singapore in 1996 and a Working Group on Trade and Competition Policy was set up in 1997. The first Chair of this Group was Professor Jenny of the French competition authority, who was Chair of the OECD Competition Law and Policy Committee.

In 1997 and 1998 the Working Group worked on a checklist of issues, of which the main elements were: the relationship between the objectives, principles, concepts, scope, and instruments of trade and competition policy and their relationship with development and economic growth; stocktaking and analysis of existing instruments, standards, and activities regarding trade and competition policy, including experience with their application; and the interaction between trade and competition policy. In 1999 the Group examined three further topics: the relevance of the fundamental WTO principles of national treatment, transparency, and most-favoured-nation treatment to competition policy and vice versa; approaches to promoting cooperation and communication among members, including in the field of technical cooperation; and the contribution of competition policy to achieving the objectives of the WTO, including the promotion of international trade.

Ultimately, the question which has to be addressed is whether a multilateral framework on competition policy should be set up under the auspices of the WTO. The US has been reluctant to go down that path whereas the EU has been a keen advocate of working through the WTO to achieve this. The EU's views were set out in a Discussion Document in March 1999, in preparation for the 1999 WTO Ministerial Conference in Seattle. The Document set out its objectives as:

a) The introduction of a competition law by significant trading partners which still lack one, and agreement that competition law should in principle cover all the sectors of the economy;

b) Ensuring that competition law, and its enforcement, are based on core principles of efficiency, transparency, non-discrimination, etc.;

---

[169] Available on the Commission's website,<http://ec.europa.eu/comm/competition/international/multilateral/oecd.html>, and on the OECD website,<http://www.oecd.org/dataoecd/7/41/35908641.pdf>

[170] <http://ec.europa.eu/competition/international/multilateral/oecd_submissions.html>.

[171] For the details, see C. Cocuzza and M. Montini, 'International Antitrust Co-operation in a Global Economy' [1998] *ECLR* 156, 160–161; E. U. Petersmann, 'International Competition Rules for Governments and for Private Business' (1996) 30 *J World Trade* 5.

c) Promoting a stricter enforcement policy in relation to anti-competitive practices with a significant impact on international trade and investment;

d) Promoting cooperation in the application of competition law to anti-competitive practices with an international dimension and limiting the risk of conflict arising from extraterritorial enforcement and fact-finding;

e) Reducing unnecessary costs and uncertainties for business arising from the application of different competition laws to the same international transactions.

In the event, the WTO meeting at Seattle collapsed. However, the US agreed to explore the idea of a multilateral framework within the WTO. The Fourth WTO Ministerial Conference at Doha in November 2001 adopted a Declaration which contained three paragraphs on competition policy. The Declaration recognised the case for a multilateral framework to enhance the contribution of competition policy to international trade and development and said that negotiations on trade and competition should take place after the Fifth Ministerial Conference at Cancun in 2003. Until then the Working Group would work on formulating certain core principles on transparency, non-discrimination and procedural fairness; hardcore cartels; modalities of voluntary cooperation; and supporting the development of competition institutions in developing countries. Competition was one of the so-called 'Singapore Issues' (the others were trade facilitation, transparency in government procurement, and the relationship between trade and investment).

The EU had high hopes for the meeting at Cancun but these were not fulfilled. The meeting was abruptly terminated amid much disagreement. Although there was certainly dispute over the 'Singapore Issues', including competition, many members of the WTO had grievances over a range of issues and the reasons for the collapse at Cancun are to do with a number of complex factors.[172] The agricultural subsidies offered by the EU and the US Government to their home producers were a cause of dissension and many developing countries had become unhappy with the concept of 'free trade' which seemed previously to have become universally accepted as the remedy for the world's ills. The WTO, like the World Bank, is seen in many quarters as part of the problem, not the remedy. The idea of a multilateral competition framework was a victim of the spirit of the times.[173] Moreover, in 2004 the General Council of the WTO abandoned any attempt to work on a set of antitrust rules.[174] It appears that this was partly due to the fears of the small or developing nations but the marked reluctance of the US was also a factor, as already noted.[175]

(iv) The International Competition Network

While attempts to put competition on the map at the WTO ran into difficulties, competition authorities from around the world have quietly been getting on with setting up procedures and mechanisms through which they can cooperate. In October 2001 the International Competition Network was established. The EU is a member. The impetus for this came from the US IPAC report (International Competition Policy Advisory Committee) in February 2000.[176] According to its website[177] the ICN 'provides competition authorities with a specialized yet informal venue

---

[172] See F. Jenny, 'Competition Trade and Development before and after Cancun' [2003] Fordham Corp L Inst (B. Hawk, ed.), 631.

[173] For an entertaining account of Cancun (yet with a serious message), see F. Jenny, 'WTO Core Principles and Trade/Competition, Policies' [2003] Fordham Corp L. Inst (B. Hawk, ed.), 703, in which he tells the tale in the guise of the plot of the film *The Third Man* (with the EU Trade Commissioner as Holly Marten and 'Trade Consensus' as Harry Lime).

[174] Doha Work Programme Decision, 1 August 2004.

[175] See E. Elhauge and D. Geradin, *Global Competition Law and Economics* (2nd edn, Hart Publishing, 2011) 1242–1247, for a discussion of this.

[176] US DOJ: available at <http:www.usdoj.gov/atr/icpac/finalreport.htm>.

[177] <http://www.internationalcompetitionnetwork.org>.

for maintaining regular contacts and addressing practical competition concerns. This allows for a dynamic dialogue that serves to build consensus and convergence towards sound competition policy principles across the global antitrust community.' The ICN facilitates procedural and substantive convergence in competition enforcement through results-based and project-orientated working groups. The ICN has proved an extremely useful and productive organisation. It has a number of very active working groups including the Merger Working Group, which has adopted 'guiding principles and recommended practices' which competition authorities should abide by when analysing mergers across several jurisdictions; the Cartels Working Group, which organises annual cartel workshops and has produced a number of reports on anti-cartel policy and a cartel enforcement manual, including a template for ICN member agencies to set out their rules governing cartel enforcement, and in 2013 is working on the creation of a common leniency waiver template for international cartel investigations; an Agency Effectiveness Working Group; an Advocacy Working Group; and a Working Group on Unilateral Conduct whose primary objectives are 'to examine the challenges involved in addressing anti-competitive unilateral conduct of dominant firms and firms with substantial market power, facilitate greater understanding of the issues involved in analyzing unilateral conduct, and to promote greater convergence and sound enforcement of laws governing unilateral conduct'.

This 'soft law' harmonisation is highly effective and the ICN is a particularly valuable resource for competition agencies from developing countries and those who have only recently adopted competition laws.

(v) A Global Competition Law Regime?

The WTO remains the most obvious framework for the establishment of some type of international competition regime and its existing dispute settlement mechanism provides a possible model. However, the problems facing the WTO vividly demonstrate how difficult it is to reach international consensus in the economic field when States are in such different stages of development and have such different interests. The requirement of the WTO is that all Member States, except the very poorest, subscribe to its rights and obligations in exchange for trade liberalisation. Prominent among the organisation's shortcomings, however, is that its rules do not sufficiently allow for socio-cultural and environmental criteria to be considered and it is argued that it is essential to take account of socio-cultural divergences in any set of competition rules which are adopted at an international level.[178] Some developing countries have come to view the WTO as a 'rich man's club', run for the benefit of the world's most powerful trading blocs, although some of the bitterest disputes to date have been between the US and the EU. Both caution and pragmatism would suggest that the present problems in the WTO need to be dealt with before a competition law element is added. However, as more and more countries adopt competition law regimes the capacity for conflict between them, should they all take extraterritorial jurisdiction, increases exponentially, at least in theory.

In the meantime EU and US competition authorities have learned, despite the occasional high-profile disagreement, to cooperate closely and bilaterally to their mutual advantage. The EU, however, remains committed to the belief that competition policy can deliver benefits to the whole global economy and that international structures are essential to enable it fully to do this. Nevertheless, at present it appears that soft law instruments, particularly within the ICN, are producing successful convergence and cooperation and spreading best practice between competition authorities from around the world. The EU is committed to these processes, which seem to hold out more promise for the globalised economy than attempts to produce international regulatory structures.

---

[178] W. Pape, 'Socio-Cultural Differences and International Competition Law' (1999) 5 *European Law Journal* 438.

7. CONCLUSIONS

1. Traditional concepts of extraterritorial jurisdiction are not well suited for use in international competition law situations.

2. Plaintiffs are understandably keen to sue in US courts when they have been victims of international cartels but the US courts are not welcoming at present and this coincides with the attempts in the EU described in Chapter 14 to develop better ways of facilitating damages actions in Europe.

3. Ideas for international competition regimes are unrealistic and over-ambitious. Bilateral agreements and friendly and cooperative relations between enforcers seem a better way ahead. While there are occasional high-profile differences, much work has been done in building up an international consensus. The best way forward at present is through soft law instruments.

4. Competition laws are now a global phenomenon. It is crucial to recognise the international dimensions of competition law and to see the EU system in a global perspective.

8. FURTHER READING

A. BOOKS

Cook, P., Fabella, R.V., and Lee, C. (eds.), *Competitive Advantage and Competition Policy in Developing Countries* (Edward Elgar, 2007)

Dabbah, M., *The Internationalisation of Antitrust Policy* (Cambridge University Press, 2003)

—— *Competition Law and Policy in the Middle East* (Cambridge University Press, 2007)

—— *International and Comparative Competition Law* (Cambridge University Press, 2010)

Elhauge, E., and Geradin, D., *Global Competition Law and Economics* (2nd edn, Hart Publishing, 2011)

Epstein, R., and Greve, M. (eds.), *Competition Laws in Conflict: Antitrust Jurisdiction in a Global Economy* (AEI Press, 2004)

Furse, M., *Antitrust Law in China, Korea and Vietnam* (Oxford University Press, 2009)

Gerber, D., *Global Competition: Law, Markets and Globalization* (Oxford University Press, 2010)

Higgins, R., *Problems and Process: International Law and How We Use It* (Clarendon Press, 1994)

Jennings, R. Y., and Watts, A. (eds.), *Oppenheim's International Law* (9th edn, Longman, 1992)

Jones, C. A., and Matsushita, M., (eds.), *Competition Policy in the Global Trading System* (Kluwer, 2002)

Kennedy, K., *Competition Law and the World Trade Organization: The Limits of Multilateralism* (Sweet & Maxwell, 2001)

Noonan, C., *The Emerging Principles of International Competition Law* (Oxford University Press, 2008)

Olmstead C. (ed.), *Extra-territorial Application of Laws and Responses Thereto* (ESC Publishing, 1984), 156

Papadopoulos, A., *The International Dimension of EU Competition Law and Policy* (Cambridge University Press, 2010)

Ryngaert, C., *Jurisdiction in International Law* (Oxford University Press, 2008)

Schachter, O., *International Law in Theory and Practice* (Nijhoff, 1991), Chap. XII

Stiglitz, J., *Globalization and its Discontents* (Penguin, 2002)

Zäch, R., and Heinemann, A. (eds.), *The Development Of Competition Law Global Perspectives* (Edward Elgar, 2010)

Zanettin, B., *Cooperation Between Antitrust Agencies at the International Level* (Hart Publishing, 2002)

B. CHAPTERS IN BOOKS

Swan, A. C., 'The Hartford Insurance Company Case; Antitrust in the Global Economy' in J. Bhandari and A. Sykes (eds.), *Economic Dimensions in International Law* (Cambridge University Press, 1997)

Wood, D. P., 'The Trade Effects of Domestic Antitrust Enforcement' in J. Bhandari and A. Sykes (eds.), *Economic Dimensions in International Law* (Cambridge University Press, 1997)

C. ARTICLES

Akehurst, M., 'Jurisdiction in International Law' (1972–1973) 46 *BYIL* 145

Bavasso, A., 'Boeing/McDonnell Douglas: Did the Commission Fly Too High?' [1998] *ECLR* 243

BISHOP, B., 'Editorial, The Boeing/McDonnell Douglas Merger' [1997] *ECLR* 417

BOWETT, D. W., 'Jurisdiction: Changing Problems of Authority over Activities and Resources' (1982) 53 *BYIL* 1

BURNSIDE, A., 'GE, Honey I Sank the Merger' [2002] *ECLR* 107

BOTTEMAN, Y., and PATSA, A., 'The Jurisdictional Reach of EU Anti-Cartel Rules: Unmuddling the Limits' (2012) 8 *European Competition Journal* 365

COCUZZA, C., and MONTINI, M., 'International Antitrust Co-operation in a Global Economy' [1998] *ECLR* 156

COLLINS, L., 'Blocking and Clawback Statutes' [1986] *JBL* 372

DI FREDERICO, G., 'The New Anti-Monopoly Law in China from a European Perspective' (2009) 32(2) *World Competition* 249

DURAND, B., FONT GALARZA, A., and MEHTA, K., 'The Interface Between Competition Policy and International Trade Liberalisation. Looking into the Future: Applying a New Virtual Anti-Trust Standard' (2004) 27 *World Competition* 3

FOX, E., 'Towards World Antitrust and Market Access' (1997) 91 *AJIL* 1

—— 'The Merger Regulation and its Territorial Reach' [1999] *ECLR* 334

GERVEN, W. VAN, ' EC Jurisdiction in Antitrust Matters: The Wood Pulp Judgment' [1989] Fordham Corp L Inst 451

GERVEN, Y. VAN, and HOET, L., 'Gencor: Some Notes on Transnational Competition Law Issues' (2001) 28 *LIEI* 195

GREWLICH, A. S., 'Globalisation and Conflict in Competition Law' (2001) *Journal of World Competition* 367

GRIFFIN, J., 'Reactions to U.S. Assertions of Extraterritorial Jurisdiction' [1998] *ECLR* 64

GUZMAN, A., 'The Case for International Antitrust' (2004) 22 *Berkeley J Intl L* 355

JENNINGS, R. Y., 'Extraterritorial Jurisdiction and the United States Antitrust Laws' (1957) 33 *BYIL* 146

JENNY, F., 'Competition, Trade and Development Before and After Cancun' [2003] Fordham Corp L Inst (B. Hawk ed.) 631

—— 'Competition Law and Policy: Global Governance Issues' (2003) 26 *World Competition* 609

KACZOROWSKA, A., 'International Competition Law in the Context of Global Capitalism' [2000] *ECLR* 117

LANGE, D. F. G., and SANDAGE, J. B., 'The Wood Pulp Decision' (1989) 26 *CMLRev* 137

LIPSKY, JR., A. B., 'Competition and the WTO: Beyond Cancun' [2003] Fordham Corp L Inst (B. Hawk, ed.) 657

MANN, F. A., 'The Doctrine of Jurisdiction in International Law' (1964) 111 *RdC* 1

—— 'Casenote' (1973) 22 *ICLQ* 35

—— 'The Doctrine of International Jurisdiction Revisited After Twenty Years' (1984) 186 *RdC* 9

MEESSEN, K. M., 'Antitrust Jurisdiction under Customary International Law' (1984) 78 *AJIL* 783

MITCHELL, A. D., 'Broadening the Vision of Trade Liberalisation' (2001) *Journal of World Competition* 367

PAPE, W., 'Socio-Cultural Differences and International Competition Law' (1999) 5 *European Law Journal* 438

PARISI, J., 'Enforcement Co-operation Among Antitrust Authorities' [1999] *ECLR* 133

PETERSMANN, E. U., 'International Competition Rules for Governments and for Private Business' (1996) 30 *Journal of World Trade Law* 5

—— 'WTO Core Principles and Trade/Competition' [2003] Fordham Corp L Inst (B. Hawk, ed.) 669

PITOFSKY, R., 'Competition Policy in a Global Economy' (1999) 3 *JIEL* 403

REYNOLDS, R. M., SICILIAN, J., and WELLMAN, P. S., 'The Extraterritorial Application of the US Antitrust Laws to Criminal Conspiracies' [1998] *ECLR* 151

ROBERTSON, A., and DEMETRIOU, M., ' "But that was in Another Country": The Extraterritorial Application of US Antitrust Laws in the US Supreme Court' (1994) 43 *ICLQ* 417

ROTH, P. M., 'Reasonable Extraterritoriality: Correcting the "Balance of Interests"' (1992) 41 *ICLQ* 245

SLOT P. J., and GRABANDI, E., 'Extraterritoriality and Jurisdiction' (1986) 23 *CMLRev* 545

TAY, A., and WILLMAN, G., ' Why (NO) Global Competition Policy is a Tough Choice' (2005) *Quarterly Review of Economics and Finance* 312

TORREMANS, P., 'Extraterritorial Application of EC and US Competition Law' (1996) 21 *ELRev* 280

WHELAN, P., 'Resisting the Long Arm of Criminal Antitrust Laws: *Norris v. US*' (2009) 72 *MLR* 272

WOOD, D. P., 'Soft Harmonization Among Competition Laws: Track Record and Prospects' (2003) 48 *Antitrust Bull* 305

INDEX

absolute territorial protection
distribution agreements 206,
207–211, 790–793
exclusive distribution
agreements 805
'object or effect' 206, 224–225
prevention, restriction
or distortion of
competition 206, 224–225
abuse of dominant position
see also **bundling; collective
dominance; discounts
and rebates; dominant
position; exclusive
purchasing contracts;
margin squeezes;
predatory prices;
refusal to supply; tying;
undertakings**
affirmative duty of dominant
undertakings 374–375
ancillary markets 393–396
anti-competitive foreclosure
concept 382–385
barriers to entry 91–92
burden of proof 388–389
bundling 485
central issues 269, 365–366
commercial interests of
undertakings, protection
of 391–392
commitments
decisions 273–274
competition on the merits
'as efficient competitor'
test 380, 399–401, 427–441
consumer welfare 381
implications 379–380
meaning 378
'no economic sense' test 381
'own efficiency' test 381
'profit sacrifice' test 381
tests 380–381
complaints 273
conditions, unfair
trading 582–583
conduct hindering inter-Member
State trade 584–591
consumer welfare 45, 381
Continental Can 367–370
definition of abuse 372–373
degree of dominance 375–376

different markets, dominance
and abuse on 393–396
discrimination
contrary to Article
102(c) 567–575
geographical price
discrimination 570–572
price discrimination 396–398,
568–572
distribution agreements 842
downstream markets, abuse
on 393–396
effect on trade between Member
States 285–286
appreciable effect 283
national courts 287
overview 283–285
part of a Member State,
covering 286
Regulation 1/2003, 287
several Member States,
covering 285
single Member State,
covering 285–286
third countries 286–287
effects-based analysis 382
enforcement
commitments
decisions 273–274
complaints 273
fines 272–273
infringement
decisions 272–273
judicial review 274–275
national competition
authorities 274
national courts 275
remedies 272–273
excessive prices 575–581
exclusionary abuse
anti-competitive foreclosure
concept 382–385
collective dominance 724
competition on the
merits 378, 379–381
conduct excluding
competitors 556
Continental Can 367–370
definition of abuse 372–373
distinguishing legitimate
and illegitimate
conduct 378–381

exclusive purchasing
contracts 450
Guidance Paper, approach of
the Commission
in 382–385, 399–401
Hoffmann-La Roche
definition 378–381
miscellaneous exclusionary
practices 556–567
prices, general principles 396,
399–401
refusal to supply 510
type of abuse 367–670
exploitative abuse
Continental Can 367–370
excessive prices 575–581
low prices on buying
side 581
prices 396
type of abuse 367–370
export bans 584–591
fines 272–273
form-based analysis 382
Guidance Paper
Background, review of Article
102 289
contents 290–291
effect 291–293
pricing policies, approach
to 399–401
review of Article 102
Hoffmann-La Roche
definition 378–381
horizontal integration 567
inefficiency 583–584
infringement decisions 272–273
intellectual property rights
acquisition of 557
AstraZeneca 558–564
misrepresentations 558–560
misuse of rights 558–564
ownership of rights 920
intention 377–378
judicial review 274–275
legal proceedings, bringing
of 564–565
legitimate conduct 378–381
less efficient competitors 378,
379–380
limiting production 583–584
low prices on buying side 581
market power 373–374

abuse of dominant position (*cont.*)
meaning of abuse
  generally 272
  importance 366
  text of Article 102, 366
meeting competition
  defence 392–393
modernisation 366
national competition
  authorities 274
national courts 275
nature of concept 376–378
objective justification
  burden of proof 388–389
  case law 386–388
  efficiencies 388, 389–391
  generally 385–386
  Guidance Paper 389–391
  meeting competition
    defence 392–393
  necessity 387, 389
  protection of commercial
    interests of
    undertaking 391–392
oligopoly
  collective
    dominance 716–723
  one or more
    undertakings 716–723
parallel imports 585–590
part of a Member State,
  covering 286
patent ambushes 563–564
pharmaceuticals 585–590
positive duty of dominant
  undertakings 374–375
post-*Continenal Can*
  position 371
price discrimination 396–398
prohibition of 271–272
purpose of Article 102, 269–270,
  370
quasi-monopolies 375
relationship with Article 101,
  293–295
relevant market 62
remedies 272–273
reprisal abuses 371–372
restrictive agreements 582–583
review of Article 102
  commissioning
    review 287–288
  Guidance Paper 289–293
  staff discussion paper 288
search engines 565–567
several Member States,
  covering 285
single market 372, 584

single Member State,
  covering 285–286
special responsibility of dominant
  undertakings 374–376
standard-essential
  patents 563–564
super-dominance 375–376
text of Article 102, 270–271
third countries 286–287
transport 282–283
travel agents 394
tying 393–394, 485
types of abuse
  categories 371–372
  Continental Can 367–370
  exclusionary abuse 367–370
  exploitative abuse 367–370
  post-*Continenal Can* 371
  reprisal abuses 371–372
  single market 372
unfair trading
  conditions 582–583
unfairly high prices 575–581
vertical integration 567
vexatious litigation 564–565

access to the file
business secrets 976
Commission Notice on, *see* Tables
complainants 976
confidentiality 973–976
exculpatory documents 971
generally 970
knowledge of case 970
national competition
  authorities 976
national courts 976
practical arrangements 970
rules 971–973
scope of right 970–973
Transparency
  Regulation 976–978
administrative procedure
first stage 938–966
investigation stage 938–966
second stage 966–979
two-stage procedure 938–939
advertising
barriers to entry 91, 92
cartels 696
dominant position 357–358
**Advisory Committee on
  Concentrations**
consultation 1180
institutional structure of EU 104
**Advisory Committee on
  Restrictive Practices and
  Dominant Positions** 104
Advocates-General
Court of Justice 105

aerospace
new economy 55
aftermarkets
dominant position 317
market definition 79–80
refusal to supply 525–526
tying 486, 489–492
agency agreements
see also **agents**
agreements (Art. 101) 151
form of agreement 774
independent economic
  operators 773
risks 774–776
single economic units 137–139,
  773–775
vertical agreements 770,
  773–776
agents
see also **agency agreements**
economic activities 137–139,
  773–774
single economic units 137–139,
  773–775
undertakings 137–139
**Agreement on the European
  Economic Area** *see* **EEA
  Agreement**
agreements (Art. 101)
see also individual agreements e.g.
  **exclusive distribution
  agreements; joint selling
  agreements; vertical
  agreements**
agency agreements 151
approval by national
  authorities 150
burden and standard of
  proof 164
categories of analysis 201–203
collective bargaining 153–154
Commission Notices 188
complex arrangements 174–179
concurrence of wills 150–151
covert agreements 149
decisions by associations of
  undertakings 172–174
defences 151
employees 163–164
existence 149
fines 149
form of agreement 150
gentlemen's agreements 150
good neighbour rules 150
hub and spoke
  arrangements 163
inferences 156
intention 150, 151
investigations 154–155

meaning 149–179
meetings 154–155
national governments, required
        by 186–187
national legislation, required
        by 150, 186–187
offers to collude 154–155
operation at different levels of
        economy 151–153
operation in separate
        markets 151–153
parallel imports 158–161
participation in
        meetings 154–155
proof 150
relocation by one party 155
single continuous
        infringements 174–179
single economic unit 151
standard conditions of sale 150
statutory powers 164
termination 150
terminology 149–150
terms of agreement 149
trade associations 150
trade marks 150
types of collusion 149
unilateral conduct 155–163
agreements of minor importance
        see **appreciable effect**
Commission Notice on,
        see Tables
agreements on standard terms
        cartels 696
        standardisation
                agreements 762–763
agriculture
        associations of
                undertakings 147
        common agricultural
                policy 110
        regulations 110
aid granted by State *see* **State aid**
allocation of cases
        Merger Regulation 1175–1176
        National Competition
                Authorities 1052–1055
allocative efficiency
        Chicago School 23–24
        consumer welfare 44–45
        meaning 8
alternative dispute resolution
        national courts 1124
ancillary restraints
        Article 101(3) Guidelines 242–243,
                244–245
        cooperatives 244–245
        examples 243–246
        franchise agreements 243
        Gøttrup-Klim 244–245

Merger Regulation 1244–1245
non-compete obligations 243
'object or effect' 242–246
objective necessity 245–246
prevention, restriction
        or distortion of
        competition 242–246
Pronuptia 243
Remia and Nutricia 243
annual reports
        European Commission 104, 119
annulment
        judicial review 1045–1046
**anti-competitive
        foreclosure** 382–385
anti-competitive practices
        see **abuse of dominant
        position; agreements;
        appreciable effect;
        Article 101; Article
        101(3) guidelines; block
        exemptions; concerted
        practices; effect on trade
        between Member States;
        extraterritoriality;
        individual exemptions
        under Article
        101(3); object or
        effect; prevention,
        restriction or distortion
        of competition;
        undertakings; vertical
        agreements**
antitrust
        meaning of 4
antitrust law, *see* **United States**
**Antitrust ManProc (DG
        Comp Manual of
        Procedures)** 932
appeals
        see also **judicial review**
        Court of Justice 1046–1048
        enforcement 1039–1041
        fines 1017, 1039–1041
        General Court 106, 1046–1048
        judicial review 1030, 1039–
                1044, 1046–1048
appreciable effect
        Commission notices 181,
                226–231
        concept 180
        economic approach 196
        exclusive distribution
                agreements 183
        Expedia 228–231
        hardcore restraints 227
        increase in trade 183
        insignificant effects 180–181
        interpretation 180–181
        joint ventures 734

market share thresholds 226
meaning 180–181
national law and EU law 186
'object or effect'
        Commission Notice on
                Agreements of Minor
                Importance 226–231
        Expedia 228–231
        hardcore restraints 227–228
        object restriction 226
        Völk v. Vervaecke 226
partitioning of the common
        market 183–184
pattern of trade test 182
third countries 183
trade between member states
        agreements operating in one
                member state 184–185
        cumulative
                conditions 185–186
        increase in trade 183
        jurisdiction 181
        national law and EU law 186
        partitioning of the common
                market 183–184
        pattern of trade test 182
        quantitative element 185–186
        restrictions on
                competition 185
        restrictions on trade 185
        tests 181–182
        turnover 186
turnover 185
vertical agreements 786–787
Völk v. Vervaecke 226
Article 4 TEU
        public undertakings 601–602
        Union loyalty 601–602
Article 49 TFEU *see* **freedom of
        establishment**
Article 101
        see also **agreements;
                appreciable effect;
                Article 101(3) guidelines;
                block exemptions;
                concerted practices;
                effect on trade between
                Member States;
                extraterritoriality;
                individual exemptions
                under Article
                101(3); object or
                effect; prevention,
                restriction or distortion
                of competition;
                undertakings; vertical
                agreements**
        background to Article
                101(1) 192–193
        burden of proof 126

Article 101 (*cont.*)
cartels
breach of Article 101, 676–678
burden of proof 676–677
individual exemptions 678
leniency 677–678
powers of
enforcement 676–677
scope 675–676
categories of analysis 201–203
central issues 122
Chapter I prohibition 189–190
competition policy 122–123
declarations of
inapplicability 124–125
exclusions 189–190
infringement 125–126
interpretation 122–123
joint ventures
appreciable effect 734
assessment 734–739
block exemptions 735
Commission Guidelines 735
Commission Notices 734–735, 738
competition policy 734, 736
economic approach 735–739
generally 734
hypothetical
possibilities 735–736
liberal policy 737–738
Optical Fibres 737–738
single economic entity 739
Vacuum Interrupters 735–736
Métropole Télévision (M6) v.
Commission 199–201
nullity 124
overview 122–123
prohibition 124
reconciling Articles 101(1) and
101(3) 193–194
relationship with Article 102
293–295
relationship between Articles
101(1) and 101(3) 192–194,
201
severance of prohibited
clauses 124, 189, 1098
standard of proof 126
structure of Article 124,
193–194
text of Article 123–124
Article 101(2)
nullity of prohibited
agreements 124, 189,
1097–1099
severance of null clauses 189,
1098

Article 101(3) exemptions
see **individual
exemptions under
Article 101(3)**
Article 101(3) Guidelines
ancillary restraints 242–243,
244–245
consumer welfare 43
modernisation 43
object or effect 233
Article 102 TFEU *see*
**abuse of dominant
position; dominant
position**
Article 106 TFEU
see also **public undertakings;
services of general
economic interest**
central issues 597
format 603–604
objectives 603
text 602–603
assignment
meaning 855
Technology Transfer Block
Exemption 877–878
associations of undertakings
see also **undertakings**
agriculture 147
Article 101, 127, 147–151
cartels 172–173
certification schemes 174
collecting societies 147
decisions 172–179
exchange of
information 173–174
governmental intervention 174
institutionalised
cooperation 147–148
meaning 127, 147
non-economic activities 148
professional associations 147
public undertakings 147
relationship with
undertakings 148–149
sporting associations 148
statutory bodies 147
trade associations 147, 173, 174
atomic energy
Euratom 110
horizontal cooperation
agreements 110
Austrian School
competition policy 32

banking
financial crisis 2–3
free market economy 3

**barriers to entry, expansion
and exit**
absolute costs advantages 89
abuse of dominant
position 91–92
advertising 91, 92
brand proliferation 92
bundled rebates 91
bundling 93
case law 348–354
Chicago School 28, 86–88
definition 86–88
dominant position 335, 347–354
economies of scale and scope 89
exclusive dealership
agreement 93
fidelity rebates 91
first mover advantages 90
Harvard School 86
high capital costs 89–90
Horizontal Merger Guidelines
(2004) 93
incumbents, strategic behaviour
by 91–92
intellectual property rights 847
legal barriers 90
licensing agreements 897
limit pricing 91
market power 335
mergers 1130
network effects 90
OECD Roundtable Report 88
opportunity costs 93
over-investment 91
patent hoarding 93
predatory pricing 91, 402
product differentiation 91, 92
rebates 91
regulatory barriers 90
reputational effects 90
role 85–86
SIEC test 1209–1211
strategic behaviour 91–92
structural barriers 89–91
sunk costs 89, 91
switching costs 93
tying 93
types of barrier 88–93
vertical integration 90–91
bid-rigging
cartels 689–690
bilateral agreements
China 1291
EU agreements 1290–1291
EU-Canada Cooperation
Agreement 1290–1291
EU-US Cooperation
Agreements 1287–1290

extraterritoriality 1287–1292
Japan-EU Cooperation
        Agreement 1291
Korea-EU Cooperation
        Agreement 1291
Partnership and Cooperation
        Agreements 1291
stabilization and association
        agreements 1291
Switzerland-EU Cooperation
        Agreement 1291
biotechnology
new economy 55
block exemptions
see also **Technology Transfer
        Block Exemption;
        Verticals Regulation
        330/2010**
black list 265
burden and standard of
        proof 250
current exemptions 263–264
direct applicability 264–265
hardcore restraints 265
horizontal cooperation
        agreements review 732
individual exemptions under
        Article 101(3) 250
interpretation of provisions 263
know-how 866
licensing agreements 866
maritime transport 111
market share 265
motor vehicles 834
overview 115–116, 263
patents 866
research and development
        agreements 742–746
safe harbours 266
scope of exemption 264
specialisation
        agreements 747–749
vertical agreements
        see also **Verticals Regulation
        330/2010**
        generally 785–786
        motor vehicles 834
        old block exemptions 817–818
white list 265
withdrawal 265–266
brand proliferation
barriers to entry 92
broadcasting
liberalisation of sector 111
bundling *see* **tying**
burden and standard of proof
abuse of dominant
        position 388–389
agreements (Art. 101) 126, 164

appraisal of
        concentrations 1184–1187
block exemptions 250
cartels 676–677
individual exemptions under
        Article 101(3) 250–251
judicial review 1036–1039
Merger Regulation 1184–1187
'object or effect' 204
parallel imports 161–162

Canada
EU-Canada Cooperation
        Agreement 1290–1291
capitalism 3
see also **Free market economy**
cartels
advertising
        generally 696
        restrictions 697–698
Article 101
        breach 676–678
        burden of proof 676–677
        individual exemptions 678
        leniency 676–678
        powers of
                enforcement 676–677
        scope 675–676
associations of
        undertakings 172–173
bid-rigging 689–690
bolstering provisions 690–691
burden of proof 676–677
collusive tendering 689–690,
        695–696
competition law 3, 673–674
complex arrangements 174–179
conclusions 729–730
customer services 697
customer sharing
        agreements 686–687
distributors 680
elimination 666–672
explicit collusion
        alignment of behaviour 663
        barriers to entry 664
        characteristics of
                markets 664–666
        coordination
                mechanisms 664–665
        demand patterns 665
        depressed conditions 665
        dispersed buyers with no
                controlling purchasing
                power 665
        fewer firms 664
        game theory 661–663
        high market
                concentration 664

homogenous goods 664
low innovation rate 665
market transparency 664
markets prone to
        collusion 664–666
meaning 659–660
objective of cartels 660
oligopolistic
        interdependence 660–663
prisoners' dilemma 661, 672
punishment of deviation 663
similar cost structures 664
fines 1019–1028
game theory 661–663
individual exemptions under
        Article 101(3)
criteria 691
generally 678
market-sharing
        agreements 695
output restrictions 693–695
price-fixing 691–693
production
        restrictions 693–695
tenders 695–696
information sharing
        agreements
advantages 699
agreements 700–701
anti-competitive
        effects 701–706
assessment of competitive
        effect 701–706
association of
        undertakings 700
business-to-business
        exchanges 708–709
concerted practices 700–701
coordinated behaviour 699
direct sharing 700–701
exchange of
        information between
        competitors 699–700
financial institutions 707–708
generally 681
horizontal cooperation
        agreements 699
indirect sharing 700–701
joint conduct 700
price coordination 699
research and development
        agreements 699
standardisation
        agreements 699
trade associations 699
unilateral conduct 700
internal enforcement
        mechanisms 663
leniency policy 671, 1019–1028

cartels (*cont.*)
market-sharing
agreements 686–687, 695
mergers 673–674
non-price trading conditions
customer services 697
generally 696
information sharing 699–709
product quality 697
prohibition 696
standard terms and
conditions 696
technical development 697
uniform terms and
conditions 696
objectives 660
oligopoly 659–660, 674, 729
output restrictions 684–688,
693–695
price-fixing
agreements 678–684
buying prices 680
distributors 680
examples 681–682
generally 678
indirect price-fixing 679–680
individual exemptions under
Article 101(3) 691–693
information exchanges 681
joint selling 680
liberal professions 682–684
professional services 682–684
resale price maintenance 680
selling prices 678–679
services sector 682
supplementary
provisions 681
target prices 679–680
product quality 697
production restrictions 684–688,
693–695
professional services 682–684
promotion restrictions 696,
697–698
relevant market 63
resale price maintenance 680
settlements 992–993
single continuous
infringements 174–179
standard terms and
conditions 696
standardisation agreements 699
tacit collusion 660, 672–674
technical development 697
tenders 689–690, 695–696
United States 674
causation
concerted practices 167–170
'cellophane fallacy'
market definition 71–72

certification schemes
associations of
undertakings 174
trade associations 174
chains of substitution
market definition 76–77,
314–315
Charter of Fundamental Rights
application to competition
law 938
general principles of EU law 107
judicial protection 101
legal status 100
purpose 100
relevant articles 938
right to an effective remedy and a
fair and public hearing 935
right to respect for private and
family life 934–935
services of general economic
interest 632
Chicago School
allocative efficiency 23–24
assessment of theories 22–28,
29–30
barriers to entry 28, 86–88
basic tenets 23–24
Chicago economics 22
consumer welfare 24, 25–26
criticisms of theory 23, 28
efficiency 19, 23, 24–25, 26–27
foundations 22–23
influence 23, 28
neo-Chicago school 29
non-political premise 27–28
politics 27–28
post-Chicago school 28–29
United States law 19, 20
Chief Economist
institutional structure of EU 103
China
bilateral agreements 1291
competition law objectives 17
**civil consequences of
prohibitions in
Articles 101 and 102** *see*
national courts
Civil Service Tribunal
establishment 107
coal and steel
European Coal and Steel
Community 110
sectoral competition laws 110
collecting societies
associations of
undertakings 147
collective bargaining
agreements (Art. 101) 153–154
exclusion from competition
law 51

collective buying *see* **joint
purchasing agreements**
collective dominance
abuse of dominant position
collective abuses 723
conclusions 726–727
conduct amounting to
abuse 723–726
excessive prices 724
exclusionary abuses 724
exploitative behaviour 724
fines 726
Flat Glass 723
generally 590–591
individual abuses 590–591
Irish Sugar 725–726
oligopoly 277–278, 716–723
one undertaking, abuse
by 725–726
remedies 726
summary 722
acceptance of concept 716–718
collective abuses 723
commitments 1250
Compagnie Maritime Belge 720–723
conclusions 726–727
conduct amounting to
abuse 723–726
development of concept 276–277,
718
examples 277–278, 277–281
excessive prices 724
exclusionary abuses 724
exploitative behaviour 724
fines 726
Flat Glass 716–718, 723
generally 590–591
importance of concept 722
individual abuses 590–591
interpretation 720–723
Irish Sugar 720–723, 725–726
Laurent Piau 720–723
licences 277
links between undertakings 718
market shares 344
Merger Regulation 719–722
non-oligopolistic collective
dominance 278–281
oligopoly 277–278, 716–723
one or more
undertakings 276–281,
716–718
one undertaking, abuse
by 725–726
remedies 726
SIEC test 1199–1208
summary 722
TACA 720–723
collusive tendering
cartels 689–690, 695–696

individual exemptions under
Article 101(3) 695–696
commercial agents
vertical agreements 770
commercialisation agreements
Article 101(1) 754–756
Horizontal Cooperation
Guidelines (2010) 754
market power 755
media rights 757
price-fixing 754–755
Commission
see also **Commission decisions**;
Commission Notices;
enforcement; inspections;
investigations
access to the file
business secrets 976
complainants 976
confidentiality 973–976
exculpatory documents 971
generally 970
knowledge of case 970
national competition
authorities 976
national courts 976
practical arrangements 970
rules 971–973
scope of right 970–973
Transparency
Regulation 976–978
administrative procedure
inter partes stage 966–979
investigation stage 938–966
two-stage procedure 938
annual reports 104, 119
Commissioners 102
communications from
Commission 118–119
Competition
Commissioners 102
damages 1050
due process 1028–1029
enforcement
access to the file 970–978
defence rights 966–967
due process 1028–1029
Hearing Officer 969
human rights 934–938
informal settlements 993–994
initiation of
proceedings 938–939
inspections 941–952
'inter partes' stage 966–979
investigation stage 939–966
meetings 967
oral hearing 978–979
powers of the
Commission 933
right to be heard 966–967

sector inquiries 1028
settlement
procedure 992–994
State of Play meetings 967
statements, Commission
power to take 953
statement of objections 968–
969, 982–983
two-stage procedure 938–939
use of powers 101–102,
1028–1029
initiation of
proceedings 938–939
institutional structure of
EU 102–104
interim measures 991–992
modernisation 42
newsletters 119
powers of the Commission 101–
102, 933
press releases 119
State of Play meetings 967
Commission decisions
see also **fines**
commitment decisions 982–990
final decisions
behavioural
remedies 980–982
Commitment
decisions 982–990
finding and termination of
infringement 979–980
findings of inapplicability 990
infringement
decisions 979–980
positive remedies 980–982
structural remedies 981–982
interim measures 991–992
overview 979–980
procedural decisions 990–991
Commission Notices
see Tables
role and status 118
commitments
mergers
abstinence from commercial
behaviour 1250
access remedies 1249–1251
behavioural
commitments 1249–1251
breach of condition/
obligation 1251
collective dominance 1250
Commission Notice on
Remedies Acceptable 1247
conglomerate mergers 1251
divestiture 1139, 1248–1249
legal basis 1245–1247
Merger
Regulation 1245–1251

modification 1251
non-structural
remedies 1250–1251
structural
remedies 1248–1249
time periods 1245–1247
types of
commitments 1247–1248
waiver 1251
commitments decisions
abuse of dominant
position 273–274
Alrosa 983–988
complainants 989–990
discretion of
Commission 983–988
effect 989
exclusive purchasing
agreements 983–988
generally 982–990
introduction of power 982
new economy 363
post-*Alrosa* position 988–990
preliminary
assessments 982–983
provisions 982
purpose 989
Statement of
Objections 982–983
third parties 989
Competition Commissioners
see also **Directorate-General for**
Competition; European
Commission
adoption of decisions 102
responsibilities 102
competition law/policy
Article 101, 122–123
assessment of objectives 18–19
Austrian School 32
cartels 3
central issues 1
Chicago School 25–26, 26–27,
27–28
competition policy 1, 18–19
conclusions 93–94
consumer welfare 41–46
contestable markets theory 31
dispersal of economic power 16
economic efficiency 4–15, 18
economic freedom 16–17
effective competition 33
'effects' based 56–57
enforcement
over-enforcement 57–58
Type 1 errors 57, 58
Type 2 errors 58
under-enforcement 57–58
European Union
agricultural sector 110–111

competition law/policy (*cont.*)
Article 3(1)(g) EC 109
Article 37 TFEU 115
Article 101 TFEU 114
Article 102 TFEU 114
Article 103 TFEU 115–116
Article 104 TFEU 116
Article 105 TFEU 117
Article 106 TFEU 114
atomic energy sector 110
block exemptions 115–116
case law 46–48
coal and steel sector 110
consumer welfare 41–46
development of law 41–52
economic analysis 58–59
effective competition 33
effects-based law 56–57
energy sector 111
enforcement 57–58
European Commission 35
free movement of goods 117
harm, theories of 56–57,
93–94
implementing legislation 115
industrial policy 48–52
liberalisation 111
main treaty
provisions 109–110
Merger Regulation 117
military equipment 113
modernisation of law 41–46
new economy 53–54
objectives 34–35, 38–52
ordoliberalism 35, 41
origins 34
over-enforcement 57–58
overview 34–35
political background 35
procedural
provisions 115–117
provisions 109–117
public policy 48–52
purpose 34–35
Regulation 17, 34
regulation, relationship
with 52–54
secondary legislation 116
sectoral regulations 110–113
single market 38–40
sport 111–113
strategy 50–51
substantive
provisions 114–115
terminology 100
transport sector 111
Treaty of Rome 34
ex post nature 53
fair competition 16–17
financial crisis 2–3, 18

'form' basis 56–57
free market economy 1, 2, 2–3,
93
free movement of goods 117
free movement of services 117
game theory 28, 30
harm, theories of 56–57, 93–94
Harvard School 21–22
horizontal cooperation
agreements 732
ideology 16
intellectual property
rights 851–853
internal market 117
international agreements 56
joint ventures 733–734
liberal democracy 16
licensing agreements 851–853
Court of Justice 860–865
evolution of Commission
policy 859–860
generally 858–859
non-territorial
restraints 865–866
limits 600–601
meaning 1, 1–4
methodology
'effects' based 56–57
'form' basis 56–57
overview 56
modernisation of law 41–46
monopolies 3
national regulatory
authorities 53–54
Neo-Chicago School 29
new economy 55
new industrial
economics 28–29
objectives
consumer welfare 14–15
dispersal of economic
power 16
economic efficiency 4–15,
26–27
economic freedom 16–17
effective competition 33
European Union law 34
fair competition 16–17
happiness 17–18
overview 15
preservation of liberty 16
productivity 17
protection of
competitors 16–17
public policy 17
single market 18
social (total) welfare 12–14
socio-political factors 17
well-being of citizens 17–18
ordoliberalism 16, 34

over-enforcement 57–58
post-Chicago School 28–29
preservation of liberty 16
productivity 17
protection of
competitors 16–17
public policy 17
public undertakings 598,
599–601
purpose 1, 3
regulation distinguished 53–54
relationship between EU and
national law 1061–1064
role of law 1, 3
single market 18, 38–40
socio-political factors 17
structure-conduct-performance
paradigm 21–22
terminology 1
transaction costs economics 31
under-enforcement 57–58
United States
background to antitrust
law 19
Chicago School 19, 20
development 20
EU and US law compared 20
Harvard School 20
influence 19–21
objectives 19–20
restrained enforcement 20
Sherman Act 19, 20
'workable competition' 20
well-being of citizens 17–18
workable competition 32
complaints
acting on complaints 1076
Commission, to 1067
EU interest 1072–1075
formal rejection 1075–1076
handling of complaints by
Commission 1067–1068
interim measures 1076
legitimate interests 1069–1070
Merger Regulation 1078
National Competition
Authorities
already dealing with
complaint 1075
complaints to NCAs 1067
options available to aggrieved
entities 1066–1067
priorities of
Commission 1072–1075
procedure 1071
rejection of
complaint 1071–1076
standing 1068–1070
statement of objections 1076
three-stage procedure 1071

where to complain 1067–1068
compliance programmes
employees' agreements 164
fining policy, relevance to 1002,
1016
market rigging 164
mitigation 1015
requirements 164, 997
computer software
intellectual property
rights 850–851
new economy 55
concentrations
see also **Merger Regulation**
abandonment 1148–1149
change in the quality of
control 1144
control 1141, 1144
decisive influence 1141–1144
definition 1140–1144
EU dimension *see* **Merger
Regulation**
joint control 1143–1144
National Competition
Authorities 1164
non-EU dimension
joint ventures 1168
national law 1168
referrals to the
Commission 1168–1171
previously independent
undertakings 1141
role of Articles 101 and 102,
1171–1172
sole control 1142–1143
concertation *see* **concerted
practices**
concerted practices
activities falling short of
agreements 164–165
causation 167–170
collusion 165
direct contact 167–170
disclosure of
information 169–170
examples 164–165
exchange of
information 169–170
frequent exchanges 167–170
hub and spoke
arrangements 171–172
implementation of
concertation 165–167
indirect contact 170–172
isolated exchanges 167–170
meaning 164–165
meetings 167–170
parallel behaviour 172
planning 165
practice of concertation on the
market 165–167

presumptions 167–170, 171
price-fixing 169
publicly sharing
information 170–172
safety net, as 164
sharing information 170–172
single meeting 168–169
strategic information 169–170
subsequent conduct 167
trade press publications 170
vertical agreements 172
confidentiality
access to the file 973–976
conglomerate mergers
see also **mergers**
commitments 1251
meaning 1132–1133
SIEC test 1230–1239
consumer surplus
economic theory 4–5
consumer welfare
abuse of dominant position 45,
381
application of standard 45–46
Article 101(3) Guidelines 43
case law 45–46, 46–48
Chicago School 24, 25–26
detriment to consumers 43–44
distributive effects 43
economic theory 12–13
efficiency 13–14, 44–45
end-users 46
European Union 41–46
generally 12
Horizontal Merger Guidelines
(2004) 43
intermediate customers 46
meaning of consumer 45–46
mergers 45, 46, 1211–1216
modernisation 42, 42–43, 45–46
Non-horizontal Merger
Guidelines 43
single market 40
social (total) welfare 43–44
State aid 46
Vertical Guidelines (2010) 43
contestable markets theory 31
cooperatives
ancillary restraints 244–245
copyright
see also **intellectual
property rights**
collective licensing 919–920
licensing agreements
collective licensing 919–920
generally 914
performance
copyright 914–919
performance
copyright 914–919
rights 849

Technology Transfer Block
Exemption 877
costs
average avoidable costs 398
average incremental cost 399
average total cost 398
average variable cost 398, 403
avoidable costs 398
levels 398–399
marginal costs 398
opportunity costs
barriers to entry 93
raising rivals' costs
economic theory 31
short-run marginal costs 398
stand-alone costs 399
switching costs
barriers to entry 93
demand-side substitution 71
total costs 398
transaction costs economics 31
Council of the European Union
delegation of powers to the
Commission 101
powers 101
purpose 101
Court of First Instance, *see now*
General Court
background 105
Court of Justice
see also **damages; EU courts;
judicial review**
Advocates-General 105
appeals from General
Court 1046–1048
interim measures 1048–1050
overturning decisions of the
General Court 106
precedent 105
preliminary references 106
role 105
**Court of Justice of the
European Union**
see also **Court of Justice;
General Court**
institutional structure 105
Croatia
accession 100
cross-elasticity of demand
meaning 6
measurement 67
cross-subsidies
economic activities 132
undertakings 132
customer allocation *see* **exclusive
distribution agreements;
exclusive supply
agreements; market
sharing**
customer services
cartels 697

customer sharing agreements
cartels 686–687

damages
Article 340 TFEU 1050
national courts
burden and standard of
proof 1120
English courts 1119–1125
EU right to
damages 1100–1111
harmonisations 1111–1118
jurisdiction 1123–1124
databases
intellectual property rights 850
dawn raids
Article 20(4)
inspections 942–945
Article 21 inspections 952
human rights 934
de minimis see **appreciable effect**
**decentralisation of competition
law** *see* **modernisation**
decisions of the Commission *see*
Commission decisions
defence *see* **enforcement**
delimitation agreements
trade marks 913
demand
cross-elasticity 6
demand curves 4–5
elasticity of demand 5–6
own price elasticity 5–6
demand-side substitution
see also **SSNIP test**
aftermarkets 317–321
banana market 306–309
buying side, markets on
the 323–325
'cellophane' fallacy 71–72
chains of substitution 76–77
characteristics of product 73–74
close trading nexus with other
companies 306–309
connected markets 79
customers 77–78
definition of relevant market 66
distinctive
characteristics 306–309
France Télécom 312–315
groups of customers 77–78
intended use of product 73–74
internet service
providers 312–315
meaning 66
measurement 67
new economy 312–315
number of product markets 317
partial interchangeability 311
price 74
primary markets 317–321

procurement markets 323–325
raw materials 321–322
relevant market 315–316
secondary markets 317–321
small but significant
non-transitory increase in
price 306
SSNIP test 67–71
structure of supply and
demand 316–317
substantial part of the
market 306–309
substitutability 306
switching costs 71
Tetra Pak II 331–334
tying dealers to
discounts 309–312
tyre market 309–312
United Brands 306–309
designs
see also **intellectual
property rights**
rights 849–850
Technology Transfer Block
Exemption 877
DG Comp *see*
**Directorate-General for
Competition**
direct applicability
block exemptions 264–265
individual exemptions under
Article 101(3) 198–201
meaning 108
direct effect
meaning 108
public undertakings
Article 106(1) 652
Article 106(2) 652–653
supremacy of EU law 108–109
**Directorate-General for
Competition**
institutional structure of
EU 102–103
responsibilities 102
statistics 1252
status 102–103
website 103–104
discounts and rebates
abuse of dominant
position 454–485
aggregated rebates 455
barriers to entry 91
British Airways 469–475
bundled rebates 455
conclusions 484–485
conditional rebates 456–457
criticisms of EU law 454
exclusionary effects 454,
469–475
exclusive purchasing 457
Guidance Paper 476–478

loyalty (fidelity) rebates 455,
456, 457–460, 469
Michelin I 460–463
Michelin II 463–468
multi-product rebates 455
progress bonuses 463–464
quantity rebates 455, 456–457,
463–469
rolled-back rebates 455, 456,
475
selective rebates 455–456
service bonuses 463
target rebates 455, 460–463,
478–483
terminology 455
Tomra 459–460, 478–483
types 455–457
United States 483–484
uses 454
Vertical Restraints Guidelines
(2000) 456
volume discounts 455
discrimination
see also **price discrimination**
abuse of dominant position
anti-competitive
effect 567–568
Article 102(c) 567–575
British Airways 572–575
competitive
disadvantage 567–568,
572–575
equivalent transactions 567
exclusionary conduct 568
generally 567–568
geographical price
discrimination 570,
570–572
price discrimination 396–398,
568, 568–572
primary line injury 567, 568
secondary line injury 567
transport 568, 568–569
selective distribution
agreements 812
distortion of competition *see*
**prevention, restriction or
distortion of competition**
distribution agreements
see also **selective distribution
agreements, vertical
agreements**
absolute territorial
protection 206, 207–211,
790–793
abuse of dominant position 842
access payments 817
cartels 680
category management
agreements 817
economic theory 777

restrictive by effect
   Delimitis 802–805
   exclusive distribution
      agreements 805–806
   exclusive purchasing
      agreements 802–805
   franchising
      agreements 815–816
   generally 801–802
   selective distribution
      agreements 806–815
   single branding
      agreements 802–805
   tying 816
exclusive customer
   allocation 817
exclusive distribution
   agreements 805–806
exclusive purchasing
   agreements 802–805
exclusive supply
   agreements 817
export bans 790–793
franchising
   agreements 815–816
independent
   distributors 771–772
methods of distribution
   agency 770
   choice of method 769
   independent
      distributors 771–772
   vertical integration 769–770
restrictive by effect
   absolute territorial
      protection 206, 207–211,
      790–793
   Allianz Hungária 793–797
   export bans 790–793
   other restrictions 793–797
   Pierre Fabre 793–797
   reform 797–801
   resale price
      maintenance 789–790
   types of restraints 788
positive effects 777–784
prevention, restriction
   or distortion of
   competition 206, 207–211
price-fixing 680
resale price
   maintenance 789–790
restraints on conduct 777
restriction of competition 777
single branding
   agreements 802–805
tying 816
upfront access payments 817
distribution networks
   dominant position 356–357

divestiture
   Commission requiring 726
   commitments 1139, 1248–1249
   oligopoly 730
dominant position
   see also **abuse of dominant**
      position; barriers to
      entry; market definition;
      product market;
      undertakings
   access to financial resources 355
   access to key inputs 355
   advertising 357–358
   aftermarkets 317–321
   air travel agency
      services 329–330
   assessment 272
   barriers to entry 335, 347–354
   conduct 358–359
   countervailing buyer
      power 359–360
   definition
      case law 298–302
      effects-based
         analysis 303–304
      generally 272
      Guidance Paper 302–303
   demand-side substitution *see*
      demand-side substitution
   distribution networks 356–357
   EAGCP (Economic Advisory
      Group for Competition
      Policy) 303–304
   economies of scale 354
   establishing dominance 304–305
   geographic market 326–331
   Guidance Paper 302–303
   high fixed costs 354
   importance of concept 297–298
   incorrect findings 272
   indications from the
      undertaking
      own assessment 345
      performance
         indicators 345–347
      prices 345–347
      profits 345
   intellectual property
      rights 355–356
   internet service
      providers 312–315
   investments 355
   legal barriers 355–356
   market definition
      demand-side substitution 306
      generally 304–305
      potential competition 306
      purpose of definition 305
      relevant market 305–306
      supply-side substitution 306

market power
   assessment 335–363, 726
   barriers to entry 335
   generally 298, 302–303, 305
   market shares 336–344
market shares
   calculation 337
   collective dominance 344
   generally 336
   Guidance Paper 340
   high market shares 337–339
   low market shares 340–344
   presumption of
      dominance 337–339
   relative market
      shares 339–340
modernisation 303
new economy 361–363
opportunity costs 358
other factors indicating
   dominance
      access to financial
         resources 355
      access to key inputs 355
      advertising 357–358
      barriers to entry 347–354
      conduct 358–359
      distribution
         networks 356–357
      economies of scale 354
      high fixed costs 354
      indications from the
         undertaking 345–347
      intellectual property
         rights 355–356
      investments 355
      legal barriers 355–356
      meaning 344–345
      opportunity costs 358
      product
         differentiation 357–358
      regulatory barriers 355–356
      reputation 357–358
      sales networks 356–357
      summary 354–359
      sunk costs 354
      superior technology 356
      switching costs 358
      trading partners 359
      vertical integration 357
performance
   indicators 345–347
prices 345–347
procurement markets 323–325
product differentiation 357–358
profits 345
prohibition 271–272
raw materials 321–322
relevant market 304–305,
   305–306

dominant position (*cont.*)
reputation 357–358
sales networks 356–357
small but significant
non-transitory increase in
price 306
substantial part of the market
meaning 281
member states 282
purpose of the
requirement 281
transport sector 282–283
volume of
production 281–282
sunk costs 354
superior technology 356
supply-side substitution 306
food packaging 325–326
generally 306
switching costs 358
temporal market 330–331
Tetra Pak II 331–334
trading partners 359
transport sector 282–283, 327
United States 298
vertical integration 357
due process
Commission, enforcement
by 1028–1029
dynamic efficiency
economic theory 8–9, 14–15
new economy 55

**EAGCP (Economic Advisory
Group for Competition
Policy)**
co-ordination of group 103
2005 Report 303–304
EC Treaty (Treaty of Rome)
see now **Treaty on the
Functioning of Europe**
ECN *see* **European Competition
Network**
economic activities
agents 137–139
cross-subsidies 132
data collection 131
employees 137
environmental
protection 130–131
health care 134–136
legal persons 137–139
meaning 127–136
natural persons 137–139
pension funds 131–132
purchasing goods/services
by entity not engaged in
economic activity 134–136
single economic units
agents 137–139

consequences 139–142
legal persons 137–139
meaning 137–139
natural persons 137–139
subsidiaries 137–142
social security 131–133
solidarity principle 133
sovereign powers 130
subsidiaries 137–142
trade unions 137
undertakings 127
economic efficiency *see*
efficiency
economies of scale and scope
barriers to entry 89
dominant position 354
economic theory 7
EEA Agreement
commencement 119
competition rules 119
EEC *see* **European Economic
Community**
**effect on trade between
Member States**
abuse of dominant position
alteration of the structure of
competition 284
appreciable effect 283
national courts 287
overview 283–285
part of a Member State,
covering 286
Regulation 1/2003, 287
several Member States,
covering 285
third countries 286–287
Article 101
agreements operating in one
Member State 184
appreciable effect 181–182,
185–186
increase in trade 183
partitioning the single
market 183
pattern of trade test 182
Commission Notice on the
effect on trade concept 185
effective competition
basis 33
economic theory 33
meaning 33
Merger Regulation 33
effective judicial protection
general principles of EU law 107
efficiency/efficiencies
allocative efficiency 8, 23–24
Article 101(3) 249–263
Chicago School 19, 23, 24–25,
26–27
competition law 4–15, 18

consumer welfare 13–14, 44–45
dynamic efficiency 8–9, 14–15
economies of scale 7
efficient market hypothesis 3
Horizontal Merger
Guidelines 1215–1216
individual exemptions under
Article 101(3) 253–254
Kaldor-Hicks improvement 13
meaning of efficiency 4
Merger Regulation 1214–1215
mergers 1129, 1130, 1133
minimum efficient scale 7
modernisation 42
monopolies 9–10
new economy 55
objective of competition
law 26–27
objective justification and
Article 102 386–388,
389–391
ordoliberalism 34
Pareto improvement 8, 13
perfect competition 7–9
potential Pareto (Kaldor-Hicks)
improvement 13
productive efficiency 8
SIEC test
cases 1216
consumer benefit 1215
consumer welfare 1211–1214
defence 1211
Horizontal Merger
Guidelines 1215–1216
Merger
Regulation 1214–1215
merger specificity 1216
verifiability 1216
single market 40
transaction costs economics 32
types 8–9
United States 19
welfare 4, 12, 94
X-inefficiency 10–11
efficient market hypothesis
economic theory 3
EFTA
role 119
EFTA Court
establishment 119
jurisdiction 119
EFTA Surveillance Authority
role 119
electronic communications
new economy 54
emergency services
public undertakings 627–628
employees
agreements (Art. 101) 163–164
economic activities 137

market rigging 164
undertakings 137
unilateral conduct 163–164
energy sector
essential facilities 522
exclusive purchasing
contracts 453
liberation of sector 111
enforcement
see also **Commission
decisions; complaints;
fines; inspections;
investigations; National
Competition Authorities;
national courts; periodic
penalty payments**
Antitrust ManProc 932
appeals 1039–1041
background 923–924
Best Practices Notice 932
central issues 922
Commission
access to the file 970–978
defence rights 966–967
due process 1028–1029
Hearing Officer 969
human rights 934–938
initiation of
proceedings 938–939
inspections 941–952
'inter partes' stage 966–979
investigations 939–966
meetings 967
oral hearing 978–979
powers of the
Commission 933
right to be heard 966–967
sector inquiries 1028
settlement
procedure 992–994
State of Play meetings 967
statements, Commission
power to take 953
statement of
objections 968–969
two-stage procedure 938–939
use of powers 1028–1029
criminalisation 1064–1066
damages under Article 340
TFEU 1050
defence rights 966–967
European Competition
Network 932
Hearing Officer 969
human rights
arbitrary intervention by
public authorities 935
competition law 936–938
criminal charges 935–936
dawn raids 934
Engel criteria 936

generally 934
inspections 934
relevant articles 934–935
right to fair trial 935–936, 955
right to independent and
impartial tribunal 935–936
right to respect for private
and family life 934–935,
950–951
individuals, sanctions
against 1064–1066
manual of procedures 932
modernisation
informal guidance 927–929
notices 932
package of Regulations and
Notices 927–932
Regulation 1/2003, 929–931
Regulation 773/2004, 931–932
White Paper 925–927
old regime under Regulation
1/2007, 924–925
oral hearing 978–979
reform of system 923–924
right to be heard 966–967
right to fair trial 935–936, 955
settlements in cartels
cases 992–993
State of Play meetings 967
statement of
objections 968–969
Engel **criteria**
human rights 936
entry onto premises
inspections 947
environmental protection
undertakings 130–131
equal treatment
fines 1017
equality
general principles of EU law 107
essential facilities
see also **refusal to supply**
conditions 518–522
criteria for abuse 518–522
definition 513, 516
development of
doctrine 514–516
elimination of
competition 518–522
energy sector 522
European Night Services 517–518
generally 513
identification of assets 516
investment 522
issues 516–517
new customers 513
newspapers 518–522
origins of concept 513
Oscar Bronner 518–522
telecommunications 522

terminology 513
terms of access 516
transport 517–518, 522
United States 513, 517
EU 2020 strategy
goals 50
EU Commission *see* **Commission**
EU Courts
see also **Court of Justice;
General Court**
case load 107
overview 105–107
precedent 105
types of action 106
EUMR *see* **Merger Regulation**
Euratom
atomic energy sector 110
establishment 99
**European Coal and Steel
Community**
coal and steel 110
establishment 99
expiry of treaty 99
European Commission *see*
Commission
European Community
background 99
subsumed in the EU 100
European Competition Network
see also **National Competition
Authorities**
enforcement 932, 1051–1057
**European Convention on
Human Rights**
accession of EU 101
international agreements 100
right to respect for private
and family life 934–935,
950–951
European Court of Justice *see now*
Court of Justice
European Economic Area *see*
EEA Agreement
**European Economic
Community (EEC)**
establishment 34, 99
expansion 99
renamed European
Community 99
European Ombudsman
election 104
institutional structure of EU 104
powers 104
European Union
see also **competition law/
policy; general principles
of EU law; institutional
structure of EU**
background 35–38
central issues 98
common market 36

European Union (cont.)
  competition policy 35
  consumer welfare 41–46
  contextual background 35–38
  creation 99
  development 36
  direct applicability 108
  establishment 36
  European Commission
      competition policy 35
  exclusive competence 38
  foundations 99
  free movement of services 117
  industrial policy 48–52
  integration of Member States 36
  internal market 36–37
  judicial system 105–107
  legal order
      Article 267 TFEU 109
      direct applicability 108
      direct effect 108
      supremacy 108–109
  legislative acts
      overview 104–105
      types 104
  Member States 100
  modernisation 99
  objectives of the EU 35–38
  ordoliberalism 35, 41
  overview 99
  principles 37
  public policy 48–52
  regulation 52–54
  Regulation 1/2003, 99
  Regulation 17 replacement
      of 99
  single market 36, 38–40
  supremacy 108–109
  three pillars 99
  Treaty on European Union
      function 100
      values 36, 100
  Treaty of Lisbon 36
  Treaty of Rome 34, 36
  undistorted competition 37
excessive prices
  abuse of dominant
      position 575–581
  collective dominance 724
exchange of information *see*
      information sharing
      agreements
exclusive competence
  European Union 38
  Merger Regulation 1157–1167
exclusive customer allocation
  distribution agreements 817
exclusive dealership agreements
  barriers to entry 93

collective exclusive dealing
      agreements 691
exclusive distribution
      agreements
  see also **distribution**
      agreements; vertical
      agreements
  absolute territorial
      protection 805
  appreciable effect 180, 183
  'object or effect' 805–806
  positive effects 805
  qualified territorial
      protection 805
  single branding 806
  STM 805–806
exclusive purchasing contracts
  anti-competitive
      effects 451–453
  case law 450–453
  commitments
      decisions 983–988
  de facto exclusivity 451
  Delimitis 802–805
  distribution
      agreements 802–805
  effects approach 452
  energy sector 453
  'English clause' 451
  exclusionary abuse 450
  generally 450
  Guidance Paper 453–454
  Guidelines on Vertical Restraints
      (2000) 450
exemptions under Article
      101(3) *see* **individual**
      exemptions under
      Article 101(3); block
      exemptions
exports
  abuse of dominant
      position 584–591
  agreements (Article 101) 157
  bans 584–591
  distribution
      agreements 790–793
  United States 1269–1270
extraterritoriality
  EU law
  Boeing/McDonnell
      Douglas 1284–1285
  Dyestuffs 1272–1278
  enforcement
      jurisdiction 1286
  GE/Honeywell 1285–1286
  Gencor 1279–1283
  generally 1271
  Merger Regulation 1278–1286
  importance of issue 188

  international agreements 1258
  international law 1270–1271
  meaning 1258–1259
  Merger Regulation 1254–1256,
      1278–1286
  United States
      effects doctrine 1260–1263
      foreign plaintiffs 1265–1269
      generally 1259–1260
      other states, reactions
          of 1263–1265
failing firm defence
  SIEC test 1217–1221
fidelity (loyalty) rebates
  see **discounts and rebates**
file, access to Commission's, *see*
      access to the file
financial crisis
  banking 2–3
  competition law 18
financial services
  information sharing
      agreements 707–708
  liberalisation of sector 111
fines
  ability to pay 1016–1017
  abuse of dominant
      position 272–273
  aggravating circumstances 1015
  appeals 1017, 1039–1041
  cartels 1019–1028
  collection 1019
  collective dominance 726
  deterrence 1015
  development of
      policy 1000–1003
  equal treatment 1017
  general principles of law 1017
  Guidelines
      2006 Guidelines 1009–1017
      adoption 1004–1005
      effect 1005–1008
      legality 1005–1008
  ignorance of infringements 999
  incorrect or misleading answer
      in investigation 948
  intentional
      infringement 997–999
  leniency policy in
      cartels 1019–1028
  liability 1018–1019
  limitation periods 994
  maximum amount 995
  mitigation 1015–1016
  negligent infringement 997–999
  ne bis in idem 1018
  payment 1019
  power to impose 994

procedural infringements 995
proportionality 1017
Regulation 1/2003, 996–997
setting fines 994, 1017
substantive
infringements 996–1019
trade associations 997
foreclosure
see also **anti-competitive
foreclosure**
abuse of dominant
position 382–385
non-horizontal mergers 1225–
1229, 1236–1238
SIEC test 1225–1229,
1236–1238
tying 508–509
franchising agreements
ancillary restraints 243
distribution
agreements 815–816
economic approach 816
meaning 815
'object or effect' 815–816
Pronuptia de Paris 815–816
**FRAND (fair, reasonable,
non-discriminatory)
terms** 510, 563, 581, 908
free market economy
banking 3
basis 2
capitalism 3
competition law 1, 93
competition policy 1, 2–3
development 2–3
economic theory 2–3
efficient market hypothesis 3
financial crisis 2–3
foundations 2
market concept 2–3
meaning 2
public institutions 3
rational expectations theory 3
Smith, Adam 2
social issues 3
supply and demand 2
theory 2, 3
free movement
intellectual property
rights 853–854
free movement of goods
competition law 117
free movement of services
competition law 117
full-function joint ventures
see also **joint ventures**
application of Merger
Regulation 734, 1145–1147
Consolidated Jurisdictional
Notice 1146–1147

coordination of competitive
behaviour 1147
criteria 1145
determining
full-functionality 1145–
1147
meaning 1145–1147
Notice on cooperative joint
ventures (1993) 733
game theory
cartels 661–663
generally 30
oligopolies and tacit
collusion 661–663
Post-Chicago school 28, 30
General Court
see also **EU courts;
judicial review**
judicial review of Commission
decisions 1029–1046
appeals from General Court to
Court of Justice 1046–1048
EU court, as 105
expedited procedure 107
precedent 105
reversal of decisions 106
role 105
specialist courts 107
general principles of EU law
Charter of Fundamental
Rights 107
effective judicial protection 107
equality 107
failure to observe 107
good administration 107
legal certainty 107
legitimate expectations 107
non-discrimination 107
proportionality 107
subsidiarity 107–108
gentlemen's agreements
agreements (Art. 101) 150
geographic market
air travel agency
services 329–330
Commission Notice on Market
Definition 82–85, 326–327
definition 64, 82–85
dominant position 326–331
telecoms 328
transport 327
tyre market 327–329
good administration
general principles of EU law 107
group exemption *see* **block
exemptions**
Guidance Paper
abuse of dominant position
background 289

contents 290–291
effect 291–293
prices 399–401
review of Article 102,
289–293
discounts and rebates 476–478
dominant position 303–304
exclusive purchasing
contracts 453–454
margin squeeze 445
market shares 340
predatory pricing 417–419
refusal to supply 511, 550–553
tying 486, 487, 489, 506–509
**guidelines issued by
Commission**
see also **Commission Notices;
Guidance Paper; Tables**
role and status 118

hardcore restrictions
appreciable effect 227
block exemptions 265
criminalisation 1064–1066
individual exemptions under
Article 101(3) 251
object restriction 227–228,
231–232
Technology Transfer Block
Exemption
competing
undertakings 885–888
customer allocation 886–888
direct restrictions 884
generally 884–885
indirect restrictions 884
market sharing 886–888
non-competing
undertakings 888–891
output limitations 886
passive sales
restrictions 889–891
price restrictions 886, 889
vertical agreements
individual exemptions
under Article
101(3) 834–837
Verticals Regulation 330/2010,
825–830
Verticals Regulation 330/2010
active sales into exclusive
territories 827–829
applicable of
regulation 825–826
components, buyers of 829
components, suppliers of 830
fixed prices 826
minimum sales prices 826
select distribution
systems 829

hardcore restrictions (*cont.*)
  territorial
    restrictions 827–829
  unauthorised distributors 829
  wholesalers 829
harm
  abuse of dominant position 367
  competition law and theories of
    harm 56–57, 93–94
Harvard School
  assessment of theory 29–30
  barriers to entry 86
  structure-conduct-performance
    paradigm 21–22
  United States law 20
health care
  economic activities 134–136
  undertakings 134–136
health insurance
  public undertakings 601
Hearing Officer
  oral hearing 978
  publication of
    decisions 978–979
  role 969, 978
Herfendahl-Hirschmann
  index 1190, 1191
horizontal cooperation
  agreements
  see also **Horizontal**
    Cooperation Guidelines
    (2010); Joint ventures
  advantages 731
  atomic energy 110
  block exemptions,
    review of 732
  central issues 731
  commercialisation agreements
    Article 101(1) 754–756
    Horizontal Cooperation
      Guidelines (2010) 754
    market power 755
    media rights 757
    price-fixing 754–755
  forms of 731
  information exchange
    agreements 741
  insurance 763
  joint purchasing agreements
    cases 752–754
    Horizontal Cooperation
      Guidelines (2010) 749–752
    nature of joint
      purchasing 749–752
    sport 765
  modernisation 732
  partnerships 732
  payment services 764
  production agreements
    Article 101(1) 746–747
    generally 746

Horizontal Cooperation
  Guidelines (2010) 746–747
  individual exemption under
    Article 101(3) 749
  specialisation
    agreements 747–749
  purposes 731
  research and development
    agreements
    Article 101(1) 741–742
    Article 101(3) 742–746
    block exemption 742–746
    Horizontal Cooperation
      Guidelines (2010) 741–742
    individual exemptions under
      Article 101(3) 746
  review of policy by
    Commission 732
  specialisation agreements block
    exemption 747–749
  sport
    generally 764–765
    joint buying 765
    media rights 765–766
    sporting rules 764–765
  standardisation agreements
    FRAND
      commitments 758–759
    Horizontal Cooperation
      Guidelines (2010) 757–763
    standard essential patents
      (SEPs) 758
    standard terms 762–763
  strategic alliances 732
Horizontal Cooperation
  Guidelines (2010)
  see also **horizontal cooperation**
    agreements
  anti-competitive effects 740
  assessment 740
  centre of gravity test 739
  commercialisation
    agreements 754
  contents 739
  de minimis thresholds 740
  general approach 739–741
  individual exemptions 741
  information exchange
    agreements 741
  insurance 763
  joint purchasing
    agreements 749–752
  market power 740
  nature and content of the
    agreement 740
  payment services 764
  potential competitors 739
  production
    agreements 746–749
  research and development
    agreements 741–742

restrictive effects 740
  specialisation
    agreements 746–749
  standardisation
    agreements 757–763
Horizontal Merger
  Guidelines (2004)
  consumer welfare 43
  efficiency 1215–1216
  forms of barriers to entry 93
  modernisation 43
  SIEC test 1187
horizontal mergers
  see also **mergers**
  countervailing buyer
    power 1209
  meaning 1131–1132
  SIEC test
    barriers to entry 1209–1211
    closeness of competition
      between merging
      firms 1193–1198
    collective
      dominance 1199–1208
    competitive
      assessment 1189–1208
    competitors increasing
      supply 1198–1199
    concentration
      levels 1190–1192
    countervailing buyer
      power 1209
    efficiencies 1211–1217
    elimination of competitive
      force 1199
    failing form
      defence 1217–1221
    guidelines 1190–1191, 1193
    Herfendahl-Hirschmann
      index 1190, 1191
    joint dominance 1199–1208
    market shares 1190–1198
    network
      industries 1221–1223
    non-coordinated
      anti-competitive
      effects 1192–1193
    overview 1189–1190
    pricing pressure indices
      (PPIs) 1192
    rescue mergers 1217–1221
    switching costs 1198
    two-sided
      markets 1221–1223
    upward pricing pressure
      (UPP) 1192
horizontal price-fixing
  see also **cartels**
  market definition 63
hub and spoke arrangements
  agreements (Art. 101) 163

concerted practices 171–172
human rights
see also **Charter on Fundamental Rights; European Convention on Human Rights; general principles of EU law**
enforcement
arbitrary intervention by public authorities 935
competition law 936–938
criminal charges 935–936
dawn raids 934
Engel criteria 936
generally 934
inspections 934
relevant articles 934–935
right to fair trial 935–936, 955
right to independent and impartial tribunal 935–936
right to respect for private and family life 934–935, 950–951
Engel criteria 936
inspections 943–945
right to independent and impartial tribunal 935–936
self-incrimination 955

improvements
licensing agreements 858, 904–905
independent distributors
vertical agreements 771–772
individual exemptions under Article 101(3)
agreements benefitting from Article 101(3) 251–252
application of article 249–250
background 192–193
block exemptions 250
burden and standard of proof 250–251
cartels
collusive tendering 695–696
criteria 691
generally 678
market-sharing agreements 695
output restrictions 693–695
price-fixing 691–693
production restrictions 693–695
tenders 695–696
collusive tendering 695–696
criteria
benefits 252–253
efficiency gains 253–254
elimination of competition 262–263

fair share of resulting benefit 258–260
indispensable restrictions 260–262
non-competition factors 254–258
direct applicability 198–201
efficiency gains 253–254
elimination of competition 262–263
evidence 250–251
fair share of resulting benefit
consumers 259
criteria 258–260
fair share 259–260
hardcore restrictions 251
indispensable restrictions 260–262
interpretation 194
market-sharing agreements 695
modernisation 198–201
non-competition factors 254–258
output restrictions 693–695
overview of exemption 124
price-fixing 691–693
production agreements 749
production restrictions 693–695
public policy 254–258
reconciling Articles 101(1) and 101(3) 193–194
relationship with Article 101(1) 192–194, 201
research and development agreements 746
role 194
unilateral action 266–267
vertical agreements
criteria 834
generally 817
old block exemptions 817–818
other restraints 837–841
industrial property rights
see **intellectual property rights**
inefficiency *see* **Efficiency**
information, Commission's power to request
Article 18 940–941
information sharing agreements
associations of undertakings 173–174
business-to-business exchanges 708–709
cartels
advantages 699
agreements 700–701

anti-competitive effects 701–706
assessment of competitive effect 701–706
association of undertakings 700
business-to-business exchanges 708–709
concerted practices 700–701
coordinated behaviour 699
direct sharing 700–701
exchange of information between competitors 699–700
financial institutions 707–708
generally 681
horizontal cooperation agreements 699
indirect sharing 700–701
joint conduct 700
price coordination 699
trade associations 699
unilateral conduct 700
financial institutions 707–708
Horizontal Cooperation Guidelines (2010) 741
prevention, restriction or distortion of competition 206
trade associations 699
infringements
abuse of dominant position 272–273
Article 101, 125–126
injunctions
English law 1126
EU right to 1125–1129
national courts 1125–1126
inspections by the Commission
Article 20 941
asking questions 948–949
assistance from NCAs/national courts 949–950
authorisation 942
copies and extracts 947–950
dawn raids 942–945
decision ordering, Article 20(4) 942
entry onto premises 947
examination of books 947
fishing expeditions 945
human rights 943–945
legal advice 951
legal professional privilege 957–966
meaning 941
national competition authorities, role of 949
national courts, role of 949–950
notice 942

**inspections by the
Commission** (cont.)
power to carry out
inspections 941–942
power to take statements 953
powers of inspectors 945–949
private premises under Article
21 952
records, examination of 947
right to respect for private and
family life 950–951
seals 948
self-incrimination 953–957
statements 953
written authorisation, Article
20(3) 942
institutional structure of EU
Advisory Committee on
Concentrations 104
Advisory Committee on
Restrictive Practices and
Dominant Positions 104
Chief Economist 103
Council of the European
Union 101–102
Directorate-General for
Competition 102–103
European Commission 102–104
European Ombudsman 104
overview 101
insurance
horizontal cooperation
agreements 763
Horizontal Cooperation
Guidelines (2010) 763
insurance companies
health insurance 601
horizontal cooperation
agreements 763
intellectual property rights
see also **licensing agreements;
refusal to supply;
Technology Transfer
Guidelines; Technology
Transfer Block
Exemption**
abuse of dominant position
abuse 920
acquisition 557
AstraZeneca 558–564
misrepresentations to patent
authorities 558–560
misuse of rights 558–564
ownership of rights 920
assignment 855
barriers to entry 847
central issues 846
competition law 851–853
computer software 850–851
copyright 849
databases 850

design rights 849–850
dominant position 355–356
free movement 853–854
importance 847
know-how 850
nature of rights 847, 848
new economy 55
overview 847–848
patents 848
plant breeders' rights 850
refusal to supply
car parts cases 526–527
disruption of previous
supply 536–548
generally 526
IMS 532–536
interface
information 536–548
Ladbroke 531–532
licensing 531–532
Magill 528–531
Microsoft 536–548
pharmaceuticals 532–536
television listings, copyright
in 528–531
royalties 855–856
semiconductor
topographies 850
trade marks 848–849
Verticals Regulation 330/2010,
822–823
interim measures
Commission decisions 991–992
complaints 1076
Court of Justice 1048–1050
judicial review 1048–1050
internal market
competition law 117
establishment 36–37
European Union 36–37
international agreements
bilateral competition law
agreements 1286–1292
European Convention on
Human Rights 100
multilateral competition law
agreements 1292
**International Competition
Network** 1294–1295
international law
extraterritoriality 1270–1271
globalisation 1295–1296
multilateral
cooperation 1292–1295
nationality principle 1270
passive personality
principle 1270
positive comity 1293
private international law 1271
territorialty principle 1270
United States 1270–1271

international organisations
globalisation 1295–1296
International Competition
Network 1294–1295
OECD 1292–1293
UNCTAD 1292–1293
WTO 1293–1294
internet
new economy 54–55
internet service providers
demand-side
substitution 312–315
dominant position 312–315
product market 312–315
telecom service
providers 312–315
investigations
fact-finding by
Commission 939–966
information, power to
request 940–941
inspections
asking questions 948–949
assistance from NCAs/
national courts 949–950
authorisation 942
copies and extracts 947–950
dawn raids 942–945
entry onto premises 947
examination of books 947
fishing expeditions 945
human rights 943–945
legal advice 951
legal professional
privilege 957–966
meaning 941
national competition
authorities 949–950
national courts 949–950
notice 942
power to carry out
inspections 941–942
power to take statements 953
powers of
inspectors 945–949
private premises 952
records, examination of 947
right to respect for
private and family
life 950–951
seals 948
self-incrimination 953–957
statements 953
written authorisation 942
Merger Regulation
conduct of
investigations 1179–1180
initial
investigation 1177–1178
phase I
investigation 1177–1178

phase II
  investigation 1178–1179
overview 939–940
requests for
  information 940–941
investments
need for as a barrier to entry 355

Japan
Japan-EU Cooperation
  Agreement 1291
joint dominance *see* **collective
  dominance**
joint purchasing agreements
cases 752–754
Horizontal Cooperation
  Guidelines (2010) 749–752
nature of joint
  purchasing 749–752
sport 765
joint selling agreements
sport 765–766
joint ventures
see also **full-function joint
  ventures**
advantages 1144–1145
appreciable effect 734
Article 101
  appreciable effect 734
  assessment 734–739
  block exemptions 735
  Commission Guidelines 735
  Commission Notices 734–735,
    738
  competition policy 734, 736
  coordination 1241–1244
  economic approach 735–739
  generally 734
  liberal policy 737–738
  Optical Fibres 737–738
  single economic entity 739
  Vacuum Interrupters 735–736
full-function joint
  ventures 1145–1147
meaning 733, 1144
Merger Regulation 732, 734,
  1144–1147, 1241–1244
Notice on cooperative joint
  ventures (1993) 733
partial function, applicable
  regimes 733
SIEC test 1241
single economic unit 739
spill-over effects 733
judicial review
abuse of dominant
  position 274–275
acts subject to challenge 1032
annulment 1045–1046

appeals from the General
  Court to the Court of
  Justice 1046–1048
appeals against
  penalties 1039–1041,
  Article 263 TFEU 1030
burden and standard of
  proof 1036–1039
failure of Commission to act
  omissions 1077
  review of acts 1077
generally 1029–1030
grounds of review 1032–1036
infringement of essential
  procedural
  requirement 1034–1035
infringement of
  treaties 1035–1036
interim measures 1048–1050
jurisdiction 1029
KME 1041–1044
lack of competence 1033–1034
locus standi 1030–1032
Merger Regulation 1253–1254
Posten Norge 1044–1045

Kaldor-Hicks improvement 13
know-how
see also **intellectual
  property rights**
block exemptions 866
meaning of 850
Technology Transfer Block
  Exemption 877
Korea
competition law 17
Korea-EU Cooperation
  Agreement 1291

legal advice
inspections 951
legal certainty
general principles of EU law 107
legal proceedings
abuse of dominant
  position 564–565
legal professional privilege
independent lawyers 959,
  961–965
inspections 957–966
meaning 957–958
procedure 965–966
protected documents 965–966
recognition 958–961
scope 957–965
legitimate expectations
general principles of EU law 107
leniency
availability of immunity 677

cartel enforcement 668,
  670–678, 1019–1028
disclosure of material 1120
effect of programme 677–678
international law, 1295
justification for policy 45
immunity from
  fines 1021–1022
model programme 1020–1021,
  1059–1060
NCAs, applications
  to 1057–1060
policy 45, 671, 677, 1019–1028,
  1059–1060
targeted inspections 1022
United States 677, 1266
liberalisation
meaning 52
public undertakings 52, 598
licensing agreements
see also **intellectual property
  rights; Technology
  Transfer Block
  Exemption; Technology
  Transfer Guidelines**
Article 101
  agreements falling outside
    TTBER 894
  analysis 895–897
  Article 101(1) 895–896
  Article 101(3) 896–897
  barriers to entry 897
  bundling 903
  captive use
    restrictions 902–903
  cross-licensing 899–900
  exclusive licences 899–900
  field of use
    restrictions 901–902
  general principles 894
  improvements 904–905
  market position 897
  maturity of market 897
  nature of agreement 897
  no presumption of
    illegality 895
  no-challenge clauses 904
  non-assertion
    agreements 905–906
  non-compete
    obligations 903–904
  other relevant factors 898
  output restrictions 901
  provisions not generally
    restrictive 898
  relevant factors to
    application 897
  royalties 898–899
  safe harbour 895

licensing agreements (cont.)
sales restrictions 900
settlement
agreements 905–906
sole licences 899–900
technology pools 906–908
Technology Transfer Block
Exemption 898–906
tying 903
barriers to entry 897
block exemptions 866
bundling 857, 903
captive use restrictions 902–903
commercial
considerations 855–858
competition law, relationship
with 851–853
competition policy
Court of Justice 860–865
evolution of Commission
policy 859–860
generally 858–859
non-territorial
restraints 865–866
copyright
collective licensing 919–920
generally 914
performance
copyright 914–919
cross-licensing 899–900
customer allocation 857
delimitation agreements 913
exclusive licences 856, 899–900
exploitation of rights 854–855
field of use restrictions 857,
901–902
improvements 858, 904–905
no-challenge clauses 858, 904
non-assertion
agreements 905–906
non-compete obligations 858,
903–904
non-exclusive licences 856
output restrictions 901
performance
copyright 914–919
prevention, restriction
or distortion of
competition 211
royalties 855–856, 898–899
sales restrictions
Article 101 999
competitors, agreements
between 900
customer allocation 857
non-competitors, agreements
between 900
territorial
restrictions 856–857
settlement agreements 905–906
sole licences 856, 899–900

technology pools 906–908
territorial restrictions on
production 856
trade marks 908–913
tying 857, 903
limitation periods
fines 994
periodic penalty payments 994
Lisbon Agenda
goals 50
replacement 50
litigation
abuse of dominant
position 564–565
vexatious litigation 564–565
loyalty (fidelity) rebates
see also **discounts and rebates**
barriers to entry 91
effects 456
meaning 455

margin squeeze
anti-competitive
effects 427–441, 448
'as efficient competitor'
test 427–441, 447
Commission decisions 426
concept 426–427
Deutsche Telekom 427–434
downstream market 434–441
encouragement from
national regulatory
authority 54, 427–434,
448–449
essential facilities 521–522
existence of abuse 427–434,
434–441
gas transmission
networks 444–445
Guidance Paper 445
harm to consumers 448
justification 434–441
meaning 426
national regulatory
authorities 54, 427–434,
448–449
operation 426
refusal to supply 434–441, 446
stand-alone abuse 427–444,
446, 447
summary 449
telecommunications 427–444,
447–449
Téléfonica 441–444
TeliaSonera 434–441
test 427–434
United States 445
marginal customers
small but significant
non-transitory increase in
price (SSNIP) test 67

market definition
see also **demand-side
substitution; SSNIP test**
abuse of dominant position 62
aftermarkets 79–80
cartels 63
chains of substitution 76–77
characteristics of product 73–74
Commission Notice on market
definition (1997)
aftermarkets 79–80
demand-side substitution 66
geographic market 82–85
product characteristics 73
relevant geographic
market 82–85
relevant product
market 65–66
SSNIP test 68
supply-side substitution 74,
75
temporal market 85
connected products 79
critical loss analysis 70
dominant position
demand-side substitution 306
generally 304–305
potential competition 306
purpose of definition 305
relevant market 305–306
supply-side substitution 306
geographic market 64, 82–85
groups of customers 77–78
horizontal price-fixing
agreements 63
importance 61–62
intended use of product 73–74
measurement 67
multi-sided markets 81
new economy 55, 78–79
pharmaceuticals 81–82
platforms 81
potential competition 66
price 74
price correlation analysis 70
procurement markets 82
raw materials 80–81
relevant geographic market 64,
82–85
relevant market
abuse of dominant
position 62
aftermarkets 79–80
buying side, markets on
the 82
cartels 63
characteristics of
product 73–74
Commission Notice
(1997) 65–66
connected products 79

definition 60, 61–66
geographic market 64, 82–85
horizontal price-fixing
   agreements 63
importance 61–62
intended use of
   product 73–74
multi-sided markets 81
pharmaceuticals 81–82
platforms 81
price 74
procurement markets 82
product market 63–64
purpose of definition 61–62
raw materials 80–81
role of definition 62–63
statutory markets 81
substitutability 63
supply and demand 79
technology markets 78–79
temporal market 85
two-sided markets 81
relevant product market 63–64
role of definition 62–63
SIEC test
Commission Notice
   (1997) 1188–1189
previous practice 1188–1189
role 1188
substitutability 63
supply and demand 79
supply-side substitution
Commission Notice
   (1997) 74, 75
meaning 66
use of definition 74–76
technology markets 78–79
Technology Transfer Block
   Exemption 881
temporal market 85
tests 69–70
time over which market
   operates 85
two-sided markets 81
Verticals Regulation 330/2010,
   824
market power
see also barriers to entry;
   dominant position;
   market definition;
   relevant market
absolute size 61
abuse of dominant
   position 373–374
assessment 60–61, 335–363
barriers to entry 335
'cellophane' fallacy 71–72
commercialisation
   agreements 755
definition 59

direct measurement 60
dominant position 298,
   302–303, 305
estimation 60
European Commission
   assessment 61
Horizontal Cooperation
   Guidelines (2010) 740
indirect measurement 60
market share 61
market shares 336–344
power over price 59
power to exclude 59–60
power to influence other
   parameters of
   competition 59
relative size 61
residual demand curve 60
SIEC test 1224
structural approach 60–61
substantial market power
   definition 59–60
market rigging
see also cartels
by employees 164
market shares
block exemptions 265
calculation 337
collective dominance 344
Commission Notice on market
   definition (1997) 337
generally 336
Guidance Paper 340
high market shares 337–339
low market shares 340–344
market power 336–344
presumption of
   dominance 337–339
relative market shares 339–340
Technology Transfer Block
   Exemption
calculation 882
competing
   undertakings 883–884
market definition 881
non-competing
   undertakings 883–884
product market 881, 882
subsequently becoming
   competitors 884
technology market 881, 882
thresholds 880–881
Verticals Regulation 330/2010
30 per cent
   threshold 823–824
calculation 833
exceeding the market
   shares 824
market definition 824
market shares cap 823–825

portfolio of products 825
market-sharing agreements
cartels 686–687, 695
individual exemptions under
   Article 101(3) 695
marketing see advertising
meetings
agreements (Art. 101) 154–155
concerted practices 167–170
Member States
see also national courts
economic integration
   into EU 36
States which are EU
   members 100
Merger Regulation
see also mergers; SIEC test
abandonment of a
   concentration 1148–1149
adoption 117
ancillary restraints 1244–1245
appeals 1253–1254
application of regulation 732,
   734
appraisal of concentrations
assessing the
   counterfactual 1184–1185
background 1180–1182
burden and standard of
   proof 1184–1187
dominance test 1181
horizontal mergers 1182–
   1184, 1187–1223
industrial policies 1239–1241
lobbying 1240
new test 1182–1184
non-competition
   factors 1239–1241
non-horizontal
   mergers 1223–1239
original test 1180–1181
political factors 1240–1241
reform of test 1181–1184
SIEC test 1182–1184,
   1187–1241
background 1134–1139
case allocation 1157–1159
collective dominance 719–722
commitments
access remedies 1249–1251
behavioural
   commitments 1249–1251
breach of condition/
   obligation 1251
Commission Notice on
   Remedies Acceptable 1247
divestiture 1248–1249
legal basis 1245–1247
modification 1251
remedy packages 1249–1251

Merger Regulation (*cont.*)
structural
remedies 1248–1249
time periods 1245–1247
types of
commitments 1247–1248
waiver 1251
complaints 1078
concentrations 1129,
1140–1144, 1148–1149
consumer welfare 45, 46
development 1134–1139
effective competition 33
efficiency 1214–1215
EU dimension
assessment 1149–1152
breach of exclusivity
provisions 1167
calculation of
turnover 1152–1156
case allocation 1157–1159
distinct markets 1159–1164
essential interests of
security 1166–1167
exclusive
competence 1157–1167
legitimate
interests 1164–1166
notification 1172–1174
number of
undertakings 1152–1156
referral to NCA 1164
review of thresholds 1152
test 1149–1152
turnover 1150–1152
exclusive
competence 1157–1167
extraterritoriality 1254–1256,
1278–1286
full-function joint ventures
application of regulation 734
investigations
conduct 1179–1180
initial
investigation 1177–1178
phase I
investigation 1177–1178
phase II
investigation 1178–1179
joint ventures 1144–1147,
1241–1244
jurisdiction
concentrations 1140–1144
extra-territorial
application 1254–1256
international
issues 1254–1256
non-EU dimension
joint ventures 1168
national law 1168

referrals to the
Commission 1168–1171
notification 1139–1140,
1172–1174
oligopoly 719–722, 727
overview 117
phase I investigation 1177–1178
phase II
investigation 1178–1179
pre-notification reasoned
submissions
background 1174
Notice on Case
Allocation 1175–1176
request for referral to the
Commission 1175
request for referral to
NCA 1174–1175
procedure
conduct of
investigations 1179–1180
initial
investigation 1177–1178
notification 1139–1140,
1172–1174
phase I
investigation 1177–1178
phase II
investigation 1178–1179
pre-notification reasoned
submissions 1174–1176
suspension 1176–1177
public policy 51
reciprocity 1256
remedies
alternative packages 1251
commitments 1245–1251
role of Articles 101 and 102,
1171
scheme of
regulation 1139–1140
scope 1139
statistics 1252
warehousing
arrangements 1147–1148
mergers
see also **Merger Regulation**
advantages of and motives
for 1130
barriers to exit 1130
cartels 673–674
central issues 1128
conglomerate mergers
meaning 1132–1133
consumer welfare 45, 46
damaging effects 1131–1133
definition 1129
efficiency 1129, 1130, 1133
failing firm defence (rescue
mergers) 1217–1221

horizontal mergers
meaning 1131–1132
industry stability 1130
large businesses, avoidance
of 1133–1134
meaning 1129
negative effects 1131–1135
positive effects 1130
purpose of control 1129–1134
role of competition law 3
sectoral control 1134
single market integration 1130
SSNIP test 72
unemployment 1134
vertical mergers
meaning 1132
military equipment
application of competition
rules 113
**minor importance, agreements
of** *see* **agreements of
minor importance**
**model leniency
policy** 1059–1060
modernisation
abuse of dominant position 366
Article 101(3) Guidelines 43
consumer welfare 42–43, 45–46
dominant position 303
effects-based law 57
efficiency 42
enforcement
informal guidance 927–929
notices 932
Regulation 1/2003, 929–931
Regulation 773/2004, 931–932
White Paper 925–927
European Commission 42
European Union 99
horizontal cooperation
agreements 732
Horizontal Merger Guidelines
(2004) 43
individual exemptions under
Article 101(3) 198–201
meaning 41–42
Métropole Télévision (M6) v.
Commission 199–201
modernisation
'package' 927–932
'more economics' approach 42,
57
national competition
authorities 104
national courts 104
Non-horizontal Merger
Guidelines 43
Regulation 1/2003
approach 198
effect of regulation 120

national competition
authorities 104
national courts 104
purpose 119
subsidiarity 108
Vertical Guidelines (2010) 43
Vertical Restraints Guidelines
(2000) 42

monopolies
see also **Merger Regulation**
competition policy 3
deadweight loss 9, 10
economic theory 9–11
efficiency 9–10
meaning 9
natural monopolies 7
objections to monopolies 9–11
perfect competition 9, 11–12
price discrimination 9
role of competition law 3
X-inefficiency 10–11

motor vehicles
block exemptions 84

**National Competition
Authorities**
see also **European Competition
Network (ECN)**
abuse of dominant position 274
access to the file 976
application of Articles 101
and 102
cooperation 1060–1061
generally 1060
application of rules 53
Article 20 inspections, role
in 949–950
assistance to Commission 949
case allocation 1052–1055
complaints
already dealing with
complaint 1075
complaints to NCAs 1067
concentrations 1164
cooperation 1052–1055,
1060–1061
designation 1051
establishment 52
freedom of Member States 1051
infringement decisions 1051
leniency
applications 1057–1060
margin squeeze 54
model leniency
policy 1059–1060
modernisation 104
national competition
law 1061–1064
non-infringement decisions,
inability to take 1051
powers 1051–1052

role 1051
scope of jurisdiction 53–54
Tele2Polska 1051
transfer of
information 1055–1057

national courts
abuse of dominant
position 275
access to the file 976
alternative dispute
resolution 1124
application of EU competition
rules 106
Article 20 inspections, role
in 949–950
assistance to Commission 949,
1094–1095
central issues 1082
compensation 1087–1088
consecutive
proceedings 1095–1097
consistent and concurrent
application of Articles 101
and 102, 1094–1095
cooperation with
Commission 1094–1095
damages
burden and standard of
proof 1120
English courts 1119–1125
EU right to
damages 1100–1111
harmonisations 1111–1118
jurisdiction 1123–1124
United States law 1124–1125
deterrents to
litigation 1086–1087
direct effect 1083–1084
duty of sincere
cooperation 1084
enforcement of infringing
agreements
Article 101, 1097–1099
Article 102, 1099–1100
illegality 1099, 1100
nullity 1097–1098, 1099
severance 1098
unenforceable
agreements 1099–1100
growth in litigation 1085–1087
judgments contrary to
Commission/NCA
decisions 1095–1097
modernisation 104
national procedural
autonomy 1083–1084
parallel proceedings 1095
preliminary references 106
principle of effectiveness 1084
private enforcement 1087–1094
public enforcement 1087–1094

remedies
alternative dispute
resolution 1124
available remedies 1085–1087
damages 1100–1125
harmonisation 1124
injunctions 1125–1126
obligatory remedies 1084
principle of effectiveness 1084
settlements 1124
settlements 1124
severance 1098
United States law 1085,
1124–1125

NCAs *see* **National Competition
Authorities**
ne bis in idem **principle**
fines 1018
Neo-Chicago School
economic theory 29
network effects
new economy 55
new economy
aerospace 55
biotechnology 55
characteristics of markets 55
commitments decisions 363
competition law 55
computer software 55
demand-side
substitution 312–315
dominant position 312–315,
361–363
dynamic efficiency 55
electronic
communications 54–55
European Commission 55
intellectual property 55
internet 54–55
market definition 55, 78–79
meaning 54–55
network effects 55
product market 312–315
regulation 55
technology markets 78–79
telecommunications 54–55,
78–79
**new industrial
economics** 28–29
non-compete obligations
ancillary restraints 243
licensing agreements 858,
903–904
selective distribution
systems 832
termination of agreement 832
vertical agreements
individual exemptions under
Article 101(3) 837–841
Verticals Regulation 330/2010,
831–832

non-discrimination
general principles of EU law 107
Non-Horizontal Merger
Guidelines
consumer welfare 43
modernisation 43
SIEC test 1187, 1223–1224
Notices, Commission *see*
Commission Notices
and Tables
notification
Merger Regulation 1139–1140,
1172–1174
pre-1 May 2004 position 195
NRAs *see* **National regulatory**
authorities

'object or effect'
see also **appreciable effect**;
prevention, restriction or
distortion of competition
absolute territorial
protection 206, 224–225
actual effect of agreement 215–
216, 222
alternative conditions 204
ancillary restraints 242–246
balancing approach 246–249
burden and standard of
proof 204
conditions 204
context of agreement's
provisions 205–211, 222–
226, 233–238
distribution agreements
absolute territorial
protection 206, 207–211,
790–793
Allianz Hungária 793–794
Delimitis 802–805
effect restriction 801–817
exclusive distribution
agreements 805–806
export bans 790–793
franchising
agreements 815–816
object restriction 788–801
other restrictions 793–797
Pierre Fabre 793–797
resale price
maintenance 789–790
selective distribution
agreements 806–815
single branding
agreements 802–805
tying 816
types of restraints 788
economic approach 195–197
effect restriction
Article 101(3) guidelines 233

Commission Notice on
Agreements of Minor
Importance 239–242
context of
agreement 233–238
distribution
agreements 801–817
exclusive distribution
agreements 805–806
franchising
agreements 815–816
inter-brand
competition 233–238
intra-brand
competition 239–240
method of analysis 233–234
rule of reason 232–233
selective distribution
agreements 806–815
single branding
agreements 802–805
tying 816
exclusive distribution
agreements 805–806
franchising
agreements 815–816
hardcore restraints 231–232
inappropriate
assumptions 222–226
industry crisis 225–226
intention of parties 215
inter-brand
competition 233–238
interpretation 179–180, 194–
195, 204
intra-brand
competition 239–240
list of object restraints
defined list, whether 212
expansion of the list 212–214
narrowing the list 215–222
list of restraints 212–214
object restriction
absolute territorial
protection 206, 224–225
actual effect of agreement 25–
216, 222
Allianz Hungária 793–794
appreciable effect 226
context of agreement's
provisions 205–211,
222–226
defined list, whether 212
distribution
agreements 788–801
expansion of the list 212–214
export bans 790–793
hardcore restraints 231–232
inappropriate
assumptions 222–226

intention of parties 215
list of restraints 212–214
narrowing the list 215–222
public policy 215–222
resale price
maintenance 789–790
subjective intention of
parties 215
proportionality 246
public policy 215–222, 246–249
resale price
maintenance 789–790
rule of reason 232–233
selective distribution
agreements 806–815
single branding
agreements 802–805
subjective intention of
parties 215
tying 816
United States 231
weighing of restraints 246–249
OECD
anti-competitive
practices 202
barriers to entry 88
international
organisations 1292–1293
oligopoly
abuse of dominant position
collective
dominance 716–727
one or more
undertakings 716–723
advance price
announcements 714–716
cartels 659–660, 729
collective dominance 277–278,
716–727
concerted practices 714–716
divestiture 730
explicit collusion 659–660
game theory 660–663
meaning 11
Merger Regulation 719–722, 727
oligopolistic
interdependence 660–661
problems 709
sector inquiries 727–729
tacit collusion
concerted practices 709–714
Dyestuffs 710–711
generally 660–662
oligopoly defence 712–714
oligopoly problem 709–710
parallel conduct 709–714
reciprocal cooperation 713
Suiker Unie 711–712
Wood Pulp 712–714
Züchner 711–712

unilateral price
announcements 714–716
opportunity costs
barriers to entry 93
dominant position 358
oral hearing
Commission
procedure 978–979
ordoliberalism
basis 33–34
competition law 16, 33–34
economic freedom 34, 41
economic theory 33–34, 41
efficiency 34
European Union 35, 41
influence 33–34, 41
meaning 33–34, 41
output restrictions
cartels 684–688, 693–695
individual exemptions under
Article 101(3) 693–695

parallel conduct
see also **oligopoly**
concerted practices 172
parallel imports
abuse of dominant
position 585–590
agreements impeding (Article
101) 158–161
burden of proof 161–162
pharmaceuticals 161–162,
585–590
single market 40
parent companies
see also **single economic unit**;
subsidiaries
presumption of decisive
influence 143–147
Pareto improvement
welfare 13
Partnership and Cooperation
Agreements 1291
patent hoarding
barriers to entry 93
patents
see also **intellectual**
property rights
block exemptions 866
nature of 848
Technology Transfer Block
Exemption 877
payment services
horizontal cooperation
agreements 764
Horizontal Cooperation
Guidelines (2010) 764
refusal to supply 523–525
penalties *see* **enforcement;**
fines; periodic penalty
payments

pension funds
undertakings 131–132
perfect competition
economic theory 7–9
performance copyright
licensing agreements 914–919
performance indicators
dominant position 345–347
periodic penalty payments
generally 994
limitation periods 994
rates 995
pharmaceuticals
abuse of dominant
position 585–590
market definition 81–82,
322–323
parallel imports 161–162,
585–590
refusal to supply 532–536
regulation 54
plant breeders' rights
intellectual property rights 850
policy *see* **competition law/**
policy
Post-Chicago School
criticism of 29
economic theory 28–29
game theory 28, 30
strategic conduct of firms 28–29
potential Pareto
improvement 13
precedent
EU Courts 105
predatory pricing
see also **costs; prices**
above-cost pricing 420–425
abuse of dominant
position 401–420
AKZO test
criteria 406–408
facts of case 404–406
aligning prices with
competitors 411–412
Areeda-Turner test 403–404
average variable cost 403,
403–404
barriers to entry,
constituting 91, 402
effects 402
France Télécom 411–412
Guidance Paper 417–419
identification 403–404
mail services 408–411
meaning 401–402
meeting competition
defence 411–412
multi-market operators 403
new economy 419–420
Post Danmark case 408–411
recoupment 412–417

sacrifice principle 417–419
selective above-cost
pricing 420–425
short-run marginal cost
(SRMC) 403–404
strategy 402–403
test 403–404
preliminary references
Article 267, national courts to
Court of Justice 106
prevention, restriction
or distortion of
competition
see also **'object or effect'**
absolute territorial
protection 206, 224–225
actual effect of
agreement 215–216
ancillary restraints 242–246
behaviour of parties 207
content of agreement's
provisions 206–211,
222–226
context of agreement 205–211
defined list of
restraints 212–214
distributors 206, 207–211
economic approach 195–197
express terms 207
industry crisis 225–226
information exchange
agreements 206, 213–214
intention of the parties 215
interpretation 179–180,
194–195
legitimate objectives 215–222
licensing agreements 211
list of object restraints
defined list, whether 212
expansion of the list 212–214
identification of
restraints 205–211
narrowing the list 215–222
objective of agreement 205–211
objective of EU law 37–38
overview 203–204
price-fixing 206, 212
public policy 215–222
reduction in capacity 206
resale price maintenance 206,
211
restrictive by object 205
selective distribution
agreements 213
subjective intention of the
parties 215
vertical agreements 207–211
price discrimination
see also **margin squeeze;**
predatory pricing;
discounts and rebates

price discrimination (*cont.*)
abuse of dominant
position 396–398
arbitrage 397
first-degree discrimination 397
goods 397
meaning 396–397
monopolies 9
persistent
discrimination 396–397
primary line injury 397–398
reservation price 397
secondary line injury 397–398
Article 102(c) 567–575
services 397
whether welfare-enhancing 397
price-fixing
see also **resale price**
maintenance
cartels
agreements 678–684
buying prices 680
distributors 680
examples 681–682
generally 678
indirect price-fixing 679–680
individual exemptions
under Article
101(3) 691–693
information exchanges 681
joint selling 680
liberal professions 682,
682–684
professional services 682–684
resale price maintenance 680
selling prices 678–679
services sector 682
supplementary
provisions 681
target prices 679–680
commercialisation
agreements 754–755
concerted practices 169
distributors 680
individual exemptions under
Article 101(3) 691–693
prevention, restriction
or distortion of
competition 206, 212
prices
see also **predatory pricing**;
price discrimination;
price-fixing
abuse of dominant position
'as efficient competitor'
standard 399–401
EU courts general
approach 401
excessive prices 575–581
exclusionary abuse 396

exploitative abuse 396
Guidance Paper 399–401
low prices on buying side 581
margin squeeze 426–449
unfairly high prices 575–581
'as efficient competitor'
standard 399–401
costs levels 398–399
dominant position 345–347
excessive prices 575–581
exclusionary abuse 396
exploitative abuse 396
Guidance Paper 399–401
limit pricing 91
low prices on buying side 581
margin squeeze 426–449
market definition 74
price discrimination 396–398
regulation 53, 54
unfairly high prices 575–581
unilateral price
announcements 714–716
private enforcement *see*
damages; national courts
procurement markets
bid-rigging 689–690
demand-side
substitution 323–325
dominant position 323–325
relevant market 82
producer surplus
economic theory 5
product differentiation
barriers to entry 91, 92
product market
see also **demand-side**
substitution; market
definition
banana market 306–309
internet service
providers 312–315
new economy 312–315
raw materials 321–322
relevant market 63–64
supply-side
substitution 325–326
tyre market 309–312
production agreements
Article 101(1) 746–747
generally 746
Horizontal Cooperation
Guidelines (2010) 746–747
individual exemption under
Article 101(3) 749
specialisation
agreements 747–749
production restrictions
cartels 684–688, 693–695
individual exemptions under
Article 101(3) 693–695

productive efficiency
consumer welfare 44–45
economic theory 8
professional associations
associations of
undertakings 147
professional services
application of competition
rules 111
cartels 682–684
profits
dominant position 345
economic theory 6–7
profit maximisation 6–7
proof *see* **burden and standard**
of proof
proportionality
general principles of EU
law 107
public enforcement *see*
enforcement
public policy
competition law 17
efficiency 51
EU competition law 48–52
individual exemptions under
Article 101(3) 254–258
Merger Regulation 51
non-welfare issues 51
'object or effect' 215–222,
246–249
prevention, restriction
or distortion of
competition 215–222
undertakings 51
public service
meaning 633
public undertakings
see also **services of general**
economic interest
approaches 600
Article 4 TEU 601–602
associations of
undertakings 147
background to
regulation 598–600
collective agreements 623–624
Commission powers
Article 106(3) 653–656
decisions 653–654
directives 654–655
legislative powers 604
policing 603, 653
scope of powers 653
supervisory powers 653
competition law/
policy 598–601
conflict of interest 611–613,
614–616, 616–618, 629
control by the State 604–605

definitions
  exclusive rights 605–607
  measures 607
  public undertakings 604–605
  special rights 605–607
direct effect
  Article 106(1) 652
  Article 106(2) 652–653
directives 654–655
economic activities
  commercial activities 600
  definition of undertaking 600
  health insurance funds 601
  social security 601
effect on trade 652
effectiveness of competition
  rules 611–613
emergency services 627–628
equality/inequality of
  opportunity 608,
  614–616, 616–618, 618–
  620, 630
exclusive rights 605–628
exercise of exclusive
  rights 608–610
extension of exclusive
  rights 611–613, 614–616,
  627–628, 629
format of Article 106
  legislative powers of the
    Commission 603
  limited immunity from Treaty
    rules 603
  policing powers of the
    Commission 603
  prohibition addressed to
    Member States 603
granting monopoly rights 607,
  620–621
health insurance 601
inability to meet
  demand 609–611, 627–
  628, 628–629
inducements to commit
  abuses 613–614
liberalisation 52, 598
measures
  definition 607
  prohibited measures 607–628
  summary 628–630
objectives of Article 106 603
possibility of abuse 614–616
pricing abuses 629–630
prohibited measures 607–628
prohibition addressed to
  Member States 603
public service obligations
  examples 598
  universal service
    obligation 598

refusal to renew
  authorisations 627–628
refusal to supply 624–626, 630
regulation 52–54
service of general economic
  interest 620–621, 624–627
services of general interest 631,
  632
social security 601
special rights 605–607
text of Article 106 602–603
unavoidable abuse 621–622
universal service obligation
  imposition 598
publication of decisions
  Hearing Officer 978–979
purchasing agreements
  see **joint purchasing**
    agreements

rational expectations theory 3
raw materials
  dominant position 321–322
  refusal to supply 511–513
  relevant product market 80–81,
    321–322
rebates *see* **discounts and rebates**
recommended resale
  prices *see* **resale price**
    maintenance
refusal to supply
  abuse of dominant
    position 510–556
  aftermarkets 525–526
  banana market 548–550
  car parts cases 526–527
  commercial interests, protection
    of 548–550
  Commercial Solvents 511–513
  constructive refusal 510
  disruption of previous
    supply 536–548
  duty to supply 510
  essential facilities 513–526
  excluding competitors
    from downstream
    markets 511–513
  exclusionary abuse 510
  financial industry 523–525
  freedom of contract 510
  Guidance Paper 511, 550–553
  intellectual property rights
    car parts cases 526–527
    disruption of previous
      supply 536–548
    generally 526
    IMS 532–536
    interface
      information 536–548
    Ladbroke 531–532

    licensing 531–532
    Magill 528–531
    Microsoft 536–548
    pharmaceuticals 532–536
    television listings, copyright
      in 528–531
  licensing 531–532
  margin squeeze 434–441, 446
  meaning 510–511
  parallel trade 550
  payment systems 523–525
  pharmaceuticals 532–536
  public undertakings 624–626,
    630
  raw materials 511–513
  remedies 511
  single market 40
  spare parts 525–526
  television listings, copyright
    in 528–531
  tying 510
  unilateral refusal 510
  United States 553–556
relevant market
  see **market definition**
remedies
  see also **commitments**;
    enforcement
  collective dominance 726
  injunctions 1125–1126
  Merger Regulation
    alternative packages 1251
    commitments 1245–1251
  national courts
    alternative dispute
      resolution 1124
    available remedies 1085–1087
    damages 1100–1125
    harmonisation 1124
    injunctions 1125–1126
    obligatory remedies 1084
    principle of effectiveness 1084
    settlements 1124
reputation
  dominant position 357–358
resale price maintenance
  cartels 680
  distribution agreements 789–790
  'object or effect' 789–790
  prevention, restriction
    or distortion of
    competition 206, 211
  reform 797–801
  United States 797–798
research and development
  agreements
  Article 101(1) 741–742
  Article 101(3) 742–746
  assignment 878
  block exemption 742–746

research and development agreements (*cont.*)

Horizontal Cooperation Guidelines (2010) 741–742

individual exemptions under Article 101(3) 746

restriction of competition *see* **prevention, restriction or distortion of competition**

right to fair trial

Commission procedure 935–936, 955

human rights 935–936, 955

self-incrimination 955

right to independent and impartial tribunal

human rights 935–936

right to respect for private and family life

Charter of Fundamental Rights 934–935

enforcement 934–935, 950–951

inspections 950–951

royalties

intellectual property rights 855–856

licensing agreements 855–856, 898–899

safe harbours

block exemptions 266

sales networks

dominant position 356–357

search engines

abuse of dominant position 565–567

selective distribution agreements

agreements (Article 101) 162–163, 806–815

characteristics of product 809–810

discrimination 812

essential restrictions 812

justifications 806–807

Metro 807–812

nature of product 809–810

necessity of restrictions 812

'object or effect' 806–815

objective justification 813–815

operation 806

Pierre Fabre 813–815

prevention, restriction or distortion of competition 213

products justifying selective distribution 810

proportionality 812

qualitative criteria 810–812

quantitative criteria 810–812

technically complex products 809–810

uniform application of criteria 810–812

unilateral conduct 162–163

Verticals Regulation 330/2010, 829–830

self-incrimination

human rights 955

inspections 953–957

right to fair trial 955

semiconductor topographies

intellectual property rights 850

services of general economic interest

see also **public undertakings**

approval of activities 635–636

background 599–600, 630–632

categorisation 633–634

Charter of Fundamental Rights 632

Commission Communications 632, 633

concept 632–634

discretion of Member States 638–641

effect on trade 652

exemption of compensation from being State aid 656

identification 638–641

institutional setting 630–632

legal status of undertaking 634

meaning 633

obstructing performance of tasks 641–651

operation of services 636–638

purpose of Article 106(2) 634

revenue-producing monopolies 634

significance 656

State aid 656

terminology 632–634

undertakings entrusted with the operation of services 634–636

services of general interest

categorisation 633–634

Commission Communications 632, 633

concept 631, 632

meaning 633

settlement agreements

assignment 878

licensing agreements 905–906

settlements

cartel cases 992–993

informal settlements 993–994

national courts 1124

severance

Article 101(2) 189, 1098

national courts 1098

null clauses 189

SGEIs *see* **services of general economic interest**

short-run marginal cost (SRMC)

predatory pricing 403–404

SIEC (significant impediment to effective competition) test

barriers to entry 1209–1211

cause of SIEC 1187

collective dominance 1199–1208

conglomerate mergers 1230–1239

consumer welfare 1211–1214

discretion of Commission 1187

efficiency

cases 1216

consumer benefit 1215

consumer welfare 1211–1214

defence 1211

Horizontal Merger Guidelines 1215–1216

Merger Regulation 1214–1215

merger specificity 1216

verifiability 1216

failing form defence 1217–1221

foreclosure 1225–1229, 1236–1238

gross upward pricing pressure index (GUPPI) 1192

guidance 1187

horizontal mergers

barriers to entry 1209–1211

closeness of competition between merging firms 1193–1198

collective dominance 1199–1208

competitive assessment 1189–1208

competitors increasing supply 1198–1199

concentration levels 1190–1192

countervailing buyer power 1209

efficiencies 1211–1217

elimination of competitive force 1199

failing form defence 1217–1221

gross upward pricing pressure index (GUPPI) 1192

guidelines 1187, 1190–1191, 1193

joint dominance 1199–1208

market shares 1190–1198

network
  industries 1221–1223
non-coordinated
  anti-competitive
    effects 1192–1193
  overview 1189–1190
  pricing pressure indices
    (PPIs) 1192
  rescue mergers 1217–1221
  switching costs 1198
  two-sided
    markets 1221–1223
  upward pricing pressure
    (UPP) 1192
joint dominance 1199–1208
joint ventures 1241
market definition
  Notice on Market
    Definition 1188–1189
  previous practice 1188–1189
  role 1188
market power 1224
Merger Regulation 1182–1184,
  1187–1241
Non-Horizontal Merger
  Guidelines 1187,
  1223–1224
non-horizontal mergers
  concentration levels 1224
  conglomerate
    mergers 1230–1239
  coordinated
    effects 1238–1239
  foreclosure 1225–1229,
    1236–1238
  guidelines 1187, 1223–1224
  market power 1224
  markets shares 1224
  other effects 1229–1330
  vertical mergers 1225–1230
overview 1187
pricing pressure indices
  (PPIs) 1192
rescue mergers 1217
vertical mergers 1225–1230
significant impediment to
  effective competition test
  see **SIEC test**
sincere cooperation duty
  national courts 1084
single branding agreements *see*
  exclusive purchasing
  contracts
single economic unit
  agents and agency
    agreements 137–139,
    773–775
  agreements (Art. 101) 151
  boundaries 143–147

consequences 139–142
joint ventures 739
legal persons 137–139
meaning 137–139
natural persons 137–139
subsidiaries 137–147
single market, *see also*
  internal market
abuse of dominant position 372,
  584
Article 101, 40
Article 102, 40
competition law objectives 18
competition policy 38–40
consumer welfare 40
efficiency 40
Guidelines on Article
  101(3) 39–40
importance 40
objective of EU 36, 38–40
parallel imports 40
refusal to supply 40
Vertical Guidelines (2010) 40
small but significant
  non-transitory increase
  in price *see* **SSNIP test**
social security
  economic activities 131–133
  public undertakings 601
  undertakings 131–133
social services of general
  interest
  meaning 633
social welfare (total welfare)
  consumer welfare 43–44
  distributive effects 43
  economic theory 12
  State aid 46
South Africa
  competition law objectives 17
sovereign powers
  undertakings 130
spare parts
  refusal to supply 525–526
special or exclusive rights,
  undertakings granted *see*
  public undertakings
specialisation agreements
  block exemptions 747–749
spill-over effects
  joint ventures 733
sport
  application of competition
    law 111–113
  horizontal cooperation
    agreements
    generally 764–765
    joint buying 765
    joint selling 765–766

media rights 765–766
sporting rules 764–765
joint purchasing
  agreements 765
joint selling
  agreements 765–766
  media rights 757, 765–766
SRMC *see* **short-run marginal**
  cost (SRMC)
SSNIP test
  adoption of test 69
  advantages of test 68–69, 71
  alternative tests 69–70
  application of test 69
  assumptions 78
  'cellophane' fallacy 71–72
  Commission Notice (1997) 68,
    69, 71, 73
  cross-elasticity of demand 67
  demand-side substitution 67–71
  dominant position 306
  marginal customers 67
  market definition 67–71
  market power 71–72
  mergers 72
  use of test 67
stabilisation and association
  agreements 1291
standard conditions of sale
  agreements (Art. 101) 150
standard of proof *see* **burden and**
  standard of proof
standard terms
  cartels 696
  Horizontal Cooperation
    Guidelines (2010) 762–763
standardisation agreements and
  standard setting
  cartels 699
  FRAND terms 758–759
  Horizontal Cooperation
    Guidelines (2010) 757–763
  standard-essential
    patents 758–760
State aid
  compensation for services
    of general economic
    interest 656
  consumer welfare 46
  social welfare 46
State of Play meetings
  enforcement 967
Statement of Objections
  Commitments
    decisions 982–983
  complaints 1076
  enforcement 968–969
statistics
  Merger Regulation 1252

strategic alliances
  horizontal cooperation
      agreements 732
  raising rivals' costs 31
sub-contracting agreements
  assignment 878
  vertical agreements 841–842
  Verticals Regulation 330/2010,
      841–842
subsidiaries
  economic activities 137–142
  independence 143–147
  influence of parent
      company 143–147
  parent company having 100 per
      cent shareholding 143–147
  presumption of decisive
      influence 143–147
  scope of principle 107–108
  single economic units 137–147
  undertakings 137–142
subsidiarity
  general principles of EU
      law 107–108
  meaning 107
  modernisation 108
sunk costs
  barriers to entry 89, 91
  dominant position 354
supply curve
  economic theory 5
  meaning 5
supply-side substitution
  dominant position 306
  Continental Can 325–326
  market definition
      Commission Notice (1997) 75
      difficulty of distinguishing from
          potential competition 74
      meaning 66, 74–76
supremacy
  European Union law 108–109
switching costs
  barriers to entry 93
  demand-side substitution 71
  dominant position 358
Switzerland
  bilateral agreements 1291

target rebates
  see also **discounts and rebates**
  abuse of dominant position 55,
      460–463, 478–483
  meaning 455
technology pools
  licensing agreements 906–908
**Technology Transfer Block
    Exemption**
  assignment 877–878

background 867–868
bilateral technology transfer
    agreements 876
copyright 877
cross-licensing 878
definition of technology transfer
    agreements 876–877
designs 877
disapplication 893
duration 894
excluded restrictions
  exploitation of
      technology 893
  generally 891–892
  improvements 892
  meaning 891
  non-challenge clauses 892
  research and
      development 893
  severance 891
  termination clauses 892
hardcore restrictions
  competing
      undertakings 885–888
  customer allocation 886–888
  direct restrictions 884
  generally 884–885
  indirect restrictions 884
  market sharing 886–888
  non-competing
      undertakings 888–891
  output limitations 886
  passive sales
      restrictions 889–891
  price restrictions 886, 889
intellectual property
    rights 855
know-how 877
market definition 881
market shares
  calculation 882
  competing
      undertakings 883–884
  market definition 881
  non-competing
      undertakings 883–884
  product market 881, 882
  subsequently becoming
      competitors 884
  technology market 881, 882
  thresholds 880–881
master licensing
    agreements 878
methodology 868–870
mixed agreements 877
non-assertion agreements 878
number of parties 876
overview 874
parties 876

patents 877
principal features 875–876
production of contract
    products 878
recitals 875
reform 874
relationship with other block
    exemptions 879
research and development
    agreements 878
safe harbour 880–884
sale and purchase of goods 877,
    878
scheme of regulation 875
scope 874, 875, 876–879
settlement agreements 878
sub-licensing 878
technology pools 878
transfer of technology 877–878
withdrawal 893
Technology Transfer Guidelines
  application of Article 101,
      872–874
  background 867–868
  general principles 870–871
  methodology 868–870
telecommunications
  essential facilities 522
  liberalisation 111
  margin squeeze 427–444
  new economy 54–55, 78–79
  regulation 54
tenders
  cartels 689–690, 695–696
territorial jurisdiction *see*
    extraterritoriality
third countries
  abuse of dominant
      position 286–287
  appreciable effect 183
third parties
  commitments decisions 989
total welfare
  economic theory 12
trade associations
  agreements (Art. 101) 150
  associations of
      undertakings 147, 173, 174
  certification schemes 174
  constitution 174
  fines 997
  information sharing
      agreements 699
  recommendations 174
trade marks
  see also **intellectual
      property rights**
  agreements (Art. 101) 150
  Campari decision 909–911

delimitation agreements 913
licensing agreements 908–913
Moosehead 912–913
rights 848–849
trade unions
economic activities 137
undertakings 137
transaction costs economics
basis 31
economic theory 31
efficiency 32
transport
competition rules 111
dominant position 282–283, 327
essential facilities 517–518, 522
geographic market 327
temporal market 331
Treaty of Amsterdam
amendments to Treaty of Rome 99
Treaty on European Union
aims 100
amended by Treaty of Lisbon 100
function 100
values 36
Treaty on the Functioning of Europe
aims 100
EC Treaty renamed TFEU 100
objectives of the EU 36–37
purpose 100
scope 100
Treaty of Lisbon
amendments to treaties 100
commencement 100
European Union 36
Treaty of Rome, EC Treaty
see also **Treaty on the Functioning of Europe**
amendments 99, 100
EEC, establishment of 34, 99
European Union 34, 36
renamed Treaty on the Functioning of Europe 36
TTBER *see* **Technology Transfer Block Exemption**
turnover
appreciable effect 185
calculation 1152–1156
Verticals Regulation 330/2010, 833
tying
abuse of dominant position 393–394
aftermarkets 486, 489–492
barriers to entry 93
case law 489–506

coercion 508
commercial rationale 487
contractual tying 486, 489–492
customer choice 508
distinct products 506–508
distribution agreements 816
economic rationale 487–489
efficiencies 509
foreclosure 508–509
generally 485–486
Guidance Paper 486, 487, 489, 506–509
Hilti 489–490
leverage 488–489
licensing agreements 857, 903
meaning 485–486
Microsoft 493–506
mixed bundling 486, 492–493, 509
multi-product rebates 509
'object or effect' 816
objections 487–489
post-*Microsoft* position 506–509
pure bundling 486
rationale 487
refusal to supply 510
technical tying 486, 493–506
Tetra Pak II 490, 491–492

UNCTAD 1292–1293
undertakings
see also **associations of undertakings**
abuse of dominant position
bodies performing public functions 276
collective dominance 276–281
meaning 276–281
public bodies 276
administrative functions 130
agents 137–139
bodies performing public functions 276
collective dominance 276–281
concept 136–137
cross-subsidies 132
definition 127
economic activities 127–136
elements 127
employees 137
entities engaged in economic activity 127
environmental protection 130–131
examples 128
form of entity 128
health care 134–136
legal persons 137–139

legal status 128
meaning 127, 276–281
natural persons 137–139
nature of activity 128, 136–137
necessary economic activities 129–133
pension funds 131–132
public bodies 276
administrative functions 130
contracting out 129–130
cross-subsidies 132
data collection 131
economic activities 129–136
environmental protection 130–131
health care 134–136
necessary economic activities 129–133
pension funds 131–132
performing non-economic public functions 129–133
public interest 130
purchasing goods/services by entity not engaged in economic activity 134–136
social security 131–133
solidarity, principle of 133
sovereign powers 130
public policy 51
purchasing goods/services by entity not engaged in economic activity 134–136
relative concept 136–137
single economic unit
agents 137–139
boundaries 143–147
legal persons 137–139
meaning 137–139
natural persons 137–139
subsidiaries 137–142
social security 131–133
sovereign powers 130
subsidiaries 137–142
trade unions 137
United States
antitrust law (competition law)
background 19
Chicago School 19, 20
development 20
efficiency 19
EU law compared 20–21
Harvard School 20
influence 19–21
objectives 19–20
restrained enforcement 20
Sherman Act 19, 20
'workable competition' 20
cartels 674
discounts and rebates 483–484

United States (*cont.*)
discovery 1269
dominant position 298
effects doctrine 1260–1263,
1269–1271
essential facilities 513, 517
extraterritoriality
cooperation agreement with
EU 1287–1290
effects doctrine 1260–1263
generally 1259–1260
other states, reactions
of 1263–1265
federal agencies 1259–1260
foreign conduct affecting
exports 1269–1270
foreign plaintiffs 1265–1269
international law 1270–1271
margin squeeze 445
national courts 1085,
1124–1125
predatory pricing, 404, 412
refusal to supply 553–556
resale price
maintenance 797–798
rule of reason 197
Sherman Act 197–198, 231,
1259
universal service obligation
imposition 598
meaning 633
upfront access payments
distribution agreements 817

vertical agreements
see also **distribution
agreements**; **Verticals
Regulation 330/2010**
abuse of dominant position 842
agency agreements 770,
773–776
agreements falling outside of
Article 101(1) 786–787
agreements under Article 101,
155–163
block exemptions
see also **Verticals Regulation
330/2010**
generally 785–786
motor vehicles 834
old block
exemptions 817–818
central issues 768
commercial agents 770
concerted practices 172
conclusions 842–844
factors affecting choice
of distribution
method 769–770

hardcore restrictions
individual exemptions under
Article 101(3) 834–837
Verticals Regulation 330/2010,
825–830
independent
distributors 771–772
individual exemptions under
Article 101(3)
criteria 834
generally 817
hardcore restraints 834–837
non-compete
obligations 837–841
old block exemptions 817–818
other restraints 837–841
methodology of
Commission 786–788
methods of distribution
agency 770
factors affecting choice 769
impact of competition
rules 773
independent
distributors 771–772
vertical integration 769–770
minor importance, agreements
of 786–787
more economic
approach 785–786
non-compete obligations
individual exemptions under
Article 101(3) 837–841
Verticals Regulation 330/2010,
831–832
parent-subsidiary
arrangements 773
positive effects 777–784
reform 785–786
sub-contracting
agreements 841–842
unilateral conduct 155–163
vertical integration 769–770
Vertical Guidelines (2010)
Article 101, 40
consumer welfare 43
modernisation 43
single market 40
vertical mergers
see also **mergers**
meaning 1132
Verticals Regulation 330/2010
application of regulation 819
background 818
commencement 834
definitions 818–820
excluded restraints
non-compete
obligations 831–832

severance of
obligations 830–831
expiry 834
hardcore restrictions
active sales into exclusive
territories 827–829
applicable of
regulation 825–826
components, buyers of 829
components, suppliers
of 830
fixed prices 826
minimum sales prices 826
select distribution
systems 829
selective distribution
systems 829–830
territorial
restrictions 827–829
unauthorised distributors 829
wholesalers 829
intellectual property
rights 822–823
main exemption
agreements between
two or more
undertakings 821
agreements falling
within another block
exemption 823
associations of retailers 822
competing undertakings,
agreements
between 821–822
distribution agreements 821
intellectual property
rights 822–823
purchasing agreements 821
vertical agreements 820–821
market definition 824
market shares
30 per cent
threshold 823–824
calculation 833
cap 823–825
exceeding the market
shares 824
market definition 824
portfolio of products 825
networks of agreements 833
non-application of the
Regulation 833
non-compete
obligations 831–832
recitals 818
selective distribution
systems 829–830
sub-contracting
agreements 841, 841–842

transitional provisions 833
turnover 833
withdrawal of the block
exemption 832
vertical restraints *see* **vertical agreements**
Vertical Restraints Guidelines (2000)
discounts and rebates 456
exclusive purchasing
contracts 450
modernisation 42

vexatious litigation
abuse of dominant
position 564–565
websites
Directorate-General for
Competition 103–104
welfare
see also **consumer welfare**
concepts 12
economic theory 12–14, 94
efficiency 12

Kaldor-Hicks improvement
(potential Pareto
improvement) 13
meaning 12
Pareto improvement 13
potential Pareto improvement 13
price discrimination 397
social (total) welfare 12
whistle-blowing *see* **leniency**
workable competition
economic theory 32
WTO 1293–1294